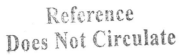

Oxford Dictionary of
National Biography

Volume 48

Oxford Dictionary of National Biography

IN ASSOCIATION WITH

The British Academy

From the earliest times to the year 2000

Edited by

H. C. G. Matthew

and

Brian Harrison

Volume 48

Rowell–Sarsfield

OXFORD

UNIVERSITY PRESS

OXFORD
UNIVERSITY PRESS

Great Clarendon Street, Oxford OX2 6DP

Oxford University Press is a department of the University of Oxford.
It furthers the University's objective of excellence in research, scholarship,
and education by publishing worldwide in

Oxford New York

Auckland Bangkok Buenos Aires Cape Town
Chennai Dar es Salaam Delhi Hong Kong Istanbul Karachi
Kolkata Kuala Lumpur Madrid Melbourne Mexico City Mumbai Nairobi
São Paulo Shanghai Taipei Tokyo Toronto

Oxford is a registered trade mark of Oxford University Press
in the UK and in certain other countries

Published in the United States
by Oxford University Press Inc., New York

© Oxford University Press 2004

Illustrations © individual copyright holders as listed in
'Picture credits', and reproduced with permission

Database right Oxford University Press (maker)

First published 2004

British Library Cataloguing in Publication Data
Data available

Library of Congress Cataloging in Publication Data
Data available: for details see volume 1, p. iv

ISBN 0-19-861398-9 (this volume)
ISBN 0-19-861411-X (set of sixty volumes)

Text captured by Alliance Phototypesetters, Pondicherry
Illustrations reproduced and archived by
Alliance Graphics Ltd, UK
Typeset in OUP Swift by Interactive Sciences Limited, Gloucester
Printed in Great Britain on acid-free paper by
Butler and Tanner Ltd,
Frome, Somerset

LIST OF ABBREVIATIONS

1 General abbreviations

AB	bachelor of arts		BCnL	bachelor of canon law
ABC	Australian Broadcasting Corporation		BCom	bachelor of commerce
ABC TV	ABC Television		BD	bachelor of divinity
act.	active		BEd	bachelor of education
A$	Australian dollar		BEng	bachelor of engineering
AD	*anno domini*		bk *pl.* bks	book(s)
AFC	Air Force Cross		BL	bachelor of law / letters / literature
AIDS	acquired immune deficiency syndrome		BLitt	bachelor of letters
AK	Alaska		BM	bachelor of medicine
AL	Alabama		BMus	bachelor of music
A level	advanced level [examination]		BP	before present
ALS	associate of the Linnean Society		BP	British Petroleum
AM	master of arts		Bros.	Brothers
AMICE	associate member of the Institution of Civil Engineers		BS	(1) bachelor of science; (2) bachelor of surgery; (3) British standard
ANZAC	Australian and New Zealand Army Corps		BSc	bachelor of science
appx *pl.* appxs	appendix(es)		BSc (Econ.)	bachelor of science (economics)
AR	Arkansas		BSc (Eng.)	bachelor of science (engineering)
ARA	associate of the Royal Academy		bt	baronet
ARCA	associate of the Royal College of Art		BTh	bachelor of theology
ARCM	associate of the Royal College of Music		*bur.*	buried
ARCO	associate of the Royal College of Organists		C.	command [identifier for published parliamentary papers]
ARIBA	associate of the Royal Institute of British Architects		*c.*	*circa*
ARP	air-raid precautions		c.	*capitulum pl. capitula*: chapter(s)
ARRC	associate of the Royal Red Cross		CA	California
ARSA	associate of the Royal Scottish Academy		Cantab.	Cantabrigiensis
art.	article / item		cap.	*capitulum pl. capitula*: chapter(s)
ASC	Army Service Corps		CB	companion of the Bath
Asch	Austrian Schilling		CBE	commander of the Order of the British Empire
ASDIC	Antisubmarine Detection Investigation Committee		CBS	Columbia Broadcasting System
ATS	Auxiliary Territorial Service		cc	cubic centimetres
ATV	Associated Television		C$	Canadian dollar
Aug	August		CD	compact disc
AZ	Arizona		Cd	command [identifier for published parliamentary papers]
b.	born		CE	Common (*or* Christian) Era
BA	bachelor of arts		cent.	century
BA (Admin.)	bachelor of arts (administration)		cf.	compare
BAFTA	British Academy of Film and Television Arts		CH	Companion of Honour
BAO	bachelor of arts in obstetrics		chap.	chapter
bap.	baptized		ChB	bachelor of surgery
BBC	British Broadcasting Corporation / Company		CI	Imperial Order of the Crown of India
BC	before Christ		CIA	Central Intelligence Agency
BCE	before the common (*or* Christian) era		CID	Criminal Investigation Department
BCE	bachelor of civil engineering		CIE	companion of the Order of the Indian Empire
BCG	bacillus of Calmette and Guérin [inoculation against tuberculosis]		Cie	Compagnie
BCh	bachelor of surgery		CLit	companion of literature
BChir	bachelor of surgery		CM	master of surgery
BCL	bachelor of civil law		cm	centimetre(s)

Cmd	command [identifier for published parliamentary papers]
CMG	companion of the Order of St Michael and St George
Cmnd	command [identifier for published parliamentary papers]
CO	Colorado
Co.	company
co.	county
col. *pl.* cols.	column(s)
Corp.	corporation
CSE	certificate of secondary education
CSI	companion of the Order of the Star of India
CT	Connecticut
CVO	commander of the Royal Victorian Order
cwt	hundredweight
$	(American) dollar
d.	(1) penny (pence); (2) died
DBE	dame commander of the Order of the British Empire
DCH	diploma in child health
DCh	doctor of surgery
DCL	doctor of civil law
DCnL	doctor of canon law
DCVO	dame commander of the Royal Victorian Order
DD	doctor of divinity
DE	Delaware
Dec	December
dem.	demolished
DEng	doctor of engineering
des.	destroyed
DFC	Distinguished Flying Cross
DipEd	diploma in education
DipPsych	diploma in psychiatry
diss.	dissertation
DL	deputy lieutenant
DLitt	doctor of letters
DLittCelt	doctor of Celtic letters
DM	(1) Deutschmark; (2) doctor of medicine; (3) doctor of musical arts
DMus	doctor of music
DNA	dioxyribonucleic acid
doc.	document
DOL	doctor of oriental learning
DPH	diploma in public health
DPhil	doctor of philosophy
DPM	diploma in psychological medicine
DSC	Distinguished Service Cross
DSc	doctor of science
DSc (Econ.)	doctor of science (economics)
DSc (Eng.)	doctor of science (engineering)
DSM	Distinguished Service Medal
DSO	companion of the Distinguished Service Order
DSocSc	doctor of social science
DTech	doctor of technology
DTh	doctor of theology
DTM	diploma in tropical medicine
DTMH	diploma in tropical medicine and hygiene
DU	doctor of the university
DUniv	doctor of the university
dwt	pennyweight
EC	European Community
ed. *pl.* eds.	edited / edited by / editor(s)
Edin.	Edinburgh
edn	edition
EEC	European Economic Community
EFTA	European Free Trade Association
EICS	East India Company Service
EMI	Electrical and Musical Industries (Ltd)
Eng.	English
enl.	enlarged
ENSA	Entertainments National Service Association
ep. *pl.* epp.	*epistola(e)*
ESP	extra-sensory perception
esp.	especially
esq.	esquire
est.	estimate / estimated
EU	European Union
ex	sold by (*lit.* out of)
excl.	excludes / excluding
exh.	exhibited
exh. cat.	exhibition catalogue
f. *pl.* ff.	following [pages]
FA	Football Association
FACP	fellow of the American College of Physicians
facs.	facsimile
FANY	First Aid Nursing Yeomanry
FBA	fellow of the British Academy
FBI	Federation of British Industries
FCS	fellow of the Chemical Society
Feb	February
FEng	fellow of the Fellowship of Engineering
FFCM	fellow of the Faculty of Community Medicine
FGS	fellow of the Geological Society
fig.	figure
FIMechE	fellow of the Institution of Mechanical Engineers
FL	Florida
fl.	*floruit*
FLS	fellow of the Linnean Society
FM	frequency modulation
fol. *pl.* fols.	folio(s)
Fr	French francs
Fr.	French
FRAeS	fellow of the Royal Aeronautical Society
FRAI	fellow of the Royal Anthropological Institute
FRAM	fellow of the Royal Academy of Music
FRAS	(1) fellow of the Royal Asiatic Society; (2) fellow of the Royal Astronomical Society
FRCM	fellow of the Royal College of Music
FRCO	fellow of the Royal College of Organists
FRCOG	fellow of the Royal College of Obstetricians and Gynaecologists
FRCP(C)	fellow of the Royal College of Physicians of Canada
FRCP (Edin.)	fellow of the Royal College of Physicians of Edinburgh
FRCP (Lond.)	fellow of the Royal College of Physicians of London
FRCPath	fellow of the Royal College of Pathologists
FRCPsych	fellow of the Royal College of Psychiatrists
FRCS	fellow of the Royal College of Surgeons
FRGS	fellow of the Royal Geographical Society
FRIBA	fellow of the Royal Institute of British Architects
FRICS	fellow of the Royal Institute of Chartered Surveyors
FRS	fellow of the Royal Society
FRSA	fellow of the Royal Society of Arts

FRSCM	fellow of the Royal School of Church Music		ISO	companion of the Imperial Service Order
FRSE	fellow of the Royal Society of Edinburgh		It.	Italian
FRSL	fellow of the Royal Society of Literature		ITA	Independent Television Authority
FSA	fellow of the Society of Antiquaries		ITV	Independent Television
ft	foot *pl.* feet		Jan	January
FTCL	fellow of Trinity College of Music, London		JP	justice of the peace
ft-lb per min.	foot-pounds per minute [unit of horsepower]		jun.	junior
FZS	fellow of the Zoological Society		KB	knight of the Order of the Bath
GA	Georgia		KBE	knight commander of the Order of the British Empire
GBE	knight or dame grand cross of the Order of the British Empire		KC	king's counsel
GCB	knight grand cross of the Order of the Bath		kcal	kilocalorie
GCE	general certificate of education		KCB	knight commander of the Order of the Bath
GCH	knight grand cross of the Royal Guelphic Order		KCH	knight commander of the Royal Guelphic Order
GCHQ	government communications headquarters		KCIE	knight commander of the Order of the Indian Empire
GCIE	knight grand commander of the Order of the Indian Empire		KCMG	knight commander of the Order of St Michael and St George
GCMG	knight or dame grand cross of the Order of St Michael and St George		KCSI	knight commander of the Order of the Star of India
GCSE	general certificate of secondary education		KCVO	knight commander of the Royal Victorian Order
GCSI	knight grand commander of the Order of the Star of India		keV	kilo-electron-volt
GCStJ	bailiff or dame grand cross of the order of St John of Jerusalem		KG	knight of the Order of the Garter
GCVO	knight or dame grand cross of the Royal Victorian Order		KGB	[Soviet committee of state security]
			KH	knight of the Royal Guelphic Order
GEC	General Electric Company		KLM	Koninklijke Luchtvaart Maatschappij (Royal Dutch Air Lines)
Ger.	German			
GI	government (*or* general) issue		km	kilometre(s)
GMT	Greenwich mean time		KP	knight of the Order of St Patrick
GP	general practitioner		KS	Kansas
GPU	[Soviet special police unit]		KT	knight of the Order of the Thistle
GSO	general staff officer		kt	knight
Heb.	Hebrew		KY	Kentucky
HEICS	Honourable East India Company Service		£	pound(s) sterling
HI	Hawaii		£E	Egyptian pound
HIV	human immunodeficiency virus		L	lira *pl.* lire
HK$	Hong Kong dollar		l. *pl.* ll.	line(s)
HM	his / her majesty('s)		LA	Lousiana
HMAS	his / her majesty's Australian ship		LAA	light anti-aircraft
HMNZS	his / her majesty's New Zealand ship		LAH	licentiate of the Apothecaries' Hall, Dublin
HMS	his / her majesty's ship		Lat.	Latin
HMSO	His / Her Majesty's Stationery Office		lb	pound(s), unit of weight
HMV	His Master's Voice		LDS	licence in dental surgery
Hon.	Honourable		*lit.*	literally
hp	horsepower		LittB	bachelor of letters
hr	hour(s)		LittD	doctor of letters
HRH	his / her royal highness		LKQCPI	licentiate of the King and Queen's College of Physicians, Ireland
HTV	Harlech Television		LLA	lady literate in arts
IA	Iowa		LLB	bachelor of laws
ibid.	*ibidem*: in the same place		LLD	doctor of laws
ICI	Imperial Chemical Industries (Ltd)		LLM	master of laws
ID	Idaho		LM	licentiate in midwifery
IL	Illinois		LP	long-playing record
illus.	illustration		LRAM	licentiate of the Royal Academy of Music
illustr.	illustrated		LRCP	licentiate of the Royal College of Physicians
IN	Indiana		LRCPS (Glasgow)	licentiate of the Royal College of Physicians and Surgeons of Glasgow
in.	inch(es)			
Inc.	Incorporated		LRCS	licentiate of the Royal College of Surgeons
incl.	includes / including		LSA	licentiate of the Society of Apothecaries
IOU	I owe you		LSD	lysergic acid diethylamide
IQ	intelligence quotient		LVO	lieutenant of the Royal Victorian Order
Ir£	Irish pound		M. *pl.* MM.	Monsieur *pl.* Messieurs
IRA	Irish Republican Army		m	metre(s)

m. *pl.* mm.	membrane(s)
MA	(1) Massachusetts; (2) master of arts
MAI	master of engineering
MB	bachelor of medicine
MBA	master of business administration
MBE	member of the Order of the British Empire
MC	Military Cross
MCC	Marylebone Cricket Club
MCh	master of surgery
MChir	master of surgery
MCom	master of commerce
MD	(1) doctor of medicine; (2) Maryland
MDMA	methylenedioxymethamphetamine
ME	Maine
MEd	master of education
MEng	master of engineering
MEP	member of the European parliament
MG	Morris Garages
MGM	Metro-Goldwyn-Mayer
Mgr	Monsignor
MI	(1) Michigan; (2) military intelligence
MI1c	[secret intelligence department]
MI5	[military intelligence department]
MI6	[secret intelligence department]
MI9	[secret escape service]
MICE	member of the Institution of Civil Engineers
MIEE	member of the Institution of Electrical Engineers
min.	minute(s)
Mk	mark
ML	(1) licentiate of medicine; (2) master of laws
MLitt	master of letters
Mlle	Mademoiselle
mm	millimetre(s)
Mme	Madame
MN	Minnesota
MO	Missouri
MOH	medical officer of health
MP	member of parliament
m.p.h.	miles per hour
MPhil	master of philosophy
MRCP	member of the Royal College of Physicians
MRCS	member of the Royal College of Surgeons
MRCVS	member of the Royal College of Veterinary Surgeons
MRIA	member of the Royal Irish Academy
MS	(1) master of science; (2) Mississippi
MS *pl.* MSS	manuscript(s)
MSc	master of science
MSc (Econ.)	master of science (economics)
MT	Montana
MusB	bachelor of music
MusBac	bachelor of music
MusD	doctor of music
MV	motor vessel
MVO	member of the Royal Victorian Order
n. *pl.* nn.	note(s)
NAAFI	Navy, Army, and Air Force Institutes
NASA	National Aeronautics and Space Administration
NATO	North Atlantic Treaty Organization
NBC	National Broadcasting Corporation
NC	North Carolina
NCO	non-commissioned officer

ND	North Dakota
n.d.	no date
NE	Nebraska
nem. con.	*nemine contradicente*: unanimously
new ser.	new series
NH	New Hampshire
NHS	National Health Service
NJ	New Jersey
NKVD	[Soviet people's commissariat for internal affairs]
NM	New Mexico
nm	nanometre(s)
no. *pl.* nos.	number(s)
Nov	November
n.p.	no place [of publication]
NS	new style
NV	Nevada
NY	New York
NZBS	New Zealand Broadcasting Service
OBE	officer of the Order of the British Empire
obit.	obituary
Oct	October
OCTU	officer cadets training unit
OECD	Organization for Economic Co-operation and Development
OEEC	Organization for European Economic Co-operation
OFM	order of Friars Minor [Franciscans]
OFMCap	Ordine Frati Minori Cappucini: member of the Capuchin order
OH	Ohio
OK	Oklahoma
O level	ordinary level [examination]
OM	Order of Merit
OP	order of Preachers [Dominicans]
op. *pl.* opp.	opus *pl.* opera
OPEC	Organization of Petroleum Exporting Countries
OR	Oregon
orig.	original
OS	old style
OSB	Order of St Benedict
OTC	Officers' Training Corps
OWS	Old Watercolour Society
Oxon.	Oxoniensis
p. *pl.* pp.	page(s)
PA	Pennsylvania
p.a.	per annum
para.	paragraph
PAYE	pay as you earn
pbk *pl.* pbks	paperback(s)
per.	[during the] period
PhD	doctor of philosophy
pl.	(1) plate(s); (2) plural
priv. coll.	private collection
pt *pl.* pts	part(s)
pubd	published
PVC	polyvinyl chloride
q. *pl.* qq.	(1) question(s); (2) quire(s)
QC	queen's counsel
R	rand
R.	Rex / Regina
r	recto
r.	reigned / ruled
RA	Royal Academy / Royal Academician

RAC	Royal Automobile Club
RAF	Royal Air Force
RAFVR	Royal Air Force Volunteer Reserve
RAM	[member of the] Royal Academy of Music
RAMC	Royal Army Medical Corps
RCA	Royal College of Art
RCNC	Royal Corps of Naval Constructors
RCOG	Royal College of Obstetricians and Gynaecologists
RDI	royal designer for industry
RE	Royal Engineers
repr. *pl.* reprs.	reprint(s) / reprinted
repro.	reproduced
rev.	revised / revised by / reviser / revision
Revd	Reverend
RHA	Royal Hibernian Academy
RI	(1) Rhode Island; (2) Royal Institute of Painters in Water-Colours
RIBA	Royal Institute of British Architects
RIN	Royal Indian Navy
RM	Reichsmark
RMS	Royal Mail steamer
RN	Royal Navy
RNA	ribonucleic acid
RNAS	Royal Naval Air Service
RNR	Royal Naval Reserve
RNVR	Royal Naval Volunteer Reserve
RO	Record Office
r.p.m.	revolutions per minute
RRS	royal research ship
Rs	rupees
RSA	(1) Royal Scottish Academician; (2) Royal Society of Arts
RSPCA	Royal Society for the Prevention of Cruelty to Animals
Rt Hon.	Right Honourable
Rt Revd	Right Reverend
RUC	Royal Ulster Constabulary
Russ.	Russian
RWS	Royal Watercolour Society
S4C	Sianel Pedwar Cymru
s.	shilling(s)
s.a.	*sub anno*: under the year
SABC	South African Broadcasting Corporation
SAS	Special Air Service
SC	South Carolina
ScD	doctor of science
S$	Singapore dollar
SD	South Dakota
sec.	second(s)
sel.	selected
sen.	senior
Sept	September
ser.	series
SHAPE	supreme headquarters allied powers, Europe
SIDRO	Société Internationale d'Énergie Hydro-Électrique
sig. *pl.* sigs.	signature(s)
sing.	singular
SIS	Secret Intelligence Service
SJ	Society of Jesus
Skr	Swedish krona
Span.	Spanish
SPCK	Society for Promoting Christian Knowledge
SS	(1) Santissimi; (2) Schutzstaffel; (3) steam ship
STB	bachelor of theology
STD	doctor of theology
STM	master of theology
STP	doctor of theology
supp.	supposedly
suppl. *pl.* suppls.	supplement(s)
s.v.	*sub verbo* / *sub voce*: under the word / heading
SY	steam yacht
TA	Territorial Army
TASS	[Soviet news agency]
TB	tuberculosis (*lit.* tubercle bacillus)
TD	(1) *teachtaí dála* (member of the Dáil); (2) territorial decoration
TN	Tennessee
TNT	trinitrotoluene
trans.	translated / translated by / translation / translator
TT	tourist trophy
TUC	Trades Union Congress
TX	Texas
U-boat	*Unterseeboot*: submarine
Ufa	Universum-Film AG
UMIST	University of Manchester Institute of Science and Technology
UN	United Nations
UNESCO	United Nations Educational, Scientific, and Cultural Organization
UNICEF	United Nations International Children's Emergency Fund
unpubd	unpublished
USS	United States ship
UT	Utah
v	verso
v.	versus
VA	Virginia
VAD	Voluntary Aid Detachment
VC	Victoria Cross
VE-day	victory in Europe day
Ven.	Venerable
VJ-day	victory over Japan day
vol. *pl.* vols.	volume(s)
VT	Vermont
WA	Washington [state]
WAAC	Women's Auxiliary Army Corps
WAAF	Women's Auxiliary Air Force
WEA	Workers' Educational Association
WHO	World Health Organization
WI	Wisconsin
WRAF	Women's Royal Air Force
WRNS	Women's Royal Naval Service
WV	West Virginia
WVS	Women's Voluntary Service
WY	Wyoming
¥	yen
YMCA	Young Men's Christian Association
YWCA	Young Women's Christian Association

2 Institution abbreviations

All Souls Oxf.	All Souls College, Oxford
AM Oxf.	Ashmolean Museum, Oxford
Balliol Oxf.	Balliol College, Oxford
BBC WAC	BBC Written Archives Centre, Reading
Beds. & Luton ARS	Bedfordshire and Luton Archives and Record Service, Bedford
Berks. RO	Berkshire Record Office, Reading
BFI	British Film Institute, London
BFI NFTVA	British Film Institute, London, National Film and Television Archive
BGS	British Geological Survey, Keyworth, Nottingham
Birm. CA	Birmingham Central Library, Birmingham City Archives
Birm. CL	Birmingham Central Library
BL	British Library, London
BL NSA	British Library, London, National Sound Archive
BL OIOC	British Library, London, Oriental and India Office Collections
BLPES	London School of Economics and Political Science, British Library of Political and Economic Science
BM	British Museum, London
Bodl. Oxf.	Bodleian Library, Oxford
Bodl. RH	Bodleian Library of Commonwealth and African Studies at Rhodes House, Oxford
Borth. Inst.	Borthwick Institute of Historical Research, University of York
Boston PL	Boston Public Library, Massachusetts
Bristol RO	Bristol Record Office
Bucks. RLSS	Buckinghamshire Records and Local Studies Service, Aylesbury
CAC Cam.	Churchill College, Cambridge, Churchill Archives Centre
Cambs. AS	Cambridgeshire Archive Service
CCC Cam.	Corpus Christi College, Cambridge
CCC Oxf.	Corpus Christi College, Oxford
Ches. & Chester ALSS	Cheshire and Chester Archives and Local Studies Service
Christ Church Oxf.	Christ Church, Oxford
Christies	Christies, London
City Westm. AC	City of Westminster Archives Centre, London
CKS	Centre for Kentish Studies, Maidstone
CLRO	Corporation of London Records Office
Coll. Arms	College of Arms, London
Col. U.	Columbia University, New York
Cornwall RO	Cornwall Record Office, Truro
Courtauld Inst.	Courtauld Institute of Art, London
CUL	Cambridge University Library
Cumbria AS	Cumbria Archive Service
Derbys. RO	Derbyshire Record Office, Matlock
Devon RO	Devon Record Office, Exeter
Dorset RO	Dorset Record Office, Dorchester
Duke U.	Duke University, Durham, North Carolina
Duke U., Perkins L.	Duke University, Durham, North Carolina, William R. Perkins Library
Durham Cath. CL	Durham Cathedral, chapter library
Durham RO	Durham Record Office
DWL	Dr Williams's Library, London
Essex RO	Essex Record Office
E. Sussex RO	East Sussex Record Office, Lewes
Eton	Eton College, Berkshire
FM Cam.	Fitzwilliam Museum, Cambridge
Folger	Folger Shakespeare Library, Washington, DC
Garr. Club	Garrick Club, London
Girton Cam.	Girton College, Cambridge
GL	Guildhall Library, London
Glos. RO	Gloucestershire Record Office, Gloucester
Gon. & Caius Cam.	Gonville and Caius College, Cambridge
Gov. Art Coll.	Government Art Collection
GS Lond.	Geological Society of London
Hants. RO	Hampshire Record Office, Winchester
Harris Man. Oxf.	Harris Manchester College, Oxford
Harvard TC	Harvard Theatre Collection, Harvard University, Cambridge, Massachusetts, Nathan Marsh Pusey Library
Harvard U.	Harvard University, Cambridge, Massachusetts
Harvard U., Houghton L.	Harvard University, Cambridge, Massachusetts, Houghton Library
Herefs. RO	Herefordshire Record Office, Hereford
Herts. ALS	Hertfordshire Archives and Local Studies, Hertford
Hist. Soc. Penn.	Historical Society of Pennsylvania, Philadelphia
HLRO	House of Lords Record Office, London
Hult. Arch.	Hulton Archive, London and New York
Hunt. L.	Huntington Library, San Marino, California
ICL	Imperial College, London
Inst. CE	Institution of Civil Engineers, London
Inst. EE	Institution of Electrical Engineers, London
IWM	Imperial War Museum, London
IWM FVA	Imperial War Museum, London, Film and Video Archive
IWM SA	Imperial War Museum, London, Sound Archive
JRL	John Rylands University Library of Manchester
King's AC Cam.	King's College Archives Centre, Cambridge
King's Cam.	King's College, Cambridge
King's Lond.	King's College, London
King's Lond., Liddell Hart C.	King's College, London, Liddell Hart Centre for Military Archives
Lancs. RO	Lancashire Record Office, Preston
L. Cong.	Library of Congress, Washington, DC
Leics. RO	Leicestershire, Leicester, and Rutland Record Office, Leicester
Lincs. Arch.	Lincolnshire Archives, Lincoln
Linn. Soc.	Linnean Society of London
LMA	London Metropolitan Archives
LPL	Lambeth Palace, London
Lpool RO	Liverpool Record Office and Local Studies Service
LUL	London University Library
Magd. Cam.	Magdalene College, Cambridge
Magd. Oxf.	Magdalen College, Oxford
Man. City Gall.	Manchester City Galleries
Man. CL	Manchester Central Library
Mass. Hist. Soc.	Massachusetts Historical Society, Boston
Merton Oxf.	Merton College, Oxford
MHS Oxf.	Museum of the History of Science, Oxford
Mitchell L., Glas.	Mitchell Library, Glasgow
Mitchell L., NSW	State Library of New South Wales, Sydney, Mitchell Library
Morgan L.	Pierpont Morgan Library, New York
NA Canada	National Archives of Canada, Ottawa
NA Ire.	National Archives of Ireland, Dublin
NAM	National Army Museum, London
NA Scot.	National Archives of Scotland, Edinburgh
News Int. RO	News International Record Office, London
NG Ire.	National Gallery of Ireland, Dublin

NG Scot.	National Gallery of Scotland, Edinburgh
NHM	Natural History Museum, London
NL Aus.	National Library of Australia, Canberra
NL Ire.	National Library of Ireland, Dublin
NL NZ	National Library of New Zealand, Wellington
NL NZ, Turnbull L.	National Library of New Zealand, Wellington, Alexander Turnbull Library
NL Scot.	National Library of Scotland, Edinburgh
NL Wales	National Library of Wales, Aberystwyth
NMG Wales	National Museum and Gallery of Wales, Cardiff
NMM	National Maritime Museum, London
Norfolk RO	Norfolk Record Office, Norwich
Northants. RO	Northamptonshire Record Office, Northampton
Northumbd RO	Northumberland Record Office
Notts. Arch.	Nottinghamshire Archives, Nottingham
NPG	National Portrait Gallery, London
NRA	National Archives, London, Historical Manuscripts Commission, National Register of Archives
Nuffield Oxf.	Nuffield College, Oxford
N. Yorks. CRO	North Yorkshire County Record Office, Northallerton
NYPL	New York Public Library
Oxf. UA	Oxford University Archives
Oxf. U. Mus. NH	Oxford University Museum of Natural History
Oxon. RO	Oxfordshire Record Office, Oxford
Pembroke Cam.	Pembroke College, Cambridge
PRO	National Archives, London, Public Record Office
PRO NIre.	Public Record Office for Northern Ireland, Belfast
Pusey Oxf.	Pusey House, Oxford
RA	Royal Academy of Arts, London
Ransom HRC	Harry Ransom Humanities Research Center, University of Texas, Austin
RAS	Royal Astronomical Society, London
RBG Kew	Royal Botanic Gardens, Kew, London
RCP Lond.	Royal College of Physicians of London
RCS Eng.	Royal College of Surgeons of England, London
RGS	Royal Geographical Society, London
RIBA	Royal Institute of British Architects, London
RIBA BAL	Royal Institute of British Architects, London, British Architectural Library
Royal Arch.	Royal Archives, Windsor Castle, Berkshire [by gracious permission of her majesty the queen]
Royal Irish Acad.	Royal Irish Academy, Dublin
Royal Scot. Acad.	Royal Scottish Academy, Edinburgh
RS	Royal Society, London
RSA	Royal Society of Arts, London
RS Friends, Lond.	Religious Society of Friends, London
St Ant. Oxf.	St Antony's College, Oxford
St John Cam.	St John's College, Cambridge
S. Antiquaries, Lond.	Society of Antiquaries of London
Sci. Mus.	Science Museum, London
Scot. NPG	Scottish National Portrait Gallery, Edinburgh
Scott Polar RI	University of Cambridge, Scott Polar Research Institute
Sheff. Arch.	Sheffield Archives
Shrops. RRC	Shropshire Records and Research Centre, Shrewsbury
SOAS	School of Oriental and African Studies, London
Som. ARS	Somerset Archive and Record Service, Taunton
Staffs. RO	Staffordshire Record Office, Stafford
Suffolk RO	Suffolk Record Office
Surrey HC	Surrey History Centre, Woking
TCD	Trinity College, Dublin
Trinity Cam.	Trinity College, Cambridge
U. Aberdeen	University of Aberdeen
U. Birm.	University of Birmingham
U. Birm. L.	University of Birmingham Library
U. Cal.	University of California
U. Cam.	University of Cambridge
UCL	University College, London
U. Durham	University of Durham
U. Durham L.	University of Durham Library
U. Edin.	University of Edinburgh
U. Edin., New Coll.	University of Edinburgh, New College
U. Edin., New Coll. L.	University of Edinburgh, New College Library
U. Edin. L.	University of Edinburgh Library
U. Glas.	University of Glasgow
U. Glas. L.	University of Glasgow Library
U. Hull	University of Hull
U. Hull, Brynmor Jones L.	University of Hull, Brynmor Jones Library
U. Leeds	University of Leeds
U. Leeds, Brotherton L.	University of Leeds, Brotherton Library
U. Lond.	University of London
U. Lpool	University of Liverpool
U. Lpool L.	University of Liverpool Library
U. Mich.	University of Michigan, Ann Arbor
U. Mich., Clements L.	University of Michigan, Ann Arbor, William L. Clements Library
U. Newcastle	University of Newcastle upon Tyne
U. Newcastle, Robinson L.	University of Newcastle upon Tyne, Robinson Library
U. Nott.	University of Nottingham
U. Nott. L.	University of Nottingham Library
U. Oxf.	University of Oxford
U. Reading	University of Reading
U. Reading L.	University of Reading Library
U. St Andr.	University of St Andrews
U. St Andr. L.	University of St Andrews Library
U. Southampton	University of Southampton
U. Southampton L.	University of Southampton Library
U. Sussex	University of Sussex, Brighton
U. Texas	University of Texas, Austin
U. Wales	University of Wales
U. Warwick Mod. RC	University of Warwick, Coventry, Modern Records Centre
V&A	Victoria and Albert Museum, London
V&A NAL	Victoria and Albert Museum, London, National Art Library
Warks. CRO	Warwickshire County Record Office, Warwick
Wellcome L.	Wellcome Library for the History and Understanding of Medicine, London
Westm. DA	Westminster Diocesan Archives, London
Wilts. & Swindon RO	Wiltshire and Swindon Record Office, Trowbridge
Worcs. RO	Worcestershire Record Office, Worcester
W. Sussex RO	West Sussex Record Office, Chichester
W. Yorks. AS	West Yorkshire Archive Service
Yale U.	Yale University, New Haven, Connecticut
Yale U., Beinecke L.	Yale University, New Haven, Connecticut, Beinecke Rare Book and Manuscript Library
Yale U. CBA	Yale University, New Haven, Connecticut, Yale Center for British Art

3 Bibliographic abbreviations

Adams, *Drama* — W. D. Adams, *A dictionary of the drama*, 1: *A–G* (1904); 2: *H–Z* (1956) [vol. 2 microfilm only]

AFM — J O'Donovan, ed. and trans., *Annala rioghachta Eireann / Annals of the kingdom of Ireland by the four masters*, 7 vols. (1848–51); 2nd edn (1856); 3rd edn (1990)

Allibone, *Dict.* — S. A. Allibone, *A critical dictionary of English literature and British and American authors*, 3 vols. (1859–71); suppl. by J. F. Kirk, 2 vols. (1891)

ANB — J. A. Garraty and M. C. Carnes, eds., *American national biography*, 24 vols. (1999)

Anderson, *Scot. nat.* — W. Anderson, *The Scottish nation, or, The surnames, families, literature, honours, and biographical history of the people of Scotland*, 3 vols. (1859–63)

Ann. mon. — H. R. Luard, ed., *Annales monastici*, 5 vols., Rolls Series, 36 (1864–9)

Ann. Ulster — S. Mac Airt and G. Mac Niocaill, eds., *Annals of Ulster (to AD 1131)* (1983)

APC — *Acts of the privy council of England*, new ser., 46 vols. (1890–1964)

APS — *The acts of the parliaments of Scotland*, 12 vols. in 13 (1814–75)

Arber, *Regs. Stationers* — F. Arber, ed., *A transcript of the registers of the Company of Stationers of London, 1554–1640 AD*, 5 vols. (1875–94)

ArchR — *Architectural Review*

ASC — D. Whitelock, D. C. Douglas, and S. I. Tucker, ed. and trans., *The Anglo-Saxon Chronicle: a revised translation* (1961)

AS chart. — P. H. Sawyer, *Anglo-Saxon charters: an annotated list and bibliography*, Royal Historical Society Guides and Handbooks (1968)

AusDB — D. Pike and others, eds., *Australian dictionary of biography*, 16 vols. (1966–2002)

Baker, *Serjeants* — J. H. Baker, *The order of serjeants at law*, SeldS, suppl. ser., 5 (1984)

Bale, *Cat.* — J. Bale, *Scriptorum illustrium Maioris Brytannie, quam nunc Angliam et Scotiam vocant: catalogus*, 2 vols. in 1 (Basel, 1557–9); facs. edn (1971)

Bale, *Index* — J. Bale, *Index Britanniae scriptorum*, ed. R. L. Poole and M. Bateson (1902); facs. edn (1990)

BBCS — *Bulletin of the Board of Celtic Studies*

BDMBR — J. O. Baylen and N. J. Gossman, eds., *Biographical dictionary of modern British radicals*, 3 vols. in 4 (1979–88)

Bede, *Hist. eccl.* — *Bede's Ecclesiastical history of the English people*, ed. and trans. B. Colgrave and R. A. B. Mynors, OMT (1969); repr. (1991)

Bénézit, *Dict.* — E. Bénézit, *Dictionnaire critique et documentaire des peintres, sculpteurs, dessinateurs et graveurs*, 3 vols. (Paris, 1911–23); new edn, 8 vols. (1948–66), repr. (1966); 3rd edn, rev. and enl., 10 vols. (1976); 4th edn, 14 vols. (1999)

BIHR — *Bulletin of the Institute of Historical Research*

Birch, *Seals* — W. de Birch, *Catalogue of seals in the department of manuscripts in the British Museum*, 6 vols. (1887–1900)

Bishop Burnet's History — *Bishop Burnet's History of his own time*, ed. M. J. Routh, 2nd edn, 6 vols. (1833)

Blackwood — *Blackwood's [Edinburgh] Magazine*, 328 vols. (1817–1980)

Blain, Clements & Grundy, *Feminist comp.* — V. Blain, P. Clements, and I. Grundy, eds., *The feminist companion to literature in English* (1990)

BL cat. — *The British Library general catalogue of printed books* [in 360 vols. with suppls., also CD-ROM and online]

BMJ — *British Medical Journal*

Boase & Courtney, *Bibl. Corn.* — G. C. Boase and W. P. Courtney, *Bibliotheca Cornubiensis: a catalogue of the writings … of Cornishmen*, 3 vols. (1874–82)

Boase, *Mod. Eng. biog.* — F. Boase, *Modern English biography: containing many thousand concise memoirs of persons who have died since the year 1850*, 6 vols. (privately printed, Truro, 1892–1921); repr. (1965)

Boswell, *Life* — *Boswell's Life of Johnson: together with Journal of a tour to the Hebrides and Johnson's Diary of a journey into north Wales*, ed. G. B. Hill, enl. edn, rev. L. F. Powell, 6 vols. (1934–50); 2nd edn (1964); repr. (1971)

Brown & Stratton, *Brit. mus.* — J. D. Brown and S. S. Stratton, *British musical biography* (1897)

Bryan, *Painters* — M. Bryan, *A biographical and critical dictionary of painters and engravers*, 2 vols. (1816); new edn, ed. G. Stanley (1849); new edn, ed. R. E. Graves and W. Armstrong, 2 vols. (1886–9); [4th edn], ed. G. C. Williamson, 5 vols. (1903–5) [various reprs.]

Burke, *Gen. GB* — J. Burke, *A genealogical and heraldic history of the commoners of Great Britain and Ireland*, 4 vols. (1833–8); new edn as *A genealogical and heraldic dictionary of the landed gentry of Great Britain and Ireland*, 3 vols. [1843–9] [many later edns]

Burke, *Gen. Ire.* — J. B. Burke, *A genealogical and heraldic history of the landed gentry of Ireland* (1899); 2nd edn (1904); 3rd edn (1912); 4th edn (1958); 5th edn as *Burke's Irish family records* (1976)

Burke, *Peerage* — J. Burke, *A general* [later edns *A genealogical*] *and heraldic dictionary of the peerage and baronetage of the United Kingdom* [later edns *the British empire*] (1829–)

Burney, *Hist. mus.* — C. Burney, *A general history of music, from the earliest ages to the present period*, 4 vols. (1776–89)

Burtchaell & Sadleir, *Alum. Dubl.* — G. D. Burtchaell and T. U. Sadleir, *Alumni Dublinenses: a register of the students, graduates, and provosts of Trinity College* (1924); [2nd edn], with suppl., in 2 pts (1935)

Calamy rev. — A. G. Matthews, *Calamy revised* (1934); repr. (1988)

CCI — *Calendar of confirmations and inventories granted and given up in the several commissariots of Scotland* (1876–)

CCIR — *Calendar of the close rolls preserved in the Public Record Office*, 47 vols. (1892–1963)

CDS — J. Bain, ed., *Calendar of documents relating to Scotland*, 4 vols., PRO (1881–8); suppl. vol. 5, ed. G. G. Simpson and J. D. Galbraith [1986]

CEPR letters — W. H. Bliss, C. Johnson, and J. Twemlow, eds., *Calendar of entries in the papal registers relating to Great Britain and Ireland: papal letters* (1893–)

CGPLA — *Calendars of the grants of probate and letters of administration* [in 4 ser.: *England & Wales, Northern Ireland, Ireland*, and *Éire*]

Chambers, *Scots.* — R. Chambers, ed., *A biographical dictionary of eminent Scotsmen*, 4 vols. (1832–5)

Chancery records — chancery records pubd by the PRO

Chancery records (RC) — chancery records pubd by the Record Commissions

CIPM	*Calendar of inquisitions post mortem*, [20 vols.], PRO (1904–); also *Henry VII*, 3 vols. (1898–1955)
Clarendon, *Hist. rebellion*	E. Hyde, earl of Clarendon, *The history of the rebellion and civil wars in England*, 6 vols. (1888); repr. (1958) and (1992)
Cobbett, *Parl. hist.*	W. Cobbett and J. Wright, eds., *Cobbett's Parliamentary history of England*, 36 vols. (1806–1820)
Colvin, *Archs.*	H. Colvin, *A biographical dictionary of British architects, 1600–1840*, 3rd edn (1995)
Cooper, *Ath. Cantab.*	C. H. Cooper and T. Cooper, *Athenae Cantabrigienses*, 3 vols. (1858–1913); repr. (1967)
CPR	*Calendar of the patent rolls preserved in the Public Record Office* (1891–)
Crockford	*Crockford's Clerical Directory*
CS	Camden Society
CSP	*Calendar of state papers* [in 11 ser.: *domestic, Scotland, Scottish series, Ireland, colonial, Commonwealth, foreign, Spain* [at Simancas], *Rome, Milan*, and *Venice*]
CYS	Canterbury and York Society
DAB	*Dictionary of American biography*, 21 vols. (1928–36), repr. in 11 vols. (1964); 10 suppls. (1944–96)
DBB	D. J. Jeremy, ed., *Dictionary of business biography*, 5 vols. (1984–6)
DCB	G. W. Brown and others, *Dictionary of Canadian biography*, [14 vols.] (1966–)
Debrett's Peerage	*Debrett's Peerage* (1803–) [sometimes *Debrett's Illustrated peerage*]
Desmond, *Botanists*	R. Desmond, *Dictionary of British and Irish botanists and horticulturists* (1977); rev. edn (1994)
Dir. Brit. archs.	A. Felstead, J. Franklin, and L. Pinfield, eds., *Directory of British architects, 1834–1900* (1993); 2nd edn, ed. A. Brodie and others, 2 vols. (2001)
DLB	J. M. Bellamy and J. Saville, eds., *Dictionary of labour biography*, [10 vols.] (1972–)
DLitB	Dictionary of Literary Biography
DNB	*Dictionary of national biography*, 63 vols. (1885–1900), suppl., 3 vols. (1901); repr. in 22 vols. (1908–9); 10 further suppls. (1912–96); *Missing persons* (1993)
DNZB	W. H. Oliver and C. Orange, eds., *The dictionary of New Zealand biography*, 5 vols. (1990–2000)
DSAB	W. J. de Kock and others, eds., *Dictionary of South African biography*, 5 vols. (1968–87)
DSB	C. C. Gillispie and F. L. Holmes, eds., *Dictionary of scientific biography*, 16 vols. (1970–80); repr. in 8 vols. (1981); 2 vol. suppl. (1990)
DSBB	A. Slaven and S. Checkland, eds., *Dictionary of Scottish business biography, 1860–1960*, 2 vols. (1986–90)
DSCHT	N. M. de S. Cameron and others, eds., *Dictionary of Scottish church history and theology* (1993)
Dugdale, *Monasticon*	W. Dugdale, *Monasticon Anglicanum*, 3 vols. (1655–72); 2nd edn, 3 vols. (1661–82); new edn, ed. J. Caley, J. Ellis, and B. Bandinel, 6 vols. in 8 pts (1817–30); repr. (1846) and (1970)
DWB	J. E. Lloyd and others, eds., *Dictionary of Welsh biography down to 1940* (1959) [Eng. trans. of *Y bywgraffiadur Cymreig hyd 1940*, 2nd edn (1954)]
EdinR	*Edinburgh Review, or, Critical Journal*
EETS	Early English Text Society
Emden, *Cam.*	A. B. Emden, *A biographical register of the University of Cambridge to 1500* (1963)
Emden, *Oxf.*	A. B. Emden, *A biographical register of the University of Oxford to AD 1500*, 3 vols. (1957–9); also *A biographical register of the University of Oxford, AD 1501 to 1540* (1974)
EngHR	*English Historical Review*
Engraved Brit. ports.	F. M. O'Donoghue and H. M. Hake, *Catalogue of engraved British portraits preserved in the department of prints and drawings in the British Museum*, 6 vols. (1908–25)
ER	*The English Reports*, 178 vols. (1900–32)
ESTC	*English short title catalogue, 1475–1800* [CD-ROM and online]
Evelyn, *Diary*	*The diary of John Evelyn*, ed. E. S. De Beer, 6 vols. (1955); repr. (2000)
Farington, *Diary*	*The diary of Joseph Farington*, ed. K. Garlick and others, 17 vols. (1978–98)
Fasti Angl. (Hardy)	J. Le Neve, *Fasti ecclesiae Anglicanae*, ed. T. D. Hardy, 3 vols. (1854)
Fasti Angl., 1066–1300	[J. Le Neve], *Fasti ecclesiae Anglicanae, 1066–1300*, ed. D. E. Greenway and J. S. Barrow, [8 vols.] (1968–)
Fasti Angl., 1300–1541	[J. Le Neve], *Fasti ecclesiae Anglicanae, 1300–1541*, 12 vols. (1962–7)
Fasti Angl., 1541–1857	[J. Le Neve], *Fasti ecclesiae Anglicanae, 1541–1857*, ed. J. M. Horn, D. M. Smith, and D. S. Bailey, [9 vols.] (1969–)
Fasti Scot.	H. Scott, *Fasti ecclesiae Scoticanae*, 3 vols. in 6 (1871); new edn, [11 vols.] (1915–)
FO List	*Foreign Office List*
Fortescue, *Brit. army*	J. W. Fortescue, *A history of the British army*, 13 vols. (1899–1930)
Foss, *Judges*	E. Foss, *The judges of England*, 9 vols. (1848–64); repr. (1966)
Foster, *Alum. Oxon.*	J. Foster, ed., *Alumni Oxonienses: the members of the University of Oxford, 1715–1886*, 4 vols. (1887–8); later edn (1891); also *Alumni Oxonienses … 1500–1714*, 4 vols. (1891–2); 8 vol. repr. (1968) and (2000)
Fuller, *Worthies*	T. Fuller, *The history of the worthies of England*, 4 pts (1662); new edn, 2 vols., ed. J. Nichols (1811); new edn, 3 vols., ed. P. A. Nuttall (1840); repr. (1965)
GEC, *Baronetage*	G. E. Cokayne, *Complete baronetage*, 6 vols. (1900–09); repr. (1983) [microprint]
GEC, *Peerage*	G. E. C. [G. E. Cokayne], *The complete peerage of England, Scotland, Ireland, Great Britain, and the United Kingdom*, 8 vols. (1887–98); new edn, ed. V. Gibbs and others, 14 vols. in 15 (1910–98); microprint repr. (1982) and (1987)
Genest, *Eng. stage*	J. Genest, *Some account of the English stage from the Restoration in 1660 to 1830*, 10 vols. (1832); repr. [New York, 1965]
Gillow, *Lit. biog. hist.*	J. Gillow, *A literary and biographical history or bibliographical dictionary of the English Catholics, from the breach with Rome, in 1534, to the present time*, 5 vols. [1885–1902]; repr. (1961); repr. with preface by C. Gillow (1999)
Gir. Camb. opera	*Giraldi Cambrensis opera*, ed. J. S. Brewer, J. F. Dimock, and G. F. Warner, 8 vols., Rolls Series, 21 (1861–91)
GJ	*Geographical Journal*

Gladstone, *Diaries*   *The Gladstone diaries: with cabinet minutes and prime-ministerial correspondence*, ed. M. R. D. Foot and H. C. G. Matthew, 14 vols. (1968–94)

GM   *Gentleman's Magazine*

Graves, *Artists*   A. Graves, ed., *A dictionary of artists who have exhibited works in the principal London exhibitions of oil paintings from 1760 to 1880* (1884); new edn (1895); 3rd edn (1901); facs. edn (1969); repr. [1970], (1973), and (1984)

Graves, *Brit. Inst.*   A. Graves, *The British Institution, 1806–1867: a complete dictionary of contributors and their work from the foundation of the institution* (1875); facs. edn (1908); repr. (1969)

Graves, *RA exhibitors*   A. Graves, *The Royal Academy of Arts: a complete dictionary of contributors and their work from its foundation in 1769 to 1904*, 8 vols. (1905–6); repr. in 4 vols. (1970) and (1972)

Graves, *Soc. Artists*   A. Graves, *The Society of Artists of Great Britain, 1760–1791, the Free Society of Artists, 1761–1783: a complete dictionary* (1907); facs. edn (1969)

Greaves & Zaller, *BDBR*   R. L. Greaves and R. Zaller, eds., *Biographical dictionary of British radicals in the seventeenth century*, 3 vols. (1982–4)

Grove, *Dict. mus.*   G. Grove, ed., *A dictionary of music and musicians*, 5 vols. (1878–90); 2nd edn, ed. J. A. Fuller Maitland (1904–10); 3rd edn, ed. H. C. Colles (1927); 4th edn with suppl. (1940); 5th edn, ed. E. Blom, 9 vols. (1954); suppl. (1961) [see also *New Grove*]

Hall, *Dramatic ports.*   L. A. Hall, *Catalogue of dramatic portraits in the theatre collection of the Harvard College library*, 4 vols. (1930–34)

Hansard   *Hansard's parliamentary debates*, ser. 1–5 (1803–)

Highfill, Burnim & Langhans, *BDA*   P. H. Highfill, K. A. Burnim, and E. A. Langhans, *A biographical dictionary of actors, actresses, musicians, dancers, managers, and other stage personnel in London, 1660–1800*, 16 vols. (1973–93)

Hist. U. Oxf.   T. H. Aston, ed., *The history of the University of Oxford*, 8 vols. (1984–2000) [1: *The early Oxford schools*, ed. J. I. Catto (1984); 2: *Late medieval Oxford*, ed. J. I. Catto and R. Evans (1992); 3: *The collegiate university*, ed. J. McConica (1986); 4: *Seventeenth-century Oxford*, ed. N. Tyacke (1997); 5: *The eighteenth century*, ed. L. S. Sutherland and L. G. Mitchell (1986); 6–7: *Nineteenth-century Oxford*, ed. M. G. Brock and M. C. Curthoys (1997–2000); 8: *The twentieth century*, ed. B. Harrison (2000)]

HJ   *Historical Journal*

HMC   Historical Manuscripts Commission

Holdsworth, *Eng. law*   W. S. Holdsworth, *A history of English law*, ed. A. L. Goodhart and H. L. Hanbury, 17 vols. (1903–72)

HoP, *Commons*   *The history of parliament: the House of Commons* [1386–1421, ed. J. S. Roskell, L. Clark, and C. Rawcliffe, 4 vols. (1992); 1509–1558, ed. S. T. Bindoff, 3 vols. (1982); 1558–1603, ed. P. W. Hasler, 3 vols. (1981); 1660–1690, ed. B. D. Henning, 3 vols. (1983); 1690–1715, ed. D. W. Hayton, E. Cruickshanks, and S. Handley, 5 vols. (2002); 1715–1754, ed. R. Sedgwick, 2 vols. (1970); 1754–1790, ed. L. Namier and J. Brooke, 3 vols. (1964), repr. (1985); 1790–1820, ed. R. G. Thorne, 5 vols. (1986); in draft (used with permission): 1422–1504, 1604–1629, 1640–1660, and 1820–1832]

IGI   *International Genealogical Index*, Church of Jesus Christ of the Latterday Saints

ILN   *Illustrated London News*

IMC   Irish Manuscripts Commission

Irving, *Scots.*   J. Irving, ed., *The book of Scotsmen eminent for achievements in arms and arts, church and state, law, legislation and literature, commerce, science, travel and philanthropy* (1881)

JCS   *Journal of the Chemical Society*

JHC   *Journals of the House of Commons*

JHL   *Journals of the House of Lords*

John of Worcester, *Chron.*   *The chronicle of John of Worcester*, ed. R. R. Darlington and P. McGurk, trans. J. Bray and P. McGurk, 3 vols., OMT (1995–) [vol. 1 forthcoming]

Keeler, *Long Parliament*   M. F. Keeler, *The Long Parliament, 1640–1641: a biographical study of its members* (1954)

Kelly, *Handbk*   *The upper ten thousand: an alphabetical list of all members of noble families*, 3 vols. (1875–7); continued as *Kelly's handbook of the upper ten thousand for 1878* [1879], 2 vols. (1878–9); continued as *Kelly's handbook to the titled, landed and official classes*, 94 vols. (1880–1973)

LondG   *London Gazette*

LP Henry VIII   J. S. Brewer, J. Gairdner, and R. H. Brodie, eds., *Letters and papers, foreign and domestic, of the reign of Henry VIII*, 23 vols. in 38 (1862–1932); repr. (1965)

Mallalieu, *Watercolour artists*   H. L. Mallalieu, *The dictionary of British watercolour artists up to 1820*, 3 vols. (1976–90); vol. 1, 2nd edn (1986)

Memoirs FRS   *Biographical Memoirs of Fellows of the Royal Society*

MGH   Monumenta Germaniae Historica

MT   *Musical Times*

Munk, *Roll*   W. Munk, *The roll of the Royal College of Physicians of London*, 2 vols. (1861); 2nd edn, 3 vols. (1878)

N&Q   *Notes and Queries*

New Grove   S. Sadie, ed., *The new Grove dictionary of music and musicians*, 20 vols. (1980); 2nd edn, 29 vols. (2001) [also online edn; see also Grove, *Dict. mus.*]

Nichols, *Illustrations*   J. Nichols and J. B. Nichols, *Illustrations of the literary history of the eighteenth century*, 8 vols. (1817–58)

Nichols, *Lit. anecdotes*   J. Nichols, *Literary anecdotes of the eighteenth century*, 9 vols. (1812–16); facs. edn (1966)

Obits. FRS   *Obituary Notices of Fellows of the Royal Society*

O'Byrne, *Naval biog. dict.*   W. R. O'Byrne, *A naval biographical dictionary* (1849); repr. (1990); [2nd edn], 2 vols. (1861)

OHS   Oxford Historical Society

Old Westminsters   *The record of Old Westminsters*, 1–2, ed. G. F. R. Barker and A. H. Stenning (1928); suppl. 1, ed. J. B. Whitmore and G. R. Y. Radcliffe [1938]; 3, ed. J. B. Whitmore, G. R. Y. Radcliffe, and D. C. Simpson (1963); suppl. 2, ed. F. E. Pagan (1978); 4, ed. F. E. Pagan and H. E. Pagan (1992)

OMT   Oxford Medieval Texts

Ordericus Vitalis, *Eccl. hist.*   *The ecclesiastical history of Orderic Vitalis*, ed. and trans. M. Chibnall, 6 vols., OMT (1969–80); repr. (1990)

Paris, *Chron.*   *Matthaei Parisiensis, monachi sancti Albani, chronica majora*, ed. H. R. Luard, Rolls Series, 7 vols. (1872–83)

Parl. papers   *Parliamentary papers* (1801–)

PBA   *Proceedings of the British Academy*

Pepys, *Diary*	*The diary of Samuel Pepys*, ed. R. Latham and W. Matthews, 11 vols. (1970–83); repr. (1995) and (2000)
Pevsner	N. Pevsner and others, Buildings of England series
PICE	*Proceedings of the Institution of Civil Engineers*
Pipe rolls	*The great roll of the pipe for . . .*, PRSoc. (1884–)
PRO	Public Record Office
PRS	*Proceedings of the Royal Society of London*
PRSoc.	Pipe Roll Society
PTRS	*Philosophical Transactions of the Royal Society*
QR	*Quarterly Review*
RC	Record Commissions
Redgrave, *Artists*	S. Redgrave, *A dictionary of artists of the English school* (1874); rev. edn (1878); repr. (1970)
Reg. Oxf.	C. W. Boase and A. Clark, eds., *Register of the University of Oxford*, 5 vols., OHS, 1, 10–12, 14 (1885–9)
Reg. PCS	J. H. Burton and others, eds., *The register of the privy council of Scotland*, 1st ser., 14 vols. (1877–98); 2nd ser., 8 vols. (1899–1908); 3rd ser., [16 vols.] (1908–70)
Reg. RAN	H. W. C. Davis and others, eds., *Regesta regum Anglo-Normannorum, 1066–1154*, 4 vols. (1913–69)
RIBA Journal	*Journal of the Royal Institute of British Architects* [later *RIBA Journal*]
RotP	J. Strachey, ed., *Rotuli parliamentorum ut et petitiones, et placita in parliamento*, 6 vols. (1767–77)
RotS	D. Macpherson, J. Caley, and W. Illingworth, eds., *Rotuli Scotiae in Turri Londinensi et in domo capitulari Westmonasteriensi asservati*, 2 vols., RC, 14 (1814–19)
RS	Record(s) Society
Rymer, *Foedera*	T. Rymer and R. Sanderson, eds., *Foedera, conventiones, literae et cuiuscunque generis acta publica inter reges Angliae et alios quosvis imperatores, reges, pontifices, principes, vel communitates*, 20 vols. (1704–35); 2nd edn, 20 vols. (1726–35); 3rd edn, 10 vols. (1739–45), facs. edn (1967); new edn, ed. A. Clarke, J. Caley, and F. Holbrooke, 4 vols., RC, 50 (1816–30)
Sainty, *Judges*	J. Sainty, ed., *The judges of England, 1272–1990*, SeldS, suppl. ser., 10 (1993)
Sainty, *King's counsel*	J. Sainty, ed., *A list of English law officers and king's counsel*, SeldS, suppl. ser., 7 (1987)
SCH	Studies in Church History
Scots peerage	J. B. Paul, ed. *The Scots peerage, founded on Wood's edition of Sir Robert Douglas's Peerage of Scotland, containing an historical and genealogical account of the nobility of that kingdom*, 9 vols. (1904–14)
SeldS	Selden Society
SHR	*Scottish Historical Review*
State trials	T. B. Howell and T. J. Howell, eds., *Cobbett's Complete collection of state trials*, 34 vols. (1809–28)
STC, 1475–1640	A. W. Pollard, G. R. Redgrave, and others, eds., *A short-title catalogue of . . . English books . . . 1475–1640* (1926); 2nd edn, ed. W. A. Jackson, F. S. Ferguson, and K. F. Pantzer, 3 vols. (1976–91) [see also Wing, *STC*]
STS	Scottish Text Society
SurtS	Surtees Society
Symeon of Durham, *Opera*	*Symeonis monachi opera omnia*, ed. T. Arnold, 2 vols., Rolls Series, 75 (1882–5); repr. (1965)
Tanner, *Bibl. Brit.-Hib.*	T. Tanner, *Bibliotheca Britannico-Hibernica*, ed. D. Wilkins (1748); repr. (1963)
Thieme & Becker, *Allgemeines Lexikon*	U. Thieme, F. Becker, and H. Vollmer, eds., *Allgemeines Lexikon der bildenden Künstler von der Antike bis zur Gegenwart*, 37 vols. (Leipzig, 1907–50); repr. (1961–5), (1983), and (1992)
Thurloe, *State papers*	*A collection of the state papers of John Thurloe*, ed. T. Birch, 7 vols. (1742)
TLS	*Times Literary Supplement*
Tout, *Admin. hist.*	T. F. Tout, *Chapters in the administrative history of mediaeval England: the wardrobe, the chamber, and the small seals*, 6 vols. (1920–33); repr. (1967)
TRHS	*Transactions of the Royal Historical Society*
VCH	H. A. Doubleday and others, eds., *The Victoria history of the counties of England*, [88 vols.] (1900–)
Venn, *Alum. Cant.*	J. Venn and J. A. Venn, *Alumni Cantabrigienses: a biographical list of all known students, graduates, and holders of office at the University of Cambridge, from the earliest times to 1900*, 10 vols. (1922–54); repr. in 2 vols. (1974–8)
Vertue, *Note books*	[G. Vertue], *Note books*, ed. K. Esdaile, earl of Ilchester, and H. M. Hake, 6 vols., Walpole Society, 18, 20, 22, 24, 26, 30 (1930–55)
VF	*Vanity Fair*
Walford, *County families*	E. Walford, *The county families of the United Kingdom, or, Royal manual of the titled and untitled aristocracy of Great Britain and Ireland* (1860)
Walker rev.	A. G. Matthews, *Walker revised: being a revision of John Walker's Sufferings of the clergy during the grand rebellion, 1642–60* (1948); repr. (1988)
Walpole, *Corr.*	*The Yale edition of Horace Walpole's correspondence*, ed. W. S. Lewis, 48 vols. (1937–83)
Ward, *Men of the reign*	T. H. Ward, ed., *Men of the reign: a biographical dictionary of eminent persons of British and colonial birth who have died during the reign of Queen Victoria* (1885); repr. (Graz, 1968)
Waterhouse, *18c painters*	E. Waterhouse, *The dictionary of 18th century painters in oils and crayons* (1981); repr. as *British 18th century painters in oils and crayons* (1991), vol. 2 of *Dictionary of British art*
Watt, *Bibl. Brit.*	R. Watt, *Bibliotheca Britannica, or, A general index to British and foreign literature*, 4 vols. (1824) [many reprs.]
Wellesley index	W. E. Houghton, ed., *The Wellesley index to Victorian periodicals, 1824–1900*, 5 vols. (1966–89); new edn (1999) [CD-ROM]
Wing, *STC*	D. Wing, ed., *Short-title catalogue of . . . English books . . . 1641–1700*, 3 vols. (1945–51); 2nd edn (1972–88); rev. and enl. edn, ed. J. J. Morrison, C. W. Nelson, and M. Seccombe, 4 vols. (1994–8) [see also *STC, 1475–1640*]
Wisden	*John Wisden's Cricketer's Almanack*
Wood, *Ath. Oxon.*	A. Wood, *Athenae Oxonienses . . . to which are added the Fasti*, 2 vols. (1691–2); 2nd edn (1721); new edn, 4 vols., ed. P. Bliss (1813–20); repr. (1967) and (1969)
Wood, *Vic. painters*	C. Wood, *Dictionary of Victorian painters* (1971); 2nd edn (1978); 3rd edn as *Victorian painters*, 2 vols. (1995), vol. 4 of *Dictionary of British art*
WW	*Who's who* (1849–)
WWBMP	M. Stenton and S. Lees, eds., *Who's who of British members of parliament*, 4 vols. (1976–81)
WWW	*Who was who* (1929–)

Rowell, George Augustus (1804–1892), meteorologist, was born at Oxford on 16 May 1804, the son of George Rowell (d. 1834), formerly of Newcastle upon Tyne. Before his tenth birthday Rowell was taken from school to assist his grandfather, a cabinet-maker; this trade Rowell himself followed for some years, but subsequently relinquished it for that of a paperhanger. Rowell's father instilled in him a passion for meteorology, and during the appearance of the comet of 1811 gave his son nightly lessons on the comet and on the apparent motion of the circumpolar stars. From his mother he received his first lessons on the cause of eclipses and on other astronomical subjects. He was specially attracted to thunderstorms and the aurora, but had little opportunity to study these subjects in books, apart from Richard Lovett's *Philosophical Essays* (1766), which dealt with electrical phenomena. He married at St Giles', Oxford, on 9 August 1829, Maria Barrett. A daughter, Elizabeth, was born in 1830; the couple had at least one other child, a son.

In 1838 Rowell attended a lecture by Professor Baden Powell and afterwards spoke to him of a theory he had worked out as to the cause of rain. Powell advised him to write down his ideas; his paper was read before the Ashmolean Society, and was published in the society's *Proceedings* for 1839. In the following year a similar paper was read by Rowell before the British Association at Glasgow, and was published in their reports. From this date Rowell published many papers and sent letters to the *Oxford Times* on meteorological subjects; his *Essay on the Cause of Rain* (1859) was well received. Rowell was appointed assistant in the Ashmolean Museum, and when the Oxford University Museum opened in 1860 he transferred to a similar position in that institution.

In middle life Rowell abandoned his studies and burned his manuscripts, from an unfounded belief that his lowly position hindered his scientific progress. But when the American professor Elias Loomis put forward a theory respecting the aurora which he considered identical with that published by himself in 1839, he issued several pamphlets drawing attention to his past work, and arguing that it was the duty of the university and of Oxford scientific men publicly to recognize his contention. In 1876 he refused an annuity voted to him the previous year by the university in consideration of his services and his scientific attainments, because his theories were still being ignored, largely because by this time the science of meteorology had advanced, leaving Rowell to hold to the outmoded ideas of his youth. He interested himself in the affairs of his native city, and was regarded as an authority on all questions relating to water supply and drainage. He died at 18 Juxon Street, Oxford on 24 January 1892.

J. B. BAILEY, rev. ANITA McCONNELL

Sources *The Athenaeum* (6 Feb 1892), 186 · Boase, *Mod. Eng. biog.* · G. A. Rowell, *Letters of meteorological phenomena* (1875–8) · G. A. Rowell, *Electrical meteorology* (1887) · d. cert.
Archives MHS Oxf., notebook relating to Ashmole | University of Lancaster, Ruskin Library, letters to John Ruskin

Rowland, Alexander (1747/8–1823). *See under* Rowland, Alexander (*bap.* 1783, *d.* 1854).

Rowland, Alexander (*bap.* 1783, *d.* 1854), perfumer, was baptized in Holborn, London, on 18 June 1783, the son of **Alexander Rowland** (1747/8–1823), perfumer. The elder Alexander Rowland was born in Holborn, the younger son of William Rowland, of the Cordwainers' Company, and his wife, Elizabeth, formerly Jones; he was apprenticed in 1763 to Mary Withybed, barber, of Snow Hill, Holborn, and joined the Barbers' Company when free of his indentures in 1770. He then ran a hairdressing establishment next to the Thatched House tavern in St James's Street, where he charged what was then the exorbitant sum of 5s. for a haircut. About 1780 he married, his wife's name being Mary; they had two sons and two daughters.

It was then not uncommon for a well-connected barber to start making his own hair preparations, and about 1793 Rowland senior offered for sale Rowland's Macassar Oil, an 'elegant, fragrant and pellucid oil' of vegetable composition. His son later stated that a relative living on the island of Celebes in the Dutch East Indies had helped by procuring the basic ingredient, which was extracted from the seeds of various species of trees near Macassar. Within two decades the oil had become hugely popular. In the first canto of *Don Juan* (1812), George Gordon, sixth Baron Byron, worked in a topical gag about the '"incomparable oil", Macassar!' Two years later the tsar of Russia was reputed to have asked for 10 guineas' worth to be sent without delay via the Foreign Office.

Rowland was by then diversifying, for example into the skin preparation Kalydor, made with oriental 'exotics', Odonto, a white, fragrant tooth powder, and Alsana extract to relieve toothache, flatulence, and spasms. His wife having died, in 1820 he married Sarah Slade, a childless widow. Rowland died at his home in Lewisham on 16 December 1823.

Rowland's elder son, Alexander, joined the firm at an early age. About 1807 he married Elizabeth (1778–1850); in addition to a son, Alexander William (b. 1808), they had several daughters. In 1816 Rowland was admitted to the livery of the Barbers' Company. More publicity-conscious than his father, he recognized that in the era of the dandy, his firm had to strive to bring perfection to gentlemen's faces and hair. However, for all its pellucidity, the oil stained the backs of padded chairs, thus leading to the widespread introduction of antimacassars to protect the upholstery.

In 1809 the younger Rowland published *An Essay on the Cultivation and Improvement of the Hair*, its puffing intention being made clear from the subtitle about the virtues of the Macassar oil. He followed this with a number of works on similar themes. By the 1840s he was widely claiming that the oil was being used by the royal family and nobility of England, as well as by several sovereigns and courts in Europe. The queen's patronage was boldly proclaimed on the double-fronted Macassar Oil and Kalydor Warehouse at 20 Hatton Garden.

In contrast with his father, Rowland actively participated in the affairs of the Barbers' Company, joining the court of assessors in 1845 and becoming master in 1851. He died in 1854, by which time his firm was spending £10,000 a year on advertising, one of the largest outlays in the country after that of Thomas Holloway. Alexander William took over the business, to be succeeded in due course by his son Alexander Frederick(*b.* 1841). In 1942 Alexander Rowland & Sons Ltd was acquired by Philip Ernest Hill and became a subsidiary of Beechams Pills Ltd.

T. A. B. CORLEY

Sources Boase, *Mod. Eng. biog.* · C. Hemstreet and M. Hemstreet, *Nooks and corners of old London* (1910), 157–8 · private information (1996) · *GM*, 1st ser., 94/1 (1824), 94 · *GM*, 2nd ser., 34 (1850), 561 · *GM*, 2nd ser., 35 (1851), 684 · parish register, Holborn, St Andrew's, 1820 [Alexander Rowland (1747/8–1823) and Sarah Slade; marriage] · parish register, Holborn, St Andrew's, June 1747 [baptism] · parish register, Holborn, St Andrew's, 18 June 1783 [baptism] · *The Times* (19 Dec 1823) [Alexander Rowland (1747/8–1823)]

Wealth at death £6000—Alexander Rowland (1747/8–1823): will, PRO

Rowland, Daniel (1711?–1790), Church of England clergyman and Methodist preacher, was born at Pantybeudy in the Cardiganshire village of Nancwnlle, the younger son of Daniel Rowland (*c.*1659–1731), rector of Llangeitho, and his wife, Janet (*d.* 1736), daughter of a local farmer, Rhys Thomas of Wenallt. There is some doubt regarding his date of birth. For many years historians advocated the year 1713, but contemporary testimony indicates 1711, a date which would mean that he was twenty-three in 1734, the age requirement for ordination.

Rowland is believed to have received his preliminary education at the Revd John Pugh's school near Llannarth in Cardiganshire, where he gained a sufficient grounding to enable him to spend some time at Hereford grammar school. He was ordained deacon by the bishop of St David's on 10 March 1734. He was installed as curate at Llangeitho and Nancwnlle, and in the same year married Elinor Davies (*d.* 1792) of Caerllugest, near Llangeitho: they had seven children, including a son, Nathaniel, who became leader of the Welsh Methodists after his father's demise. Rowland remained in these curacies for many years, serving under his brother, John Rowland, and subsequently under his own son, John.

During the year 1735 Rowland was ordained priest and underwent a spiritual conversion that was to transform his life. Tradition has it that he experienced this conversion as a result of hearing a sermon by Griffith Jones, Llanddowror, at Llanddewibrefi church. After this, the whole tenor of his ministry changed and he became known as the 'angry cleric' as a result of his vigorous chastisement of sinners (Owen, *Coffhad am y parch*, 17–18). In his elegy, William Williams hailed him as Boanerges, the son of thunder (N. C. Jones, 1.582). Under the guidance of the neighbouring dissenting minister Phylip Pugh he softened this message somewhat to include a greater emphasis on the prospect of salvation through Christ's redemption. Under his ministry Llangeitho became a centre for pilgrimage for Methodists throughout Wales, who would journey for miles to hear his services and to receive communion from his hands.

In 1737 Rowland met Howel *Harris for the first time, and this meeting marked the foundation of the Methodist

Daniel Rowland (1711?–1790), by Robert Bowyer, 1790

movement in Wales. Although they were united by their common concern to save souls, the two men possessed vastly different personalities. Despite the seriousness of his commitment to his calling, Rowland could also be relaxed and good-humoured. There were times when this lighter side to his personality proved irksome to Harris, who reproached Rowland for unbecoming levity. The tension between them became acute with the establishment of the Association, the governing body of the movement, in 1743. George Whitefield was appointed as moderator of the Association, possibly to avoid the necessity of promoting either Daniel Rowland or Howel Harris to the superior position. By the late 1740s Rowland and many of the Methodist exhorters found it increasingly difficult to tolerate both Harris's questionable doctrine and his relationship with Madam Sidney *Griffith. The final split between the two men came in 1750, with the bulk of the exhorters siding with Rowland, who thus became the effective leader of Welsh Methodism. With the support of William Williams he contrived to sustain the movement throughout the difficult years of division, and when revival broke out anew in 1762 it was significant that it was centred on his parish of Llangeitho.

Compared to Howel Harris, who left a mass of documentation behind, relatively little is known about Rowland's life and work. His papers were unfortunately lost after being sent to the countess of Huntingdon, who wished to commission a biography. Evidence suggests, however, that he had been establishing Methodist societies in the vicinity of Llangeitho at the same time as Harris was beginning his endeavours in Brecknockshire. He lacked

Harris's organizational skills, and his care for his parishioners restricted his ability to travel extensively. Yet he did not confine himself solely to his parish, but frequently ventured out on preaching tours. He preferred to concentrate his efforts on Wales and never forged such close links with Methodists elsewhere as Harris did. Nevertheless it was through the countess of Huntingdon's intercession that he was appointed chaplain to the duke of Leinster.

In the early years of the revival, in particular, Rowland composed a number of hymns, before bowing to William Williams's superior talent in that respect. His published works include several collections of his sermons and translations of religious and moral works by English authors. Among his original prose works is *Ymddiddan rhwng Methodist uniongred ac un camsyniol* (1749), a dialogue in which an orthodox Methodist repudiates the unsound notions held by Howel Harris.

There is little doubt that Rowland was held in great affection by Methodist converts the length and breadth of Wales. He was deprived of his curacies in 1763 when he refused to give an undertaking that he would limit his itinerant preaching. In order to retain his services, his parishioners built a chapel for his use at Llangeitho, which was invariably full to overflowing on communion Sundays. The vigour of his oratory and commitment to the Methodist cause remained unabated during his final years. He died on 16 October 1790 at Llangeitho and was buried on 20 October at Llangeitho church. Along with Howel Harris and William Williams, Rowland was one of the leaders of the eighteenth-century Methodist revival in Wales.

ERYN M. WHITE

Sources Trefeca papers, NL Wales, Calvinist Methodist archive · E. Evans, *Daniel Rowland and the great evangelical awakening in Wales* (1985) · D. Ll. Morgan, *Y diwygiad mawr* (1981); trans. D. Morgan as *The great awakening in Wales* (1988) · D. J. O. Jones, *Daniel Rowland, Llangeitho (1713–1790)* (1938) · G. M. Roberts, ed., *Hanes Methodistiaeth Galfinaidd Cymru*, 1 (1973) · J. Owen, *A memoir of Daniel Rowlands of Llangeitho* (1848) · J. Owen, *Coffhad am y Parch. Daniel Rowlands* (1839) · G. M. Roberts, ed., *Hanes Methodistiaeth Galfinaidd Cymru*, 2 (1978) · G. M. Roberts, 'Daniel Rowland's ordination', *Journal of the Historical Society of the Presbyterian Church of Wales*, 20 (1935), 155–6 · E. Evans, 'Daniel Rowland', *Cwmwl o dystion*, ed. E. Wyn James (1977), 60–67 · E. M. White, *'Praidd bach y bugail mawr': seiadau Methodistaidd de-orllewin Cymru, 1737–50* (1995) · J. Hughes, *Methodistiaeth Cymru*, 1 (1851) · J. Hughes, *Methodistiaeth Cymru*, 2 (1854) · J. Hughes, *Methodistiaeth Cymru*, 3 (1856) · *Gweithiau Williams Pant-y-celyn*, ed. N. C. Jones, 1 (1887)
Archives NL Wales, Calvinist Methodist archive, letters
Likenesses R. Bowyer, miniature, 1790, NL Wales [*see illus.*] · E. Griffith, statue on monument, 1883, outside chapel, Llangeitho; photographs, NL Wales · line engraving, repro. in *Gospel Magazine* (July 1778)
Wealth at death £250: inventory with wife's will, proved 14 Aug 1792, NL Wales, probate index, St David's and Cardigan

Rowland, Daniel (1778–1859), antiquary, born at Shrewsbury on 11 July 1778, was the second surviving son of John Rowland or Rowlands (*d.* 1815), rector of Llangeitho, Cardiganshire, and incumbent of Clive, Shropshire, and Mary, daughter of William Gorsuch, vicar of the Abbey parish, Shrewsbury. His paternal grandfather was Daniel *Rowland. William Gorsuch Rowland (*d.* 1851), his eldest

brother, was prebendary of Lichfield and incumbent of St Mary's, Shrewsbury.

Educated at Shrewsbury School, Daniel Rowland practised for some years as a barrister in London before moving to Frant in Sussex, where he built Saxonbury Lodge in medieval style. He devoted his leisure to literature, the fine arts, and philanthropy. At Shrewsbury he built and endowed in 1853, at a cost of over £4000, the Hospital of the Holy Cross, for five poor women. In 1846 he returned to London, settling at 28 Grosvenor Place. A fellow of the Society of Antiquaries, Rowland published a genealogical history of the Nevills of Abergavenny (1830) and an updated edition of G. B. Blakeway's *Sheriffs of Shropshire* (1831). He married, in 1818, Katherine Erskine, daughter of Pelham Maitland of Belmont, near Edinburgh. She died on 10 December 1829, leaving no children. Rowland died at Clifton, near Bristol, on 20 October 1859, and was buried in the crypt of the Foundling Hospital chapel, Guilford Street, London, of which he had been a governor.

G. Le G. NORGATE, *rev.* G. MARTIN MURPHY

Sources *GM*, 3rd ser., 8 (1860), 85–6 · M. A. Lower, *A compendious history of Sussex*, 1 (1870), 192
Wealth at death under £12,000: probate, 1 Dec 1859, *CGPLA Eng. & Wales*

Rowland, David (*fl.* 1568–1576), author and translator, who refers to himself as 'David Rowland of Anglesey', and may have been a scion of the family of Wynne of Penhesgyn Isaf, Llansadwrn, near Beaumaris. Wood states that he was educated at St Mary Hall, Oxford, but he may be identifiable with the Dominus Rowlande teaching at Corpus Christi College in 1562 (*Reg. Oxf.*, vol. 2, pt 2, p. 7). Rowland became tutor to Charles Stewart, son of the earl of Lennox, and travelled in France and Spain, obtaining some knowledge of modern languages.

Rowland's *Comfortable Ayde for Scholers* (1568; repr. 1578), dedicated to the earl of Lennox, is a collection of various English phrases rendered in Latin. Though the volume is a modified translation of Giovanni Andrea Grifoni's *Specchio della lingua latina* (Venice, 1551), schoolbooks on the principle of the phraseologia are rare before 1600 and the work represents a novel approach to teaching for its time.

In 1569 Rowland published *An Epytaphe of my Lord of Pembroke*, which does not appear to have survived, but his chief work was *The pleasant history of Lazarillo de Tormes, wherein is contained his marvellous deeds and life* (1576), a lively and colourful translation of the anonymous Spanish novel, *La vida de Lazarillo de Tormes*, which first appeared in 1554. Rowland dedicated the work to Sir Thomas Gresham, in whose Antwerp office he may have been employed for a time.

Of seminal importance in modern Western prose fiction, the original Spanish work became enormously popular and was speedily published in all the major western European languages. Rowland's English version, which was particularly influenced by Jean Saugrain's 1560 French translation, helped to propagate *Lazarillo*'s influence on English letters, and numerous reprints are testament to its own popularity. The influence of Rowland's version has been conjectured in Spenser's *Mother Hubberd's Tale* and was felt on the stage: echoes of it have been heard in Shakespeare's *Love's Labours Lost* and *Much Ado about Nothing*. In addition, as the earliest example of the picaresque genre in this language, it assisted at the birth of the early modern novel in English.

Lack of evidence for Rowland's life has led to controversy over his identity. While an attempt has been made to identify him with Richard Verstegan (formerly Rowlands), this appears implausible on account of the latter's Catholicism and the protestant stance of David Rowland.

ROSS KENNEDY

Sources Wood, *Ath. Oxon.*, new edn, 1.528 · D. Rowland, trans., *The pleasaunt historie of Lazarillo de Tormes*, ed. J. E. V. Crofts (1924) · Tanner, *Bibl. Brit.-Hib.*, 645 · W. C. Hazlitt, *Hand-book to the popular, poetical and dramatic literature of Great Britain* (1867), 387–8 · W. C. Hazlitt, *Collections and notes, 1867–1876* (1876), 492 · D. Rowland, *A comfortable ayde for scholers*, ed. R. C. Alston (1968) · *Reg. Oxf.* · G. A. Davies, 'David Rowland's *Lazarillo de Tormes* (1576): the history of a translation', *National Library of Wales Journal*, 28 (1993–4), 349–87 · D. Rowland, trans., *The life of Lazarillo de Tormes / La vida de Lazarillo de Tormes*, ed. K. Whitlock (2000)

Rowland, John (1605/6–1680), Church of England clergyman and author, was a native of Bedfordshire. He matriculated, aged fifteen, from Corpus Christi College, Oxford, in November 1621, graduated BA on 22 November 1622, and proceeded MA on 28 March 1626. In 1631 he was presented to the living at East Marsey, perhaps East Mersea, Essex. He was married twice; on 8 August 1634 Rowland as a widower received a licence to marry Ann, daughter of George Holt of Foots Cray, near Dartford, Kent, clergyman. That year he became rector of Foots Cray. By 1641 Rowland was a chaplain to Sir Jacob Astley's regiment, mobilized to fight the Scots. In a petition of 1660 he claimed to have been ejected from his rectory in 1642 and on 28 July 1643 the House of Commons sequestered his estate as a result of his complicity in the Kentish rising. According to the preface of *Pro rege*, Rowland left England for the Netherlands and began writing; in 1646 his successor at Foots Cray alleged that Rowland's wife had also gone overseas.

Through his major tracts Rowland contributed to the defence of the Church of England against puritan and dissenting voices before and after the Restoration. In 1651 he published anonymously *Pro rege et populo Anglicano apologia contra Johannis Polypragmatici (alias Miltoni Angli) defensionem destructivam regis et populi Anglicani* in response to Milton's *Defensio pro populo Anglicano* against Salmasius, the pseudonym for a group of Anglican clergy. Contemporary rumour made Joseph Jane or John Bramhall the author of this piece. In the tract Rowland exalted Salmasius and attacked Milton on several points of his *Defensio*. *Pro rege* was reprinted twice in 1652. When Milton's nephew John Phillips counter-attacked in print, Rowland issued from Antwerp a response, *Polemica sive supplementum ad apologiam anonymam pro rege etc. per Jo. Rolandum pastorem Anglicanum* (1653). In this piece Rowland claimed authorship of *Pro rege* and attacked Milton and Phillips for crediting Bramhall with the work. Surprisingly, later in the decade he published an elegy for Oliver Cromwell, *Upon the much lamented departure of the high and mighty prince, Oliver lord protector of England, Scotland and Ireland, &c.* (1658), and under Sir Robert Cotton's name, *A Choice Narrative of Count Gondamor's Transactions during his Embassy in England* (1659), an edited version of Thomas Scott's *Vox populi*.

At the Restoration Rowland re-established his credentials with *His Sacred Majesty Charles the II: his Royal Title Anagramatiz'd* (dated 22 May 1660) and *In honor of the Lord General Monck, and Thomas Allen lord major of London, for their great valour, loyalty, and prudence* (1660), both poems praising General Monck and Thomas Allen, the first in the anagram and the second in a more straightforward manner. The same year he defended John Gauden's *Analysis: the loosing of Saint Peter's bands, setting forth the true sense and solution of the covenant in point of conscience* against Zachary Crofton and the anonymous tract *The Anatomy of Dr. Gauden's Idolized Non-Sense and Blasphemy, in his Pretended Analysis* (1660) in *A Reply to the Answer of Anonymous to Doctor Gauden's Analysis of the Sense of the Covenant* (1660). Rowland's reply, written in English unlike his earlier religious materials, presents Gauden's arguments as he understands them and ridicules Crofton and the anonymous tract's criticisms. His *Saint Peter's General Petition to our Saviour, for himself and his Fellow Sufferers* (1661), a sermon on Matthew 19: 27, stated the royalist demand for rewards and preferments. Rowland had regained possession of his living the previous year; his interregnum replacement was mentioned in a letter of July 1661 as having been 'by the old debauched Vicar turned a grasing' (*Walker rev.*, 225). Rowland retained Foots Cray until his death in 1680.

JOANNA T. NEILSON

Sources Foster, *Alum. Oxon.* · *Walker rev.*, 224–5 · *CSP dom.*, 1675–6, 478 · T. D. Hardy, *Syllabus, in English, of the documents relating to England and other kingdoms contained in the collection known as 'Rymer's Foedera'*, 3 vols., PRO, 76 (1869–85) · B. Lewalski, *Life of John Milton: a critical biography* (2000) · W. R. Parker, *Milton's contemporary reputation* (1940) · W. R. Parker, *Milton: a biography*, 2 vols. (1968) · *DNB*

Rowland [*formerly* Fuhrhop], **Roland Walter** [Tiny] (1917–1998), financier, was born on 27 November 1917 at the Belgaum detention camp, Simla, India, an internment centre for enemy aliens, the third and youngest son of Wilhelm Fuhrhop, later William Frederick Rowland (1885–1974), a Hamburg-born merchant, and his Anglo-Dutch wife, Muriel, *née* Kauenhoven (1883–1944). After the war his family was initially refused entry to Britain, and instead settled in Hamburg.

Germany and England Fuhrhop was educated at Heinrich Herz Real Gymnasium, Hamburg. A big blond sportsman of robust charm, he enlisted in the Hitler Youth during the early 1930s, and served as a troop leader. Nevertheless his father's anti-Nazi sentiments led the family to leave Germany, and this time they were successful in settling in England. Roland Fuhrhop was then educated at Churchers College, Petersfield, for a year. He developed a cutglass English accent and governing-class mannerisms, although his first employer was a haulage company in Bethnal Green Road specializing in freight to and from Germany. Even in this period his dress-sense was immaculate. He repudiated his German passport and changed his

Roland Walter [Tiny] **Rowland** (1917–1998), by Jane Bown, 1981

name by deed poll to Roland Walter Rowland in October 1939. From boyhood he had been nicknamed Tiny, and he always preferred to use this sobriquet, even in official business correspondence.

Rowland was conscripted into the British army in December 1939 and assigned to the Royal Army Medical Corps in Scotland. His devotion to his mother had always been pronounced, and after she became seriously ill he went absent without leave to visit her. As a result, in 1941 he spent twenty-seven days in Glasgow's Barlinnie prison, where he was brutally treated. His parents were interned on the Isle of Man during the war and, being suspected of pro-German sympathies, Rowland was discharged from the army in 1942. Subsequently he was detained under regulation 18B on the Isle of Man, where he remained until after his mother's death. These harsh experiences, including his mother's treatment when she was dying of cancer, may have contributed to his contempt for British financial and political institutions. The prejudice against his background was persistent. Margaret Thatcher, explaining in 1987 the mutual antipathy between them, said, 'Of course, he's not English' (Wyatt, 1.306).

After leaving the Isle of Man Rowland was compelled to accept work ordained by the labour exchange as a porter at Paddington railway station. Soon he was living in Mayfair, working as a taxi driver, and operating as a spiv supplying scarce luxuries including lipstick and oranges. In

1946 he began trading in army surplus material, chiefly iron and scissors, and in 1947 started a company producing domestic refrigerators. After an initially profitable phase the business collapsed with heavy tax liabilities.

Rhodesia and Lonrho Rowland moved to Southern Rhodesia in 1948, and bought a tobacco farm and truck store at Eiffel Flats, on the main road between Salisbury and Bulawayo. Although he had the accoutrements of a prosperous man, these were frustrating years. From 1952 he lived with Irene Smith (*b.* 1912?), the wife of his business partner; it was a difficult relationship, which he left in 1963. Farming in Rhodesia did not stretch him, and he acquired the Rhodesian franchise for Mercedes Benz cars, two dubious goldmines, and an option to build an oil pipeline from the Mozambique port of Beira to Umtali in Rhodesia. These were consolidated in a holding company, Shepton Estates.

In 1961 a Scottish nobleman, Angus Ogilvy, was sent to Salisbury to revive the London and Rhodesia Mining and Land Company (L & R); formed in 1909, it had once been the most valuable company in Rhodesia. After a long decline it had come under the control of the London financier Harley Drayton. Rowland, a beguiling negotiator, convinced Ogilvy that L & R should acquire Shepton Estates. He was lavishly rewarded with 1.5 million L & R shares plus an option on a further 2 million. Rowland also became joint managing director of L & R, which subsequently changed its name to Lonrho. This arrangement was a personal masterstroke for Rowland, who in the next thirty years earned over £100 million from Lonrho in salary and dividends.

The company began building Rowland's pipeline from Beira to Umtali in 1962. Mistrusting the racial and economic policies of Southern Rhodesia well before its unilateral declaration of independence in 1965, Rowland extended Lonrho's ramifications. At a time when other white investors could see only uncertainties in postcolonial Africa, he realized that Lonrho could acquire promising assets at discounted prices. Its campaign of diversified investments began in Nyasaland in 1962. During the mid-1960s Zambia became crucial to the company's expansion. Kenneth Kaunda of Zambia, Daniel arap Moi of Kenya, and Hastings Banda of Malawi were among the African presidents who became Rowland's business allies. A major step in Lonrho's accumulating value was its acquisition in 1968 of a fifty-year lease on the Asante goldmines in Ghana. By 1970 Lonrho had assets of £198 million, with over 100,000 employees in twenty-nine countries, but debts of £117 million. Pre-tax profits were nearly £20 million by 1973 and £180 million by 1980. Its diverse interests included mines, factories, motor-car distributorships throughout Africa, hotels, trading businesses, and farms. Lonrho became the biggest food producer in Africa. Rowland travelled the continent in the company's own jet aircraft seeking or clinching deals. The hectic schedules did not seem to weary him. His fastidiousness about his own clothes, food, and drink did not extend into the corrupt, menacing, and volatile world of African business. Huge bribes were paid. Latterly he was said always to have travelled with a locked case containing £100,000 in cash for immediate expenses.

On 1 July 1968 Rowland married Josie Taylor (*b.* 1944), daughter of Lionel Taylor, who had been his farm manager in Rhodesia. He had met her when she was a little child, and had been a protective presence throughout her girlhood: reputedly he partly paid for her education. Despite unconventional elements in his courtship, he proved an exemplary husband. They had a son and three daughters.

Challenges The oil embargo imposed by the Wilson government on Rhodesia was a sham, and Tiny Rowland's remonstrations on the subject led to friction between Lonrho and the Foreign Office from 1967. He regarded United Nations sanctions against Rhodesia as both hypocritical and unenforceable: Lonrho circumvented them. The company's reputation was further injured when several of its executives were accused in South Africa of fraud over the Inyati copper mine in Rhodesia (1971–3). However, he retained the respect of black African leaders, including Nelson Mandela, while Lonrho developed large mining investments in South Africa under the Afrikaner regime.

A secretive, ruthless, and self-confident man, Rowland's consultations of board colleagues before taking big decisions were desultory or non-existent. Non-executive directors he likened to Christmas-tree decorations. He was a deal-maker, with a compelling desire to expand the business, who scoffed at the disciplined precision of accountants. The management, financial controls, and return on investment of some of the company's African interests were shoddy. In 1971, when the speed of Lonrho's expansion had strained its finances, Rowland acquired the rights to the Wankel rotary engine for the equivalent of £12 million. Most of his directors were unaware of the negotiations, and Sir Siegmund Warburg instructed his merchant bank to resign as Lonrho's financial advisers. Two directors resigned in protest, too. One of them subsequently described Rowland to Department of Trade and Industry (DTI) inspectors as:

> a man who had completely converted what was a sleep dozy company into something dynamic and who was a sort of tyrant and part madman to boot, but a brilliant one, and whose tyranny and madness had not become completely evident, and who was extremely persuasive.   (Bower, 281)

In 1972 the accountants Peat Marwick delivered a 1566 page report on Lonrho which revealed the company's poor performance. Rowland was obliged to accept outside directors, including a deputy chairman suggested by the Bank of England, Sir Basil Smallpeice. The views of Rowland and Smallpeice quickly proved irreconcilable, and after much unpleasantness, during a period when Lonrho's debts were escalating, a crisis occurred after the revelation of covert financial arrangements to benefit the chairman, Duncan Sandys. In 1973 eight directors led by Smallpeice struggled to remove Rowland as chief executive. Heavily publicized litigation revealed the payments to Sandys, which had been channelled through the Cayman Islands. This tax avoidance device was denounced in May 1973 by the prime minister, Edward Heath, who had long shown animosity against Sandys, in a phrase which forever tarnished Rowland's reputation, as the 'unpleasant and unacceptable face of capitalism' (Bower, 252). However, Rowland outmanoeuvred his critics and ultimately vanquished them at Lonrho's annual general meeting. The company's managerial idiosyncrasies and commitments in Africa meant that institutional investors had shunned it since 1971. Consequently, aside from Rowland's 20 per cent holding, the shares belonged to small investors, who showed ardent loyalty to him. He rallied them to defeat his critics, and thereafter ensured that Lonrho's directors were unable to challenge his prerogatives or question his obsessions. He was fiercely loyal to friends, but unforgiving if they failed him.

In the aftermath of the crisis of 1972–3 Kuwaiti and other groups invested in Lonrho. DTI inspectors began a long investigation of the company, paying undue attention to Lonrho's subsidies of Rowland's domestic life. In 1967, shortly before his marriage, the company bought a house for him at Hedsor Wharf on the Thames: Bourne End was a gabled brick eighteenth-century cottage which had been enlarged by Lord Boston in 1925. At Rowland's instructions the building was extended and remodelled in undistinguished neo-Georgian style in 1969–71, and the grounds extensively improved, at a total cost of £323,589. The DTI report, which was published in 1976, unsurprisingly proved hostile to Lonrho's methods. This official condemnation caused Rowland anguish, and in 1977 he began a mischievous correspondence with government departments to show up their humbug in conniving with other companies flouting its oil sanctions against Rhodesia. Subsequently he circulated a damning, authoritative dossier on the subject. His interventions forced the appointment of a government inquiry into his allegations conducted by Thomas Bingham QC. Bingham's report (issued in 1978) vindicated Rowland's claims, and exposed the worthlessness of the costly naval 'blockade' of oil to Rhodesia instituted by the Wilson government.

Feuds In the 1970s Rowland was urged to repair Lonrho's relations with the Conservative Party leadership by making donations to its funds. This he refused to do. His relations with its leaders remained poor, and he met obstacles during the 1980s that were not presented to his contemporaries. He was also urged to reduce Lonrho's dependence on Africa for its earnings. Consequently, in 1977, the company began buying shares in Scottish and Universal Trusts, the holding company of Sir Hugh Fraser's interests, which controlled 29 per cent of the House of Fraser store group, owners of Harrods. In 1979 Lonrho acquired Scottish and Universal for £56.6 million. However, the Monopolies and Mergers Commission used Lonrho's ownership of the textile firm Brentford Nylons as a pretext to stop Lonrho bidding for the House of Fraser in 1981. The commission's recommendations were obtrusively flawed and prejudiced, but Lonrho's attempts to gain control of Harrods continued to be foiled by Whitehall. In 1984 Rowland determined to lodge Lonrho's Fraser shares with an Egyptian, Mohamed Al Fayed, before making a renewed bid: 46.1 million shares were transferred to Fayed for £138 million (a profit for Lonrho of £80 million). Rowland's confidence that Fayed could not afford to buy Fraser was misplaced: Fayed raised £615 million, persuaded the government to approve his acquisition of the House of Fraser, and took over Harrods in 1985.

Rowland was justifiably aggrieved at the government's handling of the affair, and made grave allegations against Fayed. He paid for a robust campaign publicizing the anomalies and enlisted *The Observer* (which Lonrho had bought in 1981 for £6 million) in his cause. He succeeded in forcing a Department of Trade inquiry, which in 1987 vindicated many of his allegations, but the Thatcher government regarded him as an enemy and would take no steps to redress the injustice. The government's refusal to publish this report, or to refer it to the Monopolies and Mergers Commission, was unreasonable but was ultimately upheld by the judiciary. When *The Observer* published the contents of the report in a special edition issued on the day of Lonrho's annual general meeting in 1989, the attorney-general obtained an injunction against its distribution. This did not prevent widespread circulation of the report, which indicted ministers, officials, bankers, and lawyers for lax or disreputable conduct.

Revenge against the Thatcher government became a fixation for Rowland. He had no qualms about his methods: *The Observer*, for example, published offensive allegations about the financial interests of the prime minister's son. In 1986 Lonrho bought *Today* newspaper for £10 million. The newspaper was relaunched as a supporter of David Owen's Social Democratic Party, which Rowland began bank-rolling just as it went into electoral oblivion. 'Tiny Rowland had no idea what he was doing commercially when he bought *Today*', Woodrow Wyatt concluded after a discussion with Rupert Murdoch in 1987. 'He got it only as another vengeful weapon to use against Mrs. Thatcher whom he hates beyond reason' (Wyatt, 1.373).

Rowland was a dangerous adversary. During 1988 the Australian tycoon Alan Bond spent £300 million buying a 21 per cent holding in Lonrho and boasted that he was Rowland's natural successor. His 164 foot yacht *Southern Cross III* was moored in Adnan Khashoggi's marina at Antibes next to Rowland's beloved 164 foot *Hansa*, which he had bought in 1987. Bond's captain enquired of his counterpart on *Hansa* when the latter would be moving so that Bond's yacht could take the mooring. The implication was that Rowland should accommodate Lonrho's biggest shareholder. 'It was so embarrassing', Rowland supposedly said. 'It was then that I decided to destroy him' (Bower, 540). He published a ninety-three page document demonstrating in the most trenchant terms that Bond's businesses were technically insolvent and sustained only by a fragile pyramid of borrowings. Bond's bankers called in their loans, his companies collapsed, and he was briefly imprisoned.

Rowland was a formidable presence. A visitor described him in 1989:

He sits in the boardroom of Lonrho after lunch, immobile except for the occasional movements necessary to place a grape in his mouth and chew it. He is like a crocodile, steadily watching and waiting. He looks you straight in the eye. At any moment he may dismiss you as ill-informed or stupid. The jaws may snap. Meanwhile he listens and tells you without hesitation or doubt what the facts are and how they should be interpreted. (*The Spectator*)

But he became too obsessed by his feud with Fayed to protect his business. Lonrho's dividend was cut in 1991, and debts of about £1 billion necessitated the sale of various assets. Controversially, in 1992, Lonrho sold some hotels for £177.5 million to the Libyan government while the United Nations was considering sanctions against Colonel Gaddafi's regime. This deal revived doubts about Rowland's judgement and integrity. In December 1992 he arranged for the eventual sale of his 15 per cent holding in Lonrho to a German property developer, Dieter Bock, at a price substantially higher than that which small investors could hope to obtain. This raised a further outcry. Bock and Rowland shared the responsibilities of chief executive for a period, but the older man was enraged as parts of the group were sold lucratively. Among other dispersals, *The Observer* was sold in 1993 to *The Guardian*. Rowland was isolated in the titular post of president of Lonrho in 1994.

Assessment Rowland was tall, handsome, and had an authoritative (even mesmeric) presence even in old age. His names and mannerisms were somewhat artificial self-inventions, and he was blazingly intolerant of any challenges to his versions of reality. Ostentatious living or brash manners bored and repelled him. He disliked accepting hospitality from others. From the 1960s his use of the telephone was perhaps more profuse, and the political altitude of his callers more elevated, than those of any man alive. He was devious, inscrutable, manipulative, and intimidating. Cruel amusement was central to his outlook. His humour was mordant and his invective could be overpowering. He had few interests outside Lonrho, although he adored sun-bathing, liked Siamese cats, and collected African and German expressionist art. He was a superbly accomplished opportunist who was too headstrong and angry to sustain his successes. He died of cancer at the London Clinic, 20 Devonshire Place, Westminster, on 25 July 1998. He was survived by his wife, Josie, and their four children.   RICHARD DAVENPORT-HINES

Sources T. Bower, *Tiny Rowland: a rebel tycoon* (1993) • R. Hall, *My life with Tiny* (1987) • *The journals of Woodrow Wyatt*, ed. S. Curtis, 3 vols. (1998–2000), vol. 1 • *The Spectator* (8 April 1989) • S. Cronje, M. Ling, and G. Cronje, *Lonrho* (1976) • B. Smallpeice, *Of comets and queens* (1981) • Lord Young of Graffham, *The enterprise years* (1990) • N. Faith, *The Wankel engine* (1976) • P. Barry, *The rise and fall of Alan Bond* (1990) • *The Times* (27 July 1998) • *Daily Telegraph* (27 July 1998) • *The Independent* (27 July 1998) • *The Independent* (7 Aug 1998) • *The Guardian* (27 July 1998) • *The Economist* (1 Aug 1998) • m. cert. • d. cert. • b. cert. [Josie Taylor, wife]

Archives Lonmin, London, Lonrho MSS | SOUND BBC, BBC radio interviews

Likenesses J. Bown, photograph, 1981, priv. coll. [*see illus.*] • double portrait, photograph, 1984 (with Robert Maxwell), Hult. Arch. • photograph, repro. in *The Times* • photograph, repro. in *Daily Telegraph* • photograph, repro. in *The Guardian* • photograph, repro. in *The Independent* (27 July 1998) • photograph, repro. in *The*

Economist · photographs, repro. in Bower, *Tiny Rowland* · photographs, repro. in Hall, *My life with Tiny* · photographs, NPG

Wealth at death £26,087,986—gross; £25,923,190—net: probate, 1 Feb 1999, *CGPLA Eng. & Wales*

Rowlands, Sir Archibald (1892–1953), civil servant, fourth son of David Rowlands, grocer, and his wife, Sarah Thomas, was born at Twynyrodyn, Glamorgan, on 26 December 1892. Educated at Penarth county school, the University College of Wales (where he obtained first-class honours in modern languages in 1914), and as a Welsh scholar of Jesus College, Oxford, Rowlands's university career was interrupted by three years' service in the First World War, during which he reached the rank of captain, was appointed MBE, and was mentioned in dispatches. On 15 September 1920 Rowlands married Constance May (*b.* 1893/4), daughter of Philip Walter Phillips, general manager of the Swansea Harbour Trust. They had no children. In the same year he entered the administrative civil service, and was appointed to the War Office, being promoted to principal in 1923 and assistant secretary in 1936. During his service in the War Office he acted as private secretary to three successive secretaries of state, and attracted notice for his contribution to breaking down the traditional barriers between military and civilian functions in the department.

After a year at the Imperial Defence College Rowlands was seconded to the government of India as defence finance adviser in 1937, at a time when it was necessary to build up India's defence capabilities to meet possible German and Italian threats. With resources being spent freely on the Indian armed forces for the first time since 1919, Rowlands advanced his reputation for far-sighted defence thinking, and he returned to London in 1939 as deputy under-secretary, Air Ministry, and was appointed in May 1940 first permanent secretary of the Ministry of Aircraft Production under Lord Beaverbrook. This ministry, which was created from scratch with a random body of officials, technologists, and industrialists to meet the pressing needs of air defence of the United Kingdom, operated more as an immense industrial enterprise than as a conventional government department, and succeeded in producing 40,000 aircraft a year by 1944. Rowlands was made KCB in 1941 and GCB in 1947.

In 1944 Rowlands returned to India as adviser to the viceroy, Lord Wavell, with the job of co-ordinating and mitigating the impact of India's role as a base for an offensive war against the Japanese on the functioning of local ports, transport systems, and food supplies. The administrative machinery of British India was ill adapted for the requirements of total war, and even co-ordination between the many provincial and local bodies responsible for transportation and food supply was difficult to arrange. These problems had been starkly demonstrated in 1943, when a serious famine had broken out in Bengal, resulting in the deaths of more than 1 million people, as a result, in part, of serious supply problems exacerbated by the pressures of defence procurement. As well as his administrative duties Rowlands presided over the Bengal famine inquiry in 1944–5, which spotlighted various failings in wartime arrangements, and the structural difficulties of food production in an under-resourced peasant agricultural system. At the end of the war in 1945 Rowlands was appointed finance member of the viceroy's executive council, with a brief to consider issues of post-war reconstruction and social development, although any plans in these fields were constrained by the limitations of a weakening colonial administration and the sustained suspicion of powerful interests in London.

Rowlands returned to London in mid-1946 and spent the remainder of his career there as permanent secretary of the Ministry of Supply, save for a three-month assignment in 1947 as special adviser to M. A. Jinnah on the administrative structure of Pakistan after partition. The Ministry of Supply, soon amalgamated with the Ministry of Aircraft Production, had a staff of more than 100,000 and became one of the central administrative units of the post-war British economy. Thus Rowlands was required to deal with many of the crucial problems of industrial organization that resulted from the transition from war to peace, exacerbated by political battles over the nationalization and denationalization of the steel industry, the development of the atomic energy programme, and the outbreak of the Korean War. Rowlands retired from the civil service early in 1953, and died at St Andrew's Nursing Home, Henley-on-Thames, Oxfordshire, on 18 August 1953. He was survived by his wife. B. R. TOMLINSON

Sources DNB · B. R. Tomlinson, *The political economy of the raj, 1914–1947* (1979) · *CGPLA Eng. & Wales* (1953) · m. cert.

Archives BL OIOC, letters to Sir D. T. Monteath, MS Eng. D 714 · King's Lond., Liddell Hart C., corresp. with Sir B. H. Liddell Hart | FILM BFI NFTVA, news footage

Wealth at death £5137 12s. 9d.: probate, 26 Nov 1953, *CGPLA Eng. & Wales*

Rowlands, Daniel. *See* Rowland, Daniel (1711?–1790).

Rowlands, David [*pseud.* Dewi Môn] (1836–1907), Congregational minister and college head, the son of John and Margaret Rowlands, was born on 4 March 1836 at Geufron, Rhos-y-bol, Anglesey. The family were prominent in local Calvinistic Methodist circles. After a village education he was apprenticed at thirteen, and worked in shops at Holyhead and Hatfield. But with the support of the Revd W. Griffith of Holyhead, he became an independent preacher, and in 1853 entered Bala Congregational college. He went to New College, London, in 1856, before returning to Bala in 1857 for a year as assistant tutor. In 1858 he became a member of the Congregational college at Brecon, graduating BA at London University in 1860. His first pastorate was at Llanbrynmair (1861–6); he then served for four years (1866–70) as minister of the English church at Welshpool, and for two (1870–72) at the English church at Carmarthen, a crucial period in the development of English-speaking nonconformist churches in Wales. From 1872 to 1897 he was one of the tutors of Brecon College, and from 1897 principal of the institution.

Rowlands, whose bardic name was Dewi Môn, was a gifted preacher and teacher, an eloquent writer of Welsh and English verse, and a conspicuous figure in Welsh literary and political life; he frequently adjudicated at national eisteddfods. While he was an assistant tutor at Bala, he was a firm advocate for the establishment of a Welsh colony in Patagonia in Argentina.

Rowlands took an active part in the discussions concerning the implementation of the 1870 Education Act in Wales and was later to be a leading member of Brecknockshire education committee at a crucial time for the development of secondary education in the county. He also played a prominent role in the movement for the University of Wales. He served as president of the Welsh Congregational Union in 1902 and was joint editor of *Y Dysgedydd* for a period. A keen writer to music, he was literary editor of Joseph Parry's *Cambrian Minstrelsie* (1893), and contributed a number of hymns to the Congregationalist hymnbook, which he helped edit. His literary output also included two volumes on Welsh grammar, several English versions of Welsh oratorios, as well as theological tracts.

Rowlands married Mary Elizabeth, daughter of William Roberts, an ironmonger from Toxteth Park, Liverpool, on 3 March 1864; they had one surviving son, Wilfrid. After her death, Rowlands made a late second marriage in 1897 to Alice, stepdaughter of J. Prothero of Brecon. He died on 7 January 1907 in Brecon.

J. E. LLOYD, *rev.* ROBERT V. SMITH

Sources DWB · H. E. Lewis, *Cofiant a Gweithian y Prifathraw D. Rowlands* (1910) · H. T. Evans, *A bibliography of Welsh hymnology to 1960* (1972) · *Y Geninen*, 25 (1907), 176–81 · *British Weekly* (10 Jan 1907) · m. cert.

Rowlands, Henry (1551–1616), bishop of Bangor, was born in the parish of Mellteyrn, Llŷn, Caernarvonshire, the second son of a freeholder, Rolant ap Robert (*d.* 1570) of Mellteyrn, and Elin (*fl. c.*1520–*c.*1560), daughter of Gruffudd ap Robert Fychan of Talhenbont. He was educated at Penllech School and New College, Oxford, where he graduated BA in 1573, and at St Mary Hall, Oxford, where he graduated MA (1577), BTh (1591), and DTh (1605). He was ordained deacon in 1572 and became rector of Mellteyrn (1572–81) and Langton, Oxfordshire (1581–1600). About 1581 he married Frances Cotesford, *née* Hutchins (*fl. c.*1560–*c.*1620) of Langton. He obtained further preferments as prebendary of Penmynydd, Anglesey (1584–94), rector of Aberdaron, and archdeacon of Anglesey (held *in commendam* by the bishops), and dean of Bangor (1593–8), in which capacity he served as a justice of the peace.

On 16 September 1598, with Sir Robert Cecil's assistance, Rowlands was elected bishop of Bangor; he was confirmed on 11 November and consecrated at Lambeth the following day. The temporalities were restored on 15 December and he was enthroned on 19 January 1599. He held *in commendam* the livings of Trefdraeth, Anglesey (1601), Llanrhaeadr-yng-Nghinmeirch (1602), and Llanrhaeadr, Denbigh (1612). Rowlands, being aware of his see's impoverished state, devoted much of his time to repairing his cathedral church and performing charitable works. He was described by Sir John Wynn of Gwydir as a 'provident governor of his church and diocese' (Wynn, 59), and a notable benefactor who died a rich man.

Although improvements were made to the fabric of the cathedral in his time his diocese was still impoverished. He continued catechizing and exhorting, and left lands in Llansadwrn, Anglesey, to build almshouses at Bangor for six poor men selected from Penmynydd, Llangristiolus, Aberdaron, Mellteyrn, Bangor, and Amlwch. He also left lands in Eiriannell in the commote of Llifon, Anglesey, to the principal and fellows of Jesus College, Oxford, to elect two scholars, one from Botwnnog School or Friars School, Bangor, where he had influence, and the other from Beaumaris School, where he was a feoffee and executor of the founder, David Hughes.

Rowlands purchased three bells for Bangor Cathedral and, in 1611, repaired the roofs of the nave and transept. In his will (1 July 1616) he bequeathed £20 to repair the steeple, provided land valued at £30 for the foundation and maintenance of a free grammar school at Botwnnog, which opened soon after his death, and bequeathed part of his library to individuals and part to Bangor Cathedral. He supported the bards, and odes were composed for him by Huw Llŷn, Elis ap Siôn ap Morus, and 'Syr' Huw Roberts. He had a monument erected for himself and Richard Vaughan, his kinsman and his predecessor at Bangor, in the north end of the cathedral choir. He died childless on 6 July 1616 and was buried before the high altar in the cathedral choir. The spiritualities of the see were seized by the archbishop on 12 July.

J. GWYNFOR JONES

Sources NL Wales, Mostyn MS 145487 · NL Wales, Peniarth MS 7173 · NL Wales, Llanstephan MS 125560 · will, PRO, PROB 11/128, sig. 90 · *Fasti Angl.* (Hardy), 1.105–6, 110 · Wood, *Ath. Oxon.*, new edn, 2.854–6 · J. Strype, *The life and acts of … John Whitgift* (1718), 525 · B. Willis, *A survey of the cathedral church of Bangor* (1721), 24–5, 109–10, 127, 152 · *Calendar of the manuscripts of the most hon. the marquis of Salisbury*, 8, HMC, 9 (1899), 368, 470 · A. I. Pryce, *The diocese of Bangor in the sixteenth century* (1923), xxxii–xxxv, 67–75 · J. Morgan, *Coffadwriaeth am y Gwir Barchedig Henry Rowland* (1910) · R. Williams, *Enwogion Cymru: a biographical dictionary of eminent Welshmen* (1852), 461–2 · G. Williams, *Wales and the Reformation* (1997) · J. G. Jones, 'Henry Rowlands, bishop of Bangor, 1598–1616', *Journal of the Historical Society of the Church in Wales*, 26 (1979), 34–53 · M. L. Clarke, *Bangor Cathedral* (1969), 20, 97–8 · J. Wynn, *The history of the Gwydir family and memoirs*, ed. J. G. Jones (1990)

Archives NL Wales, corresp. with Wynn family, etc.

Wealth at death approx. £800: Wynn, *History of the Gwydir family*, 59

Rowlands, Henry (1655–1723), Church of England clergyman and antiquary, was the son of William Rowlands of Plas Gwyn, Llanedwen, Anglesey, and his wife, Magdaline, daughter of Edward Wynne of Penhysgyn. He was born at Plas Gwyn, home of the Rowlands family since 1600, when it had been purchased by the antiquary's great-great-greatuncle, Henry Rowlands, bishop of Bangor.

Henry Rowlands's education is unknown, but it is clear from his writing that he was fluent in Latin and Greek and had a grasp of Hebrew—one section of his *Mona* is devoted to finding similarities between Hebrew and European, especially Welsh, words. He took holy orders in 1682, and was presented on 2 October 1696 to the living of Llanidan in Anglesey on the death of the previous incumbent, John Davies (Rowlands, *Mona*, 1723, 372). Rowlands married Elizabeth Nicholas in an unknown year, and the couple had several children; two sons and three daughters, in addition to Rowlands's wife, survived him.

Like many clerics of the later seventeenth century, Rowlands developed early on an enthusiasm for local antiquities, and turned to the study of stone circles, cromlechs, and other ancient remains. And, like many of his contemporaries, he found that his direct observation of physical remains was compromised by his classical and religious training, which at this time imposed on early fieldwork a need to explain observations within a limited Judaeo-Christian chronological scheme, and with reference to ancient authorities. And, like many of his contemporaries, he took physical remains to be mainly corroborative evidence for written records and texts, rather than as the foundation for understanding the very remote past. Accordingly, he theorized that Anglesey was the ancient metropolitan seat of the druids, and ascribed the founding of Britain to the Phoenicians, a belief in which he followed a less capable observer, Aylett Sammes, but also anticipated the much greater William Stukeley. Rowlands expounded his theories in *Mona antiqua restaurata: an archaeological discourse on the antiquities, natural and historical, of the Isle of Anglesey, the antient seat of the British Druids* (1723). He seems to have been reluctant to publish his findings, having first intended his work 'for the Exercise of private thoughts and the perusal of a few friends', and in any event did not live to see it in print, dying on 21 November 1723, shortly before it appeared (Rowlands, *Mona*, advertisement to 2nd edn, 1766). The work was published by subscription and dedicated to the gentlemen of Anglesey, many of whom subscribed for multiple copies; the bishop of Derry alone signed up for forty, evidently planning to bestow copies as gifts. A second edition of *Mona* was published at London in 1766 by Henry Owen, correcting errors the author had not lived to remedy; a supplement with topographical details by Nichols Owen (1752–1811) followed in 1775. A modern edition of *Mona* appeared in 1993. The book helped establish the reputation of Anglesey as a major site of ancient druidism, influencing imaginative writings on the subject well into the nineteenth century.

Like his contemporary cleric and archaeologist the Yorkshireman Abraham de la Pryme, Rowlands's love of ancient monuments, and the more archaeological side of antiquarianism, led him to the history of the earth—a subject of great speculation in the latter part of the seventeenth century through controversial works like Thomas Burnet's *Theory of the Earth*. Rowlands contributed an unpublished treatise on geology, the whereabouts of which is not known. His close observation of agrarian life led him similarly to compose in 1704 *Idea agriculturae: the principles of vegetation asserted and defended* (first published at Dublin in 1764). Like many clerics he also conceived an interest in the history of his own county, leaving at his death a Latin manuscript entitled 'Antiquitates parochiales'. A local history of Anglesey, this was partly published in translation in *Cambro-Briton*; a fuller edition, in Latin and English versions, appeared in the first four volumes of *Archaeologia Cambrensis* in the nineteenth century, though only the hundred of Menai was completed.

Although Rowlands did not travel widely—and thus could not compare the monuments he observed with others elsewhere in the country—he was acquainted with some of the leading antiquaries of the age, including his fellow Welshman Edward Lhuyd. The great Oxford archaeologist corresponded with Rowlands and requested his help in providing details on Anglesey for his *Archaeologia* (Lhuyd to Rowlands, 1 Nov 1702, Rowlands, *Mona*, 1723, 334); some of their correspondence is printed in *Mona*. Like Lhuyd, Rowlands recognized the importance of accurate descriptions of his observations, and *Mona* is well illustrated with engravings of the objects Rowlands had encountered; these counterbalance the more fanciful depictions of druids, or of figures such as Boadicea, that he derived from such ill-advised sources as Sammes's *Britannia antiqua illustrata*.　　　　D. R. WOOLF

Sources S. Smiles, *The image of antiquity* (1994) · G. Parry, *The trophies of time: English antiquarians of the seventeenth century* (1995) · W. B. Rowlands, 'Rowlands's *Mona*', *N&Q*, 3rd ser., 3 (1863), 387, 513 · W. Gavel Jones, 'The life and works of Henry Rowlands', MA diss., U. Wales, 1936 · *DWB* · will, NL Wales, Clerk B 1723/43
Archives Bodl. Oxf., notes and papers relating to agriculture and antiquities in Anglesey, Gough Wales 2; Carte MS 108 | Bodl. Oxf., letters to Edward Lhuyd, Ashmole MS 1817

Rowlands, Richard. *See* Verstegan, Richard (1548x50–1640).

Rowlands, Samuel (*fl.* 1598–1628), satirist, first appears on the literary scene in 1598 with the publication of *The betraying of Christ; Judas in despaire; the seven words of our saviour on the crosse; with other poems on the passion*. This is a somewhat sententious biblical paraphrase. The content was largely derived unacknowledged from Antonio de Guevara's *The Mount of Calvarie* (part 1, 1595; part 2, 1597); Rowlands condensed, revised, and paraphrased Guevara's prose into verse. In the thirty years between his first and last religious publications—*Heaven's Glory, Seeke it; Eart's Vanitie, Flye it; Hell's Horrour, Fere it* (1628), a puritan-inspired plea for moral and spiritual coherence through Christ's redemptive love—Rowlands produced a considerable quantity of, mainly, verse pamphlets which are largely on satiric themes, but he continued occasionally to produce more serious reflections on the human condition.

In the prologue to *Humors Antique Faces* (1605) Rowlands offers an explanation for his choice of themes, declaring:

> Sleepe, parting from mee, gave invention light
> To finde some subject for my pen to wright ...
> When on the Sudden ...
> I was encountred by the Faerie King.
> Mortall (quoth he) I charge thee to ingage,
> Thy pen to scourge the humors of this age,
> Thou shalt not neede to make a long relation
> What thou can get by tedious observation.

His career as a satirical observer of contemporary 'humors' had, however, an inauspicious beginning. His first two satires, *The letting of humours blood in the head-vaine; with a new morisco daunced by seven satyres upon the bottome of Diogenes tubbe* (1600) and *A Mery Metinge, or, 'Tis Mery when Knaves Mete* (1600), were condemned by bishops Whitgift and Bancroft 'for that they conteyne matters unfytt to be published: they to be burnt in the hall Kytchen [of the Stationers' Company]' (Greg and Boswell, 79). They were burnt on 26 October 1600; on 29 March in the following year, twenty-nine booksellers were fined 2s. 6d. for buying these books. The publicity which this state outrage generated among the wider population seems to have worked to Rowlands's advantage, for *A Mery Metinge* (of which no original copy is extant) was reprinted as *The Knave of Clubbs* (1609), and *The Letting* appeared as *Humors Ordinarie, where a Man may be Verie Merrie and Exceeding Well Used for his Sixpence* (1603, 1607, and, under the original title, 1611 and 1613).

Rowlands argued that the object of poetry was to write:

Againste the bastard humors howrely bred
In every mad braind wit-worne, giddy head

and he condemned those poets who

stand spending your inventions treasure,
To teach Stage Parrets speak for penny pleasure
While you your selves like musick-sounding Lutes
Fretted and strung, gaine them their silken sutes

and advised them to 'Leave Cupids cut, womens face-flattering praise' for 'Loves subject growes too three-bare now adais' ('To Poets', *Humors Ordinarie*, 1604?). He is contemptuous of the absurd affectations of contemporary sonneteers and condemns those who 'on Lords and Ladies fawne' (*A Theatre of Delightfull Recreation*, 1605, 56). While he remains consistently hostile to contemporary theatre, he exhibits some nostalgia for earlier stage celebrities and speaks with obvious fondness of

When Tarlton clown'd it in a pleasant vaine,
And with conceits did good opinions gaine
Upon the stage, his merry humors shop,
Clownes knew the Clowne by his great clownish slop.
(*Humors Ordinarie*, epigram 30)

Similarly, while he may be convinced that drama is a waste of poetic talent, he is well aware of contemporary stage practice:

The gull gets on a surpliss
With a crosse upon his brest.
Like Allen playing Faustus,
In that manner was he drest.
(*Knave of Clubs*, *The Four Knaves*, ed. E. F. Rimbault, Percy Society 9, 1844, 22–3)

Much of Rowlands's satire is directed against excesses of fashion, as with him who walks

the streetes, his humors to disclose.
In the French Doublet, and the Germane hose:
The Muffes, Cloake, Spanish Hat, Tolledo blade
Italian ruffe, a Shooe right Flemish made.
Like Lord of mis-rule

and he also attacks those who use the excuse of their 'humor' to defend their pretence, for

If you question why?
His tongue is nere unfurnisht with a lye.
It is his humor too he doth protest.
(*Humors Ordinarie*, epigrams 21, 27)

He attacks the prodigal whose pride leads to 'Stretching his credit that his purse strings cracke' until 'he till death must lie in pawne for debt' (ibid., 'To the readers'). He reserves considerable anger for those who use tobacco, 'Deaths blacke dart', for

This same poison, steeped India weed,
In head, hart, lungs, doth soote & cobwebs breede.
(ibid., epigram 18)

Rowlands is always aware of current sensations to add interest to his pamphlets and refers to one Spellman, executed on 7 January 1612, who was

Upon the day of Christ's Nativitie,
In the King's Chappell, to commit felonie.
(*Knave of Hearts*, *The Four Knaves*, ed. E. F. Rimbault, Percy Society 9, 1844, 76)

He also mentions Hunckes, Stone, and old Harry—all famous bears in Paris Garden—and does not forget 'Woolner … a ravening beast' (*Knave of Clubs*, ibid., 19), who was a famous gourmand. In a similar way Rowlands was always quick to respond to topics of current interest, as with his *Sir Thomas Overbury, or, The Poysoned Knights Complaint* (1614).

Perhaps Rowlands's most controversial work was *Greene's ghost haunting conie catchers wherein is set downe the arte of humoring, the arte of carrying stones … with the conceits of Dr. Pinchbacke, a notable makeshift* (1602). The work claims to have been edited by Rowlands from Robert Greene's papers, and its publication is declared to be

for the good of the commonwealth, both for all men to see, what grosse villanies are now practised in the bright Sunne-shine, that thereby they may be forewarned to take heede how they converse with such cosoning companions: as also a just checke and controll to such wicked livers, that they perceiving their goodness set abroach, may with remorse and penitencie forsake their abominable course of life, and betake them to a more honest and civill behaviour.   (A2v)

The work, however, owes more to its borrowings from Greene's *The Blacke Bookes Messenger*, from which it derives extensive unacknowledged quotations, than to Rowlands's own invention, and it copies the cant thieves' terms which Greene had already listed. Rowlands does, however, consciously create the fiction that his work is based on papers found after Greene's death.

In *Father Hubberd's Tales* (1604), Thomas Middleton speaks of a

humerous theft,
Which seems to flow from self-conceiting breasts
(Middleton, 5.561)

implying that some hack writer stole papers from Thomas Nashe after his death, and contemporaries, as well as later scholars have suspected Rowlands of the plagiarism. It is clear, however, that Rowlands's satires do evolve from the same context as those of Nashe and Greene and he is very conversant with their work. He seems simply to borrow when it suits his convenience, as in *The Letting of Humours Blood* of 1600, which derives extensively from Lodge's *Wits Miserie* of 1596.

Rowlands's literary circle seems to have been limited: he claimed John Taylor, the water poet, as his 'loving Friend' (*Works*, 1630, commendatory verses to *The Sculler*); he was also acquainted with Thomas Andrewes and Thomas Collins, and contributed verses to works by both (*Unmasking of a Feminine Machiavell*, 1604; *Tears of Love*, 1615). In 1602 he wrote to his friend George Gaywood in *Hell's*

Broke Loose, 'My pen never was and never shall be mercenary'; his *Humors Looking Glasse* of 1608 is dedicated to 'his verie loving friend, Master George Lee'. In 1612 he contributed a poem 'In Vulponem' to W. Parkes's *Curtaine-Drawer of the World* which seems to make oblique but complimentary reference to Ben Jonson's *Volpone*. In the epistle to *The Knaves of Spades and Diamonds* (1613?) Rowlands declares that:

> For Custome sake, and for no other cause …
> I am content to use a dedication
> Not unto this, or that great mighty lord
> [but] To them that ne'er will thanke me for my paine,
> And such of whom I doe expect no gaine

and similarly, in *Greene's Ghost Haunting Conie Catchers* he speaks of his 'homely stile' and avers 'I looke for nought, nought but your loves I crave' (A3v). Again in *A Fooles Bolt* (1614) he attacks those who dedicate their works to flatter potential patrons

> that hath an expectation,
> To helpe his needy wants by dedication.
> (A3)

Despite this criticism of those who seek patronage from lords and ladies, he dedicated his first publication to Sir Nicholas Walsh, chief justice of common pleas in Ireland, and his *Famous History of Guy, Earle of Warwicke* (1607) is dedicated to Philip Herbert, earl of Montgomery. Rowlands, despite his inconsistencies, clearly appealed to a wide contemporary audience; one of his readers was the diarist John Manningham. After his final tract of 1628, however, Rowlands vanishes into the obscurity from which he had emerged some three decades earlier.　REAVLEY GAIR

Sources S. Rowlands, *Uncollected poems*, ed. F. O. Waagle (1970) • T. George, 'Samuel Rowlands's *The betraying of Christ* and Guevara's *The Mount of Calvarie*: an example of Elizabethan plagiarism', *N&Q*, 212 (1967), 467–74 • E. D. McDonald, 'An example of plagiarism among Elizabethan pamphleteers', *Indiana University Studies*, 9/8 (1911), 145–70 • E. Gosse, *Seventeenth century studies* (1883) • A. Davenport, 'Rowlands and Thomas Lodge', *N&Q*, 184 (1943), 13–16 • W. W. Greg and E. Boswell, eds., *Records of the court of the Stationers' Company, 1576 to 1602, from register B* (1930), 79 • T. Middleton, *Works*, ed. A. Dyce (1840), 5.561 and n.

Rowlands, William [*pseud.* Gwilym Lleyn] (1802–1865), bibliographer and Wesleyan Methodist minister, was born on 24 August 1802 at Llety, Bryncroes, Caernarvonshire, the eldest of six children of Thomas Rowlands, a weaver, and his wife, Eleanor. His literary name comprises the Welsh form of his first name and his place of birth on the Llŷn Peninsula. He attended schools in Bryncroes and Botwnnog before being apprenticed as a weaver. Although his parents were staunch Calvinistic Methodists, Rowlands came under the influence of Wesleyan Arminian teaching after he left home to search for work in the Tre-garth area. He joined the Wesleyan Methodists when he was eighteen, and in 1821 he began to preach. From 1821 to 1828 he was active as a lay preacher in circuits in north Wales. In 1828 he moved to the Cardigan circuit, where he offered himself as a candidate for the full-time ministry. He was admitted as a probationer minister serving in Cardiff in 1829. Thereafter he served in Merthyr Tudful (1831), Amlwch (1834), Pwllheli (1835), Newmarket (1837), Ruthin (1840), Llanidloes (1842 and 1853), Tredegar (1845 and 1856), Machynlleth (1848 and 1861), Bryn-mawr (1850), and Aberystwyth (1858). In 1834 he married Anne Andrews (1806–1880), daughter of a grocer with whom he had lodged in Cardiff. They had three sons and five daughters. He retired in 1864 and settled in Oswestry, where he died on 21 March 1865. He was buried at Caerau, near Llanidloes.

Despite having little formal education, Rowlands was a prolific writer throughout his life and contributed to many Welsh-language periodicals. His greatest gift was as a collector and organizer of information. He edited the Wesleyan journal *Yr Eurgrawn Wesleyaidd* from 1842 to 1845 and from 1853 to 1856. He was an assiduous compiler of biographies. Some of these were included by the publisher Isaac Foulkes in 1870 in his *Geirlyfr bywgraffiadol o enwogion Cymru*, containing the lives of figures from Welsh history.

Rowlands's greatest achievement was undoubtedly his pioneering biobibliography *Llyfryddiaeth y Cymry* (1869). Although the work is in Welsh, it has a separate English title-page describing it as the *Cambrian Bibliography*. The volume lists in chronological sequence books published in the Welsh language or relating to Wales from 1546, the year of publication of the first book in the Welsh language, to 1800. The bibliography is extensively annotated with biographical information about authors, translators, printers, and publishers. Since the success of the work depended on Rowlands seeing copies of books mostly in private hands in locations throughout Wales, the itinerant nature of the Wesleyan Methodist ministry proved a considerable help to him. The work still merits attention, not least because it lists some books for which no surviving copies are recorded in the standard modern bibliography by Eiluned Rees, *Libri Walliae* (1987). The author was unable to secure sufficient subscriptions to publish the work during his lifetime but it appeared posthumously under the editorship of the Anglican clergyman and scholar Daniel Sylvan Evans.　LIONEL MADDEN

Sources R. Morgan, 'Cofiant y Parch. William Rowlands', *Yr Eurgrawn Wesleyaidd*, 60 (1868) • B. Thomas, 'Gwilym Lleyn and his family', *Transactions of the Caernarvonshire Historical Society*, 45 (1984), 79–92 • D. Gwynfryn Jones, 'Y Parch. William Rowlands (Gwilym Lleyn)', *Yr Eurgrawn Wesleyaidd*, 101 (1909), 321–5, 361–9 • D. Williams, 'Gwilym Lleyn, 1802–1865', *Bathafarn*, 8 (1953), 5–23
Archives NL Wales
Wealth at death under £50: administration, 16 Aug 1865, *CGPLA Eng. & Wales*

Rowlandson [*née* White; *other married name* Talcott], **Mary** (*c.*1637–1711), colonist in America and author, was born in Somerset, probably at South Petherton, daughter of John White (1602–1673), farmer, and his wife, Joan West (1606–1654). In 1639 her parents migrated with other puritans to Salem, Massachusetts, and later moved to the inland town of Lancaster, where John White became a prosperous landowner. Here about 1656 Mary married the town's pastor, Joseph Rowlandson (1602–1678).

During the devastating war of 1675 to 1676 between the New England colonies and several Algonquian nations,

Lancaster was attacked in early February 1676, many of the inhabitants killed, and Mrs Rowlandson with her three children and other residents captured. Three months later she was ransomed and reunited with her family, lived briefly in Boston, and spent the rest of her life in Wethersfield, Connecticut, where, Joseph Rowlandson having died in 1678, she married Samuel Talcott in 1679.

In 1682 Mary's account of captivity was published in Boston and twice that year in Cambridge, Massachusetts, as *The soveraignty and goodness of God, together with the faithfulness of his promises displayed*, and the same year in London as *A true history of the captivity and restoration of Mrs Mary Rowlandson*. This pathbreaking narrative combined a puritan's testimony to God's mercy, a reluctant participant's commentary on military events, a biased reporter's ethnography of southern New England Indians, and, most poignantly, a female captive's account of physical and spiritual ordeals. With a preface probably written by Increase Mather and, in early editions, her husband's final sermon appended at the end, the book was immensely popular for more than a century and was often reprinted and imitated. Samuel Talcott died in 1691. Surviving him by twenty years, Mary Talcott died at Wethersfield in 1711.

ALDEN T. VAUGHAN

Sources M. Rowlandson, *The soveraignty and goodness of God, together with the faithfulness of his promises displayed: being a narrative of the captivity and restauration of Mrs Mary Rowlandson*, 2nd edn (1682) · N. Salisbury, introduction, in *The sovereignty and goodness of God, together with the faithfulness of his promises displayed: being a narrative of the captivity and restoration of Mrs Mary Rowlandson and related documents*, ed. N. Salisbury (1997) · A. L. White, *Genealogy of the ancestors and descendants of John White of Wenham and Lancaster, Massachusetts, 1574–1900*, 4 vols. (1900–09) · H. S. Nourse, ed., *The early records of Lancaster, Massachusetts* (1884) · K. Z. Derounian-Stodola and J. A. Levernier, *The Indian captivity narrative, 1550–1900* (1993) · M. R. Breitwieser, *American puritanism and the defense of mourning* (1990) · A. T. Vaughan and E. W. Clark, eds., *Puritans among the Indians: accounts of captivity and redemption, 1676–1724* (1981)

Rowlandson, Thomas (1757–1827), artist, was born on 13 July 1757 in the Old Jewry, London, and baptized on 23 July at St Mary Colechurch, the only son of William Rowlandson (*fl.* 1756–1789) and his wife, Mary. His father was a wool and silk merchant in the City who lost his fortune and was declared bankrupt in January 1759, when the child was only two years old. Thomas and his younger sister Elizabeth, who later married the sporting artist Samuel Howitt (1756–1822), were brought up by their uncle James, a prosperous Spitalfields silk weaver, and his wife, Jane, who had no children of their own. After his uncle died, Jane sold the business profitably and moved to Soho, where she rented apartments at 4 Church (now Romilly) Street; Thomas was then sent to school at Dr Barvis's highly respected establishment in Soho Square. Early showing an inclination to draw, he was allowed by his aunt to become an art student at the age of fifteen. Thus Rowlandson was admitted to the Royal Academy Schools in November 1772, and remained on their books until 1778; in the same month he was 'permitted to Draw' in the duke of Richmond's sculpture gallery at his house in

Thomas Rowlandson (1757–1827), by John Thomas Smith, 1824

Whitehall, a room that was arranged for the convenience of students and was then administered by the Incorporated Society of Artists.

In the late summer of 1774 Rowlandson made his first trip to Paris: his aunt, *née* Chevalier, was of French Huguenot extraction, and he himself was probably bilingual. There is no evidence, however, that he was a student at one of the drawing academies there, as stated by his obituarist in the *Gentleman's Magazine*. In 1775 he sent his first exhibit to the annual exhibition of the Royal Academy, a drawing of a biblical subject entitled in the catalogue *Dalilah Payeth Sampson a Visit while in Prison at Gaza* (no longer extant), the only subject of a conventional historical nature he is recorded as having attempted. Two years later, in 1777, he was awarded, by twenty-three votes to one, the silver medal of the academy for a figure in bas-relief. The wiry penwork of his earliest dated drawing, inscribed by him 'A Bench of Artists Sketched at the Royal Academy in the Year 1776' (Tate collection), was closely derived from that of John Hamilton Mortimer (1740–1779) and, although his academy exhibits in 1778–81 were chiefly small watercolour portraits, it was Mortimer's restless romantic imagination, interest in caricature and the macabre, and vigorous draughtsmanship that most deeply affected Rowlandson's early style.

It was unusual for a student at the Royal Academy to have developed as a draughtsman rather than as a painter, but there is no evidence that Rowlandson ever worked in oils. He was not, like so many aspiring artists, an eager devotee of the president, Sir Joshua Reynolds, but, following the Hogarth tradition, responsive to more popular forms of art, the fashion for drawing caricatures and the spread of printselling businesses at this time. A design for publication attributed to Rowlandson dates from 1774, but his *œuvre* as a printmaker does not really begin until 1780, when his works were printed by a variety of publishers, including Hannah and W. Humphrey and S. W. Fores. A close friend of James Gillray, he produced, until the end of the 1780s, numerous political as well as social caricatures, though without Gillray's venom and partisanship. After his prints lampooning the protagonists in the celebrated Westminster election had been published, he became familiar to the press as 'the ingenious *Caricaturist*' (*Morning Herald*, 25 Dec 1784).

Rowlandson was in France once again in 1778, and seems to have been in Rome in 1782: it is possible that he travelled outwards in 1781, as there is some evidence—the dependence of his great *Review* compositions of 1786 on a work exhibited by Moreau le Jeune—that he visited the Paris Salon of 1781. Inscriptions on drawings document further visits to France in 1785, 1786, and 1787; and his famous drawing *La place des Victoires* (priv. coll.) of 1783 marks a radical change both of concept and execution, influenced by French practice, which was to determine the course of Rowlandson's work as a draughtsman for the rest of his career. Up to 1780 Rowlandson had restricted himself to penwork, in one or two drawings adding grey wash to reinforce the shadows; now he began to use watercolour to supplement the wash, what the eighteenth century called a tinted drawing, at the same time developing his subject matter into a more elaborate kind of narrative, replete with interrelated incident, and combining caricature with an elegant figure style. In 1784 Rowlandson exhibited at the academy two exceptionally large and complex narrative scenes in his new manner, *Vauxhall Gardens* (V&A) and *The Serpentine River* (NMG Wales). In turn Rowlandson's work was now to influence French narrative artists such as Philibert-Louis Debucourt.

In the autumn of 1784 Rowlandson made a twelve-day journey (the *Tour in a Post Chaise*) to the Isle of Wight in the company of Henry Wigstead (1760–1800)—the genial and ambitious young painter–decorator who was a friend and executor of his aunt—possibly to see the wreck of the *Royal George*, which had foundered off Spithead in 1782. He worked up nearly seventy watercolours (Henry E. Huntington Art Gallery, San Marino, California) from drawings made on the trip, and it seems probable that, as in the case of later tours with Wigstead, to Brighton in 1789 and Wales in 1797, publication was intended, with a commentary by Wigstead (himself a caricaturist).

Rowlandson continued to live with his aunt until her death. They moved to apartments at 103 Wardour Street some time between 1775 and 1777 and, in or before 1787, to 50 Poland Street, also in Soho, where he was looked after by one of his aunt's maids, Mary Chateauvert. It was there, in April 1789, that his aunt died. Jane left her nephew, of whom she was very fond, her most substantial legacy,

which Rowlandson (accused by his obituarist of an 'uncontrollable passion for gaming') may well have gambled away (*GM*). Certainly straitened circumstances seem to have accounted for frequent moves in the 1790s, always to modest, if not positively shabby, addresses, mostly in or around the Strand. By Christmas 1791 he is reported in the press as being at his 'new habitation' at 52 Strand, and in 1793–5 in the basement of 2 Robert Street, in the Adelphi, which the rate collector described as 'dismal'. For a time, probably in the late 1790s, he had rooms adjoining George Morland (1763–1804), a boon companion of the previous decade but by then chronically inebriated and in debt, on the second floor above Mrs Lay's print shop near Carlton House. Rowlandson's last move was in 1800, to the attic of 1 James Street, Adelphi, spacious enough for a printing press, where he lived for the rest of his life.

The outbreak of the French Revolution in 1789 put an end to Rowlandson's trips to France but, in 1791–2, he was in the Low Countries and northern Germany in the company of a wealthy and congenial patron, Mathew Michell. Drawings of a Dutch packet boat, a German post house, and of The Hague, Düsseldorf, and Juliers in Westphalia are all dated 1791; and a lively study of the pier at Amsterdam is not only dated 1792 but also inscribed as having been sketched that year. Three of Rowlandson's most elaborate and detailed continental town views—of the place de Mer in Antwerp and the Stadhuis in Amsterdam (present whereabouts unknown), and the Feyge Dam and part of the fish market in the same city (Bolton Art Gallery), the first dated 1794—were probably worked up from sketches made in 1791–2 and all three were published by Rudolph Ackermann in 1797.

Michell and Ackermann were undoubtedly Rowlandson's most important patrons. Michell was a partner in the banking firm of Hodsoll, Michell, and Stirling at 345 Strand until his retirement in 1799, and lived near Rowlandson in Beaufort Buildings, on the site of the present Savoy Hotel. Subsequently Rowlandson was a constant and welcome guest at his country homes, Grove House, Enfield, and Hengar House, at St Tudy in Cornwall, and the two continued to travel together, chiefly in the west country; by the time of his death in 1818, Michell owned more than 550 of the artist's drawings.

S. W. Fores had published Rowlandson's drawings for *The Comforts of Bath* in January 1798, but from that year on it was Ackermann who kept Rowlandson in almost continuous employment producing drawings for the fine colour-plate books for which his firm, the Repository of Arts at 101 Strand, became famous. Their first major collaboration was on the *Loyal Volunteers of London and Environs* (1799). *The Microcosm of London*, for which Augustus Pugin was brought in to draw the architecture while Rowlandson supplied the figures, came out in 1808–10. *The Three Tours of Doctor Syntax: In Search of the Picturesque, In Search of Consolation*, and *In Search of a Wife*, the comic figure of the skin-and-bone cleric at the mercy of events reportedly based on an idea of Rowlandson's close friend the actor Jack Bannister, and with verses by William Combe, appeared in 1812, 1820, and 1821 respectively. Combe also provided the text for *The English Dance of Death* (1815–16) and Rowlandson's last work for Ackermann, *The History of Johnny Quae Genus* (1822). From 1806 to 1821 Rowlandson was also employed by another well-known publisher, Thomas Tegg, of 111 Cheapside, whose *Caricature Magazine* catered for the lower end of the market; for this he poured out copious satires and caricatures in collaboration with G. M. Woodward and others.

The illustrated books underline Rowlandson's extraordinary range. He was as much a master of the lyrical watercolour of rolling countryside as of the incisive caricature. A specialist in urban topography, though more interested in the picturesque than in exactitude, he was portraitist, social commentator, and sporting artist. Above all, he revelled in the comedy of everyday life, emphasizing the ridiculous and the ribald in his inventions, poking fun but avoiding emotion and satire. Much of the incident in his story-telling has to do with human appetites; eating, drinking, and amorous relationships—the last often involving a corpulent elderly man and a buxom young girl—are at the heart of Rowlandson's world. The pen and ink sketch, marked by brilliant draughtsmanship and acute observation of stance, movement, and character, was his forte.

Although Rowlandson complained as late as 1804 of his inability to secure the patronage of 'the long pursed gentry' (letter to James Heath, 1 March 1804, BL, Add. MS 29300, fol. 26), his industry and facility must surely have provided him with a good enough living; moreover he had no family responsibilities. In 1814, like so many other British artists, he visited Paris after the fall of Napoleon to see the art treasures pillaged by him assembled in the Louvre. Some time about 1820 he was in Italy, where he made careful studies from the antique, possibly with a view to publication. Several albums of drawings survive (one with pages watermarked 1821 in the Houghton Library, Harvard, and another with pages watermarked 1822 in the British Museum) which demonstrate his intention of summing up the experience of a lifetime by publishing a volume on comparative physiognomy, a subject of great interest at the time. A last sheet differentiating types of laughter is on paper watermarked 1825.

As is apparent from the drawings for *A Tour in a Post Chaise*, Rowlandson was a trim, tallish, and good-looking young man. The apple of his aunt Jane's eye, he was healthy, robust, high-spirited, and fond of pretty women. Thirty years later he referred to himself, Bannister, and Henry Angelo as 'three jolly Dogs' (letter to Angelo, 18 July 1815, formerly Hugh D. Auchincloss collection, Washington, DC). Five surviving drawings of Rowlandson chart his later appearance. Those by Bannister (formerly Auchincloss collection) and John Raphael Smith (British Museum) date from the mid-1790s (the Bannister is dated 4 June 1795) and depict him—youthfully alert in the one case, reflective in the other—still endowed with a full head of hair. The next two portraits (both NPG) show him twenty years later, with the hair both tousled and thinning. G. H. Harlow's rather romanticized drawing, which

the sitter inscribed as aged fifty-eight and dated 1814, portrays him as well built and in characteristically extrovert mood; John Jackson's pencil study, of roughly the same date, is a very credible likeness of Rowlandson, watchful and enquiring in expression. Perhaps the most vivid of the five, however (Metropolitan Museum of Art, New York), was done in the last years of the artist's life. Dated 15 June 1824, it is a study of Rowlandson sketching by John Thomas Smith, the keeper of prints and drawings at the British Museum. Bespectacled, perhaps slightly arthritic, now really balding on top, the artist is portrayed drawing intently, industrious as ever.

Rowlandson was described by his obituarist as being severely ill for two years before his death, which took place at 1 James Street, London, on 21 April 1827. He was buried in the church of St Paul's, Covent Garden, mourned by Ackermann, Bannister, and Angelo. The executor and sole legatee of his will, drawn up in 1818, was Betsey Winter (*d.* 1835), who had been his companion, probably for many years (there is a Rowlandson drawing reputedly of her dating from the late 1780s). Betsey was described as 'Mrs. Rowlandson' in the auctioneers' copy of the catalogue of the sale held at Sothebys in June 1828, and as 'Elizabeth Rowlandson' in the rate-books for 1 James Street, where she continued to live until 1829; but probate was granted to 'Betsey Winter Spinster'. Had she been married to the artist she would have been so described in Rowlandson's will. There is no evidence that Rowlandson ever had children.

Rowlandson's death attracted little attention. There was only one obituary, in the *Gentleman's Magazine*, and his drawings and watercolours fetched very low prices at the 1828 sale. The ribaldry and gusto of his social comment were soon to be replaced by the genteel humour first of John Doyle, then of *Punch*, which began to appear in 1841; so that in 1869 the Birmingham collector William Bates could write 'even among artists and professed "picturemen", few in London, none out, have ever heard of his name' ('Thomas Rowlandson, artist', *N&Q* 2 Oct 1869, 278). Except among collectors, Rowlandson's reputation was not fully restored until after the First World War. His name is now synonymous with the popular vision of late Georgian Britain.   JOHN HAYES

Sources Rowlandson sale (1828) [sale catalogue, Sothebys, 23–6 June 1828] · B. Falk, *Thomas Rowlandson: his life and art* (1949) [incl. comprehensive list of illustr. bks] · *GM*, 1st ser., 97/1 (1827), 564–5 · J. Hayes, *Rowlandson: watercolours and drawings* (1972) · R. R. Wark, *Rowlandson's drawings for 'A tour in a post chaise'* (1963) · J. Baskett and D. Snelgrove, *The drawings of Thomas Rowlandson in the Paul Mellon collection* (1977) [incl. comprehensive bibliography by C. Nicholson] · J. Grego, *Rowlandson the caricaturist*, 2 vols. (1880) [comprehensive catalogue of prints] · R. R. Wark, *Drawings by Thomas Rowlandson in the Huntington collection* (1975) · J. Riely, *Rowlandson drawings from the Paul Mellon collection* (1977) [exhibition catalogue, Yale U. CBA, 16 Nov 1977 – 15 Jan 1978, RA, 4 March – 21 May 1978] · J. Hayes, *The art of Thomas Rowlandson* (1990) [exhibition catalogue, New York, NY, Pittsburgh, PA, and Baltimore, MD, 6 Feb – 5 Aug 1990] · will, 13 Aug 1818, PRO, PROB 10/4946 · registers, RA, Royal Academy Schools · H. Angelo, *Reminiscences*, 1 (1828), 237 · parish register, St Mary Colechurch, 23 July 1757, GL, MS 4439 [baptism] · M. Payne and J. E. Payne, 'Henry Wigstead: Rowlandson's fellow-traveller', *British Art Journal* [forthcoming]

Likenesses T. Rowlandson, self-portraits, pen and watercolour drawings, 1784, Hunt. L. • J. Bannister, pencil drawing, 1795; formerly in possession of Hugh D. Auchincloss, Washington, DC • J. R. Smith, pencil, chalk, and wash drawing, *c.*1795, BM • G. H. Harlow, pencil and chalk drawing, 1814, NPG • J. Jackson, pencil drawing, *c.*1815, NPG • J. T. Smith, pen and wash drawing, 1824, Metropolitan Museum of Art, New York [*see illus.*] • mezzotint (after Bannister), BM, NPG

Wealth at death under £3000; books of prints attached to Burges Bryan sale, Sothebys, 18–21 June 1828; works by Rowlandson, some old master paintings, and several thousand old master and contemporary English prints sold at Thomas Rowlandson sale, Sothebys, 23–6 June 1828

Rowlatt, Sir **Sidney Arthur Taylor** (1862–1945), judge, was born in Cairo on 20 July 1862, the eldest son of Arthur Henry Rowlatt, a manager in the Bank of Egypt, and his wife, Amelia Caroline, daughter of Sidney Terry, general merchant, of Bombay. His younger brother, Sir Frederick Terry Rowlatt (1865–1950), became governor of the Bank of Egypt (1906–21). After schooling at Fettes College, Edinburgh, Rowlatt won a scholarship to King's College, Cambridge, in 1880. He won the Porson prize (1883), was Browne medallist (1883), was honourably mentioned for the chancellor's medal, and placed in the first class in parts one and two of the classical tripos in 1882 and 1884. For a short time after taking his degree he was an assistant master at Eton College.

In 1886 Rowlatt was elected a fellow of King's (an appointment he held until 1892), awarded a Whewell scholarship, and called to the bar by the Inner Temple (of which he became a bencher in 1908 and treasurer in 1928). He was a pupil first of F. A. Bosanquet and afterwards of Abel John Ram. Recommended by A. T. Lawrence, who knew him as a promising member of the Oxford circuit, Rowlatt became devil for R. B. Finlay, whose friendship brought him many useful contacts. On 10 April 1890 Rowlatt married Elizabeth (*d.* 1957), daughter of James Hemingway, railway contractor, of Macclesfield; they had four sons and two daughters. In 1899 he published *The Law of Principal and Surety*, which was clearly arranged, exhaustive in treatment, and recognized on more than one occasion by the courts as a work of authority.

In 1900 Finlay, as attorney-general, nominated Rowlatt for the appointment as junior counsel to the Board of Inland Revenue. It was a crucial moment in the history of taxation. The Second South African War had caused a rise in the rate of income tax and estates duty began to bite. In 1905 Rowlatt became junior counsel to the Treasury on the common-law side. In October 1912 Lord Haldane offered him a judgeship in place of Sir J. A. Hamilton, who had been made a lord justice. Rowlatt received the customary knighthood.

Rowlatt, who had already obtained some judicial experience as recorder of Windsor (1904–12), soon showed merit as a judge. Although he often took the commercial list and other non-jury cases in London and had his share of Old Bailey and circuit work, his major contribution was in revenue matters. These became ever more important with the Lloyd George budgets and the coming of the First

World War. His judgment in *Cape Brandy Syndicate* v. *Inland Revenue Commissioners* (1921) is a good example of his clear reasoning and crisp style, as applied to the interpretation of a tax statute; and over his twenty years in the King's Bench Division he helped shape the future of English tax law. In *Chibbett* v. *Joseph Robinson & Sons* (1924) war bonds paid as compensation for loss of office were held not to be taxable; in *Tollemache* v. *I.R.C.* (1926) a person occupying land under a discretionary trust had the annual value of those lands taxed; *Gimson* v. *I.R.C.* (1930) held that dividends paid out of non-taxable income of a company were not liable to assessment for tax; *Mann* v. *Nash* (1932) decided that profits from illegal 'fruit' machines were liable to tax. In general, his tax decisions were responsible and neutral, and showed none of the irresponsibility and partiality the judiciary was later to show in *I.R.C.* v. *Duke of Westminster* (1935) and later cases.

With respect to his own tax position, however, Rowlatt was less responsible. In 1931 the judges were made subject to the National Recovery Act and had their salaries reduced. The situation was not well handled by the government, but the response of the judges—or at least some of them—was embarrassing. Rowlatt was among that latter group. Rowlatt said that he and five other judges would retire at once since they would earn more retired than on the bench. Sir George Schuster, the permanent secretary to the lord chancellor, became alarmed, fearing that he could not find six silks good enough to promote to the High Court. The judges were then bought off with a favourable tax ruling and Rowlatt, in particular, was promised a privy councillorship if he agreed to stay one more year. This, however, was not an end to Rowlatt's manoeuvrings. When early in 1932 the law officers vetoed an offer the chancellor of the exchequer had made to exempt the judges from part of the cuts, Rowlatt was outraged. He wrote to Schuster, saying that he 'must accelerate the selection of a retired spot to end my days in' (Stevens, *Independence*, 58).

On his retirement later in 1932 after twenty years as a King's Bench judge, Rowlatt was made a privy councillor under the Schuster deal. Moreover with the ever increasing burden of appeals in the judicial committee of the privy council and the perennial shortage of law lords, Rowlatt was called on regularly to sit in the judicial committee. The arrangement was not a success. The most unfortunate effect was the striking down of the Canadian new deal (*Attorney-General of Canada* v. *Attorney-General of Ontario*, 1937). The panel enrolled to hear the case was not ideal. In fairness, Lord Hailsham, the lord chancellor, had tried to persuade Lord Sankey, an excellent constitutional lawyer, to preside, but he was still sulking from having been dismissed from the lord chancellorship in 1935. Lord Atkin therefore presided, and, while an excellent commercial lawyer, he had little sense of the instrumental approach needed for constitutional work. Moreover, he was a Little Englander, who disapproved of the statute of Westminster. Opposed to him was Lord Wright, but the swing vote was Rowlatt's, who incidentally, according to B. J. Mackinnon, 'sat throughout the 1937 hearings in his overcoat making neither note nor comment' (Pannick, 16). The 3:2 decision (although public dissents were not allowed) outraged Canadian public opinion, leading a member of the Bennett cabinet, M. C. H. Cahan, to refer 'to the futile efforts of this Committee of the Privy Council of the United Kingdom to revive and reassert reactionary policies' (Stevens, *Independence*, 76). The Canadian senate's O'Connor report (1939) called for abolition of appeals to London, and, while the Second World War delayed the final decision, the matter was settled and appeals were finally abolished in 1949.

Throughout the 1930s Rowlatt was a regular member of panels hearing Canadian appeals. It was not a happy arrangement. The Canadians muttered; the Australians were apparently outraged when Rowlatt appeared in an Australian panel. When faced with the rather naïve suggestion by Lord Kilmuir, Harold Macmillan's lord chancellor, of having a peripatetic final court of appeal for the Commonwealth, another normally generous former lord chancellor, Viscount Simonds, warned Kilmuir that the Australians would never accept African judges, concluding 'some will remember the row there was when … Rowlatt (Rowlatt of all people!) sat to hear some Australian appeals' (Stevens, *Independence*, 159). In short, Schuster's bribe to get Rowlatt to stay on an extra year may be said to have shortened the life of the judicial committee of the privy council.

Rowlatt was used for other public appointments as all judges are. In 1917 he was made chair of the committee on criminal conspiracies in India, which led to the passing of the Rowlatt Act in 1919, strengthening the hand of the government in dealing with those seeking independence. In recognition of his services in this connection, he was appointed KCSI in 1918. He was also chair of the royal commission on lotteries and betting (1932–3) and, in the Second World War, of the General Claims Tribunal under the Compensation (Defence) Act of 1939.

As a man Rowlatt was a witty companion, whose classical scholarship could, when the occasion demanded, produce elegant, impromptu Latin verse. In court he was from the point of view of counsel regarded as almost an ideal judge, quick to seize a point but loth to interrupt. When he spoke, it was with a cheerful almost boyish air, devoid of pomposity. He rarely reserved, and almost never wrote, a judgment. He died at Bagnor Manor, Newbury, Berkshire, on 1 March 1945. His third son, Sir John Rowlatt (1898–1956), became first parliamentary counsel to the Treasury. NORMAN S. MARSH, *rev.* ROBERT STEVENS

Sources *The Times* (23 March 1932) · *The Times* (3 March 1945) · *The Times* (7 March 1945) · *The Times* (20 March 1945) · *The Times* (24 March 1945) · *Solicitors' Journal* (10 March 1945) · *Law Journal* (10 March 1945) · *Law Times* (10 March 1945) · R. Stevens, *The independence of the judiciary: the view from the lord chancellor's office* (1993) · D. Pannick, *Judges* (1987) · R. Stevens, *Law and politics: the House of Lords as a judicial body, 1800–1976* (1978) · Lord Wright, 'Obituary for the Rt. Hon. Sir Lyman Poore Duff', *Canadian Bar Review*, 33 (1955), 1123–9 · F. R. Scott, 'Labour conventions case: Lord Wright's undisclosed dissent', *Canadian Bar Review*, 34 (1956), 114–15

Archives PRO, Lord Chancellor's Office, papers | FILM BFI NFTVA, news footage

Likenesses E. M. Hale, portrait, priv. coll.

Wealth at death £35,786 14s. 5d.: probate, 8 May 1946, *CGPLA Eng. & Wales*

Rowles, Henry (*bap.* 1777, *d.* 1841), builder, was baptized on 8 December 1777 at St Martin-in-the-Fields, Westminster, the son of James Rowles and his wife, Catherine (*née* Holland), the favourite sister of the architect Henry Holland. He was trained in Holland's office but then entered business as a builder. Presumably his family contacts stood him in good stead.

In 1804 Rowles married Adelaide Theresa Georgiana Gourdez and in that year Henry Holland leased to him the sites of twenty-one houses in Upper Cadogan Place on the Holland Park estate in west London. The largest of these houses, at the east end of the street, became Rowles's own residence. At about this time Rowles entered into a partnership with his uncle Alexander *Copland, one of the most successful of the early building contractors, and from 1811 the two men were responsible for developing part of the Tothill Fields estate belonging to the dean and chapter of Westminster Abbey. In parallel with this work Rowles entered into several major contracts on his own account. These included a saltpetre warehouse on south quay at the East India docks (1806)—Henry Holland had completed the company's headquarters in Leadenhall Street; the Theatre Royal, Drury Lane (1811), one of the first examples of a contract in gross; and the Royal Mint (1818), where Rowles was the office of works contractor for the masonry, bricklaying, and carpentry work. An estimate by Rowles dated 1807 for undertaking all the building work at East India College, Haileybury, survives in the Soane Museum, London.

About 1821 Rowles withdrew from the building industry altogether. He subsequently became a director of several dock, railway, and other companies, including St Katharine's Dock and the Rhymni ironworks. He served as managing director of the latter until his death: the ironworks was established in 1837 as successor to the Bute ironworks and its first chairman was W. J. Copland, which suggests that the earlier business connection still endured.

Rowles was one of the principal witnesses examined by the 1828 select committee on the office of works. He and another witness, William Cubitt, were described as two of the principal London general builders. In his evidence Rowles was generally critical of the method of pricing works for government contracts by 'measure and value' and strongly advocated contracts in gross as more advantageous to the employer. He commented that this system was 'very generally used now; I believe almost every new club house in London is built on the same principle' (Satoh, 38).

Rowles inherited all Henry Holland's architectural books and papers and his collection of antiquities. Many of the latter found their way into Sir John Soane's collection. The two men were on cordial terms and it seems likely that Rowles made Soane a present of the antiquities. He died in 1841. SUSIE BARSON

Sources A. Satoh, *Building in Britain: the origins of a modern industry* (1995) · S. Porter, ed., *Poplar, Blackwall and the Isle of Dogs: the parish of*

All Saints, [2], Survey of London, 44 (1994), 585 • J. M. Crook and M. H. Port, eds., *The history of the king's works*, 6 (1973) • D. Stroud, *Henry Holland, 1745–1806* (1950) • Soane's notebooks, Sir John Soane's Museum, London • parish register, St Martin-in-the-Fields, London, 8 Dec 1777 [baptism] • E. Holland, 'Collectanea genealogica', 1994

Rowlett, Thomas (1621–1652), print publisher, was the most significant figure in his profession in the seventeenth century. Everything he produced was of very high quality, and encompassed many etchings (a medium hitherto hardly exploited in England except by Wenceslaus Hollar) by most of the leading artists of the day in London. He never reprinted earlier plates bought from other publishers. The list of his publications at his 'shop neere Temple Barre' includes four engravings by William Faithorne, together with etchings by Edward Pearce (a set of ornamental grotesques), Francis Clein (a set of the *Liberal Arts* and of ornamental grotesques), Josias English (an associate of Clein at Mortlake), and Isaac de Caus (a set of views of the gardens at Wilton House). The most surprising of all his publications was a set of five imaginary landscapes etched by the diarist John Evelyn in 1649, just before his emigration to Paris.

Rowlett was apprenticed to the print publisher Robert Peake in the Goldsmiths' Company in 1636, and his name appears in a document of 1641 as a member of Peake's household. He was made free of the company on 26 February 1647. An Isaac Rowlett, perhaps Thomas's father, witnessed a will in 1632, jointly with Peake's father, William, in impeccable humanist script; this was probably the same Isaac Rowlett who served as a lieutenant under Robert Peake in the royalist garrison at Basing House.

The link with Peake explains Rowlett's career. A box of brass plates was captured with Peake at Basing House in 1645. Peake, being then imprisoned, presumably passed the plates to Rowlett to publish on his behalf. Rowlett extended the stock with new plates commissioned from the same group of royalist artists as Peake had published before the civil war, as well as from others left bereft of patronage. It was in these peculiar circumstances that so many turned their hands to print-making. In or very soon after 1649, in the aftermath of the execution of Charles, the operation was closed, and both Peake's and Rowlett's plates passed to Thomas Hinde, and thence by 1653 to Peter Stent.

A Thomas Rowlett 'gent.', of St Dunstan-in-the-West, aged twenty-two, married Marie Haines on 27 April 1643. In 1652 Elizabeth Rowlett was granted probate of Thomas Rowlett, bachelor, of the parish of St Dunstan, who had died intestate and been buried there on 3 April. Since St Dunstan is close to Rowlett's shop at Temple Bar, these almost certainly refer to the subject of this article.

ANTONY GRIFFITHS

Sources PRO, PROB 6/27, fol. 53 • Goldsmiths' Company archives, London • J. L. Chester and G. J. Armytage, eds., *Allegations for marriage licences issued by the bishop of London*, 2, Harleian Society, 26 (1887), 270 • M. Edmond, 'New light on Jacobean painters', *Burlington Magazine*, 118 (1976), 74–83, esp. 81 • M. Edmond, 'Limners and picturemakers', *Walpole Society*, 47 (1978–80), 60–242, esp. 204, no. 324 • A. Griffiths, 'The etchings of John Evelyn', *Art and patronage in the Caroline courts: essays in honour of Sir Oliver Millar*, ed. D. Howarth (1993), 51–67

Rowley, Sir Charles, first baronet (1770–1845), naval officer, born on 16 December 1770, was the fourth and youngest son of Vice-Admiral Sir Joshua *Rowley, first baronet (1730?–1790), and his wife, Sarah (*d.* 26 Dec 1812), daughter of Bartholomew Burton, deputy governor of the Bank of England, and was first cousin of Sir Josias *Rowley, baronet. He entered the navy in April 1785, served in different ships on the North American station, from November 1786 to October 1788 was with Prince William Henry (later William IV) in the *Pegasus* and the *Andromeda*; was again on the North American station, and in Newfoundland, with Vice-Admiral Milbanke, by whom, on 8 October 1789, he was promoted lieutenant and put in command of the *Trepassy*, where he remained until February 1791. In 1794 he went out to North America in the *Resolution*, flagship of Rear-Admiral George Murray, by whom he was promoted commander on 20 April, and captain on 1 August 1795. He then commanded the *Cleopatra* until May 1796, the *Hussar* until the following October, and from October 1796 to August 1798 the *Unité* in the channel. He married, on 7 December 1797, Elizabeth (*d.* 11 Jan 1838), youngest daughter of Admiral Sir Richard King, bt. They had five sons and two daughters. In 1800 Rowley was flag captain to Sir Charles Cotton in the *Prince George*. From March 1804 to November 1805 he was in the *Ruby*, for the most part in the North Sea, and from November 1805 to May 1814 he commanded the *Eagle* in the Mediterranean, in the expedition to Walcheren in 1809, off Cadiz in 1810, and from 1811 in the Adriatic, where, working with Captain Sir William Hoste, under the orders of Sir Thomas Francis Fremantle, he distinguished himself in engagements with the enemy's batteries, and especially at the capture of Fiume on 3 July, and of Trieste in October 1813. The emperor of Austria conferred on him the order of Maria Theresa, which he received permission to wear.

On 4 June 1814 Rowley was promoted rear-admiral, and on 2 January 1815 was nominated a KCB. From 1815 to 1818 he was commander-in-chief at the Nore, and at Jamaica from 1820 to 1823. He became vice-admiral on 27 May 1825, and was a lord of the Admiralty in Peel's administration of 1834–5. He stood for Portsmouth as a tory candidate, but despite official support was narrowly defeated. As a naval lord he remained wedded to the old order, asking the first lord to close down the gunnery training ship *Excellent*. He was made a GCH on 7 October 1835; a baronet on 22 February 1836; a GCB on 4 July 1840; and admiral on 23 November 1841. From December 1842 to September 1845 he was commander-in-chief at Portsmouth. He died at Brighton on 10 October 1845.

Rowley benefited from his naval family connections. He was described as a tall, dignified, rather magnificent gentleman with a fine profile. However, he spoke only slowly, which made his contribution to the debate at the board somewhat laboured. He was a fine sea commander, a tory in politics, and a reactionary in naval affairs.

J. K. LAUGHTON, *rev.* ANDREW LAMBERT

Sources J. H. Briggs, *Naval administrations, 1827 to 1892: the experience of 65 years*, ed. Lady Briggs (1898) · T. Pocock, *Remember Nelson: the life of Captain Sir William Hoste* (1977) · BL, Peel MSS · P. Mackesy, *The war in the Mediterranean, 1803–1810* (1957) · Burke, *Peerage* (1959) · O'Byrne, *Naval biog. dict.*, [2nd edn]
Archives NMM, letter and order books | BL, corresp. with Sir Hudson Lowe, Add. MSS 20107–20110, 20181, 20191–20192, 20233 · NL Scot., corresp. with Lord Melville
Likenesses J. R. Jackson, mezzotint, pubd 1848 (after G. Saunders), BM, NPG · F. S. Eastman, oils (after unknown artist), Admiralty, Portsmouth

Rowley, Charles (1839–1933), social reformer, was born on 3 November 1839 at 5 Cornwall Street, Ancoats, Manchester, the son of Charles Rowley (*fl.* 1810–1860), a warper, and his wife, Mary Jackson. A sickly child, he gained his early education largely from voracious reading, subsequently supplemented by mechanics' institute classes and a long association with the Bennett Street Sunday school. Of slight build, and continually dogged by ill health, Rowley nevertheless had a powerful presence; his insatiable curiosity, disdain for pretension of any sort, and earthy and forthright manner brought him warm friendship from an astonishing array of leading figures in late Victorian culture.

From very modest beginnings the elder Charles Rowley built up a substantial art-framing business, which employed Rowley in his youth; his occupation was recorded as 'picture frame maker' at the time of his marriage, on 11 June 1862, to Jane (1840–1913), the daughter of James Cocks, agent. There appear to have been no children. He was unfitted by both temperament and health—though he lived to be over ninety—for sustained labour (by his early thirties he had already suffered a series of nervous collapses), and his connection with the business steadily weakened. From the 1890s he seems increasingly to have survived on handouts from family and associates. However, the business brought Rowley into contact with many of the leading artists of the era, especially the Pre-Raphaelite Brotherhood, and later figures associated with the Century Guild of Artists. Strongly influenced by Ruskin, he became a leading figure in Manchester art circles and a frequent popular lecturer on art, and was active in the establishment of the municipal art gallery. He was involved in the city's decision to engage Ford Madox Brown to paint the Manchester Town Hall murals.

Although widely known as Rowley of Ancoats, Charles Rowley lived for most of his life on the outskirts of Manchester, first in Moston (which he represented on the city council, 1890–93), and later at Handforth in Cheshire. Nevertheless it was to the slum district of his birth that his energies were channelled. An advanced Liberal, Rowley had little interest in politics; instead he was preoccupied with what he saw as the degeneration of late Victorian inner-city life. While representing one of the Ancoats wards between 1875 and 1887, he promoted various activities designed to bring 'higher feeling' into the slums; these eventually coalesced into the Ancoats Recreation Committee. From 1882 the core of the movement was the winter Sunday afternoon lecture series, which quickly established itself as a significant site for the airing of progressive views, and over the subsequent forty years brought to Manchester many of the prominent intellectuals of the period. In 1888 the formation of the 'Ancoats Brotherhood' added reading groups, garden parties, summer rambles, and holidays for a wider and more prosperous membership.

Few of Rowley's ideas were novel, and he was deeply suspicious of the deadening effect of formal institutions; what marked him out was his inclusiveness, his restless search for new ways of reaching the people, and his determination to steer clear of any taint of condescension or moralizing. Despite an extensive national network of acquaintances, his orientation was emphatically local. In 1911 he published a substantial volume of memoirs, *Fifty Years of Work without Wages*, and he very occasionally contributed articles to the periodicals, but most of his writing was local and ephemeral. Perhaps for these reasons, although his activities were occasionally imitated elsewhere, he founded no national movement. His ideas were adapted by the Pleasant Sunday Afternoon brotherhoods and the Oxford Summer Schools movement of John Lewis Paton and Michael Sadler, and it was claimed that his experiences influenced the evolution of Toynbee Hall, where he was a frequent resident.

Perhaps something of the obliqueness of this success eventually rankled. Despite the large membership and substantial attendances, Rowley's Ancoats activities were never far from financial crisis, and on many occasions he spoke of suspending the lectures, but it was only in 1924 that they were finally abandoned. His first wife, Jane, had died in 1913, and he had subsequently, in 1914 or 1915, married his nurse Jean, who cared for him during the last decade of his life, during which his Handforth home, The Elms, remained a magnet for Manchester progressives. He died there, of pneumonia, on 6 September 1933, and was cremated in Manchester on 9 September, survived by his second wife.   M. Hewitt

Sources C. Rowley, *Fifty years of work without wages* (1911) · J. I. Rushton, 'Charles Rowley and the Ancoats Recreation Movement', MEd thesis, University of Manchester, 1959 · *Manchester Guardian* (7 Sept 1933) · C. Rowley, *Fifty years of Ancoats loss and gain* (1899) · biographical cuttings, Man. CL · *Manchester City News* (1870–1933) · b. cert. · m. cert. [Jane Cocks] · d. cert. · census returns, 1881 · CGPLA Eng. & Wales (1933)
Archives Chetham's Library, Manchester, letters, A.2.174 · JRL, scrapbooks | Man. CL, St Paul's Sunday school collection
Likenesses F. M. Brown, crayon drawing, 1885, Man. City Gall. · F. C. Gould, caricatures · W. Rothenstein, lithograph, Man. City Gall. · W. Rothenstein, portrait · G. Thompson, caricatures
Wealth at death £205: probate, 1933, CGPLA Eng. & Wales

Rowley, Harold Henry (1890–1969), biblical scholar, was born at 77 Earl Stowe Street, Leicester, on 24 March 1890, the fifth of six children of Richard Rowley, a foreman finisher in a shoe factory, and his wife, Emma Saunt. He was educated at the Wyggeston School, Leicester, and then at Bristol Baptist college and Bristol University, also studying as an external student of London University, where he gained the pass degree of BD in 1912. A year later he graduated BA (theology) at Bristol. He went to Oxford where he belonged to St Catherine's Society and to Mansfield College, and obtained a BLitt in 1929. In 1916 he served briefly in Egypt with the Young Men's Christian Association, but ill health forced him to return to England. On 21 May 1918 he married Gladys Barbara (b. 1891/2), daughter of Richard Arthur Shaw, commercial traveller, of Bristol. They had four children, a son and three daughters, of whom the second married another Old Testament scholar, Aubrey R. Johnson. After a time as minister of a united Baptist–Congregational church at Wells, Somerset, he went to China in 1922 as a missionary of the Baptist Missionary Society where he taught Old Testament in Shantung Christian College until 1929. His interest in China remained with him, and late in his life he published *Submission in Suffering and other Essays in Eastern Thought* (1951) and *Prophecy and Religion in Ancient China and Israel* (1956).

Rowley's first major published study was *The Aramaic of the Old Testament* (1929) which defended the critical dating of Daniel in the Hellenistic period. In 1930 Rowley became assistant lecturer in Semitic languages at Cardiff, and then, in 1935, professor of Semitic languages at Bangor. In 1945 he moved to Manchester as professor of Semitic languages and literatures, a title changed in 1949 to Hebrew language and literature. This suited Rowley's academic interests since, though perfectly competent in biblical Hebrew and in Aramaic, he did not aspire to mastery of the wider fields of the Semitic languages. The Manchester years were Rowley's great period, and the fine libraries of the city served ideally the genius of one who was meticulous in annotation and bibliography.

Rowley quickly became one of the leading figures in Old Testament studies in Britain and was able to influence the development of the subject both in England and, to an extent, abroad. As secretary responsible for foreign contacts in the Society for Old Testament Study he entered into correspondence with scholars all over war-torn Europe and did much to restore the community of scholarship which war had disrupted, for which he was gratefully remembered.

Rowley's publications were multifarious. *Darius the Mede and the Four World Empires* (1935) and *The Relevance of Apocalyptic* (1944) continued his early research interests. The Schweich lectures for 1948, published as *From Joseph to Joshua* (1950), concerned the dating of the Exodus. *The Faith of Israel* (1956) was a contribution to Old Testament theology; his last major work was *Worship in Ancient Israel* (1967). Volumes such as *The Servant of the Lord* (1952), *From Moses to Qumran* (1963), and *Men of God* (1963) collected articles previously published, many of them first given as lectures in the John Rylands Library series. Rowley was active in discussion of the recently discovered Dead Sea scrolls: his chief study was *The Zadokite Fragments and the Dead Sea Scrolls* (1952), a book later superseded by further research. He also wrote on a number of other biblical and theological themes and wrote the entry for the *Dictionary of National Biography* on T. W. Manson.

Much of Rowley's contribution, however, lay not in his own writing but in editing and planning publication. For eleven years he edited the *Book List* of the Society for Old Testament Study and made it into an internationally recognized source. The joint volume *The Old Testament and Modern Study* (1951) was extremely successful. He initiated (1956) the *Journal of Semitic Studies* and was its joint editor until 1960. Many other works of biblical and theological study were initiated, supervised, or re-edited by him, and in his retirement he undertook even wider responsibilities in advising publishers. He reviewed a vast range of theological literature, often well outside his own field, and was also a member of the Old Testament panel for the *New English Bible*. In all this he was assisted by his immense library with its notable collection of offprints, bound and indexed, which he later sold to Union Theological Seminary, Richmond, Virginia, so that it would be passed to the seminary after his death.

Rowley received honorary degrees from many universities, became a fellow of the British Academy in 1947, and was awarded the Burkitt medal in 1951. The Norwegian Academy of Science and Letters, the Royal Flemish Academy, the Royal Society of Letters of Lund, and the Society of Biblical Literature (USA) all elected him to honorary or foreign membership. He was president of the Society for Old Testament Study in 1950, and in 1955 a volume in his honour, *Wisdom in Israel and in the Ancient Near East* (Vetus Testamentum supplement 3) was published which also contained a select bibliography of his writings up to 1954. He remained active in Baptist affairs and was president of the Baptist Union in 1957–8, as well as serving the Baptist Missionary Society as chairman of its committee.

Rowley was a scholar of great competence and thoroughness rather than an original thinker. He covered all the ground and sifted the literature with extreme care, but did not initiate specific new lines of thought. He worked exceptionally hard and it was said that he thoroughly enjoyed proof-reading. His one hobby was philately. He took no sort of exercise and professed not to know that there were mountains in Wales. His health had never been robust. After retirement from Manchester in 1959 he moved to Stroud. In his retirement he had several illnesses, in the midst of which he was often to be found reading the proofs of some abstruse work. He died at Cheltenham General Hospital on 4 October 1969.

JAMES BARR, *rev.*

Sources G. W. Anderson, 'Harold Henry Rowley, 1890–1969', *PBA*, 56 (1970), 309–19 • private information (1981) • b. cert. • m. cert. • d. cert.

Archives Union Theological Seminary, Richmond, Virginia | NL Scot., corresp. with publishers

Likenesses photograph, repro. in M. Noth and D. W. Thomas, eds., *Wisdom in Israel and in the ancient Near East* (1955), frontispiece

Wealth at death £16,197: administration with will, 31 Dec 1969, *CGPLA Eng. & Wales*

Rowley, John (c.1668–1728), maker of scientific instruments and mechanic, was born in Lichfield, Staffordshire, the youngest of three sons and a daughter of William Rowley (d. 1673), sword cutler of Lichfield, and his wife, Elizabeth. On 20 October 1682 he was bound apprentice to the London mathematical and optical instrument maker Joseph Hone in the Broderers' Company, and he took his freedom in that company on 26 February 1691. Soon afterwards he established his own business, opening a shop in 1704 at the sign of the Globe, in Fleet Street in the City of London; he took five apprentices between 1699 and 1710. On 18 April 1697 he married Catherine Harding (*d.* 1756) at Wooburn, Buckinghamshire. Their daughter Elizabeth was baptized at St Bartholomew-the-Less, West Smithfield, London, on 31 May 1698.

From 1704 to 1708 Rowley enjoyed the patronage of Prince George of Denmark. He also supplied Christ's Hospital mathematical school, the Office of Ordnance, and other corporate bodies with a wide range of mathematical, drawing, surveying, and gunnery instruments. His sextant, made in 1708 and figured in John Harris's *Lexicon technicum* of 1710, together with the other instruments which he provided for the observatory at Trinity College, Cambridge, commended him to the Royal Society, which in 1711–13 asked him to report on the instruments of John Flamsteed, astronomer royal, at the Royal Observatory, Greenwich. In 1710 he made four large sundials for Blenheim Palace and three for St Paul's Cathedral, which further enhanced his reputation.

Rowley worked in brass, silver, and ivory to produce some extremely fine pieces and he was recognized as the most skilled maker of mathematical instruments and models of his day. Other craftsmen emulated him, and he was praised by scientific writers. He became the principal supplier of instruments to Charles Boyle, fourth earl of Corke and Orrery, who assembled one of the finest collections of the age. About 1712 Orrery commissioned from Rowley a mechanical model of the earth–sun–moon system, of a type constructed by the clockmaker George Graham, but larger and more sophisticated. Perhaps as a pun on the word 'horary', Rowley named it an 'orrery', still the current term for a mechanical planetarium. Rowley also made magnificent orreries for the Habsburg emperor Charles VI in 1712–13, for Peter the Great in 1714, and for the East India Company in 1714–15. George I commissioned his most elaborate model, the 'great solar system', in 1722, at a price of £1000; this may have been remodelled in 1733 by one of Rowley's former apprentices, Thomas Wright, who was also noted for his grand orreries.

On his appointment in 1715 as master of mechanics to George I, Rowley relinquished his shop to Thomas Wright and concentrated on business for the offices of Ordnance and Works, the latter being responsible for the royal palaces and other official buildings. He was charged with making and repairing water and fire engines at Kensington Palace, Hampton Court, the House of Commons, and Windsor Castle. The 'great water engine' which he built at Windsor in 1718 functioned until 1758; Rowley was its keeper by royal warrant of 1721, backdated to 1718. He constructed engines for the Tower of London and numerous fire engines for the Office of Ordnance. Appointed inspector to the Chelsea Waterworks Company, he constructed in 1725–6 a water engine which lasted until 1775. Between 1704 and 1723 he supplied the Board of Ordnance with many weighing and measuring devices, among which 'Rowley's Tower yard' later played an important

part in standardizing the English yard. His techniques for gauging cannonball weight and dimensions also led to the standardized calibration of land and sea cannon in 1715.

Rowley joined two of the earliest known art clubs, the Rose and Crown and the prestigious Virtuosi of St Luke. George Vertue has described an untraced portrait of him, painted by Jacob van Schuppen in Vienna about 1718. The 'learned and curious' often met at Rowley's Johnson's Court house, off Fleet Street, and Samuel Johnson praised him for his perpetual-motion experiments. Rowley died intestate on 14 January 1728 in London and was buried on 19 January at St Dunstan-in-the-West, Fleet Street.

JOHN H. APPLEBY

Sources J. H. Appleby, 'A new perspective on John Rowley', *Annals of Science*, 53 (1996), 1–27 · J. R. Millburn, *The ordnance records as a source for studies of instruments and their makers* (privately printed, 1994) · G. Clifton, *Directory of British scientific instrument makers, 1550–1851*, ed. G. L'E. Turner (1995) · E. W. Taylor and J. S. Wilson, *At the sign of the Orrery* (1950) · E. G. R. Taylor, *The mathematical practitioners of Tudor and Stuart England* (1954) · H. C. King and J. R. Millburn, *Geared to the stars* (1978) · M. A. Crawforth, 'Instrument makers in the London guilds', *Annals of Science*, 44 (1987), 319–77 · H. M. Colvin and others, eds., *The history of the king's works*, 5 (1976) · S. Switzer, *An introduction to a general system of hydrostatics and hydraulics*, 2 (1729) · I. Bignamini, 'George Vertue, art historian, and art institutions in London, 1689–1768', *Walpole Society*, 54 (1988), 1–148 · R. D. Connor, *The weights and measures of England* (1987) · DNB · *The British Journal, or, The Censor*, 20 (Jan 1728) · parish register (burials) St Dunstan-in-the-West, London, 1728 · minutes of the Broderers' Company, GL, MS 14657/3
Likenesses J. Van Schuppen, portrait, *c.*1718
Wealth at death see administration, PRO, PROB 6/104

Rowley, John (*c.*1768–1824), army officer, joined the Royal Military Academy, Woolwich, as a cadet on 7 October 1782, entered the Royal Artillery as second lieutenant on 28 January 1786, and was stationed at Woolwich. He was transferred to the Royal Engineers on 23 August 1787 and went to Gosport, where he was employed on the fortifications for the next two years. He went to Jersey in the summer of 1789 and was promoted first lieutenant on 2 May 1792.

In December 1793 Rowley accompanied the expedition under the earl of Moira to assist the counter-revolutionary Vendeans, but the annihilation of the Vendean army made the expedition abortive. After its return to England Rowley accompanied Lord Moira with 10,000 men to reinforce the duke of York in Flanders. On landing at Ostend on 26 June 1794 they marched through Bruges to Alost, and after a severe fight with the French retreated to Malines, fell back behind the Netthe, and joined the duke of York. Rowley was engaged in an action near Rosendael on 16 July, the action at Boxtel in September, and the siege at Nijmegen in October and November. In January 1795 the British army retreated across the dreary waste of the Weluwe district to Bremen, where, after some fighting with the French in February and March, Rowley embarked for England, arriving on 8 May.

On 15 May 1795 Rowley was appointed adjutant of the corps of engineers and military artificers at Woolwich, and continued to hold the appointment until September 1799, having been promoted captain-lieutenant on 18 June

1796. On 1 October 1799 he became aide-de-camp to the chief engineer of the kingdom at the office of the Board of Ordnance. He was promoted captain on 2 May 1800; brigade major of Royal Engineers at headquarters on 1 May 1802; regimental lieutenant-colonel and assistant inspector-general of fortifications on 1 July 1806; deputy inspector-general of fortifications on 6 December 1811; colonel in the army on 4 June 1814; regimental colonel on 20 December of the same year; and major-general on 15 March 1821. He served on various committees, and distinguished himself by his administrative ability in all his staff appointments. He was a fellow of the Royal Society (February 1809). Rowley died at Spencer Farm, Essex, the residence of the Revd Lewis Way, on 1 December 1824, while still deputy inspector-general of fortifications. Wellington, on hearing of his death, expressed, in a minute, his 'utmost concern' at the loss of so zealous and able an officer, while the Board of Ordnance recorded his services and the general regret felt at his death.

R. H. VETCH, rev. DAVID GATES

Sources PRO, War Office Records · GM, 1st ser., 94/2 (1824), 643 · W. Porter, History of the corps of royal engineers, 2 vols. (1889) · Royal Engineers records, Royal Engineers Institution, Chatham · J. Philippart, ed., The royal military calendar, 3rd edn, 5 vols. (1820) · T. C. W. Blanning, The French revolutionary wars, 1787–1802 (1996)

Rowley, Sir Joshua, first baronet (1730?–1790), naval officer, was the eldest son of Sir William *Rowley (c.1690–1768), naval officer, and Arabella (d. 1784), daughter of Captain George Dawson of co. Londonderry. As a boy he served with his father in the Mediterranean, and learned Italian and French during winters in Leghorn (Du Cane MSS, 81). On 2 July 1747 he was promoted lieutenant and in 1752 he was serving as lieutenant of the Penzance. On 4 December 1753 he was posted to the frigate Rye, apparently for rank only, and in March 1755 he was appointed to the Ambuscade, attached later on to the squadron under Sir Edward Hawke, in the Bay of Biscay. Rowley was moved into the Harwich (50 guns) in January 1756, and in October 1757 he commissioned the Montague, a new ship of 60 guns, in which he accompanied Admiral Henry Osborn to the Mediterranean, and took part in the capture of the squadron under the Marquis Du Quesne on 1 March 1758.

The Montague and Monarch pursued the Oriflamme on shore, under the walls of the castle of Aiglos. Admiral Osborn reported that, 'had it not been for violating the neutrality of Spain, they would have entirely destroyed her' (Naval Chronicle, 24, 1810, 90). Shortly afterwards Rowley returned to the channel and joined the squadron under Lord Howe. In the unfortunate affair at St Cas he commanded a division of the boats, and, having landed to direct the re-embarkation of the troops, he was wounded and made prisoner. Rowley's service was, on this occasion, highly regarded by Howe. He was shortly afterwards exchanged and reappointed to the Montague, which during 1759 he commanded under Sir Edward Hawke off Brest and in the battle of Quiberon Bay. In this year he married Sarah (d. 1812), daughter of Bartholomew Burton, deputy governor of the Bank of England.

Rowley went out with Sir James Douglas to the West Indies in 1760, moved into the Superbe in November, and returned to England in the following year. In 1762, in the Superbe, with two frigates, he convoyed the East and West Indian trade to the westward, and successfully protected it from the assault of a superior French squadron under M. de Ternay. For this service he was presented with handsome pieces of plate by the East India Company and by the City of London.

In October 1776 Rowley was appointed to the Monarch, in which in the beginning of 1778 he convoyed some transports to Gibraltar. When he afterwards put into Cadiz, he was treated with such discourtesy that he arranged with Mr Hardy the consul to escort home British merchant ships in the port, thus saving them from seizure on the declaration of war. On his return to England he was attached to the fleet under Augustus Keppel, and led the van in the action of 27 July. In January 1778 he wrote to the first lord, the fourth earl of Sandwich, thanking him for appointment as a colonel of marines (Rowley to Sandwich, 25 Jan 1778, NMM, SAN/F/12/53, not noticed in the Army List for 1778–83), but he was able to avoid involvement in the recriminations between admirals Keppel and Hugh Palliser.

At the end of the year Rowley was moved into the Suffolk, and sent to the West Indies in command of a squadron of seven ships, as a reinforcement to Rear-Admiral John Byron, whom he joined at St Lucia in February 1779. He asked to be permitted to take the Monarch's people with him: 'Most of the Monarch's men have been of my own getting and have been tried, and many of the men would not have come into the Navy if it had not been to sail with me'. He asked for Commander George Stoney as his flag-captain, but he was in fact only permitted to transfer 100 men, and was obliged to select another officer as his captain (Rowley to Sandwich, 27 and 30 Dec 1778, NMM, SAN/F/17/8, 13, 24, 33). Sandwich noted that Rowley had 'behaved with great moderation & kept clear of cabals' (Correspondence of George III, 4.225).

On 19 March Rowley was promoted rear-admiral of the blue, and in that capacity he was with Byron in the action off Grenada on 6 July. In March 1780, on the arrival of Sir George Rodney to command the station, Rowley shifted his flag to the Conqueror, in which ship he commanded the rear in the action off Martinique on 17 April, and the van in the encounter of 15–19 May. Rowley was afterwards sent to Jamaica with ten ships of the line to reinforce Sir Peter Parker, and to provide for the safety of the island and a convoy for the homeward-bound trade. In 1782 he succeeded to the command of the Jamaica station, where he remained until the peace (Rowley to Sandwich, 28 Sept 1781, NMM, SAN/F/28/87). Of his judgement in this office Lord Hood, who wrote somewhat contemptuously of him as 'our friend Jos', formed a poor opinion (D. Hannay ed., Letters Written by Sir Samuel Hood, Navy RS, 3, 1895).

Rowley had the reputation of being a good and brave officer; but he had no opportunity for distinction during his command, and after his return to England in 1783 he had no further service. Rowley was created a baronet on 10

June 1786, and promoted vice-admiral of the white on 24 September 1787. He died at his seat, Tendring Hall in Suffolk, on 26 February 1790.

Rowley's eldest son, William (d. 1832), who succeeded to the baronetcy, was sheriff of Suffolk (1791) and MP for Suffolk (1812–30). His second son, Bartholomew Samuel, was vice-admiral and commander-in-chief at Jamaica at his death on 7 October 1811; the fourth son was Charles *Rowley, naval officer. A daughter of Joshua Rowley's, Philadelphia (1763–1855), married Admiral Sir Charles Cotton. J. K. LAUGHTON, rev. NICHOLAS TRACY

Sources J. Charnock, ed., *Biographia navalis*, 6 (1798), 107 · J. Ralfe, *The naval biography of Great Britain*, 1 (1828), 170 · *Naval Chronicle*, 24 (1810), 90 · *The correspondence of King George the Third from 1760 to December 1783*, ed. J. Fortescue, 6 vols. (1927–8), also *The later correspondence of George III*, ed. A. Aspinall, 5 vols. (1962–70) · *Report on the manuscripts of Lady Du Cane*, HMC, 61 (1905), 81
Archives NMM, corresp. with Lord Sandwich, MS 91/018 SAN F/28/87; SAN F/12/53; SAN F/17/8, 13, 24, 33 · PRO, corresp. with Admiral Rodney, PRO 30/20
Likenesses G. Romney, oils, 1787–8, NMM; repro. in *Naval Chronicle*, 34, p. 89

Rowley, Sir Josias, baronet (1765–1842), naval officer, was a grandson of Sir William *Rowley and the second son of Clotworthy Rowley, barrister and sometime MP for Downpatrick, and his wife, Letitia, daughter and coheir of Samuel Campbell of Mount Campbell, co. Leitrim, and Bath. He was entered on the books of the *Monarch*, commanded by his uncle, Sir Joshua Rowley, from November 1777 to December 1778, though it is doubtful if he served in her. In December 1778 he joined the *Suffolk*, with his uncle, and went to the West Indies. In 1780 he was a midshipman of the *Alexander* (Lord Longford) in the channel, and in 1781 the *Agamemnon* (Captain Caldwell). He was promoted lieutenant on 24 December 1783 and, after service in the West Indies and the North Sea, was promoted on 14 March 1794 to command the sloop *Lark* (16 guns) in the North Sea; he was promoted captain on 6 April 1795. In April 1797 he was appointed to the *Braave* (40 guns) at the Cape of Good Hope, and in January 1799 was moved into the *Impérieuse* (38 guns), in which he went to the East Indies, and returned to England in June 1802. In April 1805 he commissioned the *Raisonnable* (64 guns), in which he took part in the action off Cape Finisterre on 22 July 1805, and at the end of the year went to the Cape of Good Hope under the command of Sir Home Riggs Popham, with whom he afterwards went to Buenos Aires and Montevideo, where he took an active part in the operations under Popham and his successors, rear-admirals Stirling and George Murray. After the failure of the expedition the *Raisonnable* returned to the Cape of Good Hope.

In September 1809, still in the *Raisonnable*, Rowley was senior officer of the little squadron in the neighbourhood of Mauritius, and concerted with the commandant of the troops at Rodrigues a plan for silencing the batteries and capturing the shipping at St Paul's on the island of Bourbon, operations successfully achieved with minimal loss on 21 September. In March 1810 he moved into the *Boadicea* (38 guns), and in July the squadron under his command

transported a strong force of soldiers, which landed on Bourbon on the 7th and 8th. The island was unable to offer any effective resistance, and the capitulation was signed on the 9th. Rowley was still at Bourbon when on 22 August he received news from Captain Samuel Pym of his projected attack on the French frigates in Grand Port, Mauritius. He sailed at once to co-operate in this, but did not arrive until the 29th, too late to prevent the disaster which overwhelmed Pym's force. He returned to Bourbon, and was still there on 12 September when the *Africaine* arrived off the island. The *Boadicea* put to sea to join her, but was still several miles distant when the *Africaine* engaged, and was captured by, the French frigates *Iphigénie* and *Astrée* in the early morning of the 13th.

With two sloops the *Boadicea* recaptured the *Africaine* the same afternoon and took her to St Paul's, followed at some distance by the two French frigates, which Rowley, in the weakened state of his squadron, did not consider it would be prudent to engage. The French frigates, on their part, considered the British too strong to attack, and they retired to Port Louis, permitting the *Boadicea* to put to sea on the morning of the 18th and capture the French frigate *Vénus*, which, with her prize, the *Ceylon* (now recaptured), appeared off the port. Rowley's force was shortly afterwards strengthened by the arrival of several frigates, and from mid-October he was able to maintain a close blockade of Port Louis, continued until the arrival of the expedition under Vice-Admiral Albemarle Bertie on 29 November and the surrender of Mauritius on 3 December. Rowley was then sent home with the dispatches, and on his arrival in England was appointed to the *America* (74 guns), which he commanded in the Mediterranean until October 1814. He had meanwhile been created a baronet on 4 December 1813 and promoted rear-admiral on 4 June 1814. On 2 January 1815 he was made a KCB. During the summer of 1815 he was again in the Mediterranean with his flag in the *Impregnable* (98 guns, Lord Exmouth), but he returned to England at the end of the war. From 1818 to 1821 he was commander-in-chief on the coast of Ireland; and from 1821 to 1826 he was MP for the potwalloping borough of Kinsale, co. Cork. On 27 May 1825 he was made vice-admiral; was commander-in-chief in the Mediterranean from December 1833 to February 1837, a command which then carried with it the GCMG, which he received on 22 February 1834; was made a GCB on 4 July 1840; and died, unmarried, at his residence, Mount Campbell, co. Leitrim, on 10 January 1842, when the baronetcy became extinct. J. K. LAUGHTON, rev. ANDREW LAMBERT

Sources D. Syrett and R. L. DiNardo, *The commissioned sea officers of the Royal Navy, 1660–1815*, rev. edn, Occasional Publications of the Navy RS, 1 (1994) · C. N. Parkinson, *War in the eastern seas, 1793–1815* (1954) · O'Byrne, *Naval biog. dict.* · J. J. Colledge, *Ships of the Royal Navy: an historical index*, 1 (1969) · J. Marshall, *Royal naval biography*, 1/2 (1823), 622–35 · *GM*, 2nd ser., 17 (1842), 325 · HoP, *Commons, 1790–1820*, vol. 2
Archives NMM, corresp. with Lord Minto · U. Durham L., letters to Viscount Ponsonby
Likenesses A. Morton, oils, 1832–3, NMM · C. Grey, ink drawing, NG Ire. · J. Kirkwood, etching, NPG

Rowley, Samuel (*d.* 1624), actor and playwright, is first evident in the 1590s when he was an actor–shareholder in the Lord Admiral's Men then performing at the Rose Playhouse on Bankside, London. He appears as 'sam' in a list of actors dated 14 December 1594 (*Henslowe's Diary*, 8). Rowley was then a young man, but seems always to have been referred to as 'sam' by Philip Henslowe (then owner of the Rose), whose *Diary* contains many mentions of Rowley. On 3 August 1597 Rowley and other actors served as witnesses of a bond (ibid., 239). Just after 8 March 1598 his name appears with the other members of the company who acknowledged a debt to Henslowe (ibid., 87). On 16 November 1598 he bound himself to perform exclusively in Henslowe's playhouse, but shortly thereafter Rowley assumed duties that pertained to the business side of the company. He was given money to 'buy divers things for to make coats for giants' in December 1598 (ibid., 102); he distributed the company's gift of 10s. to the playwrights who wrote *Sir John Oldcastle* in November 1599 (ibid., 126); and he regularly purchased plays on behalf of the Lord Admiral's Men (ibid., esp. 104). A series of letters, sent from Rowley to Henslowe in 1601, illustrates not only Rowley's involvement in business affairs, but the ways in which Henslowe managed his playhouse investment (Collier, 23, 25).

From 1597 to 1613 it is also possible to trace Rowley's acting career. The plots (one-page outlines of the plays, used during performance to remind actors which scenes they were in) of *Frederick and Basilea*, *Fortune's Tennis*, *The Battle of Alcazar*, and 1 *Tamar Cam* suggest that he performed many roles, mostly minor (*Henslowe Papers*, 152–4). However, Rowley was still listed as a player when the Admiral's Men were taken into the service of Prince Henry (1603), and he is among those on his household list in 1610 (Chambers, 2.186–8). Moreover, after the prince's death the palsgrave assumed patronage of the company: Rowley was given in the 1613 list for that company (Chambers and Greg, 1.275–7) but did not appear in subsequent lists of the Palsgrave's Men (Bentley, 1.137–9).

Rowley's career as a playwright is fraught with questions. In 1602 Henslowe paid him and a fellow actor, William Bird, 'for ther adicyones in docter fostes' (*Henslowe's Diary*, 206). It is difficult to pinpoint precisely what these 'additions' were, though literary historians commonly assume that they were the comic passages in the middle of Marlowe's play which was preserved in the 1616 text. (The Admiral's Men owned the play, performed it frequently in the 1590s, and probably revived it about this time.) The tendency of dramatists to write in collaboration was extremely common during this period. Rowley and Bird had previously finished *Judas* in 1601, possibly the unfinished play by William Haughton. Rowley collaborated with Thomas Dekker (and perhaps John Day) in the composition of *The Noble Soldier* (date unclear; Chambers, 3.472).

Yet Rowley wrote several plays on his own, including *When you See me, you Know me* (*c.*1603–5), a history play based on the reign of Henry VIII. Three additional plays, written for the Palsgrave's Men, were licensed by the master of the revels shortly before Rowley's death: *Richard III* (July 1623), *Hardshifte for Husbands* (October 1623), and *A Match or No Match* (April 1624). However, their dates of composition are unclear.

In the early part of the twentieth century H. D. Sykes argued that, using comparative stylistic analysis, Rowley's hand could be found in the prose scenes of *The Taming of a Shrew* (1588–93), *The Famous Victories of Henry V* (1583–88), the clowning passages of *Orlando Furioso* (1588–91), and the prose scenes of *Wily Beguiled* (1596–1606; Chambers, 3.472). Nevertheless, some theatre historians have challenged this theory on the basis of company provenance, as there is no known connection between Rowley and the Queen's Men, who seem definitely to have owned *The Famous Victories*, and possibly *Orlando Furioso* and *A Shrew*. Yet attribution of the two latter plays to the Queen's Men is itself a matter for debate (McMillin and MacLean, 86–90, 161–2).

Rowley's later life remains obscure. He apparently continued to work for Edward Alleyn—Henslowe's son-in-law and a theatre entrepreneur—after he retired from active involvement in acting and writing. In April 1620 it was probably Samuel Rowley who was characterized, in a letter written by one of Alleyn's lessees, as an agent who collected rent for Alleyn (*Henslowe Papers*, 94–5).

Rowley's will, proved in the commissary court of London on 4 December 1624, confirms some details of his life which formerly historians could only speculate on, as well as providing other new details (GL, MS 9171/24, fols. 355v–356v, transcribed by Somerset, and more recently by Honigmann and Brock, 138–40). Rowley was apparently the man who married Alice Coley on 7 April 1594 in the parish of St Michael, Crooked Lane. At the time when the will was written (23 July 1624) Rowley, who described himself as 'beinge visited with sicknes', was living in Whitechapel. He held property there and in nearby Stepney. Although he failed to mention any of his theatrical associates he left his brother William (*d.* 1625), also an actor–playwright, all his books. He also mentions his wife (Alice), brother (Thomas), a surviving daughter (Jane Adams), several grandchildren, and a nephew. Rowley also generously remembered 'the most needie, aged and impotent poore of the Parish of White Chappell' in his list of bequests. Rowley was buried on 20 October 1624 in the parish of St Mary, Whitechapel. It was the parish in which he had resided continuously for over twenty years. He also served in local government there. Rowley was a member of the Middlesex jury panel in 1610 and 1611, and foreman of the jury in September 1624. Additionally, he was constable of Whitechapel in 1618. S. P. CERASANO

Sources *Henslowe's diary*, ed. R. A. Foakes and R. T. Rickert (1968) · J. A. Somerset, 'New facts concerning Samuel Rowley', *Review of English Studies*, 17 (1966), 293–7 · E. K. Chambers, *The Elizabethan stage*, 4 vols. (1923) · *Henslowe papers*, ed. W. W. Greg (1907) · J. Payne Collier, ed., *The Alleyn papers* (1843) · S. McMillin and S.-B. MacLean, *The Queen's Men and their plays* (1998) · E. K. Chambers and W. W. Greg, eds., 'Dramatic records from the patent rolls', *Malone Society Collections*, 1/3 (1909), 260–84 · M. Eccles, 'Samuel Rowley', *Studies in Philology*, 79/4 (1982), 116 · G. E. Bentley, *The Jacobean and Caroline* *stage*, 7 vols. (1941–68) • E. A. J. Honigmann and S. Brock, eds., *Playhouse wills, 1558–1642: an edition of wills by Shakespeare and his contemporaries in the London theatre* (1993) • *DNB*

Rowley, William (1585?–1626), actor and playwright, is an obscure figure. Nothing is known of his parentage, place of birth, or early life, and his date of birth is conjectural. Speculation that he was a brother of Samuel Rowley, also an actor and playwright, has no firmer basis than the sharing of a common surname. Nothing is known, either, of his personal life, save that 'Grace relict of William Rowley' renounced the administration of his estate on 16 February 1626, five days after the recorded burial at St James's, Clerkenwell, Middlesex, of 'William Rowley, housekeeper'.

Early career in the theatre Rowley first appears in written records in 1607 as a playwright, as co-signatory, with John Day and George Wilkins, of an epistle, added to a second issue of *The Travels of the Three English Brothers*, and addressed to the family of the Shirleys, whose exploits the play celebrates. The first reference to him as an actor is in May 1609, as a member of a new company, the Duke of York's Men. That he was then purchasing apparel on their behalf, and that he was one of five named in a legal suit in 1610, suggests that he was a seasoned actor, and it seems possible that he was earlier a member of Queen Anne's Men, to whose repertory he contributed (besides *The Travels of the Three English Brothers*) *A Shoemaker a Gentleman* (*c.*1608) and (with Thomas Heywood) *Fortune by Land and Sea* (*c.*1608–1609).

Rowley's seniority within the Duke of York's Men, confirmed by his being named second in the list of players in the royal patent granted to the troupe in March 1610, was maintained during his long association with the company, which from November 1612, with the death of Henry, prince of Wales, was known as Prince Charles's Men. Besides acting and writing for the company, he also represented his fellows before the privy council (1615) and was payee (1610–14) for performances of plays at court. Nominally, at least, Rowley remained a member of the company until May 1625, when his name appears in the list of Prince Charles's Men granted payments for livery for the funeral of James I. But, *de facto*, he had by August 1623 become a member of the King's Men, for whom thereafter he both acted and (occasionally) wrote.

The three early plays for the Queen's Men seem to have been followed, about the years 1611 to 1614, by *A New Wonder, a Woman Never Vexed*, a comedy usually taken to be written by Rowley alone—though Darby argues cautiously for Heywood's co-authorship or revision—and by several now lost, including *Hymen's Holiday, or, Cupid's Vagaries*, performed at court on 24 February 1612. Whether these lost plays were written unaided cannot be determined, but certainly in the decade following Rowley wrote alone, so far as is known, only one play, his sole tragedy, *All's Lost by Lust* (*c.*1619).

Early dramatic collaborations, 1613–1622, and *The Changeling* Of the seven collaborative works now agreed to constitute the Rowley canon in the years 1613–22, five are from the most famous and productive of his partnerships, with Thomas Middleton. The first, *Wit at Several Weapons* (*c.*1613), was included in the 1647 folio edition of the works of Francis Beaumont and John Fletcher, but tests of authorship by Lake, Jackson, and Hoy indicate at most that there are traces of John Fletcher, and that the comedy is a Middleton–Rowley collaboration. *A Fair Quarrel*, their second joint work, and one of the two best, followed about 1617, then in 1618, it is thought, *The Old Law*. The title-page of the latter, a comedy whose main plot deals with the implications of the two meanings of the title—a law concerning the old, which requires men to be put to death at eighty and women at sixty, and the old, Mosaic, law, which requires the honouring of one's parents—credits Philip Massinger as well as Middleton and Rowley, but Massinger's involvement is disputed, and at most minor. A theatre masque, *The World Tossed at Tennis*, was performed in 1622, and the last (and incomparably the finest) of their collaborations, *The Changeling*, in the same year.

As his non-collaborative plays indicate, as a poet and playwright Rowley has major limitations. His verse is generally rough and awkward and his character depiction unsophisticated, with individuals commonly represented in terms of a single dominating trait. But working in collaboration, particularly with Middleton, he could surmount these limitations to a remarkable degree. *A Fair Quarrel*, where he is responsible not only for the 'roaring' scenes involving the foolish Chough and his servant Trimtram, but also for the sub-plot concerning Russell's attempts to prevent the marriage of his daughter Jane to the deserving Fitzallen, shows him handling a serious story line capably, but it is in *The Changeling* where Rowley is at his best. Again, he was responsible for the sub-plot, involving Isabella, the wife of the madhouse-keeper, Dr Alibius, and her suitors, a sub-plot formerly dismissed as unpleasant and irrelevant but now seen as effectively mirroring the main action. He also wrote the opening scene, with its telling first view of the lovers, Alsemero and Beatrice-Joanna, and the last, which contains, in Beatrice's farewell to her father, the most famous speech in the play. *The Changeling* is generally regarded as the finest collaborative tragedy of its era, for which Rowley deserves little less credit than Middleton.

Of the other collaborative works from this period, one, *The Birth of Merlin* (*c.*1613–15), is particularly problematic. The title-page of the 1662 quarto credits Rowley and William Shakespeare, but while Rowley's part in this mix of legendary history and romance is generally acknowledged (Merlin's parents are the Devil and Joan Goe-too't, whose brother is a typically Rowleyian clown), Shakespeare's involvement is ruled out by an entry in the records of Sir Henry Herbert, master of the revels, licensing *The Birth of Merlin* under its alternative title, 'The Child hath Founde his Father' as 'a New Play, acted by the Princes Servants at the Curtayne, 1622' (Bawcutt, 136). Jackson's summation thus best fits the situation as it stands currently: 'a poet and dramatist of stature must have participated with

Rowley in *The Birth of Merlin*, but his identity remains unknown' (Jackson, 146).

The remaining collaboration during the years 1613–22 is relatively unproblematic, since the ascription on the title-page of the 1621 quarto of *The Witch of Edmonton* to Rowley, John Ford, and Thomas Dekker is generally accepted. Their collaboration on this topical piece, which deals with the recent trial and execution for witchcraft of Elizabeth Sawyer, was clearly rewarding, since in 1624 the three, joined by John Webster, wrote another, *The Late Murder of the Son upon the Mother, or, Keep the Widow Waking*. The play is lost, but much is known of it from a lawsuit which the aggrieved son-in-law of the 'widow' in question brought against the dramatists.

Later works The remaining fruits of Rowley's last years were all, it seems, comedies. Collaboration with John Fletcher resulted in *The Maid in the Mill* (*c*.1623), and with Webster (and perhaps Heywood) in *A Cure for a Cuckold* (1624), while three or more comedies, including *The None Such*, now lost, also seem to date from this period.

Three other plays require mention. The title-page of the 1633 quarto of *A Match at Midnight* (*c*.1622) states it was 'Written by W. R.', but Hoy doubts Rowley's sole author-ship, while Young, the play's most recent editor, finds no convincing evidence of Rowley's hand. Described by Young as 'a romantic comedy of manners and intrigue decked out in the garb of City Comedy' (Rowley, *A Match at Midnight*, 38), *A Match at Midnight* is poorly constructed, with characters lacking in psychological depth; if Young is right, its omission from the Rowley canon is little loss. Nor, indeed, is there great gain if Nolan, who, in his edition of *The Thracian Wonder* (*c*.1611–12), credited on the title-page to Webster and Rowley, argues for its acceptance as a collaborative work by Rowley and Heywood, proves persuasive. With *The Spanish Gypsy* (1623) opinions are still divided, though the title-page attribution to Middleton and Rowley has been rejected. Lake considers it a Ford–Dekker collaboration, but Jackson commits himself no further than to say it is 'probably the work of Ford and another dramatist—Dekker, Rowley, or Brome' (Jackson, 159).

Non-dramatic works Rowley's non-dramatic works are few and unremarkable: a satiric pamphlet, *A Search for Money* (1609); verses on the death of Prince Henry (1612), printed in John Taylor's *Great Britain All in Black* (1612), and others in William Drummond's *Mausoleum, or, The Choicest Flowers of the Epitaphs Written on the Death of … Prince Henry* (1613); a couplet on the death of Thomas Greene, a fellow comedian in Queen Anne's Men, prefacing Joshua Cooke's comedy *Greene's Tu quoque* (1614); and a more extensive tribute to a fellow member of Prince Charles's Men, in *A Funeral Elegy on the Death of Hugh Atwell* (1621). He also contributed commendatory verses to John Taylor's *Nipping or Snipping of Abuses* (1614) and the 1623 quarto of Webster's *The Duchess of Malfi*.

Rowley's comic style As an actor Rowley seems to have specialized in comic roles, and particularly those in which his own considerable bulk was an asset. In Middleton's *Inner Temple Masque, or, Masque of Heroes* (1619) he played the part of Plumporridge, who is described as moving 'like one of the great porridge-tubs Going to the counter', and in *All's Lost by Lust* (1619) the role of 'Jaques, a simple clownish Gentleman'. Likewise, the roles of Cuddy Banks in *The Witch of Edmonton* and Bustopha in *The Maid in the Mill* seem to be tailored for Rowley's comic talents, and it is generally agreed that they were written by him, as was that of Compass in *A Cure for a Cuckold*. Reference in Jonson's *The Staple of News* (performed in February 1626) to 'the right reuerend *Archbishop* of *Spalato*', and the comment that 'He is dead, That plai'd him', makes it clear that Rowley also played the Fat Bishop in Middleton's *A Game at Chesse* (1624).

Though in collaboration Rowley specialized in comic sub-plots which included parts written for himself, the plays he wrote unaided show that there he worked over a somewhat wider range. *A Shoemaker a Gentleman* provides elements of comic realism in the portrayal of the master shoemaker, Sisley, his wife, and his men, but the main plot, drawing on English legendary history in the martyr-dom of the saints Alban, Hugh, and Gwenfrewi (Wini-fred), is in the romance tradition. So, too, is *A Woman Never Vexed*, which, loosely based on the lives of Stephen and Agnes Foster, fifteenth-century benefactors of the City of London, becomes in Rowley's hands a didactic romance, in which a widow, having been uniformly happy in her life, marries a profligate in the pious hope of suffering the share of woes promised in the Bible. He, however, is converted by marriage into an ideal husband: they prosper, and hence his wife remains 'a woman never vexed'. *A Shoe-maker, a Gentleman* and *A New Wonder, a Woman Never Vexed* no doubt pleased the unsophisticated artisan clientele at the Red Bull Theatre. *All's Lost by Lust* also met with success, being revived in the 1630s and at the Restoration. The latter is not surprising, given its subject matter, the conquest of Spain by the Moors, and its sensational handling of the personal tragedy of the Spanish general Julianus, whose daughter is raped by King Roderigo, whom he is tricked into killing by the Moors after soliciting their aid. Both the characters and dramatic situations lack subtlety, how-ever, and the verse is at best workmanlike.

The Rowley canon Although problems relating to the Rowley canon remain, computer-aided authorship tests have gone far in determining the nature and extent of his collaborative activity, often bearing out earlier studies involving verbal parallels and stylistic similarities (as, for example, his characteristic liking for 'cue-catching': link-ing a speech to its predecessor by the repetition of the final word). The canon thus revealed shows a playwright wide-ranging and adaptable, and one who developed steadily throughout his writing career. In constructional technique, this is evident in Rowley's unaided work. Where in *A Shoemaker a Gentleman* an excess of material results in a chaotically constructed play, *A Woman Never Vexed* shows a contrasting 'moderation and restraint' (Rowley, *A New Wonder*, 39). This is reflected also in *All's Lost by Lust*, where Rowley eschews opportunities to mount battle scenes in favour of more subtle effects. Improve-ment is additionally evident in his handling of language.

As Robb puts it, 'A style originally jerky, halting, crabbed, at times inarticulate—or alternatively stiffly correct—develops into one of at least competence, and finally to one which, if still insecure, at least has its moments of something approaching eloquence' (Robb, 131).

Reputation As a comic actor, Rowley was celebrated in his day, but he was not, it seems, highly regarded as a playwright. As Bentley points out, 'None of his plays was published with commendatory verses' (Bentley, 5.1017); nor indeed were most published in his lifetime. But then, of the sixteen or so extant plays with which Rowley's name is associated, only two (or at most three) are his unaided work. By preference, clearly, he worked collaboratively, and this reinforces the sense gained of a man concerned chiefly with acting and managing a theatre company. Yet even if, as Howard-Hill suggests, Rowley 'regarded himself primarily as an actor who occasionally wrote plays rather than as a dramatist' (Howard-Hill, 244–5), he none the less proves himself, in *A Fair Quarrel*, in *The Witch of Edmonton*, where he creates one of his finest clowns in Cuddy Banks, and in *A Cure for a Cuckold*, where the Compass scenes are among the play's best, to be capable of comic writing of a high order. In *The Changeling* he shares with Middleton credit for one of the tragic masterpieces of the Jacobean era.   DAVID GUNBY

Sources parish register, St James, Clerkenwell, London, 11 Feb 1626 [burial] • G. E. Bentley, *The Jacobean and Caroline stage*, 7 vols. (1941–68) • E. K. Chambers, *The Elizabethan stage*, 4 vols. (1923) • M. J. Dickson, 'William Rowley', *TLS* (28 March 1929), 260 • C. Hoy, 'The shares of Fletcher and his collaborators in the Beaumont and Fletcher canon [pt 5]', *Studies in Bibliography*, 13 (1960), 77–108 • M. P. Jackson, *Studies in attribution: Middleton and Shakespeare* (1979) • D. J. Lake, *The canon of Thomas Middleton's plays* (1975) • T. W. Baldwin, *The organization and personnel of the Shakespearean Company* (1927) • T. H. Howard-Hill, 'William Rowley', *Jacobean and Caroline dramatists*, ed. F. Bowers, DLitB, 58 (1987) • C. J. Sisson, *Lost plays of Shakespeare's age* (1936) • D. M. Robb, 'The canon of William Rowley's plays', *Modern Language Review*, 45 (1950), 129–41 • W. Rowley, *A match at midnight*, ed. S. B. Young (1980) • W. Rowley, *A new wonder, a woman never vexed*, ed. T. L. Darby (1988) • W. Rowley and T. Heywood, *The Thracian wonder*, ed. M. Nolan (1997) • W. Rowley, *The birth of Merlin*, ed. J. Udall (1991) • N. W. Bawcutt, ed., *The control and censorship of Caroline drama: the records of Sir Henry Herbert, master of the revels, 1623–73* (1996) • H. D. Gray, 'A cure for a cuckold by Heywood, Rowley and Webster', *Modern Language Review*, 22 (1927), 389–97

Rowley, Sir William (c.1690–1768), naval officer, was son of William Rowley of Whitehall, a court official under William III, and his wife, Anne. He entered the navy in 1704 as a volunteer per order in the *Orford*, with Captain Sir John Norris, and passed his examination for lieutenant on 15 September 1708. In December of that year he was posted to the *Somerset*, in which he served, mostly in the Mediterranean, until May 1713. Early in 1716 he was in Paris on a special errand for George I. This could well have been connected with the king's negotiations for a triple alliance with France and the United Provinces. Whatever the reason, Rowley's services were generously rewarded on this occasion. On 26 June 1716 he was promoted to command the frigate *Bideford* and as a consequence rose to the rank of post captain. For the next two years the *Bideford* was based at Gibraltar, cruising against the Salé pirates.

In September 1719 Rowley was appointed to the *Lively*, a small frigate employed on the coast of Ireland, mostly between Dublin and Carrickfergus, for preventing piracy and smuggling, and for raising men, with occasional visits to Bristol, Plymouth, or Portsmouth. He continued on this service for nearly nine years, and after the *Lively* was paid off in June 1728 he remained on half pay for thirteen years. About this time he married Arabella (d. 1784), daughter of Captain George Dawson of co. Londonderry. Together they had one daughter and four sons, including Sir Joshua *Rowley. Rowley became involved in business and property in Ireland as a consequence of his marriage. In September 1739 he was appointed to the *Rippon* (60 guns), but he wrote from Dublin to say that he had a lawsuit pending, which involved the possible loss of £22,000, and requested to be allowed to stay on shore.

Early in 1741 Rowley accepted command of the *Barfleur* (90 guns), in which he joined the fleet under Rear-Admiral Nicholas Haddock in the Mediterranean, remaining there under Admiral Thomas Mathews. On 7 December 1743 he was promoted rear-admiral of the white, and hoisted his flag in the *Barfleur*. In that capacity, as junior flag officer, he commanded the van in the engagement off Toulon on 11 February 1744, and was one of the few concerned whose conduct was not called into question. Indeed, while admirals Mathews and Richard Lestock faced harsh criticism upon their return to Britain, Rowley was reported to have engaged the enemy with 'the greatest vigour and resolution' (Charnock, 4.63). On 19 June 1744 he was advanced to vice-admiral of the blue, and in the following August he succeeded to the chief command of the Mediterranean Fleet. The French and Spanish had withdrawn their fleets from the area, and the work to be done was principally in concert with the allied Austrian army; but in July 1745 Rowley was summarily ordered by the secretary of state, the duke of Newcastle, to return to England. This order was due to a resolution of the House of Commons (30 April 1745) censuring the proceedings of the court martial on Captain Richard Norris, over which Rowley presided, as 'arbitrary, partial, and illegal' (Cobbett, *Parl. hist.*, 13, col. 1300).

Captain Norris, the son of Rowley's patron and former commander, now Admiral Sir John Norris, had been accused of cowardice by his junior officers while commanding the *Essex* at the battle of Toulon in 1744, and the evidence against him was certainly serious. Rowley ruled that the court martial was unable to pass judgment, as Norris had been placed upon half pay, and later left the service, but it appeared that this was a verdict conveniently engineered out of obligation to Admiral Norris. Under the existing regulations commissioned sea officers on half pay were not subject to the same discipline as those in active service. The Admiralty board under Lord Anson attempted to remedy this situation in 1749 by amending the articles of war, but many officers, including Rowley, vehemently opposed the intended changes. In the end the clear unpopularity of the proposed measure led to its abandonment, and officers wishing to avoid punishment merely had to resign their commissions.

After his recall from the Mediterranean in 1745 Rowley had no further employment at sea; but he eventually rose up the admiral's list, appointed to the post of rear-admiral of Great Britain in July 1747, and admiral of the white in 1748. On 22 June 1751 he was appointed one of the lords of the Admiralty, and in 1753 he was knighted. He was also returned to the House of Commons for the boroughs of Taunton (1750–54) and Portsmouth (1754–61) but was not an active participant in parliamentary life, and appears to have made no speeches in the house. He remained at the Admiralty until November 1756, and was again appointed to it from April to July 1757. Rowley's friendship with Lord Egremont may have played a part in his elevation to these offices. After leaving the Admiralty and the Commons Rowley seems to have concentrated upon matters at his estate in Suffolk, where he had been appointed a justice of the peace. In July 1761 he suffered a serious affront to his honour when George III promoted Anson to the rank of admiral of the fleet, despite Rowley's clear seniority. However, after Anson's death in 1762 he was belatedly appointed commander-in-chief and admiral of the fleet. Despite the incident involving Richard Norris, Rowley seems to have been regarded as a competent and mild-tempered officer. Sir Horace Mann, who did not expect to find such qualities in officers, thought him 'a man of extreme good natural parts, vastly mild and humane, and inclined to do obliging things whenever it is in his power' (Walpole, *Corr.*, 18.506). He died on 1 January 1768, leaving a vast amount of property to his family and friends. He is presumed to have been buried at Stoke by Nayland, Suffolk, and was survived by his wife who died in February 1784.

ROBERT McGREGOR

Sources DNB · J. Charnock, ed., *Biographia navalis*, 4 (1796) · *Naval Chronicle*, 22 (1809), 451 · S. R. Matthews, 'Rowley, William', HoP, *Commons*, 1715–54 · J. Brooke, 'Rowley, Sir William', HoP, *Commons*, 1754–90 · D. A. Baugh, *British naval administration in the age of Walpole* (1965) · Burke, *Peerage* (1963) · Walpole, *Corr.*, vol. 18 · GM, 1st ser., 38 (1768), 47 · [earl of Bristol], *Augustus Hervey's journal*, ed. D. Erskine (1953) · Cobbett, *Parl. hist.*, vol. 13
Archives NMM, uncatalogued letters, MSS/88/029.8 · Suffolk RO, family estate records | BL, letters to Lieutenant Hood, Add. MS 35193, fols. 15, 37 · BL, letters to duke of Newcastle, Add. MSS 32704, fol. 537; 32968, fol. 452 · BL, letter to T. Robinson, Add. MS 23819, fol. 247 · BL, letter to Lord Winchilsea, Add. MS 29589B, fol. 21 · PRO, admiral's journals, ADM 50/16 · PRO, Chancery: petty bag office: writ files; return of writs: Suffolk—Oaths of Rear-Admiral William Rowley JP, C 202/139/4 · PRO, naval commanders: Vice-Admiral Rowley, SP 42/96
Likenesses J. Faber junior, mezzotint, pubd 1743 (after C. Arnulphy), BM, NPG · J. Brooks, mezzotint, 1745, BM, NPG · oils, c.1762, NMM · J. Brooks, engraving (after C. Arnulphy, c.1745), NMM · J. Faber, engraving (after C. Arnulphy, 1745), NMM
Wealth at death over £160,000; annuities valued at £500 p.a. to be paid to various relatives; other estates entailed through the male heirs of second son, Joshua; land and manor at Tendring Hall, Suffolk; land in parish of Polstead, Suffolk; lands, investments, and manor in Barony of Loughinisland, Ulster; house in Bond Street, London: will, 1768, PRO, PROB 11/935, sig. 30

Rowley, William (1742–1806), man-midwife and surgeon, son of William Rowley of St Luke's, Old Street, London, was born in London on 18 November 1742. After apprenticeship at St Thomas's Hospital, London, he became a surgeon, and served in that capacity in the army from 1760 to 1765. In 1766 he began general practice in London, and on 23 April 1774 was created MD at St Andrews University. He became a licentiate of the Royal College of Physicians on 25 June 1784. He matriculated from St Alban's Hall, Oxford, on 28 November 1780, aged thirty-eight, and there graduated BA on 9 June 1784, MA on 24 May 1787, and MB on 17 July 1788, but was refused the degree of MD because of technical transgressions against the university statutes.

Rowley was the physician at the Marylebone Infirmary and his practice in London was considerable. He described himself on his title-pages as a man-midwife, and was consulting physician to the Queen's Lying-in Hospital, but he also practised ophthalmic and general surgery. In London he first lived in St James's Street, then in Castle Street, Leicester Fields, then at 66 Harley Street, and finally in Savile Row, where he died of typhus fever on 17 March 1806. He was buried at St James's Chapel, Hampstead Road.

Rowley gave three courses of lectures a year at Savile Row. In some controversial pamphlets he attacked William Hunter (1718–1783) for criticizing a cure for cancer practised by Rowley, and wrote against vaccination and Jenner in particular. In doing so he achieved some notoriety by supporting Benjamin Moseley's opposition to vaccination. Although some were well reviewed (see the *Gentleman's Magazine*, 1804), his books contain nothing of value, and many of them are mere advertisements. Munk concluded that 'Neither his character nor [his] career were of a kind we delight to dwell on' (2.341).

NORMAN MOORE, *rev.* ELIZABETH BAIGENT

Sources Munk, *Roll* · Foster, *Alum. Oxon.* · GM, 1st ser., 74 (1804), 1224 · GM, 1st ser., 76 (1806), 294
Likenesses C. Warren, line engraving (after miniature), BM; repro. in *Transactions of the Society of Arts* (1815)

Rowning, John (1701?–1771), natural philosopher and mathematician, was the son of John Rowning of Ashby-with-Fenby, Lincolnshire. William Rowning (d. 1757), clockmaker of Brandon, Suffolk, may have been his brother, and he was related to the Browning family, clockmakers, of Newmarket, Suffolk. He was educated at Brigg grammar school, north Lincolnshire, then from 1721 at Magdalene College, Cambridge, where he graduated BA in 1724 and MA in 1728. He held a fellowship at Magdalene, and was subsequently appointed rector of the college living of Anderby, Lincolnshire.

Rowning's interest in mechanical matters led him to devise an expanded-scale barometer, achieved by floating the tube and cistern in a liquid, with a protruding vertical rod acting as a pointer. With changing pressure, both mercury and liquid levels changed, the overall rise and fall being greater than that of the mercury alone. Though ingenious, the device was impractical, and the theory more complicated than Rowning suspected; it was, however, published in the Royal Society's *Philosophical Transactions* (38, 1733, 39–42). His chief work was his *Compendious*

System of Natural Philosophy (2 vols.), which went through seven editions between 1735 and 1772. On mathematics he published *Preliminary Discourse to an Intended Treatise on the Fluxionary Method* (1756), and in 1768 he described a complex arrangement of fixed and sliding rules and cogwheels, later published as 'Directions for making a machine for finding the roots of equations universally' (*PTRS*, 60, 1770, 240–56). Rowning and his wife, Mary (who predeceased him), had at least three sons (*b*. 1739, 1740, and 1741), who probably died young; he was survived by a daughter, Frances (*b*. 1738), who married Thomas Brown of Spalding. Rowning died at his lodgings in Carey Street, near Lincoln's Inn Fields, Westminster, London, in November 1771.   ANITA MCCONNELL

Sources W. E. Middleton, *The history of the barometer* (1964), 124–5 · A. L. Haggan and L. F. Miller, *Suffolk clocks and clockmakers* (1974), 133–4 · *Cambridge Chronicle and Journal* (17 Jan 1772) · C. Hutton, *A philosophical and mathematical dictionary*, new edn, 2 (1815), 398

Rowntree, John Stephenson (1834–1907). *See under* Rowntree, Joseph (1801–1859).

Rowntree, John Wilhelm (1868–1905), chocolate manufacturer and religious activist, was born on 4 September 1868 at Top House, St Mary's, York, the eldest of the six children of Joseph *Rowntree (1836–1925) and his second wife, (Emma) Antoinette (1846–1924), daughter of Wilhelm Seebohm of Hamburg. (Benjamin) Seebohm *Rowntree was his brother. He was educated at Bootham School, York, and Oliver's Mount School, Scarborough. In 1886 he entered his father's York cocoa works at Tanner's Moat, working in each department so as to become 'thoroughly acquainted with the *practical* side of the work' (Vernon, 88). At nineteen he reorganized the cocoa and chocolate departments; at twenty-one he became a partner and, on the firm becoming a limited company in 1897, a director, serving until his death. While not warming to business life he took a full and effective share in it, including the planning of the move in the 1890s to the Haxby Road site. He saw the firm grow from 200 employees to over 2000.

Rowntree was tall and erect in bearing, had a ready wit, and was an excellent mimic. He inherited from his mother an interest in the arts: he had some talent for painting and became passionately interested in the theatre, becoming himself a gifted amateur actor. He married on 28 July 1892 Constance Margaret Naish (1871–1928): they had five children.

At the 1893 yearly meeting of British Quakers Rowntree spoke for younger friends not reached by the language of evangelical orthodoxy. With his creative driving force he became an acknowledged leader among those urging Friends to come to terms with scientific discoveries, biblical criticism, and the social implications of the gospel. To this end he took a notable part in the Manchester conference (1895) and in the promotion from 1897 of summer schools, leading to the foundation in 1903 of Woodbrooke, Birmingham, as a permanent centre for these studies. In 1897 he met in Switzerland the American Quaker Rufus M. Jones (1863–1948): together they planned a comprehensive history of Quakerism, written after

Rowntree's death by Jones and William Charles Braithwaite (1862–1922). Rowntree also founded and edited (1899–1902) *Present Day Papers* as a vehicle of Christocentric faith freed from doctrinal narrowness: some of the society's practices he dismissed as 'Quaker caution and love of detail run to seed' (Vernon, 106).

Like his father, Rowntree was devoted to adult school work and his students found his teaching lucid and arresting but demanding. With Henry Bryan Binns (1873–1923) he wrote *A History of the Adult School Movement* (1903; reprinted with new introduction and notes, 1985). He was impatient with the 'brief and bright' approach of the Pleasant Sunday Afternoon movement. He was equally impatient with mission-minded Quakers who wished to brighten meetings for worship with congregational singing and he stressed the need for an educated lay ministry: his own gift in the vocal ministry was acknowledged by York monthly meeting in 1900.

Rowntree had been a delicate child and had early suffered from deafness (an ear trumpet had to be bought when he was only nine). In 1894 he had serious contraction of sight, diagnosed as retinitis pigmentosa, and was warned of coming and irreparable blindness. The ensuing decade of intense activity could have been, but was not, clouded by his health, despite almost daily bouts of depression. He was the only one of Joseph's children who could make his father laugh. In 1899 his doctors ordered a country life and Rowntree retired to Scalby, near Scarborough. In 1905 he sailed for his fourth visit to his American eye specialist, but contracted pneumonia on the voyage and died in a New York hospital on 9 March, his body being interred on 17 March in Friends' burial-ground, Haverford, Pennsylvania.

EDWARD H. MILLIGAN

Sources S. Allott, *John Wilhelm Rowntree, 1868–1905, and the beginnings of modern Quakerism* (1994) · J. Rowntree, 'Introductory sketch', in J. W. Rowntree, *Essays and addresses* (1905), ix–xliii · A. Vernon, *A Quaker business man: the life of Joseph Rowntree* (1958) · *Annual Monitor* (1906), 119–25 · *The Friend*, new ser., 45 (1905), 161–6, 176, 180–82, 198–9 · *British Friend*, new ser., 14 (1905), 93–7 · digest of births, 1837–1959, RS Friends, Lond. · digest registers (marriages, 1837 on), RS Friends, Lond. · digest of deaths, 1837–1961, RS Friends, Lond.
Archives RS Friends, Lond.
Likenesses photograph, *c*.1876, Joseph Rowntree Foundation, York; repro. in Allott, *John Wilhelm Rowntree* · photograph, *c*.1884, Joseph Rowntree Foundation, York; repro. in Allott, *John Wilhelm Rowntree* · F. M. Sutcliffe, photograph, *c*.1900, RS Friends, Lond.; repro. in J. W. Rowntree, *Essays and addresses*
Wealth at death £36,393 19*s*. 1*d*.: probate, 16 May 1905, *CGPLA Eng. & Wales*

Rowntree, Joseph (1801–1859), educationist, was born on 10 June 1801 at Scarborough, the sixth of the seven children of the Quakers John Rowntree (1757–1827), a master mariner, and his wife, Elizabeth, *née* Lotherington (1764–1835). He was educated at a school for the sons of Friends at Sowerby, near Thirsk. At twenty-one he started in business as a grocer in Pavement, York. On 3 May 1832 he married Sarah Stephenson (1807–1888), niece of the Quaker minister Elizabeth Robson; of their five children, one died in infancy and another was Joseph *Rowntree (1836–1925).

Rowntree's business success enabled him to devote his considerable energies to educational and social issues, discussing them almost daily with the philanthropist Samuel Tuke. He had a questioning mind and was relentlessly insistent on hard facts. Nor was he afraid of teaching by hard experience: in 1848, when his sons John and Joseph were sixteen and fourteen, he did not scruple to take them to Ireland for three weeks, where the horrors of the dead and dying in a famine-stricken countryside left on them a lasting impression that poverty was an evil which needed to be tackled by more than palliative measures.

As honorary secretary of the Quaker boys' and girls' schools in York from 1830 until his death, Rowntree was largely responsible for their moves to Bootham in 1846 and The Mount in 1857. He was also much involved with the Ackworth and Rawdon Quaker schools, and with the Flounders Institute, Ackworth, for training male teachers. With Tuke he established the Friends Educational Society in 1837 to stimulate discussion, and for thirty years he was active in promoting education among the York poor through schools under the auspices of the British and Foreign School Society. He inaugurated several schemes of municipal reform in York, becoming an alderman in 1853. Elected mayor in 1858, he declined to serve because, as chief magistrate of the city, the position would involve him in the administration of oaths.

During Rowntree's lifetime British Quakers were legally precluded from marrying non-members in meeting, and 'marriage before the priest' normally resulted in disownment. His was largely the influence which persuaded Friends (many rigidly conservative in the matter) to seek legislation, secured in 1860 and 1872, removing this limitation in England and Wales. Rowntree died at York on 4 November 1859, and was buried four days later in the Quaker burial-ground, Heslington Road.

His eldest son, **John Stephenson Rowntree** (1834–1907), was born on 2 May 1834. After schooldays at Bootham he entered his father's grocery business, remaining until his retirement in 1892. He married Elizabeth Hotham (1835–1875) on 25 August 1858, with whom he had nine children. Following her death in a carriage accident when their youngest child was nine months old, he married on 10 April 1878 Helen Doncaster (1833–1920). Like his father, he used statistics to combat emotion, and his *Quakerism Past and Present* (1859) remains a perceptive, at times scathing, analysis of certain trends in early nineteenth-century British Quakerism. He succeeded his father as secretary to the York Quaker schools and, with Lydia Rous (1819–1896), established at The Mount a training department for women teachers. He energetically promoted the higher education of women. His adult school teaching over many years was essentially practical: he was more concerned that his lessons should lead to right conduct than to theological knowledge. He was an ardent botanist, a keen archaeologist, and well versed in the history of York. He was elected lord mayor in 1880 (after making clear that he would not entertain lavishly), and during his

aldermanship devoted himself to putting the city's unsatisfactory finances on to a sound basis.

Rowntree had a keen sense of humour, but also, like his father, a streak of melancholy: a vein of sadness was evident in his ministry in York Friends' meeting (his gift had been acknowledged by the monthly meeting in 1864), but it was often based on unusual texts and incidents, and was listened to avidly by critical schoolboys and girls. He had never been robust and, weakened by successive attacks of influenza, he died at his sister's house, 314 Camden Road, London, on 13 April 1907; he was buried on 16 April in the Quaker burial-ground, Heslington Road, York.

EDWARD H. MILLIGAN

Sources J. S. Rowntree, ed., *A family memoir of Joseph Rowntree* (privately printed, Birmingham, 1868) · P. Doncaster, 'Memoir of John S. Rowntree', *John Stephenson Rowntree, his life and work*, ed. E. E. Taylor (1908), 1–94 · A. Vernon, *A Quaker business man: the life of Joseph Rowntree* (1958) · *Annual Monitor* (1860), 211–35 · *Annual Monitor* (1908), 134–46 · Yorkshire quarterly meeting births digest, RS Friends, Lond. · digest registers (marriages), RS Friends, Lond. [Lancashire quarterly meeting] · *The Friend*, 17 (1859), 228 · digest of deaths, 1837–1961, RS Friends, Lond. · digest registers (marriages, 1837 on), RS Friends, Lond. [John Stephenson Rowntree] · *The Friend*, new ser., 47 (1907), 262 [John Stephenson Rowntree]
Archives RS Friends, Lond.
Likenesses touched up photograph, c.1858, RS Friends, Lond. · double portrait, photograph, c.1870 (with John Stephenson Rowntree), Rowntree Foundation, York; repro. in S. Allott, *John Wilhelm Rowntree* (1994), 24 · double portrait, photograph, c.1890 (with John Stephenson Rowntree), repro. in Taylor, ed., *John Stephenson Rowntree*, frontispiece
Wealth at death under £12,000: probate, 23 Nov 1859, *CGPLA Eng. & Wales* · £31,138 13s. 6d.—John Stephenson Rowntree: probate, 30 May 1907, *CGPLA Eng. & Wales*

Rowntree, Joseph (1836–1925), cocoa and chocolate manufacturer, was born at Pavement, York, on 24 May 1836, the son of Joseph *Rowntree (1801–1859) and his wife, Sarah, née Stephenson (1807–1888). In 1822 his father had travelled from Scarborough to establish his grocery business, and he became prominent in civic and Quaker affairs in York, where he collaborated with Samuel Tuke to establish the Quaker Bootham and Mount schools. He led reform of the Society of Friends, and was elected an alderman of York in 1853, and lord mayor in 1858, an honour which he refused as incompatible with his Quaker principles. Initially educated at home, his son Joseph began attending Bootham School at the age of eleven, and was apprenticed to his father, aged sixteen, in 1852. In 1856 he married Julia Eliza, daughter of Benjamin Seebohm, wool merchant and prominent within the Society of Friends; they had one daughter who did not survive infancy. After Julia's death in 1863 Rowntree married her cousin, (Emma) Antoinette Seebohm (1846–1924), on 14 November 1867; they had four sons, including John Wilhelm *Rowntree, and two daughters. On his father's death in 1859 Rowntree managed the family business with his elder brother, John Stephenson, who was to accept the mayoralty of York in 1881.

In 1862 Joseph's younger brother, Henry Isaac, acquired the cocoa, chocolate, and chicory firm of his former employers and fellow Quakers, the Tukes, which he

Joseph Rowntree (1836–1925), by unknown photographer, 1878

moved to Tanner's Moat, York, two years later. He proved an inept businessman, however, and, motivated by family duty, Joseph left his successful grocery shop to become his partner in 1869. In later life, Joseph described his brother as financially 'hopelessly embarrassed' and ignorant of the essential details of the cocoa trade, despite or because of his sterling temperance work. They divided responsibilities between them: Henry Isaac oversaw manufacturing, while Joseph supervised sales and bookkeeping. Joseph was serious minded and attentive, carefully costing each line and restoring the soundness of their business, but he had joined a precarious enterprise. His new firm remained small, making losses in 1873 and 1876, and not until 1875 is Joseph Rowntree known to have described himself as a 'cocoa manufacturer'.

In 1881 the firm achieved what was to be its first breakthrough, when, with the help of a French confectioner, Claude Gaget, it began the manufacture of pastilles, previously imported from France. Adjoining premises in North Street were acquired one year later. Both Joseph and Henry Isaac were committed to the highest product quality, motivated by a Quaker duty to ethical trading and the making of socially beneficial goods. They were also suspicious of advertising and its association with deceit and quack medicines. But they were not unlike a wide variety of manufacturers, master shopkeepers, and other contemporaries, who, for business as well as ethical reasons,

held that product quality would determine long-term success. Henry Isaac died in 1883 of peritonitis, leaving no inheritance and his brother as sole partner. With sales of £51,118 and profits of £2196, Joseph Rowntree did not believe his business to be secure, and he still owed to relatives or banks £21,000 of his firm's £29,000 capital. Seven years after the first attempt, and more than twenty years after the rival Quaker firm of Cadbury, Rowntree introduced a pure cocoa essence, Elect, in 1887.

As his business continued to expand, Rowntree purchased 33 acres of land on Haxby Road, outside York, on which to build a new factory, the Cocoa Works, and he followed his success in pastilles with the manufacture of gums in 1893. The business benefited from the general expansion of demand for cocoa and confectionery products during the 1890s, and, as a result, Haxby Road was a site of continuous construction throughout the decade. Cocoa essence emerged, furthermore, as the industry's premier product, and competition persuaded a reluctant Joseph Rowntree to agree to the advertising and promotion of Elect. The firm was incorporated as Rowntree & Co. Ltd in 1897 with an issued capital of £226,200, almost wholly controlled by Joseph, his sons, and nephews. In appointing directors, therefore, he fulfilled his obligation to his own children and to those of his elder brother, John, who had financially supported his business during its early years, and to his younger brother, Henry Isaac, whose widow and successors were reliant upon him. Sales grew from £114,429 in 1890 to £463,199 by 1900 and £1,219,352 by 1910; the workforce, which numbered 200 in 1883, expanded to 894 by 1894 and 4000 by 1906, when Rowntree was Britain's eightieth largest manufacturing employer.

By 1900 Joseph Rowntree had founded a business that, in making highly prominent consumer goods, had become one of Britain's most famous companies. Like Cadbury, the firm of Rowntree also became associated in the public mind with industrial welfare and philanthropy, and it was Joseph, with his deeply held Quaker beliefs, who fostered this tradition and reputation. He was both an influential social reformer and a manufacturer. He viewed his business as a God-given trust, responsible to its employees and community as well as to its owners and shareholders. He recognized that paternalism was inappropriate to the large factory which he had established over the previous decade, as he himself was unable to maintain personal contact with so many employees, and that he would need assistance and formal schemes. A female welfare worker was appointed in 1891, and a women's employment department followed in 1896. In 1900 a welfare officer was appointed for boys, and a men's employment department was founded. Good employment conditions were deemed both good business and sound ethics: Rowntree benefited from contented, healthy workers, and charitable assistance was balanced by the maintenance of factory discipline and supervision of issues such as gambling and sexual morality. Sick and provident funds were created in 1902; a doctor's surgery was established in 1904; a savings scheme in 1905; a girls' school in 1905; a pension scheme in 1906; a boys' school in 1907; and a sick benefit scheme in 1910.

Rowntree's best-known philanthropic act occurred in 1904, when he used half of his wealth to create three trusts. He argued that he had never sought a fortune and that he did not want his children, as recipients of a large inheritance, to lead worthless lives. The Joseph Rowntree Charitable Trust was charged with supporting social research, adult education, and the Society of Friends. The Joseph Rowntree Social Trust concentrated on social and political activities that were outside the strict definition of charitable work, and the Joseph Rowntree Village Trust was given responsibility for building respectable but affordable working-class housing. By the time Rowntree died, the model village of New Earswick contained some 400 homes and was served by a range of community and educational facilities. On their founding, the Rowntree trusts held over 52 per cent of the company's shares, although the Rowntree family themselves acted as the trustees and controlled all appointments until 1941.

Rowntree believed that his business was responsible to its community, and throughout his life he fulfilled his God-given duty to society through his interest in social and political reform. In 1857 he founded the York Adult School, and followed his father on to the management committee of the Bootham and Mount schools; he also gave lifelong service to The Retreat, a mental hospital; he helped to found York's city library; he was an alderman of York from 1868 to 1874; and he held the chairmanship of the York Liberal Association. Rowntree had an abiding interest in education, and was himself well read in history, biography, travel, and natural history. In 1911, despite his reluctance to accept civic honours, he became a freeman of the city. Rowntree was an active campaigner for a number of issues. In 1899 with Arthur Sherwell he co-authored *The Temperance Problem and Social Reform*, which, with five other books in the next twenty years, argued the case for public control of the liquor trade. Rowntree believed in House of Lords reform, and, true to his pacifist Quaker values, he supported the League of Nations after the First World War. In 1903 Rowntree began purchasing a number of provincial Liberal newspapers to prevent their falling into Conservative hands, and in 1910 his Social Service Trust joined forces with George Cadbury to buy *The Star* and *Morning Chronicle*, although he soon conceded control of these titles to his fellow Quaker. Through his newspapers Rowntree indirectly sustained campaigns close to the Liberal and nonconformist conscience, over issues such as free trade, Chinese indentured labour, and licensing reform, but he was publicly embarrassed by the betting tips carried in these papers.

Rowntree was a man of mild temperament, courteous, retiring, cautious, and hardworking, with the capacity to inspire loyalty and a unity of purpose within his company. His management style was consultative, and he was willing to delegate, but his presence was always authoritative. His legacy included his philanthropy and labour policy, the model village of New Earswick, and one of Britain's great companies. His achievements were imitative rather than innovative: the welfare work, housing schemes, and the trusts were similar to those of several employers of the time, especially the Cadburys, who had begun Bournville on the outskirts of Birmingham over ten years before the Cocoa Works was conceived. His most successful products copied those of competitors, and he had been late in making a high-quality, branded cocoa essence. He was, by instinct, opposed to the advertising of this key line, cutting back the company's promotional budget between 1900 and 1905, but by necessity restoring and expanding it in 1906. Unlike Cadbury, he failed during these years to launch an alkalized, or more soluble, more 'chocolate-y', cocoa and a brand of milk chocolate bar, the demand for which he mistakenly regarded as a 'passing phase'. Rowntree closely associated the ideals of his family directors with that of his business, and, unattracted by the prospect of a soulless combine, decided against a merger with Cadbury and Fry in 1918, even though his two competitors were formally linked in 1919. But management and organization did require strengthening, and some changes were implemented in 1917, with more far-reaching reforms taking place in 1921 when his son, Benjamin Seebohm *Rowntree, much influenced by American practices, was acting company chairman. In response to the growth of trade unionism at the Cocoa Works during the First World War works councils were introduced in 1919.

When Joseph Rowntree retired as chairman in 1923 at the age of eighty-seven, his business had a turnover of over £3m and a workforce of over 7000. As the dominant personality in his company since its inception, Rowntree was one of the Victorian and Edwardian period's most successful businessmen. None the less, although the firm of Rowntree was dealing with the impact of the post-war depression, its difficulties were accentuated by an out-of-date product range that competed poorly against Cadbury lines. It was another generation, led by George Harris in the 1930s, which introduced the marketing principles and product range of the modern-day Rowntree. Joseph Rowntree had the deserved reputation of a gentle, fair-minded man, but he was also a person of deep conviction, in his private religious beliefs and in moments of public controversy. In dealing with matters of family, inheritance, and business, he revealed an unwavering, forthright but measured determination. His wife, Antoinette, died in 1924, and he died at his home, Clifton Lodge, York, on 24 February 1925. Four of his children survived him. Over two thousand people, ineligible to attend a private memorial at the Friends' meeting-house in York, gathered to remember him at the Cocoa Works, and he was buried on 28 February at the Quaker burial-ground, Heslington Road, York.

ROBERT FITZGERALD

Sources R. Fitzgerald, *Rowntree and the marketing revolution, 1862–1969* (1995) • A. Vernon, *A Quaker businessman: the life of Joseph Rowntree* (1958) • L. A. G. Strong, 'The story of Rowntree', 1948 • L. Waddilove, *One man's vision: the story of the Joseph Rowntree Village Trust* (1954) • *Confectionery Journal* (5 March 1925), 25–6 • *The Times* (25 Feb 1925), 19 • Rowntree archives
Archives Joseph Rowntree Foundation Library, York, family corresp. and papers | Labour History Archive and Study Centre, Manchester, corresp. relating to invitation to Ramsay MacDonald

to be vice-president of Temperance Legislation League · Norfolk RO, corresp. with H. W. Massingham
Likenesses photograph, 1878, Joseph Rowntree Foundation Library, York [*see illus.*] · portrait, Rowntree archives
Wealth at death £220,336 7s. 5d.: probate, 20 March 1925, *CGPLA Eng. & Wales*

Rowntree, Joshua (1844–1915), social reformer, was born on 6 April 1844 at Princess Street, Scarborough, the fourth of the five children of John Rowntree (1788–1845), grocer, and his wife, Jane, *née* Priestman (1807–1880). In 1860, on leaving Bootham School, York, he was articled to a solicitor in that city, subsequently practising from 1866 to 1886 in Scarborough. He married on 22 September 1880 Isabella Ann Tindall (1843–1929): there was one child, the social worker Maurice L. Rowntree (1882–1944).

Rowntree's interventions in municipal affairs were often unpopular: nevertheless he was chosen as mayor in 1885, relinquishing the position to stand as Liberal candidate in the 1886 parliamentary election. He entered the Commons as MP for Scarborough with his brother-in-law John Edward Ellis (1841–1910): though almost as unlike as possible in temperament and tastes, the tie between them was particularly close for there was underlying unity of aim. Rowntree was a firm home-ruler, visited Ireland on several occasions, and earned a tribute from John Dillon. He was also a temperance reformer and a vigorous supporter of the social purity campaign of Josephine Butler (1828–1906). He consistently attacked the opium traffic, and when a royal commission (1893–5) presented a report demonstrating the impossibility of stopping the trade between India and China he set to work patiently and painstakingly to examine its conclusions, which he confuted in *The Imperial Drug Trade* (1905); he lived to see his judgement accepted and acted upon.

Defeated at Scarborough in the 1892 election, Rowntree 'gave himself with whole heart and mind to the modern interpretation of Quakerism' (*Annual Monitor*, 130). He took a quiet (sometimes underestimated, but indisputably effective) part in enabling British Friends to come to terms with scientific discoveries and biblical criticism and with shaking off outdated customs—notably through the Manchester conference (1895), Scarborough summer school (1897), and the establishment in 1903 of a study centre at Woodbrooke, Birmingham, of which he and Isabella were the first wardens. He did not take part in leading Quaker worship until beyond middle life: his gift in the ministry was recorded by Pickering and Hull monthly meeting in 1896.

Rowntree was known in Scarborough simply as Joshua (accented by many on the last vowel). He was well versed in geology, botany, archaeology, and history, a lover of the moors and of the sea: he knew how to sail a boat in all weathers, he was at home with the fisherfolk and they with him, and in the last summer of his life he was rowing visitors with boyish enthusiasm. It was this breadth of interest and his ability to draw out the shy that made him so successful an adult school teacher.

Rowntree and his wife visited Friends' missions in Palestine and Syria in 1899. Concern for peace and conciliation led, in the Second South African War, to his promoting a meeting at Scarborough (March 1900) to be addressed by S. J. Cronwright Schreiner (1863–1936): this resulted in mob violence against the Rowntree families and property. With his wife and nephew Harold T. Ellis (1875–1930) he visited South Africa between December 1900 and April 1901 to investigate possible Quaker relief work, particularly in the concentration camps. Among contacts made was 'an Indian barrister, Mr Gandhi' (Hewison, 163), who spoke to him of the demoralizing conditions to which all Asian people were subjected. In 1902–3 he and his wife, who were part of a deputation on behalf of British Quakers to Friends in Australia and New Zealand, visited American Friends on their way home. Rowntree died at the home of his sister, Maria Ellis (1845–1941), at Wrea Head, Scalby, on 10 February 1915; his body was interred two days later in Scarborough cemetery.

EDWARD H. MILLIGAN

Sources S. E. Robson, *Joshua Rowntree* (1916) · *Annual Monitor* (1916), 125–37 · *The Friend*, new ser., 50 (1915), 133–5, 138–42, 152, 159–61 · H. H. Hewison, *Hedge of wild almonds: South Africa, the pro-Boers and the Quaker conscience, 1890–1910* (1989) · digest of births, 1837–1959, RS Friends, Lond. · digest registers (marriages, 1837 on), RS Friends, Lond. · digest of deaths, 1837–1961, RS Friends, Lond.
Archives RS Friends, Lond.
Likenesses Sarony, photograph, c.1885, RS Friends, Lond. · P. Bigland, oils, c.1905, RS Friends, Lond.
Wealth at death £2199 2s. 9d.: probate, 20 May 1915, *CGPLA Eng. & Wales*

Rowntree, (Benjamin) Seebohm (1871–1954), sociologist and businessman, was born at Bootham, St Olave Marygate, York, on 7 July 1871, the second son of Joseph *Rowntree (1836–1925), who then described himself as a master grocer but later became a successful cocoa and chocolate manufacturer, and his second wife, (Emma) Antoinette (1846–1924), daughter of Wilhelm Seebohm. Educated by governesses until he was ten, Seebohm Rowntree followed his father to Bootham School, York. Their exclusion from Oxford or Cambridge confirmed Quakers in their provinciality and distance from the professions. For five terms Seebohm Rowntree studied at the University of Manchester, concentrating on chemistry but without taking a degree, though in 1942 the university awarded him an honorary LLD. On 14 December 1897, at the Friends' meeting-house, Middlesbrough, he married Lydia (1868/9–1944), daughter of Edwin Potter, an engineer; they had four sons and one daughter.

The family firm of H. I. Rowntree & Co., which Seebohm Rowntree joined in 1889, was enlightened in its management, Joseph in 1902 seeing his employees as 'fellow-workers in a great industry', not as 'cogs in an industrial machine' (Briggs, 99). Both the firm and the adult school in York where Seebohm Rowntree taught for twenty years caused social reform to gain over religion among his priorities, in so far as he would have made any distinction between the two: he and his father collaborated in pushing further the firm's experiments in enlightened management, and his adult-school work prompted visits to pupils' homes. In February 1895 there followed what was

(Benjamin) Seebohm Rowntree (1871–1954), by Jane Bown, 1952

perhaps the most formative incident in his life: his visit, accompanied by a well-informed local man, to the slums of Newcastle upon Tyne. This reminder of poverty's persistence amid accumulating national wealth so sharpened his Quaker sense of personal responsibility for social ills that he spent the rest of his life in discharging it.

Poverty in York Practical and intellectual influences continuously interacted in Seebohm Rowntree's career: his personal taste for statistics and his aptitude for systematic research meshed in with the impact made by Charles Booth's social survey of London's East End. Were York's poor as badly off as Booth's poor in London? Most of 1897 and 1898 were spent away from the factory to find out, the results being published in 1901 as *Poverty: a Study of Town Life*. This, Seebohm Rowntree's most important book, soon became a classic text in the British empirical approach to sociology. As so often with his research he had several helpers, some of them paid. Rowntree and Booth were helping to detach British sociology from its earlier literary and journalistic affinities and move it towards the numerate austerities of 'social science', though without espousing unrealistic degrees of value freedom. Clearly if unexcitingly written, spare and analytic in its approach, steadfastly pursuing objectivity and precision, the book developed concepts crucial to all subsequent British social investigation: the 'poverty line' (an objective, nutritionally-based minimum), the 'poverty cycle' (bringing out both the dynamics of poverty and its extensive reach), and the distinction between a 'primary' poverty that reflected an income inadequate for efficiency and a 'secondary' poverty reflecting expenditure patterns which produced the same outcome. He also made important comparisons with European cities—on poor relief and housing, for instance. No subsequent Rowntree survey was technically so resourceful.

Poverty profoundly affected public opinion and social policy, and was reissued in cheap editions, for the time was ripe: constructive Liberalism, mobilizing intellectuals in moulding public policy, was advancing in the aftermath of the Second South African War. Rowntree's findings reinforced Booth's impact through their enhanced precision, their conciseness, and their provincial base; poverty could no longer be diagnosed as locally pathological—it was nationally endemic. Yet throughout his life, in characteristic 'New Liberal' fashion, Rowntree combined social with moral priorities, and the book he edited, *Betting and Gambling*, was published in 1905. His main purpose in *Poverty*, however, was not to blame all poverty on imprudent expenditure, but to emphasize its structural rather than moral causes. Nor was his aim to keep wages down to the minimum; on the contrary, he believed throughout his life in a high-wage economy, and—as one would expect from a Quaker—in fully realizing human potential.

Rowntree after 1906 moved gradually towards helping to mould government policy, though less in relation to urban poverty than through a characteristically Liberal preoccupation with land reform. His ambitious *Land and Labour: Lessons from Belgium* (1910) launched his long collaboration in formulating public policy with Lloyd George, to whose pre-war land scheme Rowntree contributed much. Despite their utterly contrasting qualities their partnership fuelled Liberal policy until long after the party had lost its governmental role. Lloyd George appointed Rowntree to the land inquiry committee of 1912–14, and in 1913 Rowntree collaborated with May Kendall in publishing *How the Labourer Lives*, focusing on the agricultural labourer. His *Unemployment: a Social Study* (1911), published with Bruno Lasker, showed that welfare had become a dominant interest in his life, and the First World War drew him still closer to the centre of power by highlighting the importance of his two major interests: industrial welfare and state relief of poverty.

Industrial welfare Rowntree's business career ran in parallel with, and fruitfully influenced, his career as sociologist. He became a director when the family firm was converted into a limited liability company in 1897, and was chairman from 1923 to 1941. Joseph Rowntree aimed to develop his business as a trust, and his schemes for promoting employees' welfare gained much from closely collaborating in later life with his son Seebohm. The firm helped to pioneer scientific management and industrial welfare in Britain. Seebohm Rowntree was the firm's first labour director; its eight-hour day was introduced in 1896, its pension scheme in 1906, and its works doctor first appointed in 1904. The welfare of women employees was promoted through employing 'social helpers' from 1891, and under Seebohm Rowntree's direction they ultimately became members of a fully-fledged labour department.

Works councils were set up in 1919 and in the same year a 44-hour five-day week was introduced; a psychological department was set up in 1922, and profit-sharing was introduced in the following year. Not until 1936, when his executive responsibilities ceased, did Seebohm Rowntree move from York to North Dean, his house near High Wycombe.

No self-publicist, Rowntree had no taste for political power or honours, and Beatrice Webb thought him 'too modest and hesitating in opinion to lead a committee' (*DNB*). His influence stemmed from experience and expertise valuable to early twentieth-century politicians, especially during the First World War. As director of the welfare department of the Ministry of Munitions (1915–18) and as member of the reconstruction committee in March 1917 Rowntree could propagate more widely the enlightened managerial ideas that his firm had pioneered in York. Until he retired in 1936 labour management was among his leading preoccupations—one reason why after his first visit in 1921 he regarded America as a second homeland, and why he was in some ways more influential there than in Britain. Between 1921 and 1937 he visited America sixteen times, sometimes for several weeks.

This was the background for his *Human Factor in Business* (1921), which at the time was seen as complementing his *Human Needs of Labour* (1918, revised edn 1937). These books moved on from his earlier concern with the individual as consumer to the individual at work: to the relationship between the employer's needs and the employee's opportunities, always for him reconcilable. The *Human Needs of Labour* provided a practical, down-to-earth manual of managerial best practice, as implemented in the Rowntree factory, on such matters as wages, working hours, working conditions, and employees' welfare and status. The book aimed to counter the more revolutionary proposals that were then current. Its successive editions testified (like Rowntree's successive volumes on poverty) to his success, and it influenced such important welfare texts as Eleanor Rathbone's *Disinherited Family* and Harold Macmillan's *The Middle Way*. Rowntree helped to found the Industrial Welfare Society in 1918 and the National Institute of Industrial Psychology in 1921, remaining on the latter's executive committee until 1949 and serving as chairman in 1940–47. He also founded two industrial conferences: for employers, managers, and foremen in 1919, and for the management research groups in 1927.

Here was another route into influence over national policy. Seebohm Rowntree was an independent and successful, if unacknowledged, conciliator in the railway strike of 1919; and he tried to mediate in the coal dispute in 1926, during which he strongly criticized the intervention of the churches' committee. But from the 1920s the party-political context relevant for him was that of a Liberal Party in decline, for he never established close relations with the Labour Party, and his influence suffered considerably through the Liberal/Labour split which tragically weakened the British left after 1918. His intimacy with Lloyd George again proved fruitful between 1926 and 1935 when the Liberal Party helped to generate policies which

became mainstream from the 1940s to the 1970s. He advised Lloyd George on unemployment, housing, and agriculture; participated in the Liberal industrial inquiry which published *Britain's Industrial Future* in 1928; and joined in high-level Liberal/Labour policy discussions during 1930 about remedies for unemployment. The discussions came to naught, but Rowntree did not back the National Government in 1931. His free-trade loyalty remained firm, and while repudiating the Liberal Nationals he did not join the Lloyd George Liberals. Rowntree had at first hoped that farming could help to relieve unemployment and stimulate the economy, but he was speedily disillusioned after 1934 by studying British agriculture in collaboration with William Waldorf Astor. Their first report, *The Agricultural Dilemma* (1935), challenged Lloyd George's optimism on agricultural resettlement as a remedy for unemployment, whence came a final breach with Lloyd George in that year. Failing, therefore, to back Lloyd George's 'new deal', Rowntree continued to collaborate with Astor until 1946, and together with many prominent Liberals he signed the Next Five Years Group's *Essay in Political Agreement* (1935). From the 1920s liberalism and the Liberal Party were slowly diverging; Rowntree worked with the party only for as long as seemed practicable, but he never forsook liberalism, and did much to extend its appeal and relevance.

Sociologist of the welfare state Rowntree's second survey of York, conducted in 1936 and published as *Poverty and Progress* (1941), was in effect a national stocktaking of welfare advances made since his first poverty survey. His optimism when summarizing poverty's causes is infectious: 'every one is capable of remedy without dislocating industry or our national finances' (p. 476). The survey innovated only modestly in technique: it responded to rising expectations of life by elevating the poverty line, and to changing attitudes by no longer trying to measure secondary poverty quantitatively. Drawing on more investigators than his earlier survey, this new survey could afford to be old-fashioned in its completeness of coverage, but Rowntree tested its results against what the new sample-survey techniques would have revealed, and concluded that the latter were reliable. His research was now closely geared to detailed legislative improvement, and he emphasized that 'no fact has been stated which has not a direct bearing on the steps which should be taken if the evil of poverty is to be remedied' (p. 40). Both he and Beveridge helped to pioneer family allowances, Rowntree's firm introducing its own voluntary scheme in 1940. Furthermore Beveridge showed great interest in Rowntree's new survey during winter 1941–2, and Beveridge owed much to his dialogue with Rowntree in his review of social insurance, on which he was then working. In 1944–6 Rowntree chaired the Nuffield Foundation's committee on the problems of old age, whose final report on this neglected issue, *Old Age*, was published in 1946.

Finally, in collaboration with George Russell Lavers, Rowntree produced two books in 1951. The first of these, *Poverty and the Welfare State*, the report of the third poverty survey of York, was much shorter than its two predecessors. It used the sampling techniques he had tested earlier, and focused only on examining how far public welfare had curbed poverty in York since 1936. It welcomed and probably exaggerated the claim that, despite the war, poverty had greatly declined; old age, it argued, had superseded unemployment as primary cause of such poverty as persisted. Crosland cited its optimistic view of poverty trends in his influential revisionist *The Future of Socialism* (1956), but as early as 1952 Political and Economic Planning had pinpointed the defects in the survey that later became so apparent: it was technically flawed, and it generalized from a community less representative than Rowntree supposed. So it misled its readers into thinking that a cure had been found for the problem of poverty, which had to be 'rediscovered' in the 1960s. Rowntree seems to have had little personal involvement in preparing the report, and its critics within York apparently scotched plans to conduct a fourth survey in 1953–4.

Rowntree's *English Life and Leisure* (1951), by contrast, boldly tackled controversial, unquantifiable, and largely unexplored questions of rising importance: how would the masses use the new-found relative affluence and leisure that he and others had helped them to acquire? It grew out of the long-standing interest which had produced the long thirteenth chapter in his *Poverty and Progress*. In recreation, unlike business, Rowntree had no taste for American influence: for a former Quaker entering his eighties, always unobtrusively driven forward by an intense moralism, mid-twentieth-century recreation was indeed difficult territory. The survey suffered more than his earlier books from impressionism and lack of focus, but plans for two further collaborative volumes grew out of it: *The Spiritual Life of Britain*, for which a draft was complete at Rowntree's death; and *Gambling*, for which research was done.

A colleague recalled Rowntree as 'a spare man of middle height', with a frank expression, a kindly smile, and no pretensions; not at all dominating in manner, he none the less displayed a 'quiet sense of purpose' (Wallace, 114). For several reasons Rowntree diverged from the mainstream in British life. His Quakerism was less responsible for this than it would have been earlier, for during his lifetime Quakers were steadily moving in from the fringes, very much with his help. It was his political and intellectual position that limited his influence, for three relationships congenial to Rowntree were by international standards relatively weak in inter-war Britain: a reformism powered by an undivided party of the left, an affinity between intellectual life and entrepreneurship, and a channelling of welfare to the citizen through the employer rather than through the state. Each of these was to be found elsewhere—in inter-war Scandinavia, in twentieth-century America, and in modern Japan, respectively—and it is no accident that Rowntree's intellectual concerns often drew him into overseas comparisons and collaborations. His welfare preoccupations had of course drawn him by the 1940s closer to the centre of public discussion. By other tendencies within British life, however, he was left increasingly on the margin, concerned and uncomprehending: by its growing secularization, hedonism, and materialism. Rowntree's seriousness and rationality were waning even on the left in the 1950s, let alone elsewhere, and in later decades Rowntree's political marginalization would have been completed by the disappointment of his high hopes for what the New Liberal marriage of intellect and conscience could attain. Perhaps fortunately for his peace of mind he did not survive to extreme old age, but on 7 October 1954 died of a heart attack in the wing of Disraeli's old house, Hughenden Manor, High Wycombe—his home after his wife died in 1944.

Influence and legacy Rowntree's secularized religion of civic responsibility generated in him an earnestness and consistent hard work that ensured a profound long-term and cumulative impact on many areas of British life. He was unusually skilful at drawing together the practical and the ideal, powered as he was by the optimistic and positivist conviction that through steady application and careful thought all problems could be solved. Throughout his life he readily moved on to tackle new problems: housing reform and industrial conciliation in the 1920s, the distressed areas in the 1930s, old age in the 1940s, and mass leisure in the 1950s. In 1953 he even became president of the newly founded 'War on Want', which extended his preoccupation with poverty within Britain to poverty overseas. Yet because Rowntree did not discard his earlier research interests, his social analysis was enriched by a remarkable continuity and longevity of concern. Rowntree can now be understood only by rejecting many assumptions that accumulated after 1940, during years in which paradoxically governments were implementing his ideas. These assumptions are that religion and entrepreneurship are in tension rather than mutually reinforcing; that social justice can be secured through interference by a centralized state rather than by municipal action or industrial leadership; and that an equitable distribution of wealth emerges only compulsorily through the central taxation structure rather than voluntarily through enlightened management and enhanced productivity.

The problems that had preoccupied Rowntree did not rapidly recede. Levels of welfare benefit, planning of incomes, and worker participation were major policy concerns in the corporatist politics of the 1960s and 1970s, just as unemployment and entrepreneurship moved to the fore during the Thatcherite 1980s and 1990s. And if overseas influences led academic sociology in the 1960s towards theoretical concerns which Rowntree would have found uncongenial, they never completely submerged Britain's well-established empirical and practical sociological tradition. In a more specialized world Rowntree's application of business skills to self-funded broad-ranging social investigation could hardly flourish within the universities' new sociology departments. Yet it was not long before the growth of social history and the resumed preoccupation with social welfare made Rowntree himself a subject of scholarly interest, and in his *Social Work and Social Action* (1961) Asa Briggs provided an invaluable assessment of his impact. Furthermore, Rowntree's books were quarried by the growing army of researchers into twentieth-century social and economic history, and in pioneering the scholarly study of recreation Rowntree anticipated a major late-twentieth-century intellectual concern. Briggs referred in passing to Rowntree's 'interesting and complex personality' (Briggs, 2), but did not aim to write a biography. The remarkable individual who could generate an achievement so wide-ranging demands a biography, yet the book will be difficult to write because Rowntree himself, practical and unassuming like his forebears, took little interest in himself and would have deplored the publicity.

BRIAN HARRISON

Sources A. Briggs, *Social thought and social action: a study of the work of Seebohm Rowntree, 1871–1954* (1961) · *DNB* · J. H. Veit-Wilson, 'Paradigms of poverty: a rehabilitation of B. S. Rowntree', *Journal of Social Policy*, 15/1 (Jan 1986), 69–99 · J. H. Veit-Wilson, 'Seebohm Rowntree and the poor', *New Society* (20 Jan 1983), 97–9 · S. Jenkins and A. Maynard, 'The Rowntree surveys: poverty in York since 1899', *York, 1831–1981: 150 years of scientific endeavour and social change*, ed. C. H. Feinstein (1981), 188–204 · E. P. Hennock, 'The measurement of urban poverty: from the metropolis to the nation, 1880–1920', *Economic History Review*, 2nd ser., 40 (1987), 208–27 · W. Wallace, 'A tribute to the life and work of Seebohm Rowntree, C.H.', *Yorkshire Bulletin of Economic and Social Research* (Dec 1959), 109–15 · H. Sutherland, C. G. Trinder, A. B. Atkinson, J. Corlyon, and A. K. Maynard, 'Poverty in York: a re-analysis of Rowntree's 1950 survey', *Bulletin of Economic Research*, 33/2 (Nov 1981), 59–71 · b. cert. · m. cert. · d. cert. · *CGPLA Eng. & Wales* (1955)
Archives Borth. Inst., corresp. and papers · Joseph Rowntree Foundation, York, library, corresp. and papers | HLRO, letters to David Lloyd George · NA Scot., corresp. with Lord Lothian · NMM, corresp. with Dame Katharine Furse · Nuffield Oxf., corresp. relating to Nuffield Trust for Special Areas · U. Edin. L., corresp. with Charles Sarolea · Welwyn Garden City Central Library, Hertfordshire, corresp. with Sir Frederic Osborn | SOUND BL NSA, 'Rowntree revisited', BBC Radio 4, 14 Oct 1997, H9328/1
Likenesses W. Stoneman, photograph, 1931, NPG · J. Bown, photograph, 1952, Camera Press [*see illus.*] · portrait, repro. in Briggs, *Social thought*, frontispiece
Wealth at death £90,812 2s. 3d.: probate, 12 Jan 1955, *CGPLA Eng. & Wales*

Rowse, Herbert James (1887–1963), architect, was born on 10 May 1887 at 15 Melling Road, Walton, Lancaster, the son of James William Rowse, foreman builder, and his wife, Sarah Ann, formerly Cammack. After local pupillage, in 1905 he entered the school of architecture at Liverpool University, where Charles Reilly had just been appointed Roscoe professor. Rowse gained a first-class certificate in 1907 and was joint winner of the Holt travelling scholarship, which took him to Italy and started a lifelong interest in Italian Romanesque and Renaissance architecture, and yielded a set of measured drawings which won an honourable mention in the silver medal competition of the Royal Institute of British Architects (RIBA) in 1910. He became an associate of the RIBA in 1910 while employed as an assistant to Frank Simon, who in 1912 won the competition for the Manitoba parliament building. Rowse worked in Simon's Winnipeg office in 1913. He also travelled extensively throughout North America and worked briefly in Chicago and New York. He then returned to Liverpool, where he opened his own practice in July 1914. During the First World War he worked for the Admiralty designing 'purely functional buildings'. On 29 July 1918 he married Dorothy (b. 1892/3), daughter of Thomas Parry of Crosby, and relaunched his practice with a commission for the Fairrie sugar refinery in Liverpool.

Rowse's competition-winning design for the Liverpool shipping office (the India Buildings) in 1924 was the first among a series of large-scale commercial commissions in the city, often carried out in partnership with other individuals or firms; these included Martins Bank (1927–32), Lloyds Bank (1928–32), and the Bibby Shipping Line offices (1930). The Lloyds Bank branch in Church Street was in Italian Romanesque, while for bigger buildings Rowse used a rich, eclectic classicism, often with a distinct transatlantic flavour. In 1931 he was appointed consultant to the Mersey tunnel authority, and designed the tunnel approaches, arched entrances, and ventilation towers. The largest tower, the Woodside Tower, housed the tunnel authority offices, and was a distinguished addition to the group of tall buildings at Liverpool's pierhead; it won Rowse the 1937 RIBA bronze medal. His tunnel authority schemes featured low-relief sculpture and art deco work, leaning towards the stripped classical style favoured by both European totalitarian regimes and American New Deal designers. At this time Rowse was working closely with Tyson Smith, Liverpool's leading modern sculptor. The Philharmonic Concert Hall (1936–9), with its simplified brick massing and its restrained decoration, was much closer to mainstream European modernism, and is apparently inspired by W. M. Dudok. It was this approach which informed his designs for the British pavilion at the Empire Exhibition, Glasgow (1938), the Pharmaceutical Society headquarters in Brunswick Square, London (1937), and the Pilkington Glass Company offices in St Helens, Lancashire (1938–9).

War again frustrated Rowse's professional career just when he was beginning to win substantial commissions outside Merseyside, and had purchased 1000 acres in Anglesey, where he planned to improve the estate's buildings and to modernize its husbandry. Whether he then planned to retire is unclear. Rowse served as sheriff for Anglesey during the war, and in 1947 completed the Pharmaceutical Society building (now London University's pharmacy school). In 1947 he secured the Woodchurch 2500 cottage housing scheme, in Birkenhead, upstaging his mentor Professor Sir Charles Reilly with a scheme 'traditionally English in character … modified to suit contemporary limitations and resources'. Woodchurch was one of the biggest regional projects in the era of post-war austerity, and won Rowse a bronze medal for housing from the Ministry of Health. However, the architect resigned before completion, following a dispute with the client. Rowse designed diplomatic buildings at Delhi and Karachi in 1951. He also advised the Belgians on postwar reconstruction, and was awarded the order of Leopold II in 1950. However, he took no further recorded part in British practice until he won the competition for the renovation of the 'Rows' in Chester (with Thomas Harker) just before his death at his home, Chapel House, Puddington, Cheshire, on 22 March 1963. His wife survived him. Temperamentally, Rowse was a perfectionist with meticulous attention to detail, persuading his clients to invest in the finest materials. He worked long hours and set himself high standards, demanding the same of his staff. Donald Bradshaw, writing Rowse's obituary, noted that he was fond of saying 'Never present an alternative; it shows that you have not solved your problem' (*RIBA Journal*).

SIMON PEPPER and PETER RICHMOND

Sources C. H. Reilly, *Representative British architects at the present day* (1931) · J. A. Haddy, 'Herbert J. Rowse, architect of quality, 1887–1963', M.Phil. diss., Liverpool Polytechnic, 1978 · E. Hyde, 'The life and work of Herbert James Rowse', M.Phil. diss., Liverpool John Moore's University, 1993 · *Liverpool Echo* (22 March 1963) · *Daily Telegraph* (23 March 1963) · *The Builder* (29 March 1963) · D. Bradshaw, *RIBA Journal*, 70 (1963), 421–2 · notes in biography file, RIBA BAL · associateship application form, 1910, RIBA BAL · b. cert. · m. cert. · d. cert. · CGPLA Eng. & Wales (1963)

Likenesses photograph, repro. in Reilly, 'Some young architects of today', 524–9

Wealth at death £103,109: probate, 6 Aug 1963, CGPLA Eng. & Wales

Rowse, (Alfred) Leslie (1903–1997), historian, was born on 4 December 1903 at Tregonissey, near St Austell, Cornwall, the youngest child of Richard Rowse (*d.* 1934), china clay worker and shopkeeper, and his wife, Annie, *née* Vanson (*d.* 1953). In 1907 he joined Carclaze elementary school, and in 1915 he won a scholarship to St Austell grammar school. The first volume of his autobiography, *A Cornish Childhood* (1942), was perhaps his best book, combining vividness of perception with sensitive evocation of the landscapes and spirit of his native county.

At school Rowse set his sights on Oxford. In 1921 he was elected Douglas Jerrold scholar in English literature at Christ Church. There he changed to the honour school of modern history. He made friendships with Harold Acton and Lord David Cecil, wrote poetry, and became secretary of the university Labour Club. In 1925 he obtained the second best history first of the year; shortly afterwards he was elected to a prize fellowship at All Souls College. This period of his life was covered in *A Cornishman at Oxford* (1965).

Rowse's fellowship enabled him to travel, especially in Germany, and to take time before deciding on his career. In 1931 he published *Politics and the Younger Generation*. He was adopted as Labour candidate for Penryn and Falmouth and unsuccessfully contested the seat in 1931 and 1935. His political views changed in later years but some Marxist influence was always detectable in his writings, and he remained implacably hostile to the National Government. His friendship with the Rhodes scholar Adam von Trott, later executed for involvement in the 1944 officers' plot, gave him an insight into what he regarded as the Germanic mind, and he became a notable opponent of appeasement, clashing with senior fellows of All Souls, such as Sir John Simon, Lord Halifax, and Geoffrey Dawson, on this issue. Despite some factual errors his *All Souls and Appeasement* (1961) later provided a stimulating analysis of the social and psychological roots of appeasement.

(**Alfred**) **Leslie Rowse** (1903–1997), by Denys Dawnay, 1942

He resigned as parliamentary candidate for Penryn and Falmouth in 1943; a supporter of the Suez campaign, he left the Labour Party in 1956.

Neither involvement in politics nor an undiagnosed duodenal ulcer, requiring surgery in 1938, deflected Rowse from academic and literary pursuits. He taught at the London School of Economics, worked in the Public Record Office and the British Museum, and continued to write poetry. The first of his many books on the sixteenth century, *Sir Richard Grenville of the Revenge*, appeared in 1937. Increasingly his thoughts turned to Cornwall, where he acquired a house in 1940. In 1941 he published *Tudor Cornwall*; its theme was the impact of the Reformation on the county. Above all it investigated the transformation of a remote, Celtic-speaking province into the front line of the sea struggle with Spain. His approach anticipated the post-war *Annales* school in France. The book was welcomed by scholars and placed Rowse in the front rank of English historians. Some of the themes of *Tudor Cornwall* were developed in his later works, including *The England of Elizabeth* (1950), *The Expansion of Elizabethan England* (1955), and *The Elizabethan Renaissance* (1971 and 1972). Other works included *The Early Churchills* (1956) and *The Later Churchills* (1958).

During the war years Rowse became general editor for the English Universities Press of the successful Teach Yourself History series, based on the idea of using a biography of a great man or woman to open up a significant historical theme. Rowse sometimes persuaded authors to take on figures outside their normal areas of expertise; Christopher Hill wrote on Lenin, and Basil Williams on Smuts and Botha. The results were impressive and the series prepared the way for the phenomenon of professional historians writing for mass audiences, so characteristic of the 1950s and 1960s.

In 1952 All Souls chose John Sparrow as warden in preference to Rowse, who felt a sense of rejection, a recurrent motif in his life. In later years, however, he concluded that he had had a lucky escape. He now spent more time in Cornwall and America. In 1953 he secured a lease on Trenarren, the house by the sea that he had coveted in childhood. He found life in the United States congenial and he developed a special affection for California and the Huntington Library, Pasadena. He was a successful visiting professor at numerous American universities and was prompted to write *The Cornish in America* (1969).

Rowse used several important sources hitherto unknown or neglected by historians. The diary of Arthur Throckmorton provided the basis of *Raleigh and the Throckmortons* (1961). In the 1960s, however, he embarked upon a project that dominated the rest of his life. His *William Shakespeare: a Biography* (1963) placed literary themes in the context of the political, social, and cultural life of Elizabethan England. His most controversial works concerned the sonnets. Many traditional Shakespearian scholars regarded these as literary exercises, whereas Rowse believed that they were autobiographical. In a series of books, including editions of the sonnets (1964 and 1973), *Shakespeare the Man* (1973), and *Simon Forman: Sex and Society in Shakespeare's Age* (1974), Rowse claimed to have found answers to problems that had perplexed generations of scholars. He insisted that the earlier sonnets had been addressed to the earl of Southampton, not to the earl of Pembroke. Their dedication, to 'Mr W H', was not Shakespeare's at all; the sonnets' publisher, Thomas Thorp, had dedicated them to Sir William Harvey. Most controversially Rowse claimed that the casebooks of Simon Forman had enabled him to identify the Dark Lady of the later sonnets as Aemilia Bassano, wife of William Lanier, a court musician. Rowse's claims were regarded as plausible, although doubts remained, especially about the Dark Lady. Nevertheless he was angered when some scholars denied that his evidence was incontrovertible. Longstanding friendships, such as that with his former pupil Dame Veronica Wedgwood, were broken, and the tone of Rowse's subsequent defence of his position, as in *Discovering Shakespeare: a Chapter in Literary History* (1989), became strident.

Rowse's fellowship at All Souls expired in 1974; between 1975 and 1996 he published thirty-six books. While several were devoted to Shakespeare others ranged from *Homosexuals in History* (1977) to *The Little Land of Cornwall* (1986) and *The Regicides* (1994). Some of these works indicated that his powers were undiminished. Though he was best known as a historian perhaps the finest work of his old age was his volume of poems, *A Life* (1981). One of his closest and most enduring friendships was with John Betjeman. In later years Rowse's judgements could be harsh but his generous acknowledgement of the achievements of another controversial historian, in *Froude the Historian* (1987), showed his continuing insight and sensitivity. Appropriately his last book was *My View of Shakespeare* (1996).

Rowse insisted that his many publications represented only 'the tip of the iceberg' of his writing. He was alluding primarily to the diary that he kept for most of his adult life. At breakfast in All Souls he would often tell colleagues, especially any who had displeased him, that they had been included in the entry written the night before: 'You're in it and you're in it' (personal knowledge). He made clear that his diaries contained views even more trenchant than those in his published works. He incorporated material from the diaries into his various volumes of autobiography but much remained unused. He believed that when his diaries were published he would be ranked alongside Pepys; in any event, he contended, the project would make the Yale editions of Johnson and Boswell look like a minor cottage industry. The diaries remained unpublished at his death, and those colleagues who read them agreed that full publication would require both courage and good legal advice.

In 1960 Rowse was awarded an honorary doctorate at Exeter University. He was elected to the Athenaeum, under rule 2, in 1972 and received the Benson medal of the Royal Society of Literature. In July 1996 he suffered a major stroke. He had long felt that his achievements had not received sufficient recognition but he was made a Companion of Honour in January 1997. In June the prince of Wales visited him at Trenarren, St Austell, Cornwall. He died there on 3 October 1997. It was typical of him that when his nurse smoothed his pillow and announced that her name was Shirley, not Valerie, as he supposed, he replied, 'Don't contradict ME' (private information).

Rowse could be both terrifying and charming but most people found him more agreeable than they had been led to expect. His work ranged from the lyrical to the banal. It is impossible to imagine him without either his dark or his good side; the one was necessary to the other. He was a vain man but he had few illusions about himself; Richard Ollard's biography, *A Man of Contradictions* (1999), was admirably titled.

Nowhere was the contradiction more striking than in Rowse's attitudes to sex. Despite his denunciations of the modern world he admitted that he could now acknowledge and even flaunt his homosexuality. He claimed that homosexuals are naturally more sensitive, more intuitive, and more creative than 'earth-bound' heterosexuals. Yet in old age he said, 'Of course, I used to be a homo; but now, when it doesn't matter, if anything I'm a hetero' (*The Independent*). His known opinions and general demeanour sometimes led unwary visitors to suppose that he subscribed to the view that Shakespeare himself had had homosexual leanings. Rowse would respond with fury: 'Only silly idiots believe rubbish like that; Shakespeare was two hundred per cent hetero' (personal knowledge).

JOHN CLARKE

Sources A. L. Rowse, *A Cornish childhood* (1942) · A. L. Rowse, *All Souls and appeasement* (1961) · A. L. Rowse, *A Cornishman at Oxford* (1965) · A. L. Rowse, *A Cornishman abroad* (1976) · A. L. Rowse, *Portraits and views* (1979) · A. L. Rowse, *Memories of men and women* (1980) · A. L. Rowse, *Glimpses of the great* (1985) · A. L. Rowse, *Friends and contemporaries* (1989) · A. L. Rowse, *All Souls in my time* (1993) · R. Ollard, *A man of contradictions: a life of A. L. Rowse* (1999) · *The Times* (6 Oct 1997) · *The Independent* (6 Oct 1997) · *Daily Telegraph* (6 Oct 1997) · *The Guardian* (6 Oct 1997) · *The Scotsman* (6 Oct 1997) · WWW · personal knowledge (2004) · private information (2004)
Archives BL, annotated copy of Shakespeare's *Sonnets* · University of Exeter Library, papers | King's Lond., Liddell Hart C., corresp. with Sir B. H. Liddell Hart · Shakespeare Birthplace Trust RO, Stratford upon Avon, letters and cards to Dorothy Withey · U. Sussex Library, letters to J. G. Crowther · Wightwick Manor, Wolverhampton, Lady Mander papers

Likenesses D. Dawnay, oils, 1942, NPG [*see illus.*] · photograph, 1962, repro. in *Daily Telegraph* · B. Marsden, photograph, 1993, NPG · J. Redman, photograph, repro. in *The Guardian* · photograph, repro. in *The Times* · photograph, repro. in *The Independent* · photograph, repro. in *The Scotsman*

Wealth at death £704,104: probate, 9 Dec 1997, *CGPLA Eng. & Wales*

Rowson [*née* Haswell], **Susanna** (*bap.* 1762, *d.* 1824), novelist and actress, was baptized on 25 February 1762 at St Thomas's parish church, Portsmouth, the only child of Lieutenant William Haswell, of the Royal Navy (1734–1805), and his wife, Susanna, *née* Musgrave, who died at or shortly after the birth of her daughter.

Susanna lived in Portsmouth before her father conducted her in 1766 to his home in Hull, Massachusetts, near Boston, where he collected revenue for the Royal Navy. In 1765 he had married a second wife, Rachel Woodward, and the couple had three sons. Susanna loved reading in her father's library, and she also enjoyed the attention of the American patriot James Otis, who called her his 'little pupil'. Because of her father's loyalism during the American War of Independence his property was confiscated, and for a time the family were prisoners of war. After a prisoner exchange, the family returned to England in 1778. Given her father's inability to continue serving in the Royal Navy and the young age of her half-brothers, it is almost certain that she, at the age of sixteen, became the chief financial support of the family. Based on passages in novels that she later claimed were autobiographical, scholars now assume that she served as a governess in these years, although hard evidence is lacking.

In 1786 Susanna Haswell published, by subscription, her first novel, *Victoria*, in two volumes. The novel's main plot concerns the seduction, abandonment, and death of the title character, as well as five sub-plots and several interpolated stories. In that year she also married William Rowson (*d.* 1843), a hardware merchant, trumpeter in the Royal Horse Guards, and occasional actor. They had no children, but she raised his illegitimate son. William Rowson was connected to the Covent Garden Theatre from 1782 until 1793, and Susanna Rowson, who had already written lyrics for Vauxhall Gardens, started her career as a public performer. Although she appeared in only one known London performance (15 October 1792), she and her husband probably worked provincial circuits, and she critiqued Covent Garden in a long poem published as *A Trip to Parnassus* in 1788.

Rowson and her husband were among the English actors recruited for the Philadelphia New Theatre by its manager, Thomas Wignell, in 1793. The Rowsons moved to the Federal Street Theatre in Boston in 1796, and on 17 May 1797 Susanna Rowson made her final stage appearance. In the same year she opened the Young Ladies' Academy in Boston, which she oversaw for the rest of her life. She wrote six textbooks, mostly on geography and history. She also contributed to local journals and magazines, although the long-held assumption that she edited one such journal, the *Boston Weekly Magazine*, has been called into question (Parker, 118–21).

Rowson's earliest novels, which included *The Inquisitor* (1788) and *Mary, or, The Test of Honour* (1789) in addition to *Victoria*, were reviewed scantily or negatively. *Charlotte: a Tale of Truth* (1791) brought a favourable review if no appreciable income, and it became popular in America when published in Philadelphia by Mathew Carey in 1794. In 1797, for the 'third American edition', Carey changed the title of the novel to *Charlotte Temple*, by which it is best known today. The novel, whose frail protagonist is seduced and abandoned by a British soldier, went through more than two hundred editions and was enjoyed by an estimated half million people by the mid-nineteenth century. It attained a kind of cult status, centred on the supposed tomb of the heroine in Trinity churchyard in New York city.

Rowson's other novels include *Mentoria, or, The Young Lady's Friend* (1791, 1794); *Rebecca, or, The fille de chambre* (1792), of which a revised edition came out in 1814 with a preface stating that some details were autobiographical; *Trials of the Human Heart* (4 vols., 1795); *Reuben and Rachel* (1798); and *Sarah, or, The Exemplary Wife* (1802). A sequel to *Charlotte Temple*, entitled *Charlotte's Daughter, or, The Three Orphans*, was published posthumously in 1828, with a memoir by Samuel L. Knapp. The later novels, like *Charlotte Temple*, are often didactic, stressing the consequences of filial disobedience and warning young women against yielding to the advances of would-be seducers. Such warnings are often given in somewhat intrusive fashion by the narrator, who functions as a sort of moral arbiter, especially for the young, impressionable readers envisioned by Rowson as her primary audience.

Despite her birth in Portsmouth, Susanna Rowson disliked being called British because she had automatically become an American citizen on the naturalization of her husband in 1802 (Davidson, xxvi). Her support of American individualism and civic virtue is most apparent in her plays such as *Slaves in Algiers* (1794), and songs for the stage, such as 'America, Commerce, and Freedom', which appeared in *Miscellaneous Poems* (1804). Her feminism and republicanism earned her a severe rebuke from William Cobbett, touching off a pamphlet war in 1795 between him and Rowson's defender John Swanwick.

Rowson died at Boston on 2 March 1824, and was buried in the family vault of her friend Gottlieb Graupner at St Matthew's Church, south Boston. When the church was demolished in 1866, her remains were moved to Mount Hope cemetery in Dorchester, Massachusetts. Her husband survived her.

Rowson's reputation has fluctuated since she gained widespread popularity with *Charlotte Temple*. Long derided as a mere sentimentalist, Rowson is undergoing critical reappraisal. One critic sees her 'authoritatively maternal narrative style' as the 'beginning of a trend which was to become a powerful force in American literature', marking the end of the epistolary style and signalling the rise of the 'American domestic novel' (Forcey, 240–41). Others praise her for introducing new types of fictional women, characterized by Rowson's biographer as 'independent-minded adventurers' (Parker, 123). Because Rowson both followed and modified the seduction plot common in novels of her day, she has been called an important transitional figure between 'those novelists who perpetuated and those who challenged patriarchy's ideologies, especially its inscription of woman's sphere' (Harris, 171).

STEVEN EPLEY

Sources P. L. Parker, *Susanna Rowson* (1986) · C. N. Davidson, 'Introduction', in S. Rowson, *Charlotte Temple* (1986) · B. Forcey, '*Charlotte Temple* and the end of epistolarity', *American Literature*, 63 (1991), 225–41 · S. M. Harris, ed., *American women writers to 1800* (1996) · R. W. G. Vail, *Susanna Haswell Rowson, the author of Charlotte Temple: a bibliographical study* (1933) · E. Nason, *A memoir of Mrs Susanna Rowson* (1870)
Archives American Antiquarian Society, Worcester, Massachusetts · BM · Boston PL · Brown University, Providence, Rhode Island · Harvard U. · L. Cong. · New York Historical Society · New York State Library, Albany, New York · NYPL · Trinity College, Hartford, Connecticut · University of Chicago · Yale U. | University of Virginia, Charlottesville, Alderman Library, Barrett collection
Likenesses H. W. Smith, engraving (after unknown portrait), repro. in Nason, *Memoir*, frontispiece
Wealth at death see Parker, *Susanna Rowson*, 23, 128 n53

Rowton. For this title name *see* Corry, Montagu William Lowry, Baron Rowton (1838–1903).

Roxalana. *See* Davenport, Hester, styled countess of Oxford (1642–1717).

Roxburgh, John Fergusson (1888–1954), headmaster, was born at 19 Belgrave Crescent, Edinburgh, on 5 May 1888, the second son of Archibald Roxburgh (*d.* 1906), an enterprising import and export trader, and his wife, Janet Briggs (1862–1941), daughter of John Cathcart. His paternal grandfather had been a leader in the stern persuasion of the 'Wee Frees' and although childhood was spent in Liverpool, he inherited a Scottish sense of purpose and industry. In 1901 he followed his brother to Charterhouse. His later determination to make a public school a place of enlightenment sprang from his experiences as a boy. G. H. Rendall, his scholarly headmaster, had little accord with youth; houses varied greatly in standards, and his own, Lockites, was an unaesthetic barrack-block, since demolished. Heroes of sport enforced a regime of needless rules; little was done to redeem the lives of unathletic or unusual pupils. Yet he enjoyed some exceptional teaching and from the great classicist T. E. Page learned to relish words of rich and startling aptness.

Trinity College, Cambridge, proved more liberating; Roxburgh's literary and social skills blossomed, and he spoke for liberal causes at the union and developed his talents as a photographer, especially of architecture. After achieving the first class (division three) in the classical tripos (1910), he spent a year at the Sorbonne studying for his *licence-ès-lettres*, enjoying the distinction as a foreigner of second place in the French essay.

Roxburgh's first teaching appointment was as sixth-form master at Lancing College, an excellent apprenticeship, for his mild flamboyance and his conspiracies with bright pupils to enliven school life would not have survived more eminent and crusty senior common rooms. In 1917, after rejections, he was accepted for military service and served with the signal corps of the Royal Engineers.

John Fergusson Roxburgh (1888–1954), by Elliott & Fry, 1948

His fluent French was of value in finding comfortable quarters for senior officers and he saw action in the final battles of 1918, when he was mentioned in dispatches. His experiences, and the death of his younger brother at Jutland, made him one of many who felt an obligation to educate future generations in a vision of service to honour the fallen.

Roxburgh resumed teaching and housemaster duties in 1919 and in 1923 was appointed headmaster of the recently conceived Stowe School. Post-war confusion caused shortages of places at the great public schools and there was no wish for inferior alternatives. E. H. Montauban, headmaster of The Hall, Hampstead, thought of converting the deserted palace of the former dukes of Buckingham at Stowe into a new major school and Hampstead parents were enthused by the idea that a new foundation might shed much rigidity and harshness characteristic of the old. Montauban failed to raise sufficient funds, but the Martyrs' Memorial Trust, a fierce protestant body, led by the Revd P. Warrington, seized on the plan and provided finance. Warrington, suspicious of an applicant from Anglo-Catholic Lancing, tried to mobilize votes of absentees from the trust against Roxburgh but was overruled. On 11 May 1923, Roxburgh, immaculately clad, made his first break with tradition by personally greeting each of the ninety-nine new boys on the steps of the North Front.

Within a few years Stowe had exceeded all expectations. Roxburgh conducted admission procedures and gained an astonishing knowledge of the pupils, their forenames, birthdays, and strengths and weaknesses. Encouragement was supplemented by many small thoughtful gifts from his own none-too-secure emoluments. Momentum was maintained by attracting influential parents and a display of impeccable taste in his waiting-room. He assumed the inevitability of success and nurtured contacts with great schools, epitomized in the gift of the grand avenue approach by a group of Old Etonians. Academic standards rose from humble levels, new houses were built or carved from the ducal premises, and early generations of Stoics added lustre through varied achievements. Among several royal visitors Queen Mary came in 1927 to lay the foundation stone of a chapel, appropriate to the needs of an important community.

From the start, however, J. F. had daunting struggles which drew heavily on his energy. To raise capital for indispensable facilities numbers had to be kept high and overcrowding was frequent. The absence of married accommodation increased the labours of keeping staff. The imposing buildings were draughty and difficult to convert; the grounds, potentially wonderful, were unkempt. The dust and debris of building added to health hazards. Although Warrington desired to see Stowe distinguished, his anti-Catholic crusades were embarrassing and his interference unremitting. Above all, his cross-mortgaging of schools and dubious financial rectitude brought his foundations to virtual bankruptcy in 1932. Fortunately, Legal and General, his major creditor, took over his empire and established Allied Schools, a body which gave Roxburgh freedom from financial stresses and from bigoted control. Stowe added to its reputation with strong traditions in music and art, never regarded as mere diversions. Individual sports such as golf and tennis flourished and, although J. F. sometimes affected indifference over team games, he took a keen interest in results and in the reputation of a strong cadet force which won many competitions at summer camps.

For a believer in the advance of civilization the Second World War was a grievous blow. One in eight Stoics gained decorations but one in seven lost their lives. Each death was a personal tragedy for Roxburgh, whose pupils were his extended family. His correspondence with Old Stoic families became an overwhelming burden eventually devouring his rare holidays.

Roxburgh retired in 1949. He had never discontinued his lessons which every pupil experienced at some point and through which he diffused his beliefs in fine literature and critical taste. The most spontaneous humorous comments became treasured mementoes. Yet his legacy was difficult for successors. His senior tutor, in a long wartime correspondence, vainly besought him to leave a system that did not depend upon his own personality. His second master considered resigning when boys seemed to have knowledge of Roxburgh's thoughts before masters. Firm on courtesy, J. F., in other matters of discipline, sometimes hovered on the edge of the impromptu.

On retirement the Old Stoics gave him a clock, a Sunbeam Talbot, and a large cheque. Always witty, he said he divined a purpose: 'a clock to tell him that his time was up, a motor-car to drive away and journey-money enough to take him to the Antipodes'. He gave the cheque to build workshops but took a cruise to South Africa. He moved into bachelor retirement at Great Brickhill, Buckinghamshire, where his determination never to involve himself in Stowe lent an aura of legend to the gracious liberalism he came to embody. He died at his home, Garden Cottage, Great Brickhill, on 6 May 1954; his funeral fell on the anniversary of Stowe's foundation.

Roxburgh published two books: *The Poetic Procession* (1921), literary studies based upon Workers' Educational Association lectures given as a young schoolmaster, and *Eleutheros* (1930), an imaginary discussion on public schools based upon experience of the wishes and needs of parents. A portrait by James Gunn, 'that libellous square yard' in his words, hangs at Stowe.   BRIAN REES

Sources Stowe School, archives · N. Annan, *Roxburgh of Stowe* (1965) · R. P. Croom-Johnson, *The origin of Stowe School* (1953) · DNB · private information (2004)
Archives Stowe School, archives
Likenesses Elliott & Fry, photograph, 1948, NPG [*see illus.*] · J. Gunn, oils, Stowe School
Wealth at death £44,671 8s. 8d.: probate, 29 Sept 1954, CGPLA Eng. & Wales

Roxburgh, William (1751–1815), botanist, was born at Underwood, Craigie, Ayrshire, on 3 June 1751. From the village school he proceeded to the University of Edinburgh, where he studied botany under Professor John Hope (1725–1786). Through Hope's influence, when qualified, he obtained in May 1766 an appointment as surgeon's mate on one of the East India Company's ships. After making several voyages to India and completing his medical studies at Edinburgh, he was given an appointment as assistant surgeon on the company's Madras establishment.

Roxburgh arrived at Madras in 1776, and during the following two years he was, according to a manuscript version of his *Flora Indica*, 'in large practice at the General Hospital at Madras'. In November 1780 he became full surgeon. While he was in Madras, he botanized with Johann Gerhard Koenig (1728–1785), naturalist to the nawab of Arcot and from 1778 to the Madras presidency. Koenig, a former pupil of Linnaeus, introduced Linnaean methodology to India and presumably encouraged Roxburgh in his botanical studies.

In 1781 Roxburgh was stationed at Samulcotta, some 200 miles north of Madras. The climate and the apparent fertility of the soil around Samulcotta led him to believe that pepper and coffee could be grown there commercially. He was allowed to establish experimental gardens where he planted black pepper which grew wild in the hills to the north of the town. By 1787 he had 4000 pepper plants in cultivation and by 1789 between 40,000 and 50,000. They failed to fruit, perhaps because of inappropriate methods of cultivation. He also grew coffee, sugar-cane, mulberry, and breadfruit. Some years later he stated that had his plantations not been successful he would have returned to Scotland to seek more remunerative employment. In his spare time he botanized, and in October 1789 had two Indian artists drawing some of the plants he had collected. He was an obvious candidate for the official post of naturalist in the Madras presidency (once held by his friend Koenig) when it became vacant in 1789 following the retirement of Patrick Russell. The East India Company in London approved the appointment in 1790.

In September 1790 Roxburgh sent the first of several consignments of flower drawings by his native artists together with descriptive notes and remarks on their use by Indians to Sir Joseph Banks. When Banks had received some 500 drawings by the summer of 1794, he suggested to the company that a selection of those of particular value to commerce and medicine should be engraved and published. Patrick Russell had first proposed the idea for such a work, confined to Coromandel (the east coast of Madras), the area where the plants were found, and he had nominated Banks as the best person to advise on the project. The company sponsored its publication and *Plants of the Coast of Coromandel* appeared in twelve folio parts between May 1795 and February 1820. Each of its 300 engravings had taxonomic descriptions and information on native uses in agriculture, food, and medicine.

On the death in May 1793 of Colonel Robert Kyd, the founder and manager of the Royal Botanic Garden in Calcutta Roxburgh was appointed its first salaried superintendent in November of that year. The garden had been formed in 1786 to propagate commercially viable crops as well as to grow plants of purely botanical interest. Roxburgh, with his experience of managing plantations in the south, confidently tackled his new duties. Soon seedlings of teak, Arabian coffee, Virginia tobacco, and Bengal hemp, raised in the garden, were being dispatched throughout the subcontinent for trial cultivation. Roxburgh was granted home sick leave in December 1797; on his return in the autumn of 1799 he was able to report that there were several thousand young teak trees ready for distribution. So many plants were now under cultivation that his garden was enlarged in 1805. From 1805 to 1807 he was again absent on sick leave, and further deterioration in his health forced his retirement in 1813. During his time as superintendent, the Royal Botanic Garden, Calcutta, became India's main centre for acclimatizing plants from abroad. Sir Joseph Banks through his connections with the East India Company influenced the policy of the garden which he saw as 'intended solely for the promotion of public utility and science' (Banks to East India Company, 17 Jan 1791, BL OIOC, Misc. letters received, 86, fol. 54 a–c). Roxburgh's competent management had enlarged its collections from some 300 species in 1794 to about 3500 in 1813. He had also formed a valuable collection of over 2500 flower paintings executed mainly by Indian artists, two sets of which survived, one at the Royal Botanic Garden, Calcutta, and the other at Kew Gardens.

When Roxburgh left India for good in 1813 he gave the manuscript of his *Hortus Bengalensis* to his friend at the Baptist mission in Serampore, William Carey, who was

also allowed to make a copy of the manuscript of Roxburgh's *Flora Indica*. Carey, who had a printing press in order to publish the Bible in Indian languages, printed in 1813 *A catalogue of plants described by Dr Roxburgh in his MSS Flora Indica, but not yet introduced into the botanical garden*. This was distributed in 1814 bound with the *Hortus Bengalensis*, which listed 1510 species cultivated in the botanic garden, adding the country of origin. Europeans resident in India were the principal donors but a number of plants had come from Canton, North America, the West Indies, and Britain.

The resources of his garden, both actual plants and pictorial records, had enabled Roxburgh to pursue his projected book on the Indian flora. He told Sir Joseph Banks in 1802 that it was half finished, but the government of Bengal failed to persuade the East India Company to sponsor its publication in 1805. Roxburgh himself was reluctant to publish until he had consulted botanists in Britain. On his return in 1813 he gave a copy of the manuscript to Robert Brown, an eminent botanist but a notorious procrastinator, for scrutiny. When Roxburgh died in 1815 Brown was still slowly revising it. (This manuscript, with additional notes by Roxburgh and Brown, is now in the Natural History Library, London.) In 1817, Carey, frustrated by the delay, resolved to print it himself, using the copy he had made at the time of Roxburgh's departure from India. Nathaniel Wallich, the superintendent of the botanic garden, offered to contribute descriptions of species from his own collections. The first volume of *Flora Indica* was printed by Carey at his Mission Press in Serampore in 1820. Wallich's Nepal expedition in 1820–21, and his subsequent convalescence, delayed the second volume until 1824. Many of Wallich's Nepal plants are described in volume two. A third volume promised for 1825 never materialized because, it was said, Wallich was preoccupied with other matters. Roxburgh's two sons, Bruce and James, financed the three-volume edition in 1832; this excluded Wallich's contributions to the first two volumes (1820 and 1824) but added other material in Roxburgh's manuscript. The cryptograms, edited by William Griffith, appeared in the *Calcutta Journal of Natural History* (4, 1844, 463–520). The 1832 edition and Griffith's contribution were reprinted as a single volume in 1874 by C. B. Clarke, who saw it as still meeting a demand by the amateur botanist for a compact flora. In his preface Clarke justified his decision: 'Roxburgh's work is so excellent, and his species so well conceived, that they form a solid framework, which being once put together, all the other species are easily fitted into their due places'.

Roxburgh was elected a fellow of the Linnean Society in 1799. He was also a member of the Society of Arts which thrice awarded him its gold medal for his research on Indian fibres. *Observations of the Late William Roxburgh* (1815) records his persistent attempts to find substitutes for hemp and flax. He believed he had discovered a prophylactic for malaria which he described in *A Botanical Description of a New Species of Swietenia* (1793).

Roxburgh was married three times. His first wife was a

Miss Bonté, possibly the daughter of the governor of Penang; they had a daughter, Mary. The second, Miss Huttenmann, with whom he had five sons and three daughters, was German. With his last wife, Mary Boswell, he had two daughters and a son. With so many dependants, it is not surprising that he was concerned about finding suitable husbands for his daughters and careers for his sons. Through him, in 1800, his son William was appointed as an assistant at the Royal Botanic Garden, Calcutta; he collected plants for his father in Rajmahal (1800), Chittagong (1801–2), Penang (1802), and the Moluccas and Sumatra (1803). When the elder Roxburgh was absent on sick leave between 1805 and 1807 his son deputized for him, and his father tried in vain to have him accepted as his successor as superintendent. Eventually the younger William Roxburgh became manager of spice plantations in Sumatra, where he died in 1810.

Roxburgh also had another son working with him. John Roxburgh, who was apparently illegitimate, collected plants at the Cape of Good Hope (1798–1804) and Chittagong (1810–11). His father made him overseer of the Indian flower painters about 1804. John Roxburgh was dismissed by Wallich, then acting superintendent, in July 1815, reinstated by the new superintendent, James Hare, in 1816, and dismissed once more by Wallich, by then superintendent, in March 1819.

Roxburgh died at Park Place, Edinburgh on 18 February 1815 and was buried in the family tomb of his third wife in Greyfriars churchyard in the city. A memorial to him was erected in 1823 in the Royal Botanic Garden, Calcutta, and his son, Captain James Roxburgh, had a canopy built over it in 1837. Jonas Dryander dedicated to him the genus *Roxburghia*, an evergreen Indian climber which was said to symbolize the manner in which he had made Indian botany his 'ladder of success' (*Cottage Gardener*, 6, 1851, 65).

RAY DESMOND

Sources G. King, 'A brief memoir of William Roxburgh', *Annals of the Royal Botanic Garden of Calcutta*, 5 (1895), 1–9 · R. Desmond, *The European discovery of the Indian flora* (1992) · I. H. Burkill, *Chapters on the history of botany in India* (Calcutta, 1965) · M. Archer, *Natural history drawings in the India Office Library* (1962) · J. R. Sealy, 'The Roxburgh *Flora Indica* drawings at Kew', *Kew Bulletin*, [11] (1956–7), 297–348 · J. R. Sealy, 'William Roxburgh's collection of paintings of Indian plants', *Endeavour*, 34 (1975), 84–9 · F. A. Stafleu and R. S. Cowan, *Taxonomic literature: a selective guide*, 2nd edn, 4, Regnum Vegetabile, 110 (1983) · DNB
Archives BL OIOC, corresp. and papers, MSS Eur. D 49–69 809, E 64–67, F 18 23–25 · Calcutta Botanic Garden · Delessert Herbarium, Geneva · McGill University, Montreal, Osler Library of the History of Medicine, description of *Swietenia febrifuga* · NHM, corresp. and papers · RBG Kew, corresp. and papers · RCP Lond., description of *Swietenia febrifuga* · Royal Botanic Garden, Edinburgh, catalogue of Indian plants · Royal College of Physicians of Edinburgh · RS, meteorological diary · Wellcome L., 'Flora Indica' | BL, letters to Sir Joseph Banks, Add. MSS 33977–33981 · BL, corresp. with Thomas Hardwicke, Add. MS 9869 · Linn. Soc., letters to Sir James Smith · NA Scot., letters to Francis Buchanan
Likenesses C. Warren, line engraving, BM; repro. in *Society of Arts Transactions* (1815) · engraving, repro. in King, 'A brief memoir'

Roxburghe. For this title name *see* Ker, Robert, first earl of Roxburghe (1569/70–1650); Ker, Jane, countess of Roxburghe (*b.* in or before 1585, *d.* 1643); Ker, John, first duke of Roxburghe (*c.*1680–1741); Ker, John, third duke of Roxburghe (1740–1804); Ker, James Innes-, fifth duke of Roxburghe (1736–1823).

Roxby, Robert (*c.*1809–1866), actor, was the son of William Roxby, an actor who performed under the name William Roxby Beverley and manager at one time of the theatre in Tottenham Street, Fitzroy Square. The actor Henry Roxby *Beverley and William Roxby *Beverly, the well-known scene-painter, were his brothers. After performing in provincial theatres Roxby appeared in London in 1839 at the St James's, under the management of Hooper. In 1843 he took the Theatre Royal, Manchester, where he played many leading parts in comedy. He was for some years in London at the Lyceum or Drury Lane, and was stage-manager of Drury Lane for eleven years. He acted much with Charles Mathews, and was with him and Madame Vestris at the Lyceum from 1847 to 1855. This was his brightest period. In October 1855, at Drury Lane, he played Rob Royland to the Mopus of Charles Mathews in *Married for Money*, an adaptation of Poole's *The Wealthy Widow*. On this occasion the Lyceum company had been engaged by E. T. Smith for Drury Lane. The following year at Drury Lane Roxby supported Mrs Waller, an actress from America and Australia. In March 1858 he was the original Lord George Lavender in Stirling Coyne's *The Love Knot*. He played original parts again in 1860, in Fitzball's *Christmas Eve, or, The Duel in the Snow*, founded on Gérome's famous picture, and as the first Hardress Cregan in H. J. Byron's burlesque *Miss Eily O'Connor*. In January 1863, while stage-manager at the Princess's, he was seriously burnt while fighting a fire on the stage, in which two girls in the pantomime died. On the first appearance in London of Walter Montgomery in that house as Othello, in June 1863, Roxby was Roderigo. At the close of the year he was again at Drury Lane, where, in April 1864, he played in *An April Fool* by Brough and Halliday. On 25 July 1866, after a long and painful illness, he died at the house of his brother William Roxby Beverly, 26 Russell Square, London. Roxby was a capable stage-manager and, in spite of some hardness of style and weakness of voice, a respectable actor in light comedy parts.

JOSEPH KNIGHT, *rev.* NILANJANA BANERJI

Sources *The Era* (29 July 1866) · *The life and reminiscences of E. L. Blanchard, with notes from the diary of Wm. Blanchard*, ed. C. W. Scott and C. Howard, 2 vols. (1891) · *Era Almanack and Annual* (1872) · GM, 4th ser., 2 (1866), 416 · N&Q, 8th ser., 9 (1896), 116

Roy, Camille Joseph (1870–1943), priest and scholar of French-Canadian literature, was born at Berthier-en-bas, Quebec, on 22 October 1870, the sixteenth of at least twenty children of Benjamin Roy, a farmer, and his wife, Desanges Gosselin. Of this large family five became priests and one, Paul Eugène, archbishop of Quebec. Camille, who was ordained a priest in 1894, was educated at the seminary at Quebec and at Laval University, where he was awarded a doctorate of philosophy in 1894. He also studied at the Catholic Institute in Paris, and, from 1898 to 1901, at the Sorbonne, where he came under the influence of the professor of literature, Auguste Émile Faguet.

Roy began teaching in the Quebec seminary in 1892 and in 1918 he was appointed professor of French literature at Laval. He became professor of Canadian literature in 1927 and was rector of the university four times between 1924 and 1943. His influence on education in Quebec was impressive. He introduced new faculties, including one of natural science, and founded the École Normale Supérieure there. In 1925 Roy was appointed protonotary apostolic by Pope Pius XI.

The educational and ecclesiastical aspects of Roy's life were closely connected. Although critical of a narrow and exclusive concern with religious life on the part of some Canadian writers, he was a strong supporter of a *clericaliste* literary culture which celebrated 'the high traditions of the altar, the home and the Gallic inheritance of his people' (Pierce, 545): Catholicism was therefore integral to Roy's francophone critical programme. In 1902 Roy played an important part in the creation of the Société du Parler Français au Canada, and was president of the society from 1906 to 1908. *Essais sur la littérature canadienne* (1907) and *Nos origines littéraires* (1909), the latter a collection of papers from the society's *Bulletin*, are early indications of Roy's enduring affinity with Abbé Henri-Raymond Casgrain's nineteenth-century Mouvement Littéraire du Québec; and he went on to publish a literary biography of Casgrain in 1913.

Although much wider in his sympathies than many Québecois, Roy distrusted certain tendencies in both European and American literature. He was selective in his appreciation of the French literary tradition, disliking the French Romantics, and considering the symbolist school a non-French anomaly. But if his literary taste was for the pious, austere classicism of an idealized *ancien régime*, Roy was also anxious to align his own cultural agenda with the nineteenth-century French critical tradition of Brunetière, Faguet, and Lanson. *La critique littéraire au dix-neuvième siècle de Mme de Staël à Émile Faguet* was published in 1918, the same year as his *Manuel d'histoire de la littérature canadienne-française*. This work, clearly indebted to nineteenth-century French literary historiography, went through seven editions (and some changes of title) before 1931.

Despite his undoubted services to French-Canadian literature, Roy could often appear to subordinate his support for native literature to his belief that 'French Canada had a divine mission to preserve the Christian culture of eighteenth-century France' (Story, 729). He considered Léo-Paul Desrosiers's *Nord-sud* (1931) the best native novel of the century, but would point out its inferiority to much contemporary French literature; and although he praised Pamphile LeMay as the equal of French sonneteers, his antipathy to Romanticism obliged him to qualify his approval of the 'Canadian laureate', L. H. Fréchette, whose debt to Victor Hugo was too extensive for Roy to accept uncritically.

After *A l'ombre des érables* (1924), for which he was awarded the prix David, and *Études et croquis* (1928), Roy concentrated on outlining his educational beliefs and defending his commitment to a francophone national culture in works such as *Nos problèmes d'enseignement* (1935), *Pour conserver notre héritage français* (1937), and *Pour former des hommes nouveaux* (1941).

Roy had an active professional life, preaching, speaking on formal occasions, and lecturing to French audiences in many parts of Canada and the United States. In 1933 he made a tour of the principal universities of France, giving lecture courses on French-Canadian literature. He was remembered as an independent, urbane, and essentially humanistic literary critic. He received the gold medal in French literature of the Académie Française in 1925, and honorary degrees from Ottawa and Toronto in 1927. He was elected a fellow of the Royal Society of Canada in 1904, and was president for 1928–9. He was appointed chevalier of the Légion d'honneur in 1925 and promoted officier in 1928. Roy died at Quebec on 24 June 1943.

P. J. CONNELL

Sources L. Pierce, 'Monseigneur Camille Roy', *Queen's Quarterly: a Canadian Review*, 35 (1927–8), 54–8 · personal knowledge (1958) [*DNB*] · *Proceedings and Transactions of the Royal Society of Canada*, 3rd ser., 38 (1944) · F. Ludovic, *Bio-bibliographie de Mgr Camille Roy* (1941) · W. Toye, ed., *The Oxford companion to Canadian literature* (1983) · W. S. Wallace, ed., *The Macmillan dictionary of Canadian biography*, 3rd edn (1963) · [N. Story], *The Oxford companion to Canadian history and literature*, ed. W. Toye (1967), 729 · *Revue Canadienne*, 22 (July 1918) · *DNB*
Likenesses G. Szoldatics, portrait, 1927, Laval University, Quebec, Canada · photograph, repro. in *Proceedings and Transactions of the Royal Society of Canada*

Roy, Harry [*real name* Harris Litman] (1900–1971), band leader and clarinettist, was born at 26 Kingsland Road, Shoreditch, east London, on 12 January 1900, one of at least two sons of Solomon Litman, then a master bootmaker, and his wife, Eva Okin. He changed his name by deed poll in his teens when first trying to make his way in the musical world. He was attracted to music as a boy and found his first great inspiration in the music of the Original Dixieland Jazzband, which travelled to London in 1919 to appear at the London Palladium in the revue *Joy Bells*; it was a short-lived engagement as the star of the show, George Robey, thought that the band was attracting too much attention and demanded that either they left or he would. It was the clarinettist of the band, Larry Shields, who inspired Harry Roy to concentrate mainly on the clarinet, although he also regularly played the saxophone.

For a time Harry Roy trained in business management at Beccles College, and he also worked for a while in his father's box manufacturing company. The family business lost over £28,000 and finally foundered at the end of the First World War. Consequently Roy was now free to embark on a musical career and formed a group of six players, led by his brother Sydney (always known as Sid Roy) on the piano, which they called the Darnswells and which played at the Fitzroy Galleries in Oxford Street; shortly afterwards the name of the group was changed to the somewhat grander title Original Crichton Lyricals. The group managed to get a recording contract with a minor label and had engagements at Rector's Club (in London and Paris) and at the Hammersmith Palais de Danse (succeeding the Original Dixieland Band there), at Oddenino's and the Cavour Restaurant, and, from 1927, at the Café de Paris. Its reputation grew steadily, and it toured South Africa in 1928 and then Australia, returned to tour in a show called *Variety Pie* in 1929, and visited Germany in 1930. After that the Lyricals disbanded, and Harry Roy led his own group at the Bat Club, called the Bat Club Boys, with Ivor Moreton replacing his brother as pianist. His big opportunity came when the Leicester Square Theatre in London started screening big feature films in 1931 with a live band appearance supplied as an extra attraction. The group, now known as the RKOlians, moved on to the London Pavilion in 1932 and then to the Café Anglais in 1933 before following the famous Ambrose band with an engagement at the prestigious Mayfair Hotel from March 1934 to 1936. In 1938 it made a three-month tour of South America.

Harry Roy's band made a big feature of novelty and comedy numbers and especially exploited his original love of Dixieland music, making big hits of such numbers as 'Tiger Rag'. These were sometimes performed by a small jazz group from the band, usually led by Roy, which played and recorded as Harry Roy and his Tiger-Ragamuffins. The band had a special success with pseudo-rag numbers like 'Leicester Square Rag' and 'Piccadilly Rag' in what were billed as 'modernistic' arrangements often featuring the piano duo of Ivor Moreton and Dave Kaye, who were succeeded in 1936 (when they became a music-hall turn) by Stanley Black and Norman Yarlett. 'Bugle Call Rag' was used as the band's signature tune. Regulars in the band at that time included Nat Temple on the clarinet and Joe Daniels, succeeded by Ray Ellington, on the drums. Many of the arrangements were by George Scott-Wood. Harry was featured on the clarinet and alto saxophone in a sort of vaudeville act based on the top-hatted American clarinettist Ted Lewis, and as a curiously high-pitched singer. The band became greatly popular for its corny high spirits, publicized by frequent radio broadcasts, numerous recordings with EMI and Decca, and an appearance in the film *Everything is Rhythm* in 1936. At that time he lived at 60 Park Lane, London. Harry Roy had recently got himself into the society news by marrying Elizabeth Brooke, known as Princess Pearl (*b.* 1914), the daughter of Sir Charles Vyner *Brooke, the white raja of Sarawak, on 6 August 1935. The film's slight story was loosely based on this event, and Mr and Mrs Roy led the cast and sang duets on the soundtrack. They were featured in a second film, *Rhythm Racketeer*, in 1937, and she was frequently a vocalist with the band. They had two children, but were divorced in 1947. Harry Roy remarried on 4 July 1948; his second wife was Sonia Stacpoole (*b.* 1921), the daughter of an army captain, William Edward Stacpoole.

Just after the war broke out in 1939 Roy re-formed a band for the Café Anglais and soon afterwards was featured in *Eve on Parade* at the Garrick Theatre. The band toured for ten months and then became resident at the Embassy Club. During the war it returned there on occasions and went to the Middle East to play for the forces. The big-band days did not survive for very long after the war, but Roy had a hit with 'Leicester Square Rag' in the 1950s. Harry Roy continued to lead various nightclub bands until about 1963. He was then engaged in assorted behind-the-scenes activities, including the ownership of a drinking-club in Bond Street, before re-emerging for a short time in 1969 as leader of a Dixieland band at Sherry's in Brighton and leading an interval quartet at the Lyric Theatre. Roy gave a hint during a television interview late in life that for most of his last years he experienced financial hardship. He was living at 12 Montagu Place in St Marylebone, London, when he died there of a coronary thrombosis on 1 February 1971; he was survived by his second wife.

PETER GAMMOND

Sources b. cert. · m. certs. · d. cert. · *The Times* (2 Feb 1971) · R. Orchard, disc notes, *Are you listening: Harry Roy* (1973) [World Records SH187/8] · R. Orchard, disc notes, *Bands on film* (1975) [World Records SH197] · P. Gammond, *The Oxford companion to popular music* (1991) · A. McCarthy, *The dance band era* (1971) · H. R. Schleman, *Rhythm on record* (1936) · J. Chilton, *Who's who of British jazz* (1997) · CGPLA Eng. & Wales (1971)
Likenesses photographs, 1930–37, Hult. Arch.
Wealth at death £2740: probate, 7 April 1971, CGPLA Eng. & Wales

Roy, Indra Lal (1898–1918), airman, was born on 2 December 1898 in Calcutta, India, the son of Hindu parents, Piera Lal Roy, a barrister, and his wife, Lolita. One brother, Lolit Kumar Roy (*d.* 1920), is mentioned in St Paul's School registers. Educated in Britain from the age of ten, Roy attended Colet Court preparatory school for three years and then St Paul's School (where he was a foundation scholar) for six years. A good athlete, he was captain of swimming, played rugby, and was also a motor cyclist. He was in the school cadet force from September 1914 to March 1917. Interested in flying, he read avidly about the theory of petrol engines and flying machines.

Wishing to 'do his bit in the War', Roy, who liked his school and was said to talk only in English, having 'forgotten his Indian language' (C. Roberts to General Brancker, 21 Feb 1917, PRO), left St Paul's in March 1917 for war service as a fighter pilot in the Royal Flying Corps (RFC). How difficult it had been for him to obtain a commission in the RFC is hard to judge. The 'best way' in which an Indian could enter the corps was by becoming a sergeant mechanic (ibid.). The records do not make it entirely clear whether it was the personal intervention of General Sir Sefton Brancker that enabled Roy to gain an interview for admission to the officers' cadet wing. Declared fit for military service as a pilot with the use of glasses, and appointed to a temporary commission as a second lieutenant in the RFC in July 1917, Roy was posted to 56 squadron in October 1917.

Roy's flying career did not begin well. On 6 November 1917 he crashed his aircraft and was returned to Britain for more training. After further flying he was pronounced unfit by the medical authorities. However, he managed to get the decision reversed, and on 19 June 1918 he was back in France. He joined Captain George McElroy's flight in 40 squadron, where he distinguished himself as a fighter pilot. Between 6 and 19 July 1918, in only 170 hours and 15 minutes of flying time, he shot down ten enemy aircraft, two of which he shared with McElroy. On 22 July 1918, at 8 a.m., when Roy was on observation patrol above the trenches, his aircraft was attacked, and he was killed in a fight with Fokker DVIIs of Jasta 29, as his SE 5A fell in flames over Carvin. He was buried in Estevelles communal cemetery, Pas-de-Calais, France. He was unmarried.

The only Indian fighter ace of the First World War, Roy was awarded a DFC posthumously in September 1918. In the history of British flying service his record of ten victories at the very beginning of his flying career is a unique achievement. W. A. Bishop, the Canadian ace of aces, claimed more victories—but only after long practice. Roy was still a beginner when he was killed in action.

ROZINA VISRAM

Sources R. Visram, *Asians in Britain: four hundred years of history* (2002) · C. Shores and others, *Above the trenches: a complete record of the fighter aces and units of the British empire air forces, 1915–1920* (1990) · R. Singh, *Indian Air Force: in the footsteps of our legends* (1998) · A. H. Mead and others, eds., *St Paul's School registers* (1990) · Commonwealth War Graves Commission, Maidenhead · war office records, PRO, WO 339/115198 · air ministry records, PRO, AIR 1/1222/204/5/2634/40 Sqdn

Archives PRO, WO 339/115198 · PRO, AIR 1/1222/204/5/2634/40 Sqdn · Commonwealth War Graves Commission records

Likenesses photograph, Franks Collection; repro. in Shores and others, *Above the trenches*

Roy, Manabendra Nath (1887–1954), international communist leader and ideologist, was born Narendra Nath Bhattacharya on 21 March 1887, according to family tradition, in Arbalia village, near Calcutta, the fourth child of Dinabandhu Bhattacharya, a village teacher. He was educated locally but, like many Bengali young men of the period, he held as his major concern the anti-colonial struggle, and from 1905 he became deeply involved with the revolutionary groups that had sprung up at that time. In 1915 he left India to try to arrange for the smuggling of arms from Germany. This failed, but he was able to reach California in June 1916, at which point he adopted the name Manabendra Nath Roy. He met and married there his first wife, Evelyn Trent, and at the same time came into contact with American radicals and progressives. Forced to leave the United States, he went in 1917 to Mexico, where he became involved in local politics and emerged as the effective leader of the small Mexican Socialist Party. The key event in Roy's political development was his meeting with Michael Borodin, who had arrived in Mexico in 1919 as the Comintern's emissary. Under Borodin's guidance he converted to Marxism and in August 1919 set up the Communist Party of Mexico.

Roy played a major role at the second Comintern congress in 1920 and engaged Lenin in a famous debate about the role of the 'national bourgeoisie' in the colonies in the transition to communism. Both saw the importance of anti-colonial nationalism in destabilizing the metropolitan countries such as Britain, but they diverged significantly over whether the existing colonial bourgeoisie had any long-term revolutionary potential. An immediate question was whether bourgeois parties, such as the Indian National Congress under Gandhi, should be supported. While Lenin believed they should, Roy thought that the Comintern should be more selective and seek to identify and support revolutionary movements based on the colonial working class. This reflected his more general view, set out for example in *India in Transition* (1922), that the tools of Marxist analysis could be applied universally.

From 1920 until 1929 Roy was a full-time leader of the Comintern and played a prominent part in its affairs. He was a key figure in the early history of the Communist Party of India, founded originally at Tashkent in 1920 and in India itself in 1925. His involvement in the disasters that struck the fledgeling Chinese Communist Party in 1927, however, led to his exclusion from the inner circle of leadership, while his analysis of the situation in India led him to take positions which diverged from the increasingly rigid Comintern orthodoxy. He maintained his highly critical analysis of Gandhi, but began to see the need for a tactical alliance with left-wing elements within Congress. His positions—especially his so-called 'decolonization' thesis, which saw the British establishing a working relationship with the Indian bourgeoisie at the expense of the working class and therefore implied the need for solidarity of all progressive forces—were attacked at the sixth Comintern congress in 1928 and he was expelled the following year. His personal association with figures such as Bukharin meant that there was no place for him in the Stalin-dominated Comintern thereafter. He found a spiritual home at this point with the dissident communist group in Germany led by August Thalheimer and Heinrich Brandler.

In December 1930 Roy secretly returned to India in order to establish a political base, but he was arrested by the authorities after a few months and sentenced to twelve years in prison on charges of conspiracy to overthrow the state. Although his sentence was reduced on appeal to six years, he had to endure harsh conditions in gaol, relieved only by the opportunity to read extensively. During this period he began to move beyond the orthodox Marxism of his earlier period. After his release from gaol in 1936 Roy attempted a strategy of working with the left in Congress, and established friendly relations with Jawaharlal Nehru and other progressives. However, he found little space for manoeuvre between a new generation of socialists on the one side and Gandhian activists on the other. Roy left Congress in 1940, believing that it should have agreed to support Britain in its war with Nazi Germany, and established his own Radical Democratic Party. This failed to make any electoral impact and Roy dissolved it in 1948.

Roy had separated from his first wife in 1926, and, after a relationship with Louise Geissler, in 1936 married Ellen Gottschalk. From 1946, when he settled in Dehra Dun, until his death there on 25 January 1954 he continued to develop his theories of radical humanism, which sought to apply his rationalist and materialist analysis of historical processes to the Indian context. His *magnum opus* was

Reason, Romanticism and Revolution, published in two volumes in 1952 and 1955. After his death his ideas were kept alive by a circle of devoted followers.   DAVID TAYLOR

Sources *Selected works of M. N. Roy*, ed. S. Ray, 4 vols. (1987–97) · J. P. Haithcox, *Communism and nationalism in India: M. N. Roy and Comintern policy, 1920–1939* (1971) · Sudipta Kaviraj, 'The heteronomous radicalism of M. N. Roy', *Political thought in modern India*, ed. T. Pantham and K. L. Deutsch (1986), 209–35 · S. Roy, *M. N. Roy: a political biography* (1997)
Archives Nehru Museum, New Delhi, papers
Likenesses photographs, repro. in *Selected works* · photographs, repro. in Haithcox, *Communism and nationalism*

Roy, Rammohun (1772?–1833), political and religious thinker, was born in Radhanagar, Burdwan district, Bengal, the youngest of three children of Ramkanta Roy (*d.* 1803), a *zamindar* (landholder), and his second wife, Tarini Devi. He had an elder sister, an elder brother, Jagmohan, and a younger half-brother, Ramlochan (by his father's third wife, Rammani Devi). His date of birth is uncertain. Some authorities prefer 1774, the date given by his first biographer, Lant Carpenter, in 1833, and inscribed on his tomb in 1872; and some contemporary sources give later dates. The family was of the Rarhi Brahman caste, and worshipped Vishnu. Their hereditary title was Banerji (Sanskrit form Bandyopadhyay); the princely title Roy had been conferred on Rammohun's great-grandfather by the nawab of Bengal. Rammohun himself was apparently married three times in childhood; among Rarhi Brahmans polygyny and child marriage were common and respected practices, which he later censured. Little is known of his wives, and they did not share in his social and public life. The first died young, but the third survived him; with the second, who died in 1824, Rammohun had two sons, Radhaprasad (*b.* 1800) and Ramaprasad (*b.* 1812). He also had an adopted son, Rajaram, who accompanied him to England. (Carpenter's memoir refers to him throughout as Rammohun's son, but Carpenter was later informed that he was a foundling.)

The information from contemporary sources on Rammohun Roy's early life and education is scanty and conflicting. He is said to have been sent to Patna to study Persian and Arabic, and to Calcutta or Benares for Sanskrit; what is certain is that by 1815 he was proficient in all these languages, and in English. We also know that the family moved in 1792 to Langulpara, that in 1796 he was managing his father's estates, and that later in the same year Ramkanta divided his property among his three sons, contrary to the statement of some early biographers that Rammohun was disinherited. During the next few years Rammohun was still managing his father's property, but was also in business in Calcutta, dealing in the East India Company's stock, lending money, and investing in land; he lent large sums to some of the company's British employees. His wealth grew, while his father and his elder brother fell into debt; his father died in 1803, owing rent both to the company and to the maharaja of Burdwan. Meanwhile, Rammohun's British contacts led to employment as *munshi* (translator and language teacher) and as

diwan (business manager); he was also intermittently employed by the company from 1803 to 1815, this employment taking him to various parts of Bengal and making him familiar with the English language and European ideas. In 1815 he and another Bengali, Krishnakant Basu, were sent to Bhutan by David Scott (1786–1831), who was becoming the company's expert on north-east frontier affairs. This mission is probably the foundation of the story, first recounted by Carpenter and much embroidered by later writers, of Rammohun's travels in Tibet—of which Bhutan was sometimes regarded as a part.

In 1815 Rammohun settled in Calcutta, where he published the bulk of his works. Most of these are in English and Bengali, and a few are in Sanskrit; they deal with religious, political, and legal matters, and also include his *Bengalee Grammar in English Language* (1826). In this period his European acquaintances were independent traders, journalists, and missionaries, rather than officials; he was a liberal in politics, opposed to the East India Company's monopoly but favouring independent European settlement in India. He corresponded with leading thinkers in Britain and the United States, and became known to British readers from reports in missionary journals, while his works were reviewed in British and French periodicals. He was among the pioneers of Indian journalism, founding the *Sambad Kaumudi* ('Moonlight of News') in Bengali and the *Mir'at al-Akhbar* ('Mirror of News') in Persian, both in 1822, and petitioning the government against the press regulations of 1823. In 1818–20 he contributed to the campaign against suttee (the practice whereby a wife, in principle voluntarily, burns herself with the body of her deceased husband) which culminated in a regulation forbidding the practice in 1829. Rammohun's main contribution consists of two dialogues in which he shows that suttee is not required by Sanskrit texts, as argued by its supporters, besides condemning it on humanitarian grounds. He thus joined his voice with those who rejected a feature of the Hindu tradition, while at the same time appearing as a defender of that tradition against a false interpretation. The same position can be seen in his writings against Hindu polytheism and image worship.

Some reports represented Rammohun as almost, if not quite, a Christian, others as a deist or a rationalist, but such labels do not adequately describe his religious thought. His earliest work on religion is the *Tuhfat al-muwahhidin* ('Gift to monotheists'), in Persian with an Arabic preface, published at Murshidabad in 1803–4. Here he argues that all religious traditions are true in that they teach belief in God as revealed in the design of the universe, but that they are all false in that they add unnecessary and conflicting beliefs to this common core. His later writings build on this foundation, but show a more accommodating attitude to religious traditions, particularly Hinduism and Christianity. In Hinduism (he was probably the first Indian writer to use this word) he accepted the Vedantic tradition founded on the Upanishads, but rejected image worship as contrary to a rational view of God. In Christianity he rejected the incarnation and the Trinity, thus allying himself with the Unitarians. During his residence in Calcutta he led a group which was variously known as the Atmiya Sabha ('friendly society'), Brahmos (in Bengali, *brahmya* or *brahma*, 'belonging to God', often translated as 'theist' or 'theistic'), or Hindu unitarians. After collaborating with the former Baptist missionary William Adam to form the short-lived Calcutta Unitarian Committee in 1821, he reorganized his own group as the Brahmo Sabha or Brahmo Samaj (both meaning 'theistic society') in 1828; under the latter name it became the most influential socio-religious modernizing movement of nineteenth-century Bengal, and inspired similar movements in other parts of India.

To support his view that 'the doctrines of the unity of God are real Hinduism', Rammohun translated selected Sanskrit texts into Bengali and English. He also compiled a selection from the gospels, *The Precepts of Jesus* (1820), followed by three tracts defending it against the criticism of the Baptist missionary Joshua Marshman. In a satirical series of letters published in 1823 under the pseudonym Ram Doss he proposes that trinitarian Christians and Hindu polytheists should join forces against 'this deluded sect of Unitarianism'.

In 1830 he sailed to England as ambassador of the Mughal emperor Akbar II, who conferred on him the title of raja; the East India Company refused to recognize this title, or his diplomatic status. When in Calcutta Rammohun had agreed to relinquish the title of ambassador, but he was received as such by William IV at his coronation in 1831. The purpose of the embassy was to appeal to the king for an increase in the income allowed to the emperor by the company. The actual negotiations in which Rammohun engaged were with the court of directors of the East India Company and the Board of Control (the body through which the British government controlled the company); they were partially successful. While in London Rammohun also took an active interest in Indian and British politics. He followed up his campaign against suttee by attending the meeting of the privy council on 11 July 1833, at which an appeal against the regulation of 1829 was defeated. He contributed to the discussion surrounding the renewal of the charter of the East India Company, which was completed in 1833; his submissions on this subject to the Board of Control were published in 1832 as *Exposition of the Practical Operation of the Judicial and Revenue Systems of India*. He watched the passage of the 1832 Reform Act with enthusiasm, and considered standing for parliament himself.

He was a striking figure, tall and richly dressed in Mughal style, with curly hair which remained black throughout his life. His last three weeks were spent in Bristol, among Unitarian friends. He died on 27 September 1833 of a fever accompanied by inflammation of the brain, as attested by J. B. Estlin, the physician who attended him and performed a post-mortem examination. His wealth at the time of his death was greatly reduced, partly through the collapse of his Calcutta agents. He was buried in the grounds of Stapleton Grove, the house in which he died.

In 1843 his remains were reinterred in Arnos Vale cemetery, Bristol, and in 1844 this new grave was marked with a monument in the style of a north Indian temple, as directed by his wealthy Calcutta friend Dwarkanath Tagore (grandfather of Rabindranath Tagore), who lived in England from 1842 until his death in 1846.

Rammohun Roy's reputation has suffered from the exaggerated claims of Christians and Brahmos who saw him as a prophet of light surrounded by darkness, and later of those who saw him as 'the father of modern India'. Some of his Christian contemporaries, notably Bishop T. F. Middleton, as well as secularists of his own time and later, condemned him for providing a half-way house between traditional Hinduism and their respective creeds, while Indian nationalists have deplored his enthusiasm for the British. He still occupies a unique place between India and the West, and between ancient and modern India.   DERMOT KILLINGLEY

Sources S. D. Collet, *The life and letters of Raja Rammohun Roy*, 3rd edn, ed. D. K. Biswas and P. C. Ganguli (1962) • D. Killingley, *Rammohun Roy in Hindu and Christian tradition* (1994) • M. Carpenter, *The last days in England of the rajah Rammohun Roy* (1866) • R. Chanda and J. K. Majumdar, *Selections from official letters and documents relating to the life of Raja Rammohun Roy*, 1 (1938) • L. Carpenter, *A review of the labours, opinions and character of Rajah Rammohun Roy* (1833) • B. Banerji, *Ramamohana Ray*, 5th edn 1962 [in Bengali] • I. Singh, *Rammohun Roy: a biographical inquiry into the making of modern India*, 1 (1958)
Archives BL OIOC • Harris Man. Oxf.
Likenesses H. P. Briggs, portrait, 1832, City of Bristol Museum and Art Gallery

Roy, William (*d.* in or before **1531**), Observant friar and evangelical author, was probably the son of Pety Roy, minor servant of Henry VII. He entered the convent of the Observant Franciscans at Greenwich shortly before 1516. Although his name does not appear in contemporary college records, his attendance at Cambridge is noted by Cooper. If he were there between 1519 and 1522, the dates would allow an intriguing possibility. When in 1516 Erasmus was preparing the first printed edition of the Greek New Testament, he found no Greek manuscript that included the Vulgate's verse about the 'three that bear record in heaven', 1 John 5: 7, a celebrated crux. Erasmus wrote that if he ever found a Greek manuscript containing the verse, he would insert it in later editions. He was soon sent such a manuscript, and he did include it (to his later regret). The manuscript he received, the Montfort codex, was a new copy, made between 1519 and 1522, of the Leicester codex, a manuscript owned by the Franciscan house at Cambridge, which had been originally used by Erasmus. The new copy, made in the same house, was intended to show Erasmus in error. Among its changes to the Leicester original was the inclusion of the disputed verse, which consequently appeared in all translations dependent on that Greek text (which became the 'textus receptus', long revered), including the 1611 King James Bible. The first owner of the Montfort codex was a Friar Froye, who was probably the copyist. In 1887 James Rendel

Harris argued that this name is properly 'Fratis Roye'. William Roy, Cambridge Franciscan, could have been devious enough to make this forgery.

Wolsey's visitation to the Observants in Greenwich in 1524 threatened the many absent friars, and may have provoked Roy's departure from the monastery to join English reformers on the continent. Assisted financially (like Tyndale) by the city merchant Humphrey Monmouth, Roy registered at the University of Wittenberg on 10 June 1525, though his stay was short. Tyndale, then in Cologne, later recorded in the prologue to his *Wicked Mammon* that, disappointed in his hope for help from England from 'a faithful companion', he accepted Roy's offer of assistance. Tyndale found Roy slippery, 'somewhat crafty when he cometh into new acquaintance and before he be thoroughly known and namely [especially] when all is spent' (Walter, 37–8).

In Cologne in 1525 Tyndale and Roy worked on the first English New Testament from the Greek for printing by Peter Quentel. Roy's task, reported Tyndale, was 'both to write, and to help me compare the texts together' (Walter, 38). When Tyndale came to revise his New Testament in Antwerp in 1534, he explained the need for revision as partly coming from 'lack of help at the beginning' (p. 3), which might be a judgement on the quality of Roy's assistance. Some of that Cologne New Testament had been printed when the anti-Lutheran Johannes Dobneck ('Cochlaeus') ensured that Quentel's shop was raided by the civic authorities. Warned in time, Tyndale and Roy fled up the Rhine to the safe Lutheran city of Worms, where from the printing house of Peter Schoeffer in 1526 there came the 'bare text' of the New Testament in English which was the foundation for most translations that followed.

'When that was ended', Tyndale notes, 'I took my leave, and bade him farewell for our two lives, and (as men say) a day longer' (Walter, 38). Roy went on to Strasbourg, where he translated from a Latin version the short German tract by Wolfgang Capito as *A Brief Dialogue between a Christian Father and his Stubborn Son*. To this treatise, which Roy slants in a reforming direction, he added a preface, dated 31 August 1527, in which he comments on his work with Tyndale, entirely in the light of its importance for 'every Christian man … at home in his own house', and the violent hostility it caused. He is defensive about untrue accusations that his father was Jewish, thus making his own work somehow inadequate. He has, he said, 'already translated certain books of the Old Testament' (Mozley, 42) and intends to tackle the whole. Tyndale commented on those words, 'he promiseth more a great deal than I fear me he will ever pay' (Walter, 39). Nothing has survived.

Roy was joined in Strasbourg, probably in 1528, by another apostate friar from Greenwich, Jerome Barlow. In spite of Tyndale's warning to Barlow, Roy, 'whose tongue', Tyndale wrote, 'is able not only to make fools stark mad, but also deceive the wisest … set him a-work to make rhymes' (Walter, 39). The result was *Rede me and be not Wroth* by Barlow and Roy (also known as *The Burial of the*

Mass) printed in Strasbourg in 1528. Loosely in the manner of Skelton, in 3700 lines of doggerel verse it racily attacks church practices and the burning of English New Testaments by Cuthbert Tunstall, bishop of London. The chief target is Wolsey, who is frequently and sharply vilified.

For that reason, and because Roy's reformist tracts were always high on the lists of English prohibited books (and remained so long after his death), Wolsey set his agents to hunt for Roy across the continent, without success. Roy returned clandestinely to England from December 1528 to February 1529, and again in the spring of 1529, to visit his mother in Westminster. He returned to Antwerp twice to see through the press his translations of Erasmus's prologue to his Greek New Testament, of the same author's *Paraclesis*, and of Luther on 1 Corinthians 7. By June 1529, however, Wolsey had other things on his mind than hunting heretics, and at that point Roy disappears from view. Foxe notes that he was burnt in Portugal, but gives no date. Sir Thomas More reports to the same effect, giving as his source Roy's fellow protestant Richard Bayfield, who was burnt late in 1531. DAVID DANIELL

Sources D. O. Fries, 'William Roy: a study in early-sixteenth century protestant–Lollard relationships', PhD diss., Michigan State University, 1969 · J. R. Harris, *The origin of the Leicester Codex of the New Testament* (1887) · Cooper, *Ath. Cantab.*, 1.44 · *Doctrinal treatises and introductions to different portions of the holy scriptures: by William Tyndale, martyr 1536*, ed. H. Walter, Parker Society, 42 (1848) · *Tyndale's New Testament … 1534*, ed. D. Daniell (1989) · J. F. Mozley, *Coverdale and his bibles* (1953) · St Thomas More, *The confutation of Tyndale's answer*, ed. L. A. Schuster and others, 3 vols. (1973), vol. 8 of *The Yale edition of the complete works of St Thomas More* · A. Hume, 'Wiliam Roye's "Brefe Dialoge" (1527): an English version of a Strasburg catechism', *Harvard Theological Review*, 60 (1967), 307–21

Roy, William (1726–1790), surveyor and founder of the Ordnance Survey, was born on 4 May 1726 at Miltonhead, Lanarkshire, Scotland, the second child of John Roy (*d.* 1748), factor to Sir William Gordon of Milton and, after 1737, an ordained elder of the kirk, and his wife, Mary Stewart. He had two sisters and one brother, James (1730–1767). He is known to have attended Carluke parish school and Lanark grammar school, but his career between school and his joining the military survey of Scotland in 1747 is the subject of some controversy. It has been suggested that he may have helped his father prepare estate maps, then become a surveyor of post roads for the Post Office, and then worked as a civilian draughtsman in the Ordnance office in Edinburgh. Certainly by 1747 he was highly proficient in both surveying and map making. That was the year in which, despite being a civilian, he was taken on as clerk and assistant quartermaster to Lieutenant-Colonel David Watson, deputy quartermaster-general in north Britain. Watson had been charged with opening up communication through the highlands as part of the measures to subdue the inhabitants after the Jacobite rising of 1745. In connection with this he initiated the military survey of Scotland. Roy was employed from 1747 to 1752 on the mapping of the highlands, working initially only with Paul Sandby, later famous as a watercolourist, and later with larger surveying parties. Using simple equipment (probably chains and a circumferentor) the survey traversed the land rapidly, measuring and sketching in the summer season and compiling the map from their combined results at Edinburgh in the winter months. The resulting map, known then as the 'great map' and now as the 'Roy map', exists as a protracted (working) copy and a fair copy. The former is the more accurate in detail, particularly in rural areas, while the latter is very beautiful and bears the marks of both Sandby, as draughtsman, and Roy, who was responsible for the topographic detail and lettering. From 1752 to 1755 Roy worked on the survey of southern Scotland, having charge of its western section, but the final phases of the mapping were interrupted by the Seven Years' War. No fair copy of the map of southern Scotland was made, and the surviving sheets are working maps on which Roy's is just one of many hands discernible. (A complete fair copy of the whole country was constructed between 1829 and 1864.) The maps, at a scale of 1000 yards to an inch (now in the British Library), represent an outstanding cartographic achievement by contemporary international standards. Although they were not officially commissioned (they originated in the enthusiasm of an individual, David Watson, who also footed much of the bill), they probably helped convince the military establishment of the strategic importance of having reliable and up-to-date maps, especially of troubled areas, and, as an officially produced map of a complete country (apart from its distant islands), they may be seen as a direct forebear of the Ordnance Survey maps. Watson was greatly attached to Roy and left him his mathematical instruments in his will.

While he was working on the survey of southern Scotland Roy's interest in Roman antiquities flourished. The area was rich in remains, which he sketched with increasing accuracy as he learned more about their purpose and construction. His greatest antiquarian work of the period was the most precise survey and map yet of the Antonine Wall, at a scale of 1: 36,000. He spent the period from 1755 to 1764 away from Scotland, but pursued his antiquarian works in England and visited Scotland thereafter to continue his antiquarian research. In 1776 he was elected a fellow of the Society of Antiquaries, which published his *Military Antiquities of the Romans in North Britain* (1793). It was a fine work which precisely described sites that in many cases are no longer visible; its map was finally superseded only with the Ordnance Survey's map of Roman Britain of 1924.

In December 1755 Roy had left Scotland to become a practitioner engineer, and the following month he was commissioned lieutenant in the army in the 4th King's Own regiment of foot. He continued to hold double rank in the army and the engineers during the rest of his military career. His immediate task in 1756 was a reconnaissance survey of much of southern England, mapping roads and the lie of the land in anticipation of French invasion. He worked with his fellow surveyors from Scotland, Watson and David Dundas. Roy himself surveyed much of Kent and Sussex, and because of his skills as a draughtsman he drew many maps surveyed by others.

Further reconnaissance maps followed. Roy saw active service at Rochefort under Sir John Mordaunt (at whose court martial he gave evidence) and in Germany in the Seven Years' War (1756–63). He was present at the battle of Minden on 1 August 1759, and his map of that battle was published on 29 February 1760—the day the court martial of Lieutenant-General Lord George Sackville opened; the map played an important part in that trial. From 1760 to 1761 Roy was deputy quartermaster-general of the British force under the marquess of Granby and took part in all the operations in which that force was engaged. He was appointed deputy quartermaster-general of the forces in southern Britain in 1761 and produced several more reconnaissance maps. The following year he again took up his service with the marquess of Granby in Germany.

Roy was in Scotland in 1764 collecting material for his work on Roman fortifications. He visited Ireland in 1765 and there, as throughout his military service, produced maps and plans whose technical limitations and methods of construction he was always unusually scrupulous in explaining, declaring which were the result of accurate survey and which more impressionistic. On 19 July 1765 he was appointed by royal warrant to the new post of surveyor-general of the coasts and engineer for making and directing military surveys in Great Britain. These duties were in addition to those of deputy quartermaster-general to the forces and engineer-in-ordinary. His duties involved him in considerable travel within Britain and beyond to report on engineering matters. He reached the rank of major-general in the army in 1781; his highest rank in the engineers was that of colonel.

Roy pursued his scientific interests, particularly after he settled permanently in London in 1763, and was elected fellow of the Royal Society in 1767. He was a founder member of the Royal Society Club and mixed at its dinners with the most eminent scientists of the day. When the director of the Paris observatory, Jean Dominique Cassini, proposed in 1783 that south-east England be triangulated and that the triangulation be connected to the French network to resolve the dispute over the difference in longitude between the Greenwich and Paris observatories, Joseph Banks, president of the Royal Society and a friend of Roy, suggested that Roy should supervise the task. Roy had already begun a small triangulation in his spare time in London for his 'own private amusement' but also to 'serve as a hint to the public' of the utility of a national triangulation (O'Donoghue, 44), and he undertook the project with relish. His first task was to prepare a budget to persuade the king to subvent the Royal Society's costs. He secured royal support, but, despite being a talented and experienced administrator, he significantly underestimated the final cost of the scheme, which came to over £2000. This overrunning of budget was in fact a perennial problem in mapping projects which aspired to high scientific standards. In pursuit of those high standards Roy's next task in 1784 was to commission Jesse Ramsden to make several new instruments, including a 100 foot steel chain, six glass rods each 1 metre long, and a 3 foot theodolite, since existing instruments were inadequate for the task. Roy recognized Ramsden, his colleague from the Royal Society, as the foremost scientific instrument maker of his day. Fieldwork began with the measurement of what became known as the Hounslow Heath base. This was a line starting at King's Arbour on Hounslow Heath and extending for 5 miles in the direction of Bushy Park. The work of measuring began on 16 April 1784 and excited very considerable scientific interest; it even became something of a public spectacle after the king had made a visit to the work in progress. Ramsden's glass rods and steel chains were crucial for this work, which was completed in 1784. Roy received the Copley medal of the Royal Society the following year and won international scientific acclaim for its unprecedented accuracy. However, the base-line was only the start of the work of triangulation, which could not begin without the Ramsden theodolite. The relationship between Roy and Ramsden became progressively more sour as Roy accused Ramsden of delay, dilatoriness, and negligence and Ramsden defended himself, pointing out that he had taken on the project only for the advancement of science, since it precluded his accepting more lucrative work. The Ramsden theodolite was finally delivered in July 1787, and the triangulation was carried from the Hounslow base to the Kent coast and connected with the French triangulation. A base of verification was measured on Romney Marsh under Roy's direction and was found to differ by only 28 inches from its calculated length as determined by the triangulations of the Hounslow base. Secondary triangulation followed, and the work was completed in 1789. It did not in fact resolve the immediate dispute over the difference in longitude between the Paris and Greenwich observatories, but none the less it represented a very considerable scientific advance.

Roy described the principles which guided the work in three long papers in the *Philosophical Transactions* for 1785, 1787, and 1790, from the last of which derogatory references to Ramsden by the then ailing Roy were expunged before publication. Roy's persistence and insistence on high standards had ensured that Britain acquitted itself well in the enterprise, which had as much to do with national rivalry as scientific co-operation. It was also a significant test of the use of the theodolite: the French favoured different instruments, but Roy's preference for the theodolite, despite its great weight, was vindicated in this project and shaped Ordnance Survey practice thereafter.

By the time the triangulation was completed Roy was in poor health, which a visit to Lisbon that winter failed to improve. In his absence he engaged Isaac Dalby to work on the proof of his last paper for the *Philosophical Transactions*. He returned to his military duties in April 1790 but died, having all but completed the paper, on 1 July that year, at his home, 12 (after 1820 renumbered 10) Argyll Street, London. He was buried in the parish of St James's, Westminster, on 7 July, probably at the burial-ground at Hampstead Road, which from 1887 became a public garden.

Roy, who was unmarried, left a modest estate valued at £8000 and the freehold of his house in Argyll Street. As executor he appointed his friend David Dundas, to whom he left many of his papers under the terms of his will of 17 November 1786. By far his more important legacy, however, was the establishment of what came to be called the Ordnance Survey. As early as 1763 Roy had proposed that a national survey of the kingdom be made. Inspired by the military survey of Scotland, and convinced of the advantage a map would offer at times of national danger, he proposed 'a general Survey of the whole Island at the public cost' (O'Donoghue, 41). As with so many state surveys, it was the extent of this public cost which was its downfall. Roy persisted in 1766 with a second proposal, which elaborated the strategic and scientific advantages that would flow from a national survey organized centrally under military control and based on a firm geodetic foundation, but this too came to nothing. In the triangulation of the 1780s, however, Roy quite consciously laid the foundations for such a survey by procuring from the foremost instrument maker the most advanced equipment yet produced; by establishing a base-line at Hounslow from which triangulation could be extended in all directions—not just towards France; by elaborating methods and procedures in his papers for the *Philosophical Transactions* which were suitable for both the particular Anglo-French scheme and a more general national triangulation; and, perhaps most importantly, by securing the backing of the duke of Richmond, the master-general of the ordnance, who had lent men and equipment for the triangulation. In his description of the work Roy made clear that he saw the Anglo-French triangulation as part of a larger future British project: in his 1790 paper in the *Philosophical Transactions* he recommends:

> that the trigonometrical operation, so successfully begun, should certainly be continued, and gradually extended over the whole island. Compared with the greatness of the object, the annual expense to the public would be a mere trifle … The honour of the nation is concerned in having at least as good a map of this as is of any other country. (*PTRS*, 80, 1790, 262)

In 1791 the duke of Richmond established under the auspices of the Board of Ordnance a body, known successively as the trigonometrical and the Ordnance Survey, charged with producing a general survey of the kingdom. This survey, though instituted eleven months after Roy's death, is rightly seen as his creation. At its best the survey combined a clear regard for national utility with an uncompromising adherence to high scientific standards, and for this Roy was in large part responsible. His trigonometrical work provided the technical foundations for the topographical Ordnance Survey of the south-eastern counties. Even details such as the scale of 1 inch to a mile (1: 63,360) for the early ordnance maps were the result of his choice, and the surveys continued to use the instruments he had commissioned, notably the Ramsden theodolite, which was in service until 1853. The idea of establishing a national survey board to make maps which were to be of general use, not compiled *ad hoc*, was not Roy's: such a board existed in Sweden as early as 1628. Nor was he the first to insist on high standards of mensuration and cartography, for the French were perhaps the leaders in these regards. None the less his scientific vision, his talent for administration, and perhaps above all his single-minded persistence combined to make his a unique contribution to the history of British surveying and cartography.   ELIZABETH BAIGENT

Sources Y. O'Donoghue, *William Roy, 1726–1790* (1977) · W. A. Seymour, ed., *A history of the Ordnance Survey* (1980) · J. B. Harley and Y. O'Donoghue, introduction, in *The old series ordnance survey maps of England and Wales*, Ordnance Survey, 1: *Kent, Essex, East Sussex and South Suffolk* (1975) · S. Widmalm, *Mellan kartan och verkligheten: geodesi och kartläggning, 1695–1860* (Uppsala, 1990) · S. Widmalm, 'Accuracy, rhetoric and technology: the Paris–Greenwich triangulation, 1784–88', *The quantifying spirit in the eighteenth century*, ed. Q. T. Frängsmyr, J. L. Heilbron, and R. E. Rider (1990), 179–206 · R. A. Skelton, *The military survey of Scotland* (1967) · E. Whittington and A. J. S. Gibson, *The military survey of Scotland, 1747–1755: a critique* (1986) · *DNB* · R. J. P. Kain and E. Baigent, *The cadastral map in the service of the state: a history of property mapping* (1992)
Archives BL, MS of 'Military antiquities of the Romans in north Britain', and papers relating to Hounslow Heath, Greenwich, and Paris observatories, King's MSS 247–248, 269, 271–272 · PRO, papers, MS OS 3 · S. Antiquaries, Lond., MS of his 'Military antiquities of the Romans in north Britain' · U. Durham L., military description of south-east England | BL, King George III's topographical collection · BL, King's MSS · Ordnance Survey, Southampton, King's MSS · RS, King's MSS
Likenesses cartoon (of Roy?), repro. in O'Donoghue, *William Roy*
Wealth at death £8000; plus the freehold of house in Argyll Street, London: O'Donoghue, *William Roy*, 41

Royce, Sir (Frederick) Henry, baronet (1863–1933), engineer and motor car designer, was born on 27 March 1863 at Alwalton, near Peterborough, youngest of the two boys and three girls of James Royce (1830–1872), flour miller, and his wife, Mary (d. 1904), third daughter of Benjamin King, farmer, of Edwin's Hall, Essex. When he was four his father took his two sons to London, intent upon running a metropolitan flour mill. Financial trouble followed and the young Royce became a W. H. Smith newspaper boy, first at Clapham and then Bishopsgate. When he was nine his father died, leaving under £20. Henry's schooling lapsed into irregularity and for a time he was a Post Office telegraph boy in Mayfair.

When Royce was fourteen a kindly aunt paid £20 per annum for him to be apprenticed in the Great Northern Railway Company's locomotive works in Peterborough. After three years his aunt's funds ran out but the enthusiasm and skill of a railway workshop craftsman, with whom he boarded and who taught him much about the arts of fitting and filing, had given Royce a fascination with engineering which lasted all his life. He tramped in search of work and found it with a machine tool firm in Leeds at 11s. for a 54-hour week, but soon decided that London held better prospects. In 1882 he became a tester with the London Electric Light and Power Company, which was installing electric arc and incandescent lighting in London's streets. Simultaneously he attended evening classes run by the City and Guilds Institute and others at Quintin Hogg's Polytechnic Day School in Regent Street. He sufficiently impressed his employers for them to appoint him chief electrical engineer of a subsidiary, the Lancashire Maxim and Western Electric Company, set up to introduce

Sir (Frederick) Henry Royce, baronet (1863–1933), by Peter North

electric lighting to Liverpool. Royce worked on theatre lighting until, months later, the company went into liquidation and he was thrown onto his own resources once more.

Meanwhile Royce's Liverpool work had introduced him to Ernest Albert Claremont (d. 1921), a young man with £50 capital to add to Royce's £25, and some electrical experience. In 1884 they formed F. H. Royce & Co., manufacturers of electric bell sets, lampholders, switches, fuses, and registering instruments, at Cooke Street, Manchester. Royce designed a drum-wound armature for a dynamo that had the distinct advantage of sparkless commutation in generating direct current. These dynamos were widely used in lighting cotton mills, factories, and ships and gained a strong reputation for reliability and longevity, engineering characteristics to which Royce gave high priority. The partnership was strengthened by ties of kinship and an additional £1500 capital on 16 March 1893 when Royce and Claremont married two sisters, daughters of Alfred Punt, a licensed victualler of London. With his wife, Minnie Grace (d. 1936), Royce set up home in Knutsford, in a house with a fine garden of which Royce, a dedicated rose and fruit tree grower all his life, was very proud. Shortly afterwards he brought his mother from London to live there.

In 1894 the partners converted their business into a limited company, Royce Ltd, bringing a friend with capital into the firm and appointing a young cashier and accountant, John De Looze, company secretary. De Looze freed

Royce from the minutiae of paperwork so that he could concentrate on new technical ideas. Among these were electric cranes and motors for lock gates. Royce took out an early patent for a governor to control the downward speed of the crane arm, a project prompted by his horror of accidents. Between October 1897 and February 1899 the value of the firm's orders rose from £6000 to £20,000. The directors increased the company's capital to £30,000 to finance an expansion of productive capacity. Then came setbacks. The Second South African War checked domestic investment. In his specialist market, imports of cheaper cranes from Germany and the USA (many incorporating Royce's modifications) cut into sales. Royce refused to reduce the quality of his products in order to make his prices more competitive. For several years the company's financial results deteriorated. At the same time, Royce's interest was shifting from cranes to road vehicles, a cause of some anxiety for his colleagues.

When Royce bought a second-hand 10 hp Decauville, his first motor car, early in 1903 (having previously owned a De Dion-Bouton quadricycle), French manufacturers—enthusiasts operating in scattered workshops—dominated the infant car industry. American models were appearing but Royce regarded their engineering as primitive. Initially approving the design but not the engineering of the Decauville, Royce set out to rebuild it in his spare time. He ended up redesigning it and in autumn 1903 announced to his associates that he intended to build his own motor car. The two-cylinder 10 hp model emerged from the Cooke Street works on 1 April 1904 after months of overtime in which components were ruthlessly tested by multifarious experiments. Royce made most of it himself, aided by two apprentices, T. S. Haldenby and Eric Platford, and a toolmaker, Arthur Wormald, recruited from the Westinghouse works in Trafford Park. Three examples of this model were built. In the first months they tended to break down frequently but Royce, furiously insisting on high standards all round, persisted with his improvising, innovating, testing, and fitting so that, for their day, they became unusually reliable. Claremont bought one. A newcomer to the Royce board, Henry Edmunds, who was also a member of the Automobile Club committee, saw it and sent a photograph and specifications to his friend, Charles Stewart *Rolls, who with Claude Goodman Johnson then ran an agency for French cars in London's West End. In the first week of May 1904 Rolls (who had previously approached William Weir (1877–1959) to supply a British-built car) and Edmunds went to Manchester, Royce having refused to go to London. Rolls was so impressed by the car that he agreed with Royce to become his sole agent and in this manner the famous partnership, echoing that of S. F. Edge and Montague Napier, began.

While Rolls, aristocratic and flamboyant, advertised Royce's cars in a series of reliability trials and races during 1904–6, ably understudied by Johnson, who organized sales, Royce concentrated on production. At first he manufactured a variety of models based on four chassis of 10, 15, 20, and 30 hp, the most successful being the four-cylinder 20 hp Grey Ghost. When Rolls-Royce Ltd was formed on 15 March 1906, with Claremont as chairman (as he remained until his death), Royce became chief engineer and works director with a salary of £1250 and 4 per cent of the profits above £10,000; he was the most highly paid man in the firm. After difficulties in raising capital, in December 1906 Johnson, the managing director, decided that the best way to secure a market share and cut costs would be to standardize the production of a very superior motor car. Royce set to work and designed the 40/50 hp Silver Ghost, 'his greatest achievement' (Lloyd, 1.22), which remained in production, substantially unchanged, from 1907 until 1925, when it gave way to Phantoms and Wraiths. Demand, which for Royce's cars was always ahead of supply, was strong for the Silver Ghost: 2813 were produced between 1907 and 1916, and between 1919 and 1925, 3360, the price rising from £985 to £1450 as a result of wartime inflation.

To cope with demand for the Silver Ghost, in June 1908 the motor section of the firm was separated from Cooke Street, Manchester, and transferred to Derby. By this time Royce, so long oblivious to the discipline of the balance sheet, was well recognized by the company's board as a poor production engineer but a brilliant designer. When he fell seriously ill in September 1908, his health having suffered from four years of incessant work, Johnson persuaded him to work in a drawing office at home with the assistance of a team of draughtsmen. News of Rolls's death in 1910 triggered a breakdown in Royce's health and in 1911 he underwent a major operation. Johnson, who realized that Royce's talents were the firm's greatest asset, persuaded him to live in a villa in the south of France with a drawing office and a personal staff of eight in adjacent premises. This unusual (for that time) separation of design and production lasted for the remainder of Royce's career: he divided his time between his homes at St Margaret's Bay, Kent (to which he moved in 1912) or West Wittering in Sussex (to which he moved during the First World War) in summer, and the villa at Le Canadel on the French riviera in winter, and never again came within a hundred miles of Derby. He nevertheless continued to control the main designs, keeping in close contact with experiments and other activities for another twenty years. In motor car design the original features of his work were the silent cam form of the valve-gear, the friction-damped slipper flywheel and spring drive for the timing gears, his battery ignition, the Royce expanding carburettor, and the wear-proof steering.

Although Rolls had often pressed him to design an aero-engine, he took no practical interest in the matter until the outbreak of war in 1914. Then he was persuaded by the sight of an airship struggling across the channel to modify the Silver Ghost engine for use in aeroplanes. After investigating various types of air-cooled engine, he at length characteristically made up his mind not to deviate from liquid cooling. Starting from a 12-cylinder V engine, he produced the 200 hp Eagle for the Admiralty early in 1915. This was one of two aero-engines that were neither a technical nor a production failure during the war (the other was the Hispano-Suiza). Some 6100 were ordered and it played an important part in the war. The Eagle was followed by the Falcon (2175 ordered), the Hawk in 1915, and later the Condor. Eagle engines powered the Vickers Vimy bomber which took Alcock and Brown on the first west-to-east crossing of the Atlantic in 1919. At Royce's instigation the company entered the Schneider Trophy competitions in 1929. With Ernest Walter Hives in charge of development, Royce modified the 850 hp Kestrel engine (which he designed in 1925) into the 'R' engine. Installed in the Supermarine S6 seaplane designed by R. J. Mitchell, it won the trophy. Further design work by Royce and metallurgical research at Derby improved the engine again and allowed Britain to win and keep the Schneider Trophy in 1931 (with a world speed record at 408 m.p.h.). Out of the experience gained from transatlantic and Schneider competitions, Royce laid down the prototype for the Merlin, a twelve-cylinder V engine, 'an exact scale-up of the Kestrel' (Lloyd, 2.160), which powered Spitfires and Hurricanes in the Second World War. Royce remained jealous of his position to the last. When the firm acquired Bentley Motors in 1931 he harshly subordinated W. O. Bentley, a rival designer and engineer, to the position of sales assistant in the Rolls-Royce London showroom.

Royce had only two directorships throughout his career, at Royce Ltd of Manchester and Rolls-Royce Ltd of Derby. He was a member of the institutions of mechanical, electrical, and aeronautical engineers. He was appointed OBE in 1918 and created a baronet in 1930. There were no children from his marriage. Royce died at Elmstead, his West Wittering home, on 22 April 1933. He was survived by his wife.   DAVID J. JEREMY

Sources I. Lloyd, *Rolls-Royce*, 1–2 (1978) · H. Nockolds, *The magic of a name*, 2nd edn (1950) · M. Pemberton, *The life of Sir Henry Royce: with some chapters from the stories of the late Charles S. Rolls and Claude Johnson* (1934) · D. J. Jeremy, 'Royce, Sir Frederick Henry', *DBB* · A. Bird and I. Hallows, *The Rolls-Royce motor car and the Bentleys built by Rolls-Royce*, 4th revised edn (1975) · *DNB*
Archives Inst. CE · Institution of Mechanical Engineers, London, sketches relating to automobile brakes · Rolls-Royce Enthusiasts' Club, Northamptonshire, technical corresp. and papers
Likenesses F. D. Wood, bronze statue, 1922, Arboretum, Derby · W. McMillan, bust, 1934, Rolls-Royce Ltd, Derby · P. North, photograph, Royal Aeronautical Society, London [*see illus.*] · portrait, repro. in *Engineering* (28 April 1933) · portrait, repro. in *Engineer* (28 April 1933)
Wealth at death £112,598 8s. 11d.: probate, 6 June 1933, *CGPLA Eng. & Wales*

Royden, (Agnes) Maude (1876–1956), suffragist and preacher, was born on 23 November 1876 at Mossley Hill, near Liverpool, youngest of the eight children of Sir Thomas Bland Royden, first baronet (1831–1917), shipowner and MP, and his wife, Alice Elizabeth (1844–1932), daughter of Thomas Dowdall of Liverpool. She grew up at Frankby Hall in Cheshire. Articulate and devoutly Anglican, she was educated at Cheltenham Ladies' College, and at Lady Margaret Hall, Oxford, where she established a lifelong friendship with Kathleen Courtney. Maude's decision, on leaving Oxford, to take up work in a slum settlement was not remarkable at that time for a socially aware young woman, but bold for one who had to cope with lameness from congenital hip dislocation. She began with

(Agnes) Maude Royden (1876–1956), by Elliott & Fry, 1936

high hopes, but the eighteen months she spent at the Victoria settlement in Liverpool left her worn-out and disappointed. At a low ebb, she sought advice from a man she knew to be sympathetic: the Revd (George William) Hudson Shaw (1859–1944), a lecturer and leading figure in the Oxford University extension movement. He suggested a change of scene, inviting her to help in his Rutland parish. South Luffenham thus became her base from 1902 until 1905.

She grew strongly attached to Shaw and his mentally fragile wife, Effie, helping them revive a sluggish parish. Finding she had gifts of self-expression far beyond the needs of a Sunday school class, Shaw resolved to get her extension work, lecturing on English literature. Though the Oxford delegacy then employed only male lecturers, he insisted that they try her out. This was her start in public speaking: an apprenticeship that served her well in the context of women's suffrage, where she was soon a noted speaker for the non-militant suffragists under the leadership of Mrs Fawcett.

As rising militancy shook the nation, non-militants claimed the higher ground; and none more eloquently than Maude whose feminism stemmed from Christian faith. Who but Christ had seen women as human? In her eyes the women's movement was the most profoundly moral movement since the foundation of the Christian church. It did not seem so to the Church of England. There were very few clergy members of the Church League for Women's Suffrage, which she helped to found in 1909. But leading Anglicans sought her out, for the spirituality and unselfconsciousness with which she was able to address large audiences, especially upon moral questions. In 1913 the bishop of Winchester asked her to address 2000 men at the church congress, on 'social purity'—a burning question, given the concern at that time about the white slave traffic. In 1916 Archbishop Davidson put her on the council of his national mission which was to re-Christianize wartime England. Hundreds of missioners—clergy, laymen, even laywomen—were to 'speak' to the people. But Davidson suddenly got cold feet at the thought of women 'speaking' in church, contrary to custom, and with such as Maude likely to attract large congregations. In the end it was left to the bishops, many of whom—like the bishop of London—ruled that where women must speak in church for want of other accommodation, it should be only to their own sex, and only from the foot of the chancel steps.

Were there still untouchables, Maude wrote then, that women should be barred from holy places? It moved her nearer to what one friend called ecclesiastical militancy. In 1917 when the City Temple, the great Congregational church in Holborn, offered her a preaching post, she took it. Ecumenism was not in vogue and such mingling with nonconformists shocked even liberal Anglicans. For her, however, three fruitful years in the pulpit of the City Temple so confirmed her preaching vocation that she went further: again with help from her devoted friend, Hudson Shaw. Shaw had been since 1912 vicar of St Botolph without Bishopsgate and it was at his invitation that in 1918 she spoke in church on the League of Nations and Christianity. He was rebuked by the bishop of London. In 1919 Shaw asked her to preach at the three hours' service on Good Friday. The bishop forbade it, on the grounds that this was an especially 'sacred' service. Not long afterwards the stakes were raised when the former Church League for Women's Suffrage (a cause now won) resolved to campaign not only for the preaching but the priesthood of women.

It is not known when Maude herself first thought the unthinkable, that a woman might become a priest. Probably well before the war, for she answered a discreet enquiry in 1913 with, 'I go cheerfully as far as women Bishops and Archbishops and Popes' (M. Royden to U. Roberts, 8 March 1914, Women's Library, 'Women in the church'). But she was caught up with suffrage then, and with pacifism during the war. The campaign launched in 1919, in which she took a leading part, looked to the forthcoming Lambeth conference to consider the ministry of women. Fired perhaps by post-suffrage euphoria, some of her friends now thought it likely she would become the first woman priest. But all they got was a recommendation that women be allowed to 'speak' in church, and even that was hobbled by the old restrictions. Despite these setbacks, the 1920s saw Maude at the height of her fame.

In 1921 Maude established the Guildhouse: an ecumenical place of worship, a fellowship, a social and cultural centre that soon became part of the London scene. It was a new start: for her, as preacher; for Martin Shaw, as organist and composer; and for the Revd Percy Dearmer, as professor of ecclesiastical art who transformed the big chapel in Eccleston Square. On Sunday afternoons there were talks by speakers foremost in politics and the arts. Maude preached at the Sunday evening service to a congregation from all over London. Even on weekdays the Guildhouse buzzed with its multiplicity of clubs and causes. In these unsettled post-war years Maude was in such demand to speak that, home or abroad, she was often billed as 'World famous woman preacher'. In 1923 in the USA she preached in churches and cathedrals, spoke in high schools and opera houses, to college students and businesswomen, pressing the Christian cause of peace and the need for the League of Nations. In 1928 her tour extended from the USA to New Zealand and Australia; thence to Japan and China and India. But while she was buoyed up by a sense of mission, the Guildhouse suffered from her absences. Later she regretted having turned increasingly to preaching as hopes of the priesthood faded. In 1936 when the Guildhouse closed, her sense of failure was not assuaged by her being by then a Companion of Honour and holder of honorary doctorates.

Maude supported but did not lead efforts in the anti-feminist thirties to extend the Anglican ministry of women. Peace was again her major cause and she joined Dick Sheppard's Peace Pledge Union, though in 1940 the Nazi threat led her to renounce her pacifism. In October 1944, not long after his wife's death, she married Hudson Shaw, with whom she had been in constant touch throughout all her activities. He was then eighty-five and died two months later. However, in 1947 she astounded even intimate friends with the revelation in *A Threefold Cord* of their passionate but platonic love for each other from first meeting in 1901. She died in Hampstead on 30 July 1956, leaving an adopted daughter, Helen.

SHEILA FLETCHER

Sources S. Fletcher, *Maude Royden: a life* (1989) · *DNB* · B. Heeney, *The women's movement in the Church of England, 1850–1930* (1988)
Archives Women's Library, London, corresp. and papers | BL, corresp. with Albert Mansbridge, Add. MS 65261 · Bodl. Oxf., letters to E. J. Thompson · Lady Margaret Hall, Oxford, letters to Kathleen Courtney · LPL, corresp. with H. R. L. Sheppard · Women's Library, London, letters to Dame Kathleen Courtney
Likenesses P. A. de Laszlo, oils, 1932, Lady Margaret Hall, Oxford · Elliott & Fry, photograph, 1936, NPG [*see illus.*] · H. Coster, photographs, NPG

Royden, Thomas, Baron Royden (1871–1950), shipowner, was born on 22 May 1871, at Holmefield, Mossley Hill, Liverpool, the eldest son of Thomas Bland Royden (*d.* 1917), later first baronet, and his wife, Alice Elizabeth, daughter of Thomas Dowdall, stockbroker, of Liverpool. (Agnes) Maude *Royden was his sister. His grandfather, Thomas Royden, rose from an apprenticeship in shipwrighting to control of almost 1 per cent of total UK shipbuilding capacity. His father was the founder of the Indra Line of steamers.

He was educated at Winchester College and Magdalen College, Oxford, where he gained a second class in classical honour moderations in 1892, and graduated in 1893.

He began his business career at Liverpool in 1895 in his father's firm, Thomas Royden & Sons, shipowners and managers, of which he became head, when he succeeded his father as second baronet in 1917. The aggregate tonnage of the Indra Line rose from 7579 in 1895 to 35,402 in 1906. In 1915 it was sold to Richard Holt for £750,000.

Royden's abilities, and qualities of leadership, brought him responsibility in a variety of commercial concerns. He was a director of many companies, among them the Anchor Line, Thos. and Jno. Brocklebank Ltd, the Commonwealth and Dominion (which subsequently became the Port) Line, the Midland Bank, the Shell Transport and Trading Company, the Suez Canal Company, the Phoenix Assurance Company, and the Union Marine and General Insurance Company. In 1941 he succeeded Josiah, Lord Stamp, as chairman of the London, Midland, and Scottish Railway (LMS). He was also chairman of Edmundsons' Electricity Corporation, and the Imperial Continental Gas Association.

Royden became a director of the Cunard Steam-Ship Company in 1905, and of Cunard White Star Ltd, on its inception in 1934, and he remained on the boards of both companies until his death. During his long connection with the Cunard Line he served as deputy chairman from 1909 until 1922, and was chairman from 1922 until 1930. He successfully directed the company's affairs during a period in which controlling costs and seeking new markets by the introduction of tourist class and cruises left the company in good enough shape to survive the depression. His term of office also saw the beginning of the construction of the *Queen Mary*, the first of a number of liners able to maintain the Southampton to New York service using only two ships instead of the three previously required.

During the First World War his extensive knowledge of shipping enabled him to render distinguished service to his country. In 1913 he shared in the preparation of a confidential plan for the transport of British troops and munitions across the channel, a plan which was brought into operation on the outbreak of war in August 1914. He also served as chairman of the Admiralty transport advisory committee, as a member of the shipping control committee, and as a member of the royal commission on food supplies (1916–21). When the United States entered the war in 1917, he visited that country to take part in arranging the transport of troops and war materials to Europe.

At the Paris peace conference in 1919 Royden represented the shipping controller, and in the same year was appointed CH for his public services. In 1944 he was created a baron. Recognition of his work for the allies came also from the French government, by whom he was made a commander of the Légion d'honneur, and from the government of Italy, who conferred on him the Order of St Maurice and St Lazarus. He also received the Afghan order, the Star of Afghaur.

Despite the heavy responsibilities of his commercial appointments, Royden found time and energy for many other activities. Among his public duties he was high sheriff of Cheshire in 1917, and was also deputy lieutenant for the county, as well as a justice of the peace. From 1918 until 1922 he sat as Conservative member for Bootle, but he retired from politics soon after his appointment as chairman of the Cunard Steam-Ship Company. From 1910 he was chairman of the Liverpool Steamship Owners' Association, and in 1912 president of the chamber of shipping of the United Kingdom. From 1923 he was a freeman of the Worshipful Company of Shipwrights. His lifelong interest in the sea and ships found additional expression in his work as secretary and treasurer of the training ship *Indefatigable*, while his interest in Liverpool was reflected in the work he did for the David Lewis Northern Hospital, the Mersey Mission to Seamen, the Liverpool Shipbrokers' Benevolent Society, and the executive committee of Liverpool Cathedral. In 1940 he was made a fellow of Winchester College.

In 1922 Royden married Quenelda Mary (d. 1969), widow of Charles James Williamson, of Liverpool, and daughter of Harry Clegg JP DL, of Plas Llanfair, Anglesey. There were no children of the marriage. Royden travelled extensively in the United States and in the Far East, and throughout his life retained a great interest in sport. In his younger days he was a well-known rider to hounds, a polo player, a yachtsman, an oarsman, and as a point-to-point rider gained many victories; he was also a keen shot.

Royden died at his home, 46 Brockwood Park, Bramdean, Alresford, Hampshire, on 6 November 1950. The barony lapsed upon Royden's death; but his brother, Ernest Bland (b. 1873), succeeded to the baronetcy.

F. A. BATES, *rev.* ADRIAN JARVIS

Sources *Lloyd's List* (7 Nov 1950) • Gore's *Liverpool Directories* • E. B. Royden, *Thomas Royden & Sons, shipbuilders, Liverpool, 1818–93* (privately printed, [Liverpool], 1953) • 'Our new chairman', *Cunard Magazine*, 8 (1922), 107, 115 • F. E. Hyde, *Cunard and the north Atlantic, 1840–1973: a history of shipping and financial management* (1975) • d. cert. • *CGPLA Eng. & Wales* (1951)

Archives Ches. & Chester ALSS, title deeds of Frankby Hall and estate • U. Lpool, Cunard collection

Likenesses W. Stoneman, photograph, 1919, NPG • O. Birley, oils, Cunard Steam-Ship Co. Ltd, Liverpool • F. Salisbury, charcoal and chalk drawing, Merseyside Maritime Museum, Liverpool • portrait, repro. in 'Aquitania Special Number', *The Shipbuilder* (1914), 5 • portrait, repro. in 'Mauritania Special Number', *The Shipbuilder* (1939), 5 • portrait, repro. in Royden, *Thomas Royden & Sons*, 14 • portraits, repro. in *Cunard Magazine*, 6, 12, 16 (1921–5)

Wealth at death £746,393 16s. 3d.: probate, 17 Jan 1951, *CGPLA Eng. & Wales*

Roydon [Rawdon]**, Sir Marmaduke** (1583–1646), merchant and shipowner, was baptized on 20 March 1583 at Brandsby in Yorkshire, the third of four children of Ralph Roydon of Stearsby and his wife, Jane, daughter of John Brice of Stillington in Yorkshire. At the age of sixteen he went to London and was apprenticed to Daniel Hall, a Bordeaux merchant, who employed him as a factor in France. In 1611 he married Elizabeth, daughter and heir of Thomas Thorowgood of Hoddesdon in Hertfordshire; they had sixteen children, three of whom died in infancy.

Roydon became one of the most enterprising and successful merchants in the City of London. Soon after his return from France, c.1610, he was presented with the freedom of the Clothworkers' Company. Thereafter he acquired extensive interests in the wine trade, importing large amounts of wine from France, Spain, Portugal, and the Canary Islands. In 1628 he claimed that he spent £1000 per annum on the purchase of wines. He also traded with the Netherlands and Turkey. He became a member of the French Company in 1611, the New River Company in 1619, and the Levant Company probably some time thereafter. In addition, Roydon was involved in a number of transatlantic commercial and colonial ventures. In 1614 he was involved in setting out two vessels, under John Smith and Thomas Hunt, on a trading and fishing venture to New England which acquired a cargo of furs, fish, and train oil worth nearly £1500. For a time he was interested in the search for the north-west passage. In 1628 he was the leading member of a syndicate involved in the plantation of Barbados under the auspices of James Hay, first earl of Carlisle. Roydon and his partners, to whom Carlisle was heavily in debt, were granted 10,000 acres in Barbados, on advantageous terms. Roydon's plantation was nearly lost during the civil war, but was recovered by his eldest son, Thomas, in the later 1650s. By this time the plantation was said to be of a considerable value.

During the wars with Spain and France from 1625 to 1630 Roydon was involved in promoting several privateering ventures, which included setting out one of his own vessels, the *Vintage* of London, of 140 tons, in 1627. His other recorded shipowning interests included part ownership of the *William* in 1632 and the *Marmaduke* in 1643. He probably had other interests in shipping, for which no evidence survives.

Roydon became a prominent figure in the City of London. He was a common councilman and a leading member of the Honourable Artillery Company, which had been revived about 1610. In 1631 he was elected captain-general of the company, though his election aroused opposition from various groups whose mutinous behaviour was subsequently investigated by the privy council; in 1639 he was replaced by Philip Skippon. From 1639 to 1643 he served as warden of the Clothworkers' Company.

During 1628 Roydon sat as MP for the shipbuilding town of Aldeburgh in Suffolk. He spoke in support of local shipping interests, expressing concern at the decline of shipbuilding in the realm. He also spoke against the new impositions on imported wines, but he was insistent that the king be supplied speedily with five subsidies. He served on various committees, including one to consider the best course to be taken about the bill for tonnage and poundage.

Following the outbreak of the civil war Roydon became one of the king's leading supporters in the City. In May 1643 he was involved in Waller's plot to seize the City for the king. Later in the year he joined the king's forces at Oxford, becoming colonel of a regiment that he raised at his own charge. On 28 December 1643 he was knighted for his role in the defence of Basing House. He earned the praise of one of his opponents, Captain John Play, for being 'soe noble an enemie' (Davies, 69). In 1645 he was appointed governor of Faringdon in Berkshire, where he died on 28 April 1646. He was buried in Faringdon church.

The biographer of his nephew Marmaduke Rawdon, who was employed as a factor by him for many years, portrays an enterprising, resolute, and well-connected City merchant who was proud of his commercial success. But his wealth and estate were lost as a result of his support for the king during the civil war. His house in Water Lane was sequestered and sold off by September 1645; the remainder of his estate was sold for the Commonwealth in July 1651.   JOHN C. APPLEBY

Sources *The life of Marmaduke Rawdon of York*, ed. R. Davies, CS, old ser., 85 (1863) · R. C. Johnson and others, eds., *Proceedings in parliament, 1628*, 6 vols. (1977–83) · *CSP dom.*, 1627–9; 1631–5; 1638–9; 1641–3; 1655; 1660–61 · M. A. E. Green, ed., *Calendar of the proceedings of the committee for advance of money, 1642–1656*, 1, 3, PRO (1888) · C. H. Firth and R. S. Rait, eds., *Acts and ordinances of the interregnum, 1642–1660*, 2 (1911) · *The complete works of Captain John Smith (1580–1631)*, ed. P. L. Barbour, 1 (1986) · C. T. Carr, ed., *Select charters of trading companies, AD 1530–1707*, SeldS, 28 (1913) · A. Brown, ed., *The genesis of the United States*, 2 (1890) · K. R. Andrews, *Ships, money, and politics: seafaring and naval enterprise in the reign of Charles I* (1991) · V. Pearl, *London and the outbreak of the puritan revolution: city government and national politics, 1625–1643* (1961) · R. Ashton, *The city and the court, 1603–1643* (1979) · V. T. Harlow, ed., *Colonising expeditions to the West Indies and Guiana, 1623–1667*, Hakluyt Society, 2nd ser., 56 (1925)
Archives PRO, state papers domestic · PRO, customs accounts

Roydon, Matthew (*fl.* 1583–1622), poet, in 1583 signed himself a 'maister of Arte'; a Matthew Royden graduated MA at Oxford on 6 or 7 July 1580. A Matthew Royden is identified as a student at Thavies Inn in an obligation of 6 January 1581, with Jerome and Nicholas Skyres as sureties. Eccles cites a Star Chamber action in which Nicholas Skyres—an agent for the Wolfalls, a family of vicious usurers—acknowledged he had induced into his employers' snares a '"Matthewe Royden", who (in 1593) "maketh his abode at the blacke ffryers at A showmakers howse there"' (Eccles, 'Chapman's early years', 187). The borrower Roydon may have also been a benefactor: Braunmuller transcribes a begging letter of Thomas Spelman to a 'Mr Royden' (Braunmuller, 399).

Roydon was widely connected in literary London. Eccles suggests that George Buc was Roydon's fellow student at Thavies Inn (Eccles, 'Buc', 422). In 1589 the famous scrivener Peter Bales, Matthew Royden, and Peter Ferryman were bound in debt to Edmund Peshall (Culliford, 95, citing PRO, C2 Eliz/F2/49). Ferryman, who claimed himself a servant of Sidney and Walsingham, had many literary friends, including Ben Jonson (Woudhuysen, 33–4; Braunmuller, 177, 429). In a (1609?) letter, William Strachey mentions an 'olde' friendship between Roydon and Ferryman (Culliford, 94; Braunmuller, 177, 429). Roydon may be the '*Donroy*' who harvests poetry in eclogue 3 of T[homas] L[odge]'s *A Fig for Momus* (1595) (Braunmuller, 424). This '*Donroy*' and '*Charles* the kind' excel even the élite

> fewe, (alas that they were more)
> That honour poesie, and wit adore.
> (Lodge, *A Fig for Momus*, sig. Dr)

A Matthew Royden, not necessarily the poet, married Amy Toakes at St Margaret's, Westminster, on 20 November 1595 (curiously, this record is interpolated between others for that date in the parish register, with a different ink that only began to be used a year later). The Middlesex sessions rolls contain three recognizances of 23 December 1598 of persons bound to keep the peace toward a 'Matthew Royden of Westminster clerk'.

The poet Roydon has often been labelled a 'mathematician' (Bartlett, 1941, 2; C. S. Lewis, *English Literature in the Sixteenth Century*, 1954, 466, 510; Spivak, 15; introduction to G. Chapman, *Ovid's Banquet of Sence*, facsimile, 1970, no pagination; *Poems of George Chapman*, 389). Waddington (92–4) and Bartlett (1962, iv) implicitly correct this claim, which probably derives from the bracketing of Roydon with Thomas Harriot and Walter Warner in Thomas Kyd's 1593 accusations, cited below. Warner's papers contain a reference to an 'error in Mr Royd' lettre' (BL, Add. MS 4394, fol. 381v).

Roydon participated in an outpouring of poetic grief following the death of Sir Philip Sidney, claiming friendship with Sidney in the title of his 'Elegie, or, Friends Passion for his Astrophill'. This elegy, identifiable as Roydon's by citations in *Englands Parnassus* (1600), first appeared in *The Phoenix Nest* (1593). It was reprinted with Spenser's 'Astrophel' in Spenser's *Colin Clout* (1595) and in all later editions of Spenser's works.

The only extant works signed by Roydon are two commendatory poems. His prefatory poem to Thomas Watson's pioneering *Hectompathia, or, Passionate Century of Love* (1582) gives the sequence very measured praise, suggesting that originality excuses its limitations. Roydon wrote just seven lines prefatory to G[eorge] P[eckham]'s pamphlet, *A true reporte of the late discovries, of the crowne of Englande, of the New-found landes: by that valiant and worthye gentleman, Sir Humphrey Gilbert Knight* (1583). These verses again give scant praise, noting the book's promotional purpose. They are headed 'Matthew Roydon maister of Arte, *to his fellow Student*', so a university connection may have put Roydon in touch with the first promoters of American plantation.

Roydon had, and retains, high regard as a poet. In Nashe's preface to Greene's *Menaphon* (1589), in addition to the 'divine Master *Spenser*, the miracle of wit', Roydon is named with Thomas Achlow and George Peele as among those 'extant about London' most able to 'revive Poetry, though it were executed tenne thousand times, as in *Platoes*, so in Puritans Commonwealth'. Nashe adds that Roydon 'hath shewed himselfe singular in the immortall Epitaph of his beloved *Astrophell*, besides many other most absolute Comike inventions (made more publike by every mans praise, then they can bee by my speech)' (*Works of Thomas Nashe*, 3.323). George Chapman dedicated 'The Shadow of Night' (1594), to his 'deare and most worthy friend Master Matthew Roydon', praising 'sweet *Matthew*' for taking 'delight in the deepe search of knowledge', and signing himself 'the true admirour of thy vertues' (*Poems of George Chapman*, 223–4). Chapman dedicated *Ovids Banquet of Sence* (1595) to Roydon in exactly similar terms, setting 'searching spirits' like those of 'sweet *Ma*[tthew]' apart from the 'profane multitude' (ibid., 239–40). Francis Meres in *Palladis tamia* (1598, sig. 282v) finds Roydon among other English poets equal to the greatest Italian poets. In *The Scourge of Folly* by John Davies of Hereford

(1610 or 1611, 201) Roydon is celebrated as '*the right well-deserving Mr. Mathew Royden*'. Davies in friendly exasperation describes Roydon's '*Arte*' as possessing 'abstruse' and equivocal aspects.

In his 1594 dedication to Roydon, Chapman recalls that he was cheered to learn from 'his good *Mat.*' of the studiousness of the earls of Derby and Northumberland and 'the heir of Hunsdon'. This suggests that Roydon introduced Chapman to the circle of Northumberland and Sir Walter Ralegh, which included Harriot and Lawrence Keymis.

Having these associates was to be troublesome for Roydon. Thomas Kyd was investigated in May 1593 for seditious libel, and in consequence was suspected in connection with Marlowe's supposed atheism. Kyd wrote two letters in his own defence to Sir John Puckering, lord keeper of the great seal (BL, Harley MS 6849, fols. 218–19 and Harley MS 6848, fol. 154; the matter is discussed in Harley MS 7042, fol. 206r). The first letter names '*Harriot, Warner, Royden*, and some stationers in Paules churchyard' as impiously conversant with Marlowe (BL, Harley MS 6849, fol. 218r). The second letter alleges an escape plot, claiming Marlowe 'wold perswade with men of quallitie to goe unto the k of *Scotts* whether I heare *Royden* is gon and where if he had livd he told me when I saw him last he meant to be' (Harrison, 211). These claims have inserted Roydon into a twentieth-century theory of an Elizabethan 'school of night' (a much disputed and often rejected theory; see Shirley, 359–60).

Many have wondered what writings, other than the few now known, made for Roydon's contemporary fame. No autograph manuscripts have survived, perhaps partly on account of the dangers of 1593 (when letters seem to have been destroyed in Marlowe's circle). A frequent speculation has been that Roydon wrote *Willobie his Avisa* (1594), a lengthy treatment of female chastity. It has been several times attributed to Roydon on account of its style, and of his links with the Ralegh court faction. Lewis found Roydon's authorship 'not improbable' on stylistic grounds (C. S. Lewis, *Poetry and Prose in the Sixteenth Century*, 1954, repr. 1997, 466). Harrison concluded that *Willobie* 'is the sequel to Shakespeare's *Lucrece*', having argued that Roydon wrote *Willobie* as a counter-attack on behalf of the Ralegh faction against the contrary Essex–Southampton–Shakespeare–Nashe faction (Harrison, 231).

Acheson more boldly assigned to Roydon not only *Willobie*, but at least ten other unattributed or (he thinks) misattributed poems, including *Penelope's Complaint* (1596; a response to *Willobie* by 'Peter Colse') and parts of *The Passionate Pilgrime* (1599). Acheson further alleged that Roydon and Chapman contrived the piratical *Passionate Pilgrime*, with the purpose, as in *Willobie*, of annoying Shakespeare and his friends (Acheson, *Mistress Davenant*). Following Acheson, in 1913 Professor Willy Bang concluded that certain anagrams indicate Roydon wrote *Willobie*, and possibly also *Mucedorus* (De Vocht, 213; Acheson, *Shakespeare*, 158–60).

Attempts to find Roydon parodied by Shakespeare have connected the poet with a Matthew Roydon who became fourth minor canon in St Paul's Cathedral in 1603. Acheson (*Mistress Davenant*, 142) describes Roydon as a clerical tutor or chaplain for the earl of Sussex, and (*Shakespeare*, 340n.) suggests he was buried as 'Mr. Roydon', a clergyman, at Canterbury Cathedral, on 4 October 1625. A Matthew Roydon indeed became fourth minor canon at St Paul's in 1603, then first minor canon or subdean in 1616, and the next subdean was appointed on 27 January 1625 consistent with Roydon's death in October 1625 (Hennessy, 62, 64). However, Robert Armin's dedication to Viscount Haddington and his wife of *The Italian Taylor, and his Boy* (1609) states that 'that pen-pleading Poet (grave for yeares and knowledge) Maister *Matthew Roiden*' (sig. A3r–v), aged about fifty when Armin's text was published, still profited from poetic patronage.

The 1617–22 diary of Edward Alleyn shows that the philanthropic former actor and founder of Dulwich Hospital gave a 'Mr Roydon' 8*d.* soon after 29 September 1617, and a 'Matthew Roydon' 6*d.* on 16 August 1622 (Collier, 138, 155). So the literary patronage of Sussex did not continue to the end of Roydon's life, as Armin had kindly wished.

His few known poems, and contemporary comment, suffice to show Roydon a well-connected, gregarious, perspicacious, and talented member of the extraordinary literary generation around London in the 1580s and 1590s. But, perhaps because he became an 'abstruse' writer, his early promise was unfulfilled, and Roydon's celebrity dimmed before his death. B. J. SOKOL

Sources A. Acheson, *Mistress Davenant, the Dark Lady of Shakespeare's sonnets* (1913) · A. Acheson, *Shakespeare's sonnet story* (1933) · *The collected works of Robert Armin*, ed. J. P. Feather, 2 vols. (1972) · D. Baker-Smith, A. F. Kinney, and J. van Dorsten, eds., *Sir Philip Sidney, 1586, and the creation of a legend* (1986) · *The poems of George Chapman*, ed. P. B. Bartlett (1941); repr. (1962) · A. R. Braunmuller, ed., *A seventeenth-century letter-book: a facsimile edition of Folger MS V.a.321* (1983) · J. Buxton, 'Shakespeare's *Venus and Adonis* and Sidney', *Sir Philip Sidney, 1586, and the creation of a legend*, ed. D. Baker-Smith, A. F. Kinney, and J. van Dorsten (1986), 104–10 · J. Buxton, *Sir Philip Sidney and the English Renaissance*, 3rd edn (1987) · J. P. Collier, *Memoirs of Edward Alleyn* (1842) · S. G. Culliford, *William Strachey, 1572–1621* (1965) · H. De Vocht, *Professor Willy Bang and his work in English philology* (1958) · M. Eccles, 'Sir George Buc, master of the revels', *Thomas Lodge and other Elizabethans*, ed. C. J. Sisson (1933), 409–506 · M. Eccles, *Christopher Marlowe in London* (1934) · M. Eccles, 'Chapman's early years', *Studies in Philology*, 43 (1946), 176–93 · M. Eccles, *Brief lives: Tudor and Stuart authors* (1982) · G. B. Harrison, ed., '*Willobie his avisa*', 1594, with an essay on '*Willobie his avisa*' (1926) · G. Hennessy, *Novum repertorium ecclesiasticum parochiale Londinense, or, London diocesan clergy succession from the earliest time to the year 1898* (1898) · J. C. Jeaffreson, ed., *Middlesex county records*, 4 vols. (1886–92) · *George Chapman, plays and poems*, ed. J. Hudson (1998) · *The works of Thomas Nashe*, ed. R. B. McKerrow, 5 vols. (1904–10); repr. with corrections and notes by F. P. Wilson (1958) · G. C. Moore Smith, 'Matthew Royden', *Modern Language Review*, 9 (1914), 97–8 · J. W. Shirley, *Thomas Harriot: a biography* (1983) · H. Smith, *Elizabethan poetry* (1964) · C. Spivak, *George Chapman* (1967) · R. B. Waddington, *The mind's empire: myth and form in George Chapman's narrative poems* (1974) · H. R. Woudhuysen, *Sir Philip Sidney and the circulation of manuscripts, 1558–1640* (1996)

Royle, John Forbes (1798–1858), surgeon and naturalist, was born on 20 May 1798 at Cawnpore, India, the only son of Captain William Henry Royle, in the service of the East India Company, who died while his son was a child. Educated at the Edinburgh high school, Royle was destined for the army, but while waiting at the East India Company's military academy at Addiscombe for an appointment, he became a pupil of Anthony Todd Thomson, from whom he acquired such a strong taste for natural history, and especially botany, that he declined a military appointment. Having obtained his diploma, he became an assistant surgeon in the service of the company, confident that the practice of medicine would enable him to pursue his interest in botany. In 1819 he went out to Calcutta, was placed on the medical staff of the Bengal army, and stationed first at Dum-Dum, but was subsequently sent to various parts of Bengal and the North-Western Provinces. In 1823 he was appointed superintendent of the garden at Saharanpur, having at the same time medical charge of the nearby military station. With characteristic energy he quickly carried out useful reforms in the administration of the garden. Unable to absent himself from his duties, he employed collectors and brought together a valuable collection of economic plants. He examined the drugs sold at the bazaars in India, and identified them with the medicines used by the Greeks. These researches formed the subject of Royle's *Essay on the antiquity of Hindoo medicine, including an introductory lecture to the course of materia medica and therapeutics, delivered at King's College* (1837). In this volume Royle stressed the great age and originality of Hindu medical texts and the fact that many ancient Indian remedies were efficacious. Royle also undertook singlehanded a series of meteorological observations, and obtained excellent data for determining the meteorological conditions of the climate, and for fixing one of the standard stations. In 1831 he returned to England with his collections. The results of his researches were published in his *Illustrations of the botany and other branches of the natural history of the Himalayan mountains* (2 vols., 1839). Here he recommended the introduction of cinchona plants into India, and his suggestion was approved by the governor-general of India in 1852. The following year Royle drew up a valuable report on the subject, but it was not until 1860, two years after his death, that the scheme was carried out by Sir Clements Markham.

In 1836, on the retirement of John Ayrton Paris, Royle was appointed professor of materia medica in King's College, London. He was elected a fellow of the Royal Society in 1837, and of the Linnean Society in 1833, and served on their councils. He was made MD (Munich) in 1833. Royle was also elected a fellow, and acted as secretary, of the Geological and of the Royal Horticultural societies. He was one of the founders of the Philosophical Club in 1847. On 26 August 1839 he married Annette, youngest daughter of Edward Solly, late of Curzon Street, London.

An enthusiastic and active supporter of industrial exhibitions, Royle was one of the commissioners for the City of London in the 1851 exhibition, and was selected to superintend the oriental department of the Paris Exhibition of 1855, when he was made an officer of the Légion d'honneur.

Royle's interest in manufacturing had been stimulated

by his time at the botanical garden at Saharanpur, where he had conducted research into the productivity of different species of plant. His reflections on economics and botany were later published in a number of essays including *On the Culture and Commerce of Cotton in India and Elsewhere* (1851), *The Arts and Manufactures of India* (1852), and his *Review of the Measures which have been Adopted in India for the Improved Culture of Cotton* (1857). Royle's keen awareness of the commercial potential of many Indian plants also led him to advocate state conservation of forests in his *Essay on the Productive Resources of India* (1840).

Royle's knowledge of commercial botany ensured that he was of continuing use to the East India Company which had in 1838 established a special department of correspondence relating to vegetable productions at East India House in London. This was placed under Royle's supervision. The formation and arrangement of a technical museum in connection with this undertaking had just been completed at his death, which took place on 2 January 1858 at Heathfield Lodge, Acton. He was survived by his wife. He is commemorated by the plant *Roylea wall*.

As a botanist, Royle was careful and painstaking and displayed an accuracy of observation which gave authority to his writings. He was especially successful as a writer on technical subjects.

B. B. WOODWARD, rev. MARK HARRISON

Sources R. H. Grove, *Green imperialism: colonial expansion, tropical island Edens, and the origins of environmentalism, 1600–1860* (1995) · D. Kumar, *Science and the raj, 1857–1905* (1995) · R. Desmond, *The European discovery of the Indian flora* (1992) · *Calendar of King's College, London* (1836–7), 4 · Desmond, *Botanists*, rev. edn · *GM*, 2nd ser., 11 (1839), 535 · *CGPLA Eng. & Wales* (1858)
Archives BL OIOC, report and drawings, NHDS · Merseyside Museums, plants · RBG Kew, plants | Oxf. U. Mus. NH, letters, mainly to F. W. Hope
Likenesses G. H. Ford, lithograph, repro. in Desmond, *European discovery of the Indian flora*, 109 · drawing, RBG Kew
Wealth at death under £3500: resworn administration, Dec 1863, *CGPLA Eng. & Wales* (1858)

Royston, Richard (1601–1686), bookseller and publisher, was baptized on 14 or 15 October 1601 in St Peter-in-the-East, Oxford, the son of Richard Royston, a tailor and an important civic figure in Oxford. The family of his mother, Alice, the Tidemans (or Titemans), were also tailors and influential in civic and parish affairs.

On 3 February 1617 Royston was bound for a nine-year apprenticeship to Josias Harrison in the Stationers' Company, and on 28 June 1619 turned over to John Grismond, typefounder and printer. On 6 August 1627 Royston was admitted a freeman of the Stationers' Company, and during the next year he set up shop in Ivy Lane, London, at the sign of the Angel. This remained his business address until he was burnt out by the great fire in 1666. On 26 January 1629 he entered in the Stationers' register his first publication, a broadside, *An elegie upon the death of the most hopefull Prince Henry eldest sonne to his maiestie of Bohemia*. On 6 September 1629 Royston bound his first apprentice, and by 1630 he was well launched on a career which would see him publish more than 800 books.

In the decade from 1630 to 1640 Royston built up an interesting and considerable list of publications and copyrights of important authors. Notable among these were John Donne's *LXXX Sermons* (1640) and *Fifty Sermons: the Second Volume* (1649)—in 1638 he had acted as the seller of the fifth edition of Donne's *Devotions on Emergent Occasions*, though he did not own the copyright—and the two parts of Thomas Heywood's *Fair Maid of the West* (1631).

With the outbreak of the civil war, Royston, always a staunch supporter of the church and the crown, and called 'orthodox Roystone' by John Dunton, turned to polemics. In September 1642 his *Pro-quiritatio*, an anti-parliament pamphlet, was suppressed two days after publication. Royston began to acquire the copyrights and to publish the works of a select number of high-Anglican divines, particularly Jeremy Taylor and Henry Hammond, and would become virtually their sole publisher.

John Wright, printer to the House of Lords, complained on 31 July 1645 that Royston was publishing an anti-parliament parody of Robert Ram's *Soldier's Catechism*. For this Royston was confined in Fleet prison until at least 15 October 1645, when he entered Henry Hammond's *Of Conscience* (1645). He vowed good conduct to the Lords but did not keep his vow.

In March 1646 he entered Sir Christopher Hatton's and Jeremy Taylor's *Psalter of David*, a devotional manual including the text of a portion of the Authorized Version of the Bible which was, in part, a monopoly of the Stationers' Company. On 18 January 1647 Royston appeared before the company's court, and it was agreed he could print the book, with permission, so long as he paid a fee to the company for so doing. He continued to print the book until the end of his life, but the amounts he paid were varied and uncertain. Company concern with this book was a constant in Royston's career.

By the end of 1648 the king was a prisoner of parliament and was being moved from castle to castle until he arrived at Windsor in December 1648. Shortly thereafter there appeared *Eikon basilike*, supposedly written by Charles I during his imprisonment. Royston's involvement with the publication had begun earlier and by the end of 1648 he contrived to get *Eikon* into print, using a series of printers, and began distributing it. Although it has been suggested that he was imprisoned for publishing the King's Book, there is no evidence of this. However, in October 1649, nine months after the execution of Charles I, Royston was called before the council of state and was bound in £500 to appear 'when required, and not to print or sell any unlicensed books or pamphlets in the meantime' (*CSP dom.*, 1649–50, 524).

In April 1651 Royston was reported as being the first stationer to pay a royalty, or copy money, to Henry Hammond for his *Annotations on the New Testament*. In the late 1650s Royston also began to publish the works of Peter Heylyn, an apologist for Charles I and Archbishop Laud, and was soon in trouble with the Stationers' Company. In June 1658 the court ordered all the copies of Heylyn's book against the sabbath to be burnt; nevertheless, Royston entered two more books by Heylyn on 20 August.

On 29 November 1660 Charles II granted Royston a monopoly on printing the works of Charles I, calling *Eikon* 'the most excellent discourses and soliloquies of our blessed father' (Almack, 137). From 1660 onward the crown patronized and protected Royston. On 29 November 1661 he entered *The Works of Charles I* 'by vertue of his Mats comand'. He was provisionally admitted to the livery of the company on 22 June 1662 and had several of his fines dismissed, but it took a letter from Charles II on 6 May 1663 to force Royston's membership and to have him admitted to the position of assistant. On 11 May the company complied, and thereafter Royston was hardly ever absent from a meeting of its court. By October 1663 Royston was also performing his work as a stationer to the court of Charles II, delivering account boxes, stationery, and the like. In 1665 Dr Henry Yerbury complained that 'scandalous libels [had been] published to his defamation by Rich. Royston, of London, the King's stationer, who will not discover the author' (*CSP dom.*, 5.168). This, no doubt, refers to Thomas Pierce's *True Accompt of the Proceedings* (1663), which was an account of how Pierce, as head of Magdalen College, tried to expel the Catholic Yerbury from the fellowship. The book was published without author's or publisher's names. Although Royston continued to have troubles with the Stationers' Company, on 8 May 1665 being questioned about printing the catechism which was part of the English stock, his connections with Charles II seem to have been proof against them all.

By the spring of 1666 Royston was a warden of the company and now was in a position to direct the workings of that system which had directed him, but in the first week of September the great fire of London destroyed St Paul's Cathedral and the printing and publishing industry which surrounded it. Royston, as both a stationer and a member of the government of the company, was doubly concerned. In late September Royston petitioned the king and council 'for pardon for buying some books which though unlicensed, have been freely sold for years past. Abhors all thoughts of disloyalty and is reduced to great extremity by the late fire' (*CSP dom.*, 1666–7, 172). And on 29 September the king ordered that Royston be paid £300 'in compassion to [his circumstances]' (ibid., 167). The headings of Royston's catalogues, which he had been publishing on the blank leaves at the back of his books since the 1650s, changed to such formulas as 'A catalogue of some Books Reprinted, and of other New Books Printed since the Fire, and sold by Richard Royston' (Mede).

From 1668 onward Royston became more concerned with the company's business than with his own; though he continued to publish the titles he already owned, he added very few to his list. He was, of course, busy supplying the court of Charles II with stationery: on 13 September 1668 he was paid the vast sum of £87 7s. 6d. for such supplies, and future bills would be settled for £500 in 1670 and £316 in 1684.

Royston continued to live in disharmony with his fellow stationers. In June 1673 a committee was set up to consider his long-standing differences with the company, and the company attempted to take some contentious items away from him, but with little success. But then on 5 July he was nominated for the position of master of the company and was elected, and then re-elected in 1674. No more was heard for some time of the differences between the company and Master Royston.

But Royston's stock was not dead with Charles II. On 9 April 1677 he was granted a fourteen-year monopoly to print and publish *The History of the Church of Scotland*, by John Spottiswood. At the company elections in June 1683 he acted magnanimously when he was nominated for the post of master, for he withdrew in favour of Roger Norton. Royston bound his last apprentice on 6 August 1683.

Royston attended his penultimate court meeting on 7 June 1686, when, appropriately, one of the main subjects was his infringement of the company's right by printing, yet again, Taylor's and Hatton's *Psalter of David*. In July, despite all, Royston, in his eighties, was again nominated to be master of the company, though Henry Herringman was elected. This was the last court meeting Royston attended.

Some time in November 1686 Royston died. He was buried in Christ Church Greyfriars on 15 November. His tomb bore the following inscription:

> Richard Royston, bookseller to three kings, died 1686, in the 86th year of his age. Elizabeth, wife of Luke Meredith, granddaughter of the above Richard, 1689[.] Mary Chiswell, late wife of Richard Chiswell, bookseller, another daughter of the above Richard Royston, 1689. (Nichols, 3.598)

Of Royston's wife, Margaret (*fl.* 1650–1686), there appears to be no record, but the Royston children and grandchildren continued active and irascible in the book trade well into the next century.

H. R. TEDDER, *rev.* WILLIAM PROCTOR WILLIAMS

Sources court book, Worshipful Company of Stationers and Newspapermakers, London · Arber, *Regs. Stationers* · G. E. B. Eyre, ed., *A transcript of the registers of the Worshipful Company of Stationers from 1640 to 1708*, 3 vols. (1913–14) · W. P. Williams, 'The first edition of *Holy living*: an episode in the seventeenth-century book trade', *The Library*, 5th ser., 28 (1973), 99–107 · W. P. Williams, 'Richard Royston', *The British literary book trade, 1475–1700*, ed. J. K. Bracken and J. Silver, DLitB, 170 (1996), 219–30 · D. F. McKenzie, ed., *Stationers' Company apprentices*, 3 vols. (1961–78), vols. 1–2 · E. Almack, *A bibliography of the King's Book or 'Eikon basilike'* (1896) · C. Blagden, *The Stationers' Company: a history, 1403–1959* (1960) · *CSP dom.*, 1649–71 · G. K. Fortescue and others, eds., *Catalogue of the pamphlets, books, newspapers, and manuscripts relating to the civil war, the Commonwealth, and Restoration, collected by George Thomason, 1640–1661*, 2 vols. (1908) · *The life and errors of John Dunton*, [rev. edn], 1, ed. J. B. Nichols (1818), 291–2 · *Reliquiae Hearnianae: the remains of Thomas Hearne*, ed. P. Bliss, 2 vols. (1857) · J. Mede, *The works of … J. Mede, being discourses on divers texts of Scripture* (1672) · Nichols, *Lit. anecdotes* · H. R. Plomer and others, *A dictionary of the booksellers and printers who were at work in England, Scotland, and Ireland from 1641 to 1667* (1907) · parish register, Oxford, St Peter-in-the-East [baptism], 14–15 Oct 1601 · parish register, London, Christchurch [burial], 15 Nov 1686

Ruadán mac Fergusa Birn [Ruadanus] (*d.* 584). *See under* Munster, saints of (act. c.450–c.700).

Ruaidrí ua Canannáin (*d.* 950), king of Cenél Conaill, was the grandson of Canannán, who flourished in the second half of the ninth century. Canannán was fifth in descent from Flaithbertach mac Loingsig (*d.* 765), high-king of Ireland. They were members of the Cenél Conaill, a branch of the northern Uí Néill. With the exception of a son of Ruaidrí named Niall, neither genealogies nor annals allow reconstruction of the relationships among this family during the tenth century. It is likely that the surname Ua Canannáin emerged in the decades following Ruaidrí's death.

The family's original territory lay in Mag Seiredh, a *tuath* represented by the medieval parish of Druim Tuama (Drumhome) in the north of Tír Áedha (barony of Tirhugh) in the south of the modern co. Donegal. This fertile area provided the power base for the kingship of Tír Conaill at all periods. Cenél Conaill access to the kingship was normally thwarted by their more powerful cousins the Cenél nÉogain to the north-east, the Airgialla to the south-east, and the Connachta to the south-west. The death notice of Cainnech, daughter of Canannán, in 929 is the first hint of the rising power of the family. She had been wife of Donnchad Donn mac Flainn, the reigning high-king (a member of the Clann Cholmáin of the southern Uí Néill). Donnchad's marriage may have facilitated Cenél Conaill's rise to power.

In 943 Muirchertach mac Néill of the Cenél nÉogain was killed in a battle against the vikings at Ardee in Louth. Shortly afterwards Ruaidrí seized the opportunity and killed the likely successor of Muirchertach, Máel Ruanaid mac Flainn, in a dramatic victory over the Cenél nÉogain and the vikings of Lough Foyle at 'Tracht Mugha' (unidentified) in which 300 were killed. In 944 the high-king Donnchad Donn died. The succession to the high-kingship would by custom have gone to the Cenél nÉogain but the loss of its most able member, Muirchertach, left a vacuum. The Cenél nÉogain had already lost many of its eligible members during the previous years and the killing of Máel Ruanaid mac Flainn allowed Ruaidrí to dominate the north. However, he was opposed by Congalach mac Máele Mithig, a member of the Síl nÁeda Sláine branch of the southern Uí Néill based at Knowth on the Boyne. Like Ruaidrí's family, this branch of the dynasty had been excluded from the high-kingship, holding it last in 728. In the following year Ruaidrí opened his campaign against Congalach. A party of his people were killed by Congalach and his ally, Ólaf Sihtricson (Amlaíb Cúarán in the Irish sources), the Norse king of Dublin, in Conaille (modern co. Louth). In 947 he led an army to Slane in Meath. Again Congalach and his Norse allies came against him, only to suffer a defeat in which many were killed or drowned in the River Boyne. This allowed Ruaidrí further time to consolidate in the north. In 949 he killed Flaithbertach ua Néill (son of Muirchertach), another Cenél nÉogain opponent, in Fir Lí (west of the River Bann in what is now co. Londonderry).

With the north firmly under his control, Ruaidrí made a major attempt in 950 to demonstrate that he and not Congalach was the high-king. He gained a victory over Congalach in Brega (Meath) in which the king of Fir Rois (a territory straddling the modern counties Monaghan, Louth, and Meath), Congalach mac Cellach, and others were killed. He followed up this victory by plundering all Brega and then set up camp at 'Muine Brocáin' towards the end of May. This site has not been identified but it almost certainly lay on the north bank of the Blackwater between Domnach Pátraic (Donaghpatrick), to the east of Tailtiu (Teltown), and Kells. He remained there for six months during which time he maintained severe pressure on Congalach. His superiority at this point would seem to have been recognized since one annalist tells that 'the dues of the king of Ireland were sent to him from every quarter' (*AFM*, s.a. 950). But on the feast of St Andrew, 30 November, Ruaidrí was attacked in his camp by the Norse of Dublin, almost certainly acting under the instructions of Congalach. The Norse were defeated in a battle in which, according to the annals, between 2000 and 6000 were killed, young warriors and raw recruits as well as the fighting men. Among the slain were Ruaidrí and the Norse second in command Olaf (Amlaíb). In a counter-attack Ruaidrí's son Niall also fell.

With his main rival now dead, Congalach went on a raid into Munster to demonstrate his authority as high-king. In the following years members of the Ua Canannáin family were killed: Niall Mothlach ('the Hirsute') in 951 in Cairpre Mór (around Granard, in what is now co. Longford) and Fiachra in 952 by the Cenél nÉogain. Their power was never to be as great as it had been under Ruaidrí. They frequently had difficulty in providing kings of Cenél Conaill in the face of their bitter rivalry with the Ua Máel Doraid family—a close segment of the dynasty. Their last king died in 1250.

CHARLES DOHERTY

Sources *Ann. Ulster* · W. M. Hennessy, ed. and trans., *Chronicum Scotorum: a chronicle of Irish affairs*, Rolls Series, 46 (1866) · *AFM* · S. Mac Airt, ed. and trans., *The annals of Inisfallen* (1951) · D. Murphy, ed., *The annals of Clonmacnoise*, trans. C. Mageoghagan (1896); facs. edn (1993) · T. G. Cannon, 'A history of the O'Cannons of Tir Chonaill', *Donegal Annual*, 12 (1978), 276–315 · T. Ó Canann, 'Trí Saorthuatha Mhuinntire Chanannáin: a forgotten medieval placename', *Donegal Annual*, 38 (1986), 19–46 · D. Mac Giolla Easpaig, 'Placenames and early settlement in county Donegal', *Donegal history and society: interdisciplinary essays on the history of an Irish county*, ed. W. Nolan, L. Ronayne, and M. Dunlevy (1995), 149–82 · F. Gillespie [Fearghus Mac Giolla Easpaig], 'Gaelic families of county Donegal', *Donegal history and society: interdisciplinary essays on the history of an Irish county*, ed. W. Nolan, L. Ronayne, and M. Dunlevy (1995), 759–838

Ruane, Martin Austin [*performing name* Giant Haystacks] **(1946–1998)**, wrestler, was born in St Giles's Hospital, Camberwell, London, on 10 October 1946, one of three sons of Martin Ruane and his wife, Julia Delaney. His parents were Irish immigrants from co. Mayo and the family soon moved to Salford, where Ruane grew up and attended St Thomas's School. He was a huge baby, weighing 14 lb 6 oz, and grew into an enormous man, standing 6 feet 11 inches and weighing almost 50 stone at the height of his wrestling career. He claimed to come from a family of 'giants', with a grandfather who stood 7 foot 5 inches. His two brothers were also big men, though not on his gargantuan scale. His father, a tough character in his own right, known as the Black Prince, was a foreman on an open-cast mine, and later on motorway construction, and his son followed him into heavy labouring work. He then took up work as a bouncer at a night club. This brush with the entertainment industry led him to try his hand at wrestling at the King's Hall, Belle Vue, Manchester, in 1967, just as wrestling was reinvented as a commercial spectacle. Late Saturday afternoon bouts were hosted on ITV by Kent Walton, whose commentary cleverly played up the histrionic antics in the ring.

A new generation of 'grapple fans', as Walton called them, was born and soon Ruane, in the persona of Giant Haystacks, was nationally known. This form of celebrity television wrestling was, as Roland Barthes famously observed in *Mythologies*, a crude moral drama in which a 'good' sportsmanlike competitor had to fight an 'evil' bully without compassion or decency. Ruane played the role of the brute to perfection. He would lumber into the ring, his vast bulk clothed in a dirty tunic, shaking his shaggy black beard and long hair, alternately sullen and scowling or openly roaring defiance at the jibes of the crowd. A spectator was once so infuriated that he jumped into the ring and pulled the Giant's beard before being swatted like a gnat and dispatched to the local infirmary.

Ruane's wrestling style was as primitive as his appearance, and as effective. The Giant's wrath would be roused by a blow, which would provoke him to pick up his man—no matter how big—and crash him to the ground, following up with a belly-flop to pin his opponent to the canvas. The fights were carefully choreographed, and the wrestlers were as much entertainers as sportsmen. Among this stable of celebrity wrestlers was Big Daddy [see Crabtree, Shirley]—a favourite adversary in the battle of the 'big men'—along with others such as Scrubber Daly, Bomber Roach, Cyanide Syd Copper ('rotten to the core'), and Jumping Jim Mosa, culminating in his most famous opponent, the masked Kendo Nagasaki. A popular variation involved pairing a larger and a smaller wrestler in two-man 'tag' teams. A nimble 'Jack' would taunt the Giant and then hastily tag his partner and scuttle out of the ring before Haystacks could get hold of him. Retribution, of course, would always follow, to the anguished delight of the audience.

All this attracted vast audiences—up to 18 million viewers—ranging (it was said) from royalty to elderly working-class women, who were among Giant Haystacks's most loyal fans. 'He's been a great asset to the job', as an insider remarked; 'wrestling has to have bizarre characters, it's got to have giants' (Garfield). His career, which spanned the 1970s and 1980s and was never particularly lucrative, involved driving as much as 120,000 miles a year. He always travelled alone and wrestled seriously in Europe, the Far East, and Africa as well as in the choreographed bouts in the UK. Not long before his death he had signed a contract with a friend, Hulk Hogan, to wrestle on the American circuit as the Loch Ness Monster.

In Britain, however, Ruane's career was prematurely ended not by injury but by the head of ITV entertainment, Greg Dyke, who took wrestling off the schedules on the grounds that it had the wrong image for advertisers and was losing popularity by the late 1980s. Ruane took up debt collecting—a predictable move perhaps, though apparently he secured payment not by force but because of the publicity surrounding his visits to bad debtors. For all its choreographed moves and staged confrontations, nothing could replace the thrill of the ring. 'I felt like a conductor of the Hallé Orchestra, able to play on people's emotions' (*The Guardian*, 24), as he once observed of his wrestling career in an aside which revealed his more serious and cultivated side. This dramatic power compensated for the numerous injuries he sustained and his relatively low earnings: he cleared no more than £600 a week in his prime, stayed in cheap lodgings, and took his enormous meals in transport cafés.

In private Ruane was a complex man, with a strong Catholic faith. He was devoted to his wife, Margaret Teresa (Rita) Boylan (*b.* 1943/4), whom he met in Salford and married there on 23 October 1965, and to their three children. She supported him steadfastly through his final years when his business ventures failed and nursed him through cancer from which he died at his home, 26 Bland Road, Prestwich, Manchester, on 29 November 1998.

RICHARD HOLT

Sources S. Garfield, *The wrestling* (1946) · *The Independent* (3 Dec 1998), 6 · *The Guardian* (2 Dec 1998), 24 · *The Independent* (2 Dec 1998), 9 · *Daily Telegraph* (3 Dec 1998) · b. cert. · m. cert. · d. cert.
Likenesses portrait, repro. in *The Independent* (3 Dec 1998) · portrait, repro. in *The Guardian* · portrait, repro. in *Daily Telegraph*

Rubbra, (Charles) Edmund Duncan (1901–1986), composer and pianist, was born on 23 May 1901 at 57 Cambridge Street, Northampton, the elder son (there were no daughters) of Edmund James Rubbra, journeyman shoe-last maker, clock and watch repairer, and, later, jeweller, and his wife, Mary Jane Bailey. The name Duncan was not on his birth certificate; it was the surname of his first wife and he used it after his first marriage. According to family tradition, the Rubbras originated from Bologna in Italy. He left school at fourteen and worked briefly as an errand boy and then a railway clerk. In his home there was a deep love of music and as a youngster he was much drawn to the music of Cyril Scott and Claude Debussy. Eventually he took lessons with Scott, and then went on to study composition at Reading University, where Gustav Holst taught, and counterpoint at the Royal College of Music with one of the great theorists of the day, R. O. Morris.

After leaving the college in 1925, Rubbra pursued a free-lance career as a pianist, taking whatever teaching, performing, and journalistic work came to hand. His repertory included both Arnold Schoenberg and Aleksandr Skryabin, and he was a perceptive exponent of J. S. Bach. During the 1930s he attracted increasing attention with such works as the *Sinfonia concertante* for piano and orchestra (1934) and his first symphony (1937).

During the Second World War Rubbra served in the army, as an anti-aircraft gunner in the Royal Artillery and then in the army music unit, and made an appearance in battledress at London's Henry Wood Promenade Concerts to conduct the first performance of his fourth symphony (1942). Rubbra spent much of his army service entertaining the troops with the trio he had formed with Erich

Gruenberg and William Pleeth (and was very fond of telling how the three were once introduced as being 'at the top of the tree in their various string combinations'). The Rubbra–Gruenberg–Pleeth trio continued for some years after the war until the combined pressures of Rubbra's creative work and teaching led to its demise. In 1947 he was appointed lecturer in music at Oxford University, becoming a fellow of Worcester College in 1963. He remained at Oxford until 1968. In 1961 he also joined the staff of the Guildhall School of Music, where he taught composition until 1974.

Rubbra belonged to the same generation as Sir William Walton, Sir Lennox Berkeley, and Sir Michael Tippett but had little in common with them and even less with such European contemporaries as Karl Amadeus Hartmann, Luigi Dallapiccola, and Dmitry Shostakovich. It has been said that his music was not of his time, yet could have been composed at no other. It is rooted in place—England—and, more specifically, England's musical heritage lies at its heart. There is little of the pastoral school in it, though Rubbra revered Ralph Vaughan Williams and also possessed a keen sense of nature's power, which is clearly evident in the fourth (1941–2) and seventh symphonies (1957). Rubbra's outlook was far from insular: he set to music poetry ranging from the time of the Chinese Tang dynasty and of Icelandic ballads to medieval Latin and French verse, and his interest in eastern culture, which arose in childhood, remained lifelong. In *Counterpoint* (1960), Rubbra argued that western music had grown out of melody and in particular the interaction of independent melodic lines; this was certainly a dominant principle in his own music. Such was the eloquence and quality of his vocal music that some critics spoke of his symphonies as 'motets for orchestra'. His choral music was finely fashioned and elevated in feeling, and his symphonies likewise were touched by a preoccupation with linear growth. Matter, not manner, was his central concern.

Rubbra's early symphonies are difficult, though not in the way that some contemporary music is, for the musical language itself is quite straightforward. There is nothing abstruse about the symphonies' tonality and harmony, which is basically diatonic, but they are difficult because the continuity of their melodic and polyphonic growth is logical and unremitting. The first two symphonies were composed in quick succession (both were finished in 1937) and it was obvious that, whatever their failings, Rubbra was a symphonist to be reckoned with. The third, which he finished in 1939, was a positive reaction to the experience of the second, and is outwardly the most genial and relaxed of the early symphonies. The orchestration is much cleaner and the first movement much closer to sonata form. The opening of the fourth symphony is beautiful and free from any kind of artifice, having serenity and quietude. This symphony, like the third, is not so dense contrapuntally as the first two, and though practically every idea evolves in some way or another out of the opening figure, its first movement is a sonata design. Nothing could be further removed from the grim years of the Second World War than this symphony. In 1948 came the fifth

and most often played of the Rubbra symphonies; it enjoyed something of a vogue in the 1950s. Sir Adrian Boult gave the work its première, Sir John Barbirolli recorded it, and Leopold Stokowski briefly included it in his repertory.

After the seventh symphony (1957), Rubbra's music fell on hard times and enjoyed relatively little exposure. His eighth symphony (1968) had to wait three years for a performance and the ninth (*Sinfonia sacra*, 1971–2), for soloists, chorus, and orchestra, possibly his masterpiece, also suffered relative neglect. It tells the story of the resurrection, and with its soloists and chorus would closely resemble a passion were it not for its symphonic cohesion. Like most of Rubbra's finest music, it unfolds with a seeming inevitability and naturalness, and a powerful sense of purpose that justify its inclusion in the symphonic canon. His scoring has been criticized, but conductors such as Arturo Toscanini, Eugene Ormandy, and Neeme Järvi recorded his orchestration of Brahms's *Variations and Fugue on a Theme of Handel*.

Rubbra was of medium height and was for most of his adult life bearded. He possessed a beatific smile and exercised great personal charm. Always courteous, a supportive and illuminating teacher, he radiated warmth and spirituality. His deeply religious nature shines through much of his music: the canto movement of the sixth symphony (1954), for example, and the eighth, subtitled 'Hommage à Teilhard de Chardin'. (Although he was much influenced by Buddhist teachings, Rubbra was received into the Catholic faith in 1947.) He never lost this feeling for organic growth essential to the symphony: his tenth (1974) and eleventh (1979) are highly concentrated one-movement affairs of much substance.

Rubbra's output was extensive and ran to over 160 works. Apart from the symphonies, his most important works included a viola concerto in A major, op. 75 (1952); a piano concerto in G major, op. 85 (1956); a violin concerto, op. 103 (1959); an improvisation for violin and orchestra, op. 89; four string quartets: F minor, op. 35 (1933, revised 1946), E♭ op. 55 (1952), op. 112 (1962–3), and op. 150 (1976–7); two piano trios: op. 68 (1950) and op. 138 (1973); two violin sonatas: op. 31 (1931) and op. 133 (1967); and a cello sonata in G minor, op. 60 (1946). All of his symphonies have been commercially recorded, and there is an extensive discography which includes his two masses. His last work was the *Sinfonietta* for large string orchestra, op. 163, which he completed in 1980, in his late seventies, shortly before suffering a stroke, from which he eventually died.

Rubbra was appointed CBE in 1960. He became a member of the Royal Academy of Music in 1970 and a fellow of the Guildhall School of Music in 1968. He had honorary degrees from Leicester (LLD, 1959), Durham (DMus, 1949), and Reading (DLitt, 1978). His music does not possess the dramatic power which characterizes that of Vaughan Williams and Walton but has a sense of organic continuity that is both highly developed and immediately evident to the listener. Perhaps the most distinctive and individual quality that shines through his most inspired music, such as the opening of the seventh symphony or the *Missa in honorem sancti Dominici* (op. 66, 1948), is breadth and serenity.

Rubbra's first marriage, which lasted only a few months, was to Lilian Annie Duncan. There were no children. On 25 November 1933 he married the violinist Antoinette Chaplin (*b.* 1901/2), from France, daughter of William Chaplin, engineer; they had two sons. He separated from his second wife during the 1950s and in 1975, following her death, he married Colette Muriel Marian Yardley, daughter of Harold Evans, a Sunbeam Motors salesman. They had one son. Rubbra died on 14 February 1986 in Gerrards Cross, where his home was Lindens, Bull Lane.

ROBERT LAYTON, *rev.*

Sources L. Foreman, ed., *Edmund Rubbra, composer: essays* (1977) · R. S. Grover, *The music of Edmund Rubbra* (1993) · *The Times* (15 Feb 1986) · b. cert. · m. cert. [Antoinette Chaplin] · personal knowledge (1996) · *CGPLA Eng. & Wales* (1986)
Archives BL, MS scores and papers, MS Mus. 85 | BL, corresp. with Bernard Stevens, Add. MSS 69027, 69029
Likenesses photograph, 1949, Hult. Arch.
Wealth at death £7173: probate, 16 Sept 1986, *CGPLA Eng. & Wales*

Ruben mac Connad (d. 725), scribe, is known from two references. His obituary notice of 725 in the annals of Ulster describes him as 'Rubin mac Connadh, scribe of Munster'. Ruben was probably an Irish form of the biblical name Reuben. The colophon copied inaccurately by a Breton scribe into Paris, Bibliothéque Nationale, MS Lat. 12021 tells that Ruben collaborated with *Cú Chuimne of Iona in the authorship of the *Collectio canonum Hibernensis*. According to the colophon, Ruben was from Dair-Inis, a monastery on an island in the Blackwater River not far from Youghal in Ireland. Dair-Inis was maintained by the abbey of Lismore, which had links with Iona. *Scriba* ('scribe') was used in early Ireland as a term to describe someone learned in scriptural law. Ruben came from an area in Ireland which for some time had been a centre of learning, had contacts with the continent, and where there were pioneers of the Roman Easter. Hence the decrees of the *Romani* which are referred to in the text are regarded as the decrees of this particular party in the Irish church, whereas the rulings of the *Synodus Hibernensis* refer to rules made by Irish adherents of the 'Celtic' Easter reckoning.

LUNED MAIR DAVIES

Sources *Ann. Ulster*, s.a. 725 · Bibliothèque Nationale, Paris, MS Lat. 12021, colophon · R. Thurneysen, 'Zur irischen Kanonensammlung', *Zeitschrift für Celtische Philologie*, 6 (1907–8), 1–5 · J. F. Kenney, *The sources for the early history of Ireland* (1929); repr. (1979) · K. Hughes, *The church in early Irish society* (1966)
Archives Archivio dell'Abbazia, Monte Cassino, MS 297 · Badische Landesbibliothek, Karlsruhe, MS Aug. XVIII · Biblioteca Labronica, Livorno, formerly no. 10 · Biblioteca Vallicelliana, Rome, MS t. XVIII · Bibliothèque Municipale, Orléans, MS 221 (193) · Bibliothèque Nationale, Paris, MS Lat. 12021 · Bibliothèque Nationale, Paris, MS Lat. 3182 · BL, Cotton MS Otho E.xiii · Bodl. Oxf., Hatton MS 42 · CCC Cam., MS 279 · Dombibliothek, Cologne, MS 210 · Stiftsbibliothek, St Gallen, MS 143 · Cambrai, MS 679 (619)

Rubens, Paul Alfred (1875–1917), musical comedy writer and songwriter, was born at 11 Dawson Place, Kensington, London, on 29 April 1875, the eldest son of Victor Rubens, a wealthy Berlin-born Jewish stockbroker, and his wife, Jenny, *née* Wallach. He was educated at Winchester College and studied law at University College, Oxford (1895–7), where he took part enthusiastically in university dramatics. Although he had no formal musical training, he also began writing songs in Oxford, among them a set for a stage production of *Alice in Wonderland* in which Charles Dodgson (Lewis Carroll) took a hand. He was still only nineteen when his song 'The Little Chinchilla' was accepted by the era's most important musical-theatre producer, George Edwardes, and introduced into the hit musical play *The Shop Girl* at the Gaiety Theatre.

In the years that followed Rubens contributed individual songs to a number of West End musical comedies and burlesques, but his breakthrough came when he was hired by the producer Tom Davis to provide additional numbers to Leslie Stuart's score for *Florodora* (1899). The bright, tunefully simple songs that Rubens wrote for, in particular, the show's *soubrette*, Ada Reeve ('Inkling', 'Tact', 'When I leave town'), won him his spurs, and he was swiftly put under contract by Edwardes as a supplier of supplementary songs for his productions.

Edwardes gave the young songwriter a bigger opportunity to demonstrate his talents when he mounted *Three Little Maids* (1902), a lightweight piece of musical theatre for which Rubens had written the book, the music (with Howard Talbot), and the lyrics. *Three Little Maids*, 'alternately music-hally, pretty, pale, mildly suggestive, and also successful' (Gänzl, *Encyclopedia of the Musical Theatre*, 2.1252), went on to be played around the English-singing world. It was followed by the similarly built *Lady Madcap* (1904) before Rubens surprised everyone by coming up with a work far in advance of his two recent hits in substance and quality. *Mr Popple of Ippleton* was a genuine musical comedy in the style of the French vaudeville, with a farcical and funny story and some charming and gently amusing songs which mostly avoided the rather schoolboy-naughty tone too often found in Rubens's lyrics. George P. Huntley and Ethel Irving created the lead roles of the winning tale of a country mouse (male) in the wicked city, and the piece did well enough that, after its British run, Rubens's libretto was borrowed by the American producers Comstock and Marbury to be remade as a 'new' musical play, *Nobody Home*, with songs by Jerome Kern.

Rubens returned to his habitual lightweight, light-blue style for Robert Courtneidge's successful production *The Dairymaids* (1906) and then turned out the show which was to be his most enduring success. Although he was originally scheduled to write alone what he disarmingly called the 'chatter, jingles and tunes' for *Miss Hook of Holland* (1907), the consumptive illness from which he suffered all his adult life prevented him from doing so, and the director Austen Hurgon ended by helping out with the show's libretto. *Miss Hook* was a major hit, and Rubens and Hurgon went on to provide two further pieces for its producer, Frank Curzon. *My Mimosa Maid* and *Dear Little Denmark* were, however, much less successful.

Curzon then switched Rubens away from libretto writing and teamed him instead with his newest playwriting discovery, the young Freddie Lonsdale, who had just provided the producer with a major hit in the romantic, Ruritanian costume musical *King of Cadonia* (music by Sidney Jones). Rubens's 'tunes' (this was all he ever supplied; the accompaniments had to be written for him) for *The Balkan Princess* were far from being of the quality or the musicianship of Jones's work, but—as ever—they proved to have that catchiness that makes for success. *The Balkan Princess* became a West End success, an overseas hit—produced from Broadway to Budapest to Havana—and a longtime feature of the British touring circuits.

Rubens was then signed by Edwardes as principal composer to the Gaiety Theatre, and in the years that followed he provided the famous producer with songs for *The Sunshine Girl* (1912), *The Girl from Utah* (1913), *After the Girl* (1914), *Tina* (1915), *Betty* (1915), and, above all, Fred Thompson's adaptation of the famous farce *Les dominos roses* as *Tonight's the Night* (1914). Supplied with a libretto of quality, and limited again to writing just melodies and lyrics, Rubens proved, with a singular success, that this kind of light and bright illustration of a classy comic text was what he did best. However, just as an era of such pieces was beginning in the British theatre, Rubens's illness got the better of him. He died from tuberculosis at Roscarrack, Budock, Falmouth, Cornwall, on 4 February 1917, at the age of only forty-one.

W. Graham Robertson provided a eulogy:

> That strange genius who masqueraded as a good-looking boy, wandering listlessly through life in the hope of amusing himself, and who got through more good work in his short life than many a composer of fifty has to his credit. (Robertson, 321)

Although during his lifetime the dark-featured Rubens carried an excessively public and blazing torch for several lovely actresses—notably Phyllis Dare—he never married.   KURT GÄNZL

Sources K. Gänzl, *The encyclopedia of the musical theatre*, 2 vols. (1994) • K. Gänzl, *The British musical theatre*, 2 vols. (1986) • *The Era* (29 Nov 1902), 15 • *CGPLA Eng. & Wales* (1917) • W. G. Robertson, *Time was: the reminiscences of W. Graham Robertson* (1931) • Foster, *Alum. Oxon.* • J. Parker, ed., *Who's who in the theatre*, 6th edn (1930) • b. cert. • d. cert.
Likenesses photographs, repro. in *The Era*
Wealth at death £24,128 0s. 8d.: double probate, 4 May 1917, *CGPLA Eng. & Wales* • £24,162 13s. 4d.: further grant, 29 May 1917, *CGPLA Eng. & Wales* • £12,226 3s. 6d.: further grant, 29 Oct 1917, *CGPLA Eng. & Wales*

Rubens, Sir Peter Paul (1577–1640), painter, was born on 28 June 1577 in Siegen, Westphalia, the youngest among the six children of Jan Rubens (d. 1587), a distinguished lawyer, and his wife, Maria Pypelincks (d. 1608), who had moved there from nearby Cologne. Rubens's parents were from Antwerp, in the Netherlands, which they had fled in 1568 to escape religious persecution, Jan being a protestant. Before Jan Rubens's death he and his wife officially converted to Catholicism, which became the religion of their family. In 1578 the family returned to Cologne, and in 1589, following Jan Rubens's death, Maria returned to Antwerp with Peter Paul and two of his siblings.

Rubens received a solid grounding in classical language

Sir Peter Paul Rubens (1577–1640), self-portrait, 1623

and literature both from his father and afterwards at school in Antwerp, which inspired his lifelong love of learning and provided the foundation for his prodigious knowledge and understanding of classical sources. Thereafter, following apprenticeships to three Antwerp painters, he became a master in the Antwerp painters' guild in 1598. In 1600 Rubens travelled to Italy to see and make copies of ancient sculpture and study the works of the sixteenth-century masters. For the rest of his life he drew on the stock of pictorial ideas that he encountered during these travels. He also gained his first diplomatic experience when he travelled to the Spanish court while court painter to Vincenzo Gonzaga, duke of Mantua (r. 1587–1612).

Rubens returned to Antwerp in 1608. Archduke Albert and his wife Isabella appointed him court painter, although he was permitted to live in Antwerp and not be tied to the court in Brussels. He married eighteen-year-old Isabella (1591–1626), daughter of Jan Brant, an eminent secretary of Antwerp, on 3 October 1609 and soon afterwards they settled in a house on the fashionable Wapper. In the coming years Rubens transformed his house, garden, and studio into an Italianate palazzo. His home was overflowing with various collections of books, paintings, ancient sculpture, gems, coins, and other antiquities. Here he and his wife brought up a daughter and two sons.

During the late 1610s and early 1620s Rubens was increasingly busy, completing over sixty altarpieces—

large-scale commissions—as well as pictures for individual collectors. He was also working on designs for tapestries and title-pages and supervising the creation of prints based on his paintings. While biblical subjects were his chief occupation during this decade he also became known for his historical and mythological subjects, as well as for portraits and landscapes. By the time that he had completed the ceiling decorations for the new Jesuit church in Antwerp, in 1620, Rubens's reputation as the most significant artist in northern Europe was established. In 1625 he completed a major painted cycle for the Luxembourg Palace celebrating the life of Marie de' Medici in twenty-four huge and lively images that veiled the sometimes unpleasant facts of contemporary history with a skilful blend of allegorical and mythological characters. This mix of human beings and gods, in accord with the idea of royalty by divine right, remained central to Rubens's great cycles during the next ten years.

By the mid-1620s Rubens had completed some of the most important commissions of his career. His wife and daughter had just died, leaving him with two young sons. It was at this time that the Archduchess Isabella engaged Rubens as her adviser and confidential agent to help bring about her wish (which he sincerely shared) to secure peace in the divided Netherlands. This marked the beginning of a five-year period of extensive travel for Rubens, at first on secret missions to the northern Netherlands, later on diplomatic trips to Madrid and London.

In 1628, at Isabella's direction, Rubens travelled to Madrid to begin the talks that he hoped would lead to peace between Spain and England and ultimately see his beloved Netherlands united. In the following year Isabella's nephew Philip IV, king of Spain, named Rubens secretary of the privy council of the Netherlands and sent him off to London as an envoy laying the groundwork for an Anglo-Spanish armistice. Rubens's arrival in London was greeted by the art-loving Charles I with pleasure, by the anti-Spanish faction with suspicion. He had the benefit, however, of having established ongoing relationships with many English court collectors during the previous two decades.

Sir Dudley Carleton, for instance, English ambassador to The Hague, showed interest in the great hunting pictures that Rubens produced between 1615 and 1621. In 1616 Toby Matthew, an Englishman living in Brussels who had been involved in buying works of art for Jacobean courtiers, and George Gage, a roving English agent often employed in buying artworks, visited Rubens on behalf of Carleton to acquire a hunting picture. Five years later Rubens produced *Lion Hunt* (Alte Pinakothek, Munich), for Sir John Digby, who intended to present it to the marquess of Hamilton.

In 1620 Rubens had his first contact with the fourteenth earl of Arundel, when Arundel asked him to paint a portrait of the countess, Altheia Talbot, as she stopped in Antwerp *en route* for Venice. Rubens was in frequent contact over various artistic matters with Matthew, Gage, and Carleton in the coming years. In 1623 all were involved in negotiations with Rubens on behalf of Lord Danvers (who

in turn was acting for Prince Charles), who had been keeper of St James's Palace from 1611 to 1618. Danvers had a specific request for a picture that he heard was already finished: Rubens's *Self-Portrait* (1623; Royal Collection), which hung first at St James's Palace and, later, in Charles I's bedchamber at Whitehall Palace.

Rubens was in Paris in 1625 in order to install the Medici cycle in time for the wedding of the newly crowned King Charles I and the French princess Henrietta Maria. There he met George Villiers, first duke of Buckingham. Rubens remained in contact with Buckingham from this time until the latter's death, in 1628. Their special interests—both artistic and diplomatic—fired their relationship: Buckingham wanted to acquire works by Rubens and from his collection; Rubens wanted Buckingham's help to secure peace in Europe. It was probably before Buckingham and the new British queen departed for London that Rubens made a portrait drawing of Buckingham (Albertina, Vienna) and received commissions for a large allegorical equestrian portrait and a ceiling painting celebrating the duke for York House, his London residence.

During Rubens's London sojourn Charles I commissioned him to paint nine ceiling canvases to adorn Inigo Jones's Palladian Banqueting House (1619–22), in Whitehall Palace, a project for which Rubens had lobbied ten years earlier. Rubens's first ideas for this project were set out in the remarkably free honey-coloured oil sketches *The Apotheosis of James I* (priv. coll., on loan to the National Gallery). Installed by 1636, Rubens's canvases celebrate the reign of James I (1603–25). The ceiling's thematic emphasis on peace—an imaginative combination of recent history and allegory—reflects King James's role as peacemaker as well as Rubens's own diplomatic concerns as he worked to end hostilities between Spain and England. While in London Rubens completed several portraits, most notably the dignified *Thomas Howard, Earl of Arundel* (1629–30; Isabella Stewart Gardner Museum, Boston).

Rubens's letters from London suggest that, while he frequently met Charles I, they did not establish a rapport such as the painter had enjoyed with Philip IV in Madrid. There are no portraits by Rubens of Charles I. Rubens's letters give no indication that in his meetings with the English king pictures were ever discussed, though given their shared interests such asides to politics seem likely. Rubens had been instructed to offer a truce between England and Spain that would not involve the United Provinces. He encountered some difficulty in his initial meetings with Charles, who urged him to draw up a treaty to conclude peace, not simply to negotiate a truce. By September 1629 Rubens had completed negotiations with Charles for the exchange of ambassadors. In response to Rubens's request to return to Antwerp at this point the junta directed him to remain in London until the arrival of the Spanish ambassador. The success of his diplomatic mission was praised both in London and Madrid.

The day before he set sail Rubens made one last attempt to secure peace in the Netherlands. He paid a surprise visit to the Dutch ambassador, Albert Joachimi. Given the imminent settlement of peace between Spain and England, Rubens suggested that it was a propitious moment to begin negotiations between the north and south Netherlands. He left disappointed, however, as Joachimi, feeling confident over the success of the United Provinces on the battlefield, refused to enter into any discussions concerning reunion unless the south joined the north to drive the Spaniards out.

At the end of Rubens's nine-month stay in London, culminating in the successful agreement to exchange English and Spanish ambassadors, Charles I bestowed a knighthood on him. Before leaving in March 1630 he in turn presented Charles with a painted plea for peace, *Minerva Protects Pax from Mars* (*Peace and War*; National Gallery, London) and took with him as a record of his English sojourn his *Landscape with Dragon* (*St George and the Princess*; Royal Collection). In it Charles is shown as St George saving the princess, Henrietta Maria, in a velvety, mist-enshrouded blue and green landscape, with vague references to specific London buildings.

Rubens's London mission was the last of the many visits that he made during three decades to the great courts of Europe. For Rubens the 1630s were devoted to painting and to his new wife, Hélène Fourment (sixteen when he married her, on 6 December 1630), at home in Antwerp and at Het Steen, a country haven situated between Malines and Brussels. With Hélène he spent the last ten years of his energetic life producing two more sons and three more daughters (the last born eight months after his death) and enjoying domestic tranquillity in the Flemish countryside. While he continued to receive commissions it is his mythologies and landscapes that show the marked influence of Hélène's sensuality on the one hand and the lush fertility of nature on the other—distinctive features of this period.

Rubens died, of complications suffered from gout, on 30 May 1640. That evening his body was laid out in a coffin and placed in the Fourment family vault in his parish church, St Jacob, Antwerp. The funeral service was held three days later, with a procession headed by the clergy of St Jacob, followed by members of the civic, artistic, merchant, and aristocratic circles of Antwerp. During the ensuing weeks some 800 masses celebrating Rubens's life were held in and around Antwerp. In the year following his death a funeral chapel was built for him behind the choir of St Jacob.

FIONA DONOVAN

Sources K. L. Belkin, *Rubens* (1998) · C. White, *Peter Paul Rubens* (1985) · F. Baudouin, *Peter Paul Rubens* (1977) · *The letters of Peter Paul Rubens*, ed. and trans. R. S. Magurn (1955) · F. Donovan, 'Rubens, England, and the Whitehall ceiling', PhD diss., Columbia University, 1995 · C. Ruelens and M. Rooses, eds., *Correspondance de Rubens et documents épistolaires concernant sa vie et ses œuvres*, 6 vols. (Anvers, 1887–1909) · W. N. Sainsbury, ed., *Original unpublished papers illustrative of the life of Sir Peter Paul Rubens* (1859)
Likenesses P. P. Rubens, self-portrait, oils, *c.*1609 (with his wife), Alte Pinakothek, Munich, Germany · P. P. Rubens, self-portrait, oils, 1623, Royal Collection [*see illus.*] · P. P. Rubens, self-portrait, oils, *c.*1625–1628, Rubenshuis, Antwerp, Belgium · P. P. Rubens, self-portrait, black and white chalk drawing, *c.*1639, Royal Library · P. P. Rubens, self-portrait, oils, *c.*1639, Kunsthistorisches Museum, Vienna, Austria · J. Audran, line engraving, pubd 1710 (after A. Van Dyck?), NG Ire. · B. Baron, line engraving and etching, pubd 1724 (after chalk drawing), NG Ire. · W. Hollar, portrait, NPG
Wealth at death gross assets in 1645 amounted to 283,987 florins, of which more than 96,000 florins was income from the sale of art: J. M. Muller, *Rubens: the artist as collector* (Princeton, 1989), 59

Ruck [*married name* Oliver], **Amy Roberta** [Berta] (1878–1978), novelist, was born on 2 August 1878 at Murree, Punjab, India, the eldest child of Arthur Ashley Ruck, a lieutenant in the Isle of Man regiment (8th foot), and his wife, Elizabeth Eleanor, daughter of Robert West D'Arcy, a colonel in the Bombay grenadiers. They had seven further children: three sons and four daughters. Arthur Ruck's sister Amy married Francis *Darwin and died giving birth to their son Bernard *Darwin.

Berta Ruck, as she came to be known, was brought to Britain at the age of two and lived for a while at Panlludw, near Machynlleth, Merioneth, the home of her paternal grandmother, Mary Anne Ruck (*née* Mathews), and both the place and the person were to make a deep impression on her. Her father also returned from India to an adjutancy of the Liverpool Volunteers, and the family spent some five years at residences in Fleetwood and Formby in Lancashire. In 1886 her father retired with the honorary rank of lieutenant-colonel and in 1888 was appointed chief constable of Caernarvonshire. The rest of her childhood was spent at Caernarfon, where she was educated at home, and at Bangor, where she was a boarder at St Winifred's School.

In the summer of 1892 Berta Ruck worked as an au pair in Halberstadt, Germany, and, as well as prompting what was to be a permanent liking for travel, this trip caused her to develop her latent talent for drawing. On leaving school she became a student at the Lambeth School of Art in London, with some thought of becoming a book illustrator, and on being awarded a London county council scholarship in 1901, she moved to the Slade School of Fine Art, where she studied under Henry Tonks. An extension of her scholarship in 1904 enabled her to spend a year at the Académie Colarossi in Paris, and it was there that she befriended Iris Bland, whose mother, Edith Nesbit, was an influential mentor when Berta Ruck turned to writing.

Berta Ruck's earliest published work was in the form of illustrations for magazines. (Two illustrations and a headpiece appeared in volume 23 of *The Idler* in 1903.) She also drew for the short-lived periodical *The Jabberwock*, whose editor, Brenda Girvin, encouraged her to write. From 1905 onward she began to contribute short stories and serials to magazines, much of her work appearing in *Home Chat*. On 10 June 1909 she married the novelist (George) Oliver *Onions (1873–1961), whom she had met when she was at the Slade. In 1918 Onions changed the family name to Oliver in order to protect their two sons from possible ridicule. He was afterwards known as George Oliver, although he continued to sign his works Oliver Onions.

In 1912 a *Home Chat* serial by Berta Ruck, 'His Official Fiancée', attracted the interest of a book publisher, who asked her to expand it to a full-length novel. This she did,

Amy Roberta Ruck (1878–1978), by Emil Otto Hoppé, 1927

with advice from her husband, and the book was published in 1913 under the same title as the serial. It had an immediate success in Britain and the United States and marked the start of her long career as a popular novelist. She was a prolific writer and continued to publish between one and three books per year, as well as serials and an appreciable amount of journalism, up to the early 1960s. Her last novel was *Shopping for a Husband* (1967). Most of these books had what *Home Chat* termed 'a strong love interest' and they followed a similar Cinderella motif, whereby, after many vicissitudes, a neglected or impoverished heroine gained a rich and loving husband. Her novels are lively and full of verve and she had no extravagant notion regarding the merit of her work as literature. The titles of her novels suggest their disarming innocence: *The Girls at his Billet* (1916), *The Unkissed Bride* (1929), and *He Learnt about Women* (1940). Her place as one of the leading popular romantic novelists of her day is attested, diversely, by the appearance in 1920 of a *Berta Ruck Birthday Book*, and in her inclusion, in 1930, among those best-selling authors approached by Q. D. Leavis during her work on *Fiction and the Reading Public* (1932). Barbara Cartland condensed a number of her novels. In addition to these romances Ruck celebrated her Welsh blood in four works of anecdotal reminiscences, from *A Smile from the Past* (1959) to *Ancestral Voices* (1972).

Between the wars Berta Ruck's steady life of writing was conducted in the family home, first at Henley, later at Hampstead in London—interspersed with periods of travel in Europe and the United States, where her books continued to be popular. After 1939 she moved back to Merioneth and, co-opted as a lecturer in adult education for the forces, discovered a talent for public speaking. This she continued after the war, eventually giving broadcasts on Welsh regional programmes of the BBC and appearing in BBC television's *Yesterday's Witness* series in 1970.

After her husband's death in 1961 Berta Ruck continued to live a busy life—vigour and longevity stemming, she believed, from plenty of open-air bathing, summer and winter alike. She celebrated her one hundredth birthday on 2 August 1978 and died shortly afterwards on 11 August at Bryntegawel, her home in Aberdyfi, Merioneth.

BRIAN ALDERSON, *rev.* SAYONI BASU

Sources B. Ruck, *A trickle of Welsh blood* (1967) · B. Ruck, *A storyteller tells the truth: reminiscences and notes* (1935) · Blain, Clements & Grundy, *Feminist comp.* · *The Times* (12 Aug 1978) · B. Ruck, *An asset to Wales* (1970) · B. Ruck, *Ancestral voices* (1972) · R. Anderson, 'Ruck, Berta', *Twentieth-century romance and historical writers*, ed. L. Henderson, 2nd edn (1990) · W. Bousfield, 'Onions, (George) Oliver', *Twentieth-century romance and historical writers*, ed. L. Henderson, 2nd edn (1990) · *CGPLA Eng. & Wales* (1978) · private information (1986) · m. cert.

Archives NL Wales | BL, corresp. with Marie Stopes, Add. MS 58498 · NL Wales, letters to John Cledwyn Hughes · UCL, Ogden MSS

Likenesses J. Russell & Sons, photograph, *c.*1915, NPG · E. O. Hoppé, photograph, 1927, Mansell Collection, London [*see illus.*] · O. Onions, drawing, priv. coll. · A. R. Ruck, self-portrait, priv. coll.

Wealth at death £7225: probate, 27 Oct 1978, *CGPLA Eng. & Wales*

Rucker, Sir Arthur Nevil (1895–1991), public servant, was born on 20 June 1895 at 19 Gledhow Gardens, Kensington, the only son of Sir Arthur William *Rücker (1848–1915), a physicist, and his second wife, Thereza Charlotte, *née* Story Maskelyne (1863–1941), a promoter of household science teaching [*see* Rucker, Thereza Charlotte]. A scientist of high distinction, Sir Arthur Rücker senior eventually became the first principal of the University of London. He had earlier been sought by Joseph Chamberlain for a similar post at the University of Birmingham, a fact which formed a bond between his son and Chamberlain's.

After leaving Marlborough College in the summer of 1914 Arthur Rücker joined the War Office and worked there unpaid; from 1915 to the end of the war he fought bravely in France and was twice wounded during his service with the Suffolk regiment. After a year of study at Trinity College, Cambridge, he passed the first part of the mathematical tripos, joined the Ministry of Health as an assistant principal, and informed his colleagues there that he wished to drop the umlaut from the spelling of his name. He married on 7 November 1922 Elsie Marion (1899–1991), daughter of George Broadbent, a London solicitor. They had two sons and two daughters.

At the Ministry of Health, Rucker's zeal and aptitude for business were soon noticed. Douglas Veale, then a senior figure in the ministry and later registrar of the University of Oxford, recorded: 'I have a very high opinion of Mr. Rucker's ability and enthusiasm' (note by D. Veale, January 1924, PRO, MH 107/62). Within a few years Rucker had been appointed private secretary to the minister of health, first Neville Chamberlain and then in succession

Sir Arthur Nevil Rucker (1895–1991), by Walter Stoneman, 1944

Arthur Greenwood, Chamberlain again, Sir Edward Hilton Young, and finally Sir Kingsley Wood. Promoted early to the rank of assistant secretary in 1935, and appointed CBE in 1937, he became director of establishments and public relations at the ministry in the latter year.

Just as Chamberlain admired Rucker's efficiency, industry, and acuity, so Rucker valued Chamberlain's integrity, businesslike habits, and capacity to set a high standard to the civil service. When Rucker was called to be principal private secretary to the prime minister in the spring of 1939, the minister of health wrote: 'We have all admired and appreciated your work and it is no surprise to us to perceive that others have been watching you also' (Walter Elliot to Rucker, 6 May 1939, PRO, MH 107/62). For sixteen agonizing months Rucker served Chamberlain faithfully. Like the prime minister, he believed that Britain's fault had been to let her diplomacy outrun her strength, and to threaten what she could not fulfil; he was convinced that the government had been right not to precipitate a war with Germany in the autumn of 1938, and equally right to give a guarantee to Poland in 1939. Harbouring no illusions about Russia, he was surprised neither by the Nazi–Soviet pact nor by the invasion of Finland. His junior colleague in the private office, John Colville, noted in December 1939:

> Alone with Arthur at No. 10 in the morning. He has a most endearing personality and is extraordinarily thorough. At the same time, unlike most people who are thorough and conscientious, he is full of ideas and inspired by ideals. (Colville's diary, 9 Dec 1939, Colville papers 1/1, CAC Cam.)

Having unhesitatingly elected to remain with Chamberlain when he became lord president of the council in May 1940, Rucker returned to the Ministry of Health later that year. Thence he was 'seconded for special duties' in Cairo. Churchill had decided to establish a minister of state in the Middle East, with wide-ranging tasks which included liaison with the commanders-in-chief and the British embassy in Cairo. The new minister, Oliver Lyttelton, resembled Rucker in no outward particulars, Lyttelton being enormously tall and ebullient, Rucker small and restrained. Nevertheless, Lyttelton made Rucker head of his private office and remembered gratefully his saint-like character and high ability. 'He was calm and conscientious. I learnt later that when he put his foot down, he trod on no one's toes, and his decisions did not lead to discussion and resentment' (*Memoirs of Lord Chandos*, 225). For the better part of two years Rucker threw himself wholeheartedly into complicated and delicate tasks, first under Lyttelton and then under his successor. For these exceptional services he was appointed KCMG in 1942. The only diversion of which there is a record is that he learned to fly and gained his pilot's licence after fourteen hours' instruction.

On his return to the Ministry of Health as deputy secretary in 1943, Rucker was immediately plunged into the preparations for a national health service. Tireless and inventive in seeking the compromises which would lead to an agreed scheme, he had perhaps hoped to become the permanent head of the ministry in 1945. Contrary to what has often been stated, his relations with the new minister, Aneurin Bevan, were good; but there was some incompatibility of temperament, and it is unlikely that Rucker's close association with Chamberlain eased his relations with Bevan. Rucker pressed the case for retaining the voluntary hospitals. Equally, he did not wish to remove control of other hospitals from local authorities, which would constitute the biggest reduction yet made in their powers; and he attached high importance to the close relations between them and the ministry, which they had hitherto regarded as their protector and interpreter in Whitehall. Nevertheless, Rucker entirely recognized the right of the minister to decide differently, as Bevan did when he elected to nationalize almost all hospitals. The legislation passed through parliament during 1946, but was not implemented until the summer of 1948.

Rucker had by then received the offer of a post with the United Nations. His time in Cairo had helped to fit him for this, though he and his family accepted the long separations with sadness. He became deputy director-general of the International Refugee Organization in 1948, grappling with enormous post-war problems in that context, and then deputy agent-general of the UN Korean Reconstruction Agency in 1951, where his services were warmly appreciated and eventually recognized by the award of the Korean order of Diplomatic Merit. Later he acted for six years (1956–62) as deputy chairman of the Stevenage new town corporation and then for four years (1962–6) as its chairman. To provide decent housing, not least for those in need, Rucker believed to be one of the first duties of a civilized society. He was a leading member of the committee which produced the Milner Holland report of 1965 on housing in the slums of London; this played a crucial part in persuading successive governments to support housing associations. A founder of the World of Property Housing Trust, which later changed its name to Sanctuary, he also rendered devoted service to Help the Aged, Hungarian refugees, the Commonwealth War Graves Commission, and the University of Wales, which awarded him an honorary doctorate in 1965.

To the end Rucker remained kindly, understanding of others' difficulties, and insistent upon high standards of efficiency and probity. He died at the Curridge House Nursing Home, near Newbury, Berkshire, on 12 July 1991, Lady Rucker having predeceased him by a few weeks. There is a memorial to them both at the parish church in the Berkshire village of Yattendon, Rucker's home for most of his life. They were survived by their four children. DAVID DILKS

Sources files of the ministry of health, incl. Rucker's personal file, PRO, MH 107/62, and MH 77/25, 80/30, 80/34 • J. R. Colville, *The fringes of power* (1985) • Lord Chandos [O. Lyttelton, first Viscount Chandos], *The memoirs of Lord Chandos: an unexpected view from the summit* (1962) • F. Honigsbaum, *Health, happiness and security: the creation of the national health service* (1989) • J. E. Prater, *The making of the national health service* (1981) • C. Webster, *The health services since the war*, 1 (1988) • *The Times* (17 July 1991) • *Daily Telegraph* (20 July 1991) • personal knowledge (2004) • private information (2004) • *WWW* • b. cert. • m. cert. • d. cert.
Archives Churchill College, Cambridge, diary of Sir J. R. Colville • PRO, London, records of the Ministry of Health, MH/107/62, MH77/25, 80/30/80/34 • U. Birm., papers of Neville Chamberlain
Likenesses W. Stoneman, photograph, 1944, NPG [*see illus.*] • photograph, repro. in *The Times* • photographs, priv. coll.
Wealth at death £109,567: probate, 20 March 1992, *CGPLA Eng. & Wales*

Rücker, Sir Arthur William (1848–1915), physicist, was born on 23 October 1848 at 3 Nelson Terrace, Clapham Common, Surrey, the eldest in the family of three sons and three daughters of Daniel Henry Rücker the younger (1816–1890), merchant of colonial produce, of London, and his wife, Mary Antoinette (1825–1905), eldest daughter of John D. Williams, a merchant of Coolock, co. Dublin. Educated at Clapham grammar school, Rücker went to Brasenose College, Oxford (1867), with an open mathematical scholarship, taking first-class honours in mathematical moderations and the junior university mathematical scholarship (1869), and first-class honours in mathematics (1870) and natural science (1871).

Awarded an open mathematical fellowship at Brasenose in 1871, Rücker was appointed mathematical lecturer at Brasenose and demonstrator at the Clarendon Laboratory, but when the Yorkshire College of Science was founded in Leeds in 1874 he moved to become their professor of mathematics and physics, and in 1876 he gave up his fellowship on marrying, on 5 July, Marian (1852–1878), second daughter of John Deakin Heaton, physician, of Claremont, Leeds. She died following the birth of their daughter Olive in 1878. In 1886 Rücker was appointed professor of physics at the Royal College of Science, London. He subsequently assisted the incorporation of the greater

London colleges within London University and, as a result, became the first principal in 1901, holding the position until retirement in 1908.

Rücker's research topics included thermal expansion of liquids (1876–84); properties of thin liquid films (1877–93), jointly with A. W. Reinold; and electromagnetism (1855–1901). His major contribution was undoubtedly to undertake, jointly with Thomas Thorpe, a series of magnetic surveys of the British Isles (1883–92) which significantly advanced contemporary interpretation methods, and to obtain the first measurements of the magnetic susceptibility of rocks (1890–98).

A good-humoured, patient man of great personal charm, Rücker was an energetic and skilled administrator and an excellent public speaker. His hobbies included rambling, ornithology, sketching, photography, horticulture, and astronomy, and he acquired a competency in the Welsh language. He stood unsuccessfully as a Liberal Unionist candidate for parliament in the 1885 and 1886 elections in North Leeds and the Pudsey division of Yorkshire.

In recognition of his work on thin films and terrestrial magnetism Rücker was awarded the royal medal of the Royal Society in 1891 and became president of the permanent committee on terrestrial magnetism and atmospheric electricity of the International Meteorological Conference in 1896. He was awarded the honorary degrees of doctor of science from Oxford, Cambridge, Manchester, Leeds, and Belfast and LLD from Glasgow and Edinburgh; he was knighted in 1902. Elected a fellow of the Royal Society in 1884, he was on the council (1887–9, 1894, 1898–9) and secretary (1896–1901). He was also treasurer of the British Association (1891–8) and its president (1901), and president of the Physical Society (1893–5). Rücker married, on 7 September 1892, Thereza Charlotte Story Maskelyne (1863–1941) [see Rucker, Thereza Charlotte], third daughter of Mervyn Herbert Nevil Story-*Maskelyne of Wroughton, Wiltshire, keeper of minerals at the British Museum. They had one son, Sir Arthur Nevil *Rucker (1895–1991). In retirement Rücker and his wife concerned themselves with the teaching of home science at King's College for Women. Rücker died on 1 November 1915 at his home, Everington House, Everington Lane, Yattendon, Berkshire and was buried on 5 November in the church of St Peter and St Paul, Yattendon.

RICHARD J. HOWARTH, rev.

Sources T. E. T. [T. E. Thorpe], *PRS*, 92A (1916), xxi–xlv • *The Times* (2 Nov 1915), 15c [memoir] • *The Times* (5 Nov 1915), 11b [funeral] • b. cert. • m. certs. • d. cert. • N. B. Harte, *The University of London, 1836–1986: an illustrated history* (1986)
Archives CUL, corresp. with Lord Kelvin; letters to Sir George Stokes • Oxf. U. Mus. NH, letters to Sir E. B. Poulton
Likenesses drawing (pen and ink), c.1906, repro. in *Harper's Monthly Magazine* (Oct 1906), 701 • Lafayette, photograph, U. Lond. • photograph, repro. in Thorpe, *PRS*
Wealth at death £40,224 2s. 8d.: resworn probate, 15 Jan 1916, *CGPLA Eng. & Wales*

Rucker [*née* Story Maskelyne], **Thereza Charlotte**, Lady **Rucker** (1863–1941), promoter of household science teaching, was born on 3 June 1863, at 112 Gloucester Terrace, London, the youngest of three daughters of Mervyn Herbert Nevil Story *Maskelyne (1823–1911), professor of mineralogy at Oxford, and his wife, Thereza Mary Dillwyn Llewelyn (1834–1926), daughter of John Dillwyn and Mary Llewelyn.

Although educated at home, Thereza took her studies very seriously, keeping notes of her work in a diary; she also attended classes in English literature and German at Bedford College, and took correspondence courses from Edinburgh and Oxford universities. With a lively intelligence, exemplified by an extraordinary ability to do mental arithmetic, she also assisted her father with his research and public activities. She married Arthur William *Rücker (1848–1915), first principal of the University of London, on 7 September 1892, being his second wife; they had one son, Sir Arthur Nevil *Rucker (1895–1991). Her husband was knighted in 1902.

Lady Rucker, together with Alice Ravenhill and Hilda Oakeley, was one of the main forces behind the establishment of a course in 'home science' at King's College for Women, London, in 1908. The course became a London degree subject in 1920 and led to the establishment of King's College of Household and Social Science in 1928. A devout Anglican who attended church services with unfailing regularity, she believed that women had a duty to look after their homes and families, but felt that they should be supported in those roles by having a thorough education. Her interest in the household science course, which offered a three-year scientific training combined with practical domestic arts, was underpinned by this view, as she thought that women should have the opportunity to choose a university education which had relevance for their lives as wives and mothers, but also as a professional training for the new careers opening at the time in social work, health visiting, and institutional management.

Lady Rucker was keenly interested in nature and was a talented gardener, with an encyclopaedic knowledge of wild flowers and birds. She was also a proficient pianist and needlewoman, and a lover of intellectual word games. A highly energetic and disciplined woman with a natural talent for teaching, she believed that time should not be wasted, and keenly organized games and other occupations for her grandchildren. She served for many years as president of the Women's Institute in Yattendon, and was a central figure in the area's social life. Despite her involvement in the household science movement, she was sceptical of modern inventions—she disliked motor cars, and was concerned to keep electrical plugs in their sockets in case the electricity should 'escape' onto the carpets. Slim and attractive as a young woman, in later life she dressed for warmth rather than elegance. Lady Rucker died of a heart attack at her home, Everington House, Yattendon, near Newbury, Berkshire, on 20 December 1941. There is a memorial to her at Yattendon parish church.

NANCY L. BLAKESTAD

Sources N. L. Blakestad, 'King's College of Household and Social Science and the household science movement in English higher education, c.1908–1939', DPhil diss., U. Oxf., 1994 · N. Marsh, *The history of Queen Elizabeth College: one hundred years of university education in Kensington* (1986) · V. Morton, *Oxford rebels: the life and friends of Nevil Story Maskelyne, 1823–1911* (1987) · T. Rücker, 'Lady Rücker's address', *Bedford College Magazine* (Dec 1906), 7–13 · N. L. Blakestad, 'King's College of Household and Social Science and the origins of dietetics education', *Nutrition in Britain: science, scientists, and politics in the twentieth century*, ed. D. F. Smith (1997), 75–98 · N. G. Annan, 'The intellectual aristocracy', *Studies in social history: a tribute to G. M. Trevelyan*, ed. J. H. Plumb (1955), 241–87 · M. J. Tuke, *A history of Bedford College for Women, 1849–1937* (1939) · T. Rücker, 'President's address: ATDS annual meeting, 9 May 1908', *Education* (22 May 1908), 378–80 · private information · d. cert. · m. cert. · b. cert.
Likenesses photograph, repro. in Blakestad, 'King's College of Household and Social Science'
Wealth at death £9385 7s. 5d.: resworn probate, 1942, *CGPLA Eng. & Wales*

Rud, Thomas (1667/8–1733), schoolmaster and librarian, baptized at Stockton-on-Tees on 2 January 1668, was the first son of Thomas Rudd (1641–1719), curate of Stockton, afterwards vicar of Norton and rector of Long Newton, all in co. Durham, and his wife, Alice, daughter of Thomas Watson of Stockton. After being educated at Durham grammar school, he was admitted as subsizar at Trinity College, Cambridge, on 2 February 1684, and graduated BA in 1688; he proceeded MA in 1691. From 1691 to 1699 he was headmaster of his old school at Durham. At Sherburn near Durham he married, on 8 August 1696, Isabel Hendry, daughter of Cuthbert Hendry of Shincliffe, near Durham. They had several children. From 1699 to 1709 Rud was headmaster at Newcastle grammar school, where he revived its library, and master of St Mary's Hospital. In 1700 two editions were printed at Cambridge of a Latin syntax and prosody compiled for the use of his scholars; the work was reprinted there in 1707.

In 1710 Rud returned to Durham School until 1711, when he was instituted to the vicarage of St Oswald, where he catalogued the library left to it by a predecessor, John Cock. From 1716 to 1725 he was librarian to the dean and chapter. He moved in 1725 to the vicarage of Northallerton, and in 1729 to the rectory of Washington, co. Durham. He was collated, on 9 July 1728, as prebendary of the fifth stall at Ripon collegiate church, and retained these two preferments until his death.

Rud compiled with much labour and learning, and with beautiful penmanship, a catalogue of the manuscripts at Durham Cathedral, which he completed at Northallerton on 10 November 1727. It was printed for the dean and chapter under the editorship of the Revd James Raine and, with an appendix by him, in 1825. It was one of the first such catalogues which consistently assigned an approximate dating to each volume or portion thereof, and with great reliability. Rud also, probably previously, made a catalogue of the manuscripts, and a subject catalogue of the printed books, in the episcopal (Bishop Cosin's) library, Durham.

To Thomas Bedford's edition of the chronicle of Symeon of Durham, *De exordio atque procursu Dunhelmensis ecclesiæ* (1732), there was prefixed a Latin dissertation by Rud (completed in 1722), proving, in opposition to the views of Selden, that Symeon, and not Turgot, was its author. Rud contributed several articles signed T. R., chiefly relating to Greek inscriptions, to the two volumes of *Miscellaneous Observations upon Authors, Ancient and Modern*, which were edited by John Jortin in 1731–2. A copy of Beza's New Testament (1582), at the British Library (466.9.5), has many manuscript notes by Rud and by his brother Edward Rud (1677–1727), fellow of Trinity College, Cambridge.

Rud died on 17 March 1733 aged sixty-five and was buried in Washington, co. Durham, on 19 March 1733.

W. P. COURTNEY, *rev.* A. I. DOYLE

Sources C. S. Earle and L. A. Body, eds., *Durham School register: to June, 1912*, 2nd edn (1912), 4, 21–2, 98 · Venn, *Alum. Cant.* · *GM*, 1st ser., 3 (1733), 157 · A. R. Laws, *Schola Novocastrensis*, 2 (1932), 3–6 · B. Mains and A. Tuck, *The Royal Grammar School* (1986), 43, 327–8, 330 · M. A. Rudd, *Records of the Rudd family* (1930), 233–4 · parish register (baptism), Stockton-on-Tees, St Thomas's, 2 Jan 1668 · parish register (marriage), Sherburn Hospital, 8 Aug 1696 · parish register (burial), Washington, 19 March 1733 · [J. T. Fowler], ed., *Memorials of the church of SS Peter and Wilfrid, Ripon*, 2, SurtS, 78 (1886), 315–16 · J. Brand, *The history and antiquities of the town and county of the town of Newcastle upon Tyne*, 1 (1789), 84, 95 · R. Surtees, *The history and antiquities of the county palatine of Durham*, 4/2 (1840), 107 · Nichols, *Illustrations*, 5.121–2 · *Catalogi veteres librorum ecclesiae cathedralis Dunelmi / Catalogues of the library of Durham cathedral*, SurtS, 7 (1838), 136–91 · D. F. McKenzie, *Cambridge University Press, 1696–1712: a bibliographical study*, 2 vols. (1966), vol. 1, pp. 68, 159, 165, 190, 300–01 · Wing, *STC*, R2171B–C · *VCH Durham*, 1.382–3 · J. Raine, ed., *Codicum manuscriptorum Ecclesiae Cathedralis Dunelmensis catalogus classicus* (1825)

Archives Bodl. Oxf., letters · Durham Cathedral, old catalogues, notebook, and letters · NL Wales, letters · U. Durham L., catalogues of Cosin Library and Cock Library, St Oswald's | Durham RO, church registers, Durham, St Oswald and Washington, and notebook for St Oswald's

Wealth at death left leasehold lands and tenements to son, charged with £40 p.a. to wife; £500 to daughter: will, proved 24 March 1733

Rudborne, Thomas. *See* Rodeburne, Thomas (*d.* 1442).

Rudborne, Thomas (*fl.* 1447–1454), Benedictine monk and historian, has been called junior to distinguish him from his namesake Thomas Rodeburne (Rudborne), the bishop of St David's (*d.* 1442). Recorded as a monk of St Swithun's, Winchester, in 1447, he wrote histories concerning St Swithun's and Durham Cathedral. For the latter, covering the years 1071–83, he borrowed the *Liber privilegiorum* of the church from Robert Neville, bishop of Durham (1438–57). On St Swithun's, his most substantial work was the *Historia major … ecclesiae Wintoniensis* (LPL, MS 183; Wharton, 1.179–286), finished in 1454, which traced the history of the monastery from 164. The fifteenth-century manuscript (LPL, MS 183) stops at 1138, but the work probably continued further. Rudborne also wrote the *Historia minor* (Clongowes Wood College) sometimes known as the *Breviarium* or *Medulla chronicorum*, which recounted the history of England from Brutus to 1234, with particular attention to the lives of benefactors of St Swithun's and other monasteries. In 1454 he wrote *Annales breves ecclesiae Wintoniensis*, from Brutus to Henry VI.

Another work, sometimes known as the *Epitome* of the *Historia major*, was probably by Rudborne, but is sometimes ascribed to John of Exeter. Also called the *Liber historialis*, or *Book of the Foundation*, it was cited in evidence by the monks at the time of the dissolution. The fifteenth-century scribe of the earliest extant manuscript (BL, Add. MS 29436, fols. 4–9*v*) also annotated the cartulary of St Swithun's, the Codex Wintoniensis (BL, Add. MS 15350). As Rudborne can be shown to have used the codex, as a source for the *Historia major*, it is possible that he was this annotator of the codex. If so, the fifteenth-century manuscript of the *Epitome* may be an autograph.

Rudborne utilized some documents, but mostly preferred to cite previous authors. In the *Historia major* he cited these very precisely and often quoted long passages. This feature is also noticeable in the *Epitome*. His contemporary the antiquary John Rous called him 'the most learned man of his times in the chronicles of the English' (Gransden, 322). One manuscript that he used, an Old English Bede belonging to Southwick Priory, can now be identified as part of BL, Cotton MS Otho B.xi. Although at least one of the sources he cited (Vigilantius, *De basilica Petri*) was probably a fabrication, it had been used earlier by the compiler of the *Liber de Hyda*, who also, like Rudborne, cited the work of Gerard of Cornwall, perhaps another fabrication. Elsewhere, Rudborne occasionally digressed from his main theme, tracing the origin of the Benedictine order, refuting the foundation legend of Glastonbury Abbey, or naming the English delegation to the Council of Florence (for which he is a unique source).

Rudborne's work is of more importance for the study of fifteenth-century monastic historiography than for any transmission of facts about earlier periods. He can be shown to have made interpolations into one Anglo-Saxon charter that he copied (*AS chart.*, S 818), suggesting that caution should be employed in using other texts quoted in his works.

ALEXANDER R. RUMBLE

Sources A. Gransden, *Historical writing in England*, 2 (1982), 322, 394–8, 493–4 · [H. Wharton], ed., *Anglia sacra*, 1 (1691), xxvi–viii · A. R. Rumble, 'The structure and reliability of the *Codex Wintoniensis*', 2 vols., PhD diss., U. Lond., 1980, vol. 2, pp. 5–6, 46–7 · J. Greatrex, 'Thomas Rudborne, monk of Winchester, and the Council of Florence', *Schism, heresy and religious protest*, ed. D. Baker, SCH, 9 (1972), 171–6 · J. Greatrex, ed., *The register of the common seal of the priory of St Swithun, Winchester, 1345–1497*, Hampshire RS, 2 (1978), 100 · N. R. Ker, ed., *Catalogue of manuscripts containing Anglo-Saxon* (1957), 234 · St Swithun's dissolution documents, 1530s, BL, Harley MS 358, fols. 16–17, 60–70 · *AS chart.*, S

Archives BL, Add. MS 15350 · BL, Add. MS 29436, fols. 4–9*v* · Clongowes Wood College, co. Kildare, 'Historia minor' · LPL, MS 183

Rudd, Anthony (1548/9–1615), bishop of St David's, was born in Yorkshire before 9 June 1549. He was admitted *socius minor* at Trinity College, Cambridge, on 6 September 1569, and *socius major* on 7 April 1570. He graduated BA (1566–7), MA (1570), and BTh (1577), and incorporated in that degree at Oxford on 9 July the same year. He proceeded DTh at Cambridge in 1583. At an unknown date, he married Anne Dalton; three sons, Anthony, Robert, and Richard, survived.

After a brief stay at Shudy Camps, Cambridgeshire, Rudd was rector of Stathern, Leicestershire (1579–84); and on 10 January 1584 he was installed as dean of Gloucester, an office he held until his appointment as bishop of St David's. He was consecrated by Archbishop Whitgift at

Lambeth on 9 June 1594, when his age was stated to be forty-five, and installed at St David's on 24 July 1594. He was 'A most excellent preacher, whose sermons were very acceptable to Queen Elizabeth'; and the queen on one occasion, after hearing him preach, 'commanded Archbishop Whitgift to signifie unto him that he should be his successor' (Fuller, 10.68–9). An invitation to preach for the queen in 1596 was a prelude to disaster, however. Whitgift, thought to be 'too mortified a man intentionally to lay a train to blow up this archbishop-designed', advised Rudd that the queen 'preferred plain sermons, which came home to her heart'. Choosing the text 'O teach us to number our days that we may incline our hearts unto wisdom', he 'touched on the Infirmities of Age' and bade the queen note 'how Age had furrowed her face and besprinkled her hair with its meal' (ibid., 10.69). Elizabeth declared that 'he should have kept his arithmetic to himself' and said roundly 'I see that the greatest clerks are not the wisest men' (Neale, 220). The prospect of Canterbury disappeared.

Rudd was a conscientious bishop. In his administration of the diocese he 'wrought much on the Welsh by his wisdom and won their affection' (Fuller, 10.69). On his arrival he found the bishop's palaces ruined and decayed and not fit for a bishop to use. He took part in the Hampton Court conference in 1604 and showed some sympathy for the moderate views expressed by Reynolds. Rudd opposed the oath framed against simony in the convocation of 1604, arguing that patron and clerk should both take it. On occasion, he supplied the government with information on the recusants in his diocese.

In his will, dated 25 January 1615, Rudd made many charitable bequests. He died aged sixty-six on 7 March 1615 and was buried at Llangathen church, Carmarthenshire, 'in which parish he had purchased a good estate and built a handsome seat (with a very decent chapel with a curious pulpit, ornamented with painted glass) called Aberglasney' (Yardley, 103). His wife, Anne, survived him. The estate continued in the family until 1701.

DAVID WALKER

Sources A. Rudd, *A sermon preached at Richmond before Queene Elizabeth* (1596) · E. Yardley, *Menevia sacra*, ed. F. Green (1927) · T. Fuller, *The church-history of Britain*, 11 pts in 1 (1655) · G. Williams, *Wales and the Reformation* (1997) · J. E. Neale, *Queen Elizabeth* (1934) · *DNB* · Venn, *Alum. Cant.*, 1/1
Likenesses tomb, Llangathen church, Wales

Rudd, Charles Dunell (1844–1916), businessman and associate of Cecil Rhodes, was born at Hanworth Hall, Hanworth, Norfolk, on 22 October 1844, the third son and fourth child of Henry Rudd (*b.* 1808) of Sutton Hall, Surrey, a wealthy London barrister and South Africa merchant, and his first wife, Mary, *née* Stanbridge (*b.* 1812). The Rudds were 'an ancient family of the lesser gentry' (M. A. Rudd, preface), and Henry Rudd was from the Hartley, Westmorland, branch. Rudd was educated at a private school at Wadhurst, Sussex (1853–7), and at Harrow School (1858–63) where he was a successful athlete and cricketer. Failing to win a Balliol scholarship, he went to Trinity College,

Charles Dunell Rudd (1844–1916), by unknown photographer

Cambridge (1863–5), where he won the rackets championship and played rackets for Cambridge against Oxford. He left without taking a degree. His version was that he trained for long-distance running, his health broke down, and he left on medical advice. Reportedly he was infected with tuberculosis (possibly this caused his later munificent donation to a hospital for consumptives).

Late in 1865 Rudd went to South Africa, by his own account on medical advice. He hunted and travelled, and from 1867 was involved in various business enterprises in and beyond Cape Colony, including failure as a merchant in Pietermaritzburg, and prospecting for diamonds. He was then 'a tall erect man, slender in build, having fine dark eyes, a wispy mustache, and thick fair hair, with a well-trimmed black beard' (J. T. McNish, *The Glittering Road*, 1970, p. 29). Early in 1868 he married Frances Leighton (*c.*1846–1896), daughter of Edward Chiappini, from an old Cape family. They had three sons and one daughter, Evelyn ('Doll'), who in June 1903 married Sir Eldon Gorst.

In 1871 Rudd went to the Kimberley diamond diggings and unsuccessfully dug a claim. He worked for R. E. Wallace & Co., which was involved in numerous commercial ventures, and with which his elder brother Thomas (1831–1902), a successful merchant and senior partner in Jones, Rudd & Co. of Port Elizabeth, was connected. After Wallace & Co. was liquidated in 1874 Rudd remained in Kimberley as a commission agent selling provisions from his brother's firm, and also involved in other ventures. Despite vicissitudes—including enteric fever and the theft in

1872 of a parcel of diamonds for which he was responsible, an expensive setback—he was fairly successful as a trader, insurance agent, and diamond dealer, with useful connections in Cape Town and London. In late 1871 or early 1872 he met Cecil Rhodes, and by March 1872 they had become friends and partners. Presumably Rhodes, younger and less experienced, learned from Rudd, and he relied on Rudd's steady, cautious practicality, trustworthiness, and loyalty. They worked their claims, bought more claims, dealt in diamonds, operated pumping and ice-making machinery, and sold ice-cream. On the diamond fields pumping was essential but machinery scarce, and their pumping contracts were crucial to Rhodes's and Rudd's rise. Rudd also continued his own varied business interests including insurance, wire rope, machinery, and those two staples of frontier life, alcoholic drinks and corrugated iron. While Rhodes attended Oriel College, Oxford, intermittently from 1873 to 1881, Rudd supervised their interests at Kimberley. They became rich: in 1880 they may have been worth notionally £50,000 each, though still lacking working capital. In 1880 they, with others, formed the De Beers Mining Company which, following amalgamations, became in March 1888 De Beers Consolidated Mines Ltd; Rudd was one of the directors. From 1883 to 1885 he was member for Kimberley of the legislative assembly—the 'Member for De Beers' (Wheatcroft, 94)—specifically to obtain legislation wanted by the diamond interest on the control of African labour, the compound system, liquor, and illicit diamond buying. Having achieved this he did not stand again: he wrote that he 'did not care for politics' (A. Rudd, 8). In 1881 he became a partner with Edward Wallace Tarry in E. W. Tarry & Co., the largest machinery importer on the diamond fields; when it became a joint stock company in 1884 he held a quarter interest.

In late July or early August 1886 Rhodes and Rudd went to the Witwatersrand, where gold had been discovered. Possibly owing to Rudd's caution and suspicion the area was 'salted'—Hans Sauer, who accompanied them, criticized 'the almost unbelievable stupidity of Rudd' (Wheatcroft, 90)—they missed lucrative opportunities, but acquired interests in goldmining there. Rudd became primarily concerned with gold interests, including the raising of the necessary large capital in Britain. He was largely responsible for the formation of Gold Fields of South Africa Ltd, registered in February 1887 with himself and Rhodes as managing directors and Rudd's brother Thomas, a director of the London Joint Stock Bank, as chairman. The risky flotation, without evidence of payable claims, when Rhodes was an unknown force in the City, resulted largely from Rudd's connection, through his brother, with the London Joint Stock Bank and other City firms, and gave the company 'the critical mass it needed' (Kynaston, 397). The company was so structured as to favour immensely Rhodes and Rudd, and apparently its London board knew little of some of Rhodes's activities in southern Africa. Following difficulties, and the opportunities of deep-level mining, in 1892 Charles Rudd reconstructed and revived it with new capital as Consolidated Gold Fields of South Africa, with himself still a leading director.

Rhodes, ambitious and imperialist, wanted to gain control, for himself and the British empire, of Zambezia—and especially its minerals—before the Boers, Portuguese, or Germans seized it. He hoped for a 'second Rand', and was alarmed by the July 1887 Grobler treaty obtained from Lobengula, king of the Ndebele (Matabele)—whose father Mzilikazi had conquered Matabeleland—by President Kruger's representative Pieter Grobler, which if implemented would have made the Ndebele kingdom a dependent ally of Transvaal. It was suspect, inadequately witnessed and, though kept secret by the Transvaal government, its existence was leaked. In January 1888 Rhodes sent John Larkin Fry to obtain a mineral concession from Lobengula; he failed. In August 1888 Rhodes sent a deputation, the odd trio of Rudd—possibly ignorant of Rhodes's greater purpose—Francis Robert ('Matabili') Thompson, and James Rochfort Maguire, to Lobengula. They reached Bulawayo on 20 September, and, competing with rival concession-hunters, negotiated at the royal kraal. They told the Ndebele the latter would be 'driven out of their country, if they did not get friends and arms in to help them' (C. Rudd, 62). After delays Lobengula granted them a concession (the 'Rudd concession'), signed on 30 October, by which in return for a cash income, rifles, ammunition, and an armed steamboat, the concessionaires were to receive exclusive mining, mineral, and ancillary rights (excepting the Tati concession) throughout Lobengula's domain. Rudd insisted the concession cover the territory up to the Zambezi ('Where is the Zambezi?', asked an induna), including Mashonaland. It was in the interest of Rhodes and his associates to exaggerate the extent of Lobengula's rule (though as F. C. Selous stated before being 'squared' by Rhodes with £2000, many Shona were not subject to Lobengula. Rudd and his party deceived Lobengula. According to the Revd Charles Daniel Helm of the London Missionary Society, who witnessed the concession, they said Rhodes's sole interest was in mining, and that no more than ten white men would come to work in Lobengula's country, who would obey him and be as his people. But, as Helm wrote to the society, 'these promises were not put in the concession' (Fripp and Hiller, 287). The oral version communicated to the Ndebele differed from the signed English-language document, largely drafted and handwritten by Rudd.

Returning through Bechuanaland, Rudd became lost without water, and almost died, but was saved by some Tswana, and reached Rhodes at Kimberley. Rhodes was jubilant. 'Our concession is so gigantic', he declared, 'it is like giving a man the whole of Australia' (Rotberg, 264). Lobengula attempted to repudiate the Rudd concession, sending a delegation to London and ordering the killing of Lotshe Hlabanga, the induna who had advised in favour of the concession, and his family and followers—over 300 persons. Nevertheless, despite criticism and opposition in Britain and South Africa, Rhodes used the concession to float the British South Africa Company, and to obtain from Lord Salisbury's government its royal charter in October

1889: Rudd owned 17,897 shares. The concession placed Rudd's name in history, and profited him. Contrary to what the British government and investing public had been misled into assuming—by what Lord Blake has called a '*suppressio veri* … one of Rhodes's least creditable actions' (Blake, 55)—ownership of the crucial concession was not vested in the new company, but retained by Rhodes, Rudd, and others through the Central Search Association, quietly established in 1889, which in 1890 became the United Concessions Company—in which Rudd owned 66,800 shares—from which the British South Africa Company bought the concession with a million chartered shares, worth millions of pounds on the rising market. When in 1891 Colonial Office officials realized they had been duped they advised the colonial secretary to consider revoking the concession, but neither the Salisbury government nor the following Liberal government revoked it.

Through the 1890s Rudd was mainly concerned with Gold Fields, dividing each year between its Cape Town and London offices. His role was largely raising capital and manipulating shareholders. A press report of the 1893 annual general meeting called him 'a speaker of the matter-of-fact rather than the peroration order' (A. Rudd, 50). In the 1890s Rudd disagreed with Rhodes on the running of Gold Fields and the use of its resources, and in March 1895 he protested he was no longer prepared to work with Rhodes. In October 1895 Rhodes appointed his elder brother, Colonel Frank Rhodes, as the company's Johannesburg representative, actually to assist Rhodes's plot to overthrow the Kruger regime. Rudd, though apparently unaware of this, objected to the appointment. He was apparently not involved in the conspiracy which culminated in the disastrous Jameson raid and Johannesburg rising (December 1895 to January 1896). How much he knew or suspected is not now known, but it is unlikely he was completely unaware. Possibly he turned a blind eye and waited. The Gold Fields Johannesburg organization was deeply involved: Frank Rhodes and John Hayes Hammond (their American mining engineer) were leading conspirators and used Gold Fields money, premises, and personnel, and the rebel provisional government was at Gold Fields Johannesburg headquarters. Following the raid Rudd asserted his ignorance of the conspiracy—he claimed the news 'came upon me like a thunder clap' (Macnab, 60) and that he had been 'most damnably treated' (Kubicek, 94)—and he acted quickly to dissociate himself and Gold Fields from it and to protect their interests. Though he did not fully break with Rhodes, their relations thereafter were apparently not close. Years later, according to his son, on his yacht near Mull, Rudd threw overboard a parcel and said, 'There goes the truth about the Jameson Raid' (A. Rudd, 48).

His wife died in 1896, and in 1898 Rudd married Corrie Maria (*c*.1874–1951), some thirty years younger than him, and the eldest daughter of his old Kimberley crony, Major Robert E. Wallace; they had two sons and a daughter. In 1902 Rudd retired, selling his Cape home and moving permanently back to Britain, and thereafter he enjoyed the

life of an Edwardian plutocrat. In 1896 he had bought the Ardnamurchan estate in west Argyll, and there he built two houses, Scottish baronial Glenborrodale Castle and his fishing lodge, Shielbridge, which had about twenty bedrooms. He owned a clipper-bowed, twenty-crew steam yacht, the *Mingary*, and a smaller yacht for fishing. He was reportedly 'well known in Scotland as a liberal landlord' (Fripp and Hiller, 151). He shunned publicity and, according to his son Alan, and presumably only if he gave to a political party fund, he was offered a peerage, but refused. He was a member of the Royal Company of Archers. He anonymously gave over £200,000 to the Mount Vernon Hospital (for consumptives) at Norwood, Middlesex. In summer 1916 he fell on rocks and broke several ribs. Following an operation in London on 14 November, he died on 15 November 1916 in a nursing home at 29 Wimpole Street, London, and was buried six days later at Acharacle churchyard, Argyll. His widow married William Rhodes, a nephew of Cecil Rhodes, but the marriage failed and they separated. Bevil Rudd (1894–1948), son of Rudd's eldest son, Percy (a director of De Beers), was a South African Rhodes scholar (Trinity College, 1913), served with the British army in the First World War (MC 1918), and won a gold medal (400 metres) for South Africa at the 1920 Antwerp Olympics.

Rudd was long overshadowed by Rhodes, beside whom he seemed pedestrian and limited. Oliver Ransford wrote that Rudd had 'a depressing lack of imagination' (Ransford, 181), and Thomas Pakenham that he was 'no genius' (Pakenham, 380). Yet he was a successful businessman and—though lacking Rhodes's vision, genius, and desperation—he had apparently been crucial to the rise of Rhodes, and all that that entailed. ROGER T. STEARN

Sources A. Rudd, *Charles Dunell Rudd, 1844–1916: a compendium of his life* (1981) • M. A. Rudd, *Records of the Rudd family* (1920) • R. I. Rotberg, *The founder: Cecil Rhodes and the pursuit of power* (1988) • A. Keppel-Jones, *Rhodes and Rhodesia: the white conquest of Zimbabwe, 1884–1902* (1983) • C. E. Fripp and V. W. Hiller, eds., *Gold and the gospel in Mashonaland, 1888* (1949) • DSAB • M. G. Dauglish, ed., *The Harrow School register, 1801–1900*, 2nd edn (1901) • Venn, *Alum. Cant.*, 2/5 • D. Kynaston, *The City of London*, 1 (1994) • R. Robinson, J. Gallagher, and A. Denny, *Africa and the Victorians* (1961); repr. (1967) • C. Newbury, 'Out of the pit: the capital accumulation of Cecil Rhodes', *Journal of Imperial and Commonwealth History*, 10 (1981–2), 25–49 • R. Turrell, 'Rhodes, De Beers and monopoly', *Journal of Imperial and Commonwealth History*, 10 (1981–2), 309–43 • C. Rudd, 'Diary of the trip … to Lobengula', 1887, Bodl. RH, MS Afr.s.794 • L. H. Gann, *A history of Southern Rhodesia: early days to 1934* (1965) • G. Wheatcroft, *The Randlords* (1985) • O. Ransford, *The rulers of Rhodesia: from earliest times to the referendum* (1968) • R. Blake, *A history of Rhodesia* (1977) • R. V. Kubicek, 'The Randlords in 1895: a reassessment', *Journal of British Studies*, 11/2 (1971–2), 84–103 • T. Pakenham, *The scramble for Africa, 1876–1912* (1991) • R. Macnab, *Gold their touchstone: gold fields of South Africa, 1887–1987* (1987) • 'The Gold Fields', 1887–1937, Consolidated Gold Fields of South Africa (1937) • J. Carruthers, ed., *The Jameson raid* (1996) • R. K. Rasmussen and S. C. Rubert, eds., *Historical dictionary of Zimbabwe*, 2nd edn (1990)

Archives Bodl. RH, diary of trip to King Lobengula | Brenthurst Library, Johannesburg, letters to C. J. Rhodes

Likenesses photograph, repro. in Rudd, *Charles Dunell Rudd*, frontispiece • photograph, repro. in Ransford, *Rulers of Rhodesia*, facing p. 135 • photograph, National Archives of Zimbabwe [*see illus.*]

Wealth at death £147,426 6s. 5d.: probate, 1 June 1917, *CGPLA Eng. & Wales*

Rudd, John (c.1498–1579), Church of England clergyman and cartographer, was born in Yorkshire. In 1515 he entered Clare College, Cambridge, and by 1520 had taken the degrees of BA and MA. Ordained to the priesthood in 1521, he subsequently became a fellow of St John's College, Cambridge, and graduated BTh in 1530.

During the religious changes of the 1530s Rudd initially adopted a clear anti-reformist stance, and in 1534 he was briefly imprisoned on the order of Thomas Cromwell. However, with the ascendancy of the conservative faction in the 1540s Rudd began to achieve a modest prominence, being nominated clerk of the closet, which brought him into close personal contact with Henry VIII. Before 1547 he had become vicar of the collegiate church of Norton in co. Durham, and a prebendary of Beverley, Burton upon Trent, and St Stephen's in Westminster, appointments which (with the exception of Norton) were lost owing to the dissolution of these colleges in 1548. However, Rudd appears to have gained the patronage of John Dudley, later duke of Northumberland, and he was compensated with a royal chaplaincy and prebends in the cathedrals of Durham (1550) and Winchester (1551). In 1551 he demonstrated his increasing devotion to the new doctrines by taking a wife, though this was to ensure deprivation from all his livings under Mary in 1554. However, after confessing his fault at Paul's Cross he was once more rewarded, this time with three Yorkshire livings, the vicarages of Dewsbury (1554) and Hornsea-cum-Riston (1557), and the rectory of Thornhill (1558).

Elizabeth's accession allowed Rudd to receive back his wife, along with his Durham prebend and the vicarage of Norton, on the resignation of Hornsea. In 1570 he resigned Dewsbury, having been presented to the wealthy Richmondshire rectory of Romaldkirk in 1569. It is difficult to penetrate Rudd's religious views with any certainty. Whether his survival was that of a cynical trimmer or one who had a paramount belief in the idea of the royal supremacy is impossible to determine, but he cannot have been a good parochial pastor because of his persistent plurality.

Rudd's promotions were probably attempts to remunerate a man who was of more value to the Tudor state as a cartographer than as a cleric. While he was imprisoned in 1534 he was working on a map of the Holy Land which was sent to Cromwell's confidant, Rowland Lee, in an attempt to secure his release. Rudd claimed that it was more accurate than any that had been made before, and there is a strong possibility that it is to be identified with the map which appears in the 1535 English Bible of Miles Coverdale. Released from prison, Rudd travelled round the country undertaking surveys and checking information at first hand. In 1561 he received a royal dispensation to be absent from his Durham prebend to finalize a map of England 'both fairer and more perfect and truer than it hath been hitherto' (Durham chapter records, register B, fol. 135). One of his assistants in this task was Christopher Saxton, who came from Dunningley near Dewsbury and

who was working as his servant in 1570. The completed work was possibly the map of the British Isles published by Gerardus Mercator in Duisburg in 1564.

Rudd married Isabel Whildon in 1551. They are known to have had three sons and three daughters. The eldest son, Edmund, died as a fellow of Clare College, Cambridge, in 1576. When an inventory was made of Edmund Rudd's possessions it included maps, and, perhaps significantly, an unfinished map and a drawing table, but it is not clear whether he was a cartographer in his own right, or was merely in possession of items 'on loan' from his father. John Rudd died at Durham in 1579 and was buried in the cathedral: his wife died at Durham in 1582, her inventory recording 'three maps' and 'one old map' among her possessions. DAVID MARCOMBE, *rev.*

Sources D. Marcombe, 'Saxton's apprenticeship: John Rudd, a Yorkshire cartographer', *Yorkshire Archaeological Journal*, 50 (1978), 171–5 · C. Delano-Smith, 'Son of Rudd: Edmund, another Tudor mapmaker?', *Map Collector* (1993), 38 · Durham chapter records (prior's kitchen), register B, fol. 135 · P. D. A. Harvey, *Maps in Tudor England* (1993)

Rudd [*née* Youngson], **Margaret Caroline** (b. c.1745, d. in or before 1798?), courtesan and accused forger, was born in Lurgan, co. Armagh. Much was written of her life and exploits but little can be verified. Her father, Patrick Youngson, was reported to have been an apothecary; her mother, Marjorie Stewart, was said to be the illegitimate child of a local landowner and linen merchant, John Stewart. Some accounts say that she was orphaned early and raised by her maternal uncle, the legitimate son of her mother's father. All agreed that she went to a boarding-school at Downpatrick, where she evinced both academic and flirtatious talents. At seventeen, she met and soon married Valentine Rudd, a young soldier, in Ireland as a recruiting officer. After leaving Ireland for England, the two soon spent Rudd's small patrimony, and, gossip had it, when the money was gone Mrs Rudd eloped with another young military man who was lodger in the house in which they lived.

It is unclear how and with whom Mrs Rudd spent the next several years; after her rise to fame many stories were told of this time, most of them improbable. It is likely that she set up as a courtesan, or 'demirep', of fashion, and, for a while at least, lived with Joseph Salvadore, an important international trader and merchant. In 1770 she met and soon began living with Daniel *Perreau (c.1734–1776) [*see under* Perreau, Robert], a bankrupt West Indies merchant and stock speculator of Huguenot descent. By 1775 they had had three children, and Mrs Rudd passed in the world as Mrs Daniel Perreau.

When, in March 1775, Daniel's identical twin brother, Robert Perreau, a well-established and trusted London apothecary, was found to have attempted to secure a bank loan on the basis of a forged bond, Mrs Rudd was soon implicated, and in fact denounced by both brothers, as the mastermind behind the plan. It emerged that a much more complex series of similar forgeries had occurred. When brought before the magistrates, Mrs Rudd asked for, and was granted, immunity from prosecution in order to testify against the brothers. Since forgery was a capital offence, such immunity was a valuable acquisition. Though the brothers were tried and found guilty, Mrs Rudd neither testified nor was dismissed after their trial. Instead, a case was brought against her, for, it was argued, she had been improperly given protection and was herself responsible for the crimes, of which the brothers were innocent dupes.

The brothers' executions were delayed while the judges pondered these issues. Throughout this period public interest was intense, and a prolific newspaper discussion occurred over who was to blame and what was to be done. The case provided the public with the opportunity to discuss the nature and workings of the law in general, and to consider the propriety of the magistrates' powers, the role of judges, and of capital punishment itself. Several months later, for what may have been the first time in Britain, a witness's immunity was withdrawn, and Mrs Rudd put on trial. The jury returned a most peculiar verdict, that on the basis of the evidence put before them, she was not guilty. The brothers' fate was sealed. After their executions Mrs Rudd was reported to have become the mistress of the rakish Thomas *Lyttelton, second Baron Lyttelton (1744–1779), and then disappeared from public view until the 1780s. With the publication of James *Boswell's journals, however, it is now known that she and Boswell had become acquainted shortly after the case, and that Mrs Rudd had become his mistress for some time in the mid-1780s. She briefly surfaced with the publication of a tract denouncing Lord Rawdon for his perfidy in withdrawing support from a needy member of his family, herself, and for a novel, *The Victim of Prejudice*. The press reported her death at different times, though Valentine Rudd remarried in 1798, so she may have been dead by then.

Contemporaries found Mrs Rudd's case fascinating and troubling in a series of ways. A woman of very feminine mien, it was said she possessed a 'masculine' understanding and a vigorous, sarcastic pen. Her self-defence in the press was one of the first times that a woman had written so prolifically on her own behalf under her own name. Claiming to be of aristocratic lineage and to be a much-wronged wife, she used the rhetoric of female weakness and sensibility to move the hearts and change the minds of the public. But to many she seemed to be a Circe, using and discarding men to satisfy her desires for self-promotion and material advancement. She seemed in many ways to embody both the allure and the risks of commercial credit, and to exemplify the untrustworthiness of appearance as well as the dangers of both personal and fiscal impersonation and forgery in an age of capitalism and revolution.   DONNA T. ANDREW

Sources Walpole, *Corr.* · G. Turnbull, 'Criminal biographer: Boswell and Mrs Margaret Caroline Rudd', *Studies in English Literature*, 26 (1986), 511–35 · R. Perreau, *The trials of Robert and Daniel Perreau's* (1775) · J. Langbein, 'Shaping the eighteenth century criminal trial', *University of Chicago Law Review*, 50/1 (1983), 1–162 · J. M. Beattie, *Crime and the courts in England, 1660–1800* (1986) · *Boswell: the ominous years, 1774–1776*, ed. C. Ryskamp and F. A. Pottle (1963), vol. 8 of *The Yale editions of the private papers of James Boswell*, trade edn (1950–89) · H. Bleakley, *Some distinguished victims of the scaffold: trial of Henry Fauntleroy and other famous trials for forgery* (1905)
Likenesses G. Bartolozzi junior, engraving, 1775, BM · engraving, repro. in *Lady's Magazine* (Jan 1776) · engraving, repro. in *Town and Country Magazine* (Oct 1775)

Rudd, Sayer (d. **1757**), dissenting minister and Church of England clergyman, was a minister of fluctuating religious convictions, whose first ministerial experience seems to have been as an assistant pastor in the Particular Baptist chapel in Glasshouse Street, Westminster, around the period 1716 to 1723. Later he was a member of Edward Wallin's General Baptist church at Maze Pond, Southwark, where he was ordained on 2 July 1725, as successor to Thomas Dewhurst, at Turner's Hall, Philpot Lane, London.

In 1726, upon the death of the Revd Mark Key, the congregation of the Baptist chapel in Devonshire Square, London, invited Rudd to preach to them on several occasions with the view to becoming their new pastor. In the following year a union between the Turner's Hall and Devonshire Square chapels was agreed, with the congregation of the former moving to the latter. Rudd was pastor of the united church until 1733. Shortly before this he began to entertain doubts about his Calvinist convictions and contemplated offering his services to both the Quakers and the established church. In April 1733 he announced his intention of taking a tour through France which would give him the opportunity to clarify his religious beliefs. When his congregation refused their consent he decided to go anyway and resigned his post in May. In France, he is reputed to have studied midwifery and proceeded to the degree of MD at Leiden.

On Rudd's return to London in 1734 the congregation at Maze Pond, destitute of a minister after the death of Wallin, invited him to preach on a probationary basis. The Calvinistic Baptist board, however, accused him of unitarianism and issued a minute against him. Although Rudd vigorously defended himself the board disowned him on 26 February 1735.

Rudd then preached for two years (1736–8) at a church built in Snow's Fields by a wealthy admirer, Mrs Elizabeth Ginn. After her death in June 1738, probably disillusioned at his treatment at the hands of his fellow dissenters, he conformed to the established church and was presented by Archbishop John Potter, in 1742, to the living at Walmer, Kent, and in 1752 to the vicarage of Westwell in the same county. During this time he lived near Deal, where he kept a school.

Although Rudd published a number of poems, sermons, and theological treatises he achieved no great fame as an author. Probably his best known work is *Essay on Resurrection, Millennium and Judgement* (1734), while his *Defence of the Plain Account of the Sacrament of the Lord's Supper* (1748) ran to a second edition (1752). His literary interests were not confined to theological subjects. In 1755 he published *Prodromus, or, Observations on the English Letters*, in which he advocated reform of the alphabet and the rules of spelling. Rudd, who may have been married, died at Deal on 6 May 1757. CHARLOTTE FELL-SMITH, rev. M. J. MERCER

Sources W. Wilson, *The history and antiquities of the dissenting churches and meeting houses in London, Westminster and Southwark*, 4 vols. (1808–14), vols. 1–2 · Watt, *Bibl. Brit.* · Allibone, *Dict.* · *GM*, 1st ser., 27 (1757), 241

Rudd, Thomas (1583/4–1656), military engineer and mathematician, was born at Higham Ferrers, Northamptonshire, the son of Thomas Rudd, and the sixth of that name by descent belonging to Higham Ferrers.

Nothing is known of Rudd's education or when he embarked upon a military career. He served in the Low Countries and obtained a reputation as a military engineer with the rank of captain. His description of the manner of march adopted by the prince of Orange towards the siege of Groll in 1627 was used as an example, probably based on personal experience, in his supplement to Lieutenant-Colonel Richard Elton's *The Compleat Body of the Art Military* (1650).

Such was his reputation in the Low Countries that, in 1627 at the age of forty-three, Rudd was summoned to return to England to become chief engineer of all castles, forts, and fortifications within Wales at an annual salary of £240. Subsequently he was appointed the king's principal engineer for fortifications. In this capacity he was involved in the extension of the defences of Elizabeth Castle, St Helier, Jersey, and his plan for the bastioned trace around the lower ward was forwarded to the secretary of state in August 1630 by Sir Philip de Carteret, the bailiff of Jersey.

Together with another senior engineer from the ordnance office, Thomas Heath, Rudd was sent to Portsmouth in 1634–5 to adjudicate on an issue affecting the movement of ordnance on the ramparts. In 1635–6 he received payment of £120 by way of fees and annuities. Rudd was again appointed to survey the defences of Guernsey and Jersey in 1638. This prospect led him to petition the king for five years' arrears of wages amounting to £1200. Having received these instructions, he was faced with leaving at home his wife and children 'in great poverty and debt' (*CSP dom.*, *1638–9*, 515).

The first bishops' war early in 1639 saw Rudd and another engineer of the ordnance office, John Paperill, ordered to Newcastle for service against the Scots, but in May that year Rudd was again in Portsmouth surveying its fortifications. His proposed reforms were estimated to cost £4956. In June 1639 Rudd once more petitioned for payment of arrears of salary amounting to £1300. His personal financial difficulties were taken up with the privy council by the officers of the ordnance. As well as commenting favourably on his services, they offered that: 'we observe him willing and ready to hazard his life and person, notwithstanding his old age, in any service he shall be commanded' (*CSP dom.*, *1639*, 295). He was then fifty-five years old.

In October the same year Rudd went to Dover to carry out repairs to the harbour and to the decayed Archcliffe Fort on the cliff above. After local prevarication Trinity House, in 1640, ordered that the harbour and pier be repaired according to the directions of Captain Rudd. In January 1642 Colonel George Goring, governor of Portsmouth, demanded resources to perfect the fortifications 'according to a survey taken by Captain Rudd last year' (*CSP dom.*, *1641–3*, 271).

Rudd remained loyal to the royalist cause during the civil war. He does not, however, seem to have played a conspicuous part as military engineer, but his royalist affiliations were sufficient for his estate to be decimated in 1655. His politics brought an end to his service in local government. He had been nominated and elected mayor of Higham Ferrers, but the election was disputed despite a petition in his favour in October 1640. He was a justice of the peace 'until the turbulent distracting times' (Bridges, 2.177).

Thomas Rudd was three times married. His first wife was Elizabeth, daughter of Robert Castle of Glatton, Huntingdonshire; his second Margaret, daughter of Edward Doyley of Overbury Hall, Suffolk; and his third Sarah, daughter of John Rolt of Milton Ernes, Bedfordshire, who evidently predeceased him. Rudd, with his third wife, left an only daughter, Judith. She married first a kinsman, Anthony Rudd, and secondly Goddard Pemberton.

Rudd's last years were devoted to mathematical studies and publications. *Practical Geometry*, in two parts, was published in London in 1650. The book was described on the title-page as 'a worke very necessary for all Men, but principally for Surveyors of Land, Engineers, and all Other Students in the Mathematicks'. Another book on geometry was *Euclides Elements of Geometry* in six books 'in a comendious form contrasted and demonstrated … whereunto is added The Mathematicall Preface of Mr John Dee', published in 1651. Both books were described as being by Captain Thomas Rudd, chief engineer to his late majesty. His supplement to Richard Elton's *The Compleat Body of the Art Military* (1650) embodied the duties and qualifications of all officers in an army; the enrolling, arming, and exercising of the cavalry both in posture and motion; the marching of an army, both horse and foot, with train of artillery; the designing and laying out of the quarters for the encamping of an army, both horse and foot, with the artillery train; the manner of securing the quarter by entrenchments and fortification; and some of the practical part of the art of gunnery.

Thomas Rudd died in 1656 at Higham Ferrers, aged seventy-two, and was provided with an elaborate memorial in Higham Ferrers church which incorporated several epitaphs of his own composition. His will, made on 13 December 1655, was proved on 18 February 1657, his daughter, Judith, being sole executrix. She inherited his freehold property. There were bequests to his grandchildren Richard and Mary Rudd. His sister Theodoria Cutler received some lately purchased land, and his cousin Thomas Rudd was bequeathed £100. Other beneficiaries included Francis Gray of Wellingborough, John Wright, and his four servants. There were also bequests to the almsmen at the almshouse at Higham Ferrers and to the poor of the parish. ANDREW SAUNDERS

Sources DNB · *CSP dom.*, 1634–6; 1638–43 · W. G. Ross, *Military engineering during the great civil war, 1642–9* (1984), 12 · *Professional papers of the corps of royal engineers*, Occasional Papers Series, 13 (1887) · W. Porter, *History of the corps of royal engineers*, 2 vols. (1889), 44 · J. Bridges, *The history and antiquities of Northamptonshire*, ed. P. Whalley, 2 (1791), 177 · Thurloe, *State papers* · will, PRO, PROB 11/262, sig. 68 · T. Rudd, 'A supplement to the *Compleat body of the art military*', in R. Elton, *The compleat body of the art military* (1650)

Rudder, Samuel (*bap.* 1726, *d.* 1801), topographer and printer, was baptized on 5 December 1726 at Uley, Gloucestershire, the son of Roger Rudder (*c.*1687–1771), a shopkeeper and pig-killer, and his wife, Lydia Hillier. Nothing is known of his youth or of his education, which his accomplishments suggest was at a grammar school. He was in business at Cirencester as a bookseller by 1749 and as a printer by 1752. On 22 June 1749 he married Mary Hinton (1724–1800), who was the daughter of a maltster but possibly related to Thomas Hinton, a printer in Cirencester earlier in the century. Rudder sold patent medicines and groceries and, by the 1780s, was widely employed as an auctioneer, but his press at his house in Dyer Street remained his main source of livelihood.

A short pamphlet about the late medieval windows of Fairford church, which Rudder printed, and presumably wrote, in 1763, is the earliest evidence of antiquarian interests. In February 1767 he issued a prospectus for a revised edition of the established history of his county, Sir Robert Atkyns's *Ancient and Present State of Glostershire* (1712), a project he said was suggested to him by the local magnate (and his landlord), Allen Bathurst, first Earl Bathurst, of Cirencester Park. The following year William Herbert, a London bookseller with whom Rudder had earlier discussed a collaborative effort, published an unrevised second edition of Atkyns at a lower subscription than that at which his was advertised and 'hurried to the press to come out before [Rudder's] new history could be finished' (*Gloucester Journal*, 12 Sept 1768). This setback to his plans led Rudder into a public controversy with Herbert, but it ensured that his work would be more ambitious than first planned, truly a new history of the county. It took him twelve years to complete. In 1771, when he issued a statement to quell rumours that he had abandoned the work, parts had already been printed, but he was still gathering information for the later sections in 1778. *A New History of Gloucestershire*, which had Rudder's name on the title-page only as printer, was published in June 1779.

Rudder's main sources were Atkyns's county history, often used verbatim in the manorial descents, and a detailed history of Gloucester city, left in manuscript by the Revd Richard Furney. He gathered new information by a standard printed questionnaire, by correspondence which he said 'made him a very troublesome fellow … to my friends more especially' (Austin, 244–5), and by extensive travels: he claimed to have visited every parish in the county. His annotations to a set of proofs of the *New History* record some of his experiences, meeting from Gloucestershire landowners help and hospitality and the occasional snub. The result of his methods was much useful contemporary description, particularly of local trade and industry, sometimes interspersed with the author's own views

on such things as agricultural improvement, non-resident landowners, and the proliferation of alehouses. He also seems to have had a genuine enthusiasm for antiquities, and took the trouble after publication to send out a new sheet with a fuller account of recent discoveries in his own town, the Roman Corinium. He also printed for the first time, although only a few years before John Nichols's complete edition, the Gloucestershire section of Domesday Book. His efforts to get landowners to finance views of their country houses met with a disappointing and dilatory response, and only thirteen whole-sheet plates were produced, eight of which had to be sent out after publication; most were the work of the Gloucester engraver Thomas Bonnor.

Local critics—among whom was a later historian of Gloucestershire, Thomas Rudge, then a young curate at Cirencester—and unfavourable comparison with Atkyns's book irked Rudder into adding a defensive postscript to a second issue of the *New History* in 1783; however, the book received good reviews in London periodicals, and Horace Walpole found it 'the most sensible history of a county that we have had yet' (H. Walpole, *The Letters of Horace Walpole*, ed. P. Cunningham, 1858, 7.299). The sections on Cirencester and Gloucester were published as fascicules in 1780 and 1781, and in 1800 Rudder produced a much expanded account of Cirencester (often wrongly stated to be a new edition of that of 1780).

What can be deduced of Rudder's character suggests a hard-working, conscientious, and somewhat puritanical man. His tradesman's background and down-to-earth cast of mind enabled him to avoid romantic embroidery in favour of the more practical matters of human affairs, an ingredient that has enabled the *New History* to retain its usefulness; of the several Gloucestershire antiquarian histories it is probably now the most used. He retired from business in Cirencester in 1801 and died on 15 March 1801 in Chelsea, at the house of one of his married daughters. He was buried in Cirencester on 24 March 1801. He bequeathed his papers relating to the *New History* to his eldest son, Samuel, a steel button maker in Birmingham.

NICHOLAS HERBERT

Sources N. M. Herbert, introduction, in S. Rudder, *A new history of Gloucestershire*, [new edn] (1977) · *Gloucester Journal* (1768–82) · proof copy of *New history of Gloucestershire* with author's notes in MS, Gloucester public library, Gloucestershire Collection, 35243 · prospectus for *New history of Gloucestershire*, 1767, Gloucester public library, Gloucestershire Collection, JR 1.22 · copy of questionnaire, 1767, Gloucester public library, Gloucestershire Collection, JF 1.4 · will, PRO, PROB 11/1355 · R. Austin, 'Samuel Rudder', *The Library*, 3rd ser., 6 (1915), 235–51 · F. A. Hyett and W. Bazeley, *The bibliographer's manual of Gloucestershire literature*, 3 vols. (1895–7), vol. 1, pp. 21–4; vol. 2, pp. 146–7 · E. A. L. Moir, 'The historians of Gloucestershire', *Gloucestershire studies*, ed. H. P. R. Finberg (1957) · I. Gray, *Antiquaries of Gloucestershire and Bristol*, Bristol and Gloucestershire Archaeological Society Records Section, 12 (1981), 67–9 · parish register (baptism), Uley, 5 Dec 1726 · parish register (marriage), Uley, 1754 · parish register (burial), Cirencester, 24 March 1801 · *GM*, 1st ser., 71 (1801), 285 · DNB

Archives Bodl. Oxf., cash book, incl. notes of memorials in Cirencester church · Glos. RO, corresp. and papers; MS history of Lydney parish · Gloucester Public Library, book of annotated proof sheets

Wealth at death left children twenty shares in Monmouthshire canal, original value 2000 guineas; four shares in Birmingham Copper Mining Co.: will, PRO, PROB 11/1355

Ruddiman, Thomas (1674–1757), printer, classical scholar, and librarian, was born in October 1674 at Raggel, in the parish of Boyndie, Banffshire, one of at least three sons of James Ruddiman, a farmer and staunch royalist, and Margaret, daughter of Andrew Simpson, a neighbouring farmer. He excelled in classical studies at Inverboyndie parish school, under George Morison, and when he was sixteen left home, without his parents' knowledge, to compete for the annual prize for classical learning awarded at King's College, Aberdeen. Having won the prize and obtained a bursary he matriculated in November 1690 from King's College, where he studied under William Black.

Having graduated MA on 21 June 1694 he worked as tutor to the family of Sir John Ogilvy, of Inverquharity, and then to the son of Robert Young, of Auldbar, Forfarshire. Young helped him to secure the post of schoolmaster at Laurencekirk, Kincardineshire, in April 1695. There a chance meeting in 1699 with Dr Archibald Pitcairne, who promised him his support, persuaded Ruddiman to leave Laurencekirk and try his luck in Edinburgh. Ruddiman arrived in Edinburgh early in 1700 and, through Pitcairne, began working as a copyist in the Advocates' Library. On 2 May 1702 he was appointed assistant librarian, with a salary of less than £9 a year; the following year he was rewarded for his good work with an extra allowance of £50. He supplemented his income by copying documents for Glasgow University, by teaching private pupils, and by receiving boarding pupils into his house. On 28 December 1704, in Edinburgh, he married Barbara Skolla (d. 1710), the daughter of a merchant from Kirkwall; they had three children.

1706 saw the start of Ruddiman's association with the Edinburgh printer and bookseller Robert Freebairn, who employed him as a proofreader and editor. At the same time Ruddiman's younger brother Walter (1687–1770) was engaged by Freebairn as a printer's apprentice. Ruddiman and Freebairn shared the same ideological principles, for both were staunch Episcopalians and supported the Jacobite cause. Over the next few years Ruddiman prepared for the press Sir Robert Sibbald's *Introductio ad historiam rerum a Romanis gestarum* (1706), Sir Robert Spottiswood's *Praticks of the Laws of Scotland* (1706), and a new edition of Florence Wilson's *De animi tranquillitate dialogus* (1707), to which he added a new preface and life of Wilson. He dedicated his own edition of Arthur Johnston's *Cantici Solomonis paraphrasis poetica* (1709) to his patron Pitcairne, who in return presented him with a silver cup. In 1710 he saw through the press a new folio edition of Gavin Douglas's translation of Virgil's *Aeneid*, to which he added an elaborate glossary; he was paid £8 6s. 8d. for the undertaking. On Pitcairne's death in October 1713 Ruddiman negotiated the sale of his library to Peter the Great and published, on a single sheet, an elegy, *In obitum A. Pitcarnii*; he later edited a volume of Pitcairne's verse that was published by Freebairn in 1727.

In 1710 Ruddiman considered accepting the rectorship of Dundee grammar school. This doubtless prompted the Advocates' Library to offer him an additional salary of £30 6s. 8d., which persuaded him to stay. Widowed in that year, in the following year he married Janet (d. 1728), the daughter of an Episcopalian minister. They had two children: one who died young and Thomas (1714–1747). Ruddiman co-edited with Bishop John Sage an edition of the works of William Drummond of Hawthornden, printed by James Watson in 1711, and edited the first volume of Patrick Abercromby's *The Martial Achievements of the Scots Nation* for Freebairn in 1711, and John Forrest's *Latin–English Vocabulary* (1713). In 1718 he helped to found a literary society in Edinburgh whose members included the masters of the high school and, later, Henry Home, Lord Kames. He helped Thomas Hearne to prepare his edition of John Fordun's *Scotichronicon*, which was published in Oxford in 1722.

With Freebairn's advice Ruddiman had established his own printing business by 1712 and was joined by his brother Walter. Their first publication, the second volume of Abercromby's *Martial Achievements*, appeared in 1715 but their principal business was the rapidly expanding market for schoolbooks. The most celebrated of their educational titles, Ruddiman's own *Rudiments of the Latin Tongue*, had first been published by Freebairn in 1714 but the second edition, of 1716, was 'printed and sold by the author' (title-page). This work passed through fifteen editions in his lifetime and supplanted all previous works to such an extent that it remained the standard Latin grammar in schools throughout Britain for the rest of the century. Ruddiman then embarked on the research for a work that confirmed his reputation as Scotland's foremost Latinist. Between September 1718 and November 1719 he undertook an exhaustive comparison of over seventy grammars to compile a list of rules and disputed points of grammar, and then searched the classical Latin authors to decide the correct usage in disputed cases. He presented his results in *Grammaticae Latinae institutiones* (2 vols., 1725, 1731), a demanding work that was written entirely in Latin and aimed at only the most learned of classical scholars.

Despite his high reputation Ruddiman's scholarship attracted controversy as well as praise. In 1715 Freebairn published Ruddiman's folio edition of the works of the sixteenth-century Scottish historian and Latinist George Buchanan as *Georgii Buchanani … opera omnia* (2 vols., 1715). In his Latin biographical introduction Ruddiman adversely criticized Buchanan's character and views, especially his anti-monarchical views, which were anathema to Ruddiman's Jacobite principles, but lauded Buchanan as a Latinist. Ruddiman's comments in favour of a hereditary monarchy unsurprisingly antagonized the whig and Presbyterian establishment in Scotland, especially in the year of a Jacobite rising. A number of Edinburgh professors formed a 'Society of the Scholars of Edinburgh, to vindicate that incomparably learned and pious author [Buchanan] from the calumy of Mr. Thomas Ruddiman' but their proposal to bring out a new edition of Buchanan's works, to correct Ruddiman's mistakes, was not carried out. The controversy was reignited following the Jacobite rising of 1745, when Ruddiman wrote in defence of Buchanan's paraphrase of the book of Psalms in response to William Benson, who had unfavourably compared it with the version by Arthur Johnston. In the following year the debate about hereditary succession to the throne was reopened by George Logan, a Church of Scotland minister, in his *Treatise on Government* (1746), and a pamphlet war concerning the historical precedents for succession to the Scottish crown ensued. Ruddiman defended his scholarship and political principles once again, in response to James Man's abusive attack in *A censure and examination of Mr Thomas Ruddiman's philological notes on the works of the great Buchanan* (1753). He published two equally abusive pamphlets: *Anticrisis, or, A Discussion of a Scurrilous and Malicious Libel* (1754) and *Audi alteram partem* (1756).

All Ruddiman's self-justificatory pamphlets were printed on his own presses but expression of his Jacobite views was not confined to these scholarly debates. In 1724 he took over the printing of the revived *Caledonian Mercury* for its proprietor, William Rolland, and in 1729 he acquired the whole interest in the newspaper, which remained in the family until 1772. Appearing thrice-weekly, it was a forum for moderate Jacobitism and as a consequence attracted little attention from the authorities. In fact in 1728 Ruddiman was appointed jointly with James Davidson to the University of Edinburgh. Ruddiman married, for the third time, on 29 September 1729; his bride was Anna (d. 1769), the daughter of Thomas Smith, a merchant and brewer who formerly had been a woollen draper in London. They had two children, of whom one died in infancy and the other, Alison, married James Steuart of Edinburgh and was the only child of Ruddiman's to survive him. After the rising of 1745 his only other child to survive into adulthood—his son Thomas, who by then was manager of the *Caledonian Mercury*—was imprisoned for helping to print Jacobite proclamations; he died on release, of a disease contracted in prison, on 9 September 1747. Ruddiman's nephew Walter *Ruddiman set up his own separate printing press in Edinburgh soon after 1745.

On 6 January 1730 Ruddiman was appointed keeper to the Advocates' Library, in succession to John Spottiswood. The library grew impressively in size during his twenty-two years as keeper, from about 9000 volumes in 1728 to an estimated 20,000 volumes in 1752; at least 5000 volumes were added by the time that the library catalogue was drawn up in 1737. One of Ruddiman's first achievements was to ensure that the library received the supply of books from Stationers' Hall, in London, to which it was entitled under the Copyright Act of 1710. He greatly expanded the library's general and non-legal collection, including classical authors and antiquarian and historical works; in particular he concentrated on methodically building up an unrivalled collection of early Scottish books. He did encounter some resistance from the library's five curators, who had to approve every purchase or acquisition that he made, for they did not share his enthusiasm for Scottish printing and were reluctant to buy large collections, such as Archibald Campbell's library of Scottish books and coins. Despite these restrictions Ruddiman worked well with his employers, who rewarded his many years of salary by giving him a bonus of £70 in 1737 on top of his salary of £40. This award registered the curators' gratitude to him for compiling an alphabetical and class catalogue of the library and for overseeing its printing, which was undertaken by his and his brother's firm. The first pages were printed in the spring of 1734 and, after some delays, the catalogue was finished by January 1747.

On 13 August 1739 Ruddiman resigned half of the printing business to his son Thomas and about the same time bought himself a house in Parliament Square, close to the Advocates' Library, at a cost of £300. He assisted his friend Joseph Ames in compiling the appendix on early Scottish books for his history of printing, *Typographical Antiquities* (1749). On his only trip to England, in 1737, he had been persuaded to complete for the press James Anderson's *Selectus diplomatum & numismatum Scotiae thesaurus*, which was printed in Edinburgh in 1739. In 1751 he published a superb edition of Livy, in four duodecimo volumes, but by then his sight was failing. Early in 1752 he resigned as keeper of the Advocates' Library; he was succeeded by David Hume. On 19 January 1757 he died in Edinburgh, aged eighty-two, and was buried in Greyfriars churchyard. A tablet to his memory was erected in the New Greyfriars church in 1806 by his relative Dr William Ruddiman. His library, which he had catalogued under the title 'Bibliotheca Romana', was sold in Edinburgh in February 1758. After his death Ruddiman's trustees were involved over a number of years in law suits against printers who were pirating his *Rudiments of the Latin Tongue*, which by the time of his widow's death, in 1769, had reached its seventeenth edition. Samuel Johnson, who visited Laurencekirk with James Boswell in 1773, paid tribute to Ruddiman as 'that excellent man and eminent scholar'.

A. P. WOOLRICH

Sources G. H. Johnston, *The Ruddimans in Scotland: their history and works* (1901) · G. Chalmers, *Life of Thomas Ruddiman* (1794) · D. Duncan, *Thomas Ruddiman: a study in Scottish scholarship of the early eighteenth century* (1965) · *Scots Magazine* (1747), 455 · *Scots Magazine* (1757), 54 · *Scots Magazine* (1770), 458 · B. Hillyard, 'Thomas Ruddiman and the Advocates' Library, 1728–52', *Library History*, 8 (1990), 157–70 · *N&Q*, 3rd ser., 7 (1865), 280 · *Mercurius Caledonius ...* (with historical sketch of the Caledonian Mercury to January 8, 1861) (1861) · Nichols, *Lit. anecdotes*, 3.622, 693 · Nichols, *Illustrations*, 4.235–9 · J. Boswell, *The life of Samuel Johnson*, 2 vols. (1791) · Chambers, *Scots.* (1868–70), 3.311–14 · A. Jervise, *Epitaphs and inscriptions from burial grounds and old buildings in the north-east of Scotland*, 2 vols. (1875–9), vol. 1, pp. 11, 201, 289 · *Fourth report*, HMC, 3 (1874), 532 · *Fifth report*, HMC, 4 (1876), 627 · *DNB*

Archives NL Scot., notes, corresp., and MSS · NL Scot., notes and MSS

Likenesses W. Denune, oils, 1749, Scot. NPG · F. Bartolozzi, stipple, pubd 1793, NPG; repro. in Chalmers, *Life of Ruddiman* · earl of Buchan, watercolour drawing, Scot. NPG

Ruddiman, Walter (1719–1781), printer and newspaper proprietor, was born in the parish of Alvah, by Banff on the Moray Firth, the youngest of the four sons of James Ruddiman (c.1680–c.1739), farmer, and his wife, Isabel, née Ruddiman. The will of his brother John (d. 1744), proved in Aberdeen on 11 March 1745, reveals Walter to have been then employed as a 'merchant in Banff' (cited in Johnston, *Ruddimans in Scotland*). It was shortly after this date that he moved to Edinburgh to work as a printer. That move meant that there were then two firms named Ruddiman working as printers in Edinburgh: that of Walter and the established firm of his uncles Thomas *Ruddiman (1674–1757) and Walter (1687–1770). Until the death of the elder Walter, he appears as 'Walter Ruddiman Junior' on the title-pages of his publications. On 11 September 1754 he was admitted a burgess of Edinburgh, and about that time he married Janet Bradfute (d. 1776), with whom he had four children: Thomas (1755–1825), with whom he entered partnership and who inherited his printing firm; John (d. 1816); Walter (1762–1823), a lieutenant in the Scots brigade in the Netherlands; and Janet (1761–1849).

In July 1757 Ruddiman began publishing the *Edinburgh Magazine*, a periodical in octavo bearing the imprint 'Edinburgh:/Printed by Walter Ruddiman Junior and Company,/Morocco's Close, Lawn - Market'. Ruddiman abandoned the project in 1762, after publishing the sixth volume. His most significant undertaking was to publish the *Weekly Magazine, or, Edinburgh Amusement*. The first issue was published on 7 July 1768, and the periodical claimed to offer 'The Essence of all the Magazines, Reviews, Newspapers, &c. published in Great Britain: Also Extracts from every new Work of Merit, whether political, literary, serious, or comical, being a Register of the Writings and Transactions of the Times'. It was a tremendous success, quickly establishing itself as the most popular weekly publication in Edinburgh, selling as many as 3000 copies per week. By 1770 Ruddiman had moved his business to Forrester's Wynd in Edinburgh's Lawnmarket, and from that location came the edition of the *Weekly Magazine* (7 February 1771) that carried the first published poem of Robert Fergusson (1750–1774). Ruddiman's son Thomas became a partner in the following April, and it is with the imprint 'Printed by Walter and Thomas Ruddiman' that the first edition of *Poems by Robert Fergusson* appeared in January 1773, the only edition to appear in the poet's lifetime. In his versified will Fergusson bequeathed his portrait to Ruddiman, concluding with the request that his will be printed:

> patent may it be, and seen,
> in Walter's Weekly Magazine.

By the mid-1770s the *Weekly Magazine* was a runaway success, not least because of its appealing mix of reviews, literature, and news. Newspapers carried stamp duty at the time; 'literary' periodicals did not. The presence of news in the *Weekly Magazine* was brought to the attention of the exchequer, which found it liable to stamp duty on this account. In response Ruddiman in 1777 divided the magazine into two separate publications: a new octavo newspaper entitled *Ruddiman's Weekly Mercury*, costing 3d. and attracting tax at a halfpenny per copy, and the *Weekly Magazine*, now a weekly miscellany free of news and tax,

which from the forty-seventh volume (30 December 1779) became the *Edinburgh Magazine, or, Literary Amusement*. Ruddiman's restructuring of his publications effectively divided his market: in 1780 the *Edinburgh Magazine* had a circulation of some 1400 copies, the *Weekly Mercury* between 1800 and 2000. The action brought against Ruddiman, together with his response, had an important influence in clarifying the distinction between newspapers and other periodical forms that is common today. Predeceased by his wife, who had died on 21 May 1776, Walter Ruddiman died in Edinburgh on 16 June 1781, and was buried on 19 June at the city's Greyfriars churchyard.

HAMISH MATHISON

Sources G. H. Johnston, *The Ruddimans in Scotland: their history and works* (1901) · G. H. Johnston, *Notes on the Ruddimans* (1887) · G. Chalmers, *The life of Thomas Ruddiman* (1794) · D. Duncan, *Thomas Ruddiman: a study in Scottish scholarship of the early eighteenth century* (1965) · I. C. Walker, 'Scottish verse in the *Weekly Magazine*', *Studies in Scottish Literature*, 5/1 (1967), 3–13 · 'The record book of Kincaid and Creech, "Weekly Magazine accounts, 1768–1773"', U. Edin. L., MS La. III 752 · T. Ruddiman, letter to John Cumming, 14 May 1782, U. Edin. L., MS La. II 82 · invoice from Walter Ruddiman to Kincaid and Donaldson for printing of Livy, 1756, U. Edin. L., MS Add. II 508 · Duke of Buckingham [G. Villiers], *The rehearsal* (1753) · *Edinburgh Magazine* (1757–62) · *Weekly Magazine, or, Edinburgh Amusement* (1768–79) · *Edinburgh Magazine, or, Literary Amusement* (1779–83) · *Ruddiman's Weekly Mercury* (1777–83) · bur. reg. Scot., Greyfriars, Edinburgh, 16 and 19 June 1781
Likenesses W. Turner, oils
Wealth at death son inherited business

Rudé, George Frederick Elliot (1910–1993), historian, was born on 8 February 1910 in Oslo, Norway, the second of two sons of Jens Essendrop Rude (1875–1942), an engineer and inventor, and his wife, Amy Geraldine Elliot (1873–1943), daughter of George Augustus Elliot, lieutenant-colonel in the British army, later a banker, and Blanche Wilhelmina Barnard, a descendant of George Barnard, librarian to George III. In 1919 the family settled permanently in England, living on the mother's small private income. Young George was educated at Seabrook Lodge in Hythe, Kent, at Shrewsbury School, and at Trinity College, Cambridge, where he read modern languages. He received honours in French and German and took his BA in 1931.

For the next eighteen years, Rudé taught modern languages at Stowe and St Paul's schools. He displayed no special interest in politics until 1932, when he visited the Soviet Union on a six-week guided tour. Rudé reportedly 'came back a committed communist and anti-fascist' (Stretton, 44). After immersing himself in the writings of Marx and Lenin, he joined the British Communist Party in 1935. He pursued his teaching career while participating in lower-level political activity and took part in the so-called battle of Cable Street on 4 October 1936 against Oswald Mosley's blackshirted marchers. During the Second World War, Rudé served in the London region of the National Fire Service. He also contributed to the war effort by publishing a pamphlet, *Why Russia is Strong* (1942). He warmly praised the military and economic power of the Soviet Union and lauded its leader, Joseph Stalin, for waging a courageous struggle against the Nazi invader.

Meanwhile, on 16 March 1940, Rudé married Dorothy (Doreen) Frances Claire Therese de la Hoyde, the daughter of a banker, born at Dublin in 1910. They had no children.

After the war Rudé turned his attention to historical studies. He received a BA (1948) and a PhD (1950) at the University of London. His doctoral dissertation, 'The Parisian wage-earning population and the insurrectionary movement of 1789–91', was based on extensive research undertaken in the Paris archives. It demonstrated both his scholarly abilities and his concern for the popular classes. The latter, in turn, reflected Rudé's strong Marxist sympathies, which would colour all his future historical writings. From 1946 until 1956 he participated actively in the Communist Party historians' group, with its class-conflict approach to English history. Rudé's research in France brought him into contact with the eminent scholar Georges Lefebvre, who encouraged his work on revolutionary crowds and published his articles in *Annales Historiques de la Révolution Française*. In Britain, Rudé conducted research at the Guildhall Library and the Public Record Office, contributing to various English-language journals. He was awarded the Alexander prize by the Royal Historical Society for an article on the Gordon riots of 1780. By 1953, perhaps to establish his identity as a French scholar, he began to accent his surname: Rudé.

The Crowd in the French Revolution, a substantially revised and expanded version of Rudé's doctoral dissertation, appeared in 1959. The book demonstrated his mastery of the archival sources as well as his understanding of revolutionary crowds, their composition, motives, and action. Favourably reviewed, it firmly established his reputation as a specialist in the revolutionary period. However, Rudé's overt involvement with the British Communist Party cost him dearly. Compelled to resign from St Paul's School in 1949, he was unable to find a university post. He spent the next decade teaching history at Sir Walter St John's and Holloway comprehensive schools. Finally, in 1960, he accepted a senior lectureship at the University of Adelaide, going into 'exile' in Australia and quietly severing his ties to communism. But his earlier affiliation induced the Australian security intelligence organization to monitor his activities.

Continuing to pursue his research in French and English social history, Rudé published an important number of works. In *Wilkes and Liberty* (1962) he examined the political agitation provoked by the radical John Wilkes and the social composition of the crowds who rioted in his name. *The Crowd in History* (1964) traced popular disturbances, particularly the food riot, in England and France between 1730 and 1848. He wrote a general synthesis of the French Revolutionary and Napoleonic era in his *Revolutionary Europe, 1783–1815* (1964), in which he placed special emphasis on the dimensions of social change. With E. J. Hobsbawm he produced *Captain Swing* (1968), a detailed account of the failed uprising of rural labourers in 1830. On his own Rudé issued *Paris and London in the Eighteenth Century* (1969), a collection of studies that dealt with popular protests and revolts, the result of two decades of archival research.

Rudé's growing scholarly reputation earned him posts as visiting professor at Columbia University (1965) and the University of Tokyo (1967). He also spent the spring term of 1968 teaching at the University of Stirling before he returned to Australia as a professor at Flinders University in Adelaide. In 1970 he removed to Montreal, Canada, to teach at Sir George Williams (later Concordia) University. He would remain in 'exile' there for seventeen years.

With undiminished energy Rudé conducted archival research and published extensively. In 1971 appeared his *Hanoverian London, 1714–1808*, a detailed analysis of social and political conditions in the crowded English capital, and in the following year his *Europe in the Eighteenth Century*, an account of the growing conflict between aristocracy and bourgeoisie that prefigured the French Revolution. He turned his hand to biography in *Robespierre: Portrait of a Revolutionary Democrat* (1975), a sympathetic life of the Jacobin leader, whom he considered the first champion of democracy and the people's rights. In *Protest and Punishment* (1977) he detailed the fate of thousands of individuals transported to Australia for having protested or rebelled against social conditions. Examining radical political thought, his *Ideology and Popular Protest* (1980) explained the motives that impelled riots and rebellions from the middle ages to the mid-nineteenth century. His *Criminal and Victim* (1985) explored the causes and repression of criminality in England during the early 1800s, viewing it as a form of class warfare.

After retiring to his home in England, Rudé completed his final work, *The French Revolution*, in 1988. In a clear, straightforward style he defended the revolution's accomplishments against its detractors. His once robust health declined, and he died of pneumonia at Battle Hospital, Battle, Sussex, on 8 January 1993 and was cremated the same day. His wife survived him.

Tall, athletic in build, and elegant in attire, Rudé always remained a gentleman in behaviour. As his friend E. J. Hobsbawm observed, he 'loved wine and good food, … swimming, Piero della Francesca, eighteenth-century painting and … music'. These aristocratic traits were balanced by his firm commitment to Marxist ideology, expressed in his numerous sympathetic studies of the popular classes, history 'seen from below'.

JAMES FRIGUGLIETTI

Sources H. Stretton, 'George Rudé', *History from below: studies in popular protest and popular ideology in honour of George Rudé*, ed. F. Krantz (1985), 43–54 · E. Hobsbawm, 'George Rudé: historian from below', *The Guardian* (12 Jan 1993) · 'George Rudé', *Perspectives on the European past: conversations with historians*, ed. N. F. Cantor (1971), 40–61 · H. Kaye, 'A face in the crowd', *Times Higher Education Supplement* (31 March 1989) · J. Cohen and others, *George Rudé, 1910–1993, Marxist historian: memorial tributes* (1993) · J. Friguglietti, 'How George Frederick Elliot Rude became the historian George Rudé', *The sphinx in the Tuileries and other essays in modern French history*, ed. R. Aldrich and M. Lyons (1999) · d. cert. · private information (2004) · WWW, 1991–5 · m. cert.

Likenesses J. Bauer, photograph, 1970, repro. in G. Rudé, *Paris and London in the eighteenth century* (1970), jacket · J. Bauer, photograph, 1988, repro. in G. Rudé, *The French Revolution* (1988), jacket · photograph, 1989, repro. in *Times Higher Educational Supplement*

Wealth at death under £125,000: probate, 9 Aug 1994, *CGPLA Eng. & Wales*

Rudellat, Yvonne Claire (1897–1945). *See under* Women agents on active service in France (*act.* 1942–1945).

Rudge, Edward (1763–1846), botanist and antiquary, was born in Evesham on 27 June 1763, the son of Edward Rudge (1717–1790), a merchant and alderman of Salisbury, and his wife, Elizabeth Long (*d.* 1820). His father possessed a large portion of the abbey estate at Evesham. Rudge matriculated from Queen's College, Oxford, on 11 October 1781, but took no degree. On 27 July 1791 he married Anne (*d.* 1836), only daughter of Peter Nouaille of Great Ness House, Kent. The couple had three sons and a daughter. Their eldest son was Edward John Rudge [*see below*].

Rudge's attention was early turned to botany, through the influence of his uncle, Samuel Rudge (*d.* 1817), a retired barrister who formed a herbarium which passed to his nephew. His uncle's encouragement, and the purchase of a fine series of plants from Guiana, collected by M. Martin, led Rudge to study the flora of that country, and to publish between 1805 and 1807 *Plantarum Guianae rariorum icones et descriptiones hactenus ineditae*. He was also interested in antiquities, and between 1811 and 1834 conducted a series of excavations in those portions of the Evesham Abbey estate under his control. Details of the relics and ruins he unearthed were published (with a memoir by his son) by the Society of Antiquaries in *Vestuta Monumenta*. In 1842 Rudge erected an octagon tower on the battlefield of Evesham, commemorating Simon de Montfort, earl of Leicester.

Rudge was an early fellow of the Society of Antiquaries, and was elected to the Linnean Society in 1802, and to the Royal Society in 1805. In 1829 he was sheriff of Worcestershire. In addition to *Plantarum Guianae rariorum* Rudge was author of some seven botanical papers in the Royal and Linnean societies' publications, and of several papers in *Archaeologia*. Following the death of his first wife, he married, in 1841, Margaret, widow of Daniel Bazalgette. Rudge died at his home, the Abbey Manor House, Evesham, on 3 September 1846. A genus of the botanical order Rubiaceae was named *Rudgea* in his honour by Richard Anthony Salisbury in 1806.

Edward John Rudge (1792–1861), antiquary, was born in London on 30 May 1792. He was educated at Chiswick and Westminster, before going up to Gonville and Caius College, Cambridge, in 1811. He graduated BA in 1815 and MA in 1818, and was called to the bar on 21 May 1819. On 29 August 1825 he married Felizarda, daughter of Charles van Notten-Pole of Wick Hill House, Gloucestershire.

Rudge was elected a fellow of the Society of Antiquaries in 1834, and of the Royal Society in 1847. He was the author of *Some Account of the History and Antiquities of Evesham* (1820) and *Illustrated and Historical Account of Buckden Palace* (1839). He died at Evesham on 29 January 1861.

B. B. WOODWARD, *rev.* PETER OSBORNE

Sources Desmond, *Botanists*, rev. edn, 598 · Burke, *Gen. GB* · Venn, *Alum. Cant.* · *Proceedings of the Linnean Society of London*, 1 (1838–48), 315, 337 · *GM*, 2nd ser., 26 (1846), 652 · *GM*, 2nd ser., 27 (1847), 181 · J. Britten and G. S. Boulger, eds., *A biographical index of British and Irish botanists* (1893) · *Catalogue of scientific papers*, Royal Society, 5 (1871) · catalogue [BM]

Archives NHM
Likenesses engraving, RS

Rudge, Edward John (1792–1861). *See under* Rudge, Edward (1763–1846).

Rudge, Thomas (*bap.* 1753, *d.* 1825), topographer and writer on agriculture, was baptized on 13 June 1753 at the church of St Mary de Lode, Gloucester, the son of Thomas Rudge (1725/6–1809), attorney and writing master, and his first wife, Anne (1719/20–1759). His father was deputy registrar of the consistory court of Gloucester diocese from the early 1770s. The younger Thomas attended Gloucester's College School (the cathedral school), and was admitted to Merton College, Oxford, in 1770, at the age of sixteen; he acquired the degree of BA (1780), and from Worcester College proceeded MA (1783) and BD (1784). After ordination he had no difficulty in securing livings in his home diocese. In 1777 he was instituted to the vicarage of Frampton-on-Severn, with which he held in 1779 a stipendiary curacy at Cirencester and from 1780 the vicarage of Haresfield. In 1784 he resigned Frampton and became rector of a Gloucester city parish, St Michael, which he then held in plurality with Haresfield for the rest of his life. Between 1788 and 1803 his income from the two benefices (about £120 a year in 1784), was supplemented by the mastership of the Crypt Grammar School at Gloucester, a post that gave him a small annual income from the foundation but freedom to take private boarding pupils on his own account. During the first part of his career he lived at Gloucester but served both his parishes, since Haresfield was within a short ride of the city. He married in 1778 Sarah King (1755/6–1821) from Iron Acton, Gloucestershire.

Rudge also sought a role in the legal and administrative sphere of diocesan work, presumably influenced in this by his father, whose bequests to Thomas at his death in 1809 included his law books, and by an elder brother, James (*d.* 1786), who practised as a proctor in the Gloucester consistory court. By 1788 Thomas himself was regularly presiding over that court as surrogate (deputy) to the diocesan chancellor. Such experience helped towards his appointment in 1814 as archdeacon of Gloucester, with which came yet another benefice, the rectory of Dursley, and in 1817 as chancellor of Hereford diocese; both those appointments he owed to George Huntingford, bishop of Gloucester until 1815 when translated to the see of Hereford. The archdeaconry involved much visitational work as well as legal functions. In his last years, when he also served as a JP for Gloucestershire, Rudge had a formidable workload for a man aged over seventy. Haresfield, where he rebuilt the vicarage house, was his principal residence during the last part of his career and he continued to serve that parish in person, appointing curates for his other benefices.

Rudge also found time to produce three books on his native county. He may have had antiquarian interests by 1779, when he annoyed Samuel Rudder by retailing, with apparent relish, criticism of the latter's new county history. Little is known, however, of the genesis of Rudge's own county history, entitled *The History of (the County) of Gloucester, Compressed and Brought Down to the Year 1803* and published in two volumes in February 1804 (although 1803 is given on the title-page). A third volume, on Gloucester city, was then said to be ready but was not published until 1811 as a separate title, *The History and Antiquities of Gloucester*. His aims were modest, to provide in a concise form and update the information in Sir Robert Atkyns's history of Gloucestershire (1712); he made no claim to original research in the records. He saw it as a virtue to include nothing that would 'hurt the feelings of the living, insult the memory of the dead, or pass the slightest censure on any public institution or establishment' ('Preface' to *The History of (the County) of Gloucester*) and his presence as author is almost imperceptible in his books or the publicity for them. In this he provides a marked contrast to a contemporary Gloucestershire historian, the Revd Thomas Fosbrooke, who had a confrontational attitude to criticism, real or imagined. The two men were competitors for subscribers, and on at least one occasion advertisements for their county histories appeared in the local newspaper next to each other, though Fosbrooke's was not published until three years after Rudge's.

It is unclear how and why Rudge came to be chosen as author of the *General View of the Agriculture of the County of Gloucester*, which was published in 1807 as one of the second and revised series of county surveys produced for the board of agriculture. The result, showing a detailed knowledge of farming practice and an able grasp of the economy of the county as a whole, was a vast improvement on the board's first survey for Gloucestershire, a slight work of 1794 by George Turner, and was more comprehensive even than a substantial treatise on the county produced by the professional agriculturist William Marshall in 1789.

Rudge died at Haresfield on 3 March 1825 and was buried in Haresfield church on 10 March. His surviving children included Charles, who adopted as a surname his mother's maiden name (King), Henry Rudge, a surgeon at Leominster in 1830, and the Revd Frederick Rudge, his father's curate at Dursley and in 1816 vicar of Eardisland, Herefordshire. A nephew (and former pupil under Thomas at the Crypt Grammar School), the Revd James Rudge, became incumbent and lecturer of Limehouse, Middlesex, and published several sermons.

Nicholas Herbert

Sources Hockaday abstracts, Gloucester Library, 85, 186, 200, 219, 233 · parish registers, Glos. RO, P154; P163 · *Gloucester Journal* (24 March 1788) · *Gloucester Journal* (6 Sept 1802) · *Gloucester Journal* (13 Feb 1804) · *Gloucester Journal* (25 May 1807) · *Gloucester Journal* (3 Aug 1807) · *Gloucester Journal* (22 April 1811) · PRO, PROB 11/1502, fol. 267v–269; 1698, fol. 169r–v · Glos. RO, GDR, B3/3,19, 22, 28, 35 · *Gloucestershire Notes and Queries*, 2 (1884), 372 · Rudge family monument, Gloucester Cathedral · Foster, *Alum. Oxon.* · *VCH Gloucestershire*, 2.349–50; 10.196 · I. Gray, *Antiquaries of Gloucestershire and Bristol*, Bristol and Gloucestershire Archaeological Society Records Section, 12 (1981), 72–3 · Gloucester Library, Gloucestershire collection, S 18.12 · parish register, Iron Acton, 1778, Bristol RO [marriage] · Glos. RO, GDR, VI/63 · Glos. RO, D 936/E12/12, fol. 60; E 12/18, fol. 42 · R. Austin, 'Letters of Thomas Dudley Fosbrooke', *Transactions of the Bristol and Gloucestershire Archaeological Society*, 37 (1914), 135–84, esp. 150

Wealth at death property at Bosbury, Herefordshire, expected to raise at least £1600 at its sale; some property in Gloucester; legacies totalling £300; plus other unspecified assets expected to purchase annuities totalling £80: will, PRO, PROB 11/1698, fols. 169r–169v

Rudhall, Abraham, the elder (1657–1736), bell-founder, was born on 1 September 1657, the son of Quaker parents, Henry (d. 1685) and Grizell (d. 1674) Riddall. He was the first of a noted family of bell-founders active in Gloucester from 1684 to 1830, during which time they cast over 4500 church bells. Details of Rudhall's early career remain fragmentary. In 1677 he seems to have been in Gloucester as a carpenter. His name appears in the accounts of St Mary de Crypt, where he may well have been assisting the bell-founders William Coey and Richard Purdue III (1653–1686). However, the earliest ring of bells that he himself cast was for St Nicholas, Oddington, in 1684, as is stated in a series of advertisements listing his bells, beginning in the *London Postman* of 20 February 1705. The same advertisement states that he had also, by this time, cast one ring of ten, ten rings of eight, thirty-two sixes, twenty-five fives, and others, totalling 547 in all. With his son Abraham [see below], he went on to cast many more, including the rings of ten for St Bride's, Fleet Street (destroyed in the Second World War), and St Martin-in-the-Fields (subsequently removed to Australia). Rudhall's bells were admired in his own time for their good musical qualities—indeed, one of the Bodleian Library's copies of the catalogue of Rudhall's bells, printed in Oxford in 1705 by Leonard Lichfield, has a handwritten addition naming Rudhall as 'the greatest Bell-Founder of this age'.

Rudhall married Elizabeth Jennings (1658–1699) of Hempsted in 1677, although there is some suggestion that he had a former wife named Grace. Elizabeth had eight children, including Grizell (d. 28 April 1684), Issac (d. April 1697), Jacob (d. 4 Oct 1699), Joseph (d. 11 Oct 1761), Priscilla (d. July 1741), Alicia (d. 28 June 1735), who married William *Hine, organist of Gloucester Cathedral, in 1711, and Abraham. After Elizabeth's death Rudhall married Margaret (d. 1717). Rudhall was made a freeman of the city of Gloucester in 1691; he joined the College Youths' Society of Bellringers at Bath in 1699. He retired in 1718, and died on 25 January 1736, aged seventy-eight. He was buried on 28 January in Gloucester Cathedral, where the memorial to him reads: 'Abraham Rudhall, bellfounder, famed for his great skill, beloved and esteemed for his singular good nature and integrity'.

Abraham Rudhall the younger (1680–1735) was his father's eldest son. Although he took over from his father only in 1718, the first bell to bear his name was cast for Tredington, and is dated 1700. He died on 17 December 1735 and was buried in the churchyard of St John the Baptist, Gloucester, leaving all his 'workhouses and appurtenances' to Abel Rudhall (1714–1760), one of the four sons and three daughters of himself and his wife, Eleanor (d. 13 July 1751), who began to cast bells under his own name in 1736. Three of Abel's sons successively carried on the business, namely: Thomas Rudhall (1740?–1783); Charles Rudhall (1746–1815); and John Rudhall (1760–1835), the last bell-founder of the name. The Gloucester foundry was nominally closed in 1828, but bells bearing John Rudhall's name are found with later dates, up to his death in 1835.

L. M. MIDDLETON, *rev.* GILES HUDSON

Sources M. Bliss and F. Sharpe, *Church bells of Gloucestershire* (1986), 57–77 · B. Frith, 'Locally-cast bells still ring in USA', *The Citizen* (6 Jan 1977), 9 · H. T. Ellacombe, *The church bells of Gloucestershire* (privately printed, Exeter, 1881), 5–8 · Grove, *Dict. mus.* · [W. I. R. V.], 'Abraham Rudhall, bell-founder', *N&Q*, 8th ser., 3 (1893), 134

Rudhall, Abraham, the younger (1680–1735). *See under* Rudhall, Abraham, the elder (1657–1736).

Ruding, Rogers (1751–1820), numismatist, was born at Westcotes, Leicester, on 9 August 1751, the fourth child and younger son of Rogers Ruding (*bap.* 1710), receiver-general of taxes for Leicestershire from 1758, and of Anne (*fl.* 1745–1751), daughter of James Skrymsher of Hill Hall, Staffordshire. On 21 June 1768 the younger Rogers (known as Rory by his father) matriculated at Merton College, Oxford, where his uncle Walter Ruding was a fellow. Ruding took his BA in April 1772 and on 2 August 1774 was elected a probationer fellow. He became a full fellow in 1775 and proceeded MA in that year. He was ordained deacon on 2 June 1776 and priest on 15 June 1777; in 1782 he took the degree of BD and in 1788 was appointed to the college living of Wolford, Warwickshire. His tenure of his fellowship ended in 1793. He was presented to another college living, that of Malden, Surrey, on 23 March and married his cousin Charlotte, fourth daughter of his uncle John Ruding of Great Russell Street, Bloomsbury, London, on 16 May 1793. They had three sons and two daughters.

While at Oxford, Ruding developed interests in the history of his college and its founder, Walter de Merton. From about the time of his move to Malden, he started to work on the history of English coinage. From 1796 the *Gentleman's Magazine* published many contributions from him about coins, and he also published articles in *Archaeologia*. Coinage reforms were proposed by him in a pamphlet of 1798; his *Annals of the Coinage*, a chronological account of English coinage which was published in four quarto volumes in 1817, combined his interests in historical and contemporary numismatics and, he hoped, would help to prevent counterfeiting. He concentrated on the accurate recording of information, and among the notable features of his work are his use of medieval records then not readily available to scholars and of works printed in the sixteenth, seventeenth, and eighteenth centuries. The edition quickly sold out and was republished in 1819 and again in 1840.

Ruding was elected a fellow of the Society of Antiquaries on 11 June 1807; he was also an honorary member of the Literary and Philosophical Society of Newcastle upon Tyne. He died, deeply in debt, on 16 February 1820 in Malden, where he was buried on 24 February. His wife survived him.

SARAH BENDALL

Sources H. E. Pagan, 'Presidential address', *British Numismatic Journal*, 55 (1985), 208–19, esp. 211–19 · *GM*, 1st ser., 90/1 (1820), 278 · K. N. Ross, *A history of Malden* (1947) · Foster, *Alum. Oxon.* · *DNB* · Nichols, *Lit. anecdotes*, 9.218

Archives BL, papers relating to *Annals of the coinage of Britain*, Add. MSS 18072–18096 · LUL, papers relating to *Annals of the coinage of Britain*, MS 154 | Bodl. Oxf., MS Don. d. 90 · Bodl. Oxf., MS Eng. Lett. c. 364 · Bodl. Oxf., MS Eng. Lett. c. 372
Likenesses L. Vaslet, pastel drawing, 1789, Merton Oxf.
Wealth at death in debt for at least £775: Pagan, 'Presidential address'

Rudler, Gustave (1872–1957), French scholar, was born in Besançon, France, on 11 January 1872, the son of a teacher at the local *lycée*, and educated at the Lycée Louis-le-Grand and the École Normale Supérieure in Paris. Taking the first place nationally in the *agrégation*, he was appointed as professor of rhetoric at, successively, *lycées* in St Étienne, Caen, and finally his old school of Louis-le-Grand. In 1908 he successfully defended his doctoral thesis, 'La jeunesse de Benjamin Constant, 1767–1794'. When published, this work achieved the distinction of being *couronné* by the Académie Française, being seen as a pioneering study in the field of Constant literature and remaining authoritative on this early period of the author's life.

Rudler was briefly a lecturer at the Sorbonne until in 1913 he was appointed professor of French at Bedford College in the University of London. The rest of his professional life was spent in England. The tenure of the chair, however, was interrupted by the obligations of military service in the First World War. He subsequently returned to Bedford College, remaining there until 1920, when he was elected to the newly created Marshal Foch chair of French literature at the University of Oxford, which carried with it a fellowship at All Souls College. He held this chair until his retirement in 1949, then returned to Paris, dying there on 17 October 1957. His wife, Madeleine, had predeceased him in 1946.

Rudler's scholarship is strongly marked by the influence of the famous French scholar and critic Gustave Lanson, who had directed his doctoral research, and he came to see himself as Lanson's disciple. Indeed, his lavish praise for Lanson's work aroused intense irritation in such opponents as Charles Péguy in the years preceding the First World War. Like Lanson, he held a fervent belief in the importance of clear order and logical thinking in literary criticism, via the traditional French methods of *explication de texte* and *dissertation* (essay writing), allied to a lucid and exactly accurate analysis of literary texts. In pursuit of this objective, he wrote a primer on textual criticism, *L'explication française: principes et application* (1902), and, for more advanced students, *Les techniques de la critique et de l'histoire littéraire* (1923), which he dedicated to Lanson. These works carried the Lansonian gospel to Britain, with consequences that, in the view of many, unduly encouraged a 'scientific' approach to French studies in this country.

Rudler's own scholarly publications ranged widely, but had a particular emphasis on Benjamin Constant. His *thèse complémentaire* for the doctorate had been a 'Bibliographie critique des oeuvres de Benjamin Constant', which was published, like his main thesis, in 1908. He later provided a critical edition of Constant's most well-known work,

Adolphe (1919), and over the years he composed several articles and lectures on the author. But he also wrote a two-volume study, *Michelet: historien de Jeanne d'Arc* (1925–6), and a critical edition of Michelet's eponymous work on Joan of Arc (1927). Late in his career he provided important editions for the Blackwells French Texts series of Racine's *Mithridate* (1943) and Molière's *Le misanthrope* (1947). In addition, he wrote articles on themes and authors as widely ranging as the correspondence of Guez de Balzac, the political content of Chateaubriand's *Les martyrs*, the historical sources of Mme de Lafayette's *La princesse de Clèves*, and the portrait scene in Victor Hugo's *Hernani*. His published writings extended over a half-century, from 1898 to 1947.

Rudler edited the *Revue universitaire* and the *Revue critique des livres nouveaux* (both 1910–13), and later the *French Quarterly* (1919–32), the first English periodical devoted to French literature, thought, and art, of which he was the founder (with A. Terracher). He was warmly remembered at Oxford for his devotion to scholarship and teaching alike; a former pupil recalled that he lectured rapidly and entirely in French, firing at students in the audience questions that had to be answered in the language. While lecturing on plays he acted out certain scenes, on one occasion hiding under a table when the plot required it. In 1952 a Festschrift was presented to him, *The French Mind*, edited by Will Moore, Rhoda Sutherland, and Enid Starkie, with a foreword by Alfred Ewert that describes the book as 'a token of gratitude and admiration for the scholar and of esteem and affection for the man'.   HAYDN MASON

Sources *French Studies*, 12 (1958), 1–4 · *The Times* (18 Oct 1957) · *WWW* · Oxf. UA · A. Compagnon, *La troisième république des lettres, de Flaubert à Proust* (1983) · P. Mansell Jones, *The assault on French literature and other essays* (1963) · 'Reminiscences of H. R. Lloyd-Jones', Brasenose College, Oxford, archives, accession 129

Rudolf, Edward de Montjoie (1852–1933), social reformer, was born at 63 Pleasant Place, West Square, Lambeth, London, on 11 April 1852, the second son of Major William Edward Rudolf (1785–1871) and his second wife, Susan Amy Goodin (1832–1910). He was educated mainly at home, and owing to his elderly father's failing eyesight spent much of his childhood assisting with the latter's translation work to supplement the family's income. In his thirteenth year he became the family's sole wage earner when he began work as an office boy. The years between 1865 and 1880 saw the development of the three interests that were to influence the rest of his life—education, the church, and child welfare.

While working, Rudolf continued his education, even denying himself meals to buy books. In 1871 his perseverance was rewarded when he passed the first open civil service examination and obtained a post in the office of works. He became official private secretary to the first commissioner, G. J. Shaw-Lefevre (afterwards Lord Eversley), and to his successor, Lord Rosebery. At this time Rudolf was also involved in the popular education movement in south London, and between 1869 and 1875 he established several working men's classes and night schools.

The second and third of Rudolf's interests were inextricably linked. In 1872 he became superintendent of the Sunday school at St Anne's Church in South Lambeth, and in 1874 his growing social awareness and desire for a clerical career came together when he joined the Guild of St Alban. In 1880 the experience of finding two of his Sunday school children begging following the death of their father convinced Rudolf of the need for a children's home, run by the Church of England, which would assist homeless and impoverished children. With the support of local clergymen and businessmen, such as Canon J. Erskine Clarke and Mark Beaufoy, afterwards MP for Kennington, he formed the Church of England Central Home for Waifs and Strays on 21 March 1881. Following a deputation from Rudolf and his supporters, the archbishop of Canterbury became the society's first president in August 1881.

The organization grew rapidly: the first home was opened in 1882. In 1919, 4531 children were cared for in 113 homes; by the time of Rudolf's death 37,000 children had been assisted. In 1893 the society became known as the Church of England Incorporated Society for Providing Homes for Waifs and Strays. In 1946 it became the Church of England Children's Society, now popularly known as the Children's Society. From the first Rudolf insisted on the children having as normal a life as possible; he did not want them to become institutionalized through residential care. Many were boarded out with foster parents, and those who were not lived in small homes, where they were not segregated or distinguished by a uniform.

Rudolf acted as honorary secretary until he was appointed full time in 1890. He was an able administrator who dealt with all aspects of the society's work. In addition, he wrote for and edited the society's supporter magazine and travelled widely, attending fund-raising events and committees, opening new homes, and visiting staff and children in the homes. In 1903, for example, he made thirty-one tours around the country on society business. Whenever he visited a home he always tried to spend some time with the children, joining in with their activities. He also did his best to keep in touch with young people previously in the society's care, and wanted them to feel they had a friend in him long after they had left the homes. Although poor health caused him to resign the secretaryship in 1919, he remained a keen member of all committees.

Rudolf's activities were not confined to the Waifs and Strays Society. In July 1884, with Benjamin Waugh, he was elected joint honorary secretary of the newly formed London Society for the Prevention of Cruelty to Children. He held this position until May 1889, when the London Society became the National Society for the Prevention of Cruelty to Children. He maintained his links with the new body by serving on both its central executive committee from 1889 to 1892 and its council in 1893. Rudolf was strongly in favour of registration and inspection of all voluntary institutions for children: at the International Congress for the Welfare and Protection of Children held in London in 1902 he argued that 'it might become a stepping-stone to the greatest advantage of all—the establishment of a State Children's Department' ('Proposed government registration and inspection of voluntary schools').

Rudolf gave evidence to numerous parliamentary committees, including Lord Shaftesbury's inquiry in 1885 into children employed by circuses, for the Mundella report in 1896, and to the Daylight Saving Bill committee in 1908. In 1892 he put forward proposals for the Church of England to develop an old-age pension scheme for elderly people unable to support themselves. However, his main interest outside the welfare of children was the League of Nations Union, of which he was a member of the executive and finance committees. In 1915, with the support of the bishop of Lichfield, Rudolf published a declaration on the limitation of war, stating that, in order to prevent further wars, 'the universal Christian church without reference to nationality should make its voice heard' and demand a peace settlement overseen by an effective international tribunal ('Declaration of the limitation of war').

Rudolf finally realized his ambition to become a clergyman when he was ordained as a deacon in 1898 and as a priest in 1907. In 1911 he became a prebendary of St Paul's Cathedral. He was appointed CBE in 1931, and in the same year the honorary degree of MA was conferred upon him by Oxford University.

Rudolf married Emma Bulmer (1861–1929) on 6 July 1881; they had four sons, two of whom predeceased him, and three daughters. Rudolf died at 8 Victoria Mansions, Eastbourne, on 29 May 1933. By his own wish, his body was cremated on 31 May and the ashes were buried in his wife's grave in Ocklynge cemetery.

C. DE M. RUDOLF, *rev.* IAN WAKELING and
NOEL DE MONTJOIE RUDOLF

Sources [E. de M. Rudolf], *The first forty years: a chronicle of the Church of England Waifs and Strays Society* (1922) · C. de M. Rudolf, 'Rudolf of the Waifs', c.1951, The Children's Society Archive, 85. 123 · J. Stroud, *Thirteen penny stamps: the story of the Church of England Children's Society from 1881 to the 1970s* (1971) · E. de M. Rudolf, 'My early days', 1931, priv. coll. · *Our Waifs and Strays Magazine* (July 1933) · *Sussex Daily News* (30 May 1933) · E. de M. Rudolf, 'Declaration of the limitation of war', 1915, priv. coll. · E. de M. Rudolf, Letter presented to children leaving the care of the Society, 1920, The Children's Society Archive, XX/Polloc/1/1 · 39th Annual Report of Church of England Incorporated Society for Providing Homes for Waifs and Strays, 1919 (1920), The Children's Society Archive · H. Ward, 'The charitable relationship: parents, children and the Waifs and Strays Society', PhD diss., University of Bristol, 1990 · E. de M. Rudolf, 'Proposed government registration and inspection of voluntary schools', proof copy, Proceedings of the Congress for the Welfare and Protection of Children, 1902, priv. coll. · m. cert. · d. cert.
Archives Children's Society, London, archive · priv. coll. | LPL, Tait MSS
Likenesses S. A. Walker, photograph, 1888, Children's Society archive, London · Brown, Barnes & Bell, photograph, 1890–99, Children's Society archive, London · Elliott & Fry, photograph, 1910–19, Children's Society archive, London · J. Russell & Sons, photograph, 1920–29, Children's Society archive, London · E. Pearce, oils, 1930, Edward Rudolf House, London · Elliott & Fry, photograph, 1932, Children's Society archive, London · T. C. Dugdale, oils, priv. coll.
Wealth at death £4469 0s. 5d.: probate, 22 July 1933, *CGPLA Eng. & Wales*

Rudyerd, Sir Benjamin (1572–1658), politician and poet, was born on 26 December 1572, the third son of James Rudyerd and Margaret Kidwelly. He was educated at Winchester College and matriculated at St John's College, Oxford, on 15 January 1588, although he apparently left without taking a degree. He was admitted to the Middle Temple on 18 April 1590 and was called to the bar on 24 October 1600. At an unknown date he married Mary Harrington, and in 1610 he obtained a licence to travel abroad for three years. After his return he was knighted, on 30 March 1618; shortly afterwards, on 17 April, he was appointed surveyor of the court of wards for life. He held that lucrative office until the court's abolition in February 1646, whereupon the Long Parliament voted him £6000 as compensation. In 1619 he was also granted an annuity of £200 which was apparently still being paid in the 1640s.

Poetry and the Pembroke connection Rudyerd's political career did not really begin until 1621, and his earlier years were notable mainly for his accomplishments as a poet. His associates included Ben Jonson, who in 1616 printed three epigrams dedicated to Rudyerd. Rudyerd wrote 'Le prince d'Amour, an account of the revels of the Society of the Middle Temple in 1599', and also a series of poems, some written in the form of exchanges with verses by his friend and patron William Herbert, third earl of Pembroke. All these works were published posthumously in 1660.

Rudyerd's friendship with Pembroke, and with his younger brother, Philip Herbert, earl of Montgomery, who became fourth earl of Pembroke, was a crucial influence on his career. He owed his appointment as surveyor of the wards to the third earl. He sometimes answered letters for the third and then the fourth earl, and also acted as a surety for some of their legal transactions such as indentures conveying land. Similarly, his return to parliament for Portsmouth (1621, 1624, 1625), and then for the Wiltshire constituencies of Old Sarum (1626), Downton (1628–9), and Wilton (1640–48) was directly due to the earls of Pembroke, whose seat was at Wilton House. During this period the earls of Pembroke nominated both members for Wilton and at least one for each of the three other constituencies that Rudyerd represented.

The parliaments of the 1620s Throughout his parliamentary career Rudyerd co-operated closely with his patrons. During the parliaments of the 1620s he consistently advocated careful collaboration between members of the two houses, and this was reflected in the alignment of his own attitudes with those of the third earl of Pembroke on several key issues. He has been described as 'the chief House of Commons spokesman for Pembroke' (C. Russell, *Parliaments and English Politics, 1621–1629*, 1979, 13). Both men were, first of all, strongly committed to godly protestantism. Vehemently anti-Catholic, they both advocated a pan-protestant, pro-Dutch, anti-Spanish foreign policy, and were prepared to contemplate a French alliance if that helped to isolate Spain. Rudyerd's view of diplomacy was guided primarily by his horror that 'our religion was battered abroad' (Manning, 62). At home this outlook translated into a deep concern about 'scandalous livings as well as scandalous ministers' (Cobbett, *Parl. hist.*, 2.45) and a wish to alleviate the poverty of the church. In January 1629, for example, he told the Commons committee on religion that 'scandalous livings cannot but have scandalous ministers' and 'though christianity and religion bee established generally throughout this kingdome, yet untill it bee planted more particularly, I shall scarce thinke this a Christian Commonwealth' (*Sir Benjamin Ruddierd's Speech in Behalfe of the Cleargy*, 1628/9, 4). He believed that until parliament took radical steps the church's economic problems could not be resolved.

Rudyerd was one of a small minority in the Commons—which also included Sir Nathaniel Rich, Sir Dudley Digges, and John Pym—who sought an overhaul of crown revenues. They aimed both to enlarge the monarch's income and to safeguard the future of parliaments. Rudyerd was the least radical of these members, and throughout the 1620s he mainly confined himself to advocating the grant of a generous number of subsidies. For example, in 1621 he moved:

> that this House would consider of a present supply of the army in the Palatinate, that that business and the dangers which may come thereby be not wound up on delays till they break, and so our supply come too late.   (Manning, 62–3)

Or again, on 17 March 1628:

> the way to show that we are the wise counsellors we should be is … by giving a large and ample supply, proportionable to the greatness and importance of the work in hand; for counsel without money is but a speculation.   (ibid., 116)

He recognized that parliament's 'power of the purse', if pushed too far, could force the king to resort to non-parliamentary means of raising money: this fear lay behind his celebrated warning to the Commons, earlier in that same speech, that 'this is the crisis of Parliaments: we shall know by this if Parliaments live or die' (ibid., 114).

Rudyerd's repeated calls for generous supply closely resembled Pembroke's own views, and their attitudes towards Buckingham were similarly aligned. Throughout, they remained at heart suspicious of the duke, but they were prepared to co-operate with him for tactical reasons, especially after 1623–4 when Buckingham became committed to an anti-Spanish foreign policy. But this reconciliation was only skin-deep: it was a member of the Pembroke interest, Dr Turner, who launched the attack on Buckingham in the 1626 parliament, and Rudyerd was among the sixteen members of the Commons appointed to assist the managers of the duke's impeachment. A further attempt at reconciliation, in the form of a marriage agreement concluded on 3 August 1626 between Buckingham's daughter and Pembroke's nephew, appears to have had some effect, and probably explains why both Rudyerd and Pembroke took a moderate line in the debates over the petition of right in 1628,

and in particular opposed naming the duke in the petition.

The third earl of Pembroke died on 10 April 1630. Rudyerd shared the interest of his new patron, the fourth earl, in colonial enterprises, and on 4 December 1630 became one of the original incorporators of the Providence Island Company. Although this company was not the hotbed of puritan opposition that has sometimes been claimed, many of its members shared Rudyerd's commitment to godly protestantism. Little further can be discovered about his activities during the years of Charles I's personal rule, but it is likely that his work as surveyor of the court of wards kept him busy, and in June 1637 he complained to the earl of Leicester of having 'so many employments of my vocation' (Manning, 141–2).

Protestant orator in the 1640s This obscurity came to an abrupt end when parliament was recalled in 1640. Rudyerd took a characteristically moderate line in the Short Parliament, and on 16 April reportedly warned the Commons that 'it is wisdom in us to preserve temper and moderation': 'if temper and moderation be not respected by us, beware of having the race of Parliaments rooted out' (Manning, 151). Parliament was 'the bed of reconciliation between King and people', and Rudyerd continued to regard the speedy and generous granting of supply as essential to achieve this: 'Before the ending of the Parliament (the untimely breaking of which would be the breaking of us), I doubt not but His Majesty's revenue may be so settled, that he may live plentifully at home and abroad' (ibid., 150). Yet the parliament was dissolved after only three weeks. When the Long Parliament met the following November, his rhetoric became rather more forceful, yet his two central concerns—religion and supply—remained the same.

In a remarkable speech on 7 November 1640 he declared: 'let religion be our *primum quaerite*, for all things else are but *etcaeteras* to it'. He bitterly denounced Laudian innovations on the grounds that moderate, loyal 'conformists' like himself now found themselves branded puritans:

> under the name of Puritans, all our religion is branded … Whosoever squares his actions by any rule, either divine or humane, he is a Puritan. Whoever would be governed by the King's laws, he is a Puritan. He that would not do whatsoever other men would have him do, he is a Puritan. Their great work, their masterpiece, now is, to make all those of the religion to be the suspected party of the kingdom.   (*The Speeches of Sir Benjamin Rudyer*, 3)

He lamented the

> disturbance [that] hath been brought upon the Church for vain, petty trifles. How the whole Church, the whole kingdom, hath been troubled where to place 'a metaphor'—an altar. We have seen ministers, their wives, children, and families undone, against all law—against conscience—against all bowels of compassion—about not dancing upon Sundays … These inventions are but sieves made on purpose to winnow the best men, and that's the devil's occupation.   (ibid., 2)

He further denounced the Laudians on 15 December, claiming that they 'have turned so many out of the way of truth, *via tuta* they have stopt up, but *via devia* they have enlarged and left open, as appears by their crooked canons' (Manning, 175).

Equally, Rudyerd remained sympathetic to the crown's financial problems. Once what he called the 'subverting, destructive counsels', who rang 'a doleful, deadly knell over the whole kingdom' (Manning, 162), had been removed, he then wanted the houses to grant generous supply. Thus, on 23 December he asserted:

> the principal part of this business is money; and now we are about it, I shall be glad we may give so much as will not only serve the turn for the present, but likewise to provide that it comes not quick upon us again. (ibid., 166–7)

He continued to regard the 'reciprocation' between monarch and people as 'the strongest, the sweetest union' (ibid., 164), and he later praised the constitutional reforms of the early months of the Long Parliament as 'a dream of happiness' (ibid., 230).

The parliament's initially high degree of unity began to disintegrate from mid-1641 onwards, particularly over the issue of religious reformation. Rudyerd's godly protestantism and hatred of Laudianism were typical of many who became parliamentarians in the civil wars; where he was unusual was in his continuing attachment to the institution of episcopacy and his mistrust of root and branch reform. On 27 May 1641, in response to Sir Edward Dering's bill demanding the abolition of episcopacy, he argued that 'it now behoves us to restrain the bishops to the duties of their functions, as they may never more hanker after heterogeneous, extravagant employments' (Manning, 185). However, 'when they are thus circumscribed, and the public secured from their corruptions, then shall I not grudge them a liberal, plentiful subsistence' (ibid., 186). He regarded bishops as 'the most primitive, the most spreading, the most lasting government of the Church' and he questioned 'whether a popular democratical government of the Church … will be either suitable or acceptable to a regal monarchical government of the State' (ibid., 186).

Rudyerd returned to these issues in a further speech on 15 June 1641. He rejected the view that 'there can be no reformation without destruction', and was emphatically not 'of their opinion who believe that there is an innate ill quality in episcopacy, like a specifical property': 'I hope there is no original sin in episcopacy; and though there were, yet may the calling be as well reformed as the person regenerated'. He hoped that bishops might be 'reduced according to the usage of ancient churches in the best times' (Manning, 188–9). He summed up his position thus: 'I am as much for reformation, for purging and maintaining religion, as any man whatsoever: but I profess, I am not for innovation, demolition, nor abolition' (Cobbett, *Parl. hist.*, 2.835).

Advocate of peace From the late summer of 1641 such an attachment to a moderate, primitive episcopacy inclined many members of the Long Parliament to rally to the king. Yet Rudyerd remained at Westminster, and his long-standing commitment to godly protestantism may well have contributed to this decision. He broadly shared this religious outlook with the fourth earl of Pembroke, who became progressively more estranged from the court and was dismissed as lord chamberlain of the king's household in July 1641. The close political alignment between Rudyerd and Pembroke was particularly apparent in 1641–2. Both supported Strafford's attainder and ultimately sided with parliament; but equally, as war approached, both tried desperately to promote an accommodation between the crown and the two houses.

In November 1641 Rudyerd took an ambivalent view of the grand remonstrance. He accepted that it was 'requisite we should publish a declaration, because there are so many depravers of this Parliament'. However, he then continued:

> my vote goes along in general with the narrative historical part of it; but for the prophetical part, to foresee the whole work of this Parliament to come, and to bind it up by anticipation and engagement of votes beforehand, for ought I know, Sir, we have no such custom. (Manning, 221–3)

In the summer of 1642 both Rudyerd and Pembroke remained at Westminster while continuing to urge an accommodation. On the morning of 9 July Pembroke made a speech 'laying open the means for that happy union' (*A Perfect Diurnall of the Passages in Parliament, from 4 to 11 July 1642*, 1642, 6), while later that day Rudyerd begged the houses 'to compose and settle these threatening ruining distractions' and 'make a fair way for the King's return hither'. He urged parliament not to 'contend for such a hazardous, unsafe securitie as may endanger the losse of what we have already' and, in a memorable phrase, warned that they could never 'make a mathematicall securitie' (*A Worthy Speech Spoken in The Honourable House of Commons, by Sir Benjamin Rudyerd, this Present July, 1642*, 1642, 2–4).

During the civil war Rudyerd remained a passionate advocate of peace negotiations. On 17 February 1643, for example, he implored the Commons to consider 'who shall be answerable for all the innocent bloud which shall be spilt hereafter, if we doe not endeavour a peace, by a speedy treaty' (*Sir Benjamin Rudyerd his Speech in the high Court of Parliament the 17 of February [1643], for a Speedy Treaty of Peace with his Majestie*, 1643, 5). Like other moderate parliamentarians such as Sir Simonds D'Ewes, Bulstrode Whitelocke, and John Selden, he advised talks at every possible opportunity. He also remained committed to godly reformation and was appointed a lay member of the Westminster assembly on 12 June 1643.

Rudyerd's links with Pembroke continued to be close. Both were appointed commissioners for the English colonies and plantations on 2 November 1643. On 14 June 1645 Rudyerd brought two letters to the committee of both kingdoms, one directed to himself and the other to Pembroke. In his will, dated 1 May 1649, Pembroke stipulated that Rudyerd was to continue to occupy the premises in Kent that the earl had assigned to him by an indenture of 21 February 1639. At his death in January 1650 Pembroke owed Rudyerd a debt of £260, which was discharged shortly afterwards by the earl's executors (Sheffield Archives, Elmhirst MS, Pye deposit, EM 1358/1, EM 1358/2, EM 1360; Hatfield House, accounts, 168/2, 22, 28).

In the autumn of 1648 Pembroke was one of the parliamentarian commissioners appointed to negotiate with the king at Newport, while back in London, on 5 December, Rudyerd voted that the talks should continue. The next day he was among those arrested, and briefly imprisoned, by Colonel Pride. Immediately after his release Rudyerd, who was then just short of his seventy-sixth birthday, retired to his seat at Westwoodhay in Berkshire. He lived out his remaining years there very quietly, and died there on 31 May 1658. He was buried in the chancel of the church at Westwoodhay.   DAVID L. SMITH

Sources J. A. Manning, *Memoirs of Sir Benjamin Rudyerd* (1841) • Keeler, *Long Parliament*, 329 • W. Notestein, F. H. Relf, and H. Simpson, eds., *Commons debates, 1621*, 7 vols. (1935) • R. C. Johnson and others, eds., *Proceedings in parliament, 1628*, 6 vols. (1977–83) • W. B. Bidwell and M. Jansson, eds., *Proceedings in parliament, 1626*, 4 vols. (1991–6) • *The journal of Sir Simonds D'Ewes from the beginning of the Long Parliament to the opening of the trial of the earl of Strafford*, ed. W. Notestein (1923) • W. H. Coates, A. Steele Young, and V. F. Snow, eds., *The private journals of the Long Parliament*, 3 vols. (1982–92) • *JHC*, 2–8 (1640–67) • PRO, state papers domestic, Charles I, SP 16 • Cobbett, *Parl. hist.*, vols. 1–2 • *The speeches of Sir Benjamin Rudyer in the high court of parliament* (1641) • *Sir Benjamin Rudyerd's speech concerning bishops, deans and chapters* (1641) • *Two worthy speeches spoken in the honourable House of Commons by Sir Benjamin Rudyerd* (1643) • D. L. Smith, *Constitutional royalism and the search for settlement, c. 1640–1649* (1994)
Archives BL, Harley MSS, parliamentary speeches, etc.
Likenesses D. Mytens, oils, 1627, Gov. Art Coll.; repro. in Manning, *Memoirs* • W. Hollar, etching (after D. Mytens), BM, NPG • J. Payne, line engraving (after D. Mytens), BM, NPG

Rudyerd, John (*fl.* 1703–1709), builder of the second Eddystone lighthouse, was one of a large and poor family. Little is known of his origins, except that he was born in Cornwall, probably near Plymouth. There he was in the service of a gentleman, who caused him to be educated.

In the early eighteenth century Rudyerd was in business as a silk mercer in Ludgate Hill, London, when he was engaged by Captain John Lovel or Lovet, the lessee, to act as 'architect and surveyor' for a lighthouse on the Eddystone Reef near Plymouth, to replace the one built by Henry Winstanley, which had been swept away by a storm in 1703 after only five years. Assisted by Norcott and Smith, Woolwich shipwrights, he carried out a tremendous feat of engineering. Using a shore base at Empacombe, he first anchored his structure to the rocks in a novel and successful way. Then, using layers of oak balks between much thicker layers of granite to give mass for stability, he built the tower round a central timber mast, to a height of 61 feet. The whole was encased in heavy oak timbers, caulked and pitch-covered like a ship, to a total height of 92 feet.

The light, which had twenty-four candles, was first shown on 28 July 1708, and the lighthouse was completed in 1709. It stood successfully in its very exposed position until December 1755; it was then totally destroyed by fire, which started in the lantern roof and, despite the efforts of the keepers, spread down through the timbers, driving the men out upon the rocks, whence they were rescued next day.

John Smeaton expressed the greatest admiration for Rudyerd's work, which greatly benefited him when he built the third Eddystone light. Rudyerd was the builder of the first successful sea-rock lighthouse in the world, but nothing more is known of him. Smeaton presumed that he died soon after completion of the work.

JAMES HODGE, *rev.*

Sources J. Smeaton, *A narrative of the building and a description of the construction of the Edystone lighthouse with stone*, 2nd edn (1793) • J. Hodge, *Four Cornishmen, their contribution to science and engineering: University of Exeter, the second Kemp memorial lecture … 23 March 1988* [1988] • T. Rowatt, 'Notes on original models of the Eddystone lighthouses', *Transactions* [Newcomen Society], 5 (1924–5), 15–23 • A. W. Skempton, ed., *John Smeaton FRS* (1981) • D. B. Hague and R. Christie, *Lighthouses: their architecture, history and archaeology* (1975)
Archives Royal Scottish Museums, Edinburgh, Eddystone lighthouse models and drawings • RS, Smeaton Drawings

Rue, de la, family (*per. c.*1820–1923), stationers and printers, came to prominence with **Thomas de la Rue** (1793–1866), born in La Forêt, Guernsey, and apprenticed to the master printer Joseph Antoine Chevalier at St Peter Port in Guernsey in 1803. On finishing his apprenticeship, Thomas took up with Tom Greenslade of Bishop's Nympton in Devon, who was related by marriage to Thomas's future wife, Jane Warren: in 1802 they launched a newspaper, *Le Publiciste*. After only a few months Thomas walked out on the partnership and, with a determination and audacity that were to characterize his business life, raised funding from John Campion, husband of his sister Rachel, to publish his own rival newspaper, *Le Miroir Politique*. This was so successful that after only a few months he advertised for an apprentice. Thomas's interest in the quality of printing and in other types of publication, such as editions of the litany and Psalms, indicated the future direction of his career.

In March 1814 de la Rue married Jane Warren (1789–1858) of Bishop's Nympton. Their first child, Warren de la *Rue (1815–1889), was born at St Peter Port in January 1815. In that summer de la Rue left the *Miroir Politique*, and after his father's death in November 1816 he and his family left Guernsey. They may have moved first to Barnstaple before settling in London, where Thomas set up business in Finsbury Square manufacturing straw hats, a skill perhaps learned in Guernsey through family connections. His second son, William Frederick [*see below*], was born in London soon after. Millinery still allowed de la Rue to experiment with different printing techniques and dyes for paper bonnets during the 1820s; however, a reference to playing cards in his notebooks for 1828 signalled what was to become a lucrative new line. Two years later he was in business with Samuel Cornish and William Frederick Rock, calling themselves 'Cardmakers, Hot Pressers and Enamellers'.

The new decade brought mixed fortunes. The first few years were prosperous: in 1831 de la Rue registered an ace of spades at the Stamp Office, Somerset House, as was

Thomas de la Rue (1793–1866), by Wilhelm Trautschold, 1857

required for purposes of duty on playing cards; the following year he received royal letters patent for improvements in the colour printing and decoration of playing cards. His specification contained descriptions of two methods of applying colour by surface-printing, one employing typography from raised wooden or metal blocks, the other lithography, printing from stones. In each case separate blocks or stones were used for different colours and Thomas paid particular attention to methods of fitting the design together in perfect register, with no overlap or gap between colours. Not all his innovations were successful: attempts to add character to the expressions on the face cards were unpopular—instead, Thomas applied creativity to decoration on the back of the cards. In 1835 the business moved to the address that became the seat of its empire, 110 Bunhill Row in the City, with the family living next door at number 108. However, the commercial depression of 1837 caused serious financial difficulties for the firm and the partnership—now de la Rue, James, and Rudd—was dissolved. Things were so bad that late in May de la Rue was arrested for debt, and though it was in his creditors' interest to bail him out, they drove a hard bargain to do so, running the business for a while as a trust with de la Rue as a paid employee, and negotiating a low price to buy his patent for the production of white lead. The family pulled together to weather the storm: by 1837 both de la Rue's sons were working in the business, and his wife and eldest daughter also helped out. Warren de la

Rue had joined the firm some two years earlier, and was already proving the worth of his scientific interests; indeed, another scientist with whom he had collaborated, Charles Button, lent de la Rue money to help clear his debts. In 1839 both Warren and Charles Button were made partners in the firm, and in the following year Warren married Georgiana Bowles (1819–1918), who travelled with him on business and helped him throughout his career. Typically, Thomas de la Rue bounced back from his problems, celebrating Victoria's coronation in June 1838 by employing 100 staff for six days to gild a special edition of the *Sun* newspaper.

For several decades both family and business flourished as established lines and new products were developed with shrewd collaboration and constant experiment, and were rewarded with public recognition. Warren de la Rue combined scientific experiment with business travel, as well as superintending building works and devising an improved boiler for making tea for the workmen. Playing cards became a cornerstone of the business, the more expensive packs distinguished by the work of Owen Jones (1809–1874), who in an association lasting several decades produced over 170 designs for playing cards alone, including a pack for the royal family, as well as for diaries and calendars. The cards and their manufacture earned the praise of Charles Dickens in his *Household Words* (vol. 6, 1853), and their influence was indirectly acknowledged by the family long after the business had diversified: referring to the number of cards in a pack, William Frederick left £52 in his will to Owen Jones, while Warren's younger son, Thomas Andros de la Rue [*see below*], had the houses of Cadogan Square renumbered so that his would be number 52.

In an early venture into overseas markets in the early 1840s Thomas de la Rue established his younger brother, Paul, in St Petersburg to oversee the tsar's playing card business, for which De La Rue supplied machinery. Railway tickets and visiting cards were added to the range of printed goods, and the range of social stationery expanded. Such activities followed on from existing business, but as early as 1840 de la Rue took out a printing patent which contained hints of two key areas of future development, in a reference to 'banknotes, post office envelopes or any work requiring great difficulty of invention'. At this date the firm was not yet directly engaged in the security printing of currency or stamps, but among several valuable contacts, Warren was friendly with Edwin Hill, the brother of Rowland Hill who introduced the pre-paid penny postage in 1840. Capitalizing on the market opened up by the increase in post, De La Rue initially moved into the manufacture of envelopes, cut mechanically by a machine invented by Warren de la Rue and Edwin Hill.

This venture was just one feature of the accolade published in *Chambers's Edinburgh Journal* in July 1846: recounting his experience in 'A day at De La Rue's', the writer found 'an amusing hive of industry; steam-engines, machinery and animated beings, commingling in restless and varied movement' to produce playing cards, mourning stationery and marriage cards, needle-books, and even a portable chessboard. The description shows that inventive production was matched by economies of scale and good management: the firm made and repaired their own machinery, while the productivity of some 300 employees was maximized by such paternalistic measures as replacing beer breaks with a shorter working day and establishing a library and a sickness fund. The article described the firm as the largest of its kind in the world—journalistic exaggeration, perhaps, but indicative of status which was recognized and enhanced at the Great Exhibition of 1851.

With the help of good contacts—Warren had by now been elected to the Royal Society and Owen Jones was superintendent of works for the Great Exhibition—De La Rue had a prime site and attracted huge crowds to their display, of which the envelope-making machine was the centrepiece. Other items included portable writing-desks, designed by William Frederick, and playing cards with coloured pips to assist those with poor sight; the latter were not a success at the time, though similar devices are now a common feature on paper currency, of which the present-day De La Rue is a major producer. Thomas, Warren, and the firm won medals for their contributions to the exhibition, which were also rewarded by good publicity in the exhibition catalogue, the *Illustrated London News*, and in Henry Selous's painting of Victoria opening the exhibition, which included Thomas and Warren among the onlookers—indeed, the family bought the painting, later presented to the Victoria and Albert Museum. At the exhibitions in New York and Paris in 1853 and 1855 the firm won further honours and Thomas was made chevalier of the Légion d'honneur.

William Frederick de la Rue (1825–1870), Thomas's younger son, was born on 3 April 1825; he began working for the firm in 1837 and became a traveller in 1840. He was made a partner in 1850 and married Emma Tanner on 20 May of the following year. For some time they lived in the family house next door to the business in Bunhill Row before moving to Harley Street in 1864. Known as Colonel Billy because of his close association with a militia regiment, the 4th Tower Hamlets, William Frederick applied his administrative skills to complement Warren's scientific interests. Over the next twenty years they introduced two important new lines: postage stamps and paper money. In 1853 the firm received a four-year contract from the Inland Revenue to produce adhesive revenue stamps for drafts and receipts. The surface-printing techniques De La Rue used for playing cards enabled them to offer benefits of cost and security over their rivals, Perkins, Bacon & Co., who had hitherto had the Inland Revenue business. In the next few years this advantage was pressed further, helped by a chemist, Hugo Müller, whom Warren had brought to the firm and who worked on perfecting secure printing inks. In 1855 De La Rue produced their first postage stamp, the fourpenny carmine; two years later they received a further contract for the 1s. and 6d. stamps. Another major market opened up in 1854 with the order

for stamps for the East India Company, a contract which led to further postal business for the whole of India, including the supply of government stationery.

A second breakthrough came in 1858 when the crown agents asked De La Rue to produce stamps for the British colonies. Once again, De La Rue's gain was Perkins Bacon's loss: disapproving of their lack of consultation, the new agent general for the crown agents established a good relationship with William Frederick, who was given the courtesy title 'Engraver to the Agents General for the Crown Colonies'. The potential offered by colonial business was boosted further in 1859 when Mauritius placed an order for paper currency, a line of security printing anticipated in the patent of 1840. In 1860 banknotes for Mauritius were printed from copper plates. For the immediate future postage stamps were the greater area of growth for the firm, but these developments were the seeds of greater things to come, for in the twentieth century supplying stamps and banknotes to the British empire was a major part of De La Rue's business.

During the 1850s Thomas de la Rue continued to work on improvements in paper and printing inks, still maintaining his determination to stay ahead of the field; thus in 1856 and 1857 he took John Dickinson & Co. to court for infringing the patent for the envelope-making machine, and won. In 1858 his wife, Jane, died; some months later he married a young Swedish woman, Alice Marie André. Soon afterwards he retired from the firm, having negotiated a generous settlement which included lending money to his sons at high interest. In valuing his own achievement in founding the business above that of his sons in developing it, Thomas created a bitterness that was not resolved; thus his career ended as it had begun, with a successful partnership turning sour. After a few weeks of illness, he died in London in summer 1866.

Following Thomas's retirement the firm's business continued to expand at home and abroad. Perhaps through William Frederick's friendship with American cousins, De La Rue in 1862 was given the contract to print postage stamps for the Confederate states. William Frederick and Warren were both active in travelling to solicit new business. They won orders for stamps and railway tickets in Italy, latterly helping the Italians to set up their own printing plant. Two letters from William Frederick at Bunhill Row to Warren in Italy in 1862 are a mix of family concerns—Emma, William Frederick's wife, was ill—and business, including a promising new order from the raja of Mysore. Postal contracts continued for India, and were established for Portugal and in South America. At home output and sales of playing cards and railway tickets rose impressively, research continued into improving paper and watermarks, and the stationery business flourished, including the ever popular Improved Indelible Diary and Memorandum, almost a miniature almanac, and calendars and diaries embellished with Owen Jones's exquisite decoration—also to be found on labels for Whitbread's stout and Huntley and Palmers' biscuits. To accommodate this growth, the firm opened offices in Liverpool and Paris (the effects of the Civil War led to the early closure of a New York office) and expanded their London property.

In 1870 William Frederick died at forty-six from cancer of the liver, leaving a distraught family. Warren, who had retired some months earlier, came back to run the firm with the help of his two sons, Warren William (1847–1921) and **Sir Thomas Andros de la Rue**, first baronet (1849–1911), both of whom had joined the firm on finishing their education. From the 1870s to the 1890s the firm built on existing foundations, again acquiring new property to meet orders from the crown agents and the Board of Inland Revenue, who in 1879 gave De La Rue the order for the 1*d.* stamp, thus putting the country's entire postage stamp business into their hands. As in the past, production was backed by research, to prove, for example, that the red ink used on the penny stamp was not harmful. The continued growth probably owed much to Warren's presence, for after his retirement in 1880 and death in 1889 the picture changed considerably.

Warren de la Rue's sons showed strong family loyalty, helping at home when their father was ill, but their contrasting personalities—William Warren pedantic and humourless and Thomas Andros urbane and extrovert— were markedly less successful in business than their father and uncle, though Warren William's thoroughness at least protected the firm's interests for a time. Accounts differ on how long Warren William remained active in the firm; it seems likely, however, that his involvement diminished after a riding accident in 1896, if not before, and that Thomas Andros was effectively in control of the business after their father's death. On 1 February 1876 he married Emily Maria Speed (1848–1904), with whom he had three sons; he conducted a glittering social life with a passion for theatre and parties. In 1898 he was made a baronet (in recognition of his work as governor of the Royal Chest Hospital) and he turned the firm into a public company, with most of the shares owned by the family and friends. Having inherited a spectacularly successful business, Thomas Andros proceeded to run it with complacency and short-sightedness, caring less for the welfare of staff and more for profit. His attitude towards major customers suggests some of the first Thomas's stubbornness, but without his drive towards invention and investment to develop new lines and maintain the firm's competitive edge. Thomas Andros alienated two crucial clients: the relationship with the crown agents deteriorated, and the Inland Revenue became concerned about De La Rue's monopoly of stamp production, noting that their prices did not fall to reflect cheaper manufacturing costs. In 1911 the Inland Revenue proposed splitting their contract between De La Rue and Harrisons; there may also have been a request that De La Rue lower their prices: either way, Thomas Andros refused to compromise, and the whole contract went to Harrisons.

This major loss was the start of a serious decline in the fortunes of the De La Rue firm. Thomas Andros died a few months later in April 1911, leaving the business in the hands of his sons, Evelyn, Ivor, and Stuart. They inherited a diminished empire and their lack of flair and harmony failed to restore it. Though the scarcity of gold during the First World War led to contracts for printing 10*s.* and £1 notes, these orders were shared with another firm, Waterlow Brothers and Leighton; Stuart de la Rue entered into a dubious arrangement with a third company, Waterlow & Sons, with mutual promises of financial compensation should either receive future contracts. His two older brothers having joined the army, Stuart was left in charge, recklessly acquiring new and unprofitable businesses. By 1921 De La Rue was approaching bankruptcy: ten years after the loss of the Inland Revenue contract Stuart repeated his father's stubborn short-sightedness and lost the government's postal and stationery business for India because he was not prepared to set up a printing office there. Two years later, in 1923, a court battle with the now combined Waterlow firms culminated in public scandal when it emerged that Thomas Andros had long since had a private agreement with Waterlows to share out remuneration from postal contracts. Unable to restore confidence, his youngest son was now forced to leave, ending the family's control of the firm.

Under new management, retrenchment was eventually followed by the revival, marked by the establishment of a prestigious annual dinner in 1932, and the negotiation of substantial and lucrative banknote contracts from the minister of finance in China. In 1939, with war again imminent, De La Rue undertook to safeguard this production by building printing works in Shanghai and Rangoon, rediscovering the initiative which had been evident in the 1840s and which would again carry them forwards. By the start of the twenty-first century the firm still bearing the family name De La Rue has become the world's largest commercial security printer, operating internationally to provide currency for over 150 countries, cash-handling systems, and security documents. With this dynamism in developing technology and searching out new business, the modern firm still bears witness to the legacy of its founding father, Thomas, and his sons Warren and William Frederick.

VIRGINIA HEWITT

Sources L. Houseman, *The house that Thomas built: the story of De La Rue* (1968) • U. Reading L., De La Rue archive, MS 937 • 'A day at De La Rue's', *Chambers's Edinburgh Journal*, 133 (1846), 33–6 and 57–60 • W. A. Wiseman, *Great Britain: the De La Rue years, 1878–1910*, 2 (1990) • record of baronets, Coll. Arms, 11, p. 109 • Burke, *Peerage* • IGI • Specification of patents, old series, 1832, BL, nos. 6231–6238 • 'Visit to Messrs. De la Rue's card manufactury', *Bradshaw's Journal*, 24 (16 April 1842)

Archives Post Office, London, archive • U. Reading, MSS

Likenesses W. Trautschold, portrait, 1851 (William Frederick de la Rue), repro. in Houseman, *House that Thomas built* • W. Trautschold, portrait, 1857 (Thomas de la Rue), repro. in Houseman, *House that Thomas built* [*see illus.*] • Fuchs, portrait, 1902 (Sir Thomas Andros de la Rue), repro. in Houseman, *House that Thomas built*

Wealth at death under £40,000—Thomas de la Rue: resworn probate, 1867, *CGPLA Eng. & Wales* (1866) • £60,000—William Frederick de la Rue: Houseman, *House that Thomas built* • £787,566 9*s.* 11*d.*—Sir Thomas Andros de la Rue: resworn probate, 1911, *CGPLA Eng. & Wales*; U. Reading, archive

Rue, Sir Thomas Andros de la, first baronet (1849–1911). *See under* Rue, de la, family (*per.* c.1820–1923).

Rue, Thomas de la (1793–1866). *See under* Rue, de la, family
(*per. c.*1820–1923).

Rue, Warren de la (1815–1889), chemist and astronomer,
was born on 18 January 1815 in Guernsey, the elder son of
Thomas de la *Rue (1793–1866), printer, and his wife, Jane
Warren (1789–1858) [*see under* Rue, de la, family]. The family moved to London not long after his birth, but he was
subsequently sent to the Collège de Sainte-Barbe in Paris
to be educated. He returned to London in his teens and
entered his father's business, which, by this time, was
establishing itself as a major producer of stationery. He
followed his father in being interested in technical innovation, and studied privately relevant areas of science,
more especially chemistry. On 17 February 1840 de la Rue
married Georgiana (1819–1918), the third daughter of
Thomas Bowles from Guernsey. They had four sons and
one daughter.

Successful chemistry, 1836–1850 De la Rue's paper relating
to the chemistry of electric batteries (a lifelong interest)
appeared in 1836. The work derived from his concern for
the use of electrotypes in printing, a process which he was
one of the first to introduce on a large scale. In 1845, when
the Royal College of Chemistry was founded in London by
the German chemist, August Wilhelm Hofmann, de la Rue
became one of the first to study there. Besides meeting a
number of future leaders of British chemistry at the college, he became a close friend of Hofmann himself, and
helped him edit chemical translations from the German.
De la Rue's scientific work benefited from skills developed
as part of his business activities. Good draughtsmanship
was one example. Another was mechanical aptitude. On
the business side, this led him to invent, along with Edwin
Hill, the first envelope making machine, which became
one of the exhibits at the Great Exhibition of 1851. Both de
la Rue and his father were jury members at the exhibition,
and for the former his involvement proved highly significant both in terms of business and of science. On the business side, de la Rue became interested in another of the
exhibits—a patent candle. He subsequently carried out
chemical studies which led to improvements in this product. For this he received a substantial payment from its
manufacturers. In 1850 de la Rue's scientific activities
were recognized by his election to the Royal Society.

Astronomy Though de la Rue carried out a number of
investigations into organic chemistry in the latter part of
the 1850s and the early 1860s, his research time was
increasingly taken up by astronomy. In 1840 he came into
contact with James Nasmyth, a successful engineer, who
had developed an interest in astronomy and, more especially, in the construction of an altazimuth reflecting telescope. He inspired de la Rue and cast two speculum mirrors for him; de la Rue developed his own methods for fig-
uring and polishing them. Nasmyth was in close contact
with another wealthy amateur astronomer, William Lassell, who not only provided de la Rue with additional suggestions for polishing mirrors, but also pointed out to him
the value of equatorial mountings for reflecting telescopes. The major outcome of all this advice was that by

Warren de la Rue (1815–1889), by Maull & Polyblank, 1855

1849 de la Rue had constructed a 13 inch equatorial
reflector which he installed in a small observatory at his
home in Canonbury, Middlesex, and used for a number of
studies in subsequent years. Lassell's interest in Saturn
also communicated itself to de la Rue. His first astronomical publication for the Royal Astronomical Society was
based on a drawing he made of that planet which showed
its newly discovered inner ring.

At the Great Exhibition de la Rue saw daguerreotypes of
the moon sent from Harvard College observatory. Astronomical photography had an immediate appeal for him,
combining as it did his interests in chemistry, astronomy,
and instrumentation. The timing was also propitious. The
daguerreotype process was slow and inconvenient, and
the plates were unable to record faint objects. In 1851 a
new wet collodion process was brought into use. As the
name suggests, this entailed exposing plates immediately
after they had been sensitized by chemical immersion.
Though the plates were not entirely convenient to handle
this allowed much fainter details to be recorded. De la Rue
applied the new process to taking pictures of the moon,
obtained several useful images, and enlarged them. However, his telescope had to be accurately guided by hand
during exposures, and this proved to be difficult.

In 1857 de la Rue moved from Canonbury to Cranford,
Middlesex, where he remounted his telescope with a
mechanical drive. He soon produced not only better pictures of the moon, but also photographs of Jupiter, Saturn, and a bright double star. One important result to
emerge was the extent to which the photographic images

of the moon and planets differed from their visual appearances. Since the photographic plates were more sensitive to blue light than the human eye, these differences indicated variations in colour. De la Rue further realized that the moon could be photographed from slightly different angles as it pursued its path round the earth. This allowed him to combine photographs taken at different times to provide the first stereoscopic pictures of an astronomical body. Like his earlier work on telescope making, this new advance was warmly praised by the leading British scientist Sir John Herschel.

The observatory at Kew had come under the control of the British Association in the 1840s, and Herschel suggested that it should be used to obtain daily photographs of the sun. De la Rue was the obvious person to consult on this matter, so the Kew committee of the British Association asked him to examine the requirements for constructing a photo-heliograph. Funds for the construction were provided by the Royal Society. De la Rue inaugurated the new instrument at Kew in 1858, where it remained in operation—with a short period at de la Rue's own observatory—until 1872. In 1859 Balfour Stewart was appointed to take charge of the Kew observatory. Over the next few years de la Rue, Balfour Stewart, and the assistant at the observatory, Benjamin Loewy, were involved in an intensive series of solar studies.

In 1860 de la Rue took the photo-heliograph to Spain where a total solar eclipse was visible. His photographs played an important part in demonstrating that prominences were undoubtedly genuine features hovering above the sun's surface. De la Rue described this work in his Bakerian lecture to the Royal Society in 1862. Meanwhile, in 1861, he applied his stereoscopic methods to photographs of the sun. The results, along with other observations at Kew, supported the suggestion made by Alexander Wilson in the eighteenth century that sunspots represent depressions in the solar surface. It also appeared that the bright solar faculae occupied positions above, and often behind, the sunspots as the sun rotated. These observations were important for current discussions of the sun and its atmosphere. However, the main reasons for obtaining frequent photographs of the sun were twofold: to investigate in more detail the solar cycle, discovered by the German amateur astronomer, Heinrich Schwabe in the 1840s, and to relate this to the solar–terrestrial interaction affecting the earth's magnetic field, detected in the early 1850s by Edward Sabine. The Kew studies, which covered an entire solar cycle, provided the best statistical data on sunspots then available, and were used to examine the variations in spot numbers in considerable detail. More speculatively, de la Rue and his colleagues tried to relate the incidence of sunspots to the motions of the planets.

Balfour Stewart resigned from Kew in 1871. De la Rue's photo-heliograph was transferred to the Royal Observatory, beginning its operations there in 1873 (though it returned to Kew a few years later). Nevertheless, in November 1872 de la Rue withdrew from the Royal Astronomical Society council because of their deference to Airy's opposition to an independent solar observatory. However, de la Rue continued to be involved in the Kew observatory until his death. With the departure of the photo-heliograph he started preparing for the forthcoming transit of Venus in 1874 but, his eyesight a problem, he finally decided he was no longer fit enough to carry out intensive astronomical observations. In 1873, having heard from Charles Pritchard that Oxford University was to fund a new observatory, he offered his telescope and other equipment on the understanding that it would be installed and used. By this he became co-founder of the new observatory, and a vital benefactor of it, and so maintained his interest in observational astronomy at Oxford. In 1887 he paid for a photographic refractor so that the observatory could participate in the new international *carte du ciel* project.

Late chemistry In 1873 de la Rue moved house to Portland Place in central London. Here he reverted to his chemical interests, setting up a laboratory in which he and his friend, Hugo Müller, carried out a series of investigations. Müller had worked with him earlier on organic chemistry, but by the end of the 1860s they had turned their attention to the study of electrical discharges through gases. De la Rue's interest in them may well have stemmed from Balfour Stewart, who suggested that aurorae, one of the phenomena affected by solar–terrestrial interaction, might be electrical discharges. The topic of discharges became increasingly important as the century progressed, and de la Rue continued working on it until a few years before his death. To obtain the voltage required, he returned to his development of electrical batteries. By the time he finished his experiments he was using a battery containing 15,000 cells. One of the key figures in understanding discharges, J. J. Thomson, subsequently declared that de la Rue and Müller had taken some of the best photographs of striated discharges ever made. Unfortunately, a proper understanding of the discharge phenomenon, and hence of the photographs, came only after de la Rue's death.

Public life De la Rue was one of the wealthy amateurs who played a vital role in nineteenth-century British science. In part this was by direct donation. Apart from his interest in Oxford he offered financial support for other scientific enterprises. One example was the expedition by David Gill in 1877 to Ascension Island in order to make a new determination of the sun's distance. Equally, de la Rue devoted a good deal of his time to the organization of science. In terms of his two main concerns—chemistry and astronomy—he was, in the former field, a founder member of the Chemical Society and its president from 1867 to 1869 and in 1879–80. In astronomy he was an honorary secretary of the Royal Astronomical Society from 1855 to 1862, president from 1864 to 1866 and a member of its council for most of the time from 1866 until his death. He was also president of the London Institution for many years, retiring from this position in 1878, when he became secretary of the Royal Institution. He was much in demand as a committee member throughout his life, for he was regarded as tactful, kindly, and generous.

Many honours came to de la Rue from both home and abroad. He was awarded the gold medal of the Royal Astronomical Society in 1862, a royal medal of the Royal Society in 1864, and the prix Lalande of the Académie des Sciences in 1865. He was a corresponding member of a number of foreign societies, but his closest ties were with Paris, which he continued to visit throughout his life. Like his father before him, he was appointed to the Légion d'honneur.

Having worked in the family business all his life de la Rue became head of the firm on his father's death in 1866. He tried to retire in 1869, but was forced to return in the following year on the death of his brother. He finally retired in 1880, when the business activities devolved on his sons. He suffered from poor health in his later years, which curtailed his activities. Following a bout of pneumonia he died at 73 Portland Place, Marylebone, London, on 19 April 1889. He was survived by his wife.

P. J. Hartog, *rev.* A. J. Meadows

Sources *Monthly Notices of the Royal Astronomical Society*, 50 (1889–90), 155–64 · *The Times* (22 April 1889) · *Nature*, 40 (1889), 26–9, esp. 27 · A. M. Clerke, *A popular history of astronomy during the nineteenth century* (1885) · C. A. Young, *The Sun* (1881) · A. J. Meadows, *Science and controversy: a biography of Sir Norman Lockyer* (1972)
Archives CUL, papers · NHM, autobiographical notes · RS, papers · U. Reading L., Guernsay estate corresp. and papers | Birr Castle, Offaly, letters to earls of Rosse · Bodl. Oxf., Pritchard corresp. · CUL, corresp. with Sir George Airy · CUL, corresp. with Sir George Stokes · Inst. EE, letters to Michael Faraday · RAS, letters to Richard Hodgson · RAS, letters to Royal Astronomical Society · RS, letters to Sir John Herschel
Likenesses Maull & Polyblank, photograph, 1855, NPG [*see illus.*] · E. Edwards, photograph, pubd 1865, NPG · Lock & Whitfield, woodburytype photograph, pubd 1882, NPG · Spy [L. Ward], caricature, chromolithograph, NPG; repro. in *VF* (2 Aug 1894) · photograph (as president of RAS), RAS · photograph, RAS, ADD. MS 91/1/120 · photograph, RAS, ADD. MS 94/66
Wealth at death £305,956 7s. 9d.: resworn probate, March 1890, *CGPLA Eng. & Wales* (1889)

Rue, William Frederick de la (1825–1870). *See under* Rue, de la, family (*per. c.*1820–1923).

Ruff, William (1801–1856), sporting journalist, was born in London. He was educated for the law, but soon after 1820 he succeeded his father as the turf editor of *Bell's Life in London and Sporting Chronicle* and reporter of sporting intelligence to the principal London newspapers. He brought to this task not only many exclusive sources of information, but also an indefatigable zeal to provide the earliest and most reliable information. To ensure his reports reached London as speedily as possible he pioneered the use of pigeon expresses: it was reckoned, for example, that a good bird could fly the 55 miles from Goodwood in about one hour fifteen minutes. His race accounts were 'like "potted soup", the largest amount of facts in the smallest amount of space' (*Sporting Magazine*, 77), but they were also accurate and impartial, and his honesty and integrity were never questioned in over a quarter century's involvement with the turf. It seems probable that the reason he was able to maintain this reputation, at a time when horse racing was far from honest, was that he was known never to bet. Ruff also provided racing intelligence to leading owners, including George IV, by whom he was owed £100 at the time of the king's death.

In 1843 Ruff published for the first time *The Guide to the Turf, or, Pocket Racing Companion*. Initially published annually, and containing details of entries in races to come, lists of past winners, and analyses of the performances of two-year-olds, this rapidly became one of the standard reference books of the turf; much respected, it is still published by the *Sporting Life* today. Ruff retired in the spring of 1854, and never visited a racecourse again. For many years before his retirement he had suffered from ill health, partly brought on by 'over-zealous and constant attention to his harassing and laborious duties' (*Bell's Life*, 4). Towards the end of 1856 he contracted phthisis, and he died on 30 December at his home, 33 Doughty Street, London. Ruff was unmarried and had no children. His half-brother John, also a sporting journalist with *Bell's Life*, had died less than six months before, and both were buried in the same grave at Brookwood cemetery, Woking.

John Pinfold

Sources *Bell's Life in London* (4 Jan 1857), 4 · *Sporting Chronicle* (4 Jan 1857) · *GM*, 3rd ser., 2 (1857), 247 · *Sporting Magazine*, 3rd ser., 29 (1857), 77 · The Druid [H. H. Dixon], *The post and the paddock: with recollections of George IV, Sam Chiffney, and other turf celebrities*, rev. edn (1880) · A. Ross, *The turf* (1982) · will · d. cert.
Likenesses R. Ansdell, group portrait (*The Waterloo coursing meeting of 1840*), Walker Art Gallery, Liverpool
Wealth at death £12,000: probate records

Ruffhead, Owen (*c.*1723–1769), legal writer, was probably born in London, the son of James Ruffhead, of Westminster, baker to George I. His father paid for his education with the proceeds of a winning lottery ticket, and he was admitted to the Inner Temple on 2 December 1742. He was called to the bar in June 1754 and was admitted to the Middle Temple in July 1761.

Ruffhead developed a practice in special pleading and in drawing parliamentary bills, but found his chief work as a writer. He was the first book reviewer for the *Gentleman's Magazine*, and contributed to Ralph Griffiths's *Monthly Review*. In 1756 he began the *Con-Test*, of which Dr Johnson had 'yet heard no great commendation' (Chalmers), a short-lived periodical paper in support of the government and in opposition to Arthur Murphy's equally short-lived *Test*, which supported Henry Fox, afterwards Lord Holland. In 1760 appeared a pamphlet entitled *Reasons why the Approaching Treaty of Peace should be Debated in Parliament*, in the form of a letter addressed to William Pitt. Later in the same year came *Ministerial usurpation displayed, and the prerogatives of the crown, and the right of parliament and of the privy council, considered*, responding to published remarks against the former pamphlet. Ruffhead had edited two volumes, the first of which appeared in 1758, continuing, to the thirteenth year of George III, John Cay's *The statutes at large from Magna Charta to the thirtieth year of King George the Second inclusive*, and in 1762 appeared Ruffhead's own *The Statutes at Large from Magna Charta to the End of the Last Parliament, 1761*, completed by a ninth volume to the fourth year of George III in 1765. This edition appeared again in 1769, and was several times re-edited. Ruffhead's statutes appeared in the same year as the first volume of Danby Pickering's edition of the statutes, Ruffhead and Pickering each borrowing material from the other. In 1763 appeared a further political pamphlet, *Considerations on the Present Dangerous Crisis*, criticizing both Lord Bute's conduct of the government and the conduct of the opposition. A reply for Lord Bute, perhaps written by Horace Walpole, appeared in the same year. Returning to legal writing, in 1766 Ruffhead completed the fifth volume of Mathew Bacon's *New Abridgment*, and on 26 February that year received the LLD degree of the University of Edinburgh.

In the following year William Warburton, bishop of Gloucester, commissioned Ruffhead to produce Warburton's long-awaited life of Warburton's friend Alexander Pope, providing Ruffhead with materials, and making corrections to the proofs. The resulting *Life of Alexander Pope, Esq. Compiled from Original Manuscripts* appeared in 1769. It was several times re-issued, and translated into French, but the reviews were unfavourable and it never found an admirer, Dr Johnson remarking that Ruffhead 'knew nothing of Pope, and nothing of poetry' (Hill, 2.166). At this time also appeared a further political pamphlet, *The Case of the Late Election for the County of Middlesex Considered*, defending the government's conduct in respect of John Wilkes's expulsion from parliament.

Ruffhead's promised reward for his partisan pamphleteering, a place as one of the chief secretaries of the Treasury, was pre-empted by his death in London on 25 October 1769, attributed to a cold caught while pleading in a crowded court room. After a legacy to his sister, Mrs Ann Campion, the bulk of his estate, including his chambers in Pump Court in the Temple, was left to his son James Thompson Ruffhead (c.1753–1798), who took holy orders and died as curate of Prittlewell, Essex. At the time of his death Ruffhead had been under an agreement to produce a new edition of Chambers's *Cyclopedia*, though nothing was done and the proprietors recovered their money from Ruffhead's estate and concluded a replacement agreement for a new edition with the Revd Dr John Calder in 1773. Two of Ruffhead's works appeared after his death, both in 1772: a ninth edition of Giles Jacob's *A New Law-Dictionary* (with John Morgan) and *A complete index to the statues at large, from Magna Charta to the tenth year of George III inclusive*. N. G. JONES

Sources GM, 1st ser., 39 (1769), 511 · GM, 1st ser., 69 (1799), 283, 387 · J. Noorthouck, *An historical and classical dictionary*, 2 (1776) · A. Chalmers, ed., *The general biographical dictionary*, new edn, 32 vols. (1812–17) · H. A. C. Sturgess, ed., *Register of admissions to the Honourable Society of the Middle Temple, from the fifteenth century to the year 1944*, 1 (1949) · F. A. Inderwick and R. A. Roberts, eds., *A calendar of the Inner Temple records*, 4 (1933) · F. A. Inderwick and R. A. Roberts, eds., *A calendar of the Inner Temple records*, 5 (1936) · O. Ruffhead's will, PRO, PROB 11/952/393 · F. J. G. Robinson and others, *Eighteenth-century British books: an author union catalogue*, 4 (1981) · A. Luders and others, eds., *Statutes of the realm*, 11 vols. in 12, RC (1810–28), vol. 1 · J. Spence, *Observations, anecdotes, and characters, of books and men*, ed. J. M. Osborn, new edn, 1 (1966) · Nichols, *Illustrations*, vol. 4 · J. D. Cowley, *A bibliography of abridgments, digests, dictionaries and indexes of English law to the year 1800* (1932) · Boswell, *Life*, vol. 2

Ruffside. For this title name *see* Brown, Douglas Clifton, Viscount Ruffside (1879–1958).

Rufus, Geoffrey. *See* Geoffrey Rufus (d. 1141).

Rugby. For this title name *see* Maffey, John Loader, first Baron Rugby (1877–1969).

Rugeley Poisoner, the. *See* Palmer, William (1824–1856).

Rugg, Thomas (d. 1670), diarist, was probably connected with the Norfolk Rugges, as his diary reveals a particular interest in that region. He lived in Covent Garden for much of his life: in 1661 he notes that he had lived there for fourteen years. On 4 July 1650 he married Elizabeth Cox, 'of Covent Garden' (parish register of St Clement Danes). Four children were born to Thomas and Elizabeth Rugg between 1653 and 1662. He was a barber by trade, and was employed at knights of Bath ceremonies in this capacity.

Rugg's diary, rather like that of Narcissus Luttrell, is a compendium of newsbooks, pamphlets, broadsides, newsletters, and personal letters and observations, and is entitled 'Mercurius politicus redivivus, or, A collection of the most materiall occurances and transactions in public affaires since Anno Domini 1659 untill—serving as an annuall diurnall for future satsifaction & information. Together with a table.' His language is that of the newsbooks. A major theme of the first part is the restoration of Charles II, and he chronicles events leading up to the coronation in detail: half the entries in the diary are from the years 1660 to 1661. He is conscious of his role as amateur historian, summarizing ephemeral printed pieces in order to preserve them, and recording events he considers to be of national importance, usually with a London perspective. He is a conservative, strongly royalist and Anglican: he is an admirer of fellow Covent Garden dweller Roger L'Estrange, who became the rabidly tory surveyor of the press.

Rugg maintained his diary and his business to the end of his life, bequeathing 'the instruments and goods properly belonging to my shop and trade' to his son Thomas. His bequests show him to have been moderately prosperous. He was buried on 16 March 1670 at St Paul's, Covent Garden: his wife, Elizabeth, was executor. The manuscript of the diary belonged to Thomas Grey, earl of Stamford, in 1693, and is now in the British Library (BL, Add. MSS 10116–10117). It is in two large quarto volumes: the first volume is mostly autograph, the second showing an increasing use of scribes. After his death entries continue sporadically until 1672. ELIZABETH R. CLARKE

Sources 'Mercurius politicus redivivus, or, A collection of the most materiall occurances and transactions in public affaires since Anno Domini 1659', BL, Add. MSS 10116–10117 · *The diurnal of Thomas Rugge, 1659–1661*, ed. W. L. Sachse, CS, 3rd ser., 91 (1961) · DNB · parish register, St Clement Danes, City Westm. AC, 4 July 1650 [marriage] · will, PRO, PROB 11/332/40

Archives BL, diary, Add. MSS 10116–10117 [with additions after his death]

Wealth at death bequests to children; remainder to wife; money to be redistributed to children if she remarries, providing £40 each; therefore estate worth min. £320: will, PRO, PROB 11/332/40 [1670]

Rugg, William [*name in religion* William Repps] (*d.* **1550**), bishop of Norwich, was the son of William Rugg of North Repps in Norfolk, whence he took his surname on entering Norwich Cathedral priory, before progressing to Gonville Hall, Cambridge, in 1509, where he graduated BTh that year and DTh in 1513. In 1514 Rugg was sacrist of Norwich priory; six years later he was prior of Norwich's cell at Great Yarmouth, and in 1526 he was sub-prior of Norwich. At the visitation that year he was accused of undue familiarity with 'the wardroper's wife', but the charge was probably malicious and was not pursued by the bishop. At the beginning of 1530 he was instrumental in persuading Cambridge University to support the king's divorce, for which he was rewarded in April with the abbacy of St Benet of Hulme, Norfolk. Rugg's rule as abbot was lax, and he was more concerned to please the king and line his own pocket than to govern his fellow monks. By 1532 the abbey's debts amounted to more than a year's income, and in 1536 it was noted that he had been granting away lands expecting the dissolution of the house. That year his continued support for the king, and his freedom with the house's property, saw him elevated to the bishopric of Norwich as part of an exchange of property between the crown and the see. By act of parliament in February 1536 (27 Hen. VIII c. 45) the revenues of the see were transferred to the crown, and the estates of the abbey of Hulme and the priory of Hickling were conferred on the see as its new endowment. Rugg was consecrated bishop on 11 June 1536; the temporalities were restored on 19 July following.

As bishop, Rugg supported the king's policies towards the papacy: in July 1536 he upheld the right of secular princes to summon a general council, and in the summer of 1538 he took part in proceedings against Anthony Browne, a former observant friar convicted of denying the royal supremacy, trying (though in vain) to persuade Browne of the error of his opinions. On other matters, however, Rugg was a staunch conservative, increasingly at odds with Cromwell and Cranmer. With other conservatives he drafted a defence of shrines and pilgrimages which, however, was rejected from the final text of the Bishops' Book; in 1539 he was listed as one of the conservatives maintaining transubstantiation and auricular confession; in 1540 he supported the six articles. Cranmer complained in 1537 that Rugg 'doth approve none to preach in his diocese that be of right judgement' (MacCulloch, 456), and the following year Cromwell tried, in vain, to persuade Rugg to resign with the offer of a pension. He and the archbishop could only try to protect the godly in East Anglia and berate Rugg for his treatment of them. The bishop, however, remained entrenched with the firm support of the duke of Norfolk. The duke's fall in 1547 may have weakened Rugg's position, but he remained a champion of the traditionalist cause under Edward VI, uniting with other conservative bishops to defend the real presence and the Latin mass, and voting against communion in both kinds for the laity, the dissolution of the chantries, clerical marriage, and the new liturgy.

Meanwhile Rugg's economic fortunes had seriously deteriorated. Not only had the exchange of 1536 left the episcopal revenues diminished by about £300 a year, but the estates which had formerly belonged to St Benet's had been wasted by Rugg's own improvidence as abbot, earning him the posthumous reputation as a 'varlet' and 'a destroying abbot' (Barton, 1.13). Moreover, if his critics are to be believed, Rugg failed to make any economies and tried to live in the same state as his considerably richer episcopal predecessors. To make ends meet, he adopted a number of disastrous expedients. He acceded to three further exchanges of episcopal estates in 1542, 1543 and 1545, and in 1548 he agreed to grant the palace at Norwich and eleven of the best remaining estates of the see to Sir Francis Brian. This last grant, however, was never effected and may have been security for a loan, for by February 1549 Rugg was heavily in debt, owing £890 to the crown, having been forced to divert the clerical taxes that he had collected to cover his own expenditure.

Despite his financial embarrassments and being mocked by his own servants as a 'ragged' bishop, too indebted to maintain the palace or pay their wages, Rugg clung on to power, and even drew up articles for a visitation of his diocese. His downfall came in the wake of Ket's rebellion in Norfolk in the late summer of 1549. Rugg's actions during the rebellion, like those of several other East Anglian magnates and clergy, are obscure, but it was alleged in the immediate aftermath of the suppression of the rebellion that he had given money to the rebels and had three times had a secret conference with Ket himself. Rugg's indictment 'for comforting the traytors of Norffolk' was said in September 1549 to be imminent ('Letters of Richard Scudamore', 90–91). Instead, by 26 January 1550 Rugg had resigned his episcopate in return for a brace of pardons, a £200-a-year pension, and the cancellation of all his debts. The prodigal bishop did not enjoy his retirement for long however: he died on 21 September 1550 and was buried in Norwich Cathedral.

IAN ATHERTON

Sources F. Blomefield and C. Parkin, *An essay towards a topographical history of the county of Norfolk*, [2nd edn], 11 vols. (1805–10), vol. 3, pp. 547–50 • *LP Henry VIII* • 'The letters of Richard Scudamore to Sir Philip Holby, September 1549 – March 1555', ed. M. Dowling, *Camden miscellany, XXX*, CS, 4th ser., 39 (1990), 90–91 • *CPR, 1548–53*, esp. 1549–51 • Anthony Harrison's account of William Rugg, Bodl. Oxf., MS Tanner 228, fols. 177–80 • A. Jessopp, *Visitations of the diocese of Norwich, A.D. 1492–1532*, 2nd ser., CS, 43 (1888) • D. MacCulloch, *Thomas Cranmer: a life* (1996) • S. M. Lyons, 'The resignation (1549) of William Rugg: a reconsideration', *Catholic Historical Review*, 73 (1987), 23–40 • Venn, *Alum. Cant.*, 1/3.497 • *Fasti Angl., 1541–1857*, [Ely], 37 • G. Burnet, *The history of the Reformation of the Church of England*, rev. N. Pocock, new edn, 7 vols. (1865) • *The Registrum vagum of Anthony Harison*, ed. T. F. Barton, 1, Norfolk RS, 32 (1963), 13 • G. R. Elton, *Policy and police: the enforcement of the Reformation in the age of Thomas Cromwell* (1972) • W. K. Jordan, *Edward VI, 1: The young king* (1968)

Rugge, Thomas. *See* Rugg, Thomas (*d.* 1670).

Ruggle, George (*bap.* **1575**, *d.* **1621/2**), Latin playwright, was baptized on 3 November 1575 at Lavenham, Suffolk, the fifth and youngest son of Thomas Ruggle, a clothier, and his wife, Marjory (*d.* 1613). George Ruggle was educated at

Lavenham grammar school, and matriculated as a pensioner at St John's College, Cambridge, on 2 June 1589. He became a scholar of Trinity College, Cambridge, in 1593; he graduated BA in the same year and MA in 1597. In 1598 he was elected a fellow of Clare College, where he remained for the rest of his academic career. His skill as a tutor is said to have attracted Nicholas Ferrar to Clare.

Ruggle's literary reputation rests on a single work, his Latin comedy *Ignoramus* (1615); nevertheless, he deserves a fairly high place among British neo-Latin authors, for *Ignoramus* is by some distance the most successful of all the university plays, both in its initial reception and its later history of performance and publication. It remained well known, and was periodically revived on stage, throughout the eighteenth century, only falling into obscurity (along with most other British Latin works) in the nineteenth and twentieth. Scenes from it (edited and produced by David Money, directed by Cressida Ryan) were performed in Latin at Peterhouse Theatre, Cambridge, on 3 August 2000, as part of the congress of the International Association for Neo-Latin Studies. This version was revived in February 2002.

Ignoramus is a satire on common lawyers; the subject was in part prompted by a local Cambridge dispute in 1611–12 which had led to friction between Francis Brakin, the town recorder, and the university. Ruggle's model was an Italian comedy, *La trappolaria* (1596) by Giambattista della Porta, itself modelled on Plautus; Ruggle uses many familiar comic devices, but also adds many scenes to Porta's original. In particular, Ruggle's Latin word play is original. He uses the barbarous law-Latin of Ignoramus himself to great comic effect. The rascally lawyer Ignoramus (a satirical portrait of the recorder Brakin) woos the heroine, Rosabella, with legalistic verses: '*dabo fee simple*' in return for '*love's pretty dimple*' (act I, scene v), while intending to take immoral advantage of her. The tables are turned in later scenes: Ignoramus is threatened with a pig gelder's terrifying equipment, and finally exorcized by fake monks. The exorcism scene (act IV, scene xi) is one of the funniest in the play, and best calculated to appeal to an audience suspicious of Catholics and witchcraft. Every law term Ignoramus shouts out is taken for the name of another devil that has possessed him.

Ignoramus was performed on 8 March 1615 in Trinity College (where the king and prince were staying); seating was fitted in the hall to accommodate a huge audience of courtiers and academics, allegedly as many as 2000 people. The expenses were considerable. Some spectators found that the play's extreme length, over five hours, detracted from its delightfulness. King James, however, was full of enthusiasm, and requested a repeat performance at Royston on 13 May 1615. London lawyers, including the lord chief justice, resented Ruggle's attacks on their profession; indignant pamphlets flew about, and *Ignoramus* became one of the best-known and most controversial of Jacobean plays, its title character becoming proverbial for folly. The actors in the first performance of *Ignoramus* (as in many revivals) were eager, and in many cases aristocratic, students. Samuel Fairclough, however,

refused to wear women's clothes for the part of Surda, the old woman; as his puritan biographer noted, 'Thus did this youth choose to lose the smiles of the court, and to bear the frowns of the Vice-Chancellor, rather than to hazard the loss of the light of Gods countenance' (Nelson, *Records*, 543).

Ruggle resigned his fellowship of Clare College in 1620 (when he was third in the list of seniority); he appears to have taken a position as tutor to the sons of Toby Palavicino (and grandsons of Sir Horatio Palavicino) of Babraham. He may already have been in poor health. His will is dated 6 September 1621, and was proved on 3 November 1622. The precise date and cause of his death are uncertain.

Ignoramus was preserved in manuscript, and first printed in 1630; many further editions followed, even in 1658 and 1659, before the Restoration and reopening of London theatres. In 1662 an English imitation by Ferdinando Parkhurst was performed in London in the presence of Charles II; the same year saw a rival, more accurate, translation by Robert Codrington, which was adapted in 1678 by Edward Ravenscroft, as *The English Lawyer*. The original Latin was performed at Westminster School several times in the eighteenth century, providing a welcome modern variation to the usual diet of Plautus and Terence. A few other schools did likewise: Bury St Edmund's in 1731, for instance, and Merchant Taylors' in 1763. At Westminster in 1747 Ignoramus was played by Hamilton Boyle, later earl of Cork and Orrery; the Latin elegiac prologue (printed in Mure, Bull, and Scott, 79) mentions the 1745 rising, and the campaigns of Marshal Saxe. A fourth, extra performance was demanded, and the players were complimented in the *Gentleman's Magazine*. A thorough critical edition, explaining all the legal jokes, appeared in 1787 (ed. J. S. Hawkins).

Ruggle is said to have written other, English, comedies. He was a major donor of books to the library at Clare: the fellows' library still holds his large collection of plays in Italian, as well as Latin treatises on various subjects. He donated at least eleven works of neo-Latin literary prose, including the *Turkish Letters* of Augerius Busbequius (1595), which introduced to western scholars the great inscription at Ankara containing the *Res gestae* of the emperor Augustus. His book collection suggests a man of wide culture, particularly interested in the Italian literature that played such a large part in moulding the Elizabethan stage.

D. K. MONEY

Sources E. F. J. Tucker, ed., *George Ruggle: Ignoramus* (1987) [facsimile of MS] · E. F. J. Tucker, *A critical edition of Ferdinando Parkhurst's 'Ignoramus: the academical lawyer'* (1987) · A. H. Nelson, *Records of early English drama: Cambridge* (1989) · A. H. Nelson, *Early Cambridge theatres* (1994) · J. W. Binns, *Intellectual culture in Elizabethan and Jacobean England: the Latin writings of the age* (1990) · G. Ruggle, *Ignoramus*, ed. J. S. Hawkins (1787) · H. Kallendorf and C. Kallendorf, 'Exorcism and the interstices of language' [paper delivered at IANLS congress, August 2000] [forthcoming in *Acta Conventus Neolatini Cantabrigiensis*] · DNB · D. K. Money, programmes for performance of *Ignoramus*, Cambridge, 3 Aug 2000, 15–16 Feb 2002 · D. K. Money, 'Neo-Latin literature in Cambridge', *Order and connexion*, ed. R. C. Alston (1997), 77–95 · J. Sargeaunt, *Annals of Westminster School* (1898) · J. Mure, H. Bull, and C. B. Scott, eds., *Lusus alteri*

Westmonasterienses (1863) • F. W. M. Draper, *Four centuries of Merchant Taylors' School* (1962) • E. F. J. Tucker, *Intruder into Eden* (1984) • D. Greenwood, 'The staging of Neo-Latin plays', *Educational Theatre Journal*, 16 (1964), 311–23
Archives Clare College, Cambridge, books
Likenesses line engraving, NPG

Ruggles, Thomas (1745–1813), author and barrister, was born on 28 January 1745 at Bradford Street, Bocking, Essex, the only surviving son of Thomas Ruggles (1709–1758), cloth exporter, and his wife, Ann (1715–1748), eldest daughter of Joshua Brise, a London merchant who retired to Clare, Suffolk, and purchased several estates in that neighbourhood, and his wife, Elizabeth. His father was the second son of Thomas Ruggles of Bocking, Essex, a wealthy manufacturer and clothier who purchased several estates in Essex. In 1776, upon the demise of his cousin John, he inherited the mansion and lands of Spains Hall in Finchingfield, near Braintree, Essex, from his uncle Samuel Ruggles.

Ruggles's first wife, Elizabeth, daughter of Joseph Sayer, died childless on 28 November 1776. In March 1779 he married Jane Anne (d. 1822), daughter of John Freeland of Cobham, Surrey. With his second wife he had eight children, three of whom predeceased him: John, Samuel (d. 1807), Shandrach-George (d. 1804), Maria, Ann (d. 1812), Jane, Francis-Brise, and Sophia-Lydia.

Ruggles was educated as a barrister at the Temple, an inn of court, and eventually became a bencher of Lincoln's Inn and of the honourable society of the Inner Temple. In addition, he became a fellow of the Antiquarian Society. After inheriting Spains Hall he became an active magistrate, high sheriff, and deputy lieutenant in the counties of Essex and Suffolk. In the 1790s he published two substantial works that are of importance to legal, social, and economic historians. The first was entitled *The Barrister, or, Strictures on the Education Proper for the Bar* (1792). In twenty-six short essays addressed to students attending the inns of court, Ruggles aimed 'to preserve the proper dignity of the bar, and a knowledge of the honourable means of advancement in the profession' (p. 269). In addition to offering advice on proper manners and moral behaviour, he also counselled his audience on oratorical eloquence and logical argument. His major educational recommendation was that admission to the inns of court be contingent on the completion of a bachelor's degree in arts or law at Cambridge or Oxford. Only such a background—particularly in ancient and modern languages, philosophy, history, and poetry—would allow barristers and practisers to rise above their own self-interest and develop integrity of mind. The second work, *The history of the poor, their rights, duties, and the laws respecting them. In a series of letters* (2 vols., 1793–4), was an important contribution to the debate on poverty in late eighteenth-century England. The influential political economist J. R. McCulloch included this title in *The Literature of Political Economy* (1845) and the modern historian J. R. Poynter gave it deserved attention in *Society and Pauperism* (1969). Ruggles, deeply intent on improving the deplorable condition of the poor, eventually concluded that poverty stemmed

from the indolence, improvidence, and moral laxity of the labouring class, especially 'the baneful and seducing habit of drinking strong liquors' (*History of the Poor*, 2.182). The old poor law which provided relief to the destitute should remain in force but was sadly in need of reform. Houses of industry, he contended, should teach the poor, especially children, habits of industry and improved morals. In addition, voluntary contributory organizations such as friendly societies should be promoted to encourage labourers to save, and thus reduce the number of relief recipients. Ruggles, a close friend of Arthur Young, was called in to advise Prime Minister William Pitt on the Poor Law Bill of 1796 and claimed that his *History of the Poor* had inspired Pitt to take action (Poynter, 63). Although Pitt's bill never passed, many of Ruggles's ideas foreshadowed the new poor law of 1834.

Ruggles died at Spains Hall on 17 November 1813 and was buried at St John the Baptist Church, Finchingfield. His will bequeathed Spains Hall to his wife, Jane Anne. His only surviving son, John, inherited the estates in Suffolk and upon the death of his mother on 22 November 1822 he received Spains Hall. JAMES P. HUZEL

Sources DNB • Burke, *Gen. GB* (1833) • Burke, *Gen. GB* (1939) • PRO, B11/1551ff (1814) • GM, 1st ser., 77 (1807) • GM, 1st ser., 83/2 (1813) • J. R. Poynter, *Society and pauperism: English ideas on poor relief, 1795–1834* (1969) • J. R. McCulloch, *The literature of political economy: a classified catalogue* (1845) • W. Berry, *County genealogies: pedigrees of Essex families* (1840) • private information (2004) [T. E. Ruggles-Brise, Sir John Ruggles-Brise]

Ruiséal, Tomás Ó Néill. *See* Russell, Thomas O'Neill (1828–1908).

Rule, Gilbert (c.1629–1701), Church of Scotland minister, is of unknown parents and background. Nothing is known of his early years, but in 1647 he was a student at the University of St Andrews, and in 1651 he became a regent at King's College, Aberdeen. In 1652 he was appointed sub-principal of the college after the removal of the previous incumbent in a Cromwellian purge. He married Janet Turnbull (d. 1699) on 4 February 1655; the marriage produced three sons and two daughters. About 1657 Rule moved to England and became curate at Alnwick in Northumberland.

At the Restoration conflict arose between Rule and one of his churchwardens, Major Orde, over Rule's refusal to use the prayer book. This led to Rule's indictment by Orde in August 1660 at Newcastle assizes for defaming the Book of Common Prayer. However, Orde was killed by a fall from his horse before the trial, which was regarded by Rule's partisans as a divine judgment. In the absence of a prosecutor, Rule was acquitted.

Rule was ejected from his parish by the Act of Uniformity of 1662. He returned to Scotland, where he preached for a time. This attracted the unfavourable attention of the authorities, forcing Rule to leave Scotland. He travelled in France and the Netherlands and studied medicine at the University of Leiden, where he was awarded the degree of MD on 9 February 1666.

In 1679 Rule was at Berwick upon Tweed, where he practised medicine. He also continued to preach at conventicles in both England and Scotland. The presbyterian earl of Haddington fitted up a meeting-house for him at Linton Bridge in the parish of Prestonkirk, which was indulged by the privy council on 18 December 1679. However, Rule broke the conditions of the indulgence by holding a presbyterian service in the church of St Giles in Edinburgh, where he baptized the child of his niece. Although this was done with the consent of the episcopalian minister of St Giles, Archibald Turner, Rule was arrested and, by an order dated 8 April 1680, was confined in the Bass Rock prison. There he fell seriously ill, and petitioned the privy council for his release in July 1680. This was granted, on condition that he left Scotland within eight days, under a bond of 5000 marks.

Rule moved to Dublin, where he served as minister to the presbyterian congregation of Wood Street church with his friend Daniel Williams. The revolution of 1688 restored the pre-eminence of presbyterianism in Scotland, and Rule received a call to the charge of Old Greyfriars in Edinburgh on 7 December 1688. After returning to Scotland he was confirmed in his new position by Edinburgh council on 24 July 1689. In 1690 he was appointed to a commission for purging the University of Edinburgh. As a result of the purge, the principal, Alexander Monro, was removed and on 26 September 1690 Rule was elected to replace him. On 13 or 14 November 1691 Rule and other ministers were appointed by the general assembly to present the presbyterian case to William III in London. On 26 January 1691 Rule reported that the king had assured the delegation of his commitment to the protection of presbyterianism.

After 1689 Rule produced several written works, mostly defences of presbyterianism against its episcopalian slanderers, including Alexander Monro. These included *A Rational Defence of Non-Conformity* (1689), and vindications of the Church of Scotland. In 1697 his *Good Old Way Defended* again spoke up for presbyterian practice. Rule also appears to have been an eloquent preacher. On one occasion, he is supposed to have encountered a ghost in a deserted house, who led him to the skeleton of a murdered man. On the following Sunday, Rule preached about the matter in such moving language that an old man in the congregation confessed to the murder. Rule died in Edinburgh on 7 June 1701, having outlived his wife by two years.   ALEXANDER DU TOIT

Sources *Fasti Scot.*, new edn, 1.39 • E. Calamy, ed., *An abridgement of Mr. Baxter's history of his life and times, with an account of the ministers, &c., who were ejected after the Restauration of King Charles II*, 2nd edn, 2 vols. (1713), vol. 2, pp. 514–18 • A. Grant, *The story of the University of Edinburgh during its first three hundred years*, 2 vols. (1884), vol. 2, pp. 257–9 • A. Bower, *The history of the University of Edinburgh*, 3 vols. (1817–30), 1.312–21 • R. Wodrow, *The history of the sufferings of the Church of Scotland from the Restoration to the revolution*, ed. R. Burns, 4 vols. (1828–30), vol. 3, pp. 194–5 • J. Armstrong, 'An appendix, containing some account of the Presbyterian churches in Dublin', in J. Armstrong and others, *Ordination service … of the Rev. James Martineau* (1829), 69–70 • R. Wodrow, *Analecta, or, Materials for a history of remarkable providences, mostly relating to Scotch ministers and Christians*, ed. [M. Leishman], 4 vols., Maitland Club, 60 (1842–3), vol. 1, pp. 201–2, 215; vol. 4, pp. 88–90 • P. J. Anderson, ed., *Officers and graduates of University and King's College, Aberdeen, MVD–MDCCCLX*, New Spalding Club, 11 (1893), 26, 41 • R. W. Innes Smith, *English-speaking students of medicine at the University of Leyden* (1932), 200 • *DNB*

Archives BL, Birch collection • U. Edin., Laing collection

Rule, William Harris (1802–1890), Methodist minister and historian, born at Penryn, Cornwall, on 15 November 1802, was the son of John Rule and his wife, Louisa, daughter of William Harris, a Cornish Quaker. The father, a native of Berwick upon Tweed, was of Scottish parentage. While a surgeon in the army he was captured and imprisoned for some years in France; after his release he entered the naval packet service and was stationed in the West Indies. A strict and severe father, when his son was seventeen years old he turned him out of the house, and young Rule took refuge for a time with an aunt. His education was much neglected, but he received some instruction in Latin from the rector of Falmouth, Thomas Hitchens. He left Cornwall, and eked out a living as a portrait painter in Devonport, Plymouth, Exeter, and finally in London. Early in 1822, influenced by the Treffry and Osborn families, he left the Church of England for the Wesleyan Methodists, and became a village schoolmaster at Newington in Kent. On 24 February 1826 he married Mary Ann Dunmill (d. 1873), only daughter of Richard Barrow of Maidstone, with whom he had several children. He was ordained a Wesleyan minister on 14 March 1826. During his probation he devoted much time to classical study.

On 22 March 1826 Rule left England with his new wife on a projected mission to the Druze of Mount Lebanon, which, however, had to be abandoned. Rule acted for more than a year as resident missionary in Malta. During this time he studied Italian and learned some Arabic. While in the island he was several times stoned by the mob as a protestant and supposed freemason. On 31 May 1827 he left Malta. He was sent in November 1827 by the Wesleyan Missionary Society to the island of St Vincent. In March 1831 he came home, and was next year sent to Gibraltar, where he founded the first charity school, besides four day and evening schools, and had both English and Spanish congregations. He also lectured in Spanish on protestantism, prepared Spanish versions of the four gospels, the Wesleyan Methodist catechism, and Horne's 'Letter on toleration', and compiled a Spanish hymnbook, which obtained a large circulation in Spanish America. A Wesleyan mission established by Rule at Cadiz was suppressed by the Christinist government in 1839; but with the help of Sir George William Frederick Villiers (afterwards Lord Clarendon), the English ambassador, he obtained a royal order repealing the edicts which prohibited foreigners from taking part in Spanish education. Rule returned to England in July 1842. In 1878 he again visited Spain to report on Wesleyan missions at Gibraltar and Barcelona.

From 1842 to 1868 Rule ministered in England. From 1851 to 1857 he acted as joint editor at the Wesleyan conference office. From 1857 to 1865 he was minister to the Wesleyan soldiers at Aldershot, and obtained an official recognition of their worship by royal warrant in 1881. After 1868 he acted as supernumerary minister at Croydon until April 1873. He was elected member of the Croydon school board in 1871. On 10 March 1874, following the death of his first wife, Rule married Harriette Edmed of Maidstone. He died in Clyde Road, Addiscombe, on 25 September 1890.

Rule was a scholarly preacher and a prolific writer, and is said to have been master of ten languages. He received the degree of DD from Dickenson College (Methodist Episcopal church), Ohio, in July 1854. His principal work, published in 1868, and reissued in two volumes in 1874, was a *History of the Inquisition from the Twelfth Century*, based on the best contemporary Roman Catholic authorities. Although a staunch protestant and an early committee member of the Protestant Alliance, Rule produced a well-researched piece of historical scholarship, avoiding mere polemic. In 1870 Rule published a *History of the Karaite Jews*, the first attempt to deal with the subject in England. He afterwards rewrote the work, but the new version was not published. Between 1871 and 1873, with the help of M. J. Corbett Anderson as illustrator, Rule began to issue a work on biblical monuments. All the copies were destroyed by fire at the binder's, but the work was reissued in an extended form as *Oriental Records, Monumental and Historical, Confirmatory of the Old and New Testament* (2 vols., 1877).

C. H. Kelly, himself a very distinguished Wesleyan minister, described Rule as 'the most remarkable man with whom I ever came into contact' (Kelly, 110). Small of stature, in the course of a lengthy ministry he stood his ground in controversy with West Indian plantation owners, Roman Catholic prelates, Spanish officials, the hierarchy of the British army, and those within Methodism who were horrified by his high-Wesleyan ecclesiology and enthusiastic adoption of cassock, bands, gown, and surplice. A contemporary obituarist, noting that Rule was sometimes 'bold beyond the bounds of prudence', concluded that 'his character was of exceptional force' (*Minutes of Conference*, 22–3).

G. Le G. Norgate, *rev.* Martin Wellings

Sources DNB · W. H. Rule, *Recollections of my life and work* (1886) · *Minutes of several conversations at the yearly conference of the people called Methodists* (1891), 22–3 · C. H. Kelly, *Memories* (1910)

Likenesses photograph, repro. in Rule, *Recollections*, frontispiece

Rumbold, Sir (Horace) Algernon Fraser (1906–1993), civil servant and historian, was born on 27 February 1906 at North Berwick, East Lothian, the eldest of four children (three sons and a daughter) of Colonel William Edwin Rumbold (1870–1947), Royal Artillery officer, and his wife, Elizabeth (Bessie) Gordon Cameron (*d.* 1948), daughter of the Revd Robert James Cameron of Burntisland, Fife. He was educated at Wellington College and Christ Church, Oxford, from where he graduated with a second-class degree in modern history in 1927. His father's family had links with the Foreign Office stretching back to 1790. His grandfather was Sir Horace *Rumbold, eighth baronet (1829–1913), diplomatist, and his uncle, Sir Horace George Montagu Rumbold, ninth baronet (1869–1941), was British ambassador in Berlin from 1928 to 1933, played golf with

Algy in his youth, and encouraged his keen appetite for history. Rumbold joined the India Office in 1929 and served as private secretary to a succession of parliamentary under-secretaries including Rab Butler, then to the permanent under-secretary, Sir (Samuel) Findlater Stewart. He subsequently served at the desk dealing with India's northern neighbours and it was he who in 1943 briefed Sir Anthony Eden before a crucial meeting with T. V. Soong, the Chinese foreign minister, at which Britain's view on the status of Tibet was spelt out in its most authoritative form: while Britain recognized Tibet as having enjoyed *de facto* independence since 1911, she had always been prepared to recognize Chinese suzerainty over Tibet, but only on the understanding that Tibet was regarded as autonomous. In Britain's view that term involved not only Tibet's complete internal freedom but also the right to conduct her own external relations with other countries without reference to China. On 19 January 1946 Rumbold married (Margaret) Adel (Dale) Hughes (*b.* 1916), only daughter of Arthur Joseph Hughes, of Chigwell, Essex. They had two daughters, Sarah Josephine (*b.* 1948) and Caroline Elizabeth (*b.* 1950).

On Indian independence day in 1947 Rumbold moved to the Commonwealth Relations Office and served as deputy high commissioner in South Africa between 1949 and 1953. He spent the rest of his official career in Whitehall, becoming an assistant under-secretary in 1954 and, four years later, a deputy under-secretary with responsibility for economic policy. He was deeply involved in negotiations over Commonwealth preferences in the European Free Trade Association (EFTA), but his vigorous hostility to the Common Market led to his being bypassed by Duncan Sandys at the time of the Macmillan government's unsuccessful attempt to secure British entry. Rumbold retained a passionate concern over the affairs of the Indian subcontinent and, when Tibet lost its freedom in 1959, he joined with other old India hands like Sir Olaf Caroe (a former foreign secretary to the Indian government) to found the Tibet Society of the United Kingdom, which conducted active propaganda for Tibetan independence.

In 1965, when fighting, which had broken out between India and Pakistan over the Rann of Cutch, spread to the Punjab and threatened Kashmir, Rumbold was directly involved in advising Harold Wilson, then prime minister, to issue a statement blaming the Indians for crossing the border and calling for an end of hostilities. As the Indians were reacting to what they saw as flagrant Pakistani provocation on the Kashmir front and were winning at the time, this statement caused a serious crisis in Anglo-Indian relations. Disclosure by *The Times* that the British government was considering economic sanctions and a forecast on the BBC World Service of an early oil embargo against both parties further angered New Delhi. Wilson claimed in his memoirs that he had been 'taken for a ride' by a pro-Pakistani faction in the Commonwealth Relations Office, but added that it had not remained there long—a reference identifiable as Rumbold and implying his early retirement (Wilson, 133–4). As Rumbold had left

Whitehall in 1966 on reaching normal retirement age Wilson later apologized, though he still contended that he had been the victim of wrong advice—the facts being too much in dispute.

Rumbold defended himself in a letter to *The Times*. He said he was strongly of the view that officials should be silent, but when politicians defended changes in their views by passing judgement on their officials, whose advice at the time they accepted, the situation altered. There had been powerful international reasons, 'well known to Mr Wilson at the time', why it was important to bring the fighting quickly to a close. Historians would be able to see for themselves when the full papers were made available in 1996 (*The Times*, 5 Aug 1971). The full papers were not in fact released in 1996, some being extracted and closed for a further ten years. It is clear, however, that Rumbold's overriding concern was that China should not be afforded an opportunity to 'fish in the troubled waters of Kashmir'. Wilson used just this phrase when speaking to the Pakistan high commissioner on 7 September, the day after issuing his statement.

Though Lord Wilson made no reference to the subject in his memoirs, it was his friend Professor Thomas Balogh who on 8 September proposed an oil embargo. It fell to Rumbold to chair an inter-departmental committee of officials to consider this and other possible economic measures. The committee was told that the prime minister had asked that all cargo of use for the war should be stopped if possible. A BP tanker carrying aviation spirit was due at Karachi, but the representative of the Ministry of Power told the committee that they were 'dead against any interference by HMG': it was a situation in which the position of the US oil companies had to be considered (PRO, POWE 61/350). The committee's broadly agreed conclusions, formulated a week later, were that an oil embargo would not have an immediate effect; that both countries could get crude oil from elsewhere; that an embargo would mean the loss of £100 million of British company assets in the subcontinent, plus the loss of an outlet for crude oil; and that there would be difficulties in the Middle East. This advice, over Rumbold's signature, must have been unwelcome to the prime minister and his circle.

In retirement Rumbold remained active. He became an adviser on development to the Welsh Office and was deputy chairman of the Air Transport Licensing Board in 1971–2. He had joined the governing body of the School of Oriental and African Studies in 1965 and sat on it until 1980. From 1977 to 1988 he was president of the Tibet Society and wrote frequently to *The Times*, often attacking China's treatment of Tibet and the prevailing bias of British policy in favour of the Chinese interpretation of events in that country. In 1979 he published an erudite study, *Watershed in India: 1914–22*, which was favourably reviewed by A. J. P. Taylor, among others.

Rumbold was a scholarly and somewhat austere public servant, of great personal integrity. He was a stickler for detail and accuracy, outspoken in denouncing misrepresentation of facts. He was appointed CIE in 1947, CMG in 1953, and KCMG in 1960. He died of a heart attack on 23 October 1993 at his home, Shortwoods, West Clandon, Guildford, Surrey, and was cremated; he was survived by his wife and two daughters.   BROOKS RICHARDS

Sources *The Times* (28 Oct 1993) · *The Independent* (6 Dec 1993) · H. Wilson, *The labour government, 1964–1970: a personal record* (1971) · PRO, PREM 13/393, 394, 395 · PRO, POWE 61/350 [India/Pakistan hostilities, September 1965] · private information (2004) [Mrs Caroline Keevil] · personal knowledge (2004) · *WWW, 1991–5* · Burke, *Peerage*
Archives PRO, Commonwealth Relations Office, India Office, Prime Minister's Department, and other government records
Likenesses photograph, repro. in *The Times* · photograph, repro. in *The Independent*
Wealth at death £183,772: probate, 1 Feb 1994, *CGPLA Eng. & Wales*

Rumbold, Sir Arthur Carlos Henry, fifth baronet (1820–1869). *See under* Rumbold, Sir George Berriman, second baronet (1764–1807).

Rumbold, Sir George Berriman, second baronet (1764–1807), diplomatist, born on 17 August 1764 at Fort William, Calcutta, was the second son of Sir Thomas *Rumbold, first baronet (1736–1791), governor of Madras, and his first wife, Frances (*d.* 1764), only daughter of James Berriman. He was admitted a pensioner of Christ's College, Cambridge, on 13 January 1781, afterwards becoming a fellow-commoner. His elder brother having died in 1786, he succeeded as second baronet in 1791. He entered the diplomatic service, and in 1803 was appointed ambassador to the Hanse towns and minister-resident of Great Britain at Hamburg. On the night of 25 October 1804, on the direct orders of Fouché in Paris (who suspected a conspiracy), a detachment of French troops landed in boats on the Hamburg Berg, proceeded to the Grindel, Rumbold's country residence, forced the door, and compelled him to deliver up his papers. He was taken to Hanover in a guarded coach, and thence to Paris. Prussian protests were instrumental in gaining his release, and he was escorted to Cherbourg, from where he travelled to Portsmouth. He returned to Hamburg and retired from the service in 1806.

Rumbold married, in November 1783, Caroline, only child of James Hearn of Waterford. Rumbold died of fever at Memel on 15 December 1807. Two years later, his widow married Sir W. Sidney Smith; she died in 1826. Rumbold and his wife had two sons and four daughters. Of the latter, Caroline (*d.* 1847) married Colonel Adolphe de St Clair of the *garde du corps*; Maria (*d.* 31 Dec 1875) was the wife of Rear-Admiral Arabin; and Emily (*d.* 1861) married Ferdinand, Baron de Delmar. The elder son, Sir William Rumbold (1787–1833), third baronet, married Henrietta Elizabeth, second daughter and coheir of Thomas Boothby, first Baron Rancliffe. Their surviving sons, Cavendish Stuart Rumbold (1815–1853), Arthur Carlos Henry Rumbold (1820–1869), Charles Hale Rumbold (1822–1877), and Horace *Rumbold (1829–1913), the last of whom became ambassador at Vienna, were successively fourth, fifth, seventh, and eighth baronets.

Of these, **Sir Arthur Carlos Henry Rumbold**, fifth baronet (1820–1869), army officer and colonial administrator, was born on 25 September 1820. He entered the army in 1837 as an ensign in the 51st foot, but afterwards exchanged into the 70th. In July 1848 he was appointed a stipendiary magistrate in Jamaica, but in 1855 joined the allied army in the Crimea. He served with the Osmanli cavalry as brigade major to Major-General C. Havelock. He held the rank of colonel in the imperial Ottoman army, and for his services in the war received the order of the Mejidiye, fourth class. On 4 March 1857 he was appointed president of Nevis in the Leeward Islands, and on 17 November 1865 of the Virgin Islands. From January to April 1867 he acted as administrator of St Kitts and Anguilla. He died on 12 June 1869, having been twice married (first, in 1846, to Antoinette, *née* de Kerven, who died in 1867; second, in 1868, to Helen Eliza, *née* Hopewell). In 1848 he published an English version of F. Ponsard's tragedy *Lucrèce*.   G. LE G. NORGATE, *rev.* H. C. G. MATTHEW

Sources GM, 1st ser., 74 (1804), 1063–4, 1159–60 · GM, 1st ser., 78 (1808), 270 · *ILN* (17 July 1869) · *Army List* (1868) · Boase, *Mod. Eng. biog.* · Burke, *Peerage* · *CGPLA Eng. & Wales* (1869)
Archives Archives Nationales, Paris, corresp. and papers · NRA, priv. coll., corresp. and papers | Harrowby Manuscript Trust, Sandon Hall, Staffordshire, letters to Lord Harrowby · NL Scot., corresp. with Robert Liston · PRO, corresp. with Francis Jackson, FO 353
Wealth at death under £1500—Sir Arthur Carlos Henry Rumbold: will, 1869

Rumbold, Henry (*bap.* 1617, *d.* 1690). *See under* Rumbold, William (1613–1667).

Rumbold, Sir Horace, eighth baronet (1829–1913), diplomatist, the fifth son of Sir William Rumbold, third baronet (1787–1833), and his wife, Henrietta Elizabeth, second daughter and coheir of Thomas Boothby, first Baron Rancliffe, was born in Calcutta on 2 July 1829. His father had served on the staff of the second earl of Moira (afterwards marquess of Hastings), governor-general of Bengal. Horace was sent home from India when he was three years old, and was privately educated in Paris, where he had many relatives among the old French aristocracy. No examinations being then required, he was introduced into the diplomatic service by Lord Palmerston in 1849.

In the next ten years Rumbold held appointments in Washington and Piedmont (1849), Paris and Frankfurt (1852), Stuttgart (1854), and Vienna (1856). In December 1858 he was appointed secretary of the legation in China on the staff of Frederick William Adolphus Bruce and went to China in March 1859. Bruce sent him back to England in January 1860 to report to the government the active resistance which was offered to the progress of the British mission to the Chinese capital. This report led to the Anglo-French expedition to Peking (Beijing) in that year. Promotion came slowly to Rumbold, and he held in succession a long series of minor diplomatic posts. After serving at Athens (1862, 1866–7), Bern (1864), St Petersburg (1868–71), and Constantinople (1871), he became consul-general in Chile (1872–8), minister at Bern (1878), and envoy-extraordinary to Argentina (1879–81), Sweden and Norway (1881–4), Greece (1884–8), and the Netherlands (1888–96). In 1896 he was appointed ambassador at Vienna. To his friends' congratulations he replied that it was 'not promotion but reparation', and four years later he retired.

Rumbold occupied his leisure in writing accounts of his wide experience as a diplomatist. He was the author of *The Great Silver River: Notes of a Residence in Buenos Ayres* (1887), *Recollections of a Diplomatist* (1902), *Further Recollections* (1903), and *Final Recollections* (1905). In 1909 he published *The Austrian Court in the Nineteenth Century*, a book which created some sensation and was regarded as a grave indiscretion at a time when high officials had not acquired the habit of writing memoirs.

Rumbold succeeded his brother, Sir Charles Hale Rumbold, as eighth baronet, in 1877 (the baronetcy having passed in turn, since his father's death in 1833, to his three elder surviving brothers and a nephew). He was sworn of the privy council in 1896 and made GCB in 1897. He married twice: first, in 1867 Caroline Barney (1847–1872), daughter of George Harrington of Washington, the USA's minister at Bern, with whom he had three sons; second, in 1881 Louisa Anne (*d.* 1940), daughter of Thomas Russell *Crampton, and widow of Captain St George Francis Robert Caulfeild, 1st Life Guards, with whom he had one son. Rumbold died at Vicar's Hill, Lymington, on 3 November 1913. He was succeeded in the baronetcy by his eldest son, Horace George Montagu *Rumbold (1869–1941), who, despite his father's disappointments, followed him into the diplomatic service.

VALENTINE CHIROL, *rev.* H. C. G. MATTHEW

Sources *FO List* (1913) · personal knowledge (1927)
Archives NRA, priv. coll., corresp. and papers | Bodl. Oxf., corresp. with Lord Kimberley; corresp. with H. G. M. Rumbold · Lpool RO, corresp. with fifteenth earl of Derby
Likenesses P. N., wood-engraving, NPG
Wealth at death £35,535 19s. 7d.: probate, 28 Feb 1914, *CGPLA Eng. & Wales*

Rumbold, Sir Horace George Montagu, ninth baronet (1869–1941), diplomatist, was born on 5 February 1869 at St Petersburg, the eldest of the three sons of Sir Horace *Rumbold, eighth baronet (1829–1913), and his first wife, Caroline Barney, *née* Harrington (1847–1872), daughter of George Harrington, United States minister at Bern. Rumbold's mother died when he was not yet four years old, and his father married, second, Louisa Anne (*d.* 1940), daughter of Thomas Russell Crampton and widow of Captain St George Francis Robert Caulfeild. There was a further son from this second marriage. Rumbold's father, a distinguished diplomatist himself, having been brought up on the continent, determined that his son was to have an exclusively English education. At the age of ten he was sent to the Revd John Hawtrey's preparatory school, Aldin House near Slough, which was known locally as Little Eton. From there he went to Eton College three years later. His time at Eton was a formative period and, in his manner, conduct, and appearance, he remained discernibly Etonian all his life.

In June 1888 Rumbold was appointed an honorary

Sir Horace George Montagu Rumbold, ninth baronet (1869–1941), by unknown photographer, c.1900

attaché at the Hague legation, where his father was minister. In February 1891 he passed first in the competitive entrance examination for the diplomatic corps. For the next few years he followed the usual routine of younger members of the service and was posted to the missions at Cairo (December 1891 – June 1895), Tehran (July 1895 – July 1897), and Vienna (July 1897 – November 1900), where he once again served under his father. In November 1900 he returned to Cairo, where he remained for the next seven years, reaching the rank of first secretary in April 1904. In later life Rumbold looked back on his long spell at Cairo as the high point of his early career. None the less, his relations with his chief, the British agent and *de facto* ruler of the country, the earl of Cromer, were often strained. He held Cromer's abilities in high regard, yet profoundly disagreed with his policy of gradually introducing Egyptians into responsible positions within the government of the country. On 18 July 1905 he married Etheldred Constantia (1879–1964), the younger daughter of Sir Edmund Douglas Veitch *Fane, of Boyton Manor, Wiltshire, diplomatist. They had three children: Constantia Dorothy (b. 1906), (Horace) Anthony Claude (b. 1911), and Bridget Margherita (1914–1918).

From Cairo Rumbold was posted in December 1906 to Madrid where he remained until December 1908, when he was transferred for a brief and uneventful period as chargé d'affaires to Munich. In February 1909 he was promoted to counsellor of embassy and posted to Tokyo. He remained in the Far East for four years, until November 1913. At Tokyo, in April 1911, he played a crucial, albeit ultimately unsuccessful, role in trying to persuade the Foreign Office against the renewal of the 1905 Anglo-Japanese alliance. The Foreign Office dismissed his warning that Japan would soon pursue a bellicose policy in Asia, and Rumbold, now in charge of the embassy, was instructed to bring the negotiations for the renewal to a conclusion. His talks with Komura, the Japanese foreign minister, continued throughout the early summer, but Rumbold was able to remove the last remaining obstacles and the alliance was signed in July 1911.

In November 1913 Rumbold succeeded his father to the baronetcy. Professionally, however, he had made little progress. He was offered the posts of minister-resident at Guatemala city and Lima in August and October 1913. Fearing prolonged 'exile' in South America, however, he refused both offers and was transferred to Berlin, still a counsellor, in November 1913. In view of his father's well-known criticisms of German policy in the *National Review* in 1902 his appointment was perhaps not very judicious. Rumbold himself had long come to regard Germany with suspicion ever since he had gained firsthand experience of German commercial rivalry in Egypt. Within nine months of his arrival he found himself in the eye of the storm unleashed by the assassination at Sarajevo. Once again he was in charge of an embassy at an important juncture; and in light of Britain's crucial role during the later stages of the July crisis 'the British "chargé" here is almost as big a bug as he was in Japan' (incomplete letter by Rumbold, c.mid-July 1914, Rumbold MSS, dep. 16). His efforts to persuade the German government to accept an international conference to mediate between Austria and Serbia were to no avail. The civilian authorities in Berlin, he concluded one month after the outbreak of war, had lost control and Germany had been dragged into the war by Austria. In retirement, he recorded his version of the events of July 1914 in his thoughtful *War Crisis in Berlin, July–August 1914* (1940).

Rumbold spent the first half of the war at the Foreign Office where he was in charge of prisoner-of-war affairs. In September 1916 he was appointed minister at Bern. It was there that Rumbold won his reputation as an extremely able diplomat. From his vantage point in Switzerland he was an important source of information about the internal conditions of the central powers. These conditions were considerably worsened by the allied economic blockade, of which Bern was the southern cornerstone. For his blockade work Rumbold was appointed KCMG in 1917.

After the Paris peace settlement Rumbold was made Britain's first minister to the newly independent Poland, in September 1919. Already during the war, at Bern, he had been the Foreign Office's link with Polish nationalists. He had very much wished for this post, but his year-long spell at Warsaw was fraught with difficulties. Despite Britain's general support for Poland's independence, Polish designs to extend their eastern frontier at the expense of Russia soured Anglo-Polish relations. As military fortunes alternated in the Russo-Polish war, Rumbold continued to exert a moderating influence with a view to facilitating a negotiated settlement. His adroit handling of the situation quickly justified his appointment. None the less his position was frequently difficult, never more so than after Lloyd George's commitment to Poland at the Spa conference in July 1920. As Lloyd George had not deigned to inform the Foreign Office, Rumbold found himself in the humiliating position of not being able to confirm or deny accounts of the conference.

After one arduous year in Poland, Rumbold was anxious for a transfer. Lord Hardinge, the permanent under-secretary of the Foreign Office, wanted him to become Britain's first post-war ambassador to Berlin, but his advice was ignored by Lloyd George and Lord Curzon, the foreign secretary. Instead Rumbold was sent to Constantinople as high commissioner and ambassador in November 1920. If anything, his new post was even more difficult than Warsaw had been. The Near Eastern peace settlement had unravelled after the treaty of Sèvres proved abortive, and Rumbold's relations with the Turkish authorities were highly anomalous, with the former based at Constantinople, accredited to the sultan's withering regime, and the latter, wielding the real power in Turkey and denounced as bandits by the allied powers, now removed to Ankara. Dissension among the British, French, and Italian governments, and Turkish intransigence, culminating in the Chanak crisis in September 1922, only added to Rumbold's woes. Indeed, he found himself in profound disagreement with the government's hard line towards the Kemalist forces. Judging that talks were still possible and on his own initiative, he withheld the ultimatum he had been instructed to deliver. This incurred him the wrath of the cabinet in London, but he had judged the situation correctly. Mustafa Kemal was prepared to negotiate, and from Constantinople Rumbold directed the ensuing talks which resulted in the convention of Mudanya.

In view of his work during the Chanak crisis Rumbold was asked by Lord Curzon to act as his deputy at the first, abortive Lausanne peace conference (November 1922 – February 1923) and then as chief delegate at the second conference. In the course of his three-year involvement in Turkish affairs Rumbold, unlike many allied diplomatists, had come to respect Kemal's qualities as a statesman. His position as chief delegate at the second conference, however, was rendered more difficult by the wish of a section of the new government under Bonar Law for a speedy evacuation of the British occupation along the Turkish straits and the impatience of the more radical members of the nationalist grand assembly at Ankara to retake Constantinople. Still, with characteristic calm, Rumbold set out to remove the remaining stumbling-blocks. Nearly four months of painstaking negotiations resulted in the treaty of Lausanne of 24 July 1923. That the negotiations were ultimately brought to a successful conclusion was largely due to 'the moderation and patience with which … Rumbold created concord out of dissonance' (Rumbold, xxvii). As a reward for his services at Constantinople and Lausanne he was sworn of the privy council in 1921 and promoted GCMG in 1923.

Rumbold's next appointment, in February 1924, was as ambassador to Madrid, where he spent four years, although he briefly returned to the Near East in November 1925 as chairman of the international commission on the Graeco-Bulgarian frontier. His ambassadorship at Madrid was less onerous than his previous two posts. Spain itself had changed considerably since his two-year spell there seventeen years previously. A series of domestic political crises, compounded by colonial difficulties in Spanish Morocco, had resulted in Primo de Rivera's *de facto* military dictatorship. Throughout his four years at Madrid Rumbold largely confined himself to observing how de Rivera's dictatorship developed, while trying to do what he could to shore up what remained of monarchical power.

In August 1928 Rumbold was transferred to his last post, as ambassador to Berlin. He arrived in Berlin on 3 August 'exactly fourteen years to the day almost—i.e. August 4 1914—when he was Counsellor & crept out of Berlin under cavalry escort & amid the booings of a crowd' (H. Nicolson to V. Sackville-West, 3 Aug 1928 (copy), Rumbold MSS, dep. 44). Still, after four years of de Rivera's military dictatorship he found the Weimar authorities easier to work with. He struck up a particular rapport with Gustav Stresemann, the already ailing foreign minister of the republic. In Stresemann and the president, von Hindenburg, he saw the only two reliable pillars of German democracy. He was by no means a Germanophile, but he realized that in the interest of European stability the Weimar republic had to be assisted. He believed that the outstanding questions in relations with Germany, such as the reparations issue or the Rhineland evacuation, could be solved diplomatically, thus lending greater authority to the republican regime and perhaps preventing a recrudescence of militarism. After the death of Stresemann in 1929 and the collapse of the last democratic government in the following year he urged his government to support the minority administration under Dr Brüning with a view to raising German morale. The chancellor was 'a man of great determination and his honesty and sincerity are almost worthy of Baldwin' (Rumbold to Nicolson (personal), 30 Nov 1930, Rumbold MSS, dep. 38). The only ones to profit from the collapse of Brüning's government, he argued, would be Adolf Hitler and his Nazi party, the growth of which movement Rumbold followed with some concern. The Nazi take-over coincided with Rumbold's own retirement from diplomacy, in August 1933. In his lengthy farewell dispatch he offered his analysis of Nazi ideology and warned of early signs of German preparations for a comprehensive rearmament programme, adding the ominous words that 'Hitlerism has eradicated [Germany's inferiority complex], but only at the cost of burdening Europe with a new outbreak of nationalism' (Rumbold, 343–58).

On his retirement Rumbold was appointed GCB. In 1935 he was Britain's chief representative at the Geneva refugee conference. In the following year he served as vice-chairman of Lord Peel's royal commission on Palestine. At the outbreak of the Second World War he joined the Ministry of Economic Warfare and served as chairman of the 'black list committee', which was set up to groom German refugees as a possible alternative government. In early

1941 he was taken ill, and in April had to give up his work. On 24 May 1941 he died at his home, Pyt House, Tisbury, Wiltshire. He was succeeded as tenth baronet by his son, Anthony.

Harold Nicolson, who twice served under Rumbold, described him in the following terms:

> The eye-glass in his eye, the vagueness of response, even the half-opened mouth indicated an attitude of mind which the English could recognise as post-Etonian but which the unwary foreigner sometimes mistook for lack of alertness ... he had merely trained himself to appear more English than any Englishman had ever seemed before. And if his manner ever misled a foreigner into underrating his intelligence, that foreigner was quickly disabused. (Rumbold, xxiv)

Nicolson dedicated the first edition of his *Diplomacy* to Rumbold as 'an ideal diplomatist'.   T. G. OTTE

Sources Bodl. Oxf., MSS Rumbold · M. Gilbert, *Sir Horace Rumbold: portrait of a diplomat* (1973) · G. P. Gooch and H. Temperley, eds., *British documents on the origins of the war, 1898–1914*, 8 (1932); 11 (1926) · W. N. Medlicott and others, eds., *Documents on British foreign policy, 1919–1939*, 1st ser., 11: *Upper Silesia, Poland and the Baltic States, January 1920 – March 1921* (1961); 1st ser., 18: *Greece and Turkey, September 3 1922 – July 24 1923*; ser. 1a, 7: *German, Austrian and Middle Eastern questions, 1929–1930* (1975); 2nd ser., 5: *1933* (1956) · CUL, Hardinge MSS, box 43 · H. Rumbold, *The war crisis in Berlin, July–August 1914*, 2nd edn (1944) [with introduction by H. Nicolson] · P. Lowe, *Great Britain and Japan, 1911–1915* (1969) · WWW, 1941–50 · FO List · Burke, *Peerage* · CGPLA Eng. & Wales (1941) · *The Times* (25 May 1941)
Archives Bodl. Oxf., journals, corresp., and papers | CUL, corresp. with Lord Hardinge · Herts. ALS, letters to Lady Desborough · HLRO, letters to David Lloyd George · Nuffield Oxf., corresp. with Lord Cherwell · PRO, Foreign Office archives, FO 371 | FILM IWM FVA, actuality footage
Likenesses photograph, c.1900, NPG [*see illus.*] · W. Stoneman, two photographs, 1919–36, NPG · P. A. de Laszlo, portrait, priv. coll. · photographs, repro. in Gilbert, *Sir Horace Rumbold*
Wealth at death £45,212 5s. 2d.: probate, 26 Aug 1941, CGPLA Eng. & Wales

Rumbold, Richard (c.1622–1685), conspirator, joined the parliamentarian army early in the civil war at the age of nineteen, losing an eye in the conflict, so that in later life he was known as Hannibal after the one-eyed Carthaginian general. Though still a private soldier he was chosen as one of the guards surrounding the scaffold when Charles I was executed in January 1649. A month later he displayed his radical views when, with seven other private soldiers, he petitioned Sir Thomas Fairfax, the army commander, for the re-establishment of ordinary soldiers' representatives—the 'agitators'—on the army's general council. For this act half of the petitioners were cashiered from the army but Rumbold survived, possibly because he subsequently disowned the petition, since his name does not appear in the version which the Levellers printed. He went on to serve in the Dunbar and Worcester campaigns, evidently with some distinction, for by 1651 he had achieved the rare feat of being promoted from the ranks to the position of lieutenant in Cromwell's own regiment. He remained in the army through the 1650s and may have been promoted to captain, the rank by which he was subsequently known, just before the Restoration.

Dismissed from the army at the Restoration, Rumbold married the widow of a well-to-do maltster and carried on this trade from the residence he acquired with the business, the 'Rye House' near Hoddesdon in Hertfordshire. He had the reputation of being a bluff honest soldier, though a government informer described him as a 'Brisk man & of Interest' (*CSP dom.*, *1683*, 185). His business may have been in decline by 1682, for in that year he took legal advice on recovering a debt of £10 contracted in 1651. He was also by then making regular payments to a woman named Jane Suner, possibly charity, possibly blackmail. A man of action, he proposed on one occasion to knock on the head a fellow conspirator of doubtful loyalty. He held strong Baptist views, and on the scaffold in 1685 denounced both episcopacy and Catholicism as 'superstitious and pernicious' (Wodrow, 2.552). Rumoured to have been involved in republican plots against the monarchy in the 1670s, he was certainly by 1682 discussing with some other desperate whigs and exclusionists an attack on Charles II and the duke of York as the two returned from the Newmarket races to London. The road followed by the royal coach went past Rumbold's Rye House in Hertfordshire, and the plan was for some forty armed horsemen to gather there. Half would ambush the king's guards, and the rest under Rumbold would attack the royal coach. The plot was abandoned in March 1683, when the royal party unexpectedly returned early to London. There is evidence that Rumbold, though participating actively in the early discussions, had by 1683 turned cold on the plan, principally because John Wildman, an experienced plotter who had first recruited him, was becoming sceptical of its success. When the government first received information of the plot, from Josiah Keeling in June 1683, it delayed briefly before issuing arrest warrants, enabling Rumbold and other conspirators to escape to the continent.

Early in 1685 Rumbold, like most other English exiles, joined the duke of Monmouth when the latter began preparing an expedition to depose the newly crowned James II. Though the duke desperately needed men with military experience Rumbold's regicide plotting was probably the reason why he was sent off with Argyll's expedition to the Scottish highlands as a liaison officer. Argyll promoted him to the rank of colonel, intending him to command a regiment when his small force was swollen by successful recruiting: in the meantime he commanded the rebels' sole troop of horse. He successfully held off loyalist militia when Argyll with the main force tried to attack Inveraray, and was a cool reconciling voice in the earl's heated and divided counsels. At the end, when the rebel force went astray in a bog and panicked as they crossed the River Clyde into Renfrewshire, Rumbold was sent to the head of the column to try to restore order. Discipline, however, was poor; the force was fragmented, and was completely routed when attacked by the militia. Captured after being badly wounded, he was paraded through Edinburgh, and because of the gravity of his wounds was tried on 26 July 1685 and executed on the same day. At his trial and on the scaffold he freely admitted his complicity in Argyll's rebellion, but absolutely denied intending the death of Charles II in the Rye House plot. He furthermore denied being a republican, saying that a strictly limited monarchy was the best form of government; though misbehaviour by the king was grounds for lawful resistance. His last words were a memorable assertion of political equality: 'I am sure there was no man born marked of God above another; for none comes into the world with a saddle upon his back, neither any booted and spurred to ride him' (State trials, 9.873–81). By James II's personal direction Rumbold's quarters were not mounted in Scotland, but were put on display near the Rye House, and in Kent where his family had connections. His brother William, who had taken part in Monmouth's rebellion and contributed £100 to it, was pardoned by James II in 1688.

ROBIN CLIFTON

Sources R. L. Greaves, *Secrets of the kingdom: British radicals from the Popish Plot to the revolution of 1688–89* (1992) • J. F. McGregor, 'Rumbold, Richard', Greaves & Zaller, *BDBR* • R. Clifton, *The last popular rebellion: the western rising of 1685* (1984) • D. J. Milne, 'The Rye House plot with special reference to its place in the exclusion contest and its consequences till 1685', PhD diss., U. Lond., 1949 • R. Wodrow, *The history of the sufferings of the Church of Scotland from the Restauration to the revolution*, 2 vols. (1721–2) • C. J. Fox, *History of the early part of the reign of James the second* (1808) • G. H. Rose, *A selection from the papers of the earls of Marchmont*, 3 vols. (1831) • *CSP dom.*, 1650–85 • J. Ferguson, *Robert Ferguson the plotter: the secret of the Ryehouse conspiracy and the story of a strange career* (1887) • *DNB* • *State trials*, vols. 9, 11
Wealth at death very little

Rumbold, Richard William John Nugent [*pseud.* Richard Lumford] (**1913–1961**), author, was born on 24 June 1913, probably at Dowth Hall, co. Meath, Ireland, second of the three children of Charles Edmund Arden Law Rumbold (1872–1943), sometime captain 2nd dragoon guards, and Anne Christian (1881–1928), daughter of the Hon. Richard Anthony Nugent and his wife, Henrietta Gradwell. An elder brother died at birth and he had a sister, Rosemary, three years younger. His mother was from an ancient Norman-Irish family, the earls of Westmeath. His father was English, wealthy, descended from the famous nabob Sir Thomas Rumbold, governor of Madras; also from the Ardens, relatives of Shakespeare. Rumbold's autobiographical book *My Father's Son* (1947), with fictional names and under the pseudonym Richard Lumford, was a brave and cathartic account of his wretched childhood, and revealed him as a gifted writer dominated by a bullying father. This work also included an account of the suicide of his mother. It was reissued in 1958 under his own name, with an introduction by Harold Nicolson, his long-suffering mentor and constant support. His second cousin William Plomer was to confirm that the description of the father was no exaggeration: 'only a Balzac or a Dickens could dream up such a character'. Rumbold was handsome and physically well built, with blue eyes. His father attacked him constantly for 'effeminacy', and regarded intellectuals as 'half-baked'. Just as the father was constantly on the move from house to house, so Rumbold was sent to a number of schools, in England, France, and Germany. For a while, to 'knock out the softness', he was a cadet on a naval training ship, an unhappy experience. However, he passed into Christ Church, Oxford, where he revived and ran a literary club, arranging talks by such personalities as Lord Alfred Douglas, Frieda Lawrence, W. B. Yeats, and Charles Morgan; many of these speakers became loyal friends. Rumbold had been brought up a Roman Catholic, but by this time he was becoming disillusioned with Catholic dogma. In 1933 he published a novel, *Little Victims*, which he dedicated to Richard Aldington. This bitter, ill-judged, obviously autobiographical book was a *succès de scandale*, lashing out at the church, his parents, public-school homosexuality, and Oxford aesthetes. He was refused the sacrament by the university chaplain, Ronald Knox. Furious, he decided to abjure Roman Catholicism. Very soon afterwards he spat blood and tuberculosis was diagnosed. He left Oxford without taking a degree in 1934.

Rumbold travelled a great deal and on a cruise met a well-off American, Hilda Byrne Young, who for much of his life acted as a doting substitute mother, amazingly tolerant of his homosexuality and sometimes treated as a servant. On Harold Nicolson's suggestion that he should interest himself in other people's problems, he visited the London docklands and Welsh coalmines, and became genuinely obsessed with a desire to help the underdog. When war came he joined up as a private in the Royal Army Service Corps, but soon transferred to the Royal Air Force. He was exhilarated by the experience of his training as a pilot, not only the flying but the sense of comradeship. His lyrical descriptions are outstanding in *My Father's Son*. Later, bombing raids upset his conscience, and he applied to become a fighter pilot. Some foolhardy escapades ended with flying under the Menai Bridge, for which he was court-martialled. Once more he spat blood.

Desperate for literary recognition, brooding over imagined slights, deeply serious, longing for the true love he could never achieve, Rumbold first began treatment for schizophrenia in Switzerland and then began visits to a psychiatrist, Denis Carroll, who encouraged him to write his autobiography. He wrote articles, and edited a somewhat skimpy collection of Flaubert's letters in 1950. He took up riding a motorcycle, at tremendous speeds. His ecstatic discovery of flying led to a biography of Saint-Exupéry, *The Winged Life* (1953), written in collaboration with Lady Margaret Stewart. Hilda Young accompanied him to Ceylon, where he hoped to find 'sensual liberation and spiritual reconciliation'. His interest in Buddhism took him to Japan, where he was a part-time postulant in a Zen monastery. Back in England, after an operation, his obvious inner turmoil increased, to the concern of many devoted friends, partly as a result of a further disaster in his family, the death of his sister. Rumbold went to Sicily, accompanied by Hilda Young, and by Archibald Colquhoun, the translator of *The Leopard*, who himself had recently returned to the Roman Catholic faith. Rumbold still regarded the church as the enemy of freedom and pleasure, especially for its stance on homosexuality, but reluctantly agreed to attend mass daily; Harold Nicolson maintained that he was refused confession and communion, the priests presumably having been told by Colquhoun of the original interdict. All the time he was desperately working on two books.

On 10 March 1961, at a hotel in Palermo, while Hilda Young was typing in another room, Rumbold fell from a window, possibly accidentally, and was killed. He was permitted a Roman Catholic funeral in the graveyard of the Anglican church of Watton-on-Stone in Hertfordshire, the village where his ancestor Sir Thomas Rumbold had built his splendid house. One recalls Rumbold's own description of Saint-Exupéry: 'He remained to the end an idealist, an anguished idealist, ceaselessly searching for a faith for his idealism, and for inner peace'. Extracts from his diaries, with some meditations on Zen, were movingly—and to some extent discreetly—edited by William Plomer in *A Message in Code* (1964).   RALEIGH TREVELYAN

Sources R. Lumford [R. Rumbold], *My father's son* (1949); repr. with introduction by H. Nicolson (1958) · *A message in code: the diary of Richard Rumbold, 1932–60*, ed. W. Plomer (1964) · *The Times* (11 March 1961) · *The Times* (8 April 1961) · personal knowledge (2004) · private information (2004) · J. Lees-Milne, *Harold Nicolson: a biography*, 2: *1930–1968* (1981) · P. F. Alexander, *William Plomer: a biography* (1989)

Likenesses photograph, repro. in Plomer, ed., *Message in code*, frontispiece

Wealth at death £133,402 6s. 4d.: probate, 20 July 1961, *CGPLA Eng. & Wales*

Rumbold, Sir Thomas, first baronet (1736–1791), administrator in India, was born on 4 January 1736 at Low Leyton, Leytonstone, Essex, the third son of William Rumbold and his wife, Dorothy (d. 1753), widow of John Mann and daughter of Richard Cheney of Hackney. Thomas's father was a purser on the East India Company ship the *King George* when he married Dorothy at Calcutta in 1726. The Rumbolds returned to England and settled at Leytonstone. However, gambling debts forced William to seek a return to India to repair his fortune. His request to be allowed to return in the company's service was granted in February 1743, when he was appointed a factor on the Bombay establishment. He sailed for India, leaving his wife and children in the care of his sister Elizabeth.

East India service, 1752–1778 The East India connections of the family procured Thomas Rumbold an entry as a writer in the company's Madras civil service on 8 January 1752. Soon after his arrival there he changed from the civil to the military service, where he served as a lieutenant under Stringer Lawrence at Trichinopoly in 1754. On 22 June 1756 Rumbold married Frances (d. 1764), daughter of James Berriman, with whom he had one daughter, also Frances, and two sons, before she died on 22 August 1764. Some months after his marriage Rumbold accompanied Lord Clive to Calcutta. He was wounded in the attack on the nawab's camp on 7 February 1757, was made a captain, and was Clive's aide-de-camp at Plassey four months later.

On being superseded in the military service by John Gowen, who was transferred from Bombay and appointed major on Clive's decision, Rumbold and seven other captains resigned their commissions on 31 August 1758. Rumbold now tried his luck in the Bengal civil service. By late 1760 he was third in council at Chittagong, undertaking the revenue administration of that province recently ceded to the company with his colleagues Harry Verelst

and Randolph Marriott. Rumbold acted as collector in charge of gathering the land revenue. Important private advantages could be reaped from the revenue administration in the early years after Plassey and were considered particularly rewarding to people in Rumbold's position with direct access to the men at the bottom of the revenue hierarchy.

Rumbold, Marriott, and Verelst, in partnership, also extensively engaged in private trade. They owned several 'country' ships, that is, ships built in India for Asian trade, and set up their own shipyard at Bakarganj, where a first ship was completed in 1762. The partners pioneered setting up a commercial venture shipping goods to Arracan, now Myanmar. Their most important trade was in salt, produced on the island of Sandwip. By 1762 the partnership traded on a capital of more than £30,000.

In 1763 Rumbold was appointed chief at the company's Patna factory. This position was reputed to be very valuable because of the possibilities for private trade it offered and because of the potential profits the administration of the Bihar revenue could bring its occupant. No doubt profiting from his experience as a collector at Chittagong, Rumbold here laid the foundations of his substantial fortune and his reputation as one of the period's most notorious nabobs.

Clive's return to Bengal in 1765 brought Rumbold into the Bengal council. He took up his seat in 1766, and as a member of the council continued to be occupied with the collection of the land revenue. In 1768 he accompanied Shitab Rai, the Indian administrator of the province, on a tour through Bihar with a view to establishing a more exact estimate of the revenue it could yield. A year later he was allowed an extra share (percentage on the revenue proceeds) 'in consideration of the additional trouble and attention he has as a Supravisor of the Bahar collections' (Datta and others, 5.520). In December 1769 he resigned from the company's service and embarked for Britain.

On arrival Rumbold immediately set out to acquire an influence in the company and a seat in parliament. Helped by the strength of his purse, he succeeded in both. In 1770 he became MP for the notoriously corrupt and expensive borough of New Shoreham. Acquiring large stockholdings to further his company career, he became an East India director in 1772. Unfortunately for him, the crisis the company faced that same year severely discredited the sitting directors, of whom only Laurence Sulivan dared to stand for re-election in 1773. It was not until 1775 that Rumbold resumed a seat in the company's directorate.

Rumbold was believed to be worth between £200,000 and £300,000 when he returned home in 1769. However, he had left an important part of this fortune invested in India awaiting later remittance to Britain. Deteriorating economic circumstances in Bengal after the great famine (1770) endangered the recovery of this part of his fortune, a consideration that must have induced him to seek a new career in India almost immediately after his return to Britain. In 1771 he was mentioned as a candidate for the governorship of Bengal before the choice ultimately fell on Warren Hastings. In 1773, with the company's approval, he envisaged returning to Bengal as second in council but finally decided to await a better opportunity. In 1775, following the recall of the governor of Madras, Alexander Wynch, Rumbold eagerly canvassed to take his place. He obtained the support of Lord North's administration and of the court of directors but was finally defeated by his opponent, Lord Pigot, at the general court of proprietors by a margin of only four votes. Two years later, on the news of Pigot's death, he finally satisfied his ambition by receiving the governorship, returning to India, where he arrived in early February 1778.

Governor of Madras, 1778–1781 The affairs of the company's settlement at Madras had been worrying the directors for some time because of the involvement of their servants in the affairs of the nawab of Arcot, to whom many were creditors. Company servants were thus inclined to promote policies which enlarged the nawab's landholding and increased the security of their loans. Lord Pigot had tried to put a stop to this but had been suspended from his governorship and imprisoned by a faction of the Madras council. Despite his experience and expertise in land revenue matters, the wisdom of the choice of Thomas Rumbold as Pigot's successor can be doubted. His principal ambitions for his Madras governorship were not in the field of public policy.

Four months after his arrival rumours of war with France reached Bengal. Rumbold received orders to besiege the French settlements of Pondicherry and Mahé. Pondicherry capitulated in October 1778, Mahé in March 1779. Rumbold hoped that these successes would obtain him 'some mark of distinction from the Crown'. He sent home his eldest son, William Richard, who had gone out with him to India, to carry the good news, and wrote to all his 'friends among the great … to forward this business' and set his government 'in a favourable point of view' (Thomas Rumbold to Edward Law, Madras, 25 Oct 1778, BL OIOC, Rumbold papers). Though Rumbold succeeded in his first ambition and was created a baronet on 23 March 1779, subsequent dealings with the nizam of Hyderabad and brushes with Haidar Ali of Mysore eventually prevented him from making his government appreciated at home.

Rumbold angered the nizam of the Deccan by concluding a treaty with his brother Basalat Jang without giving the nizam prior notice. In this treaty the company would lease the Guntur district from Basalat Jang, paying him a stipulated rent, while obtaining the permission to station troops on his territory. After its conclusion Rumbold wrote to the nizam asking his permission for an army detachment to cross his lands to be stationed in his brother's district. The nizam took offence at Rumbold's direct dealing with his brother and answered that he would resist any attempt to march troops through his territory by force. Rumbold superciliously answered that the nizam would do well not to risk a break of friendship with the British. He added to the insult by instructing John Hollond, his emissary at the nizam's court, to negotiate the remission of all rents still due to the nizam by virtue of a treaty concluded between him and the company in 1768,

and to induce him to dismiss a French-officered contingent he had in his pay. Hollond was to offer no concessions in return but to work on the nizam's apprehensions. After thus evoking the nizam's resentment, Rumbold tried to pass his troops to the Guntur district over a strip of land recently conquered by Haidar Ali. Their passage was blocked by Haidar's troops, who forced them to retreat.

Both the negotiations of Hollond and the attempt at passing company troops over Haidar's territory had been effected without consulting Hastings and the Bengal council. Having been informed of the matter by Hollond himself, Hastings put an immediate stop to Hollond's negotiations until he received new instructions from Bengal. Rumbold reacted by recalling Hollond from the nizam's court and by writing to Hastings that the affair was not within the controlling power of the Bengal government. This affair did little good to the already strained relationship between Rumbold and Hastings.

Rumbold also attracted the dislike of many civil servants by personally negotiating the leases for the collection of the land revenue with the zamindars, or landholders. He in fact wished to substitute the existing system of annual leases for a system of tenancies of three years at a lower rent. Before he summoned the zamindars to Madras for settling their leases directly with him, the chiefs of the subordinate factories had conducted most of these negotiations. Negotiating leases with the zamindars was often very lucrative as they were ready to pay substantial bribes to those in a position to bestow them. Rumbold meant to introduce stability and to counter corruption in the revenue administration by his reforms. In keeping with his general interest in accruing wealth from his appointment, it is virtually certain that he, and his friends, profited personally from the measures he took.

Rumbold's cavalier policy in his relations with inland powers and his attempts at reforming the collection of the land revenue made him enemies. Thomas Palk, serving at Madras, wrote that he was blind and deaf to every consideration but that of establishing an interest at home. The notorious bon vivant William Hickey, however, arriving in Madras in July 1779, 'found the inhabitants of the settlement exceedingly gay, chiefly owing to the cheerful example given by the Governor … and his Lady. There was scarce an evening without some great entertainment'. Hickey was introduced to Rumbold, and describes him as 'a man of good address and fashionable appearance' (*Memoirs*, 2.194). With Rumbold to Madras had come his second wife, Joanna (*d.* 1823), daughter of Edmund Law, whom he had married in England on 23 May 1772. Shortly upon their arrival Joanna gave birth to their second son. To her brother she wrote that they had intended to call him Edmund, after their father, but that the nawab of Arcot had insisted on the boy being called Anwar. The boy was baptized Anwar Henry Rumbold according to the nawab's wish. Rumbold thus seems to have entertained lavishly and to have been on good terms with the nawab of Arcot.

Rumbold's governorship was also plagued with illness. In October 1778 he wrote to his brother-in-law that he had thought his 'worldly cares … near at an end' (Thomas

Rumbold to Edward Law, Madras, 25 Oct 1778, BL OIOC, Rumbold MSS). In April the following year his wife feared again for his life, and Rumbold suffered another attack only one month later. In January 1780 he announced his return to the directors on the score of his ill health and embarked for Britain on 6 April. Three months later Haidar Ali and his allies invaded the Carnatic.

Later career On arrival in England in January 1781, Rumbold faced a storm of criticism, culminating in the demand for a parliamentary inquiry. Determined to enter parliament before his case was brought on, he bought a seat at Yarmouth from Edward Rushworth and also obtained a parliamentary seat for his eldest son, William Richard. When, in April 1781, a committee of secrecy was proposed by Lord North to inquire into the cause of the war in the Carnatic, Rumbold voted in favour of the motion, affirming that the more the matter was probed, the more evident it would appear that his conduct in India had been justifiable in every part of it. By December he was complaining that though the committee was called secret, he found its proceedings publicly commented on in terms highly injurious to his character. He also regretted not yet having been allowed to utter one word in his defence. On 29 April 1782 the House of Commons agreed to the committee's resolutions condemning his conduct. The chairman of the committee, Henry Dundas, moved for a bill for inflicting pains and penalties on Rumbold, accompanied by a bill restraining him from leaving Britain and obliging him to pay a £100,000 security for himself.

The main charges were corrupt dealings with the zamindars and with the nawab of Arcot and a charge that Rumbold's undiplomatic dealings with the country powers had provoked the war in the Carnatic. Rumbold severely resented the restraining bill, deeming that such restrictions on a man's liberty and property was indeed a punishment. He repeated his objection that he had not yet been permitted to make any defence and said 'he could not call that justice, which inflicted punishment on a man who had not been heard in his defence' (HoP, *Commons, 1754–90*, 3.383). Many members of parliament, like Horace Walpole, probably thought him guilty. Walpole wrote to George Hardinge, conducting Rumbold's defence with great ability: 'It is not your fault if you have not yet made Sir Thomas white as driven snow to me ... nature has providentially given us a powerful antidote to eloquence' (Walpole, *Corr.*, 35.623). However, they had misgivings about the constitutional propriety of the proceedings, and in particular the restraining bill, which came under heavy fire for the reasons advanced by Rumbold. As early as May 1782 Charles James Fox sensed 'a real tenderness for the person accused, which if it be the real temper of the House at large must make it impossible to carry on the prosecution with effect' (HoP, *Commons, 1754–90*, 3.384). In the end the bill was allowed to lapse.

Parliamentary prosecution had failed to be successful against Clive a decade earlier, failed against Sir Thomas Rumbold in 1783, and would eventually also fail in the case of Warren Hastings's impeachment a decade later.

Many reasons can be assigned for this failure, of which the difficulty of producing evidence proved a significant factor. The principal contribution of Rumbold's prosecution, as was the case with the parliamentary proceedings against Clive and Hastings, was that the publicity they generated raised a public and political consciousness about the need for reforms in India.

Rumbold's eldest son, William Richard, died while still in his twenties, and Rumbold's baronetcy eventually devolved upon his second son, George Berriman *Rumbold, later a diplomatist and minister residentiary of Great Britain in Hamburg. George Berriman quarrelled with his father in 1785, having given offence to Rumbold's second wife. Rumbold probably never forgave his son's faux pas. In his will he left his entire estate to Joanna and the four sons and three daughters he had with her, leaving only an annuity of £300 to his eldest surviving son.

After his return from Bengal in 1770 Rumbold commissioned Thomas Leverton to build him a house in Palladian style on his estate at Woodhall Park in Hertfordshire. It was there that he died on 11 November 1791, and he was buried in the church at Watton.

WILLEM G. J. KUITERS

Sources *DNB* · K. K. Datta and others, eds., *Fort William–India House correspondence*, 5 (1962); 7 (1971) · L. S. Sutherland, *The East India Company in eighteenth century politics* (1952) · ER, 30.896–8 · P. J. Marshall, *East Indian fortunes: the British in Bengal in the eighteenth century* (1976) · V. C. P. Hodson, *List of officers of the Bengal army, 1758–1834*, 3 (1946) · Burke, *Gen. GB* · M. M. Drummond, 'Rumbold, Thomas', HoP, *Commons, 1754–90* · BL OIOC, J/1/1, fols. 219–220; B/67; 1 Feb 1743 · BL OIOC, N/2/1, fol. 271, N/1/2, fols. 85, 99, N/1/1, fols. 63, 66 · *Memoirs of William Hickey*, ed. A. Spencer, 2 (1918) · A. M. Serayuddin, *The revenue administration of the East India Company in Chittagong* (1971) · J. H. Phillips, 'Parliament and southern India, 1781–1783: the secret committee of inquiry and the prosecution of Sir Thomas Rumbold', *Parliamentary History*, 7 (1988), 81–97
Archives BL OIOC, family corresp., MS Eur. D 788 · BL OIOC, papers, MS Photo Eur. 099 · Herts. ALS, estate papers | BL, corresp. with Warren Hastings and papers, Add. MSS 29140–29193 · BL OIOC, corresp. relating to India
Likenesses W. Angus, line engraving (after T. Stothard), BM; repro. in *European Magazine* (1782)
Wealth at death insolvent: BL OIOC, D/151, auditor's references

Rumbold, William (1613–1667), courtier and royalist conspirator, was born at or near Burbage in Leicestershire, the son of Thomas Rumbold (*d.* in or after 1617) and Catherine Ripplinghame (*d.* in or after 1617). His family, a branch of the Rumbolds of Hertfordshire, had been settled in Burbage for three generations by the time of his birth. Nothing is known of his early years or education, but in 1629 he obtained a subordinate post in the great wardrobe office, in which he was still employed on the outbreak of the civil war. He was the officer sent to London to fetch the royal standard set up at Nottingham, and was in attendance on Charles I until after the battle of Naseby, when he joined his brother Henry Rumbold [see below] in Spain.

Rumbold returned to England on the execution of the king, and from 1653 or 1654 acted briefly as Charles II's financial agent and secretary to the secret royalist council or Sealed Knot, using as cover an address 'at Mr. Townsends house on Puddle Wharfe Hill neare to the Wardrobe'

(Underdown, 129). Allegedly denounced to Cromwell by Sir Richard Willis on the suppression of Penruddock's rising (March 1655) and amid rumours of a plot to assassinate the protector he was confined first in the Gatehouse and afterwards with more strictness in the Tower. Nevertheless he contrived to keep up, under the aliases Robinson and Wright, an active correspondence with Sir Edward Hyde and James Butler, twelfth earl of Ormond. He warmly supported Charles II's alliance with Philip IV of Spain concluded by the treaty of Brussels in 1656. His imprisonment lasted more than two years during which time he was an active intermediary between the Leveller, John Wildman, and royalist conspirators. On Rumbold's release in 1658 he was one of the prime movers in Sir George Booth's plot, and afterwards co-operated with John Mordaunt, Baron Mordaunt of Reigate, in the hazardous enterprise of securing the adhesion of Monck and the City of London to the royal cause. On the Restoration he was made clerk of the great wardrobe, and in December 1663 surveyor-general of the customs. He was also one of the commissioners for tracing the dispersed regalia and personal estate of the late king and his family. He married, at an unknown date, Mary (d. 1667), daughter of William Barclay, esquire of the body to Charles I.

Rumbold died at his house at Parson's Green, Fulham, on 27 May 1667. His remains were interred in All Saints', Fulham. With his wife, who survived him but a few months, he had three daughters, of whom Mary, the eldest, married James Sloane, MP for Thetford (1696–8), brother of Sir Hans Sloane, and a son, Edward, his successor in the surveyor-generalship of the customs, who married Anne, daughter of George, Viscount Grandison, and died without issue at Enfield in 1726.

Henry Rumbold (bap. 1617, d. 1690), merchant and diplomat, and younger brother of William Rumbold, was baptized at Burbage on 19 January 1617. During the civil war, and except for a visit to his brother William in London in 1653, during the interregnum, he lived in Spain, being in partnership as a wine merchant at Puerto Santa Maria with Anthony Upton, John Thurloe's brother-in-law; Sir Benjamin Bathurst afterwards succeeded him in the firm. More loyal than patriotic he communicated to the court of Madrid intelligence (obtained through Upton) of the movements of Blake's fleet (1656–7), and used the interest which he thus made to facilitate the recognition of Henry Bennet (afterwards Lord Arlington) as the accredited representative of the king of England (1658). Through Bennet's influence he obtained on the Restoration the consulate of Cadiz and Puerto Santa Maria; and while holding this post provisioned, at his own risk, Lord Sandwich's fleet and the town of Tangier during the interval between the cession of that place to the British crown and its occupation. He also furnished supplies and recruits to the garrison after the occupation. After resigning the consulate he returned to England, in 1663, and was sworn in as gentleman of the privy chamber in extraordinary (December). He also held for a time a commissionership of prizes, and the consulate of Malaga, San Lucar, and Seville, the latter post as a sinecure, for he continued to live in England.

Rumbold married twice, in both cases according to the rite of the Catholic church. His first wife, married in 1663, was Isabel de Avila (d. 1663); his second, married in the same year and shortly before his return to England, was Francisca Maria, daughter of Bryan I'Anson, merchant of Cadiz and grandee of Spain, second son of Sir Bryan I'Anson, created baronet by Charles II in 1652. He died in London in March 1690 and was buried at All Saints', Fulham, on 28 March. His younger brother Thomas acted as his deputy, and afterwards as consul at San Lucar, where he died on 19 January 1706. Rumbold had at least two children.

With his first wife he had a son, Henry (d. 1689), who served with distinction as a cavalry officer in Tangier between 1662 and 1671, when he was sent home as escort to Lady Middleton. An engagement of marriage which he formed on the voyage with a daughter of Sir Robert Paston was apparently broken off by the lady's family. He was, however, twice married, and his widow married John Cotton Plowden, younger brother of Francis Plowden, comptroller of the household to James II. A son of Rumbold's second marriage was the grandfather of Sir Thomas Rumbold. J. M. RIGG, *rev.* SEAN KELSEY

Sources H. Rumbold, 'Notes on the history of the family of Rumbold in the seventeenth century', *TRHS*, new ser., 6 (1893), 145–65 · *Calendar of the Clarendon state papers preserved in the Bodleian Library*, ed. O. Ogle and others, 5 vols. (1869–1970), vols. 4–5 · D. Underdown, *Royalist conspiracy in England, 1649–1660* (1960) · IGI · will, PRO, PROB 11/324, fols. 196v–197r
Wealth at death see will, PRO, PROB 11/324, fols. 196v–197r

Rumford. For this title name *see* Thompson, Sir Benjamin, Count Rumford in the nobility of the Holy Roman empire (1753–1814).

Rumold [St Rumold, Rombaut] (*fl.* **7th–8th cent.**), martyr, is associated with Malines, in modern Belgium, where he is said to have been martyred. Rumold's cult, centred on his grave in St Stephen's Chapel in the abbey at Malines (of which he was purported to be the founder), was already flourishing at the beginning of the ninth century. His name appears among those of the martyrs in mass books from places as far apart as Cologne, Bavaria, and St Denis, near Paris. The only remotely reliable sources for the narrative of his life, however, are a charter of the west Frankish king, Charles the Simple, of 913; the *Gesta episcoporum Cameracensium*, written by Balderic of Noyon between 1041 and 1043; and the life of St Gummar, written between 1130 and 1175. All three describe Rumold as a stranger to Malines who lived as a hermit there and was later murdered.

The first to elaborate on this story, and to attribute to Rumold the, by then, common hagiographical trait of Irish origin, was Thierry, abbot of St Trond, who, about 1100, wrote the *passio* of St Rumold, which survives in many manuscripts, and also Rumold's *miracula*. Without revealing his sources, Thierry related that Rumold had been a priest, born in Ireland, who, returning from a pilgrimage to Rome, settled in Malines. Later, he received from a Count Ado a piece of land on which to build a monastery, in gratitude for having brought Ado's son back to life. An interpolated version of this *passio* in a Utrecht manuscript, Codex Ultraiectensis, adds the names of Rumold's parents, his royal filiation, and the fact that he was a bishop. A later life, written between the mid-thirteenth and the mid-fifteenth centuries, and extant in copies of the fifteenth and sixteenth centuries, goes further, by making Rumold a bishop of Dublin and giving his death date as 24 June 775. Since this was also the feast of St John the Baptist, Rumold's day is more commonly commemorated on 1 July (as in the martyrology of Donegal), or 3 July (in the Roman breviary). At the end of the thirteenth century, an office for St Rumold was composed, inspired by the interpolated version of the *passio*, and by the *miracula*, and followed at Malines, Liège, Brussels, and Antwerp. In 1227 Rumold's relics were translated from St Stephen's Chapel to the recently built church of St Rombaut. From the fifteenth century onwards, his legend, as described in the later life, became one of the most popular sources of painting and play writing in the Netherlands.

NATHALIE STALMANS

Sources *Acta sanctorum: Julius*, 1 (Antwerp, 1719), 215–37 · C. Perier-d'Ieteren, 'Précisions iconographiques et historiques sur la série de la légende de S. Rombaut', *Handelingen van de Koninklijke Kring (…) van Mechelen*, 79 (1975), 113–32 · J. Laenen, *Saint Rombaut, ses reliques et son culte* (1919) · L. Réau, *Iconographie de l'art chrétien*, 3/3 (1959), 1166–7 · B. de Gaiffier, 'Attestations anciennes sur la culte de S. Rombaut', *Sacris Erudiri*, 26 (1983), 51–5

Rumsey, Henry Wyldbore (1809–1876), medical practitioner and writer on sanitary reform, was born on 3 July 1809 in Chesham, Buckinghamshire, the eldest of five children of Henry Nathaniel Rumsey, surgeon, and his wife, Elizabeth Frances Catherine, daughter of Sir Robert Murray. Rumsey's early education was conducted by various tutors. At the age of sixteen he began formal medical studies with John Attenburrow at Nottingham Hospital. Rumsey completed his training at St George's Hospital, London, where he was a house pupil of the eminent surgeon Caesar Hawkins. He became a member of the Royal College of Surgeons in 1831 and a fellow in 1844.

In 1831 Rumsey briefly worked as physician to Lord Dillon in Oxfordshire before returning to Chesham to take over his father's practice. There, in 1835, he married Frances Sophia Langston, who survived him. In 1838 Rumsey took up a practice in Gloucester, and also served as surgeon to the town dispensary. In 1851, partly to recover from a breakdown in his health brought on by his work as a cholera inspector, Rumsey moved to Cheltenham, where he built up a select practice.

Rumsey made his intellectual reputation, though not his fortune, through public health. His unique talent in sanitary reform was to grasp the need for rational organization at a time when old paternalist mechanisms for health care through charity and the old poor law had broken down and were being replaced by the ruthless efficiency of the new poor law, and while piecemeal public health legislation struggled to keep up with the problems posed by an industrial urban environment. His lifelong concerns were clearly expressed in his first sphere of interest, the provision of health care to the poor.

Rumsey was involved with a self-supporting dispensary—a form of friendly society through which the poor could pay for medical services by small, regular subscriptions—early in his career. His first publication, *Medical Relief for the Labouring Class on the Principle of Mutual Insurance* (1837), set out a model of best administrative practice for such institutions, which prevented patients or practitioners from abusing the system to acquire unnecessary care or inflated fees. In 1835 Rumsey became honorary secretary to the sick poor committee of the Provincial Medical and Surgical Association, one of the largest and most influential professional societies. In this post he gathered materials for a series of reports on medical relief for the poor which provided the basis for an unsuccessful bill for the better regulation of medical relief. By 1838 his expertise was such that he was called as a witness before the poor-law committee of the House of Commons. He also testified before the 1844 select committee on medical poor relief.

By the 1850s Rumsey's interest in health care provision had broadened to encompass comprehensive government control of medical services. He published widely on the subject, and his ideas were drawn together in his most famous work, his *Essays on State Medicine* (1856). Rumsey made unfavourable comparisons between the rational organization of state medicine in continental Europe, especially Germany and France, and the English lack of system which bred piecemeal and often ill thought out legislation and overlapping systems of government inspection, and gave substantial public health responsibilities to an unpopular autocratic lay poor-law board. Instead, Rumsey advocated that all medicine should be controlled through a central council of health, and operate through evenly sized districts rather than the existing patchwork of parish and civic authorities. The council would oversee the content and standards of medical education and determine the appropriate number of practitioners. It would supervise systematic medical care for the poor, funded through local taxes (a system partly modelled on the Irish dispensaries), and the application of comprehensive programmes of action against epidemics. Rumsey continued to criticize poor-law medical relief, arguing that medical care was in no way pauperizing, and should be made readily available. An address to the British Medical Association in 1867, later published as *On State Medicine in Great Britain and Ireland* (1867), succinctly reiterated his criticisms of the lack of system in public health and demanded a rational, national organization of trained state physicians to oversee the health care and the accurate registration of deaths—the inadequacies of the system and the problems of basing policy on the statistics derived from this source became one of Rumsey's favourite topics in his later years. This paper inspired the formation of a joint committee of the British Medical Association and the Social Science Association to call for a reorganization of sanitary administration. Rumsey was duly appointed to the resulting royal sanitary commission in 1868.

Rumsey's work brought him considerable recognition in his own lifetime. Obituarists ranked his skills in sanitary theory as second only to those of John Simon and William Farr. In 1863 Rumsey was nominated a member of the General Medical Council, in 1867 he received an honorary MD from Trinity College, Dublin, and in 1874 he was elected to the Royal Society. Rumsey was also an honorary member of the Metropolitan Association of Health Officers and a fellow of the Royal Medico-Chirurgical Society. Towards the end of his life Rumsey got into financial difficulties; these were eased in 1875 by a testimonial fund, chaired by William Farr, which raised over £1000 and obtained a civil-list pension of £100 per annum. By this time Rumsey was too ill to receive the grant in person. He suffered a stroke in January 1875 and died on 23 October 1876, at 1 Tatchley Villas, Prestbury, near Cheltenham.

DEBORAH BRUNTON

Sources *BMJ* (4 Nov 1876), 596; (11 Nov 1876), 638–9 • V. G. Plarr, *Plarr's Lives of the fellows of the Royal College of Surgeons of England*, rev. D'A. Power, 2 (1930), 252–4 • *The Lancet* (9 Dec 1876), 841–2 • A. Stewart and E. Jenkins, *Medical and logical aspects of sanitary reform* (1969), 20–23 • d. cert. • *CGPLA Eng. & Wales* (1877)
Wealth at death under £5000: administration, 27 Jan 1877, *CGPLA Eng. & Wales*

Rumsey, John (*fl.* 1660–1686), conspirator, is of unknown parentage, and served as a cornet in the New Model Army. After the Restoration he served with English forces in Portugal for seven years under Lord Schomberg, achieving the rank of lieutenant-colonel. According to Burnet 'he did a brave action in that service, and Schomberg writ a particular letter to the king setting it out' (*Burnet's History*, 2.357). Rumsey returned from Lisbon in 1667. Following a trip to Jersey in late February he was ordered to join the forces fighting the Dutch. When they were disbanded several months later his return to Portugal was delayed by illness. In 1669, while awaiting another military assignment, Rumsey was awarded an allowance of £200 a year to be paid out of Queen Catherine's portion for his former 'merit and behaviour' in his majesty's services (*CSP dom.*, 1668–9, 152). By April 1673 he had become the collector of customs at Bristol on the recommendation of the earl of Clarendon. In 1675 Rumsey wrote to Secretary Williamson warning the court of 'the disadvantage that the persecution' of Bristol dissenters would bring upon his majesty (*CSP dom.*, 1673–5, 517). While in Bristol, Rumsey married Anna Smyth, the widow of his friend Sir Hugh Smyth. She was the daughter of the royalist John Ashburnham.

By 1670 Rumsey had become acquainted with the first earl of Shaftesbury and was active in the latter's mining enterprises. At one point he was the chief steward of the mines with a salary of £100 and a free share of the company. In the late 1670s and early 1680s, as Shaftesbury increasingly became the vortex of opposition, Rumsey was ever by his side. Burnet described him as one of 'lord Shaftesbury's creatures' (*Burnet's History*, 2.373). The Scottish conspirator William Carstares called Rumsey and Robert Ferguson Shaftesbury's 'retainers' (*State Papers and Letters Addressed to William Carstares*, Edinburgh, 1774, 9). Amid the exclusion crisis Rumsey moved to Soho and joined the notorious Green Ribbon Club. In 1680 he helped to plan the duke of Monmouth's west country progress. He also went to Bristol with Shaftesbury and Monmouth to help Nathaniel Wade organize the whigs there.

In summer and autumn 1682 Rumsey and Ferguson served as Shaftesbury's envoys to a small circle of whig leaders, including William, Lord Russell, Lord Grey of Werk, Colonel Algernon Sidney, Arthur Capel, earl of Essex, and Lord Howard of Escrick, as well as a larger cabal of former soldiers, barristers, and artisans. According to later confessions in those months a series of discussions took place concerning the leading of a general insurrection against the government. Rumsey and Wade were to lead the rising in Bristol; Monmouth and Russell in Cheshire; John Trenchard in Taunton, and lords Howard and Grey in Essex. But in December Shaftesbury learned that the government was preparing to arrest him and he went into hiding. A month later he left England for the last time, seeking refuge in Amsterdam and taking Rumsey, Ferguson, and Captain Thomas Walcott with him.

After Shaftesbury's death in January 1683 his servants returned to London and the discussion of sedition among the whig conspirators was revived. Further, more serious consideration was now given to a plan to assassinate Charles II and his Catholic brother, the duke of York, at Rye House mill as they returned from the races at Newmarket. According to Burnet 'Rumsey, Ferguson, and West were often talking of the danger to executing this [an insurrection], and that the shorter and surer way was to kill the two brothers' (*Burnet's History*, 2.359). All their talk, however, came to nothing, when, on June 12, their plans were betrayed to Secretary Jenkins by one of their own, Josiah Keeling.

Aware that their discussions had been exposed several of the plotters including Rumsey met one last time on 17 June. Nathaniel Wade proposed that they immediately muster what men they could and lead a rising 'here or in the west to die like men than be hanged like dogs'. But Rumsey flatly declared that their situation was hopeless, 'The hearts of the people are down and our great men are good for nothing' (*State trials*, 9.409). On 23 June a proclamation offered a reward of £100 apiece for the apprehension of Rumsey, Walcott, Wade, and others. The next day Rumsey surrendered to the duke of Albemarle and was interrogated by the privy council. As an associate of Shaftesbury's he may have felt he was a marked man and so along with the barrister Robert West he began to recount the story of the Rye House plot, as it soon became known. Charles II himself examined Rumsey on 27 June.

According to Ormond, Rumsey was 'highly obligated by the King and the Duke that he has made himself a good fortune … and he seemed to me to be more concerned for the infamy of such ingratitude than for his own life, of which all men say he was upon service very little careful' (*Ormonde MSS*, new ser., 7.53–4). Rumsey also faced family pressure. The week of his arrest his wife, Anna, was extremely sick and her daughter, Elizabeth Smyth, persuaded Rumsey to confess all he knew for her mother's sake. In the subsequent treason trials Rumsey testified against Captain Walcott, Lord Russell, and Algernon Sidney, all three of whom were executed. Rumsey was also used as a witness, following Monmouth's failed rebellion, in the trials of Henry Cornish and Lord Brandon in 1685. In July 1686 Rumsey tried to bribe a yearly pension out of Thomas Grey, earl of Stamford, a former associate of Shaftesbury's, in return for which Rumsey agreed to withhold evidence of Stamford's complicity in the Rye House plot. Both were arrested, and Stamford was committed to the Tower though he was eventually pardoned.

Needless to say Rumsey's willingness to turn king's evidence earned him a poor reputation among fellow whigs. Burnet recounted how Lord Russell had told him that every time he saw Rumsey 'he felt such a secret aversion to him, that he was in no danger of trusting him much'. Burnet and others also asserted that Rumsey was 'a spy of the court's which some suspected he was all along' (*Burnet's History*, 2.357–8). Fellow conspirator Richard Rumbold declared, 'I am convinced [Rumsey] hath been the Duke of Yorks spie and trepan managed by the Duke of Beaufort ever since he was the little Lords privado' (PRO, SP 29/430/16). Apparently the court never trusted Rumsey either. He was excepted from James II's general pardon in March 1686 and sent to St Nicholas Island a month later for the remainder of his life. MELINDA ZOOK

Sources CSP dom., 1667–79; 1685 • N. Luttrell, *A brief historical relation of state affairs from September 1678 to April 1714*, 1 (1857), 266 • *Bishop Burnet's History of his own time: with the suppressed passages of the first volume*, ed. M. J. Routh, 6 vols. (1823), vol. 2, pp. 357–8 • *Report on the manuscripts of the earl of Egmont*, 2 vols. in 3, HMC, 63 (1905–9), vol. 2, pp. 41, 44–6 • *Calendar of the manuscripts of the marquess of Ormonde*, new ser., 8 vols., HMC, 36 (1902–20), vol. 7, pp. 53–4 • *Report on the manuscripts of the marquis of Downshire*, 6 vols. in 7, HMC, 75 (1924–95), vol. 1, pp. 56, 59–60 • *State trials*, vol. 9 • R. L. Greaves, *Secrets of the kingdom: British radicals from the Popish Plot to the revolution of 1688–89* (1992) • R. Ashcraft, *Revolutionary politics and Locke's two treatises of government* (1986) • K. H. D. Haley, *The first earl of Shaftesbury* (1968), 229, 714, 716–18, 720–22, 728 • M. Zook, *Radical whigs and conspiratorial politics in late Stuart England* (1999), 10, 21, 95n., 103, 104, 109, 111, 116, 141, 146n., 199
Archives PRO, SP 29 | BL, Middleton collection, Add. MS 41, fols. 809–21 • BL, Wade's confession, Harley MS 6, fol. 845

Rumsey, Walter (1583/4–1660), barrister, was born at Llanofer, near Abergavenny, the second son of John Rumsey (*fl. c.*1555–1610), a former fellow of Oriel College, Oxford, and Anne (*fl. c.*1560–1610), daughter of Thomas David of Usk, Monmouthshire. He entered Gloucester Hall (now Worcester College), Oxford, on 17 October 1600 at the age of sixteen. He subsequently entered Gray's Inn on 16 May 1603 and was called to the bar on 3 June 1608. Popularly nicknamed 'the picklock of the law', Rumsey proceeded to build a large and lucrative practice.

Through his marriage to Barbara Prichard Rumsey acquired an estate at Llanofer. He served as deputy steward of Hereford in 1623 and in September 1631 he became puisne justice of the great sessions for the counties of Brecon, Glamorgan, and Radnor at a salary of £50 per annum. He became a bencher of his inn on 16 November

1631 although he did not assume his seat until 25 April 1634. His inn chose him as Lent reader on 8 November 1633 and as dean of the chapel on 6 November 1640. In the Short Parliament of 1640 Rumsey sat as one of the knights of the shire for Monmouthshire but appears to have played a minor role in the proceedings of that brief assembly, speaking seldom and then very briefly. He was possibly chosen again to serve in the Long Parliament, but refused. Upon the outbreak of the civil war in 1642 Charles I made Rumsey a commissioner of array for Monmouth and he appears to have remained staunchly loyal to the king. On 18 December 1645 parliamentary forces captured him upon entering Hereford. Information was laid against him that he had recently fled to Hereford with fellow Welsh royalist judge David Jenkins, had been taken by clubmen, and that he had three rooms filled with goods at Gray's Inn. The Long Parliament removed him from his judicial post in 1647.

Rumsey appears to have had diverse interests outside the law including gardening, agriculture, the playing and composing of music, and medicine. He was an intimate of John Aubrey who visited his house and whom he also served as legal counsel in Brecknockshire on a suit involving a disputed entail. However, Rumsey is perhaps best remembered for his medical experiments. Troubled by phlegm, he invented the 'provang' or whalebone instrument. This device, used to clean the throat and stomach by inducing vomiting, subsequently enjoyed some popularity both in Britain and abroad. Aubrey recorded that although he himself could never make it go down his throat, he had seen Rumsey use the device on several occasions and 'for those that can 'tis a most incomparable engine' (Aubrey, 274). Rumsey also published in 1657 a brief treatise outlining both this instrument's use and his other experiments entitled *Organon salutatis: an instrument to cleanse the stomach, as also divers new experiments of the virtue of tobacco and coffee; how much they conduce to preserve humane health*. This work was reprinted in 1659 and 1664.

Rumsey resumed his judicial career at the Restoration in 1660. He was made keeper of the judicial seal for Brecknockshire, Glamorgan, and Radnorshire and was nominated as one of the intended knights of the Royal Oak. He died later that year at his Llanofer estate aged seventy-six and was buried at the parish church in the family vault. A son, Edward Rumsey, attorney, survived him.

D. A. ORR

Sources DNB • DWB, 897 • Foster, *Alum. Oxon.*, 1500–1714, 4.1289 • Wood, *Ath. Oxon.*, new edn, 3.509–10 • J. Aubrey, *Brief lives: a modern English version*, ed. R. Barber (1982), 274 • W. R. Prest, *The rise of the barristers: a social history of the English bar, 1590–1640* (1986), 200, 389 • *The Short Parliament (1640) diary of Sir Thomas Aston*, ed. J. D. Maltby, CS, 4th ser., 35 (1988), 111, 113, 119 • E. S. Cope and W. H. Coates, eds., *Proceedings of the Short Parliament of 1640*, CS, 4th ser., 19 (1977)

Runcie, Robert Alexander Kennedy, Baron Runcie (1921–2000), archbishop of Canterbury, was born on 2 October 1921 at 3 Little Crosby Road, Great Crosby, a suburb of Liverpool, the youngest of the four children of Robert Dalziel Runcie (1879–1946) and Anne, *née* Benson (d.

Robert Alexander Kennedy Runcie, Baron Runcie (1921–2000), by Snowdon, 1981

1950). His father was a Scottish electrical engineer in charge of the power plant of Tate and Lyle, and his Norfolk mother had Irish antecedents. When family duties permitted she signed on as a hairdresser on Cunard Line cruises. Neither of his parents was a churchgoer but he was baptized and confirmed. His elder brother Kenneth taught him a love of games. His sister Kathleen took him to St Faith's Anglo-Catholic Church, whose distinctive worship attracted him. This happy, energetic family was disrupted when his father went blind and had to retire, and they moved to a smaller house in 1940. By then Runcie was a tall (soon to be over 6 feet), slim, sandy-haired, athletic young man regarded as very good company.

Education and war service Unusually for a future archbishop, Runcie's education began at the council's Coronation Road primary school, followed by Merchant Taylors' School, Liverpool. The headmaster, Dr Charles Russell, a fellow of Pembroke College, Cambridge, and a friend of William Temple, took a special interest in Runcie. In 1940 Runcie obtained a Squire scholarship from Oxford and a Harrison foundation scholarship from his school and gained a place at Brasenose College, which also welcomed him as a sportsman. At school he had become captain of cricket and played in the first rugby fifteen as well as becoming a leading and popular sixth-former, already appreciated as a mimic and raconteur. His headmaster had given him the idea that it is possible both to be religious and to wrestle with the problems of suffering and evil. He continued to attend St Faith's.

During the Second World War, Brasenose was evacuated

to Christ Church, where Runcie read Greats, concentrating on the study of ancient history rather than on the linguistic requirements of Latin and Greek. Eventually, after a break of five years' war service (1941–6), he returned to Oxford and obtained a first. His lifelong ability to see two sides of a question was sharpened by his struggles to remain a believer in an atmosphere dominated by the atheistic philosopher A. J. Ayer. Later he found the thinking of the Christian philosopher Donald McKinnon and the writings of Søren Kierkegaard congenial, but confessed he was 'pretty well seduced by the arguments of the Logical Positivists'. Wittgenstein with 'his mixture of ascetic rationality combined with a sort of mysticism' he saw as 'a way in which I could hold together a fundamental scepticism with religious devotion' (Carpenter, 88). His first was a tribute to his ability to work in vacations, as his term time was much given to hospitality, its inevitable debts, and his friendships with many men and women.

'War hero for Archbishop' was how some London posters were to greet Runcie in 1980, but he remembered burying friends and looking at dead young Germans and wondering how their girlfriends and parents would take the news. Awaiting call-up at Oxford in October 1941, he was surprised when the adjutant of the university Officers' Training Corps suggested an interview with the Scots Guards in London. He was accepted and after Pirbright and Sandhurst was commissioned. The guards had a brigade in the western desert and another in Italy but their main effort was the formation of an armoured division to serve in Europe, where Runcie was in action. On 2 May 1945 he was awarded the Military Cross for his part in the attack on the strongly defended town of Winnekendonk. The citation for knocking out German tanks, which were blocking the British advance, also briefly mentions Runcie's rescue of a soldier trapped in a smouldering tank who had to be hauled out after moving the turret. As Germany collapsed he took the surrender of a U-boat, saw the horrors of Belsen, and ultimately was attached to the Italo–Yugoslav boundary commission which had the task of drawing the national boundaries between Italy, Yugoslavia, and Austria, in particular in relation to Trieste. Here in August 1946 he was demobilized and returned to Oxford.

Ordination To the surprise of many of his guards and university friends, Runcie followed Oxford with training for ordination at Westcott House, Cambridge. However, the possibility had lurked at the back of his mind since his confirmation when he was fourteen. Like many of the post-war generation in all the churches, in France as well as in Britain, he was in his own words 'carried along by the feeling that there was work to be done, because there was a world to rebuild—rebuilding church life after what had been dismantled during the war, and industrial missions and worker priests … and new religious orders, with the beginning of Taizé' (Carpenter, 115). The theological questions, later highlighted in very different ways by John Robinson, Don Cupitt, and David Jenkins, were not questions which troubled him: he never took a theological degree. The prayerful devotion of his training with the daily offices carried him through to ordination as deacon by the bishop of Newcastle on Christmas eve 1950. Three-quarters of his fellow students at Westcott House ('two idyllic years', he said in a contemporary letter to the writer of this article) had served in the war. These colleagues, friends, and pupils included Ronald Bowlby, Peter Bradshaw, Hugh Montefiore, Simon Phipps, Barry Till, Bill Vanstone, Stephen Verney, Kenneth Woollcombe, and Frank Wright, all leaders in reconstructing the post-war church. Runcie's Newcastle curacy (he said of this at the time, 'for two years I gave myself as I've never given myself to anything'; Carpenter, 117) was followed by a return to the staff of Westcott House where his gifts for friendship, teaching, enlivening, and amusing a whole community were used to the full. In 1956 he became dean of Trinity Hall and there he married, on 5 September 1957, (Angela) Rosalind (known as Lindy; b. 1931/2), daughter of J. W. Cecil Turner, a notable teacher of law and since the First World War a declared atheist. Lindy was the only member of the family to go to church, though always an outspoken critic, famously declaring when her husband became archbishop, 'Too much religion makes me go pop'. She wanted a life of her own, had studied at the Royal College of Music, gave music lessons, and became a concert performer.

In 1960 Runcie became principal of Cuddesdon, an Anglican theological college near Oxford, in hopes that he would humanize the institution and strengthen its links with the university as well as care for its village. He and Lindy slowly modified its monastic rules, which had included keeping the students' wives 2 miles away (nicknamed the Principal's Safety Belt), but opening the college to women staff and students was left to his successors. He encouraged ordinands to learn the elements of social care and to share in the work of Littlemore, a progressive hospital for treating mental illness. He gave the Teape lectures in Delhi, Calcutta, and Bangalore and visited the Holy Land. He defined his aim at Cuddesdon as training ordinands to become priests who could face the questions of the modern secular world. He argued against using such phrases as 'the Bible says' or 'the church teaches', insisting that this was no substitute for hard thinking.

St Albans From 1970 to 1980 Runcie was bishop of St Albans, where he was popular and effective. He spent time with those he met by chance in the cathedral, and parishes felt his encouragement and liveliness. Thanks to Canon Eric James, he started the St Albans' ministerial training scheme to produce a more articulate and better-informed laity and later (much against Runcie's will) a larger number of non-stipendiary clergy. Runcie recognized that his 'both-and' style of leadership, emphasizing the authority of professional competence, needed the work of Eric James and others prepared to face the conflict involved in bringing Anglican ways up to date. Runcie was notably kind to priests with relational problems.

Runcie also undertook two major tasks with serious consequences for his future. He became co-chairman of the Anglican–Orthodox joint doctrinal discussions and simultaneously chairman of the Central Religious Advisory Council for the BBC and Independent Broadcasting Authority. The first was to commit him to argue the case against the ordination of women because of the Orthodox objections, the second led him to be criticized for being easy-going in surrendering some of the time previously reserved for religious broadcasting, 'the God slot'. But his ten years at St Albans revealed him as a prominent bishop in the church, gifted, with charm and style, prepared to work hard even when bored by the details of ecclesiastical life. His 'cut-glass' accent diminished his media influence, but he was felt to encourage quiet and conservative change. He seemed to know everyone and spoke from wide experience, rescuing 'churchy' occasions often entertainingly from being enclosed in an ecclesiastical ghetto. He hoped that those he served could recognize that holiness and humour belong together. He did not support the radical sixties' reports (Paul and Tiller) designed to prepare the church for the coming crises in numbers and finance.

Canterbury On 25 March 1980 Runcie was enthroned as 101st archbishop of Canterbury, an appointment accepted after five weeks' hesitation. He was the first archbishop appointed on the recommendation of the Crown Appointments Commission, a body largely elected by the general synod, set up to give the church greater freedom in the appointment of its bishops. James Callaghan and the other political leaders had accepted this change but were allowed to have their patronage secretary present at all discussions, to the great regret of Michael Ramsey. Margaret Thatcher, now prime minister, despite many disagreements with Runcie never broke the letter of this change. Dioceses had more initiative and in Runcie's case this method of appointment assured him that he had the goodwill of the general synod, the diocese of Canterbury, and the laity of the church represented by Sir Richard O'Brien, who was the chairman of the commission for Runcie's appointment.

Summing up the achievements of his ten years at Canterbury, his *Times* obituarist wrote:

Robert Runcie was a successful and at times even brilliant leader of the Church of England and the Anglican Communion. He presided over both and held them together in the face of strong theological, geographical and political forces which would have defeated many of his predecessors. Occupying an office from which far more is expected than can usually be realised, he deployed his personal gifts of charm, patience and charity to maintain a sense of Anglican coherence and cohesiveness in England and abroad.

That he did not single-handedly reverse the long-term decline in church membership nor give to the public face of Anglicanism one clear, unambivalent image measures the extent to which the Church's problems were beyond human ingenuity to solve. His singular achievement was to teach the Church of England that these were facts of life to be lived with, not early signs that the gates of hell were about to prevail. (*The Times*, 13 July 2000)

Roman relations Runcie differed from his immediate predecessors, archbishops Michael Ramsey and Donald Coggan, by being lukewarm about efforts to unite with the Methodists and the free churches; nor did he continue the financial reforms which Archbishop Fisher had achieved at no. 1 Millbank, the headquarters of the church commissioners. Financial problems were to haunt his successor. Runcie underestimated the deeply traditional culture of Vatican and Eastern Orthodox leadership. But he developed a strong personal friendship with Cardinal Basil Hume, the archbishop of Westminster, and also with Professor Adrian Hastings, the liberal-minded Roman Catholic historian, whose *Robert Runcie* (1991) was the most acute and sympathetic of Runcie's biographies. Both courageously defended him in public when there seemed to be a concerted plot to undermine his leadership. The reception of Pope John Paul II at Canterbury Cathedral in 1982, just after the Falklands service at St Paul's, when he had quoted the pope on the evil of war, was the high point of his relations with Rome. The Vatican later distanced itself, as did the Orthodox, over the ordination of women. One of the most painful events in his primacy was in March 1982 in Liverpool when 'protestant' demonstrators with boos and hisses greeted him with placards 'Rome Rules Runcie' and accused him of being a Judas.

The Falklands service Runcie was neither a pacifist nor a jingoist, and always supported the British government's right to defend the Falkland Islands and the islanders from the Argentine invasion. But he was determined after the war, with the other church leaders, to emphasize the pope's message, delivered at Coventry, that war is evil. Runcie's sermon at St Paul's, much attacked by the right wing, urged reconciliation and shared mourning by both British and Argentinian families who had lost relatives. 'A shared anguish can be a bridge of reconciliation. Our neighbours are indeed like us.' Many felt that he deserved a bar to his Military Cross for this sermon (full text in Runcie, *Windows*; account of the service itself in A. B. Webster, *Reaching for Reality*, 2002). Margaret Thatcher, the prime minister, was critical and was restrained from taking the matter up in the House of Commons only by the personal intervention of the duke of Edinburgh.

Women and the sacrament Runcie paid less attention to the ordination of women, which was slowly being accepted in the Anglican communion around the world. But Rome and the Orthodox were officially not even discussing this question. He tried delaying tactics and in 1982 he became the first archbishop to attend the annual festival at Walsingham, which was an Anglo-Catholic rallying point. In 1981 he had spoken at an international ecumenical conference at Sheffield and with 'a snide Oxbridge note' had tried to be amusing about the religious role of women; this 'almost had him booed off the platform' (Hastings, 78). He would not attend the Westminster Abbey service celebrating the Revd Florence Li Tim Oi, the pioneer Anglican priest, or the eucharist at Canterbury Cathedral in 1986 for the ministry of women in England and in the Anglican communion. He had at first agreed to celebrate, then reneged on the advice of some of his closest colleagues. He had fine political advisers at Lambeth but had no one on the staff who was versed in feminist theology, Catholic and protestant, or with experience of sacramental life and worship led by women.

Some felt that Runcie had abdicated his authority to lead the church in the new world culture where women as well as men held positions of leadership. He preferred to distance himself and leave the decision on women's ordination to his successor. Dame Christian Howard commented, 'What matters is what is right, what is doctrine, not what is expedient' (see M. C. F. Webster, *A New Strength, a New Song*, 1994). In 1988 Runcie spoke in favour in the general synod but voted against; he declared that he agreed with the principle but was against putting it into practice. This led moderate speakers to urge that the church should not nail its colours to the fence for ever or make fudge its only diet. But in the House of Lords debate of 1993, which gave overwhelming parliamentary approval to women's priesthood, when he was no longer archbishop, Runcie supported his successor by commending women's ordination as 'a model of the priest as the Good Shepherd'. It was sad for the archbishop and for his many admirers that his reluctant hesitation lasted so long, though some thought him 'the pilot that weathered the storm' (A. Hastings, *The Tablet*, 15 July 2000, 922).

Collegiality Runcie's reluctance to commit himself was encouraged by the growth of party conflict both in British politics and in the life of the church. Highly organized groups, the Anglo-Catholics led by Bishop Graham Leonard, who later left the Church of England to become a Roman Catholic, as well as a few extreme evangelicals, made collegiality, especially in the house of bishops and in the standing committee of the general synod, impossible. Though bishops take an oath of obedience to the archbishop, Leonard ignored Runcie's request not to interfere in the difficulties of the parish of Tulsa in the USA, where Leonard had no jurisdiction. It was noticed that when Runcie was attacked in the press and Mrs Runcie made a successful settlement out of court for libel by a London paper, the archbishop received more public support from Cardinal Basil Hume and ecumenical friends than from the standing committee. This internal disloyalty increased Runcie's insecurity, especially when he contrasted it with the coherence of his army experience. He sadly reflected, 'it is part of an archbishop's task to prevent the Church trying to sting itself to death like a demented scorpion' (quoted by A. Hastings, *The Tablet*, 15 July 2000, 972). Seven days before his death, discussing his time as archbishop, he said sadly to his son James: 'I could have done a better job if only I had been allowed to'.

Pleasures and pressures For most lay people Runcie was an admirable church leader with his experience of a short-of-cash upbringing, the guards and the war, academic teaching, and family life with a wife very much her own person and two happy and questioning children. His courage and wit with well-researched speeches made Christianity intellectually and personally attractive. Easily bored himself, he became an outstanding after-dinner speaker, avoiding simplistic clichés. Like other national figures he employed speechwriters both for sermons and speeches in the House of Lords, general synod, Mansion House and for many other occasions, but he took great time and trouble to personalize what he said. At the heart of his thinking was a profound acceptance of the pattern of Christ's teaching, crucifixion, and resurrection. In his last message to fellow clergy shortly before his death, he urged them to value the other great religious approaches, especially Jewish, Muslim, and Eastern. He had a special gift for seeing both sides of questions and felt that those without a sense of humour should never be put in charge of anything.

Perhaps Runcie attempted too much. He travelled extensively, ten times to Africa and frequently to America, and western and eastern Europe. This pressurized life, and his commitment to tolerance, contributed to a low point in his episcopate. In 1987 Canon Gareth Vaughan Bennett, an Oxford don and traditionalist supporter, disappointed of a further career move and angered by what he saw as a liberal tendency in the church, published an anonymous attack in Crockford, an official church publication, on Runcie's moral character—asserting that he was a mere pragmatist, a person without principle. Bennett at first denied authorship and then when harried by the media committed suicide. It was a painful episode, front-page news in the tabloids. Dr John Habgood, the archbishop of York, gallantly and to his own cost, drew the media away from Runcie, when London Anglican church leaders, lay and clerical, were not publicly supportive. Runcie maintained a sad but dignified silence. The vicious attacks damaged both the church and Runcie.

Faith in the city This wounding campaign did not dampen Runcie's commitment to remain archbishop. He ignored those who demanded his resignation in favour of a hardline, illiberal, and authoritarian archbishop. Instead he showed great skill and energy in facing the real needs of the inner cities, as riots disclosed the suffering of the unemployed and the dangers of poor schools and neglected housing in semi-derelict estates. The prime minister and her party appeared to think that 'There is no such thing as Society' and to be abdicating responsibility. Church people and family members living in the inner cities and housing estates knew that England was in crisis.

Urged on by the urban bishops, especially David Sheppard of Liverpool and Jim Thompson of Stepney, with Canon Eric James as gadfly and Sir Richard O'Brien as determined but diplomatic chairman, Archbishop Runcie's report *Faith in the City* (1985) became a banner for those with a sense of duty to society. It was initially denounced by a government minister as 'marxist' but led to the church raising over £20 million for its urban fund. Runcie's speech in the Bank of England on 27 January 1987, at a meeting organized by St Paul's Cathedral and chaired by the governor, to involve the financial City, was passionate and powerful. The report came to be seen as a manifesto for the change in national policy which the 1997 general election finally effected. Some had realized that Runcie was the surrogate leader of the opposition. Diehards, such as Alan Clark MP, described him as a 'wimp'.

Lambeth conference The Lambeth conference of 1988 was a triumph for Runcie's leadership, which had included so many visits to overseas churches. He took great trouble to get it well prepared and organized (in contrast to the 1978 and 1998 conferences). He held together the different views over the ordination of women and prevented the Anglican communion from dividing into opposing factions. He was seen at his best as a wise, eirenic, witty, and humane leader, pleading against isolated or alienating decisions. In South Africa, by early action on the Crown Appointments Commission, he had cleared the way by bringing home an English bishop, so that Archbishop Desmond Tutu could be appointed to give inspired leadership at Cape Town. Runcie's success at the Lambeth conference was achieved despite his anxiety over Terry Waite, his Anglican communion staff officer, who had been on several Middle East rescue missions, the first in Iran and Libya with remarkable success. Waite went where no one else would go. During the last mission, undertaken against Runcie's advice, Waite became involved with Colonel North, the dubious American agent, and endured nearly five years in captivity before his release after Runcie's own retirement. In attempts to rescue Waite, negotiations and prayers never ceased and valuable Iranian contacts developed.

Assessments Christians in England of all churches felt that Runcie was an outstanding Anglican leader, relaxed about doctrinal differences, personally committed to a catholic but liberal spiritual life, no manipulator, sharing with them the challenges to faith of a secular and scientific environment, even though some hesitated about his chameleon-like quality of being all things to all people. He reflected the influence of Westcott House where he had been both a student and a staff member. Here in those immediately post-war years he had experienced a community loyal to each other where all types of Anglican believers learned, worked, and prayed together. He did not join friends in contributing to Kenneth Carey's collection entitled *The Historic Episcopate* (1954), viewing it as not sufficiently Anglo-Catholic. In later years he developed a more tolerant personality, which attracted people who were looking for religious guidance without sectarianism.

Runcie retired at the end of January 1991 as Baron Runcie of Cuddesdon in the county of Oxford and made his home in his former diocese, St Albans. He remained an engaging letter-writer with all his self-deprecating and whimsical humour, and continued his brilliant Swan Hellenic cruise lectures. He became an active president of the Classical Association, and as high steward of the University of Cambridge raised large sums for the imaginative reconstruction of the divinity faculty. He also supported the Emmaus project for the destitute.

In 1996 Runcie was much criticized over his invitation to Humphrey Carpenter to write an authorized biography, *Robert Runcie: the Reluctant Archbishop* (1996), largely based on selected tape recordings. Runcie had urged his colleagues and friends to take part on the understanding that nothing would be published for many years. He failed to see that what he described as 'burbling' (Carpenter, 385) would be so hurtful to his colleagues, friends, and their wives when it appeared so rapidly in a sensational biography. Carpenter concluded the work with Runcie's defence that there was 'much I never expected to see in print' (ibid., 385).

A week before Runcie's death from prostate cancer, he recorded an extended television interview with his son, James, where the sincerity of this sensitive, self-critical man shone through the severity of his final illness. He pointed to the complexity of the human personality and noticed how hard Jesus Christ was on clergymen. He died at his home, 26A Jennings Road, St Albans, on 11 July 2000. At his funeral in St Alban's Abbey on 22 July Bishop Graham James, formerly on his staff, preached on the text 'I have become all things to all people … for the sake of the Gospel'. He was buried in the churchyard of the abbey. The memorial service on 8 November, attended by the prince of Wales and many members of the royal family, was in Westminster Abbey with the bishop of London, Richard Chartres, preaching. Both services drew national leaders as well as believers from many faiths, who respected the archbishop who had said in his 1980 enthronement sermon: 'The way of Jesus means reverencing people whether they belong to our party or not. The strategy of Jesus means changing lives with love.' He belonged to and led a church struggling in a self-confident, scientific society and was admired for attempting so much while admitting insecurity. Runcie was alert to the spiritual hopes and fears of many outside all the churches, and fulfilled the increasingly complex task of archbishop of Canterbury with determination, wit, and faith. The archbishop was survived by his wife, Lady Runcie, his son, James, and daughter, Rebecca.   ALAN WEBSTER

Sources M. Duggan, *Runcie: the making of an archbishop* (1983) · H. Carpenter, *Robert Runcie: the reluctant archbishop* (1996) · J. Mantle, *Archbishop* (1991) · A. Hastings, *Robert Runcie* (1991) · R. Runcie, *Windows onto God* (1983) · *General synod of the Church of England* (1980–90) [printed proceedings] · *Conversations and correspondence, 1946–2000* · S. Platten, ed., *Runcie: on reflection* (2002) · D. Cohn-Sherboh, ed., *Traditional unity* (1991) · H. Clark, *The church under Thatcher* (1993) · *Faith in the city* (1985) [archbishop's report] · *The Times* (13 July 2000) · *Daily Telegraph* (13 July 2000) · *The Independent* (13 July 2000) · *The Guardian* (13 July 2000) · *The Scotsman* (13 July 2000) · *The Tablet* (15 July 2000) · private information (2004) [Anthony Howard, Barry Till] · personal knowledge (2004) · b. cert. · m. cert.
Archives LPL · NRA, priv. coll., papers
Likenesses photographs, 1970–91, Hult. Arch. · D. Poole, portrait, 1981, LPL · Snowdon, photograph, 1981, priv. coll. [*see illus.*] · photograph, 1982 · photograph, repro. in Hastings, *Robert Runcie*, following p. 112 · photograph, repro. in Runcie, *Windows onto God*, front cover · photographs, LPL

Runciman, Alexander (1736–1785), artist, was born in Edinburgh on 15 August 1736, the eldest child of James Runciman, 'freeman wright in Portsburgh' ('Register of Edinburgh Apprentices'), and Mary Smith, and was baptized in the Canongate Kirk, Edinburgh. He was the brother of John *Runciman (1744–1768/9). From 4 April 1750 to 21 October 1762 he was apprenticed to the decorative landscape painter Robert Norie and later became

partner in the Norie family firm. But Runciman was ambitious to be more than a decorative painter and sent paintings to the Free Society of Artists in London as early as 1762. He also worked for the Edinburgh Theatre as stage painter and was an early member of the Cape Club, formed around the theatre, where he was known as Sir Brimstone, a name that suggests his fiery temperament. Chambers records more mildly, however, that he was 'remarkable for [his] candour and simplicity of manners' (Chambers, *Scots.*, 4.213). He may have studied with the printmaker Richard Cooper senior, for he was an accomplished etcher and was friendly with Richard Cooper the younger. David Herd, collector of folk-songs, and James Cumming, antiquarian and fellow apprentice with Robert Norie, were also close friends. An undated, wild, and expressive drawing, *Lear on the Heath*, parallels John Runciman's painting *King Lear* (both National Gallery of Scotland, Edinburgh), which is dated 1767. Both works reflect a precociously Romantic reading of the play.

In 1766 Runciman was employed by Sir James Clerk to paint the portico of his new house at Penicuik, near Edinburgh, in grisaille. The commission to paint the saloon and staircases followed. The payment of £150 to both brothers was in advance. Sir James Clerk noted it was 'the sum promised by me to them during their stay in Italy' (Clerk). Runciman arrived in Rome in June 1767 and lodged in the via Gregoriana. The banker Robert Alexander also supported him and he had realized all his own assets, but his correspondence reflects constant financial anxiety. Some vigorous landscape drawings of Rome and its environs suggest he may have hoped to capitalize on these. His brother, John Runciman, joined him in September. Persecuted by rivals, John Runciman left Rome and at some time in the winter of 1768–9 Runciman was called to Naples where his brother was ill. James Barry volunteered to accompany him (Barry). John had died before they arrived, but the two painters formed a friendship. Runciman was also friendly with the sculptor Tobias Serghells, who made a portrait medallion of him, and with Henry Fuseli, who in a letter to Mary Moser described him as 'the best painter among us here in Rome' (27 April 1771, Smith). The death of his brother spurred Alexander to realize his own ambitions; inspired by Gavin Hamilton, he embarked on a very large painting, *Ulysses and Nausicaa* (exh. RA, 1772). He also proposed to Sir James Clerk to decorate the saloon at Penicuik with the life of Achilles (Runciman to Clerk, 16 May 1770, GD18, 4680). A number of drawings record this project. His drawing style is idiosyncratic, but original. He was among the first to use Greek vase painting as a model and two of these drawings, *Achilles and Pallas* (c.1769) and the elaborate *Marriage of Peleus and Thetis* (c.1771; both National Gallery of Scotland, Edinburgh) are in outline, the first example of this neoclassical version of the primitive style. *The Origin of Painting* (1773; priv. coll.) is the epitome of this ideal, but most characteristic of Runciman's precocious interpretation of the primitive is his dramatically expressive drawing *Ossian Singing* (c.1770; National Gallery of Scotland, Edinburgh).

Runciman returned to Scotland in October 1771. He

visited London in the spring, but in July 1772 began work at Penicuik. By mid-October he had painted both the saloon and one staircase, twenty-one full-sized paintings in oil on plaster, an astonishing season of work. Destroyed by fire in 1899, the ceiling is recorded in photographs, in a small nineteenth-century watercolour copy, and in a number of his own etchings of individual compositions. His final choice of subject was MacPherson's *Ossian* and the room became famous as Ossian's Hall. MacPherson's champion, Hugh Blair, characterized the poetry as 'abounding with vehemence and fire' (Blair, 1.4). Runciman's painting matched this. Vigorously painted, rich in colour, and highly unorthodox in drawing and composition, in its stress on spontaneity and primitive, imaginative vigour at the expense of 'correctness', it had an important place in the early history of modern art. He also painted four scenes from the life of St Margaret in one staircase. The other staircase was completed later by John Bonnar.

On 25 November 1772 Runciman was appointed master of the Trustees' Academy, Edinburgh, and held the post until his death. Among his pupils were Alexander Nasmyth and George Walker. According to William Robertson (Dunlop, l.395) both he and Henry Raeburn also studied informally with Runciman. In 1773 Runciman painted the *Ascension* and four subsidiary pictures in the new Episcopalian Chapel in Edinburgh on the same scale as his work at Penicuik. He also provided decorations for the Theatre Royal and the Royal Infirmary and continued to exhibit ambitious pictures in London with subjects from Milton, Shakespeare, and ancient and modern history. During his lifetime he enjoyed a great reputation as a landscape painter. Some of his fine landscape drawings survive (National Gallery of Scotland, Edinburgh); his most important landscape painting is the *Allegro* (1773; priv. coll.), an interpretation of Milton's poem which closely parallels his friend Robert Fergusson's contemporary poem 'Hame Content'. He painted a strange, visionary portrait of Fergusson (n.d.; Scot. NPG) and his own self-portrait with John Brown painted for the earl of Buchan (1784; Scot. NPG) is equally unorthodox. The two are arguing in front of his easel and the heat of their exchange is conveyed, not only by expression and gesture, but by the way it is painted. Runciman was also history painter to the Society of Antiquaries of Scotland founded by Buchan. He lived in Chapel Street, Edinburgh, in a modest second-floor flat (now 19 West Nicholson Street) with his partner. He collapsed and died on the corner of the street on 21 November 1785, and was buried in the Canongate Kirk.

DUNCAN MACMILLAN

Sources J. D. Macmillan, 'The earlier career of Alexander Runciman and the influences that shaped his style', PhD diss., U. Edin., 1973 · D. Macmillan, *Painting in Scotland: the golden age* (1986) [exhibition catalogue, U. Edin., Talbot Rice Gallery, and Tate Gallery, London, 1986] · D. Macmillan, 'Alexander Runciman in Rome', *Burlington Magazine*, 112 (1970), 23–30 · Graves, *Soc. Artists* · D. Wilson, *Memorials of Edinburgh in olden times*, 2nd edn, 2 vols. (1891), vol. 2, p. 174 · C. B. B. Wood, ed., *Register of Edinburgh apprentices, 1701–1755*, Scottish RS, 61 (1929), 75 · Chambers, *Scots.* (1855) · Roll of the knights companions of the most sovereign and social order of the Cape and Sederunt book of the knights companion of the Cape, NL Scot., MSS 2003, 2004 · Penicuik accounts, Register House, MS GD18 · [W. Ross], *Description of the paintings in the Hall of Ossian at Pennycuik near Edinburgh* (1773) · J. M. Gray, *Notes on art treasures at Penicuik house Midlothian* (privately printed, Edinburgh, 1889) [repr. from *The Scottish Leader*] · J. Clerk, 'Journal of expenses of my new house', Register House, Penicuik MSS, MS GD18, 1758a · letters of Alexander Runciman to James Cumming and to Robert Alexander, U. Edin. L., Laing MS, La.iv.26 · letters of Alexander Runciman to Sir James Clerk, Register House, Penicuik MSS, GD18, 4680 and 4682 · J. Barry, *Works*, ed. E. Fryer, 3 vols. (1806), vol. 1, p. 114 · J. T. Smith, *Nollekens and his times*, 1 (1828), 68 · H. Blair, 'On the poems of Ossian', *The poems of Ossian*, 2 vols. (1775) · W. Dunlop, *History of the rise and progress of arts and design in the USA*, 2 vols. (1834), vo. 1, p. 395 · J. Ingamells, ed., *A dictionary of British and Irish travellers in Italy, 1701–1800* (1997)

Archives General Register Office for Scotland, Edinburgh, MSS · NL Scot., MSS · U. Edin. L., MSS

Likenesses J. Baxter?, portrait, c.1770, NG Scot. · A. Runciman, self-portrait, oils, 1784 (with J. Brown), Scot. NPG · J. Brown, pencil drawing, 1785, Scot. NPG · J. Stewart, stipple, pubd 1802, BM · J. Brown, pencil drawing, NG Scot. · J. Runciman, pencil drawing, NG Scot. · pencil and chalk drawing, Scot. NPG

Runciman [*née* Stevenson], **Hilda**, Viscountess Runciman (1869–1956), politician, was born at 64 Wellington Terrace, Westoe, co. Durham, on 28 September 1869, the fifth daughter of James Cochran *Stevenson (1825–1905), a chemicals manufacturer and member of parliament for South Shields, and his wife, Elisa Ramsay Anderson. Her aunts, Flora Clift Stevenson and Louisa Stevenson, were active in the women's movement in Scotland. She was educated at Notting Hill high school and at Girton College, Cambridge, where she held a scholarship awarded for achieving first place in the senior Cambridge local examination. After obtaining first-class honours in the history tripos (1890), she became an assistant mistress at St Leonards School, St Andrews. On 23 August 1898 Hilda married Walter *Runciman (1870–1949), later Viscount Runciman, with whom she had five children: (Walter) Leslie *Runciman (1900–1989), the politician, Margaret (*b.* 1901), James Cochran Stevenson (Steven) *Runciman (1903–2000), the historian, Ruth (*b.* 1907), and Katharine (*b.* 1909).

The combination of a politically active family, a nonconformist upbringing, and a university education led Hilda Runciman into public affairs in her twenties. In 1897 she became the first woman to be elected to the Newcastle school board, and was a co-opted member of the Northumberland county education committee from 1903 onwards. A forceful and confident speaker and an experienced canvasser, she took a particular interest in education, social work, and housing. But until the First World War her efforts were chiefly devoted to her children and to supporting her husband's political career.

During the 1920s, however, Hilda Runciman adopted a more public role. She served as a JP in both London and Northumberland and was president of the Women's National Liberal Federation in 1919–21, sitting on its executive for many years; she was also president of the

Hilda Runciman, Viscountess Runciman (1869–1956), by Bassano, 1927

Women's Free Church Council, a member of the executive of the League of Nations Union, chair of the Westminster Housing Association, and a founder of the Westminster Housing Trust. In Liberal Party politics she took a strong Asquithian line, and under her presidency the Women's National Liberal Federation advocated the maintenance of independent Liberalism and an end to the Lloyd George coalition. However, in spite of her appetite for politics she refused invitations to stand for parliament. 'Politics as a profession will never appeal to any great extent to women', she insisted (*South Wales News*, 27 March 1928). Indeed, she professed not to know what women's questions were. On the other hand, her anti-feminism may well have stood her in good stead when she eventually contested a rural constituency in 1928.

The occasion arose because Walter, who currently represented Swansea, had been adopted as a candidate by the Liberals of St Ives in Cornwall. With this in mind the Runcimans spent the summer of 1927 sailing round the Cornish coast in their yacht, which enabled them to visit many places in the new constituency. However, the retirement of the sitting member (John Anthony Hawke) caused an unexpected by-election in St Ives, which Walter wished to avoid for fear of forcing another contest on the Liberals in Swansea. As a result Hilda was nominated as a stop-gap candidate until the general election. She turned the situation to advantage by emphasizing her role as a loyal wife; her husband, five children, and father-in-law all campaigned for her. The constituency was flattered by the promise that it would effectively enjoy two members in parliament if Hilda were elected. 'It is right and proper that women should agree with their husbands on all questions', she once remarked, 'but if you have Conservative husbands, I implore you to think for yourselves' (*Express and Echo*, 24 May 1929). At this time the Liberal Party was enjoying a revival engineered partly by Lloyd George and his bold programme of interventionism for reducing unemployment. Hilda, however, ignored this and stood as a traditional free-trade Liberal. Indeed, she followed her husband in expressly repudiating Lloyd George, who was not even invited to speak in the by-election. Despite this schismatic approach and the intervention of a Labour candidate, she gained the seat from the Conservatives (March 1928).

In her brief spell in the Commons, Hilda Runciman concentrated on issues, such as fishing, tin mining, and china clay, which were of concern in Cornwall, as well as housing and unemployment. She attracted praise for her 'clear dulcet tones ... perfect enunciation ... and soft and musical voice' (*Yorkshire Post*, 11 Aug 1930). At the general election in May 1929 she withdrew from St Ives in favour of Walter; but, her appetite now whetted and her reputation enhanced, she contested Tavistock, in Devon, which she only narrowly failed to gain from the Conservatives. This, however, was Hilda's last election. Had she wished she could clearly have enjoyed a longer parliamentary career and a higher political profile. The rest of her life was divided between the family home at Doxford, in Northumberland, and a London residence, 73 Portland Place, where she died of heart failure on 28 October 1956.

MARTIN PUGH

Sources U. Newcastle, Robinson L., Walter Runciman MSS • M. Pugh, *Women and the women's movement in Britain, 1914–1959* (1992) • *The Times* (9 Nov 1956) • *The Times* (16 Nov 1956) • *The Times* (24 Nov 1956) • *Women's Liberal Magazine* (1919–25) • *Women's Liberal News* (1925–35) • b. cert. • m. cert. • d. cert. • K. T. Butler and H. I. McMorran, eds., *Girton College register, 1869–1946* (1948)
Archives U. Newcastle, Robinson L., diaries, corresp., and papers | U. Newcastle, Robinson L., Walter Runciman MSS | FILM BFI NFTVA, news footage
Likenesses Bassano, photograph, 1927, NPG [*see illus.*]
Wealth at death £54,284 5s. 7d.: probate, 20 Nov 1956, *CGPLA Eng. & Wales*

Runciman, James (1852–1891), schoolteacher and journalist, was born at Cresswell, a village near Morpeth in Northumberland, on 1 August 1852. He was the youngest of the five sons and two daughters of Walter Runciman, a coastguard and formerly a sea captain, and his wife, Jane, daughter of John Finlay; Walter *Runciman, later first Baron Runciman, was his elder brother. He attended the village school at Ellington before spending two years (1863–5) in the naval school at Greenwich, London, becoming afterwards a pupil teacher at North Shields ragged school. He then spent two years at the British and Foreign School Society's Training College for Teachers in Borough Road, London, where he excelled in every subject. His first teaching post was at Hale Street, Deptford, a particularly rough area where parents were hostile to the board school. He was subsequently promoted to other schools run by the London school board, at South Street, Greenwich, and at Blackheath Hill. He proved a successful teacher, encouraging individuality and helping able boys to prepare for scholarships.

At night Runciman continued his own studies and attempted journalism. He soon wrote regularly for *The Teacher*, *The Schoolmaster*, and *Vanity Fair*; of the last paper he became sub-editor in 1874. In January 1874 he matriculated at the University of London, and passed the first bachelor of science examination in 1876. About 1880, while continuing teaching, he was sub-editor of *London*, a clever but short-lived little newspaper, edited by W. E. Henley. Although noted in early manhood as a vigorous figure, with a ruddy countenance and a mass of fair hair, Runciman's health gave way under the strain of combining two occupations. He gave up teaching to concentrate on journalism. As a writer on social or ethical topics (including temperance, a cause which his Wesleyan Methodist family promoted), he was vigorous and versatile. His *Schools and Scholars* (1887) was the most influential of his sometimes pungent and bitter writings on the working conditions of elementary schoolteachers in the period of 'payment by results', when their livelihoods were at the mercy of school inspectors and their caprices. His best literary work described the life of the fishermen of the North Sea, with whom he spent many of his vacations. An admirable series of seafaring sketches, which he contributed to the *St James's Gazette*, was reprinted in 1883 as *The Romance of the Coast*. Of his *Dream of the North Sea* (1889), a vivid account of the fishermen's perils, the queen accepted the dedication. Runciman died prematurely, of consumption, at his home, Tyneside, Minerva Road, Kingston upon Thames, Surrey, on 6 July 1891. An appeal was mounted to secure a pension for his widow and children, who were left in straitened circumstances.

G. C. BOASE, rev. M. C. CURTHOYS

Sources J. F. Runciman, ed., *Side-lights of James Runciman* (1893) · *The Schoolmaster* (11 July 1891), 44–5 · *ILN* (18 July 1891), 71 · *Pall Mall Gazette* (9 July 1891), 6 · A. Tropp, *The school teachers* (1957) · *Wellesley index* · b. cert. · Boase, *Mod. Eng. biog.*
Likenesses portrait, repro. in *ILN*, 67

Runciman, Sir James Cochran Stevenson [Steven] (1903–2000), historian, was born on 7 July 1903 in Northumberland, the second son and third of the five children of Walter *Runciman (1870–1949), politician, and later first Viscount Runciman of Doxford, and his wife, Hilda *Runciman, *née* Stevenson (1869–1956), politician. His parents were the first married couple to sit together (as Liberals) in the Commons, and his mother's family contained a number of progressive and intelligent women. His paternal grandfather founded a shipping line and his maternal grandfather owned a chemical works in Jarrow. He was educated first at home, then successively at Summer Fields, Eton College (where he was a King's Scholar), and Trinity College, Cambridge, where he held a scholarship (1921) and gained a first in history in 1924. His historical interests were accompanied by an early gift for languages, and cemented by a memorable first visit to Istanbul in 1924 in his grandfather's yacht, in which he had

earlier also travelled to Scandinavia. He became a fellow of Trinity in 1927, after more travel, this time to China via the Suez Canal, but resigned his fellowship in 1938 on coming into an inheritance from his grandfather; he was made an honorary fellow in 1965. His knowledge of Bulgarian had persuaded the Cambridge Byzantine historian J. B. Bury to accept him as a pupil, and in 1940 it led to his being recommended by Guy Burgess, his own first pupil in Cambridge, for the post of press attaché at the British legation in Sofia, which entailed travelling there via Cape Town and Cairo. When the Germans entered Bulgaria in 1941, he left with the rest of the legation and travelled (not without incident) to Istanbul and thence to the British embassy in Cairo, where he was charged with setting up news broadcasts in Balkan languages. From there he was moved to Jerusalem, but spent 1942–5 as professor of Byzantine art and history in the University of Istanbul, his only professorial appointment, and one which allowed him to build up a firsthand knowledge of the remains of Byzantine civilization. This was followed by a period (1945–7) as representative of the British Council in Greece during the difficult post-war period. The rest of his life was spent as a private scholar, travelling and writing, at first mostly at his house on the island of Eigg, and from 1966 onwards at the border tower that became his home at Elshieshields. As well as books and academic articles, he gave many lectures at home and abroad, including many series: the Waynflete (1953–4), the Gifford (1960–62), the Birkbeck (1966), the Wiles (1968), the Robb, at Auckland (1970), the Regents', at Los Angeles (1971), and the Weir, at Cincinnati (1973). He was invited to be Alexander White professor at Chicago in 1963. He also played a wider role, serving on the councils or boards of many bodies. These included the national trusts for Scotland and Greece, the Scottish National Museum of Antiquities, the Scottish Ballet, the British Institute of Archaeology at Ankara, the Royal Historical Society, the British Museum, the Victoria and Albert Museum, the Anglo-Hellenic League (which established a prize in his honour), and the London Library. While his wit could be sharp on occasion, he was a kind friend and loyal supporter of younger Byzantinists, and generously gave his time to help them establish the subject more firmly in British universities. He was president of the Society for the Promotion of Byzantine Studies from its foundation in 1983, and chaired every annual general meeting. Similarly, always staying at the Athenaeum, he attended every one of the Runciman lectures named after him at King's College, London. He was made honorary president of the International Committee for Byzantine Studies in 1976. At the end of his life his connection with the monasteries on Mount Athos gave him particular satisfaction. This connection was reinforced by his presidency since their inception in 1992 of the Friends of Mount Athos. He used the Onassis Foundation award for culture, which he received in 1997, to help to restore the Protaton at Karyes, visiting the Holy Mountain by helicopter in July 2000, only months before his death, for the inauguration of the new museum that had been created inside the tower. He memorably describes his first visit to

Athos in 1937 (after two earlier but unsuccessful attempts) in his book *A Traveller's Alphabet: Partial Memoirs* (1991). In view of his passionate interest in Byzantium and deep sympathy with the later Orthodox world, many expected him to convert to Orthodoxy. But while this affection and respect for Orthodoxy continued throughout his life, he remained a member of the Church of Scotland in which he had been brought up. Runciman received many honours. He was elected a fellow of the British Academy in 1957 and of the Society of Antiquaries in 1964; he was knighted in 1958 and made a Companion of Honour in 1984 and a CLit in 1987. Among his foreign honours were the Greek order of the Phoenix (1961) and the Bulgarian order of the Madara Horseman (1993). The more exotic included becoming an honorary whirling dervish and being named grand orator of the great church. He received honorary degrees from thirteen universities, British, American, and Greek.

Steven Runciman's first two books, *The Emperor Romanos Lecapenus* (1929) and *The First Bulgarian Empire* (1930), emerged from his fellowship dissertation at Trinity, Cambridge, and from his work with J. B. Bury. They were quickly followed in 1933 by *Byzantine Civilization*, the first of the many books by him which brought Byzantium to a wider reading public. His activities during the war years brought a pause, but *The Medieval Manichee* was published in 1947 and was followed by *The Eastern Schism* (1955) and *The Great Church in Captivity* (1968), the latter a pioneering study of the state of the Greek Orthodox church under Ottoman rule. He thus came into his own as a historian of religion, to which he brought the personal and humane vision that is characteristic of all his writing. This was continued in his three-volume *History of the Crusades* (1951–4), a major achievement of narrative history infused by passion and at times romanticism, as a result of which he has been compared to Macaulay. Inherent in the work is regret at the deplorable failure of the crusading West to understand Byzantium and the East. Runciman's style of writing, and perhaps also his detachment from the narrow confines of academic life, gave him access to a wide cultivated readership, much of which had hitherto been quite unfamiliar with Byzantium. Though he did not write again on the scale of *The History of the Crusades*, he went on to produce several more smaller studies, each of them highly personal, and each beautifully written: *The Sicilian Vespers* (1958), *The Fall of Constantinople, 1453* (1965), *The Last Byzantine Renaissance* (1970), *Byzantine Style and Civilisation* (1975), *The Byzantine Theocracy* (1977), and *Mistra* (1980). *Paradise Regained*, privately printed in 1992, is a moral fable set in Kurdistan which he had written in 1935. It is dedicated to Dadie Rylands, a colourful member of his set at Eton and Cambridge.

Runciman's taste for travel had begun with childhood journeys to France and Germany. He was also a man of immense curiosity. *The White Rajahs* (1960) grew out of a request from the Colonial Office to write a history of Sarawak. In a revealing comment, he wrote that he had never wanted to be commissioned to write a book, but that on this occasion the idea of some extended travel appealed to him after his mother's recent death, and typically he took it on. Other journeys led, for example, to an interest and affection for Bahrain which continued to the end of his life. Since he was also extremely well-connected, he had many fascinating and often unique experiences, which he enjoyed to the full and loved to recount. As is clear from the descriptions in *A Traveller's Alphabet*, the closest he came to writing autobiography, this extraordinarily wide experience in turn fed into and influenced his historical writing.

As well as making so significant a contribution to the history of Byzantium, and to civilized letters, Steven Runciman was an immensely kind and attentive friend. He never married, but he continued to keep up his correspondence with a number of friends to the last and his talk was always fascinating (and at times acerbic). He died after a fall on 1 November 2000 at the home of his great-nephew in Radway, Warwickshire, and was buried at Lochmaben near Lockerbie. A memorial meeting was held at the Gennadius Library in Athens on 12 December 2000 and another at Mistra in May 2001, and a memorial service at St Columba's (Church of Scotland), in Pont Street, London, on 25 January 2001.   AVERIL CAMERON

Sources S. Runciman, *A traveller's alphabet* (1991) · *The Times* (2 Nov 2000) · *Daily Telegraph* (2 Nov 2000) · *The Independent* (2 Nov 2000) · *The Guardian* (3 Nov 2000) · *The Scotsman* (3 Nov 2000) · Lord Jellicoe, 'Sir Steven Runciman', *Anglo-Hellenic Review*, 23 (2001), 3 · A. Bryer, 'Sir Steven Runciman: the spider, the owl and the historian', *History Today*, 51/5 (May 2001), 4–6 · A. Bryer, 'Sir Steven Runciman', *Bulletin of British Byzantine Studies*, 27 (2001), 82–4 · *Friends of Mount Athos Annual Report* (2000) · Burke, *Peerage* · WWW · personal knowledge (2004) · private information (2004)
Archives Hants. RO, Wickham MSS · King's Cam., Rylands MSS
Likenesses S. Conroy, oils, 1990, Scot. NPG; repro. in *The Times* · M. Macleod, photograph, *c.*1990, repro. in *The Guardian* · photograph, repro. in *The Scotsman*
Wealth at death £7,214,844.84: confirmation, 22 June 2001, *CCI*

Runciman, John (1744–1768/9), painter, was born in Edinburgh, the son of James Runciman, 'freeman wright in Portsburgh', and Mary Smith. He was the younger brother of Alexander *Runciman (1736–1785), by whom he was presumably trained as nothing else is known of his education. An etching by John, *Taking Down of the Netherbow Port*, of the demolition of a historic building in 1764, certainly shows a precocious talent. It also reflects the brothers' links with antiquarians such as George Paton, who contributed this image to Richard Gough's *British Topography* (1780, 2.678), and James Cumming, and suggests that, like Alexander, John had learned to etch with the printmaker Richard Cooper senior. Even more remarkable is a group of small panel paintings that John Runciman evidently painted before he left Edinburgh in 1767. These all have biblical subjects, such as the *Flight into Egypt* (NG Scot.) and the *Adoration of the Shepherds* (priv. coll.), unfashionable at the time. It was equally unfashionable to turn for inspiration to artists such as Teniers, Rubens, Rembrandt, and even Dürer, as Runciman did in these pictures. The latter interest, however, he shared with his contemporary, the miniature painter John Donaldson, who was closely associated with Cooper. Runciman's paintings suggest he was searching for an expressive style. His few surviving drawings from these years, now in the National Gallery of Scotland, Edinburgh, are as intense in feeling and as unfashionable in style as these paintings. The only painting by him that is dated, however, is *King Lear* from 1767 (NG Scot.). It shows Lear with Kent, Edgar, and the Fool beside a stormy sea and so does not illustrate a scene in the play, but appears to be an epitome of it. If so, it reflects a precociously Romantic reading, presenting its subject as Lear's rediscovery of nature in himself.

In 1767 Sir James Clerk commissioned Alexander and John Runciman to paint the saloon and staircases of his new house at Penicuik, near Edinburgh, in return for an advance payment of £150 to help fund their visit to Italy (Clerk, 'Journal', GD18, 1758a). Robert Alexander, an Edinburgh banker, also assisted with the finance for their journey (letters of Walter Ross concerning the Runcimans, transcribed by David Laing, Edinburgh University Library, La.IV.25). John followed his brother, staying in London until at least 18 October, when he drew money on a draft from Walter Ross (Walter Runciman's account with Walter Ross), and arriving in Rome some time before 5 December (A. Runciman to J. Cumming, 5 Dec 1767). The brothers lodged together in the via Gregoriana (Archive of the Diocese of Rome, San Giovanni in Laterano, Stato degli Animi, Santa Maria del Popolo, Easter 1768). John left Rome for Naples in late 1768 or early 1769 and his brother indicated that the reason for his departure was a spiteful campaign by the painter James Nevay (A. Runciman to J. Cumming, September 1769). Nevay's motives are unclear, but Alexander clearly held him responsible for John's death. When Alexander was told of his brother's illness, James Barry volunteered to accompany him to Naples, though when they arrived he was already dead (A. Runciman to R. Alexander, 20 July 1769; J. Barry to E. Burke, n.d., Barry, 1.114).

Before he left Rome John Runciman 'destroyed his best things' (A. Runciman to R. Alexander, 20 July 1769), but what little survives makes it plain that Nevay had reason to be jealous. The only painting clearly done in Rome is his self-portrait (Scot. NPG), but it is a remarkable picture. John's face is half-hidden beneath the shadow of his hat. He appears to be pondering Michelangelo's figure *Day* visible behind him. Internalized and Romantic in spite of its early date, it anticipates Fuseli's famous portrait of John Cartwright leaning on a book (formerly believed to be a self-portrait), and it is likely that Fuseli, as a close friend of Alexander, knew it. A small etching of an unknown subject, and one or two drawings, show that he was indeed turning to Michelangelo as a source of inspiration for a new emotional and expressive kind of art in a way that was followed by Fuseli and by others, including his own brother Alexander, who was deeply affected by his death which occurred in Naples, probably early in 1769. John was consumptive (J. Barry to E. Burke, n.d., Barry, 1.114) but his death appears to have been precipitated by a cold (A. Runciman to J. Clerk, 12 Jan 1771).

DUNCAN MACMILLAN

Sources J. D. Macmillan, 'The earlier career of Alexander Runciman and the influences that shaped his style', PhD diss., U. Edin., 1973 · J. Ingamells, ed., *A dictionary of British and Irish travellers in Italy, 1701–1800* (1997) · [J. Barry], *Works*, ed. E. Fryer, 3 vols. (1806) · J. Clerk, 'Journal of expenses of my new house', General Register Office for Scotland, Edinburgh, Penicuik MSS, GD18, 1758a · Alexander Runciman's account with Walter Ross, U. Edin. L., Laing MSS · A. Runciman, letter to James Cumming, 5 Dec 1767, U. Edin. L., Laing MSS · A. Runciman, letter to James Cumming, Sept 1769, U. Edin. L., MS La.IV.26 · A. Runciman, letter to Robert Alexander, 20 July 1769, U. Edin. L., MS La.IV.26 · A. Runciman, letter to Sir James Clerk, 12 Jan 1771, NA Scot., Penicuik MSS, GD18, 4682
Archives Archive of the Diocese of Rome, S. Giovanni in Laterano, letters of Alexander Runciman · General Register Office for Scotland, Edinburgh, Penicuik MSS, Sir James Clerk, 'Journal of expenses of my new house'
Likenesses J. Runciman, self-portrait, oils, 1767, Scot. NPG

Runciman, (Walter) Leslie, second Viscount Runciman of Doxford (1900–1989), shipowner, was born in Newcastle upon Tyne on 26 August 1900, the eldest of five children and elder son of Walter *Runciman, first Viscount Runciman of Doxford (1870–1949), shipowner, Liberal MP, and president of the Board of Trade, and his wife, Hilda *Runciman (1869–1956), later an MP, daughter of James Cochran *Stevenson, chemical manufacturer and MP for South Shields. The younger son, James Cochran Stevenson (Steven) *Runciman, became a well-known scholar of the Byzantine period. Leslie Runciman grew up at Doxford and was educated at Eton College, where he was a King's scholar, and at Trinity College, Cambridge, also as a scholar. He once remarked, however, that he learned good manners from a gamekeeper. At Cambridge he took part one in classics in 1920 and achieved a second class (division two) in part two of the economics tripos in 1922.

After a year with the Blue Funnel Line in Liverpool Runciman went into the family firm of Walter Runciman & Co., shipowners. Here he learned the basics of shipping affairs from his formidable grandfather, Sir Walter *Runciman (later first Baron Runciman), who had begun life as a boy in small merchant sailing vessels. In due course Leslie Runciman became chairman of the company and six other shipping and banking concerns. He was for fifty years a member of the chamber of shipping and a very successful president in 1952. He was also for many years a UK delegate to the international chamber of shipping. He was president of the Royal Institution of Naval Architects in 1951–61 and chairman of the trustees of the National Maritime Museum from 1962 to 1972, a role for which his interests fitted him exactly, and of the government advisory committee on historic wreck sites from 1973 to 1986. He was an honorary elder brother of Trinity House. Like his grandfather, he was also a very practical seaman, cruising far and wide, first in the family's three-masted schooner *Sunbeam* and later in his motor ketch *Bondicar*. He succeeded Prince Philip, duke of Edinburgh, as commodore of the Royal Yacht Squadron in 1968–74. He was also a keen shot and an enthusiastic skier.

As a young man in the 1920s Runciman became interested in aviation. He qualified as a pilot, had some success in the king's cup air races of the period, and founded his own aviation company. He raised and commanded the Durham squadron of the Auxiliary Air Force and in 1937 was awarded the Air Force Cross. He joined the boards of both Imperial Airways and British Airways in 1938 and played a prominent part in their amalgamation into the British Overseas Airways Corporation. In 1939 he became its first director-general, but he resigned in 1943 in protest at the government's somewhat negative attitude to civil aviation. From 1943 to 1946 he was air attaché at the British embassy in Tehran, with the rank of air commodore, and he was a member (later vice-chairman) of the Air Transport Advisory Council from 1946 to 1954. His family shipping interests supplanted those of aviation when his father died in 1949 and he succeeded as second viscount and third baronet. He became increasingly involved in the affairs of the Moor Line, Walter Runciman & Co., Runciman (London) Ltd, the Doxford Co. Ltd, and the Anchor Line.

Runciman's other interests included forty years of service on the board of Lloyds Bank, of which he was a deputy chairman from 1962 to 1971. He was among other things chairman of the committee on horticultural marketing (which determined the future location of Covent Garden market) in 1955–6, prime warden of the Goldsmiths' Company, and chairman of the British Hallmarking Council from 1974 to 1982.

Runciman was a tall and very handsome man with great personal charm. He carried natural authority which, however, he never used to overawe or dominate his colleagues and subordinates, and which, surprisingly, masked a certain diffidence. He was a natural chairman and finder of the middle way who gained the immediate respect of those with whom he worked. He was a doer, who became deeply involved in all his commitments. He was also an intellectual, an omnivorous reader, and chairman of the Horatian Society in 1970–88, whose conversation was constantly illuminated with quotation. He greatly enjoyed opera at Glyndebourne. Unfailingly courteous to all with whom he came into contact, he was very attractive to women. His attitude to them was that of his generation and background and he did not see them as members of the board. To work closely with him engendered not only respect, but also affection—and occasional mild exasperation with his insistence on the detached view. He was appointed OBE in 1946 and deputy lieutenant of Northumberland in 1961, and was awarded an honorary DCL by Durham University in 1937.

In 1923 Runciman married Rosamond Nina *Lehmann, novelist, daughter of Rudolph Chambers *Lehmann, journalist and MP. The marriage was dissolved in 1928 and in 1932 he married Katherine Schuyler, younger daughter of William R. Garrison, of New York, and Constance Clementine Schuyler, née Coudert. They had one son. Runciman died, following serious injury in an accident three years before, from which he never fully recovered, in King Edward VII Hospital in London on 1 September 1989. His body was cremated at Golders Green crematorium. He

was succeeded in the viscountcy by his son, Walter Garrison Runciman (b. 1934), the sociologist. A memorial service was held in St Clement Danes, London, on 29 November 1989.   BASIL GREENHILL, rev.

Sources *The Times* (2 Sept 1989) · *The Times* (30 Nov 1989) · *The Independent* (21 Sept 1989) · Burke, *Peerage* · private information (1996) · personal knowledge (1996) · *CGPLA Eng. & Wales* (1990)
Wealth at death £1,792,084: probate, 2 Feb 1990, *CGPLA Eng. & Wales*

Runciman, Margaret. *See* Fairweather, Margaret (1901–1944).

Runciman, Walter, first Baron Runciman (1847–1937), shipowner, was born at Dunbar, East Lothian, on 6 July 1847, the fourth son of Walter Runciman, master of a schooner and later in the coastguard service, and his wife, Jane, eldest daughter of John Finlay, shipowner, of Dunbar. He was elder brother of James *Runciman. The family moved to the coastguard station at Cresswell, Northumberland, to which the father had been appointed, and where Runciman's brother was born in 1852. In 1859, after attending a church school, young Walter ran away from home to seek a career at sea.

Runciman was bound apprentice for six years in the brig *Harperley*, 450 tons, which sailed with coal from the Tyne to Mozambique. After a few voyages he broke his indentures and, tramping from Troon to the Tyne, joined the brig *Maid of Athens*. He later served in four other small sailing ships, attended a nautical school in 1867, and obtained a mate's certificate. After further sea service he gained a master mariner's certificate in 1871, and in 1873 was appointed master of the barque *F. E. Althausse*, holding this command until 1877. Runciman then transferred from sail to steam, becoming master of the steamer *Coanwood*, 1650 tons, until 1885. He saved from his earnings and did some trading on the side.

After over twenty-five years at sea Runciman, partly for reasons of health, began a new career as a shipowner at South Shields, Durham. His training in both sail and steam was valuable to him in the shipowning business. His first ship, the steamer *Dudley*, 1200 tons, did well for him during a period of depressed trade, and, as business improved, he gradually acquired eleven other second-hand steamers. In 1889, at South Shields, Runciman built his first new steamer, the *Blakemore*, which was the foundation of the Moor Line Ltd of cargo steamships. By 1895 the Moor Line, now based in Newcastle upon Tyne, owned twenty-five steamers, and by 1914 about forty. This company was liquidated in 1919, after which Runciman became senior partner in Walter Runciman & Co. Ltd of Newcastle and London. By 1924, Runciman's company, owners of a new Moor Line, had twenty-three steamers in service. Runciman in 1935 acquired a controlling interest in the Anchor Line Ltd of Glasgow. He was also chairman or director of many other shipping companies and combines.

Runciman was president of the chamber of shipping of the United Kingdom in 1910–11. In 1932, on the death of James Lyle Mackay, earl of Inchcape, he succeeded to the

Walter Runciman, first Baron Runciman (1847–1937), by Lafayette, 1927

presidency of the Shipping Federation, serving until his own death. The federation had been formed in 1890 to combat the Seamen's and Firemen's Union, but Runciman admired, and was sympathetic towards, the union's leader, Joseph Havelock Wilson.

In middle life Runciman was a strong, if independent, Liberal. He was chairman of the executive of the Northern Liberal Federation from 1904 to 1926, but resigned in protest against what he considered the Liberal Party's subservience to David Lloyd George. From 1914 to 1918, Runciman was Liberal MP for Hartlepool. In 1931, he declared that free trade had outlived its usefulness and afterwards favoured tariff reform.

A keen yachtsman, in 1922 Runciman bought, as his first yacht of note, the *Sunbeam*, famous for the voyages of its former owner, Thomas, Lord Brassey. It was succeeded by *Sunbeam II*, an auxiliary three-masted schooner built for Runciman, and launched in 1929. He was a member of several yacht clubs and commodore of the Royal Northumbrian yacht club. In 1937, Runciman became honorary commodore of the Royal Naval Volunteer Supplementary Reserve.

Runciman, a man of strong character and striking appearance, was respected throughout the shipping industry for his individualism, geniality, and kindliness. Although disliking most labour and welfare legislation, he was a popular employer and was interested in good industrial relations. He was a life-long teetotaller, and involved in the temperance movement. Runciman was an

admirer of Napoleon Bonaparte, collected books about him, and wrote two. He also wrote several books about sailing ships, as well as an autobiography, *Before the Mast—and After* (1924), which are valuable depictions of nineteenth-century seafaring life. Runciman was an ardent Methodist and a lay preacher in Northumberland.

On 26 March 1869 Runciman married Anne Margaret (d. 1933), daughter of John Lawson, ship's captain, of Blakemoor, Northumberland; they had one child, Walter *Runciman (1870–1949). Runciman was created baronet in 1906, and Baron Runciman of Shoreston in 1933. His wife predeceased him on 20 February 1933 and he died at his home, Fernwood House, Clayton Road, Newcastle upon Tyne, on 13 August 1937.

A. E. JOHNSTONE, *rev.* D. M. CREGIER

Sources *The Times* (14 Aug 1937) · W. G. Runciman, *Before the mast—and after: the autobiography of a sailor and ship owner* (1924) · personal knowledge (1949) · D. J. Rowe, 'Runciman, Walter', *DBB* · *CGPLA Eng. & Wales* (1937) · m. cert. · d. cert. · *WW* · *WWBMP*
Archives NMM, corresp. and papers relating to Royal Mail Group | BLPES, letters to A. G. Gardner · U. Newcastle, Robinson L., corresp. with his son Walter Runciman
Likenesses Lafayette, photograph, 1927, NPG [*see illus.*] · H. Furniss, caricature, pen-and-ink sketch, NPG · photograph, repro. in W. Runciman, *Collier brigs & their sailors* (1926)
Wealth at death £2,388,453 11s. 1d.: probate save and except settled land, 11 Sept 1937, *CGPLA Eng. & Wales* · £18,440: further grant limited to settled land, 11 Oct 1937, *CGPLA Eng. & Wales*

Runciman, Walter, first Viscount Runciman of Doxford (1870–1949), politician, was born at South Shields on 19 November 1870, the only child of Walter (later Baron) *Runciman (1847–1937), shipowner, and his wife, Anne Margaret Lawson (d. 1933). He was educated privately and then at South Shields high school from 1881. In 1889 he went to Trinity College, Cambridge, where he graduated in history in 1892. He then entered his father's shipping firm, which was renamed the Moor Line in 1895. Runciman married Hilda Stevenson (1869–1956) [see Runciman, Hilda], the daughter of James Cochran *Stevenson, a wealthy chemicals manufacturer and former MP for South Shields, on 23 August 1898. They had three daughters and two sons; (Walter) Leslie *Runciman, the elder, succeeded to the title, and James Cochran Stevenson *Runciman became an eminent historian.

Walter Runciman grew up in a typical provincial Victorian Liberal family. His father was a self-made shipping entrepreneur who believed strongly in free trade and individualism and was hostile to trade unions. Both parents were Wesleyan Methodists. Walter became a lifelong teetotaller. Though he played a part in his father's business, he evidently became set on a political career at an early age. In 1898 he was elected to Newcastle school board. After contesting a tory seat at Gravesend in 1898 he won a by-election in the two-member marginal constituency of Oldham in 1899. Though in some ways an orthodox Liberal, the young Runciman experienced a wide range of influences in the form of the Rainbow Circle, Fabianism, and the ideas of 'national efficiency', and also through friendships with young politicians such as Charles Trevelyan and Herbert Samuel. As a result he soon displayed his

Walter Runciman, first Viscount Runciman of Doxford (1870–1949), by Olive Edis

frustration with the traditional Gladstonian leadership of the party. During the late 1890s he became associated with the Liberal Imperialists, which was less an indication of any desire to expand the empire than a symptom of his concern for a more imaginative and interventionist domestic programme. Despite his pro-war stance, however, Runciman was narrowly defeated by Winston Churchill at Oldham in the general election of 1900. By 1902 he had gained the nomination for a much safer Liberal seat at Dewsbury, though in the face of disapproval from the party leaders in London. Campbell-Bannerman described him as 'a pugnacious, sectional partisan who will be, as in the past, a mutineer whenever mutiny is possible' (Campbell-Bannerman to Herbert Gladstone, 30 Oct 1901, Herbert Gladstone MSS, BL Add. MS 45987). This penchant for party infighting certainly recurred during Runciman's long career and eventually damaged his prospects of office.

However, once back in the Commons in 1902 Runciman rapidly worked his way into the mainstream of Liberal politics by taking up the defence of free trade and the attack on the Balfour Education Act. As a young backbencher he gained a reputation for his skill as a platform speaker, in particular for his ability to express complex arguments with clarity. He also benefited from a close association with a prominent north-eastern Liberal, Sir Edward Grey, who was both friend and patron for many years. As a result Runciman received junior office as parliamentary secretary to the Local Government Board in the new Liberal government formed at the end of 1905, and was financial secretary to the Treasury, 1907–8. In this role he demonstrated a sure grasp of administrative detail, and his personal knowledge of business also made

him an asset in an administration dominated by lawyers. Consequently, when H. H. Asquith became prime minister in 1908 he promoted Runciman to the cabinet as president of the Board of Education. However, the Board of Education was an awkward post for a Liberal at this time, caught between the expectations of nonconformists, keen to modify the 1902 act which had abolished school boards, and the Church of England, backed by the Conservative peers in the House of Lords. Arguably the most competent of the series of education ministers before 1914, Runciman negotiated patiently with Randall Davidson, the archbishop of Canterbury, but his bill was eventually withdrawn because of obstructionism in the Lords. Eventually Runciman escaped to the Board of Agriculture and Fisheries in 1911. Here he revealed the interventionist side of his politics by making use of the funds available under the Development Commission, which was established in the 1909 budget, for agricultural research and improvement schemes. He was also a key figure, if overshadowed by Lloyd George and his famous land campaign, in devising schemes for the building of rural houses and for the introduction of minimum wages for agricultural labourers to be determined by regional wages boards. This episode puts Runciman squarely in the mainstream of new Liberalism. Though he had criticized the 'people's budget' in detail, he had backed the political strategy behind it. His later reputation as an orthodox Gladstonian was thus not fully justified; it arose largely from his role during the inter-war period as a bitter opponent of Lloyd George.

The outbreak of war in 1914 interrupted Runciman's domestic agenda and derailed his entire career. Regarded as a 'navalist', he saw the entente with France as a danger to peace and was very loath to enter the war. However, he was not for unconditional peace, and reluctantly agreed to British entry in the hope that her contribution would be essentially a naval one. Ministerial resignations in August 1914 led to his move to the Board of Trade, a post for which he was well equipped. Here, however, he faced the problem of rising food prices and food shortages exacerbated by the requisitioning of merchant vessels by the Admiralty and attacks by German submarines. In this situation Runciman took steps to discourage hoarding, banned the export of some food items, and secretly bought meat and wheat supplies with a view to releasing them onto the domestic market and thus limiting price rises. In January 1916 his department also took over the building of merchant ships, a move which bore fruit in 1917 after he had left office. Runciman was no believer in the 'business-as-usual' approach to war. On the other hand, he understood the limitations of state interventionism; it was impossible, in his view, for Britain to control world prices, and to some extent he accepted the necessity for them to rise. 'There was only one thing worse than high prices' he declared, 'and that was having no food' (*The Times*, 29 Sept 1916). However, he received little credit for his efforts. He became a victim of attacks by the tory press designed to portray the Liberal ministers as ineffective in wartime. Moreover, as a shipowner himself he offered a target for criticism in view of the big profits shippers were enjoying.

Wartime experience made Runciman acutely aware of Britain's reliance on imports, and in the long run this began to undermine his free trade convictions. At the time, however, he appeared to be a highly orthodox Liberal. He was among the ministers who believed in running the war by voluntary recruiting rather than conscription, on the grounds that the loss of manpower to the army would eventually be so damaging to industrial output as to be counter-productive. Consequently, when Asquith was displaced as prime minister in a coup by Lloyd George in December 1916, Runciman joined the majority of his Liberal colleagues in refusing to serve in the new coalition. He had remained in office partly in order to check the drift towards a continentalist strategy which was now unstoppable.

Runciman's prominent role on the opposition front bench for the remainder of the war made it inevitable that he would be opposed by the Lloyd George coalition at the general election in December 1918. In a three-cornered contest at Dewsbury he came bottom of the poll. At this stage he allowed himself to be diverted by his business interests for a time. In 1920 he became vice-chairman of a new shipping company founded after the sale of the Moor Line in 1919; he also served as a director of the *Economist* from 1920 and as chairman of the UK Temperance and General Provident Institution. But he soon attempted to revive his political career by contesting Berwick in 1922 and Brighton in 1923 before winning a seat at Swansea in 1924.

However, Runciman was now handicapped partly by association with the failures of the Asquith administration, and also by his own penchant for partisanship. He and Hilda devoted much of their efforts between the wars to futile attempts to exclude Lloyd George from all influence within the Liberal Party. In parliament Runciman became chairman of the radical group, which refused to accept Lloyd George as chairman of the parliamentary party after 1926; and after 1927 he was active in the Liberal council, which aimed to keep the party in the country out of Lloyd George's hands. 'I do not regard Lloyd George as an enemy', he said in 1928, 'I regard him as a millstone. He is drowning the Liberal Party as well as debasing it' (Runciman to Harcourt Johnstone, 30 Oct 1928, Runciman MSS, vol. 218). Unfortunately this attitude antagonized many Liberal activists and it was a factor in encouraging Runciman to leave his Swansea constituency for St Ives in Cornwall. When the St Ives seat fell vacant in 1928 Runciman felt reluctant to force an unnecessary by-election at Swansea, so Hilda stood in his place and withdrew in his favour at the general election in 1929. Both flatly repudiated Lloyd George and his programme for reducing unemployment.

In the process Runciman became very detached from the Liberal Party. When Ramsay MacDonald offered him the deputy chairmanship of the Royal Mail Group, the world's largest shipping group, in November 1930, he accepted and decided to leave the Commons at the next election. During the 1920s Runciman had gradually moved to the right in the sense that he accepted the orthodox Treasury view of the economy rather than the Keynesian alternative. Thus, when the National Government was formed in 1931 he was a natural candidate for inclusion in the new cabinet; but he had become so isolated by this time that he had no claim on the posts allocated to the Liberals. He did, however, consolidate his position by making public pronouncements which suggested that he was about to abandon free trade. As a result he was returned unopposed as MP for St Ives at the 1931 general election; during the campaign he made the notorious claim, in a speech at South Shields, that the deposits of savers at the Post Office Savings Bank would be at risk under a Labour government. Subsequently he was reappointed to the Board of Trade in the National Government (though he had hoped for the exchequer), in which capacity he presided over the adoption of a protectionist policy. It was an uncomfortable experience, though he claimed to have exercised a moderating influence on the Conservatives. He lost this office in May 1937 when Neville Chamberlain replaced Baldwin as prime minister, and vacated his St Ives seat on his elevation to the peerage (10 June 1937) as first Viscount Runciman of Doxford. The title was taken from the country house at Doxford, Northumberland, which the Runcimans had bought in 1909. He received the honorary degrees of LLD from Manchester University in 1911 and Bristol in 1929, and the DCL from Oxford in 1934.

Runciman's final contribution to public life, and the single episode for which he is best-known, came in July 1938 when Lord Halifax, the foreign secretary, asked him to go to Prague in an attempt to mediate between the rival claims of the Sudetenland Germans and the Czechoslovak government. An unsympathetic British observer described his arrival in Prague on 3 August 1938: 'a stooping, bald-headed man with a clean-shaven, beak-nosed face emerged, carrying a brief-case' (Wheeler-Bennett, 77). In a series of patient negotiations he succeeded in extracting some concessions from the reluctant Czechs. However, the Runciman mission never enjoyed full backing from the prime minister, and was eventually sabotaged by an aggressive speech from Hitler on 12 September. Shortly after this Runciman returned home. His report was published on 28 September. In October 1938 he rejoined the government as lord president of the council, and served for nearly a year. He resigned soon after the outbreak of war, suffering from insomnia and depression. After a long illness he died at his home at Doxford on 13 November 1949. His wife survived him.

In a long and distinguished career Runciman had not quite attained the high offices which his abilities and experience would have justified, and his achievements fell short of his potential. He had often been overshadowed by more flamboyant characters; he had the misfortune to reach his peak just as his party entered upon its decline; and he became diverted by years of political infighting.

MARTIN PUGH

Sources J. Wallace, 'The political career of Walter Runciman, first Viscount Runciman of Doxford (1870–1949)', PhD diss.,

U. Newcastle, 1994 · U. Newcastle, Robinson L., Walter Runciman MSS · *The Times* (15 Nov 1949) · *DNB* · W. G. Runciman, *Before the mast—and after: the autobiography of a sailor and ship owner* (1924) · W. Runciman, *Liberalism as I see it* (1927) · J. W. Wheeler-Bennett, *Munich, prologue to tragedy* (1948) · E. L. Woodward and R. Butler, eds., *Documents on British foreign policy, 1919–1939*, 3rd ser., 2 (1949) · *CGPLA Eng. & Wales* (1950) · BL, Herbert Gladstone MSS

Archives PRO, MSS relating to Czechoslovakia, FO 800/304–8 · U. Newcastle, Robinson L., corresp. and papers | BL, corresp. with Arthur James Balfour, Add. MS 49716, *passim* · BL, corresp. with John Burns, Add. MS 49716, *passim* · BL, corresp. with Lord Gladstone, Add. MSS 46060–46086 · BL OIOC, letters to Lord Reading, MSS Eur. E 238, F 118 · BLPES, letters to A. G. Gardiner · Bodl. Oxf., corresp. with H. Asquith · Bodl. Oxf., letters to Margot Asquith · Bodl. Oxf., letters to Lewis Harcourt · Bodl. Oxf., corresp. with Lord Selborne · Bodl. Oxf., corresp. with Lord Simon · CAC Cam., corresp. with Leslie Hore-Belisha · CAC Cam., corresp. with A. Hurd · HLRO, letters to David Lloyd George · HLRO, corresp. with Andrew Bonar Law · HLRO, corresp. with H. Samuel · NA Scot., corresp. with Lord Lothian · Norfolk RO, corresp. with H. W. Massingham · Nuffield Oxf., corresp. with Lord Emmott · PRO, corresp. with Lord Kitchener, PRO 30/57; WO 159 · PRO NIre., corresp. with Edward Carson · TCD, corresp. with Erskine Childers · U. Newcastle, Robinson L., corresp. with C. P. Trevelyan | FILM BFI NFTVA, documentary footage · BFI NFTVA, news footage · BFI NFTVA, propaganda footage (Hegworth Manufacturing Company)

Likenesses B. Partridge, ink caricature, 1908 (*The cabinet cherubs*), NPG; repro. in *Punch* (22 April 1908) · W. Strang, print, drypoint, 1913, NPG · J. Russell & Sons, photograph, *c*.1915, NPG · Matt, pen-and-ink caricature, 1924, NPG · E. Kapp, charcoal caricature, 1929, Barber Institute of Fine Arts, Birmingham · R. G. Eves, oils, 1937, General Council of British Shipping · Vandyk, photograph, *c*.1937, NPG · O. Edis, photograph, NPG [*see illus.*] · O. Edis, photographs, NPG

Wealth at death £976,659 17*s.* 1*d.*—save and except settled land: probate, 6 Jan 1950, *CGPLA Eng. & Wales* · £61,675—limited to settled land: probate, 6 Feb 1950, *CGPLA Eng. & Wales*

Runcorn, (Stanley) Keith (1922–1995), geophysicist, was born at 186 Duke Street, Southport, Lancashire, on 19 November 1922, the only son of William Henry Runcorn, a monumental mason, and his wife, Lily Idena, *née* Roberts (*b.* 1895). He was educated first at the King George V Grammar School in Southport, then in 1940 entered Gonville and Caius College, Cambridge, where he graduated BA in engineering in 1942. In lieu of military service he was posted to the Radar Research and Development Establishment at Malvern. His academic career began in 1946 with his appointment as an assistant lecturer in physics at Manchester University. Although he was initially interested in cosmic ray physics, he was lured into geophysics through the immense enthusiasm of the head of department, Patrick Blackett, whose new geomagnetic theory connected the origin of the field with the rotation of the earth, and thence required the sources of the geomagnetic field to be distributed throughout the whole body of the earth, in contrast with geodynamo theories, then being initiated by W. M. Elsasser, which place the sources deep within the earth's liquid core.

For his PhD thesis Runcorn, following a remark of E. C. Bullard, calculated the variation of geomagnetic field strength with depth expected for the two types of theory. Then, advised by W. Bullerwell of the geological survey, he went on to measure the field down deep coalmines using

(Stanley) Keith Runcorn (1922–1995), by Nick Sinclair, 1993

standard survey magnetometers. Crucially the results were consistent with 'core' type rather than 'distributed' theories. Meanwhile Blackett had designed and constructed a highly sensitive astatic magnetometer to detect the extremely weak magnetic field that his theory predicted should exist in the vicinity of a rotating gold sphere. This experiment yielded a negative result, so the magnetometer became available for other research. In 1950 Runcorn was appointed an assistant director of research at the department of geodesy and geophysics, University of Cambridge, and several Manchester undergraduates whose appetite for geophysics had been whetted during the mine experiment joined him as research students.

Impressed by Jan Hospers's investigations in 1950 on the remanent magnetism of the Icelandic basalt lava flows, Runcorn put forward the axial dipole hypothesis to describe the time-averaged character of the geomagnetic field, and importantly he interested Sir Ronald Fisher (they were both fellows of Gonville and Caius College) in developing statistical methods for spherical distributions. He resolved to extend palaeomagnetic research to weakly magnetized sedimentary rocks, making use of Blackett's magnetometer. In 1951 he took on Edward Irving, a Cambridge geology graduate, and they selected the nicely bedded and finely laminated Precambrian Torridonian sandstones as the subject of study.

Irving's first results yielded a well-defined palaeomagnetic axis strongly oblique to the present axial dipole with normal and reversed directions, and their potential relevance to Alfred Wegener's (then controversial) proposals on polar wander and continental drift was quickly appreciated. So, later in 1951, Runcorn took on Kenneth Creer to build an astatic magnetometer at Cambridge and to begin a palaeomagnetic survey of the geological column. By mid-1954 Irving and Creer had assembled enough data to construct a palaeomagnetic polar wander curve for the UK.

In 1955 Runcorn was appointed to the chair of physics at King's College, Newcastle (then part of the University of Durham). Several of his former postgraduate students, including Frank Lowes, Raymond Hide, and Kenneth Creer, joined him as university lecturers. He made frequent lecture tours to the USA, disseminating the broadranging and highly original geophysical work of his young research team. In particular the department became the global focal point for palaeo/rock magnetism through the 1960s. Runcorn himself was interested mainly in the deep-seated physical processes that occur in the core and mantle rather than the directly observable near-surface geology. A favourite idea of his, which stemmed from Hide's PhD work on thermal convection in rotating fluids, involved the concept of a growing inner core which, he argued, would produce successive and rather sudden incremental changes in the number of lobes in the pattern of mantle convection, and thus explain why long, relatively quiescent geological periods have been interrupted by shorter phases of continental drift. Importantly all this happened chronologically a decade before the development of the sea-floor spreading hypothesis and the conception of plate tectonics.

Thereafter Runcorn's prime interests moved to lunar and planetary physics. Together with David Collinson he was appointed by NASA to participate in the study of lunar samples from the Apollo programme. Through the late 1960s, 1970s, and 1980s he organized many major international conferences at Newcastle, some under the auspices of NATO as 'institutes of advanced study'. Committee work and administration bored him and he played little part in university politics. Rather, his drive and energy were fuelled by his frequent visits to the USA. At Newcastle he became known (with some affection) as the visiting professor.

Besides his election as fellow of the Royal Society (1965), Runcorn was honoured by many learned societies around the world and awarded honorary degrees by numerous universities. He held short-term appointments at the Dominion Observatory, Ottawa (1955); the California Institute of Technology (1957); the University of Miami (1966); Pennsylvania State University (1967); and the University of California at Los Angeles (1975). After retirement from Newcastle in 1988 he divided his time between the University of Alaska, as Sydney Chapman professor in physical science, and the Space Studies Group at Imperial College. He was visiting professor at Kiel University (1992) and at the Max Planck Institute, Mainz (1994). Runcorn was a sincere, thoughtful, and kindly person. He was a keen rugby player through his late fifties and remained an enthusiastic squash player into his seventies. He never married. He died on 5 December 1995 as a result of being attacked in his room at the Hotel San Diego in San Diego, California, where he was visiting fellow geophysicists on his way to the autumn meeting of the American Geophysical Union. K. M. CREER

Sources The Independent (16 Dec 1995) · The Times (18 Dec 1995) · WWW · personal knowledge (2004) · private information (2004) · b. cert.

Archives CAC Cam., corresp. with Sir Edward Bullard · CUL, corresp. with Joseph Needham · RS, corresp. with Lord Blackett
Likenesses N. Sinclair, bromide print, 1993, NPG [see illus.] · photograph, repro. in The Independent

Rundall, Francis Hornblow (1823–1908), administrator in India, was born at Madras on 22 December 1823, the youngest son of the seven children of Lieutenant-Colonel Charles Rundall, judge advocate-general of the Madras army, and his wife, Henrietta Wryghte. Educated at Kensington grammar school and at the East India Company's military seminary at Addiscombe (1839–41), he was gazetted to the Madras engineers on 10 December 1841, and reached India on 23 December 1843. He was adjutant of the Madras sappers and miners for a few months, but in September 1844 joined the public works department as assistant to General Sir Arthur Thomas Cotton, who was then engaged in surveying the Godavari delta to prepare major irrigation works. He assisted Cotton in the construction of the Godavari works from 1845 to 1851 and came to share his chief's almost religious belief in the efficacy of irrigation and navigable canals in transforming the Indian economy. He was appointed district engineer of Vizagapatam and Ganjam in 1851 (when also he was promoted captain) and district engineer of Rajahmundry in May 1855, a position which gave him charge of the further Godavari works then in progress.

In 1859 Rundall became superintending engineer of the northern circle and departmental secretary to the Madras government. He also served as consulting engineer to the government for the works of the private Madras Irrigation Company. In 1861 he was promoted lieutenant-colonel and granted special leave to be chief engineer to the East India Irrigation and Canal Company, then constructing the Orissa canals on plans laid down by Cotton. Though water was supplied from 1865, the works were not sufficiently advanced to be effective in the famine of the following year, but under Rundall they provided an important form of relief labour. Eventually completed, the canals proved a financial failure and were taken over by the government in 1869. However, they remained of great value in time of drought.

From July 1867 Rundall was chief irrigation engineer and joint secretary to the Bengal government, and the Son canals, which had also been projected by the East India Irrigation and Canal Company and watered half a million acres, were commenced under his orders. From April 1872 he was inspector-general of irrigation and deputy secretary to the government of India, and was thus brought into close touch with the development of irrigation throughout the country. He gained a reputation for enthusiasm and only once took home leave during a service which eventually terminated in April 1874.

Rundall, who had been promoted colonel in June 1868 and major-general in March 1869, was created a CSI in December 1875, and was made colonel commandant of the Royal Engineers in 1876. He became lieutenant-general at the end of 1878, and general in November 1885, being placed on the unemployed supernumerary list in July 1881. On 8 December 1846 he had married Fanny Ada, daughter of Captain W. G. Seton-Burn, 3rd light dragoons; they had a family of three daughters and two sons.

In 1876–7, at the invitation of the Khedive Ismaʿil, Rundall surveyed the delta of the Nile and submitted plans and estimates for irrigation. His proposals, which included the construction of a mighty dam not far from that eventually built at Aswan, were frustrated by Egypt's bankruptcy. Rundall's services were also engaged by a syndicate formed in 1883 to construct a Palestinian canal facilitating the passage of large vessels between the Mediterranean and the Red Sea, by way of the Jordan valley and the Gulf of ʿAqabah, but the project did not mature. After retirement he lectured on Indian irrigation at the Chatham school of military engineering. He completed a *Review of Progress of Irrigation Schemes in Relation to Famine Aspects* for the parliamentary select committee on Indian famine in 1878.

Rundall died at St Ninian's, Moffat, Dumfriesshire (his son-in-law's house), on 30 September 1908, and was buried at Moffat cemetery.

F. H. BROWN, *rev.* DAVID WASHBROOK

Sources *India Office List* (1908) · *The Times* (1 Oct 1908) · F. M. Rundall, 'General F. H. Rundall', *Royal Engineers Journal*, new ser., 8 (1908), 383–4 · Lady Hope [E. R. C. Hope], *General Sir Arthur Cotton: his life and work* (1900)
Wealth at death £2006 10s. 4d.: resworn probate, 29 Oct 1908, *CGPLA Eng. & Wales*

Rundall, Mary Ann (d. 1839), educational writer, was the head of a school for young girls in Bath known as Percy House Seminary. Her sister, Elizabeth, a teacher of dancing, married the actor Robert William *Elliston and had a large family. In 1815 Miss Rundall published *Symbolic Illustrations of the History of England*. Dedicated to Princess Elizabeth, it was intended to help students remember important historical events by means of symbols based on the mnemonics of Gregor von Feinagle, who had visited Britain in 1811 and published *The New Art of Memory* with a London publisher in the following year. *Symbolic Illustrations* was favourably reviewed in the *Gentleman's Magazine*: 'the greater part of [the symbols] exhibit, each in a compact diagram, short narrations or histories; and thus, not only identify, but compress the objects of study' (*GM*, 1st ser., 85/2, 1815, 611). A critic for the *Quarterly Review*, however, was far less complimentary, and described *Symbolic Illustrations* as 'by far the most absurd book that has ever fallen into our hands' (*QR*, 418), highlighting the fact that 700 pages of letterpress were required to explain the thirty-nine plates of symbols. The complexity of the symbols certainly seems to justify the reviewer's criticism, and it is surprising to find a riposte in the *Gentleman's Magazine*: this contributor, who identifies himself as a teacher, praises the *Symbolic Illustrations* as 'a most happy auxiliary' to the teaching of history and lauds Miss Rundall's 'ingenuity and application' (*GM*, 1st ser., 87/1, 1817, 34).

Mary Ann Rundall's subsequent publications—*An Easy Grammar of Sacred History* (1810) and a *Sequel to the Grammar of Sacred History* (1824)—did not excite such controversy as *Symbolic Illustrations* had done. By the time of the publication of the *Sequel* Miss Rundall may have been living in

London, possibly at Wanstead. She was still running a school: the *Sequel* contains an advertisement revealing that she received 'a few pupils' whom she instructed in 'every useful Science and elegant Accomplishment'. She died in Lower Bedford Place, London, on 2 October 1839.

ELIZABETH LEE, *rev.* ROSEMARY MITCHELL

Sources [J. Watkins and F. Shoberl], *A biographical dictionary of the living authors of Great Britain and Ireland* (1816), 302 · *GM*, 1st ser., 85/2 (1815), 611–2; 87/1 (1817), 33–4; 2nd ser., 12 (1839), 545 · review, *QR*, 30 (1816), 418

Rundell [*née* Ketelby], **Maria Eliza** (1745–1828), writer on cookery, was the only child of Abel Johnson Ketelby (d. 1756), a barrister of the Middle Temple, resident at Ludlow, Shropshire. She married, on 30 December 1766, Thomas Rundell, a surgeon practising at Bath, where they lived. They raised two sons and three daughters. Thomas Rundell died, after a long and painful illness, on 30 September 1795. Mrs Rundell then moved to Swansea, confiding her two younger daughters to the care of their uncle and aunt in London.

Mrs Rundell began collecting recipes and household tips for her daughters. She sent the manuscript to the publisher John Murray, of whose family she was an old friend, and it was published in 1806 under the title of *Domestic Cookery*; a second amplified edition was completed at Ambleside where Mrs Rundell was living with her married daughter. The book had an immediate success, 5000–10,000 copies were printed annually, and succeeding editions were enlarged and embellished by engravings. It became one of Murray's most valuable properties and in 1812, when he bought the lease of his premises in Albemarle Street, the copyright of *Domestic Cookery* formed part of the surety. As the earliest manual of household management with any pretensions to completeness, it called forth many imitations.

In 1808 Murray presented Mrs Rundell with £150. She replied, 'I never had the smallest idea of any return for what I considered a free gift to one whom I had long regarded as my friend'. In acknowledging a copy of the second edition, Mrs Rundell begged Murray not to think of remunerating her further, and in the preface to the edition of 1810 she expressly stated that she would receive no emolument. But in 1814 Mrs Rundell accused Murray of neglecting the book and of hindering its sale. After obtaining an injunction in the vice-chancellor's court to restrain Murray from republishing the book when the rights expired, she in 1821 offered an improved version of it to Messrs Longman for publication. Murray retaliated by obtaining an injunction from the lord chancellor to prevent Mrs Rundell from publishing the book with any of his additions and embellishments. On 3 November the lord chancellor dissolved the injunction against Murray, but gave right to neither party, declaring that a court of law and not a court of equity must decide between them. After long delay, Mrs Rundell accepted Murray's offer of £2000 in full discharge of all her claims. The book continued to earn its keep. It was translated into German in 1841 and the sixty-fifth English edition appeared in the same year.

Mrs Rundell's son Edmund Waller Rundell joined the eminent London silversmith Philip *Rundell (to whom his father had been related) and later became a partner in his firm, which was then known as Rundell, Bridge, and Rundell. Mrs Rundell, who was peripatetic throughout her long years of widowhood, enjoyed the hospitality of her many friends and married offspring. In 1827 she was a considerable beneficiary in Philip Rundell's will. She subsequently travelled to Lausanne, Switzerland, and died there on 16 December 1828.

ELIZABETH LEE, rev. ANITA McCONNELL

Sources *Memoirs, journal and correspondence of Thomas Moore*, ed. J. Russell, 5 (1854), 118–19 · *GM*, 1st ser., 65 (1795), 881 · 'London and its vicinity', *GM*, 1st ser., 91/2 (1821), 465 · *GM*, 1st ser., 99/1 (1829), 94 · S. Smiles, *A publisher and his friends: memoir and correspondence of the late John Murray*, 1 (1891), 90; 2 (1891), 120–25 · *The Times* (5 Nov 1821), 3b · *The Times* (7 Nov 1821), 3a · *The Times* (22 Nov 1827), 3b · *The Times* (26 Nov 1827), 3a · S. Tanner, 'A man who never was', *Silver Society Journal*, 2 (1991), 89–102 · *Memoirs of the late Philip Rundell Esq* (1827) · M. A. Rundell, *Letters addressed to two absent daughters* (1814) · will, Bank of England will extracts, 1829/6808
Archives Wellcome L., MS manual on pregnancy and children
Wealth at death under £9000: will, 1828, Bank of England will extracts, 1829/6808

Rundell, Philip (1746–1827), jeweller and millionaire, was born on 15 January 1746 and baptized on 8 February 1746 at Norton St Philip, near Bath, Somerset, one of the large family of Richard Rundell, victualler or maltster, and his wife, Ann Ditcher. Shortly after his fourteenth birthday, on 10 May 1760 Rundell was apprenticed in Bath to the jeweller William Rogers. After serving his time he found employment in the late 1760s, probably through the influence of family connections in the City of London, with William Pickett, the retail goldsmith of the Golden Salmon, Ludgate Hill. The youthful Rundell appears to have shown his aptitude for business so rapidly that within three or four years Pickett, admittedly increasingly preoccupied by aldermanic affairs on his way to becoming lord mayor in 1789, made him a partner. Rundell was made free of the Drapers' Company by redemption on 15 May 1771.

The firm of Pickett and Rundell survived until February 1786, when Rundell, taking sole charge, agreed to buy Pickett out. In December the following year the firm's name was altered from Philip Rundell to Rundell and Bridge upon John Bridge becoming the new partner. Under these two men the concern became pre-eminent in the British goldsmiths' trade. For nearly forty years they formed what seems to have been the perfect working partnership, each attending to that part of the business to which their very different characters suited them best. Rundell, hard-working, often irascible, and steadfast in striking a bargain, and also regarded by London contemporaries as the keenest judge of diamonds, superintended the firm's jewellery and other manufacturing departments. Bridge, on the other hand, was possessed of an urbanity of manner which proved of the greatest importance, especially in the firm's dealings with George III and other members of the royal family.

About 1798 Rundell arranged to purchase the old-established jewellery business of John Duval, Sons & Co.; by this means Rundell and Bridge became the crown jewellers. A further change occurred in 1804–5 when the firm's style was altered to Rundell, Bridge, and Rundell following the admission of the senior partner's nephew, Edmund Waller Rundell (1768?–1857), son of Maria Eliza Rundell, into the business. By now Rundells was in a dominant position with many of the finest workshops, including that of Paul Storr, at its disposal, together with the services of artists such as William Theed, John Flaxman, and Thomas Stothard. Besides a stock of both new and antique silver, much of Rundells' business depended upon the sale and purchase of precious stones, pearls, jewellery, gold boxes, and objects of virtu. By 1812–13 Rundell was furthermore actively engaged in buying a steam engine for a diamond-cutting subsidiary in Spitalfields.

Although never married, according to the article on him in the *Annual Biography and Obituary* for 1828 Rundell

> always manifested much pleasure in the enjoyment of female society, for which the comeliness of his person, his conversational powers, and his habitual attentiveness, naturally fitted him. He was unassuming in his manners, and when relieved from the cares of business, was a cheerful and agreeable companion. He was fond of music, had a tolerable voice, and sang with taste. (p. 323)

During the last twenty years of his life, however, he suffered from increasing deafness and the effects of an internal complaint, in consequence of which 'he withdrew much from society, and lived very retired' (p. 324). Other, less charitable accounts of Rundell's character, conduct, and the acquisition of his great personal wealth have survived, the more unpleasant of which, perhaps significantly, were written by former employees.

Rundell retired on 29 September 1823. Throughout most of his working life he lived above the shop at 32 Ludgate Hill, although latterly he occupied a house nearby in The Crescent, New Bridge Street, Blackfriars. On his retirement he took up residence in a small house at South Bank, Regent's Park, in order, according to one authority, to be near his medical advisers. Others claim that this was the abode of Rundell's mistress, Mrs Elizabeth Wartridge. His health began to deteriorate seriously towards the end of 1826 and he died at South Bank on 17 February 1827. He was buried in Hendon parish churchyard, the grave being marked by a stone tomb erected in his memory by Joseph Neeld junior.

JOHN CULME, rev.

Sources *Memoirs of the late Philip Rundell, Esq. ... by a gentleman many years connected with the firm* (1827) · *Annual Biography and Obituary*, 12 (1828), 317–32 · S. Bury, 'The lengthening shadow of Rundell's [pts 1–3]', *The Connoisseur*, 161 (1966), 79–85, 152–8, 218–22 · A. G. Grimwade, *London goldsmiths, 1697–1837: their marks and lives, from the original registers at Goldsmiths' Hall*, 3rd edn (1990), 648, 766 · private information (1993)

Rundle, Sir (Henry Macleod) Leslie (1856–1934), army officer, was born at Newton Abbot, Devon, on 6 January 1856, the second son of Captain Joseph Sparkehall Rundle RN, and his wife, Renira Catherine, daughter of Commander Walter Wemyss Leslie RN. On leaving the Royal Military Academy, Woolwich, he was gazetted to the Royal Artillery in August 1876. He first saw active service in 1879 in the Anglo-Zulu War with Sir Evelyn Wood's flying column, serving at the battle of Ulundi (4 July), and being mentioned in dispatches. In 1881 he took part in the First South African War and was wounded at Potchefstroom.

Rundle's military reputation rests mainly upon his services in Egypt and the Sudan. In 1882 he was at the battle of Tell al-Kebir, and in 1883 began fifteen years' service with the Egyptian army. He served under Lord Kitchener with the Nile expedition (1884–5), when he was engaged in guarding the Nubian Desert with a force of Ababda Arabs. He was mentioned in dispatches and promoted captain and brevet major in 1885. It was during this time that he formed a lasting friendship with Kitchener. In the same year he was posted to the Sudan frontier field force (1885–7), and while with that unit he was awarded the DSO (1887) and the Osmanieh medal (third class). In 1889, on the Sudan frontier, he commanded the artillery at the battle of Toski, was mentioned in dispatches, promoted brevet lieutenant-colonel, and awarded the Mejidiye medal (second class). In 1891, as assistant adjutant-general, he was engaged in the recapture of Tokar; the next year he became adjutant-general in the Egyptian army, and then spent nearly five years at Cairo, receiving his brevet colonelcy in 1894. With the Dongola expeditionary force, as Kitchener's chief of staff, in 1896 he was present at the engagements of Firket and Hafir; he was promoted major-general (supernumerary) in November 1896 and the same year was appointed CMG. After the battle of Omdurman on 2 September 1898 he took Kitchener's place during his absence at Fashoda and led a column up the Blue Nile to relieve Gedaref, and for these services was appointed KCB and received the special thanks of parliament in 1898. He married in 1887 Eleanor Georgina, eldest daughter of Captain Henry Jermyn Montgomery Campbell, Royal Artillery, of Thurmaston Hall, Leicestershire; they had no children.

In 1898 Rundle returned home to command the south-eastern district (1898–9) and the following year (1899–1900) became deputy adjutant-general to the forces, at the War Office. In 1900 he was given command of a division at Aldershot, but in March was ordered to South Africa, where he commanded the 8th division (1900–02). He conducted the Dewetsdorp operations and commanded at the battles of Biddulphsberg and Wittebergen, and later fought and was wounded at the Brandwater basin, where Prinsloo surrendered. In 1900 he was appointed KCMG.

In 1902 Rundle returned again to England and assumed command of the 5th division, 2nd army corps. In November 1903 he was appointed major-general in command of the north-eastern district and acting general officer commanding-in-chief northern command until April 1905, when he was promoted lieutenant-general and general officer commanding-in-chief (second class). On relinquishing the northern command in November 1907, he remained without appointment until in July 1909 he was made governor and commander-in-chief of Malta, being promoted general in September of that year. In 1911 he was appointed GCB, in 1912 GCVO, and in 1914 GCMG. He remained at Malta until February 1915, when

he returned to England and succeeded Sir Ian Hamilton as commander-in-chief, central force, organized for home defence. He relinquished this post in May 1916 and was without appointment until his retirement from the army in May 1919. He was honorary colonel, 3rd battalion, the Buffs, from 1899 to 1907, and was appointed colonel-commandant, Royal Artillery, in 1907. He was a JP and county councillor for Hertfordshire.

Rundle was a handsome man of smart appearance. During his long military career he earned a reputation for thoroughness and caution. Although scrupulously fair, he was outwardly somewhat unapproachable, except to children, with whom he had a warm rapport. He died at 8 Beaumont Street, Marylebone, London, on 19 November 1934, and was survived by his widow.

C. V. OWEN, rev. JAMES FALKNER

Sources Army List · The Times (20 Nov 1934) · Hart's Army List · J. F. Maurice and M. H. Grant, eds., History of the war in South Africa, 1899–1902, 4 vols. (1906–10) · E. W. C. Sandes, The royal engineers in Egypt and the Sudan (1937) · WWW · CGPLA Eng. & Wales (1934)
Archives Bodl. Oxf., corresp. · U. Durham L., papers | PRO, letters to Lord Kitchener on recruiting and manpower, PRO 30/57/73 · U. Durham L., corresp. with Sir Reginald Wingate
Likenesses W. Stoneman, photograph, NPG · photograph, repro. in Army and Navy Illustrated (1 July 1899) · photograph, repro. in The Sketch (14 March 1900) · wood-engraving, NPG
Wealth at death £8696 0s. 3d.: probate, 20 Dec 1934, CGPLA Eng. & Wales

Rundle, Thomas (1687/8–1743), Church of Ireland bishop of Derry, was born at Milton Abbot, Devon, the son of Thomas Rundle, an Exeter clergyman. After passing through the grammar school at Exeter under John Reynolds, uncle of Sir Joshua, he matriculated as a commoner of Exeter College, Oxford, on 5 April 1704, at the age of sixteen. He took the degrees of BCL in 1710 and DCL in 1723.

In 1712 Rundle made the acquaintance of William Whiston, to the formation of whose 'society for promoting primitive Christianity' Rundle and his tutor Thomas Rennel were well disposed. In the same year he became tutor to the only son of John Cater of Kempston, near Bedford. Here Whiston visited him, and, finding him proficient in the fathers, set him upon a critical examination of the Sibylline oracles, a task of which he soon tired. When Rundle informed Whiston that he intended to take holy orders, a breach, lasting for many years, ensued between them. Whiston sharply reproached Rundle for want of principle. It appears, however, that Rundle had begun to lose faith in Whiston's judgement on matters of antiquity. He was now more attracted to the Arian theology of Samuel Clarke (1675–1729).

Rundle was ordained deacon on 29 July and priest on 5 August 1716, by William Talbot (1659–1730), then bishop of Salisbury, whose younger son, Edward, had been Rundle's most intimate friend since Oxford days. The bishop at once made Rundle his domestic chaplain and gave him a prebend at Salisbury. Rundle became incumbent also of two Wiltshire livings in the bishop's gift, Inglesham (1719) and Poulshot (1720). Bishop Talbot also appointed him archdeacon of Wiltshire (1720) and treasurer of Sarum (1721). During his residence at Salisbury, Rundle became well acquainted with the deist Thomas Chubb, of whose publications (up to 1730) he thought highly.

Although Edward Talbot died in December 1720, his family continued to patronize Rundle. Bishop Talbot, on being promoted to Durham, collated him to a stall in his cathedral (23 January 1722), and preferred him to a better one before the end of the year; he gave him also the vicarage (1722) and rectory (1724) of Sedgefield, co. Durham, and appointed him (1728) to the mastership of the hospital of Sherburn, 2 miles from Durham. Rundle lived at the palace as resident chaplain from September 1722 until Bishop Talbot's death on 10 October 1730. Whiston intimates that his high living at Durham permanently injured his heath; however, he 'lived very abstemiously afterward', for when he became resident in Dublin, Jonathan Swift complained: 'His only fault is that he drinks no wine, and I drink nothing else' (Dallaway, cxxv). Thomas Secker, future archbishop of Canterbury, was Rundle's fellow chaplain from 1722 to 1724. Pope commented later in the second dialogue of his *Epilogue to the Satires*, 'Ev'n in a Bishop I can spy desert—Secker is decent, Rundle has a heart.'

In December 1733 Rundle was nominated to the see of Gloucester by the lord chancellor, Charles Talbot, eldest son of Bishop Talbot, who had made him his chaplain. Although the appointment was published in the newspapers, Edmund Gibson, bishop of London, interposed. The real objection was to Rundle's ecclesiastical politics, but the opportunity was taken to misrepresent his relations with Chubb and to raise the cry of deist. Rundle pointed out that Talbot had both asserted 'the injustice of the charge' and detected 'the sinister means that were made use of to support it' (Dallaway, lii). Crucial to the charge was the misrepresentation of a private conversation between Rundle and Robert Cannon which had been overheard by Gibson's henchman in London, Richard Venn, rector of St Antholin's. Of Gibson himself, Rundle said: 'it is not me, but the phantom represented to him under my name, that he so vehemently opposes' (ibid., lxxv). There was impressive countervailing influence. Arthur Ashley Sykes published a defence of Rundle; a protégé of Gibson, John Coneybeare, also defended him; and Whiston, who had 'come into a kind of Friendship again' with Rundle, interceded on his behalf (*Memoirs of the Life and Writings*, 1.273). The facts, moreover, spoke for themselves. Rundle had not only preached against deists, but had led a discussion against Matthew Tindal and Anthony Collins at the Grecian Coffee House. The matter was eventually compromised by giving the see of Gloucester to Martin Benson, a friend of Rundle, while Rundle himself was appointed to Derry.

There was an inevitable fall-out in Ireland. The primate, Hugh Boulter, wrote to the viceroy regretting Rundle's appointment, but did not protest against it. In his strategy of achieving English ascendancy in Irish appointments Boulter's concern was that 'it will give a handle to some clamour here'; yet he accepted that Irish affairs 'must give way to the more weighty concerns in England' (Boulter, 2.105–6). Swift's ire was aroused by overt dissatisfaction on the part of some Irish bishops, and was expressed in his spirited lines:

> Rundle a bishop! Well he may—
> He's still a Christian more than they!
> I know the subject of their quarrels—
> The man has learning, sense, and morals.

Rundle's patent to the see of Derry was dated 17 July 1735, and on 3 August he was consecrated at Dunboyne by the primate and the bishops of Meath and Kilmore. Given his public duties, he lived chiefly in Dublin, where he rebuilt his town house. His published letters—mostly addressed to Barbara Sandys (1685–1746) of Miserden, Gloucestershire—complement those of Boulter and Edward Synge. They reveal his contentment. 'At Dublin, I enjoy the most delightful habitation, the finest landscape, and the mildest climate … I have a house there rather too elegant and magnificent; in the north an easy diocese, and a large revenue': Derry was, in fact, a wealthier see than Gloucester. Rundle ruled it with a gentle hand and won the affection of his clergy. He wrote that he had thirty-five incumbents, all of good 'general learning', and 'rather more curates, who are allowed by their rectors such a stipend, as hath, alas! tempted most of them to marry', some supporting eight or ten children on £40 a year (Dallaway, clx–cxii).

Rundle received George Whitefield courteously in Dublin. In his sermon (one of four which he published) in Christ Church Cathedral in 1735, on the anniversary of the Irish rising of 1641, he noted that 'Severity irritates, and hardens in Opposition', and recommended apostolic 'gentleness, meekness, and patience in teaching the Truth' to Roman Catholics (T. Rundle, *Sermon*, 1735, 30). Swift wrote that he was esteemed 'as a person of learning and conversation, and humanity; but he is beloved by all people' (Dallaway, cxxvii). Rundle died, unmarried, at Dublin on 15 April 1743, and was buried in St Peter's churchyard, Dublin. He bequeathed most of his fortune of £20,000 to John Talbot, second son of the lord chancellor.

ALAN R. ACHESON

Sources DNB · J. Dallaway, introduction, in *Letters of the late Thomas Rundle … to Mrs Barbara Sandys, of Miserden, Glocestershire*, 1 (1789) · *Memoirs of the life and writings of Mr William Whiston, containing memoirs of several of his friends also, written by himself*, 3 vols. (1749–50) · H. Boulter, *Letters*, 2 vols. (1770) · R. Mant, *History of the Church of Ireland from the revolution to the union of the churches*, 2 vols. (1840), vol. 2, pp. 537–43 · H. Cotton, *Fasti ecclesiae Hibernicae*, 3 (1849) · W. A. Phillips, ed., *History of the Church of Ireland*, 3 vols. (1933–4), vol. 3, pp. 215–17

Archives LPL, letters to William, Earl Talbot

Likenesses oils, Durham Cathedral · oils, LPL

Wealth at death £20,000: DNB

Runge [*née* Hasluck; *other married name* Ross], **Norah Cecil** (1884–1978), politician, was born on 27 September 1884 at 39 Sutherland Gardens, Kensington, London, the daughter of Lawrence Hasluck, a chartered accountant, and his wife, Lucy, *née* Williams. She was educated privately. On 31 May 1906 she married Julius Joseph Runge (1878/9–1935), of Craven Hill, Middlesex, the son of Charles Hermann Runge. They had three sons and a daughter; one son was

Sir Peter Runge (d. 1970), chairman of the British National Export Council.

Norah Runge was superintendent of the soldiers' and sailors' free buffet at Paddington Station, 1915–19, and was appointed OBE in 1918 in recognition of this work. She chaired the women's branch of Rotherhithe Conservative Association from 1927 to 1932, and was president of the full association from 1932 to 1946. She was adopted as the Conservative candidate for the Rotherhithe division of Bermondsey at the 1931 general election. It was a contest that she was not expected to win: her opponent was the long-serving Labour member Ben Smith, who had first won the seat in 1923, and whose majority in 1929 was over 10,000. The absence of a Liberal candidate in 1931, however, improved Runge's chances, as did the high level of unemployment in Rotherhithe, which housed docks and several big factories. Undeterred by the size of the task she campaigned energetically, holding open-air meetings. Her hard work paid off with a remarkable victory by 130 votes, less than 1 per cent of those cast.

Of the sixteen Conservative women candidates at this election a record number of thirteen were elected, and Runge proved among the most active in parliament. She registered the most appearances of any woman in the division lists of the Commons, 1933–4, voting 224 times. She also regularly tabled questions, many of them affecting her constituency. In August 1935 she asked for a statement on policy regarding 'propagandist teaching' in schools, having learned that Bermondsey borough council was recommending the removal from classroom walls of pictures on patriotic themes such as the death of Nelson and the charge of the light brigade. Whatever the truth of the report it revealed the depth of political antagonism in the borough, and Runge's determination to fight socialism in any guise.

Though Runge's social background was very different from that of her constituents she was an effective member in their interests. Her experience of greyhound racing, both as an owner and (on a modest scale) as a punter, led her to support in December 1932 a bill to improve regulation of the industry, which must be made 'as clean, honest and straight as possible' (The Times, 3 Dec 1932). And in April 1932 she made her maiden speech in support of Sunday cinema opening, a popular form of entertainment with working people, but one which religious groups strongly opposed. Runge believed that the question should be viewed in terms of its benefits to the community as a whole, and not as a purely religious issue. She held no brief for the cinema proprietors—'I have seldom been to one of their entertainments without wishing that I were elsewhere' (Hansard 5C, vol. 264, col. 883)—but understood that a visit to the cinema gave working-class families a chance to escape the cramped and often colourless conditions in which they lived. Having argued cogently in favour of the bill, Runge inexplicably entered the division lobby against it.

Slum clearance was another primary concern, and Runge identified the lack of temporary accommodation for displaced residents as the main obstacle. She wrote to The Times in March 1933 calling for a co-ordinated approach to the problem, but the lack of any advance compelled her to renew her appeal a year later. There was genuine urgency in her plea that temporary housing be made available 'in parks, public places, passenger vessels, and indeed on any vacant space' (The Times, 24 March 1934). On unemployment benefit, another key issue for her constituents, Runge declared herself 'a whole-hearted supporter of the means test' (Hansard 5C, vol. 289, cols. 1164–5). But she was also aware of the many injustices in its administration, particularly in assessing family resources. In working-class households there could often be an extended family living together, and in such circumstances she believed it was unreasonable to expect those who were earning a wage to keep those who were not: 'A big slice of those who form part of the household should be disregarded' (Hansard 5C, vol. 289, cols. 1164–5). She was less liberal, though, over an amendment to the India Bill, in May 1935, to include more women in the electorate there: 'Because I am a woman I suppose I shall be expected to support this amendment, but I am not going to do anything of the sort. I expect I shall be called a traitor to my sex' (ibid., vol. 301, col. 1796). Remarkably, given the controversy she expected would be caused by her opposition, she gave no reason for it, beyond expressing blind faith in the government to 'do the best … for the women of India' (ibid.).

At the general election of 1935 Labour made a recovery from the débâcle of 1931, and at Rotherhithe, Runge was decisively beaten by 4665 votes by Ben Smith. She afterwards turned her attention to local politics, serving as an alderman of London county council, 1937–61, and as deputy chair of the council, 1951–2. She was also active in party organization, becoming chairman of the London area women's advisory committee of Conservative associations, 1938–43, and president, 1943–5; she served as vice-chairman of the central women's advisory committee of Conservative associations, 1941–2, and as vice-chairman of the London Conservative Union Council, 1940–47. At the general election of 1945 Runge again contested Rotherhithe, but was well beaten (again by Ben Smith, recently knighted), and in the following year she stood down to make way for a younger candidate; she was then sixty-one.

After the death of her first husband Runge quietly married, on 4 September 1939, Dr Thomas Arthur Ross (1874/5–1941), a psychiatrist who was also a widower. During the Second World War Runge was active in civil defence in Bermondsey, and worked for the prisoner of war department of the Red Cross, 1941–5. She later chaired the Horton Hospital management committee from 1948 to 1952, and was a member of the board of governors of Bethlem Royal and Maudsley Hospital from 1948 to 1960. After retiring from her public and political commitments in 1961 she set up an antique shop in Chelsea, which she ran until a few years before her death. She died on 6 June 1978 at her home, 1A St John's House, Smith Square, Westminster.

MARK POTTLE

Sources WWW · WWBMP · *The Times* (29 Sept 1931) · *The Times* (13 Oct 1931) · *The Times* (29 Oct 1931) · *The Times* (14 April 1932) · *The Times* (17 Nov 1932) · *The Times* (3 Dec 1932) · *The Times* (24 March 1933) · *The Times* (24 March 1934) · *The Times* (10 May 1934) · *The Times* (16 May 1935) · *The Times* (6 Sept 1939) · *The Times* (12 Oct 1946) · *The Times* (8 June 1978) · *Hansard 5C* (1932), 264.883–6; (1933), 274.42; 276.2366, 2518; (1934), 289.1164–5; (1935), 301.1796; 304.2995 · F. W. S. Craig, *British parliamentary election results, 1918–1949*, rev. edn (1977) · P. Brookes, *Women at Westminster: an account of women in the British parliament, 1918–1966* (1967) · C. Rallings and M. Thrasher, *British electoral facts, 1832–1999* (2000) · b. cert. · m. cert. [Julius Joseph Runge] · m. cert. [Thomas Arthur Ross] · d. cert.
Likenesses photograph, repro. in *The Times* (29 Oct 1931)
Wealth at death £205,312: probate, 25 Sept 1978, *CGPLA Eng. & Wales*

Runnington, Charles (1751–1821), serjeant-at-law, was born on 29 August 1751 in Hertfordshire, and was probably the son of John Runnington, mayor of Hertford in 1754. He was educated under private tutors, and after some years of special pleading was called to the bar at the Inner Temple in Hilary term 1778. He was made serjeant-at-law on 27 November 1787, and held for a time the office of deputy judge of the Marshalsea court. On 27 May 1815 he was appointed to the chief commissionership in insolvency, which he resigned in 1819.

Runnington was twice married. His first marriage, in 1777, was to Anna Maria, youngest sister of the lawyer Sir Samuel Shepherd. The couple had a son and a daughter. In 1783 he married Mrs Wetherell, widow of Charles Wetherell of Jamaica. Runnington's only son, Charles Henry Runnington, died on 20 November 1810.

Runnington was the editor of a number of well-known legal works, including *The Statutes at Large* (1786, rev. edn), and also of Sir Matthew Hale's *History of the Common Law* (1779). He was author of *A Treatise on the Action of Ejectment* (1781), which was subsequently recast and revised as *The history, principles, and practice of the legal remedy by ejectment, and the resulting action for mesne profits* (1795). Runnington died on 18 January 1821 at Brighton.

J. M. RIGG, rev. ROBERT BROWN

Sources J. Watkins, *The universal biographical dictionary*, new edn (1821) · J. Gorton, *A general biographical dictionary*, 3 vols. (1841) · J. Haydn, *The book of dignities: containing lists of the official personages of the British empire*, ed. H. Ockerby, [new edn] (1890) · *Complete encyclopaedia of modern British biography … the Georgian era*, 4 vols. (1835) · *GM*, 1st ser., 57 (1787), 119 · *GM*, 1st ser., 80 (1810), 591 · *GM*, 1st ser., 85/1 (1815), 560 · *GM*, 1st ser., 91/1 (1821), 87–8 · *LondG* (22 Nov 1787) · *LondG* (27 May 1815)
Likenesses T. Blood, stipple, 1817, BM, NPG; repro. in *European Magazine*

Runting, Ernest George Virgo (1861–1954), chiropodist, was born on 26 December 1861, at 68 South Audley Street, London, the son of William Runting (*d.* 1881), dentist, and his wife, Fanny Maria Potter (1832–1882), chiropodist, who followed her parents in the craft. Educated privately, Runting at fifteen was apprenticed as a cadet to a three-master ship, the *Suffolk*, and he served for five years, making many trips to North America. On the death of his father in 1881 his mother bought him out of the service and trained him and his brother William in chiropody.

In 1884 Runting started his own practice in Elm Park Terrace, South Kensington, London. He built a large connection and followed his mother, who was chiropodist to Queen Victoria, with royal appointments to Queen Alexandra and Queen Mary. From earning fee receipts of £64 10s. in 1884 he went on to average £2000 per annum from 1897 to 1927, having the leading practice in the country, but treating the needy free.

Runting's ambition was to make the craft of chiropody a profession, and he had contact with developments in America from 1895, when chiropodists were first licensed in New York. A patient, the Revd Dr Arnold Whittaker Oxford (1855–1948), was impressed by Runting and suggested in 1912 that they should form a society of chiropodists. Oxford had been the high-church vicar of St Luke's, Beswick Street, for sixteen years, but becoming uncertain of his ecclesiastical position had trained in medicine. A wealthy man, Oxford found medicine the medium for his humanitarian activities. In addition to being a Greek scholar, an author of books on antiquarian subjects, an untiring worker in the hospital and charitable fields, and a leading freemason, he was so impressed by Runting's skills as a chiropodist that he was determined that such benefits be brought within the reach of everyone. A meeting was called of thirty-five chiropodists (the leading practitioners from England and Scotland) and held at Runting's home and place of practice, 7 New Burlington Street, London, on 14 November 1912, when the decision was taken to form the National Society of Chiropodists, with Runting as president and Oxford as honorary treasurer.

In 1913 the society opened the Silver Street Pedic Clinic (later the London Foot Hospital), near the British Museum, for the free treatment of the necessitous poor. A journal, *The Chiropodist*, was started in January 1914; a library was begun, and lectures and clinical training were established. A school of chiropody was due to open in 1914 (Oxford had persuaded several medical practitioners to help), but the outbreak of war prevented it. During the war servicemen were treated free at the clinic, and short courses were provided for soldiers sent by the War Office who then served as battalion chiropodists. The school was eventually opened at the clinic in April 1919, and Runting headed the staff (all giving their services free) and was active in developing the academic course and clinical teaching. Runting and Oxford are regarded as the founders of the London Foot Hospital School of Podiatric Medicine. Runting had contributed a chapter to the first multi-authored work of its kind, *Textbook of Chiropody* (1914); and the first of his own books, *Battalion Chiropody Training and Practice*, was published in 1918.

Runting's classic *Practical Chiropody* was published in 1925 and received good reviews from the *Medical Times* and *The Lancet*. The book reached its eighth edition in 1952, and there were seven reprints; a revised, ninth edition was published in 1956, after Runting's death, and there were several American editions as well as one in Spanish. *The Lancet* had printed an article by Runting on the treatment of corns in 1927, and in many of his other writings Runting built on the work of Lewis Durlacher (1792–1864), developing the use of silver nitrate, the treatment of verrucae, toenail problems, the rational approach to the treatment of corns, and the importance of considering 'the chiropodist's handicap—the shoe'. From its beginnings in 1914 *The Chiropodist* had a monthly page of jottings by Runting, under the pen-name Old Chiro, which continued until 1945 and did much to influence the development of the profession. A selection appeared as *Chiropody Jottings* in 1932.

Runting and his wife, Mabel (1851/2–1932), had a son and two daughters (one in practice with him). Runting devoted his life to chiropody, and, generous of his time and money to needy patients, his colleagues, and his church, he died a poor man. He was a member of All Souls Church, Langham Place, London, for many years, and was elected people's warden of St Peter's in 1946. Runting died as a result of acute bronchitis at his home, 155 Chiltern Court, Baker Street, London, on 16 January 1954. A thanksgiving service was held at All Souls on 22 January.

J. C. DAGNALL

Sources J. C. Dagnall, 'E. G. V. Runting — "Old Chiro" — and the first society', *British Chiropody Journal*, 22 (1957), 9–14 · J. C. Dagnall, 'A history of chiropody-podiatry and foot care', *British Journal of Chiropody*, 48 (1983), 137–83 · J. C. Dagnall, 'The London Foot Hospital, 1913–1988: an outline history', *British Journal of Chiropody*, 53 (1988), 185–99 · J. C. Dagnall, 'The origins of the Society of Chiropodists and Podiatrists and its history, 1945 to 1995', *Journal of British Podiatric Medicine*, 50 (1995), 135–41, 151–6, 174–81 · *The Chiropodist*, 9 (1954), 43–44 · 'Mrs Runting's death', *The Chiropodist*, 19 (1932), 155 · The rector's letter, Feb 1954, All Souls Church, London · letters from Miss M. C. Virgo Runting, 1954–61, to F. Paul French, collection of J. C. Dagnall · private information (2004) [M. R. Witting] · b. cert. · d. cert. · d. cert. [Fanny Runting] · d. cert. [Mabel Runting] · m. cert. [William and Fanny Runting]
Archives London Foot Hospital, MSS · priv. coll., material illustrating the development of chiropody, books, and journals · Society of Chiropodists and Podiatrists, London, MSS
Likenesses photographs, priv. coll. · portrait, London Foot Hospital
Wealth at death £2725 6s. 7d.: probate, 26 Feb 1954, CGPLA Eng. & Wales

Rupert, prince and count palatine of the Rhine and duke of Cumberland (1619–1682), royalist army and naval officer, was born on 18 December 1619 NS, the son of Frederick V (1596–1632), elector palatine of the Rhine, and his wife, *Elizabeth (1596–1662), the daughter of James VI and I of Great Britain. He was born in Prague, where his parents were in residence as the king and queen of Bohemia, and was baptized in the palace chapel on 31 March 1620 NS. The name given to him reflected the ambitions of his family, for the only elector palatine to be elected to the imperial crown of Germany had been a Rupert, two centuries before. In 1618 the Bohemian estates had invited the Calvinist elector to accept a crown normally reserved for the heir of the Austrian Habsburgs. Despite the opposition or inactivity of fellow protestants, many Lutheran rather than Calvinist, and including Elizabeth's cautious father, Frederick consented. Within a year, however, his

Rupert, prince and count palatine of the Rhine and duke of Cumberland (1619–1682), by Sir Peter Lely, c.1665–6

supporters were defeated by the Habsburg forces at the battle of the White Mountain (November 1620), and in the confusion of the family's flight from Prague the new baby was almost left behind. He was thrown into the boot of the departing coach at the last moment.

Exile and early military career The Rhine palatinate, with its capital of Heidelberg, was one of the richest and most cultivated principalities within the empire, and its ruler—known then in England as the palsgrave—the prime elector of Germany. The loss of the Bohemian throne was followed by the military conquest of the Rhine electorate by the allies of the Habsburgs. The exiled palatines, among the earliest victims of what was to become known as the Thirty Years' War, found sanctuary in The Hague, at the court of the prince of Orange, Frederick Henry. There Rupert was brought up with his many siblings. His eldest brother drowned in 1629, his father died three years later, and Rupert found himself second in line to his brother, the new elector, *Charles Lewis. These tragic events aroused sympathy for Elizabeth, the celebrated 'queen of Hearts' of the English court before her marriage, still styled queen of Bohemia by protestant Europe; her household remained at the centre of much diplomatic and occasional military activity thereafter.

Frederick, even in less tragic circumstances, had been a chilly, morose, and ungracious man, often an embarrassment to his courtiers, but his wife was, like her father, clever, vivacious, spendthrift, and a reckless, untiring hunter. The children shared these differing characteristics in varying proportions. To them their mother was an adored but distant figure. She had fourteen children—several died in childhood—and housed them for a time at Leiden, three days' journey from The Hague. She viewed them dispassionately, showing greater concern for her even more numerous pet monkeys and dogs. The children were brought up in a harsh atmosphere of family illnesses and deaths, political crises, looming poverty, and continual disappointment. The family was dependent on the generosity not only of the house of Orange but also of the English government—Elizabeth's brother *Charles I provided a pension of £20,000 a year. The wealthy and eccentric Sir William Craven, a follower of the queen who aspired to be a soldier and courtier, subsidized them on occasion.

Despite these handicaps and the stiff formality of the court the children contrived to enjoy themselves. They were talented and boisterous, none more so than Rupert. Even his mother remarked on Rupert's angelic appearance, so much at variance with his wayward conduct. Badly behaved, headstrong, and impetuous, he acquired the family nickname Robert le diable (Robert the devil). He may have inherited his ungovernable temper from his maternal grandfather. But he was an infant prodigy: at an early age he had mastered all the major European languages, and had precociously developed musical and artistic tastes. He and his sister Louise learned from the Utrecht painter Gerrit van Honthorst, who lived in the household and portrayed the family members frequently. A good mathematician as well as linguist, Rupert was keenly interested in all things military. It was said that among his tutors in these years was the leading English soldier Sir Jacob Astley, also of the household. At the age of eighteen Rupert was over 6 feet tall, and according to his sister was blessed with a double portion of good health and physical stamina.

As well as money, Charles I offered hospitality to Charles Lewis and Rupert. They arrived in England in 1636 and were feted everywhere, visiting Oxford for a student play, receiving honorary MAs, and having their portraits painted by Van Dyck. Of practical help to recover their patrimony they received only vague promises of English aid, and the advice to have 'a little patience' (Bromley, 297). Rupert in particular, apparently suppressing his natural moroseness better than his brother, was much admired. As well as being tall and strong, he was handsome and athletic, an excellent tennis player, and an accomplished dancer. He dressed well, even fashionably. Charles Lewis, a cautious young man, deplored the energetic way his younger brother played tennis, which made him sweat. It confirmed the view that whatever Rupert did he did to extremes.

Many vied to gain Rupert's attention and win his support. A plan to mount an expedition to Madagascar, as yet uncolonized, was mooted, which would have the advantage of providing honourable employment for the prince. Thomas Howard, earl of Arundel, who had led an embassy to Vienna to plead the palatines' cause, acted as patron. Rupert was enthusiastic, but his mother was more realistic: she termed it his 'romance of Madagascar', and

quashed the plan (CSP dom., 1636–7, 559). It was strongly felt he should marry, and a wealthy Huguenot noblewoman, heir of the duc de Rohan, France's leading protestant nobleman, was suggested. But Rupert spurned this match. He was also targeted by Charles's queen, Henrietta Maria, as a likely convert to Roman Catholicism. The church was regaining territory and minds at this time, particularly in ruling circles, and Elizabeth feared that her son would succumb—a potential political blow of great consequence for such a high-profile protestant family. Later four of Rupert's siblings would embrace the old religion, so her fears were justified. She recalled him in the winter of 1636–7, perhaps for that reason.

Rupert rejoined his brother in March 1637, but they stayed in England for only a further three months, before Elizabeth, advised by Archbishop Laud among others, found more suitable employment for both Rupert and *Maurice, his next younger brother. She had no illusions but that they would have to carve out a career for themselves at the point of a sword. Even in his teens Rupert had gone campaigning with the prince of Orange's army. He had already met some of the leading British soldiers of fortune, such as George Goring, serving in the Netherlands. Now in the autumn of 1637 he showed his mettle at the siege of Breda. The following year with English volunteers, money, and ships the elector landed in north Germany, near Bremen, close to the Dutch border, in a move which it was hoped would bring pressure on the emperor. But he had omitted to co-ordinate his campaign with the Swedish or Dutch forces in the area, and his little army was soon overwhelmed by the imperialists, between Lemgo and Vlotho on the River Weser in October. Charles Lewis narrowly escaped but Rupert was captured.

For almost three years, 1639–41, Rupert was held a prisoner in the castle at Linz, in Austria, on the Danube. At first he suffered hard usage but the visiting Archduke Leopold, the emperor's brother, befriended him and bettered his condition. His imperial guardians worked hard to persuade him to change sides, convert to Rome, and otherwise ease his captivity. His mother again feared for him: 'I wish him rather dead then in his ennemies hands' (Letters of Elizabeth, Queen of Bohemia, 110). But, for a twenty-year-old, Rupert showed strength of character and was able to assure his mother of his steadfastness to the cause. Instead he set himself to study the theory of war, interested himself in gunnery—the start of a lifelong passion—took up the art of engraving, and acquired the rare white poodle Boye, given to him by the earl of Arundel. The diplomatic efforts of his uncle, Charles I, at Vienna eventually secured his release in October 1641, on the promise that he would not again take up arms against the empire.

Rupert did not remain long with the family at The Hague. His thoughts turned again to England, no longer a haven of peace in war-torn Europe. It was rumoured early in 1642 that he might gain a command in the army to be raised by the Long Parliament to be sent to Ireland, where the rising of the Catholic Irish had broken out. In February he sailed to Dover but, meeting the queen about to depart for the Netherlands, was advised to journey back with her. The king no doubt thought that the presence of his hot-headed young nephew would harm his fragile political position. But with Henrietta Maria and her daughter, Mary, the bride of the stadholder's son, at The Hague, the recruitment of money, men, and armaments for a coming civil war in England proceeded apace. Rupert and his brother Maurice set sail, with a large entourage of British and foreign soldiers and military experts, for the north of England, and reached the king, who had raised his standard at Nottingham, in August.

Cavalry commander: Edgehill and Brentford, 1642 Rupert was now unreservedly welcomed by the king and his supporters, working hard to build an army in the more favourable political climate of summer 1642. The Order of the Garter was conferred on him, and he was immediately commissioned by the king to command the cavalry. Henrietta Maria had warned her husband that the prince, despite the good impression he had made at Whitehall earlier, was 'very young and self-willed' (C. Oman, *Elizabeth of Bohemia*, 1938, 351). But Charles was a dynast, a believer in the importance of family ties, and shared to the full the contemporary association of high birth with natural authority, especially in military command, and with natural ability. Rupert's closeness to the king would ensure his loyalty. Despite his years he was a fully trained professional soldier, well known and respected by the many British and foreign volunteers who now flocked from the Netherlands and Germany to the royal banner.

If the cavaliers around the king viewed Rupert as a great catch—in the same way that their opponents delighted in the appointment of a great aristocrat, Robert Devereux, earl of Essex, to command their forces—his mother and his elder brother were dismayed. Charles Lewis was in London and, ever cautious, had remained on good terms with the Long Parliament. It controlled, along with all the king's other revenues and expenditure, the subsidy to the elector's family. Advised by their correspondent in London, the MP Sir Thomas Roe ('honest fat Tom' to the queen of Bohemia), they issued a declaration deploring the conduct of Rupert and Maurice, and expressing their wish to reconcile both sides. Thereafter the elector would give tacit support to the Long Parliament, continue to receive his pension, and occasionally be viewed as the Stuarts' reversionary interest if the main line should fail or be politically proscribed.

Whatever the view of his family and his opponents, Rupert's appointment had an electrifying effect on the morale of his supporters. Richly attired—the prince was 'always very sparkish in his dress' (Scott, *Rupert*, 74)—and superbly mounted on a charger, he cut an impressive figure. As Sir Philip Warwick, the herald and an eyewitness, put it: 'Of so great virtue is the personall courage and example of one great commander … he put that spirit into the King's Army that all men seemed resolv'd' (P. Warwick, *Memoires of the Reigne of King Charles I*, 1701, 226–8). In the pike-and-musket era the individual general led from the front and his pay reflected his value: 300 times that of the common soldier. His headquarters was small (Rupert had only sixteen staff officers, with fifty-two horses at their disposal), and the line of command was simple and direct. Such primitive arrangements meant that the army commander had also to be a military entrepreneur, constantly bargaining for scarce supplies and pacifying—or harshly disciplining—his men. But a favoured prince like Rupert or his brother could also enjoy wide powers of patronage: of appointing and promoting their own nominees, commissioning regiments, creating semi-independent satrapies, and making deals with civilian authorities.

Rupert was in a special position from the beginning. Charles's favour to his nephew extended to the powers conferred by his command of the horse. Rupert was to obey the lord-general of the army, Robert Bertie, earl of Lindsey, and orders from the council of war which the king had created, but also 'to advise as you shall think fit' (Scott, *Rupert*, 61). The most active, youthful, and talented of the king's followers flocked to take service with their most glamorous and independent leader. Another young gifted soldier, of Anglo-Irish background, Henry Wilmot, was appointed his second-in-command. Within a few weeks the cavalry arm was 2500 strong, in an army of 12,500, and remained thereafter the hard core of the royalists' fighting machine. Rupert's reputation, already high, was further raised when he fell on a reconnoitring party of roundhead horse near Worcester, and destroyed it. The morale of Essex's army dropped correspondingly. Before the first set-piece battle of the war, Edgehill, 23 October 1642, he quarrelled with Lindsey over the elderly peer's plan of attack. Lindsey had been trained many years before in the Dutch school, while Rupert had the latest ideas drawn from Swedish practice. The lord-general resigned, preferring to fight on foot alongside his men. Rupert's innovations extended to the method of engagement for the cavalry. He ordered the horse to charge 'as close as was possible, keeping their Ranks with Sword in Hand' (R. Bulstrode, *Memoirs and Reflections upon the Reign and Government of King Charles the 1ˢᵗ*, 1721, 81), rather than halt to discharge their pistols. His cavalry, although not heavily armoured (Rupert's own regiment, seven troops strong at Edgehill, was one of cuirassiers), would rely henceforth on shock tactics, a reversion to the past in modern form. This plan worked, for both wings, sweeping down the slopes of Edgehill, scattered their opponents, plundered the baggage train, and captured Essex's guns and even his coach. But neither could be brought back to help the hard-pressed foot in the centre of the field, which suffered great losses. The battle ended inconclusively, although the king's men were at the end of the day between Essex and his London base, and Rupert may well have advocated a rapid march on the capital, to be overruled by wiser—or more cautious—politicians in council. But it showed that the king had a war-winning element in his cavalry, described by one eyewitness as 'the greatest pillar' of his army (Davies, 43).

Nevertheless, Essex's much-mauled forces got back in time to block—with the massive reinforcement provided by the London trained bands—the great west road to London at Turnham Green on 13 November 1642. While the king received ambassadors for peace from parliament, Rupert had broken through and destroyed the regiment guarding the Thames at Brentford. The supposed treachery of this action, its bloodiness, and the general terror inspired by Rupert, help to explain Londoners' determined resistance. Already press and pulpit in the capital were ringing with denunciations of the prince. Printed propaganda, on the scale now displayed, was new and unfamiliar in England, and all the more effective for that reason. Rupert was a convenient hate figure for the popular press, which enthusiastically depicted him throughout the war as 'Prince Robber', a German mercenary, a callous freebooter, and a betrayer of the protestant cause.

The campaigns of 1643 The royal army withdrew to Oxford, which became for almost four years the king's capital. The cavalry was dispersed around the Berkshire and Oxfordshire villages: Rupert chose Abingdon as his headquarters, while taking quarters himself in St John's College, Oxford, at least for a time. The king had set up a council of war, of his leading advisers and military men, which accompanied him on campaign but otherwise met frequently at Christ Church. Both Rupert and Maurice were members of it. Rupert attended most meetings when he was with the king at Oxford or in the main army—twenty-four of the fifty-two with recorded membership. He was, however, often distant with his own forces until November 1644 when he was made supreme commander, and tensions would mount when decisions made in council conflicted with his own wishes. From the start he did not like or trust his deputy, Henry Wilmot. Nor did his uncle, devoted though he was to Rupert's interests, always take the advice offered either by the prince or council. Beset by clamorous lobbyists, agents of foreign powers, and offers of help from various quarters, the king often relied on differing small and secret groups of advisers, or his own or his wife's judgement alone, the resulting action on occasion carried out clandestinely by his household servants.

In the first winter of the war, while a ring of defensive garrisons and strongholds was created round Oxford, Rupert worked tirelessly at mundane tasks. He turned out to be not only a brilliant cavalry leader, but also hardworking, abstemious, and a meticulous organizer with an eye for detail. He exercised the horse, expanded their quarters, and probed the enemy positions in Buckinghamshire and Berkshire. To the west there was a solid block of hostile territory based on the parliamentarian control of the county towns, especially the second city of the realm, Bristol. But Sir Ralph Hopton, a follower of the queen of Bohemia in his youth, was building up a strong force for the king in Cornwall, which would prove the roundhead hegemony of the west country vulnerable. In the north William Cavendish, earl of Newcastle, was putting together a powerful alliance for the king, and in February Queen Henrietta Maria herself, with much needed supplies from the continent, landed in Yorkshire. Even the allegiance of London to the parliamentarian cause

seemed doubtful at this time, and the king promoted several 'fine designs' to exploit this. Only shortage of arms and munitions at Oxford, until the queen's train arrived in May 1643, prevented bolder strategies being pursued.

The initiative until then was taken by Rupert and the horse. There was almost a personal duel with the most active general on the other side, Sir William Waller, to take towns and territory. Maurice was sent to the west to contain his activities. Rupert's main task was to clear the lines between Newcastle's advancing forces, or at least the queen's little army with its abundant supplies, and Oxford. He first rescued a parlous situation in the west midlands by raising the siege of Lichfield, then sacked Birmingham. He raided into parliamentarian quarters in Buckinghamshire, an incursion that failed of its purpose—the capture of an enemy convoy of money—but had an important result, the death of the opposing commander, John Hampden. He met the queen at Stratford upon Avon later in June, and accompanied her to a meeting with the king on the battlefield of Edgehill on 13 July 1643. Oxford's armouries were now more adequately stocked.

Waller's army was finally routed at Roundway Down on the same day. Hopton's Cornish foot had fought its way out of Cornwall and linked with elements of the Oxford horse under Prince Maurice and William Seymour, Lord Hertford, the nominal commander in the west, to score this decisive victory. It paved the way for an outright attack on Bristol and Gloucester, all the easier because Essex, despite his success in capturing Reading, was immobilized in the Thames valley by sickness and discontent in his army. Rupert called up the main force of infantry from Oxford, placed the Cornish under Hopton and his brother on the south side of Bristol, and began a ferocious assault on 26 July. His stormtroopers used firepikes to terrify the defenders, and a breach was made on the northern line. The city was vulnerable, with a long and undulating defensive line, thinly manned. While the marshy conditions on the south side, and a shortage of adequate scaling ladders, frustrated the Cornish attack, the parliamentarian governor had no option but to surrender. Rupert had been foremost in the taking of a regional capital, second only to London, and a major port for overseas supplies.

Rupert had earlier pressed the king for independent command for his brother Maurice, and was irked that the latter had been subordinated to Hertford in the recent campaign. When the peer claimed the right to appoint the governor of Bristol (he nominated Hopton), the prince objected. With the merger of the two armies Maurice would lose status, reverting to the command of his own regiment only. The solution was to make Rupert himself governor, with Hopton his deputy, and remove Hertford to Oxford. The prince took over a strong regiment of foot, his bluecoats, to add to the Bristol garrison. Maurice was therefore released to follow up the capture of Bristol with the conquest of most of Dorset and Devon.

In the consolidation and expansion of royalist territory that marked the success of the king at this stage of the war the city of Gloucester presented a major obstacle. Rupert was probably not the main influence on the decision to besiege it; lengthy sieges were a matter for the infantry and artillery. But the prince and the horse were blamed in some quarters for failing to stop Essex, with a new army recruited in London, marching to its relief across the Cotswolds, good cavalry country. The siege was raised on 5 September 1643. Rupert was successful, by a lightning attack on some of Essex's horse, in delaying their homeward journey. The royal forces were able to take up a strong position at Newbury, through which Essex had to pass. At the battle that followed (20 September 1643) his tired and straitened army fought at a disadvantage, extricating itself with difficulty to regain the London road. The City trained bands of foot played an important role in standing firm against the fierce onslaught of Rupert's cavalry.

Despite the setback at Gloucester, and the indecisive nature of the battle of Newbury, the cavaliers remained strong and confident, not least in their mounted arm. While Hopton advanced through Hampshire, Newcastle moved on Hull, and Maurice was ordered to besiege Plymouth, Rupert was commissioned on 28 October to take command of forces to be raised in the counties of the eastern association, the heartland of the opposition. This was an ambitious objective, and it soon came to a halt. Rupert was repulsed before Aylesbury, where George Digby, the king's secretary of state, had promised that the governor was ready to open the gates to him. The blood of Rupert's men left in the snow, in January 1644, was a warning not to trust all of the secretary's many projects. The royalists were forced on the defensive. The entry of the Scots into the war, on the side of parliament, Newcastle's defeat by the Yorkshire forces under Ferdinando Fairfax, Lord Fairfax, at Winceby, and Maurice's failure before Plymouth darkened the prospects for the king in early 1644.

Newark and Marston Moor, 1644 Charles continued to place his faith in Rupert. When an assembly of the king's supporters among MPs, a counter-parliament to that at Westminster, was summoned in the new year, Charles raised his nephew to the English peerage as earl of Holderness and duke of Cumberland, on 24 January 1644. There is no evidence that Rupert sat in the upper house that met at Oxford in the weeks following, but his new title allowed London propagandists to open a fresh line of attack on the prince as 'duke of Plunderland'. Instead he was posted to Wales, vital to royalist recruitment. On 5 February he was appointed president of Wales, a title which had lapsed with the abolition of the council of Wales before the civil war. His post cut across the existing command structure, was bitterly resented by the generals on the spot, and does not appear to have been fully implemented. But the king assured his nephew that 'I meane not to trust you by halfes' (Day, 4). Based at Shrewsbury for most of March–May 1644, the prince revived royalist fortunes in a crucial area. He inspected garrisons and fortresses from north Wales to Ashby-de-la-Zouch, aiding John Byron, Lord Byron, at Chester, replacing local worthies with professional soldiers, and raising military taxation.

The increasing pressure on royalist territory north of the Trent had resulted in a threat to Newark, one of the key points in their control of the region. Rupert was ordered to relieve the town on 12 March 1644. With what scratch units he could gather from surrounding garrisons and by means of forced marches (the last one at night) he surprised and divided the besieging force under the veteran Scottish soldier Sir John Meldrum. In the mêlée that followed he was surrounded by enemy horsemen and nearly killed. But Meldrum surrendered on humiliating terms, even abandoning all his guns. Newark survived as a royal stronghold for another two years. The king himself congratulated Rupert on this spectacular feat of arms; it was, he declared, 'no less than the saving of all the north' (Warburton, 2.397). Supplies that had previously been diverted to other theatres of war were now made available to the prince, whose success was the one bright spot in the encircling gloom. He persuaded the king and the high command to field a mainly cavalry force for the summer's campaign and remain on the defensive in the south with the foot in strengthened garrisons. But no sooner had he returned to Shrewsbury than this plan was reversed, and Essex and Waller were able to invade Oxford-controlled areas, and threaten the royal capital itself.

The contradictions apparent in the official responses to the prince's activities and advice at this stage of the war reflected his strengths and weaknesses, and those of the high command. The royalist council of war was an uneasy mixture of soldiers and politicians: it was quickly divided into factions, and the perennial scarcity of military resources led to fierce competition. For his part, Rupert made a unique contribution of discord to this dismal scene. His virtues—courage and daring, great energy, and drive, especially in the field, combined with good organizational powers and a meticulous grasp of detail—were not effective in the council chamber. Clarendon's verdict is well known: 'The prince was rough and passionate, and loved not debate; liked what was proposed as he liked the persons who proposed it' (Clarendon, *Hist. rebellion*, 3.443). He was 'so great an enemy' (ibid.) to the two most influential in council, George Digby (an erstwhile follower, now alienated) and Sir John Colepeper, that deadlock resulted. Ignorant of British politics and personalities, he could not win over those of a contrary view. He blamed any shortcomings in the execution of his plans on personal deficiencies or political hostility. His later naval career was marked by the same impatience with officialdom and rival commanders or subordinates.

Rupert had now to turn his attention to the north. The Scottish advance had penned Newcastle into the city of York, and the northern horse under George Goring, Lord Goring, had been worsted by Lord Fairfax and his son Sir Thomas at Selby. The king's chief supporter in Lancashire, James Stanley, earl of Derby, pleaded with Rupert to rescue his wife, besieged in Lathom House, but as he crossed the Mersey Rupert heard strong rumours that some courtiers and generals at Oxford were plotting against him. Some, it was said, were indifferent whether the prince or the Scots prevailed that summer. For a few days it was uncertain whether—in his anger and frustration—he would continue his march or resign his commission. In the end he pressed on with his mission, but no doubt was ready to back any scheme that would topple his known enemies at court.

Lancashire royalism, quelled since the beginning of the war, was revived by the triumphant progress of the prince's army in May 1644. Fighting on foot at the head of his troops he stormed Bolton and put many to the sword. He captured Liverpool, weakly defended, and relieved Lathom. With Derby's assistance he recruited his army, especially the foot. He was now in a better position to achieve his objectives. But what were these? He received an important letter that the king and some of his councillors had jointly penned on 14 June, urging him in uncompromising terms to relieve York: 'if York be lost I shall esteem my crown little less'. To avert this calamity the prince must, furthermore, 'beat the rebels' army of both kingdoms, which are before it' (Warburton, 2.437–9). The king had just, with difficulty, eluded the clutches of Essex and Waller, and his letter was panicky and confused. But it was, however interpreted, a direct command of a kind that he had never sent his nephew before.

Rupert crossed the Pennines at the head of 7000 horse, after Goring's men had joined him, and as many foot. Skilfully avoiding the much larger number of English and Scottish forces that had maintained a close siege for ten weeks, he crossed the Ouse north of York and entered the city on 1 July. The besiegers hurriedly decamped westwards and Rupert—no doubt mindful of the king's letter—followed. Late on 2 July the allied generals turned on their pursuers. The garrison of York scarcely had time to join Rupert on the field of Marston Moor when the battle began. In the course of two hours of a thundery summer evening the biggest and bloodiest encounter of the civil war was fought, with the outcome so uncertain that most of the generals on both sides had abandoned the stricken field by the end. Goring had swept all before him, on one wing. But Oliver Cromwell, christened Old Ironsides by Rupert, had controlled the parliamentarian left wing, and eventually borne back the opposing cavalry, which had stood for a long time 'like an iron wall' (P. Young, *Marston Moor*, 1970, 129). Despite severe casualties, including his favourite bitch, Boye, most of Rupert's men escaped, the prince hiding for a time, it was said, in a beanfield; but Newcastle's foot was taken or killed to a man. It was a prime disaster for the royalist cause: York surrendered within two weeks, and the north was lost.

Captain-general, 1644–1645 Yet the first consequences of Marston Moor were not as unfavourable to Rupert or the royal cause as the king had predicted. The prince brought his still substantial body of cavalry to bolster a shaky position in the south, though not in time to assist the main army at the second battle of Newbury (27 October 1644). There the king, faced by the combined strength of three armies, had been fortunate to survive but had extricated himself, his army, and his guns with great skill. The summer's campaign had not been fruitless; the infantry of Essex's army had been cornered in Cornwall and forced to surrender en bloc. At the same time Rupert's enemies, Wilmot and Henry Percy, Lord Percy, blamed by the prince, probably unfairly, for withholding supplies of arms, had been dismissed the service. The part that he himself played in this coup, unpopular with the officers of the 'old horse' regiments (the first twenty raised), is unclear. He consented, however, to the replacement of Wilmot with Goring. This cleared the way for the king to promote his nephew to supreme command. Under the nominal suzerainty of the fifteen-year-old prince of Wales, Rupert was appointed captain-general of all forces in England and Wales, on 7 November (confirmed on 30 November) 1644.

Patrick Ruthven, Lord Forth, the previous commander-in-chief, was old and deaf, and a younger man was needed. The king had created a separate council for the war in the west, also nominally under the prince of Wales, which removed from Oxford and the main army several politicians and soldiers unfriendly to Rupert, including Hyde, Colepeper, and Hopton. Nevertheless Rupert's promotion, described by Hyde sourly as 'no popular change', was controversial (Clarendon, *Hist. rebellion*, 3.443). It reinforced the charge of nepotism at court. 'The malice of some to the prince' in the summer seemed to be justified by his loss of the north; his brother's failure to take the small port of Lyme was added to the charge against the palatines (Carte, 1.58–60). And it was, typically, accompanied by dissension, for the new captain-general was initially denied the command of the guards, the small, socially exclusive, body of cavalry closest to the king. The prince resented this omission. Rupert also suspected, with reason, that the creation of a separate command structure for the west, involving Goring, the hero of Marston Moor, under the aegis of the new council at Bristol, was to act as 'a counterpoise' to the Oxford army.

In the winter months Rupert worked hard to rebuild the royalist war effort after the setbacks of the summer. There was much to do. The exorbitant demands of the royalists had provoked an armed response in some areas, such as the Clubmen in the Welsh borders. Desertion from existing units was rife, and even some of Rupert's own regiment of horse were reported 'straggling' in Somerset. He had local as well as national authority in several key areas. He was governor of Bristol and president of Wales, and his brother Maurice was made lieutenant-general in Wales and the marches. With characteristic energy, determination, and ruthlessness Rupert repeated his round of inspections of garrisons, fortifications, and centres of arms production, supplying deficiencies and conscripting thousands to replace the runaways. He promoted his own followers, often young career soldiers, rough but effective and with few local ties, in place of any remaining civilian officials or gentry commanders who had proved incompetent. Some were popular and successful, such as William Legge, governor of Oxford; others harsh and unacceptable, like Charles Gerard in south Wales. Viewing Charles's inflated entourage as redundant (and hostile to himself), he asked Legge to 'desire the King to bring as few scullions and beefeaters with him' on the coming campaign (Warburton, 3.73).

Naseby, the fall of Bristol, and court martial, 1645 In April 1645 the king conferred on his nephew the honorific title of master of the horse, and at last (after a six-month delay) gave him command of the guards. Unimportant in themselves, these actions seemed to confirm a trend. 'All is governed by P. Rupert, who grows a great courtier … Certainly the Lord Digby loves him not', reported an agent at Oxford (Carte, 1.90). In refashioning the crown's military machine, and removing some of his rivals, the prince made enemies. The chief of these was the secretary, still close to the king at Oxford and in the field. Both in effect headed rival parties, which supplied each with damaging information about the other. When at last the army was ready for the summer campaign, in May, and about to face its biggest test, the New Model Army just created under the able command of Sir Thomas Fairfax, the counsels of the king were bitterly divided. It is probable that Rupert, intent on marching to the relief of Chester and possibly regaining the north (and the reputation dented at Marston Moor), did not want immediately to challenge the larger parliamentarian force. Goring's western army, and Gerard's force in south Wales, were still distant. While the royalist cavalry continued to be (at over half the total) the dominant element in the main army, Rupert commanded only 9000 men against Fairfax's force of 14,500. But the two sides collided in Northamptonshire just north of the village of Naseby, and battle was joined the next day, 14 June 1645.

Rupert took the initiative by advancing his whole force across the broad moor that separated the two armies. He fought with the right wing of horse and, as in so many earlier encounters, his massed ranks, in close order, broke through their opponents' lines, in this case General Henry Ireton's horse, but only after intense hand-to-hand fighting. On the other wing the remnants of the northern horse, whole regiments reduced to the size of troops, and discontented with their continued absence from home, were no match for Cromwell's cavalry, which had greater discipline, higher morale, and weight of numbers on its side. The well-led and veteran royalist foot in the centre fought valiantly but in the end were borne down by the combined infantry and cavalry of the New Model. Most were captured, the rest killed. The king was willing to lead a final charge, but was dissuaded; his coach and secret papers were taken. Rupert's men fled to Bristol, Charles and his court to south Wales.

Recriminations followed, eagerly embraced by the two parties that divided the high command. While the king, with Digby in attendance, vainly attempted to recruit a new army in Wales, Rupert was, for the first time in his civil war career, inactive, even defeatist. He was no doubt disillusioned by the publication of the king's secret correspondence with Irish parties and foreign powers. He had seen the quality of the New Model at first hand: once it had defeated Goring's army (10 July 1645) no other royalist force could withstand it. Bristol, the city he governed, was

an empty shell, devastated by plague and economic catastrophe. He spent his time, it was said, dallying with the young and beautiful Mary Stuart, duchess of Richmond, the wife of his best friend at court. He wrote to her husband James to remonstrate with the king, that he 'hath no way left to preserve his posterity, kingdom and nobility, but by a treaty' (Warburton, 3.149). This was an entirely reasonable assessment, reflecting the view of many of the king's leading supporters, whose estates were being wasted by the prolonging of the war. It was also the view of a soldier of fortune who saw no point in continuing an unprofitable struggle, and wished to fight another day.

The king rejected the advice proffered, and Digby was able to exploit the first doubts his sovereign now had about the loyalty of his nephew. The secretary blamed Rupert for abusing the supreme power he had gained. The crown, he wrote, had been 'absolutely given away' to him (BL, Add. MS 33596, fols. 9–12). Rumour-mongers at Oxford, London, and the queen's court at Paris feverishly speculated that Rupert was plotting with his elder brother, the elector palatine—prominent in the capital as an ally of the Long Parliament—the replacement of the senior line of the Stuarts with the German branch. These fears seemed confirmed when, on the assault of Bristol by the New Model, Rupert surrendered the city on 10 September. 'Clad in scarlet, very richly laid in silver lace, and mounted upon a very gallant black Barbary horse', he was shown every respect by Fairfax and Cromwell, and reciprocated this feeling. He saw what a formidable fighting force parliament had created, and told his captors he would persuade the king to 'a happy peace' (Scott, *Rupert*, 182–3). For his part, however, Charles, believing that Rupert had been capable of saving Bristol, was outraged by his nephew's action. Prompted by the secretary he saw an international conspiracy to betray his cause. He dismissed Rupert; and his followers, Maurice, Legge, Gerard, and the rest of the prince's nominees, were either cashiered or resigned in sympathy. The king ordered his nephews to depart the realm.

But the drama was not over. Gathering some 200 followers the two princes sought justice and satisfaction from the king at Newark. Digby fled to the north, in the hope of joining James Graham, marquess of Montrose, hitherto successful in Scotland. A court martial at Newark, hastily constituted, cleared Rupert of treason but not of 'indiscretion', and in a famous scene the aggrieved former generals confronted Charles and gave vent to their pent-up rage, but went away empty-handed. For them the war was over. When, by December, no proof of any conspiracy was produced, the king was reconciled to his nephew at Oxford, through the good offices of Legge. Rupert, however, heartily disapproved of the king's negotiations with the Scottish covenanters, and opposed his secret journey to the Scottish army. He and Maurice took advantage of the terms for the surrender of Oxford to Fairfax (20 June 1646) to slip out of England. Rupert sailed to France; his brother returned to the Netherlands. The most important chapter of his life was ended. Since his first arrival in England in August 1642 Rupert had occupied the highest military offices the king could bestow; he had given life to the war effort in all parts of the realm; and he had campaigned unceasingly throughout the seasons, in which, the journal of his marches reveals, he had ridden 5750 miles. His reward, for the moment, was exile and penury.

Rupert was well received at the French court and its appendage, the household of Henrietta Maria at St Germain, to which the prince of Wales had now fled. King Charles had written to his wife to welcome him, in August 1646: 'for albeit his passions may sometimes make him mistake, yet I am confident of his honest constancy and courage, having at last behaved himself very well' (J. Bruce, ed., *Charles I in 1646*, CS, 63, 1856, 58). The French queen regent and Cardinal Mazarin appointed him a *maréchal de champ* and commander of the English in French service. In this role he joined the French marshal Gassion, on the north-east frontier, where he faced a strong Spanish force which included Lord Goring and many English. The skirmishing on the border was inconclusive, but during one episode the prince was shot in the head, a wound which troubled him later. He returned to St Germain in September 1647.

The little court of the exiled Prince Charles was wracked by quarrels. In the misery, poverty, and enforced leisure of their defeated state the cavaliers sought to settle old scores, blaming each other for the collapse of their cause. As well as the continuation of the disputes that had marked the later stages of the civil war, there was plenty of new combustible material. The leading participants circulated in manuscript or in print justifications of their actions, and the secret correspondence of the king and Digby, captured and now published by their enemies, contained startling revelations of double dealing and character assassination. While still at Oxford Rupert had challenged one of the peers of the council. He now required satisfaction from Digby, above all, but the guards at court intervened and stopped the duel. He did, however, meet and wound Lord Percy. Several other aggrieved cavaliers took part in a more general mêlée, though none was killed. Later the long-running dispute with Colepeper (now Lord Colepeper) flared up in the council, then at The Hague, over one of the prince's less reputable followers. Colepeper was physically assaulted by the man, whom he had described as 'a shark'.

Naval war, 1648–1653 The prospects for the young prince of Wales were transformed early in the summer of 1648. Widespread discontent at the lack of a political settlement following the royalist defeat had led to a reaction in favour of the imprisoned king, and a Scottish invasion on his behalf. Disturbances on the Kent coast spread to the fleet, and eleven vessels sailed to the Netherlands to join the prince. There he and Rupert went aboard, to the acclamation of the sailors. It seemed likely that the appearance of this part of the parliamentarian navy at the anchorages in the Thames might threaten London's trade, overawe the capital's mercantile élite, and persuade the rest of the fleet to join them. Much of the country was aflame, the New Model Army was preoccupied, and the

Scots were on their march south. But the leadership of the revolted ships was divided over its objectives. The Scots wanted them to sail north to assist their invasion, and in any case Rupert and Maurice were politically unacceptable to them. Rupert advised a landfall on the Isle of Wight to rescue the king, who was at Carisbrooke Castle. He grew impatient at the unwillingness of Admiral William Batten, who had brought a first-rate ship of the line over to their side, to engage the enemy fleet. The forts that guarded the Downs, on which the ships depended, fell to parliamentarian sympathizers, and Rupert was forced to return to the Netherlands. The defeat of the Scots at Preston, the fall of Colchester, and the general collapse of the risings elsewhere in this second civil war confirmed their failure.

Rupert still stood high with the young Charles, who had grown up before and during the civil war to admire his glamorous and courageous cousin, and that affection was reciprocated. The court shifted to The Hague and despite the attentions of the parliamentarian fleet Rupert worked hard to prepare what remained of the revolted squadron again for the sea. He had taken an interest in naval affairs since the Madagascar project of 1636, and command at sea—where the captain 'fought' the ship and a trained seaman/master 'sailed' it—was commonly given to soldiers. He never overcame, however, his proneness to seasickness. No money was available and he had to use strong-arm methods to put down mutinies, holding one ringleader over the side of the ship until he got his way. He bargained with merchants, raised credit on his mother's jewels, and improvised as best he could, in the same energetic way as he had prepared for the campaigns of the civil war. He had the advantage that he had been granted the same extensive command as then. He and his brother, however, were still excluded from participation in any future Scottish alliance (Rupert was friendly to Montrose, not the presbyterian leadership).

Instead Ireland was thought to offer better prospects. There James Butler, marquess of Ormond, was struggling to defend royal interests against several warring parties. In January 1649 Rupert and Maurice sailed with eight ships to Kinsale, intent chiefly on maintaining themselves by commerce raiding. In this they were so successful that marine insurance rates in London increased by 400 per cent. They were incapable of aiding Ormond in Dublin, however, and the conquest of much of Ireland by Cromwell's army after August, especially the city of Cork's change of allegiance, made their position precarious. They managed to evade Robert Blake's fleet and set sail for Portugal, whose king, like most crowned heads, had expressed sympathy for the royal cause on the execution of Charles I. They arrived at the mouth of the Tagus in November 1649.

At first the little fleet was well received by the king in Lisbon. Rupert was able to sell prize goods and buy supplies locally. But the arrival of Blake's powerful flotilla and a diplomatic representative from the new English Commonwealth changed attitudes: the Lisbon government feared for its overseas trade. A strongly worded declaration by the prince against parliament provoked the English envoy to describe Rupert as 'this Vagabond Jerman, a Prince of Fortune … his Principality meere piracye … cudgelled out of England from his trade of plundering' (Gardiner, 18). He was prevented by Blake from leaving the Tagus on more than one occasion but eventually eluded him and made for the Mediterranean in September 1650.

Without a base on the Atlantic or Mediterranean coasts, a regular source of income, or even much accreditation in the form of letters of marque from a recognized power, Rupert's sea adventures thereafter were construed by most nations and their merchants as 'mere piracy'. His ships preyed on English merchantmen in Spanish ports, and on Spanish ships as those of a country allied to the English Commonwealth. Even governments hostile to the new republic feared reprisals, as the Portuguese had done, if they harboured a pirate presence, for the Rump was strengthening the navy and exerting its power. Many of its new admirals were highly competent and experienced, veterans of the New Model Army. Faced with such difficulties one of Rupert's captains lamented: 'We plough the sea for a subsistence, and, being destitute of a port, we take the confines of the Mediterranean Sea for our harbour; poverty and despair being companions, and revenge our guide' (Warburton, 3.313). 'Robert le diable' was a suitable leader of such an expedition.

For twenty months the flotilla, harried by Blake's powerful squadron, scoured the shipping lanes for prizes to sustain its activities. In November 1650 at Cartagena it was able, by selling or pawning some of its valuable bronze cannon, to refit one or two ships and replace others. It called at Malaga in the new year and bought stores at Toulon on credit in May 1651, debts outstanding years later. Rupert wanted to sail to the West Indies, where some royalists were still active and the pickings might be greater, but his crews preferred to remain close to the Azores for much of 1651. There his flagship was lost. Rupert then sailed south to pillage the west African coast. In a daring raid he rescued his close associate Robert Holmes from almost certain death, and was struck by an arrow, which he cut out of his chest himself. At last in summer 1652 he was able to cross the Atlantic, with only four ships, and prepare to attack shipping there. But the last royalist enclave, Barbados, had been extinguished and in a hurricane near the Virgin Islands, which lasted four days (13–16 September), he lost most of the fleet and his brother Maurice. In a family wracked by quarrels of all kinds Rupert's devotion and closeness to the younger brother, who had shared all dangers at his side for ten years, was remarkable, and Maurice's death was a devastating blow. Over a decade later Rupert was still seeking news of him. Only two ships returned to France in March 1653. Since first setting out from the Netherlands in 1649 Rupert had sailed 15,000 miles in 1500 days, and taken thirty-one prizes. He came back ill and exhausted: he lay sick at Nantes for some time before rejoining the court at Paris. It was a tribute to his expert seamanship (and endurance of seasickness), extraordinary stamina, and physical fitness that he had survived, when so many of his shipmates had succumbed to the perils of long sea voyages. To frequent storms at sea, rotting victuals, stagnant drinking water, scurvy and other common diseases of the sailing ship era, were added the acute dangers of a piratical career, constant fighting, mutinous crews, and fear of capture. Ironically, having avoided these obvious hazards, he nearly lost his life in the calmer waters of the Seine in June; he went for a swim and almost drowned.

Exile and wanderings, 1653–1660 Rupert's reception at court was all that could be desired, at first. Lean, dark, and weather-beaten, he cut an exotic and intriguing figure, for among his household were 'richly-liveried Blackamoors', parrots and monkeys, and—a fashionable appendage—a small negro boy (Warburton, 3.425). Although his old enemy, Lord Percy, was a dominant figure, his cousin the king, Hyde, and even the queen mother were friendly. In part the welcome of the impoverished court was inspired by the hope that the prize money he had brought—it was thought to be worth £14,000—would relieve their wants. His follower Sir Edward Herbert, despite his unsuitability for the post, was made lord keeper, and Rupert was restored to his old position of master of the horse. But the pirate treasure proved illusory, and tempers worsened. The prince had returned with only one ship and a captured prize, and both were rotten. The cannon he brought were of value, but had been pledged to bankers and the unpaid sailors. A huge quarrel ensued, which involved the king and Hyde, Mazarin and the French government, the prince and his creditors. The outcome was that neither Charles II nor Rupert benefited, for Mazarin claimed the right to sell the guns and did so at a low price. The sailors were paid but the rest of the prince's creditors were not.

The political position of the prince was not strong enough to overcome these disputes at the exiled court. His much reduced faction included such weak or disreputable creatures as Herbert, Robert Holmes, and Charles, Lord Gerard, and it was only loosely attached to the influential Louvre group around the queen mother, which would not exert itself to save him. He had the good sense not to back the wildest schemes designed to overthrow Hyde, but nevertheless found no way back to the good graces of the king. He left the court in June 1654 when it was also preparing to leave Paris for Germany. Followed by a small entourage, which included Holmes and Gerard, he was thereafter friendless, a wanderer exiled from a court itself in penurious exile.

The European situation had changed since the end of the Thirty Years' War. The treaty of Munster, 1648, had restored Rupert's elder brother, Charles Lewis, to the lower Palatinate and the electoral title, if not to the rest of his ancient domains. Rupert no doubt hoped that, travelling to Heidelberg and Vienna as a prince of the empire, he might recover some part of his inheritance. The emperor, it was said, owed him 30,000 rix dollars under the terms of the treaty, and his brother a part of the electoral territory. But Charles Lewis faced many problems, including marriage difficulties, and more pressing obligations in his ruined lands. He soon quarrelled with both his mother, perennially bankrupt, and his brother over their legacies. Despite visits to Heidelberg Rupert was refused any recompense; claims to money owed were matched by demands for return of goods allegedly taken. The prince had only the consolation of knowing that he, rather than, as before, his elder brother, was the favourite of his mother.

Rupert was equally denied compensation at the court of the emperor. He had fewer opportunities for employment even as a soldier of fortune, his enemies' former description of him. The main conflict in Germany was over, and as a prisoner of the emperor twenty years before he had given a pledge not to take up arms against him. Little is known of his activities in these years. He may have treated with Modena for a general's place in 1655, and was later in negotiations with the king of Hungary for a similar purpose. But neither of these came to anything, and even Cromwell's spies in Germany could not trace his movements for much of the time. The only fighting he saw was apparently on the Baltic coast of Germany, when he had command of an imperial expedition into Swedish Pomerania in the winter of 1659–60.

The Restoration With the triumphant return to England of his cousin Charles II in May 1660, Rupert's prospects potentially improved. Despite the quarrel of 1654 he had kept in touch with the new king, and he had a good friend at court in the person of William Legge, the most respected of his followers and newly appointed lieutenant-general of the ordnance. But Rupert arrived late, no doubt uncertain of his reception. Not until 29 September did Pepys note: 'I hear Prince Robt. is come to Court; but welcome to nobody' (Pepys, 1.255). Clearly if he was to take his place in the new regime there were problems to overcome. One was the position of his mother, Elizabeth of Bohemia, already refused permission to come to England from The Hague. Another was to find a suitable job and a means of subsistence, given his failure so far to gain his inheritance. Charles immediately provided him with an annual pension of £4000 (later increased to £6000), and in the following year consented to send him on a diplomatic mission to Vienna, as a cover for Rupert's hope of entering imperial service as a general of horse in the war against the Turks. From April to November 1661 the prince moved around European capitals but the deal—if that is what it was—fell through.

Rupert's mission accomplished something, however. Subsidized by his mother's old courtier Lord Craven he negotiated terms for her return to England. He was able to speak for the new British regime at the imperial court. He inspected the latest fortifications and recruited engineers to assist such works at home. He even found time and funds to send back a quantity of Hungarian and Rhenish wine for the royal household. What success he had was due in part to the support of the new king and the chancellor Hyde, now earl of Clarendon, obtained, probably, by Legge. The queen of Bohemia died in London in February 1662. As it was Rupert, not the Elector Charles Lewis, who inherited her collection of jewels worth £4500, a complete breach with his elder brother duly followed.

Relations with the king and his brother, James, duke of York, remained uneasy. Rupert had been accused of taking the part of James against Charles on occasion during the exile. Though the royal brothers were passionate about ships and seafaring and no doubt admired their cousin's knowledge and experience of naval affairs, Rupert in his middle age was a difficult man to like. He had the sardonic, even embittered, air of an ageing dandy and was thought to be more saturnine, severe, and short-tempered than ever. Nevertheless, on his return from Vienna he began to rise at court. In 1662 he became a privy councillor, and the following year a governor of the mines royal. He helped to gain royal patronage for a new company to trade with the west coast of Africa, the Company of Royal Adventurers of England Trading into Africa (commonly called the Royal African Company). His hopes of profits in Guinea gold and slaves were mixed with resentment at native hostility and Dutch dominance. It was natural that when a fleet was prepared to make good English claims there he was chosen admiral. He was furious when this appointment was cancelled, but his right-hand-man, Robert Holmes, went instead; the disturbances that ensued contributed to the outbreak of the Second Anglo-Dutch War in 1665.

The Second and Third Anglo-Dutch wars, 1665–1667 and 1672–1674 Rupert no doubt expected that he would play a leading role in the new war, although in October 1664, while inspecting one of his warships at Portsmouth, a block of the mainyard rigging had fallen on his head. The blow reopened the old wound in his skull made years before by a pistol shot in France. He was forced to retire for six months while doctors scarified his scalp. In January 1665 Pepys noted that Rupert had a hole in his periwig, to relieve pressure on his head. This, and the pain the prince was enduring, gave rise to rumours that he was suffering from syphilis. But, physically strong as ever, he made a partial recovery, and was ready for action shortly after war was declared in March 1665.

Rupert, James, duke of York, and Edward Montagu, earl of Sandwich, shared the command of the navy this year. The Restoration government had built on the solid foundations of sea power created in the interregnum, and Britain now had a sizeable battle fleet. The Dutch had been worsted in the first war, and had learned from their mistakes. They met the new tactics of line abreast with equal discipline and seamanship, if inferior gunnery. On 3 June 1665 they lost seventeen ships at the battle of Lowestoft, and would have lost more had the British high command not given up the chase. In a bloody encounter Rupert and James had had lucky escapes and the king decided to recall them both. Rupert rejected the king's request, in July, to share command with Sandwich.

In the following June, however, Rupert was happy to co-operate with George Monck, duke of Albemarle, another distinguished soldier turned sailor. The Dutch position this year was strengthened by their alliance with France, and it was the belief that a French squadron was sailing from Toulon to join the main Dutch fleet in the channel that prompted the two admirals to detach Rupert and twenty ships to deal with it. Monck, in consequence, fought for three days (1–3 June 1666) against a more powerful force; messages to recall Rupert did not reach him; and it was not until he heard the gunfire of the battle itself that he sailed back. Arriving on the fourth day he was in the thick of the action, forced to change his flagship three times; in the end he turned a defeat into a draw, both sides suffering great losses. Any disadvantage was reversed at the battle on St James's day, 25 July, when Albemarle and Rupert won a narrow victory.

It was while Rupert was admiral that the new 'fighting instructions' were issued, which gave authority and permanence to line abreast tactics. His hand can be detected too in the careful preparations for Robert Holmes's attack on north Holland's coastal towns and shipping ('Holmes's bonfire') in August. Although he was still viewed warily by the royal brothers, Rupert's success at sea gave him greater stature at home. With the support of James for a time he acted as the patron of several former cavalier sea-officers, matching Sandwich's promotion of old Cromwellians. Aggression on the high seas and the seizure of rival trading stations (the capture of New Amsterdam, renamed New York, at the start of the war, is wrongly attributed to Holmes) also had an impact on domestic politics, with Clarendon losing ground to courtiers and soldiers promoting the war. Among the chancellor's leading critics were some of Rupert's favourites, such as Holmes (knighted that year), Sir Frescheville Holles, and Sir Edward Spragge.

Rupert's head wound still troubled him, and to relieve the pressure on his brain he was twice trepanned by the king's doctors in February 1667. The improved method of trephining was employed and, according to Pepys, who gave a graphic description of it, the patient felt no pain. With the main fleet laid up that year he had time to convalesce, passing the time making improvements to the medical forceps used for his scalp dressing. But when in June the Dutch sailed up the Medway and destroyed or captured part of the fleet moored there, including the flagship the *Royal Charles*, the king sent for Rupert to report on and repair the defences that had proved so ineffective. He had gained popularity with his criticisms of naval administration after the 1666 campaign, and he avoided blame for the Medway disaster.

Charles II's alliance with France led to the Third Anglo-Dutch War in 1672. As with the earlier conflict it was heralded by the aggressive actions of Sir Robert Holmes, in this case, along with Spragge, an unprovoked (and unsuccessful) attack on the Smyrna convoy. When Sandwich was killed at Solebay on 28 May 1672 and James was forced to retire under the terms of the Test Act of 1673, Rupert was appointed first lord of the Admiralty on 9 July (remaining until 14 May 1679) and given command of the combined Anglo-French fleet at sea. He showed his usual boldness by sailing across the shoals at the mouth of the Thames to break the Dutch blockade. But in two indecisive engagements with De Ruyter in May and June, off the Dutch coast, few ships were lost on either side, and Rupert

was criticized for poor communications with his subordinates and with his French allies. He had certainly failed to clear the narrow seas with his more numerous, bigger, and newer first rates, and it was increasingly unlikely that the large invasion force assembled in England for a Dutch invasion would be able to join the French armies occupying most of the United Provinces.

Already Rupert had quarrelled with the duc de Schomberg, the French-nominated general of these forces, despite the fact that the latter was a native of the Palatinate. Relations with the French reached their nadir at the battle of the Texel, on 11 August. Rupert, with the red squadron in the centre, grappled with De Ruyter, but the heaviest fighting involved Spragge and the blue. Although again no big ships were lost, Spragge was drowned and the Dutch forced the allies to retire. Rupert was furious with this unsatisfactory result and made his criticisms public; a vituperative pamphlet war ensued. He blamed factionalism at court for the inadequate provisioning of the fleet, and the king's too detailed orders for the frustration of his plans. It was rumoured that he caned some of the officials involved: Pepys had always feared him. He attacked the French admiral d'Estrees for not engaging the enemy, and the conveniently dead Spragge for disobedience. Public opinion was aroused against the French, and Rupert became, for once, a popular hero. The king was obliged to make peace with the Dutch in 1674. But among the sailors Rupert had lost respect, and he was compared unfavourably with the duke of York.

'Country' politics The war and the ensuing controversy marked a shift in Rupert's politics. He began to be known for his 'zeal for the Reformed Protestant Religion' (J. Davies, *Gentlemen and Tarpaulins*, 1991, 165), and his anti-French stance. His agent, Holmes, and the duke of York's secretaries, like their masters, had had a constantly shifting, sometimes antagonistic, working relationship, a rivalry reflected in their choice of officers. James's conversion to Catholicism and his marriage to an Italian princess were no more approved of by Rupert than Charles II. He was angered by the promotion of Spragge (no longer his but the duke's protégé) and the non-selection of Holmes. The growing power of Louis XIV in Europe must have alarmed him; his sister Sophia, a favourite, was married to the protestant elector of Hanover, and her son—the future George I—was a possible future successor to the British throne.

Rupert, along with public opinion, had in the 1660s identified the seapower of the Dutch as one of the obstacles to British overseas trade and the acquisition of colonies; the exploits of Holmes had demonstrated as much. Ten years later, as a member of the council for trade and plantations, he saw that France had become the main rival. The unpopularity of the French alliance, and the sterility of the Third Anglo-Dutch War, simply confirmed him in this view. In 1670 he accepted the governorship of the Hudson's Bay Company, which presented a challenge to the French monopoly of trade, mainly in prime beaver skins, in northern Canada. His secretary, Sir James Hayes, became secretary and a leading member of the company, and the prince invested money. One of the first ships to be built for the company was named the *Prince Rupert*, and the huge tract of territory around Hudson Bay was to be called Rupertsland. Maritime exploration interested him, and he kept the logbooks of some of the ships involved in his library.

Among others on the board were Lord Craven, the old family friend, and Anthony Ashley Cooper, Lord Ashley, earl of Shaftesbury from 1672 and a prominent member of the privy council. He shared other business interests, such as in silver mining, with Rupert. He was linked with the prince in the patent for the development of a new type of iron cannon, and his family kept this connection into the 1690s. Rupert's close associate Legge had died in 1670 but he continued to work with his successor at the Ordnance office on a number of projects. In this endeavour the prince was also in competition with France. When Shaftesbury was dismissed from office in 1673 Rupert supported him, and was angered by the king's hostile attitude to parliament. Increasingly he was identified with anti-popish sentiment, encouraging 'country party' MPs to attack the earl of Danby, and advocating a French war to ambassadors and politicians in the late 1670s. In the exclusion crisis of 1679–81 he backed the publication of a protestant tract, acted as a bridge between some of the oppositionist peers and the king, opposed the sacking of Shaftesbury, and dined with him on his dismissal in 1681. It was widely rumoured that he visited Andrew Marvell in secret at this time. He suggested that, to secure the protestant succession, his nephew George should marry James's younger daughter, Anne.

The virtuoso: art and science Politics occupied Rupert only some of the time. Apart from his naval career, nothing was more important and time-consuming than the development of his intellectual, artistic, and scientific interests. Something of a mathematical genius in his youth, he never lost his practical bent, the fascination with things mechanical, especially methods and weapons of war, and his belief in the need to experiment and observe. In this he was a man of his time, which was the age of the virtuosi. The catalogue of his library made in 1677, however, showed how far beyond the conventional educated gentleman's reading he had gone. It contained over 1000 volumes, in English, French, German, Dutch, and Italian; classical authors were in translation. Scientific textbooks and manuals—in mathematics, anatomy, the art of war, chemistry, and physics—were as strongly represented as editions of modern poets and playwrights, and the standard collections of maps and plates, chronicles and histories. Engravings of works by famous artists, including Van Dyck, and journals of exploration, were exceptional items. He was himself a competent artist. In his youth he had made etchings of some merit. In 1658 he experimented with the new process of mezzotint engraving and three years later he demonstrated it 'with his owne hands', for the benefit of the diarist John Evelyn (Evelyn, 3.274). If he was not the inventor, a matter still debated, he was the earliest practitioner in England. Fine examples of his prints survive.

In 1664 Rupert was made, along with his royal cousins, an honorary founder member of the new Royal Society. Although he did not attend meetings—and the main objective for the society was social acceptance—he was a frequent contributor to its scientific discussions and experiments, through the president, Sir Robert Moray, himself an old foreign service, professional soldier. His research was wide-ranging. He submitted for testing a gunpowder eleven times stronger than normal; a novel water pump; an early machine gun; a perspective aid for artists; and improved sea charts and navigational instruments. His projected expedition to the Guinea coast in 1664 was to have been partly scientific in purpose. As described, he experimented in the dressing of his own head wound, and presented papers on the healing process, including the treatment of burns, to the Royal Society. John Locke was among those who took note of Rupert's experiments.

One of the prince's major research interests was metallurgy. It was frequently noticed, not always approvingly, that, clad in a sooty apron, he directed work at furnaces and in laboratories he had set up at Chelsea and at Windsor, where he was governor of the castle. He had probably borrowed from France the new techniques employed there to make plate glass, which required high-temperature furnaces. Chelsea residents complained of the pollution caused by his 'glass houses', situated on the site of the present royal hospital. Some of the results were on a minor scale. He developed an alloy of iron and zinc (Prince's metal) used in the making of small ware, and experimented in the production of perfectly round lead shot. It is probable that the unbreakable tadpole-shaped bubbles of glass, well known then and later as Rupert's drops, were a product. John Evelyn mentioned them in 1661.

But other of Rupert's experiments were major projects, involving established industries. He had always been passionate about gunnery and fortification—the geometry of war—and used his standing with the government and his direct line to the ordnance office, through his friendship with Legge and his successors, to begin experiments in the improvement of iron cannon. If by refining the casting and finishing process iron pieces could be made as strong and accurate as bronze there would be a considerable saving in expense. There was also the competition with France where similar, and secret, developments were taking place. Industrial spies were active in both countries and several of Rupert's technicians were foreign. In 1671 he was granted a patent to make the new guns.

The new cannon required a higher standard of iron ore, involved much wastage, and needed careful boring. They were consequently up to three times more costly than the normal cast-iron ordnance. Some 550 were produced in the iron works of the Browne family in the Kentish Weald before 1676: they were distinctive, bearing the inscription 'Rupert Inven.[it]'. The misreading of this as 'Rupertinoe' gave these cannon the name they were formerly known by. But the experiment eventually lapsed. In France it had been a failure, and in Britain it was found that in the end the patented guns were not appreciably better than the standard cheaper variety. The Browne family went bankrupt, and at his death Rupert was owed money he had invested in the project.

Love and death Rupert never married, in the event rejecting the various overtures, some of political or diplomatic importance, suggested to him by his uncle and others. Nevertheless, he enjoyed several relationships with women. As a captive twenty-year-old at Linz he had the company of the daughter of the castle governor. He may have been in love with the duchess of Richmond during the civil-war years. Surviving letters seem to indicate a liaison with a French woman in 1653–4. His wandering life as a soldier and sailor, without a permanent home until his middle age, may have hindered a settled relationship, but after the Restoration he met Francesca (1645/6–1708), the daughter of an old follower, Henry Bard, Lord Bellamont. A son, Dudley Bard (b. 1667), followed his father's profession in arms and was killed at the siege of Buda in 1686. A purported marriage certificate, dated at Petersham, Surrey, 30 July 1664, has been located, but if such a contract existed it was never acknowledged by the prince.

When the court was at Tunbridge Wells in summer 1668 Rupert met and was charmed by the diminutive young actress Margaret Hughes (d. 1719). She, the court gossips said, 'brought down and greatly subdued his natural fierceness' (Hamilton, 101). She was soon set up as his mistress, and a daughter, Ruperta, was born in 1673. The prince provided her with a magnificent riverside mansion at Hammersmith, and in his will he left the bulk of his personal property to 'Mrs Hughes' and her daughter.

Rupert lived in his last years at his house in Spring Gardens, at the entrance to Whitehall. He also had lodgings in the palace itself, opposite those of the duke of York. As governor of Windsor Castle since 1668 he had rooms in the Round Tower, and it was Rupert, with his expertise in fortification, who supervised the repair and rebuilding of part of the castle, which was ruinous. He also, according to John Evelyn, reporting a visit in 1670, handsomely adorned his hall 'with a furniture of Armes'—a patterned display of weapons and armour on the walls—which contrasted pleasingly with the softer tone of the tapestries and pictures in his bedroom (Evelyn, 3.560). Rupert was among the first to introduce this form of martial decoration into England.

Rupert died in Spring Gardens on 29 November 1682, a few days after catching a chest infection at the theatre. For some time before he had found difficulty in walking because of an ulcerated leg. A post-mortem concluded that he had also suffered from kidney stones, a hard growth in the brain, a probable result of his head wound, and a 'bone' in his heart, no doubt some calcification of the tissue. He was buried in Henry VII's chapel in Westminster Abbey on 6 December. Lord Craven acted as executor of his will. Having received £6000 per annum from the king for twenty years, and frequent free gifts, as well as the profits of the offices he held, Rupert was well off and could provide for his dependants. The jewels he inherited from his mother, including the celebrated 'great pearl necklace', were bought by Nell Gwyn for £4500.

Assessment Prince Rupert enjoyed a remarkably varied reputation during his long career. His closeness to both Charles I and his sons allowed him to demonstrate at an early age his great talents as a cavalry leader, and later as a naval commander. He embodied the transition from the age of the Renaissance prince, knowledgeable in many fields, to that of the modern 'mathematical' general or admiral, who understood the geometry of war. Royal birth was also, however, a handicap, in the jealousies it aroused. He was dogged by court and party faction during every stage of his career, and he was temperamentally incapable of overcoming it. He was too irascible, tactless, and impatient to be an effective politician, unjustly blaming subordinates for lack of support and the hostility of rival commanders for any failures. A poor judge of character, he was too influenced by disreputable followers, and alienated many who might have helped him.

Since his death Rupert's name has been associated chiefly with the more positive aspects of his career. He is seen as a highly competent, courageous, and energetic soldier, who became an equally successful sailor. The terrifying effect of his thunderbolt charges has entered popular legend. His youth and good looks, well preserved in the early portraits of Van Dyck and Honthorst, have prettified the image. He is the subject of several historical novels, one of which is Margaret Irwin's *The Stranger Prince*.

IAN ROY

Sources E. Warburton, *Memoirs of Prince Rupert and the cavaliers*, 3 vols. (1849) • E. Scott, *Rupert, prince palatine* (1899) • E. Scott, *The king in exile: the wanderings of Charles II from June 1646 to July 1654* (1905) • *The letters of Elizabeth, queen of Bohemia*, ed. L. M. Baker (1953) • G. Bromley, ed., *A collection of original royal letters* (1787) • Clarendon, *Hist. rebellion* • R. Scrope and T. Monkhouse, eds., *State papers collected by Edward, earl of Clarendon*, 3 vols. (1767–86) • *The life of Edward, earl of Clarendon … written by himself*, 2 vols. (1760) • W. A. Day, ed., *The Pythouse papers* (1879) • C. H. Firth, ed., 'The journal of Prince Rupert's marches, 5 Sept 1642 to 4 July 1646', *EngHR*, 13 (1898), 729–41 • *DNB* • R. von Liliencron and others, eds., *Allgemeine deutsche Biographie*, 56 vols. (Leipzig, 1875–1912) • L. C. O'Malley, 'The whig prince: Prince Rupert and the court vs. country factions during the reign of Charles II', *Albion*, 8 (1976), 333–50 • K. Dewhurst, 'Prince Rupert as a scientist', *British Journal for the History of Science*, 1 (1963), 365–73 • G. Martin, 'Prince Rupert and the surgeons', *History Today*, 40 (1990) • Evelyn, *Diary*, vol. 3 • Pepys, *Diary* • S. B. Bailey, *Prince Rupert's patent guns* (2000) • T. Birch, *The history of the Royal Society of London*, 4 vols. (1756–7) • J. R. Powell and E. K. Timings, eds., *The Rupert and Monck letter book, 1666*, Navy RS, 112 (1969) • J. G. Nichols and J. Bruce, eds., *Wills from Doctors' Commons*, CS, old ser., 83 (1863) • *A collection of original letters and papers, concerning the affairs of England from the year 1641 to 1660. Found among the duke of Ormonde's papers*, ed. T. Carte, 2 vols. (1739) • R. Symonds, *Diary of the marches of the royal army*, ed. C. E. Long and I. Roy, Camden Society Reprints, 3 (1997) • *CSP dom.*, 1636–82 • C. Petrie, ed., *King Charles, Prince Rupert, and the civil war from original letters* (1974) • J. Charnock, ed., *Biographia navalis*, 6 vols. (1794–8), vol. 1, pp. 124–35 • A. Hamilton, *Memoirs of Count Grammont*, ed. G. Goodwin (1908) • M. A. E. Green, *Elizabeth, electress palatine and queen of Bohemia*, rev. S. C. Lomas (1909) • *The letters, speeches and declarations of King Charles II*, ed. A. Bryant (1968) • *Memoirs of the life and death of Prince Rupert* (1683) • G. Davies, 'The battle of Edgehill', *EngHR*, 36 (1921), 30–45 •

S. R. Gardiner, ed., 'Prince Rupert at Lisbon', *Camden miscellany, X,* CS, 3rd ser., 4 (1902) **Archives** BL, catalogue of library, Sloane MS 555 · BL, corresp., Add. MS 21506 · BL, household accounts, Add. MS 29767 · BL, letters and papers · BL, narratives towards a biography, Add. MSS 62084B, 62085A, 62085B · BL, official corresp. relating to civil war, Add. MSS 18980–18982 · BL, Pythouse papers, Add. MS 62083 · BL, voyage to West Indies, Add. MS 30307 · BL, Add. MS 62086 · Bodl. Oxf., draft orders and nautical memoranda · Bodl. Oxf., official corresp. [transcripts] · V&A NAL, royal letters | NA Scot., letters to first marquess of Montrose · Staffs. RO, Dartmouth papers, Legge letters, D (W) 1778 I · Suffolk RO, Bury St Edmunds, letters to Sir John Granville · Yale U., Beinecke L., letters to William Legge **Likenesses** M. J. van Miereveldt, oils, 1625, Royal Collection · A. Van Dyck, oils, 1631–2, Vienna, Kunsthistorisches Museum · G. Honthorst, oils, *c.*1632–1634, Louvre, Paris · A. Van Dyck, double portrait, oils, *c.*1635–1640 (with Prince Charles Lewis), Louvre, Paris · A. Van Dyck, portrait, *c.*1637, National Gallery, London · attrib. G. Honthorst, oils, *c.*1641, NPG · group portrait, oils, *c.*1642–1664 (after W. Dobson), Ashdown House, Oxfordshire · W. Dobson, group portrait, *c.*1644; at Ombersley Court in 1960s · W. Dobson, portrait, *c.*1644, repro. in P. Young, *Marston Moor, 1644: the campaign and the battle* (1970) · P. Lely, portrait, *c.*1665–1666, Royal Collection [*see illus.*] · P. Lely, portrait, *c.*1667 (*Flagmen of Lowestoft*), NMM · S. Cooper, miniature, *c.*1670, Buccleuch estates, Selkirk · P. Lely, oils, *c.*1670, Euston Hall, Suffolk; version, NPG · oils, *c.*1670, Knebworth House, Hertfordshire · J. M. Wright, oils, 1672, Magd. Oxf. · J. D'Agar, oils, *c.*1678, Corporation of New Windsor · J. Dwight, stoneware bust, *c.*1680, BM · C. P. Dienssart, bust (as young man), AM Oxf. · G. P. Harding, pen and wash drawing, NPG · G. Honthorst, portrait, Landesgalerie, Hanover · miniature (after P. Lely), NPG

Rupp, (Ernest) Gordon (1910–1986), ecclesiastical historian, was born on 7 January 1910 in Islington, the only son and elder child of John Henry Rupp, counting-house clerk, and his wife, Sarah Thomas, nurse. He learned to read at the Methodist Sunday school in Islington and, after an elementary education at Owen's School, became a messenger boy to a furniture dealer and then a bank clerk. At the bank he used his wage to buy one Everyman volume a week and so read many great novels and fell in love with the English language. He went out to Finsbury Park to preach on a box and became a Methodist local preacher. He decided to be a teacher, and the Methodist community gave him the money to spend a year at the London Institute of Education, and then a further year, studying history, at King's College, London. The Methodist church then wanted him as a minister and sent him to Wesley House at Cambridge in 1933–6, where he gained a first class in both parts of the theology tripos (1935 and 1936). He was afterwards sent for a year to the universities of Strasbourg and Basel.

In 1938 Rupp married Marjorie (*d.* 1988), daughter of Frank Hibbard, toolmaker; they had one son. From 1938 to 1946 Rupp was a Methodist minister at Chislehurst, and from 1947 to 1952 a tutor at the Methodist college in Richmond. He gained a Cambridge BD in 1946 and DD in 1955.

Rupp was a born pamphleteer and was threatened with prosecution by Hilaire Belloc for a wartime article in the *Record*. In 1944, replying to a pamphlet which accused Martin Luther of causing the rise of Hitler, because Luther was responsible for the German cult of the state, he published *Martin Luther, Hitler's Cause—or Cure?* This counter-pamphlet was persuasive and funny and its author was not afraid to pillory Archbishop William Temple; he also disclosed a rare knowledge of Luther's original texts, thereby showing Rupp to be a potential academic historian. As a result of his pamphlet, Rupp was invited to give the Birkbeck lectures in Cambridge in 1947, which drew large audiences. In the same year he wrote *Studies in the Making of the English Protestant Tradition*. In 1952 Norman Sykes, who had taught him at London, found him a lectureship in Reformation history at Cambridge, which he held from 1952 to 1956. He subsequently became the first professor of ecclesiastical history at Manchester in 1956–67. In 1968 he was appointed Dixie professor at Cambridge, with a fellowship at Emmanuel College (until 1977). But the professor at Manchester was also the deputy pianist at the Sunday school in Chorlton-cum-Hardy, as well as an observer at the second Vatican Council, and the professor at Cambridge was also the principal of Wesley House from 1967 to 1974 and for the year 1968–9 the president of the Methodist conference and a frustrated leader in the plan to unite the Methodists and the Anglicans. His university colleagues occasionally grumbled that, when they needed him for a meeting, he was speaking in a little chapel 300 miles away.

As a historian Rupp reintroduced the British to Luther's thought with the publication in 1953 of his Birkbeck lectures, *The Righteousness of God*. He did not overstress the importance of Luther in the Reformation (he also studied other leading radicals in *Patterns of Reformation*, 1969) and he thought that social causes were given too much emphasis, to the detriment of the religious and theological ideas which lay at the heart of the Reformation. He was the first Briton to read the complete critical texts of Luther's works, and to understand the different interpretations in the two Germanies, whether Marxist or not. He also made himself familiar with Swedish Lutheran scholarship.

John Wesley was almost as consuming an interest. Rupp was among the editors of the *History of the Methodist Churches in Great Britain* (4 vols., 1965–88) and his last book centred on the age of Wesley—*Religion in England, 1688–1791* (1986). He was elected a fellow of the British Academy in 1970. An honorary fellow of King's College, London (1969), Fitzwilliam and Emmanuel colleges, Cambridge (1969 and 1983), Rupp had honorary degrees from Aberdeen, Manchester, and Paris.

Rupp never lost his simple tastes, retaining a liking for fish and chips and ginger beer. In an age when sermons had become much shorter, he was the supreme master of that art form. He had a husky voice and was small and impish, with a delightful command of satire and barbed wit. He was no man for tidy structures but looked to the heavens to probe the mystery of religion. He lit up with humour, historical example, and humane insight all that he encountered. Rupp died in Cambridge on 19 December 1986, his wife and son surviving him.

OWEN CHADWICK, *rev.*

Sources *The Times* (22 Dec 1986) · P. N. Brooks, 'Ernest Gordon Rupp, 1910–1986', *PBA*, 80 (1993), 493–8 · D. Thompson, *Cambridge*

Review (June 1987), 91–2 • P. Brooks, ed., *Christian spirituality: essays in honour of Gordon Rupp* (1975) [incl. a list of Rupp's writings to 1973] • J. M. Turner, 'Gordon Rupp … as historian', *Epworth Review* (Jan 1991), 70–82 • personal knowledge (1996) • J. Vickers, ed., *Dictionary of Methodism in Britain and Ireland* (2000) • *Methodist Recorder* (1 Jan 1987) • *Methodist Recorder* (8 Jan 1987) • *Wisdom and wit: an anthology from the writings of Gordon Rupp*, ed. J. Vickers [n.d., 1993?]

Archives Wesley House, Cambridge, papers

Likenesses photograph, repro. in Brooks, 'Ernest Gordon Rupp', 494

Wealth at death £15,125: probate, 11 March 1987, *CGPLA Eng. & Wales*

Rusden, George William (1819–1903), educationist and civil servant in Australia, was born on 9 July 1819 at Leith Hill Place, near Dorking, the second son of the eleven children of the Revd George Keylock Rusden (1784–1859) and his wife, Anne, the only daughter of the Revd Thomas Townshend. Educated in his father's school at Leith Hill Place until he was fourteen, when his family emigrated to Australia, Rusden later read widely in English, French, German, and classical literature. The Rusdens arrived in Sydney on 1 May 1834; during the voyage Rusden met Charles Nicholson, and later managed properties for the wealthy physician, learning much about the pastoral industry and Aboriginal culture.

In 1847 Rusden visited China seeking business success, but returned to Sydney in 1849 little richer. On 28 May 1849 he became an agent of the national board of education (of which Nicholson was a member), entrusted with establishing non-denominational elementary schools in remote districts and competing for government funds with the denominational board, which favoured doctrinal instruction. The dedicated Rusden covered 10,000 miles on horseback in two and a quarter years.

The travel and salary disputes caused his resignation. In 1851 he became chief clerk in the colonial secretary's office, Melbourne, and in 1852 clerk of the lieutenant-governor's advisory body, formed when Victoria separated from New South Wales in 1851. In 1856 he reluctantly accepted the clerkship of the upper house of the parliament established that year. His annual salary of £1000 brought financial security, especially as he remained unmarried. A staunch tory, Rusden found the council's ultra-conservative politics congenial.

Rusden retired in 1882, though in 1862 he visited China to assist his youngest brother Alfred's business. He meticulously recorded his own Chinese investments in clothing, cotton, rice, silk, and opium as well as his domination of the billiard table at the exclusive Melbourne Club. In its convivial rooms he could advocate colonial hereditary honours, the introduction of British flora and fauna (he belonged to the Acclimatisation Society), and strong municipal government—he was mayor of the council of Brighton in 1860, 1861, and 1872.

Rusden's educational concerns remained. In 1853, untypically for a devout Anglican, he defended non-denominational, state-supported schooling in *National Education* and became a commissioner of Victoria's national board. Dedicated, willing to juggle the truth or the board's finances, and doggedly attending meetings his colleagues neglected, Rusden became its *de facto* director. The national and denominational boards were dissolved in 1862. The substituted single board failed and the 1872 Education Act, to Rusden's horror, made state schooling secular and withdrew aid from church schools. Rusden also served on the University of Melbourne's council from its establishment in 1853 until 1882, helping to shape its regulations and resisting attempts to admit women. Largely through him, the Shakespeare scholarship was established in 1864.

Rusden wrote books, pamphlets, and occasional verse on many topics, sometimes under the pseudonyms of 'Vindex' and 'Yittadairn'. He published *Moyarra: an Australian Legend, in Two Cantos* (1851), a poem about two Aboriginal lovers, *The Discovery, Survey, and Settlement of Port Phillip* (1871), and *Curiosities of Colonization* (1874). He retired with an annual pension of £500 to England and published *History of New Zealand* (1883). This work showed his sympathy for the Maori, and provoked a libel case for its attack on the minister for native affairs. Rusden criticized this ex-farmer for his part in the New Zealand wars. Two hearings resulted in Rusden paying damages of about £2500. Also in 1883 he published *History of Australia*, which is distorted by dogmatic anti-democratic views and personal prejudices, but saved by his intimate knowledge of Victorian politics.

In 1893 Rusden returned to Melbourne for health reasons. Shortly before his death, on 23 December 1903, he published *William Shakespeare: his Life, his Works, and his Teachings*. His estate was divided equally between the children of his surviving sisters and brother. He bequeathed his home to the Church of England, having already donated £8000 in 1889. On 31 December an obituary in *Melbourne Punch*, as A. G. Austin noted, bade farewell to

> cheery and worthy G. W. Rusden, with his pleasant crab-apple face and long legs … We don't know any Australian resident so distinctly English. Yet he did not live much in England … What a delicious bundle of prejudices was Rusden. A walking Westminster Abbey. And honest as the day.

R. J. W. SELLECK

Sources A. G. Austin, *George William Rusden and national education in Australia, 1849–1862* (1958) • W. Bate, *A history of Brighton*, 2nd edn (1983) • A. Blainey and M. Lazarus, 'Rusden, George William', *AusDB*, vol. 6 • P. de Serville, *Pounds and pedigrees: the upper class in Victoria, 1850–80* (1991) • Board of National Education, New South Wales, fair minutes, 1848–53, Mitchell L., NSW • minutes of the national board of education, Victoria, 1851–62, Public Record Office of Victoria, Laverton, Victoria • M. Pawsey, 'Backroom politics and educational reform: the national board and Victoria's Common Schools Act', *History of Education Review*, 12/2 (1983), 29–42 • R. Wright, *A people's counsel: a history of the Parliament of Victoria, 1856–1990* (1992) • University of Melbourne, Trinity College, Rusden MSS • d. cert.

Archives State Library of Victoria, Melbourne • University of Melbourne, Trinity College | Public Record Office, Victoria, Australia, minutes of the national board of education

Likenesses photograph, repro. in Austin, *George William Rusden*; priv. coll.

Wealth at death £18,000: probate, Melbourne

Rush, Anthony (1537–1577), dean of Chichester, was either the heir of Arthur Rush of Sudbourne, Suffolk, and grandson of Sir Thomas Rush of Sudbourne, who was knighted by Henry VIII in 1533, or, more likely, the third son of Sir Thomas and his first wife, Anne, and Arthur's brother. Anthony became the ward of Thomas Wriothesley, first earl of Southampton, who in 1550 bequeathed him his leasehold estates in Suffolk. Educated at King's School, Canterbury, Rush went up to Oxford with the financial support of Nicholas Wooton, dean of Canterbury. He graduated BA at Magdalen College on 4 July 1554, immediately becoming a probationer fellow. He was ordained subdeacon by Edmund Bonner, bishop of London, on 21 March 1556 as of the diocese of Norwich and fellow of Magdalen. But he soon appears to have embraced protestantism, since in 1557 he was punished for disobedience to the vice-president of his college, apparently for refusing to attend mass. He nevertheless proceeded MA on 20 June 1558, but thereupon resigned his fellowship.

His conversion to protestantism apparently led Rush into the orbit of Thomas Radcliffe, third earl of Sussex, and he presumably went to Ireland as Sussex's chaplain when the earl became successively lord-deputy and lord lieutenant there (1556–65), since one Anthony Rushe received letters patent on 2 October 1560 for the vicarage of Donsoghlin in the diocese of Meath. Early in 1561 Wooton suggested him to Archbishop Parker as a suitable candidate for the mastership of King's School, Canterbury. Parker agreed, provided that Dean Alexander Nowell of St Paul's was also prepared to commend him, and he also granted Rush a preaching licence at this time. During his mastership Rush collaborated with John Bale, then a prebendary of Canterbury, in the production of anti-Catholic plays with a cast of schoolboys.

Thereafter Rush's promotions were many and varied. He resigned from King's in 1565 but was instituted rector of Woodham Walter, Essex, at Sussex's presentation in June that year, and also received the prebendal rectory of Brightling, Sussex. In 1566 he proceeded DTh at Cambridge, was installed canon of Windsor on 29 July, and was made rector of Calverton, Buckinghamshire. That year also he published *A president for a prince. Wherein is to be seene by the testimonie of auncient writers, the duetie of kings*, with a dedication to the queen, whose chaplain he later became. In May or June 1566 Sussex recommended Rush for a prebend at Canterbury, and on 7 February 1567 for the deanery of York. On 29 March 1568 he was granted letters patent as canon of the second prebend at Canterbury, which he held until his death, and received the rectory of Orgarswick, Kent, the same year. He was appointed rector of St Olave's, Southwark, in 1569.

On 10 June 1570 Rush was installed dean of Chichester, where the bishop, Richard Curteys, was at odds with his cathedral chapter. At first Rush sided with Curteys. His clandestine and irregular chapter meetings (he spent most of his time at Windsor), held when most of the chapter could not attend and often convened without quorums, even involved picking the lock of the chapter

strongbox to make use of the capitular seal. This behaviour eventually led to Curteys enacting statutes directed particularly against such practices. Rush regularly had leases made which were much to the detriment of the bishop: one of them leased a property to the dean's own servant for eighty years, and eventually had to be modified by the chapter. Rush died on 1 April 1577 and was buried in St George's Chapel, Windsor, where his widow (her identity is unknown) erected a monument with a long memorial inscription.

GARY W. JENKINS

Sources Wood, *Ath. Oxon.*, new edn, 1.429 · Tanner, *Bibl. Brit.-Hib.* · *Correspondence of Matthew Parker*, ed. J. Bruce and T. T. Perowne, Parker Society, 42 (1853) · R. B. Manning, *Religion and society in Elizabethan Sussex* (1969) · A. Foster, 'The dean and chapter, 1570–1660', *Chichester Cathedral: an historical survey*, ed. M. Hobbs (1994), 85–100 · W. D. Peckham, ed., *The acts of the dean and chapter of the cathedral church of Chichester, 1472–1544*, Sussex RS, 52 (1952) · A. R. Rush, *Benjamin Rush, M.D. (1745–1813): his origins and ancestry* [n.d.] · W. C. Metcalfe, *A book of knights banneret, knights of the Bath and knights bachelor* (1885) · J. R. Bloxam, *A register of the presidents, fellows … of Saint Mary Magdalen College*, 8 vols. (1853–85), vol. 2 · J. Morrin, ed., *Calendar of the patent and close rolls of chancery in Ireland, of the reigns of Henry VIII, Edward VI, Mary, and Elizabeth*, 1 (1861) · P. Collinson, 'The protestant cathedral, 1541–1660', *A history of Canterbury Cathedral, 598–1982*, ed. P. Collinson and others (1995), 154–203 · GL, MS 9535/1, fol. 57r

Wealth at death income presumably large; held numerous ecclesiastical livings

Rush, Benjamin (1746–1813), physician and university professor, was born on 4 January 1746 in Byberry, Pennsylvania, the fourth of the seven children of John Rush (1712?–1751), a farmer and gunsmith, and Susanna Harvey, *née* Hall (1717?–1795). When Rush's father died at the age of thirty-nine in 1751, his mother, whom Rush remembered as a woman of 'uncommon talents and address in doing business' (*Autobiography*, 27), sold the gunsmith shop and ran a country store in Philadelphia to support herself and her children. From 1754 to 1759 Rush attended the Nottingham Academy, a boarding-school in Maryland run by his uncle the Revd Samuel Finley, a Presbyterian minister schooled by the revivalist William Tennent. Rush admired Finley's 'apostolical prudence', and judged the Nottingham Academy to be the 'most respectable and flourishing' preparatory school in the middle colonies (ibid., 29, 31). In 1759 Rush joined the junior class of the College of New Jersey, and upon receiving his AB degree in 1760 thought about becoming a lawyer. Finley, however, frowned upon a profession so 'full of temptations' (ibid., 37) and suggested that Rush pursue a career in medicine instead. Acting on the advice of his 'venerable preceptor' (ibid., 33), Rush was apprenticed under John Redman, Philadelphia's leading physician, from 1761 to 1766.

Some time in the last years of his apprenticeship, probably at the urging of Dr Redman, Rush decided to continue his medical education at the University of Edinburgh, the premier medical centre of the latter half of the eighteenth century. He left Philadelphia in August and, after a brief stay in Liverpool, arrived in Edinburgh in November 1766. The ensuing two years he spent listening to medical lectures and engaging in private conversations with his professors were, Rush later wrote, the 'most important in their influence upon my character and conduct of any period of my life' (*Autobiography*, 43). Then in 1768, medical degree in hand, Rush relocated to London, to work at St Thomas's Hospital and to attend the lectures and dissections of William Hunter, the celebrated Scottish anatomist and surgeon. Finally, on 26 May 1769, after an abbreviated tour of Paris, where he was unimpressed by the medical knowledge of leading French physicians, he boarded the *Edward* bound for New York.

Rush rose quickly within the ranks of the medical establishment of Philadelphia, but he was less than candid when he declared in his autobiography that his successes were entirely of his own making. One of the highlights of his stay in London was the pleasure he took in the 'paternal friendship' (*Autobiography*, 74) of Benjamin Franklin. Also, prior to his departure from London, he secured from Thomas Penn, proprietor of Pennsylvania, a letter of recommendation to the trustees of the College of Philadelphia. The influence of such highly placed friends helped. On 1 August 1769, the very day he saw his first patient, Rush received notice from the trustees of the College of Philadelphia of his appointment to the medical faculty. Aged twenty-three, Rush became the first professor of chemistry in America. The appointment, Rush admitted, 'made my name familiar to the public ear much sooner than it would [otherwise] have been' (ibid., 81).

Rush supposedly resolved on the day of his arrival in Philadelphia not to 'perpetrate matrimony' until he was certain that a 'family would be no impediment to his farther progress' (Hawke, 81). By 1775, having established himself as a person of some renown in the city, he was ready for marriage. On 11 January 1776 Rush married Julia Stockton (1759–1848), the eldest daughter of old friends, Richard and Annis Boudinot Stockton of Princeton. Julia, not quite seventeen years old at the time of her marriage, proved to be 'everything to me that a friend, a companion, and a wife should be to any man' (*Letters*, 1.531). Had he 'yielded to her advice upon many occasions', Rush said, he would have 'known less distress from various causes in [his] journey thro' life' (*Autobiography*, 166). Together for thirty-seven years, Rush and his 'Dearest Life', his 'dearest Jewel', his 'Best Half' (*Letters*, 1.99, 105; 2.928), had thirteen children. Four of the children died in infancy.

For Rush domestic concerns were unavoidably intertwined with the evolving imperial crisis. That he was by 1776 an advocate of independence comes as no surprise. A decade earlier he had been outspoken in his opposition to the Stamp Act, and during his stay in Edinburgh he had come to question the authority of kings and to adopt republican principles. Having been elected to the second continental congress in July 1776, Rush was a signer of the Declaration of Independence. He lost his seat in congress in 1777, but was soon named physician-general of the middle department of the continental army. Although Rush welcomed this appointment, his prickly temperament and criticism of the management of the army's hospitals brought him into collision with his superior, William Shippen jun., the director-general of the continental army's hospital department. Convinced that maladministration and outright corruption ran rampant, and unable to gain satisfaction from the commander-in-chief, George Washington, Rush urged friends in congress to intervene. In desperation he began to question the competence of Washington himself. Washington responded by accusing Rush of duplicity. With few allies and formidable adversaries Rush's position became untenable. After a congressional committee in January 1778 formally heard his charges and Shippen's rebuttal, and decided in favour of the latter, Rush resigned his commission.

Disillusioned by the circumstances of his 'retirement' from the army, Rush was determined to devote himself 'exclusively to the duties of [his] profession' (*Autobiography*, 138). He immersed himself in his medical practice, and by 1787 was the best-known physician in America. He found it impossible, however, to abandon the world of politics altogether. Influenced by the medical ideas of William Cullen, his revered 'master' (ibid., 80) at Edinburgh, Rush believed that life and health were sustained by stimuli acting upon the nervous system. And because the force of stimuli generated by social conditions were as consequential as those associated with nature, he was alive to the medical implications of local customs and institutions. He was especially interested in the influence of government upon health. After surveying the health deficiencies of despotic governments and limited monarchies, he concluded that only under the influence of those simple virtues and gentle stimuli associated with well-constructed republican governments could life flourish.

Thus inspired, Rush was a critic of the Pennsylvania constitution of 1776 and the articles of confederation. Both frames of government were defective because they were drafted at a time when Americans, 'intoxicated' with the 'first flowings of liberty' (*Letters*, 1.137), were unwilling to check the potential excesses of popular rule. Although he was not a delegate to the constitutional convention, and therefore not privy to its secret deliberations, Rush publicly recommended the new federal government even before the convention had completed its work. At the Pennsylvania ratifying convention he was second only to James Wilson in representing the federalist position. His hope was that the constitution 'like a new continental wagon will overset our state dung cart' (ibid., 1.440). To this end, in 1789 he was a principal player in the campaign that netted more than 10,000 signatures endorsing a legislative motion calling for a state convention. The resulting convention crafted the 1790 Pennsylvania constitution which overturned the most controversial elements of the 1776 frame—replacing the unicameral assembly with a bicameral legislature and the executive council with a single executive.

That ratifying the constitution and overturning the 1776 state constitution formed two parts of the same struggle for Rush is a reflection not only of his medical theories but of his understanding of the meaning of the revolution. 'The revolution is not over!' Rush insisted in 1787 (*Selected Writings*, 31). Republican forms of government had been or were being perfected, but the manners and morals of the people still needed to be shaped to accommodate these perfected forms. Rush's contributions as an educator and social reformer thus complemented his involvement in state and national politics. He championed the cause of free schools for children of the poor; proposed an expanded curriculum of studies for women; helped establish Dickinson College (1783), in Carlisle, Pennsylvania; was a charter trustee of Franklin College (1787) in Lancaster, Pennsylvania; and called for the founding of a post-baccalaureate federal university in the nation's capital. Rush's drive to improve the morals of the people also extended to his self-proclaimed campaign to combat their 'vulgar errors' (*Letters*, 1.481). He cautioned against the use and abuse of tobacco and alcohol; condemned the resort to corporal punishment in schools; enlarged the 'empire of humanity' (ibid., 1.417) to cover penal reform; led the opposition to the death penalty; fostered a more compassionate view of mental illness and its treatment; decried the evils of the slave trade; and, after belatedly freeing his slave, William, in 1788, became a leader in the anti-slavery movement.

In the 1790s and the first decade of the nineteenth century Rush continued to experience his share of successes and set-backs. His tireless dedication during the yellow fever epidemic of 1793, when he saw some 50 to 150 patients a day and nearly succumbed to the disease himself, increased his popularity among the citizens of Philadelphia. His regimen of bleeding and purging the sick, however, exposed him to the 'long and loud complaints' (*Letters*, 2.735) of his colleagues. Stung by their criticism, Rush resigned from the College of Physicians, a medical society he had helped found six years earlier. But the 'scourge of tongues' (ibid., 2.741) did not derail his career as a professor of medicine. After the College of Philadelphia and the University of the State of Pennsylvania merged in 1791 to form the University of Pennsylvania, Rush became its first professor of the institutes of medicine (1792). In 1796 he received the additional appointment of professor of the practice of physic in the new university, and his classes enrolled ever larger numbers of pupils. From 1792 until 1812 Rush taught approximately 3500 students, more than any other professor of medicine in America at the time. His influence as a teacher, coupled with the publication of an enlarged four-volume edition of his *Medical Inquiries and Observations* (1796) and his famous *Medical Inquiries and Observations upon the Diseases of the Mind* (1812), gained him international fame and secured his position as America's foremost physician. Rush died in Philadelphia on 19 April 1813, and was buried three days later at the town's Christ Church burial-ground.

MELVIN YAZAWA

Sources The autobiography of Benjamin Rush, ed. G. W. Corner (1948) · Letters of Benjamin Rush, ed. L. H. Butterfield, 2 vols. (1951) · N. G. Goodman, Benjamin Rush: physician and citizen, 1746–1813 (1934) · D. F. Hawke, Benjamin Rush: a revolutionary gadfly (1971) · D. J. D'Elia, Benjamin Rush: philosopher of the American revolution (1974) · C. Binger, Revolutionary doctor: Benjamin Rush, 1746–1813 (1966) · H. G. Good, Benjamin Rush and his services to American education (1918) · Selected writings of Benjamin Rush, ed. D. D. Runes (1947) · R. B. Sullivan, 'Rush, Benjamin', ANB · R. H. Shryock, 'Rush, Benjamin', DAB, 16.227–31

Archives College of Physicians, Philadelphia · Hist. Soc. Penn., MSS · Johns Hopkins University, Baltimore, William H. Welch Medical Library · Ridgway Library, Philadelphia · University of Pennsylvania, Philadelphia
Likenesses C. W. Peale, oils, 1783, Frick Art Reference Library · St-Memin, engraving, 1802, Corcoran Gallery of Art, Washington, DC · W. Haines, portrait, 1805, University of Pennsylvania Medical School · M. Furst, medallion, 1808 (after bronze), Museum of the American Numismatic Society

Rush, James Blomfield (d. 1849). *See under* Jermy, Isaac (1789–1848).

Rushbrooke, James Henry (1870–1947), Baptist minister and secretary of the Baptist World Alliance, was born on 29 July 1870 at 39 Cudworth Street, Bethnal Green, London, the son of James Rushbrooke, later a stationmaster at Thorpe-le-Soken, Essex, and his wife, Sarah Jane Pegram. He had a brother and five sisters, and was educated at the national school at Thorpe-le-Soken and then at Walsingham grammar school. Rushbrooke moved back to London at the age of fifteen to take up employment as a clerk with Willesden district council. He attended the local parish church as a child, but became a Baptist in London. Baptized as a believer in 1887, he joined the Baptist church at Westbourne Park, Paddington, where John Clifford exercised a very remarkable ministry. Here he espoused a liberal evangelicalism which combined commitment to the expansion of new knowledge, the urgency of human need, and imaginative evangelism. Admitted to the New Connexion General Baptist College in Nottingham to train for the ministry in 1894, he also took advantage of studies at the newly opened University College. Winning the Pegg scholarship allowed him to complete his education in Marburg, Halle, and Berlin (1899–1901).

On 16 August 1892 Rushbrooke married Kate (b. 1864/5), daughter of James Partridge, gardener. A music teacher from Thorpe-le-Soken, she died later that year shortly after giving birth to a son, who also died. He met his second wife, Dorothea (Dora) Weber (d. 1944), daughter of the distinguished portrait painter Professor Anton Weber, in Germany and married her there on 16 June 1902. Thus his sympathies were early engaged with the wider world, equipping him for a career devoted to the needs of the world church. In these very human relationships lay his concern for Anglo-German friendship and understanding, leading in turn into his passion for peace. His study in Germany brought him into contact with theologians such as Alfred von Harnack and Albrecht Ritschl, exponents of that liberal protestantism which arose out of their wrestling with theological issues in the context of philosophical and critical developments. Rushbrooke attended von Harnack's lectures entitled *What is Christianity?* and was much stimulated by them, while retaining his commitment in the Baptist tradition to an evangelical outlook.

Rushbrooke's first pastorate was at St Mary's Gate, Derby (1902–6), in the east midland heartlands where the New Connexion influence on Baptist life was greatest. After three years at Archway Road, Highgate (1906–10), he became the first minister of the new Hampstead Garden Suburb Free Church, a pioneering venture in ecumenical

James Henry Rushbrooke (1870–1947), by Lafayette, 1928

partnership. The church had Lutyens as its architect and one of the foundation stones, laid by Henrietta Barnett, the originator of the vision of the garden suburb, had inscribed on it 'God is larger than the creeds'. Rushbrooke served there as a much respected minister until 1920.

For the next quarter of a century Rushbrooke worked tirelessly for the benefit of the recently founded Baptist World Alliance (BWA). He spoke at the first European Baptist conference in Berlin (1908) and at the second BWA congress in Philadelphia (1911). He made two visits to Budapest to try to help the Hungarian Baptists overcome local divisions and was organizer of the second European Baptist conference in Stockholm in 1913. In 1914 he and his family had the misfortune to be caught in Germany on the outbreak of the First World War, after attending a protestant peace conference at Constance. Although initially interned, they were allowed to return to England in October 1914 as part of an exchange of ministers.

After the First World War Rushbrooke was asked by the alliance in 1920 to undertake, with Dr Charles Brooks of New York, a three-month investigatory tour of Europe to assess post-war needs, reporting back to a conference in London which brought together the leaders of the continental churches together with representatives from Britain, USA, Canada, and Australia. It was this conference that issued the invitation to Rushbrooke to take up the post of Baptist European commissioner in 1921. This enabled him fully to exploit his many gifts: of encouragement of those who were in difficulties, of negotiation with civil authorities, of persuasion towards those who in

North America had access to the necessary funds, and of effective administration and communication.

In 1925 Rushbrooke added the 'eastern' secretaryship to his work as commissioner, the two offices becoming one full-time position. At this time he also served as president of the Baptist Union of Great Britain and Ireland (1926–7). In 1928 he was the natural candidate for appointment as the first full-time general secretary of the BWA, serving the whole worldwide fellowship. Eleven further years of distinguished service followed until in 1939, on the eve of his seventieth birthday, he was elected president of the alliance, only the second British Baptist in that office. Because of the war, Dr W. O. Lewis, Rushbrooke's successor, was confined in North America, and the new president looked remarkably like the old secretary in terms of the responsibilities Rushbrooke, ever the peacemaker and reconciler, still had to carry. As general secretary, Rushbrooke had become the human face of Baptists worldwide. As champion of religious freedom and encourager of Baptists in their missionary task, he gave himself tirelessly to detailed administration and costly advocacy of evangelical minorities, especially in eastern and Latin Europe.

During the quarter-century following his experimental interdenominational pastorate in Hampstead, Baptist participation in ecumenical conversations developed at a different pace on different sides of the Atlantic: in North America there was considerable suspicion of British interest in ecumenical initiatives. Rushbrooke was torn in different directions: the pioneer of the Hampstead initiative had now to heed a wider constituency. Thus in 1927 on Rushbrooke's initiative British Baptists declined to be represented at the Lausanne meeting of faith and order, sending only a greeting. Rushbrooke was apparently concerned about the BWA losing the confidence and the crucial financial support of the Southern Baptist Convention. To hold Baptists together in worldwide fellowship was for Rushbrooke in the second half of his life a sufficient goal in itself. Early in 1947 he sustained a fatal stroke which led to his death on 1 February at his home, 3 Pembroke Vale, Clifton, Bristol. He received honorary doctorates from universities in Canada (McMaster, 1921, and Acadia, 1939) and the USA (Bates, 1931). J. H. Y. Briggs

Sources E. A. Payne, *James Henry Rushbrooke: a Baptist greatheart* (1954) · B. Green, *Tomorrow's man: a biography of James Henry Rushbrooke* (1997) · F. T. Lord, *Baptist world fellowship: a short history of the Baptist World Alliance* (1955) · B. Green, '"Earnest to make others free": J. H. Rushbrooke and religious liberty', *Baptist Quarterly*, 36 (1995–6), 108–19 · b. cert. · m. cert. · d. cert. · *CGPLA Eng. & Wales* (1947)

Archives Regent's Park College, Oxford, letters and papers | Baptist World Alliance, Virginia, Baptist World Alliance reports · Regent's Park College, Oxford, Baptist World Alliance reports

Likenesses Lafayette, photograph, 1928, NPG [*see illus.*] · L. D. M. Purser, oils, Hampstead Garden Suburb Free Church, London · photographs, Baptist Church House, Didcot; repro. in Green, *Tomorrow's man* · photographs, Headquarters of the Baptist World Alliance; repro. in Green, *Tomorrow's man*

Wealth at death £6119 14s. 4d.: probate, 9 Oct 1947, *CGPLA Eng. & Wales*

Rushbury, Sir **Henry George** [Harry] (1889–1968), painter and engraver, was born on 28 October 1889 at Harborne, Warwickshire, then still a country village on the outskirts of Birmingham, the younger son of G. Norbury Rushbury, a clerk, and his wife, Naomi Fennell. The father, when unsuccessfully job-hunting, used to take his son with him on visits to churches and other old buildings, thereby developing the boy's powers of observation and kindling what was to be a lifelong and essential interest in immediate surroundings.

At the age of thirteen Rushbury gained a scholarship to Birmingham School of Art, where, from 1903 to 1909, studying at first gold- and silversmith's work and later stained-glass design and mural decoration, he came under the stimulating influence of the headmaster, R. M. Catterson Smith, who encouraged the students to make quick drawings of figures in movement rather than highly finished studies of posed models, but also subjected them to the strict discipline of painting in tempera. Thus, while still very young, and despite the poverty at home, Rushbury was well equipped to perceive and record accurately his environment, particularly townscapes with people going about their daily business, which gave liveliness and scale to his works.

On leaving Birmingham, Rushbury worked in the Cotswolds for a time, as assistant to Henry Payne at St Loe's, near Stroud in Gloucestershire, making designs for stained glass and helping with a series of tempera paintings for William Lygon, Earl Beauchamp, at Madresfield Court, Worcestershire. In 1912 he settled in London, sharing lodgings in Chelsea with his friend Gerald Brockhurst, who had been a fellow student under Catterson Smith. There he met Francis Dodd, who taught him the techniques of etching and drypoint.

In 1914 Rushbury married Florence Harriet, the daughter of Herbert W. Lazell, a lay preacher. After war broke out he joined the army in 1915 and was later transferred to the Royal Flying Corps. His draughtsmanship was soon put to good use and he became an official war artist, producing various documentary drawings which are now in the Imperial War Museum.

After the war Rushbury spent a few months studying under Henry Tonks at the Slade School of Fine Art, London, but soon continued a busy life of drawing and engraving which involved extensive travelling on the continent each year, particularly in France and Italy. He had first exhibited at the Royal Academy in 1913 and, with scarcely a break in the sequence, continued to do so throughout his career, amassing a total of more than 200 works. Their titles alone are evidence of the broad coverage of his interests—for example, *The Brewery, Sandwich* (1915), *Walls of Siena* (1923), *Quai des Belges, Marseille* (1929), *A Street in Gerona* (1936), *Stirling Castle* (1946), *Market, Concarneau* (1955), *Tenby Harbour* (1962), and *Orvieto* (1968). Rushbury was a master of the mood of the moment—early morning, a busy forenoon, a drowsy afternoon in the sunlight, or a sultry evening. He was far more than an accomplished topographical draughtsman, for he always seemed to be able to portray the spirit of his subject.

Some of Rushbury's best work was used to illustrate Sidney Dark's *Paris* (1926), *Rome of the Renaissance and Today* (1932), by Sir James Rennell Rodd (later Lord Rennell), and *Fenland Rivers* (1936), by Iris Wedgwood. All three books, excellent as they are in their texts, are greatly enhanced by the clarity and warmth of the drawings, which bring the places visually to life, always maintaining the monumental qualities of the dominant subjects but setting them in the local climatic and social conditions. This was achieved not only by the artist's unerring choice of viewpoints and his skilful use of light and shade but also frequently by including human figures and their transport—as, for example (in the *Rome* book), *The Pantheon*, with groups of people chatting, carriages, and tramway cars, and *Palazzo Farnese*, with its horses and carts and the fountain playing.

Rushbury was fortunate to be able to depict such scenes before they were despoiled by excessive motor traffic. His output was considerable, as is evident in mixed and one-man exhibitions over a long period of years, and his works, with their blend of scholarly interest and sympathetic rendering, were extremely attractive and, in scale, very suitable for rooms of reasonable size. He also undertook a series of mural decorations for Chelmsford town hall in 1937.

Rushbury was again an official artist during the Second World War, recording the production side of the war effort. At sixty years of age, in 1949, he was elected keeper of the Royal Academy and, as head of its schools until his retirement in 1964, did much to encourage the students through his experiences and to help them to tread their own paths.

Rushbury exhibited regularly with several societies and became a member of the New English Art Club in 1917, of the Royal Society of Painter-Etchers in 1921, and of the Royal Society of Painters in Water Colours in 1922. He was elected an associate of the Royal Academy in 1927 and a Royal Academician in 1936 and was made an honorary associate of the Royal Institute of British Architects in 1948. He was appointed CVO in 1955, CBE in 1960, and KCVO in 1964.

In personality Rushbury was most friendly and club-loving, being a staunch supporter of both the Arts Club and the Chelsea Arts Club. Sir Alfred Munnings said that 'Henry could charm a bird off a tree'. In appearance he was somewhat Pickwickian—short and sturdy in stature but with sharp features and alert blue eyes. He was rubicund, kindly, and an enlivening companion. He died in Lewes, Sussex, on 5 July 1968, survived by his widow (who died later that year) and their two daughters.

S. C. HUTCHISON, *rev.*

Sources R. H. W., *Draughtsmen* (1924) · H. *Rushbury* (1928) [incl. introduction by M. C. Salaman] · *The Times* (6 July 1968) · *Daily Telegraph* (6 July 1968) · RA · private information (1981) · personal knowledge (1981) · *CGPLA Eng. & Wales* (1969) · S. Wildman, *Sir Henry Rushbury* (1989) [exhibition catalogue, Birmingham, Sheffield, and London, 22 July–15 Dec 1989; incl. memoirs by John Ward and Trevor Halliday]

Archives RA, MSS, minutes, records | SOUND broadcast dialogue with Stanley Casson (1889–1944), before 1933
Likenesses M. Lambert, terracotta bust, 1959, RA · T. C. Dugdale, group portrait, oils (*Lunch at the Chelsea Arts Club*), Chelsea Arts Club, London · T. Ramos, portrait, repro. in *The Times* (26 June 1961); priv. coll.
Wealth at death £46,563: probate, 7 March 1969, *CGPLA Eng. & Wales*

Rushcliffe. For this title name *see* Betterton, Henry Bucknall, Baron Rushcliffe (1872–1949).

Rushook, Thomas (*d.* 1393), bishop of Chichester, was prior of the Dominican house at Hereford by 1352 and still in 1354. Presumably he was professed there and was probably of a local family, there being the village of Rushock in the county. Where he obtained his degree of DTh is unknown, and it is not mentioned until as late as April 1383. By 1373 he was provincial of his order in England, when he was asked by the crown for his opinion on the pope's claim to churches' temporalities. In June 1378, together with the other officers of the English province, he was deposed in a general council of the order at Carcassonne after a dispute with the master-general. On 10 November the crown authorized him to appeal to the pope, and all English Dominicans were prohibited from impeding him in the continued exercise of his office or in his appeal. On 25 August 1379, after a hearing of the case by Cardinal Nicolò Carracciolo and benefiting from the circumstance of the great schism, Rushook was restored to his office by Urban VI. Perhaps this crisis brought him to the attention of the royal court. By 5 May 1379 he had been appointed confessor to the boy king, Richard II. On 6 October 1380 he was granted for life the office of chirographer of the common bench, but the appointment was reversed on 20 December because the incumbent was still alive. In November 1381 there was a petition in parliament that he should not 'come to or live in the king's household save only at the four principal feasts of the year' (*RotP*, 3.101); this was rejected by the government, but such open criticism is early testimony to the dislike Rushook could inspire and of his perceived influence with the young king: John Gower later described him as 'a fawning confessor and a professor of evil who lay hidden under the wings of the king, a friar black within and without' (Wright, 1.421).

Rushook resigned his office as provincial on becoming archdeacon of St Asaph on 9 June 1382; his new office was a personal gift from the king, quite anomalous and even uncanonical for a friar to hold. On 14 or 15 January 1383 he was papally provided as bishop of Llandaff and consecrated in the Blackfriars house in London on 3 May. On 18 October he was given the rectory of Newland, Gloucestershire, to supply an adequate income. He remained in attendance on the king as his confessor. Apart from one or two personal favours for friends, there is no official sign of his influence. However, on 16 October 1385 he was translated on the king's nomination to Chichester, against the election of Richard Scrope by the chapter, who may well have been indicating their explicit dislike for Rushook.

While continuing as king's confessor Rushook can be seen travelling and working in his diocese at least in December 1386 and June–August 1387; no register survives to give a clearer picture. However, Rushook was among those who gave formal witness to the decision of the leading judges in Richard II's favour at Nottingham on 25 August 1387, against the establishment by the Wonderful Parliament in the previous year of a supervisory commission over his rule. Hostile sources even said that Rushook was to the fore in threatening the justices if they decided otherwise. Unsurprisingly, he suffered when leading magnates took military action and had Richard's advisers purged in the Merciless Parliament. In January 1388 Rushook was one of those ordered from court. Not without courage, he still attended the parliament. On 6 March he was attacked so fiercely by the Commons there that, had the clergy present not stood firm on his privilege, he might have faced capital punishment. He was impeached for treason, tried in person, and on 12 May found guilty; his goods were held forfeit to the crown as of 1 October 1387, as too the temporalities of his see. Rushook himself was sentenced to exile in Cork in Ireland, with a maximum subsistence of £26 6s. 8d. p.a., 'if any of his friends wish to give him as much' (*RotP*, 3.244). On 8 July he received a safe conduct to be at Bristol by 1 August and in Cork by 29 September.

The king's opponents were thorough; by 17 November 1388 they had had Rushook translated to the see of Kilmore, which although in Ireland was well outside English control. However, armed with information from friends of the bishop about his misery, and now somewhat recovered in personal authority, on 10 March 1390 Richard II granted him an annuity of £40. He was paid for the last time on 25 January 1393, so probably he died soon afterwards. As a Dominican, he could make no will. He was, for no obvious reason, buried at Seal in Kent. Although Richard had not dared recall him as confessor, he made his position clear enough by employing Rushook's young companion and chaplain from the Hereford house, John Burghill, instead. He was to attract similar abuse. It should be pointed out, however, that those close to Richard II were rarely parasites or incapable; indeed usually he favoured talent. Rushook's sins seem those of unpopular loyalty rather than of personal demerit.   R. G. DAVIES

Sources R. G. Davies, 'The episcopate in England and Wales, 1375–1443', PhD diss., University of Manchester, 1974, 3.ccxxxviii–ccxl · C. F. R. Palmer, 'The king's confessors', *The Antiquary*, 22 (1890), 265–6 · *RotP*, 3.101, 243–4 · T. Wright, ed., *Political poems and songs relating to English history*, 1, Rolls Series, 14 (1859)

Rushout, Sir John, fourth baronet (1685–1775), politician, born on 6 February 1685, was the fourth son of Sir James Rushout, first baronet (1644–1698), of Milnst-Maylards, Essex, and his wife, Alice, the daughter and heir of Edward Pitt, of Harrow on the Hill, and the widow of Edward Palmer. His grandfather, a Flemish merchant, settled in England in the early seventeenth century and was naturalized in 1634. His father bought an estate near Evesham in the 1640s, and represented that borough in two parliaments.

Rushout was educated at Eton College. He became a captain in the Horse Guards in 1710, but retired from the service two years later. He succeeded his nephew Sir James Rushout as fourth baronet on 21 September 1711; the manor of Maylards, however, passed out of the family. At a by-election in April 1713 he entered parliament for the borough of Malmesbury, a seat he held until 1722. In that year he was chosen for both Malmesbury and Evesham, but having been defeated on petition for the former constituency he sat for Evesham, which he continued to represent until he retired from parliament at the dissolution of 1768. By then he had attained the position of father of the House of Commons. On 16 October 1729 he married Anne (d. 1766), the sixth daughter of George Compton, fourth earl of Northampton; they had one son and two daughters.

Rushout was a frequent though apparently boring speaker in the house. Following his traditional whig principles, he voted against the Septennial Act but for the repeal of the Occasional Conformity and Schism Acts. He initiated the Commons inquiry into the Atterbury plot, and was a leading figure in the impeachment of Lord Macclesfield in 1725. That same year, he followed his friend William Pulteney (later Lord Bath) into opposition, where he remained for the rest of Walpole's administration. Rushout acted as Pulteney's second in the latter's duel with Lord Hervey in St James's Park on 25 January 1731. He served as teller for the opposition against the convention in 1739, and was chosen as one of the committee of secrecy appointed, on 26 March 1742, to inquire into Walpole's conduct during the last ten years of his ministry. In February 1742 he accepted office in the ministry of Lord Carteret (afterwards Earl Granville) as a lord commissioner of the Treasury with a salary of £1600 a year, and in December 1743 was promoted to the very lucrative post of treasurer of the navy. He was admitted to the privy council on 19 January 1744, but was dismissed on the formation of the 'broadbottom' administration in the following December.

Rushout then joined the Leicester House group with others of the Bath–Granville connection, and was expecting a peerage when Frederick acceded. After the death of the prince of Wales he gravitated towards the duke of Newcastle with the hope of obtaining a title, but he became less active in the house. He had to fight a contest at Evesham, however, in both the 1754 and 1761 general elections, which cost him dearly in both money and effort. He supported Wilkes in the privilege debates of 23 and 24 November 1763, and voted against Grenville's government on general warrants the following year. He declined standing for re-election at Evesham in 1768, 'on account of his age', but later did become a candidate to thwart a possible opposition to his son, John, who continued to represent Evesham until 1796. He died, aged eighty-nine, on 2 February 1775.   W. R. WILLIAMS, rev. M. E. CLAYTON

Sources HoP, *Commons, 1754–90* · R. R. Sedgwick, 'Rushout, Sir John', HoP, *Commons, 1715–54* · HoP, *Commons, 1690–1715* [draft] · A. S. Foord, *His Majesty's opposition, 1714–1830* (1964) · C. Jones, ed., *Party and management in parliament, 1660–1784* (1984) · Walpole, *Corr.*

Archives Worcs. RO, papers

Likenesses J. F. Moore, bust, 1769, Worcester Infirmary · J. M. Rysbrack, bust on monument, c.1775, St Peter and St Paul Church, Blockley, Gloucestershire

Rushout, John, second Baron Northwick (1769–1859), collector and art connoisseur, was born on 16 February 1769, the eldest son in the family of two sons and three daughters of Sir John Rushout (d. 1800), later first Baron Northwick, and his wife, Rebecca, daughter of Humphrey Bowles of Wanstead in Essex. He was descended from a Flemish family, who moved to London as merchants in the reign of Charles I and settled at Northwick, Worcestershire. Rushout's father chose an unconventional education for him: instead of a public school followed by university, he was sent to a school in Hackney and then to Neufchâtel.

Rushout spent a year in Spain before travelling in September 1793 to Italy, where he remained until 1800 as an attaché to the ambassador to the king of Naples. He travelled extensively throughout Italy; his 'voyage de catalogue' (priv. coll.) records places and dates but gives little information about the impression the cities made on him. He made friendships among many of the most eminent men of the day, including Edward Gibbon, Horatio Nelson (Viscount Nelson), Sir William Hamilton and his wife, Richard Payne Knight, Antonio Canova, and Vincenzo Camuccini. He later wrote that he had developed:

> an unbounded admiration for the works of the most refined art in painting, sculpture and architecture, with which [Rome] then abounded … These were the seductive amusements of my youth: they have clung to me through a long life, and they are now the solace of my old age. (Ingamells, 830)

The classical scholar J. B. S. Morritt recorded that when he met Rushout in Naples in 1795 the latter's collection of medals had already reached 12,000, and that Rushout had given up 'his whole time to it [collecting] from morning to night' (ibid.).

Rushout returned to England on succeeding his father as second Baron Northwick in 1800, and was able to devote himself to the formation of the collection for which Northwick Park became famous. In his introduction to the catalogue of Northwick pictures (1921), Tancred Borenius wrote that Lord Northwick was a:

> collector of very high intelligence and discrimination. Living at a time when the value of works of art in the market was one of taste and appreciation rather than of mere commerce, he was able to avail himself of an ample fortune to buy the finest specimens of the Fine Arts which came into the market.

He also planted beeches, firs, and larches on the Northwick estate, and created ornamental cascades along the brook which flowed through his woodlands.

Northwick was a catholic collector, and bought actively at auctions for over half a century. He acquired pictures of all schools, especially Italian pictures from all periods, Flemish pictures, and contemporary British paintings. His pioneering interest was in Italian pictures of the fifteenth and early sixteenth centuries. So extensive did his collection become that he built a special picture gallery at Northwick Park in 1832, and some years later acquired Thirlestane House in Cheltenham, the guide to which in 1846 listed over 500 pictures. By 1859 the collection exceeded 1400 pictures; sculpture, bronzes, antique gems and cameos, enamels, coins, carvings, miniatures, and manuscripts also formed part of the collection. Of liberal disposition, he opened Thirlestane House to the public and it became one of the greatest attractions of Cheltenham. Northwick was an initial subscriber to the British Institution, founded in 1805; a member of the Society of Dilettanti; and a fellow of the Society of Antiquaries.

Northwick died, unmarried and intestate, at Northwick Park on 20 January 1859. He was succeeded as third Baron Northwick by his nephew, George Rushout-Bowles MP. As his property had to be divided equally among his nearest kin, it was necessary for Thirlestane House and the famous collections to be sold. The auction was conducted by Harry Phillips, auctioneer of New Bond Street, London, in July and August 1859 and raised some £95,000 in eighteen days: four pictures were bought by the National Gallery, and others by collectors of the calibre of William Douglas, eleventh duke of Hamilton, Walter Scott, fifth duke of Buccleuch, the fourth marquess of Hertford, and Baron James de Rothschild. However, a considerable part of the collections was bought by George, third Baron Northwick, and was taken to Northwick Park.

CHARLES SEBAG-MONTEFIORE, *rev.*

Sources *Annual Register* (1859) · T. Borenius, *The Northwick pictures* (1921) · J. Ingamells, ed., *A dictionary of British and Irish travellers in Italy, 1701–1800* (1997) · G. F. Waagen, *Treasures of art in Great Britain*, 3 vols. (1854) · memorial, Gloucestershire, Blockley church
Archives priv. coll., MSS, 'voyage de catalogue' | Bodl. Oxf., letters to Sir T. Phillipps
Likenesses A. Kauffmann, oils; Christies, 25 June 1965
Wealth at death under £160,000: resworn probate, Aug 1860, *CGPLA Eng. & Wales* (1859)

Rushton, Benjamin (1785–1853), hand-loom weaver and radical agitator, was born at Dewsbury in Yorkshire, but later moved to Halifax, where he found employment as a fancy-worsted weaver, residing at Friendly Fold in the village of Ovenden. He married Mary Helliwell (*b.* 1786) of Ovenden at Halifax parish church on 16 August 1809, but by 1851 was a widower, living with his daughter, son-in-law, grandchildren, and sons. His sons, Zimri and Henry Hunt Rushton, bore respectively the names of an obscure Old Testament rebel leader and a celebrated contemporary radical orator, while his grandchildren's names commemorated the Chartist leader Henry Vincent and the legendary Swiss freedom fighter William Tell, reflecting the radical sympathies of this weaving family across two generations.

At a public meeting in Halifax in January 1838, well before the publication of the People's Charter, Rushton supported a resolution calling for five of its six points, maintaining that 'until they had universal suffrage the aristocracy would continue to rob them'. He also proposed a motion for the repeal of the new poor law, lamenting the prospect of ending his days in a 'bastille' (*Halifax Guardian*, 23 Jan 1838). He later addressed a vast Chartist open-air demonstration at Hartshead Moor in support of the first national petition in May 1839; harangued meetings of rioters in Halifax in August 1842, for which he was arrested and imprisoned; chaired a Chartist rally on Skircoat Moor in April 1848 in support of the third national petition; spoke at a mass meeting at Blackstone Edge on the eve of the return of Ernest Jones to Halifax, following his release from prison in July 1850; and served as treasurer for the West Riding Chartists.

Rushton was remembered by contemporaries as a passionate speaker with a tendency to use 'rather broad language' (Wilson, 220). Occasionally his tone was menacing, for example, when he unambiguously advocated armed action and openly expressed sympathy with continental revolutionaries following the rejection of the third Chartist petition in May 1848; but the imagery and rhetoric of his public oratory drew heavily on the Bible. He observed cynically at a general election meeting in 1841 that all the candidates were promising 'plenty of gold and silver like the stones in the Jerusalem streets and loaves as large as Goliath of Gath' while the banner of the Ovenden weavers proclaimed 'Be not ye afraid of them, remember the Lord, who is great and terrible, and fight for your brethren, your sons and your daughters, your wives and your houses' (*Halifax Guardian*, 3 July 1841).

Rushton was received into membership of the Methodist New Connexion at Salem, North Parade, Halifax, on 19 February 1815, and subsequently supported the development of the cause at Ovenden, serving as a Sunday school teacher and popular local preacher, appearing at chapel anniversary services in a clean brat, patched knee-breeches, highly polished clogs, and a tall hat. However, he became increasingly critical of organized religion and vociferously anti-clerical. At an anti-poor law meeting in Halifax in 1837 he criticized the whig government's provision of a salary of £15,000 for the archbishop of Canterbury and later seconded a resolution at Hartshead Moor binding the meeting 'not to attend any place of worship where the administration of services is inimical to civil liberty' (Yeo, 120). He probably withdrew from the Methodist New Connexion around the time of William Cobbett's appeal to Methodists to refuse to pay their dues, later declaring that 'he had given nothing to the parsons since 1821', but continued to preach on Methodist property until the end of the decade, to the growing consternation of the Methodist authorities (E. P. Thompson, 438). Thereafter he occupied the pulpits of radical and secessionist congregations across the West Riding, taking as his text 'The poor ye have with you always' on one documented occasion at the Chartist chapel at Littletown in the Spen valley (ibid., 439). His Methodist background and predominantly radical sympathies were characteristic of a generation of popular preachers who brought radical instincts into Methodism and Methodist insights into radicalism until expulsion or withdrawal severed their increasingly tenuous links with the Methodist movement. Indeed, before his death he pointedly requested that no paid minister be allowed to speak at his funeral.

By 1847, in order to supplement his meagre earnings from weaving and enable him to buy shares in the Chartist land company, Rushton had acquired the additional occupation of tea dealer. He continued weaving into his late sixties and was observed by the Chartist Ernest Jones working on intricate patterns at his loom shortly before his death. Rushton died on 17 June 1853 at Friendly Fold, Ovenden, Halifax. He died, as he had lived, in poverty. The local Chartist executive decreed that he should have a public funeral at their expense on Sunday 26 June 1853 and that, in accordance with his wishes, a petition calling for the People's Charter should be adopted 'over his remains' (*Halifax Courier*, 25 June 1853). In the event, the petition was adopted at a rally held immediately after the funeral ceremony, which was conducted at the Halifax general cemetery, Lister Lane, by R. G. Gammage of the Chartist national executive and members of the Ovenden Oddfellows, of which Rushton had been an honorary member, with a eulogy hailing Rushton as 'a noble patriot' delivered by Ernest Jones (Vincent, 220). Rushton was borne to the grave by a hearse drawn by beplumed horses along a route lined, as Ernest Jones observed, by 'a continuous wall of human beings ranged for a length of two miles on either side of road' (Epstein and Thompson, 329). Five special trains brought Chartists from Bradford, and attendance at the funeral, estimated by the *Halifax Guardian* at between 6000 and 10,000, was greater than that at the funerals of national Chartist leaders. The Chartist historian Dorothy Thompson has concluded that 'Rushton epitomised the type of West Riding local leader', the majority of whom were weavers, 'earning their living at their work but always taking time to attend, and very often chair great demonstrations or local meetings' (D. Thompson, 225–6).   JOHN A. HARGREAVES

Sources *Halifax Courier* (25 June 1853) · *Halifax Courier* (2 July 1853) · *Halifax Guardian* (25 June 1853) · *Halifax Guardian* (2 July 1853) · D. Thompson, *The Chartists: popular politics in the industrial revolution* (1984) · J. A. Hargreaves, 'Religion and society in the parish of Halifax, *c.*1740–1914', PhD diss., Huddersfield Polytechnic, 1991 · B. Wilson, 'The struggles of an old chartist', *Testaments of radicalism*, ed. D. Vincent (1977), 193–242 · K. Tiller, 'Late chartism: Halifax, 1847–1858', *The Chartist experience: studies in working-class radicalism and culture, 1830–60*, ed. J. Epstein and D. Thompson (1982), 311–344, esp. 327 · Halifax parish church, marriage register, D53 1/45 · census returns for Halifax, 1841, 1851 · d. cert. · E. V. Chapman, *John Wesley and Co.* (1952) · G. R. Dalby, 'The chartist movement in Halifax', *Transactions of the Halifax Antiquarian Society* (1956) · F. Peel, *Spen Valley: past and present* (1893) · E. Yeo, 'Christianity and chartist struggle, 1838–1842', *Past and Present*, 91 (1981) · *Halifax Guardian* (23 Jan 1838) · E. P. Thompson, *The making of the English working class* (1963)

Wealth at death died poor: Wilson, 'Struggles of an old Chartist'

Rushton, Edward (1756–1814), poet and slavery abolitionist, was born on 13 November 1756 in John Street, Liverpool, the son of Thomas Rushton, a Liverpool victualler. He entered Liverpool Free School at the age of six and by

eleven was apprenticed to Messrs Watt and Gregson, a Liverpool shipping company with West Indian interests. At the age of sixteen he showed great courage while still an apprentice when he took the helm of a ship which the captain and crew were about to abandon. He guided the vessel back into the safety of the port of Liverpool. This act of bravery was endorsed on his indenture of apprenticeship and he was promoted to second mate.

In 1773, while on a slave ship to Guinea, Rushton survived a sinking, then later that year on a slaver heading for Dominica he became so sickened by the brutal treatment of the slaves that he was charged with mutiny after remonstrating with the captain. Many of the slaves had contracted the highly contagious ophthalmia, which had spread like wildfire in the appalling conditions. Rushton took pity on them and tried to bring what relief he could. He caught the disease himself, entirely lost the sight of his left eye, and suffered from an opacity of the right cornea.

Meanwhile Rushton's father had remarried and when Edward returned he was turned out of the family home by his new stepmother. He was taken in by his sister and his father continued to support him with an allowance of 4*s.* a week, out of which he paid a young boy 3*d.* a week to read to him.

The experience of his travels and the injustices he had witnessed led to the publication in 1782 of Rushton's first poem, *The Dismembered Empire*, a condemnation of the American War of Independence. In 1797 he wrote to former President George Washington questioning his hypocrisy in retaining slaves for his own use while fighting for liberty and independence. He wrote in similar fashion to Thomas Paine but both turned a deaf ear and did not reply. His abhorrence of the slave trade was reflected in *The West Indian Eclogues*, the first of his poems on the subject published in 1787. So well known had Rushton's reputation and views become that Thomas Clarkson sought him out while on a visit to Liverpool to credit his contribution to the abolitionist cause.

About 1782 Rushton's father established Edward and his sister in a tavern at 19 Crooked Lane, Liverpool. Rushton was unsuited to the work, and after his marriage about 1784 to Isabella Rain (*d.* 1811) he moved on to become the editor of the *Liverpool Herald*. This career was also to be short-lived. Concerned with the excessive barbarism of the press-gang Rushton attacked the practice in the *Herald*. His partner, worried about a local backlash resulting from Rushton's allegations, suggested a retraction, but Rushton resigned rather than compromise. His views on press-gang brutality inspired his poem *Will Clewline*, published in 1806.

A short while later Rushton became a bookseller at 44 Paradise Street, but yet again his outspoken views made him enemies and lost him valued custom. In what was a period of revolution in France and social unrest in England, Rushton made no attempt to moderate his radical thoughts. At length his business recovered and he was able to live out his life in relative comfort while raising a family.

In the late 1780s Rushton regularly met a dozen or so

associates in a society which is thought to have been the forerunner of the ill-fated radical Debating Society formed by William Roscoe and the surgeon James Currie in 1795. Here, with the help of his companions, Rushton formulated the idea of raising funds to provide care for the numerous local blind paupers. The Liverpool School for the Indigent Blind, the first of its kind in the country, opened in 1791, although Rushton does not appear to have played any further part in its operation. His literary output continued with the publication of a collection of poems in 1806, which also included his letter to Washington and an *Essay on Causes of the Dissimilarity of Colour in the Human Species.*

Rushton regained his sight in 1807 following an operation by the Manchester surgeon Benjamin Gibson, and was thus able to see his wife and children for the first time. His wife, Isabella, died a short time later in 1811 as well as one of his daughters. Rushton died of paralysis on 22 November 1814 at his home in Paradise Street and was buried in St James's cemetery, Liverpool.

Edward Rushton (1795–1857), the eldest of the Rushtons' four children, was born on 22 September 1795 and became a prominent figure in Liverpool politics. He was called to the bar on 18 November 1831 and was appointed stipendiary magistrate of Liverpool on 17 May 1839. He was an ardent social reformer, advocating Catholic emancipation and prison reform, including humane treatment of juvenile offenders, and opposing capital punishment. He died on 4 April 1851, aged fifty-five, at his home, Parkside House in Liverpool, and was buried in St James's cemetery, Liverpool.   MICHAEL ROYDEN

Sources W. Shepherd, 'Sketch of a life of the author', in E. Rushton, *Poems and other writings* (1824) • M. G. Thomas, *Edward Rushton*, N.I.B. Biographies, 1 (1949) • M. W. Royden, *Pioneers and perseverance* (1991) • H. Smithers, *Liverpool: its commerce, statistics and institutions* (1825) • E. Rushton jun., 'Biographical sketch of Edward Rushton', *Belfast Magazine* (Dec 1814) • W. L. Rushton, *Edward Rushton Jnr: letters of a Templar (1820–1850)* (1903) • R. W. Proctor, *Literary reminiscences and gleanings* (1860), 141 • T. W. M. Lund, *Blindness, or, Some thoughts for sighted people* [sermon preached in the chapel of the Royal School for the Blind, Liverpool, 20th Feb 1887; includes appx A, *A sketch of the life of Edward Rushton, the blind poet* (1887)] • J. A. Picton, *Memorials of Liverpool* (1878), 1.426; 2.166, 215 • A. Bowker, 'In memoriam', or, Funeral records of Liverpool celebrities (1876) • S. Bannister, *Worthies of the working classes* (1854), 7 • H. Gawthrop, *Fraser's guide to Liverpool and Birkenhead* (1855), 289–92 • IGI

Archives U. Lpool, letters to William Rathbone [Edward Rushton, 1795–1857]

Likenesses Gibson, bust, 1815, repro. in Royden, *Pioneers and perseverance*; copy, Royal Liverpool School for the Blind, Wavertree, Liverpool • E. Smith, line engraving, pubd 1815, BM • S. Gambardella, oils (Edward Rushton, 1795–1857), Walker Art Gallery, Liverpool • cameo print, repro. in Royden, *Pioneers and perseverance* • portrait, Royal Liverpool School for the Blind, Wavertree, Liverpool; repro. in Royden, *Pioneers and perseverance*, ix

Rushton, Edward (1795–1857). *See under* Rushton, Edward (1756–1814).

Rushton, Robert (1793–1833), servant, the son of Samuel Rushton, a tenant farmer at Newstead, Nottinghamshire, was introduced to Byron by William Fletcher in April 1804

and was soon taken into his household. Byron paid for his education locally and had him vaccinated against smallpox (*Byron's Letters and Journals*, 1.187, 189). His appearance, 'slim, with light auburn hair and dark eyes' (Peach, 27), is immortalized in George Sanders's double portrait of 1807–8, now in the Royal Collection. Apart from Mrs Mule, a bedmaker, Byron employed only Rushton, Fletcher, one footman, and a groom, at his London bachelor establishment. In May 1809 Rushton was dismissed in disgrace and Fletcher sacked when caught frequenting prostitutes (*Byron's Letters and Journals*, 1.203). Quickly forgiven, they accompanied Byron and John Cam Hobhouse to Portugal in the following month. Rushton appears as 'my little page' in 'Childe Harold's Goodnight' (Lord Byron, *Childe Harold's Pilgrimage*, I.XIII–XIV). With Byron, Hobhouse, and Sanguinetti (another servant), Rushton rode from the Tagus to Puerta Santa Maria in Spain via Seville and Cadiz between 20 July and 3 August (Fletcher and the luggage went by sea). On 15 August he returned to England from Gibraltar, his master lubriciously alleging to his mother, Catherine Byron, that '*boys* are not *safe* amongst the Turks' (*Byron's Letters and Journals*, 1.221–2). In January 1812 Rushton again caused vexation by openly objecting to the elevation of Byron's lover, Susan Vaughan, above all other Newstead servants. Susan was soon sent home to Wales, and Rushton was ordered to continue studying '*Accounts* and Land-Measurement, etc' (ibid., 2.232). On 7 September 1813 he went to work for James Wedderburn Webster at Aston Hall, Rotherham, but was back with Byron by April 1816, again accompanying him abroad, travelling as far as Geneva, now 'treated rather as a secretary than a servant' (*Literary Gazette*, 364n.). He returned to England with Scrope Davies 'and various manuscripts of Byron's' (Marchand, 2.647), on 5 September 1816.

In Nottingham on 7 May 1817 Rushton married Elizabeth Bagnall (d. 1846), 'a woman of very pleasing manners and lively conversation', with whom he subsequently 'lived at Arnold, kept a boys' school and a lodge garden' (Beardall MS, 37). As a gardener he was famous for skilful grafting of roses. In 1832 Thomas Wildman, keen to patronize an associate of Byron's, bestowed on him the tenancy of a farm at Newstead. Rushton also joined Colonel Wildman's Sherwood Rangers yeomanry. His tragic and premature death in 1833 was provoked by an overdose of Trooper's ointment taken for a sore throat that had been started by breathing in bonfire smoke. He was buried in his wife's family vault at St Peter's churchyard, Nottingham, on 5 May 1833. Rushton's widow returned to Arnold, but the school had failed by 1840 when she took over the keeper's lodge at Newstead, where she continued until her death in 1846. The youngest son, George, was appointed butler to Thomas Wildman, but suffered the ultimate Byronic fate: drowning in the Newstead lake just five months after his mother's demise. The only daughter, Eliza Ann, remained on the estate until 1850 (Newstead rental, NA 999).

Searching in March 1816 for evidence of 'unnatural crimes' committed by Byron, Stephen Lushington heard from Lady Caroline Lamb 'that Rushton was one of those whom he had corrupted' (Lovelace MS 129, fol. 87). Lushington was well aware of the unreliability of that particular witness, though Byron's myriad feebler biographers make it a fact. None of Byron's erotic lyrics were inspired by Rushton, nor was there anything unusual in their master–mentor, servant–protégé relationship. Its platonic nature is best confirmed by the fact that Rushton did not accompany Byron to Greece.   RALPH LLOYD-JONES

Sources Notts. Arch., Beardall papers, DD 721/1 · *Byron's letters and journals*, ed. L. A. Marchand, 12 vols. (1973–82), vols. 1–2 · L. A. Marchand, *Byron: a biography*, 3 vols. (1957) · A. Peach, 'Portraits of Byron', *Walpole Society*, 62 (2000), 1–144 · *Literary Gazette* (7 June 1828) · Newstead rental MSS, Newstead Abbey, Nottinghamshire · Lovelace MSS, Bodl. Oxf.
Likenesses G. Sanders, double portrait, oils, 1807–8 (with Byron), Royal Collection

Rushton, William Albert Hugh (1901–1980), neurophysiologist, was born in London on 8 December 1901, eldest of the three children and the elder son of William Rushton, a dentist from Liverpool, and his wife, Alice Louise Jane Amsler, granddaughter of the Swiss engraver Samuel Amsler. Alice Amsler was a good pianist and Rushton thought he acquired his love of music from her.

Rushton was educated at Gresham's School, Holt, at Emmanuel College, Cambridge (1921–8), and at University College, London (1932–5). He gained a college scholarship in 1923, a second class in part one of the natural sciences tripos in 1924, and a first class in part two of the same tripos in 1925 (physiology). He was awarded the George Henry Lewes studentship in 1926, and in 1928 obtained his PhD for research under E. D. Adrian on the electrical excitability of peripheral nerves. His major contribution was to analyse the spatial spread of excitability, and he did the groundwork upon which Alan Hodgkin and Andrew Huxley built the ionic theory of nervous conduction a few years later. He continued this line of work until about 1950, and it was on the strength of it that he was elected FRS in 1948. Rushton married Marjorie Glasson (b. 1903/4), geography lecturer and daughter of William Norman Kendrick, a colliery sales manager of Cardiff, on 30 July 1930. They had five children, of whom one died in infancy.

Rushton gained his medical qualifications, MRCS and LRCP, only in 1937 after numerous attempts, and he expressed dissatisfaction with his early research achievements. Nevertheless, he was awarded a visiting fellowship with Detlev Bronk at the Johnson Foundation, Philadelphia (1929–31), was elected research fellow of Emmanuel College for two years in 1932 and again in 1935, and was appointed to a university lectureship at Cambridge in the latter year. In 1938 he became staff fellow and director of medical studies at Trinity College, where he remained a fellow for the rest of his life. He spent the years 1942–7 in psychoanalysis with Susan Isaacs, and said afterwards that the process had 'renewed' him. At the age of forty-seven he started his renewed career as a visual physiologist with R. Granit in Stockholm on a sabbatical year, in

1948–9. He ultimately chose to measure the photosensitive visual pigments in the living human eye. He also succeeded in providing the first direct confirmation that colour blindness was caused by lack of photosensitive pigments. His revitalization of the psychophysical side of vision research was even more important. While noteworthy advances were being made in the photochemistry and neurophysiology of vision, Rushton sought for explanations of the whole process, from incident photon to effective vision, and his ingenious psychophysical experiments set an example that the world attempted to follow.

Rushton's basic character was introspective and thoughtful, but at the same time he was intensely interested in other people, and responded with great personal warmth to anyone who displayed intelligence or originality on the topics in which he was interested. He sometimes cut a flamboyant figure, both to the undergraduates he taught and at scientific meetings, yet the purpose behind his outrageous questions and witty comments was clear, for he constantly championed the reasoning power of the intellect against the mere dull amassing of facts.

Rushton gained numerous honours for his work on vision, including foreign honorary membership of the American Academy of Arts and Sciences. He was awarded the Prentice medal of the American Academy of Optometry in 1963, the Feldberg prize in 1967, membership of the Royal Swedish Academy of Sciences in 1968, the royal medal of the Royal Society in 1970, and the Proctor medal in 1971. He was appointed professor of visual physiology at Cambridge in 1966 (he had become reader in physiology in 1953), and after retirement in 1968 he spent eight more very active years as distinguished research professor in psychobiology in Tallahassee.

Rushton took great pride in his family, who shared his musical accomplishment, his wife playing the piano and oboe, and his children (two sons and two daughters) the cello, horn, clarinet, and flute, while Rushton himself played the bassoon, viola, and violin. The youngest son, Julian, later became professor of music at Leeds. Rushton died on 21 June 1980 at his home, Shawms, Conduit Head Road, Cambridge, and was survived by his wife.
HORACE BARLOW, *rev.*

Sources H. B. Barlow, *Memoirs FRS*, 32 (1986), 421–59 · W. A. H. Rushton, 'From nerves to eyes', *The neurosciences: paths of discovery*, ed. F. G. Worden (1975) · *The Times* (23 June 1980) · *Vision Research*, 22 (1975) · private information (1986) · personal knowledge (1986) · d. cert. · m. cert.
Archives Wellcome L., corresp. and notes | CAC Cam., corresp. with A. V. Hill
Wealth at death £162,454: probate, 5 Nov 1980, *CGPLA Eng. & Wales*

Rushton, William George [Willie] (1937–1996), cartoonist, comedian, and author, was born on 18 August 1937 at 3 Wilbraham Place, Chelsea, the only child of John Atherton Rushton (d. 1958), a publisher, and his Welsh wife, Veronica Hannah Gilbert James. Willie Rushton was educated at Shrewsbury School, where his contemporaries included Richard Ingrams, Christopher Booker, and Paul

William George Rushton (1937–1996), by Tim Cuff

Foot. With Ingrams and Booker he produced *The Wallopian*, a satirical version of the school magazine, to which he contributed cartoons. Along with commentary on schoolmasters that was more barbed than the authorities found acceptable, their chief targets were pseudo-intellectuals, for whom they coined the term 'pseuds', which later gained common currency in *Private Eye*. Academically undistinguished, Rushton claimed to have failed O-level maths seven times; confronted with a specimen in a bottle during a biology exam and asked 'What's this?', he answered, 'Disgusting'. His theatrical talent found an outlet at Shrewsbury: he recalled that when he played Lord Loam in *The Admirable Crichton*, 'the audience wondered which elderly member of staff had been dragooned into playing Loam' (*The Independent*, 13 Dec 1996).

Rushton did his national service in the army, among the last generation to do so. He failed the officer selection board, and served in the ranks. An anti-authoritarian, he found the army absurd, but welcomed the egalitarian ideas he developed as a trooper in Bad Oeynhausen. He left the army in 1952 and worked for a short time in a solicitor's office. The occasional cartoons he sent to *Punch* were rejected. He left the law firm after narrowly missing being knocked down by a bus, vowing that he would not waste another day of his life doing something he did not enjoy. His contemporaries from Shrewsbury had gone on

to university: at Oxford, Ingrams was editing two magazines, *Mesopotamia* and *Parson's Pleasure*, to which Rushton contributed cartoons. The idea for a London-based satirical magazine was developed in a Chelsea pub, and the first issue of *Private Eye* appeared on 25 October 1961. Early issues of the paper were put together in Rushton's bedroom in his mother's house at 28 Scarsdale Villas, Kensington: he alone mastered the art of laying out Christopher Booker's copy and his own cartoons, which were then taken to Neasden to be printed by the then revolutionary photolitho process. *Private Eye* was well received, and favourably reviewed in *The Observer*, and its success was assured. Rushton was more than a cartoonist for the magazine. He supplied jokes, puns, and *doubles entendres*, and had a genius for inventing names for *Eye* characters, such as Lunchtime O'Booze, the archetypal hard-drinking journalist.

Also in 1961 Rushton made his professional acting début, in Spike Milligan's *The Bed-Sitting Room*, at the Marlowe Theatre, Canterbury; the critic Kenneth Tynan deemed his performance brilliant. Shortly afterwards, he joined Ingrams, John Wells, and Barbara Windsor in a bizarre cabaret at the Room at the Top (of a department store) in Ilford, where he was recruited by Ned Sherrin, the producer of the satirical BBC television show *That Was The Week That Was* (or *TW3* as it was familiarly known). Rushton had already started writing whimsical songs, like 'Neasden', 'The Bum Song', and 'Fornicazione … is Italian for Love'. On *TW3* (1962–3) he was an immediate success. His weekly impressions of tory politicians have been called 'masterpieces of refined cruelty' (*The Times*, 12 Dec 1996), although he did not really do impressions of individuals so much as impersonations of types: he excelled as the embodiment of pompous, overbearing establishment figures, ripe for knocking down. In 1963 he was persuaded to run against Alec Douglas-Home in the Kinross by-election, a decision he regretted. He won forty-five votes. He was unhappy with the sequel to *TW3*, and left after a few shows. He was put to better use in *Not Only … But Also* (1965–6), which starred Peter Cook and Dudley Moore. In 1968 he married the actress Arlene Dorgan, with whom he had a son; there were two stepsons from her previous marriage.

Rushton's theatrical career continued fitfully (he appeared in *Gulliver's Travels* at the Mermaid in 1971 and again in 1979, and in Eric Idle's *Pass the Butler* at the Globe in 1982), and in 1996 he toured with *Two Old Farts in the Night*, an anarchic run of one-night stands with his fellow radio panellist Barry Cryer. He had a series of cameo roles in films, including *Those Magnificent Men in their Flying Machines* (1965) and *Monte Carlo or Bust* (1969). On television he took the parts of Plautus in Frankie Howerd's comic foray into ancient Rome, *Up Pompeii* (1970), and Major Trumpington in the drama *Colditz* (1974). He never had a satisfactory vehicle to showcase his own talents: *Rushton's Illustrated* (1980) had only one season. He was a regular panellist on the television quiz show *Celebrity Squares* (1985–9) and a popular reader on the children's story programme *Jackanory*. Perhaps his widest following was gained through the cult BBC Radio 4 'antidote to panel games', *I'm Sorry I Haven't a Clue*; he joined it in 1974 and appeared in each yearly series until his death. The show's formula, in which the teams of (usually) Tim Brooke Taylor, Barry Cryer, Graeme Garden, and Willie Rushton were given 'silly things' to do by the chairman, Humphrey Lyttelton, admirably suited Rushton's humour; even his silences could leave the audience rocking with laughter.

Rushton remained prolific as writer, cartoonist, and illustrator. His commitment to *Private Eye* diminished, but he continued to supply it with cartoons, especially to illustrate the regular 'Mrs Wilson's Diary' item, and Auberon Waugh's 'Diary'. He also illustrated Waugh's 'The Way of the World' column in the *Daily Telegraph*, and contributed to his *Literary Review*. As well as illustrating the work of others, he published a number of humorous books, including *Pigsticking, a Joy for Life: a Gentleman's Guide to Sporting Pastimes* (1977), *Bureaucrats: how to Annoy Them* (under the pseudonym R. T. Fishall) (1981), and *Willie Rushton's Great Moments in History* (1984). The original drawings from the latter work found a permanent home in the Victoria and Albert Museum. His cartoons were distinctive, 'distinguished by their clean line and bold use of black and white' (*Daily Telegraph*, 12 Dec 1996), and his caricatures are readily identifiable with their subjects. In his later years he began to work brilliantly in colour. Cricket was a personal passion. His father had sent him for coaching at Lord's before he went to Shrewsbury, and in later life he played for the Lord's Taverners. He wrote a novel, *W. G. Grace's Last Case* (1984), based on a fictional episode in the life of the great cricketer.

Rushton was diagnosed with diabetes in the early 1980s, and gave up beer; he became, according to Richard Ingrams, 'quite grumpy as a result, but his grumpiness had an admirable and jaunty quality to it' (*Daily Telegraph*, 13 Dec 1996). His sudden death profoundly shocked his friends and contemporaries. He went into hospital for heart surgery, and died from complications on 11 December 1996, in the Cromwell Hospital, Kensington.

NED SHERRIN

Sources private information (2004) · personal knowledge (2004) · *Daily Telegraph* (12 Dec 1996) · *The Times* (12 Dec 1996) · *The Independent* (13 Dec 1996) · *The Guardian* (12 Dec 1996) · b. cert. · d. cert.
Archives FILM BFI NFTVA, documentary footage |SOUND BL NSA, performance recording
Likenesses photographs, 1963, Hult. Arch. · T. Cuff, photograph, Apex Photo Agency Ltd, Exeter [*see illus.*] · W. Rushton, self-portrait, caricature, repro. in *The Independent*
Wealth at death £400,929: probate, 12 March 1997, CGPLA Eng. & Wales

Rushworth [Rushforth], **John** (*c*.1612–1690), historian and politician, was born at Acklington Park in the parish of Warkworth, Northumberland, about 1612 according to his own testimony, the eldest child of Lawrence Rushworth (*d*. 1640/42) of Acklington Park and Margaret, daughter of Cuthbert Carnaby of Halton. His father was the eldest son of Alexander Rushworth, son and heir to John Rushworth of Coley Hall, near Halifax. The family name was also referred to as Rushforth; in John's case this could also be

an allusion to his celerity. The Rushworths had a history of financial difficulties. Coley Hall was sold in 1572; Lawrence was imprisoned for debt in 1629; his son would sell the lease of Acklington Park and end his life in debtor's prison. Rushworth was well connected in Yorkshire, whence both of his parents were descended, and he claimed to be 'Neare of kin to Sr Thomas Fairfax' (Bodl. Oxf., MS Wood F.39, fols. 383–4). Rushworth was educated at Oxford, probably at Queen's College, but did not matriculate. He married Hannah, possibly the daughter of Lewis Widdrington of Cheeseburn Grange and sister to Sir Thomas *Widdrington, speaker of the House of Commons. They had four daughters.

Lawyer, parliamentarian, and supplier of news During the 1630s Rushworth began to document significant events and:

> did personally attend and observe all Occurrences of moment during the Eleven years Interval of Parliament, in the *Star-Chamber*, *Court of Honour*, and *Exchequer-Chamber*, when all the Judges of *England* met there upon extraordinary Cases; at the Council Table, when great Causes were heard before the King and Council. (Rushworth, *Collections*, pt 1, sigs. b4r, bv)

He took notes in shorthand, and these records formed the basis of his subsequent history of the period. On 13 April 1638 Rushworth was appointed solicitor to the town of Berwick at £4 per annum, an appointment which he still held in 1671, and on 25 April 1640 he was appointed clerk-assistant to the House of Commons at the request of Henry Elsing, the clerk. He was at this time forbidden to take notes, except at the order of the house (*JHC*, 1640–42, 12). Following the dissolution of the Short Parliament he was admitted, on 14 August 1640, to Lincoln's Inn; the admissions register suggests that his father was then deceased. In 1643 he was appointed cursitor of chancery for Yorkshire and Westmorland. He was called to the bar in 1647.

After the meeting of the Long Parliament, Rushworth continued to work as clerk-assistant, and was increasingly employed as a messenger conveying news and documents between Westminster and the army camps in the north. In his twilight years he recorded: 'it so fell out I Ride 10 severall times with that Expedition between London and Yorke being one hundred and fifty miles in 24 hours at a time' (Bodl. Oxf., MS Wood F.39, fol. 384). Mayors and other officers were ordered to assist Rushworth with resources, including fresh horses. On one occasion Tom Elliot, while secretly taking the great seal to the king at Oxford, encountered Rushworth carrying a message to York. To avoid suspicion he appealed to Rushworth's sense of self-importance by saying that it was fit Rushworth should make haste, and accordingly gave him his horse. In a letter of August 1641, describing the progress in disbanding the Scots at York, Rushworth mentioned that he had overtaken Fairfax on his journey thither, who was himself hastening to York to advance the business; this can be read as an extravagant notice of his expeditiousness (Bodl. Oxf., MS Tanner 66, fol. 139r). Rushworth's initial fame derived from his ability as a messenger: one contemporary described him as 'o^r nimble Mercury Mr Rushforth' (Bodl. Oxf., MS Tanner 63, fol. 43). A 1643 newsbook reported:

> His diligence and speed in faithfully observing these commands of Parliament hath beene well knowne, for he was imployed neere twenty times this last Sommer betweene *York* and *London*, and seldom above twenty foure hours in riding of it, God speed him well, and send him safe backe. (*Kingdoms Weekly Intelligencer*, 13, 21–8 March 1643, 102)

In 1641 Rushworth began to buy news pamphlets and periodicals; from December 1641 he usually bought one newsbook a week and formed an impressive collection of these early periodicals, which he annotated, underlined, and commented on. They subsequently formed one element of his major work, *Historical Collections*.

On 4 January 1642, when Charles I violated the privileges of parliament by entering the lower house with an armed guard to demand the five members impeached of treason, Rushworth disobeyed the parliamentary injunction against taking notes and recorded the exchange. The king sent for Rushworth, who subsequently wrote:

> his Majesty Commanded him, to give him *a Copy of his Speech* in the House, Mr. *Rushworth* humbly besought his Majesty (hoping for an Excuse) to call to mind how Mr. *Francis Nevil* … was committed to the *Tower*, but for telling his Majesty what words were spoken in the House … to which his Majesty smartly replied, *I do not ask you to tell me what was said by any Member of the House but what I said my self*. Whereupon he readily gave Obedience to his Majesties Command, and in his Majesties presence in the Room, called the *Jewel House*, he Transcribed his Majesties *Speech* out of his Characters, his Majesty staying in the Room all the while. And then and there presented the same to the King, which his Majesty was pleased to command to be sent speedily to the *Press*, and the next Morning it came forth in Print. (Rushworth, *Collections*, pt 3, 1.478)

Rushworth did not return to the royalist cause until 1659, though he personally assisted Yorkshire royalists in the interim.

On 11 April 1644 the House of Commons appointed Rushworth licenser to the press with responsibility for pamphlets and newsbooks. Rushworth probably did not edit any newsbook, but he oversaw the production and was involved in the supply of news in the interest of parliament as much as the censoring of content. When Sir Thomas Fairfax was appointed general of the New Model Army, his kinsman and fellow Yorkshireman Rushworth became secretary to the general and the army's council of war. In this position he wrote correspondence on Fairfax's behalf and more generally, with his secretary Samuel Clark and assistant Gilbert Mabbott, worked to promote the reputation of the army through news of its successes. He wrote the accounts of battles which Fairfax communicated to the House of Commons, and many of these were published as news pamphlets with Rushworth's name appended. Rushworth was therefore associated with news in a range of prominent roles: messenger, intelligencer, licenser, and reporter.

When Fairfax was busy Rushworth also wrote personal letters to his father Ferdinando, Lord Fairfax. In one letter of 18 May 1647 Rushworth expressed the general's weariness and desire to resign his command, continuing only through his patience and public spirit. Those who sought to influence Fairfax saw Rushworth as an intermediary. Accompanying Fairfax to Oxford, he was created an MA on 21 May 1649 (he was described as a member of Queen's College), and was subsequently appointed as a delegate to consider relations between city and university. When Fairfax resigned his command on 25 June 1650, he sent his resignation to the Commons by Rushworth. Soon afterwards Rushworth rebuffed approaches by royalists hoping to secure the co-operation of Fairfax and himself.

After Fairfax's resignation Rushworth returned to the practice of law and soon accumulated a number of offices. In January 1651 he was appointed to a committee investigating the reformation of the common law. On 11 August he and Captain Bishop were instructed by the council of state 'to take care to maintain intelligence between Council and the armies'; the intelligencers were given substantial sums of money to accomplish this, and their accounts were examined not long afterwards, perhaps under some suspicion (*CSP dom.*, *1651*, 317). Rushworth was made a freeman of Newcastle upon Tyne in 1652, and remained an agent to the city at least until 1671. In June 1653 he was appointed to the committee to examine fees and profits of the court of probate and wills. In July 1654, with William Rowe, he became registrar to the admiralty court. Much of his business in this period involved the admiralty court and the navy. The act that founded a college at Durham in May 1656 named Rushworth as a 'visitor' responsible for overseeing its management.

Historian and politician During the 1650s Rushworth worked on his *Historical Collections*, a documentary history of the civil wars beginning in 1618 (some royalist historians were suspicious of those who traced the history of the war back in time), written, he claimed in his preface, without commentary or opinions, 'a bare Narrative of matter of Fact, digested in order of time' (Rushworth, *Collections*, pt 1, sig. b*v*). He submitted the manuscript of the first volume to the council of state in October 1657. He may have been seeking patronage, but it is likely that this was a condition of his privileged access to council and parliamentary papers: after Cromwell's death the council ordered him to return their books, though they granted him continuing access. The council appointed readers for the manuscript. Bulstrode Whitelocke saw it in January 1658, as, according to Whitelocke, Cromwell had ordered. The first part of the *Historical Collections* was published in 1659, with a dedication to Richard Cromwell, no doubt a disappointing replacement for his father.

In 1657 Rushworth became an MP, being returned by the town of Berwick to replace the deceased Colonel George Fenwick. He was also returned to Richard Cromwell's parliament in 1659. Again approached by royalists, this time he was more compliant, supplying Lord Mordaunt with information concerning Fairfax and General Monck early in 1660. Sir Edward Hyde briefly doubted his integrity, but

Lord Mordaunt assured the king that Rushworth was 'honest' (*Clarendon State Papers*, 570). When Monck restored the members who had been excluded in December 1648, Rushworth, 'the darling agent of the secluded members', was appointed secretary to the new council of state. In this capacity he expressed its obedience to Monck. Now clearly in favour of a restored monarchy, Rushworth was again returned to the Convention Parliament in 1660. In June he restored to the privy council records which he claimed to have protected 'during the late unhappy times', and was thanked by the king (*Fourth Report*, HMC, 231).

The Restoration did not pass entirely without incident for one so closely associated with regicides. On 24 July 1660 the House of Lords examined Rushworth over what he knew of a meeting at which the king's death was contrived; he indicated a remote knowledge of such an event. Another story was later recorded by Alice Thornton. She implicated Rushworth in a meeting of a 'cabal', all disguised, including Lord Baltimore and William Lilly, at her uncle's house on 29 January 1649. The cabal apparently intended to persuade the king to repent and admit the justice of the high court's proceedings. The story should probably be regarded with some suspicion. Rushworth's past, however, was not in his favour and in the 1661 elections he stood down and was replaced by Edward Grey. He continued as agent for Berwick and for Newcastle, and continued to write newsletters, and in an intercepted letter of June 1667 he remonstrated against a 'great gown man' (presumably Hyde, now earl of Clarendon), who obstructed the calling of a parliament, and the 'bishops and papists' who cheated the king. The discoverer wrote to Sir Joseph Williamson, secretary to Lord Arlington, that 'The King may look for little obedience so long as such men are agents for corporations' (*CSP dom.*, *1667*, 188, 290).

Rushworth's wife, Hannah, and their four daughters are not mentioned in his correspondence, though a letter by the youngest suggests that he was a caring father. The presumed eldest daughter, Hannah, born about 1646, married Sir Francis Fane of Fulbeck in 1664. Rebecca, born about 1649, married Robert Blayney of Kinsham, Hereford, in 1667. Margaret, the third daughter, was a pallbearer at the funeral of Mary, Lady Markham, in 1683. Rushworth was Mary's guardian after the death of her father, Sir Thomas Widdrington, in 1664 and presumably gave consent for her marriage to Sir Robert Markham in 1665, as well as for her sister Ursula's wedding in 1668. Katherine, Rushworth's youngest daughter, wrote a letter to the duke of Newcastle in 1691 thanking him on her father's behalf for a gift of £20 he had given to Rushworth two years before his death, and petitioning him for the fulfilment of his offer of further charity. She observed that she and her three sisters had 'the education of gentlewomen', which made their financial extremities the harder to bear (*Portland MSS*, 2.164–5).

On the appointment of Orlando Bridgeman as lord keeper of the great seal in 1667 Rushworth was made his secretary. When Bridgeman was removed from office in 1672, Rushworth's prospects went into decline. His finances were further damaged by the bankruptcy of Samuel Hartlib the younger, his fellow agent for Newcastle. In 1674–5 he was for a while employed by the Massachusetts assembly as their London agent on a retainer of 12 guineas a year, 'yet is not all he hath done worth a rush … he is old and full of business, and hath but small interest at Court' (HoP, *Commons, 1660–90*, 3.357–9). His correspondence in the 1670s included persistent requests for financial assistance. Rushworth was able to help the imprisoned opposition peer Shaftesbury in February 1678: when shorthand notes of words spoken by the earl in the king's bench were produced as evidence against him, Rushworth produced his own shorthand notes of the same words, and the texts so differed that the testimony seemed inconclusive and the case failed (*Ormonde MSS*, 4.408). Grey's death in 1676 opened the Berwick seat but, despite petitioning against the election of Peregrine Osborne, Rushworth did not gain the seat until the 1679 elections. He was a moderately active MP in the Exclusion parliaments, though only one speech is recorded, on 9 May 1679, producing precedents for denying counsel to the impeached lord treasurer, the earl of Danby. He voted in favour of exclusion.

Further publications, decline, and death A surreptitious second edition of the first part of *Historical Collections* appeared in or about 1675, perhaps responding to contemporary concerns about encroaching popery and arbitrary government. An effort was made to conceal its belatedness: some copies even contained the dedication to Richard Cromwell, though a note referring to the end of monarchy was omitted. Rushworth finished the second part of *Historical Collections* in 1677 and dutifully submitted it to the licensers. He wrote to his fellow MP Thomas Thynne in September that the secretary of state had returned the manuscript and 'excepted against nothing but some passages in the beginning of the Parlament the 3ᵈ of November 1640' (BL, Add. MS 32095, fol. 36). The secretary pointed out that Rushworth's inclusion of these passages seemed to endorse their reflections on bishops, whereas the general method of the collections was to avoid commentary. They agreed that the book would conclude with the meeting of the Long Parliament. Rushworth was ordered to produce a scribal copy of the manuscript for the secretary's keeping, to ensure that the printed copy did not introduce amendments: this was a standard procedure, though it incurred a significant expense and delayed production.

Historical Collections: the Second Part, in two volumes, did not appear until 1680, when press controls were relaxed. Rushworth commented in the preface: 'The *Reader* should not have staid so many Years in the Dark, … if I could have bin sooner permitted to have sent him through the Press' (Rushworth, *Historical Collections*, 2, 1.Ar). The volumes covered the dissolution of the parliament of 1628–9 to the meeting of the Short Parliament in 1640, plus a selection of speeches from the Long Parliament. These were probably not the same as those he had intended in 1677: in 1681 he wrote to Harbottle Grimston, master of the rolls, that these 'I huddled up of a suddaine into that parte, not intending the same att first, fearing then alsoe an interruption of the presse' (*Verulam MSS*, 82–3). The excerpts reveal how Rushworth's collection of documents was organized to offer an interpretative narrative of the approach to civil war, as the struggle between creeping royal prerogative and parliamentary privilege. His selection of passages—most taken from a previously published collection of speeches—show future royalists speaking in favour of the delinquency of judges in the ship-money cases, of local grievances against the burden of ship-money, and of frequent parliaments. Rushworth validates those issues over which, in his grand narrative, the war was to be fought. The House of Lords is not represented. To consolidate this ideological account he weaves into his main text contentious cases from Star Chamber in 1625–8, based on his own notes, relegating the more ordinary cases to a large and significant appendix. Through selection and careful organization Rushworth was able to suggest a politically charged interpretation, despite the absence of comments and reflections. In 1680 he published *The Tryal of Thomas Earl of Strafford*, mainly based on his own observations of proceedings and dedicated to George Savile, earl of Halifax, in an edition uniform with his *Collections*, and often treated as a fourth volume in that series.

Despite his many offices and his legal and financial business, and notwithstanding the inheritance in 1657 of an estate from a royalist friend whom he had helped in exile, financial difficulties overtook Rushworth. Anthony Wood suggested that Rushworth had husbanded his wealth carelessly. In a letter of 1675 he mentions his age as sixty-three. In the following year he suffered a fall, preventing him for some time from crossing town and thus slowing down his work. In 1680 Acklington Park, his family estate, was granted on lease to another. Sir William Dugdale wrote to Anthony Wood in November 1681 that he had not seen Rushworth for a year, 'though I was many times at his lodging, early and late, they always denied him. I doubt he is now very poore, wch is the reason y^t he thus doth abscond' (Bodl. Oxf., MS Wood F.41, fol. 148r). By 1687 Rushworth was imprisoned for debt at the king's bench. A note by John Aubrey dated between July 1687 and June 1689 suggests that he had been there for three or four years, though there is no evidence of Rushworth's activities between 1684 and 1687. He was aided by a gift from the earl of Newcastle. In June 1689 John Aubrey visited Rushworth and afterwards wrote to Wood: 'he hath quite lost his Memory with drinking Brandy: remembred nothing of you &c: his Landlady wiped his nose like a child' (Bodl. Oxf., MS Wood F.39, fol. 386v). The poet Andrew Marvell had noted as early as 1674 that Rushworth was not averse to a pint of wine with amenable conversation, and that too much wine might interfere with conversation. Before his death on 12 May 1690 at Rules Court, London, he had so far declined that, Aubrey noted, 'He had forgot his children' (ibid., fol. 405r). He was buried on 14 May at the church of St George in Southwark.

Posthumous works and reputation The third part of *Historical Collections*, dealing in two volumes with November 1640 to the end of 1644, was finally published in 1691. Rushworth claimed in one letter in May 1681 that it would be published later that year; in another letter in July 1687 he wrote that 'the time favers not ye Comeing of it forth' (Bodl. Oxf., MS Wood F.39, fol. 383v). By the time the revolution of 1688 created a more benign atmosphere Rushworth was probably beyond seeing it through the press. The fourth part, also in two volumes, appeared in 1701, and covered 1645 through to the execution of the king. Rushworth had been appropriated to whig history at this point, but the fourth part was less original and useful than the former parts; the final 1000 pages or so derived directly from Samuel Pecke's newsbook *Perfect Diurnal of the Passages in Parliament*. Rushworth's editing of this material was so lackadaisical that he failed to omit book advertisements and other anomalies.

Rushworth's reputation as a historian was assailed in his lifetime, notably by John Nalson, who began his *Impartial Collection* (1682–3), a royalist counter-compilation, in 1681. Only two volumes, reaching 1641, were completed. Nalson contended that Rushworth used unreliable sources for his documents, and transcribed them inaccurately; that he was partial in his selection of these documents; and that, contrary to his stated method, he did interweave reflections on his materials. By contrast, Nalson eschewed 'the Rules of a Bare Collector', which would leave his readers 'groping in the dark and unpleasant Night of Conjectures' (J. Nalson, *An Impartial Collection of the Great Affairs of State*, 2 vols., 1682–3, 1.ii) and offered fierce and bitter reflections on the politics of his opponent. The contrast in styles speaks to Rushworth's moderation and to the modest nature of his interpolations. In practice Rushworth did use sources that were unreliable, and appears not to have sought multiple versions of documents; however, Nalson failed to make stick his accusation that this resulted in severe bias. Certainly the most useful sections of Rushworth's history are those based on his own notes of events to which he was an eyewitness; and the later sections based on printed newsbooks are of limited use to a modern historian.

Nalson's criticisms do ring true on the allegations of selectivity: it is the brilliance of the *Historical Collections* to lay the burden of interpretative narrative on a series of documents, declarations, and speeches, as if the evidence will speak for itself. Some later readers, notably Rapin de Thoyras, defended Rushworth and his documentary method, noting that the rhetorical intensity of the tory criticism of Rushworth was not matched by sustained practical demonstration of his shortcomings. *Historical Collections*, much resorted to as a repository of documents, was influential on subsequent historians. Rushworth wrote to Wood:

> I gave ye first President of my method in writing & declaring onely matter of fact in Order of time without obeservation or Reflection? Dr Nalson a Learned man finds fault with me but I Leave it to Posterity to Judge.   (Bodl. Oxf., MS Wood F.39, fol. 383r)

JOAD RAYMOND

Sources Bodl. Oxf., MS Wood F. 39, fols. 148, 383–4, 386, 405 · Bodl. Oxf., MSS Arch. H e. 108, 109 · Bodl. Oxf., MS Tanner 66, fol. 139r · Bodl. Oxf., MS Tanner 63, fol. 43 · BL, Add. MS 32095, fol. 36 · BL, Add. MS 18979 · G. Hampson, 'Rushworth, John', HoP, *Commons, 1660–90* · J. Raymond, *The invention of the newspaper: English newsbooks, 1641–1649* (1996) · J. Rushworth, *Historical collections*, 5 pts in 8 vols. (1659–1701) · J. Rushworth, *The tryal of Thomas earl of Strafford* (1680) · JHC · CSP dom., 1651–4; 1657–9; 1672–3 · Cobbett, *Parl. hist.*, vol. 23 · B. Whitelocke, *Memorials of English affairs*, new edn, 4 vols. (1853) · *Calendar of the Clarendon state papers preserved in the Bodleian Library*, 4: 1657–1660, ed. F. J. Routledge (1932) · *Fourth report*, HMC, 3 (1874) · *The manuscripts of his grace the duke of Portland*, 10 vols., HMC, 29 (1891–1931), vols. 5–10 · *Manuscripts of the earl of Egmont: diary of Viscount Percival, afterwards first earl of Egmont*, 3 vols., HMC, 63 (1920–23) · *Calendar of the manuscripts of the marquess of Ormonde*, new ser., 8 vols., HMC, 36 (1902–20) · *Fifth report*, HMC, 4 (1876) · *Report on the manuscripts of the earl of Verulam*, HMC, 64 (1906), 82–3 · N&Q, 2nd ser., 11 (1861), 263–4 · *The manuscripts of the House of Lords*, new ser., 12 vols. (1900–77), vol. 11 · *The manuscripts of the marquess of Abergavenny, Lord Braye, G. F. Luttrell*, HMC, 15 (1887) · W. P. Baildon, ed., *The records of the Honorable Society of Lincoln's Inn: admissions*, 1 (1896) · Foster, *Alum. Oxon.* · Wood, *Ath. Oxon.: Fasti* (1815), 2 · J. L. Chester and G. J. Armytage, eds., *Allegations for marriage licences issued by the dean and chapter of Westminster, 1558 to 1699; also, for those issued by the vicar-general of the archbishop of Canterbury, 1660 to 1679*, Harleian Society, 23 (1886) · *The poems and letters of Andrew Marvell*, ed. H. Margoliouth, rev. P. Legouis, 3rd edn, 2 vols. (1971) · F. Henderson, '"Posterity to judge": John Rushworth and his *Historical collections*', *Bodleian Library Record*, 15 (1996), 246–59 · C. R. Markham, *A life of the great Lord Fairfax* (1870) · *Diary of Thomas Burton*, ed. J. T. Rutt, 4 vols. (1828) · J. W. Clay, ed., *Abstracts of Yorkshire wills in the time of the Commonwealth*, Yorkshire Archaeological Society, 9 (1890) · *Kingdoms Weekly Intelligencer*, 13 (21–8 March 1643) · R. de Thoyras, *The history of England*, trans. N. Tindal, 2nd edn, 2 vols. (1732–3) · *A history of Northumberland*, Northumberland County History Committee, 15 vols. (1893–1940) · *The autobiography of Mrs Alice Thornton*, ed. [C. Jackson], SurtS, 62 (1875)
Archives Bodl. Oxf., newsbooks and pamphlets in marginalia, Arch. H e.108, 109 · CKS, letters to Lord Fairfax
Likenesses R. White, line engraving, 1692, BM, NPG; repro. in Rushworth, *Historical collections*, vol. 1, frontispiece

Rushworth, John (1669–1736), surgeon, was the son of Thomas Rushworth, vicar of St Sepulchre, Northampton, and later vicar of Guilsborough, Northamptonshire. John Rushworth qualified as a surgeon and lived in Northampton, where he had a considerable practice. His most memorable achievement was the discovery of the efficacy of cinchona bark in cases of gangrene, a finding which was utilized by John Ranby some years later. Rushworth first made this discovery known to Sir Hans Sloane in 1721, but he subsequently disclosed it to the master and wardens of the Company of Barber-Surgeons for the use of the profession at large.

Rushworth shares with Samuel Garth the honour of being one of the first to suggest the foundation of infirmaries and dispensaries in the centre of every county and town. He was especially keen that they should be established in Northamptonshire, but the infirmary for that county was not established until 1743, some seven years after his death. Rushworth was particularly anxious to advance the status of surgery, which he called the 'ancientest and certainest part of physic'.

Rushworth's publications include *A Letter to the Mrs. or Governors of the Mystery and Commonalty of Barber-Surgeons* (1731), *A Proposal for the Improvement of Surgery Offered to the Masters of the Mystery of Barbers and Surgeons at London* (1732), and *Two Letters Showing the Great Advantage of the Bark in Mortifications* (1732). Rushworth died on 6 December 1736 and was buried in the church of All Saints, Northampton, where a tablet was erected to his memory, and to that of his wife, Jane; she was the heir of Daniel Danvers of Northampton, doctor of medicine, and sister of Knightly Danvers, recorder of Northampton, and had died on 3 July 1725. The names of the ten children of the family are recorded on the tablet.

D'A. POWER, rev. MICHAEL BEVAN

Sources GM, 1st ser., 6 (1736), 749 · GM, 1st ser., 86/1 (1816), 643 · G. Baker, *The history and antiquities of the county of Northampton*, 2 vols. (1822–41) · private information (1897)

Rushworth [Richworth; *alias* Robinson]**, William** [*alias* Charles Rosse] (*c.*1594–1637), Roman Catholic priest and religious controversialist, was born in Lincolnshire. In June 1612 he started his studies for the priesthood by entering the English College at Douai, where he went by the name of Charles Rosse. He was ordained at Arras on 19 December 1615. At Douai he was a contemporary of the martyr Thomas Maxfield, who mentions him in his last letter before his execution in 1616 as his 'deare friend' (Pollen, 57). On 8 March 1618, having completed his theological studies, Rushworth became prefect of the college, a post he filled for only half a year. On 18 August 1618 he left for the mission in England via a stop at Brussels. A year later he returned for a short visit accompanying four English boys to Douai. In England he worked in several places but mainly in Lincolnshire.

Rushworth was interested in mathematics as is clear from his correspondence (under the alias Robinson) with the well-known mathematician William Oughtred. Apart from a discussion of mathematical problems and controversies there are complaints by Rushworth about his physical condition and a characterization of the kind of life he led:

> my natural genius led me to physic and mathematics, in both which I should have had some insight, if a more serious calling had not diverted me. God's will be done; my life is solitary, my companions books, my liberty retiredness, so that how I should be cured of this infirmity I well know not, but refer all to his blessed will. (Rigaud, 1.19)

Rushworth died in England in 1637 and left behind a manuscript dealing with his 'more serious calling', theology. This is a tract in the form of three dialogues between an uncle and his nephew in which they discuss the controversial issue as to whether God's revelation to man was revealed through scripture alone or also through tradition. The work is a defence of the Roman Catholic position that attaches great importance to tradition; it also, interestingly, pleads for a plain manner of reading the Bible as opposed to seeing it as a theological puzzle to be solved by specialists. The manuscript was edited by Rushworth's friend and fellow controversialist Thomas White and published at Paris under the title *The Dialogues of William Richworth, or, The Judgmend of Common Sense in the Choise of Religion* (1640). A reprint appeared in 1648, and in 1654 White prepared a new extended edition which involved adapting the style, writing a new preface, and adding a fourth dialogue. Rushworth's work was the starting point of a long controversy in the following decades. His book became quite famous with many protestant replies by theologians such as John Tillotson, Matthew Poole, William Chillingworth, Lucius Falkland, and Henry Hammond. Some of Rushworth's critics were answered by White in his *An Apology for Rushworth's Dialogues* (Paris, 1654) and by John Belson, who belonged to Thomas White's circle of friends, in his *Tradidi vobis* (London, 1662).   F. BLOM and J. BLOM

Sources *Rushworth's dialogues … corrected and enlarg'd by T. White* (Paris, 1654), preface • B. C. Southgate, 'A note on the authorship of Rushworth's *Dialogues*', *N&Q*, 226 (1981), 207–8 • E. H. Burton and T. L. Williams, eds., *The Douay College diaries, third, fourth and fifth, 1598–1654*, 1–2, Catholic RS, 10–11 (1911) • 'The life and martyrdom of Mr Maxfield, priest, 1616', ed. J. H. Pollen, *Miscellanea, III*, Catholic RS, 3 (1906), 30–58, esp. 55, 57 • C. Dodd [H. Tootell], *The church history of England, from the year 1500, to the year 1688*, 3 (1742), 92 • S. P. Rigaud and S. J. Rigaud, eds., *Correspondence of scientific men of the seventeenth century*, 1 (1841), 6, 8, 11, 14–20 • G. Anstruther, *The seminary priests*, 2 (1975), 266–7 • G. H. Tavard, 'Scripture and tradition among seventeenth-century recusants', *Theological Studies*, 25 (1964), 343–85 • G. H. Tavard, *The seventeenth century tradition: a study in recusant thought* (1978)

John Ruskin (1819–1900), by Sir John Everett Millais, 1853–4

Ruskin, John (1819–1900), art critic and social critic, was born on 8 February 1819 at 54 Hunter Street, Brunswick Square, London, the only child of John James Ruskin (1785–1864), a sherry importer, and Margaret Cox, formerly Cock (1781–1871), the daughter of a Croydon publican. His parents were first cousins: the intensity of the triangular relationship between father, mother, and son was to have both a creative and a destructive influence on the course of Ruskin's life. Contradiction governed a career driven by a search for synthesis.

Although the immediate social context of the Ruskin family was Edinburgh during the commercially and intellectually flourishing period at the close of the eighteenth century, and these Scottish roots always remained important, the Ruskins were by origin English. John Ruskin's grandfather, John Thomas Ruskin (1761–1817), had moved to Edinburgh from London after an uncompleted apprenticeship to a vintner, and set up as a grocer, later giving himself the superior classification of 'merchant'. In Edinburgh in or about 1783 he married Catherine Tweddale, the daughter of a Presbyterian minister, who later brought an inheritance to the family. John Thomas was sometimes irascible and depressive, and not good at business, characteristics also to be found in his grandson. After John James Ruskin graduated from Edinburgh Royal High School in 1801, he was sent to London to find work as a clerk in a mercantile house, rather than being allowed to study law as he had hoped.

John James Ruskin's future wife, Margaret, was the daughter of John Thomas's elder sister, who took over the management of a Croydon public house on her husband's death in 1787. At or about the time that John James Ruskin was sent to London, Margaret travelled north to become a companion to his mother, Catherine Ruskin. Margaret adopted the firm religious principles of her

aunt, and modified her surname to the more genteel Cox. In 1808 John Thomas failed in business, but his son shouldered the debt, so avoiding the slur of bankruptcy. In 1809 John James and Margaret became engaged, but the marriage was postponed because of John Thomas's debts and his opposition to the marriage. John Thomas moved to Perth with Catherine, and was cared for by Margaret, but his mental health deteriorated to the point of insanity.

John James, however, prospered in the sherry trade. In 1815 he became chief partner in the new firm of Ruskin, Telford, and Domecq, importing and distributing sherry and other wines. Domecq supplied the sherry from his vineyards near Jerez, Telford supplied the capital, and John James the salesmanship, effort, and acumen. In 1817 his mother suddenly died, and his father shortly afterwards, almost certainly a suicide. John James and Margaret were thus, after a nine-year engagement, free to marry, which they did, without celebration, early in 1818. The circumstances of their engagement, and the character of John James's parents, were to have an enduring effect in creating an atmosphere of duty, hard work, and suppressed anxiety in the Ruskin household. While John James became increasingly wealthy and successful, his father's debts were not finally cleared until 1832.

Childhood and education In 1823 the Ruskin family moved from 54 Hunter Street (dem. 1969) and took a lease on a semi-detached house with a large garden, at 28 Herne Hill, Herne Hill, Surrey (dem. *c*.1912). Ruskin was educated by his parents, with the help of private tutors, until the age of fourteen. The account of his childhood he gives in his unfinished and deliberately selective memoirs, *Praeterita* (1885–9), is far from trustworthy. On the one hand he suggests that it was paradisaical, but on the other that he was toyless and friendless. While *Praeterita* does reflect the close intensity of the atmosphere at Herne Hill, the isolation he describes is intended to explain his independence of mind, while the frustration and deprivation he evokes is more that of his old age than his of youth. He had plenty of toys and pets, including a dog that bit and scarred his lip for life. In 1828 he was joined from Perth by his cousin Mary Richardson, whose mother had died, and who remained a member of the family until her marriage in 1848.

Ruskin's world was enclosed by his parents. From his father he learned his Romanticism: the tory medievalism of Scott, the self-dramatization of Byron, and the nature worship of Wordsworth. From his mother he learned his religion. John James appears to have continued his own interrupted education alongside his son, resolving his intellectual frustration by investing in his offspring's creativity. He also passed on to him a love of drawing, having had a number of lessons when a youth from the Edinburgh landscape artist Alexander Nasmyth. From an early age Ruskin was encouraged both to draw and to write, and to take an interest in geology, beginning a handwritten mineralogical dictionary at the age of twelve. His early efforts at verse were generously rewarded by his father, at a farthing, later a halfpenny, a line.

This paternal literary and artistic encouragement was, however, tempered by maternal constraint, for the pleasures of imaginative expression were confined by a strongly evangelical self-discipline. As Helen Viljoen wrote:

> whereas John James Ruskin reverently acquiesced to the articles of faith, Margaret participated in Catherine's [her aunt, John James's mother] doctrine with her *heart*, so that within her own personality a religious creed became emotionally, imaginatively, wedded to experience. Margaret's temperament was truly religious, as John James's was not. And it was this temperament which Ruskin would share with his mother—a temperament which largely shaped his own experience of life and never changed with creed. (Viljoen, 93)

Ruskin's certainty in the rightness of his views and independence from received opinion—his critics might say his dogmatism—is attributable to his mother's cast of mind. Yet the conflict between his father's expressive desire and his mother's cautious restraint was to undermine his apparent confidence throughout his life.

Ruskin was baptized at home on 20 February 1819 by a Presbyterian chaplain from the recently founded Caledonian Chapel in Hatton Garden; in south London the Ruskins attended the services of an evangelical Congregationalist, Edward Andrews, who was also Ruskin's first tutor. The Ruskins, however, had become evangelical Anglicans by the time their son entered Christ Church, Oxford, where he was confirmed into the Church of England in April 1837, at the urging of his tutor, the Revd W. L. Brown. Every morning, from the age of three, his mother made him read from the Bible and learn passages by heart. It was a literary and intellectual as well as religious education, for the sonorities of the King James Bible and the eighteenth-century verse of the Scottish paraphrases of

the psalms were to inform his prose, and the texts to supply a bedrock of reference throughout his life. The evangelical interpretative practice of typology shaped his understanding both of nature and of art, while the profound appreciation that he gained of the wisdom of Solomon from the Old Testament—later joined by his reading of Plato—inclined him to be a law-giver on his own account. The puritanism of his religion was in conflict with the sensual appeal of much of the art that he was to study, and inhibited the enjoyment of his own body.

Ruskin's private education was enhanced by regular summer coaching tours, first to see the picturesque scenery and visit the country house collections of Britain, and then, from 1833 onwards, to see France, Switzerland, and Italy. Between 1833 and 1835 he spent his mornings at a day school run by the Revd Thomas Dale of St Matthew's Chapel, a Church of England establishment in Denmark Hill. In 1836 he attended lectures at King's College, London, where Dale had become the first professor of English literature. In October of that year he matriculated as a gentleman commoner at Christ Church, Oxford.

Ruskin was already a published author before going up to Oxford, with geological essays for J. C. Loudon's *Magazine of Natural History* in 1834. He published his first poetry in the *Spiritual Times* in August 1829 and contributed verses to the annual *Friendship's Offering* for the first time in 1835. At Oxford he wrote a series of essays linking architecture and nature for Loudon's *Architectural Magazine*, later republished as *The Poetry of Architecture* (pirate American edition 1873, authorized edition 1893).

The domestic intensity of Ruskin's early life developed, but was not the source of, a distinctive talent. He wrote in a draft for *Praeterita* that he had 'a sensual faculty of pleasure in sight, as far as I know unparalleled' (*Works*, 35.619). Ruskin's perceptual sensibility, and his ability to deploy it both as a draughtsman and a visual analyst, marks him out from his more book-bound peers. He made only a few experiments in oil painting; his drawing skills were encouraged by a traditional drawing master, Charles Runciman, and refined by tutors of celebrity, Anthony Van Dyke Copley Fielding and then the more progressive James Duffield Harding. He continued to learn from contemporary artists until the 1860s. In 1873 he was elected an honorary member of the professional Old Watercolour Society, yet although his drawings would justify the appellation, he never considered himself an artist, emphasizing always that he drew in order to gain certain facts, and he exhibited rarely. None the less, Ruskin's drawings are a remarkable achievement, both as a record of his mind, and as works of great beauty. His ability visually to depict architecture and landscape was matched by his genius for the verbal description of works of art.

Ruskin's love of art was stimulated by his father's growing collection of works, chiefly by members of the Old Watercolour Society, through which Samuel Prout became a family friend. The most important artist to enjoy the Ruskins' patronage was J. M. W. Turner. Father and son did not acquire their first watercolour by Turner until 1839, but Turner's work was well known to Ruskin from the vignette illustrations to the second edition of Samuel Rogers's poem *Italy*, published in 1830 and given to him for his thirteenth birthday in 1832. Ruskin produced imitations of both the illustrations and the travel verse. When Turner's new paintings in the 1836 Royal Academy summer exhibition were attacked in *Blackwood's Magazine*, Ruskin wrote a riposte intended for publication, but John James sent the piece to Turner, who did not wish the matter taken further.

Oxford When Ruskin went into residence at Christ Church in January 1837, the grandson of a grocer and a publican stood on the threshold of the upper-middle class, with every prospect of becoming established in that social position by being ordained in the Church of England. His father's wealth and social aspiration meant that his enrolment as gentleman commoner gave him equal college status with members of the aristocracy. Yet he was not to be released from home, for his mother moved into lodgings in the High Street, and his father joined them at weekends. Ruskin, by now 5 feet 10 inches tall, slimly built, with brown hair and striking blue eyes, was delicate, and prone to bouts of depression, so that his health was to break down, but it is possible that his mother was at Oxford to keep an eye on his spiritual as much as his physical health. The university was in the grip of the controversies surrounding the Oxford Movement; however, Ruskin showed no sign of being touched by high-church fervour, apart from becoming a member of the mildly ecclesiological Oxford Society for the Preservation of Gothic Architecture.

Unlike his aristocratic companions, Ruskin was a 'reading man', making him unpopular with some, but he made important friendships with the future classical archaeologist Charles Newton, and with Henry Acland, who was to play a key role in his lifelong relations with the university. He was encouraged by a young senior member of Christ Church, Henry Liddell, who was also to influence his future Oxford career. Though reading classical Greats, Ruskin attracted the attention of the geologist and natural theologian Dr William Buckland, and made drawings for his lectures. He spoke at the Union, and put considerable effort into the Newdigate poetry competition, winning at the third attempt in 1839. He met Wordsworth when presented with the prize. Ruskin's poetic impulse was to fade in the 1840s, however, and he was not appreciative of his father's decision privately to publish a selection of his verse, *Poems*, in 1850.

In the autumn of 1839 Ruskin was advised to sit for an honours degree the following April, but the twenty-year-old was troubled by an adolescent passion for the daughter of his father's partner, Pedro Domecq. Adèle, a Roman Catholic partly educated in England, was the subject of Ruskin's youthful verse, but clearly not a prospect for marriage. In December 1839 he was devastated when he learned of her engagement, and was studying intensely for his examinations under a private tutor, the Revd Osborne Gordon, when in April 1840, shortly after Adèle's marriage, he coughed blood, and had to withdraw from the university.

Ruskin's academic and projected church career was blighted by this breakdown, but when after convalescence he sat for a pass degree in April 1842, he achieved the unusual distinction of an honorary double fourth, taking his MA in October 1843. Ruskin deprecated his early Oxford career in *Praeterita*, but it is significant that he chose to publish the first two volumes of *Modern Painters* under the pseudonym 'a Graduate of Oxford'.

From *Modern Painters*, volume 1, to *The Stones of Venice*
Ruskin's initial hopes of returning to Oxford in the autumn of 1840 had been dashed by further slight haemorrhages, so his parents took him abroad, on a long continental tour from September 1840 to October 1841. The party travelled as far south as Naples, and spent two periods in Rome; Ruskin liked neither city. In Rome, however, he met Joseph Severn, the friend of Keats, whose son Arthur would marry Ruskin's cousin Joan Agnew and become his heir and unsympathetic guardian. Severn introduced Ruskin to a fellow painter, George Richmond, who became a firm family friend and made portraits of both Ruskins, father and son. Richmond, with his brother Tom, took the eager but naïve student in hand as regards the Italian old masters, and was to be regularly consulted during the composition of *Modern Painters*.

At Oxford Ruskin's knowledge of Turner and the collection of his drawings had grown. He is believed to have first met the artist in June 1840, and Turner was soon on sufficiently good terms to accept the Ruskins' hospitality and attend birthday dinners in honour of their son. In 1842 father and son became patrons as well as collectors, when Turner's dealer Thomas Griffith included them in an invitation to Turner's circle of patrons to commission finished watercolours based on preliminary sketches. This opportunity, repeated in 1843, gave Ruskin a valuable insight into Turner's creative process, but his desire to acquire more drawings than his father would sanction became a matter of contention between them. Ruskin's own drawing style, partly under the influence of J. D. Harding, with whom he began lessons in 1841, was developing from the conventional picturesque in the manner of Prout towards a greater naturalism, a shift dramatized by two epiphanic moments in *Praeterita* (*Works*, 35.311, 314), the first describing drawing a piece of ivy at Herne Hill, the second an aspen at Fontainebleau, although there is no independent evidence that they in fact occurred.

On returning to England in 1841 Ruskin spent six weeks at Leamington Spa, undergoing Dr Jephson's celebrated cure. In early summer 1842 the Ruskins once more went abroad, with Switzerland as their principal destination, returning via the Rhine. In Geneva Ruskin read an English newspaper review of that year's Royal Academy, attacking Turner's contributions. According to a letter to his former tutor Osborne Gordon, Ruskin 'determined to write a pamphlet and blow the critics out of the water' (*Works*, 3.666). This was the origin of *Modern Painters: their Superiority in the Art of Landscape Painting to the Ancient Masters*, a work in five volumes that would not be completed until 1860. The first two volumes were completed at the Ruskins' new home, 163 Denmark Hill (dem. 1947), a large detached house in 7 acres to which the family moved in the autumn of 1842, a mile from Herne Hill and overlooking Camberwell and Dulwich. Though dependent on his father's patronage, Ruskin was able to begin and sustain a career as a writer without any of the economic considerations that normally circumscribe literary life.

Ruskin's ruling theme in the first, unillustrated volume of *Modern Painters* was Turner's adherence to truth, but to a truth that extended beyond the mere factual appearance of landscape: 'There is a moral as well as material truth,— a truth of impression as well as of form,—of thought as well as of matter' (*Works*, 3.104). Such truths depended on a clarity of perception that was free of the pictorial conventions of the seventeenth-century Italian and Dutch masters who set the norm for received taste in landscape painting, and whose works were represented in Christ Church, the National Gallery, and Dulwich Picture Gallery. Ruskin substituted a different way of seeing, that of the geologist and botanist, deploying the accuracy of observation encouraged by the classificatory sciences that did not conflict with natural theology. Ruskin demonstrated his own ardent study of nature in the first volume of *Modern Painters*, and argued that Turner 'is the only painter who has ever drawn a mountain, or a stone' (ibid., 3.252).

The first edition, however, published in May 1843, stopped short of criticizing Turner's contemporaries, who worked in the convention of the picturesque. These were Ruskin's teachers, and his father's friends. It was not until the third edition, published in 1846, also the year of the first publication of volume 2, that blame was substituted for praise. The tone and direction of volume 2 had been significantly influenced by Ruskin's visit to France, Switzerland, and Italy in 1845, the first time he had travelled on the continent without his parents. He had been able greatly to expand his knowledge of European painting by studying in the Musée du Louvre. In Pisa and Florence he began to examine early Italian painters such as Fra Angelico, the so-called 'primitives' who were beginning to attract scholarly attention thanks to Alexis Rio's *De la poésie chrétienne dans son principe, dans sa matière, et dans ses formes* (1836), which Ruskin read on the journey. After a recuperative break in the hills at Macugnaga and a visit to examine the site of Turner's drawing of the pass of Faido, which he had commissioned in 1843, he and Harding, who had joined him, travelled on to Venice. Not only did Ruskin, whose own drawing style was now a modified version of Turner's, begin to see through the conventional methods of his companion; in Venice he was confronted by the revelation of the true greatness of the Venetian masters, above all the paintings by Jacopo Tintoretto in the Scuola di San Rocco. It was further evident to Ruskin that the city was suffering the effects of both modernization and decay.

The second volume of *Modern Painters* adopted a different style from that of the first. Ruskin wished to show that truthful perception of nature led to an experience of beauty that was also an apprehension of God. It was necessary to prove that beauty rested on an absolute, divine basis, not custom or subjective association. To this end he devised the concept of the 'theoretic faculty'—derived from the Greek *theoria*, or contemplation—a faculty which mediated between eye and mind, and which allowed an instinctual, emotional (in Ruskin's terminology, moral) as opposed to conscious and rational, apprehension of beauty: 'this, and this only, is the full comprehension and contemplation of the Beautiful as a gift of God' (*Works*, 4.47).

Ruskin divided beauty into two categories, 'vital' and 'typical'. Vital beauty, in accordance with natural theology, expresses God's purpose in the harmonious creation of the world and its creatures, including man. Typical beauty, in accordance with evangelical typology, expresses the immanence of God in the natural world through the presence of 'types' to which man responds as beautiful. These types are qualities rather than things: infinity, unity, repose, purity, and symmetry. They are associated with divine qualities and can be found in nature and in art, but though abstract themselves, they have a real presence that it is the artist's duty truthfully to represent. Through his mother's training and the sermons he heard every Sunday, Ruskin had absorbed the evangelical practice of treating objects as both real and symbolic at the same time, a key critical practice that remained a feature of his writings throughout his life.

Ruskin completed the ground plan of his critical and aesthetic theories in volume 2 of *Modern Painters* with a discussion of the imagination. Where the theoretic faculty perceived, the imagination created. He posited three orders of truth: of fact, of thought, and of symbol, with their corresponding imaginative faculties. The penetrative imagination saw the object or idea, both its external form and its internal essence. The associative imagination enabled the artist or writer to convey the truth perceived and so his thought. The contemplative imagination turned these truths into symbolic form. Thus it is perfectly legitimate for an artist to change or rearrange what he has truthfully observed and penetratively imagined, as Ruskin demonstrated in *Modern Painters*, volume 4 (1856), in his discussion of Turner's drawing of the pass of Faido (*Works*, 6.34–41). There was a higher truth than natural fact, but it took Ruskin until the completion of *Modern Painters* volume 5 (1860), via a discussion of the 'Symbolical Grotesque' in *The Stones of Venice*, volume 3 (1853), fully to develop a theory of the imagination that successfully synthesized the dialectic of the real and the symbolic.

The second volume of *Modern Painters* was published in April 1846 (and the third, revised edition of volume 1 in September). The defence of Turner was incomplete— indeed, he was little discussed in the volume—while the range of reference to Renaissance and pre-Renaissance artists is much wider. The critical reception of these first two volumes was mixed: there were approving remarks from Charlotte Brontë, Wordsworth, and Elizabeth Gaskell, but Ruskin's challenge to an aesthetic orthodoxy derived from Sir Joshua Reynolds and Sir George Beaumont drew strong disapproval from the Revd John Eagles in *Blackwood's* (54, October 1843, 485–503) and from George Darley in *The Athenaeum* (3 and 10 February 1844).

None the less, Ruskin was launched on a literary and intellectual career: he was invited to the breakfasts of Richard Monckton-Milnes and Samuel Rogers, while to his father's table came a conservative mixture of artists, collectors, and evangelical clergymen. During 1847 he experienced a period of depression and uncertainty, and took another cure with Dr Jephson of Leamington. His mind was turning towards architecture. The visit to Italy in 1845 had made him aware of the beauty and decay of Italian Romanesque and Gothic. The Gothic revival, and its Romanist tendencies, was also attracting his interest. In 1844 Ruskin had been involved with the architect Gilbert Scott's rebuilding of a local church, St Giles, Camberwell, in the Gothic revival style. He and a friend made at Thomas Dale's school, Edmund Oldfield, who was to join Ruskin in helping to found the Arundel Society in 1849, designed the painted glass for the east window. In 1853 Scott also consulted Ruskin about remodelling the Camden Chapel (damaged by fire 1907, des. *c.*1940) in Romanesque style. On a visit to Venice during the now almost ritual family tour in the summer of 1846 Ruskin read Robert Willis's *Remarks on the Architecture of the Middle Ages, Especially of Italy* (1835), and continued the development of the more analytical style of architectural drawing that he had begun in 1845.

Ruskin published two lengthy review articles in the *Quarterly Review*: on Lord Lindsay's *Sketches of the History of Christian Art* (81/159, June 1847, 1–57)—in which he discussed architecture as well as art for the first time—and Sir Charles Eastlake's *Materials for a History of Oil Painting* (82/164, March 1848, 390–427). He now concentrated on architectural research, visiting Salisbury Cathedral in July 1848 before making a tour of the churches of Normandy from August to October. Ruskin had married Euphemia Chalmers Gray (1828–1897), usually known as Effie, on 10 April 1848; northern France was as far as they could travel that year, because of the political disturbances in France, and the Venetian revolt against Austrian occupation and the ensuing siege of the city.

The Seven Lamps of Architecture was published in May 1849, the first of Ruskin's works to carry his name, and the first to be illustrated, with fourteen plates drawn and etched by him. A reference in the preface to the depredations of 'the Restorer, or Revolutionist' (*Works*, 8.3n.) made Ruskin's position clear. He wished to protect what survived, and draw from it certain principles which would influence the direction of the Gothic revival, notably towards the use of Gothic in secular buildings. His purpose was both to secularize and make protestant the movement, drawing it away from the Roman Catholic influence of Augustus Welby Pugin. His intervention was theoretical rather than practical: the 'lamps' of architecture were moral categories—sacrifice, truth, power, beauty, life, memory, and obedience. Like the types of typical beauty in *Modern Painters*, volume 2, they are abstract notions in themselves, but for Ruskin were manifested in particular Gothic buildings in Italy and northern France.

The timeliness of Ruskin's intervention, and his growing reputation, meant that the book received considerable, if mixed, attention; his moral purpose was appreciated but his technical knowledge was questioned. *The Seven Lamps of Architecture*, however, proved only the prelude to a much larger work, *The Stones of Venice* (3 vols., 1851–3), which had a political as well as an aesthetic dynamic. Ruskin's opening remark in *Praeterita* carries an important, if exaggerated, truth: 'I am, and my father was before me, a violent Tory of the old school' (*Works*, 35.13). Although John James Ruskin's commercial interests made him a free-trader, he belonged to the ultra-tory school of thought which had not been reconciled to Catholic emancipation or the Reform Act of 1832. The ultra-tories had strong links to the evangelicals, several of whose preachers were friends of the Ruskin family. The first volume of *The Stones of Venice* was published against the background of the 'papal aggression' crisis of 1850, when the Roman Catholic church restored the Catholic episcopal hierarchy in England. Ruskin's admiration for Venice in part stemmed from its traditional resistance to the authority of Rome, and in his opening sentences he drew political as well as moral and cultural parallels between the lost maritime empires of Tyre and Venice, and the threatened empire of England:

> Since first the dominion of men was asserted over the ocean, three thrones, of mark beyond all others, have been set upon its sands: the thrones of Tyre, Venice, and England. Of the First of these great powers only the memory remains; of the Second, the ruin; the Third, which inherits their greatness, if it forget their example, may be led through prouder eminence to less pitied destruction.   (ibid., 9.17)

The three volumes of *The Stones of Venice* were the product of the most concentrated period of study in Ruskin's life, including two long winters spent in Venice, from November 1849 to March 1850, and September 1851 to the end of June 1852. On both occasions Ruskin was accompanied by his wife, Effie, who the first winter also had a companion, Charlotte Ker. The siege of 1849 had ended only three months before, and the Ruskin party staying at the Hotel Danieli must have been some of the first foreign visitors. The winter was arduous, but Ruskin threw himself into a systematic study of Venetian architecture. He explained in the first volume:

> To my consternation, I found that the Venetian antiquaries were not agreed within a century as to the date of the building of the facade of the Ducal Palace, and that nothing was known of any other civil edifice of the early city … Every date in question was determinable only by internal evidence; and it became necessary for me to examine not only every one of the older palaces, stone by stone, but every fragment throughout the city which afforded any clue to the formation of its styles.   (*Works*, 9.3–4)

Ruskin set about establishing, by drawing and measurement, an architectural typology that would account for the evolution of Venetian Gothic from the Romanesque, and also reveal within the Gothic itself the first signs of the decadence that overtook the city's architecture as it turned to Renaissance forms. This typology, while conforming to the archetypal trope of rise, efflorescence, decline, and fall, was considered still largely valid 150 years later. The first volume of *The Stones of Venice*, *The Foundations*, written in the intervening summer and winter of 1850–51, and published in March 1851, was taken up principally with a theoretical discussion of the elements of architectural construction and decoration, as a prelude to a cultural study of Venice itself in the following two volumes. It was illustrated with woodcuts and engravings, and supported by a folio-sized part-publication: *Examples of the Architecture of Venice*. The technical prose was as ill received as the technical examples. The first volume sold slowly while the folio publication, intended to run to a dozen parts, was halted after the issue of only three (one in May and two in November 1851), with fifteen plates published.

When Ruskin and his wife returned to Venice in 1851 economic life had revived, and the young and attractive Mrs Ruskin much enjoyed the social life afforded by the Austrian military authorities in Venice and Verona. The Ruskins rented a set of rooms in the Casa Wetzler on the Grand Canal (which became the Gritti Palace Hotel). Ruskin continued his research, placing more emphasis on archival work, where he was much helped by an English resident, the antiquarian Rawdon Brown, whom the Ruskins had first met in December 1849. (While Ruskin had adequate French, his Italian was always limited.) Ruskin was drafting parts of the second volume, and it is evident both from the manuscript and from his correspondence with his father that he was under parental pressure to adopt a more elevated and less technical style.

One solution to the problem of Ruskin's excessive production of text, already adopted in volume 1, was to thrust unwieldy or technical material into appendices. In the case of volume 1, one appendix was expelled from the book altogether and was issued on 6 March 1851 as *Notes on the Construction of Sheepfolds*, an evangelical intervention on the proper relation between clergy and laity which argued that the true church consisted of both, and called upon all Church of England (and Church of Scotland) factions to unite in resistance to Rome. Ruskin partly acknowledged the difficulties of volume 1 in 1879 when he issued a travellers' edition which compressed the whole work into two volumes (vol. 2, 1881) and omitted most of the first volume. Ruskin also regretted in later life the strongly protestant tone of the work.

Although equally encumbered with appendices, volume 2, *The Sea-Stories* (issued July 1853), and volume 3, *The Fall* (issued October 1853), benefited from John James Ruskin's editorial intervention. Ruskin traced the history of Venice from its origins among the late Roman refugees on Torcello, describing this as the 'Byzantine Period' which lasted until the 'Serrar del Consiglio' at the beginning of the fourteenth century, when the Venetian oligarchy was established, and of which St Mark's was the key building. The Gothic period, of which the ducal palace formed the focus, closing volume 2, lasted until the mid-fifteenth century. Ruskin could be polemically exact when situating the ensuing decline: 'I date the commencement of the Fall of Venice from the death of Carlo

Zeno, 8th May 1418' (*Works*, 9.21), but this date was subject to revision, and while criticizing the decline of architecture which began with the corruption of the Gothic itself, Ruskin expressed his admiration for painters of the Renaissance such as Tintoretto, Bellini, Titian, Giorgione, and Veronese. The third volume, divided between 'Early Renaissance', 'Roman Renaissance', and 'Grotesque Renaissance', traced 'the moral temper of the falling Venetians … from pride to infidelity, and from infidelity to the unscrupulous *pursuit of pleasure*' (ibid., 11.135). Ruskin was prepared to acknowledge the qualities of the classical, sixteenth-century Casa Grimani by Michele Sanmicheli, but not that of Andrea Palladio's San Giorgio Maggiore, completed in 1610, which he found 'gross … barbarous … childish … servile … insipid … contemptible' (ibid., 11.381).

The importance of *The Stones of Venice* lies not in its hostility to the Renaissance, but in its celebration of the Byzantine and the Gothic, which had an immediate effect on Victorian architects, who began to introduce Romanesque forms and Venetian and Veronese colour and sculptural features into their designs. Ruskin's reputation was such that, unusually, *The Times* devoted three long review articles to the second and third volumes. Ruskin's dialectical argument by contrasts was a technique possibly borrowed from Pugin, whom Ruskin affected not to have read, but certainly knew. The contrast between an English cathedral close and St Mark's Square, for example, supports the fundamental contrast Ruskin draws between the fates of the Venetian and British empires (*Works*, 10.78–84).

The 'critical medievalism' of Thomas Carlyle's *Past and Present* also contributed to Ruskin's world view, Ruskin having met Carlyle for the first time in 1850, and he was thus drawn into the beginnings of his social and economic criticism, where Carlyle remained an influence and a support. In the chapter 'The nature of Gothic' (*Works*, 10.180–269) Ruskin argued that under conditions of industrialization and the division of labour, social disharmony and industrial unrest were bound to occur, because the previously expressive craftsman—Ruskin's ideal working man—had been reduced to the condition of a machine:

> the great cry that rises from all our manufacturing cities, louder than their furnace blast, is all in very deed for this—that we manufacture everything there except men; we blanch cotton, and strengthen steel, and refine sugar, and shape pottery; but to brighten, to strengthen, to refine, or to form a single living spirit, never enters into our estimate of advantages. (ibid., 10.196)

Such a view was not inconsistent with Ruskin's toryism, for his ideal society, represented by the creative, harmonious, noble, and imperialist Venice of the fifteenth century that he imagined, was one of hierarchy and order, rights and responsibilities, privileges and duties. But it is significant that this chapter was twice separately reprinted in his lifetime, first for the inauguration of the London Working Men's College in 1854, and second by William Morris in 1892. In his introduction to the Kelmscott edition, Morris wrote: 'To some of us when we first read it, now many years ago, it seemed to point out a new road on which the world should travel' (*Works*, 10.460).

Ruskin's marriage On 25 April 1854 Ruskin accompanied his wife to King's Cross railway station to see her off on a visit to her parents in Scotland. He was about to make another continental journey, with his own parents, but without her. That evening Ruskin was served with a legal citation at Denmark Hill, claiming the nullity of the marriage. Following an undefended hearing in the ecclesiastical commissary court of Surrey on 15 July 1854, the marriage was annulled on the grounds that 'the said John Ruskin was incapable of consummating the same by reason of incurable impotency' (Lutyens, *Millais*, 230). Ruskin was in Chamonix with his parents on the day of the hearing.

There is little that is certain about the intimate details of Ruskin's marriage to Euphemia Chalmers Gray beyond the fact that it was never consummated. A medical examination confirmed Effie's virginity, but in a legal deposition that was not introduced in court, Ruskin stated: 'I can prove my virility at once' (Lutyens, *Millais*, 192). This was never put to the test, but it seems likely that Ruskin was referring to masturbation. Again, there is no confirmation of this, but a letter to a confidante, Mrs Cowper, in 1868 in which he wrote 'Have I not often told you that I was another Rousseau?' (*Letters … to Lord and Lady Mount-Temple*, 167) has been taken as a discreet reference to the practice. At this same time he told a male friend that he had been capable of consummating his marriage, but that he had not loved Effie sufficiently to want to do so (Burd, *John Ruskin*, 115).

Effie was the daughter of a Perth lawyer, George Gray. A family friend and business associate of John James Ruskin, in 1829 Gray had moved into the former Ruskin family home, Bowerswell, Perth, the scene of John Thomas Ruskin's probable suicide, although the house was rebuilt in 1842. Effie first met her future husband when she was twelve, on a visit to Herne Hill. The following year, 1841, on a second visit, she challenged him to write a fairy story. This became Ruskin's only published work of fiction, and one of his most popular books, when *The King of the Golden River* was published in 1850 with illustrations by Richard Doyle. The tale, in the manner of the brothers Grimm, deployed imagery that was to resurface in Ruskin's writings on political economy.

It took Ruskin a time to recover from his infatuation with Adèle Domecq. In 1846 he began to show an interest in Charlotte Lockhart, granddaughter of Sir Walter Scott, and daughter of James Lockhart, editor of the *Quarterly Review*. This tentative attraction, however, was transferred to Effie, who came to stay at Denmark Hill at the time of her nineteenth birthday in May 1847. Ruskin, as has been seen, was suffering from nervousness and depression at this time, but after another cure with Dr Jephson, he travelled to Scotland to visit a new friend, William Macdonald, at Crossmount. The journey provided an opportunity for courtship when he called on the Grays at Perth in October, where he decided he was in love. Ruskin did not propose to Effie, however, until he had returned to London, and both offer and acceptance were by letter.

Ruskin's parents raised no objections to the marriage, possibly fearing a repetition of the breakdown that followed Adèle Domecq's marriage, but preparations for the wedding in the following year were marred by Gray's near bankruptcy as a result of railway speculation. So there was no dowry, while Ruskin himself became anxious at the prospect before him.

The wedding took place at Bowerswell on 10 April 1848, but neither John James nor Margaret Ruskin was present, being uncomfortable with the associations of the house. The first night was spent at Blair Atholl. In a letter to her father in 1854, revealing the extent of the marriage's failure, Effie said that she had been sexually ignorant and that Ruskin 'was disgusted with my person the first evening' (Lutyens, *Millais*, 156). This has been interpreted as meaning that Ruskin was equally innocent, especially in the matter of female pubic hair, but this seems unlikely, as he had seen erotic images belonging to fellow undergraduates at Oxford. There is also speculation that Effie's menstrual cycle interfered with consummation (Hilton, *John Ruskin: the Early Years*, 119), which is plausible but not provable.

It is evident that innocence, combined with anxiety, together with a mutual desire to travel without the encumbrance of pregnancy, led to an agreed postponement—according to Effie, until her twenty-fifth birthday. Outwardly the newlyweds became a fashionable and cultivated young couple, returning from their honeymoon to live at Denmark Hill, before the eleven-week summer tour of Normandy. On their return they moved into a rented house at 31 Park Street, Mayfair, although Ruskin, who was working on *The Seven Lamps of Architecture*, continued to use his study at Denmark Hill. In France, Effie had witnessed Ruskin's self-absorption, and there was already friction with his parents which became serious at new year 1849 when she fell ill. In February 1849 she returned to her parents and did not see her husband for nine months, while he took his parents to Switzerland in the summer. In Scotland she consulted a gynaecologist, while her father tried by letter to prise her husband from his parents. In September Ruskin somewhat reluctantly travelled north to collect her. Three weeks later they set out for Venice.

The two long stays in Venice of 1849–50 and 1851–2 appear to have been the happiest for the couple, for Effie was able to enjoy Austro-Venetian society, and Ruskin was able to work, while the senior Ruskins were at a distance. Ruskin began to experience religious doubt while on the second visit to Venice, writing a long commentary, now lost, on the book of Job; but this was kept from his public writings. In the intervening sixteen months they continued to live at Park Street, and Ruskin to work at Denmark Hill. During this period their social and intellectual circle continued to widen. They were on calling terms with Sir Charles Eastlake, president of the Royal Academy and director of the National Gallery, and his wife, Elizabeth. While Ruskin disapproved of Sir Charles's taste, Lady Eastlake formed an alliance with Effie. Through friendship with F. J. Furnivall, Ruskin came into contact with the Christian socialist F. D. Maurice. Ruskin was also friendly with the poet Coventry Patmore, and it was through Patmore that he became acquainted with the Pre-Raphaelite circle, notably John Everett Millais.

During his second winter in Venice in 1852 Ruskin tried unsuccessfully to persuade the National Gallery to buy paintings by Tintoretto. The Ruskins' Venetian stay ended in scandal and inconvenience after the theft of Effie's jewels. An Englishman attached to the Austrian army was suspected, their departure was delayed, and Ruskin had to decline a challenge to a duel. The case remained unsolved. In June 1852 they returned, not to Park Street, but to a new address, 30 Herne Hill (dem. 1912), which John James Ruskin had leased and furnished at his own expense, and to his own taste. It was now clear to Effie that Ruskin did not intend to consummate the marriage, and she felt trapped by the close proximity of Ruskin's parents, who were increasingly critical of her alleged extravagance. She spent seven weeks with her own parents at Bowerswell from September 1852, and told them of her unhappiness, though not the full reasons for it.

In the spring of 1853 Ruskin rented a house at 6 Charles Street, Mayfair, for a few weeks at the start of the London season, apparently to satisfy Effie's taste for London society. They were together at the private view of the Royal Academy summer exhibition in May, where Millais was showing *The Order of Release, 1746*, for which Effie had posed as the freed Jacobite prisoner's wife. Ruskin, who saw himself as Millais's mentor and champion, repeated an invitation, first made to Millais in 1851, to holiday with him, this time not in the Alps, but in Scotland. Through the artist John Frederick Lewis, whom Ruskin also patronized, he had been invited to lecture at the Philosophical Institution in Edinburgh that autumn, a first public appearance on the lecture platform that alarmed his parents. The holiday party was intended to include Millais's brother William, and the artist Holman Hunt. Hunt however declined, as he was preparing to go to the Holy Land.

In June Ruskin's party travelled north, visiting the house of the intellectual, amateur scientist, and antiquarian Sir Walter Trevelyan at Wallington in Northumberland. Ruskin had known the cultivated Pauline, Lady Trevelyan, since 1847, and they enjoyed a close friendship until her death, while travelling abroad with her husband in Ruskin's company, in 1866. At the beginning of July they arrived at the hamlet of Brig o'Turk, Glenfinlas, near Stirling, staying first at a hotel, and then in a rented cottage, where Millais and Effie were thrown much together, and fell in love. A project to paint Effie's portrait at the castle of Doune was abandoned (although oil sketches of her and many drawings were produced), and Ruskin's portrait was commissioned instead, a full-length posed in the bed of a rocky stream (priv. coll.). Ruskin was preparing the index to *The Stones of Venice* and writing his Edinburgh lectures, for which Millais helped to draw large diagrammatic illustrations.

In November, the portrait still unfinished, the party broke up at Edinburgh as Ruskin gave his lectures. Effie went to Bowerswell, and Millais to London. After the Ruskins returned to London in late December he continued to pose for Millais so that the head and figure could be put into the portrait, which was not finally completed and paid for until December 1854, after Millais had made a second trip to the site in June. Ruskin did not break with Millais until then. His marriage, however, had effectively ended in the autumn of 1853. Effie had given up any pretence of being able to get on with Ruskin's parents; Millais had written to Effie's mother attacking Ruskin. For Ruskin what followed was a convenient way out of a failed relationship. On 7 March Effie finally wrote to her father telling him the truth about her marriage. Lawyers were consulted, and on 25 April Effie left Ruskin for good. She married Millais on 3 July 1855.

Critic of contemporary art 'Be assured I shall neither be subdued, nor materially changed, by this matter. The worst of it for *me* has long been passed' (*Works*, 36.165). This comment in a letter to F. J. Furnivall, of 24 April 1854, demonstrates not only that the difficulties of Ruskin's marriage were already the subject of gossip before the rupture, but that he was determined to ignore them as far as possible. It is ironic that the scandal should have broken just as he was becoming a public figure, and it is indicative of his determination that during the 1850s Ruskin established himself as a contemporary art critic, with a commitment to social as well as aesthetic reform. This is demonstrated by his support for the Pre-Raphaelite painters, the London Working Men's College, and the University Museum, Oxford—all interlocking projects. It was only when he came to complete his defence of Turner at the end of the decade that doubt, even despair, broke in.

Turner, Gothic architecture, and the Pre-Raphaelites were the topics of Ruskin's four Edinburgh lectures of 1853, published the following year in revised form as *Lectures on Architecture and Painting*. A writer for the *Edinburgh Guardian* recorded this impression of Ruskin's first public appearance as a lecturer:

> Mr Ruskin has light sand-coloured hair; his face is more red than pale; the mouth well cut, with a good deal of decision in its curve, though somewhat wanting in sustained dignity and strength; an aquiline nose; his forehead by no means broad or massive, but the brows full and well bound together; the eye we could not see … Mr Ruskin's elocution is peculiar; he has a difficulty in sounding the letter 'r'; but it is not this we now refer to, it is the peculiar tone in the rising and falling of his voice at measured intervals, in a way scarcely ever heard except in the public lection of the service appointed to be read in churches. These are the two things with which, perhaps, you are most surprised,—his dress and his manner of speaking,—both of which (the white waistcoat notwithstanding) are eminently clerical.   (*Works*, 12.xxxi–xxxii)

The only feature missing from this description apart from Ruskin's distinctive eyes is the light blue cravat that became his personal emblem.

Ruskin's association with the Pre-Raphaelites was complicated by the public and private agendas of the personalities involved. He was doubly powerful, being a private patron (and adviser to other buyers such as the Trevelyans, Lady Waterford, Ellen Heaton, and Francis

McCracken) as well as being a public critic. There was self-interest on both sides: Ruskin sought friendship while expecting an affirmative response to his critical views; the artists had their careers to serve. In a letter to Tennyson in 1857 Ruskin referred to himself in terms of 'we PRBs' (*Works*, 36.265), he was a member of the Hogarth Club (1858–61), and he helped with the organization of a Pre-Raphaelite exhibition at Russell Place. But his decade in seniority made him more patron than brother-in-arms and his break with Millais divided an already fissiparous group of artists. His initial influence was indirect, but his emphasis on rejecting conventional picture making, accurate observation of nature, and the symbolic possibilities of natural fact were part of the Pre-Raphaelite programme. Holman Hunt read the second volume of *Modern Painters* in 1847 and drew Millais's attention to the writer's ideas. A reading of *The Stones of Venice* by William Morris and Edward Burne-Jones when Oxford undergraduates in 1853 was similarly significant. But Ruskin had not appreciated Millais's *Christ in the House of his Parents* with its high-church iconography when he saw it at the Royal Academy in 1850. Architecture and Venice were his principal preoccupations at the time of the Pre-Raphaelite Brotherhood's most cohesive activity.

When the Pre-Raphaelite paintings in the 1851 Royal Academy were again critically assaulted, Millais decided to make an appeal to Ruskin through their mutual acquaintance Coventry Patmore. Ruskin may also have been more directly engaged, for his father expressed an interest in buying Millais's *The Return of the Dove to the Ark*. The result of Patmore's appeal was two letters from Ruskin to *The Times* on 13 and 30 May 1851, defending works by Millais, Hunt, and Charles Collins, though by no means over-praising them, and warning against their Tractarian tendencies. The personal friendship with Millais followed, and Ruskin's decision to promote and try to mould the young artist.

The public expression of this came in additions to *Modern Painters* and the pamphlet *Pre-Raphaelitism*, issued in August 1851. The title may appear opportunistic, for the principal subject was Turner, and the most important statements about the Pre-Raphaelites were relegated to a footnote. Yet Ruskin understood the potential of the movement and its radical intentions: 'the Pre-Raphaelites imitate no pictures: they paint from nature only' (*Works*, 12.357n.). In Millais he saw a successor to the ageing Turner, as another, though stylistically different, seeker of visual and imaginative truth. (The programme of Millais's Glenfinlas painting was the intended synthesis of a Turnerian landscape subject with Pre-Raphaelite attention to detail in a contemporary portrait.) Arguing always that the Pre-Raphaelites represented only a first step, he welcomed them as potential founders of 'a new and noble school in England' (ibid., 12.358n.).

Ruskin had come to appreciate the extent to which Millais was not Turner by the time his portrait was complete and their friendship became impossible, though Ruskin was still ready, as late as 1886, to recognize aspects of his talent (*Works*, 14.495–6). In 1854 Ruskin again wrote twice to *The Times*, this time on the subject of Holman Hunt's Royal Academy pictures *The Light of the World* (5 May) and *The Awakening Conscience* (25 May). Hunt was away in the Holy Land, and as Hunt was a close associate of Millais at this time, Ruskin's friendship with the most 'Ruskinian' of the Pre-Raphaelites did not develop until after 1869. Instead Ruskin turned his enthusiasm to Dante Gabriel Rossetti, a very different kind of painter and a very different personality, whose work he had first seen in 1853. He bought and commissioned drawings from Rossetti, and from his future wife, the ailing Elizabeth Siddal. He sought medical help for her from his friend Henry Acland, now established with a medical practice and an academic career at Oxford, and in 1855 made her an allowance of £150 a year, an arrangement that appears to have ended in 1857. He guaranteed Rossetti an income from purchases, and in 1858 advanced £100 towards the publication of the artist's *Early Italian Poets* (1861). He encouraged commissions from his American friend Charles Eliot Norton and from the Leeds collector Ellen Heaton.

Although Rossetti took advantage of Ruskin's patronage, his bohemian ways did not conform to his patron's values, and from 1857 onwards the friendship began to cool. Rossetti resented Ruskin's scoldings, while Ruskin found Rossetti's Romantic medievalism increasingly morbid. In 1862 when, following Siddal's death, Rossetti moved to 16 Cheyne Walk, Ruskin tentatively suggested that he too might take rooms there, but the idea came to nothing. There was a dispute over the circulation of a joint portrait photograph, with William Bell Scott, taken at the house in 1863. By 1865 the increasingly quarrelsome Rossetti was falsely accusing Ruskin of selling his drawings, and Ruskin, now out of sympathy with the turn the artist's work had taken, ended their connection. He did, however, pay tribute to Rossetti in his lectures *The Art of England* (1883) after the artist's death in 1882.

Although no longer obliged to 'go into society', Ruskin sought intellectual companionship with writers as well as artists. In 1853 he met the Edinburgh physician and Turnerian Dr John Brown for the first time, although their correspondence ran from 1846 until 1882. In 1854 he met the public health reformer Dr John Simon, who became a close friend and nursed him after his first mental breakdown. In 1855 he first met the Bostonian Charles Eliot Norton, who was to promote Ruskin's ideas in America and become his literary executor and, with Joan Severn, the burner of much material relating to Rose La Touche. Ruskin regularly visited Thomas Carlyle at this period, who introduced him to the historian J. A. Froude. Ruskin was a visitor to Mrs Henry Prinsep's salon at Little Holland House, the home of George Frederick Watts who had made a portrait drawing of Effie Ruskin, and who was also to be celebrated in *The Art of England*. Tennyson was also a frequenter of the salon. Coventry Patmore introduced Ruskin to his fellow poet William Allingham and to Robert and Elizabeth Browning during their visit to England in 1855, with whom an important friendship developed.

A supporter of the Architectural Museum since 1851, at the end of 1854 Ruskin became involved in two parallel projects, the University Museum, Oxford, and the London Working Men's College, neither initiated by him, but providing opportunities for participation and patronage. The University Museum had been promoted by Acland, and once Ruskin had met the architect, Benjamin Woodward, he became closely involved in not only raising funds for the decoration of the building, but in the decorative scheme itself, proposing designs and encouraging the employment of Pre-Raphaelite artists such as the sculptors Alexander Munro and Thomas Woolner. He had hoped that Rossetti would also undertake work there, but instead Rossetti chose to lead the decoration of the new Oxford Union library and debating hall, also designed by Woodward. As a secular building devoted to the natural sciences, the University Museum was a contemporary expression of Ruskin's views on Gothic architecture; he carried his aesthetic principles into the social sphere by lecturing to the craftsmen who were building it. Woodward's tuberculosis threw increasing responsibility onto Acland and Ruskin; when Woodward died in 1861 the decorative scheme, though not the building, was still incomplete, and Ruskin lost interest in the project.

Ruskin's connection with the London Working Men's College lasted somewhat longer, although he was most active between 1854 and 1858, when he gave regular classes. The college had been founded by a group of Christian socialists, with F. D. Maurice as principal. Ruskin's political views did not conform to its founder's: he said his aim was 'directed not to making a carpenter an artist, but to making him happier as a carpenter' (Works, 13.553). But he was pleased to conduct an elementary drawing class where his emphasis on shading and on sketching from natural objects was in contrast to the methods instilled in the government schools of design, of which he was becoming increasingly critical. He recruited Rossetti to teach a class in figure-drawing and painting. It was through the college that Edward Jones (later Burne-Jones) met Rossetti in early 1856, at the same time as he came into contact with Ruskin, the beginning of a third Pre-Raphaelite friendship.

Ruskin taught drawing, largely by letter, to private correspondents as well as at the Working Men's College. Among these at various times were Louisa, marchioness of Waterford, Ellen Heaton, Louise Blandy (the daughter of his dentist), Ada Dundas, and the artists Anne Mutrie, Anna Blunden, and Isabella Jay. Octavia Hill, who was to run a philanthropic housing scheme with Ruskin's support in the 1860s before falling out with him, first met him as a pupil. It was his reputation as a teacher that led to the fatal introduction to the La Touche family in 1858. In 1859 he became an unofficial patron and teacher at Margaret Bell's progressive school for girls at Winnington in Cheshire. His teaching methods were synthesized in *The Elements of Drawing* (1857) in which he argued that: 'the sight is a more important thing than the drawing' (Works, 15.13). He followed this popular riposte to contemporary drawing manuals with the far less successful *Elements of Perspective* in 1859 and wrote again on drawing in the uncompleted

Laws of Fiesole in 1879. Ruskin's opposition to the mechanical methodology of the government schools led him to found his own school of drawing at Oxford when he began to lecture as the first Slade professor in 1870.

Besides allowing Ruskin to develop his teaching principles in practice, the London Working Men's College was the recruiting-ground for a number of Ruskin's assistants, most notably his future publisher, George Allen. William Ward was to be employed by him to facsimile Turners, J. W. Bunney to record threatened architecture, Arthur Burgess to assist with work at Oxford, and Henry Swan to become curator of the Museum of the Guild of St George.

Between 1855 and 1859 Ruskin was also engaged in the annual production of his *Academy Notes*—brief and highly selective notices of paintings that had caught his eye in the Royal Academy summer exhibition, the Watercolour societies, the Society of British Artists, and the French exhibition. These pamphlets were rapidly produced and went through changing editions; they were idiosyncratic, but attempted to steer the middle-class buyer through the dense patchwork of paintings and drawings displayed. He praised works which in his view conformed to Pre-Raphaelite aspirations as he understood them, within a broadly realist aesthetic. He also criticized those whom he supported, notably J. F. Lewis, and John Brett, whose *Val d'Aosta* (1859) had been painted virtually to Ruskin's instructions but which none the less was pronounced a disappointment (though he subsequently bought the picture). Other artists, among them Alfred William Hunt and J. C. Hook, received important encouragement. Ruskin abandoned the series in 1859, partly because of the low standards that year, partly for more general reasons of disenchantment with the art market, but he issued one more number devoted to the Royal Academy of 1875.

Ruskin's active engagement in so many different aspects of the contemporary art world helped to delay the completion of *Modern Painters*, although there were other contributory factors. The death of Turner, with whom he had never had an easy relationship, at the end of 1851 presented difficulties, for now the entire contents of his studio were open to inspection. Ruskin, perhaps also projecting some of his own experience onto the artist, began to discover a darker message in his work. Faced with the entanglements of Turner's will, he quickly resigned as an executor (an appointment to be taken as an acknowledgement of his service to the artist). When the legacy of paintings and drawings was released to the National Gallery in 1856, however, he campaigned to be allowed to make a representative selection of watercolours from the 20,000 works on paper. Once given permission in 1857, Ruskin placed 400 in cabinets of his own design, thus making them available for public inspection in the National Gallery. In 1856 he also contributed the letterpress to the dealer Ernest Gambart's publication of Turner mezzotints, *The Harbours of England*. Work on the Turner bequest—cleaning, mounting, and framing as well as cataloguing—continued until May 1858. He published a commentary on the oil paintings placed on display at Marlborough House in January 1857, and followed this with a privately printed selection of works on paper for the trustees of the National Gallery. He then published a further catalogue of works on paper arranged for display at Marlborough House (1857, rev. edn 1858). He completed his arduous task with a printed report to the trustees in 1858. Among the many sketchbooks and drawings were discovered a number which both Ruskin and the National Gallery authorities deemed to be obscene. Fearing that possession of such drawings might be illegal, the keeper, Ralph Wornum, proposed their destruction. Ruskin and the authorities agreed, and he witnessed the burning although he ensured that a small number of sketchbooks were preserved.

The third volume of *Modern Painters* appeared in January 1856, the fourth in April, but the final volume was not published until June 1860. The natural world was still Ruskin's touchstone, and Turner still his artist-hero, but both were seen in an altered context as Ruskin tried to come to terms with the waning of his dogmatic evangelical belief and the correlative loss of a spontaneous joy in landscape. His critical yardstick was still an artist or writer's fidelity to truth, 'but truth so presented that it will need the help of the imagination to make it real' (*Works*, 5.185). Taken as a whole, these volumes constituted an attempt to establish a satisfactory theory of the imagination that rested on the material facts of the natural world, but which showed not only that these facts also carried a profound symbolic truth, but that that truth could equally be conveyed in symbolic form. The crowded symbolism in Holman Hunt's minutely realistic *The Awakening Conscience* and the entirely imaginary, though equally realistically depicted, image of Christ in Hunt's *The Light of the World* must serve here as shorthand examples.

As Ruskin developed his theories from the notion of the 'grotesque' in *The Stones of Venice* his interest in the symbolic meanings contained in both art and literature became central. Devising the term 'the pathetic fallacy' (*Works*, 5.201), he rejected Romantic notions of a personal identification between the artist and the external world, but increasingly he saw the artist as a seer-mediator between God and man. Fallen man is necessarily a flawed lens, but Ruskin discovered a tragic nobility in this state. As he began to adopt a more humanistic approach, conscious of his own fallibility and even sensuality, he developed a system of mythographic interpretation, assisted by Max Müller's philology, which drew both on Judaeo-Christian and Hellenic traditions. These myths existed in nature, and in the contemporary world. They were also susceptible to a psychological reading, as expressions of the moral conflicts in the mind of man.

Turner was finally presented as the interpreter of these myths, attesting both to the spiritual condition of the artist, and of the nineteenth century. Ruskin wrote of *The Garden of the Hesperides* (1806):

Such then is our English painter's first great religious picture; and exponent of our English faith. A sad-coloured work not executed in Angelico's white and gold; nor in Perugino's crimson and azure; but in a sulphurous hue, as

relating to a paradise of smoke. That power, it appears, on the hill-top, is our British Madonna.   (*Works*, 7.407–8)

The dragon crouched above the garden is also the serpent in the Christian paradise, and a symbol of the moral and industrial pollution of Britain.

A mid-life crisis

Once I could speak joyfully about beautiful things, thinking to be understood;—now I cannot any more; for it seems to me that no one regards them. Wherever I look or travel in England or abroad, I see that men, wherever they can reach, destroy all beauty.   (*Works*, 7.422–3)

This comment towards the close of *Modern Painters* volume 5 is evidence of the gloomier state of mind in which the great project of the first half of Ruskin's life was completed, and shows the direction that his thoughts were taking in his fortieth year. It has been customary to treat 1860 as a watershed, with the publication of four essays on political economy in the *Cornhill Magazine* as a new beginning. But the change of subject matter—already suggested in *The Nature of Gothic*—had been adumbrated in 1857, and the relationship between the aesthetic economy and the moral climate remained a pivotal issue. 1860 is the central point of a process lasting several years on either side of that date. The key elements were a change in religious position, a new view of the Italian masters of the Renaissance, increasingly strained relations with his parents, and the stirrings of sexual desire. During this process Ruskin once more experienced depression and uncertainty. In a letter to Elizabeth Barrett Browning in November 1860 he wrote: 'I am divided in thought between many things, and the strength I have to spend on any seems to me nothing' (ibid., 36.350).

As early as 1851 Ruskin had begun to see that the natural theology that sustained his evangelical Romanticism was threatened by the advances of science and biblical criticism. He privately confessed to Acland:

If only the Geologists would let me alone, I could do very well, but those dreadful Hammers! I hear the clink of them at the end of every cadence of the Bible verses—and on the other side, these unhappy, blinking Puseyisms; men trying to do right, and losing their very Humanity.   (*Works*, 36.115)

His initial response to doubt was to suppress it by an act of faith, but in the summer of 1858 he travelled to Switzerland and Italy alone, in order to recuperate from his intense and disturbing work on the Turner bequest. He stayed for six weeks in Turin, spent enjoyable nights at the opera, and for the first time broke his strict sabbatarianism by drawing on a Sunday. He worshipped with the local protestant Waldensian community, but was struck by the contrast between the narrow plainness of the services and their setting, and the visual splendour of Veronese's *Solomon and the Queen of Sheba* which he was studying in the Turin municipal gallery. In later accounts he described the change of heart that followed as an epiphanic moment that left him 'a conclusively *un*-converted man' (ibid., 29.89). That day, he later wrote in his autobiography, 'my evangelical beliefs were put away, to be debated of no more' (ibid., 35.496).

While we may accept Ruskin's account as an

'un-conversion', it is clear that this was not a sudden event, nor was it a change to outright atheism, though for a time Ruskin lost faith in the hope of an afterlife. His fundamentally religious cast of mind remained the same, and it is significant that for some years after their first meeting in 1857 a favourite opponent in private religious debate was the evangelical Baptist Charles Haddon Spurgeon. The Bible remained a sacred text, but its wisdom now formed part of a wider literature of divine inspiration.

Ruskin's relaxation of his previously narrow religious views had an important relation to the change in his ideas on art and artists. Indeed, each is a consequence of the other. The emphasis was now less on the pure and spiritual than on the human and the physical. A note written during his work in the Turin gallery, and shared with his father, read: 'A good, stout, self-commanding, magnificent Animality is the make for poets and artists' (*Works*, 7.xl). This view was arrived at through the knowledge gained from the Turner bequest, but also from the study of Giorgione, Veronese, and Titian, who with Turner became the principal figures in *Modern Painters*, volume 5. This turn towards the Venetian colourists of the sixteenth century, as opposed to the painters of the preceding Gothic period, had a broader significance. His interest in the Gothic revival waned at this period, and he became critical of the Romantic medievalism of Rossetti and his circle. At the same time his belief in the continuity of the highest tradition in Western art, derived from classical antiquity, pointed not only forward to the founding principles of the Pre-Raphaelites, but back to the Greeks themselves.

The young artist Edward Burne-Jones, imbued though he was with a morbid medievalism, was a beneficiary of Ruskin's 'Venetian' period. He had first corresponded with Ruskin in January 1856, and then came into regular contact through the London Working Men's College and Little Holland House, gradually replacing Rossetti in Ruskin's affections. In 1859 Burne-Jones travelled in Italy at Ruskin's expense, studying the artists of whom his patron approved. Ruskin commissioned and bought work from him, and in 1861 became godfather to the artist's son Philip. In 1862 he and his wife, Georgiana, again travelled in Italy, at Ruskin's expense and for some of the time in his company, patron and artist both making copies of Ruskin's latest 'discovery', the early sixteenth-century Lombard painter Bernardino Luini. Burne-Jones became a frequenter of Winnington Hall School, making designs for a tapestry to be embroidered there for Ruskin, but never completed. In 1863 Ruskin commissioned him to make designs intended for the published version of his second series of essays in political economy, *Munera pulveris* (1872). During the 1860s Ruskin enjoyed a happy relationship with Burne-Jones, who seemed the contemporary artist most in sympathy with the classical and mythological bent of his current writings; but there was a falling-out, never quite repaired, in 1871. Burne-Jones had become a devotee of Michelangelo, whose violent mannerism Ruskin attacked in his lecture *The Relation of Michael Angelo to Tintoret* (1872), to Burne-Jones's anger.

At first, until Georgiana Burne-Jones succeeded in charming him, John James Ruskin disapproved of his son's favour for the artist—another bone of contention, along with the family's collection of Turners, between father and son. It is significant that in March 1861 Ruskin gave forty-eight Turner drawings from his collection to the Ashmolean Museum, Oxford, and a further twenty-five to the Fitzwilliam Museum, Cambridge, in May—a gesture of personal divestment as much as of public generosity. John James, feeling his age and in declining health, put heavy moral pressure on his son to complete *Modern Painters*. In 1859 parents and child made their last continental journey together, visiting Cologne, Berlin, Dresden, and Munich so that Ruskin could make good his deficient knowledge of their galleries, and make further studies of Veronese and Titian. It was not a happy tour, and Ruskin's religious views no longer accorded with his mother's fiercely held beliefs. To make matters worse, in September 1860 she broke her thigh, while his father's health began to trouble him.

Characteristically, Ruskin responded to domestic and other difficulties by proposing to withdraw into private research. In February 1861 he spoke of this in a letter to Charles Eliot Norton, describing:

> almost unendurable solitude in my own home, only made more painful to me by parental love which did not and never could help me, and which was cruelly hurtful without knowing it; and terrible discoveries in the course of such investigation as I made into grounds of old faith. (*Works*, 36.356)

He certainly withdrew from his parents' company. From 1859 until 1868 he regularly sought recreation and refuge at Winnington Hall School, John James disapproving of his financial support for Miss Bell. He was also much abroad, for he had a long-term project to write a history of Swiss towns, an idea that produced many drawings, but no text.

Ruskin spent much of the summer of 1861 at Boulogne, and was in Switzerland until Christmas; from May to November 1862 he was in Italy, Switzerland, and then across the border in Savoy, returning to Mornex in Savoy in December where he had rented a house and installed his assistant George Allen with an etching press. After a visit to England in the summer of 1863 he returned to Chamonix. All this time he was contemplating exile, telling Norton in 1862: 'I must find a home' (*Works*, 36.407). To that end in 1863 he seriously considered buying land in order to build a house high on the Brezon above Bonneville in the Savoy Alps. He was dissuaded from this impracticality, but he did buy land at Chamonix, subsequently disposed of. In November 1863 he returned to England, but remained as peripatetic as ever, his wanderings only brought to an end by the final illness of his father, who died on 3 March 1864.

The political economy of art Ruskin's inheritance was £157,000, pictures worth at least £10,000, and property in the form of houses and land. He immediately began to disperse this fortune in charitable and philanthropic schemes—notably placing Octavia Hill in charge of some of his houses—but made the unfortunate choice of the fraudulent artistic entrepreneur Charles Augustus Howell as secretary and almoner, although he had seen through him by 1869. He remained tied to his mother (aged eighty-three in 1864), living at Denmark Hill, but the burden was eased by the arrival of his young second cousin once removed Joan (Joanna) Agnew, who became his mother's companion. In death, as in life, John James's money allowed his son to live and write as he wished, but the concomitant parental censorship was removed. Ruskin's epitaph on his father's tomb—'He was an entirely honest merchant' (*Works*, 17.lxxvii)—had an unconscious irony, for it was a merchant's money that allowed Ruskin to devote the latter half of his life to a critique of the creation and distribution of wealth, and an attempt, by word and deed, to enforce its redefinition.

Ruskin's engagement with political economy came through art and architecture, as *The Nature of Gothic* had shown. In 1857 the great Manchester Art Treasures Exhibition gave him an opportunity to make a more direct intervention, when he was invited to give two lectures which he half-satirically entitled *The Political Economy of Art* (1857, reprinted, with additions, as *A Joy for Ever*, 1880). Just as his pamphlet of 1854, *The Opening of the Crystal Palace*, used the re-erection of the Crystal Palace at Sydenham to plead for the preservation of old buildings, Ruskin's Manchester lectures subverted the display of masterpieces by speaking of art in economic terms. Like further lectures in Manchester and Bradford reprinted as *The Two Paths* (1859), they were concerned with issues of production and distribution within the aesthetic sphere. What linked them to political economy was a labour theory of value derived from Adam Smith and David Ricardo; for artists, like Gothic craftsmen, were workers, creating the pictorial wealth celebrated by the Manchester exhibition.

Although Ruskin's criticism of orthodox utilitarian economics became increasingly direct as he moved from the field of cultural production on to the manufacturers' home ground, he repeated a trope of his writings on art and architecture by casting himself as an outsider, claiming, in this case quite rightly, to have little theoretical knowledge of economics. It was this independent position that gave him his sense of moral authority, although it means that Ruskin's political economy must be distilled from a wide range of writings on both art and society. In Manchester, the home of *laissez-faire*, he stated: 'the "Let-alone" principle is, in all things which man has to do with, the principle of death' (*Works*, 16.26). The word 'death' was not a rhetorical flourish. Throughout his economic writings and social commentary it bore the full weight of Ruskin's absolute distinction between good and evil. The countervailing image was life, as in his celebrated statement in *Unto this Last* (1862): 'THERE IS NO WEALTH BUT LIFE' (ibid., 17.105). Wealth was expressed, not by the economist's value in exchange, but the moralist's value in use.

The principle that governed the creation and distribution of wealth was both aesthetic and political: 'Government and co-operation are in all things and eternally the laws of life. Anarchy and competition, eternally, and in all things, the laws of death.' This 'Law of Help', appeared twice in Ruskin's writing. In *Modern Painters*, volume 5, it was applied to principles of composition (*Works*, 7.207), whereas in *Unto this Last* it was applied to economic relations (ibid., 17.75). In spite of the socialist-sounding reference to co-operation, Ruskin's anti-capitalism was profoundly conservative. His admiration for the Venetian republic and his own upbringing reinforced a strict, if benevolent, paternalism that rested on notions of an implacable divine justice rather than a calculated equity. This conception of justice lay behind his active support for Carlyle and other fellow members of the Governor Eyre Defence and Aid Fund in 1865–6, in opposition to the Jamaica Committee led by John Stuart Mill, as his speech on the Jamaica insurrection showed (ibid., 18.552–4).

Ruskin's first two attempts to convey his moral principles in political economic terms initially were failures, much derided in the establishment press, but they laid the foundations for the creation of a much wider constituency for Ruskin's ideas that was to keep his values in circulation even when he himself had fallen silent. The first of these was the articles published in the *Cornhill* in 1860, an outlet deliberately chosen because of its middle-class appeal. To the editor Thackeray's embarrassment, Ruskin's attack on the utilitarian *homo economicus* caused an outcry that led to the series being abbreviated, although Ruskin was allowed more space for his fourth and final contribution. The articles were reprinted, without significant alteration, as *Unto this Last* in 1862, and at first sold very badly. A further four articles, this time for Froude in *Fraser's Magazine* in 1862–3, attempted to build on the new definitions offered in *Unto this Last* and were also stopped. They were not published in volume form until 1872, as *Munera pulveris*, dedicated to Carlyle. Ruskin's persistence in attacking the conventional business ethics of his day inevitably exacerbated tension with his merchant father.

From Ruskin's Manchester lectures of 1857, his confidence as a lecturer grew, for he relished the direct contact with an audience, the opportunity to extemporize, and the persuasive effect the immediacy of his presence and delivery had. Such lectures and addresses could then be gathered up, revised, and issued in volume form, and throughout the 1860s this was his method of publication. These lectures should be read as a continuous and developing discourse, rather than as closed studies of fixed subjects. They were critiques both of contemporary culture and of the society that produced that culture. In the two lectures, 'Of kings' treasuries' and 'Of queens' gardens', delivered in Manchester in 1864, and reprinted as *Sesame and Lilies* (1865; with a third lecture, 'The mystery of life and its arts', 1871), Ruskin evoked images of kingship and queenship, which in their respective public and domestic spheres offered male leadership and female care, an ideal of moral and social responsibility in contrast to the selfish anarchy of *laissez-faire*. He pursued similar themes in the three lively and contentious lectures republished as *The*

Crown of Wild Olive in 1866 (issued with a fourth lecture and other matter, 1873).

In 1867 Ruskin experimented with another form of public yet personal discourse which he was to use increasingly frequently—the letter to a newspaper. In this case the letters were addressed, not to an editor, but to Thomas Dixon, a cork-cutter in Sunderland who arranged for their republication in the *Leeds Mercury* and the *Manchester Examiner*. The letters, ranging freely over the issues of the day, and particularly the agitation for reform, were reprinted as *Time and tide, by Weare and Tyne: twenty-five letters to a working-man of Sunderland on the laws of work* in 1867. Their form anticipated that of *Fors Clavigera* from 1871 onwards.

A leading theme developing throughout Ruskin's writings of the 1860s was the importance of education. This too grew out of his earlier art criticism, since it was his intention to educate both artist and patron; but the issue broadened to the purpose and methods of education in general. At Winnington Hall School his informal teaching in person and by letter extended far beyond that of a drawing master. In 1866 he again experimented with discursive form by dramatizing himself in the persona of the 'Old Lecturer (of incalculable age)' (*Works*, 18.207), in a series of Socratic dialogues with a dozen girls modelled on his favourite pupils at Winnington: *The Ethics of the Dust*. Here crystallography is deployed as the ruling metaphor in lectures that are part games, part moral lessons, and which convey the pleasure he took in his young audience's company.

Ruskin did not neglect more straightforward issues of art criticism, though his lectures and articles no longer respected any boundary between the categories of aesthetics, literature, philosophy, political economy, or natural science. He published a series of nine articles in the *Art Journal* in 1865–6 under the general title 'The Cestus of Aglaia', gave the lecture 'Modern art' at the British Institution in 1867, and gave the Rede lecture at Cambridge, 'The relation of national ethics to national arts', the same year, on the occasion of receiving an honorary doctorate from the university. (He was to receive an honorary DCL from Oxford in 1893.) He gave the lecture 'The flamboyant architecture of the valley of the Somme' in 1869 at the British Institution and arranged an exhibition of paintings and drawings by himself and others in illustration. He adopted a similar procedure the following year, after an extended visit to Verona for the Arundel Society, in 1869, with his lecture 'Verona and its rivers', in which he advocated extensive damming to control the flood waters of the Alps.

The most significant of this group of works was published in 1869 as *The Queen of the Air*, three 'lectures' on the Greek myths of Athena assembled from various sources, including material from his *Art Journal* articles. Deploying philology, botany, colour theory, economics, and moral philosophy as well as his distinctive form of mythography, Ruskin presented a modern myth of Athena, an emblematic figure who stood for the healing and creative powers of the imagination, and of nature. Her counter-type was the serpent, a symbol of pollution, whose coils might be found in drains, or in the wreaths of black smoke that darkened the sky and drew obscurity over the lecture he gave in Dublin in 1868, 'The mystery of life and its arts'. The female principle represented by Athena had particular personal significance for Ruskin, and it is necessary to turn to the events in his private life that overshadowed all his public work of the 1860s, and beyond.

Rose La Touche   In January 1858 Ruskin called for the first time at the London residence of Mr and Mrs John La Touche, as a result of an introduction effected by Louisa, marchioness of Waterford. John La Touche was a wealthy Irish banker of Huguenot extraction, who had a large estate at Harristown, co. Kildare. He was a follower of Spurgeon, by whom he was to be baptized as an evangelical Baptist in 1863. Maria La Touche did not share her husband's evangelicalism, had published two novels, and was a member of an aristocratic circle of cultivated Anglo-Irishwomen. It was the La Touche habit to spend a Christmas and spring season in London, which accounted for the pattern of journeys between Harristown and London in the following years. Mrs La Touche wished to lionize Ruskin, and did so by asking him to give drawing lessons to her daughters Emily (1844–1867) and Rose (1848–1875). Ruskin at first demurred, but a friendship began. It was thus just after her tenth birthday, on 3 January 1858, and just before his thirty-ninth on 8 February, that the tragic relationship between Rose and Ruskin began.

Initially Ruskin appears to have been interested equally in Mrs La Touche and her daughters. Mrs La Touche began as one more of Ruskin's married confidantes, and it was during a visit to Harristown in August 1861 that he told her of his changed religious position. She asked him not to make this public for ten years. By the autumn of 1861 Ruskin felt deeply drawn towards Rose, but that October she fell ill for the first time from the psychosomatic disorder (possibly the as yet unrecognized condition *anorexia nervosa*) which eventually killed her. Rose was strongly under her father's religious influence, and published a volume of devotional poetry, *Clouds and Light*, in 1870. Ruskin's preference for daughter over mother may have caused some tension, and Ruskin was out of sympathy with the father, so that his continental wanderings from 1862 to 1864 were partly driven by a desire to avoid their London visits. He did not see Rose between the spring of 1862 and December 1865, though Mrs La Touche did not break off contact. Rose had further bouts of illness in 1862 and 1863.

Like other men of his class and culture—for instance, his future Oxford colleague Charles Dodgson—Ruskin enjoyed the company of young girls, as his happiness at Winnington testified. It was their purity that attracted him; any sexual feelings were sublimated in the playful relationship of master and pupil that characterized his letters to several female correspondents. These flirtations continued in parallel to his more profound feelings for Rose. In 1887, after his mental health had broken down more than once, a tutelary friendship with a young art student, Kathleen Olander, developed into a fantasy of marriage on his part, before her parents intervened. It is possible to see a sad reprise of the relationship with Rose in this final passion.

Rose was no flirtation. Just after her eighteenth birthday in January 1866, with Ruskin about to turn forty-seven, he proposed marriage. Her answer was not a refusal, but a request to wait for three years. The La Touches became alarmed by the love that was apparent on both sides, but did not entirely sever communications. Ruskin was forced to rely on intermediaries, the first of whom was Georgiana Cowper, *née* Tollemache. He had seen her in Rome in 1840, and met her again in 1854. In 1848 she had married William Cowper, a stepson of Lord Palmerston, who acknowledged this patrimony by changing his name to Cowper-Temple in 1869, becoming Lord Mount-Temple in 1880. In 1865 he had inherited Palmerston's estate, Broadlands in Hampshire. The second intermediary was George MacDonald, a friend of Mrs La Touche who had been forced by his unorthodox views to give up holy orders and become a writer. The third was Joan Agnew, only two years older than Rose, who between August 1866 and September 1867 was engaged to the La Touches' son Percy (1846–1921), and who was sometimes allowed to see Rose when Ruskin was not.

Ruskin endured the waiting. In May 1868, at a time when there had been reassuring letters from her, there was an opportunity to see Rose in Dublin, where he had travelled to give his lecture 'The mystery of life and its arts'. But there was no meeting, and communications became expressly forbidden. The reason was that Mrs La Touche had consulted Ruskin's former wife, Effie, about his character and about her view of the legal position. The fear was that a consummated marriage with Rose would render the previous grounds for annulment void, and so make the second marriage bigamous. The three years' wait passed, and Rose's bouts of illness continued. It was not until 7 January 1870 that Ruskin met her accidentally at the Royal Academy. Covert communication was resumed and Rose assured him of her love, though alluding to the religious obstacles between them, for Ruskin's position had been known to her since 1862, and her own religious devotion was extreme.

In October 1870 Mrs La Touche showed Rose the results of further correspondence with Effie Millais, which had the desired damaging effect. Ruskin for his own part sought legal advice which concluded that a marriage was possible, and communicated this to Rose in the summer of 1871. She however rejected him. Both Rose and Ruskin became ill, he experiencing a physical and mental breakdown at Matlock Bath in Derbyshire in July. In 1872 Rose initiated a reconciliation through MacDonald and the Cowper-Temples which brought an initially reluctant Ruskin hurrying back from Venice at the end of July. There were a few days of happiness, but Ruskin pressed his case for marriage and Rose refused. In 1873, by which time Rose's condition was deteriorating, it was Ruskin's turn to reject a possible meeting. At the beginning of 1874,

estranged from her parents, Rose travelled to London in search of medical treatment. Joan Agnew was allowed to see her, but Ruskin not. In September, when she was again in London, her parents relented, and Ruskin was able to visit her regularly until her return to Ireland in December. In January 1875 she was back in London, but extremely ill, and Ruskin saw her for the last time on 15 February, before she was taken to Dublin in April. She died on 25 May, aged twenty-seven. Ruskin heard the news on 28 May. He was broken-hearted.

The role played by religion in this tragedy was cruelly ironic, for Ruskin's abandonment of his evangelical beliefs in the very year that he had first met Rose had proved an insurmountable obstacle. Yet Rose, through those associated with her, was to help restore Ruskin's faith. Mrs Cowper and her husband were devotees of the spiritualist movement. Persuaded by her, Ruskin attended his first séance in February 1864 and in April had several séances with the American medium Daniel Dunglass Home, who impressed him. He saw Home again in July 1866, and through the Cowpers maintained an interest in spiritualist manifestations of the afterlife. In March 1868, however, he attended a séance with the Cowpers that disillusioned him with the charlatanism associated with mediums, and he abandoned the practice, but not his interest.

In March 1874 Ruskin left England for Italy, where he had been asked to supervise the making of copies of frescoes by Giotto in the church of St Francis in Assisi for the Arundel Society. He visited Rome, where he made a study of Botticelli's *Zipporah* in the Sistine Chapel, travelled to Naples, and then crossed to Sicily. He returned to Rome and in early June settled at Assisi until the end of July, when he moved on to Lucca, and Florence. Here he prepared the guidebook *Mornings in Florence* (1875–7) before returning to England at the end of October, via Chamonix.

In Assisi Ruskin made use of the sacristan's cell and engaged in religious disputes with the friars, while continuing private Bible reading. His chief interest was not the frescoes in the upper church being copied for the Arundel Society, but works in the lower church that he attributed to Cimabue and Giotto. He made a careful study of *The Marriage of Poverty and St Francis*, where the roses above Poverty's head provoked home thoughts from abroad. His study of pre-Renaissance painters continued in Florence, and brought about a shift in his appreciation that recognized the spiritual as distinct from the technical achievement of their work. It also produced a shift in his religious views, back to a renewed sense of faith that was to make his work 'much more distinctly Christian in its tone' (*Works*, 29.86).

Grief at the death of Rose La Touche in 1875 left him once more open to the attractions of spiritualism. In December 1875 he went to stay with the Cowper-Temples at Broadlands, where a medium convinced him that she had seen Rose in communication with him, although he himself saw and heard nothing. He was thus predisposed to believe in the possibility of receiving some sign from

Rose when the following year he spent the winter in Venice, making a close study of Carpaccio's cycle of paintings on the life of St Ursula in the Accademia Gallery. Permitted to have *The Dream of St Ursula* in a private room, as the anniversary of the Broadlands 'teachings' approached, Ruskin increasingly identified Rose with the dead virgin saint. At Christmas a series of coincidences, including reading a letter from Mrs La Touche to Joan Severn, convinced him that Rose was in communication with him, and that he should be reconciled with her mother. In a state of exaltation, he became a '"Catholic"', though 'no more … a *Roman*-Catholic, than again an Evangelical-Protestant' (*Works*, 29.92).

The professor The private distress caused by the seventeen-year relationship with Rose La Touche undermined Ruskin's mental stability: there are many coded references to her in his public writings. None the less, by the end of the 1860s Ruskin was established as a prominent, if controversial, commentator on art and social issues, with a growing following. His position received institutional recognition when he was elected Oxford's first Slade professor of fine art in August 1869. The election was engineered by Acland. In 1858 Ruskin had been made an honorary student (that is to say, fellow) of Christ Church; Acland had promoted his candidacy for the professorship of poetry in 1866, and in 1867 suggested he became a curator of the University Galleries (now the Ashmolean Museum).

The Slade professorship came at a domestically eventful time for Ruskin: in April 1871 his mother's companion, Joan Agnew, married Arthur Severn, and moved into the former Ruskin home at 28 Herne Hill. His old nurse, Anne Strachan, died. During that summer he bought, unseen, the small house at Brantwood, across the lake from the then Lancashire village of Coniston, from the radical pamphleteer William Linton. On 5 December his mother died, so he was free to give up the house at Denmark Hill, and to begin to enlarge and improve Brantwood, into which he formally moved in September 1872. Having been made an honorary fellow of Corpus Christi College in April 1871, he began to divide his time, when not travelling on his familiar paths abroad, between his rooms in Corpus, Brantwood, and Herne Hill, where he occupied his former nursery.

Ruskin's activities in the 1870s attempted to synthesize his intentions and beliefs. The teaching at Oxford ran in parallel with a wider mission of social reform, addressed to the world at large through the medium of his monthly publication, begun in January 1871, *Fors Clavigera: Letters to the Workmen and Labourers of Great Britain*. Significantly, he recast his relationship with his audience by taking over his publishing activities from Smith, Elder & Co., and placing them in the hands of his assistant George Allen. Allen became not only responsible for *Fors Clavigera*, but in 1871 began to publish an accumulative edition of Ruskin's works which presented him in terms of his later social writing, rather than the 'fine' writing of before 1860. Ruskin's insistence on a fixed retail price for his books was to lead in time to the establishment of the net book agreement, which lasted until the 1990s. By 1873 Ruskin was in full control of his publishing activities, and released a stream of publications, usually in part form, across the field of natural science, cultural history, political economy, and art criticism. The thrust of his writing, however, was to try to extend his arguments into practical action. None of these projects achieved more than partial success, yet they stood as examples of what might be aspired to: as always with Ruskin, the parts represented a greater whole.

Ruskin's initial appointment as Slade professor was for three years at a salary of £360 a year—the only money he ever earned, apart from the sale of his books. This was renewed twice before his first resignation in 1878. He gave eleven series of lectures during this period. Most were subsequently published, although the printed versions do not fully reflect the liveliness, humour, and sometimes anger of their delivery, nor the effect of the varied and ingenious illustrations and demonstrations that accompanied them. Many had to be delivered twice because of their popularity. The printed versions do, however, indicate the free range of his mind. After the controlled and helpfully didactic inaugural *Lectures on Art* (1870, delivered February and March 1870), they cover the whole spread of Ruskin's interests. The chief series were *Aratra Pentelici: Six Lectures on Sculpture* (1872, delivered November and December 1870); *Lectures on Landscape* (1897, delivered January and February 1871); *The Eagle's Nest: Ten Lectures on the Relation of Natural Science to Art* (1872, delivered February and March 1872); *Ariadne Florentina: Six Lectures on Wood and Metal Engraving* (1876, delivered November and December 1872); *Love's Meinie: Lectures on Greek and English Birds* (1881, delivered March and May 1873, published together with two given at Eton College); *Val d'Arno: Ten Lectures on … Tuscan Art* (1874, delivered October and November 1873); *Deucalion* (1879, geological essays, including four lectures delivered in October and November 1874, and to which are related the botanical studies published as *Proserpina*, issued in parts between 1875 and 1886). Ruskin's course 'Twelve studies in the *Discourses* of Sir Joshua Reynolds', delivered in November 1875, and his 'Twelve readings in *Modern Painters*', delivered in November and December 1878, were not published. He took leave of absence in Venice in the winter of 1876–7.

Ruskin's principal intention was to instruct Oxford undergraduates in their responsibilities as future leaders, and as patrons of art. He carried his polemic into the practical field, by in 1871 taking over the existing government-sponsored Oxford School of Art in the University Galleries, and reconstituting it as a drawing school, to be run according to his own principles, and administered by a drawing-master (the school's existing incumbent, Alexander MacDonald) whose post he endowed with £5000. He accumulated a collection of visual aids, drawn from his lectures, which he developed in successive catalogues for use as a course of instruction. The materials included his own drawings, works by Turner from his original gift of

1861, to which he added more, works by artists he patronized and assistants he employed, engravings, woodcuts, and photographs, and even pages from an illuminated missal, for it was ever Ruskin's habit to cut up and distribute parts of the medieval manuscripts he collected throughout his life. These materials were framed and housed in mahogany cabinets of his own design, arranged in three principal series: the 'Standard and reference' series, holding 200 frames, and the 'Rudimentary' and 'Educational' series, holding 300 frames each. These valuable collections (which were in a constant state of rearrangement), together with plaster casts, books, and other works of art, were kept in the gallery used by the drawing school, and formally given to the university in 1875.

Ruskin's many other projects, however, and his absences from Oxford, meant that the Ruskin School of Drawing did not function as he would have wished. Indeed, Ruskin began to feel a certain disenchantment with Oxford, both in his relations with the senior members, who envied his reputation and did not respond to his calls for reform, and with the undergraduates, who in the main sustained a hearty philistinism. In March 1874, as an antidote to rowing and cricket, he called for volunteers to help drain and surface a muddy track in the nearby village of Ferry Hinksey. This project, which ended the following summer, attracted public ridicule, but proved to be a valuable recruiting ground for a new generation of followers, among them Arnold Toynbee, H. D. Rawnsley (with Octavia Hill a future founder of the National Trust, Ruskinian in inspiration), his future editor and literary executor Alexander Wedderburn, and his devoted interpreter and first biographer, William Gershom Collingwood.

The notion of healthy labour was a direct link to the principles enunciated in *Fors Clavigera*, its title a play on the notion of fortune as key or fateful hammer. The pamphlet's serendipitous theme allowed Ruskin, by pricking the conscience of the world, to justify his private pleasure in art and collecting. The free form enabled him to address public and private events, while the response of his correspondents engendered a virtual dialogue with his audience. His work for the Mansion House committee for the relief of Paris during the Franco-Prussian War was an early topic.

Through the pages of *Fors Clavigera* Ruskin was able to develop the idea of a utopian society, or treasure-store, initially launched in 1871 as the St George's Fund with £7000 of his own money. It would hold land, promote education, and eschew industrial life and the steam engine. A first gift of houses in Barmouth was made in 1875 by an admirer, Mrs Fanny Talbot, and other gifts and supporters were found through *Fors Clavigera*. In its legal and constitutional form, the Guild of St George did not come into existence until 1878, or meet until 1879. Ruskin was appointed master, with absolute authority over a strictly hierarchical order of society that reflected his ideal image of Venice. The guild acquired little land and built no schools, nor was its membership ever large; yet it served as a focus for Ruskin's most earnest disciples, and remains the one direct link with his ideas.

The most practical expression of the guild's values was a museum, placed in a cottage in the Walkley district of Sheffield. The property was bought in November 1875 at the instigation of a former pupil of the London Working Men's College, Henry Swan, who had gathered a group of working men interested in launching a collective farming experiment at nearby Totley—again paid for by Ruskin. The museum was multiform and multipurpose, serving as a library and teaching collection including casts, drawings, prints, and geological specimens. When in 1876 Ruskin became alarmed by the destructive restoration of buildings in Venice and elsewhere, it became the repository of the copies and studies he commissioned from a small group of English and Italian copyists regularly employed by him. The crowded cottage was extended in 1884, and in 1890 the collection moved to a house provided by Sheffield corporation at Meersbrook Park, by which time Ruskin was no longer actively in control of his affairs.

Ruskin continued the monthly production of *Fors Clavigera* even when abroad, and regular publication was maintained until letter 87 of March 1878, when Ruskin had his first complete mental collapse. His themes and moods were many, but there was an ever-stronger note of reiteration, as autobiographical material began to appear more frequently. Matter from *Fors Clavigera* was drafted into *Praeterita*, begun in January 1885. Another sign of reiteration was his increasing use of baby talk in his private letters to Joan Severn. In 1875 he asserted the values of an earlier form of transport by commissioning a new posting carriage.

In 1876, tired of Oxford and grieving for Rose La Touche, Ruskin returned to Venice for the first extended stay since 1853. His intention was to revise *The Stones of Venice* (another turning back), possibly adding a fourth volume. Distracted, however, by his many projects and his obsession with the St Ursula–Rose connection, he produced another guidebook, *St Mark's Rest* (1877–84), a *Guide to the Principal Pictures in the Academy of Fine Arts at Venice* (1877), and contributed the preface to a book by a Venetian curator, Count Alvise Zorzi, that protested against the proposed restoration of the façade of St Mark's. Ruskin carried this campaign to England and used the Guild of St George as a conduit for support, commissioning a large painting of the façade from his copyist J. W. Bunney. These protests proved successful and the proposed restoration was stopped.

After his return to England at the end of May 1878 Ruskin delivered his extempore 'Readings in *Modern Painters*' at Oxford in the autumn and began to prepare an exhibition of his collection of Turners, together with a selection of his own drawings, for display at the Fine Art Society in London the following February. This too was an act of reiteration, recalling as it did both his youthful work on Turner and his relationship with his father, with whom he had created the collection. At new year he was a guest at Windsor Castle of Prince Leopold, a trustee of the Ruskin School of Drawing, and followed this with a visit to the Gladstone family at Hawarden. (This personal encounter caused Ruskin to soften his attacks on Gladstone in *Fors Clavigera*, but there was no disguising the difference between Ruskin's ultra-tory views and Gladstone's Liberalism.) Ruskin's mental balance was slipping, and on 20 February 1878 he broke down completely: '*Mere* overwork or worry, might have soon ended me, but it would not have driven me crazy. I went crazy about St Ursula and the other saints,—chiefly young-lady saints' (*Correspondence of … Ruskin and … Norton*, 412).

The storm cloud of the nineteenth century Ruskin's delusions during his first attack of what has been characterized as either manic depression or 'paranoid schizophrenia' (Hunt, *The Wider Sea*, 370) were violent and extreme, revealing hostility to Joan Severn. Yet he was recovering by 8 April, and was able to complete his Turner catalogue. But although able to travel, he did not attend the hearing in London in November of the suit for libel brought against him by James McNeil Whistler, pleading ill health. The previous June he had visited the newly opened Grosvenor Gallery, and in an ensuing number of *Fors Clavigera* he praised the work of Burne-Jones but attacked Whistler's 'Nocturnes', accusing him of 'Cockney impudence' for asking 200 guineas 'for flinging a pot of paint in the public's face' (*Works*, 29.160). Whistler won a derisory farthing's damages, while Ruskin's legal costs were met by a subscription of his friends; but Ruskin found it a convenient reason for resigning the Slade professorship.

The portrait of Ruskin drawn by Hubert von Herkomer in 1879 shows the toll the previous years had taken. While his hair never went entirely grey, he let his side-whiskers grow, and after further illness in 1881 they became a full beard, so that as he aged, and his body became bent, he took on increasingly the appearance of a sage. It was at this period that Ruskin began to acquire self-conscious disciples, partly through the Guild of St George, and partly through the formation of organizations such as the Ruskin Society of Manchester (1879) and the Ruskin Reading Guild (1887). His preferred means of communication, *Fors Clavigera*, resumed publication in March 1880.

Ruskin carried on desultory work on a number of part-publications as his recovery continued. In March 1880 he gave a lecture on snakes at the London Institution and in the summer worked on a somewhat eccentric series of articles for the *Nineteenth Century* published in 1880–81 as 'Fiction, fair and foul'. He made two visits to France, and on the second in October began work on *The Bible of Amiens* (1880–85), a mythographic history combined with close analysis of the sculpture of Amiens Cathedral that was intended as part of a larger unfinished work, *Our Fathers have Told Us: Sketches of the History of Christendom. Arrows of the Chace*, a collection of his letters to the press, edited by Alexander Wedderburn, was also published in two volumes in 1880.

Foreshadowed by troubling thoughts of Rose, on 19 February 1881 Ruskin suffered a second and violent attack at Brantwood, and attendants had to be called. He recovered by 22 March, and spent the rest of the year at his house, doing little work, but spending freely on the guild. He adopted the ladies' teacher-training college Whitelands in

Chelsea as the site of a May queen festival, a version of a former event at Winnington, and in 1885 the ceremony of choosing a rose queen was replicated at the High School for Girls in Cork. A companion, that is to say member, of the Guild of St George successfully established a wool mill on the Isle of Man on Ruskinian lines, and another began to revive the Langdale hand-spinning and weaving industry. In February 1882 Ruskin prepared a *General Statement Explaining the Nature and Purposes of St George's Guild* (1882), but in March he was struck down for the third time.

This third attack, which took place while Ruskin was staying at Herne Hill, was less serious than the previous two. He remained under Joan Severn's care until August, when he began a tour to France, Switzerland, and Italy until December, accompanied by W. G. Collingwood. Work was undertaken to enlarge Brantwood in order to accommodate the Severns, and his financial resources became overstretched. In Florence in October he met the American artist Francesca Alexander. He was enthused by her studies of peasant life, and helped the publication of her *Story of Ida* (1883), *Roadside Songs of Tuscany* (1885—for which he bought and gave away many of the original drawings), and *Christ's Folk in the Apennine* (1888). He was already in contact by letter with Kate Greenaway, who was to visit Brantwood in the spring of 1883 and receive praise in his next Oxford lectures, but her feelings for him were not reciprocated. Having indicated that he was prepared to return to Oxford, on 2 January 1883 he was re-elected Slade professor.

1883 was spent mainly at Brantwood, where Ruskin was visited by Mr and Mrs La Touche, except for excursions to London, to Scotland in September, and to Oxford in March, May, and November to deliver the lectures published as *The Art of England* (1884). In restrained tones, Ruskin reviewed the work of the artists he had known, and praised a group of contemporary women illustrative artists. But he was unwell by the end of the year, and the state of his mind was revealed in the late *tour de force*, *The Storm Cloud of the Nineteenth Century* (1884), based on a lecture given twice at the London Institution in February of that year. It was an extraordinary collision between the public and the personal. Following fifty years of amateur meteorological observation, he stated that since 1871 a new 'plague-wind' (*Works*, 34.31) had begun to blow which had darkened the skies and, by implication, the mind of man. He found a moral metaphor in the foul winds recorded in his diaries which had an objective correlative in industrial pollution, but which was also a figure for his own mind. In the printed version, the second lecture is an annotation of and private commentary on the first.

Ruskin's attack in the lecture on the '*deliberate* blasphemy of science' (*Works*, 34.73) signalled the approach of the climax of his long battle with contemporary scientists, whose values he sought to counter with the mythopoeic botany, geology, and ornithology of *Proserpina*, *Deucalion*, and *Love's Meinie*. In the field of geology he defended the theories on the movement of glaciers of James Forbes (whom he had met in 1844) against the attacks of John Tyndall, an associate of T. H. Huxley. His principal quarrel was with the approach to scientific knowledge represented by Charles Darwin's *On the Origin of Species*, the subject of a symbolically important debate between Huxley and Bishop Wilberforce in 1860. The location for this debate, the University Museum, Oxford, was of special significance for Ruskin. Not only had the debate emblematized the end of the natural theology upon which the building's decoration was premised, Ruskin used its lecture hall as Slade professor, where he found himself increasingly at odds with the 'Darwinian Theory' (*Works*, 26.99).

Ruskin had known Darwin since 1837, and Darwin, whom he respected, visited Brantwood in 1879 and 1881, but his attacks on Darwinism became increasingly intemperate, while he expressed an ever deeper revulsion against anatomy. These matters came to a head at Oxford in 1884. Wounded by the university's refusal to support his plans to expand the drawing school, he revoked a bequest made the year before. At the same time he was drawn into the controversy surrounding the proposal to equip a laboratory in the museum for the new professor of physiology, Sir John Burdon-Sanderson, who held a licence to practise vivisection. His Michaelmas lectures, titled 'The pleasures of England', were largely extempore disquisitions on the English character which gave free rein to his anger and disappointment, and became a spectacle for the undergraduates. He was forcibly dissuaded by the vice-chancellor, Benjamin Jowett, from giving two announced lectures on science and atheism. When on 10 March 1885 the university agreed to fund the new physiology laboratories, Ruskin resigned his chair, and demanded the return of many of the additional works that he had placed in his school.

Praeterita and after   With letter 96, at Christmas 1884, Ruskin formally ceased publication of the now desultory *Fors Clavigera*, in order to concentrate his remaining energies on an autobiography whose title encapsulated his ever stronger mood of reiteration. Its subtitle—'Outlines of scenes and thoughts perhaps worthy of memory in my past life'—underlined his intention to recall only what pleased him, so that for instance his marriage received no mention. The work began to be published as it was composed, intermittently and in parts, in July 1885, and was never finished. In May 1886 he added another autobiographical dimension by publishing some of his raw material as *Dilecta: Correspondence, Diary Notes, and Extracts from Books Illustrating 'Praeterita'* (1886, 1887, 1900), which also remained unfinished.

Praeterita is a delightful work, a rewriting of Ruskin's life that makes it unreliable as a source of biographical fact, yet an accurate portrait of the author's mind. That it remained unfinished shows that the contradictions of that mind never achieved their desired synthesis, though this version is the best that could be achieved, and makes it a significant work of literature, most especially in his Wordsworthian evocation of the power of nature on the growth of a young mind. The conscious manipulation of memory had been intended to be therapeutic, but there were memories and hurts that could not be suppressed,

and as Ruskin struggled to bring them out he found himself fighting a double battle: to retain his sanity, and to control the composition of a work that increasingly alarmed Joan Severn.

At the end of July 1885, just as the first two sections of *Praeterita* describing his family background and early childhood appeared, Ruskin had a fourth, longer, and more severe attack of madness. Joan Severn responded by regulating his correspondence and contacts, and attempting to manage his finances, which were by now dependent on the sale of his books. Faced with the prospect of losing all control over his affairs through permanent insanity, Ruskin reluctantly prepared to make over Brantwood to Joan and Arthur Severn, and appointed Joan, C. E. Norton, and Alexander Wedderburn his literary executors. Ruskin resumed publication of *Praeterita* in September and continued until July 1886, by which time his account had reached 1844, but there was increasing tension with the Severns over money. In July 1886 he became violently mad again, but published two further sections in October, one in January and one in March 1887, bringing the account up to 1847.

In May 1887, however, Ruskin quarrelled violently with the Severns and temporarily left Brantwood for the nearby Waterhead Hotel. The cause was once more control over his estate and over the composition of *Praeterita*. In spite of a reconciliation, in August Ruskin, accompanied by his servant Peter Baxter, left Brantwood with the intention of going abroad, but instead he stopped at Folkestone, and then settled in nearby Sandgate, where he lived in reduced circumstances until June 1888, forced to borrow money from his publisher George Allen, who disapproved of Joan Severn's treatment of him. He made occasional visits to London, where he met Kathleen Olander. More parts of *Praeterita* appeared in June and November 1887 and May 1888, in the last of which he gave an account of his 'unconversion' of 1858 (*Works*, 35.496).

1858 was also the year he had first met Rose La Touche, making this a dangerous moment both for Ruskin and the Severns, who feared for his reputation. In June 1888, accompanied by Arthur Severn, Ruskin travelled to Abbeville and then in August, accompanied by the young architect Detmar Blow, set out on his old paths through Switzerland to Italy, writing an 'Epilogue' to *Modern Painters* at Chamonix (*Works*, 7.461–4). While visiting Francesca Alexander at Bassano he composed the chapter of *Praeterita* in which he described his first meeting with Rose. Upset by the past, and the rupture of his relationship with Kathleen Olander, Ruskin became increasingly depressed and by the time he reached Venice in October his mind was giving way again. He had returned as far as Paris in December when Joan Severn was called to fetch him home.

In May 1889 Ruskin left Brantwood for the last time, accompanied by Joan Severn, travelling to Seascale on the Cumberland coast where he struggled to continue *Praeterita*, composing what proved to be the final section, 'Joanna's Care', devoted to the woman who had become his keeper. In June 1889 the previous chapter, introducing Rose, was published, followed by 'Joanna's Care' in July, but in August he suffered another devastating breakdown which lasted until August the following year, bringing any hope of further work to an end.

The years until Ruskin's death were spent at Brantwood, in the Severns' protective custody, anxiously monitored by his neighbour, W. G. Collingwood. He was able to receive visitors, but gradually retreated into silence, saying little, and writing few letters. On the occasion of his eightieth birthday in 1899 he was able to receive a national address of congratulation sponsored by almost all the organizations with which he had been associated, read by the secretary of the Birmingham Society, John Howard Whitehouse, who was to protect his legacy in the lean years of Ruskin's reputation in the first half of the twentieth century.

On 18 January 1900, now confined to his bedroom, Ruskin caught influenza from one of the servants, and he died peacefully in the afternoon of 20 January. Although a burial in Westminster Abbey was offered, Ruskin was buried in accordance with his wishes in Coniston churchyard on 25 January 1900.

Ruskin's legacy During Ruskin's final years his reputation as a sage steadily grew and his values were absorbed by a wide range of early twentieth-century reformers. In 1903 publication began of the monumental Library Edition of his complete works in thirty-nine volumes, edited by E. T. Cook and Alexander Wedderburn. Although biographically reticent and presenting a liberal version of Ruskin, this became the foundation for future Ruskin scholarship. The edition was not a commercial success, however, as Ruskin's reputation sank into a trough as a result of generational change and a reaction against Victorian ideas. The Severns had immediately begun to disperse their inheritance, a process accelerated after Joan Severn's death in 1924, and completed after Arthur's in 1931, which left Brantwood empty, its treasures scattered in Britain, America, and Japan.

Brantwood was bought by J. H. Whitehouse. In 1919 he had founded Bembridge School on the Isle of Wight, on Ruskinian principles. There in 1929 he built the Ruskin Galleries to house a growing collection of Ruskin manuscripts and other material. Brantwood was opened as a public memorial to Ruskin in 1934. Over the years many of the objects dispersed from Brantwood were returned and the house began to present changing displays featuring Ruskin's drawings and aspects of his ideas. In the 1990s work began on restoration of the gardens and the development of the estate to reflect Ruskin's views on ecology and conservation.

Whitehouse's collection continued to grow even after his death in 1955 when chairmanship of the Education Trust Ltd, owner of the collection, passed to R. G. Lloyd (later Lord Lloyd of Kilgerran). In 1957 J. S. Dearden was appointed curator. Shortly before Lord Lloyd's death in 1991 agreement was reached with Lancaster University for the transfer of the Bembridge archive to a purpose-built building on the campus, and in 1993 the Ruskin Foundation was created to manage the collection, on loan from the Education Trust. The Ruskin Library opened at Lancaster in 1998.

Although he was always the object of biographical interest, scholarly study of Ruskin did not begin to revive until the late 1950s, a revival confirmed by a conference at Brantwood in 1969. From the 1970s critical studies, biographies, and exhibitions multiplied, so that when the centenary of his death was celebrated in 2000, interest in his ideas—though now in a completely different context—stood almost as high as it had in 1900. Through the widespread diffusion of his ideas on social reform, and the interdisciplinary nature of his art criticism, Ruskin can fairly be said to have had a hand in shaping the culture of the twentieth century, just as he did that of the nineteenth. The reason for his lasting appeal was his combination of moral certainty and intellectual openness, summed up by his abiding paradox: 'No true disciple of mine will ever be a "Ruskinian"!' (*Works*, 24.371).

ROBERT HEWISON

Sources The works of John Ruskin, ed. E. T. Cook and A. Wedderburn, library edn, 39 vols. (1903–12) · V. A. Burd, ed., The Ruskin family letters, 2 vols. (1973) · The letters of John Ruskin to Lord and Lady Mount-Temple, ed. J. L. Bradley (1964) · The Winnington letters: John Ruskin's correspondence with Margaret Alexis Bell and the children at Winnington Hall, ed. V. A. Burd (1969) · The correspondence of John Ruskin and Charles Eliot Norton, ed. J. L. Bradley and I. Ousby (1987) · H. G. Viljoen, Ruskin's Scottish heritage (1956) · T. Hilton, John Ruskin: the early years (1985) · T. Hilton, John Ruskin: the later years (2000) · D. Leon, Ruskin: the great Victorian (1949) · Effie in Venice: unpublished letters of Mrs John Ruskin written from Venice between 1849–1852, ed. M. Lutyens (1965) · M. Lutyens, Millais and the Ruskins (1967) · M. Lutyens, The Ruskins and the Grays (1972) · V. A. Burd, John Ruskin and Rose La Touche (1979) · V. A. Burd, Ruskin, Lady Mount-Temple and the spiritualists (1982) · J. L. Bradley, ed., Ruskin: the critical heritage (1984) · J. D. Hunt, The wider sea: a life of John Ruskin (1982) · The diaries of John Ruskin, ed. J. Evans and J. H. Whitehouse, 3 vols. (1956–9) · The Brantwood diary of John Ruskin, ed. H. G. Viljoen (1971) · Ruskin in Italy: his letters to his parents, 1845, ed. H. I. Shapiro (1972) · Ruskin's letters from Venice, 1851–52, ed. J. L. Bradley (1955) · Letters from the continent, 1858, ed. J. Hayman · Sublime and instructive: letters from John Ruskin to Louisa, marchioness of Waterford, Anna Blunden and Ellen Heaton, ed. V. Surtees (1972) · P. Walton, The drawings of John Ruskin (1972) · J. S. Dearden, Facets of Ruskin (1970) · J. S. Dearden, John Ruskin's Camberwell (1990) · J. S. Dearden, Ruskin, Bembridge and Brantwood: the growth of the Whitehouse collection (1994) · J. S. Dearden, The portraits of John Ruskin (1999) · M. D. Wheeler, Ruskin's God (1999) · J. L. Bradley, Ruskin: a chronology (1977) · G. P. Landow, The aesthetic and critical theories of John Ruskin (1971) · G. P. Landow, Ruskin (1985) · R. Hewison, John Ruskin: the argument of the eye (1976) · R. Hewison, Ruskin and Venice (1978) · R. Hewison, Ruskin and Oxford (1995) · R. Hewison, I. Warrell, and S. Wildman, Ruskin, Turner and the Pre-Raphaelites (2000) [exhibition catalogue, Tate Gallery, London, 9 March – 28 May 2000] · D. Birch, ed., Ruskin and the dawn of the modern (1999) · R. B. Stein, John Ruskin and aesthetic thought in America, 1840–1900 (1967)

Archives AM Oxf., MSS · BL, letters [copies] · Bodl. Oxf., corresp. and literary papers; letters · Boston PL, letters · Brantwood, Coniston, MSS · Col. U., letters and literary MSS · Cumbria AS, Kendal, corresp. and papers; sermon notes · Duke U., Perkins L., letters · FM Cam., literary papers and letters · Guild of St George, Sheffield, papers relating to Guild of St George · Hunt. L., letters and literary MSS · JRL, corresp. and papers · Morgan L., MSS · NRA, priv. coll., letters · Princeton University Library, New Jersey, letters and literary MSS · Ransom HRC, corresp. and literary MSS · Ruskin Museum, Coniston, papers · University of Arizona, Tucson, letters · University of Lancaster, Ruskin Library, corresp., literary MSS, and family papers · University of Strathclyde, Glasgow,

MSS · University of Surrey, Roehampton, London, Whitelands College, letters · Yale U., Beinecke L., MSS | Armitt Library, Ambleside, letters to Armitt family · Balliol Oxf., letters to Miss Fortescue and Charles Newton · BL, letters to Katherine Bradley, Add. MS 46867 · BL, corresp. with Rawdon Brown, Add. MS 36304 · BL, letters to Mary Gladstone, Add. MS 46246 · BL, letters to Elizabeth Murray, Add. MS 37021 · BLPES, letters to Frederic Harrison · Bodl. Oxf., letters to Henry Acland and family; letters to George Allen; letters to John Brown and Rawdon Brown; letters to Ada Dundas and her parents; letters to Marcus Huish; letters to Alice C. Owen; letters to Mark Pattison; letters to George Richardson; letters to Smith, Elder & Co.; corresp. with Sir J. G. Wilkinson [incl. copies] · Col. U., letters to George Allen · Cornell University, Ithaca, New York, letters to Alfred William Hunt; letters to Margaret Raine Hunt · Cumbria AS, Kendal, corresp. with H. Fletcher and H. D. Rawnsley · FM Cam., letters to Edward Burne-Jones and Georgina Burne-Jones; letters to Robert Chester · Hammersmith and Fulham Archives and Local History Centre, London, letters to A. Wickham · Harvard U., Houghton L., letters, mainly to Charles Eliot Norton; letters to William Roffe; letters to Walter Severn · JRL, letters to Augusta Hayes · Keswick Museum and Art Gallery, letters to Jeanette Foster · LUL, letters to Grace Allen · McGill University, Montreal, McLennan Library, letters to Elizabeth White and literary MSS · Mitchell L., Glas., letters to James R. Anderson · Mitchell L., NSW, letters to Adelaide Ironside · NL Scot., letters to Thomas Carlyle · NMM, letters to Robert Leslie [copies] · Notts. Arch., letters to Henrietta Carey · Sheff. Arch., letters, mainly to John F. Moss, relating to Ruskin Museum · Trinity Cam., letters to Lord Houghton · U. Hull, Brynmor Jones L., letters to H. Fletcher · U. Leeds, Brotherton L., letters to Evelyn Noyes and Charlotte Noyes · U. Newcastle, letters to Sir Walter Trevelyan and Lady Trevelyan · U. St Andr. L., letters to James Forbes and George Forbes · UCL, letters to Walter Lucas Brown · W. Sussex RO, corresp. with Frederick Maxse · Watts Gallery, Guildford, corresp. with George Frederic Watts

Likenesses J. Northcote, oils, 1822, NPG · G. Richmond, portrait, 1842, Bembridge School, Isle of Wight, Ruskin Galleries · G. Richmond, chalk drawing, c.1843, NPG · G. Richmond, engraving, 1843, Lancaster University, Ruskin Library · J. E. Millais, pencil and watercolour drawing, 1853, Bembridge School, Isle of Wight · J. E. Millais, pencil drawing, 1853 (for his 1853–4 portrait), AM Oxf. · J. E. Millais with W. Millais, pencil, pen, and ink drawing, 1853, Bolton Museum and Art Gallery · J. E. Millais, oils, 1853–4, priv. coll. [*see illus.*] · D. G. Rossetti, chalk drawing, 1861, AM Oxf. · J. Ruskin, self-portrait, watercolour, 1861, Morgan L. · W. Downey, group portrait, photograph, 1863, Lancaster University, Ruskin Library · W. Bell Scott, watercolour drawing, 1864, Wallington, Northumberland · J. Ruskin, self-portrait, watercolour, 1873, Morgan L. · J. Ruskin, self-portrait, pencil, 1873–4, Brantwood Trust, Coniston · J. Ruskin, self-portrait, pencil, 1874, Lancaster University, Ruskin Library · J. Ruskin, self-portrait, watercolour drawing, 1874, Wellesley College, Massachusetts · C. L. Dodgson, photograph, c.1875, NPG · J. E. Boehm, marble bust, 1879, Ruskin School of Drawing, Oxford · H. J. von Herkomer, watercolour, 1879, NPG · J. E. Boehm, terracotta cast from marble bust, c.1880–1881, AM Oxf. · J. E. Boehm, plaster cast, 1881, NPG · C. Dressler, terracotta bust, 1885, Tate collection · T. B. Wirgman, pencil drawing, c.1886, NPG · C. Dressler, bronze bust, 1888, NPG · Elliott & Fry, photograph, 1891, NPG · photograph, 1893 (after Miss Acland), NPG · F. Hollyer, photograph, 1894, V&A · J. McCleland, photograph, 1895, NPG · W. G. Collingwood, oils, 1897, Ruskin Foundation · C. Dressler, bronze bust, 1903, Bournville School of Art and Crafts, Birmingham · Barraud, photograph, NPG; repro. in *Men and Women of the Day*, 1 (1888) · Barraud, photographs, NPG · H. J. Brooks, group portrait (*Private view of the old masters exhibition, Royal Academy, 1888*), NPG · W. Burton, etching, BM · L. Caldesi & Co., photograph, NPG · A. Cecioni, preliminary studies and chromolithograph, NPG; Uffizi, Florence · A. Cecioni, watercolour caricature, South London Art Gallery; repro. in *VF* (17 Feb 1872) ·

W. & D. Downey, photograph, NPG · Elliott & Fry, photograph, NPG · H. C. Fehr, marble bust, South London Art Gallery · E. O. Ford, memorial bust, Westminster Abbey · Lock & Whitfield, photograph, NPG; repro. in T. Cooper and others, *Men of mark: a gallery of contemporary portraits* (1882) · A. C. Lucchesi, plaster medallion, CCC Oxf. · G. Pilotell, drypoint, BM · miniature, Brantwood Trust, Coniston · photographs, Bembridge School, Isle of Wight · prints, BM, NPG

Wealth at death £10,660 2s. 8d.: probate, 9 May 1900, CGPLA Eng. & Wales

Ruspini, Bartholomew [Bartolomeo] (1730–1813), dentist and prominent freemason, was born on 21 February 1730 at Ca Bonoré, Romacolo, in the parish of Grumello de' Zanchi 18 km north of Bergamo, Italy, the eldest of the eight children of Giovanni Andrea Ruspini (1707–1769) and his wife, Bartolomea (1708–1788). By his own account he qualified as a surgeon in Bergamo as a young man, but it seems more likely he turned to dentistry after failing to do so. He claimed to have studied with J.-F. Capperon, dentist to Louis XV. By at least 1752 Ruspini was practising dentistry in England, and in the early 1750s he visited Scotland and Ireland. In 1757 he was in London, where on 19 February he married Elizabeth Stiles. However, much of his early career in Britain was based in Bath and Bristol. From about 1766, reputedly under the patronage of George III's mother, Augusta, he established himself on a more permanent basis in London, moving to 32 St Albans Street, opposite Carlton House. On 6 April 1767 he made a somewhat surprising second marriage, to the much younger Elizabeth Ord (b. 1747), daughter of Francis Ord of Langridge Hall, near Berwick, and second cousin to Edwin Lascelles, builder of Harewood House. The marriage produced four sons and five daughters. Three of Ruspini's sons followed him into dental practice: James Bladen (1768–1840)—his partner from 1787, George Bartholomew Holwell (b. 1769), and William (1780–1812). James and George were pupils at Westminster School. Ruspini's daughter Jane-Amelia married the physician John Taylor *Warren.

In 1767 or 1768 Ruspini published his *Treatise on the Teeth*; this went through numerous editions but was essentially a promotional booklet. The contents, while sensible, were largely traditional and remained unchanged.

The marketing of dental products countrywide constituted a considerable part of Ruspini's business and generated a great deal of newspaper advertising. In 1783 he was the first person to be summonsed under the Medicines Stamp Act, accused of selling medicines without paying the tax imposed on non-medically qualified vendors. He thereupon produced a surgical diploma from Bergamo (surprisingly dated 18 June 1758) and the case was dismissed. Ruspini went on to launch his haemostatic styptic in 1785, together with the pamphlet *Concise Relation of the Effects of an Extraordinary Styptic Recently Discovered*. After this styptic was used by the prince of Wales in 1787, Ruspini was appointed his dentist. A further publication, *Short Observations on the Teeth*, appeared in 1795.

Ruspini became a freemason through the Bush Lodge in Bristol in 1762 (he had been unsuccessful in Bath in 1759)

Bartholomew Ruspini (1730–1813), by Ozias Humphry, 1776

and soon rose to prominence in masonic circles. At different times he belonged to and held office in eight different London lodges as well as being a Royal Arch mason. In 1777 he was a founder of the Nine Muses Lodge; its distinguished members included aristocrats, past grand masters, foreign dignitaries, and prominent figures from the world of the arts such as Giovanni Cipriani, Francesco Bartolozzi, Johann Christian Bach, and Johann Zoffany. In 1787 Ruspini introduced the future George IV to freemasonry and was a founder member of the Prince of Wales Lodge, membership of which was restricted to those under the prince's patronage. The following year, although a 'modern', he joined the Grand Master's Lodge (Antients). Despite this, at the direction of the prince he became grand sword-bearer for life in 1791. Ruspini was made a knight of the papal order of the golden spur in 1789, allegedly for support given to the Italian community in London. Thereafter, unlike Mozart who received the same decoration in 1770, he always styled himself 'chevalier'.

Ruspini's outstanding contribution to freemasonry was his role as 'institutor' in 1788 of the Royal Cumberland Freemasons' School (later the Royal Masonic Institution for Girls), which annually commemorated his name. The 'orphans' attended his funeral, which took place five days after his death on 14 December 1813 at 32 St Albans Street, Pall Mall, London. He was buried in St James's churchyard, Piccadilly. His wife survived him.

To some Ruspini was a flamboyant opportunist, missing few openings for self-publicity; this made him the target of a number of attacks and won him the nickname of 'Duke of Tuscany'. To others he was the soul of kindness, generosity, hospitality, conviviality, spontaneity, probity, and above all, charity. His delight in dancing and display made him an excellent masonic master of ceremonies. A good-looking man, he moved in fashionable circles and was accepted by the highly influential, despite (or perhaps because of) the bizarre nature of some of his contacts, who included Cagliostro and J. A. Starck. A well-known public figure (he instructed his brother to address letters 'Ruspini, England' since he was often out of London), he was portrayed and caricatured a number of times by eminent artists and was mentioned in contemporary memoirs and letters. On his death his effects were valued at under £450. This relatively low figure has been attributed to Ruspini's philanthropy and opulent lifestyle.

CHRISTINE HILLAM

Sources J. M. Campbell, 'The Chevalier Bartholomew Ruspini, 1728–1813', *Dental Magazine and Oral Topics* (Dec 1953), 402–22 · 'Sketch of the life of the Chevalier Ruspini, GSB', *Freemasons' Magazine*, 1 (1793), 576–8 · P. J. Dawson, 'The Chevalier Bartholomew Ruspini, 1728–1813', *Ars Quatuor Coronatorum*, 86 (1973), 87–99 · G. B. Abbott, *History of the Royal Masonic Institution for Girls*, 2nd edn (1889) · parish register (marriages), 19 Feb 1757, St Bartholomew the Great, London · parish register (marriages), 6 Apr 1767, St James's, Westminster · parish register (burials), 19 Dec 1813, St James's, Westminster · [provincial and London press] (1750–1813) [hundreds of advertisements] · membership lists of Prince of Wales Lodge (no. 412), 1787–1804, Freemasons' Hall, Library · membership list of Lodge of Nine Muses, 1777–82, Freemasons' Hall, Library · GM, 1st ser., 83/2 (1813), 701 · M. K. Schuchard, 'William Blake and the promiscuous baboons', *British Journal for Eighteenth-Century Studies*, 18 (1995), 185–200 · Royal Arch. · death duty register, PRO, IR 27/150, fol. 610 · parish register, Grumello de' Zanchi

Archives Freemasons' Hall, London, artefacts · Royal College of Physicians of Edinburgh, artefacts | BL, Lyson collection, artefacts, D2 733, 1804 · Sci. Mus., Wellcome collection, artefacts

Likenesses attrib. N. Hone, group portrait, oils, c.1775, Royal College of Surgeons, Edinburgh · O. Humphry, drawing, 1776, AM Oxf. [*see illus.*] · engraving, c.1784 (after *The London dentist* by Dighton), British Dental Association, London · M. W. Peters, pastel drawing, c.1785, Royal College of Surgeons, Edinburgh · T. Rowlandson, engraving, 1787 (*Transplanting of the teeth*), British Dental Association, London · G. Romney, oils, c.1790, Statens Museum for Kunst, Copenhagen · lithograph, c.1790 (after G. Romney), Royal College of Surgeons, Edinburgh · M. W. Peters, pastel drawing, 1793, Royal Masonic School for Girls, Ricksmansworth, Hertfordshire · Lancy, engraving, Jan 1794 (after Romney?), repro. in *Freemasons' Magazine*, 577 · I. Jenner, engraving, 1800, BL · W. Ridley, engraving, 1800, Royal College of Surgeons, Edinburgh · W. Ridley, stipple, 1800, Wellcome L. · T. Stothard, oils, 1802, Royal Masonic School for Girls, Ricksmansworth, Hertfordshire · J. Hopwood, engraving, 1811 (after Smith), Royal College of Surgeons, Edinburgh · statue, 20th cent., Royal Masonic School for Girls, Rickmansworth, Hertfordshire · F. Bartolozzi, engraving (after Stothard, 1802), Royal College of Surgeons, Edinburgh, Menzies Campbell collection · W. S. Leney, stipple, Wellcome L. · T. Rowlandson and A. Pugin, aquatint (after Stothard, 1802), repro. in R. Ackermann, *Microcosm of London* (1808) · F. C. Stoute, mezzotint (after Jenner, 1800)

Wealth at death under £450: PRO, death duty register, IR 27/150, fol. 610

Russ, (Richard) Patrick. *See* O'Brian, (Richard) Patrick (1914–2000).

Russ, Sidney (1879–1963), physicist, was born on 2 December 1879 at 27 Clifton Hill, St John's Wood, London, the fourth son of Charles Russ, a furrier, and his wife, Emily, formerly Callaway. He went to Shebbear College, north Devon, and graduated BSc with first-class honours from University College, London, in 1905, after which he became a demonstrator at the University of Manchester, working under Rutherford after the latter arrived there in 1907. In 1909 he obtained a DSc from University College, London, in 1910 he became Beit memorial fellow at the cancer research laboratories, Middlesex Hospital, and in 1913 he was appointed physicist to the hospital. In 1919 he changed to the medical school and in 1920 he accepted the newly instituted Joel chair of physics which he held to his retirement in 1946. He joined the Röntgen Society in 1910, of which he was president in 1919–20. Russ was a member of the British radium and X-ray protection committee, secretary of the Medical Research Council radiology committee, and scientific secretary of the National Radium Commission from 1928 to 1934. He was an original member of the King Edward's Hospital Fund radium committee which kept a stock of radium at the Middlesex in the care of Russ. This was loaned to other hospitals in London as required, together with help and advice on applications and dosimetry. The Medical Research Council also put Russ in charge of a radon organization which supplied nine facilities in the United Kingdom from 1924 to 1939. Russ served on various committees of the British Empire Cancer Campaign in its early years. He was appointed CBE in 1931 for his services to radium work, and he became the first chairman of the Hospital Physicists' Association, which was launched in 1943. Russ was married to Mary Priestley, eldest daughter of Major F. N. Priestley of Leeds; they had three children.

When diploma courses were established for radiology after the First World War, Russ became responsible for the physics syllabus of the courses at Cambridge University and the University of London, thus teaching a substantial part of a generation of British radiologists. He wrote two textbooks, *Physics for Medical Students* (1928) and *Physics in Medical Radiology* (1928). He has been called a hard taskmaster, and his teaching style has been called conscientious, concise, pedantic, firm but always sympathetic, precise and autocratic but genuinely kind and understanding.

Russ's main role was in certification of radiation and people. He worked to spread precision measurement throughout medicine in general, and radiology in particular. Dosage problems and radiation protection were the immediate motivations for precision measurement, creating a need for quality instrumentation, safe practices, and constant control and calibration. Before the age of clinical trials this kind of work can be seen as facilitating the replication of clinical practices and the communication of clinical results. However, Russ, along with most physicists working in medicine, thought of his work not merely as a handmaiden for clinicians but rather as bringing science to bear upon the whimsical and unmethodical work of medical doctors. Russ's ambitions for the role of medical physics must be said to have failed in the sense

that it is now a mere tool upon which clinical medicine can draw.

Russ was a driving force at the centre of the diffusion of precision measurement of radiation in Britain both of X-rays and of radioactive radiation. The two were very different. When contained in airtight vials radioactive samples were known to radiate constantly (or at least to come to do so after radioactive equilibrium was achieved). Thus they had to be measured only once, after which they could travel with a certificate designating the value. A certificate was meaningful only if this singular measurement was not doubted; the onus was on Russ to inspire trust. X-ray dosage was necessarily different because X-ray tubes do not emit unchanging radiation. Trustworthy measurement in any given location required the presence on the ground of reliable instruments and people. Russ measured, educated people in measurement, and lobbied for routine calibration of instruments, centred upon the National Physical Laboratory (this is one of the points of the co-authored book with Hector Colwell: *X-Ray and Radium Injuries*, 1934). His research, teaching, and committee work were all a part of this building of an infrastructure.

Early on Russ also did research on irradiation of human tissue, especially cancer. He attempted to categorize the clinical effect of particular kinds of radiation (different wavelengths and intensities of X-rays; different intensities of gamma rays). His collaboration with Hector Colwell, *Radium, X-Rays, and the Living Cell* (1915 and 1924), is an indication that work could still span both physics and medicine. By contrast the foundation of the Hospital Physicists' Association was symptomatic of a division of labour where physicists deal with measurement of radiation only and not with diagnosis, therapy, or clinical research.

After his retirement to Bognor Regis in 1946 Russ wrote popular books on cancer. *Cancer: Where we Stand* (1950) was supported by the British Empire Cancer Campaign. It was thought to reduce the resistance in the public to cancer examinations, and thus to the application of therapy at an earlier stage when chances of success would be markedly increased. *Smoking and its Effects* (1955) is an argument that a strict causation of lung cancer by tobacco had not been proven. In it Russ declared himself a keen smoker, marshalled statistical evidence, and discussed the problems of statistical inference at length. Russ died of carcinoma of the bronchus at his home, The Hut, Fish Lane, on 27 July 1963. ARNE HESSENBRUCH

Sources WWW, 1961–70 · *The Lancet* (10 Aug 1963), 309 · *BMJ* (10 Aug 1963), 391 · *Nature*, 199 (1963), 851–2 · *British Journal of Radiology*, 36 (1963), 702, 862–3 · E. H. Burrows, *Pioneers and early years: a history of British radiology* (1986), 229–30 · D. Ranger, *The Middlesex Hospital medical school* (1985), 30–31, 98 · *History of the Hospital Physicists' Association, 1943–1983*, Hospital Physicists' Association (1983), 126 · b. cert. · d. cert.
Archives British Institute of Radiology, London · Central Middlesex Hospital, London
Likenesses photograph, repro. in *British Journal of Radiology*, 702 · photograph, repro. in Hospital Physicists' Association, *History of*

the Hospital Physicists' Association · photograph, British Institute of Radiology

Wealth at death £7679 7s. 8d.: probate, 21 Nov 1963, *CGPLA Eng. & Wales*

Russel, Alexander (1814–1876), newspaper editor, was born on 10 December 1814 at Edinburgh. His father, John Russel, a solicitor and a Liberal in politics, died when he was very young. His mother, Mary, a daughter of John Somerville, clerk in the jury court, lived until he was fifty. After attending the classical school kept by the Revd Ross Kennedy in St James's Square, Edinburgh, young Russel was apprenticed to a printer. John Johnstone, later editor of the *Inverness Courier*, was one of his fellow apprentices. Johnstone's wife, Christian Isobel Johnstone, had a large share in editing *Tait's Edinburgh Magazine*, and gave Russel the opportunity of contributing to it. As a youth Russel split from his family, who attended the established church, by attending the services of the evangelical John Brown (1784–1858). In later life he attended Greyfriars Kirk in Edinburgh.

In 1839 Russel was appointed editor of the *Berwick Advertiser*, where he learnt the techniques of his profession. Having learnt shorthand in boyhood, he was able to act as reporter as well as to write articles. From an early stage he was an active Liberal. While at Berwick he made the acquaintance of David Robertson of Ladykirk, later Lord Marjoribanks, and with him took an active share in Northumbrian political contests. In 1842 he left Berwick for Cupar, where he edited the *Fife Herald*. In Fife he was again active in Liberal politics, working with Admiral Wemyss and Edward Ellice, the elder and younger. After his hard work in Cupar, Russel became editor of the *Kilmarnock Chronicle*, a new Liberal newspaper. John Ritchie, one of the founders of *The Scotsman*, was impressed by his articles and invited him to become assistant to Charles Maclaren, the editor of *The Scotsman*.

In March 1845 Russel returned to his native city to fill an important position in the office of its principal newspaper. Maclaren recognized Russel's energy and ability, and from the end of 1845 effectively gave the position of editor to Russel, who formally succeeded him in 1849. Russel quickly showed considerable social passion, with an inquiry into highland destitution published in articles in *The Scotsman* and the *Edinburgh Review*. He was a vigorous free-trader and supporter of the Anti-Corn Law League, but in 1853 he strongly attacked the manifesto of the National Association for the Vindication of Scottish Rights, which was supported by Duncan McLaren, the leading Liberal in Edinburgh. In 1856 McLaren sued Russel and *The Scotsman* for libel over a festering quarrel dating from disputes over T. B. Macaulay's candidacy for Edinburgh in elections since 1847; Russel had called McLaren a snake and accused him of engaging in an 'unholy alliance'. McLaren was awarded £400 and costs; a public subscription paid for both sums.

Despite this set-back *The Scotsman* prospered under Russel's editorship, and from June 1855 it was published daily (instead of twice weekly), priced 1d. By 1865 its circulation was 17,000, and by 1877 it had risen to 50,000, the greatest circulation of any paper outside London. Russel thus gained his paper a British as well as a Scottish reputation. He was a hard taskmaster, and unwilling to admit a good article to be a colleague's work. Asked to congratulate one of the staff, he replied: 'Man ... I can't. I can't praise anybody; I never could' (*The Glorious Privilege*, 50). 'His professional pride', his obituarist remarked, was 'far too high to allow him to indulge in anything like journalistic Bohemianism' (*Alexander Russel*, 32). Even so, he was popular in Edinburgh and London Liberal circles, and was elected to the Reform Club in London in 1875.

Russel was twice married—first to Jessie McWilliam, and next to a widow, Helen de Lacy Evans, *née* Carter (*b*. 1833/4) [*see* Russel, Helen de Lacy Evans, *under* Edinburgh Seven]; there were children from both marriages. His second wife was one of the students involved in the campaign to secure medical education for women in Edinburgh, in which campaign Russel had also been active.

Russel disliked travelling out of Scotland (though he attended the opening of the Suez Canal in 1869) and his passion was angling. He was a founder of regular journalism on angling; some of his articles were collected in *The Salmon* (1864). He also disliked speaking in public and in 1872 declined to become a candidate for the lord rectorship of Aberdeen University. In 1868 his eyesight began to fail and in 1872 he developed symptoms of heart disease. He died on 18 July 1876 at 9 Chester Street, Edinburgh, of angina pectoris following pleurisy and was buried in the Dean cemetery. He was survived by his second wife, and by at least two sons and a daughter. His daughter from his second marriage was Helen Alexander *Archdale (1876–1949), feminist and journalist.

Russel made a considerable contribution to Scottish life. He widened the Scottish view of political matters and was religiously broadminded in an often intolerant culture. He hated jobbery and narrow toryism but, as his quarrel with McLaren showed, avoided the worst aspects of unyielding Liberalism.   H. C. G. MATTHEW

Sources *Alexander Russel* (1876) · H. G. Graham, 'Russel of *The Scotsman*', *Fraser's Magazine*, new ser., 22 (1880), 301–17 · [M. Magnusson and others], *The glorious privilege: the history of The Scotsman* (1967) · d. cert. · DNB

Archives NL Scot., corresp. | NL Scot., corresp. with Blackwoods; letters to J. Burton; corresp. with G. Combe; letters to E. Ellice · U. Leeds, Brotherton L., letters to Evelyn Noyes and Charlotte Noyes

Likenesses W. Brodie, marble bust, Scot. NPG · wood-engraving (after photograph by Truefitt Brothers), NPG; repro. in *ILN* (10 March 1860) · wood-engraving, NPG; repro. in *ILN* (12 June 1875)

Wealth at death £46,778 5s. 10d.: confirmation, 19 Sept 1876, *CCI*

Russel, George (1728–1767), poet, son of Christopher Russel, was born in Minorca. His father, who was born in 1670 and died at Ciudadela in Minorca in 1729, was a distinguished officer of the 19th regiment of foot, who had served in Flanders and in the wars of Queen Anne. George Russel is said to have been educated at Westminster School. He matriculated from St Mary Hall, Oxford, on 28 May 1746, graduating BA in 1750. Through the influence of John Boyle, fifth earl of Cork and Orrery, with whose son,

Hamilton Boyle, he was on familiar terms, Russel obtained the rectory of Schull, co. Cork, Ireland, in 1753. There he died in 1767. Russel wrote much verse from 1744 until his death, including a number of poems that celebrate the Boyle family. He seems to have spent time at their Marston estate, where he may have met Thomas Southerne.

In 1769 Russel's poetry was published in two volumes in Cork, under the title of *The Works of the Revd George Russel, Rector of Skull, in the Diocese of Cork*. Among his poems is the popular fable called 'The Chameleon', which is generally attributed to James Merrick. Edmond Malone claimed that Russel's poems had 'considerable merit' (p. 508). Chalmers concurs with this, attributing Russel's poetic obscurity to the publication of his work in Ireland only. Arthur Sherbo speculates that Russel edited *The Student, or, Oxford and Cambridge Monthly Miscellany* (1750–51), to which he had contributed pieces.

D. J. O'DONOGHUE, rev. JEFFREY HERRLE

Sources A. Chalmers, ed., *The general biographical dictionary*, new edn, 26 (1816), 483 · D. J. O'Donoghue, *The poets of Ireland: a biographical dictionary with bibliographical particulars*, 1 vol. in 3 pts (1892–3), 406 · *The critical and miscellaneous prose works of John Dryden*, ed. E. Malone, 3 vols. (1800), vol. 1, pp. 508–10 · Foster, *Alum. Oxon.*, 1715–1886, 3.1236 · A. Sherbo, *Christopher Smart, scholar of the university* (1967), 279
Archives Yale U., copy of *The Student, or Oxford and Cambridge Monthly Miscellany* owned by subject, and MS note

Russel, Helen de Lacy Evans (b. 1833/4). *See under* Edinburgh Seven (act. 1869–1873).

Russel, John (1740/41–1817), Church of Scotland minister, was a native of Moray, the son of Thomas Russel and Catharine Cumming. After a university education, details of which are unknown, he was appointed parochial teacher at Cromarty, where he remained some years after being licensed to preach by the presbytery of Chanonry on 21 June 1768. His strictness and severity as a disciplinarian earned him the nickname of 'hard dominie'; according to Hugh Miller 'never was a schoolmaster more thoroughly feared and detested by his pupils'. Miller tells the story of how a woman who had endured his classes as a child fainted at his sudden appearance as a visiting preacher (Miller, 415–16). In this role, however, he was popular even in Cromarty for his enforcement of the terrors of the law and for his depiction of the 'miseries of the wicked in a future state' (ibid., 413).

On 30 March 1774 Russel was ordained minister of the Kilmarnock chapel of ease. As a minister he did not belie the reputation he had gained as a schoolmaster. A strict sabbatarian, he was accustomed on Sundays to go out, staff in hand, 'full in the middle of the road', and forcibly turn back—being strong as well as determined—any parishioner about to indulge in the sin of Sunday walking; it is said that at the sound of his heavy cudgel in the streets everyone disappeared (Miller, 419). His stentorian voice, aided by his dark and gloomy countenance, lent such effect to his fanatical denunciations that few even of the most reckless parishioners listened to him unmoved. Russel was twice married, first to Mary MacFarlane with

whom he had one son, Andrew, and then, following her death, to Catherine Cunningham (1744/5–1819). This marriage, which took place on 22 April 1782, produced three children: Mary (b. 1783), John (b. 1785), who later became minister of Muthill, Perthshire, and Alexander (b. 1786).

On 18 January 1800 Russel was called to the second charge of Stirling where he remained for the rest of his life. He published several sermons expounding a Calvinism of the most forbidding type but gained celebrity through the satire of Robert Burns, being one of the combatants in the *Twa Herds, or, The Holy Tulsie* (1784/5); Black Jock, the state physician of 'Glowrin Superstition' in the *Epistle to John Goldie* (1784/5); 'the Lord's ain trumpet' in *The Holy Fair* (1784/5); the 'misca'er of common sense' in *The Ordination* (1786); and Rumble John in *The Kirk of Scotland* (1789). He died at Stirling on 23 February 1817, aged seventy-six. T. F. HENDERSON, *rev.* CAROL McGUIRK

Sources *Fasti Scot.*, new edn · H. Miller, *Scenes and legends of the north of Scotland*, 14th edn (1876) · *The poems and songs of Robert Burns*, ed. J. Kinsley, 3 vols. (1968)

Russel, Richard (1685–1756), journalist, was baptized on 7 August 1685 in Dallington, Sussex, the eldest of three sons of Richard Russel (c.1644–1700), vicar of Dallington, and his wife (probably his third), Susannah Hawes. At the age of twelve Russel entered University College, Oxford, from where his father had matriculated; he graduated BA in 1702, and proceeded MA in 1705.

The next decade proved crucial for Russel. He began his career in the church in 1710, as vicar of Alfriston and minister of Selmeston, Sussex. At the end of 1711 he revealed his acerbic style and unyielding tory politics in *The Impeachment, or, The Church Triumphant*, a long poem on the Sacheverell affair which, an enemy later claimed, simply appeared like a ghost in a white sheet, 'frighted the house with a dismal groan and vanished' (Henley, 18 May 1731). Ten months later, on 11 September 1712, Russel married Juliana Franckwell (*bap.* 1686), of Eastbourne; they had four daughters and three noteworthy sons: Richard *Russel (1714?–1771) [see under Russell, Richard (1687–1759)], a physician; James (c.1720–1763), a painter and antiquary; and William (b. c.1721), a bookseller.

Russel's life changed dramatically on 23 January 1716 when he was deprived of his livings because he had refused to take the oaths, a decision he defended in a farewell sermon, *The Obligation of Acting According to Conscience* (1716). Thereafter his religious life was focused on the secret world of nonjurors; he became a friend of leading figures such as Thomas Hearne, Richard Rawlinson, Thomas Brett, and Hilkiah Bedford, and was active in controversies within the group over prayers and rituals. Meanwhile, needing other means to support his growing family, he took up farming, a business which he found unsuitable to his temperament and education. At the same time he was involved in scholarly projects which both added income and were compatible with his nonjuring convictions. In 1716 he translated seventeenth-century Latin lectures by Robert Sanderson on the nature of oaths. Then he began collecting subscriptions to support his translation, *The New Testament with Moral Reflections*, of the work by the Jansenist Pasquier Quesnel; subscribers to his four volumes (1719–25) included a host of well-known nonjurors and Jacobites as well as friends in Sussex.

Yet Russel's main importance today rests not on religious writing but on his role as editor, primary writer, and major shareholder of the satirical newspaper the *Grub-Street Journal* (1730–37). By 1729 he had met two men who were instrumental in shaping and producing the paper, Lawton Gilliver and John Martyn. Gilliver, a young bookseller who became a leading partner in the *Journal* and had close connections with Alexander Pope, was already involved in two of Russel's projected editions. Martyn, who co-edited the paper in its early years and then dropped out, was also a lay nonjuror, and his friendship with Russel seems to have come from their common religious background.

That background is also reflected in the anti-Walpole and occasionally Jacobite bias of the *Journal*, a paper aptly characterized by one of its enemies as 'universally condemn'd, and yet universally read' (*Weekly Register*, 8 July 1732). Its main purpose, as Russel saw it, was to 'restrain the enormities' of authors, printers, and booksellers (Russel, ix), a purpose to which he easily adapted his gift for sardonic language and his scholarly habit of mind. Enemies soon abounded, but they were seldom a match for the paper's aggressive and querulous wit. In its early years the *Journal* attacked the same targets as Pope and Swift, figures such as Colley Cibber and the hack writers who were the personages of Pope's *Dunciad*. Indeed it was widely assumed, then and later, that Pope had been instrumental in setting up and managing the periodical, an illusion which the 'Grubs' saw no reason to dispel. But although Russel printed a few of Pope's epigrams and dedicated to the poet his edition of Vida (1732), he did not know Pope, who had no personal connection with the *Journal*.

Since his paper by design ridiculed the exaggerations, falsehoods, and triviality of contemporary journalism, Russel was in constant war with other journalists. Over the years the main targets were the *London Journal*, John Henley's *Hyp-Doctor*, Eustace Budgell's *Bee*, Aaron Hill's *Prompter*, and the *Gentleman's Magazine*. But non-journalistic figures who seemed either fraudulent or immoral or heterodox were also fair game, from the quack Joshua Ward to the playwright Henry Fielding. All this time the 'runt' Russel, as Henley dubbed him, was reportedly living at various addresses near Smith Square, Westminster, and running a boarding-house for the sons of nonjurors who attended Westminster School. When the end came for the *Grub-Street Journal* in 1737, supposedly driven out by the popularity of the monthly magazines, he published a selection of the first 138 numbers as *Memoirs of the Society of Grub-Street*.

Russel had directed the wittiest and most original periodical of the 1730s, but he never again matched that success. After its demise he continued preparing an edition of the writings of the apostolic fathers, which finally appeared in 1746, published by his son William, at whose shop he increasingly spent his time. His final project was to edit the letters from Italy written to the family by his son James, which appeared in two volumes (1748–50) as *Letters from a Young Painter Abroad to his Friends in England* and which dwelt at length on Roman antiquities. Russel's manuscript copies of the original letters reveal his last years to have been marked by unrelenting Jacobitism, worries over money, and urinary disease. He died on 3 January 1756 in the parish of St Clement Danes and was buried at St Anne's, Soho, on 9 January. Failure seemed to follow him even to the grave: apparently all that remains of a plan to publish by subscription two volumes of his miscellaneous pieces 'for the Benefit of his Widow' is a copy of the printed title-page of the proposal itself.

BERTRAND A. GOLDGAR

Sources BL, Add. MS 41169 • B. A. Goldgar, 'Pope and the *Grub-Street Journal*', *Modern Philology*, 74 (1976–7), 366–80 • *Remarks and collections of Thomas Hearne*, ed. C. E. Doble and others, 11 vols., OHS, 2, 7, 13, 34, 42–3, 48, 50, 65, 67, 72 (1885–1921), vols. 6, 8, 10–11 • H. Broxap, *The later nonjurors* (1924) • [J. Henley], *The Hyp-Doctor* (1731–3) • [R. Russel], *Memoirs of the society of Grub-Street*, 2 vols. (1737) • 'The minute book of the partners in the *Grub Street Journal*', *Publishing History*, 4 (1978), 49–94 • J. T. Hillhouse, *The Grub-Street journal* (1928) • BL, Add. MS 5383 (51) • *IGI* • parish register, E. Sussex RO [baptism] • parish register, St Anne's, Soho, City Westm. AC, 9 Jan 1756 [burial]

Archives BL, Add. MS 41169 • Bodl. Oxf., MS Eng. Th. C26, fols. 223–4; Rawlinson D373, fols. 106–8

Wealth at death letters a few years before death spoke of financial trouble (unable to supply daughter's dowry); edition of his writings proposed for widow's benefit

Russel, Richard (1714?–1771). *See under* Russell, Richard (1687–1759).

Russel, Theodore. *See* Russell, Theodore (*bap.* 1614, *d.* 1689).

Russel, William (*d.* 1702), General Baptist minister and religious controversialist, was the son of John Russel, a Baptist pastor of Waddesdon, Buckinghamshire. Probably educated at Cambridge, he graduated in arts and in 1688 received the degree of MD by royal command. In 1662 he was living at Chesham, Buckinghamshire. By 1670 he had settled in St Bartholomew's Close, West Smithfield, London, becoming a prominent figure within the Goswell Street General Baptist Church until he left with other members in 1697. Russel subsequently became minister of a new church established at High Hall, West Smithfield.

From about 1680 it appears that Russel practised as a physician, his one medical tract, *De calculo vesicæ, or, A discourse concerning stone in the bladder, wherein is demonstrated, that the dissolution thereof* (*by internal remedies*) *is grounded upon reason and experience* (1691), giving an account of some success in treating bladder stone. However, Russel was primarily renowned as a religious controversialist, publishing works throughout his life in defence of his General Baptist faith and ecclesiology. His first foray came in 1663 when he launched an attack on sabbatarian doctrine in *No Seventh Day Sabbath Commanded by Jesus Christ*. This treatise was confuted by Edward Stennet in *The Seventh Day is the Sabbath of the Lord* (1664) and by William Saller in *A Preservative Against Atheism and Error* (1664). Ten years later, when an explosion in Baptist–Quaker controversy occurred, Russel turned his pen against the former Baptist William Loddington's *The Twelve Pagan Principles Held by the Quakers Seriously Considered*. Russel's anti-Quaker tract, *Quakerism is Paganism* (1674), was answered by Loddington in *Quakerism No Paganism* (1674). In 1676 Russel confirmed his anti-paedobaptist stance in an *Epistle Concerning Infant Baptism*, an issue which would re-emerge in later conflicts.

Russel's most active period as a disputant came in the late 1690s. Opposing congregational psalm singing, his publication of *Some Brief Animadversions on Mr. Allens Essay* (1696) occasioned the Baptist minister Richard Allen's reply *A Brief Vindication from Dr. Russel's Animadversions* (1696). An *Answer* to this was duly penned by Richard Claridge (including an epistle by Russel), with the dispute being taken up by Isaac Marlow in *The Controversie of Singing Brought to an End* (both 1696).

Around this time, Russel also engaged in altercations further afield. In *A Vindication of the Baptized Churches* (1697) he championed General Baptists in the midlands involved in a contention over baptism incited by Michael Harrison, the Presbyterian minister at Pottersbury, Northamptonshire. Russel's notable reputation as a learned controversialist was further affirmed in the famous Portsmouth disputation of 22 February 1699. Brought in from London, he led the defence of the Gosport Particular Baptist Church against Portsmouth Presbyterians objecting to members of their own congregation becoming Baptist converts. A royal licence (the last of its kind) was granted permitting a public debate to settle the matter but, after a day of arguing, both sides managed to proclaim themselves victorious. A minor publication frenzy followed, in which Russel produced *A True Narrative of the Portsmouth Disputation* (which went to three editions in 1699) as well as *Infant Baptism is Will Worship* (1700). Among subsequent attacks, he faced Thomas Hewerdine's *Some Plain Letters in the Defence of Infant Baptism* (1699), which Russel answered in *A Just Vindication of the Doctrine and Practice of […] Water Baptism* (1701). Hewerdine replied in turn with *A Just Vindication of Some Plain Letters in the Defence of Infant-Baptism* (1702).

Russel married early, it seems, and the death of his son Jabez (1662–1671) prompted him to publish *The Life and Death of Jabez Eliezer Russel* (1672). Nehemiah (*b.* 1663) appears to have been his only child to have reached adulthood. William Russel died in London on 6 March 1702. He must be distinguished from William *Russell (1634–*c.*1696), a physician who was, more famously, 'chymist in ordinary' to Charles II and who manufactured a 'royal tincture'. Some histories of seventeenth-century English Baptists have mistakenly confused the two, treating them as the same person.   MICHAEL DAVIES

Sources DNB · Greaves & Zaller, *BDBR*, 3.121 · T. Crosby, *The history of the English Baptists, from the Reformation to the beginning of the reign of King George I*, 4 vols. (1738–40), vol. 3, pp. 259–61; vol. 4, pp. 312–53 · J. Ivimey, *A history of the English Baptists*, 4 vols. (1811–30), vol. 1, pp. 555–9; vol. 2, pp. 77, 212–13, 600–03 · D. C. Sparkes, 'The Portsmouth disputation of 1699', *Baptist Quarterly*, 19 (1961–2), 59–75 · W. Russel, *The life and death of Jabez Eliezer Russel* (1672) · T. L. Underwood, *Primitivism, radicalism, and the Lamb's war: the Baptist–Quaker conflict in seventeenth-century England* (1997) · W. Wilson, *The history and antiquities of the dissenting churches and meeting houses in London, Westminster and Southwark*, 4 vols. (1808–14), vol. 3, pp. 391–5 · A. C. Underwood, *A history of the English Baptists* (1947) · W. T. Whitley, *A history of British Baptists* (1923) · W. T. Whitley, ed., *A Baptist bibliography*, 2 vols. (1916–22) · J. Smith, *Bibliotheca anti-Quakeriana, or, A catalogue of books adverse to the Society of Friends* (1873) · Venn, *Alum. Cant.*, 1/3.501 · W. Hustler, ed., *Graduati Cantabrigienses* (1823), 407 [for the years 1659–1823] · *BL cat.* · *Early nonconformity, 1566–1800: a catalogue of books in Dr Williams's Library, London*, 12 vols. (1968)

Russell. For this title name *see* individual entries under Russell; *see also* Arnim, Mary Annette von [Mary Annette Russell, Countess Russell] (1866–1941).

Russell [*née* Somers-Cocks], **Adeline Mary**, duchess of Bedford (1852–1920), penal reformer, was born on 24 May 1852, the second daughter of Charles Somers Somers-Cocks, third earl of Somers (1819–1883) and his wife, Virginia (*d.* 1910), daughter of James Pattle. Her education and upbringing were directly supervised by her powerful and devoted mother. On 24 October 1876 she married George William Francis Sackville Russell (1852–1893), styled the marquess of Tavistock, who sat as a Liberal member of parliament for Bedfordshire (1875–85). They lived at their London home, 37 Chesham Place, and their country home, Oakley House, Oakley, Bedfordshire.

Adeline Russell's husband succeeded his father as tenth duke of Bedford in 1891. He was said to be a reclusive and dictatorial man with a penchant for high formality, and their two years at Woburn Abbey were dogged by his ill health. On 23 March 1893 he died of diabetes. The couple were childless. Benjamin Jowett, master of Balliol College, Oxford, where her husband had been an undergraduate, was a friend and correspondent of Adeline in the early 1890s. He urged her not to shrink from the responsibilities of her rank but to see these as God-ordained and requiring harmonious co-operation between all classes to secure moral and social improvement. On the death of her husband she left Woburn Abbey to live for the rest of her life at Woodside House, Chenies, Buckinghamshire.

The duchess of Bedford became one of those aristocratic and middle-class Victorian and Edwardian women who distinguished themselves in charity work, one of the few fields of public activity open to women. Early in her married life she led a movement to rescue women who were street dwellers or prostitutes around Victoria Station, London. At this time she was closely involved with the Associated Workers' League, which was concerned with the well-being of women at work.

In 1895 the Gladstone committee on prisons recommended that there should be a female presence at the London-based Prison Commission headquarters. This body governed all English and Welsh prisons, and the new chairman, Sir Evelyn Ruggles-Brise, did not want salaried professional women there. Therefore he sought a female volunteer adviser and consultant for this role. In addition, in the late nineteenth century there was a strong movement to provide 'lady visitors' for female prisoners and to befriend and educate women prisoners and plan their aftercare, a function seen as very important by Victorian penologists who believed women were especially vulnerable to male predators when released friendless into society.

From 1897 the duchess of Bedford, assisted by Lady Battersea, visited Aylesbury convict prison for women fortnightly. They placed young female convicts in 'homes' designed to be less institutional than the refuges previously used for women released on parole licence ('ticket-of-leave'). She also visited the State Inebriate Reformatory opened at the prison in 1902 and was closely involved in founding the borstal wing of Aylesbury prison, opened in 1908. In 1900 she became the first president of the national Lady Visitors' Association, a position she held until her death. The association aimed to secure lady visitors at each prison holding women, to befriend, assess, and educate them, and to provide aftercare.

Ruggles-Brise selected the duchess of Bedford as consultant and worked closely with her until 1920. First she advised on controversial issues regarding custody of women. For example, in 1919 she chaired an extensive inquiry into allegations of gross neglect of mothers in labour in Holloway prison. Her report was direct and critical. Second, she gave advice on new projects for women prisoners: for example, plans for aftercare of borstal girls were laid at her house in the late nineteenth century, and the 1897 prison commissioners' report extensively discussed her ideas on 'homes' for young women offenders. Third, she published on the moral and occupational training of women prisoners in such journals as *Nineteenth Century and After* and gave addresses to international congresses of women. Last, she intervened in the matter of hunger-striking suffragettes in prisons between 1908 and 1914. She visited these and put it to them that they were committing sin in so risking their lives, and was thus identified by the suffragette movement as a collaborator with penal repression. They particularly resented her public glossing of the suffering inflicted by force-feeding in the prisons.

During the First World War the duchess of Bedford worked on a joint committee of the Red Cross and the order of St John of Jerusalem to provide nursing care for wounded service personnel. Between 1918 and 1920 she helped to establish a Sunshine Home for blind babies at Chorleywood near her home. She died at Mexborough House, Dover Street, London, on 12 April 1920, of influenza, and was buried on 17 April at Chenies, Buckinghamshire. She was a devout Anglican Christian all her life. Although prominent in London high society for over forty years, she was uncomfortable and unconfident in these circles. However, as Jowett had counselled, she put aside her reticence to further her social-work objectives. She was skilled at reconciling sharply differing opinions to secure a workable compromise. She was a good linguist and painter and a keen gardener. BILL FORSYTHE

Sources *The Times* (14 April 1920), 14g, 16e · *The Times* (15 April 1920), 18d · M. Richardson, *Laugh a defiance* (1953) · PRO, HO45-10429-A53867; HO45-9750-A58684; P.Com7/57; P.Com7/174 · Burke, *Peerage* · GEC, *Peerage* · E. Ruggles-Brise, *The English prison system* (1921) · L. Zedner, *Women, crime and custody in Victorian England* (1991) · 'Directors of convict prisons', *Parl. papers* (1897–1920) [annual reports] · W. Forsythe, *Penal discipline, reformatory projects and the English prison commission* (1991) · S. McConville, *English local prisons, 1860–1900: next only to death* (1995) · L. Radzinowicz and R. Hood, *A history of English criminal law and its administration from 1750*, rev. edn, 5: *The emergence of penal policy in Victorian and Edwardian England* (1990) · private information (2004) [archivist, Woburn Abbey] · E. Abbott and L. Campbell, *The life and letters of Benjamin Jowett*, 2 vols. (1897) · L. Trowbridge, *Memories and reflections* (1925) · *CGPLA Eng. & Wales* (1920)

Likenesses E. Roberts, pastel drawing, Woburn Abbey, Bedfordshire · G. F. Watts, oils, Woburn Abbey, Bedfordshire

Wealth at death £104,863 18s. 8d.: probate, 6 May 1920, *CGPLA Eng. & Wales*

Russell, Alexander (1714–1768), physician and naturalist, was born in Edinburgh on 8 September 1714, the third son of John Russell of Braidshaw, Edinburghshire, writer to the signet, and his second wife, Ursulla Alexander, with whom he had nine children. Through his third marriage, to Mary, daughter of the Revd Anderson, minister of West Calder, he had four sons, one of whom was Patrick *Russell (1727–1805), who also became a physician. Alexander Russell was educated at Edinburgh high school and the University of Edinburgh, attending lectures at the latter from 1732 to 1734, while apprenticed to an uncle, a surgeon, possibly Alexander Russell, author of several medical works published in Edinburgh. In 1734 Russell was one of the founder members of the Medical Society of Edinburgh University.

In 1735 Russell went to London, and in 1740 went to Aleppo in Syria as physician to the English factory. There, as he wrote in his *Natural History of Aleppo* (1756), he established an 'extensive practice among all ranks and degrees of people'. He learned to speak Arabic fluently, and acquired great influence with the pasha. In 1750 he was joined by his younger half-brother Patrick, and in 1753 he resigned, returning to England by way of Naples and Leghorn, in order to supplement his study of the plague at Aleppo by visiting the lazarettos at those places. Russell had sent home to his fellow student and correspondent John Fothergill seeds of the true scammony, which were raised successfully by Peter Collinson and James Gordon of Mile End. Russell published a description of the plant, and the native method of collecting it, in the first volume of *Medical Observations*, issued in 1755 by the Medical Society of London, which he had helped to found in 1752. He also introduced *Arbutus Andrachne*.

Russell reached London in February 1755; following encouragement from Fothergill, he published his *Natural History of Aleppo* the next year. This work, which was described by John Pinkerton as 'one of the most complete pictures of Eastern manners extant', was reviewed by Samuel Johnson in the *Literary Magazine*, and was translated into German. A second edition was published by Patrick Russell in 1794.

In May 1756 Alexander Russell was elected a fellow of

the Royal Society, and in 1757 and 1766 he was consulted by the privy council about quarantine regulations, because of the outbreak of the plague at Lisbon; in 1760, having become a licentiate of the Royal College of Physicians and, in 1748, an MD of Glasgow, he was appointed physician to St Thomas's Hospital, London. He was one of the members of the Society of Physicians who in 1767 formed the separate Society for Collegiate Physicians which aimed to win voting rights for licentiates of the Royal College of Physicians (Lawrence, 264). Russell died of a putrid fever on 28 November 1768 at his house in Walbrook, London. He was attended by his friends Fothergill and William Pitcairn. After his death, a eulogistic essay on his character was read by Fothergill before the Royal College of Physicians: in this Russell is described as 'in respect of stature rather tall than middling, well reade, of a fresh sanguine complexion' (Fothergill, 437). He is commemorated by the plant *Russelia* Jacq.

G. S. Boulger, rev. Patrick Wallis

Sources J. Fothergill, 'An essay on the character of the late Alexander Russell', *The works of John Fothergill*, ed. J. C. Lettsom, 3 (1784) · W. I. Addison, *A roll of graduates of the University of Glasgow from 31st December 1727 to 31st December 1897* (1898) · G. Clark and A. M. Cooke, *A history of the Royal College of Physicians of London*, 3 vols. (1964–72) · Munk, *Roll* · *GM*, 1st ser., 38 (1768), 109 · S. C. Lawrence, *Charitable knowledge: hospital pupils and practitioners in eighteenth-century London* (1996) · J. Pinkerton, ed., *A general collection of the best and most interesting voyages and travels in all parts of the world*, 17 vols. (1808–14) · Desmond, *Botanists*, rev. edn · b. cert.
Archives NHM, plants
Likenesses T. Trotter, line engraving (after N. Dance), Wellcome L. · T. Trotter, stipple (after N. Dance), NPG · portraits, Carnegie Mellon University, Pittsburgh, Hunt Botanical library

Russell, Sir Andrew Hamilton (1868–1960), sheep farmer and army officer, was born on 23 February 1868 at Napier, New Zealand, the second of the eight children and the elder son of Andrew Hamilton Russell (1837–1916), a sheep farmer and former army officer in the 58th regiment, and his wife, Katherine Sarah (1843–1886), the daughter of a Sedgwick nail manufacturer, Thomas Tinsley, and his wife, Eliza. The fourth in line to carry the names Andrew Hamilton, Russell was known from infancy as Guy. A reluctant and undistinguished pupil at Twyford School, near Winchester (1878–81), and at Harrow School (1882–5), he redeemed himself by securing second place in the entrance examination to the Royal Military College, Sandhurst, in 1886. After graduating with the sword for general proficiency in 1887, he joined the 1st battalion, the Border regiment (in which both his father and grandfather had served). Much of the period 1888 to 1892 was spent in India, either with his regiment or on attachment to the Indian staff corps. He served in Burma in both 1890 and 1892. Back in Europe in mid-1892, and disliking the prospect of garrison service, he resigned his commission and returned to New Zealand.

Russell began the year 1893 as a farm cadet on the properties at Tunanui and Twyford, near Hastings, in Hawke's Bay, jointly owned by his father (now residing in Switzerland) and his uncle William Russell Russell and managed by the latter. Following the dissolution of the partnership

he took over the management of his father's properties on 1 April 1896, and eventually, between 1906 and 1910, acquired all his father's assets in New Zealand. On 5 August 1896, at Hastings, he married Gertrude Mary Beetham Williams (1873–1964), the daughter of a prominent Hawke's Bay landowner; they had three daughters and two sons. A series of natural disasters, including a major flood in 1897, tested his farming capacities to the full.

In 1890 Russell resumed his military career by forming, and commanding, a volunteer mounted rifles unit. By 1909 he held the rank of major in the New Zealand volunteer force. Having made his mark as commander, from 17 March 1911, of the Wellington mounted rifles brigade in the new Territorial Force, he was the obvious choice to command the New Zealand mounted rifles brigade formed as part of the New Zealand expeditionary force following the outbreak of the First World War. He left New Zealand as the highest ranked territorial officer in the force. During the fighting at Gallipoli, to which his brigade was committed on 12 May 1915, he made his mark as a determined and effective commander, being later described by the commander-in-chief, Sir Ian Hamilton, as 'beyond doubt the outstanding personality on the Peninsula' among those who survived (Waite, xiii). The site of his headquarters on a plateau at Anzac became known as Russell's Top. Shortly after being appointed a KCMG, on 27 November 1915, he assumed command of the New Zealand and Australian division, and he oversaw the final stages of the successful evacuation from the Peninsula.

In April 1916 Russell took his division, now a purely New Zealand formation, to France for service on the western front. An active divisional commander, he placed heavy emphasis on adequate training and direct supervision; he also insisted on firm discipline. At some considerable risk—his scalp was creased by a sniper's bullet in 1917—he made a practice of visiting units in the front line. Combining the practical common sense of a colonial farmer, a familiarity with western Europe unusual among his divisional colleagues (he spoke French, German, and Latin), and some background in the British army, he proved an inspiring commander.

Undemonstrative, self-effacing, straight talking, responsible, determined, Russell epitomized the New Zealand citizen soldier of the First World War. He demanded a high standard of his men, who in turn appreciated his concern for their welfare. His particular pains to prepare his division for its major operations were rewarded with impressive, though costly, performances on the Somme in September–October 1916 and at Messines in June 1917. His most significant failure occurred at Passchendaele on 12 October 1917, when an attack failed, with the division's heaviest loss of life of the campaign; Russell later blamed himself for not verifying that preparations were adequate. During 1918 his division played a key role in the stemming of the German onslaught, and then, later in the year, in the allied counter-offensive. An offer of a corps command in June 1918 came at an inopportune time, with sick leave in England in the offing, and the possibility had evaporated by the time Russell returned to the front. With his health badly affected, he relinquished command of the New Zealand division, now in Germany, on 1 February 1919. His service in France was recognized by his appointment as a CB (1916) and a KCB (1918), as well as numerous allied decorations; he was mentioned in dispatches nine times.

Back at Tunanui in 1919, Russell applied himself to the welfare of former servicemen and was president of the New Zealand Returned Soldiers' Association for all but two of the years between 1921 and 1935; on his retirement he was made an officer of the association. A bid to enter parliament as a Reform Party candidate in 1922 failed. As a sheep farmer he successfully withstood the recurring financial vicissitudes of the inter-war years while supporting a variety of conservative causes and taking a prominent role in many community organizations. As honorary colonel of a regiment, he retained a connection with the Territorial Force, and he lobbied the government on defence matters as president of the National Defence League. The Second World War brought an even more active role: in between serving on the war council in 1940 and 1941–2, he was an energetic inspector-general of the forces from 23 September 1940 to 31 July 1941, and from 10 October to 28 December 1940 he was acting chief of the general staff. His younger son was killed in action in Libya on 5 September 1942. A conscientious member of the Church of England, he drew comfort from his faith in later life. He died of heart failure at Tunanui on 29 November 1960; after his funeral with full military honours two days later, he was cremated at Hastings.

IAN MCGIBBON

Sources R. F. Gambrill, 'The Russell family saga', NL NZ, Turnbull L., 5 vols., qms-0821 · 'Russell, Andrew Hamilton', New Zealand Defence Force, Wellington, Defence Department file D2/555 · F. Waite, *The New Zealanders at Gallipoli* (1921) · H. Stewart, *The New Zealand division, 1916–1919* (1921) · C. Pugsley, 'Russell, Andrew Hamilton', *DNZB*, vol. 3 · C. Pugsley, 'Russell, commander of genius', *Defence Quarterly Magazine*, 23 (1998), 25–9 · T. Seddon, NL NZ, Turnbull L., MS papers 1619, fol. 215 · Field Marshal M. Wilson to T. Seddon, 11 Dec 1960, NL NZ, Turnbull L., MS papers 1619, fol. 154 · b. cert. · m. cert. · d. cert.
Archives priv. coll., MSS
Likenesses photographs, NL NZ, Turnbull L.

Russell [*née* Worsley], **Anna** (1807–1876), botanist, was born in Arnos Vale, Bristol, in November 1807, one of five daughters and at least two sons of Philip John Worsley (1769–1811), a sugar refiner in that city. Brought up in a Unitarian family in which the children were given every encouragement to develop their talents, she and her brother Samuel (1803?–1888) showed a keenness for natural history. While he collected fossils, her interest lay initially in insects; after some years, though, she turned increasingly to botany, perhaps influenced in this by a brother-in-law, the Revd Thomas Butler (1806–1886), a keen amateur botanist and father of the novelist Samuel Butler, to whom she was to become godmother. A long list of localities for the rarer plants of her home district contributed by her, indirectly, to H. C. Watson's *New Botanist's Guide* (1835) first brought her botanical ability to wider notice and won her the respect of its unsparingly critical

author, who in later years was to acclaim her diligence and accuracy with unwonted warmth. Visits to the Butlers in Nottinghamshire and to another botanist relative, Dr Joseph Bunny (1798–1885), at Newbury in Berkshire extended her acquaintance with the British flora and led to her producing a list of plants local to Newbury which was published in 1839 as an appendix to an anonymous history of that town (since revealed to have been edited by Edward William Gray). More than sixty species in this were first records for the county. Soon after, both she and Butler joined the Botanical Society of London and for many years she was active in contributing specimens to its annual exchanges of herbarium material. Some of these were collected for her by a friend, Frederick Russell; their botanical friendship culminated in marriage in 1844.

After some years at Brislington, on the outskirts of Bristol, the couple moved, in 1856, to Frederick Russell's home town of Kenilworth in Warwickshire. There Anna's interest turned to fungi, on which she brought to bear an early facility with pen and brush, eventually building up a collection of over 730 drawings, most of them of Warwickshire species.

As able and as quietly productive as her several female contemporaries who won comparable distinction in marine algology, Anna Russell nevertheless shared their diffidence at venturing into print, preferring to restrict knowledge of her work to a limited circle and leave it to intermediaries to publish her discoveries. She died at Kenilworth on 11 November 1876, her husband having predeceased her. Her herbarium and a collection of birds' eggs were bequeathed by her to the Birmingham and Midland Institute, but neither can now be traced.

D. E. ALLEN

Sources D. E. Allen, 'The botanical family of Samuel Butler', *Journal of the Society of the Bibliography of Natural History*, 9 (1978–80), 133–6 · J. E. Bagnall, *Flora of Warwickshire* (1891), 505 · J. W. White, *The flora of Bristol* (1912), 78–9 · D. E. Allen, 'Samuel Butler and natural history: a supplementary note', *Archives of Natural History*, 10 (1981–2), 153–4 · G. C. Druce, *The flora of Berkshire* (1897), cxvii–cxviii · wills index, Principal Registry of the Family Division, London
Wealth at death under £7000: resworn probate, March 1877, *CGPLA Eng. & Wales* (1876)

Russell, Anthony (1663?–1743). *See under* Russell, Theodore (*bap.* 1614, *d.* 1689).

Russell, Sir Archibald Edward (1904–1995), aircraft design engineer, was born on 30 May 1904 at Bradley Street, Wotton under Edge, Gloucestershire, one of the four sons of Arthur Hallett Russell (*d.* 1961), schoolmaster, and his wife, Edith Maud Richards. Archibald aspired to be an engineer from the age of six, when he first played with Meccano. He went to East Dean grammar school, Cinderford (1914–19), where his father was headmaster, and Fairfield secondary school, Bristol (1919–21), before winning a scholarship to the University of Bristol. In 1924 he graduated with a BSc in automotive engineering.

Russell was initially employed as a fitter at the Bristol bus maintenance depot, but in May 1925 he became assistant stress calculator at the Bristol Aeroplane Company at Filton. Promoted chief stress calculator a year later, he soon found himself engaged on pioneering work. During the mid-1920s steel strips were replacing wooden struts in the primary structure of aircraft. In the absence of any significant literature Russell had to rely on the laws of physics and his own ingenuity in planning test programmes. His efforts contributed to the success of the Bristol Bulldog, a fighter biplane, whose sales sustained the firm during the slump. Russell married Lorna Lilian Mansfield (d. 1984), a 24-year-old secretary, on 5 September 1929. They had one son and one daughter.

The introduction of aluminium alloys in the early 1930s brought fresh professional challenges. As chief technician (1931–8), working under Frank Barnwell and Leslie Frise, Russell helped to develop metal-covered aircraft with stiffened shells intended to buckle harmlessly under normal loads. The first important application of the 'stressed skin structure' was the type 142 Britain First, commissioned by Lord Rothermere to show up the deficiencies of existing RAF aeroplanes. Its military version, the Blenheim, was rushed into production in 1936; the RAF had a thousand by September 1939. In the interim Russell was alerted to the fact that his friendly Norwegian neighbour in Falcondale Road, Westbury-on-Trym, was a German spy.

Russell shared his expertise with the stressed-skin committee of the Royal Aeronautical Society in 1939, which established design data for the new structural form. Variants of the Blenheim were needed as long-range fighters and for coastal reconnaissance and anti-submarine patrols during the Second World War. Russell also worked on the Beaufort torpedo bomber and the Beaufighter. Within the Bristol Aeroplane Company his official title advanced from technical designer (1938–44) to chief engineer (1944–60), though formalities counted for little in the drawing office. Russ (as he was known), a burly, vigorous man, with a sense of humour and a fiery temper, remained the sort of engineer who liked to get his hands dirty.

The military demands on British aircraft designers relaxed when the USA entered the war. By 1944 Russell was preoccupied with post-war civil aviation and plans for a luxury airliner capable of flying the Atlantic without refuelling stops. The Brabazon I prototype, which flew in 1949, was by far the largest aeroplane ever built in Britain, but serious fatigue cracking led to its abandonment in 1953. Bigger faster aircraft required thick non-buckling skins, and Russell and his team devised new long-life structures. Their Britannia airliner, created for the British Overseas Airways Corporation, was a technical success, yet, by the time it entered service on the transatlantic route in 1957, its turboprop engines had been overtaken by turbojets. Britain lost its lead in airliner development to the American company Boeing.

Russell won international recognition in aviation circles after giving the Wright Brothers memorial lecture in New York in 1949. He received an honorary doctorate from Bristol University (1951) and a CBE (1955). From 1951 he sat on the board of the Bristol Aeroplane Company, which renamed itself Bristol Aircraft Ltd in 1956 before becoming a part of the British Aircraft Corporation (BAC) in 1960. Always drawn to new problems in aerodynamics and metallurgy, Russell served on the supersonic transport aircraft committee (STAC) of the Ministry of Transport and Civil Aviation from 1956 to 1959, when Bristol was commissioned to produce the feasibility study for a British supersonic transport (SST). His plans for a 130-passenger long-range Mach 2 SST, known as the type 198, struck the ministry as too large and expensive, but BAC was given the design contract for a smaller SST in 1960 on condition that it seek a foreign collaborator to share the development costs. On 29 November 1962 the British and French governments agreed to finance a joint project by BAC and Sud Aviation. The radically innovative high-speed aeroplane would be named Concorde (which the British spelt Concord until 1967).

As technical director (1960–66), managing director (1966–7), and chairman of the Filton division of BAC (1967–9), Russell devoted the remainder of his working life to Concorde. Two Anglo-French committees ran the project, with the division of responsibility between Britain and France set at 40:60 on the airframe committee and 60:40 on the engine committee. Thus, while heading the 2000–strong British airframe design team, Russell was deputy technical director on the airframe committee, whose main technical director was Pierre Satre of Sud Aviation. They frequently argued. Russell always advocated a large intercontinental SST on the lines of his type 198 design; Satre wanted a smaller transcontinental SST like his own Super Caravelle design. The original plan was to make two different Concordes—one long-range, one medium-range—but this proved unviable. The compromise model, a long-range aircraft for eighty passengers, still seemed far too small to Russell. Working methods also diverged: Satre decreed that the technical directors should confine themselves to policy, but his deputy itched to get involved in practical detail (to the fury of Lucien Servanty, the chief engineer of Sud Aviation). Russ made a habit of challenging technical decisions, often late in the day, with a vehemence that could upset people unused to his adversarial style. He encouraged competition between the British and French teams: sharp criticism of each other's work ensured high standards, he believed, despite complaints from some quarters that this approach wasted time and deprived the project of strategic leadership. That said, he grew friendly with Louis Giusta of Sud Aviation, with whom he jointly chaired the Concorde executive committee (1965–9).

The British prototype of Concorde (002) made its first flight at Filton on 9 April 1969. Technical necessity had twice compelled the French to agree to the enlargement of the compromise design (after heavy expenditure on tools for smaller models that were never built). The final production version of Concorde conformed so closely to his original specifications in respect of size, speed, weight, and range that Russell hardly knew whether to laugh or cry. In retirement (after 1969), he never ceased to point out that his type 198 design should have been adopted in the first place. Elected a fellow of the Royal

Society in 1970, he received a knighthood in January 1972.

Concorde was an engineering triumph. It cruised at 1350 m.p.h., reducing the flying time between London and New York to less than four hours. However, the development costs had spiralled from a projected £95 million to around £2 billion, and the oil shock of 1973–4 made supersonic flight largely uneconomic. Only sixteen production Concordes were ever built. Russell remarked that every new aeroplane amounted to a commercial act of faith.

Widowed in 1984, Sir Archibald Russell married Judith Coutsoubos, *née* Humphrey, a 43-year-old divorcée, on 22 September 1986 and moved from Bristol to Cornwall. He died of pneumonia and prostate cancer at his home, Runnymead, 21 Riverside, Angarrack, Hayle, Cornwall, on 29 May 1995. His career in aviation embraced about thirty distinct prototypes, stretching from biplanes to supersonic airliners. Many called him 'the father of Concorde'.

JASON TOMES

Sources A. Russell, *A span of wings* (1992) · *The Times* (31 May 1995) · *The Independent* (1 June 1995) · *The Daily Telegraph* (1 June 1995) · *The Guardian* (31 May 1995) · W. J. Strang, 'Sir Archibald Edward Russell, CBE', *Royal Society Memoirs*, 42 (1996), 380–84 · G. Knight, *Concorde: the inside story* (1976) · K. Owen, *Concorde: new shape in the sky* (1982) · B. Trubshaw, *Concorde: the inside story* (2000) · J. Edwards, 'Concord will likely be the first and the last', *Daily Mail* (29 Sept 1992) · C. Orlebar, *The Concorde story* (1986) · b. cert. · m. certs. · d. certs.
Likenesses photograph, repro. in *The Times* · photograph, repro. in *The Independent* · photograph, repro. in Strang, *Royal Society Memoirs*, p. 380

Russell, Arthur Tozer (1806–1874), Church of England clergyman and hymn writer, elder son of Thomas *Russell or Cloutt (*c*.1781–1846), a Unitarian minister, was born at Northampton on 20 March 1806. John Fuller *Russell was his brother. He received his early education at St Saviour's School, Southwark, and Merchant Taylors' School, London. Having read some writings of Thomas Belsham, he wished to qualify for the Unitarian ministry. Belsham got him an exhibition, under the name of Russell, on the Hackney College fund, with a view to his entrance as a divinity student at Manchester College, York. The exhibition was temporarily withdrawn because of his hostility to dissenters; however, he entered Manchester College, on the Hackney foundation, in September 1822, under the name of Cloutt, among his fellow entrants being Robert Brook Aspland and James Martineau. At the annual examination, on 30 July 1824, he delivered a Latin oration, under the name of Russell. He then left York without finishing his course.

Russell made the acquaintance of Francis Wrangham, archdeacon of Cleveland, and decided to study for ordination in the Church of England. In 1825 he entered as a sizar at St John's College, Cambridge, and won the Hulsean prize in his freshman year with *The Law* (1826). After becoming a scholar of St John's (1826), he was ordained deacon (1829) by John Kaye, bishop of Lincoln, and curate of Great Gransden, Huntingdonshire, 1829–30. In 1830 he was ordained priest and became vicar of Caxton, Cambridgeshire; in 1831 he graduated LLB. In 1852 he

became vicar of Whaddon, Cambridgeshire, exchanging this benefice in 1863 for the vicarage of St Thomas, Toxteth Park, Liverpool, whose patron was W. E. Gladstone. Gladstone thought well of him and refused him permission to transfer to another parish in 1866. In 1868, however, he became vicar of Wrockwardine Wood, Shropshire. His last preferment was to the rectory of Southwick, Sussex, in 1874, but his health was broken. As a clergyman he was exemplary; his brief incumbency in Liverpool was noted for his educational work in his parish. His theological views underwent several modifications, but he kept an open mind, and his love for the writings of St Augustine gave both strength and breadth to his views.

Russell's career as a hymn writer began early, his first hymns being included in the third edition of his father's *Collection*. Hymns by him, original and translated, were published in *The Christian Life* (1847), *Psalms and Hymns* (1851), *The Choral Hymn-Book* (1861), and other collections. In 1851 he added a sixth verse, designed to improve its theology, to the well-known hymn 'Nearer my God, to thee' (1841) by Sarah Fuller Adams. He published also *Hymn Tunes, Original and Selected* (1843). In all he produced about 140 original and 130 translated hymns.

Russell published sermons and remarks on sermons, translated John Jewel's apology in 1834, and wrote several memorials of Caroline churchmen, notably one of Lancelot Andrewes (1863). He wrote critical articles on the Greek Testament for the *British and Foreign Evangelical Review* in 1862–3 and left an unpublished history of the bishops of England and Wales.

Russell's wife's name is unknown. He died at Southwick rectory on 18 November 1874, and was survived by his daughter, Lucy Stainforth Russell.

ALEXANDER GORDON, rev. H. C. G. MATTHEW

Sources Crockford (1874) · *Christian Reformer, or, Unitarian Magazine and Review*, new ser., 3 (1847), 64 [obit. of Thomas Russell] · 'Manchester College, York', *Monthly Repository*, 17 (1822), 773 · 'Manchester College, York', *Monthly Repository*, 19 (1824), 426 · Venn, *Alum. Cant.* · J. Julian, ed., *A dictionary of hymnology* (1892) · *Roll of students entered at the Manchester Academy* (1868) · Gladstone, *Diaries* · *CGPLA Eng. & Wales* (1875)
Archives BL, corresp. with W. E. Gladstone, Add. MSS 44358–44413
Wealth at death under £800: probate, 20 Jan 1875, *CGPLA Eng. & Wales*

Russell, (Muriel) Audrey (1906–1989), radio broadcaster, was born on 29 June 1906 in Dublin, the only child of John Strangman Russell, director of the family woollen mill, of Dublin, and his wife, Muriel Metcalfe, sister of E. Dudley (Fruity) Metcalfe, the closest friend of the prince of Wales (later Edward VIII and duke of Windsor). From an Anglo-Irish protestant background, her parents were part of Dublin society, and her father led the life of a country gentleman. She was educated at home by governesses, and later at Southlands, a private boarding-school in Harrow, before going to a finishing school at the Villa St Georges in Neuilly, Paris.

Back in London, Audrey Russell trained as an actress for

(Muriel) **Audrey Russell** (1906–1989), by unknown photographer, 1953

six months at the Central School of Speech and Drama, and then worked for several years as a theatre dogsbody, preparing stage meals, understudying, and taking walk-on parts. She was assistant stage manager for Rodney Ackland's play *After October*, which ran for a year in 1936, and then became stage manager for the Group Theatre, an avant-garde theatre club at the Westminster Theatre.

With the outbreak of the Second World War imminent, Audrey Russell joined the London Fire Brigade (later the London Auxiliary Fire Service). She fought fires throughout the blitz. Stationed in Manchester Square, she was close to the BBC, and after she had been interviewed on the effects of the air raids she was asked to do a series of broadcasts on the work of the Auxiliary Fire Service, which included a description of the worst night of the blitz, 10 May 1941, when the House of Commons was bombed. This led to a secondment to the Air Ministry for six weeks, to do a series of talks on the work of the Women's Auxiliary Air Force.

In 1942 the BBC asked to have Audrey Russell released from national service in order to join the magazine programme *Radio Newsreel*. For two years she travelled all over the country, broadcasting from army camps, bomb sites, and rescue stations, interviewing those whose homes had been destroyed, and reporting on the damage done by flying bombs and rockets. On D-day she was in Trafalgar Square interviewing people on their reactions to the Normandy landings. In 1944 she was accredited as a British war correspondent by the War Office, and went with the war reporting unit to Europe to send back dispatches from Belgium, the Netherlands, Germany, and Norway. Suffering from influenza she returned home in March 1945 and spent the rest of the war in London.

Determined to make a career in broadcasting rather than go back to the theatre, Audrey Russell accepted a post as a reporter in the new Home Service reporting unit, but she really wanted to be a commentator rather than a reporter. She was attracted by the tightrope quality of doing a live commentary, describing the action as it happens, which was very different from the work of a reporter, who could read from a script. She succeeded in 1947, when she was asked to join the outside broadcasts team commentating on the wedding of Princess Elizabeth, to cover the 'women's angle', describing the wedding dress and clothes worn by the guests.

Audrey Russell decided in 1948 to leave the news division and join the outside broadcasts department on a contract basis. She became one of the principal royal commentators on state occasions, covering eight royal weddings between 1947 and 1981. She covered the Festival of Britain in 1951, and went on the first of many royal tours in 1952. At the coronation in 1953 she was in Westminster Abbey to describe the processions, and then accompanied the six-month royal tour around the world by sea. Every year she broadcast from the royal Maundy service. She covered the funerals of Sir Winston Churchill and Victoria (Mary), the princess royal, in 1965, and described the silver jubilee in 1977 and the eightieth-birthday celebrations for the queen mother in 1980. In recognition of her work the queen gave her a hand-embroidered chair. Although she was never tempted to leave radio broadcasting for television, she did a series of programmes on BBC television in the 1960s on the opening of the Queen's Gallery, Buckingham Palace, in 1962 and the first ten exhibitions held there.

Audrey Russell was the only woman to be an accredited war correspondent in the Second World War, and the first woman news reporter when she joined the Home Service in 1945. Her voice was instantly recognizable, and she was to radio coverage of state occasions what Richard Dimbleby was to television. She became a freeman of the City of London in 1967, and was appointed MVO in 1976.

Audrey Russell was tall, blonde, and elegantly dressed, with a beautiful, calm speaking voice, with the slightest tinge of an Irish accent. She loved painting in oils, and collected art, as well as lecturing on art and antiques. She was unmarried, having broken off her engagement to Brent Grotrian, the heir to a baronetcy. He was later killed in Burma, in 1941. She died on 8 August 1989 of Alzheimer's disease in Woking, Surrey.

ANNE PIMLOTT BAKER, rev.

Sources *The Times* (10 Aug 1989) · A. Russell, *A certain voice* (1984) · L. Miall, *Inside the BBC: British broadcasting characters* (1994) · *CGPLA Eng. & Wales* (1989)

Archives SOUND BL NSA

Likenesses photograph, 1953, BBC Picture Archives, London [*see illus.*] · photograph, repro. in L. Miall, *Inside the BBC* (1994), facing p.

71 · photographs, repro. in A. Russell, *A certain voice* (1984), including 'The author as war correspondent', p. 53

Wealth at death £427,795: probate, 9 Nov 1989, *CGPLA Eng. & Wales*

Russell, Sir Baker Creed (1837–1911), army officer, was born at Ravensworth, New South Wales, on 7 December 1837, the son of Captain the Hon. W. Russell of the 73rd foot and his wife, Mary, eldest daughter of Dr Martin of the 73rd. Commissioned as an ensign in the 6th dragoon guards on 2 November 1855, Russell joined his regiment in India. Promoted lieutenant on 1 August 1856, Russell was stationed at Meerut in 1857 at the outbreak of the mutiny. He saw action at Karnaul and distinguished himself with Sir Thomas Seaton's column at Gungaree and Patiali, the recurring casualties among senior officers propelling Russell into squadron command. In 1858 he served in central India with the Agra field force in its pursuit of Tantia Topi. Promotion to a captaincy by purchase was on 18 February 1859 and, following transfer to the 13th hussars in 1862, Russell received a brevet majority on 24 January 1865. In 1866 he married Pauline Henrietta, daughter of Captain Henry Hunter of the 5th dragoon guards. A striking woman, Pal, as she was known to Lady Wolseley, apparently had a somewhat stormy relationship with Russell.

Regimental service followed until, in September 1873, Russell's reputation as a good fighting man led to selection as a special service officer on Sir Garnet Wolseley's Asante expedition: he commanded one of two locally raised native regiments and played a prominent part in the action at Abrakampa on 5 November. Subsequently his regiment formed part of the advance guard during the march on Kumasi. Wolseley wrote, 'I wish I had a hundred men like him here' (Wolseley to Lady Wolseley, 27 Nov 1873, W/P 3/15). To H. M. Stanley, then a war correspondent, Russell appeared 'a resolute, hard-handed man, with vim and nerve in him, a sharp sword for an enemy, and a soft tongue for a friend' (Temple, 124). For his services Russell received a brevet lieutenant-colonelcy on 1 April 1874 and the CB.

Russell was now identified as one of the *Wolseley ring (*act.* 1873–1890), which was advantageous and disadvantageous. He was assured of employment on expeditions commanded by Wolseley, as in July 1878 when he accompanied Wolseley to Cyprus as assistant military secretary, although staff work was not his strength. However, Wolseley's opponents in the military establishment obstructed his advancement, and in March 1879 he resigned his Cyprus appointment rather than be seconded from his regiment. Later in 1879 Russell joined Wolseley in South Africa for the closing stages of the Anglo-Zulu War, employed primarily as a column commander operating against the Pedi chief Sekukuni, against whose final stronghold Russell personally led the assault, having his horse shot under him. However, Russell was able to remain in South Africa only by Wolseley's refusal to return him to his regiment in India. Russell had been promoted major on 15 July 1878 and he was now created KCMG but was not given the further promotion for which Wolseley strove on his behalf. Russell was given the

unattached rank of colonel on 18 February 1880 and regimental rank as lieutenant-colonel on 29 September 1880.

In 1882 Wolseley wanted Russell for his Egyptian expedition, but opposition from the commander-in-chief, the duke of Cambridge, and the prince of Wales restricted his initial appointment to assistant adjutant-general to the cavalry division. Once in Egypt, however, Wolseley promptly gave Russell local rank as brigadier-general and appointed him to command the 1st cavalry brigade. Again Russell showed great skill as a cavalry commander—he had once remarked that the purpose of cavalry was 'to look pretty in time of peace and to get killed in war' (Lehmann, *First Boer War*, 227)—again having his horse shot under him, at Qassasin on 9 September. Russell's reward was the KCB.

Egypt was Russell's last campaign, since in 1884 Wolseley was unable to find a place for him on the Gordon relief expedition, with a resulting cooling of their relationship. In 1886 Russell became inspecting officer of auxiliary cavalry but took up the command at Shorncliffe later that year. He was promoted major-general on 1 April 1889 and took command of the cavalry brigade at Aldershot from 1890 to 1895. He commanded north-west district from 1895 to 1898, receiving promotion to lieutenant-general on 20 January 1897. His final appointment before retirement was at southern command from 1898 to 1904. He had become colonel of the 13th hussars on 20 January 1904 and received promotion to full general on 19 December 1903. He was made GCB in 1900. Russell died at his home, 10 Trinity Crescent, Folkestone, on 25 November 1911, survived by his wife.   IAN F. W. BECKETT

Sources Wolseley to Lady Wolseley, Hove Central Library, Sussex, Wolseley Collections, S.A.2 W/P · letters from Baker Russell, Hove Central Library, Sussex, Wolseley Collections, LW/P 3/7/72, M3/1/117 · Ashanti journal, PRO, Wolseley MSS, WO 147/3 · Cyprus journal, PRO, Wolseley MSS, WO 147/6 · South African journal, PRO, Wolseley MSS, WO 147/7 · letters from Baker Russell, University of Natal, South Africa, Killie Campbell Africana Library, Wood MSS, KCM 89/9, 89/9/22/5, 89/9/23/14, 89/9/27/13 · letter from Baker Russell, Brenthurst Library, Parktown, Johannesburg, Alison MSS, Acc 6399 · A. Temple, *Our living generals* (1900) · J. H. Lehmann, *The model major-general: a biography of Field-Marshal Lord Wolseley* (Boston, 1964) · *The South African journal of Sir Garnet Wolseley, 1879–1880*, ed. A. Preston (1973) · *Army List* · *WWW* · J. H. Lehmann, *The First Boer War* (1972) · C. N. Robinson, *Celebrities of the army*, 18 pts (1900) · Burke, *Peerage* · *CGPLA Eng. & Wales* (1911)

Archives Hove Central Library, Sussex, Wolseley collections, letters, LW/P 3/7/72, M3/1/117 · PRO, Wolseley MSS, Ashanti journal; Cyprus journal; South African journal, WO 147/3, 146/6, 147/7 · University of Natal, South Africa, Killie Campbell Africana Library, Wood MSS, letters, KCM 89/9/22/5, 89/9/23/14, 89/9/27/13

Wealth at death £307 1s. 6d.: probate, 22 Dec 1911, *CGPLA Eng. & Wales*

Russell, Bertrand Arthur William, third Earl Russell (1872–1970), philosopher, journalist, and political campaigner, was born on 18 May 1872 at Ravenscroft, Trelleck, Monmouthshire, the youngest among the three children of John *Russell, Viscount Amberley (1842–1876) (the eldest son of the first Earl Russell, previously Lord John Russell), and his wife, Kate, daughter of the second Baron Stanley of Alderley [see Russell, Katharine Louisa, Viscountess Amberley (1842–1874)]. John Francis Stanley

Bertrand Arthur William Russell, third Earl Russell (1872–1970), by Ida Kar, 1953

(Frank) Russell (1865–1931), who succeeded as the second Earl Russell, was his elder brother.

Childhood and adolescence Russell's early childhood was marred by tragedy and bereavement. When he was two, his mother and his sister, Rachel, died of diphtheria. Just eighteen months later his father, too, died, leaving him and his brother Frank in the care of their grandparents, Earl and Countess Russell, who lived in Pembroke Lodge, a grace-and-favour house in Richmond Park granted to Lord Russell by Queen Victoria. When Russell was six his grandfather died, after which, he recounted in his autobiography, he used to lie awake at night wondering when his grandmother too would die and leave him.

Russell's grandmother did not die until he reached adulthood, and throughout his childhood and adolescence she was without doubt the person who exerted the greatest influence on him. From her he acquired a devout religious faith and, more lastingly, a deep respect for the role his family had played in the political history of Britain since the time of Henry VIII. His understanding of himself as inheritor of a tradition of opposition to tyranny and authority that went back hundreds of years played a large role in giving him the personal courage that characterized his own political activities. While Frank was sent away to Winchester College, young Bertie (as he was known within the family and, later, to close friends) received from private tutors an education fit for the future prime minister his grandmother hoped and expected him to become. In keeping with the self-conscious progressiveness that characterized the Russell family, this education

concentrated, not on Greek and Latin, but on modern languages, economics, constitutional history, science, and mathematics, in all of which Russell excelled. Though he remained comparatively uneducated in music and the pictorial arts, he acquired from his grandmother a deep love of English literature, especially its poetry, that stayed with him for the rest of his life.

Of equal importance for Russell's formative years was the furtive secrecy his grandmother maintained on the subject of his parents. After their deaths she discovered that his mother, Kate, had had, with his father's approval, sexual relations with Douglas Spalding, a tutor they had hired to teach their children (he was terminally ill and she slept with him in order to grant him his wish that he should not die celibate). Lady Russell's shock at this was so great that she hardly mentioned Russell's parents to him, and, on the few occasions that she did so, hinted that he had had a lucky escape in not being brought up by such wicked people. As a result, Russell later said, he 'vaguely sensed a great mystery' (Schilpp, 3) about his parents and would spend much time alone in the garden at Pembroke Lodge wondering what sort of people they had been and why his grandmother was so disapproving of them. He also dwelt on something else he noticed about his grandmother: that she trembled whenever insanity was mentioned.

It is against this background of loss, uncertainty, mystery, and the frustrated yearning to know something about his parents that one must regard what Russell himself saw as the turning point in his childhood intellectual development: his introduction, at the age of eleven, to Euclidean geometry. 'I had not imagined', Russell later wrote, 'that there was anything so delicious in the world … [It was] as dazzling as first love' (Russell, *Autobiography*, 1.36). What he found so delightful was the intoxicating discovery that some things at least could be demonstrated to be true beyond all possible doubt, their truth being independent of all opinion and all authority, and immune from any kind of uncertainty. This, then, became his model of what human knowledge could, and should, be like—irrefutable, demonstrable, and, above all, certain—and his philosophical career might be seen as a long series of failed attempts to show how such knowledge might be possible. The seeds of his later work on the philosophy of mathematics are discernible in his disappointment at eleven that, though Euclid's theorems could be demonstrated from his axioms, these axioms themselves had to be taken on trust. What he dreamed of was a mathematics in which even the axioms were demonstrable; he further hoped to find that the natural, and even the human, sciences could be founded on such a mathematics. Only then, he thought, would the joy he experienced at discovering the axiomatic method be completely justified and only then could he, and the rest of humanity, claim to really know anything.

Early support for this attitude came from W. K. Clifford's *Common Sense of the Exact Sciences*, which Russell read as a teenager and which became an enormously important book to him. Clifford's creed, expressed pithily in his lecture 'The ethics of belief' (1877), was that: 'It is wrong always, everywhere, and for any one to believe anything upon insufficient evidence' (Clifford, *Lectures and Essays*, 1879, 31). It was a view embraced enthusiastically by the adolescent Russell and one which inevitably corroded the religious faith he had acquired from his grandmother.

Russell's earliest surviving philosophical reflections are contained in a diary he began shortly before his sixteenth birthday and centre on the doubts that had begun to assail him concerning religious belief. Knowing that these doubts would offend his grandmother, he disguised his thoughts by writing them in Greek letters, using a system of phonetic transliteration that he had invented himself, and entitling his diary 'Greek exercises'. The first entry confesses: 'I have been irresistibly led to such conclusions as would not only shock my people, but have given me much pain' (Russell, *Collected Papers*, 1.3). Among those conclusions were that immortality, the efficacy of prayer, free will, and even the existence of the soul, were illusory. He was prepared to accept the existence of God, but only as the controlling law of nature, not as a personal deity with a love of mankind, nor as the foundation for morality.

These thoughts served only to alienate Russell still further from his grandmother, and to increase his sense of isolation. 'After the age of fourteen', he writes in his autobiography, 'I found living at home only endurable at the cost of complete silence about everything that interested me' (Schilpp, 7). When, at sixteen, he was sent to a 'crammer' school in London to prepare him for the scholarship examination at Cambridge, he hoped, at last, to find friends, but found instead a group of rambunctious boys (most of them future army officers) towards whom he felt only contempt.

In December 1889 Russell was awarded a minor scholarship to read mathematics at Trinity College, Cambridge, to prepare for which he spent the following six months studying the infinitesimal calculus with a private tutor in London. In his last diary entry before he left Pembroke Lodge for Cambridge he announced, with a note of tragedy but also, one senses, with a sense of relief, that he had by this time lost his faith entirely. His earlier view that God had to exist as the provider and controller of nature's laws had, it seems, been undermined by his reading of John Stuart Mill's *Autobiography*.

Cambridge, 1890–1893 At Cambridge, Russell, aged eighteen, found what he had been looking for all his life until then: companionship. Within a few months of arriving at Trinity he formed a circle of friends with whom, in stark contrast to his home, he could discuss everything that mattered to him. Most of these friends belonged to the famous Cambridge discussion group the Apostles, which, at the prompting of Russell's mathematics tutor, Alfred North Whitehead, elected Russell as a member. 'The Society' (as it was known to its members) quickly became the focal point of Russell's undergraduate life. Through it he was introduced to some of the most influential philosophers of the day, including, most notably, John Ellis

McTaggart, who, together with the Oxford philosopher F. H. Bradley, was one of the leading members of the neo-Hegelian movement which then dominated the younger generation of British philosophers.

In May 1893 Russell took part one of the mathematics tripos and was placed seventh wrangler, after which, inspired by his discussions with the Apostles, he abandoned mathematics in favour of philosophy, devoting the next year to studying for part two of the moral sciences tripos. His tutors for this were James Ward, Henry Sidgwick, and G. F. Stout, though the biggest influence on his philosophical development remained McTaggart. Russell had been bitterly disappointed by his undergraduate mathematics course, which he felt, by teaching the subject as a series of techniques rather than as a body of truth, had failed to do justice to the delight he had felt at the age of eleven on discovering Euclid's axiomatic system. Significantly, the highlight of his undergraduate philosophical career was an essay he wrote for James Ward on the threat posed to Kant's theory of mathematics by the construction of non-Euclidean systems of geometry, a subject which allowed him to discuss the very question which had bothered him at eleven: how can one know whether Euclid's axioms are true or not? When, in summer 1894, Russell was awarded a starred first in moral sciences and invited to submit a fellowship dissertation, he chose as his topic 'the epistemological bearings of metageometry'.

The dissertation was written within a year, and on the basis of it Russell was awarded a five-year fellowship at Trinity, beginning in 1895. Two years later a revised version was published as *An Essay on the Foundations of Geometry*, Russell's first philosophical book, in which he provides a partial defence of Kant's theory that the truth of geometry is a necessary condition of all possible experience. This, Russell argues, is correct, though not of Euclidean geometry but of the more abstract and comparatively modern system of 'projective geometry'. The truth or otherwise of the specifically Euclidean axioms Russell regards as an empirical matter. In a more general sense, however, Russell agrees with Kant in locating the foundations of geometry in the structure of our spatial intuitions. Russell later dismissed the book as a foolish and immature work, and its central claims have not been accepted by either mathematicians or philosophers. None the less, principally through being reviewed at length and with great respect by the eminent French mathematician Henri Poincaré, it served to establish Russell's professional reputation and led to his being invited to deliver a paper at the prestigious International Congress of Philosophy held in Paris in 1900, an event that profoundly affected his career.

First marriage and early philosophical work On 13 December 1894, at twenty-two, Russell married Alys Whitall (*c*.1867–1951), daughter of Robert Pearsall Smith, a rich American Quaker, who left Philadelphia to settle in Surrey after scandal had forced him to relinquish his career as a charismatic evangelist. The literary scholar (Lloyd) Logan Pearsall Smith was her brother. Russell's grandmother vehemently opposed the marriage and, in an effort to dissuade him from going ahead with it, explained to him why she trembled at any mention of insanity. There was, she claimed, inherited madness in the Russell family, and if the marriage went ahead it was sure to produce insane children. In support of this claim she revealed to Russell something that had hitherto been carefully concealed from him: his uncle William had been confined to a lunatic asylum since 1874. His aunt Agatha and even his own father, Lady Russell alleged, had also shown signs of mental instability. Though she failed to dissuade Russell from marrying, Lady Russell did instil into her grandson a deep and lasting horror of madness. In a diary entry of the time he records that, after his grandmother's revelations, he felt 'haunted by the fear of the family ghost, which seems to seize on me with clammy invisible hands' and that Pembroke Lodge had begun to seem to him like a vault 'haunted by the ghosts of maniacs' (Russell, *Collected Papers*, 1.65). The fear of madness transformed his personality and caused him, he later said, 'to avoid all deep emotion and live, as nearly as I could, a life of intellect tempered by flippancy' (Russell, *Autobiography*, 1.85).

For their honeymoon Russell and Alys travelled to Berlin, where Russell attended lectures on economics and took time to study the doctrines and methods of the Social Democratic Party, then the most influential Marxist movement in Europe. The result was *German Social Democracy* (1896), Russell's first political book, which, though sympathetic to the reformist aims of the German socialist movement, included some trenchant and far-sighted criticisms of Marxist dogmas. In Berlin, Russell formulated for himself an ambitious scheme of writing two series of books, one on the philosophy of the sciences, the other on social and political questions. 'At last', as he later put it, 'I would achieve a Hegelian synthesis in an encyclopaedic work dealing with theory and practice' (Schilpp, 11). He eventually wrote on all the subjects he intended, but not in the form that he envisaged, for, shortly after finishing his book on geometry, he abandoned the metaphysical idealism that was to have provided the framework for this grand synthesis.

Russell's abandonment of idealism is customarily attributed to the influence of his friend and fellow Apostle, G. E. Moore, but a much greater influence on his thought at this time was in fact the work of a group of German mathematicians that included Karl Weierstrass, Georg Cantor, and Richard Dedekind, who, through the analysis of the fundamental concepts of mathematics, sought to provide it with logically rigorous foundations. Their success in this was, Russell considered, of enormous philosophical as well as mathematical significance; indeed, he described it as: 'the greatest triumph of which our age has to boast' (*Mysticism and Logic*, 2nd edn, 1917, 82).

Throughout his mathematical studies at Cambridge, Russell had remained ignorant of this body of work. However, in 1896 he was asked by Stout to review for *Mind* a book by the French philosopher and historian of science Arthur Hannequin called *Essai critique sur l'hypothèse des atomes dans la science contemporaine*, which contained a discussion of Georg Cantor's theory of transfinite numbers. Though Russell expressed agreement with Hannequin's criticisms of Cantor's theory, he was sufficiently intrigued to make a close study of Cantor's work. Later in that same year, during a visit to America, the importance of Weierstrass's work on the theory of functions was impressed upon him by the mathematicians Frank Morley and James Harkness, and on his return to England he made a study, not only of Weierstrass but also of Dedekind's classic works *Continuity and Irrational Numbers* and *Nature and the Meaning of Numbers*. From his reading of Cantor, Weierstrass, and Dedekind, Russell discovered that there were putative mathematical solutions to the problems of continuity and infinity that previously he had thought required neo-Hegelian philosophy to solve.

During his short-lived neo-Hegelian phase Russell had believed that the notions of infinity, continuity, and the infinitesimal introduced contradictions into mathematics which it was, by itself, unable to resolve. These contradictions, he thought, suggested not that mathematics needed to be rebuilt upon more secure foundations, but that it was inherently flawed as a means of understanding reality. Much better, he considered, was the Hegelian approach of overcoming contradiction through a process of dialectical synthesis which led, stage by stage, to the single, indivisible absolute, the reality of which underlay all appearance and the understanding of which was available only to philosophy. Now that he had become convinced by the work of Cantor, Dedekind, and Weierstrass that the differential calculus could be recast without the need for infinitesimals and that the notions of infinity and continuity could be given mathematical definitions that were free from contradiction, this particular motive for embracing Hegelian metaphysics was removed, and Russell adopted the view, which he held for the rest of his life, that analysis, not synthesis, was the surest method for the philosopher and that, therefore, all the grand system building of previous philosophers—including himself—was misconceived.

The Principles of Mathematics Inspired by the work of the mathematicians whom he had come so greatly to admire, Russell conceived the idea of demonstrating that mathematics not only had logically rigorous foundations but that it was in its entirety nothing but logic. In this he was influenced by Alfred North Whitehead's book *A Treatise on Universal Algebra with Applications* (1898), which argued that mathematics ought to be understood not, as tradition would have it, as the 'science of quantity', but rather as the study of 'all types of formal, necessary, deductive reasoning' (Whitehead, *A Treatise on Universal Algebra*, vi). In his understanding of what logic was, however, he was influenced still more by G. E. Moore's article 'The nature of judgment' (1899), from which Russell took a peculiar notion of the nature of propositions that was to bedevil his philosophical thinking for many years.

On Moore's understanding a proposition is not, as the Hegelians would have it, a unity that defies analysis;

rather, it is a complex that invites analysis into its constituent parts, which Moore called 'concepts'. These concepts, however, are not, on Moore's theory, elements of thought, but rather the building blocks of the world. Thus a proposition is not a linguistic entity but, as Moore put it, an 'existent', something whose being is independent of thought, and to analyse a proposition is not to investigate a portion of language, but to carve up a piece of the world itself. Logic, the analysis of the relations between propositions, is on this understanding indistinguishable from metaphysics; it is, in other words, an investigation into the most abstract and general features of reality. What follows from this view, and what became a characteristic feature of Russell's method of philosophy, is the conviction that the grammar of linguistic utterances can just as readily disguise as reveal the real logical structure of propositions and, therefore, of reality.

This conception of logic was expressed by Russell with great force and elegance in his widely acclaimed book *The Philosophy of Leibniz*, which arose out of a series of lectures he gave at Cambridge in Lent term 1899. In this he presents what he describes as 'a reconstruction of the system which Leibniz *should* have written' (Russell, *The Philosophy of Leibniz*, 2), two fundamental tenets of which are that 'all sound philosophy should begin with an analysis of propositions' (ibid., 8) and that 'every proposition has a subject and a predicate' (ibid., 14). The first of these Russell accepts, the second he rejects, leading him to claim that if Leibniz had admitted the existence of relational propositions, he would have had no case for denying, as he did, the reality of relations.

In summer 1900 Russell went to Paris to deliver at the International Congress of Philosophy a paper called 'The notion of order and absolute position in space and time', in which he argued (against Kant, the Hegelian tradition, and his former self) that temporal and spatial relations were part of reality and not merely of 'appearance'. By this time Russell had already begun work on a large book he entitled *The Principles of Mathematics*, the aim of which was to show that the notions of continuity, infinity, space, time, matter, and motion can all be understood arithmetically, as relations between numbers, both numbers and relations being understood by him to have an objective existence independent of thought and, in particular, of the 'structure of intuition' to which he had appealed in his earlier book on geometry.

At Paris, Russell met the Italian mathematician Giuseppe Peano, the head of a movement whose ultimate goal was to construct a single axiomatic system upon which the whole of mathematics could be founded. In pursuit of this aim Peano had invented a special symbolism which he used to construct a system of mathematical logic, at the heart of which is the now-familiar notion of a 'propositional function'. Using this system, Peano and his colleagues had shown that arithmetic could be founded on a single elegant formal theory which used only three basic ideas (zero, number, and successor) and five initial axioms. Inspired by his meeting with Peano and his study of Peano's work, Russell returned from Paris with an almost ecstatic conviction that he knew the way ahead: if he could show that all mathematical notions were fundamentally arithmetical and that Peano's system was fundamentally a system of logic, then he would have succeeded in his stated aim of demonstrating that mathematics was logic. For this the crucial step would be to show that Peano's axioms could be founded upon a system of logic.

With this in mind Russell developed a theory of 'classes', in which a class is understood as the extension of a propositional function (the propositional function 'x is a man', for example, has as its extension the class of men), and then used that theory to define numbers. In this way, he hoped, Peano's three basic ideas could be shown to be founded upon nothing more than the purely logical notion of 'class'. Excited by these ideas and working at a frenetic pace, Russell set about rewriting *The Principles of Mathematics*, which he finished on the last day of the year 1900 in a mood of almost limitless confidence and triumph. 'I invented a new subject', he wrote that night to his friend Helen Thomas, 'which turned out to be all mathematics, for the first time treated in its essence' (Monk, *Spirit*, 133). Finishing this draft of the book was, Russell later said, the highest point of his life, an 'intellectual honeymoon such as I have never experienced before or since' (Russell, *Philosophical Development*, 73).

Principia mathematica The draft of *The Principles of Mathematics* that Russell finished in a state of exaltation at the end of 1900 was never published. In spring 1901 he discovered a contradiction in its basic logical theory that threatened to undermine the entire project. The contradiction, subsequently known as Russell's paradox, arises from the following considerations: some classes are members of themselves (for example, the class of all classes), and some are not (for example, the class of men), so it ought to be possible to construct the class of all classes that are not members of themselves. But, now, if one asks of this class, 'Is it a member of itself?' one becomes enmeshed in an apparently inescapable contradiction: if it is, then it is not, and if it is not, then it is. It is rather like defining the village barber as 'the man who shaves all those who do not shave themselves' and then asking whether he shaves himself or not.

At first this paradox seemed trivial, but the more Russell reflected upon it, the deeper the problem seemed, eventually persuading him that there was something fundamentally wrong with the notion of a class as he had understood it in *The Principles of Mathematics*. After wrestling with the problem inconclusively for about a year, Russell, in summer 1902, rewrote parts of the book, adding to it a discussion of the contradiction together with a frank admission that he had no satisfactory solution to it. All he could offer was a sketch of a possible solution, with which, he made clear, he was not entirely content. This sketch, to which he gave the name 'the theory of types', has as its basic idea the thought that a class cannot be a member of itself since a class and its members are of different logical types. Therefore there is, contrary to what he had said earlier, no such thing as the 'class of all classes' and the contradiction does not arise. Russell offered this 'solution' only as the basis for discussion, a gesture which imparted to the whole book—which in its 1900 manifestation had been quite magisterially self-confident—a tentative and unresolved note.

In May 1902 Russell delivered the book to the Cambridge University Press, and shortly afterwards began a close study of the works of Gottlob Frege, who was then unknown among philosophers, despite having already published the works that are among the classics of the analytic tradition in philosophy: *The Foundations of Arithmetic* and the series of essays that include 'Sense and reference' and 'Concept and object'. Belatedly Russell discovered that Frege had in these works anticipated the main lines of his own philosophy of mathematics. He decided immediately to write an appendix to his book, outlining Frege's doctrines, acknowledging the importance and the priority of Frege's work, and indicating where he and Frege agreed and disagreed with each other.

In many ways Frege's work was not only an anticipation of Russell's work but also an advance on it. However, his system too was threatened by the paradox that Russell had discovered, and on 16 June 1902 Russell wrote to him informing him of the fact. In reply, Frege wrote that Russell's discovery had left him 'thunderstruck' (Monk, *Spirit*, 153), since it undermined not only his foundations of arithmetic but, as far as he could see, all possible foundations. While Frege sank into a deep depression, Russell set about repairing the damage by constructing a theory of logic immune to the paradox. Like a malignant cancerous growth, however, the contradiction reappeared in different guises whenever Russell thought that he had got rid of it.

If Russell's delight in contemplating the world of mathematics could be regarded—as he himself was inclined to regard it—as a kind of religion, then these paradoxes brought him to the brink of atheism. He felt about them, he later said, 'much as an earnest Catholic must feel about wicked Popes' (Russell, *Philosophical Development*, 212). The analogy is not as fanciful as it might appear. For Russell, as for the pre-Socratic philosopher Pythagoras, the contemplation of mathematical objects was the noblest exercise of the intellect that life had to offer, and the access it gave to a world of infinite totalities was, in Russell's view, the nearest thing to religion that was consistent with fidelity to the truth. It was thus crucially important for him to believe that the objects of mathematics, that is, classes, were real. By showing that the notion of class as used in *The Principles of Mathematics* was contradictory, the paradox threatened to reveal Russell's Pythagorean faith in mathematical certainties to be as ill-founded as his grandmother's faith in a loving God. When Russell described his philosophical development after the discovery of the paradox as a 'retreat from Pythagoras', therefore, he was hinting at a process of disillusionment every bit as devastating as the loss of his childhood faith in Christianity.

In seeking a solution to the problems raised by the paradox Russell was helped by his old tutor, Alfred North Whitehead, with whom he had agreed to collaborate in the production of a massive work of logic and mathematics that would serve as the second volume not only to *The Principles of Mathematics*, but also to Whitehead's *Treatise on Universal Algebra*. The extraordinarily ambitious aim of this book was to demonstrate the truth of the thesis that mathematics was logic by actually deriving, one by one, the theorems of mathematics from an axiomatic system of logic.

The problem that bedevilled this project from the start was that of deciding what, in the light of Russell's paradox, that system of logic should be. Between 1903 and 1909 Russell struggled with this problem, and in the process abandoned one element after another of the Pythagorean view of logic that lies at the heart of *The Principles of Mathematics*. At an early stage he decided that classes did not, after all, exist. They were 'logical fictions', the appearance of which was generated by the construction of propositional functions. Related to this is Russell's argument in his seminal article 'On denoting' (1905) that what, in *The Principles of Mathematics*, he had called 'denoting concepts' did not exist. Denotation, on Russell's early view, was the logical (rather than linguistic) relation between a concept and an object; characteristic of denotation is that in language it is achieved through descriptions rather than names. For example, 'the next prime after 7' is a concept that denotes the number 11. Such concepts occupy a central place in *The Principles of Mathematics*, because classes are typically identified by denoting phrases ('the class of all men', for example). In seeking to solve the paradox Russell came to the conclusion that one of the central problems was that, in language, it is possible to construct denoting phrases to which no object corresponds, such as 'the present king of France' or, more relevantly, 'the class of all classes that do not belong to themselves'.

The solution presented to this problem in 'On denoting' is characteristically radical. Denoting concepts, Russell now believed, are as illusory as classes, and all denoting phrases are, by themselves, meaningless. Like classes, denoting concepts are logical fictions, and denoting phrases are 'incomplete symbols' that acquire a meaning only in the context of a proposition. According to the celebrated 'theory of descriptions' outlined in 'On denoting', the descriptive phrase 'the present king of France' is meaningless. A proposition which contains it, however, such as 'the present king of France is bald', is not meaningless but false, since, when understood properly, it is not, as appearance would suggest, a single proposition predicating baldness of a non-existent entity; rather it is a conjunction of three propositions:

> The propositional function 'x is at present king of France' is not always false. If the propositional function 'y is at present king of France' is true for any y, then y is identical to x (that is, there is only one present king of France). x is bald.

By means of this rather convoluted analysis, then, 'The present king of France is bald' is shown to be a meaningful, but false, assertion.

Dispensing with classes and denoting concepts was, Russell considered, a large step forward in constructing a logical theory that would withstand the threat posed by the paradox, but it did not, by itself, entirely solve the problem, since, as he discovered at an early stage, a paradox exactly analogous to the one about classes that he had discovered in 1901 can be generated using the notion of a propositional function in place of that of a class. Immediately after finishing 'On denoting' Russell attempted to deal with this problem through the construction of a formal system—to which he gave the name 'substitution theory'—in which there are no propositional functions, but only propositions. In place of the variables characteristic of propositional functions, one would have, in this theory, a technique of substituting one individual for another in propositions that share the same form.

For the first half of 1906 Russell was confident that in the 'substitution theory' he had found the solution to his problem. By the autumn, however, he had rejected it, having discovered that it, too, generated contradictions analogous to the original paradox. His reaction was to develop a theory according to which propositions, like classes and denoting concepts, were 'logical fictions', and the sentences expressing them, like denoting phrases, 'incomplete symbols'. Truth, Russell now maintained, was not a relation between a proposition and a fact, but rather a relation between a judgment and a fact, a judgment being not an abstract Platonic entity (such as he had earlier conceived propositions), but a mental act.

In the following year Russell developed what has become known as the 'ramified theory of types', which he and Whitehead adopted as the basic logical structure of *Principia mathematica*. Whereas the earlier 'simple' theory of types had posited a hierarchy of objects—individuals, classes of individuals, classes of classes of individuals, etc.—the ramified theory establishes a hierarchy of judgments or, more precisely, of 'levels of truth'. The result is a logical theory of dizzying complexity: statements about numbers are reduced to statements about classes, which are, in turn, reduced to the theory of propositional functions, which is, ultimately, grounded in a hierarchy of judgments. Nevertheless, Russell and Whitehead considered themselves to have found the theory they were looking for, and in 1909 the colossal manuscript of *Principia mathematica* was delivered to the Cambridge University Press, to be published in three volumes between 1911 and 1913.

On the day when he delivered it Russell wrote to his friend Helen Flexner: 'I imagine no human being will ever read it through' (Monk, *Spirit*, 194). It is indeed unreadable, but it is nevertheless one of the most impressive intellectual monuments of the twentieth century. To Russell's satisfaction, it demonstrated its central thesis—that mathematics is a branch of logic—but an important question to which it gave only a confused answer is: what is logic? In the decade following the publication of *Principia* Russell was provided with what he came to regard as a definitive answer to this question by his pupil Ludwig Wittgenstein,

an answer that was to complete the 'retreat from Pythagoras'.

The deterioration of his first marriage The personal background to Russell's herculean labours on *Principia mathematica* was a married life that was bleak, joyless, and in the end unbearable. In the years immediately after their marriage, Russell and Alys lived in a small house called The Millhanger in Fernhurst, Sussex, close to where Alys's parents lived. Within a few years, Russell came to loathe Alys's mother, whom he considered vindictive and cruel. Alys, however, to Russell's great irritation, remained steadfastly loyal to her mother and Russell began to seek out the attentions of other women, not least Alys's sister, Mary, to whom he had been attracted even before his marriage. About the time of his visit to Paris in 1900, he fell in love with Evelyn Ada Maud Rice Whitehead, *née* Willoughby-Wade (1865–1950), his colleague's wife, a love which he kept scrupulously hidden. During Lent term 1901 the Russells and Whiteheads lived together in a house in Cambridge, where Russell, while witnessing Evelyn suffering from an angina attack, underwent what he later described as 'a sort of mystic illumination' that, he claimed, transformed him into 'a completely different person' (Russell, *Autobiography*, 1.146). The 'life of intellect tempered by flippancy' into which he had settled suddenly seemed to him unendurable and was replaced by a conviction that 'in human relations one should penetrate to the core of loneliness in each person and speak to that'.

What he meant, he made clear in a letter years later to Ottoline Morrell, was that he was seized with an overwhelming desire to relieve what he considered to be Evelyn Whitehead's loneliness. In summer 1901 Russell announced that he could no longer bear to live close to Alys's mother, and he and Alys moved into the Whiteheads' home in Grantchester. There, in new year 1902, Russell in another moment of sudden illumination came to realize that he no longer loved his wife. Though he did not then tell her this, his attitude towards her changed to one of coldness. The effect on Alys was devastating and, after falling into a deep depression, she moved to Brighton to take a 'rest cure', while Russell remained with the Whiteheads. When Alys returned to Fernhurst in the summer, she asked Russell directly whether he still loved her, and it was then that he told her that his love was dead and could never be revived. He and she could stay married, he said, and they could live together, but he no longer wished to share a bedroom with her. In a rather unsettling diary entry of the time, Russell describes how, that night, he listened to 'her loud, heart-rending sobs, while I worked at my desk next door', and how, by keeping her hopes of reconciliation 'alive but unfulfilled', he considered himself to have 'effected a great moral reformation in her' (Russell, *Collected Papers*, 12.22–3).

For the next nine years Russell and Alys lived together in a dreadful hollow shell of a marriage, during which time Alys never gave up hope that Russell's love for her would revive, while Russell grew increasingly cold and irritable towards her. Russell's absorption in abstract work provided some kind of consolation from this wretched state of affairs, as did a semi-religious philosophy of life he outlined in an unpublished manuscript called 'The pilgrimage of life', according to which wisdom consists in pursuing the truth, even though an understanding of the truth is not compatible with happiness. The same thought is expressed in 'The free man's worship', which was published in 1903 and which became one of his best-known and most anthologized essays.

In spring 1905 Russell and Alys moved to Bagley Wood, just south of Oxford, where the unhappiness of their lives became so acute that both of them, at different times, spoke of death as a welcome relief. Four years later, after finishing *Principia mathematica*, Russell devoted himself with great energy to the campaign for re-election of his local Liberal MP, Philip Morrell, during which he became entranced by Morrell's wife, Lady Ottoline Violet Anne *Morrell (1873–1938). As a result of his campaigning, Russell, in 1910, was asked to consider becoming the Liberal candidate for the constituency of Bedford. The idea that he might, at this stage in his life, abandon his philosophical career in favour of politics was not as surprising as it might at first appear. He did not at this time have an academic position, and, feeling intellectually worn out by the effort of finishing *Principia mathematica*, he was tempted to change tack and become a member of parliament. He had, after all, stood for parliament before, in May 1907, when he had been a women's suffrage candidate (though, admittedly, with no danger of actually being elected) at a by-election for the Wimbledon seat. After careful deliberation, however, he declined the offer of the Bedford candidature, and chose instead to accept an offer from Trinity College, Cambridge, of a five-year lectureship. One of the attractions of this was that it would allow him and Alys to live separately, he in Nevile's Court and she in Fernhurst.

The impact of Ottoline Morrell and Ludwig Wittgenstein Less than a year into his five-year lectureship Russell began an affair with Ottoline Morrell, which transformed his personality and his career. He left Alys, and, for a few years, made his love for Ottoline the very centre of his life. In place of the contemplation of abstract truth, he now substituted an equally intense absorption in his own emotional life, and in place of the austere ethic of 'The free man's worship' he substituted a rather different (though closely related) kind of mysticism—expressed in an unpublished book called 'Prisons'—according to which each of us is offered the chance of escaping the prison of our selves, first through love of another human being and then through contemplation of the infinite. He also, partly under Ottoline's influence, largely lost interest in technical philosophy and began to write in a different, more accessible style. Through writing a best-selling introductory book called *The Problems of Philosophy* (1912) Russell discovered that he had a gift for writing on difficult subjects for the general public and began increasingly to address his work to that public rather than to the tiny handful of people capable of understanding *Principia mathematica*.

In the year in which he began his affair with Lady Ottoline, Russell met Ludwig Wittgenstein, who arrived in Cambridge to study logic with Russell. Fired with intense enthusiasm for the subject, Wittgenstein made great progress, and within a year Russell began to look to him to provide the next big step in philosophy and to defer to him on questions of logic. Wittgenstein's own work, however, eventually published in 1922 as *Tractatus logico-philosophicus*, undermined the entire approach to logic that had inspired Russell's great contributions to the philosophy of mathematics. Russell became persuaded by it that there were, after all, no 'truths' of logic at all, that logic consisted entirely of tautologies. Previously he had believed that logic investigated certain abstract and general features of reality; now he was convinced that it was concerned only with the structure of language. This was to be the final step in the 'retreat from Pythagoras' and a further incentive for Russell to abandon technical philosophy in favour of other things.

Not that this abandonment happened suddenly; rather, throughout the period from 1911 to 1914, Russell's interests swung pendulum-like between technical philosophy and his love for Ottoline, the ebb and flow of these vacillations coinciding more or less with the turbulent course of his relationship with Ottoline. What he was singularly unable to sustain, however, was an interest in the question about the nature of logic that *Principia mathematica* had left unsettled. In 1912 he began a paper called 'What is logic?' in which he made a half-hearted attempt to defend and elucidate the idea that the objects of logic are 'forms', but, discouraged and dissatisfied by his inability to arrive at a coherent view, he left the paper unfinished. After that he felt inclined to leave the question to Wittgenstein. In 1913 he began a large book called 'The theory of knowledge', in which he committed himself both to the view (of which he had become persuaded by Wittgenstein) that there were no such things as logical objects and to the apparently incompatible claim that there had to be 'something which seems fitly described as "acquaintance with logical objects"' (Russell, 'Theory of knowledge', 97). This book, too, was abandoned after its theory of judgment—a refinement of the theory at the heart of *Principia*—was severely criticized by Wittgenstein.

These abortive attempts to write something on the problem he considered to be the most pressing philosophical question of the time induced in Russell something of a crisis of self-confidence. In any case he was not entirely sure that he wanted any longer to devote himself to logic. 'Oddly enough,' he wrote to his friend Lucy Donnelly in January 1912, 'I have developed a certain nausea for the subtleties and distinctions that made up good philosophy; I should like to write things of human interest, like bad philosophers, only without being bad' (Monk, *Spirit*, 245). In pursuit of this aim he adapted some of the material he had written for 'Prisons' into an article entitled 'The essence of religion', which aroused such vehement criticisms from Wittgenstein that Russell quickly lost faith in it. He then tried his hand at fiction and produced an autobiographical short story called 'The Perplexities of John

Forstice', which, like so much he wrote during these years, he left unpublished.

By summer 1913 a combination of Wittgenstein's attacks on his philosophical work and the frustrations of his largely unreciprocated passion for Ottoline had left Russell close to a nervous breakdown. In the autumn, however, Wittgenstein left Cambridge for Norway, and Russell and Ottoline agreed to see less of each other. Russell's sanity and self-respect were further restored by a meeting with the novelist Joseph Conrad (for whom Russell had an almost limitless admiration), which led to a friendship between the two that was of immense importance to Russell, if not to Conrad. Turning from logic to epistemology, and with Wittgenstein out of the way, Russell was finally able to produce some publishable philosophy. In a series of essays and a book entitled *Our Knowledge of the External World*, he expounded a form of empiricism according to which the external world is a 'construction' out of sense-data. In spring 1914 Russell travelled to Harvard to take up a visiting lectureship and to deliver the Lowell lectures, in preparation for which he had written *Our Knowledge of the External World*. While at Harvard he befriended T. S. Eliot, who was among his students and who, in his poem 'Mr Apollinax', drew a vivid and memorable impression of both Russell and of the effect he had on Harvard society.

After his time at Harvard came to an end Russell visited other American universities and, while in Chicago, met a professor's daughter called Helen Dudley, with whom he spent a night, after which he took the extraordinary step of inviting her to England to become his wife. The emergence of a rival seems to have rekindled Ottoline's passion, and when Russell returned home in June she set out, successfully, to win him back. The unfortunate Miss Dudley set sail for England on 3 August, but by that time Russell had lost any interest he might have had in becoming her husband.

The First World War On the day after Helen Dudley's ship set sail from New York, Great Britain declared war on Germany. As jubilant crowds gathered in London to celebrate the news, Russell and Ottoline walked among them despairingly, clinging to each other for comfort and support.

At the outbreak of the First World War, Russell became a more or less full-time political agitator, demonstrating the courage in resisting the state which was characteristic of his political activities throughout his long life and which commanded admiration even among those who disagreed with his politics. During the first year of the war his energies were directed at denouncing what he regarded as the betrayal of liberalism by Asquith's government in committing Britain to a war against Germany. His view, shared by the Union of Democratic Control (UDC), of which he became a member, was that the foreign policy which had led to the war was fundamentally misguided and had been constructed without appeal to popular or even parliamentary opinion. In a UDC pamphlet called *War, the Offspring of Fear*, he described the war as a 'great race-conflict' between the Teutonic and Slavic peoples, in which Britain's interests lay in supporting the Germans and Austrians rather than the Russians.

In an article called 'The ethics of war' which he published in the new year of 1915, Russell made clear that his objections to the war did not rest on any general pacifism. He did not think war was always wrong. Indeed, the position he took justifies a surprising amount of bloodshed. His general principle was that, if a war furthered civilization, it was justifiable, but otherwise not. Thus wars of colonization and wars of principle (in defence of, for example, democracy) were generally justifiable, and wars of self-defence sometimes so (when, for example, they were fought against inferior civilizations), but wars of prestige—of which the war against Germany was an example—were hardly ever justifiable. If attacked by a civilized country, Russell suggested, the best response would be one of non-resistance, since defeat in such a war would hurt only one's pride, and would not threaten one's civilization.

Shortly after writing this article Russell conceived the ambitious idea of writing a large, two-volume work on the history, principles, and practice of foreign policy, the first volume of which would be a study of how the Liberal government elected in 1906 had betrayed its supporters through its construction of a policy designed to lead to war with Germany, while the second volume would contain a more general account of European history since 1870, pointing to the need for some kind of international reform of diplomatic relations. In pursuing this project Russell enlisted the help of Irene Cooper-Willis, with whom he shared a curiously tepid flirtation which was brought to an end when she rebuffed his advances. After this he lost interest in the project and the proposed two-volume work never appeared, though some of the material gathered for it was used in a booklet called *The Policy of the Entente, 1904–1914* that Russell published at the end of 1915.

Russell, like most people at the time, expected that the war would be over in a few months. When this did not happen and the war dragged on, its horror escalating at every turn, Russell's concerns shifted from the analysis of foreign policy to the more fundamental question of how Western civilization might be rebuilt after the war had all but destroyed it. To concentrate on this question Russell took two terms' leave from his academic duties at Cambridge. After meeting D. H. Lawrence and being impressed by his psychological insight, he decided to spend the bulk of this time on a joint project with Lawrence in which the two of them would think through anew the nature and function of all social and political institutions—the state, marriage, morality, property, and so on—with the aim of laying the foundations for a happier and more peaceful world. These ideas they would deliver in a series of public lectures from which, they hoped, would arise an exciting new social movement. When, however, Russell showed Lawrence the synopsis of the lectures he intended to deliver, the two discovered that they had been at cross purposes and there followed an acrimonious falling-out, with Russell accusing Lawrence of having no mind and

Lawrence accusing Russell of having nothing but a mind. Russell went ahead with his lectures, which were a great success and were published as *Principles of Social Reconstruction* (1916), a book Russell continued throughout his life to regard as the 'least unsatisfactory' expression of his 'own personal religion'.

In January 1916 the British government, fearing that the war would be lost through lack of available men, passed the Military Service Bill, which introduced compulsory conscription for all single men aged between eighteen and forty-one. Russell reacted to this with outraged horror and he threw himself with great passion into the campaigns led by the No-Conscription Fellowship to defend the rights of conscientious objectors. In May 1916 Russell's leave of absence from Trinity ended and he resumed his lectures. Within a few weeks, however, he was summoned to court to be charged with impeding recruiting and discipline on account of a leaflet he had written in support of the No-Conscription Fellowship. He was found guilty and fined £100, as a result of which he was sacked from his lectureship.

Now without an academic position, Russell during the following year continued to give public lectures, outlining his increasingly radical political stance. In *Political Ideals* in 1917 he announced himself a supporter of the guild socialist movement, and when the Russian Revolution broke out he greeted it with unrestrained enthusiasm. In June 1917 Russell spoke at a conference of revolutionary sympathizers in Leeds and supported its resolution calling for the establishment throughout Britain of Soviet-style workers' councils. In the following month, however, he was shocked at the violence he witnessed at a meeting in London, where the attempt to elect such a workers' council led to a riot, after which Russell decided to retire from politics and return to philosophy.

In autumn and winter 1917–18 Russell gave two sets of public lectures on philosophy, the first on mathematical logic and the second on the 'philosophy of logical atomism', both of which showed a determination to return to the issues he had abandoned under the impact of Wittgenstein's criticisms in 1913. 'The chief thesis I have to maintain', Russell announced in these lectures, 'is the legitimacy of analysis' (*Lectures on Logical Atomism*, 49). The kind of analysis he had in mind is one which seeks to understand the forms of facts, such forms being understood as very general and abstract features of the objective world.

During a rare break from philosophical thinking and writing during this period Russell wrote an article for *The Tribune* in which he alleged that American troops would be employed in Britain to break up strikes. It was a foolish and unfounded suggestion, for which Russell was again taken to court, this time charged with prejudicing Britain's relations with its ally, an offence for which he received a six-month prison sentence. While in prison Russell worked his lectures on mathematical logic into a book called *Introduction to Mathematical Philosophy*, which was intended to serve as a popular introduction to the system of *Principia mathematica*. He also began a study of

behaviouristic psychology which was to influence much of the work that he produced after the war, most notably his book *The Analysis of Mind* (1921).

Second marriage On Russell's release from prison in September 1918 (just two months before the end of the war), his life, both professionally and personally, was in an unsettled state. During the war, after Helen Dudley had returned to America, his relations with Ottoline had come to an end and several affairs—including one especially tangled one with T. S. Eliot's wife, Vivien (1888–1947), a writer—had come to nothing, he fell deeply in love with the actress and peace campaigner Lady Constance Mary Malleson (1895–1975), to whom he always referred to by her stage name, Colette O'Niel. He found Colette's commitment to sexual freedom, however, unbearable, and was thrown into fits of jealous rage whenever she was—or he imagined her to be—with another man.

Seeking refuge from this emotional turmoil, Russell moved into Garsington, the country home of Ottoline Morrell, with whom he remained friends even after they had ceased to be lovers; there, for a few months, he concentrated on philosophy. During this time he prepared a set of lectures that became *The Analysis of Mind*, and wrote a long paper for the Aristotelian Society called 'On propositions', in which he rejected his earlier theory of judgment in favour of a causal theory of meaning that seeks to understand the nature of propositions through an analysis of the events in the world and in our minds that cause them and are caused by them.

These ideas were elaborated in Russell's series of eight lectures on the analysis of mind in the early summer of 1919, and expanded still further in *The Analysis of Mind*, which was published two years later. Underpinning Russell's causal theory of meaning was a metaphysic that he (following William James) called 'neutral monism', which asserts that the basic 'stuff' from which the world is constructed is neither mental nor physical but something neutral between the two. According to this view 'mental' events such as perceptions, thoughts, and beliefs are spatially located inside our heads and are caused by 'physical' events taking place in world, the apparent difference in kind between the two being an illusion. In later years Russell abandoned neutral monism, in favour of a curious combination of physicalism and solipsism (a mixture of Berkeley and modern physics, he liked to say), according to which, as he put it in *My Philosophical Development* (1959): 'we *can* witness or observe what goes on in our heads and … we cannot witness or observe anything else at all' (Russell, *Philosophical Development*, 26).

At the time of giving these lectures Russell found a new lover: Dora Black (1894–1986) [*see* Russell, Dora Winifred], a 25-year-old Cambridge graduate with left-wing political opinions and a forthright disregard for conventional morality. When his lectures were finished in June, he took a three-month holiday in Dorset, during which he was joined at various (and sometimes overlapping) occasions by both Colette and Dora. In November he received an invitation from Trinity to be reinstated as a lecturer; after his experiences of public lectures and freelance writing, however, he was unsure whether he could bear to return to academic life.

At the end of 1919 Russell, accompanied by Dora, travelled to The Hague to meet Wittgenstein in order to go through the text of *Tractatus logico-philosophicus*, Wittgenstein having sent a copy of the manuscript to Russell in the summer. The meeting proved an important turning point in Russell's life since he became persuaded by Wittgenstein to adopt a linguistic view of logic that undermined not only the view of his early work on the philosophy of mathematics, but also the view he had been expounding in his lectures since 1917. Logic, Russell was now convinced (and remained so for the rest of his life), is concerned not with objectively existing forms, but only with symbols. To understand a logical proposition is not to grasp an abstract truth, but rather merely to understand the meanings of words. On accepting this view, Russell considered his 'retreat from Pythagoras' to be complete, and the moral he drew from it is that neither logic nor mathematics (since he continued to believe that mathematics was logic) had the philosophical significance he had previously ascribed to them.

In spring 1920 Russell visited Russia as part of a trade delegation. What he hoped to find there was a socialist state that could serve as a model for the West, but, to his great disillusionment, what he found instead was a cruel and despotic régime. The visit left him with a deep and abiding loathing for Soviet communism which he expressed in *The Practice and Theory of Bolshevism* (1921), a brave and penetrating analysis of the situation in Russia that, Russell knew, would be welcomed by his political opponents and hated by his political friends.

Waiting for Russell on his return from Russia was an invitation to spend a year in China as a visiting lecturer at the University of Peking. Russell at once accepted, and wrote to Trinity asking for a year's leave of absence before his resuming his lectureship there. In fact, he never did resume his Trinity post, since, while he and Dora were in China together, Russell wrote resigning his lectureship. Shortly afterwards, to Russell's unfettered delight, Dora became pregnant. As soon as they returned home in summer 1921 Russell obtained a divorce from Alys and married Dora, on 27 September 1921, just in time to secure the legitimacy of his son, John Conrad, who was born in November.

With his second marriage and the birth of his son, Russell's life entered a new phase. In order to provide for his family (a daughter, Katherine, was added in 1923), Russell produced a staggering amount of journalism, published a series of pot-boiling books, and underwent several gruelling lecture tours of the United States. In the process the quality of his writing inevitably suffered and, to the dismay of those who admired his early work in philosophy, he frequently published views on subjects about which he knew very little and opinions which were hasty, ill-considered, and contradictory.

Russell was aware of this falling-off of standards but, for a while, he did not mind it, so long as the commissions for his work kept arriving, which they rarely failed to do. Not that he wrote entirely for money. He was also concerned to influence public opinion. He and Dora saw themselves as leaders of a progressive socialist movement that was stridently anti-clerical, openly defiant of conventional sexual morality, and dedicated to the reform of education. They did not just write about these things: they also sought to influence policy through political participation. In 1922 and 1923 Russell stood for parliament as a Labour candidate for Chelsea, and the following year Dora did likewise. They were also active in many political campaigns, including those for women's rights and for birth control. However, in the pursuit of these aims, Russell often blinded himself to how second-rate his work on political themes actually was.

The lectures and journalism Russell and Dora wrote while in China and soon afterwards formed a jointly published book, *The Prospects of Industrial Civilization* (1922), which presents a view that Russell repeated many times in many places afterwards, namely that the establishment of international socialism is necessary to save civilization from destroying itself through war. The same message also underlies *The Problem of China*, published in the same year, in which Russell collected the various articles he had published expressing his love of the Chinese people and his desire to see the more industrially advanced countries learning from them rather than destroying them. In 1923 Russell's gift for the lucid explanation of technical ideas was put to good use in *The ABC of Atoms*, which he followed two years later with the more popular *The ABC of Relativity*.

Still more popular were *On Education* (1926), *Marriage and Morals* (1929), and *The Conquest of Happiness* (1930), all of which enjoyed a wide sale and helped to establish Russell in the eyes of the general public as a philosopher with important things to say about the moral, political, and social issues of the day. Meanwhile, his public lecture 'Why I am not a Christian', delivered in 1926 and reprinted many times, became a *locus classicus* of atheistic rationalism.

In the midst of all this Russell managed for short periods to dedicate himself to technical philosophy, but the results—the second edition of *Principia mathematica* in 1925 and *The Analysis of Matter* in 1927—failed to satisfy many. In the revised edition of *Principia* Russell introduced a new system of logic, influenced by both Wittgenstein and Frank Ramsey, which, however, was unable to do the job required of it. *The Analysis of Matter* presents a very sophisticated theory of 'structural realism', the fundamental ideas of which were decisively refuted in a devastating critique written by the mathematician M. A. Newman.

In 1927 Russell and Dora set up their own school, Beacon Hill, as a pioneering experiment in primary education, to pay for which Russell undertook several lucrative but exhausting lecture tours of the United States of America. During these years Russell's second marriage came under increasing strain, partly because of overwork but chiefly because Dora chose to have two children with another man, whom she insisted on raising alongside John and

Kate. In 1932 Russell left Dora for a young Oxford undergraduate called Patricia Helen (known by her friends and relations as Peter) Spence, and for the next three years his life was dominated by an extraordinarily acrimonious and complicated divorce from Dora, which was finally granted in 1935.

Return to philosophy In the following year, on 18 January 1936, Russell married Peter, who was the daughter of Harry Evelyn Spence. In 1937 they had a son, Conrad. By this time his faith in many of the ideals that he and Dora had championed together had been severely weakened and he no longer felt able to speak with dogmatic certainty about education, marriage, morals, and the pursuit of happiness. Worn out by years of frenetic public activity and tired of writing pot-boilers, he longed to return to serious intellectual work. For a while he considered becoming a full-time (though non-academic) historian, but after the lukewarm reception given to *Freedom and Organization* (1934), his study of European history from 1814 to 1914, he abandoned the idea. In 1936 he published *Which Way to Peace?*, a plea for Britain to avoid war with Germany, which argued that the best way of dealing with the Nazi threat would be to pursue a policy of complete non-resistance. Understandably, Russell later became embarrassed by this book and never allowed it to be reprinted.

On the death of his brother Frank in 1931, Russell inherited the family earldom, and in 1937 he paid homage to his parents by editing, together with his third wife, *The Amberley Papers*, a two-volume collection of unremarkable, and surprisingly dull, family correspondence. Though he was encouraged by, among others, Beatrice Webb to use his title to promote the Labour cause in the House of Lords, he chose not to, preferring instead to abandon politics altogether in favour of a return to academic philosophy.

In 1935 Russell wrote 'On order in time', a formidably technical paper that demonstrated that, at the age of sixty-two and with a long break from academic life, he had not lost the ability to wrestle with abstruse and abstract issues. In the following year he published 'The limits of empiricism', which showed him for the first time in years engaging with the work of contemporary philosophers, in particular the work inspired by the later Wittgenstein. On the basis of these and other publications (including a revised edition of *The Principles of Mathematics*, published in 1937), Russell felt able, despite his advanced years, to apply for academic posts in philosophy. After being rebuffed by Princeton and Cambridge, he was invited in 1937 to give a series of lectures at Oxford called 'Words and facts'. Though this did not, as he had hoped, lead to the offer of a permanent post, it helped to bring him back into academic circles, and for the year 1937–8 he was elected president of the Aristotelian Society, delivering as his presidential address a paper called 'On verification'. In this, as in a paper delivered to the Aristotelian Society in the summer of 1938 called 'The relevance of psychology to logic', Russell defended the thesis that all knowledge has,

as its foundation, 'basic propositions'; that is, propositions that are derived, not from other propositions but from direct experience. These propositions, Russell argued, cannot be shown to be true, but it is nevertheless, psychologically, impossible to doubt them.

By the time he delivered the second of these papers, Russell had at last succeeded in securing an academic appointment, albeit a temporary one: a one-year visiting professorship at the University of Chicago, starting in 1938. Russell hoped that it would be renewed but, despite the success of his seminars, which were attended by many notable philosophers, including Rudolf Carnap, Russell was obliged in 1939, at the age of sixty-seven, to seek work elsewhere. This time he found a three-year appointment at the University of California, Los Angeles, but within a few months of taking up this position he was applying for other jobs, dissatisfied with both the standard of his students and the autocracy of the university's management. He hoped to find something on the east coast, and was much gratified when, in 1940, he was invited to deliver the prestigious William James lectures at Harvard, lectures which were published as *An Inquiry into Meaning and Truth*. In the same year he was offered and accepted a professorship at the College of the City of New York, but in a much publicized case he was prevented from taking this up because of objections to the views on sex and marriage that he had published in the 1920s. He was then saved from financial ruin by securing a position teaching the history of philosophy at the Barnes Foundation in Philadelphia. Though he soon fell out with the notoriously difficult Dr Barnes and was sacked, Russell was able to turn these lectures into *History of Western Philosophy*, which proved to be a best-seller and was for many years the main source of his income.

Post-war political activism Russell's life in the United States during the Second World War was extraordinarily difficult, not only because he was unable to find an employer with whom he got on well, but also because his third marriage deteriorated into bitter acrimony. Partly under the strain of the public controversies in which Russell became embroiled and the consequent threat of financial ruin, and partly also because of what she perceived as his coldness towards her, Peter developed a ferocious hatred of Russell and became increasingly bad-tempered with both him and his children John and Kate, who had come to live with their father at the outbreak of war. By 1943 family life had become all but unendurable.

In the midst of this gloom Russell, to his great delight, received an invitation to return to Cambridge to take up a five-year fellowship at Trinity College, beginning in autumn 1944. This allowed him to write what became his last major contribution to philosophy, *Human Knowledge: its Scope and Application*, published in 1949, in which he developed at length his view that certainty in human knowledge was impossible and that the best to be hoped for was the probable truth afforded us by what he called 'postulates of scientific inference'. At Cambridge during this time Russell was dismayed to discover how far he had fallen out of favour among the younger generation of

British philosophers, for whom Wittgenstein was now the greatest influence. To his great chagrin, *Human Knowledge* was reviewed without any great respect. In the 1950s Russell hit back with a series of polemical attacks on 'Oxford ordinary language philosophy', but these served only to widen the gulf between him and the leading philosophers of the day.

Once again the pendulum between politics and philosophy swung the other way and Russell devoted most of his last years to political campaigning, For a short period between 1945 and 1950 he, for once in his life, found himself in favour with the authorities, and he received many official tributes, including membership of the Order of Merit in 1949 and the Nobel prize for literature in 1950. During this period his political views were belligerently anti-communist, and on several occasions he urged upon the Western powers a policy of threatening Russia with atomic bombardment if they resisted the call to submit to international authority. So embarrassed did he later become by this advice that he later denied having made it, despite the public record to the contrary.

In 1949 Peter finally left Russell, taking their young son Conrad with her. From 1950 to 1953 Russell shared a house in Richmond with his son John, who, by this time, had a wife and three children. During these years Russell led a quiet life, and, forsaking both philosophy and politics, dedicated himself to literary writing, first his autobiography and then two collections of short stories, *Satan in the Suburbs* (1953) and *Nightmares of Eminent Persons* (1954). His autobiography—or, at any rate, its first volume—is widely, and justly, considered a masterpiece, but not so his short stories, which have been generally greeted, even by his admirers, with an uncomfortable and puzzled silence. Extracts from the autobiography were broadcast as radio talks and published as *Portraits from Memory* in 1956, and three years later Russell published a separate intellectual autobiography, *My Philosophical Development*, which provides a fascinating account of his 'retreat from Pythagoras' and the impact Wittgenstein made on his philosophical career.

Family life in Richmond, which had been fairly happy for the first years or so, came to an abrupt end in 1953 when John and his wife Susan walked out of the house, never to return. In the previous year, on 15 December 1952, Russell had married, as his fourth wife, Edith (*d.* 1978), daughter of Edward Bronson Finch, of New York, and at last found marital happiness, somewhat alloyed by the sudden responsibility of caring for John's three daughters. At the end of 1954 John was diagnosed as schizophrenic, after which Russell had almost nothing to do with him and fought a bitter legal battle with Dora—horribly reminiscent for all concerned of their divorce battles of the 1930s—to keep control of the three girls. In 1956 he moved to north Wales, taking the girls with him, hoping to provide for them the kind of stable family life that John had been so manifestly unable to provide. He was unable, however, to prevent a series of heartbreaking tragedies: John never regained his mind, Susan became insane and spent most of the rest of her life in psychiatric care, and,

of the three granddaughters, one committed suicide, one became schizophrenic, and the third left England for New Mexico, hoping to leave all traces of her Russell background behind.

The abrupt end of the Richmond household coincided with a dramatic re-entry into public life, heralded by Russell's powerful 1954 radio broadcast, 'Man's peril', in which he argued that the Bikini H-bomb tests illustrated the need for war itself to be abolished. This led the following year to the 'Einstein–Russell manifesto', which called upon scientists throughout the world to testify to the futility of attempting to 'win' a nuclear war. The Pugwash movement (called after the place of its first conference) of scientists which attempted to carry out this manifesto elected Russell as its president, but after a few years he began to think more direct action was necessary to avert global catastrophe, and in 1958 he became one of the founders of the Campaign for Nuclear Disarmament, backing its calls for British neutrality in *Common Sense and Nuclear Warfare* (1959).

In 1960 Russell became convinced by the American radical Ralph Schoenman that mass civil disobedience was required to change the British government's policy on nuclear weapons, and together they formed the Committee of 100, which organized well-publicized mass campaigns of illegal protest activities designed to have as many people imprisoned as possible. One of those imprisoned was Russell himself, who in September 1961, at eighty-nine, was sentenced to two months (later shortened to a week) in Brixton gaol. The sight of the frail but defiant and distinguished philosopher being sent to prison was a major propaganda coup for the anti-nuclear movement, and throughout the 1960s the image of Russell—impossibly old, white-haired, small, and bony, his jaw jutting out in implacable defiance—became a familiar and popular icon of political protest.

In the following year Russell, aided by Schoenman, made an attempt to intervene personally in the Cuban missile crisis by sending urgent telegrams to all the world leaders involved. In *Unarmed Victory* (1963) the (surely false) impression is given that these telegrams played some role in the ending of the crisis and, encouraged by Schoenman, Russell began to imagine himself as a force to be reckoned with in international politics, a fantasy which fuelled the creation in 1963 of the Bertrand Russell Peace Foundation. The credibility of this latter foundation as a peacemaking organization was undermined by the intemperate and belligerent nature of its statements. In these, using the language and the slogans of Trotskyist revolutionaries, Russell announced his support for Che Guevara's call for a series of guerrilla wars in order to defeat 'US imperialism'. The international war crimes tribunal organized by the foundation in 1967 was similarly compromised, as was Russell's last book, *War Crimes in Vietnam*, a series of articles that it is practically impossible to believe were written by Russell himself.

In 1969 Russell finally broke with Schoenman, but he was by that time very frail, and on 2 February 1970, a few months before his ninety-eighth birthday, he died of acute bronchitis at his home, Plas Penrhyn, Penrhyndeu-draeth, Merioneth.

Historical significance When he died Russell was better known as an anti-war campaigner than as a philosopher of mathematics. At this distance, however, it is possible to see that it is principally for his great contributions to philosophy that he will be remembered and honoured by future generations. In some respects, as Russell himself often lamented, his philosophical work was a failure. He failed to find what he had set out to find—a solid basis for certain, indubitable knowledge—and he failed, too, to demonstrate that mathematics was but a branch of logic. However, in searching for these things he left a legacy that has profoundly influenced the way in which philosophy is pursued, particularly in the English-speaking countries.

In its use of techniques borrowed from mathematical logic, its concern to identify the 'logical form' of linguistic expressions hidden by 'surface' grammatical structures, and its conception of itself as a quasi-technical discipline analogous to scientific enquiry, analytic philosophy at the close of the twentieth century probably owes more to Russell than to any other twentieth-century philosopher. The Cambridge philosopher Frank Ramsey summed up the attitude to Russell's chief contribution to philosophy that has remained prevalent in the profession when he described the theory of descriptions as a paradigm of philosophy.

Far less enduring have been Russell's contributions to epistemology. The 'neutral monism' espoused in *The Analysis of Mind* still enjoys some support among contemporary philosophers of mind, but the notion that the external world is a 'construction' out of sense-data and the claim that all the objects of our knowledge are literally 'inside our heads' have largely fallen out of favour.

Some of Russell's popular works, in particular *On Education*, *Marriage and Morals*, and *The Conquest of Happiness*, continue to sell well, as do *The Problems of Philosophy* and *History of Western Philosophy*, but most of his writings on political themes are now out of print and are likely to remain so. *The Principles of Mathematics* and 'On denoting', however, continue to be studied and debated by successive generations of philosophers, and it is as the author of these that Russell's permanent place in the history of ideas is assured.   RAY MONK

Sources B. Russell, *Autobiography*, 1 (1967) · B. Russell, *Autobiography*, 2 (1968) · B. Russell, *Autobiography*, 3 (1969) · B. Russell, *My philosophical development* (1959) · B. Russell, *Collected papers*, 1 (1983) · B. Russell, *Collected papers*, 12 (1985) · P. A. Schilpp, *The philosophy of Bertrand Russell* (1944) · R. Monk, *Bertrand Russell: the spirit of solitude* (1996) · R. Monk, *Bertrand Russell: the ghost of madness* (2000) · Burke, *Peerage* (2000) **Archives** BL, corresp. with Society of Authors, Add. MS 63323 · BLPES, diary of visit to Berlin · McMaster University, Hamilton, Ontario, William Ready division of archives and research collections, corresp. and papers · Wellcome L., papers relating to Family Planning Association | BL, corresp. with Marie Stopes, Add. MS 53556 · Bodl. Oxf., corresp. with Gilbert Murray · Bodl. Oxf., letters to Lord Ponsonby · CAC Cam., corresp. with Lord Gladwyn · CUL, letters to G. E. Moore · Cumbria AS, Carlisle, letters to Catherine Marshall and papers relating to No Conscription Fellowship · Harvard U., Houghton L., letters to R. C. Marsh · JRL, letters to the *Manchester Guardian* · King's AC Cam., letters to J. M. Keynes · Labour History Archive and Study Centre, Manchester, corresp. with R. Palme Dutt · McMaster University, Hamilton, Ontario, William Ready division of archives and research collections, letters to Constance Malleson · Norfolk RO, corresp. with H. W. Massingham · Rice University, Houston, Texas, Woodson Research Center, corresp. with Sir Julian Huxley · U. Newcastle, Robinson L., corresp. with C. P. Trevelyan | FILM BFI NFTVA, 'Reputations' (2 parts), BBC2, May 1997 · BFI NFTVA, current affairs footage · BFI NFTVA, 'Wise Elders', 1953; 'Reputations', BBC1, 28 May 1997, BBC 2, 4 June 1997; current affairs footage; documentary footage; news footage; recorded lectures | SOUND BL NSA, 'Speaking personally', 11 April 1961, T7786/01 · BL NSA, 'Three passions of Bertrand Russell', BBC, 16 March 1967, M1269WC1 · BL NSA, 'Bertrand Russell', BBC Radio 4, 4 April 1970, T3645WC1 · BL NSA, 'Passionate involvement: Bertrand Russell and the 20th century', BBC Radio 4, 14 April 1970, NP1500W, P501WC1 · BL NSA, 'Bertrand Russell: a reassessment', BBC Radio 4, 3 June 1981, T2790W · BL NSA, 'Bertrand Russell', 4 Nov 1992, C125/226 BD2 · BL NSA, documentary recordings · BL NSA, oral history interviews · BL NSA, recorded lectures [Reith lectures] · BL NSA, recorded talk **Likenesses** R. Fry, oils, *c*.1925, NPG · E. L. Edwards, bust, 1953 · J. Epstein, bust, 1953 · I. Kar, photograph, 1953, NPG [*see illus.*] · P. Halsman, photograph, 1958, NPG; repro. in R. W. Clark, *The life of Bertrand Russell* (1975) · L. Bassingthwaighte, oils, 1969 · D. Griffiths, oils, 1969 · M. Quinton, bust, 1980, Red Lion Square, London · W. Rothenstein, drawing, repro. in K. Matthews, *British philosophers* (1943) **Wealth at death** £69,243: probate, 23 Oct 1970, *CGPLA Eng. & Wales*

Russell, Sir Charles, third baronet (1826–1883), army officer, was born on 22 June 1826, the son of Sir Henry Russell, second baronet (*d.* 1852), of Swallowfield, the resident at Hyderabad, and his second wife, Marie Clotilde (*d.* 1872), daughter of Benoit Mottet de la Fontaine. Sir Henry *Russell (1751–1836) was his grandfather. After education at Eton College, he was commissioned ensign in the 35th foot on 25 August 1843, became lieutenant on 9 June 1846, and served with his regiment in Mauritius. In 1847 he exchanged into the Grenadier Guards, and on 13 September 1853 became lieutenant and captain. He succeeded to the baronetcy on 19 April 1852.

In 1854 Russell went to the Crimea with the 3rd battalion, was at the battle of the Alma, and served through the siege of Sevastopol. During the latter part of it he was deputy assistant quartermaster-general to the 1st division. He received the brevet rank of major (2 November 1855), the Légion d'honneur (knight), and the Mejidiye (fifth class). In 1857 he was among the first recipients of the Victoria Cross, for bravery at the battle of Inkerman.

Russell became captain and lieutenant-colonel on 23 April 1858, and retired on 13 June 1868. On 4 July 1877 he was appointed honorary colonel of the 23rd Middlesex volunteers. He was a JP and deputy lieutenant for Berkshire, and a Conservative MP for that county from July 1865 to November 1868, and for Westminster from 1874 to 1882. He died at his residence, Swallowfield Park, near Reading, on 14 April 1883. He was unmarried, and was succeeded by his brother George.

E. M. LLOYD, *rev.* JAMES LUNT

Sources A. W. Kinglake, *The invasion of the Crimea*, [new edn], 6 (1877) · *The Times* (16 April 1883) · J. Foster, *The peerage, baronetage, and knightage of the British empire for 1883*, 2 [1883] · F. W. Hamilton,

The origin and history of the first or grenadier guards, 3 (1874) • C. Hibbert, *The destruction of Lord Raglan* [1961]

Archives Bodl. Oxf., corresp. and papers relating mainly to investments for development of guano in Peru

Likenesses Ape [C. Pellegrini], caricature, watercolour study, NPG; repro. in *VF* (2 Feb 1878) • L. W. Desanges, oils, Grenadier Guards, London

Wealth at death £39,433 10s. 10d.: probate, 13 Sept 1883, *CGPLA Eng. & Wales*

Russell, Sir Charles, first baronet (1863–1928), lawyer, was born on 8 July 1863, probably in London, the second of five sons and third of ten children of Charles Arthur *Russell (1832–1900) and his wife, Ellen Mulholland (1836–1918) and brother of the judge Francis *Russell. His father received a life peerage as Baron Russell of Killowen shortly before becoming lord chief justice in 1894. Russell was educated at Beaumont College, Berkshire, and abroad. His admittance as a solicitor in 1888 enabled him to marry, in 1889, Adah Walmsley (1867–1959), daughter of William Williams, and granddaughter of Sir Joshua Walmsley. They had one daughter.

Having practised for three years on his own account at Mincing Lane, Russell in 1891 entered a partnership with Edward Day at 37 Norfolk Street, off the Strand. When this partnership was dissolved in 1898, Russell continued the firm of Charles Russell & Co. in the same premises. He was supported by the advice and connections of his father, whom he venerated. His work in the Bering Sea arbitration of 1893 led to his appointment as solicitor for the dominion government of Canada in 1896. The most prolonged issue in which he represented Canada was its Labrador boundary dispute with Newfoundland. Russell was involved even before this was submitted in 1907 to the judicial committee of the privy council, but terms of reference were not agreed until 1922 and the decision (in Newfoundland's favour) was delivered in 1927. The Grand Trunk Railway arbitration also required Russell's attention, but was less protracted.

Russell reached wider prominence in 1895, when the ninth marquess of Queensberry, having provoked a writ for criminal libel from Oscar *Wilde and finding that his solicitor Sir George Lewis preferred to withdraw from the case, strode up the Strand determined to enlist the first solicitor whom he could find working on a Saturday. Russell assembled the evidence and mustered the witnesses that accomplished Wilde's ruin. He had first briefed Edward Carson in 1893, and their collaboration in this *cause célèbre* promoted both their reputations. Henceforth Russell became a distinguished consultant in complicated family affairs. Observant, constructive, and discreet in his personal dealings, he was dominating and persistent in his office, which had the apt telegraphic address of 'Toilful'. His practice, as it developed after 1895, is best compared with that of Sir George Lewis. Both baronets were repositories of professional secrets from highly placed individuals; both succeeded in keeping many delicate cases out of court; both were meticulous in their preparations for trials, and had an intuitive anticipation of jurymen's minds. Russell was less flamboyant than Lewis, and less implacable in the destruction of his antagonists.

The Education Bill introduced in 1906 portended, as George Wyndham wrote in April, 'the biggest fight since 1640' between contending religious creeds (*Letters of George Wyndham*, 2.184). In this verbal battle Russell proved a stalwart champion of Roman Catholic interests. At numerous meetings in northern England and London (including a rally at the Royal Albert Hall on 6 May) and as chief secular spokesman of a deputation to the marquess of Lansdowne on 29 November, he insisted on the desire of Roman Catholics that their children should receive authentic Catholic teaching from Roman Catholics. One sequel to his work on the executive of the Catholic Education Council was his publication of a pamphlet entitled *The Catholics of London and Public Life* (1907). It vexed Russell that for reasons of prejudice his 250,000 co-religionists in the capital were under-represented in municipal government. In an effort to redress this injustice he became first president of the Federated London Catholic Associations (1908–10), and himself represented Bermondsey for the Progressive Party on London county council from 1910 to 1913. As the descendant of Ulster Roman Catholics, Russell was interested in adjusting Irish grievances, and during the home rule controversy in 1914 suggested that northern protestants might be conciliated either by the proposed Irish parliament alternating its meetings between Dublin and Belfast, or by the erection of an equivalent of Washington, DC, on the shores of Strangford Lough, near his ancestral Newry.

In the general election of 1895 Russell was defeated by 312 votes as the Liberal candidate at Central Hackney (his father had represented an adjoining constituency until the previous year). When he again contested a parliamentary seat, South Salford, in December 1910, he failed by the even narrower margin of 227 votes. For several years he served on the political committee of the Eighty Club, a Liberal Imperialist group in which his father had been active. His patriotism was such that when Sir Roger Casement was brought to London under escort in 1916, and appealed to Russell as a solicitor with a large Irish Catholic connection, Russell declined to act for him, and sent his clerk to the Tower of London to tell Casement so.

During the European war Russell was chairman of the collections committee of the British Red Cross Society. Family pride and loyalties counted for much with him: when he was raised to a baronetcy in the new year honours of 1916, he secured a special remainder to the heirs male of the body of his father. His only child, Monica, in 1917 married her cousin Alec Russell, who inherited the baronetcy, but this union was dissolved by divorce in 1932. Russell was also created KCVO in 1921. He was a kindly, companionable man who shone in conversation and was a polished host. At the age of about forty he renounced polo for the less strenuous game of golf: in 1921 his handicap was 13. He also yachted. The stewards of the Jockey Club, to whom he was solicitor from 1903, were specially congenial clients, for like his father he dearly loved a good horse. In one of his last cases, *Wright v. Gladstone* (1927), he gave Herbert and Henry Gladstone the shrewd advice not to offer their father's journal in evidence during their defence of the late prime minister's reputation. He died of pneumonia on 27 March 1928 at the Hospital of St John and St Elizabeth, Grove End Road, St John's Wood, London. His funeral service was held at Westminster Cathedral on 30 March. He was survived by his wife.

RICHARD DAVENPORT-HINES

Sources *The Times* (28 March 1928) · *The Times* (29 March 1928) · E. Oldmeadow, *Francis, Cardinal Bourne*, 2 vols. (1940–44) · *The diary of Beatrice Webb*, ed. N. MacKenzie and J. MacKenzie, 4 vols. (1982–5), vol. 3 · Lord Newton [T. W. Legh], *Retrospection* (1941) · *Letters of George Wyndham, 1877–1913*, ed. G. Wyndham, 2 (privately printed, Edinburgh, 1915) · d. cert. · H. C. G. Matthew, *Gladstone, 1875–1898* (1995) · C. J. Parry, *Index of baronetage creations* (1967), 141 · GEC, *Peerage* · WW

Archives Bodl. Oxf., letters relating to libel case between the Globe and Margaret Asquith | LPL, corresp. with Gladstone family, MSS 2759, 2772–2773

Likenesses photograph, 1915, repro. in *ILN* (8 Jan 1916), 53 · Lafayette, photograph, NPG · P. A. de Laszlo, oils, priv. coll. · Spy [L. Ward], caricature, watercolour study, NPG; repro. in *VF* (10 April 1907)

Wealth at death £73,528 2s. 3d.: probate, 6 June 1928, *CGPLA Eng. & Wales*

Russell, Charles Arthur, Baron Russell of Killowen (1832–1900), judge, was born on 10 November 1832 at Newry, co. Down, Ireland, the eldest son of Arthur Russell (1785–1845) and his wife, Margaret, daughter of Matthew Mullin and widow of John Hamill, a merchant of Belfast. After his father's death in 1845 Russell, along with his siblings, was brought up by his mother and their paternal uncle, Dr Charles William *Russell, then a professor at and afterwards president of St Patrick's College, Maynooth. The Russells were a recusant family and the children were brought up in the Catholic faith. Russell attended a diocesan seminary in Belfast as his first school, was then taught at a private school in Newry, for two years, and finally spent one year at St Vincent's College, Castleknock, co. Dublin. He seems to have worked reasonably hard at school, but was not particularly distinguished. Although he later matriculated at Trinity College, Dublin (1856), he never graduated.

Early career In January 1849 Russell began his legal training under Cornelius Denvir, a solicitor at Newry. After Denvir's death in 1852, his articles were transferred to Alexander O'Rorke of Belfast. Russell was admitted a solicitor in January 1854 and took charge of an office of O'Rorke's in Londonderry for six months. He then returned to Belfast, and practised in the county courts of Down and Antrim. Around that time extreme protestant sentiment had led to riots and other civil disturbances. When the resulting case came before the magistrates, Russell spoke well and defended the Catholics who had been involved in the violence. His speeches were reported in the provincial newspaper and public opinion swung strongly in his favour. His success on this occasion, along with the encouragement and recommendation of those among whom he practised, confirmed his resolve to become a barrister in London.

On 6 November 1856 Russell entered at Lincoln's Inn and moved permanently to London. In 1857 he became a pupil of Henry Bagshawe, then an equity junior with a

Charles Arthur Russell, Baron Russell of Killowen (1832–1900), by John Singer Sargent, 1900 [replica]

large practice at the chancery bar. Remembered at this time as being grave, reserved, and hard-working, he acquired a considerable knowledge of real property law, but conveyancing and equity drafting did not interest him, and he left to join the common-law bar. He never attended the chambers of a pleader as the common-law procedure acts had largely removed the need for such specialization. He found time to write for newspapers and magazines, and contributed a weekly letter on current politics to the Dublin *Nation*. Though unsuccessful as a candidate for the inns of court studentship in 1858, he was awarded a certificate of honour. On 10 August 1858 he married Ellen (1836–1918), eldest daughter of Joseph Stevenson Mulholland MD of Belfast. In the Hilary term of 1859 he again competed for the studentship, which was awarded to Montague Cookson, afterwards Crackanthorpe KC.

On 26 January 1859 Russell was called to the bar and joined the northern circuit. He practised in the passage court, Liverpool, and within four years of being called to the bar was making £1000 per annum. He soon began to be known in London, and argued a case before Lord Westbury with such ability that he was offered a county court judgeship. He was knighted on 8 March 1866.

Judge and MP In 1872 Russell took silk at the same time as Farrer, afterwards Baron Herschell, with whom he effectively divided all of the business cases on the circuit. In commercial cases, where rights mainly depended on written evidence, Russell's knowledge of business and of the law enabled him to go straight to the point and get through a long list quickly. However, where there was a conflict of evidence, his style of advocacy was open to criticism and complaint. He was not thought to be a pleasant antagonist. Despite a quick temper and a tendency to allow matters to become personal between himself and opposing counsel he was popular on circuit and said to treat witnesses fairly. With experience his methods became less aggressive; and it is said that he always had a helping hand for his juniors. His particular strengths were best displayed when fraud, perfidy, or malice were to be exposed. An aggressive cross-examiner, he was well able to deal with the dishonest witness. He also carried great sway when addressing a jury, not so much through oratorical brilliance as his exercise of a compelling moral authority. He was thorough in his preparation for difficult cases and expected high standards of his juniors and instructing solicitors, although he was sometimes faulted for impetuosity, in consultation as well as in court.

In 1875 Russell was invited to stand for the parliamentary seat of Durham but withdrew his candidacy once it became clear that his Catholicism might cause difficulties, suggesting instead that Farrer Herschell should take his place as the Liberal candidate. In 1876, on the death of Percival A. Pickering QC, he applied with other leaders of the circuit for the vacant judgeship of the court of passage at Liverpool but all lost out to Mr T. Henry Baylis QC. In 1880, after two further unsuccessful attempts, he was eventually returned to parliament, as an independent Liberal, for Dundalk, co. Louth, being opposed by home-rulers and Parnellites. He had been warned that he might be in physical danger if he stood, and one attempt at assault was indeed made, but his obvious courage and strength in self-defence deterred any further acts of violence.

Irish nationalism When Russell entered parliament Irish nationalism was represented in the House of Commons by only a small minority of the Irish members. It was not until the franchise was expanded by the act of 1884, and as many as eighty-five members returned from Ireland to support the demand for an Irish parliament, that he pledged himself, together with the majority of Liberals, to the policy of home rule. Russell was nevertheless always a firm supporter of the Irish cause, and well before Gladstone and Parnell made their alliance frequently spoke in debates on Ireland and usually voted with the nationalists. In February 1881 he opposed W. E. Forster's Coercion Bill which involved the imprisonment of many men of good repute and was badly applied. Russell's opposition to the bill and the fact that many respectable men were imprisoned because of the bill meant that in Ireland the title 'ex suspect' became one of distinction. In March 1882 Russell opposed the proposal for an inquiry into the working of the Land Act, and in the following April he supported the government in the change of policy which led to the release of Forster's prisoners. He was outspoken against the measure of coercion which followed the Phoenix Park murders, renewing the hostility between the government and the Irish MPs, and sought by various amendments to mitigate the severity of the government proposals. In 1883 he delivered a long speech in the debate on the address, complaining that the legitimate demands for

the redress of Irish grievances were disregarded; and in 1884 he spoke in support of an inquiry into the Maamtrasna trials. He seldom spoke in debates other than those connected with Ireland, but in 1883 he spoke in favour of a bill for creating a court of criminal appeal, contending that the interference of the home secretary with the sentences of judges was unconstitutional; and he also supported the granting of state aid to voluntary schools.

In 1882 Russell was offered a judgeship, which he was tempted to accept since he had no hope of retaining an Irish seat. He declined the offer, however, and decided to look for an English constituency. In 1885 he was returned for South Hackney, and was appointed attorney-general in Gladstone's government of 1886. His re-election upon taking office was opposed by the Conservatives, but he was again returned. He then threw himself into the home rule struggle with energy and determination. The alliance between Liberals and Parnellites enabled him to give full play to his enthusiasm, and he travelled all over England addressing public meetings, great and small, in every part of the country. His speeches in the House of Commons on the Home Rule Bill were probably his best parliamentary performances. In supporting the second reading he referred to 'the so-called loyal minority' as not being an aid but a hindrance to any solid union between England and Ireland, since he saw their loyalty as being strongly based on their self-interest. At the general election of 1886 he was again returned for South Hackney, defeating his opponent, C. J. Darling (afterwards a judge of the High Court), by a small majority. In 1887 he resisted the passing of the Coercion Bill of that year in a powerful speech.

In 1888 the Parnell Commission Act was passed. Its declared object was to create a tribunal to inquire into charges and allegations made against certain members of parliament and other persons by the defendants in the recent *O'Donnell* v. *Walter* case. Three of the judges were appointed commissioners, and the sittings began on 22 October. Russell appeared as leading counsel for Parnell, and the attorney-general, Sir R. Webster (afterwards Lord Alverstone and lord chief justice), was on the other side. The cross-examination of many of the Irish witnesses called by the attorney-general devolved upon Russell, and was successfully conducted in very difficult circumstances. He had no notice of the order in which they would appear, and had little information about them. Yet it was said that few witnesses left the box without being successfully attacked and disparaged. His famous speech for the defence occupied six days, and was concluded on 12 April 1889. It was well suited to the occasion and to the tribunal, and was undoubtedly his greatest forensic effort, although reputedly lacking in oratorical flourish.

Later years In 1889 Russell involved himself in a criminal case and defended Mrs Florence *Maybrick on the charge of poisoning her husband. The controversial case aroused a great deal of interest; Russell failed to prevent Maybrick's conviction, but her sentence was commuted from death to penal servitude. In 1890 he spoke in the debate in the House of Commons on the report of the special commission, his speech being described half-humorously in *The Times* as a blend of argument, invective, cajolery, and eloquent appeals to prejudice or sentiment so skilful that it added up to a very able speech.

On Gladstone's return to power in 1892 Russell was again appointed attorney-general, and was once more returned for Hackney by a large majority. In 1893, together with Sir R. Webster, he represented Great Britain in the Bering Sea arbitration. The case concerned the denial by Great Britain of the United States' exclusive jurisdiction over the sealing industry in the Bering Sea. Independently of this title (allegedly 'purchased' from Russia in 1867), the United States claimed jurisdiction as lawful protectors of seals bred in the disputed area on the basis of 'principles of right', or rules on which civilized nations ought to be agreed. This was stated to be international law. Russell and Webster contended that international law consisted of the rules which civilized nations had agreed to treat as binding. These rules were not to be ascertained by reference to 'principles of right', as counsel for the United States had argued, but were to be found in the records of international transactions. It was argued that, apart from actual consent, so ascertained, there was no universal moral standard; Russell and Webster won on this point. The discussion as to the future regulations for the management of the sealing industry occupied eight days. Russell's services were recognized by the award of the grand cross of St Michael and St George.

On 7 May 1894 Russell succeeded Charles Synge Christopher, Lord Bowen, as lord of appeal, and was raised to the peerage for life by the title of Russell of Killowen. In June of the same year, on the death of John Duke, Lord Coleridge, he was appointed lord chief justice. As chief justice he was reputed to be patient, courteous, and dignified. His extensive knowledge of the law was admired widely. No judge won the confidence and goodwill of the public more quickly or fully.

Russell took an interest in legal matters outside his immediate judicial duties. In 1895 he supported the judges of his division in the endeavour to establish the court for the trial of commercial causes, a project which for many years had been met by the strenuous and successful opposition of Lord Coleridge. In the same year he delivered an address in Lincoln's Inn hall on legal education. He dwelt at length on the failure of the existing system, and insisted that no student should be admitted to the degree of barrister who had not given proof of his professional competency. He bestowed faint praise on the Council of Legal Education, and urged that there should be a charter of a school of law with a senate not wholly composed of benchers and lawyers. His comments were resented and entirely disregarded.

In 1896, after gaining the conviction of the Jameson raiders and firmly laying down the law with clarity and force, Russell visited the United States for the purpose of delivering to American lawyers assembled at Saratoga in New York state an address entitled *Arbitration: its Origin, History, and Prospects*. In it he adhered to the view which he had laid before the Bering Sea arbitrators that international law was neither more nor less than what civilized nations have agreed shall be binding on one another. Amid great applause he expressed hopes for the peaceful settlement of disputes between nations.

In 1899, on the death of Farrer, Lord Herschell, Russell was appointed in his place to act as one of the arbitrators to determine the boundaries of British Guiana and Venezuela under the treaty of 2 February 1897. The arbitration was held in Paris, Great Britain being represented by Sir R. Webster and Sir R. Reid, and Venezuela by American counsel. Although Russell took little part in the discussion, he directed attention to the points at issue. The unanimous verdict was in favour of an award for Great Britain.

Death and assessment In July 1900 Russell left London for the north Wales circuit. At Chester he suffered an attack of illness and was advised to go home. In a few days it became clear that something serious was wrong. After an attempt to save him through an operation, he died on 10 August at his home, 2 Cromwell Houses, Kensington. He was buried at Epsom, Surrey, on 14 August. He was survived by his wife and five sons, including Sir Charles *Russell and Francis Xavier Joseph *Russell, and four daughters.

Russell's keen intellect and resolute will helped him to unite much respect and even enthusiasm. Despite his often cold and forbidding manner, there was great kindliness in him as seen in his consideration for others. No reader, he was an indefatigable player of whist and piquet. He was also a familiar figure on racecourses, and was both interested in and knowledgeable about bloodstock. Russell was a large-minded man and his intimate friends included those who differed widely from him and each other in social class and position, politics, and religion.

When hard at work Russell shut himself up at his chambers at 3 Brick Court, Temple, or at his country house, Tadworth Court, near Epsom, but when free he was fond of socializing. He readily accepted invitations to address public meetings on politics, education, or for charitable projects. Even after he became chief justice he was ready to preside over public occasions, and especially at charity dinners. While he never failed to interest his audience his style was sombre, and, although well informed, he was inclined to dwell more on perceived shortcomings than to emphasize achievements.

Russell had a strong view of his obligation to enforce the duty of honesty and good faith in commercial transactions. His protests from the bench against fraud in the promotion of companies and the practice of receiving commissions were offered courageously, and he believed that good results would follow. The Secret Commissions Bill which he introduced in the House of Lords in 1900 required of him much effort, the collection of the necessary materials involving him in a personal correspondence with public bodies and individuals all over the kingdom.

Among his published works were *New Views of Ireland, or, Irish Land: Grievances, Remedies*, reprinted from the *Daily Telegraph* (1880); *The Christian Schools of England and Recent Legislation Concerning them* (1883); *Address on Legal Education*

(1895); and *Arbitration: its Origin, History, and Prospects: an Address to the Saratoga Congress*, (1896).

Russell earned a great deal of money at the bar. His fee book shows that from 1862 to 1872 he made as junior on an average £3000 a year. In the ten years after he took silk in 1872 he made approximately £10,000 per annum; from 1882 to 1892 his annual earnings averaged nearly £16,000, and from 1893, when he was again appointed attorney-general, until he became a lord of appeal in April 1894, he received £32,826.

Russell was granted an honorary LLD by Trinity College, Dublin, in 1894, by Laval University, Canada, in 1896, and by Edinburgh University and the University of Cambridge in 1897. Lord Russell is remembered as a great judge and a man of personal integrity. The best likeness of him is the portrait by J. S. Sargent RA, now in the possession of his family, a replica of which is housed in the National Portrait Gallery.   J. C. MATHEW, rev. SINÉAD AGNEW

Sources *The Times* (11 Aug 1900) · R. B. O'Brien, *The life of Lord Russell of Killowen* (1901) · L. G. Pine, *The new extinct peerage, 1884–1971: containing extinct, abeyant, dormant, and suspended peerages with genealogies and arms* (1972), 245 · Gillow, *Lit. biog. hist.* · Boase, *Mod. Eng. biog.* · J. Foster, *Men-at-the-bar: a biographical hand-list of the members of the various inns of court*, 2nd edn (1885), 406 · W. P. Baildon, ed., *The records of the Honorable Society of Lincoln's Inn: admissions*, 2 (1896), 274 · *Leading men of London: a collection of biographical sketches* (1895), 5–6 · *Men and women of the time* (1899) · A. T. C. Pratt, ed., *People of the period: being a collection of the biographies of upwards of six thousand living celebrities*, 2 (1897), 339 · L. C. Sanders, *Celebrities of the century: being a dictionary of men and women of the nineteenth century* (1887), 881 · J. Hutchinson, ed., *A catalogue of notable Middle Templars: with brief biographical notices* (1902), 211–12 · Allibone, *Dict.* · 'Russell', *The Weekly Gallery of Celebrities*, 1 (1891), 6–7 · GEC, *Peerage* · Burke, *Peerage* (1900) · A. P. Quinn, 'A brief encounter with Lord Russell of Killowen', *Irish Law Times and Solicitors' Journal*, new ser., 13/4 (1995), 94–6 · E. Kilmurray, *Dictionary of British portraiture*, 3 (1981) · *The Times* (11 Aug 1900) · *Law List* · personal knowledge (1901) · *CGPLA Eng. & Wales* (1900)
Archives BL, corresp. with W. E. Gladstone, Add. MSS 44463–44524, *passim* · Bodl. Oxf., corresp. with Sir William Harcourt; letters to various members of the Lewis family · NL Scot., corresp. with Lord Rosebery
Likenesses R. Lehmann, drawing, 1891, BM · J. D. Penrose, oils, 1896, Gov. Art Coll. · J. S. Sargent, oils, 1900 · J. S. Sargent, oils, replica, 1900, NPG [*see illus.*] · Barraud, photograph, NPG; repro. in *Men and Women of the Day*, 2 (1889) · T. Brock, marble statue, Gov. Art Coll. · W. & D. Downey, woodburytype photograph, NPG; repro. in W. Downey and D. Downey, *The cabinet portrait gallery*, 2 (1891) · H. Furniss, caricature, pen-and-ink sketch, NPG · S. P. Hall, pencil sketches (Parnell Commission sessions), NPG; repro. in *The Graphic* (2–11 March 1889) · F. Pegram, pencil sketches, V&A · Quiz, chromolithograph, NPG; repro. in *VF* (29 March 1890) · F. Verheyden, caricature, watercolour study, NPG; repro. in *VF* (5 May 1883) · E. Ward, oils, Reform Club, London
Wealth at death £149,062 4s. 3d.: probate, 29 Oct 1900, *CGPLA Eng. & Wales*

Russell, Charles Ritchie, **Baron Russell of Killowen** (1908–1986), judge, was born on 12 January 1908 at 68 Elm Park Gardens, Chelsea, London, the youngest in the family of one son and two daughters (a third daughter died in infancy) of Francis Xavier Joseph *Russell, Baron Russell of Killowen (1867–1946), lord of appeal, and his wife, Mary Emily Ritchie (d. 1956). On his father's side Russell's family were Ulster Catholics who settled in Ireland about 1300.

His grandfather, Charles Arthur *Russell, Baron Russell of Killowen, became lord chief justice. Russell's father was a Chancery judge and a member of the Court of Appeal before being appointed to the House of Lords. On his mother's side Russell was descended from a Scottish family; his maternal grandfather was Charles Thomson *Ritchie, first Baron Ritchie of Dundee, chancellor of the exchequer. Russell followed his father to Beaumont College and Oriel College, Oxford, where he was awarded a half blue in golf and a third class in jurisprudence in 1929. He claimed to prefer the cinema to study and golf to both.

After being called to the bar in 1931 by Lincoln's Inn, Russell worked hard in Old Buildings, where he quickly repaired any deficiencies in legal learning. During the Second World War he became a major in the Royal Artillery, was attached to the 6th airborne division, and on D-day flew into the Orne valley by glider. He subsequently took part in another glider drop over the Rhine and suffered abdominal wounds from shell fire. For his exploits on active service Russell was mentioned in dispatches and awarded the Croix de Guerre with star.

After the war Russell returned to the bar and took silk in 1948. He quickly became one of a triumvirate of distinguished Chancery counsel: Andrew Clark pulverized witnesses and some judges, E. Milner Holland was successful with sweet reason, and Russell was the most formidable advocate. Russell was handsome, tall, slim, and elegant; he was dark with expressive eyes and a sensitive, sometimes sardonic expression. He was possessed of a warm melodious voice which made his well structured arguments almost irresistible. In 1960 he was appointed a judge of the Chancery Division and was knighted; two years later he went up to the Court of Appeal and was sworn of the privy council. As a judge Russell was urbane, courteous, and aloof; his flashing wit disconcerted some who were not suffered gladly. His judgments were models of analysis and lucidity, well suited to the complicated commercial and property disputes with which he was mainly concerned. Out of court he was kind and amusing to people of all ages and backgrounds. He was not very interested in the arts and his light reading was confined to Jane Austen, and the novels and biographies of the nineteenth century, especially the works of Anthony Trollope. He enjoyed claret, partridge, and a good cigar, but was not a gourmet. He was a sound bat and subtle bowler for Wisborough Green in village cricket as late as his forties. He played golf to a handicap of eight until he became lame in his seventies. He much enjoyed the Bar Golfing Society meetings at Sandwich, Rye, and Deal. He was tolerant towards his weaker partners and enjoyed the company of the young; he was a sparkling member of the Garrick Club.

Lincoln's Inn appealed to Russell's sense of history and he became treasurer in 1972. In his approach to the law, Russell was a firm believer in certainty and a follower of precedent; he did not approve of the purposive construction of statutes and did not admire the intellectual flexibility which enabled Lord Denning to his own satisfaction to temper the wind to the shorn lamb. Russell took refuge sometimes in a cold reserve and patrician arrogance, fortified on occasions by alcohol, which led to his suffering a great humiliation. In 1960 he pleaded guilty in a magistrate's court to driving with an unlawful level of alcohol. He was fined £25 and costs and his licence was suspended for a year. The incident was a severe blow to Russell. He was passed over in 1971 when a vacancy occurred in the House of Lords; he behaved with dignity and his work in the Court of Appeal did not suffer. When he had completed thirteen years' hard labour in that court the authorities relented and in 1975 he was appointed lord of appeal, to his surprise and to the relief of his friends. Russell took the same title as his father and grandfather. His work in the House of Lords followed the pattern of his earlier judicial career. The appellate committee was in 1975 dominated by lords Wilberforce and Diplock. Russell was prepared to follow their lead, but he was not slow to dissent when he concluded that precedent was threatened.

On 4 August 1933 Russell married Joan Elizabeth (1911/12–1976), daughter of James Aubrey Torrens, consulting physician; she was a graduate of Somerville College, Oxford, keenly interested in literature and poetry, and was a help and companion to Russell when he was at the bar and on the bench. There were two sons and one daughter of the marriage. Another daughter died at the age of eight months. Joan died in 1976 and in 1979 Russell married Elizabeth Cecilia, the young widow of Edward Hey Laughton-Scott, circuit judge, and daughter of William Foster MacNeece Foster, air vice-marshal. She introduced her own children and her family and a wide circle of friends, and Russell perceptibly mellowed. He died in Southampton General Hospital on 23 June 1986, after a fall at home in which he struck his head on the fireplace.

TEMPLEMAN, *rev.*

Sources *The Times* (24 June 1986) · personal knowledge (1996) · private information (1996) · *CGPLA Eng. & Wales* (1986) · m. cert. [J. E. Torrens] · d. cert.
Wealth at death £166,854: probate, 7 Aug 1986, *CGPLA Eng. & Wales*

Russell, Charles William (1812–1880), college head, was born on 14 May 1812 at Killough, co. Down, the seventh of nine children of Charles Russell (1760–1828), merchant and farmer, and his second wife, Anne (1776–1839), daughter of Thomas McEvoy of Drogheda and his wife, Anne. His father, descended from an Anglo-Norman baronial family, had prospered as a merchant in Killough. His stepbrother was the father of Charles Russell, later lord chief justice and Baron Russell of Killowen.

Russell was educated at a classical school in Downpatrick, and at Drogheda grammar school. He entered St Patrick's College, Maynooth, in 1826, completed his theological studies, joined the postgraduate department in 1832, and was ordained priest in 1835. A few weeks before ordination he was appointed to the chair of humanity in the college. Ten years later he was appointed professor of ecclesiastical history, when that chair was established as a result of Peel's increased endowment of Maynooth.

In 1836 Russell began writing for the *Dublin Review* which had just been founded by Daniel O'Connell, Nicholas Wiseman (later cardinal), and Michael Quin as the Catholic counterpart to *The Edinburgh* and *The Quarterly*. Until his last years he remained its most regular and prolific correspondent, writing especially on historical, religious, and literary matters. In 1842 he was appointed vicar apostolic of Ceylon but successfully declined the office. When his name headed the list of candidates proposed for the office of coadjutor bishop in his native diocese of Down and Connor in 1859, he again begged to be excused from consideration by Rome, and he renewed this appeal successfully seven years later when the parish priests of Armagh made him their second choice in their list of preferences for succession to the primatial see.

In 1841 Russell began a correspondence with John Henry Newman, who, with John Keble and Edward Pusey, was spearheading a revival in the Anglican church by their *Tracts for the Times*. The Tractarians sought to rejuvenate their church by situating it firmly in the apostolic traditions, distinguishing between these and Roman accretions, and defending its position as a *via media* between popery and dissent. They rejected the role given to the Madonna and saints in the Roman Catholic church. Russell passed on to Newman copies of Catholic prayer books and sermons to enable him to get a fairer grasp of Catholic devotional practices, and he visited him at Oxford in 1843. In 1845 Newman became a Catholic, and some twenty years later in his *Apologia pro vita sua* revealed that Russell had, perhaps, more to do with his conversion than anyone else, remarking that his friend had always been 'gentle, mild, unobtrusive, uncontroversial'.

In 1857 Russell became president of Maynooth. In 1858 he published his life of Cardinal Mezzofanti, the celebrated Italian linguist, who had died in 1849. Favourably reviewed, it was translated into Italian, French, and German. With a Maynooth colleague he had already translated Carl von Schmid's *Tales Designed Chiefly for the Young*, in 1845–6, and in 1850 he had produced a translation and commentary on Leibnitz's *System of Theology*. He also wrote several articles for the *Edinburgh Review* and the *North British Review*, contributed extensively to *Chambers's Encyclopaedia* (1860–8), and was responsible for three entries in the *Encyclopaedia Britannica* (1853–60) and for several in the *English Cyclopaedia* (1854–70). With a colleague, J. P. Prendergast, he helped select for transcription and report on the voluminous papers of Thomas Carte in the Bodleian Library (1865–71), and together they then calendared the state papers of James I relating to Ireland (1869–76); the fifth and last volume of James's papers was published after Russell's death. When the Royal Commission on Historical Manuscripts was established in 1869, Russell was the only Irish scholar appointed to it.

During his last years at Maynooth, Russell made arrangements for the addition of a large collegiate chapel to complete the gothic buildings. He was appointed a domestic prelate to Pope Pius IX in 1877, the same year in which he was partially incapacitated as a result of a riding accident. Russell died on 26 February 1880 at 22 Upper Fitzwilliam Street, Dublin, and was buried in the college cemetery at Maynooth on the 28th. AMBROSE MACAULAY

Sources A. Macaulay, *Dr Russell of Maynooth* (1983) · [M. Russell], 'Dr Russell of Maynooth', *Irish Monthly*, 20–22 (Jan 1892–June 1894) [in 20 pts; see also 'Dr Russell's literary work', 22 (1894), 632–42] · P. J. Corish, 'Newman and Maynooth', *Newman and Gladstone centennial essays*, ed. J. Bastable (1978) · L. C. Casartelli, 'Our diamond jubilee', *Dublin Review*, 118 (1896) · J. H. Newman, *Apologia pro vita sua* (1864) · CGPLA Eng. & Wales (1880)
Archives St Patrick's College, Maynooth, Maynooth College archives, corresp. and papers | Archives of the Irish Province of the Society of Jesus, Dublin, Matthew Russell MSS · Archives of the Sacred Congregation for the Evangelization of Peoples, Rome · Birmingham Oratory, letters to J. H. Newman · BL, corresp. with W. E. Gladstone, Add. MSS 44392–44443, *passim* · CUL, letters to Lord Acton · Irish College, Rome, Cullen MSS · NL Ire., letters to Lord Emly · Westm. DA, Bagshawe MSS · Westm. DA, corresp. with Wiseman
Likenesses Gagliardi, oils, 1883, St Patrick's College, Maynooth
Wealth at death under £4000: probate, 1880, *CGPLA Eng. & Wales*

Russell, Sir David (1809–1884), army officer, was the eldest son of Colonel James Russell of Woodside, Stirlingshire, and Mary, daughter of John Stirling of Kippindavie, Perthshire. He was born at Woodside on 27 May 1809, was educated at Edinburgh and Dresden, and entered the army on 10 January 1828 as a cornet in the 7th light dragoons. He became lieutenant on 1 October 1829 and captain on 5 April 1833. On 10 April 1835 he exchanged to the 84th regiment, in which he became major on 7 July 1845, lieutenant-colonel on 10 December 1847, and brevet colonel on 28 November 1854.

Russell's first and only active service was in the Indian mutiny. At the second relief of Lucknow, under Sir Colin Campbell, he commanded the 5th brigade. He covered the left of the relieving force as it fought its way to the residency, and captured Banks's house, but was wounded and disabled in the attack on the hospital (14–17 November 1857). After the relief he remained with Outram at the Alambagh, commanding the 1st brigade. In the siege and capture of Lucknow, in March 1858, he commanded the 2nd brigade in Franks's division, which took part in the attack on the *kaisarbagh*. He was mentioned in dispatches, received a reward for distinguished service, and was made CB (24 March 1858).

On 31 August 1858 Russell was appointed inspecting field officer for recruiting, and on 3 September 1862 he became major-general. He was employed in Canada during 1867, and from July 1868 to 1871 he commanded the south-eastern district. He became lieutenant-general on 25 October 1871 and general on 1 October 1877. He was given the colonelcy of the 75th highlanders on 18 January 1870, and transferred to the 84th regiment on 24 October 1872. He was made KCB on 20 May 1871. He died at his residence, 3 Elvaston Place, South Kensington, London, on 16 January 1884. E. M. LLOYD, *rev.* JAMES FALKNER

Sources *Army List* · *The Times* (17 Jan 1884) · *LondG* (16 Jan 1858) · *LondG* (25 May 1858) · *Hart's Army List* · Boase, *Mod. Eng. biog.* · Kelly, *Handbk*
Wealth at death £9960 6s. 3d. in UK: probate, 26 March 1884, *CGPLA Eng. & Wales*

Russell [*née* Black], **Dora Winifred** (1894–1986), writer and campaigner for women's rights, was born on 3 April 1894 at 1 Mount Villas, Luna Road, Thornton Heath, Croydon, the second of three daughters and second of four children of Sir Frederick William Black (1863–1930), clerk in the Admiralty and later senior civil servant, and his wife, Sarah Isabella Davisson. She was educated at Sutton high school and Girton College, Cambridge, where she was awarded a first class in the medieval and modern languages tripos in 1915. She began research on eighteenth-century French philosophers at University College, London, but in 1917 went to the United States as personal assistant to her father, who was head of a special government mission to persuade the American government to re-route some of its oil tankers to Britain. She was appointed MBE for this in 1918. Shortly after her return she was elected to a fellowship by Girton, and returned to Cambridge in 1918.

In 1916 Dora had met Bertrand Arthur William *Russell (1872–1970), already famous as a mathematician and philosopher, and notorious as a pacifist. Bertrand Russell was the son of John *Russell, Viscount Amberley (1842–1876), MP for Nottingham. He became third Earl Russell in 1931. They began an affair in 1919. She visited Russia in 1920, and on her return took to wearing peasant-style clothes. She remained an enthusiastic supporter of the Soviet Union all her life. In 1921 she wrote 'The soul of Russia and the body of America', which was finally incorporated in *The Religion of the Machine Age* (1983). She resigned her Girton fellowship in 1920 in order to accompany Russell to Russia and China.

Russell was married, although separated, and had no children. Although Dora disapproved of marriage she agreed to marry him when she became pregnant, as he was anxious to produce a legitimate heir. On their return from China he divorced his wife and married Dora in the same month, September 1921, two months before their son John (1921–1987), later fourth Earl Russell, was born.

They bought a house in Chelsea, and Dora soon became aware of the difficulties involved in being married to a much older, famous man. Although Russell supported women's suffrage, he believed that women were less intelligent than men, and that their main function was to be wives and mothers. His friends adopted a patronizing attitude towards Dora, assuming that any ideas she might express came from him. She was determined to have an identity separate from that of her husband, and to escape from the shadow of his reputation. She joined the Labour Party, and stood unsuccessfully as Labour candidate for Chelsea in the autumn of 1924. She helped to form the Workers' Birth Control Group in 1924, and threw herself into the campaign for birth-control advice to be given to all women. In 1925 she published *Hypatia, or, Women and Knowledge*, followed by *The Right to be Happy* in 1927.

In 1927 Dora and Bertrand Russell started Beacon Hill School at Telegraph House, on the South Downs, in order to educate their own children in the company of others, because no existing school seemed satisfactory. The plan

Dora Winifred Russell (1894–1986), by Jane Bown, 1984

was to do away with excessive discipline, religious instruction, and the tyranny of adults. It was a joint venture, although Dora was responsible for the day-to-day organization, while Bertrand financed it through writing popular books and lecture tours in the United States. The school was ridiculed in the press, and Bertrand Russell later claimed it was a failure, but it embodied many progressive ideas. Dora published *In Defence of Children* in 1932.

Bertrand Russell left Dora, and the school, in 1932, after she had had two children with Griffin Barry, an American journalist. Although they had always insisted on their freedom to have affairs with other people, Russell could not accept her extending this to the freedom to have another man's child. They were divorced in 1935. She managed to carry on the school alone, moving several times after leaving Telegraph House in 1934. She had a brief affair with a communist, Paul Gillard, before he was murdered, and on 29 June 1940 married his friend, Gordon (Pat) Grace (*b.* 1909/10), a working-class Irish communist who was helping her to run the school. He was the son of Patrick Grace, clothier, and he died in 1949.

Dora closed the school in 1943, and went to London to work at the Ministry of Information, moving to the Soviet relations division in 1944 to work on *British Ally*, a weekly paper published by the British government in Moscow. When the paper was closed down in 1950 she lost her job. Unable to find another, she devoted herself to feminist causes and the women's peace movement. She was a member of the Six Point Group (a discussion and political pressure organization) and the Married Women's Association. She attended peace conferences, and went to New York in 1954 to the United Nations Commission on the Status of Women, on behalf of the Women's International Democratic Federation. In 1958 she organized the Women's Caravan of Peace, a group of women who travelled across Europe to Moscow and back, protesting against nuclear weapons and calling for total disarmament, with the banner 'women of all lands want peace'.

In 1962 Dora returned to Cornwall, to Carn Foel, Porthcurno, the house she and Russell had bought in 1922. She

devoted most of her time to writing, and to the care of her son John, who had had a mental breakdown in 1954. She continued to campaign for peace, leading a London Campaign for Nuclear Disarmament rally in a wheelchair at the age of eighty-nine, and just before her death she took part in an anti-nuclear demonstration at the Royal Air Force base at St Mawgan, Cornwall. Dora Russell died on 31 May 1986 at home in Porthcurno. She was cremated at Penmount crematorium, Truro, on 9 June and her ashes were scattered in her garden at Carn Foel. She had four children, one son and one daughter from her first marriage, and one son and one daughter with Griffin Barry. The younger son was injured in a mining accident in 1952 and was an invalid until his death in 1983.

Dora Russell loved campaigning, enjoying public speaking—she had always wanted to be an actress—and writing letters to the press. A chain-smoker, she was small, red-haired, and untidy, and claimed to have been one of the first women in England to wear shorts, in the 1920s. Throughout her life she campaigned for sexual freedom for women. She believed passionately that hope for the future lay in women. Many of her ideas anticipated those of the feminist movement of the 1970s and 1980s.

ANNE PIMLOTT BAKER, *rev.*

Sources D. Russell, *The tamarisk tree*, 3 vols. (1975–85) · D. Russell, *The Dora Russell reader: 57 years of writing and journalism, 1925–1982* (1983) · D. Spender, *There's always been a women's movement this century* (1983) · B. Russell, *The autobiography of Bertrand Russell*, 2 (1968) · C. Moorehead, *Bertrand Russell* (1992) · R. Monk, *Bertrand Russell: the spirit of solitude* (1996) · m. cert. [G. Grace] · K. Tait, *Carn Voel: my mother's house* (1998) · *The Times* (5 June 1986)
Archives Feminist Archive, papers, especially papers relating to Women's Caravan for Peace · Internationaal Instituut voor Sociale Geschiedenis, Amsterdam, corresp. and papers
Likenesses J. Bown, photograph, 1984, priv. coll. [*see illus.*] · Pinchot, photograph, repro. in *The autobiography of Bertrand Russell* (1968), vol. 2, facing p. 145 · photograph, repro. in K. Tait, *Carn Voel* (1998)

Russell, Dorothy Stuart (1895–1983), pathologist, was born on 27 June 1895, in Sydney, Australia, the second daughter of Philip Stuart Russell, bank clerk, and his wife, Alice Louisa, daughter of William Cave. She was orphaned when she was three, by the death of her father, and at the age of eight, by the death of her mother, who had remarried. She and her sister were sent to their aunt, who was married to Alexander Campbell Yorke, the rector at Fowlmere, near Cambridge. She attended the Perse High School for Girls in Cambridge and, from 1915, Girton College, qualifying for first-class honours in part one of the natural sciences tripos in 1918. Russell then entered the London Hospital medical college, where she was influenced by Hubert Turnbull, professor of morbid anatomy. She qualified MRCS (England) and LRCP (London) in 1922 and MB BS (London) in 1923, with the Sutton prize in pathology, and began work under Turnbull, first as a junior Beit fellow from 1923 to 1926, and later while supported by the Medical Research Council. From 1933 to 1946 she was a member of the council's scientific staff. Her first major work was *A Classification of Bright's Disease* (MRC Special

Reports, 142, 1929), which was the basis of her London MD, awarded in 1930, with the university medal.

Hugh Cairns, the neurosurgeon at the London Hospital, encouraged Russell into neuropathology and, with a Rockefeller travelling fellowship in 1928–9, she visited Frank B. Mallory in Boston and Wilder Penfield in Montreal, returning in 1930 to the London Hospital. In 1939 she joined Cairns, now Nuffield professor of surgery in Oxford, at the wartime hospital in St Hugh's College, a move partly enforced by the evacuation of many medical departments from London. Pio del Rio-Hortega was briefly a colleague before he departed for Buenos Aires in 1940.

Russell's wartime period at Oxford was one of intense productive work, and her *Observations on the Pathology of Hydrocephalus* (MRC Special Reports, 1940; 2nd edn, 1967) became a definitive account of the subject. Her major life work was on brain tumours, their staining and classification, and her masterpiece was the first edition in 1959 of her book, with L. J. Rubinstein, entitled *Pathology of Tumours of the Nervous System*. Russell gained a Cambridge ScD in 1943. In 1944 she returned from Oxford to the London Hospital and in 1946 succeeded Turnbull as professor of morbid anatomy and director of the Bernhard Baron Institute of Pathology, the first woman to occupy such a prestigious position, in which she remained until her retirement in 1960. These were golden years for her contributions to neuropathology, and to morbid anatomy, for she always considered herself a general pathologist.

Russell's outstanding achievements brought many honours. She was an honorary fellow of Girton College, Cambridge, St Hugh's College, Oxford, the Royal Microscopical Society, the Royal College of Pathology, and the Royal Society of Medicine. She received honorary doctorates of the universities of Glasgow and McGill, the John Hunter medal and triennial prize of the Royal College of Surgeons, and the Oliver-Sharpey prize of the Royal College of Physicians, of which she was a fellow (MRCP 1943, FRCP 1948). She delivered the Bryce memorial lecture at Somerville College, Oxford, the foundation lecture of the Association of Clinical Pathologists, and the Hugh Cairns and Schorstein lectures at the London Hospital. She was the first woman member of the Medical Research Society.

Russell's personality had two paradoxical sides. Her penetrating mind, combined with a rigorous training in morbid anatomy, lent her writings and utterances a clarity and thrust which few of her contemporaries equalled. Consequently, in scientific circles, she was regarded with a degree of respect amounting to awe, and in debate was feared because of her customary trenchant exposition of her views. Yet in private she was reserved and shy, sometimes expressing a humble opinion of her own abilities and attainments. She suffered from epilepsy, a disability made generally known, at her request, after her death. To her friends and close colleagues, and to her disciples, with whom she remained in touch, she extended a warm friendship, embracing also their families.

Russell was active in her retirement at Westcott, near Dorking, Surrey, for, although she seldom attended meetings, many friends and former pupils visited her and she was in regular correspondence with former colleagues. She died on 19 October 1983 in Dorking General Hospital. She was unmarried. J. T. HUGHES, *rev.*

Sources *The Times* (20 Oct 1983) · *The Lancet* (29 Oct 1983), 1039 · *BMJ* (12 Nov 1983), 1477–8 · Munk, *Roll* · B. Wootton, *In a world I never made* (1967) · private information (1990) [Dr A. H. T. Robb-Smith, Dr H. V. Smith] · personal knowledge (1990) · K. T. Butler and H. I. McMorran, eds., *Girton College register, 1869–1946* (1948) · *CGPLA Eng. & Wales* (1983) · J. F. Geddes, 'A portrait of "The Lady": a life of Dorothy Russell', *Journal of the Royal Society of Medicine*, 90 (1997), 455–61 · D. S. Russell, 'Personal view', *BMJ* (27 July 1968), 248 · 'The powers of the Perse. 1: the head girl and netball captain', *The Persean* (1914), 230

Wealth at death £289,760: probate, 15 March 1984, *CGPLA Eng. & Wales*

Russell, Edward, earl of Orford (1652–1727), naval officer, was born at Chiswick, Middlesex, son of Edward Russell, younger brother of William Russell, fifth earl and later first duke of Bedford (1613–1700). His mother was Penelope, daughter of Sir Moyses Hill of Hillsborough, co. Down, and widow of Sir William Brooke. Orphaned early, in 1666 Russell was admitted at St John's College, Cambridge, as a fellow-commoner, but he entered the navy in the same year and his later correspondence suggests a meagre academic competence. He was appointed lieutenant of the *Advice* in 1671, fought at Solebay in May 1672 as lieutenant of the *Rupert* under Sir John Holmes, and was rewarded with his first command, the forty-two gun *Phoenix*. Following the Test Act of 1673, James, duke of York, resigned as lord high admiral, but the favour Russell continued to enjoy from him (though even Pepys, no friend to 'gentlemen officers', later conceded Russell's professional merit) helped him to secure several peacetime captaincies, and he also held an army commission until 1682. He commanded the *Reserve* in 1676 in the Mediterranean under Narborough and then Herbert, and the *Defiance* in 1677, when he was also appointed a groom of York's bedchamber. He then commanded the *Swiftsure* in 1678 and in 1680 the *Newcastle*, in which he served on the Tangier station. Here, like his fellow commanders, Russell acquired a substantial fortune through illicit trading.

Diplomatic activities Pepys believed that it was Russell's Tangier profits which enabled him to resign his command after the Rye House plot of 1683. But Pepys's censoriousness overlooked the trauma, for all members of the Bedford family, of the execution in July 1683 of William Russell, Russell's cousin. Just over forty years earlier Russell's grandfather, Francis Russell, fourth earl of Bedford (*bap.* 1587, *d.* 1641), had been in the forefront of opposition to Charles I, and it was natural for Russell to leave the duke of York's service after the 'murder' of 'a man I passionately loved' (letter to William Russell's widow, 2 Sept 1718, *Letters of Lady Rachel Russell*, 1853, 2.182). Also about 1683 Russell seems to have made his first marriage, though his wife is unidentified.

Russell discovered in himself a bent for opposition, which placed him in the van of those whigs who could discern in William of Orange Britain's best, perhaps only, hope, for safeguarding protestantism and liberty. And

Edward Russell, earl of Orford (1652–1727), by Sir Godfrey Kneller, *c*.1705–10

Russell had the means to hand: between March and May 1687 he collaborated with Dijkfelt, William of Orange's emissary to James II, through Lady Russell's friendship with Mary of Orange and through William Russell's sister Catherine Harbord, now in the Netherlands. The culmination of a year of intense but necessarily undocumented activity for Russell as a go-between led to his being one of the seven signatories of the invitation to William of 30 June 1688. The following November, having crossed again to the Netherlands, he served as William's secretary in his invasion of England, and was soon rewarded by a parliamentary seat at Launceston, through William Harbord's Bedford interest, and the treasurership of the navy.

These rewards were rapidly followed by flag rank in May 1689, and appointment as *custos rotulorum* in both Cambridgeshire and Caernarfon. But Russell was bitterly jealous of Arthur Herbert, commander of William's invasion fleet and, after May 1689, earl of Torrington, and this soon brought forth those 'ill qualities of vanity and pride' (Snyder, 1207) which Marlborough remarked on to his wife in 1709. Russell did valuable service in the channel in 1689 in enforcing a total blockade of France, and then had the ungrateful task of escorting a new consort for Charles II of Spain from Flushing to Corunna between January and April 1690 which, he claimed, left him severely out of pocket. Hitherto, Herbert's preferment was the main focus for Russell's discontents, but this jealousy became transferred by degrees to the high church earl of Nottingham until he, in his turn, left William's ministry in late 1693 in the wake of the Smyrna convoy debacle—when the fleet escorting the convoy in June was disastrously scattered by the French off Cape St Vincent. Though Russell left the Admiralty board in December 1690 he had already been promoted admiral of the fleet, and he was active at sea in 1691. Yet his differences with the present ministry and the lack of financial reward from William for his past services led him to seek some reassurance from James II. Such an approach could only encourage Louis XIV in his invasion plans for 1692, but Russell's motivation was the self-perceived slight and did not impair his professionalism: the navy played its part in bringing the war in Ireland to an end in October 1691.

Naval commands His first wife having died after December 1688, Russell married in November 1691 Lady Margaret Russell (*d.* 1701), sister of the revered William Russell. The following year brought the event which crowned his career at sea and gained him lasting eminence: the five-day battle of La Hogue. Russell had thus far avoided engaging the French fleet, but on 19 May they were sighted approaching the position of his Dutch and English fleets, some 20 miles north-east of Cape Barfleur. The French commander, Tourville, had only forty-five ships of the line, but ran down to engage because, in the hazy weather, he failed to realize that he was considerably outnumbered. The allied fleet was standing towards the south, led by the Dutch, who were contained by the French and prevented from coming to action. The French centre and rear, locally superior in numbers, fell upon the English centre, the Red squadron, with Tourville's *Soleil Royal* attacking Russell's *Britannia*. The fight was evenly balanced until the wind veered west-north-west, allowing the rear of the Red squadron to break through the French line, and a little later the Blue squadron passed to windward. By four o'clock the English fleet had enveloped the French centre and rear. The wind then dropped, and a dense fog came on, so that firing ceased. Towards six a light breeze lifted the fog, at which the French ships fled in disorder, pursued by the English throughout that night and the next day. Apart from some isolated vessels which escaped through the channel or into the North Sea, numerous ships were driven westward, some passing through the Race of Alderney. Of the remainder, three were burnt at Cherbourg and another twelve, plus eight or ten transports, were followed into the Bay of La Hogue and there burnt on 23 and 24 May.

Having declined a peerage on grounds of insufficient income to support it, Russell, now sitting for Portsmouth, had considerable support in the Commons, and as he had no command in 1693 he avoided any direct responsibility for the Smyrna convoy's fate. In November 1693 he succeeded in obtaining substantial parliamentary votes for the navy, and in May 1694 he became first lord of the Admiralty when the power of the whig electoral magnates, the incipient junto, was growing. Among these men, Wharton, Somers, Charles Montague (a distant relative), Russell could already count himself an equal.

In June 1694 Russell commanded the fleet of some sixty-three ships sent to the Mediterranean to keep the French from attacking the Catalan coast. He wintered at Cadiz, and returned to a station off Barcelona the following spring; in August he attempted to recover Palamos, occupied by the French, but learning that a large fleet gathered at Toulon was ready to sail he re-embarked his troops and went to meet it. However, the French ships did not venture from port, and in the autumn Russell returned from sea for the last time, with a notably enhanced prestige. This prolonged Mediterranean command was without precedent, and had helped keep Savoy within the alliance against France.

The reluctant politician Returned for Cambridgeshire in the 1695 election, Russell now had a parliamentary following of naval officers and officials who looked primarily to him for favours. In 1696, despite the allegations of Jacobite loyalties stemming from the Fenwick conspiracy against William III, Russell strove to counter French invasion. A year later he was raised to the peerage as Baron Shingay, Viscount Barfleur, and earl of Orford, testimony to both his national standing and his electoral strength, the latter only surpassed within the junto by Wharton. Yet dragons' teeth had been sown at Cadiz: the discretion he had necessarily been given in disbursing moneys for maintenance of the fleet led in 1701 to charges of malversation of funds which featured in the impeachment process against him and which, it was alleged, had enabled his massive expenditure on his property at Chippenham near Cambridge. He and other members of the junto feared to be in office when Charles II of Spain died. In the elections of 1698, with the war now ended, they all sensed a widespread resistance to the war taxation, and were aware of William's own desire to be freed from their frequently arrogant counsels. Orford was pressured into resigning both treasurership and Admiralty in 1699, and it was only because the upper and lower houses fell out over the impeachment processes, coupled to a darkening scene abroad, that in June 1701 he escaped total ruin. The experience was as formative for him as William Russell's death eighteen years earlier, and determined all his future actions.

The junto survived these inter-war vicissitudes but Orford's frequently expressed distaste for the hurly-burly of Westminster marked him out from his colleagues. He did not serve again at sea after 1695 but he could never be wholly relied upon to pull his political weight, for all his electoral power, though he showed brutality enough in dispensing with naval officers he disliked. Confederates avoided visiting him at Chippenham, and the conviviality of the Kit-Cat Club was not for him, as it was for the others. From 1689 or 1690 Orford resided also at 43 King Street, Covent Garden, and in 1697 he took a twenty-one-year lease on the house. On obtaining a new lease in 1716 he was required to pull down the property and rebuild it, and this was done in 1716–17, the architect probably being Thomas Archer. A shrill and well-informed critic of George of Denmark as lord high admiral after 1702, Orford naturally earned Anne's antipathy, but by 1705 he had found in the young Robert Walpole an able protégé, a favour Walpole lastingly acknowledged. In 1706 Orford

took a leading part in the negotiations for the union with Scotland, personally appointing as the English commissioners' secretary George Dodington, who had been on his staff in the Mediterranean (and subsequently served as an Admiralty commissioner) and attending some two-thirds of the commission's meetings in London. Orford established his own patronage among the new Scottish MPs but, beyond virtually dictating the terms upon which he returned to the Admiralty in October 1709, nominating his board and requiring parliamentary approval of it, he took little part in the bruising whig politicking of the period. Marlborough favoured Orford for the Garter, which he might not have spurned, but the defeat of the whigs in 1710 cut off this prospect. Joining the protesters against the 'restraining orders' of the summer of 1712, Orford, already named as a regent by Georg Ludwig of Brunswick-Lüneburg, could expect a return of political fortune at the hands of the new king, along with those other juntoists who had sufficient health to serve George I.

Hanoverian navy politics In taking the first lordship of the Admiralty for a third time on George I's accession, Orford was probably aiming to prepare the navy to resist another Jacobite attempt to recover the crown. Like George's other British ministers, such as Townshend, Walpole, or Stanhope, Orford could not know what other challenges lay ahead for the ministry through Britain's link with the electorate of Hanover. There were insuring clauses of the Act of Settlement against any Hanoverian employment of British forces without parliament's prior consent, but no way to gauge how far the need for an unprecedented demonstration of naval power in the Baltic, tolerably clear even before George I reached his new kingdom because of the intensity of Swedish privateering against all merchantmen, might activate parliamentary concern. Little was known in London about Hanoverian territorial aspirations against Sweden in north-west Germany at this stage of the Great Northern War, but two convoying seasons in the Baltic soon disclosed to Orford and others the Hanoverians' preparedness and ability to circumvent the Act of Settlement by entering into naval arrangements with Denmark, a power with which Britain was not in military alliance any more than she was at war with Sweden. Orford, only too aware of being answerable to parliament, went to great lengths to ensure that the potential value of the two convoying squadrons to Hanover could only be modest and their armament merely in line with the role of neutral broker between Denmark and Sweden, which the navy had last played at Copenhagen in 1700. His success in frustrating the hopes aroused in the Danes by illicit Hanoverian promptings, of which George I, as elector, was fully apprised, emerges plainly in the dispatches sent to Copenhagen by the Danish representative in London, Söhlenthal. This clash of British and Hanoverian interests was, however, transcended in the autumn of 1716 by a dramatic deterioration in Hanover's relations with Peter the Great of Russia, whose ambitions in north

Germany were prejudicial to Hanover's territorial integrity. The acute differences between Orford, Townshend, and Walpole on the one hand and Stanhope and Sunderland (the latter spurred on by his aggrieved father-in-law, Marlborough) on the other, over how British and Hanoverian aims in the north might best be reconciled, brought the collapse of George I's first British ministry in the spring of 1717 and Orford's resignation from the Admiralty in April. Though George I tried hard to forestall Walpole's simultaneous resignation he knew better than to try to retain Orford. It is almost certain that in the course of 1716, especially after George I and Stanhope left for Hanover in May, Orford buttressed Townshend and Walpole in their misgivings over the consequences for British interests of Hanoverian designs in the Great Northern War. In late summer 1717 Orford attended George I at Newmarket and received him at Chippenham, but these were probably little more than formal courtesies.

Apart from occasional appearances in the Lords as a whig dissident, Orford now retired from public life. 'Cherry-cheeked Russell' (Ehrman, 271), choleric, denigratory, sulkily retiring, has an equivocal place in the politics of his time and, in spite of La Hogue, an oddly disconnected naval record which still defies evaluation. But his Russell blood, and a tradition of opposition to dubiously directed power, flowed strongly in him. No children survived from either of his marriages, and on his death at Chippenham in 1727 his title lapsed until its revival, in its second creation, by Walpole in 1742. Orford was buried in the Russell vault at Chenies.   D. D. ALDRIDGE

Sources E. L. Ellis, 'The whig junto', MLitt diss., U. Oxf., 1962 • E. Cruickshanks, 'Russell, Edward', HoP, Commons, 1660–90, 3.359–60 • J. Ehrman, *The navy in the war of William III, 1689–1697* (1953), esp. chaps. 12 and 14 • E. B. Powley, *The naval side of King William's war* (1972) • D. D. Aldridge, 'Admiral Edward Russell: pre- and post-Barfleur', *Guerres maritimes, 1688–1713* [Portsmouth 1992], ed. Journées franco-britanniques d'histoire de la marine (Vincennes, 1996) • P. Aubrey, *The defeat of James Stuart's armada, 1692* (1979) • D. D. Aldridge, 'Russell: La Hogue, 1692', *Great battles of the Royal Navy*, ed. E. Grove (1994) • R. Walcott, *English politics in the early eighteenth century* (1956) • H. Horwitz, *Parliament, policy and politics in the reign of William III* (1977) • R. H. Irrmann, 'Gallia Frustra', *Essays in honour of W. T. Morgan*, ed. J. J. Murray (Bloomington, Indiana, 1951) • M. Spufford, *A Cambridgeshire community* (1965) • J. J. Murray, *George I, the Baltic, and the whig split* (1968) • D. D. Aldridge, 'Admiral Sir John Norris and the British naval expeditions to the Baltic Sea, 1715–1727', PhD diss., U. Lond., 1971 • *The Marlborough–Godolphin correspondence*, ed. H. L. Snyder, 3 (1975), 1207 • BL, Egerton MSS, 2621, fol. 77
Archives Cambs. AS, household accounts • Cumbria AS, Carlisle, naval corresp. • NMM, accounts • NRA, accounts • Woburn Abbey, Bedfordshire, dispatches | BL, reports of commission, Add. MSS 17761–17765 • CKS, corresp. with Alexander Stanhope • HLRO, corresp. with Admiralty • Leics. RO, corresp. with earl of Nottingham • LPL, summary of Russell's activities connected with the battle of La Hogue, 1692 • Mount Stuart Trust, Isle of Bute, corresp. with Loudon • Northants. RO, corresp. with duke of Shrewsbury • U. Nott. L., letters to first earl of Portland, and other MSS
Likenesses G. Kneller, oils, c.1693–1697, NMM • G. Kneller, oils, c.1705–1710, NMM [see illus.] • G. Vertue, line engraving, 1716 (after T. Gibson), BM, NPG • W. Elder, line engraving (when Admiral Russell; after W. Wissing), NPG • attrib. T. Gibson, oils, NMM • R. White, line engraving, BM • mezzotint, BM, NPG

Russell, Lord Edward (1805–1887), naval officer, was born on 24 April 1805, the second son of John *Russell, sixth duke of Bedford (1766–1839), and his second wife, Lady Georgiana, fifth daughter of Alexander Gordon, fourth duke of Gordon; John *Russell, first Earl Russell, was his half-brother. He entered the navy in January 1819, passed his examination in 1825, and on 18 October 1826 was promoted lieutenant on the brig *Philomel*, in which he was present at the battle of Navarino on 20 October 1827. He was then for a short time in the *Dartmouth*, but returned to the *Philomel*, and from her was promoted commander on 15 November 1828. In November 1830 he was appointed to the *Britomart*, but in the following January was moved to the *Savage*, and in April 1832 to the *Nimrod*, on the Lisbon station. He was invalided from her in August 1833, and on 19 November was advanced to post rank over the heads of at least 100 older officers. From November 1834 to 1838 he commanded the *Actaeon* in South America.

In 1839 Russell became private secretary to his half-brother, Lord John Russell. From 1841 to 1847 he was whig MP for Tavistock (the family borough), and one of the queen's naval aides-de-camp from 1846 to 1850. He was at that time well known as a patron of the turf.

Following the sudden death of Captain Henry Blackwood, in January 1851, Russell was appointed to the *Vengeance* for service in the Mediterranean. Here he had the benefit of a brilliant first officer, William Mends. Shortly after arriving in the Mediterranean, Russell was sent, in 1851, on a mission to the pasha of Egypt to support British efforts to build a railway between Alexandria and Cairo. After returning to England in late 1852, the *Vengeance* went out to reinforce the Mediterranean Fleet as the Eastern crisis developed. During a prolonged period spent at anchor in Besika Bay, Russell was seriously ill with malaria. In 1854 the allied fleet entered the Black Sea; Russell oversaw the landing of the British army at Varna, and on 17 October 1854 took part in the attack on the sea forts of Sevastopol. In the summer of 1855 the *Vengeance* was paid off, and on 5 July, Russell was made a CB. He had no further service, but became rear-admiral on 17 October 1856, vice-admiral on 27 April 1863, and admiral on 20 March 1867. On 8 February 1860 he married Mary Ann (d. 16 Oct 1874), daughter of Aaron Taylor of Montpelier Street, Kensington, London; they had no surviving children.

On 1 April 1870 Russell retired. He died at the Royal Yacht Squadron club house, Cowes, on 21 May 1887. Russell's career was made by his father and brother, his periods of service coinciding with those of whig governments. He was an amateur aristocratic officer who served only at home or in the Mediterranean, and more than once had to rely on his relatives to avoid problems.

J. K. LAUGHTON, *rev.* ANDREW LAMBERT

Sources B. S. Mends, *Admiral Sir W. R. Mends* (1899) • A. D. Lambert, *The Crimean War: British grand strategy, 1853–56* (1990) • W. Sussex RO, Lyons papers • Cumbria AS, Carlisle, Graham MSS • C. Penrose-Fitzgerald, *Sir George Tryon* (1898) • J. Prest, *Lord John Russell* (1972) • Burke, *Peerage* (1959) • CGPLA Eng. & Wales (1887)
Archives NMM, papers
Wealth at death £1394 9s. 11d.: probate, 22 July 1887, CGPLA Eng. & Wales

Russell, Edward Richard, first Baron Russell of Liverpool (1834–1920), newspaper editor and proprietor, born on 9 August 1834 at the Barbican, London, was the son of Edward Haslingden Russell (1809–1851) and Mary Anne Crook (d. 1851). He received an elementary education to the age of fourteen, and thereafter taught himself. Orphaned at sixteen, he was already so well launched upon a career in journalism that he was soon appointed editor of the *Islington Gazette*. However, Russell's unwonted enthusiasm for radical politics led to the newspaper being successfully sued for libel and him consequently forfeiting his job. This proved a temporary set-back for, in 1860, at the precociously early age of twenty-six, Russell accepted the invitation of the owner, Michael Whitty, to become assistant editor of the *Liverpool Daily Post*. He stayed six years, but resigned when refused a limited partnership by Whitty. For the next four years he freelanced in London, and was deputy editor and chief leader writer for Justin McCarthy's *Morning Star*. The intelligence, shrewdness, and judgement he demonstrated in his political commentaries won glowing tributes from the leaders of the Liberal Party. Early in the 1860s, in an obscure magazine, *Every Month*, Russell became the first to canvass the name of W. E. Gladstone as the future Liberal leader.

In 1869 Russell returned to Liverpool as editor of the *Daily Post*. Shortly after Whitty's death in 1873, with A. G. Jeans, Russell became the newspaper's co-proprietor. In 1879 the two men started a complementary evening newspaper, the *Liverpool Echo*. In 1905 the *Liverpool Daily Post* merged with the *Daily Mercury*, and continued to flourish throughout the half century that Russell was its editor. A Liberal newspaper in a tory stronghold, the *Post* owed much of its distinction and popularity to Russell's writing. He was a perspicacious literary and theatre critic. His parliamentary reporting demonstrated an intimate knowledge of Westminster. He explained complex and divisive issues to his readers with a felicity and sureness of touch. His writing, like his public speaking, was informed, fluent, sensible, and convincing rather than brilliant.

An advanced Liberal, Russell early espoused home rule and profoundly admired Gladstone. Ireland's political future sundered relations between Joseph Chamberlain and Russell. The ambitious politician had assiduously cultivated the editor as an important ally in the provincial press who could explain and help popularize his new policies, a process that culminated with the publication of Chamberlain's so-called 'unauthorized' programme in 1885. Russell nurtured parliamentary ambitions himself. The *Pall Mall Gazette* (3 July 1885) asserted that it was infinitely more important for Russell to be an editor than an MP. Nevertheless, Russell stood and was elected as Liberal member for the Bridgeton division of Glasgow in November 1885. He was successfully re-elected as a Gladstonian Liberal in July 1886, but took the Chiltern Hundreds the following year, possibly because of pressure of work. He had not been long enough in the house to make a reputation, but his best, most persuasive speeches were on home rule, making plain his disappointment at Chamberlain's 'betrayal'.

Russell remained an important figure in Liberal politics, and an influential friend to successive Liberal leaders. In local affairs he enjoyed an enormous personal following that breached conventional party political loyalties. Never was this better demonstrated than in 1905 when he was carried upon the shoulders of a cheering throng from St George's Hall where he had won a famous victory at the assizes. He had been charged with criminal libel for asserting that certain tory licensing justices were too friendly to the drink trade.

Russell took a prominent part in Liverpool's educational and cultural life as president of the city's Literary and Philosophical Society and a life member of the university's court. A great theatre enthusiast, he was a founder of the Liverpool Repertory and remained a director until 1917.

Russell married twice. His first marriage was on 16 December 1858 to Eliza Sophia, daughter of Stephen Bradley of Bridge, Kent. They had two sons. Eliza died on 22 January 1901. On 30 April 1902 Russell married Jean Stewart (*née* Macdonald), widow of Joseph M'Farlane. Russell was fearless and uncompromising in public life, but at home in his later years was somewhat cowed by his dour second wife, who died in 1927.

In 1893 Russell was knighted. Somewhat paradoxically, as a radical Liberal who had long considered the hereditary principle in the House of Lords doomed, he accepted a barony in 1919. Ironically the king twice opposed Russell's elevation as too great a step for a 'mere knight bachelor' and because of his great age. The creation was approved, reluctantly, only because Lloyd George insisted. Russell had eagerly anticipated renewing his parliamentary career, interrupted in 1887, but he died on 20 February 1920 at his home, The Gables, at 5 Croxteth Road, Toxteth Park, Liverpool. He was buried on 23 February at Childwall.

Born to neither wealth nor privilege, in a long life Russell, by his intelligence and industry, gained both fame and fortune. He was always content to remain in the background 'pulling the strings that made others dance his tune' (*Liverpool Post*, 21 Feb 1920). The doyen of provincial newspaper editors, Russell was blessed with 'the sweetest disposition, a generous nature and an even temperament'. To the end of his very long life, an admiring colleague, Sir Henry Lucy, observed, 'like Peter Pan, he never seemed to grow old' (Russell, 65–6).   A. J. A. MORRIS

Sources Lord Russell [E. R. Russell], *That reminds me* (1959) • L. W. Brady, 'A Victorian editor and high policy: Sir Edward Russell and Joseph Chamberlain in the 1880's', *Journal of Newspaper and Periodical History*, 5 (1988–9), 14–22 • WW • WWBMP • P. F. Clarke, *Lancashire and the new liberalism* (1971) • A. J. Lee, *The origins of the popular press in England, 1855–1914* (1976) • T. H. S. Escott, *Masters of English journalism* (1911), 293 • Lucy Brown, *Victorian news and newspapers* (1985), 194 • S. E. Koss, *The rise and fall of the political press in Britain*, 1 (1981) • GEC, *Peerage* • d. cert. • M. A. Beaverbrook, *Men and power, 1917–1918* (1956), 244–5
Archives BL, corresp. with Sir Henry Campbell-Bannerman, Add. MSS 41234–41241 • Lpool RO, corresp.; corresp. and papers • U. Birm. L., corresp. with Joseph Chamberlain | BL, letters to W. E. Gladstone, Add. MSS 44415–44519, *passim* • HLRO, letters to David Lloyd George • NL Scot., corresp., mainly with Lord Rosebery

Likenesses oils?, repro. in Russell, *That reminds me*, facing p. 34
Wealth at death £63,686 10s. 5d.: resworn probate, 8 April 1920, *CGPLA Eng. & Wales*

Russell, Edward Southwell, twenty-sixth Baron de Clifford (1907–1982), racing driver, dog-food salesman, and the last peer to be tried by the House of Lords, was born on 31 January 1907, the only son of Jack Southwell Russell, twenty-fifth Baron de Clifford (1884–1909), an Irish landowner, and his wife, Evelyn Victoria Anne (*b.* 1886/7), a Gibson girl whose stage name was Eva Carrington; she was the daughter of Walter Robert Chandler of Dalgan Park, Shrule, Tuam, sometime orderly room clerk to Colonel Fred Burnaby. In infancy Russell succeeded to the title and an impoverished Irish estate (12,000 acres in co. Mayo and co. Galway, worth £5691 a year in 1883 but valued at £100,000 in 1909) when his father was killed in a motor accident at Bramber, Sussex, on 1 September 1909. He was educated at Eton College and Imperial College, London, where he studied engineering. His early years were associated with fast cars and fast women. On 11 March 1926, aged nineteen, he married Dorothy (Dolly) Evelyn Meyrick (1902–1987), dance hostess daughter of the shady nightclub manageress Kate *Meyrick, and was promptly fined £50 for making a false oath to obtain the marriage certificate, claiming that he was aged twenty-two and the son of Jack Russell, engineer; he feared that his mother, who was his legal guardian and by then on her third husband, George Vernon Tate, might have withheld her consent. He was lucky, the lord mayor stated, in imposing the fine, to have escaped a prison sentence.

Nine years later de Clifford was luckier still to escape prison. On 21 August 1935 he was charged with 'feloniously killing and slaying Douglas George Hopkins by driving a motor recklessly at the Kingston Bypass road'; he stated that the other car, driven by Hopkins, another racing driver, returning at 3.30 a.m. from a dance in Datchet with his sister and girlfriend, had been out of control, on the wrong side of the road, and going at a tremendous speed, so that he, de Clifford, had swerved to avoid it and thus also ended up on the wrong side of the road. This was not considered a convincing defence. A peer—and indeed any peeress, whether noble by birth or by marriage—accused of felony had to be tried by his peers—a privilege, or procedure, that could not be waived. These trials had become exceedingly rare so that the first action of the House of Lords was to set up a select committee to scrutinize the precedents and establish the proper form for turning itself into a court, which it drew from the last trial, that of the second Earl Russell for bigamy, in 1901.

The Russell trial had been a big social occasion, with much demand for ringside seats; again, in 1935 admission to de Clifford's trial was by ticket only, issued to privileged categories of peers electing not to take a full part in the trial, peeresses, eldest sons of peers, Scottish and Irish peers, and a limited number of MPs. While there was a full house on 12 December 1935 it was not, however, treated as a second Ascot, unlike the 1901 event, which had chanced to fall in July. There was some preliminary debate on whether it was obligatory for peers to wear cocked hats, and on the definition of a cocked hat; it was decided that all peers wishing to be full members of the trial had to be properly dressed and hatted, but ordinary spectators could be less formally dressed. After this considerable build-up the trial itself, while quite spectacular as pageant, was very brief. Sir Henry Curtis Bennett KC advanced the extraordinary argument that de Clifford had no case to answer, since the mere fact that a motorist was on the wrong side of the road, as he admitted he had been, was no evidence of negligence, let alone of criminal negligence. The trial peers listened to this in the royal gallery (fitted out as a court), trooped out to their chamber to debate it, and returned to the court to pronounce in turn, starting with the most junior baron, that de Clifford was not guilty. The charge against him of dangerous driving still stood, in theory to be heard in the ordinary courts; but it was quietly dropped and no further charges were pursued.

These occasional trials by peers tended to produce theatrical performances of a carefully choreographed and half-remembered costume drama—Dorothy Sayers, no doubt inspired by accounts of the Russell trial, gave a graphic description of a fictitious trial by peers in her *Clouds of Witness* (1926)—and bizarre verdicts. The de Clifford acquittal was in the tradition of the perverse conviction of Earl Russell for bigamy (he spent three months in Holloway prison) on the grounds that his divorce from his outrageously impossible first wife, perfectly validly performed at Reno, Nevada, was not recognized under English law, and of the even more outrageous acquittal of Lord Cardigan in 1841, because the evidence that he shot Harvey Tuckett in a duel did not prove that he had shot the Harvey Garnet Phipps Tuckett named in the indictment. The lord chancellor in 1935, Hailsham, praised the trial as a fine example of maintaining a glorious tradition, while at the same time acknowledging that the whole archaic ritual was an anachronistic and inherently unfair procedure. Nothing was done about it, however, until after 1945, when a section of the law reforms in the 1948 Criminal Justice Act abolished trial by peers.

For de Clifford the publicity of his trial and the curious basis of his acquittal meant his withdrawal from public life. He perhaps appreciated the irony that he had begun to build a reputation as a road safety expert in the Lords from his maiden speech, at the age of twenty-one, proposing driving tests for all applicants for driving licences and—years before its time—suggesting that road deaths and injuries of children could be curbed by having policemen outside schools to help them in crossing roads. In the early 1930s, between visits to Brooklands racetrack, he maintained a steady stream of short speeches on road safety, pressing for the introduction of driving tests because it was 'unfair that the majority of motorists should be penalised for the minority of careless drivers' (*The Times*, 3 June 1932) and welcoming speed limits in built-up areas, urging that 'there were places in larger towns where even 30 miles an hour would be too great' (ibid., 11 July 1934). He gave this up after 1935 and never spoke in the Lords again. He also gave up racing, using his engineering training with armoured cars in the Territorial Army and then with the Royal Electrical and Mechanical Engineers (REME) during the Second World War; he transferred to the regular army in 1942, was appointed OBE (military) in 1955, and retired as lieutenant-colonel.

De Clifford's marriage survived his appearance as co-respondent in a divorce case in 1936 but he and his wife separated after the war and were finally divorced in 1973; on 4 December 1974 he married Mina Margaret, only daughter of George Edward Sands. For a while he lived in Wrantage, near Taunton, Somerset, running a quarantine kennel and selling dog food door-to-door, and then moved to The Birches, Silvington, Cleobury Mortimer, Shropshire, where he died on 3 January 1982, leaving £437. He was survived by his second wife, and was succeeded in the title by his elder son, John Edward Southwell Russell, who was born in 1928.   F. M. L. THOMPSON

Sources *The Times* (8 Jan 1982) · *The Times* (4 Oct 1982) · *Daily Telegraph* (25 Sept 1987) [obituary of Dorothy, Lady de Clifford] · *Hansard 5L* (1928), 70.43; (1928), 71.905–7; (1932), 84.576–7, 85.920–24, 931, 1111; (1934), 93.441–4, 670, 824–5, 833, 846–7, 984–5 · Burke, *Peerage* · *WW* · Kelly, *Handbk* · R. F. V. Heuston, *Lives of the lord chancellors, 1940–1970* (1987), 482–3
Wealth at death £437: *The Times* (4 Oct 1982)

Russell, Edward Stuart (1887–1954), biologist, was born on 25 March 1887 in Port Glasgow, Renfrewshire, the youngest of the eight surviving children of the Revd John Naismith Russell, minister in the Free Church of Scotland, and his wife, Helen Cockburn Young, the daughter of a blacksmith from East Lothian. He was educated at Jean Street School in Port Glasgow, and won a scholarship to Greenock Academy, where he was a pupil from 1898 to 1904. His school reports describe his diligence as 'excellent' and his progress as 'great'. He went to Glasgow University in 1904, and in his first year studied Greek, Latin, and chemistry. He graduated MA in 1907 and BSc in 1909. He was awarded the degree of DSc by the university in 1921.

While a student, Russell became interested in marine biology and was influenced in his thinking by J. Arthur Thomson and Patrick Geddes. In 1909 he was appointed to the Board of Agriculture and Fisheries as inspector for international investigations. From 1 April of the following year he was based at 43 Parliament Street in London; he retained an office there for most of his working life. In 1911 he married Jehanne Aurélie, the daughter of Charles Owen Minchin, who had been a chief clerk in the estate duty office of the Inland Revenue.

By 1914 Russell was one of five naturalist inspectors, and then an inspector of fisheries employed by the Ministry of Agriculture and Fisheries. One of his qualities was the ability to put together a whole picture from fragments of information. He used this gift in interpreting fishery statistics. During the First World War he was sent to Cornwall to work with the local fishermen, both collecting data and helping them to adhere to wartime regulations. In 1921 he was appointed director of fisheries investigations—a title later changed to chief scientific officer, Ministry of Agriculture and Fisheries, fisheries branch. In the early 1930s,

at a time when statistics were reluctantly used by biologists, he published a paper on the overfishing problem in the *Journal du Conseil International pour l'Exploration de la Mer* for 1931, in which he presented an extremely simple equation which took into account the various factors which could influence fish yields. Russell himself was surprised by the enthusiasm for this paper, as the concepts were so straightforward. He also proposed set areas in which to quantify fish catches, rather than the previously diffuse ones. He was interested in fish behaviour, and his 1937 article on fish migrations in *Biological Review* is interesting not only for the evidence of his wide reading, but for the frequency with which he highlights unresolved problems.

Russell did not like interference in his work and assumed others did not either. Thus he administered the Lowestoft laboratory from his London office, and visited Lowestoft at fortnightly intervals. This gave the research workers considerable freedom to develop their own lines of enquiry. In 1943–4 Russell was the fisheries adviser to the secretary of state for the colonies. He was fisheries scientific adviser from 1945 to 1947, when he retired.

Russell had a very active mind and enjoyed research. Using his strong classical background he was able to investigate early ideas on development. *Form and Function* (1916) was the result of much detailed reading and was subtitled 'a contribution to the history of animal morphology'. Two other major works were *The Interpretation of Development and Heredity* (1930) and *The Directiveness of Organic Activities* (1945), which argues that the 'central concept of functional biology must be organism, not mechanism' (*Directiveness*, 185).

From 1926 to 1940 Russell was the first editor of the *Journal du Conseil*, and he was thereby able to exert considerable influence on the development of European fisheries. He was a member of council of the Marine Biological Association for four terms of three years between 1927 and 1943, and a vice-president from 1948 until his death. He was president of the Linnean Society from 1940 to 1942, and an honorary member of the Dutch Zoological Society.

From 1932 to 1947 Russell was an honorary lecturer in animal behaviour in the department of zoology and comparative anatomy at University College, London. *The Behaviour of Animals* (1934) is based on the lectures he gave in 1933. In it he said that 'it is far more important nowadays to work out the life-history and habits of a beetle or a caddis-fly than to form extensive collections or make new "records"' (*Behaviour*, vi). In 1934 he was president of section D (zoology) when the British Association for the Advancement of Science held its annual meeting in Aberdeen. His presidential address was on the study of behaviour. This was a time in biology when ecology, the study of living organisms in their habitats, was just beginning to develop into a science. Russell was able to encourage students into being questioning observers of animal behaviour. He was a kindly and humble person, yet he had a quiet determination to see an idea through when he felt it was the right one. He was made an OBE in 1930. He died at the East Sussex Hospital in Hastings on 24 August 1954, and was buried six days later at Hollington Church-in-the-Wood; he was survived by his wife.

CATHARINE M. C. HAINES

Sources M. Graham, 'E. S. Russell, 1887–1954', *Journal du Conseil International pour l'Exploration de la Mer*, 20 (1954), 135–9 · *The Times* (26 Aug 1954), 8f · letter, *The Times* (28 Aug 1954), 9b · A. J. Lee, *The ministry of agriculture, fisheries and food's directorate of fisheries research: its origins and development* (1992), 71–82 · E. S. Russell, 'Fish Migrations', *Biological Review*, 12 (1937), 320–27 · A. Hardy, *The open sea: its natural history*, 2: *Fish and fisheries* (1959), 247–55 · Greenock Academy, archives · UCL, records office · Marine Biological Association of the United Kingdom, Plymouth, records · E. S. Russell, *The interpretation of development and heredity: a study in biological method* (1930) · *CGPLA Eng. & Wales* (1954) · *Hastings and St Leonard's Observer* (28 Aug 1954), 2

Archives Marine Biological Association of the United Kingdom, Plymouth, letters to E. T. Browne

Likenesses photograph, repro. in *Journal du Conseil International pour l'Exploration de la Mer*, 135

Wealth at death £3946 1s. 7d.: probate, 23 Nov 1954, *CGPLA Eng. & Wales*

Russell [née Cooke], **Elizabeth**, **Lady Russell** [other married name Elizabeth Hoby, Lady Hoby] (**1528–1609**), linguist and courtier, was the third of five learned daughters of Sir Anthony *Cooke (1505/6–1576) of Gidea Hall, Essex, tutor to Edward VI, and his wife, Anne, daughter of Sir William Fitzwilliam. Through her father's influence she became skilled in languages. On 27 June 1558 she married Sir Thomas *Hoby (1530–1566) of Bisham Abbey, Berkshire, translator of Castiglione's *Il Cortegiano* into English as *The Courtier*. A son, Edward, and two daughters, who died young, were born between 1560 and 1564. She accompanied her husband to France on his appointment as ambassador in March 1566, where he died on 13 July. Shortly afterwards she gave birth to a second son, Thomas Posthumous. In Bisham church she created the Hoby Chapel, where she interred the bodies of her husband and his elder brother, Philip, in a joint monument with effigies and epitaphs in Greek, Latin, and English.

On 23 December 1574 Elizabeth married John, Lord Russell (d. 1584), heir to Francis *Russell, second earl of Bedford. Two daughters were born, Anne and Elizabeth, and one authority records a son who died in 1580. The tradition at Bisham that her ill treatment caused a son's death (and the appearance of her repentant ghost) cannot be verified. Lord Russell predeceased his father, dying on 24 July 1584, so denying her the title of countess of Bedford. She erected a monument to him in Westminster Abbey, again revealing her linguistic skills in the accompanying inscriptions.

Through access to those in power, Elizabeth could offer patronage to others. She gave support to the composer John Dowland (but opposed Richard Burbage's proposal in 1596 to convert property near her Blackfriars home into a playhouse). From the 1560s to the 1590s her patronage was frequently sought in matters ranging from the shrievalty of Buckinghamshire to a knighthood for the duke of Somerset's son-in-law. She, in turn, relied on the support of her brother-in-law William Cecil, Lord Burghley, and her nephew Robert Cecil. When her despised son Thomas

Posthumous fled in 1586 to avoid having to study law, she begged Burghley to take him into his service. (In 1588 Thomas was admitted to Gray's Inn as Burghley's protégé.) Apart from her alleged poverty, her concern in 1593 was that her daughters had been cheated of their Russell birthright by their aunt, Lady Warwick—a view with which Burghley sympathized. She also sought his help in a dispute with one Lovelace, lieutenant of Windsor Forest and Castle, which had erupted into violence. In 1595 Burghley was unsympathetic, causing her to note his 'mutterings, which stick fast by me' (*CSP dom.*, 1595–7, 147). Occasionally the process was reversed. On Burghley's behalf in 1596 she tackled Anthony Bacon, nephew to both, questioning his loyalty and his associates' religion.

In 1599, after numerous disputes, Lady Russell complained to Robert Cecil of being 'beggared by law' (*Salisbury MSS*, 9.339) and was angered by her daughter Elizabeth's 'presumptuous disobedience' in supporting a plan to be rid of Russell House—a link with her second husband. She wrote repeatedly to Cecil in 1601 about Justice Warburton's revoking of a judgment against a former servant, metaphorically refusing to be 'bearded by a girl's tearing out of my teeth' (*Salisbury MSS*, 11.563–4). From 1603 she disputed the earl of Nottingham's right to the lease of Donnington Castle, Berkshire, requiring Cecil's presence when the Star Chamber hearing began in 1606. Constantly interrupting the court, she lost the case.

For much of her life Elizabeth enjoyed royal patronage. The queen was reputedly godmother to two of her children, and after Lord Russell's death she paid debts and provided for both daughters, eventually granting them posts at court. In 1592 the queen, court, and privy council were entertained at Bisham Abbey, but in 1595 Lady Russell found she could only see the queen when 'going to God's house' (*CSP dom.*, 1595–7, 147–8). She was back in favour in June 1600, when the queen attended the marriage of her daughter Anne to Henry, Lord Herbert, son of the earl of Worcester, at Blackfriars. Her younger daughter died a few days later, allegedly from a needleprick in her left forefinger. She wrote to Robert Cecil in 1601 that the girl had not been given as honourable a burial as 'meaner maids' (*Salisbury MSS*, 11.562) in the queen's service, while her own uncomfortable farewell from court had 'killed a courtier' in her.

Lady Russell retained her linguistic skills over the years, adding Latin verses and quotations to letters, and translating from the French *A way of reconciliation touching the true nature and substance of the body and blood of Christ in the sacrament* (printed in 1605). She dedicated this to her surviving daughter. In her will she claimed to eschew 'vain ostentation or pomp' (PRO, PROB 11/113, fol. 435r) for her funeral, but wrote to Sir William Dethick, Garter king of arms, about the number of mourners and appropriate display for her status. She also left money for seventy poor widows to be provided with funeral clothes. Her will reveals that apart from her Berkshire and London holdings (inherited by her son Edward) she had tithes from eight Worcestershire parishes and property in Gloucestershire. The latter went to Thomas Posthumous, whose wife was Margaret Hoby (*née* Dakins), the diarist. She died in May or June 1609, and was buried at Bisham church on 2 June. Her memorial in Bisham church depicts her kneeling at a priedieu and wearing a coronet, with the figures of children from both marriages around her.

PAMELA PRIESTLAND

Sources *Calendar of the manuscripts of the most hon. the marquis of Salisbury*, 7, HMC, 9 (1899), 87, 281; 9 (1902), 77–8, 321, 339–40, 358–9, 383; 11 (1906), 423–4, 562–4; 13 (1915), 265, 515; 14 (1923), 192; 18 (1940), 436–7 · *CSP dom.*, 1547–80; 1591–7; addenda, 1566–79 · BL, MS Egerton 2148, 4v, 184–5 · T. Hoby, 'The travels and life of Sir Thomas Hoby', ed. E. Powell, *Camden miscellany, X*, CS, 3rd ser., 4 (1902), ix, opposite xvi · G. Ballard, *Memoirs of several ladies of Great Britain* (1752), 194–201 · P. Compton, *The story of Bisham Abbey* (1973), 68–87, 103–6 · D. Du Maurier, *Golden lads: a study of Anthony Bacon, Francis and their friends* (1975), 171–5 · will, PRO, PROB 11/113, fols. 435r–436r · *VCH Essex*, vol. 7 · D. Lysons and S. Lysons, *Magna Britannia: being a concise topographical account of the several counties of Great Britain*, new edn, 1 (1813), 243, 450–51 · *The letters of John Chamberlain*, ed. N. E. McClure, 1 (1939), 101, 105 · J. Nichols, *The progresses, processions, and magnificent festivities of King James I, his royal consort, family and court*, 1 (1828), 258, 274 · D. Englander, D. Norman, R. O'Day, and W. R. Owens, eds., *Culture and belief in Europe, 1450–1660* (1990), 212 · J. Foster, *The register of admissions to Gray's Inn, 1521–1889, together with the register of marriages in Gray's Inn chapel, 1695–1754* (privately printed, London, 1889) [entries for 3/1588] · 'Cooke, Sir Anthony', *DNB* · 'Hoby, Sir Thomas', *DNB* · D. Poulton, *John Dowland* (1972), 390, 424–6

Likenesses oils, *c*.1590, Bisham Abbey, Buckinghamshire; repro. in Compton, *Story of Bisham Abbey*, frontispiece · alabaster tomb effigy, 1609, All Saints' Church, Bisham, Buckinghamshire

Wealth at death £2816 2s.: will, PRO, PROB 11/113, fols. 435r–436r

Russell [*née* Cromwell; *other married name* Rich], **Frances**, **Lady Russell** (*bap.* 1638, *d.* 1720), daughter of Oliver Cromwell, was born in Ely and baptized in St Mary's Church there on 6 December 1638, the youngest of nine children and four daughters of Oliver *Cromwell (1599–1658), the future lord protector, and his wife, Elizabeth *Cromwell, *née* Bourchier (1598–1665), daughter of Sir James Bourchier. Frances and her sister Mary [*see* Belasyse, Mary, Countess Fauconberg] remained in the parental home long after their surviving siblings married and moved away. Thus she was living with them when they became protector and protectress, was assigned apartments at Whitehall and Hampton Court, and was often referred to as Lady or Princess Frances. During the 1650s her name was linked with several alleged suitors until in November 1657 she married Robert Rich (1634–1658), grandson of Robert Rich, second earl of Warwick (1587–1658), and only son and heir of Robert Rich, Lord Rich (1611–1659). The courtship had been long and difficult, with reservations from both families. The groom's father, Lord Rich, a former royalist of doubtful loyalty to the regime, was heavily in debt, and his relations with both his father and his son were strained, tensions heightened by Cromwell's 'high' demands for the marriage settlement (*Frankland-Russell-Astley MSS*, 21–2). Cromwell was also concerned by rumours, eventually discounted, that the proposed bridegroom was 'vicious' and 'given to play' (Thurloe, *State papers*, 5.146). But Frances was determined to proceed, a settlement was eventually agreed, and on 11 November

1657 in a civil service at Whitehall Palace they were married in the presence of protector, protectress, Lord Rich, the earl of Warwick, and others. The earl of Clarendon alleges that a second marriage was conducted privately by an ordained minister in accordance with the prayer book. The wedding feast on the following day was particularly exuberant, and celebrations continued intermittently for several days more. Rich, already ill at the time of the marriage, died at Whitehall on 16 February 1658. There were no children of the marriage.

Frances, styled Lady Rich, continued to live at Whitehall and Hampton Court. After the collapse of the protectorate in spring 1659 she apparently lived for a time at the house of her brother Richard *Cromwell at Hursley in Hampshire, for it was there on 7 May 1663 that she married her second husband, John Russell (1632–1670), of Chippenham in Cambridgeshire, who in April 1664 succeeded to his father's baronetcy. There was already a close connection between the two families, for Frances's brother Henry *Cromwell had married Russell's sister. After their marriage the couple lived at Chippenham, though Sir John was frequently in London on business and many of his letters seek to revive his wife, to reassure her, and to allay her 'melancholy'. The couple had five children (three sons—William, Richard, and John—and two daughters—Christian and Elizabeth) before the marriage was ended by Sir John's death in March 1670.

Frances, Lady Russell, never remarried and instead embarked upon half a century of widowhood. She remained close to her sister Mary and her husband Fauconberg, corresponding with them and spending time with them in London and Yorkshire. The attachment was strengthened when Frances's favourite daughter, Elizabeth, married Fauconberg's nephew Thomas Frankland, though temporary difficulties in the marriage also for a time led to tension between Frances and Fauconberg. By the late 1680s Frances's eldest son and heir, Sir William Russell, was in financial difficulties and had sold Chippenham. Frances, too, was reporting that, despite her earlier strong financial position—although she lost some property at the Restoration, she claimed to have brought property and £2000 into her marriage in 1663 (*Frankland-Russell-Astley MSS*, 203) and she had been well provided for under her husband's will—she was in some difficulty, writing of her 'unhappy circumstances' and seeking 'any employment that might become a gentlewoman' (ibid., 69). However, support from her sister, not least a very substantial bequest in her will, seems to have given her greater security in old age. On 27 August 1717, describing herself as 'Dame Frances Russell of St Giles in the Fields', she drew up her will. She left cash bequests totalling well over £3000, principally to her surviving children and grandchildren, but the bulk of her estate was to pass to her son-in-law Frankland. Having outlived all her siblings, Frances, the last surviving child of Oliver Cromwell, died in London in her eighty-second year, on 27 January 1720. According to her wishes, as recorded in her will, she was buried in Chiswick church, 'near to the body of my dear sister the late Countess Fauconberg'.   PETER GAUNT

Sources *The writings and speeches of Oliver Cromwell*, ed. W. C. Abbott and C. D. Crane, 4 vols. (1937–47) • J. Waylen, *The house of Cromwell and the story of Dunkirk* (1897) • M. Noble, *Memoirs of the protectoral-house of Cromwell*, 2 vols. (1787) • R. W. Ramsey, *Studies in Cromwell's family circle* (1930), chap. 7 • R. Sherwood, *Oliver Cromwell: king in all but name, 1653–58* (1997), esp. chap. 9 • *Report on the manuscripts of Mrs Frankland-Russell-Astley of Chequers Court, Bucks.*, HMC, 52 (1900), 69, 203 • *CSP dom.*, 1656–8 • Thurloe, *State papers* • will, PRO, PROB 11/572, sig. 39 • will of Sir John Russell, PRO, PROB 11/333, sig. 68 • will of Mary Belasyse, countess of Fauconberg, PRO, PROB 11/533, sig. 130 • Clarendon, *Hist. rebellion*, 4.34 • F. Peck, ed., *Desiderata curiosa*, 2 (1735), bk 13, p. 18 • GEC, *Peerage* • GEC, *Baronetage*
Archives BL, letter-book of Henry Cromwell, Lansdowne MSS 821–823 • Bodl. Oxf., Thurloe state papers, MS Rawl.
Likenesses S. Cooper, watercolour miniature, 1653 (either Elizabeth or Frances Cromwell), repro. in D. Foskett, *Samuel Cooper and his contemporaries* (1974), no. 41 [exhibition catalogue, NPG, 1974] • J. M. Wright, oils, c.1658–1659, Glasgow Art Gallery and Museum • J. Riley, oils, Cromwell Museum, Huntingdon • oils, Chequers Trust
Wealth at death over £3000; plus property: will, PRO, PROB 11/572, sig. 39

Russell [née Elliot], **Frances Anna Maria** [Fanny], **Countess Russell** [formerly Lady John Russell] (**1815–1898**), political wife, was born on 15 November 1815 at Minto House, Roxburghshire, the second daughter and third child in the family of five sons and four daughters of Gilbert Elliot Murray *Kynynmound, second earl of Minto (1782–1859), and his wife, Mary Brydone (1786–1853). Lady Fanny spent her childhood at Minto and was brought up with a strong sense of obligation and responsibility towards her large family. Her father's political career began in earnest in 1832, when he was sent by the whig government to Berlin as minister, taking his family with him. They remained there until 1834, and in 1835 Minto's appointment as lord privy seal took the family to London, just at the time when Lady Fanny was ready to be launched into society.

It is difficult to assess the impact made by Lady Fanny Elliot on the whig society she joined in London. In her own diary, she repeatedly comments on how 'it is so impossible for anybody ever to admire my looks or think me agreeable' (MacCarthy and Russell, 25), and laments her social awkwardness. Others were less critical, and portraits from the 1840s and 1850s show an attractive woman with abundant glossy brown hair and a trim figure. Lady Fanny was clearly a highly intelligent woman, although she was not troubled with a systematic education. Her interest was early captured by politics—not, as was more common, by the personalities of the politicians she came to know, but by the great issues of the day, and by the truly whiggish belief in the value and necessity of public service. Her religious convictions were strong: brought up in the Presbyterian Church of Scotland, she disliked ritual and the priestly caste as much as the evangelical conviction of the necessity for personal conversion. In later life she became a Unitarian. These characteristics, along with her protectiveness and sense of obligation towards her family, were to define her public role.

The leading whig Lord John *Russell (1792–1878) was well known to the Elliots. A widower with two daughters, and four children from his wife's previous marriage, he was more than twenty years older than Fanny Elliot. Two years after his first wife's death, he fell in love with his colleague's daughter, and he proposed to her in writing on 3 September 1840. To the relief of her mother, Lady Fanny refused: the age difference was too great (and the burden of the inherited children would be no small consideration). But Lord John literally haunted her dreams, and unavoidably they continued to meet in London. On 8 June 1841 her hesitation was overcome, and they were engaged. Lady Minto had long been won over—'it was not an ordinary person that could suit her … it is evident how fully he appreciates the singular beauty of her character' (MacCarthy and Russell, 43)—and his family accepted the match, with reservations: 'The family are not liked and are considered jobbers, but I hear a good report of her … I expect he ought to be the best judge of his own happiness' (G. Blakiston, *Lord William Russell and his Wife, 1815–1846*, 1972, 449), wrote his brother. Perhaps as importantly, Lady Fanny was approved at Holland House: 'good tempered and sensible' was Lady Holland's verdict. On 20 July 1841 they were married at Minto, and a month later the whigs fell from office.

Lady John found great happiness in her marriage, which helped to reconcile her to the loss of her beloved Scotland and to the overnight acquisition of six children, a household to manage, and the public gaze which inevitably focused on the wife of so prominent a politician. Unlike many of her contemporaries, such as Emily Palmerston, Mary Anne Disraeli, and Catherine Gladstone, Lady John Russell never came to relish her position at the political centre. Her health was not good during the 1840s—she had a number of miscarriages, as well as giving birth to four children between 1842 and 1853, including (Francis Albert) Rollo *Russell. She was also notoriously anxious about the effects on her husband's health of holding office. Her hostility towards London life, in particular, was undisguised, and although she carried out the social obligations of a political wife, she always viewed it as 'a sacrifice of private happiness to public duty' (MacCarthy and Russell, 73). Fiercely proud of her husband and his reputation, she told him in 1845, 'My ambition is that you should be the head of the most moral and religious government the country has ever had' (ibid., 72); it was ironic, then, that his connection with her family led to accusations of jobbery and of undue influence exercised over him by both his wife and his father-in-law. Lady John was widely blamed by politicians for the failings of her husband, who vacillated over forming or joining ministries, but her real weakness was an inability (and unwillingness) to play by the rules of the political game. 'I shall not behave like an angel any more', she threatened her father in 1851, 'but say what I think everywhere & to every-body & do a great deal of mischief & break up the ministry' (Reynolds, 181). In particular, she has been blamed for the souring of relations between Russell and Gladstone (whom in later life she came to admire greatly for his commitment to Ireland). The relief she felt at her husband's final retirement from active politics in 1868 (he had been created Earl Russell in 1861) was intense.

Lady John's interest in political issues and her commitment to a radical whig agenda never wavered. Her letters (particularly to her husband, father, and sons) show a clear understanding of the questions of the day, and a passionate conviction that justice should be done. She believed in liberty for Italy, home rule for Ireland, and parliamentary reform for Westminster; she supported religious liberty (although she fervently disliked 'theology' and ritual, and especially Roman Catholicism) and women's rights (although she believed that in some respects 'women's wrongs' had been exaggerated); and, a true whig, she had her reservations about monarchy: 'I consider Princes & Princesses as unmitigated evils—Sovereigns have their use in the world, but nobody has ever yet told me of any good purpose served by the existence of these offshoots of Sovereignty' (Lady John to Rollo Russell, 13 March 1863, Bodl. Oxf., MS Eng. lett. e. 111, fols. 226–8).

After Russell's retirement he and his wife continued to live at Pembroke Lodge in Richmond Park, the home provided for them by the queen. There Lady Russell entertained politicians, men of letters and science, and international visitors; unfettered by the demands of active politics, Pembroke Lodge became a place of pleasant resort and Lady Russell an agreeable hostess. The death of their widowed eldest son, Lord Amberley, in 1876, brought their two grandsons Frank and Bertrand *Russell to live permanently with the Russells, but Lord Russell himself died in 1878. Lady Russell survived him by twenty years, during which her interests continued unabated. Among her close friends and correspondents at this time were the positivist Frederic Harrison and the Irish home rule MP Justin McCarthy. The latter described her insatiable desire for knowledge: 'she appears to have felt that whenever she came into converse with any fellow being she was in communication with one who could tell her something which she did not already know' (MacCarthy and Russell, 296). Lady Russell died at Pembroke Lodge on 17 January 1898, and was buried with her husband at Chenies in Buckinghamshire four days later.   K. D. REYNOLDS

Sources D. MacCarthy and A. Russell, eds., *Lady John Russell: a memoir* (1910) · NA Scot., Minto papers · Bodl. Oxf., MS Eng. lett. e. 111 · K. D. Reynolds, *Aristocratic women and political society in Victorian Britain* (1998) · J. Prest, *Lord John Russell* (1972) · J. Prest, 'Gladstone and Russell', *TRHS*, 5th ser., 16 (1966), 43–63
Archives BL, letters, RP 2342 [copies] · Bodl. Oxf., corresp. and papers, MS Eng. lett. d 271, e 111–115; Eng. misc. b 100 · NL Scot., Minto papers · PRO, corresp., PRO 30/22 | BL, letters to W. E. Gladstone, Add. MSS 44393–44520, *passim* · NL Scot., letters to Alexander Campbell Fraser · U. Durham L., letters to Maria, Lady Grey
Likenesses Thorburn, miniature, 1844, repro. in MacCarthy and Russell, eds., *Lady John Russell* · M. Severn, watercolour, 1854, repro. in MacCarthy and Russell, eds., *Lady John Russell* · photograph, 1884, repro. in MacCarthy and Russell, eds., *Lady John Russell*
Wealth at death £27,945 12s. 7d.: probate, 23 March 1898, *CGPLA Eng. & Wales*

Russell, Francis, second earl of Bedford (1526/7–1585), magnate, only son of John *Russell, first earl of Bedford (d. 1555), and Anne (d. 1559), daughter of Sir Guy Sapcotes of Huntingdonshire, was educated at King's College, Cambridge, although he did not take a degree. The family were of Dorset origin although by Francis's birth they were seated at Chenies in Buckinghamshire, an inheritance of Francis's mother. His father had given long service to the first two Tudors, and by the 1550s had risen to the highest circle of power, privy councillor and lord privy seal. He was one of the captains of the royal army in the Boulogne campaign of 1544, and it was here under his father's command that Francis entered royal service. Sheriff of Buckinghamshire in 1547, he headed one of the enclosure commissions in 1548 and accompanied his father in the campaign to suppress the western rebellion in 1549. This began a connection with west-country affairs which lasted a lifetime. In 1559 he was appointed lord warden of the stannaries, a post he held until 1580.

Russell sat for Buckinghamshire in the 1545 parliament (at age eighteen) and again for the same constituency in 1547. In 1550, upon his father's creation as earl of Bedford, he was styled Lord Russell, and in 1553 he was summoned to the Lords as Baron Russell. At the coronation of Edward VI in 1547 he was knighted, one of the forty knights of the Bath. He seems already to have been committed to the reformed religion and attended the conference on the eucharist at the houses of Sir Richard Morison and William Cecil. In 1553 both father and son signed the document settling the succession on Lady Jane Grey: the earl passed unscathed into the new Marian regime, retaining all his offices, but his son suffered a brief detention in the sheriff of London's hands before a pardon was issued on 12 September 1554. In the aftermath of Wyatt's rebellion, Russell admitted having carried a letter from Wyatt to Elizabeth. It was probably at this time that his connection with her entourage began. He became a close friend of William Cecil, to whom he gave letters of attorney on his departure to the continent.

That event followed his father's death in 1555, when Russell became second earl of Bedford. He had licence from the crown to travel and a letter to the emperor at Brussels. His stay there was brief; anxious to continue his travels, he showed no enthusiasm to see Charles. But after an interview, he had permission to set out for Italy. Arriving at Venice, he lingered there long enough to forge ties with the Venetian élite and to learn Italian. His tour took him to Rome and Naples; there survives a letter to Cecil written from Ferrara. Moving back over the Alps, he spent the winter of 1556–7 in Zürich under the tutelage of the reformer Henry Bullinger, with whom he developed a warm relationship.

In 1557 Bedford returned to England at peace with the Marian regime. He was appointed lord lieutenant of Dorset, Devon, Cornwall, and Somerset, succeeding his father in this post. The latter had acquired large lands in Devon, partly monastic properties, partly those of the forfeited Courtneys, so that the family's west-country eminence rested on both estate and office.

Privy councillor and diplomat Bedford was one of a group to whom Elizabeth sent messages the day before her accession, and on 21 November 1558 he was sworn of the privy council. He was a constant attender in the first year of the reign, and a busy participant in the urgent business of those months. As the only peer who had consorted with continental reformers in the late reign, he was a forthright supporter of a return to the Edwardian religious regime. He was also one of the leading regional magnates and a close collaborator of the new secretary.

The official programme for re-establishing the English liturgy soon foundered in the House of Lords. In the angry debates on this measure, Bedford engaged in a slanging match with the bishop of Ely and Lord Montague, alleging that in their mission to Rome under Mary, the cardinals had offered them the services of whores. The bill failed and a new strategy had to be devised. When the measure again reached the upper house, it was steered by a committee which included Bedford. When the new order was in place, he sat on the commission for receiving oaths of loyalty to the royal supremacy.

In December 1560 François II of France died and was succeeded by his brother Charles IX, a minor. The decline of Guise influence in the French court opened the way for improving Anglo-French relations, but Mary Stuart's reappearance on the marriage market opened up new complications. A special envoy of rank was to be dispatched to Paris on a nominal mission of condolence. Bedford, proposed by the new ambassador, Nicholas Throckmorton, and backed by Cecil, was chosen for the job. Throckmorton urged the earl's wisdom, piety, and honour, adding significantly that he was a member of no faction. Bedford's competence in Italian, Catherine de' Medici's native tongue, was an added advantage.

The earl's instructions, written by Cecil, gave him three tasks. He was to secure the queen of Scots's signature to the treaty of Edinburgh, which had sealed English victory in the struggle to oust the French from her kingdom. Secondly, he was to sound out her intentions as to possible remarriage. Lastly, he was to dissuade the French from sending representatives to the revived Council of Trent. Unofficially he was to sound out the leaders of the nascent protestant party in the French court and to assess their present or possible role in its fraught politics. He crossed to France in January 1561, where he was hospitably received and had extensive conferences with the queen mother and all the leading courtiers. On the subject of Trent, Catherine was elusive. With Mary Stuart he had little success, either in persuading her to sign the treaty or in giving him any clue as to her marital intentions. In his contacts with the pro-reform leaders, he found the king of Navarre lukewarm in religion and irresolute in action. Admiral Coligny, however, was warm in his response and with him Bedford initiated a lasting relationship between the English government and the Huguenot leadership (Bedford may have been in correspondence with Coligny before his French trip). During the mission Bedford collaborated cordially with Throckmorton, offering to mediate between Throckmorton and Robert Dudley.

On 27 August 1562 Bedford's wife, Margaret Gostwick, daughter of Sir John St John of Bletsoe, whom he had married as her second husband in 1546, died in the smallpox epidemic of that year. She had borne him seven children. In 1566 Bedford married Bridget, daughter of John, Lord Hussey, and widow of Sir Richard Morison and of Henry Manners, second earl of Rutland. She survived him, and died on 12 January 1601.

Warden of the Scottish marches Back at the council board, Bedford shared in responsibilities connected with the Le Havre expedition of 1562–3. He acted as host to the vidame de Chartres, the Huguenot agent with whom he had had previous correspondence and on whom he bestowed a ring. In 1561 the queen had appointed Bedford to the council of the north, of which he was an absentee member for several years. Then in September 1563 she nominated him governor of Berwick and warden of the east marches towards Scotland, although his commission was not issued until 2 February 1564. He was at Berwick by March, and was nominated for the Garter the following month. Although his responsibilities were mainly local—the maintenance of order in an area of endemic disorder—he was necessarily drawn into the troubled relations between the two kingdoms, most particularly the question of Mary's remarriage. In autumn 1564 the queen appointed him, jointly with Thomas Randolph, the English agent in Scotland, to broach a proposal for Mary's marriage to Robert Dudley, the newly coined earl of Leicester. They were to make this proposal to Maitland and Moray, whom they met secretly in November. They received a cool response and had to endure the royal displeasure. Bedford seems to have had no further involvement in this abortive scheme. He was then summoned to court for the council's discussions which followed on Mary's decision to marry.

In August 1565 the queen appointed Bedford lieutenant-general in the north with military authority in Northumberland, Westmorland, and co. Durham. He promptly became further involved in Scottish affairs when Moray strongly opposed the Darnley match, celebrated in July 1565, and along with other lords took to arms against his queen. Bedford espoused their cause, hoping the queen would wink at his clandestine support for the rebel lords. To this she consented and sent £3000, of which £1000 was to be given to Moray. Bedford, rejoicing in the decision, thanked Cecil for his support. The queen's action, according to the earl, redounded to God's glory and her honour. As Moray's position became more desperate, Bedford advanced a scheme by which the Scottish earl should cross the border and then be reinstated in Scotland by English arms. In the end he fled to England in October, where Elizabeth offered refuge but refused arms. She rebuked Bedford when he allowed Moray to go to London. He could only express his bitter disappointment with royal policy. He wrote to Leicester for support, thanking him for his 'friendly, honourable, and gentle letter … If I could tell or devise which way to become more bound unto you than I am already, I would not let to confess and acknowledge same' (Wright, 1.215).

The tie with Leicester was strengthened by the marriage of Bedford's daughter Anne to Ambrose Dudley, earl of Warwick. The queen's liberality on that occasion was gratifying. Even more satisfying was her letter of January

1566 expressing her good judgement of his true and faithful service. Bedford went north as Elizabeth's representative at the baptism of the future James VI and I in December. On that occasion he conferred with Moray, re-established since the Rizzio murder.

Bedford found border service irksome and his letters contain repeated requests for recall. As often as possible he was absent from his post for intervals of several months, earning a royal rebuke. He was, in fact, away in the south when the crisis of Mary's deposition exploded in summer 1567. Disorder became rampant on the borders. Bedford, desperately needing authority to deal with the rebel lords, sought Leicester's intervention at court, but the queen obstinately refused to recognize them and accused Bedford of affection for their cause. The indignant earl declared that he had done nothing but as directed, but 'in wishing them well he has favoured them and their actions for he sees it good and honourable ... the [Scottish] queen's doings to be abominable and to be detested' (*CSP for., 1565–8*, 308). His pleas for recall now grew shriller; he declared his health was failing. Elizabeth finally took pity; the earl left the borders for the last time in October 1567, although he was not formally removed from office until Hunsdon's appointment in August 1568.

After Bedford's return south he remained firmly fixed at court for the next decade, a regular attender at council. There were no more major assignments from the queen. He served on the trial of Norfolk in 1572 but otherwise his appearance in the records of state business is limited to the council register.

The west-country career The year 1577 marked a significant change in the earl's public role. From August of that year to January 1579, Bedford was absent from the council board. In following years the pattern continued; he was spending more than half his time away from court in the west country. His name, however, was still conspicuous in the council records, not as a member attendant, but as the recipient of a stream of letters from Westminster to Exeter, where Bedford now resided in his capacity as lord lieutenant of the three western counties and the city itself.

Bedford had inherited both his west-country estates and his local offices from his father. When Elizabeth came to the throne, she renewed the lieutenancy of the western counties (omitting Somerset) granted by Mary in 1557. In 1572 she added the high stewardship of the duchy of Cornwall to the stannary post he already held. His father had built a house in Exeter which Bedford used as his headquarters. His role in the west became a kind of informal counterpart to the regional presidencies of the Welsh marches and the north (his father had filled the short-lived western presidency). The west country did not have the governmental problems of these other areas, but its distance from the capital made a regional representative of rank useful to the council.

Much of Bedford's activity in the west is made clear by the council correspondence. It frequently asked him to settle disputes among local gentry, acting as mediator, but with authority to enforce a legal settlement. He was called on to assemble and equip soldiers for service in Ireland and to inspect fortifications. Piracy and smuggling were constant preoccupations on these coasts, as was the collection of intelligence from overseas merchants. He chaired the regional committee on the restraint of grain and victuals and was ordered to apprehend, imprison, and examine law-breakers, some of whom would then be passed on to Westminster. In the last year of his life Bedford also held the office of chief justice of forests south of the Trent.

Besides all these administrative and semi-judicial activities, Bedford found time for a straightforward political task—the management of parliamentary elections. In 1571 and 1572 the privy council asked him to manage the elections in Devon and Cornwall, and in 1572 in Buckinghamshire as well. Apart from such formal arrangements, the earl played a major part in the return of borough members throughout the western region. The three counties of his lieutenancy (plus Wiltshire) returned 60–70 members to parliament, the largest such concentration in the country. Numbers grew as new constituencies were enfranchised; with Cecil's aid, Bedford was able to enfranchise four Cornish boroughs. His predominant position, both as landholder and as official, gave him a powerful voice, which he used to the full. It would be misleading, however, if he were visualized as disposing at his pleasure of a tidy clutch of pocket boroughs. Arrangements were much more complex and untidy, a matter of bargaining and persuasion, much affected by local circumstance and varying from parliament to parliament. There were a few cases of unvarying control by the lord lieutenant, but most boroughs wished to keep control of at least one seat in their own hands. In 1562 Exeter flatly refused their lieutenant either seat. In some cases the borough's choice was also the earl's, or a borough, not having a particular nominee for a particular parliament, would yield to the lord lieutenant's request. Consequently a Bedford nominee might sit for different constituencies in different parliaments. The earl might nominate in a particular borough in one parliament, but not in the next. What best describes his overall role is influence rather than patronage in the strict sense.

That influence varied from one parliament to another, but the volume of the *History of Parliament* for 1558–1603 estimates that, of 346 members returned by the three western counties in Elizabeth's first four parliaments, 138 (40 per cent) were associated with Bedford either by direct nomination or, more frequently, by indirect influence. In Dorset's case the percentage in the four parliaments was 50 or over. The earl's influence was perceptibly waning in 1584, the last election in which he participated.

What was his purpose in this electoral enterprise? He was not attempting to build a Bedford bloc in the Commons or to pursue the advancement of some special interest. His perspective was that of a privy councillor who was also a great regional magnate, using his commanding local position to further the purposes of central government, or, more particularly, of William Cecil. In his election management over many decades, Bedford collaborated closely with the minister. Their joint object was to place in the Commons men who could be useful in serving on committees or as spokesmen on the floor in pursuing government policy goals. Bedford was, of course, concerned that they should share his views, particularly in religious matters, as committed adherents of the reformed faith, zealous for the advancement of the gospel. Concrete examples of the latter concern were the earl's care to find seats for spokesmen of evangelical bent, such as Laurence Tomson, Walsingham's secretary in 1572 and 1584.

Religious and intellectual life Contemporaries viewed Bedford as a stalwart and outspoken supporter of a vigorous evangelical protestantism. It was manifest in his continuing connections with the continental reformers, who regarded him as their spokesman at the English court. He was able, for instance, to persuade the queen to invite Pietro Martire Vermigli (Peter Martyr) to England although the invitation was declined by the divine. Correspondence with continental reformers continued. At the very end of his life he headed a list of contributors to a fund for the relief of Geneva, while the French church in London found him a protector.

Of Bedford's domestic interests in religious matters, there remains surprisingly little direct evidence. He took the ardent evangelical William Whittingham with him on his Paris mission. There is a clue to his religious outlook in a letter from Berwick in the course of which he deplores the use of surplice and caps, asserting that such requirements would lose the services of good pastors, all too scarce. Locally he won the applause of Bishop Alley of Exeter for his liberality, and he was a patron to the Marian exile John Woolton, consecrated bishop of Exeter in 1579. What is surprising is the lack of evidence of Bedford's role in the agitation for further reform in parliament and elsewhere from the 1560s on.

More can be gleaned of the man's inner life from a list of Bedford's library at Chenies prepared in 1584. It numbered 221 volumes (with allowance for duplicates, 162 titles). They included some 165 religious, 21 literary, and 12 political works. Twelve were in Italian. Calvin, Beza, Jewel, and Zwingli were numbered among the theologians; Foxe was there as well. Contemporary affairs were represented by histories of Italy and France and of the Low Countries along with a report on recent occurrences in Ireland. More interesting still are authors' dedications of their works to Bedford; they numbered twenty-three (outdoing in number both Leicester and Philip Sidney). They include works by Thomas Gibson, John Becon, and John Udall, and translations of Ralph Gualter, along with a report on the colloquy of Poissy. Several express gratitude for Bedford's patronage. Most surprising is George Willes's dedication of his edition of Eden's *Voyages in the East and West Indies*. Willes, himself an overseas traveller, writes warmly of the support given him by the earl—and the pension granted by the countess.

Assessment Bedford stands somewhat apart from his fellows in the council. The inheritor of an earldom and a large landed estate, and of greater regional eminence than virtually any other councillor, he had less to strive for in personal advancement in office or wealth. Significantly he held no court office but he was a zealous servant of the crown, in the council and then, reluctantly, on the borders. Then, in the final decade of his life, he chose to spend as much time as possible away from the centre of power, a risk no other courtier would take. Doubtless he felt that the confidence of the queen, his close alliance with Cecil, and his freedom from factional alliance or intrigue guaranteed his position. He was, of course, by no means idle during his west-country sojourns. His personal commitment to evangelical protestantism was probably greater than that of any other councillor save Francis Knollys.

Bedford's main seat, Chenies in Buckinghamshire, was a comfortably short journey from London where he maintained another house in St Clement Danes parish. Another house at Woburn in Bedfordshire was used to some extent. He died in his London home, Russell House, the Strand, on 28 July 1585 and was buried on 14 September at Chenies, where an alabaster tomb was erected in the chapel. He left money to the University of Oxford and building stone to Corpus Christi College, Cambridge. He had a large family. Three sons predeceased him, the last of these, Francis, having been killed on the borders only hours before his father's death. This son was father to Edward, the third earl. The second earl's surviving son, William *Russell (d. 1613), had a distinguished military career, served as lord deputy of Ireland, and was created Lord Russell of Thornhaugh. Three daughters were married to peers—Anne to Ambrose Dudley, earl of Warwick, Elizabeth to William Bourchier, earl of Bath, and Margaret [see Clifford, Margaret] to George Clifford, earl of Cumberland.

A modern estimate of the Bedford estates' gross rentals (as of 1602) placed annual return in the range of £3600–£5399, somewhere among the dozen wealthiest peers. Bedford received only minor grants from the crown; he purchased Kingston Lacey in Dorset, and much energy went into the buying and exchange of lands. Nevertheless he died heavily in debt.   WALLACE T. MacCAFFREY

Sources J. F. Wiffen, *Historical memoirs of the house of Russell* (1833) · C. H. Garrett, *The Marian exiles: a study in the origins of Elizabethan puritanism* (1938) · *Calendar of the manuscripts of the most hon. the marquis of Salisbury*, 1–2, HMC, 9 (1883–8) · T. Wright, *Queen Elizabeth and her times* (1838) · *A collection of state papers … left by William Cecill, Lord Burghley*, ed. S. Haynes, 1 (1740) · W. Camden, *Annales, or, The historie of the most renowned and victorious Princesse Elizabeth*, trans. R. N. [R. Norton], 3rd edn (1635), 71 · HoP, *Commons, 1509–58*, 3.230–31 · APC, 1547–82 · GEC, *Peerage*, new edn, 2.75–6
Archives Woburn Abbey, Bedfordshire, MSS
Likenesses H. Holbein the younger, chalk drawing, c.1540–1542, Royal Collection · M. Gheeraerts, etching (*Procession of garter knights, 1576*), BM · oils, Woburn Abbey, Bedfordshire

Russell, Francis, fourth earl of Bedford (*bap.* **1587**, *d.* **1641**), politician, was baptized on 19 October 1587 at St Mary's, Watford, Hertfordshire, the son and heir of William *Russell, first Baron Russell of Thornhaugh (c.1553–1613), lord deputy of Ireland, and Elizabeth (*d.* 1611), daughter and heir of Henry Long of Shingay, Cambridgeshire.

Early life and political career As a youth Russell attended his father in Ireland; he was knighted in 1607. Two years later, on 26 February 1609, he married Catherine (d. 1657), daughter of Giles Bridges, third Baron Chandos. All the outward signs suggest that the marriage was a happy one. She was an executor in all his draft wills save that of 1621, when she was an overseer, and 1624, made while she was pregnant, and in the will eventually admitted to probate. In his draft wills of 1621 and 1624 he left her the large sum of £100 to buy a ring 'which I desire her to wear in the remembrance of me until she shall marrye one that she shall conceive worthie to be her husband' (Bedford MS XI i, 196). This is much more sensitive and more generous than the normal attitude of Stuart gentlemen to the remarriage of their wives. He also anticipated Locke in noting that the words 'honour … thy mother' in the fifth commandment indicated that women could have some place in government.

Russell and his wife had ten children, of whom eight grew to adulthood. Of the four sons the eldest was William *Russell, first duke of Bedford. The second son, Francis, died about a month before his father and Edward (d. in or before 1666), the third son, was the father of the first earl of Orford. John (d. 1687) had a lengthy career as a royalist and as commander of Charles II's regiment of foot guards. Of the four daughters Diana (1624–1695), the youngest, married Francis Newport, later earl of Bradford, shortly after her father's death. The remaining daughters were all married in their father's lifetime: Margaret (d. 1676) to James Hay, second earl of Carlisle; Anne (d. 1697) to George *Digby, son of the earl of Bristol; and Catherine (c.1618–1676) to Robert *Greville, second Baron Brooke of Beauchamps Court. These three marriages just about boxed the political compass. Yet all three sons-in-law seem to have been on excellent terms with their father-in-law, and received rings in his wills. One of Russell's peculiarities, especially when set beside others who ranked as parliamentary leaders in 1640, is the politically and theologically eclectic character of his social circle. And this is particularly evident in the various individuals he named as executors and overseers of his draft wills, ranging from John Pym to Sir John Strangways.

Russell was elected to the House of Commons for Lyme Regis, Dorset, at a by-election in 1610, but left no mark on its proceedings. After succeeding his father in 1613 he sat in the Lords from 1614 to 1626 as Lord Russell of Thornhaugh; he rapidly established himself as a very regular attender and a hard-working committee man, but a rare speaker. This is less significant than it might have been in the Commons. The quiet word with interested parties, and the tidy adjustment in committee, were much more effective weapons in the Lords than skill in oratory. The growing frequency and importance of Lord Russell's committee nominations before he inherited the earldom suggests that he was trusted and respected in the house. From 1621 onwards he was normally on the committee of privileges and its subcommittee to view the journal book of the Lords. He was equally consistently on committees for bills of arms, in which, as lord lieutenant of Devon and Exeter from 1623 and a soldier's son, he took a serious interest. In 1621 he was also heavily involved in the Mompesson case, and slightly less so in those of Bacon, Bennet, and Floyd, and in the monopolies bill. Again in 1621 he acted as sponsor for Lionel Cranfield when he took his seat as Baron Cranfield. In 1625 he also acted as sponsor for William Fiennes when he was introduced as Viscount Saye and Sele, and for Lord Robartes. In 1626 he showed more desire to appear above the parapet, and spoke in favour of the motion to limit peers to two proxies each. This aligned him clearly with the duke of Buckingham's enemies, as did his speech of 8 May in favour of allowing counsel to the earl of Bristol. He was on the committee to take examinations in the Bristol case, which means the house trusted his discretion. Moreover, he was on the even more sensitive committee to decide on the questions for the judges about the king's desire to appear as a witness against Bristol.

Having inherited the earldom of Bedford in 1627, the new earl left a very brief diary of the 1628 parliamentary session. This indicates the serious interest in procedure which marks most successful parliamentarians, and a deep interest in Sir Benjamin Rudyerd's speech which, fearing that parliament's 'power of the purse' could lead the king to resort to non-parliamentary means of raising money, warned that 'This is the crisis of Parliaments: we shall know by this if Parliaments live or die' (C. Russell, *The Crisis of Parliaments: English History, 1509–1660*, 1971, 299). The diary also contains a rare personal note: 'I would give, if it were possible, more to prerogative than is yet, so as I knew what it were' (M. F. Keeler, M. Jansson, and W. B. Bidwell, eds., *Lords' Proceedings, 1628*, 1983, 728). This does as much as anything to indicate Bedford's position in the late 1620s. He wanted to get back to the position which had been normal in 1610, that the scope of the prerogative was bounded by law. It represents a desire that the king's power should be under control and not arbitrary, rather than one that it should be effectively reduced. In 1628 Bedford was against the duke of Buckingham and against a power outside the law, but both positions seem to indicate a desire to get back to things as they had been before, rather than to introduce anything new. That and the desire to act as reconciler are clear. There is no evidence in the parliamentary record of the 1620s to indicate Bedford's attitude on questions of religion.

From the 1630s there is no word from Bedford of public comment on the major issues of dispute. It must be presumed from silence that he paid his ship money. However, it seems significant that his client and favourite Oliver St John acted as counsel for John Hampden, who refused to pay the levy. Hampden was already associated with Bedford and it is unlikely that St John, whose commons and chamber at the inns of court were paid by Bedford, took on the case without Bedford's approval. The generous treatment of St John contrasts with that of the later MP Robert Scawen. He is referred to in the 1634–5 will as 'my servant Scawen', having earlier complained bitterly of

Bedford's persistent failure to pay him. Pym was called in to mediate several times, but failed to produce a settlement, so Scawen decamped to the service of the earl of Northumberland, taking with him a large quantity of Bedford's working papers which now form Alnwick Castle MS Y III.

The Bedford inheritance After the death of his father Francis Russell inherited an estate which he valued in 1628 at £3450 per annum 'all rackt land'. Since this figure appears in a letter asking for a reduction of his subsidy assessment, it is unlikely to be an overestimate. Russell was the grandson of the second earl of Bedford, his father being the second earl's youngest son, and when his cousin Edward Russell, the third earl, died in 1627 Francis found himself the heir to the title. However, the *inquisition post mortem* of the third earl found that Francis Russell had been in possession of his predecessor's estates since 23 March 1619. He had effectively enjoyed the power and position of an earl of Bedford since that date.

While the cadet Thornhaugh line was flourishing the elder Bedford line had been suffering a series of misfortunes. The second earl's eldest son was shot some twelve hours before his father's death, leaving the second earl's grandson, Edward, as heir to the title. Unfortunately, this left the estate subject to a wardship and the legal problems of an out-of-date will, which immediately gave rise to a lawsuit in the court of wards. When the third earl came of age, he rapidly aligned himself with the earl of Essex, and became involved in his rebellion of 1601. His life was spared but a fine of £10,000, coming on top of the wardship and the lawsuit, got the earl off on the wrong financial footing. Moreover, he did not succeed in living within his income. His wife Lucy Harrington, one of the greatest literary patrons of her day, is unlikely to have come cheap, and he himself does not appear to have had much head for business. In 1607 the earl of Salisbury wrote to Lord Russell of Thornhaugh to ask for his consent to a sale of some of the entailed estates, and received a brusque refusal. The earl was then made to take out a bond in heavy sums not to sell his entailed estate. It appears to have been Sir William Russell, treasurer of the navy and customs farmer, who found the solution to this problem. He was not only a kinsman of the fourth earl, but also one of the richest men in England and one of the king's principal creditors. The solution was for the third earl to sell out to his heir, and one may conjecture that Sir William may have lent much of the money for the purchase. The estates had been saved for the family, but it had been a very considerable strain. In his letter asking for a reduction in his subsidy assessment in 1628, the fourth earl claimed that the Bedford estate had been worth £5000 per annum, but that since then there had been very considerable sales. It is likely that what he inherited was encumbered, and that rents may have been kept low in return for entry fines. Financial recovery was a high priority, but it was recovery from a very solid platform, and of a potentially very valuable estate.

It seems likely that at all stages of his life after 1619 Bedford's income was in the range of £5000–£10,000, and moving unevenly upwards within this. The overall impression suggests his careful attention to land management, and above all he seems to have had the ability, highly unusual among the peerage, to reduce expenditure when under financial pressure. He continued for a while after acquiring his new estates to live in the old Russell of Thornhaugh house in Chiswick. His centre of gravity shifted very slowly to Bedford House in the Strand, influenced by the demands of politics and of the Covent Garden development. Woburn, which before and after was the family's main base, was at first a focus of only occasional interest. It reveals much of his sense of duty that when he was summoned back to Oxford for the resumed session of the 1625 parliament, he went.

The estate was divided into several blocks. There was a large amount of land in Devon and Cornwall, much of it designed to sustain the first earl in the dignity of president of the council of the west. During Francis Russell's tenure of the earldom the emphasis was shifting slowly away from Devon and Cornwall towards a new interest in the east of England and the Fen country. He was made *custos rotulorum* in 1619 and lord lieutenant of Devon and Exeter in 1623, in his predecessor's lifetime, and held the latter post until his death, later jointly with his eldest son. Yet though he was conscientious and hard-working, his interventions are normally in the form of letters from Chiswick or later Bedford House. There is almost no evidence of his discharging his place in person.

Woburn in Bedfordshire was a dilapidated building when Bedford inherited it, and the centre of a rather small block of land. It did, however, present the prospect of consolidation with the Thornhaugh estates, centring on Thorney. In the 1630s Bedford had Woburn rebuilt by Inigo Jones, and after that it was much nearer the centre of his interests. In addition there was ancestral land in Dorset where the family had been country gentry before they first came to court, Gloucestershire land which had come to Bedford with his wife, who brought a portion of £7000, and a considerable number of scattered manors around the country. His draft will of 1634–5 refers to lands in Cambridgeshire, Northamptonshire, Bedfordshire, Buckinghamshire, Hertfordshire, Middlesex, Huntingdonshire, Cornwall, Dorset, Hampshire, Wiltshire, Devon, and the city of Exeter. In addition there was the Covent Garden estate, which, like the fen property, was to become first a headache and then a goldmine. Its development was to become a major focus of Bedford's interests in the 1630s.

The portions set down for Bedford's daughters in his various wills range from £3000 to £5000, and provide some suggestion of prosperity. Perhaps the best evidence of prosperity during the 1620s is that he was not borrowing money but lending it. That this was a deliberate economic decision, and not just friendship, is suggested by a note in his draft will of 1624, which directs that money may be lent, if his overseers thinks safe, at no more charge than borrowers will willingly give, and otherwise the money is to go into the chamber of London. He wished to encourage barren metal to breed.

Reading and thinking Among clergy Bedford's sympathies span the spectrum with acrobatic skill. In his early wills he leaves a ring to Dr Senhouse, bishop of Carlisle, and his funeral sermon is to be given by one or other of his household chaplains. Dedications from Cornelius Burges, vicar of Watford, where Bedford owned land, indicate a sympathy with the Westminster assembly wing of the church, and the choice of James Ussher, archbishop of Armagh, to preach a series of lectures at St Paul's, Covent Garden, indicates a rapport with its Calvinist episcopalian centre. On the other hand, the claim of Edward Hyde, earl of Clarendon, that Bedford used to dine with Archbishop Laud indicates an ability to make friends with the Arminian wing of the church. Bedford is probably almost the only man in England who could come to the Long Parliament in 1640 claiming the personal friendship of both Pym and Laud. The clergyman whose private conversation seems to figure most largely in his commonplace books is John Williams, bishop of Lincoln, lord keeper to King James. Perhaps it is the scholarly ecumenism of a good Jacobean which comes nearest to Bedford's ecclesiastical position. In terms of public opinion it was still a popular position, but it commended itself neither to Pym, nor to Charles I, nor to the Scottish covenanters. It underlines the point that in January 1640 two of Bedford's sons took part in the masque for William Davenant's *Salmacida spolia*.

The massive body of his commonplace books accounts for some 90 per cent of the surviving material about Bedford, and they are very hard to use. They are essentially notes on Bedford's reading and on what he heard in conversation. Material from his reading is often acknowledged, but is not always so. It is thus easy to confuse material Bedford has read with his own opinions. For example, material on Arminianism turns out to come from Francis Rous's *Testis veritatis*. There are three possible ways of arriving at Bedford's own opinion. The first is from his occasional notes expressing his own opinion. If they are initialled 'F.R.' he takes personal responsibility for them. His occasional annotations, usually confined to the word 'NO' in enormous capitals, are equally clear. The passages in his copy of Pym's parliamentary diary for 1625 asking for more lenient treatment for nonconforming ministers and Charles I's declaration against the Scots of the summer of 1640 both receive this treatment. The second is from the index headings in the fair volumes. Since these were classified jointly by Bedford and his secretaries during his lifetime, he may be assumed to have some share in responsibility for the index. Entries such as 'Antichrist—see Popes', 'Popes—see Antichrist' tell their own story, and serve as a reminder that the one gap in the ecumenical character of Bedford's friendships is a singular lack of Roman Catholics. The fact that most of the material on Arminianism appears under the entry 'heretikes' is suggestive. The third and least certain way is when the balance of notes on a subject appears to run very clearly one way.

Bedford was a zealous reader of poetry with a particular affection for John Donne, George Herbert, and Francis Quarles. The combination of some of Donne's most predestinarian material, from sermons as well as divine poems, with Herbert on communion, again indicates the ecclesiastical sympathies of a Jacobean. The two conspicuous absentees are Jonson and Shakespeare. Bedford shows a lively interest in science, and was fascinated by William Harvey's discovery of the circulation of the blood, on which he took copious notes. He was equally intrigued both by Reginald Scot's *The Discovery of Witchcraft*, and by Aristotle on wind, showing all the naturalistic fallacies which infuriated Galileo. He was also intrigued by astrology but not sure of it.

Religious material in the commonplace books accounts for some 40 per cent of the total and shows an eclecticism. The view of the advocates of limited episcopacy, that a bishop should exercise jurisdiction with the advice of his priests, is ascribed, with Bedford's characteristic contempt for categories, to the Council of Trent. Radical protestantism is represented by Tom Tell-Troth and Thomas Beard's *Theatre of God's Judgements*, and Arminianism by copious quotation from Lancelot Andrewes, but the overwhelming bulk of his reading seems to be in good Jacobean Calvinist conformist episcopalians such as Joseph Hall, John Davenant, George Carleton, and Robert Sanderson. It is hard to resist the impression that this is the ecclesiastical school with which Bedford felt most at home, even if his tolerance extended outwards on both sides of it.

Constitutional ideas Bedford enjoyed history, and expressed regret at 'our having forborne to make historie an expresse profession' (Bedford MS XI i, 88). The framework of his constitutional thinking is drawn out of English history on the one hand, and the tradition of good counsel which goes back to Aquinas and Aristotle on the other. His constitutional thinking is focused, not on changing the balance between institutions, but on securing good counsel to the king. The poles of Bedford's constitutional thinking are in the English medieval dimension of king, counsellors, and baronage. His mental world is closer to that of Simon de Montfort than it is to that of his grandson the whig martyr William, Lord Russell. For him the deposition of Rehoboam because he had relied on evil counsellors was a paradigm. The big danger against which he was guarding was not that of kings trying to be tyrants, but that of counsellors, 'flattering earwigs', in his phrase, tailoring their advice to please the king. One of his longest, and most crucial, quotations was designed to protect the independence of the council from the king:

> Kings must take heed of striking too much feare into their counsellors, lest they make them with drawe themselves from the liberty of advising they must not declare their owne opinions least that declaration become a rule to other men's reasons and soe they rather vote then advise, they must not often bee present at the counsel board, when things are in debate, but only when they are ripe for resolution, least their counsellors be over ayed [awed] with their presence, and reade their kings disaffecting of their advises in the eyes of their princes.   (Bedford MS XI i, 44)

These are the views of a man who remembered that two

out of the three previous earls of Bedford had been members of the council, and may have felt a calling to follow in their footsteps. It is tempting to read a wistfulness into his quotation from Robert Sanderson that 'God will not call any man to that, whereto he will not open him a fair and orderly passage' (ibid., XI i, 58). If so, he was not the only Caroline peer to fail to obtain the position he thought his status entitled him to: it was a side-effect of the inflation of honours.

It is in line with this that one of the savagest, and most uniform, sections of the commonplace books is that on favourites. Bedford quotes Mariana, that 'the kings favour is tyrannie, when by that favour a man rules over them in fact, that can plead neither election nor succession to that power'. He concludes ruefully that, if there must be favourites, there should be competition: 'a king should have more than one favourite, emulation will make them walke the fairer wayes' (Bedford MS XI i, 56, 58). Only a quotation from Andrewes that Daniel was a good favourite runs against the stream. It is clear that among Pym's parliamentary activities, those which captured the earl's attention were those which were directed at bad ministers and evil counsellors: Mompesson, Manwaring, Buckingham, and Strafford.

In international affairs Bedford quoted the earl of Salisbury, whom he seems to have admired, in favour of alliance with France: 'France his feare of Spaines growth and greatnes will always solder that linke with England which religion breakes'. He was also pro-Scottish, noting that 'Scotland's alliance to us better than any nation for whose ayde wee must expect tides and windes' (Bedford MS XI i, 165). This is not the ecclesiastical loyalty to brethren of Francis Rous or John Hampden, but the politic pro-Scottishness of the Cecils. Finally, the commonplace books contain fascinating fragments of political gossip, such as the remark attributed to Henry Howard, earl of Northampton, that 'King Jeamses hope of the commonwelth wase like top [to] be cast away upon Edwin Sandys instead of Goodwin Sands', or Gondomar's remark to Bristol that 'he woud undoe hime self with resoun' (ibid., XXV, unfoliated).

Covent Garden and fen drainage The development of Covent Garden and the plan to drain the fens preoccupied Bedford for most of the 1630s. The former stretched from what was described in 1633 as 'a little lane … lately called Russell Street' on the west, to Long Acre on the north, down to the Strand on the south (*CSP dom.*, 1633–4, 168–9). When the population of the area was growing so rapidly that in 1629 the parish church of St Martin-in-the-Fields was 2000 short of being able to hold all its inhabitants, there was a large potential market if the problems of development could be overcome. The earl having been granted a licence to build in 1631, his tenements in Covent Garden and Long Acre became sublet and subdivided, failing to produce the smart area the king required. However, in the piazza, Inigo Jones contributed the design of the church and much more, satisfying the king's desire to beautify London. A survey of 1635 attempted to check the number of subtenants. Where there were eighty-eight

prime tenements, they found 428 subtenants, indicating that the king was right that multi-occupation had become a problem. By 1641 the problems seem to have been over, and the property was yielding nearly £1000 a year. Yet Bedford seems to have been unfortunate with water. His first attempt at introducing a water supply ended with losing a chancery lawsuit with the bishop of Durham, and he ended by having a terrible row with Lady Worcester, who said her water was 'poyson'd by a dead, stinking, rotten, and we fear poyson'd katte'. Attempts to make peace ended with her accusing him of 'expressions wch I thought should never have passed the penn of so noble a personage as my Lord of Bedford' (Alnwick Castle MS, Y III 2(4), envelope 9). It is naturally impossible to establish the rights and wrongs of this dispute. What is clear is that urban development in the early seventeenth century was a hazardous business.

Bedford carried on two of his father's interests. One was the active interest in matters of arms. The second was an interest in fen drainage. In 1590 his father had brought over Dutch drainage engineers to attempt the drainage of the fens around Thorney, starting an interest the family was to keep up for two centuries. However, Bedford's fen drainage project was even more hazardous than the Covent Garden development because of the vast capital investment involved, the complex ecological balance of the fenland, the variety of conflicting property interests, and the limited understanding of the effects of altering the flow of water in such nearly flat country. The plan was to drain 95,000 acres, making them, like the Low Countries, worth a mark an acre. To this end Bedford's company of adventurers planned to allocate 40,000 acres to Bedford, and 12,000 to the king, in the hope that the work would be an addition to the crown's revenue: the company spent £100,000, of which the king contributed £20,000, but want of money and fears that the scheme might not be as legal as it should be brought work to a stop. The ground was drained sufficiently for use in summer, but not enough to keep it dry in winter. Thus the scheme was summarized by the earl of Manchester, in a memorandum probably designed for a committee of the House of Lords in 1641.

Part of the difficulty in tracking down the funding and success or failure of the drainage work is that it seems to have been split into a number of different adventures, centred on the Nene, the Ouse, the Welland, and the Isle of Ely. The investment was spread among a large number of the great ones of the kingdom, backed up by a number of substantial local gentlemen. Bedford was closely assisted by Sir William Russell as treasurer and Oliver St John who handled much of the legal business. Because those funding it were far richer than those funding the Providence Island Company, it seems to have been possible to carry losses until the work was eventually declared complete in 1653 (twelve years after Bedford's death), and rents began to come in.

Politics and plans for settlement, c.1638–1641 If the fen business marks the triumph of muddling through, Bedford's contribution to the Long Parliament and to the events preceding the English civil war marks the failure of meticulous planning. This story has always been seen through the eyes of Clarendon. He said that among 'the great contrivers and designers' the first was:

> the earl of Bedford, a wise man, and of too great and plentiful a fortune to wish a subversion of the government; and it quickly appeared, that he only intended to make himself and his friends great at Court, not at all to lessen the Court itself.   (Hyde, earl of Clarendon, 1.241)

Clarendon states that Bedford and Pym were engaged to see the king's revenue 'liberally provided for', and to settle tonnage and poundage (ibid., 1.280). The king's objectives in doing business with them were 'to save the life of the earl of Strafford and to preserve the church from ruin'. He claims that 'in that of the Church, the major part even of these persons would have been willing to have satisfied the King' (ibid., 1.282). Bedford, he claims, wanted no alteration in the government of the church. In return for these efforts Bedford was to be lord treasurer, Pym chancellor of the exchequer, and high office was to be found for a number of other members of the parliamentary junto, among whom Clarendon mentions Hampden, Robert Devereux, third earl of Essex, and Edward Montagu, Viscount Mandeville.

Nevertheless, Clarendon's account, however accurate, is out of perspective and sometimes misleading. In the first place, he completely glosses over the concessions in matters of policy the king would have had to make to achieve such a settlement. In religion a church run by Ussher or Williams, though still episcopal, would have been very different from one run by Laud and Richard Neile. The foreign policy of such a government might have been closer to Cromwell's after 1655 than to Charles's before 1640. Perhaps most important, it would have been clear that the king was the servant, not the master, of what the thirteenth century had called 'the community of the realm'—something more enduring and less institutional than a parliament. To this end the relations between the king and his council would have needed to change fundamentally. If Clarendon's best source was the king, it is understandable that this is not what he heard, but Edward Hyde in 1641 had known it well enough.

The other dimension which does not appear in Clarendon's account is that this, as much as those of 1215, 1258, and 1388, was to be a coerced settlement. It was commonly understood that, if the king had not been facing superior military force in the hands of the Scots, he would never have so much as discussed any settlement on this line. The junto leaders knew perfectly well that in 1215 and 1258 it had been necessary to fight to preserve the settlement against an attempt by an angry king to break out of his leading strings, and after 1388 some of the lords appellant had ended up executed or murdered. Those who coerced a king did so at their own risk. It was therefore necessary to make the Scots guarantors of any final settlement, and therefore any settlement which was to be secure needed their consent. Anyone who accepted a lesser settlement was taking a great risk with his life.

Since the king's two non-negotiables, the future of the church and the life of Strafford, were both equally non-negotiable to the Scots, the junto was always likely to be faced with the need to make a choice between the king and the Scots. Hyde had known this well enough, and on 27 February 1641 brilliantly attempted to force the junto to that choice, only to get a weak evasion from Hampden that 'we are all of a mind in desiring what is best' (M. Jansson, ed., *Two Diaries of the Long Parliament*, 1984, 12). Since the conflict between the king and the Scottish covenanters, unlike any rift in English public opinion, was beyond the reach of negotiation, this choice was never going to go away.

In order to get into this position in the first place Bedford and the junto needed to keep up a relationship with the Scots before their invasion and after it which came perilously close to the collusive. Bedford appears personally in this process in a meeting at Warwick Castle, arranged by his son-in-law Lord Brooke, where he may have met and talked with Scottish ministers. There is no proof that Bedford and Scottish ministers were present on the same occasion. The presence of Bedford and Pym is recorded in September 1638, and of 'Dr Rutterford, a Scot', probably Samuel Rutherford, on 29 December 1639. Bedford was accompanied by his heir, Lord Russell, his son-in-law George Digby, Richard Knightley, and John Pym. Digby, later a prominent anti-Scot, may well have been unhappy with this approach. On 19 July 1640 he wrote to Bedford thanking him for his good counsels, and saying '*in this I shew an obedience* to you only in that wherein *mine own reason* hath a share *in the command*', and denying that he was swallowed up in contemplative studies (Bedford MSS, fourth earl, family papers). The italicized passages are underlined in a pen so clumsily heavy that it may be confidently taken as Bedford's. Bedford had heard the warning, and was to hear it again many times in the next eight months.

Bedford first expressed his views in public in the petition of the twelve peers, on 28 August 1640. This was the same day on which the Scots crossed the Tyne and defeated the English army at the battle of Newburn. The peers are unlikely to have known this, but communication was close enough to make the coincidence of dates more than purely coincidental. Their action therefore came perilously close to aiding and abetting the enemy in time of war. The petition was drawn up at a meeting at Bedford House in the Strand. It was subsequently said to have been drafted by Pym and St John. The signatories formed a list wide enough to panic the privy council, especially when further peers put their names to it even after the news of Newburn. The most alarming signature was the earl of Hertford, who was not only the brother-in-law of Essex, but also the son of Arabella Stuart and the grandson of Katherine Grey. His presence raised the spectre of the one thing the peers' strategy lacked: a pretender. It was Hertford and Bedford with whom the privy council chose to negotiate on 7 September. From then on, much of the privy council was directed to withdrawing Charles from an exposed position, with or without his consent.

But Bedford's settlement plans must be set in a similar context. They were not an opposition programme, but an attempt, with backing from inside the heart of government, to drag the king kicking and screaming into the real world, and thereby to reunite the country.

Meanwhile, Bedford was named a commissioner to negotiate with the Scots at the treaty of Ripon. When the treaty led only to an interim settlement to pay the Scottish army while a parliament was called, Bedford and his fellow commissioners were transformed into commissioners to negotiate the treaty of London for a final peace with the Scots, acting, to Charles's dismay, as commissioners from the parliament as well as from the king. Bedford produced his usual indefatigable attendance record, save for the period 9 December 1640 to 5 January 1641, when the minutes record him as sick. One interesting intervention of his was recorded by Richard Dyott in a letter of 25 September 1640: Bristol had proposed that the king be absent from 'these consultations', and Bedford, taking exactly the opposite line from the one he took in his commonplace book, said he would count him unworthy to live that should be afraid to say anything in the king's presence (Staffs. RO, Stafford, D 661/11/1/5).

The king seems to have been finally persuaded that he needed to negotiate about Christmas 1640, and serious negotiation seems to have begun from the privy council meeting of 15 January, which agreed to restore the church to the state it had been in Queen Elizabeth's time. This was a good slogan of uncertain meaning, but a useful place from which to begin negotiation. The council seem also to have persuaded the king of the need for a new law for the militia, something Bedford and Pym had wanted at least since 1628, but to which Charles was very reluctant to agree. They also got the king to agree to a serious attempt to restore his revenue by parliamentary means, and to a triennial act. The day before this meeting Lucy Carlisle, whose ear was very close to the ground, reported that 'I now beleeve wee shall have great change of officers, and contrary to what I thought … Bedford will be treasurer' (Russell, 243). The conclusions of this meeting were announced to parliament by the king in a speech of 23 January, in which he offered, in words he was to live to regret, that 'what parts of my revenue that shall be found illegal or grievous to the public, I shall willingly lay down, relying entirely upon the affections of my people'. He was clearly ready to trust Bedford's financial offers. More work ahead was suggested by his declared opposition to any plans 'that bishops shall be no better than cyphers' (*JHL*, 4.142). More trouble was suggested by Temple's report that all that would be done for the Scots was to pay them £200,000 as a 'Brotherly Assistance' and 'so to cleare them away presently' (ibid., 247). It was a programme which might stir anger in the Scots and fear in the junto.

Serious negotiations on the ecclesiastical issue began with the king's meeting, on 21 January 1641, with Archbishop Ussher, Richard Holdsworth, and Ralph Brownrigg. Some of the work of this group survives, and it shows a real attempt to bridge the gap between Charles and the Scots. The fact that Ussher happened to be on the spot because he was lecturing at St Paul's, Covent Garden, and that Brownrigg was married to Pym's niece, suggests this group may have been collaborating with Bedford and Pym. They attempted to narrow the gap between presbytery and episcopacy by taking up the line of John Reynolds and Richard Hooker, that bishops needed to act with the advice of their clergy. It is the line Bedford, in his commonplace book, had traced back to the Council of Trent. If they hoped that the combined provenance of Trent and Richard Hooker might persuade Charles that this was not merely a puritan idea, they were unsuccessful. Equally, there is no sign that the Scots, who had learned under James VI where limited episcopacy might lead, had the least sympathy with these proposals.

For Bedford as putative lord treasurer the financial side of the negotiation was his special responsibility, and this is better preserved on paper than any other part of the negotiation. He enjoyed the assistance of a formidable team of experts. The balance sheets, the essential tool for reform, were drawn up by his old friend Sir Edward Wardour, clerk of the pells in the exchequer, and Sir Robert Pye, auditor of the exchequer, whose son married Hampden's daughter. On the customs he relied on the help of his old standby Sir William Russell, treasurer of the navy and former customs farmer, as well as Sir John Harrison who was a current customs farmer. On land revenue he of course relied on the help of Pym. It is worth noting that in this list Pym was the only one who was clearly parliamentarian in the civil war. The most fully developed plans related to the customs, which were by far the biggest source of revenue. It is an area in which Bedford had been thinking for a very long time, and one early blueprint can be shown from context to date back to before 1630. The key point was to make the king a legal grant of tonnage and poundage, as had not been done in 1625. This was to be combined with a reversal of the judgment in *Bate's Case*, reasserting the principle that no customs duties could be imposed except by act of parliament. This clearly made it necessary to compile a new book of rates uprating the values at which goods were to be assessed for customs. Increases in revenue were to be delivered through the uprating of the values in the book of rates. The book of rates was finally delivered in 1642. It was too late for it to be approved, but it was put into use in 1660, when it justified the work which had been put into it.

The granting of this much legal revenue to the king raised a question of security, since there was no wish to make the king able to govern without parliaments and without taking account of the wishes of others. This was solved with great ingenuity. Tonnage and poundage was to be voted for three years at a time, lapsing each time a new parliament was due under the Triennial Act. The next problem was to prevent the king from doing what he had done in 1625, and continuing to collect the money after his legal authority had lapsed. This was to be solved, to the alarm of some in the Commons, by voting tonnage and poundage to commissioners to the king's use. These commissioners were to be taken from the parliamentary leaders themselves, who, under the cloak of the old system of customs farming, were to gain the power to withhold the king's revenue whenever his legal right to it ceased. This conferred a real stranglehold on executive power. Next came two major proposals for increasing the king's landed income, both preserved among Bedford's papers ('The project upon the wardes' and 'The project upon the clergie and colledges'). Evidently these did not remain confined to Bedford's papers, since a vehement denunciation of them in the foulest of Edward Nicholas's foul hand is extant. The first was a revival of the proposal of the great contract to compound for wardship, though not for purveyance until after Bedford's death. This proposal avoided the arguments of 1610 about the horrors of a land tax by putting the cost directly on those who got the benefit, those whose land had been held by knight service in chief. Their land was to be regranted to be held in common socage, which created no liability for wardship. They were to pay a rent and an entry fine for the new grant, and the value of the land was to be uprated by a formula in which there was some scope for adjustment. The balance between rent and fine could be adjusted according to the needs of the moment at which the bargain was concluded. The immediate proposal offered the king an increase in income of £48,000 per annum, and a capital windfall of £239,000. This would have helped to fill what proved the major gap in the Restoration financial settlement: provision for paying the king's debts and starting with a clean slate. The other proposal out of the same stable was for confiscation of the lands of deans and chapters as what Sir Simonds D'Ewes called the 'new abbies'. Here again uprating of the land was to be used to raise both income and capital for new leases of what was to become crown land. The proposal was for an increase in income of £120,000 and a capital sum in entry fines of £420,000. There was never any possibility that Charles would consent to this, and he implicitly ruled it out by his declaration at the council meeting of 24 January that 'the k. would rather starve than have any of the church lands or livings' (Russell, 245).

There were also a number of proposals about the parliamentary subsidy. The lump sum assessment used for ship money was transferred to the subsidy. This meant that it was impossible to reduce the total yield by under-assessment. Under-assessment of one payer now meant over-assessment of another. Certificates, freeing people from tax in one place because they had paid it in another, were to be abolished. This was another ship money innovation imported into parliamentary finance. The commissioners for collecting the subsidy, formerly named under the great seal, were now named in the act of parliament itself, and held office by parliamentary authority. Clarendon also said Bedford had a project to introduce an excise. For many years this statement had been unsupported. However, Edward Nicholas's tirade against the abolition of wardship contains an aside referring to possibilities 'if the k. consents to exchange it for the Excise' (Russell, 254). This, together with the fact that Pym subsequently did introduce it in 1643, is probably sufficient. If so, it was a proposal to fill what, by comparison with continental states, was the biggest gap in the English financial system.

Failure and death All these were good proposals, yet, though some were aired in the Commons, they waited on conclusion of the negotiations on religion. There were some optimistic signs during February 1641. On 19 February the king appointed seven new councillors, Bedford, Hertford, Saye, Essex, Mandeville, Savill, and Bristol. Of these, only Bedford, Saye, Essex, and Mandeville were still in the junto network, and they might have taken warning from the fact that as soon as they were put on the council the frequency of its meetings dropped sharply. Also in February, Oliver St John was appointed solicitor-general. He subsequently gave the credit to Hamilton, but since Hamilton at the time was negotiating to marry his son to Bedford's daughter, this is not incompatible with the general belief that Bedford was responsible for his preferment.

The negotiations began to go sour with the publication of the Scots' paper of 24 February 1641, in which they insisted on the abolition of episcopacy, 'the cause of all our broyles', and demanded the execution of Strafford on the ground that 'better one perish than unitie' (Thomason tract, BL E 669, fol. 3 (4)). This moved Charles to such rage that Johnston of Wariston commented that 'the king hes run starke mad' (Russell, 197). From this moment on it was crystal clear that the junto could only secure a settlement by ditching their Scottish allies. It will never be known whether they would have accepted the continuation of episcopacy or the life of Strafford as issues in their own right. The question was whether they had the option. In the impeachment of the five members, Charles was later to try to charge them with treason for their correspondence with the Scots during 1640. It did not take great intelligence for them to work out that Charles might consider this option, and the junto's problem, in Clarendon's words, is that 'they could not think themselves secure in his favour' (Hyde, earl of Clarendon, 1.254). They could not risk losing Scottish protection. There is some evidence that this issue may have caused a split, with Bedford possibly, as Clarendon believed, in a group which would still have settled. However, he was no use to Charles unless he could bring the others with him. Unfortunately he could not and from about the second week of March 1641 there was no possibility of a settlement whatsoever. Bedford had failed.

Bedford lived to be the first in the junto to hear of the army plot, in which Charles, having given up hope of negotiation, turned to force to rid himself of this turbulent parliament. Bedford's self-epitaph was that he was 'trusted by King Charles in his most secret counsels' (Bedford MSS, fourth earl, family papers). He must have known by this point that it was no longer true, if it ever had been. In the first week of May 1641 he fell sick of the smallpox, and died on 9 May. He was buried at Chenies in Buckinghamshire. In a rare gesture of honour the Commons adjourned all its committees to allow members to attend his funeral. Bedford was the only person to be given this honour by the house under the early Stuarts. The French ambassador described him as 'homme de grande vertu, également aimé de la noblesse et du peuple, à qui l'on avait destiné la charge du Grand Tresorier' ('a man of great virtue, equally loved by the nobility and the people, who was destined to become Lord Treasurer'; PRO, 31/3/72, fol. 555). Great honour was no substitute for success. For many years, Bedford was remembered as the man who might have prevented civil war. He might have done, but he did not. The attempt had finally failed some two months before his death.

There was a personal failure as well. The endless succession of draft wills was designed to avoid the fate of the second earl, who put the estate in chaos by dying with an out-of-date will. Bedford, in spite of all his efforts, did the same. He was told at the beginning of his last illness that his second son, Francis, had predeceased him, but his smallpox precluded the making of a new will. Edward, his third son, was under eighteen and could not consent to deeds changing the inheritance, and so it was necessary to settle the estate by a private act of parliament. Since a parliament was in session, there was no difficulty in getting the act through. It left the task of dividing Francis's share between the widow, the heir, and Edward, to Sir Alexander St John, Oliver St John, Lord Brooke, the earl of Bristol, George Digby, the earl of Elgin, Sir John Strangways, John Glanville, and John Pym, 'all of them neere and especiall friends of the said Earl' (PRO, C 204, bundle 3, no. 1). This is a snapshot of Bedford's inner circle at the moment of his death—four royalists (Bristol, Digby, Strangways, and Glanville), three parliamentarians (St John, Brooke, and Pym), and two who are not easily classifiable. Bedford's heir was to change sides twice during the war. The fourth earl's circle, like his culture and his career, gives absolutely no clue to what side he would have taken if he had lived to take sides in the civil war.

Reputation Bedford's reputation rests on two things. The first is that he was the leading figure in the junto of parliamentary leaders in 1640. He was host and presided over the drafting of the petition of the twelve peers, requesting the recall of parliament, on 28 August 1640. He was the patron of John Pym and Oliver St John, and the parliamentary leaders' candidate for the post of lord treasurer in any compromise settlement. The second is that he is credited by Clarendon with being the one man who, if he had lived, could have prevented the civil war from taking place. The first reputation is true. The second, if the phrase is permissible, is deserved but untrue. Bedford devoted all his efforts to making a compromise settlement, but it was clear some eight weeks before he died that his attempt had failed. Neither the king nor the Scottish covenanters wanted peace enough to pay the necessary price. Nothing in the surviving evidence enables today's commentators to judge with any confidence what Bedford would have done if he had lived to the beginning of the civil war in August 1642.

He died as he had lived, absolutely on the fault-line which was to divide the two sides in that conflict. When the war came people such as he had to decide, not which way their beliefs inclined—for they inclined both ways—but which part of their beliefs mattered more than another. People rarely know how they will make that choice until they know the circumstances and mood in which the choice is to be made. Bedford was a Calvinist episcopalian with no great love for nonconformity. He was one who did not trust Charles I with power, while not being wedded to Cokeian doctrines of law and ancient constitution. He was a peacemaker by temperament, who died before it could be discernible whom he blamed for his failure to make peace.

It was not Bedford's settlement, which was ideally designed to reunite the English body politic, which was to blame. It would have had enemies on both sides, and disappointed adherents on both sides, but there were few indeed who could not have lived with it. John Lilburne and Francis Kynaston would doubtless have protested, but Pym and Laud could have lived with it. The problem in avoiding the English civil war was not to reunite the English body politic: that was not where the problem lay. The country was not, even in May 1641, split into two hostile camps. If Bedford's problem had been merely how to reunite England, he would have succeeded.

Bedford's problems were twofold: they were the king and the Scottish covenanters. The king simply did not accept the proposition that he had to rule in a way his subjects found acceptable. He had to be coerced into it. All the past history of baronial crises should have taught Bedford that deposition was the only answer to this problem. He did not have that option, first, because the prevailing English culture put a taboo on deposition which the crisis was not yet grave enough to overcome, second, because the vast majority of the English, and even many of the privy council, insisted on pretending the king was less inflexible than he was, and third, because there was no pretender. It was soon clear that Hertford was unwilling, and the elector palatine, who alarmed everyone by going to stay with the earl of Essex, was warned off it by his mother. The only way to deal with the king was by a foreign army, and that army had demands, many of which were as unacceptable as the king's. The attempt to coerce the king by means of the Scots created even worse problems than it prevented. Bedford had fallen at the one hurdle no peacemaker can overcome: the desire of the parties to go on fighting. Next time a foreign army was called in to deal with an impossible king, it brought its pretender with it. That was a viable policy. Bedford's was not.

CONRAD RUSSELL

Sources G. S. Thompson, *Life in a noble household, 1641–1700* (1937) · E. Hyde, earl of Clarendon, *The history of the rebellion and civil wars in England*, 3 vols. (1702–4) · *CSP dom.*, 1607–41 · Trustees of the Bedford Settled Estates, Woburn Abbey, Bedfordshire, Bedford MSS [incl. the fourth earl's family papers, commonplace bks, and draft wills] · *JHL*, 2–4 (1578–1642) · BL, Add. MSS 26637; 26639 · W. B. Bidwell and M. Jansson, eds., *Proceedings in parliament, 1626*, 4 vols. (1991–6) · E. S. Cope, 'The earl of Bedford's notes on the Short Parliament of 1640', *BIHR*, 53 (1980), 255–8 · Alnwick Castle, Northumberland, Alnwick Castle MS Y III · C. Russell, *The fall of the British monarchies, 1637–1642* (1991) · GEC, *Peerage* · *Notes of the debates in the House of Lords, officially taken by Henry Elsing, clerk of the parliaments, AD*

1624 and 1626, ed. S. R. Gardiner, CS, new ser., 24 (1879) · parish register, Watford, St Mary, Herts. ALS, 19 Oct 1587 [baptism] · PRO, PROB 11/188/29 · PRO, C204, bundle 3, no. 1 · A. Searle, ed., *Barrington family letters, 1628–1632*, CS, 4th ser., 28 (1983) · E. R. Foster, ed., *Proceedings in parliament, 1610*, 2 vols. (1966) · C. M. Andrews, *The colonial period in American history*, 1 (1934) · *Calendar of the manuscripts of the most hon. the marquis of Salisbury*, 24 vols., HMC, 9 (1883–1976) · UCL, Ogden MS 7/7 · PRO, C142/435/118 · A. Hughes, 'Thomas Dugard and his circle in the 1630s—a "parliamentary–puritan" connexion?', *HJ*, 29 (1986), 771–93 · *The parliamentary diary of Robert Bowyer, 1606–1607*, ed. D. H. Wilson (1931) · Cambs. AS, Huntingdon, Manchester MS 32/5/10 · PRO, wards 15 · *DNB*

Archives Trustees of the Bedford Settled Estates, Woburn Abbey, Bedfordshire, papers · Woburn Abbey, Bedfordshire, papers **Likenesses** attrib. R. Peake, oils, *c*.1600, Woburn Abbey, Bedfordshire · A. Van Dyck, oils, 1636, Woburn Abbey, Bedfordshire · attrib. C. Johnson, oils, Woburn Abbey, Bedfordshire · after A. Van Dyck, portrait, priv. coll. · double portrait, alabaster tomb effigy (with wife), St Michael's Church, Chenies, Buckinghamshire, Bedford Chapel **Wealth at death** substantial: will, PRO, PROB 11/188/29

Russell, Francis, fifth duke of Bedford (1765–1802), agriculturist and politician, was born on 23 July 1765 and baptized on 20 August 1765 at St Giles-in-the-Fields, London, the eldest child of Francis Russell, marquess of Tavistock (1739–1767), politician, and Lady Elizabeth Keppel (1739–1768), daughter of William Keppel, second earl of Albemarle. His father was killed by a fall from his horse on 22 March 1767 and his mother died of consumption at Lisbon on 2 November 1768 at the age of twenty-eight. In 1771 he succeeded his grandfather, John *Russell, fourth duke of Bedford. He was educated at Loughborough House, near London, and at the age of nine he entered Westminster School, going on to Trinity College, Cambridge, in 1780. He went on the grand tour in 1784 and returned in August 1786. He took his seat in the House of Lords on 5 December 1787. He had shown little interest in study, and was reputed hardly ever to have opened a book before he was twenty-four. In 1793, according to Lord Holland, he confessed that he was afraid to speak in the Lords for fear of not expressing himself in correct English.

Bedford's lifelong interest was in agriculture and estate management. The Bedford properties, scattered over eleven counties, were among the greatest estates of the period and they were already highly organized and efficiently run. Bedford became known as a leading promoter of agricultural improvement. The seventh duke claimed in 1897 that he was 'among the first to initiate an agricultural system which was designed, some years later, to make the agricultural industry of Great Britain a model for the whole civilized world' (Bedford, 26–7). He was an original member of the board of agriculture set up in 1793, and the first president of the Smithfield Club in 1798. He practised what he preached and established a model farm of 4000 acres at Woburn where he carried out pioneering experiments breeding cattle and sheep and growing crops; these were recorded by Arthur Young in his *Annals of Agriculture* (1795) for imitation by others. He was caricatured by Gillray as 'the Bedfordshire Ox' in his satire *The Promised French Invasion* in 1797. He instituted an annual agricultural fair at Woburn which lasted for several days and attracted farming enthusiasts from all over

Francis Russell, fifth duke of Bedford (1765–1802), by John Hoppner, exh. RA 1797?

the country. These fairs were famous for their exhibitions of sheep-shearing, ploughing competitions, and other inducements to 'improvement', which he rewarded with prizes. His numerous guests were entertained at banquets at the end of the week's events, and he was a paternalistic landlord to his tenants and labourers who benefited from his benevolence. His successor continued these practices; the cost of pensions and other charities on his Bedfordshire and Buckinghamshire estates amounted in 1816 to over £44,000 (Beckett, 355).

Bedford was not only a model agricultural landlord but also a promoter of urban development. His London estates, totalling some 119 acres in the West End, Bloomsbury, Bedford New Town, and Covent Garden, had been marked out for development by his grandfather and, after the latter's death, his widow and her agent, Robert Palmer, embarked on ambitious building projects centred on what became Bedford Square, described by a modern architectural historian as 'one of the most valuable relics of Georgian London' (Summerson, 152). In 1800 Bedford obtained two acts of parliament for developing the Bloomsbury estate. Under the architect and developer James Burton and his later successor Thomas Cubitt, Bloomsbury Square, Russell Square, Tavistock Square, and the surrounding streets became a classic example of Georgian townscape, sadly diminished by modern alterations. By 1819, the rents of the London estates were yielding half of the family's considerable total income. The duke's great wealth made him a target for the satire of *The Anti-Jacobin* when he was accused of trying to evade the assessed taxes on twenty-five of his servants.

The Bedfords were already one of the leading whig political clans and the fifth duke was naturally drawn into that world. He was attracted to whig society, like many other young aristocrats of his day, at Devonshire House where Georgiana, duchess of Devonshire, her sister Lady Duncannon, and Lady Melbourne ruled the fashionable *ton*. They were captivated by Bedford's good looks, charm, and manners and nicknamed him Loo. He was a faithful friend to them all, and tried to help and advise them in their financial troubles, brought on by their addiction to gambling, and, in Lady Duncannon's case, her fraught relationship with Granville Leveson-Gower. She referred to him as 'the truest and most steady of friends' (Leveson-Gower, 1.99). His connection with their society also confirmed his attachment to Charles James Fox, who became his closest political mentor. Bedford disapproved of Grey's Association of the Friends of the People and its cause of parliamentary reform but, during the wilderness years for the Foxite whigs that followed the secession of the Portland whig leaders to Pitt, he remained true to Fox in opposition to Pitt's repression of popular liberties, despite Fox's praise of the French Revolution which, if it were introduced into England, would presumably have stripped him of his noble status. Fox was grateful for his support, and described him as 'one of the main pillars of the party', which was reduced to a handful in the House of Lords (*Memorials and Correspondence*, 3.67). In 1793 Bedford was one of the leading subscribers to a fund to pay Fox's debts and on his death in 1802 he left £5000 to Fox and an annuity of £250 to Miss Armitstead.

Overcoming his earlier diffidence, Bedford now became the Foxites' leading spokesman in the upper house. He was not a witty speaker, being too 'intolerably prolix and heavy in style, to hold his audience' (Turberville, 90). Lord Holland thought that he seemed 'to treat the understandings of his adversaries with contempt', but he paid tribute to his 'fluency, his readiness in argument, and … above all, his intrepid avowal of every opinion which he held'. Despite 'the absence of all sprightliness or classical ornament, and with the fault of prolixity, he became … a leading debater in the House, as well as a considerable man in the country' (Holland, 1.145, 80–81). Bedford was also one of the intimate friends of the prince of Wales, and on 8 April 1795 was one of the two unmarried dukes who supported him (only too literally) at his wedding to Princess Caroline of Brunswick-Wolfenbüttel, when the bridegroom was evidently in a state of intoxication. In June 1795 on the prince's annuity bill he defended the prince's conduct, despite his extravagance, on the grounds of 'his age, the situation in which he was placed, and the insufficiency of his income to support the splendour necessary

for his rank', saying that the ministers should have liquidated his debts and his father should have contributed to do so (Cobbett, *Parl. hist.*, 22.128).

Bedford supported all Fox's initiatives from the House of Lords. He signed the protest against the suspension of habeas corpus on 22 May 1794, and on the 30th proposed the motion for peace with France which had been previously introduced in the Commons by Fox. In October 1795 he opposed the address, describing the ministry as 'if not corrupt and despotic, at least weak and inefficient' (Cobbett, *Parl. hist.*, 32.193). In November he opposed Pitt's Treasonable Practices Bill which extended the law of treason to the advocacy of radical reform as 'a daring attack and flagititious outrage on the liberty of the subject' (ibid., 32.257). He also objected to the Seditious Meetings Bill which restricted the holding of political meetings, reminding his audience that the 'lower orders' would mainly be affected 'but recollect that we are dependant on their labours for all desirable aspects of our situation— riches, honour and power' (ibid., 32.249–50, 548–9). In May 1797 and March 1798 he moved for the dismissal of ministers, losing on both occasions by large majorities. He opposed the suspension of cash payments by the Bank of England in 1797, and in 1798 he joined Grey and Lauderdale in persuading Fox to secede from parliament as a protest against Pitt's regime, although he himself occasionally returned to the Lords. He did so in 1798 to vote against the income tax and to protest against the methods used to suppress the Irish rising as 'a system of coercion … enforced … with a rigour shocking to humanity', involving torture and burning of houses—'practices so disgraceful to the British name' (ibid., 34.204–7, 33.1517–18). In January 1801 he co-operated with Grey and Fitzwilliam in drawing up the opposition's amendment to the address, and after Pitt's resignation he advocated a coalition government, to include Addington and Fox, and was nominated for the office of lord president of the council, but the scheme came to nothing.

Perhaps Bedford's most famous intervention during the war years was his scathing criticism of Burke, whom the Foxites saw as an apostate for having accepted a pension from Pitt's government in 1796. His attack drew forth Burke's celebrated pamphlet *A Letter to a Noble Lord* (1796), in which he contrasted his pension as a reward for services to his country with the grants received in the past by Bedford's family, which 'were so enormous as not only to outrage economy, but even to stagger credibility' (*Writings and Speeches*, 9/1.164). He described his adversary as

> the leviathan among the creatures of the crown. … His ribs, his fins, his whalebone, his blubber, the very spiracles through which he spouts a torrent of brine against his origin, and covers me all over with the spray—everything of him and about him is from the Throne. Is it for him to question the dispensation of the Royal favour?   (ibid.)

In contrast to Burke, Bedford had been 'swaddled and rocked and dandled into a legislator': his support of (alleged) revolutionary principles endangered 'the safety of that Constitution which secures his own utility or his own ignificance' (ibid., 9/1.160, 171).

Bedford did not marry but he had two children with a mistress, Mrs Palmer. In 1802, at the age of thirty-six, to the great distress of the ladies at Devonshire House, he announced his engagement to Lady Georgiana Gordon, daughter of Jane, duchess of Gordon, the former intimate of Pitt. Within a month, however, he was dead, having died at his seat, Woburn Abbey, on 2 March 1802 from a strangulated hernia, sustained when playing tennis. He bequeathed his personal estate to his brother and heir, Lord John *Russell (1766–1839), who became the sixth duke and who married his brother's intended bride in 1803. He was buried at night on 10 March at Chenies, Buckinghamshire, one of his properties. Fox and Sheridan eulogized him in the House of Commons, and Lord Holland paid tribute to his judgement, integrity, talents, and personal qualities: 'His heart was affectionate, and he joined to all these qualifications great firmness of mind and the purest simplicity of manners that I ever knew … he was truth itself, … always plain, undisguised truth and real benevolence' (Holland, 1.146). Lady Bessborough praised his patriotism: 'I am convinced that … he would sacrifice his fortune and life to what he thought his duty and the real good of the country' (Leveson-Gower, 1.208). Bedford's statue by Westmacott was erected in Russell Square in 1809, and shows him with one hand resting on a plough, the other holding some ears of corn.

E. A. Smith

Sources GEC, *Peerage* · A. S. Turberville, *The House of Lords in the age of reform, 1784–1837* (1958) · H. R. Vassall, Lord Holland, *Memoirs of the whig party during my time*, ed. H. E. Vassall, Lord Holland, 2 vols. (1852–4) · Cobbett, *Parl. hist.* · *Memorials and correspondence of Charles James Fox*, ed. J. Russell, 4 vols. (1853–7) · L. G. Mitchell, *Charles James Fox* (1992) · J. V. Beckett, *The aristocracy in England, 1660–1914* (1986) · *Lord Granville Leveson Gower: private correspondence, 1781–1821*, ed. Castalia, Countess Granville [C. R. Leveson-Gower], 2nd edn, 2 vols. (1916) · H. A. Russell, duke of Bedford, *A great agricultural estate, being the story of the origin and administration of Woburn and Thorney*, 3rd edn (1897) · A. Young, ed., *Annals of agriculture and other useful arts* (1795) · J. Summerson, *Georgian London*, rev. edn (1962) · *The writings and speeches of Edmund Burke*, ed. P. Langford, 9 vols. (1981–) · C. Edmonds, ed., *The poetry of the Anti-Jacobin*, new edn (1854) · *DNB*
Archives BL, Charles James Fox MSS · BL, corresp. with Lord Holland, Add. MS 51660 · Hants. RO, Tierney MSS · NL Ire., letters from him and members of his family to Lord Upper Ossory · U. Durham L., Grey MSS
Likenesses J. Reynolds, group portrait, oils, 1776 (*St George and the dragon*), Osterley Park, London · J. Sayers, caricature, engraving, pubd 1795, BM · I. Cruikshank, caricature, engraving, pubd 1796, BM · J. Gillray, caricature, aquatint, pubd 1796, BM · J. Hoppner, oils, exh. RA 1796, Woburn Abbey, Bedfordshire · J. Hoppner, oils, exh. RA 1797?, Royal Collection [*see illus.*] · W. Kimpton, silhouette, c.1800, NPG · J. Gillray, group portrait, line and stipple print with watercolour, pubd 1801 (with the Union Club), NG Ire. · J. Nollekens, bust, 1802, Woburn Abbey, Bedfordshire · J. Nollekens, bust, 1803, Holkham Hall, Norfolk · W. Grimaldi, watercolour miniature (after Hoppner), NPG · J. Hoppner, oils, second version, Petworth House [NT], Sussex · W. Lane, pencil drawing, NPG · J. Nollekens, bust, Royal Collection · R. Westmacott, bronze statue, Russell Square, London

Russell, Francis Charles Hastings, ninth duke of Bedford (1819–1891). *See under* Russell, Lord George William (1790–1846).

Russell, Francis Xavier Joseph [Frank], **Baron Russell of Killowen** (1867–1946), judge, was born in London on 2 July 1867, the fourth son of Charles Arthur *Russell, later Baron Russell of Killowen (1832–1900), lord chief justice of England, and his wife, Ellen Mulholland (1836–1918). Frank Russell was the second of three consecutive generations of Russells to reach the highest rank of the judiciary, that of lord of appeal in ordinary.

Educated at Beaumont College, Berkshire, and at Oriel College, Oxford, as an undergraduate Russell distinguished himself both in the Oxford Union, where in 1887 his brilliant speech in favour of home rule caused A. V. Dicey, notwithstanding his disapproval of the proposed reform, to write a letter of congratulation to Russell's father, and academically, obtaining in 1890 a first in jurisprudence.

In 1893 Russell was called to the bar by Lincoln's Inn and practised at the Chancery bar in the chambers of the future Mr Justice Joyce. He achieved immediate success, helped by his family connections—his elder brother, Sir Charles *Russell, was an eminent solicitor—but he had the ability to succeed without that advantage. The privy council case in which the British South Africa Company sought to limit the crown's rights in the territory of Lobengula, the Matabele (Ndebele) chief, contributed to his rapid advancement. On 17 February 1900 he married Mary Emily (d. 1956), daughter of Charles Thomson *Ritchie, first Baron Ritchie of Dundee; they had one son, Charles Ritchie *Russell, later also Baron Russell of Killowen, and three daughters.

In 1908 Russell took silk, and as was then the custom he attached himself to the court of Mr Justice Swinfen Eady, and later to that of Mr Justice Astbury. In 1918 he joined the select band of Chancery 'specials', silks who for a special fee went into any court. As a devout Roman Catholic, appropriately he appeared in *Bourne* v. *Keane* (1919), persuading the House of Lords to overrule previous authorities to declare that a bequest for masses for the dead was a valid charitable gift and not void as being to superstitious uses.

The lord chancellor, Lord Birkenhead, who presided in that case, was sufficiently impressed to cause Russell to be appointed to fill the next Chancery vacancy in 1919. Unusually, Russell declined the knighthood customarily offered to a High Court judge, on the ground that as a peer's son he already outranked a mere knight. His decisions were rarely reversed on appeal and in 1928 he was elevated to the Court of Appeal and sworn of the privy council. Only a year later he was appointed a lord of appeal in ordinary, with a life peerage, taking the same title as his father. For the next sixteen years he sat regularly in the House of Lords and the privy council.

Well respected though he was, Russell was not an outstanding contributor to the development of the law, showing himself to be conservative in his social and religious views both judicially and in his occasional speeches in debates. On A. P. Herbert's Matrimonial Causes Bill he spoke strongly against the measure, declaring that the

Francis Xavier Joseph Russell, Baron Russell of Killowen (1867–1946), by Lafayette, 1928

Lord Hailsham at the start of his second term as lord chancellor, described Russell as 'Quick, first rate, but occasionally inclined to be narrow in outlook' (Heuston, 481).

Russell retired at the beginning of 1946 through ill health. He had a small compact figure and a strong, intelligent, and broad-browed face. Described by Lord Simon as 'a serene spirit of rare quality' (*The Times*, 23 Dec 1946), he was a kindly, companionable, and genial man with a sharp wit, which made him much in demand as an after-dinner speaker. Elected a bencher of Lincoln's Inn in 1915, he became treasurer in 1936. For years he was the chairman of trustees of the Garrick Club and president of the Beaumont Union and of the Thomas More Society. In 1928 he was elected an honorary fellow of Oriel College. He died on 20 December 1946 at his home, Lane End, Walton on the Hill, Surrey, and was buried at Epsom. He was survived by his wife, son, and two daughters.

PETER GIBSON

Sources *The Times* (23 Dec 1946) · *Law Times* (4 Jan 1947) · A. W. B. Simpson, ed., *Biographical dictionary of the common law* (1984) · R. F. V. Heuston, *Lives of the lord chancellors, 1885–1940* (1964) · R. Stevens, *Law and politics: the House of Lords as a judicial body, 1800–1976* (1979), 312 · *DNB* · *Daily Telegraph* (23 Dec 1946) · G. Lewis, *Lord Atkin* (1983) · *WWW, 1897–1915* · *WWW, 1941–50* · Burke, *Peerage* (1939) · *CGPLA Eng. & Wales* (1947)

Likenesses Lafayette, photograph, 1928, NPG [*see illus.*] · W. Stoneman, photograph, 1929, NPG · R. G. Eves, oils, 1937, Lincoln's Inn, London · R. G. Eves, oils, Garr. Club

Wealth at death £62,886 2*s.* 2*d.*: probate, 22 April 1947, *CGPLA Eng. & Wales*

question of divorce was a religious one and that as a Catholic he could not approve the facilitation of divorce. He dissented in the matrimonial case *Fender* v. *St John-Mildmay* (1937), saying: 'The institution of marriage has long been on a slippery slope' and 'what was once a holy estate enduring for the joint lives of the spouses is steadily assuming the characteristics of a contract for a tenancy at will'. In *Alderman* v. *Great Western Railway Company* (1937) he construed narrowly the scope of employment of a workman. A staunch defender of property rights, he favoured a strict and literal construction of fiscal legislation, saying in *IRC* v. *Duke of Westminster* (1936):

> I view with disfavour the doctrine that in taxation cases the subject is to be taxed if, in accordance with a Court's view of what it considers the substance of a transaction, the Court thinks that the case falls within the contemplation or spirit of the statute.

In *Regal (Hastings) Ltd.* v. *Gulliver* (1941), he took a stern view of a director profiting from his fiduciary position, saying: 'The profiteer, however honest and well-intentioned, cannot escape the risk of being called to account.' But his dissenting judgment in *Banco de Portugal* v. *Waterlow & Sons Ltd.* (1932), supporting Lord Justice Scrutton in the Court of Appeal, showed characteristic robustness of thought, and his lucidity and power of concise and precise statement were much admired. He was Lord Atkin's 'most formidable adversary in the House' (Lewis, 76), each being capable of expressing himself in the forceful language of the advocate. Lord Dunedin, writing confidentially to the first

Russell, Sir Frederick Stratten (1897–1984), marine biologist, was born on 3 November 1897 at Bridport, Dorset, the younger son and second of three children of William Russell, schoolteacher, of Bridport, and his wife, Lucy Binfield, daughter of Henry Newman of Liverpool. He was educated at Oundle School from 1909, and was awarded an open scholarship to Gonville and Caius College, Cambridge, in 1915. His academic career was interrupted by the First World War, in which he served with distinction as an observer in the Royal Naval Air Service. He was awarded the DSC, DFC, and Croix de Guerre (with palm). He took up his scholarship to Caius in 1919 and received a first-class honours degree in natural science (zoology) in 1922. The following year he married Gweneth Evans (d. 1979), who was employed at the Ministry of Labour. She was the daughter of John Moy Evans of Swansea. They later had one son.

After a brief period as assistant director of fisheries research for the Egyptian government Russell joined the staff of the Marine Biological Association in Plymouth as an assistant naturalist in 1924. There, his skills as an observer and his ability to unravel the significant patterns from a mass of information enabled him to make rapid progress in his research. Field studies in the English Channel led to the publication of a series of classic papers explaining the vertical distribution of young fish and small animals (zooplankton) in the sea in terms of their sensitivity to light.

In 1928–9 Russell worked in Australia on the Great Barrier Reef expedition and, on his return to Plymouth, he began to study the patterns of biological change in the English Channel. He recognized the importance of certain indicator species as heralds of environmental change and contributed to the identification of the seasonally cyclical nature of plankton abundance in the channel. He also studied the life cycles of the Medusae (jellyfish), in many instances culturing these delicate animals in the laboratory with the assistance of W. J. Rees. Having learned the art of watercolour sketching from his father and having also received training as a photographer in the First World War, his papers were beautifully illustrated. He developed his talents to produce and edit a series of keys, which is still widely used for the identification of planktonic (drifting) animals. His skills were most eloquently used in the magnificent illustrated volumes on the British Medusae begun at this time.

In 1940–45 Russell served as a wing commander in air staff intelligence. Immediately after the war he was invited to return to Plymouth as the director of the laboratory—a challenge he accepted somewhat reluctantly because of the administrative duties involved. He served as director from 1945 to 1965, a period considered by his contemporaries as the golden age of the laboratory. Although he had a relaxed and kindly nature he was energetic and decisive and provided firm direction. His policy of recruiting able and dedicated staff and allowing them to develop their own ideas attracted a wide range of distinguished scientists. During his directorship the laboratory facilities were improved by a carefully planned building programme and by the purchase of an ocean-going research vessel (RV *Sarsia*). Despite the considerable energy that he devoted to his role as director, Russell continued his research. Volume 1 (Hydromedusae) of his superbly illustrated work, *The Medusae of the British Isles*, was published in 1953 and the second volume (Scyphomedusae) in 1970.

Russell retired from the directorship of the Marine Biological Association in 1965 but he retained a room at the laboratory and continued his work on the Medusae and on the distribution of young fish and the significance of biological changes in the English Channel. He published *The Eggs and Planktonic Stages of British Marine Fishes* in 1976. His studies of biological variability continued in collaboration with his colleagues in Plymouth. This work led to the recognition of large periodic changes in the English Channel (the Russell cycle), related to the rise and fall of the herring fishery, that are extremely important for attempts to assess man's impact on the environment.

Russell was elected FRS in 1938. In 1955 he was appointed CBE and in 1957 he was elected an honorary fellow of the Institute of Biology and an honorary LLD at the University of Glasgow. He was awarded honorary DSc degrees at the universities of Exeter (1960), Birmingham (1966), and Bristol (1972). He received the gold medal of the Linnean Society in 1961 and was knighted in 1965. He was elected an honorary fellow of Gonville and Caius College, Cambridge, in 1965. He was a foreign member of the Royal Danish Academy and was an honorary member of the Physiological Society, the Challenger Society, and the Fisheries Society of the British Isles.

Although deeply affected by the sudden death of his wife in 1979, Russell continued to work with vigour at the Plymouth laboratory until he moved to Thames Bank Nursing Home in Goring in 1980. He died there on 5 June 1984. MICHAEL WHITFIELD, *rev.*

Sources E. J. Denton and A. J. Southward, *Memoirs FRS*, 32 (1986), 461–93 · personal knowledge (1990) · *The Times* (6 June 1984) · *CGPLA Eng. & Wales* (1984)

Archives Marine Biological Association of the United Kingdom, Plymouth, personal and scientific corresp. and papers · NMM, pilot's logbook | CAC Cam., letters to A. V. Hill · Marine Biological Association of the United Kingdom, Plymouth, corresp. with E. T. Browne · NHM, letters to Charles Maurice Yonge

Wealth at death £227,099: probate, 29 Aug 1984, *CGPLA Eng. & Wales*

Russell, Lord George William (1790–1846), army officer and diplomatist, was second son of John *Russell, sixth duke of Bedford (1766–1839), and his first wife, Georgiana Elizabeth (d. 11 Oct 1801), second daughter of George Byng, fourth Viscount Torrington. Lord John *Russell (later Earl Russell) was his younger brother. He was born in Harley Street, London, on 8 May 1790, and was educated with Lord John at Dr Moore's private school at Sunbury, by the Revd John Smith at Woodnesborough, near Sandwich, and at Westminster School for just over a year. In 1839, after reading *Nicholas Nickleby*, he wrote that Dotheboys Hall reminded him of his own schooling: 'the blows and starvation came back to my recollection' (Blakiston, 420). To his brother Lord John he was through life warmly attached. He entered the army as cornet in the 1st (Royal) Dragoons on 5 February 1806, and became lieutenant on 11 September. He took part in the expedition to Copenhagen in 1807 as aide-de-camp to Sir George Ludlow.

On 25 March 1808 Russell became captain in the 23rd light dragoons, and went with the regiment to Portugal in 1809. In the charge on Villette's column at Talavera, which cost the regiment so heavily, he was wounded and nearly taken prisoner. He returned to England with the regiment at the end of the year. In 1810 he went back to the Peninsula as aide-de-camp to General Graham at Cadiz, and was present at the battle of Barossa (5 March 1811). In 1812 he became aide-de-camp to Wellington, and was on his staff at Vitoria, Orthez, and Toulouse. He was sent home with dispatches after Toulouse, and received a brevet lieutenant-colonelcy and medal for that battle (12 April 1814). He had become major in the 102nd regiment on 4 February 1813. Harriette Wilson described him as 'a gentlemanlike little fellow' (Blakiston, 14). Russell married, on 21 June 1817, Elizabeth Anne (1793–1874), only child of Captain the Hon. John Theophilus Rawdon (d. 1808), the brother of Francis, first marquess of Hastings, and his wife, Frances *née* Stevenson, who was generally considered 'a tiresome gossiping fool' (Blakiston, 30). Educated on the continent, Elizabeth was a rootless polyglot cosmopolitan. Beautiful and vivacious, it was to her that Byron alluded in 'Beppo' as the only one he had ever seen 'whose bloom could, after dancing, dare the dawn'. Arrogant, selfish, and pushy, she dominated her relatively gentle, unconfident husband, and was hostile to his family, especially his stepmother. She had lifelong tory sympathies, and was distrusted by the whigs: Brougham called her 'that cursed woman' (Blakiston, 266). She and Russell had three sons, of whom the youngest was Odo William *Russell, Baron Ampthill.

Soon after his marriage in 1817 Russell went to Paris as aide-de-camp to Wellington, who was then ambassador. From 1812 to 1830 he was MP for Bedford. He was a staunch whig, regarded by his family as radical, later privately encouraging Lord John Russell's opposition to the corn laws. In 1826 he urged his brother to master the Irish question and identify himself with it. In 1830 the duke of Bedford wrote to Russell that the latter could not again stand for Bedford, as he had alienated local support by his 'non-efficiency as a member' (Blakiston, 212).

Russell and his wife spent much time on the continent, which she preferred, though his family urged him to return to England. On 28 October 1824 he obtained the command of the 8th (Royal Irish) hussars, and held it until November 1828. He advocated a revision of the cavalry regulations, and wrote to Wellington on this, arguing partly from his own experience in the Peninsula; Wellington expressed his agreement. In 1829 and 1830 Russell briefly commanded (as lieutenant-colonel) the 90th regiment at Corfu, spending much of his time on leave elsewhere. He became colonel in the army on 22 July 1830, went on half pay in 1831, and became major-general on 23 November 1841, but had no further military employment. He was aide-de-camp to William IV in 1830–37 and to Victoria in 1837–41.

When the whigs came into office in 1830 a diplomatic career opened for Russell. He was attached to the mission of Sir Robert Adair to Belgium in July 1831. In 1832 he was sent on a special mission to Portugal, during the struggle between Don Miguel and Donna Maria. He wrote to Palmerston urging British intervention in support of Donna Maria. In April 1834 he returned to England, and in November was transferred to Stuttgart, Württemberg; on 24 November 1835 he succeeded Lord Minto as ambassador at Berlin. Disillusioned with his wife, in 1835, at Baden-Baden and elsewhere, Russell had an affair with a German Jew, probably Henrietta Marx, a widow and the daughter of Baron Salomon von Haber, a wealthy banker. There was a public scandal; Lady Russell felt humiliated by 'l'infâme Juive' and left her husband. Though they were apparently reconciled, she lived mostly apart from him on the continent until his death. In September 1841, when Peel returned to power, Russell was recalled. He received the GCB (civil) on 19 July 1838, and the order of Leopold (first class) in 1841. The delicate health of his elder brother and of his nephew at times suggested that he might inherit the dukedom, but they outlived him. Russell was shy, witty, and naturally lazy—his career largely the result of aristocratic jobbery.

Russell died at Genoa on 16 July 1846, and was buried in the Bedford Chapel at Chenies church, Buckinghamshire,

on 29 July. His wife returned to England in 1850, living in Audley Square, London. She was received into the Church of Rome in 1860, and died on 10 August 1874.

The eldest son, **Francis Charles Hastings Russell**, ninth duke of Bedford (1819–1891), agriculturist, was born in Curzon Street, London, on 16 October 1819. He entered the Scots Fusilier Guards in 1838, but retired when he married, on 18 January 1844, Lady Elizabeth Sackville-West (d. 22 April 1897), eldest daughter of George John Sackville-*West, fifth Earl De La Warr [see under West, John, first Earl De La Warr]. She was a bridesmaid, and subsequently mistress of the robes (1880–83), to Queen Victoria.

Russell was Liberal MP for Bedfordshire from 1847 to 1872, when (26 May) he succeeded to the dukedom on the death of his first cousin, William, eighth duke, the son of Francis and grandson of John, sixth duke. In 1879 he succeeded the prince of Wales as president of the Royal Agricultural Society, and he carried out costly experiments at his Woburn estate on manure fertilizing. Valuable results were obtained on an experimental farm. The duke himself had a keen practical knowledge of ensilage and stock breeding. Although caustic-tongued, he was shy and took little part in politics. He chiefly occupied himself in superintending the management of his vast properties, covering about 90,000 acres in Bedfordshire, Devonshire, Cambridgeshire, Northamptonshire, Dorset, Buckinghamshire, Huntingdonshire, and Cornwall. He presented a statue of Bunyan and other gifts to the town of Bedford, built a town hall, and devised many improvements on his property in and around Tavistock and on his estates in the fens, but he was taunted by the press (especially *Punch*) for neglecting Covent Garden market and important properties in its vicinity. Over £1 million was added to the ducal revenues in his time by the fines exacted on the leases falling due upon his Bloomsbury estate.

Russell was created KG on 1 December 1880. Formerly a Liberal, in 1886 he broke with the Gladstonian party and from then was Unionist. In later life he became a hypochondriac, and, suffering from pneumonia, he shot himself through the heart 'while temporarily insane' (GEC, *Peerage*, 87) at his house at 81 Eaton Square, London, on 14 January 1891; he was cremated at Woking and his ashes were buried at Chenies church.

Russell was succeeded by his eldest son, George William Francis Sackville Russell, who was born at Eaton Place West on 16 April 1852, graduated BA from Balliol College, Oxford, in 1874, and was called to the bar from Lincoln's Inn. He married on 24 October 1876 Lady Adeline Mary Somers-Cocks, second daughter and coheir of Charles, third Earl Somers. He was Liberal MP for Bedfordshire from 1875 to 1885, and died suddenly of diabetes on 23 March 1893 at 37 Chosham Place, leaving no children. He was succeeded by his brother Herbrand Arthur *Russell, eleventh duke (1858–1940).

E. M. LLOYD and THOMAS SECCOMBE, *rev.*
JAMES FALKNER

Sources G. Blakiston, *Lord William Russell and his wife, 1815–1846* (1972) · *Army List* · *The Times* (15 Jan 1891) · *The Times* (19 Jan 1891) ·

GM, 2nd ser., 26 (1846), 316 · R. Cannon, ed., *Historical record of the eighth, or the king's royal Irish regiment of hussars* (1844) · *ILN* (24 Jan 1891) · *Hart's Army List* · *Supplementary despatches (correspondence) and memoranda of Field Marshal Arthur, duke of Wellington*, ed. A. R. Wellesley, second duke of Wellington, 15 vols. (1858–72) · *The Spectator* (7 March 1891) · GEC, *Peerage* · Burke, *Peerage* · HoP, *Commons*
Archives Woburn Abbey, Bedfordshire, corresp. and papers | BL, corresp. with Lord Holland, Add. MS 51676 · Lambton Park, Chester-le-Street, co. Durham, letters to first earl of Durham · NL Scot., letters to Lord Lynedoch · PRO, corresp. with Lord John Russell, PRO 30/22 · U. Southampton L., corresp. with Lord Palmerston
Likenesses G. Hayter, oils, exh. RA 1820, Woburn Abbey, Bedfordshire · J. Maguès, drawing, 1839, repro. in Blakiston, *Lord William Russell*, facing p. 463; priv. coll. · R. Westmacott, bust, 1843, Woburn Abbey, Bedfordshire · G. Richmond, portrait, 1869 (Russell, Francis Charles Hastings), Woburn Abbey, Bedfordshire · G. Hayter, group portrait, oils (*The trial of Queen Caroline*, 1820), NPG
Wealth at death £230,970 2s. 3d.—Francis Charles Hastings Russell: probate, 1892, resworn

Russell, George William [*pseud.* A. E.] (1867–1935), journalist, poet, and agricultural economist, was born on 10 April 1867 at William Street, in the Ulster town of Lurgan, the youngest of three children of Thomas Elias Russell (1822?–1900), a bookkeeper employed by Bell & Co., a Quaker firm of cambric manufacturers, and his wife, Marianne, *née* Armstrong, of Drumgor (1836?–1897). His sister, Mary Elizabeth, died at the age of eighteen; his brother, Thomas Matthew, predeceased him by only a few years.

'The strayed angel', 1867–1890 Although born in Lurgan, an Ulster town noted for its sectarian tensions, Russell was raised in the semi-rural surroundings of Lord Lurgan's estate. At the age of four he was enrolled in the local model school, where he soon gained a reputation as a bright, gentle student with artistic talents. For the next six years his childhood seems to have been as pious as it was peaceful. His parents were devout members of the Church of Ireland, while his bookkeeper father, who had evangelical leanings, sometimes sought additional fellowship with the Primitive Methodists. In time George William Russell would also come to value this kind of alliance between practical business and a desire for spiritual fulfilment free of commitment to a single institution.

Shortly after Russell turned eleven his father accepted an offer of employment with a Dublin firm of accountants. The family lived first at 33 Emorville Avenue, the boy attending Dr Power's school in Harrington Street from 1878 until 1882. His gift for painting persuaded his parents, when he turned thirteen, to send him to evening classes at the Metropolitan School of Art for three months. Early in 1882 he was enrolled at Rathmines College, where he completed his sixth form. The reminiscences of fellow pupils suggest that he was both well-regarded and high-spirited.

But change was about to intrude itself. While staying with relatives in Armagh, a visit he had been making every second summer since he moved south, Russell suddenly began to experience supernatural visions that left him dazzled and bifurcated between a self that seemed confident, and one that was stammering and introverted.

George William Russell (1867–1935), by John Butler Yeats, 1903

So urgent were these revelations for visual expression that when he re-enrolled in evening classes at the art school in October 1883, he would suddenly spurn the assigned task and begin to paint with enviable fluency vivid interpretations of eternity. It was either then, or at the day classes he attended once he had left Rathmines College in 1884, that he came to know the painter Oliver Sheppard, the sculptor John Hughes, and a lanky, bearded art student, poet, and occultist, William Butler Yeats.

The ensuing friendship between the seventeen-year-old Russell, whom the Yeats sisters dubbed 'the strayed angel', and the nineteen-year-old Yeats both challenged and threatened to overwhelm the younger man. It brought, for example, invitations to Katharine Tynan's literary gatherings—where after one visit they were lampooned for their mutual admiration in the Dublin *Evening Telegraph* of 14 January 1888—and it brought invitations to meetings of the Contemporary Club, a non-sectarian group formed late in 1885 to discuss the 'social, political and literary questions of the day'. Yet Russell was determined to preserve a measure of independence, and refused to associate with Yeats's campaign for a literary expression of Irish nationality. He also refused to join both his friend's Hermetic Society, founded in 1885, and Charles Johnston's Theosophical Society, founded a year later. His first publication, an article entitled 'The speech of the gods', which he co-authored with Johnston for the December 1887 issue of Madame Blavatsky's *The Theosophist*, carries a signature quite deliberately free of institutional commitment.

Some time late in 1887, in his quest for detachment, Russell burnt all his manuscripts. Shortly after, he withdrew from art school to devote himself to meditation and to an intense study of spiritual texts, particularly the sacred literature of India, for which he retained a lifelong reverence. Sensing that such spiritual turbulence was somehow representative, Yeats published a pen-sketch of his friend entitled 'An Irish visionary' in the *National Observer* on 3 October 1891. Thereafter entitled 'A Visionary', it was collected in *The Celtic Twilight* (1893, 1902, 1914, 1921).

A. E. at large, 1891–1896 Having served seven years of spiritual apprenticeship, Russell now embarked on seven years of personal consolidation. In August 1890 he took a regular job as a clerk at Pims, a large drapers in South Great George's Street. At the end of the year he joined the esoteric section of the Theosophical Society, and four months later he moved out of his parents' home to join a small community of fellow theosophists at 3 Upper Ely Place, affectionately known as The Household. It was to become the pivot of his life until 1897.

The Household stimulated Russell's creativity and provided him with a social life, though it insulated him from the wider world. The defining event of 1891 for him was not Parnell's death but Madame Blavatsky's. In the summer of 1892 he began to paint a series of murals, portions of which still survive, depicting the journey of the pilgrim soul. He also served as librarian, auditor, and vice-president. And in a pamphlet entitled *To the Fellows of the Theosophical Society* (1894) he took his first step in his career as a polemicist, defending William Quan Judge, one of the founders of the Theosophical Society, against allegations of psychic fraud. The pamphlet was printed by the *Irish Theosophist*, a weekly journal which The Household had decided to launch on 15 October 1892 and to which Russell regularly contributed poems, stories, and articles as G. W. R. and Æ or A. E.—derived from Aeon, which, according to the gnostics, was the generic name for the earliest beings separated from the deity, one of whom Russell believed had incarnated in him.

Several of Russell's poems captured the attention of an enterprising friend, Charles Weekes, who decided to found his own publishing company to give them a wider public. A. E.'s *Homeward: Songs by the Way* appeared in June 1894. It enjoyed considerable success, selling in Ireland, England, and America and being reprinted five times in a total run of approximately 4000 copies. In acknowledging this achievement and their friendship, Yeats dedicated 'Crossways', the first section of his *Poems* (1895) to him, Russell returning the compliment with a laudatory review of the volume in the *Irish Weekly Independent* for 26 October 1895. Confident of the integrity of his own voice, and urged on by Yeats to declare his literary nationality, Russell promptly joined the Irish Literary Society, Dublin.

Russell's confidence was further buttressed by a programme of meditation (which among other things helped him to overcome his stammer), begun under the tutelage of an American theosophist, James Pryse, who had joined The Household in February 1895. In December 1896 the

lease on 3 Upper Ely Place expired, and The Household was obliged to move to 13 Eustace Street. Shortly after, it disbanded. Russell, now approaching thirty, returned to live with his parents at 5 Seapoint Terrace, Monkstown, where they had moved in 1892.

Forced back on his own resources, but fired up by Madame Blavatsky's chiliastic prophecies and his recent discovery of Standish O'Grady's mythological histories, Russell launched himself on a programme of propaganda. In February he announced the imminence of the new age in a pamphlet entitled *The Future of Ireland and the Awakening of the Fires* (1897), and in May he launched an attack on the hegemony of the Catholic church with *Ideals in Ireland: Priest or Hero?* (1897). Bouts of fervid street preaching followed. Early that summer while down at Bray, O'Grady was astonished to hear his writings being proclaimed from the sea-wall during a passionate oration about the return of the ancient gods.

For more than a year Russell had been writing excitedly to Yeats about such a possibility, and late in June 1897 the two men set out for the west to find a site for a school of the mysteries; in the course of their search they stayed at Coole Park, Russell's first visit marking the start of a lifelong friendship with Lady Gregory characterized by deep mutual respect. His almost fanatical commitment to harnessing the spiritual forces of the new age at this time prompted Yeats to use him as one of the models for the symbolic Michael Robartes, and dedicate *The Secret Rose* (1897) to him. In September Russell published *The Earth Breath and other Poems* (1897), which, though well received, revealed that his verse risked becoming stylized. In October he began contributing regularly to *The Internationalist*, a journal intended to continue the work of the *Irish Theosophist*, which had ceased publication on 15 September 1897. Recalling him at this period, a friend described Russell as 'aflame with Theosophy, a red hot missionary'. Yet this zeal was about to be harnessed with considerably greater effect for an utterly different cause.

Evoking the national being, 1897–1917 Early in November 1897 news reached Yeats that Russell was being urged to emigrate to America to work as an editor for the theosophists. Determined to secure his friend for Ireland and for literature, Yeats brought him to Horace Plunkett, the founder of the Irish Agricultural Organisation Society (IAOS) and, with assistance from Lady Gregory, arranged for him to accept a post as an organizer of rural banks along Raiffeisen lines in the Congested Districts. For the next six months Russell travelled extensively throughout the west, infusing a visionary fervour into the fledgeling co-operative movement. As his correspondence shows, he found the work by turns demanding, lonely, exhilarating, depressing, and immensely challenging.

All the patterns of Russell's old life began to break up, and new ones began to form. In March 1898 he seceded from the Theosophical Society, and devoted his energies to his own Hermetic Society, over which he presided for the next thirty-five years. On 9 June 1898 he took an hour off work to marry Violet North (1869–1932), an English theosophist with literary gifts who had come to live at The

Household early in 1895. And in October he was given a Dublin-based job as an assistant secretary to the IAOS. At first the Russells lived at various addresses in Rathmines. Their first son, Bryan Russell, was born on 30 January 1899 (and not in March of that year, as has previously been stated). He died in childhood, and the Russell's second son was named Brian Hartley. Their third child, a daughter, died a month after she was born in July 1901. Their fourth, a son, Diarmuid Conor, was born on 17 November 1902. By then the Russells had moved to 25 Coulson Avenue, Rathgar, where they continued to live until early in 1906, when they bought a small house at 17 Rathgar Avenue, Rathgar, the last of their Dublin addresses.

Now settled, Russell began to take a greater interest in the Irish literary movement. Towards the end of 1898 he became embroiled in a controversy about the relationship between drama and nationality with John Eglinton, Yeats, and William Larminie in the columns of the Dublin *Daily Express*, subsequently published as *Literary Ideals in Ireland* in May 1899. Against the advocates of cosmopolitanism, which he presciently linked with cultural imperialism, Russell argued for a drama that would foster nativist idealism. Two years later he contributed 'Nationality and Imperialism' to a volume, *Ideals in Ireland* (1901), edited by Lady Gregory. His essay caught the attention of a fellow contributor, George Moore, and when the novelist moved to Dublin in 1901, Russell not only found him a house at 4 Upper Ely Place, but for the next decade became one of its most regular visitors. In Moore's three-volume memoir *Hail and Farewell* (1911, 1912, 1914) Dublin society is summed up as 'AE and the rest'.

For his part, Moore delighted and infuriated Russell. In 1902, when he felt that the novelist's collaboration with Yeats on *Diarmuid and Grania* had denigrated the ancient legend, Russell wrote his own play *Deirdre* as a corrective. Staged with Yeats's *Kathleen ni Houlihan* at the hall of St Teresa's Total Abstinence Association, Clarendon Street, on 2, 3, and 4 April 1902, it launched the Irish National Theatre Society, succeeding the Irish Literary Theatre to become the precursor to Ireland's most famous theatre company, the Abbey. Russell was invited to be president, but deferred to Yeats whom he unselfishly served in a variety of roles, even though their different aims—a fully professional company versus an amateur society that would foster local talent—increasingly enmeshed them in conflict. Eventually Russell resigned from the theatre early in 1908 and broke off contact with Yeats for five years. In the event, *Deirdre* was his only play, though he planned several others and just before the First World War drafted a political comedy, *The Hon. Enid Marjoribanks*.

Although he had felt thwarted in his attempts to foster dramatic talent, Russell established an enduring reputation for nourishing young writers. In his early years these included Seumas O'Sullivan, Padraic Colum, and James Stephens. His benevolence was both specific and general. Specifically, he edited *New Songs* in 1904, an anthology of young poets' work which sold over 1000 copies and whose politics of inclusion and exclusion were immortalized in James Joyce's *Ulysses* (1922). Generally, he magnanimously dispensed hospitality, books, and advice every Sunday evening at 17 Rathgar Avenue for almost a quarter of a century.

Russell's own creative output increased markedly during these years. In 1903 he published *The Nuts of Knowledge: Lyrical Poems Old and New* with the Yeats sisters' Dun Emer Press for which he acted as a business adviser. And early the next year he published *The Divine Vision and other Poems* (1904) with Macmillan, who also published a collection of early theosophical fantasies entitled *The Mask of Apollo and other Stories* (1905). Other poetry from this period included another volume with Dun Emer, *By Still Waters: Lyrical Poems Old and New* (1906). Other prose included *Some Irish Essays* (1906), which contained his contributions to the *Express* controversy, and reprints of earlier theosophical articles issued as pamphlets, *The Hero in Man* (1909) and *The Renewal of Youth* (1911).

From 1905 Russell began the custom of regularly exhibiting his paintings, their sale supplementing his rather meagre salary from the IAOS. Yet most of his energies were devoted to realizing its aims—'better farming, better business, and better living'. In 1905 he was appointed editor of the weekly *Irish Homestead*, and for the next eighteen years, week after week, he produced a vigorous leading article on a current issue, several columns of admonitory and cultural notes, and technical advice and agricultural news for an ever-increasing audience (by 1909, for example, IAOS membership numbered 100,000 of an estimated 500,000 Irish farmers). Ably assisted by Susan Mitchell, a lively redhead with a wicked wit, the *Homestead* provided Russell with a further opportunity to foster young writers, the most notable being James Joyce, three of whose short stories he first published. In time Russell became widely acknowledged as one of the leading journalists of his day.

The apogee of Russell's influence was marked by the combination of his work on the *Irish Homestead*; the publication of his *Collected Poems* (1913), which went into five editions and ten reprints; and the appearance of his collection of essays, *Imaginations and Reveries* (1915), which went into three editions and two reprints. Predictably, the bulk of his publications from this period were polemical, ranging over social and political issues, particularly as they related to agrarian reform. They include: *Ireland and Tariff Reform* (1909); *The Building up of a Rural Civilisation* (1910); *Co-Operation and Nationality* (1912); and *The Rural Community* (1913). The issue that most provoked him was the great lock-out of 1913, when William Martin Murphy's Dublin United Tramways Company refused to employ members of James Larkin's and James Connolly's Irish Transport and General Workers' Union. Russell not only spoke at the London rally organized to protest at the organizers' imprisonment and designed a flag for the civilian militia raised to protect the workers, but he also hit back with three masterpieces of political invective: *To the Masters of Dublin* (1913); *The Tragedy of Labour in Dublin* (1913); and *The Dublin Strike* (1913). His intrepid eloquence won him many admirers, including Yeats, with whom he effected a reconciliation.

The growing violence both at home and abroad saw Russell speak out on a wide range of issues. As a co-operator he argued that the First World War confronted Irish farmers with a sacred duty and an economic challenge, a view put forward in *Ireland, Agriculture and the War* (1915) and *Talks with an Irish Farmer* (1916). As a poet and pacifist, he rebuked Kipling for his militant unionism in an open letter to the London *Daily News* (15 April 1912), while he repudiated violence in *Gods of War, with other Poems* (1915) and political coercion in *Conscription for Ireland* (1918). And as a nationalist and theosophist he sought both to understand and to influence the emerging polity with *The National being* (1916). The Easter rising horrified and excited him, inspiring a long poem, 'Salutation', privately printed as a pamphlet in January 1917 and then published in full in the *Irish Times* that December. Nominated as a nationalist delegate to the subsequent peace conference, he sought to effect a reconciliation between the major antagonists by impartially analysing their positions in *Thoughts for a Convention* (1917), but resigned when he failed.

An Irish statesman, 1918–1935 The more Ireland descended into chaos, the more Russell sought to ennoble it through public exhortation, and through enquiries into his own spirituality. The first was *The Candle of Vision* (1918), a prose meditation on the sources and nature of his own hypnagogic revelations. Published just three weeks before the armistice, it was reprinted five times within two years despite its somewhat mannered style. Early the following year he began *The Interpreters* which, like *The National being*, examines the conviction that emerging nations take their character from some determining ideal. Towards the end of 1919 he put it aside to work on his finest long poem, *Michael*, which explores the same idea though within the context of the Easter rising. *The Interpreters*, rapidly overtaken by events, was eventually published in 1922.

By then, Russell needed all the spiritual strength he could muster, as the appointed peace-keepers, the Black and Tans, began wantonly destroying creameries on the pretext that they harboured terrorists. A protest to the British government, *A Plea for Justice* (1920), fell on deaf ears. As the country slid inexorably into civil war, Russell fought to combat despair by arguing passionately for his ideal of Ireland as a co-operative commonwealth in the *Homestead* and in three pamphlets: *The Inner and the Outer Ireland* (1921); *Ireland and the Empire at the Court of Conscience* (1921); and *Ireland, Past and Future* (1922).

On 7 January 1922 the Dáil ratified the treaty. Offered a seat in the new senate, Russell declined, though Sir Horace Plunkett persuaded him to accept the editorship of the *Irish Statesman*, a pro-treaty weekly mainly financed by American money. Susan Mitchell, his close colleague for seventeen years at the *Homestead*, joined him as his assistant. The first number appeared in September 1923. Now at the height of his journalistic powers, Russell dispensed advice and provoked debate about issues ranging from the Lane bequest to the border dispute, from censorship to hunger strikes. The paper also enabled him to foster a new generation of young writers, including Austin Clarke, Oliver St John Gogarty, Patrick Kavanagh, Frank O'Connor, and Monk Gibbon.

Despite his busy schedule, Russell found poetic inspiration returning, with the result that he was able to bring out four slim volumes during his time as editor: *Voices of the Stones* (1925), *Midsummer Eve* (1928), *Dark Weeping* (1929), and *Enchantment and other Poems* (1930). In recognition of his achievements, Yale University made him an honorary DLitt in 1928 and Trinity College followed suit in 1929. Early that year his younger son Diarmuid emigrated to New York, having worked as an assistant editor to his father following Susan Mitchell's death in 1926. His replacement, Irene Haugh, was appointed in May 1929. The previous January Russell had gone on a three-month fund-raising visit to America to ensure the *Statesman*'s survival, but a combination of the 1928 stockmarket crash and a libel action over a music review closed the paper on 12 April 1930.

A fund was promptly launched for its unemployed editor, and on 3 September 1930 the governor-general of the Free State presented Russell with a cheque for £800 for his retirement. Ten days later he sailed for America for an eight-month lecture tour, in part to earn money to pay for the treatment of his wife's cancer. Despite a hectic schedule, Russell found time to compile *Vale and other Poems* (1931), which was published in London while he was still abroad. Returning to Dublin in May 1931, he discovered that his wife was gravely ill. She died on 3 February 1932. Russell withdrew to a London hotel by himself for a week to mourn. For a time it seemed he was being stalked by loss: the following month Sir Horace Plunkett died; in May Lady Gregory died; and in January 1933 George Moore died. That July Kingsley Porter, his Donegal host for several years, drowned the day Russell arrived for his summer holiday.

Yet Russell derived some consolation from painting and from literary work. Partly from his own sense of public duty and partly at Yeats's insistence, he helped to organize the Irish Academy of Letters. In 1932 he published *Song and its Fountains*, in which he examined the provenance of his poetry in terms of those visions that had invaded his consciousness nearly half a century before. The following year he published *The Avatars: a Futurist Fantasy* (1933), in which he attempted to recapture the fervid anticipation of 1896, when he was passionately convinced that Ireland was poised to enter a new age of spirituality. Nothing could be further from thirties Ireland, de Valera's holy homeland of pious peasants, and the difference was brought sharply into focus for Russell by the orchestrated piety of the Eucharistic Congress of 1932.

Disillusioned, Russell sold 17 Rathgar Avenue in July 1933 and gave away most of his belongings. After holidaying in Donegal he responded to an invitation to advise the American secretary of agriculture on the ways that co-operation might be utilized in Roosevelt's New Deal. Again, despite a demanding itinerary, he compiled a volume of poems, *The House of the Titans and other Poems* (1934). After three months in America, Russell fell ill. He hurried back to England, where he was admitted to the Stagsden Nursing Home at 14 West Cliff Road, Bournemouth, dying of bowel cancer soon after 11 p.m. on 17 July 1935. Three days later he was buried in Mount Jerome cemetery, Dublin. His *Selected Poems* (1935), which was then in press, was published two months later. *Some Passages from the Letters of Æ to W. B. Yeats*, selectively edited by the poet, was published by the Yeats sisters at the Cuala Press in 1936.

Russell bulked large in the imagination of his contemporaries, and it is their writings which best summarize his role in the Ireland of his day. George Moore's *Hail and Farewell* (1911, 1912, 1914) praises the delicate charm of his poetry and prose and his practical kindness. In his memoirs A. E. lives as a writer, teacher, and conversationalist who exercised a profound but immeasurable spiritual influence on his country. James Joyce's *Ulysses* (1922) provides a more astringent portrait of the urban A. E.—the beard, the bicycle, the co-operative watch, and the patronage of literary endeavour that prompted many a young writer to say like Stephen Dedalus, 'A.E.I.O.U.'. Yeats in *The Trembling of the Veil* (1922) pays tribute to the spiritual and political power of Russell's magnanimity, but suspected it was dissipated in woolly benevolence. Simone Téry's *L'isle des bards* (1925) praises the breadth of his interests and his intense intellectual vitality. Sean O'Casey's *Autobiographies* (1956) provide a compendium of the criticism, particularly of a style that became increasingly repetitive and a spirituality that bordered on arrogance. Finally, Frank O'Connor's *My Father's Son* (1968) depicts the ageing Russell as a creature of habit, a generous but shrewd mentor, a figure poignantly at odds with an Ireland which increasingly ignored him despite his being one of its best-known journalists, poets, painters, mystics, agricultural economists, and elder statesmen.   PETER R. KUCH

Sources H. Summerfield, *That myriad-minded man: a biography of George William Russell 'A.E.', 1867–1935* (1975) • A. Denson, *Printed writings by George W. Russell (AE): a bibliography, with some notes on his pictures and portraits* (1961) [information on MSS holdings] • *Letters from AE*, ed. A. Denson (1961) • *The descent of the gods: comprising the mystical writings of G. W. Russell 'A.E.'*, ed. R. Iyer and N. Iyer (1988) [pt 3 of the *Collected works*] • *Collected edition of the writings of G. W. Russell*, ed. H. Summerfield, 1–2 (1978) • P. R. Kuch, 'A critical edition of G. W. Russell (A. E.)'s writings on literature and art', DPhil diss., U. Oxf., 1988 • P. R. Kuch, *Yeats and AE: 'the antagonism that unites dear friends'* (1986) • M. Gibbon, ed., *The living torch* (1938) [sels. from the *Irish Statesman*] • E. Doyle Smith, 'Index to the *Irish Statesman*', PhD diss., University of Washington, Seattle, 1966 • R. F. Foster, *The apprentice mage, 1865–1914* (1997), vol. 1 of *W. B. Yeats: a life* • R. B. Davis, *George William Russell ('AE')*, Twayne's English Authors series, 208 (1977) [short biography] • J. Eglinton [W. Kirkpatrick Magee], *A memoir of G. W. Russell (A.E.)* (1937) • G. Moore, *Ave* (1911) • G. Moore, *Salve* (1912) • G. Moore, *Vale* (1914) • W. B. Yeats, *Autobiographies* (1955) • F. O'Connor, *My father's son* (1968) • J. Joyce, *Ulysses* (1922) • S. O'Casey, *Autobiographies*, 2 vols. (1956) • S. Téry, *L'isle des bards* (1925) • E. Boyd, *Ireland's literary renaissance* (1916) • *The collected letters of W. B. Yeats*, ed. J. Kelly and others, [3 vols.] (1986–) • d. cert. • *CGPLA Eng. & Wales* (1935)

Archives Armagh County Museum, letters, poems, MSS • Indiana University, Bloomington, Lilly Library, papers • Indiana University, Bloomington, Birmingham MSS • NL Ire., MSS • NL Ire., papers • Ransom HRC, MS of *The house of the Titans*, notebooks • TCD, sketchbooks • University of Victoria, corresp. | Armagh County Museum, letters to Charles Weekes • BL, corresp. with Macmillans, Add. MS 55002 • BL, corresp. with George Bernard Shaw, Add. MS 50548 • Colby College, Waterville, Maine, James A. Healy collection • NA Scot., letters to Philip Kerr • NL Ire., letters to Alice Stopford Green • NL Ire., letters to Joseph O'Neill • NL Ire., letters to Seumas O'Sullivan • NRA, priv. coll., letters to Eva Gore-Booth • NYPL, Henry W. and Albert A. Berg Collection of English and American Literature, MSS • Plunkett Foundation, Long Hanborough, Oxfordshire, corresp. with Sir Horace Plunkett • TCD, corresp. with Thomas Bodkin • TCD, corresp. with Erskine Childers and Mary Childers • TCD, corresp. with Thomas McGreevy • TCD, letters to Carrie Rae • University College, Dublin, letters to Constantine P. Curran • University College, Dublin, letters to D. J. O'Donoghue • University of Kansas, Lawrence, P. S. O'Hegarty collection

Likenesses J. Hughes, plaster bust, *c*.1885–1886, Hugh Lane Gallery of Modern Art, Dublin • J. B. Yeats, pencil drawing, 1898, NG Ire. • S. H. Purser, oils, *c*.1902, NG Ire. • J. B. Yeats, oils, 1902, repro. in W. M. Murphy, *Prodigal father: the life of John Butler Yeats* (1978) • C. D. Markiewicz, oils, *c*.1903, Hugh Lane Gallery of Modern Art, Dublin • J. B. Yeats, oils, 1903, NG Ire. [*see illus.*] • J. B. Yeats, oils, 1905, Abbey Theatre, Dublin • J. B. Yeats, oils, 1912, Abbey Theatre; repro. in W. M. Murphy, *Prodigal father: the life of John Butler Yeats* (1978) • M. Duncan, lithograph, *c*.1912–1913, NPG • D. O'Brien, oils, *c*.1914, Abbey Theatre, Dublin • O. Sheppard, sandstone bust, 1916, NG Ire. • E. Kapp, drawing, 1919, U. Birm. • W. Rothenstein, drawing, 1921, NG Ire. • T. Spicer-Simson, plasticine medallion, 1922, NG Ire. • J. Keating, group portrait, oils, *c*.1924 (*Homage to Hugh Lane*), Hugh Lane Gallery of Modern Art, Dublin • J. Connor, bronze bust, *c*.1926, Public Art Gallery, Limerick • H. Roberts, oils, 1929, Ulster Museum, Belfast • J. Hare, bronze bust, *c*.1931, NPG • D. Gilbert, bronze bust, *c*.1933, Ulster Museum • A. H. Fisher, etching, *c*.1934, Carlisle City Art Gallery • S. O'Sullivan, chalk drawing, 1935, Municipal Gallery of Modern Art and Public Art Gallery, Limerick • E. C. Purdy, two photographs, 1935, repro. in Denson, *Printed writings* • L. Davidson, oils, U. Texas • N. Newton, oils, NG Ire. • T. Spicer-Simson, bronze cast, NG Ire. • J. B. Yeats, pencil drawing, U. Texas

Wealth at death £2449 1*s*. 7*d*.: resworn probate, 27 Aug 1935, *CGPLA Eng. & Wales*

Russell, George William Erskine (1853–1919), politician and writer, was born in London on 3 February 1853, the youngest of six children (two sons and four daughters) of Lord Charles James Fox Russell (son of John *Russell, sixth duke of Bedford), and his wife, Isabella Clarissa, daughter of William Davies of Pen-y-lan, Carmarthenshire. Lord Charles was an MP from 1832 until 1848, and was then appointed serjeant-at-arms attending the House of Commons, and Russell's childhood was spent in the official lodgings in Speaker's Court. It was there, he said, that he acquired the three enthusiasms of his life—politics, religion, and books. He was a lame and sickly child; at Harrow School, where he was sent as a home-boarder, he could play no games. He went as a scholar to University College, Oxford, in 1872; there he combined studiousness with acquiring a reputation as a 'riding man', and was elected to Vincent's Club. In 1874 his physical ailments were compounded by myelitis; he described himself as 'maimed for life, with all hope of academic distinction at an end'. He took a pass degree at Oxford.

Russell was elected to parliament as member for Aylesbury in 1880. Although born in the very purple of whiggery, he displayed independence of judgement, and, in spite of his personal admiration for W. E. Gladstone (tempered by a certain irreverence), he attached himself to the

George William Erskine Russell (1853–1919), by Elliott & Fry

Christian socialists, especially Charles Kingsley and F. D. Maurice. He was a regular workhouse and hospital visitor, conducted Bible classes, and was active in Christian missions. A prominent figure in purity movements, he was chairman of the National Vigilance Association in 1885, and one of the founders of the White Cross Society. After he retired from parliament, he was invited by Edward Talbot, bishop of Rochester, to do practical work in south London. In 1898 he became a diocesan lay reader. He maintained excellent relations with the dissenting movements, and spoke frequently at PSA (Pleasant Sunday Afternoon) meetings. He was strongly in favour of Church of England services for men only, as a means of introducing working men to church.

Russell wrote throughout his adult life (he first appeared in print at the age of thirteen, with some verses on a volunteer encampment). He was a regular contributor to many of the leading newspapers and periodicals; his weekly articles for the *Manchester Guardian* were republished in two series of *Collections and Recollections* (1898). His religious opinions were set out in *A Short History of the Evangelical Movement* (1915), and his personal interpretation of whig philosophy in *Politics and Personalities* (1917). He edited the letters of Matthew Arnold, and wrote a number of biographies and memoirs, including those of Gladstone, Sydney Smith, E. B. Pusey, Bishop King of Lincoln, and H. P. Liddon.

Russell was one of the founders of the National Liberal Club. He was awarded an LLD by the University of St Andrews in 1899, and became a privy councillor in 1907. He died, unmarried, on 17 March 1919 at his house, 18 Wilton Street, London. G. H. L. LE MAY, *rev.*

Sources G. W. E. Russell, *One look back* (1911) • *The Times* (18 March 1919) • Gladstone, *Diaries* • E. J. Bristow, *Vice and vigilance* (1977) • H. L. Malchow, *Agitators and promoters in the age of Gladstone and Disraeli: a biographical dictionary* (1983)
Archives BL, letters to G. K. Chesterton, Add. MS 73239, fols. 173–185v • BL, H. J. Gladstone MSS • BL, corresp. with W. E. Gladstone, Add. MSS 46048–46074, *passim* • BL, corresp. with Macmillans, Add. MS 55031 • BLPES, letters to A. G. Gardiner • Bodl. Oxf., letters mainly to Pakenham T. Beatty • Bodl. Oxf., corresp. with Lord Kimberley • JRL, letters to C. P. Scott • King's Cam., letters to Oscar Browning • NL Scot., corresp. with Lord Rosebery
Likenesses Elliott & Fry, photograph, repro. in A. Gardiner, *Pillars of society* (1913), facing p. 218 [*see illus.*]
Wealth at death £1703 5s. 4d.: probate, 20 May 1919, *CGPLA Eng. & Wales*

radical section of the Liberal Party. This caused him many difficulties with the duke of Bedford, and his constituents. He wrote articles for the *Fortnightly Review*, favoured the disestablishment of the Church of England, and was sympathetic to the 'unauthorized programme' of Joseph Chamberlain. In June 1883 he was appointed as parliamentary secretary to the Local Government Board; his investigations of the London slums were partly responsible for the appointment of a royal commission on the housing of the poor in 1884.

Russell lost his seat in 1885. In 1889 he was chosen as an alderman of the newly established London county council, in the Progressive interest. He served until 1895, being particularly active in the movement to raise the tone of the London music-halls by prohibiting sales of alcohol on the premises. He was re-elected to parliament in 1892, as member for North Bedfordshire, and was appointed under-secretary for India, and then, in 1894, under-secretary in the Home department. He retired from politics in 1895, and devoted himself to his other two enthusiasms, religion and books.

From early life Russell was deeply interested in evangelical Christianity (he published, anonymously, a religious tract at the age of fourteen), and he had an abiding belief in personal social service. While at Oxford he taught at a Sunday school in Cowley and a night school at St Frideswide's Church. After Oxford he was influenced by the

Russell, Sir (Sydney) Gordon (1892–1980), designer and craftsman, was born on 20 May 1892 in Elm Grove, Cricklewood, the eldest of three sons of Sydney Bolton Russell (1866–1938), a bank clerk who became a renowned hotel keeper, and his wife, Elizabeth Shefford (1864–1956), whose family were farmers at Winkfield, near Windsor. Gordon Russell became a pivotal figure in twentieth-century British design, as both a practitioner and a public spokesman, providing a unique link between the arts and crafts movement and design for industry.

Early years and Cotswold influence Russell's early childhood was spent at 35 Tooting Bec Road, a 'smart, hard, ugly and monotonous little suburban house' (Russell, 20),

Sir (Sydney) **Gordon Russell** (1892–1980), by Carel Weight,
*c.*1967

the antithesis of the design ideals he promulgated later in
life. He was nine when the family moved to the country,
first to Repton, where his father worked as agency manager to Samuel Allsopp, brewers of Burton upon Trent,
and then, in 1904, to the picturesque village of Broadway
in Worcestershire where his father took over the local
Lygon Arms and aggrandized it into the first English
'country house' hotel. Gordon Russell came to share his
entrepreneurial father's passion for ancient buildings,
antique furniture, and out-of-the-way objects, helping in
the hotel's own furniture repair shop while he was still a
boy.

In the first decade of the twentieth century the Cotswolds were an active centre of the arts and crafts movement. William Morris himself had strong connections
with the area. His followers, the furniture makers Ernest
Gimson and Sidney and Ernest Barnsley, had settled in
Sapperton. Russell's attendance as a weekly boarder at
Chipping Campden grammar school brought him into
direct contact with the Guild of Handicraft, the community of metalworkers, enamellers, wood carvers, furniture
makers, and printers brought by C. R. Ashbee from east
London to Chipping Campden in 1902. Russell was
inspired not only by the inherent architectural quality of
Cotswold towns and villages, with their excellent vernacular traditions of craftsmanship, but also by the way in
which these arts and crafts designers were intelligently
reinterpreting the past.

By the time Russell left school he was 'a voracious gazer'

(Russell, 38). His appetite for new sights was stimulated
further when his uncle, a sea captain with the Lamport
and Holt Line, took him on as purser on the SS *Veronique*,
sailing to South America. On his return he was put in
charge of the repair shop at the Lygon, assisted by three or
four joiners, and entrusted with buying antiques for the
hotel. He now set up his own experimental workshop,
making wooden moulds to produce his version of the
medieval leather blackjack or drinking pot, and cutting
his own goose quills for formal script writing. What would
be a lasting interest in lettering and printing was encouraged by Katherine Adams, a neighbour in Broadway,
where she ran the Eadburgha Bindery, and by Sydney
Cockerell, the connoisseur who had been secretary to
Morris's Kelmscott Press.

Russell's natural progression as a craftsman–designer
was cut short by the First World War. He served with the
Worcester regiment, mainly in the front line, enduring
the horrors of the Somme, Ypres, and Passchendaele, of
which he commented with characteristic pragmatism
'one had to live for the day and take things as they came'
(Russell, 99). He became an officer in 1917 and was
awarded the Military Cross for the counter-attack he
organized in February 1918, when one of his posts was
rushed by a storming party. In the final German offensive
of the following month, he was shot in the left arm and
invalided home. Russell's war experience heightened his
awareness of the importance of discipline and planning:
he was to bring to the cause of British design something of
the precision of the military campaign. The experience of
mass destructiveness focused his ambitions on creating a
new post-war aesthetic. He now came to view modern
design as a necessary act of reparation: 'I felt strongly that
my generation, which had destroyed so much lovely
work, had a constructive duty to perform' (ibid., 117).

Gordon Russell furniture, 1919–1939   Gordon Russell's early
furniture was clearly influenced by the Cotswold arts and
crafts designers, particularly Ernest Gimson. One of his
first pieces was the monumental panelled walnut bed
designed for his own marriage, on 8 August 1921, to Constance Elizabeth Jane Vere Denning (1897–1981), always
known as Toni, resilient and witty daughter of an Irish
doctor. Russell began to make his name with surprisingly
confident and often elaborate craftsman-made pieces in
which the deep chamfers, bevelled panels, and flamboyant inlays exploited the qualities of English timbers Russell favoured: oak, walnut, laburnum, cherry, cedar, chest-
nut, yew.

In 1922 Gordon Russell exhibited his furniture for the
first time, at the Cheltenham exhibition of Cotswold arts
and crafts. The following year, he was asked to design a
'model' café for an exhibition at the Victoria and Albert
Museum: an appropriate commission for a man with so
robust an appreciation of food and drink. In 1924 Gordon
Russell's furniture was included in the Palace of Arts at
the British Empire Exhibition at Wembley, and in 1925 he
won a gold medal at the Paris Exhibition for the now famous English walnut inlaid cabinet and stand with barley-
sugar stick legs, first of a series of designs inspired by

eighteenth-century examples. By now there were about thirty craftsmen in the Broadway workshop, including two skilled cabinet-makers, and the scope had expanded to include decorative metalwork and designs for table glass.

While espousing modernism, Russell remained emotionally rooted in the past. Like William Morris, he saw the understanding of old techniques and standards of workmanship as a means of revitalizing the present: 'it was my great love for old things that made me wish to design new ones' (Russell, 117). By the mid-1920s he was experimenting with much plainer and more evidently machine-made forms of furniture, expressive of his own conviction that mechanization, used unapologetically, could be a force for good, and stimulated by Russell's personal contacts with such important patrons of modern design as Frank Pick, Ambrose Heal, and Allen Lane, fellow members of the Design and Industries Association. Russell's earliest design in the new functional style was his severely rectilinear boot cupboard in Honduras mahogany of 1925. As his firm gradually gravitated towards machine production, Russell also continued to design his one-off craftsman-made pieces, putting into practice the theory of interdependence of hand and machine on which his whole design philosophy was based.

In less than a decade Russell's combination of English country doggedness with visionary zeal had developed his small rural craft workshop into a small factory equipped with machinery for series production. He had created a contract market for his products as well as growing demand for Gordon Russell furniture among the middle-class progressive intelligentsia. In 1929 a London retail shop, precursor of the crusading 'contemporary' design shops of the post-war period, was opened first at 28 and later 40 Wigmore Street. Here the German émigré art historian Nikolaus Pevsner worked for three years as buyer. By 1930, the year later described by Pevsner as the company's *annus mirabilis*, Gordon Russell furniture 'suddenly turned modern in the sense and on the aesthetic model of the best of continental furniture' (Pevsner, 1968, 2.218). Russell's achievement was remarkable in the context of the general level of British taste in household furnishings, then veering between the neo-Georgian and spurious 'moderne'.

Up to 1930 Gordon Russell had himself carried out all designing for Gordon Russell Ltd. This changed with the return to Broadway of his younger brother R. D. (Dick) *Russell from four years' training as an architect at the Architectural Association (AA) in London, a plan instigated by Gordon himself. Dick, his wife, Marian *Pepler [see under Russell, Richard Drew], a textile designer, and other modernist AA-trained designers, took over the design of Gordon Russell products. Gordon moved into the role a later generation would define as creative director. The company survived the slump by manufacturing radio cabinets for Murphy. These clean-lined timber cabinets, designed by Dick Russell, are now considered classics of the period. In 1935 Gordon Russell Ltd opened a new factory at Park Royal, west London, specifically for Murphy production. This experience of production in huge quantities—200,000 cabinets being manufactured in 1937 alone—gave the company new flexibility and adeptness in precision engineering. Gordon Russell stayed in business through the war by making ammunition boxes, high precision aircraft models for wind tunnel testing, and parts for the wings of RAF mosquito planes.

Russell maintained that 'Design affects the whole pattern of life and good design was an essential part of life' (Russell, 129). His practical idealism found tangible expression in the building of Kingcombe, the Cotswold stone house commissioned from the architect Leslie Mansfield soon after his marriage and Russell's ruling passion for over fifty years. The almost hand-built house and garden, on the crossroads half-way up to Dover's Hill, above Chipping Campden village, resembled William Morris's Red House in that it was not simply a living place but a statement of belief. With its unshowy beauty, its attention to fine detail, unselfconscious combinations of the old and new, Kingcombe encapsulated Gordon Russell's predilection for the simple and the stalwart. His personal aesthetic was subsumed into official 'good design' as promoted by the government, under Russell's aegis, after the Second World War.

Utility furniture, 1940–1946 In 1942 Gordon Russell was invited by Dr Hugh Dalton, president of the Board of Trade, to join the wartime utility furniture committee advising the government on furniture to be made available on coupons to people such as the bombed-out or newly married categorized as in special need. Russell's subsequent appointment the following year as chairman of the Utility Furniture Design Panel made him the guiding spirit in a national initiative of some significance as an unprecedented example of state intervention in the setting of mandatory standards for all furniture manufactured in Britain until the scheme wound down in 1947. Russell rose to the challenge with alacrity, seeing in utility the opportunity to introduce a much wider public to the principles of simple, rational design that he believed in: 'I felt that to raise the whole standard of furniture for the mass of the people was not a bad war job' (Russell, 200).

The government directive was for soundly made furniture of the best available materials and of pleasant design. The first designers appointed by Russell's design panel—H. J. Cutler and Edwin Clinch—were both from High Wycombe, traditional centre of the furniture trade, and their straightforward professional approach resulted in a practical range of furniture capable of being manufactured by 600 firms of variable capacities and skills.

Wartime privations favoured Russell's purist ideology. The acute shortage of timber, and the lack of labour for decorative carving, dictated rigorous simplicity of style, recalling the most basic quasi-arts and crafts furniture produced by Heals and indeed Gordon Russell's own experimental boot cupboard of 1925. When utility furniture began appearing in the shops early in 1943, it was criticized by the intelligentsia for being too conservative, and by the furniture trade for being too advanced, a divergence of opinion Russell took to be encouraging. As the scheme developed, the design panel was expanded. Jacques Groag, a Czech émigré architect, worked closely with Russell on developing early post-war utility furniture; Enid *Marx designed furnishing fabrics. If utility did not achieve the total volte-face for which Russell had hoped, since once restrictions were lifted a large section of the public reverted to imitation antique, his initiative made a potent contribution to the English design tradition that extends from Gimson and the Barnsleys to Terence Conran and mid-1960s Habitat.

Gordon Russell's war work kept him mainly in London, gaining valuable experience in dealing with government departments. His bluff country farmer appearance was misleading, concealing a sharp, retentive mind. His progressive outlook proved useful to the official post-war reconstruction committees set up before war ended. He was appointed to the Board of Trade furniture production committee and the design committee of the furniture trade working party. In 1944 he became a member of the Council of Industrial Design, a newly formed government body for the promotion of higher standards of design in British industry.

The Council of Industrial Design, 1947–1956 In 1947 Gordon Russell became director of the Council of Industrial Design (COID) (later renamed the Design Council), succeeding S. C. Leslie, a civil servant seconded from the Ministry of Home Security. It was Russell, with the depth of his own knowledge as a craftsman and manufacturer and his proselytizing zeal, who established the principles and ethos of the council, which remained largely unchanged over the next four decades. The COID was to be the model for numerous design councils across the world.

Public interest in the potential of 'contemporary' design had already been awakened by the exhibition 'Britain can make it' at the Victoria and Albert Museum in 1946. But Russell saw that permanent improvement would necessitate sustained action on three fronts: better training and increased status for designers; education of retailers (of which he already had experience through his involvement in the late 1930s with the Good Furniture Group of shopkeepers willing to endorse the modern); and stimulation of consumer taste by means of exhibitions of exemplary design since, as Russell argued, people could not be expected to demand something they had never seen. Most crucially, Russell was intent on bettering the everyday lives of ordinary people through influencing national standards in public buildings, public transport, and streets and highways, embracing for the COID his own holistic vision of design.

Russell's successes at the COID relied on close convivial networks of like-minded individuals, many of them fellow members of the Royal Society of Arts' faculty of royal designers for industry to which Russell was elected in 1940. He served as master of the faculty from 1947 to 1949. He had strong personal links within the Royal College of Art (RCA), newly reorganized under Robin Darwin, a young rector who believed in training designers to work

in industry. Gordon's brother Dick became first RCA professor of wood, metal, and plastics. Russell also co-operated closely with Hugh Casson, chief architect of the festival of Britain in 1951 at which thousands of products from the '1951 stock list' of manufactured goods meeting the COID's requisite design criteria were unveiled.

Russell expanded the COID's influence patiently and systematically, following his trusted principles of 'limited advance and then consolidation' (Russell, 199). He established a corps of industrial officers to spread the message of 'good design' to manufacturers throughout the country. British modern design was impressed on public consciousness by a programme of design weeks in the provinces; the opening, in 1956, of a permanent showroom, the Design Centre, in the Haymarket, London; the well-publicized annual Design Centre awards; and the black and white triangular swing ticket 'As selected for the Design Centre', soon familiar enough to be the subject of cartoons. Though Russell's methods were later to appear unacceptably paternalistic, and his assumption of absolute standards of aesthetic correctness was challenged in the less doctrinaire decade to come, his approach to design was still in the ascendant when he retired from the COID in 1956. He handed over to his deputy, Paul Reilly, later Baron Reilly. Russell had been appointed CBE in 1947, and was knighted in 1955.

Retirement, death, and reputation Russell was a large-framed man of tremendous physical energy. As described by his daughter Kate and his son-in-law Ken Baynes, 'To have seen him at home, up to his knees in mud excavating his garden canal next to an Irish casual labourer and an expert joiner, was to experience something almost feudal in character' (Baynes and Baynes, introduction). His authoritarianism and emotional reticence made for an uneasy family life. None of his three sons—Michael (b. 1922), Robert (b. 1924), Oliver (b. 1926)—followed him into the family business, and a tragic history of mental illness dogged the family. But Gordon Russell's relations with his grandchildren were happier, and in his old age Russell enjoyed initiating them into the idiosyncratic spaces of the house and gardens at Kingcombe which he had created with such delight.

In retirement Russell returned to letter-cutting in stone and to designing hand-made furniture. The English yew wood dining table of 1977, in Jacobean style reinterpreted by Russell, is his *tour de force*. He continued with his writing: a panoramic visual history *Looking at Furniture* was published in 1964. In April 1978 motor neurone disease was diagnosed. Although visibly flagging, illness did not prevent him from delivering the royal designers for industry annual address in the following November. This address, entitled *Skill*, was Russell's final and most compelling statement of his view 'that we deprive man of his skill at our peril' (*Skill*, c.1979, 2).

Gordon Russell died at home at Kingcombe on 7 October 1980 and was buried on 10 October at the church of St James the Great, Chipping Campden. By the end of the century it had become apparent that Russell's was one of the truly original voices of his time, the twentieth-century successor to John Ruskin in his towering energy in defence of art, craft, and the environment. He summed up his own career with typical laconic understatement as 'pushing a tank uphill' (Russell, 318). Examples of Russell's furniture are in the Victoria and Albert Museum; others from the utility range are in the collection of the Geffrye Museum, London.   FIONA MACCARTHY

Sources G. Russell, *Designer's trade: autobiography of Gordon Russell* (1968) · K. Baynes and K. Baynes, *Gordon Russell* (1981) · J. Myerson, *Gordon Russell: designer of furniture* (1992) · N. Pevsner, 'Patient progress two: Gordon Russell', *Studies in art, architecture and design*, 2: *Victorian and after* (1968), 210–25 · J. Gloag, 'Gordon Russell and Cotswold craftsmanship', *Architects' Journal* (15 Aug 1928), 219–26 · J. Gloag, 'Gordon Russell', *ArchR*, 168 (1980), 260–61 · P. Reilly, *An eye on design* (1987) · R. Allwood and K. Laurie, *R. D. Russell, Marian Pepler* (1983) [exhibition catalogue, Geffrye Museum, London, 9 Sept – 23 October 1983] · R. Sword, *Utility furniture and fashion, 1941–1951* (1974) [exhibition catalogue, Geffrye Museum, London] · personal knowledge (2004) · private information (2004) [K. Baynes]
Archives Cheltenham Art Gallery and Museum, archive · Gordon Russell Trust, Broadway, Worcestershire, archive | University of Brighton, Design Council archive
Likenesses C. Weight, oils, *c.*1967, NPG [*see illus.*]
Wealth at death £49,738: probate, 21 Nov 1980, *CGPLA Eng. & Wales*

Russell, Sir Guy Herbrand Edward (1898–1977), naval officer, was born in London on 14 April 1898, the second son in the family of four sons and one daughter of (Arthur) Oliver Villiers *Russell, second Baron Ampthill (1869–1935), later governor of Madras, and his wife, Lady Margaret Lygon (1874–1957), daughter of Frederick *Lygon, sixth Earl Beauchamp. His elder brother was John Hugo *Russell, third Baron Ampthill (1896–1973). Entering the navy in 1911 from Stonehouse School, he went to the Royal Naval College at Osborne and Dartmouth. On the outbreak of war in 1914 he went to sea as a midshipman aged sixteen in the *Implacable*. He was present at the Dardanelles campaign and escorted the Royal Fusiliers to 'X' beach on the day of the assault. Later he served on the *Royal Oak* at the battle of Jutland. He was mentioned in dispatches for his services during the war.

Russell had a more varied career than falls to the lot of most naval officers. Eschewing technical specialization which he contended restricted service experience, he remained a 'salt horse'. Up to the time of his comparatively early promotion to commander in 1931, he had seen service in destroyers, training establishments, cruisers, and battleships, and on the staff of the commander-in-chief, Mediterranean, at a time of recurring crises. He proved himself both adaptable and imaginative in all these posts. In 1931 he completed the naval staff course at Greenwich and returned to the Mediterranean as the executive officer of the *Queen Elizabeth*, the fleet flagship of Admiral Sir William Fisher. He soon made a reputation as an outstanding executive officer, and was universally admired, being promoted to captain in 1936 at the early age of thirty-eight. After promotion he returned to England for a course at the Imperial Defence College, which was followed by a number of staff appointments. In 1939

Russell married the Hon. (Helen) Elizabeth (*b.* 1908), daughter of (George) Rowland Blades, first Baron Ebbisham, MP for Epsom (1918–28) and lord mayor of London (1926–7); they had two sons and one daughter.

After the outbreak of war in 1939 Russell held two sea appointments; first as commanding officer of the *Protector*, a net layer, and then of the *Cumberland*, a cruiser employed in the north Atlantic on trade protection. At the end of 1941 he joined Viscount Gort, governor of Gibraltar, as naval liaison officer, and transferred with him to Malta as his chief of staff during the time of the siege of Malta. Few more competent and resolute characters than Gort and Russell could have been chosen to command Malta during this crucial period of the war in the Mediterranean.

After Malta was relieved, Russell became captain of the battleship *Nelson*, then of the *Duke of York*, fleet flagship of the Home Fleet in the action off the North Cape in December 1943, when she sank the German battle cruiser *Scharnhorst*. For this he was appointed to the DSO for great gallantry, determination, and skill, having already been mentioned in dispatches twice since the start of the war. On his return to the Admiralty a year after the action he was appointed naval assistant to the chief of personnel, a post for which he was admirably suited. Promoted to rear-admiral in 1945 he soon made his way to the top of the admirals list. Back again at the Imperial Defence College (1946–8), then commanding the 2nd cruiser squadron (1948–9), he earned the lasting admiration of the commander-in-chief of the Home Fleet, Admiral Sir Rhoderick McGrigor.

After a period with the reserves from 1949 to 1951, Russell was appointed commander-in-chief, Far East station (1951–3), where he did outstandingly well during the Korean War and the troubles in Malaya. He became an admiral in 1952. After this he served as second sea lord and chief of naval personnel from 1953 to 1955, a time of much change during which his wide experience and sympathies for officers and ratings alike had full scope. From 1956 to 1958 he was commandant of the Imperial Defence College, where he was able to give students of all services the benefit of his wide experience.

Russell retired in 1958 and devoted himself wholeheartedly to training young people and running schools. He soon made an impact with his breadth of vision and strength of character. He was chairman of the National Association of Boys' Clubs (1958–63) and of the Missions to Seamen (1960–65). He served on the governing bodies of Wellington College, Cranleigh School, and Gordon Boys' School, and was chairman of Radley College for six years.

Russell was an imposing and handsome figure who at first sight perhaps awed an onlooker, unless he detected the twinkle in his eye. Behind a bluff exterior he had an acute intelligence, which soon saw through any pretensions. He was gifted with great common sense and brought to bear a splendid sense of the ridiculous on unwise propositions. His sense of humour delighted his friends and confounded his opponents. In Admiralty board meetings he could always be relied upon to deflate plausible but unwise suggestions, to the delight of his supporters. He was a modest and kind-hearted man. A magnificent oarsman, which delighted his father, who was also a great oarsman, he was in addition a very good shot and an enthusiastic golfer.

Russell was appointed CBE (1943), CB (1948), KCB (1951), and GBE (1953). He died on 25 September 1977 at his home, Cleve Cottage, Wisborough Green, Sussex.

WILLIAM DAVIS, rev.

Sources The Times (27 Sept 1977) · S. W. Roskill, The war at sea, 1939–1945, 3 vols. in 4 (1954–61) · personal knowledge (1986) · Burke, Peerage (1980) · WWW · CGPLA Eng. & Wales (1977)
Archives FILM IWM FVA, actuality footage
Wealth at death £51,933: probate, 11 Nov 1977, CGPLA Eng. & Wales

Russell, Hastings William Sackville, twelfth duke of Bedford (1888–1953), evangelical Christian and pacifist, was born on 21 December 1888 at Cairnsmore House, Minnigaff, Kirkcudbrightshire, the only child of Lord Herbrand Arthur *Russell, later eleventh duke of Bedford (1858–1940), and his wife, Mary Du Caurroy *Russell (1865–1937) [see under Russell, Herbrand Arthur], daughter of the Ven. W. H. Tribe, archdeacon of Lahore. His childhood was lonely. His father was forbidding, aloof, and autocratic; his mother (the famous Flying Duchess, who was to take up aviation in her sixties) was deaf, short-tempered, and dismissive of anything short of perfection. He shared, however, his parents' interest in wildlife, and was later to produce publications on birds of the parrot family.

In 1893, when his father became duke, Russell took the courtesy title of marquess of Tavistock. At Eton College (1905–7) he was bullied and unhappy. At Balliol College, Oxford (1907–11), where he obtained a fourth in history, he developed the strong evangelical Christian beliefs that were to dominate the rest of his life. In 1912, at his father's wish, he joined the Middlesex regiment but, hating the experience, resigned his commission. At the outbreak of the First World War he refused to rejoin the regiment, and his father disinherited him; they did not see each other again for twenty years. Through Robert Whitwell, an Oxford don interested in the YMCA, he became in 1914 a helper at a camp near Portsmouth, where he worked for five years (his bad eyesight saving him from military service). On 21 November 1914 he married Whitwell's daughter, Louisa Crommelin Roberta Jowitt (1893–1960). They were to have two sons and one daughter.

From 1919 Tavistock immersed himself in Christian and social work. Concerned at the effects of the economic situation, he became a supporter of social credit, on which he wrote extensively. His personal life, meanwhile, suffered. In 1935 he and his wife separated, after a highly public lawsuit in which she had unsuccessfully sued for restoration of conjugal rights; and in 1939 he disinherited his elder son because of what he saw as an unsuitable marriage.

In 1938–9, campaigning against the approaching war,

Tavistock became associated with the pro-Nazi and antisemitic fringe, becoming in 1939 president of the openly antisemitic British People's Party (whose programme included monetary reform and peace with Nazi Germany). Its general secretary was John Beckett, co-founder of William Joyce's National Socialist League. Like many pre-war pacifists Tavistock may have acted through naïvety; his letters and memoirs betray ignorance of the implications of antisemitism. After the outbreak of war he became chairman of the British Council for a Christian Settlement in Europe, with Beckett as secretary, and also took part, in late 1939, in secret meetings with Oswald Mosley and representatives of other extremist organizations. In January 1940 certain peace proposals were conveyed to him via the German legation in Dublin. Tavistock, despite official scepticism, went to Dublin, and returned with peace terms that were ridiculed by the press, which stressed his 'fascist' connections. He remained convinced that a real chance had been thwarted by governmental apathy.

On 27 August 1940 Tavistock succeeded his father as twelfth duke of Bedford. Throughout the war, in numerous pamphlets and in the House of Lords, he continued his peace campaign, attacking Churchill's belligerence, and 'the attempt, by the moneylending financiers and big business monopolists, to destroy the relatively sane financial system of the Axis Powers' (Hansard 5L, 2 June 1942). His internment was often demanded (and considered seriously by the war cabinet), but never activated.

After the war, with John Beckett, Bedford revived the British People's Party, drawing in various members of pre-war organizations such as the Imperial Fascist League and the Nordic League; it had little success. On 9 October 1953 he died of gunshot wounds, described by the coroner as accidentally inflicted, on his Endsleigh estate in Devon. After a funeral at Efford, Plymouth, on 14 October, his ashes were interred in the family vault at Chenies, Buckinghamshire.

Described by his son as 'the loneliest man I ever knew' (John, duke of Bedford, 86–7), Bedford appears to have been an unworldly, sincere, but opinionated man, whose naïvety led him into association with people and ideas that blended ill with his very real Christian ideals.

RICHARD GRIFFITHS

Sources H. W. S. Russell, twelfth duke of Bedford, The years of transition [1949] [autobiographical] · J. R. Russell, thirteenth duke of Bedford, A silver-plated spoon (1959) · The Times (12 Oct 1953) · Marquess of Tavistock, The fate of a peace effort (1940) · Hansard 5L (1940–44) · Home office and cabinet office files, PRO · R. Griffiths, Patriotism perverted: Captain Ramsay, the Right Club and British anti-Semitism (1998) · R. Thurlow, Fascism in Britain: a history, 1918–1985 (1987) · b. cert. · m. cert. · d. cert. · Burke, Peerage (1998) · CGPLA Eng. & Wales (1953) · WWW, 1929–40 · The Times (15 Oct 1953)
Archives Mitchell L., Glas., corresp. with Guy Aldred and Ethel Macdonald | BL, corresp. with Marie Stopes, Add. MS 58557 · CAC Cam., corresp. with Sir Ralph Hawtrey · HLRO, letters to David Lloyd George · U. Hull, letters to C. W. Brook
Likenesses photograph, repro. in Russell, Years of transition, frontispiece · photographs, repro. in Russell, Silver-plated spoon, facing p. 86

Wealth at death £802,252 19*s.* 9*d.*—save and except settled land: probate, 7 Nov 1953, *CGPLA Eng. & Wales* • £4,990,000—limited to settled land: probate, 8 Dec 1953, *CGPLA Eng. & Wales*

Russell, Sir Henry, first baronet (1751–1836), judge in India, born at Dover on 8 August 1751, was the third son of Michael Russell (1711–1793), merchant of Dover, and his wife, Hannah (*d.* 1796), daughter of Henry Henshaw. The earl of Hardwicke nominated him in 1763 to the foundation of Charterhouse School, and he was educated there and at Queens' College, Cambridge (BA, 1772; MA, 1775). He was admitted a member of Lincoln's Inn on 20 June 1768, and about 1775 was appointed by Lord Bathurst to a commissionership in bankruptcy. He married, on 1 August 1776, Anne, daughter of John Skinner of Lydd, Kent; she died in 1780, and she and their son Henry, who died in 1781, were buried at Lydd, where there is a monument to her memory by Flaxman. Russell remarried on 23 July 1782; his second wife was Anne Barbara (*d.* 1 Aug 1814), fifth daughter of Sir Charles Whitworth, and sister of Charles, Earl Whitworth.

Russell was called to the bar on 7 July 1783. In 1797 he was appointed a puisne judge in the supreme court of judicature in Bengal and was knighted. He reached Calcutta on 28 May 1798. In 1807 he was appointed chief justice of the supreme court in place of Sir John Anstruther. The judges of the supreme court were appointments of the crown, not of the East India Company, under the Regulating Act of 1773, and Russell's tenure did much to enhance the appointment's dignity after the quarrels dating back to Warren Hastings as to whether the court had jurisdiction not only over Calcutta and over Europeans resident in Bengal (which in Russell's time was extended to include the Benares area), but also over Indians who lived throughout the territories controlled by the company. On 8 January 1808 he pronounced a judgment that attracted great attention because of his unusual concern for the rights of a poor Indian. John Grant, a company cadet, was found guilty of maliciously setting fire to an Indian's hut. In sentencing him to death, Russell said: 'The natives are entitled to have their characters, property, and lives protected; and as long as they enjoy that privilege from us, they give their affection and allegiance in return' (*Asiatic Annual Register*, 1808, 24–7).

Russell's house at Calcutta stood in what is now called after him Russell Street (*Calcutta Review*, December 1852). In his gossipy *Memoirs*, William Hickey describes how Lady Russell's beautiful young niece Rose Aylmer, who had come to India in search of a suitable husband, was a great centre of attraction at parties there. Her death from cholera after six months in Calcutta was memorialized in Walter Savage Landor's once famous poem 'Rose Aylmer'.

By patent dated 10 December 1812 Russell was created a baronet. On 9 November 1813 he resigned the chief justiceship, and on 8 December, at a public meeting in the town hall, Calcutta, he was presented with addresses from the European and Indian residents, the latter comparing his attributes 'with those of the great King Nooshirvan the

Just' (*Calcutta Gazette*, December 1813). Writing to him privately on 8 November 1813 the governor-general, Lord Moira, spoke of his 'able, upright, and dignified administration of justice', and testimony to his merits was formally recorded in a general letter from the Bengal government to the court of directors, dated 7 December 1813 (letters received from Bengal, 1808–13). Russell left Calcutta two days later, and on his return to England the East India Company awarded him a pension of £2000 a year. After his retirement he declined his brother-in-law Lord Whitworth's offer of a seat in parliament, as member for East Grinstead, a pocket borough of the Sackville family, on the ground that he 'did not choose to be any gentleman's gentleman'. On 27 June 1816 he was sworn a member of the privy council. His remaining years were mainly spent at his country house, Swallowfield Park, Reading, where he died on 18 January 1836.

Russell and his second wife had five sons (including William Whitworth *Russell) and five daughters. Three of the sons entered the East India Company service. Sir Henry (1783–1852), the second baronet, was resident at Hyderabad in 1810; Charles (*d.* 1856), after leaving India, was member of parliament for Reading; and Francis Whitworth (1790–1852) died at Chittagong on 25 March 1852.

STEPHEN WHEELER, *rev.* AINSLIE T. EMBREE

Sources 'Bengal occurrences', *Asiatic Annual Register*, 10 (1808), 24–7 • *Calcutta Gazette* (Dec 1813) • letters received from Bengal, 1808–13, BL OIOC • *Memoirs of William Hickey*, ed. A. Spencer, 4 vols. (1913–25) • S. C. Hill, ed., *Catalogue of the home miscellaneous series of the India Office records* (1927) • *GM*, 2nd ser., 6 (1836), 96–7 • private information (1897) [Sir George Russell, subject's nephew]

Archives Bodl. Oxf., corresp. and papers | BL OIOC, home miscellaneous series

Likenesses F. Chantrey, bust, 1822, AM Oxf. • G. Chinnery, portrait; known to be at high court, Calcutta, India, in 1897 • J. Jackson, portrait; known to be at Swallowfield Park, Reading, in 1897 • S. W. Reynolds, mezzotint (after G. Chinnery), BM, NPG • Romney, portrait; known to be at Swallowfield Park, Reading, in 1897 • portrait, BL OIOC • portrait, repro. in *Memoirs of William Hickey*, frontispiece

Russell, Henry (1812×14–1900), song writer and entertainer, was one of several sons of Moses Russell (1762/3–1857), a government officer, and his wife, Sarah, *née* Levin, a niece of the British chief rabbi, Solomon Hirschel. When Henry was still a small child the family moved to London, where he studied music with Charles M. King. In 1828 he sang at the Surrey Theatre with R. W. Elliston's Children's Opera, with which he claimed to have appeared before George IV in Brighton. He then went to Italy to complete his musical education as an external student of the Bologna conservatory, and met Rossini, Donizetti, Bellini, Balfe, and other musical celebrities.

Back in London, Russell became chorus master at the King's Theatre, and on 20 April 1835 he married Isabella Lloyd (1811?–1887) of the banking family. By now, however, he had decided to seek his fortune as an entertainer in Canada. He initially experienced little success in Toronto when performing songs by the classical masters, and he supported himself as organist and choirmaster at the First Presbyterian Church in Rochester, New York.

Henry Russell (1812x14–1900), by Claude Jacquand, 1841

Then, inspired by the great Kentucky orator Henry Clay, he began composing descriptive ballads, which he performed at the piano. Following his first New York recital in October 1836, he won huge success around North America. He reckoned that his songs had an influence on such issues as the abolition of slavery and (with 'The Maniac', 1840) the private lunatic asylum. His other songs included 'Woodman! Spare that Tree!' (1837), 'The Ivy Green' (1838), 'A life on the ocean wave' (1838), and 'The Old Arm Chair' (1840), which are regarded as an important element in the evolution of an American popular song tradition. Russell himself has been described as the most important American songwriter before Stephen Foster.

Seeking to repeat his success in Britain, Russell made his London début on 23 February 1842, exciting astonishment at the notion of concerts by a single performer, and arousing admiration for his fine baritone voice, his clear enunciation, and the narrative force of his delivery. After a further brief visit to America he settled in Britain, and found audiences around the country. As well as composing further successful songs, such as 'There's a good time coming, boys' (1848) and 'Cheer! Boys, Cheer!' (1851), in 1851, with Dr Charles Mackay, he staged the entertainment 'The far west, or, The emigrant's progress from the Old World to the New', which had a significant influence on emigration to America. He abandoned regular public performance in 1857 and retired with his family to Boulogne, but remained active as a moneylender and bill broker.

With his first wife, Isabella Lloyd (1811?–1887), Russell had at least two daughters and four sons, including the novelist William Clark *Russell (1844–1911). On 21 August

1888 he married Hannah de Lara (1844–1922), an illustrator known also as Emma Landon Ronald, with whom he already had two sons, the conductor, composer, and pianist Sir Landon *Ronald (1873–1938), and the singing teacher and opera impresario Henry Russell (1871–1937), father of Sheridan William Robin *Russell [see under Russell, Katherine]. His first family was raised as Christian, his second in the Jewish tradition.

Russell composed some 600 to 800 songs, including a series on Scott's *The Lady of the Lake*, scripture melodies, dramatic scenes, and cantatas. In 1889 'A life on the ocean wave' was adopted as the regimental march of the Royal Marines, and in 1891 Russell was honoured by a celebration at Covent Garden Theatre, at which he made a speech. In 1895 he published a volume of fanciful and unreliable memoirs, *Cheer! Boys, Cheer!* In old age he occupied himself in his carpentry workshop at his home at 18 Howley Place, Harrow Road, Maida Vale, London, where he died on 7 December 1900. He was buried on 10 December in Kensal Green cemetery, where his stone memorial is in the form of an 'old arm chair', recalling one of his most popular songs.   ANDREW LAMB

Sources H. Russell, *Cheer! boys, cheer!* (1895) · *Musical Treasury*, 4 (1846) · *Jewish Chronicle* (11 Dec 1900) · C. Hamm, *Yesterdays: popular song in America* (1979) · *ILN* (19 April 1851) · *ILN* (9 Sept 1854) · *ILN* (15 Dec 1900) · *BL cat.* · M. W. Disher, *Victorian song: from dive to drawing room* (1955) · A. de Lara, *Finale* (1955) · B. Duckenfield, *O lovely knight* (1991) · 'A man of many melodies: the late Henry Russell', *The Sphere* (15 Dec 1900), 302 · *DNB* · *WWW* · J. A. Stephens, 'Russell, Henry', *New Grove* · *MT*, 42 (1901), 27, 93 · m. cert. · d. cert.

Archives BL, music collection

Likenesses portrait, *c.*1838, repro. in *Strand Magazine* (1891) · R. Street, lithograph, *c.*1840, repro. in Hamm, *Yesterdays* · C. Jacquand, portrait, 1841; Bonhams, 20 March 1986, lot 21 [see illus.] · daguerreotype, *c.*1853, repro. in *Strand Magazine* (1891) · Mayall, daguerreotype, *c.*1854, repro. in *ILN* (9 Sept 1854) · Barrauds Ltd, photograph, *c.*1891, repro. in Russell, *Cheer! boys, cheer!*, frontispiece · Elliott & Fry, photograph, *c.*1895, repro. in *ILN* (15 Dec 1900) · Mr Caswell Smith, photograph, repro. in *The Sphere* (15 Dec 1900) · H. Furniss, pen-and-ink drawing, NPG · E. Walker, portrait, repro. in *Musical Treasury* · two prints, BM

Wealth at death £1297 15s. 7d.: probate, 19 Jan 1901, *CGPLA Eng. & Wales*

Russell, Henry Chamberlain (1836–1907), astronomer, born at West Maitland, New South Wales, Australia, on 17 March 1836, was the second son of the Hon. Bourn Russell (1794–1880), sometime mariner and storekeeper, later a politician, and his wife, Jane, *née* Mackreth. After education at the West Maitland grammar school and at Sydney University, where he graduated BA in 1859, he was appointed (1 January 1859) an assistant to William Scott, director of the new Sydney observatory. In 1861 he married Emily Jane (d. 1923), the daughter of Ambrose Foss of Sydney; they had one son and four daughters. He succeeded to the position of government astronomer on 12 July 1870.

The first years of Russell's directorship were devoted to the enlargement and re-equipment of the observatory, and to the increase in weather stations, from forty-three when he took over in 1870 to nearly 1000 by 1889, staffed by volunteer observers using equipment often designed by Russell himself. He exchanged weather data by telegraph and in 1877 sent daily weather maps to the press. He was a pioneer of the global view of meteorology and wrote extensively on southern hemisphere systems. His claim that the River Darling lost far more water than could be accounted for by discharge and evaporation, though incorrect in detail, encouraged studies which stimulated knowledge of the underground water systems of the country.

Russell and R. L. J. Ellery of Victoria organized an expedition to Cape Sidmouth to observe the solar eclipse of 1871. In 1874 Russell observed the transit of Venus from Sydney and in 1881 he organized parties to observe the transit of Mercury. Cloudy skies prevented his observing the 1882 transit of Venus. He represented Australia at the congress held in Paris in 1887 to consider the preparation of a photographic chart of the sky. He promised the co-operation of the Sydney observatory, and at once ordered the necessary telescope objective, but with characteristic resource decided to construct the mounting at his observatory. The committee of the astrographic chart entrusted the zone of south declination 54° to 62° to him, and this task, considerable for an observatory of modest resources, fully occupied the later years of his directorship. It was well on the way to completion when he retired in 1905.

Russell took an active part in initiating technical education in New South Wales; he was a fellow of the University of Sydney and vice-chancellor in 1891. He was three times president of the Royal Society of New South Wales, and first president of the Australasian Association for the Advancement of Science. He was the first graduate of Sydney University to be elected FRS, in 1886, and was created CMG in 1890. He was responsible for the many volumes of astronomical and meteorological observations issued from the Sydney observatory, and he also published numerous papers in the memoirs and monthly notices of the Royal Astronomical Society, the Royal Society of New South Wales, and other scientific societies.

Russell suffered a severe illness in 1903, and after a year's leave of absence he retired. He died at Sydney observatory on 22 February 1907, and was buried in the Anglican section of Waverley cemetery.

A. R. HINKS, rev. ANITA MCCONNELL

Sources R. Bhathal, 'Henry Chamberlain Russell', *Journal and Proceedings of the Royal Society of New South Wales*, 124 (1991), 1–21 · G. P. Walsh, 'Russell, Henry Chamberlaine', *AusDB*, vol. 6 · F. W. D., *PRS*, 80A (1907–8), lx-lxiii · *Monthly Notices of the Royal Astronomical Society*, 68 (1907–8), 241–3 · J. D. North, 'Russell, Henry Chamberlaine', *DSB*
Archives RAS, letters to Royal Astronomical Society
Likenesses photograph, repro. in Bhathal, 'Henry Chamberlain Russell'

Russell, Herbrand Arthur, eleventh duke of Bedford (1858–1940), agriculturist and philanthropist, was born on 19 February 1858 in London, the younger son in the family of two sons and two daughters of Francis Charles Hastings *Russell, ninth duke of Bedford (1819–1891) [see under Russell, Lord George William] and his wife, Lady

Herbrand Arthur Russell, eleventh duke of Bedford (1858–1940), by unknown photographer, c.1910

Elizabeth (d. 1897), eldest daughter of George John Sackville-West, fifth Earl De La Warr. He was educated at home, and matriculated at Balliol College, Oxford, in 1877, but did not take a degree. In 1879 he joined the Grenadier Guards and served in the Egyptian campaign of 1882. From 1884 to 1888 he was aide-de-camp to the viceroy of India, Frederick Temple Hamilton-Temple Blackwood, first marquess of Dufferin and Ava. In 1888, at Barrackpore in India, he married Mary Du Caurroy [see below], younger daughter of Walter Harry Tribe, archdeacon of Lahore, India, and his wife, Sophie, daughter of Charles Lander, formerly consul-general in the Dardanelles. They had one son. In 1893 he succeeded his elder brother as duke of Bedford.

Seven years later Bedford was called upon to make a decision which set the keynote for his subsequent career. In October 1900 Lord Salisbury, reconstructing his cabinet after the general election, submitted the duke's name to the queen for the office of under-secretary of state for war. In his memorandum Lord Salisbury spoke highly of the duke's practical and military abilities, but in refusing this and at least one subsequent offer of office (a colonial appointment) the duke was acting upon a conviction already reached, and one which grew stronger with the years, that personal management of his estates and a political career could not be combined.

Bedford loved his estates and the countryside, and he

was no townsman, despite his important London properties. Although he was proud of his office as lord lieutenant of Middlesex (1898–1926), and of being chosen in 1900 as first mayor of Holborn, neither appointment gave him the same degree of pleasure and the same opportunities as did his chairmanship from 1895 to 1928 of the Bedfordshire county council. He enjoyed country pursuits such as fishing and shooting, but as a countryman he was also profoundly interested in science. This early interest had been much stimulated by the kindness shown him as a boy by F. T. Buckland, and even more by his visits to T. H. Huxley, with whom he studied physiology. After his succession to the dukedom his vast inheritance gave him the opportunity to apply science to his estates, particularly to Woburn Abbey in Bedfordshire, where he set up forestry and arboriculture research stations.

Bedford's chief scientific interest was zoology, however, and his investigations at Woburn were closely associated with work for the Zoological Society. He was elected a fellow of the society in 1872, and served as president from 1899 to 1936, when he was awarded a gold medal. During that time the development and care of the private collection of living creatures in the park at Woburn went along with the development and care of the collection at London Zoo in Regent's Park, where by the duke's share in a guarantee of a sinking fund the construction of the aquarium in the gardens of the society was made possible. He was responsible for the introduction into the zoo of Przhevalsky's horse, the only genuine wild horse in existence. He also secured for Woburn Park, in the years following the Boxer riots, the only surviving specimens of Père David's deer, a species of unknown origin, which had formerly been the property of the emperors of China. In 1908 Bedford's work was recognized by his election as FRS, for his patronage of research and his contribution to the increase of zoological knowledge.

The duke commanded the 3rd (militia) battalion of the Bedfordshire regiment from 1897 to 1908, and on the outbreak of the First World War he rejoined the regular army. In 1914 he established a Bedfordshire training depot in Ampthill Park, which became, after the Military Service Act of 1916, a command depot, with the duke as colonel-commandant. At the same time part of the abbey and adjacent buildings were turned into a base hospital for wounded men direct from the firing line. Provision made, at the sole expense of the duke, in both camp and hospital, for special and new methods of treatment demonstrated the importance which he and his wife attached to medical and surgical as well as to other research. In recognition of his war services the duke, who had received the Garter in 1902, was in 1919 appointed KBE. His other great public service was to act as president of the Imperial Cancer Research Fund, which office he held from 1910 to 1936.

The period after 1918 saw the duke more than ever absorbed by his country interests. The main achievement of the latter years of his presidency of the Zoological Society of London was the creation, first thought of in 1926, of a zoological park at Whipsnade in Bedfordshire for the breeding of wild animals, to celebrate the centenary of the Zoological Society. He worked closely with the society's secretary, Peter Chalmers Mitchell, and five years after the purchase of 480 acres of the Whipsnade estate, in December 1926, the Whipsnade Park Zoo opened in May 1931. The duke of Bedford planted a beech tree at the end of Duke's Avenue, to commemorate the opening of the park, and he presented the zoo with a pair of muntjacs, several other deer, and three turkeys. At Woburn he helped to save the survivors of the European bison herds which were almost extinct in their native haunts in Lithuania and the Caucasus as a result of the war.

Dame Mary Du Caurroy Russell [*née* Tribe], duchess of Bedford (1865–1937), nurse and hospital manager, was born on 26 September 1865 at Stockbridge, Hampshire, where her father was rector. Her parents went to India when her father was appointed to a position in the North-Western Provinces in 1867, and she and her sister were brought up in Sussex by relatives. She was educated at Cheltenham Ladies' College in 1877 and 1879–81, spending 1878–9 in Zürich. In 1881 she joined her parents in Lahore, and lived there until her marriage. In the early years of her married life she developed a severe and distressing form of deafness, probably as a result of typhoid fever, which she caught soon after her arrival in India.

Since her childhood Mary had wanted to become a nurse, and after her marriage she studied nursing at the London Hospital. In 1898 she opened a small cottage hospital in Woburn, and in 1903 this was replaced by a model hospital, medical and surgical, under her supervision. Gradually, however, both she and the professionals with whom she came into contact realized that her real interest was in surgery. The First World War offered her, in middle age, the opportunity for which she herself said that she had long waited. Her model hospital became a military hospital which worked in conjunction with the base hospital at the abbey. The duchess supervised both establishments and at the same time trained in theatre work, so that in 1917 she was able to undertake the post of surgeon's assistant. She then trained in radiography and radiology, in both of which, already a photographer, she attained a remarkable degree of proficiency. After the closing of the abbey hospital in 1920, the duchess devoted all her attention to her own model hospital, determined that it should profit by all that she had learned in her war service. It was reorganized as a civilian hospital for surgical cases, and became the Woburn Surgical Hospital. The duchess was both chief theatre sister and radiologist. She was appointed DBE in 1928.

The duchess had for a long time wanted to learn to fly. In June 1926, at the age of sixty, she took her first flight and began to receive instruction as a pilot. Flights with a co-pilot, Captain Barnard, to India in 1928 and 1929 and to South Africa in 1930, the last two being record flights, were regarded as pioneer ventures in travel by air. She gained her pilot's licence in 1933.

The duchess died in an aeroplane accident off the east coast of Britain on 22 March 1937. The duke of Bedford died at Woburn Abbey on 27 August 1940. He was succeeded as twelfth duke by his only child, Hastings William Sackville *Russell.

G. S. THOMSON, rev. ANNE PIMLOTT BAKER

Sources P. C. Mitchell, *Obits. FRS*, 3 (1939–41), 499–502 · J. Gore, ed., *Mary, Duchess of Bedford, 1865–1937* (1938) · P. Chalmers Mitchell, *Centenary history of the Zoological Society of London* (1929) · *WWW* · Burke, *Peerage* · L. Pendar, *Whipsnade wild animal park* (1991)
Archives Beds. & Luton ARS, household accounts | Hitchin Museum and Art Gallery, Hertfordshire, letters to K. D. Little · Richmond Local Studies Library, London, corresp. with D. Sladen
Likenesses photograph, c.1910, Hult. Arch. [*see illus.*] · J. Collier, oils, 1913, Guildhall, London · W. Stoneman, photograph, 1921, NPG · F. C. Gould, caricature, pen-and-ink drawing (*Birds of a feather*), Woburn Abbey, Bedfordshire · S. P. Hall, pencil drawing, NPG · G. Reid, oils, Woburn Abbey, Bedfordshire · J. H. Walker, oils, Woburn Abbey, Bedfordshire · photograph, repro. in *Obits. FRS* · photograph, repro. in Gore, ed., *Mary, Duchess of Bedford*
Wealth at death £3,239,130: resworn probate, 11 Dec 1940, CGPLA Eng. & Wales

Russell, James (c.1720–1773), surgeon and university professor, was born in Edinburgh, the son of the surgeon Francis Russell and his wife, a daughter of Robert Gordon of Halhead, Aberdeenshire. Little is known of Russell until 21 January 1747, when he was made a burgess and guild brother of Edinburgh by right of his father. Eight days later he became a member of the Surgeons' Company, and in 1752–3 he was head of the Incorporation of Surgeons. He served on Edinburgh town council from 1753 to 1755, and in 1761 was appointed by the council to a committee responsible for improving the city's water supply.

Russell's links with the town council, as well as his family connections, also eventually secured him a teaching position at the University of Edinburgh. In June 1759 the Edinburgh natural philosophy chair came vacant and, after much back-room manoeuvring, his cousin Adam *Ferguson was elected, despite the fact that Russell was the more qualified candidate. But those who managed the election had decided to place Ferguson in the university with a view to transferring him to the moral philosophy chair at the earliest opportunity, and to bring in Russell as his successor. This scheme duly came to fruition in 1764, and on 23 May of that year Russell was finally ratified as the professor of natural philosophy.

During his brief tenure in the chair, Russell taught a course of natural philosophy that differed significantly from those offered at the other Scottish universities in this period. Rather than simply surveying the individual sciences of astronomy, mechanics, pneumatics, hydrostatics, magnetism, electricity, and optics, as was done elsewhere, Russell rooted his discussion of these subjects in an account of our cognitive faculties and an enumeration of the various attractive and repulsive powers of matter. Drawing on his medical experience, he detailed the mental mechanisms by which humankind acquires knowledge, and because of his philosophical bent he was one of the first Edinburgh professors to introduce the ideas of Thomas Reid into his lectures. He also seems to have been less reliant on spectacular experimental demonstrations than were his Scottish counterparts, and in

his course he placed greater emphasis on the natural theological implications of the physical sciences than was the norm.

Russell was highly clubbable, and much admired by David Hume and the Edinburgh literati. Having joined the Edinburgh Musical Society in November 1744, he then became an early member of the Select Society in 1754, and subsequently took part in the *Poker Club, which was founded in 1762 by a group led by Hume and Ferguson that campaigned for the formation of a Scottish militia. He was also active in the Edinburgh Philosophical Society, and apparently served as its secretary from 1762 until his death. Known for his mechanical dexterity, he acted as the society's expert on electrical theory.

Russell married Margaret Balfour (1720–1785), the sister of the Edinburgh professor James Balfour of Pilrig. He died in Edinburgh on 17 October 1773.   PAUL WOOD

Sources [J. Russell], *Of natural philosophy* (Edinburgh, [1770]) · Edinburgh City Archives, Edinburgh town council records, 26 Dec 1759 to 7 Oct 1761 and 16 May 1764 to 20 Feb 1765, MSS SL7/1/76; SL7/1/80 · senate minutes, vols. 1–2, 1733–1811, U. Edin. L., Dup. 436 · C. B. B. Watson, ed., *Roll of Edinburgh burgesses and guild-brethren, 1701–1760*, Scottish RS, 62 (1930) · B. Balfour-Melville, *The Balfours of Pilrig* (1907) · A. Bower, *The history of the University of Edinburgh*, 3 vols. (1817–30) · *The letters of David Hume*, ed. J. Y. T. Greig, 2 vols. (1932) · *New letters of David Hume*, ed. R. Klibansky and E. C. Mossner (1954) · *The correspondence of Adam Ferguson*, ed. V. Merolle, 2 vols. (1995) · D. Stewart, *Account of the life and writings of Thomas Reid* (1802) · R. L. Emerson, 'The Philosophical Society of Edinburgh, 1768–1783', *British Journal for the History of Science*, 18 (1985), 255–303 · R. B. Sher, 'Professors of virtue: a social history of the chair of moral philosophy at Edinburgh', *Studies in the philosophy of the Scottish Enlightenment*, ed. M. A. Stewart (1990), 87–126
Likenesses D. Martin, double portrait, oils, 1769 (with his son James), Scot. NPG

Russell, James (1754–1836), surgeon, was born in Edinburgh, the son of James Russell, professor of natural philosophy at Edinburgh University, and Margaret, daughter of James Balfour of Pilrig. Russell was educated in Edinburgh and spent his entire career there. He took courses in medicine at the university but did not graduate. He became a fellow of the Royal College of Surgeons of Edinburgh on 11 July 1777. By the 1790s Russell, together with Benjamin Bell and Andrew Wardrop, was part of a surgical partnership which specialized in training apprentices. Russell was a staunch defender of the prerogatives and reputation of the college throughout his long career, and he took a particular interest in the college's museum and in developing its educational role. On 21 September 1798 Russell married Eleanor, daughter of William Oliver, a landowner; they had five sons and four daughters.

Along with five other fellows of the Royal College of Surgeons, Russell was, on 23 December 1800, appointed one of the first surgeons-in-ordinary to the Royal Infirmary of Edinburgh. This measure marked a radical change in the organization of the surgical service at the infirmary. Since November 1786 Russell had been responsible for another innovation at the infirmary: he took it upon himself to give a series of clinical lectures in surgery at the hospital.

He regarded this course as a partial remedy for the inadequate surgical instruction at that time provided by the university medical school. Russell's method of instruction was explicitly modelled on the clinical lectures on medical cases already given at the infirmary. For the remainder of his career he delivered one or two courses a year at the hospital, and despite being a somnolent lecturer he attracted between 170 and 180 students annually.

In 1793 Russell petitioned Robert Dundas, the lord advocate, in favour of the establishment of a 'clinical and pathological' chair of surgery at Edinburgh University, of which he would be the first incumbent. Although nothing came of this initial approach, another petition, addressed this time to the town council, led to the creation in June 1803 of a regius chair of clinical surgery in the university with an annual endowment of £50. The crown's willingness to fund this new chair may have been due to a desire at a time of war to secure a supply of adequately trained surgeons to serve in the armed forces.

Russell's course was, however, handicapped by the fact that it was not mandatory for students wishing to take the MD to attend it. In 1824 Russell addressed a pamphlet, entitled *Argument in favour of requiring every candidate for a degree in medicine to attend a course of clinical lectures on the practice of surgery*, to the principal and professors of the university. In this publication Russell sought to show the specious and disingenuous character of the objections raised by the medical professors to giving his teaching equal status to the lectures in clinical medicine delivered at the infirmary. He maintained that physic and surgery were so intimately connected that it was necessary for every medical student to be educated in both divisions of the healing art; moreover, 'A Student, by thus studying the appearance of disease in local external affections, is acquiring an accurate knowledge of fundamental principles of diseased action, which may be easily transferred to explain the nature of similar morbid affections of the internal parts' (Russell, *Argument*, pp. 4–5). In 1834 Russell sold his chair to James Syme for £300 a year for his lifetime.

As well as his polemical publications Russell produced a number of clinical and pathological texts, including *A Treatise on Scrofula* (1808). He was a member of the Philosophical Society of Edinburgh and became one of the original fellows of the Royal Society of Edinburgh in 1783. In his younger days Russell was identified with the whig party in Edinburgh, but later he became known for the conservatism of his political views. He died at his country home, Bangholm Bower, on 14 August 1836, and was buried in Old Greyfriars churchyard.

Russell had a keen interest in art and literature; he acquired an excellent collection of paintings, and was something of an artist himself, sketching in crayons and sepia. Sir Walter Scott was an acquaintance.

L. S. JACYNA

Sources DNB · L. S. Jacyna, *Philosophic whigs: medicine, science and citizenship in Edinburgh, 1789–1848* (1994) · L. Rosner, *Medical education in the age of improvement: Edinburgh students and apprentices, 1760–1826* (1991) · A. Logan Turner, *Story of a great hospital: the Royal Infirmary of Edinburgh, 1729–1929* (1937)
Archives Royal College of Physicians of Edinburgh, casebooks | U. Edin., New Coll. L., letters to Thomas Chalmers
Likenesses D. Martin, double portrait, oils, 1769 (with his father), Scot. NPG · W. Gordon, portrait, priv. coll.

Russell, James (1786–1851), surgeon, was born on 19 November 1786 at 1 New Hall Street, Birmingham, the son of George Russell, at one time a prosperous merchant in Birmingham but later ruined by the outbreak of the American War of Independence, and Martha, daughter of John Skey and sister to James Skey of Upton. He was the grandson of Thomas Russell, low bailiff of Birmingham. His father and others of his family were Unitarians, and prominent members of Joseph Priestley's congregation; the house of his uncle (James Russell) at Showell Green was burnt during the Priestley riots of 1791, and his father's house was threatened.

After attending a private school near Warwick, Russell became the pupil of John Blount, a Birmingham surgeon, on 17 November 1800, and about 1806 he travelled to London, where he entered as a student at Guy's Hospital. He received his diploma from the Royal College of Surgeons on 6 May 1808, and obtained the post of visiting apothecary to the Birmingham Dispensary. This post he resigned on 30 September 1811. He spent the winter of 1811–12 in London, attending John Abernethy's lectures. He had to borrow money in order to pay the expenses of his education, but paid it off at the earliest opportunity. In 1812 he settled in practice at 67 New Hall Street as successor to a Mr Lardner; he moved to no. 63 in 1821, and later established a partnership with a Mr Vickers. On 18 January 1815 Russell was elected honorary surgeon to the Birmingham Dispensary, a post which he held until 9 November 1825; he also held the office of surgeon to the town infirmary, but he failed to obtain election on the staff of the general hospital, owing mainly to his outspoken religious opinions.

When sanitary inspectors were appointed for the borough, Russell was selected, together with his lifelong friend Mr Hodgson, for the office he held until his death. He was the originator of many important improvements in the sanitary condition of Birmingham, especially those in relation to drainage and ventilation. In 1851 he wrote an elaborate report, 'The sanitary condition of Birmingham', and he gave evidence before the parliamentary committee concerning the Birmingham improvement bill. Throughout his career, in addition to the time and energy which he gave to charitable institutions, as surgeon to the Protestant Dissenters' Charity School and the Asylum for the Deaf and Dumb at Edgbaston, Russell devoted much of his time to helping the sick poor. He gave special attention to midwifery, on which he accumulated a large amount of statistical information. He left behind him notes of more than 2700 cases of midwifery that he had attended, and he published in the *Edinburgh Medical and Surgical Journal* a paper on the results of his midwifery practice.

Russell took an active part in the establishment of the

Medical Benevolent Society in Birmingham, and many of the city's literary and scientific institutions benefited from his assistance—in particular, the Philosophical Institution, of which he was treasurer for many years. He delivered several lectures before the Philosophical Institution and the Literary Society, including 'The influence of certain occupations on the health of the workpeople', 'The nature and properties of the atmosphere', 'Natural and artificial ventilation', and 'On some of the more aggravated evils which affect the poorer classes'. He also read papers in 1840 and 1841 on infanticide, before the Literary Society, and a paper entitled 'The natural history and habits of the Tereti Navalis'. He took a prominent part in establishing the Birmingham Geological Museum.

Russell was a Liberal in politics and took an active interest in the passing of the Reform Bill. When Earl Grey left office in 1831 he at once—at great risk to his practice—publicly enrolled himself as a member of the Birmingham Political Union, under the leadership of Thomas Attwood. On the institution of the fellowship of the Royal College of Surgeons in 1843 he was selected as an honorary fellow.

On 5 May 1817 Russell had married Sarah Hawkes of Birmingham, with whom he had three children; the eldest, James Russell (d. 1885), was for many years physician to the Birmingham General Hospital. Russell himself died of heart disease at 63 New Hall Street, Birmingham, on 24 December 1851. He was buried in the family vault under the old meeting-house on 31 December.

W. W. WEBB, rev. PATRICK WALLIS

Sources The Lancet (10 Jan 1852) • GM, 2nd ser., 37 (1852), 196–7 • London and Provincial Medical Directory (1853) • d. cert. • private information (1897)
Likenesses oils, 1897, priv. coll.

Russell, James (1790–1861), law reporter, was the eldest son of the James Russell of Stirling. After graduating with distinction at Glasgow University, he was called to the English bar from the Inner Temple in June 1822. Having been introduced by Henry Lascelles, second earl of Harewood, to Lord Eldon, he was appointed in the following year a reporter in the courts of the lord chancellor and master of the rolls. In 1824 he became sole authorized reporter and continued reporting until 1834. In April 1839 he married Maria, eldest daughter of Robert Cholmeley, rector of Wainfleet, Lincolnshire; they had three sons and five daughters. He gradually acquired a large chancery and bankruptcy practice, and took silk in 1841. He ultimately became leader of Vice-Chancellor Knight Bruce's court, but gradually lost his sight, and for some years before his death he was blind. He was on four occasions asked to become a candidate for parliament, but declined each invitation. While not a brilliant pleader, Russell held a high position at the bar, owing to his learning and acuteness.

Besides contributing to the *Quarterly Review*, Russell, together with his younger brother, John Russell of the Scots bar, was for some years editor of the *Annual Register*.

James Russell died at his home, Roxeth House, near Harrow, on 6 January 1861, and was buried at Kensal Green. He was survived by his wife.

G. LE G. NORGATE, rev. ERIC METCALFE

Sources Solicitors' Journal, 5 (1860–61), 188 • Law Times (16 Feb 1861) • Annual Register (1861), 488 • J. W. Wallace, The reporters, 4th edn (1882) • Allibone, Dict. • CGPLA Eng. & Wales (1861)
Likenesses T. Lupton, mezzotint (after E. Coleman), BM, NPG
Wealth at death £100,000: probate, 25 Feb 1861, CGPLA Eng. & Wales

Russell, James Burn (1837–1904), medical officer of health, was born on 5 May 1837 at 16 Robertson Street, Glasgow, the elder child of David Russell (1808–1871), printer, and his wife, Agnes (1816–1839), daughter of John Cassels, a grain merchant of the burgh of Calton (now part of Glasgow), and his wife, Jean Harvie. His mother died when he was aged two and his father emigrated to Australia several years later. Russell and his sister were brought up in Rutherglen, near Glasgow, in the home of their grandfather James Russell, Glasgow's first steamboat harbour-master and veteran of the battle of Waterloo.

Russell attended Glasgow high school before entering Glasgow University in 1854 and graduating BA in 1857. He showed literary flair, winning prizes for essays, writing verse, and teaching himself Anglo-Saxon. His natural philosophy teacher was Professor William Thomson (later Lord Kelvin), who recruited him as his assistant on his 1858 expedition to lay an Atlantic cable; they were nearly lost at sea during a storm of exceptional ferocity. On his return Russell enrolled in Glasgow University medical school, where his teachers included Joseph Lister. After graduating MD CM in 1862 he worked as a houseman at Glasgow Royal Infirmary and then as assistant medical officer of Glasgow poorhouse, with responsibility for the fever wards.

In 1865 Professor William Gairdner, who three years earlier had become the city's first medical officer of health, put Russell in charge of the city's first municipal fever hospital, and in 1870 he was given command also of the new Belvidere Fever Hospital. Russell's marriage to Helen Fenton Davidson (1842–1884), daughter of the Revd Peter Davidson, minister of Queen Street United Presbyterian Church, Edinburgh, took place on 3 September 1868, and a son and two daughters were born in the 1870s; but soon afterwards his wife was committed to Glasgow Royal Asylum at Gartnavel, where she died in 1884.

It was as Glasgow's first full-time medical officer of health, from 1872 to 1898, that Russell made his greatest contributions to public health. He was selected from a field of forty-five candidates after the town council had decided to rescind Gairdner's part-time appointment and replace him with a full-time medical officer of health—the first such appointment in Scotland. Russell faced a formidable task amid the squalor and overcrowding created by Glasgow's rapid industrial expansion. No other city in Britain had as high a proportion of one-room and two-room houses. However, by the time Russell left his post

James Burn Russell (1837–1904), by T. & R. Annan & Sons

Glasgow was internationally renowned for its public health services; mortality had dropped from 29 to 21 per 1000 and was lower than that of Liverpool and Manchester. Deaths from tuberculosis and other respiratory diseases had declined more sharply than in the rest of Scotland and the city led the fight against childhood diseases.

Russell initially had no medical staff but worked through the sanitary inspectors, particularly the epidemic inspectors, widening the scope of their work. Taking a scientific approach he established a set of small-area health statistics unmatched in Britain, and propounded the law of occupancy, relating death rates to room density. He used his literary skills to overcome public apathy and ignorance, writing prolifically and becoming a moving public speaker, this despite a crippling shyness which made it difficult for him to speak even at committee meetings. In the 1880s his lectures, 'The Children of the City' and 'Life in one room', prepared the way for reform by opening middle-class eyes to the realities of slum life. Russell worked closely with a group of enlightened town councillors on the health committee to initiate local legislation on public health and building standards, and he energetically enforced existing laws—tracking down smallpox vaccination defaulters, warring with irresponsible landlords, pouncing on jobbing butchers who were selling suspect sausages, denouncing industrialists for polluting the environment, and pursuing the miscreants through the law courts with a regard to detail that made him almost invincible.

Russell's influence extended beyond the city. In a series of investigations which did much to establish the connection between enteric fever and infected milk he travelled by train and gig to inspect waterlogged farm steadings, and his memorandum on the sanitary requirements of dairy farms, issued in 1888, was widely circulated. His paper on tuberculosis, published in 1896, which typified Russell's broad, environmentally conscious approach to public health, received international recognition. In the 1890s Russell was a key figure in Glasgow's great age of municipal enterprise, which attracted civic delegations from the United States. Yet his outspokenness attracted controversy, and the strong statutory powers that he and the health committee wielded made them a target for criticism, particularly among opponents of sanitary reform.

In 1898 Russell resigned to become medical member of the Local Government Board for Scotland, where he rigorously enforced the provisions of the Scottish Public Health Act of 1897. Despite deteriorating health he remained at his post—sometimes working from his bed—until his death at a private hospital at 41 Drummond Place, Edinburgh, on 22 October 1904. Glasgow sanitary inspectors formed a guard of honour at the Glasgow necropolis on 26 October, following a funeral service held at Morningside Congregational Church, Edinburgh. A memorial service was held at Elgin Place Memorial Church, Glasgow, on 6 November.

Russell was a committed Congregationalist and, from 1886, an active Liberal Unionist. He was a president of the Royal Philosophical Society of Glasgow. In 1889 he received the first Bisset-Hawkins memorial medal of the Royal College of Physicians of London for zeal in promoting public health. He declined a knighthood. In addition to numerous contributions to the *Glasgow Medical Journal* (which he edited for several years) and the *Sanitary Journal*, he was the author of *The Evolution of the Function of Public Health Administration* (1895). A posthumous collection of his writing, *Public Health Administration in Glasgow*, edited by his successor as medical officer of health, A. K. Chalmers, was published in 1905.   EDNA ROBERTSON

Sources Glasgow medical officer's reports, Mitchell L., Glas., Glasgow City Archives · health committee of Glasgow, police board minutes, Mitchell L., Glas., Glasgow City Archives · private information (1998) · A. K. Chalmers, *The health of Glasgow, 1818–1925* (1930) · *Glasgow Herald* (24 Oct 1904) · *The Scotsman* (24 Oct 1904) · *Glasgow Medical Journal*, new ser., 62 (1904), 431–7 · *The Lancet* (12 Nov 1904), 1387 · B. White, 'James Burn Russell, M.O.H., Glasgow, 1872–1898', *Proceedings of the Scottish Society of the History of Medicine* (1985–6), 1–8 · C. I. Pennington, 'Mortality, public health and medical improvements in Glasgow, 1855–1911', PhD diss., Stirling University, 1977 · d. cert. · m. cert.

Archives Mitchell L., Glas., Glasgow City Archives · NL Scot. · priv. coll., family papers · Wellcome L., corresp. | Bodl. Oxf., James Bryce MSS

Likenesses T. & R. Annan & Sons, photograph, Wellcome L. · T. & R. Annan & Sons, photograph, repro. in J. B. Russell, *Public health administration in Glasgow* (1905), frontispiece [see illus.] ·

bronze bust, Greater Glasgow Health Board · marble bust, Glasgow Art Galleries and Museums

Wealth at death £10,675 17s. 1d.: confirmation, 9 Dec 1904, *CCI*

Russell, John (*d.* 1437), administrator and speaker of the House of Commons, was a kinsman, perhaps even an illegitimate son, of Sir John Russell (*d.* 1405) of Strensham, Worcestershire, master of the horse and councillor to Richard II, in whose property in Buckinghamshire he had an interest in remainder. Yet although closely linked with Sir John, who named him as his executor, he forged an independent career, and established himself as a landowner in Herefordshire, where he most likely lived at Aymestrey. After becoming an apprentice-at-law and member of Lincoln's Inn, Russell was a frequent pleader in the royal courts, and from 1403 until 1421 was retained as counsel to the duchy of Lancaster. He served for twenty years without break as a JP in Herefordshire from 1407, and was active in a judicial capacity in south Wales too, where between 1409 and 1417 he held county courts and petty sessions for Edward, duke of York, and his heir, and presided as a justice in the duchy of Lancaster lordships. An interest in parliamentary affairs led to his appointment as proxy for the abbot of Gloucester in the parliaments of 1410, 1411, and 1417, as well as to his own frequent elections to the Commons. He sat at least thirteen times as representative for Herefordshire between 1414 and 1433. In 1420 he was an unsuccessful candidate for the speakership, narrowly losing by four votes to another lawyer, Roger Hunt, but in 1423, his eighth recorded parliament, he succeeded in obtaining the office, and when, on 17 November of that year, Henry VI (not yet two years old) made his first ever appearance before the assembled houses, it fell to Russell to deliver a fulsome speech of welcome, praising the new monarch, his father Henry V, his uncles, the dukes of Bedford and Gloucester, and the royal council.

Over the years Russell had been engaged by several members of the nobility in the capacity of legal adviser, feoffee, estates' steward, or executor, among them Blanche Mowbray, Lady Poynings, Joan Beauchamp, Lady Bergavenny, John, Lord Harington, and James, Lord Berkeley. Of greater significance was his association with Duke Edward of York, who granted him an annuity for life, and employed him as a feoffee of his estates and overseer of his will, tasks which kept him occupied for several years after the duke's death at Agincourt. For an undefined period he served on the council in England of John of Lancaster, duke of Bedford, the regent of France. He acted as steward of the lordship of Usk for Anne, the widowed countess of March, and having been involved in property settlements contingent upon her marriage to John Holland, earl of Huntingdon, he may well have been responsible for a petition to the parliament of 1430 made on the couple's behalf. His second election as speaker, in the parliament of 1432, may have owed something to his links with Bedford and with Humphrey, earl of Stafford (*d.* 1460), whom he served as a justice in his Welsh lordships, and most probably as a councillor too. It may also have been helped by his continuing involvement as a trustee in

the affairs of the young Richard, duke of York (*d.* 1460), who in this parliament successfully petitioned for livery of seisin of his inheritance. In both the parliaments in which Russell officiated as speaker the Commons declined to vote more than a minimal grant of taxation, which may explain why he gained little or nothing from the crown when parliament was dissolved. He sat in the Commons one more time, in 1433, before he died in 1437. His widow, Isabel, took a vow of perpetual chastity in Hereford Cathedral on 25 March 1437. The identity of his heir is not recorded.   LINDA CLARK

Sources HoP, *Commons, 1386–1421* · R. A. Griffiths and R. S. Thomas, *The principality of Wales in the later middle ages: the structure and personnel of government, 1: South Wales, 1277–1536* (1972), 135, 137 · J. S. Roskell, *The Commons and their speakers in English parliaments, 1376–1523* (1965), 63–4, 78–9, 180–82 · A. T. Bannister, ed., *Registrum Thome Spofford … AD MCCCCXXII–MCCCCXLVIII, CYS, 23 (1919) · Calendar of the fine rolls, PRO, 16 (1936), 300

Russell, John (*fl.* in or before 1447), author or compiler of a manual of household practices, describes himself in the *Boke of Nurture* (as it is styled in BL, MS Harley 4011), as sometime a servant with Humphrey, duke of Gloucester (1391–1447), as usher in chamber and marshal in hall. But now age has come on him: 'croked age hathe compelled me & leue court y must nede' (Russell, ed. Furnivall, l. 1217). If he made his poem while he was in service there it must have been done before 1447, the date of Duke Humphrey's death. Nothing further is known about Russell: a possible identification with an Oxford Magister John Russell who appears in documents of 1445–7 has been suggested, but there does not seem to be any obvious connection between the two. An apparent inconsistency with the announcement at the beginning, 'an vsshere y am', may be explained as a dramatic convention of the genre of courtesy books, in which the instructor speaks directly to his pupil or 'son'. Alternatively, it may be a confusion caused by the uncertain transmission of this kind of material, in which matter is reused or adapted freely.

The relationship between Harley 4011 (the only manuscript to ascribe the work to Russell) and the other four manuscripts that contain versions of it is far from clear. It may well be that Russell was not the original author, but adapted and revised an earlier work (the instructor at one point says that he has tested 'this treatise' in his youth). However the *Boke* was made or developed, it remains a fascinating document. In its 1250 lines of irregular verse in monorhyming quatrains a young man is instructed in the duties of various offices, including those of chamberlain, usher, and marshal, the method of laying the table (and how to wrap up the lord's bread 'stately'), and the art of carving. There are descriptions of feasts, and of the 'sotiltes' (confections of pastry or sugar made into figures or scenes) that accompanied each course. The 'tables of precedence' which are supplied suggest some of the problems that might be faced by a marshal—where to put a former mayor of London or the mayor of Calais, or a lady of royal blood who has married a knight, or a lady of lower blood who has married royalty, and so on. Russell's *Boke* is a detailed guide to the practices and rituals of the fifteenth-century household. DOUGLAS GRAY

Sources F. J. Furnivall, ed., *Early English meals and manners*, EETS, original ser., 32 (1868) · J. Nicholls, *The matter of courtesy: medieval courtesy books and the 'Gawain' poet* (1985), esp. 159–60, 191 · Emden, *Oxf.*

Archives BL, MS Harley 4011

Russell, John (*c.*1430–1494), administrator and bishop of Lincoln, was probably born, from the chronology of his career, about 1430, in the parish of St Peter, Cheeshill, Winchester. He may have been the son of John Russell of Winchester, barber, and Margery his wife, who made an enfeoffment in 1466 in a transaction witnessed by various prominent courtiers at a time when the future bishop was a rising royal official. He was admitted as a scholar of Winchester College in 1443, and proceeded to New College, Oxford, in 1447. He became a fellow there in 1449 and subwarden in 1461, leaving Oxford a year later. He was admitted BCL in 1454–5; he was described as BCnL and BCL in March 1459, and as DCnL in the following December. About this time he finally took orders—he was ordained acolyte in May 1458, subdeacon a year later, and deacon in September 1459. It is not known when he was ordained priest, but this was probably before he was granted a canonry and prebend at Salisbury on 24 February 1461. He received several benefices in various dioceses, including the archdeaconry of Berkshire in 1466, before entering the episcopate as bishop of Rochester in 1476.

Like other men with legal training Russell took his talents into royal rather than episcopal service. Although he was still a regent doctor in canon law at Oxford in 1462, he had probably already been attracted into the king's service when he was appointed to a prebend in the royal chapel of St Stephen, Westminster, on 27 April 1461. The details of his early governmental career are not known, but in September 1467 he was one of the envoys who negotiated the marriage of Edward IV's sister, Margaret of York, to Charles, duke of Burgundy. This may not have been his first diplomatic mission, for he was in Bruges earlier that year, when he bought a copy of Cicero's *De officiis*. He may have been a protégé of Bishop Richard Beauchamp of Salisbury, who headed the September embassy, and may indeed have modelled his career on Beauchamp's, as both men were administrators rather than politicians. Russell served on various embassies in the late 1460s, particularly to the Burgundian court, and it was probably not a coincidence that he delivered an oration when Charles of Burgundy was admitted to the Order of the Garter on 4 February 1470. During Henry VI's readeption in 1470–71, however, he remained a royal agent, serving as an envoy to negotiate a truce with France in February 1471, while after Edward IV's return he continued to be employed in negotiations with the Burgundians, the Hanse, and the Scots. In Edward's later years he was not involved in diplomacy, probably because his services were needed elsewhere, but Richard III in 1484 and Henry VII after 1485 both drew on his expertise as an ambassador.

Administrative obligations probably explain why in 1468 the pope dispensed Russell for twelve years to visit his archdeaconry by deputy, although before this period expired, in 1476, he had been promoted bishop of Rochester—the pope provided him on 15 July, the temporalities were restored on 6 September, and he was consecrated on the 22nd. In 1469 he was appointed secondary in the privy seal office, and in 1474 became keeper of the privy seal. It is not known how active he was in diocesan administration, for his Rochester register has not survived, although one of his *acta* there, preserved in a Lincoln formulary, refers to him conducting the visitation of a nunnery. But departmental responsibilities inevitably kept him near the centre of royal administration at Westminster; in 1479 he was involved in a suit in the Star Chamber there, and in the same year a letter from him to Archbishop Thomas Bourchier is dated from his house at Lambeth Marsh. On 7 July 1480 Russell was translated to the greater see of Lincoln, the temporalities being restored on 9 September following. Most indications of his location after his promotion suggest that public duties kept him close to London, with occasional visits to his diocese. Although most of his ordinations were conducted by a suffragan, he officiated in one at his cathedral in April 1482 and is noted at one of his episcopal manors in the following month. He also attended convocation in 1481 and 1482. As a bishop he had secular as well as spiritual duties, serving (at least nominally) on the commission of the peace for Kent while he was at Rochester, and on fifteen other commissions while at Lincoln.

He was present at court when Edward IV died on 9 April 1483, and assisted during the funeral, but in the following month he was thrust to the front of the political stage when Richard of Gloucester appointed him to replace Archbishop Thomas Rotherham of York as chancellor on 10 May, following the latter's dismissal on account of his close associations with the Woodvilles and particularly with the queen. Such a promotion of the keeper of the privy seal to chancellor was not unusual and represented a minimal change in the administration. During Gloucester's protectorate Russell was involved in the administration of Edward IV's will, and in preparing for the coronation and first parliament of the young Edward V. Some punning allusions to 'Rivers' in the speech he drafted for opening the young king's parliament suggest that he was willing to take an anti-Woodville point of view. He presided over one half of the council that met at Westminster to discuss coronation arrangements on 13 June, while the other half at the Tower of London saw the arrest and execution of Lord Hastings. There were precedents for such a division of the council, and it is not clear whether or not Russell was aware of Richard's plans. He was present three days later when the young duke of York was removed from sanctuary and handed over to the protector. Although he did not participate actively in the manoeuvres before Richard's usurpation, he clearly acquiesced in them, for he was confirmed as chancellor on the day after the new king's accession, participated in his coronation, and attended the subsequent banquet. It is doubtful if he had any real alternative, although one might note that the archbishop of Canterbury did absent himself from the coronation banquet.

As chancellor during Richard III's reign, Russell was heavily involved in official routine, which included giving judgment in the court of chancery. The king evidently trusted him in matters of some delicacy, because he asked him to try to persuade his solicitor Thomas Lynam not to marry Edward IV's former mistress, Elizabeth Shore. There is little reason, however, to think that Russell was a strong partisan of Richard, for he seems to have been an administrator rather than a politician, and in moments of crisis may well have been left to keep the routine work of government going. He was not always at court—during the rebellion in the autumn of 1483 he surrendered the great seal to the king for a month, probably because Richard wished to have possession of it as a vital tool of government during the crisis. Russell may have suffered from ill health, although it is uncertain if this was physical or diplomatic. The king again took possession of the seal in July 1485, shortly before Bosworth, and retained it until his death, but there is no clear evidence that Russell was dismissed because his loyalty was suspect—indeed it is not clear when he ceased to hold the chancellorship. In Russell's later years there are some indications of physical frailty: in 1486 he petitioned the pope successfully for a faculty to resign his office, reserving a pension, because he was too infirm to continue as bishop (although in fact he did not take advantage of this); in 1492 he glossed a manuscript of excerpts from anti-heretical writings with the comment that he was tired with many heretics; and in 1494 he tried to resign as chancellor of Oxford University. One bequest in his will, to a member of his diocesan registry staff, was specifically stated to have been made in return for the legatee's attending him in his sickness. However, as Russell remained quite active in public affairs throughout this period, a hypochondriacal streak in him may be suspected.

After Bosworth, Russell rapidly came to terms with Henry VII, although the new king restored Rotherham to the chancellorship as one of two interim appointments before promoting John Morton. He was a trier of petitions in the new king's first parliament, and Henry used his services in negotiations with both the Scots and the Bretons in 1486. He did, however, spend more time in his diocese than previously, although some of his *acta* are still dated from London. He still left most ordination duties to his suffragan, only occasionally officiating himself, but he did play a part in resolving a long-standing dispute between Crowland and Peterborough abbeys over rights to certain lands and the appropriation of a benefice (spending some ten days at the former house during the proceedings in April 1486), in redrafting the statutes of the Newarke College at Leicester, to which he later made a bequest in his will, in settling a question of payments due from inhabitants of an almshouse at Stamford, and in uniting two chantries which were no longer financially viable. His compilation of anti-heretical material suggests that Russell was also concerned with the threat of Lollardy in the

diocese. He also was appointed a papal judge-delegate in an assortment of cases dealing with testamentary, matrimonial, and tithe disputes.

Perhaps Russell's main concern in these years was the affairs of Oxford University, of which he had been elected chancellor in late 1483, possibly because the university then saw him as a valuable ally in high places. He played an active part in raising money for a new canon-law school, and for the rebuilding of the nave of St Mary's Church. He had a reputation for learning—the Italian humanist Domenico Mancini commented on this in 1483, and a generation later Sir Thomas More referred to him as one of the most learned men in England of his time. His literary interests were wide-ranging, to judge by the books that he owned or gave to colleges in Oxford, which included various humanist works. Among the classical texts were works of Virgil, Cicero, Statius, Pliny, and Plutarch, and there were more recent writings by Boccaccio (from which he proposed to quote in a draft speech for Edward V's parliament), Guarino da Verona, and Leonardo Aretino. But he also owned various medieval works, including Matthew Paris's *Historia Anglorum*, books of both canon and civil law, a volume of the acts of the Council of Basel, and Bonaventure's commentary on the first two books of the *Sentences*. It has been suggested that he was the author of the so-called 'civil service' continuation of the Crowland chronicle, but recent scholarship has suggested that there are more objections to this theory than arguments in support of it.

John Russell died at his episcopal manor of Nettleham on 30 December 1494, shortly after making his will, and was buried in Lincoln Cathedral. His will, dated to the day of his death, suggests that he was a man who was more involved in the life of institutions than in personal relationships. He made no provision for the souls of relatives or benefactors, and most of his personal bequests were to his chaplains and members of his diocesan staff. Indeed the only provision that he made for his own soul consisted of two endowments of anniversary services, in perpetuity in the Newarke at Leicester, and for ten years in his cathedral at Lincoln. The only indication of a tie of friendship was a bequest to the daughter of Viscount Welles, to whom he was godfather. Gifts were made to various religious houses in his diocese, more particularly to those burdened with pensions to the bishop, and to churches appropriated to the episcopal *mensa*. His interest in learning was reflected in gifts, often of books, both to individuals and to institutions. Bequests to New College and the cathedrals of Rochester and Lincoln mirror his career, and suggest that at the end he put behind him the secular world to which he had given so much of his life.

JOHN A. F. THOMSON

Sources Lincoln episcopal registers, Lincs. Arch., register 22 (Russell's register) · *Chancery records* · Rymer, *Foedera*, 1st edn, vols. 11–12 · Emden, *Oxf.* · *CEPR letters*, vols. 12–16 · will, PRO, PROB 11/10, fols. 164v–165v · Lincoln formulary 3, Lincs. Arch. · *The usurpation of Richard the third: Dominicus Mancinus ad Angelum Catonem de occupatione regni Anglie per Ricardum tercium libellus*, ed. and trans. C. A. J. Armstrong, 2nd edn (1969) [Lat. orig., 1483, with parallel Eng. trans.] · *Three books of Polydore Vergil's 'English history'*, ed.

H. Ellis, CS, 29 (1844) · H. Anstey, ed., *Epistolae academicae Oxon.*, 2, OHS, 36 (1898) · *Registrum Thomae Bourgchier … 1454–1486*, ed. F. R. H. Du Boulay, CYS, 54 (1957) · *The register of John Morton, archbishop of Canterbury, 1486–1500*, ed. C. Harper-Bill, 1–2, CYS, 75, 78 (1987–91) · J. Gairdner, ed., *Letters and papers illustrative of the reigns of Richard III and Henry VII*, 1, Rolls Series, 24 (1861) · St Thomas More, *The history of King Richard III*, ed. R. S. Sylvester (1963), vol. 2 of *The Yale edition of the complete works of St Thomas More* · R. Horrox and P. W. Hammond, eds., *British Library Harleian manuscript 433*, 4 vols. (1979–83)

Archives Lincs. Arch., episcopal register 22 · Lincs. Arch., formulary 3

Wealth at death over £625; plus value of books; bequests in kind; residue of goods: will, PRO, PROB 11/10, fols. 164*v*–165*v*

Russell, John, first earl of Bedford (*c*.1485–1555), courtier and magnate, was probably born in Dorset, the son and heir of James Russell (*d*. 1505/6), landowner, of Kingston Russell, Dorset, and his first wife, Alice, daughter of John Wise of Sydenham, Devon. Russell's father died between December 1505 and February 1506, but he did not come into full possession of his inheritance until the death of his stepmother, Joan Russell, in 1523. A Dorset family with ties to both Dorchester and Weymouth, the Russells in the fourteenth century had engaged in commercial activities, including the Bordeaux wine trade, while making profitable marriages and gradually increasing their property. Russell's grandfather was probably John Russell (*d*. 1505), who sat as knight for the shire in 1472 and held the Dorset manor of Berwick. He was a member of the royal household to both Edward IV and Henry VII, and this improved the prospects for other members of his family. Little is known about John Russell the younger's early life, but he was fluent in French and Italian, and possibly Spanish, and in the seventeenth century Thomas Fuller claimed he had been 'bred beyond the Seas' (Willen, 3). His linguistic proficiency, along with his innate shrewdness, served Russell well in establishing a career at court.

Courtier and envoy, 1506–1526 According to legend, credible but unsubstantiated in contemporary sources, Russell's introduction to the Tudor court came unexpectedly. On 17 January 1506 a storm at sea forced Philip and Joanna, king and queen of Castile, to land at Melcombe Regis in Dorset. Sir Thomas Trenchard, one of the Dorset gentry entertaining Philip, had ties to the Russell family and allegedly requested John Russell to act as interpreter and escort the king to the royal court at Windsor Castle in Berkshire. Once there, Russell came to the attention of Henry VII and won appointment as a gentleman of the chamber in 1507. On 11 May 1509 he participated in Henry's funeral procession as a gentleman usher. At court he was able to cultivate a successful relationship, eventually a friendship of sorts, with the new king, Henry VIII, who was only six years his junior. He took part in the jousting at court during the 1510s, reinforcing his ties with the young circle about the king.

Russell served Henry VIII loyally, industriously, and unobtrusively. Like other courtiers, he fulfilled military, diplomatic, and administrative duties, as the occasion demanded or the opportunity arose. In 1513, identified as

John Russell, first earl of Bedford (*c*.1485–1555), by Hans Holbein the younger, late 1530s

a gentleman usher of the king's chamber, he was appointed a spear to serve in Calais for 18*d*. per day. He may well have participated in the sieges of Thérouanne and Tournai, for he remained as a captain in the Tournai garrison, paid 4*s*. per day and responsible for eighty men. In 1514 he travelled to Paris to witness the marriage of Louis XII to Princess Mary on 9 October. Coming to the attention of Thomas Wolsey, archbishop of York, during this period, Russell participated in various schemes aimed against Richard de la Pole, claimant to the throne, and carried messages from Tournai to Wolsey. Engaged in diplomacy that was often underhand, he none the less disliked the isolation and expense associated with life in the garrison. In 1518 he was the first to sign a letter of complaint that the captains addressed to Wolsey. As envoy to Charles Somerset, first earl of Worcester, in 1519 he served in the delegation negotiating the surrender of the garrison at Tournai. He re-entered the royal household, probably as a gentleman usher, in 1519 at an annual salary of £33 6*s*. 8*d*., and in 1520 accompanied Henry VIII to France at the Field of Cloth of Gold.

Maintaining the confidence of both Henry and Wolsey, Russell gradually advanced at court during the 1520s. In 1522 he participated in a naval expedition under the command of Thomas Howard, earl of Surrey, and lost the sight of his right eye through an arrow wound at the siege of Morlaix on 2 July. Surrey knighted Russell that day, commending him for his 'hardyness and noble courage', one of the few times in his military career that Russell won such praise (Willen, 8). On 28 June 1523 he was named knight marshal of the household, but his primary responsibilities were increasingly diplomatic. Between about 30

June and 20 September 1523 he was a special ambassador in France. In August he travelled incognito to Bourg-en-Bresse to negotiate final terms of alliance between Henry and Charles Bourbon (III), duc de Bourbon and constable of France. Upon Russell's return to court in September, Sir Thomas More reported that the king took 'great pleasure' in Russell's 'well acheved errand' (*State Papers, Henry VIII*, 1.135).

Having returned to the continent in October 1523, Russell spent most of the next two years abroad as a royal envoy, usually acting in secret to convey and distribute English funds on behalf of Bourbon. He contacted Bourbon about 1 November and acted as paymaster for the constable's troops. Russell was paid £2 per day for carrying out this sensitive mission. His first assignment, to travel to the imperial city of Besançon with £12,000 to support German mercenaries, miscarried because the soldiers had dispersed before his arrival. Wolsey wrote in November asking for the return of the funds, but these instructions did not reach Russell until January 1524. Russell was briefly in England in April, only to return to the continent in May 1524 with £20,000 to distribute to Bourbon for his enterprises against François I. Russell travelled as a merchant, even hiding funds in bales of oats as he went through Geneva, before reaching Chambéry in July. His innate caution meant that he carried out his mission with care and this provoked Richard Pace, the English envoy accompanying Bourbon, who regarded Russell as too slow. Not until August did the funds reach Bourbon at Marseilles. Wolsey instructed Russell and Pace to distribute an additional £10,000 to assure Bourbon's victory but warned that the money not be 'spent in vayne' (*State Papers, Henry VIII*, 6.332). Again acting cautiously, Russell travelled to Rome to consult the English envoy there, John Clerk. He arrived on 8 October and apparently visited Clement VII. Russell and Clerk suggested to Wolsey that the money provided for Bourbon's return to England. Upon further instruction from Wolsey, Russell joined Bourbon's army and participated in the battle of Pavia on 24 February 1525, reporting in March on the imperial victory and the capture of François. He remained with Bourbon, whom he came to admire, and for the next few months provided Henry and Wolsey with intelligence. Wolsey now regarded Russell as one of his circle. Wanting courtiers whom he could trust in close proximity to the king, in January 1526 Wolsey included Russell in the Eltham ordinances as one of the gentlemen of the privy chamber.

Courtier and landowner, 1526–1536 At some point between November 1525 and October 1526 Russell, as he entered his forties, married Anne (*d.* 1559), daughter and heir of Sir Guy Sapcote of Huntingdon and his wife, Margaret. She was the widow of John Broughton, with whom she had three surviving children, and of Sir Richard Jerningham. The match undoubtedly pleased Henry and Wolsey, and while personal papers do not survive, evidence suggests the marriage was stable and successful. Anne Jerningham brought with her three manors valued at £70 per annum. One of these, Chenies in Buckinghamshire, Russell enlarged and made their family residence. The king

bestowed Amersham, another Buckinghamshire manor, as a wedding gift, valued at £43 per annum. By 1527 Russell's lands and fees were assessed at £134 6s. 8d., making him a wealthy gentleman. His only child and heir, Francis *Russell, second earl of Bedford (1526/7–1585), was born about this time, and in 1528 his stepson, John Broughton, died while in service to Wolsey. Adding to Anne Russell's distress at the death of her son was the status of her youngest daughter, Katherine, 'all her Joy in this world' (PRO, SP 1/49, fol. 63r). Sir Thomas Cheyney, supported by Anne Boleyn, blocked Russell's efforts to purchase the child's wardship.

On 2 January 1527 Russell was sent as special ambassador to Clement VII. English diplomatic strategy changed as the imperial alliance was abandoned in favour of supporting the French, the papacy, and their Italian allies against Charles V and Bourbon. It was a frustrating and ultimately unsuccessful mission. Accompanied by Sir Thomas Wyatt the elder, Russell had an audience with the pope on 8 February. He delivered 30,000 ducats to Clement and assured Henry of the pope's appreciation. Yet, the next few months brought little positive result. Russell negotiated with the imperial viceroy of Naples but could not gain favourable terms for the papacy, then broke his leg *en route* for Venice. He and Sir Gregory Casale, English envoy at Rome, insisted, when writing to Wolsey, that they were discouraging the pope's desire for a truce. By March, Russell requested his own recall and managed to depart from Rome in late April, just days before the city was sacked by imperial troops.

Russell possibly returned on a diplomatic mission to Italy in January 1528, but as Henry became increasingly preoccupied with his divorce from Katherine of Aragon, Russell's continental assignments came to an end. He was sheriff of Dorset and Somerset from 1527 to 1528, an indication that he retained property and standing in the western counties. His prominence at court increased with his appointment as a knight of the body by 1527. Wolsey then inserted him as a gentleman of the privy chamber in 1527 in an attempt to increase his own influence at court. In 1529 he was designated honorary member of Lincoln's Inn. He continued his service in the privy chamber and acted frequently as intermediary between the king and Wolsey. He remained on good terms with Wolsey even as the cardinal fell from favour. In July 1529 he wrote to cheer Wolsey and predicted that the cardinal would soon regain the king's goodwill. George Cavendish reported that on 1 November Henry dispatched Russell on a secret midnight visit to reassure Wolsey that 'the kyng commendyth hyme unto you/ And delyverd hyme a great Ryng of gold with a Turkkas [turquoise] for a tokyn/ And willyd you to be of good chere/ who lovythe you as well as ever he dide' (*The Life and Death of Cardinal Wolsey by George Cavendish*, ed. R. S. Sylvester, EETS, 243, 1959, 111). Russell kept Henry's confidence, yet his continued support for Wolsey alienated Anne Boleyn and probably impeded his career. She persuaded the king to recall Russell from a diplomatic mission *en route* for France in May 1529. When Russell publicly defended Wolsey in February 1530, Anne showed her displeasure by not speaking to him for a month.

In his mid-forties Russell proved able to bide his time. He sat as knight of the shire for Buckinghamshire in the parliament of 1529. He may have been an MP in a previous parliament but nothing is known of his activities in the Reformation Parliament. In October 1532 he accompanied Henry to Calais for a meeting with François and inspected English fortifications there. In 1533, however, he rejected an offer to become deputy governor of Calais and also suggested that his friend Arthur Plantagenet, Viscount Lisle, decline the post too: advice that was rejected. Russell deliberately avoided the isolation from court that he had earlier experienced at Tournai. Also in 1533 Russell was appointed JP for Bedfordshire, Buckinghamshire, Hertfordshire, Huntingdonshire, and Northamptonshire, and was reappointed to these commissions of the peace for the rest of his life.

Councillor and nobleman, 1536–1547 After Anne Boleyn's fall, Russell's court career revived its progress, helped by events in 1536. On 30 May he attended the wedding of Henry and Jane Seymour. He wrote to Lisle that the 'kyng hath come out of hell into heaven for the gentellness of this [Jane] and the cursidness and unhappyness in the other [Anne]' (PRO, SP 3/7, fol. 28r). In October he fought to suppress the rebellion in Lincolnshire and the Pilgrimage of Grace. His soldiering won Russell no accolades, yet secured him military prominence as one of Henry's chief commanders. Days after the outbreak of the rebellion in Lincolnshire, Sir William Parr of Horton, Northamptonshire, and he led a small force at Stamford, where they were joined by Charles Brandon, first duke of Suffolk, Sir Frances Bryan, Richard Cromwell, Sir William Fitzwilliam, and a large contingent of troops. The king, and perhaps Sir Thomas Cromwell, may have been uneasy with Russell's initial, hesitant response at Stamford. Russell defended himself against charges of 'slackness', and Suffolk and Fitzwilliam confirmed shortages of men and supply (Willen, 26–7). After the suppression of the Lincolnshire revolt, Russell was dispatched in November first to defend Newark, Nottinghamshire, then to join Surrey (now third duke of Norfolk) at Doncaster in Yorkshire. In December he acted as intermediary between Henry in London and Norfolk and George Talbot, fourth earl of Shrewsbury, still in Doncaster. He delivered the king's pardon to the rebels, but in Henry's mind did so prematurely. None the less, as the rebellion ended, Russell remained in favour with both Henry and Sir Thomas Cromwell.

Late in 1536 Russell was appointed to the reorganized council. On 18 October he became comptroller of the royal household, an office previously held by his friend Sir William Paulet, now named treasurer. When Jane died on 24 October 1537, John and Anne Russell were among those granted jewels belonging to the late queen. Russell was now a wealthy man. Joyce Youings calculated his income as £551 19s. 4d. by 1539, the result of fees, annuities, grants, and other properties collected from his marriage and a career at court spanning thirty-three years. He was on good terms with Cromwell, as earlier he had been with Wolsey, but his success was tied to his relationship with the king. He understood Henry's temperament and needs, and in 1538 Gaspard de Coligny, sieur de Castillon, the French ambassador, commented on the close relationship that existed between the king and his councillor. Earlier, Thomas Darcy, Baron Darcy, claimed that Russell was among those who 'dare and wyll speke to the king the tryth' (LP Henry VIII, 11, no. 1086). Lord and Lady Lisle relied upon him as a friend at court to advance numerous suits throughout the decade.

Russell's status and responsibilities took a dramatic step forward in spring 1539 when Henry elevated him to the peerage. On 9 March he was created Baron Russell and on 24 April was elected knight of the Garter (installed on 18 May). Also in April he became lord president of the council of the west, an administrative body newly created by Cromwell to promote stability in the western counties. The crown felt the need to respond to the political vacuum in the west created by the execution of Henry Courtenay, marquess of Exeter. On 4 July the king, to promote Russell's influence, granted him about 30,000 acres, drawn primarily from the former monastery of Tavistock in Devon and valued at £648 12s. per annum. Russell was unique in receiving lands from Henry to build 'territorial power in the interests of the crown' (Miller, 246). The grant doubled Russell's income, making him a regional magnate of some note. To underscore his special status in the west, the crown, also on 4 July, named him steward of the duchy of Cornwall and lord warden of the stannaries. By summer 1539, according to Richard Grenville, the Courtenays were 'never more esteemed nor better beloved in this parts than his lordship is' (The Lisle Letters, ed. M. St C. Byrne, 6 vols., 1981, 5.639). To bolster his position Russell was appointed JP for Cornwall, Devon, Dorset, and Somerset. The council of the west did not survive Cromwell's fall, but Russell's association with the western counties endured, a source of wealth and status for his family and by the 1550s a source of stability there for the crown.

Russell was an active participant in Henry's campaigns and policies of the 1540s. In the aftermath of Cromwell's fall he was appointed lord high admiral on 28 July 1540 and then, on 3 December 1542, lord privy seal—a position which he retained for the remainder of his life and which brought him a yearly salary of £365. In 1541 he was commissioned to levy and transport 4000 men to Calais, and subsequently travelled with William Fitzwilliam, earl of Southampton, to Calais and Guînes to inspect fortifications and provide intelligence reports. In 1542 he travelled with the king within England and hosted a session of the privy council at his home at Chenies in October. On 7 November 1542 he was named high steward of Oxford University. In December Russell was involved in the proceedings against Katherine Howard. Throughout these years Russell's relationship with Henry remained secure.

In 1540 he had been among the first to learn of Henry's disenchantment with Anne of Cleves. In 1543, when the conservatives on the privy council turned on Thomas Cranmer, archbishop of Canterbury, Russell insisted he knew 'right well' that Henry would protect him (Willen, 33). In 1545 the Venetian ambassador, Giacomo Zambon, singled out Russell as a regular companion to the king.

Regarded as a friend by the empire, Russell was one of the commissioners who negotiated the alliance with Charles against France in 1543. In 1544, during the campaign against France, he was commander of the vanguard, consisting of 13,000 men. Norfolk and he joined forces in the unsuccessful siege against Montreuil and by autumn were forced to retreat, first to Boulogne, then to Calais. Throughout the summer Russell expressed dissatisfaction with Norfolk's siege strategy, and he was among those privy councillors expressing unease with Henry's general commitment to the war. He complained to the king himself that it was an expensive 'wyld war … without any gayne' (PRO, SP 1/189, fol. 151r). Back in England by November 1544, Russell served as lord lieutenant in June 1545, responsible for supervising coastal defences and for recruiting mariners and ships in the south-west.

Russell's success rested on a blend of personal qualities that served him well in the midst of the intrigue and vicissitudes of court politics. A contemporary likeness from these years survives at Windsor: a drawing by Hans Holbein the younger of the late 1530s shows him in a skullcap and with a full beard. His face is drawn in partial profile to hide his right eye, which had been injured years earlier, and his expression is serious and determined. Russell, however, remains in some respects an elusive figure. He could be outspoken and frank, as in 1544 when he wrote to the king and questioned his campaign against France or, in a separate episode that year, when he argued with Edward Seymour, earl of Hertford, over rights to a leasehold. Yet Russell was always pragmatic and sensitive to political realities. In 1540, during Cromwell's fall, the French ambassador, Charles de Marillac, predicted correctly that Russell, one of Cromwell's few friends, would offer no real assistance since he had 'long learned to bend to all winds' (Willen, 34). Russell advocated no policies of his own and expressed no religious preferences. While historians like John Strype, A. F. Pollard, and W. K. Jordan, have classified him as a protestant, others, including G. S. Thomson and Diane Willen, question this interpretation. Associated with the protestant Miles Coverdale during Edward VI's reign, under Mary I he befriended the Catholic Dr John Feckenham, abbot of Westminster, who witnessed his will and later preached at his widow's funeral. In fact, neither his friendships nor his patronage were bestowed along religious lines. Loyalty to the crown and Erastianism in religion remained guiding principles of his career.

Service under Edward VI and Mary I, 1547–1555 Henry bequeathed £500 to Russell and designated him one of the sixteen executors to sit on Edward's regency council. On 31 January 1547, just three days after Henry's death, the regency council proclaimed Hertford lord protector and governor of the king's person. Russell was not an instigator of these events, but was one of thirteen who signed the council's minute that day. He supported Hertford without closely allying with him. On 15 February eight privy councillors received new titles, offices, and lands allegedly granted in Henry's unfulfilled gift clause, but in effect awarded by the new regime. Henry's list of prospective recipients had originally included Russell, and Edward's government considered him for an earldom; a list dated 15 February names him earl of Northampton, with a grant of lands worth £200 per annum. Instead Russell chose, or at least was willing to accept, a reversionary grant to Woburn Abbey in Bedfordshire, itself a handsome acquisition worth £100 per annum and, after his death, the family seat. He was high steward at Edward's coronation on 20 February and continued as lord privy seal. In March Russell, Sir William Paget, John Dudley, earl of Warwick, and Thomas Seymour, Baron Seymour of Sudeley, negotiated with the French, in sessions held at his house on the Strand in London, over the status of fortifications in Boulogne and the possibility of a treaty of amity. In 1548 he warned Seymour against plans to marry Princess Elizabeth, and in January 1549 provided evidence used in the act of attainder against him. Russell's most significant role came after the outbreak of rebellion in Devon in June 1549 when he was commissioned, as lord lieutenant, to suppress the rebels and then, with Sir William Herbert, deployed his army in October to seal the fate of the lord protector.

W. K. Jordan blamed Russell for the instability that persisted in the west after Henry's grants of 1539. Although many among the western gentry liked Russell, he had been a peer for only a decade by the time the western rebellion broke out. His interventions in local affairs had been sporadic and confined to times of military crises. In 1549 trouble began at Bodmin in Cornwall on 6 June and soon spread to Plymouth, then the rest of Devon, as mobs protested at the new Book of Common Prayer. The privy council dispatched Russell and instructed him on 24 June to use persuasion before raising soldiers. Reaching Somerset, Russell recognized the seriousness of the revolt and began to argue with the beleaguered privy council for more men and supplies. As he lingered outside Honiton in Devon, the privy council grew exasperated with his inaction, especially after 2 July when rebels besieged Exeter. After the arrival of reinforcements, Russell's forces were victorious at the battle of Fenny Bridges on 29 July but prematurely stopped pursuit of the rebels. On 16 August, with additional troops under William Grey, thirteenth Baron Grey of Wilton, the king's forces achieved victory at Sampford Courtenay. Russell relieved Exeter on 6 August but again allowed rebels to escape. The arrival of 1000 Welsh under Herbert on 17 August assisted in the final suppression of the uprising on 29 August.

Russell's innate conservatism hindered his effectiveness during the western rebellion and irritated a privy council overwhelmed with uprisings elsewhere. Yet, the events of 1549 proved a turning point in Russell's relationship with the west. Acting as lord lieutenant, he assumed judicial and administrative functions 'reminiscent of the former lord president … Some of the purpose, if not the substance, of the Council of the West was resurrected' (Willen, 76, 81). He showed concern for the 'oppressyon' of the commons and instructed west-country JPs in September 1549 to ensure that 'justice and equite (without respect of persons) shall appertayne' (ibid., 77). He strengthened his relationship with Exeter and, according to John Hooker, was instrumental in securing the manor of Exe Island for the city in 1550. During Warwick's ascendancy, again as lord lieutenant, Russell addressed judicial, administrative, and military concerns in the west. He had 'a lively interest' in parliamentary patronage, and as in Henry's reign, used his very extensive influence in selection of MPs for seats in the south-west (HoP, *Commons, 1509–58*, 3.236). Indeed, Russell probably controlled more parliamentary patronage than anybody else.

Russell directly contributed to Warwick's ascendancy and was compensated in turn. Having refused to disband his troops in September 1549, Herbert and he were still in the west country when Thomas Wriothesley, first earl of Southampton, and Warwick led the October coup against Somerset. In response to Somerset's request on 5 October, Russell and Herbert advanced with their army to Andover in Hampshire. On 8 October, however, citing the 'woful Clamytie' of civil war, they refused Somerset's subsequent pleas to bring their troops to Windsor Castle (Pocock, 91). Their decision determined Somerset's fate and the protectorate was dissolved on 13 October. Russell was appointed as one of six 'attendant lords', two of whom would attend the king at all times (APC, 1547–50, 344–5). His greatest reward came on 19 January 1550, when he was created earl of Bedford and received lands worth nearly £340 per annum. Two days later Paget, Sir John Mason, Sir William Petre, and he left for France to negotiate the return of Boulogne. They began peace negotiations on 19 February and did not conclude their mission until the end of March. Bedford held a series of legal and administrative commissions under Warwick and continued to attend both the privy council and the House of Lords regularly. He was involved with trade issues and in 1552 spoke bluntly to the imperial ambassador, Jehan Scheyve, on behalf of English trading interests in the Low Countries. Further reward followed, including the grant on 4 May 1552 of Somerset's Long Acre estate in Middlesex, which included the site of Covent Garden.

Bedford was a reluctant participant in the scheme devised by Warwick, now duke of Northumberland, to alter the succession. In spring 1553 he was uncharacteristically absent from parliament and the privy council. In June he accepted gifts in land and endorsed the 'device' for the succession, but the imperial ambassador reported the lord privy seal's opposition. On 13 July, one week after the death of the king, Bedford and six other privy councillors secretly consulted with Scheyve. On 19 July, given Princess Mary's support in the provinces, Bedford was among those who proclaimed her queen. True to his nature, he acted cautiously throughout the crisis, all the more so since Northumberland had entrusted his son, Francis Russell, Baron Russell, with Windsor Castle. Bedford's support for Mary was, however, consistent with both his Erastianism and his long-standing loyalty to the Tudor dynasty. His relationship with Mary went back to the 1530s, when his wife had attended the princess and he had advocated her cause at court, a dangerous course at the time.

Bedford attended privy council meetings as Mary's lord privy seal as early as 17 August 1553, yet acted cautiously. Russell, who had opposed Mary openly and was well known for his protestantism, was not pardoned until November. During the rebellion of Sir Thomas Wyatt the younger, Bedford assisted in holding London Bridge against the rebels and briefly became active in privy council affairs again. Russell, implicated in the rebellion, was again pardoned on 12 September 1554. Although Bedford initially petitioned Mary to make an English marriage, the imperial ambassador, Simon Renard, solicited his support with a generous pension. Bedford now performed his final mission for the crown: he was sent as special ambassador to Spain with Thomas Radcliffe, Baron Fitzwalter, from 12 March to 20 July to witness ratification of the marriage treaty and arrange for Philip of Spain's arrival in England. He spared his clients in the west country the trouble and expense of receiving the Spanish retinue by arranging Philip's landing at Southampton on 19 July. Bedford was one of the peers who participated in the wedding ceremony on 25 July. After parliament convened in November, however, his attendance both at the privy council and in the Lords was irregular. Historians, including M. A. R. Graves and Jennifer Loach, debate the motivation for his absences, particularly the question of whether he opposed the Regency Bill and influenced members of the Commons to support him against it. Poor health may have been reason enough for his absences. He last attended the privy council on 11 January 1555 and drew up his will on 2 February.

On 14 March 1555, at or about seventy years old, Bedford died at his house on the Strand. Despite his instructions for a simple funeral, he was buried in a lavish ceremony 'with three hundred horse all in black' on 20 March at Chenies (Thomson, 195). 'Greatly perturbed' about his son's involvement in Wyatt's rebellion, he took the unusual step of transferring the whole of his estate to jointure. His executors were his wife, his son, and his longtime friend Paulet (now first marquess of Winchester). His widow subsequently built a chapel to house his fine tomb at Chenies. She died on 14 March 1559 and was buried with her husband at Chenies on 21 March 1559.

Bedford's legacy was both personal and public. Beginning with modest property inherited in Dorset and Somerset, he possessed impressive personal wealth by the time of his death. His holdings included lands from Tavistock Abbey (1539), Woburn Abbey (1547), and Thorney Abbey in Cambridgeshire (1551). Beyond these grants from the crown, he entered the land market in the early 1540s, and by 1558 the Bedford estate collected annual rentals exceeding £2000. His investments included mercantile and mining ventures: he was a shipowner in the 1540s and in 1553 became a shareholder in the Muscovy Company. However impressive, his success was slow in coming, the result of hard work, political shrewdness, and carefully cultivated personal relationships, most notably with Henry VIII. Known for his honesty as well as for his pragmatism, Russell belongs among a handful of Henricians whose loyal service significantly contributed to the stability of the Tudor dynasty.   DIANE WILLEN

Sources G. S. Thomson, *Two centuries of family history: a study in social development* (1930) · D. Willen, *John Russell, first earl of Bedford, one of the king's men* (1981) · HoP, *Commons, 1509–58*, 3.234–6 · H. Miller, *Henry VIII and the English nobility* (1986) · C. G. Cruickshank, *The English occupation of Tournai, 1513–1519* (1971) · J. Youings, *Devon monastic lands: calendar of particulars for grants, 1536–1558*, Devon and Cornwall RS, new ser., 1 (1955) · E. W. Ives, *Anne Boleyn* (1986) · *DNB* · N. Pocock, ed., *Troubles connected with the prayer book of 1549: documents … in the record office*, CS, new ser., 37 (1884) · J. Loach, *Parliament and the crown in the reign of Mary Tudor* (1986) · D. M. Loades, *The reign of Mary Tudor: politics, government and religion in England, 1553–58* (1979) · M. Graves, *The House of Lords in the parliaments of Edward VI and Mary I* (1981) · R. M. Warnicke, *The marrying of Anne of Cleves: royal protocol in Tudor England* (2000) · *LP Henry VIII* · *State papers published under … Henry VIII*, 11 vols. (1830–52) · W. K. Jordan, *Edward VI, 1: The young king* (1968) · W. K. Jordan, *Edward VI, 2: The threshold of power* (1970) · R. Strong, *Tudor and Jacobean portraits*, 2 vols. (1969) · J. Youings, 'The council of the west', *TRHS*, 5th ser., 10 (1960), 41–59

Archives Bedford Office, London, papers · Beds. & Luton ARS, estate MSS · Devon RO, estate MSS, W 1258, L. 1258 | BL, Add. MSS · BL, letters to A. Browne, Add. MSS 32648, 32648 · BL, letters to bishop Gardiner and bishop Thirlby, Add. MS 25114 · BL, Harley MSS · BL, letters to Lord Hertford, Add. MS 32654 · BL, Lansdowne MSS · BL, Royal MSS · BL, Sloane MSS · BL, Cotton MSS, letters to Wolsey, etc. · Inner Temple, London, Petyt MS 538/47 · Longleat House, Wiltshire, Seymour MSS · PRO, Chancery papers; duchy of Lancaster papers; lord chamberlain's accounts; Exchequer papers; Privy Council papers; Privy Seal Office papers; ministers' and receivers' accounts; state papers

Likenesses H. Holbein the younger, chalk drawing, 1536–9, Royal Collection [*see illus.*] · oils, *c.*1540 (after H. Holbein the younger), Woburn Abbey, Bedfordshire · double portrait, alabaster tomb effigy, 1555 (with his wife), St Michael's Church, Chenies, Buckinghamshire, Bedford chapel · oils, *c.*1555, Woburn Abbey, Bedfordshire · group portrait, oils on panel, *c.*1570 (*Edward VI and the pope*), NPG

Wealth at death family lands brought over £2000 p.a. in rentals by 1558: L. Stone, *The Crisis of the aristocracy, 1558-1641* (1965), appx VIII, 760 · Youings, *Devon monastic lands*, 5, n.1 · grants and other acquisitions: Willen, *John Russell*, 82–126

Russell, John (*c.*1550–1612), lawyer and author, probably came from a Fife family, but nothing is known of his parents. He is first recorded in 1566, when he received a bachelor's degree from St Leonard's College, in the University of St Andrews; this suggests he was born about 1550. In 1568 he received his MA, and on 28 August 1571, when he was granted a crown pension, he was still described as a student at St Leonard's. He was probably studying law, for on 24 March 1575 he joined the Faculty of Advocates. However, he does not appear to have practised much at first; instead he began to teach, and on 23 March 1580 was called 'doctor utriusque juris' ('doctor of civil and canon law').

From the early 1580s Russell's practice at the bar expanded greatly. In Scotland, unlike in England, a lawyer could plead for clients in criminal cases, and Russell became a criminal specialist. Pitcairn's *Ancient Criminal Trials*, selected from manuscript sources, shows Russell in fifty-eight cases between 1580 and 1612, more than any other lawyer. He appeared in some of the most famous and important trials in Scottish history, including the witchcraft trials of Barbara Napier and Euphame MacCalzean, and the 1593 treason trial of the earl of Bothwell. He also had a flourishing civil practice. In 1599 he successfully defended the Edinburgh minister Robert Bruce when James VI tried to deprive him of his pension. On 19 May 1590 he made a Latin oration at Queen Anne's entry into Edinburgh. In 1604 he wrote a tract entitled *A Treatise of the Happie and Blissed Unioun*, supporting further union between England and Scotland. It survives in two manuscripts, one a first draft, the other an Anglicized version sent to the king in London; the Scottish version was printed in 1985 by the Scottish History Society.

Russell's is one of the longest of twenty-eight surviving treatises that formed part of the union debate in Scotland and England between 1603 and 1605. It is organized as a three-part dialectic, containing arguments first against the union, then in favour of it, and finally refuting the contrary and affirming the positive positions. An appendix contains some practical suggestions. The principal reason given for a union is the increased strength that this will give a united Great Britain, in both religion and secular policy. But Russell approaches his topic as a patriotic lowland Scot. Any union must treat the two countries as equals and not subordinate Scotland to England: 'God forbid! Bettir that we of this age had nevir bein borne, than to sie that miserie in our tyme, thairby to amit [lose] that libertie quhilk our predicessoris have sua lang enjoyit' (Russell, 84). The treatise reveals Russell's characteristics in many other fields, as a committed protestant with an abiding hatred for 'Papistis, falselie callit catholiques' (ibid., 117), and as a well-read man able to quote classical authors from Plato to Eusebius, and moderns such as Machiavelli and Bodin. As befits a doctor of civil and canon law, he mentions various Roman law writers, and cites papal decretals. He decries the lawlessness and disobedience of borderers, highlanders, and princely nobles who think themselves above the law. He produces some astute analyses. He predicts that if the king does not return to reside from time to time in Scotland, the result will be 'ane aristocracie' and the loss of 'the heartis of his people heir' (ibid., 102), a fair description of what happened in the covenanting revolution of 1637–41.

Russell emerges in both his career and his treatise as an honest but difficult person. In 1602 he ruthlessly pursued three people whom he suspected of burning his house. On 13 May 1609 he refused to obey a direct command from the privy council ordering him to defend Sir James MacDonald of Dunyvaig in a criminal trial. In the treatise, while Russell heaps praise on King James, he also scatters criticisms and unwelcome advice throughout the text; much of this was eliminated from the final draft, but some remained. This may help explain why Russell was rarely employed on public business. Russell had at least two sons, John (born before 4 March 1584), who became a lawyer, and James. He married Marion Carmichael on 17 November 1596, but must have had an earlier wife who was John's mother. He was successful enough to acquire the lands of Wester Granton in Edinburghshire. He died on 7 October 1612. In his inventory, his library was valued at £133 Scots and the king owed him £1200 Scots. His total estate, exclusive of his lands, was worth £2386 Scots.

MICHAEL WASSER

Sources J. Russell, 'A treatise of the happie and blissed unioun', *The Jacobean union: six tracts of 1604*, ed. B. R. Galloway and B. P. Levack, Scottish History Society, 4th ser., 21 (1985), 75–142 • F. J. Grant, ed., *The Faculty of Advocates in Scotland, 1532–1943*, Scottish RS, 145 (1944) • R. Pitcairn, ed., *Ancient criminal trials in Scotland*, 7 pts in 3, Bannatyne Club, 42 (1833) • J. M. Anderson, ed., *Early records of the University of St Andrews*, Scottish History Society, 3rd ser., 8 (1926) • B. R. Galloway and B. P. Levack, 'Introduction', *The Jacobean union: six tracts of 1604*, ed. B. R. Galloway and B. P. Levack, Scottish History Society, 4th ser., 21 (1985), ix–lxxx • commissary court of Edinburgh, NA Scot., CC8/8/47, fols. 294r–294v • *CSP Scot.*, 1589–95; 1597–1603 • J. M. Thomson and others, eds., *Registrum magni sigilli regum Scotorum / The register of the great seal of Scotland*, 11 vols. (1882–1914), vols. 4, 6 • M. Livingstone, D. Hay Fleming, and others, eds., *Registrum secreti sigilli regum Scotorum / The register of the privy seal of Scotland*, 6–8 (1963–82) • *Reg. PCS*, 1st ser., vol. 6 • J. Bain, ed., *The border papers: calendar of letters and papers relating to the affairs of the borders of England and Scotland*, 2 vols. (1894–6), vol. 1 • D. Calderwood, *The history of the Kirk of Scotland*, ed. T. Thomson and D. Laing, 8 vols., Wodrow Society, 7 (1842–9) • D. Stevenson, *Scotland's last royal wedding* (1997)
Archives BL, MS treatise, Royal MS 18.A.LXXVI • NL Scot., MS treatise, Advocates' MS 31.4.7
Wealth at death £2386 Scots excl. lands: NA Scot., commissary court of Edinburgh, CC8/8/47, fols. 294r–294v

Russell, John, fourth duke of Bedford (1710–1771), politician, was the second son of Wriothesley Russell, second duke of Bedford (1680–1711), landowner, and his wife, Elizabeth (1681/2–1724), daughter and heir of John Howland of Streatham, Surrey, and Elizabeth Child. He was born in Streatham on 30 September 1710 and was known as Lord John Russell until he succeeded to the dukedom on the death of his elder brother, on 23 October 1732. After being educated at home he went, at the age of nineteen, on the grand tour. On 11 October 1731 he married Lady Diana Spencer (1710–1735), youngest daughter of Charles *Spencer, third earl of Sunderland (1674/5–1722), politician, and Lady Anne Churchill (1683–1716), second daughter of the first duke of Marlborough. She died of consumption on 27 September 1735, their only son having died on the day of his birth, 11 November 1732. On 2 April 1737 Russell married Lady Gertrude Leveson-Gower (1718/19–1794), the eldest daughter of John Leveson-*Gower, first Earl Gower (1694–1754), politician, and his first wife, Evelyn Pierrepont (1691–1727). His second wife took a keen interest in politics and exerted a certain amount of influence over her husband's decision-making. They had two sons and a daughter. The younger son died in infancy; the daughter, Caroline (1743–1811), married, on 23 August 1762, George *Spencer, duke of Marlborough (1739–1817); the elder son, Francis (1739–1767), styled marquess of Tavistock from birth, married, in 1764, Elizabeth, youngest

John Russell, fourth duke of Bedford (1710–1771), by Thomas Gainsborough, c.1770

daughter of William Keppel, second earl of Albemarle. Tavistock died on 22 March 1767, leaving his eldest son, Francis, to succeed his grandfather as fifth duke of Bedford.

The fourth duke of Bedford was not tall; Chesterfield referred to him as his 'bright little grace'. Lord Charlemont commented: 'The duke, a man of excellent parts, though deficient in common sense, was in the highest degree passionate, but perfectly good natured' (*Charlemont MSS*, 1.10). Bedford had a keen sense of his own importance, and his pride and arrogance frequently caused offence. He was certainly strong-willed. But he also had an unwavering sense of duty, though this did not always transform itself into willingness to complete the more mundane tasks connected with the ministerial offices that he held.

Though much of Bedford's life was dominated by his political career he devoted much time to his estates, employing Philip Millar, the eminent botanist, as an assistant. He took an interest in improving the streets around his London residence and supported the paving of Regent Street; he also introduced turnpike bills. He was of a convivial disposition and enjoyed the leisure pursuits offered in both Bedfordshire and London. He regularly attended the opera and the theatre, and patronized David Garrick and Gainsborough. He and his second wife also indulged in amateur theatricals, and the duchess was said to have been particularly fond of acting at Woburn. A keen sportsman, Bedford enjoyed watching cricket, hunting, and yachting—he owned a yacht himself. Throughout much of his life, however, he suffered from ill health;

he was plagued by gout and regularly took the waters at Bath. In later years he was nearly blinded by cataracts.

Early political career Arrangements had been made for Russell to enter the House of Commons but, following his brother Wriothesley's death in 1732 without an heir, he succeeded as fourth duke. He initially devoted time to restoring the family fortune, concentrating on improving the family estates and its London properties, and developing commercial interests; in time he became one of the wealthiest men in Britain, with an estimated income of £30,000. He quickly became engrossed in affairs of state, and began his political career as a follower of William Pulteney and Lord Carteret, in opposition to Walpole. In 1734 he introduced his first motion in the Lords, against corrupt practices in the election of Scottish peers; it was defeated but he revived the issue in 1735. He backed Carteret's motion supporting the prince of Wales's right to £100,000 a year from the civil list, and in 1738 he spoke against Walpole's determination to retain peaceful relations with Spain, taking the side of London merchants. After Walpole's fall in 1742 he declared his hope 'that obnoxious men might now be removed, good men put into their room and a change of measures brought about as well as men' (Wiffen, 2.343). He was not invited to join the new ministry dominated by Carteret, and remained in opposition. In February 1743 he attacked the government's plan to fund 16,000 Hanoverian troops, and in April 1744 he opposed the extension of the law of treason.

First lord of the Admiralty Bedford joined the new Pelham ministry, formed in the wake of Carteret's retirement after the collapse of his foreign policy. In November 1744 he was appointed first lord of the Admiralty and on 25 December he was sworn of the privy council. In 1746 he was rewarded with the post—linked to the navy—of wardenship of the New Forest. His period at the Admiralty was not unsuccessful, although it is probable that its major achievements were largely due to the talents of Lord Sandwich, his protégé, and to Admiral Anson, whom he appointed to the Admiralty board. Measures were taken to pension off elderly officers, enabling the navy to look to younger men. The navy also went through a major refit, which was undoubtedly a decisive factor in its successful capture of the fortress of Louisbourg on the island of Cape Breton in 1745. Of less immediate military significance was the introduction of official naval uniforms, supposedly inspired by an outfit worn by the duchess. Bedford did not shirk from disciplining his admirals, and he dismissed Admiral Vernon, who wanted to appoint officers without reference to the board and was accused of criticizing the Admiralty in print. It is also clear that Bedford was keen to address the hardships endured by the ordinary sailor; having left the Admiralty he condemned press gangs as 'detrimental to trade and to the liberty of the subject' (*Correspondence*, 2.13). He also supported Grenville's bill of 1757 for the punctual payment of seamen.

During the Jacobite rising of 1745 Bedford was responsible for initiating a scheme—against the inclination of the Pelhams—for landowners to raise volunteer regiments at their own expense. However, ill health prevented him from accompanying his own regiment, in which he held the rank of colonel, although he did join it in Edinburgh, after Culloden. The gap between Bedford and the Pelhams was further illustrated, in 1746, by the cabinet's rejection of his plan for the conquest of Canada.

Secretary of state In February 1748 Lord Chesterfield resigned as secretary of state for the north. Newcastle eventually replaced him; Bedford became southern secretary and Sandwich took the Admiralty. In 1749 Bedford was made knight of the Garter and in 1751 lord lieutenant of Devon, having received the same honour, in 1745, in his home county of Bedfordshire. Bedford and the Pelhams formed an uneasy partnership. Henry Pelham was clearly frustrated by the amount of time that Bedford spent at his seat in Woburn, enjoying the diversions provided by his estate and sporting pursuits. Newcastle's relationship with Bedford was even more strained, making co-operation between the two secretaries very difficult. They clashed over Sandwich's peace mission to The Hague; Newcastle expected to be consulted first but Sandwich usually chose to turn to Bedford. During these negotiations Bedford strongly favoured peace, occasionally against the national interest; he even went as far as suggesting that Gibraltar should be ceded to Spain in order to hasten negotiations. He was also concerned that further campaigning might undermine the peace talks. That said, he did criticize Newcastle for 'too strong and too implicit a reliance on the good faith of France' (*Correspondence*, 1.453).

Newcastle rapidly lost patience with Bedford, who was unwilling to allow any interference in his office. Newcastle was also uneasy about Bedford's close relationship with the king, George II, and the duke of Cumberland. When the king went to Hanover, Newcastle accompanied him, taking the opportunity to influence him against Bedford, who was accused of inattention to the duties of his office. The king refused to dismiss Bedford but in 1751 the Pelham brothers circumvented his opposition by removing Sandwich, fully realizing that Bedford would resign in protest. Having done so Bedford was offered the presidency of the council, which he refused, realizing that it was impossible for him to work with the Pelhams. By then he was head of a political faction soon to comprise a dozen peers and rather more MPs.

Opposing the Pelhams Though not a natural opponent of the king's measures Bedford quickly warmed to the task of combating Pelham and Newcastle. In 1752 he stood alone in denouncing the scheme for a new subsidiary treaty with Saxony. In March he attacked the ministry on the bill for purchasing Scottish forfeited estates. On Hardwicke's Marriage Bill of 1753 he argued that 'clandestine marriages … are marriages of love and more likely to be productive of useful subjects than the prudential marriages made by parents' (G. F. Thomas, 35). He also attacked the Jewish Naturalization Act and demonstrated that he was willing to take his opposition outside parliament. Allying himself with William Beckford he employed James Ralph to set up *The Protestor*, which ran from June to November 1753, feeding public hostility towards the 'Jew Bill'.

After the duke of Newcastle had become head of the administration, on the death of his brother Pelham in 1754, Bedford formed an alliance with Henry Fox, who was made secretary of state in the autumn of 1755. Fox succeeded in persuading Bedford to take a more sympathetic attitude towards the government. As a result Bedford agreed to support the Russian and Hessian subsidiary treaties, though he refused to take office. However, as relations with France deteriorated Bedford accepted that war was likely and allowed his supporters, who included Sandwich, Richard Rigby, and Gower, to accept posts in the ministry. Yet he remained resolute in his views on the way that the campaign should be fought. He strenuously resisted the payment of subsidies to continental allies, preferring to back a predominantly naval campaign.

Lord lieutenant of Ireland Bedford was involved in the ministerial negotiations of 1756, although he failed in his bid to effect an alliance between Pitt and Fox. He eventually accepted the office of lord lieutenant of Ireland on 15 December 1756, in a Pitt-dominated ministry with the duke of Devonshire as its titular head. Though displeased by the Pitt–Newcastle ministry of June 1757 he did not tender his resignation and refused to be dislodged when Pitt attempted to replace him with Temple. Before leaving for Ireland his support in parliament for the Militia Bill involved him in disturbances in Bedfordshire, where as lord lieutenant he was responsible for organizing the militia; in June 1757 crowds gathered to resist militia recruitment and even threatened Woburn Abbey.

Bedford and Pitt were not on cordial terms at the beginning of the viceroyalty, and Bedford's relationship with Newcastle was also decidedly chilly. Newcastle admitted that there was no 'great personal confidence, or regard' between Bedford and himself (BL, Add. MS 32873, fol. 188). Though Bedford was an experienced politician it does seem that he underestimated the challenge facing him in Ireland. He was certain that a new approach to Irish government could ensure a peaceful session, and his recipe for success was to govern Ireland without favouring any of the Irish parliamentary managers—or undertakers, as they were known. He did consider governing through a single undertaker but his choice was Lord Kildare, whose following was not large enough to provide a majority in the Commons and who was not reliable on popular questions. Both methods of government proved unacceptable to the other senior undertakers, John Ponsonby and Primate Stone.

The first session of Bedford's administration was dominated by controversy over the Irish pension list. A pension awarded to the princess of Hesse-Cassel on the Irish establishment aroused anger in Ireland, and Bedford compounded this by securing a stipend for his sister-in-law Lady Betty Waldegrave. This was a calamitous error of judgement. The Commons drew up a remonstrance,

threatening to reject the session's money bill if Bedford refused to transmit it to London. After the supporters of Stone and Ponsonby deserted government on a trial vote Bedford was forced to comply. He wrote to Pitt, requesting that he should be allowed to make dismissals, but Pitt, who was friendly with Stone, insisted that he adopt a more temperate approach. A government investigation of abuses at the revenue board—the fiefdom of John Ponsonby—further alienated Stone and Ponsonby and they refused to attend any further government meetings at Dublin Castle. At the end of the session Bedford considered ways of avoiding appointing Ponsonby and Stone as lords justices, such as extending his own residency or naming a lord deputy. But these were deemed impractical, and following pressure from the British ministry and the point-blank refusal by Kildare to co-operate with the other undertakers Bedford was forced to give way and nominate Stone and Ponsonby, along with Lord Shannon. The triumph of the Irish political magnates over Bedford owed much to the unwillingness of Pitt and Newcastle to stir up another Irish crisis while Britain was at war. But Bedford's deficiencies in character, ability, and connections also played their part in his failure.

Bedford's second session, beginning in October 1759, saw Stone and Ponsonby continuing as the chief parliamentary managers. However, the independent MPs John Hely-Hutchinson and Edmund Sexton Pery attacked the government with some success. Hely-Hutchinson played a part in fomenting a violent demonstration by the Dublin crowd against British cattle buyers. But this was overshadowed by an anti-union riot on 3 December 1759. The riot was reputedly provoked by a rumour that the Commons was implementing legislation to facilitate the passing of an act of union between Britain and Ireland. Richard Rigby, Bedford's chief secretary, was forced to flee Dublin. Bedford claimed that the crowd had been composed primarily of Presbyterian weavers but Pitt refused to accept this explanation, preferring to blame Catholic insurgents. Bedford was eventually forced to capitulate and accept the version fabricated by the British government.

Bedford returned to England in June 1760 but continued to be plagued by Irish difficulties. In December the lords justices refused to transmit a money bill that did not originate in the Irish commons. Stone and Ponsonby again took a lead in this affair. Bedford, with the support of Fox, Bute, and the king, was against a compromise but Pitt carried the day and another Irish crisis was avoided through a British concession. Bedford's tenure as viceroy was not impressive; his treatment of the undertaker factions had been inconsistent and he had frequently displayed a lamentable lack of judgement, although it is clear that his task was hindered by an irresolute and divided British ministry. When Bedford was offered the court post of master of the horse in place of the lord lieutenancy Stone deemed it to be particularly suitable for his talents: 'human creatures certainly ought not to be subjected to him; but to have made him keeper of the lions in the

Tower would yet have been more unexceptionable' (*Beaufort MSS*, 230). Yet Bedford's sympathetic attitude towards Ireland's oppressed Catholic majority must be commended. This was not a popular stance, given that in 1760 the French commander Thurot made a temporarily successful landing at Carrickfergus. Moreover despite the somewhat ignominious end to his viceroyalty Bedford was invited to return to Ireland in September 1768 to be installed as chancellor of Trinity College, Dublin, replacing the duke of Cumberland. His reception was warm, possibly because the corn bounty that he had introduced in 1758 had reaped generous rewards for Ireland.

Peace negotiator During his time as viceroy Bedford's relationship with Pitt had been less than harmonious, and tension between the two men was increased by their wildly divergent views on the conduct of the Seven Years' War. As early as 1759 Bedford had begun to have doubts about the wisdom of continuing hostilities. British forces had already seen some considerable success, notably General Wolfe's victory in Quebec. Bedford felt that the wisest move at this point would be to secure a peace and that extending the war could prove disastrous. In the new reign, of George III, he formed a loose attachment with Bute on the grounds that they both favoured a cessation of hostilities. In 1760 he tried to persuade Newcastle to remain in the ministry, fearing the effects that it would have on the peace negotiations were he to resign. Bedford did not have an official office in government, although he still maintained contact with ministers, and on the instructions of the king he continued to be sent state papers. Indeed his influence increased as peace became more popular within the government, and he was regularly summoned to the cabinet by the peace party, who knew that he would stand up to the chief war hawks, Pitt and Temple.

Bedford's views on the proposed peace between Britain and France were out of touch with public opinion but in many ways he demonstrated a shrewd understanding of foreign relations. First, he pointed out the dangers of removing the French threat from America:

> I don't know whether the neighbourhood of the French to our North American Colonies was not the greatest security for their dependence on the mother country, which I feel will be slighted by them when their apprehension of the French is removed.   (Corbett, 2.173n)

Bedford also warned that a harsh peace treaty punishing France would not guarantee peace in Europe for long. He observed:

> at the same time we are fair to ourselves, let us be just to others, and not think to impose such terms on France, as we are sure she cannot long acquiesce under and which, when she has taken breath she will take the first opportunity of breaking.   (BL, Add. MS 32922, fol. 452)

At the same time he argued:

> to drive France entirely out of any naval power is fighting against nature, and can tend to no one good to this country, but on the contrary must excite all the naval powers in Europe to enter a confederacy against us.   (Ayling, 284)

Bedford questioned whether Canada should be retained. He was also willing to be flexible on Guadeloupe, Senegal, Goree, and exclusive rights to the Newfoundland fisheries. In Namier's view 'he had declared against a strengthening of the British position … in every single corner of what was the classical Empire diagram in 1761' (Namier, 276). He even appeared to doubt the value of British victories; at one point he warned that 'another victory in either of the Indies would undo us' (Ayling, 284).

In August 1761 Bedford refused to attend any further cabinet meetings after Pitt subjected his colleagues to a particularly violent harangue on the need to step up the war. Hardwicke said that 'the Duke of Bedford stood by us very manfully' (Ayling, 288). For Bedford the make-up of the ministry was becoming increasingly unpalatable. He regarded the influence enjoyed by Bute, the king's favourite, as unconstitutional. But as Bute and the king favoured peace Bedford was willing to stand by them, and following Pitt's resignation on 25 November 1761 he became privy seal. Owing to a fit of gout he was not involved in the decision to declare war on Spain, although Temple berated him in the Lords over his lukewarm views on this. In February 1762 he introduced a motion against the continuation of the war in Germany. Bute, though implicated with Bedford in keeping the peace preliminaries secret from Fredrick II, opposed the motion. In July 1762, when it was determined that Bedford should take charge of the peace negotiations, the abandoning of Prussia became a reality.

Bedford arrived in Paris on 12 September 1762. His mission did not get off to an auspicious start, for he had been hissed as he went through the streets of London. Moreover he was incensed by the need to submit the preliminaries to the king prior to approval. Lord Egremont, who was hostile to Bedford, was probably behind this decision—he referred to Bedford as one 'who for our misfortune is irrevocably our plenipotentiary in Paris' (Smith, 1.480)—although Bute was most likely also responsible. Bedford was also angered by indirect communications sent by British ministers to the duc de Nivernais, the French ambassador in London.

Bedford's handling of the negotiations clearly demonstrated his flaws as a politician. He was stubbornly determined to follow his own instincts, and as a result exceeded his instructions. Indeed his desperation for peace came near to costing Britain the benefits of important naval victories. Walpole observed:

> Bad as that peace proved, it was near being concluded on terms still more disadvantageous; for France, receiving earlier intelligence than we did of the capture of the Havannah had near prevailed on the Duke of Bedford to sign the Treaty.   (Walpole, 1.157)

Bedford certainly found the capture of Havana embarrassing but he was able to use it to gain Florida. His Francophilia, his enlightened approach to trade, and his determination not to impose an unrealistic treaty explain some of the more generous elements in the peace preliminaries signed by him on 3 November 1762; the final treaty was signed in Paris on 10 February 1763. Bute, with not a little insincerity, stated that 'no man had ever rendered so great a service to his king and country and that there was not a man in the kingdom could have done it but the Duke of Bedford' (*Correspondence*, 3.201). Bedford, however, having felt that he had been betrayed during the peace negotiations, reserved a good deal of his animosity for Bute and would spend much of the remainder of his political career fighting against the secret influence supposedly wielded by the royal favourite.

The Grenville ministry Before his return from Paris, Bedford was informed by Bute of his resignation and urged to take office as president of the council. Bedford refused the offer, suggesting that certain great whig lords—namely Newcastle, Devonshire, Hardwicke, and Grafton—should be invited to join the ministry. Bedford was more amenable after Egremont's death but his attempts to negotiate a return alongside Pitt came to nothing, as he found that Pitt would no longer agree to co-operate with him. As a result the incensed Bedford agreed to join George Grenville's ministry. On 9 September 1763 he was made lord president of the council, on the condition that Bute would not play a role in government. In the debate on the address in November he defended the peace against Temple's criticisms. On 6 December he attacked the City of London for not being more assertive against the Wilkite rioters. Bedford's relationship with Grenville was somewhat stormy; they disagreed over the distribution of patronage, and Bedford's attendance at cabinet meetings became less regular. Historians have seen Bedford's determination to secure the lion's share of patronage on behalf of his supporters as the guiding principle of his political career.

During the regency dispute of April 1765 Bedford successfully opposed Northington's wish to include the princess dowager in any possible regency, primarily because he feared that this would allow Bute to dominate. In May Bedford's willingness to support free trade was further illustrated by his opposing a prohibitive duty on foreign silks. Despite being the sole speaker he persuaded the house to reject the bill and was said to have spoken with 'uncommon harshness' of the Spitalfields weavers (*Annual Register*, 1765, 8.42). London's weavers reacted angrily and a riot occurred on 15 May; Bedford's coach was attacked and he was hit on the temple with a stone. On reaching his house he permitted two of the leaders a personal interview. However, he failed to satisfy the protesters, and on 17 May they surrounded his house in Bloomsbury Square, preventing him from leaving. Troops were eventually required to disperse the crowd, although further riots occurred outside his house on 20 May. Both the duke and duchess believed that Bute was to blame for inciting the disorder.

The king's dissatisfaction with his ministers—particularly Bedford, whose intervention in the regency dispute had not been welcome—led him to seek assistance from Pitt. But Pitt's negotiations to form a new ministry failed, and on 23 May Grenville and Bedford issued a number of conditions for their remaining in office. These included the proscription of Bute and the acceptance of Weymouth—a Bedford supporter whose private life was frowned upon by George III—as lord lieutenant of Ireland.

The king's anger was more pronounced following a meeting with Bedford on 12 June. Bedford presented the king with a list of minutes—effectively non-negotiable demands—going through them point by point. He announced to George III in very plain language that if Bute were not excluded from the king's circle of advisers he should consider the ministry to have tendered its resignation. He also implicitly accused the king of breaking his word with regard to Bute. Bedford's blunt manner, willingness to dictate terms to the king, and inability to let the matter drop, even after Bute had been excluded, led the king to resolve to deny Bedford future ministerial office. He referred to 'the insolent treatment I have met with, unexampled before' and 'the late arrogant declaration of the Duke of Bedford in the name of his colleagues in which my favour was insisted on and my very deportment regulated' (*Correspondence of George III*, 1.123). Bedford certainly overstepped the mark but he must be given credit for standing against the king when many of his ministerial colleagues, though holding the same views, avoided the responsibility. He was dismissed as lord president on 12 July, when George III removed the Grenville ministry.

The American crisis Bedford's opposition to the incoming Rockingham ministry focused on its American policy, and in particular the planned repeal of the Stamp Act passed by Grenville in 1765 to tax the colonies. Though never a warmonger Bedford believed in firm control over Britain's colonies, and in his view the resistance of the Americans denied the authority of the British parliament. He was active in the Lords, disrupting the Rockinghams by tabling motions and calling for papers relating to the American crisis. He also sought another audience with George III in a bid to persuade the king not to countenance repeal of the Stamp Act. In this case, however, the king refused to intervene in a matter that was before parliament.

When in July 1766 the Rockinghams were replaced with a ministry led by Pitt (now raised to the peerage as earl of Chatham) Bedford entered into negotiations, but Chatham would not accede to the Bedfords' patronage demands. At the same time Bedford's chief parliamentary man of business, Richard Rigby, made it clear that he would prefer an alliance in opposition with the Grenvilles. Bedford, however, had no desire to oppose. As Grenville put it: 'He thought the melancholy and disordered state of the kingdom such as required all the assistance it could receive; and therefore he doubted whether he and his friends should disturb the government' (Smith, 3.380–81). George III was happy to take the Bedfords into government, but as individuals rather than as a party. Again the Bedfords have been condemned for their greed, but party unity and securing senior offices was obviously of primary importance, particularly to success in shaping policy. On 25 February 1767 Bedford moved for papers relating to America. However his interest in politics was disrupted by the death of his son, the marquess of Tavistock, who had been thrown from his horse. Bedford was attacked for lack of emotion when he returned to politics in April, a criticism that was more applicable on the death of his daughter-in-law shortly afterwards. He entered that fact in his diary and then went to the opera.

Matters came to a head in April 1767, when Bedford attacked the part of the Massachusetts Act that constituted a pardon for those resisting British taxation. He had not informed the Rockinghams and so did not receive their support. George III was also displeased, describing Bedford's motion as ill timed and unprecedented. Yet some unity among the opposition groups persisted, and Bedford was using the sort of language that would certainly have appealed to the Rockinghams. He said that his party's aim 'was to restore the strength and energy to the king's Government upon a constitutional footing free from *favouritism* and the *guidance* of a minister not in responsible employment'. He talked of the opposition uniting 'to rescue his Majesty and this country out of the hands of the Earl of Bute' (*Correspondence*, 3.373–4). Bedford's negotiations with the other opposition parties continued, and he came near to closing a deal with the Rockinghams in July 1767. However, any such alliance would have involved a fudge on America. The two parties also disagreed on who should lead the Commons. Bedford, very reasonably, was willing to take a Rockinghamite but would not have Henry Conway, and suggested Dowdeswell in his place. Conway was probably rejected, not because he was soft on the American colonies but because he had already shown his weakness as Commons leader.

Return to government The failure of the Rockingham alliance, and Grafton's realization that his ministry's stability depended on the accession of a group like the Bedfords, enabled Bedford to return to government, although he did not take up office himself. By 18 December 1767 the negotiations with Grafton, acting prime minister since Chatham was unwell, were complete and George III was forced to accept the Bedfords—as a party, not individuals—into office. For the Bedfords a return to government was the most sensible step; being a junior partner in government was preferable to being a junior partner in opposition. At the same time Bedford's age made the comforts of government more attractive, and some of his more place-hungry supporters were getting restless.

On 20 December Bedford underwent an operation on his cataracts that was only partially successful. From this point his role in public affairs was minor, although he continued to attend the Lords, taking a hard line on America. He also maintained his active social life and constant supervision of his estates. In July 1769 he visited Devon, where he was lord lieutenant and had extensive lands, to prevent a pro-Wilkite petition from being drafted. While being granted the freedom of Exeter he was met by a hostile crowd and was forced to escape from the cathedral via a secret passage. He continued on his tour, visiting Okehampton and Tavistock, but when he reached Honiton his coach was attacked and its windows smashed. From 1769 his health deteriorated rapidly, and in the spring of 1770 he became partially paralysed. He died at Bedford House, Bloomsbury, on 15 January 1771 and was buried in the family vaults at Chenies, Buckinghamshire, five days later.

Conclusions As a politician Bedford had an inflated view of his own capabilities. However, he was not unintelligent and was capable of forming his own views. He was certainly not the puppet of Richard Rigby and his wife, as some historians have suggested. Though not a brilliant speaker he was a capable orator and performed reasonably well in the Lords; he was usually well versed in the subject matter under discussion. However, he did not always take his responsibilities as a minister seriously and was easily distracted by the attractions of Woburn. At the same time his political instincts occasionally failed him, and in admittedly difficult circumstances he performed poorly as viceroy in Ireland. His American policy should be judged less harshly; he was prepared to take a hard line and in many cases his views were not so divergent from politicians of other parties—indeed, they reflected British public opinion. Moreover it is evident that for much of his political career he was an advocate of peaceful relations with Britain's continental neighbours.

Accusations of rapacity are also wide of the mark. The Bedfords did ask for better places and made fewer conditions about policy than their rivals but their low numbers made this strategy essential. Though a smaller group than the Rockinghams the Bedfords certainly acted as a party and practised collective resignation. In many ways they were much better organized as a party than their opponents, although this was mostly due to the skills of Richard Rigby. Bedford himself worked tirelessly on behalf of his followers, and in the later stages of his career had no ambition to take office himself. In the final years of his political life he was able to stand up to the king and force him to admit the Bedfords into government as a party rather than as individuals. Ultimately his strength as leader ensured that the Bedford group survived his death by more than ten years.   MARTYN J. POWELL

Sources DNB · *Correspondence of John, fourth duke of Bedford*, ed. J. Russell, 3 vols. (1842–6) · G. F. Thomas, 'John, fourth duke of Bedford', PhD diss., U. Wales, 1953 · M. J. Powell, 'An early imperial problem: Britain and Ireland, 1750–1783', PhD diss., U. Wales, 1997 · J. Brooke, *The Chatham administration, 1766–1768* (1956) · P. Lawson, *George Grenville: a political life* (1984) · N. A. M. Rodger, *The insatiable earl: a life of John Montagu, fourth earl of Sandwich* (1993) · P. D. G. Thomas, *British politics and the Stamp Act crisis: the first phase of the American revolution, 1763–1767* (1975) · P. D. G. Thomas, *The Townshend duties crisis: the second phase of the American revolution, 1767–1773* (1987) · R. Pares, *King George III and the politicians* (1953) · P. Langford, *A polite and commercial people: England, 1727–1783* (1989) · *The manuscripts of the duke of Beaufort … the earl of Donoughmore*, HMC, 27 (1891) · *The Grenville papers: being the correspondence of Richard Grenville … and … George Grenville*, ed. W. J. Smith, 4 vols. (1852–3) · H. Walpole, *Memoirs of the reign of King George the Third*, ed. G. F. R. Barker, 4 vols. (1894); repr. (1970) · *The correspondence of King George the Third from 1760 to December 1783*, ed. J. Fortescue, 6 vols. (1927–8) · *The manuscripts and correspondence of James, first earl of Charlemont*, 2 vols., HMC, 28 (1891–4) · S. Ayling, *The elder Pitt* (1976) · J. S. Corbett, *England in the Seven Years War*, 2 (1907) · L. Namier, *England in the age of the American revolution*, 2nd edn (1961) · J. H. Wiffen, *Memoirs of the house of Russell*, 2 vols. (1833) · Newcastle papers, BL, Add. MSS 32873, 32922 · GEC, *Peerage*

Archives PRO NIre., transcripts · Woburn Abbey, Woburn, Bedfordshire, MSS | BL, Newcastle papers · BL, corresp. with Lord Bute, Add. MSS 38191 · BL, corresp. with George Grenville, Add. MS 57811 · BL, corresp. with 1st and 2nd earls of Hardwicke, Add. MSS 35465–35692 · BL, corresp. with Lord Holland, Add. MS 51385 · BL, corresp. with Lord Holderness, Eg. MS 3413 · BL, corresp. with duke of Newcastle, Lord, Albemarle etc., Add. MSS 32689–33079 *passim* · Derbys. RO, corresp. rel. to Ireland · Derbys. RO, letters to Lord Lieutenant of Ireland · Mount Stuart Trust Archive, corresp. with Lord Bute · NMM, corresp. with earl of Sandwich · PRO, corresp. as minister in Paris, 30/50 · PRO, letters to Lord Chatham, 30/8 · Sheff. Arch., corresp. with Lord Rockingham · Trustees of Chatsworth Settlement, letters to dukes of Devonshire · U. Nott., corresp. with duke of Newcastle, Henry Pelham, Lord Sandwich, Sir T. Robinson, col., Yorke, B. Keene, Mr Durand

Likenesses G. Knapton, oils, 1747, Brooks's Club, London, Society of Dilettanti · J. Reynolds, oils, c.1759–1762, Woburn Abbey, Bedfordshire · T. Gainsborough, oils, 1764, Woburn Abbey, Bedfordshire · T. Gainsborough, oils, c.1770, NPG [see illus.] · J. Reynolds, engraving (after T. Gainsborough, 1764), repro. in Russell, ed., *Correspondence of John*, vol. 1

Russell, John (1745–1806), portrait painter and astronomer, was born on 29 March 1745 at 32 High Street, Guildford, the second child of John Russell (1711–1804), book- and printseller, five times mayor of Guildford, and an artist himself (his *Prospects of Guildford* were engraved and published in 1759 and 1782), and his wife, Ann Parvish (1719–1775).

Early career and religious conversion John Russell was baptized in the ruins of Holy Trinity Church, Guildford, and educated at the local grammar school before winning premiums at the Society of Arts in 1759 and 1760. He was then apprenticed to the painter Francis Cotes, who became a friend and mentor, and painted a miniature of his promising pupil. This happy relationship was frequently endangered by Russell's religious 'conversion', which began with an entry on the title-page of his diary, decorated with a stony desert and a view of Golgotha in the background: 'John Russell converted September 30, 1764, aetat. 19, at about half an hour after seven in the evening' (Russell). This prompted an evangelical ardour. For example, while painting Lord Montagu's portrait at Cowdray House in 1767, Russell not only annoyed the household by his intrusive fanaticism but excited such ill feeling among the many Anglicans and Roman Catholics of the neighbourhood that on his return journey he was refused accommodation at all the inns in Midhurst. Even his fellow citizens of Guildford rioted in protest.

In 1768 Russell settled in London, first in Portland Street, where he painted, in 1769, an oil portrait of the notorious forger Dr William Dodd (NPG). Here he met another celebrated Methodist, Selina Hastings, countess of Huntingdon, who tried unsuccessfully to make him give up painting and to lure him to her religious community. On 5 February 1770 he married one of his 'converts'—Hannah Faden (1745–1816), daughter of a map- and printseller at Charing Cross—and moved to 7 Mortimer Street, Cavendish Square. They lived contentedly there, moving later to Newman Street, and produced twelve children, their religious enthusiasm gradually subsiding.

John Russell (1745–1806), self-portrait, c.1780

Portraits and fancy pictures At about this time Russell turned from oils to pastel, a medium in which he excelled, forming his style on that of Rosalba Carriera. A stream of portraits followed, exhibited first at the Incorporated Society of Artists, then in 1769 at the first exhibition of the Royal Academy, where he continued to show annually until his death in 1806. His pastel portraits are technically and aesthetically brilliant, easily surpassing those of his master, Francis Cotes. They are usually laid on blue paper, the pastel colours vivid, a striking *sfumato* effect achieved by blurring with the finger and crayon, and the details accented with black chalk. In 1770 he showed his *Portrait of George Whitefield* and his large figure *Aquarius* won the Royal Academy's gold medal. He also painted the eleven-year-old William Wilberforce (the work is in the National Portrait Gallery, London), the first of many oil and pastel portraits of the philanthropist who later described Russell as 'A religious man, very high-church indeed.' (R. I. Wilberforce and S. Wilberforce, *The Life of William Wilberforce*, vol. 1, 1838, 5–6). Marriage may have softened Russell's militant evangelicalism but his diary bears daily witness to anxiety for his spiritual welfare. He would not work on a Sunday nor would he allow anyone to enter his studio. He was afraid to go out to dinner on account of the loose and blasphemous conversation he might hear. He was on good terms with Sir Joshua Reynolds, with whom he dined at the Royal Academy, the Dilettanti Society, and the Literary Club, but on these and other festive occasions he always left early.

Dozens of fancy pictures followed, specially of children with dogs, cats, foxes, squirrels, rabbits, and owls. One of these, *Girl with Cherries* (1781), is in the Louvre, and two others, *Fortune-Teller* and *Girl with Cat* (1790 and 1791), are in the Tate Collection. Russell produced hundreds of portraits, many exhibited at the Royal Academy, beginning with three or four a year, and working up to seventeen in 1789 and twenty-one in 1790. One oil, *Charles Wesley* (1771), hangs in Wesley's Chapel, City Road, London; his *Countess of Huntingdon* (1772) was lost in a shipwreck on a voyage to Georgia, and another, *John Wesley* (1773), was also lost but both survive in engravings. From 1781 he tried his hand at painting miniatures, exhibiting nine in the next five years. They are scarce and painted in watercolour or gouache on ivory with broad sweeping strokes of the brush. One of George IV when prince of Wales, is a miniature variant of a pastel in the Fogg Art Museum, Harvard University, which in turn is closely related to his full-length oil of the prince in the uniform of the royal Kentish bowmen, in the Royal Collection. Another is at Corsham Court and two, attributed to Russell, are at Petworth House.

Patronage and technique In 1788 Russell was elected a Royal Academician and in the following year, as a result of his portraits of the king's physician, Dr Willis, and Queen Charlotte and her family, he was appointed painter to the king and the prince of Wales, also to the duke of York. In 1796 he painted the princess of Wales with the little Princess Charlotte on her knee, seen in Russell's house by Joseph Farington, who described 'the manner of the Princess as very affable, witht. the least of German hauteur' (Farington, *Diary*, 11 Nov 1796). His large pastels (91 × 71 cm) of the two famous bathing attendants at Brighton, *John 'Smoaker' Miles* and *Martha Gunn*, were commissioned by the prince of Wales, and both are still in the Royal Collection.

Royal patronage and his own prolific output assured Russell relative affluence. A small freehold estate in Dorking was left him in 1781 by a cousin. His diary records an income of £600 in 1786 and £1000 in 1789, 'and probably on the increase'. He appears to have been well employed as long as he lived, charging about the same high prices as Sir Joshua Reynolds, but he never became a fashionable artist; most of his sitters were connected with the throne, the pulpit, or the stage where, curiously enough, he had many friends. In the latter part of his life he spent much of his time in Yorkshire, specially at Leeds, where he also had many friends and painted some of his best works. Among his pastel portraits, interesting for their subjects, are: *Philip Stanhope*, son and recipient of Lord Chesterfield's letters; *John Bacon*, the sculptor and an intimate friend; *Bartolozzi*, the engraver; *William Cowper*, the poet; *William Wilberforce*, the philanthropist; *Admiral Bligh* of the *Bounty*; *Mrs Jordan*, *Mrs Siddons*, and *Jack and Elizabeth Bannister* of the stage; and *Richard Brinsley Sheridan* (NPG).

In 1772 Russell published his excellent and detailed *Elements of Painting with Crayons*, purporting to explain the technique of Francis Cotes but in fact a handbook to the art of pastel painting. He revised and enlarged it in 1777, and it became popular throughout the nineteenth century. He recommended a strong blue paper, the thicker the better and mounted on linen. The posture he advised was 'sitting with the box of crayons in his lap'. The smudging or *sfumato* effect he described as 'sweetening with the finger'. He made his own crayons, mixing the colours with spirits of wine on a grindstone, then rolling them quickly 'into pastils in the left hand with the ball of the right, first forming them cylindrically and then tapering them at each end' (Williamson, 93-4).

Between 1797 and 1807 Dr Robert John Thornton published *The New Illustration of the Sexual System of Linnaeus*, a great work which included *The Temple of Flora*, illustrated by Philip Reinagle and others. Russell made the frontispiece, and also pastel portraits of Thornton himself (exh. RA, 1799), Mrs Thornton, and other botanists, including Sir James Edward Smith, founder of the Linnean Society (oil), and Dr A. B. Lambert, both in the society's collection in Piccadilly, London.

Russell was also an astronomer: about 1784 he was introduced to Sir William Herschel, whose portrait, holding a diagram of the Georgian planet (Uranus) and its satellites, he painted in 1794 (Science Museum, London). Another sitter was the astronomer royal, Nevil Maskelyne (1804), and several fellows of the Royal Society, including William Hey, Thomas Martyn, and George Keate. His portrait of Dr John Jeffries (NMM) shows the American loyalist crossing the English Channel, with the French astronaut Jean-Pierre Blanchard in an air balloon equipped with scientific instruments. But his interest in astronomy began long before when, as a young man, he was struck by the beauty of the moon seen through a telescope belonging to a friend, the sculptor John Bacon. This developed into serious lunar studies which produced the largest and most accurate picture of the moon to date, a mechanical moon bearing an engraved lunar map (the selenograph), a relief map of the moon, and an engraving of the full moon maps, the lunar plenispheres. In his portrait *Sir Joseph Banks* (oil), the president of the Royal Society is shown holding one of the moon maps. An album in the Museum of the History of Science, Oxford, contains working drawings, with the first sketch labelled: 'Drawn about the Year 1764. This is the first drawing I ever made from the Moon. J. R. in the Garden of John Bacon RA, 17 Newman Street' ('Russell's drawings', fol. 1, appx 3). Joseph Farington took tea with Russell in 1793,

> and was highly gratified by seeing the different representations he has made of the appearance of the Moon—he told us he had been about 7 years engaged in this undertaking … He described to us the manifest errors which have been given by others. That of Cassini is very incorrect. (Farington, *Diary*, 9 Dec 1793)

Last years Russell's diary, kept in the Victoria and Albert Museum Library, was written in the Byrom shorthand system, and deciphered and indexed by his grandson, the Revd S. H. Russell, in 1871. A specimen page is illustrated in

Williamson (p. 96). It begins with his conversion on 30 September 1764 and ends on 4 January 1801. In December 1800 Russell injured himself by a fall through a broken cellar-flap, and early in 1801 he caught his finger in a steel trap which prevented his working for some weeks. In 1803 he became deaf after an attack of cholera, but he was none the less able to produce what is believed to be the largest pastel picture ever painted, *Lady Johnstone and her Family and a Greyhound* (185 x 140 cm; priv. coll., Yorkshire). In 1805 he complained of 'having the stone' (Farington, *Diary*, 14 April 1806). Early in 1806 he went to Hull where he was visited by the poet Kirk White who earlier had described him as 'a complete artist … inclined to Hutchinsonian principles' (White to B. Maddock, 31 Jan 1805, Williamson, 83). He died there of typhus on 20 April 1806 and was buried under the choir stalls of Holy Trinity, Hull.

His third son, **William Russell** (1784–1870), born on 26 November 1784, who was with him when he died, exhibited pastels at the Royal Academy and the British Institution from 1805 to 1809, and the oil portraits *Lord Erskine* (exh. RA, 1808) and *Judge Bailey* (NPG). He was educated at the Revd George Gibson's school, London. He was ordained on 21 May 1809, giving up painting for fear it might interfere with his spiritual duties, and became, for forty years, rector of St Nicholas, Shepperton, Middlesex. He married Laetitia Ann Nichols. He died on 14 September 1870 at 5 The Grove, Highgate, Middlesex.

R. J. B. WALKER

Sources G. C. Williamson, *John Russell R. A.* (1894) [based on Russell's diary, in the V&A] · W. F. Ryan, 'John Russell, R. A., and early lunar mapping', *Smithsonian Journal of History*, 1 (1966), 27–48 · Farington, *Diary* · E. Edwards, *Anecdotes of painters* (1808); facs. edn (1970) · O. Millar, *The later Georgian pictures in the collection of her majesty the queen*, 2 vols. (1969) · B. Scott, 'Childhood in crayons: John Russell's portraits', *Country Life* (11 Nov 1982), 1470–71 · R. R. M. See, 'Portraits of children of the Russell family by John Russell', *The Connoisseur* (Dec 1918), 182–92 · B. Stewart and M. Cutten, *The dictionary of portrait painters in Britain up to 1920* (1997) · I. C. Rhodes, *John Russell RA (1745–1806), 250th Anniversary exhibition of pastel portraits* (1995) [exhibition catalogue, Guildford House Gallery] · J. Russell, diary, V&A
Archives V&A, English MSS · V&A NAL, diaries and travel journal
Likenesses J. Russell, self-portrait, black chalk, *c*.1780, NPG [*see illus.*] · J. Russell, self-portrait, pastel, 1794, Borough of Guildford Museum, Surrey · G. Dance, pencil drawing, *c*.1795, RA · H. Singleton, group portrait, oils (*The Royal Academicians, 1793*), RA · process block (when young), BM
Wealth at death under £14,000—William Russell: probate, 20 Oct 1870, *CGPLA Eng. & Wales*

Russell, John, sixth duke of Bedford (1766–1839), landowner, was born on 30 September 1766 at Bedford House, Bloomsbury, London, the second son of Francis Russell, marquess of Tavistock (1739–1767), and his wife, Lady Elizabeth Keppel (1739–1767), sixth daughter of William Anne *Keppel, second earl of Albemarle, and the grandson of John Russell, fourth duke of Bedford (1710–1771). His father was killed by a fall from his horse when Russell was six months old; his mother died of consumption, in Lisbon, when he was thirteen months old, and it does not appear that his grandparents, engaged in high politics,

John Russell, sixth duke of Bedford (1766–1839), by Sir Thomas Lawrence, exh. RA 1822

had much time to spare for his upbringing. He is said to have become an officer in the Bedfordshire militia when he was twelve, in 1778, and more certainly he served as an ensign in the 3rd regiment of foot guards between 1783 and 1785. On 21 March 1786 he married Georgiana Elizabeth (1768?–1801), second daughter of George Byng, fourth Viscount Torrington, the ceremony being performed first in Brussels in March and then again in the Russell family church in Streatham in April. He was said to have neglected Georgiana, but they contrived to have three sons, Francis, seventh duke (1788–1861), George William *Russell (1790–1846), and Lord John *Russell (1792–1878), statesman and prime minister. Like his elder brother, Francis *Russell, he was a radical Foxite whig, advocating parliamentary reform, and a member of the Society of the Friends of the People. He entered the Commons in 1788, sitting for the family borough of Tavistock from then until 1802, but spoke infrequently. On occasion, as when he opposed the abolition of the slave trade arguing with time-honoured casuistry that it would be harmful to the interests of the slaves to exclude the humane British from the trade because it would then be carried on by more brutal foreign traders, his stance was less than convincingly radical.

Russell's first wife died at Bath in October 1801, in March 1802 he succeeded to the dukedom when his brother Francis died unmarried, and on 23 June 1803 he married another Georgiana (1781–1853), the 21-year-old fifth daughter of Alexander *Gordon, fourth duke of Gordon. He was kind to his second Georgiana where he had been indifferent to the first, and they had ten children, including Lord Edward *Russell, the last born in 1826 when she was forty-five. She was high-spirited, enlivening Woburn which was oppressed by the silence and shyness of the duke, by having pillow fights, pelting her guests with apples and oranges, and organizing games of blind man's buff. As well as finding time for all the children, to whom the couple were devoted, and the three sons of the first marriage with whom the duke kept in close touch, the duchess engaged in a long-lasting liaison with the painter Edwin Landseer whom she first met in 1823. She was dubbed 'une coquette comme la lune' by her step-daughter-in-law, and 'a bold bad woman with the remains of beauty' by Le Marchant in 1833 (Aspinall, 366).

Disillusioned by the war with France and the collapse of radical hopes, Bedford retreated from politics into the life of a country gentleman, like his bachelor brother before him, who had adopted the role of a leading agricultural improver. This had cost him a great deal of money and obliged him to sell the potentially prime estate at Streatham. John, with his new wife, placed agricultural improvement a shade below the gratification of Georgiana's desires. First, though, he enjoyed a brief taste of office as Irish viceroy in the 1806–7 'ministry of all the talents', which was marked by his vigorous advocacy of the need to conciliate the Catholics, most notably with the bill to give Catholic officers equal treatment in the army, which caused the fall of the ministry when George III declined to accept the measure. After this he virtually disappeared from the political scene, seldom speaking in the Lords, though he did protest against the suspension of habeas corpus in 1817 and took Queen Caroline's side in 1820; in further proof of his consistent whiggery he fought a duel with the duke of Buckingham in Kensington Gardens in May 1822 because he objected to Buckingham's public apostasy (Blakiston, 62). It is thus a little surprising that in July 1830 Wellington offered Bedford the lord chamberlain's office and that he was 'much gratified but declined on ground of his health' (Ellenborough, 2.308). This apparent wobble in his political allegiance may have stemmed from a belief that it had become acceptable to rally behind Wellington in the aftermath of his concession of Catholic emancipation, but it was nevertheless felt that Bedford had 'quitted Lord Grey' (Letters of Dorothea, 280), and with him, presumably, his own son Lord John Russell. By November 1830 he was back on the whig rails with the Garter given to him by Grey, and warmly backing his son's accession to office. Within a year or two he was enthusiastically supporting Lord John as 'Jack the Giant Killer' (Blakiston, 335), trusting that he would try to purge the government of 'a few black sheep such as Palmerston' (Bourne, 545).

By this time Woburn had resumed its traditional place as a leading centre of country-house politics. Thanks to the duchess it was also at the leading edge of fashionable country-house parties, and she persuaded the duke to introduce the new-fangled technique of the battue for the mass shooting of pheasants to keep the fashionable gentlemen amused. Greville spent the 1820 new year at Woburn and enjoyed it immensely, recording that 'the chasse was brilliant, in five days we killed 835 pheasants … The Duchess was very civil and the party very gay' (Greville, Diary, 1.27). Bedford's son Lord William Russell wrote in 1825 that 'to shoot at Woburn and dance at Almack's, those two things were the ne plus ultra of fashionability' (Blakiston, 135). At the duchess's behest Bedford rented from his father-in-law a lodge and estate, the Doune of Rothiemurchus, Inverness, which was used every autumn for the grouse and fishing. Her influence, too, was behind the development on the Tavistock estate of the family holiday complex of Endsleigh, where the building of the Gothic 'cottage' ornée and its attendant dairy and ducal picnic shelter was so expensive that the duke had to economize by discontinuing the annual sheep-shearings at Woburn, on the grounds that these had fulfilled their purpose and were no longer beneficial. About the same time he resigned from the Smithfield Club, of which he had been president in succession to his brother the founder-president, declaring that no further improvements in animal husbandry were desirable. This was a fair measure of his interest in farming and agricultural improvement, although he did agree to become a vice-president of the newly formed (Royal) Agricultural Society of England in 1838. Nevertheless, neither the agricultural nor the London estates were neglected in his time. On the Thorney estate work on the Bedford Level main drain went ahead, and in London the development of the Bloomsbury estate following the demolition of Bedford House was started, and Covent Garden was provided with a handsome market building, by Charles Fowler, in 1828–30. These appear to have been the work of agents whose ideas were generally approved. The duke's personal interests were horticultural and botanical, rather than agricultural. He experimented at Woburn with different grasses, heaths, willows, pines, and ornamental plants and shrubs, of which he caused several catalogues to be published.

Having been in poor health for several years Bedford died at the Doune on 20 October 1839 and was brought, 'by steam' from Inverness, for burial in the family mausoleum at Chenies in Buckinghamshire on 16 November. Greville, forgetting the hospitality he had enjoyed in 1820, gave the duke a poor character as incorrigibly self-centred and self-indulgent, claiming that: 'A more uninteresting and weak-minded selfish character does not exist than the Duke of Bedford' (Greville Memoirs, 4.247–8). His family had a more tolerant view, but his eldest son said of him 'he had not the power or resolution to hold his hand, whenever money was within his reach' (Blakiston, 433), and was not a little upset to discover that during his father's time the debts on the Bedford estate had doubled to nearly half a million, despite the huge annual income. Having thirteen children, a passion for collecting pictures and sculpture, and a wife with extravagant tastes, Bedford had not done the Russell fortunes much service.

F. M. L. THOMPSON

Sources G. Blakiston, *Lord William Russell and his wife, 1815–1846* (1972) · DNB · *The Greville memoirs, 1814–1860*, ed. L. Strachey and

R. Fulford, 8 vols. (1938) · *The Greville diary*, ed. P. W. Wilson, 2 vols. (1927) · *Early correspondence of Lord John Russell*, ed. R. Russell, 2 vols. (1913?) · W. Cobbett, ed., *Parliamentary debates: 1803–20*, 41 vols. (1803–20) · GEC, *Peerage* · D. Spring, *The English landed estate in the nineteenth century: its administration* (1963) · A. Aspinall, ed., *Three early nineteenth-century diaries* (1952) [extracts from Le Marchant, E. J. Littleton, Baron Hatherton, and E. Law, earl of Ellenborough] · H. A. Russell, duke of Bedford, *A great agricultural estate, being the story of the origin and administration of Woburn and Thorney* (1897) · E. Law, Lord Ellenborough, *A political diary, 1828–1830*, ed. Lord Colchester, 2 vols. (1881) · K. Bourne, *Palmerston: the early years, 1784–1841* (1982) · *Letters of Dorothea, Princess Lieven, during her residence in London, 1812–1834*, ed. L. G. Robinson (1902)

Archives Bloomsbury estate office, MSS · Devon RO, corresp. with solicitors relating to Camelford elections · NL Ire., letters relating to Ireland · NRA, priv. coll., corresp. and MSS · Woburn Abbey, corresp. and papers | Beds. & Luton ARS, letters to Samuel Whitbread · BL, corresp. with Lord Grenville, Add. MSS 58956–58957 · BL, corresp. with Lord Hardwicke, Add. MSS 35646–35766, *passim* · BL, corresp. with Lord Holland and Lady Holland, Add. MSS 51661–51673 · BL, letters to second Earl Spencer · BL, letters to Arthur Young, Add. MSS 35128–35130, *passim* · Keele University Library, letters to duchess of Bedford · Linn. Soc., letters to Sir James Smith · NL Scot., corresp. with Edward Ellice senior · NL Scot., corresp. with William Elliot · NL Scot., letters to Lord Lynedoch · NRA Scotland, priv. coll., corresp. with William Adam · NRA, priv. coll., letters to George William Russell · NRA, priv. coll., corresp. with Samuel Whitbread · PRO, corresp. with Lord John Russell, PRO 30/22 · RA, corresp. with Thomas Lawrence · Staffs. RO, corresp. with Lord Bradford · U. Durham L., letters to second Earl Grey

Likenesses J. Reynolds, group portrait, oils, 1776 (*St George and the dragon*), Osterley Park, London · W. Beechey, oils, 1790, Woburn Abbey, Bedfordshire · G. Garrard, group portrait, oils, 1804 (*Woburn sheep shearing*), Woburn Abbey, Bedfordshire · G. Garrard, etching, pubd 1806, BM, NPG · W. Grimaldi, watercolour miniature, 1808, Woburn Abbey, Bedfordshire · J. Nollekens, marble bust, 1808, Woburn Abbey, Bedfordshire; copy, Royal Collection · J. D. Ingres, pencil drawing, 1815, City Art Museum, St Louis · G. Hayter, pen and sepia wash drawing, c.1815–1820, NPG · H. Raeburn, oils, exh. RA 1820, Longleat House, Wiltshire · G. Hayter, group portrait, oils, 1820–23 (*The trial of Queen Caroline, 1820*), NPG · T. Lawrence, oils, exh. RA 1822, Woburn Abbey, Bedfordshire [*see illus.*] · G. Hayter, oils, 1826, Woburn Abbey, Bedfordshire · J. Francis, marble bust, 1832, Woburn Abbey, Bedfordshire · G. Hayter, group portrait, oils, 1833–43 (*The House of Commons, 1833*), NPG · J. Doyle, lithograph, pubd 1836, NG Ire. · R. J. Lane, lithograph, pubd 1836 (after E. Landseer), BM, NPG · G. Hayter, group portrait, oils, 1838 (*The coronation of Queen Victoria*), Royal Collection · recumbent figure on tomb, Chenies parish church, Buckinghamshire, Bedford chapel

Wealth at death under £250,000: will, 1840; GEC, *Peerage*, 2.85

Russell, John (1786–1863), headmaster, was born on 23 September 1786 at Helmdon, Northamptonshire, the eldest son of the Revd John Russell (*d*. 26 April 1802), rector of Helmdon and of Ilmington, Warwickshire. A younger brother, William Russell (1787–1831), became a fellow of Magdalen College, Oxford. Educated at Charterhouse from 1796 to 1803, being gold medallist there in 1801, John Russell entered Christ Church, Oxford, in 1803. One of only three names to appear in the Oxford class list for Easter term 1806 under the newly created system of honours, he graduated BA in 1809 and MA in 1810. He was assistant master at Charterhouse from 1806 to 1811, and married in 1808 Mary Augusta, eldest daughter of Revd Eusebius Lloyd, curate of Silchester, Hampshire, and a

cousin of Russell's Christ Church contemporary Charles Lloyd. He was ordained deacon in 1807 and priest in 1810.

Russell succeeded Dr Matthew Raine as master of Charterhouse in 1811, the statute which required that the master should have attained twenty-seven years of age being set aside on this occasion. A sound classical scholar, he wrote *Rudiments of the Latin Language* (1813; 3rd edn, 1827), followed in 1833 by an *English Grammar* (9th edn, 1840). He was a bold innovator in his pedagogic methods. Soon after his appointment he introduced Andrew Bell's Madras system of monitorial instruction, whereby much of the teaching was devolved to older boys (*praepositi*); in 1821 there were only five masters in charge of some 431 boys. He persisted with the experiment, though it was later dropped. In 1818 he attempted to replace corporal punishment with monetary fines; uproar among the boys at the threat to their pockets forced a reinstatement of the old system, marked, as Augustus Page Saunders (1800–1878), a pupil and later Russell's successor recalled, by a mass birching of the demonstrators (*Public Schools Commission*, 4, 1864, 21–2). His attempt in 1814 to open some of the places on the foundation to competition, as opposed to nomination by the governors, was narrowly defeated. Despite these set-backs the school became extremely popular during the early years of his administration, pupil numbers reaching a peak of 480 by 1825. Subsequently numbers began to fall. An active supporter of the Society of Schoolmasters (as was his predecessor), Russell was one of a generation of headmasters who viewed their responsibilities as limited mainly to instruction. Residing at Blackheath, some distance from the school, he exercised little personal supervision over the boarders. By abolishing some traditional customs, but failing to devise alternative methods of keeping order in the vast dormitories, he allowed much bullying to prevail. Among his pupils were George Grote, Sir Henry Havelock, and William Makepeace Thackeray, who immortalized the school as Grey Friars in *Vanity Fair*, *The Newcomes*, and other of his works, and outlined Russell's portrait in the stern but wise headmaster 'of our time'.

Russell held the livings of Burbage, Wiltshire, and Hurstbourne Tarrant, Hampshire, from 1814 to 1818. In 1827 he was made a prebendary, and afterwards canon residentiary, of Canterbury. He resigned the headmastership in 1832 on being presented by C. J. Blomfield, bishop of London, to the rectory of St Botolph without Bishopsgate, which he held until his death. He was president of Sion College in 1845 and 1846, treasurer of the Society for the Propagation of the Gospel, and a capable administrator of other societies including the Clergy Orphan Association. He published in 1850 an edition of *The Ephemerides* of Isaac Casaubon, followed in 1859 by *The History of Sion College*. Russell died at The Oaks, Canterbury, Kent, on 3 June 1863. He was survived by two daughters, Augusta and Mary, and two sons, Francis (1815–1891), recorder of Tenterden, Kent, and William (1817–1898), a clergyman, two other sons having predeceased him.

M. C. CURTHOYS

Sources *The Times* (5 June 1863) · T. Mozley, *Reminiscences, chiefly of Oriel College and the Oxford Movement*, 2 vols. (1882) · W. Haig Brown, *Charterhouse past and present* (1879) · Venn, *Alum. Cant.* · R. L. Arrowsmith, ed., *Charterhouse register, 1769–1872* (1974)
Archives LPL, diary · Sion College, London
Likenesses W. Say, mezzotint, pubd 1829 (after B. R. Faulkner), BM, NPG
Wealth at death under £35,000: probate, 3 July 1863, *CGPLA Eng. & Wales*

Russell, John [*formerly* Lord John Russell], **first Earl Russell** (1792–1878), prime minister and author, born at Hertford Street, Westminster, on 18 August 1792, was the third son of Lord John *Russell (1766–1839) and his first wife, Georgiana Elizabeth (1768?–1801), second daughter of George Byng, fourth Viscount Torrington, and his wife, Lady Lucy Boyle, only daughter of the fifth earl of Cork and Orrery. Lord John was a seven months' child, and fully grown he stood under 5 feet 5 inches tall. Throughout his life he was subject to colds and felt faint in 'hot rooms, late hours and bad air' (G. W. E. Russell, 11). He was his mother's last and favourite child, and he had just been sent away to school for the first time when she died, on 11 October 1801, when he was nine. In 1802 his father succeeded Lord John's uncle as sixth duke of Bedford. In 1803 the duke married Georgiana (*d.* 1853), fifth daughter of Alexander *Gordon, fourth duke of Gordon. There were seven sons and three daughters of the new union.

Education Lord John entered Westminster School in 1803 and fagged for his elder brother, Francis. The school was 'too much' for his health, and his stepmother had him brought home and entrusted to the domestic chaplain, Edmund Cartwright, inventor of the power-loom, for his lessons. From 1805 to 1808 he was a living-in pupil of the Revd John Smith, the vicar of Woodnesborough, near Sandwich. In 1806, when the whigs were in office, Lord John passed the summer in Dublin with his father, who was the lord lieutenant. There, as in London, he loved the theatres. In 1807 he accompanied his father on a tour through Scotland, and met Sir Walter Scott. In 1808 Lord and Lady Holland, who 'kept a knife and fork' for him at Holland House, took him to Lisbon, Seville, and Cadiz, where they instructed Spanish insurgents in British constitutional practices. In 1809 Lord John's father, observing that 'nothing was learned' in the English universities, proposed to send his son to Edinburgh. Lord John did not wish to go, but Lord and Lady Holland persuaded him to attend. He lodged for three years with Professor John Playfair, heard lectures by Dugald Stewart, joined the Speculative Society, and met Francis Jeffrey, the editor of the *Edinburgh Review*. Frail as he was, Lord John had acquired a taste for travel. In the long vacation of 1810 he returned to the Peninsula to visit his elder brother William, who was a soldier, and witnessed the Cortes in session. In 1811 Professor Playfair took him on a tour through the manufacturing districts, Birmingham, Liverpool, Manchester, Sheffield, and Leeds. In 1812–13 he paid another extended visit to Spain, and examined the fields of Barossa and Talavera, where William had been in action. He joined his brother

John Russell [Lord John Russell], **first Earl Russell** (1792–1878), by George Frederic Watts, *c.*1852

upon the last hill in Spain and gazed into France, where, but for the wars, his grand tour would have begun. In 1814 he sailed to Italy, and on Christmas eve he had a private audience with Napoleon in Elba. In 1815, when the wars finally came to an end, he set off for Paris, and continued all his life to visit France as often as he could, and Italy as well.

A thorough whig In 1813, while Lord John was abroad, he was returned to parliament for the family borough of Tavistock. On 12 May 1814 in his maiden speech he argued against compelling the Norwegians to unite with the Swedes. In the years which followed, when the whigs were in opposition and he had no prospect of official employment, he began lifelong friendships with Tom Moore, the Irish poet, Sydney Smith, the witty priest, and Samuel Rogers, the poet. For occupation, he turned to writing. He started with *The Life of William Lord Russell* (1819), one of the whig martyrs who had been executed in 1683. The next year he published *Essays and Sketches of Life and Character by a Gentleman who has Left his Lodgings* (1820); a novel, *The Nun of Arrouca* (1820); and a five-act play, *Don Carlos, or, Persecution* (1820), which was written in blank verse and dedicated to Lord Holland. These were followed by *An Essay on the History of the English Government and Constitution, from the Reign of Henry VIII to the Present Time* (1821; enlarged edn, 1823; rev. edn, 1865 and 1873), *Memoirs of the Affairs of Europe from the Peace of Utrecht* (1824), *Establishment of the Turks in Europe* (1828), a second volume of *Memoirs of the Affairs of Europe* (1829), and *The Causes of the French Revolution* (1832).

History contributed a strange mixture of depth and anachronism to Lord John's politics. He had been born into a great whig house, where he was taught that the aristocracy occupied a middle place between crown and people and held their great estates in trust for the preservation of the constitution. The defining moment in his politics, which occurred nine years before he was born, was George III's dismissal of Charles James Fox in 1783. Throughout his life he worked with a statue of Fox on his desk, and like Fox he thought that even in an age of revolutionary societies and tumults a wilful monarch posed a greater threat to parliament than the people, who were slow. He acknowledged that the French Revolution had been accompanied by acts of violence and outrage. It taught us that 'great changes accomplished by the people were dangerous, although sometimes salutary'. But on whom to lay the blame of their excesses? As he said in the preface to his *Essay on the History of the English Government and Constitution* (1821), the monarchies of the continent of Europe had been, generally speaking, 'so ill-adapted to make their subjects virtuous and happy, that they require, or required, complete regeneration' (p. iii). But 'the government of England ought not to be included in this class; ... it is calculated to produce liberty, worth, and content ... whilst its abuses easily admit of reforms consistent with its spirit' (p. iv). Tories attributed the popular discontent of the war and post-war period to wickedness, Lord John to misgovernment. The composition of the lower house had remained unchanged since the revolution of 1688. Now there was a need for 'great changes', and these, provided they were accomplished by the aristocracy, at the desire of the people, would prove to be 'at once salutary and safe'.

Political apprenticeship In February 1817 Lord John spoke against the suspension of the Habeas Corpus Act. Shortly afterwards, being unwell, he resigned his seat. He was returned again, unopposed, for Tavistock at the general election of 1818, and for Huntingdonshire in 1820. In 1826 he lost his seat and took refuge in Bandon, an Irish borough controlled by the duke of Devonshire, with whom he had been at school at Woodnesborough. During the 1820s Lord John took up the cause of parliamentary reform. As he saw it, Liverpool's government lived in fear of the large unrepresented towns, and relied for its majority upon the members for small boroughs who voted with government in return for patronage. In 1819 he condemned the Peterloo massacre, which would never have taken place, he thought, had there been elections at Manchester. In 1820–21 he pursued the disfranchisement of Grampound for gross corruption. The ministry refused to transfer the seats to Leeds, or to any other large town (they went to Yorkshire). In the House of Commons, on 25 April 1822, Lord John advocated reform in a speech which passed into the annals of English oratory:

> At the present period the ministers of the Crown possess the confidence of the House of Commons, but the House of Commons does not possess the esteem and reverence of the people. ... The ministers of the Crown, after obtaining triumphant majorities in this House, are obliged to have recourse to other means than those of persuasion, reverence for authority, and voluntary respect, to procure the adherence of the country. They are obliged to enforce, by arms, obedience to acts of this House—which, according to

every just theory, are supposed to emanate from the people themselves. (*Hansard 2*, 7.73–5)

He proposed to take one member away from each of 100 small boroughs, and redistribute 60 of the seats to the counties and 40 to the large towns. His motion was lost by 269 votes to 164, and in 1826, when he tried again, he was defeated by a larger majority.

On 26 February 1828 Lord John tasted success for the first time when he brought forward a motion to repeal the Test and Corporation Acts. Characteristically, he used the exact words employed by Fox in 1790, and was thrilled when fifteen tory ultras changed sides and the motion was carried by 237 to 193. Catholic emancipation followed (from a different chain of events) in the ensuing year. In the meantime, Lord John campaigned to transfer the two seats taken from Penryn, which was disfranchised after the 1826 election, to Manchester. Disappointed in this, he proposed to enfranchise Manchester, Leeds, and Birmingham immediately, without waiting for more seats to become vacant. That was the position when George IV died in 1830. At the general election which followed Lord John stood for Bedford. His opponent publicized a passage from *Memoirs of the Affairs of Europe* in which Lord John animadverted upon the irrational behaviour of Methodists, and he was defeated. He departed for Paris, and was still out of parliament on 16 November when Wellington announced the resignation of the ministry. Lord John was back in the family borough at Tavistock, canvassing the electors, when Earl Grey invited him to become paymaster of the forces.

The Great Reform Act A few days after Lord John had been returned unopposed, Lord Durham asked him to join a committee of four to draft a reform bill. The people complained of the sale of boroughs, nomination by individuals and closed corporations, and the expense and corruption of elections. The committee agreed that a reform bill must be substantial enough to settle the question for a generation. Lord John suggested that this meant they should redistribute 150 seats, and it seems to have been his draft they worked to. Boroughs with fewer than 2000 inhabitants were to lose both members, those with between 2000 and 4000 were to lose one. That would stop boroughmongering. Then, the ancient rights voters were to be extinguished, condemned for their venality. Seats were to be redistributed to the large towns and to the populous counties. In the towns the test of fitness to vote was to be the occupation of a house of a certain value. In the counties the existing electorate of 40 shilling freeholders was to be enlarged by the addition of some leaseholders and copyholders. A register of electors was to be established and revised every year in order to eliminate the time spent examining claims during a poll, and the duration of a poll and the opportunities for carnival and drunkenness were to be reduced from fourteen days to two.

The constitution was to be restored and a new era of virtuous politics inaugurated. But there was to be no revolution. Lord John aimed to forestall what he termed 'reform upon a principle', and to baffle the 'fanatics' who demanded universal suffrage and annual parliaments. On one issue, the introduction of the secret ballot, he disagreed with the other members of the committee. Non-electors had a right to know how electors voted. Without it, they would raise an irresistible cry for universal suffrage. The secret ballot was among the recommendations submitted to the cabinet by the committee. But the cabinet threw it out, and Lord John's view prevailed. It was an issue upon which he never changed his mind, and his opposition was probably decisive in delaying its introduction for forty years until his political career was over.

The whig leader in the House of Commons, Lord Althorp, was a poor speaker, and Lord John was invited, even though he was not a member of the cabinet, to introduce the bill to the House of Commons on 1 March 1831. After all the intense speculation of the preceding weeks, he passed over the arguments which he had developed at length in 1822, and went straight into 'a clear and intelligible statement' of the proposed changes. The announcement that 168 constituencies were to disappear stunned the house, and changed the mental map of a whole generation. In contrast to Pitt's proposals in 1785, there was to be no compensation to the owners of rotten boroughs which were abolished.

The second reading was carried, by one vote, on 22 March 1831. In April, when his ministry was defeated, Lord Grey appealed to the country. Lord John was re-elected for Tavistock and elected for Devonshire, and he chose the county seat. By the time the new parliament met, the duke of Bedford and Lord Holland had prevailed upon Grey to take Lord John into the cabinet. On 24 June he introduced a second Reform Bill. The committee stage lasted until 7 September, and a month later the Lords rejected the bill. When Nottingham Castle was burnt, and the centre of Bristol sacked, everything underlined the whig case that small adjustments made voluntarily in the 1820s would have saved the nation from much larger changes conceded in the face of excitement now. Replying to an address from the Birmingham Political Union, Lord John wrote that it was 'impossible that the whisper of a faction [the House of Lords] should prevail against the voice of a nation' (*Hansard 3*, 8.599). The phrase upset the king. On 12 December Lord John introduced the third Reform Bill. Towards the end of his life he said that the crisis which followed, in May, when the king dismissed Grey and sent for Wellington, was the only moment of real peril to the country that he could recall. The bill received the royal assent on 7 June 1832. The Lords had reinstated the ancient rights voters, but little else. Writing in the *Edinburgh Review* in January 1846, Lord John said that the tories had been wrong in thinking the bill could be rejected, the whigs had been wrong in foreboding failure for so extensive a measure, and the radicals had been wrong in supposing that 'so large a ruin must lead to a more uniform construction. The authors of the plan were alone justified by the event'.

The condition of Ireland Lord John headed the poll for South Devonshire in December 1832. The paymaster's duties being so light, he began to look around him for something to do in the reformed parliament. In 1826 his brother William had drawn his attention to 'suffering, ill-used Ireland', adding that 'the gratitude of millions, the applause of the world would attend the Man who would rescue this poor Country' (*Early Correspondence*, 1.253). In the summer of 1833 Lord John visited Ireland, and concluded that, even after Catholic emancipation, Ireland under the protestant ascendancy resembled 'nothing so much as Spain in 1810, in the occupation of the French' (Russell to Grey, 2 Oct 1833, Grey MSS). The entire population was required to pay tithes to the established church, which was the church of one-tenth of the population, and soldiers were used to repress the disturbances which occurred and collect the money. In 1834 there would have to be a new tithe act. The sums involved were large, and Lord John believed that, after the needs of the protestant church had been met, there would be a surplus which could be used to pay the Catholic clergy or, if the Roman Catholic hierarchy would not allow their clergy to become clients of the state, to subsidize the education of all classes of Christians. In the cabinet the resistance to what came to be known as 'appropriation' was led by Lord Stanley, who had been Irish secretary from 1830 to 1833, and was now colonial secretary. Stanley had just carried the act to emancipate the slaves, and he was at this stage more highly esteemed in the cabinet than Lord John. But Lord John had the ear of Lord Althorp and the support of the reform party. On 6 May 1834 he announced in the House of Commons that once parliament had vindicated the state's right to legislate for the church's property in tithes he would be 'prepared to assert his opinion with regard to their appropriation' (Walpole, 1.199). Johnny had, as Stanley said, 'upset the coach', and on 27 May Stanley, Graham, Richmond, and Ripon resigned.

Lord John took no part in the intrigues which caused Grey to give up the premiership in disgust. Melbourne became prime minister, and in November, when Althorp succeeded to his father's title and went to the House of Lords, Lord John was the obvious choice to succeed him as leader in the House of Commons. Lord John's father doubted whether his son's constitution would bear the strain. Grey warned that he must learn 'a little discretion both in speaking and writing', and Lord Holland acknowledged that he did not take the requisite pains 'to collect the opinions of others' (Prest, *Russell*, 72). Even his friends sometimes felt they had been snubbed. His enemies supposed he was a dangerous radical, who proposed to undermine the established church. On 14 November William IV dismissed the ministry while it still enjoyed a huge majority in parliament and sent for the duke of Wellington, who in turn advised him to summon Peel.

The Lichfield House compact The king's action was a bolt from the past, a rerun of 1783, and the whigs were determined that it should not be followed by another fifty years of almost uninterrupted tory rule. Peel dissolved parliament, and while Lord John was in south Devon, where he was returned unopposed, he met and courted Adelaide Lister, Lady Ribblesdale (1807–1838). She was the daughter of Thomas Henry *Lister, the author of *Granby*, a novel published in 1826 which referred, in a manner Lord John would have warmed to at the time, to a ministerial borough called Rottentown. Adelaide was now a very youthful-looking widow (her husband, Thomas Lister, second Baron Ribblesdale, died in 1832) of twenty-seven with four children. Inspired by this brightening of his fortunes, Lord John took up his new role as leader of the opposition in the House of Commons. He decided to avenge the party on the king by opposing the re-election of the speaker, Charles Manners-Sutton, who had collaborated in the royal *coup d'état*. On 18 February, the eve of the opening of parliament, members of the three opposition groups, whigs, radicals, and Irish, met Lord John in Lichfield House. The agreement reached then implied co-operation thereafter. Manners-Sutton was ousted by 316 votes to 306, and on 25 February Lord John carried an amendment to the address expressing support for the ministry which William had dismissed in November. But the margin was small, 294 to 287, and Peel did not resign. Moderates wanted Peel to be given a fair trial, and Lord John dare not initiate a motion of no confidence. When Peel brought in an Irish tithe bill, Lord John was warned that if he did not move the appropriation question it would be raised from the back benches. There were two more meetings at Lichfield House on 12 and 23 March. Early in April Peel was defeated three times, and on 8 April he resigned. In his first trial as leader Lord John had ejected Peel, the greatest politician of the age, and he had vindicated the constitution. It was his finest hour. On 11 April 1835 Melbourne began the formation of a new ministry, and Lord John and Lady Ribblesdale were married, and went to live in 30 Wilton Crescent, London.

The Melbourne administration, 1835–1841 Lord John (or the Widow's Mite, as he was dubbed) now had the opportunity to construct a whig future upon the foundation of an unexpectedly relevant whig past, and he chose the Home Office from which to do it. In May, when Lord John sought re-election in South Devon at the obligatory by-election, he was opposed and defeated by 3755 votes to 3128, and was obliged, for a third time, to take refuge in a small borough, Stroud. As home secretary he had overall responsibility for the government of Ireland. The wrongs of centuries could not be put right in a year, but Lord John was determined to speak in 'the language of conciliation' and to treat the Irish Catholics as 'the free subjects of a free country'. The ministry was committed to an appropriation bill. But the whigs' dependence upon the Irish members was not popular in England, and this allowed the House of Lords, one quarter of whose members were connected to the protestant ascendancy in Ireland, to wreck the ministry's Irish legislation. The Lords would not pass an appropriation bill, and until that was dropped they would not allow any other measure of reform for Ireland to pass either. In 1836 Lord John pressed Melbourne, unsuccessfully, to request the king to create sufficient peers to get the bill through. The stalemate lasted until William IV died on 20 June 1837. At the general election which followed Lord John retained his seat at Stroud.

When parliament met he took the view that the new parliament was not committed to the appropriation clause, and after consulting the authorities in Dublin, he abandoned it in 1838. But his opponents were remorseless. They allowed him to introduce a poor law into Ireland. But they threw out a bill to enable the state to construct the main lines of railway. In the Commons, they introduced a motion to expunge the appropriation resolution from the journals of the house. Then, on 21 March 1839, after the lord lieutenant, the earl of Mulgrave, had returned to England as the marquess of Normanby, the Lords set up a select committee to inquire into the whole course of Irish government since 1835. They continued to hold up the Municipal Corporations Bill for Ireland until 1840, when the ministry appeared to be approaching its end, and Lord John was forced to settle, in the sixth bill in six years, for an act which re-formed a handful of corporations and extinguished the rest.

The whigs could scarcely legislate for Ireland. But Lord John was saved from the fate he dreaded, of 'being responsible for the government of Ireland without having any thing just or kind to offer' (Russell to Palmerston, 24 July 1843, Palmerston papers). Ireland was governed through soldiers, police, magistrates, courts, and judges, and the executive had many powers and much patronage. Inspired by Lord John, the lord lieutenant, with Morpeth the chief secretary and Thomas Drummond the private secretary, stopped using troops to collect the tithe. Catholics were recruited into the police, protestant policemen were dismissed if they attended Orange lodges, stipendiary magistrates were appointed to counteract the bias of protestant magistrates, the crown stopped challenging Catholic jurors, Catholic solicitors were employed to conduct crown cases, and as vacancies arose the judiciary was remodelled. The result was that, as O'Connell wrote to Henry Warburton on 29 December 1836, the ministry was 'for the first time in History conquering the "Anti-Saxon" spirit of Ireland and adding eight millions to the King's subjects' (O'Connell to Warburton, 29 Dec 1836, Russell papers, PRO).

In Great Britain as in Ireland Lord John sought to eliminate causes of disaffection by modernizing the country's institutions. Hitherto they had been 'lax, careless, wasteful, injudicious in the extreme'. Now he wanted to introduce 'system, method, science, economy, regularity, discipline' (R. A. Lewis, *Edwin Chadwick and the Public Health Movement, 1832–1854*, 1952, 321). Melbourne's government inherited a backlog of contentious issues relating to civil and religious liberty. First, in 1835, came the bill to reform the municipal corporations in England and Wales (those in Scotland had been reformed in 1833). Many of the ancient corporations exercised influence over elections to parliament, and it was time to expose them to popular (householder) feelings. Towards the end of the session Russell and Peel came to a bargain across the floor of the house. Lord John disappointed his radicals, Peel the House of Lords, and the bill passed. Simultaneously, Melbourne allayed fears that he and Lord John were hostile to the Church of England. Certainly Lord John took a utilitarian view of organized religion, as a form of social cement and a tool for the reduction of crime. But he was not a scoffer, and he was attached to the gospel. He enjoyed a good sermon, and when in London attended services either at St Paul's, Knightsbridge, or at the Belgrave Chapel. He valued the historic role of the dissenting sects in the creation of a pluralistic and tolerant society. But he also esteemed the established churches in both England and Scotland, and held a consistent opinion in favour of the compulsory collection of church rates. Peel had appointed an ecclesiastical commission, and Melbourne and Lord John agreed with the archbishop of Canterbury that the church would be allowed to set its own house in order. Provided it eliminated sinecures and equated salaries to responsibilities, the whigs would defend it from the radicals. Tithe, however, was not within the remit of the commission, and in 1836 Lord John arranged for the tithe in England and Wales to be commuted into a fixed rent charge. Next he instituted a system of national registration of births, marriages, and deaths, and followed it with an act enabling dissenters to be married in their own chapels.

In Britain as in Ireland the results of the general election of 1837 imposed new constraints upon government policy. The radicals began a fresh agitation for the secret ballot. Lord John responded with a speech at Stroud in August 1837, in which he refused to reconsider the provisions of the 1832 Reform Act. The confirmation of this stance upon the opening of parliament in November earned him the nickname Finality Jack. In 1838 the economy went into recession and the Chartist movement was born. On 1 November Lady John died after giving birth to their second daughter, two-year-old Georgiana's sister, Victoria. The three and a half years Lord John had spent with Addy were the happiest period in his life. For several weeks he was unable to attend to business. When he resumed work he was determined not to become responsible for another Peterloo, and he refused to contemplate emergency legislation against the Chartist leaders. Instead, in an inspired move, he sent Fox's nephew, General Sir Charles Napier, to take command of the northern districts. The crisis came in May 1839, and passed, and the permanent under-secretary at the Home Office, Samuel March Phillipps, remarked how 'Lord John in his quiet way, without parade, but with a steady decided hand, and a most undisturbed temper' had steered the ship among the breakers (S. M. Phillips, 17 Oct 1839, Russell papers, PRO).

Even while speaking against the Chartist petition Lord John was trying to establish a universal system of schooling all over the country. He dismissed fears of the tories 'seizing hold of the [proposed] Education Boards, as they do of all other machinery', because 'education in the end must have a liberal tendency [and] this evil ought to be submitted to, rather than leave such multitudes in ignorance' (Russell to Brougham, 27 Aug 1837, Brougham papers). The cabinet preferred to go on working through the voluntary societies, but Lord John did secure the creation of a committee of council on education and the appointment of school inspectors, though his plan for a normal school for training teachers fell victim to Anglican

jealousy. He found it easier, in the climate of 1839, to pass an act permitting the justices in quarter sessions to establish rural police forces complementing those which the new town councils were already required to maintain.

Religion, schooling, and justice all had a part to play in Lord John's ideal society. He secured pardons for the Dorchester labourers. He appointed manufacturers to balance the landed gentlemen on the justices' bench. He attempted to coax the legal profession towards the codification of English law. He attended to the criminal law, and abolished the death penalty for forgery and other offences. He distinguished between serious offenders, who were to be transported, and the remainder, who were to be imprisoned in the United Kingdom. He established a prison inspectorate, opened a prison for young offenders at Parkhurst, and prepared the way for the construction of model prisons at Pentonville and Perth, and the phasing out of the hulks.

By the time Normanby left Ireland in 1839, there was a crisis in Canada. The ministry had already suspended the constitution in Lower Canada in 1837, and was now engaged on a bill of indemnity for the members of Lord Durham's administration. Normanby accepted the Colonial Office on the understanding that he would be allowed to exchange departments with Lord John at some future date. Before that could happen Peel attacked the ministry's policy towards Jamaica. Lord John argued that 300,000 former slaves must be protected from the misbehaviour of 2000 white landowners, but the government majority fell to five, and Melbourne resigned. The queen sent for Peel, who asked her, if he was to form a new ministry, to dismiss some of the whig ladies of the bedchamber. When she refused, the partisan in Lord John was too strong for the constitutionalist to agonize about the manner in which the whigs returned to office. Towards the end of the session Poulett Thomson agreed to go to Canada to implement the union of Upper and Lower Canada provided he was to be responsible to Lord John, and Normanby and Lord John did at last change places (August 1839). A few weeks later Lord John's father died, and his elder brother became duke of Bedford.

Sir James Stephen, the permanent under-secretary at the Colonial Office, said that Lord John was 'one of the very few men in the World, who in the exercise of great political power, is filling the precise function for which nature designed, and education qualified him' (Knaplund, 16). Lord John began thinking about ridding New South Wales of its penal character, and annexed New Zealand in order both to forestall the French and to save the indigenous population from uncontrolled British settlement. But the great issue was Canada, and much of the session of 1840 was devoted to a new Canada act. Thomson secured agreement to the union of Upper with Lower Canada, and solved the problem of the lands reserved for the clergy of the different denominations. In this way, he wrote to Lord John, he had carried 'the Reform Bill and Irish Church [Bill] of Canada' (*Letters from Lord Sydenham*, 47). It then fell to Lord John to carry these measures through the United Kingdom parliament. Once again, just as he had done the year before over the Chartist petition, O'Connell faithfully delivered the votes of the Irish members, and the government survived.

The Irish members now stood between the Conservatives and power. Parliamentary electors in Ireland were registered for eight years at a time, there was some impersonating of the removed and the dead, and Stanley took a leaf out of Lord John's book and brought in a bill to assimilate Irish practices to British ones (equal treatment under the Union) and insist upon an annual registration. The effect would be to injure the O'Connellites, who invoked the Lichfield House compact and called upon the whigs to save them from disaster. Lord John did not find the case for electoral impurity an easy one to argue, and the session was nearly over before he was able to outwit Stanley and persuade him to give up for that year. The recess brought the first serious disagreement with Palmerston, about the crisis in the Near East. Stanley would return with another Irish Registration Bill in 1841, and Lord John began to look for ways of getting politics onto new ground. Hence his decision to invite parliament, in 1841, to substitute a fixed duty of 8s. a quarter on corn for the sliding scale of 1828. Before the ministry could unfold its plan, Peel defeated it on 18 May over the sugar duties, and then, on 4 June, won a motion of no confidence by one vote. Melbourne dissolved parliament and prepared for a general election. The whigs and the Irish parted. In his electioneering Lord John emphasized that the corn laws were an issue Peel could not handle: 'the blockheads of their party will make their insurrection' (27 Oct 1841, *Later Correspondence*, 1.49).

Peel's ministry, 1841–1846 Lord John was invited to stand for the City of London with its four members. He was elected, but he came fourth. The whigs lost the election, but Melbourne waited to meet parliament, and the change of ministry took place at the end of August. In the meantime, on 20 July 1841, Lord John was married to Lady Fanny Elliot [see Russell, Frances Anna Maria (1815–1898)], daughter of the second earl of Minto. Fanny made a home in Lord John's new London house at 37 Chesham Place for the four Ribblesdale children and for Georgiana and Victoria, and brought them all up together with her own children, John *Russell, Viscount Amberley (1842–1876), George Gilbert William (Willy; b. 1848), Francis Albert Rollo *Russell (1849–1914), and Mary Agatha (b. 1853). Fanny also suffered miscarriages, and was often laid up for months on end. She was not a very successful political hostess, but she was ambitious for her husband, and Bertrand *Russell, her grandson, thought that a meticulous conscientiousness was preached to his grandfather at home with 'unfortunate' results.

Lord John passed his time editing the *Correspondence of John, Fourth Duke of Bedford* (3 vols., 1842–6) and reading works of political economy. In 1842 Peel's revision of the sliding scale for corn imports and his tariff reforms were so successful that it began to look as though the difference between the parties might after all remain Ireland. Peel abandoned the whig policy of appointing Catholics to offices, and O'Connell revived the repeal movement. Lord John concluded that Peel and the good government of Ireland were a contradiction in terms, and that the great object now must be 'to prevent the establishment of a settled hatred between the two nations' (Walpole, 1.395). But Peel then appointed a commission to inquire into the problem of land tenure. Lord John responded with chagrin; 'if we had thus thrown the subject loose ... we should have been charged with endangering all property' (Russell to Palmerston, 26 Aug 1843, Palmerston papers). In 1845 Peel proposed to increase the annual grant to the Roman Catholic seminary at Maynooth. The tory party split, and Lord John lent Peel his support, the measure being carried by whig votes. By this time the scenario envisaged by Lord John in 1841 was beginning to unfold. In 1843 the Canada Corn Act alarmed tory back-benchers. In 1844 Lord John doubted whether Peel was prepared to stand the test of even one bad harvest. In the Commons on 10 June 1845 he challenged ministers to deny 'that the present Corn Law is intended to, and does in the opinion of political economists, add to the rent of the landlords. Only conceive the effect of this impression working on the minds of the people for many years' (*Hansard 3*, 81.368).

In the autumn of 1845 the potato failed. While Peel's cabinet dithered Lord John was in Edinburgh with Lady John who was unwell. Without consulting any of the other whig leaders he penned an Edinburgh letter announcing his conversion to complete free trade. This was published in the *Morning Chronicle* on 26 November 1845. On 8 December he received a summons from the queen. On 11 December he reached Osborne, where he was invited to form a new ministry, and thus became the leader of the party. While Lady John fantasized about his forming the most religious and moral government the country had ever known, her husband presided over a week of indecision. The whigs were in a minority. If they formed a ministry and proposed immediate suspension of the corn laws followed by gradual abolition would Peel support them? Peel could not say. That being so the whigs decided, with an eye on the constituencies, to adopt total and immediate repeal. But when Lord John moved on to discuss the allocation of offices Grey raised insuperable objections to Palmerston's going back to the Foreign Office. On 19 December Lord John abandoned his first attempt to form a government. It was Peel who was to have the honour of repealing the corn laws—with whig support—and not the other way round. Peel's party split. In April 1846 Lord John overcame a mutiny by whig peers hoping to revert to a fixed duty. On 25 June the bill to repeal the corn laws passed all its stages with whig support, and in the early hours of 26 June the protectionists and the whigs together defeated Peel upon his Irish Coercion Bill.

Prime minister, 1846–1852 The queen sent for Lord John on 28 June 1846, and in due course she lent him Pembroke Lodge, at Petersham, where he could relax away from London. It remained his country home for the rest of his life. Lord John's cabinet had many strengths. Palmerston returned to the Foreign Office, and Grey, who did not renew his objections to Palmerston, accepted the Colonial

Office. Sir George Grey took the Home Office, where he was much less accident-prone than his predecessor Sir James Graham. Lord Bessborough, who became lord lieutenant of Ireland, died a year later and was succeeded by Lord Clarendon. Sir Charles Wood became chancellor of the exchequer. Lord Lansdowne held the lead in the House of Lords. But in other respects the prospects were not so bright. Lord John's brother William died in 1846. His other brother, Francis, the seventh duke of Bedford, helped with Lord John's expenses, but meddled in his politics and unsettled him. The whigs were in a minority, and the Peelites refused Lord John's overtures. Within the cabinet Lord John depended upon Lansdowne to help him resolve differences of opinion with Palmerston. But upon Ireland, where the ministry was faced, as Lord John said, with a thirteenth-century famine acting upon a nineteenth-century population, Palmerston and Lansdowne, who were both Irish landlords, presented a common front against Lord John.

Twice, in 1841 and 1844, Lord John had exposed the sophistry of striking moral attitudes about the importation of slave-grown sugar without a word said about the country's reliance upon slave-grown cotton. Now he used the one chance which any new ministry has of carrying out a coup, to reduce the duties upon foreign sugar, and prepare the way for the gradual equalization over five years of the duties upon foreign and colonial sugar. Next, he began to plan measures for the relief and regeneration of Ireland. The potato was failing again. There could be no repetition of Peel's purchase of maize the year before, and delegations to Downing Street were told that the government could not undertake to provide a supply of food. The ministry did however introduce a Labour Rate Act, to last for one year, to employ the destitute upon works of public utility and pay them wages with which to buy food. Under this act the Treasury advanced £10 million, and Lord John continued to the end of his life to deny that his government had allowed the Irish to starve. The act was intended to hasten the development of a modern economy. Cottiers whose potato grounds had failed would become wage labourers, and a new class of shopkeepers would arise to supply their wants. Before the act expired the government would amend the Irish Poor Law Act of 1838 to bring it into line with that in England and Wales, with less eligibility and a right to relief.

The principal measure of the 1847 session, then, was the enlargement of the Irish poor law. Other measures involved finding distinctively Liberal solutions for unresolved problems inherited from previous parliaments. Lord John spoke up in favour of John Fielden's Ten Hours Act. He himself brought forward a bill to reconstruct the English poor-law commission and make it responsible through a minister to parliament. He excelled at constitutional issues of this kind and his solution was accepted. A public health bill prepared by Morpeth proved to be too much for the digestion of a dying parliament, but education fared better. Lord John believed 'that you never could effectually raise education in this country till you raised the condition and prospects of the schoolmaster' (*Hansard*

3, 91.957–8, 19 April 1847). Henceforward teachers were to be allowed to select apprentices from among their best pupils, and teachers with fifteen years' service were to be entitled to pensions. The Methodists were brought within the scope of the privy council grants (followed by the Roman Catholics the year after). Then there was the creation of a bishopric at Manchester. Peel had established no new sees. Lord John did the right thing by the Church of England by creating one, and soothed the radicals by declining to add to the number of bishops in the House of Lords and inventing the formula according to which the bishops are elevated to the upper house in order of seniority.

After the general election of August 1847 party ties were loose and Lord John could not command a regular majority, though he hoped, by drafting his measures to attract Peelite support, to be able to muster 395 supporters of moderate progress. The election was scarcely over before the country faced a financial crisis, and Lord John and Sir Charles Wood (who had consulted Peel) had to authorize the Bank of England to break Peel's Bank Act of 1844. In Ireland, the famine now continued into another year. Further relief was restricted to donations in aid of soup kitchens manned by voluntary organizations. Destitute Irish were thrown, as planned, upon the new poor law. In order to reduce the rates, landlords responded with clearances which led to a wave of highly publicized assassinations. The new parliament met in November 1847, and Lord John was obliged to consider an emergency powers act. Before he would agree to that he insisted that the cabinet's measures must bear upon both sides in the contest. Tenants should be given security of tenure, and in order to bring new capital into Ireland distressed landlords should be sold up through an Encumbered Estates Act. To keep the priests loyal, the court of St James should establish diplomatic relations with Rome. The Crime and Outrage Act passed before Christmas. In 1848 security of tenure was sidetracked into a select committee for fear it would cross the water. The Encumbered Estates Act passed, but parliament amended the Diplomatic Relations Act to insist, insultingly, upon the pope's ambassador being a layman. Soon 1848 became a miserable year. Supporters of cheap government attacked the income tax, and the government was able to renew it for only one year at a time. Unemployment consequent upon the financial crisis of 1847 led to a revival of Chartism, which was now centred upon London. The climax came on 10 April, when Feargus O'Connor MP planned to lead a march upon the houses of parliament. The duke of Wellington attended a meeting of the whig cabinet, Sir George Grey kept calm, and the crowd on Kennington Common was persuaded to disperse. For a few weeks, while most of Europe appeared to have fallen into the hands of revolutionaries, alarm gave way to a mood of pride in the people's loyalty to parliamentary institutions. But this ended in July with Smith O'Brien's rising in Ireland. The year did, however, bring one great success in the Public Health Act, which established a general board of health and laid down the conditions, some compulsory others voluntary, under which towns (excluding, as was unkindly noticed, Lord John's London constituency) were to be made or allowed to cleanse themselves.

The parliament elected in 1847 never recovered from its bad beginning. That being so, it is remarkable how much useful work it did in the years that followed. In 1849 the ministry repealed the navigation laws, and thus extinguished the old colonial system. So far as Irish legislation was concerned it became a listening government. The Irish MPs were offered a choice between an income tax and a rate in aid of emigration, which was passed. Peel broke a long silence and pointed out that the Irish court of chancery was not equal to the work of the Encumbered Estates Act. Taking their lead from him the ministry created a new court of three encumbered estates commissioners. The procedures were draconian, and already, by 1858, one-tenth of the land of Ireland had been sold up and passed into the hands of new owners, many of whom were native Irish. In 1850 the ministry passed an Irish Representation of the People Act, to enlarge an electorate reduced by the famine, and an act which began to combine the separate colonies into a self-governing dominion of Australia. Tackling one of the last great untouched interests, Lord John set up a commission of inquiry into Oxford and Cambridge universities.

Towards the end of the session of 1850 Palmerston's stock rose with the Don Pacifico debate, and Peel died. Lord John's authority within the party and in parliament began to weaken, and his judgement became less sure. He had already been taken aback, towards the end of 1847, by the bishops' response to his appointment of Renn Dickson *Hampden, an academic theologian with latitudinarian views, to the see of Hereford. He had since been rattled by the high-church reaction to the Gorham judgment, and by the hostility expressed by the new archbishop of Armagh, Paul Cullen, to the British government at the Synod of Thurles. In October 1850, when the pope divided England into twelve sees, whose bishops would assume titles taken from English place names, Lord John wrote another letter, this time to the bishop of Durham, denouncing the pope for his 'aggression' and the Puseyite spies within the gates for corrupting the established church with 'the mummeries of superstition'. Once again, none of his colleagues had been consulted. Russell's 'Durham letter', as it was at once called, brought applause, but it was an intemperate and undignified epistle and it lost him the confidence of the Irish members and of the Peelites. All his life Lord John had spoken up in favour of toleration. He appeared now to have compromised his character, and he was never to be so useful again.

The session of 1851 began with a debate upon Locke King's motion to equalize the county and borough franchises. Lord John undertook, if the motion was withdrawn, to bring in a reform bill of his own the following year. Instead, it was the government that was defeated, on 20 February, by 100 votes to 54, and their resignation was followed by a ministerial crisis. Stanley could not form a government, and the Ecclesiastical Titles Bill was an insuperable obstacle to a junction between the Peelites and Lord John. Russell was forced to continue, without any addition of strength, and all through the early summer, while crowds flocked to the Crystal Palace to witness the marvels of modern technology, the British parliament was busy with the committee stages of a bill more relevant to the sixteenth century than the nineteenth. The protectionists voted with Lord John, and the second reading was carried by 438 votes to 95. But the act belonged to the strange world of post-1846 politics, where a small minority might hold up important legislation and a large majority might be assembled in support of something which meant little or nothing at all. The act was a dead letter, and was repealed by Gladstone in 1871. After the session was over, however, Lord John did succeed in bringing two Peelites, Lord Seymour [see St Maur, Edward Adolphus] and the second Viscount Granville, and Frederick Peel, the son of the deceased prime minister, into the administration.

As in 1840–41 Lord John's last hope was to find an issue which would carry the ministry onto new ground and enable the march of modernization to continue. Experience had shown that even the Reform Act of 1832 was not perfect. It had not solved the imbalance between the two houses, and it had led to town versus country politics and a sense of exclusion among the working classes. He had taken the matter up again for the first time in 1848, after the Chartist demonstrations. Action, he had argued, might bring on a revolution, but inaction must do so. His colleagues had not been impressed. Life peers, whose introduction Russell favoured, would lower the tone of the House of Lords, and the representation of the working classes through guilds would satisfy no one. Since then, Lord John had given his hasty undertaking when resisting Locke King's motion. In the autumn of 1851 he persuaded an unenthusiastic, if not actually mutinous, cabinet to set up a committee to draft a reform bill. Then, in December, he was obliged to dismiss Palmerston, whose calculated insubordination at the Foreign Office he could no longer restrain. He appointed Granville in his place. Before parliament met he made another fruitless effort to persuade the duke of Newcastle and other Peelites to join his ministry. In February he introduced the Reform Bill. A few days later, on 20 February 1852, Palmerston enjoyed his 'tit for tat with Johnny Russell', when the government was defeated by 136 votes to 125 upon an amendment to its Militia Bill. Lord John resigned, and was replaced on 23 February by Derby.

Achievement Having already done so much between 1835 and 1841 to remove the obstacles to a union of hearts between Britain and Ireland, Lord John had not been able, in the wake of the famine and the deaths, to complete the work he had begun. But looking back over the whole period between 1835 and 1852, it is clear that he had made the whig creed relevant to the modern world, and saved the party from dying of its former languid and indifferent worldly wisdom. His voice was 'small and thin', his pronunciation was archaic, and he scarcely knew, when speaking, where 'to dispose of his hands or feet'. But 'there was something manly and even vigorous in his bearing'. 'He held his head erect', and he was heard with attention by a full house. When Joseph Parkes, the whig whip, found himself staring into the abyss of a probable defeat, he consoled himself with the thought that 'Johnny counts for 25 himself, which so balances parties' (Parkes to Ellice, 5 July 1841, Ellice papers). Lord John had been, by common consent, the only man who could lead the party. He had neglected his supporters, and he had refused to curry favour with the editors of newspapers. But he took a relaxed view of colleagues whose conduct was wayward or whose thoughts were unorthodox (such as Lord Brougham and Joseph Hume). He understood that opinions could not be coerced, and he had faith in the power of discussion to move men forward in the end. Bills of his which had to be abandoned or modified were not, as his enemies suggested, a stain upon the reputation of government, but waves advancing little by little upon a shore where a Liberal tide was coming in. His opponents mistrusted his feeling that history was on his side, and accused him of being partisan, and it was true that he espoused the novel view that the whigs, when in office, were just as much entitled to govern and to make appointments, on whig principles, as the tories, when they were in office, were on tory principles. In this and other ways he offered an alternative to Peelite Conservatism. He was not Peel's equal in the ordered sequence of a set speech, but he had a sharper turn of phrase, a gift for riposte, and a feeling for everything enlightened and rational. Here, as the portrait by Sir Francis Grant in the National Portrait Gallery shows, was 'a man of mind, of thought, and of moral elevation'. Above all, he was absolutely without fear of change (only of no change). When he became leader in 1835 it was still not certain that the Reform Act was going to lead to a revolution in government. By the time he ceased to be prime minister in 1852 there was hardly an institution remaining which had not been reformed, apart from the army. The anxieties of the war and postwar years had yielded to the march of intellect and an almost universal preference for modernity and progress.

Quarrels with colleagues, 1852–1859 Out of office, Lord John honoured a dead friend in editing eight volumes of Tom Moore's *Memoirs, Journal, and Correspondence* (1853–6). Simultaneously he began preparing *The Memorials and Correspondence of Charles James Fox* (4 vols., 1853–7) and the *Life and Times of Charles James Fox* (3 vols., 1859–66) for publication. But he did not abandon politics. At the general election held in July 1852 he came second in the poll for the City of London. With Palmerston refusing ever to serve under Lord John again, the whigs devised a plan for union under Lord Lansdowne, as prime minister. In December, when Lansdowne declined the role assigned to him, Lord John was manoeuvred by his brother into agreeing to serve under Lord Aberdeen. Lord John believed that Aberdeen had given an undertaking to retire in his favour in due course, behaved as though Aberdeen and he were the twin heads of the administration, and argued bitterly over the allocation of cabinet places between Peelites and whigs. He accepted the lead in the Commons, but could not make up his mind whether to become foreign secretary or to

remain a member of the cabinet without portfolio. In the event he opted for the first course, and then, bewilderingly, changed his mind and insisted, when parliament met in February, upon the other, and gave up his office after eight weeks on 21 February 1853. Aberdeen humoured him, and the ministry, thanks to Gladstone's budget, which Lord John described as 'large, honest, and framed for duration', came through its first session with credit.

Aberdeen promised that, in 1854, Lord John should be allowed to bring in a reform bill, and faithfully supported him against all Palmerston's objections. The bill proposed to extend the franchise to £10 occupiers in the counties and to reduce the borough franchise from £10 to £6. Fifty-five seats were to be redistributed to the large counties and large towns. The bill also contained novel proposals for fancy franchises, which would allow property, intelligence, and station extra influence, and for the creation of three-member two-votes constituencies, which would facilitate the representation of minorities, of the tories in the large towns and of the whigs in the counties. But the prospect of war with Russia was working on Palmerston's side. The bill was received with a mixture of indifference and hostility, and Lord John was obliged to abandon it before the second reading.

Lord John turned to the conduct of the war. He urged Aberdeen to separate the war department from the Colonial Office, and to remove the duke of Newcastle from the war department. But Aberdeen would not sacrifice the duke to Lord John, so the duke kept the war department and Sir George Grey accepted the colonies. In May Lord John capriciously insisted upon resuming office himself and becoming lord president of the council (an office which, as the queen said, had not been held by a commoner since the reign of Henry VIII). Granville was ejected from the cabinet to make room for him, and Gladstone thought the whole transaction worthy of a set of clowns. The one achievement of the session was Gladstone's act setting up a body of executive commissioners to reform Oxford University—thus continuing a process initiated by Lord John in 1850. The summer brought news of defeats in the Crimea, and by November Lord John was in a state of excited desperation. He pressed Aberdeen to take control of the war effort, and said that unless this was done he could not go through with another session. When parliament met in January 1855, and J. A. Roebuck gave notice of a motion to inquire into the conduct of the war, Lord John deserted his colleagues, and resigned on 24 January 1855. By the time the vote took place five days later, he was so incensed by the reproaches of old friends that he actually contemplated voting with the majority which brought the coalition down.

The third person to be invited to form a new ministry, after Lord Derby and Lord Lansdowne, was Lord John. There was no possibility of his succeeding, but it was necessary to bring home to him how isolated he had become, and clear the way for his rival, Palmerston. The new prime minister wondered what to do with Lord John, and decided to send him to Vienna, where the Austrian government was about to host a conference which, it was hoped, would lead either to a negotiated peace or to Austria's entering the war upon the allied side. In February 1855, when he was on his way, the Peelites resigned from the ministry, and Palmerston offered him the post of colonial secretary. Lord John accepted the office and continued to Vienna. He was instructed to insist upon a limit to Russian armaments upon the Black Sea. The Russians would not accept this, and the Austrians proposed that the allies should be allowed to keep as many warships there as the Russians. Lord John said he thought this was reasonable. In the meantime the French and British governments had changed their war aim to the neutralization of the Black Sea. When Lord John returned to London he allowed Palmerston to talk him out of resignation, and supported the demand for neutralization. The Austrians exposed his inconsistency. The British press then fell on him for having been willing to truckle to the Russians, and for deceiving the House of Commons.

Lord John was forced out of office, and resigned on 13 July 1855. He was on the verge of a breakdown, and bought Rodborough Manor near Amberley in Gloucestershire. He had only one engagement that autumn, when he addressed the YMCA on the causes which have retarded moral and political progress. The 1856 session brought the country back 'to the old do-nothing days of Castlereagh' (Russell to Minto, 30 July 1856, Minto papers), and Lord John moved resolutions in favour of putting education within the reach of every child. In 1857 he acted together with Cobden and the Peelites to condemn the Second Opium War and defeat the government. Palmerston dissolved parliament and Lord John survived an attempt to oust him from his City seat. In 1858 he delivered an inaugural address, 'The improvement of the law: health, education, and morals of the people', to the meeting of the National Association for the Promotion of Social Science. In the House of Commons he voted in the majority which defeated Palmerston's Conspiracy to Murder Bill. When Derby became prime minister in February 1858, Lord John encouraged him to allow the bill for the government of India to be shaped by resolution of the house. There could, therefore, be no question of a government defeat leading to the immediate restoration of Palmerston. By 1859 Lord John was recovering influence in the house. Derby brought in a reform bill, and Lord John drafted an amendment which was carried on 31 March by 330 votes to 291. At the general election which followed Lord John himself was returned without a contest. But the margin between the parties was close, and it was time for Palmerston and Lord John to bury their differences. Each agreed to serve under the other, but not under a third, the Peelites united with the whigs and Liberals, and on 10 June 1859 Derby was ejected by 323 votes to 310.

Foreign secretary, 1859–1865 The queen selected Palmerston to lead the new administration, and Lord John chose the Foreign Office. He had been there before, but only for a few weeks in 1853, when the issue of the holy places in Palestine was being handled in the traditional diplomatic terms of the concert of Europe and the balance of power.

Now the powers themselves were being turned inside out by their component nationalities, and there were, during Lord John's six-year tenure, two players with an interest in redrawing the map of Europe, Napoleon III and Bismarck.

Palmerston, to whom Lord John turned for advice, believed that Napoleon III wished to avenge his uncle's defeat at Waterloo. In 1859 there was a panic about a possible French invasion. While Palmerston wanted to fortify the arsenals and Gladstone tried to lower war fever by concluding a commercial treaty with France, Lord John supported both camps and thus helped to avert a breach in the cabinet. Elsewhere in Europe, France and Britain often found themselves on the same side of the fault lines which divided the liberal powers from the autocracies. The immediate issue was Italy. Both Napoleon III and Lord John wished to see Italy freed from Austrian rule. When Lord John took office in 1859 Austria had already declared war on France, and the problem was how to encourage the Italians without enabling France to alter the balance of power. In March 1860 Lord John condemned the French annexation of Nice and Savoy. In July, when Garibaldi invaded Sicily, Cavour sent Sir James Lacaita on an urgent mission to Lord John, to persuade the British government not to prevent the insurgents from crossing the Strait of Messina and invading the kingdom of Naples. Lord John complied, and when Cavour annexed the whole of southern and central Italy, and other powers withdrew their ministers from Turin, Lord John sent his famous dispatch of 27 October 1860 informing the world that the people of southern Italy had had good reasons for throwing off their allegiance to their former governments. Instead of censuring them her majesty's government would 'turn their eyes rather to the gratifying prospect of a people building up the edifice of their liberties, and consolidating the work of their independence, amid the sympathies and good wishes of Europe'. In 1861 Britain officially recognized the new kingdom of Italy.

In 1860, while Lord John was associating Britain with the creation of the new Italian state, he was also busy with another reform bill. The formula was much the same as before, as was the response. He rued the mood of the country, which, as he said, was to 'rest and be thankful'. In 1861 his brother the duke of Bedford died, and Lord John inherited the Ardsalla estate on the banks of the Boyne in co. Meath. This had been gifted to the Russell family by the third and last Earl Ludlow in 1842. It was too late for Lord John to become a model landlord. As Palmerston was still 'as fresh as a four year old' and Gladstone was becoming the star of the young Liberals, Lord John then asked for a peerage. Palmerston had tried to persuade the Lords to accept a life peer in 1856, and failed. There was nothing for it but to become a hereditary one, and Lord John became Earl Russell of Kingston Russell, and his eldest son became Viscount Amberley of Amberley and Ardsalla. Commentators were surprised, because young John was ardently interested in Liberal politics, and could now look forward to no more than an abbreviated career in the House of Commons.

By the time he went to the Foreign Office Russell had become the thinking person's politician, and any fine Sunday a stream of visitors might be seen making their way out of town to Pembroke Lodge. Macaulay came, until his death in 1859, and after him Alexander Kinglake and Edward Lecky. Dickens and Thackeray, whose works Russell read aloud to his children, were frequent guests; Tennyson a more occasional one. Mrs Beecher Stowe and Longfellow made a point of calling when they were in Europe. Dean Stanley had a short train journey from Westminster, and Charles Dodgson, Goldwin Smith, and H. G. Liddell a slightly longer one from Oxford. Another Oxford visitor, Benjamin Jowett, found that, notwithstanding his shyness, Russell could talk to you 'on any subject of history or philosophy like a real man' (Jowett to R. Morier, 10 May 1861, E. Abbott and L. Campbell, *Letters of Benjamin Jowett*, 1899, 58). On the lawn they mingled somewhat incongruously with the ambassadors of foreign powers accredited to the court of St James. Abroad as at home Russell wished to promote the development of representative institutions, and the didactic tone of his dispatches constituted 'une littérature diplomatique tout à fait nouvelle' (Walpole, 2.328). British ambassadors abroad, who were versed in the traditional circumlocutions, like Lord Cowley, were horrified when Russell likened King Victor Emmanuel to William III, and referred the emperor of Austria to the authority of 'that eminent jurist Vattel' for his opinion on a subject's right to resist his sovereign. Their opposite numbers in London, Charles Francis Adams, Count Apponyi, Count Bernstorff, and M. de Persigny, seem to have taken Russell's cheek in good part. Their worry was that they scarcely dare let Russell out of their sight, because there was no knowing what he might do next.

Russell enjoyed his years at the Foreign Office, but he did not achieve a second success equal to his Italian one. Like other members of the cabinet he was in two minds about the American Civil War. When a Northern cruiser took two Southern agents off the British ship *Trent* his peppery dispatch had to be toned down at the instance of Prince Albert, and when told that a ship being built in Laird's yard in Birkenhead, the *Alabama*, was being armed in order to prey upon Northern shipping, he delayed stopping it until too late. In 1863, when the Russians suppressed the insurrection in Poland, he found himself unable to concert a joint remonstrance with France. In 1864 he hosted a conference in London aimed at defusing the Schleswig-Holstein crisis. Palmerston had encouraged the Danes to believe that they would not stand alone, but the cabinet refused to sanction military intervention, and Lord John came before the conference empty-handed. This was one of the most significant failures of British foreign policy during the nineteenth century, and it led to a defeat, upon a motion of censure, in the House of Lords (July 1864).

Prime minister, 1865–1866 There was a general election in 1865, and Palmerston died on 18 October before the new parliament met. Russell was invited to carry on the existing government, and Gladstone took the lead in the House of Commons. Here was the alliance of whigs and Peelites under Russell's leadership for which he had hoped since 1846. When the cabinet met, Russell committed the ministry to another reform bill. In the months which followed London society appears to have been bitterly hostile to Russell's flirtation with 'democracy' and the wildest rumours circulated about what was taking place in cabinet. The work, as Russell realized, now fell upon Gladstone, who introduced the bill on 12 March. There were no redistribution of seats clauses, ministers were told they had not shown their hand, and the second reading was carried by only 318 to 313 votes. In May they brought in a redistribution bill which proposed to take one member away from small two-member constituencies, and to group other small boroughs. But thirty-five 'liberals' formed a 'Cave of Adullam' and voted against the bill. On 18 June the government was defeated, and on 26 June they resigned. In the meantime Amberley had entered parliament at a by-election and witnessed the last seven weeks of his father's government. Russell himself took it all very well, merely remarking that it was nice weather to go out in, and forecasting that his successor would have to bring in another bill 'like ours' with 'some of Dizzy's elixir' infused into the dose (Russell to Gladstone, 31 Aug 1866, BL, Add. MS 44293, fols. 197–198).

Final years, 1866–1878 When the winter came both the Russells and the Gladstones went off to Italy, where they met at Russell's request and discussed the Irish church. In 1867 Russell visited his estate in Ireland. In December he was 'determined to make a move about education', and brought a series of resolutions before the House of Lords in which he asserted the moral right of every child to the blessings of education (*Dear Miss Nightingale*, 417). He addressed a *Letter to the Right Hon. Chichester Fortescue on the State of Ireland*, followed by a second *Letter* and a third, arguing, as ever, in favour of concurrent endowment. He announced his retirement from politics, or did he?; no one was quite sure. He took no part in the general election of 1868, but followed Gladstone's campaign in the newspapers, or, as he put it, 'drank a quart bottle of Gladstone every morning' (Russell to Gladstone, 24 Oct 1868, BL, Add. MS 44294, fols. 137–138). Russell criticized the Gladstone ministry's new course in foreign policy, and attacked the submission of the *Alabama* claims to arbitration. Gladstone himself was 'more sorry than surprised' by all this. He reassured Russell that the bill to disestablish and disendow the Irish church was founded 'upon principles of which you were the expositor long ago', and that in all that related to the constitution he looked upon him as his oracle and master (Walpole, 2.437). In 1869–70 and again in 1871–2 Lord and Lady Russell spent the winter in the south of France, but in 1873 they proceeded no further than Dieppe. In 1874 Russell finished dictating his *Recollections and Suggestions*. His last years were saddened by the illness of his sons Rollo and William, and the death in June 1874 of Kate Amberley and her daughter, his granddaughter. In January 1876 Lord Amberley died. In 1878 Russell himself fell ill. Gladstone went to Pembroke Lodge and found him 'a noble wreck' (Gladstone, *Diaries*, 8.308). He was 'quite ready to go now'. He died at Pembroke Lodge on 28 May 1878, and was buried on 4 June in the family vault at Chenies, Buckinghamshire.

Historical reputation Russell should have retired in 1852. But he had insisted upon carrying on, and behaved with a mixture of mortification and petulance which cost him a great reputation. By the time he died, there was only one person who might have been able to write a *Life* that would have restored Russell in the public estimation, and that was John Morley. But Russell had never been businesslike, his archives were in confusion, and Morley refused. After a delay the commission passed to Spencer Walpole and the *Life* was published in 1889. But by that time the world was moving on. Asquith and Lloyd George had not been brought up to revere Russell in the way that he had revered Fox. In the century after Spencer Walpole wrote, there were only three more biographies of Lord John, and when books were written about the whigs it was to treat them as dinosaurs—wonderful, but extinct. Towards the end of the twentieth century, however, when British politicians appeared to have much to learn from other more prosperous nations about civil rights, the toleration of dissent, and respect for education, there was a revival of interest in the whigs. The works of Richard Brent (1987), Peter Mandler (1990), and Jonathan Parry (1993) struck an increasingly appreciative note. Nineteenth-century whigs, it was then clear, got many things right. They had a rational understanding of the relationship between the past and the present. They dismissed the political superstitions of Edmund Burke, and welcomed new ideas and the dialectical turns of debate. They favoured inquiry and the collection of statistics. They took a positive and realistic view of what could be achieved by legislation and government. For a generation they—and Lord John Russell most of all—practised a high-minded and disinterested form of politics which stands to this day as the high-water mark of parliamentary government.   JOHN PREST

Sources S. Walpole, *The life of Lord John Russell*, 2 vols. (1889) • J. M. Prest, *Lord John Russell* (1972) • *Selections from speeches of Earl Russell, 1817 to 1841, and from despatches, 1859 to 1865*, 2 vols. (1870) • J. Russell, *Recollections and suggestions, 1813–1873* (1875) • *Early correspondence of Lord John Russell*, ed. R. Russell, 2 vols. (1913?) • *The later correspondence of Lord John Russell, 1840–1878*, ed. G. P. Gooch, 2 vols. (1925) • J. D. MacCarthy and M. A. Russell, *Lady John Russell: a memoir, with selections from her diaries*, 3rd edn (1926) • G. W. E. Russell, *Collections and recollections* (1898) • *The Honourable Adelaide Drummond: retrospect and memoir*, ed. B. Champneys (1915) • *Recollections of Lady Georgiana Peel*, ed. E. Peel (1920) • *The Amberley papers: the letters and diaries of Lord and Lady Amberley*, ed. B. Russell and P. Russell, 2 vols. (1937) • *The Roman question: extracts from the despatches of Odo Russell from Rome, 1858–1870*, ed. N. Blakiston (1962) • G. Blakiston, *Lord William Russell and his wife, 1815–1846* (1972) • W. M. Torrens, *Memoirs of William Lamb, second Viscount Melbourne*, new edn (1890) • A. P. Donajgrodski, 'The home office, 1822–48', DPhil diss., U. Oxf., 1973 • R. B. O'Brien, *Thomas Drummond, under-secretary in Ireland, 1835–40: life and letters* (1889) • D. A. Kerr, 'A nation of beggars'? Priests, people, and politics in famine Ireland, 1846–1852 (1994) • W. P. Morrell, *British colonial policy in the age of Peel and Russell* (1930) • *Letters from Lord Sydenham, governor-general of Canada, 1839 to 1841, to Lord John Russell*, ed. P. Knaplund (1931) • P. Knaplund, *James Stephen and the British colonial system, 1813–1847* (1953) • O. A. Kinchen, *Lord Russell's Canadian policy* (1945) • H. G. Grey, *The colonial policy of Lord John Russell's administration*, 2 vols. (1853) • *The Greville memoirs, 1814–1860*, ed. L. Strachey and R. Fulford, 8 vols. (1938) • D. Southgate, *The passing of the whigs, 1832–1886* (1962) • A. V. Mitchell, *The whigs in opposition, 1815–1830* (1967) • R. Brent, *Liberal Anglican politics: whiggery, religion, and reform, 1830–1841* (1987) • P. Mandler, *Aristocratic government in the age of reform: whigs and liberals, 1830–1852* (1990) • Gladstone, *Diaries* • J. Parry, *The rise and fall of liberal government in Victorian Britain* (1993) • J. Parry, 'Past and future in the later career of Lord John Russell', *History and biography: essays in honour of Derek Beales*, ed. T. C. W. Blanning and D. Cannadine (1996) • G. F. A. Best, 'The whigs and the church establishment in the age of Grey and Holland', *History*, new ser., 45 (1960), 103–18 • F. A. Dreyer, 'The whigs and the political crisis of 1845', *EngHR*, 80 (1965), 514–37 • J. Prest, 'Gladstone and Russell', *TRHS*, 5th ser., 16 (1966), 43–63 • J. P. Ellens, 'Lord John Russell and the church rate conflict: the struggle for a broad church, 1834–1868', *Journal of British Studies*, 26 (1987), 232–57 • U. Durham L., archives and special collections, Grey of Howick collection • U. Southampton L., Palmerston MSS • UCL, Brougham MSS • NL Scot., Ellice MSS • NL Scot., Minto MSS • *Dear Miss Nightingale: a selection of Benjamin Jowett's letters to Florence Nightingale, 1860–1893*, ed. V. Quinn and J. Prest (1987)

Archives BL, corresp. and literary papers, Add. MS 38080, 47598–47601 • BL, letters, RP2342 [copies] • Bodl. Oxf., letter-book, letters and notes • Duke U., Perkins L., political letters and memoranda • Hunt. L., letters • McMaster University, Hamilton, Ontario, diary • NL Scot., corresp. • NL Wales, letters • PRO, general and official corresp. and papers, PRO 30/22 • U. Mich., Clements L., corresp. and papers • UCL, literary and political papers | Althorp, Northamptonshire, Spencer papers • Balliol Oxf., corresp. with Sir Robert Morier • BL, corresp. with Lord Aberdeen, Add. MSS 43066–43068 • BL, letters to Lord Broughton, Add. MSS 47226–47229 • BL, corresp. with A. J. Fraser, Add. MSS 44912–44913 • BL, corresp. with W. E. Gladstone, Add. MSS 44291–44294 • BL, Halifax papers • BL, corresp. with third Baron Holland and Lady Holland, Add. MSS 51677–51680 • BL, corresp. with fourth Baron Holland, Add. MS 52006 • BL, corresp. with Sir Austen Layard, Add. MSS 38959–39118 • BL, corresp. with Sir Robert Peel, Add. MSS 40400–40603 • BL, corresp. with fifth marquess of Ripon, Add. MS 43512 • BL, letters to Lord Stanmore, Add. MS 49272 • BL, corresp. with first Baron Strathnairn, Add. MS 42799 • BL, corresp. with Charles Wood, Add. MS 49531 • Bodl. Oxf., letters to fourth earl of Clarendon • Bodl. Oxf., corresp. with Sir John Fiennes Crampton • Bodl. Oxf., letters to Disraeli • Bodl. Oxf., letters to Sir William Harcourt • Bodl. Oxf., corresp. with Lord Kimberley • Bodl. Oxf., corresp. with Sir Thomas Phillipps • Bodl. Oxf., corresp. with Samuel Wilberforce • Bodl. RH, corresp. with Thomas Buxton • Borth. Inst., corresp. with first Viscount Halifax • Bowood House, Wiltshire, Lansdowne papers • Bucks. RLSS, letters to twelfth duke of Somerset • Cambs. AS, Huntingdon, letters to fifth duke of Manchester • Castle Howard, Yorkshire, Carlisle papers • Chatsworth House, Derbyshire, letters to dukes of Devonshire • CKS, letters to Lord Stanhope • CKS, corresp. with William Tapley • Cumbria AS, Carlisle, corresp. with Sir James Graham • Devon RO, corresp. with second Earl Fortescue • Harrowby Manuscript Trust, Sandon Hall, Staffordshire, letters to Lord Harrowby and Lady Harrowby • Herts. ALS, corresp. with first Baron Lytton • HLRO, corresp. with Speaker Brand • JRL, letters to Sir James Kay-Shuttleworth • LPL, corresp. with William Howley • LPL, corresp. with Lord Selborne • LPL, corresp. with A. C. Tait • Lpool RO, letters to fourteenth earl of Derby • NA Scot., corresp. with first earl of Dalhousie • NA Scot., letters to Charles Augustus Murray • NL Scot., letters to Edward Ellis sen. • NL Scot., corresp. with George Gleig • NL Scot., letters to Minto family • NL Scot., letters to Sir Andrew Rutherford • NL Wales, corresp. with Lord Clive • NL Wales, corresp. with Sir George Cornewall Lewis • Norfolk RO, corresp. with Sir Henry Lytton Bulwer • NRA, corresp. with first earl of Durham • NRA, priv.

coll., letters to first marquess of Anglesey · NRA, priv. coll., letters to first Baron Hammond · NRA, priv. coll., corresp. with Lord Seymour · NRA, priv. coll., letters to E. J. Shirley · PRO, corresp. with Stratford Canning, FO 352 · PRO, corresp. with first Earl Cowley, FO 519 · PRO, letters to first Baron Hammond, FO 391 · PRO, corresp. with Odo Russell, FO 918 · PRO NIre., corresp. with Lord Dufferin · St Deiniol's Library, Hawarden, letters to fifth duke of Newcastle · Staffs. RO, letters to first Baron Hatherton · Suffolk RO, Ipswich, notes to George Keppel · Surrey HC, letters to Sir T. D. Acland · Trinity Cam., letters to Lord Houghton · U. Durham L., corresp. with second Earl Grey; corresp. with third Earl Grey; corresp. with Hon. Charles Grey · U. Nott. L., corresp. with Sir Andrew Buchanan · U. Nott. L., letters to J. E. Denison · U. Nott. L., corresp. with fifth duke of Newcastle and others · U. Southampton L., corresp. with Lord Melbourne · U. Southampton L., corresp. with Lord Palmerston · U. Southampton L., letters to duke of Wellington · UCL, corresp. with Lord Brougham · UCL, corresp. with Sir E. Chadwick · UCL, letters to Society for the Diffusion of Useful Knowledge · UCL, Parkes papers · W. Sussex RO, corresp. with Richard Cobden · W. Sussex RO, letters to fifth duke of Richmond · W. Sussex RO, letters to sixth duke of Richmond · W. Sussex RO, corresp. with John Abel Smith and Sir James Brooke · W. Yorks. AS, Leeds, letters to first marquess of Clanricarde · Warks. CRO, letters to Dormer family · Wilts. & Swindon RO, corresp. with Sidney Herbert and Elizabeth Herbert · Woburn Abbey, Bedfordshire, letters to dukes of Bedford · Woburn Abbey, Bedfordshire, letters to Lord George William Russell

Likenesses G. Hayter, oils, c.1815, Longleat House, Wiltshire · D. Maclise, pencil drawing, 1831, V&A · J. Francis, marble bust, 1832, NPG; on loan to House of Lords · G. Hayter, oils, 1832, Woburn Abbey, Bedfordshire · J. Bromley, mezzotint, pubd 1836 (after G. Hayter), BM, NPG · J. Francis, bust, 1838, Royal Collection · R. Westmacott junior, bust, c.1843, Woburn Abbey, Bedfordshire · G. F. Watts, oils, c.1851, NPG · G. F. Watts, chalk drawing, c.1852, NPG [*see illus.*] · F. Grant, oils, 1853, NPG · T. J. Barker, group portrait, oils, c.1861 (*Queen Victoria Presenting a Bible in the Audience Chamber at Windsor*), NPG · J. E. Boehm, statue, 1880, Palace of Westminster; related marble bust, Westminster Abbey, London · J. E. Boehm, terracotta head, c.1880 (study for statue, Palace of Westminster), NPG · F. C. Gould, pen-and-ink drawing, c.1901, NPG · Ape [C. Pellegrini], caricature, coloured lithograph, NPG; repro. in *VF* (5 June 1869) · Ape [C. Pellegrini], lithograph, repro. in *VF* (5 June 1889), pl. 18 · W. Beechey, oils (as a boy), Woburn Abbey, Bedfordshire · I. Bruce, aquatint (after unknown silhouettist), NPG · S. F. Diez, drawing, Staatliche Kupferstichkabinett, Berlin · J. Doyle, caricature drawings, BM · J. Gilbert, group portrait, pencil and wash (*The Coalition Ministry, 1854*), NPG · G. Hayter, group portrait, oils (*The trial of Queen Caroline, 1820*), NPG · G. Hayter, group portrait, oils (*House of Commons, 1833*), NPG · J. Partridge, group portrait (*The Fine Arts Commissioners, 1846*), NPG · J. Phillip, group portrait, oils (*The House of Commons, 1860*), Palace of Westminster, London · H. W. Phillips, group portrait, oils (*The Royal Commissioners for the Great Exhibition, 1851*), V&A · Sartain, engraving, repro. in *Eclectic Magazine*, 52 (1861), 289 · Thorburn, miniature · D. Wilkie, group portrait, oils (*The first Council of Queen Victoria, 1837*), Royal Collection · Wilkie, portrait, repro. in *Les Lettres*, 2 (1887), 286 · T. C. Wilson, lithograph (after his earlier work), NPG · Window and Bridge, carte-de-visite, NPG

Wealth at death under £80,000: probate, 2 July 1878, *CGPLA Eng. & Wales*

Russell, John [Jack; *called* the Sporting Parson] (1795–1883), Church of England clergyman and sportsman, was born on 21 December 1795 at Dartmouth, Devon, the eldest son of John Russell (1760–1847), rector of South Hill, near Callington, Cornwall, and later of Iddesleigh, Devon, and his wife, Nora, *née* Jewell. His father's family, the

John [Jack] **Russell** (1795–1883), by Joseph Brown, pubd 1870 (after Button & Sons)

Kingston-Russells, had lived in Devon since 1551. He was first educated at his father's small school and subsequently attended Plympton grammar school and (from 1809) Blundell's school at Tiverton. He matriculated from Exeter College, Oxford, in 1814, and graduated BA in 1818. He was ordained deacon the following year, and priest in 1820. He was appointed curate at George Nympton, near South Molton, and then became his father's curate at Iddesleigh in 1826. In 1832 he moved to Tordown in the parish of Swimbridge, near Barnstaple, and the next year was appointed by the dean of Exeter perpetual curate of Swimbridge and Landkey. He remained there contentedly until 1879, when he reluctantly accepted from Lord Poltimore the more valuable living of Black Torrington, near Hatherleigh.

Russell began hunting as a boy, with his father's pack of hounds, and was a passionate hunt follower until the last year of his life; he pursued everything from hares and foxes to otters and stags, so that a quarry was available all year round. At school in Tiverton he kept ferrets for ratting and rabbiting, and with a friend he acquired his first pack of four and a half couple of scratch hounds, boarded at the local blacksmith's, for hare-hunting. At Oxford University Russell—a strong man, 6 feet tall—fished, rowed, took boxing lessons, and hunted the fox and stag at every opportunity, with some of the most prestigious hunts, including those of the duke of Beaufort and Sir Thomas Mostyn.

It was in Oxford that Russell acquired the first of the fox terriers for which he became famous and which have since borne the name Jack Russell terriers. He recognized the potential of this dog, Trump, when he saw her with a milkman, and promptly purchased her; she was the progenitor of this particular breed, which drove the foxes out of their earths for the foxhounds. After Oxford, although he worked hard in his parish, he found the life of a rural parson very quiet, and as the South Molton area was inhabited by otters, he resolved to hunt them. He achieved no success, however, until he added to his pack a large foxhound, Racer, which had been rejected as too fast or mute for fox-hunting. That season he was delighted to kill thirty-five otters and subsequently realized that hounds have no natural instinct to pursue the otter, perhaps because the water where they live carries no scent, and the hounds need to be trained to this prey while young. This pack was trencher-fed by his parishioners. He also hunted the fox with the hounds of a neighbouring parson, John Froude (d. 1852), vicar of Knowstone.

On 30 May 1826, at Swimbridge, Russell married Penelope Incledon Bury, the daughter of Admiral and Mrs Bury, an influential local family, of Dennington House, Barnstaple. They had two sons, one of whom died in infancy. They were a devoted couple who shared a keen interest in hunting, and were often seen hunting together, on Exmoor ponies. At Iddesleigh he had the opportunity to form his own fox hunt and he was given a slice of two neighbouring hunts to create his territory. It was the custom in this area for people to ring the church bell when a fox was located, so that they could assemble and kill it for sport, with axes or sticks. When Russell discovered this, he stood up to the crowds and requested that he should be allowed to kill the foxes in a more English way; eventually word spread and he was allowed to hunt the foxes. He joined his pack to that of C. A. Harris, of Okehampton, Devon, in 1827 and hunted successfully on two days each week. They built artificial earths for fox cubs, which were fed until they were big enough to be hunted, thus providing fox-hunting to order. He parted with his hounds on his appointment to Swimbridge, but after two years there, encouraged by his wife, he started a fresh pack which he kept for almost thirty-seven years, despite incurring the wrath of Henry Phillpotts, the bishop of Exeter. Russell was summoned by the bishop and accused of neglecting his duties in favour of hunting, but the charge was proved false, and the bishop was powerless to prevent his sport.

Russell had excellent judgement of a hound's potential and could, like many hound owners, recognize each animal individually. He also acted as his own huntsman. In 1845, with Sir Walter Carew and a Mr Trelawny, Russell formed a fox-hunting club at South Molton; the three packs met for a fortnight, in spring and autumn, at The George inn and provided hunting for the neighbourhood. Many landowners destroyed foxes but Russell always managed to preserve enough to provide twelve good days' sport. He also helped to revive the Exmoor stag hunt. A keen agricultural improver in a part of the country where farming methods were considered backward, he attended the Royal Agricultural Society's Plymouth meeting in 1865, where he met the prince of Wales. In 1873 he was invited to join the prince and princess at Sandringham.

After his wife died in 1875, Russell busied himself by becoming an honorary hospital governor, and chaplain to the high sheriff of Cornwall. In 1882, the year before he died, Russell went out stag-hunting and travelled to Ascot races, and to Sandringham, but his health rapidly deteriorated and he died on 28 April 1883 at Black Torrington. A thousand people attended his funeral on 3 May at Swimbridge. In addition to his hunting prowess, Russell's enthusiastic promotion of Devon cream and cider, and his keen support for Devon wrestlers against their Cornish rivals, made him a popular county figure. His 'full-flavoured Devonian speech' was

> garnished with picturesque west-country phrases, and illuminated by a pungent wit … In the pulpit he tried to reform conduct rather than to expound doctrine, being a stern denouncer of bad language, strong drinks, and the 'filthy habit of smoking'. (DNB)

IRIS M. MIDDLETON

Sources E. W. L. Davies, *The out-of-door life of the Rev John Russell* (1883) · Foster, *Alum. Oxon.* · *DNB* · *The Times* (30 April 1883) · *ILN* (12 May 1883) · Ward, *Men of the reign*, 783 · *Sporting and Dramatic News* (5 May 1883) · *Sporting and Dramatic News* (12 May 1883) · *The Field* (5 May 1883) · *The Russell album. A memorial of the late Rev. John Russell, containing a series of twelve hunting sketches by T. M. B. Marshall* (1885) [intro. by C. A. M. Harris] · C. W. Boase, ed., *Registrum Collegii Exoniensis*, new edn, OHS, 27 (1894), 216 · F. J. Snell, *Blundell's: a short history of a famous west country school* (1928)
Likenesses J. Brown, stipple, pubd 1870 (after photograph by Button & Sons), NPG [*see illus.*] · engraving, repro. in Davies, *Out-of-door life of the Rev John Russell*, frontispiece · process block print (after S. J. Carter), NPG

Russell, John, Viscount Amberley (1842–1876), politician and writer, was born on 10 December 1842 at 37 Chesham Place, London, the eldest of the four children of Lord John Russell (1792–1878) [see Russell, John, first Earl Russell], and his second wife, Frances Anna Maria *Russell (1815–1898), daughter of Gilbert Elliot Murray *Kynynmound, second earl of Minto, and his wife, Mary. He became Viscount Amberley when his father took a peerage as Earl Russell in July 1861. He was educated at home until 1857 and then at Harrow School, Edinburgh University, and Trinity College, Cambridge, which he left prematurely in February 1863, disliking Cambridge's social tone and mathematical orientation.

Short in stature and black-haired, Amberley was serious, shy, and self-conscious, and had a hunger for truth, especially on religious questions. In the early 1860s he came to reject the notion of the divinity of Christ and became an agnostic, though he remained reverential in spirit. For over ten years from 1864 he made a careful comparative study of religions, with a view to separating out the transitory and man-made components of each from universally applicable truths. The resulting work, *An

John Russell, Viscount Amberley (1842–1876), by John Watkins

Analysis of Religious Belief, was published posthumously in 1876. In periodical articles between 1863 and 1867 Amberley argued that, since the Church of England had been established in order to serve national purposes, its clergymen should be given unfettered freedom of expression, so as to make it truly comprehensive and advance religious understanding. He became a follower and friend of John Stuart Mill. On 8 November 1864, at Alderley, Cheshire, he married Katharine Louisa (1842–1874) [*see* Russell, Katharine Louisa], daughter of Edward John Stanley, second Baron Stanley of Alderley; she was a woman of high spirits and intellectual curiosity, who encouraged him to mix with advanced philosophical liberals.

Amberley's father was anxious for him to enter parliament; he stood unsuccessfully for Leeds in 1865 but was elected for Nottingham in May 1866. His major contribution in parliament was the introduction of a bill in 1867 to allow secularists and others to charge for Sunday evening lectures of a decorous and uplifting nature. Though supported by Mill, the bill was defeated. Mill regarded Amberley as one of his most promising political heirs, but he was defeated at the South Devon election of 1868. His unwise choice of a county constituency reflected his high-minded and inflexible attitude to practical politics: he disliked the compromises with ignorance and money required in many large boroughs, while his views were too unorthodox for most smaller seats. His defeat was assisted by controversy over his support for birth control as a means of checking downward pressure on wages; opponents suggested that he lacked commitment to marriage and supported abortion.

Amberley retired from politics to concentrate on his religious studies, though he continued to advocate various radical causes in speeches and articles. These included women's suffrage, an international federation charged with preventing wars, and a secular solution to the religious difficulty thrown up by the 1870 Education Act. In 1870 he and his wife bought Ravenscroft, a property near Chepstow in Monmouthshire (where he was a magistrate), and, still very much in love, retreated into a more isolated domestic life, much of which was spent reorganizing the grounds and communing with nature. But, though essentially contented, Amberley was constitutionally weak and low-spirited, and suffered from epilepsy in 1873. He was plunged into severe depression by the death of his wife and daughter from diphtheria in the summer of 1874. Without Lady Amberley's practical vivacity he took little interest in living, and he died of bronchitis at Ravenscroft on 9 January 1876. In accordance with his instructions, on 13 January he was buried with his wife and daughter in a vault in the grounds of his house, though his family later had the three bodies removed to the Russell vault at Chenies, Buckinghamshire.

Amberley left his two sons, John Francis Stanley Russell and Bertrand *Russell (the philosopher), the second and third earls Russell, in the charge of two guardians of heterodox views and habits. But his deeply pious mother had this instruction challenged and won custody of them. Bertrand Russell, with his wife, edited his parents' papers in two volumes (1937), with an interesting commentary on them and on the Russells generally. Though Amberley died when his famous son was only three, his life and political views were clearly a strong posthumous influence, and helped to link Bertrand to J. S. Mill's philosophy and politics.   JONATHAN PARRY

Sources *The Amberley papers: the letters and diaries of Lord and Lady Amberley*, ed. B. Russell and P. Russell, 2 vols. (1937) · Earl Russell [J. F. S. Russell], *My life and adventures* (1923) · *Wellesley index* · D. MacCarthy and A. Russell, *Lady John Russell* (1910)
Archives Harvard U., Houghton L. · McMaster University, Hamilton, Ontario, corresp. and papers | NL Scot., letters to Alexander Campbell
Likenesses photograph, 1860–64, repro. in Russell and Russell, eds., *The Amberley papers*, 1.242 · G. Howard, sketch, 1864, repro. in Russell and Russell, eds., *The Amberley papers*, 1.322 · J. Watkins, photograph, NPG [*see illus.*] · portrait, repro. in *ILN*, 68 (1876), 76
Wealth at death under £10,000: probate, 9 Feb 1876, *CGPLA Eng. & Wales*

Russell, Sir (Edward) John (1872–1965), agricultural scientist, was born on 31 October 1872 in Frampton-on-Severn, the eldest of the nine children of Edward Thomas Russell and his wife, Clara Angel, daughter of Captain Samuel Hallet. His maternal grandfather owned barges and had a wharf in Lambeth; his paternal grandfather was in the coal business. His father was a schoolmaster, whose disagreements with employers led to frequent moves around

Sir (Edward) John Russell (1872–1965), by Howard Coster, c.1940

the country and, ultimately, lay appointments at churches in Leicester and Birmingham.

After attending a large number of schools, Russell went, at the age of thirteen, to the recently opened technical school in Birmingham, where he decided that chemistry would be his vocation. He did very well at that school, but his parents moved to London when he was fourteen, and he was obliged to find work. He was apprenticed to a homoeopathic chemist in London, which he found unrewarding, but he made good use of evening classes and private reading. Having matriculated he entered the Presbyterian college in Carmarthen in 1891. After a year he went with a scholarship to University College, Aberystwyth, and thence, in 1894, to Owens College, Manchester. Having graduated BSc with first-class honours in chemistry in 1896, he started research on rates of reaction in thoroughly dried gases. He was awarded a DSc by London University in 1901.

Intense exposure to nonconformist religion, various missions and charities, and his father's republican sympathies, made Russell dissatisfied with the condition of the urban poor. Pure chemistry was beginning to seem too limited a subject. He therefore went to Copenhagen in 1900 to learn about agricultural co-operatives and the biochemistry of yeast. In 1901 he was appointed lecturer at Wye Agricultural College in Kent and there found his vocation. Russell soon realized that agriculture was not a large-scale solution to town unemployment, requiring, as it did, a highly skilled workforce.

On 15 September 1903 Russell married Elnor (1878–1965), whom he had met two years earlier at the Manchester Mission, the daughter of Walter Oldham of Manchester, formerly a merchant of Penang and Singapore. They had five sons and two daughters. One of the sons died in 1926 at the age of sixteen, after a road accident, and another was killed in action in 1945, at the age of twenty-seven. One of the surviving sons, (Edward) Walter *Russell, became professor of soil science at Reading University.

In 1907 Russell moved to Rothamsted Experimental Station, where he became director in 1912. Agricultural research at that time was moribund: the president of the Board of Agriculture and Fisheries 'could not conceive of circumstances in which the Board would concern itself with research' and expressed the view that British agriculture was 'dead and it was the Board's business to bury it'. Under Russell, however, Rothamsted grew steadily in size and influence. In 1910 a £1 million development fund was set up for agriculture, part of which went to Rothamsted. When war began in 1914 Russell became a member of various committees concerned with government-financed research; this brought more grants to the experimental station. Government finance continued after the war and enabled new departments to be established. However, it was an uphill task for there were those in influential positions who thought that Rothamsted should become an institute for routine soil analysis. Russell showed skill, amounting to genius, in obtaining money from private sources most dramatically when he managed in seven weeks to raise enough money to buy the Rothamsted estate, which the public trustee was proposing to sell for development in 1934. His detestation of money lying idle led to useful, but disconcerting, flexibility in Rothamsted finances.

Chance observation while at Wye led Russell and collaborators to a detailed examination of the beneficial effects of partially sterilizing soil. Although not practical on a field scale, the method was extensively used in glasshouses. After his appointment as director he had little time for research, and travelled widely to give advice and to gain experience of agriculture in other climates. He remained an enthusiastic traveller until nearly the end of his life and visited at least twenty countries. During a visit to Sudan in 1934 he was disturbed by the lack of information exchange between that country and Britain, and, as a result, he initiated the Imperial (later Commonwealth) Agricultural Bureaux.

Russell retired in 1943, but went on working in his new home near Woodstock, writing papers on research, and publishing many lectures, addresses, and reports on his travels. Among his many books were *Soil Conditions and Plant Growth* (1st edn, 1912; 7th edn, 1937), *World Population and World Food Supplies* (1954), *A History of Agricultural Science in Great Britain, 1620–1954* (1966), and *The Land Called Me* (1956), an autobiography. He was elected FRS in 1917, was appointed OBE in 1918, and was knighted in 1922. He was awarded gold medals from five bodies, and honorary degrees from eleven. Russell was rather short and, in his prime, lean. He moved quickly and walked leaning slightly forward and a little jerkily. His bright blue eyes always retained an expression of innocent candour. He died in a nursing home at Thames Bank, Goring-on-Thames, on 12 July 1965, surviving his wife by only a few weeks. N. W. PIRIE, rev.

Sources E. J. Russell, *The land called me* (1956) · H. G. Thornton, *Memoirs FRS*, 12 (1966), 457–77 · personal knowledge (1971) · m. cert.
Archives Rothamsted Experimental Station, Harpenden, corresp. and papers · U. Reading L., corresp., diaries, and papers · Wye College, Kent, diaries and papers | RS, corresp. with Sir Frederick Bawden
Likenesses W. Stoneman, photographs, 1923–42, NPG · H. Coster, photograph, *c*.1940, NPG [*see illus.*] · W. Bird, photograph, *c*.1959, RS · E. Hall, portrait, 1959 · W. Stoneman, photograph, RS
Wealth at death £4869: probate, 5 Nov 1965, *CGPLA Eng. & Wales*

Russell, John Fuller (1813–1884), ecclesiastical historian, born on 15 August 1813 in Middlesex, was the son of Thomas *Russell (*c*.1781–1846) and the brother of Arthur Tozer *Russell. He was educated at Mill Hill and the Merchant Taylors' School, London, and was admitted a pensioner of Peterhouse, Cambridge, on 4 June 1832. In 1836, while an undergraduate there, he entered into a correspondence with Edward Bouverie Pusey, and was one of the first sympathizers with the Oxford Movement at Cambridge. He became a regular correspondent of Pusey, and in 1837 visited him at Christ Church. Pusey advised him regarding Catholic principles in the church, and later warned Russell against excess with regard to the ornaments rubric. Russell was ordained deacon in 1838, and appointed to the curacy of St Peter's, Walworth, Surrey. In 1839 he graduated LLB, and in the same year was admitted into priest's orders, becoming curate of St Mary's, Newington Butts. He held the perpetual curacy of St James, Enfield, from 1841 to 1854, and in 1856 was presented to the rectory of Greenhithe, Kent, by Sidney Sussex College, Cambridge. He died on 6 April 1884 at his house at 4 Ormonde Terrace, Regent's Park, London, and was survived by his son, Edward Meadows Russell; no details of his marriage are known.

Russell was a member of the council of the Society of Antiquaries, of the central committee of the Royal Archaeological Institute, and of the committee of the Ecclesiological Society; he was vice-president of the Royal Archaeological Institute. He kept a collection of fourteenth-century ecclesiastical pictures at his home near Enfield. He was an expert witness before the ritual commission, having published *Strict Observance of the Rubric Recommended* in 1838. His evidence was published as *Oral and written evidence in regard to the post-Reformation symbolical use of lights in the Church of England* in the second report of the ritual commission (1867). His other publications focused on issues of high-church doctrine and discipline, particularly the authority of the clergy.

He was co-editor with Dean Hook of the *Voice of the Church* (2 vols., 1840), and with Dr W. J. Irons of *Tracts of the Anglican Fathers* (1841). He was also editor of *Hierurgia Anglicana, or, Documents and extracts illustrative of the Church of England after the Reformation* (1848).

THOMPSON COOPER, rev. ELLIE CLEWLOW

Sources *The Times* (10 April 1884) · Venn, *Alum. Cant.* · Boase, *Mod. Eng. biog.* · H. P. Liddon, *Life of Edward Bouverie Pusey*, ed. J. O. Johnston and others, 4th edn, 4 vols. (1894–8) · *CGPLA Eng. & Wales* (1884)
Archives Enfield Local History Unit, London, notebook · Pusey Oxf., corresp. and papers
Wealth at death £14,767 9s. 2d.: probate, 18 June 1884, *CGPLA Eng. & Wales*

Russell, John Hugo, third Baron Ampthill (1896–1973), naval officer and company director, was born at his father's London house, 109 Park Street, Mayfair, on 4 October 1896, the eldest in the family of four sons and one daughter of (Arthur) Oliver Villiers *Russell, second Baron Ampthill (1869–1935), and his wife, Lady Margaret Lygon (1874–1957), daughter of Frederick *Lygon, sixth Earl Beauchamp. His younger brother, Sir Guy Herbrand Edward *Russell (1898–1977), became an admiral.

Russell's childhood was spent in India where his father was governor of Madras and interim acting viceroy. After going through the Royal Naval College at Osborne and Dartmouth as a cadet, Russell joined the navy as a midshipman in 1912. Nicknamed Stilts on account of his height (6 feet 2 inches), he was from the outset a dedicated sailor and popular with superiors and subordinates alike. He served throughout the First World War, initially in HMS *Defence*, which was sunk at Jutland with no survivors a week after he had left her to join a sloop in the Mediterranean on promotion to sub-lieutenant. Later in the war he qualified as a submarine officer and took part in numerous underwater patrols in the North Sea. Soon after the war he retired from the service for domestic reasons. Most of the interwar years he spent with Carrier Engineering and Gallaher Limited, the tobacco manufacturing company in Belfast, of which he became a director in 1937, particularly interesting himself in the welfare of its employees. He succeeded his father in 1935.

Recalled to the navy with the rank of commander on the outbreak of the Second World War, Ampthill served throughout, first in the torpedo and mining department of the Admiralty and then on the staff of Admiral Sir Bertram Ramsay, allied naval commander-in-chief of the expeditionary force under General Eisenhower. As senior administrative officer with the rank of captain, Ampthill played an important part behind the scenes in the planning and execution of the naval aspects of the allied landings in north Africa and Europe. For his services in these campaigns he was created CBE (1945) and chevalier of the Légion d'honneur, besides being awarded the Croix de Guerre with palms and the US order of the Legion of Merit.

Immediately after the war Ampthill returned to Gallahers as an executive director and he remained on the board of the company until his retirement in 1966. From 1949 until his death he was also a member of the council of the Industrial Welfare Society, later the Industrial Society, and from 1964 to 1969 he was its chairman. Meanwhile, he continued to take a keen part in defence debates in the House of Lords as a staunch supporter of the Royal Navy and also in debates on industrial welfare.

Ampthill married first, in 1918, Christabel Hulme (1895/6–1976), second daughter of Lieutenant-Colonel John Hart, Leinster regiment, and his wife, Blanche Anstruther Erskine, of Broadhurst, Heathfield, Sussex. They had one son, Geoffrey Denis Erskine, who was born on 15 October 1921. A year later Ampthill petitioned for a divorce on the grounds of his wife's adultery, denying that he was Geoffrey's father. The jury disagreed, but at the re-hearing of the case in 1923 the petitioner was granted a decree nisi. After Christabel Russell's appeal had been dismissed by the Court of Appeal, she appealed to the House of Lords, who by a majority of three to two in May 1924 allowed her appeal on the grounds that her husband's evidence in the court below was inadmissible. Having thus established her son's legitimacy, judicially confirmed in 1926, Lady Ampthill's marriage was dissolved by divorce on her petition in 1937.

In the same year Ampthill married, second, Sibell Faithfull, daughter of Thomas Wilkinson Lumley, chief constable of Leicestershire. She died in 1947 without children. In 1948, he married, third, Adeline Mary Constance, eldest daughter of Canon Henry Evelyn Hone, vicar and rural dean of Godalming, Surrey. They had a son and a daughter. After a successful business career in London, Ampthill's first wife, Christabel, who was noted for her good looks, high spirits, and prowess in the hunting field, spent her later years in Ireland where she died on 16 February 1976, in Galway, at the age of eighty.

The House of Lords judgment in the so-called Russell baby case in 1924 was of considerable social as well as legal importance. It established the principle (reversed by parliament in 1949) that no evidence can be given by a husband and wife in any legal proceedings, if the effect of such evidence would be to bastardize a child born in wedlock. It also led to the passing two years later of the act of parliament restricting the reporting of divorce proceedings in England and Wales to the identity of the parties, the grounds for the petition, the judge's summing up, and the verdict.

Ampthill died on 3 June 1973 at his London home, 6 Springfield Road, St John's Wood. His elder son Geoffrey's claim to succeed him in title and sit in the upper house as fourth baron was contested by his younger son, John. The matter came before the House of Lords committee of privileges which after hearing legal argument upheld the elder son's claim.   H. MONTGOMERY HYDE, rev.

Sources *The Times* (4 June 1973) · *The Times* (18 Feb 1976) · *Law reports: appeal cases* (1924), 687 · E. Hunter, *Christabel: the Russell case and after* (1973) · private information (1986) · Burke, *Peerage* (1980) · *CGPLA Eng. & Wales* (1973)

Wealth at death £100,049: probate, 16 Aug 1973, *CGPLA Eng. & Wales*

Russell, John Scott (1808–1882), engineer and naval architect, eldest son of David Russell, a Scottish clergyman, and

his wife, Agnes Clark (*née* Scott), was born at Parkhead, near Glasgow, on 8 May 1808. He was baptized John and added his mother's maiden name when he left home. At the age of twelve he began to study for the church at St Andrews University but a year later he matriculated at Glasgow University, where his interests became increasingly scientific and he was awarded his MA in 1825. He moved to Edinburgh and took a number of teaching posts, culminating with a temporary appointment to carry out the duties of the professor of natural philosophy in 1832.

In 1834 Russell designed and built six large steam carriages which cruised at 14 m.p.h., carrying twenty-six passengers and a crew of three. They ran for a short time between Glasgow and Paisley and were said to be very comfortable but, following continual opposition and an accident, they were soon withdrawn.

At the same time Russell was working for a company operating a passenger service on the canal between Edinburgh and Glasgow. His first paper, to the British Association in 1835, showed how the wave of translation could be used to reduce the resistance of barges moving fast in a restricted waterway. In the course of his canal work he had built four experimental vessels of differing form to test his theory. The first of these, *Wave*, of about 60 feet length, had very hollow waterlines at the bow but was very lightly built and showed signs of weakness. This was remedied in the second vessel, *Storm*, of 120 feet length. In this ship the stiffeners were arranged longitudinally, supported by fairly closely spaced bulkheads instead of the traditional transverse framing. For a given weight, this is a stronger method of construction, and its introduction may be seen as Russell's greatest contribution to shipbuilding. The final two had further variations in form.

Russell believed that this work could be extended to the wave-making resistance of ships in the open sea and this led him to propose his 'wave-line' theory, which he was to develop over much of his career. It was a semi-empirical approach based on the idea of pushing the water aside with minimum loss of energy which led him to recommend very hollow waterlines forward, based on a sine curve. In his later writings he modified this slightly, suggesting that the distribution of sectional area should follow a sine curve, a variation which he sometimes described as the wave-form theory. At this time and later he carried out a large number of model tests but was unable to derive a consistent interpretation. Ships designed on this approach were generally fast and economical since, though his theory was fallacious, it none the less led to fine ends which were appropriate to the speed–length ratios of ships of the day. There was at that time no way of estimating the power required to drive a new ship at its design speed, and between 1838 and 1866 five major British Association committees attempted to solve the problem. Russell's reputation ensured that he was a member of each of them.

In 1836 Russell married Harriette, the second daughter of Lieutenant-Colonel and Lady Osborne; they had three daughters and one son. In 1838 he became a manager at Caird's engine works in Greenock. During this time he designed several ships on his wave-line theory which were engined by Caird. His fame was growing and in 1841 he was invited to write the section on shipbuilding for the *Encyclopaedia Britannica*. There seemed little prospect of advancement in the family firm of Caird and in 1844 Russell moved to London as editor of the *Railway Chronicle*. The following year he was persuaded to become secretary of the then almost defunct Royal Society of Arts. The society took the initiative in proposing a national exhibition and it was in no small degree due to Russell's efforts as joint secretary (1850) that this became a success as the Great Exhibition of 1851. The final stages were run by an executive committee and Russell was not greatly involved, so that his efforts in the earlier stages were overlooked. He was also much involved in the move of the Crystal Palace to Sydenham after the exhibition closed.

In 1847 Russell and partners had taken over the old Fairbairn shipyard at Millwall on the River Thames, which took up an increasing amount of time particularly from 1851, when he took sole control of the yard. In 1850 he designed a yacht, *Titania*, for Robert Stevenson which had very hollow bowlines but was constrained by British yacht-racing rules. In 1851 *Titania* was the only yacht to accept the challenge of the US yacht *America*; her defeat inaugurated the America's cup races.

In 1851 Russell was invited by the Australian Royal Mail Co., for which I. K. Brunel was chief engineer, to tender for two big mail steamers of 3000 tons and carrying 200 passengers. The two great engineers got on well together and the two ships, *Adelaide* and *Victoria*, were successful, the latter winning a prize for the fastest passage to Australia: sixty days. By the spring of 1852 Brunel was discussing plans with Russell for a truly enormous ship which was to become the *Great Eastern*. Before building work could begin, Russell's shipyard was devastated by a serious fire but was only partially covered by insurance.

The overall concept of the *Great Eastern* was due to Brunel, Russell's contribution being the hull form, the design of the paddle engines, and, last but not least, the actual building of the monster. She was to be 600 feet long and of 20,000 tons, figures which were not exceeded until nearly half a century later. Though the form was claimed to be in accordance with the wave-line theory, it was much modified and, by Russell's equations, optimized for about 24 knots, far greater than the 14 knots expected. There were problems from the start, owing to Brunel's frequent changes and insistence on approving every detail, difficult to reconcile with the delegation of detail design authority which every shipyard then practised. Russell's financial backer died and, during the Crimean War, wage rates on the Thames trebled. Russell had several fixed-price contracts for warships and these together with another fire, added to his financial problems and his shipyard, like several other Thames builders, failed in February 1856. He remained in charge of building the *Great Eastern* under a new contract. The ship was a technical success but a commercial failure, like so many of Brunel's projects.

Before the Crimean War Russell had designed some paddle gunboats for Prussia, and two of these were taken over for the Royal Navy; later, two more somewhat similar vessels were ordered. During the war Russell was involved with an Austrian engineer, Wilhelm Bauer, who was trying to develop a submarine. Bauer was afraid that Russell was stealing his ideas and went to Russia, where his submarine was built. Russell was, indeed, working on a submarine vehicle, but his was more of a diving bell inside which the crew of two walked along the bottom.

Russell had long advocated armoured warships and was encouraged by his experience in building Admiralty-designed, armoured batteries for attacking Russian coastal forts. There were many problems to be overcome before seagoing, armoured ships became practical, particularly in the behaviour of iron under the impact of gunshot. His claims to have assisted in the design of *Warrior* seem incorrect though the Admiralty designer, Watts, was probably influenced both by Russell's structural style and by the wave-line approach.

Russell was elected FRS in 1849 and he was a member of council (and sometime vice-president) of both the Institution of Civil Engineers and the Institution of Mechanical Engineers. In the autumn of 1859 he held a small dinner party which led to the formation of the Institution of Naval Architects. In all three institutions he was active in debate until he was driven to resign from the 'Civils' in 1867 following unproven allegations of professional misconduct. He opposed William Froude's theory of rolling in 1863 and was worsted in a long and generally good-natured debate. His own problems with model tests led him to oppose William Froude's proposals for a ship tank but eventually he accepted the results gracefully. His chief publication, *The Modern System of Naval Architecture for Commerce and War*, appeared in three volumes between 1864 and 1865 and remains the most complete record of naval architecture and of shipbuilding of the time.

In a paper to the Institution of Naval Architects in 1863 Russell had pressed for an Admiralty school of naval architecture to replace two earlier schools which, though successful in producing outstanding graduates, had been closed by cost-saving politicians. This new school was set up at South Kensington in 1864 and is the direct ancestor of the current school at University College, London. From 1867 onwards he pressed for a much improved system of technical education in the United Kingdom.

Russell continued to practise, and designed a train ferry for Lake Constance in 1868. The draught of this vessel was limited to 6 feet, which forced him into a novel structural design using the superstructure to carry stress. He also designed the great rotunda for the Vienna exhibition in 1873. The failure of his shipyard was only the first of his major financial problems; an unwise business deal to supply guns during the American Civil War left him with heavy debts and much of his property was sold. The collapse of his son's shipyard on the Taff in 1869 caused further losses.

A happy family life did much to compensate for declining income in later years. The last two of Russell's twenty-one papers to the Institution of Naval Architects were read in 1882 but he was too ill to take part in the discussion and died at Ventnor, Isle of Wight, on 8 June 1882. He was survived by his wife.

Russell was a brilliant, intuitive engineer but, though better-educated than many of his contemporaries, appears to have lacked the mathematical ability either to develop his ideas or to expose fallacies. He was very clear both in writing and in speech and seems to have been well liked. His business ventures were unlucky rather than unskilled. Perhaps his greatest achievement lay in his contribution to debate both in engineering institutions and in the British Association committees which stimulated so many of his contemporaries. DAVID K. BROWN

Sources DNB · G. S. Emerson, *John Scott Russell* (1977) · K. C. Barnaby, *The Institution of Naval Architects* (1960) · T. Wright, 'Ship hydrodynamics, 1710–1880', PhD diss., CNAA, Sci. Mus., London, 1983
Archives Sci. Mus., engineering notebooks and registers relating to steam and the *Great Eastern* | U. Edin. L., letters to David Ramsey Hay
Likenesses Lock & Whitfield, woodburytype photograph, NPG; repro. in T. Cooper, *Men of mark: a gallery of contemporary portraits* (1878) · W. H. Mote, stipple (after photograph by Mayall), NPG · H. W. Phillips, group portrait, oils (*The royal commissioners for the Great Exhibition, 1851*), V&A · H. W. Phillips, oils, Scot. NPG

Russell, Joseph (1760–1847), agriculturist, born in Ashow, was one of seventeen children of Richard Russell, who kept the forge in the adjacent village of Blackdon, Lillington, Warwickshire. Very little is known about his mother or his early life. According to Colvile's *Worthies of Warwickshire*, his early education consisted of a twelve-month period in Birmingham and about 1780 he moved to Cubbington, where he rented a farm of 320 acres from Edward Leigh, fifth Baron Leigh. He is also credited with purchasing two blocks of land amounting to 110 acres in the surrounding parishes. According to the Leigh archives, however, he does not appear at Cubbington in the 1784 rental accounts but is there by 1792, the date of the next surviving volume. In 1806 he increased the size of his holding by becoming tenant of part of the farm of the late Thomas Sabin.

Colvile portrayed Russell as an enterprising farmer, responsible for pioneering the cultivation of crops such as asparagus and flax, from which he made a precarious living. He successfully introduced Leicester sheep to Warwickshire, and Talavera wheat into England as early as 1810. Russell is also credited with improving the subsoil plough and developing a cloverhead gathering machine. A model of this machine was sent to the Society for the Encouragement of Arts, Manufacture, and Commerce, where it received a mark of honour and was exhibited in the society's room for many years. It was not the practice of the society, however, to provide prizes for specific innovations but for outstanding qualities. Moreover, in spite of Russell's attempts to present himself as a progressive farmer, there are no references to these improvements or innovations in his correspondence with his landlord which was a prelude to terminating his tenancy in 1821. Until 1815 Russell appeared to be a reasonably competent farmer but, following the end of the French and Napoleonic wars and the collapse in grain prices, his rent was increasingly in arrears. His financial problems compelled him in 1821 to move to London where, according to Colvile, he embarked upon an unspecified business adventure with two of his sons. Like many of his farming innovations this was a commercial disaster and in 1829 he returned to Warwickshire with his wife, Frances, and fourteen of their seventeen surviving children. His children were dispersed among his friends or left to develop careers for themselves. He lived for a number of years at various lodgings in Kenilworth, and was employed in valuing buildings and estates primarily for the new poor-law system. Colvile claims that he was very successful in this, particularly in Bedford, where the rector of the parish gave him £20 in addition to his fees.

In 1830 Russell's first work, *A Treatise on Practical and Chemical Agriculture*, was published. This was followed by *Observations on the Growth of British Corn* (1832) and *A New System of Agriculture* (1840). All his texts were dedicated to his previous landlord, Lord Leigh, whom Russell described in the preface as 'the ardent and steady friend of the British farmer'. His writings were reasonably popular, advocating a number of controversial suggestions for improving agricultural productivity.

Russell's reputation reflected the fact that he was considerably more enterprising than his contemporaries who, in Warwickshire, were mainly small farmers who cultivated intractable soils and who were often little educated, suspicious, and highly resistant to new ideas. His reputation was also significantly enhanced by the writing and publication of three texts which, although neither very profound nor scientific, enabled him to gain national recognition even though Colvile exaggerated his importance. It is not surprising that innovative individuals like Russell were so widely acclaimed by their patrons who stood to benefit most from agricultural modernization. In spite of his literary endeavours, he made a very precarious living from the sale of his books, and required financial support from his friends in the last few years of his life. He died suddenly on 7 March 1847 soon after moving to his daughter's home at Abbey Hill, Kenilworth, and was buried near his family on the south side of Ashow church. He was survived by his wife. JOHN MARTIN

Sources F. L. Colvile, *The worthies of Warwickshire who lived between 1500 and 1800* [1870] · Leigh archives, Shakespeare Birthplace Trust RO, Stratford upon Avon, DR 18/17/47/24 · Sir Joseph Banks MSS, RSA · Warks. CRO, Greville papers, CR1880 · M. Overton, *Agricultural revolution in England: the transformation of the agrarian economy, 1500–1850* (1996) · J. D. Chambers and G. E. Mingay, *The agricultural revolution, 1750–1880* (1966) · private information (2004) · DNB
Archives Suffolk RO, Bury St Edmunds, papers mainly relating to research into history of the parish of Rattlesden | Shakespeare Birthplace Trust RO, Stratford upon Avon, Leigh archives

Russell, Joseph (1834–1917), shipbuilder, was born on 8 April 1834 at Blackheath, London, the son of Joshua Russell, a solicitor in Southwark, and his second wife, Jane Ann Russell. In 1835 the elder Russell gave up his legal practice to become the Baptist minister of Melksham in Wiltshire. He was comfortably off since his father, Archibald Russell, also a solicitor, had speculated successfully in the London property market. In 1844 the family returned to Blackheath and the young Joseph Russell was sent to Mill Hill School, Middlesex.

After leaving school in 1848 Russell attended classes at King's College, London, and was then apprenticed in 1850 to J. W. Hoby & Co., engineers, iron-founders, and ship-builders at Renfrew on the River Clyde. This firm had been established by his stepsister's husband, J. W. Hoby, a partner in the Birmingham civil engineering firm of Fox and Henderson. During 1854 Hoby's business collapsed and was taken over by its creditors. Russell completed his apprenticeship the following year and on gaining his majority was given £1000 by his father. He was immediately appointed manager of the works. In 1858 he married Elisabeth (Bessie) Wright; they had three sons and six daughters.

Russell left Renfrew in 1859 to take over the lease of the Ardrossan dockyard in Ayrshire, building over the next six years about thirty small vessels. In May 1865 he gave up the lease as the owner would not sell the yard to him. In May 1866 he accepted the post of manager of Lawrence Hill's shipyard at Port Glasgow on the lower Clyde, investing £4000 in the business. Over the next three years he built twenty-nine ships but left in 1869 because Hill was a poor businessman. He returned to London in that year in order to care for his father, who died in 1870. He spent the next three years looking after his inherited property interests in London, before returning to Scotland in 1873 to start a new shipbuilding firm, Russell & Co., at Port Glasgow in partnership with Anderson Rodger and William Todd Lithgow.

Russell & Co. was an immediate success, building large sailing vessels to semi-standard designs with interchangeable parts, in which the partners were prepared to take investments to encourage custom. However, Joseph Russell was dealt a serious setback when the City of Glasgow Bank failed in the autumn of 1878. He held £300 of stock, on which he was forced to pay calls of £8271. Nevertheless, in 1879 the firm expanded its facilities by acquiring J. E. Scott's bankrupt Cartsdyke yard in Greenock. This was followed by the construction of an entirely new yard at Kingston in Port Glasgow at the end of 1881. The business continued to prosper throughout the 1880s, despite the uncertainties that affected most of the shipbuilding industry. This success in part reflected the partners' willingness to experiment with new technology. In 1886 they introduced a standard 3000 ton class of sailing vessel equipped with auxiliary engines and brace halyard winches. Russell retired from the firm in 1891, loaning it nearly £123,000 and leaving Lithgow in control of the Kingston and Cartsdyke yards.

Aged only fifty-seven, Russell was not ready entirely to retire from business concerns. He continued to assist Lithgow, particularly in looking after the financial side of the firm, and he also sought commercial opportunities for his sons William Russell and Archie Russell. He purchased a large country house, Seafield, at Ardrossan, where he could indulge his passions of shooting and riding. He had always travelled regularly to the continent and now began to go for longer periods. More of his time was devoted to work for the Free Church of Scotland and the Port Glasgow school board, and he gave regular Bible classes, as well as serving on the church's Foreign Missions, Highland, and Livingstonia committees. He played an active part in the negotiations leading up to the amalgamation of the Free Church with the United Presbyterian church in 1900.

During the 1890s Russell began to speculate heavily in the property market, acquiring houses and land, and making loans for development in the west of Scotland. Lithgow fell seriously ill in 1907 and, although his loan to the firm had been paid off, Russell helped Lithgow's sons run the company. He managed the financial side of the business for them until 1913, when he finally retired. He died on 3 June 1917 at Seafield House, Ardrossan. His wife died in 1921.

MICHAEL S. MOSS

Sources private information (2004) · M. Moss, 'William Todd Lithgow: founder of a fortune', *SHR*, 62 (1983), 47–72 · U. Glas., Archives and Business Records Centre, Lithgow MSS · M. Moss, 'Russell, Joseph', *DSBB*
Archives priv. coll., diaries | U. Glas., Archives and Business Records Centre, Lithgow MSS

Russell [*née* Stanley], **Katharine Louisa**, Viscountess Amberley (1842–1874), radical and suffragist, was born on 3 March 1842 at Alderley Park, Cheshire, into the strong-minded and eccentric family of the Stanleys of Alderley. She was the fifth daughter and eighth child in the family of seven girls and three boys of Edward John *Stanley, second Baron Stanley of Alderley and first Baron Eddisbury of Winnington (1802–1869), magnate and Liberal politician, and Henrietta Maria *Stanley (1807–1895), eldest daughter of Henry Augustus Dillon-*Lee, thirteenth Viscount Dillon, commonly referred to as Lady Stanley of Alderley. Kate, as she was always called, was a prepossessing, lively girl, educated at home and later assiduously self-educated. When she was twenty-one she met John *Russell, Viscount Amberley (1842–1876), eldest son of Lord John *Russell, and they were immediately mutually smitten. His family was unenthusiastic about the Stanleys, and a six-month separation of the young lovers was exacted. On 8 November 1864, the moratorium over, they were married. It was a very happy (if unorthodox) marriage: 'ever since I have known my own one, life has been perfect, blissful and full of meaning, joy and purpose … were there more marriages such as ours life would indeed be bright', she wrote in April 1872 (Moorehead, 14). They both believed fervently in self-improvement to fit them to fulfil their duty to improve the world. They lived first at Rodborough Manor, near Stroud, in Gloucestershire, and there her first child, John Francis (Frank) Stanley Russell, was born on 12 August 1865. On 17 August 1867 Kate and her husband left for a tour of the United States, meeting and being fêted by radicals from Boston to Chicago. They returned on 4 January 1868. On 2 March Kate gave premature birth to twins, only one of whom, Rachel Lucretia (named for the American women's rights activist Lucretia Mott), survived.

Early in 1865 Kate Amberley had met Helen Taylor and her stepfather, John Stuart Mill, whom Kate greatly

Katharine Louisa Russell, Viscountess Amberley (1842–1874), by George Howard, ninth earl of Carlisle, 1864

admired. Through them, she became involved with the Langham Place circle of women's rights activists, lending her support to their campaigns for women's education and women doctors, and serving on the committee promoting the Married Women's Property Bill. She was also active in the suffrage movement. Encouraged by Mill and Taylor and primed by Mill's gift of his *Subjection of Women*, she spoke on 'The claims of women' (published in the *Fortnightly Review*, 9, 1871, 95–110) in the Subscription Rooms at Stroud under the auspices of the mechanics' institute on 25 May 1870. It was this public appearance that brought her the much publicized snub from the duchess of Cambridge:

> I know you, you are the daughter in law but now I hear you only like dirty people & dirty Americans. All London is full of it; all the clubs are talking of it. I must look at your petticoats to see if they are dirty. (*Amberley Papers*, 2.499)

The queen herself was moved by hearing of the speech to a tirade against 'this mad, wicked folly of "Woman's Rights"', concluding that 'Lady —— ought to get a *good whipping*'. Fortunately for all concerned the tirade was in a private letter to Sir Theodore Martin and was not publicly known at the time (Martin, 69–70).

In 1870 Amberley's father decided to sell Rodborough, and the young couple bought Ravenscroft, near Chepstow

in Monmouthshire. Bertrand Arthur William *Russell was born there on 18 May 1872. Taylor and Mill agreed to stand in the place of godparents, 'for there is no one in whose steps I would rather see a boy of mine following in ever such a humble way, than in Mr. Mill's' (K. Amberley to H. Taylor, 16 June 1872, Mill/Taylor Collection).

On 12 June 1873 Amberley had an epileptic fit. Concern for his health led Kate the following winter to make a six-month tour in Europe with her husband. Rachel and Bertrand were left with the Russell grandparents; the troublesome Frank and his consumptive tutor, Douglas Spalding, accompanied the Amberleys. Bertrand Russell wrote:

> Apparently on grounds of pure theory, my father and mother decided that although he [Spalding] ought to remain childless on account of his tuberculosis, it was unfair to expect him to remain celibate. My mother therefore, allowed him to live with her, though I know of no evidence that she derived any pleasure from doing so. (Russell, *Autobiography*, 1.17)

On their way home Frank developed diphtheria. He recovered but no sooner had they reached Ravenscroft than Rachel sickened. Four days later, on 25 June, Kate caught the disease through her desperate attempts to save her daughter. On 28 June 1874 Katharine Louisa Russell, Viscountess Amberley, died; Rachel died the next day. Mother and daughter were buried side by side at Ravenscroft.   ANN P. ROBSON

Sources McMaster University, Hamilton, Ontario, Canada, Russell Archives, Amberley Family MSS · *The Amberley papers: the letters and diaries of Lord and Lady Amberley*, ed. B. Russell and P. Russell, 2 vols. (1937) · BLPES, Mill–Taylor collection · B. Russell, *The autobiography of Bertrand Russell*, 1 (1967) · *DNB* · *The later letters of John Stuart Mill, 1849–1873*, ed. F. E. Mineka and D. N. Lindley, 4 vols. (1972), vols. 14–17 of *The collected works of John Stuart Mill*, ed. J. M. Robson and others (1963–91), vols. 3–4 · N. Mitford, ed., *The ladies of Alderley* (1967) · C. Moorehead, *Bertrand Russell: a life* (1992) · L. Holcombe, *Wives and property: reform of married women's property law in nineteenth-century England* (1983) · O. Banks, *The biographical dictionary of British feminists*, 1 (1985) · T. Martin, *Queen Victoria as I knew her* (1908)

Archives McMaster University, Hamilton, Ontario, corresp. and papers | BLPES, Mill–Taylor collection · NL Scot., corresp. with Thomas Carlyle · NL Scot., letters to Alexander Campbell Fraser

Likenesses G. Howard, ninth earl of Carlisle, drawing, 1864, repro. in Russell and Russell, eds., *The Amberley papers*, vol. 1, facing p. 307 [*see illus.*] · photographs, repro. in Russell and Russell, eds., *Amberley papers*

Russell [*née* Stewart], **Katherine Frances** [Kit] (1909–1998), social worker and university teacher, was born at 20 Southwell Gardens, Kensington, London, on 6 April 1909, the eldest of the four daughters and second of the seven children of Sir Francis Hugh (Frank) Stewart (1869–1921), a partner in Gladstone, Wyllie & Co., merchants, of London and Calcutta, and his wife, Frances Henrietta (1885–1962), eldest daughter of Arthur George Rickards, barrister. Sent home at the age of five from India in 1914, Kit Stewart did not see her parents again for five years. In 1921, and only eight months after he had retired, her father died. Widowed at thirty-seven with seven children under fourteen to support, Lady Stewart worked as the organizing secretary of the St Pancras Housing Association. Her connection with this and other voluntary organizations proved an important influence on the path in life her eldest daughter was to follow, as also was Olive Willis, founder and first headmistress of Downe House, the independent girls' boarding-school Kit Stewart attended. On leaving the school at the age of seventeen, she at first combined running the family household with voluntary work outside the home. This early work in the impoverished dockside area of Bermondsey, in Southwark, was at Time and Talents, a settlement started in 1887 by Christian society ladies. In 1931 she went to the London School of Economics (LSE) and in 1933, having gained the certificate in social science, she became the warden of the Time and Talents club house in Dockhead. She remained a devoted supporter of the settlement and admirer of Bermondsey people until the very end of her life.

In 1937 Kit Stewart was recruited by the London Council of Social Service to organize community activities on the new Honor Oak housing estate in Lewisham, but following the outbreak of the Second World War she moved in 1940 to become warden of a youth centre in Southampton, a city by then suffering heavily under the blitz. Three years later she joined her former LSE tutor and great friend Eileen Younghusband, with whom for some years she shared a flat, in work for the British Council. Their task was to train 'allied nationals' for the social welfare work that would be needed in shattered western Europe, then still occupied. In 1945, the war over, she took charge of five emergency courses run by the Institute of Almoners to ease the shortage of hospital social workers in Britain that the war had engendered, and in 1949 moved on to the social science department at the LSE, first as practical work organizer, later as senior lecturer. She retired from the LSE in 1973, but continued as president of the LSE Society for many years. She was appointed OBE in 1976, and made an honorary fellow of the LSE in 1978. Although more interested in people than in research, after her retirement in 1973 she drafted and sent a detailed questionnaire to 2000 past LSE social administration students, and largely by personal follow-up got a 90 per cent response. The book from the study, *Changing Course* (1981), was described by Ralf Dahrendorf as 'a story of professionalisation, a story of social mobility, a story of career patterns, a story of the role of women, and a story of the imprint of individuals and their initiative' (Russell and Barnes, 255).

Tall, slim, and with silky golden hair always worn in a loose bun, Kit Stewart was classically beautiful, and remained so into old age. At forty-eight she married Sheridan Russell, described 'as a bright-eyed elfin figure of warmth and wit' (*The Guardian*, 17 July 1998). Recruited in 1945 to the first emergency course as the first male student in an entirely female profession, he soon became a close friend, but they did not marry until 1 June 1957. Commenting on marriage ten years earlier, she had written to one of her students about to marry, 'I do *so* believe in marriage. It must be the perfect maximum giving and receiving' (personal knowledge). So it proved to be with her own marriage, which led to a remarkable partnership that Dame Eileen Younghusband described as 'proving that

one and one sometimes adds up to much more than two' (Russell and Barnes, 241).

Born on 23 March 1900 at 61a Curzon Street, Mayfair, London, **Sheridan William Robin Russell** (1900–1991) was the younger son of Henry Russell (*c*.1870–1937), professor of singing, and his wife, Nina, *née* Andrade (*b*. 1870). Music was a prominent theme in his family: Russell's father became artistic director of first the San Carlo and later the Boston Opera companies; his uncle, Sir Landon *Ronald (1873–1938), was a composer and conductor, as was his paternal grandfather, Henry *Russell (1812×14–1900). His mother was the daughter of a Spanish leather merchant and his Portuguese wife. Both parents were of partly Jewish descent. Sheridan Russell grew up in Rome, Paris, Boston, and London, with little formal education but on familiar terms with singers and composers of the times. He became a young virtuoso cellist, but because of a hearing defect (first noticed by Debussy) had later to abandon this career—although not his musical and artistic interests. Fluent in French, English, and Italian, he was recruited for work at Bletchley Park and later in the war was transferred, with the rank of captain, to work with the Italian partisans. His change to social work after the war led to another distinguished career as head almoner at the National Hospital for Nervous Diseases. While there he started the flourishing and nationwide Paintings in Hospital charity—to which in its early days he persuaded Matthew Smith, among other well-known painters, to contribute works.

Until late old age Sheridan Russell never abandoned his cello playing, and in their drawing room at 100 Cheyne Walk the Russells held nearly 300 soirées of chamber music. They called on Russell's many professional musician friends to take part, and 'entertained thousands of LSE students and staff and an eclectic circle of friends from social services and government, the arts and the sciences' (*The Guardian*, 17 July 1998). Sheridan Russell died at home on 9 April 1991. After his death Kit organized the preparation and private publication of a book, *Sheridan's Story* (1993). All 1800 copies were sold. Kit Russell's warmth and kindness were legendary and underpinned by her profound Christian belief; but she could be exacting on behalf of the commitments she cared for and put so much into. She died on 9 July 1998 at St George's Nursing Home, Westminster, of old age and was buried at Christ Church, Flood Street, Chelsea.   PHYLLIS WILLMOTT

Sources K. Russell and W. Barnes, eds., *Sheridan's story: Sheridan Russell, 1900–1991* (privately printed, 1993) · *The Times* (28 July 1998), 3 · *The Guardian* (17 July 1998) · K. Jones, *Eileen Younghusband: a biography* (1984) · M. Daunt, *By peaceful means: the story of Time and Talents, 1887–1987* (1989) · personal knowledge (2004) · private information (2004) [Catherine Graham-Harrison] · b. cert. · b. cert. [Sheridan Russell, husband] · m. cert. · d. cert. · d. cert. [Sheridan Russell, husband] · Burke, *Peerage*

Likenesses photograph (Kit and Sheridan Russell), repro. in *The Guardian* · photograph, repro. in *The Times* · photographs, priv. coll. · photographs, repro. in Russell and Barnes, eds., *Sheridan's story*

Russell, (Edward Frederick) Langley, second Baron Russell of Liverpool (1895–1981), military lawyer and author,

(Edward Frederick) Langley Russell, second Baron Russell of Liverpool (1895–1981), by Bassano, 1933

was born on 10 April 1895, at 6 Abercromby Square, Liverpool, the only child of Richard Henry Langley Russell (1861–1899) and his comedy-actress wife, Mabel Suffolk Younge (1865?–1956). He was reared by his grandfather, Edward Richard *Russell, who was the doyen of provincial journalists and who, on 9 October 1919, in the fiftieth year of his editorship of the *Liverpool Daily Post*, received the barony which his grandson inherited four months later in February 1920. Langley Russell, as he was known, was educated at Greenbank School (1902–4), Liverpool College (1904–12), and St John's College, Cambridge (1913–14). He joined the 6th battalion, the King's Liverpool regiment, as a rifleman in August 1914 and was gazetted to the regular army in July 1915. During unforgettable experiences of trench warfare he was thrice wounded; he received the MC in 1916 and two bars in 1918. His lungs never recovered from being gassed. He saw active service against the IRA in co. Cork in 1920–1, and transferred to the 20th lancers, Indian army in 1925, but he was compelled by ill health to send in his papers in 1930.

Russell was called to the bar at Gray's Inn (1931) and joined the Oxford circuit but never acquired a substantial practice, possibly because his peerage made him seem a dilettante. He therefore sought a living as military assistant to the judge advocate general (JAG) of HM forces (1934–43). He was promoted deputy judge advocate general in 1943, and after JAG appointments in France and north Africa, was based in Naples (1944–5). At the end of the war he became responsible for all courts martial, war crime trials, and questions of military law in the British-occupied zone of Germany. A lifelong Francophile, gastronome, and wine connoisseur, Langley Russell had mistrusted Germans (and British appeasers) before 1939. He was revolted by the atrocities which were revealed under his auspices in trials of German war criminals in British military courts in occupied Germany (1946–50) and at heart believed that because of their war depravities the German people existed on a different level from the rest of humanity. In March 1951 he and his wife were assaulted by a mob in the German village of Vlotho. During the controversy that followed he felt inadequately supported by the British government: 'I shall never forget the scurvy treatment which led to my departure', he wrote after he was recalled to London on 1 May (Russell, 200). The next three years (1951–4), during which he worked in London as assistant judge advocate, were the most frustrating of his career. At his wife's suggestion he compiled a detailed account of Nazi war criminality which Cassell agreed to publish as *The Scourge of the Swastika*. On the intimation of the lord chancellor, Simonds, that publication was incompatible with Russell's judicial office, he resigned. In 250 pages the book recounted in as moderate language as possible appalling stories of murder and torture. Over 250,000 copies of *The Scourge of the Swastika* were sold internationally after its publication in 1954. Its popularity displeased those seeking to restore the West German republic's position in the international community, and a few complained of its sensationalism. In fact Russell tried to be fair: a more tenable criticism is that he treated war crimes as an exclusively Teutonic phenomenon, though other nations had also perpetrated war barbarities.

In retirement Russell wrote prolifically in trenchant, unpretentious prose. His second book, *Though the Heavens Fall* (1956), was a potboiler about celebrated legal cases such as the Tichborne claimant and the slander action brought in 1891 over the Tranby Croft baccarat scandal. *The Knights of Bushido* (1958) was an account of Japanese war atrocities which, together with *The Scourge of the Swastika*, fascinated the Moors murderers Ian Brady and Myra Hindley before their arrest in 1965. Russell in 1966 was awarded £5000 damages against *Private Eye* which had dubbed him 'Lord Liver of Cesspool' while suggesting that he exploited war atrocities. Russell published a collection of amiable but disconnected memories in *That Reminds me* (1959). His knowledge of German genocide made him a pronounced Zionist; his pro-Jewish sympathies are evident in *The Trial of Adolf Eichmann* (1962). His visits to Africa are reflected in *The Tragedy of the Congo* (1962) and in *South Africa Today—and Tomorrow?* (1963). He opposed the Afrikaner policy of apartheid with a vigour that was perhaps unusual among his generation, and does credit to his sense and feelings. In *Deadman's Hill* (1965) he painstakingly examined the evidence arrayed against James Hanratty for the murder in 1961 of Michael Gregsten and convincingly concluded that the wrong man was hanged; this book is further testimony to Russell's independent, stubborn sense of justice. His other books include *If I Forget thee* (1960), *The Royal Conscience* (1961), *The Knight of the Sword* (1964), and *Return of the*

Swastika? (1968). A convivial, good-hearted man, Russell was chairman of the Authors' Club for 1961–2.

Having lost money in farming ventures, and after long difficulties with the Inland Revenue and repeated shifts of residence, Russell was obliged to move to France in 1967 and was adjudged bankrupt in 1972. He married first, on 21 June 1920, Constance Claudine (*d.* 1974), daughter of Colonel Philip Cecil Harcourt Gordon; they had one son and a daughter. This marriage was dissolved on her petition in 1933. On 5 July 1933 he married (Joan) Elizabeth, nicknamed Betty, daughter of Dr David Ewart; they had one daughter. After the dissolution of this marriage in 1946 he married, on 27 May 1946, Alix, widow of Comte Bernard de Richard d'Ivry, and daughter of the marquis de Breviaire d'Alaincourt. After her death in a motor accident in France in 1971 he married, on 3 November 1972, Selma Marian (1907/8–1977), the widow of A. W. Brayley and daughter of James S. Kennedy, civil engineer. Having suffered a severe stroke, Russell died on 8 April 1981, in a Hastings nursing home, and was cremated on 13 April.

RICHARD DAVENPORT-HINES

Sources *The Times* (10 April 1981) · E. F. M. Russell, *That reminds me* (1959) · D. Healey, 'Lord Russell and the Germans', *The Spectator* (20 Aug 1954), 217–18 · m. cert. · GEC, *Peerage*
Archives Bodl. RH, corresp. with Sir R. R. Welensky and some papers relating to Rhodesia
Likenesses Bassano, photograph, 1933, NPG [*see illus.*] · photograph, *c.*1958, repro. in Russell, *That reminds me*, frontispiece

Russell, Sir (Edward) Lionel (1903–1983), educational administrator, was born at 35 Sotheby Road, Islington, London, on 8 May 1903, the son of Edward Russell, an analytical chemist, and his wife, Kate. He was educated at Clifton College and at Christ's College, Cambridge, where he gained a first in part one of the mathematical tripos (1923) and a second in English (1925). Following a lectureship at the University of Lund, Sweden (1925–31), and a period as assistant master at Charterhouse School (1932–5), Russell moved into local education authority administration, as assistant director of education in Liverpool (1935–8), the career he was to follow for the rest of his life. He was assistant education officer in Birmingham (1938–46) and chief education officer for the city from 1946 to 1968.

A manager rather than an educational theorist, Russell was soon recognized as an astute and reliable administrator with a practical and humane approach to educational policy. At Birmingham he instituted a strong sense of civic pride and emphasized the obligations of the education service to the city and its inhabitants. He acquired a reputation as a demanding chief, committed to the highest standards and to meticulous administrative efficiency. Throughout his career he had a strong interest in and commitment to adult and further education. He was closely involved, for example, in the evolution of the University of Aston (1966) from its origins in the Birmingham College of Technology.

Nationally, Russell was from the 1950s onwards a prominent member of influential public bodies concerned with education: the University Grants Committee (1954–63), the Council for National Academic Awards (1964–70), and, as president, the Association of Chief Education Officers (1955–7). He was called upon frequently as a private adviser to education ministers and was seen as a wise counsel and a safe pair of hands. It was therefore no surprise when in 1969 he was invited by the secretary of state for education, Ted Short, to chair a committee of inquiry to review the provision of non-vocational adult education in England and Wales. However, by the time the report, entitled *Adult Education: a Plan for Development*, appeared in 1973, the political situation had changed markedly (Margaret Thatcher was now secretary of state for education in Edward Heath's Conservative government), and economic crisis was imminent.

Events therefore overtook and effectively submerged what was in reality a reasonable, practical, and mildly progressive programme for adult education recommended by the report. The Russell report suggested no fundamental changes to structures or provision, but rather a general expansion, a greater emphasis upon adult education in the further education sector, and a higher priority in the adult education provision of the Workers' Educational Association (WEA) and the universities for work with disadvantaged communities. With some prescience, given the emphasis upon lifelong learning in the later 1990s and beyond, Russell envisaged a more accessible, flexible, inclusive, and learner-centred system of post-compulsory education and training.

At the time, however, the Russell report and the liberal, welfare state world view it reflected, was overwhelmed by larger forces. Adult education in all sectors was fundamentally and systematically undermined through the late 1970s and the 1980s by a series of spending cuts and restructuring. Despite rhetorical support for adult education and its liberating mission, none of the political parties gave material support to adult education as such, let alone to the modest developmental proposals of the report. It was not only ignored, in effect, by the political parties: the professional field was generally critical of Russell's perceived caution and pragmatic, evolutionary tenor. Through the 1970s, therefore, the report had few friends. However, with the hindsight of almost thirty years, the report and its recommendations had considerable resonance.

Russell's professional values and personal qualities were well symbolized by the report's pragmatic liberalism. He was a very private man, dedicated to liberal educational values and the highest standards of public service. He was meticulous and particular, not least in the drafting of documents, and was well known for ravaging the drafts of his subordinates. He was a rather heavy, formal, and seemingly austere figure. Yet his shyness concealed a kindly and considerate man who treated with courtesy everyone with whom he had contact.

One of the leading figures in English education during the quarter of a century following the 1944 Education Act, Russell was appointed CBE in 1953 and knighted in 1962. He never married. One of his few interests outside his work was cricket, for which he had a passion, particularly in Gloucestershire. He died at Manor Park Hospital, Bristol, on 26 December 1983. RICHARD TAYLOR

Sources The Times (30 Dec 1983) · WWW · R. Aldrich and P. Gordon, Dictionary of British educationists (1989) · R. Fieldhouse, A history of modern British adult education (1996) · b. cert. · d. cert.
Archives LUL, committee on adult education papers
Wealth at death £59,501: probate, 3 Feb 1984, CGPLA Eng. & Wales

Russell [née Harington], **Lucy, countess of Bedford** (*bap.* **1581**, *d.* **1627**), courtier and patron of the arts, was baptized on 25 January 1581 at St Dunstan and All Saints, Stepney, Middlesex, the elder daughter of John *Harington, first Baron Harington of Exton, Rutland (1539/40–1613), and Anne (*c.*1554–1620), daughter of Robert Kelway, surveyor of the court of wards and liveries, and his second wife, Cecily, daughter of Edward Bulstrode.

Education and early years at court Little is known about the countess's early life—probably spent at Combe Abbey in Warwickshire, her parents' principal residence until 1592—but she was well educated. The dedication to her by Claudius (de Sainliens) Holiband of his *Campo de fior, or, The Flowrie Field of Foure Languages* (1583) when she was two years old refers to 'the good will [her parents] will beare to learning, & the earnest inclination they have to bring you up in such vertuous exercise as is most meet for your tender yeares' (sig. Aij). John Florio, in the dedicatory epistle of his Italian–English dictionary (*A Worlde of Wordes*, 1598), praised her for her ability to understand, read, write, and speak Italian, French, and Spanish.

On 12 December 1594, a month before her fourteenth birthday, Lucy was married to the 21-year-old Edward Russell, third earl of Bedford (1572–1627), at St Dunstan and All Saints, Stepney. During their long marriage the countess gave birth to only two children, a son, Francis, Lord Russell, who died in February 1602 within a month of his birth, and a daughter, born 5 September 1610, who lived for only two hours.

The youthful Lady Bedford and her husband participated in the social life of the Elizabethan court and the aristocracy in London in the late 1590s, accumulating large debts. These debts were compounded by the fine of £10,000 which the earl attracted by his implication in the rebellion of the earl of Essex in February 1601. Bedford was also confined to a 6 or 7 mile radius of Chenies, his house in Buckinghamshire. Queen Elizabeth's death on 24 March 1603, and the smooth accession of James VI as James I, provided an opportunity for the Bedfords to be restored to favour, an opportunity that the countess exploited to the full.

Lady Bedford's first step was to secure a post in the privy chamber of James's consort, Anne of Denmark, and to establish herself as soon as possible in the new queen's favour. This she achieved by travelling north with several female relatives ahead of the official party sent to attend Queen Anne from Scotland. The countess secured a coveted bedchamber post, which she retained throughout the queen's life despite an occasional loss of the high favour she enjoyed with her royal mistress. The queen's

Lucy Russell, countess of Bedford (*bap.* 1581, *d.* 1627), attrib. William Larkin, *c.*1615

death on 2 March 1619 freed Lady Bedford from bedchamber service which, as her letters to her friend Jane, Lady Cornwallis, attest, had become increasingly irksome to her during the 1610s through ill health and disaffection with royal service, the queen, and the court. Nevertheless, she continued to attend the court to conduct business.

Set-backs and solutions at court, 1610–1620 In her early thirties the countess suffered a series of serious set-backs, familial and political. The death of her short-lived daughter in 1610 and the miscarriage of another child in 1611 were followed by a serious illness, possibly a stroke, in November 1612 (*De L'Isle and Dudley MSS*, 4.229; *Letters of John Chamberlain*, 1.306; Birch, 1.211). During her illness she reportedly 'in a manner' vowed never to return to court, but nevertheless had done so by 1 August 1613. Misfortune then struck her immediate Harington family, dissolving their significant royal connections in the space of a little over twelve months. On 23 August 1613 her father died of fever at Worms after escorting Princess Elizabeth to Heidelberg following her marriage to the elector palatine of the Rhine. In February 1614 Lady Bedford's brother, the second Lord Harington, died of smallpox: his own close association with Prince Henry had already ended with the prince's death in November 1612. Death also deprived Lady Bedford of her powerful patron, Robert Cecil, first earl of Salisbury, secretary of state and lord treasurer. After he died in May 1612 she was obliged to find a new patron in order to cope with the financial and political repercussions of these events.

From 1614 onwards much of the countess's energy at court was directed towards dealing with the Harington estate, which was heavily encumbered with debts amounting to £40,000. The extent of these debts shaped her activities in the sphere of court politics and patronage. After Salisbury's death she developed a network of powerful male patrons, friends, and associates at court to assist her in gaining the grants necessary to offset these debts. This network included her kinsman, William, third earl of Pembroke (lord chamberlain from 1615), and James's Scottish favourites, James Hay, Viscount Doncaster, and James, marquess of Hamilton, both gentlemen of the king's bedchamber. From about 1618 Hamilton, in particular, performed the critical function of presenting her suits to the king, joined with her in a number of grants and ventures, and otherwise supported her interests. Through Salisbury she had secured the patent for the manufacture of gold and silver thread in 1611; in 1616, with the duke of Lennox, she gained her father's patent for coining farthing tokens. In 1619 Hamilton secured a grant of Newcastle sea coal revenue for her and in 1624 joined with her in a grant of the royal mines in Pembrokeshire.

With Pembroke the countess was involved in the patronage of 'place' at court, notably the chancellorship of the duchy of Cornwall in 1618 and the groom-portership of the royal household in 1619. While they mediated successfully with Buckingham on Sir Humphrey May's behalf for the former post, the latter ultimately went to one of Buckingham's 'creatures' (*Letters of John Chamberlain*, 2.275). Lady Bedford was also able to exercise limited household patronage through her privileged position in the queen's bedchamber. She obtained places in the bedchamber for a Harington first cousin, Lady Markham, and maternal kinswomen Cecilia and Dorothy Bulstrode.

The countess was also active in colonial ventures. She was included in the list of adventurers in the letters patent for further plantations in Virginia in March 1612 and appears to have taken over her father's interest in the Bermuda Company after his death in 1613. She was given land in Bermuda in the grant to the company's adventurers in 1615 but later transferred that land to Hamilton 'upon some secretts' (Lefroy, 105–6). These 'secretts' may have been part of the negotiations she was conducting with Hamilton for the marriage of her only niece, Anne Chichester, to Hamilton's son, the earl of Arran (which did not eventuate).

From 1620 Lady Bedford interested herself in the affairs of Princess Elizabeth, the exiled electress palatine and queen of Bohemia, who had been entrusted to the guardianship of the countess's parents from 1603 until her marriage in 1613. This interest associated Lady Bedford even more closely with Pembroke, Hamilton, and the 'puritan party' which had 'discovered a new focus' in the restoration of the Palatinate (Adams, 142–3). The countess's active political involvement is clear from her surviving correspondence with Sir Dudley Carleton, then resident ambassador in The Hague, where the Bohemian royal family had settled. Lady Bedford passed on information to Elizabeth and offered her political advice, both directly and through Carleton. In July and August 1621, she visited Elizabeth in The Hague.

Lady Bedford as patron In the dedicatory epistle of Sir Arthur Gorges's translation of *Lucans Pharsalia* (1614), Carew Gorges described Lady Bedford as 'an honourable lover and Patronesse of learning and the Muses, an instinct naturally ingrafted in your excellent spirit, by that worthy blood of the Sydneyes' (her paternal grandmother was Lucy Sidney, aunt of Sir Philip Sidney and Mary Sidney Herbert, countess of Pembroke). The countess was closely associated with some of the leading poets, playwrights, and translators of the day, notably Michael Drayton, John Florio, Samuel Daniel, John Donne, and Ben Jonson (who also eulogized her as his muse in three *Epigrammes* to her). She received numerous dedications of literary works, but a number of these dedications were shared with her mother, her husband, and other court women. According to John Florio, in his dedicatory epistle of the first book of Montaigne's essays addressed to her and her mother, Lady Bedford encouraged him to complete his translation in her house. She read the manuscript and her husband and members of her Harington family provided Florio with financial assistance (*The Essayes … of … Michaell de Montaigne*, 1603). If she is the faithless Selena in the eighth eclogue of Drayton's *Poems Lyrick and Pastoral* (1605?), her association with Drayton came to an end about this time because he was jealous that she had transferred her patronage to another writer.

A close relationship between the countess and John Donne lasted from *c*.1607 to 1615. Lady Bedford gave him permission to name his daughter Lucy in 1608 and, during their association, Donne wrote several poems to or for her. However, their relationship foundered in 1615 when the countess was not moved by his elegy on her brother's death to pay Donne's debts. Religious disagreement may have been the cause, perhaps influenced by Dr Burges, a Puritan divine and physician who had attended Lady Bedford during her serious illness in 1612 (*Life and Letters of John Donne*, 2.73; Thomson, 331–5).

An undated letter to Lady Bedford from Donne clearly indicates that she wrote poetry herself (*Life and Letters of John Donne*, 1.217–18). None survives that can confidently be attributed to her authorship. However, Grierson notes that the elegy 'Death be not proud, thy hand gave not this blow', attributed to Donne, is headed 'By L. C. of B.' and 'By C. L. of B.' in two manuscripts (*The Poems of John Donne*, 1912, 1.422).

As a Calvinist and a prominent member of two deeply religious godly protestant families the countess attracted a number of dedications of religious works: twenty-two between 1597 and 1621. Once again the majority are shared with other members of her family or other court women; several are by the Bedfords' domestic chaplain. These dedications indicate that her patronage was acknowledged in the context of her family connections and the Bedfords' 'dispositions to patronize and countenance' religious treatises (Peter Allibond, trans., *The Golden Chayne of Salvation*, 1604, sig. A3). There is no evidence that she secured royal chaplaincies or preaching posts at court for ministers of religion.

Lady Bedford's broader cultural patronage included music, masques, and art collecting. She also created gardens at More Park, the Bedfords' house near Rickmansworth in Hertfordshire. Sir William Temple praised these gardens in his essay, *The Gardens of Epicurus*, as 'The perfectest Figure of a Garden I ever saw, either at home or abroad … made … with very great care, excellent Contrivance, and much Cost' (*Miscellanea: the Second Part*, 1696, 117). The lutenist John Dowland dedicated his *Second Booke of Songes or Ayres* to her in 1600, honouring her for her 'knowledge of Musicke' (sig. Aij). Lady Bedford was an enthusiastic participant in court masques: she danced in all of Queen Anne's masques but one (*Tethys' Festival*, in June 1610, as she was six months pregnant) and in *Hymenaei*, Ben Jonson's masque at court for the wedding of the earl and countess of Essex in 1606. She also promoted the writing and performance of masques at court and elsewhere. In 1603–4, she preferred Samuel Daniel to Queen Anne to write the first extant court masque, *The Vision of the Twelve Goddesses*, performed by the queen and eleven ladies-in-waiting at Hampton Court on 8 January 1604. In 1617 the countess furthered and encouraged the presentation of a masque (*Cupid's Banishment* by Robert White) 'By the young Gentlewomen of the Ladies Hall In Deptford at Greenwhich The 4th of May'.

Lady Bedford revealed her avid interest in art collecting, developed later in life, in an undated letter (*c*.1624) to Lady Cornwallis (later Bacon): 'though I be but a late beginner, I have prety store of choise peeses'. Declaring that she was 'a very diligent gatherer of all I can gett of Holben's or any other excellent master's hand', the countess anxiously sought to obtain some paintings by Holbein from the estate of Lady Bacon's father-in-law who 'was like to die', before the earl of Arundel, one of the greatest collectors of the period, heard about them. Arundel had already cousened her 'of some pictures promissed me' (*Private Correspondence*, ed. Braybrooke, 51, 50). She also commissioned a picture from Lady Bacon's husband, Sir Nathanial Bacon, and gave two portraits—one a miniature—to Charles I.

The countess died on 26 May 1627 at More Park, shortly after the death of her husband. She was buried with her Harington family at Exton, in Rutland.

HELEN PAYNE

Sources APC, 1600–04 · H. Sydney and others, *Letters and memorials of state*, ed. A. Collins, 2 vols. (1746) · *The private correspondence of Jane, Lady Cornwallis, 1613–1644*, ed. Lord Braybrooke (1842) · *The letters of John Chamberlain*, ed. N. E. McClure, 2 vols. (1939) · [T. Birch and R. F. Williams], eds., *The court and times of James the First*, 2 vols. (1849); repr. (1973) · W. Notestein, F. H. Relf, and H. Simpson, eds., *Commons debates, 1621*, 7 vols. (1935) · [N. Butler?], *The historye of the Bermudaes or Summer Islands*, ed. J. H. Lefroy, Hakluyt Society, 1st ser., 65 (1882) · *Liber famelicus of Sir James Whitelocke, a judge of the court of king's bench in the reigns of James I and Charles I*, ed. J. Bruce, CS, old ser., 70 (1858), 17–18 · E. Gosse, *The life and letters of John Donne, dean of St Paul's*, 2 vols. (1899) · P. Thomson, 'John Donne and the countess of Bedford', *Modern Language Review*, 44 (1949), 329–40 · M. Maurer, 'The real presence of Lucy Russell, countess of Bedford, and the terms of John Donne's "Honour is so sublime perfection"', *ELH: a Journal of English Literary History*, 47 (1980), 205–34 · F. B. Williams, *Index of dedications and commendatory verses in English books before 1641* (1962) · PRO, State papers domestic, SP 14 [correspondence] · PRO, State papers Holland, SP 84 [correspondence] · S. L. Adams, 'Foreign policy and the parliaments of 1621 and 1624', *Faction and parliament: essays on early Stuart history*, ed. K. Sharpe (1978), 139–70 · *The complete works in verse and prose of Samuel Daniel*, ed. A. B. Grosart, 5 vols. (1885–96); repr. (1963) · *Ben Jonson*, ed. C. H. Herford, P. Simpson, and E. M. Simpson, 11 vols. (1925–52) · 'Abraham van der Doort's catalogue of the collections of Charles I', ed. O. Millar, *Walpole Society*, 37 (1958–60), esp. 109, 118 · *The poems of Ben Jonson*, ed. B. H. Newdigate (1936) · *Report on the manuscripts of the marquis of Downshire*, 6 vols. in 7, HMC, 75 (1924–95), vol. 2, p. 412 · S. P. Cerasano and M. Wynne-Davis, eds., *Renaissance drama by women* (1996)

Likenesses attrib. school of Robert Peake the elder, oils, *c*.1604, NPG · attrib. J. de Critz, oils, *c*.1606, Woburn Abbey, Bedfordshire; repro. in R. Strong, *The English icon: Elizabethan and Jacobean portraiture* (1969), pl. 243 · attrib. W. Larkin, oils, *c*.1615, Nationalmuseum, Gripsholm Castle, Stockholm [*see illus.*] · attrib. J. Priwitzer, oils, *c*.1620, repro. in *British paintings, 1500–1850* (1997), pl. 15 [Sothebys sale catalogue]; version, Woburn Abbey, Bedfordshire; repro. in *Ben Jonson*, ed. Herford, Simpson, and Simpson, 8, facing p. 60 · attrib. M. Gheeraerts, oils, St Edward's Hall, Stow on the Wold, Gloucestershire · I. Oliver, miniature, NPG; repro. in *Important portrait miniatures including masterworks from the Edward Grosvner Paine Collection* (1996) [sale catalogue, Christies, 15 Oct 1996] · I. Oliver, miniature, bodycolour and watercolour on vellum and card, FM Cam.; repro. in K. Hearn, ed., *Dynasties: painting in Tudor and Jacobean England, 1530–1630* (1995), 140 [exhibition catalogue, Tate Gallery, London, 12 Oct 1995 – 7 Jan 1996] · S. de Passe, line engraving, BM, NPG; repro. in A. M. Hind, *Engraving in England in the sixteenth and seventeenth centuries*, 2 (1955), pl. 148(b)

Wealth at death estates inherited on death of father in 1613 and brother in 1614 were heavily encumbered with debt · administration, PRO; GEC, *Peerage*

Russell, Mary Annette. See Arnim, Mary Annette von (1866–1941).

Russell, Dame Mary Du Caurroy (1865–1937). See under Russell, Herbrand Arthur, eleventh duke of Bedford (1858–1940).

Russell, Matthew (1834–1912), poet and editor, was born in Ballybot, near Newry, co. Down, Ireland, the sixth and youngest child of Arthur Russell (1785–1845), a master in the merchant marine, and his wife, Margaret Hamill, *née* Mullan (d. in or after 1845). On his marriage to the widowed Margaret Hamill, Arthur Russell purchased a brewery in Newry. The Russells, who traced their descent from an Anglo-Norman ancestor who arrived in Ireland with Strongbow, were comfortable but not rich, and when Arthur Russell fell ill in the late 1830s, he leased the brewery and moved his family to Seafield House, a small farm at Killowen on Carlingford Lough, where the children were educated by a governess. Both parents were enthusiastic supporters of Daniel O'Connell, and both, particularly Mrs Russell, were strict Catholics; the children had to read from Alban Butler's *The Lives of the Saints* every day. Matthew Russell's uncle Charles William *Russell, who became president of St Patrick's College, Maynooth, in 1857, was instrumental in converting Newman to Catholicism, as well as helping Cardinal Wiseman to edit the *Dublin Review*. Arthur Russell died in May 1845 and the family returned to Newry, although they continued to spend summers at Killowen. Russell's three surviving sisters all became nuns in the order of Mercy, while his brother Charles Arthur *Russell (1832–1900), a barrister, rose to be lord chief justice of England in 1894.

Matthew Russell was educated at Castleknock College and St Patrick's College, Maynooth; he entered the Society of Jesus in 1857 and in 1864 was ordained priest. Until 1873 he did school and church work in Limerick, but in that year he moved to Dublin and founded (and edited until his death) the *Irish Monthly*, subtitled the 'Irish Catholic'. Its first editorial announced that it was 'devoted to the service of the Faith and the Fatherland after which it is named', and that it would be Catholic and national in tone, with the emphasis on Catholic. Although theologically orientated in its early years, Russell began to hope that it might be 'the forerunner of a Catholic literature in Ireland', which he saw as 'the essential want of this country', since over the previous century 'Genius and Intelligence' had been 'hostile to, or estranged from Catholicity', and he gradually opened the magazine to literature and even to non-Catholic writers such as Oscar Wilde and W. B. Yeats. As well as serializing stories by living writers such as Rosa Mulholland and publishing poems by Katharine Tynan, Rose Kavanagh, Dora Sigerson, and Ellen O'Leary, it also printed correspondence, work, and recollections of earlier Irish writers and politicians, including Charles Kickham, Gerald Griffin, and Thomas Davis.

In addition to editing the *Irish Monthly*, Russell published numerous volumes of religious and secular poems, a series of very popular devotional works, a biography of his three sisters and of the Blessed John Eudes, and an edition of Rose Kavanagh's poetry. He was also in demand as a lecturer and particularly concerned himself with speaking in support of the temperance movement. From 1877 to 1886 he served as a priest at St Francis Xavier's Church in Gardner Street, Dublin, and from 1886 to 1903 taught at University College, St Stephen's Green, before returning to his sacerdotal duties in Gardner Street until his death. W. B. Yeats described Russell in January 1889 as 'a Catholic priest of a most courteous, kindly, and liberal kind' (*Collected Letters*), and these qualities are evident both in his editorial policy and in his attitude towards his contributors and parishioners. Russell performed many quiet acts of charity and was particularly understanding when Katharine Tynan, one of his most assiduous contributors and correspondents, married a protestant in 1893. He died at 20 Mountjoy Square, Dublin, on 12 September 1912.

JOHN KELLY

Sources *The collected letters of W. B. Yeats*, ed. J. Kelly and others, [3 vols.] (1986–) · *Irish Book Lover*, 4/3 (1912) · D. J. O'Donoghue, *The poets of Ireland: a biographical and bibliographical dictionary* (1912) · W. J. Paul, *Modern Irish poetry*, 2 (1897) · Matthew Russell papers, Archivae Provincia Hibernia, Dublin · M. Russell, *The three sisters of Lord Russell of Killowen and their convent life* (1912) · d. cert.

Russell, Michael (1781–1848), bishop of Glasgow and Galloway, was born in Edinburgh on 12 August 1781, the eldest son of John Russell of Edinburgh and Euphan, *née* Hamilton. He matriculated at Glasgow University in November 1800, and graduated MA in 1806. Afterwards he was appointed second master of the grammar school at Stirling whence his family appear to have moved by 1791; but, having become a convert to episcopalianism, he resigned and opened a school of his own. In 1808 he was ordained a deacon in the Scottish Episcopal church, and given charge of the small congregation at Alloa. Like most incumbencies in the Episcopal church the position was poorly paid, so he retained his school until his appointment in 1809 to the charge of St James's Chapel, Leith. In 1820 he received the degree of LLD from the University of Glasgow. Russell maintained a constant stream of publications covering a wide range of concerns in which he was an interested rather than an original thinker. For many years he was a contributor to the *Encyclopaedia Metropolitana* and the *British Critic*. He was also editor of the *Scottish Episcopal Review and Magazine* for some years. Russell was also a contributor to a number of popular serial publications, including the *Edinburgh Cabinet Library* and *Constable's Miscellany*. Particularly interested in education and church history, he published a *History of the Church of Scotland* (2 vols., 1834). His religious opinions were mildly liberal which caused his orthodoxy to be questioned by the more intolerant among his high-church brethren. Despite this, he became dean of the diocese of Edinburgh in 1831, and on 8 October 1837 he was ordained bishop of Glasgow and Galloway, on the separation of that diocese from Edinburgh and St Andrews. As a bishop he published a number of single sermons and charges in which he enthusiastically and carefully defended episcopalianism. In his diocesan administration he was conciliatory and concerned, although, like many of his contemporaries among the Scottish bishops, he was introvert in character, instinctively preferring books to active social engagement. It was in large part due to Russell that the Scottish church was indebted for the bill passed in 1840 removing some religious disabilities from episcopalian clergy officiating in England. In 1842 the University of Oxford conferred on him the honorary degree of DCL. As a theologian Russell was more in the mould of the English high-churchmen than the nonjuring version predominant in the north of Scotland, with its attachment to the Scottish communion office. He disliked the possibility of the revival of the latter in his own diocese when it was advocated by some clergy and laity under Tractarian influence. Russell was made increasingly aware during the 1840s of the massive influx of Anglican English and Irish into Glasgow, and attempted to make arrangements for their pastoral care through the establishment of episcopalian missions. He died suddenly on 2 April 1848 in Edinburgh, probably from cardiac arrest, and was buried at Restalrig following the funeral on 11 April. A marble slab was erected in his memory in St James's Chapel, Leith.

T. F. HENDERSON, *rev.* ROWAN STRONG

Sources W. Walker, *Three churchmen* (1893) · R. Strong, 'Coronets and altars: aristocratic women's and men's support for the Oxford Movement in Scotland during the 1840s', *Gender and Christian religion*, ed. R. N. Swanson, SCH, 34 (1998), 391–403 · *IGI*
Archives NL Scot., letters to Alexander D'Orsey
Likenesses portrait, repro. in Walker, *Three churchmen*, facing p. 9

Russell, Odo William Leopold, first Baron Ampthill (1829–1884), diplomatist, was born on 20 February 1829, at Casa Bianca, Florence, Italy, the third and youngest son of Major-General Lord George William *Russell (1790–1846), British ambassador at Berlin (1835–41), and his wife, Elizabeth Anne Rawdon (1793–1874). As a child and youth he travelled widely on the continent. He was educated briefly at Westminster School, but chiefly by foreign tutors and his mother, who held original views on education. As a result he had nothing of the muddied English oaf about him. He seldom took exercise. He spoke French, Italian, and German with exceptional purity, though his English accent was always tinged with continental inflexions. He had a good tenor voice, which he took the trouble to train, and a fine musical sensibility. He sought the acquaintance of scholars, and secluded himself with his books to relieve the tensions of his official life. His literary tastes were discriminating and intellectually challenging. He enjoyed reptiles, animals, birds, and fish both as companions and as objects of scientific interest.

Early diplomatic career At the age of twenty, in March 1849, Russell was appointed attaché at the British embassy in Vienna. He worked at the Foreign Office in 1850–52 under Palmerston and then Granville. In September 1853 he became second paid attaché at Paris under Lord Cowley, and was promoted first attaché at Constantinople in August 1854. He was described at this time as 'charming—a poet, full of *esprit*, and entirely without fatuity or pride' (Ross, 2.11). Twice during 1855 he took charge of the embassy during visits to the Crimea by his chief, Lord Stratford de Redcliffe, whose bullying never cowed him; he was the ambassador's only subordinate who did not find the working conditions intolerable. In 1857 he worked at the Washington legation under Lord Napier. Russell was a stickler for diplomatic formalities who 'classed his time so methodically that he found means to do twice as much work as most men, and with half the fuss' (*The Times*, 26 Aug 1884, 6c). His dispatches were strong and terse without ambiguities or embellishments; his diplomatic telegrams too were succinct and definitive.

Russell and the Roman question From November 1858 until August 1870 Russell was attached to the legation at Florence, but resided in Rome, for his real work was as an unaccredited envoy to the Vatican. The Roman beau monde soon succumbed to his charm: he joined Signor Alari's music class and acted in Mrs Plowden's private theatricals in order to maintain contacts with English Roman

Odo William Leopold Russell, first Baron Ampthill (1829–1884), by Camille Silvy, 1864

Catholics. 'Fort bien vu de tous dans la société romaine, homme du monde, aimable et séduisant, il ne néglige aucune coterie' ('Well-regarded by all Roman society, a man of the world, pleasant and attractive, he neglected no social circle'; d'Ideville, 42). He was attached to Henry Elliot's special mission of 1859 to Francis II, king of the Sicilies, and was promoted second secretary in October 1862, but declined a secretaryship at Constantinople in 1864. This was a critical period in British relations with the Vatican, and Russell had undivided responsibility in delicate and critical work. Initially he was charged with bringing before the curia the official British version of Irish affairs and with emphasizing the parallels between Fenians and Garibaldians. But the unification of Italy in 1861, the collapse of the papacy's temporal power, and the machinations surrounding the First Vatican Council of 1869–70 were momentous events in which Russell was as much a protagonist as an observer.

Like all Russells he was an immaculate protestant, but his mother's conversion to Rome had empowered him with an intellectual conception of the Catholic faith. According to a French observer:

> His intimacy with Cardinal Antonelli enabled him to acquire a thoroughly Italian subtlety seldom to be met with in an

Englishman. A close observer by nature, he has learnt by experience how to observe still more closely: he has discovered how to weigh the characters of men, to discern their weaknesses, and to profit by their meannesses and susceptibilities. (*The Times*, 27 Aug 1884, 5b)

During the Vatican Council, Pope Pius IX, appreciating Russell's discretion, granted Cardinal Manning dispensation to disclose secret information to him so that the British government might be kept authoritatively informed, partly in the hope that the British would rescue the pope if the Vatican was invaded. Without Russell's aid, Manning might have been unable to foil the efforts of J. J. I. von Döllinger and Lord Acton to achieve European diplomatic intervention against the pope and the Vatican Council. Manning enabled Russell to supply the Foreign Office with accurate reports of proceedings of the Vatican Council, which often contradicted the information supplied by Acton to Gladstone. 'You stand *very high*', Clarendon reported from the cabinet to Russell on 7 February 1870. 'There is no business however urgent that would not be suspended if I announced that I had a despatch from O. R. to read' (N. Blakiston, 389). Russell's sympathy with the pontiff has been exaggerated by Roman Catholic propagandists. He was ironical about the stupidity, credulity, and prudery of many of the prelates, and contemptuous of what he called in 1861 'the small pious frauds through which the Court at Rome still delight to exercise their power' (ibid., 180). Pius's momentous encyclical of 1864, with its Syllabus of Errors, was deplored by Russell for proclaiming 'unbounded pretensions to absolute control over the souls and bodies of mankind' (p. 299) and for placing 'the Pope at the head of a vast ecclesiastical conspiracy against the principles which govern modern society' (p. 303). He welcomed the consequences of Manning's appointment as archbishop of Westminster (1865) as 'detrimental to popery in England' (p. 315) and wrote to Derby in 1884, 'The Pope has made his Church ridiculous by the proclamation of the Immaculate Conception, of the Syllabus and of his own infallibility' (Taffs, 31).

On 5 May 1868 Russell married Lady Emily Theresa Villiers (1843–1927), third daughter of George William Frederick *Villiers, fourth earl of Clarendon, to whom for many years he addressed dispatches as foreign secretary. She was a gracious and intelligent woman, with a shrewd knowledge of international politics. She was left inconsolable at his death, after which she was appointed lady of the bedchamber (1885–1901) by Queen Victoria. The Russells had four sons, including (Arthur) Oliver Villiers *Russell, and two daughters. On the succession of his brother Francis Charles Hastings *Russell [see under Russell, Lord George William] as ninth duke of Bedford, Odo Russell received royal warrant of precedence as the son of a duke (25 June 1872). Following the death of his father-in-law, to whom he was devoted, Russell returned to London on leave of absence in July 1870 and was appointed assistant under-secretary at the Foreign Office in August. He was on a special mission to the German army headquarters at Versailles from November 1870 until March 1871. He conferred with Bismarck on the crisis created by Russia's

opportunistic denunciation (at the nadir of French power) of those clauses in the treaty of Paris of 1856 prohibiting Russia and Turkey from building warships on the Black Sea. Russell prevented this abrupt violation of a solemn pact by insisting on his own initiative that if Russia persisted, Britain would go to war with or without its allies. The direct result of Russell's mission was a peaceful solution of the immediate problem at the London conference of January 1871.

Ambassador in Berlin Russell's personal success with Bismarck led to his appointment as ambassador at Berlin in October 1871. Always prudent, discreet, and just, his conduct of the embassy stood in distinct contrast to that of his predecessor, Lord Augustus Loftus, 'foolish … pompous and inclined to swagger' (Derby, diary, 10 Nov 1884, Stanley MSS, Lpool RO). Russell admired the new Germany and liked Germans: during his thirteen years in Berlin he never forfeited the confidence of Bismarck. Just as he had understood his Constantinople chief, Stratford de Redcliffe, and had never been broken by his suspicious rages, so too he achieved a sympathetic understanding of Bismarck. He withstood the Iron Chancellor's rages about real or imaginary plots, dispelled his darkest suspicions of British policy, and penetrated to the core of Bismarckian motives and strategy. Russell was trusted by Crown Princess Frederick and the Hohenzollerns, but his cordiality to Bismarck's enemies was never tainted by the suspicion of intrigue. Nor was the objectivity of his dispatches compromised by his private belief that *Kulturkampf* must fail, or by his revulsion at Bismarck's persecution of Roman Catholicism. From the outset, he recognized Germany's colonial aspirations, though his appreciation of this complex situation was imperfect. In 1879 he was responsible for the novelty of attaching a commercial expert to the Berlin embassy staff.

The Congress of Berlin During the Far Eastern crisis of 1875–7 Russell acted with promptitude and tact upon his instructions, despite regarding British policy as vacillating and misjudged. It was in recognition of his discreet and patient work that Russell in June 1878 was appointed third British plenipotentiary, after Beaconsfield and Salisbury, at the Berlin congress. There he tendered discreet and solid advice to Beaconsfield on tactics and personalities. He worked chiefly on committees, meeting in private, which settled the agenda for the sittings of the congress or addressed vexatious boundary disputes that might delay agreement. Russell was afterwards much involved in such details of the implementation of the treaty of Berlin as the Montenegrin frontier question. The congress occasioned the apogee of his public reputation. Sir Charles Dilke declared in 1879, 'Odo Russell always easily the first wherever he goes' (Gwynn and Tuckwell, 1.292). 'Lord Odo R is certainly an extremely agreeable man, so well-informed and able to bring out his information in so pleasant and interesting a manner', Edward Walter Hamilton noted in 1880 (Hamilton, 1.69). Visiting Berlin in 1881, George Joachim Goschen found him 'lively, witty, broad-minded, cultured, even-tempered, and with an immense knowledge of men and things' (Elliot, 1.209). Friedrich von Holstein judged him 'a man with extremely pleasant manners but with considerable self-esteem' (Rich and Fisher, 1.67).

Privately, in 1871 Russell denounced Lord Granville's incapacity at the Foreign Office, and by 1873 he aspired to be foreign secretary in a Liberal administration. He continued to find Granville both doctrinaire and vacillating in the early 1880s, but by then his hopes of a cabinet appointment had probably receded. Although his father-in-law, Clarendon, had been envoy at Madrid fifteen years before taking the foreign secretaryship in 1853, the obstacles to a career diplomat assuming this political post were surely weightier than Russell's talents and family connections. He was made GCB in 1874 and GCMG in 1879, and accepted a barony offered by Beaconsfield after the Congress of Berlin, but afterwards withdrew his acceptance, on learning that Gladstone thought it disloyal to the Liberal Party. His brother, the duke of Bedford, certainly urged the impropriety of accepting a coronet from the Conservatives, and refused to endow his peerage (Russell had hitherto received a yearly charge upon the Bedford estates in Bloomsbury). Bedford however agreed in September 1880 to settle £100,000 on him so that Gladstone might recommend him for a peerage. He was created Baron Ampthill (11 March 1881) on the occasion of the marriage of Prince Wilhelm of Prussia (afterwards Kaiser Wilhelm II), and henceforth regularly attended the House of Lords when in London. At this time he considered substituting *With or without allies* as his heraldic motto instead of the Russells' *Che sera, sera.*

During the Egyptian crisis of 1882, Ampthill skilfully tracked the course of Bismarck's intrigues, and a fortnight before the British fleet's bombardment of Alexandria, advised, 'Prince Bismarck will side with us, because his sympathies are always on the side of force' (Fitzmaurice, 2.262). In his own words, Ampthill was crucial in helping Granville steer 'out of "entangling alliances" into the independent prosecution of a truly British national policy' (ibid., 2.268). Although for ten years Bismarck had vehemently disclaimed colonial ambitions to Ampthill, the last phase of the Berlin embassy was characterized by German claims in Fiji (1883) and west Africa (1884), and by related ebullitions of anti-British feeling.

Ampthill was short, liverish, and stout from early manhood. He had an enormous head, a genial face, glinting golden spectacles, a generous mind, suave manners, and a gentle disposition. He was a heavy eater, though temperate in drink. He died of peritonitis on 25 August 1884, at his summer villa at Potsdam, and was interred on 3 September in the Bedford vault at Chenies. Bismarck thought him irreplaceable.

'He was eminently fit for the life he led, having by nature the easy unimpassioned temper which belongs to a diplomatist', recorded Lord Derby on 26 August 1884.

He told stories, and conversed, admirably well: there were few pleasanter companions. His health was never strong, and latterly failed a good deal owing to sedentary habits …

He had an art both in writing and talking, more than any man I have known, of insinuating what he did not think it desirable or prudent to say openly: so that you knew what he thought, yet could hardly assert that he had given an opinion. (Vincent, 101–2)

RICHARD DAVENPORT-HINES

Sources *The Times* (26 Aug 1884) · *The Times* (27 Aug 1884) · *The Times* (3 Sept 1884) · *The Times* (4 Sept 1884) · *ILN* (6 Sept 1884), 235 · N. Blakiston, ed., *The Roman question: extracts from the despatches of Odo Russell from Rome, 1858–1870* (1962) · W. Taffs, *Ambassador to Bismarck: Lord Odo Russell* (1938) · *A selection from the diaries of Edward Henry Stanley, 15th earl of Derby (1826–93), between March 1869 and September 1878*, ed. J. R. Vincent, CS, 5th ser., 4 (1994) · E. G. Petty-Fitzmaurice, *The life of Granville George Leveson Gower, second Earl Granville*, 2nd edn, 2 (1905) · J. A. Ross, *Three generations of Englishwomen: memoirs and correspondence of Mrs John Taylor, Mrs Sarah Austin and Lady Duff Gordon*, 2 vols. (1888) · H. A. d'Ideville, *Journal d'un diplomate en Italie, 1862–1866: notes intimes pour servir a l'histoire du second empire* (Paris, 1873) · A. D. Elliot, *The life of George Joachim Goschen, first Viscount Goschen, 1831–1907*, 2 vols. (1911) · N. Rich and M. H. Fisher, eds., *The Holstein papers*, 1 (1955) · *The later Derby diaries … selected passages*, ed. J. Vincent (privately printed, Bristol, 1981) · S. Gwynn and G. M. Tuckwell, *The life of the Rt. Hon. Sir Charles W. Dilke*, 2 vols. (1917) · J. R. Rodd, *Social and diplomatic memories*, 1 (1922) · *The diary of Sir Edward Walter Hamilton, 1880–1885*, ed. D. W. R. Bahlman, 2 vols. (1972) · W. N. Medlicott, *The Congress of Berlin and after* (1938) · Gladstone, *Diaries* · G. Blakiston, *Lord William Russell and his wife, 1815–1846* (1972) · GEC, *Peerage* · K. Urbach, *Bismarck's favourite Englishman: Lord Odo Russell's mission to Berlin* (2000)

Archives PRO, corresp. and papers, FO 918 · UCL, autograph collection | Balliol Oxf., corresp. with Sir Robert Morier · BL, corresp. with W. E. Gladstone, Add. MSS 44093–44467, *passim* · BL, corresp. with Sir Austen Layard, Add. MSS 38993–39130, *passim* · BL OIOC, letters to Sir Mountstuart Grant-Duff, MS Eur. F 234 · Bodl. Oxf., letters to fourth earl of Clarendon · Bodl. Oxf., Russell MSS · CUL, corresp. with Lord Acton · Lpool RO, corresp. with fifteenth earl of Derby · Nationaal Archief, The Hague, letters to Donald Mackay · National Archives of Malta, corresp. with Sir John Gaspard Le Marchant · PRO, corresp. with second Earl Granville, PRO 30/29 · PRO, letters to Lord Hammond, FO 391 · PRO, corresp. with Lord John Russell, FO 364/1–11 · PRO, letters to Sir William White, FO 364/1–11 · PRO NIre., letters to Lord Dufferin

Likenesses Kriehuber, lithograph, 1847, repro. in Blakiston, ed., *Roman question*, facing p. xxx · L. Guterbock, oils, 1860–1869?, repro. in Blakiston, ed., *Roman question*, facing p. 211 · C. Silvy, photograph, 1864, NPG [*see illus.*] · R. T., pen-and-ink sketch, 1880–89, repro. in *ILN*, 220 · C. Holroyd, oils, *c*.1885 (posthumous), repro. in Taffs, *Ambassador to Bismarck*, facing p. 245 · R. C. Clouston, mezzotint (after C. Holroyd), BM · relief marble tablet, St Michael's Church, Chenies, Buckinghamshire, Russell chapel

Wealth at death £45,994 15*s.* 4*d.*: probate, 17 Dec 1884, CGPLA Eng. & Wales

Russell, (Arthur) Oliver Villiers, second Baron Ampthill (1869–1935), administrator in India, was born at the Palazzo Chigi, Rome, on 19 February 1869, the eldest child of Lord Odo William Leopold *Russell, first Baron Ampthill (1829–1884), and his wife, Lady Emily Theresa (1843–1927), third daughter of George William Frederick *Villiers, fourth earl of Clarendon. Born into two of the great whig dynasties, Oliver Russell, as he was known, had a charmed upbringing. He was tall, handsome, and well-built, a natural favourite at his two schools, Chignell's and Eton College (1883–8), and in his final two years at the latter he captained the boats and presided over Pop, the Eton society. At New College, Oxford, he continued his distinguished

(Arthur) Oliver Villiers Russell, second Baron Ampthill (1869–1935), by Walter Stoneman, 1921

oarsmanship, rowing in the victorious university eights of 1890 and 1891 and also in the victorious Leander eight in the Grand Challenge Cup at Henley in 1891, and, with Guy Nickalls, winning the silver goblets at Henley in 1890 and 1891. In 1891, the year of his graduation with third-class honours in modern history, he was president of both the university boat club and the union.

On 6 October 1894 Ampthill (who had succeeded to the title ten years previously, in 1884) married Lady Margaret (1874–1957), third daughter of Frederick *Lygon, sixth Earl Beauchamp, an energetic woman ideally suited to the role of aristocratic consort, and with whom he was to have five children. In 1895 he was appointed assistant secretary to Joseph Chamberlain at the Colonial Office, with elevation to private secretary following in 1897. Like Chamberlain, Ampthill's instinctive liberalism was gradually subsumed by an appreciation of empire, especially after 1900, when, newly created GCIE, he was appointed to succeed Sir Arthur Havelock as governor of Madras. He was young for the job and initially the viceroy, Lord Curzon, found him arrogant, allergic to criticism, and addicted to pomp and ceremony—flaws, of course, which many contemporaries thought Curzon's own. The two men disagreed over Curzon's attempts to curb the racism of British soldiers and when Ampthill reacted with insufficient outrage to the killing by one of his aides of an Indian (by 'a push with the foot'), Curzon forced the man's resignation. Nevertheless, in covering for Curzon when he went on leave in 1904, Ampthill proved himself a loyal deputy and repeatedly frustrated St John Brodrick's efforts at the India

Office to use the interregnum to push through a batch of anti-Curzonian policies. He was no match, however, for Lord Kitchener, Curzon's petulant commander-in-chief, and allowed him to strip the military department of its control of supply and transport, thus readying Kitchener for his ultimate triumph over the viceroy's military member as Indian war supremo.

Upon returning to England in 1906 Ampthill took up the cause of Indians in South Africa. He also chaired an advisory committee on Indian students in Britain convened by John Morley, the Liberals' Indian secretary, but had little sympathy with Morley's proposals for Indian political reform, an attitude which may have cost him the viceroyalty. Ampthill claimed to favour far more liberal advances than Morley did, but, given his dislike of parliamentary intervention in the ruling of India, it seems that personal, paternalistic relations would have dominated any reforms that won his support. With each subsequent stage of reform, as India drew further away from the empire, so Ampthill's outspoken opposition increased. In 1909 he had written a fulsome introduction to Joseph Doke's booklet *M. K. Gandhi: an Indian Patriot in South Africa*, and until his death in 1935 he persisted in his argument that it was Britain's failure to treat Indians throughout the empire equally that had encouraged them to repudiate British suzerainty.

In the run-up to the First World War Ampthill fostered the Territorial Army in Bedfordshire, home of his country residences, Milton Ernest Hall and, afterwards, Oakley House. During the war he commanded in France the 13th battalion of the Leicestershire regiment and subsequently the 3rd and 8th battalions of the Bedfordshire regiment, and was twice mentioned in dispatches. For a year (1917–18) he was Indian Labour Corps adviser at general headquarters on the western front. In 1919 he was promoted to brevet-colonel.

Since his undergraduate days Ampthill had been a prominent freemason and in 1908 the duke of Connaught appointed him pro-grand master of English freemasonry, an office he held until his death. He was also a JP and sometime chairman of Bedfordshire county council. He died of pneumonia, at the Bath Club in Dover Street, London, on 7 July 1935, and was buried at Chenies, Buckinghamshire, on 10 July. He was survived by his widow, who was created GCVO in 1946, and their five children: John Hugo *Russell (1896–1973), lieutenant-commander RN, who succeeded his father as third Baron Ampthill; Guy Herbrand Edward *Russell (1898–1977); Edward Wriothesley Curzon (*b.* 1901); Leopold Oliver (*b.* 1907); and Phyllis Margaret (*b.* 1909).   KATHERINE PRIOR

Sources D. Gilmour, *Curzon* (1994) · *The Times* (8 July 1935), 16 · *The Times* (9 July 1935), 8 · *The Times* (11 July 1935), 19 · *The Times* (12 July 1935), 16 · M. N. Das, *India under Morley and Minto* (1964) · Burke, *Peerage* (1959) · J. J. Doke, *M. K. Gandhi: an Indian patriot in South Africa* (1909) · *The historical register of the University of Oxford … to the end of Trinity term 1900* (1900) · H. E. C. Stapylton, *Second series of Eton school lists … 1853–1892* (1900) · *DNB*

Archives BL OIOC, corresp. and MSS, MS Eng. E 233 | BL OIOC, Curzon collection · BL OIOC, letters to Arthur Godley, MS Eur. F 102 · BL OIOC, corresp. with Lord George Hamilton, MSS Eur. C

125–26, D 508–510, F 123 · BL OIOC, corresp. with Sir Henry Richards, MS Eur. F 122 · CUL, corresp. with Lord Hardinge · HLRO, letters to Willoughby Debroke · NL Aus., letters to Alfred Deakin · PRO, letters to Lord Kitchener, PRO 30/57; W0159
Likenesses W. Stoneman, photograph, 1921, NPG [*see illus.*] · A. S. Cope, oils, *c.*1925, Freemasons' Hall, London · H. Leslie, silhouette, 1926, NPG · photograph, 1930, NPG
Wealth at death £15,377 0s. 9d.: probate save and except settled land, 8 Aug 1935, *CGPLA Eng. & Wales* · £41,015: probate limited to settled land, 20 Sept 1935, *CGPLA Eng. & Wales*

Russell, Patrick (1629–1692), Roman Catholic archbishop of Dublin, was born in Rush in northern co. Dublin. His father, James Russell, appears to have been a man of some substance, but no details survive; neither has his mother's name been preserved. A visitation in 1630 recorded that all the parishioners were recusants, with two mass-houses served by a priest, Patrick Duff. There are, however, no details of Patrick Russell's early life and education: he is first recorded as a student of the Irish seminary of St Patrick in Lisbon, where he was ordained priest on 12 June 1654. This would imply that he had gone to Lisbon about the year 1648. It would not have been possible for him to return to Ireland until after the Restoration in 1660. He is first recorded in 1675, but clearly had been working in Dublin for a considerable time, for he is described as vicar-general and parish priest of St Nicholas, officiating at the chapel recently built in Francis Street. Enforcement of the laws against recusancy varied in severity, but a real storm broke out when Titus Oates sprang the Popish Plot in 1678. Archbishop Peter Talbot, appointed in 1669, was arrested and died in prison on 15 November 1680.

Russell was now in charge of the diocese, and in July 1683 he was appointed archbishop. It was still necessary for him to live discreetly, and no record of his consecration has survived. All changed, however, with the accession of James II. Richard Talbot, brother of the deceased archbishop, was created earl of Tyrconnell and appointed lord lieutenant. Roman Catholic bishops received an annual pension from the king, and they and their clergy exercised their functions openly. Russell presided over a number of synods called to reorganize the church. Early in 1689 he could report that a number of churches had been taken over, together with the cathedral of Christ Church. Developments speeded up when James II went to Ireland in March 1689, and as archbishop of the capital city Russell had a prominent role. On 6 June, for example, he installed a community of Benedictine nuns in Channel Row in the presence of the king and his court. In consequence, he had little hope of escape after the defeat of James at the battle of the Boyne on 1 July 1690. He was imprisoned in Dublin Castle, where he died on 14 July 1692. At his own request, he was buried in the cemetery of his parish church at Lusk, beside his birthplace, Rush.

PATRICK J. CORISH

Sources L. F. Renehan, *Collections on Irish church history*, ed. D. McCarthy, 1 (1861), 223–34 · N. Donnelly, *A short history of some Dublin parishes*, vol. 2, pt 6, section 1 (1906); facs. repr., pt 6, section 1 (1979), 33–4 · *Constitutiones provinciales et synodales ecclesiae metropolitanae et primatialis Dubliniensis* (1770), 80–128 [no author given] · P. F. Moran, ed., *Spicilegium Ossoriense*, 2 (1878) · W. Carrigan, ed., 'Catholic episcopal wills in the Public Record Office, Dublin, 1685–1812', *Archivium Hibernicum*, 4 (1915), 66–7 · H. Fenning, ed., 'Irishmen ordained at Lisbon, 1587–1625, 1641–60', *Collectanea Hibernica*, 31–32 (1989–90), 103–17 · 'Archbishop Bulkeley's visitation of Dublin, 1630', ed. M. V. Ronan, *Archivium Hibernicum*, 8 (1941), 56–98 · J. D'Alton, *The memoirs of the archbishops of Dublin* (1838), 446–57 · N. Donnelly, 'The diocese of Dublin in the eighteenth century', *Irish Ecclesiastical Record*, 3rd ser., 10 (1889), 721–32, esp. 731–2 · inscription on plate fixed to his coffin
Archives Sacra Congregazione di Propaganda Fide, Rome
Likenesses oils, archbishop's house, Dublin
Wealth at death modest: Carrigan, ed., 'Catholic episcopal wills'

Russell, Patrick (1727–1805), physician and naturalist, was born in Edinburgh on 6 February 1727, the fifth son of John Russell, a lawyer of Braidshaw, Edinburghshire, and his third wife, Mary, daughter of the Revd Anderson, minister of West Calder. The half-brother of Alexander *Russell (1714–1768), he is said to have graduated MD. In 1750 he joined his brother Alexander at Aleppo, and in 1753 succeeded him as physician to the factory of the English Levant Company. He was much respected there, and the pasha granted him the privilege of wearing a turban. From the date of the publication of his brother's *Natural History of Aleppo* (1756) until Alexander's death in 1768 Patrick forwarded many emendations for the work. The epidemic of plague at Aleppo in 1760, 1761, and 1762 gave him exceptional opportunities of adding to his brother's studies of the disease, and in 1759 and 1768 he sent home accounts of destructive earthquakes in Syria, and of the method of inoculation practised in Arabia, which were published in the *Philosophical Transactions* for 1760 and 1768 respectively. In 1771 he left Aleppo, returning, as his brother had done, through Italy and France, in order to examine the lazarettos established for those impounded in quarantine at Mediterranean ports. Reaching home in 1772, he at first thought of practising as a physician in Edinburgh, but, on John Fothergill's advice, settled in London. He was elected FRS in 1777.

In 1781, after his younger brother Claud had been appointed administrator of Vizagapatam, Russell accompanied him to India, and in November 1785 he succeeded the Dane John Gerard Koenig as botanist to the East India Company in the Carnatic. In this capacity he made large collections of specimens and drawings of the plants, fishes, and reptiles of the country; and he proposed to the governor of Madras in 1785 that the company's medical officers and others should be officially requested to collect specimens and information concerning useful plants of the various districts of India. In 1787 he drew up a preliminary memoir on the poisonous snakes of the Coromandel coast, which was printed officially at Madras, and in 1788 he sent Sir Joseph Banks an account of the siliceous secretion in the bamboo known as tabashír, which was printed in the Royal Society's *Philosophical Transactions* for 1791. While in India, Russell also arranged the materials he had collected on the plague. These he sent home in 1787 for the revision of his friends William Robertson, Adam Ferguson, and Adam Smith.

Russell left India with his brother Claud in January 1789,

placing his collections of plants and fishes in the company's museum at Madras. His *Treatise on the Plague* appeared in 2 volumes in 1791. In this work Russell struck a balance between 'contagionist' theories of plague, which stressed its communicability in merchandise and from person to person, and 'miasmatic' theories, which saw plague as arising from an unhealthy state of the air. Thus, unlike some of his younger contemporaries such as Charles Maclean, Russell was steadfast in his opposition to the removal of quarantine, in the Mediterranean and in Britain itself. Nevertheless, Russell acknowledged that the immunity of the British Isles from plague for over twenty-five years owed as much to improved hygiene and housing as to *cordons sanitaires*.

In 1794 Russell issued a much enlarged edition, in two volumes, of his brother's *Natural History of Aleppo*, which incorporated some of his brother's previously unpublished work. The following year, he wrote the preface to the *Plants of the Coast of Coromandel* by William Roxburgh, a sumptuous work published at the expense of the East India Company, and one outcome of his own recommendations made ten years before. In 1796 he published on the same scale, at the cost of the company, the first fascicle of his *Account of Indian Serpents Collected on the Coast of Coromandel* in folio, with forty-six plates, forty-four of which were coloured. It was the first publication on this branch of Indian zoology—the product of a huge collaborative enterprise in which Russell enlisted the help of other company servants. Russell's *Account* also relied heavily on Indian knowledge, although he subjected local wisdom to the trial of experiment and his own observations. A second fascicle, comprising twenty-two coloured plates, issued in 1801 and 1802, and twenty-four issued in 1804, was all that appeared during his lifetime; but the third fascicle was published in 1807, and the fourth in 1809, the latter reprinting two papers by him from the *Philosophical Transactions* for 1804, and accompanied by a memoir and a portrait of the author in his fifty-fifth year.

In 1799 Russell was consulted by the privy council as to quarantine regulations after a fresh outbreak of plague in the Levant. In 1803 he published, 'by order of the court of directors', *Descriptions and Figures of Two Hundred Fishes; Collected [by him] at Vizagapatam* in two folio volumes. He died at his house in Weymouth Street, London, unmarried, on 2 July 1805.   G. S. BOULGER, *rev.* MARK HARRISON

Sources P. Russell, 'Preface', in W. Roxburgh, *Plants of the coast of Coromandel* (1795) · Desmond, *Botanists*, rev. edn · *GM*, 1st ser., 75 (1805), 683 · *The record of the Royal Society of London*, 4th edn (1940) · 'Memoir', P. Russell, *Account of Indian serpents collected on the coast of Coromandel*, 4th fasciculus (1809)
Archives BL OIOC, catalogue of plants, MS Eur. E 54 | BL, letters to Sir Joseph Banks, Add. MSS 33977–33979 · NHM, Aleppo plants and drawings · NHM, Indian plants
Likenesses pencil drawing, 1794 (after G. Dance), RCP Lond. · W. Daniell, soft-ground etching, pubd 1811 (after G. Dance), BM, NPG · Evans, engraving (after Varlet), repro. in *PTRS* (1804) · W. Ridley, stipple (after L. Vaslet), BM, NPG; repro. in *European Magazine* (1811) · portrait, Hunt Botanical Library, Pittsburgh, Pennsylvania

Russell [*née* Wriothesley; *other married name* Vaughan], **Rachel, Lady Russell** (*bap.* **1637**, *d.* **1723**), noblewoman,

Rachel Russell, Lady Russell (*bap.* 1637, *d.* 1723), by unknown artist

was baptized on 19 September 1637 at the parish church of St Peter in the village of Titchfield in Hampshire, the daughter of Thomas *Wriothesley, fourth earl of Southampton (1608–1667), an adviser and friend of Charles I, and Charles II's lord treasurer. Her mother was Southampton's first wife, the strikingly beautiful Rachel (1603–1640), eldest daughter of Daniel de Massüe, seigneur de Ruvigny, and widow of Elysée de Beaujeu, seigneur de la Maison Fort; she was a devout Huguenot, and her brother, the first marquis de Ruvigny, was appointed lord deputy general of protestants in France in 1653; he later served as a special envoy to the Stuart court. Rachel's mother died in childbirth in 1640 leaving another daughter, Elizabeth (1636–1680), who married Edward Noel, later first earl of Gainsborough. In 1642 Southampton married Elizabeth, eldest daughter of Francis Leigh, Lord Dunsmore. Only one of their four daughters, yet another Elizabeth (1646–1690), survived childhood. Rachel regarded her full sister Elizabeth as a 'delicious friend', whose 'conversation and tender kindness' were precious to her (*Letters*, 37, 168). She was also close to her half-sister Elizabeth, and 'ever loved her tenderly' (*Letters*, 168). The two older girls were no doubt educated together by tutors at Titchfield, where the atmosphere was high-minded, 'like ours at Cambridge' wrote a visitor (G. C. M. Smith, *Henry Tubbe*, 1915, 12). Rachel developed a legible handwriting, a competent orthography, and a talent for forthright, engaging expression. She learned to write French effortlessly and presumably to speak it well, skills no doubt strengthened by a visit to France. Sisterly affection not only enriched the personal lives of these three women but also enlarged their political connections and made possible the harmonious division of their father's property.

First marriage, 1654–1667 In October 1654, at the age of seventeen, Rachel accepted an arranged marriage with Francis, styled Lord Vaughan (1638–1667), a young man of limited promise, the eldest son of Richard *Vaughan, second earl of Carbery (1600?–1686). The marriage contract provided £900 a year to the couple and guaranteed that amount to Rachel for life should Francis predecease her. During this thirteen-year union Rachel Vaughan lived mostly at Golden Grove in Wales, the Carberys' principal seat, and after 1660, when the earl became lord president of the marches of Wales, at Ludlow Castle. She kept in touch with the larger world, however: she visited her father in London and her sister at Titchfield and spent a holiday at Bath with her cousin Margaret, who was married to Anthony Ashley Cooper, later the first earl of Shaftesbury (1621–1683).

The Carberys provided a stimulating cultural and intellectual environment, presided over by the earl, a patron of poets, and his third wife, Alice Egerton, much admired for talent in music and dance. Jeremy Taylor, author of devotional literature which Rachel Vaughan treasured, served as chaplain. Correspondence indicates that Rachel was already interested in politics. In 1660 the Restoration brought office and wealth to the men in the Carbery and Southampton families and gave Rachel entrée to high social and political circles in London and Wales. Her personal life was marred, however, by illness and death; in 1657 she was stricken with measles and in 1660 with smallpox; she suffered a miscarriage in 1657; two babies, one born in 1659, the other in 1665, died. On 2 March 1667 Francis died of the plague, her father two months later.

Appearance and personality With the death of her husband and father Rachel Vaughan was transformed into a wealthy and independent widow; defying convention she almost immediately circulated in London society and was much admired for her beauty, personality, and wealth. A handsome woman with a high forehead, light brown hair, shown in a portrait in ringlets at the ears and drawn up in a large chignon, and dark brown eyes, she possessed a regular nose and a wide mouth with full and somewhat sensuous lips. Warm, vivacious, and quick, Rachel was also a person of sound judgement. She had a voluble manner of speaking: Gilbert Burnet recorded that her 'thoughts furnish so fast for her in discourse that she [is] sometimes as it were choked with them, and can scarce fetch them all out' (H. C. Foxcroft, *A Supplement to Burnet's 'History of my Own Time'*, 1902, 117); an admirer thought that he 'never knew man nor woman speak better' (*Letters*, dedication, lxvii). Her wealth also drew suitors. Her father had left his huge estate to be divided among the three sisters; by the luck of the draw to determine which portion of it would go to which sister, Rachel received the most valuable portion: the manor of Bloomsbury in London on which stood a recently completed mansion built by her father, Southampton House (in which, at the time, her

stepmother held a life interest), and manors in Hampshire, the most important being Stratton House. To this was added income from her first marriage.

Second marriage, 1669–1683 Within three months of Lord Vaughan's death gossips reported that William *Russell (1639–1683) had a 'great desire' to win Rachel Vaughan's hand (Chatsworth House, letters, 15.1). Russell was the third (but second surviving) son of William Russell, fifth earl and later first duke of Bedford (1613–1700), and his wife, Anne Carr (1615–1684), daughter of Robert, earl of Somerset (1586–1645), and his wife, Frances Howard, the former countess of Essex. Russell was a tall, good-looking, socially prominent man, who was well liked. Two years Rachel Vaughan's junior, he was also impetuous, extravagant, heedless of the consequences of his actions, and known to be a womanizer. He and Rachel fell passionately in love. She sought to encourage Russell by writing him 'expressions of love' (Woburn, Bedford estate office, HMC 40A, 17) and 'testimonies of affection' (Chatsworth House, Russell MSS, uncatalogued box 1). Painfully aware of the disparity in their wealth—as a second son, his prospects of inheriting the Bedford wealth and title were uncertain—William insisted that gaining Rachel's fortune was of no interest to him; ''tis her person and that alone I adore and admire' (Woburn, Bedford estate office, HMC, 39, 34–5). After a long courtship they married on 20 August 1669. The marriage settlement made them a very wealthy couple. From Bedford came cash in the form of an allowance of £2000 a year, this amount guaranteed to Rachel should William predecease her. Rachel brought to the marriage additional cash income, land, and houses, notably the Bloomsbury property in London, including Southampton House (now cleared of Lady Southampton's life interest), and manors in Hampshire, including Stratton House.

Marriage changed both of them. William became generally a model husband and father. Rachel's horizons were broadened: they included her husband, children, two households, a new sense of personal responsibility for public affairs, and a heightened religious sensibility. The Russells lived mostly at Stratton House, spending a portion of each year (after 1675) in London at Southampton House, with visits to Rachel's sister at Titchfield and William's family at Woburn Abbey. Deeply attached to William, Rachel poured out her affection in letters written when they were apart. 'My best life' she wrote in 1672, 'you that know so well how to love and oblige, make my felicity entire' (Berry, 6). In 1682 she declared, 'I know as certainly as I live, that I have been … as passionate a lover as ever woman was' (ibid., 65). Rachel bore four children: Anne (born 13 December 1671, died four months later), Rachel (1674), Katherine (1676), and Wriothesley (1680). The little children's conversation and antics were a staple of her letters: she described two-year-old Wriothesley prancing about 'mad, winking at me, and striking with his drumstick whatever comes to his reach' (Berry, 65). She ended one letter with a short, very effective word picture of the nursery: 'Boy is asleep, girls singing abed' (ibid., 56).

In 1678 Russell's elder brother died and William became

heir to the Bedford title and fortune; he assumed the courtesy title of Lord Russell. This change in his position and prospects elevated his social standing and augmented his political influence. Rachel took his name, now that his rank was equal to that of her first husband, becoming Lady Russell. Rachel's interest in politics expanded as William's political visibility grew. She undertook to keep her husband informed of political developments when he was out of town, gathering news because she wanted 'to be as useful and acceptable' to Russell as possible (Berry, 19). She was able to tap into many sources thanks to her many friends and family relations in high places; unabashedly she vowed 'to suck the honey from all if they will be communicative' (ibid., 49). Lady Russell introduced her husband to her French uncle, Henri de Ruvigny, and her cousin, also Henri de Ruvigny. Russell met the latter early in 1678 to discover the true intentions of Louis XIV and Charles II. The meetings were reported in dispatches from the English ambassador to France, Lady Russell's brother-in-law, Montague, and revealed to the House of Commons by Thomas Osborne, first earl of Danby (1632–1712), the lord treasurer, to document that the parliamentary opposition was in league with France. These revelations could have destroyed Russell's career, but his reputation and popularity were so strong that they did not. Rachel also brought William into contact with Shaftesbury, her cousin by marriage, and Russell became Shaftesbury's chief lieutenant in the House of Commons. As she became increasingly alarmed for William's safety she cautioned him, urged an accommodation with James, duke of York, and argued with him for ten hours about a course of action she wanted him to take. Her more level-headed view of politics, however, did not moderate her husband's rashness.

Russell's arrest, trial, and execution On 26 June 1683 Russell was arrested and sent to the Tower charged with conspiring with other whig leaders in schemes to raise rebellion by seizing the king's guards. On 13 July he was tried as a traitor before the court of king's bench at the Old Bailey and found guilty. On 21 July he was executed in Lincoln's Inn Fields. Lady Russell played a prominent role in these terrible events. She successfully petitioned the government to ease the conditions of Russell's confinement, permit visits from his family, and allow him to consult lawyers (an unusual favour). She also kept William informed of events and wrote him notes, enclosing at least one in a cold chicken. She acted as an intermediary between Russell and his lawyers and his friends, and helped to persuade eleven men to testify to his good character. She eagerly agreed to, and carried out, a scheme his friends devised to have her appear at his trial to take notes for him. The purpose in making her visible in this unprecedented way was to remind the court, the king, the jury, and the public of the Russells' well-known marital felicity and also of the services Rachel's father had rendered to both Charles I and Charles II. The presiding judge, Sir Francis Pemberton (1625–1697), chief justice of the court of common pleas, who had served the Russells as their lawyer, was sympathetic to William and insistent that the

law and legal procedures be observed, as indeed they were. But the evidence against Russell was compelling, his defence weak and unconvincing, and his protests about the jury and the requirement of two witnesses to the same act of treason not conformable to the law as it stood in 1683. The jury deliberated for a little over an hour and returned a verdict of guilty.

Lady Russell spent the next week in a frenzy of purposeful activity trying to win for William a pardon or at least a reprieve. She and others bombarded the king, who alone had the power of pardon, with petitions and at the same time implored the duke of York to intervene with Charles on William's behalf. She won a personal interview with the king, at which she implored him, perhaps weeping at his feet, to grant a delay in the execution. Charles refused, saying that had it been in Russell's power, he would not have granted him six hours. She consulted William about his scaffold speech, assisted him to copy out five 'original' copies, and arranged for timely widespread distribution. On the last night of his life Rachel had dinner with him, conversed normally, and left, after a fond embrace, without shedding a tear, an act of great self-control for this spirited woman.

Widowhood In the aftermath of Lord Russell's execution Lady Russell was 'amazed' (Letters, 6)—meaning crazy—with grief; indeed, 'wild and sad thoughts' (Letters, 60) tormented her for years. Until her own death she wore black, draped her private rooms at Southampton House and Stratton in black, and sanctified the days of William's arrest, trial, and execution with prayer, remembrance, and withdrawal. Writing letters, reminiscences, and reflections became an obsession. She poured out her grief to her most important correspondent, the Revd John Fitz-William, who responded with counsel and comfort. These poignant letters were full of adoration for William as an 'inestimable treasure' (Letters, 32), memories of their happy marriage, and her struggle to accept God's will. She also directed attention towards defending and preserving a positive memory of Lord Russell, overseeing business affairs, and supervising the education and marriage arrangements of her children. She persuaded the king not to confiscate William's private estate, and to allow her to set up an escutcheon in William's honour, unprecedented in the case of a condemned traitor, and considered ways to counter tracts written against William by friends of the government.

Lady Russell managed her business affairs independently of the earl of Bedford, her father-in-law; as a feme sole she had the authority to do so. Vowing in 1684 to 'converse with none but lawyers and accountants' (Letters, 196), she appointed her own business manager, opened her own account with Child and Rogers, goldsmith bankers, oversaw the development of Bloomsbury Square, and called in lawyers to redesign trusts to settle her properties in her own and her son's interest. She also drew upon the best legal advice available to assure that Wriothesley would inherit his grandfather's title and fortune.

Lady Russell's most abiding concern was her three children. Dismissing objections she hired a Huguenot refugee to serve as a French master, and forced herself in winter 1684–5 to return to Southampton House, 'a place of terror' (*Letters*, 32) because of the memories it held, so that her son might be in London for medical treatment. In 1687 she managed to return to Stratton; thereafter she spent winters in London and other months at either Stratton or Woburn. With William Cavendish (1641–1707), her husband's dear friend, she negotiated, after five months of hard bargaining in 1687, a settlement between her daughter, Rachel, and his son, William Cavendish (1663–1729), who became the second duke of Devonshire. Lady Rachel enjoyed comparable success in 1692–3 in making arrangements for Katherine; after persuading herself that an old scandal in the Manners family had lost significance she settled Katherine with John Manners (1676–1721), who became the second duke of Rutland. As any patriarch might have done, she wrote joyfully of having joined her daughters to the 'two best fortunes in England' (*Letters*, 189). In the case of Wriothesley, now Lord Tavistock, Rachel chose great money over ancient lineage. After a year of negotiations in 1693–4 which involved so much property that a parliamentary act was required to settle matters Wriothesley was betrothed to Elizabeth Howland (1682–1724), the granddaughter of Sir Josiah Child, the wealthy merchant and officer of the East India Company, and daughter of the late John Howland, a rich landowner in Surrey. The dowry was the enormous sum of £50,000. Wriothesley became the second duke of Bedford at the death of the first duke in 1700. The activities associated with her children were a powerful antidote to her sorrow.

The revolution of 1688–9 changed Lady Russell's life. She ardently supported the prince and princess of Orange, praying for their success, and wishing she could do more. When they became King William III and Queen Mary II and the whigs, for a time, were dominant Rachel enjoyed a renewed social and political position. The reversal of Lord William Russell's attainder in the spring of 1689 and the elevation in 1694 of his father to a dukedom, largely on grounds of Lord Russell's suffering, brought Rachel a respected place as 'grande dame' of the whigs. With her wide contacts and her energetic nature she exercised some influence in political and ecclesiastical affairs; she championed the appointment of William Cowper as king's counsel; encountering difficulties, she wrote that she did not 'like to be baulk'd' (*Letters*, 123); she had a role in the appointment of the new archbishop of Canterbury, petitioned Queen Mary in 1691 to grant a post in Wales to her candidate, and in 1703 orchestrated efforts to achieve a dukedom for the earl of Rutland. In 1694 and 1695 she underwent two cataract operations, both successful. Her advancing years were marred by personal tragedies: Wriothesley died of smallpox on 26 May 1711 and Katherine of complications in childbirth on 30 October 1711. Her principal correspondent now became her French cousin, the duke of Galway; together they tried to recover his property in France.

Lady Russell died, probably of a stroke, at 5 a.m. on 29 September 1723 at Southampton House, at the age of eighty-seven; she was buried, as her will directed, at Chenies, next to her husband. Thanks to her business acumen her landed properties had increased in value; the Bloomsbury rentals by 33 per cent to about £3000 a year, and the Hampshire properties by 66 per cent, also to about £3000 a year. The bulk of her property, silver plate, and money went to her surviving children and grandchildren. Her wealth is indicated by the generous legacies she left to Thomas Sellwood, her steward, and to at least fourteen other servants: a year's salary for all and, variously, property, silver plate, and household goods. Among other beneficiaries were the poor of the parish of St Giles-in-the-Fields, poor French refugees, and a charity school for the poor. Galway, relations from her first marriage, and the widow of the minister at Micheldever also felt her largesse. Sellwood went through Rachel's papers sent to Chatsworth House, finding among them her correspondence with FitzWilliam, and put the letters in order. This made it possible on short notice to publish the letters in 1773 to rebut the damaging revelations of the historian Sir James Dalrymple about Lord Russell's meeting with French envoys in 1678.

Lady Russell has inspired admiration over the centuries: her letters to FitzWilliam appeared in 1773, intimate letters edited by Mary Berry in 1819; both sets of letters were well received and helped to revive and rehabilitate the memory of Lord Russell. Five biographical sketches came out, one by Berry, another by François Guizot, the French protestant historian and statesman. All stressed her piety, devotion to husband and family, and forbearance in the face of personal tragedy. Lady Russell exemplifies these qualities, to be sure, but following her husband's execution she is also properly seen in broader dimensions, as a well-regarded, independent, intelligent feme sole, exercising authority as head of her family, overseeing the education of and negotiating favourable marriage contracts for her children, managing her property and business affairs, carrying on a large correspondence, and exercising some influence on behalf of whig interests in the revolution of 1688–9 and on appointments to political and religious offices. Her long life helps to reveal more fully the complex nature of aristocratic female culture in late Stuart and early Georgian England.   LOIS G. SCHWOERER

Sources L. G. Schwoerer, *Lady Rachel Russell (1637–1732): 'One of the best of women'* (1988) • L. G. Schwoerer, 'William, Lord Russell: the making of a martyr, 1683–1983', *Journal of British Studies*, 24 (1985), 41–71 • M. Berry, *Some account of the life of Rachael Wriothesley Lady Russell … followed by … letters from Lady Russell to her husband, William Lord Russell, from 1672 to 1682* (1819) • *Letters of Lady Rachel Russell: from the manuscript in the library at Woburn Abbey* (1773) • *Bishop Burnet's History* • *The speech of the late Lord Russell* (1683) • will, PRO, PROB 11/594, fols. 152v–157r • parish register, St Peter, Titchfield, 19 Sept 1637, Hants. RO [baptism] • GEC, *Peerage*, new edn, vol. 11 • letters, diaries, and papers, Bedford estate office, Woburn • parish register, St Peter, Titchfield, 20 Aug 1669, Hants. RO • tombstone, Chenies, Bedford chapel • *Weekly Journal, or, British Gazetteer* (5 Oct 1723)

Archives Bedford estate office, Woburn, letters, papers, and diaries • Chatsworth House, Derbyshire, corresp. • Chatsworth House, Derbyshire, uncatalogued, Box 1; Box 2 • U. Nott. L., letters

Likenesses W. Derby, drawing, 1829 (after miniature by S. Cooper), Woburn Abbey, Bedfordshire · oils, Woburn Abbey, Bedfordshire · oils, Woburn Abbey, Bedfordshire; repro. in Schwoerer, *Lady Rachel Russell* [*see illus.*] · portrait (as young matron), repro. in Schwoerer, *Lady Rachel Russell*

Wealth at death very rich: will, PRO, PROB 11/594, fols. 152v–157r; Woburn Abbey, Bedfordshire, MSS Sa 1 'An accompt of the whole Personal Estate of the Rt. Honble Rachel Lady Rusel as the same stood on 29th day of Septem: 1723 being the day of her Ladyship death'

Russell, Richard (1630–1693), diplomat and Roman Catholic bishop in Portugal, was born in Buckland, Berkshire, the son of Richard Russell, a Roman Catholic. At the age of twelve he became a servant to Edward Pickford alias Daniel, newly appointed president of the English College, Lisbon, and devoted himself so much to study that on 14 August 1647 he was admitted as a student there. Despite an offer in 1651 of early ordination and a mission to England, he went instead to Douai College, arriving there in December the same year. He was ordained priest at Valenciennes on 20 September 1653 and studied for two further years at Paris, before being recalled in December 1655 to Lisbon where he was made procurator at the college.

According to Crowley, Russell 'rapidly became a well-known and influential figure in Lisbon' (Crowley, 17/2, 13). He was particularly involved in the diplomatic manoeuvrings between Portugal and England at this time; a letter by an English spy in 1657 describes him as 'a certain English priest, no great politician for witt, yet was a great informer against the late treaty … a short fatt man' (Crowley, 17/2, 15). In August 1657 Russell accompanied the Portuguese ambassador, Francisco de Mello, to England. With the agreement of the English chapter of the secular clergy, he remained with the ambassador until they both returned in 1660; by that time, it was claimed that Russell had helped to convert some 3000 people in England.

Probably in January 1660, Russell was made a canon of the English chapter. Following the restoration of Charles II, Russell was closely involved, with de Mello (now marquess of Sande), in the marriage negotiations between the English king and Catherine of Braganza. Russell brought to Britain the portrait of the infanta that apparently convinced the king of her beauty, and he worked with Sir Richard Fanshawe, envoy-extraordinary, in the drawing up of the marriage treaty itself (concluded in the summer of 1661) that included a dowry of £300,000 and the colonies of Tangier and Bombay. On his return to Lisbon, Russell was thanked by the queen regent, Luísa de Gusmão, for his 'singular assistance and fidelity in promoting the interests of her kingdom' (Kirk, Croft, and Gillow, *Lit. biog. hist.*, 37); a high recommendation from Charles II may have further influenced Luísa to nominate Russell as the bishop of the Cape Verde Islands on 6 August 1661, with the promise of the first vacant see in Portugal—an offer Russell declined.

Russell accompanied Catherine to England in May 1662 and was deputed by the English chapter to act as the witness at the couple's private Catholic wedding ceremony. That same year he was nominated for the bishopric of Portalegre, though the reluctance of Rome to recognize the legitimacy of the newly independent regime in Portugal meant that Russell was not formally consecrated for more than a decade. In the meantime he continued to travel between Lisbon and London, dealing with difficult diplomatic problems, while the English chapter hoped he would soon resign his Portuguese see and become head of the English clergy as the position of the vicar-apostolic in England had long been unfilled. During this time Russell was also drawn into conflict with the secretary of the English chapter, John Sergeant, over the vexed question of the relationship between the chapter and Rome in regard to the appointment of bishops in England; Sergeant, who Russell had described as 'a troublesome spirit' in a letter of 1667, was eventually removed from the secretaryship (Sharratt, 'Bishop Russell', 28). Russell still felt that Sergeant was a dangerous influence on the English College, and several years later he felt obliged to intervene to dispel suspicions that the college was sympathetic to the unorthodox beliefs of Thomas White alias Blacklo.

Russell was consecrated as bishop of Portalegre on 27 September 1671 at the English College (Portuguese sources claim this took place in the royal chapel), but did not take possession of the see until January 1672. Portalegre was one of the smallest dioceses in Portugal and had suffered almost twenty years without a bishop. Russell set out to improve its situation, and in 1674 a friend observed that he was 'in very great esteem there, with all, especially in his own diocese, which he has reduced to good order' (Crowley, 18/2, 18). On 10 September 1685 Russell was made bishop of Viseu. He brought to this larger and more significant diocese the same energy and motivation that he had exhibited in Portalegre, summoning a synod in order to reorganize the diocese. He kept a strict but simple household, and was well known for his conversation and humour; he was also feared as a severe examiner of candidate priests. He refused to wear silk and forbade the display of his coat of arms on public buildings. Remarkably generous, he concluded his final account of his administration to Pope Innocent XI by saying:

> In these and similar works I have spent and exhausted the whole income of my church, so that after twenty-two years of the episcopal charge, I am able truly to say (not in pride but in the humility of a grateful heart be it spoken) gold and silver I have not. (Crowley, 18/3, 20)

'Bispo Inglez' (as Russell was known) died at Fontel Farm, Viseu, on 15 November 1693 and was buried later the same month in the cathedral under the floor of the choir (Crowley, 18/2, 21). He left some furniture, clothing, and books to his nephew Nicholas Waldegrave, an English priest in Portugal, and some money legacies to be distributed among his household and priests. He also had a sister in the English Brigittine house of Syon, then in Lisbon.

M. LEONOR MACHADO DE SOUSA

Sources Gillow, *Lit. biog. hist.*, vol. 5 · J. Kirk, W. Croft, and J. Gillow, *Historical account of Lisbon College* (1902) · R. Macaulay, *They went to Portugal too* (1990) · L. de Sousa, 'Memorias chronologicas dos bispos de Viseu', Viseu City Library, Portugal, MS 1767 · F. de Gouveia e Sousa, 'D. Ricardo Russell—mu Inglês bispo de Viseu', *Beira Alta*, 9 (1950), 323–60 · E. M. Rosenthal, 'Lisbon College', *Anglo-Portuguese News* (20 July 1940), 10, b. 10 [4th year] · I. Ramos and

I. Lousada, 'O Colégio dos Inglesiuhos em Lisboa', *Revista de Estudos Anglo-Portugueses*, 5 (1995), 9–44 · M. Sharratt, ed., *Lisbon College register, 1628–1813*, Catholic RS, 72 (1991), 164–7 · J. J. Crowley, 'Dr Richard Russell (1630–1693), bishop of Vizeu', *The Lisbonian*, 17/2 (1933), 11–16; 17/3 (1934), 9–16; 17/4 (1934), 11–21; 18/1 (1935), 12–16; 18/2 (1935), 17–22; 18/3 (1936), 17–20 · M. Sharratt, 'Bishop Russell and John Sergeant', *Ushaw Magazine*, 253 (1979), 22–37 · J. Sergeant, *An account of the chapter erected by William, titular bishop of Chalcedon*, ed. W. Turnbull (1853) · C. Dodd [H. Tootell], *The church history of England, from the year 1500, to the year 1688*, 3 (1742)

Archives District Archives, Viseu, Portugal · Ushaw College, Durham, Lisbon College archives, corresp. and MSS, incl. diplomatic MSS and letters to the president of the college
Likenesses portrait, Ushaw College, Durham
Wealth at death took to Viseu estimated £10,000 money and estimated £10,000,000 in furniture, church objects, clothing, and books: District Archives, Viseu, Portugal

Russell, Richard (*b.* before **1640**, *d.* **1686×97**), translator of alchemical and iatrochemical treatises, prepared chemical medicines with his brother William *Russell (1634–*c.*1696) who was chemist-in-ordinary to Charles II and author of *A Physical Treatise, Grounded, not upon Tradition, nor Phancy, but Experience* (1684). While there is no positive evidence to identify him with any one of the Richard Russells who matriculated from various colleges at Oxford between about 1620 and 1666, he may have been so affiliated.

The primary source of information on Russell's work as translator is his address to the reader included in *The works of Geber, the most famous Arabian prince and philosopher, faithfully Englished by Richard Russel a lover of chymistry* (1678, reissued 1686). In this preface, dated 'May 3d. 1678, *From my House at the Star in New-Market in Wapping, near the Dock*', Russell states that it had been his original intention to conceal his identity as Geber's translator, as he had done in four previously published translations: Oswald Croll's *Bazilica chymica, & praxis chymiatricae, or, Royal and Practical Chymistry* (1670), described as his 'first *Essay* in that kind of *Learning*'; the *Tyrocinium chymicum, or, Chymical essays, acquired from the fountaine of nature, and manuall experience, by John Beguinus* (1669); *The golden calf, which the world adores, and desires: ... written in Latin by John Frederick Helvetius doctor and practitioner of medicine* (1670); and *Basil Valentine, his triumphant chariot of antimony, with annotations of Theodore Kirkringius, MD* (1678). He further notes that a volume of the works of Ramon Lull is ready for printing and that he has 'compleated two of [Paracelsus's] three *Volumes*, and about half the third'. The translations of Lull and Paracelsus were never printed. However, even without these, Russell's published works represent an important contribution to the store of alchemical and iatrochemical translations that were appearing in the last half of the seventeenth century in response to the increasing popularity of chemical medicines and the growing number of practitioners who were not expert in Latin.

Russell was married but his wife's name is not known. Valuable information on his practice of iatrochemistry in association with his brother William is included in *Arcana philosophia, or, Chymical secrets, containing the noted and useful chymical medicines of Dr Wil. and Rich. Russel chymists ...* publish'd by John Headrich, *philo-chymicus, and formerly operator to Dr. Richard Russel* (1697). Published after the deaths of the Russells and avowedly Paracelsian in orientation, Headrich's book speaks of the high regard enjoyed by the Russells, whose clients included 'that discerning Monarch K. *Charles* the II' and other members of the court. As one who had learned the secret of the Russells' tincture through assisting in Richard's laboratory, Headrich seeks to vindicate their reputations from possible debasement resulting from circulation of counterfeit medicines following their deaths; clearly his assertion of the authenticity of his own preparations was an attempt to promote their sale. Richard Russell died at some time between 1686 and 1697. Headrich also reports that he continued to serve as laboratory operator for Russell's widow.

STANTON J. LINDEN

Sources R. Russell, 'Address to the reader', in *The works of Geber, the most famous Arabian prince and philosopher*, trans. R. Russell (1678); repr. (1686) · *Arcana philosophia, or, Chymical secrets, containing the noted and useful chymical medicines of Dr Wil. and Rich. Russel chymists ... publish'd by John Headrich, philo-chymicus, and formerly operator to Dr Richard Russel* (1697) · W. Russell, *A physical treatise, grounded, not upon tradition, nor phancy, but experience* (1684) · C. Webster, *The great instauration: science, medicine and reform, 1626–1660* (1975) · J. Ferguson, *Bibliographia Paracelsica*, pt 3 (1890) · C. E. Whiting, *The University of Durham, 1832–1932* (1932)

Russell, Richard (1687–1759), physician, was born on 26 November 1687 at the High Street (at a house now numbered 77), Lewes, Sussex, the eldest of the seven children of Nathaniel Russell (1657–1713), apothecary, and his wife, Mary (1659–1737?), daughter of Drew Ellis, yeoman, of Southerham, near Lewes. He attended the town's grammar school and was probably apprenticed to a surgeon in London, where he also assisted the physician George Howe (1654/5–1710). As a surgeon practising in Lewes, in 1713 he reported a case to the Royal Society and commanded the high premium of £80 for an apprentice. But his practice and interest extended more widely, as it was with a thesis on epilepsy in children, promoted by Hermann Boerhaave, that in December 1724 he graduated MD at the University of Leiden, a mere two months after matriculation. After a few further months in Rotterdam he returned to Lewes by October 1725, to take over the practice of Peter White, just deceased. Russell quickly established himself as the leading physician in east Sussex, soon prosperous enough to invest in property. On 4 December 1719 he married—despite her parents' opposition—Mary (1698–1764), only child of William Kempe, gentleman, and his wife, Mary, of Malling deanery, in South Malling, near Lewes. Nevertheless on Kempe's death in January 1721 his estate passed to his daughter, and Russell lived there for the rest of his life. He and his wife had five daughters and two sons between 1720 and 1735, all of whom outlived him. His sister Hannah was the mother of Sir Lucas Pepys.

In the 1720s Russell observed how people living on the coast drank sea water to cure diseases of the lower belly, and at Leiden he was considering how to treat glandular secretions. From the 1730s Brighton, 8 miles from Lewes, was attracting visitors for informal recreation by the sea and on the South Downs, and patients were there following Russell's regime of sea water bathing and drinking, some of them referred by London physicians. He distilled his experience in *De tabe glandulari, sive, De usu aquæ marinæ in morbis glandularum dissertatio* (1750). After the proprietor of a London mineral water warehouse published a pirated English translation in 1752 (fifth edition, 1769), Russell issued his own the following year, as *A Dissertation Concerning the Use of Sea Water in the Diseases of the Glands*. Demand for his treatment encouraged him in 1753–4 to buy tenements on the low cliff at the eastern edge of Brighton, and build a substantial five-bay house for the reception of patients. In many cases the virtue of Russell's sea water treatments lay not in the water itself, but in the dietetic and hygienic routine and discipline imposed in Brighton's attractive surroundings. Russell's success helped to popularize such treatments and contributed to Brighton's emergence as Britain's first fashionable seaside resort.

Professional recognition came with election as a fellow of the Royal Society on 13 February 1752, and, two years later, with the MD degree from the University of Cambridge granted by royal licence on the recommendation of the Royal College of Physicians and the university's chancellor, the duke of Newcastle. For the degree he submitted a synopsis of *The Oeconomy of Nature in Acute and Chronical Diseases of the Glands* (Latin and English editions, 1755). Russell had long supported Newcastle's political interest in Sussex and benefited from his patronage.

Russell died on 21 December 1759, and was buried at South Malling Church three days later. His eldest son and heir, William, a lawyer, took the surname of Kempe, as required by his grandfather's will if he was to enjoy the estate settled on his mother; his inheritance included about 1300 acres of land in east Sussex. The greater part of Russell's practice at Brighton passed to Dr Anthony Relhan.

This Richard Russell has previously been confused with **Richard Russel** (1714?–1771), physician, possibly born on 18 December 1714 at Selmeston, Sussex, the son of the Revd Richard Russel MA, vicar of Alfriston and of Selmeston, and his wife, Juliana. After eight years at Westminster School Russel studied medicine for seven years, in hospitals and with an apothecary in London, by taking the MD degree at Rheims in June 1738, and finally with the famed man-midwife Gregoire in Paris. He started to practise at Hoddesdon, Hertfordshire, and in early 1741 was appointed physician to the branch of Christ's Hospital at Ware, Hertfordshire, but failed to obtain the appointment at the Hertford branch in 1742. On 4 August 1741 he married Elizabeth Wilkins of Hoddesdon at Christ Church, Newgate Street, London, and he was admitted an extra licentiate of the Royal College of Physicians, London, on 23 July 1742. About 1747 he moved to Henley-on-Thames, Oxfordshire, and about 1750 to Reading, Berkshire. There he became involved in a dispute with Anthony Addington, the father of Lord Sidmouth, in connection with which he published two pamphlets, *A letter to Dr. Addington of Reading, on his refusal to join in consultation with a physician, who had taken his degree abroad, and was approved and licensed by the*

College of Physicians (1749), and *Letter to Mr. Thomas Bigg, late surgeon of St Bartholomew's Hospital, occasioned by his having written a defamatory letter to Dr. Addington against Dr. Russel of Reading* (1751). He died at Reading on 5 July 1771.

JOHN H. FARRANT

Sources W. H. Challen, 'Richard Russell, M.D.', *Sussex Notes and Queries*, 14 (1954–7), 73–8 · E. W. Gilbert, *Brighton, old ocean's bauble* (1954) · R. W. Innes Smith, *English-speaking students of medicine at the University of Leyden* (1932) · E. Sussex RO, SAS/G 34/93–116, SAS/WS 105–106, SAS/PN 173–175, SAS/BRI 57–58 [Russell's landed property] · correspondence with Thomas Birch, BL, Add. MS 4317 · letters to Sir Hans Sloane, BL, Add. MS 4076 · letters to the duke of Newcastle, BL, Add. MSS 32688, 32719, 32724, 32884 · *GM*, 1st ser., 29 (1759), 606 · *GM*, 1st ser., 41 (1771), 335 · parish register, Lewes, St Michael's, E. Sussex RO [birth, baptism, marriage] · parish register, South Malling, E. Sussex RO, marriage, burial · parish register, Lewes, St John sub Castro, E. Sussex RO [marriage] · J. Houghton, 'Desent of High Street properties', E. Sussex RO, Sussex Archaeological Society [typescript] · R. Russel, *A letter to Dr. Addington of Reading, on his refusal to join in consultation with a physician, who had taken his degree abroad, and was approved and licensed by the College of Physicians* (1749) · R. Russel, *Letter to Mr. Thomas Bigg, late surgeon of St Bartholomew's Hospital, occasioned by his having written a defamatory letter to Dr. Addington against Dr. Russel of Reading* (1751) · parish register, Selmeston, E. Sussex RO [baptism]
Archives BL, corresp. with Thomas Birch, Add. MS 4317 · BL, letters to the duke of Newcastle, Add. MSS 32688, 32719, 32724, 32884 · BL, letters to Sir Hans Sloane, Add. MS 4076
Likenesses H. Wilkin, watercolour (after B. Wilson), Wellcome L. · attrib. B. Wilson, oils (in later years), Brighton Art Gallery

Russell, Richard Drew [Dick] (1903–1981), architect and furniture designer, was born in Repton, Derbyshire, on 21 December 1903, the third son of Elizabeth Shefford (1864–1956) and Sydney Bolton Russell (1866–1938), a hotelier. From the age of six weeks he and his family—including his older brothers, Gordon *Russell and Don—lived in the Lygon Arms in the Cotswold village of Broadway in Worcestershire. His father owned the hotel which was to provide the background to Dick's early life, and a means of his entering the area of work in which he became so successful.

During his long career as an architect and designer Russell worked as a member of the British modern movement which, in response to developments in Germany, Scandinavia, and elsewhere, evolved in the middle decades of the twentieth century into a simple, functional design aesthetic. He was a contemporary of architects and designers such as Wells Coates, Serge Chermayeff, and Robert Goodden but embraced the more conservative end of the spectrum. Although his work was always simple and machine-made he never abandoned the use of wood in furniture nor the idea of quality that emanated from the craftsman. As such he epitomized English modernism, which, along with its Scandinavian counterpart, was never as austere or radically forward-looking as German modernism.

A striking tall, blonde, and handsome man, Dick Russell was educated at Dean Close School, Cheltenham. He was introduced to furniture design in the repair shop of the Lygon Arms; in 1919 he joined his brother Gordon to work in the shop and within four years they had produced furniture items which went on display at London's Victoria and

Richard Drew Russell (1903–1981), by Sylvia Redding

Albert Museum. Aware that a training in design was necessary to move the furniture forward he went to study at the Architectural Association Schools in London where he came under the strong influence of contemporary Danish design through the teaching of Steen Eiler Rasmussen, who instilled in his pupils the importance of wedding tradition to the present. Indeed a strong Scandinavian influence was to remain with Russell throughout his career. The Stockholm Exhibition of 1930 and the 1931 exhibition of Swedish arts and crafts held at London's Dorland Hall both reaffirmed for him a belief in the importance of combining the quality of craft manufacture with the democratic possibilities of machine production.

Russell became a director of Russell Workshops Ltd in 1928 (the firm changed its name to Gordon Russell Ltd in the following year) and for the next few years worked alongside his brother, moving from the French-inspired 'modernistic' style to the simpler forms of modernism by the early 1930s. Among the landmarks of these years was a range of furniture and interiors created for Claridges Hotel. Russell also tried his hand at architecture in this period, producing in 1932, with his wife-to-be—Marian Pepler [see below]—a house named Lobden which was clearly influenced by European modernism.

1931 marked the start of Russell's collaboration with Murphy Radio Ltd which lasted right up to the late 1940s and which resulted in some of his most striking and lasting modern designs. He worked on a wide range of wireless, radiogram, and television cabinets which helped bring about their transition from furniture items to machines. Still using wood (unlike Coates and Chermayeff who used bakelite for their designs for Ekco) he produced a wide range of forms which were characteristically simple and modern. The best known of his designs include his A40C wireless console of 1937, the façade of which was a simple rosewood veneered rectangle with a circle and smaller rectangle cut out for the speaker and the wavelengths section respectively, with four chunky knobs positioned carefully alongside. The Baffle radio of 1946 was a much larger, free-standing object characterized, none the less, by the same minimal approach.

In 1932 Russell left the Cotswolds for London, where he continued to work for his brother's firm alongside other commissions until 1935 when he became an independent consultant from his Vigo Street office. He returned to Gordon Russell Ltd in 1939 just before being called up for war service as a member of the camouflage unit of the Royal Naval Volunteer Reserve.

The post-war years proved equally as productive as the pre-war period and marked the peak of Russell's career. He was made a royal designer for industry in 1944 and became the professor of wood, metal, and plastics at the Royal College of Art four years later. He remained there until 1964 developing a teaching method which owed much to that of the Danish designer Kaare Klint at the Academy of Applied Arts in Copenhagen. During his years at the college he continued to practise as a designer, contributing furniture and interiors to the key exhibitions of those years ('Britain can make it' of 1946 and the Festival of Britain of 1951 in particular) and creating furniture and interiors for offices, boardrooms, schools, hostels, and luxury hotels. His work was still modern in spirit and made of wood—rosewood mostly—and he favoured unit furniture and built-in storage. His bedroom furniture for the Scottish Co-operative Wholesale Society of about 1948, for example, was designed along these lines. Through the 1950s and 1960s his design practice—from 1959 it was named Russell, Hodgson, and Leigh— remained active and two younger designers, Mary Shand and Robin Wade, came to work for him. In 1965 the practice worked on room interiors for the University of Essex. A number of furniture designs—both one-offs and ranges—also emanated from this fertile period, notable among them the chair Russell designed for Coventry Cathedral which was commissioned by Basil Spence. It quickly became a familiar interior component of many modern built churches in this era. Examples of his furniture are in the Victoria and Albert Museum, London.

Russell met his wife (they married on 1 December 1933) at the Architectural Association Schools where they both studied architecture. On graduating **Marian Pepler** (1904–1997), who was born on 24 August 1904 at Sanderstead, Surrey, the daughter of the architect and subsequently town planner Sir George Lionel *Pepler and his wife, (Edith) Amy Bobbett, and the niece of (Douglas) Hilary Pepler, the founder of the Ditchling Press, went to Broadway to seek work at Gordon Russell Ltd. Throughout her life Marian—a very attractive, quiet, small-featured woman—remained a determined but self-effacing character happy to let her husband occupy the centre-stage and to stay in the wings herself. She took on the roles of wife and mother—the couple had two sons and a daughter—with a sense of pleasure and great commitment although she remained professionally active in one capacity or another for most of her adult life. In 1930 she designed her first rug and in the same year she attended classes at the London School of Weaving to learn how to make rugs. From the start, however, she, like her husband, was committed to machine production and to a simple, modern look. The manufacturers she worked with through her career, which lasted, albeit with a break to bring up their three children, into the 1960s, included Wilton Royal and Tomkinson. The Russell company used many of her designs in their interiors over the years and for a short period from 1933 to 1935 she acted as a buyer for the firm's London shop at 28 Wigmore Street, quickly expanding her role to include Broadway as well. While she was mainly occupied with acquiring fabrics she also moved into other components of the interior including ceramics and glass. When illness forced her to abandon this role she was superseded by the architectural historian Nikolaus Pevsner, who later described her work as possessing 'a sensitivity and a quiet perfection not surpassed anywhere in Europe' (*The Independent*, 25 Oct 1997). Pepler then became a consultant for the Gordon Russell firm, advising on furnishings and, in particular, colour. It was a role which she undertook again for her husband's practice after the war.

Pepler's rugs were all characterized by soft, earthy colours and simple, abstract decoration. She used mostly fawns and browns in the early 1930s but moved to include blue, green, and yellow a little later. *Aquamarine*, a rug of 1932, for example, had wavy lines and circles on its surface and it combined aquamarine, yellow, raisin brown, and natural in its subtle colour scheme. Throughout her career she was inevitably compared with the more flamboyant rug designer Marian Dorn, but Pepler's main purpose in designing a rug was to use it to bring together all the elements of the room and, for her, restrained colours did this more effectively. Her approach emanated from her training in architecture. In 1947 Pepler was elected a fellow of the Society of Industrial Artists, recognition that she had reached the peak of her profession. She continued to design, concentrating more and more on carpets. Post-war work of note includes rugs for the interior of the *Oriana*, produced in the mid-1950s.

The designs of Russell and Pepler shared a common goal and achieved the same standards although, as with so many designer couples, the work of the former is much more widely recognized. The consistently high quality of her work which came through at an exhibition of their work which was held at the Geffrye Museum in 1983 surprised many people who had not realized her full artistic capacity, however. They both played a key role in formulating a peculiarly British brand of modernism in the middle years of the century and in ensuring that with the enthusiasm for all things new the past was not entirely forgotten. Russell died on 16 October 1981 and Pepler outlived him by sixteen years which were spent with her son, Daniel, and family, designing cushions and creating a small garden. She died on 13 October 1997 at Eynsham, Oxfordshire.

PENNY SPARKE

Sources R. Allwood and K. Laurie, *R. D. Russell, Marian Pepler* (1983) [exhibition catalogue, Geffrye Museum, London, 9 Sept – 23 October 1983] · G. Russell, *Designer's trade: autobiography of Gordon Russell* (1968) · W. Carrington, *Design and decoration in the home* (1938) · N. Pevsner, 'Broadcasting comes of age: the radio cabinet, 1919–1940', *ArchR*, 87 (1940), 189–90 · R. Carter, *Designer*, 11 (Dec 1981) · C. G. Tormley, 'Contemporary British rug design', *Design for Today*, 43 (April 1935), 135–9 · H. Read, *Art and industry* (1934) · M. Farr, *Design in British industry* (1955) · G. Naylor, *A history of Gordon Russell Ltd, Broadway* (1976) · CGPLA Eng. & Wales (1981) · *The Independent* (25 Oct 1997) · *The Independent* (20 Oct 1997)

Archives Gordon Russell Ltd, Broadway, Worcestershire, MSS

Likenesses S. Redding, photograph, priv. coll. [*see illus.*] · double portrait, photograph (with Marian Pepler), RSA

Wealth at death £41,436: probate, 17 Dec 1981, *CGPLA Eng. & Wales*

Russell, (William) Ritchie (1903–1980), neurologist, was born in Edinburgh on 7 February 1903, the eldest of three sons and fourth of the six children of William Russell, professor of medicine at Edinburgh University, and his wife, Beatrice, daughter of James Ritchie, civil engineer. She was a graduate in medicine of the University of Brussels. Two of his sisters and one brother also became doctors. Russell was educated at Edinburgh Academy and later at Edinburgh University, graduating MB, ChB, in 1926. After holding resident appointments at the Royal Infirmary, Edinburgh, and, in 1928–30, at the National Hospital for Nervous Diseases, Queen Square, London, he was appointed in 1934 as assistant physician at the Royal Infirmary, Edinburgh, working in internal medicine with an interest in neurology. He was awarded the gold medal for his MD thesis in 1932. In the same year he married Jean, daughter of Robert Stuart Low, an engineer. They had one son, later a general practitioner, and a daughter.

In 1938 Russell was appointed lecturer in neurology at Edinburgh University and began to confine his practice largely to neurological medicine. In 1940 he joined the Royal Army Medical Corps as a specialist neurologist, ultimately attaining the rank of brigadier. He was closely associated with the Military Hospital for Head Injuries established in Oxford at St Hugh's College and at Wheatley for much of the Second World War, but for a time in 1943 he served as consultant in neurology to the Middle East forces. It was during this time that he developed his major interest in head injury and in the effects of wounds on the brain. After demobilization, he was appointed in 1945 as consultant neurologist to the United Oxford Hospitals and in 1949 became lecturer in clinical neurology in the University of Oxford. In 1948 he was appointed honorary consultant in neurology to the army. In Oxford, in collaboration with Sir Hugh Cairns, he studied in detail the thousand or more British war pensioners suffering from focal brain wounds. Some of this work was carried out at the Ministry of Pensions Hospital at Stoke Mandeville and at Headington Hill Hall rehabilitation centre.

In 1966 Russell became the first holder of the chair of

clinical neurology in Oxford, where he built up a strong academic department of neurology and established an increasingly effective regional neurological service, his administrative ability and doggedness securing for neurology its due place in the teaching hospital. Besides inspiring and teaching others, he continued research into the effects of closed head injury, multiple sclerosis, and poliomyelitis. It was largely his work which drew attention to the deleterious effects of injections and of tonsillectomy in the preparalytic stage of poliomyelitis, and his book on this topic *Poliomyelitis* (c.1952) clearly analysed the effects of exercise and trauma on the extent and distribution of paralysis in this disease.

Russell was also one of those who initiated the scientific investigation of methods of assisted respiration and of their value in neurological disease, and in his later years he did important work on speech and memory, editing with M. L. E. Espir *Traumatic Aphasia* (1961). He also wrote *The Traumatic Amnesias* (1971) and *Explaining the Brain* (1975). For many years a member of the Association of British Neurologists, he was its president from 1970 to 1972, and also edited the *Journal of Neurology, Neurosurgery and Psychiatry* from 1948 to 1969.

As a clinician, Russell was also outstanding; his words on diagnosis, treatment, or prognosis, though never the loudest, were often the last. Those who got to know him well appreciated the kindliness, generosity, and quick humour behind his solemn countenance. In his later years his work on behalf of the neurologically disabled won increasing international renown.

Russell became FRCP in 1943. He was appointed CBE in 1952 and his publications won him an Oxford DSc in 1955. In 1953 he was president of the section of neurology at the British Medical Association annual meeting and in 1963 was elected an honorary member of the American Neurological Association. He retired in 1970. Russell died by his own hand at his home at Ritchie Court, 380 Banbury Road, Oxford, on 8 December 1980.   JOHN WALTON, *rev.*

Sources *BMJ* (3 Jan 1981), 78 · *The Lancet* (20 Dec 1980) · private information (1986) · personal knowledge (1986)
Likenesses photograph, repro. in *The Lancet*, 1385 · photograph, repro. in *BMJ*
Wealth at death £27,675: probate, 7 April 1981, *CGPLA Eng. & Wales*

Russell, Robert (1757–1822), carrier, was baptized on 8 November 1757 at Burstock, near Beaminster, Dorset, the fifth of the six children of Robert Russell. His father died at Boomer, near North Petherton, Somerset, in 1775 or 1778. His uncle Thomas Russell (1730–1799) became, in the 1760s, a partner in a firm of carriers by horse-drawn wagon between Exeter and London. This firm was thenceforth managed by four generations of Russells, and the name Russell became synonymous with west country carrying. Thomas Russell ran the firm from Andover, but appears to have taken on Robert Russell as his partner at Exeter by 1780. Robert married Sarah Lathbury (c.1754–1816) there on 29 April 1780. In 1785 the partners took over the other Exeter carrying firm, which made them the dominant carriers in the area.

When Thomas Russell retired in 1792, Robert Russell took over as sole proprietor, which he remained for the next twenty-four years, running the business from the former Bear inn, South Street, Exeter. The firm had about 220 horses, up to thirty wagons, and sixty or seventy staff, spread out along more than 300 miles of road. There were daily services between Exeter and London, with wagons drawn by teams of eight horses, travelling day and night, and carrying up to 6 tons of goods, and less frequent services with smaller wagons and teams between Exeter and Plymouth and Falmouth. At each intermediate place the firm had premises and staff.

Russell's was probably the largest carrying firm ever under the control of one man, apart from Pickfords under Joseph Baxendale in the 1820s and 1830s. It is clear that he prospered, as he purchased property in several counties, rebuilt the firm's Exeter headquarters and other premises, and was one of the founders of the Devon County Bank in 1807, contributing £5000 to its stock. His success was helped by the weakness of carrying competition in the west country, war with France (which discouraged the use of coastal vessels), the East India Company's demand for west country cloth (which it exported from London), and a virtual monopoly in conveying to London the bullion brought to Falmouth by the Post Office packet boats. In 1806 Russell was described as a person of 'loyalty, patriotism and respectability' ('Select committee … highways', 2.304).

However, Russell's grip on the concern slackened in the last years of his ownership, by which time he was spending only three or four days a week at Exeter, and the remainder at his house at Exmouth. His retirement from carrying, at the end of June 1816, was probably an acknowledgement that he could no longer provide the unremitting attention required by a large carrying firm. The firm was sold to a partnership of eight men, mostly employees but including Russell's only surviving son, Thomas (1783–1841), who became one of the firm's Exeter partners, and after whom the firm was now named. However, Thomas Russell was sightseeing in Naples at the time (he was once described as 'a young art dilettante' (Lefebure, 436)), and did not return until 1818, so his father continued to play a part in the carrying business on his behalf.

Sarah Russell died on 29 October 1816. In 1819 Robert Russell married Anne Browne Crosse (d. 1831), whose property in the parish of Llanbrynmair, Montgomeryshire, was, in the late twentieth century, still occupied by his descendants. He died on 23 September 1822 at Exmouth, aged sixty-four, leaving one son and three daughters. His widow died in April 1831, aged seventynine.

Thomas Russell remained a partner in the carrying firm until 1837, when a new partnership took over, including his own son, Robert Henry Russell (b. 1811) who gave his name to the firm. This partnership was broken up in consequence of the actions of the Great Western Railway in 1843, when the Russell connection with carrying ended.

DORIAN GERHOLD

Sources D. Gerhold, *Road transport before the railways: Russell's London flying waggons* (1993) • *Trewman's Exeter Flying Post* (26 Sept 1822), 4b • PRO, C 112/91, no. 336 • monument to Anne Russell, Llanbrynmair • 'Select committee on … regulations for preservation of turnpike roads and highways', *Parl. papers* (1808), 2.304, no. 77 • M. Lefebure, *Samuel Taylor Coleridge: a bondage of opium* (1974), 436 • *GM*, 1st ser., 86/2 (1816), 470
Archives PRO, letters to the London partners, C 112/91–94
Wealth at death approx. £24,000: PRO, death duty registers, IR 26/969, pp. 217–20, in Gerhold, *Road transport*, 36, 257

Russell, (Francis Albert) Rollo (1849–1914), meteorologist, was born on 11 July 1849 at Pembroke Lodge, Richmond, Surrey, the third son of Lord John *Russell, later the first Earl Russell (1792–1878), and his second wife, Frances Anna Maria Elliot *Russell, later Countess Russell (*d.* 1898). Educated privately by a tutor until the age of fourteen, Russell went on to Harrow School and from 1869 to Christ Church, Oxford. Graduating in 1872 with distinction in natural science he took up a clerkship at the Foreign Office, but he was plagued by very poor eyesight and found office life unendurable. A naturally reticent and reclusive person Russell withdrew to the family home on the outskirts of Richmond Park, and devoted himself to scientific and natural historical observation and writing. He resigned from the civil service in 1888.

Following the sudden and tragic deaths of his brother, sister-in-law, and niece during an eighteen-month period in 1875 and 1876 Russell was appointed, together with his mother, legal guardian to his nephews Frank and Bertrand *Russell. This proved an utterly unsatisfactory arrangement. Frank detested the religious solemnity of Pembroke Lodge more intensely than Bertrand, but in later life both brothers remembered their uncle Rollo as a timid and obsequious man who invariably conformed to his mother's quietly repressive and puritanical demands.

Like nearly every Russell of his generation Rollo experienced traumatic personal grief. In 1885 he married Alice Sophia, daughter of Thomas Spragging Godfrey of Balderton Hall, Nottinghamshire, with whom he had a son. But within a year Alice had died. In 1891 he married Gertrude Ellen Cornelia, daughter of Henry Joachim of Haslemere, Surrey, and sister of Harold Joachim, the Oxford idealist philosopher, author of *The Nature of Truth*, and influential tutor to the young graduate T. S. Eliot. They had a son and a daughter.

Russell had been elected a fellow of the Royal Meteorological Society at the precocious age of nineteen in 1868 and became vice-president in 1893 and 1894. A countryman at heart, he was nevertheless fascinated and appalled by the urban condition and more particularly by the terrible fogs, or smogs, which afflicted London with extraordinary severity between the 1870s and the 1890s. Convinced that atmospheric pollution would hasten an already predetermined drift towards social and biological degeneration, in 1880 Russell wrote a best-selling pamphlet, *London Fogs*. This became a touchstone for a number of predominantly aristocratic and upper middle-class pressure groups which campaigned for a reduction in the consumption of domestic fuel, the replacement of the late Victorian hearth by gas heating, and controlled experiment with smokeless grates. The cause was not, however, a popular one. Russell therefore felt impelled to return throughout the following decades to the related themes of atmospheric pollution and the social costs attributable to environmental degradation in the capital and other urban centres. By the mid-Edwardian period, however, the annual metropolitan fog season between November and March had become less intense. The meteorological community, Russell included, was puzzled by an improvement which proved no more than temporary: between the end of the First World War and the catastrophic smog of 1952 London was once again intermittently visited by dense and life-threatening fog.

When not involved in environmental pamphleteering, Russell dedicated himself to more deeply considered academic work. But his *Epidemics, Plagues and Fevers* (1892), *Atmosphere in Relation to Human Life and Health* (1896), and *Strength and Diet* (1905) are characterized by a tendency towards geographical and meteorologial determinism and a conviction that a rejuvenated countryside would eventually prove itself superior to, and might even replace, the troubled conurbations of the late nineteenth and early twentieth centuries. This anti-urban utopianism was articulated in numerous books, articles, and poems, which sang the praises of a largely imagined rural life and deplored the collapse of charitable and paternalistic ties in the working-class areas of great cities. Convinced that it was possible to detect connections between European town life and susceptibility to medical conditions, and allegedly racially determined traits normally encountered in the tropics, Russell committed himself wholeheartedly to agrarian revivalism.

Russell did not scorn the possibility of social improvement through explicitly party political intervention, and he wrote a brief history of the Liberal Party and of Liberalism in the nineteenth century. Just before his death from septicaemia Russell completed an edition of the early correspondence of his father. He died at his London home, 43 Holland Street, Kensington, on 30 March 1914. He was survived by his second wife.

BILL LUCKIN

Sources R. Monk, *Bertrand Russell: the spirit of solitude* (1996) • E. Gaskell, *Surrey leaders, social and political* (privately printed, London, [n.d., 1908?]) • A. T. C. Pratt, ed., *People of the period: being a collection of the biographies of upwards of six thousand living celebrities*, 2 vols. (1897) • Burke, *Peerage* • *WWW* • *Symons's Meteorological Magazine*, 49 (1914), 47–8 • *Quarterly Journal of the Royal Meteorological Society*, 40 (1914), 246–7 • *The Times* (1 April 1914) • *The Times* (3–4 April 1914) • *The Times* (5 May 1914) • d. cert. [Alice Sophia Russell] • d. cert. [Francis Albert Rollo Russell] • *CGPLA Eng. & Wales* (1914)
Archives Bodl. Oxf., letters to F. A. R. Russell, MS 41707, fols. 168–207 • Bodl. Oxf., letters to F. A. R. Russell, MSS 41709–41711 • Bodl. Oxf., letters to F. A. R. Russell, MS 41714, fols. 1–2, 53–78
Wealth at death £22,422 19s. 2d.: probate, 30 April 1914, *CGPLA Eng. & Wales*

Russell, Samuel Thomas (1766–1845), actor, the son of Samuel Russell, a provincial actor, was born in London. As a child he acted juvenile parts in the provinces and toured with a conjuror named Breslaw, and in 1782 performed at the Royal Circus and Equestrian Philharmonic opened by

Charles Dibdin and Charles Hughes on the site later occupied by the Surrey Theatre. About 1790 he began playing leading business with a 'sharing company' at Eastbourne. In Dover he married the daughter of Mate, a printer who was also an actor and the manager and proprietor of the theatre. At Margate, where Russell acted, his father was a member of the same company, and was famous for his Jerry Sneak in Samuel Foote's *The Mayor of Garratt*. The prince of Wales took an interest in the latter's performance in 1795 and, on his recommendation, Russell's father was offered an engagement by King at Drury Lane. The son, however, was (through a trick, it is said) engaged instead. Russell accordingly appeared at Drury Lane on 21 September 1795, as Charles Surface in *The School for Scandal* and Fribble in *Miss in her Teens*. Although he disapproved of Russell's Charles Surface, the prince commended his Fribble. Russell made a success, in May 1796, in an original part in an anonymous unprinted farce called *Alive and Merry*. In June he took a benefit jointly with Robert Palmer, the pieces being *Hamlet* and *Follies of a Day*. During the summer months Russell took the Richmond Theatre, at which he played leading business, and he also acted as a star in the provinces. Between 1797 and 1799 he was, at Drury Lane, among other characters, the first Robert in Reynolds's *The Will*, the original Jeremy Jumps in O'Keeffe's unprinted *The Nosegay of Weeds, or, Old Servants in New Places*, and the original Diaphanous in *The Ugly Club*, a dramatic caricature taken from no. 17 of *The Spectator*, and announced as by Edmund Spenser the younger.

In 1812 Russell served as stage-manager at the Surrey under Robert William Elliston. He was later stage-manager at the Olympic, where he played a variety of roles, from Jerry Sneak and Peter Pastoral in *Teasing Made Easy* to Rover and Joseph Surface. In August 1814 he moved to the Haymarket. He remained there for about five years, performing original roles as well as parts in such revivals as *The Beaux' Stratagem*, in which he was Archer. He returned to Drury Lane in February 1819. That autumn Elliston appointed him stage-manager at Drury Lane, and there he played the first Sir Marmaduke Metaphor in *The Disagreeable Surprise*, an anonymous adaptation from Beaumont and Fletcher (December 1819), and Dominie Sampson in *Guy Mannering* (April 1820). The part of Mercutio in *Romeo and Juliet* was allotted him the following season, with Motley in *The Castle Spectre* and Tom Shuffleton in *John Bull*. After that, for about eight or ten years Russell managed the Brighton Theatre. In 1837 and 1838 he was stage-manager at the Haymarket, and in the latter year became, under Alfred Bunn, stage-manager for a second period at Drury Lane. In 1840 he played at Her Majesty's his great part of Jerry Sneak to William Dowton's Major Sturgeon. He took a benefit at the Haymarket in 1842. Russell was supposed to be a wealthy man. However, the proceeds of his benefit were misappropriated by a dishonest broker, and he was reduced to poverty. He died at Gravesend, in the house of one of his daughters, on 25 February 1845. He had married a second time, and had three daughters.

Russell's greatest part was Jerry Sneak, though he was unsurpassed in the Copper Captain, and excellent in Paul Pry and many other characters. He also had a reputation for being a prince of hoaxers and for playing tricks, principally on his friend and associate William Dowton.

JOSEPH KNIGHT, rev. NILANJANA BANERJI

Sources T. Gilliland, *The dramatic mirror, containing the history of the stage from the earliest period, to the present time*, 2 vols. (1808) · W. C. Russell, *Representative actors* (1896) · *The thespian dictionary, or, Dramatic biography of the present age*, 2nd edn (1805) · Hall, *Dramatic ports.* · Mrs Mathews, *Tea-table talk, ennobled actresses, and other miscellanies*, 2 vols. (1857) · *GM*, 2nd ser., 23 (1845), 446 · T. Dibdin, *Reminiscences* (1837) · Genest, *Eng. stage*

Likenesses S. De Wilde, group portrait, exh. RA 1810, Garr. Club · S. De Wilde, watercolour drawing (as Jerry Sneak in Foote's *The mayor of Garratt*), Garr. Club · eight prints, Harvard TC · portrait, repro. in *British Stage* (Sept 1818)

Russell, Sheridan William Robin (1900–1991). *See under* Russell, Katherine Frances (1909–1998).

Russell [Roussel, Russel], **Theodore** (*bap.* 1614, *d.* 1689), portrait painter, was born in London and baptized at the Dutch church, Austin Friars, on 9 October 1614, the son of Nicasius Roussel (or Russell), a goldsmith and jeweller from Bruges, and his second wife, Clara. His father had settled in London about 1567, and on 21 April 1590 married, at the Dutch church, Jacomina Wils of Meessene. They had a son, John, who is probably identical with Jan Rossel or Russel, resident at Mortlake from 1629 to 1645, and probably connected with the tapestry works there. Nicasius married, secondly, at the Dutch church on 27 November 1604, Clara, the daughter of Cornelis and Johanna Jansz and the sister of Cornelius Johnson (Janssen van Ceulen; 1593–1664), the renowned portrait painter. The Russell, Gheeraerts, de Critz, Johnson, and Oliver families, who produced some of the most important artists and miniaturists of the Stuart period, were all immigrants related by marriage. Theodore Russell resided in Blackfriars and married in January 1649. His son Anthony [*see below*] provided information for George Vertue, stating that his father trained under Cornelius Johnson for nine years and then spent a year with Van Dyck. Securely signed and dated work by Russell is rare, but that which does survive bears witness to the debt he owed to Johnson. His *Portrait of a Man*, signed and dated 1644, at Knebworth House, Hertfordshire, shows him working in the distinctive, sensitive manner of Johnson though lacking his uncle's refinement. Four further portraits of young female sitters at Knebworth are unsigned but attributed to Russell. All clearly show a distinctive style with careful attention to facial features. A portrait of Ellis Woodrofe of Helperley (priv. coll.) is also convincingly attributed to Russell. Anthony Russell told Vertue that his father copied Van Dyck's 'pictures on small pannells' (Vertue, *Note books*, 1.79), but contemporary evidence does not necessarily support such a tradition. The style and manner of his paintings of 1644 is very different from that of the small-scale 'cabinet' pictures by the copyist Van Leemput. Many of Van Leemput's copies have been traditionally attributed to Russell, but these bear little resemblance to the Knebworth group. Vertue also claimed that Russell was a 'lover of Ease and his Bottle' (Vertue, *Note books*, 2.12).

Anthony Russell (1663?–1743), is said to have trained with John Riley, and like his father gained a reputation as a portrait painter. His portrait of the religious controversialist Dr Henry Sacheverell (1710) was engraved in mezzotint by John Smith. He was an intimate friend of Vertue, who engraved some of his portraits, and he supplied Vertue with many biographical notes, concerning artists of the seventeenth century, which are now embodied in Horace Walpole's *Anecdotes of Painting*. Russell died in London, aged about eighty.   L. H. CUST, rev. ANN SUMNER

Sources Vertue, *Note books*, 1.26, 42, 66, 79; 2.1, 12, 73; 4.55 · M. Edmond, 'Limners and picturemakers', *Walpole Society*, 47 (1978–80), 60–242 · O. Millar, *The age of Charles I: painting in England, 1620–1649* (1972), no. 167 [exhibition catalogue, Tate Gallery, London, 15 Nov 1972 – 14 Jan 1973]

Russell, Thomas (*bap.* 1762, *d.* 1788), poet, was baptized at Beaminster, Dorset, in March or October 1762, the second son of John Russell (1725–1808), a prosperous attorney of Beaminster, and his wife, Virtue (1743–1768), daughter of Richard Brickle of Shaftesbury. His father's family had been for generations merchants and shipowners at Weymouth. His elder brother John Banger had antiquarian tastes, and contributed to the second edition of Hutchins's *Dorset* (1796–1803). After attending the grammar school at Bridport, Russell entered Winchester College as a commoner in 1777, and before the end of the year was already in sixth book and fifteenth boy in the school. In 1778 he entered college, and the following year was senior in the school; he gained medals for Latin verse and Latin essay (1778–9), and was elected to New College, Oxford, in 1780, being second on the roll. He graduated BA in October 1784, was ordained deacon in 1785, and priest in 1786. In the *Gentleman's Magazine* (1st ser., 52, 1782, 574, and 53, 1783, 124), under the signature A. S., he wrote two erudite papers on the poetry of Mosen Jordi and the Provençal language, defending his former master Thomas Warton against Joseph Ritson's ill-tempered 'Observations' on the 'History of poetry'. A career of brilliant promise was cut short by phthisis, of which Russell died at Bristol Hotwells on 31 July 1788. He was buried near his mother in the churchyard of Powerstock, Dorset, a mural tablet being erected to his memory in the tower of the church.

Until shortly before his death Russell was engaged in correcting his poems, and a volume entitled *Sonnets and Miscellaneous Poems* appeared in 1789, dedicated to Warton by the editor William Howley. The most noteworthy feature of the little volume is the excellence of Russell's sonnets. Together with William Lisle Bowles, a fellow Wykehamist of kindred sympathies, he may claim an important place in the revival of the sonnet in England. Wordsworth not only wrote with warm appreciation of Russell's genius as a sonneteer, but in his sonnet 'Iona (upon Landing)' he adopted four lines from Russell, as conveying his feeling better than any words of his own could do. Another sonnet of Russell's seems to have suggested an exquisite passage in Byron's 'O snatch'd away in beauty's bloom'; and of a third, 'supposed to be written at Lemnos', Landor wrote that it alone authorized Russell to

join the shades of Sophocles and Euripides. Coleridge, Cary, and Bowles applaud this Miltonic sonnet, which was much anthologized after Russell's death. Russell lacked the originality of genius, but, says Cary, 'his ear was tuned to the harmonies of Spenser, Milton, and Dryden, and fragments of their sounds he gives us back as from an echo, but so combined as to make a sweet music of his own' (Cary, *Memoir*, 1847, 2.297–8).

THOMAS SECCOMBE, rev. M. CLARE LOUGHLIN-CHOW

Sources E. Partridge, 'Introduction', *The poems of Cuthbert Shaw and Thomas Russell* (1925) · E. Blunden, *A Wessex worthy: Thomas Russell* (1960) · *GM*, 1st ser., 58 (1788), 752–3 · Foster, *Alum. Oxon.* · T. F. Kirby, *Winchester scholars: a list of the wardens, fellows, and scholars of … Winchester College* (1888), 270 · *The lounger's common place book*, 3 (1805), 121 · *N&Q*, 4th ser., 10 (1872), 472 · *N&Q*, 4th ser., 11 (1873), 23 · *N&Q*, 8th ser., 9 (1896), 145–6 · *N&Q*, 8th ser., 9 (1896), 214 · *N&Q*, 8th ser., 9 (1896), 450 · C. W. Holgate, 'Memoir', *Wykehamist* (31 July 1888)

Russell, Thomas (1767–1803), Irish nationalist, was born on 21 November 1767 in Drommahane townland, Kilshannig parish, co. Cork, the fifth and youngest child of John Russell (*c.*1720–1792), a native of co. Kilkenny and a lieutenant in the 83rd foot regiment, and his wife, whose maiden name was O'Kennedy (*d.* 1786). Although Russell was brought up as a protestant in the Church of Ireland, his mother was probably a Roman Catholic and his paternal grandmother certainly was. She was a member of the O'Clear family—a Catholic gentry family from the co. Kilkenny/Queen's county border—who had lost their lands because they had espoused the Jacobite cause in the 1690s. The family moved in the 1770s to Dublin, where John Russell was a captain of invalids at the Royal Hospital, Kilmainham. The family was deeply religious, and Thomas received his religious education from his elder sister, Margaret (1752–1834); his father supervised his education at home. Thomas intended to enter the church but instead, in 1783, he joined his brother Ambrose (*c.*1756–1793) in India, where Ambrose was a lieutenant in the 52nd foot regiment. He had two other brothers: John Russell (*c.*1748–*c.*1815), a political radical who moved to London in 1792 and obtained a lieutenancy in the West London militia in 1794, and William (*fl.* 1793–1796), a lieutenant in the 63rd regiment and the black sheep of the family.

In 1783 Thomas Russell was appointed an ensign, first in the 100th foot regiment, then in the same regiment as his brother Ambrose. They fought together at the battle of Cannanore, one of their commanders being Colonel John Knox, member of a prominent political family that later befriended and supported Russell. In 1786–7 Thomas returned to Ireland as an officer on half pay. Once again he contemplated taking holy orders and seems to have paid a visit to the Isle of Man, with this in view. However, nothing appears to have come of this, and in August 1790 he was made an ensign in the 64th foot regiment and posted to Belfast in September.

Early political involvement and personality While observing a session of the Irish House of Commons in July 1790, Russell met and befriended Theobald Wolfe Tone. Thus began one of the legendary friendships of Irish history. Russell

Thomas Russell (1767–1803), by unknown artist

spent the rest of that summer with the Tones in their holiday cottage at Sandymount, south of Dublin, where he helped Tone refine an earlier project for a British military colony on the Sandwich Islands. Russell is a key figure in Tone's journals, sharing and influencing his political ideas and becoming both a family friend and Tone's closest associate. Indeed, Tone's celebrated journals grew out of the friendship, for the two men agreed to keep such jottings for each other's amusement. He appears under the nickname chosen by Tone, 'P. P. clerk of this parish', taken from a satirical essay attributed to both Jonathan Swift and Alexander Pope that tells the story of a pious young man led astray by women and pleasure. Unfortunately Russell's journals were no match for his friend's, being disjointed, infrequent, and difficult to read.

Russell had a complex personality: convivial, gracious, and thoughtful towards others, he was also deeply religious and introspective; his seriousness and intense self-criticism became the object of Tone's gentle mockery. Russell's pursuit of the virtuous ideal frequently involved him in Rousseauistic musings on the imperfections of human nature, particularly his own. He was an exceptionally tall and handsome man; even the warrant for his arrest in 1803 was complimentary, describing him as 'a tall, handsome man' of 'dark complexion, aquiline nose, large black eyes, with heavy eye-brows, good teeth, full-chested, walking generally fast and upright, and having a military appearance … with a clear distinct voice, and … a good address' (Elliott, *Wolfe Tone*, 94). He never married, though his character and good looks made him an object of fascination with a number of *femmes de lettres*, notably Mary Ann McCracken and William Drennan's sister, Martha McTier. He frequently resorted to prostitutes and casual partners, yet his idealization of pure love seems to have prevented him from successfully wooing the object of his love, Eliza Goddard. It seems that recognition of his

own lack of financial prospect also restrained him from proposing marriage to her.

Russell was an unworldly man and as a result was constantly in financial distress. This was deepened by high moral principle. In July 1791 he had to sell his ensigncy because of the financial difficulties in which he found himself after a friend, the American Thomas Digges, for whom he had gone security, absconded. At the end of that year—through the good graces of the Knoxes—he was appointed seneschal of the manor court in Dungannon, co. Tyrone, only to renounce the position in September 1792 because of the sectarianism which he witnessed in his fellow magistrates. He then thought of trying his fortune in revolutionary France, of which he was a passionate admirer. But his father's death on 5 December 1792 threw the responsibility of providing for his sister upon him, and effectively terminated such plans and deepened his financial embarrassment. Although he was appointed librarian of the Belfast Society for Promoting Knowledge in January 1794, imprisonment (1796–1802) for his political activities left him in straightened circumstances for the rest of his life, and dependent on the generosity of his Belfast friends, notably Dr James McDonnell, John Templeton, Martha McTier, and, most of all, Mary Ann McCracken.

Russell made friends among Belfast's radicals and literati. Among these were the botanist John Templeton and the Irish music collector Edward Bunting, as well as members of the largely Presbyterian merchant class, who later founded the United Irish Society. Russell was a typical Enlightenment man of letters, with a keen interest in the pursuit of knowledge. His jottings—often chronicling his extensive tours on foot through Ulster and north Leinster—reflect his interest in natural science in particular. He was also one of the very few United Irishmen with an interest in Gaelic culture. He took Irish lessons from the noted Gaelic scholar Patrick Lynch, assisted in the editing of an Irish-language dictionary, and was involved in the Belfast harpers' festival of 1792.

United Irishman It is possible to chronicle Russell's political involvement from the time of his meeting with Tone. He became a corresponding member of a political club which Tone formed in Dublin in 1790, with the intention of contributing essays on religious tolerance and Catholic emancipation. Although these did not materialize, his notes show advanced ideas which were to influence Tone's pamphlet *An Argument on Behalf of the Catholics of Ireland* (1791). It was Russell who invited Tone to draw up the resolutions for a new political society to be founded in Belfast on 14 July 1791. Tone responded in a letter which stated that privately he supported the idea of constitutional separation from England, but realized then was not the time to pursue it. The letter fell into government hands and caused Russell to be questioned before a House of Lords secret committee two years later. The setting up in Belfast of the new society—to be called the Society of United Irishmen—was delayed until October 1791, when Russell and Tone became founding members. Tone's account of their two-week stay in Belfast, charting the serious and not-so-serious activities of the two friends, is perhaps the most amusing part of his diaries. At the end of that month Russell and Tone travelled to Dublin to help found the Dublin Society of United Irishmen. But apart from his role in a dispute in late 1791 or early 1792 over whether members should take a secret oath or 'test', Russell's involvement in the Dublin society was intermittent. Indeed, such was his work on behalf of Catholic emancipation in these years—particularly when Tone was employed by the Catholic committee in 1792–3—that he alienated some United Irishmen by refusing to communicate developments, anxious as he was not to jeopardize the Catholic campaign by giving its enemies the excuse of denouncing it as allied with dangerous radicals. His friends in Belfast thought the Catholic committee ungenerous in not recognizing his contribution.

When war broke out between Britain and revolutionary France in February 1793, the Irish authorities clamped down on societies such as the United Irishmen, and Russell was one of those summoned to appear before a secret committee of the Irish House of Lords in March 1793. For a while that spring he also acted as secretary to the Dublin Society of United Irishmen and was one of the committee appointed to draw up their plans for parliamentary reform (1793–4). But the society was in some disarray because many of its leaders had been arrested, and Russell and Tone despaired of reform in Ireland and talked of going to live in America. But they remained and tried to pull the remnants of the society back together.

With the exception of Henry Joy McCracken, Russell was the only major United Irish leader with a genuine sympathy and understanding for the common people. In his lengthy walks in Ulster he often spoke with them and believed that their political ideas were more advanced and pro-French than the middle-class United Irishmen gave them credit for. He was instrumental in persuading Tone that a revolution in Ireland was feasible. In May 1795 he was one of the small group which gathered at McArt's Fort on the Cave Hill, Belfast, to send Tone off on his voyage to the United States of America, and took a famous oath to overthrow British rule in Ireland. When Tone was thinking of settling as a farmer in America, Russell reminded him of his undertaking to use his exile as a channel to negotiate military aid from France. Tone's disillusionment with American politics was plain in his correspondence with Russell and shattered Russell's longstanding admiration for the country.

Russell also provided the bridge that brought the middle-class United Irish leadership into communication with lower social elements in the north, where the restructuring of the United Irish Society as an underground revolutionary movement began in 1795–6. In 1796 he was appointed its military commander in co. Down. It was with good reason that the government considered Russell one of the most dangerous of the United Irish leaders. He was one of the inner trio of leaders to whom Tone sent his younger brother, Arthur, in December 1795, to announce his departure for France, in pursuit of French military aid for Ireland.

Arrest and imprisonment Russell was a regular contributor to the United Irish newspapers the *Northern Star* and the *Press*, his most notable contributions being poems against slavery and on the defeat of Gaelic Ireland at the battle of Aughrim (1691). He was proposed for the editorship of a sister paper in Dublin—the *National Journal*—but declined. In 1793 he co-wrote with William Sampson a satirical pamphlet in mock-epic form, *Review of the Lion of Old England*, which attacked the myth of the 'glorious revolution', showing how Britain's current war policy had aligned it with the most autocratic monarchs of Europe. The following year he contributed to a critique of Thomas Paine's *Ages of Reason*. In his 1796 pamphlet *A Letter to the People of Ireland on the Present Situation of the Country*, he openly proclaimed himself one of the United Irishmen, by then a banned seditious organization. He argued that the ordinary people had been betrayed by the Irish gentry, backed by England, and he championed the cause of the Catholics. The pamphlet was deemed seditious and a warrant was issued for his arrest. He surrendered himself voluntarily on 16 September 1796 and was taken from Belfast to Newgate prison in Dublin. Because he refused to give sureties for his good behaviour, he was not bailed and remained in prison until 1802, the longest detention without trial of any of the state prisoners. When Lord Edward Fitzgerald was wounded and arrested on 19 May 1798, he was brought to Newgate, where Russell was the only United Irishman to see him. When Tone was captured and capitally convicted in November 1798, it was Russell who tried to mobilize support to have him reprieved.

Russell was unenthusiastic about the state prisoners' compact with government in August 1798 (the Kilmainham treaty), which was designed to stop the executions after the failed 1798 rising. He believed the government had broken the compact by altering its statement and continuing to detain the prisoners. He was one of those who reorganized the United Irish Society from within prison, while younger leaders still at liberty—notably Robert Emmet and Russell's niece's husband, William Henry Hamilton—reconstructed it as a more secretive military organization. In March 1799 he was sent with the other state prisoners to Fort George in Scotland, and was released to Hamburg in June 1802. The split which had occurred within the United Irish leadership before 1798 continued through their imprisonment, and Russell remained with the group which accompanied Thomas Addis Emmet to Amsterdam and finally to Paris by September 1802.

Last days Of all the former United Irish leaders, Russell was the most eager to reopen negotiations with France. But he was also the most mistrustful of the new regime under Napoleon Bonaparte. It was this mistrust which now began to dictate the nature of plans for another rising, for although the United Irishmen knew that no rising in Ireland could be successful without French help, they sought to ensure that the French would be given no excuse to take control of the country. Robert Emmet raised the funding in Ireland, while Russell recruited among the Irish exiles in France and returned to Ireland, via London, in April 1803. Russell's undoubted sympathy for the lower orders had left him with an unrealistic belief that the ordinary people were quite capable of rising without the French. On 18 July 1803 he travelled north from Dublin with Hamilton and James Hope, the Templepatrick weaver who had already played a key role in recruiting the artisans of Belfast and Dublin into the movement. The number of people who harboured them, and reports that men were being drilled in the areas in co. Antrim and co. Down where they visited, gave some support to Russell's belief. But the middle classes who had led the rising in 1798 were cool, and—as with the plans for the south—the northern rising was aborted by news of the failure of Emmet's premature rebellion of 23 July 1803. Russell travelled to Dublin by boat in an effort to rescue Emmet, but was captured there on 9 September, the formal identification being made by his old patron, George Knox.

Russell was returned to the north and tried by special commission at Downpatrick, co. Down, on 19 October. A melancholy and fatalistic man, he refused to offer any defence, but delivered a speech which spoke of his religious feelings, called on the rich to look after the poor, and declared that many gentlemen of the jury had once shared the beliefs for which he was about to die. Russell was executed at Downpatrick prison on 21 October and buried that day in the nearby Church of Ireland churchyard. A plain slab—organized and paid for by his friend Mary Ann McCracken, who had likewise supported him financially throughout his imprisonment and trial—marks his place of burial.

Only in recent years has the significance of Russell within the United Irish movement been explored fully, though he was central to Tone's autobiography, first published in 1826, and figured prominently in R. R. Madden's seminal study of the United Irishmen in 1843–6. Like Henry Joy McCracken, he has always had the status of folk-hero in the north, particularly in south co. Down—a reputation reflected in the celebrated dialect poem by Florence Wilson 'The Man from God Knows where' (1918).

MARIANNE ELLIOTT

Sources TCD, Madden MS 873 · TCD, Sirr MS 868/9 · TCD, Tone MSS, MSS 2041–2050, 3805–3809 · NA Ire., Rebellion MSS, MS 620 · letters, PRO NIre., Drennan MSS, D 591, D 729 · Memoirs of Miles Byrne, ed. F. Byrne, 3 vols. (1863) · The Drennan–McTier letters, ed. J. Agnew, 3 vols. (1998–9) · State trials, vols. 28–9 · M. MacDonagh, The viceroy's post-bag (1904) · Northern Star (1792–7) · Journals and memoirs of Thomas Russell, ed. C. J. Woods (Dublin, 1991) · W. T. W. Tone, Life of Theobald Wolfe Tone, 2 vols. (Washington, DC, 1826) · The writings of Theobald Wolfe Tone, 1763–98, ed. T. W. Moody, R. B. McDowell, and C. J. Woods, 1 (1998) · B. Clifford, Thomas Russell and Belfast (1988) · M. Elliott, Partners in revolution: the United Irishmen and France (1982) · M. Elliott, Wolfe Tone: prophet of Irish independence (1989) · S. N. MacGiolla Easpaig, Tomás Ruiséil (1957) · M. McNeill, The life and times of Mary Ann McCracken, 1770–1866: a Belfast panorama (1960) · R. R. Madden, The United Irishmen: their lives and times, 3rd ser., vol. 2 (1846) · J. Morgan, 'Sketch of the life of Thomas Russell', Ulster Magazine, 1 (1830), 39–60 · C. J. Woods, 'The place of Thomas Russell in the United Irish movement', Ireland and the French Revolution, ed. H. Gough and D. Dickson (1990), 83–100 · D. Carroll, The man from God knows where: Thomas Russell, 1767–1803 (1995) · private information (2004) · J. Quinn, Soul on fire: a life of Thomas Russell (2002)

Archives NA Ire., letters, notebooks, and papers · TCD, corresp., diary fragments, and papers
Likenesses engraving, NL Ire.; repro. in Elliott, Partners, 311 · group portrait, coloured lithograph (The United Irish Patriots, 1798), NPG · miniature, priv. coll. [see illus.] · portrait, repro. in Madden, United Irishmen

Russell [formerly Cloutt], **Thomas** (c.1781–1846), Congregational minister, was born at Marden, Kent. His father, whose surname was Cloutt or Clout, and grandfather were members of the Church of England, and Thomas was confirmed as an Anglican, but was educated for the independent ministry at Hoxton Academy (1800–03) under Dr Robert Simpson. His first post was at Tonbridge, Kent, in 1803. In 1806 he became minister of Pell Street Chapel, Ratcliffe Highway, Smithfield, London, which was built in 1805 after the previous chapel had been demolished to make way for the London docks, but he did not achieve popularity as a preacher.

About 1820 Cloutt started to use the name of Russell, and in 1823 officially changed his name. Soon afterwards he received an MA from one of the Scottish universities. When Pell Street Chapel closed, a few years before his death, he became minister of Baker Street Chapel, Enfield, Middlesex. He was a trustee of Coward College and, from 1842, a trustee of the foundations of Dr Daniel Williams. He was also secretary of the Aged Ministers' Relief Society. Unusually for a Congregationalist, Russell was a supporter of the Dissenters' Chapels Act of 1844.

Under the name of Cloutt he published four sermons (1806–18) and a Collection of Hymns (1813). In 1823 he began his edition of the works of Dr John Owen, published in twenty-one volumes in 1826. In 1828 he began work on an edition of The Works of the English and Scottish Reformers, but only three volumes were published, in 1828, containing works of William Tyndale and John Frith. He also edited some of the works of Richard Baxter, and revised the end of William Orme's The Life and Times of Richard Baxter (1830).

Russell was married, and his children included the clergymen Arthur Tozer *Russell and John Fuller *Russell. He died on 10 December 1846 at his home in Penton Row, Walworth, Surrey.

ALEXANDER GORDON, rev. ANNE PIMLOTT BAKER

Sources W. D. Jeremy, The Presbyterian Fund and Dr Daniel Williams's Trust (1885), 208 · Congregational Year Book (1846), 177 · Christian Reformer, or, Unitarian Magazine and Review, new ser., 3 (1847), 64
Archives DWL, corresp. | Bodl. Oxf., corresp. with Sir Thomas Phillipps

Russell, Thomas (1830–1904), financier and land speculator, was born in Cork, the first of six children of Thomas Russell (1808–1873), carpenter, and Mary Roberts (1811–1847), ward of a Church of Ireland rector. The Russells left Ireland with the infant Thomas in 1833. After seven years in New South Wales the family settled in Auckland, the new capital of New Zealand. In 1844 young Thomas was articled to Auckland's foremost lawyer, Thomas Outhwaite. While undergoing legal training, he became an enthusiastic lay worker for the then powerful Wesleyan denomination. Licensed to practise at twenty-one, he had grown into a tall, energetic man of persuasive personality. As ambitious as he was able, he set up as a sole solicitor. The Wesleyans helped him by putting much church and mission work his way. On 18 July 1854 he married Emeline Vercoe; they had seven children.

During the later 1850s Russell rose to be a powerful figure in the Auckland business community, as an activist in the progress party (the political arm of the local merchants), and as a foremost conveyancing solicitor. Determined and plausible, he established an ascendancy over the settlement's capitalists which endured for three decades. In 1859 he took the initiative in forming the New Zealand Insurance Company, and two years later was the driving force behind the creation of the Bank of New Zealand. In the same year he formed a legal partnership with Frederick Whitaker, renowned counsel and politician. Whitaker and Russell soon became the most profitable practice in the land. In an era when business advantage was inseparable from political influence, Russell entered the general assembly in 1861. Within a year he was taken into the cabinet, holding office until late 1864 in two successive ministries. As minister of defence in the second administration, he pressed for an uncompromising military reckoning with Maori during the land wars, and for confiscation of all 'rebel' lands, policies which cause, even today, undiminished anguish and resentment among the Maori people.

When the capital was shifted to Wellington in 1865 Russell withdrew from politics to concentrate on his multifarious business interests. He was the chief promoter in the same year of the New Zealand Loan and Mercantile Agency Co. Ltd, incorporated in London. This company raised mortgage debentures in Britain to finance short-term advances to squatters secured by a lien on the season's wool clip, and more importantly to take over some troublesome long-term mortgage advances of the Bank of New Zealand. During the Thames gold rush Russell was a heavy investor in mines, batteries, and goldmining companies. By 1874 he had so prospered that he went to live in England as an expatriate rentier, entrusting his extensive interests in New Zealand to his partner Whitaker and to local agents. He realized, as few did, that by living in London he could take advantage of the capital market there at times when investors were 'on the feed' to finance first the development of extensive landed estates run by syndicates, of which he was the key figure, and second the Bank of New Zealand and its loan company whose directorates he now dominated. A rural collapse in New Zealand and the well-founded suspicion of British debenture holders that colonial borrowers could no longer service their debts brought down Russell's landed companies in the later 1880s and imperilled the financial institutions he had created. Russell himself would have been ruined had he not shuffled off some of his debts to the shoulders of others, and invested in the highly profitable Waihi Goldmining Company formed in 1887.

Russell remains a controversial figure. He was extraordinarily self-regarding. A chancery judge investigating the affairs of Russell's insolvent Loan and Mercantile Company in 1894 identified him as the chief culprit; the evidence showed 'irresistibly' that the other directors had the 'fixed belief that everything recommended by Mr Russell must be right and for the interest of the company … They left him absolute master of the situation' (Mennell, 71–2). Yet he was admirably forward-looking. His policy of making use of readily available nineteenth-century British capital to develop the infrastructure of the colonial economy has few detractors today, although most historians agree that his sanguine temperament often led him to mistake the right time to invest. He died at Farnham, Surrey, where he had lived from 1897, on 2 September 1904.   R. C. J. STONE

Sources R. C. J. Stone, *Makers of fortune* (1973) · New Zealand Loan and Mercantile Agency Co. Ltd MSS, NL NZ · P. Mennell, ed., *The New Zealand Loan and Mercantile Agency Co. Ltd* (1894) · F. Larkworthy, *Ninety-one years* (1924) · R. C. J. Stone, *The making of Russell McVeagh* (1992) · H. J. Hanham, 'New Zealand promoters and British investors, 1860–1895', *Studies of a small democracy: essays in honour of Willis Airey*, ed. R. Chapman and K. Sinclair (1963), 56–77 · private information (2004) · *The Observer* [Auckland] (13 Nov 1880), 73 · m. cert. · d. cert.

Archives NL NZ, New Zealand Loan and Mercantile Agency Co. Ltd MSS

Wealth at death £160,778: probate

Russell, Thomas Baron (1865–1931), advertising consultant, was born on 15 November 1865 at 12 Avenue Terrace, Avenue Road, Camberwell, London, the son of Thomas Russell, librarian of a circulating library, and his wife, Mary, *née* Everett. Russell's father encouraged the boy's reading and he developed a love of literature which he intended to pursue at university, but was prevented by his father's serious illness. He was obliged to leave school and, after several jobs, in January 1882 obtained a post with John Morgan Richards Ltd, a firm of importing chemists.

Morgan Richards was an importer of American patent medicines and the firm's success depended on advertising. In his twenty-three years with the firm, Russell gained practical experience in this side of their business, both at home and on his business trips to the USA, Canada, India, and Australia. He created the memorable advertisements for Carter's Little Liver Pills. Aware of the influence of advertising magazines, he wrote regularly for the American *Printer's Ink*, under the editorship of his friend John Irving Romer, and from 1901 in the new *Advertising World* edited by William Ewert Berry. Russell disapproved of the way in which the advertising business was then organized, with agents receiving commission from the newspaper, the vendor of space, rather than from the advertiser. He urged that advertisers should pay a net rate, free of all discounts and commissions, and that the agents should receive an agreed fee.

In 1905 Russell was persuaded by Horace Hooper, the paper's new advertising director, to join *The Times* as its advertising manager. During his three years at the newspaper, Russell inaugurated the Times Book Club and increased the amount of illustrated display advertising. He was the originator of *The Times*'s 'gold brick' advertisements, whose information, having been researched by

Times staff, was held up as reliable. When Hooper bought the *Encyclopaedia Britannica* from Adam and Charles Black, Russell cultivated a new readership by selling it in instalments and by mail order. After he left *The Times* he organized the promotion of other books and encyclopaedias.

In 1910 Russell set himself up as an advertising consultant—arguably the first such in Britain. In contrast to agents, who bought advertising space on behalf of their clients, the consultant was paid by fee or annual retainer to prepare the advertising material and generally advise on aspects of the business—in Russell's words, 'functioning exactly as a consulting physician' (Nevett, 108). The Incorporated Society of Advertisement Consultants, which he founded in 1910 and presided over for twenty-one years, prescribed the codes of conduct and standards expected of its members. He was later involved with the Publicity Club, and was the first recipient of its cup, awarded for distinguished services to advertising.

Respected for his high standards and personal integrity, Russell was often hired to arbitrate on disputes in the advertising field. He was one of the first professionals to venture into the political arena: the Liberal Party hired him in 1910, and during the First World War he advised a government committee on recruiting campaigns and was also involved with advertising the War Loan of 1915. After the war he delivered the first lectures on advertising to be delivered as a university course at the London School of Economics. Ill health forced his retirement in 1931. He died at his home, Highwood, Batts Corner, Binsted Road, near Farnham, Surrey, on 31 December 1931. He was survived by his wife, Olga Hutteman, and by their three sons and three daughters.   ANITA MCCONNELL

Sources *Advertisers' Weekly* (24 Sept 1931) · *Advertisers' Weekly* (19 Nov 1931) · *Advertisers' Weekly* (7 Jan 1932) · T. R. Nevett, *Advertising in Britain: a history* (1982) · A. Garth, *History of the Publicity Club of London* (1978) · *Advertising World* (Dec 1901) · [S. Morison and others], *The history of The Times*, 3 (1947) · T. B. Russell, *Wisdom in advertising* (1901) · T. B. Russell, *Force in advertising* (1904) · T. B. Russell, *Advertising methods and mediums* (1910) · T. B. Russell, *Commercial advertising*, 2nd edn (1925) · T. B. Russell, *Retail advertising*, 3rd edn (1925) · *Times, Financial and commercial supplement* (1905) · *CGPLA Eng. & Wales* (1932) · D. J. Jeremy, 'Russell, Thomas Baron', *DBB* · b. cert. · d. cert.

Likenesses photograph, repro. in *Advertisers' Weekly* (7 Jan 1932)

Wealth at death £3878 3*s*. 3*d*.: resworn probate, 7 April 1932, *CGPLA Eng. & Wales*

Russell, Thomas Macnamara (*b.* before **1740**, *d.* **1824**), naval officer, may have been the son of an Englishman who settled in Ireland and married into the Macnamara family from Ballyally, co. Clare. After a period in the merchant service he entered the navy about 1766, when he joined the guardship *Cornwall* at Plymouth, and in her, and afterwards in the *Arrogant*, he served for nearly three years as an able seaman. He was then for about two years midshipman or second master of the cutter *Hunter*, employed on preventive service in the North Sea, and for about eighteen months master's mate in the guardship *Terrible* at Portsmouth, with Captain Marriot Arbuthnot, of whom

he became a committed follower. He passed his lieutenant's examination on 2 December 1772, being then described in his certificate as 'more than 32'.

In 1776 Russell was serving on the coast of North America, and on 2 June he was promoted lieutenant of the sloop *Albany* by Rear-Admiral Molyneux Shuldham. He was moved to the *Diligent*, and on his return to England appointed to the *Raleigh*, with Captain James Gambier. Russell was present at the relief of Jersey in May 1779, and at the capture of Charlestown. At Charlestown on 11 May 1780 he was promoted by Arbuthnot to the command of the sloop *Beaumont*, from which, on 7 May 1781, he was posted to the *Bedford*. Apparently this was for rank only, and he was almost immediately appointed to the *Hussar* (20 guns), in which he cruised on the coast of North America with marked success, making several prizes.

On 22 January 1783 Russell fell in with the French frigate *Sibylle* (32 guns), which had been roughly handled by the *Magicienne* three weeks before, and afterwards, in a violent gale, had been dismasted, and obliged to throw twelve of her guns overboard. When she sighted the *Hussar* she hoisted the British flag over the French, the recognized signal of a prize, and at the same time, in the shrouds, another British flag, union downwards, the signal of distress. Russell accordingly bore down to her assistance, but as he drew near, his suspicions being roused, he was able to bear away in time to avoid the full effect of a raking broadside. On this the *Sibylle*, under British colours, attempted to board the *Hussar*, but was beaten off with great loss, and when the *Centurion*, attracted by the firing, came within gunshot, the *Sibylle* surrendered. Indignant at the treacherous conduct of her captain, Thibaut-René, comte de Kergariou-Locmarin, Russell broke his sword and made him a close prisoner, with a sentry over him. When he brought the prize into New York he reported the circumstance, but, as peace was then on the point of being concluded, the affair was hushed up. Kergariou threatened to demand personal satisfaction, and after the peace Russell went to Paris to meet him, but he returned on finding that his would-be enemy had gone to the Pyrenees. Russell modestly declined a knighthood, which his small fortune could not support.

In 1789 Russell was appointed to the frigate *Diana* on the West Indian station, and at the end of 1791 he was sent to St Domingo with a convoy of provisions for the French. He learned that a British officer, Lieutenant John Perkins, was imprisoned at Jérémie, on a charge of having supplied the black insurgents with arms. Perkins, known as Jack Punch, was in fact an intelligence officer. Russell was convinced that the charge was false, went round to Jérémie, and secured Perkins's release by threatening a bombardment of the town. He returned to England in 1792, and on 16 June married Elizabeth Phillips (*d.* 1818) at Arundel, Sussex; the couple had no children. Four years later Russell was appointed to the *Vengeance* (74 guns), again for service in the West Indies, where, under Rear-Admiral Henry Harvey, he took part in the reduction of St Lucia and Trinidad. The *Vengeance* returned to England in the spring of 1799, and formed part of the Channel Fleet during the summer, after which she was paid off, and in the following April Russell was appointed to the *Princess Royal*, which he commanded until his promotion to the rank of rear-admiral on 1 January 1801.

On the renewal of the war in 1803 Russell hoisted his flag on the *Dictator*, under the orders of Lord Keith in the Downs. On 9 November 1805 he was promoted vice-admiral, and in 1807 he was appointed commander-in-chief of the squadron in the North Sea. In September, on the news of war having been declared by Denmark, he took possession of Heligoland, which during the war continued to be the principal depot of the British trade with Germany in defiance of Napoleon's continental system.

Russell became an admiral on 12 August 1812. He died suddenly in his carriage near Poole on 22 July 1824.

J. K. LAUGHTON, *rev.* NICHOLAS TRACY

Sources GM, 1st ser., 94/2 (1824), 369 · *Naval Chronicle*, 17 (1807), 441 · *Naval Chronicle*, 18 (1807), 233–6 · J. Marshall, *Royal naval biography*, 1 (1823), 137, 606 · R. Beatson, *Naval and military memoirs of Great Britain*, 2nd edn, 6 vols. (1804), vol. 5, p. 552; vol. 6, p. 349 · O. J. Troude, *Batailles navales de la France* (1867) · IGI
Archives NMM, letters to Lord Keith, KEI/28/71–78
Likenesses engraving (after portrait by C. G. Stuart), repro. in *Naval Chronicle*, 17

Russell, Thomas O'Neill [Tomás Ó Néill Ruiséal; *pseud.* Reginald Tierney] (**1828–1908**), a founder of the Gaelic League, was born in May 1828 at Lissanode, Moate, co. Westmeath, the youngest of the four sons and five daughters of Joseph Russell (1762–1837), a member of the Religious Society of Friends and an extensive farmer, and his wife, Sarah Boardman (1791–1873). One of his grandmothers was Mary Neale Watson, a gaelicized version of whose patronymic he adopted as his middle name.

Having received a sound elementary education at a local national school, Russell helped in the running of the family farm, where he doubtless heard Gaelic spoken among the workers. He later told Douglas Hyde that he had attended the Christmas market in Athlone a couple of years before the great famine, when he would have been fifteen or sixteen years old. He estimated that there were some fifty thousand people present, and that he heard as much Gaelic spoken as English, or perhaps more. It was very likely this experience that awakened his love for the language, of which he became an ardent propagandist at home and abroad. S. J. M. Brown's *Ireland in Fiction* and Liam Cox's *Moate* say that Russell was devoted to the revival from about 1858; he himself tells us in his *Teanga thíoramhuil na hÉireann* that he had been interested in Gaelic from his boyhood.

While still in his early twenties Russell went to work in Dublin for a fellow Quaker named Jacob, whose small firm expanded in course of time to become W. and R. Jacob & Co. Ltd, Ireland's premier biscuit manufacturers. Russell soon began to travel for the firm, and D. J. O'Donoghue (1866–1917), who knew him, said that he subsequently followed the same calling for other houses in Ireland, France, and America. In 1858 he wrote a series of letters for the *Irishman* periodical in support of a Gaelic revival. His first book, the novel *Dick Massey*, published in Glasgow in 1860

under the pen-name Reginald Tierney, paints a faithful picture of social life in rural Ireland in the decades before the great famine. Gaelic in concept and 'altogether on the side of the peasant', it was several times reprinted.

About 1865 Russell emigrated to the United States and there he remained for nearly thirty years, visiting every state of the union in the course of his work as a commercial traveller. With his interest in Irish language and culture still undiminished, he availed himself of every opportunity to advance the cause of Gaelic among the Irish in the United States; but his sincere efforts were not always attended with the desired results, for, according to Hyde, his somewhat brusque manner and his pedantry often antagonized people. Yet he was an eloquent and a forceful speaker, with a commanding presence and splendid physique. He contributed voluminously to the press, both in prose and verse, but chiefly for propagandist purposes: his relations with editors were sometimes strained because of the contrariety of his views.

During his self-imposed exile Russell paid occasional visits to Ireland, and he was in the forefront of every Irish cultural organization between 1876 and 1893, the year in which he settled in Dublin. He married Laura Garrier, a Scandinavian, with whom he conversed much in French as she knew little or no English. They had one son. Russell was one of those present when the Gaelic League was founded in Dublin in July 1893: he afterwards served on council and was also a founder member of the Feis Cheoil (Irish music festival) in 1897. He published eleven works in Gaelic and English, most of which were written after his return to Ireland, the last being *Is Ireland a Dying Nation?* (1906), which alienated many old friends and relatives. He died at 49 Synge Street, Dublin, on 15 June 1908, and was buried two days later in Mount Jerome cemetery, Harold's Cross, Dublin.

SÉAMAS Ó SAOTHRAÍ

Sources D. J. O'Donoghue, *The poets of Ireland: a biographical and bibliographical dictionary* (1912), 408 · D. Hyde, *Mise agus an Connradh* (1937), esp. 162–7 · D. Breathnach and M. Ní Mhurchú, *1882–1982 Beathaisnéis a trí* (1992), 148–50 · L. Cox, *Moate county Westmeath: a history* (1981), 150–53 · S. J. M. Brown, *Ireland in fiction*, 2nd edn, repr. 1969 (1919), 269 · S. Fenton, *It all happened* (1949), 276ff · G. Moore, *Hail and farewell: salve!* (1933), 84ff. · DNB · M. Ní Mhuiríosa, *Réamhchonraitheoirí* (1968), 39–52 · M. Keaney, *Westmeath authors: a bibliographical and biographical study* (1969), 168–9 · J. Sheehan, *South Westmeath farm and folk* (1978), esp. 80–82 · *Evening Herald* (16 June 1908) · *Freeman's Journal* [Dublin] (16 June 1908) · *Irish Independent* (16 June 1908) · *Irish Times* (16 June 1908) · *Dublin Evening Mail* (17 June 1908) · *Irish Times* (18 June 1908)

Russell, Sir Thomas Wallace, first baronet (**1841–1920**), politician, was born on 28 February 1841 in Cupar, Fife, the third son of David Russell (*d.* 1862), a stonemason, and his wife, Isabella Wallace (*d.* 1847). He was educated at Madras Academy, Cupar, and migrated to Ulster in 1859. He settled in Donaghmore, co. Tyrone, where he held various positions, including a clerkship in a soap factory and a sales assistantship in a drapery store. He married Harriet, daughter of Thomas Agnew of Dungannon, on 29 September 1865; the couple had two daughters. Harriet died in 1894. On 23 May 1896 he married Martha Catherine Keown (*d.* in or after 1939), daughter of Lieutenant-Colonel Henry

Keown of Castleroe, Londonderry, with whom he had a son and a daughter. His son and heir, a lieutenant in the Royal Dublin Fusiliers, was killed on the western front in November 1916.

Russell was a self-made man of formidable political and administrative talents. He was an effective polemicist and journalist; he was also an unflagging and popular platform speaker who—along with the more conservative Edward Saunderson—did much to represent the Irish unionist case to British audiences in the 1880s. Later in his career he demonstrated considerable ability as a junior minister, and held office under both Lord Salisbury and H. H. Asquith. He applied his talents within three main fields: temperance, unionism, and land reform. These were the governing principles of much of his career, and the foundation for all three was an evangelical Presbyterian faith. This provided biblical vindication for sobriety, and stimulated Russell to defend the political interests of Irish protestants, and especially of the Presbyterian farming community.

Russell's advocacy of temperance laid the foundations for his later emergence as a politician of national significance. In 1863 he was elected secretary of the Dungannon Temperance Society, and used the post as a springboard to a full-time career within the temperance movement: in 1864 he was appointed as agent of the Irish Temperance League in Dublin, with a brief to convert the whole of the south of Ireland to the cause. Temperance brought Russell a training in public oratory and in polemical journalism; it also brought financial security, for in the mid-1870s he and his wife opened what would become a highly successful temperance hotel in central Dublin.

Although Russell had little regard for landlordism and some tacit sympathy for Irish national aspirations, his Scottish Presbyterian roots and temperance convictions led him naturally into the Liberal Unionist ranks in the mid-1880s. His first attempt to get into the Commons, as the Liberal candidate at Preston in 1885, was a failure; but he found greater electoral favour in his home territory of South Tyrone, where in July 1886 he defeated the leading Parnellite William O'Brien. (O'Brien was both an opponent of the union and of temperance reformers, whom he designated as 'that sect of Puritans'.) Russell held the constituency until January 1910: thereafter (1911–18) he represented North Tyrone. Between 1886 and 1900 he was a highly effective, if independent-minded, advocate of the Unionist cause, addressing some 1400 meetings and working closely with the Irish Loyal and Patriotic Union (Irish Unionist Alliance). Gladstone considered Russell's contribution to debate on the second Home Rule Bill (1893) as among the best delivered in the Commons. Other Liberals (such as A. E. Pease) recognized the threat that Russell represented as a stump orator.

However, Russell's loyalty to unionism depended upon the movement's capacity to satisfy his farmer support. This loyalty survived, albeit in a bruised form, until 1900. Russell launched a rural agitation in 1894–5 designed to bolster farmer support for a Liberal land bill: this outraged his Conservative critics within the Unionist alliance. In 1895, on the formation of Lord Salisbury's third ministry, Russell was silenced with junior office (the parliamentary secretaryship of the Local Government Board) and by the promise of a Unionist land bill. But in the late 1890s Russell was moving towards a more radical settlement of the Irish land question; and in September 1900 at Clogher, co. Tyrone, he declared in favour of compulsory land purchase. This speech led to his dismissal from the government, and to a period of independent dissent and political reorientation.

Between 1900 and 1906 Russell challenged mainstream unionism for the command of the protestant farmer vote. His supporters won two by-elections, wresting East Down (1902) and North Fermanagh (1903) from Unionist control and provoking panic within the Unionist movement as a whole. The early success of Russell's agitation had profound repercussions. It further chivvied the Unionist government towards a sweeping measure of land purchase, and it stimulated a comprehensive overhaul of Ulster Unionist electoral machinery. These measures simultaneously underlined the seriousness with which Russell was viewed, and helped to deflate the agitation that he had created.

In the wake of Wyndham's Land Act (1903) and the creation of the Ulster Unionist Council (1904–5), Russell's land movement began to flounder. Having been estranged from unionism, and having failed to create a lasting independent movement, he joined the Liberal Party in 1906: his most significant publication, *Ireland and the Empire* (1901), looked forward to this development. In 1907 he succeeded Sir Horace Plunkett as vice-president of the Irish department of agriculture and technical instruction. He held this office until 1918. He was sworn of the Irish privy council in 1908, and awarded a baronetcy in 1917. He died in Dublin on 2 May 1920, aware that the final collapse of British rule in Ireland was approaching, and was buried in Mount Jerome cemetery, as he had wished, three days later.

Russell was a Victorian faddist—a radical nonconformist who combined unwavering conviction with very considerable political skill. The crusading zeal that he had applied to the cause of temperance was transferred to the land question. But his passion and eloquence were not always accompanied by political realism or even tact. He made demands of the Unionist alliance that, given the alliance's fissile nature, could not be granted. He was too idiosyncratic to be restrained by any one party, and yet too able to be denied access to party politics. That he held ministerial rank under both a Unionist and a Liberal administration is a reflection of both his talents and his obtuseness.

ALVIN JACKSON

Sources A. Jackson, 'Irish unionism and the Russellite threat, 1894–1906', *Irish Historical Studies*, 25 (1986–7), 376–404 · J. Loughlin, 'T. W. Russell, the tenant-farmer interest and progressive unionism in Ulster, 1886–1900', *Éire–Ireland*, 25/1 (1990), 44–63 · A. Jackson, *The Ulster party: Irish unionists in the House of Commons, 1884–1911* (1989) · E. Malcolm, 'Ireland sober, Ireland free': drink and temperance in nineteenth-century Ireland* (1986) · Burke, *Peerage* · WW · WWW · will · *Irish Times* (6 May 1920)

Archives PRO NIre., papers | Hatfield House, Hertfordshire, Salisbury MSS • PRO NIre., Irish Unionist Alliance MSS • TCD, corresp. with John Dillon

Likenesses S. P. Hall, pencil drawing, 1886, NG Ire. • F. C. Gould, caricature, chalk sketch, NPG • W. Orpen, drawing, Hugh Lane Gallery of Modern Art, Dublin • S. Purser, oils, NG Ire. • Spy [L. Ward], caricature, watercolour study, NPG; repro. in *VF* (24 March 1888) • B. Stone, photographs, NPG

Russell, **Sir Thomas Wentworth** (1879–1954), police officer in the Egyptian service, was born on 22 November 1879 at Wollaton rectory, fourth child and third son of the Revd Henry Charles Russell (1842–1922), grandson of the sixth duke of Bedford, and his wife, Leila Louisa Millicent Willoughby (*d.* 1886), daughter of the eighth Baron Middleton, whose Nottinghamshire property comprised Wollaton with 800 acres of deer park. From the rector, who combined the functions of parson and squire, Russell learned, in an atmosphere of religious assurance and sporting affluence, to box, shoot, hunt, and fish until, like his father, 'there was nothing he could not catch'.

Russell was educated at Cheam School, Haileybury College, and Trinity College, Cambridge (1899–1902), contriving throughout to gratify his passion for field sports. He was awarded a BA in 1902. His choice of career was settled when, on vacation at Applecross in Ross-shire, another Willoughby 'paradise' with 80,000 acres reserved for sport, he was invited to visit Cairo by Percy Machell, a distant cousin, then adviser to the Egyptian minister of the interior. He came home to graduate, entering Egyptian service in October 1902.

After apprenticeship with the Alexandria coastguards Russell was appointed provincial sub-inspector in January 1903 and served, later as inspector, in every Egyptian province, thus acquiring unrivalled knowledge of local officials, while directing police activities which ranged from coping with the consequences of Nile floods and plague epidemics to pitched battles against Bedouin brigands; their depredations were virtually eliminated by the police camel corps formed on Russell's initiative in 1906. In 1911 he was appointed assistant commandant of police in Alexandria where he enjoyed a foretaste of dealing with city demonstrations, 'sporting evenings' raiding gambling dens, and an interlude in command of western desert anti-contraband operations. He was transferred to Cairo as assistant commandant in 1913.

In 1917, following a line of British notables, Russell was appointed commandant of the Cairo city police with rank of lewa (major-general) and title of pasha. By then Egypt was a British protectorate; under war stress British power, far from withering away, was everywhere in irritating evidence; smouldering Egyptian resentment, fully comprehensible to 'Russell Pasha', flared into violence in March 1919; a clash between hysterical mobs determined to demonstrate and British troops committed to enforce a ban seemed inevitable; but, thanks to Russell's inspired intervention, the demonstrations were converted into orderly processions which he led through Cairo streets, standing in an open car or on foot, with a pause for brandy-and-soda at the Turf Club.

After Egyptian independence in 1922 Russell served under twenty-nine different ministers of interior; opposition leaders were government quarry, but, by adroit manoeuvre combined with personal charm, he mitigated the violence of internecine political warfare, notably in 1932 when, reducing crisis to comedy, he avoided using force against the entire shadow cabinet of the Wafd party. While retaining the esteem of most politicians, he deplored their quarrels, which seemed, in his perhaps over-simplified view, to hamper the real progress of a nation he loved.

Russell's own talents were increasingly diverted to the scourge of growing drug addiction. He pressed evidence on the prime minister, and in 1929 the Egyptian Central Narcotics Intelligence Bureau was formed. As director, operating with small capital resources and hereditary enthusiasm, he hunted the sources of supply; tracks led to Switzerland, France, Bulgaria, Turkey, and Greece. At Geneva he bluntly presented his findings. Moral pressure, backed by incontrovertible evidence, was so effective that by 1939, when he was elected vice-president of the League of Nations advisory committee on opium traffic, most European bases of supply were destroyed. In 1940 Cairo again became the pivot of British military operations. Egyptian police discipline, buttressed by Russell's presence, held firm under strain; co-operation with the visiting army was close, surviving even the use of British tanks to compel King Farouk to change his ministers in February 1942, a controversial expedient that pained and surprised Russell. In 1946, still popular, he retired, the last British officer in Egyptian service. He was appointed OBE in 1920, CMG in 1926, and KBE in 1938. He also held numerous foreign decorations.

Amid the conflict of Egyptian nationalism, British exigencies, and European minority pretensions, Russell remained an impartial guardian of law and order, justly renowned for professional expertise. Although political assassinations were all too prevalent, the murderers rarely contrived to escape. He was a remarkable and solicitous police chief, a link in the best British tradition with Egypt, and, by his campaign to suppress drug traffic, a pioneer in an important international cause.

In 1911 Russell married Evelyn Dorothea Temple (*d.* 1968), daughter of Francis Moore, stockjobber. They had one son, Sir John Wriothesley Russell, who became ambassador to Spain in 1969, and one daughter, Camilla Georgiana, who married Christopher Sykes. Tall and commanding, a sportsman, a dandy, a horseman who made history by riding his camel over fences, as much at ease in his wife's salon as in any desert company, ready for any discomfort on an ibex trail but a bon viveur in town, finding humour in everything and friends everywhere, Russell was a legend in his lifetime. Some of the flavour was happily preserved in his own published reminiscences, *Egyptian Service* (1949). He died at Fitzroy House, 16 Fitzroy Square, London, on 10 April 1954.   P. J. V. ROLO, *rev.*

Sources T. W. Russell, *Egyptian service* (1949) • private information (1971) • *The Times* (12 April 1954) • Venn, *Alum. Cant.* • *WWW* • Burke, *Peerage* (1969) • *CGPLA Eng. & Wales* (1954)

Archives St Ant. Oxf., Middle East Centre, corresp. and MSS [mainly photocopies]
Likenesses W. Stoneman, photograph, 1949, NPG · J. Ward, oils, 1956 (posthumous), Haileybury and Imperial Service College
Wealth at death £17,608 11s. 7d.: probate, 18 June 1954, CGPLA Eng. & Wales

Russell, (Edward) Walter (1904–1994), soil scientist, was born on 27 October 1904 at 1 Camden Villas, Wye, Kent, the eldest of the five sons and two daughters of Sir (Edward) John *Russell (1872–1965), soil scientist, and his wife, Elnor, née Oldham (1878–1965), daughter of Walter Oldham of Manchester, formerly a merchant of Penang and Singapore, and his wife, Elnor, née Brennand. Russell's father was director of Rothamsted Experimental Station, Harpenden (1912–43), and from 1917 a fellow of the Royal Society. Russell was educated at Oundle School and at Gonville and Caius College, Cambridge, where he studied mathematics and physics. In the mid-1920s his interest turned to soils and he travelled first to Zürich to work with Wiener on the behaviour of clay colloids and then to Georgia to study pedology with Polynov. These early travels set the scene for much of his later work in terms of both the breadth of his study and the international contact he had with leading workers and their research groups.

In 1930 Russell joined the physics department at Rothamsted under the leadership of Bernard Keen and it was there that he undertook the scientific research for which he was best-known. He conducted a series of field investigations into the effects of cultivation, and especially deep ploughing, on soils used for cereal production, and combined these with laboratory studies of the inter-particle forces contributing to soil aggregation. During the Second World War the results were directed towards the saving of tractor fuel, but in many ways the work was ahead of its time. It demonstrated that a major benefit of cultivation was weed control, and when herbicides became more widely available the results laid the basis for the minimum tillage methods and the 'post-green revolution' techniques of no-till.

Russell married (Alice) Margaret Webster (b. 1906/7), daughter of Sir Hugh Calthrop Webster, chartered surveyor and official arbitrator, on 1 July 1933. They had a son, John (b. 1935), and two daughters, Ann (b. 1938) and Sally (b. 1942). Russell travelled widely and was active in the early years of the International Society of Soil Science and in the formation of the British Society of Soil Science, of which he was the first secretary (1947–55).

In 1948 Russell was appointed reader in soil science and fellow of Brasenose College, Oxford, where he devoted his time to the advancement of students. He ran a special course for agricultural cadets in the colonial service and opened his laboratory to students from diverse sciences and countries. Many of these students went on to have distinguished careers. In 1950 Russell published a rewritten version of his father's book, *Soil Conditions and Plant Growth*. This, the eighth edition, while preserving his father's aim of highlighting the importance of soil as a medium for plant growth, brought together much new material gained from Russell's own travels, and from his ability to talk with scientists from a range of disciplines impinging on soils.

In 1955 Russell became director of the East African Agriculture and Forestry Research Organization, working with colonial service scientists in support of the research needs of Kenya, Uganda, and Tanganyika. The scientists were located in scattered, small laboratories, in departments directed by agricultural generalists who were reluctant to commit funds to research. For the high commission Bernard Keen had established research committees which were brought to life by Russell's enthusiasm and ability to win co-operation. From his base at Muguga, Russell worked hard to promote sound scientific research to underpin the agricultural development aspirations in east Africa. For this work he was appointed CMG in 1960. In 1970 he was awarded an honorary doctorate by the University of East Africa.

Russell returned to Britain in 1964 to be the first head of the newly formed department of soil science at Reading University. There he set to with characteristic energy to attract staff and students and to build a strong department (the only one in Britain to survive into the twenty-first century as an independent entity). His interest in the detail of research enthused many of his students and co-workers. He was remembered as a gentleman, treating everyone with kindness and respect, and for asking key questions at the end of seminars despite occasionally appearing to have slept through them. While at Reading he was called on to lecture and advise in many countries, and chaired many committees and advisory groups in the UK. He produced the ninth (1961) and tenth (1973) editions of *Soil Conditions and Plant Growth* before asking his former colleagues in the department (led by Alan Wild) to undertake revisions for the eleventh edition, which appeared as *Russell's Soil Conditions and Plant Growth* in 1988. Russell's percipience in applying a broad base of science to the study of soils allowed the department of soil science at Reading to be both 'the basement of the plant sciences' and the 'attic of the earth sciences' (*Independent*, 17 Nov 1994).

Russell retired as professor of soil science at Reading in 1970, becoming professor emeritus. He died of renal failure at his home, 592 Fox Hollies Road, Hall Green, Birmingham, on 22 October 1994. He was survived by his three children, his wife having predeceased him. A laboratory was named after him at the University of Reading, housing the computational models that summarize current scientific expression of our knowledge of soils.

PETER J. GREGORY

Sources *The Independent* (17 Nov 1994) · *The Times* (1 Nov 1994) · personal knowledge (2004) · private information (2004) [family; Dennis Greenland, Sir Charles Pereira, Alan Wild] · *WWW*, 1991–5 · m. cert. · d. cert.
Likenesses photograph, repro. in *The Independent*
Wealth at death £451,536: probate, 6 Jan 1995, CGPLA Eng. & Wales

Russell, Sir Walter Westley (1867–1949), painter and art teacher, was born on 31 May 1867 at Forest Gate, Essex, the son of William Henry Russell, a bookbinder, and his wife,

Sir Walter Westley Russell (1867–1949), by Ambrose McEvoy

Charlotte Emily Bradley. In his early twenties he studied painting at the Westminster School of Art, London, under Frederick Brown. Like Henry Tonks and other promising students of the period, he gained from Brown a sound training in drawing and painting and an interest in the movement in British art which was influenced by the discoveries of the French impressionists, and was in revolt against the Royal Academy and Victorian conventions.

Russell's early work consisted of illustrations and etchings reminiscent of the work of the illustrators of the 1860s, and of portraits and interiors which he exhibited at the New English Art Club from 1893. He became a member of the club in 1895, and in the same year joined the staff of the Slade School of Fine Art under Brown, who had been appointed Slade professor in 1893. With Tonks and P. Wilson Steer he became one of a team whose teaching had much influence on British painting at that time. He taught as assistant professor at the Slade School until 1927, apart from a period of war service (1916–19) when, as a lieutenant in the Royal Engineers, he worked alongside Leon Underwood in the camouflage corps. He was mentioned in dispatches. In 1900 he married Lydia Burton (1881–1944), daughter of William Nelson Burton, of Wooburn Green, Buckinghamshire; there were no children.

Russell first exhibited at the Royal Academy in 1898. In 1920 he was elected an ARA and in 1926 an RA, and in 1927 he was elected keeper of the Royal Academy. Under the president and council he now became responsible for the schools, at a time of important change in the teaching organization. This was the abolition of the visitor system, whereby members and associates taught on rota for two or three months at a time, and the substitution for it of a permanent teaching staff. Russell in his quiet way was no doubt instrumental in bringing this about, hoping thus to gain greater continuity in teaching and to carry on those principles of teaching learned from Brown and developed so successfully at the Slade School. This was in fact what he was able to do, adding his individual contribution of sound, if somewhat laconic, criticism which, together with his own personal and professional integrity, had a definite influence on his students. On becoming a senior academician he retired from the keepership in 1942.

Meanwhile, Russell worked in his studio at 107 Cheyne Walk, Chelsea, steadily producing portraits, interiors, and landscapes. His portrait of Mr Minney (c.1920, Tate collection) was exhibited at the Royal Academy summer exhibition in 1920, when the humour and pathos of this elderly gentleman in a bulging white waistcoat were noted. In later years Russell was usually represented in the first room of the Royal Academy's exhibition by small paintings of female figures and portraits in domestic settings, such as The Amber Beads (1926) and Cordelia (1930), both of which are in the Tate collection. These paintings are marked by static poses and somewhat blank expressions, but also by his masterly draughtsmanship and a brilliant finish throughout the composition.

Among the earlier paintings Donkeys and Kites (c.1912, Tate collection) was perhaps one of Russell's most important landscapes. In 1926 he painted a series of Venetian scenes, the prelude to an increasing interest in the effect of light on atmosphere. He also painted many landscapes, beach scenes, and seascapes in oil and watercolour, often done at Shoreham by Sea, Sussex, and at Blakeney, Norfolk, which he visited in the summer with Sir William Llewellyn, then president of the academy. These paintings are mostly very light in tone, the oils somewhat resembling watercolours, and reminiscent of Steer. Many of Russell's best watercolours were shown at the exhibitions of the Society of Painters in Water Colours, of which he was made a member in 1930. He was appointed a trustee of the National Gallery in 1927 and of the Tate Gallery in 1934; in 1931 he was appointed CVO and in 1935 was knighted. Five of his pictures in the Tate collection were purchased out of the Chantrey bequest, and he is represented in the Hugh Lane Municipal Gallery of Modern Art, Dublin, the Walker Art Gallery, Liverpool, and other public and corporate collections. He died on 16 April 1949 at his home, 4 Pembroke Road, Kensington, London.

W. T. MONNINGTON, rev. BEN WHITWORTH

Sources C. H. Collins-Baker, 'The paintings of Walter W. Russell', The Studio, 50 (1910), 171–8 · M. C. Salaman, 'The art of Walter W. Russell', The Studio, 83 (1922), 80–88 · WW (1938) · A. Jarman and others, eds., Royal Academy exhibitors, 1905–1970: a dictionary of artists and their work in the summer exhibitions of the Royal Academy of Arts, 5 (1981) · Graves, RA exhibitors, vol. 3 · archive material, Courtauld Inst., Witt Library · Index to registers of births and deaths, Family

Record Centre · *CGPLA Eng. & Wales* (1949) · *The Times* (22 April 1949) · personal knowledge (1959)
Likenesses G. C. Beresford, photographs, 1922, NPG · A. McEvoy, watercolour drawing, RA [*see illus.*]
Wealth at death £13,860 12s. 1d.: probate, 7 Oct 1949, *CGPLA Eng. & Wales*

Russell, William (*d.* 1374), abbot of Rushen and bishop of Sodor and Man, was a native Manxman. Russell was for about eighteen years abbot of the Cistercian foundation Rushen Abbey, the premier religious house on the Isle of Man. In 1348 he was elected bishop of Sodor and Man by the clergy of Man in St German's Cathedral, Peel. He cemented his position by gaining papal provision to the diocese of Sodor and Man, and was consecrated at Avignon by Bertrand, cardinal-bishop of Ostia by 6 May 1349.

The writer of the episcopal list, which is appended to the chronicle of the kings of Sodor and Man and the Isles, states, mistakenly, that Russell was consecrated by Pope Clement VI in person and claims, again mistakenly, that all his predecessors had been confirmed and consecrated by the archbishop of Nidaros, Norway (the metropolitan).

Unfortunately, it is impossible to evaluate the power of the Norwegian metropolitan over the diocese of Sodor and Man, because the Norwegian records have been lost. It is notable, however, that although the papal camera informed Arno, archbishop of Nidaros, of the appointment of Russell as bishop of Sodor and Man, Pope Clement VI granted Russell exemption from undertaking the perilous sea voyage to pay obedience to his metropolitan in person.

The diocese of Sodor and Man had suffered badly during the Anglo-Scottish wars. In 1349 Pope Clement VI allowed Russell to encumber himself and the Sodor church with a mortgage of 1200 gold florins, to claim and receive the majority of the goods and debts of his predecessor, Bishop Thomas, and promised a charitable subsidy in support of his diocese. Despite these favours, Russell was late in paying his common and petty services to the apostolic chamber. In 1363 he complained to Pope Urban V that his cathedral church and its precincts had been occupied as a fortress, that the bishops had greatly suffered, and that divine services had ceased. As in 1349, he received papal dispensation to consecrate eight illiterate persons to benefices, because so few literate persons were to be found on account of the wars.

At its fullest extent, the diocese of Sodor and Man included the Outer Hebrides, the Inner Hebrides (excluding Lismore, Kerrera, Seil, Luing, and the Cumbraes), and the Isle of Man. The scant evidence for Russell's episcopate relates mainly to his activities in Man, emphasizing the rift between the Hebrides and Man, which culminated in the division of the diocese between two bishops in 1387.

The synodal statutes attributed to Russell in three interrelated manuscripts of the sixteenth and seventeenth centuries are described as being made on 23 February 1351 by Russell and all the clergy of Man, but no mention is made of the Hebrides. The six chapters relate to keeping order in the parishes and churches, and to the duty of the clergy to expound the Catholic faith to the laity. The statutes stipulate that the laity should be persuaded to learn the apostolic creed in their mother tongue which, in the mid-fourteenth century, was probably Manx Gaelic.

William Russell died on 21 April 1374 at Ramshead in Lancashire and was buried at the monastery of Furness, the mother house of Rushen Abbey.

EMMA CHRISTIAN

Sources E. B. Fryde and others, eds., *Handbook of British chronology*, 3rd edn, Royal Historical Society Guides and Handbooks, 2 (1986) · A. W. Moore, *Sodor and Man* (1895) · J. Dowden, *The bishops of Scotland ... prior to the Reformation*, ed. J. M. Thomson (1912) · G. Broderick, ed. and trans., *Cronica regum Mannie et Insularum / Chronicles of the kings of Man and the Isles* (1979) · P. A. Munch and A. Goss, eds., *Chronicon regum Manniae et Insularum / The chronicle of Man and the Sudreys*, 2 vols., Manx Society, 22–3 (1859–1907)
Archives BL, Cotton MS Julius A.vii, fols. 50*r*–52*r* · Bodl. Oxf., Add. MS C 64 (SC 28419), fols. 55*r*–57*r*, 58*r*–66*v*, 113*r*–116*r* · Gon. & Caius Cam., MS 793, pp. 53–79 · Manx Museum, Douglas, Isle of Man, MS 2042A, fols. 1*r*–10*v*

Russell, William, first Baron Russell of Thornhaugh (*c.*1553–1613), lord deputy of Ireland, was born at Chenies, Buckinghamshire, the fourth son of Francis *Russell, second earl of Bedford (1526/7–1585), administrator, and his first wife, Margaret (*d.* 1562), daughter of Sir John St John, of Bletsoe, Bedfordshire, and his wife, Margaret. His elder brothers, Edward (*d.* 1573), John (*d.* 1584), and Francis (*d.* 1585), were, successively, Lord Russell. He had three younger sisters, including Margaret (1560–1616), who married George Clifford, third earl of Cumberland. He was much influenced by his tutor at Magdalen College, Oxford, the Calvinist divine Dr Laurence Humphrey, but did not graduate. He continued his education by travelling through Europe between 1575 and 1579. The University of Oxford did not confer the degree of MA on him until July 1595. His father settled much land on him while young, including the manor of Thornhaugh in Northamptonshire.

Service in Ireland and the Netherlands, 1580–1594 Russell was elected MP for Fowey, Cornwall, in 1572 (a seat controlled by his father), and probably attended the first session of parliament. He was appointed a gentleman pensioner from about 1572 to 1593 or 1596. Shortly after his return to England in 1579 he was sent to Ireland. He was given command of a company of recruits raised by the clergy in October 1580 to help contain the rebellion led by James Eustace, Viscount Baltinglass, and Feagh McHugh O'Byrne, the firebrand of the Wicklow Mountains. Their forces had already routed those of Arthur Grey, fourteenth Lord Grey of Wilton, the lord deputy, at Glenmalure on 20 August 1580. On 4 April 1581 Russell and the soldier of fortune Sir William Stanley made a spirited incursion into O'Byrne's lands and succeeded in burning down his house at Ballinacor and slaughtering some of his followers. Russell's first services in Ireland brought rewards; he got the lease of Baltinglass Abbey, co. Wicklow, and its manors in co. Carlow. Russell was licensed to return to England on 4 September and was knighted by Grey on 10 September.

In November 1581 Russell performed a joust and tilt

before Elizabeth I on the occasion of the courting visit of Francis Valoris, duc d'Alençon. His career is uncertain for the next three or four years. On 13 February 1585 he married Elizabeth (d. 1611), daughter and heir of Henry Long, of Shingay, Cambridgeshire, and his wife, Dorothy, at Watford, Northamptonshire. This marriage brought more land in Cambridgeshire, Bedfordshire, and Hertfordshire, and Russell acquired yet more in Buckinghamshire and Northamptonshire at the death of his brother Francis. He was now a substantial gentleman. Russell wrote a reform tract on how Ireland should be governed, advocating force and strength and that 'the sword be bent naked over their heads' (BL, Cotton MS Titus B, xii, fol. 352r).

Robert Dudley, earl of Leicester, gave Russell his first major appointment as lieutenant-general of horse in his Netherlands campaign in December 1585. Russell's military reputation was enhanced by outstanding valour in the battlefield. In April 1586 he returned to England to raise a band of horse. He led these reinforcements in the engagement at Warnsfeld before the prolonged skirmish at Zutphen on 22 September 1586. Russell seems to have led the attack, despite being hopelessly outnumbered by highly professional Spanish tercios, or infantry, and 'charged so terribly that after he had broke his lance, he with his curtle-axe so played his part that the enemy reputed him a devil and no man' (M. W. Wallace, *Life of Sir Philip Sidney*, 1915, 379). In token of his comradeship Sir Philip Sidney bequeathed Russell his best gilt suit of armour; Russell also succeeded Sidney as governor of the cautionary town of Flushing on 1 February 1587. In June he was able to get supplies through to Sluys, which Messandro Farnese, duke of Parma, was about to blockade, which proved vital to the relief force. Russell continued to serve effectively until 1589 and supported the anti-Spanish, anti-Catholic cause fervently. However, in December 1587 he was censured by the states general for supporting the citizens of Campveer and Arnemuyden, who wished to put themselves under the protection of Elizabeth. His critics argue that his support for Leicester was a cloak for his ambition to be the governor of Walcheren. Russell denied personal ambition. That he was considered a satisfactory governor of Flushing is attested to by the clamour of the protestant churches in the Netherlands for him to be continued in his post when Leicester's successor, Peregrine Bertie, Lord Willoughby de Eresby, tried to oust him. Despite great difficulties, such as inadequate payments for his garrison at Flushing, mutiny was prevented by Russell, who paid out of his own pocket.

While he was governor of Flushing, Russell's close associates in England were Leicester and Sir Francis Walsingham, principal secretary. He asked Walsingham to be godfather to his son in 1587. He made many pleas to Leicester and Walsingham for money, support, and provisions and, as his difficulties mounted, it was to them that he begged to be recalled from a post 'wherein I neither reap profit, honour nor content' (HoP, *Commons, 1558–1603*, 310). He vainly hoped to be appointed master of the ordnance, an office long held by his brother-in-law Ambrose Dudley, earl of Warwick. He returned to the life of a country

gentleman on his recall from Flushing in June 1589. He had been appointed JP for Northamptonshire about 1586, and he was named of the quorum for Cambridgeshire and Middlesex about 1592. His second surviving son and eventual successor, Francis *Russell, second Baron Russell of Thornhaugh and fourth earl of Bedford (*bap.* 1587, *d.* 1641), was born in 1593.

Lord deputy of Ireland, 1594–1597 Russell was appointed lord deputy of Ireland on 16 May 1594 and sworn in on 11 August. He was selected because of his extensive military experience, previous knowledge of Ireland, connections, and wealth. He assumed the government of Ireland at a crucial phase as Hugh O'Neill, second earl of Tyrone, and his confederates were well set on all-out rebellion. Russell found that the widespread discontent in Ulster was spreading 'to the peril of the whole realm' (*Calendar of Carew MSS*, 3.92–5). Russell had no detailed knowledge of Ireland and, with the deaths of Leicester and Walsingham, was devoid of powerful friends at court. Although a soldier was once again at the head of Irish affairs, Russell was overshadowed by the presence of Sir John Norris, president of Munster and the most experienced English military commander of the age. His appointment as general-in-chief of all the Irish forces became a rival threat to the authority of the new lord deputy, and the two men became mutually and overtly antagonistic. However, within days of assuming office Russell was astonished by Tyrone's arrival in Dublin on 15 August to tender humble submission and promise to restore peace. Despite Tyrone's enemies accusing him of treason, Russell and the Irish privy council permitted him to return home in safety. The decision earned them a severe public censure from the queen and a private letter reproaching Russell; she wrote, 'no one has more forgotten or mistaken our directions than you have done … we enjoined you not to dismiss the Earl [O'Neill] if he once came to you till our pleasure were known' (*Calendar of Carew MSS*, 3.101). Nevertheless, Russell could not be accused of inaction, for within a week of arriving in Ireland he set out in person on 18 August, leading a force of about 1000 infantry and 200 cavalry to relieve the garrison at Enniskillen, co. Fermanagh, then under siege, where he arrived on 30 August. Ten days later he returned to Dublin via Cavan, where he strengthened the garrison and complained that there were too many Irish employed, 'these garrison bands being in effect the strength of the realm, so long as they were continued English' (PRO, SP 63/176/11). Realizing how Tyrone had duped him, Russell tried in vain to get him to come to Dublin by promising, perhaps disingenuously, a truce. By December, despite opposition from members of the Irish privy council, he decided against all temporizing with the rebels and wanted a vigorous military policy, including substantial reinforcements. To his chagrin, the queen responded to his request for a military subordinate by appointing Norris, with a special patent which gave him independent military control in Ulster. Russell resented what was virtually a co-ordinate authority and equal pay. At a delicate juncture in negotiations with the Gaelic chiefs these squabbles within the English leadership in Ireland were exploited by Tyrone.

Meanwhile O'Byrne was dealt with. On 16 January 1595 Russell, ostensibly on a hunting journey into Wicklow, attacked his headquarters at Ballinacor. The result was the same as it had been fourteen years previously—while possession was taken of the house the occupants escaped into the glens and recesses of Dromkitt. Russell continued to pursue him for two and a half years and the fighting in the Wicklow hills was vicious. O'Byrne's wife, Rose O'Toole, was captured and sentenced to be burnt, yet she was kept alive. Eventually, on 8 May 1597 O'Byrne was betrayed and killed. This action temporarily quelled disorder in the south.

Russell's obsession to quell the Wicklow rebels meant that affairs in the north became more threatening, and Tyrone's victory at Clontibret, co. Monaghan, against Sir Henry Bagenal's forces in June 1595 shocked him into a combined set of operations, with Norris setting out for Newry. Russell advanced to Armagh and set up a garrison there, before marching on to relieve Monaghan. He then withdrew his forces to the pale and watched the situation in Connaught, where Sir Richard Bingham, his forceful commander in the west, was hard pressed by Hugh Roe O'Donnell and the Mayo Burkes. By leaving Norris in charge of the war in Ulster, the divided command exposed the weakness of the state against the now confident confederate rebels and paralysed the government. Tyrone was convinced that any further peace proposals to Russell would be treated with understandable contempt, as indeed they were in August 1596, and was aware that Norris and Sir Geoffrey Fenton were overcoming the other rebels through setting one against another and by seeking accommodation with one, while attacking another. This attitude only increased the lord deputy's difficulties as the warfare become desultory. Russell set out for Connaught in November and was received in state in Galway. At Athlone, co. Westmeath, he sat in council to deliberate on the host of complaints against Bingham's vigorous prosecution of the war—of which Russell approved. He sensibly made a short-lived truce with the Burkes and returned to Dublin before Christmas. In March of the same year the Mayo Burkes with their Scottish mercenaries laid waste lands east of the Shannon, taking over lands belonging to the family of MacCoughlan and Cloughan Castle. Russell repulsed them and recovered the castle. To his great annoyance Norris managed to secure the English government's approval of yet another truce with Tyrone and, even more galling to him, got them to recall his supporter Bingham. Norris then openly protested at Russell's pursuit of the O'Byrnes in Wicklow, claiming that this would endanger the safety of the entire realm. Russell was getting bogged down in Irish politics and warfare. Richard Beacon acted as his mentor in Ireland, writing in his allegorical treatise on reform, *Solon his Follie*, in 1594, that pretence of madness was necessary to govern Ireland effectively. From the queen's and privy council's standpoint neither war nor peace was being properly managed in Ireland. Thus they wisely decided to replace Russell with Thomas Burgh, Lord Burgh, and temporarily removed Norris; both in any case wanted to be out of Ireland.

Final years, 1597–1613 Burgh took up the lord deputyship on 22 May 1597, and Russell returned home to the London residence of his nephew, Edward Russell, third earl of Bedford, Bedford House, 'very fat, they say, both in body and purse' (*Letters of John Chamberlain*, 1.30). In writing to Sir Robert Cecil, principal secretary, and the privy council on 25 June he expressed his worries that he was 'tormented on being denied the queen's presence for whose services I have ever wished to sacrifice my best endeavours'. He confided to Cecil that he had written to the queen, as William Cecil, Lord Burghley, the lord treasurer, had advised, 'and sent unsealed by my sister [countess of Cumberland] to show to you' (*Salisbury MSS*, 7.269–70). He did not return to England with any new appointment pending. He was an unsuccessful contender with Sir Robert Sidney for the vacant governorship of Berwick, a post held by Russell's father in the 1560s. Furthermore he failed in his bid against Sir Walter Ralegh for the governorship of Jersey.

It is surprising that as late as 1603 the privy council consulted Russell on Irish affairs. However, in summer 1599, a time of threatened Spanish invasion, he put forward a practical resistance plan and was duly appointed commander of the forces in the western counties. At the same time he was made a freeman of the town and county of Southampton. Russell's bellicosity was unabated; he wrote to Cecil in August that year:

> My desire and affection flieth, but my body is massy, but if I may reach those insolent beggars [the Spaniards] either upon their landing or presently after, I will give my dear Sovereign such an account of our day's service as hath not been performed in the kingdom of England. (*Salisbury MSS*, 9.339)

Russell's remaining years were spent at Northall in Buckinghamshire. His last public appearances were the entertainment of the queen at his house in Chiswick, Middlesex, in September 1602, his creation as Baron Russell of Thornhaugh, Northamptonshire, by James VI and I on 21 July 1603, and his attendance at the funeral of Henry, prince of Wales, on 5 November 1612. It is said that Russell avoided the Jacobean court on account of its immorality and waste, especially of public money, and that he had hoped Henry would restore virtue and good government had he lived.

In his will made in October 1612, Russell affirmed his Calvinism. He died at Northall, on 9 August 1613. He made many generous bequests to his relatives but also to the poor of Thornhaugh, Northall, and Chiswick and gave three years' wages to all his servants. His only surviving son, Francis, was his successor and chief beneficiary. Russell was buried in the church at Thornhaugh in a tomb he had built for himself. While none can question his personal bravery as a soldier in the Netherlands and in Ireland or the efficient administration of his government of Flushing, his term of office as lord deputy of Ireland is considered among the least satisfactory of the century.

J. J. N. McGURK

Sources J. S. Brewer and W. Bullen, eds., *Calendar of the Carew manuscripts*, 3: *1589–1600*, PRO (1869), 95–187, 220–60 [Russell's journal in Ireland] · *CSP Ire.*, *1592–99* · *Calendar of the manuscripts of the most hon. the marquis of Salisbury*, 24 vols., HMC, 9 (1883–1976), vols. 3–4 · 'Calendar of fiants, Henry VIII to Elizabeth', *Report of the Deputy Keeper of the Public Records in Ireland*, 7–22 (1875–90), appxs, nos. 3745, 5879, 5891, 5938, 6054, 5896, 5898, 5900 (6103–6105 n.d.) · J. H. Wiffen, *Historical memoirs of the house of Russell*, 2 vols. (1833) · R. Bagwell, *Ireland under the Tudors*, 3 vols. (1885–90); repr. (1963), 242–79 · *APC*, *1588–9* · G. Parker, *The army of Flanders and the Spanish road* (1972) · G. Scott-Thomson, *Two centuries of family history* (1930) · W. T. MacCaffrey, *Elizabeth I: war and politics, 1588–1603* (1992) · *The letters of John Chamberlain*, ed. N. E. McClure, 1 (1939) · H. Morgan, *Tyrone's rebellion: the outbreak of the Nine Years' War in Tudor Ireland*, Royal Historical Society Studies in History, 67 (1993), 179–87 · C. O'Brien, ed., *Feagh McHugh O'Byrne, the Wicklow firebrand*, Rathdrum Historical Society (1998) · I. Cassidy, 'Russell, William', HoP, *Commons, 1558–1603* · *AFM*, 6.1955, 1989, 2019

Archives Beds. & Luton ARS, deeds and estate MSS; title deeds, manorial records, and estate MSS · BL, arms of knights created by him as lord deputy, Harley MS 1386, fol. 100 · BL, MSS, Egerton MSS 2713–2722 · BL, transcripts of MSS, Add. MS 4728, fols. 4–113 · LPL, journal relating to his governorship of Ireland · Som. ARS, MSS relating to Ireland, Carew of Crowcombe MSS DD/TB/56/51/8 · Woburn Abbey, Bedfordshire, papers as lord deputy of Ireland | BL, reform treatise to the privy council relating to Ireland, MS Cotton Titus B xii, 347–352 · LPL, Bacon MSS 647–662, esp. MS 651, MSS 655–656

Likenesses attrib. G. Gower, oils, *c*.1580, Woburn Abbey, Bedfordshire · portrait, *c*.1580, NG Ire. · oils, *c*.1588, Woburn Abbey, Bedfordshire · G. P. Harding, watercolour (after portrait, *c*.1580) · portrait (the Woburn Abbey painting), priv. coll. · print (after watercolour by G. P. Harding), NG Ire.; repro. in G. P. Harding, *Ancient historical pictures* (1844)

Wealth at death bequests incl. best horse and sword to nephew, three years' wages to servants, jewels and plate to sister, nieces, and cousins; also £10 each to the poor of Thornhaugh, Northall, and Chiswick: Cassidy, 'Russell, William'; Wiffen, *Historical memoirs*, 2.89–93; *VCH Northamptonshire*, 1.419–20, 2.532

Russell, Sir William, first baronet (*c*.1575–1654), merchant and naval administrator, was, as evidence submitted by him to chancery suggests, born about 1575, the eldest of the five sons of William Russell (*d*. 1591) of Egham, Surrey, and Joan Saunders. A slender inheritance comprising a property in Windsor and £20 in cash undoubtedly inclined him towards a mercantile career. He was in Russia during the 'time of troubles', apparently as an agent for the Dutch, and left Moscow in March 1605, subsequently writing a short account of the overthrow of Boris Godunov entitled *The Reporte of a Bloodie and Terrible Massacre in the Citty of Mosco*, which was published anonymously in London (1607). In 1605 he joined the Levant Company, and was appointed an executor of the will of Sir Francis Cherry, a leading London merchant who died that April and whose daughter Elizabeth (*bap*. 1588) he later married. On 21 October 1609 he was sworn a freeman of the East India Company, having first bought up the shares formerly held by Cherry, and by the following year he was a member of the Russia Company, supplying cordage to the navy. In July 1612 he was appointed a director of the newly formed North-West Passage Company. On 19 April 1613 he and his brother-in-law John Merrick were appointed special ambassadors to Russia, their embassy lasting until the following autumn. He became a director of the

East India Company on 5 July 1615, but in 1617–18 he sold stock in the company, presumably to help finance his purchase of the treasurership of the navy from Sir Robert Mansell in April 1618. He was dignified with a knighthood on 29 April, and formally appointed to office on 10 May, but his membership of the Navy Board was abruptly ended in the following November, when the board was suspended for maladministration. Russell himself was beyond reproach and was permitted to continue as treasurer, but until April 1625 he was excluded from membership of the navy commission, which assumed the board's executive functions.

Russell and his first wife had no children and she died some time before 1618. By that time Russell owned the Cambridgeshire manor of Chippenham, and had married Elizabeth (*d*. 1626), daughter of Thomas Gerard of Burwell, Cambridgeshire; they had six sons and three daughters. In 1622 and 1623 Russell was recommended by the king to the ailing Virginia Company, but on neither occasion was he elected its treasurer. Around the same time he withdrew from the Russia Company after losing confidence in its management. In April 1625 he was recommended for election to parliament as member for New Windsor by the lord admiral, who mentioned that he had been born not far from the borough, but his nomination was received too late. However, New Windsor returned him to the second Caroline parliament (1626).

Russell's finances were stretched to breaking point by the outbreak of war with Spain in 1625. By April he had raised more than £34,000 to meet the cost of naval preparations, but a near-empty exchequer meant that he was not speedily reimbursed, although he was promised £3000 in addition to the customary interest, and was granted (with his brother Killiphet) the farm of the impositions on silk for life (14 May). On 15 July he complained that 'I am already too deeply engaged', and he warned that 'if I can get fairly off this time I shall be well advised hereafter how I come in' (*Cowper MSS*, 207). Over the winter of 1626–7 his London residence in Tower Street was besieged by mobs of unpaid sailors, who on one occasion broke down his gate 'and would have plucked him out by the ears had he not given them fair words' (Birch and Williams, 1.175). Fearing for his safety, perhaps, he subsequently surrendered his patent to Sir Sackville Crowe (5 April 1627). Crowe's slender resources meant that he continued to bankroll the navy, however, most notably in February 1628 when he furnished it with more than £95,500 to pay off arrears. Moreover, he remained an active member of the navy commission until its dissolution in February 1628.

On 12 April 1628 Russell married thirdly Elizabeth, the widow of John Wheatley of Catsfield, Sussex, and coheir of Michael Smallpage of Pevensey, Sussex; they had two sons. He purchased a baronetcy on 19 January 1629. One year later, with the end of the Spanish war in sight, he returned to office as treasurer of the navy on improved financial terms. Once again he proved his value as a banker. In 1633, for instance, he advanced more than £30,000 to help clear the navy's wartime debts. However, he was increasingly afflicted by gout, and by the beginning of 1639 his hands and feet were so affected that the younger Henry Vane was appointed as co-treasurer. Russell's wealth and credit nevertheless remained an essential element of naval finance, and therefore the House of Commons was dismayed in March 1641 when Russell proved reluctant to advance the sum of £20,000 to meet the navy's immediate needs. An angry Sir Simonds D'Ewes contrasted the disrepair of the navy with those who had 'gotten their heads to be crowned with coronets and have in a short space heaped up vast estates' (*Journal*, ed. Notestein, 499–500).

Russell reverted to his former position as sole treasurer following Vane's dismissal in December 1641. He seems to have been briefly imprisoned by the king in January 1642, but on the outbreak of civil war he was regarded with disdain by parliament, which appointed Vane as sole navy treasurer on 8 August 1642. Four days later the king conferred the treasurership jointly on Russell and Sir John Penington, but Russell probably avoided active involvement with the royalist cause, as his estates were never sequestrated. In 1645 he and other members of the New Barbary Company, which had been established in 1638, petitioned the House of Lords for stay of execution in a sentence obtained against them in the admiralty court. He died intestate early in 1654, and was buried at Chippenham on 3 February. A monument in his memory was erected in Burwell parish church in 1663. He was succeeded by his heir Francis, his son by his second marriage, who served as an MP in the 1640s and 1650s. Francis's son, John, married Oliver Cromwell's daughter, Frances, and his daughter Elizabeth married Henry Cromwell. Russell must be distinguished from Sir William Russell, bt, of Strensham, sheriff of Worcestershire in 1643 and royalist governor of Worcester during the civil war, who died on 30 November 1669.   ANDREW THRUSH

Sources CSP dom., 1611–43 · APC, 1618–31 · The manuscripts of the Earl Cowper, 3 vols., HMC, 23 (1888–9), vols. 1–2 · Sixth report, HMC, 5 (1877–8), 86 · CSP col., vol. 2 · The letters of John Chamberlain, ed. N. E. McClure, 2 (1939), 158, 161 · Rymer, Foedera, 3rd edn, 8/1.9–10 · Sir Thomas Smithe's voiage and entertainment in Rushia (1605) · G. M. Bell, A handlist of British diplomatic representatives, 1509–1688, Royal Historical Society Guides and Handbooks, 16 (1990), 224 · J. Turrim, 'Noticeable entries in the parish registers of Allhallows, Barking', N&Q, 3rd ser., 2 (1862), 423–5, esp. 424 · PRO, PROB 11/77, fol. 372 [father's will] · PRO, PROB 11/105, fol. 270 [Sir Francis Cherry's will] · [T. Birch and R. F. Williams], eds., The court and times of Charles the First, 1 (1848), 175 · The journal of Sir Simonds D'Ewes from the beginning of the Long Parliament to the opening of the trial of the earl of Strafford, ed. W. Notestein (1923), 499–500 · W. H. Black, ed., Docquets of letters patent (1837), 334 · N. Dews, The history of Deptford (1883), 931 · J. Burke and J. B. Burke, A genealogical and heraldic history of the extinct and dormant baronetcies of England, Ireland, and Scotland (1838), 455–6 · T. K. Rabb, Enterprise and empire: merchant and gentry investment in the expansion of England, 1575–1630 (1967), 369 · W. A. Shaw, The knights of England, 2 (1906), 168 · PRO, C24/595/22, fol. 22 · PRO, C24/601/pt 1, no. 83, fol. 63 · PRO, C24/565/4, fol. 14 · PRO, C24/638/pt 1, no. 13, fol. 8 · S. M. Kingsbury, ed., The records of the Virginia Company of London, 2 (1906), 28; 4 (1935), 90 · The visitation of London, anno Domini 1633, 1634, and 1635, made by Sir Henry St George, 2, ed. J. J. Howard, Harleian Society, 17 (1883) · M. Jansson and W. B. Bidwell, eds., Proceedings in parliament, 1625 (1987), 694 · 'Russell, Sir William', HoP, Commons [draft] · R. Ashton, 'The disbursing official under the early Stuarts', BIHR, 30 (1957), 162–74 · GEC, Baronetage

Likenesses M. Gheeraerts, oils, 1625, Woburn Abbey, Bedfordshire

Russell, William, first duke of Bedford (1616–1700), politician, was born in August 1616, the eldest son of Francis *Russell, second Baron Russell of Thornhaugh, and later fourth earl of Bedford (*bap.* 1587, *d.* 1641), and his wife, Catharine (*c.*1589–1657), daughter and coheir of Giles *Brydges, third Baron Chandos [*see under* Brydges, Edmund]. He was created a knight of the Bath at Charles I's coronation in February 1626 and, according to Clarendon, attended Magdalen College, Oxford. In or about 1635 he travelled to Madrid, where he hoped to learn Spanish, but had returned to England by 11 July 1637 when he married Anne (1615–1684), the sole heir of Robert *Carr, earl of Somerset (1585/6?–1645). William's father's opposition to the match was overcome only by the provision of a £12,000 dowry for his new daughter-in-law. The marriage itself was to be a fruitful one, producing eleven children.

Russell followed his father's example in the crisis preceding the outbreak of civil war, siding with the king's opponents. He represented the family borough of Tavistock in both the Short and Long parliaments; John Pym was the borough's other member. Russell made little impact in the lower house, for his stay there was brief. In April 1641 he served on a conference committee charged with preparing a list of grievances for the king. Only a month later his father died unexpectedly of smallpox, translating Russell to the Lords as fifth earl of Bedford. Although he was still comparatively young at twenty-four, parliament gave Bedford considerable responsibility. He was named as a commissioner to treat with the king in Scotland in August 1641 (though he never served). More significantly, parliament awarded him the lord lieutenancy of the important counties of Devon and Somerset in February and March 1642. In July that year he assumed command of parliament's horse, and in September he led a campaign against the marquess of Hertford in the west. Hertford, attempting with little success to raise royalist troops, was poorly prepared to defend himself against Bedford's 3300 men, but nevertheless parliament's forces performed badly. Bedford complained that nearly half of his men had deserted, and that the rest were disobedient cowards: 'If a bullet come over their heads they fall flat on their bellies' (Tenth Report, HMC, 147). Hertford escaped and Bedford returned to London, where he endured criticism for his lacklustre generalship.

Bedford's failure in the west and the enmity of some of the more radical parliamentarians such as Henry Marten seem to have impelled him to rethink his political position. Though he fought with Essex at Edgehill on 23 October 1642, by the summer of 1643 he had allied himself with the earls of Holland and Clare, advocates of a settlement with the king. In early August, Lord General Essex rejected the advice of the peace party, and Bedford acted. He joined Charles I at Oxford, and the king pardoned him for his offences. He fought with the royalists at the siege of Gloucester and the battle of Newbury on 20 September, but he was soon dissatisfied with his new colleagues. Some royalists distrusted Bedford, and while the king himself welcomed him to his side, his place in Charles's counsels was a minor one at best. Disillusioned, in December 1643 he wrote to the speaker of the House of Lords explaining his desertion as an attempt at personal negotiation with the king. As that effort had failed, he said, he asked for parliament's forgiveness. He was gaoled briefly, but parliament soon relented and ended the sequestration of his estates in July 1644. But Bedford's brief career as a royalist ensured that his parliamentarian fellows no longer fully trusted him, and they refused him permission to return to his seat in the Lords. Several attempts failed—on one occasion, in February 1647, by a single vote. In May 1647, after another fruitless effort, Lord Willoughby of Parham summed up the feelings of the house. Arguing against Bedford's readmission he said that the earl deserved no favours, 'having deserted us … when we were in our lowest condition, and' having 'lately before taken an oath not to do anything against the Parliament' (*De L'Isle and Dudley MSS*, 6.566). In any case, the increasingly radical course of the army and parliament alienated Bedford, who withdrew to his estate at Woburn. Although he took the engagement in 1650 he played no important political role during the interregnum. He avoided royalist conspiracy and concentrated upon maintaining his estate. He oversaw the completion of his father's massive fen drainage project, the Bedford level, a work that sparked resistance and riots in 1653.

Described as a leader of the presbyterian faction Bedford resumed his seat in the Lords on 25 April 1660. Cavaliers suspected him of a desire to impose conditions upon Charles II's restoration, a scheme which failed in any event. Bedford was never close to the court during Charles II's reign, even though he bore the sceptre at the coronation. The king made an effort to win him over in the run-up to the Third Anglo-Dutch War: in 1671 he named him governor of Plymouth, and on 29 May 1672, the day after the battle of Sole Bay, he was elected a knight of the Garter. In 1673 he was a joint commissioner of the office of earl marshal, but the failure of the king's overtures to dissenters ended his courtship of Bedford.

Although Bedford attended his parish church he also maintained a presbyterian chaplain, and his wife was arrested at a conventicle in London in March 1675. There was little likelihood that he would fall in with Danby's plan to establish a royalist Anglican dominance in the state, and from 1675 Bedford was in opposition. He allied himself with Shaftesbury during the battle over exclusion, but his enthusiasm for confrontation was limited. In December 1679 he joined ten peers in petitioning Charles for a new parliament, but claimed illness when his colleagues went to court to present the document. In November 1680 he was on a committee that drafted a protestant association bill, and in January 1681 he and twenty-five other exclusionists petitioned against assembling parliament in Oxford.

The king turned his hand against Bedford in 1682 when the family borough of Tavistock lost its charter, but worse was to come. The earl's son and heir, William *Russell, Lord Russell, was ensnared in the Rye House plot in 1683. Although Bedford allegedly offered the duchess of Portsmouth £50,000 to use her influence to save his son, Charles was implacable, and Russell went to the block on 21 July 1683. This bitter blow caused Bedford once more to retire temporarily from politics.

The earl did not re-emerge until after the revolution of 1688. He once again carried the sceptre, at the coronation of William and Mary, and in February 1689 joined the privy council. He replaced his Jacobite rival, the second earl of Ailesbury, as lord lieutenant of Bedfordshire, and was also lieutenant of Cambridgeshire, and of Middlesex from 1692. Bedford allegedly declined the offer of a dukedom in 1692, but accepted one in May 1694, when he became first duke of Bedford, and also marquess of Tavistock; in the following year he was also created Baron Howland of Streatham.

In William and Mary's reign Bedford's political importance was greater than ever, but he was never a politician of the first rank. He remained keenly interested in advancing his estate, which by 1700 was very substantial indeed; his grandson and heir calculated the first duke's income at some £20,000 per annum. In addition to his country estates Bedford continued to develop his London property and invested in overseas trade.

Ailesbury, who was no great admirer of the duke, but a good judge of character, described him as

> a graceful old nobleman, and his outside was all. He always had lived to himself, and his company in the summers were only his relations from London, or else wh[ere] and sometimes some lords and gentlemen, lovers of bowling and cards, for about a week, but few or none of the country gentlemen ever went thither … This lord had no interest in the county [Bedfordshire] but what was called the Presbyterian one; he went to the Parish church on Sunday morning, but had a Presbyterian chaplain, and no common prayer in his chapel. (*Memoirs of … Ailesbury*, 1.182)

Bedford died on 7 September 1700 aged eighty-four at his London home, Bedford House in the Strand, and was buried on 17 September at Chenies, Buckinghamshire. His wife had predeceased him, dying in 1684, and he was succeeded as second duke by his grandson, Wriothesley Russell.   VICTOR STATER

Sources GEC, *Peerage* · N. Luttrell, *A brief historical relation of state affairs from September 1678 to April 1714*, 1–3 (1857) · Clarendon, *Hist. rebellion* · G. S. Thomson, *The Russells in Bloomsbury, 1669–1771* (1940) · *Memoirs of Thomas, earl of Ailesbury*, ed. W. E. Buckley, 1, Roxburghe Club, 122 (1890), 182 · *Calendar of the manuscripts of the marquess of Ormonde*, new ser., 8 vols., HMC, 36 (1902–20), vol. 4, p. 566 · *Tenth report*, HMC (1885); repr. (1906), 147 · *Report on the manuscripts of Lord De L'Isle and Dudley*, 6, HMC, 77 (1966), 476, 562–63, 566 · *The memoirs of Anne, Lady Halkett and Ann, Lady Fanshawe*, ed. J. Loftis (1979), 113 · *Report on the manuscripts of his grace the duke of Buccleuch and Queensberry … preserved at Montagu House*, 3 vols. in 4, HMC, 45 (1899–1926), vol. 1, p. 321 · *The manuscripts of his grace the duke of Portland*, 10 vols., HMC, 29 (1891–1931), vol. 3, p. 481

Archives V&A NAL, household bills · Woburn Abbey, Bedfordshire, papers

Likenesses J. Priwitzer, oils, 1627, Woburn Abbey, Bedfordshire · A. Van Dyck, double portrait, oils, *c*.1633 (with second earl of Bristol), Althorp, Northamptonshire · P. Lely, oils, 1676, Woburn Abbey, Bedfordshire · J. Kerseboom, oils, *c*.1685, Hardwick Hall,

Derbyshire · G. Kneller, oils, c.1692, NPG · E. Lutterel, miniature, chalk drawing, 1698, NPG · attrib. F. Bird, effigy on monument, marble, c.1701, St Michael's Church, Chenies, Buckinghamshire · A. Van Dyck, double portrait, oils (with his wife), Wilton House, Wiltshire

Wealth at death income est. at approx. £20,000 p.a. in 1700: Thomson, *Russells in Bloomsbury*, 101

Russell, William (1634–c.1696), chemical physician and apothecary, about whom details of family background remain obscure, was in all likelihood the brother of Richard *Russell, a practitioner in chymical medicine and translator of alchemical works, with whom he ran a pharmacy business in Little Minories, and later in Goodman's Fields. Russell produced a 'royal tincture', which was used by the king and other members of the aristocracy, and on the title-page of his one major work, *A Physical Treatise, Grounded, not upon Tradition, nor Phancy, but Experience* (1684), he described himself as pharmacist and chemist-in-ordinary to Charles II. It was no doubt in connection with this treatise that Russell was proposed as a fellow of the Royal Society in January 1681 by John Houghton, apothecary and tea dealer. Russell failed, alongside two other candidates of Houghton's, to be elected, and his somewhat uncertain professional status may account for it.

Russell claims in *A Physical Treatise* that a providential awakening in his early years set him on the road of curative physic. He underlines his support for chemical medicines that consist of universal rather than particular remedies; particularly good examples are those 'Mineral and Metalick Virtues, [that] being more concentrate, have more universal Dispositions' (p. 7), as opposed to their external properties. In the last part of the work, however, Russell describes cures he has used without the frequent assistance of chemical remedies from the shops of apothecaries, perhaps to emphasize as much his own independent practices as their limited effectiveness. One should note in this regard the publication soon after Russell's death of John Headrick's *Arcana philosophia, or, Chymical Secrets, Containing the Noted … Chymical Medicines of Dr. Wil. and Rich. Russel* (1697), as well as the thrust of his brother's alchemical preoccupations as expressed in *The Works of Geber … of the Investigation and Perfection of the Philosophers-Stone* (1686). Although the precise date of Russell's death is unknown it is thought that he died about 1696.

MALCOLM OSTER

Sources M. Hunter, *The Royal Society and its fellows, 1660–1700: the morphology of an early scientific institution*, 2nd edn (1994), 59 · M. Hunter, *Establishing the new science: the experience of the early Royal Society* (1989), 344 · C. Webster, *The great instauration: science, medicine and reform, 1626–1660* (1975), 531 · *DNB*

Russell, William, Lord Russell [called the Patriot, the Martyr] (1639–1683), politician and conspirator, was born on 29 September 1639, the third but second surviving son of William *Russell, fifth earl and later first duke of Bedford (1616–1700), nobleman, and his wife, Anne (1615–1684), daughter of Robert *Carr, earl of Somerset (1585/6?–1645), and his wife, Frances *Howard, the former countess of Essex.

William Russell, Lord Russell (1639–1683), by unknown engraver, c.1683 (after Sir Godfrey Kneller, 1680–83)

Education, interests, and early career Russell and his elder brother, Francis, were educated privately at Woburn Abbey in Bedfordshire (the fifth earl's principal estate) by John Thornton, the family's nonconformist chaplain. Their studies focused on religious works that praised nonconformity and abhorred Roman Catholicism. In 1655 Russell entered Trinity College, Cambridge; he matriculated from Magdalene College. He spent the next several years travelling with Francis and a French tutor around France, Switzerland, Italy, and Austria. He suffered a severe illness in Paris in March 1658 which 'put him at death's door' (Bedford office, Woburn Abbey, HMC 36, fol. 6). In December 1659, citing his 'inclination to the warres', Russell laid plans to join the army of the Swedish king, but nothing came of them (Chatsworth, Russell MSS, box 2). In travel diaries and letters Russell revealed that he enjoyed dancing and bathing at night in Lyons where the ladies wore masks and not much else; and that Queen Kristina, whom he admired, looked like a man and 'resembled a woman only in her inconstancy' (Chatsworth, Russell MSS, box 1).

Russell did not develop broad intellectual interests. As an adult he confined his reading to religious texts, newssheets, and current political tracts. He was, moreover, 'no great reader of statutes' (Grey, 4.71). His private conversations, according to Gilbert Burnet, centred on domestic politics and the 'affaires of Europe' ('Dr Burnet's relation', Chatsworth, Russell MSS, box 1). But without doubt he also talked about religion; clergymen were among his many friends and in 1679 he appointed as his chaplain Samuel *Johnson, a radical preacher and pamphleteer, whose political studies he encouraged. No doubt Russell's commitment to the principles of nonconformity, limited monarchy, and the right of resistance was strengthened by Johnson. In public Russell was a man of few words. Burnet described him as 'a slow man, and of little discourse', but insisted that he had 'true judgment when he considered things at his own leisure' (*Bishop Burnet's History*, 2.365).

With the restoration of the Stuart monarchy in 1660 Russell began to play a minor role in public affairs. Because of Francis's failing health he marched in the procession at Charles's coronation, held some local offices in Bedfordshire, and won election to the Convention Parliament in 1660 for the family borough of Tavistock in Devon. Tavistock returned him to the Cavalier Parliament in 1661, and he represented it for the next eighteen years. In 1663 the house made him promise neither to send nor to receive a challenge from Robert Spencer, the second earl of Sunderland, who had jilted Russell's cousin, Lady Anne Digby. In 1667 and 1668 Russell won modest recognition, being appointed for the first time as a teller and selected with others to present an address to the king.

Appearance, character, and marriage William was a tall (about 5 feet 10 inches), handsome man, rather heavy set, with brown hair, light brown eyes, a strong, slightly bulbous nose, and a wide, sensuous mouth. He possessed a pleasing manner, a usually cheerful and smiling countenance, and a 'generous and obliging temper' (*Bishop Burnet's History*, 2.83). An impulsive person with extravagant tastes and a commitment to chivalric ideals William borrowed money throughout his life to support spendthrift ways. His youthful behaviour was not unblemished: in 1663 and 1664 he engaged in duels, explaining that he was honour bound to do so; in 1665 he and his uncle (Colonel John Russell, of the king's guards) pursued a woman to whom the duke of York was also attracted. A row ensued and the two of them landed in the Tower for several days; they won release only after an abject apology and the payment of a fine.

When he was almost thirty years old William married Rachel, Lady Vaughan [*see* Russell, Rachel (*bap.* 1637, *d.* 1723)], the wealthy widow of Francis, Lord Vaughan (1638–1676), eldest son of Richard *Vaughan, second earl of Carbery. Her parents were Thomas *Wriothesley, fourth earl of Southampton (1608–1667), Charles II's lord treasurer, and his first wife, Rachel (1603–1640), daughter of Daniel de Massue, seigneur de Ruvigny, a French Huguenot.

Rachel Vaughan and Russell fell passionately in love, but the courtship was protracted; painfully aware of the disparity in their wealth Russell insisted to his mother that 'it is not [Rachel's] fortune I look after … 'tis her person and that alone I adore and admire' (Bedford office, Woburn Abbey, HMC, 39, pp. 34–5). He declared that if he failed to win her he would abandon the world. Rachel spared him this fate and they married on 20 August 1669. The marriage settlement made the couple very wealthy, with a generous annual income, a mansion in London, and properties in several shires. They lived first at Stratton House in Hampshire and after 1675 spent a portion of each year in London at Southampton House in Bloomsbury.

They had four children: Anne (*b.* 13 Dec 1671, *d.* shortly thereafter); Rachel (*b.* 17 Jan 1674, *d.* 1725), who married William Cavendish, later second duke of Devonshire; Katherine (*b.* 23 Aug 1676, *d.* 1711), who married John Manners, later second duke of Rutland; and Wriothesley (*b.* 1 Nov 1680, *d.* 1711), who married Elizabeth Howland and became the second duke of Bedford. Russell continued his reckless behaviour: in 1671 he sought to vindicate the reputation of his wife's half-sister, Elizabeth Percy, countess of Northumberland, a widow, whose ardent suitor, Henry Savile, had entered her bed chamber at one o'clock in the morning to declare his passion. The countess fled. When the story got out Savile, fearing for his life, rode to London and sailed for France, pursued by Russell and others; only Russell continued the chase overseas. There was, however, a softer side to Russell: he was a tender and loving husband, an indulgent father, and a loyal friend.

Parliamentary career From 1673 onwards Russell's career in the House of Commons falls into two major parts: his movement from obscurity in 1673 to importance in 1678 when the Popish Plot broke, and his ascent to eminence from 1678 to 1681 during the exclusion crisis. A reckless streak characterized his politics, just as it did his personal behaviour. William shared with others the fear that Charles's policies signalled that the government favoured France, Catholicism, and absolute power. On 31 October 1673, for the first time, Russell opened a major debate in a committee of the whole house on supply to continue the Third Anglo-Dutch War. Declaring that he 'would rather be thought to mean well, and speak ill, than to betray the trust of his country' (Grey, 2.198), Russell asserted that the money given to fight the Netherlands endangered the nation and protestantism. He hinted that the king's ministers had betrayed their trust and urged the house to refuse a supply. Moderate views prevailed, but this speech launched his career.

Russell continued to assault the king's ministers: in January 1674 he supported a motion to remove from the king's presence and counsels the duke of Buckingham; he charged that Buckingham was close to a 'knot of persons' who 'turn our Saviour and Parliaments into ridicule and contrive prorogations' (Grey, 2.256). In the 1675 session he called for the impeachment of the earl of Danby, the lord treasurer, on grounds of financial mismanagement and inclinations towards arbitrary government, citing Danby's alleged remarks that 'a new proclamation is as good as an old law' (Grey, 3.41). He reignited antagonism to standing armies, declaring intemperately that with a standing army, 'we cannot be secure in this House, and some of us may have our heads taken off' (Grey, 2.393). He favoured banning Catholics from the house and was teller for the bill to place the revenue for building warships in the chamber of London, instead of the Treasury, a slap at Danby. By the time Charles prorogued parliament in November 1675, Russell was identified with extremists in the country party; a friend hoped that before parliament reconvened Russell's two brothers-in-law 'might do some good with him' (*CSP dom.*, 1676–7, 287).

When parliament reopened in February 1677 Russell

and Anthony Ashley Cooper, first earl of Shaftesbury, his wife's relation by marriage, had formed a close connection. Shaftesbury was a principal organizer and tactician in the House of Lords of the emerging country opposition and then the whig party. Russell became his most trusted and dependable ally in the Commons. As Shaftesbury directed, Russell supported the proposition that parliament was dissolved on the ground that ancient laws, dating back to the fourteenth century, required parliament to meet at least once a year; the prorogation had lasted fifteen months. The argument threatened a prerogative of the crown to call and dissolve parliament at its pleasure, and four peers, including Shaftesbury, were sent to the Tower for their part in the action. Russell, however, escaped punishment.

Russell's social and political position was enhanced on 14 January 1678 when his brother Francis died and he assumed the courtesy title of Lord Russell and the position of heir to the Bedford title and fortune. He continued to oppose the court's domestic and foreign policies in 1678 as he had in 1677. The opposition distrusted Charles II, fearing that he would raise men and money for war against France and then, with the connivance of Louis XIV, arrange a peace and use the troops to destroy parliamentary liberties and protestantism. To discover the real intentions of the British and French kings Russell and Denzil, Lord Holles, met in February and March 1678 with Henri de *Massue de Ruvigny, Lady Russell's cousin, who was sent by Louis XIV to persuade the parliamentary opposition not to grant money for a French war. Russell indignantly rejected Ruvigny's suggestion of bribing MPs, saying that he 'should be very sorry to have any commerce with people capable of being gained by money' (Dalrymple, 2.133). In April Russell and Holles, joined by Buckingham and Shaftesbury, met the French ambassador for further conversations to the same ends. The talks testify to Russell's moral strength regarding bribery; he neither accepted nor distributed money.

In October 1678 the political situation changed dramatically when Charles told the opening session of parliament about the revelations of a popish plot to kill him and elevate the duke of York to the throne. Russell sincerely believed in the reality of the plot and co-operated with Shaftesbury in exploiting it for political ends. On 2 November 1678 Russell introduced a motion asking the king to remove his brother from his counsels and his presence, declaring in an 'unusually able speech' (Foxcroft, 1.135) that 'all our danger proceeded from the duke of York, who is perverted to popery, and from him only' (Grey, 6.133). In December Danby, to demonstrate that the parliamentary opposition was in league with France, unveiled letters that Ralph Montagu, the unscrupulous English ambassador to Louis XIV and Lady Russell's brother-in-law, had written about Ruvigny's mission. But the ploy failed. Russell, the only one named in the dispatches, was not above using a duplicitous remark to protect himself. He said, 'I defy any man alive to charge me with any dealing with the French. My actions here have given sufficient testimony to the contrary' (Grey, 6.360).

The prevailing view was that the court had produced the letters 'with some design against' Russell (Grey, 6.364), and members decided not to enter the letters in the journal lest they stain William's reputation. One member, however, worried that although 'we here very well understand Lord Russell's character ... how after ages may understand it, I know not' (Grey, 6.364). Within a fortnight Charles prorogued parliament, dissolved it on 30 January 1679, and called for new elections.

The elections that took place in the next three years testified to Russell's newly elevated status. In early 1679 he was returned as knight of the shire for both Bedfordshire and Hampshire, an unusual honour; Russell chose Bedfordshire. In September 1679 he again won re-election in both counties and again he declined Hampshire. In the elections to the third Exclusion Parliament in 1681 he was returned for Bedfordshire; this time the gentlemen of Hampshire made no effort to have him represent them.

On 27 April 1679 Russell addressed the house in a speech of undeniable rhetorical strength. Declaring that if the succession were not changed 'we must resolve when we have a Prince of the Popish Religion to be Papists, or burn', William defiantly exclaimed, 'And I will do neither' (Grey, 7.147). Expressing utter scorn of Roman Catholicism as a 'ridiculous and nonsensical Religion' (Grey, 7.148), he denied that ownership of abbey lands influenced his anti-Catholicism. His motion to appoint a committee to prepare a bill to secure the nation 'in case of a Popish Successor' (Grey, 7.148), the first Exclusion Bill, followed in May. The exclusion of York, rather than limitations on the crown, became William's central political goal. To defeat the bill the king prorogued parliament at the end of May.

In the meantime Russell accepted Charles's invitation to join the newly constituted privy council, which was designed to involve opposition members in the government. William remained on the council for nine months, further irritating the king by insulting his ministers. On 26 January 1680, when Charles prorogued parliament again, Russell, with three others, following Shaftesbury's direction, resigned in a body from the council, the king granting them permission to withdraw 'with all my heart' (Luttrell, 1.33). Privately Charles expressed contempt for them.

In June 1680 Russell participated in Shaftesbury's 'sensational gesture' (Haley, 580): the presentation to the Middlesex grand jury of an information against York for recusancy. Lord Chief Justice Scroggs dismissed the jury to sabotage the plan, and this move ignited Russell's ire against him. On 26 October 1680, with a rhetorical flourish, William told the house that 'this Parliament must either destroy popery, or they will destroy us; there is no middle way to be taken, no mincing the matter' (Grey, 7.358). On 2 November Russell moved a second Exclusion Bill and, as the first member appointed to the committee, probably served as chairman. Debates, amendments, and delays in the Lords sorely tested his patience. On 15 November Russell's 'impetuous temper and exceeding ardour ... hurried him on with such violence' that he seized the bill and ran with it to the Lords, followed by other house members (HoP, *Commons, 1660–90*). The defeat of the second Exclusion Bill was a severe disappointment: Russell said that if his father had voted against the bill he would 'have thought him an enemy to the king and kingdom' and declared that if he could not live a protestant he hoped to die as one (Grey, 8.13). In subsequent weeks Russell's steps embarrassed the government; he opposed money for Tangier because the 'chief Person that manages affairs is a Papist and a slave to the Pope' (Grey, 8.13). He participated in attacks on highly placed officials: Sir George Jeffreys, recorder of London; Sir Francis North, lord chief justice of the court of common pleas; Scroggs; and Laurence Hyde, a lord of the Treasury and York's brother-in-law. He was involved in bringing to trial the five Roman Catholic peers charged with complicity in the plot; the house convicted the aged William Howard, Viscount Stafford, of treason. It was said that Russell opposed the king's commuting the terrible sentence for treason to beheading; his friends explained that, if true, it was because Russell feared that if Charles commuted the sentence without being challenged he might commute the verdict. At about this time Russell adopted the idea of charging York with treason for his alleged part in the Popish Plot, bringing him to trial, and executing him, reasoning that York would take revenge on men who had opposed him.

In December Russell and others negotiated with Charles to win him over to exclusion. Gossip reported a deal: in exchange for excluding York, Charles would receive ample supplies and the power to name his own successor; whig leaders would win offices—for Russell the governorship of Portsmouth. But the deal collapsed; Charles dissolved parliament and ordered new elections. Parliament convened in Oxford on 21 March 1681. On the 26th Russell seconded the motion for the exclusion of York, declaring that 'nothing but excluding the duke … can secure us' (Grey, 8.310); he was principally responsible for the 'rejection of the king's terms' (*DNB*). The third Exclusion Bill was ordered to be read a second time on 28 March, but before that happened Charles dissolved parliament, leaving disgruntled whigs without a legitimate political forum.

Russell did not retire to Stratton, as has been said, but made himself visible as a loyal friend of radical whigs: he invited Prince William of Orange to meet at Southampton House in July 1681, opposed the court-supported candidate for mayor of London in September, and contributed to the bail for Shaftesbury's release from prison in November. In 1682 he was dubbed the Prince of Whigland (*Heraclitus Ridens*, nos. 64, 70). He also engaged in secret conversations with whig leaders about how to achieve their ends. After Shaftesbury had escaped to the Netherlands, where he died in January 1683, a council of six, which included Russell, continued to hold conspiratorial talks. On 12 June 1683 Josiah Keeling, one of the lesser conspirators, informed the government of what he knew; on the 15th he implicated Russell. Russell learned that he had been named, but declined to flee. At this time he undoubtedly destroyed his political papers.

Arrest, trial, and execution On 26 June 1683 Russell was arrested and sent to the Tower charged with conspiring with others in a scheme, known as the Rye House Plot, to raise rebellion by seizing the king's guards and thereby, in law, to kill the king. He was not charged with plotting to murder the king physically. William remained in the Tower for two weeks, seeing family and many friends, and consulting lawyers about his defence. On Friday 13 July William was tried in the court of king's bench at the Old Bailey. Presiding was the lord chief justice of the court of common pleas, Francis Pemberton, who was sympathetic to Russell, even-handed in addressing the jury, and insistent that the law be strictly observed. Sir George Jeffreys and others assisted by Sir Francis North, managed the prosecution. Russell, as planned, tried to delay the proceedings, brought forward Lady Russell to take notes for him, using her as a symbol of his good character and of her father's services to Charles II and his father, and questioned the jurors' status as freeholders, a point inapplicable in treason cases. Russell's formal defence was weak: he appealed to the sympathy of the court, claimed that his acts, if proven, did not fall within the law of treason (they did), maintained that two witnesses to the same act of treason were required (not true at the time), tried to discredit the testimony of plea bargainers, and brought in witnesses to testify to his good character but not to answer his accusers. The jury deliberated for over an hour and brought in a verdict of guilty of high treason. The next day Russell was sentenced to die.

During the following week Russell devoted himself to saying farewell to friends, family, and Lady Russell; talking with Burnet, who stayed with him at the request of Lady Russell and who kept a journal of these days; composing his scaffold speech; and, with Rachel's help, writing out five 'original' copies of it. William, his wife, his father, Rachel's French relatives, and others spared no effort—and his father no money—to persuade the king and York to pardon or at least grant him a short reprieve—all to no avail. On 21 July he was executed in Lincoln's Inn Fields, the king having commuted his sentence to beheading. Chivalrous to the end Russell refused to be blindfolded; he flinched as the axe fell and it took two more blows to sever his head. People dipped their handkerchiefs in his blood. His body was buried that night in the family vault at Chenies in Buckinghamshire.

Russell died a traitor without a will, so the value of his personal estate is unknown, but it was heavily encumbered with debts. At the petition of his wife Charles did not confiscate his personal estate.

Made a martyr Until recently the view of Russell as a man and of his trial depended upon the viewer's personal connections and political inclinations. On the one hand Lady Russell, his family, and his political associates, for emotional and political reasons, claimed that he was innocent. Russell's speech (which his wife insisted he had written) laid out the argument—that clever crown lawyers had twisted the law and unqualified jurors had unjustly convicted him. Incapable of violence against the person of the king—whatever others might have planned—Russell was a martyr to true English liberties and religion. The speech was immediately and widely distributed. On the other hand, the government maintained in equally powerful tracts, notably *An Antidote Against Poison* (1683) by Sir Bartholomew Shower, and *Considerations upon a Printed Sheet* (1683) by Sir Roger L'Estrange, that Russell's speech was ghost written, the evidence against him incontrovertible, and the trial proceedings exemplary in law. Russell was a 'Stomackful, huffing Cavalier' (R. L'Estrange, *Considerations upon a Printed Sheet*, 1683, 12).

It took the success of the revolution of 1688 to seal the perception of Russell as a martyr. His attainder was removed in March 1689; his father was elevated to a dukedom in 1694, a tribute to Russell, 'the ornament of his age', the patent indicated (G. Thomson, *Family Background*, 1949, 195). Whig-inclined historians nurtured this conviction through the centuries. Plays, the publication of Lady Russell's letters, accounts of the Bedford family, a sympathetic biography by John, Lord Russell, and a magnificent commissioned painting of the trial by Sir George Hayter sustained the interpretation. Even Dalrymple's revelations about Russell's dealings with the French did not destroy it. A few historians questioned this flattering picture (for example, David Hume, in *History of Great Britain*, 2 vols., 1754–7; Alfred Havinghurst, in 'The judiciary and politics in the reign of Charles II', *Law Quarterly Review*, 66, 1950, 62–78, 229–52; and David Ogg, in *England in the Reign of Charles II*, 3rd edn, 1961); but no dispassionate examination of the Rye House Plot or of Russell's trial appeared until the late twentieth century, when studies by M. S. Zook and L. G. Schwoerer concluded that the one was real and the other according to the law in 1683.

Russell was a handsome, genial, popular man, with a reckless streak, a commitment to chivalric ideals, a bravado attitude, and a naïve understanding of politics. During the exclusion crisis he played a leading role in keeping emotions at boiling point, ruling out compromise. In 1683 the publications of his wife, family, and political friends transformed him into a martyr; over the years his family continued to perpetuate his reputation as the Patriot and the Martyr, successfully obscuring the man behind the image for some two hundred years.

Lois G. Schwoerer

Sources L. G. Schwoerer, *Lady Rachel Russell (1637–1723): 'One of the Best of Women'* (1988) · L. G. Schwoerer, 'The trial of Lord William Russell (1683): judicial murder?', *Journal of Legal History*, 9 (1988), 142–68 · L. G. Schwoerer, 'William, Lord Russell: the making of a martyr, 1683–1983', *Journal of British Studies*, 24 (1985), 41–71 · A. Grey, ed., *Debates of the House of Commons, from the year 1667 to the year 1694*, 10 vols. (1763) · *CSP dom.* · *Calendar of the manuscripts of the marquess of Ormonde*, new ser., 8 vols., HMC, 36 (1902–20), vols. 4, 7 · *State trials*, vol. 9 · *Bishop Burnet's History* · L. Naylor, 'Russell, Hon. William', HoP, *Commons, 1660–90* · K. H. D. Haley, *The first earl of Shaftesbury* (1968) · *JHC* · *JHL* · *The life and letters of Sir George Savile ... first marquis of Halifax*, ed. H. C. Foxcroft, 2 vols. (1898) · N. Luttrell, *A brief historical relation of state affairs from September 1678 to April 1714*, 1 (1857) · J. Dalrymple, *Memoirs of Great Britain and Ireland*, 2 vols. (1771–3) · GEC, *Peerage*, new edn · John, Lord Russell, *The life of William Lord Russell* (1819) · *Speech of the late Lord Russel [sic]* (1683) · *DNB* · Venn, *Alum. Cant.* · *Seventh report*, HMC, 6 (1879), 374 · M. S. Zook, *Radical whigs and conspiratorial politics in late Stuart England* (1999) ·

PRO, PRO 31/3/147, fol. 379; 31/3/155, fol. 85v · L. Brown, *The first earl of Shaftesbury* (1933) · coffin plate, Bedford chapel, Chenies · private information (2004) [archivist, Woburn Abbey, Bedfordshire] · Russell correspondence, Woburn Abbey, Bedford Office, Bedfordshire, HMC 36, 39 · *Weekly Journal, or, British Gazetteer* (5 Oct 1723) · G. S. Thomson, notes, William, Lord Russell and Lady Rachel (personal), Woburn Abbey, Bedford Office, Bedfordshire · parish register, Titchfield, 19 Sept 1637 [baptism; Rachel Wriothesley] · parish register, Titchfield, 20 Aug 1669 [marriage] · travel diaries and correspondence, Chatsworth House, Derbyshire, Russell MSS, boxes 1–2

Archives Chatsworth House, Derbyshire, MSS, uncatalogued, box 1 · Chatsworth House, Derbyshire, MSS, uncatalogued, box 2 | BL, Add. MS 21406, fol. 22 · BL, Add. MS 8127, fols. 62–8 · BL, Add. MS 34526, fols. 16–19v · Bodl. Oxf., MS North 6.1, fols. 280–81 · Bodl. Oxf., MS Rawl. C. 983, fol. 61 · East Kent Archives Centre, Dover, papers about his execution · PRO, SP 29/429, pt 1, pp. 144–9 · Woburn Abbey, Bedford Office, Bedfordshire, HMC 36, 38, 39, 40 · Woburn Abbey, Bedford Office, Bedfordshire, G. S. Thomson, notes, William, Lord Russell, and Lady Rachel (personal)

Likenesses C. Lefevre, oils, c.1659, Woburn Abbey, Bedfordshire · G. Kneller, oils, c.1680, Woburn Abbey, Bedfordshire · G. Bower, silver medal, 1683, BM · P. Vanderbank, line engraving, c.1683 (after G. Kneller), BM, NPG · mezzotint, c.1863 (after G. Kneller, 1680–83), BM, NPG [*see illus.*] · J. Fittler, engraving, repro. in Schwoerer, *Lady Rachel Russell* · attrib. T. Flatman, miniature, NPG · miniature (after S. Cooper), Woburn Abbey, Bedfordshire

Wealth at death personal estate heavily encumbered with debts

Russell, William (1740–1818), merchant and reformer, was born in Birmingham on 11 November 1740, the eldest son of Thomas Russell (1696–1760), ironmaster and merchant, and his wife, Frances (1713–1767), daughter of Thomas Pougher of Leicester. He was educated for a mercantile life. The family business in Birmingham had been founded by his great-grandfather Thomas, and was continued by his grandfather William (d. 1742) and father, Thomas. Its principal activity after 1783 was the large-scale export of Birmingham and Sheffield ironware, particularly to Russia, Spain, and North America. Russell's grandfather was also an original investor in the Principio iron company, the first in Maryland. At some date between 1717 and 1724 Thomas Russell went out to Maryland, where he took a leading role in building the first furnace and organizing the company, soon the largest iron firm in the thirteen colonies. By about 1751 the firm owned four furnaces in Virginia and Maryland, and two forges, and accounted for about half the iron then exported from the colonies to England. Apart from the two Augustine Washingtons, father and brother of George, the partners in the firm were all English. At his death in 1760, Russell's father left him his landed property in England and America plus half his interest in the Principio company. The other half was left to his second son, Thomas (1743–1786), who emigrated to Maryland to become general manager of the firm there. In 1780 the state of Maryland confiscated the property of the Principio company except for the small shares of Augustine Washington's heir and Thomas Russell, by then a citizen there.

William Russell was active as a skinner, threadmaker, and general domestic and foreign trader. In September 1762 he married Martha Twamley (1741–1790), daughter of

Josiah Twamley of Kidderminster, ironmonger and Independent. They had a son, Thomas Pougher Russell (1775–1851), later a banker in Gloucester, and four daughters. Russell was recognized as one of the most eminent merchants and public-spirited residents of Birmingham. A member of the local commercial committee, he participated in the successful efforts to improve roads, streets, and lighting and to establish a hospital and subscription library. He was also recognized as the leading figure in the local Presbyterian–Unitarian congregation and was a particular friend and patron of its minister, Joseph Priestley. At the national level, he was a member of the select Society for Constitutional Information from 1783 and a midlands regional leader in the agitation of 1787–90 for the repeal of the Test and Corporation Acts. His principal residence was at Showell Green in the parish of Yardley, 2 miles from Birmingham, and he served as a justice of the peace in Worcestershire. That did not protect him at the time of the Church and King riots in Birmingham in July 1791, ostensibly provoked by his sponsorship of a public dinner, attended by many prominent dissenters, to celebrate the second anniversary of the fall of the Bastille. The rioters attacked and burned Priestley's chapel, home, and laboratory as well as Russell's country house. The local justices of the peace were conspicuously inactive during the initial phase of the riot and only after vigorous lobbying was Russell able to obtain for the sufferers some compensation assessed against property owners within the hundred. However, he no longer felt comfortable among his former neighbours and withdrew to Gloucester, leaving his Birmingham interests in the care of his youngest brother, George.

In the years following the end of the American War of Independence in 1783, Russell, Russell, and Smith (the firm of William and George Russell) exported on a large scale to the United States and were owed substantial balances there, especially in Pennsylvania, whence remittances were difficult, particularly after the start of the British–French war in 1793 disrupted American trade with France and the West Indies. In an effort to collect these recent commercial debts and to investigate the possibility of recovering part of his lost inheritance in Maryland, Russell resolved to go to America. This was, however, not only a business trip; he imagined that he might find life more congenial in America (whither Priestley had already withdrawn) and took his son and two of his daughters with him. The American vessel on which the Russell family embarked in 1794 was stopped by a French man-of-war and they were detained for a year at Brest and Paris until the intercession of the American minister obtained their release. During that year, Russell became involved in some speculative activities in France which left him the proprietor of a secularized church estate in Normandy. On arrival in America in 1795 he settled his family at Middletown, Connecticut, but himself travelled extensively, visiting Priestley in Pennsylvania and George Washington in Virginia (the Russells had had business connections with the Washingtons from the 1720s). He was unsuccessful in obtaining redress from the state of

Maryland but did collect some debts in Pennsylvania, paid partly in land. From such payments and other purchases, he accumulated holdings of over 35,000 acres there.

Russell's children did not in the end find America sufficiently congenial, and he resolved to return to Europe in 1801. He went first to Hamburg, where he had commercial matters to settle, and then, after the Peace of Amiens (1802), to France. He delayed his return to England in part because of a fear that he might have violated British law when he acquired his estate in France in wartime. When the conflict resumed in 1803, he could not leave France and was forced to settle on his Norman estate for the duration of hostilities; he did not return to England until 1814. He died on 26 January 1818 at The Hyde, near Upton-on-Severn, Worcestershire, the residence of his son-in-law James Skey. He was reported to have been much concerned with religion in his last years. He was buried in his family vault in St Philip's Church, Birmingham.

Jacob M. Price

Sources S. H. Jeyes, *The Russells of Birmingham in the French revolution and in America, 1791–1814* (1911) · T. R. [T. Russell], *Monthly Repository*, 13 (1818), 141, 153–5 · R. P. Stearns, 'The library: a description of the Russell papers', *Pennsylvania Magazine of History and Biography*, 62 (1938), 205–12 · J. Money, *Experience and identity: Birmingham and the west midlands, 1760–1800* (1977) · W. G. Whitely and H. Whitely, 'The Principio Company: a historical sketch', *Pennsylvania Magazine of History and Biography*, 11 (1887) · J. M. Swank, *History of the manufacture of iron … from 1585 to 1885* (1884) · 'A churchman', *An authentic account of the late riots in Birmingham* (1791) · notes by R. P. Stearns on W. Russell, BL, Add. MS 45022 · BL, W. Russell MSS, Add. MSS 44998–44999

Archives Birm. CA, corresp. and papers · BL, corresp. and family papers, Add. MSS 44992–45022, 29600 · Hist. Soc. Penn., business and family papers

Likenesses miniature, photograph, Assay office, Birmingham · portrait (after miniature), repro. in Jeyes, *Russells of Birmingham*, facing p. 96 · watercolour, repro. in Jeyes, *Russells of Birmingham*, frontispiece

Russell, William (1746–1793), historian, son of Alexander Russell, farmer, and his wife, Christian Ballantyne, was born at the farm of Windydoors, Edinburghshire. He was at school at Inverleithen, Peeblesshire, until 1756, when he went to Edinburgh and studied writing and arithmetic for ten months, after which he was apprenticed to the bookselling and printing firm of Martin and Witherspoon.

As a journeyman Russell joined in 1763 the Miscellaneous Society, composed of university and other students. His friends revised a translation by him of Crébillon's *Rhadamisthe et Zénobie*, which he unsuccessfully submitted to David Garrick for representation. He was invited to spend the autumn of 1765 with Lord Elibank at his seat in Haddingtonshire and, hoping for Elibank's patronage, abandoned his trade. He then lived with his father until May 1767, when he left for London, hoping to live as a man of letters. In this he was disappointed and he was forced to take a job as corrector of the press for William Strahan. In 1769 he became printing overseer to Messrs Brown and Adlard, but soon after 1770 appears to have managed to live exclusively by literary work. In that year his first successful publication, *Sentimental Tales*, appeared, followed by further works in 1772 and 1774. In 1780 he visited Jamaica to secure money as his brother's heir, and on his return resumed his literary career in London.

Russell achieved his chief reputation as a historian. The first of his works to meet with any success was *The History of America, from the First Discovery by Columbus to the Conclusion of the Late War*, which was completed in 1779. In the same year he issued, anonymously, the first two volumes of his *History of Modern Europe, in a Series of Letters from a Nobleman to his Son*. Three further volumes, with the author's name, appeared in 1784, and the whole work was published in five volumes in 1786. His *History of Ancient Europe, with a View of the Revolutions in Asia and Africa* (1793) was a fragment, and had indifferent success. Thomas Cadell arranged to pay him £750 for a history of England from the accession of George III to the end of the American War of Independence, but this was not begun. Russell also published poetry, essays, an unsuccessful play, and a tribute to Sarah Siddons, the actress.

In 1787 Russell married a Miss Scott, and returned to Scotland. He settled at Knottyholm, a farm near Langholm, Dumfriesshire, belonging to the duke of Buccleuch. In 1792 he received the honorary degree of LLD from St Andrews University. His health was poor, and this was made worse by constant arguments with booksellers. He died suddenly of a stroke at his home on 25 December 1793, and was buried in the churchyard of Westerkirk, Langholm. His wife and one daughter survived him and continued to live at Knottyholm.

T. W. BAYNE, *rev.* ALEXANDER DU TOIT

Sources D. Irving, *Lives of Scotish authors: viz Fergusson, Falconer, and Russell* (1801) · A. Chalmers, ed., *The general biographical dictionary*, new edn, 26 (1816), 483–5 · Chambers, *Scots.* (1855)
Archives BL, Gladstone MSS, digest of his *History of modern Europe* · NL Scot., Watson collection · U. Edin. L., Laing collection
Likenesses engraving?, repro. in Irving, *Lives of Scotish authors*, frontispiece
Wealth at death farm at Knottyholm still occupied by wife and daughter after his death; but farm belonged to duke of Buccleuch, and Russell was presumably only tenant: Irving, *Lives of Scotish authors*

Russell, Sir William, first baronet (1773–1839). *See under* Russell, Sir William, second baronet (1822–1892).

Russell, William (1777–1813), organist and composer, the son of William Russell, an organ builder, was born in London on 6 October 1777. From his eighth year he was taught by the organists William Cope, William Shrubsole, and John Groombridge. Between 1789 and 1793 he was deputy to his father, who was organist to St Mary Aldermanbury, London. In 1793 Russell was appointed organist to the Great Queen Street Chapel; cathedral services were performed there until 1798, when the chapel became a Wesleyan meeting-house. In September 1798 he was elected organist at St Anne's, Limehouse, and in 1801 he was elected to a similar post at the Foundling Hospital.

About this time Russell resumed his musical studies under Samuel Arnold, through whose influence he obtained employment at various London theatres. Between 1800 and 1804, he composed the music for nearly twenty pantomimes for Sadler's Wells and several pieces for the Royal Circus; he also wrote music for Covent Garden, where he acted as accompanist. His settings of Christopher Smart's 'Ode on St Cecilia's Day' (1800) and *The Redemption of Israel* were both probably performed by the Cecilian Society, of which he was a member. A volume of psalms, hymns, and anthems was compiled for the Foundling Chapel in 1809. In 1808 he graduated BMus from Magdalen College, Oxford, and began acting as an organ inspector, on some occasions looking over instruments built by his father. He further published *Twelve Voluntaries for the Organ or Pianoforte* and a *Second Book of Voluntaries* (1812), while *Job*, an oratorio of his adapted for organ or piano by S. S. Wesley, was issued in 1826. Russell died on 21 November 1813 at Cobham Row, Cold Bathfields, London.

L. M. MIDDLETON, *rev.* NILANJANA BANERJI

Sources *New Grove* · Brown & Stratton, *Brit. mus.* · W. H. Husk, *Musical celebrations on St. Cecilia's Day* (1857) · Foster, *Alum. Oxon.* · *GM*, 1st ser., 83/2 (1813), 625 · D. Baptie, *A handbook of musical biography* (1883) · C. F. A. Williams, *Degrees in music* (1894) · [J. S. Sainsbury], ed., *A dictionary of musicians*, 2nd edn, 2 vols. (1827)

Russell, William (1784–1870). *See under* Russell, John (1745–1806).

Russell, Sir William, second baronet (1822–1892), army officer, was born on 5 April 1822 at Calcutta, the only son of **Sir William Russell**, first baronet (1773–1839), physician, of Charlton Park, Gloucestershire, and his second wife, Jane Eliza, daughter of Major-General James Doddington Sherwood of the East India Company service.

The father, born at Edinburgh on 29 May 1773, was the sixth son of John Russell of Roseburne, near Edinburgh, a writer to the signet. An Edinburgh MD, he went to Calcutta, where he acquired a large practice. On returning to London he distinguished himself during the 1832 cholera epidemic, and was created a baronet (9 April 1832).

The son, who succeeded to the baronetcy on his father's death on 26 September 1839, was commissioned cornet in the 7th hussars on 2 July 1841 and became lieutenant on 27 February 1846, captain on 16 April 1847, and major on 13 August 1857. He was master of the horse (1849–50), and aide-de-camp (1850–52) to Lord Clarendon when lord lieutenant of Ireland. During the Crimean War he served on the staff. From 1857 to 1859 he was Liberal MP for Dover.

Russell saw much active service during the latter part of the Indian mutiny. The 7th hussars joined the force under Outram at the Alambagh in February 1858, and were at the siege of Lucknow. After its capture they formed part of the column with which Sir Hope Grant defeated the rebels at Bari on 13 April. Russell was in command of the regiment, and was mentioned in dispatches. At Nawabganj, the 7th hussars, under Russell, charged twice through the enemy and dispersed them. They formed part of the field force under Horsford in the latter part of 1858, and particularly distinguished themselves on 30 December in the pursuit of the enemy to the Rapti. They crossed the Rapti and helped to drive the rebels into Nepal in February 1859. Russell was made brevet lieutenant-colonel on 20 July

1858, and became lieutenant-colonel of his regiment on 12 November. He was made CB on 11 May 1859.

After returning to England, Russell was Liberal MP for Norwich from 1860 to 1874. In 1861 he exchanged from the 7th to the 14th hussars, and on 29 November 1864 was placed on half pay. On 1 January 1863 he married Margaret (d. 21 May 1900), the only child of Robert Wilson of Aberdeen.

In 1871 Russell published his *Scheme for the Reorganisation of the Land Forces*, in which he proposed a general militia enlisted for one year, from which men would pass either into the standing army for twelve years or into the local militia for five years, and from both these bodies into the reserves. He became lieutenant-general on 1 July 1881. Russell died at his home, 66 Gloucester Street, Warwick Square, London, on 19 March 1892, and was buried at Highgate cemetery on 24 March. He was succeeded by his eldest son, William. E. M. LLOYD, rev. JAMES LUNT

Sources W. H. Russell, *My Indian mutiny diary*, ed. M. Edwardes (1957) · J. M. Brereton, *The 7th queen's own hussars* (1975) · C. R. B. Barrett, *The 7th, queen's own, hussars*, 2 vols. (1914) · *The Times* (22 March 1892) · J. W. Kaye and G. B. Malleson, *Kaye's and Malleson's History of the Indian mutiny of 1857–8*, 6 vols. (1888–9) · Fortescue, *Brit. army*, vol. 13 · J. Foster, *The peerage, baronetage, and knightage of the British empire for 1883*, 2 [1883] · *Bulletins of the campaign* (1843–8) [taken from issues of *London Gazette*] · Boase, *Mod. Eng. biog.* · Burke, *Peerage* · WWBMP · CGPLA Eng. & Wales (1893)

Wealth at death £78: probate, 11 March 1893, *CGPLA Eng. & Wales*

Russell, William Armstrong (1821–1879), bishop of north China, son of Marcus Carew Russell and Fanny Potts, was born at Ballydavid House, Littleton, co. Tipperary, and educated at Midleton School, Cork, and at Trinity College, Dublin. He was ordained by Bishop C. J. Blomfield in 1847, and went that year as a missionary to Ningpo (Ningbo) in China, with the Church Missionary Society; he was accompanied by Robert Henry Cobbold, afterwards archdeacon of Ningpo. They were assisted by a Miss Aldersey; these three were the first English missionaries in Ningpo.

On 30 September 1852 Russell married Mary Ann (d. 1887), daughter of Charles William Leisk. She was fluent in Chinese and assisted in missionary work. Russell translated into the local dialect of Ningpo the greater part of the New Testament, portions of the Old Testament, and the Book of Common Prayer, besides writing many tracts and essays. He was appointed the first missionary bishop of north China in November 1872, and on 15 December was consecrated in Westminster Abbey. After his return to China he admitted four Chinese men to deacons' and priests' orders; he confirmed nearly 300 Chinese Christians, and dedicated several mission churches. He died at Shanghai on 5 October 1879. His widow continued to work at Ningpo until she died on 25 August 1887.

G. C. BOASE, rev. H. C. G. MATTHEW

Sources *The Record* (17 Oct 1879) · *The Times* (18 Oct 1879) · *The Guardian* (18 Oct 1879) · *Register of missionaries ... from 1804 to 1904*, Church Missionary Society (privately printed, c.1905)

Archives Church Missionary Society Library, London, letters to Church Missionary Society · LPL, corresp. with A. C. Tait and related papers

Russell, William Clark (1844–1911), novelist, born at the Carlton House Hotel, Broadway, New York, on 24 February 1844, was the son of Henry *Russell (1812x14–1900), vocalist, composer, and songwriter, and his first wife, Isabella Lloyd (1811?–1887), the daughter of Charles Lloyd of Bingley Hall, Birmingham. He inherited his taste for literature from his mother, who was a relative of the poet William Wordsworth, and herself a writer of verse. After education at private schools at Winchester and Boulogne he joined the British merchant service in 1858 and served as an apprentice on the sailing-vessel *Duncan Dunbar*. He made several voyages to India and Australia, and while off the coast of China in 1860 he witnessed the capture of the Taku (Dagu) forts by the combined British and French forces. His eight years on board ship were marked by privations which seriously undermined his health. Nevertheless, from these early experiences he gathered the material which was to be his literary stock-in-trade.

In 1866 Clark Russell retired from the merchant service, and after a few months in a commercial calling he adopted a literary career. He began by writing a tragedy in verse, which was produced at the Haymarket Theatre, London, in 1866, but this proved a failure. Subsequently he took up journalism. In 1868 he was editor of *The Leader*, and in 1871 he wrote for the *Kent County News*. In 1868 he married Alexandrina, daughter of D. H. Henry of the Institution of Civil Engineers and niece of Sir Thomas Henry, police magistrate. They had one son, Herbert Russell (1869–1944), a writer on naval subjects, and three daughters. Clark Russell soon turned to writing nautical tales of adventure, which was henceforth his main occupation. One of his first novels, *John Holdsworth, Chief Mate* (1875), at once attracted attention, and the still more popular *Wreck of the Grosvenor* (1877; new edn, 1900) established his reputation as a graphic writer of sea stories. While these early works brought him little profit owing to the sale of the copyright to the publishers, they served as useful advertisement. For thirty years a constant stream of more or less successful novels flowed from his fertile pen, some, such as *The Little Loo* (1878), appearing under the pseudonym Sydney Mostyn, and others, including *A Dark Secret* (1875), under the name Eliza Rhyl Davies. Together with those works published under his own name, in all he produced fifty-seven volumes.

Sir Edwin Arnold called Clark Russell 'the prose Homer of the great ocean' and Algernon Swinburne described him as 'the greatest master of the sea, living or dead'. His novels rendered similar benefits to the merchant service to those of Frederick Marryat to the Royal Navy in stimulating public interest and reform. While his descriptive powers were considerable, his characterization was not so successful. His nautical interests are also seen in his nonfiction. He wrote admirable biographies of William Dampier (1889), Horatio Nelson (1890), and Cuthbert Collingwood (1891) and edited the dispatches and correspondence of Marryat and Nelson (1890). His poems and naval ballads were collected into *The Turnpike Sailor, or, Rhymes on the Road* (1907; 3rd edn, 1911, as *The Father of the Sea*).

Meanwhile Clark Russell continued to contribute articles on sea topics to the leading journals. In 1880 he received an invitation from Joseph Cowen to join the staff of the *Newcastle Chronicle*, and later for a brief period he was editor of *Mayfair*. In 1882 he accepted the offer of a post on the *Daily Telegraph* and for seven years was a regular contributor to that paper under the pseudonym of A Seafarer. The tragedies and comedies of the sea were his principal themes, and his masterly account of the wreck of the *Indian Chief* on the Long Sand (5 January 1881) enhanced his growing reputation as a descriptive writer. Many of his fugitive articles in the *Daily Telegraph* were reprinted in volume form under such titles as *My Watch Below* (1882) and *Round the Galley Fire* (1883).

A zealous champion in the press of the grievances of the merchant seamen, Clark Russell urged that the hardships of their life had remained practically unchanged since the repeal of the Navigation Acts in 1854, and that despite the Merchant Shipping Act of 1876 ships were still sent to sea undermanned and overladen. Partly in response to this agitation further acts of parliament to prevent unseaworthy vessels putting to sea were passed in 1880, 1883, 1889, and 1892. In the *Contemporary Review* in 1885 Clark Russell protested against seamen and firemen not being represented on the shipping commission appointed by Chamberlain. In 1896 the duke of York (afterwards George V) expressed his opinion that the great improvement in the conditions of the merchant service was due in no small degree to Clark Russell's writings.

Latterly severe attacks of rheumatoid arthritis considerably reduced Clark Russell's literary activity and compelled him to retire, first to Ramsgate and subsequently to Deal. His last years were spent at Bath. Although crippled by disease, he continued working up to the last. He died at his home, 9 Sydney Place, Bath, on 8 November 1911.

G. S. WOODS, rev. SAYONI BASU

Sources *The Times* (9 Nov 1911) · *The Athenaeum* (11 Nov 1911), 595 · *Men and women of the time* (1899) · W. J. Ward, 'A national asset', in W. Clark Russell, *The father of the sea* (1911) · *Daily Telegraph* (9 Nov 1911) · R. R. Bowker, 'London as a literary centre, second paper: the novelists', *Harper's New Monthly Magazine*, 77 (1888), 17 · A. T. C. Pratt, ed., *People of the period: being a collection of the biographies of upwards of six thousand living celebrities*, 2 vols. (1897)

Likenesses P. Naumann & R. Taylor & Co., group portrait, wood-engraving (*Our literary contributors—past and present*), BM, NPG; repro. in *ILN* (14 May 1892) · portrait, repro. in Ward, 'A national asset' · wood-engraving (after photograph by Elliott & Fry), NPG; repro. in *Harper's Magazine* (June 1888)

Wealth at death £19,427 17s. 4d.: probate, 18 Dec 1911, *CGPLA Eng. & Wales*

Russell, Sir William Howard (1820–1907), journalist, was born at Lily Vale, in the parish of Tallaght, co. Dublin, on 28 March 1820. His father, John Russell (*c*.1796–1867), from a family long settled in co. Limerick, was agent in Dublin for a Sheffield firm. His mother was Mary (1803/4–1840), daughter of John Kelly, known as Captain Jack Kelly, a grazier, who owned a small property at Lily Vale. Near the house where Russell was born some ruins, known as

Sir William Howard Russell (1820–1907), by Roger Fenton, 1855

Castle Kelly, suggested a family prosperity, which by 1820 was only a legend. John Russell was protestant, and his wife Roman Catholic. In the early years of William's life John Russell's business failed and he moved to Liverpool. Unsuccessful, he at various times had a small business, was an editor, and was a shopwalker in a Liverpool store, which William regretted as 'a post unfit for a gentleman' (Hankinson, 89). William Russell was brought up first by his grandfather Kelly, and then in Dublin by his paternal grandfather, also William Russell. John Russell's wife and younger son, John Howard Russell, both died in Liverpool. Russell was brought up a member of the Church of Ireland and, influenced by his paternal grandparents' ascendancy Orangeism, was a lifelong, if sometimes unconventional, Conservative. He was educated at private schools, including E. J. Geoghegan's school in Hume Street, Dublin (1832–7). Always interested in military matters, in 1835 he attempted unsuccessfully to join the auxiliary legion raised by Sir George de Lacy Evans to fight in Spain. In October 1838 he entered Trinity College, Dublin. He left in 1841 without a degree, yet he acquired a knowledge of the classics and a liking for them, which continued through his life. His tutor frequently spoke of the possibility of his taking a fellowship.

In 1841 his cousin Robert Russell arrived in Ireland to organize for the reporting of the Irish general election by *The Times*, the largest-circulation daily paper, and he hired Russell as a reporter. Russell was ignorant of journalism, except for some slight work on the Dublin *Evening Mail*. At Longford, seeking information from both sides on events he had missed, he went to the hospital, where he found the information he wanted, and more. After the election, one of the middle-class 'micks on the make' (Foster, 284), he went to London to read for the bar, learned shorthand, did occasional journalism for *The Times*, and in 1842 was for a term junior mathematical master at Kensington grammar school, a proprietary school in Kensington Square. In 1843 J. T. Delane, the editor of *The Times*, sent him to report the repeal agitation in Ireland. Russell attended 'monster meetings' and had amusing encounters with O'Connell, who good-humouredly denounced the 'Times' Server'. His vivacious reporting was so appreciated by Delane that he became attached to *The Times* regularly as a reporter. He reported O'Connell's 1844 trial and the 'railway mania', and worked in the House of Commons press gallery. In 1845 he joined the staff of the *Morning Chronicle*. On 16 September 1846 he married at Howth an Irish Catholic, Mary (*c*.1816–1867), second daughter of Peter Burrowes of Warren Lodge, co. Dublin: they had two daughters and two sons. The marriage was initially happy but later marred by her illnesses and mental condition. Following years of illness, she died on 24 January 1867.

In April 1848 Russell enrolled as a special constable against the Chartists, and that autumn he rejoined *The Times*. In June 1850 he was called to the bar at the Middle Temple, but never applied himself enough to succeed, though it was some years before he ceased to take an occasional brief. In 1850 he accompanied the Schleswig-Holstein forces in their campaign against the Danes and was present at the decisive Danish victory of Idstedt (25 July). Convivial and amusing company, Billy Russell spent much time at clubs, especially the Garrick, and enjoyed brandy, billiards, and whist. He became the friend of Dickens, Thackeray, Jerrold, and other writers.

Russell's great opportunity came when Delane sent him as one of the *Times* correspondents to report the impending war with Russia. He left England on 23 February 1854 and was away nearly two years. He joined the army at Malta and went with it to Gallipoli, then Varna, and in September to the Crimea, where he reported the battles and the siege of Sevastopol. Unwelcomed and obstructed by Lord Raglan, senior officers (except de Lacy Evans), and staff, yet neither banned, controlled, nor censored, Russell made friends with junior officers, and from them and other ranks, and by observation, gained his information. He wore quasi-military clothes and was armed, but did not fight. He was not a great writer but his reports were vivid, dramatic, interesting, and convincing. His description of the 93rd highlanders at the battle of Balaklava (25 October 1854) as 'that thin red streak tipped with a line of steel' (Lambert and Badsey, 110) was later much quoted as the 'thin red line'. His reports identified with the British forces and praised British heroism. He exposed logistic and medical bungling and failure, and the suffering of the troops, especially in the winter of 1854–5, though he also gained credit for revelations actually by others, notably Thomas Chenery. However, Russell did not emphasize officer privileges and the contrast between officers' and other ranks' conditions. He criticized Raglan, unjustly scapegoating him, and other senior officers. He wrote privately to Delane—in November 1854 alleging 'Lord Raglan is utterly incompetent to lead an army' (Sweetman, 263)—

who used his letters in editorials and contacts with ministers. In May 1855 Russell accompanied the allied amphibious force to Kerch, at the entrance to the Sea of Azov. The operation was successful, but marred by vandalism and looting. Russell condemned the 'destruction and barbarous violence' (Lambert and Badsey, 205) and blamed the British commander, Sir George Brown, for not preventing it.

Russell's reports had a great impact on the British public and politicians. They contributed to the sending of Florence Nightingale and her nurses and of many 'comforts' to the troops, and to the authorities' improving supplies and conditions. They also, by arousing public, especially middle-class, indignation, contributed to the demand for military and administrative reform and to the fall of the Aberdeen ministry (30 January 1855): the duke of Newcastle told Russell, 'It was you who turned out the government' (Hankinson, 84). However his reports also, as Raglan stated, revealed military information potentially useful to the enemy. Yet, Sir Evelyn Wood wrote, Russell 'saved the remnant' of the army.

Russell 'rose like a meteor in the Crimean War' (Bullard, 31). He returned as Balaclava Russell or Crimean Russell, famous and lionized. In 1856 Trinity College, Dublin, awarded him an honorary LLD, and from then until knighted he was known as Dr Russell. From his reports he compiled *The War: from the Landing at Gallipoli to the Death of Lord Raglan* (2 vols., 1855, 1856), and thereafter he published a succession of books, mostly compiled from his war, travel, and other reporting. In 1857, advised by Dickens, he lectured on the Crimean War in England, Scotland, and Ireland, and gained £1600. Fame won him entry to aristocratic society; his charm and entertaining company ensured he continued there. He became a friend of the second duke of Wellington and of the third duke of Sutherland.

In December 1857 *The Times* sent Russell to India to report the mutiny war and investigate rebel atrocities; he reached Calcutta in January 1858. He accompanied Sir Colin Campbell (Lord Clyde), who welcomed and assisted him, on the 1858 campaign, and narrowly escaped being killed by a rebel. Russell criticized British snobbery as well as attitudes to and treatment of Indians, and advocated leniency and conciliation. His *Times* articles were attacked by the Anglo-Indian press. Delane attributed the cessation of indiscriminate executions to Russell's first report from Cawnpore. He left India in March 1859 and returned home.

From 1860 to 1901 Russell was founder editor and variously part and sole owner of the *Army and Navy Gazette*, which he partly wrote and to which he attracted distinguished contributors. He advocated army reforms, breech-loading artillery, and conscription. His attitudes were largely continentalist: 'he took the characteristically Continental view of an Army rather than the characteristically English view' (Atkins, 2.357).

In March 1861, with war there imminent, *The Times* sent Russell to the United States, paying £1200 a year and expenses. He opposed slavery and favoured the north. Initially he was lionized: one paper called him 'the most famous newspaper correspondent the world has ever seen' (Atkins, 2.8). However, after he described the Federal disorderly retreat after the first battle of Bull Run (21 July 1861), condemning the 'disgraceful rout' (Russell, *My Diary*, 2.238), he was nicknamed Bull Run Russell, vilified, and his life threatened, and he was forbidden to accompany the Federal army. He returned to England without warning in April 1862, much to the displeasure of Delane. He received a pension of £300 a year from *The Times* in 1863, and continued an occasional contributor until his death.

In 1866 Russell reported for *The Times* the last phase of the Austro-Prussian War, including the battle of Königgrätz (Sadowa) on 3 July. Much impressed by the Prussians' bolt-action Dreyse 'needle-gun', which he considered crucial to the Prussian victory, he urged the British rearm with a fixed-ammunition breech-loading rifle.

In 1870–71 Russell reported for *The Times* the Franco-Prussian War. He accompanied the army of the Prussian crown prince and was treated with much consideration. He failed to adopt new faster methods, especially telegraphing, and was repeatedly scooped by his rivals, notably Archibald Forbes of the *Daily News*. Mowbray Morris, the *Times* manager, told Russell, 'The D. N. has beaten us hollow, and continues to do so' (Atkins, 2.216). In 1871 Russell was awarded the Iron Cross, second class.

In 1879 Russell wanted to report the Anglo-Zulu War. Rejected by *The Times* and *The Standard*, he was employed by Edward Levy-Lawson of the *Daily Telegraph*, which had overtaken *The Times* in circulation if not in prestige. He accompanied Sir Garnet Wolseley, who despised but cultivated journalists, and arrived after the Anglo-Zulu War was essentially over. He opposed the policies of Frere and Wolseley. In November 1879 he reported alleged drunkenness, robbery, and other misconduct by British troops in the Transvaal. Wolseley denied this and there was public controversy between them. Privately Wolseley considered Russell 'no gentleman … the scoundrel and low snob' (Spiers, *Late Victorian Army*, 196), an 'ass' ignorant of war, and accepted socially only because he was 'a buffoon and professional jester' (Preston, 202). In 1882 Russell was visiting Egypt when the British invaded: Wolseley forbad him to accompany the troops. In 1884 in the *Army and Navy Gazette* Russell denounced Wolseley's Nile route for the Gordon relief expedition. Ostensibly their relations were amicable.

In the 1868 general election—partly financed by the duke of Wellington and other friends, and allegedly partly by his inept fellow candidate Charles James Freake—Russell unsuccessfully contested the two-member Chelsea constituency as 'a Conservative on independent Liberal principles' (Atkins, 2.151), opposed to Irish disestablishment and to compulsory education. Top of the poll was Charles Wentworth Dilke. Russell was invited but declined to stand again.

Allegedly in the 1870s Russell enjoyed a secret mistress, with whom he had three children. In 1883 he met at a house party in Scotland, and on 18 February 1884 married at the British embassy in Paris, an Italian Catholic, Countess Antoinette Mathilde Pia Alexandra Malvezzi (c.1847–1918)—Russell called her Titi—daughter of Count Malvezzi. They had no children and the marriage was happy.

From about 1868 Russell was a member of the prince of Wales's circle, though his relationship with the prince fluctuated, and he deplored the depravity and obscenity of some of his set. Russell sometimes dined with the duke of Cambridge, who disagreed with him and teased him. He accompanied the prince on his tours through the Near East in 1869 and India in 1875–6 (for which *The Times* paid Russell £300 a month plus expenses) and published books on them. In 1881, with the duke of Sutherland, he revisited Canada and the United States, and in 1889 went as the guest of Colonel John Thomas North, the Nitrate King, who paid him £1000, to South America.

Russell considered himself 'a gentleman by birth and education' (Hankinson, 31). He was about 5 feet 7 inches, portly, with blue eyes. He had a pleasant baritone and retained his Irish brogue. In the Crimea and India he was bearded, later only moustached. Latterly he was overweight. Sociable, affectionate, charming, lively, amusing, and a raconteur, he was considered 'the best company in the world' (Atkins, 2.127), but in private was sometimes anxious and depressed. He was brave, impulsive, moved by indignation and pity, and sometimes outspoken. However, he was sometimes careless, unfair, and—as apparently with Raglan—motivated by a personal grudge. He continued to spend much time at his clubs, which included the Carlton and the Marlborough, and he ate and drank much. Despite his post-Crimea substantial income, he spent extravagantly and was repeatedly in debt.

Though only a small minority of his working life was spent reporting wars, Russell's greatest achievement was as a war correspondent, a term he disliked. Though not the first person to report a war for a newspaper, in the Crimea he established the concept and credibility of the war correspondent and strong public support for the role. Largely because of him war correspondence emerged as a new branch of journalism, and he largely set the pattern for British war correspondents.

Russell was knighted on Lord Rosebery's recommendation in 1895, and was created CVO in 1902. He was awarded British campaign medals and French, Prussian, Austrian, Turkish, Greek, and Portuguese orders, and was deputy lieutenant for Tower Hamlets. He died on 10 February 1907 at his home, 202 Cromwell Road, Kensington, London, and was buried at Brompton cemetery, London. His widow, who survived him, in 1912 received a civil-list pension of £80. On 9 February 1909 a bronze memorial bust of Russell by Bertram Mackennal was unveiled in the crypt of St Paul's Cathedral; the inscription read 'the first and greatest of War Correspondents' (Atkins, 2.388).

ROGER T. STEARN

Sources J. B. Atkins, *The life of Sir William Howard Russell C.V.O., LL.D: the first special correspondent*, 2 vols. (1911) • A. Hankinson, *Man of wars: William Howard Russell of 'The Times'* (1982) • Burke, *Peerage*

(1967) · *WWW* · Burtchaell & Sadleir, *Alum. Dubl.*, 2nd edn · L. Brown, *Victorian news and newspapers* (1985) · F. L. Bullard, *Famous war correspondents* (1914) · W. H. Russell, *The great war with Russia: the invasion of the Crimea*, 2nd edn (1895) · W. H. Russell, *My diary north and south*, 2 vols. (1863) · [S. Morison and others], *The history of The Times*, 2 (1939) · C. Hibbert, *The destruction of Lord Raglan* [1961] · private information (1912) · J. Sweetman, *Raglan: from the Peninsula to the Crimea* (1993) · S. M. Mitra, *The life and letters of Sir John Hall* (1911) · *In relief of Gordon: Lord Wolseley's campaign journal of the Khartoum relief expedition, 1884–1885*, ed. A. Preston (1967) · E. M. Spiers, *Radical general: Sir George de Lacy Evans, 1787–1870* (1983) · A. Lambert and S. Badsey, *The war correspondents: the Crimean War* (1994) · *The letters of Charles Dickens*, ed. M. House, G. Storey, and others, 8 (1995) · E. M. Spiers, *The late Victorian army, 1868–1902* (1992) · P. Knightley, *The first casualty: the war correspondent as hero, propagandist and myth maker from the Crimea to Vietnam* (1975); pbk edn (1978) · R. F. Foster, *Paddy and Mr Punch: connections in Irish and English history* (1995) · R. T. Stearn, 'War correspondents and colonial war, c.1870–1900', *Popular imperialism and the military, 1850–1950*, ed. J. M. MacKenzie (1992) · A. D. Lambert, *The Crimean War: British grand strategy, 1853–56* (1990)

Archives News Int. RO, papers | BL, letters to Sir A. H. Layard and others · Hove Central Library, letters to Lord Wolseley and Lady Wolseley · Hunt. L., letters · NL Scot., letters to Lord William Hay, MS 14467 · NL Scot., letters to Lord Rosebery · Sheff. Arch., letters to Lord Wharncliffe

Likenesses R. Fenton, photograph, 1855, V&A [*see illus.*] · L. Dickinson, oils, c.1860, News Int. RO · H. N. O'Neil, group portrait, oils, 1869 (*The billiard room of the Garrick Club*), Garr. Club · B. Mackennal, memorial bust, 1909, St Paul's Cathedral, London · Ape [C. Pellegrini], caricature, watercolour study, NPG; repro. in *VF* (16 Jan 1875) · T. Cranfield, carte-de-visite, NPG · C. D. Fredericks & Co., carte-de-visite, NPG · H. Furniss, caricature, pen-and-ink sketch, NPG · Lock & Whitfield, photograph, woodburytype (oval, for *Men of Mark* (1876)), NPG · London Stereoscopic Co., photograph, carte (seated), NPG, Album 40 · Mayall, photograph, carte, NPG · Schier & Schoefft, photograph, carte, NPG, X8722 · woodcuts, NPG

Wealth at death £4343 3s. 2d.: probate, 2 May 1907, *CGPLA Eng. & Wales*

Russell, William James (1830–1909), chemist and educationist, was born on 20 May 1830 at Gloucester, the third child of Thomas Pougher Russell (1775–1851), a banker at Gloucester, and his wife, Mary (1790–1877), fourth daughter of Colonel James Skey and his second wife, Eleanor. His paternal grandfather, William *Russell (1740–1818), was a close friend of Joseph Priestley. He attended private schools—Dr Wreford's at Bristol and later Mr Bache's at Birmingham. In 1847 he entered University College, London, to study chemistry under Thomas Graham and Alexander Williamson (1824–1904). From 1851 to 1853 he was assistant to Edward Frankland at Owens College, Manchester, before proceeding to Heidelberg University to study under Robert Bunsen. He graduated PhD and returned to England in 1855.

During the next fifteen years Russell held various appointments, which sometimes overlapped. He taught for two years at the Midland Institute, Birmingham, and in 1857 became assistant to Williamson in London, an appointment which lasted until about 1867. However, in 1860–70 he was also professor of natural philosophy at Bedford College for Women, and from 1865, lecturer in chemistry at the Royal Albert Veterinary College. In 1868–70 he was at St Mary's Hospital medical college. Finally, in 1870, he became lecturer in chemistry at St Bartholomew's Hospital medical college, remaining there until his retirement in 1897.

On 21 August 1862 he married Fanny (1833/4–1871), daughter of Abraham Follett *Osler, glass manufacturer of Birmingham. They had one son and one daughter; the latter married Alexander Scott FRS.

Russell was a pioneer both in the chemical education of medical students, which he sought to make much more relevant to medicine than had been the case before, and in the scientific education of women. At the start of his time at Bedford College he opened the first science laboratory accessible to women students. During his long career his researches covered many topics. His earliest research was on methods of gas analysis and he wrote the article on this topic for Watts's *Dictionary of Chemistry* (1868, 1888). In 1863 and 1869 he made important accurate determinations of the atomic weights of cobalt and nickel. He devised a new method for the quantitative analysis of urea and made pioneering studies of the absorption spectra of solutions. For many years he analysed the air at several sites in London, in order to achieve a better understanding of fog formation. After he retired from teaching he continued research at the Davy–Faraday Laboratory of the Royal Institution.

Russell kept extensive diaries from the age of fifteen until shortly before his death, but their whereabouts is unknown. He did much voluntary work for education and chemistry. He was on the council of Bedford College in 1878–1903, and was chairman from 1887. Much development of the college occurred during his time. In 1851 he was elected a fellow of the Chemical Society and at various times was a member of council, treasurer, and vice-president; he was president in 1889–91, when the society celebrated its golden jubilee. He was a founder member of the Institute of Chemistry in 1877 and served in various offices, including president in 1894–7. Russell was elected FRS in 1872, served as vice-president in 1897–9, and gave the Bakerian lecture in 1898. He was prominent in the chemical section (section B) of the British Association for the Advancement of Science, was the founder secretary of the B Club in 1860, and was president of the section for the Bradford meeting in 1873.

According to an obituary Russell was 'quiet but genial in manner and … was very highly valued by a large circle of friends' (*PRS*). Wealthy, scientific, and from a Unitarian background, Russell was very much the kind of person for whom University College, London, was created, and he in turn did a great deal to further the expansion of quality higher education in the capital.

Russell died, after a short illness, at his country home, St Ives House, near Ringwood, on 12 November 1909.

JOHN SHORTER

Sources *JCS*, 113 (1918), 339–50 · *Nature*, 82 (1909–10), 101–2 · *PRS*, 84A (1910–11), xxx–xxxi · J. R. Brown and J. L. Thornton, 'William James Russell (1830–1909) and investigations of London fog', *Annals of Science*, 11 (1955), 331–6 [incl. bibliography] · K. R. Webb, 'William James Russell, 1830–1909: sixth president, 1894–1897', *Journal of the Royal Institute of Chemistry*, 84 (1960), 272–4 · *The Times* (13 Nov 1909) · M. J. Tuke, *A history of Bedford College for Women, 1849–*

1937 (1939) · *St Bartholomew's Hospital Reports*, 45 (1909), xlix–lvi · d. cert. · m. cert.

Archives NL Scot., lecture notes · Royal Holloway College, Egham, Surrey · RS, letters and referees' reports on articles | NAM, Burn-Murdoch MSS

Likenesses group portrait, photograph, c.1890 (with the Chemical Society Jubilee), Royal Society of Chemistry, London · photograph, c.1890, Royal Society of Chemistry, London, presidential portraits; repro. in Brown and Thornton, 'William James Russell' · H. Olivier, portrait, Royal Holloway College, Egham, Surrey

Wealth at death £85,993 12s. 1d.: administration with will, 29 Dec 1909

Russell, Sir William Oldnall (c.1784–1833), legal writer and judge in India, was the eldest son of Samuel Oldnall, rector of St Nicholas, Worcester, and of North Piddle, and Mary, daughter of William Russell, of Powick. In 1816, in accordance with the will of his maternal grandfather, he took the surname of Russell, retaining Oldnall as a forename. He matriculated from Christ Church, Oxford, on 22 December 1801, and was a student of the college until 1810, graduating BA in 1804 and MA in 1807. He was admitted as a member of Lincoln's Inn on 12 November 1805, was called to the bar on 19 June 1809, and became a serjeant-at-law on 25 June 1827. He married, in 1825, Louisa Maria, daughter of John Lloyd Williams, and they had children.

In 1819 Russell published a *Treatise on Crimes and Misdemeanours* (2 vols.), by far the most significant event of his professional life. The *Treatise* went through twelve editions, the last published in 1964. After Russell's own second edition (1826), the work was revised by a succession of legal editors, initially practising barristers and latterly academic lawyers. Russell's *Treatise* (along with J. F. Archbold's *Law and Practice Relating to Pleading and Evidence in Criminal Cases*, first published in 1822) was the most influential and enduring of nineteenth-century general practitioner works on the criminal law. The *Treatise* was innovatory both structurally and substantively. Its substance was largely a skilful synthesis of authoritative institutional works, including those of Hale, Hawkins, Foster, and Blackstone, combined with previously unpublished judicial manuscripts. Most significantly, and unlike any other practitioner work of the period, Russell's *Treatise* incorporated much of Blackstone's general conceptual treatment of the basis of criminal responsibility in its opening chapter. Additionally, Russell broke ranks with earlier and contemporary writers on criminal law in respect of the expositional hierarchy or ordering of offences. In particular, instead of adopting the convention of first dealing with religious offences followed by an account of those relating to treason, Russell jettisoned the former and radically pruned the latter, describing them as 'offences principally affecting the government, the public peace or public rights' (*Treatise*, 'Preface'). The work went through seven American editions between 1824 and 1853. More generally, subsequent nineteenth- and early twentieth-century editions suffered from the unwillingness of editors to combine the integration of new authorities with the systematic excision of redundant accounts

of case law. It was a characteristic which provoked the later criminal theorist Fitzjames Stephen to comment:

> The cases as they stand in Russell are like the stores at Balaclava in the winter of 1854 ... Everything is there, nothing is in its place, and the few feeble attempts at arrangement ... only serve to bring the mass of confusion to light. (Stephen, 366)

Russell also published *Practice in the Court of Great Sessions on the Caermarthen Circuit* (3 parts, 1814), and with Edward Ryan, *Crown Cases Reserved and Decided, 1799–1824* (1825).

Russell's contemporary influence and reputation as a criminal lawyer and author were fulsomely acknowledged during a parliamentary speech of Peel in relation to Peel's criminal law reform programme:

> There is one gentleman ... to whom I must make this public return of my acknowledgement ... Mr. Russell, a gentleman who has rendered important service to the law by most valuable publications, and who has offered suggestions with respect to many provisions included in these bills that are entitled to every attention. (*Hansard 2*)

In the previous year Russell had written to Peel emphasizing the importance for the functioning of the criminal justice system of Russell and Ryan's *Crown Cases Reserved and Decided*, and requesting Peel's permission to make him the work's dedicatee.

In January 1832 Charles Grant, president of the India board, appointed Russell chief justice of Bengal, whereupon Russell was knighted (22 February 1832). Grant believed that, 'after much enquiry', he had selected 'the fittest person for the duty', and he was surprised that a man of such calibre accepted the post, notwithstanding the enormous annual salary of £8000 attached to it, which was equal to that of the lord chief justice of England (Philips, 2.1066, Grant to Bentinck, 13 May 1833). Russell's former co-author, Sir Edward Ryan, then a puisne judge at Calcutta, was bitterly disappointed not to get the job himself, but he had not long to wait. Russell arrived in Calcutta in July 1832, but he sickened soon afterwards. He died on board the steamer *Enterprize* off the coast of Prince of Wales Island (Penang), where he had gone for his health, on 22 January 1833, and was buried on the island on the same day. Ryan was made chief justice in his stead.

K. J. M. Smith

Sources W. P. Baildon, ed., *The records of the Honorable Society of Lincoln's Inn: admissions*, 2 (1896) · W. P. Baildon, ed., *The records of the Honorable Society of Lincoln's Inn: the black books*, 4 (1902) · Foster, *Alum. Oxon.* · *DNB* · *East-India Register and Directory* (1833–4) · *Hansard 2* (1826), 14.1238 · 'Return of the number of persons appointed to judicial or legal offices in ... the East Indies since January 1832', *Parl. papers* (1847–8), 51.203, no. 473, 51.205, no. 473-II · J. F. Stephen, *Digest of the criminal law* (1877), 366 · D. Duman, *The English and colonial bars in the nineteenth century* (1983) · BL, Peel MSS, Add. MSS 40379, fol. 204; 40386, fol. 63; 40387, fol. 288 · Sir E. Cotton, *Memories of the supreme court at Fort William in Bengal, 1774–1862* (1925) · 'Charles Grant to Lord Bentinck, 13 May 1833', *The correspondence of Lord William Cavendish Bentinck, governor-general of India, 1828–1835*, ed. C. H. Philips, 2 (1977), 1064–6 · Bengal ecclesiastical records, BL OIOC, N/1/65, fol. 22

Archives BL, Peel MSS

Likenesses T. George?, sketch, 1832, Lincoln's Inn, London · F. C. Lewis, stipple (after T. George), Lincoln's Inn, London

Wealth at death Rs56,568 [£5657] Indian estate: Bengal Inventories, BL OIOC, L/AG/34/27/103, p. 185; will, BL OIOC, L/AG/34/29/52, fols. 157–64

Russell, William Whitworth (1795–1847), prison reformer, was born at Eltham, Kent, on 17 September 1795, the fourth son of five sons and five daughters born to Sir Henry *Russell (1751–1836), chief justice of Bengal, and his wife, Anne Barbara (d. 1814), daughter of Sir Charles Whitworth. He was educated at Harrow School and matriculated at St John's College, Cambridge, on 7 June 1814. He graduated BA in 1818 and MA in 1822. He was ordained deacon on 20 December 1818 at Lincoln and priest on 19 December 1819. Russell married Frances Carpenter (d. 1873), a vice-admiral's daughter, on 6 April 1824 and they had two sons and a daughter.

From 1825 to his death Russell was vicar of Chiddingly, Sussex, but his life's work lay elsewhere, for in 1830 he was appointed chaplain to Millbank penitentiary from a strong list of applicants. This had opened in 1816 as a showcase prison on the banks of the Thames, and was designed to house up to 1000 prisoners of both sexes whose sentences of transportation had been commuted conditional on a long sentence at Millbank. It was the only British prison directly administered by central government at this time. The chaplain was salaried at £400 p.a. and lived in the prison. He was responsible for ministry to prisoners and staff, and was required to hold two Sunday services weekly, visit infirmary patients daily, supervise the education of prisoners in morality, numeracy, and literacy, and visit prisoners in their cells to catechize, admonish, and exhort them. Indeed the chaplain at Millbank had scarcely less authority than the governor, Captain Chapman, and Russell focused particularly on delivering moral and religious education which he saw as indispensable to reformation of character, devising systems of communal instruction to bolster his services, sermons, and cell visits. Russell demonstrated at this time a remarkable enthusiasm for lecturing to groups of prisoners and praise was lavished on him for his educational work. The prison under his influence also moved decisively towards cellular separation of prisoners. Russell's intense enthusiasm for long and detailed scriptural exposition of obscure texts to prisoners led to ridicule and hostility among some. For example, they would collectively intone 'Ba-a-lamb' at mention of Balaam of the book of Numbers and in unison hurl prayer books at his head as he preached to them.

In 1831 Russell gave evidence to the select committee of the House of Commons on secondary punishments. He focused on the glorification of vice and crime which, in his view, arose when prisoners were permitted to associate, and favoured cellular confinement of prisoners to combat what he saw as the corrupting, undisciplined, and brutal regimes in the prisons of his day. In 1835 he was back before the House of Lords select committee on prisons advocating rigorous uniform severity within a framework of single cellular confinement. However, in the meantime he had read William Crawford's report of 1834 on the American prison system. He decidedly agreed with Crawford on the merits of cellular confinement—the separate system at Philadelphia—as opposed to collective discipline with brutally enforced prohibition of communication—the silent system at Auburn—but he was concerned that complete cellular confinement would impede collective worship and education. He clung also to his belief in the value of the chaplain instructing small groups. Another focus of his evidence was the importance of preventing any manipulation of conditions by prisoners, for example, the discretionary reduction of sentence for good behaviour, because he was certain that human punishment, like divine, should be certain, rigorous, unmanipulable, and awful. The planks of his vision, therefore, were cellular separation, religious instruction, rigorous penal deterrence, and certainty of punishment—all intended to model the reality of a wrathful God who will inevitably meet and condemn all who do not repent. He was sure that promiscuous assemblage of grossly ignorant and sinful people in criminogenic communities was the ground from which the individual progressed from vice to crime to hell.

Russell thus argued in favour of a separate cell for each prisoner with instruction, worship, and hard labour carried out in partitioned cubicles within purpose-built chapels and treadmills, with only the chaplain in his pulpit or the supervisor in his dais visible to the prisoner at worship or hard labour. Masks would be worn by prisoners whenever outside the cell, for example on the way to chapel, to prevent recognition or communication. The prison would consist of a central headquarters and chapel from which would radiate lines of tiered cells approached by corridors between each line and on each tier. This would, in his view, prevent collective subornation of the project for the spiritual and moral reform of prisoners. In the cell the lonely prisoner would listen to conscience, dwell on past sins and betrayed family, reflect on the satanic horror of the criminal community and neighbourhood, and receive with joy the message and knowledge delivered by chaplain and officers of the prison. Indeed, by 1838 Russell was pressing for trade training and instruction in the cell rather than the penal treadmill. Overall permanent learning, he envisaged, would erase old habits of self-indulgence and wickedness, and new skills would be taught. Thus would be ingrained in the prisoner a wholly new view of religion and human obligation, by a system severe enough to break resistance and hardness of heart, but yet able to win over the individual with kindness, and thus be at the same time magnificently deterrent and reformative.

In 1835 Russell and William Crawford were appointed prison inspectors for London and the home counties under the 1835 Prison Act. There were five of these inspectors covering the whole country but Russell and Crawford were the senior team. They were paid more than the other three and given nationwide responsibilities for statistical reporting, investigating abuse, and advising the home secretary on policy and on his new duty of authorization of new prison rules and plans. Under this remarkable piece of centralizing legislation Russell and Crawford were indefatigable. Parliament published their long annual reports, which were dogmatic propaganda for the separate system. They devised new laws, demanded new regulations, and argued publicly with local magistrates and prison governors, such as George Laval Chesterton of Coldbath Fields house of correction in Middlesex, many of whom did not want utopian and expensive new programmes of prison discipline. In this extraordinary plethora of administrative activity Russell outran Crawford who, in more diplomatic frame, sought to repair damage done. Russell made a deep impression on prison policy in the late 1830s with his irascible, fundamentalist, and immensely energetic approach.

In 1838 Russell and William Crawford published their most detailed and polemical annual report. A few months before, Joshua Jebb, a royal engineer, had begun secondment to the Home Office as a prison surveyor. Conflict swiftly developed between the ideological, inflexible, and visionary Russell and the severely pragmatic Jebb, initially over their respective powers and duties, with Crawford trying to mediate. Clearly between 1837 and 1839 Russell was hugely overworked with plans to build other centrally governed prisons, such as Parkhurst (for juvenile convicts, which opened in late 1838) and Pentonville (a model separate system prison opened in 1842). He was convinced that Jebb was stealing his thunder by plagiarizing his and Crawford's architectural designs, and as the decline of transportation led to increased demand for home-based disposal of convicts in the 1840s, their rivalry intensified. Jebb favoured a new type of prison in which public works using convict labour would be a leading feature, and in which conditions could be varied according to conduct and point in sentence, with discretionary remission of part of the sentence held out as a further incentive to good behaviour. All this was of course anathema to separatists. As the 1840s wore on Russell lost ground to Jebb, who came more and more to the fore as the Home Office expert on the design and management of what came to be called convict prisons. In 1844 Jebb became surveyor-general of prisons.

By the mid-1840s Russell was exhausted by these struggles, and he was also speculating unwisely in railways to pay for the extravagant habits of his daughter, Fanny, who was going into society. In 1844 Russell, Crawford, and one other inspector had effectively been constituted the superintending board of Millbank. Two years later, serious allegations were made of excessive severity towards defiant prisoners (punishments of 100 lashes), of drunkenness on the governor's part, and of the authoritarian treatment of staff. These led to a parliamentary inquiry, before which Russell gave evidence. While the inquiry's report of January 1847 did not find the major allegations proved, it did find 'defects and faults' in governance, and Sir George Grey, the home secretary, criticized the prison board. Shortly thereafter, in April 1847, Crawford died of a heart attack in Pentonville model prison, and on the evening of August 2 of the same year Russell shot himself with a pistol in the board-room of Millbank penitentiary. The coroner's jury heard that he had been unwell for some days and found him to have been of 'unsound mind' at the time of his death. His historical significance is as a major public official spearheading a penal revolution aimed at radical reformation of the prisoner and general deterrence; *si monumentum requiris, circumspice* ('if you seek a monument, look around you'). BILL FORSYTHE

Sources Venn, *Alum. Cant.*, 2/5 · *GM*, 2nd ser., 28 (1847), 550 · E. Stockdale, 'The rise of Joshua Jebb, 1837–1850', *British Journal of Criminology*, 16 (1976), 164–70 · S. McConville, *A history of English prison administration*, 1: *1750–1877* (1981), 1 · L. Radzinowicz and R. Hood, *A history of English criminal law and its administration from 1750*, rev. edn, 5: *The emergence of penal policy in Victorian and Edwardian England* (1990) · Burke, *Peerage* (1999) · 'Inspectors of prisons for the home district', *Parl. papers* (1835–47) [reports 1–13] · 'Select committee on secondary punishments', *Parl. papers* (1831), 7.22–8 [evidence given by W. W. Russell] · 'Select committee … on gaols and houses of correction: first report', *Parl. papers*, 11 (1835), 11.31–65, no. 438 · 'Report of the committee of the general penitentiary at Millbank', *Parl. papers* (1835–40) [annual reports] · A. Griffiths, *Memorials of Millbank* (1884)

Russen, David (*fl.* 1702–1703), author, was in 1702 resident at Hythe, Kent. In 1703 he published *Iter lunare, or, A Voyage to the Moon*. It was reissued in 1707. The book consists of a detailed account and criticism of Cyrano de Bergerac's *Selenarchia*, which Russen had read with 'abundance of Delight' in the English version by Thomas St Sere (D. Russen, *Iter lunare*, 1703, 1). He held Bergerac's view that the moon was inhabited, and he proposed to ascend to it by means of

> a Spring of well-tempered steel, one end of which would be fastened to the top of a high mountain, the other to a frame or seat: this Spring being with Cords, Pullies, or other Engins bent, and then let loose by degrees by those who manage the Pullies. (ibid., 44–5)

The moon must be at the time of ascent 'in the full in *Cancer*' (ibid., 46).

Russen also published *Fundamentals without foundation, or, A true picture of the Anabaptists in their rise, progress, and practice* (1703). A reply by Joseph Stennett appeared in 1704. Russen made insinuations against the private character of Benjamin Keach, the Baptist preacher. A rejoinder to Stennett by James Barry was published with his *Brief and Plain Discovery* in 1715.

G. LE G. NORGATE, *rev.* FREYA JOHNSTON

Sources *GM*, 1st ser., 47 (1777) · ESTC

Rust, Cyprian Thomas (1808–1895), Church of England clergyman, was born at Stowmarket, Suffolk, on 25 March 1808, and was educated in a boarding-school at Halesworth. He became a Baptist preacher in London, and in 1838 was ordained minister of Eld Lane Chapel, Colchester. In 1849 he joined the Church of England, and entered Queens' College, Cambridge, where he graduated LLB in 1856. He was ordained deacon in 1852 and priest in 1853. After a brief curacy at St Mary's, Rockland, Norfolk (1852–3), he was licensed to the perpetual curacy of St Michael at Thorn, Norwich, where he remained until 1865. He then served for three years as rector of Heigham, just outside Norwich. When, in 1868, this huge parish was divided into three, Rust chose for himself the newly constituted parish of Holy Trinity, South Heigham. In 1875 he was presented to the rectory of Westerfield, near Ipswich, which he resigned in 1890. He died at Soham, Cambridgeshire, on 7 March 1895 in the house of John Cyprian Rust (1841–1927), vicar of the parish and the only child of Cyprian's marriage to the daughter of Samuel *Warren QC.

Rust was an accomplished Hebrew scholar and published several works, including *Essays and Reviews: a Lecture* (1861); *The higher criticism: some account of its labours on the primitive history—the Pentateuch and book of Joshua* (1878) was a treatise criticizing the writings of H. G. A. Ewald, and was entirely rewritten and republished under the same title in 1889 in order to deal with the theories of Julius Wellhausen and Abraham Kuenen.

THOMPSON COOPER, *rev.* L. E. LAUER

Sources Crockford (1860) · Crockford (1892) · Venn, *Alum. Cant.* · *The Times* (15 March 1895), 10
Wealth at death £3656 11s. 5d.: probate, 23 April 1895, *CGPLA Eng. & Wales*

Rust, George (*c*.1628–1670), Church of Ireland bishop of Dromore, was born in Cambridge. He matriculated as a sizar at St Catharine's College, Cambridge University, at Easter 1644, graduating BA in 1647. Rust then migrated to Christ's College, probably in order to study with Henry More and Ralph Cudworth. He was elected fellow of Christ's in 1649, a position which he held until 1659. He proceeded MA in 1650. In 1655 he delivered a Latin discourse in St Mary's, Cambridge, in answer to Pilate's question 'What is truth?' At the commencement of 1658 he maintained in the same place the thesis that scripture teaches the resurrection of the soul and that reason does not refute it. His reputation for learning was such that Ralph Cudworth, then master of Christ's, could describe him in 1656 as 'an understanding pious and discreet man … of exceeding good parts and a generall scholar' (Peile, 1.486). He proceeded BD in 1658, and must have taken his doctorate soon afterwards.

After the Restoration, Rust was invited by Jeremy Taylor, bishop of Down and Connor, to take up the vacant deanery of Connor. He was ordained deacon and priest on the same day, 7 May 1661, and travelled to Ireland in the company of Viscount Conway and his wife, Anne, in July, landing at Dublin in August; he was instituted as dean of Connor on the 31st of the same month. The trip appears to mark the beginning of close ties of friendship and patronage between Rust and the Conways. The year 1661 also saw the anonymous publication of Rust's most notorious work, *A Letter of Resolution Concerning Origen*. He made a controversial defence of Origen's heretical notion of the pre-existence of the soul. His aim was to stress the essential justice of God's initial creation of souls, and human freedom and responsibility for sin. He was clearly influenced by More's teachings on the subject, but his former teacher did not discover the pamphlet's author. The *Letter* earned the censure of the vice-chancellor of Cambridge, Theophilus Dillingham, who, according to More, regarded it as 'a dangerous book' (Nicolson and Hutton, 195). In 1662 Rust obtained further ecclesiastical preferment from the crown, becoming rector of Island Magee. On 20 October 1663, he preached at the funeral of Hugh Montgomery,

first earl of Mount Alexander, where he emphasized the necessity of a future state. In 1664 he became rector of Lisburn, where the Conways lived. At about this time, together with More, he recommended Valentine Greatrakes, 'the Stroker', to the Conways with a view to curing Anne Conway's debilitating headaches. Greatrakes travelled to the Conways' residence at Ragley in Warwickshire in January 1666 where, in front of Rust, More, Cudworth, and a distinguished academic audience, he tried but failed to cure Lady Conway of her illness. Back in Ireland, Jeremy Taylor, Rust's ecclesiastical patron, died in August 1667, and Rust preached a well-known funeral sermon. He was appointed bishop of Dromore, a diocese administered by Taylor since 1661, by patent on 8 November 1667 and was consecrated in Christ Church, Dublin, on 15 December. He fell ill in October 1670 and never properly recovered, succumbing to a fever on 30 November 1670. He died at Lisburn, and was buried in the same vault as Jeremy Taylor in Dromore Cathedral. He had been married but nothing is known of his wife.

Many of Rust's works were published posthumously by his friends and admirers. His *A Discourse of Truth* was published together with Joseph Glanvill's *The Way of Happiness and Salvation* in *Two Discourses* (1677), republished with annotations by Henry More in Glanvill's *Two Choice and Useful Discourses* (1682). Henry Hallywell, one of Rust's students at Christ's, edited, translated, and annotated Rust's *A Discourse of the Use of Reason in Matters of Religion*, a piece targeting the views of enthusiasts and deists, in 1683. Hallywell also edited Rust's *Remains* in 1686, which includes several sermons and discourses composed by him in the 1650s. His philosophical views were very close to those of his mentors More and Cudworth, and his contemporary and friend Joseph Glanvill. As a Cambridge Platonist, he consistently defended the use of reason in religion, emphasizing God's essential justice and rationality. He strenuously opposed atheism, enthusiasm, and deism. He reconciled this philosophical rationalism with adherence to the established church and claimed that he would 'sooner choose to be of the Communion of the Church of England, than any Church that I know in the Christian world' because it required conformity to only a few outward rites and left considerable latitude in matters of speculation (G. Rust, *A Sermon Preached at New-Town*, 1664, 37). This was a position which he felt accorded with the institutions of the primitive Christian church, in which he retained an abiding interest. According to Joseph Glanvill, he had given a new direction to Cambridge studies:

> He had too great a Soul for the Trifles of the Age, and saw early the nakedness of Phrases and Phancies; He out-grew the pretended Orthodoxy of those days, and addicted himself to the Primitive Learning and Theology, in which he even then became a great Master. (Glanvill, 161)

JON PARKIN

Sources DNB · J. Peile, *Biographical register of Christ's College, 1505–1905, and of the earlier foundation, God's House, 1448–1505*, ed. [J. A. Venn], 1 (1910), 486 · Venn, *Alum. Cant.*, 1/3 · J. Glanvill, *Two choice and useful treatises* (1682), sigs. N8r–O2v [pp. 159–64] · *The Conway letters: the correspondence of Anne, Viscountess Conway, Henry More, and their friends, 1642–1684*, ed. M. H. Nicolson, rev. edn, ed. S. Hutton

(1992), viii, 6, 44, 49, 118–20, 171, 173, 176, 186, 188, 191–2, 194–7, 208–9, 212, 215n, 220, 222–3, 246, 256, 261, 266–7, 286–7, 290, 321, 326, 471, 473, 501 · *CSP Ire.*, 1663–5, 645; 1666–9, 449–50, 451, 455, 457, 472–3, 530, 567–8; 1669–70, 110–11, 141, 245–7, 281–2, 285, 300, 305, 309, 320–21, 620 · E. Berwick, *Rawdon papers* (1819), 208, 247 · H. Cotton, *Fasti ecclesiae Hibernicae*, 3 (1849), 253, 281 · W. C. De Pauley, *The candle of the Lord: studies in the Cambridge Platonists* (1937), 177–85 · *The diary and correspondence of Dr John Worthington*, ed. R. C. Christie, 2/2, Chetham Society, 114 (1886), 118, 134, 301, 305, 312, 331 · C. H. Cooper, *Annals of Cambridge*, 3 (1845), 545–6 · P. C. Almond, 'The journey of the soul in seventeenth century English Platonism', *History of European Ideas*, 13/6 (1991), 775–91

Rust, William Charles (1903–1949), political activist and journalist, was born on 24 April 1903 at 5 Eastdene Street, St George's Road, Camberwell, London, the son of Frederick George Rust, journeyman bookbinder, and his wife, Eliza Rogers. He left school at fourteen and worked as an office boy at Hulton's press agency, from where he was sacked for exposing the trade union leader J. T. Brownlie as one of Hulton's labour correspondents. Rust also worked briefly at Sylvia Pankhurst's *Workers' Dreadnought* and shortly after its formation in 1920 he joined the British Communist Party.

Unlike most of that first generation of communist leaders Rust never really experienced life as anything other than a party functionary. Initially active as an unemployed organizer in Camberwell, he joined the party's executive as early as 1923 as representative of the Young Communist League, and its political bureau two years later. In the same capacity he made the first of his many trips to Moscow to attend the Fifth Congress of the Communist International. Though he was in many respects a model party bureaucrat, that did not necessarily make for comfortable office routines. In 1925 Rust was among twelve communist leaders imprisoned for sedition, in his case for twelve months, and several times before the war he had to uproot himself to perform party duties both at home and abroad. What his dependence on the apparatus did mean, however, is that he was to be noted even among his fellow communists for his quite exceptional devotion to Moscow.

That may in part have been a matter of ambition. In 1928–9 Stalin made much use of communist youth movements to undermine the older or less tractable elements still prominent in several communist parties. Rust, then working in Moscow for the secretariat of the Young Communist International, could scarcely have been better placed for such a role. One lasting result was an intense rivalry and distrust between Rust and Harry Pollitt, the latter then emerging as the party's secretary, while Rust was installed as editor of the party newspaper launched in 1930, the *Daily Worker*. There is much anecdotal evidence from his second spell as editor, from 1939 to 1949, that Rust regarded the paper not least as a vehicle for his own leadership ambitions.

By this time Rust had a formidable record as a party organizer. Ending his first stint at the *Worker* in 1932, he then put in spells as a party representative in Moscow, a district organizer in Lancashire, and a base commissar (technically the *Daily Worker*'s correspondent), with the

William Charles Rust (1903–1949), by unknown photographer

International Brigades in Spain. The occasion for his resuming the paper's editorship was a fierce controversy within the party leadership over Moscow's instructions that it oppose the war with Germany. As always Rust kept close to the Moscow line, and for the twenty months in which the communists maintained an anti-war stance he was one of a three-man secretariat which replaced Pollitt. After the Russians entered the war in June 1941 Rust retained his editorship of the *Worker*, and on the lifting of its temporary wartime ban in September 1942 he embarked on what many regarded as a quixotic project: the establishment of his communist news-sheet as a fully professional, mass circulation daily.

Rust himself was to recount these events in his *Story of the Daily Worker* (1949). Harnessing the goodwill the communists then enjoyed, both within the labour movement and on Fleet Street, the paper recruited a team of impressively talented young journalists, transferred ownership to a non-party co-operative society, and equipped itself with a new printing press and premises. To great fanfares and a torchlight procession, the 'new' *Daily Worker*, was, after considerable delays, finally launched on 1 May 1948. Briefly it held a six-figure circulation, but in truth its moment of opportunity had passed. With the onset of the cold war not only did many of its erstwhile friends desert it, but the paper itself was now subjected to the tighter political disciplines that the continuing reality of communist control allowed. The paper's long decline had already begun by the time of Rust's sudden death. He was taken ill at an executive meeting of the Communist Party and died from a haemorrhage at Charing Cross Hospital, London, on 3 February 1949.

Even among fellow communists Rust was not widely liked. Of deceptively Pickwickian countenance, he lacked nothing in self-regard and yet displayed a sedulous deference to the Moscow overlords who alone could further his considerable ambitions. Colleagues at the *Worker*, several of them indebted to him for their start in journalism, remembered him more positively. Certainly there was no doubt as to the energy and ability with which, not even a journalist by training, he took on the might of Fleet Street. As to his hidden complexities, these may never be fully revealed.

Rust's first marriage, to Kathleen Taylor (originally O'Shaughnessy), produced a daughter, Rosa, born in the USSR in 1925 and remaining there after her parents returned home. Caught up in the wartime deportation of the Volga Germans before coming to Britain in 1944, Rosa's very existence was unsuspected by most of her father's colleagues. Rust, meanwhile, had met his second wife, Tamara Kravets, a Soviet citizen and daughter of a Russian architect who, like so many others, came under suspicion during the terror. The circumstances in which Tamara was allowed to leave the USSR, herself to become a leading member of the British Communist Party, have since prompted considerable speculation among former associates. Rust's career, even more than those of most of his colleagues, may yet be further illuminated by materials from the Russian archives.   KEVIN MORGAN

Sources W. Rust, *The story of the Daily Worker*, ed. A. Hutt (1949) · K. Morgan, 'The communist party and the *Daily Worker*, 1930–1956', *Opening the books: essays on the social and cultural history of British communism*, ed. G. Andrews, N. Fishman, and K. Morgan (1995), 142–59 · A. Macleod, *The death of Uncle Joe* (1997) · M. MacEwen, *The greening of a red* (1991) · N. Barron, *History of the communist party of Great Britain, 1927–1941* (1985) · L. J. Macfarlane, *The British communist party: its origin and development until 1929* (1966) · B. Alexander, *British volunteers for liberty: Spain, 1936–39* (1982) · private information (2004) · *Sunday Worker* (25 Oct 1925) · *Daily Worker* (4–5 Feb 1949); (9–10 Feb 1949) · b. cert. · d. cert.
Archives People's History Museum, Manchester, communist party archives, MSS · Russian State Archive of Socio-Political History (RGASPI), Moscow, Communist International archives, MSS | FILM BFI NFTVA, documentary footage · BFI NFTVA, propaganda film footage
Likenesses photographs, People's History Museum, Manchester [*see illus.*]
Wealth at death £499 7s. 6d.: administration, 13 April 1949, *CGPLA Eng. & Wales*

Rustat, Tobias (*bap.* 1608, *d.* 1694), courtier and benefactor, was baptized on 17 September 1608 in Barrow-on-Soar, Leicestershire, the last of seven children of the Revd Robert Rustat (1567–1637) and Alice Snoden (*d.* 1660?), sister of Robert Snoden, bishop of Carlisle. Heraldic evidence suggests the name Rustat is probably a variant of Ruste or Russe. Although two elder brothers became vicars, Tobias became apprentice to a London barber–surgeon before

Tobias Rustat (*bap.* 1608, *d.* 1694), by Sir Godfrey Kneller, 1682

joining the household of Basil, Viscount Feilding, appointed ambassador to Venice in 1634. Feilding's secretary, Thomas Raymond, commented on Rustat's sobriety, piety, and his 'being so unlearned that he needed help in his writing and indicting' (*Autobiography*).

Feilding initially backed the parliamentarians, so Rustat moved across to the young duke of Buckingham, then being educated with Prince Charles. During the civil war, Raymond says, 'Rustat's abode was sometimes with the King, otherwhiles with the Queen and Prince'. Raymond and Rustat met again in Calais when Rustat was being interrogated while carrying a message, hidden in a hollowed-out cane, from the queen to the king in Oxford, for which he was paid £30 in September 1643 by the privy seal 'for service'.

According to a letter from the Revd Tobias Rustat (1716–1793) to William Cole, Rustat went with Buckingham and Lord Holland in 1647 to help the escape of Charles from Hampton Court. He also took part in the royalist rising in Kent, where he saved the life of Buckingham, whose helmet got tangled in a tree. Family legend says he witnessed the execution of Charles.

When Charles II went to Scotland, the small retinue he was permitted included Buckingham and Rustat. After the battle of Worcester, Charles fled in disguise and Rustat took away his sword and buff-coat, which became prized Boscobel mementoes. Five weeks later 'Toby Rustitt' was, somewhat surprisingly, given permission by the council of state to cross the channel. Rustat now became essentially the exiled king's valet, being appointed yeoman of the robes in 1659, which brought appreciable income from the fees arising from the granting of knighthoods and other honours. He also became under-housekeeper at Hampton Court, which provided further opportunities, such as petitioning for estates of convicted murderers forfeited to the crown. Two years into the Restoration he was lending money to other courtiers, using the king's authority to ensure priority repayment. He became a director of the Royal African Company and the record of his banking transactions with Edward Backwell still survives.

Being unmarried, with few household responsibilities, Rustat gave widely to charity. Over £10,000 was dispersed among Leicestershire churches, St Paul's Cathedral, Chelsea Hospital, St John's Hospital, Bath, St John's College (Oxford and Cambridge), Cambridge University Library, and particularly Jesus College, Cambridge, his father's college, where he is buried and where an annual Rustat Feast is still celebrated. In 1669 he and Sir William Boreman proposed founding a hospital at Greenwich. His benefaction to St John's College, Oxford, to distribute £3 p.a. to thirteen deserving fellows and scholars also endowed lectures on subjection and obedience and on the unlawfulness of subjects' taking up arms against their princes, to be delivered on the anniversaries of the king's execution and the battle of Edgehill respectively. The benefaction to the university library at Cambridge, to provide £50 p.a. for the purchase of books, was intended 'to return towards the Advancement of the true religion now established in this Realme, good learning and the honour of God' some part of the estate which he had acquired through God's special favour in 'his Majesties my most gracious master's miraculous restauracion' (Lewin and Renfrew, 19). Evelyn confirms that Rustat's bounty owed much to this sense of gratitude and loyalty. The books so bought were to be bound in the same way with Rustat's arms stamped in gold on the cover, kept in one place in the library, and recorded in a vellum book. His most important endowment at Cambridge was for eight scholarships for the sons of deceased Anglican clergymen. His £1000 gift towards the building of the Royal Hospital at Chelsea made him the largest single private benefactor to the institution. The king, Sir Stephen Fox recalled, 'said with discontent that he saw nobody in this age for building hospitals but Toby and himselfe' (ibid., 20).

Rustat commissioned three royal statues from Grinling Gibbons, all in Roman costume—Charles II, at Chelsea; Charles II on a horse, in Windsor Castle; and James II, now in Trafalgar Square. In Jesus College, where Rustat is buried, is a marble memorial, probably by Gibbons, which Rustat stored in his house for eight years. The college also has a portrait painted by Kneller, dated 1682. In the British Museum is a rare engraving, apparently based on this portrait, but incorporating a charity motif.

Rustat's total loyalty was lampooned in a 1673 mock auction which included 'Lott 43. The Travels of Charles II with the witty pranks of making knights of the legends written by Toby Rustan, Historiographer Royall' (Raymond, *Poems on Affairs of State*). Evelyn summed him up as 'a very simple, ignorant, but honest and loyal creature' (Evelyn, 4.207). Having sworn allegiance to William and Mary in

1689 to secure his pension, he still visited the earl of Clarendon imprisoned in the Tower in 1690 for his opposition to William.

Rustat died on 15 March 1694, aged eighty-five, in Westminster, and was buried in Jesus College, Cambridge, eight days later. He left over £20,000, principally to his brother's grandson Tobias Rustat of Withersfield (1668–1744), together with a cabinet which came from Charles I and three pairs of tennis socks.   PHILIP LEWIN

Sources P. Lewin and J. Renfrew, 'Tobias Rustat, best of royal servants', 1999, Jesus College, Cambridge [incl. appx: T. Rustat to W. Cole, 1743] · [J. Guise], *Autobiography of Thomas Raymond, and Memoirs of the family of Guise of Elmore, Gloucestershire*, ed. G. Davies, CS, 3rd ser., 28 (1917), 9–80 · W. Hewett, *Memoirs of Tobias Rustat* (1849) · T. Rustat, letters to Edmund Boldero, 1670–1677, Jesus College, Cambridge · Evelyn, *Diary*, vol. 4 · Edward Backwell's ledgers, 1663–70, Royal Bank of Scotland Archives · J. M. Renfrew and M. Robbins, *Tobias Rustat and his monument in Jesus College Cambridge* (1991) · *CSP dom.*, 1643–85 · parish register, Barrow-on-Soar, 17 Sept 1608, Leics. RO [baptism] · G. F. Farnham, ed., *Quorndon records* (1912), 324–43 · PRO, Lord Chamberlain's department records · PRO, Lord Steward's department records · Royal Arch. · J. C. T. Oates, *Cambridge University Library: a history from the beginnings to the Copyright Act of Queen Anne* (1986) · K. G. Davies, *The Royal African Company* (1957) · F. Peck, ed., *Desiderata curiosa*, new edn, 2 vols. in 1 (1779) · *Poems on affairs of state ... by the greatest wits of the age*, 3 (1704)

Archives CUL, papers and letters | Bodl. Oxf., MSS Rawl., letters · Jesus College, Cambridge, letters to Edmund Boldero

Likenesses G. Kneller, oils, 1682, Jesus College, Cambridge [*see illus.*] · attrib. A. Quellin, marble medallion, *c*.1685, Jesus College, Cambridge · W. Gardiner, engraving, 1796 (after G. Kneller); copy, BM · J. H. Lynch, engraving, 1849, repro. in Hewett, *Memoirs* · engraving (after G. Kneller), BM

Wealth at death £20,000: *Rustat v. Heron* (1698), bill of complaint by John Rustat against Tobias's executors · will, PRO, PROB 11/419, 64–5 (fols. 152*v*–155*v*)

Rusticus. *See* Newman, Edward (1801–1876).

Ruston, Joseph (1835–1897), engineer and manufacturer, was born in February 1835 at Chatteris, Cambridgeshire, son of Robert Ruston (*d*. 1850/51), farmer. He was educated at Wesley College, Sheffield, and was apprenticed in the cutlery firm of Wolstenholme & Son. Opportunities for advancement in this old-established firm were limited, so he sought a partnership elsewhere, having some capital inherited from his father, who had died when Joseph was fifteen.

On 1 January 1857 Ruston entered the partnership of Burton and Proctor at Lincoln. This firm, subsequently styled Ruston, Burton, and Proctor, was a small business of millwrights and general smiths. They made and repaired various types of machinery, including ploughs, threshing machines, and a few steam engines. Ruston brought energy, enthusiasm, and new business acumen to the firm. He persuaded his partners to make a more vigorous entry into the market for portable steam engines by building for stock. The first machines were well received at shows, and Ruston was keen to increase production. The pace of change was too great for Burton, who sold his share to Ruston in July 1857 for £8000. In 1864 Proctor retired, and Ruston became sole proprietor of Ruston,

Proctor & Co. (and the firm retained that name until 1918).

Joseph Ruston toured widely across Europe, and as far afield as Russia, to win business. He had a readiness to seize market opportunities and to innovate. As a result, while steam engines, threshing machines, and grinding mills remained principal products during the nineteenth century, there was early diversification into pumping and irrigation equipment for overseas, and into railway locomotives and pit winding engines. By the end of the century the firm had joined the leading manufacturers of gas and oil engines. The acquisition of the rights to manufacture mechanical excavators, known as steam navvies, led to a profitable development of the business. Their successful use in the construction of the Manchester Ship Canal established the reputation of these machines. The firm was turned into a limited liability company in 1889, with a capital of £500,000. Ruston served as chairman of the company until his death; but he also had other business activities, including the chairmanship of Joseph Rogers & Son Ltd, cutlers in Sheffield, and of the Lincolnshire Publishing Company Ltd, newspaper publishers.

Elected to Lincoln city council in November 1865, Ruston represented the lower ward until 1874, when he was made an alderman. In 1869 he was appointed chief magistrate for the city, and he was a justice of the peace for the city from 1871 and for Lindsey from 1885. He was mayor of the city of Lincoln for the year 1869–70. He was appointed deputy lieutenant for Lincolnshire in 1889, and was high sheriff of Lincolnshire for 1891, in which year he was also made a freeman of the city, the first to be accorded such an honour. Ruston entered national politics in 1884, being returned as Liberal MP for Lincoln at a by-election. He was elected again at the general election the following year. However, he parted company with the Liberal Party over home rule for Ireland, voted against Gladstone's bill of 1886, and declined to stand at the election called that year.

Ruston married Jane, daughter of Mr W. Brown of Sheffield, in 1859. The couple had two sons and six daughters. In 1873 Ruston bought Monks Manor, Lincoln, where he housed an extensive collection of art. A member of Newland Congregational Chapel, Ruston was a deacon of the church from 1865 onwards. He was a supporter of the church's mission work, and he made financial contributions for mission chapels at South Bar and Croft Street, Lincoln, and for the Newland chapel's new building. Other charitable work included involvement with the Lincoln branch of the YMCA—he served as president and contributed to a new gymnasium. He was president of the Lincoln committee of the NSPCC. In 1892 he paid for a new children's ward at the city hospital. He provided a drill hall for the Lincoln Volunteers in 1890, and underwrote the restoration of Queen Eleanor's tomb in the cathedral. He was involved in educational development in Lincoln through his position on the city council. He encouraged the development of the city's grammar school, and supported the extension fund for elementary schools. He served as chairman of the Lincolnshire Agricultural Society in 1892.

Joseph Ruston's spirit of enterprise became legendary in the late nineteenth-century engineering world. When he first became a partner in the firm in 1857 the business employed twenty-five men. At his death it employed more than 2500 people, and there was a branch in Budapest and agencies throughout the world. Ruston died of heart disease on 10 June 1897 at Monks Manor, Lincoln, survived by his wife. He was buried at Eastgate cemetery, Lincoln. One of his sons, Joseph Seward Ruston, was chairman of the engineering company from 1901 to 1939.

JONATHAN BROWN

Sources B. Newman, *One hundred years of good company: published on the occasion of the Ruston centenary, 1857-1957* (1957) • F. Hill, *Victorian Lincoln* (1974) • N. R. Wright, *Lincolnshire towns and industry, 1700–1914* (1982) • *The Engineer* (18 June 1897) • *Lincolnshire Echo* (11 June 1897) • *Implement & Machinery Review*, 23 (1897–8), 21754–6 • private information (2004)
Likenesses photograph, *c.*1886, repro. in *Implement and Machinery Review*, 21755 • photographs, Ruston Gas Turbines company archive, Lincoln • portrait, Usher Art Gallery, Lincoln • portraits, repro. in Newman, *One hundred years*
Wealth at death £912,303 4*s.* 4*d.*: probate, 6 Aug 1897, *CGPLA Eng. & Wales*

Ruthall, Thomas (*d.* 1523), bishop of Durham, is said by John Leland to have been a native of Cirencester; his parents may have been John Ruthall and his wife, Alicia (whose surname may have been Avelyng). He was educated at Oxford, where he took the degrees of BCL by 1488, licentiate in canon law in 1490, and DCnL probably by 1 July 1493, when a papal dispensation referred to him as doctor of decrees. By then he was rector of St Peter's, Barnsley, Gloucestershire, having been ordained acolyte on 13 September 1488 and deacon on 10 April 1490, in both cases at Worcester. In 1494 he was admitted to the fraternity of Christ Church, Canterbury, and a Canterbury connection is also suggested by his being collated to the rectory of Bocking, Essex, by Archbishop John Morton on 29 November 1495 (the living was a Canterbury peculiar). It may well have been Morton who brought Ruthall into government circles.

On 10 June 1495 Ruthall was in Rome, where he inscribed his name in the *Liber fraternitatis* of the Hospital of the Holy Spirit and St Mary in Sassia. On 24 April 1496 he was commissioned to treat with the French for redress of injuries, on 28 August 1497 was appointed an envoy to treat with Louis XII of France, and in June 1498 went on a mission to the papal curia. On 14 June 1499 he was made a papal protonotary. Secular promotion came the following year, when he was appointed secretary to the king; he retained this position until 1516. In 1504 he became a privy councillor. Meanwhile he had begun to accumulate benefices, being admitted rector of Monks Risborough, Buckinghamshire, on 10 October 1500, and of Southam, Warwickshire, on 12 November following. On 10 September 1502 Ruthall was admitted dean of Salisbury, on 7 December 1503 he was collated to the archdeaconry of Gloucester, and he subsequently obtained prebends in Wells, Lincoln, and Exeter cathedrals, together with the deanery of

Wimborne Minster. In 1503 he was elected chancellor of Cambridge University (where his degrees had been incorporated in 1499/1500), but resigned in 1504.

On 11 January 1509 Ruthall was made bishop of Durham by papal provision. The death of Henry VII on 21 April delayed his consecration, which eventually took place on 24 June at York House, Westminster, under a papal bull issued on the 12th, after Henry VIII had confirmed the appointment. The temporalities were restored on 5 July. Ruthall resigned his other preferments. He acted as an executor of Henry VII's will, and in 1513 accompanied the king to France with a hundred men, but was sent back to England when the Scottish king, James IV, threatened war. Ruthall took a leading part in preparing the defences of the borders, superintending the fortifying of Norham Castle (which nevertheless fell to the Scots after a five-day siege, greatly to his distress), and having St Cuthbert's banner brought out to bring victory, probably the last time it went to war with the levies of the palatinate. At the battle of Flodden, on 9 September, the bishopric's men, led by Sir William Bulmer, fought in the vanguard of the English army, and after the victory King James's banner was set beside the shrine of St Cuthbert, as Ruthall himself reported to Wolsey, in a dispatch describing the English triumph as 'the most happy that can be remembered' (LP Henry VIII, 1/2, no. 2283). A year later, on 30 July 1514, he was a witness when the king's sister Mary renounced her marriage to Charles, prince of Castile; he later accompanied her to France and was present at her marriage to King Louis XII at Abbeville on 9 October.

On 18 May 1516 Ruthall became keeper of the privy seal, an office he held until his death. A hard-working official who did much of the interviewing necessary in diplomatic negotiations, he co-operated closely with Thomas Wolsey, to the extent of being described by the Venetian ambassador Sebastiano Giustiniani as Wolsey's *alter ego* in the conducting of foreign affairs, and as 'singing treble to the Cardinal's bass' (LP Henry VIII, 2/1, no. 2205). In July 1518 he made a welcoming oration when Cardinal Campeggi arrived in London with Wolsey's commission as papal legate *a latere*, while in December he was among the ambassadors who went to France to negotiate the betrothal of Henry VIII's daughter Mary to the dauphin, Charles. In 1520 he was present with Wolsey at the Field of Cloth of Gold, and a year later attended him to Calais for negotiations with imperial ambassadors. He was present as secretary when Henry VIII examined the third duke of Buckingham, suspected of treason. On 19 June 1522 he witnessed the anglo-imperial treaty of Windsor. And in the meantime, when there was a renewed threat of Scottish attack in the north, he once more concerned himself with the defences of Norham.

Ruthall died, unmarried, at Durham Place, London, on 4 February 1523 and was buried in St John's chapel in Westminster Abbey. An effigy later placed over his tomb represents him as mitred and vested, with an epitaph stating that he died in 1524. His episcopal registers have not survived. Although he was seldom in his diocese a long letter from his chaplain in June 1518, reporting that 'The Bishop has won the hearts of all the country by restoring it to order' (LP Henry VIII, 2/2, no. 4258), suggests that he governed it effectively through subordinates, who by deliberate policy were more likely to be members of gentry families than local magnates like the Nevilles and Lumleys. It also indicates that he was concerned for his revenues, as does the surely apocryphal story, retailed by a Durham monk, that when Henry VIII ordered Ruthall to compile an account of the crown lands and revenues throughout England, the bishop also drew up an account of his own wealth, and had both reports identically bound in white vellum. But he accidentally gave the wrong volume to Wolsey, who passed it on to the king with the remark that he need look no further for money than Bishop Thomas Ruthall. The latter was so mortified that he died.

In 1509 Ruthall provided for the repair of the southern third of the bridge over the Tyne at Newcastle, and of the town walls. He also began to build a dining hall at his palace of Auckland Castle, and made provision for its completion after his death. It has been claimed that he added to the endowment of Cirencester grammar school, but evidence is lacking, while Leland records that Ruthall promised much for rebuilding the parish church nave, but died before he could give anything. Nevertheless the bishop's arms appear in the roof, while his maternal aunt Alice Avelyng gave 100 marks towards building the porch, to which his mother also contributed. The dedicatee of Thomas More's translation of Lucian, Ruthall was also acclaimed by Andrea Ammonio, who in one ode praised his eloquence, judgement, and tenacious memory.

MARGOT JOHNSON

Sources Emden, *Oxf.*, 3.1612–13 · Emden, *Cam.*, 447–8 · Cooper, *Ath. Cantab.*, vol. 1 · E. B. Fryde and others, eds., *Handbook of British chronology*, 3rd edn, Royal Historical Society Guides and Handbooks, 2 (1986) · J. Gairdner, ed., *Letters and papers illustrative of the reigns of Richard III and Henry VII*, 2 vols., Rolls Series, 24 (1861–3), vol. 1 · *CSP Venice, 1202–1509* · *LP Henry VIII*, vols. 1–3 · C. Wriothesley, *A chronicle of England during the reigns of the Tudors from AD 1485 to 1559*, ed. W. D. Hamilton, 1, CS, new ser., 11 (1875), 12 · *Historiae Dunelmensis scriptores tres: Gaufridus de Coldingham, Robertus de Graystanes, et Willielmus de Chambre*, ed. J. Raine, SurtS, 9 (1839), 151–2, 155 · *The itinerary of John Leland in or about the years 1535–1543*, ed. L. Toulmin Smith, 11 pts in 5 vols. (1906–10), 1/2.129; 2.50–51 · *VCH Dorset*, 2.113 · *VCH Berkshire*, 2.29 · R. Surtees, *A history and antiquities of the county palatine of Durham* (1810), lxv–lxvi · *CEPR letters*, vol. 16 · *Andreae Ammonii carmina omnia*, ed. C. Pizzi, Nuova collezione di testi umanistici inediti o rari, 9 (1958) · M. James, *Family, lineage and civil society: a study of society, politics, and mentality in the Durham region, 1500–1640* (1974) · G. R. Elton, *Reform and Reformation: England, 1509–1558* (1977)

Archives PRO, state papers of [Richard III], Henry VII, and Henry VIII

Likenesses recumbent effigy on tomb, 16th cent., Westminster Abbey, St John's chapel

Rutherford [Rutherfurd], **Andrew, earl of Teviot** (*d.* 1664), army officer, was the fifth and youngest son of William Rutherfurd (*d.* 1624) of Wrightslands and of Easter and Wester Quarrelholes in the barony of Restalrig, near Edinburgh, merchant burgess of Edinburgh, who came of a cadet branch of the Rutherfords of Hunthill, and his wife, Isobel, daughter of James Stewart of Traquair.

Rutherford attended the University of Edinburgh, but early on chose a military career, taking advantage of the network of Scots already in French service to enter the regiment of the *gardes ecossaises*, newly founded in 1642 under the colonelcy of James Campbell, earl of Irvine. Rutherford distinguished himself at the siege of Thionville in 1643 and the battle of Lens in 1648. He remained loyal to the French crown during the civil wars of the Fronde, and served for much of the 1650s under the command of Maréchal Turenne. In consequence he was in regular contact with James, duke of York, who also served in the army corps commanded by Turenne until the Stuarts shifted their alliance to the king of Spain in 1656.

Following the death of Campbell, and largely thanks to the strong support of Jacques d'Etampes, marquis de La Ferté-Imbault, *colonel général des Ecossais*, Rutherford succeeded to the colonelcy, in which capacity he served until the Franco-Spanish peace of the Pyrenees in 1659. He was described by Samuel Pepys as

> the boldest adventurer of his person in the world, and from a mean man in few years was come to this greatness ... only by the death of all his officers, he many times having the luck of being the only survivor of them all, by venturing upon service for the king of France that nobody else would. (Pepys, 5.170)

Contrary to some accounts, Rutherford never rose beyond the rank of colonel in French service, and was certainly not promoted to the prestigious rank of *lieutenant général*.

Although the regiment of *gardes ecossaises* was not officially disbanded until 1662, it was subjected to a substantial *réformation* of its effective strength after the peace of the Pyrenees, and Rutherford returned to Scotland in 1660. Despite his association with the Franco-Cromwellian military alliance, he seems to have had little difficulty in attracting the favour of the Restoration regime. On 10 January 1661 he was created Lord Rutherford with the right to nominate whomsoever he saw fit as his successor, a right that was especially significant in that, though Rutherford had married Susanna de Melville (who eventually survived him) in France in 1651, the marriage had produced no children. In March 1661 Charles II selected Rutherford to succeed Sir William Lockhart as governor of Dunkirk. Dunkirk was sold to Louis XIV in 1662, and in April 1663 Rutherford was transferred to Tangier as governor and in succession to Vice-Admiral Henry Mordaunt, earl of Peterborough. Pepys was hostile to the appointment, citing Rutherford's Catholicism when 'all the rest of the officers almost are such already', and suggesting that he was only appointed 'to prevent the Irish having too great and the whole command there' (Pepys, 3.282–3, 4.116). Prior to this appointment, in February 1663, Rutherford had been created earl of Teviot, though with succession limited to heirs male of his body.

Teviot's governorship of Tangier was marked by efforts to improve the fortifications, and a series of skirmishes against the surrounding Moorish populations. Pepys considered him 'cunning' and extremely adept at serving his own financial interests in supplying both the garrisons at Dunkirk and Tangier (Pepys, 5.275–6). On 4 May 1664 Rutherford, some four hundred soldiers, and most of his garrison officers were killed in a Moorish ambush about a mile and a half outside the town. His successor as governor, John, Baron Belasyse, was one of the five Catholic peers to be impeached during the Popish Plot. Lacking a male heir, the earldom of Teviot became extinct with Rutherford's death, but he had already made provision by his will in December 1663 for the transfer of his estates and other titles to Thomas Rutherford of Hunthill, who was created Lord Rutherford on 16 December 1665.

DAVID PARROTT

Sources M. Pinard, *Chronologie historique militaire*, 7 vols. (Paris, 1760–64) · G. Daniel, *Histoire de la milice françoise*, 2 vols. (Paris, 1721) · L. Susane, *Histoire de l'ancienne infanterie française*, 8 vols. (Paris, 1849–53) · F. Michel, *Les Ecossais en France*, 2 vols. (1862) · A. M. Ramsay, *Histoire du vicomte de Turenne*, 2 vols. (The Hague, 1738) · L. Addison, *A discourse of Tangier under the government of the earl of Teviot* (1685) · Pepys, *Diary*, vols. 3–5, 8–9 · *Scots peerage* · GEC, *Peerage* · E. M. G. Routh, *Tangier: England's lost Atlantic outpost, 1661–1684* (1912)

Archives NL Scot., papers | BL, letters to Lord Lauderdale, Add. MSS 23116–23121

Rutherford, Daniel (1749–1819), physician and chemist, born at Edinburgh on 3 November 1749, was the son of John *Rutherford (1695–1779), physician, and his second wife, Anne, *née* Mackay, and half-brother of Anne, the mother of Sir Walter Scott (1771–1832). Educated at first at home, he was sent, when seven years old, to the school of James Mundell, afterwards to an academy in England, and then to the University of Edinburgh, where, after graduating MA, he began his medical studies. He studied under William Cullen and Joseph Black, and obtained his MD on 12 September 1772, his inaugural dissertation being 'De aere fixo dicto aut mephitico'. This tract owes its importance to the distinction, clearly established in it, between carbonic acid gas and nitrogen. It opens with an account of the work of Black and of Henry Cavendish on 'fixed' or 'mephitic' air (carbonic acid). Rutherford proceeds to point out (p. 17) that 'by means of animal respiration' pure air not only in part becomes mephitic, but also undergoes another singular change in its nature; for even after the mephitic air has been absorbed by a caustic lye from air which has been rendered noxious by respiration, the residual gas (atmospheric nitrogen) also extinguishes flame and life. The mephitic air he supposes to have been probably generated from the food, and to have been expelled as a harmful substance from the blood, by means of the lungs. He found experimentally that air passed over ignited charcoal and treated with caustic lye behaves in the same way as air made noxious by respiration; but that when a metal, phosphorus, or sulphur is calcined in air (probably in the case of the sulphur in the presence of water), the residual gas contains no 'mephitic air', but only undergoes the 'singular change' above referred to. It follows then 'that this change is the only one which can be ascribed to combustion'. Rutherford gave no name to the residual gas (which has since been called nitrogen), but supposed that it was 'atmospheric air as it were united with and saturated with phlogiston'. John Mayow had

Daniel Rutherford (1749–1819), by William Holl, 1804 (after Sir Henry Raeburn, exh. RA 1802)

already conjectured that the atmosphere was composed of two constituents, of which one remained unchanged in the process of combustion, and had supported this view by experiments. Moreover, practically all the facts and views recorded by Rutherford are to be found in Priestley's memoir published in the *Philosophical Transactions* for 1772, and read six months before the publication of Rutherford's tract; but Priestley's exposition is less methodical and precise. Rutherford mentions (p. 25) that he had heard of Priestley's researches on the action of plants on mephitic air, but makes no other reference to Priestley's work, which he had quite possibly not seen. Neither of the two chemists regarded the gas as an element at this time. Rutherford's comparison of putrefaction to slow combustion (p. 24) is interesting, although Priestley had also previously shown the similarity of the two processes.

Having published this paper and completed his university course, Rutherford travelled in England, went to France in 1773, and then went on to Italy. He returned in 1775 to Edinburgh, where he began to practise. He became a licentiate of the Royal College of Physicians of Edinburgh on 6 February 1776, and a fellow on 6 May 1777. He was president of the college from 1 December 1796 to 5 December 1798. He married, on 13 December 1786, Harriet, youngest daughter of John Mitchelson of Middleton. Their daughter Margaret was the wife of James Alexander Haldane, and mother of Daniel Rutherford Haldane. They had at least one other daughter and two sons.

On 1 December 1786 Rutherford succeeded John Hope as professor of botany in the university and keeper of the Royal Botanic Garden at Edinburgh. Rutherford's interest in botany was, however, limited and his course attracted few medical students. These low numbers may have stemmed from the poor reviews his course received in *A Guide for Gentlemen Studying Medicine at the University of Edinburgh* (1792). According to this work, the vegetable preparations presented in Rutherford's class could be obtained in local shops, while the information Rutherford imparted to his students simply reiterated material found in a variety of popular materia medica treatises. This criticism of his course led Rutherford to engage in a public debate with James Hamilton, who was widely believed to have written this text. A letter by Rutherford directed to Hamilton appears in *Correspondence relative to the publication of a pamphlet, entitled A guide for gentlemen studying medicine at the University of Edinburgh*.

Rutherford's appointment as professor of botany brought him into contact with the Royal Infirmary, and on the death of Henry Cullen in 1791 he was elected a physician-in-ordinary to that establishment. Rutherford's clinical lectures were given in tandem with Andrew Duncan and Francis Home. He was elected a fellow of the Philosophical (afterwards the Royal) Society of Edinburgh in 1788, and of the Linnean Society in 1796. He was also a member of the Aesculapian, Harveian, and Gymnastics clubs.

Rutherford's publications were both few in number and highly derivative. Although he was traditionally credited with the authorship of *Characteres generum plantarum* (1793), this work was probably written by John Hope. Rutherford's contribution to this work was simply the inclusion of new material, all of which was drawn from other botanical works. His article 'An account of the morbid appearances observed in two cases of diabetes mellitus', published in the *Edinburgh Medical and Surgical Journal* (1805), simply described an autopsy with no new theories regarding diabetes being introduced. An earlier article entitled 'A description of an improved thermometer' was published in the *Transactions of the Royal Society of Edinburgh* (vol. 3, 1794).

Rutherford died suddenly in Edinburgh on 15 November 1819, leaving his wife and three children. He was buried on 20 November at St John's Chapel, Edinburgh. According to a letter written by Rutherford's nephew, Sir Walter Scott, his uncle

> had breakfasted without intimating the least illness and was dressd to go out and particularly to visit my mother when just while he was playing with his cat which you know he was very fond of he sunk backwards and died in his daughter Annes arms, almost without a groan and in the course of a single minute. (*Letters*, 6.51)

Scott went on to say that

> Dr Rutherford was a very ingenious as well as an excellent man more of a gentleman than his profession usually are for he could not take the back-stairs mode of rising in it. Otherwise he might have been much more wealthy. He ought to have had the Chemistry class as he was one of the best Chemists in Europe but superior interest assignd it to another who though a neat experimentalist is not to be compared to poor Daniel for originality of genius. Since you knew him his health was broken and his spirits dejected which may be traced to the loss of his eldest son on board the

East India-man and also I think to a slight paralytic touch which he had some years ago.   (ibid., 52–3)

B. B. WOODWARD, *rev.* ALEXANDRA M. LORD

Sources B. Henrey, *British botanical and horticultural literature before 1800*, 3 vols. (1975) · J. Johnson, *A guide for gentlemen studying medicine at the University of Edinburgh* (1792) · G. B. Risse, *Hospital life in Enlightenment Scotland: care and teaching at the Royal Infirmary of Edinburgh* (1986) · L. Rosner, *Medical education in the age of improvement: Edinburgh students and apprentices, 1760–1826* (1991) · private information (1897) · *The letters of Sir Walter Scott*, ed. H. J. C. Grierson and others, centenary edn, 12 vols. (1932–79), vols. 1, 6

Archives National Institute of Health, Bethesda, Maryland · NL Scot. · Royal Botanic Garden, Edinburgh, corresp. and papers · Royal College of Physicians of Edinburgh, notes on clinical cases · U. Edin. L., lecture notes · University of British Columbia, Woodward Biomedical Library, lecture notes

Likenesses W. Holl, stipple, 1804 (after H. Raeburn), NPG [*see illus.*] · W. Holl, stipple, second version, Wellcome L. · H. Raeburn, portrait; copy by H. Kerr, Royal College of Physicians of Edinburgh · bust, Royal College of Physicians of Edinburgh

Wealth at death approx. £2000: Scott, *Letters*, vol. 6, p. 82

Rutherford, Ernest, Baron Rutherford of Nelson (1871–1937), physicist, was born on 30 August 1871 between the settlements of Brightwater and Spring Grove, near Nelson, New Zealand, the fourth child and second son of the twelve children of James Rutherford (1838/9–1928), wheelwright, railroad tie-cutter, engineer, and farmer, and his wife, Martha (1843–1935), daughter of Charles Edwin Thompson (*d.* 1853) and his wife, Caroline.

New Zealand, 1871–1895 The New Zealand of Rutherford's youth was an agrarian society, settled by Europeans for only a few generations. Yet they brought to the antipodes their Scottish and English values of hard work, thrift, and a respect for education, and endeavoured to create the institutions that would reward their pioneering activities. Rutherford absorbed these qualities, exhibiting the energy and resourcefulness of his father and the thirst for knowledge of his mother, a former teacher. The family moved to Foxhill in 1875, Havelock in 1882, and Pungarehu, on the North Island, in 1886. Rutherford attended the state schools in these rural communities, benefiting from the Education Act of 1877 which mandated free schooling between the ages of seven and thirteen. A bright student, Rutherford won a board of education scholarship to Nelson College, a privately run secondary school near his former home on South Island. By the time he enrolled in 1887 he had tinkered with mechanical devices and perused a copy of Balfour Stewart's popular science textbook, but had given no evidence that he inclined toward a career in science. This would have been an unrealistic goal in any case, given the dearth of scientific jobs in New Zealand. William S. Littlejohn, a charismatic mathematics and science master at the college who provided extra instruction, was responsible for the youth's unlikely choice. Rutherford won prizes in almost every subject, but valued most those taught by Littlejohn.

Another competitive scholarship allowed Rutherford in 1890 to enter Canterbury College in South Island's largest municipality, Christchurch. If Nelson College was pseudo-Eton, then the city of Christchurch was simulated England, and Rutherford's horizons expanded culturally as

Ernest Rutherford, Baron Rutherford of Nelson (1871–1937), by Sir Oswald Birley, 1932

well as intellectually. The college, one of four that comprised the University of New Zealand, had a faculty of eight, and numbered about 170 students. Most important for Rutherford were the upright Charles H. H. Cook, who provided him with a solid, conventional mathematical education, and the outrageous Alexander W. Bickerton, whose contagious enthusiasm drew the student away from his initial mathematical inclinations to the wonders of the physical sciences. Rutherford's genial personality meshed as well with the probity of the pious professor as with the eccentricities of the anti-clerical socialist. More to the point, Bickerton was the first really creative scholar Rutherford encountered. Balanced by the level-headed, proof required mathematical approach of Littlejohn and Cook, Bickerton's spark ignited not a momentary scientific flare but a long burning flame.

At the end of 1892 Rutherford received the BA degree and won a mathematical scholarship for a postgraduate year at Canterbury, during which he earned the MA with double first-class honours in mathematics and mathematical physics and in physical science. This mathematical ability is notable, for during his career he rarely made significant use of it, with the major exception of the calculations that led to the nuclear atom model in 1911. Rutherford was encouraged to remain for the 1894 academic year; by this time he was captured by physics and began his first independent research. He had additional cause to linger in Christchurch, for his heart was captivated by Mary Newton, daughter of the woman in whose house he roomed.

The research, undertaken in a basement cloakroom, dealt with the magnetization of iron by a high-frequency discharge. This was a topic of some interest, both scientifically and economically. The radio waves predicted by James Clerk Maxwell's electromagnetic theory had been detected by Heinrich Hertz several years before and still held the keen attention of many physicists. Such waves were produced by a rapidly alternating electric current, as found in the discharge of a Leyden jar. Rutherford recognized that an already magnetized needle lost some of its strength in an alternating field, making it a detector of wireless signals, a device with commercial potential. He then endeavoured to extend the range and sensitivity of his apparatus. Two papers from this period were published in the *Transactions of the New Zealand Institute*, which rarely received submissions in physics. Rutherford earned the BSc in 1894 and applied for an 1851 Exhibition scholarship, an award funded by the profits from that successful event in London. He came in second among the New Zealand competitors, but received the prize when the winner declined it. A condition of the award was attendance at a different institution; Rutherford chose the Cavendish Laboratory of Cambridge University, whose director, Joseph John Thomson, dominated the study of electromagnetic phenomena.

Cambridge, 1895–1898 The university had recently changed its statutes to allow graduates of other institutions to qualify for a degree after two years of residence and the completion of a significant investigation. It was a measure of the increasing prominence of science in British—and indeed Western—society. Enrolling in the autumn of 1895 Rutherford was the first research student, and his success confirmed the wisdom of the change. He continued to improve his radio detector and soon was able to receive signals over a distance of half a mile. But he was diverted from this subject, never really to return to it. What commerce lost, science gained. The loss, it must be admitted, was not large, for there were other, more practical, types of detectors being developed, and Rutherford did not have the entrepreneurial vision and skills of a Marconi.

Two months after Rutherford's arrival in Cambridge X-rays were discovered in Germany by Wilhelm Conrad Röntgen. The new radiation had marked effect upon the discharge of electricity in gases, a subject in which Thomson was greatly interested. Rutherford could not decline the flattering invitation when his professor asked him to join in the investigation. Their collaboration yielded a classic paper in 1896 on the theory of ionization. The X-rays, they said, split apart atoms or molecules of the gas into positive and negative components called ions. The ions then were attracted to electrodes of the opposite polarity, their flow constituting a measurable current. Rutherford provided experimental data that quantified

the subject, while the theory, presumably, was crafted largely by Thomson.

This work continued through much of 1896 and 1897, with Rutherford examining the ions' velocities, their rates of recombination, the electrification of different gases, and other characteristics of the phenomenon. Thomson independently determined the charge-to-mass ratio of the most commonly found ion, a particle soon to be called the electron. His student, also independently, chased down other forms of radiation that produced ions, examining first ultraviolet light and then uranium rays.

Uranium radiation, or radioactivity, had been discovered in early 1896 in Paris by Antoine Henri Becquerel, who explored the phenomenon so thoroughly that it appeared there was little left to do with it. Then both Marie Curie and Rutherford, taking a more quantitative approach, looked at the emitters and their emissions and found there was much to investigate. Rutherford, who was always interested in the latest scientific discoveries, had the gift of recognizing those of singular significance and was creative enough to design rather straightforward experiments to tease out the details. Numbers mattered.

Gerhard C. Schmidt in Germany and Marie Curie in Paris found that the element thorium also was radioactive. Curie, with her husband, Pierre, and a chemist named Gustave Bémont, then discovered radioactive substances that they named polonium and radium and claimed to be new elements. The attention of the world's scientific community was now riveted to radioactivity, not to leave it for decades. Rutherford, however, was not captured by these siren songs of 1898; his flirtation with radioactivity began the year before, even before thorium's activity was noted. And his work alone, even without the notoriety of radium, would have sufficed to alert physicists and chemists to the significance of radioactivity. For the next four decades Rutherford and his students pursued radioactivity through its connections with atomic physics and its branching into nuclear physics and nuclear chemistry, he as the dominant figure in this science and the science recognized as one of the most important parts of physics.

It began with Rutherford examining the radiation from uranium. Absorption experiments in which the rays fell upon varying thicknesses of foil revealed one type that was readily stopped, though it was very efficient in causing ionization, and another that penetrated further through the foil but was a less effective ionizer. Rutherford often joked that he was a simple man and liked simple experiments and explanations. He named the two radiations alpha and beta, for simplicity.

From his electrical wave detector, through the electrification of gases due to X-rays, ultraviolet rays, and uranium rays, to the study of radioactivity itself, Rutherford published alone five substantial papers from his stay in Cambridge. His 1851 Exhibition scholarship was renewed for a singular third year and he was awarded Trinity College's Coutts Trotter studentship, worth £250. But Rutherford needed to think of salaried employment rather than term-limited appointments, especially if he hoped to marry. A physics professorship at McGill University in Montreal became vacant in the summer of 1898 and representatives of the school visited Cambridge to seek Thomson's advice. Although he felt he had little chance because there were older and more experienced candidates, the 26-year-old Rutherford was chosen. McGill, with a well-equipped laboratory, placed its priority on original investigation, and Thomson had pronounced Rutherford the best student in research he had ever had.

Montreal, 1898–1907 At McGill, Rutherford quickly won over those colleagues who thought that he could not fill the shoes of his predecessor, Hugh L. Callendar. The physics department's chairman, John Cox, was so impressed that he himself taught some of Rutherford's classes to allow him the maximum time for research; the laboratory was perhaps the best in North America. In Cambridge, Rutherford's primary attention had been upon uranium. Now he examined thorium's radioactivity. With more ideas for experiments than time (and sometimes special expertise) to conduct them, he looked to faculty colleagues for collaboration until he built up his own band of research students. The professor of electrical engineering, R. B. Owens, obtained erratic ionization measurements until Rutherford traced the cause to air currents in the room, and recognized that something from thorium was being blown about. Uncertain if it was a gas or a cloud of particles, Rutherford in 1900 called it thorium 'emanation', and European physicists soon discovered emanations from radium and actinium.

Rutherford added other radioactive substances to the list. The emanation itself was radioactive and deposited a layer, also radioactive, upon surfaces it touched. It was called 'active deposit' and eventually was resolved into a number of components, labelled thorium A, B, C, and so on. Rutherford noticed the deposit when insulators broke down: ionization produced by the radioactive materials allowed charges to leak away. He also observed that a number of substances, such as thorium emanation, radium emanation, their active deposits, and polonium decreased in activity over time, in contrast to uranium, thorium, and radium, whose strength appeared constant. For those that varied, the time to achieve half strength—the half-life—was unique for each substance and provided a means of identification.

The London chemist William Crookes doubted that the long-known elements uranium and thorium were intrinsically radioactive; there must be something entrained in them that emitted the ionizing rays. By a tedious series of dissolutions and recrystallizations of uranium nitrate, in 1900 he separated uranium that failed to expose photographic plates and a substance he called uranium X that succeeded in this alternative test for radioactivity. But belief in the stability of uranium crashed when Becquerel, who repeated Crookes's procedure, looked at his materials a year and a half later and found the uranium vigorous once more and the uranium X inactive. The first several years after Becquerel discovered radioactivity in 1896 were devoted largely to study of the radiations; it was

meat and potatoes for physicists. After about 1900, however, with the accumulation of many new radioactive substances, the emitters themselves increasingly came under observation, and their chemical identity was naturally the realm of chemists. Rutherford was alert to this change and found a new demonstrator in the chemistry department named Frederick Soddy who was willing to join him.

They repeated the Crookes–Becquerel work using thorium and the same thing occurred: the freshly prepared inactive thorium recovered its original level of activity in a few weeks and the initially active thorium X lost it. Graphs of the rise to double value and fall to half value showed the same time period for each, suggesting a more fundamental connection than mere entrainment. This was the key to Rutherford's foremost accomplishment at McGill, the explanation of radioactivity that he formulated with Soddy. The discoverer of the phenomenon, Becquerel, interpreted it as a form of long-lived phosphorescence, though even he found that unpersuasive by the early twentieth century, when he spoke opaquely of 'molecular transformations'. In keeping with the British tradition of visualized mechanical models, Crookes divined a 'Maxwell demon' acting as a gatekeeper to segregate faster moving air molecules and from them extract their excess energy, which appeared as radiation. The views of the Curies evolved, and in the early 1900s they strongly favoured the idea that an unknown ethereal radiation pervaded space, causing a resonance in the heaviest elements which resulted in the emission of alpha, beta, and gamma rays as secondary radiations. It was a clever idea, but as untestable as the others and thus worthless. The suggestion closest to the views of Rutherford and Soddy was offered by Julius Elster and Hans Geitel, who rejected external causes and placed the source within the atom itself.

Rutherford and Soddy agreed with the interpretation of radioactivity as an atomic phenomenon. But they sidestepped speculation and supported their case with evidence. Their theory, called at different times transformation, disintegration, and transmutation, asserted that the atomic process involved spontaneous chemical changes that produced new substances. Thus, thorium 'decayed' into thorium X, while thorium emanation decayed sequentially into thorium A, B, C, and so on. Each was a different chemical element. It is not difficult to sense their anxiety that they would be labelled as daft, for alchemy had been exorcised from the science of chemistry in the eighteenth century and it appeared that they were attempting to bring it back.

And bring it back they did, but in a modern, acceptable form. The graphs of the rise and decay of activity were interpreted as measures of each radioelement's quantity and half-life. When a mineral was mined the radioelements it contained were in equilibrium; in a given time the same number of atoms of the parent decayed into the daughter as those of the daughter decayed into the granddaughter, and so on until an inactive end product was reached. However, the quantity of each family member in the rock varied widely, there being many atoms of those with long half-lives and fewer of those with short half-lives. When a parent and daughter element were chemically separated, as in the experiment performed by Crookes, it would take time for the parent's activity to rise, as it formed more daughters, while maintaining its own numbers constant from the grandparent (unless it was the very first radioelement in the family, whose numbers can only decrease). Simultaneously, the separated daughter, deprived of its infusion of atoms from the parent, could only decline in activity as its own numbers decreased.

What explained the apparently constant activities of uranium, thorium, and radium? Rutherford and Soddy saw that they actually had half-lives, though they were very long compared with human lifetimes, meaning that they contained relatively enormous numbers of atoms. If they were the Adam or Eve of a family their numbers and activities were actually declining, even if the changes could not then be measured. This insight allowed Rutherford and Soddy to overcome an obstacle to any theory of radioactivity: it must conform to the law of conservation of energy. This meant that the energy's source must be identified, be it sunlight, moving air molecules, an aethereal radiation, or within the atom. It meant further that the source could not be inexhaustible. By saying that *all* radioelements, including uranium, ultimately would change into an inactive end product, they satisfied this cornerstone of nineteenth-century physics.

This revolutionary theory of 1902–3 was received with a minimum of contention. Few besides Lord Kelvin, by now aged and fixed in his ideas, and Henry Armstrong, a chemist of the old school who delighted in battle, rose to challenge it. Most chemists probably decided to reserve judgement, for it was hard to jettison their long-held belief in the stability of the atoms arrayed in the periodic table of elements, yet it was equally difficult to refute Rutherford's and Soddy's experimental evidence.

A good theory explains a range of scientific data; it also suggests further investigations to test likely consequences. The transformation theory was bountiful. McGill's benefactor, William Macdonald, donated to it a liquid air machine, then a novel forerunner of the 'big science' that involved scientific apparatus built by industry. With it Rutherford and Soddy showed that emanation was a gas, by condensing it at low temperatures. Interest in emanation was heightened even more when it was seen that it belonged in that remarkable family of inert gases found recently by William Ramsay. Soddy in 1903 joined Ramsay in London, where by spectroscopic examination of the substance they found that emanation produced helium, another of the inert gases.

Helium was never thought to be a radioactive body, but its identity was uncertain. The beta ray had been proven to be identical to the electron by Becquerel. The alpha ray also was a particle and of positive charge, as Rutherford found in 1903. Yet, charge-to-mass (e/m) measurements were sufficiently imprecise that the alpha might be a charged atom of hydrogen or helium. Rutherford inclined

toward the latter identification, though in either case he saw the alpha as the vehicle for changes in atomic weight as one radioelement transformed into another. It was especially fascinating to him because he could visualize the enormous speed and energy with which it was ejected from a decaying atom. Rutherford measured other characteristics of the alpha, including the number emitted each second from a gram of radium, a value important in calculating the half-life of the element. He tried again in 1906 to determine e/m of the alpha, but failed to resolve its identity; this would remain a task for the future.

Soddy had convinced Rutherford of the value of skilled chemical assistance, so he was delighted in 1904 to make the acquaintance of Bertram Boltwood, soon to teach at Yale University. Boltwood proved circumstantially that uranium and radium were related, thereby linking two radioactive families into one, and in 1907 discovered ionium, the immediate parent of radium. He was a major contributor to an understanding of the detailed sequence of the decay series. Their collaboration was by mail and focused on the amount of radium in each gram of uranium in many different mineral samples. Rutherford also suggested that if the inactive end product of the decay series could be identified, its quantity measured, and its rate of formation determined, the age of the mineral would be known. Boltwood, noting the universality of lead in uranium minerals, measured its quantity. Then, using Rutherford's value of radium's half-life and their joint figure for the amount of radium in a gram of uranium, he calculated lead's rate of formation. His oldest rocks were over a billion years. Geologists and evolutionary biologists in the nineteenth century had insisted upon a very long period for the age of the earth; the processes they studied required immense epochs. But physicists, led by Lord Kelvin's calculations of the rate of decay of heat from a once molten planet, produced ages of the earth as small as tens of millions of years. Rutherford's idea and Boltwood's quantitative execution of it changed the paradigm of this subject.

In the summer of 1900 Rutherford travelled to New Zealand, and in September married his fiancée, Mary Newton; they had a daughter, Eileen. His growing fame attracted research students to his laboratory from Europe and the United States, as well as from Canada. The German chemist Otto Hahn, who had discovered the radioelement radiothorium, and who decades later received the Nobel prize for the discovery of nuclear fission, came for the 1905–6 year. From the first Rutherford was hospitable to women in his laboratory, Harriet Brooks being a notable representative in a period when gender prejudice remained strong. Honours accumulated: election to fellowship of the Royal Society of London in 1903, its Rumford medal and Bakerian lectureship in 1904, the Silliman lectures at Yale in 1905, and the Nobel prize for chemistry in 1908. Rutherford laughed about the last, saying that he had observed many rapid transformations among radioelements, but none so rapid as his transformation from a physicist into a chemist. He was conscious of his worth and proud of his honours, but not vain. He lectured widely and had opportunities to join the faculties of several universities in the United States and England. He summarized knowledge of the field in his text *Radio-Activity*, first published in 1904 and greatly expanded in subsequent editions, sometimes with modified titles, as the field grew.

Manchester, 1907–1919 Although he was happy and well treated in Montreal, the world's scientific centre of gravity remained in western Europe and sooner or later Rutherford was bound to be attracted to it. The occasion arose when Arthur Schuster chose to retire early from his chair at the University of Manchester, on the condition that Rutherford would succeed him. Schuster had built a new physics laboratory and encouraged research activities such that, if the Cavendish Laboratory ranked as the finest in Britain, Manchester easily was the second best. Rutherford accepted the appointment in 1907. The independently wealthy Schuster also left to the laboratory his personal assistant, Hans Geiger, and endowed it with a readership in mathematical physics, filled successively by Harry Bateman, Charles G. Darwin, and Niels Bohr. These and others whose names became prominent in science were attracted to Rutherford, for now he had a secure reputation for fundamental discoveries and as the leader of a research team. Indeed, four men from Germany alone came to study with Rutherford during his first year in Manchester.

Rutherford was a master of the sealing wax and string school of investigation, preferring to make or reuse apparatus, rather than buy it off the shelf. In this tradition of thrift he rarely sought large and highly active quantities of radioactive materials for himself and his students. He had made do with only a few milligrams of radioelements in Montreal. Now the highly considerate Austrian Academy of Sciences sent, from the Joachimsthal uranium mines under its control, about 350 milligrams of radium chloride, intended as a joint loan to Ramsay in London and Rutherford. The recipients recognized that the strong sample should not be divided, but Ramsay wanted to hold it indefinitely, being willing periodically to send Rutherford a vial of the emanation that evolved. The Austrian Academy ultimately resolved the dilemma by providing Rutherford with a radium source for his exclusive use.

The volume of emanation in equilibrium with a gram of radium had been determined by Ramsay and a colleague, but their value contradicted other data. Rutherford repeated the experiment, purifying the emanation in liquid air, and arrived at a value that restored harmony. Once Soddy finished his work with Ramsay the latter turned from a meticulous experimenter into a frequently careless one, and a few times it became Rutherford's unpleasant chore to set the record straight. Though possessed of a vigorous and forthright personality, Rutherford usually preferred to settle differences privately; he may have had a distaste for controversy and he certainly preferred to spend his time in more productive ways. With Ramsay, and also with Becquerel, his opposition was

public. That they were both scientists of an older generation, and Rutherford a modest and tactful person with his seniors, suggests that he was pushed beyond his point of forbearance.

Rutherford, whose investigations progressed across a wide front, stayed close to his favourite object: the alpha particle. Beta particles were too common and minute, having a mass only about one two-thousandth that of an atom of the lightest element, hydrogen. But alphas were massive, of atomic dimension, and might be a key to the ultimate goal of physicists, a greater understanding of the nature of matter. With Geiger he built a long brass tube having an insulated wire along the axis connected to an electrometer. When alphas entered the partially evacuated cylinder they created ions, but the effect of a single alpha was barely measurable. By placing a high voltage on the wire, however, the ions were drawn rapidly to it, themselves creating more ions along the way. Ionization by collision provided the means of registering individual alphas directly, instead of calculating their number from the total charge recorded.

This experiment of 1908 confirmed that each alpha caused a flash of light to occur when it struck a luminous screen, such as one composed of zinc sulphide crystals. Scintillation counting, known for a few years as a means of recording events, was now validated as reliable. It was also more convenient than the primitive device that evolved into the justly famous Geiger counter and the later Geiger–Müller counter, so Rutherford and Geiger for a time dropped the electrical method and became expert in registering scintillations. Useful information resulted. For example, they measured the charge from a radium sample and divided it by the number of alphas emitted to obtain the charge of each particle. This established the most accurate value of the basic unit of charge, e, before Robert A. Millikan performed his oil drop experiment. That their result was about double the best previous estimation of e increased Rutherford's conviction that the alpha bore two charges and thus was helium, but the identity still remained to be proven.

Success in this came in 1908, thanks to the skills of two members of the Manchester laboratory. Otto Baumbach, the laboratory's glass-blower, made a tube so thin that alpha particles, which could be stopped by a sheet of paper, were able to pass through the glass. Emanation was pumped into the tube and the alphas from its decay were allowed to accumulate in an outer, thicker evacuated envelope. Thomas Royds sparked whatever collected in the space between the tubes and, to Rutherford's delight, recorded the spectrum of helium.

Skilled radiochemists also were attracted to Manchester, including Rutherford's friend from Yale, Boltwood, and in 1909–10 they redetermined the rate of production of helium by radium. This was a useful piece of work, for by combining it with counting results they could calculate Avogadro's number more directly than had been done before. Other chemical work with major consequences was accomplished in the laboratory, though Rutherford only observed the research from afar. Alexander Russell,

Kasimir Fajans, and Georg von Hevesy each contributed to an understanding of the group displacement laws and the concept of isotopy. After the Rutherford–Soddy transformation theory, these ideas may be considered the most fundamental in the explanation of radioactivity, for they elaborated the steps through the periodic table taken in alpha and beta decay, and recognized that more than one substance was to be found in many of the table's boxes. Fajans deserves credit for the final interpretation, although Soddy is often incorrectly given primacy.

Experiments at McGill had shown Rutherford that alphas were scattered slightly when they impinged upon thin metal foils or sheets of mica, and his mind awakened to the intense electrical forces in the atom. He noticed the phenomenon again when he and Geiger fired alphas into the residual air in their electrical counter. Both because scattering made measurements less precise and because it might reveal more about how alphas and betas were absorbed by matter, Geiger examined it quantitatively. He found that the scintillations caused by scattered alphas increased with the atomic weight and thickness of the foil target, until the projectiles could no longer penetrate the foil. Geiger looked only at small deflections and, as expected, observed fewer scintillations at larger angles from the beam.

The undergraduate honours programme at Manchester was unusual in having students in their final year perform a real investigation instead of repeat classical experiments. The task given to Ernest Marsden in 1909, to look for large-angle scattering of alpha particles, appeared unpromising. One wonders why Rutherford assigned it, for he knew intuitively how unlikely it was for a massive and fast moving alpha to be deflected appreciably, even by the accumulation of many small scatterings. On the other hand, Rutherford's success was based in part on his open-mindedness, including his willingness to try what could be described as 'any damn fool experiment' on the chance that it might work. To everyone's amazement, Marsden observed occasional scattering at angles greater than 90°, whereupon Geiger excitedly joined him to complete the investigation. Rutherford's reaction, no doubt improved by repetition over the years, is famous: 'It was almost as incredible as if you fired a 15-inch shell at a piece of tissue paper and it came back and hit you' (E. Rutherford, 'Forty years of physics', in Background to Modern Science, ed. J. Needham and W. Pagel, 1938, 68).

What did it mean, though? There were several pictures of the atom current at the time, including Philipp Lenard's dynamide and Hantaro Nagaoka's saturnian models, both of which proposed some sort of massive centre to a larger atom, but lacked sufficient detailed evidence to be credible. The most widely accepted view was that of J. J. Thomson, called the plum pudding model because it pictured negative electron plums arranged uniformly in a spherical atomic pudding of positive electrification. With this model Thomson made many comparisons between predicted and experimental consequences of small-angle scattering.

The model broke down, however, for large-angle scattering. Any high-energy projectile was thought to encounter many atoms in a foil, no matter how thin the target, and be deflected by each one. Yet the probability was minute that the projectile's final path would differ markedly from the entry beam, even after multiple deflections. It took Rutherford well over a year of cogitation before he could say that he knew what the atom looked like. In early 1911 he revealed a new model, the nuclear atom, which is regarded as the greatest accomplishment of his career. Alphas, he maintained, were bent from their paths by encounters with single atoms of the target. For this to occur the electrostatic attraction or repulsion (for the mathematics, it does not matter which) must be concentrated in a volume that was tiny compared with the volume of the entire atom. The atom that emerged was like our solar system, mostly empty space in which electron satellites orbited a minute and dense nucleus sun. Further calculations of the probability of single scattering at various angles were confirmed in subsequent experiments by Geiger and Marsden. Outside Manchester the discovery was received without excitement; even Rutherford was unaware of its significance.

This changed in 1913 when Niels Bohr published his interpretation. He had visited the laboratory in 1912, and returned as a staff member in 1914–16. At home in Denmark he wove together radioactivity, atomic physics, spectroscopy, quantum theory, and chemistry. Radioactivity arose in the nucleus, he said, while ordinary chemical and physical properties were dependent upon the electrons in orbit. The orbits were stable, a contradiction of classical electrodynamics, and the angular momentum of electrons in them was quantized. Lined spectra were due to quantized energy absorption or emission as electrons jumped from one stable orbit to another. This grand scheme attracted attention to the nuclear atom, as did contemporary work of another student of Rutherford. Henry G. J. Moseley determined the wavelength of a particular line in the X-ray spectrum of many elements and showed that these values varied regularly with the order of the elements in the periodic table. Only one thing, he felt, changed so constantly: the charge on the nucleus. Mendeleyev's table had been created according to the atomic weight of the elements; Moseley now showed that the atomic number, or nuclear charge, was really the underlying factor.

The impact of the research connected to the Manchester laboratory was enormous: nuclear physics arose, atomic physics expanded, radioactivity decayed as its major questions were answered, and chemistry was now seen by some as merely a branch of physics. Rutherford's influence on his 'boys' (and some girls) was equally strong. He generally made daily rounds, stopping at the workbench of each student to discuss an experiment, and he carefully reviewed publications submitted from the laboratory. Rutherford's travels and honours continued apace: he visited Winnipeg in 1909 as president of section A of the British Association for the Advancement of Science, attended prestigious conferences such as the Radiology

Congress in Brussels (1910) and Solvay conferences in the same city (1911, 1913), frequently attended meetings of the Royal Society in London, to whose council he was elected (1910), and delivered the Hale lectures of the National Academy of Sciences in Washington (1914). In 1914 he was knighted.

The First World War nearly emptied the laboratory, as able-bodied men saw it as their patriotic duty to enlist. Rutherford consulted for the Admiralty board of invention and research on anti-submarine warfare and engaged in research on underwater acoustics himself. A large water tank was installed in the Manchester laboratory and Rutherford made frequent trips to a research facility established at Aberdour; he even participated in some sea trials. For a while he led British efforts in submarine detection, visited Paris to learn of French accomplishments, and was part of an Anglo-French mission to Washington, but his duties lightened as W. H. Bragg took on full-time responsibility for Aberdour and later A. S. Eve headed research at Harwich. At this point Rutherford resumed his study of the nucleus.

When alphas entered a tube of gas Rutherford saw scintillations beyond the range of these projectiles. This was expected, as the alphas transferred momentum to gas particles they hit. Inexplicably, however, the scintillations were alike, whether hydrogen or nitrogen filled the tube. Why should a recoil atom of nitrogen look like a proton? Rutherford's explanation in 1919 stands as the third of his great contributions, along with the nuclear atom and the transformation theory. The alpha, he argued, broke apart the nitrogen nucleus, and the proton was a piece of debris.

Cambridge, 1919–1937 The artificial transformation of elements occupied Rutherford for the rest of his career. He was chosen in 1919 to succeed Thomson as director of the Cavendish Laboratory. With him from Manchester came James Chadwick, who became his closest collaborator and his laboratory deputy, sharing in the increasingly heavy administrative duties. Together they drew up annual lists of the investigations to be assigned to the laboratory's research students. They also dealt with finances, always a difficult matter. Outside sources provided some funds, but the university's grant to the Cavendish (derived mostly from student fees) was the major amount. This was spent on salaries, wages, apparatus, materials, and utilities, and rose from nearly £9000 p.a. in 1921 to over £16,000 in 1935.

During the early 1920s Rutherford and Chadwick succeeded in disintegrating several of the lighter elements, but unresolved was the question whether the alpha escaped the explosion unscathed or combined with the target nucleus before the latter transformed. Patrick M. S. Blackett in 1925 used the cloud chamber apparatus developed by Charles T. R. Wilson to photograph the tracks of some 400,000 alpha encounters. Most were ordinary elastic collisions, but eight involved disintegrations. Leaving the point of disintegration were two tracks, disintegration fragments, proving that the alpha had been absorbed into a compound nucleus.

Rutherford and Chadwick failed to disrupt any heavier elements and realized that their alpha projectiles from naturally decaying radioelements, carrying a positive charge of two, were repelled by the large positive charges on the nuclei of elements with larger atomic numbers. Experiments began in the Cavendish with accelerated electrons and protons. A new breed of research student arose, with engineering experience, such as Thomas Allibone, Peter Kapitsa, and John D. Cockcroft. Cockcroft and Ernest T. S. Walton constructed the most successful accelerator, capable of hurling protons across several hundred thousand volts. Thanks to a visit by George Gamow, who explained that wave mechanics predicted the possibility that a projectile of relatively low energy could tunnel through the potential barrier of the nucleus instead of going over it, they ceased trying to raise the voltage and in 1932 did the experiment. Not only did they disintegrate atoms, they offered experimental proof of Einstein's long-famous relationship $E = mc^2$. This convinced Rutherford that quantum and wave mechanics were valuable, even if he did not understand them. It also inclined him to invest in the future, in the form of a cyclotron, which was developed by Ernest O. Lawrence in California and which could more easily attain high voltages, and a commercially built two million volt linear device. Higher voltages were needed to split the heavier elements.

In his Bakerian lecture of 1920 Rutherford predicted the existence of a neutral particle of mass similar to that of the proton. Chadwick searched for it often in the 1920s, finally succeeding in 1932 when he recognized that unusually penetrating gamma rays described by the Joliot-Curies in Paris were actually neutrons. Norman Feather in the Cavendish soon showed that neutrons could initiate nuclear disintegrations.

The main effort in generating such disintegrations remained, however, with the cyclotron and linear accelerator. These were large machines, symbolic of the new 'big science'. Rutherford, who hoped to leave the rebuilding of the Cavendish to his successor, was reluctantly drawn into plans for the future; he felt the obligation to provide the tools demanded for nuclear research. Fortunately his relations with industry were excellent, not least because of his chairmanship for seven years of the advisory council of the Department of Scientific and Industrial Research (DSIR). Occasionally some of his DSIR colleagues chided Rutherford for the 'useless knowledge' in basic science that flowed from DSIR grants to his students, but his belief in the value of science to industry remained unshaken. The value of industry to science was initially less obvious to him, but that too became clear. In particular, Metropolitan-Vickers sent to his laboratory some well-trained research students, and collaborated in constructing high voltage machines. Installation of these new research instruments created problems, for the old Cavendish buildings were already overcrowded and the rooms often too small. Rutherford disliked the task of seeking funds (indeed, he once declined a sizeable grant, presumably because he wanted to be under no obligation to justify his expenditures each year), but he did orchestrate the plans for a new building in the Cavendish complex. In 1936 Sir Herbert Austin provided the entire sum of £250,000 in a single gift. But neither the building nor the particle accelerating machines were completed by the time of Rutherford's death in 1937.

Rutherford was seen by many as the most accomplished experimenter since Michael Faraday. While there may be some truth in this accolade it obscures the case that may be made for Rutherford as a significant theorist. He was by no means a mathematical physicist, but it must be recognized that, of his three greatest contributions, only the artificial disintegration of 1919 was an experimental discovery. The transformation theory of 1902–3 and the model of the nuclear atom of 1911, while based on experimental evidence, were theoretical concepts. And, contrary to his frequent jocular criticism of theoreticians, he sincerely appreciated their value and encouraged their role in his laboratories. In the Cavendish, Ralph Fowler, his son-in-law, was most conspicuous, but for lesser periods Rudolf Peierls, Neville Mott, and Maurice Goldhaber were in residence.

In his career Rutherford published some 180 research papers and five texts. He was awarded over two dozen honorary degrees and was elected to membership of most of the national academies of science in the world. The Royal Society presented him with its highest award, the Copley medal, in 1922, he was president of the British Association in 1923, George V conferred on him the Order of Merit in 1925, he served as president of the Royal Society (1925–30), and he was raised to the peerage in 1931 as Baron Rutherford of Nelson. In this busy life he had little time for activities far removed from the laboratory or scientific organizations, but he did serve as president of the Academic Assistance Council from 1933 (a rare instance of Rutherford involving himself in a political issue, since the body was created to help scientists who fled Nazism), and he played golf occasionally.

Rutherford's personality was overpowering and his humour often heavy-handed. When his students' work went well he was warmly appreciative; when it went badly he was critical and unsympathetic, an unfortunate circumstance for a sensitive student. The vast majority, however, remembered him with affection. They in large measure chaired the physics departments of Britain and its former empire, in part because they came from the most famous laboratory but also because nuclear physics was the most prominent science in the world. In the 1930s Rutherford commented that efforts towards the practical extraction of the energy known to be locked up in the atom, with the tools at their disposal, was fruitless; 'moonshine' he called it (*New York Times*, 12 Sept 1933). He did not live to see the discovery of nuclear fission in 1938, which provided the missing tool, nor the Anglo-American project during the Second World War to construct nuclear weapons and nuclear reactors, in which his students played significant roles. He died in the Evelyn Nursing Home, Cambridge, on 19 October 1937 of complications following an operation for a strangulated hernia; he was cremated on 25 October and his ashes were placed in Westminster Abbey. He was survived by his wife.

LAWRENCE BADASH

Sources D. Wilson, *Rutherford: simple genius* (1983) · A. S. Eve, *Rutherford* (1939) · N. Feather, *Lord Rutherford* (1940) · E. N. da C. Andrade, *Rutherford and the nature of the atom* (1964) · J. B. Birks, ed., *Rutherford at Manchester* (1962) · M. Oliphant, *Rutherford: recollections of the Cambridge days* (1972) · L. Badash, ed., *Rutherford and Boltwood: letters on radioactivity* (1969) · A. S. Eve and J. Chadwick, *Obits. FRS*, 2 (1936–8), 395–423 · *The collected papers of Lord Rutherford of Nelson*, ed. J. Chadwick, 3 vols. (1962–5) · d. cert.
Archives CAC Cam., notebooks · CUL, corresp., notebooks, and papers · McGill University, Montreal, department of physics, apparatus · Sci. Mus., corresp. [copies] · U. Cam., Cavendish Laboratory, apparatus | CAC Cam., letters to Sir James Chadwick · California Institute of Technology, Pasadena, letters to G. E. Hale · Canterbury Museum, Christchurch, New Zealand, corresp. with A. W. Bickerton · CUL, letters to A. B. Wood · HLRO, letters to Herbert Samuel · JRL, corresp. with R. S. Hutton · Lincoln College, Oxford, corresp. with Nevil Vincent Sidgwick · Nuffield Oxf., corresp. with Lord Cherwell · Ransom HRC, letters to Sir Owen Richardson · Royal Institution of Great Britain, London, letters to Royal Institute of Great Britain · RS, corresp. with Sir Joseph Larmor · RS, letters to Sir Arthur Schuster · TCD, letters to John Joly · Trinity Cam., corresp. with Joseph John Thomson · University of Copenhagen, Niels Bohr Institute for Astronomy, Physics, and Geophysics, corresp. with Niels Bohr · Yale U., Sterling Memorial Library, letters to B. B. Boltwood
Likenesses O. Edis, photograph, *c*.1920–1930, NPG · W. Stoneman, photograph, 1921, NPG · P. A. de Laszlo, oils, 1924, Trinity Cam. · W. Rothenstein, sanguine and pencil drawing, *c*.1925, NPG · R. Schwabe, pencil drawing, 1928, Trinity Cam. · O. Birley, oils, 1932, RS [*see illus.*] · J. Gunn, oils, 1932, NPG · E. Gill, relief portrait on stone plaque, *c*.1933, U. Cam., Mond Laboratory · F. Dodd, chalk drawing, 1934, NPG · F. Dodd, charcoal drawing, 1934, FM Cam. · F. L. Emanuel, oils, 1936, Nelson College, New Zealand · B. Anrep, mosaic sculpture, National Gallery, London
Wealth at death £7402 6s. 4d.: probate, 21 March 1938, *CGPLA Eng. & Wales*

Rutherford, John (*c*.1520–1577), philosopher and Church of Scotland minister, was born in Jedburgh, Roxburghshire, the second son of Andrew or Archibald Rutherford, a canon of the Augustinian house at Jedburgh, and a daughter of the Douglas family of Bonjedward. Rutherford studied under Nicolas de Grouchy at the Collège de Guyenne in Bordeaux before accompanying him and George Buchanan to the new college of arts at Coimbra in Portugal in 1547. After receiving his licence in arts, Rutherford lectured at Coimbra and then, about late 1551, went to Paris, where he was incorporated as a master in the university. By 1553 he was associated with the Collège de Sainte-Barbe, and on 27 August 1554 he was listed as a quaestor or bursar of the German nation at the University of Paris. In December 1553 Rutherford declined an invitation to join the staff of St Mary's College, St Andrews, but in 1555 he accepted a position in the Montaigne household near Périgueux as tutor of Michel's younger brother Thomas. Rutherford had been studying medicine, but his friends urged him to complete a compendium of logic on which he had been working since at least February 1553.

Rutherford had been in the Montaigne household four months when John Hamilton, archbishop of St Andrews, and John Douglas, provost of St Mary's, invited him to teach humanity at St Mary's. He took up his new post on 1 November 1556, and the following spring Hamilton instructed him to lecture on rhetoric and the Greek and Latin humanities. Rutherford's major work, *Commentariorum de arte disserendi libri quatuor*, with an epistle dedicatory to Hamilton, was published in Paris in 1557. Rutherford claimed one of his students had given the manuscript to a careless printer without his authorization, but this seems unlikely since it includes a letter by the author dated 22 November 1555. Written in Ciceronian Latin with some Greek, the treatise is a commentary on Aristotle's logic which in the humanist manner attempts to understand the philosopher on his own terms and is critical of what Rutherford deemed the sophistry of modern critics. Instead he favoured classical commentators such as Themistius and Simplicius, and he also thought well of the Italian philosopher Agostino Nifo, a critic of Lorenzo Valla.

Probably shortly after his return to Scotland, Rutherford married Christian Forsyth. Having embraced reformed protestant principles by this time, he was deemed fit for the ministry by the general assembly on 20 December 1560. Two months earlier, on 22 October, he had succeeded William Cranston as provost of St Salvator's College, St Andrews, a position he would occupy until shortly before his death. He was also an elder in the St Andrews kirk session by 1561. When Rutherford complained that John Balfour was unqualified to be the minister at Cults, near Cupar, Fife, and offered to be its pastor, the general assembly concurred on 25 June 1563. Although the assembly admonished him on 5 March 1571 for neglecting his cure, he served the church until 1574. Over the years he undertook various responsibilities for the assembly, including membership on committees to assess the church's jurisdiction (1564) and to determine whether the Leith articles (a financial compromise between crown and church which led to the introduction of protestant bishops) conformed to scripture (1572). In September 1566 he was a signatory of a letter to Theodore Beza approving the second Helvetic confession, excepting only the celebration of the holy days associated with Christ's life.

Rutherford became involved in a number of controversies in the 1570s. Criticized early in the decade both by the students of St Leonard's College and by John Knox for failing to support the king's party, Rutherford was in turn offended by Knox's refusal to participate in the induction of John Douglas as archbishop of St Andrews on 10 February 1572, and accused him of coveting the post himself. Then in March 1574 he was embroiled in the dispute over John Davidson's *Ane Dialog or Mutuall Talking Betuix a Clerk and ane Courteour*, which attacked the earl of Morton's distribution of ministers and, Rutherford believed, contained unfavourable references to himself. He was also at odds with the Melvilles, criticizing Andrew Melville's adherence to Ramist views which Rutherford had rejected. The Melvilles for their part disliked Rutherford's support of the establishment; James Melville acknowledged his erudition but castigated him as envious and corrupt.

A second edition of Rutherford's *Commentariorum*, which he finished on 5 May 1576, was published at Edinburgh in 1577. A more positive treatment of Plutarch is the only significant change from the first edition. Because of advancing age Rutherford resigned his provostship at St Salvator's on 29 August 1577, and he died between 20 September and 18 December that year. His eldest son, John, a graduate of St Andrews who became principal master of St Salvator's (3 September 1579) and minister of St Andrews (July 1584), died of plague in October 1585. A younger son, William, skipper of a ship at Leith, was the grandfather of Andrew Rutherford, earl of Teviot.

RICHARD L. GREAVES

Sources *Fasti Scot.*, new edn, 5.138, 231; 7.411; 8.441, 456, 468 · T. Thomson, ed., *Acts and proceedings of the general assemblies of the Kirk of Scotland*, 3 pts, Bannatyne Club, 81 (1839–45) · J. Durkan, 'John Rutherford and Montaigne: an early influence', Bibliothèque d'Humanisme et Renaissance, 41 (1979), 115–22 · J. Durkan, 'Education: the laying of fresh foundations', *Humanism in Renaissance Scotland*, ed. J. MacQueen (1990), 123–60, esp. 135–5 · D. E. R. Watt, ed., *Fasti ecclesiae Scoticanae medii aevi ad annum 1638*, [2nd edn], Scottish RS, new ser., 1 (1969), 384 · R. Bannatyne, *Memoriales of transactions in Scotland, 1569–1573*, ed. [R. Pitcairn], Bannatyne Club, 51 (1836), 257–63 · *The autobiography and diary of Mr James Melvill*, ed. R. Pitcairn, Wodrow Society (1842), 26–7 · A. Broadie, 'Philosophy in Renaissance Scotland: loss and gain', *Humanism in Renaissance Scotland*, ed. J. MacQueen (1990), 75–96, esp. 85–5 · J. Kirk, '"Melvillian" reform in the Scottish universities', *The Renaissance in Scotland: studies in literature, religion, history, and culture offered to John Durkan*, ed. A. A. MacDonald and others (1994), 276–300, esp. 283–4 · H. Robinson, ed. and trans., *The Zurich letters, comprising the correspondence of several English bishops and others with some of the Helvetian reformers, during the early part of the reign of Queen Elizabeth*, 2, Parker Society, 8 (1845), 362–5 · G. R. Hewitt, *Scotland under Morton, 1572–80* (1982), 85–6 · M. Livingstone, D. Hay Fleming, and others, eds., *Registrum secreti sigilli regum Scotorum / The register of the privy seal of Scotland*, 7 (1966), no. 1218 · D. Calderwood, *The true history of the Church of Scotland, from the beginning of the Reformation, unto the end of the reigne of King James VI* (1678), 29, 56

Rutherford, John (1695–1779), physician, son of John Rutherford, minister of Yarrow, Selkirkshire, was born on 1 August 1695. He was educated at Selkirk grammar school, then the University of Edinburgh (1709–10), and after the ordinary arts course, was apprenticed to Alexander Nesbit, an Edinburgh surgeon, with whom he remained until 1716.

Rutherford then moved to London, and attended the various hospitals, hearing lectures by James Douglas on anatomy and by Nathanael St André on surgery. From London he went to Leiden, which Boerhaave was then making famous as a centre of medical teaching. Boerhaave emphasized that medicine must be taught at the bedside, a lesson Rutherford did not forget. He obtained his MD from Rheims on 31 July 1719, and passed the winter in Paris, attending the private demonstrations of Winslow.

In 1720 Rutherford returned to Britain, settled in Edinburgh in 1721, and with the doctors Andrew Sinclair, Andrew Plummer, and John Innes, started a laboratory for the preparation of compound medicines, an art then little known in Scotland. They also taught the rudiments of chemistry, and afterwards, on Boerhaave's advice, lectured on other branches of physic. On 9 February 1726 they all became professors in the University of Edinburgh. Rutherford had been elected FRCP, Edinburgh, in 1724, and was appointed to the chair of the practice of physic. He delivered his lectures in Latin, which he spoke more fluently than his native tongue.

Rutherford is important because he started the clinical teaching of medicine in the University of Edinburgh, the first place in Britain to teach in this way. In 1748 he was permitted to give a course of clinical lectures in the Royal Infirmary, to supplement bedside teaching. He encouraged his pupils to bring patients to him on Saturdays, when he made a diagnosis and prescribed a course of action in the presence of the class. The success of this innovation was so great, and the number of students increased so rapidly, that by 1750 he had a special ward of his own with twelve beds. A new era had begun. In 1765 Rutherford resigned, and was succeeded by John Gregory.

Rutherford was married twice. His first wife was the daughter of Sir John Swinton of Swinton. Their daughter Anne (d. 1819) married Walter Scott, writer to the signet; they were the parents of Sir Walter Scott. Rutherford's second wife was Anne Mackay, a descendant of the family of Lord Rae. Daniel *Rutherford was their son. John Rutherford suffered from gout, as did his father and his son Daniel. Sir Walter Scott described his grandfather as 'an excellent anatomist as well as physician', and 'a man distinguished for professional talent, for lively wit, and for literary acquirement' (Lockhart, 1.15, 10).

Rutherford died in Edinburgh in 1779 and was buried on 10 March 1779 in Greyfriars churchyard, Edinburgh.

D'A. POWER, rev. JEAN LOUDON

Sources A. Chalmers, ed., *The general biographical dictionary*, new edn, 26 (1816), 497–9 · T. G. Stewart, 'History of the Royal Infirmary', *Edinburgh Hospital Reports*, 1 (1893), 1–10 · R. W. Innes Smith, *English-speaking students of medicine at the University of Leyden* (1932) · *Annual Biography and Obituary*, 5 (1821), 138–48 [obit. of Daniel Rutherford] · J. G. Lockhart, *Memoirs of the life of Sir Walter Scott*, 1 (1837) · A. S. MacNalty, *Sir Walter Scott: the wounded falcon* (1969), 165–7 · private information (1897) · private information (2004) · *Medical and Philosophical Commentaries*, 6 (1779), 236 · D. Laing, ed., *A catalogue of the graduates ... of the University of Edinburgh*, Bannatyne Club, 106 (1858), xxi–xxii

Archives McGill University, Montreal, Osler Library of the History of Medicine, lecture notes · Royal College of Physicians and Surgeons of Glasgow, clinical lectures at Royal Infirmary · Royal College of Physicians of Edinburgh, case and lecture notes · U. Edin. L., clinical lecture notes · Wellcome L., transcripts of clinical lectures

Likenesses oils, Abbotsford, Melrose; copy by H. Kerr, Royal College of Physicians of Edinburgh

Rutherford [*married name* Stringer Davis], Dame **Margaret Taylor** (1892–1972), actress, was born in Balham, London, on 11 May 1892, the only child of William Rutherford (formerly Benn), a traveller in silks in India, and his wife, Florence Nicholson. She was taken to India as a baby, but when, at the age of three, she suffered the death of her mother, she was returned to England to live with an aunt, Bessie Nicholson. Her father died shortly afterwards. She was educated at Wimbledon high school and Raven's

Dame Margaret Taylor Rutherford (1892–1972), by Rolf Mahrenholz

Croft School in Seaford, Sussex. She qualified as a licentiate of the Royal Academy of Music and became a music teacher, doing nothing to further her wish to act professionally until, at the age of thirty-three, she inherited a small income when her aunt died. A letter of introduction from John Drinkwater enabled her to join the Old Vic company as a student in 1925, the year in which Edith Evans played the leading parts there, but this did not lead to more work in the theatre and she returned to teaching at Wimbledon, where she spent two more years before being engaged as an understudy at the Lyric, Hammersmith, by Sir Nigel Playfair.

From Hammersmith, Margaret Rutherford went to Croydon, Epsom, and Oxford, playing in weekly repertory, and at Oxford she met the director Tyrone Guthrie. His eagle eye picked out her strikingly original personality and talent, and he directed her soon afterwards at Her Majesty's in London. In 1935 she played for Guthrie in an ill-fated but star-studded drama, *Hervey House*, with Fay Compton, Gertrude Lawrence, and Nicholas Hannen, and in Robert Morley's comedy *Short Story*. On this latter occasion she won a spirited battle against the redoubtable Marie Tempest, who was none too pleased with a newcomer's success in her own established field of light comedy. She attempted to thwart Margaret Rutherford by distracting the attention of the audience in their scenes together, but Marie Tempest finally capitulated good-humouredly when she found her rival had the courage to stand up to her. In 1938, in an Irish comedy, *Spring Meeting*, by Mollie Keane, under the direction of John Gielgud, she had a big personal success as a comic aunt, Miss Bijou Furse, exchanging racing tips with the old butler (played by Arthur Sinclair), extracting a tiny hot-water bottle from the depths of her capacious cardigans, and devouring her breakfast egg with unconcealed relish and delight. The director had had considerable difficulty in persuading her to undertake the part, since she saw little humour in the play when it was first given to her to read. 'Don't you think that as we are living in such gloomy times', she wrote, 'that people want to laugh?'

Margaret Rutherford's solemnity was, of course, an invaluable asset in her acting of farce. With an unfailing instinct for execution and timing, there was always a hint of sadness, as in many of the greatest comedians, behind the comicality of her performances. In herself a deeply serious person, she loved music and poetry, and her beautifully spoken poetry readings for the Apollo Society and elsewhere were important to her.

In 1939 (a year before she somewhat improbably created the part of the malevolent housekeeper, Mrs Danvers, in Daphne Du Maurier's *Rebecca* at the Queen's Theatre) Margaret Rutherford appeared as Miss Prism in John Gielgud's production of Oscar Wilde's *The Importance of being Earnest* for some special matinées. For the run of the play at the Globe in London which followed, she accepted the offer to repeat her performance but only on condition that she might also understudy Edith Evans (playing Lady Bracknell)—an unheard-of stipulation for an important actress. Her Miss Prism contrasted her class-conscious humility and terror of Lady Bracknell's imperious demands with her rapturous recognition of her beloved handbag (on which the dénouement of the play rested). When, in 1947, the production was taken to the United States, Edith Evans did not wish to go, and Margaret Rutherford was invited to replace her, which she did with notable success, though the director thought her 'Lady Mayoress rather than the Queen Mary' of Edith Evans. She was a versatile member of the company and fitted in with the production with skill and versatility. As the spiritualist Madame Arcati in Noël Coward's *Blithe Spirit* she suffered great agonies in fearing to make mock of a cult which she knew to be taken very seriously by its devotees, and at the end of its long stage run at the Piccadilly in 1941 she suffered a nervous breakdown as a result. Continually in demand as the years went by, she conjured up a series of superb sketches of domineering but endearing lady dragons.

Margaret Rutherford had a notable career in films, beginning in 1938 in *Dusty Ermine*, directed by Bernard Vorhaus. Her film credits included the Ealing comedy *Passport to Pimlico* (1949), Frank Launder's and John Dighton's school farce *The Happiest Days of your Life* (1950), and reprises of Madame Arcati in *Blithe Spirit* directed by David Lean (1945) and Miss Prism in Anthony Asquith's film version of *The Importance of being Earnest* (1952). She achieved transatlantic popularity for her portrayal of Agatha Christie's Miss Marple in several films, beginning with *Murder she Said* (1961). In 1964 she won an Oscar as best supporting actress for *The VIPs*, playing alongside Richard Burton and Elizabeth Taylor. Her success in films did not perhaps give her very great satisfaction, though she was always touchingly appreciative of praise and popularity.

On 26 March 1945 Margaret Rutherford married an actor, James Buckley Stringer Davis, who was devoted to her. She always insisted on his being engaged to play small parts in every film, stage, or television production in which she appeared. A most modest and dedicated actress, who adored her husband and who was infinitely kind, unassuming, and intensely professional, she was perhaps increasingly disturbed to find herself famous as a figure of fun. As she began to age, she began to lose her confidence. She insisted on continuing to fulfil commitments after she was already seriously ill, and she failed to complete a film, from which she retired, after some humiliation at the hands of the impatient director, with the greatest dignity. Her last appearance, as Mrs Malaprop, at the Haymarket with Sir Ralph Richardson in Sheridan's *The Rivals*—an engagement she was finally obliged to give up after a few weeks—was a most poignant struggle against her obviously failing powers. She died on 22 May 1972 in the Chalfont and Gerrards Cross Hospital, Chalfont St Peter, Buckinghamshire. Not long before her death her friends were approached by a journalist who was endeavouring to help her complete her autobiography. Dame Margaret (she was appointed OBE in 1961 and DBE in 1967) had been incapacitated by illness, and neither she herself nor her husband was able to complete the assignment, and the ghost writer was at a loss how to gain the further material which she needed and was trying to fill the gaps with tributes from some of her friends and colleagues. But it appeared in the course of detailed researches that a certain amount of information had come to light about Margaret Rutherford's earlier life, involving an unhappy family background and recurrences of mental disturbance which would be pointless and painful to bring to light, and the book was finally cobbled together as well as possible under these unhappy circumstances, and published in 1972.

Never slender or good-looking, Margaret Rutherford had extraordinary charm. Light on her feet, she moved with grace and distinction, taking the stage with confidence and apparent ease. She wore costume to perfection, and her phrasing and diction, whether in William Congreve, R. B. Sheridan, or Oscar Wilde, were equally impeccable. On the night she left the cast of *The School for Scandal* at the Haymarket in 1962, in which she had been a memorable Mrs Candour, she gave a party on the stage after the last performance, leaving a happy memory of her dancing joyously up and down the stage hand in hand with the stage carpenter. Kenneth Tynan had a recollection of her:

> Playing Lady Wishfort in Congreve's *Way of the World* [at the Lyric, Hammersmith, in 1953], Miss Rutherford can act with her chin alone. I especially cherish the chin commanding, the chin in doubt and the chin at bay. My dearest impression

is a vision of Miss Rutherford, clad in something loose, darting about her Boudoir like a gigantic Bumble Bee at large in a hothouse.

JOHN GIELGUD

Sources M. Rutherford and G. Robyns, *Margaret Rutherford: an autobiography* (1972) · E. Keown, *Margaret Rutherford* (1956) · *The Times* (23 May 1972) · *WWW* · *British Theatre* [yearbook, P. Noble] (1946?) · personal knowledge (2004) · *CGPLA Eng. & Wales* (1972) · *DNB*
Archives FILM BFI NFTVA, performance footage | SOUND BL NSA, 'Margaret Rutherford, 1892–1972', Channel 4, 5 Oct 1993, V2444/2 · BL NSA, 'Art of Margaret Rutherford', BBC Radio 3, 10 Dec 1975, NP2653W C1 · BL NSA, performance recordings
Likenesses M. Noakes, pencil drawing, 1970, NPG · R. Mahrenholz, photograph, NPG [*see illus.*]
Wealth at death £13,850: administration, 10 Aug 1972, *CGPLA Eng. & Wales*

Rutherford, Mark. *See* White, William Hale (1831–1913).

Rutherford, Samuel (*c.*1600–1661), Church of Scotland minister and political theorist, was born about 1600 in Nisbet, near Crailing, in south-east Scotland. His first biographer wrote that he was 'a gentleman by extraction' (McWard, preface), and Robert Wodrow claimed that he was 'the son of an heretor' (Wodrow, 3.88).

Family and early career Rutherford's parents are unknown, but he had two younger brothers: George became a schoolteacher in Kirkcudbright, and James served as a soldier on the continent. They were all almost certainly educated at Jedburgh grammar school. A key influence on the young Rutherford was the presbyterian controversialist David Calderwood, who became minister of Crailing in 1604. Calderwood was an unyielding opponent of episcopacy and 'popish' ceremonies, and he was eventually deprived of his charge in 1617 for protesting against royal ecclesiastical policies. However, Rutherford later claimed that in his birthplace 'Christ was scarce named, as touching any reality or power of godliness' (*Letters*, 680).

Rutherford entered the University of Edinburgh in 1617 and graduated in 1621. In 1623 he was appointed regent of humanity. In Edinburgh he seems to have associated with the radical presbyterian merchants John Mein and William Rigg, who led protests against the five articles of Perth and organized illegal conventicles. However, according to an entry in the burgh records of Edinburgh for 3 February 1626, it had been 'declaired by the principall of the colledge that Mr Samuell Rutherfuird, regent of humanitie, hes fallin in furnicatioun with Euphame Hamilton, and hes committit ane grit scandle in the college' (Wood, 296). A child was born to Hamilton and Rutherford in April 1626, by which time they may well have married, but the sexual scandal lost Rutherford his position as a regent. Chastened, he turned his thoughts towards parish ministry.

In 1627 Rutherford became the minister of Anwoth in Kirkcudbrightshire at the invitation of the local nobleman and presbyterian sympathizer Sir John Gordon of Lochinvar. According to Rutherford's biographer he entered his charge 'without giving any engagement to the bishop' (McWard, preface), possibly because Bishop

Andrew Lamb was willing to ordain him alongside a group of presbyters. Before Rutherford's arrival, his parishioners later wrote, 'our soules were under that miserable extreame femine of the word, that we had onlie the puir help of an sermone everie second Sabboth, by reasone of ane most inconvenient unione with uther twa kirkis' (Murray, 355). Rutherford transformed this situation. 'He used ordinarily to rise be three a clock in the morning', wrote John Livingstone, and 'was the instrument of much good among a poor ignorant people, many of which he brought to the knowledge and practise of religion' (Tweedie, 1.320). However, Rutherford was 'diseased of a fever tertian for the space of thirteen weeks' and his wife died in June 1630 (*Letters*, 53). The children of their marriage seemed to have died before their mother.

Presbyterian activism Despite these personal tragedies Rutherford's activism was undiminished. He established a network of connections with the gentry of south-west Scotland and became a close friend of Jane Campbell, the wife of Sir John Gordon and the sister of Lord Lorne. From his base in Anwoth, Rutherford orchestrated a presbyterian campaign against royal ecclesiastical policy. He disseminated political information, intervened in burgh elections, wrote his own catechism, organized seasons of fasting and prayer for the corruption of the church, wrote a Latin treatise against Arminianism, and circulated manuscript treatises he had written to justify conventicles. In June 1630 he was summoned before the high commission for his nonconformist activities and though he was not prosecuted, he was now a marked man. When Charles I visited Scotland for his coronation in 1633, Rutherford's patron, Sir John Gordon, was created Viscount Kenmure and Lord Lochinvar, and out of gratitude to the king withdrew from the parliament which was passing anti-presbyterian legislation. When Kenmure was on his deathbed a year later Rutherford chided him for this betrayal of the presbyterian cause. In 1634 the young Scottish 'Canterburian' Thomas Sydserff succeeded Lamb as bishop of Galloway. Sydserff wasted little time in moving against nonconformists, and in 1636 Rutherford was brought before the high commission in Edinburgh, deprived of his charge, and sentenced to be confined to Aberdeen.

Rutherford arrived in Aberdeen in September 1636 and in November his brother George was forced to resign from his post as schoolmaster of Kirkcudbright because of nonconformity. Rutherford complained that he was pointed out in the streets as 'the banished minister' and was 'openly preached against in the pulpits' (*Letters*, 189). He was soon engaged in disputation with the 'Aberdeen doctors', whose moderate Calvinism he regarded as sheer Arminianism. Although he was visited by sympathizers, he confessed 'My dumb Sabbaths stick in my throat' (*Letters*, 268). Frustrated at his confinement in 1636 and 1637 he released a torrent of letters to nobles, lairds, burgesses, and ministers all over Scotland, many of which have survived. Besides containing devotional encouragement the letters also urged recipients to stand up for the purity of the kirk of Scotland and resist the Caroline innovations.

Among those to whom Rutherford wrote were Lord Balmerino, Lord Loudoun, and the earl of Casillis, leading covenanters after 1638.

Covenanter leader About a month after the signing of the national covenant in February 1638 Rutherford left Aberdeen and returned to Anwoth. In November the Glasgow assembly exonerated him from all church censures, and he also had the satisfaction of acting as a witness against Sydserff, who was deposed along with the other bishops. Rutherford was now at the heart of the Church of Scotland, and meeting regularly with other covenanter leaders like Loudon, Alexander Henderson, and Robert Baillie. Although he returned to Anwoth the 1639 general assembly determined that he should become professor of divinity at New College, St Andrews.

Rutherford arrived in St Andrews in October 1639 and set about overturning the episcopalian legacy. In December he was preaching for the English puritan Lord Brooke at Warwick (the first record there is of his travelling outside Scotland). On 24 March 1640 he married Jean McMath (d. 1675); they later had a number of children. On the eve of the second bishops' war in August he preached a series of crusading sermons to the Scottish army. Back in St Andrews he and his close friend Robert Blair provoked a storm of protest from the local presbytery by opposing the appointment of Andrew Afflect as a minister because his ministry was not 'so spirituall and powerfull as the case of St Andrews required' (*Letters and Journals of Robert Baillie*, 2.49). Rutherford and Blair were so unhappy that they applied for removal elsewhere, but in the end they both stayed on. Then, in 1643, Rutherford was appointed a Scottish commissioner to the Westminster assembly of divines, along with Baillie, Henderson, and George Gillespie.

Residence in London and publications Rutherford took up his seat in the assembly in November 1643 and remained in London until November 1647. In these four years he participated fully in the assembly's debates over church government and published a number of major works, including *Lex, rex, or, The Law and the Prince* (1644), a lengthy and sometimes bitter defence of armed resistance to Charles I. It was written in response to *Sacro-sancta regum majestas* (1644) by the deposed bishop of Ross, John Maxwell, and drew on Calvinist resistance theory and the political theory of Spanish neo-scholastics. It argued that legitimate government was grounded in a covenant between king and people. Because Charles I had violated his covenant with the Scottish people by trying to force idolatry upon them, they had been duty bound to resist him by force under the authority of lesser magistrates.

Rutherford's main responsibility in London was to advance the presbyterian cause. He had begun with great hopes of building 'the waste places of Zion in another kingdom' (*Letters*, 615), but was soon disillusioned by the state of English puritanism. He complained of 'Multitudes of Anabaptists, Antinomians, Familists, Separatists' and wondered if he was any more likely to find 'a sound Christian' in London than in Spain (*Letters*, 618–19). Within the assembly Erastians and Independents led a spirited campaign against the Scottish model of divine-right presbyterianism. Rutherford had already offered a critique of New England congregationalism in *A Peaceable Plea for Paul's Presbytery* (1642), but he now followed this up with two more major works against Independency and Erastianism, *The Due Right of Presbyteries* (1644) and *The Divine Right of Church Government and Excommunication* (1646).

By the end of his stay in London, Rutherford was becoming more concerned about sectarian heresies. In *A Survey of Spiritual Antichrist* (1648), he traced back the varieties of contemporary heresy to sixteenth-century radicals, and argued that the subjectivism of the sects would recreate the anarchy associated with the early Anabaptist movement. In *A Free Disputation Against Pretended Liberty of Conscience* (1649) he condemned radical puritan tolerationists, and reasserted the traditional protestant doctrine of religious coercion. The book has been described as 'the ablest defence of religious persecution written in the seventeenth century' (O. Chadwick, *The Reformation*, 1964, 403). The increasing harshness of Rutherford's tone during the 1640s reflects his growing pessimism about the English situation. Although he witnessed the formal abolition of episcopacy and parliament's adoption of a somewhat diluted system of presbyterian church government, he was aware that the Independents were growing in strength. By the time he prepared to return to Scotland in November 1647 his hopes of a presbyterian international were receding, and the retreat to presbyterianism in one country had already begun.

Leadership and division in Scotland, 1648–1661 A month after Rutherford's return to Scotland the moderate covenanters signed the engagement with Charles I. Rutherford was resolutely opposed to this alliance, and as a regular attender at the commission of the kirk he helped to orchestrate a campaign against it. In March 1648 he presented a declaration against the engagement to the Scottish parliament. The defeat of the engagers' army at Preston in August 1648 opened the way for the radical presbyterians. In the Whiggamore raid conventiclers from south-west Scotland marched on Edinburgh and helped to establish a militant kirk party regime. Rutherford was now at the height of his influence in Scotland. He drafted an act for the abolition of patronage, aimed at securing the right of congregations to choose their own pastor; this was passed by parliament in March 1649. He was also elected to professorships at Edinburgh University and at the new University of Harderwyck in the Netherlands. However, he chose to remain in St Andrews and assist the cause of reformation in Scotland. After the execution of Charles I in January 1649 the covenanters had proclaimed his son king of Great Britain and Ireland. The author of *Lex, rex* was deeply suspicious of the young king, and when Charles visited Scotland in July 1650 he was subjected to a lengthy speech from Rutherford 'running mutch upon what was the dewtie of kings' (*Diary of Mr John Lamont*, 20). As the covenanters prepared to fight Cromwell's army Rutherford was convinced that victory for the cause was imminent. The defeat at Dunbar in September

1650 came as a shattering blow. But his diagnosis of the problem was simple: although the army had been purged of ungodly 'malignants' before the battle, the purging had not gone far enough. He persuaded Colonel Gilbert Ker that a small force of pure men, like Gideon's army, would meet with military success. In December, Ker attacked the English at Hamilton, only to suffer a crushing defeat.

Rutherford was profoundly demoralized by this debacle, but he remained hostile to any attempt to readmit 'malignants' to the covenanter armies or offices of state, as did the militant authors of the western remonstrance. When the general assembly ruled that purges of the army could be relaxed a division opened up between the remonstrants (later protesters) and the moderate resolutioners who comprised the majority within the kirk. The division deepened when Charles II was crowned at Scone in January 1651. By May there was a veritable civil war within the church and Rutherford was organizing a separate religious fast from that of his old friend, Robert Blair, who had refused to take sides on the issue. Rutherford felt so strongly about the dispute that he turned down two offers of a professorship at Utrecht in 1651. The decisive break with the resolutioners came at the St Andrews general assembly of July 1651. Rutherford handed in a protestation against the lawfulness of the assembly and then left. He was never again to attend a general assembly of the Church of Scotland. Attempts to heal the divisions between protesters and resolutioners came to nothing. Despite having defended presbyterian polity throughout the 1640s Rutherford now refused to submit to the judgments of its highest court. For the last decade of his life he was almost a semi-separatist. A few protesters in Aberdeen actually broke with the Church of Scotland altogether and became Independents, and Rutherford tried with no success to reclaim them. In 1658 he stoked the flames of controversy by attacking the resolutioners in the preface to his *Survey of the Survey of that Summe of Church Discipline Penned by Mr Thomas Hooker*. In St Andrews, Rutherford's zeal for the protesters was so contentious that his colleague James Wood left New College for St Salvator's. Despite these bitter disputes Rutherford continued to preach to large crowds at protester communion festivals and occasionally in Edinburgh. His wife gave birth to three more children after his return from London, but Agnes, born in 1649, was the only child to survive him.

the restoration of Charles II in 1660 augured ill for Rutherford. In September the committee of estates issued a declaration against *Lex, rex* and copies of the book were burned in Edinburgh and outside New College in St Andrews. Rutherford was deprived of his position in the university, his charge in the church, and his stipend, and was confined to his own house. He was cited to appear before parliament on a charge of treason and his friends feared that he might well face execution. However, early in 1661 Rutherford fell seriously ill. On 8 March he issued a last will and testimony, and near the end of the month he died, at St Mary's College, St Andrews. He was buried in the cathedral graveyard.

Rutherford's legacy Rutherford was perhaps the leading theorist of the Scottish covenanters, but he was always on the militant wing of the movement. He was never appointed moderator of the general assembly, and as a defender of conventicles and a protester he stoked controversy in the kirk. In England, however, he earned a place in one of Milton's sonnets (*On the New Forcers of Conscience, c.*1647) as a prime defender of Scottish presbyterianism and proponent of persecution.

Rutherford's posthumous reputation rested on his letters, which were first published in the Netherlands in 1664, and quickly became a classic of evangelical protestant piety. They were lavishly praised by Richard Baxter and Charles Spurgeon, and were republished no fewer than eighty times in various English editions, and at least fifteen times in Dutch. Rutherford became known as the Saint of the Covenant, and devout evangelicals even made pilgrimages to Anwoth. Meanwhile, Rutherford's controversial writings gathered dust and were largely forgotten. The exception was *Lex, rex*, which was republished in the mid-nineteenth century and celebrated as a great defence of whig liberties. In the early 1980s *Lex, rex* was published again by supporters of the American religious right, who incorrectly claimed that it had influenced the American founding fathers and used it to justify civil disobedience over abortion. In 1982 an American lawyer established the Rutherford Institute to defend religious liberties under threat from the secular state. The institute gained notoriety in the late 1990s by funding the Paula Jones sexual harassment case against President Bill Clinton; its founder claimed that he wished to demonstrate that *lex* still took priority over *rex*. JOHN COFFEY

Sources *Letters of Samuel Rutherford*, ed. A. A. Bonar, 3rd edn (1891) · J. Coffey, *Politics, religion and the British revolutions: the mind of Samuel Rutherford* (1997) · *The letters and journals of Robert Baillie*, ed. D. Laing, 3 vols. (1841–2) · W. K. Tweedie, ed., *Select biographies*, 2 vols., Wodrow Society, 7 (1845–7) · T. Murray, *The life of S. Rutherfurd* (1828) · R. McWard, in S. Rutherford, *Joshua redivivus, or, Mr Rutherfoord's letters* (1664) [preface] · R. Wodrow, *Analecta, or, Materials for a history of remarkable providences, mostly relating to Scotch ministers and Christians*, ed. [M. Leishman], 4 vols., Maitland Club, 60 (1842–3) · A. Peterkin, ed., *Records of the Kirk of Scotland* (1838) · J. Gordon, *History of Scots affairs from 1637–1641*, ed. J. Robertson and G. Grub, 3 vols., Spalding Club, 1, 3, 5 (1841) · *Diary of Sir Archibald Johnston of Wariston*, ed. G. M. Paul and others, 3 vols., Scottish History Society, 61, 2nd ser., 18, 3rd. ser., 34 (1911–40) · 'Fragment of the diary of Sir Archibald Johnston, Lord Wariston, 1639', ed. G. M. Paul, *Wariston's diary and other papers*, Scottish History Society, 26 (1896), 1–98 · *The diary of Mr John Lamont of Newton, 1649–1671*, ed. G. R. Kinloch, Maitland Club, 7 (1830) · M. Wood, ed., *Extracts from the records of the burgh of Edinburgh, 1604–1626*, [7] (1931)

Archives NL Scot., MSS 16475, 15948 Acc. 9270 as.3 · U. Edin. L., La. III. 69/5, La. II. 394, Dc. 5.30–31 · U. St Andr. L., BS.540 R8.10, MS 30386

Likenesses R. Walker, oils, 1640–49, U. St Andr., St Mary's College

Wealth at death £2923 Scots, incl. books value £1800 and debts owed to Rutherford: will, 1661, Murray, *Life of S. Rutherfurd*, 359–60

Rutherford, William (1797/8–1871), mathematician, was probably born in Northumberland or co. Durham. He was a master at a school at Woodburn, Northumberland, from 1822 to 1825. During this time he married, and a daughter,

Mary Fenwick Rutherford, was born to him and his wife, Elizabeth, and baptized on 11 March 1823 at Birdhope Craig Presbyterian Chapel. Rutherford then went to Hawick, Roxburghshire, and later (1832–7) was a master at Corporation Academy, Berwick. In 1838 he obtained a mathematical post at the Royal Military Academy, Woolwich, where he was always popular with his pupils. His contemporaries recorded that he was a skilful teacher with the ability to explain mathematics and its practical applications remarkably clearly.

Rutherford was a member of the council of the Royal Astronomical Society from 1844 to 1847, and honorary secretary in 1845 and 1846. He is said to have been well versed in both theoretical and practical astronomy, and interested in the proceedings of the society, but did not contribute to its *Transactions*. He sent many problems and solutions, and occasional papers, to the *Ladies' Diary* from 1822, to the *Gentleman's Diary*, and, from 1841, after the two merged, to 1869, to the combined *Lady's and Gentleman's Diary*. He always delighted in what he called a 'pretty problem' (Dunkin), by which he meant something requiring careful mathematical reasoning for its solution.

Rutherford's mathematical studies were remembered as being of the old north-country type. He was a friend of W. S. B. Woolhouse, a mathematical prodigy, also from north-east England. He was the editor, in conjunction with Stephen Fenwick and (for the first volume only) with Thomas Stephen Davies, of *The Mathematician*, to which he contributed many papers. Three volumes were published, in 1845, 1847, and 1850. He edited many other works, including *Simson's Euclid* (1841, 1847) and Hutton's *Course of Mathematics*, which he remodelled for use in the Royal Military Academy. The book must have been well received since four editions appeared, between 1840 and 1860. He was responsible for editions of Bonnycastle's *Algebra*, with William Galbraith (1848); Thomas Carpenter's *Arithmetic* (1852, 1859); and Tyson's *Key to Bonnycastle's Arithmetic* (1860). He produced about fifteen published papers and pamphlets, the best-known of which was a pamphlet on the solution of spherical triangles. He calculated the value of π to 440 decimal places (*Abstracts of Papers … of the Royal Society*, 6, 1850–54, 274). His papers were of a fairly elementary nature, most concerning geometry, algebra, or differential and integral calculus. They appeared from 1841 to 1859 in both journals and more popular magazines.

Rutherford retired from his post at Woolwich about 1864, and died on 16 September 1871, at his home, Tweed Cottage, Maryon Road, Charlton, London, at the age of seventy-three. W. F. SEDGWICK, *rev.* JULIA TOMPSON

Sources *Monthly Notices of the Royal Astronomical Society*, 32 (1871–2), 146–7 · Allibone, *Dict.* · E. Dunkin, *Obituary notices of astronomers: fellows and associates of the Royal Astronomical Society* (1879) · *CGPLA Eng. & Wales* (1871)
Archives RS, corresp. and papers
Wealth at death under £800: probate, 14 Oct 1871, *CGPLA Eng. & Wales*

Rutherford, William (1839–1899), physiologist, was born at Ancrum Craig in Roxburghshire on 20 April 1839, the seventh and youngest son of Thomas Bunyan Rutherford,

a farmer and landowner, and his wife, Elizabeth (*née* Bunyan). He was educated at Jedburgh grammar school and then entered the University of Edinburgh, where he graduated MD in 1863, receiving a gold medal for his thesis. He acted as house physician at the Royal Infirmary to Daniel Rutherford Haldane, and as house surgeon to James Spence. For a year he was assistant demonstrator of anatomy at Surgeons' Hall under John Struthers, after which he went abroad to perfect his knowledge of experimental physiology. He spent the winter of 1864–5 in Berlin, working under Professor Du Bois-Reymond, to gain a special insight into electrical physiology. From there he travelled to Dresden, Prague, Vienna, and Leipzig, where he worked with C. F. W. Ludwig, and then went on to Paris. In 1865 he returned to Edinburgh, and was appointed assistant to John Hughes Bennett, then professor of the institutes of medicine in the University of Edinburgh. Bennett had already introduced classes in practical physiology, and these were further developed by Rutherford and Bennett's other assistants. Rutherford also carried out research on the effect of the vagus nerve on the circulatory system, and made histological examinations of the brains of insane people. In 1869 Rutherford was appointed professor of physiology in King's College, London, where he introduced courses in practical physiology and established a properly equipped laboratory. He did not follow the usual custom for the professor to have a clinical post at University College Hospital. Rutherford's lectures were illustrated by attractive diagrams and by the performance of precise and delicate experiments. During 1871 and 1872 thirteen of his lectures were published in *The Lancet*. Above all, Rutherford's students were made to prepare microscopical sections for themselves, and to carry out the easier manipulations in connection with physiological chemistry and experimental physiology. In 1871 Rutherford also lectured as Fullerian professor of physiology at the Royal Institution.

In 1874 when Hughes Bennett resigned because of ill health, Rutherford returned to Edinburgh as professor of physiology, and was the first occupant of the chair to eschew medical practice and clinical teaching. He was elected a fellow of the Royal Society of Edinburgh in 1869, and a fellow of the Royal Society of London in 1876.

The science of histology owes much to Rutherford; he was one of the first teachers in Britain to introduce the improvements which had been found most serviceable in foreign laboratories. He modified a microtome, invented by A. B. Stirling, adding to it a freezing chamber. This enabled him to cut enough sections for the largest class of students very quickly. The apparatus rapidly came into extensive use, and proved of great service in the study both of histology and pathology. As a physiologist he was interested in the recondite problems of electrophysiology, and in the physiological action of drugs on the secretion of bile. The latter work led him into controversy with anti-vivisectionists, and a delay of four years in obtaining permission to carry out certain experiments. Later in life he moved into less contentious areas. He investigated the structure of crustacean muscle and the human special senses.

Rutherford devoted much valuable time to perfecting his lectures on physiology. This care rendered him one of the most successful and brilliant lecturers to have held a professorial chair in the University of Edinburgh. He was also a good musician, with a fine baritone voice, and for some time he acted as secretary of the University of Edinburgh Musical Society. He served on the board of Edinburgh Royal Infirmary.

As a student Rutherford cultivated refined manners, correcting his border accent and adopting a formal mode of speech which lasted throughout his life. His mannerisms were accentuated after his return to Edinburgh from London and were regarded by some as symptoms of superciliousness, vanity, and disregard of the feelings of others. Rutherford's admirers, however, explained his behaviour as an attempt to hide his exceptional shyness. He was extremely sensitive to criticism and the controversies with anti-vivisectionists led to a nervous breakdown. This, and his interest in oriental religions and metaphysical speculation, resulted in moves to remove him from the chair at Edinburgh, which he successfully resisted. At the same time there was a serious rift between Rutherford and the wider community of physiologists. In 1889 and 1898 the Physiological Society refused invitations from Rutherford to meet in Edinburgh. Both the Physiological Society, of which Rutherford was a founder, and the Royal Society failed to publish biographical memoirs.

Rutherford's publications include *Notes of a Course of Practical Histology for Medical Students, Given in King's College, London* (1872), *Outlines of Practical Histology* (1875), *An Experimental Research on the Physiological Actions of Drugs on the Secretion of Bile* (1880), and *A Textbook of Physiology* (1880). He was also co-editor of the *Journal of Anatomy and Physiology* (1875–6), and of the *Journal of Physiology* (1878). He died from influenza at his home, 14 Douglas Crescent, Edinburgh, on 21 February 1899, and was buried on the 25th at Ancrum church. He was unmarried.

D'A. POWER, *rev.* DAVID F. SMITH

Sources *BMJ* (4 March 1899), 564–7 · W. J. O'Connor, *Founders of British physiology: a biographical dictionary, 1820–1885* (1988), 188–9, 198–202 · *The Lancet* (25 Feb 1899), 538–41 · S. Richards, 'Conan Doyle's "Challenger" unchampioned: William Rutherford, FRS (1839–99) and the origins of practical physiology in Britain', *Notes and Records of the Royal Society*, 40 (1985–6), 193–217 · d. cert. · personal knowledge (1901) · private information (1901)

Archives RCS Eng., lecture notes · Royal College of Physicians of Edinburgh, lecture notes · U. Edin. L., laboratory papers and lecture notes · U. Edin. L., notebook relating to physiological apparatus

Likenesses Barraud and Jerrard, U. Edin., medical faculty · W. Hole, etching, NPG, Wellcome L.; repro. in W. Hole, *Quasi cursores: portraits of the high officers of the University of Edinburgh at its tercentenary festival* (1884) · J. Hutchison, bust, U. Edin., medical faculty · Maull & Fox, photograph, Wellcome L. · photograph, repro. in *BMJ* · photograph, repro. in *The Lancet*

Wealth at death £22,981 9s. 8d.: confirmation, 28 April 1899, *CCI*

Rutherford, William Gunion (1853–1907), classical scholar, was born at Glasgow on 17 July 1853, the second son of Robert Rutherford, minister of the United Presbyterian church at Mountain Cross, in Peeblesshire, and his wife, Agnes, daughter of William Gunion, a Glasgow merchant. After receiving Latin lessons from a dominie, William was sent to Glasgow high school, and from there to St Andrews University, where Lewis Campbell was Greek professor. In April 1873 he went to Oxford as an exhibitioner of Balliol, and in 1874 was in the first class in classical moderations, but he chose natural science for his final school (in which he took a second class), reading at the same time much Greek on his own account. He graduated in December 1876, and at once became a classical master at St Paul's School, London.

In 1878 Rutherford published a *Greek Accidence* (which was later revised and expanded) and in 1881 *The New Phrynichus*, in which the text of the second-century Atticist was copiously illustrated with many examples of Attic forms and lengthy discussions of usage. This was followed in 1883 by an edition of Babrius with critical dissertations and notes. In the same year he was elected fellow and tutor of University College, Oxford. Before he went into residence the headmastership of Westminster School fell vacant, and at the instigation of Benjamin Jowett, Rutherford became a candidate for the post. He was elected and took up office in September 1883. On 3 January 1884 he married Constance Gordon, daughter of John Thomson Renton, of Bradston Brooke, Surrey.

Rutherford went to Westminster as a reformer. He introduced a modern side and a termly personal interview with each boy, and began regular morning services in Poets' Corner in Westminster Abbey. He caused opposition from boys and old boys (but not from masters) by his abolition of rowing, but his view of Westminster as a day school was shared by few. By 1894 there were only thirty-one boarders who were not scholars, but opposition to his attempt to abolish College (the boarding-house for foundation scholars) led to the compromise of twenty additional day-boy scholarships. He was a figure of awe to many pupils, both as teacher and preacher (he had taken orders on assuming the headmastership), and, although he was not universally popular, his reforms (together with those of his successor, James Gow) were very influential in the development of the school. Rutherford's health began to fail and early in 1899 he went with his wife on a voyage to New Zealand. The benefit which he gained from the voyage, however, was not lasting, and in July 1901 he gave up his headmastership and retired to Little Hallands, near Bishopstone, which had been for some years his country house.

In 1889 Rutherford published an edition of book iv of Thucydides in which he attempted to show that the current texts of Greek authors were corrupted by the incorporation of large numbers of marginal or interlinear glosses. Few of his corrections are any longer accepted. His text of the newly discovered *Mimiambi* of Herondas (1892) has been described by the most recent editor as 'a mass of conjectures, some correct, the majority rash and ill-considered'. An edition and translation of the scholia to Aristophanes (2 vols., 1896) is unfortunately almost devoid of value because of its dependence on a single inferior manuscript. In a third volume entitled *A Chapter in the History of Annotation* (1905), he attempted a fuller discussion of his ideas on interlinear interpolation. Although the theory is no longer accepted in the terms stated by Rutherford, the volume includes a vast amount of recondite information about education and the history of Greek scholarship in antiquity and the middle ages.

Rutherford was profoundly dissatisfied with the revised version of the New Testament. His sense of Hellenistic Greek told him that the author of the Pauline epistles thought in one language and wrote in another. In 1900 he brought out a new translation of the epistle to the Romans. He began a new translation of the epistles to the Thessalonians and to the Corinthians. He had completed the work as far as 2 Corinthians 8: 24 when he died somewhat suddenly at Little Hallands on 19 July 1907. He was buried in Bishopstone churchyard. His last work was published posthumously with a biographical sketch by his friend Spenser Wilkinson.

JOHN SARGEAUNT, rev. RICHARD SMAIL

Sources *The Times* (20 July 1907) · S. Wilkinson, preface, *St Paul's epistles to the Thessalonians and to the Corinthians: a new translation*, trans. W. G. Rutherford (1908) · J. Field, *The king's nurseries: the story of Westminster School* (1987)
Archives NAM, letters to Professor Spenser Wilkinson on literary matters
Likenesses S. Lucas, chalk drawing, exh. RA 1895, Westminster School, London · S. Lucas, oils, 1901, Westminster School, London · S. Lucas, crayon, Westminster School, London · Spy [L. Ward], chromolithograph caricature, NPG; repro. in *VF* (3 March 1898)
Wealth at death £9303 15s. 8d.: probate, 24 Sept 1907, *CGPLA Eng. & Wales*

Rutherforth, Thomas (1712–1771), moral philosopher, was born at Papworth, St Agnes, Cambridgeshire, on 13 October 1712, the son of Thomas Rutherforth (*b.* 1674/5), Church of England clergyman. He was educated at school at Huntingdon and at St John's College, Cambridge, where he was admitted as a sizar on 6 April 1726. He graduated BA in 1730, and proceeded MA in 1733, BD in 1740, and DD in 1745. He was also elected a fellow in 1733, a position he held until 1752, and was ordained priest by the bishop of Bristol on 23 September 1737.

Rutherforth's strong interest in the natural sciences led to his election to the Gentlemen's Society at Spalding in 1742 and to the Royal Society in 1743. Within Cambridge he taught physical science privately, publishing in 1743 his *Ordo institutionum physicarum*, an outline of his firmly Newtonian course of instruction which was further developed with great clarity in his *A system of natural philosophy, being a course of lectures in mechanics, optics, hydrostatics, and astronomy* (1748), which became a popular textbook.

Together with Rutherforth's teaching in natural philosophy went a strong interest in moral philosophy, and his lectures in this area were published in two volumes as the *Institutes of Natural Law* (1754 and 1756). It is a work that draws heavily on Grotius and considers morality chiefly in terms of its social consequences, a form of utilitarianism

that was later to influence his younger Cambridge colleague William Paley. Earlier, in *An Essay on the Nature and Obligations of Virtue* (1744), Rutherforth offered a critique of the other dominant schools of moral philosophy active within Britain at the time, chiefly the hedonist views of Mandeville, the rationalist views of Clarke and Balguy, Shaftesbury's theory of the disinterestedness of virtue, and the Hutchesonian conception of an innate moral sense. As an alternative he developed a form of Christian utilitarianism, arguing that good actions advanced one's happiness in both this world and the next. Such a view prompted the strictures of Catharine Cockburn who maintained that 'by denying … to the duties of religion or virtue any foundation but the *prospect of a reward*; he highly injures and dishonours both' (*Works*, 2.105).

Public recognition of Rutherforth's influential role within the university came with the award of the degree of DD in 1745. His theses on that occasion reflected both his interest in biblical studies, especially of the Old Testament, and in natural theology. For the first he dealt with the sacrifice of Isaac as a type of Christ's death and for the second the role of miracles in proving the existence of God. A few years later he returned to these issues in two influential pamphlets. In 1750 he defended Christianity by recourse to the prophecies of the Old Testament in a pamphlet defending Thomas Sherlock, bishop of London, against the attacks of Conyers Middleton; and in the following year he returned to the theme of miracles in a work directed against David Hume's sceptical essay on that subject.

Such works brought increasing advancement. Rutherforth became chaplain to Frederick, prince of Wales, and afterwards to the princess dowager. In 1751 he became rector of Barley, Hertfordshire, and rector of Brinkley, Cambridgeshire, and in 1752 he became archdeacon of Essex. Further preferment later followed, with appointments as rector of Somersham, Huntingdonshire, in 1756 and rector of Shenfield, Essex, in 1767. His rising status was also evident in his marriage to Charlotte Elizabeth Abdy (*d.* 1771), daughter of Sir William Abdy, fourth baronet (*d.* 1750), of Albyns in Essex, and his wife, Mary Stotherd (*d.* 1743), on 11 April 1752. They had two sons, one of whom died in infancy while the other, Thomas Abdy Rutherforth (*d.* 1798), Church of England clergyman, became heir to the Abdy estates.

Rutherforth remained active in Cambridge affairs. After atoning for his support for Prince Frederick when he stood for the chancellorship of Cambridge in 1748, he gained the favour of Cambridge's chancellor, the duke of Newcastle, who aided him in obtaining the regius chair of divinity in 1756. His clear exposition of arguments in defence of Christianity and the church establishment— particularly in regard to maintaining the obligation to subscribe to the Thirty-Nine Articles (the subject of three of his pamphlets)—led to his being described by the antiquary William Cole as 'the great and unrivalled ornament of the Divinity Scholes' (Winstanley, 360). Cole was, however, less flattering in his personal description of Rutherforth, portraying him as 'pitted with the smallpox, and very yellow or sallow complexioned' (ibid.). Rutherforth died in the house of his wife's brother, Sir Anthony Abdy, on 5 October 1771, and was buried in the chancel of Barley church.   JOHN GASCOIGNE

Sources Nichols, *Lit. anecdotes*, 2.196–8, 705; 6.361 · *GM*, 1st ser., 41 (1771), 475 · *GM*, 1st ser., 50 (1780), 226 · *GM*, 1st ser., 68 (1798), 913 [death of son] · H. Hubbard, 'Journal of matters relating to the university', BL, Add. MS 5852, 112 · *The works of Mrs Catharine Cockburn, theological, moral, dramatic and poetical*, 2 vols. (1751) · D. A. Winstanley, *Unreformed Cambridge: a study of certain aspects of the university in the eighteenth century* (1935), 360 · T. Rutherforth, *Ordo institutionum physicarum* (1743) · T. Rutherforth, *An essay on the nature and obligations of virtue* (1744) · T. Rutherforth, *A system of natural philosophy, being a course of lectures in mechanics, optics, hydrostatics, and astronomy*, 2 vols. (1748) · T. Rutherforth, *Institutes of natural law*, 2 vols. (1754–6) · Venn, *Alum. Cant.* · Burke, *Peerage*
Archives CUL, speeches · Glos. RO, corresp. | BL, corresp. with duke of Newcastle, Add. MSS 32866–33072, *passim* · BL, letters to Charles Yorke and Lord Hardwicke, Add. MSS 35608–35658, *passim* · Glos. RO, corresp. with Granville Sharp

Rutherfurd [*formerly* Greenfield], **Andrew, Lord Rutherfurd** (**1791–1854**), judge and politician, was born Andrew Greenfield on 21 June 1791 in Edinburgh, the son of William Greenfield and his wife, Janet Bervie. His mother was descended from the old Scottish family of Rutherfurd, which name he adopted some time before the commencement of his public career. He was educated at Edinburgh high school and the University of Edinburgh, though his name does not appear in the university's published roll of graduates. He passed advocate on 27 June 1812, and rapidly acquired a large junior practice. He married, on 10 April 1822, Sophia Frances (*d.* 1852), youngest daughter of Sir James Stewart, baronet, of Fort Stewart, Ramelton, co. Donegal.

On 6 June 1833 Rutherfurd was appointed a member of the commission of inquiry into the state of the laws and courts of Scotland. He was described by Lord Cockburn in November 1834 as 'beyond all comparison the most eminent person now in the profession' (H. Cockburn, *Journal*, 1874, 1.77). He succeeded John Cunninghame as solicitor-general for Scotland in Lord Melbourne's second administration on 18 July 1837 (*London Gazette*, 1837, 2.1833). He was made lord advocate (in the room of Sir John Archibald Murray) on 20 April 1839 and in the same month was elected to the House of Commons as member for Leith burghs, which he continued to represent until his elevation to the judicial bench.

In the Commons, Rutherfurd made his maiden speech during a debate on Scottish business on 3 July 1839 (*Hansard 3*, 48, 1158, 1168–70). During this session he conducted the bill for the amendment of the Scottish law of evidence (3 & 4 Vict. c. 59) through the House of Commons. He resigned office with the rest of his colleagues on the accession of Sir Robert Peel to power in September 1841. Cockburn considered that Rutherfurd had made an 'excellent' lord advocate, but that overall he had 'scarcely fulfilled the expectations which his reputation had excited as a parliamentary debater or manager … Yet the House of Commons contains few more able or eloquent men' (H. Cockburn, *Journal*, 1874, 1.307).

In March 1843 Rutherfurd prophesied that unless the petition of the general assembly of the Church of Scotland was granted, 'a schism would almost inevitably be created in Scotland which would never be cured' (*Hansard 3*, 67, 394–411). In 1844 he supported Fox-Maule's bill for the abolition of tests in Scottish universities (ibid., 74, 480–86), and in April 1845 he spoke in favour of the Maynooth grant, with an admission that 'he knew that he was delivering an opinion against the sentiments of many of his constituents' (*Hansard 3*, 79, 831–3). On the 1st of the following month he brought in a bill for regulating admission to the secular chairs of the Scottish universities. So effective was his speech on this occasion that 'it had the rare effect of changing the previously announced resolution of government to refuse the leave' (H. Cockburn, *Journal*, 2.111). The bill was, however, subsequently defeated on its second reading in spite of Macaulay's eloquent appeal on its behalf. Rutherfurd had, on 15 November 1844, been chosen lord rector of Glasgow University. On 2 December 1845 he and Macaulay addressed a public meeting in Edinburgh in favour of the abolition of the corn laws. Earlier he had indicated an antipathy towards their immediate abolition: this and his opposition to the ballot and to any further extension of the suffrage show him as belonging to the conservative wing of his party.

Rutherfurd was reappointed lord advocate on the formation of Lord John Russell's first administration (6 July 1846). His five acts of Scottish law reform were passed during the following session. These were about services of heirs (10 & 11 Vict. c. 47), the transference of heritages not held in burgage tenure (c. 48), the transference of those held in burgage (c. 49), the transference of heritable securities for debt (c. 50), and crown charters and precepts from chancery (c. 51). The use of Latin in legal documents largely ended in Scotland at this time as an indirect result of this raft of legislation. Rutherfurd failed, however, to pass his Registration and Marriage bills. On 28 June 1847 he was nominated to the commission appointed to inquire into the laws of marriage: later, on 20 June 1849, he supported the second reading of Stuart-Wortley's resultant bill to amend them, and on 9 July he urged the house to pass the Scotch Marriage Bill. On 24 February 1848 he had moved for leave to bring in a bill to amend the law of entail in Scotland, the object of which, he explained, was 'to get rid of an absurd and preposterous system which had been the curse of the country for 160 years' (*Hansard 3*, 96, 1307–13). This important measure, which received the royal assent on 14 August 1848 (11 & 12 Vict. c. 36), was perhaps his most significant achievement. During the 1850 session he conducted the Scotch Police and Improvement of Towns Bill (13 & 14 Vict. c. 33) through the Commons. He spoke for the last time in the house on 16 May 1850 (*Hansard 3*, 111, 146–7).

In early 1851 Rutherfurd was afflicted by severe illness. On 7 April 1851 he was appointed an ordinary lord of session in the place of Sir James Wellwood Moncreiff, and he was sworn a member of the privy council on 5 May (*London Gazette*, 1851, 1.981, 1196); he took his seat on the bench with the title of Lord Rutherfurd on the 23rd of the same month. He died at his residence in St Colme Street, Edinburgh, after an illness of some months, on 13 December 1854, and was buried on the 20th in the Dean cemetery, Edinburgh, under a pyramid of red granite. His wife had predeceased him, dying at Lauriston Castle, Kincardineshire, on 10 October 1852; there were no children of the marriage. His nephew, Lord Rutherfurd Clark, was a judge of court of session from 1875 to 1896. The fine library which Rutherfurd formed at Lauriston was sold in Edinburgh by T. Nisbet in March and April 1855.

Although Rutherfurd's manner could seem affected and artificial, he was an admirable speaker and a powerful advocate. Sir Archibald Alison wrote: 'In legal acuteness and argument, for which his peculiar powers gave him a great predilection, he was superior to both his friends, Cockburn and Jeffrey' (A. Alison, *Life and Writings*, 1883, 1.280). He was a profound lawyer, a successful law-reformer, and an accomplished scholar. He could read Greek with ease, and he possessed an extraordinary knowledge of Italian. According to Sir James Lacaita, Rutherfurd and Gladstone were the only two Englishmen he had ever known who 'could conquer the difficulty of obsolete Italian dialects' (*Recollections of Dean Boyle*, 1895, 27). In private life he was a delightful companion, but as a public man he incurred unpopularity owing to his unconciliatory and somewhat haughty demeanour.

G. F. R. BARKER, rev. H. J. SPENCER

Sources F. J. Grant, ed., *The Faculty of Advocates in Scotland, 1532–1943*, Scottish RS, 145 (1944) · M. Gordon, *Christopher North, a memoir of John Wilson* (1862), vols. 1 and 2 · Anderson, *Scot. nat.* · J. Grant, *Cassell's old and new Edinburgh*, 3 vols. [1880–83], vols. 2, 3 · *The Scotsman* (16 Dec 1854) · *The Times* (16 Dec 1854) · *ILN* (23 Dec 1854) · *Annual Register* (1854), appx to 'Chronicle', 373 · *GM*, 2nd ser., 38 (1852), 656 · *GM*, 2nd ser., 43 (1855), 194–5, 391, 502 · *Edinburgh Magazine and Literary Miscellany*, 89 (1822), 694 · Irving, *Scots.* · WWBMP · N&Q, 2nd ser., 12 (1861), 442 · N&Q, 8th ser., 7 (1895), 367 · J. Haydn, *The book of dignities: containing lists of the official personages of the British empire*, ed. H. Ockerby, 3rd edn (1894); repr. as *Haydn's book of dignities* (1969) · C. Rogers, *Monuments and monumental inscriptions in Scotland*, 1 (1871), 131

Archives NL Scot., corresp. and papers | Bodl. Oxf., letters to Sir William Napier · Glos. RO, letters to Daniel Ellis · NA Scot., letters to Lord Panmure · NRA Scotland, priv. coll., letters to Lady Moncreiff · PRO, corresp. with Lord John Russell, PRO 30/22

Likenesses W. Brodie, marble bust; known to be at Parliament House, Edinburgh, in 1897 · B. W. Crombie, watercolour drawing, Scot. NPG · J. W. Gordon, chalk drawing, Scot. NPG · J. W. Gordon, oils, NG Scot. · J. W. Gordon, portrait, Leith Town Council · G. Harvey, group portrait, oils, Scot. NPG · C. Smith, oils; known to be at Parliament House, Edinburgh, in 1897

Rutherston, Albert Daniel (1881–1953), painter and illustrator, was born on 5 December 1881 in Bradford, Yorkshire, the youngest child of Moritz Rothenstein (1836–1914), a wool manufacturer, and his wife, Bertha Henriette Dux (1844–1912), both Jewish immigrants from northern Germany who married on 7 June 1865 in Hildesheim. In 1916 Albert and his brother **Charles Lambert Rutherston** (1866–1927), who was born in Bradford on 21 October 1866, Anglicized their surname to Rutherston, while their other brother, William *Rothenstein (1872–1945), retained the family name. Moritz Rothenstein arrived in

Bradford in 1859 and joined an established stuff and woollen merchants firm called Schlesinger, which he eventually took over. He settled in the city, and following his marriage became a naturalized British subject, on 27 November 1867. The eldest son, Charles, entered the family business in the 1880s and used his inherited wealth to create an impressive collection of modern, mostly British, art, as well as ceramics. In 1925 he donated most of his art collection to the city of Manchester's art gallery as the nucleus of a loan collection to circulate around northern educational institutions to promote understanding and appreciation of contemporary art. An early patron of Henry Moore, Charles Rutherston also supported both his artist brothers, of whom William became the better known. He married in 1900 Harriet Fiero, an American, and secondly, on 14 October 1925, Essil R. Elmslie (1880–1952), an artist and owner of the Redfern Gallery, London. Charles Rutherston died at Frinton-on-Sea, Essex, on 28 December 1927. The Rothensteins and their heirs, as artists, writers, collectors, and connoisseurs, exercised a significant influence on twentieth-century British art.

From 1898 to 1902, after matriculating from Bradford grammar school at the age of sixteen, Albert Rutherston studied at the Slade School of Fine Art, London, where, because of his youth and height (5 feet 5 inches), he was nicknamed Little Albert. At the Slade he was befriended by Augustus John and William Orpen. The Three Musketeers, as William Rothenstein coined them, drew and painted together, frequented the theatre and music halls in search of subjects and models, and visited France. In Paris they met Charles Conder, whose fan designs on silk influenced Rutherston's later work. Orpen and Rutherston were close, sharing rooms in London; Rutherston also briefly occupied a house with Wyndham Lewis. Other friends were Walter Sickert and Spencer Gore. In 1909, with the core of the British avant-garde, Rutherston rented part of 19 Fitzroy Square, which became an influential artistic centre. In 1919 he married the actress Marjorie Holman (c.1898–1957), with whom he had two sons. Shortly afterwards he took up teaching, first at the Camberwell School of Arts and Crafts and afterwards as director of the Oxford School of Painting and Drawing. The school amalgamated with the Ruskin School of Drawing in 1922, and thereafter Rutherston taught there as a visitor with Paul Nash. From 1929 to 1949 he was Ruskin master of drawing at Oxford. During the 1920s Rutherston was also involved with publishing, editing a series of monographs on contemporary British artists published by Ernest Benn, including one on himself. In 1936—along with Vanessa Bell, Duncan Grant, Nash, Ben Nicholson, Graham Sutherland, and others—he founded the Pottery Group; its designs, produced on Foley bone china ware, were exhibited and sold at Harrods.

Rutherston had first exhibited in 1900 at the New English Art Club, where he was elected a member in 1903 and contributed to exhibitions regularly until 1941, often serving on the selection jury and the executive and hanging committees. He was also elected an associate of the Royal Watercolour Society in 1934 and became a full member in

1942. Besides participating in group exhibitions, he had one-man shows at the Carfax Gallery, London (1910, 1913); Leicester Galleries, London (1921, 1926, 1934, 1953); Oxford Art Club (1934); Stafford Gallery, London (1939); and Oxford University Arts Club (1949). He also painted a screen for the British pavilion for the 1937 Paris exhibition 'Arts et techniques dans la vie moderne' (now in the V&A) and undertook several other, less successful, public art commissions.

Artistically, Rutherston's interests encompassed painting, drawing, printmaking, and book illustration. Believing that there should be no distinction between fine and commercial art (he was registered with the National Registry for Industrial Art), he also accepted design commissions for calendars, catalogue covers, packaging, and London Underground posters. His early portraits and figurative paintings of street life and working women (usually using costerwomen as models) are well observed, realistic, and subdued in hue in the manner of the Slade—for example, *Laundry Girls* (1906; Tate collection). These were followed by landscape watercolours similar to those of his brother Will and by decorative watercolours, often on silk and using the fan shape or other form specially designed for inclusion in furniture such as mirrors or fire screens. Imaginative theatre and costume designs were praised following creative collaborations with H. Granville Barker on several productions, including *The Winter's Tale* (1912) and Shaw's *Androcles and the Lion* (1913–14). Other notable successes were the set and costumes for Anna Pavlova's ballet *Le réveil de Flore* (1914). Although influences from Augustus John, Leon Bakst, and Aubrey Beardsley may be detected in his decorative work, Rutherston's style is nevertheless distinctive.

Rutherston was extrovert and dandyish, but kindly in nature. He suffered from general ill health and hypochondria throughout his life following several operations for unrecorded illnesses, as well as a nervous breakdown in 1909. Following his marriage, a more ordered existence supplanted the wild bohemianism of the early years of his career. He always loved the company of friends and enjoyed holding court with his students. His thirteen-year relationship with one, Patricia Koring, significantly affected his life and work in old age. He returned to oil painting in the 1940s in a series of portraits and figure studies which rank among his best works, for example, *Patricia No. 2* (1948) and *Reclining Nude* (1942). After leaving his comfortable home in Bradford, he lived mostly in London and the Cotswolds, and died of a heart attack in Ouchy, Lausanne, Switzerland, on 14 July 1953, aged seventy-one. He was cremated in Switzerland. Examples of his works are held in Manchester City Art Galleries; Bradford Museums and Art Galleries; the Fitzwilliam Museum, Cambridge; the Ashmolean Museum, Oxford; Leeds City Art Gallery; and the National Portrait Gallery and the Victoria and Albert Museum, London.

SANDRA MARTIN

Sources M. Rutherston, *Albert Rutherston* (1988) [incl. extensive bibliography] • W. Rothenstein, *Men and memories* (1931–9) • R. Speaight, *William Rothenstein* (1962) • papers, Tate collection • artist's file, archive material, Courtauld Inst., Witt Library • R. M. Y. Gleadowe, *Albert Rutherston* (1925) • A. Rutherston, *Sixteen designs for the theatre* (1928) • *The Studio* [various vols., see Max Rutherston bibliography] • J. Johnson and A. Greutzner, *The dictionary of British artists, 1880–1940* (1976), vol. 5 of *Dictionary of British art* • G. M. Waters, *Dictionary of British artists, working 1900–1950* (1975) • *Burlington Magazine* (Aug 1945) • *Apollo* (July 1969) • *CGPLA Eng. & Wales* (1953)

Archives Bradford Museums and Art Galleries, papers • Man. City Gall., papers • Manchester Metropolitan University, papers • Tate collection, papers | NL Wales, letters to Michael Salaman • Tate collection, corresp. with Lord Clark

Likenesses W. Rothenstein, chalk drawing, 1889, repro. in Speaight, *William Rothenstein* • A. D. Rutherston, self-portrait, oils, c.1898, Ferens Art Gallery, Kingston upon Hull • G. Chowne, group portrait, oils, 1910, Bradford City Art Gallery • Elliott & Fry, photograph, repro. in Gleadowe, *Albert Rutherston* • W. Rothenstein, red chalk?, repro. in W. Rothenstein, *Twenty-four portraits* (1923)

Wealth at death £4323: probate, 1953

Rutherston, Charles Lambert (1866–1927). *See under* Rutherston, Albert Daniel (1881–1953).

Ruthquist [*née* McKay], **Alexina** (1848–1892), missionary, was born on 8 September 1848 at Fordyce, Banffshire, the third child of the Revd Murdoch McKay, Free Church of Scotland minister at Rhynie, and his wife, Alexina Robertson. She had at least two sisters. Alexander McKay (1849–1890), CMS missionary to Uganda, was her cousin. She was educated at home and later at Miss Milne's seminary in Edinburgh. While at school she expressed a desire to become a missionary. Her mother, however, was unwilling to give her permission; in accordance with her wishes, Alexina agreed to defer her ambition and wait for a definite 'call' to mission work.

Mrs McKay was convinced of her daughter's vocation in 1876, when a family friend recommended the McKay daughters to the Ladies' Society for Female Education in India and South Africa of the Free Church of Scotland. Her mother's approval secured, Alexina was sent to Nagpur as zenana agent (a missionary employed specifically to evangelize women) of the Free Church Mission there; she arrived in India in November 1877.

Travelling with an interpreter and a Biblewoman, Alexina visited the homes of all who would allow her entrance, offering lessons in English, needlework, reading, and the harmonium, as well as religious instruction. She was said to have had a beautiful singing voice which she used to good effect, punctuating lessons with hymns in Marathi. Unwilling to confine her ministry to women, she made temperance visits to the local soldiers' camps. Her sister Maggie joined her at Nagpur in early 1881. Alexina spent 1883 on furlough in Britain conducting missionary meetings on behalf of the society; she declined a proposal of marriage, and returned to India. From 1880 she wrote under the pen name Phoebe for the magazine for Free Church of Scotland zenana agents, *Jottings by Busy People*.

In March 1884 Alexina's sister married a Swedish missionary and moved to Narsingphur. Alexina continued as zenana agent but resigned on her own marriage, which took place in Bombay on 13 October 1888, to the Revd Johan Ruthquist, also of the Swedish Mission. The couple settled in Amarwara and on 3 November 1889 their only child, Mary Juanita, was born; she lived for twelve days. With few domestic duties Alexina was able to accompany her husband as he toured the district. Her talent for singing, used before to keep the attention of her zenana pupils as well as to impart simple biblical messages, was now employed to draw audiences in the villages they visited. When in Amarwara she held Bible classes, visited village women, and distributed medicine.

Although failing in health, Alexina offered to accompany a widowed Swedish missionary to Stockholm with his two children, one a sickly infant. While the ship was in the Red Sea she became ill. After lying unconscious for two days, she died at Elektra on 5 September 1892, and was buried at Suez.   L. E. LAUER

Sources Mrs J. W. Harrison, *A. Mackay Ruthquist, or, Singing the gospel among Hindus and Gónds* (1893) • *The helpmeet: a record of women's work in heathen lands in connection with the Free Church of Scotland* (Jan 1893) • b. cert.
Likenesses engraving, repro. in Harrison, *A. Mackay Ruthquist*, frontispiece

Ruthven raiders (*act.* **1581–1585**), political faction, arose following the replacement of the government of James Douglas, fourth earl of Morton, by one headed by two of his leading opponents, James Stewart, earl of Arran, and Esmé Stewart, duke of Lennox. None the less, as a result of an amalgam of religious, political, and personal factors, the Arran–Lennox government quickly found itself under extreme pressure. Hence the Ruthven raid on 23 August 1582, when James VI was seized by William *Ruthven, first earl of Gowrie, and the other raiders. These consisted principally of Archibald *Douglas, eighth earl of Angus, Patrick *Lindsay, sixth Lord Lindsay of the Byres, Thomas *Lyon, master of Glamis, and John *Erskine, eighteenth or second earl of Mar. The raiders remained in control of the country for the next ten months, during which time the king was under house arrest in Ruthven Castle, Arran was imprisoned at Stirling, and Lennox departed for France, where he died in May 1583.

The coup was in part inspired by growing concern among the members of the kirk at the religious policy of the Arran–Lennox regime. Here there had been, for example, little progress in a scheme devised by the general assembly for the erection of presbyteries, while a new archbishop of Glasgow, Robert Montgomerie, had been appointed in controversial circumstances. This upset not only the church but also those among the raiders with strongly protestant feelings. In this category could be included Angus, Lindsay, and to some extent Mar, as well as some others such as James *Cunningham, sixth earl of Glencairn [*see under* Cunningham family], and Sir William Douglas of Lochleven. A further complication was the long-standing political rivalry between the Stewarts and the Douglases. Morton's downfall had resulted in many of his followers, notably Angus, being forfeited. Significantly, one of James VI's first actions while under the control of the raiders was to pardon Angus and various other members of the Douglas family.

Finally, some of the raiders had strong personal reasons for becoming involved. Thus Ruthven, despite his elevation to the earldom of Gowrie in August 1581, was apparently seriously aggrieved about certain substantial sums of money that the crown owed him from the time he served as treasurer in the Morton and Arran–Lennox administrations. As for Glamis, further unruly behaviour by him in pursuit of an interminable family feud with the Crawfords had recently been punished by a highly unpopular and hefty fine by the government.

Although the raiders certainly had the backing of the kirk within Scotland, where their seizure of power was described 'as the late action of the reformation' (*Acts and Proceedings*, 2.594), they received, despite their pronounced protestant and Anglophile leanings, little support from the English authorities. An attempt in April 1583, for instance, to negotiate an alliance whereby Elizabeth would restore the English estates of the Lennox family to James VI, came to nought. An annual subsidy of £3000 sterling was eventually agreed in May, but was never paid because of the collapse of the raiders' regime. Instead the English preferred a policy characterized by putting pressure on the Ruthven administration through a threat to release Mary, queen of Scots, and allow her to become joint sovereign with her son, the arrangement sometimes referred to as the 'association'.

Meanwhile George Gordon, sixth earl of Huntly, David Lindsay, eleventh earl of Crawford, Colin Campbell, sixth earl of Argyll, and Andrew Leslie, fifth earl of Rothes, former supporters of Arran and Lennox, were conspiring to free James VI from the raiders' custody. This they achieved in June 1583, when the king succeeded in escaping from Ruthven Castle and joined the counter-revolutionaries at St Andrews. Gowrie's regime had ended.

Undoubtedly the main beneficiary of this upheaval was Arran, who quickly assumed control of the country. Most of the former raiders were forced into exile in England, Ireland, or in the case of Angus the north of Scotland. An attempt in April 1584 by Angus, Glamis, Lindsay, and Mar, in partnership with the Hamilton family, to stage another coup by besieging the king and Arran at Stirling was a failure, with the rebels being compelled to retire once more to England. The following month Gowrie, who had been arrested beforehand, was executed for his alleged involvement in the affair.

The former raiders remained in exile for another eighteen months before Elizabeth released them and ensured the downfall of Arran in November 1585. Thereafter the careers of most of the raiders flourished. Angus, until his death in 1588, was a key figure in the administration of the borders, and the earldom of Morton was restored to him in 1587; Glamis was appointed treasurer in the new government, a position he retained for the next decade; Mar, the king's old school companion, remained on friendly terms with James, ultimately becoming the guardian of his son Prince Henry, and much later a royal treasurer; Lindsay was freed from Tantallon Castle, where he had been imprisoned by Arran, though he was not a prominent figure in the few remaining years of his life. Consequently the Ruthven family was the only one adversely affected. The execution of the first earl of Gowrie marked the start of an unfortunate era for that family. It culminated in the deaths in 1600 of two of his sons, in the abortive attempt at seizing James VI known as the Gowrie conspiracy.

G. R. HEWITT

Sources D. Calderwood, *The history of the Kirk of Scotland*, ed. T. Thomson and D. Laing, 8 vols., Wodrow Society, 7 (1842–9), vol. 3 · *CSP Scot.*, 1571–81 · *Reg. PCS*, 1st ser., vols. 2–3 · *Scots peerage* · *DNB* · G. Donaldson, *Scotland: James V–James VII* (1965) · T. Thomson, ed., *Acts and proceedings of the general assemblies of the Kirk of Scotland*, 3 pts, Bannatyne Club, 81 (1839–45) · C. Donnachie and G. Hewitt, *A companion to Scottish history* (1989)

Ruthven, Alexander, master of Ruthven (1580?–1600), nobleman and alleged conspirator, was probably born in December 1580; he was baptized in Perth on 22 January 1581, the third son of fourteen children born to William *Ruthven, first earl of Gowrie (c.1543–1584), and his wife, Dorothea Stewart. John *Ruthven, who became third earl in 1588 on the death of his brother James, was Alexander's elder brother. Following his initial education at Perth grammar school, Alexander entered the University of Edinburgh, where his education continued under the superintendence of the principal, Robert Rollock. He was described by the English ambassador to Scotland, Sir William Bowes, as 'a learned, sweet and hurtless young gentleman' (*CSP Scot.*, 1597–1603, 702) and by an anonymous Scottish chronicler as 'a gallant man' (Pitcairn, 2.297).

Although Alexander Ruthven aspired to become a gentleman of the chamber to James VI, and was apparently in good favour with the king, he never received an official nomination to the office, nor did he ever appear as such in the royal household accounts. Rumours abounded that he was a favourite of James's queen, Anne of Denmark, though no evidence exists to substantiate such a claim. Even less likely is the suggestion that he was the queen's lover. One widely recounted story suggests that Anne presented Alexander with a ribbon that had been given to her by the king. Apparently, while strolling through the gardens of Falkland Palace one warm day, James noticed the said ribbon upon the chest of a snoozing Alexander. One of the queen's gentlewomen, possibly Alexander's sister Beatrix, saw the king's reaction, removed the ribbon from Alexander's breast, and returned it to the queen before the king could question her. Although the exact reason for his departure is unclear, Alexander left court about May 1600 and was present with his brother John in July for the hunting at Strathbraan, where he stayed until the beginning of August. What happened next has become one of Scottish history's great unsolved mysteries.

According to James VI's official account of the events that transpired at Gowrie House, Alexander Ruthven approached the king outside Falkland Palace's stables some time before seven in the morning on Tuesday 5 August 1600, just as the king was preparing to mount for the day's buck hunting, and stated that he had made a sudden departure from Perth in order to impart vital information, intended for the king's ears alone. The story, which took about fifteen minutes to relate, was that Ruthven had met a mysterious man carrying a large pot of coined gold. Haste was imperative as he had left the man, and the gold, locked in Gowrie House, his brother's home, situated in the south-east corner of Perth, on the banks of the River Tay, and wished the king to interview the man before the earl could. Although James claimed to have been sceptical of the story, he convinced himself that the unidentified man was a Jesuit priest carrying foreign coin; therefore, the money would default to the royal coffers.

An alternative story, transmitted through English channels, was that Gowrie had discovered a great treasure in an old tower in his Perth home, and knowing the king's current financial difficulties had sent Alexander to escort James immediately to Gowrie House. A third suggestion, preferred by those historians who see the events at Gowrie House as a plot by the king to murder the Ruthven brothers, is that James sent a message to the master of Ruthven requesting his presence that morning in Falkland; the treasurer's accounts indicate that a boy was indeed sent from Falkland in July, with a private letter from the king to the master. An earlier letter had been sent by the king, while still in Edinburgh, to the earl of Gowrie.

Whatever the reason for the journey, the master is said to have pressed the king for an answer without delay. He had ridden to Falkland early in the morning accompanied by a servant, Andrew Ruthven, and his brother's chamberlain of Scone, Andrew Henderson, both of whom were to ride back to Gowrie House with advance word of the king's arrival. Halfway through the hunt James informed Alexander that he would return to Gowrie House with him but not until the hunt was finished, which occurred at approximately eleven o'clock. Immediately after the kill, and with no time allowed for the king to procure a fresh horse, James and Alexander departed.

The official account states that Ruthven wished the king to tell no one of this activity, neither the second duke of Lennox nor the second earl of Mar, and to bring no attendants apart from domestic servants. James, suspicious of these requests, asked Lennox, whose first wife had been married to Ruthven's sister Sophia, to accompany him. During the ride to Perth the king imparted the entire story to the duke and requested his opinion. Although Lennox considered Alexander 'ane honest discrete gentilman' (Pitcairn, 2.171), he found the story unbelievable. Not wishing to be excluded, the rest of the hunting party, including Mar, Mar's cousins Sir Thomas and James Erskine, and at least ten other courtiers and their servants, as well as several of the king's servitors, changed horses at Falkland and caught up with the king 4 miles outside Perth.

Nearly two hours after leaving Falkland the royal entourage approached the town of Perth. As they neared the town Alexander Ruthven left the royal party and rode ahead, stating that he wished to inform his brother of the king's imminent arrival. At some point before the king's arrival at the residence, Ruthven encountered his brother's steward, George Craigengelt, on the stairs and was asked a twofold question: Why was Alexander wearing boots? And why had the king suddenly arrived at Perth? Ruthven made no mention of his ride to Falkland, but simply stated that he had been on an errand. As for the reason for the king's visit, Ruthven suggested that James had come to ensure that Gowrie's debt to Robert Abercrombie, the king's saddler, was settled.

Meanwhile, Gowrie and his dining companions went directly to the South Inch, where they greeted the king and his entourage and escorted them to Gowrie House. The apparently unexpected guests were made to wait an hour before the king's meal was served in a private chamber, attended by the brothers. When James had progressed to his dessert, Gowrie left the chamber and invited the rest of the king's entourage to dine in the hall. The courtiers had almost finished their meal when they saw James and Ruthven pass through the hall and up the main stair of the house.

Before following Ruthven from the private chamber, the unarmed king apparently requested that Sir Thomas Erskine be brought to him: a request that was never carried out. Ruthven and the king ascended the stairs and progressed through the gallery to a small study where a man, later identified as the aforementioned Henderson, waited with a dagger. Both the king's account and Henderson's affidavit stated that, upon entering the room, Ruthven locked the door, took the dagger from the other man's girdle, and held it to the king's breast, threatening his life as retribution for his part in the execution of Ruthven's father. Suddenly claiming the need to speak to his brother, Ruthven appointed Henderson to be the king's keeper, warned the king not to open any windows, and left the study.

Not long thereafter, and with the earl nowhere in sight, Ruthven returned to the study only to discover that a window had been opened, albeit by Henderson. The opened window led to an argument and struggle between Ruthven and the king. It was at this point that James stuck his head out of the window and shouted for help. It was obvious to most of the king's entourage in the courtyard below, who were at that moment attempting to determine whether the king had ridden off (as had been reported), that James was struggling physically with the master. Thus they ran back into the house through the main door, up the stairway, and through the gallery, only to be stopped by a locked door. The first person to gain access to the little study, by way of a small turnpike stair, was John Ramsay, the king's page of honour, who dashed in, still holding one of the king's hawks. Ramsay struck Ruthven several times with a dagger to the head and neck before the injured master was pushed down the stairs, apparently by the king. Henderson claimed to have left the turret room soon after Ramsay entered; therefore, it is not surprising that Ramsay only vaguely remembered having seen another man in the room.

Next upon the scene were Sir Thomas Erskine, one of the king's trusted childhood friends, Dr Hugh Herries, the king's physician, and George Wilson, a servant to James Erskine, all of whom encountered a bleeding Alexander Ruthven on the turnpike stairs. Sir Thomas gave a fatal sword thrust to the master before continuing up the stairs to the aid of the king. Ruthven's dying words were purportedly, 'Allace! I had na wyte [blame] of it!' (Pitcairn, 2.182). It was said later that neither sword nor dagger could be found near Ruthven's body (which was subsequently dismembered as that of a traitor), only a rapier rusted to virtual immobility in the scabbard.

One of the greatest mysteries of the events at Gowrie House was the origin of the struggle between the king and the master, and the nature of their discussion in the study. Unfortunately, only the king's account of the event exists, and the reports of Henderson, who claimed to be the man in the tower, viewed with much suspicion. One suggestion, which places an unfavourable light on the king's actions, was that James had made a pass at the handsome young nobleman and a struggle had ensued. However, the most commonly proposed cause of the struggle was an argument over the king's role in the execution of Ruthven's father, the first earl of Gowrie, in 1584. It has been suggested that the king could never have suspected the master of wishing to harm him in any way. But whether or not he was harmless, or had any preparatory role in the events of the day, Alexander Ruthven played a vital part in events as they developed at Gowrie House on 5 August 1600. John and Alexander Ruthven were posthumously condemned for treason and their bodies, forbidden burial by the king, were hanged, drawn, and quartered at Edinburgh on 17 November 1600. Their heads remained exposed in Edinburgh, and their arms and legs were taken to be exposed in Perth.

AMY L. JUHALA

Sources R. Pitcairn, ed., *Ancient criminal trials in Scotland*, 2, Bannatyne Club, 42 (1833) · D. Calderwood, *The history of the Kirk of Scotland*, ed. T. Thomson and D. Laing, 8 vols., Wodrow Society, 7 (1842–9), vol. 6 · *CSP Scot.*, *1597–1603* · M. Lee jun., 'The Gowrie conspiracy revisited', *The inevitable union and other essays on early modern Scotland* [forthcoming] · W. F. Arbuckle, 'The Gowrie conspiracy [2 pts]', *SHR*, 36 (1957), 1–24, 89–100 · A. Lang, *James VI and the Gowrie mystery* (1902) · W. Roughead, *The riddle of the Ruthvens and other studies* (1919) · L. Barbé, *The tragedy of the Gowrie House* (1887) · G. M. Thomson, *A kind of justice: two studies in treason* (1970) · S. Cowan, ed., *The Ruthven family papers* (1912) · J. Spottiswoode, *History of the Church of Scotland*, ed. M. Napier and M. Russell, 3 vols., Spottiswoode Society, 6 (1847–51); repr. (NY, 1973), vol. 3 · Edinburgh City Archives, Edinburgh council treasurers' accounts, vol. 1596–1612 · *Scots peerage*, 4.263–8

Ruthven, Alexander Gore Arkwright Hore-, first earl of Gowrie (1872–1955), army officer and governor-general of Australia, was born on 6 July 1872 at The Hermitage, Clewer, near Windsor, Berkshire, second son and third of five children of Walter James Hore-Ruthven, eighth Lord Ruthven of Freeland in the Scottish peerage, later first Baron Ruthven of Gowrie in the peerage of the United Kingdom (1838–1921), and his wife, Lady Caroline Annesley Gore (1848–1915), daughter of the fourth earl of Arran. Known as Sandie or Sandy, Alexander had a military heritage: his father, a soldier's son, had fought in the Indian mutiny, the Crimea, and Abyssinia; the eighth baron and his three surviving sons were all to serve in the British

Alexander Gore Arkwright Hore-Ruthven, first earl of Gowrie (1872–1955), by James Russell & Sons, *c.*1945

army during the First World War. After schooling at Westward Ho! (1882), Winton House, Winchester (1883–5), and Eton College (1886–8), Alexander joined the militia—3rd battalion, Highland light infantry—about 1893. On 28 February 1899, while a captain temporarily attached to the Egyptian army in the Sudan, he was awarded the VC for a gallant action at the battle of Gedaref on 22 September 1898 when he rescued a wounded Egyptian officer from the advancing dervishes. This was the first VC to be awarded to a militia officer and earned the young soldier repute in Britain as an imperial hero and a commission in the British army: he was gazetted to the Cameron Highlanders on 17 May 1899.

Hore-Ruthven returned to Egypt for the Sudan campaign, in which he was thrice mentioned in dispatches; he was a special service officer in Somaliland in 1903–4, and then joined his regiment in Dublin. From 1905 to 1908 he was military secretary to the lord lieutenant of Ireland, Lord Dudley, and his successor Lord Aberdeen; and he was promoted into the 1st (King's) dragoon guards as captain on 11 April 1908. On 1 June of that year, at St George's, Hanover Square, London, Hore-Ruthven married Zara Eileen Pollok (1879–1965), daughter of John Pollock, a landowner from Galway. The newly-weds soon left for Sydney where Hore-Ruthven took up duty in September as military secretary to Dudley, recently appointed governor-general of Australia.

After a short detachment to the staff of Lord Kitchener, Hore-Ruthven was appointed to Staff College, Quetta,

India, in 1911. On the outbreak of war in 1914 he sailed to France with the Meerut division; he was brigade major in the 8th cavalry brigade, British expeditionary force, from 20 November 1914 to 23 March 1915 and on 2 April became major in the Welsh Guards. He served at Gallipoli from June to September 1915, and was awarded the DSO for an action in which he was severely wounded at Suvla in August. Following a twelve-month recuperation he joined the guards division and served in France. He was (temporary) brigadier-general, 7th army corps, from December 1917 and in July 1918 became commander of the 26th infantry (Highland) brigade. Having been appointed CMG in 1918, he was awarded a bar to his DSO and appointed CB in 1919. By the war's end he had been five times mentioned in dispatches. He commanded the Welsh Guards from 1920 to 1924 and the 1st (infantry) brigade of guards at Aldershot from 1924. In 1926 he and his troops were stationed in London during the general strike. He retired from the army in 1928.

Lacking an independent income but having royal patronage, Hore-Ruthven looked to the colonies for a career, and from 1928 to 1934 happily found a billet as governor of South Australia for which he was promoted KCMG. Tall and good-looking, with a trim moustache, a soldierly carriage, an affable personality, and a ready smile, Gowrie was a dignified representative of the crown in Australia. During the political and economic crises of the depression years, like his colleagues in government houses throughout the dominion he leaned naturally towards the conservative rather than the Labor side of politics. In Adelaide he antagonized trade union leaders by some of his public statements during labour unrest. While on leave in Great Britain in 1933 he helped to mediate between Australia and the Marylebone Cricket Club over the bodyline controversy.

With a conservative government in office in New South Wales, Hore-Ruthven was an ideal choice to succeed Sir Philip Game as governor in the senior Australian state, and after a short visit to England he arrived in Sydney for this purpose in February 1935. By then, however, the question of finding a British-born governor-general for Australia in succession to the Australian-born Sir Isaac Isaacs was exercising the minds of both the Conservative Australian prime minister (Joseph Lyons) and the king. Having failed to persuade George V to allow the duke of Kent to take the post, Lyons acceded to the king's suggestion of the experienced Hore-Ruthven who, after being raised to the peerage as Baron Gowrie of Canberra and Dirleton in 1935 and promoted GCMG, took up office in Canberra as governor-general on 23 January 1936. He was sworn of the privy council in the following year.

During Gowrie's residence at Yarralumla (Government House, Canberra) he was to have five prime ministers: Lyons, Robert Menzies, Earle Page, Arthur Fadden, and John Curtin. As economic circumstances improved Gowrie cautiously increased the public activities of the office, which had been curtailed during the depression under Isaacs. In 1938, unusually for a governor-general of

Australia, he visited the Dutch East Indies, *en route* to England. He had originally intended to serve for only four years. The death of George V had removed the impediment to the selection of a royal governor-general, and the duke of Kent was designated as Gowrie's successor, to take office in November 1939. But the outbreak of war led to the new appointment being postponed, and the duke's war duties and his death in 1942 led to further extensions of Gowrie's term.

Wartime brought restricted ceremonial and social duties but increased visits to hospitals, munitions factories, and military establishments. Lady Gowrie was an active gubernatorial wife, playing a prominent role in the kindergarten movement, the Australian Red Cross Society, and other organizations. By the time they left Australia, on 10 September 1944, the Gowries had become well-liked on all sides of politics. Labor leader Curtin regarded them highly. The Gowries' simple sincerity and soldierly willingness to do their duty was widely recognized, and their sharing in the nation's wartime sufferings was accentuated by the death of their surviving son (Alexander Harding) Patrick, a commando and poet, in 1942. When he was succeeded by the duke of Gloucester on 30 January 1945, Gowrie had spent nine years as governor-general, a record term of office.

Having been raised in the peerage to Viscount Ruthven of Canberra and Dirleton in 1944 and earl of Gowrie in 1945, Gowrie was appointed deputy constable and lieutenant-governor of Windsor Castle from 1945. Here he and his wife welcomed many Australian visitors. He became honorary colonel of the Welsh Guards and in 1948–9 was president of the Marylebone Cricket Club. In 1953 he retired from public life. He was a member of the London boards of several companies. Gowrie died on 2 May 1955 at Hodgis Barn in Shipton Moyne, Tetbury, Gloucestershire, survived by his wife, who died on 19 July 1965, and by two grandsons, the elder of whom succeeded him and was to become a minister in the cabinet of Margaret Thatcher. The first earl of Gowrie had been the most successful member of an old Scottish aristocratic family that had re-established its position through soldiering and imperial proconsulship. One of the most popular of the imported governors-general of Australia, he had played a positive part in its political and social life and as a 'visible link' with Britain.   CHRISTOPHER CUNNEEN

Sources J. Blanch, *Gowrie, V.C.* (1998) · *AusDB* · NL Aus., Gowrie MSS, MS 2852 · *The Times* (4 May 1955) · *The Times* (1 March 1921) · *The Times* (22 July 1965) · *ILN* (11 March 1899), 333 · Burke, *Peerage* · C. Cunneen, *Kings' men* (1983) · Burke, *Gen. Ire.* · *Debrett's Peerage* · *WWW* · *Sydney Morning Herald* (12 Feb 1933) · *Sydney Morning Herald* (4 April 1938) · *Sydney Morning Herald* (16 Nov 1943) · *Sydney Morning Herald* (22 July 1944) · *Sydney Morning Herald* (4 May 1955) · *The Argus* [Melbourne] (1 March 1941) · *Army List* · O'M. Creagh and E. M. Humphris, *The V.C. and D.S.O.*, 1 [1920] · b. cert. · m. cert. · d. cert. · *CGPLA Eng. & Wales* (1955)

Archives NL Aus., Gowrie MSS, MS 2852 | FILM BFI NFTVA, documentary footage · BFI NFTVA, news footage

Likenesses W. Stoneman, photograph, 1922, NPG · J. Russell & Sons, photograph, *c*.1945, NPG [*see illus.*] · P. Fitzgerald, oils, Cavalry and Guards Club, London · C. Wheeler, oils, Parliament House, Canberra

Wealth at death £11,087 0*s*. 3*d*.: probate, 11 July 1955, *CGPLA Eng. & Wales*

Ruthven [*formerly* Trotter]**, Edward Southwell** (1772?–1836), politician, was the eldest of the three sons of Edward Trotter (*d*. 1777), a clergyman of the established church in co. Down, and his wife, Mary, daughter of the Very Revd James Dickson, dean of Down. John Bernard *Trotter was a younger brother, and the third son, Ruthven Trotter, became a major in the army and was killed at Buenos Aires in 1807. After three years (1787–90) at Trinity College, Dublin, Edward Southwell Trotter entered Wadham College, Oxford, as a fellow-commoner in October 1790, but he left the university without a degree. He was admitted to the Middle Temple in 1791. On 12 March 1794 he married Harriet Jane, daughter of Francis Price MP, of Saintfield, co. Down. They had three sons and four daughters. His son Edward, of Ballyfan House, Kildare, was MP for co. Kildare in 1832–7, as a repealer.

The Trotter family claimed descent from the earls of Gowrie, and in 1800 Edward Southwell assumed the name Ruthven. Having succeeded to his father's estates at Oakley, co. Down, he successfully contested the parliamentary representation of Downpatrick, against John Wilson Croker, in November 1806. Ruthven's uncle William Dickson, bishop of Down, had been a lifelong friend of Charles James Fox, and in 1806 Edward's brother John Bernard Trotter became the whig leader's private secretary. Ruthven was thus closely associated with the whigs, and his return was aided by the whig peeress Lady Downshire. He made his maiden speech on 11 January 1807, but parliament was dissolved in the following April, and in the general election of May, Croker succeeded in ousting Ruthven from Downpatrick. Ruthven stood again unsuccessfully for Downpatrick in 1815, 1818, and 1820, but did not enter parliament again until 7 August 1830, when he was re-elected for Downpatrick as a supporter of O'Connell. He was re-elected for the same constituency on 9 May 1831, but on 17 December 1832 was, with the support of the national political union, returned with O'Connell as member for Dublin. From this time he took an active part in parliamentary debates, but was often criticized for verbosity and eccentricity. He acted with O'Connell and generally supported Hume and the radicals, frequently moving for reductions in the estimates. He made many speeches in favour of the Reform Bill of 1831, but demanded a large increase in the number of Irish members. Although a protestant, he also supported Earl Grey's Irish church legislation, though he did not consider it went far enough. On 12 February 1833 he proposed reducing the number of Irish bishops to four; he approved of the abolition of church rates, and maintained that church lands were public property, and ought to be appropriated to the education of the people and maintenance of the clergy of all sects. Outside parliament he was an active supporter of the anti-tithe agitation. During the session of 1834 he acquired notoriety by moving the adjournment of the house night after night, and members made an organized attempt to prevent his being heard by coughing and yawning, until Ruthven threatened to find a cure for their coughs outside the house; he fought a duel with Louis Perrin.

In January 1835 Ruthven was again returned with O'Connell for Dublin, but a petition was presented; the inquiry was prolonged until May 1836, when O'Connell and Ruthven were unseated. Meanwhile Ruthven had died on 31 March 1836 at his lodging in North Street, Westminster. He was buried in Glasnevin cemetery, Dublin, his funeral being the occasion of a popular demonstration; a monument, of which the foundation-stone was laid by O'Connell, was erected to his memory.

A. F. POLLARD, rev. PETER GRAY

Sources HoP, *Commons* · O. MacDonagh, *The emancipist: Daniel O'Connell, 1830–47* (1989) · A. D. Macintyre, *The Liberator: Daniel O'Connell and the Irish party, 1830–1847* (1965) · *GM*, 2nd ser., 5 (1836), 664–5

Ruthven, John, **third earl of Gowrie** (1577/8–1600), magnate and alleged conspirator, was born in 1577 or 1578 in Perth, the second son of William *Ruthven, first earl of Gowrie (*c*.1543–1584), and his wife, Dorothea Stewart. He succeeded to the earldom in 1588 on the death of his older brother, James.

Education and travels In 1591, after completing his studies at Perth grammar school, Gowrie entered the University of Edinburgh where he studied under the guidance of William Rind, his private tutor (and a Perth native), and Robert Rollock, principal of the university. There he was considered 'of great expectatioun, and much respected by the professors' according to David Calderwood, who graduated with Gowrie in 1594 (Calderwood, 6.27).

Gowrie was elected as provost of Perth in 1592, a position that he held until his untimely death. That same year parliament ratified his possession of the earldom of Gowrie and the abbacy of Scone, despite his father's having been executed for treason in 1584. But although Gowrie owed his dignity and living to the king, he was neither a friend to James nor an ardent supporter of his government. Through the activities of his mother and sister he was linked with the raid on Holyrood Palace led by the first earl of Bothwell in July 1593. Three months later, Gowrie, Bothwell, Montrose, and others were named in a letter from the fifth earl of Atholl, Gowrie's brother-in-law, to Queen Elizabeth, stating their support of her policies and position in Scotland.

In August 1594 Gowrie notified the town council of Perth of his intention to pursue further studies on the continent. He travelled to Padua with William Rind and enrolled in the University of Padua, where eventually he was elected rector for one year. While in Italy he received a letter from the king and replied, on 24 November 1595, with a message expressing gratitude and support. These years in Italy were later used to his disadvantage by the king's minister, Patrick Galloway, who claimed that the earl would 'not have attempted such a treason' had he remained in Scotland (Calderwood, 6.78). Having completed his education, Gowrie embarked on a continental tour, visiting Rome and Venice before arriving in Geneva about the end of 1599. In Geneva he stayed at the home of Theodore Beza for nearly three months and apparently

made a favourable impression on the reformer, who later 'never heard nor made mention of [Gowrie's] death but with tears' (ibid., 67). Gowrie's next destination was Paris, where he made the acquaintance of the English ambassador, Sir Henry Neville. According to Neville's report to Sir Robert Cecil, Queen Elizabeth's secretary, the young earl was 'exceedingly well affected to the cause of religion, devoted to Elizabeth's service, and a nobleman of whom, for his good judgment, zeal, and ability, exceeding good use could be made on his return' (Pitcairn, 2.315).

The earl, approximately twenty-two years of age, 'of comely personage', and described as 'one of the best accomplished for his age, both for learning, travel and good qualities' (*CSP Scot.*, *1597–1603*, 630), arrived in London on 3 April 1600 to a warm welcome from Elizabeth, with whom he had several meetings. His stay at the English court could not have lasted much longer than three weeks as Gowrie arrived in Edinburgh in early May, where he was welcomed by a large group of friends: this gathering of supporters prompted the king to comment that 'there were more with his father when he was convoyed to the scaffold' (Calderwood, 6.71). Scottish court politics, in particular the chamber faction who wished to strengthen their opposition to the earl of Mar, had brought him home. After some time in Edinburgh, Gowrie returned to Perth, on 20 May.

Relations with James VI On his return the young earl had petitioned the court of session for a protection from his debt for one year, as he was unable to pay off his creditors. The request was given royal approval and granted on 20 June 1600. The king himself was in debt to Gowrie for approximately £48,000 Scots, money loaned to the crown by Gowrie's father while treasurer. The earl owed his debt protection in large measure to the inability of the king, who was trying to cope with a nearly empty treasury, to repay the large amount he owed the Gowrie estate.

While in Edinburgh, Gowrie performed his requisite court attendance. All signs are that this was an unpleasant time for the earl: mounting factional conflicts among the king's courtiers, primarily over control of the Scottish kirk and the English succession, led to heightened suspicions and explosive tempers. A convention of estates was convened—again on 20 June—with the purpose of deciding what, if any, preparations should be undertaken to ensure James's succession to the English throne. Gowrie took this opportunity to become one of the more vocal opponents of the king's taxation plan, which called on the estates to raise 100,000 crowns for the maintenance of an army. His reply to the royal request was that it was dishonourable to ask for more than the country could give. This interference greatly irritated James, who had granted Gowrie's debt-protection request with the primary objective of gaining the earl's support on the issue of taxation.

Death at Gowrie House In early July 1600 Gowrie travelled to his hunting estate in Strathbraan, accompanied by his brother, Alexander *Ruthven, and a cousin, James Wemyss of Bogie. During his stay Gowrie received letters from the king, and purportedly from the queen, requesting that he join the royal court on its hunting activities in Falkland, letters which were allegedly found in the earl's pocket at his death but later destroyed. Although there is no material proof of this royal correspondence, the treasurer's accounts contain two entries of payments to messengers sent with private letters to both the earl and his brother during July.

Gowrie returned to Perth on 2 August and supposedly planned to continue onwards to Dirleton Castle on 5 August to visit his mother and younger brothers but delayed his departure to await his brother's return from Falkland. Whatever led to the events at Gowrie House, in the south-eastern corner of Perth, nothing had been done to prepare for a royal guest, and Gowrie's skeletal domestic staff was thrown into turmoil in an attempt to prepare a meal for the king and his accompanying courtiers. To make matters worse, Gowrie's steward, George Craigengelt, was ill in bed.

The first news that Gowrie received of the approaching royal party seems to have come from his brother, who had galloped into town ahead of the royal train. Gowrie, apparently surprised, rose from his meal and went out to greet the king and his courtiers at the South Inch, accompanied by the men who had been dining with him. The official account suggests that the earl was ill at ease during the king's visit. Not only had Gowrie received some earlier correspondence from the king, but he had also incurred the king's enmity as a vocal opponent of the June taxation plan. Consequently, it is by no means surprising that Gowrie should have been uncomfortable, whether from guilt or from the shock of an unexpected royal arrival.

Food was hastily arranged and James was served dinner one hour after his arrival, in a private room, while the rest of the king's entourage waited in the hall. Following a royal prompt, Gowrie excused himself from the king's service in order to propose a toast to his majesty's health in the presence of the hunting party. The toast completed, the duke of Lennox noticed the king leave the dining room with Alexander Ruthven, but when he questioned the earl the reply was that James had simply gone on 'a private errand'. Following their dinner Lennox, Mar, and the accompanying twenty or so courtiers and servitors exited to the estate's gardens to enjoy some cherries.

While they were lounging around the gardens, one of Gowrie's servitors, Thomas Cranston, entered and informed the earl that the king had just left the estate through the back gate. Gowrie immediately cried for horses, though he was informed by Cranston that his own horse was still in Scone. Heading to the stables, the group was met by Gowrie's porter, Robert Christie, who assured them that the king could not have departed as the back gate was still locked. Gowrie, who refused to believe his own porter, repeatedly stated that he was sure the king had departed. Interestingly, not one of the courtiers or servitors seems to have considered checking the stables to verify the presence, or lack thereof, of the king's horse.

As the concerned courtiers were milling about the inner courtyard, they heard the king's voice cry: 'I am murdered! Treason! My Lord Mar, help! Help!' They then glimpsed the king's reddened face in the window of the turret above. At this unexpected development Sir Thomas Erskine and his brother James seized Gowrie and threatened him with the words, 'Traitor, this is thy deed. Thou shalt die', but were fought off by Andrew Ruthven of Forgan. While Lennox and most of the courtiers rushed back into the main hall, Gowrie ran up the street into town, stopped, drew two swords from his scabbard—a habit he had developed on the continent—and returned to the mêlée, proclaiming that he 'would gang into his own house or die by the way' (Pitcairn, 2.173).

The king's account states that Gowrie and seven servants ran up the back stairs to confront the king. Most likely far fewer servants accompanied the earl, as only four of the king's men—Sir Thomas Erskine, Dr Hugh Herries, John Ramsay, and George Wilson—were in the small study with the king, who was locked into the turret room for safety. On his way up the turnpike stair Gowrie passed the dead body of his brother. Thus the earl, spurred to vengeance by the death of his brother and by all accounts an expert swordsman, rushed into the study and began to attack the king's retainers with raw fury. Using the king's removal to his advantage, Ramsay, the king's page of honour, exclaimed 'You have killed the king our master, and will you also take our lives?' (Spottiswoode, 3.86). This one statement so stunned the earl that he quit fighting and lowered the points of his swords. James's retainers took advantage, and either a shocked Gowrie allowed Ramsay's rapier to find its target to his chest or he was stabbed from behind by one of the others. Either way, the young earl was killed instantly. With his death and that of his brother, the ability to decipher clearly the facts behind the events of the day was eliminated.

Aftermath The bodies of Gowrie and his brother were forbidden burial and brought to Edinburgh, under tight guard, to be put on posthumous trial for treason during the parliament held in early November. Edinburgh's town council covered the costs of hosting the bodies, which included payment to four men to carry the bodies to trial and back, incense candles from an apothecary to be burnt over the bodies, and candles for the night watchmen. However, with Gowrie and the master both dead, there was no one to stand as witness in their defence. Most of the evidence collected for the trial came either from courtiers and servitors loyal to the king or from Gowrie's servitors, whose depositions were taken under either torture or threat of torture. To no one's surprise, parliament declared the deceased earl and his brother guilty of treason on 15 November: their lands and livings were annexed to the crown, the earl's posterity was disinherited, and their bodies were hanged, drawn, and quartered, with their heads displayed at Edinburgh's Tolbooth and their arms and legs placed at various locations around Perth. An annual day of celebration on 5 August was decreed; it was later also observed in England.

The king's determination to rid himself of any reminders of the troublesome family was highly unusual:

he insisted that the name of Ruthven be banned, refused to allow any of that name to come within 10 miles of the court, and was relentless in his pursuit of Gowrie's brothers William and Patrick. The events at Gowrie House had tentacles that reached into the royal household and marriage. Queen Anne, whose favourite lady of the bedchamber was Beatrix Ruthven, sister to the two dead men, received her husband's proclamations, on the events in general and the Ruthvens in particular, with very bad grace. She reportedly said that James should imprison her also, but requested that he be careful what he 'mintit' at because she was not the earl of Gowrie.

Speculations What actually transpired that fateful day in August will never be known. Scholars discredit the king's story—that he was drawn to Perth by the lure of gold—as a last-minute concoction to conceal the true reason for his journey. It is made even more implausible by the suggestion that the Ruthvens were willing to share their good fortune with the penurious king. The king's story was publicly disbelieved at the time by the ministers of Edinburgh, especially Robert Bruce, who got into serious trouble by refusing to retract his scepticism.

As to why the king rode to Perth that day, ideas vary widely. Some scholars have suggested a plot by the earl to kill a king with whom his family had a long-standing history of conflict: Gowrie's grandfather and father had both been involved in the murder of Mary's secretary, David Riccio; and his father had spearheaded a successful kidnapping of the teenage king in August 1582, and had links with another attempted coup, the Stirling raid of 1584, which resulted in his execution. Other scholars have argued that it was a plot devised by James to eliminate the troublesome but exceedingly popular young earl. Not only had Gowrie been involved with the treasonable activities of Bothwell and Atholl, but more importantly he was being actively wooed both by Scotland's ultra-protestant ministers and by the pro-English party within the court: in short, he was a potentially dangerous young nobleman from an untrustworthy family. However, apart from the delivery of royal letters to Gowrie and Alexander Ruthven, there is no evidence to link the king with the plot, and the fact that one of the king's captains, Murray of Tullibardine, arrived that day in Perth with a small, private army is simply coincidental. On the other hand, the case against Gowrie has more weight, even though damaging testimonies from the earl's servitors were probably gained through torture and even though the letters, supposedly in the hand of Robert Logan of Restalrig, which came to light several years later and suggested a plot by Logan and Gowrie to kidnap the king and hold him at Logan's impregnable fortress of Fast Castle, are widely viewed as forgeries.

It is unlikely that the aim of the conspiracy was to take the king's life. Kidnapping, on the other hand, was a tried and true method of bringing about change within an administration and had been successfully used by Gowrie's father. If the earl's goal was to kidnap the king, adjust his policy towards England, and remove the Roman Catholic element in his government that the kirk and ministers found so very upsetting, then something went drastically wrong; but the obvious attempt to lure James away from his bevy of courtiers and servitors at Gowrie House accords nicely with the suggestion of a kidnap plot, as does the cry, by one of Gowrie's servants, that the king had ridden off alone. However, this explains neither the actions in the tower room nor the subsequent death of the young master. Perhaps the king made a pass at the handsome young nobleman and a struggle ensued. The more likely scenario is that Ruthven, angry and vengeful over the execution of his father and the king's part in it, lost his composure and attacked his monarch. By all accounts Gowrie was completely stunned by three events: the king's cry from the tower window, his brother's demise, and Ramsay's shout that the king was dead. Gowrie's responses reinforce the suggestion that the king's death was not the ultimate objective.

The two most recent studies of the conspiracy give some possible explanations for events. W. F. Arbuckle's study of 1957 suggests that the aim was to secure the king's person with the intention of thereby influencing royal policy on either the kirk or the English succession. It provides evidence for Gowrie's strict views on secrecy in relation to political plots, his insistence that the king had departed, and the suggestion that Alexander was not fully aware of all that his brother intended. However, Arbuckle attributes the outcome of events to accident: a sudden quarrel between the king and the master. Maurice Lee jun. proposes a political reason for James's abrupt flight from the sport he loved to the home of a man he despised. Citing the unstable political situation at the time, the king's financial difficulties, and Gowrie's friendly relations with England, Lee suggests that secret information from England, delivered through Gowrie, is what drew James to Perth; hence the ridiculous cover story of the pot of gold. The king was not expected to arrive with an entire entourage, but by then it was too late to alter the plans. Rather than an accidental quarrel, Lee proposes that Alexander was in such despair over the apparent failure of the plot, and so determined to avenge his father's death, that he took matters into his own hands and attempted to murder his sovereign.

All these suggestions must remain hypothetical. Owing to a lack of evidence on both sides and the possibly sensitive nature of the events, a true and complete story of what transpired at Gowrie House on Tuesday 5 August 1600, and the planning and motives behind the actions, will never be known.   AMY L. JUHALA

Sources R. Pitcairn, ed., *Ancient criminal trials in Scotland*, 2, Bannatyne Club, 42 (1833) · D. Calderwood, *The history of the Kirk of Scotland*, ed. T. Thomson and D. Laing, 8 vols., Wodrow Society, 7 (1842–9), vol. 6 · *CSP Scot., 1597–1603* · M. Lee jun., 'The Gowrie conspiracy revisited', *The inevitable union and other essays on early modern Scotland* [forthcoming] · W. F. Arbuckle, 'The Gowrie conspiracy [2 pts]', *SHR*, 36 (1957), 1–24, 89–100 · A. Lang, *James VI and the Gowrie mystery* (1902) · W. Roughead, *The riddle of the Ruthvens and other studies* (1919) · L. Barbé, *The tragedy of Gowrie House* (1887) · G. M. Thomson,

A kind of justice: two studies in treason (1970) • S. Cowan, ed., *The Ruthven family papers* (1912) • J. Spottiswoode, *History of the Church of Scotland*, ed. M. Napier and M. Russell, 3 vols., Spottiswoode Society, 6 (1847–51); repr. (NY, 1973) • Edinburgh City Archives, Edinburgh council treasurers' accounts, vol. 1596–1612 • *Scots peerage*, 4.263–8 • *Reg. PCS*, 1st ser., vol. 6

Ruthven, Patrick, third Lord Ruthven (*c.*1520–1566), magnate, was the eldest son of William *Ruthven, second Lord Ruthven (*b.* before 1513, *d.* 1552), and Janet, eldest daughter and coheir of Patrick, Lord Haliburton of Dirleton. The belief that he was educated at the University of St Andrews is an old one, but no documentary evidence of his attendance there seems to exist. He makes his first appearance in the public records in March 1541, sitting in parliament as master of Ruthven. An anonymous note of April 1544 among the Hamilton papers notes that the English ships entering the Firth of Forth at that time might do well to receive him and take him on board for his advice. Whether he advised the English then it is impossible to say, but it is certain that he was in Perth the following June, when Cardinal David Beaton and the third earl of Arran, governor of Scotland, attempted to intervene in the affairs of the town by capitalizing on a feud between the Ruthven and Gray families. Possibly as a result of his decisive action in routing the Gray faction and preserving his family's dominance within the burgh, Patrick Ruthven was entered burgess and guild brother of Perth in October 1544, having been chosen provost of the town at Michaelmas.

Re-elected to that office in 1547, Ruthven entered into negotiations with the English for the delivery of Perth into English hands. Matters moved slowly while his loyalty to the English cause was tested, and by September 1548 it was clear that his dependability was questionable. Meanwhile, during the spring of 1548, he was briefly deprived of his provostship of Perth by the earl of Erroll and others, and he only succeeded in regaining his position with the help of his father. This threat to his family's authority in Perth may have weakened Ruthven's commitment to the English, for the following July he was granted a respite for his dealings with them, and he later received a precept of remission for the same.

Ruthven may have showed Anglophile leanings through his first marriage, before August 1546, to Janet Douglas, illegitimate daughter of the eighteenth earl of Angus and Margaret Stewart; Angus was for several years a leader of the pro-English faction. Janet was the mother of all Ruthven's recorded children, six sons and two daughters. She died after 1554, and in 1557 Ruthven contracted to marry Janet Stewart, daughter of John Stewart, earl of Atholl, and widow of Henry Stewart, Lord Methven; they had no children.

Ruthven was in Paris in March 1551. He became third Lord Ruthven on 6 October 1552 when he was entered as heir to his father. At the end of the year he was named as a leader of footsoldiers in a force which it was proposed to send to France. At Michaelmas 1553 he was once more chosen provost of Perth, and before his term ended the town authorities enacted that he should be provost for

seven years to come, though the formality of an election was to be continued yearly. In return Ruthven promised a faithful administration, and he remained provost until his death in 1566. He kept his undertaking, for between 1555 and 1557 the burgh of Perth and its provost engaged in a lengthy series of confrontations over the act of parliament Against Craftsmen in Burghs. Ruthven played a critical role in upholding the interests of Perth's craftsmen burgesses and in negotiating a compromise with the queen regent, Mary of Guise, which protected at least some of the craft privileges. His actions appear to have won him crucial support in the burgh, especially among the craftsmen burgesses, support which persisted into 1559 and the conversion of Perth to the Reformation.

Patrick Ruthven's protestant sympathies seem to have stemmed from his Anglophile associations of the 1540s. His letters from this period contain a number of quotations from the vernacular Bible, suggesting an attachment to one of the key elements in the evangelical cause. His associates among local lairds in the 1550s became committed protestants, while some of his most ardent supporters in Perth had clearly documented ties to 'crypto-protestants' in the town. All this probably accounts for his confident refusal to the queen regent's request of April 1559 that he suppress the new religious practices there and compel orthodox Catholic devotions at Easter time. According to Knox, Ruthven told the regent that it was quite useless for him to try to change the minds of the townspeople in the matter of religion, though he could command their physical subjugation. Knox subsequently preached his famous sermon 'vehement against idolatry' (*History of the Reformation*, 4.162) in the parish kirk in Perth and on 10 May 1559 the destruction of the religious houses in and around Perth ensued. That all this was countenanced by the provost and magistrates is shown by the fact of Mary of Guise's feeling compelled to re-establish her personal control over the town. To this end she entered Perth with French troops and dismissed Lord Ruthven and his allies, replacing them with men of her own persuasion. Lord Ruthven had joined the regent before she entered the town, but he quickly left her camp and returned to supporting the activities of the lords of the congregation against her. The occupation of Perth ended on 24 June 1559, with Ruthven taking part in the attack and subsequent negotiations and recovering his position as provost.

In the months that followed Ruthven mediated between the regent and the lords of the congregation. When English aid to the congregation was obtained in February 1560, Ruthven accompanied Lord James Stewart to Berwick and took part in the negotiations with the duke of Norfolk. Ruthven signed the bond of 27 April 1560 and attended the Reformation Parliament in August 1560. He supported the marriage proposal between Arran and Queen Elizabeth, but thereafter absented himself from Edinburgh until the following January.

On 16 November 1560 Ruthven was at Scone, receiving a feu charter to former abbey lands from the commendator, Patrick Hepburn, bishop of Moray. However, his long absence from the centre of power and his associations with some of Queen Mary's supporters brought his loyalty to the congregation under suspicion. Although Ruthven returned to Edinburgh and sat with the council throughout the spring and summer of 1561, the English ambassador Thomas Randolph noted that he was not trusted by all of his peers. His unpopularity increased over the years, and by 1563 he was only serving on the council because of the influence of William Maitland of Leithington. Randolph reported that both the queen and the earl of Moray disliked him, yet he continued a staunch defender of protestantism and John Knox. His influence remained equally strong in and around Perth and he was confirmed as sheriff-clerk of Perth in May 1564.

In 1565 Ruthven supported the proposed marriage of Queen Mary to Lord Darnley, and consequently became more prominent on the queen's council. A convention of estates was summoned to Perth in June that year and the queen and her party spent time in the burgh as well as at Ruthven's castle just outside the town. Ruthven sat on the council for a few months after the marriage of the queen, but his deteriorating health seems to have kept him away from court throughout December and January 1565–6. He claimed to have been bedridden for three months that winter suffering from 'an inflammation of the liver and a consumption of the kidneys' (Keith, 3.260).

In February 1566, despite the fact that he 'was scarcely able to walk twice the length of his chamber' (ibid.), Ruthven was recruited by George Douglas (his first wife's half-brother) to take part in the removal of the queen's secretary David Riccio from her household and her confidence. Ruthven and the earl of Morton entered into a bond with Lord Darnley whereby the latter promised that in return for their complicity in the matter, he would protect them should it be necessary to commit a crime in the removal of Riccio. Subsequently on the evening of 9 March 1566 Ruthven made a dramatic appearance in the queen's chamber in Holyroodhouse while Mary was at supper with her friends. Ash-white from his illness, visibly wearing full armour under his nightgown, he demanded, 'Let it please your majesty that yonder man David come forth of your privy chamber where he hath been overlong' (Fraser, 252), before giving a barely coherent recitation of the secretary's misdeeds. His accomplices then dragged Riccio out of the room and stabbed him to death, after which Ruthven returned to the queen's presence and asked for wine.

Ruthven remained on guard with his men at the palace for two days, assuring the queen's attendants and the burgesses of Edinburgh that no harm was intended to the queen. Furthermore, he reassured those who questioned what was happening by telling them that he was acting at the instance of Lord Darnley. Mary soon escaped, however, and regained the upper hand, and Darnley equally quickly denied any part in or knowledge of the affair. Consequently Ruthven and his accomplices were forced to flee to England, after which they were tried in absentia and subjected to forfeiture for treason and non-compearance. While he was in exile Ruthven wrote an account of

Riccio's murder entitled *Ruthven's Relation*. The narrative was intended to justify his recent actions, and claimed that he was upholding the honour of Lord Darnley who had been cuckolded by his wife. It was directed to Queen Elizabeth, whose favour Ruthven required if he was to remain in exile in England. The memoir claims an important role in the affair for its author, while glossing over the criminal and treasonable nature of the act itself. Ruthven's exile was not long. He died at Newcastle about 16 May 1566, aged forty-six. He had suffered from a debilitating disease for some time and this probably caused his death. On 24 December following a posthumous precept of remission was granted for his part in the death of Riccio.

Patrick Ruthven was succeeded by his second son, William *Ruthven, who became fourth Lord Ruthven, his elder brother having died before November 1560.

MARY BLACK VERSCHUUR

Sources burgh records: court books, guild court book, convenor court book, Perth · protocol books of Sir Henry Elder, NA Scot. · J. Scott, *A history of the life and death of John, earl of Gowrie* (1818) · R. Keith, *History of church and state in Scotland* (1844), appx XI, 3.260–78 [*Ruthven's relation*] · J. M. Thomson and others, eds., *Registrum magni sigilli regum Scotorum / The register of the great seal of Scotland*, 11 vols. (1882–1914), vols. 3–4 · *Reg. PCS*, 1st ser. · *CSP Scot.*, 1547–63, 1 · J. Bain, ed., *The Hamilton papers: letters and papers illustrating the political relations of England and Scotland in the XVIth century*, 1, Scottish RO, 12 (1890) · *CSP for.*, 1563–8 · *LP Henry VIII*, vols. 4, 16, 18 · *John Knox's History of the Reformation in Scotland*, ed. W. C. Dickinson, 2 vols. (1949) · *The Scottish correspondence of Mary of Lorraine*, ed. A. I. Cameron, Scottish History Society, 3rd ser., 10 (1927) · *Scots peerage*, 4.289–62 · GEC, *Peerage*, new edn, 11.247–9 · A. Fraser, *Mary, queen of Scots* (1969) · private information (2004) [N. Reid]

Archives BL, 'A discourse of the late troubles happend in Scotland between the Queen's Matie and the king her husband and certain of the nobility', Add. MS 33256, fols. 134–49 · BL, papers and corresp. concerning internal affairs and relations with England, Add. MS 33256, fols. 2–103 | BL, corresp. of English officers and others concerning the siege of Haddington and affairs of the border, 1548, Add. MS 32657, fols. 104–33

Ruthven, Patrick, earl of Forth and earl of Brentford

(d. 1651), royalist army officer, was the second son of William Ruthven (d. 1603) of Ballindean, Perthshire, and his wife, Katherine Stewart. His father was the son of a younger son of William *Ruthven, first Lord Ruthven; his mother was the daughter of John Stewart, first Lord Innermeath. Patrick is generally taken to have been born about 1573, though on somewhat uncertain grounds; a portrait of him commissioned in 1623, now in Skokloster Castle, Sweden, gives his date of birth as 1586.

Swedish service Like many a younger son Ruthven sought his fortune abroad and entered the Swedish service, where he was serving as an officer by 1608. By 1615 he was a captain in Samuel Cockburn's regiment of Scots, ordered to levy and conduct 1000 foreign soldiers (presumably Scots) to Narva during the Swedish campaigns in Russia. The following year he acted as governor of Pskov and was given command of an East Gotland company of 300 men. He became colonel of a regiment of 1200 men from Småland in 1618 and from Kronsberg in 1622. Ruthven had begun to make his reputation, both as a soldier and a hard drinker. According to Gustavus Adolphus's eighteenth-century biographer Walter Harte, Ruthven was reputedly able to 'drink immeasurably and preserve his understanding to the last', whereby he wormed a good deal of information out of less hardened drinkers (W. Harte, *The History of the Life of Gustavus Adolphus*, 2 vols., 1759, 1.177). More tellingly, however, his colleagues punningly nicknamed him Pater Rotwein ('father red wine').

Rather more creditably, Ruthven distinguished himself in a number of battles, in Sweden's war with Poland in the 1620s and later in its intervention in the Thirty Years' War. His compatriot Robert Monro, while admiring Ruthven's capacity for drink, also praised him as a brave and successful warrior, who served the Swedish crown:

> long and valorously … carrying the marks of his valour in his body, being above the waste full of tokens of valour, credibly gotten in his Masters service; for as he was couragious before his enemy, he was also fortunate in his Conduct, in obtaining victory beyond his fellowes: and being often singled out, man to man, to make his courage the more undoubted, he always gave testimony in this kinde of his valour, answerable to the externall shew and hansome frame of his body, being in personage inferior to no man, for strength and comely stature.   (Monro, 249–50)

Ruthven was present at the siege of Riga in 1621 and served in the campaigns of 1621–2. In 1623 he was given joint command in the defence of Kalmar against an expected Polish landing, with orders to torch the city and withdraw to the castle if necessary. His actions at the battle of Dirschau on 8 August 1627 led to his being honoured by Gustavus Adolphus the following month on the occasion of the Swedish king receiving the Garter from Charles I. He fought at the capture of Strasbourg in 1628 and the battle of Breitenfeld (or Leipzig) on 2 September 1631. In 1630 he was reported as colonel of a Scots regiment and garrisoned at Elbingen. In January 1632, Monro recalled, he was governor of Marienburg, colonel of a Dutch regiment, and the oldest Scottish colonel in Swedish service. On the surrender of Ulm the following month he was appointed governor of the fortress with a garrison of 1200 men. By April he had subjugated the surrounding area to Swedish authority. The king granted him the nearby estate of Kirchberg and promoted him major-general in May.

Ruthven had already been married twice by this time. The name of his first wife is unknown. He married, second, Jean (or Joanna), the sister of Sir John *Henderson, another Scot in Swedish service. By the early 1630s he had at least four children: one son, Alexander, afterwards Lord Ettrick, who died in the 1640s, and three daughters, Elspeth, Jean (or Janet), and Christian. About 1633 he was married a third time, to Clara Berner (*d.* 1679) of Sackendorf, Mecklenburg. Their first child was born in 1634: none of their three children survived Ruthven.

After taking part in various petty operations in southern Germany, Ruthven was sent to England on a diplomatic and recruiting mission in 1634. He returned to the continent in time to be present at the disastrous Swedish defeat at Nördlingen on 6 September. Appointed lieutenant-general in the small army of Marshal Banér, the only remaining Swedish force of any significance left in Germany after the battle, he played a notable part in its operations against the Saxon and Brandenburg allies of the emperor. But already by 1636 he wished to return to Britain, and in June 1637 received Queen Kristina's farewell letter of commendation to King Charles.

The king's service: from Edinburgh to Edgehill In July 1637 Charles I ordered Ruthven to return to Sweden on a diplomatic mission. However, with the deteriorating political situation in Scotland his services were needed in Britain. Opposition to the king was growing in Scotland and both sides were recruiting every professional soldier they could find. Ruthven does not seem to have returned to Sweden, and by December had been appointed muster master-general in Scotland. At the prompting of a former colleague, James Hamilton, marquess of Hamilton, he was appointed in 1639 governor of Edinburgh Castle. His début was inauspicious. Denied entrance to his castle, he retired to Newcastle upon Tyne, but as a mark of the king's continuing confidence he was created Lord Ruthven of Ettrick in April 1639. After the so-called pacification of Berwick, however, he was at last allowed to take possession of Edinburgh Castle, with a garrison of 300 men, and on 11 November was instructed by the king to hold it at all costs. This he proceeded to do when hostilities again broke out between the king and the Scottish government in 1640, but he was eventually forced to surrender on 15 September 1640 after a siege of some seven months. Ruthven himself was described at the time as 'spoiled with the scurvy, his legs swelled, and many of his teeth fallen out'. His long defence of Edinburgh Castle was the only creditable action in the war, which ended disastrously for Charles I in the rout at Newburn and subsequent capture of Newcastle upon Tyne by the Scots. Ruthven therefore remained high in the king's favour and was created earl of Forth on 27 March 1642.

Obstinacy aside, however, Ruthven had not so far had much opportunity to display his talents, but at the outbreak of the English civil war he joined the king at Shrewsbury and was appointed marshal-general of the cavalier army. As such one of his principal duties was the marshalling or deployment of that army on the field of battle. The first opportunity to do so occurred at Edgehill on 23 October 1642, and it was marked by a furious row with his immediate superior, Robert Bertie, earl of Lindsey. The latter wanted the infantry brigades drawn up in the modern Dutch or German manner with pikemen massed in the centre and musketeers on either side. Notwithstanding, Ruthven instead insisted on deploying them in a supposedly outmoded Swedish arrowhead formation with pikemen in front. In this he was undoubtedly right for at this stage in the war the royalists were desperately short of both firearms and ammunition and Ruthven's 'Swedish' brigades therefore allowed them to make the optimum use of the pikemen who comprised the greater part of their infantry. The king supported Ruthven in the quarrel, Lindsey promptly resigned and got himself killed fighting in the front rank, and Ruthven was consequently appointed lord general in his place.

Lord general, 1642–1644 Hotly contested on both sides, the battle of Edgehill ended indecisively, but afterwards the parliamentarian army led by the earl of Essex withdrew northwards, leaving the road to London open. The royalist cavalry commander, Prince Rupert, thereupon proposed leading a flying column to seize the capital, but although strongly supported by Ruthven, the plan was rejected by the still shell-shocked council of war, and as it turned out parliament had already raised a second army, led by Philip Skippon, for the defence of London. On 12 November 1642 the royalist advance guard reached Brentford. Prince Rupert's cavalry were initially beaten off, but then Ruthven brought up an infantry brigade and successfully stormed the town. When the main field armies closed up to each other on Turnham Green shortly afterwards, however, the royalists found themselves heavily outnumbered and retired to Oxford, which then became the king's headquarters for the remainder of the war.

In April 1643 Reading, one of the outer ring of fortresses established to protect Oxford, was besieged by the earl of Essex. Unfortunately, although the largest of the outlying garrisons, it was also the most vulnerable for it lay on the wrong side of the Thames. Ruthven's efforts to raise the siege were also hampered by the fact that a considerable part of the royalist field army had been trapped in the town and it took some time to assemble a proper relief force. By that time the acting governor, Richard Fielding, had already agreed to surrender and a last-minute attempt by Ruthven to cross the Thames at Caversham Bridge on 26 April failed when Fielding refused to break an agreed cease-fire. Fielding initially was condemned to death for his lack of co-operation, but pardoned, probably at Ruthven's instigation, when it was realized that by sticking to the surrender terms he had ensured the repatriation of the regiments trapped in the town.

Later that year Ruthven was wounded in the head during the siege of Gloucester, but when the earl of Essex's army tried to return to London after raising the siege he conducted a skilful campaign which culminated in the royalists blocking the parliamentarians' retreat at Newbury on 20 September 1643. Unfortunately, while he was a very able strategist, Ruthven was becoming too old, slow, and deaf to function as an effective tactical commander. A failure of co-ordination as much as exhaustion prevented the royalists from attaining an outright victory, and having run out of ammunition they were compelled to withdraw northwards during the night, leaving the London road clear. In March 1644 Ruthven superseded the overrated Ralph, Lord Hopton, as royalist commander in Hampshire, but was badly beaten by Sir William Waller at Cheriton on 29 March. He had taken up an excellent ridgetop position which initially discomfited the parliamentarians, but later in the day he failed to restrain Hopton from launching a series of unco-ordinated attacks into the valley below, which resulted in the total defeat of the royalist

cavalry. Ruthven and Richard Fielding did, however, succeed in executing an orderly retreat with the infantry and artillery.

After this defeat it was agreed that the king's army would remain within the Oxford defences until such time as Prince Rupert could raise a new army at Shrewsbury, but he was diverted instead to fight the Scots and in his absence, both Reading, which had been reoccupied after the battle of Newbury, and Abingdon were abandoned. This enabled the parliamentarians to mount an offensive against Oxford, from which the king fled at the head of a flying column in June 1644. Ruthven, who had been created earl of Brentford on 27 May, was initially left behind, probably because of his increasing infirmities, but rejoined the king with substantial reinforcements on 26 June. At this stage the king's main preoccupation was to maintain a clear line of communication to a proposed rendezvous with Prince Rupert at Worcester, but in a confused action at Cropredy Bridge, near Banbury, Sir William Waller's army was defeated and it was decided to march into the west country in pursuit of the main parliamentarian army, led by the earl of Essex. This campaign revealed Ruthven at his very best, and culminated in the surrender of Essex's army at Lostwithiel on 2 September, after a very carefully co-ordinated converging attack. Unfortunately, at the subsequent second battle of Newbury on 27 October 1644 Ruthven was again wounded in the head and had to be left behind at Donnington Castle when the rest of the royalist army broke out of its encirclement that night.

Last years While at Donnington, Ruthven is said to have been unsuccessfully urged to change sides by Sir John Hurry, but although he refused he was shortly afterwards superseded as lord general by the king's nephew, Prince Rupert. According to the earl of Clarendon this was because:

> he was now much decayed in his parts, and, with the long-continued custom of immoderate drinking, dozed in his understanding, which had never been quick and vigorous, he having been always illiterate to the greatest degree that can be imagined. He was now become very deaf, yet often pretended not to have heard what he did not then contradict, and thought fit afterwards to disclaim. He was a man of few words and of great compliance, and usually delivered that as his opinion which he foresaw would be grateful to the King. (Clarendon, *Hist. rebellion*, 3.345)

While there is no doubt that Ruthven was in poor health and had insufficient mental agility to handle a rapidly changing tactical situation, he had on the whole acquitted himself extremely well in the militarily challenging and politically sensitive post of lord general. The king normally insisted on leading his army in person and consequently historians, including Clarendon, have tended to cast Ruthven in a purely advisory role. In reality it was Ruthven's strategic skill and careful planning which very nearly brought about the defeat of the earl of Essex's army during the Newbury campaign of 1643 and brilliantly encompassed its destruction at Lostwithiel in 1644. By contrast after Ruthven's replacement by Rupert in November 1644 the royalist army lacked any real strategic direction. Not only did Rupert blunder into a defeat at Naseby in June 1645, but while Ruthven, in similar circumstances, had managed to extricate both infantry and guns from the defeat at Cheriton, Rupert failed to save either and so turned a serious reverse into a total catastrophe.

In the meantime when the prince of Wales was given his own court in the west country in March 1645, Ruthven was appointed his chamberlain and afterwards accompanied him to exile in France. Despite his age he actively solicited assistance for the royalist cause, pledging his Swedish estates to purchase arms, and in the summer of 1650 he accompanied Charles II to Scotland. The Scottish parliament responded by including him in an act of 4 June 1650 prohibiting certain named individuals from entering the country. Ruthven, however, had a long history of ignoring pronouncements from that quarter. On 10 June 1640 an act of forfeaultry (forfeiture) had been passed against him, and on 25 July 1644 he had been declared a traitor and his estates again forfeited. After he had defiantly come ashore yet another act was passed on 27 June, rather plaintively ordering him to leave. He responded by taking up residence in Perth, where in December 1650 he was included in a rather belated coalition formed by royalists and covenanters in the wake of Cromwell's victory at Dunbar, but took no further part in public affairs. Ruthven died at Dundee on 2 February 1651. He was buried in the Grange Durham's aisle of Monifieth church, Forfarshire. His estates in Selkirkshire, Sweden, and Mecklenburg, encumbered with debt and legal entanglements, proved a source of protracted dispute between his widow and his three daughters for many years.   STUART REID

Sources W. D. Macray, ed., *Ruthven correspondence: letters and papers of Patrick Ruthven, earl of Forth and Brentford, and of his family, AD 1615 – AD 1662*, Roxburghe Club, 90 (1869) • Clarendon, *Hist. rebellion* • S. Reid, *All the king's armies: a military history of the English civil war* (1998) • *The historical works of Sir James Balfour*, ed. J. Haig, 4 vols. (1824–5) • P. R. Newman, *Royalist officers in England and Wales, 1642–1660: a biographical dictionary* (1981) • B. Asker, 'Patrick Ruthven', *Svenskt biografiskt lexikon*, 150.770–74 • GEC, *Peerage* • *Scots peerage* • S. Reid, *The campaigns of Montrose: a military history of the civil war in Scotland, 1639–1646* (1990) • S. Murdoch and A. Grosjean, 'Scotland, Scandinavia and Northern Europe, 1580–1707', www.abdn.ac.uk/ssne/ • R. Monro, *Monro his expedition with the worthy Scots regiment (called Mac-Keyes regiment) levied in August 1626* (1637); new edn, with introduction by W. S. Brockington (1999) • P. Gordon, *A short abridgement of Britane's distemper*, ed. J. Dunn, Spalding Club, 10 (1844) • J. Gordon, *History of Scots affairs from 1637–1641*, ed. J. Robertson and G. Grub, 1, Spalding Club, 1 (1841) • J. Spalding, *Memorialls of the trubles in Scotland and in England, AD 1624 – AD 1645*, ed. J. Stuart, 2 vols., Spalding Club, [21, 23] (1850–51) • APS • DNB • J. Balfour, *Annals of Scotland*

Archives NA Scot., corresp. and MSS • NA Scot., letters and MSS • Royal Archives, Stockholm, Oxenstierna MSS

Likenesses G. G. Kräill, oils, 1623, Skokloster Castle, Sweden • P. Paul, etching, BM, NPG • mezzotint (after unknown artist), BM, NPG • oils, Bodl. Oxf.

Ruthven, William, of that ilk, first Lord Ruthven (*b.* in or before **1448**, *d.* **1528**), landowner and administrator, was the only son and heir of Sir Patrick Ruthven of that ilk and his wife, a daughter of Sir Thomas Cranstoun of that ilk. He had succeeded his father as head of this important east Perthshire family by 12 July 1480, when he resigned his lands of Ruthven to his own son and heir, William. By 1484 the older William's local status had been recognized in his appointment as chamberlain of the royal lordship of Methven and as a conservator of the three-year truce with England. He was also a knight by this date. Loyal to James III in the crises of 1482 and 1488, he was created Lord Ruthven in parliament on 29 January 1488, probably as a royalist counter to the Perthshire rebel Laurence, Lord Oliphant, and to Ruthven's equally disaffected neighbour in west Angus, Andrew, second Lord Gray (*d.* 1514). In May 1488, after a confrontation at Blackness, James III, who may have passed through Ruthven's lands on his way south from Aberdeen, surrendered Ruthven as one of four hostages to the rebels. Ruthven was ransomed for £1000, a sum for which he was pursued in 1488–9 by Lord Oliphant, who also took Ruthven's sheriffdom of Perth.

But in 1501 Ruthven's heir, William, was sheriff of Perth, a post which Ruthven himself later occupied (after his son died at the battle of Flodden in 1513) and which involved him in much litigation, notably with the burgh of Perth. In favour with both James IV and James V, Ruthven received royal grants of the lands of Strathbraen (1500), Rait (1506), Kynnard (1512), and the barony of Innernity (1528) in Perthshire, and the land of Strathmiglo in Fife (1522).

Ruthven's liaison with Isabel Livingston of Saltcoats (widow of Walter Lindsay of Beaufort), whom he married about July 1480, produced two sons, William and John, who were legitimated in 1480; a daughter, Isabel, was born after their marriage. Following his first wife's death Ruthven married Christian, daughter of William, third Lord Forbes. They had a son, William, the ancestor of the earls of Forth, and a daughter, Elizabeth, who married twice. Ruthven died an octogenarian in 1528. His heir was another William Ruthven, his grandson from his eldest son's second marriage.   MICHAEL A. PENMAN

Sources J. M. Thomson and others, eds., *Registrum magni sigilli regum Scotorum / The register of the great seal of Scotland*, 11 vols. (1882–1914), vols. 2–3 • G. Burnett and others, eds., *The exchequer rolls of Scotland*, 9–12 (1886–9) • APS, *1424–1567* • T. Dickson and J. B. Paul, eds., *Compota thesaurariorum regum Scotorum / Accounts of the lord high treasurer of Scotland*, 1–4 (1877–1902) • [T. Thomson] and others, eds., *The acts of the lords of council in civil causes, 1478–1503*, 3 vols. (1839–1993) • [T. Thomson], ed., *The acts of the lords auditors of causes and complaints, AD 1466–AD 1494*, RC, 40 (1839) • S. Cowan, ed., *The Ruthven family papers, the Ruthven version of the conspiracy and assassination at Gowrie House* (1912) • *Scots peerage* • N. Macdougall, *James III: a political study* (1982) • N. Macdougall, *James IV* (1989)

Ruthven, William, second Lord Ruthven (*b.* before **1513**, *d.* **1552**), nobleman, was the son of William Ruthven, master of Ruthven (*d.* 1513), and Katherine Buttergask. His father was killed at Flodden, and as a result William succeeded his grandfather the first Lord Ruthven some time between July and September 1528. Before 10 March 1520 he had married Jonet, eldest daughter and coheir of Patrick, Lord Haliburton of Dirleton. They had twelve children—five boys and seven girls.

In 1524, while he was still master of Ruthven, William Ruthven was identified as a supporter of James V and in July 1528 he was entered a burgess and guild brother of

Perth. It was doubtless his loyalty to the king which at this time led to his appointment as provost of Perth with permission to remain in that office throughout the 1528–9 electoral year. (He became second Lord Ruthven between the date of the initial grant of the office of provost and the Michaelmas head court.) The lords Ruthven were hereditary sheriffs of Perth and custodians of the king's lodging in the town, and throughout his life his interests were closely allied with Perth and some of its most prominent families.

Ruthven rendered Perth's bailie accounts to the treasurer in 1530 and continued to serve as provost until Michaelmas 1531. He refused to appear on the assize called to the first trial of Lady Glamis in 1532, when she was accused of poisoning her husband, but otherwise he remained a loyal supporter of King James, for which he was rewarded with various grants and privileges. He was admitted an extraordinary lord of session in 1533, and was one of the king's commissioners to investigate slaughters and anarchy on the borders in 1541. He does not appear to have gone with the king's army to Solway Moss, however, though a summons directing him to join the king 'with diligence' (J. Cameron, 314) was issued on 20 November 1542, just four days before the battle. Under the circumstances it seems unlikely that he received the summons in time.

Ruthven attended the parliament of 1543, and along with Henry Balnaves represented the laity in the debate over the introduction and use of the scriptures in the vernacular. Ruthven's own religious position is hard to assess—his support of a vernacular Bible is one of the few indications he gave of friendliness towards reform. At the same assembly he was named to the governor's secret council and appointed one of the guardians of the young Queen Mary. His subsequent loyalty to her and to her mother suggests that his primary loyalty was given to the maintenance of established authority. He appears to have played a key role in arranging the reconciliation between Mary of Guise, Cardinal Beaton, and the regent Arran soon afterwards. It was he who escorted the English envoy Sir Ralph Sadler to the conference between these parties in September 1543, and he was named one of the proposed negotiators for peace with England in 1544.

Some time during the 1540s (the date is illegible on the bond) Ruthven gave his bond of manrent for life to Mary of Guise, and throughout the last decade of his life he remained a trusted and loyal supporter of the dowager and her daughter. He held the town of Perth firmly in its loyalty to the queen. Attempts by Beaton and Arran to intervene in the affairs of the burgh by capitalizing on a feud between Ruthven and Patrick, fourth Lord Gray, failed to dislodge the former from his position vis-à-vis either the town or the queen and her mother. He acted likewise in maintaining the constancy of the burgh when his eldest son, Patrick *Ruthven (now master of Ruthven), was bargaining with the English occupants of Broughty Castle for the delivery of Perth to the English forces during 1547 and 1548.

Lord Ruthven was appointed keeper of the privy seal on 8 August 1546. He became hereditary custodian of the queen's lodging in Perth in the following month, and was appointed keeper of the town's artillery in November 1548. He regularly attended privy council meetings until just a few months before his death, making his last recorded appearance there on 20 March 1552. He also continued to play an active role in the political life of Perth, sometimes exercising control over the town personally, sometimes acting through deputies. He served as provost in 1528, 1530, and 1546, and from 1548 and until his death in 1552. His son Henry had been installed as parish clerk of Perth in May 1548.

Perth burghs records indicate that Ruthven died shortly before the end of the 1551–2 electoral year—that is, in late August or early September 1552. His eldest son, Patrick, was entered as his heir on 6 October 1552.

MARY BLACK VERSCHUUR

Sources Perth burgh records: court books, miscellaneous ecclesiastical records, guild court book, convenor court book, NA Scot. • protocol books of Sir Henry Elder, NA Scot. • J. M. Thomson and others, eds., *Registrum magni sigilli regum Scotorum / The register of the great seal of Scotland*, 11 vols. (1882–1914), vols. 3–4 • *Reg. PCS*, 1st ser., vol. 1 • *CSP Scot.*, 1547–63 • J. Bain, ed., *The Hamilton papers: letters and papers illustrating the political relations of England and Scotland in the XVIth century*, 1, Scottish RO, 12 (1890) • *LP Henry VIII*, vols. 4, 16, 18 • *The Scottish correspondence of Mary of Lorraine*, ed. A. I. Cameron, Scottish History Society, 3rd ser., 10 (1927) • R. Pitcairn, ed., *Ancient criminal trials in Scotland*, 1, Bannatyne Club, 42 (1833) • J. Wormald, *Lords and men in Scotland: bonds of manrent, 1442–1603* (1985) • *Scots peerage*, 4.259–61 • J. Cameron, *James V: the personal rule, 1528–1542*, ed. N. Macdougall (1998) • J. Scott, *A history of the life and death of John, earl of Gowrie* (1818)

Ruthven, William, fourth Lord Ruthven and first earl of Gowrie (*c*.1543–1584), magnate and politician, was the second son of Patrick *Ruthven, third Lord Ruthven (*c*.1520–1566), and his first wife, Janet (*d*. 1555×7), an illegitimate daughter of Archibald Douglas, eighteenth earl of Angus. By November 1560, following the death of his elder brother, Patrick, he was known as the master of Ruthven. On 17 August that year he married Dorothea (*d*. in or after 1605), daughter of Henry Stewart, first Lord Methven, and his second or third wife, Jane Stewart (who as a widow had married the third Lord Ruthven in 1557). They had five sons and eight daughters. On 4 April 1562 William Ruthven and his wife were granted certain lands in the barony of Ruthven, which his father had resigned in their favour.

King's man Like his father the master of Ruthven supported Queen Mary against the chaseabout raid, the earl of Moray's rebellion in 1565. Again with his father Ruthven was a leading participant in the murder of David Riccio on 9 March 1566, and he subsequently fled to England. On 19 March he was summoned before the privy council to answer for his actions; failing to compear, he was denounced as a rebel on 1 June. Twelve days later his father died at Newcastle, and William succeeded as fourth Lord Ruthven. Along with the other leading murderers of Riccio he was pardoned that December and permitted to return to Scotland. On 1 May 1567 Ruthven subscribed the

Stirling bond to defend Prince James against the murderers of his father, Lord Darnley, and he was with the confederate lords who opposed the queen at Carberry. Ruthven first attended a meeting of the privy council on 21 June that year, and he remained a member thereafter almost without intermission until 1583.

Having signed the order committing Mary to Lochleven, Ruthven conveyed her there and was one of her guardians during her imprisonment. In early July 1567, however, it was claimed that 'Ruthven is employed in another commission, as he began to show great favour to her [Mary] and give her intelligence' (*CSP Scot.*, 1563–9, 350). Mary herself claimed that he made protestations of love to her. Nevertheless, on 24 July he and Patrick Lindsay, fourth Lord Lindsay of the Byres, were given the responsibility of securing the queen's abdication, and on the 29th they publicly presented, on Mary's behalf, documents declaring that she had abdicated and had appointed Moray as regent, and claimed that she had done so voluntarily. Ruthven was present at James's coronation later that day and was one of the councillors who witnessed Moray's acceptance of the regency on 22 August. That year he was elected provost of Perth, so maintaining his family's dominance in that town.

Ruthven was with the regent's forces when they defeated the queen at Langside on 13 May 1568. In April 1569, after Lord Herries had had an audience with Moray to discuss a possible peace between the supporters of James and Mary, Lindsay and Ruthven took him to be imprisoned in Edinburgh Castle, and both men also voted against Mary's petition to divorce Bothwell in the convention which met at the end of June. On 24 November Ruthven was appointed lieutenant of Perth and bailie and justice of the lands of Scone; on 7 December he received a grant of lands in South Kinkell. Following Moray's assassination on 23 January 1570, Ruthven was one of the bearers of the regent's body at his funeral.

During the civil war which followed Moray's murder Ruthven was active, both politically and militarily, on behalf of the king's party. In 1570 he assisted in the capture of Brechin from troops loyal to the queen. That September he was appointed warden of the Scottish east march, a position which he held until November 1573, and which from January or February 1572 he combined with a general lieutenancy for all the Scottish marches. It is a measure of Ruthven's perceived ability that on 24 June 1571, though not yet thirty, he was also made treasurer for life. He was present when John Erskine, earl of Mar, was elected regent on 5 September following, and was regularly with the king's forces at their base in Leith as they attempted to reduce Edinburgh Castle, in the hands of Marian diehards, during 1571 and 1572. In February 1572 Ruthven formed part of the escort for the English ambassadors Sir William Drury and Thomas Randolph when they entered Leith, and he also occasionally led troops in action. In February 1572 he was sent to defend Jedburgh against an attack by Sir Thomas Kerr of Fernihurst, in which he was successful, and two months later he was involved in a heated skirmish in Edinburgh after all the

mills for 4 miles round had been destroyed in an attempt to starve the town into submission. These services notwithstanding, Ruthven was said in 1572 to be one of those who favoured peace, and in November that year he was sent as a commissioner to Perth to negotiate terms. He subscribed the settlement known as the pacification of Perth on 23 February 1573, and his brother Alexander was later offered as one of the hostages to ensure the safe surrender of Edinburgh. In April 1573 William Ruthven negotiated with Sir William Drury the terms whereby the latter would bring English troops and guns north to besiege Edinburgh Castle; the castle surrendered on 28 May, so bringing the civil war to an end.

Relations with Morton On 24 November 1572 Ruthven was present at the convention which elected James Douglas, fourth earl of Morton, as regent. Ruthven voted with the majority, though later he was associated with the beginnings of opposition to Morton. In July 1577 the English ambassador Robert Bowes reported that John Stewart, fourth earl of Atholl, Ruthven, Lord Lindsay of the Byres, and others had confederated themselves by oath for maintenance of the king. This development had arisen from a bitter dispute between Atholl and the sixth earl of Argyll. Having decided that Morton was unwilling to resolve it, the two earls came to terms and together turned on the regent. Ruthven continued to support Atholl, and, though he did not attend the first meeting of the convention which met at Stirling on 8 March 1578 to remove Morton from the regency, he was present four days later when the convention ratified Morton's resignation. On the 15th Ruthven was one of the lords who went to Edinburgh to require Morton's surrender of the castle. About the same time he was again made lieutenant of all the marches.

Morton's exclusion from office did not last, and on 12 June 1578 Ruthven was among the delegates to a convention who voted that the former regent should be restored to the privy council, with first place at its meetings; he was said by an English source to be content with Morton's rule. Ruthven also attended the parliament held by Morton at Stirling in July 1578, and on 25 November he was appointed an extraordinary lord of session. Perhaps because he was a committed protestant, Ruthven had in 1575 been described as prominent among the enemies of the Roman Catholic Hamiltons, and when Morton launched an attack on them in spring 1579 Ruthven showed that his position had not changed. He signed the order for the prosecution of the Hamiltons on 30 April, and two days later was appointed as one of the commissioners empowered to implement it. He was among the besiegers of Hamilton Castle in May and was thanked for his actions later that month. After the forfeiture of the Hamilton lands in November, some of their lands were reported to have remained in Ruthven's hands.

Despite his support of Morton, Ruthven became attached to the faction which crystallized round the king's favourite Esmé Stewart, seigneur d'Aubigny, who arrived in Scotland in September 1579 and was granted the earldom of Lennox in the following March. This probably assisted his brother Alexander's appointment as a gentleman of the bedchamber on 24 September 1580. At the same time Ruthven's relations with Morton were visibly deteriorating. On 1 November that year, as he was returning from the wedding of John Erskine, second earl of Mar, Ruthven was attacked by the master of Oliphant, with whose family he was on bad terms. One of his party was shot and killed and, following Ruthven's petition, Oliphant was tried for the murder. He was acquitted, however, with Morton taking his part. Morton was arrested on 31 December 1580 and charged with complicity in the murder of Darnley, and it was said afterwards that Ruthven had known of the plans to move against the former regent but had failed to inform him of them; he was also reported to be against Morton in 1581. During consultations at Morton's trial at Dalkeith in May, Ruthven apparently became ill through drinking bad beer, and it was rumoured that he had been poisoned. But he recovered, and following Morton's execution on 2 June and the forfeiture of his estates Ruthven and two of his brothers received valuable financial windfalls. Nor was that the limit of his advancement during this year, for in August (perhaps on the 23rd) he was made earl of Gowrie, with a territorial endowment created on 20 October from the lands of Scone Abbey (which he had held as commendator since 1571).

The Ruthven raid Lennox was unable to maintain himself in power for long, despite the favour of King James, who made him duke of Lennox on 5 August 1581. Both his suspected papistry and his links with France made him a contentious figure at a time when Scottish church policy was increasingly anti-Roman and when important elements favoured closer links with England. On both these grounds Gowrie was a leading figure in the opposition to the duke, and he also had personal reasons for resenting the pre-eminence of Lennox, with whom he quarrelled over patronage and crown revenues. The duke's regime had spent lavishly on the royal household, moreover, and as treasurer Gowrie was obliged to cope with the resulting deficits, to the extent of having to wadset his own lands in order to support the financial burdens of his office. The result was the *coup d'état* of 23 August 1582 known as the Ruthven raid [see Ruthven raiders], whereby Gowrie, supported by the earls of Angus and Glencairn and by many lairds and ministers, seized the person of the king and ousted Lennox from power. As befitted the man who gave his name to the raid, Gowrie was a leading figure in the regime that followed. He took steps to protect his own interests—one of the purposes of a tax imposed in April 1583 was to repay the crown's debts to himself—but his administration also made efforts to control royal household expenditure.

James Stewart, earl of Arran, who had been Lennox's right-hand man, tried to rescue the king from the Ruthven raiders at the time of their coup, but he was captured and might have been killed, so it was said, had it not been for Gowrie's intervention. Arran was placed in Gowrie's custody until December 1582, when Gowrie requested that he be set at liberty, subsequently agreeing, however, that he should remain in confinement until it was certain that

Lennox had left the country. However, the divisions among the Scottish élites were such that Gowrie's regime proved no more stable than Lennox's had done. The militant presbyterianism of the Edinburgh ministers and their followers, which largely defined the religious policy of the new regime, soon proved too radical for the town's merchant community. King James received French ambassadors and looked for independence, and Gowrie found that the material support he had hoped for from Elizabeth was not forthcoming. When in June 1583 James escaped from his confinement at Falkland there were reports that Gowrie had colluded in his flight, even though it brought the Ruthven administration to an end. While many of those associated with the Ruthven raid fled to England, Gowrie himself initially retained the king's favour. He received a pardon and full remission for his part in the raid, and remained a member of the privy council until August 1583.

Downfall and death Following Arran's return to prominence in August 1583, however, Gowrie's position became more precarious, until in February 1584 he was licensed to leave the country. He was still in Scotland in April, first at Perth and then at Dundee, where he had ostensibly gone to take ship, but was increasingly suspected of conspiracy, and the suspicions seemed to be warranted when other malcontents, formerly members of the Ruthven regime who were acting with English encouragement, attacked Stirling Castle later that month in the hope of once more capturing the king. By then Gowrie was himself in custody. He seems to have known in advance about the proposed coup, but dithered over joining it. On 13 April Colonel William Stewart went to Dundee with a warrant for his arrest; at first Gowrie barricaded himself in his lodgings, but on the 15th he surrendered to Stewart. He was brought first to Edinburgh, then to Kinneill, before being taken to Stirling where he was tried at the beginning of May. In addition to treason he was accused of witchcraft and conferring with a sorcerer, charges which he denied and which were not pursued. Condemned for treason, Gowrie was beheaded at Stirling on 4 May 1584 and his lands were forfeited. He died with impressive fortitude.

Gowrie was a cultivated man, who had a picture gallery in the fine town house built for him in Perth, and was devout in religion, the minister of Perth reporting early in 1584 how 'his Lordship resortit daylie to my sermons' (Brown, 232). As he faced death he also showed himself a considerate husband; according to an account of his trial, Gowrie spoke to a gentleman:

> desiring him to comend him to his wife, & to conceale his death from her, requestinge, also, that his frendis might comfort her, & put her in good hope of his life till she were stronger in bodie, for she was even at this instant weakened throughe the deliverie of his cheild. (Bruce, 35)

His widow, who had recently given birth to their thirteenth child, experienced considerable financial hardship owing both to Gowrie's indebtedness and his forfeiture, which was not rescinded until 1586. In that year their eldest son, James (*bap.* 1575), became second earl, but he died in 1588 and was succeeded by his brother John *Ruthven

(1577/8–1600). The third earl, along with his younger brother Alexander *Ruthven (1580?–1600), was killed in mysterious circumstances at Gowrie House on 5 August 1600, and all his honours were forfeited, this time irrevocably.

SHARON ADAMS

Sources GEC, *Peerage* · *Scots peerage* · G. Hewitt, *Scotland under Morton, 1572–1580* (1982) · G. Donaldson, *All the queen's men: power and politics in Mary Stewart's Scotland* (1983) · *Memoirs of his own life by Sir James Melville of Halhill*, ed. T. Thomson, Bannatyne Club, 18 (1827) · *CSP Scot.* · *Reg. PCS*, 1st ser. · J. Bruce, ed., *Papers relating to William, first earl of Gowrie* (1867) · M. Lynch and J. Goodare, eds., *The reign of James VI* (2000) · K. M. Brown, *Noble society in Scotland: wealth, family and culture from Reformation to revolution* (2000) · M. Lynch, *Edinburgh and the Reformation* (1981) · T. I. Rae, *The administration of the Scottish frontier, 1513–1603* (1966) · A. Fraser, *Mary, queen of Scots* (1970)
Archives Glos. RO, Gloucester, letters to Sir George Carey

Rutland. For this title name *see* Manners, Thomas, first earl of Rutland (*c*.1497–1543); Manners, Henry, second earl of Rutland (1526–1563); Manners, Edward, third earl of Rutland (1549–1587); Manners, Roger, fifth earl of Rutland (1576–1612); Manners, Francis, sixth earl of Rutland (1578–1632); Manners, John, eighth earl of Rutland (1604–1679); Manners, John, first duke of Rutland (1638–1711); Manners, Charles, fourth duke of Rutland (1754–1787); Manners, Mary Isabella, duchess of Rutland (1756–1831); Manners, Charles Cecil John, sixth duke of Rutland (1815–1888); Manners, John James Robert, seventh duke of Rutland (1818–1906); Manners, (Marion Margaret) Violet, duchess of Rutland (1856–1937).

Rutledge, Andrew (*c*.1709–1755), lawyer and politician in America, was descended from the Rutledges of Ireland, where it is believed his father owned and operated a farm in co. Cavan, in Ballymagied near Baronlog. The names of his parents and exact location of Andrew's birth are unknown. He entered Trinity College, Dublin, about 1724, taking his BA in 1728, and migrated to America about 1730. In South Carolina his legal training and ability prompted Governor Robert Johnson in 1732 to describe him as 'a lawyer of very good repute'. Nicholas Trott, formerly a member of the council and chief justice of South Carolina, aided Rutledge in his law practice. In 1735 he acquired a 1000-acre land grant in Williamsburg township, Craven county, and a town lot in Kingston. That year he married Sarah (*d*. 1743), daughter of John Boone and his wife, Elizabeth Paley, and widow of Hugh Hext. Andrew and Sarah resided on the Wando Neck plantation in Christ Church parish, part of the estate she inherited from her father and first husband. Although they had no children, a stepdaughter, Sarah Hext, married in 1738 Andrew's younger brother, Dr John Rutledge, who had arrived in Charles Town in 1735.

The Rutledge brothers served in the lower chamber of the colonial legislature, the Commons house of assembly, Andrew from 1733 to 1752 and John from 1743 to 1750. Andrew became known as a champion of the privileges and rights of the assembly against royal authority. In a dispute between Commons house and the chief justice, Robert Wright, Andrew, although a new arrival to the assembly, led the effort to deny the judge his salary. Himself a staunch supporter of the Church of England establishment, he nevertheless in July 1740 represented the Anglican evangelist the Revd George Whitefield against charges levelled by the bishop of London's commissary, the Revd Alexander Garden, rector of St Philip's parish, Charles Town. This trial is believed to have been the first in an Anglican ecclesiastical court in a British colony. His defence of the assembly's claim that money bills could not be amended in council helped pave the way for his election to the highest elected office in the colony, speaker of the house, which he held from 1749 to 1752. In local affairs he was adjutant-general of the militia, justice of the peace for Berkeley county, vestryman for Christ Church parish, commissioner for the creation of St Michael's parish, and commissioner for the importation of Indian corn. He held membership in the St Andrew's Society, and both brothers were charter members of the Charles Town Library Society.

Andrew Rutledge became a surrogate father to his brother's children upon John's death in 1750. Described as lanky and dignified in appearance, he was noted as one who 'always discharged his Trust with Honour'. Andrew died on 19 November 1755 and was buried the next day in St Philip's churchyard, Charles Town, South Carolina. His sister-in-law, Sarah, and her children received his estate, valued at £12,000. Nephews John, Hugh, and Edward followed their uncle into the practice of law and service in the assembly. Edward signed the Declaration of Independence in 1776, and John signed the US constitution in 1787.

FREDERICK V. MILLS, SR.

Sources R. Barry, *Mr. Rutledge of South Carolina* (1942) · M. E. Sirmans, *Colonial South Carolina* (1966) · J. Haw, *John and Edward Rutledge of South Carolina* (1997) · W. B. Edgar and N. L. Bailey, eds., *Biographical directory of the South Carolina house of representatives*, 2 (1977) · R. B. Clow, 'Edward Rutledge of South Carolina, 1749–1800', PhD diss., University of Georgia, 1976 · L. Tyerman, *The life of the Rev. George Whitefield*, 2 vols. (1876–7) · E. McCrady, *The history of South Carolina under the royal government, 1719–1776* (1899) · M. L. Webber, 'Dr John Rutledge and his descendants', *South Carolina Historical and Genealogical Magazine*, 31 (1930), 7–25, 93–106 · J. P. Greene, *The quest for power: the lower houses of assembly in the southern royal colonies, 1689–1776* (1963)
Archives Charleston Library Society, South Carolina, family MSS · Duke U., family MSS · L. Cong., family MSS · South Carolina Historical Society, Charleston · University of North Carolina, Chapel Hill, family MSS · University of South Carolina, Columbia, family MSS
Wealth at death approx. £12,000: Charleston county wills, vol. 7, pp. 399–400, South Carolina Archives and History Center, Columbia

Rutledge, Edward (1749–1800), planter and revolutionary politician in America, was born on 23 November 1749 in Charles Town, South Carolina, the seventh and youngest child of the Irish immigrant John Rutledge (*d*. 1750) and his wife, Sarah Hext (1724–1792). His father, a physician and planter, died when Edward was one year old, but his young, wealthy mother employed a tutor to instruct him in the classical languages and allowed him to study law with his elder brother John *Rutledge. Having trained in the law at the Middle Temple of the inns of court in London from 12 January 1767 to 3 July 1772, Edward was called to the English bar in 1772. He returned to South Carolina in 1773, accepted a 640 acre plantation from his mother, and quickly established himself in Charles Town society. On 1 March 1774 he married Henrietta Middleton (d. 1792), the daughter of Henry Middleton. They had three children.

A small man and a mediocre orator, Edward Rutledge was intelligent and had a charming personality that suited him for the role of mediator during the debates that led to American independence. After parliament imposed the 'Intolerable Acts' (1774) upon the colonies in response to the Boston tea party, he became the youngest of the five delegates from his state to the first session of the continental congress in 1774, joining his moderate brother John, Henry Middleton, Thomas Lynch senior, and the radical Christopher Gadsden. He made a poor impression upon John Adams, who found him 'young and zealous, a little unsteady and injudicious, but very unnatural and affected as a speaker' (Works of John Adams, 2.396). Offended by the arrogant Massachusetts statesman, Rutledge still worked for a bill of rights that would give British Americans permanent relief from taxes. He also favoured a complete cessation of trade with Britain, except for South Carolina's rice, if parliament did not repeal the objectionable laws. After the congress adjourned on 26 October 1774, he returned home to serve in the first and second provincial congresses of South Carolina in 1775 and 1776. The provincial congress of 1775 reappointed the same five men to return to the second session of the continental congress.

At the continental congress in May 1775, Rutledge spoke for reconciliation with Great Britain despite the growing military confrontation, but he changed his mind by the autumn. Early in 1776, after his brother John and Christopher Gadsden left the congress to participate in the war in South Carolina, he controlled the remaining South Carolina delegation. He persuaded them on 2 July to vote for independence. Distrustful of the New England radicals in the congress, he wanted a confederation rather than a strong central government.

In November 1776 Rutledge served as a captain in the Charles Town battery of artillery, and later saw action at Beaufort in February 1779. Meanwhile, in addition to his military career, his parish in Charles Town elected him to the state house of representatives in 1778. There he mediated between patriots and dissenters, a thankless task that preserved sufficient unity for the state to continue the war. The next year the state house returned him to the continental congress. Before he could leave South Carolina, however, the British captured Charles Town, arrested him, and imprisoned him at St Augustine, Florida. From September 1780 to July 1781 he languished in the old Spanish fort with other prominent military and civilian prisoners. After the American victory at Yorktown, Virginia, in 1781, his captors released him. He returned to the state house of representatives in January 1782, where he argued for lenient treatment of the loyalists.

A popular attorney after the war, Rutledge represented Charles Town (from 1783 Charleston) in the state house of representatives from 1782 to 1796, and in the state constitutional conventions of 1788 and 1790; in the latter he wrote the law abolishing rights of primogeniture. He became a national federalist and served as a presidential elector in 1788, 1792, and 1796. On 22 April 1792 Henrietta died. On 28 October of the same year Rutledge married Mary Shubrick (d. 1829?), widow of Nicholas Eveleigh, the comptroller of the currency for George Washington; they had no children.

Wealthy before the war, Rutledge lost most of his assets during the conflict, but rebuilt and enlarged his fortune in the 1790s. In 1794 he declined President George Washington's offer of an appointment as associate justice of the United States supreme court, because he needed to stay at home to tend to his expanding financial affairs. Nevertheless, he thought that men of virtue and means should render public service. In 1796 he broke with his party because he did not like its candidate, John Adams, and cast his vote for South Carolina's Thomas Pinckney and the democratic republican Thomas Jefferson. He remained politically active until the end of his life, and he served two terms in the state senate, 1796 and 1798. By the time he was elected governor in 1798, he was broken in health. He died, a hero, at his desk, in the governor's office in Columbia, on 23 January 1800.

A planter and slave owner, as well as an attorney, Rutledge had a particular interest in promoting agriculture, often serving on committees, experimenting with new crops, and carrying on lively correspondence with others on the subject. Active in numerous social and civic clubs, he joined the Friendly Brothers of St Patrick, a South Carolina society for attorneys of Irish extraction that promoted educational and charitable activities, and served as a vestryman in St Michael's Church. He was buried on 25 January 1800 in St Philip's churchyard in Charleston, South Carolina.   E. STANLY GODBOLD JR.

Sources Duke U., Rutledge MSS · University of South Carolina, Columbia, South Caroliniana Library, Edward Rutledge papers · L. Cong., manuscript division, Edward Rutledge MSS · South Carolina Historical and Genealogical Magazine, 17/1 (1916) · South Carolina Historical and Genealogical Magazine, 22/1 (1921) · South Carolina Historical and Genealogical Magazine, 31/1 (1930) · South Carolina Historical Magazine, 64/1 (1963) · Charleston inventories and wills, South Carolina Department of Archives and History, Columbia · J. Haw, John and Edward Rutledge of South Carolina (1997) · E. S. Godbold and R. H. Woody, Christopher Gadsden and the American Revolution (1982) · The works of John Adams, second president of the United States, ed. C. F. Adams, 10 vols. (1850–56) · E. C. Burnett, ed., Letters of members of the continental congress, 10 vols. (1921–36) · W. B. Edgar, N. L. Bailey, and A. Moore, eds., Biographical directory of the South Carolina house of representatives, 5 vols. (1974–92) · E. McCrady, The history of South Carolina in the revolution, 2 vols. (1901–2) · D. Ramsay, The history of South Carolina: from its first settlement in 1670, to the year 1808, 2 vols. (1809) · P. H. Smith and others, eds., Letters of delegates to congress, 1774–1789, 26 vols. (1976–2000) · D. D. Wallace, The history of South Carolina, 4 vols. (1934) · M. L. Webber, 'Dr John Rutledge and his descendants [pt 1]', South Carolina Historical and Genealogical Magazine, 31 (1930), 7–25 · South Carolina Gazette (7 March 1774) · South Carolina Gazette (25 Jan 1800) · State Gazette of South Carolina (1 Nov 1792)

Archives Duke U., papers · L. Cong., papers · University of South Carolina, Columbia, papers
Likenesses oils, Charleston Museum, South Carolina
Wealth at death wealthy; 600 acres; 230 slaves: Charleston inventories and wills, South Carolina Archives and History Center, Columbia

Rutledge, John (1739–1800), revolutionary politician in America, was born in Charles Town, South Carolina, in September 1739, the oldest of the seven children of the Irish immigrant John Rutledge (*d.* 1750) and his fifteen-year-old wife, Sarah Hext (1724–1792). The senior Rutledge was a planter and physician who gained his wealth through his wife's dowry. Their youngest child, Edward *Rutledge, signed the American Declaration of Independence and enjoyed a public career similar to that of his brother John. As a child John had three teachers—the Anglican minister of Christ Church parish, Charles Town, a tutor in the classics, and his father. He studied law at the Middle Temple in London from 1758, and was called to the English bar in 1760. He immediately returned to South Carolina, and soon thereafter used his knowledge of British law to argue for the rights of Americans within the empire. On 1 May 1763 he married Elizabeth (*d.* 1792), the daughter of Frederick Grimké, and they became the parents of ten children.

John Rutledge began his public career in 1761, when Christ Church parish elected him to the South Carolina Commons house of assembly. At the age of twenty-three he chaired the committee that indicted Governor Thomas Boone in the Christopher Gadsden election controversy, a dispute that elevated the power of a local assembly over that of the royal governor. At the Stamp Act congress of 1765 he chaired the committee that petitioned the House of Lords politely but firmly for redress of grievances, but he did not favour the severance of ties with the mother country.

Witty, an eloquent orator, tall, grave, and impatient, John Rutledge served with his brother Edward in the first session of the continental congress in 1774. Using English constitutional precedents, he argued for colonial self-government without independence. A staunch defender of the interests of the southern colonies, he successfully argued to exempt South Carolina's rice from the list of goods the colonists refused to sell to England until it repealed the 'objectionable' tax laws. At the second session of the continental congress in 1775–6, he supported the establishment of new governments in all of the colonies. He left Philadelphia on 5 November 1775 to assume leadership in his home province.

After Rutledge served on the committee that wrote the South Carolina constitution of 1776, the general assembly elected him president and commander-in-chief of South Carolina. A knowledgeable man of courage and dedication, but quick-tempered, he assumed this awesome task at the beginning of the colonies' war for independence. After a British attempt to capture Charles Town failed in June 1776, the state enjoyed two years of war-free prosperity under his leadership. In 1778, however, when democratic elements led by Rawlins Lowndes of the upcountry

forced a revision of the constitution that instituted an elected senate and disestablished the Episcopal church, Rutledge resigned.

When the state faced invasion again in January 1779, it elected John Rutledge governor. His desperate attempts to raise troops for generals Benjamin Lincoln and William Moultrie borrowed time, but ultimately proved inadequate to repel the massive British invasion in the spring of 1780. Shortly before British troops occupied Charles Town in May, Rutledge slipped away to lead a government in exile and wage unrelenting war against them, thus escaping capture and imprisonment. By letter and in person, Rutledge begged General George Washington for help. Washington sent General Nathanael Greene to defend the southern colonies, but Rutledge also encouraged the South Carolinians Thomas Sumter, Andrew Pickens, and Francis Marion to wage guerrilla war against the British troops as they fanned upward across the state. In August 1781 he sold indigo in Philadelphia to buy military supplies, restored civilian government, pardoned many citizens who had supported the British, and called for the election of a legislature to meet in January 1782. That assembly honoured him by adopting all of his proposals, including one that called for the confiscation of the property of loyalists in lieu of harsher punishment. As president of his state from 1776 to 1778, during the controversial early years of independence, and as governor from 1779 to 1781, when the colonies finally achieved independence, he justly achieved the highest honour of any citizen in the history of his state. Ineligible to succeed himself, he left the governorship on 29 January 1782. He served in the state house of representatives until 1790, attended the continental congress from May 1782 to September 1783, and in 1784 was elected to the South Carolina chancery court.

John Rutledge helped to write the constitution of the United States and to establish the new nation. As chairman of the committee on detail at the constitutional convention in Philadelphia in 1787, he argued points dear to the 'aristocratic' south. He wanted to protect the slave trade, make wealth the basis for representation, have the national government assume the state debts, and establish a legislature that would dominate the government. According to legend, during that hot summer in Philadelphia, he asked a slave to prepare him a cool drink. That slave's effort produced the south's first fabled mint julep, a concoction of sugar, crushed mint leaves, and straight bourbon whiskey over crushed ice. Once the new government took effect and George Washington became president, Washington appointed him senior associate of the supreme court.

Because of his declining health and the raging political disputes in South Carolina and the nation, John Rutledge's judicial career became more honorary than distinguished. He resigned from the supreme court before he actually served in order to become chief justice of South Carolina in February 1791. In 1795 he asked George Washington to appoint him chief justice of the United States to replace John Jay of New York, who was resigning. Washington made the appointment, but Rutledge soon found himself in the middle of a heated debate that would guarantee that he would not win confirmation by the United States senate. At a public meeting in St Michael's Church in Charleston (as Charles Town had been renamed in 1783) he vehemently and erratically attacked Jay's treaty of 1794 with Great Britain. He thought it discriminated against the south and should not be ratified. At Washington's request the senate ratified it anyway, but did not confirm Rutledge as chief justice. While waiting for confirmation he presided over one term of the supreme court, but the mental instability that had affected him since 1792 had become so obvious that his public career ended.

In private life John Rutledge owned plantations, slaves, and an elaborate town house in Charles Town, most of which he lost during the American War of Independence. Although he enjoyed watching his children grow into successful careers, his own declined in the 1790s. He was hopelessly bankrupt and finally devastated by the deaths of his mother and his wife, both in 1792. Plagued by bouts of melancholia and often suicidal, he had no chance to retrieve his fortune or public career. Unable to accept the death of his younger brother Edward on 23 January 1800, John Rutledge died at his home in Charleston of unspecified causes (possibly suicide) in a state of deep depression on 18 July 1800. Eulogists mentioned his extraordinary service during the revolution, but his funeral did not attract the elaborate public attention comparable to that of Edward, then governor, six months earlier. He was interred in St Michael's churchyard in Charles Town.

E. STANLY GODBOLD JR.

Sources J. Haw, *John and Edward Rutledge of South Carolina* (1997) • E. S. Godbold and R. H. Woody, *Christopher Gadsden and the American Revolution* (1982) • H. Flanders, *The lives and times of the chief justices of the supreme court of the United States*, 2 vols. (1881) • R. W. Gibbes, ed., *Documentary history of the American revolution*, 3 vols. (1853–7) • W. E. Hemphill and W. A. Wates, eds., *Extracts from the journals of the provincial congresses of South Carolina, 1775–1776* (1960) • E. A. Jones, *American members of the inns of court* (1924) • E. McCrady, *The history of South Carolina in the revolution*, 2 vols. (1901–2) • D. Ramsay, *The history of the revolution in South-Carolina, from a British province to an independent state*, 2 vols. (1785) • P. H. Smith and others, eds., *Letters of delegates to congress, 1774–1789*, 26 vols. (1976–2000) • J. Drayton, *Memoirs of the American Revolution*, 2 vols. (1821) • W. Moultrie, *Memoirs of the American Revolution*, 2 vols. (1802) • R. M. Weir, *Colonial South Carolina: a history* (1983) • M. L. Webber, 'Dr John Rutledge and his descendants [pt 1]', *South Carolina Historical and Genealogical Magazine*, 31 (1930), 7–25

Likenesses portrait, South Carolina Historical Society, Charleston, South Carolina

Wealth at death bankrupt: Charleston inventories D, 1800–10, South Carolina Archives and History Center, Columbia

Rutlidge, James [John James; Jacobite Sir James Rutlidge, second baronet] (1742–1794), writer and publicist, was born, probably at Dunkirk, France, the son of Walter Rutlidge (*d.* 1779), a banker and shipowner who had assisted the Young Pretender during the Jacobite rising of 1745, for which he had been created a baronet. James (sometimes known as John James) accordingly styled himself chevalier or baronet. Of French–Irish descent—his paternal grandfather was an Irish Jacobite who settled in France—he was brought up to speak both French and English, although it is unlikely that he ever visited Britain. He entered, without pay, the duke of Berwick's Franco-Irish cavalry regiment, but on its being disbanded in 1762 he returned to Dunkirk, where he married a shipowner's daughter, about whom no details are known. In 1772 he moved to Paris, where he intended to live on the money raised from selling the reversionary interest in his father's property near Rheims. However, his family ensured that the expected proceeds were not forthcoming, and he was forced to earn his living from writing.

Rutlidge's principal claim to fame was his promotion of English literature in France. In *Observations à messieurs de l'Académie française* (1776) he provided a spirited defence of Shakespeare's superiority over French dramatists, attacking Voltaire for his earlier criticisms of the English writer. Rutlidge also corresponded with Oliver Goldsmith, sending him a French version of *The Deserted Village*, which he published along with Goldsmith's reply, as well as trying his hand at a series of essays, *Le babillard* (3 vols., 1778), in the style of Addison and Steele. Other works included a *Mémoire sur le caractère et les moeurs des François comparés à ceux des Anglois* (1776) and *La quinzaine angloise*, purportedly a posthumous study by Lawrence Sterne, which was translated as *The Englishman's Fortnight in Paris* (1777); a sequel, *Le second voyage de milord*, was published in 1779.

Rutlidge's disputatious character was well suited to the factionalism that resulted from the French Revolution. He became a champion of the Paris bakers and in the *affaires des boulangers* accused Louis XVI's minister, Necker, of conspiring to deprive the capital of bread. He was arrested and imprisoned at the Châtelet in November 1789. Released in the following January, he continued his attacks on Necker, for which he was rewarded with membership of the Cordeliers' Club but refused entry into the Jacobin Club on account of his reputation for slander. Between January and August 1791 he published a number of pieces of political journalism for the periodical *Le Creuset* but was soon after expelled from the Cordeliers' Club. After the death on 13 July 1793 of Marat, who had applauded his denunciations, he seems to have fallen into obscurity only to be denounced by the poet Fabre d'Églantine and arrested and imprisoned by the committee of general security in October of that year. He remained in Paris, where he died six months later in March 1794.   J. G. ALGER, *rev.* PHILIP CARTER

Sources R. Las Vergnas, *Le chevalier Rutlidge, 'gentilhomme anglais', 1742–1794* (Paris, 1931) • J. G. Alger, *Englishmen in the French Revolution* (1889)

Rutt, John Towill (1760–1841), politician and writer, born in London on 4 April 1760, was the only son of George Rutt, at first a druggist in Friday Street, Cheapside, and afterwards a wholesale merchant in drugs in Thames Street, who married Elizabeth Towill. In early childhood he was placed for some time under the care of the Revd Dr Joshua Toulmin at Taunton (J. T. Rutt, *The Life and Correspondence of Joseph Priestley*, 2 vols., 1831–2, 1.154), and on 1 July 1771 he was admitted to St Paul's School, London, under Dr Richard Roberts. The headmaster recommended he be sent to university, but his parents were strict non-conformists and opposed the advice. The lad went into his father's business, and did not wholly withdraw from mercantile pursuits until late in life. But for his literary taste and public zeal he would have died a man of great wealth.

In 1780 Rutt joined the Society for Constitutional Information, founded by Major John Cartwright. With the onset of the French Revolution, he became a founder member of, and was active in, the Society of the Friends of the People, to which Lord Grey, Erskine, and other prominent whigs belonged. The sufferings of the Scottish reformers Muir, Palmer, and Skirving aroused his sympathy; he visited the convicts on board the hulks, when awaiting orders to sail, and sent papers and pamphlets to them in New South Wales (Belsham, 524). He married in June 1786 Rachel, the second daughter of Joseph Pattisson of Maldon, Essex; they had a family of thirteen children. Rutt's religious convictions gradually became Unitarian, and by 1796 he was a leading member of the Gravel Pit congregation at Hackney, of which T. Belsham was the pastor. He was an intimate friend of Priestley and Gilbert Wakefield. He gave much help to the former after the riots at Birmingham, and acted as one of Wakefield's bail, assisting him after his incarceration in Dorchester gaol. Another intimate friend was Henry Crabb Robinson.

After his partial withdrawal from business about 1800, Rutt dwelt for some years at Whitegate House, near Witham in Essex, and then alternately at Clapton and Bromley by Bow, before finally settling at Bexley. He aided in founding the *Monthly Repository*, was a regular contributor to its columns, and occasionally acted as its editor (Aspland, 191, 566). He also wrote in the *Christian Reformer*, the other journal of the Unitarians. In 1802 he edited for that religious body a *Collection of Prayers, Psalms, and Hymns*. As a member of the Clothworkers he worked energetically in the management of the company's charities, and he laid the first stone of the Domestic Society's school and chapel in Spicer Street, Spitalfields. He promoted vaccination, following its discovery by Edward Jenner, and sought to overcome the prejudice against it. His public speaking was vigorous, his conversation was animated, and his verses showed facility and playful humour. He died at Bexley on 3 March 1841. Seven of his children, with his widow, survived him. Rachel, the eldest daughter, married Sir Thomas Noon Talfourd.

Rutt was the author of a small volume of poetry, entitled *The Sympathy of Priests, Addressed to T. F. Palmer, at Port Jackson, with Odes* (1792). In conjunction with Arnold Wainewright, he published in 1804 an enlarged edition, brought down to the date of death, of the *Memoirs of Gilbert Wakefield*, originally published by Wakefield in 1792. The years between 1817 and 1831 were chiefly spent in editing the *Theological and Miscellaneous Works of Dr Priestley* in twenty-five volumes, portions of which were subsequently issued separately. The first volume Rutt issued separately as *The Life and Correspondence of Joseph Priestley* (2

vols., 1831–2). He also edited with extensive notes, historical and biographical, *The Diary of Thomas Burton, M.P., 1656 to 1659* (1828), *Calamy's Historical Account of my Own Life, 1671–1731* (1830), and *The life, journals, and correspondence of Samuel Pepys, with a narrative of his voyage to Tangier* (1841) (cf. W. D. Macray, *Annals of the Bodleian Library*, 2nd edn, 1890, 236–7). He contributed several articles to the *Encyclopaedia metropolitana*, including the one on the history of Greece.

W. P. COURTNEY, rev. PETER SPENCE

Sources *Memorials of the late John Towill Rutt* (1845) · *GM*, 2nd ser., 15 (1841), 437–8 · *Christian Reformer, or, Unitarian Magazine and Review*, 8 (1841), 122, 261–2 · R. B. Gardiner, ed., *The admission registers of St Paul's School, from 1748 to 1876* (1884) · *Diary, reminiscences, and correspondence of Henry Crabb Robinson*, ed. T. Sadler, 3 vols. (1869) · R. B. Aspland, *Memoir of the life, works and correspondence of the Rev. Robert Aspland* (1850) · *The life and correspondence of Major Cartwright*, ed. F. D. Cartwright, 2 vols. (1826) · T. Belsham, *Memoirs of the late Reverend Theophilus Lindsey* (1812) · J. A. Casada, 'Rutt, John Towill', *BDMBR*, vol. 1

Archives Dudley Archives and Local History Service, letters | DWL, corresp. with Joseph Priestley, family, etc. · DWL, corresp. with Henry Crabb Robinson

Rutter, Francis Vane Phipson [Frank] (1876–1937), art critic and museum curator, was born on 17 February 1876 at 4 The Cedars, Putney, the youngest son of Henry Rutter (d. 1896), a solicitor, and his wife, Emmeline Claridge Phipson. He was educated at Merchant Taylors' School and at Queens' College, Cambridge, graduating in 1899 with a BA degree in Semitic languages. After minor successes as a journalist, in 1901 Rutter became sub-editor of the *Daily Mail* and then editor of *To-Day* (1902–4). Leonard Rees, recognizing his versatility, had appointed him art critic of the *Sunday Times* in 1903, and he learnt his trade on the job and in Paris, where café life in the Latin quarter facilitated discussions with the leaders of the fast changing new art movements. When the French art dealers Durand-Ruel staged a superb impressionist exhibition in London in 1905, Rutter initiated a *Sunday Times* fund to buy for the National Gallery. The gallery rejected a Monet; however, a Boudin, *The Entrance to Trouville Harbour* (National Gallery), was later accepted, following the intervention of Sir Claude Philips and D. S. McColl.

In Paris in 1907 Rutter was persuaded that French-based artists would exhibit in London under a non-juried society similar to the Société des Artistes Indépendants and persuaded his progressively minded friends from the Fitzroy Street Group (founded in the same year), Walter Sickert, Harold Gilman, and Spencer Gore, to back the formation of the Allied Artists' Association. With Lucien Pissarro advising, Rutter, a born organizer, collected some eighty members, and in July 1908 exhibited over 3000 works in the Albert Hall. For four years he ran this successful but unprofitable international London salon which 'discovered' Walter Bayes, Robert Bevan, and Charles Ginner, and gave Brancusi, Epstein, and Kandinsky their first London showings. He also edited its mouthpiece, the *Art News*, until financial pressures caused his resignation. On 30 August 1909 he had married Thirza Sarah (Trixie; b. 1887/8); she was the daughter of James Henry Tiernan of the New Zealand constabulary. In 1912 he accepted the £300 a year curatorship of Leeds City Art Gallery.

Encouraged by G. B. Shaw, Rutter became a Fabian Society member; he was also a supporter of the suffragettes. In 1910 his efforts to end the isolation of British art were eclipsed by an establishment figure, Roger Fry, who had 'an immense *succès d'exécration*' with his 'Manet and the post-impressionists' exhibition, which introduced Cézanne, Gauguin, and Van Gogh to an outraged public (Rutter, *Art in my Time*, 145). In support, Rutter rushed out a small book, *Revolution in Art* (expanded in 1926 into *Evolution in Modern Art*); the title was inspired by Gauguin's declaration that 'in art there are only revolutionists or plagiarists' (F. Rutter, *Revolution in Art*, 1910, 30). From Leeds, Rutter continued to champion innovation in his *Sunday Times* 'Round the galleries' column, and in October 1913 the Doré Gallery in Bond Street commissioned him to organize the Post-Impressionist and Futurist Exhibition. Arranged chronologically from Camille Pissarro to the vorticists, led by Wyndham Lewis (who had quarrelled with Fry), Rutter's selection showed his unrivalled knowledge of European developments in modern art; his foreword to the exhibition catalogue explained the variety of work that had been loosely labelled 'post-impressionist'.

In Leeds, Rutter's intention to build a modern art collection had already been dashed by the attitude of 'boorish' ruling councillors, and his standing slumped in June 1913 after his wife (whom he was to divorce about 1920) connived in the escape of a suffragette arsonist, Lilian Lenton. Before he resigned in 1917 to work at the Admiralty in London, he combined with Michael Sadler—a collector of Gauguins and Kandinskys and vice-chancellor of Leeds University—to found a Leeds Art Collections Fund. This assisted with purchases and exhibitions, including the first major Constable exhibition and a post-impressionist exhibition in June 1913 which was held at the Leeds Art Club. The two outsiders had reinvigorated the club, originated by Holbrook Jackson and A. R. Orage, who now edited the *New Age*. Young Herbert Read, critic and theorist of modern art, was greatly influenced by Rutter and by club discussion of new art movements; in 1917 he joined Rutter as co-editor of *Art and Letters*. This quarterly failed in 1920, despite support from Osbert Sitwell. Read was also attracted by Rutter's plan for an authors' co-operative on the lines of the Allied Artists' Association, where Rutter resumed the reins from 1915 to 1919. Rutter opened his Adelphi Gallery in London in 1919, showing small works by David Bomberg, Edward Wadsworth, and Ginner, but, valuing above all his 'liberty and leisure', he soon turned to concentrate on writing, publishing some twenty books and numerous additional articles in *Apollo*, the *Burlington Magazine*, *The Studio*, *The Times*, and the *Financial Times*.

Tall, with an emphatic manner, Rutter cared passionately about art and artists. Before his death from bronchitis at his home, 5 Litchfield Way, London, on 18 April 1937, he owned some eighty paintings, the finest by his friends, the 'lovable' Gore, Gilman, Ginner, and Lucien Pissarro, who all supported his Leeds activities. He left his estate to his second wife, Ethel Dorothy (*b*. 1894/5), daughter of William Robert Bunce, a coal merchant, whom he had married on 29 March 1920. Rutter was buried on 21 April 1937 at Hampstead. FELICITY OWEN

Sources F. Rutter, *Since I was twenty-five* (1927) • F. Rutter, *Art in my time* (1933) • T. Steele, *Alfred Orage and the Leeds Arts Club, 1893–1923* (1990) • W. Baron, *The Camden Town Group* (1979) • A. G. Robins, ed., *Modern art in Britain, 1910–14* (1997), 116–30 [exhibition catalogue, Barbican Art Gallery, London] • J. King, *The last modern* (1990) • H. Read, *The contrary experience: autobiographies* (1993) • F. Owen, 'Introducing impressionism: Frank Rutter, Lucien Pissarro and friends', *Apollo*, 138 (1993), 212–16 • J. B. Bullen, ed., *Post-impressionists in England* (1988) • B. Dolman, ed., *A dictionary of contemporary British artists* (1929) • *The Times* (19 April 1937) • b. cert. • m. cert. • *CGPLA Eng. & Wales* (1937)
Archives AM Oxf., Pissarro family archive
Likenesses G. Kelly, oils, *c*.1908, Hugh Lane Municipal Gallery of Modern Art, Dublin
Wealth at death £4985 2*s*. 0*d*.: probate, 17 June 1937, *CGPLA Eng. & Wales*

Rutter, John (1796–1851), topographer and local political agent, was born in Castle Street, Bristol, on 10 April 1796, the youngest of seven children of Thomas Rutter (1741–1800), a Quaker bellows and brushmaker, and Hester Farley (1750–1806). Orphaned in 1806 he was brought up as a Quaker by two elder sisters and apprenticed in 1811 to a linen draper in Shaftesbury, Dorset, a trade he later described as 'only fit for women' (*Chitty* v. *Knowles*, Dorset Lent assize, 1834, 129–30). In 1817, with the paternal legacy held in trust until his majority, he set up as a printer. A year later (7 July 1818) he married Ann Burchett Clarence, a Quaker, and the daughter of a London draper. They had six children, of whom four survived to adulthood.

Rutter's first publication, in 1818, was a pamphlet summarizing the history of Cranborne Chase, at that time a subject of intense public controversy over the ending of a franchise for the preservation of deer. In the course of twelve years as printer, author, illustrator, and bookseller Rutter established himself as a topographer of importance. Invited to Fonthill by William Beckford, he published *Delineations of Fonthill Abbey* in 1822, followed by *History of Wardour Castle* in 1823. His interest in the Cranborne Chase area adjoining Shaftesbury then gave way to his earlier interest in, and familiarity with, his native Somerset. *Delineations of Northwestern Somerset* (1829) is notable for the wide-ranging knowledge that this largely self-educated man had accumulated by judicious reading, correspondence, and acute observation, and puts particular emphasis on geology and environmental interests. Some sections also appeared individually as guides to Weston-super-Mare, Clevedon, and the Banwell bone caverns.

With Rutter's stubborn temperament and radical principles, he was inevitably drawn into the struggle over corruption and reform in Shaftesbury's local government (1820–35). As a 'close' corporation, its governing body was self-perpetuating, with no public elections and its membership limited to Church of England communicants. Rutter emerged as a leader of the increasingly articulate forces of dissent in their opposition to the misuse of the town's finances and the corrupt tactics of bribery and intimidation of tenants in its parliamentary elections. Following the Reform Act of 1832 he served as political agent for the successful reform candidate John Poulter (MP for Shaftesbury, 1832–8). The Municipal Corporations Act of 1835 replaced close corporations with elected town councils, and Rutter was elected to the new authority. During the long campaign he had begun to study law in order to defend himself in the courts; he eventually articled himself to a solicitor and was able to set up his own practice.

A feature of Rutter's religious life was his support for the Bible Society as secretary of its local branch. His holding of Bible-reading classes for the children of working men, regardless of denomination, was frowned upon by the Quakers; when he refused to refrain they disowned him (Society of Friends, register of members, 10 Aug 1841) but he continued to worship with them. He died suddenly on 2 April 1851 after a road accident in which he was thrown from his coach; his wife survived him. He was interred in the Quaker burial-ground in Shaftesbury.

DESMOND HAWKINS

Sources W. W. Huggins, *The family of the Le Roter or Rutter* (1966) · Shaftesbury Museum, Dorset, Shaftesbury Historical Society, Rutter archive · F. C. Hopton, *Corruption and reform* (1975) · B. Innes, *Shaftesbury* (1992) · D. Hawkins, *Cranborne Chase* (1980) · Society of Friends, Bristol and Somerset register

Archives Bodl. Oxf., descriptive sketches of Somerset, drafts for 1829 *Delineations* · Bodl. Oxf., prospectuses for work on Fonthill · Dorset RO, MS history of Shaftesbury, notes relating to Dorset and Wiltshire, corresp. relating to elections · Shaftesbury Museum, Dorset, Shaftesbury Historical Society

Likenesses miniature, priv. coll. · portrait, repro. in Innes, *Shaftesbury*, 66

Rutter, Joseph (*bap.* 1610?), playwright and translator, was probably the Joseph Rutter who was baptized on 21 February 1610 in the parish of St Mary Somerset, London, the son of William Rutter. In 1635 he published *The shepheards holy-day: a pastorall tragi-comaedie acted before both their majesties at White-hall, by the queenes servants*. Ben Jonson supplied a commendatory poem in which he described Rutter as 'a deare Sonne, and right-learned Friend' (*Ben Jonson*, 8.414). Jonson used his commendatory verses to create a group who constituted the Tribe of Ben, although some, such as Sir Thomas Salusbury of Lleweni, sought to elect themselves. For Jonson and his 'sons', there was a specific standard of ethical behaviour to be observed both in social conduct and in composition, and as far as Jonson was concerned, Rutter conformed to these requirements.

Jonson declares that the 'whole piece' of Rutter's play was 'spun by nature, off the fleece', but approval was evidently not universal for Jonson also alludes to

> deepe-grounded, understanding men,
> That sit to censure *Playes*

whom Rutter, like Jonson, has encountered (*Ben Jonson*, 8.414–15). Rutter insisted that his play was

> well-meaning … with intent
> To defame none

and he disclaims both satire and 'Looseness of speech' for

> A Shepheard's Muse gently of love does sing,
> And with it mingles no impurer thing.
> (*Shepheard's Holy-Day*, sig. B2r)

His pastoral is a good example of the genre, preoccupied as it is with the themes of love, marriage, honour, and, in this case, mourning. An elegy on the death of Lady Venetia Digby, who died on 1 May 1633, is appended to the published edition of the play, and the grief of her husband, Sir Kenelm Digby, is reflected in the character of Thyrsis. It would seem that Rutter spent some time living in the Digby household. The epilogue dedicates the play to Charles I and Henrietta Maria.

As far as Rutter was concerned, Jonson was in all respects his poetic mentor, for in his own elegy on Jonson, published in the 1638 collection of elegies concerning Jonson, *Jonsonius verbius*, Rutter affirms that the master had left behind:

> A *stock* for *writers* to set up withall:
> That out of *thy full Comedies*, their *small*
> And *slender wits* by vexing much *thy writ*
> And their owne braines may draw good *saving wit.*

He declares that he is 'not the latest' of those who are seeking to exploit Jonson's legacy but all may benefit for there is of learning 'great store for us to feed upon' (*Ben Jonson*, 11.460).

For some years Rutter was tutor to the two sons of Edward Sackville, fourth earl of Dorset, and the earl 'commanded' him to translate Corneille's *Le Cid*; it was published in 1637 as *The Cid, a Tragicomedy*, having been 'acted before their Majesties at Court, and on the Cock-pit stage' (*The Cid*, 1637, sig. A2r). Rutter declares that he has 'followed close both the sense & words of the Author' but has omitted two scenes 'as being soliloquies and little pertinent to the business'; he also warns the reader that 'Some places in the Originall I have changed, but not many' and admits 'some things I have added' (ibid., sig. A4r). His translation is in blank verse but, without Corneille's grandiloquence, the characters become diminished, almost commonplace. However, Rutter's translation, which includes some translation by his pupils, is vastly superior to the literal ones by Sir William Lower, *Polyeuctes* (1655) and *Horatius* (1656), the only other pre-Restoration versions of Pierre Corneille's works in English. Rutter translated the second part of *Le Cid* in 1640, at the request of Charles I. Nothing is known about the rest of his life, or the date and circumstances of his death.

REAVLEY GAIR

Sources *Ben Jonson*, ed. C. H. Herford, P. Simpson, and E. M. Simpson, 8 (1947), 414–15; 11 (1952), 459–60 · D. F. Canfield, *Corneille and Racine in England* (New York, 1904) · M. Kerr, *The influence of Ben Jonson on English comedy, 1598–1643* (New York, 1912) · A. Lefevre, 'Au temps de la reine Henriette-Marie: *Le Cid* à Londres', *Revue de Littérature Comparée*, 45 (1971), 74–90 · NL Wales, MS Peniarth 5390 D · IGI

Rutter, Samuel (*d.* 1662), bishop of Sodor and Man, was, according to tradition, the grandson of John Rutter, the miller on the Stanley family estate in Burscough, Lancashire, supposedly a descendant of the Rutters of Kingsley, Cheshire; his parents' names are unknown. By 1623, when he was elected from there to Christ Church, Oxford, he was a pupil at Westminster School, and he was king's scholar at the school from some time before March 1624 until at least 1626. There is no record of his matriculation at university or of his graduation.

In 1630 Rutter was appointed rector of Waberthwaite, Cumberland. He was a close friend of James Stanley, Lord Strange, subsequently seventh earl of Derby, whom he served as chaplain. He was also entrusted with the education of Derby's son and heir, Charles. Through the Stanley connection in 1640 he secured the archdeaconry of the Isle of Man and with it the rectory of Andreas parish there. As was common among English clergy appointed to the senior positions in the Manx church, Rutter did not immediately take up residence in the island. After Derby's departure for the island in June 1643 to deal with unrest among the inhabitants Rutter remained with Charlotte, countess of Derby, at the royalist Stanley stronghold of Lathom House during its first siege by parliamentarian forces, which commenced shortly thereafter. However, following the death of Richard Parr, bishop of Sodor and Man, in March 1644 and Derby's decision not to nominate a replacement, he became in effect the chief ecclesiastical officer for the island, and when the siege of Lathom was temporarily lifted on 27 May that year Rutter made his first journey there in the company of Countess Charlotte. Although he administered an oath of loyalty to the Manx clergy in July 1644, Rutter apparently went back to Lathom and was present during the second siege, which began the same month. He returned to the island after Lathom fell into parliamentarian hands in December 1644. Perhaps as a result of Rutter's personal involvement the Stanley chronicler, John Seacome, ascribed the authorship of an anonymous account of the first siege of Lathom to Rutter, who certainly turned his hand to writing during his time in the Isle of Man, producing a number of songs and poems. Among his other works he wrote an ode 'To the Glorious Memory of the Blessed Martyr, James Earle of Derby' after the execution of his friend and patron in October 1651.

In church matters in the island Rutter and Derby are said to have 'worked steadily by ancient rules, not forgetting "godly discipline" and the prayer book' (Keble, 1.133). Despite an apparent tolerance in the island of some practices which contemporaries would have readily described as popish, they shared a dislike of Arminian practices. Although his active tenure in office was comparatively short, Rutter, together with Derby, is credited with doing more to settle the church in the island than any bishop before Thomas Wilson (1663–1755). When a force under Colonel Robert Duckenfield arrived off the Isle of Man in October 1651 Rutter was nominated as one of the commissioners to treat with the parliamentarians on behalf of the countess. Following the surrender of the island Rutter accompanied Countess Charlotte on her return to England. He remained close to her and was a witness to her will, drawn up on 2 May 1654, though she outlived him.

After the Restoration, Rutter was, on 29 November 1660, appointed prebendary of Longdon in Lichfield Cathedral.

In October 1661, after being nominated by Charles Stanley, now earl of Derby, to the long-vacant see of Sodor and Man, he was confirmed as bishop. Rutter was consecrated on 24 March 1662. He did not live long after his elevation to the episcopacy and died, unmarried, in the Isle of Man on 30 May 1662. He was buried in St German's Cathedral within Peel Castle.   J. R. DICKINSON

Sources W. Harrison, 'Samuel Rutter, bishop of Sodor and Man', *Mona miscellany*, Manx Society, 16 (1869), 225–30 · James, seventh earl of Derby, *The Stanley papers, pt 3*, ed. F. R. Raines, 3 vols., Chetham Society, 66–7, 70 (1867) · W. Ffarrington, *The Stanley papers, pt 2*, ed. F. R. Raines, Chetham Society, 31 (1853) · J. R. Dickinson, 'Musical and dramatic entertainment in the Isle of Man', *Records of early English drama: Lancashire*, ed. D. George (1991), 267–81 · *Old Westminsters*, vol. 2 · *Walker rev.* · W. Harrison, *An account of the diocese of Sodor and Man*, Manx Society, 29 (1879) · Foster, *Alum. Oxon.* · *Report of the Deputy Keeper of the Public Records*, 46 (1885), appx 2 · *Fasti Angl.* (Hardy), vol. 3 · J. Keble, *The life of the right reverend father in God, Thomas Wilson*, 1 (1863) · J. Seacome, *Memoirs; containing a genealogical and historical account of the ancient and honourable house of Stanley, from the conquest to the death of James late earl of Derby, in the year 1735, as also a full description of the Isle of Man, etc.* (1741) · will, [n.d.], Manx Museum Library, MF/EW16/382–393

Likenesses W. Dobson, oils, Manx Museum, Douglas; repro. in G. D. Kinley, 'Laughton V. Lord Bishop of Sodar and Man: the great libel case of 1870 re-examined', *Journal of the Manx Museum*, 6 (1965), pl. 256

Wealth at death £140: will and inventory, Manx Museum Library, MF/EW16/382–393

Ruttledge, Hugh (1884–1961), mountaineer, was born on 24 October 1884, the son of Lieutenant-Colonel Edward Butler Ruttledge, of the Indian Medical Service, and his wife, Alice Dennison. He went to schools in Dresden and Lausanne and to Cheltenham College, before going in 1903 as an exhibitioner to Pembroke College, Cambridge. In 1906 he obtained a second-class degree in the classical honours tripos.

Following success in the Indian Civil Service examination in 1908 and an obligatory probationary year at London University studying Indian law, police regulations, and Indian history and languages, Ruttledge sailed for India late in 1909. After assistant postings in Roorkee and Sitapur, he was made city magistrate at Agra, where he married Dorothy Jessie Hair Elder in 1915. He was promoted city magistrate of Lucknow in 1917 and deputy commissioner there in 1921 during a period of turbulence. He enjoyed polo, big game-hunting, and pig-sticking until a serious riding accident in 1915, which left him with a compacted hip bone and spinal curvature. His injuries in no way diminished his love of mountains, however, and his appointment in 1925 as deputy commissioner of Almora district brought him right into the Himalayan foothills, within sight of the great peaks. Determined to get to know every part of his dominion, he embarked, with Mrs Ruttledge, on a rigorous series of explorations of glaciers and peaks on the Tibetan frontier. By the time of his early retirement at the end of 1929, he and his wife had climbed or crossed no fewer than twelve high passes, six of them over 18,000 feet.

The highest peak in the British empire, Nanda Devi, had never been approached at that time, being encircled by a formidable ring of peaks, all above 21,000 feet. Between them, no depression existed lower than 17,000 foot— except in the west, where the Ganges had carved one of the world's most terrific and impenetrable gorges. In 1925, with Colonel R. C. Wilson and Dr T. Howard Somervell (of Everest fame), the Ruttledges reconnoitred the area to the north-east of Nandi Devi, hoping to gain its inner sanctuary via Milam and the Timphu glacier. They saw enough to realize it would be far too hazardous to force a way over the rim here with laden porters.

The following year, with Wilson, on an official trade mission to Tibet, they took the opportunity to complete a circuit of holy Mount Kailas, the first Europeans to perform this ritual pilgrimage, or *parikarma*. On the way back, they accomplished the first recorded crossing of Traill's Pass between Nanda Devi and Nanda Kot, from the north. In 1927, with Dr T. G. Longstaff and a small band of Sherpas, they reconnoitred glaciers of the Nandakini valley and crossed a 17,500 foot pass between Nanda Ghunti and Trisul. Dr Longstaff remarked afterwards on the great esteem in which the various peoples of Ruttledge's huge district held their deputy commissioner—not least for his devotion to their sacred *himachal*. His *parikarma* may have been 'unblessed by his official superiors', Longstaff said (Longstaff, 419), but it greatly added to his standing locally. Somervell, too, has remarked on Ruttledge's professional 'frustrations', believing these to be a major factor in Ruttledge's premature departure from the Indian Civil Service: 'He was so tired of making plans that he knew to be right, to find that the Government always thought they knew better than the man on the spot' (Longland, Somervell, and Wilson, 398).

Ruttledge returned to the UK in 1929 and almost immediately began organizing a further trip to Nanda Devi. In spring 1932, with the alpine guide Emile Rey, he explored the head of the Sundardhunga valley on the southern rim of the sanctuary, only to find once more that the serac-threatened col presented too great a risk for his Sherpas. So ended his quest: a couple of years later mountaineers forced a way into the inner sanctum through the gorge of the Ganges. One of them wrote that Ruttledge's 'generous and genuine delight' at their success 'showed clearly the kind of man he was' (Shipton, 124).

In 1933 permission was obtained from Tibet for a fresh British attempt to climb Mount Everest, which Ruttledge was invited to lead. Nine years had passed since the last expedition, on which G. L. Mallory and A. C. Irvine had disappeared, and an almost completely new team was called for. Ruttledge consulted widely before putting together a highly talented group. Frank Smythe and Eric Shipton were the most experienced Himalayan mountaineers of the day, to whom were added thrusting young alpinists, mostly of Oxbridge background, confident and opinionated, and a handful of seasoned military campaigners. Jack Longland, one of the younger members, has testified to the delight of travelling with Ruttledge across the Tibetan uplands:

> He had a keen interest in the strange topography, in the unusual customs of hospitality and bargaining, and in the animals and birds, whose lack of timidity he revelled in. He had a sure and friendly touch when dealing with the Dzongpens (governors), the muleteers, and the sherpa and other porters, as well as a natural authority, tempered by a real liking for those who lived in wild places. (DNB)

In a more clement season the disparate traditions and disciplines within the party might have caused little friction. As it was, failure to establish Camp V on a rare fair day (20 May) proved disastrous. The three climbers sent up for the task—one of the young thrusters and two military men—dumped their loads and retreated with their porters 1000 feet short of the target. In the ensuing acrimony two vital days were lost and the expedition missed its chance of improving significantly on the height gained by the expedition of 1924.

Upon its return, an inquiry was held by the Mount Everest committee (comprising representatives of the Royal Geographical Society and the Alpine Club) into all aspects of organization and leadership. Confidential statements were taken from several expedition members. Though almost unanimous in their expression of affection for Ruttledge, many felt his very niceness prevented him from being a strong leader. Even so, most were not averse to serving under him again in 1936. There was an abortive challenge to his leadership, with Ruttledge resigning the offered post several times before eventually consenting to return. This second trip proved far happier, although the team was squarely defeated by an exceptionally early monsoon.

Ruttledge had arrived on the Everest scene at a time of great change and high aspirations. After several failed attempts and with national pride at stake, the pressure on him to succeed was great. He put heart and soul into organizing an efficient pair of expeditions, bringing together some of the finest climbers for the task. The potential was there, which made the outcome all the more bitter for those involved, but it is worth remembering that no lives were lost in either effort. Still, as Raymond Greene remarked of the Camp V incident several decades later, 'it may be that we lost not two days but twenty years' (private information).

In 1932 Ruttledge had purchased the tiny island of Gometra, off the coast of Mull, which he planned to farm. When called upon to prepare for his second Everest expedition, he moved to London, by which time he was coming round to the idea that a life afloat would provide the ideal retirement environment. He bought a 42 foot converted Watson lifeboat, which he replaced with a larger sailing cutter on his return from the Himalaya. In this he made several adventurous voyages, and it remained the family home until the end of the war. Other yachts followed and the Ruttledges were not persuaded ashore until 1950, when they set up home on the edge of Dartmoor. Ruttledge died in Stoke, Plymouth, on 7 November 1961, leaving his wife, one son, and two daughters. He wrote *Everest 1933* (1934) and *Everest: the Unfinished Adventure* (1937).   AUDREY SALKELD

Sources J. Longland, T. H. Somervell, and R. Wilson, 'Hugh Ruttledge, 1884–1961', *Alpine Journal*, 67 (1962), 393–9 • E. Shipton, 'Hugh Ruttledge', *GJ*, 128 (1962), 124–5 • *The Times* (9 Nov 1961) •

DNB • private information (2004) • T. G. Longstaff, 'The Nanda Devi group and the sources of the Nandakgini', *GJ*, 71 (1928), 417–30 • *CGPLA Eng. & Wales* (1962)

Archives RGS, corresp. | FILM BFI NFTVA, record footage
Likenesses portraits, RGS
Wealth at death £1964 6s. 4d.: probate, 14 Feb 1962, *CGPLA Eng. & Wales*

Rutty, John (1698–1775), physician, was born in Melksham, Wiltshire, on 25 December 1698. He was a younger son of John and Esther Rutty, a Quaker couple who had two other sons and three daughters. The occupation of John Rutty senior is variously recorded as cheesemonger, maltster, and shopkeeper. After attending several non-Quaker schools from the age of thirteen to eighteen, the younger John Rutty matriculated at the University of Leiden on 14 March 1722. He studied medicine under Boerhaave and graduated MD on 23 July 1723 with a thesis, *De diarrhoea*, dedicated to his cousin William Rutty (1687–1730), an eminent London physician who was secretary of the Royal Society 1727–30.

In 1724 Rutty settled in Dublin, where he was to practise medicine throughout his life. In the same year he initiated two long-term projects: a detailed study of materia medica and a systematic record of the weather of Dublin. In 1729 he enrolled as a licentiate fellow of the King and Queen's College of Physicians in Ireland. The following year the intercession of his cousin gave Rutty the opportunity to present the first of many papers to the Royal Society.

Rutty was extremely active in Dublin's intellectual life for the next three decades. In 1744 he was a founder member of the Physico-Historical Society which aimed to produce a detailed survey of each of the counties of Ireland. Rutty contributed a chapter to a volume on co. Down and was given the task of preparing the survey for co. Dublin in 1747, though the latter project was unfinished when the society became defunct five years later. In 1756 he was a founding member of the Medico-Philosophical Society of Dublin and in time would contribute 99 of the 230 papers given to the society. He also appears to have played an important role in the Botanical Society of Dublin, which was defunct before 1756.

Much of Rutty's work was concerned with the composition of mineral waters. His researches resulted in his large *A Methodical Synopsis of Mineral Waters* (1757), which did not sell well, and numerous shorter works (including five articles for the *Philosophical Transactions of the Royal Society*). He also had a prolonged dispute with Charles Lucas concerning the detection of sulphur (hydrogen sulphide) in mineral waters. Related to Rutty's interest in waters were his experiments concerning the composition of different types of milk. Despite his cat—'a delicate pampered animal'—devouring a number of specimens, Rutty's researches resulted in the tract *The Analysis of Milk* (1762).

The last five years of Rutty's life saw an increase in the volume of his published work as he feared he might die before he had completed several key projects. The first to reach fruition was *A Chronological History of the Weather and Seasons, and of Diseases in Dublin for Forty Years* published in 1770. Begun in 1724 as an annual record of weather and disease in the city, this work also has the first reliable description of relapsing fever. In 1772 Rutty published *An Essay towards a Natural History of the County of Dublin*, in two volumes, completing the project begun in 1747. Rutty's *Natural History* includes the earliest notice of the brown rat (*Rattus Norvegicus*) coming to Ireland.

Late in 1772 Rutty suffered a stroke which left him unable to speak, walk, or write. This created only a hiatus in his work. Rutty, somewhat recovered by May 1774, expressed his thanks for the 'exemption from the anxiety and cares of attending practice; and for the opportunity it [the stroke] gave … to revise, correct and improve former labours' (RS Friends, Lond., Robson MSS, vol. 93, no. 27, 16). His efforts were largely directed to completing his researches on materia medica initiated in 1724. The result was *Materia medica antiqua et nova* of 1775, a large treatise on drugs written in Latin with a foreword by Professor Van Royen of Leiden. This work appears to have sold poorly and to have been considered outdated in its approach.

Rutty, who had been brought up as a member of the Society of Friends, was deeply religious. An elder of the Friends' meeting-house, Dublin, he regularly visited local Quaker families and held monthly meetings with the pupils of the Friends' school. He voraciously read devotional works, lived ascetically, and often gave his medical services to the poor. Rutty knew many of the leading Quakers of his day including John Fry. He also knew John Wesley. Rutty distinguished himself as a historian of the Society of Friends through his revision and extension of the unpublished work of Thomas Wright of Cork (1640–1724). Over fifteen years in preparation, Rutty's *A History of the Rise and Progress of the People called Quakers in Ireland* was published in 1751. It had run to four editions by 1811, and was still judged 'valuable and comprehensive' in the late nineteenth century (Webb, 58).

Rutty also published a number of religious works, the best known of which is *A Spiritual Diary and Soliloquies* (2 vols.), published in 1776. It consists of short daily entries, most of which are concerned with his religious practice, spiritual ideas, and self-criticism. Rutty had hoped that the work, compiled from 13 September 1753 until December 1774, would excite piety and virtue, and show that 'sanctification is not the work of a day, nor a week, nor a year' (1.v). Unfortunately Rutty's repetitive cataloguing of his faults, mostly 'swinishness in eating and doggedness of temper', is principally remembered as a subject for the wit of Samuel Johnson (*Boswell's Life of Johnson*, 852–3). Rutty died in Dublin on 27 April 1775 and was buried there at the Quaker burial-ground at St Stephen's Green.

MAX SATCHELL

Sources digest registers of births, marriages, and burials, RS Friends, Lond. [Gloucestershire and Wiltshire quarterly meeting] • J. Rutty, correspondence with W. Clark, 1732–74, RS Friends, Lond., MS vol. 290 • J. Osborne, 'Illustrious physicians and surgeons in Ireland, no. IV: John Rutty MD', *Dublin Quarterly Journal of Medical Science*, 3 (1847), 500–76 • A. J. Webb, *A compendium of Irish biography* (1878) • *Boswell's Life of Johnson*, new edn, ed. R. W. Chapman (1953) • J. Rutty, correspondence with J. Fry, 1761–74, RS

Friends, Lond., Temp MS 745, vols. 48, 60, 93 • J. Rutty, correspondence with T. Fowler, 1761–6, RS Friends, Lond., MS vol. 311 • J. Rutty, correspondence to William Rutty, 1729–30, RS, EL 3342–3 • R. W. Innes Smith, *English-speaking students of medicine at the University of Leyden* (1932) • G. L. H. Davies, 'The making of Irish geography: IV, The Physico-Historical Society of Dublin, 1755–1752', *Irish Geography*, 12 (1979), 92–8 • W. F. Harvey, 'John Rutty, of Dublin, Quaker physician', *Friends' Quarterly Examiner*, 68 (1934), 28–45, 115–27 • 'History of periodic medical literature in Ireland, including notices of the medical and philosophical societies of Dublin', *Dublin Quarterly Journal of Medical Science*, 1 (1846), i–xlviii • W. T. Sharpless, 'Dr John Rutty of Dublin and his *Spiritual diary and soliloquies*', *Annals of Medical History*, 10 (1928), 249–57 • N. Penney, 'Quakerism in Wiltshire', *Wiltshire Notes and Queries*, 3 (1901), 547 • K. F. Kiple, *The Cambridge world history of human disease* (1993) • C. Lever, *The naturalized animals of the British Isles* (1977) • J. Smith, ed., *A descriptive catalogue of Friends' books*, 2 (1867), 523

Archives RS Friends, Lond., corresp. with John Fry, Thomas Fowler, and William Clarke, MD

Wealth at death not very wealthy: Osborne, 'Illustrious physicians', 569

Rutty, William (1687–1730), physician, was born in London and was admitted to the Merchant Taylors' School on 10 September 1701. He matriculated as a pensioner at Christ's College, Cambridge, in December 1707, and graduated there MB in 1712 and MD on 17 July 1719. He was admitted a candidate or member of the Royal College of Physicians on 30 September 1719, and was elected a fellow on 30 September 1720. On 13 August 1720 he was a candidate for the osteology lecture at Barber-Surgeons' Hall, and again on 30 October 1721; he was successful when a candidate for the third time on 29 March 1721. On 20 August 1724 he was elected to the viscera lectureship at the same place, and on 15 August 1728 to the muscular lectureship. In March 1722 he delivered the Goulstonian lectures at the Royal College of Physicians on the anatomy and diseases of the urinary organs, and published them in 1726 as *A Treatise of the Urinary Passages*, with a dedication to Sir Hans Sloane. The lectures contain a clear account of contemporary knowledge of the subject, and relate two interesting cases, not to be found elsewhere: one in the practice of John Bamber, lithotomist to St Bartholomew's Hospital, of calcified concretions in the caecum giving rise to symptoms resembling renal colic, and the other of double renal calculus in the daughter of Sir Hugh Myddelton, from a note by Francis Glisson. Rutty was elected a fellow of the Royal Society on 30 June 1720, and became second secretary on 30 November 1727. He died on 10 June 1730.   NORMAN MOORE, *rev.* MICHAEL BEVAN

Sources Munk, *Roll* • S. Young, *The annals of the Barber-Surgeons of London: compiled from their records and other sources* (1890) • T. Thomson, *History of the Royal Society from its institution to the end of the eighteenth century* (1812) • Venn, *Alum. Cant.*

Archives RS, corresp., EL3344–3380

Ruvigny. For this title name *see* Massue de Ruvigny, Henri de, earl of Galway, and marquess of Ruvigny in the French nobility (1648–1720).

Ruxley [Rokesley], **Gregory of** (*d.* 1291), merchant and mayor of London, took his name from Ruxley in north Kent; the Robert whose manor of Ruxley was confiscated by King John may have been his ancestor. A goldsmith by

profession, Gregory belonged to that group of leading London merchants engaged in all aspects of trade. Active as a merchant on the king's behalf, from 1258 he supplied the court with goods and lent money to the king, culminating in a loan of £1000 in 1290. He exported corn to Gascony in 1272 and to Ireland in 1281, while his activity in the wool trade explains his nomination as a commissioner to settle the dispute of the early 1270s with Flanders. In the 1280s he dealt in wine, even attempting to reduce the brokerage rate on it, while in 1285, with other leading merchants, he became involved in a dispute with the men of the Cinque Ports over the issue of jettison—the right to goods thrown overboard during storms at sea.

Ruxley was a leading figure in the government of late thirteenth-century London. Alderman of Dowgate ward from 1265 to 1291, he was sheriff in 1263–4, 1265, and 1270–1, and mayor in 1274–81 and 1284–5. As an alderman he had supported the mayor, Henry le Waleys (*d.* 1302), in 1273 leading the attack directed by Waleys on the charters granted to the craft guilds in the 1260s by Walter Hervey, and his own mayoralty saw a codification of city custom, improvements in the administration of the city, for instance in measures to improve public hygiene by the creation of a corps of scavengers, and the constitution of a guild of lawyers. But his activities as mayor were clearly less innovative and wide-ranging than those of Waleys earlier in the 1270s, and he came under increasing criticism for the ineffectiveness of his administration, especially with regard to law and order. In 1281 he lost the mayoralty. In 1284 opposition to Waleys, who had replaced him, allowed Ruxley to secure re-election, but in the summer of 1285 the king set up a commission to examine the issue of lawlessness in London, and allowed the canons of St Paul's to enclose the site of the old folkmoot (where the citizens had once held courts and assemblies), to the north-east of the cathedral, on the grounds that it was the haunt of evil-doers. These royal attacks on the city's liberties led to Ruxley's resigning the mayoralty on 30 June 1285, whereupon the city was taken into the king's hand.

Although Ruxley stood up for the city's liberties, he cannot be regarded as a systematic opponent of the king. He had been named as a royalist in 1264, when London was in baronial hands, and a plot against him and other leading citizens was actually prevented by the royalist victory at Evesham in 1265. Afterwards he frequently benefited from royal favour, in such forms as exemption from tallage in 1268, a valuable wardship in 1273, the grant of free warren in his Kentish manor of Lullingstone in 1279, the keepership of the royal manor of Banstead, Surrey, in 1282, and gifts of game. Furthermore, he was frequently involved in the operations of royal government. The king's butler from 1275 to 1278, he was appointed to over thirty judicial commissions between 1276 and 1291. When Edward I decided on a recoinage in 1279, Ruxley was appointed one of the two keepers of the exchange of London and Canterbury, and he was still active in this capacity in 1290. On several occasions in the 1270s and 1280s he was ordered to administer in London the edicts against the clipping and forging of money. In 1282 and 1283 he audited the accounts of the Irish exchange, and he was also the keeper in London of the customs duties known as the 'new aid'. Appointed keeper and protector of the Jews in London in 1266, he examined their accounts in 1276, while in 1278 he was responsible for the collection of the tallage assessed on them. In 1279 he and Giles de Oudenarde were ordered to take into the king's hand all the houses and rents belonging to certain Jews for the use of Queen Eleanor, and in 1290 he was adviser for the sale of Jewish property in London.

Gregory of Ruxley died on 12 July 1291, and his will was proved in the court of husting on 23 July following. A tenant-in-chief, he held five manors in Kent as well as one in Surrey and another in Sussex, while his extensive London property was scattered over several parishes. His first dwelling house in London was in the parish of All Hallows-the-Great, towards the Ropery, but he later moved to a large mansion in Lombard Street, Cornhill, which in 1318 passed to the Bardi. Surviving correspondence alludes to his aristocratic lifestyle. A patron of the mendicant friars, he was buried in the choir of the church of the Franciscans, whose dormitory he had built and furnished. He was also the financial agent of the Dominicans in the building of their convent, and left chantries in the parish churches of All Hallows-the-Great and St Mary Woolnoth, where his wife, Avice, who had predeceased him, was buried. Ruxley had no children, and his lands outside London went to his nephew, Roger Ruislip, who then changed his name to Ruxley. His London property was divided among the rest of his family, including the children of his brother Robert, also an alderman. The London Ruxleys in the generation after Gregory were all involved in Hanseatic trade, but after the middle of the fourteenth century the family slipped into obscurity. FRÉDÉRIQUE LACHAUD

Sources CLRO · CLRO, Husting rolls, 20/57 · *Chancery records* · G. A. Williams, *Medieval London: from commune to capital* (1963), 330–31 · T. Stapleton, ed., *De antiquis legibus liber: cronica majorum et vicecomitum Londoniarum*, CS, 34 (1846) · W. Stubbs, ed., 'Annales Londonienses', *Chronicles of the reigns of Edward I and Edward II*, 1, Rolls Series, 76 (1882), 1–251 · C. L. Kingsford, *The Grey friars of London*, British Society of Franciscan Studies, 6 (1915) · L. B. L., 'Ancient letters of men of Kent', *Archaeologia Cantiana*, 2 (1859), 233–5 · A. B. Beaven, ed., *The aldermen of the City of London, temp. Henry III–[1912]*, 2 vols. (1908–13) · W. Kellaway, 'The coroner in medieval London', *Studies in London history presented to Philip Edmund Jones*, ed. A. E. J. Hollaender and W. Kellaway (1969) · M. D. Lobel, ed., *The British atlas of historic towns*, 3 (1989), 83 · M. Weinbaum, *London unter Eduard I und II*, 2 vols. (1933) · J. Stow, *A survey of London*, rev. edn (1603); repr. with introduction by C. L. Kingsford as *A survey of London*, 2 vols. (1908), 198–203 · CIPM, 2, no. 824 · *Calendar of the fine rolls*, PRO, 1 (1911)

Wealth at death various properties in London, five manors in Kent, a manor in Sussex and a manor in Surrey: CLRO, Husting roll 20; CIPM, 2, no. 824

Ruxton, Buck (1899–1936), physician and murderer, was originally named Bukhtyar Rustomji Rantanji Hakim. A Parsi native of Bombay, he was a bachelor of medicine of the universities of Bombay and London, and a bachelor of surgery at the University of Bombay. After qualifying in 1922 he served in the Indian Medical Service (IMS) at

Basrah and Baghdad, and as a ship's doctor at sea. During this period he was known as Captain Buck Hakim. He had medical experience in London, but failed in the examination for the fellowship of the Royal College of Surgeons of Edinburgh. He apparently had a wife living in India when about 1927 he met Isabella Van Ess, *née* Kerr (1901–1935), manager of Fairley's restaurant in Edinburgh and separated from her Dutch husband. Early in 1928 she left her job, and they went to live together in London. They never married, though she took the surname Ruxton, but they had two daughters and one son. They made a contrasting couple: he was a small man with delicate, darkly handsome features; she was considerably taller, and of a mannish appearance. Following his assuming by deed poll the name of Buck Ruxton *c*.1929, they settled in 1930 at 2 Dalton Square, Lancaster, where he built up a prosperous medical practice. His gentlemanly and sympathetic manner ensured his success as a physician; he treated his patients with consideration (he once drove home a patient disabled by multiple sclerosis), and was agreeable and attentive to children. However, in his domestic life he was ferociously jealous. He uttered wild threats against his partner, used violence against her, held knives to her throat, and kept a revolver in their bedroom. 'We were the kind of people who could not live with each other and could not live without each other', he claimed. 'Who loves most chastises most' (Blundell and Haswell Wilson, 202). Twice the police were called to their house. In 1932 she tried to gas herself, and in 1934 she fled to Edinburgh. Finally he became morbidly suspicious of her friendship with a local man, Bobbie Edmondson.

On 14 September 1935 Isabella returned about midnight from a day in Blackpool. There was a livid row, which concluded with her being strangled. Mary Rogerson (b. 1915), their children's nursemaid, was murdered at the same time (perhaps while attempting to defend her). Ruxton drained their bodies of blood into the bath, dismembered them, and removed evidence of identity. Among several grave mistakes, on 15 September he gave bloodstained stair carpets, stair pads underneath them, and a bloodstained blue suit to his patient Mary Hampshire, whom he had asked to help prepare the house for decorators. Other attempts to erase traces of his murders proved equally clumsy. Dustmen found bloodstained carpets, clothes, and towels in the backyard on 16 September. Ruxton motored to Moffat in Dumfriesshire, where he threw the bundles of human remains into a stream called Gardenholme Linn. To friends, patients, and others he gave contradictory and often overblown explanations for the disappearance of the two women. When he made an ill-judged visit to the Lancaster police on 24 September to complain that he was being unfairly investigated for the murder of a Mrs Smalley at Morecambe, his speech was of incoherent rapidity. His manner in the ensuing days was voluble, self-pitying, tearful, and unconvincing.

On 29 September four bundles were found in Gardenholme Linn. These contained maggot-ridden human remains, including two heads (one wrapped in a child's woollen rompers), and subsequently other portions were found in the vicinity. On 9 October Mary Rogerson's stepmother reported her disappearance to the Lancaster police. By 10 October Ruxton was increasingly frantic about the incriminating material that he had given Mrs Hampshire. He became distraught as suspicions against him intensified, and made many implausible statements and improbable accusations, until on 13 October he was charged with the murder of Mary Rogerson. On 5 November he was charged with Isabella Ruxton's murder.

After police court proceedings at Lancaster between 26 November and 15 December Ruxton's trial for the latter crime opened on 2 March 1936 at Manchester assizes before Sir John Singleton. Counsel for the crown included Maxwell Fyfe (afterwards earl of Kilmuir) and Hartley Shawcross. Leading counsel for the prisoner was Norman Birkett. The reconstruction of the bodies was undertaken by Professor James Brash, and proved a gruesome affair when recounted in court. The evidence of Brash and other medical witnesses was not convincingly disputed. Among many telling facts it was proved that a copy of a special edition of the *Sunday Graphic*, which was found with the mutilated body fragments at Gardenholme Linn, had been delivered to the Ruxton house. The romper suit was definitely identified too. The only witness called for the defence was the prisoner (11–12 March). Hysterical outbursts and paroxysms of weeping punctuated his testimony. Crown witnesses he denounced as liars. Overpowering circumstantial evidence, together with his own guilty, panic-stricken demeanour, ensured his conviction on 13 March. His appeal (27 April) was dismissed by Lord Chief Justice Hewart, sitting in the court of criminal appeal with du Parcq and Goddard.

Shortly afterwards Ruxton sold his confession to a Sunday newspaper for £3000, which he put towards his legal costs. The fact that a physician had committed two murders, that he was an Indian living in the English provinces with a white woman, and the grisly nature of his crimes, gained him high and enduring notoriety. Ruxton remained a bogeyman in Lancashire long after his execution on 12 May 1936 at Strangeways prison, Manchester.

RICHARD DAVENPORT-HINES

Sources private information (2004) [Mrs Rose Hayhurst] · R. H. Blundell and G. Haswell Wilson, eds., *Trial of Buck Ruxton* (1937) · D. Bardens, *Lord Justice Birkett* (1962), 228–42 · H. M. Hyde, *Norman Birkett* (1964), 428–49 · H. Shawcross, *Life sentence* (1995), 29–30 · *CGPLA Eng. & Wales* (1936) · *The Times* (13 May 1936), 7e
Likenesses Associated Newspapers, photograph, 1935, repro. in Hyde, *Norman Birkett* · Keystone, photograph, 1935, repro. in Blundell and Haswell Wilson, eds., *Trial of Buck Ruxton* · photograph, 1935, repro. in Bardens, *Lord Justice Birkett*
Wealth at death £1765 7s. 10d.: probate, 10 June 1936, *CGPLA Eng. & Wales*

Ryall, Henry Thomas (1811–1867), engraver, was born in August 1811 in Frome, Somerset. Of his parents nothing is known. He was a pupil of the celebrated mezzotint engraver Samuel William Reynolds (1773–1835). Early in his career Ryall employed the techniques known (due to the effect of broken line characteristic of crayon drawing) as chalk or stipple engraving, and he produced many small-scale plates for the illustration of such publications as Edward Lodge's *Portraits of Illustrious Personages of Great Britain* and Charles Heath's *Book of Beauty*.

However, Ryall is best-known for the many larger reproductive engravings (of which there are more than forty examples in the Victoria and Albert Museum) in which he used the skilful combination of techniques conveniently labelled mixed mezzotint. In these works the composition is usually established with etched line and the texture and chiaroscuro are achieved through a subtle interplay of stipple, mezzotint, and engraving with the burin. He reproduced in this way the pictures of many eminent artists, including Sir George Hayter's *Coronation of Queen Victoria* (produced with the assistance of Henry Bryan Hall and published in 1842); C. R. Leslie's *The Christening of the Princess Royal* (the publication of which was declared by Francis Graham Moon in 1849 to the newly established Printsellers' Association, and which gained for Ryall the honorary appointment of historical engraver to Queen Victoria); Richard Ansdell's *The Fight for the Standard* (declared by Hering and Remington in 1854); and Sir Edwin Landseer's *The Life's in the Old Dog Yet* (published in 1865 jointly by Robert Grundy in Liverpool and Goupil in Paris and Berlin). These examples alone confirm that Ryall was regarded by the leading print publishers of the day as in the top rank of his profession. *The Fight for the Standard*, a depiction of an actual episode at Waterloo, is arguably his masterpiece, Ansdell's flashing brushwork translated with equivalent verve into the language of engraved and bitten line, tone, and texture. Ryall's expressive power (related to the painter's, of course, though in an important sense independent) is also evident in the pair of plates after Claude Marie Dubufe's *Adam* and *Eve* (*The Temptation* and *The Fall*), declared for publication by the enterprising London-based Belgian Ernest Gambart (who later acted as Ryall's executor) in May 1861.

Ryall's versatility is demonstrated by the very wide variety of subjects he undertook: in addition to the depictions of royal life, of battle, and of the hunt, his engravings range from the pastoral scenes of Rosa Bonheur, such as *Landais Peasants Going to Market*, via the history pictures of Sir David Wilkie (for example *Christopher Columbus at the Convent of La Rabida*) and the high drama of Jean Léon Gérome's *A Duel after a Bal masqué*, to Sir Frederick Burton's gentle *The Blind Girl at the Holy Well*.

Despite his evident eminence, Ryall's work was exhibited at the Royal Academy on only two occasions. He died at his home, Park House, Cookham, Berkshire, on 14 September 1867 leaving a widow, Georgiana. Examples of his prints are in the British Museum.

ANTHONY DYSON

Sources *An alphabetical list of engravings* (Printsellers' Association, 1892) · R. K. Engen, *Dictionary of Victorian engravers, print publishers and their works* (1979) · J. H. Slater, *Engravings and their value*, 6th edn (1978) · H. Beck, *Victorian engravings* (1973) · B. Hunnisett, *An illustrated dictionary of British steel engravers*, new edn (1989) · Graves, *Artists*, new edn · A. Dyson, *Pictures to print* (1984) · *DNB* · *CGPLA Eng. & Wales* (1867) · *Art Journal*, new ser., 6 (1867), 249

Wealth at death under £2000: probate, 16 Nov 1867, *CGPLA Eng. & Wales*

Ryan, Daniel Frederick (*c*.1762–1798), army officer and magistrate, was born at Ballynaclash, co. Wicklow, the son of Dr Ryan of Wexford and his wife, Mary, the daughter of William Morton of Ballynaclash. He was educated at Trinity College, Dublin, and served as lieutenant and assistant surgeon in the 103rd regiment during the American War of Independence. He returned to Dublin in 1783 to practise as a surgeon and, in 1784, married Catherine Bishopp of Kinsale, co. Cork. Some time after 1788 he began writing for the pro-government newspaper *Faulkner's Dublin Journal*, owned by an uncle, the loyalist zealot John Giffard. Ryan joined the Irish yeomanry in 1796, serving first as a private in the St Stephen's Green corps and then, from 9 February 1797, as first lieutenant in the St Sepulchre's infantry. He was promoted captain on 27 April 1797.

Ryan was a magistrate and served as deputy town major of Dublin. He was also a prominent Dublin Orangeman. On 13 May 1798 he assisted the town major, Henry Charles Sirr, with the seizure of several cannon belonging to the United Irishmen and, on 18 May, was involved in a fracas in Watling Street with members of Lord Edward Fitzgerald's bodyguard, which saw the arrest of William Putnam McCabe. The following day Ryan and another magistrate, William Bellingham Swan, accompanied Sirr and a party of soldiers to arrest Fitzgerald in a house on Thomas Street. The arrest was accomplished after a severe struggle in an upstairs room during which both Swan and Ryan were wounded. Stabbed fourteen times, with one abdominal wound so grievous that he was virtually disembowelled, Ryan was treated by a surgeon called Adrien; although he rallied for a while, he died on 30 May. Accounts of the precise circumstances of the struggle leading to the arrest vary; one, by Ryan's son, published in *The Times* (9 January 1839), implied that Swan lacked resolution and overreacted to his wounds, which turned out to be superficial. Swan's own deposition in the Home Office papers, while it in no way diminishes Ryan's role, shows that he, Swan, was wounded in the side and on the fingers after having seized Fitzgerald's dagger, and was still at close quarters when Ryan rushed in and grappled with Fitzgerald, who cut at him repeatedly. This tallies with Sirr's description of what he saw on entering the room, and can be regarded as accurate, as the viceroy, Lord Camden, considered Swan's account authoritative and Ryan's information 'not very material' (PRO, HO 100/100/76, fol. 203).

Ryan was buried at St Mary's Church, Dublin, on 1 June 1798 and, with the rebellion raging, became something of a loyalist martyr, his funeral being attended by about 1500 Dublin yeomen and 300 Orangemen. Yeomen from the St Sepulchre's corps fired over his grave. In recognition of his sacrifice, the government paid all Ryan's debts and granted his widow an annuity of £200 for life, transferable on her death to their two daughters, Catherine and Jane, for their lives. Ryan's son, Daniel Frederick, then aged about eight, was also provided for, and eventually became assistant secretary at the Excise Office in London—possibly through the influence of Sir Robert Peel, who took an interest in his career.

ROBERT DUNLOP, rev. A. F. BLACKSTOCK

Sources *Faulkner's Dublin Journal* (22 May 1798) · *Faulkner's Dublin Journal* (30 May 1798) · *Faulkner's Dublin Journal* (2 June 1798) · PRO, Home Office 100 vol. 76, fols. 203 and 206–7; vol. 197, fols. 232–3 · *Dublin Gazette* (7–9 Feb 1797) · *Dublin Gazette* (25–7 April 1797) · *The Times* (20 Dec 1838) · *The Times* (9 Jan 1839) · *The journal and correspondence of William, Lord Auckland*, ed. [G. Hogge], 4 vols. (1861–2), vol. 3, pp. 413–15 · R. Musgrave, *Memoirs of the different rebellions in Ireland* (1801), 206–8 · *GM*, 1st ser., 68 (1798), 539, 720 · W. J. Fitzpatrick, *Secret service under Pitt* (1892), 133 · R. R. Madden, *The United Irishmen: their lives and times*, 2nd edn, 2nd ser. (1858), 433–7 · W. E. H. Lecky, *A history of England in the eighteenth century*, 8 vols. (1879–90), vol. 8, pp. 42–3, 46–7 · T. Reynolds, *The life of Thomas Reynolds*, 2 vols. (1839), vol. 2, pp. 230–36 · S. Tillyard, *Citizen lord: Edward Fitzgerald, 1763–1798* (1997), 271–3 · T. Moore, *The life and death of Lord Edward Fitzgerald* (1831), 2.87–90 · abstracts of wills, PRO NIre., T 559/33 · private information (1897) · H. Gifford, letter to T. Welby, 20 May 1798, NL Ire., MS NLI 4607 [copy, 1831]
Likenesses engraving? (the arrest of Fitzgerald), NG Ire.; repro. in R. Kee, *Ireland: a history* (1980), 67
Wealth at death probably not wealthy; government had to pay debts and provide for wife and children: *GM*

Ryan, (Michael) Desmond Henry (1816–1868), drama and music critic, the son of Michael *Ryan (*fl.* 1784–1831), a well-known physician [see under Ryan, Michael (1800–1840)], was born at Kilkenny, Ireland, on 3 March 1816. He studied medicine at Edinburgh University from early in 1832, but had to leave when he found he could not cope with activities in the dissecting room. In 1836 he went to London, equipped with his knowledge of literature, music, fine art, and the theatre, and concentrated on a literary career, writing articles and poems. His first notable efforts were 'Christopher among the Mountains', a satire on Professor Wilson's criticism of the last canto of *Childe Harold*, and a parody of the *Noctes Ambrosianae*. He met and became a lifelong friend of J. W. Davison, editor of the *Musical World* from 27 April 1843 to March 1855, and became a contributor to the journal in 1844; he was sub-editor from mid-August 1845 until the year of his death. In addition, he became music and drama critic with the *Morning Post*, the *Morning Chronicle*, the *Morning Herald*, *The Standard*, and other journals. In 1849 he wrote the libretto for G. A. Macfarren's *King Charles II* (produced at the Princess's Theatre under Edward Loder) and for a spectacular opera, *Pietro il grande* (translated from the English by Maggioni), commissioned by the French conductor Louis Jullien, which was produced at the Royal Italian Opera, Covent Garden, on 17 August 1852. In collaboration with Frank Mori he wrote an opera, *Lambert Simnel*, intended for John Sims Reeves, but never produced. He also wrote the words to a very large number of songs, including *Songs of Even*, with music by F. N. Crouch (1841), a set of twelve *Sacred Songs and Ballads* by Edward Loder (1845), and a collection of *Songs of Ireland*, in which, in conjunction with Crouch, he added new words to old melodies. He died, after a long illness, at his home, 21 Tavistock Road, Hyde

Park Gardens, London, on 8 December 1868. He was married twice and left a widow and eight children. A son, Desmond Lumley Ryan (1851–1888), who wrote the article on his father in the first edition of Grove's *Dictionary of Music and Musicians*, was a music critic for *The Standard* and editor of *The Gem* until 1885. He also composed some works, including songs and a toy symphony (1885), and wrote several librettos.   J. C. HADDEN, *rev.* DAVID J. GOLBY

Sources D. L. Ryan, 'Ryan, Michael Desmond', Grove, *Dict. mus.* · J. W. D., *Musical World* (12 Dec 1868), 846 · Brown & Stratton, *Brit. mus.* · L. Langley, 'The English musical journal in the early nineteenth century', PhD diss., University of North Carolina, 1983

Ryan, Edward (*d.* 1819), Church of Ireland clergyman and author, was born in Ireland, the second son of John Philip Ryan and his wife, whose maiden name was Murphy. He entered Trinity College, Dublin, as a scholar in 1767, and graduated BA (1769), MA (1773), LLB (1779), BD (1782), and DD (1789). He was curate of St Anne's, Dublin, from 1776. On 16 June 1790 he became vicar of St Luke's, Dublin, and prebendary of St Patrick's Cathedral, where he remained for the rest of his life. Although some of his family were Roman Catholics, Ryan published a critical account of Catholicism in his *History of the Effects of Religion on Mankind*, the first volume of which appeared in 1788 and was followed by a second five years later; a French translation, *Bienfaits de la religion*, was published in 1810. Ryan donated the proceeds of his book to the poor of the parish of St Luke's. His other works include *A Short but Comprehensive View of the Evidences of the Mosaic and Christian Codes* (1795); *An Analysis of Ward's Errata of the Protestant Bible* (1808), which prompted John Milner's *An Inquiry into Certain Opinions Concerning the Catholic Inhabitants of Ireland* (1808); and a *Letter to G. Ensor … to which are Added Reasons for being a Christian* (1811). Ryan died in January 1819.

CHARLOTTE FELL-SMITH, *rev.* PHILIP CARTER

Sources H. Cotton, *Fasti ecclesiae Hibernicae*, 1–2 (1845–8) · Burtchaell & Sadleir, *Alum. Dubl.* · *GM*, 1st ser., 89/1 (1819), 92 · Nichols, *Illustrations* · [J. Watkins and F. Shoberl], *A biographical dictionary of the living authors of Great Britain and Ireland* (1816)

Ryan, Sir Edward (1793–1875), judge in India and civil service commissioner, was born on 28 August 1793, the eldest son of John Burke Ryan, of Grosvenor Place, London. He matriculated at Trinity College, Cambridge, in autumn 1810 and graduated BA in 1814, MA in 1817. At Cambridge he befriended John F. W. Herschel, Charles Babbage, and George Peacock, all future fellows of the Royal Society, and in February 1820 his acquaintance with Herschel prompted him to join the Royal Astronomical Society.

In 1814 Ryan married Louisa (*d.* 1860), sixth daughter of William Whitmore of Dudmaston Hall, Bridgnorth, Shropshire; they had at least four sons and two daughters. On 21 June 1817 he was called to the bar at Lincoln's Inn and began practising on the Oxford circuit. In 1825 he published, with William Oldnall Russell, *Crown cases reserved for consideration and decided by the twelve judges of England from the year 1799*. In November 1826 he was appointed a puisne judge of the supreme court at Calcutta and knighted (27 November). He arrived in Calcutta in 1827, having already prepared, with William Moody, another

Sir Edward Ryan (1793–1875), by Frederic Leighton, Baron Leighton, *c.*1872

book for the press, *Reports of cases determined at nisi prius, in the courts of king's bench and common pleas, and on the Oxford and western circuits, … 1823 … 1826* (1827).

In Calcutta Ryan rapidly established a reputation as both a genial host and an informed and generous patron of intellectual endeavour. The young French botanist Victor Jacquemont, who was his guest in the summer of 1829, revelled in his scientific understanding. He was president of the agricultural and horticultural society and a founder member of Calcutta's first ice house. He also keenly supported attempts to make Western knowledge available to Indians through instruction in English, and funded the reprinting in Calcutta of a range of publications from the Society for the Diffusion of Useful Knowledge. His enthusiasm for educational reform won him the affection of two veterans of the campaign for English-language instruction in India: T. B. Macaulay, the first law member of the governor-general's council, and Macaulay's brother-in-law, Charles Trevelyan. In March 1835 Ryan joined Macaulay and Trevelyan on the government's general committee of public instruction and, after they departed for England in early 1838, he carried on their education programme as president of the committee.

Both Macaulay and the governor-general, Lord William Bentinck, respected Ryan for his legal acumen, and Macaulay was especially appreciative of his friendliness to the new penal code that he was drafting for India. In 1832 Ryan had been disappointed to be passed over for the position of chief justice in favour of his former co-author, William Russell, but Russell died in January 1833 and Ryan succeeded him. Bentinck was delighted at his elevation.

He had commended him fulsomely to Charles Grant, president of the Board of Control, explaining that Ryan was regarded in Calcutta as 'the sergeant major of the march of the intellect'—a 'zealous and active contributor' to 'all the societies for the encouragement of agriculture, the arts and sciences'. In short, he was 'one of the most *useful* men in India' (Bentinck to Grant, 18 Dec 1832, *Correspondence of … Bentinck*, 2.536). Ryan returned the compliment by naming one of his younger sons William Cavendish Bentinck. He had a stately figure to match his place in Calcutta society, although it was the comic salience of his 'high nose and attenuated calves' that appealed most to the caricaturist's pen wielded by a young William Tayler (Tayler, 1.89).

During his chief justiceship Ryan several times narrowly escaped death from fever. In January 1843 he resigned the post and returned to England. On 10 June 1843 he was sworn a privy counsellor, in order to assist as an assessor when the council's judicial committee was hearing Indian appeals. From 1850 to November 1865 he was a permanent member of the judicial committee. In 1845 he was appointed to a royal commission to consolidate the digests an earlier commission had produced on English criminal law. He was gazetted a railway commissioner on 4 November 1846, and served as assistant controller of the exchequer from 1851 to 1862. On 21 May 1855 he embarked on a new career as one of the first unpaid commissioners of the new civil service commission, and in April 1862 he became first commissioner and a salaried officer. The initial appointment probably owed much to the involvement of his old Indian friends Trevelyan and Macaulay in matters of domestic and Indian Civil Service reform. Charles Trevelyan had become assistant secretary to the Treasury in 1840, and in 1853, with Stafford Northcote as his co-author and Gladstone as his patron, he had written a crusading report calling for appointments to the home civil service to be thrown open to examination-based competition. The report's assault on patronage stirred a furious backlash against change, but over the next fifteen or so years Ryan, who had noticeably more tact than either Gladstone or Trevelyan, oversaw the gradual expansion of the commission's remit, from an initial system of tests for nominees, to experimentation with limited competition in 1860, and finally to the introduction of open competition in 1870. In addition, from 1858 the commission conducted the examinations for entry to the Indian Civil Service and also for admissions to the army. Ryan had maintained his reputation as a cautious but essentially liberal reformer in matters of Indian governance by addressing in 1850 a letter, co-written with Charles Hay Cameron, to the East India Company's directors calling on them to take decisive steps to open the covenanted services to Indians. Reform could begin, Ryan and Cameron suggested, with the appointment of Dr S. C. G. Chuckerbutty, a British-trained doctor, as an assistant surgeon in the Bengal medical service.

Ryan's interest in education found numerous outlets in England. A bencher of Lincoln's Inn from 1844, in 1852 he was appointed a member of the Council of Legal Education. He was a member of the senate of the University of London from 1846 until his death, and from 1871 to 1874 was the university's vice-chancellor. He was also a member of the council of University College, London, an institution to which his good friend George Grote had devoted himself. He was elected FRAS in 1820, FGS in 1846, and FRS on 2 February 1860. He was secretary and president of the Dilettanti Society.

Ryan's London residence was at 5 Addison Road, Kensington. He died at Dover, Kent, on 22 August 1875. He was survived by five of his children, including colonels Edward Moody Ryan (b. 1824) and William Cavendish Bentinck Ryan (b. 1833) of the Bengal army, and Sir Charles Lister Ryan (1831–1920), comptroller and auditor-general.

KATHERINE PRIOR

Sources W. P. Baildon, ed., *The records of the Honorable Society of Lincoln's Inn: the black books*, 4 (1902); 5, ed. R. Roxburgh (1968) · W. P. Baildon, ed., *The records of the Honorable Society of Lincoln's Inn: admissions*, 2 (1896) · *The correspondence of Lord William Cavendish Bentinck, governor-general of India, 1828–1835*, ed. C. H. Philips, 2 vols. (1977) · V. Jacquemont, *Letters from India* (1834) · W. Tayler, *Thirty-eight years in India*, 2 vols. (1881) · W. W. Rouse Ball and J. A. Venn, eds., *Admissions to Trinity College, Cambridge*, 4 (1911) · 'Select committee on Indian territories: first report', *Parl. papers* (1852–3), vol. 27, no. 426 · *The Times* (25 Aug 1875), 1, 7 · *The Times* (8 Oct 1875), 3 · J. Cline, *Thomas Babington Macaulay: the shaping of the historian* (1973) · Boase, *Mod. Eng. biog.* · W. A. Shaw, *The knights of England*, 2 (1906), 326 · *DNB*

Archives Shrops. RRC, corresp. and papers | BL, Charles Babbage MSS, Add. MS 37194, 37197–37198 · BL OIOC, Malkin collection, MS Eur. D 1203 · U. Nott., Hallward Library, duke of Portland family MSS · U. Nott. L., letters to Lord William Bentinck, PWJ 1982–2028

Likenesses F. Leighton, Baron Leighton, oils, c.1872, Brooks's Club, London [*see illus.*] · F. R. Say, oils, Town Hall, Calcutta · M. A. Shee, oils, Judges Library, Calcutta

Wealth at death under £50,000: probate, 17 Sept 1875, CGPLA Eng. & Wales

Ryan, Elizabeth Montague (1892–1979), tennis player, was born at Anaheim, a suburb of Los Angeles, on 5 February 1892, the younger daughter and younger child of Francis George Ryan, who had emigrated from London to California and invested shrewdly in land (on a census form he described himself as 'a capitalist'), and his wife, Matilda Brooks, of San Francisco. Her father died in 1898, after the family had moved to Santa Monica. She and her sister, Alice, born in 1890, learned to play tennis there and soon established themselves as determined match players, meeting the strongest Californians of the day and even travelling to tournaments in Canada.

They made their most important journey, however, in 1912. After Mrs Ryan's second marriage had ended in disappointment, she decided to take her daughters to England. Elizabeth Ryan was to live there for most of the rest of her life. The trip began as a holiday but soon the sisters were competing enthusiastically in British tournaments. Disconcerted at first by the difference between the pace and bounce of Californian cement courts and English grass, the younger Miss Ryan adapted her game with sufficient success to play at Wimbledon. She was only the sixth overseas player—and the third American—to enter the women's singles and may have been regarded as brash and over-confident, but she reached the fourth round and held two match points against Mrs Hillyard, six times the champion, before losing 3–6, 8–6, 6–3. If she came to England as a stranger, she learned its geography from the map of the tournament circuit. In that first year she won prizes at Liverpool, Malton, Warwick, Winchester, Edgbaston, Lincoln, Tunbridge Wells, Saxmundham, Felixstowe, Chichester, Eastbourne, and Hythe. Partnered by many of the best players of the day and invariably playing singles, doubles, and mixed at each tournament, she had begun to amass her huge collection of trophies and titles. An American journalist who interviewed her soon after she turned professional in 1935 estimated that during her years of play Ryan won or was runner-up in 1500 events. London was her base. She returned only occasionally to the United States but she competed frequently in the major European tournaments.

It seemed that Ryan played whenever she could and her performances were remarkable for dedication, skill, and strength, for endurance and sheer appetite for competition. Her range of shots was formidable. If Hazel Wightman was the first woman to use the volley, at a time when players generally felt safer at the back of the court, Elizabeth Ryan took matters further by showing that the volley could be a central part of a woman's technique by playing at the net consistently and forcefully. Alice Marble, speaking for the next generation, called her the greatest woman volleyer of all time: 'I never saw her make a really defensive volley. Hugging the net, hitting high volleys like rifle shots, she had every angle known to the game at her command.' She had been forced to learn to volley, she told Ted Tinling, during a final against her sister at Vancouver when she was fifteen. Alice was making the ball bounce awkwardly from a rough patch and she decided that the only way to stop this was to meet the ball before it bounced. She possessed a most effective drop shot and a chop, which was notoriously difficult to take on wet grass. As for her smash, Fred Perry said that of all the women who played mixed doubles in the 1930s only Elizabeth Ryan could kill an overhead against a man waiting behind the baseline.

Ryan played in two Wimbledon singles finals but, unable to overcome either Suzanne Lenglen or Helen Wills and injured in 1931, a year when the field was weaker than usual, she was generally regarded as 'unlucky' in singles. In doubles, however, she was dominating. 'Miss Ryan, in my humble opinion, is the best player in ladies' doubles since lawn tennis was invented', said Commander G. W. Hillyard in 1924, writing from long experience as a player and an observer of the championships. She won the first of her nineteen Wimbledon doubles titles—twelve women's and seven mixed—with Agatha Morton in 1914. She and Suzanne Lenglen, whom she partnered for the first time on the Riviera in 1913 when Miss Lenglen, at thirteen, was just about to be recognized as the prodigy of the circuit, held the title from 1919 to 1923, and lost only one set in five years. Then, after a year when Miss Lenglen withdrew through illness, they

regained it in 1925. Elizabeth Ryan was also champion with Mary K. Browne (1926), Helen Wills Moody (1927 and 1930), and Simone Mathieu (1933 and 1934). In mixed doubles she won the title with Randolph Lycett (1919, 1921, and 1923), Francis Hunter (1927), Patrick Spence (1928), Jack Crawford (1930), and Enrique Maier (1932). She won the French doubles title four times and the American doubles and mixed in 1926 and the American doubles title again in 1933.

'Of late years it had become almost a certainty that the ladies doubles would go to Miss Ryan and her partner, whoever that partner might be', wrote F. R. Burrow, the Wimbledon referee, after her last appearance in the championships.

> It was unfortunate that the years when she was at her best as a singles player were just the years when Miss Lenglen was dominating the courts. But for the French girl, it is fairly certain that Miss Ryan would have had a couple of wins in the singles to add to her successes in the doubles.

She returned to the centre court during Wimbledon's centenary celebrations in 1977, when she and Toto Brugnon were invited to represent Wimbledon's doubles winners at the champions' parade.

There was a final irony. For more than forty years her nineteen titles stood as the highest total gained by any player at Wimbledon, but every year she was more and more conscious of the fact that Billie Jean King, another remarkable Californian, was approaching her record. On 8 July 1979, the penultimate day of that year's championships and the day before Mrs King gained her twentieth title, Elizabeth Ryan collapsed and died at the All England Lawn Tennis Club at Wimbledon. Some time before she had told friends that she hoped she would take her record to the grave. She died as she had played, determined not to be beaten. She was unmarried.   DAVID GRAY, *rev.*

Sources *Ayres' Lawn Tennis Almanack* · *Lowe's Lawn Tennis Almanack* · E. Tinling, *Love and faults* (1979) · F. G. Lowe, *Gordon Lowe on lawn tennis* (1924) · F. R. Burrow, *The centre court and others* (1937) · G. W. Hillyard, *Forty years of first-class lawn tennis* (1924) · personal knowledge (1986) · *CGPLA Eng. & Wales* (1979)
Archives FILM BFI NFTVA, news footage
Wealth at death £21,387—in England and Wales: probate, 7 Sept 1979, *CGPLA Eng. & Wales*

Ryan, Frank (1902–1944), Irish nationalist, was born on 11 September 1902 in Elton, near Knocklong, co. Limerick, the seventh of the nine children of national school teachers Vere Francis Ryan (1870–1946) and Anne Slattery (1874–1944). Educated at Elton national school and at St Colman's College, Fermoy, he joined the IRA's East Limerick brigade in late 1920. An opponent of the treaty settlement, he was interned during the civil war. After his release Ryan completed a degree in Celtic studies at University College, Dublin, in 1925.

Ryan's imposing physique and charismatic, if pugnacious, personality marked him out as a leader at republican demonstrations. He was a proficient propagandist and edited numerous republican newspapers, including the IRA's *An Phoblacht*. Appointed adjutant of the IRA's Dublin brigade (1926) and elected to the IRA executive

(1929), Ryan was prominent among the left of the IRA leadership in the early 1930s—notably in campaigns against the pro-treaty Cumann na nGaedheal and the fascistic Blueshirt movement.

Along with a growing minority within the IRA, Ryan believed the organization should change its focus from physical force to socialist agitation. He was greatly influenced by another IRA leader, Peadar O'Donnell, who stressed the necessity for economic, as well as political, revolution to achieve a united Ireland. In 1931 Ryan was associated with Saor Éire, a left-wing political initiative within the IRA, which collapsed against a background of government repression, clerical hostility, and limited support from the IRA leadership. Imprisoned by the Cumann na nGaedheal government in 1932, Ryan was released upon the election of Fianna Fáil, Eamon de Valera's moderate republican party. After a split between left-wing republicans and the IRA leadership, Ryan and a substantial minority of the IRA formed Republican Congress in April 1934 which aimed to unite workers, small farmers, and other potential radicals. The congress, however, soon split because of tensions between its republican and socialist objectives. Ryan supported the majority faction, which called for a united front of republicans rather than a workers' republic.

Ryan remained joint secretary of the declining congress from 1934 to 1936. After the outbreak of the Spanish Civil War—viewed in Ireland predominantly as a conflict between Christianity and communism—Ryan, although personally a devout Catholic, supported the Spanish government. In December 1936 he left Ireland with the first contingent of the 200 Irishmen who would fight in the International Brigades. The most senior Irish officer in the republican army, he was attached to the 15th International Brigades headquarters. Although primarily involved in propaganda work he was injured while fighting in the battle of Jarama in February 1937. After a brief convalescence in Ireland he returned to Spain, where he was appointed adjutant of the 15th brigade with the rank of major. Captured by nationalist forces at Calaceite, near Gandesa, on the Aragon front in March 1938, he remained incarcerated at San Pedro de Cardeña prison long after the release of other international prisoners, despite intense diplomatic and public pressure from Ireland.

In July 1940 Admiral Canaris, head of German intelligence, persuaded General Franco to permit Ryan's 'escape' in order to strengthen German links with the IRA. With the approval of the Irish minister in Spain, Ryan—now severely deaf and in poor health—was brought to Berlin and reunited with Sean Russell, the IRA's chief of staff, who was due to return to Ireland to foment anti-British agitation. Russell, however, died on a German submarine off the Irish coast, and Ryan—despite his anti-fascism and former criticism of the IRA's militarism—agreed to return to Berlin to take Russell's place as the IRA's representative in Germany. Although sometimes depicted as a captive of Nazi Germany, Ryan was well treated, occasionally providing advice on Irish affairs to German officials. In January 1943 he suffered a stroke;

he died, unmarried, in Loschwitz Sanatorium, near Dresden, on 10 June 1944. He was buried in Loschwitz cemetery on 14 June but, after appeals to the German Democratic Republic, Ryan's remains were taken to Ireland and reinterred in Glasnevin cemetery, Dublin, on 22 June 1979.   FEARGHAL MCGARRY

Sources S. Cronin, *Frank Ryan: the search for the republic* (1980) • M. O'Riordan, *Connolly Column* (1979) • D. Keogh, *Ireland and Europe, 1919–48* (1988) • Aodh Ó Canainn, ed., 'Eilís Ryan in her own words', *Saothar*, 21 (1996), 129–46 • R. English, *Radicals and the republic* (1994) • T. P. Coogan, *The IRA*, 4th edn (1995)
Archives NA Ire., corresp. from Spain and Germany • priv. colls., letters
Likenesses photographs, repro. in Cronin, *Frank Ryan*

Ryan, Frederick Michael (1873–1913), playwright and journalist, was born at 8 Brunswick Place, Dublin, on 12 October 1873, the son of John Ryan, a bookkeeper, from whom he inherited his radicalism, and Catherine Davis. On leaving school he became a clerk in the civil service in London, where he frequented Fabian Society lectures and performances of Ibsen's plays. He resigned his position after a year because of ill health and joined the Dublin accountants Craig, Gardner & Co., where the stage-struck Frank Fay was a fellow clerk.

On 6 March 1896 Ryan was elected a member of the Celtic Society, founded by Arthur Griffith and William Rooney to stimulate debate on Irish affairs, and a forerunner of the Sinn Féin party. Later that year he also joined James Connolly's Irish Socialist Republican Party (ISRP), although he did not remain an active member of either society for long; the factionalism in the ISRP frustrated him, and he found himself growing out of sympathy with Griffith's bourgeois nationalism and racialism.

Ryan's friendship with Frank and William Fay led him to join their amateur Ormonde Dramatic Society in 1901, and in April 1902 he took a small part in their production of plays by George Russell and W. B. Yeats which led to the establishment of the Irish National Theatre Society. Ryan was elected secretary of the new society on 8 August, a position he held with great efficiency until 1904, when he became treasurer. He also turned his hand to playwriting, and his Ibsenite drama, *The Laying of the Foundations*, on the theme of municipal corruption, was produced on 12 October 1902, revived early in December, and performed on the Irish National Theatre Society's first visit to London on 2 May 1903.

Being secretary to the theatre did nothing to stem Ryan's constant flow of letters and articles to the Dublin and London press, usually under his pen-name Irial or Finian. His contributions to Griffith's *United Irishman* criticized the paper's refusal to see the Irish struggle from an international perspective, and in 1904 he vigorously attacked Griffith's antisemitism. Growing weary of the orthodoxy and superficiality of Irish journals, he and John Eglinton launched *Dana*, 'A Magazine of Independent Thought' in 1904, to promote the interchange of progressive ideas. The work of many leading writers of the Irish literary revival appeared in this monthly, including a poem by James Joyce—although the editors rejected an early version of *A Portrait of the Artist*. The magazine folded after less than a year, but Ryan had contributed enough articles in this time to make up his only book, *Criticism and Courage* (1906), and, deprived of his own journal, he continued to publish in *The Nationist* and the *New Age*.

Meanwhile Yeats was transforming the Irish National Theatre Society into a professional company, with power vested in three directors. Although opposed to this suppression of democracy, Ryan helped redraft the constitution, but voted against its adoption at the general meeting and subsequently resigned from the society. He helped other seceders set up a rival Theatre of Ireland in 1906 but, tired of theatrical quarrels, soon withdrew altogether from the Irish dramatic movement. His attempts with like-minded colleagues to establish a 'national democratic committee' in 1906 were abandoned with the sudden death of Michael Davitt, the proposed chairman, and as an alternative Ryan set up the Dublin Philosophic Society, which arranged a series of public lectures on rationalist themes. Early in 1907 he started the *National Democrat* with Francis Sheehy-Skeffington to carry on the committee's work in another form; this penny monthly ran for seven issues and its demise left Ryan much out of pocket.

With the failure of this venture Ryan left Dublin for Cairo to take up the assistant editorship of the anti-imperialist *Egyptian Standard*, but returned to Ireland in April 1909 to write against vested commercial and clerical interests in the *Irish Nation*. In June 1909 he helped William O'Brien reorganize the Socialist Party of Ireland of which he subsequently became secretary. He also served as secretary to the committee of the Young Ireland branch of the United Irish League. When James Connolly returned permanently to Ireland in July 1910, he immediately called on Ryan, who later found him supplementary employment which subsidized his trade union work. Early in 1911 Ryan returned to London to edit Wilfrid Scawen Blunt's monthly review *Egypt*, but on 3 April 1913, while in Sussex to discuss the future of the periodical with Blunt, he was taken ill with appendicitis. He died on 7 April at New Buildings Place, Shipley Road, Billingshurst, after an emergency operation. Although a confirmed agnostic, he was buried in the Crawley monastery churchyard.

JOHN KELLY

Sources J. Kelly, 'A lost Abbey play, Frederick Ryan's *The laying of the foundations*', *Ariel*, 1/3 (July 1970) · F. Sheehy-Skeffington, 'Frederick Ryan: the saint of Irish rationalism', *Irish Review* (May 1913) · b. cert. · d. cert. · Abbey Theatre prompt books, NL Ire., MS 10950 · NL Ire., Skeffington papers, MSS 21616–22656 · NL Ire., Abbey Theatre papers, MS 13068 · J. Holloway, diaries, NL Ire. · University College, Dublin, D. J. O'Donoghue papers · Harvard U., Widener Library, George Roberts papers · F. Ryan, *Criticism and courage* (1906) · W. S. Blunt, *My diaries: being a personal narrative of events, 1888–1914*, 2 vols. (1919–20) · M. Davis, 'The Abbey Theatre's first secretary', *Irish Independent* (14 Jan 1955)
Archives Harvard U., Widener Library, George Roberts papers · NL Ire., Abbey Theatre prompt books · NL Ire., Skeffington papers · NL Ire., Abbey Theatre papers · NL Ire., Joseph Holloway's diaries · University College, Dublin, D. J. O'Donoghue papers

Ryan, James (*c*.1770–1847), mining engineer and inventor, was born in Ireland. His early years are obscure but he had 'from a youth, a powerful predilection for the study of minerals, and their various geological character and position' (J. Ryan, 'Address to coal owners of Tyne and Wear', 15 Nov 1843, 2). By 1800 he was employed as 'mineral surveyor' to the Grand Canal Company of Ireland. In 1803, the company became involved in establishing the Doonane collieries at Castlecomer, in the hope of building up trade on the canal. By late April 1804 Ryan was based at these collieries, the site of the first Newcomen and Watt steam engines in Ireland. About this time Ryan was also involved with north Welsh collieries, including that at Bagillt, Flintshire. His involvement in mining seems to have inspired his invention of a new mine-boring apparatus, first reported at a meeting of the Dublin Society on 19 April 1804. The device brought up cores from potential mining sites using a cylindrical trepanning cutter. With the encouragement of the Dublin Society and a loan from the Grand Canal Company (to which he was now named engineer), Ryan obtained an English patent for his corer on 28 February 1805. The device was used for mineral exploration near Clonmel and Wexford in Ireland, but after a report on their Doonane collieries, the Grand Canal Company decided it had no further use for Ryan's services.

Ryan moved to mainland Britain where his invention was demonstrated to the board of agriculture and the British Mineralogical Society in 1807, and to members of both the Royal Society and the Geological Society of London in 1808. All these groups reported favourably on its novelty. The 1808 demonstration to the Geological Society was arranged by James Sowerby (1757–1822), an early advocate of the importance of William Smith's stratigraphic discoveries. This introduced Ryan to Smith's methods, and Ryan sent stratigraphically arranged suites of geological specimens both to Sowerby, for use in his *Mineral Conchology* project, and to the Geological Society from 1808. In this same year Ryan's device was used in exploratory borings for Richard Trevithick's Thames Tunnel project.

In 1806 Richard Lovell Edgeworth had noted that Ryan's invention could be used in boring special wide passages to improve mine ventilation. This application was soon put into practice in the particularly dangerous south Staffordshire coalfield, and Ryan lectured on his new methods at the Royal Institution in 1810. With the foundation of the Society for Preventing Accidents in Coal Mines in 1813, mine ventilation became a highly political matter. Views were polarized as to whether better illumination (with the Davy and Stephenson 'safety' lamps) or better ventilation (as encouraged by Ryan) was more needed. The Royal Society and Royal Institution favoured the first, while the Society of Arts favoured the second, awarding Ryan 100 guineas with a gold medal in 1816.

In 1818 Ryan moved to Montgomeryshire to mine lead and then feldspar for the Staffordshire pottery industry. This involvement was to cause Ryan major financial embarrassment, and litigation was still continuing in 1840. Nevertheless, Ryan had by 1831 erected a school there for instructing 'young men in my System of mining'

(Wedgwood MS 21874). This was the first such purpose-built school in Britain. Ryan's last years were spent continuing to promote his scheme of mine ventilation. In 1840 this had drawn praise from a Belgian director of mines and the 1842 *Report of the South Shields Committee* was also very favourable. Yet another disaster, in a poorly ventilated mine at Haswell, Durham, in 1844, inspired a commission of inquiry under Charles Lyell and Michael Faraday. Ryan was not allowed to speak at the inquest but Faraday noted that Ryan's 'principle seems very beautiful' (M. Faraday, 'The ventilation of mines', *Civil Engineer and Architects' Journal*, 8, April 1845, 118).

Ryan died on 21 July 1847 at the house of Mr Brooke, Wolverhampton Street, Dudley, the town which he had made his home since 1808. He was buried on 25 July at St Thomas's, Dudley. He had latterly been receiving an annual pension of £50 from the revenues of Lord Ward's mines, whose safety he had so much promoted. He had married in or before 1811 (his wife's name was Mary), and, following his death, his only child, Mary Jane, was allowed a reduced pension of 10s. a week. Ryan's last moments none the less were 'comparatively those of a pauper' (Johnson, 194), his reward for developing a mine system which was more expensive than the one it should have replaced and, perhaps, for being Irish.

H. S. TORRENS

Sources H. S. Torrens, 'James Ryan (c. 1770–1847) and the problems of introducing Irish "New Technology" to British mines in the early nineteenth century', *Science and society in Ireland: the social context of science and technology in Ireland, 1800–1950*, ed. P. J. Bowler and N. Whyte (1997), 67–83 • R. Delany, *The Grand Canal of Ireland* [1973] • c.1831, Keele University, Wedgwood MSS 21874–21888 • J. Farey, 'Coal and colliery', in A. Rees and others, *The cyclopaedia, or, Universal dictionary of arts, sciences, and literature*, 45 vols. (1819–20) • 'Select committee on accidents in mines', *Parl. papers* (1835), vol. 5, no. 603 • *Mining Journal* (14 Dec 1839), 186 • *Mining Journal* (2 May 1840), 138 • M. Berman, *Social change and scientific organization: the Royal Institution, 1799–1844* (1978) • H. Johnson, 'On the mode of working the thick or 10 yard coal of South Staffordshire', *Transactions of the North of England Institute of Mining Engineers*, 10 (1862), 183–97 • parish register, St Thomas, Dudley, Warwickshire • *Mining Journal* (24 July 1847)
Archives Durham RO, Society for Preventing Accidents in Coal Mines archives | BGS, Bell collection • NHM, Sowerby MSS • University of Bristol, Eyles MSS
Wealth at death comparatively a pauper: Johnson, 'On the mode of working', 194

Ryan, James (c.1799–1875), tightrope walker and circus proprietor, was said to be the cousin of Charles Adams, an equestrian actor, and grandson of the circus proprietor Henry Adams. Billed as the 'Young Hibernian', he was seen at Birmingham in May 1815 performing on the tightrope. At Astley's Amphitheatre in London in 1822 he turned a previously unequalled number of somersaults, and in 1823 he was billed to turn forward and backward somersaults on the tightrope without the aid of a balance pole.

Early in 1828 Ryan's Arena was operating in Chelsea; this business on his own account succeeded, and later in that year he erected a substantial amphitheatre in Bradford Street, Birmingham, with an arena and a stage. He later had premises in Sheffield, Halifax, Bristol, and other

large cities, but kept Birmingham as his headquarters. During the 1830s considerable animosity existed between Ryan and Andrew Ducrow, and Ryan opened many of his circuses in opposition to Ducrow. In 1841 he opened a brick-built circus, which led to his financial ruin, and in 1842 he was forced to sell his buildings. He continued to perform in other proprietors' arenas, and appeared as late as 1859 with Madame Macarte's circus at Stourbridge. He retired shortly after this, and for some years lived in Bromsgrove Street, Birmingham. In later years he was said to be eccentric, and was described as a short, thick-set man, of fine build and appearance. He remained healthy and vigorous, though he partly lost the sight in one eye. In 1873 he joined his daughter Susannah, a popular equestrian performer, at her home in Paris. He died there in poverty on 13 November 1875.

Ryan was remembered as a kind-hearted, energetic performer, with a fund of stories of circus life. At the height of his career he was a real benefactor to his equestrian performers, and was known for rewarding talent with proper remuneration.   JOHN M. TURNER

Sources J. M. Turner, *Gloucestershire history* (1991) • Boase, *Mod. Eng. biog.* • C. Keith, *Circus life and amusements* (1879) • T. Frost, *Circus life and circus celebrities* (1875) • D. Salberg, *Ring down the curtain* (1980) • A. H. Saxon, *The life and art of Andrew Ducrow* (1978) • S. Wild, *Old Wild's* (1888) • W. F. Wallett, *The public life of W. F. Wallett* (1870) • C. W. Montague, *Recollections of an equestrian manager* (1881) • *World's Fair* (17 Jan 1925) • *World's Fair* (18 Jan 1930) • *World's Fair* (13 Feb 1932) • *Birmingham Journal* (13 May 1837) • *The Era* (4 May 1845)
Wealth at death extreme poverty: Montague, *Recollections*

Ryan, Lacy (c.1694–1760), actor, was born in the parish of St Margaret, Westminster, the son of Daniel Ryan, a tailor of Irish descent. Educated at St Paul's School, he was encouraged by his father to pursue a career in law, and he was consequently sent into the office of his godfather, a Mr Lacy, who was a solicitor. But he quickly abandoned this occupation, and on 1 July 1710, at Greenwich, under William Pinkethman, he took the role of Rosencrantz in *Hamlet*. He must, however, have previously appeared at the Haymarket, since Thomas Betterton, who died on 4 May 1710, saw him as Seyton in *Macbeth* there, and is said to have commended his work while chiding John Downes, the prompter, for sending on a child in a full periwig to take on a man's part.

On 3 January 1711 Ryan appeared for the first time at Drury Lane as Lorenzo in *The Jew of Venice*, Lord Lansdowne's alteration of *The Merchant of Venice*. The role of Granius in Thomas Otway's *Caius Marius* followed on 17 March 1711, and on 17 August Ryan was the original Young Gentleman in Elkanah Settle's *A City Ramble, or, A Playhouse Wedding*. He created a number of original performances, including the first Valentine in Charles Johnson's *The Wife's Relief, or, The Husband's Cure* later in 1711 and the original Ensign Standard in Charles Shadwell's *The Humours of the Army* in 1713. On the recommendation of Sir Richard Steele he was assigned the part of Marcus in the original production of Joseph Addison's *Cato* on 14 April 1713, and on 12 May he was the first Astrolabe in John Gay's *The Wife of Bath*.

Ryan's reputation grew rapidly, and by 1714 his name was appearing with regularity on playbills in roles of all sizes. On 5 January 1714 at Drury Lane he played the original Arcas in Johnson's *The Victim*, and later appearances that year included Ferdinand in *The Tempest*, Sir Andrew Tipstaff in *The Puritan, or, The Widow of Watling Street*, Loveday in Edward Ravenscroft's *The London Cuckolds*, and Lovewell in James Shirley's *The Gamester*. In 1715 he is listed as having taken the parts of Laertes, Richmond in *Richard III*, Lucius in *Titus Andronicus*, Edgeworth in Ben Jonson's *Bartholomew Fair*, the Prince of Tanais in Nicholas Rowe's *Tamerlane*, and Bonario in Jonson's *Volpone*. Among other original roles were Sussex in Rowe's *Lady Jane Gray* in 1715, Learchus in Susannah Centlivre's *The Cruel Gift* in 1716, and Osmyn in Johnson's *Sultaness* and Vortimer in Mary de la Rivière Manley's *Lucius*, both in 1717. By the autumn of that year he was acting in Bullock and Leigh's booth at Southwark fair.

While eating his supper at the Sun tavern in Bedford Street, Covent Garden, on 7 June 1718, Ryan was assaulted by a notorious tippler and bully named Kelly, whom in self-defence he ran through with his sword and killed. That he was not taken to trial, unlike his fellow actor James Quin, who on 10 July of the same year was found guilty of manslaughter for killing William Bowen under similar circumstances, may in some way be taken as an indication of the esteem in which Ryan was held. He was no stranger to violence; in the spring of 1713 he had been assaulted by a group of Thames watermen, and his wound began to bleed the same evening on stage—appropriately as he was brought in on a bier during act IV of *Cato*. The bad luck continued: on 1 May 1725 he was wounded in the cheek during an on-stage sword fight in the last act of *Richard III*. More seriously, on Saturday 15 March 1735 he was shot in the face and robbed by a footpad in Great Queen Street, when he sustained severe injury to his upper jaw and lost four teeth. On 17 March, when his name was on the bill for Loveless, he wrote to the *Daily Post* expressing his fear that he would never be able to appear again, and apologizing to his patrons for not being able to be present at his benefit, organized to take place three days later. The benefit was, however, a great success. The prince of Wales sent 10 guineas, and there was a crowded house for which, on 22 March, in the same paper, Ryan expressed his gratitude. He reappeared on 25 April as the original Bellair in William Popple's *Double Deceit, or, A Cure for Jealousy*.

On 1 March 1718 Ryan made his first appearance at the Lincoln's Inn Fields Theatre as Cassius in *Julius Caesar*. He was to remain at that playhouse for nearly fourteen years. The list of roles he took on during his time there is a lengthy one, as he shared with his lifelong friend James Quin the lead in both tragedies and comedies. Most notably, these included Banquo, Hamlet, Richard II, Iago, Benedick, Hotspur, Macduff, Julius Caesar, Buckingham in *Henry VIII*, Lysimachus in Nathaniel Lee's *The Rival Queens*, Portius in Addison's *Cato*, Courtwell in Richard Savage's *Woman's a Riddle*, Oroonoko in Thomas Southerne's play of that name, and Amintor in Beaumont and Fletcher's *The Maid's Tragedy*.

On the opening of the new house in Covent Garden on 7 December 1732 by the Lincoln's Inn Fields company, Ryan took the part of Mirabell in the performance of William Congreve's *The Way of the World*. He was to continue performing there for the remainder of his career. On 7 February 1760 he was seen for what seems to have been the last time as Eumenes in John Hughes's *The Siege of Damascus*. On 1 March he advertised that he had been for some time much indisposed, and had postponed his benefit until 14 April in the hope of being able to make a personal appearance then. For that benefit Thomas Arne's *Comus* and Otway's *The Cheats of Scapin* were played, though it does not appear that Ryan took part in either piece. He died on 15 August 1760 at his house in Crown Court, Charles Street, Westminster. Another account, however, locates his death as having occurred in Bath on the 14th or the 18th.

Little is known about Ryan's wife and family. About 1719 he married the daughter of a grocer in the Strand. The couple had two sons, one of whom may have been the Anthony Ryan who had a brief stage career in the 1730s and who died on 3 October 1740.

Ryan, whose voice had a drawling, croaking accent as a result of the injury to his jaw, which had also distorted his naturally handsome features, was one of the actors whom David Garrick, in his early and saucy mimicries, derided on the stage. In later years Garrick went to see Ryan in order to mock his ungraceful and ill-dressed figure in *Richard III*, but instead found unexpected excellence in the performance and consequently modified and improved his own work. Following his early success in the role of Marcus in Addison's *Cato*, Ryan was to enjoy for three decades an undisputed reputation for his performances as villains and lovers in tragedy and fine gentlemen in comedy. Thomas Davies, in his *Memoirs of the Life of David Garrick*, however, described Ryan as possessing an awkward deportment and manner of moving his head. Indeed, he appeared at times extravagantly ridiculous in comic characters, and, though he had been long held in high esteem, by the 1750s he could no longer credibly sustain the younger roles to which his name had long been attached. His most important original part was Falconbridge in Colley Cibber's *Papal Tyranny in the Reign of King John* (15 February 1745). His best performances were as Edgar in *King Lear*, Iago, Mosca in Jonson's *Volpone*, Ford, and Dumont. He was considered excellent as Macduff in the fourth act of *Macbeth* and his mad scene in Lewis Theobald's *Orestes* won high commendation, though he had to contend with considerable rivalry from Spranger Barry. He was far too old when he played Alonzo in Edward Young's *The Revenge* but showed power in the scenes of jealousy and distraction, and as Captain Plume in George Farquhar's *The Recruiting Officer*, one of his last interpretations, he displayed great spirit. Without ever quite achieving the first rank, he approached very near it and was one of the most genuinely useful actors of the day.   MARK BATTY

Sources Genest, *Eng. stage* • Mr Dibdin [C. Dibdin], *A complete history of the English stage*, 5 vols. (privately printed, London, [1800]) • T. Davies, *Memoirs of the life of David Garrick*, 2 vols. (1808) • T. Davies,

Dramatic miscellanies, 3 vols. (1784) · T. Wilkinson, *Memoirs of his own life*, 4 vols. (1790) · J. Doran and R. W. Lowe, *'Their majesties' servants': annals of the English stage*, rev. edn, 3 vols. (1888) · W. C. Russell, *Representative actors* [1888] · Highfill, Burnim & Langhans, *BDA* · *DNB*

Ryan, Michael (*fl.* 1784–1831). *See under* Ryan, Michael (1800–1840).

Ryan, Michael (1800–1840), surgeon and writer on medicine, of unknown parentage, was probably born in Ireland. He studied medicine in Dublin and Edinburgh, where he took his degree and became a member of the College of Surgeons of Edinburgh. He spent several years in practice in Kilkenny before moving to London about 1829, where he became a member of the Royal College of Physicians and gave clinical instruction at the Metropolitan Free Hospital. In 1830 he was a candidate for the chair of toxicology in the Medico-Botanical Society and that same year he read a paper to the society, 'The use of the secale cornutum or ergot of rye in midwifery'. He lectured on medical jurisprudence at the medical theatre, Hatton Garden, and on obstetrics at the North London school of medicine, and was lecturer in medicine and midwifery at the Hunterian School of Medicine, Great Windmill Street, until it closed in 1838. Parts of these courses of lectures were later published.

Ryan wrote several very popular works including *Manual of Medical Jurisprudence* (1831; 2nd edn, 1836) which was also published in Philadelphia in 1832 with notes by R. E. Griffith, and *Manual of Midwifery … Comprising a New Nomenclature of Obstetric Medicine* (3 edns, 1831), which appeared in Burlington, Vermont, in 1835. An enlarged and rewritten *Manual of Midwifery* (1841) included an atlas of obstetrics which Ryan had first published in 1840. Further works included *The Philosophy of Marriage in its Social, Moral and Physical Relations* (8 vols., 1837; 12th edn, 1867), *Prostitution in London, with a Comparative View of that of Paris and New York* (1839), and *The Medico-Chirurgical Pharmacopoeia* (1837; 2nd edn, 1839). Between 1832 and 1838 Ryan edited the *London Medical and Surgical Journal*; he also edited and augmented T. Denman's *Obstetrician's Vade-mecum* (1836) and translated and added to *Le nouveau formulaire pratique des hôpitaux* by Milne-Edwards and Vavasour. An obituarist commented, however, that Ryan's 'writings were more characterized for great industry and talent of compilation than for any originality of matter' (*Provincial Medical and Surgical Journal*, 207).

Ryan was one of the earliest members of the British Medical Association. He married young, and when he died at his home in Charlotte Street, London, on 11 December 1840, his widow, Ellen, and their four young children were left unsupported apart from a modest sum subscribed by his medical colleagues.

Another **Michael Ryan** (*fl.* 1784–1831), physician, graduated MD at Edinburgh in 1784 with a thesis on the palsy known as raphania. He was a fellow of the Royal College of Surgeons in Ireland and practised for some years at Kilkenny, and afterwards at Edinburgh, where he was described as a fellow of the Scottish Society of Antiquaries, though his name is not in the lists. His *Enquiry into the Nature, Causes, and Cure of Consumption of the Lungs etc* (1787) discussed Cullen's *First Lines of the Practice of Physic* and in the appendix Ryan opposed the views contained in Reid's essay on phthisis pulmonalis. Other writings included *Observations of the History and Cure of the Asthma* (1793), *On Peruvian Bark* (1794), and several articles for the *London Medical and Physical Journal*, including 'Observations on the medical qualities of acetate lead', 'Remarks on the cure of autumnal fever', 'Observations on the influenza of 1803', and 'An account of an epidemic at Kilkenny in 1800'. Ryan was a member of the Royal College of Surgeons of London and eventually entered the colonial service. His widow died at Ranelagh, Dublin, in 1851, leaving a son, (Michael) Desmond Henry *Ryan (1816–1868), a drama and music critic. G. Le G. Norgate, *rev.* Stephanie J. Snow

Sources J. F. Clarke, *Autobiographical recollections of the medical profession* (1874) · list of members, RCS Eng. · *GM*, 1st ser., 100/1 (1830), 351, 450 · *GM*, 2nd ser., 15 (1841), 105 · *GM*, 2nd ser., 36 (1851), 555 · *Provincial Medical and Surgical Journal* (1840–41), 207–8 · PRO, PROB 6/218 fols. 338–9 · P. Vaughan, *Doctors' Commons: a short history of the British Medical Association* (1959), 126

Ryan, Richard (1796–1849), biographer and writer, was born in Cork, the son of Richard Ryan, a Camden Town bookseller. In 1830, his father and mother had both died, and Ryan junior took over the family business. He did not, however, merely content himself with his father's profession, but also found time to write a wide range of literary works. These included comic plays, several of which were later printed in an 1825 anthology of plays edited by J. Cumberland; a series of poems and ballads on subjects ranging from sacred texts to the superstitions of the Irish peasantry; and songs which were set to music by some eminent Victorian composers.

Ryan is best remembered for his many biographical works, often containing engravings, which included popular and anecdotal depictions of various scenes, situations, and adventures from the history of the theatre, and also collections of the choicest anecdotes relating to poets of different ages and nations. Of more lasting value was his *Biographia Hibernica*, a biographical dictionary of Irish worthies, from the earliest periods to the early nineteenth century, which was published in two volumes between 1819 and 1821. Ryan's heart was, however, increasingly not in the work. Of the many entries the work contains, more than half occur in the letters A to D.

Ryan died at his home, 5 Pratt Street, Camden Town, on 20 October 1849. Many of his drinking songs and his more 'gossipy and pleasant' works remained popular after his death. The reputation of the *Biographia*, however, fell into a steady decline throughout the nineteenth and early twentieth centuries, and along with it Ryan's name. Jason Edwards

Sources Allibone, *Dict.* · D. J. O'Donoghue, *The poets of Ireland: a biographical dictionary with bibliographical particulars*, 1 vol. in 3 pts (1892–3), 220 · d. cert.
Archives Cork City Library, letters to T. C. Croker

Ryan, Vincent William (1816–1888), bishop of Mauritius, was born in Cork barracks, Cork, on 18 December 1816, the son of Captain John Ryan of the 82nd regiment, and his wife, Harriet, daughter of Pierre Gauvain, judge, of Alderney. Before the age of three he went with his parents to Mauritius. He returned to England in time to begin at Gosport College, and then went to university at Magdalen Hall (afterwards Hertford College), Oxford, in 1838. He graduated BA in 1841 and MA in 1848. He took the degree of DD in 1853. After ordination he became curate to St Anne's parish, Alderney, and then incumbent from 1842. In 1847 he became curate of Edge Hill, near Liverpool, and vice-president of the Liverpool Collegiate Institute. He became principal of the Church of England Metropolitan Training Institution at Highbury, Middlesex, on 1 July 1850. In 1854 he was nominated bishop of Mauritius, a post for which his knowledge of French particularly suited him. He set sail for Mauritius on 15 March 1855, and landed at Port Louis on 12 June, accompanied by a catechist from the Society for the Propagation of the Gospel.

Although the London Missionary Society was represented in other ports of Mauritius, Ryan found only two clergymen in Port Louis, along with one missionary in the country districts. Notwithstanding, he took full advantage of the awakening interest in evangelical Christianity there. On 8 January 1856 he consecrated a new church at Mahébourg. Later in the year (on 11 October) he made his first visit to the Seychelles, which were included in his diocese. In 1859 he visited the islands again, and consecrated the new church at Mahé. He was particularly interested in the schools in his diocese and in the Hindu population.

In June 1860 Ryan visited England to raise further funds for his missionary work. On 12 July 1862 he went with the special commissioner to Madagascar, to explore the possibility of establishing a new mission there. He visited the capital and the scene of the massacres of Christians, and returned to Mauritius in poor health. In October 1862 he revisited the Seychelles after the hurricane of that year. He paid a second visit to England in the spring of 1863. In 1867 he finally left Mauritius.

After acting as archdeacon of Suffolk for four months, Ryan became rector of St Nicholas, Guildford, and commissary of Winchester. In May 1870 he was transferred to the vicarage of Bradford, Yorkshire, where his ministry was marked by developments in parish work. He was rural dean from 1870 to 1876, and in 1875 became archdeacon of Craven and commissary to the bishop of Ripon. In 1872 he went on a special mission to Mauritius. In August 1880 Ryan became vicar of St Peter's, Bournemouth, and in 1881 rector of Middleham; in 1883 he became rector of Stanhope in co. Durham. Ryan was married to Elizabeth Dowse, daughter of Charles Atkins of Romford, Hampshire; they had two sons, one named Vincent John and both of whom became clergymen, and one daughter, all of whom survived him. Ryan died at the rectory, Stanhope, on 11 January 1888, and was buried in St Thomas's churchyard on 14 January.   C. A. HARRIS, *rev.* LYNN MILNE

Sources *Colonial Church Chronicle*, 7 (1854–5), 70, 278, 320, 394 · V. W. Ryan, *Mauritius and Madagascar* (1864) [extracts from his journals] · W. M. Egglestone, *Bishop Ryan* (1889) · *CGPLA Eng. & Wales* (1888) · d. cert. · Boase, *Mod. Eng. biog.*

Archives LPL, letters to Baroness Burdett-Coutts; corresp. with A. C. Tait and related papers

Likenesses oils, 1854, Hertford College, Oxford · portrait, repro. in *Home Words* (Feb 1882), 38

Wealth at death £2834 4*s.* 4*d.*: probate, 7 March 1888, *CGPLA Eng. & Wales*

Rycaut, Sir Paul (1629–1700), diplomat and author, was born in November or December 1629, probably in London, the eleventh child and tenth successive son of Peter (later Sir Peter) *Rycaut or Ricaut (1578–1653) and his wife, Mary van der Colge or Vercolge (*d.* in or after 1660). He was baptized on 23 December in the parish church of St Christopher-le-Stocks, London, a year after his brother Thomas.

Early career With Thomas, Rycaut matriculated in 1646 as a pensioner at Trinity College, Cambridge, and in 1647 was elected to a scholarship. He graduated BA in 1650, and the following year went to Madrid with his eldest brother, Peter, to try to recover a large debt owed to their father by the Spanish government. While his brother pursued this he enrolled at the nearby University of Alcalá de Henares, which he found more intellectually stimulating than Cambridge. As an exercise in Spanish he translated into English the first part of *El criticón*, an allegorical novel by a Jesuit professor, Baltasar Gracian y Morales, about a child raised in a cave on St Helena and his subsequent reactions to the world and to human society. After returning to England he was admitted, in 1652, to Gray's Inn.

After his father's death Rycaut was involved, along with his brothers, in further attempts to retrieve the Spanish debt through diplomatic channels or by letters of marque. In 1655 he joined Robert Blake's fleet in Italy for a punitive expedition against the privateers of Tunis, who had seized a shipload of currants belonging to his brother Philip, and he was present on 4 April when Blake burned the Tunisian war galleys in their winter harbour at Porto Farina. On 18 December he attended the public conference in Whitehall on the resettlement of the Jews in England, and left the principal surviving account of Oliver Cromwell's speech in favour, which he always thought the best he ever heard. This did not prevent him from becoming actively involved in royalist intrigues, which in 1658 took him to his father's native city, Antwerp, where he still had cousins. Although the family estate at Aylesford in Kent had had to be sold, the Rycauts were by then well connected in the county, and on the recommendation of Sir Edward Dering, second baronet, Paul was hired as a private secretary in the summer of 1660 by the new lord lieutenant, Heneage Finch, third earl of Winchilsea, who had just been appointed ambassador to the Porte.

Constantinople and early publications The principal secretary of embassy and chancellor elect of the Levant Company's factory at Constantinople, Robert Bargrave, fell sick on the voyage out to Turkey and died at Smyrna. From the time of his arrival at Constantinople in January 1661 Rycaut therefore acted as chancellor as well as private secretary, and was soon confirmed in this much more important post. In addition he replaced Winchilsea's steward, who was sent home with dispatches, and as his Turkish

Sir Paul Rycaut (1629–1700), by Johann Rundt, 1691

improved he took over much of the embassy's ordinary business from the unreliable first dragoman. He was also entrusted with several independent missions. In August 1663 he was dispatched by frigate to the three Ottoman regencies of Tripoli, Tunis, and Algiers with the sultan's ratifications of treaties concluded the year before. When Algiers refused to confirm its treaty he continued on to London and represented the need for reprisals; a punitive expedition sailed in response. He also presented Charles II with an Arab horse from Winchilsea, and received in return a gold chain and medal for himself. He arrived back in Constantinople in March 1664, and in April 1665 was sent to seek redress for the English factory at Aleppo over a customs dispute from the grand vizier, Fazil Ahmad Köprülü, then encamped with the Ottoman army at Belgrade. He accompanied the army on its homeward march. In December he was sent again to London, and for the first leg of the journey retraced his steps through the Balkans in the company of a hundred released Austrian prisoners of war, hearing the same battlefield stories from the other side.

All this helped to fill the blank notebooks which Rycaut had brought out to Turkey, for he had always intended to be the chronicler of his time there. The eventful voyage out in 1660–61, and Winchilsea's favourable reception by the vizier and sultan, were described in *Narrative of the success of the voyage of the right honourable Heneage Finch, earl of Winchelsea*, published anonymously in London in 1661, but from internal evidence clearly Rycaut's work. Next came an edition of the new treaty negotiated at Adrianople in

January 1662, *The capitulations and articles of peace between the majestie of the king of England, Scotland, France and Ireland &c. and the sultan of the Ottoman empire*, printed on the press of a Jewish printer settled at Smyrna, and published at Constantinople in 1663. It was the first work ever to appear in English in Turkey, and was dedicated to the Levant Company—although when Rycaut reached London later that year he substituted a hastily printed dedication to the king in the copies earmarked for the government.

Rycaut's first major work was *The Present State of the Ottoman Empire*, a three-part analysis of Ottoman government and society. The first part discussed the constitution, the education of the ruling classes, the principal offices, and the relationship between the central government and the outlying provinces, Balkan satellites, and foreign states. The second part dealt with religion and morality; the third, with the armed forces. Although the title-page was dated 1667 it was actually published in 1666 just before the fire of London, which destroyed most of the stock. However, it earned Rycaut election to the Royal Society in December 1666 and was quickly reprinted. From 1670 translations began to appear, and by 1678 it was a bestseller in English, French, Dutch, German, Italian, and Polish. A Russian translation followed in 1741, and it was also paraphrased in other languages, notably the Hungarian letters of Kelemen Mikes (published 1794), and a Latin treatise on Islam by Dimitrie Cantemir, which appeared originally in a Russian translation and, in 1977, in Romanian. Attractively illustrated by costume drawings, the *Present State* was nevertheless intended for serious study by policy makers, and its strength lay in the exceptional range and accuracy of the information obtained by Rycaut from his contacts in the Ottoman bureaucracy. It shaped European perceptions of the Ottomans for a century, and historians continued to see it as unusually fair-minded in its approach, until towards the end of the twentieth century it began to draw criticism for subscribing to the myths of oriental despotism.

Smyrna and later publications Rycaut's next publication was an anonymous account of the movement led by the Jewish pseudo-messiah Sabbatai Zevi, which had erupted at Smyrna in 1665. It was published initially in 1669 in the *History of the Three Late Famous Impostors* edited by John Evelyn, and was reprinted many times in English, German, French, and even Welsh, as well as being reclaimed by Rycaut himself for later publication in his own *History*. Initial circumspection had been needed because in September 1667 he took up appointment as British consul at Smyrna, remaining there until April 1678.

Smyrna (modern Izmir) was a rapidly growing entrepôt with sixty or seventy resident Levant Company factors or apprentices. A quarter of England's total cloth export went to Turkey, and principally to Smyrna, where it was exchanged for the raw silk, mohair, and cotton which were also vital to English manufacturing industry. Rycaut's term of office coincided with a golden age for this valuable trade, from a combination of Ottoman goodwill and stability under the Köprülü regime, maritime security, sound financial practices, difficulties encountered by competitors, and the harmony prevailing in the English factory. Both the Ottoman and the English authorities had devolved substantial powers to the consul, who had to be able to deal effectively with a wide range of problems. Rycaut spoke nine languages, and was as proficient a mediator in commercial and diplomatic affairs as in interpreting one culture to another through his pen. His growing literary reputation was itself an asset; many travellers' accounts mention the universal respect in which he was held, and pay tribute to his civility and learning. He added to his reputation in 1670 by leading an expedition which rediscovered the lost site of Thyateira, one of the seven churches of Asia addressed in the Book of Revelation, as was confirmed by inscriptions among the ruins.

After six months in Italy sightseeing and collecting further inscriptions Rycaut arrived home shortly before Christmas 1678. He was elected to the Levant Company's board of assistants and was asked to see through the press a new edition of the *Capitulations*, incorporating additional articles granted in 1675. This appeared in April 1679. In May there followed *The Present State of the Greek and Armenian Churches, Anno Christi, 1678*, and in November (with a title-page postdated 1680) *The history of the Turkish empire* [in later editions *History of the Turks*] *from the year 1623 to the year 1677*. Both works were well received, as much for Rycaut's clear, lively, and judicious style as for the wealth of inside information he brought to bear, and were again widely translated. Next came his old translation from the Spanish, *The Critick* (1681), and a new translation from Greek of the life of Numa Pompilius for the John Dryden edition of Plutarch's *Lives* (1683). He was then commissioned by his publisher to write a continuation of a work by Baptista Platina, alias Bartolomeo Sacchi, which together with an anonymous translation of the original (often credited to Rycaut owing to an ambiguous title-page) was published as *Lives of the Popes* in 1685. As Platina had only reached 1471 Rycaut's continuation had to cover two centuries of European history from the standpoint of the Vatican, and was a synthesis of printed sources in Latin, French, and Italian. The last of these commissions was another translation from the Spanish, the classic history of the Incas by Garcilaso de la Vega, which eventually appeared as *Royal Commentaries of Peru* in 1688. The common element in these very different enterprises was Rycaut's interest in human societies and how they were shaped by external factors—geography, climate, diet, wealth—for he believed that 'the rational soul of man … in all mankind is of little difference in it self' (*The Present State of the Ottoman Empire*, 1667, 2.ix). His translations as well as his original writings were to influence students of human nature from Racine, Leibniz, and John Locke to Daniel Defoe, Montesquieu, and Byron.

Later political career Rycaut had taken the gamble of resigning his consulship in the hope that he would secure the next vacancy in the embassy, but when this arose in 1680 he was unsuccessful. Known still as Consul Rycaut he continued to act as a government consultant on Ottoman affairs and in 1682 was approached for a secret mission. He was to travel to Algiers in disguise and end the war then raging by concluding a peace before the French could intervene. He was about to leave when news arrived that Vice-Admiral Arthur Herbert had already negotiated a treaty. He had to wait another three years for employment. At last in October 1685 he was knighted and appointed chief secretary in Ireland, with special responsibility for Leinster and Connaught and a seat on the Irish privy council. Together with the new lord lieutenant, Henry Hyde, second earl of Clarendon, he crossed to Dublin in January 1686. He was soon able to report to his friend Archbishop William Sancroft 'that I never was more happy, nor more contented then I am at present' (Bodl. Oxf., MS Tanner 31, fol. 287). His brother Thomas was by then a prosperous Dublin lawyer, and his widowed sister-in-law Grace Rycaut came out to keep house for him, an arrangement that lasted until her death eleven years later. He was elected to the council of the Dublin Philosophical Society and appointed a judge of Admiralty in Ireland (the patent was renewed in 1691). Clarendon's administration, however, was swiftly undermined by James II's policy of Catholicization and his connivance in the intrigues of the earl of Tyrconnell. The position became untenable and Clarendon and Rycaut were formally relieved in February 1687.

Back in London Rycaut found a new patron in George Savile, first marquess of Halifax. Both men were old opponents of French expansionism. Indeed, in 1671 the secretary of the French embassy at the Porte had thought it necessary to circulate an anonymous rebuttal of the derogatory remarks about France in *The Present State of the Ottoman Empire*. Louis XIV's reunion policy and his revocation of the edict of Nantes had only hardened Rycaut's conviction that the French were 'the common fire-brands of Germany, and Incendiaries of all the World' and their king 'a Tyrant, and the Enemie of Mankind' (BL, Add. MS 34095, fols. 212–13). Throughout the revolution crisis Halifax and Rycaut met regularly to discuss the latest news, and early in 1689 the marquess recommended Rycaut for appointment as William and Mary's resident at the three Hanse Towns of Hamburg, Lübeck, and Bremen.

Rycaut reached Hamburg in August 1689 and remained there until May 1700. He felt the cold bitterly until he discovered the duvet, which he is credited with introducing to England, for he sent his friends 6-pound bags of eider-down for Christmas complete with instructions for use: 'the coverlet must be quilted high and in large panes, or otherwise it will not be warme' (BL, Add. MS 37663, fol. 19). Although he missed his London friends he was back in his element as the hospitable patron of a privileged community of English merchants, in this case the Merchant Adventurers. In 1697, on the express instructions of William III, he defeated the attempts of the king's Scottish subjects to establish a rival factory in the same port; his memorial in French to the senate of Hamburg disowning the commissioners of the Scots Company for Trading with Africa and the Indies (later better known as the Darien Company) was published several times in English translation by the justly indignant Scots. His principal duties, executed with equal zeal, were to prevent contraband trade with France and to promote the grand alliance. Hamburg was an important staging post for agents and news, and he was kept busy until after the advent of peace in 1697. He then had leisure to send the under-secretary of state an illustrated account of lemmings and their migrations which was published in *Philosophical Transactions* in 1699. His large postbag from south-east Europe had meanwhile allowed him to keep his Turkish history up to date, and a continuation from 1679 to 1699 was published in 1700 shortly before his return.

Rycaut had a stroke on 9 November, spent a week supervising from his sickbed the arrangements for his funeral and monument, and died in his rented house in Wardour Street, London, on 16 November 1700. He was buried on 27 November beside his parents in the church of St Peter and St Paul, Aylesford. He had never married, perhaps on account of his sister-in-law, whose death in 1697 he described as the greatest affliction of his life, 'having as I may say, lost my true friend, and my companion' (BL, Add. MS 46533, fol. 266). Comparison of the portraits of Rycaut by Lely *c.*1679 and by Rundt in 1691 shows how much he had mellowed since she came into his life. His heir was the nine-year-old great-grandson of his eldest brother. Much of the inheritance was embezzled before it could be claimed, but his legacy survives in his writings, still essential sources for the study of the Ottoman empire in the seventeenth century.   SONIA P. ANDERSON

Sources S. P. Anderson, *An English consul in Turkey: Paul Rycaut at Smyrna, 1667–1678* (1989) • BL, Lansdowne MSS 1153A–1153E; Add. MSS 19514–19515, 37663 • PRO, SP 71/1; SP 82/17–19; SP 97/17–19; SP 104/194–200; SP 105/112–14, 151–5, 175; C 6/354/65, 71; C 6/359/4; C 33/308–320 • will, PRO, PROB 11/458, fol. 183 • Leics. RO, Finch papers • *Report on the manuscripts of Allan George Finch*, 5 vols., HMC, 71 (1913–2003) • Bodl. Oxf., MS Rawl. A. 482; MS Eng. lett. C. 8; MSS Smith 53, 65; MS Tanner 31 • *CSP dom.*, *1651–1702* • *CSP Venice, 1661–6* • RS • Longleat House, Wiltshire, Coventry MSS 4, 5, 49, 69; Thynne MS 12 • S. P. Anderson, 'Sir Paul Rycaut FRS (1629–1700): his family and writings', *Proceedings of the Huguenot Society*, 21 (1965–70), 464–91 • S. P. Anderson, 'Paul Rycaut and his journey from Constantinople to Vienna in 1665–1666', *Revue des Études Sud-Est Européennes*, 11 (1973), 251–73 • All Souls Oxf., MS 240 • BL, Add. MSS 7021, 22910, 34095, 46533 • Bibliothèque Nationale, Paris, Fonds Français n.a.7478 [holograph tract by the Sieur de la Croix] [copies are in the Bibliothèque de l'Arsenal, Paris and BL, Add. MS 72560] • W. A. Shaw, *The knights of England*, 2 vols. (1906); repr. (1971) • E. Freshfield, ed., *Register book of the parish of St Christopher le Stocks*, 1 (1882), 17 • Venn, *Alum. Cant.* • J. Foster, *The register of admissions to Gray's Inn, 1521–1889, together with the register of marriages in Gray's Inn chapel, 1695–1754* (privately printed, London, 1889), 260 • N. Luttrell, *A brief historical relation of state affairs from September 1678 to April 1714*, 4 (1857), 708–9 • P. Rycaut, the translator to the reader, in L. Gracian, *The critick* (1681) • P. Melvin, 'Sir Paul Rycaut's memoranda and letters from Ireland, 1686–1687', *Analecta Hibernica*, 27 (1972), 123–82 • C. Heywood, 'Sir Paul Rycaut, a seventeenth-century observer of the Ottoman state: notes for a study', repr. with revisions in C. Heywood, *Writing Ottoman history: documents and interpretations* (2001), no. 4 • B. H. Beck, *From the rising of the sun: English images of the Ottoman empire to 1715* (1987) • A. Grosrichard, *The sultan's court: European fantasies of the East* (1998)

Archives BL, Lansdowne MSS 1153A–1153E ['A collection of Sir Paul Rycaut's papers'] • BL, letter-books and papers, Add. MSS 19514–19515, 37663 • Bodl. Oxf., MS Rawl. A.482 [Rycaut's letter-book] | All Souls Oxf., letters to Sir L. Jenkins • BL, letters to W. Blathwayt, Add. MS 21490 • BL, letters to Sir W. Colt, Add. MSS 34095, 36662 • BL, letters to J. Ellis, Add. MSS 28897–28905 • BL, letters to Lord Lexington, Add. MS 46553 • BL, letters to G. Stepney, Add. MS 7060 • Bodl. Oxf., letters to W. Blathwayt, MS Eng. lett. e 5 • Bodl. Oxf., letters to Lord Clarendon, MS Eng. lett. C. 8 • Leics. RO, corresp. with earls of Winchilsea and Nottingham, Finch papers • Princeton University, New Jersey, corresp. with W. Blathwayt • PRO, SP 71/1, SP 82/17–19, SP 97/17–19, SP 104/194–200, SP 105/112–14, 151–5, 175 • Yale U., misc. papers and letters to W. Blathwayt

Likenesses P. Lely, oils, *c.*1679–1680, NPG • J. Rundt, oils, 1691, RS [*see illus.*] • R. White, line engraving (after P. Lely, 1679), BM, NPG; repro. in P. Rycaut, *History of the Turkish empire* (1680), frontispiece

Wealth at death 'about £5700', mainly investments in securities (Malt Lottery and Million Lottery tickets, Bank of England stock, an Old East India Company bond, exchequer bills): Anderson, *An English consul*, appx. 3; will, PRO, PROB 11/458, fol. 183; PRO, C 6/354/65, 71; C 6/359/4; C 33/312, fol. 216; C 33/316, fol. 449

Rycaut, Sir Peter (1578–1653), merchant and financier, was born at Antwerp, the son of Andrew Rycaut (son of Peter Rycaut of Brabant) and his Spanish wife, Emerentia, daughter of Garcia Gonsala. He settled in London in 1600 and used his connections in Spain, Portugal, Italy, and the Low Countries to build up a thriving Mediterranean trade. He also allied himself with leading Dutch merchants in London through his marriage to Mary (*d.* in or after 1660), daughter of Roger van der Colge (or Vercolge) and stepdaughter of Walter Artson the elder. Their ten sons and three daughters were baptized between 1611 and 1634; ten children survived into adulthood, including the youngest son, Paul *Rycaut. The couple were active in the Dutch, French, and Italian reformed churches in London, as well as in their local Anglican parish of St Christopher-le-Stocks after moving from St Swithin's Lane to Cornhill.

By the 1620s Rycaut was a multiple shipowner, with a controlling interest in the *Centurion*, *St George*, *St Peter*, *Peter and Andrew*, *John and James*, *Benjamin and John*, and other substantial ships. He had also become a merchant banker, corresponding in particular with his Annony relatives in Antwerp and the Spinolas in Genoa, part owners in his ships. He came accordingly under suspicion of being a front for foreign interests, or at least a pawn, vulnerable through his birth as a Spanish subject. In 1621 he lent a large sum to his friend Gondomar, the Spanish ambassador in London, to enable him to purchase and ship to Lisbon 100 pieces of ordnance for the service of the king of Spain. The arrangements for repayment in Portugal failed, and subsequent attempts to recover the debt with interest were to preoccupy the Rycaut family for more than forty years. When their cause was taken up by Cromwell, it was to contribute to the breach with Spain in 1655. In the shorter term Peter Rycaut's attempts to attach goods at Genoa belonging to Gondomar's successor led the Spanish viceroy of Naples to seize his 500 ton flagship, the *St George*, and Rycaut was suspected of selling her clandestinely to Spain. It took four years to clear his name; but he then defended himself so ably that it proved a turning point in his career.

Henceforth Rycaut's money and contacts were increasingly employed in the government's service. As an agent for the *asentistas* he helped to arrange that Spanish silver for Flanders, formerly routed via Genoa, was instead brought to Dover, where two-thirds was unladen and reminted in London against bills of exchange redeemable in the Low Countries. This resulted in a regular flow of silver into the kingdom from 1631 to 1647. In 1635 he headed the group of merchants granted a monopoly to import and refine the gold and silver used in the manufacture of wire thread. He invested substantially in the government's West Indies venture of 1636. He was the treasurer of the royal fishing association, at considerable personal loss, while both in his own name and indirectly he lent heavily to the crown in 1639–40. In return he received letters of denization on 27 July 1637 (although his naturalization bill was lost in committee in 1641), and was knighted on 30 April 1641. Shortly afterwards the husband of his eldest daughter, Mary, John Mayney, received a knighthood and baronetcy, and his eldest son, Peter, was contracted to the sister of a crown ward, Viscount Strangford. Rycaut himself had joined the landed gentry in 1639 with the purchase of two fine properties of 500 acres each: The Friars, Aylesford, a former Carmelite priory on the Medway near Maidstone, in Kent; and King's Barns Manor, Upper Beeding, in Sussex, on the Adur beside Bramber Castle.

Rycaut was arrested at The Friars in August 1642 when parliamentary troops led by the notorious Colonel Sandys discovered arms and plate hidden in the roof. He was taken under guard to Upnor Castle and thence to London, where he managed to purchase his release. But in 1643, after raising a royalist troop of five hundred horse and lending £1000 to Sir John Mayney to buy arms in Holland, he had to escape to Rouen, which remained the family's continental base for some years. He was declared a delinquent and his estate sequestered, the first £5000 of his assets going straight to Sir William Waller's army. Over £2000 of this sum was in East India goods; and a further £1600 in the form of a bond by the East India Company (to which he had sold the *Peter and Andrew*) was also surrendered. Rycaut retaliated with actions to arrest the company's goods in Genoa, Venice, and Leghorn, which gave his friends on the board an excuse to resist further parliamentary demands.

Letters from Rycaut were captured at Naseby in 1645 and he was exempted by name in the Newcastle propositions of 1646 from holding office or approaching the court again. His London house and the priory were both turned into parliamentary magazines, and the latter also served as headquarters for the committee of Kent—plans for recapturing it played a large part in royalist conspiracies. Nevertheless he was allowed in 1647 to return to England, and then to The Friars, and his sequestration was lifted in 1648 after he had taken the covenant and compounded for a sixth of his remaining estate. But in 1650 the family was suspected (rightly) of remitting money to Charles II, and his books were again impounded. He died in Cornhill, London, on 22 February 1653 and was buried on 1 March in the church of St Peter and St Paul at Aylesford, where his wife later joined him. What little remained of his great wealth was mismanaged by his sons, and in 1657 they had

to sell The Friars. As they complained at the Restoration, probably with little exaggeration, but to equally little avail, 'Sir Peter for his Services and Loyaltie … was sequestred his houses rifled plundred and his Family turned out of doores, soe that he suffred in his Estate to the value of One Hundred Thousand Pounds' (SP 29/17, fol. 91). SONIA P. ANDERSON

Sources S. P. Anderson, 'Sir Paul Rycaut FRS (1629–1700): his family and writings', *Proceedings of the Huguenot Society*, 21 (1965–70), 464–91 · S. P. Anderson, *An English consul in Turkey: Paul Rycaut at Smyrna, 1667–1678* (1989) · *The registers of the French church, Threadneedle Street, London*, 1, ed. W. J. C. Moens, Huguenot Society of London, 9 (1896) · R. E. G. Kirk and E. F. Kirk, eds., *Returns of aliens dwelling in the city and suburbs of London, from the reign of Henry VIII to that of James I*, Huguenot Society of London, 10/2–3 (1902–7) · W. A. Shaw, ed., *Letters of denization and acts of naturalization for aliens in England and Ireland, 1603–1700*, Huguenot Society of London, 18 (1911) · *Le Neve's Pedigrees of the knights*, ed. G. W. Marshall, Harleian Society, 8 (1873), 399–400 · *The visitation of London, anno Domini 1633, 1634, and 1635, made by Sir Henry St George*, 2, ed. J. J. Howard, Harleian Society, 17 (1883) · J. B. Whitmore and A. W. Hughes Clarke, eds., *London visitation pedigrees, 1664*, Harleian Society, 92 (1940), 117 · E. Freshfield, ed., *The register book of the parish of St Christopher le Stocks*, 3 vols. in 1 (1882) · E. Freshfield, ed., *Accomptes of the churchwardens of the paryshe of St Christofers [sic] in London* (1885) · E. Freshfield, ed., *Minutes of the vestry meetings and other records of the parish of St Christopher* (privately printed, London, 1886) · E. Freshfield, ed., *Wills, leases, and memoranda in the book of records of the parish of St Christopher le Stocks in … London* (privately printed, 1895) · *CSP Venice, 1615–56* · *CSP col.*, vols. 3–4, 6, 8 · *CSP dom.*, 1623–70, passim · M. A. E. Green, ed., *Calendar of the proceedings of the committee for advance of money, 1642–1656*, 3 vols., PRO (1888) · M. A. E. Green, ed., *Calendar of the proceedings of the committee for compounding … 1643–1660*, 5 vols., PRO (1889–92) · E. B. Sainsbury, ed., *A calendar of the court minutes … of the East India Company*, 11 vols. (1907–38), vols. 1–5 · *JHC*, 2–6 (1640–51) · PRO, HCA 13/44–62, passim · PRO, HCA 16/636 · PRO, SP 23/113 · PRO, SP 29/17, fol. 91 · PRO, SP 29/142B, fol. 249 · PRO, SP 29/412, fols. 98 ff. · PRO, SP 46/101, fols. 147–64 · PRO, SP 94/33–43, passim · PRO, SP 97/10, fols. 117–25 · PRO, SP 97/11, fols. 123–7 · BL, Add. MS 5685, fol. 173 · BL, Add. MS 36448, fols. 33–4 · BL, Lansdowne MSS, 1153 C–D · CKS, Banks papers, U234/A1–2 · *A perfect diurnall of the severall passages in our late journey into Kent* (1642) · *A true relation of the late expedition into Kent* (1642) · *Fifth report*, HMC, 4 (1876), 46, 162 · *The manuscripts of the Earl Cowper*, 3 vols., HMC, 23 (1888–9), vols. 1–2 · J. H. Hessels, ed., *Archives of the London-Dutch church* (1892), 46 · K. R. Andrews, *Ships, money, and politics: seafaring and naval enterprise in the reign of Charles I* (1991) · will, made 22 Feb. 1653, proved, 21 April 1653, PRO, PROB 11/231, sig. 321 · further grant, 16 Feb 1662, PRO, PROB 11/307, sig. 26

Archives BL, papers of Sir John Coke, Add. MSS 64881–64898 · PRO, records of the committee for compounding, SP 23/113, pp. 1065–1156

Likenesses A. Van Dyck, oils, c.1640, Kedleston Hall, Derbyshire

Wealth at death £7123 bequests incl. £2000 each to three sons: will, proved, 21 April 1653, PRO, PROB 11/231, sig. 321

Rychard [Richardys], **Thomas** (d. 1563/4), prior of Totnes and printer, was a student of theology at Gloucester College, Oxford, for eight years; he petitioned for admission to the degree of BTh on 28 June and 29 October 1515.

By 1525 Rychard was a monk at the Benedictine monastery at Tavistock, in which year he was responsible for the first product of the first printing press in Devon. His edition of John Walton's English verse translation of Boethius's *De consolatione philosophiae* was printed for Robert Langdon. Rychard supplied some additions to the prose commentary for this volume and also attempted to revise Walton's language for the sixteenth-century reader, consulting both the Latin text and Chaucer's English version.

On 27 February 1528 Rychard was elected prior of Totnes in Devon; he is perhaps the Richard who is recorded as prior at its suppression. Sir Peter Edgcumbe, whose father had become patron of the priory under Henry VII, described the last prior in a letter to Thomas Cromwell as 'a man off goode vertuus conversacyon and a good viander' (Wright, 118). The *Short Title Catalogue* suggests Rychard may also have printed a 1534 edition of the statutes of the Devon stannary. Rychard was subsequently rector of St George's in Exeter from 1535 until his death, which took place between 10 August 1563 when he drew up his will and 14 April 1564 when it was proved. The will no longer survives.

CHARLOTTE FELL-SMITH, *rev.* P. BOTLEY

Sources Boethius: *De consolatione philosophiae*, ed. M. Science, trans. J. Walton, EETS, orig. ser., 170 (1927), xviii–xx, xxiv–xxx, xliii–xlv, 364–79 · Dugdale, *Monasticon*, new edn, 4.629 · Emden, *Oxf.*, 4.484 · G. Oliver, *Monasticon dioecesis Exoniensis, being a collection of records and instruments illustrating the ancient conventual, collegiate and eleemosynary foundations, in the counties of Cornwall and Devon* (1846), 109, 240 · T. Wright, ed., *Three chapters of letters relating to the suppression of monasteries* (1843), 117–18 · D. P. Alford, *The abbots of Tavistock with views beyond* (1891), 137–8, 337–8 · *Reg. Oxf.*, 1.97 · *STC, 1475–1640*

Ryck, William de (1635–1697×9), history painter, was born in Antwerp, where he was a pupil of Erasmus Quellinus. He trained as a goldsmith, and was still in Antwerp in 1684. According to Vertue a

> Print [a large sheet] the Story of St. Catherine. several figures. the Judges of the lawes pronouncing sentence against her.—designd painted and *Engraved* < a sort of scrach'd etching. Touch'd up > by Will De Rijck [was] dedicated to Ferdinand Van Beughem Bishop of Antwerp. (Vertue, *Note Books*, 4.20)

He took up painting when in England where he had arrived by 1688. Two paintings signed by de Ryck and dated 1688 are known to have been painted in England. Waterhouse reproduced examples of portraits by de Ryck and noted that he painted 'in a style like that of Riley' (Waterhouse, 237). His only known recorded work was *Tarquin and Lucretia*. De Ryck died in London between 1697 and 1699. He had a daughter, Catharina, who also became a painter. SUSAN COOPER MORGAN

Sources Redgrave, *Artists* · *Allgemeines Künstlerlexikon internationale Künstlerdatenbank*, K. G. Saur Verlag, 8th edn (Munich, 1999) [CD-ROM] · E. K. Waterhouse, *The dictionary of British 16th and 17th century painters* (1988)
Archives Courtauld Inst., Witt Library, cuttings, MSS notes, and photographs

Ryde, John Walter (1898–1961), physicist, was born at Brighton on 15 April 1898, the only child of Walter William Ryde, artists' colourman, of Brighton, and his wife, Hannah Louise Buckland, who was related distantly to William Buckland FRS (1784–1856), geologist and sometime dean of Westminster. Ryde's father died in 1908, whereafter he and his mother moved to South Kensington. He was educated at Brighton grammar school and at

St Paul's School, which he left in 1913 to continue his education abroad. After a year in France he was forced by the outbreak of war to return to England, where he joined Finsbury Technical College, to study under Professor Silvanus P. Thompson. In 1916 he volunteered for service in the Royal Engineers, being posted in due course to France, and receiving a commission just before the 1918 armistice.

After demobilization Ryde was appointed to the scientific staff of the research laboratories of the General Electric Company Ltd (GEC), then in process of formation under Clifford C. Paterson. He was soon promoted in this organization in recognition of his outstanding abilities. His scientific interests covered a range so extensive as to be quite unusual in this age of specialization. He possessed the gift of being able to familiarize himself with a fresh field of study very rapidly, following this up quite often by a significant contribution to the advancement of the subject. Much of his work was theoretical but he was also a skilled experimenter, a talent he retained throughout his career. His work at the GEC Wembley laboratories was thus not confined by departmental boundaries, his final appointment, in 1953, being to the new post of chief scientist. In 1930 he married Dorothy, daughter of Thomas Edward Ritchie, electrical engineer. They had one son.

Ryde's early work was concerned with electric discharge in gases, thermionic emission, spectrophotometry, spectroscopic analysis, optical projection systems, and the optical properties of diffusing media. The work on discharge in gases took a sudden turn in a very practical and commercially significant direction in the early 1930s when he and his team developed the first successful high-pressure mercury vapour lamp, later widely adopted for the lighting of streets and industrial installations. This work occupied a major part of his effort for several years, but by the time war came in 1939 the scientific problems were largely solved and he was free to turn his attention to other, more pressing, problems of that time.

It was now that Ryde's various leisure-time interests—astronomy, geology, microscopy, mathematical studies—proved of such value; not only was he heavily engaged in various aspects of war work at the Wembley laboratories, but he was able to make a number of significant personal contributions to defence matters. A particularly important theoretical investigation, undertaken jointly with his wife—also a skilled mathematician—was concerned with the effect on centimetric radio waves (for example in radar) of meteorological conditions such as rain, hail, cloud, and dust storms. The calculation of the attenuation and echo intensities involved a prodigious amount of computational work which was fully rewarded when their theoretical predictions were, some years later, confirmed to a most satisfactory degree by direct measurements.

Ryde's interest in astronomy also enabled him to make another significant personal contribution during the war. There was a need for information regarding the illumination from natural sources during hours of darkness and

Ryde devised a means for calculating and presenting this information in a form readily usable by those responsible for military operations. The issue of 'Ryde night illumination diagrams' by the hydrographic department of the Admiralty continued until 1947.

After the war Ryde continued to exercise his general influence over the whole of the scientific work at the GEC laboratories, in which organization he was still active at the time of his death. In 1948 he was elected to fellowship of the Royal Society. He was also a fellow of the Royal Astronomical Society, a fellow of the Institute of Physics, and, for a number of years, played an important part in the affairs of the Royal Institution as chairman of its Davy Faraday committee. He died at Savernake Hospital, Marlborough, on 15 May 1961. His wife survived him.

B. S. COOPER, rev.

Sources R. Whiddington, *Memoirs FRS*, 8 (1962), 105–17 · *The Times* (19 May 1961) · personal knowledge (1981) · *CGPLA Eng. & Wales* (1961)
Likenesses photograph, repro. in Whiddington, *Memoirs FRS*, facing p. 105
Wealth at death £14,945 7s. 7d.: probate, 1961

Ryder. *See also* Rider.

Ryder, Sir Alfred Phillipps (1820–1888), naval officer, born on 27 November 1820, was the seventh son of Henry *Ryder (1777–1836), bishop of Lichfield, and his wife, Sophia, daughter of Thomas March Phillipps of Garendon Park, Leicestershire. He entered the navy in May 1833, passed his examination in July 1839, and in the special competitive course at the Royal Naval College, Portsmouth, won his commission as lieutenant on 20 July 1841. He was then appointed to the frigate *Belvidera* (42 guns), in which he served in the Mediterranean until she was paid off in 1845. On 15 January 1846 he was promoted commander, and in May 1847 was appointed to the steam sloop *Vixen*, on the North America and West Indies station, from which he was promoted on 2 May 1848, for brilliant service at the capture of Fort Serapique on the San Juan River.

From 1853 to 1857 Ryder commanded the frigate *Dauntless* in the channel, and afterwards in the Baltic and the Black Sea during the Crimean War. While in the Baltic, Ryder allowed a prize to escape, and damaged the engines of his ship, earning the wrath of Sir Charles Napier. Napier wanted to court-martial him, but the Admiralty refused to support this course of action. From 1863 to 1866 he was controller of the coastguard, and was promoted rear-admiral on 2 April 1866. He was second in command of the Channel Fleet in 1868–9, and was afterwards naval attaché at Paris. Perhaps the most intelligent advocate of the ram as a major weapon of war, Ryder contributed to the extensive debate on naval tactics and design that dominated the early 1870s. In 1871 he served on the Admiralty committee on designs, and, with George Elliot, submitted a dissenting report, stressing the need to retain sail power and improve seaworthiness.

On 7 May 1872 Ryder became vice-admiral; he was commander-in-chief in China from 1874 to 1877, became admiral on 5 August 1877, and from 1879 to 1882 was

commander-in-chief at Portsmouth. On 24 May 1884 he was nominated a KCB, and on 29 April 1885 was promoted admiral of the fleet. After resigning the Portsmouth command he lived mostly at Torquay, Devon. His health, never robust, was impaired, and he suffered from depression. In April 1888 he went to London for medical treatment, and while taking a trip on the river on 30 April was drowned near Vauxhall pier. He was buried on 5 May at Hambleden, near Henley-on-Thames, Oxfordshire.

Ryder was a man of high attainments, and made persistent exertions to raise the standard of education in the navy. He devoted much of his time on shore to scientific study, and was the author of some pamphlets on professional subjects, including one on a new method of determining distances at sea. A brilliant officer of considerable promise, he was a pioneer in the development of naval doctrine and supported the work of John Laughton, which was based on a combination of historical study and technical analysis.

J. K. LAUGHTON, rev. ANDREW LAMBERT

Sources S. Sandler, *The emergence of the modern capital ship* (1979) · *Admiralty committee on ship designs, 1871* (1872) · A. D. Lambert, *The Crimean War: British grand strategy, 1853–56* (1990) · personal knowledge (1897) · *Journal of the Royal United Service Institution* [various] · P. H. Colomb, *Memoirs of Admiral the Right Honble. Sir Astley Cooper Key* (1898) · *CGPLA Eng. & Wales* (1888)
Archives Hants. RO, corresp. · Harrowby Manuscript Trust, Sandon Hall, Staffordshire, corresp. and papers | BL, letters and reports to Sir Charles Napier, Add. MSS 40024–40025, 40042 · LPL, corresp. relating to Church of England Purity Society
Likenesses wood-engraving (after photograph by Symonds & Son), NPG; repro. in *ILN*, 92 (12 May 1888), 510
Wealth at death £33,992 10s. 3d.: resworn probate, Nov 1888, *CGPLA Eng. & Wales*

Ryder, Charles Henry Dudley (1868–1945), surveyor in India, was born at St Servan, Brittany, on 28 June 1868, the seventh son of Lieutenant-Colonel Spencer Charles Dudley Ryder (1825–1873) and his wife, Julia (d. 1902), daughter of the Revd William Money, chaplain at St Servan. His father was grandson of Nathaniel Ryder, first Baron Harrowby.

From Cheltenham College, Ryder was gazetted in July 1886 to the Royal Engineers. In November 1891, after three years in the Indian public works department, he joined the survey of India. A year later, on 27 December 1892, he married Ida Josephine (1872/3–1948), eldest daughter of Lieutenant-Colonel Edward Evans Grigg of the Indian staff corps. Three daughters were born to them in the old century and three sons in the new.

Between 1898 and 1900, with Henry Rodolph Davies, Ryder surveyed the whole of China's south-western Yunnan province. After mapping more than 1400 miles of new routes, he travelled down the Yangtze (Yangzi) to reach Shanghai in July 1900 in time to participate in the relief of the foreign legations at Peking, who were besieged by the Boxers.

In 1904 Ryder took charge of the survey party accompanying Francis Younghusband's mission to Tibet. He extended the triangulation of India up to Lhasa and then, in September 1904, embarked with Captain C. G. Rawlings and thirty assistants on a survey across Tibet from Gyantse to Gartok and thence back over the Himalayas to Simla. With winter coming on, the expedition was a race against time, impeded by treacherous terrain, extreme cold, and uncertain supplies, but the party reached Simla safely on 11 January 1905, having surveyed the Brahmaputra to its source and mapped the upper Sutlej, the Manasarowar Lake region, and the Gartok branch of the Indus. Back in Europe, Ryder was awarded the patron's medal of the Royal Geographical Society and the silver and gold medals of the Scottish and Paris geographical societies. Younghusband recommended him for the CIE, but he was rewarded instead with the DSO and promotion to major.

In 1907 Ryder became superintendent of the survey of the north-west frontier and in 1913–14 headed the British survey party with the Turco-Persian frontier commission. After a century of international shilly-shallying over the border, the work of the commission proved unexpectedly smooth and good-humoured, something which the leader of the British delegation, Arnold Wilson, attributed partly to the trust that the Russian, Persian, and Turkish commissioners placed in Ryder, permitting him to correct and alter their maps. By 27 October 1914 the commission had demarcated 1180 miles of the frontier from the Persian Gulf to Mount Ararat. Two days later Ryder and Wilson crossed the border into Russia, just hours short of Turkey's entry into the war.

Ryder was created CIE in 1915, and in 1916 became superintendent of the map publication office in Calcutta. In 1917 he returned to the Middle East with the Mesopotamia expedition force and in May 1918, with the rank of colonel, became deputy director of surveys in Baghdad. A year later he was promoted to surveyor-general of India, in which post he remained until his retirement in September 1924. He was made a CB in 1922.

Ryder was of stocky, squarish build, and exuded an air of reliability. His colleagues spoke of him as efficient, dependable, and tactful, an ideal travelling companion. Much of his efficiency stemmed from the good relations he cultivated with his Indian technical staff; he treated them courteously, as like-minded professionals, and in his reports readily acknowledged their expertise.

Ryder died on 13 July 1945 at his home, 85 The Fairway, Aldwick Bay, Bognor Regis, Sussex, survived by his wife, daughters, and youngest son. He was buried on 16 July in Pagham parish church, Sussex. His two elder sons had been killed in the war: Major Lisle Charles Dudley Ryder of the Norfolk regiment, in May 1940, in Belgium, and Major Ernle Terrick Dudley Ryder of the 1st Gurkha rifles, in February 1942, off the coast of Sumatra. Ryder's third son, Robert Edward Dudley *Ryder (1908–1986), captain in the Royal Navy and Conservative MP for Merton and Morden (1950–55), was awarded the VC for his part in the attack on St Nazaire in March 1942.

R. N. RUDMOSE BROWN, *rev.* KATHERINE PRIOR

Sources *India Office List* (1926) · C. G. Rawlings, *The great plateau* (1905) · A. Wilson, *SW Persia: a political officer's diary, 1907–1914* (1941) · P. Landon, *Lhasa*, 2 vols. (1905) · *The Times* (16 July 1945) · Burke, *Peerage* (1959) · ecclesiastical records, BL OIOC · E. S. Skirving, ed., *Cheltenham College register, 1841–1927* (1928) · C. H. D. Ryder, 'Exploration and survey with the Tibet frontier commission, and from Gyangtse to Simla via Gartok', *GJ*, 26 (1905), 369–91 · F. Younghusband, *India and Tibet* (1910)

Likenesses photograph, 1905, RGS · group photograph (British delegation to the Turco-Persian frontier commission, 1913–14), repro. in G. E. Hubbard, *From the Gulf to Ararat* (1916)

Wealth at death £11,919 18s. 5d.: probate, 17 Nov 1945, CGPLA Eng. & Wales

Ryder, Sir Dudley (1691–1756), judge, was born on 4 November 1691, the second son of Richard Ryder (d. 1733), a Cheapside linen draper living at Hackney in Middlesex, and his wife, Elizabeth, daughter of William Marshall of Lincoln's Inn. His paternal grandfather, the Revd Dudley Ryder (d. 1683), was a nonconformist minister in Bedworth, Warwickshire, ejected after the Act of Uniformity. John *Ryder (c.1697–1775), archbishop of Tuam, was a cousin.

Early life and beginnings at the bar, 1691–1730 Ryder followed the usual pattern of education for dissenters, attending a dissenting academy at Hackney before going on to the universities of Edinburgh (where he does not appear in the published list of graduates) and Leiden. It is possible that he was intended originally for the nonconformist ministry, but on 22 June 1713 he was admitted to the Middle Temple, and he began to eat dinners there three years later. His student diary, commencing in 1715, gives a vivid picture of the unstructured regime followed by law students, consisting of desultory reading, attendance in Westminster Hall, and self-help mooting groups, together with the extra-curricular activities typical of young men who aspired to politeness but were tempted by the pleasures of the town. (The edition of the diary published by William Matthews in 1939 omits most of the references to his legal studies.) He was called to the bar on 8 May 1719 and, like most barristers, took work where he could find it, in his case in king's bench and chancery, and on circuit. Even as a student, however, Ryder found equity more congenial than common law because it 'depends less upon precedents and arbitrary laws and more upon good sound reason and sense' (*Diary*, 1715–16, ed. Matthews, p. 429) and by 1728, the year in which his name first appears in the reports, he was concentrating on chancery. No doubt an added attraction was his affinity with the incumbent lord chancellor, Peter, first Baron King, who was also the son of a dissenting tradesman, and who made a point of patronizing young men from nonconformist families. Certainly in 1725, the year when King became chancellor, he migrated (on 26 July) to Lincoln's Inn, where chancery out-of-term sittings were held, and the reports show that he was in good practice there by 1730.

Law officer and parliamentarian, 1733–1754 King may have been the agent for Ryder's introduction into politics. Ryder was brought in for St Germans, a government borough, on a vacancy in March 1733, and he was made solicitor-general in the legal promotions undertaken in November. In the latter month he married Anne, the daughter of Nathaniel Newnham of Streatham, a rich

Sir Dudley Ryder (1691–1756), by James Cranke

West India merchant. In future years she spent much of her time at Bath, but Ryder wrote her letters full of affectionate expressions, and described her as 'the best of women' in his will, made over twenty years later (will, fol. 212r). He transferred to Tiverton at the general election of 1734, and ultimately established a strong family interest there, but he was not mentioned in debates until 9 June 1737, when he spoke briefly in favour of the bill against the provost and city of Edinburgh, arising out of the Porteous riots. He became attorney-general in January 1737, but turned down an offer of the mastership of the rolls in 1738, after his application for an increase in the salary was rejected. He was knighted on 12 May 1740. As the senior law officer he was expected to lead for the government in the introduction of public legislation, but he generally sought to appear as moderate and principled:

> I am sometimes tempted to attack the enemies of the administration in a severe manner, but I check myself in that design. I am more fitted to act the part of candour, mildness, sincerity and good nature and reasoning. My own disposition leads me to this. It will give me more credit in the World. It will better hide my infirmity and want of ability in any respect, and I think my talents are rather better suited to it. It will better, likewise, secure me against enemies, and fall in more with my talents, which are not formed for bustle and controversy, management and design. It is indeed as much the reverse as can well be. I should therefore keep out of all scrapes, all enmities.   (Ryder's diary, 22 Aug 1741, Harrowby MSS)

When aroused Ryder was liable to give severe judgments in defence of the establishment, however. In December 1740 he spoke sternly against a libel which had been distributed at the door of the Commons, arguing that they needed no assistance 'from the informations of these officious instructors, who ought … rather to be taught by some parliamentary censure to know their own station, than to be encouraged to neglect their own employments, for the sake of directing their governors' (Cobbett, *Parl. hist.*, 11.887–8). In March 1741 he made several contributions to debates on the Seamen's Bill, opposing the increase of wages for volunteers, and defending impressment as 'not only founded on immemorial custom, which makes it part of the common law, but is likewise established by our statutes' (ibid., 12.69). And he was certainly loyal to the government, even making a 'glorious speech' defending Sir Robert Walpole in January 1742 (Walpole, *Corr.*, 17.297). On 28 April 1744 he moved for the suspension of the Habeas Corpus Act for two months on the grounds of the threat of invasion by the Pretender, James Stuart, saying:

> fully convinced as he was of the importance of that invaluable law towards the preservation of our liberties, he should as soon have consented to cut off his right hand, as stand up to make that motion, if he was not fully persuaded that it was absolutely necessary to secure all the invaluable blessings we enjoyed.   (Cobbett, *Parl. hist.*, 13.671–2)

And on 3 May 1744 he explained at length the Lords' amendments to the bill for making it high treason to correspond with the Pretender, which centred upon attainting his sons, defending the practice by which traitors' estates were forfeit to the crown with arguments from civil law authorities and medieval history. The younger Philip Yorke (later second earl of Hardwicke) said it was one of the best speeches on the government side in 'a warm and long debate' (ibid., 13.857). Indeed, Ryder undertook this task in the Commons as the mouthpiece of Yorke's father, Lord Hardwicke, who was the author of the amendments, and for the remainder of his career he appears normally to have acted on the chancellor's instructions, as a loyal functionary of the government. But he tended to be over-conscientious: while admitting his 'singular goodness and integrity', Horace Walpole said that 'he wearied the audience by the multiplicity of his arguments; resembling the Physician who ordered a medicine to be composed of all the simples in a meadow, as there must be some of them at least that would be proper' (Walpole, *Memoirs*, 1.123–4).

In December 1747 Ryder spoke against the bill to prohibit the sale of insurance to French ships during the war, evincing a characteristically eighteenth-century attitude towards warfare, wherein armed hostility should not be allowed to interrupt profitable trade with the enemy; however, the bill passed. He was more plausible in May 1751, when he made a good speech in support of the Regency Bill occasioned by the death of Frederick, prince of Wales, wherein he demonstrated considerable knowledge of medieval and Tudor history, arguing the dangers of establishing a sole regent. On 14 May 1753, in what was arguably his best speech, he moved for the committal of Hardwicke's Marriage Bill, revealing traces of his dissenting background while insisting on the positive sovereignty of parliament. Arguing for the nullification of clandestine marriages, he condemned the notion that a marriage solemnized by a priest could not be annulled because it was 'firmly established by the divine law', and exclaimed, 'Thank God! We have in this age got the better of this, as well we have of a great many other superstitious opinions', adding that:

> primitive and pure Christianity always was consistent with common sense; but additions have been since made to it, many of which are inconsistent with common sense, and of these I take the old opinion relating to marriage to be one; for I think nothing can be more inconsistent with common sense than to say, that the supreme legislature of a society cannot put contracts of marriage, as well as every other contract, under what regulations they think most conducive to the good of that society.　(Cobbett, *Parl. hist.*, 15.6)

This was his last major speech in parliament. Later he said he thought the bill was justified, but he was so 'zealous' in it because he supported Hardwicke against attack from Henry Fox (Ryder's diary, 13 April 1756, Harrowby MSS).

Ryder was not highly experienced in crown law, and although he was a law officer for over a decade, his name is not mentioned in the state trials before 1746, when he conducted the proceedings against the Jacobite rebels who were tried in London. Most of the ordinary cases were so straightforward that the crown counsel had little to do, but Ryder answered some legal points raised by the defence ably enough. The case against Simon Fraser, eleventh Lord Lovat, tried by impeachment in March 1747, was more complex, because Lovat had not appeared for the Pretender in person, but was accused of secretly aiding him over several years. Ryder appeared as the principal manager for the Commons, and made a long speech, adroitly summarizing the evidence. He explained why this prosecution was not undertaken by indictment in the usual way, affirming the need for 'the people in general' to take a general view of the rebellion:

> and learn this certain truth, which should be imprinted, in everlasting characters, on the mind of every Briton; that there is no effectual security against those determined and perpetual enemies, but in a vigilant and firm union of honest men.　(*State trials*, 18.577)

He also countered all Lovat's frequent objections to the admissibility of the evidence with cogent legal arguments, and was accused of 'great warmness' by the defendant, who was found guilty unanimously (ibid., 18.819).

In some cases, however, Ryder seems to have gone beyond professional duty. In 1749 he resisted the discharge of a man who had been committed on the warrant of a secretary of state and held for two years without trial on suspicion of treason, although he admitted there was no evidence against him (*R. v. Fitzgerald*). And in July 1752 he failed to secure a verdict in the case of a bookseller, John or William Owen, whom he prosecuted on behalf of the Commons for selling a pamphlet reflecting on their committal of Alexander Murray for contempt. The defence insisted that it was not sufficient in a case of libel merely to prove that Owen had printed and sold the book, and that the jury should consider that seditious intent was not proved. Against the chief justice's summing-up they duly returned a verdict of not guilty and stuck to it, although Ryder tried to persuade them to find only on the fact of publication, which would have entailed a guilty verdict under current judicial interpretations. He suffered further embarrassment on leaving the court. In his opening address he had said, 'The House of Commons are the good people of England, being the representatives of the people. The rest are what?—nothing—unless it be a mob?' (*State trials*, 18.1221), and after the trial he was abused by the mob, becoming the butt of a popular song:

> Mr. Attorney's grim wig, though awfully big,
> No more shall frighten the nation;
> W'ell write what we think, and to Liberty drink,
> And defy his *eggs-off*. Information.
> (*London Magazine*, 1753, in Campbell, *Chief Justices*, 2.233)

Chief justice, 1754–1756　*R. v. Owen* was the last major trial that Ryder conducted as attorney-general. He had been offered the rolls again in December 1749, and almost accepted on the vague promise of a peerage, but his wife intervened, being 'much against my acceptance of this without additional salary, and [she] thinks my sleepy disposition will make me unfit for the office' (Ryder's diary, 18 Dec 1749, Harrowby MSS). By 1752, having been in office for nearly twenty years, he was thinking of retirement with 'a peerage and some place, which is but reasonable considering my long service' (ibid., 1 June, 1752). However, the chief justiceship of king's bench became vacant with the death of Sir William Lee in April 1754, and Ryder was appointed on 2 May. During his brief tenure of office he did not preside at any major state trials, although he took his turn with the other judges in trying criminal cases at the Old Bailey and on circuit. As a chancery specialist he was concerned about his competence in common law, but studied to refresh his memory, and seems to have given general satisfaction, without distinguishing himself. He desperately wanted to be a peer, and was supported in his pretensions by the bar, but at his appointment the proposal was put off by the king on the grounds that it would create a precedent. He persevered, and by 1756 the prospect had improved: the duke of Newcastle wanted to strengthen the government's debating capacity in the Lords, and Hardwicke admitted he needed assistance in hearing appeals. Ultimately the prize eluded him, however: he contracted a fever and died suddenly on 25 May 1756, probably at his home in Streatham, Surrey, after the king had authorized a warrant creating him Baron Ryder of Harrowby, but before the process was complete. An attempt to execute the letters patent for the barony in the name of his son came to nothing.

Despite his consciousness of his achievements as a leading lawyer and parliamentarian, Ryder's diaries reveal a man of little self-confidence who struggled to maintain his public reputation. He realized his success depended upon making himself useful, and studied to ingratiate himself with social superiors, sometimes acting against his better judgement. For example, in 1748–9, although reluctant, he served Hardwicke and Newcastle by filing two *ex officio* informations against the vice-chancellor of Oxford University for not proceeding against a Jacobite demonstration, even though the evidence was insufficient, and the prosecutions were maintained only 'for the vindication of the government' (Oldham, 168). He also tended to be governed by his wife, who seems to have been avaricious. Indeed he was accused of pressing his pregnant sister-in-law into making a will favourable to her family, contrary to the interests of her husband, by leaving all her marriage portion and interest thereupon to her brothers and sisters.

Ryder could not avoid some scrapes and humiliations, but he struck most of his contemporaries as a man of honesty and integrity. He did his best for his family, and died possessed of a great estate, which he had valued in 1752 at about £110,000 in cash, stocks, securities and £3000 a year in land. His will was a remarkably elaborate document, even for a successful lawyer: he not only entailed his real estate in the usual way and provided many individual legacies, but also left detailed limitations for the provision of jointures and portions which might be paid out of it by his heirs. He was buried at Grantham in Lincolnshire, near the site of Harrowby, his principal estate, with the grand monument for which he had allowed 'a sum not exceeding three hundred pounds' (will, fol. 214r–v). His shorthand diaries have proved to be a valuable source for historians.

Ryder's only son, **Nathaniel Ryder**, first Baron Harrowby (1735–1803), was born on 3 July 1735, was admitted to Clare College, Cambridge, in 1753, and graduated MA in 1756. He was MP for Tiverton from 1756. In parliament he normally supported the government, and spoke occasionally. On 22 January 1762, at Lambeth, Surrey, he married Elizabeth (*bap.* 1739, *d.* 1804), daughter and coheir of Richard *Terrick, bishop successively of Peterborough and London, and his wife Tabitha, *née* Stainforth. He applied for a peerage as early as 1766, and on 20 May 1776 was created Baron Harrowby. Like his father, he kept a diary, and although his career did not reach comparable heights to his father's, despite the consolation of a peerage, the diary provides some insight into the parliamentary politics of the 1760s and 1770s. Harrowby used the same shorthand in his diary as did his father, which has been fully deciphered only by late twentieth-century historians.

Harrowby died at Bath on 20 June 1803, and was buried in Bath Abbey on 25 June. He was survived by his wife, his daughter Elizabeth (*d.* 1830), and his three sons, Dudley *Ryder, first earl of Harrowby (1762–1847), Richard *Ryder (1766–1832), and Henry *Ryder (1777–1836). Another daughter, Anne, had died in 1801.　　　DAVID LEMMINGS

Sources Cobbett, *Parl. hist.*, vols. 10–15 · *State trials*, vol. 18 · D. Ryder, diaries and correspondence, Sandon Hall, Staffordshire, Harrowby MSS · *DNB* · E. Foss, *Biographia juridica: a biographical dictionary of the judges of England … 1066–1870* (1870) · R. R. Sedgwick, 'Ryder, Dudley', HoP, *Commons, 1715–54* · John, Lord Campbell, *The lives of the chief justices of England*, 3rd edn, 4 vols. (1874) · will, PRO, PROB 11/823, sig. 177 · ER, vols. 2, 24, 94, 95 · J. Brooke, 'Ryder, Nathaniel', HoP, *Commons, 1754–90* · *The diary of Dudley Ryder, 1715–1716*, ed. W. Matthews (1939) · J. Oldham, 'The work of Ryder and Murray as law officers of the crown', *Legal record and historical reality: proceedings of the eighth British legal history conference*, ed. T. G. Watkin (1989), 157–73 · H. Walpole, *Memoirs of the reign of King George the Second*, ed. Lord Holland, 2nd edn, 3 vols. (1847) · Walpole, *Corr.*, vol. 17 · D. Lemmings, *Professors of the law* (2000) · D. Lemmings, *Gentlemen and barristers: the inns of court and the English bar, 1680–1730* (1990) · L. Way, letters, Bucks. RLSS, Way MSS D/W/77/1–27 · Holdsworth, *Eng. law*, vol. 12 · Sainty, *Judges* · W. P. Baildon, ed., *The records of the Honorable Society of Lincoln's Inn: admissions*, 1 (1896) · Sainty, *King's counsel* · private information (2004) [P. D. G. Thomas] · GEC, *Peerage* · Burke, *Peerage* (1999)

Archives Bodl. Oxf., notes on European history · L. Cong., letter-book, MS 818 [copy] · Lincoln's Inn, London, Harrowby MSS, diaries and legal notes [transcript] · Lincoln's Inn, London, shorthand legal notebooks, incl. political and parliamentary material · Sandon Hall, Staffordshire, Harrowby Manuscript Trust, corresp. and family and legal papers; shorthand diary [transcript] | BL, opinions of lawyers, Egerton MS 1074 · BL, letters to first earl of Hardwicke, Add. MSS 35447–35591, *passim* · BL, corresp. with duke of Newcastle, Add. MSS 32699–32858, *passim*

Likenesses H. Cheere, relief portrait medallion, St Wulfram's Church, Grantham · J. Cranke, oils, Lincoln's Inn, London · J. Cranke, portrait, Sandon Hall, Staffordshire [*see illus.*] · J. Faber junior, mezzotint (after J. Cranke), BM

Wealth at death very large personal estate in money, stocks, and securities (nearly £110,000 in 1752); also over £3000 p.a. in real estate

Ryder, Dudley, first earl of Harrowby (1762–1847), politician, was born in the parish of St George, Hanover Square, London, on 22 December 1762, the eldest of the three sons of Nathaniel *Ryder (1735–1803), member of parliament for Tiverton from 1756 until he was created Baron Harrowby on 20 May 1776 [*see under* Ryder, Sir Dudley (1691–1756)], and his wife, Elizabeth (*bap.* 1739, *d.* 1804), daughter of Richard *Terrick, bishop of Peterborough (1757–64) and London (1764–77). Dudley Ryder was educated privately before going on to Harrow School (1774–9) and St John's College, Cambridge (1779–82). At the general election of 1784, three months after coming of age, he was returned to parliament for Tiverton, the family borough, where he sat undisturbed throughout his Commons career. He showed promise in debate and attached himself devotedly to Pitt, the premier, who became his personal friend and political patron. In August 1789 Pitt forced Ryder's appointment as under-secretary at the Foreign Office on the secretary of state, the duke of Leeds, who would have preferred someone of his own choosing. He had to resign after six months on account of doubts about the legality of two under-secretaries from the same department sitting in the Commons, but he was handsomely compensated with appointments as comptroller of the household and a commissioner of the Board of Control and admission to the privy council (3 March 1790). That month he was made a member of the Board of Trade, and in October 1790 he was promoted to be its vice-president. He remained in that place for eleven years and in 1791, when he gave up his household and India board offices, became also a joint paymaster-general. In the summer of 1800 he exchanged this post for the treasurership of the navy, having declined the mastership of the Royal Mint a year previously. Ryder, who chaired the finance committee in 1791 and the coin committee in 1800,

Dudley Ryder, first earl of Harrowby (1762–1847), by Thomas Phillips, 1810

showed considerable aptitude for routine business. In the sessions of 1795–6 and 1800–01 he was responsible for steering through the Commons measures to deal with corn scarcities. As a member of the 1797 secret finance committee, he wrote a report on the Treasury and worked closely with Pitt in assessing the implications of the committee's findings. Beyond his departmental brief he was an effective and combative debater, who readily defended the government's repressive domestic policies and conduct of the war. He was, however, favourable to abolition of the slave trade and to Catholic emancipation. He was Pitt's second in his duel with Tierney on 27 May 1798. On 30 July 1795 he had married Lady Susan Leveson-Gower (1772–1838), daughter of Granville Leveson-*Gower, the first marquess of Stafford, with whom he had four sons and five daughters. His first son, who succeeded him, was Dudley *Ryder (1798–1882).

At Pitt's earnest request, Ryder remained in office under Addington, although he refused to take the foreign secretaryship. A serious illness in the summer of 1801, which seemed at one point likely to be fatal, prompted him to surrender his places in the autumn. He grew increasingly uneasy with the ministry's feebleness and, anxious for Pitt's reinstatement, defected from it in May 1803. On his father's death on 20 June 1803, he succeeded to the peerage and the family's Staffordshire estates at Sandon, near Stone. On Pitt's return to power in May 1804 Harrowby became foreign secretary, but an accident in December, when he sustained head injuries after falling downstairs at the Foreign Office, compelled him to resign. He had recovered by July 1805, when Pitt made him chancellor of the duchy of Lancaster. In November Pitt sent him on a special mission to Berlin in a bid to forge a new continental coalition against France. His nerves soon gave way and he begged to be recalled, but Pitt kept him steady and he was able to effect an alliance with Prussia before Bonaparte's victory at Austerlitz put an end to the project. He resigned with his colleagues after Pitt's death and did not take office in the duke of Portland's tory administration until July 1809, when he was appointed president of the Board of Control. On 19 July that year he was created earl of Harrowby. From November 1809 he sat in Perceval's cabinet without holding office until June 1812, when on the formation of Lord Liverpool's ministry he was made lord president of the council. He had a deep interest in the church, and on 9 March 1813 he introduced to the Lords a bill to provide for stipendiary curates, which became law on 20 July (53 Geo. III c. 149). In April 1815 he and William Wellesley Pole went on a brief special mission to Brussels to confer with the latter's brother the duke of Wellington at army headquarters. In 1819 he chaired the Lords committee on the currency and prepared its report. It was at his London house in Grosvenor Square that the Cato Street conspirators planned to massacre the cabinet in February 1820, when the plot was betrayed to him. He remained in place under Canning in April 1827 but retired on the formation of Lord Goderich's administration in August. On Goderich's first resignation in December 1827 he declined the premiership, as he later claimed to have done twice previously. He was never again in office, but became a member of the judicial committee of the privy council in 1833.

Harrowby made his last and arguably most significant political exertion as joint leader, with Lord Wharncliffe (whose son John Stuart Wortley had married his daughter Georgiana in 1826), of the tory waverer peers during the reform crisis of 1831–2. He decided to oppose the second reading of the Grey ministry's bill, and did so in an accomplished speech on 4 October 1831, pleading in effect for a delay in order that a compromise might be reached, while indicating his willingness to support the enfranchisement of large towns and an enhancement of the county representation at the expense of rotten boroughs. He then tried to promote agreement on a modified measure. He, his eldest son, and Wharncliffe began negotiations with the government, the bishops, and leading figures in the City, but their efforts had failed by the end of November 1831. In January 1832 Harrowby drafted a circular to opposition peers outlining the waverers' preferred policy of supporting the second reading of the revised bill in order to avoid a mass creation of peers to force it through, and of then using their numerical superiority to secure amendments in committee. On 26 March and 10 April he stated the waverers' case in the Lords and on 13 April he voted for the second reading, which was carried by 184 votes to 175. He and his associates reluctantly acquiesced in the opposition leaders' decision to vote for postponement of the borough disfranchisement clauses, failing to realize that ministers would call their bluff by resigning when they were defeated on this on 7 May. In the ensuing brief crisis Harrowby refused to try to form a tory ministry to carry a modified reform. The failure of Wellington's attempt to do so and the return to power of the Grey ministry marked the ultimate failure of Harrowby's efforts (Brock, 240–41, 243–7, 260–62, 271–3, 275–7, 279, 281, 283, 285–6, 289–90, 294). He took little part in politics thereafter.

In 1801 Lord Glenbervie had this to say of him:

Ryder is … a man of parts, and has certainly a good deal of information, and he … means to be a good sort of man. But his manner is not advantageous to him. His little circular pursed-in mouth, a sort of ruddiness and smoothness of face, and a weak short kind of articulation, make him appear both in private and in public what has been called *missey*, and there appears to be a certain quickness in his temper which, when he fails in venting it in a species of captious smartness or repartee, renders him what by another familiar expression is called *miffy*. (*Diaries of Sylvester Douglas*, 1.193)

Liverpool, his former chief at the Board of Trade, wrote in 1804:

Few know Lord Harrowby better than myself. He has a very sharp understanding, but a wretched mind, or a very distempered body which operates on his mind … This last circumstance disqualifies him for business … I have heard that he has a bad temper; but this temper never showed itself to me, so that I know nothing of it. Though reasonably rich, he is interested. (*Journal and Correspondence of … Auckland*, 4.226)

Henry Fox felt in 1824 that he:

would be a more agreeable man, if nature had benevolently given him a larger mouth. His knowledge is great, his quickness lively, and his opinions just and moderate. His articulation is too rapid and precise, and his temper is peevish. (*Journal of … Fox*, 198)

His sister-in-law Lady Harriet Leveson-Gower described him in 1810 as:

certainly agreeable and well informed, and disposed to communicate his knowledge in the most pleasant manner, without any pretension or display; but … the whole thing is too *tight*, and it would improve him to go a great deal into a warm bath. He would come out so relaxed and upon a more enlarged scale, which would be an unspeakable improvement to both body and mind. (*Private Correspondence*, 2.361)

Greville, who noted that despite his bad health he had lived to be the last survivor of his political generation, wrote after his death at Sandon Hall on 26 December 1847:

He was at the top of the second-rate men, always honourable and straightforward, generally liberal and enlightened, greatly esteemed and respected … He was remarkably well informed … but his precise manner and tart disposition prevented his being agreeable in society. He was very religious, very generous, and a man of the strictest integrity in private and in public life. (*Greville Memoirs*, 6.1)

D. R. FISHER

Sources D. R. Fisher, 'Ryder, Dudley', HoP, *Commons, 1790–1820* · M. Brock, *The Great Reform Act* (1973) · J. Ehrman, *The younger Pitt*, 3: *The consuming struggle* (1996) · *The diaries of Sylvester Douglas (Lord Glenbervie)*, ed. F. Bickley, 1 (1928), 193 · *The journal and correspondence of William, Lord Auckland*, ed. [G. Hogge], 4 vols. (1861–2), vol. 4, p. 226 · *The journal of the Hon. Henry Edward Fox*, ed. earl of Ilchester [G. S. Holland Fox-Strangways] (1923), 198 · *Lord Granville Leveson Gower: private correspondence, 1781 to 1821*, ed. Castalia, Countess Granville [C. R. Leveson-Gower], 2nd edn, 2 (1916), 361 · *The Greville memoirs, 1814–1860*, ed. L. Strachey and R. Fulford, 8 vols. (1938),

vol. 6, p. 1 · D. Ryder, *Autobiography* (privately printed, 1891) · D. Ryder, first earl of Harrowby, *Family reminiscences, etc.* (privately printed, 1891) · GEC, *Peerage*
Archives Hants. RO, family corresp. · Sandon Hall, Staffordshire, Harrowby Manuscript Trust, corresp. and papers; corresp. relating to Tiverton | All Souls Oxf., corresp. with Charles Richard Vaughan · BL, corresp. with Lord Aberdeen, Add. MS 43230 · BL, corresp. with Lord Grenville, Add. MS 58961 · BL, corresp. with first and second earls of Liverpool, Add. MSS 38226–38354, 38472, 38565–38580, *passim* · BL, corresp. with Sir Arthur Paget, Add. MS 48390 · BL, corresp. with Sir Robert Peel, Add. MSS 40254–40422, *passim* · PRO, letters to William Pitt, PRO 30/8 · PRO NIre., corresp. with Lord Castlereagh · Sheff. Arch., letters to Lord Wharncliffe
Likenesses T. Phillips, portrait, 1810, priv. coll. [*see illus.*] · J. S. Agar, stipple, 1813 (after T. Phillips), BM, NPG; repro. in *The British gallery of contemporary portraits* (1814) · R. Dighton, coloured etching caricature, pubd 1818, NPG · J. Doyle, pen and pencil caricature, 1832, BM · H. B. Hall, stipple, 1837 (after Meunier), BM, NPG; repro. in H. T. Ryall, *Portraits of eminent conservatives and statesmen* [in pts, 1836–46] · J. Doyle, pen and chalk caricature, BM · G. Hayter, group portrait, oils (*The trial of Queen Caroline, 1820*), NPG · K. A. Hickel, group portrait, oils (*The House of Commons, 1793*), NPG
Wealth at death under £60,000: PRO, death duty registers, IR 26/1805/155

Ryder, Dudley, second earl of Harrowby (1798–1882), politician, was born at the army pay office, Whitehall, London, on 19 May 1798, the eldest son of Dudley *Ryder, first earl of Harrowby (1762–1847), and his wife, Lady Susan Leveson-Gower (1772–1838), sixth daughter of the first marquess of Stafford. He was known until his father's death in 1847 as Viscount Sandon. As a child, Sandon had a severe stammer, which caused his parents to send him to a variety of private schools and tutors, including John Thelwall, the radical turned elocutionist (HoP, *Commons*). By the time he was eighteen his stammer had largely gone. He matriculated from Christ Church, Oxford, on 19 October 1816, and in 1819 gained a double first-class degree, the first hereditary peer to do so. He graduated BA on 10 February 1820, MA on 21 June 1832, and was created DCL on 5 July 1848. Among his personal friends at Oxford were Edward Stanley (afterwards fourteenth earl of Derby), Henry Labouchere (afterwards Lord Taunton), Lord Ossington, and Lord Francis Egerton (afterwards Lord Ellesmere). In 1819, while still an undergraduate, he was elected for the family borough of Tiverton. He was re-elected in 1820, 1826, and 1830. On 15 September 1823, at the British embassy in Bern, he married Frances Stuart (1801–1859), fourth daughter of John Stuart, first marquess of Bute, and his second wife, Frances, *née* Coutts. She was a striking beauty. They had four sons and two daughters.

In 1827 Sandon was appointed a lord of the Admiralty in Lord Liverpool's administration, but resigned next year, believing that the duke of Wellington, who then became premier, would oppose Catholic emancipation. Though a Conservative, he held, like his father, many liberal opinions. He voted for the inquiry into the civil list which overturned the Wellington administration (1830). But on 18 December in the same year he again accepted office, as secretary to the India board. He voted for the Reform Bill on 20 April 1831, but resigned as secretary to the board a few days later. Despite this resignation, his reforming position was unacceptable to his constituents and he did not stand for Tiverton in 1831, but was returned instead for Liverpool at a by-election in October 1831 and again at the general election of 1832, being supported there by the Gladstone family and the West India interest. He thus moved from a backwater into the mainstream of commercial politics. He supported the Reform Bill 'as a measure of peace' (Lord Sandon, *Address to the Electors of Liverpool*, 1834). His election in 1832 was the subject of an unsuccessful petition (W. E. Gladstone's maiden speech being made in Sandon's support), and his re-election in 1835, 1837, and 1841 (when he defeated Lord Palmerston) was always closely contested. His fellow Liverpool MP was first William Ewart (a Liberal), then, from 1837, Cresswell Cresswell (a fellow tory).

In the 1832 parliament Sandon represented the claims to compensation of the West India planters as the whigs ended slavery there. He proposed the loyal address on the king's speech in 1835 and was appointed commissioner for inquiring into punishments in the army, a subject then the focus of much reforming interest. Sandon began to move in the Peel circle, attending social occasions at Drayton (Peel's house, not far from the Harrowby estate in Staffordshire). He became friendly with Gladstone, sharing some of his religious as well as his political interests and co-operating with him in the campaign for a diocesan system of education and in the Anglican agitation against Russell's educational proposals in 1839. In 1840–41 Sandon was privy to the party meetings which culminated in the defeat of the whig government by an amendment which he moved on the sugar duties on 7 May 1841, the precursor to the government's defeat in the vote of confidence on 5 June 1841.

Sandon might well have expected office in Peel's government of 1841. But he remained on the back benches, from which he supported the prime minister in his disputes with his tory followers. Sandon supported the Maynooth grant, though a strong protestant, and the increasingly free-trade budgets of Peel and Gladstone. He was considered for the Board of Trade on Gladstone's resignation in January 1845, but declined it fearing constituency opposition to his support for the Maynooth grant. He voted with the government on the vital vote to repeal the corn laws on 15 May 1846. He did not stand at the election of 1847, and on his father's death on 26 December 1847 he succeeded to the title. In the Lords he was seen as a bridge between the Peelites and the tories and in 1852 he acted as a mediator between the two on free trade.

During the Crimean War, Harrowby was strongly pro-war, and began to distance himself from the Peelites, though Gladstone made him one of the commissioners for Oxford University under the 1854 act. When the Peelites left the government, he entered it, becoming Palmerston's chancellor of the duchy of Lancaster on 31 March 1855 and being sworn of the privy council. He was chancellor until 5 December 1855, when he became lord privy seal. He strongly supported Palmerston's conduct of the war and of the peace. The standing committee of the cabinet on the conduct of the war, set up at his suggestion, was an important innovation. In 1857, however, his health declined and forced him to resign office on 3 February 1858. He was given the Garter on 28 June 1859 on Palmerston's return to office.

Harrowby's chief public interest became the established church. He was a firm but moderate evangelical and a friend of Lord Shaftesbury. He served on the ecclesiastical commission from 1847 to 1880. He moved in June 1869 the rejection in the Lords of Gladstone's bill to disestablish the Church of Ireland, his motion and the consequent amendments leading to a wrangle, eventually resolved, between the two houses. In 1880, when the Liberals returned to power, Harrowby acted as mediator on the vexed question of the Burials Bill, the eventual compromise being partly of his making. Harrowby was a member of various royal commissions, on Maynooth (as chairman 1853–5), ritual, and the clergy. He was a governor of the Charterhouse and of King's College, London. He was active in his locality as a magistrate in Staffordshire and Gloucestershire and took a keen interest in prison reform. As a speaker, he was 'solid, sensible, and reasonable, remarkable for independent thought and felicity of expression, without attempting oratorical display' (*DNB*). He was quite active in the area of science, being elected to the Royal Society on 24 November 1853 and frequently attending it; he was president of the British Association in 1854 for its meeting at Liverpool. He was one of the early members of the Geographical and Statistical societies and was president of the Royal Society for the Prevention of Cruelty to Animals. On his estates he was known as a reforming landowner and as a promoter of county agricultural societies, being president of that in Staffordshire.

Harrowby was a cultivated man who spoke good French and Italian. In his later years he lived a good deal in Rome, where he became something of a connoisseur of art. He died at his seat, Sandon Hall, Stone, Staffordshire, on 18 November 1882 and was buried at Sandon on 23 November. His first son having died at birth, he was succeeded by his second, Dudley Francis Stuart *Ryder (1831–1900).

Having overcome considerable youthful disability, Harrowby might have expected to have played a greater part in high political life than he did; his absence of flamboyance perhaps disadvantaged him among the Peelites, though it was the virtue which, rather too late, made him a useful member of Palmerston's cabinet.

H. C. G. MATTHEW

Sources DNB · GEC, *Peerage* · *The Times* (21 Nov 1882) · *Morning Post* (21 Nov 1882) · *Staffordshire Advertiser* (25 Nov 1882) · Gladstone, *Diaries* · N. Gash, *Sir Robert Peel: the life of Sir Robert Peel after 1830* (1972) · S. G. Checkland, *The Gladstones: a family biography, 1764–1851* (1971) · P. A. Symonds, 'Ryder, Dudley', HoP, *Commons* · A. Aspinall, ed., *Three early nineteenth-century diaries* (1952) [extracts from Le Marchant, E. J. Littleton, Baron Hatherton, and E. Law, earl of Ellenborough] · D. Ryder, second earl of Harrowby, *Reminiscences* (privately printed, 1891) · D. Ryder, first earl of Harrowby, *Family reminiscences, etc.* (privately printed, 1891) · J. Wolffe, *The protestant crusade in Great Britain, 1829–1860* (1991) · *CGPLA Eng. & Wales* (1883) ·

P. J. Waller, *Democracy and sectarianism: a political and social history of Liverpool, 1868–1939* (1981)

Archives Hants. RO, family corresp. • Sandon Hall, Staffordshire, Harrowby Manuscript Trust, corresp. and papers; corresp. relating to Tiverton | BL, corresp. with Lord Aberdeen, Add. MSS 43241–43252 • BL, corresp. with W. E. Gladstone, Add. MSS 44354–44527 • BL, corresp. with Sir Robert Peel, Add. MSS 40412–40585 • Bodl. Oxf., corresp. with Sir Thomas Phillipps • Keele University Library, letters to Sneyd family • LPL, letters to A. C. Tait • Lpool RO, letters to fourteenth earl of Derby

Likenesses Ape [C. Pellegrini], lithograph, repro. in *VF* (1871), 3, pl. 81 • G. Hayter, group portrait, oils (*The House of Commons, 1833*), NPG • F. C. Lewis, stipple (after J. Slater), BM • E. Richmond, portrait, Sandon Hall, Staffordshire • H. Robinson, stipple and line engraving, NPG • carte-de-visite, NPG

Wealth at death £49,510 9s. 7d.: probate, 17 Jan 1883, *CGPLA Eng. & Wales*

Ryder, Dudley Francis Stuart, **third earl of Harrowby** (1831–1900), politician, the second son of Dudley *Ryder, second earl of Harrowby (1798–1882), and Lady Frances Stuart, fourth daughter of John Stuart, first marquess of Bute, was born at Brighton on 16 January 1831. He was educated at Harrow School and the University of Oxford, where he matriculated from Christ Church on 31 May 1849, graduated BA in 1853 with a pass degree, and proceeded MA in 1878. On leaving the university Viscount Sandon, as he was styled from 1847 until 1882, toured the East with his college friend Henry Herbert, later fourth earl of Carnarvon, visiting Syria and Lebanon (see H. H. M. Herbert, *Recollections of the Druses of the Lebanon*, 1860). On his return to England he did garrison duty as captain in the 2nd Staffordshire militia regiment during the period of the Crimean War and the Indian mutiny. He entered parliament in 1856, being returned (30 May) for Lichfield as a supporter of Lord Palmerston (whose cabinet his father soon entered), and gained experience of public life as private secretary to Henry Labouchere (afterwards Lord Taunton) at the Colonial Office. Defeated at Stafford at a by-election in August 1860, he remained without a seat until 1868, when he was returned (19 November) as third member for Liverpool (his father's former constituency), which seat he held until his father's death in 1882. He was a member of the select committees on the Hudson's Bay Company (1857) and the Euphrates valley (1871–2), and continued throughout life to devote much time and attention to the study of imperial and colonial questions. On 3 October 1861 he married Lady Mary Frances (1832–1917), daughter of Brownlow Cecil, second marquess of Exeter, and his wife, Isabella, *née* Poyntz; they had no children.

Sandon's election for Lichfield associated him with a strong tradition of urban Conservatism, to which he responded. He came 'closer than anyone in the Conservative party to embodying the Disraelian ideal of a socially-conscious aristocracy' (Smith, 124). He supported the presence of some working men in the Commons, but he had a clear view of the trusteeship of the aristocracy. He played a part in what became known as the New Social Alliance (between aristocracy and people) in 1871. From the start of his time in politics he had stressed the importance of education—not usually a Conservative political priority—and

Dudley Francis Stuart Ryder, third earl of Harrowby (1831–1900), by London Stereoscopic Co., 1885?

he was a member of the first London school board, taking an active part in it both as chairman of the statistical committee and as a firm but even-handed supporter of voluntary schools and religious instruction. He was a member of the National Society and the National Education Union and a supporter of compulsory education, largely on the grounds that this would secure the position of the voluntary schools and remove the need for school boards in the country areas. He attempted to reverse Liberal legislation on endowed schools. His appointment in 1874 as Disraeli's vice-president of the council thus followed his natural development; he was sworn of the privy council but he was not a member of the cabinet. He noted in his diary that he and Richard Cross 'are the people in fact who brought the Govt. into power' (Shannon, 188). He soon urged upon a sceptical cabinet the importance of compulsory education and of religious education. Despite acrimonious difficulties with the lord president, the duke of Richmond, in the course of which he threatened to resign, he played a part in drafting the Education Bill of 1876, which excluded his religious educational ideas and his own proposals for compulsory education but made a move towards indirect compulsion. Derby thought his conduct at this time showed 'his weakness and narrowness of brain: though he is assiduous and I believe accurate in business' (Vincent, 182). The bill passed, setting up school attendance committees. Sandon did not take his ideas further. Richmond was keen to remove his subordinate from his department. Sandon was offered but declined the Admiralty and the Irish secretaryship (giving family reasons for being unable to live in Ireland). Anxious about his constituents' opinion, he requested an announcement that he was declining offers and not being passed over. On 4 April 1878 he was moved to the Board of Trade, without initial cabinet membership, though it quickly became available; he held the post for the rest of the government. His view that the agricultural depression was transient was not shared by the electorate at the 1880 general election. As well as the trade depression, Sandon found himself dealing with the controversial question of the merchant navy and the conditions of its seamen, but made no significant progress with it before the fall of the government. During the 1874–80 government he played some part in the allocation of ecclesiastical patronage; like his father he was a moderate evangelical.

On his father's death in 1882 Sandon became earl of Harrowby. He returned to office as lord privy seal in Lord Salisbury's minority government of 1885–6 (which he accepted not realizing that it carried no salary) and was a member of the royal commission on education appointed in January 1886. Like his friend Carnarvon, he inclined to some form of distinct representative government for Ireland, but he opposed Gladstone's home-rule proposals. He made it clear to Salisbury that he wished to retire from government and he was not considered for office when Salisbury formed his second government in July 1886. That year he became president of the British and Foreign Bible Society and representative of the Lichfield diocese in the laymen's house of convocation. He was first chairman of Staffordshire county council in 1888, but his health declined and in later years he suffered from chronic bronchitis, from which he died at his seat, Sandon Hall, Staffordshire, on 26 March 1900; he was buried at Sandon on 30 March. Dying childless, he was succeeded as fourth earl by his only brother, Henry Dudley Ryder (1836–1900), who died on board his yacht at Algiers nine months later.

H. C. G. MATTHEW

Sources GEC, *Peerage* • P. Smith, *Disraelian Conservatism and social reform* (1967) • G. Sutherland, *Policy-making in elementary education, 1870–1895* (1973) • R. Shannon, *The age of Disraeli, 1868–1881: the rise of tory democracy* (1992) • A. B. Cooke and J. Vincent, *The governing passion: cabinet government and party politics in Britain, 1885–86* (1974) • *The diaries of E. H. Stanley, 15th earl of Derby, 1869–1878*, CS, 5th series, 4 (1994) • *CGPLA Eng. & Wales* (1900)
Archives Sandon Hall, Staffordshire, Harrowby Manuscript Trust, corresp. and papers | BL, corresp. with Lord Carnarvon, Add. MSS 60863, 61024 • Bodl. Oxf., letters to Benjamin Disraeli • Hants. RO, letters to Arthur Bower Forwood • LPL, corresp. with E. W. Benson
Likenesses G. Richmond, chalk drawing, 1860, NPG • London Stereoscopic Co., photograph, 1885?, NPG [*see illus.*] • H. Herkomer, oils, 1899, British and Foreign Bible Society, London • Ape [C. Pellegrini], caricature, watercolour study, NPG; repro. in *VF* (28 Nov 1885) • H. C. Balding, stipple and line engraving (after photograph by H. Barraud), NPG • Lock & Whitfield, woodburytype photograph, NPG; repro. in T. Cooper, *Men of mark: a gallery of contemporary portraits* (1878)
Wealth at death £183,848 1s. 2d.: resworn probate, Feb 1901, *CGPLA Eng. & Wales* (1900)

Ryder, Henry (1777–1836), bishop of Lichfield and Coventry, was born at Streatham, Surrey, on 21 July 1777, the youngest son of Nathaniel *Ryder, first Baron Harrowby (1735–1803), of Sandon in Staffordshire [*see under* Ryder, Sir Dudley], and his wife, Elizabeth (*bap.* 1739, *d.* 1804), daughter and coheir of Richard *Terrick, bishop of London. Dudley *Ryder, first earl of Harrowby, and Richard *Ryder were his elder brothers. He was educated at Harrow School before being admitted in 1795, as a fellow commoner, at St John's College, Cambridge, where he gained a reputation for literary taste, studious habits, and irreproachable conduct. He graduated MA in 1798 and DD in 1813.

In 1800 Ryder was ordained to the curacy of Sandon, a living in the patronage of his own family. In 1801 he was presented by the crown to the rectory of Lutterworth in Leicestershire, a living which from 1805 he held in plurality with the neighbouring vicarage of Claybrook. On 15 December 1802 he married Sophia (*d.* 1862), daughter of Thomas March Phillipps of Garendon Park, Leicestershire, with whom he had ten sons and three daughters, all of whom survived him except one son, Charles, who was drowned at sea in 1825. Their third son, George Dudley Ryder, the brother-in-law of Henry Wilberforce and Henry Manning, became a convert to Roman Catholicism in 1846. Their seventh son was Sir Alfred Phillipps *Ryder, the admiral. Their eldest daughter, Anna Sophia, married Sir George Grey, the evangelical whig politician.

While participating fully in the fashionable social life expected of a clergyman of his means and connections, Ryder seems, from the beginning, to have taken his pastoral charge at Lutterworth and Claybrook with great seriousness. His naturally amiable temperament facilitated relations with his parishioners, and he was notable for his attention to the poor and the sick and for the diligence with which he undertook the catechizing of the young. He well illustrates the point that pluralism in the Hanoverian church did not always result in pastoral neglect, since he took great care in the employment of his curates, choosing men whom he respected for their personal piety and pastoral abilities and conferring regularly with them about the spiritual condition of his parishioners.

Ryder took care to develop his own theological education, entering on a course of reading in the early fathers and a critical study of the Bible with the assistance of commentaries in the tradition of the orthodox high-church school of divinity, of which, at this time, he was an adherent. He was also attentive to the development of personal piety and to that of his family, whom he regularly assembled for the reading of prayers. His connections and his attention to his duty guaranteed further preferment, and in 1808 he was presented to a canonry of Windsor. His sermons in St George's Chapel were greatly admired by George III, who said that they reminded him of the divinity of former days.

Ryder's initial reaction to the evangelical school in the church was one of suspicion, and he took the opportunity to attack evangelical principles when, in 1807, he preached a sermon at the archdeacon's visitation at

Henry Ryder (1777–1836), by Henry William Pickersgill, 1818

Leicester in the presence of Thomas Robinson, vicar of St Mary's, the most prominent local evangelical. However, he was impressed by Robinson's forbearance in declining to reply to this attack when called upon to preach the visitation sermon in the following year, and the two clergymen developed a friendly acquaintance which seems to have been the catalyst for a gradual change in Ryder's religious views. His reading expanded to include a number of evangelical devotional and apologetic works, including John Newton's *Cardiphonia* and *Letters to a Nobleman* as well as the biblical commentaries of Matthew Henry and Thomas Scott.

By 1811 Ryder was prepared not only to be identified as an evangelical but also to take the chair at a meeting of the Leicester branch of the most controversial of evangelical organizations, the Bible Society. His new theological convictions influenced Ryder's own practice of family worship, which became a daily event and featured Bible reading as well as prayer. They also led to an extension of his parochial ministry, as he introduced a cottage meeting at Claybrook and a weekly lecture in a factory at Lutterworth. He gradually came to the view that his earlier work in the parish, for all its conscientiousness, had been defective because it had not centred on evangelical preaching and teaching. Ryder's open avowal of evangelicalism made his appointment as dean of Wells in 1812 a matter of some controversy, and he continued as dean to associate freely with prominent local evangelicals, including Hannah More and Thomas Gisborne. He also introduced an evening service with preaching at a church in

the city, and became, in 1814, the first dignitary of the church to preach the annual sermon of the Church Missionary Society (CMS).

The elevation of Ryder to the see of Gloucester in 1815, the first evangelical to be appointed to the bench, was even more controversial, being opposed by, among others, the archbishop of Canterbury. The appointment may have owed much to the efforts of his brother, the earl of Harrowby, then lord president of the council and an influential member of Liverpool's administration. It must also have been eased, however, by the particular form of Ryder's evangelical doctrine. As his sermon on the death of Thomas Robinson, preached in 1813, makes clear, while sharing the evangelical sentiments of his friend Ryder did not adhere to the Calvinist theology which was so objectionable to many members of the church, not least Lord Liverpool himself.

The moderation of Ryder's evangelicalism was combined with a firm attachment to the Church of England. As a bishop he sought to combine an evangelical agenda with a non-partisan approach which aimed to unify the clergy of his diocese. Thus, in his first two visitation charges of 1816 and 1819 he quoted authorities as broadly acceptable as Paley and Horsley in favour of preaching for conversion, advocated support for both the Society for Promoting Christian Knowledge and the Bible Society, and referred his clergy to the examples of Laud and Andrewes in favour of departing from the approved form of prayer when visiting the sick. He encouraged his clergy to place a high value on personal devotion, centred on the Bible, as the foundation of a public ministry which should be characterized not merely by high professional standards but also by an urgency and a warmth of feeling flowing from personal experience of the benefits of the gospel. He recommended both the punctilious performance of the established offices of the church, including the baptism and communion services, and the preaching of a second sermon in the evening each Sunday, as well as the development of new pastoral measures including catechetical lectures and the introduction of day, evening, and Sunday schools for the particular benefit of the poor.

As a diocesan administrator Ryder was vigorous. He used the statistics gathered from visitation returns to gain a fuller view of the state of his diocese, and sought to take full advantage of the legislative changes of the early nineteenth century to reduce the level of non-residence among the clergy, improve the lot of curates, and provide additional church accommodation in areas of rising population. He also promoted voluntary societies, including the Gloucester Diocesan Society for the education of the poor, which he established in 1816.

In 1824 Ryder was translated to Lichfield and Coventry despite the reservations of the king. He was thus enabled to deploy the same skills and vigour in a larger diocese rapidly being transformed by urbanization and industrialization. He organized a diocesan church building society, and in 1832 was able to announce that seats for an additional 36,000 people were being provided in new and enlarged church buildings and that significant improvements were also being made in the provision for education. However, perhaps the most characteristic feature of his episcopates was the high level of personal attention which he devoted to his charge. Not only was he liberal in personal charity and in endowing parish churches from the revenues of his sees, he was also, at the cost of considerable effort, a conscientious pastor to his clergy and people. At Gloucester, for example, he often preached three times on a Sunday as well as giving a weekly lecture at one of the city churches and instructing the children of the national school. It was entirely characteristic that his final illness seems to have been exacerbated by his undertaking Sunday duty for the curate of a parish near his episcopal residence who had been unavoidably detained in London by the death of his father. In addition to his diocesan work Ryder maintained a lively interest in other evangelical causes, particularly the CMS, of which he became a vice-president and for which he became the first bishop willing to ordain agents directly for the mission field without requiring that they first serve a curacy in England.

Perhaps worn out by overwork Ryder died on 31 March 1836 at Hastings, Sussex, where he was buried. His published works were limited to a few individual sermons and visitation charges. A monument to the bishop was erected in Lichfield Cathedral, but he would probably have appreciated more the new church built in his memory in a populous suburb of Birmingham. MARK SMITH

Sources *Christian Observer* (1836), 315–18, 503–8, 566–73, 629–36 · *Annual Register* (1836) · *GM*, 2nd ser., 5 (1836), 658–9 · Venn, *Alum. Cant.* · G. C. B. Davies, *The first evangelical bishop* (1958) · *DNB*
Archives Harrowby Manuscript Trust, Sandon Hall, Staffordshire, letters and papers
Likenesses R. W. Sievier, stipple, pubd 1817 (after W. Behnes), NPG · H. W. Pickersgill, portrait, 1818, priv. coll. [*see illus.*] · F. Chantrey, statue, 1841, Lichfield Cathedral; model for statue, 1841, AM Oxf. · T. Woolnoth, stipple (after H. Pickersgill), BM, NPG; repro. in *Christian Keepsake* (1836)

Ryder, John (*c*.1697–1775), Church of Ireland archbishop of Tuam, was born at Nuneaton, Warwickshire, the son of Dudley Ryder, a haberdasher. His grandfather also was Dudley Ryder (*d.* 1683), the ejected rector of Bedworth, Warwickshire. He was educated at Charterhouse School and, from 1712, at Queens' College, Cambridge, whence he graduated BA (1716), MA (1719), and DD (1741), and where he was a fellow of the college from 1718 to 1721. He was ordained deacon at Peterborough on 13 March 1720, and priest at Lincoln on 14 May 1721. On 15 May 1721 he became vicar of Nuneaton, and held the living until his appointment to the see of Killaloe, by patent of 30 January 1742; he was consecrated in St Bridget's, Dublin, on 21 February. He was translated to the see of Down and Connor, by patent of 1 May 1743, and was further promoted, on 14 March 1752, to archbishop of Tuam and bishop of Ardagh. His rise in the church was due to the influence with the Pelham ministry of his cousin the attorney-general, Dudley *Ryder. At the same time he was a devoted bishop whose views were evangelical and whose disposition was courteous and kindly.

Ryder married, first, Alice, daughter of John Wilmot of Osmaston, Derbyshire, with whom he had two sons. She

died on 21 December 1744, and in July 1748 Ryder married Frances, widow of Dean John Hamilton and daughter of Bishop Francis Hutchinson; she died on 29 April 1750. Both Ryder's sons, John (1723–1791) and Dudley Charles, entered the Church of Ireland.

Ryder's latter years were spent at Nice, where he died on 4 February 1775 from the effects of a fall from his horse. He was buried on 6 February in a ground near the shore purchased for protestant burials by the British consul. His will, made on 1 December 1774, left £500 to his sons.

ALEXANDER GORDON, *rev.* EOIN MAGENNIS

Sources J. B. Leslie and H. B. Swanzy, *Biographical succession lists of the clergy of diocese of Down* (1936) · Venn, *Alum. Cant.* · H. Cotton, *Fasti ecclesiae Hibernicae*, 3 (1849) · PRO NIre., Wilmot MSS · *GM*, 1st ser., 102/1 (1832), 563
Archives Sandon Hall, Stafford, Staffordshire, Harrowby Manuscript Trust, letters to family | BL, Egerton charters, Nuneaton patent, EG. CH 7730 · BL, Add. MSS 32704, 32776 · Derbys. RO, corresp. with R. Wilmot · PRO NIre., corresp. with Sir R. Wilmot
Likenesses oils, Queens' College, Cambridge
Wealth at death £500; plus plate: Leslie and Swanzy, eds., *Clergy*

Ryder, John Nicholas Robins (1814–1885), actor, born in the Isle of Thanet on 5 April 1814, had already shown his promise in the provinces before being engaged by W. C. Macready for Drury Lane in 1842. He took part in most of Macready's productions, including *As You Like It*, as Duke Frederick (1 October 1842), and Sheridan Knowles's *The Secretary* (24 April 1843), as the original King. In September 1843, and again in 1848–9, he accompanied Macready to America. The second visit culminated in the Astor Place riot, which forms the core of Richard Nelson's *Two Shakespearean Actors* (1990), in which Ryder achieves the status of a dramatic character. More than once in his reminiscences Macready expressed his contentment at his choice of a companion, saying that without him he 'could not have got through' (*Macready's Reminiscences*, 2.222). Macready also admitted to cutting down Ryder's parts. At the Princess's Theatre, Ryder was Claudius to Macready's Hamlet (31 October 1845), the original Sir Adam Weir in James White's *The King of the Commons* (20 May 1846), Van den Bosch in Macready's abridgement of Taylor's *Philip Van Artevelde* (22 November 1848), and Œnarus in Oxenford's version of Corneille's *Ariane* (28 January 1850).

Just as in the 1840s Ryder had given stalwart support to Macready, so in the 1850s did he to Charles Kean. At the Princess's, where initially Kean shared the management with Robert Keeley, Ryder's powerful physique and voice provided a contrast with Kean's relatively naturalistic style. Lavish Shakespearian revivals were the centrepiece of Kean's management. Unlike those of some members of the company, Ryder's performances were not swamped by the scenic excesses. His Shakespearian credits included Antonio in *Twelfth Night* (28 September 1850), Pistol in *The Merry Wives of Windsor*, Hubert in *King John* (a great success, more than once repeated), Macduff, Buckingham in *King Henry VIII*, Polixenes, Bolingbroke in *Richard II*, Caliban, Edgar in *King Lear*, Williams in *Henry V*, and Bassanio. Outside Shakespeare, he created the characters of Aymer de la

John Nicholas Robins Ryder (1814–1885), by unknown photographer, pubd 1879

Roche in A. R. Slous's *The Templar* (9 November 1850), Colonel Boswell in Lovell's *Trial of Love* (7 June 1852), and John Dymond in Jerrold's *Heart of Gold* (9 October 1854). In Kean's lavish revival of Byron's *Sardanapalus* (13 June 1853) Ryder carried the acting honours as Salamenes.

In August 1854 Ryder absented himself from the Princess's to inaugurate Lydia Pearce's management of the Bower Saloon, playing Othello, Macbeth, and *The Stranger* (by B. Thompson). On Kean's retirement from the Princess's, Ryder remained under Augustus Harris senior, and created the roles of Giovanni Orseolo in Falconer's *Master Passion* (2 November 1859), an adaptation of *Les noces vénitiennes* of Victor Séjour, and Mark Beresford in *Gossip*, an adaptation by T. J. Williams and A. Harris of *L'Enfant terrible*. He was the first Timothy Crabstick in England in Brougham's *Playing with Fire* (28 September 1861). He also played Kent in *King Lear*, and was Iago to Fechter's Othello in October 1861. He later played Othello to Fechter's Iago, Falstaff in *The Merry Wives of Windsor*, and Jaques, and was the original Colonel Lambeth in Brougham's *Angel of Midnight* (15 February 1862).

At Astley's, renamed the Westminster, Ryder was David Deans in Boucicault's *The Trial of Effie Deans* (26 January 1863). He had previously appeared at Drury Lane as the Rajah Gholam Bahadoor in Boucicault's *The Relief of Lucknow* (19 September 1862). At Drury Lane he also played in Falconer's *Nature above Art* (12 September 1863), as the Abbot of Saint Maurice in Phelps's revival of *Manfred* (10 October 1863), and as Santoni, a monk, in Falconer's *Night and Morning* (8 January 1864).

On 22 October 1864, at the Lyceum under Fechter, Ryder was the first Baron d'Alvares in *The King's Butterfly*, an adaptation of *Fanfan la Tulipe*. Don Salluste in *Ruy Blas* followed at the same house, and on 11 November 1867, in consequence of the sudden illness of Fechter, he assumed the title role for four acts of *Hamlet*, having appeared as the Ghost in act 1. In 1869 he was the original Javert in Bayle Bernard's *The Man with Two Lives*, and the first Dr Mortimer in F. C. Burnand's *The Turn of the Tide*, at Drury Lane and the Queen's, respectively. In this latter house he also created the part of Sir Norwald in Burnand's *Morden Grange*. In Tom Taylor's *'Twixt Axe and Crown* (22 January 1870) he was the first Simon Renard, and in Taylor's *Joan of Arc* (10 April 1871) the first Raoul de Gaucourt, his son, William, who was for a short time on the London stage, playing the Count de la Trémouille. On 8 July 1872 he was the first Creon in Wills's *Medea in Corinth*. He created the part of Chevalier Malcorne in Sir Charles Young's *Montcalm*, and, still at the Queen's, was the original Ireton in Bate Richard's *Cromwell*. On 15 December 1874 he was Friar Lawrence at the Lyceum, and in April 1875, at the Gaiety, Leonato in *Much Ado about Nothing*. He played Banquo for a benefit at Drury Lane on 12 November 1882, and on 6 October of the same year was, at the Adelphi, the original Colonel Wynter in *In the Ranks* by Sims and Pettitt, but had to give up the part through illness. He died, in relative poverty (he left less than £200), on 27 March 1885 at his home, 84 Barrington Road, Brixton, London, survived by his daughter.

A serviceable actor in secondary roles, Ryder was noted for his powerful voice, his tall and imposing physique, and his masterly make-up. He features in many of the Martin Laroche photographs of Charles Kean's Princess's Theatre productions. The stereophotograph (in the Mander and Mitchenson Collection) group from *The Winter's Tale* carries the caption 'Arranged by Mr Ryder'—indicating that he was one of the first actors to exploit the potential of this new medium. Friar Lawrence and Hubert were his best characters. He was a good stage manager and a competent instructor. Among the many pupils whom he trained and brought onto the stage were Stella Colas and Lilian Adelaide Neilson.

JOSEPH KNIGHT, rev. RICHARD FOULKES

Sources C. E. Pascoe, ed., *The dramatic list*, 2nd edn (1880) · *Macready's reminiscences, and selections from his diaries and letters*, ed. F. Pollock, 1 (1875) · J. W. Cole, *The life and theatrical times of Charles Kean ... including a summary of the English stage for the last fifty years*, 2 vols. (1859) · *The Era* (28 March 1885) · *Era Almanack and Annual* (1868) · *The life and reminiscences of E. L. Blanchard, with notes from the diary of Wm. Blanchard*, ed. C. W. Scott and C. Howard, 2 vols. (1891) · J. Coleman, *Players and playwrights I have known*, 2 vols. (1888) · E. Stirling, *Old Drury Lane*, 2 vols. (1881) · T. E. Pemberton, *Life and writings of T. W. Robertson* (1893) · R. Nelson, *Two Shakespearean actors*

(1990) · D. Mullin, ed., *Victorian actors and actresses in review: a dictionary of contemporary views of representative British and American actors and actresses, 1837–1901* (1983) · *CGPLA Eng. & Wales* (1885) · d. cert.

Likenesses photograph, pubd 1879, NPG [*see illus.*] · Laroche, photographs, priv. coll.; repro. in *Theatrephile*, 2 (1987), 29–33 · four prints, Harvard TC

Wealth at death £186 2s.: probate, 15 May 1885, *CGPLA Eng. & Wales*

Ryder, Nathaniel, first Baron Harrowby (1735–1803). *See under* Ryder, Sir Dudley (1691–1756).

Ryder, Richard (1766–1832), politician, second son of the politician Nathaniel *Ryder, first Baron Harrowby (1735–1803) [*see under* Ryder, Sir Dudley], and his wife, Elizabeth (*bap.* 1739, *d.* 1804), daughter and coheir of Richard *Terrick, bishop of London, was born on 5 July 1766. Dudley *Ryder, first earl of Harrowby, and Henry *Ryder were his brothers. Throughout his life he suffered from debilitating headaches. After being educated at Neasden and at Harrow School, he proceeded in 1784 to St John's College, Cambridge, where he graduated MA in 1787. He was admitted a student of Lincoln's Inn on 9 February 1788, and was called to the bar on 19 November 1791. He was active in the militia during 1797–8. Having entered parliament in February 1795, at a by-election, for the family borough of Tiverton, he retained the seat for thirty-five years, retiring at the dissolution in 1830. He was a loyal Pittite and a friend of George Canning. He married, on 1 August 1799, Frederica, daughter and heir of Sir John *Skynner, kt, lord chief baron of the exchequer; she died on 8 August 1821. They had one surviving daughter, Susan.

Ryder continued to practise as a lawyer and, on turning down the Irish secretaryship in 1804, was appointed second justice of the great sessions for the counties of Carmarthen, Cardigan, and Pembroke, in July 1804, and continued to act as a Welsh judge until 1807. He also took office under the duke of Portland as a lord commissioner of the Treasury on 16 September 1807, but found the strain of the meetings too great. He was sworn of the privy council on 25 November 1807, and was promoted judge-advocate-general on 4 December following. In the ministry of Spencer Perceval, from 1 November 1809 to June 1812, he was secretary of state for the Home department, and was *ex officio* a commissioner of the Board of Control for the affairs of India. Like Perceval, he was a devout evangelical, but with none of that tendency's steely self-discipline.

As home secretary, Ryder 'was soon seen to be out of his depth' (HoP, *Commons, 1790–1820*, 5.80), and in 1810 Perceval had, in effect, to take over his secretaryship; he subsequently rallied, but again had to be relieved by Perceval during the Luddite disturbance. Ryder combined personal feebleness with reaction, opposing Romilly's attempts to reform capital punishment and opposing Catholic relief and the Maynooth grant. He resigned after Perceval's assassination and 'took to his bed' (ibid.). Ryder made an error in being persuaded into the home secretaryship through personal loyalty to Perceval: neither his health nor his character were adequate. Though those close to

him saw merits, his reputation lingered as one of the least adequate holders of a secretaryship of state.

Ryder was elected a bencher of Lincoln's Inn in 1811, and served as treasurer in 1819. For many years he held, too, the lucrative appointment of registrar of the consistory court, and he received £2000 p.a. as estate auditor for his brother's father-in-law, Lord Stafford. He succeeded to the seat of his relative Thomas Ryder, Westbrook Hay, Herefordshire, and died there on 18 September 1832.

W. R. WILLIAMS, *rev.* H. C. G. MATTHEW

Sources GM, 1st ser., 69 (1799), 716 · HoP, *Commons, 1790–1820* · D. Ryder, *Autobiography* (privately printed, 1891) · D. Gray, *Spencer Perceval: the evangelical prime minister, 1762–1812* (1963) · Venn, *Alum. Cant.*

Archives BL, letters and papers relating to Catholic emancipation, Add. MS 49187 · Bodl. Oxf., corresp., MS Eng. lett. c. 665 · Sandon Hall, Staffordshire, Harrowby Manuscript Trust, corresp. and papers; corresp relating to Tiverton | BL, corresp. with third Lord Hardwicke, Add. MSS 35644–35757, *passim* · BL, corresp. with C. P. Yorke, Add. MS 45038 · NL Scot., corresp. with Lord Melville · PRO NIre., corresp. with Lord Castlereagh · Royal Arch., letters to George III

Ryder, Robert Edward Dudley (1908–1986), naval officer, was born on 16 February 1908 at Dehra Dun, India, the third and youngest son of the six children of Colonel Charles Henry Dudley *Ryder (1868–1945), army officer, explorer, and surveyor-general of India, and his wife, Ida Josephine (1872/3–1948), daughter of Lieutenant-Colonel E. E. Grigg, Indian staff corps, of Stevenage, Hertfordshire. He was the scion of a distinguished family, with Bishop Ryder and Admiral Ryder also among his forebears. He attended Hazlehurst School, at Frant, near Tunbridge Wells, and Cheltenham College (1921–5) before joining the Royal Navy in January 1926 as the top cadet among public-school entrants. After training (and winning the king's dirk) on HMS *Erebus* he served as midshipman on HMS *Ramillies* (1927–9) before completing submarine training and joining the China station on board HMS *Olympus* in 1930. Already a keen ocean-racing yachtsman, in 1933–4 he sailed with four friends from Hong Kong to Dartmouth, via the Aleutian Islands and the Panama Canal. This voyage in the 30 ton ketch *Tai-Mo-Shan* (which Ryder had designed) did much to develop his mental and physical endurance as well as his seaman's skills. After this he was selected as skipper of the *Penola*, the three-masted schooner that served as the base for the British Graham Land expedition between 1934 and 1937. The strongly self-disciplined Ryder was somewhat taken aback by the amateurish sailing ways of his colleagues and felt his responsibilities as master of the ship underrated by the expedition's leader, John Rymill. Nevertheless his impressive navigational skills enabled him to play a full part in the expedition's important surveying in the Antarctic and he was awarded the Polar medal with clasp.

Ryder returned to general service in August 1937, on board the battleship HMS *Warspite*, the flagship of the Mediterranean Fleet, but on the outbreak of the Second World War he immediately volunteered to join the 'Q' ships. This promised him the opportunity for adventure used much initiative and imagination in planning and organizing the raid. The naval forces successfully rammed the lock gates, despite coming under intense fire, while commandos led by Lieutenant-Colonel Newman completed various demolition tasks on shore. Ryder himself directed operations until the last possible moment, when he withdrew on a motor boat laden with dead and wounded. The next day the *Campbeltown* exploded, successfully wrecking the dock while incidentally killing many German soldiers. Of 615 men who left Falmouth 169 were killed and 215 taken prisoner but this cost was accounted small for an operation whose 'calculated boldness in conception … steadfastness of purpose in execution, and … unflinching courage of performance' (Roskill, 173) recalled Britain's best naval traditions. Its success lay too in shaking the confidence of the Germans while boosting the resistance of the French and the morale of the English at a time when the fortunes of war seemed doubtful.

Ryder's outstanding bravery was duly recognized by the award of one of five VCs, although his own account of the raid, *The Attack on St Nazaire* (1947), was written in his characteristically modest, unassuming, yet thoroughly professional manner. After this climax of his career he took part in the planning and conduct of the Dieppe raid in August 1942, for which he was mentioned in dispatches, but other combined operations that he planned were all cancelled. By 1944—with the large ships of the future having little appeal—he sought a role in post-war naval intelligence. But at that time his seaman's skills were indispensable and, after leading the assault on Berniers-sur-Mer during the D-day landings, he commanded the destroyer HMS *Opportune* in its anti-enemy boat and Arctic convoy missions. Forced out of sea service by illness at the end of the war, he was posted to the Admiralty's tactical and staff duties division before taking up a long expected appointment as naval attaché in Norway in 1948. While this proved an agreeable diplomatic post, helping to persuade Norway to join NATO, it set back rather than advanced his hopes of a career in naval intelligence. The view from abroad also convinced him that Britain's achievements under Churchill were being rapidly eroded by socialism under Attlee. Though promoted captain in 1948 he now contemplated a political career as the best way to serve his country.

Ryder was adopted as Conservative candidate for the new constituency of Merton and Morden in December 1948; having won the seat in the general election of February 1950 he was obliged to leave his post at Oslo and resign from the navy. He was to retain the constituency, with a greatly increased majority, in 1951. Motivated by sincere antipathy to socialism rather than by narrow party loyalty he was a hard-working and conscientious MP, specializing in London matters and defence issues while also writing a nautical thriller, *Coverplan* (1953). But he did not find the Commons much to his liking, nor did it provide the income that he needed to support his family; he therefore stood down in 1955. Ryder then considered a number of careers, hankering above all for some role in cold war intelligence, but this never materialized. Eventually he

Robert Edward Dudley Ryder (1908–1986), by Elliott & Fry, 1949

but his first command, the HMS *Williamette Valley*, a converted Cardiff tramp, after roaming the north and south Atlantic was torpedoed in June 1940, leaving Ryder to survive, clinging to a wooden spar for four days. He then took charge of HMS *Fleetwood*, a frigate engaged in east coast convoys, and was promoted commander in December 1940. On 26 April 1941, during the fitting out of his next command, he married the charming and supportive Constance Hilaré Myfanwy (1918–1982), third daughter of the Revd Lumley Green-Wilkinson of Lovel Hill, Windsor Forest, and his wife, Caroline Myfanwy, in a ceremony at which the archbishop of Canterbury officiated. The couple had a son and a daughter. In June, Ryder rejoined HMS *Prince Philippe*, a converted cross-channel ferry turned troop carrier, but after only one month, in July 1941, he lost his ship in a collision in the Firth of Clyde.

Having incurred the displeasure of the Admiralty, Ryder seemed doomed to a career ashore and was made naval liaison officer to General Alexander, chief of southern command. Known as a redoubtable and expert, if hitherto unlucky, seaman, in February 1942 he was unexpectedly called by Mountbatten (whom he did not greatly admire) to combined operations headquarters and was appointed to lead one of the war's most daring raids, the attack on St Nazaire. The French Loire port, it was feared, might become the base for Germany's most powerful battleship, the *Tirpitz*, and so threaten Britain's Atlantic sea lanes. To forestall this Ryder was charged with disabling the lock, using HMS *Campbeltown*, loaded with explosives charged to detonate after the British forces had withdrawn. Ryder resorted to a well-paid but humdrum job as joint managing director of John Lewis's Oxford Street store; this he cordially hated but endured for three years. At a loss for a new career he then built up a small chain of newsagents in west London; this proved even less to his liking but its lucrative sale in the mid-1960s enabled him to retire to Norfolk and, later, to Berkshire. His political and business careers therefore proved anticlimactic, yet he found consolation—and his greatest pleasure—in sailing, regularly cruising with his wife, children, and friends. A firm Anglican, a dog lover, a ready shot, and a talented artist, he lived quietly in the countryside, playing some part in both the Royal National Lifeboat Institution and the Royal Cruising Club. His concern over the dangers of socialism recurred strongly in the early 1970s but his constitutionalism led him to reject the lure of extremist politics. Ryder, trim, strong, and angular in appearance, remained a dutiful, kindly man with a keen sense of fun. While an adventurous and heroic sailor and the epitome of the service aristocracy, he consistently valued private happiness above public fame. He died, fittingly, on his boat off Guernsey on 29 June 1986. He was cremated at Oxford, after a funeral at Inkpen, Berkshire, on 10 July.   A. C. Howe

Sources personal knowledge (2004) · priv. coll., Ryder papers · R. E. D. Ryder, naval papers, IWM · R. E. D. Ryder, MS diary of the British Graham Land expedition, 1934–7, Scott Polar RI · M. Sherwood, *The voyage of the Tai-Mo-Shan* (1935) · J. Rymill, *Southern lights* (1938) · R. E. D. Ryder, *The attack on St Nazaire* (1947) · J. Dorrian, *Storming St Nazaire* (1998) · PRO, DEFE2/125–133 [operation Chariot] · *The Times* (1 July 1986) · C. E. Lucas Phillips, *The greatest raid of all* (1958) · S. W. Roskill, *The war at sea, 1939–1945*, 2 (1956) · *CGPLA Eng. & Wales* (1986)
Archives IWM, naval papers · priv. coll., papers · Scott Polar RI, diary, corresp., and papers of the British Graham Land expedition | FILM BBC WAC · BFI NFTVA, 'St Nazaire greets war heroes, British News, 11 Aug 1947 · NMM, British Graham Land expedition, 1934–7 | SOUND IWM SA, 2 March 1946, 25731
Likenesses Elliott & Fry, photograph, 1949, NPG [*see illus.*] · portrait, *c.*1949, repro. in Dorrian, *Storming St Nazaire* · S. Ryder, oils, *c.*1975, priv. coll.
Wealth at death £157,822: probate, 4 Sept 1986, *CGPLA Eng. & Wales*

Ryder, (Margaret) Susan [Sue], **Baroness Ryder of Warsaw** (1924–2000), founder of the Sue Ryder Foundation and social worker, was born on 3 July 1924 at Belmont Nursing Home, Leeds, the daughter of Charles Foster Ryder (*d.* 1942), a farmer and landowner (formerly a brewer), of Scarcroft Grange, Thorner, near Leeds, and Thurlow, in Suffolk, and his second wife, Mabel Elizabeth, *née* Sims. Charles Ryder had five children from his first marriage, and Sue Ryder, as she was always known, was the youngest of the four children from his second marriage. She was educated at home and at Benenden School, Kent. Religion was central to her upbringing and she learned from her mother especially the value of Christian compassion. A short distance from the comfortable family home at Scarcroft were terrible slum dwellings, where her mother undertook social work. Accompanying her on visits there the young Sue Ryder witnessed poverty at first hand and was shocked by what she saw. She later recalled

(Margaret) Susan Ryder, Baroness Ryder of Warsaw (1924–2000), by Snowdon, 1984

that she had grown up in the shadow of the First World War, and that on reading the poetry of Julian Grenfell, Rupert Brooke, Siegfried Sassoon, and Wilfred Owen she felt that society had betrayed these authors and those for whom they had written. Her need to commemorate the sacrifice of a war generation was powerfully reinforced during the Second World War and was the chief inspiration of her later charity work.

After the outbreak of war in 1939 Ryder joined the First Aid Nursing Yeomanry. She was subsequently attached to the newly formed Special Operations Executive, where she worked principally as a driver and radio operator. She came into contact with agents of all nationalities—she called them 'bods'—but grew especially close to those from Poland, a country she came to love. Her duties included driving the agents to airfields from which they would be flown into occupied Europe. Their bravery left an indelible mark upon her and she searched for some way of perpetuating the qualities that they represented: 'the qualities of endurance, of courage, of faith and optimism' (Ryder and Cheshire, 10). About 1942 Ryder married a young naval officer who was killed in action soon afterwards. In the following year she was sent overseas with the Special Operations Executive, first to north Africa and then to Italy. After the war she volunteered to work with a relief unit in northern France, and she drove a mobile clinic with the Croix Rouge. Ryder worked wherever she perceived the need, and was instinctively drawn to the neglected. In German prisons she found many non-Germans harshly sentenced by military courts for crimes ranging from petty theft to murder. Ryder took up the cause of these forgotten men, who were often the survivors of concentration camps, and fought doughtily against official obstruction to improve their conditions. She visited some 130 prisons regularly and also established, briefly, a holiday home in Denmark for concentration camp survivors and those with long-term illnesses. This scheme was later put on a more permanent footing with the establishment of two holiday homes in England.

In winter 1951–2 a shortage of funds forced Ryder to return to Britain. In 1953, 'with the help of a small legacy, credit from the bank and much optimism', she established the 'Sue Ryder Foundation for the sick and disabled of all age groups' (Ryder, *And the Morrow is Theirs*, 105). This was to be the 'living memorial' that she first conceived while working with the Special Operations Executive. According to its charter the foundation was dedicated to the millions lost in both world wars:

> This is an international foundation devoted to the relief of suffering on the widest scale. It seeks to render personal service to those in need and to give affection to those who are unloved, regardless of age, race or creed, as part of the Family of man.   (Ryder and Cheshire, 16)

The foundation took as its symbol a sprig of rosemary to signify remembrance. In this new enterprise Ryder was staunchly supported by her mother, whose home in Cavendish, Suffolk, became the foundation's administrative headquarters and first residential home. The first patients—Ryder called them 'bods' in memory of the agents of the Special Operations Executive—were referred by local authorities on the basis of physical disability or psychiatric illness. Cavendish was run by professional and voluntary carers, and paid for by government funds and charitable donations. It set the pattern on which other homes would be established. Four decades later the Sue Ryder Foundation ran 80 homes in a dozen countries, with 28 in Poland and 22 in Yugoslavia. All kinds of fund-raising initiatives kept this huge enterprise afloat. A television appeal in 1966 raised over £40,000 and the 18,000 individuals who donated money were each thanked with a letter that Ryder characteristically signed herself: she understood well the importance of showing gratitude. Press interest in the foundation made her a national figure and she was a reluctant 'victim' of the television programme *This is Your Life*. But although she professed to shrink from this kind of publicity she was driven by an undeniable egoism, and 'Sue Ryder' became a household name through a chain of about 500 high-street charity shops.

In February 1955 (Geoffrey) Leonard *Cheshire VC, later Baron Cheshire (1917–1992), founder of the Cheshire Homes for the physically disabled, invited Sue Ryder to visit his new home at Ampthill. Neither knew of the other's work, but each recognized a kindred spirit: both were converts to Roman Catholicism and had built their foundations 'without funds and on faith' (Ryder, *And the Morrow is Theirs*, 119). They became specially close during a visit to India in 1957 when they planned a joint venture at

Dehra Dun in Uttar Pradesh; the Ryder–Cheshire centre that opened there included a large unit for the care of non-infectious lepers. They announced their engagement in February 1959, having previously reassured the staff of both their foundations: 'our sole aim is still the good of the work' (ibid., 122). They were married on 5 April 1959 in a simple ceremony in the private chapel of Cardinal Valerian Gracias in Bombay. After an all too brief honeymoon in India they began their married life with an arduous joint fund-raising tour of Australia and New Zealand. Mother Teresa of Calcutta had once told them that they would find the sacrifices that marriage entailed worthwhile, and so it proved. Together they shared happiness, as well as the enormous demands placed upon them by their respective foundations, to which each was a willing martyr.

On their return to Britain they lived in a small flat at Cavendish. A son and daughter were born in 1960 and 1962 but Ryder did not allow pregnancy to interrupt her work. She preferred action to delegation and was happiest when driving through the night to open a new home or deliver aid. Last-minute hitches gave her a chance to take centre stage: 'She loved to be able to prove that there was a need for her to dig deeper than anyone else, to keep going when others flagged' (*The Independent*, 4 Nov 2000). Small, thin, and neatly dressed, with characteristic headscarves, she seemed to have no interest in food, and at Cavendish 'tripped and skipped from prayers in the chapel to kitchen to post-room, chivvying someone as she went' (ibid.). Her family background lent a grandeur to her manner that she never lost, in spite of the simplicity of her tastes and the frugality of her lifestyle. And behind the piety there was a lively character with a hint of flirtatiousness.

In 1979 Sue Ryder was created a life peer: her title, Baroness Ryder of Warsaw, was a personal tribute to the people of Poland. She played an active and independent part in Lords debates, and proved a trenchant social commentator. In 1992 Leonard Cheshire died, ending a unique partnership. Her last years were overshadowed by a bitter dispute with the trustees of the Sue Ryder Foundation over their plans to modernize the charity—a case of what some in the sector unkindly, if aptly, called 'founder member syndrome'. The dispute caused great distress to Lady Ryder, and damage to the charity that she had created, and reached a sad conclusion in 1998 when Sue Ryder severed links with the Sue Ryder Foundation. In September 2000 the charity relaunched itself as Sue Ryder Care. Shortly before this Lady Ryder began the Bouverie Foundation, for the relief of poverty, sickness, and disability. She died after a lengthy illness at Bury St Edmunds, Suffolk, on 2 November 2000, and was survived by her son and daughter.

Sue Ryder was appointed OBE in 1957 for her work with German prisoners, and made CMG in 1976. She held numerous honorary doctorates from British universities, as well as decorations from foreign governments, including one of Poland's highest honours, the officer's cross of the order of Polonia Restituta Poland (1965), and the commander's cross (1992). In 1975 she published an autobiography, *And the Morrow is Theirs*, much of which was incorporated in *Child of My Love* (1986; revised, 1998). Her memoirs recount how a prisoner once flung at her the reproach 'I think you could have done more—that is what you are here for', which she accepted with Christian humility: 'I believe that these words apply to my entire life and to all that I have tried to do' (Ryder, *And the Morrow is Theirs*, 227). This is, though, a wholly unsatisfactory epitaph for Sue Ryder, one of the greatest Christian charity workers of her time.   MARK POTTLE

Sources S. Ryder, *And the morrow is theirs* (1975) · S. Ryder, *Child of my love* (1986); new edn (1998) · S. Ryder and L. Cheshire, *The hope of the disabled person* (1983) [the Royal Society of Medicine Stevens Lecture for the Laity, 1982] · *WWW* · Burke, *Peerage* · *Electronic Telegraph* (25 Sept 1998); (27 Sept 2000) · *Sunday Times* (23 July 2000) · *The Guardian* (2 Aug 2000); (3 Nov 2000) · *The Independent* (3–4 Nov 2000) · *The Times* (3 Nov 2000) · *Daily Telegraph* (3 Nov 2000) · *Marketing Week* (21 Sept 2000) · *Leicester Mercury* (22 Sept 2000) · *The Scotsman* (4 Nov 2000) · *The Herald* [Glasgow] (4 Nov 2000) · b. cert.
Likenesses R. Cuthbert, oils, 1982, NPG · Snowdon, photograph, 1984, NPG [*see illus.*] · N. Sinclair, photograph, 1991, NPG · double portrait, photograph (with Leonard Cheshire), repro. in *The Times*, 25 · double portrait, photograph (with Leonard Cheshire), repro. in *Daily Telegraph*

Ryder, Thomas (1735–1791), actor and theatre manager, was possibly born in Nottinghamshire, the first of the two sons of the provincial actor and manager Preswick Ryder (d. 1771) and his wife, the actress Sarah Ryder, *née* Darby. His brother, Samuel (1738–1771), was an actor in Ireland. There is some suggestion that Ryder performed on the Yorkshire circuit, and he certainly appeared in Scotland before moving to Ireland, where he achieved significant long-term success. The range of his early roles in Edinburgh—which included Aimwell in George Farquhar's *The Beaux' Stratagem*, Tom in Richard Steele's *The Conscious Lovers*, Bedamar in Thomas Otway's *Venice Preserv'd*, Razor in John Vanbrugh's *The Provoked Wife*, and Sir Andrew Aguecheek in *Twelfth Night*—set the tone of variety, adaptability, and, indeed, solid reliability that marked the whole of his acting career.

Ryder's first appearance in Ireland was in Dublin on 7 December 1757, as Captain Plume in a Smock Alley production of Farquhar's *The Recruiting Officer*. Ireland's first house was then under the management of Thomas Sheridan, whose company was both critically and popularly celebrated. Ryder continued to play the Smock Alley winter seasons through the subsequent stewardship of Brown and the management of Henry Mossop (1761–71), again appearing in a broad range of roles that embraced Tressel in *Richard III*, Lord Aimworth in Isaac Bickerstaff's *The Maid of the Mill*, and Scrub in *The Recruiting Officer*. He also appeared at the Crow Street Theatre in 1759–60.

In spring 1764 Ryder married the actress Rosetta Comerford (d. 1794), who had made her Smock Alley début in 1752. She was possibly the daughter or a sister of the actor Henry Comerford. The couple is known to have had three daughters—a Miss E., Mary (d. April 1791), and Rose (d. 1801)—and one son. At least two of the daughters followed their parents onto the stage, making their débuts at Covent Garden on Ryder's own benefit night of 16 April 1790. Their son, John, acted when a child but joined the Sligo militia and was killed in a duel in Kinsale in 1796, when he was just nineteen years of age.

Through the late 1760s and into the very early 1770s Ryder began to experiment with theatrical management, leading tours to Ireland's county towns of Limerick, Waterford, Londonderry, Kilkenny, Drogheda, Sligo, and Belfast, where on 30 April 1770 he opened a small theatre. When Mossop quit Smock Alley for England in 1771 Ryder was in a strong position to assume management of the company. This he did in 1772 and on 24 April 1773 he also purchased the lease of the theatre. He continued in management at Smock Alley until 1782, sometimes also operating and acting at the Crow Street Theatre and, in the summer, performing in London at Ranelagh Gardens. His company was good and successful, but Ryder himself was increasingly victim to profligacy and ill-judged extravagance, particularly in his domestic arrangements: he kept both a country house and a town house as well as fashionable equipage. In 1782 he lost the lease of Smock Alley to one of his own actors, Richard Daly. Nevertheless, from 1783 to 1786 he continued to perform in what was now Daly's company, adding a typical range of outside engagements that included in the summer of 1783 performances at Edinburgh, Cork, and Limerick.

Plagued by debt, and the victim of some degree of misfortune, Ryder finally left Dublin and made his London stage début at Covent Garden, as Sir John Brute in *The Provoked Wife*, on 28 October 1786. There his career was solid and seemingly settled. Over nearly five winter seasons—both at Covent Garden and in one summer season (1790) at the Haymarket—he expanded his acting repertory to include roles in new comic operas and pantomimes, as well as in the repertory pieces: Heartwell in William Congreve's *The Old Bachelor*, the anonymous interlude *Lady Pentweazle in Town*, in which he played Lady Pentweazle, and Peachum in John Gay's *The Beggar's Opera*. However, on 19 November 1790 he made his final appearance on the London stage and left the Covent Garden company halfway through their season. There is reasonable speculation that he may have quarrelled with the manager, Thomas Harris. However, by 4 December he was working again, acting at the Theatre Royal, Edinburgh, where he shortly, if rather briefly, took over management. He expanded the Edinburgh company—his daughters were principal players—and again extended his own repertory to take in, for example, the new roles of Sir Peter Teazle in Sheridan's *The School for Scandal* and Touchstone in *As You Like It*. He continued in management at Edinburgh until the spring of 1791, when he formed a new company (which again included his daughters) to tour Ireland. His final engagement was on 14 September for eight nights at the Rosemary Lane Theatre in Belfast. Thereafter, with his health failing, he retired to Dublin, where he died at Sandymount on 26 November 1791; he was perhaps buried in the churchyard of Drumcondra.

Although Ryder was never a playwright proper he did

adapt four old plays for contemporary production. *Like Master, Like Man* was an updating of Vanbrugh's *The Mistake, or, The Connaught Wife*, and he made alterations, of John Hippisley's *A Journey to Bristol: Such Things have Been*; of Isaac Jackman's *The Man of Parts*; and (probably) of John Crowne's *Sir Courtly Nice*, renamed *Opposition*.

John Genest mentions Ryder as 'a good actor, particularly in low Comedy' (Genest, *Eng. stage*, 7.35), while Thomas Snagg(e) comments on the range of his acting roles, concluding that 'He was as universal an actor as ever graced the board'. He was certainly a ubiquitous man of the theatre who could act a range of roles, sing, dance, run a company, stage a tour, and plan a programme. His style was hearty and somewhat bluff, and altogether a little too vulgar and unsophisticated—a little too coarse according to some critics—for him to be admitted to the first rank of London actors.   ADRIENNE SCULLION

Sources Highfill, Burnim & Langhans, *BDA* · R. Hitchcock, *An historical view of the Irish stage from the earliest period down to the close of the season 1788*, 2 vols. (1788–94) · W. S. Clark, *The Irish stage in the county towns, 1720–1800* (1965) · J. C. Dibdin, *The annals of the Edinburgh stage* (1888) · Genest, *Eng. stage*, vol. 7 · *The thespian dictionary, or, Dramatic biography of the eighteenth century* (1802) · E. K. Sheldon, *Thomas Sheridan of Smock-Alley: recording his life as actor and theater manager in both Dublin and London* (1967) · S. Whyte, *A miscellany* (1796) · *Memoirs of Charles Lee Lewes, containing anecdotes, historical and biographical, of the English and Scottish stages during a period of forty years* (1805)
Likenesses W. Angus, engraving (as Lovergold in *The miser*; after C. R. Ryley), repro. in *New English theatre*, 8 vols. (1776) · J. Ford, engraving (after M. A. Shee), BM; repro. in Highfill, Burnim & Langhans, *BDA* · W. N. Gardiner, engraving (as Sir John Restless in *All in the wrong*; after E. Harding, 1787), Harvard TC; repro. in *Universal Magazine and Review* (Dec 1791) · Loftis, watercolour drawing (as Falstaff in *Henry IV, Part I*), repro. in Highfill, Burnim & Langhans, *BDA* · J. Roberts, drawing, Garr. Club · engraving (as Ben in *Love for love*) · portrait (as Sir John Restless in *All in the wrong*), NL Ire.; repro. in *Hibernian Magazine* (Jan 1773)

Ryder, Thomas (*bap.* 1750, *d.* 1810), engraver, was baptized at St Faith's under St Paul's, London, on 20 January 1750, the son of Thomas Ryder of Paternoster Row, London, a bookbinder, and his wife, Alice. He was apprenticed in August 1765 to the elder James Basire (1730–1802), printmaker, in the Stationers' Company, and trained as a line engraver. In 1766 and 1767 he exhibited drawings with the Free Society: for the first he won a prize from the Society of Arts for a drawing by an artist aged under sixteen. His address was given at this time as Basire's house, Great Queen Street, Lincoln's Inn. Ryder was said to have been a student at the Royal Academy Schools, although there is no record of his enrolment unless he was the Thomas Ride entered in 1772. However, Ryder may have there met Simon Watts, who became his principal publisher in the 1780s. During that decade he engraved a number of attractive stipples after such contemporary artists as Bigg, Cipriani, Cosway, Ryley, and Shelley, and a few line engravings, notably *The Politician* (a portrait of Benjamin Franklin), after S. Elmer, published by Torre in 1782.

The name of Ryder's wife is unknown, but a son, another Thomas Ryder, was born in 1789, when Ryder was living at 43 Great Titchfield Street, from where he sold his own engravings. About 1790 he engraved a group of prints after Henry Bunbury as well as Thomas Lawrence's portrait of Bunbury. Ryder was a mainstay of Boydell's edition of Shakespeare, engraving nine of the large plates as well as the whole-length portrait of Queen Charlotte after William Beechey that was prefixed to the second volume. He did not work frequently for the Boydells, but his other prints for them, *The Captive*, after Joseph Wright, *The Murder of James I of Scotland*, after John Opie, and *The Last Supper*, after Benjamin West, were also on a grand scale. Engravers were paid 300 guineas for each Shakespeare plate, so Boydell's commissions would have maintained Ryder through the 1790s. The firm's decline and John Boydell's death must have come as a serious blow to him. Ryder's last major print, in line, was *Vortigern and Rowena* (1803), after Angelica Kauffman. He died in 1810.
               TIMOTHY CLAYTON and ANITA McCONNELL

Sources T. Dodd, 'Memoirs of English engravers', BL, Add. MS 33404, fol. 100 · Redgrave, *Artists* · D. F. McKenzie, ed., *Stationers' Company apprentices*, [3]: *1701–1800* (1978) · W. H. Friedman, *Boydell's Shakespeare Gallery* (1976) · parish register, St Faith's under St Paul's, GL [baptism]

Ryder, Sir William. *See* Rider, Sir William (*c.*1544–1611).

Rye, Edward Caldwell (1832–1885), entomologist, was born on 10 April 1832 at 16 Golden Square, London, one of the nine children of Edward Rye, a London solicitor and book collector of Norfolk descent, and his wife, Maria Tuppen. His sister, Maria Susan *Rye (1829–1903), was a social reformer who founded in 1861 the Female Middle-Class Emigration Society; his younger brother Walter *Rye (1843–1928) became a Norfolk antiquary and sports administrator. Originally intended to succeed to the family legal business, Rye was educated at King's College School, London, and then articled to his father. Despite having no wish to pursue a career in the legal profession, and quietly entertaining the hope of a position in the British Museum's zoological department, he continued in his father's office before becoming managing clerk to a barrister at Lincoln's Inn.

Early in life Rye exhibited great artistic talent, and this served to augment his clerk's salary on occasion. He excelled in drawing entomological specimens, and cultivated a fondness for the subject in the process. His earliest work, on the Lepidoptera, formed the basis for a piece in the *Entomologist's Weekly Intelligencer* (2.44) in 1857. However, he later became interested in the British Coleoptera, of which he formed valuable collections, and on which he contributed articles to the *Weekly Intelligencer* and *The Zoologist*. In 1859 Rye joined the Entomological Society of London (he later resigned, but was re-elected in 1876). He also wrote a series of articles on British Coleoptera for the *Entomologist's Annual* between 1863 and 1874. In 1864 he was offered a position on the editorial staff of the *Entomologist's Monthly Magazine*. He was also the author of a work entitled *British Beetles*, which was issued in 1866 and accompanied by a catalogue of indigenous Coleoptera. From 1870 he was a contributor to the *Zoological Record*, a publication of which he subsequently became editor.

On 20 August 1867 at Bloomsbury, London, Rye married

Isabella Sophia (*bap.* 1837), second daughter of the naturalist George Robert *Waterhouse (1810–1888) and his wife, Elizabeth. The couple had four children. In 1874 Rye was elected a fellow of the Zoological Society. In the following year he became librarian at the Royal Geographical Society, a post which he held until his death. He was a regular contributor to the *Field* newspaper, which he edited along with *Travel*. He was also for many years recording secretary at the meetings of the geographical section of the British Association.

Rye was an enthusiastic water sportsman who won numerous prizes in boat races on the Thames. On 30 July 1881 he suffered serious injury when his boat was crushed by a steamer, but in time he made a full recovery. He died of smallpox on 7 February 1885 at the Fever Hospital, Stockwell, Surrey. He was survived by his wife and their four children. YOLANDA FOOTE

Sources private information (1897) · Boase, *Mod. Eng. biog.* · *Entomologist's Monthly Magazine*, 21 (1885), 238–40 · *CGPLA Eng. & Wales* (1885) · IGI
Likenesses C. Mackechnie-Jarvis, portrait, repro. in *Proceedings and Transactions of the British Entomological and Natural History Society*, 8 (1976), 103
Wealth at death £2442 2s. 5d.: administration, 8 July 1885, *CGPLA Eng. & Wales*

Rye, Maria Susan (1829–1903), social reformer and promoter of emigration, was born on 31 March 1829 at 2 Lower James Street, Golden Square, London, the eldest of the nine children of Edward Rye, a solicitor and bibliophile, and his wife, Maria Tuppen of Brighton. She was educated at home. From the age of sixteen she undertook parochial work in the parish of St Luke's, Chelsea, where Charles Kingsley's father was vicar. She briefly became secretary of the committee to promote the Married Women's Property Bill, introduced in 1856, but found herself at odds with some of the group's views on the suffrage issue. Sympathizing with the plight of educated middle-class women, for whom there was little employment outside teaching, she was a founder member of the Society for Promoting the Employment of Women, formed in 1859. She opened a law-copying office at 12 Portugal Street, Lincoln's Inn Fields, founded the Victoria Press (with Emily Faithfull), established a telegraph school (with Isa Craig) in 1860, and opened a register office. That these ventures were commercially successful reflects the determination, leadership qualities, and entrepreneurial abilities that she was to utilize in other ventures.

Maria Rye's interest in emigration began when she independently assisted twenty-two women whom she could not place in work to emigrate to the colonies. In a paper read to the Social Science Congress in Dublin she suggested that the emigration of educated women to the colonies would both relieve England of the problem of distressed gentlewomen and at the same time lead to an 'elevation in morals' in the colonies (*English Woman's Journal*, 168). In the following year she founded the Female Middle-Class Emigration Society with Jane Lewin. Over the next seven years she travelled extensively, escorting parties of women and girls to Australia, New Zealand, and Canada, whose senior emigration agent in England considered her no more than 'a passenger agent of the sharpest description' (Parr, 30). In 1865 she collected information about immigration barracks in Australia and tried to correct abuses in hospitals, especially at the Tarban Creek Lunatic Asylum, on which subject she corresponded with Florence Nightingale and Lord Shaftesbury.

On a visit to North America, Maria Rye encountered the work of Charles Loring Brace and Mr Van Meter, who had established homes in New York for destitute and homeless children. This persuaded her to transfer her considerable energies to the emigration of orphan children, leaving female emigration to Jane Lewin. She proposed the emigration of the 'gutter children' of England's cities to rural Canada and the western states of America (*The Times*, 29 March 1869), and in June 1869 she took her first party of three children to Canada. The emigration of children began in earnest when, on 28 October 1869, she embarked from Liverpool with a party of seventy-five girls aged between four and twelve, including fifty from the Kirkdale Industrial School. In the following year Annie *Macpherson took out a party of 100 boys to Canada. These two women dominated the field for almost a decade until Dr Barnardo, William Quarrier, and other agencies became involved. Both determined women and natural leaders, they had much in common, but made no attempt to co-operate. Annie Macpherson's organization was more efficient and less controversial, but Maria Rye's tireless pen and influential supporters ensured that she achieved the higher profile.

Rye established a home in Peckham, London, and a receiving home in Canada in a converted gaol and court house which she had acquired at Niagara-on-the-Lake, called Our Western Home. She lobbied influential people and obtained the support of Lord Shaftesbury, the archbishop of Canterbury, and William Rathbone MP. Shaftesbury was instrumental in persuading the poor law board to allow the emigration of pauper children to Canada under the care of Rye and Macpherson. Financial support for the scheme came from readers of *The Times*, a civil list pension granted in 1871, the poor law authorities, and grants from the Canadian and provincial governments; its critics, prompted by the appearance of Rye's fund-raising appeal, *Our Gutter Children* (1809), included Charles Dickens and George Cruikshank. Rye published a number of pamphlets outlining the progress of the children, but from other sources in Canada came disturbing reports about the treatment and character of some of the children, together with suggestions that Maria Rye was personally profiting from the British and Canadian public funds applied to her work. The Local Government Board initiated an inquiry and in 1874 sent Andrew Doyle to Canada to investigate the distributing homes and to interview the children. Serious deficiencies in the training, welfare, and aftercare of the children were uncovered. Impatient of criticism, Maria Rye entered into a rancorous debate with Doyle. The doubts over child supervision, combined with better economic conditions at home, led to the suspension of the emigration of pauper children until 1883. Criticism was not confined to Maria Rye's endeavours, however; J. J. Kelso, the Canadian inspector of juvenile immigration agencies, considered her home 'responsible for a good deal of the odium that now attaches to child immigration in this country' (Wagner, 156). In spite of such strictures, she continued to receive support to maintain her work, and over a period of twenty-five years she made innumerable journeys across the Atlantic and was responsible for placing some 4000 girls in Canadian homes. In 1895 she retired to Baconsthorpe, Hemel Hempstead, and transferred the freehold of her homes at Peckham and Niagara to the Waifs and Strays Society; she subsequently served on the society's emigration committee. Maria Rye, a woman of very strong character and physique, held intense religious convictions. She died, unmarried, at Marlowes, Hemel Hempstead, on 12 November 1903, of intestinal cancer, from which she had suffered for four years. She was buried in the cemetery at Hemel Hempstead on 16 November 1903.   JUDY COLLINGWOOD

Sources J. Parr, *Labouring children* (1980) · G. Wagner, *Children of the empire* (1982) · *Our Waifs and Strays* (Jan 1904) · 'Report … on the emigration of pauper children to Canada', *Parl. papers* (1875), 63.255, no. 9 · 'Reply of Mr. Doyle to … report on emigration of pauper children', *Parl. papers* (1877), vol. 71, no. 263 · *English Woman's Journal*, 8 (1861), 165–71 · *The Times* (3 April 1862) · *Chambers biographical dictionary of women* (1996) · *Europa biographical dictionary of British women* (1983) · Mrs S. Wortley, 'Emigration', in Baroness Burdett-Coutts, *Woman's mission: a series of congress papers* (1893) · will · *CGPLA Eng. & Wales* · d. cert. · *DNB*
Archives BL, Add. MS 45799, fols. 178–207 · priv. coll., corresp. and papers by her nephew · Women's Library, London, autograph letter collection | Public Archives of Ontario, Toronto, corresp. with William Kirby · Women's Library, London, Nightingale papers, Female Middle-Class Emigration Society, 1862–86
Likenesses group portrait, photograph (with children), Niagara Historical Society · photograph, repro. in *Our Waifs and Strays*, 215 · photograph, Niagara Historical Society
Wealth at death £3555 13s.: resworn probate, 16 Dec 1903, *CGPLA Eng. & Wales*

Rye, Walter (1843–1928), athlete and antiquary, was born on 31 October 1843 at 14 King's Parade, Chelsea, the seventh child of Edward Rye, a London solicitor and bibliophile, and his wife, Maria Tuppen. His siblings included Maria Susan *Rye, the social reformer, and Edward Caldwell *Rye, the entomologist. It was always Walter Rye's boast that, although born in London, he was part of one of the oldest families in Norfolk, the Ryes having been mentioned in the Domesday Book.

Rye left school at fourteen, and entered his father's office at 16 Golden Square, Westminster, as a clerk, continuing his studies with evening classes at King's College, before becoming articled to his father in June 1861, and qualifying as a solicitor in May 1866. In 1870 he married Georgina Eliza, adopted daughter of George Sturges. Rye continued to practise in Golden Square until his retirement in 1900, when he passed the business to his sons and moved to Norwich, a city he had visited for many years, and where he had helped to save some of the most historic buildings from destruction. In 1908–9 he was mayor of

Norwich—an uncommon honour for a man resident in the city for only eight years. Always a controversialist, Rye refused to don the traditional mayor's frock coat when the king visited Norwich. The king, dressed in the full uniform of a field marshal, was welcomed by Rye dressed in a grey morning suit. 'Did you see the man's trousers?' the king is said to have remarked, while a local newspaper commented in an obituary, 'Walter Rye was Mayor when the King came and he was Walter Rye when he left' (Ryan, 46).

Rye, a 'determined combative character', had two great passions in life, antiquarianism and athletics, and he pursued both with amazing energy. He produced over eighty works on Norfolk local history and topography, and bequeathed his collection of historic manuscripts to the county library, of which he was a co-opted member of the committee. The manuscript collection became the Rye MSS. Rye contributed to the Victoria county history of Norfolk and was well known as an expert on local affairs, including the future of the Norfolk broads, of whose protection society he was founder member and honorary solicitor.

Rye's interest in athletics began with a series of long walks at the age of fifteen with the purpose of collecting descriptions of plants and insects for a diary of natural history finds. The nature of these walks soon shifted to tests of speed and endurance and by seventeen Rye was entering running and walking races for gentleman amateurs, and had become one of the best walkers in the London area. The *Sporting Gazette* recorded on 20 September 1873 that Rye was, 'we believe, the only amateur who has walked 7 miles in an hour, and run a mile inside five minutes in public'. Rye was also a member of the Thames Rowing Club, and it was through this connection that he advertised the first 'handicap paper hunt' of the Thames Hare and Hounds in *The Sportsman* on 3 October 1868, to be held on Saturday 17 October, from the King's Head, Roehampton. This became known as the Thames Handicap Steeplechase no. 1, beginning a series of such races which marked the first organized cross-country running events to be held outside schools.

By 1870 Rye was a powerful figure in the world of athletics administration. He was secretary of the London athletic club and the Thames Hare and Hounds, as well as the athletics correspondent of the *Sporting Gazette*, which allowed him to indulge his taste for controversial comment on a wide variety of issues, most notably on the definition of the 'gentleman amateur'. For a long while Rye was in favour of the clause which restricted the involvement of 'mechanics, artisans and labourers', and confined competition to those who were 'gentlemen by position and education', but, under the influence of his friend Montague Shearman, his silence on the issue at the meeting which formed the Amateur Athletics Association in 1880 was an important factor in the acceptance of a broader definition of amateur status by the new body.

Rye continued as life president of the Thames Hare and Hounds, but in his later years had little to do with the sport of which he was termed the 'father'. He took to tricycling, and carried out a series of long rides around Norfolk, some of which are described in his *Autobiography of an Ancient Athlete and Antiquary* (1916), and then to archery, in which he competed into his eighties. His wife, whom he described as 'the prettiest and pluckiest creature I have ever met', died in 1910. They had seven sons and three daughters. All of the six sons who survived to adulthood became involved in cross-country running, and Frank Gibbs Rye (1874–1948), a solicitor and Conservative MP, succeeded his father as life president of the Thames Hare and Hounds. Rye died at his home, 66 Clarendon Road, Norwich, on 24 February 1928, and was buried in Lamas, near Buxton, Norfolk. M. A. BRYANT

Sources J. Ryan, *The annals of Thames Hare and Hounds, 1868–1945* (1968) · *The Times* (26 Feb 1928) · G. A. Stephen, *Walter Rye: memoir, bibliography, and catalogue of his Norfolk manuscripts in the Norwich public libraries* (1929) · W. Rye, *An autobiography of an ancient athlete and antiquary* (1916) · *Cox's county who's who series: Norfolk, Suffolk, and Cambridgeshire* (1912) · H. F. Pash, ed., *Fifty years of progress, 1880–1930: the jubilee souvenir of the Amateur Athletic Association* [1930] · P. Lovesey, *The official centenary history of the Amateur Athletics Association* (1979) · C. R. J. Currie and C. P. Lewis, eds., *English county histories: a guide* (1994) · m. cert.
Archives Ancient House Museum, Thetford, his typescript index to Thomas Martin's history of Thetford · Norfolk RO, collected notes and papers on Norfolk history · Norfolk RO, corresp. and papers · NRA, priv. coll., corresp. and papers | LUL, letters to J. H. Round · W. Sussex RO, corresp. with Oswald Barron
Likenesses portrait, repro. in Stephen, *Walter Rye* · portrait, repro. in Ryan, *Annals of Thames Hare and Hounds*, 66
Wealth at death £12,420 5s. 10d.: probate, 10 April 1929, CGPLA Eng. & Wales

Rye, William Brenchley (1818–1901), librarian, born at Rochester, Kent, on 26 January 1818, was one of the three sons of Arthur Rye (d. 1832), a doctor, and his wife, Amelia (d. 1861). He was educated at the Chatham and Rochester classical and mathematical school, but the death of his father (aged fifty) left him with little money, and in 1834 he moved to London and entered the office of a solicitor. He met John Winter Jones, afterwards principal librarian of the British Museum, who in 1838, soon after his own appointment there, obtained for Rye employment as a transcriber in the library. Rye's efficiency earned him the good opinion of Antonio Panizzi, then keeper of printed books, who in 1840 secured his appointment as a supernumerary assistant, and in 1844 he was placed on the permanent staff. On the bequest to the nation of the splendid library of Thomas Grenville, Rye was entrusted with its removal to the British Museum in January 1847, and afterwards with its arrangement there. He compiled the third part of the catalogue, which was published in 1872. He selected, arranged, and catalogued the collection of reference books in the new reading-room, opened in 1857, and he drew up the plan showing the placing of the books which was in use for many years. He became an assistant keeper in the department of printed books in 1857, and succeeded Thomas Watts in the keepership in 1869, but failing health and eyesight compelled him to retire in July 1875. He compiled a report on the way in which the collections of the department had developed since the purchase

grant was increased in 1846–7; this impressed the trustees, but Rye was probably even more gratified by the fact that Panizzi (who had retired in 1866) congratulated him on it. The Weigel sale of block-books and incunabula in 1872, at which some important purchases were made, was another significant event in his term of office.

Rye's interests were antiquarian rather than literary, and he was well informed on Old English literature, and medieval architecture and antiquities. He also practised etching. He edited for the Hakluyt Society in 1851, with an introduction and notes, Richard Hakluyt's translation of Fernando de Soto's Portuguese narrative of the *Discovery and Conquest of Terra Florida*, but his principal work was *England as Seen by Foreigners in the Days of Elizabeth and James the First* (1865), a collection of the narratives of foreign visitors, with a valuable introduction, and etchings by himself. He contributed to the early volumes of *Notes and Queries*, and wrote papers for the *Archaeologia Cantiana* and the *Antiquary*. The etchings that he contributed to the *Publications of the Antiquarian Etching Club* (5 vols., 1849–54) were brought together in a privately issued volume in 1857. His collections for a 'History of Rochester', in three quarto volumes, are in the British Library.

Rye married twice: the identity of his first wife is unknown; his second wife, whom he married on 13 December 1866, was Frances Wilhelmina (d. 1923), youngest daughter of William Barker of Camberwell; they had two sons and one daughter, Mary Frances.

Rye, who in his last years was totally blind, died at his home, 41 Lancaster Road, West Norwood, Surrey, from an attack of bronchitis, on 21 December 1901. He was buried in Highgate cemetery on 27 December. The elder of his sons by his second marriage, William Brenchley Rye (1873–1906), became an assistant librarian in the John Rylands Library, Manchester; the younger, Reginald Arthur Rye (1876–1945), was Goldsmiths' librarian of the University of London from 1906 to 1944, and author of *The Libraries of London* (3rd edn, entitled *Students' Guide to the Libraries of London*, 1927).

R. E. GRAVES, *rev.* P. R. HARRIS

Sources *Library Association Record*, 4 (1902), 48–51 · *The Athenaeum* (4 Jan 1902), 18 · P. R. Harris, 'The acquisitions system of the department of printed books in the 1870s', *British Library Journal*, 7 (1981), 120–35
Archives BL · BM · LUL, *England as seen by foreigners in the days of Elizabeth and James I* (1895) with MS corrections and annotations, and a volume of press cuttings
Likenesses photograph, BL
Wealth at death £520 10s. 5d.: probate, 23 Jan 1902, CGPLA Eng. & Wales

Ryerson, (Adolphus) Egerton (1803–1882), educationist and Methodist minister in Canada, was born at Charlotteville township, Norfolk county, Upper Canada, on 24 March 1803, the fifth son of Colonel Joseph Ryerson (1761–1854) and his wife, Mehetabel Stickney (1766–1850). John Ryerson and William Ryerson, Methodist ministers, were his brothers, as was George *Ryerson, a minister of the Catholic Apostolic church. Joseph Ryerson, his father, who was born at Paterson, New Jersey, served as an officer in the loyalist side during the American War of Independence. Afterwards he settled near Fredericton, New Brunswick, whence he moved to Port Ryerse, near Long Point, Norfolk county, Upper Canada, and, with his three elder sons, fought against the United States as a militiaman in the Anglo-American War of 1812–14.

Egerton Ryerson (as he was invariably known) was educated at the London district grammar school, Vittoria, and subsequently worked on his father's farm near Vittoria. He became an assistant teacher in his old school in 1821, the year in which he followed his elder brothers John and William into the Methodist communion. This caused a breach with his father, a staunch Anglican; the latter's adoption of Methodism effected a reconciliation two years later. After a further spell of study was interrupted by serious illness, Egerton Ryerson entered the Methodist ministry in March 1825, and served his apprenticeship in York (Toronto), and on the Credit River mission. He was fully ordained in 1827, and spent the next two years as a travelling preacher on the Cobourg and Ancaster circuits in Ontario. In 1826 he made his first tilt at Anglican ascendancy in Canada, in a published reply to Archdeacon John Strachan, who had imputed disloyalty to the crown to nonconformists. Throughout his life he remained an energetic pamphleteer and newspaper correspondent on political, educational, and religious matters, and was capable of pure invective, particularly if he felt himself to have been slighted. In 1829 he was selected by the Methodist conference as founding editor of the York-based *Christian Guardian*, a post he held, with gaps while he went on his travels to Europe, until 1840. Under his stewardship the paper became one of the most influential in the colony. During this period he also helped to establish the publishing concern that would later become the Ryerson Press.

Ryerson was married, first, on 10 September 1828, at Hamilton, Upper Canada, to Hannah Aikman (d. 1832); their two children both died young. With his second wife, Mary, the daughter of J. R. Armstrong of York, to whom he was married on 8 November 1833, he had two more children, Charles Egerton and Sophia, who survived him. As a delegate at the English Methodist conference in 1833, he helped to unite the Methodist church in Canada (to which he belonged) and the Canadian outpost of the English body. He made a second visit to England in 1835 to raise funds for Victoria College, the Methodist academy in Cobourg, whose foundation he supervised between November 1835 and June 1837, becoming principal in 1841.

In politics Ryerson pursued an independent course that more than once brought on his head accusations of inconsistency and apostasy: after his return from England in the autumn of 1833 he used his own newspaper, and the columns of *The Times*, to attack the Canadian reformer William Lyon Mackenzie and his English allies Joseph Hume and John Arthur Roebuck. This angered Canadian reformers with whom he had been formerly aligned, and he

went on to condemn the rebellion of 1837 in no uncertain terms. Subsequently, having been initially supportive, he became disillusioned with the autocratic (and Anglican-leaning) governorships of Francis Bond Head and his successor Sir George Arthur, and backed the devolved government proposals of the earl of Durham, for whose landmark report of 1838 he supplied information. Yet his faith in the British constitution and his support for the maintenance of the colonial link remained constant, and he backed the governorship of Charles Poulett Thomson, Lord Sydenham (1839–41), who he believed had solved the conundrum 'that a people may be colonists and yet be free' (Gidney, 787). He spent summer 1840 in Britain with his brother William, negotiating the dissolution of the union with the English Methodist conference, among which there was a widespread belief—in marked contrast to the views of most of his Canadian detractors—that the *Christian Guardian* had given succour to colonial radicalism under his stewardship.

Early in 1844 Ryerson was offered the post of superintendent of schools in Upper Canada, which he took up in September of that year, having—with typical controversialist zeal—published a vigorous defence of the governor Charles Theophilus Metcalfe in a series of letters to the *British Colonist*. His 1847 report into education, written after extensive fact-finding tours of Europe and the United States, bore the mark both of his Methodism and empire loyalism: his preference was for a universal, Christian, non-denominational schooling (although on pragmatic grounds he defended the existence of Roman Catholic separate schools). The substance of his plans, and his place in office, survived the election of a reform government in 1848. Major educational legislation was enacted under his aegis in 1846, 1850, and 1871; the last provided for free tuition and a degree of compulsory attendance. In office he was a voluminous and methodical correspondent, wrote school textbooks, and edited the *Journal of Education for Upper Canada* (1848–75). He undertook educational tours of the province, promoted school libraries, and created a museum of art and science. Grammar schools were given public funding and prescribed a broad curriculum, and a system of local schools inspection was set in place. In higher education he defended denominational colleges (such as the one he had helped to set up), which during his later years in office set him against those who wished to see a comprehensive university in the province.

Ryerson retired in February 1876, having struggled against intermittent poor health for the previous decade and a half (at the age of nearly sixty, his typically robust response to the onset of illness was to take up sailing and rowing). His achievement was to impose a strong centralized authority upon the patchwork structure he had inherited, and so to establish 'the first effective social service bureaucracy in the province's history' (Gidney, 790). Three honorary degrees acknowledged his efforts, but he still made enemies—usually on the liberal side. Sometimes he handed his opponents ammunition, as in 1855-7, when it emerged that he had creamed off the interest on public funds held in his name—not then illegal, but increasingly thought unacceptable.

Having been estranged from the church for a time in 1854–5, Ryerson was made the first president of the Canadian Methodists in 1871, and published a history of Canadian Methodism in 1882. An abiding interest of his retirement was the history of American loyalism, which bore literary fruit in *The Loyalists of America and their Times*, (2 vols., 1880). He died at Toronto on 19 February 1882 and was buried in Mount Pleasant cemetery. His autobiography, which lay incomplete at his death, was edited by John George Hodgkins and published in 1883 as *The Story of my Life*. H. J. SPENCER

Sources *DNB* · R. D. Gidney, 'Ryerson, Egerton', *DCB*, vol. 11 · Allibone, *Dict.*

Archives University of Toronto, United Church Archives, corresp. | NA Canada, John A. Macdonald papers · Public Archives of Ontario, Toronto, papers of the education department · Public Archives of Ontario, Toronto, John George Hodgkins papers, corresp., MSS 1375–1381

Likenesses statue, 1889, grounds of the education department, Toronto

Ryerson, George (1791–1882), preacher and minister of the Catholic Apostolic church, was born at Maugerville, near Fredericton, New Brunswick, Canada, on 7 March 1791. He was the son of Joseph Ryerson (1761–1854), farmer and soldier, and his wife, Mehetabel, *née* Stickney (1766–1850). He was the eldest brother of Egerton *Ryerson. The family soon moved to Charlotteville, near Vittoria, Ontario, and Ryerson attended the London district grammar school. As an officer under his father in the 1st Norfolk militia he assisted in the capture of Detroit (1812), but severe wounds received in a later engagement permanently impaired his speech. Hoping to take orders he studied for a time at Union College, Schenectady, New York (though the college has no record of him), and after repeated rejections by the Anglican authorities he followed his brothers into the Methodist ministry. In 1820 he married Sarah Rolph, the settlement of whose mother's estate later took him to England. Appointed a justice of the peace for London, Ontario (1821), he was an unsuccessful reform candidate in the general election of 1824. In England on family business in 1828, he presented, on behalf of the Canadian Methodists, a petition for recognition in the field of education to the House of Commons in May and June.

On returning to his previous work in the Indian reserves, Ryerson was active in the Credit River and Grand River missions, during which time his wife died, on 10 July 1829. Following his earlier experience in England and his informed contributions to the *Christian Guardian*, Ryerson was chosen to present further petitions in England where, in June 1831, he put to the colonial secretary, Lord Goderich, the case for opening the University of Upper Canada to non-Anglicans. However, his disillusion with British Methodism, the apparent godlessness of London, the cholera, and the current political crisis were all pushing Ryerson towards the extreme apocalypticism of Edward Irving and the emerging Catholic Apostolic church. On 29 September 1832 he was imprisoned with a fellow Irvingite, James Evill, for open-air preaching at Charing Cross— an episode unknown to his Canadian biographers. Ryerson's subsequent decision to withdraw from public life deprived his brother Egerton, whose remonstrances were unavailing, of a shrewd and perceptive counsellor. On 15 June 1836 he married Sophia (d. 1849), the daughter of Edward Symes of London. On returning home he became a leading figure in the Canadian Catholic Apostolic church, serving as the angel (bishop) in Toronto from 1837 to 1872. In 1853 he married Isabella Dorcas, the daughter of Judge Ansel Sterling. The *Toronto Globe*'s report of his death at 317 Church Street, Toronto, on 19 December 1882 epitomized the tranquil obscurity of his later life by misnaming him William Ryerson, an error repeated in the *Dictionary of National Biography*. His widow died exactly ten years later. TIMOTHY C. F. STUNT

Sources C. Dougall, 'Ryerson, George', *DCB*, vol. 11 · A. W. Ryerson, *The Ryerson genealogy* (1916), 111 · G. S. Ryerson, *Looking backward* (1924), 18–22 · C. B. Sissons, *Egerton Ryerson: his life and letters* (1937), 1–167 · S. Newman-Norton, 'A biographical index of those associated with the Lord's work', Bodl. Oxf., MS facs b.61 [Ryerson, George; Evill, James] · E. Ryerson, *The loyalists of America and their times*, 2 (1880), 257 · *The Globe* [Toronto] (21 Dec 1882)

Likenesses photograph, repro. in Sissons, *Egerton Ryerson*, vol. 1, facing p. 32 · photograph (aged ninety), repro. in Ryerson, *Looking backward*, facing p. 18

Rygge, Robert (d. 1410), theologian and university principal, was presumably a native of Devon or Cornwall who must have become a scholar at Oxford shortly before 1360, since he was admitted a fellow of Exeter College in 1361. He remained a fellow until about 1365, and retained his connections with both college and diocese: as founder of a loan chest in the college, its benefactor in his will, and as one of its visitors appointed in 1378 by Thomas Brantingham, bishop of Exeter; and as executor of the bishop at the latter's death in 1394, as vicar-general to his successor, Edmund Stafford (d. 1419), from 1400, and as successively canon of the cathedral (18 December 1392), archdeacon of Barnstaple (16 February 1395), and chancellor of Exeter (30 January 1400). However it was at Oxford that he was briefly to become notorious. He was elected a fellow of Merton College in 1365, and took his turn as one of its bursars between 1371 and 1374. Among his colleagues was Mr John Aston, later one of the radical Dr John Wyclif's most ardent supporters, and a younger fellow, Mr William James, described by an unsympathetic observer in 1382 as *familiarissimus* with Rygge, who would devote many years to propagating Wyclif's cause. In these circumstances it is probable that as opinion polarized in Oxford for or against Wyclif's criticisms of church endowments, hostility to the friars, and rejection of the doctrine of transubstantiation during the 1370s, Rygge came to be one of the evangelical doctor's admirers if not a disciple. Like Wyclif he had turned to theology, and was already bachelor by 1378 and doctor by 1381 at the latest. He was therefore qualified to sit on the committee of twelve appointed by the university chancellor, Dr William Barton, to examine the orthodoxy of Wyclif's teaching on the eucharist in 1380 or 1381; the committee duly condemned Wyclif's doctrines, some time before May 1381, but evidently not unanimously, as Wyclif himself referred to the 'six or seven distorters of the truth' (Wyclif, 89) whose opinion had formed the majority. Rygge was presumably one of the minority who opposed the condemnation.

Rygge was himself elected chancellor probably shortly before 1 June 1381. Although he is not known to have defended Wyclif in his last months in Oxford, he gave active support to Wyclif's remaining associates, Dr Nicholas Hereford and Mr Philip Repingdon (d. 1424), in their onslaught on the friars in Hilary term 1382, and ignored the protests of the Benedictine John Wells (d. 1388) and the Carmelite Peter Stokes (d. 1399); he appointed Hereford to preach the Ascension day (15 May) sermon in St Frideswide's churchyard, and Repingdon that for Corpus Christi day (5 June). He was probably aware that the friars had the backing of the new archbishop of Canterbury, William Courtenay (d. 1396), but in spite of the archbishop's direct mandate chose not to publish either his official inhibitions or the list of propositions condemned at Courtenay's Blackfriars council held in May of that year, relying on the university's immunity from ecclesiastical jurisdiction. He was therefore summoned with his colleague Mr Thomas Brightwell before Courtenay and his councillors at Lambeth, examined, and after some argument induced to submit; he published the council's decrees in Oxford on 15 June, forcing the Wycliffite masters to face prosecution. Nevertheless Rygge did his best to prevent their Oxford opponents from attacking them, suspending the Cistercian Dr Henry Crump for describing them as 'Lollards'. For this he was again summoned to London, this time before the king's council, and required both to reinstate Crump and to inquire into any heretical opinions held within the university (13–14 July). By November, when Courtenay held a session of convocation in Oxford, Rygge had entirely submitted, and used his influence to induce other Wycliffite masters to conform.

Rygge claimed in his defence only to be maintaining university privileges, and his animus against the friars was traditional in Oxford. If his associations with Wycliffites suggest that his sympathy with them was more than his representative role demanded, he showed no further sign of unorthodoxy, and was probably responsible for the marked absence of theological controversy in Oxford during the 1380s. In this stance he received full support from his colleagues, being re-elected chancellor every year until 25 May 1388, when, having failed to control riots among the northern and southern scholars, he was removed by order of parliament. Archbishop Courtenay worked with him, and was possibly influential in procuring for him the prebend of Dultingcote at Wells in August 1386, which he held for the rest of his life. But it was from Exeter in Devon that he was summoned with other elder statesmen of the university to advise the crown on the papal schism in January 1399. Rygge died,

probably at Exeter, between 24 March and 10 April 1410. His abandonment of radicalism was no more opportunistic than that of other Wycliffites such as Philip Repingdon and Nicholas Hereford themselves, both of whom prospered in the established church after their eventual submissions. One book of his survives: a copy of the encyclopaedia of Bartholomaeus Anglicus, *De proprietatibus rerum* (Bodl. Oxf., MS Bodley 749), one of the volumes he bequeathed to Exeter College.   JEREMY CATTO

Sources Exeter College, Oxford, rectors' accounts · Merton Oxf., records, 3698–9, 3701–6, 3708–9, 3713, 4171b, 4172–3, 6048–50 · Bartholomaeus Anglicus, 'De proprietatibus rerum', Bodl. Oxf., MS Bodley 749 · will, PRO, PROB 11/2A, sig. 21 · F. C. Hingeston-Randolph, ed., *The register of Thomas de Brantyngham, bishop of Exeter*, 2 vols. (1901–6), vol. 1, pp. 124, 155; vol. 2, p. 748 · F. C. Hingeston-Randolph, ed., *The register of Edmund Stafford, 1395–1419* (1886), 166, 311, 379 · *CPR, 1385–9*, 208 · *CClR, 1396–9*, 367–8 · [T. Netter], *Fasciculi zizaniorum magistri Johannis Wyclif cum tritico*, ed. W. W. Shirley, Rolls Series, 5 (1858), 110–13, 272–82, 292–319 · D. Wilkins, ed., *Concilia Magnae Britanniae et Hiberniae*, 3 (1737), 171 · A. Hudson, 'Wycliffism in Oxford, 1381–1411', *Wyclif in his times*, ed. A. Kenny (1986), 67–84 · J. I. Catto, 'Wyclif and Wycliffism at Oxford, 1356–1430', *Hist. U. Oxf.* 2: *Late med. Oxf.*, 175–261 · Emden, *Oxf.* · J. Wyclif, *De blasphemia*, ed. M. H. Dziewicki (1893)

Ryland, Arthur (1807–1877), lawyer and local politician, was born on 23 August 1807 at Edgbaston, Birmingham, the fifth of six children of John Ryland, wire manufacturer. After attending the Revd D. N. Walton's School in Cherry Street, Birmingham, and a spell in his father's business, he was articled to William Palmer in 1823. On admission in 1828 he practised alone and with his elder brother Timothy, before entering into partnership with Thomas Martineau in 1851. He was married twice. His first wife, and mother of his daughter, Frances, was the daughter of Thomas Tyndall. After her death he married his cousin Anna Smith Phipson.

Ryland belonged to an old Unitarian Birmingham family which had long held a leading position in the town. He occupied a prominent place in the public life of Birmingham from the 1840s to the 1870s. His public role was shaped by his religious beliefs, family influence, occupation, and professional ideology. He quickly built up a successful practice, attracting work from private clients, companies, and public bodies. He held several important legal appointments, such as clerk to the justices and clerk to the guardians of the assay office. In 1852 he published a treatise on the law relating to the assay of precious metals. Questions of law reform also occupied his time. Ryland was active in local and national professional organizations and played an important part in their development. In 1831 he founded the Birmingham Law Library Society. He was president of the Birmingham Law Society in 1873 and again in 1876. He was influential in the creation of the Metropolitan and Provincial Law Association, and in 1863 was the first provincial solicitor elected to the council of the Incorporated Law Society, London.

Ryland's professional training and acumen, wide social circle, reforming zeal, and personal beliefs made him the ideal 'committee man'. He had firm views on the duty owed by professionals, especially solicitors, to devote their skills and knowledge freely to the service of the community. These views found their most concrete expression in an address to the Birmingham Law Students' Society in 1861.

Ryland was a staunch Liberal, being connected with the Political Union, the incorporation movement in the 1830s, and the agitation that saw the town council replace the older, oligarchic municipal bodies in 1851. He first entered the council in 1854 at a time when it was dominated by the parsimonious 'economist' party. Ryland orchestrated a campaign both within and outside the council to change the nature of municipal government. He remained on the council until 1874 (as mayor in 1860 and alderman from 1861) and made a large contribution to establishing the basis from which Joseph Chamberlain could build the 'civic gospel'.

Ryland was instrumental in the foundation, administration, and support of numerous local charities and institutions. His major achievement was the establishment in 1853 of the Birmingham and Midland Institute to rectify the dearth of adult education facilities and literary culture in Birmingham. The plan drew widespread support, including that of Charles Dickens, who performed the first public readings of *A Christmas Carol* to raise funds.

Ryland began to retire from public life in 1874. He left Edgbaston and built a house near Bromsgrove, Worcestershire. Although in bad health he took a holiday at Cannes, France, where he died on 24 March 1877 as the result of inflammation of the lungs. He was buried at Cannes.

ANDREW ROWLEY

Sources T. Martineau, 'Mr Arthur Ryland', *The Institute Magazine* (Dec 1892), 49–56; (Jan 1893), 74–81 • 'Arthur Ryland', *Edgbastonia*, 2 (1882), 76–9 • G. H. Osborne, newspaper cuttings: Birmingham biography 1, BRL 60534 • G. H. Osborne, obituary notices: Birmingham and district 1, BRL 243129 • R. Waterhouse, 'Arthur Ryland's First Journal', *Central Literary Magazine*, 39 (1961), 10–17 • M. McGowen, 'Arthur Ryland of Birmingham and some new Dickens letters', *The Dickensian*, 74 (1978) • *Solicitors' Journal*, 21 (1876–7), 417–18 • Boase, *Mod. Eng. biog.*
Likenesses J. W. Gordon, oils; Sothebys, 1978 [previously on loan by council of Midland Institute to Birmingham Museums and Art Gallery] • engraving, repro. in *Edgbastonia* • engraving, repro. in *The Institute Magazine* (Dec 1892), 49–56
Wealth at death under £30,000: probate, 23 April 1877, *CGPLA Eng. & Wales*

Ryland, Herman Witsius (*c.*1759–1838), colonial official, born probably at Northampton or Warwick, was the younger son of John Collett *Ryland (1723–1792), a Baptist minister, and his wife, Elizabeth Frith (*d.* 1779) of Warwick, and the brother of John *Ryland. He was trained for the army and in 1781 was assistant deputy paymaster-general to the British forces in North America. At the end of the war he returned to England with Sir Guy Carleton, who had negotiated the peace. Nothing is known of his activities in the following ten years until in 1793 he became civil secretary to Carleton, by then Lord Dorchester and governor of Lower Canada. The position brought him considerable influence and a salary which enabled him to marry, on or about 26 December 1794, Charlotte Warwick, an English woman to whom he had

been betrothed for about ten years. Ryland remained civil secretary to Dorchester's successor, Robert Prescott, but resigned after a quarrel in 1798 and returned to England, where he worked for the recall of Prescott. In 1799 Prescott was replaced by Robert Shore Milnes, and Ryland returned to Lower Canada as his civil secretary. After 1807 he continued as civil secretary under Sir James Henry Craig, with whom he worked particularly closely. As well as receiving a substantial salary as civil secretary, he held an array of well-paid influential posts, notably that of clerk of the executive council from 1796. In 1811 he was also appointed to the legislative council.

Ryland worked to establish the supremacy of the crown and the furthering of British interests in Canada, in part by securing the position of the Church of England and particularly by reducing the power of the Roman Catholic church, to which as a Baptist he was also personally opposed.

In 1810 Craig sent Ryland to London to obtain acceptance for a wide range of proposals designed to increase executive influence in the colony and to justify the repressive measures which the Francophobic Craig had taken during what the Canadians described as a 'reign of terror'. One of these proposals was a reunion of the Canadas. However, Ryland achieved little and he returned to Canada in 1812 to find that Craig's successor, Sir George Prevost, had effectively displaced him as civil secretary. In 1813 he was compelled to resign, although he retained his lucrative post as clerk of the executive council. For the next two decades Ryland used his position in the legislative council to thwart any efforts to conciliate the assembly of Lower Canada, but only during the brief administration of Sir Francis Nathaniel Burton did he exercise much direct influence on executive policy. Gradually his official positions were stripped from him, although he remained clerk of the executive council until shortly before his death.

From about 1834 Ryland was in poor health, and he died on 20 July 1838 at Beauport, Lower Canada, where he had held an estate since 1805. Of his nine children only four survived him. He was an old-fashioned placeman with an insatiable appetite for lucrative posts, but he was competent and apparently scrupulously honest. He was an extreme tory, increasingly out of touch with political realities in the colony and in the mother country. Intensely hostile to the Roman Catholic church and to the rise of French-Canadian nationalism, he recommended extreme policies which were partly responsible for the rebellions of 1837–8. C. A. HARRIS, *rev.* ELIZABETH BAIGENT

Sources *DCB*, vol. 7 • R. C. Dalton, *The Jesuits' estate question* (1968) • R. Christie, *A history of the late province of Lower Canada*, 6 vols. (1848–66)
Archives NA Canada, corresp. and papers | BL, letters to the second Earl Spencer • NA Scot., corresp. with Lord Dalhousie
Likenesses portrait, NA Canada

Ryland, John (1716/17–1798), friend of Samuel Johnson, was born in London, but spent his early years at Stratford upon Avon. Though trained for the law he entered commerce, and for many years was a West India merchant on

Tower Hill, London. As a young man he spent much of his time with John Hawkesworth, and subsequently married his sister. Through this relationship he contributed to the *Gentleman's Magazine*, and during Hawkesworth's occasional absences from London he saw the periodical through the press.

Ryland was acquainted with Samuel Johnson for many years, and was the last surviving friend of his early life. He belonged to the old club that met weekly in 1749 at the King's Head in Ivy Lane and was broken up about 1753, and he was one of the four surviving members who dined together in 1783. He also belonged to the Essex Head Club, which Johnson formed at the close of his life. He constantly visited Johnson in his last illness, he supplied John Nichols with several of the particulars which are inserted in the article in the *Gentleman's Magazine* for 1784 (p. 957), and attended the funeral. Several of Johnson's letters to him are included in the correspondence edited by G. B. Hill, but he is seldom mentioned by Boswell, possibly because these letters were withheld from publication in Boswell's *Life*. In religion a dissenter, in politics a staunch whig, Ryland was a good scholar, and expressed himself well both in speech and in writing. He died at Cooper's Row, Crutched Friars, London, on 24 June 1798, aged eighty-one. W. P. COURTNEY, *rev.* MICHAEL BEVAN

Sources *Boswell's Life of Johnson*, ed. G. B. Hill, 6 vols. (1887), vol. 1, p. 242; vol. 4, pp. 360, 435–6 · *GM*, 1st ser., 68 (1798), 629–30 · Nichols, *Lit. anecdotes*, 9.500–02

Ryland, John (1753–1825), Baptist minister and theologian, was born at Warwick on 29 January 1753, the elder son of John Collett *Ryland (1723–1792), Baptist minister and schoolmaster, and his first wife, Elizabeth Frith (*d.* 1779) of Warwick. His brother, Herman Witsius *Ryland, was a civil servant in British North America. His father was a 'burly and explosive' Calvinist who was suspicious of any suggestion of Arminianism, notwithstanding a genuine evangelical experience. Young Ryland, who was educated at his father's school, was a precocious child. He could read Psalm 23 in Hebrew when only five years old and by the time he was nine had read through the Greek Testament. As a teenager it was clear that his ability was matched by spiritual understanding and maturity rare in someone so young. On 13 September 1767 he was baptized in the River Nene near Northampton. Before he was fifteen he began to assist his father in his school at Northampton, where he became pastor in 1759. Then in 1781 he was associated with his father in the Northamptonshire pastorate. On his father's retirement in 1786 he became sole pastor. Ryland was one of a group of ministers within the Northamptonshire Association who were beginning to throw off the shackles of hyper-Calvinism. He himself had been brought up in a Calvinistic home and in the College Lane Chapel, which were dominated by his father's strong convictions; so it was natural that he imbibed some of his father's views, especially his Calvinism. In addition, when preaching at Andrew Fuller's funeral in 1815, Ryland acknowledged the influence of 'Newton and the first Robert Hall who were the counsellors of my youth'

John Ryland (1753–1825), by unknown engraver

(Champion, 'Theology of John Ryland', 17). Robert Hall senior, who was minister of the church at Arnesby (1753–91), modified his basic Calvinism in writing his *Help to Zion's Travellers* (1781), while John Newton, vicar of Olney (1764–79) and rector of St Mary Woolnoth (1779–1807), kept in touch with Ryland, writing to him two or three times a year between 1774 and 1807. Newton remained a strict Calvinist, yet interpreted it with a warm personal piety. It was, however, Ryland's study of the Bible and the writings of Jonathan Edwards which chiefly brought about his change of viewpoint. On 23 April 1784 he received a parcel of books from John Erskine of Edinburgh. Among them was a pamphlet by Edwards, *An humble attempt to promote explicit agreement and visible union of God's people in extraordinary prayer*. This pamphlet had a profound influence on Ryland and his two close friends Andrew Fuller and John Sutcliff, and through them it affected the thinking of the whole Northamptonshire Association. This was particularly significant, as the churches comprising the association agreed to meet monthly for united prayer for the revival of religion at home and 'the spread of the Gospel to the most distant parts of the habitable globe' (Stanley, 5).

Ryland and Sutcliff were both founder members of the Baptist Missionary Society (BMS) and both were frequently consulted by the secretary, Andrew Fuller. When Fuller died in 1815 it was perhaps natural, amid the crisis about his successor, that John Ryland should be chosen, serving first with James Hinton of Oxford and latterly with John Dyer, who became the society's first full-time salaried secretary. Ryland left Northampton for Bristol within a year of the formation of the BMS, and as a principal of Bristol Baptist College did not hesitate to put the claims of the society to his students. In fact no less than twenty-six of his students served with the Baptist mission during his principalship. It is to Ryland that the BMS owes its earliest links with the West Indies. Moses Baker, a man of mixed race from New York working on the plantations, teaching the slaves the elements of the gospel, encountered the fury of the planters. He entered into a correspondence with Ryland, who then consulted with Wilberforce. The result was that in December 1813 the BMS sent John Rowe, a student of Ryland's, to Jamaica.

There was one further occasion when Ryland was actively involved in the affairs of the mission. This was in 1819. Dyer had written to William Carey about the criticisms of Joshua Marshman by the younger missionaries, and Carey had replied to the charges. Carey was deeply hurt when two letters arrived from Ryland, one to Carey, the other to Marshman, repeating the charges brought against Marshman by the junior missionaries. Although Ryland had died before the break with Serampore, this intervention by him marked the beginning of the end of the BMS's relations with the mission at Serampore.

In 1793 Ryland became president of the Bristol Baptist College and minister of Broadmead Chapel at Bristol, having been made a DD by Brown University in the previous year. About 200 students passed through his hands during his principalship. At the same time, the college moved to new premises at Stokes Croft at a total cost of over £12,000. In addition to Hebrew, Greek, and Latin, he taught his students theology, church history, sacred antiquity, rhetoric, and logic by the 'seminar method', rather than by producing any lectures of his own. He published numerous sermons and charges and wrote many recommendatory prefaces for religious works and for biographies of his friends. He was also a popular hymn writer, though of the ninety-nine hymns he wrote, only three were in common use by the twentieth century, and only one, 'Let us sing the king messiah', at the end of the century.

Ryland was twice married. On 12 January 1780 he married Elizabeth Tyler, daughter of Robert Tyler of Banbury; she died on 23 January 1787, a few weeks after the birth of their only child. Two years later, on 18 June 1789, he married Frances Barrett of Northampton, who survived him. They had three daughters and one son, Jonathan Edwards *Ryland, who was secretary of Bristol Baptist College for two years (1823–5).

Ryland promoted evangelical views among Baptists in the west country, guarding against 'Pelagian pride' on one hand and 'Antinomian licentiousness' on the other. Essentially a scholar, he was widely read, concerned about accuracy in detail, and interested in subjects outside his own field, including natural history. As a teacher he moulded the thinking of many of the early BMS missionaries. Shy, gentle in manner, and charitable in judgement, he was a man of deep piety. He had friends in other denominations, including Toplady, Newton, and Scott,

and was an advocate of 'mixed communion'. Ryland died on 25 May 1825 at Bristol and was buried on 2 June in the burial-ground adjoining Broadmead Chapel.

E. F. CLIPSHAM

Sources J. Culross, *The three Rylands: a hundred years of various Christian service* (1897) · N. S. Moon, '"Widening the horizons", 1792–1825', *Education for ministry: Bristol Baptist College, 1679–1979* (1979), 27–39 · L. G. Champion, 'The theology of John Ryland, its sources and its influences', *Baptist Quarterly*, 28 (1979–80), 17–29 · L. G. Champion, 'The letters of John Newton to John Ryland', *Baptist Quarterly*, 27 (1977–8), 157–63 · H. W. Robinson, 'The experience of John Ryland', *Baptist Quarterly*, 4 (1928–9), 17–26 · B. Stanley, *The history of the Baptist Missionary Society, 1792–1992* (1992) · DNB · G. F. Nuttall, 'Northamptonshire and The modern question: a turning-point in eighteenth-century dissent', *Journal of Theological Studies*, new ser., 16 (1965), 101–23 · W. Newman, *Rylandiana* (1835)

Archives Northants. RO, corresp., notebooks, MSS · Regent's Park College, Oxford, Angus Library, corresp. | Bodl. Oxf., corresp. with William Wilberforce

Likenesses W. Walker, engraving, 1815 (after portrait, Bristol Baptist College) · N. C. Bramwaite, engraving, 1824 (after portrait, Bristol Baptist College) · J. Goldgar, engraving · Granger, engraving · R. Houston, engraving (after J. Russell, 1775) · J. Thornthwaite, engraving (after J. Burgniss) · engraving, NPG [*see illus.*] · portrait, Bristol Baptist College

Ryland, John Collett (1723–1792), Baptist minister and schoolmaster, the son of Joseph Ryland (d. 1748), a farmer and grazier of Lower Ditchford, Gloucestershire, and his wife, Freelove Collett (d. 1728), and grandson of John Ryland, yeoman, of Hinton on the Green, was born at Bourton on the Water on 12 October 1723. His mother came from a farm named Slaughter in the same parish and was a collateral descendant of John Colet, dean of St Paul's. She died when Ryland was five. He was baptized on 2 October 1741 by Benjamin Beddome, who was instrumental in sending him about 1744 to Bernard Foskett's academy at Bristol to prepare for the ministry. After considerable spiritual conflict he left Bristol about 1746 and was ordained pastor of the Baptist church in Warwick on 26 July 1750; John Brine preached at his ordination service. He also kept a school in St Mary's parsonage, which he rented from the rector, Dr Tate, who, when criticized for harbouring a dissenter, used to retort that he had brought the man as near the church as he could, though he could not force him into it.

Ryland married, on 23 December 1748, Elizabeth Frith (d. 1779) of Warwick. They had five children: their eldest child, who died very young, Elizabeth (d. 1821), James, John *Ryland (1753–1825), and Herman Witsius *Ryland (c.1759–1838). In 1751 he compiled an extensive register of Baptist congregations in England and Wales. Perhaps owing to disagreements over closed communion he left his Warwick congregation in October 1759 and moved to Northampton, where he lived for twenty-six years as minister and schoolmaster. His school had premises in Horsemarket, Sheep Lane, and Market Street, and his pupils, who often numbered as many as ninety, included Samuel Baxter and Robert Hall the younger. The newly founded Brown University in Providence, Rhode Island, conferred on him an MA in 1769. Following his wife's death he married, on 13 February 1782, Mrs Stott, the widow of an army officer. On 2 July 1784 he delivered at sunrise over the grave of Andrew Gifford in Bunhill Fields an oration which was published and twice reprinted (1834 and 1888).

In 1786 Ryland resigned the care of his church to his son John, who had been co-pastor since 1781, and moved his school to Enfield, where it grew and flourished. Several of his assistant teachers followed him into the Baptist ministry, such as William Newman. Ryland frequently preached in the neighbourhood, often at the countess of Huntingdon's chapel at Chaseside, but he did not have a pastoral charge. Massive in stature, he had a singing voice like the roaring of the sea. He had a quick apprehension, a lively imagination, and fine memory, but tended to be a little eccentric. He is said to have once addressed from a coach-box, wearing a seven-storied wig, holiday crowds assembled on the flat banks of the Lea, near Ponder's End.

Ryland had a passion for publishing and his output was considerable. Once or twice this involved him in financial difficulties, which were one factor in the move to Enfield. Neither printer, publisher, nor engraver could turn out their work half fast enough for him. As his friends James Hervey and Augustus Toplady told him, he would have done more had he done less. His range of publications included poetry, biography, essays, theological tracts, and a grammar for the Greek New Testament. With the astronomer James Ferguson he published two scientific works on mechanics and optics. He also contributed to the *Baptist Annual Register*, edited by John Rippon, wrote many of the articles for Buck's *Theological Dictionary* (1802), and edited works by Edward Polhill, John Quarles, Jonathan Edwards, and Cotton Mather. He belonged to the influential group of Baptist ministers in Northamptonshire that formed an association in 1764. Calvinist in theology, he was not narrow in his views, and wrote under the pseudonym of Pacificus *A Modest Plea for Free Communion* in 1772. He was a passionate supporter of the American cause in the War of Independence. He read widely and voraciously, and it is his chief merit to have done more than perhaps any man of his time to promote learning among Baptists and orthodox dissenters.

Ryland died at Enfield on 24 July 1792 and was buried at Northampton, his funeral sermon being preached by John Rippon; an elegy on his death was published by Legatus in 1792. He was survived by his wife.

CHARLOTTE FELL-SMITH, *rev.* S. L. COPSON

Sources W. Newman, *Rylandiana* (1835) · J. Rippon, *The gentle dismission of saints from earth to heaven* (1792) · 'The life of the Rev. John Ryland', *Evangelical Magazine*, 8 (1800), 397–405 · *GM*, 1st ser., 62 (1792), 678 · *Baptist Annual Register* (1790–93), 124–5, 329 · *DCB*, vol. 7 · P. J. Wallis, 'A check-list of the writings of John [Collett] Ryland, 1723–1792', Newcastle upon Tyne, 1972
Archives Northants. RO, commonplace books
Likenesses R. Houston, mezzotint (after J. Russell), BM; repro. in Witsen, *Oeconomia* (1775)

Ryland, Jonathan Edwards (1798–1866), translator and writer, was born at Northampton on 5 May 1798, the only son of John *Ryland (1753–1825), Baptist minister, and his second wife, Frances, eldest daughter of William Barrett. His earlier years were spent in Bristol. He was educated at Bristol Baptist College, over which his father presided, and at Edinburgh University, where he was a pupil of Dr Thomas Brown. For a time he was mathematical and classical tutor at Mill Hill College, Middlesex, and for a short period he taught at Bradford College, at Bradford in Yorkshire. On 4 January 1828 he married Frances, daughter of John Buxton of Northampton. He afterwards moved to Bristol, and in 1835 went to Northampton, where he remained for the rest of his life.

Ryland was well acquainted with Hebrew, Latin, Greek, and German, but he was shy and reserved in manner, and did not do himself justice; he chiefly edited and translated the works of others. His earliest compositions appeared in *The Visitor* (1823); he was a writer for the *Baptist Magazine*, and he edited volumes 9–12 of the fifth series of the *Eclectic Review*. He wrote for Kitto's *Cyclopaedia of Biblical Literature*, and he published in 1856 a memoir of Kitto. In 1864 he produced *Wholesome Words, or, One Hundred Choice Passages from Old Authors*, and to the eighth edition of the *Encyclopaedia Britannica* he contributed memoirs of John Foster, Andrew Fuller, John Kitto, Robert Robinson, Friedrich Schleiermacher, and Schwartz, and the articles on Northampton and Northamptonshire.

Ryland's translations included *Justin Martyr: his Life, Writings, and Opinions* (1843), after Semisch; *Guido and Julius* (1836), after Tholuck; *The Weaver of Quelbrunn* (1851), after Barth; the *Life of Christ* (vol. 2, 1864), after Lange; two treatises by Hengstenberg; and several volumes by Neander on the history of the church (1842).

Ryland edited the *Pastoral Memorials* of his father (1826–8), and the *Life and Correspondence of John Foster* (1846). He also edited Foster's *Essays* and *Lectures*.

In 1852 the degree of MA was conferred on Ryland by Brown University, Rhode Island. He died of pneumonia and heart disease at Waterloo, Northampton, on 16 April 1866.   W. P. COURTNEY, *rev.* JAMES EDGAR BARCUS, JR.

Sources J. Culross, *The three Rylands* (1897) · *GM*, 4th ser., 1 (1866), 771 · *The Freeman* (27 April 1866), 263, 269, 279 · Boase, *Mod. Eng. biog.* · d. cert.
Wealth at death under £300: administration, 26 Oct 1866, *CGPLA Eng. & Wales*

Ryland, William Wynne (bap. 1733, d. 1783), engraver, baptized on 2 December 1733 in St Martin Ludgate, London, was the eldest of seven sons of Edward Ryland (d. 1771?), engraver and copperplate printer, and his wife, Mary. It is said that Sir William Watkins Wynne was his godfather. In 1748 he was apprenticed to his father in the Stationers' Company, and under him learned much about the business of print production; he also studied drawing at the St Martin's Lane Academy and engraving under the immigrant history engraver François Ravenet. He went to France to complete his training by studying figure drawing under François Boucher and etching under Jacques Philippe le Bas. The German engraver Johann Georg Wille noted in his journal that he had got to know Ryland when he was in Paris about 1757–8. He was married to his wife

William Wynne Ryland (*bap.* 1733, *d.* 1783), by D. P. Pariset (after Pierre Étienne Falconet, 1768)

Mary by June 1759, when their first daughter was baptized. At the time of his death there were six children, four of whom were being educated in France.

In 1758 Ryland accepted the commission, previously refused by Robert Strange, to engrave Allan Ramsay's full-length portraits of the prince of Wales and Lord Bute. For these he was paid £50 per quarter and a further 100 guineas for his drawings and the copyright in the prints. When he presented the first finished engraving to the soon-to-be-crowned monarch in 1761 he was appointed engraver to the king with a pension of £200 p.a. for eight years. The portrait of Bute (1763) was followed by state portraits of the king and Queen Charlotte in coronation robes. Ryland received a further £100 p.a. pension from the queen. Thus richly endowed with royal favour, Ryland launched simultaneous careers as an artist and as a printseller.

In 1762 Ryland took a first apprentice, William Pym, and in 1764 a second, Joseph Strutt. The next year, 1765, he went into partnership in a print shop with Henry Bryer, who had just completed an apprenticeship with Ryland's father. Their shop sign, the King's Arms, boasted their royal connection, and from its prestigious site opposite the Royal Exchange in Cornhill they published contemporary paintings. Ryland was one of the earliest printsellers to buy paintings that had created a stir at the new exhibitions held by the Society of Artists in order to make prints of them, and it would appear that the firm of

Ryland and Bryer also dealt more broadly in paintings. During the late 1760s they encouraged and exploited a new enthusiasm for contemporary British art and their firm was one of the most significant publishers in this field. Ryland was able to make good use of business connections that he had established during his training in Paris and from the first it is likely that he was importing and exporting prints and perhaps paintings too. He was also empowered to purchase art on behalf of the king. On a visit to Wille in May 1765 he bought a series of the finest impressions of Wille's historical prints for George III. At this date Ryland's home address in Stafford Row, near the queen's palace, was conveniently situated for attendance at court, where his fluency in French stood him in good stead with the queen and her German entourage. His engraving of Francis Cotes's portrait of Queen Charlotte with the royal princesses was published in 1770.

Ryland's reputation as an artist was founded on his excellent royal portraits, but he advertised his cosmopolitan sophistication at the Society of Artists' 1761 exhibition with a print after Boucher. He was elected a fellow of the society upon its incorporation in 1765 and was a director in 1768–9, but was expelled in 1772 after exhibiting with the Royal Academy. His familiarity with the latest French methods for facsimile reproduction of drawings was put to good use between 1762 and 1768 in fifty-three prints of old-master drawings in British collections commissioned by Charles Rogers and involving 'several new Inventions and various Methods of Handling' (Rogers, 246).

In 1771 Ryland's affairs suffered a sudden and serious reverse when a cargo of pictures destined for sale in India returned unsold. It would appear that, somewhat rashly, Ryland and Bryer had guaranteed a 50 per cent profit to the seamen to whom the cargo had been entrusted, which they were now obliged to pay even though the goods had not been sold. This brought on a bankruptcy that caused the dissolution of the partnership and the shop. Although Ryland later claimed to have repaid all his creditors in full, his career was forcibly turned into a new channel and possibly rescued through his courtly connections. In 1772 he commissioned Thomas Burke to engrave mezzotints after a series of paintings by Angelica Kauffman, a popular new arrival in England and a favourite of the queen. The first was entitled *Queen Charlotte Raising the Genius of the Fine Arts*. This association with Angelica Kauffman proved mutually beneficial and was maintained throughout his life. In 1774 Ryland engraved and published the first of a long series of dotted prints after Kauffman that were designed to look like red chalk drawings. Ryland interpreted Kauffman's designs with sensitivity and improved her draughtsmanship in the translation. Usually circular, and printed in red or brown or sometimes in colours, his prints looked most attractive in gold frames, and these beautiful neo-classical designs proved very popular in Britain and on the continent. Ryland published little else until Kauffman left England in 1781, when he gave up his shop at 159 Strand and retired to his suburban house in Knightsbridge. There he continued to work on a pair of major engravings after John Hamilton Mortimer and another after Kauffman.

Ryland's financial position at this time is uncertain. He may still have been burdened with debts from the bankruptcy of 1771, but the weight of evidence suggests otherwise. His lifestyle was one of apparent affluence, and he remained a respectable figure in his profession. He was one of the leading engravers who petitioned for a stronger copyright act in 1777, and in 1783 he certified with Francesco Bartolozzi and William Woollett that Jane Hogarth had not had her husband William's engraved plates retouched since his death. But Ryland seems to have been unable to resist the lure of the capital markets and later in 1783 he came badly unstuck. A warrant was issued for his arrest for issuing two forged bills drawn on the East India Company. From accounts of his trial it is far from clear that he was guilty of any knowledge of the forgery, but his conduct in fleeing his house and then attempting suicide when discovered told against him. The forgery itself (of which Ryland was not accused) was so convincing that it took a papermaker's evidence to prove that one of the bills was false. Ryland's plea that it was fear of the vindictive power of the company and of the difficulty of proving his innocence that had driven him to run failed to impress the jury, and he was sentenced to hang. He asked that his case be laid before the king but his plea for clemency fell on deaf ears. On 29 August 1783, after a delay caused by a thunderstorm, Ryland was executed at Tyburn, together with a horse-thief, several robbers, and a man who had impersonated a sailor to get his prize-money.

Ryland was said to be of 'quakerish simplicity in his personal appearance' (*Memoirs and Recollections of … Raimbach*, 6). The announcement advertising a reward for his apprehension in 1783 described his appearance more fully:

> about fifty years of age, about five feet nine inches high, wears a wig with a club or cue, and his own hair turned over in front; a black complexion, a thin face with strong lines; his common countenance very grave, but, whilst he speaks, rather smiling, and shows his teeth and has great affability in his manner.

A portrait of him by Pierre Falconet was published in 1768 and several less reliable likenesses appeared at the time of his trial. Ryland was unsurpassed for the delicacy of his touch and the elegant restraint of his work in stipple. His execution removed one of the foremost exponents of the art of engraving.   TIMOTHY CLAYTON

Sources *A catalogue of the very capital collection of etchings, fine proof prints touched and finished by A. Kauffman, some mezzotints, finished and unfinished plates of a late celebrated artist* (1784) [sale catalogue, Christie and Ansell, 7 April 1784] • *A catalogue of twenty capital copper plates, and a part of the genuine and valuable stock of modern prints of Mrs Ryland, printseller, of New Bond Street* (1799) [sale catalogue, Christies, 3 March 1799] • H. Bleackley, *Some distinguished victims of the scaffold* (1905) • Farington, *Diary* • C. Rogers, *A collection of prints in imitation of drawings* (1778) • *GM*, 1st ser., 41 (1771), 572 • *GM*, 1st ser., 48 (1778), 593–4 • *GM*, 1st ser., 53 (1783), 26, 710, 714 • *GM*, 1st ser., 78 (1808), 87 • *Court and City Register* (1775), 73 • H. Hayward and P. Kirkham, *William and John Linnell: eighteenth-century London furniture makers* (1980) • 1771 bankruptcy, PRO, B 1/77/320–33 • *Memoirs and recollections of the late Abraham Raimbach*, ed. M. T. S. Raimbach (1843) •

J. Dennistoun, *Memoirs of Sir Robert Strange … and of his brother-in-law Andrew Lumisden*, 2 vols. (1855) • *Mémoires et journal de Jean-Georges Wille*, ed. G. Duplessis, 2 vols. (1857) • W. W. Roworth, ed., *Angelica Kauffman: a continental artist in Georgian England* (1992) • T. Clayton, *The English print, 1688–1802* (1997) • Graves, *Soc. Artists* • parish register, St Martin Ludgate, 2 Dec 1733, GL [baptism]
Likenesses D. P. Pariset, medallion, chalk manner, 1768 (after drawing by P. É. Falconet), BM • engraving, 1784, repro. in *Authentic memoirs of William Wynne Ryland* (1784) • D. P. Pariset, stipple (after P. É. Falconet, 1768), BM, NPG [*see illus.*]

Rylands [*née* Tennant]**, Enriqueta Augustina** (1843–1908), founder of the John Rylands Library, Manchester, was born on 31 May 1843 in Havana, Cuba, one of the five children of Stephen Cattley Tennant (1800–1848), a partner in a Liverpool mercantile firm, and Juana Camila Dalcour (1818–1855), the second daughter of Francesco Lalande Dalcour (1782–1838). Stephen Tennant retired from business in 1848 and took up residence in Liverpool, but died in the same year. His widow migrated to Paris, where she married a Polish pianist and friend of Chopin, Jules Fontana (1810–1869); she died suddenly in 1855. Enriqueta Tennant attended a convent school in New York and finishing schools in London and Paris.

Almost nothing is known of the first twenty years of the life of Enriqueta Tennant, and very little of the next fifteen years. She abandoned the Catholic faith of her mother and became a Congregationalist, perhaps through the agency of the Revd Thomas Raffles of Liverpool. In the early 1860s she became a companion to Martha (1806–1875), second wife of John *Rylands (1801–1888), Manchester's wealthiest merchant, who had established his country seat at Longford Hall, Stretford, in 1857. Joseph Parker, the minister at Cavendish Congregational chapel from 1858 to 1869, found her to be 'young, vivacious, accomplished' (Parker, 142). Eight months after the death of Martha Rylands, Enriqueta Tennant married, on 6 October 1875, the 74-year-old John Rylands, all of whose seven children had died prematurely. She herself remained childless but adopted two children, Arthur and Maria. She gave a new impetus to the philanthropic activity of her husband, in Britain and abroad, and co-operated closely in the publication of his *Paragraph Bible* and his hymnbooks. In December 1888 Rylands died and Enriqueta, as his main legatee and chief executor, became the chief shareholder in Manchester's two leading firms, Rylands & Sons Ltd and the Manchester Ship Canal Company, advised only by a small group of trusted associates.

Enriqueta Rylands determined to commemorate her husband appropriately, and in particular to reflect his profound commitment to the study of the Bible. Her original ambition, to create a large theological library in Manchester for the use of Noncomformist ministers and laity, was eventually transformed by the purchase in 1892 of the 40,000-volume library from Althorp, which had been built up over thirty years from 1790 by the second Earl Spencer. The general perception of Manchester as a cultural desert was changed by this great acquisition which began to broaden the whole basis of the developing memorial collection. Mrs Rylands discovered that in order to insure her new possession she had to have it catalogued, and appointed Edward Gordon Duff as her librarian.

One of the city's most notorious slums was deliberately chosen as the site for the new library building. Its construction stimulated a wave of local improvements and helped to make Deansgate into a main civic thoroughfare. The library took ten years instead of three to complete, and also cost three times as much as the original estimate, £224,086 against £78,000. The John Rylands Library was formally inaugurated on 6 October 1899, the anniversary of the marriage of the founder. On the same day Mrs Rylands was admitted to the freedom of the city of Manchester, the first woman to be so honoured. One year later the resignation of her librarian sent a shock wave through the literary world of Lancashire. Duff's relations with his employer had never been harmonious: his interests lay in the sphere of the higher bibliography, and he does not seem to have understood the deep attachment of Mrs Rylands to her own creation, nor to have shared her profound devotion to the Bible. His first catalogue, printed in 1895, proved to be not at all what Mrs Rylands had expected. It listed all the rare and beautiful books predating the year 1640 from the Spencer library, but devoted only two and a half pages to an unannotated enumeration of some sixty-nine bibles and testaments. Evidence suggests that Mrs Rylands immediately forbade the publication of the catalogue, although stocks had already been printed (Farnie, 'John Rylands', 60). She also decided to dispense with Duff's services as soon as feasible, and Duff remained in office only in order to prepare a full catalogue. That work failed to appear in time for the official inauguration and was published six months later, in March 1900. Thirty-six pages of entries on the Bible were to Mrs Rylands the most significant by far of the 1986 pages, which filled three volumes. The catalogue was savagely criticized in *The Times* (23 April 1900), and within another four months Duff was ousted from office.

Duff was succeeded by Henry Guppy, an active Methodist as well as an assiduous cataloguer. He enabled the library to survive a dearth of readers during its early months. In 1901 Mrs Rylands purchased for £155,000 the manuscripts of the Bibliotheca Lindesiana formed by the earls of Crawford and Balcarres: they numbered 6000 rolls, tablets, and codices, acquired since 1840, and were predominantly oriental. Discovering that the manuscripts were useless unless they were catalogued, she agreed to employ nine eminent scholars to undertake the task. Three catalogues duly appeared in 1909, 1911–15, and 1921, but four others were not published until 1932, 1933, 1934, and 1938. Together the Spencer library and the Crawford manuscripts transformed Mrs Rylands's foundation into one of the world's great libraries. Within Manchester, the John Rylands Library increased its share of the volumes held by all libraries from 9 per cent in 1897 to 21 per cent in 1923.

Enriqueta Rylands resembled her husband in her formidable abilities, in her strength of will, and in her profound philanthropic disposition. Inspired by a strong sense of duty, she eschewed society and chose to live laborious days in the stoical pursuit of her aims. She had a passion for secrecy and abhorred publicity. Throughout her life she remained the sole executor of her own purposes, exercising a comprehensive supervision of the construction, equipment, and iconography of her library. She devised the regulations for its administration and chose the motto for the coat of arms, *Nihil sine labore*. She gave full support to the Forward Movement, launched in 1905–6 by the sixty Congregational churches of Manchester and Salford, since she regarded the religious life of Manchester as the most important of all its activities. With her aid, mission halls were opened in Salford in 1907, in London in 1908, and in Manchester in 1911 in the hope of creating 'one city, one church'. Since the 1890s she had been afflicted by what at first seemed to be rheumatism and had undertaken a series of annual tours of the continent. She drew up her first will in 1894 and bought a villa, Fairholme, in Torquay in 1905, eighteen months after the diagnosis of a malignant disease. She died there on 4 February 1908. Her funeral in Manchester on 10 February was attended by eighteen family members, including Joseph Reece Rylands (1864–1917), the grandnephew of John Rylands. After cremation her ashes were interred beside the remains of her husband in the unconsecrated portion of the southern cemetery in Manchester, beneath the Rylands memorial. From her estate of £3,448,692 she made charitable bequests totalling £448,000, or treble the £157,000 bequeathed by her husband to religious, educational, and charitable institutions.

Enriqueta Rylands was especially generous in her legacies to hospitals, ragged schools, women's charities, and educational foundations. The John Rylands Library received £200,000. It remained the most fitting of memorials to Mrs Rylands, as well as to her husband, even though the trust of 1900 was abrogated in 1972 as the library was absorbed into the library of the University of Manchester; the Rylands lectures were discontinued, after eighty-seven years, in 1987. An auction sale of ninety-eight 'duplicate' early books proved controversial and adversely affected the reputation of the library. Nevertheless, from 1988 Manchester had two libraries, and an associated research institute, bearing the name of John Rylands.

D. A. FARNIE

Sources D. A. Farnie, 'Enriqueta Augusta Rylands, 1843–1908, founder of the John Rylands Library', *Bulletin of the John Rylands University Library*, 71 (1989), 3–38 · D. A. Farnie, 'John Rylands of Manchester', *Bulletin of the John Rylands University Library*, 75 (1993), 3–103 · D. A. Farnie, 'The Wiener thesis vindicated: the onslaught of 1994 upon the reputation of John Rylands of Manchester', *Religion, business and wealth in modern Britain*, ed. D. J. Jeremy (1998), 86–107 · J. Parker, *A preacher's life* (1899), 142–58 · C. S. Horne, *Christian World* (6 Feb 1908) · C. S. Horne, *British Congregationalist* (13 Feb 1908) · W. Huckett, *Lancashire Congregational Year Book* (1908) · A. S. Peake, *British Weekly* (13 Feb 1908) · [H. Guppy], *Bulletin of the John Rylands University Library*, 1 (1903), 47–8 · W. S. Coker and T. D. Watson, *Indian traders of the southeastern Spanish borderlands* (1986) · W. Hardynski, 'Jules Fontana', *Polski slownik biograficzny* (1948), 7.58–9 · *The Red Earl: the papers of the fifth Earl Spencer, 1835–1910*, ed. P. Gordon, 2, Northamptonshire RS, 34 (1986) · N. Barker, 'The rape of the Rylands', *Book Collector*, 37 (1988), 169–84 · *Books from the John*

Rylands University Library of Manchester (1988) [sale catalogue, Sothebys, London, 14 April 1988] • private information (2004)

Archives JRL, accounts and residuary papers | JRL, corresp. with Champneys and Linnell • JRL, E. G. Duff MSS • JRL, H. Guppy MSS • Poynton, Cheshire, Linnell MSS

Likenesses R. Hall, photograph, *c.*1899, Manchester Guardian archives; repro. in *Lancashire Congregational Year Book*, 103 • R. Hall, photograph, *c.*1899, Manchester Guardian archives; repro. in *Christian Herald* (27 Feb 1908) • J. Cassidy, statue, 1907, JRL • J. Adams-Acton, double portrait, marble medallion, 1910 (with John Rylands), Cheadle Hulme School, Cheshire • R. Durrant of Torquay, photograph, repro. in *The Christian* (13 Feb 1908), 12 • maquette of statue, JRL, Elizabeth Stott Centre

Wealth at death £3,448,692 15*s.*: probate, 24 March 1908, *CGPLA Eng. & Wales*

Rylands, George Humphrey Wolferstan [Dadie] (1902–1999), literary scholar and theatre director, was born on 23 October 1902 at the Down House, Tockington, Gloucestershire, the second of three children of Thomas Kirkland Rylands, land agent, and his wife, Bertha (Betha) Nisbet Wolferstan, *née* Thomas, daughter of a Marlborough College housemaster. He also had one half-brother from his father's first marriage. His paternal grandfather manufactured wire in Lancashire and was a Liberal MP. Rylands later inherited a fortune from an uncle. Everyone knew him as Dadie, from his early mispronunciation of 'baby'.

Educated at Durnford's Preparatory School, Rylands liked to say that he only just won a scholarship to Eton College. He was awarded both Loder prizes for declamation, the Shakespeare gold medal, was the first boy to direct a play in College Hall (*Twelfth Night* with himself as a memorable Viola), and was a king's scholar (1920). Provost J. T. Sheppard invited him to attend King's College, Cambridge, from January 1921 to perform as Electra in *The Oresteia*. He changed from classics to read English (1922) and was the first student of F. L. (Peter) Lucas. His prolific undergraduate acting with the university's Marlowe Dramatic Society included playing the Duchess of Malfi (1924). He graduated with a starred first.

A member of the exclusive Cambridge Apostles, with universally adored good looks—thick canary-coloured hair, pastel blue eyes, 'pussy-cat smile' (his own words), and open expression—he caught the fancy of Lytton Strachey, who introduced him to the Bloomsbury group; it was a time for high-spirited parties and exploring further his homosexuality. In 1924 he worked for six months with Leonard and Virginia Woolf at the Hogarth Press. They were especially fond of him, and as well as two volumes of his verse, *Russet and Taffeta* (1925) and *Poems* (1931), they also published his fellowship dissertation (initially rejected by King's) as *Words and Poetry* (1928). After he was elected a fellow of King's in 1927, Dora Carrington and Douglas Davidson decorated his Old Lodge rooms, which are parodied by Virginia Woolf in *A Room of One's Own* (1929). Famous for effortlessly stylish hospitality, he lived there for the rest of his life. His college offices included (before the war) lay dean and steward and (during the war) assistant bursar, praelector, and director of studies. After the war he continued to serve on the council, the board of the fellowship electors, and estates committee.

As a teacher Rylands inspired generations of undergraduates with his unforgettable lectures and his belief that literature should move the heart. As director of the Marlowe Society, he was not a natural actor, but his voice held an audience with its crisp and easy precision. His productions were admired for their transparent clarity, musical power of the verse speaking, and sensitive dramatic rhythms. Notable productions in the 1920s and 1930s included *King Lear* (1929), *Antony and Cleopatra* (1933), *Hamlet* (1936), and *Macbeth* (1939). During this period he also published *Shakespeare the Poet* (1934) and his immensely popular Shakespeare anthology, *The Ages of Man* (1939; which later provided Sir John Gielgud with the content and arrangement for his famous solo recital from 1957).

Many of the undergraduates Rylands directed became very influential in British theatre, including John Barton, Sir Peter Hall, Sir Derek Jacobi, Sir Ian McKellen, Trevor Nunn, and Sir Michael and Corin Redgrave. In 1944 he was asked by Gielgud to direct him in his fifth, and some thought best, *Hamlet*, with Dame Peggy Ashcroft as Ophelia; Oxford published his edition of the play in 1947. In 1945 he became a governor of the Old Vic; he was also made chairman of the Apollo Society in 1946 (a post he held until 1972), and was a member of the Cheltenham College council from 1946 until 1976. After the death of John Maynard Keynes he became chairman of the Cambridge Arts Theatre in 1946 (remaining so until 1982), for which he was a tireless fund-raiser and a major benefactor. In 1948 Rylands was made a member of the advisory board of the *Shakespeare Survey* and toured Berlin during the airlift with productions of *The White Devil* and *Measure for Measure*, in which he played Angelo, his favourite role.

In 1951 Rylands delivered the British Academy Shakespeare lecture, 'Shakespeare's poetic energy' (1951). By this time he was so well known that he was caricatured by Noël Coward in *Star Quality* (1951). Having directed *Troilus and Cressida* three times in the 1940s and 1950s, he also directed it for a BBC television production in 1954. From 1957 to 1964 he directed audio recordings of the entire Shakespeare canon for the British Council. Although uneven in quality, the pioneering project drew wide acclaim and brought together amateur and professional talent. His radio work consisting of talks on Shakespeare spanned forty years (1930s–1970s).

Rylands was appointed CBE in 1961 and made a Companion of Honour in 1987. Cambridge honoured him with a LittD (1975) and Durham with a DLitt (1988). In 1988 BBC Radio 4 broadcast 'The life of Rylands', and there were theatrical tributes to him in Stratford upon Avon in 1992 and London in 1996.

Rylands did not publish much; his ideas spread through his genius for friendship, encouragement, and conversation. He travelled widely to Egypt, America, Palestine, and India. Outliving all the friends of his own age, except Frances Partridge, he gradually became a legend in the college, although he considered leaving King's in later life. For the last two years he needed professional care, but was always visited by friends. They sat next to him, as they always had done, in his window-seat, overlooking the south-west of King's College chapel. He died peacefully in his rooms on 16 January 1999 and after cremation on 25 January his ashes were interred in the chapel at King's. He was unmarried. The bulk of his £1 million estate was left in trust to his college.   PAUL EDMONDSON

Sources *The Independent* (20 Jan 1999) · *The Guardian* (19 Jan 1999) · *Daily Telegraph* (19 Jan 1999) · *The Times* (18 Jan 1999) · *George Rylands, 1902–1999: a memoir printed for King's College* (2000) · personal knowledge (2004) · private information (2004) · G. H. W. Rylands, *Words and poetry* (1928) · G. Rylands, 'The poet and the player', *Shakespeare Survey*, 7 (1954), 25–34 · R. Christiansen, ed., *Cambridge Arts Theatre: celebrating sixty years* (1996) · *WW* (1993) · b. cert. · d. cert.
Archives King's AC Cam., corresp. and MSS | BLPES, corresp. with editors of *Economic Journal* · King's AC Cam., letters to R. Kahn; letters to Sir J. T. Sheppard · U. Reading, letters to G. Bell & Sons; letters to Hogarth Press · U. Sussex, corresp. with L. Woolf · U. Sussex, corresp. with Virginia Woolf | SOUND BBC WAC · BL NSA
Likenesses L. Le Breton, oils, 1933, King's Cam. · J. Bell, oils, 1981, King's Cam. · R. Behrens, oils, 1994, priv. coll. · attrib. L. Le Breton, oils, King's Cam. · photographs, repro. in *George Rylands* · photographs, repro. in Christiansen, ed., *Cambridge Arts Theatre*
Wealth at death £995,197—gross; £991,145—net: probate, 18 May 1999, *CGPLA Eng. & Wales*

Rylands, John (1801–1888), textile merchant and philanthropist, was born on 7 February 1801 in the village of Parr, near St Helens in Lancashire, the third and youngest son of the five children of Joseph Rylands (1767–1847) and Elizabeth Pilkington Rylands (1761–1829), both of old Lancashire stock. After attending St Helens grammar school he followed the family tradition by becoming, in 1817, a manufacturer of linens for the home trade on the hand-loom. In 1819 the firm of Rylands & Sons was established by Joseph Rylands and his three sons, enabling John to acquire the skills of the retail draper and commercial traveller. John Rylands opened a warehouse in Manchester in 1822 and extended the operations of the firm successively from linen manufacture into dyeing and bleaching in 1824, into cotton spinning in 1830, and into power-loom weaving as well as coal mining in 1839. Until the death of his mother in 1829 he was inclined to attach too much importance to the acquisition of wealth. Thereafter his religion ceased to be conventional: he was baptized at the age of twenty-nine and resolved to live for the good of others and to create a great and profitable business as a source of secure employment. In his new incarnation as a Christian capitalist he prospered more than ever before. He became the sole proprietor of the firm from 1842, opened a warehouse in London in 1849, and withdrew from linen manufacture in 1854 in order to concentrate upon the cotton industry. By then he had become a self-made millionaire, being the first native of Lancashire to attain that status. After the death of James Morrison (1789–1857) of London he became the greatest textile merchant in the land. During the crisis of the cotton famine he profited by the low prices of mills and machinery to expand his operations further. In 1863–5 he built model mills at Wigan. Thus he became the largest manufacturer in the cotton industry as well as Manchester's first multimillionaire.

In 1873 the firm was incorporated as a limited company, with a capital of £2 million, which remained the largest single capital in the trade until the creation of the Coats combine in 1896. John Rylands as 'governor' retained supreme power within the company but extended the privilege of shareholding to both its draper clients and its chief employees, in harmony with the contemporary enthusiasm for 'industrial partnership'. From 1872 the firm expanded into the manufacture of ready-made clothing upon the sewing machine. From 1874 it launched a determined export drive in both Europe and America and began to display its wares at international exhibitions, winning prizes at Cape Town in 1877 and at Paris in 1878. Its hands increased sixfold in number, from 2000 in 1860 to 12,000 in 1875. With seventeen mills and forty-two departments within its warehouses the firm had become, in manufacture, in finishing, and in distribution, 'the recognized and undisputed head and leader of the cotton trade' (*Manchester of Today*, 1888, 79). That trade was the country's leading industry and was then at the zenith of its influence in the world.

Rylands & Sons was not a representative cotton-manufacturing firm. It stood apart from other concerns by virtue of its immense size, its integrated operations, its primary dependence upon the home market, and, above all, its merchanting functions. Its successful expansion in the face of constantly renewed opposition was a remarkable achievement and can only be attributed to the unresting enterprise of John Rylands, whose daily hours of work averaged nineteen in 1820 and still numbered twelve during the 1870s. He developed normal mercantile abilities to the point of genius. A superb organizer and an exceptional judge of character, he excelled in financial acumen. He rigorously controlled costs and compelled each department to stand upon its own feet. Above all, he built up a high reputation for the quality of his wares and maintained that reputation through the use of trade marks. His individual efforts raised standards throughout the whole of the trade, especially in the manufacture of unbleached calico. The greatest tribute to his capacity was paid after his death, when no successor as 'governor' was appointed: the chairmanship of the board was placed in commission and devolved in rotation during 1889–1900 upon his three ablest lieutenants, Reuben Spencer (1830–1901), William Carnelley (1821–1919), and James Horrocks (1832–1895). The foundations of the firm had been laid so well that it enjoyed the unusually long lifespan of 170 years (1819–1989). John Rylands became Manchester's greatest merchant-manufacturer during the golden age of the cotton industry. In 1878 he declined to accept office as sheriff of London, a position which would have made him eligible to become lord mayor of London: no other Manchester merchant is known to have been so honoured. In 1886 he performed an important civic duty by rescuing the newly founded Manchester Ship Canal Company from financial crisis and so enabled it to survive and to fulfil its aim of creating the port of Manchester.

Rylands became one of the most notable philanthropists of the age, proving that he knew how to use money as well as how to make it. His extensive charitable activity never became obtrusive and his largest benefactions remained secret. He became a large benefactor to the townships of Ainsworth, Gorton, Greenheys, and Stretford, and, bearing in mind his own bereavements, made special provision for orphans, for widows, and for the aged poor. His benefactions to the poor of Rome in the 1870s were so liberal as to secure the award in 1880 of a knighthood of the order of the Crown of Italy. His own religious faith became increasingly supradenominational. A staunch nonconformist of the Congregational denomination by birth, with Baptist leanings, he developed a catholic sympathy with all other believers. Some sixty years before the birth of the ecumenical movement proper, he sought to foster a spirit of unity throughout the whole of 'the church universal'. Such an unusual approach was inspired by five ministers: the Baptists John Birt (1787–1862), Dr Samuel G. Green (1822–1905), and Alexander McLaren (1826–1910) and the Congregationalists Dr Robert Halley (1796–1876) and Dr Joseph Parker (1830–1902). A profound believer in the value of education, Rylands sought to free it from its denominational constraints. He supported non-sectarian Christian societies as well as the New Union Church, founded in Stretford in 1864. As an ardent student of scripture he made strenuous efforts to free the Bible from sectarian interpretation and to restore it to the individual believer. Thus he published three editions of the Rylands Paragraph Bible (1863, 1878, 1886) with an extensive 226-page index volume, as well as French and Italian editions of the New Testament (1867, 1869). Increasingly he came to recognize in hymns the inner unity and hidden harmony of the churches of Christendom which could not find embodiment in their creed. He built up a collection of hymns, which doubled in size from 30,000 in the 1860s to 60,000 in the 1880s. From that collection were published between 1864 and 1887 four hymn books, the most notable being *Hymns of the Church Universal* (1886). Rylands approximates closely to the ideal type of capitalist studied by both Max Weber and J. A. Schumpeter: he remains a striking example of the innovating entrepreneur inspired by a profound belief in the truths of Christianity, especially as expounded in the New Testament, and in their essential relevance to daily life.

Rylands died at his home, Longford Hall, Stretford, on 11 December 1888 at the age of eighty-seven, and was buried on 15 December at the southern cemetery, Manchester. He left a personal estate of £2,574,922, including bequests totalling £157,000 to religious, educational, and charitable institutions. That estate represented the largest fortune left by any cotton manufacturer to that date and furnished a striking contrast to the estates left respectively by his father in 1847 (£26,829), his brother Joseph in 1853 (£90,000), and his brother Richard in 1863 (£5000). He was married three times, first, on 17 March 1825, to Dinah Raby (1801–1843). Their seven children all died, between 1830 and 1834 and between 1861 and 1872. There were no children of his marriage, on 4 January 1848, to Martha Carden (1806–1875). She was a fervent supporter of his religious and philanthropic activity. His third wife, whom

he married on 6 October 1875, was Enriqueta Augustina Tennant (1843–1908); they adopted a son and a daughter. Enriqueta was the executor of his will and inherited the bulk of his wealth. She erected a permanent memorial to her husband in the form of the John Rylands Library, which was opened in 1899. Despite investing £1 million in the library, she still left in 1908 an estate of £3,607,056. The library was merged in 1972 with the library of the University of Manchester, which then itself adopted the name of the John Rylands University Library of Manchester. D. A. FARNIE

Sources D. A. Farnie, 'The Wiener thesis vindicated: the onslaught of 1994 upon the reputation of John Rylands of Manchester', *Religion, business and wealth in modern Britain*, ed. D. J. Jeremy (1998), 86–107 · D. A. Farnie, 'John Rylands of Manchester', *Bulletin of the John Rylands University Library*, 75 (1993), 3–103 · D. A. Farnie, 'Enriqueta Augusta Rylands, 1843–1908, founder of the John Rylands Library', *Bulletin of the John Rylands University Library*, 71 (1989), 3–38 · D. A. Farnie, 'Rylands, John', *DBB* · R. Spencer, 'Principal Manchester firms—their rise and progress, no. 5: Messrs Rylands & Sons', *Manchester City News* (1 April 1865); (8 April 1865); (15 April 1865) · R. Spencer, *The home trade of Manchester* (1890), 145–61 · S. G. Green and J. W. Kiddle, *In memoriam John Rylands* (privately printed, Manchester, 1889), 21, 55 · S. G. Green, 'The late Mrs John Rylands of Manchester', *Sunday at Home* (23 March 1889), 181–6 · J. Parker, *A preacher's life* (1899), 142–58 · G. H. Pike, *Dr Parker and his friends* (1904), 48–64 · Lesser Columbus [L. Cowen], 'A Lancashire lesson', *Commerce* (5 July 1893), 17–23 · A. W. B. Simpson, 'Legal liability for bursting reservoirs: the historical context of *Rylands* v. *Fletcher*', *Journal of Legal Studies*, 13 (1984), 209–64 · W. R. Credland, 'The Althorp Library', *Manchester Quarterly*, 12 (1893) · d. cert.
Archives JRL, archives of John Rylands & Sons Ltd · JRL · Wigan Archives Service, Leigh, deeds of Joseph Rylands [father] | JRL, English MSS 1140, 1185 (2 vols.)
Likenesses oils, 1869, JRL · A. Debenham Ryde, photograph, 1882, repro. in Green, 'The late Mrs John Rylands of Manchester', 185 · H. Hills, engraving, 1884 (after photograph), JRL · photograph, 1887, repro. in Green and Kiddle, *In memoriam John Rylands*, frontispiece · J. Cassidy, statue, 1894, JRL · W. G. Baxter, cartoon, repro. in *Momus*, 3/63 (15 May 1899), 8 · portraits, repro. in Farnie, 'John Rylands of Manchester'
Wealth at death £2,574,922 5*s.* 8*d.*—effects in England: probate, 1 March 1889, *CGPLA Eng. & Wales*

Rylands, Peter (1820–1887), steel manufacturer and politician, born in Bewsey House, Warrington, on 18 January 1820, was the youngest son of John Rylands, manufacturer, and his wife, a daughter of the Revd James Glazebrook, vicar of Belton, Leicestershire. He was educated at the Boteler grammar school in Warrington. As a boy he had a passion for politics, and in 1835 presided at a whig banquet of 200 sons of Warrington electors, who had taken part in a mock election. Up to the age of twenty-one his time was chiefly passed in studying and writing papers on natural history and phrenology. However, in 1841 he discovered that his father's means had shrunk, owing to the diversion of the manufacture of sailcloth from Warrington, and that the manufacture of steel and iron wire, another business conducted by his father, had ceased to pay. With his brothers, Rylands reconstituted the latter business, and within a few years returned it to prosperity. In 1864 he established an ironworks, which became the Pearson and Knowles Coal and Iron Company.

Originally a nonconformist, Rylands later joined the

Church of England and in 1845 he published a little pamphlet on *The Mission of the Church*. A larger work, on *The Pulpit and the People*, appeared in 1847. He also took an active part in politics, and became a working member of the Anti-Corn Law League. Active in obtaining the incorporation of Warrington in 1847, he was elected mayor of the town in 1852, and in 1859 he was invited to become a Liberal candidate in opposition to Gilbert Greenall; but he declined owing to the pressures of business. With Mr McMinnies and the Revd R. A. Mould, he contributed a series of letters to the *Warrington Guardian*, signed Oliver West, which attracted wide attention, and animated local Liberal sentiment. The authorship was not disclosed until after Rylands's death. Rylands became MP for Warrington in 1868, but was defeated there and in South-East Lancashire in 1874. In 1876 he was elected to the Commons as member for Burnley, and represented that constituency until his death.

In parliament Rylands proved himself an earnest and hard-working but independent radical. He persistently drew attention to rising government expenditure, which he deplored. In 1886 he joined the Liberal Unionists in opposition to Gladstone's policy of home rule for Ireland. However, he was a strong supporter of Gladstone's opposition to Disraeli's Near Eastern foreign policy in 1876–8. Outside parliament he was a vice-president from 1870 to 1885 of the Central Association for Stopping the Sale of Intoxicating Liquors on Sundays and a vice-president in 1880–81 of the National Association for the Repeal of the Contagious Diseases Act.

Rylands married twice. His second wife, whom he married in 1861, was Caroline, daughter of William Reynolds of Warrington. She survived him after his death on 8 February 1887 at their home, Massey Hall, Thelwall, Cheshire. They had three sons, of whom the youngest was Sir (William) Peter *Rylands.   W. F. RAE, rev. MATTHEW LEE

Sources *Correspondence and speeches of Mr Peter Rylands*, ed. L. G. Rylands, 2 vols. (1890) • Boase, *Mod. Eng. biog.* • Walford, *County families* (1875) • H. L. Malchow, *Agitators and promoters in the age of Gladstone and Disraeli: a biographical dictionary* (1983) • Gladstone, *Diaries* • *CGPLA Eng. & Wales* (1887)

Archives W. Sussex RO, corresp. with Richard Cobden

Likenesses R. T., wood-engraving (after photograph by Russell & Sons), NPG; repro. in *ILN* (19 Feb 1887) • Spy [L. Ward], caricature, watercolour study, NPG; repro. in *VF* (25 Jan 1879) • portrait, repro. in *Correspondence and speeches*, ed. Rylands

Wealth at death £89,257 7s. 10d.: probate, 4 May 1887

Rylands, Sir (William) Peter, baronet (1868–1948), wire manufacturer, was born at Bewsey House, Warrington, Lancashire, on 23 October 1868, third and youngest son of the politician Peter *Rylands (1820–1887) of Massey Hall, Grappenhall, Thelwall, near Warrington, and his second wife, Caroline Wright (1841–1920), daughter of William Reynolds of Penketh House, Warrington, and Pinhoe, Devon. He was educated at Charterhouse School (1881–7) and at Trinity College, Cambridge (1887–90), and in 1891 visited Mashonaland in Africa to hunt big game. He was called to the bar at the Inner Temple, London, in 1894, and in that year he married Nora Mary (1865–1946), daughter of David de Angelis, a Parisian with business interests in

the Bradford wool trade; they had no children. Rylands practised on the northern circuit and in 1895 edited *Thomas Terrell on the Law and Practice Relating to Letters Patent for Inventions*.

On his thirtieth birthday, following the death of his uncle John Rylands (1814–1898), Peter Rylands, as he was always known, became managing director of the family wire business of Rylands Bros. He was an intelligent, broad-minded, well-read, and adaptable businessman whose company faced a complicated market structure as well as strong German competition and obstructive trade unionism. He gave a full analysis of its business in evidence to the tariff commission on 1 June 1904: his testimony is that of a clear, persuasive speaker with considerable mental agility. In 1898 he also joined the board of the Pearson and Knowles Coal and Iron Company of Warrington and Wigan, in which his family had a large interest. It was proof of his belief in the necessity of large-scale amalgamated enterprise to maintain competitiveness that Rylands Bros. was bought in 1906–7 by Pearson Knowles. He ran Rylands Bros. as the wire department of Pearson Knowles, and was concerned in the erection of the group's new Partington steelworks in 1910–13.

Rylands deplored the absence of business experience in British political leadership, and he advocated trade associations, manufacturing combinations, and tariff protection to prevent the diffusion of effort and wasting of resources. He was president of the Iron and Steel Wire Manufacturers' Association from 1900, and in 1912 was one of the promoters of the Employers' Parliamentary Association to lobby for the Lancashire business interest. He was a founder member of the Federation of British Industries (FBI) in 1916 and was a crucial figure in establishing it as a national institution, though he was not forgiven by some Lancashire leaders for his part in the absorption of the Employers' Parliamentary Association by the Birmingham-led FBI. He was chairman of the FBI's labour committee in 1917–18, of its overseas trade and consular committee in 1918–22, and president of the FBI for an unprecedented two-year stint in 1920–22. He was dexterous in seeking united expressions of business opinion on public issues, and was much involved in other forms of industrial politics. He was appointed to the government's tariff advisory committee in 1923 and to its committee on industry and trade of 1925–30 chaired by Sir Arthur Balfour. He was also president of the Iron and Steel Institute (1926–7) and the Federation of Iron and Steel Manufacturers (1930–31). He was not a mercenary man, but regarded money as a means of production rather than as an ultimate personal aim. His taste for paradox and philosophical speculation alarmed some of his cruder business colleagues. His opinions were independent and tenacious, but his outlook was moderate and constructive, and he disliked sectionalism of any kind.

In 1920 Rylands Bros. and Pearson Knowles were bought by the Newcastle armourers Armstrong Whitworth. Armstrong's overbearing chairman, Sir Glynn West, excluded Rylands from the head board and managed these acquisitions so badly that by 1926 the Armstrong companies were insolvent. After intervention by the Bank of England, Pearson Knowles and Rylands Bros. were merged in 1930 in the new Lancashire Steel Corp., of which Rylands became a director. He was nevertheless sceptical of the benefits of the 'rationalization' movement promoted by the Bank of England to rescue Britain's declining staple industries.

Like his father and namesake Rylands was prominent in his district. He was a magistrate in Lancashire from 1905 and in Cheshire from 1906, and was high sheriff of Cheshire in 1935–6. He abandoned his father's political allegiances and was sometime chairman of the Warrington Conservative Association, though it is hard to imagine him at ease among diehards. Among many voluntary local offices he was president of the Warrington chamber of commerce and life governor and benefactor of Warrington Infirmary. Even in his social and sporting interests Rylands proved his talent as an initiator. He was the founder and first master of several masonic lodges, and founder secretary of Lymm Golf Club near his home. Keen on shooting and fishing, he was characteristically deliberative at croquet. In appearance he was quiet, dapper, and shrewd; for his portrait (c.1921) for the FBI he wore a pince-nez and spotted bow-tie.

Rylands was knighted in 1921 and received a baronetcy in 1939. He died of heart failure on 22 October 1948 at his home, Massey Hall, Grappenhall, Thelwall. This was the eve of his eightieth birthday, which would also have been the fiftieth anniversary of his becoming managing director of Rylands Bros.; he had spent his last day at his office in Warrington finalizing arrangements for a celebratory party, but died at home. His baronetcy became extinct, and he was buried on 27 October at All Saints', Thelwall.   RICHARD DAVENPORT-HINES

Sources *Warrington Guardian* (27 Oct 1948) • C. Tennyson, *Stars and markets* (1957) • R. P. T. Davenport-Hines, 'Rylands, Sir William Peter', *DBB* • Burke, *Peerage* (1949) • R. P. T. Davenport-Hines, *Dudley Docker: the life and times of a trade warrior* (1984) • *The Times* (1948) • b. cert. • d. cert.
Archives BLPES, Tariff Commission MSS, TC3 1/27 • Tyne and Wear Archives Service, Newcastle upon Tyne, Armstrong Whitworth MSS • U. Warwick Mod. RC, Confederation of British Industry MSS
Likenesses portrait, *c.*1921, Confederation of British Industry; repro. in Davenport-Hines, 'Rylands, Sir William Peter'
Wealth at death £192,199: Davenport-Hines, 'Rylands, Sir William Peter'

Ryle, Gilbert (1900–1976), philosopher, was born in his family's home in Brighton on 19 August 1900. His twin sister, Mary, and he were the eighth and ninth of the ten children of Reginald John Ryle MD, general practitioner, and his wife, Catherine Scott. John Alfred *Ryle, professor of medicine, was an elder brother. His grandfather John Charles *Ryle was the first bishop of Liverpool. Both his parents had shed the strict evangelicalism of their upbringing, and Ryle himself was without religious beliefs. He was educated at Brighton College and at the Queen's College, Oxford, to which he won a classical scholarship (1919) and where he gained first-class honours in, successively, classical honour moderations (1921) and

Gilbert Ryle (1900–1976), by Hubert Andrew Freeth, 1952

the honour schools of *literae humaniores* (1923) and philosophy, politics, and economics (1924). He was invited to sit the final examination in this latter, new school in order to set a standard for first-class performance in it. Joining athletic to academic achievement, he was captain of the Queen's College boat club in 1923 and rowed in the university trial eights in that year. In 1924 he was appointed lecturer in philosophy at Christ Church, Oxford, and in 1925 was elected a student and tutor in philosophy in that college. He served the college both as junior and as senior censor, and was junior proctor of the university in 1937–8. In 1940 he was commissioned in the Welsh Guards and was employed on intelligence work until demobilized in 1945 with the rank of major. From 1945 until his retirement in 1968 he was Waynflete professor of metaphysical philosophy and fellow of Magdalen College, Oxford. He edited *Mind*, in succession to G. E. Moore, from 1947 to 1971.

As he says in the autobiographical introduction to a collection of critical essays on his work (1971) Ryle was, from the start of his Oxford career, 'philosophically eager'. Finding the local philosophical atmosphere, in the early and middle 1920s, distinctly tepid, he turned to the work of Bertrand Russell, at that time an object of disapproval or neglect in Oxford, taught himself German, and read Frege, Husserl, Brentano, Bolzano, and Meinong. Towards the end of the decade he made the acquaintance of the Cambridge philosophers Moore and Ludwig Wittgenstein, and became a friend of the latter. During this period, in which he helped to start an informal discussion group of the younger Oxford philosophers, he formed the conviction, which remained with him, that philosophical questions were essentially questions about the meaning or 'logical grammar' of expressions. Above all, he thought it was important to establish the distinction, and the rationale of the distinction, between what collocations of expressions made sense and what made, perhaps unobviously, nonsense. Philosophical error and perplexity typically arose from treating expressions belonging to one logical type or category as if they belonged to another. Such confusions, often encouraged by superficial grammar, could be exposed by pressing them to the limit of obvious absurdity.

The most influential of Ryle's pre-war papers on these logical and meta-philosophical themes were 'Systematically misleading expressions' (1932) and 'Categories' (1938). In this latter essay and in his inaugural lecture as Waynflete professor ('Philosophical arguments', 1945) he appeared to be aiming at a precise and general theoretical account of the notion of a logical type or category. This attempt, if it was one, was imperfectly successful and he later (*Dilemmas*, 1954) disavowed the belief that his notion of a logical category was capable of a precise and general explication; an admission that disturbed him little, if at all, since he remained convinced of the philosophical utility of the notion and became increasingly concerned with the practice, rather than the theory, of his method.

Ryle found a major field for the application of that method in what he described as the 'official', or Cartesian, theory of the mind, which formed the target of attack in his principal work, *The Concept of Mind* (1949). Calling it, 'with deliberate abusiveness', the myth of 'the ghost in the machine', he described the official theory as embodying one big category-mistake, ramifying into a family of related category-mistakes: the mind was conceived of as a ghostly analogue of the body, and mental operations as private and immaterial counterparts of public and physical operations. Ryle saw his task as a twofold one: destructively, he was to exhibit the absurdities which followed from the official doctrine; constructively, he was to establish the true logical character of 'mental-conduct concepts', that is, of the words we use when we speak of mental faculties, qualities, and performances. In successive chapters he dealt with intelligence, the will, emotion, self-knowledge, sensation, imagination, and intellect. He repeatedly succeeded in showing that many expressions which, on the official view, were taken to refer exclusively to private inner episodes or processes are in fact dispositional or semi-dispositional in character, where the dispositions in question are dispositions to overt and observable behaviour. Not all his analyses were equally successful; his treatment of some topics, notably sensation, imagination, and thinking, gave some ground for the suspicion that he really wished, quite implausibly, to deny the existence of private, subjective experiences altogether. His chapter on the intellect elicited from J. L. Austin, who reviewed the work in the *Times Literary Supplement*, the comment: '"Ponderings", once firmly distinguished from what they are not, are thenceforward left in the air, where they are surely not more happily located than "in the mind"' (*TLS*, 7 April 1950, xi).

Ryle's next book, *Dilemmas* (1954), was a slightly modified version of the Tarner lectures which he delivered in Trinity College, Cambridge, in the previous year. In it he demonstrated, in a number of diverse cases, how specialist and non-specialist accounts of what is in some sense the same subject matter may generate apparent conflicts in the speculative mind if the concepts concerned are allowed to become detached from the background of their working employment. The resolution of such conflicts then calls for the reimposition of 'category-disciplines' by the critical philosopher. In this way, for example, we are delivered from the threat of being forced by classical logic into fatalism, or by simple mathematics into Zeno's paradox of Achilles and the tortoise, or by the discoveries of natural science into the repudiation of our common-sense picture of the world.

Throughout his philosophical career Ryle produced a steady stream of articles and reviews. Many were concerned with the philosophy of language, the theory of meaning, or the nature of philosophy itself; some reflected his early interest in phenomenology; others were devoted to his great predecessors or contemporaries, Locke, Moore, and Wittgenstein; yet others to questions in the philosophy of mind, particularly, in his later years, to the topic of thinking. Most of those which were published in his lifetime were assembled in the two large volumes of *Collected Papers* (1971). Plato, whose *Parmenides* he made the subject of an important and original study published in 1939, continued to fascinate Ryle throughout his life; it was to him that he devoted his last unitary book, *Plato's Progress* (1966), a piece of ingenious detective work on the life of the philosopher. Novel and brilliant as Ryle's theories were, they were received with scepticism by classical scholars, whose general view was that adequate materials for a life of Plato did not exist.

A posthumously published collection of papers, *On Thinking* (ed. K. Kolenda, 1979), reflected the preoccupation of Ryle's later years and his own dissatisfaction with his earlier treatment of the topic. He described his 'long-range objective' as that of finding out 'how to talk sense about the thinking that Le Penseur is occupied in doing' without falling into the category-errors of behaviourism on the one hand or Cartesianism on the other. He approached the question by considering what it is that distinguishes thoughtful from thoughtless performances of ordinary overt activities such as climbing, driving, or dissecting; found the distinction in a variety of adverbial qualifications such as 'vigilantly', 'carefully', 'noticingly', 'experimentally', and so on; and concluded that there is no one specific type of *content* essential to Le Penseur's doing (it may, but need not, consist in experimental inner speech or in imagining modifications of a studied situation), but that, whatever the specific content may be, it is essentially *qualified* in the same way as thoughtfully conducted overt activities.

In these last essays, as in all his work, the distinction and originality of Ryle's thought and style were abundantly manifest. The dominant characteristics of that style were verve and brilliance, concreteness and wit, and an utter freedom from pretentiousness or jargon. Striking epigram, balanced antithesis, and memorable phrase were combined with homely illustration and analogy to illuminate each recalcitrant topic in turn. His *œuvre* as a whole remains a brilliant and lasting contribution both to philosophy and to English letters.

During the years which followed the Second World War, Oxford University emerged once more as a distinguished centre of philosophy in the Western world. Ryle, at the centre of this centre, played a greater part in this development than any other individual. He contributed to it not only by his writings, lectures, and classes, influential as these were. He was also primarily responsible for the introduction, by a statute of 1946, of the new postgraduate degree of bachelor of philosophy, which was first examined in 1948. This innovation led to an expansion and flourishing of graduate philosophical study in Oxford, attracting students from outside as well as inside the United Kingdom, particularly from Australia and the United States, and greatly stimulating the philosophical activity of Oxford tutors. In contrast with the degree of doctor of philosophy, which required the student to produce a dissertation on a single subject, the new degree demanded that he or she show competence, in written papers, over a relatively wide area of problems, besides submitting a shorter thesis on a chosen topic. Ryle held, correctly, that the fulfilment of these requirements formed a better preparation for the aspirant teacher of the subject than the premature concentration on a single issue which was demanded of the student who proceeded directly from undergraduate studies to reading for a doctorate. In the decades that followed, and as the British university system expanded, new and already established philosophy departments were increasingly staffed by holders of the Oxford BPhil.

Always impatient of pretentiousness, fashion, or mere orthodoxy, always ready with sharp and pertinent criticism both of style and of content, Ryle was at the same time untiring in his encouragement of young, and thus far unknown, philosophers. As editor of *Mind* he tended to prefer the offerings of philosophers with unfamiliar names, often from unfamiliar places, to those of the well-established, who could easily find outlets for their writings elsewhere. This tendency was not without its critics; but the journal flourished. The number of members of the Mind Association more than trebled during his editorship. The brisk unfussiness of his conduct of the periodical was exemplary.

Ryle was little interested in the arts, except the literary arts—more specifically the writing of prose. The exception is important. Though the relatively abstract problems of philosophy and the furtherance of philosophical studies were, throughout his life, his dominant concern, he was a man of great literary and moral sensitivity. The former kind of sensitivity was amply evidenced in his own writing and in the criticism which he privately offered of the drafts of others; but the union of both kinds is admirably displayed in his fine essay 'Jane Austen and the moralists' (1966). Of the works of that author, indeed, he was a devoted admirer. (Once, when asked whether he ever read novels, he is said to have replied: 'Oh yes, all six of them, every year.')

Ryle's most strongly marked personal characteristics were directness, friendliness, candour, and a strong sense of justice. He was uncompromising in his judgements and could be brusque. He had no use for gossip. He was tall, slim, and soldierly in appearance.

Ryle received many academic honours: he was a foreign honorary member of the American Academy of Arts and Sciences (1968), an honorary student of Christ Church, and an honorary fellow of Queen's and Magdalen colleges; he was awarded honorary doctorates by the universities of Birmingham, Warwick, Sussex, Hull, Keele, Trent (Ontario), and Trinity College, Dublin.

On retirement from the Waynflete chair Ryle lived in Islip, near Oxford, with his twin sister, who survived him. He suffered a stroke and died on 6 October 1976 while on holiday in Yorkshire. He was unmarried. In his will he left a considerable sum of money to Hertford College, chosen as being less well endowed than those colleges with which he was more closely connected.   P. F. STRAWSON, *rev.*

Sources O. P. Wood and G. Pitcher, eds., *Ryle: a collection of critical essays* (1971) · G. J. Warnock, 'Preface', in G. Ryle, *On thinking*, ed. K. Kolenda (1979) · G. J. Warnock, 'Gilbert Ryle's editorship', *Mind*, new ser., 85 (1976), 47–56 · personal knowledge (1986) · private information (1986)
Archives Bodl. Oxf., corresp. with R. G. Collingwood · Nuffield Oxf., corresp. with Lord Cherwell |SOUND BL NSA, *Conversations with philosophers*, BBC Radio 3, 27 Dec 1970, P596W C1 · BL NSA, documentary recording · BL NSA, recorded lecture
Likenesses H. A. Freeth, drawing, 1952, NPG [*see illus.*] · A. Sorrell, group portrait, oils, 1954, Magd. Oxf. · R. Whistler, oils, Magd. Oxf. · portrait, Magd. Oxf.
Wealth at death £82,573: probate, 17 Jan 1977, *CGPLA Eng. & Wales*

Ryle, Herbert Edward (1856–1925), dean of Westminster and biblical scholar, was born in Onslow Square, London, on 25 May 1856, the second son of John Charles *Ryle (1816–1900), bishop of Liverpool, and his second wife, Jessie Elizabeth, the eldest daughter of John Walker, of Crawfordton, Dumfriesshire. Herbert Ryle was three years old when his mother died, and in 1861 his father married Henrietta, daughter of Lieutenant-Colonel William Legh Clowes, of Broughton Old Hall, Lancashire; she proved to be a loving mother to her stepchildren. Ryle and his brothers and sisters were brought up in their father's country parishes in Suffolk, first at Helmingham and after 1861 at Stradbroke. Ryle continued to love the countryside throughout his life, and though he moved away from the evangelical conservatism of his childhood home he remained close to his father.

After attending school at Hill House, Wadhurst, Sussex, Ryle went in 1868 to Eton College, where after a year as an oppidan he became a scholar ('colleger'). In 1875 he won the Newcastle scholarship, and in the same year he proceeded to King's College, Cambridge, as a classical scholar. A football accident in 1877 prevented him from further involvement in athletics and he took an *aegrotat* degree in

1879. Between 1879 and 1881, however, he won every distinction open at Cambridge to students of theology, including a first class in the theological tripos. He was elected a fellow of King's College, Cambridge, in April 1881, and began a career of twenty years as a teacher. He was ordained deacon in 1882 and priest in 1883. On 15 August 1883 he married Nea Hewish Adams. They had three sons, the eldest of whom died at birth; the youngest, aged only eight, died in 1897.

Ryle spent an interlude of eighteen months (from September 1886 to March 1888) as principal of St David's College, Lampeter, but apart from this administrative post his work until 1901 continued in teaching at the University of Cambridge, where he returned from Lampeter in 1887 to become Hulsean professor of divinity, succeeding F. J. A. Hort. Ryle's main academic interest lay in Old Testament studies, and he had a belief, which he sought to convey to his students, in the integrity of biblical criticism. The clarity of his delivery made him a popular lecturer and a number of his students spoke with gratitude of his teaching. During these years Ryle published a number of books connected with his academic interests, including *The Early Narratives of Genesis* (1892), *The Canon of the Old Testament* (1892), and *Philo and Holy Scripture* (1895). After his election as president of Queens' College, Cambridge, in 1896, he found little time for writing. He was, however, responsible for the edition of Genesis in the Cambridge Bible (1914), when he was dean of Westminster.

In his work on the Old Testament, Ryle sought to expound the results of continental critical scholarship, particularly the work of Julius Wellhausen. But while Wellhausen's religious viewpoint was regarded with mistrust, Ryle presented Wellhausen's historical-critical theories within the tradition of liberal Anglican scholarship, thus contributing to the gradual appropriation of critical ideas within British scholarship. Ryle's tone was reverent, with an emphasis on the spiritual (rather than the literal) truth of the Old and the New Testament. As his pupil A. H. M. McNeile wrote, Ryle 'drew the minds of thinking men to realise that the historical study of the Old Testament, so far from upsetting faith, was its only safe intellectual background' (Fitzgerald, 98). Along with S. R. Driver and A. P. Kirkpatrick, Ryle at that time 'represented to many people English higher criticism of the Old Testament' (ibid., 97). The respect he earned was due in part to his accessible personality, and the popularity of his wife, Nea. Among their friends were the Cambridge New Testament scholars, Brooke Foss Westcott and F. J. A. Hort.

In December 1900 Ryle was appointed bishop of Exeter, and he was consecrated in Westminster Abbey in January 1901. He became bishop of Winchester in the spring of 1903. In his short time at Exeter he won the trust and affection of both clergy and laity, but at Winchester he was less fortunate. Having been greatly overworked at Exeter, in January 1904 he suffered an attack of angina pectoris, followed by appendicitis. Also, as a reflection of his broad-church principles, he had issued early on a letter to the diocese of Winchester which alarmed high-churchmen

by forbidding certain ritual practices. This, together with a mistaken impression that his health compromised his ability to fulfil his episcopal duties, hindered him in winning the confidence so readily given to him at Exeter. Nevertheless, he steadily overcame these misgivings over the next eight years, and his resignation in 1911 was regretted throughout the diocese. Ryle was a good administrator, and he left the diocese in a higher state of efficiency than it had ever attained before. He was appointed honorary chaplain to the queen in 1896 and chairman of the commission sent to Sweden in 1909 by the archbishop of Canterbury to investigate the possibility of closer relations between the English and Swedish churches.

In December 1910 Ryle accepted the offer of the deanery of Westminster. For several months he had been handicapped by a lame foot, and he reluctantly decided to exchange episcopal work for less exacting duties. He was installed in the abbey in April 1911, at a time when the building was being prepared for the coronation of King George V. He was created CVO in the same year. Circumstances never allowed him to resume academic work; nevertheless the years he spent at Westminster turned out to be among the most fruitful of his career. Under his guidance and with the help of his advisers, the dignity of the abbey services was notably increased, and his work was commemorated by the Dean Ryle Fund, a sum of £170,000 raised for the maintenance of the abbey in response to an appeal issued by him in 1920. During the First World War, Ryle used to take the midday service of intercession personally, and he was responsible for the many special services held in wartime. His carefully prepared sermons were simple in form and direct in style, and Archbishop William Temple wrote that he had never 'heard such exquisitely beautiful preaching of the simple Gospel' (Fitzgerald, 295).

Apart from in his duties as dean, Ryle was taken up with committee work. As chairman of the so-called 'grand committee' of the Representative Church Council, he did much to prepare the way for the passing of the Enabling Act of 1920; and from 1919 to 1925 he was prolocutor of the lower house of the convocation of Canterbury, presiding over the prolonged debates over the revision of the Book of Common Prayer. He was created KCVO in 1921. Ryle had never been strong and he had a history of heart trouble; in the autumn of 1924 his health broke down. After five months in a nursing home at Bournemouth he returned in May 1925 to the deanery, where he died on 20 August. He was buried on 25 August in Westminster Abbey in a spot close to the tomb of the 'unknown soldier'. His wife survived him.

Ryle was a courteous man of fine presence, with a quick sense of humour and a ready sympathy. But there was also an element of reserve in his character, and he disliked pretentiousness and self-advertisement. In ecclesiastical matters his standpoint was that of a broad-churchman. Ryle was a man of common sense and strong simplicity of faith. Bishop Francis Paget described him as 'a past master in equity' and Archbishop Davidson declared that his 'lucid vision and Christian common sense … gained for him the quite exceptional confidence of his brother bishops' (Fitzgerald, xi and xii).

M. H. FitzGerald, rev. Joanna Hawke

Sources M. H. Fitzgerald, *A memoir of Herbert Edward Ryle* (1928) · *Men and women of the time* (1899) · C. A. M. Press, *Hampshire and Isle of Wight leaders: social and political* (1903)
Archives Westminster Abbey, library, corresp. and papers as dean of Westminster | BL, corresp. with Macmillans, Add. MS 55111 · King's AC Cam., letters to Oscar Browning
Likenesses photograph, 1910, repro. in Fitzgerald, *Memoir of Herbert Edward Ryle*, frontispiece · W. Carter, oils, exh. RA 1913, Farnham Castle, Surrey · M. Beerbohm, caricature drawing, 1924 (*Our abbey*), Art Gallery of New South Wales, Sydney, Australia · H. G. Riviere, oils, Queens' College, Cambridge · WH, chromolithograph caricature, NPG; repro. in *VF* (27 March 1912) · print, NPG
Wealth at death £10,675 4s. 6d.: probate, 8 Oct 1925, *CGPLA Eng. & Wales*

Ryle, John Alfred (1889–1950), physician, was born on 12 December 1889 at Northland, Hadley Green, Barnet, the eldest son of the eleven children of a Brighton physician, Reginald John Ryle, and his wife, Catherine (formerly Scott). He was a grandson of John Charles *Ryle, bishop of Liverpool, and nephew of H. E. Ryle, bishop of Exeter and of Winchester. His younger brother, Gilbert *Ryle, became Waynflete professor of metaphysics at Oxford. John's father rejected Christianity in favour of becoming what late Victorians chose to call a 'rationalist'; a friend of the Huxley family, a devoted disciple of Darwinian evolutionary theory, a member of the Aristotelian Society, and a committed pacifist, Reginald Ryle had a profound influence upon John's development.

Ryle was educated at Brighton College. Unable to go to Oxford for financial reasons, like his father he trained for medicine and studied at Guy's Hospital in London before war broke out. After serving in Belgium and France with the Royal Army Medical Corps in the First World War, he returned to Guy's in 1919 as medical registrar; in the same year he became MRCP and MD (London) with gold medal. He became assistant physician in 1920, and later consultant physician; he was made a fellow of the Royal College of Physicians in 1924. On 23 October 1914 he married Miriam Power Scully (*b.* 1893/4), daughter of William Charles Scully, a civil servant in Cape Town, Cape Province. They had five children.

Ryle set up practice in Wimpole Street, London, in 1922. By the early 1930s he had become one of the city's most eminent physicians, with an international reputation for the invention of a gastro-investigative tube and, together with Izod Bennett, the standardization of the fractional meal test. His Goulstonian lectures were published as *Gastric Function in Health and Disease* in 1926. Ryle seemed destined to become president of the Royal College of Physicians, but in 1935 he was invited to become the regius professor of physic at Cambridge. There he established a new medical department and developed links with investigative clinical research at Addenbrooke's Hospital. His years at Cambridge proved to be frustrating, however, as the pace of change was too slow. Ryle was given only very limited access to beds for research patients at Addenbrooke's and, perhaps more importantly, his political consciousness became increasingly left-wing. Pre-war Cambridge had a large enough group of radicals to have encompassed him but Ryle was not a clubbable man. Elected a fellow of Gonville and Caius College in 1936 he was uncomfortable with college life and was not content simply to intellectualize about social problems. Furthermore the Cambridge chair had traditionally been occupied by elderly men at the end of their clinical career and all had been Cambridge graduates. Ryle was young, a successful London clinician, and an outsider. He was thus perceived as a threat by the local clinical élite. On the other hand, having had no experience of the laboratory he was rejected by some of the scientific community. Despite this his achievements were not insignificant at Cambridge, as the later careers of his postgraduate students testify. His *Natural History of Disease* was published in 1936.

Ryle was more politically active by the late 1930s. He helped to organize relief for victims of the Spanish Civil War and employment for medical refugees. He stood, unsuccessfully, as an Independent Progressive parliamentary candidate for Cambridge University in 1940. From his twenties he was a pacifist, like his father, and he became president of the Medical Peace Campaign. He spoke before meetings of the Socialist Medical Association but did not become a member. When war broke out he renounced strict pacifism in favour of the need to resist fascism, and in 1941 he joined the Anglo-Soviet Friendship Committee. War dispersed the members of his Cambridge department and Ryle returned to Guy's, living in a workman's flat in the borough of Southwark, to serve throughout the blitz, and to become a chief consultant to the Ministry of Health within the Emergency Medical Service. The strain of his duties led to his first coronary thrombosis in 1942.

The following year Ryle resigned his position at Cambridge, and on 1 April 1943 he took up the chair at the newly established Institute of Social Medicine at Oxford. The creation of the institute was set in motion when Sir Arthur MacNalty, the chief medical officer to the Ministry of Health, proposed in 1939 that a new chair of social medicine be established at his old university of Oxford. Once established the institute acted as both a research and a teaching institution. It had a committee consisting of representatives from the Nuffield Trust, including Ernest Rock Carling, and from the Oxford medical faculty, including Arthur Ellis and Leslie Witts. The institute provided courses in social medicine for medical students, and lectures were also open to all graduate students and to medical social workers and health visitors. Eventually it took over all undergraduate public-health teaching for clinical students after Sir Arthur MacNalty retired from lecturing in 1946. A number of medical officers of health, factory officers, and others in the field were also recruited to provide lectures. In 1946 Ryle suggested that social medicine was reforming the preclinical curriculum by placing a stronger emphasis on principles and paying close attention to social factors in aetiology. The institute's courses stressed the value of statistical methods and what Ryle termed 'social diagnosis and the importance of social case-taking in follow-up inquiries of hospitalized sickness' (Institute of Social Medicine, Oxford, *Second Annual Report 1946*, 1947, 12).

A wide range of research projects was pursued at the institute: a child health survey and a radiographic survey of child development; numerous statistical analyses, such as the correlation between skin cancer or TB and occupational and other social factors, and the analysis of the correlation between stillbirth rates and nutritional factors; a large survey of peptic ulcer among the employees of Morris Motors; an investigation of fluorine hazards to humans and animals; a survey of uncertified illness among local factory women; and, in co-operation with the Medical Research Council, research on goitre and iodine prophylaxis. Ryle initially had three senior members of staff and a number of junior faculty, but he added more staff every year and continually hosted numerous visiting scholars from abroad.

Between 1946 and 1948 Ryle gave a number of lectures in the United States, Canada, and Britain which defined the new academic discipline of social medicine. He published these lectures as a single volume, *Changing Disciplines* (1948), intended as a manifesto for a new medical creed. He promoted clinical science as a field rather than a laboratory study which incorporated social science into the explanation of disease causation, and he returned the 'whole patient' to the centre of medical practice. Although he dedicated the remainder of his life to social medicine, Ryle felt that he had never ceased to be a clinician. In creating social medicine as a discipline, he believed he was forging a renaissance in the clinical art, changing it from within, expanding its boundaries, and making it a new humanistic science for the twentieth century.

The primary method of social medicine was social pathology, which analysed the morbid processes at work among human groups and populations in the same way as clinical pathology examined the morbid processes within the body of the individual. As the clinical pathologist used a scalpel so the social pathologist used the tools of statistics, sociology, and epidemiology. Ryle asserted that the science of social pathology was inherently bound to the science of what he called 'hygieology'—the study of the causes of health. According to Ryle, health and disease knew no sharp boundary: there was only the normal range of variability and its extremes were determined by environmental conditions. Health was created by the interrelations of ancestry and environment.

For Ryle social medicine also had a moral task. Its social conscience and scientific intent would help to establish scientific humanism as a new secular ethic, governing social, economic, and political behaviour. He wrote a book on the new humanism, *Fears may be Liars* (1941), in which he stated that life must be brought under human control through the rational direction of human evolution and that the science of life must be utilized to bring about a better social organization and 'a humane and scientific elaboration of the natural principle of mutual aid' (p. 41). Designing an equality of opportunity for health was, he believed, one of its tasks; assisting the establishment of a religion of rationalism in a new social order was another.

Ryle was awarded the honorary degrees of MD at Cambridge, in 1935, and DSc at McGill, in 1947. He was appointed physician-extraordinary to the king in 1935, having previously been physician to the royal household. He was a member of the Medical Research Council from 1935 to 1939; president of the Association of Physicians of Great Britain and Ireland in 1942; member of the commission on higher education in the colonies from 1943 to 1945; and member of the double-day, shift-working committee of the Ministry of Labour and National Service from 1945 to 1946.

Ryle died on 27 February 1950 from a coronary thrombosis at his home, Barkhale, Sutton Pulborough, Sussex. He left his widow, Miriam, and their five children. Their second son, Martin *Ryle, won a Nobel prize for astronomy.   DOROTHY PORTER

Sources *The Lancet* (11 March 1950), 471–3 · *BMJ* (11 March 1950), 611–13 · Munk, *Roll* · C. Symonds, 'John Alfred Ryle', *Guy's Hospital Reports*, 4th ser., 29 (1950), 209–22 · private information (1997) · J. A. Ryle, *Changing disciplines* (1994) · D. Porter, 'John Ryle: doctor of revolution?', *Doctors, politics and society: historical essays*, ed. D. Porter and R. Porter (1993), 229–47 · D. Porter, 'Changing disciplines: John Ryle and the making of social medicine in the 1940s Britain', *History of Science*, 30 (1992), 137–64, esp. 119–47 · *DNB* · b. cert. · m. cert. · *CGPLA Eng. & Wales* (1950) · A. MacNalty, *The reform of the public health services* (1943)

Archives JRL, letters to the *Manchester Guardian* · priv. coll. · U. Oxf., Wellcome Unit for the History of Medicine | Wellcome L., letters to the Eugenics Society · Wellcome L., letters to Carlos Paton Blacker · Wellcome L., letters to the Pioneer Health Centre, Peckham · Wellcome L., letters to Frederick Parkes Weber

Likenesses photograph, repro. in *The Lancet* · photograph, repro. in *BMJ*

Wealth at death £28,093 14s. 10d.: probate, 26 May 1950, *CGPLA Eng. & Wales*

Ryle, John Charles (1816–1900), bishop of Liverpool, was born on 10 May 1816 at Park House, Macclesfield, the fourth child and elder son of John Ryle, banker and MP, and his wife, Susanna, daughter of Charles Hurt of Wirksworth. He had four sisters and one brother. Ryle's mother was the granddaughter of Sir Richard Arkwright and the family fortunes were made in the silk trade. In the early nineteenth century the Ryles took up banking, and at the same time the family's Methodist sympathies were replaced by unenthusiastic conformity to the Church of England. John Ryle, a supporter of parliamentary reform, was MP for Macclesfield between 1832 and 1837. The younger John was sent to school with the Revd J. Jackson at Over, Cheshire, from 1824 to 1827 and proceeded to Eton College in 1828. In 1834 he went up to Christ Church, Oxford, where he was Fell exhibitioner (1835) and Craven scholar (1836). A distinguished academic record, culminating in a first class in *literae humaniores* in 1837, was matched by athletic prowess as captain of the university cricket eleven. He graduated BA in 1838 and, declining

John Charles Ryle (1816–1900), by Barraud, pubd 1888

invitations to stand for a fellowship, returned to Maccles-field to prepare for a career in business and politics.

The decisive event in Ryle's life took place in June 1841, when his father's bank collapsed. The family estates and income were swept away and the household broken up. Ryle, who had turned to evangelical Christianity during his final summer in Oxford, decided to take holy orders, recording later, 'I became a clergyman because I felt shut up to do it, and saw no other course of life open to me' (*J. C. Ryle, a Self Portrait*, 59). He was ordained deacon in 1841 and priest in 1842, serving as curate of Exbury, Hampshire, from 1841 to 1843. After five months as rector of St Thomas's, Winchester (1843–4), where he 'filled [the] church to suffocation and turned the parish upside-down' (ibid., 67), Ryle was preferred to the living of Helming-ham, Suffolk. In 1861 increasing difficulties with the pat-ron, John Tollemache, led him to accept Bishop Pelham's offer of the vicarage of Stradbroke in the same county, where he remained until 1880. Ryle was appointed rural dean of Hoxne in 1870 and honorary canon of Norwich in 1872. He was select preacher at Cambridge in 1873–4 and at Oxford in 1874–6 and 1879–80. He took his MA in 1871 and was created DD in 1880. The years at Helmingham and Stradbroke, both small country parishes, saw Ryle rise to prominence within the evangelical school. Standing 6 feet 3½ inches tall, his commanding presence, combined with lucid oratory, made him a popular preacher, while regular visits to London for his wife's health gave him easy access to metropolitan pulpits. While proposing schemes of church reform he denounced in 1868 Gladstone's plan to disestablish the Church of Ireland. An advocate of evan-gelical unity, he also called for involvement in the wider life of the Church of England and spoke regularly at the annual church congresses. Although he combined this with staunch protestantism, unflinching opposition to ritualism, and a moderate Calvinist theology it earned him the epithet 'neo-evangelical' from the ultra-conservatives. It was, however, as an author of tracts that Ryle made his greatest impact, writing some 200 titles which sold 12 million copies during his lifetime. Whether devotional, evangelistic, or polemical Ryle's tracts were always models of forceful argument and limpid prose. Apart from his homiletical volumes, *Expository Thoughts on the Gospels*, most of Ryle's books were collections of his tracts. These included *Knots Untied* (1877), which has had continuing influence as a presentation of the evangelical position, and *Holiness* (1877, 1880), which expressed Ryle's opposition to the teaching of the Keswick Movement. His appearance on the convention platform at Keswick in 1892 marked only a partial reconciliation between differ-ent strands of Holiness teaching within evangelicalism.

In 1880 Ryle was offered the deanery of Salisbury, but while still dean-designate he was persuaded to accept the see of Liverpool. As the first bishop of this geographically compact but densely populated see, Ryle's priorities were the provision of more clergy ('living agents') and places of worship. Finance for diocesan institutions remained a problem, and disputes about sites, compounded by a lack of money, delayed progress on the scheme for a cathedral. As a well-known evangelical Ryle was bound to be a con-troversial bishop, and his reluctant acquiescence in the prosecution of the Revd James Bell Cox for ritual irregu-larities (1885–92) brought criticism not only from high-churchmen but also from those who thought him lacking in protestant zeal. After several periods of ill health in the 1890s Ryle announced his resignation in October 1899, with effect from 1 March 1900. On retirement he moved to Lowestoft.

Ryle was married three times. He married first, on 29 October 1845, at Helmingham, Matilda Charlotte Louisa, daughter of John Pemberton Plumptre, MP, of Fredville, Kent, who died in June 1847 leaving a daughter, Georgina Matilda; second, on 21 February 1850, at Tor Mohun, Tor-quay, Jessie Elizabeth, daughter of John Walker of Craw-fordton, Dumfriesshire, with whom he had four child-ren—Jessie, Reginald, Herbert Edward *Ryle (later bishop of Winchester), and Arthur, and who died after prolonged illness in May 1860; and third, on 24 October 1861, Henri-etta Amelia, daughter of Lieutenant-Colonel William Legh Clowes of Broughton Old Hall, Lancashire. Henrietta Ryle died in April 1889 without issue. Ryle died at his home, Helmingham House in Lowestoft, on 10 June 1900. His funeral took place at All Saints', Childwall, Liverpool, on 14 June, and he was buried in All Saints' graveyard.

MARTIN WELLINGS

Sources *J. C. Ryle, a self portrait: a partial autobiography*, ed. P. Toon (1975) · P. Toon and M. Smout, *John Charles Ryle: evangelical bishop* (1976) · *DNB* · M. H. Fitzgerald, *A memoir of Herbert Edward Ryle* (1928) · I. D. Farley, 'J. C. Ryle—episcopal evangelist', PhD diss.,

U. Durham, 1988 • M. L. Loane, *John Charles Ryle, 1816–1900: a short biography* (1953) • *The Record* (27 Oct 1899) • *The Record* (17 Nov 1899) • *The Record* (15 June 1900) • *The Times* (11 June 1900) • *WWW* • J. Bentley, *Ritualism and politics in Victorian Britain* (1978), 114–16 • P. J. Waller, *Democracy and sectarianism: a political and social history of Liverpool, 1868–1939* (1981), 172–7

Archives Lpool RO, letters to A. J. Tomlin

Likenesses Ape [C. Pellegrini], caricature, watercolour study, NPG; repro. in *VF* (26 March 1881) • Barraud, photograph, NPG; repro. in *Men and Women of the Day*, 1 (1888) [*see illus.*] • Delany & Co., two cartes-de-visite, NPG • W. Holl, stipple (after photograph), NPG • Lock & Whitfield, woodburytype photograph, NPG; repro. in T. Cooper, *Men of mark: a gallery of contemporary portraits* (1883) • oils, Eton • photograph, NPG • stipple, NPG

Wealth at death £26,662 4s. 8d.: probate, 18 Oct 1900, *CGPLA Eng. & Wales*

Ryle, Sir Martin (1918–1984), radio astronomer, was born on 27 September 1918 at Brighton, Sussex, the second son and second child in a family of three sons and two daughters of John Alfred *Ryle (1889–1950), a professor of medicine, and his wife, Miriam Power (1893/4–c.1986), the daughter of William Charles Scully, a civil servant, of Cape Town, who came from a landowning family in co. Tipperary. His father was to become regius professor of physic at Cambridge and, after the Second World War, the first professor of social medicine at Oxford. An uncle, Gilbert Ryle, was professor of philosophy at Oxford.

Ryle's early education was entrusted to a governess, who taught him and his siblings at the family home at 13 Wimpole Street, London. He then attended Gladstone's Preparatory School in Eaton Square before entering Bradfield College at the age of thirteen. His ability with his hands was fostered at home, where regular instruction was provided to him and his elder brother by a professional carpenter. In 1936 he went to Christ Church, Oxford, where he obtained first-class honours in physics in 1939. His enthusiasm for radio engineering and electronics was already apparent. By the time he left school he had built his own radio transmitter and acquired a Post Office licence to operate it. At Oxford, he and E. Cooke-Yarborough, a fellow undergraduate, set up the university amateur radio station.

Wartime service In 1939 Ryle joined J. A. Ratcliffe's ionospheric research group at the Cavendish Laboratory, Cambridge. On the outbreak of the Second World War, Ratcliffe joined the Air Ministry Research Establishment, later to become the Telecommunications Research Establishment (TRE), and Ryle followed in May 1940. For the first two years he worked mainly on the design of antennae and test equipment. In 1942 he became the leader of group 5 of the newly formed radio countermeasures division, whose task was to provide jamming transmitters against the German radar defence system and radio-deception operations. Among the latter was the electronic 'spoof-invasion' on D-day, which led the German high command to believe that the invasion was to take place across the Strait of Dover.

Radar techniques developed at an astounding pace during these years, and Ryle and his colleagues worked in a frantic atmosphere, constantly having to find immediate practical solutions for the electronic defence of the RAF's bomber fleet. Sir Bernard Lovell remarked that 'Ryle's extraordinary inventiveness and immediate scientific insight were of great importance in this work and often led him to be intolerant of those not similarly blessed' (*DNB*). But he also learned how to motivate groups of research workers. In a letter to the present writer, written only two months before his death, he said:

> Presumably I knew some physics in 1939—but this evaporated during the six succeeding years—though it was replaced by other things. But six years of designing/ installing/flying boxes of electronics gave one 'state of the art' electronics, a fair intimacy with aircraft and the ability to talk constructively with Air Vice-Marshals—or radar mechanics—and above all gave one the privilege of flying with the in-between-operational-tours aircrew who flew our aircraft.

According to Sir Francis Graham-Smith, perhaps Ryle's greatest achievement was to discover a vulnerable element in the V-2 rocket radio guidance system. The system developed by Ryle and his old college friend Cooke-Yarborough successfully disrupted the accurate aim of the V-2 rockets and probably contributed to the abandonment of radio control only a few weeks later.

Solar radio-emission After the war Ryle returned to Cambridge on a fellowship from Imperial Chemical Industries, and soon turned his energies to understanding the nature of the radio emissions from cosmic sources which had interfered with anti-aircraft radars. The pioneer radio astronomer J. S. Hey had found that the jamming was caused by intense radio outbursts from the sun, apparently associated with large solar flares and sunspot groups. The angular resolving power of the radio antennae available at that time was not sufficient to resolve the disc of the sun, let alone locate the origin of the radio emission. Ryle and D. D. Vonberg adapted surplus radar equipment and developed new receiver techniques for metre wavelengths to create a radio interferometer, the antennae being separated by several hundreds of metres in order to provide high enough angular resolution. Only later was it realized that they had reinvented the radio equivalent of the Michelson interferometer. A massive sunspot occurred in July 1946, and their observations showed conclusively that the radio emission originated from a region on the surface of the sun similar in size to that of the sunspot region.

In addition to the emission from the sun, Hey had discovered a discrete source of radio emission in the constellation of Cygnus, and Ryle and Graham-Smith adapted the solar interferometer to observe the radio source, which became known as Cygnus A. In 1947 the source was successfully observed, and in addition another even more intense discrete source was found in the nearby constellation of Cassiopeia. By 1950 Graham-Smith had measured very precisely the position of Cygnus A, and it turned out that the source was associated with a distant massive galaxy.

During the time in which the fledgeling radio group began to take shape, Ryle married (Ella) Rowena Palmer, the youngest sister of Graham-Smith's wife, Elizabeth, on 19 June 1947. It was a wonderfully happy marriage, and they had three children, Alison (*b.* 1949), John (*b.* 1951), and Claire (*b.* 1952). Somewhat to his surprise, midway through his fellowship Ryle was appointed a university lecturer (1948). In 1952 he was elected a fellow of the Royal Society.

Radio interferometry Ryle appreciated that radio interferometry was the way to overcome the problem of the low angular resolution of single-dish radio antennae, and over the next twenty-five years he and his colleagues developed a series of radio interferometers of increasing complexity and ingenuity which enabled surveys of the sky to be carried out and the structures and nature of the radio sources to be unravelled. His contribution of genius was the development of the concept of aperture synthesis, the technique by which images of radio sources can be created by combining interferometric observations made with modest-sized radio telescopes located at different interferometer spacings. The technical problem was to measure both the relative amplitudes and the phases of the incoming signals, which contain all the information needed to reconstruct the distribution of radio intensity on the sky.

Throughout the 1950s and 1960s, one of Ryle's major objectives was to produce reliable catalogues of all the bright radio sources in the northern sky. In his review of the new science of radio astronomy published in 1950, he had believed that most of the 'radio stars' belonged to our own galaxy, but increasingly it became clear that, in directions away from the Milky Way, the bulk of them were associated with distant galaxies. The bombshell was dropped in 1955 in his Halley lecture at Oxford, when he announced the results of the second Cambridge survey of radio sources. This survey had found vastly more faint radio sources than could be explained by any of the standard cosmological models—Ryle inferred that the only reasonable interpretation of these observations was that the universe had changed with time, so that there had been many more radio sources in the distant past. This interpretation flew in the face of the steady state theory, propounded by Bondi, Gold, and Hoyle in 1948, according to which the universe should have the same overall appearance at all cosmic epochs. It soon became apparent that the intensities of the faintest sources had been systematically overestimated because of the effects of source confusion. An acrimonious dispute resulted, not only with the proponents of steady state theory, but also with the Sydney radio astronomers, who did not observe the excess of faint sources found by Ryle in their surveys of the southern sky. The correct answer was discovered by Ryle's colleague Peter Scheuer, who analysed the survey records statistically and found that there was indeed a significant excess of faint sources, but not to the extent originally claimed. In the 1960s the revised third and fourth Cambridge catalogues showed that Ryle's interpretation was correct.

The Mullard Observatory These events had positive and negative impacts on the work of the Cambridge radio astronomy group. The negative side was that the group became more defensive in its interaction with outside groups. The positive side was that new astrophysical and cosmological opportunities were opened up. In 1956 the radio observatory moved to a disused wartime Air Ministry bomb store at Lord's Bridge, near Cambridge, and, in acknowledgement of a grant of £100,000 from the electronics company Mullard Ltd, the new observatory was opened in 1957 as the Mullard Radio Astronomy Observatory.

Aperture synthesis In 1959 Ryle was appointed professor of radio astronomy. At the same time his most ambitious experiment was under way—the use of the rotation of the earth to carry telescopes at fixed points on the earth about each other as observed from a point on the celestial sphere. The germ of this idea had already appeared in his notebooks in 1954. By 1959 digital computers were fast enough to cope with the demands of this form of synthesis mapping, and, in a classic set of observations, Ryle and Ann Neville created the first earth-rotation aperture synthesis map of a region of sky about the north celestial pole. The angular resolution of the survey was 4.5 minutes of arc and the sensitivity eight times greater than that of the original antenna system. The success of this project pointed the way to the future. The succeeding generations of aperture synthesis arrays employed fully steerable antennae—the One-Mile Telescope completed in 1965 and the Five-Kilometer Telescope in 1972. Both of these telescopes were far ahead of the radio astronomical capability of any other telescope system in the world. Ryle was personally involved in every aspect of these very complex telescope systems. As remarked by Scheuer, the development of aperture synthesis:

> was the story of one remarkable man, who not only provided the inspiration and driving force but actually designed most of the bits and pieces, charmed or savaged official persons according to their deserts, wielded shovels and sledgehammers, mended breakdowns, and kept the rest of us on our toes.

Intellectually, he relied almost completely on his well-honed physical intuition as the way to solve any problem, be it in engineering, astrophysics, or cosmology—indeed, he believed this was the only way research should be conducted. Ryle was knighted in 1966.

The Nobel prize These telescopes were central to understanding the nature of the radio sources. Radio astronomy has played a crucial role in the realization that high-energy astrophysical activity involving supermassive black holes and general relativity are part of the large-scale fabric of the universe.

From the beginning, led by the dynamism and vision of Ryle, the Cambridge radio astronomy group developed a remarkably coherent and focused research programme. Ryle was fortunate in being supported by an outstanding group of physicists. Among these, Antony Hewish had played a central role in the development of aperture synthesis and in 1964 had begun the study of the flickering, or scintillation, of radio sources due to irregularities in the outflow of material from the sun—what is known as the solar wind. A remarkable by-product of these studies was the discovery of pulsating radio sources, now called pulsars, by Hewish and his graduate student Jocelyn Bell. These objects were soon convincingly identified as rapidly rotating, magnetized neutron stars, which had been predicted to exist on theoretical grounds. Their serendipitous discovery at long radio wavelengths was a crucial event for all astronomy. In 1974 Ryle and Hewish were awarded jointly the Nobel prize for physics, the citation explicitly describing the development of aperture synthesis as Ryle's major contribution. His list of honours was extensive, including foreign memberships of the Royal Danish Academy (1968), the American Academy of Arts and Sciences (1970), and the USSR Academy of Sciences (1971). Among many medals were the gold medal of the Royal Astronomical Society (1964), the Popov medal of the USSR Academy of Sciences (1971), and the royal medal of the Royal Society (1973).

Anti-nuclear campaigns In 1972 Ryle was appointed astronomer royal, the first time the post had been separated from the directorship of the Royal Greenwich Observatory. This coincided with a period of grave deterioration in his health, originating from a malfunctioning heart and aggravated by stress. Medical examination exposed lung cancer, for which he had surgery in 1977. Over the same period his main preoccupations shifted away from radio astronomy. His acute awareness of the dangers of nuclear power fuelled a passionate ethical sense of crusade concerning the potential misuse of science. His conviction was that man breaks the natural laws at his peril. His deep concern for alternative energy sources led to an enthusiasm for wind energy, a natural outcome of his expertise as a sailing-boat designer, and he began a successful research and development programme at Lord's Bridge involving the construction of wind-powered generators. He was passionate about the proliferation of nuclear weapons and wrote a monograph, *Towards the Nuclear Holocaust*, which, as expressed by Graham-Smith,

> is partly a cry of pain and a desperate plea for a halt in the arms race, and partly an indictment of all those concerned with the civil nuclear programme, which he regarded as sustainable only on account of its production of plutonium for military purposes. (Graham-Smith, 517–8)

Ryle died on 14 October 1984 at the family home, 5A Herschel Road, Cambridge, and was cremated at Cambridge crematorium. His legacy went far beyond the technical brilliance of his contribution to radio astronomy. When he began his career after the war, the UK could not compete with the United States in observational astronomy. Through his technical and scientific contributions, as well as his inspiring leadership, Ryle played a major role in rejuvenating British astronomy and bringing it to the forefront of world astronomy.   MALCOLM S. LONGAIR

Sources F. Graham-Smith, *Memoirs FRS*, 32 (1986), 497–524 · B. Lovell, *Quarterly Journal of the Royal Astronomical Society*, 26 (1985), 358–68 · 'Martin Ryle', *Les prix Nobel en 1974* (1975), 80–99 · P. A. G. Scheuer, 'Radio source counts', *Modern cosmology in retrospect*, ed. B. Bertotti and others (1990), 331–45 · M. S. Longair, 'Astrophysics and cosmology', *Twentieth century physics*, ed. L. M. Brown, A. Pais, and B. Pippard, 3 (1995) · M. Ryle, N. Kurti, and R. L. F. Boyd, *Search and Research*, ed. J. P. Wilson (1971) · J. S. Hey, *The evolution of radio astronomy* (1973) · W. T. Sullivan III, ed., *The early years of radio astronomy* (1984) · W. T. Sullivan III, *Classics of radio astronomy* (1982) · *DNB* · personal knowledge (2004) · private information (2004)

Archives CAC Cam., further corresp. and papers; papers · U. Cam., Cavendish Laboratory, corresp. and MSS | Nuffield Oxf., corresp. with Lord Cherwell | FILM U. Cam., Cavendish Laboratory | SOUND BBC Archives, talks

Likenesses E. Leigh, photograph, 1974, repro. in Graham-Smith, *Memoirs FRS* · photographs, U. Cam., Cavendish Laboratory

Wealth at death £4267: probate, 11 July 1985, *CGPLA Eng. & Wales*

Ryley, Charles Reuben (*c*.1752–1798), painter, son of a trooper in the horseguards, was born in London. He suffered from poor health and a physical deformity. Showing an early inclination towards art, he first studied engraving, for which he received a premium in 1767 from the Society of Arts. He later turned to painting, becoming a pupil of John Hamilton Mortimer RA and in February 1769 a student at the Royal Academy Schools, where he obtained a silver medal in 1770, and a gold medal in 1778 for his painting *Orestes on the Point of being Sacrificed by Iphigenia*. He exhibited annually at the Royal Academy from 1778 until his death, showing drawings and small paintings of mainly literary subjects, some of which were engraved.

Ryley's initial promise as a history painter was affected by his bad health, and during the 1790s he was forced to fall back on teaching in schools, designing trade cards, and illustrating books. He also worked as a decorative painter on a number of country houses, including that of the duke of Richmond at Goodwood. After beginning life with strict Methodist views, Ryley fell into irregular habits, which affected his already fragile health and brought about his death on 13 October 1798, at his home in New Road, Marylebone, Middlesex.

L. H. CUST, rev. ROSIE DIAS

Sources E. Edwards, *Anecdotes of painters* (1808); facs. edn (1970) · Redgrave, *Artists* · Graves, *RA exhibitors* · S. C. Hutchison, 'The Royal Academy Schools, 1768–1830', *Walpole Society*, 38 (1960–62), 123–91 · will, PRO, PROB 11/1314

Wealth at death £200 in bequests; residue to half-sister: will, PRO, PROB 11/1314

Ryley [Riley], **John** (1747–1815), mathematics teacher, was born on 30 November 1747 at Old-Coats, near Pudsey, in the West Riding of Yorkshire, the son of Samuel Ryley, a farmer and weaver. After a village education he worked at home as a husbandman and weaver, devoting his leisure to mathematics.

In 1774 Ryley was appointed mathematical master at Drighlington grammar school. He continued to study, going on his half-days as pupil to John Crookes of Leeds, 'the most famous mathematician' in the area (Nichols, 101). In 1775 he opened his own school at Pudsey, where he married Miss Dawson of Topcliffe. The next year he became assistant at a school in Beeston, near Leeds. He contributed to several periodicals, sending solutions to the *Ladies' Diary* from 1786 (and questions from 1791), and winning many prizes. His pseudonyms were Ferdinando, Rylando, and Mr Brookes.

In 1789 Ryley was made headmaster of the Blue Coat School in Leeds, retaining the post until death. He also taught, about 1800–02, in Leeds grammar school, and took private pupils, several of whom distinguished themselves at Cambridge. The eminent Liverpool geometer J. H. Swale was taught by him. He pioneered the *Leeds Correspondent, a Literary, Mathematical, and Philosophical Miscellany*, and edited the first volume (four numbers, 1814–15). He also compiled *The Leeds Guide*, containing a history of Leeds and environs (1806, 1808).

Ryley was described as tall and stout, with an intense expression; according to James Nichols, his physical 'form, size, and countenance' were 'not much unlike Dr Johnson'. To those who knew him, however, he was a 'modest, clever, and communicative person' (Nichols, 250). Ryley died, in Leeds, suffering from gout, on 22 April 1815. He had three sons, the eldest probably Samuel Riley of Armley Mills, and the second John Riley (c.1784–1809), a bookseller and 'a most accomplished young man' (ibid., 246); there were two surviving daughters.

W. F. SEDGWICK, *rev.* RUTH WALLIS

Sources J. N. [J. Nichols], 'John Ryley', *Leeds Correspondent*, 2 (1816), 97–103; 242–50 • R. C. Archibald, 'Notes on some minor English mathematical serials', *Mathematical Gazette*, 14 (1928–9), 379–400, esp. 393 • R. V. Taylor, ed., *The biographia Leodiensis, or, Biographical sketches of the worthies of Leeds* (1865) • R. V. Taylor, ed., *Supplement of the Biographia Leodiensis, or, Biographical sketches of the worthies of Leeds* (1867) • S. Rayner, *History and antiquities of Pudsey*, ed. W. Smith (1887) • *Wright's Leeds Intelligencer* (April 1815) • *Pudsey Almanac* (1873)

Ryley, Sir Philip (*d.* 1733). *See under* Ryley, William (*d.* 1667).

Ryley [*formerly* Romney]**, Samuel William** (1759–1837), actor and author, was born in London, the son and only child of Samuel Romney, a wholesale grocer. He was educated first at a day school in Kensington and then at a similar establishment in Fulham. When he was six the family left London, and young Romney was next placed at the grammar school in Chester. His parents intended him for the wool trade, and he commenced an apprenticeship with William Kenworthy of Quickwood, Saddleworth, Yorkshire, but these plans were cast aside when Romney ran away with his master's daughter Ann (*bap.* 9 Dec 1759). They married at Gretna Green on 15 September 1776, and afterwards confirmed their vows in the parish church at Clifton, near Preston, probably on 10 October.

From Sir William Heathcote, his mother's uncle, Romney had inherited the considerable sum of £4000, but this money was soon exhausted. Reckless, ardent, and unfortunate, he assumed the name of Ryley and entered upon the career which was to shape his life.

In February 1783, at Newcastle upon Tyne, Ryley joined on sharing terms Austin's and Whitlock's company of actors and played the lead role of George Barnwell in George Lillo's *The London Merchant*. Having left this engagement about £20 the poorer, he was next found with William Powell's company, touring in the west of England. With typical impetuosity, Ryley advanced £200 to join Powell in management (Worcester, 1784). In the *Gloucester Journal* of 31 May 1784 it is stated that he had purchased the

Worcester, Gloucester, Ludlow, and Wolverhampton theatres from Messrs Powell and Pero, a purchase made with borrowed money. The investment failed, and, struggling with debts, Ryley soon returned to the ranks as a strolling actor.

For several years thereafter the Ryleys travelled in the provinces, making the occasional fruitless sortie to London, the mecca of the provincial stage. Ann Ryley, after discovering a talent for acting, began to appear alongside her husband, in particular as Fanny to his Lord Ogleby in Colman and Garrick's comedy *The Clandestine Marriage*. Ryley wrote and performed songs on topical themes which had some success. At Manchester in 1792 he produced the musical farce *The Civilian, or, The Farmer Turned Footman*, and the following year a comic opera, *Roderic Random*, drawn from Smollett's novel. However, since these ventures did not answer to his expectations, Ryley abandoned the stroller's life for a time 'to commence tradesman in the spirit line'. When this also failed he returned to the stage, in Tate Wilkinson's company, to present a lively medley entitled *New Brooms*, written by himself.

With *New Brooms* Ryley transferred to Francis Aickin's company at Liverpool and then to Stephen Kemble's at Newcastle upon Tyne. He was in Kemble's company at Edinburgh on 16 January 1797, on which occasion 'Mr Ryley from Liverpool' was noted as giving his popular entertainment *New Brooms* between the play and the farce.

Ryley's life exhibits, with painful clarity, the precarious existence of the supporting actor of his day—snatching, at one moment, at dreams of fame and, at the next, facing the reality of poor shelter and meagre rations. In 1808 his *The Itinerant, or, Memoirs of an Actor* was published in London in three volumes; this semi-autobiographical work reveals the reality of that shifting life, and its humours, in the sometimes brutal setting of Georgian England. It is not, however, to be relied upon for biographical accuracy.

The Itinerant was well enough received to permit of a second series, published in 1816 and 1817; a third series, *The Itinerant in Scotland* (1827), is a rare work. Encouraged by the reception given to *The Itinerant*, Ryley wrote two plays, *The Old Soldier* and *The Irish Girl*, which he took to London. Neither was accepted for publication. He also, on 13 February 1809, made a belated appearance on the London stage, at Drury Lane, playing Sir Peter Teazle in Sheridan's *The School for Scandal*. The *Monthly Mirror* was disparaging, describing him as 'a thin gentleman of about fifty', whose delivery might make him respectable in the country. A further period of struggling provincial management followed.

Mrs Ryley, also, was active with her pen; her three-volume romance *Fanny Fitz-York, Heiress of Tremorne*, published in 1818, sold well. Husband and wife collaborated to write a further play, *The Castle of Glyndower*, which was produced at Drury Lane on 2 March 1818. The cast was good, but the play was not; it was damned at the end of the second act and not revived.

In December 1819 Charles Mathews, describing him as

'poor old Ryley, penniless and melancholy as usual' (Mathews, 3.105), gives us a glimpse of the ageing actor and author at Liverpool. His modest home, known as Ryley's Castle, at Parkgate on the River Dee, became increasingly the centre for his regional operations. Mrs Ryley died there on 27 March 1823; Ryley later married her niece, who had also been her nurse.

The Irish Girl was first performed at the Theatre Royal, Liverpool, on 25 February 1825, for Ryley's benefit; in a prologue the author himself says that it was 'to keep the wolf from the door'. There were occasional revivals, also mainly for Ryley's benefit. In old age Ryley continued, in Lancashire and Cheshire, to play Sir Peter Teazle, Lord Ogleby, and other character parts. In addition he was active in the formation of debating societies in Liverpool and as an actors' coach, but the public enjoyed him best in his new role as showman to an entertainment of dancing and grimacing pasteboard figures. Ryley kept time on the violin and sang a song of his own devising, punctuated with the chorus 'Make faces'. He died after a painful illness on 12 September 1837 at Ryley's Castle, and was buried at Neston parish church, Cheshire.   MARK SORRELL

Sources DNB · Highfill, Burnim & Langhans, *BDA* · *Gloucester Journal* (31 May 1784) · A. Mathews, *Memoirs of Charles Mathews, comedian*, 2nd edn, 4 vols. (1838) · private information (2004) [B. C. Frith]
Likenesses engraving, repro. in S. W. Ryley, *The Itinerant, or, Memoirs of an actor*, 4 (1816)

Ryley, William (*d.* 1667), herald and writer, was the son of William Ryley (*d.* 1634). His early life is obscure but he is believed to have been a native of Lancashire. He may have been a brother of Thomas Ryley, who was educated at Westminster School and Cambridge, but William Ryley's own education is unknown, although he later claimed an address in the Middle Temple. According to a petition from his son, Ryley 'served in the Records' from 1626, presumably as clerk of the records in the Tower, under Sir John Borough, Garter king of arms. However, in another petition for the post of Bluemantle, presumably when soliciting the post he obtained in 1633, he mentioned being educated by his father for twelve years in the records and in heraldry. Ryley was appointed Rouge Rose pursuivant on 31 July 1630, apparently due to the influence of the earl of Arundel, and Bluemantle pursuivant on 4 September 1633. Thus he was involved in the visitations of Buckinghamshire and Oxfordshire in 1634, and signed many funeral certificates between 1634 and 1640. In 1637–8 he was clerk of the iters, under the chief justice in eyre south of the Trent, the earl of Holland. On 11 April 1638 he was admitted to Lincoln's Inn, at the request of the reader William Rigby. He was appointed Lancaster herald on 11 November 1641.

Along with the other heralds Ryley accompanied Charles I to Oxford. The House of Commons on 6 April 1642 ordered Borough to ensure that Ryley was in London in order to attend parliament with records as necessary; on 7 July 1642 he was ordered £25 by the Commons for transcribing documents relating to the commission of array. On 31 July 1643 Charles I ordered Ryley to stay in London to look after the records in Borough's absence. On 8 September 1643 he had his tax assessment for the twentieth remitted by parliament for good service. According to Bulstrode Whitelocke, Ryley was imprisoned in January 1644 for 'intelligence with Oxford' (Whitelocke, 1.232) but released shortly afterwards. He should not be confused with Theophilus Ryley, who was accused before the committee of examinations at Westminster of plotting with Sir Basil Brooke to create a rift between parliament and the City of London, and to divert the Scottish advance.

Following the sequestration of Borough's office and the appointment of John Selden to succeed him on 27 October 1643, Ryley was continued as clerk of the records. On 11 April 1645 he petitioned the committee for the king's revenue for arrears of his salary. On 26 June 1645 he was deputed to record all the ensigns and cornets captured after the battle of Naseby. On 24 January 1646 he petitioned the House of Lords as a counter-measure to the petition to the House of Commons of Rupert Browne, which accused him of 'keeping up intelligence with the enemy at Oxford' (*Sixth Report*, HMC, 95). As a herald Ryley was employed to preside over the state funeral of the parliamentarian general Robert Devereux, third earl of Essex, in Westminster Abbey, being created Norroy king of arms on 20 October 1646, two days before the ceremony. A petition of August 1648 to the Commons did yield £200 for his maintenance. In August 1651, when the office of keeper of the records in the Tower was abolished, Ryley was proposed for a post under the master of the rolls with responsibility for the records, at a salary of £200 p.a. Henceforth there were many references to him in the council papers.

In 1653 the old charge of Ryley being in contact with royalists in Oxford, or even in arms for the king, was revived, but he was able to take advantage of the Act of Oblivion. On 19 April 1654 he was appointed agent to the commission for the sale of royal forests. He attended the funeral of Oliver Cromwell and the installation of Richard Cromwell in his capacity as a herald. In July 1658 he obtained the assistance of Bulstrode Whitelocke in securing his salary by promising to help in calendaring the records in the Tower. On 25 February 1659 he was appointed Clarenceux king of arms. He proclaimed Charles II through Westminster on 8 May 1660. Following the Restoration, Ryley was demoted to Lancaster herald, but the chapter made him their registrar on 13 December 1660. He officiated at the coronation of Charles II. The appointment of William Prynne as keeper of the records saw Ryley and his son named as deputies, although Ryley clearly did not find relations easy with Prynne.

In 1661 William Ryley [*see below*] 'of the Middle Temple' published *Placita parliamentaria, or, Pleadings in parliament, with judgements thereon in the reign of Edward the First and Edward the Second*. A second version appeared later in 1661 under the name of William Ryley 'of the Inner Temple' (W. Kennet, *A Register and Chronicle Ecclesiastical and Civil*, 1728, 487), Ryley junior dedicating his edition to Clarendon and Finch. In May 1664 Samuel Pepys recorded meeting old Ryley, the herald, and his son; and spoke to his son, who told me in very bad words concerning Mr Prin, that the king had given him an office of keeping the Records, but that he never comes thither, nor had been there these six months— so that I perceive they expect to get his employment from him.   (Pepys, 5.149)

However, Ryley senior died in July 1667, with Prynne still in post. He was buried on the 25th in Westminster Abbey. The identity of his wife is unknown, but, in addition to William, he had two other sons (one of whom predeceased him) and two daughters.

William Ryley (d. 1675), archivist, was the son of William Ryley. He claimed to have been educated at Westminster School under Busby, and then at Christ Church, Oxford; however neither assertion can be verified. In a petition Ryley claimed to have been a clerk in the records office from 1647, and to have been wounded at the battle of Worcester while fighting on the royalist side. He entered the Inner Temple on 26 April 1652, and was called to the bar on 12 February 1665. Before 1660 Ryley married Elizabeth (bap. 1637), daughter of Sir Anthony Chester, second baronet, of Chicheley, Buckinghamshire. Relations between Ryley and Prynne may have improved after his father's death, as he was remembered with the bequest of a book in Prynne's will. However, Ryley failed in his quest to succeed Prynne as keeper of the records in 1669, and thereafter he was reduced to submitting a succession of petitions on his financial plight, including one shortly before his death which referred to having 'lost all preferments to attend to the study of the records, wherein I took my delight, and now, after all my endeavours and constant service to his Majesty, must by sad experience die a beggar' (DNB). In May 1675 he was reported to be 'in a languishing' condition (CSP dom., 1675–6, 121). He was buried on 12 November 1675 at St Peter ad Vincula, near the Tower.

Sir Philip Ryley (d. 1733), son of William Ryley the younger, may have received some benefit from his father's importunities because on 1 November 1684 he was appointed a serjeant-at-arms at the Treasury. On 8 December 1686 he was appointed one of four agents for arrears taxes, and by December 1687 he was dealing with petitions relating to royal forests, suggesting that he was already surveyor-general of woods south of the Trent. The revolution of 1688 proved to be no bar to further bureaucratic advancement. He was reappointed one of four agents for arrears taxes in March 1689 (a post which he held until 1700); in April his post as serjeant-at-arms was renewed, and he continued as surveyor of forests. On 15 July 1696 he was elected a member of the Royal Society, but he was never admitted. As a consequence of place legislation many excise commissioners laid down their places in the summer of 1700 and, on 22 June, Ryley was appointed to the new commission, a place he retained until November 1715. Towards the end of William III's reign Ryley surrendered his serjeant's office to his brother Reginald, but he was reappointed on 11 January 1706. On 30 May 1711 he was named a commissioner for collecting the new leather duties. He was knighted on 26 April 1728.

He died at Norwich on 25 January 1733. His will of August 1732 demonstrated the extent of his property interests, encompassing as it did Great Hockham, Norfolk, and houses at Thetford and Hampstead, plus a lease on a residence in Dover Street in London. His son Reginald having predeceased him, Ryley named his grandson Philip Reginald Ryley as his executor, together with several trustees, including Sir Thomas Hanmer, fourth baronet.

STUART HANDLEY

Sources J. E. Bailey, *The troubles of William Ryley, Lancaster herald, and of his son, clerk of the records in the Tower* (1879) · M. Noble, *A history of the College of Arms* (1804) · R. E. C. Waters, *Genealogical memoirs of the extinct family of Chester of Chicheley*, 2 vols. (1878), 1.174–81 · *CSP dom.*, 1629–76 · J. C. Sainty and R. Bucholz, eds., *Officials of the royal household, 1660–1837*, 1: *Department of the lord chamberlain and associated offices* (1997) · B. Whitelocke, *Memorials of English affairs*, new edn, 4 vols. (1853); vol. 1, p. 232 · W. P. Baildon, ed., *The records of the Honorable Society of Lincoln's Inn: admissions*, 1 (1896), 236 · W. A. Shaw, ed., *Calendar of treasury books*, 15, PRO (1933), 385 · G. Holmes, *Augustan England* (1982), 249, 260 · *Sixth report*, HMC, 5 (1877–8), 95 [House of Lords] · Pepys, *Diary*, 5.149 · N. Luttrell, *A brief historical relation of state affairs from September 1678 to April 1714*, 6 vols. (1857) · M. Hunter, *The Royal Society and its fellows, 1660–1700: the morphology of an early scientific institution* (1982), 244–5 · PRO, PROB 11/659, fol. 170 [Philip Ryley]

Ryley, William (d. **1675**). *See under* Ryley, William (d. 1667).

Rymer, James (*fl.* **1770–1842**), naval surgeon, born in Scotland, was said to be related to the family of Thomas Rymer, editor of the *Foedera*. James's father died when he was young, and he was educated by his mother. Having served an apprenticeship to a surgeon and apothecary, he studied anatomy and medicine at Edinburgh University. In 1770 Rymer left Edinburgh for London. He was appointed surgeon's mate on HMS *Montreal*, on which he made two voyages in the Mediterranean and the Levant. Soon afterwards he joined the *Trident*, the ship of Rear-Admiral Sir Peter Denis, and subsequently he went on a voyage to Nevis in the West Indies. In December 1775 he became surgeon to the sloop *Hazard* and in this same year he published *A Description of the Island of Nevis*.

Rymer soon transferred to the *Surprise*, commanded by Captain Robert Linzee, which reached Quebec in May 1776, and he then accompanied Admiral Montagu's squadron to St John's, Newfoundland. On the return voyage, in November 1776, putrid fever broke out. Rymer was next attached as surgeon to the sloop *Alderney*, which was stationed at Great Yarmouth. While there he wrote *A Sketch of Great Yarmouth, with some Reflections on Cold Bathing* (1777). In 1778 he was transferred to the *Conquistador*, which was stationed at the Nore for the reception and distribution of conscripts and volunteers. After fifteen months' service he was transferred to the *Marlborough*, which was ordered for foreign service. Rymer, who attributed his transfer to the dislike of his commanding officer, wrote a scurrilous pamphlet under the title *Transplantation, or, Poor Crocus Pluckt up by the Root* (1779).

Rymer remained in the navy until 1782. He published a number of works, including in 1793 an essay on scurvy, in 1778 a book entitled *The Practice of Navigation*, and in 1780 *Observations and Remarks Respecting the More Effectual Means of*

Preservation of Wounded Seamen. He also published works on more general medical subjects, such as gout and indigestion. In 1828 he published *A Treatise on Diet and Regimen*, which was dedicated to the surgeon John Abernethy.

In Rymer's later years he practised at Reigate and Ramsgate, living at the latter in 1841–2. The date of his death is uncertain. Rymer's last surviving daughter died in Brighton in 1855.

G. Le G. Norgate, *rev.* Claire E. J. Herrick

Sources [J. Watkins and F. Shoberl], *A biographical dictionary of the living authors of Great Britain and Ireland* (1816) • Watt, *Bibl. Brit.* • J. Rymer, *Transplantation, or, Poor crocus pluckt up by the root* (1779) • *GM*, 2nd ser., 44 (1855), 331

Rymer, James Malcolm [*pseuds.* M. J. Errym, Malcolm J. Merry] (1803/4–1884), novelist and journal editor, was the son of Duncan Rymer, engraver and printseller, and his wife, Louisa, a wholesale milliner. He went to London from Scotland about 1838, when his father set up business in Bloomsbury. His first interests were in mechanics; in 1840 he was granted a patent for an improved furniture castor, and in 1841 was listed as a civil engineer living at 42 Burton Street, St Pancras. He soon became, however, one of the most prolific writers of popular fiction in mid-nineteenth-century Britain, although he never published under his own name, choosing instead to employ a number of pseudonyms, the most common of which were M. J. Errym and Malcolm J. Merry, but which also included Marianne Blimber, Nelson Percival, J. D. Conroy, Septimus R. Urban, Bertha Thorne Bishop, and Captain Merry USN. Rymer also appears to have had skills as an engraver, as in 1854, with his son Francis Chadwick, he ran Rymer & Co., lithographers, at 16 Red Lion Square. Some of his own fiction was illustrated by woodcuts with distinctive quality and panache, probably indicating the hand of the author.

In the late 1830s the publisher Edward Lloyd was pioneering fiction for the expanding working-class urban readership, a public which by his profession Rymer knew well. In 1841 Lloyd published Rymer's *Adeline, or, The Grave of the Forsaken*, a vivid 'domestic' tale, and two years later *Ada the Betrayed, or, The Murder at the Old Smithy* became the lead serial in *Lloyd's Penny Weekly Miscellany* for 1843. The success of the novel in this serialized format helped establish the popularity of the penny issue form and Lloyd's fortune. Rymer combined powerful melodrama with narrative skills learned from mainstream writers, and Ada, in particular, has a touch of Dickens's Oliver Twist about her as, with parentage unknown, she preserved her innocence through the perils of a criminalized city. Rymer's successive works showed range as well as suspenseful plotting. *The Black Monk, or, The Secret of the Grey Turret* (1844) updated both Ann Radcliffe and Walter Scott for his semi-literate readers, while he supplied a contemporary interest in social issues with *The White Slave: a Romance for the Nineteenth Century* (1845). Over the years 1846–7, writing anonymously, and adapting some earlier sources, Rymer created two of the most enduring icons of Victorian popular culture. *Varney the Vampyre, or, The Feast of Blood*, distantly related to John Polidori's *The Vampyre* (1819), created

a sensation when serialized by Lloyd in penny numbers, and established the aristocratic vampire in the public imagination. Contemporaneously, Rymer wrote *A String of Pearls, or, The Barber of Fleet Street*, a work often attributed to Thomas Peckett Prest, for Lloyd's *People's Periodical and Family Magazine*. This innocuously titled tale introduced the cannibalistic Sweeney Todd and Mrs Lovett into popular fiction and drama. The success of these two works probably helped release Rymer from bankruptcy in February 1847. Rymer now was one of Lloyd's most prolific writers.

In the 1850s Lloyd's publications were becoming superseded for the adult market by the more sophisticated popular fiction offered by the publisher John Dicks, in particular the novels of G. W. M. Reynolds. In 1858 *The Life Raft: a Tale of the Sea* by 'M. J. Errym' appeared in *Reynolds's Miscellany*. Rymer became one of Dicks's major authors. His most popular titles exploited the current taste for criminal historical romances, but he remained versatile. It is claimed, on the strength of his accurate delineation of American scenes, that he visited the United States, and from the early 1860s his stories appear in the expanding genre of American dime novels. These were published under a bewildering variation of pseudonyms and titles. *The Raft and the Spray* was reissued four times, with different titles and attributions. The pseudonyms appear to be Rymer's own invention, suggesting that he himself was milking the market.

Rymer was said by Thomas Catling to have written up to ten stories simultaneously, and has been credited with over 120 titles, mostly published anonymously or under pseudonyms. Rymer also edited a number of periodicals, including the *Queen's Magazine* (1842), *Lloyd's Weekly Miscellany* (1845), the *Illuminated Magazine* (1845–6), and the *London Miscellany* (1857–8). On his death he left two scrapbooks inscribed 'Tales and Sketches Contributed by James M. Rymer to Various Periodicals'. These indicate a very different style from that of *Varney the Vampyre*—essays in the style of Leigh Hunt, and some accomplished short stories, suggesting that through his pseudonyms he deliberately concealed his successful career as a sensational author. He died on 11 August 1884 at Lawn Cottage, Shepherd's Bush Green, London, leaving £7859 2s. 10d. He was survived by his widow, Sara Rebecca.

Louis James

Sources E. F. Bleiler, 'Introduction', in J. M. Rymer, *Varney the vampyre* (1972), v–xviii • A. Block, *The English novel, 1740–1850: a catalogue including prose romances, short stories and translations of foreign fiction*, new edn (1961) • T. Catling, *My life's pilgrimage* (1911) • M. Dalziel, *Popular fiction 100 years ago* (1957) • L. James, *Fiction for the working man, 1830–1850* (1963) • F. Jay, *Peeps into the past* (1918–19) [suppl. to *Spare moments*] • A. Johanssen, *The house of Beadle and Adams* (1950) • 'List of patents', *Mechanic's Magazine*, 873 (2 May 1840), 69 • J. Medcraft, *Bibliography of penny bloods of Edward Lloyd* (1945) • V. E. Neuberg, *Popular literature: a history and guide* (1977) • J. M. Rymer, 'Tales and sketches' [scrapbooks in personal collection of L. James] • J. M. Rymer, 'Last will and testament', 1884, Principal Registry of the Family Division, London, 734 • M. Rymer, 'Popular writing', *Queen's Magazine*, 1 (1842), 99–100 • M. Summers, *A Gothic bibliography* (1940) • E. S. Turner, *Boys will be boys*, rev. edn (1957) • J. J. Wilson, 'M. J. Errym', *Bootle Times* (9 June 1916) • d. cert. • private information (2004) [Frank Algar] • *London Directory* • H. R. Smith,

New light on Sweeney Todd: Thomas Peckett Prest, James Malcolm Rymer and Elizabeth Caroline Grey (2002) · 'Court of bankruptcy: Rymer', *Lloyd's Weekly London Newspaper*, 222 (21 Feb 1847)
Archives priv. coll., notebooks
Wealth at death £7859 2s. 10d.: probate, 24 Sept 1884, *CGPLA Eng. & Wales*

Rymer, Thomas (1642/3–1713), literary critic and historian, the son of Ralph Rymer (*bap.* 1601, *d.* 1664), lord of the manor of Brafferton, Yorkshire, was probably born at Yafforth, in the same county. His father, although at one time treasurer of his district during the Commonwealth, was arrested on 12 October 1663 for participating in the presbyterian rising, and on 7 January 1664 was condemned for treason and hanged. For eight years, from 1651 to 1659, Thomas attended the Northallerton Free School kept by Thomas Smelt.

Early years and literary work Rymer was admitted a *pensionarius minor* at Sidney Sussex College, Cambridge, on 29 April 1659, aged sixteen, and left the university in 1662 without a degree. He entered Gray's Inn on 2 May 1666 and became a barrister on 16 June 1673. Shortly after his being called to the bar, in 1674 his *Reflections on Aristotle's Treatise of Poesie*, translated from the French of René Rapin, was published, in the preface of which he demonstrated his intimate knowledge of English and continental writers, as well as of Greek and Latin authors. Rymer did not, however, mention Shakespeare; nor did he mention Francis Beaumont and John Fletcher, authors to whom he was soon to devote his attention. He took occasion in his preface to compare two descriptions of night, one from the French of Pierre Le Moyne's epic poem *St Louys* (1658) and this from Dryden's *The Indian Emperour, or, The Conquest of Mexico*:

> All things are hush'd, as Nature's self lay dead,
> The Mountains seem to Nod their drowsie head,
> The little Birds in dreams their Songs repeat,
> And sleeping flowers beneath Night-dew sweat,
> Even Lust and Envy sleep.

'In this description', Rymer wrote, 'four lines yield greater variety of matter, and more choice thoughts than twice the number of any other Language' (*Critical Works*, 15). Samuel Johnson declared that Rymer had made the passage famous; Rymer was not, it is evident, incapable of some critical *aperçus*.

From 1674 to 1677 Rymer was engaged on his verse drama *Edgar, or, The English Monarch: an Heroick Tragedy*, dedicated to the king, based on William of Malmesbury's *De gestis regum Anglorum* and adhering to the dramatic unities. The play was licensed on 13 September 1677, printed in 1678, and may have been performed in October of the earlier year in opposition to Edward Ravenscroft's *King Edgar and Alfrida*. In the 'Advertisement' prefatory to the play, Rymer wrote:

> The Tragedy ends Prosperously; a sort of Tragedy that rarely succeeds; man being apter to pity the Distressed, than to rejoyce with the Prosperous. Yet this sort seems principally to have pleased *Euripides*; and is necessary here for the Design ... Rhyme is the more proper for this sort of Tragedy, which ends happily.

Addison, among others, saw nothing praiseworthy in the

Thomas Rymer (1642/3–1713), by unknown engraver, pubd 1819 (after contemporary caricature)

play (*Spectator*, no. 592). *The Tragedies of the Last Age Consider'd* (1678), Rymer's substantial critical essay in the form of a letter to Fleetwood Sheppard, opens with his selecting for comment 'the choicest and most applauded *English Tragedies* of that last age; as *Rollo*; *A King and No King*; the *Maid's Tragedy*, by *Beaumont and Fletcher*; *Othello*, *Julius Cæsar*, by *Shakespeare*; and *Cataline* by Worthy Ben'. Rymer managed to rehearse the plots of the first three plays (*Rollo* is of uncertain authorship) and to analyse the plays according to his views on how tragedy should be written. He advocated strict compliance with the theory of decorum—characters were stereotyped, with soldiers being courageous; women, modest. Poetical justice demanded that the good be rewarded, the evil punished. Plots should not be improbable; plays should have a moral. He promised to come later to *Othello* and the other plays, with reflections on *Paradise Lost*, a work of which he thought little. Rymer sent a copy of his *Tragedies* to John Dryden in 1677, and in a letter to the earl of Dorset, Dryden wrote of receiving the book, which he described as 'the best piece of Criticism in the English tongue; perhaps in any other of the modern ... and think my selfe happy he has not fallen upon me, as severely and as wittily as he has upon Shakespeare and Fletcher' (*Letters of John Dryden*, 13, 14). Dryden used the endpapers of his copy of the *Tragedies* for a number of 'Heads of an Answer to Rymer', taking much issue with him but remaining respectful of his achievement (*Works of John Dryden*, 17.185–93). Dryden was, however, ambivalent about Rymer as critic in later pronouncements, no longer regarding him so highly as he did in the letter of 1677.

Pope told Joseph Spence that 'Chaucer and his contemporaries borrowed a good deal from the Provençal poets, the best account of whom, in our language, is in Rymer's piece on Tragedy', and that Rymer is 'generally right, though rather too severe in his opinion of the particular plays he speaks of; and is, on the whole, one of the best critics we ever had' (Spence, 117). Dr Johnson, along with Dryden foremost in the hierarchy of English literary critics, took occasion in his life of Dryden to compare him as critic to Rymer:

> The different manner and effect with which critical knowledge may be conveyed was perhaps never more clearly exemplified in the performances of Rymer and Dryden. ... With Dryden we are wandering in quest of Truth, whom we find, if we find her at all, drest in the graces of elegance; and if we miss her, the labour of the pursuit rewards itself: we are led only through fragrance and flowers. Rymer, without taking a nearer, takes a rougher way; every step is to be made through thorns and brambles, and Truth, if we meet her, appears repulsive by her mien and ungraceful by her habit. Dryden's criticism has the majesty of a queen; Rymer's has the ferocity of a tyrant. (Johnson, 1.412–13)

T. S. Eliot, a better poet than himself a critic of the drama, has made the remarkable statement that he has never 'seen a cogent refutation to Rymer's objections to *Othello*' (Eliot, 121).

Historian Rymer reverted to the second of his major interests, the documentary study of history, his *General draught and prospect of government in Europe ... shewing the antiquity, power, and decay of parliaments* being published in 1681 and variously titled thereafter. The work was in the form of a 'Letter to Tho. Benskin', author of *Disputatio medica inauguralis, de hydrope ascite* (1679), an unexpected acquaintance or friend. The *General Draught* may have been in answer to Sir Robert Filmer's *Patriarcha, or, The Natural Power of Kings*, published in 1680 and discussed by Rymer in his own work. Almost surely because of the publication of the *General Draught* and the later, 1689, edition of the same work, Rymer was appointed historiographer to the king in 1692, succeeding Thomas Shadwell and enjoying thereafter an annual sum of £200. Almost equally surely, Rymer's putative friendship with Lord Somers and Charles Montagu, later earl of Halifax, did not harm his chances for the succession to Shadwell. In any event, when the English government under William III decided to have all the public alliances, treaties, and confederacies of England with other countries transcribed and published, an undertaking sponsored by Montagu and Somers, with the former as the probable initiator of the project, Rymer was chosen for the task. He was to spend the rest of his life working on the project. His appointment as editor of *Foedera* was no sinecure, however, and he soon found himself in need of more funds for his work, so that in the period from the inception of the project to August 1698, five years later, he was out of pocket by some £750. He was given a salary of £200 a year in May 1703, but that was not enough to keep him from suffering extreme poverty until his death ten years later.

The progress of the work was sluggish, with the first volume appearing in November 1704, eleven years after it had begun. Volumes 2, 3, and 4 came out in the next three yeas. In 1707, with the completion of volume 4, Robert Sanderson (1660–1741), clerk of the rolls in the Rolls Chapel, Rymer's assistant from 1696 to 1707, became associate editor. Volumes 5–15 came out at somewhat regular intervals, and when Rymer died Sanderson was given the authority to complete the work, which ran to twenty volumes. His editing of volume 16, largely prepared by Rymer, to volume 20 has been adversely criticized.

Leibnitz's *Codex juris gentium diplomaticus* (1693) served as model for *Foedera*, and Rymer also relied heavily on the Elizabethan manuscript 'Book of abbreviations of leagues' by the distinguished antiquary Arthur Agard (1540–1615). He was helped more directly by correspondence with Leibnitz and with Bishop William Nicolson, archbishop of Cashel (1655–1727), compiler of *The English, Scotch, and Irish Historical Libraries* (originally published separately and then posthumously together in 1756), which listed and described 'most of our historians, either in print or manuscript'. Sir Thomas Duffus Hardy prepared a *Syllabus* to *Foedera*, incorporating many corrections (3 vols., 1869–85). One of the major faults of Rymer's editing was his inclusion of documents not germane to his purpose. There were other editorial blunders, many of them pointed out by his contemporaries. However, modern scholars are agreed as to the importance of Rymer's achievement. *Foedera* proved to be a success, praised both in England and abroad. Rapin, in what may be termed a display of reciprocity, abridged each volume in French, as it came out, for Le Clerc's *Bibliothèque choisie*. The abridgements were translated back into English and published by Stephen Whately under the title of *Acta regia* (4 vols., 1731). The work even attracted attention in less scientific circles.

Poet Rymer wrote poetry of various kinds, verse epistles, commemorative poems, translations from Ovid, and light verse. Most of his light verse appeared posthumously in 1714 in a collection of poetry whose title can be usefully abbreviated as *Curious Amusements*, now a very rare work. His contribution ran to thirty-one poems, three of them addressed to Mary, the illegitimate daughter of Charles Sackville, earl of Dorset, under the pastorally derived name of Dolorissa. He also addressed poems to the family of Thomas Grey, second earl of Stamford. His efforts in the realm of light verse have been likened to those of some of his friends, Sir Fleetwood Sheppard, George Stepney, John Somers, and Charles Montagu. Indeed, it was almost surely Sheppard, also of Gray's Inn, who introduced Rymer to the London literary circle, for Sheppard numbered among his friends Charles Sedley, Charles Sackville, sixth earl of Dorset, and John Wilmot, earl of Rochester. Rymer met Dryden through the agency of Dorset, and he evidently knew Thomas Hobbes and Edmund Waller. Indeed, he contributed two poems to a collection of *Poems to the Memory of that Incomparable Poet Edmond Waller, Esquire* (1688), and he also wrote the preface to an edition of Rochester's poems, with the tragedy *Valentinian* (1691).

Rymer wrote, in 'The preface to the reader', that Rochester's 'Satyr upon Man' is 'commonly taken to be a Translation from *Boileau*'. He then proceeded to quote fourteen lines from Boileau's 'Epître III, A M. Arnauld Docteur de Sorbonne', beginning 'De tous les Animaux qui s'elevent dans l'Air', John Oldham's translation of Boileau's poem, and seven lines from Rochester's poem, beginning:

Were I (who, to my cost, already am,
One of those strange, prodigious Creatures, Man),

and concluded:

My Lord *Rochester* gives us another Cast of Thought, another Turn of Expression, a strength, a Spirit, and Manly Vigour, which the *French* are utter strangers to. Whatever Giant *Boileau* may be in his own Country, He seems little more than a Man of Straw with my Lord *Rochester*.

He translated 'Penelope to Ulysses' for *Ovid's Epistles, Translated by Several Hands* (1680), edited by Dryden and including translations by, among others, Thomas Otway and Samuel Butler. He also translated the life of Nicias for the collaborative edition of Plutarch's *Lives* (1684), with translations of a number of other lives by writers associated with Cambridge, also edited by Dryden, as well as a translation of Ovid, *Amores*, iii.6, for Dryden's *Miscellany Poems* (1684). It is obvious that the two remained on friendly terms for some years.

Value as a critic Students of the early English drama, particularly of the plays of Shakespeare, will remember Rymer (for he should so be remembered) as the author of *A short view of tragedy; it's original, excellency and corruption, with some reflections on Shakespear, and other practitioners for the stage*, published in 1692 but dated 1693. The *Short View*, Rymer's most ambitious effort as literary critic, is divided into two almost equal parts in number of pages, the first six chapters being devoted to the origin, excellence, and decline of tragedy, and the final two chapters to Shakespeare and other practitioners for the stage. Some two-thirds of the last two chapters are given over to the now famous or infamous analysis of *Othello*. Given Rymer's insistence upon probability in the drama, as well as upon poetic justice, a term first used by him, essentially meaning that the good shall be rewarded and the evil punished, it is understandable why he rounded upon Shakespeare for the obvious breaches of probability, something more modern critics have also pounced upon. In a prefatory synopsis to chapter 7, Rymer emphasized Shakespeare's failure to follow the principle of decorum, noting:

Nothing of the Moor in Othello, of a Venetian in Desdemona. Of a Souldier in Iago. Venetians no sense of Jealousie. Thoughts, in Othello, in a Horse, or Mastiff, more sensibly exprest. Ill Manners. Outragous to a Nobleman, to Humanity. (*Critical Works*, 131)

Within a short space he drew three morals from the plot, or fable:

I. First. This may be a caution to all Maids of Quality how, without their Parents consent, they run away with Blackamoors. ... Secondly. This may be a warning to all good Wives, that they look well to their Linnen. Thirdly. This may

be a lesson to Husbands, that before their Jealousie be Tragical, their proofs may be Mathematical. (ibid., 132)

And there is the follow-up to the synopsis in the sentence 'In the *Neighing* of an Horse, or in the growling of a Mastiff, there is a meaning, there is as lively expression, and, may I say, more humanity, than many times in the Tragical flights of *Shakespear*' (ibid., 136). And, Rymer concludes, 'There is in this Play, some burlesk, some humour, and ramble of Comical Wit, some shew, and some *Mimickry* to divert the spectators: but the tragical part is, plainly none other, than a Bloody Farce without salt or savour' (ibid., 164). What has largely been forgotten is that the first six chapters of the *Short View* are a valuable literary-historical narrative of the origins and progress of tragedy up to the time of Shakespeare.

Rymer died at his house in Arundel Street, the Strand, London, on 14 December 1713, in almost dire poverty, and was buried four days later in the parish church of St Clement Danes. In his will, dated 10 July 1712, he left what property he had to Mrs Anna Parnell, spinster, presumably his housekeeper, who sold his 'Collectanea' to the Treasury for £215. There is no record of any marriage.

ARTHUR SHERBO

Sources *The critical works of Thomas Rymer*, ed. C. A. Zimansky (1956) • J. M. Osborn, 'Thomas Rymer as rhymer', *Poetry Quarterly*, 54 (1975), 152–77 • G. Reedy, 'Rymer and history', *Clio*, 7 (1978), 409–22 • S. Johnson, *Lives of the English poets*, ed. G. B. Hill, [new edn], 3 vols. (1905) • J. Spence, *Anecdotes, observations, and characters, of books and men*, ed. S. W. Singer (1820); repr. with introduction by B. Dobrée (1964) • T. S. Eliot, *Selected essays* (1932) • W. Van Lennep and others, eds., *The London stage, 1660–1800*, pt 1: 1660–1700 (1965) • Venn, *Alum. Cant.* • *The letters of John Dryden*, ed. C. E. Ward (1942) • *The works of John Dryden*, ed. E. N. Hooker, H. T. Swedenberg, and V. A. Dearing, 20 vols. (1956–2000)
Archives BL, papers, Add. MSS 4573–4630, 18911
Likenesses line engraving, BM, NPG; repro. in J. Caulfield, *Portraits, memoirs and characters of remarkable persons*, 4 vols. (1819–20) [see illus.]

Rymington [Rimston], **William** (d. in or after 1385), Cistercian monk, theologian, and religious controversialist, presumably took his name from Rimington, in the West Riding of Yorkshire, and is first recorded as a monk of Salley Abbey, Yorkshire, who received papal dispensation to hold dignities in his religious order, in spite of his illegitimacy, in July 1358. He must subsequently have been sent to read theology at Oxford, but nothing further is known of him before his chancellorship of the university (probably from Whitsuntide 1372 to about March 1373). He preached at the York convocations of 1371 and 1373; his two sermons survive in the collection of Richard Hertford, a Cistercian of Whalley. Rymington was made prior of Salley before 1380, and held the office until his death at an unknown date in or after 1385. During these years he attacked the unorthodox opinions of John Wyclif, especially on ecclesiastical authority and the religious orders, in his *Conclusiones XLV*, relying on the authority of patristic writers and the canonists. Wyclif replied intemperately in his *Responsiones* (1383–4), to which Rymington made a rejoinder (c.1385, after Wyclif's death), imperfectly preserved. He also wrote a meditation, *Stimulus peccatoris*, which circulated with Richard Rolle's works and achieved some popularity in the fifteenth century. He was buried at Salley Abbey, where his tombstone was found and excavated in the nineteenth century, revealing a tall and athletic figure.   JEREMY CATTO

Sources 'Conclusiones', and rejoinder to Wyclif, Bodl. Oxf., MS Bodley 158 · 'Stimulus peccatoris', Bodl. Oxf., MS Bodley 801 · sermons, Bibliothèque de l'Université, Paris, MS 790, fols. 105v–120 · W. Rymington, *Stimulus peccatoris*, ed. R. O'Brien, *Cîteaux: Commentarii Cistercienses*, 16 (1965), 278–304 · R. O'Brien, 'Two sermons at York synod of William Rymyngton, 1372 and 1373', *Cîteaux*, 19 (1968), 40–67 · J. Wyclif, *Opera minora*, ed. J. Loserth, Wyclif Society (1913), 201–57 · Bale, *Index*, 147–8 · Tanner, *Bibl. Brit.-Hib.*, 633 · J. R. Walbran, ed., *Memorials of the abbey of St Mary of Fountains*, 1, SurtS, 42 (1863), 63 · J. McNulty, ed., *The chartulary of the Cistercian Abbey of St Mary of Sallay in Craven*, 2, Yorkshire Archaeological Society, 90 (1934), 183–5, 205–7 · J. McNulty, 'William of Rymington, prior of Salley Abbey', *Yorkshire Archaeological Journal*, 30 (1930–31), 231–47 · J. McNulty, 'Stephen of Eston, abbot of Salley, Newminster, and Fountains', *Yorkshire Archaeological Journal*, 31 (1932–4), 49–64, esp. 62–4 · Emden, *Oxf.* · A. Hudson, *The premature reformation: Wycliffite texts and Lollard history* (1988), 45–6
Archives Bibliothèque de l'Université, Paris, MS 790, fols. 105v–120 · Bodl. Oxf., Bodley MS 158 · Bodl. Oxf., Bodley MS 801

Rymsdyk, Andrew van (1753/4–1786). *See under* Rymsdyk, Jan van (d. 1790).

Rymsdyk, Jan van (d. 1790), artist, was born in the Netherlands. Of his parents, nothing is known. He contributed to the great English obstetric atlases of the eighteenth century and was particularly active as an anatomical illustrator in London in the 1750s, working primarily in red chalk and pastels. By 1750 Rymsdyk was in London providing drawings (Hunterian collection, Glasgow University Library) for the plates to William Hunter's *The Anatomy of the Gravid Uterus*, eventually published in 1774.

Familiar with his work for Hunter, William Smellie employed Rymsdyk to contribute preparatory drawings to his *A Sett of Anatomical Tables*, illustrated with life-size obstetric plates. The book is dated 1754 but did not appear until the following year. Most of Rymsdyk's drawings for Smellie were completed by 1752 and were later purchased by Hunter in Smellie's posthumous sale on 29 June 1770 (Hunterian collection, Glasgow University Library). Rymsdyk's portrait of Smellie is known only from the print after it by Charles Grignion.

Rymsdyk was also employed by John Hunter, William's brother. All of the illustrations to *The natural history of the human teeth: explaining their structure, use, formation, growth, and diseases* were drawn by Rymsdyk 'under the Author's direction'. Although published in London 1771, the book is based on work done by Hunter before 1755, and some of Rymsdyk's preparatory drawings, in the library of the Royal College of Surgeons, London, bear this date. Rymsdyk's exceptionally attractive red-chalk drawings of the entire skull for the book were truncated in the finished plates, since only the teeth and jaw area were of relevance.

Rymsdyk's reputation as an anatomical draughtsman brought him to the attention of Charles Nicholas Jenty. Rymsdyk provided drawings for the mezzotint illustrations to Jenty's *An Essay on the Demonstration of the Human Structure* (1757). In Jenty's opinion:

> none imitated Nature better than Mr. Van Riemsdyk; who … has been for some Time employed by the Doctors Smellie and Hunter in Pieces of Midwifery, &c. and is well known to be the ablest Person we have in London, in anatomical Performances.   (pp. 6–7)

In the same year, six life-size mezzotint plates to Jenty's *The Demonstrations of a Pregnant Uterus of a Woman at her Full Time* were published. These are described in the title as 'Done from the pictures painted, after dissections, by Mr Van Riemsdyk', although the first plate bears the signature of Thomas Burgess. Pastel drawings by Rymsdyk for Jenty, one dated 1755, were sent to the Pennsylvania Hospital, Philadelphia, by John Fothergill for teaching purposes, arriving in 1762.

Despite his success in this genre, it is known from Rymsdyk's later comments in his *Museum Britannicum* of 1778 that he felt that his talents as an artist had not been properly recognized. In 1758 he sought a change in career and moved to Bristol, where he advertised himself as a portrait painter and a drawing teacher in *Felix Farley's Bristol Journal* (16 December 1758). Some of his subsequent sitters belonged to the Bristol medical community. Richard Smith recorded one such portrait of the surgeon John Page (1713–1792), now in the boardroom of the Bristol Royal Infirmary ('Bristol Infirmary biographical memoirs', 2.190). Rymsdyk failed to achieve financial success in Bristol and is described by Smith as being reduced to wearing the cast-off clothing of William Barrett, man-midwife and local historian (ibid.). A portrait of Barrett attributed to Rymsdyk (c.1764) is in the Bristol Museum and Art Gallery.

By 1764 Rymsdyk had returned to London, where he was residing at Wych Street, Drury Lane, with his son Andrew [*see below*], and was again in the employ of William Hunter as an anatomical draughtsman. On 16 July 1772 Rymsdyk first obtained permission from the British Museum for access to the exhibits to make drawings (Add. MS 45869, fol. 49v). In 1778 the *Museum Britannicum, being an exhibition of a great variety of antiquities and natural curiosities* was published, illustrated with prints after drawings by Rymsdyk and his son Andrew of a selection of objects in the British Museum. A second edition appeared posthumously in 1791. The text is by Jan van Rymsdyk and the extensive annotations frequently reveal his wide range of interests as well as a difficult and petulant character. There are several references to what he considered his lost career as a painter and his lengthy servitude to those who did not fully appreciate him, an allusion to William Hunter. The preparatory drawings, mainly in delicate coloured wash, are in the British Museum print room. The book, according to a supplementary obituary notice of Andrew van Rymsdyk, was not a financial success (*GM*, 1145). Jan van Rymsdyk's last works were drawings for Thomas Denman's *A collection of engravings, tending to illustrate the generation and parturition of animals, and of the human species* (1787) and an *Introduction to the Practice of Midwifery* (1801).

Further anatomical, pathological, and natural history drawings and pastels by Rymsdyk are in the Royal College of Surgeons, London, the British Museum, and the Hunterian collection, University of Glasgow, including those for illustrations to papers in the journal *Medical Observations and Inquiries*. Few of his prints survive. He contributed only one engraved figure to Hunter's *Gravid Uterus* and one plate to the *Museum Britannicum*, preferring instead to hire engravers for the latter book for which he advertised in the *Daily Advertiser* (20 September 1775). Rymsdyk was also a collector of old-master drawings, those that he owned identifiable by the mark 'Rymsdyk's Museum'. These are now in various collections, including the British Museum.

Rymsdyk had two sons, **Andrew van Rymsdyk** (1753/4–1786) and John (*fl.* 1778–1790). At the age of eleven, in 1765, Andrew (or Andries) was awarded a premium prize for drawing from the Society of Arts, and again in 1766 and 1767. He exhibited at the Society of Arts (1769, 1776) and the Royal Academy of Art, London (1775), and contributed drawings to the *Museum Britannicum*. In the 1780s he advertised as a miniature painter (misleadingly claiming to be a member of the Royal Academy) in the local press of Norwich, Chester, and Bath, where he died on 13 November 1786. Miniatures by him, *The Seventh Earl of Athlone* (1783) and *Sarah Siddons* (1783), are in the National Gallery of Ireland, and two miniatures of unidentified sitters, male and female, are in the Victoria and Albert Museum, the latter signed and dated 1780. The 'Rymsdyk Jr.' who exhibited two enamels at the Royal Academy in 1778 has been identified as Andrew but is more likely to have been his brother, John van Rymsdyk, who is mentioned in his father's will of 1790.

By 1775 Jan van Rymsdyk had moved to Charles Street, off St James's Square, London, and this is where he was resident with his sister, Maria, and second son, John, when he drew up his will on 14 February 1790. He died there shortly afterwards, on 20 February 1790.

MONIQUE KORNELL

Sources J. L. Thornton, *Jan van Rymsdyk: medical artist of the eighteenth century* (1982) · 'Richard Smith (1796–1843)', Bristol RO, Bristol Infirmary biographical memoirs, vols. 1–2 · 'Persons admitted to reading room, Jan 12th 1762 to March 2nd 1781', BL, Add. MS 45869, fol. 49v · *Felix Farley's Bristol Journal* (16 Dec 1758) · *Felix Farley's Bristol Journal* (13 Jan 1759) · *Daily Advertiser* [London] (20 Sept 1775) · D. Foskett, *A dictionary of British miniature painters*, 2 vols. (1972) · F. Lugt, *Les marques de collections de dessins et d'estampes* (Amsterdam, 1921), no. 2167 · C. H. Brock, *Dr William Hunter's papers and drawings in the Hunterian collection of Glasgow University Library: a handlist* (1990) · B. C. Corner, 'Dr Ibis and the artists: a sidelight upon Hunter's atlas, *The gravid uterus*', *Journal of the History of Medicine and Allied Sciences*, 6 (1951), 1–21 · G. Munro Smith, *A history of the Bristol Royal Infirmary* (1917) · R. Dossie, *Memoirs of agriculture, and other oeconomical arts*, 3 (1782), 404, 430 · Graves, *Artists* · GM, 1st ser., 56 (1786), 1003, 1145 · *Norfolk Chronicle* (13 Oct 1781) · *Adams's Weekly Courant* (22 July 1783) · *Bath Chronicle* (22 Feb 1781) · *Bath Chronicle* (16 Oct 1783) · *Bath Chronicle* (28 Oct 1783) · *Bath Chronicle* (2 Nov 1783) · *Bath Chronicle* (18 Nov 1783) · *Bath Chronicle* (24 Aug 1786) · will, PRO, PROB 10/3142 · J. van Rymsdyk and A. van Rymsdyk, *Museum*

Britannicum, being an exhibition of a great variety of antiquities and natural curiosities, belonging to … the British Museum (1778)

Wealth at death under £5000: will, PRO, PROB 10/3142

Ryrie, Sir Granville de Laune (1865–1937), army officer and politician in Australia, was born on the sheep station of Micalago, Michelago, New South Wales, on 1 July 1865, the fourth of the nine children of Alexander Ryrie (1827–1909), a grazier and later a member of the legislative council, and his wife, Charlotte (1827–1913), elder daughter of Captain Alured Tasker Faunce, of the 4th King's Own regiment.

Ryrie was educated at Oatlands preparatory school, Mittagong (1875–7), and at the King's School, Parramatta (1878–83), and at the age of sixteen he went as jackeroo to Goonal station in north-west New South Wales. He became an excellent bushman and judge of horses, gained considerable skill at carving and boomerang throwing, and learned the local Aboriginal language. Returning to Micalago as the sheep station manager, Ryrie entered fully into the local life. His interests were sporting and social rather than intellectual and bookish. He bred good horses and raced them, played football, and was twice runner-up in the New South Wales amateur heavyweight boxing championship. His excellent physique, his fine tenor voice, his whistling, and his clever mimicry of the lyre-bird were gifts that won him wide popularity. Ryrie married on 18 February 1896 Mary Gwendolyn Frances, second daughter of Alfred McFarland, judge of the district court of New South Wales; they had twin daughters in 1897 and a son in 1911.

Ryrie joined the local light horse volunteers as a trooper and rose to be commissioned second lieutenant in 1898. In April 1900 he embarked for South Africa as a captain in the 6th New South Wales imperial bushmen, and was wounded at Wonderfontein (September), promoted major (November), and awarded the queen's medal with four clasps. In June 1901 he returned home with his regiment.

More popular for his boxing and singing than his political oratory, Ryrie held the Queanbeyan seat in the New South Wales legislative assembly from 1906 to 1910, but failed to gain the Cootamundra seat in 1910. In 1911 he was elected to the commonwealth parliament for North Sydney, a seat he held until 1922. He remained, however, a citizen soldier, commanding the 3rd light horse regiment from 1904 to 1911 as lieutenant-colonel. He embarked for Egypt in December 1914 as brigadier-general commanding the 2nd light horse brigade. Serving through the Gallipoli campaign from May until the evacuation in December 1915, he was severely wounded on 29 September. With little love for military forms or textbooks he nevertheless gained a reputation as a skilful regimental soldier. Ryrie was an expert judge of ground with a sure sense of the possibilities of a situation and a marked unwillingness to waste the lives of his troops. These skills he displayed most notably during the August offensive at Gallipoli and during the first battle of Gaza in Palestine in March 1917. Ryrie led his brigade in Sinai, Palestine, and Syria from 1916 to 1918. Throughout he achieved steady, consistent

Sir Granville de Laune Ryrie (1865–1937), by Lafayette, 1929

success for which he was five times mentioned in dispatches, and appointed CMG in 1916, CB in 1918, and KCMG in 1919. Overlooked for divisional command during the war, and probably unsuited to it, he was nevertheless, in 1919, promoted major-general commanding the Australian troops in Egypt. His success rested not only on his strictly military gifts, but equally on the devotion which this brusque, humorous, sixteen-stone giant inspired in his men, for he shared their rough life, their rations, and their dangers. They knew him affectionately as 'the Bull' and 'the Old Brig'.

Back in Australia, Ryrie held the position of assistant minister for defence from 1920 to 1921, and introduced 'Ryrie's rise', an improvement in pay rates for the permanent forces. In 1922 he was returned unopposed to the commonwealth parliament for Warringah, a seat which he held until he became high commissioner in London. He occupied this latter position from July 1927 until July 1932. Ryrie was not at his best as a diplomat, with his bluntness and lack of political judgement often landing him in trouble. For example, he caused a furore when he publicly recommended American farm vehicles over British for Australian conditions. And on another occasion he was exposed painfully for not mastering his brief when called upon to defend Australia's record in New Guinea before the permanent mandates commission in Geneva. Still, he worked hard and effectively, first in promoting trade and immigration, and later in the difficult financial negotiations that came with the great depression. In these London years his health was not good, and on his return to Australia he retired from public life.

Ryrie died of uraemia and cardiac arrest at the Royal Prince Alfred Hospital, Sydney, on 2 October 1937, and was buried in October at Michelago Anglican Church after a state funeral in Sydney.

Ryrie's greatest contribution to Australian public life was as a military leader. Honest and fearless in politics, his outspokenness did not help his advancement. Ryrie exemplified what was best in the Australian country tradition and was consequently a military leader of the kind most fitted to get the best out of the commonwealth's citizen

forces. The value of his work in this field has been fully recognized in the official records of Australia's part in the First World War.   HERBERT BURTON, rev. CARL BRIDGE

Sources P. Vincent, *My darling Mick: the life of Granville Ryrie* (1997) • *AusDB* • P. Dennis and others, *The Oxford companion to Australian military history* (1995) • [A. H. Chisholm], ed., *The Australian encyclopaedia*, [new edn], 7 (Sydney, 1963) • B. P. Attard, 'The Australian high commissioner's office: politics and Anglo-Australian relations, 1901–1939', DPhil diss., U. Oxf., 1991 • *Sydney Morning Herald* (4 Oct 1937) • *The Argus* [Melbourne] (4 Oct 1937) • *The Times* (4 Oct 1937) • C. E. W. Bean, *The story of Anzac: from the outbreak of war to the end of the first phase of the Gallipoli campaign, May 4, 1915*, 2nd edn (1933), vol. 1 of *The official history of Australia in the war of 1914–1918* • C. E. W. Bean, *The story of Anzac: from 4 May, 1915, to the evacuation of the Gallipoli peninsula* (1924), vol. 2 of *The official history of Australia in the war of 1914–1918* • H. S. Gullett, *The Australian imperial force in Sinai and Palestine, 1914–1918* (1923), vol. 7 of *The official history of Australia in the war of 1914–1918* • P. L. Murray, ed., *Official records of the Australian military contingents to the war in South Africa* (1911)
Archives NL Aus.
Likenesses Lafayette, photograph, 1929, NPG [*see illus.*] • G. Lambert, pencil sketch, Australian War Memorial, Canberra, Australia • C. Wheeler, oils, Australian War Memorial, Canberra, Australia • H. Woolcott, oils, Australian War Memorial, Canberra, Australia

Rysbrack, (John) Michael [*formerly* Johannes Michiel] (1694–1770), sculptor, was born in Antwerp on 24 June 1694, and baptized there on 27 June 1694 at St George's. His father, Peeter Rijsbrack (*bap.* 1655, *d.* 1729), a Catholic, was a landscape painter who had worked in London with Nicolas de Largillière, but who moved to Paris in 1675, where he married a Frenchwoman, Geneviève Compagnon (*d.* 1719), widow of Phillippe Buyster, a Flemish sculptor working at Versailles. The couple subsequently settled in Antwerp, and had eleven children, among them the painters Peter Andreas, James (or Jacques), and Gerard. Michael was the eighth or ninth child. Rysbrack was given the Christian names of a godparent, whose surname, Lodgwick, suggests he may have been English. Despite his baptismal names he was known, after settling in England, as Michael Rysbrack. He invariably signed himself thus and contemporaries referred to him so; from 1732 he appears consistently as Michael in the Marylebone rate books, though the spelling of Rysbrack varies considerably until 1737. It may be as a result of his first entry in the *Dictionary of National Biography* (1897) that the custom developed of referring to him as John Michael, as his name appears in his will.

Education and arrival in England Although he does not appear in the apprenticeship lists of the Guild of St Luke in Antwerp, it is likely that Rysbrack trained under the leading Antwerp sculptor Michael Van der Voort (Vervoort or van der Vorst) from 1706 to 1712. He is noted among the masters of the guild in 1714–15, and in 1716 '(Jan.) Michiel Rysbrack' is recorded as taking two apprentices. No work has been attributed to him during this period, and much of it is likely to have been assigned to his master.

Rysbrack emigrated to England in 1720. The precise reasons for this are not known. The restrictive practices of

(John) **Michael Rysbrack** (1694–1770), by Andrea Soldi, 1753

the guild system of Flanders, whose corporate ethos operated at the expense of the individual, may have contributed to his decision to move to London. They may in turn explain why, unlike Peter Scheemakers and Louis-François Roubiliac, he did not join an established workshop on arrival, nor ever take a partner or apprentices. The reasons may also have been economic, for Flanders in the early eighteenth century saw a decline in the grand projects encouraged by the creative energy of the Counter-Reformation, and a number of Flemish sculptors, among them Laurent Delvaux and Scheemakers, also sought employment in London. Further, they may have been personal, for Rysbrack came with his elder brother Peter, who had already worked in London, and who had been widowed the previous year. It is not known where Rysbrack lived during his first five years in London. From October 1725 until his death he lived and worked in Vere Street, 'near the Oxford Chappel' (now St Peter's), Oxford Road (now Oxford Street), on the Harleian estate owned by one of his earliest patrons, Edward Harley, second earl of Oxford, and developed by James Gibbs. George Vertue's account of his 'unreasonable gripeing usage' at the hands of Gibbs (Vertue, *Note books*, 3.17) may reflect the sculptor's youthful self-esteem, rather than any serious rift, because Rysbrack continued to work with Gibbs long after he had established an independent reputation. It was a trait neatly encapsulated in Horace Walpole's description of Rysbrack as 'no vain man' in his essay on the sculptor in *Anecdotes of Painting*. Both his public and private lives were marked by a loyalty to patrons, family, and friends.

When he arrived in London aged twenty-six, Rysbrack was an independent master with a distinctly individual

and innovatory style. His independence of spirit and his strong sense of identity were characteristics which were able to flourish in the Britain of the 1720s and 1730s. He achieved almost immediate recognition and, until his retirement in 1764, maintained a position as one of the leading sculptors in a period when the status of sculpture outshone that of painting. Alone of all the arts in Britain, sculpture could compete with work being produced on the continent. Rysbrack's reputation was founded on his skill as a modeller. Vertue's first mention of him in October 1720 notes his 'moddels in Clay are very excellent & shows him to be great Master *tho' young*' (Vertue, *Note books*, 1.76). His pleasure and pride in his models continued throughout his life. He would not part with the model for the Stourhead *Flora* to Sir Edward Littleton in 1758, as 'I Expect to work after [it] sometime or other' (Webb, 199), and another letter to the same patron expresses evident distress at damage to a terracotta goat (Anglesey Abbey, Cambridgeshire), modelled in the 1720s for a life-size version for Lord Burlington (Chatsworth, Derbyshire), which he had only parted with to Littleton in 1765. When his fortunes appeared to fluctuate in the 1740s in the face of rivalry from Scheemakers and Roubiliac, it was to terracotta that he resorted. The *Rubens* of 1743 (priv. coll.) and the *Hercules* of 1744 (Stourhead, Wiltshire) are virtuoso performances in the medium.

Rysbrack was innovative in monumental, architectural, garden, and portrait sculpture, and in all these areas he immediately found influential patrons, a position he was to sustain throughout a long working career. His Catholicism may have led to his initial introduction to his co-religionists George Vertue and James Gibbs, but it did not preclude his working also for leading protestant architects, among them Lord Burlington and William Kent, nor from finding favour at court. As the *Free Briton* pointed out (16 August 1733): 'I know not whether Rysbrack be a Whig or a Tory, I know him to be a good statuary, and I believe him to be an honest man and impartial Sculptor.'

Early years Rysbrack's first completed public work in England was the monument to Matthew Prior designed by Gibbs, which incorporates the portrait bust of the poet by Antoine Coysevox. The monument, with supporting figures of the muses Clio and Euterpe, for which Rysbrack was paid £35 each, was set up in the most public of positions in Westminster Abbey in 1721. Rysbrack's semi-recumbent effigy of the merchant Edward Colston for All Saints', Bristol (begun in 1723), set new standards for likeness, animation, and execution (both monuments are recorded in Gibbs's *Book of Architecture*, 1728, pls. 112–13). His range in this area never fails to impress, from the flamboyant high baroque of the polychromatic monument to John Churchill, first duke of Marlborough, at Blenheim Palace, Oxfordshire (1733), to the startling simplicity of the classicism of his monument to Sir Isaac Newton (1731; Westminster Abbey). Both of these monuments were designed by William Kent, the latter being described by James Ralph in 1734 as 'exceedingly venerable, bold, and majestick' (*A Critical Review of the Public Buildings, Statues, and Ornaments in, and about London and Westminster*, 69).

Besides grand set pieces Rysbrack's workshop also supplied handsome chimneypieces and solid monuments, in large numbers, which followed a formula set out by Gibbs in *A Book of Architecture*, such as the wall tablet and bust to the Revd Sir John Tynte, bt (1742; Goathurst, Somerset).

In the 1720s Rysbrack worked for Lord Burlington in the gardens at Chiswick (recorded in a series of paintings by his brother Peter in 1729); for Kent at Kensington Palace; and at Stowe, Buckinghamshire, for Richard Temple, first Viscount Cobham. The seven Anglo-Saxon deities for Stowe (1727, dispersed in 1921) introduced an element of antiquarian accuracy, and are the most important sculptural programme carried out in England in the period. At Kensington Palace the relief *A Roman Marriage* (1723) in the cupola room was the first of a series of architectural reliefs by Rysbrack. These were integral to the interior decorative schemes that were part of the innovative character of English Palladian domestic architecture, and Rysbrack has been credited with their introduction. Among the most distinguished are those for Kent's stone hall and marble parlour at Houghton Hall, Norfolk (1726–30), and for Leoni's hall at Clandon Park, Surrey (1731–5). Their subject matter is almost always after the antique.

Contemporaries commented on the rise in popularity of the portrait bust, and in 1747 R. Campbell reported in the *London Tradesman* that 'The Taste of Busts … prevails much of late years, and in some measure interferes with Portrait Painting: The Nobility now affect to have their Busts done that Way rather than sit for their pictures' (p. 139), and continued 'Mr Rysbrack may be said to be eminent in his Way' (p. 140). Rysbrack was the only sculptor to be mentioned by name here. He set the fashion for the two most distinctive types of portrait bust, the informal presentation of the sitter *en négligé*, that is in indoor dress, and the severely classical presentation of the sitter *all'anticà*, as if he were a Roman senator or general. Although not the earliest example, Rysbrack's Daniel Finch, second earl of Nottingham (1723; V&A), is in the most radical classical manner. The bust of Finch established his reputation and ensured his employment. Thirty-five years later his portrait of Benjamin Franklin (priv. coll., Australia) is as incisive and impressive as any. By 1732 Vertue had recorded sixty models for busts in the sculptor's studio and declared 'his superior meritt to other Sculptors is very aparent in his Modells of portraits—from the life none equallizing for truth of Likeness and property of ornaments or head-dress &c.' (Vertue, *Note books*, 3.84). The sculptor was equally innovative in two important subgroups: the historical bust and child portraiture. In the former group Rysbrack created a number of important icons, among them Shakespeare, Milton, and Newton, the earliest of these dating from the mid-1720s at Stowe, and resited c.1735 in the Temple of British Worthies (Stowe School, Buckinghamshire). This series of busts at Stowe was highly influential both as a visual expression of the political propaganda of the day and in defining an age which had developed a new awareness of history and an antiquarian patriotism.

Although it has been generally accepted that the genre of child portrait sculpture was developed in France and made famous by Jean-Antoine Houdon and Augustin Pajou in the 1770s, the epitome of the genre, and the earliest, are Rysbrack's bust and relief roundel *Peggy* (1723; priv. coll.), whose subject was the eight-year-old Margaret Cavendish Holles Harley, daughter of the second earl of Oxford. There are numerous other examples by Rysbrack, such as *Edward Salter* (1748; AM Oxf.). Significantly, they are not confined to the heirs and scions of aristocrats, but record the appearance of the children of the newly emergent professional middle classes. They are a visual expression of a change in understanding of the nature of childhood itself, and it has been suggested that William Hogarth may have responded to the popularity of this genre, and specifically to Rysbrack's contribution, in his own radical departure in the presentation of children in the 1740s.

Middle years Rysbrack's fame was assured in 1735 when Queen Caroline visited his 'work house', to see the great bronze equestrian statue of William III before it was put on board ship for Bristol. It had been commissioned in 1731, by subscription among the city's merchant oligarchy, after a competition in which a version submitted by Peter Scheemakers had been rejected. It was a gesture of qualified loyalty to the Hanoverian dynasty, one not lost on the queen who herself promptly commissioned a series of kings and queens from Rysbrack for her new library at St James's, then being built by William Kent. This same year Rysbrack was steward of St Luke's, described by Vertue 'as the Tip top Clubbs of all, for men of the highest Character in Arts & Gentlemen Lovers of Art' (Vertue, *Note books*, 3.120). In the same year he was portrayed in *A Conversation of Virtuosi* painted by Gawen Hamilton (NPG), the only sculptor in a group of thirteen which included Vertue, Gibbs, Kent, John Wootton, and Charles Bridgeman.

The arrival of Roubiliac and the return of Scheemakers from Rome in the early 1730s provided competition for Rysbrack and threatened his position as the foremost sculptor in England. By the 1740s he was losing out: Scheemakers completed the monument to Shakespeare designed by Kent, paid for by subscription, and erected in Westminster Abbey in 1741, while Roubiliac, whose reputation had been established by the figure of George Frideric Handel for Vauxhall Gardens in 1738 (V&A), won the prestigious commission for the monument to John Campbell, second duke of Argyll, in Westminster Abbey in 1745.

It was at this time that Rysbrack became involved with Thomas Coram's foundling hospital, whose royal charter had been granted in 1739. Rysbrack was proposed as a governor and guardian in December 1744 and elected in March 1745. He provided a marble relief for the court room entitled *Charity Children Engaged in Navigation and Husbandry*, and inscribed it 'M. Rysbrack Fecit et Donavit'. Rysbrack was the first member of a sub-committee of artists to be recruited by Hogarth to consider further embellishments for the hospital, and was a regular attender of the annual feast held there on St Luke's day, those convivial gatherings of artists that led to the founding of the Royal Academy. Though a founder member, Rysbrack was prevented by ill health from attending the first meetings of the Royal Academy in 1769.

Late work In the mid-1740s Rysbrack's fortunes appeared to flag. It was at this point that 'finding himself somewhat at leisure business not being so brisk' (Vertue, *Note books*, 3.121), he made a 2 foot high model of Hercules, which Vertue informs us was made up from 'at least seaven or 8 different men' (Vertue, *Note books*, 3.122). In 1747 Henry Hoare commissioned for £300 a full-size version in marble for the gardens at Stourhead. It was not completed until 1756, but Hoare built a temple, the Pantheon, to house it, and paid Rysbrack £50 'beyond y Contract' (Wilts. & Swindon RO, Stourhead papers, 383.6). The Hoares were among Rysbrack's most loyal patrons. He visited them at Stourhead, and in his will left the terracotta model of the Hercules to Henry Hoare.

Evidence of Rysbrack's undiminished invention is to be found in the figure of John Locke commissioned for the staircase of the new library at Christ Church, Oxford, and completed in 1756, in which the philosopher is presented as a latter-day baroque saint. It is significant that Robert Adam, intending to impress his patron, John Hope, second earl of Hopetoun, with a design for a chimneypiece in an innovatory style, entrusted Rysbrack with its execution, on the advice of Joseph Wilton (chimneypiece, 1756; Hopetoun House, Linlithgowshire). Adam and Rysbrack also collaborated on monuments to Admiral Edward Boscawen (1763; St Michael Penkevil, Cornwall) and Sir Nathaniel Curzon (1764; Kedleston Hall, Derbyshire), when the sculptor was already sixty-nine.

Old age Rysbrack suffered increasingly from a 'dropsical disorder', or fluid retention, and from 1756 there are a number of references to its development, without a hint of self-pity, in his letters to Sir Edward Littleton, the patron of his later years: 'When I am in my room I am always indisposed, which makes me chuse exercise' (31 July 1756; Webb, 195). Rysbrack's remedy, characteristic of a life marked by hard work and industry, was to 'take Exercise in the Shop for my own health' (6 May 1758; ibid., 200). When in 1764 illness finally got the better of him, Rysbrack did not retire to the country of his birth with a handsome capital, as did Peter Scheemakers. Instead he devoted himself to drawing for pleasure; a custom that had developed out of his practice of providing a number of highly finished designs from which his patrons could choose, whether of funerary monuments or chimneypieces:

> From time to time he would amuse himself with making high-finished Drawings in an admirable taste; these are generally of his own invention, designed with a smart pen, washed with bister, and heightened with white. This Amusement he continued to the last days of his life.

wrote the connoisseur and collector Charles Rogers (Rogers, 2.228), a compliment Rogers underlined by including *Time* by Rysbrack, alone among contemporary artists to be represented by his own work. This esteem was echoed by J. T. Smith, the first keeper of prints at the British Museum, who exempted Rysbrack from his criticism of the draughtsmanship of other eighteenth-century sculptors. These drawings, done for 'Amusement', were often intended as presents to friends and patrons: *Time* had been given to Rogers as a new year's gift in 1765. On 19 May 1764, the year Rysbrack retired, he wrote to his most loyal patron, Henry Hoare, repeating a request to draw for him subjects 'Great and Noble, and something surprising, which will give me the Greatest Pleasure in the World' (Wilts. & Swindon RO, Stourhead papers, 383.6). These were collected by contemporaries and mounted as old master drawings and were given individual lots in the sales that marked his retirement.

In contrast to Peter Scheemakers, Rysbrack died in relative poverty. This was partly due to his generosity to his less successful relations and their dependants, and partly, as Rogers averred, to 'the fury with which he made his Collections' (Rogers, 2.228). His collection of prints and drawings was vast, catholic, and full of surprises. It included works by and after Michelangelo and Raphael, Titian, Veronese, the Carracci, Rubens, Claude, and Poussin; more remarkable were works by Watteau, Edme Bouchardon, and Jean-Baptiste Greuze, and by his contemporaries Hogarth, Gainsborough, and Benjamin West. Their dispersal took ten days at a sale held by Langfords in 1764, and a further three days at a sale held by Christies ten years later. Rogers himself bought at these sales, and reproduced two of Rysbrack's Guercinos and a Salvator Rosa in *Prints in Imitation of Drawings*. Rysbrack may in a small way have been a dealer in casts after the antique and old master paintings, as his paternal grandfather had been before him.

Rysbrack's contribution to British sculpture set it on a par with the best being executed anywhere in Europe at the time, and his influence on the work of native English sculptors such as Henry Cheere, Thomas Carter, and William Tyler was considerable. He was held in high esteem by his contemporaries, but his death coincided with a reaction against the robust Roman classicism of the Augustan age and the work of Robert Adam, and an increasing interest in Greece as the embodiment of the classical ideal. His reputation further suffered at the hands of John Flaxman, a sculptor of a younger generation. Flaxman's animadversions, given in his *Address to the president and members of the Royal Academy on the death of Thomas Banks, R.A., sculptor* (1803), relegated Rysbrack to a 'mere workman, too insipid to give pleasure, and too dull to offend greatly' (Flaxman, 289).

Although he was an immigrant whose entire known work was executed in Britain, who made it his abode for fifty years, and who appears not to have sought naturalization either by letters patent or by a private act of parliament, Rysbrack contributed significantly to the establishment of a British national identity. He had assimilated the aspirations of his adopted country and had been assimilated in turn by its inhabitants, eliciting loyalty and affection from all with whom he engaged. Rysbrack was a joiner, an active member of the clubs and coteries of the day, including the learned Spalding Gentleman's Society. He was clearly a most engaging character and very good company. Henry Angelo in his *Reminiscences* (1830) recalled the painter James Barry telling Dr Johnson of a propensity of Rysbrack the 'celebrated sculptor' to fits of laughter. He recounted how, invited to dine with Sarah, duchess of Marlborough, and seated near her, Rysbrack developed one of his fits of laughter and had the whole dinner table in convulsions, none of them quite knowing why (Angelo, 1.491–5). This capacity for good humour did not desert him. Charles Rogers, who visited him two days before he died, remarked 'nor would he even now refuse to laugh when the conversation took a gay turn'. Rogers declared that 'it would be superfluous to raise a Monument over him whose Memory will be observed, so long as Marble shall last, by the many noble Monuments he has erected over others' (Rogers, 2.228). He died of dropsy on 8 January 1770, six years after his final retirement, at home in Vere Street, Marylebone, where he had paid rates since 1725. He was buried in the parish church of St Marylebone on 11 January, and his will was proved on the 26th of that month.   KATHARINE EUSTACE

Sources Vertue, *Note books* · C. Rogers, *A collection of prints in imitation of drawings* (1778) · H. Walpole, *Anecdotes of painting*, ed. M. Berry (1798), vol. 3 of *The works of Horatio Walpole, earl of Orford*, ed. M. Berry, Lord Holland, and J. Croker (1798–1825) · P. Rombouts and T. Van Lerius, *De liggeren en andere historische archieven der Antwerpsche Sint Lucasgilde*, 2 (The Hague, 1876); repr. (Amsterdam, 1961) · J. T. Smith, *Nollekens and his times*, 2 vols. (1828) · K. Eustace, *Michael Rysbrack: sculptor, 1694–1770* (1982) [exhibition catalogue, City of Bristol Museum and Art Gallery, Bristol, 6 March – 1 May 1982] · K. Eustace, 'The Hopetoun chimneypiece, Adam Clerisseau and Rysbrack', *Burlington Magazine*, 139 (1997), 743–52 · K. Eustace, 'The politics of the past: Stowe and the development of the historical portrait bust', *Apollo*, 148 (July 1998), 31–40 · Marylebone rate books, City Westm. AC · M. Baker, *Figured in marble* (2000), 108–18, 129–43 · G. Balderston, 'The genesis of Edward Salter aetatis 6', *Georgian Group Journal*, 10 (2000), 175–205 · M. Whinney, *Sculpture in Britain, 1530 to 1830*, rev. J. Physick, 2nd edn (1988) · J. Flaxman, *Lectures in sculpture* (1838) · H. Angelo, *Reminiscences*, 1 (1828) · M. Webb, *Michael Rysbrack: sculptor* (1954) [incl. letters]
Archives Glos. RO · Som. ARS · Wilts. & Swindon RO
Likenesses attrib. J. Vanderbank, oils, *c*.1728, NPG · J. Faber junior, mezzotint, pubd 1734 (after J. Vanderbank), BM, NPG · G. Hamilton, group portrait, oils, 1735 (*A conversation of virtuosi … at the King's Arms*), NPG · A. Soldi, oils, 1753, Yale U. CBA, Paul Mellon collection [*see illus.*] · Finden, engraving (after J. Vanderbank), repro. in Walpole, *Anecdotes of painting* · attrib. J. Richardson, pencil drawing, V&A

Ryse, Philipp. *See* Philip ap Rhys (*fl.* 1547–1559).

Ryssheton [Rishton], **Nicholas** (*d.* 1413), canon lawyer and diplomat, was probably a native of Lancashire, where he had a brother, Henry Rishton, one of whose sons, also Nicholas (*d.* 1463), emulated his uncle's career. The elder Nicholas held a prebend in Crediton collegiate church, Devon, in 1385, and the rectories of Warfield, Berkshire, and Astbury, Cheshire, the latter by papal provision, in 1389. By that year, too, he had gained canonries with expectations of prebends in St Paul's and Lincoln (neither of which he ever made good) from the pope, and on 12 November gained a like grace in Lichfield at the petition of Cardinal Angelus of San Lorenzo in Damaso. None of

these was immediately or ever profitable, but the last in particular suggests that Ryssheton was already known personally in the curia. He was an MA by 7 March 1389, when he was granted a three-year licence by Bishop Waltham of Salisbury to study at an English university. However, on 9 June 1391 he was in the papal curia working for Bishop Waltham in a suit against the Salisbury Cathedral chapter, and perhaps then resumed rather than began academic studies in Italy. By 26 November 1396 he was a licentiate in canon law of Bologna, at which point the pope dispensed him to take the degree elsewhere since he could not afford to return. It was no doubt his experiences in the curia and Italy that inspired him to make a determination on the ending of the papal schism in the theology faculty at Oxford University about this time. He was a doctor in both laws by 1398, but of which university must remain doubtful, for by that time he was working as a papal chaplain and auditor of causes in the curia. He still enjoyed this title in 1404. In August 1399 he gave way to the crown's candidate for a prebend in Beverley collegiate church, Yorkshire, despite the pope's affirming his right to provide him to it.

On 8 February 1400 Archbishop Arundel appointed Ryssheton as his auditor of causes in the court of Canterbury, a position he held until 1408, and on 25 March 1401 collated him to the rectory of Cliffe, Kent. The archbishop had a remarkable eye for quality. On 28 September 1401 in Coventry, Ryssheton acted as proctor in giving fealty for the see of Bath and Wells to Arundel on behalf of Henry Bowet, the first time this had ever been permitted by deputy. From late 1402 he was appointed to a series of English delegations to negotiate with France and Flanders, and was certainly on such missions at Calais from 14 November 1403 to 6 April 1404, from 16 August to 29 October 1404 (returning to inform the king at Coventry of the complete lack of progress even as to an agenda), from 2 December 1404 to 18 February 1405, and from 10 March to 4 June 1405. Curiously, he still relied altogether on the papacy for preferment, and by 11 November 1404 had been provided ineffectively to the archdeaconry of Buckingham and with expectative graces to prebends in York and Salisbury. On 19 October 1405 he was even given full dispensation to shuffle any present and future benefices as he wished; in reality he only had Cliffe and the Crediton prebend. On 4 June 1408 he was at last collated by the newly promoted Bishop Robert Hallum, his former Canterbury colleague, to the prebend of Netheravon in Salisbury.

In January 1408 Ryssheton dined at New College, Oxford, and, having retired as auditor of causes soon after, he was sent by the crown at the end of the year to speak with Pope Gregory XII. He was present at the Council of Pisa in 1409, although his function is unclear. Thereafter, he seems to have lived in Kent, probably even at Cliffe. He composed some sermons. He was a member of the council of the prior of Christ Church, Canterbury, in 1412, and in his will he revealed that he was a member of no fewer than nine major monastic confraternities, indicative of his considerable usefulness as a canon lawyer and one familiar with the curia. He made this will on 5 June 1413, requesting burial on the right-hand side of the altar in Cliffe church. His nephew was to have his copy of the *Provinciale* of his Canterbury colleague William Lyndwood, an important reference because the definitive version of this great work was said by its very compiler to have been created only between 1422 and 1430. Ryssheton bequeathed his copy of *Legenda aurea* to Cobham collegiate church. His will was admitted to probate as early as 15 June 1413.   R. G. DAVIES

Sources Emden, *Oxf.*, 3.1619–20 · *DNB* · I. J. Churchill, *Canterbury administration: the administrative machinery of the archbishopric of Canterbury*, 2 vols. (1933), vol. 1, pp. 265, 488; vol. 2, pp. 243, 245 · PRO, Prerogative Court of Canterbury, wills, Marche 26 · F. C. Hingeston, ed., *Royal and historical letters during the reign of Henry the Fourth*, 1, Rolls Series, 18 (1860)

Ryther, Augustine (d. 1593), map engraver and maker of scientific instruments, is of unknown origin. The *Dictionary of National Biography*, apparently following the Yorkshire antiquary Ralph Thoresby, suggested that he was a native of Leeds; however, no firm evidence can now be found for this, and the idea perhaps rests on his later association with Christopher Saxton, who came from and worked in the West Riding of Yorkshire. Ryther was admitted to the Grocers' Company of London, whose arms decorate some of his maps: he was the first of the remarkable number of Elizabethan instrument makers who were free of that company. In 1590 he worked close to Leadenhall, next to the sign of the Tower. He was the first English map engraver to be important by international standards and sometimes emphasized his nationality by signing his work Augustinus Ryther Anglus (for example on his maps for Saxton), to distinguish his work from that of Flemish engravers who were pre-eminent in the field. Some two dozen of his maps and charts survive and are catalogued in detail by Turner. The best known are his engravings of maps for Saxton: Durham and Westmorland (1576), Gloucester and York (1577), and England; his three new engravings for *The Mariners Mirror*, Anthony Ashley's version (1588) of Lucas Janszoon Wagenaer's collection of charts *Spiegel der zeevaerdi*; and eleven engravings of Robert Hood's charts showing the invasion of the Spanish Armada in 1588, published in 1590 with a description of the invasion by Petruccio Ubaldini, translated by Ryther. His engraving in 1588 of Ralph Agas's bird's-eye view of Oxford, his two planispheres and a chart of the north-east Atlantic for Thomas Hood, and his playing cards showing the counties of England and Wales are also widely known. His last commission was probably his very large engraving of John Hamond's map of Cambridge on nine copper sheets, published in 1593.

Turner suggests that Ryther turned to instrument making relatively late in life in response to the growing demand for navigational and surveying instruments, and his two surviving instruments attest to his skill in this field (descriptions and plates in Turner, 173–7). His compendium (1588; Science Museum, London) combines the names and latitudes of thirty European towns, an equinoctial sundial, and a magnetic compass, and his altazimuth theodolite (1590; Museo di Storia della Scienza, Florence) is one of only three extant Elizabethan theodolites. He was buried at St Andrew Undershaft, London, on 30 August 1593. Suggestions that he was the Mr Ryther who was held in the Fleet in 1594 and 1595 are shown by the burial register and the administration of his estate in 1593 to be wrong. There is no known record of his having married. His apprentice Charles Whitwell (apprenticed 1582, made free 1590) went on to become one of the foremost instrument makers of his day.   ELIZABETH BAIGENT

Sources G. L'E. Turner, *Elizabethan instrument makers: the origins of the London trade in precision instrument making* (2000) · E. G. R. Taylor, *The mathematical practitioners of Tudor and Stuart England* (1954) · J. Brown, *Mathematical instrument makers in the Grocers' Company, 1688–1800* (1979) · A. M. Hind, *Engraving in England in the sixteenth and seventeenth centuries*, 1 (1952) · *DNB* · administration of estate, GL, commissary court MSS, 9168/14, fol. 273v
Wealth at death see administration of estate, GL, commissary court MSS, 9168/14, fol. 273v

Ryther, John (1631x5–1681), clergyman and ejected minister, the son of John Rither (d. 1673), a tanner of York who later turned Quaker, was born in Yorkshire. There is uncertainty over his date of birth: he was said to be forty-nine when he died in 1681, suggesting that he was born in 1631 or 1632, but his reported age of fifteen at matriculation would suggest 1634 or 1635. Educated at Leeds grammar school, he entered Cambridge on 25 March 1650, aged fifteen, as a sizar at Sidney Sussex College. From 25 March 1655 until his ejection in 1660 he was vicar of Frodingham, including Bromby, Lincolnshire. He then obtained the vicarage of North Ferriby, Yorkshire, only to be turned out by the Act of Uniformity in 1662. He continued to preach in his house at Brough, in the neighbouring parish of Elloughton, and for this spent several months confined in York Castle. Forced from home by the Five Mile Act in 1666, he eventually settled as pastor of the Independent church at Bradford-dale in 1668. In the following year he preached there as well as at the Halifax chapelries of Cross Stone, Sowerby, and Coley, for which he was again imprisoned. In 1669 he sought refuge in London. His new flock, which included many sailors, built him a meeting-house at Wapping, Middlesex, where he was ordained an Independent minister on 6 February 1670. Almost immediately he was convicted for illegal preaching; warrants were issued against him but he managed to escape. The sailors became so devoted to the Seaman's Preacher, as Ryther was known, that they reportedly prevented his apprehension by intimidating the arresting officers.

Ryther published numerous works between 1672 and 1680, including *The Morning Seeker* (1673), a series of sermons on the advantages of early religion. In dedicating this to the godly Lady Dorothy Norcliffe of Langton, Yorkshire, and her daughters, Lady Elizabeth Bright and Lady Katherine Wentworth, Ryther acknowledged the support they had given him and other ejected ministers. In addition to *A Funeral Sermon* (1674) for his close friend James Janeway, the Presbyterian minister at Rotherhithe,

Surrey, Ryther edited Janeway's posthumous *Legacy to his Friends, Containing Twenty-Seven Instances of Sea-Dangers and Deliverances* (1675). Ryther's best-known work, *A Plat for Mariners* (1672, 1675, 1780, 1803), several sermons on Jonah's voyage, included an epistle by Janeway. The evangelical John Newton (1727–1807), himself a former sailor, added a preface in 1780. Ryther aimed at a popular rather than scholarly audience. Employing an affecting style which earned him the nickname Crying Jeremy, he pleaded with sinners to awaken from their spiritual lethargy and respond to Christ's call while there was still time.

Ryther and his wife, Margaret, who survived him, had one son, John [*see below*], and a daughter, Rachel Dale. He died in June 1681, leaving his house in Stepney, Middlesex, to his son. He remembered his 'honoured mother' with 20*s*. a year for life (PRO, PROB 11/367, fol. 130). He was buried in his chapel in Wapping. Shortly after his death, government informers reported finding a supply of guns and powder hidden near 'Ryder's' meeting-house, though whether he was at all linked to this cache is not known (*CSP dom.*, *1680–81*, 365).

John Ryther (d. 1704), Independent minister, son of John Ryther, served as chaplain on ships trading to the East and West Indies. The journal he kept during his voyages from 1676 to 1681 was given to the antiquarian Ralph Thoresby by William Moult, the Independent minister at Leeds. In 1686 Ryther became minister of the Castle Gate Independent Church in Nottingham. For most of his career he co-operated amicably with the Nottingham Presbyterians. He joined with them in at least two ordinations, and had his children baptized by John Whitlock the elder, of the High Pavement Presbyterian Church. In *A Defence of the Glorious Gospel* (1703), however, Ryther threatened this harmony by accusing John Barret, the Nottingham Presbyterian, of Arminian errors. He also published a *Sermon Preached before the Society of Reformation of Manners* (1699). Ryther died at Nottingham on 27 January 1704. The name of Ryther's wife is not known, but his daughter Anne married Robert Kippis and was the mother of Andrew Kippis, the Unitarian divine and biographer. JIM BENEDICT

Sources *Calamy rev.*, 421 • Greaves & Zaller, *BDBR*, 127 • E. Calamy, ed., *An abridgement of Mr. Baxter's history of his life and times, with an account of the ministers, &c., who were ejected after the Restauration of King Charles II*, 2nd edn, 2 vols. (1713), vol. 2, pp. 448, 833 • B. Dale, *Yorkshire puritanism and early nonconformity*, ed. T. G. Crippen [n.d., c.1909], 134–5 • J. Ryther, 'preface', *The morning seeker* (1673) • Ryther's will, PRO, PROB 11/367, sig. 111 • *CSP dom.*, *1663–4*, 300; *1680–81*, 365 • A. Gordon, ed., *Freedom after ejection: a review (1690–1692) of presbyterian and congregational nonconformity in England and Wales* (1917) • G. F. Nuttall, 'The emergence of nonconformity', in G. F. Nuttall and others, *The beginnings of nonconformity* (1964), 9–32, 16 • D. L. Wykes, 'After the happy union: presbyterians and Independents in the provinces', *Unity and diversity in the church*, ed. R. N. Swanson, SCH, 32 (1996), 283–95 • *The nonconformist's memorial ... originally written by ... Edmund Calamy*, ed. S. Palmer, [3rd edn], 3 (1803), 463–4 • J. G. Miall, *Congregationalism in Yorkshire* (1868), 240 • *The Rev. Oliver Heywood ... his autobiography, diaries, anecdote and event books*, ed. J. H. Turner, 2 (1883), 289–90, 295 • A. R. Henderson, *History of the Castle Gate Congregational Church, Nottingham 1655–1905* (1905), 139–50 • R. Thoresby, *Ducatus Leodiensis, or, The topography of ... Leedes* (1715), 526 • J. H. Turner, T. Dickenson, and O. Heywood,

eds., *The nonconformist register of baptisms, marriages, and deaths* (1881), 138, 140 • W. Wilson, *The history and antiquities of the dissenting churches and meeting houses in London, Westminster and Southwark*, 4 vols. (1808–14), vol. 4, p. 103 • Venn, *Alum. Cant.*

Archives BL, sermon notes, Add. MS 45671, fols. 8b–57b • BL, sermon notes, Add. MS 45675, fols. 5–194b

Wealth at death 'goods and chattels' to wife; house; library; 20*s*. in mourning gifts; 20*s*. p.a. to mother: will, PRO, PROB 11/367, sig. 111, proved 19 July 1681

Ryther, John (d. 1704). *See under* Ryther, John (1631x5–1681).

Ryves [Reeve], **Bruno** [Bruen] (c.1596–1677), dean of Windsor and journalist, was the fourth son of Thomas Ryves of Damory Court, Dorset; Sir Thomas *Ryves (d. 1652) was his first cousin. As Bruen Ryves, the version of his name he often preferred, on 21 October 1610 he subscribed as a clerk at New College, Oxford. He graduated BA on 26 October 1616 and in 1617 became a clerk at Magdalen College, a position he retained for the next twelve years. He proceeded MA on 9 June 1619.

In 1628 Ryves became rector of St Martin Vintry, London. On 14 October that year at St Mary Magdalen, Old Fish Street, as Brume Rives he married Katherine, daughter of Sir Richard Waldram of Charley, Leicestershire, who brought with her land in Ireland; they had five children who survived to adulthood. Ryves proceeded BD on 30 June 1632 and was admitted to Gray's Inn in 1634. His career prospered during the Laudian ascendancy. On 25 June 1639 he proceeded DD and that year became vicar of Stanwell, Middlesex, where he was 'a noted and florid preacher' (Wood, *Ath. Oxon.*, 3.1110–11). A Lent preacher at court in 1639 and 1640 he was appointed in October 1639 to serve as a royal chaplain the following year, and between 1641 and 1644 served the October turn.

During the rebellion of 1641 the Ryves's Irish land, worth £40 a year, was lost. About June 1642 Ryves joined the royalist army, serving on the council of war. On 3 July his Stanwell parishioners petitioned the House of Lords, complaining of his royalist and anti-sectarian preaching. The Lords sequestered him from St Martin on 21 February 1643, citing his absence in the army, and admitted Nathaniel Salloway; he was subsequently sequestered from Stanwell too, and with his wife and four children, 'Taken out of their Beds at Midnight, Turned out of doors, all his Goods seized, and all that Night lay under a Hedge in the Wet and Cold' (*Walker rev.*, part 2, 12). In response Charles I asked Bishop John Prideaux to place Ryves in Salloway's living at Severn Stoke, Worcestershire, but Lord Arundel, who immediately on hearing of their plight had taken in the Ryves family, charitably continued to support them for some years at Shafton, Dorset.

As part of the royalist war effort Ryves turned to journalism. The first issue of *Mercurius rusticus* was published on 20 May 1643; it appeared irregularly for twenty-one issues, the last on 16 March 1644. Printed in Oxford this royalist newsbook detailed the murders, robberies, plunderings, and other outrages suffered by the king's subjects, and the

Bruno Ryves (*c*.1596–1677), by unknown artist

sacrileges committed upon the cathedral churches of England by parliamentarian troops. It was reprinted as a single volume (not concealing its periodical origins, and probably using the newsbook as the copy text) in 1646, and was reprinted in 1647, in 1648 (as *Angliae ruina*), 1685, and 1723. The collected editions were published with a fine engraved frontispiece featuring ten scenes from the civil wars. Ryves's concern with recording the facts for posterity led him to write also *Mercurius Belgicus* (1646), a chronology of the war from 1641 to 1645, which was eventually extended into the more detailed *Micro-chronicon* (1647). These were published with various editions of the textually mutable *Mercurius Rusticus*; Ryves was not the author of *Querela Cantabrigensis*, therewith published. Ryves's works all exhibit a resentment of religious heterodoxy and a concern with social status and the monetary value of property.

When the first civil war concluded in 1646 Ryves compounded, though his fine remained unpaid in 1653. He continued to preach: Henry Hammond mentions a sermon given by Ryves at St Martin Orgar, London, on 20 May 1649. His *Two Sermons* (1652), on the perils of covetousness, blamed the love of money for rebellion, treason, and sacrilege. He preached at Lincoln's Inn on 9 May 1654 and was elected preacher there; in that capacity he delivered, on 15 July 1655, a funeral sermon for Ferdinando Leigh, son of Lord Leigh of Stonelergh, published in 1656, on the importance of steadfastness in faith. His ministry was appreciated by the benchers, who extended his salary and voted him a gratuity after he was ejected from his place by Oliver Cromwell on 4 November 1656. Despite this disfavour he assisted in Brian Walton's polyglot Bible by

arranging the lifting of tax on the paper; Ryves also assisted Walton in his inquiry into London tithes. At some point during the 1650s Ryves appears to have travelled abroad to transport money (from Sir Lancelot Lake) to Charles Stuart in exile.

Ryves found notable success in the Restoration church. He had been appointed dean of Chichester (and master of the hospital there) by royal patent on 8 June 1646, and was finally established there on 12 July 1660, but by patent dated 25 August he was appointed dean of Windsor and installed on 3 September. Probably in August he was also made minister at St Giles Cripplegate, which belonged to the dean and chapter at St Paul's. Correspondence suggests that he was living at St Paul's Churchyard at this time. Sworn register of the Garter on 14 January 1661, in this capacity he dealt with petitions from poor knights of Windsor. He composed at least one hymn for Garter ceremonies. He also undertook the compilation of the records of the order, from the year 1638 to the present, entitling it *Liber Carolinus* and completing it in 1670. In this connection he corresponded extensively with Elias Ashmole. His letters during these years suggest a personal stiffness and irritability. He felt under pressure from the king and from prospective patrons and clients, and repeatedly expressed concern over payments for various expenses incurred. Soon after his appointment as register he was presented to the rectory of Acton in Middlesex. In his absence he appointed a curate to preach. Richard Baxter reports that this young man spent too little time in the pulpit and too much in the alehouse. When Baxter resorted to preaching at his own house after church service, in defiance of the Conventicle Act, Ryves assisted (as he later supposedly confessed) in Baxter's arrest and six-month imprisonment for speaking seditious words, thereby earning the resentment of his parishioners. Also in early 1661 Ryves became rector of Haseley, Oxfordshire. He persuaded the king that this living should be annexed to his deanery, although the connection was never formally established. Baxter's accusations of pluralism were therefore accurate in the spirit as well as the letter of the law.

Ryves's political views remained constant. In a sermon before the House of Commons on 15 January 1662, at a fast held because of the unusually clement weather that threatened to bring plague, he revealed 'how the neglect of exacting Justice on offenders (by which he insinuated such of the old *Kings* murderers, as [were] yet reprievd, & in the Tower) was a maine cause of Gods punishing a Land &c' (Evelyn, *Diary*, 3.311–12). John Evelyn does not commend Ryves's artistry, and there is no evidence that his sermon was printed.

Of Ryves's sons, Brune (the eldest) and (probably) Thomas became merchants; Joseph was eminent in the Restoration church. His daughter Jane married Robert Sewell or Seawell, whom Ryves valued greatly; his other daughters, Dorothy Cooke and Katherine Keate, were also mentioned in his will. There is a mystery of some conflict within his family: one letter suggests an expulsion in 1660 of one Doll (Dorothy?) from his household, and forbids his daughter(s) or daughters-in-law from visiting her. Ryves died at Windsor on 13 July 1677, 'aged 81', and was buried, like his wife before him, in the alley aisle on the south side of St George's Chapel. Despite the financial concerns he expressed he left a significant estate. A long Latin inscription on the wall over his grave characterized him as 'fide, zelo, Affectu in rebus Regis, Ecclesiae, Regni promovendis' ('advancing the cause of king, church and monarchy with faith, zeal and love'; J. Pote, *The History and Antiquities of Windsor Castle*, 1769, 365).

JOAD RAYMOND

Sources Walker rev. • Foster, *Alum. Oxon.* • J. Hutchins, *The history and antiquities of the county of Dorset*, 3rd edn, ed. W. Shipp and J. W. Hodson, 4 vols. (1861–74) • will, PRO, PROB 11/356, sig. 7 • *Reliquiae Baxterianae, or, Mr Richard Baxter's narrative of the most memorable passages of his life and times*, ed. M. Sylvester, 1 vol. in 3 pts (1696) • Wood, *Ath. Oxon.*, new edn, 3.1110–11 • *Elias Ashmole (1617–1692): his autobiographical and historical notes*, ed. C. H. Josten, 5 vols. (1966 [i.e. 1967]) • J. H. Todd, *Memoirs of the life and writings of the Right Rev. Brian Walton* (1821) • Z. Grey, *An impartial examination of the third volume of Mr Daniel Neal's 'History of the puritans'* (1737) • PRO, LC 5/134, pp. 342, 364, 396, 432 • N. W. S. Cranfield, 'Chaplains in ordinary at the early Stuart court: the purple road', *Patronage and recruitment in the Tudor and early Stuart church*, ed. C. Cross (1996), 120–47 • J. Walter, *Understanding popular violence in the English revolution: the Colchester plunderers* (1999)

Archives Bodl. Oxf., MSS Ashmole • Pembroke College, Oxford, corresp. with John Hall relating to Clapcot tithe

Likenesses R. Earlom, mezzotint, pubd 1810, BM, NPG • portrait, c.1836 • oils, St George's Chapel, Windsor [see illus.]

Ryves, Elizabeth (1750–1797), writer, was born in Ireland in 1750 and was descended from an old Irish family connected with that of Bruno Ryves (c.1596–1677). She owned some property, but, being cheated out of it 'by the chicanery of the law', fell into poverty, and went to London to petition the king in 1775 and to earn a living by her pen. She wrote political articles for newspapers, verses, plays, and learned French in order to produce translations. She translated into English Rousseau's *Social Contract*, Raynal's *Letter to the National Assembly*, and Delacroix's *Review of the Constitutions of the Principal States of Europe* (1792); she also attempted to translate Froissart, but gave it up as too difficult. For some time she is said to have conducted the historical and political portions of Dodsley's *Annual Register*. In 1777 she published her *Poems on Several Occasions*.

Ryves's dramatic efforts, *The Prude* (1777), a comic opera in three acts, and *The Debt of Honour*, were accepted by a theatrical manager, but were never acted; she received £100 as compensation. She wrote one novel, *The Hermit of Snowden, or, Memoirs of Albert and Lavinia* (1789), said to be an account of her own life. Her other works include *The Triumph of Hymen* (1777), *Ode to the Rev. William Mason* (1780), *Dialogues in the Elysian Fields* (1785), and *The Hastiniad, an Heroick Poem* (1785). She died unmarried and in poverty on 29 April 1797 in Store Street, Tottenham Court Road, London. Isaac D'Israeli, to whom she was personally known, expended much pity on her fate in his *Calamities of Authors* (1812). ELIZABETH LEE, *rev.* REBECCA MILLS

Sources [I. D'Israeli], *Calamities of authors*, 1 (1812), 297–309 • Blain, Clements & Grundy, *Feminist comp.* • J. Todd, ed., *A dictionary of British and American women writers, 1660–1800* (1984) • D. E. Baker, *Biographia dramatica, or, A companion to the playhouse*, rev. I. Reed, new edn, rev. S. Jones, 1/2 (1812), 619 • D. J. O'Donoghue, *The poets of Ireland: a biographical dictionary with bibliographical particulars*, 1 vol. in 3 pts (1892–3), 221 • A. J. Webb, *A compendium of Irish biography* (1878), 461 • J. S. Crone, *A concise dictionary of Irish biography*, rev. edn (1937), 225 • *GM*, 1st ser., 65 (1795), 540 • *GM*, 1st ser., 67 (1797), 445, 522 • Watt, *Bibl. Brit.*, vol. 2 • R. Hogan, ed., *Dictionary of Irish literature*, rev. edn, 2 (1996)

Ryves, George Frederick (1758–1826), naval officer, was born on 8 September 1758, the son of Thomas Ryves and his second wife, Anna Maria, daughter of Daniel Graham. He was educated at Harrow School and joined the Royal Navy in February 1774, surviving an explosion on his first ship, the Plymouth guard vessel *Kent*, which killed eleven men, in July of that year. In April 1775 he was sent to the West Indies in the flagship of Vice-Admiral James Young, and was there appointed to command the *Tartar* (8 guns), a small vessel of thirty-three men. He had a successful career in her, capturing over fifty enemy vessels, some of them privateers whose armament more than matched that of his own ship.

Ryves returned to England in May 1778 and a year later was appointed to Vice-Admiral Thomas Arbuthnot's flagship, the *Europe*. He was made a temporary lieutenant in September 1779, a promotion confirmed in November 1780, when he returned to Jamaica for two years. He was then to sail to the East Indies, but his vessel was dismasted in a gale, and when peace was signed in March 1783 he was placed on half pay. Ryves used the peace to tour parts of Europe, before being taken back into active service at the time of the Nootka Sound incident. On 3 January 1792 he married Catherine Elizabeth (d. c.1804), the third and youngest daughter of the Hon. James Edward Arundel, of Ashcombe, Wiltshire. They had four children: two sons, George Frederick and Henry Wyndham; and two daughters, Harriet and Catherine Elizabeth.

In early 1795 Ryves was appointed to the *Aurora* and then to command the *Bulldog*, which was stationed in the West Indies. He was unable to meet up with her, but instead volunteered to serve ashore with a naval party during the attack on St Lucia. His efforts to organize the movement of heavy guns to assist in the assault were greatly appreciated by Sir Hugh Christian, his commander. Ryves stayed in the West Indies until September 1797, when he returned to England. He was promoted to captain's rank in May 1798 and spent some time off Newfoundland before, in 1801, he was dispatched to the Mediterranean. His work there, transferring troops to and from Egypt on his ship, the *Agincourt*, was highly praised by his contemporaries, who did not fail to note that on the return journey he had entertained some of his passengers at his own expense.

Ryves was sent to Corfu in March 1802, and then to Maddalena Island which he surveyed; for this work Nelson personally thanked Ryves after making the island his base in 1803. He also received gifts from the kings of Naples and Sardinia. The crew of Ryves's next vessel, the *Gibraltar*, were unhappy at being kept on despite the peace of Amiens, but he was able to restore discipline. At the beginning of 1804 he received news that his wife had died, but Ryves remained in the Mediterranean until June of that year, and returned to Britain only at the end of July, when his vessel at last paid off. In 1806 Ryves married again. His second wife was Emma, daughter of Richard Robert Graham, of Chelsea Hospital. They had five children: four sons, Charles Graham, Walter Robert, Edward Augustus, and Herbert Thomas; and one daughter, Mary Emma.

Ryves himself saw active service on only one other occasion. In March 1810 he was appointed to command the *Africa*, which he took to the Baltic. Despite severe gales, he was able to bring both the *Africa* and the convoy she was escorting back safely, a not inconsiderable achievement in the circumstances. He saw no further active service, though he was promoted to flag rank on 27 May 1825. He died at his family home, Shrowton House, Dorset, on 20 May 1826.   J. K. LAUGHTON, rev. MICHAEL PARTRIDGE

Sources GM, 1st ser., 96/1 (1826), 640–43 · J. Marshall, *Royal naval biography*, 2 (1824), 136–45 · Naval Service Records, PRO, ADM 9/2 · O'Byrne, *Naval biog. dict.* [George Frederick Ryves and Herbert Thomas Ryves] · *The dispatches and letters of Vice-Admiral Lord Viscount Nelson*, ed. N. H. Nicolas, 7 vols. (1844–6)

Ryves, Lavinia Janetta Horton (1797–1871). *See under* Serres, Olivia (1772–1835).

Ryves, Sir Thomas (d. 1652), civil lawyer, was the eighth son of John Ryves (1536–1587) of Damory Court, Blandford, Dorset, and his wife, Elizabeth (c.1537–1609), daughter of Sir John Mervyn of Fonthill, Wiltshire. George (1569–1613), the second son, became warden of New College, Oxford; William (d. 1660), the sixth, became attorney-general of Ireland in 1619 and judge of the king's bench in 1636. Thomas was also a first cousin of Bruno Ryves (c.1596–1677), author of *Mercurius Rusticus* and eventually dean of Windsor. He was educated at Winchester School from 1590, and New College, Oxford, from 1598, where he graduated BCL on 7 February 1605 and DCL on 21 June 1610. Several of the terms that were allowed to count towards his Oxford degree were in fact spent in the law schools of French universities, although it is not clear which one or ones he attended.

Ryves was admitted to Doctors' Commons in 1611, and in the following year went to Ireland with Sir John Davies, whose wife was sister to Ryves's aunt. He was involved in 1613 in the struggle for the speakership of the Irish parliament between Davies and Sir John Everard; his account of this ended up in the state papers. In October 1613 Ryves obtained the reversion of the office of judge of faculties in the prerogative court of Ireland, eventually succeeding Sir Daniel Donne in this position in 1617. However, the Irish bishops, notably Ussher and the bishop of Meath, demanded that one of their own should fill the position, and although Ryves attempted to defend his position for some time, he eventually resigned the office, which was given to the archbishop of Dublin in 1621. Perhaps not surprisingly in the light of this dispute, Ussher had a poor opinion of Ryves, considering him dishonest.

Ryves returned to England and began to practise in the London courts in 1622. He practised in the court of delegates until 1624 but also began to take on admiralty cases, for example appearing alongside the attorney-general

against Sir Henry Mervyn and Sir William St John in April 1623. He remained one of the most prominent lawyers in the high court of the admiralty throughout the 1620s and 1630s. In July 1623 he was appointed assistant to Arthur, Lord Chichester, going to the peace conference at Cologne that was intended to solve the Palatinate crisis; Ryves was to receive 40s. a day for the service, but does not appear to have set out. Instead, he was sworn advocate-general to James I, and continued in the same position after the accession of Charles I, to whom he was additionally appointed master of requests extraordinary in June 1626. Also in 1626 he delivered the opinion on the king's right to translate bishops, and opposed the appointment of unqualified diocesan chancellors. He became a commissioner of the vice-admiralty of Dorset in 1628 and a commissioner against piracy for the Cinque Ports in 1630 and 1638, holding a similar position for Dorchester in 1631 and for Dorset in 1639. He was appointed dean of Shoreham and Croydon in 1633, and in the following year was placed on a commission to visit the schools and churches in the diocese of Canterbury. He became judge of the admiralty of Dover in 1635 and of the Cinque Ports in the following year. He last appears to have practised law in 1643, and tradition recounts that he then fought for the king, despite his age, and was wounded several times. However, no account of him has been found in various listings of royalist officers. He was knighted by the king on 19 March 1644 and in September 1648 was employed as one of the king's intermediaries in the Newport negotiations, the final abortive attempt to arrange a settlement between king and parliament before the army engineered Pride's Purge and the execution of Charles. Ryves died in London on 2 January 1652 and was buried at St Clement Danes. He had married Elizabeth Waldram (bap. 1609, d. 1673/4), a daughter of Sir Richard Waldram of Oadby, Leicestershire; her elder sister Katherine married his cousin Bruno. The marriage seems to have been childless, for neither Ryves's will, made on 31 December 1651 and proved on 5 January 1652, nor his widow's mentions any surviving children. In his will Ryves confirmed his lifelong royalism by referring to 430 acres in Wainfleet, Lincolnshire, that he had purchased from 'his Majesty'. One of his nephews was bequeathed a small ring, 'praying him not to measure my love by the smallness of the legacy' (will, fol. 96v).

Ryves wrote a number of historical and polemic works. *The Poore Vicars Plea* (1620) supported the claims of the Irish clergy to tithes. *Regiminis Anglicani in Hibernia defensio adversus* [*David Rothe's*] *analecten* (1624), sought to defend James I's policies in Ireland. He also published *Imperatoris Justiniani defensio adversus Alemannum* at London in 1626 and Frankfurt in 1628. His *Historia navalis antiqua, lib. iv*, published in London in 1633, incorporated the *Historia navalis, lib. i* that had been published in 1629, and went down to the creation of the Roman empire. *Historia navalis media, lib. iii* (1640) continued the history to the fall of Constantinople in 1453. In 1683 Samuel Pepys praised Ryves's *Historia navalis* in fulsome terms,

> there being not anything I know of extant in history, so much to the honour of our country as this piece of Sir

Thomas Reeves, I am sure, nor so edifying to me upon the subject which above all others I am covetous of information in. (*Downshire MSS*, 1.18)

J. D. DAVIES

Sources B. P. Levack, *The civil lawyers in England, 1603–1641* (1973) · will, PRO, PROB 11/220, fol. 96v · *CSP dom., 1619–43* · *CSP Ire., 1611–25* · *Report on the manuscripts of the marquis of Downshire*, 6 vols. in 7, HMC, 75 (1924–95), vol. 1, p. 18 · will, PRO, PROB 11/344, fol. 76v [Elizabeth Ryves] · *IGI*
Archives PRO, High Court of Admiralty papers, HCA 24/79–98 · PRO, state papers, domestic, and Irish, SP 14/137–185 (domestic), SP 63/231–240 (Irish)
Wealth at death 430 acres at Wainfleet, Lincolnshire; also lands at Harlaxton: will, PRO, PROB 11/220, fol. 96v

Saadat Ali (*d.* 1814). *See under* Oudh, nawab wazirs of (*act.* 1754–1814).

Sabatier, John (*d.* 1779/80), silk weaver, was baptized Jean Sabatier, the son of Jean Sabatier (*d.* 1745), a silk weaver. His date and place of birth are unknown; the family arrived in England as Huguenot refugees and settled in the district of Spitalfields on the eastern flank of the City of London. The younger John Sabatier (known outside his community by the Anglicized form of his name) was apprenticed to his father in 1719, and took his freedom in the Weavers' Company, of which he became a liveryman in 1743. He was living at 16 Princes Street when he married on 1 June 1736 Susanne Pouget (*c.*1718–1798), also a foreign-born Huguenot refugee; the couple had several children, but most died in infancy and only two sons and two daughters outlived their father.

The Sabatiers were among the small class of weavers of flowered silks, damasks, brocades, and velvets, acknowledged as highly skilled craftsmen and relatively wealthy. In 1745, when the army of the Young Pretender was marching towards London, Sabatier was one of the loyal weavers willing to take up arms in defence of the king—he offered thirty-four men, a gesture which in the event was not needed. He appears to have traded independently from the late 1740s, probably after his father's death, running fifty looms, which, with four men to a loom, suggests that he was employing 200 men. During this time he was exporting silks to the value of £2000 to £3000 from Chester to Ireland. Sabatier was a major customer of the designer Anna Maria Garthwaite from 1747 to 1756, and bought some ninety designs from her. He ran several types of loom, producing the fabrics known as tabbies, tobines, satins, and damasks. Between 1750 and 1757 he took as a partner David Delavau; they had some hundred looms, and took orders from most of the leading London mercers. But this was the height of their prosperity, and, as Sabatier testified to the parliamentary commissions of 1750, 1765, and 1766, the Spitalfields trade was severely hit by imported silks. He himself reduced the number of looms to eighty in 1764 when he ceased to receive orders for the spring trade in lighter fabrics, and to forty-eight by the time of his testimony, and even so he had not disposed of the heavier winter stock woven the previous year.

From 1749 Sabatier regularly attended meetings of his local vestry of Christchurch, and in the 1750s he served as auditor, commissioner, and treasurer on several of the committees which ran local affairs. In 1752–3 he was among those actively promoting a bill in parliament for the erection of a parish workhouse to relieve unemployment; when the act was passed he served as one of the overseeing governors and directors. He was a director of the French protestant hospital and an elder of the French church in Threadneedle Street in the City.

Sabatier leased various properties according to the number of looms under his control. By 1750 he had 14 and 16 Princes Street, one or both of which later passed to Delavau. In 1755 he leased 84 Commercial Street, which he kept until his death, and also in 1755 he negotiated with the Christchurch vestry to build a property in Church Street abutting on their wall. He retained a number of London properties when he retired, probably about 1777, to a fine house in East Street, Chichester, Sussex, where he died, either late in 1779 or early in 1780. His wife, Susanne, died on 1 July 1798 and was buried at St Peter-the-Less, Chichester.

ANITA MCCONNELL

Sources *JHC*, 30 (1765–6), 208, 724–5 · P. A. Bezodis, *Spitalfields and Mile End new town*, Survey of London, 27 (1957), 186, 216–17 · London Borough of Tower Hamlets Archives, Christchurch vestry minutes, 1743–55, 1754–6 · Middlesex land registry, LMA, 1755/4/67 · N. K. A. Rothstein, 'The silk industry in London, 1702–66', MA diss., U. Lond., 1961 · *LondG* (5–8 Oct 1745), 7 · *GM*, 1st ser., 68 (1798), 633 · will of Jean Sabatier, senior, proved, 2 July 1745, PRO, PROB 11/741, sig. 206 · will of J. Sabatier junior, proved, 19 Feb 1780, PRO, PROB 11/1062, sig. 106 · A. Plummer, *The London Weavers' Company, 1600–1970* (1972), 159 · Weavers' Company apprenticeships, GL, 4657A/3 · GL, Royal Exchange Insurance Co., 7253/3
Wealth at death approx. £3000: will, PRO, PROB 11/1062, sig. 106

Sabatini, Rafael (1875–1950), novelist, was born on 29 April 1875 in Jesi, Italy, the only son of Maestro-Cavaliere Vincenzo Sabatini and his English wife, Anna Trafford, both opera singers. He was educated at the *école cantonale* in Zug, Switzerland, and in Portugal at the *lycée* of Oporto and at Coimbra. He settled in England as a young man, and married Ruth Goad Dixon (*b.* 1877/8) on 9 August 1905; he became a British citizen in 1918. His first novel, *The Tavern Knight*, was published in 1904, and for the next forty-five years his books appeared with almost annual regularity to an increasingly receptive public, while his short stories found a ready market in popular magazines. He was adept at using the same basic plot in various forms, and a number of his short stories were eventually expanded into full-length novels.

Sabatini's early work showed the influence of the late Victorian romancers, Stanley Weyman in particular. As his writing matured and he acquired that extensive knowledge of European history which informed all his work, he developed a highly distinctive narrative technique in which the romantic element, while always present, was often the handmaiden of the history which was his passion. Fiction was his forte, but he also produced two notable historical works: *The Life of Cesare Borgia* (1912), and *Torquemada and the Spanish Inquisition* (1913). There was biography too: *Heroic Lives* (1934), and three volumes of short studies, *The Historical Nights' Entertainments* (1918,

1919, and 1938), in which he investigated numerous historical controversies and personalities. He wrote six plays, none of which proved as popular as his books.

It was while Sabatini was serving in War Office intelligence during the First World War that he had his first major success, with *The Sea Hawk* (1915), a swashbuckler *par excellence* about an Elizabethan Englishman who becomes a leader of Barbary corsairs. It established Sabatini not only as a leading historical novelist, but as the foremost exponent of the pirate story, a reputation confirmed in 1922 with *Captain Blood*, and its two sequels, *The Chronicles of Captain Blood* (1931), and *The Fortunes of Captain Blood* (1936).

In *Captain Blood* Sabatini demonstrated his mastery of the art of blending fiction with soundly researched historical fact. It is based on two real lives, that of Henry Pitman, an English surgeon who escaped to the West Indies after being condemned by Judge George Jeffreys for complicity in the Monmouth rising, and of Sir Henry Morgan, whose piratical exploits Sabatini adapted from Alexander Esquemelin's firsthand account, *The Buccaneers of America*, and attributed to his fictional hero, Dr Peter Blood. He used this technique time and again—'history disguised as fiction', as his publicists called it, not unjustly, for if he took occasional liberties with the letter of historic truth, he was never false to its spirit. The backgrounds to his stories, the detail of customs and manners, no less than the greater matters of politics, religion, and warfare, were as accurate as long study and careful research could make them.

Scaramouche (1921), which is rivalled only by *Captain Blood* as Sabatini's most popular work, is a case in point. The story of a young lawyer who, in pursuit of vengeance on a murderous aristocrat, becomes in turn a political agitator, an itinerant actor, and a fencing-master, provides a genuinely instructive survey of the early days of the French Revolution; it also earned Sabatini a curious accolade. He was meticulous about opening and closing sentences, and Yale University inscribed on a college building the first words of *Scaramouche*: 'He was born with a gift of laughter, and a sense that the world was mad.'

While there were few periods from the thirteenth century to the Victorian era which Sabatini did not touch, the French Revolution was one of his favourite settings, as was Renaissance Italy. Nowhere was he more at home than among the *condottieri*, whose subtleties and stratagems were reflected in his own ingenious plots, and if there was a historic figure he admired, perhaps to excess, it was Cesare Borgia.

In 1927 Sabatini's son and namesake, Rafael, was killed in a car accident, and in 1932 Sabatini and his wife were divorced. On 5 March 1935 he married Christine, *née* Wood (*b.* 1891/2), formerly the wife of Hugh Wainwright Dixon. They made a home for themselves at Clock Mills, Clifford, Herefordshire, where Sabatini enjoyed fishing in the River Wye, although he also retained his memberships at the Garrick, Savage, and Author's clubs in London.

The success which Sabatini's books enjoyed was immensely enhanced by motion pictures. *The Sea Hawk*, *Scaramouche*, and *Bardelys the Magnificent* were made into successful silent films, but it was with the sound version of *Captain Blood* (1935), starring the fledgeling Errol Flynn, that Sabatini reached a worldwide audience. There followed *The Black Swan* (1942), and remakes of *The Sea Hawk* (1940) and *Scaramouche* (1952), featuring such leading players as Tyrone Power, George Sanders, Flora Robson, and Stewart Granger.

Sabatini's popularity did little for his literary reputation. The critical establishment tended to dismiss him as a romantic swashbuckler, but he was admired and respected by fellow authors for his mastery of narrative and plot construction, the accuracy of his character studies (among them a merciless portrait of Frederick the Great in *King in Prussia*, another of James I in *The Minion*, and memorable cameos of Wellington, Elizabeth I, Danton, Drake, Henry VIII, and many others), and his inimitable style. It was urbane, sardonic, faintly academic, and occasionally elaborate, but always clear, the style of a man who knows exactly what he is talking about and assumes, without condescension, that his reader knows too. These were virtues enough to set against the charge of romanticism, but his greatest gift was the ability to bring the past to life in vivid and convincing colours, and to enthuse millions of readers with his own love of history.

'Admirers who met Sabatini in the flesh found a tall, well-built, likable, approachable and unaffected man with reddish hair, flashing hazel eyes, and the features of one of his own Cesares' (Kunitz and Haycraft, 1218). Sabatini died after a skiing accident on 13 February 1950 at the Nevada Palace Hotel, Adelboden, Switzerland. He was survived by his wife, Christine.

GEORGE MacDONALD FRASER

Sources DNB · *The Times* (14 Feb 1950) · L. Henderson, ed., *Twentieth-century romance and historical writers*, 2nd edn (1990) · S. J. Kunitz and H. Haycraft, eds., *Twentieth century authors: a biographical dictionary of modern literature* (1942) · m. certs. · d. cert. · *CGPLA Eng. & Wales* (1951)

Archives University of Bristol Library, corresp. and literary papers | BL, corresp. with Society of Authors, Add. MS 56797

Wealth at death £49,011 4s.: probate, 26 Jan 1951, *CGPLA Eng. & Wales*

Sabie, Francis (*fl.* 1587–1596), poet, was a schoolmaster at Lichfield in 1587. He published three volumes of verse: two in 1595 and one in 1596. His earliest publication, in two parts, was entitled *The Fisher-Mans Tale: of the Famous Actes, Life, and Love of Cassander, a Grecian Knight* (1595), and *Flora's Fortune: the Second Part and Finishing of the 'Fisher-Mans Tale'* (1595). The work was a paraphrase in blank verse of *Pandosto: the Triumph of Time* (afterwards renamed *Dorastus and Fawnia*), a romance by Robert Greene. The first part was dedicated to Henry Mordaunt, and the second to Frances Tresham (who was later involved in Essex's rebellion and the Gunpowder Plot). Both were from Catholic Northamptonshire families and in the dedications Sabie talks of the benefits he and his parents had received from the dedicatees and their families.

Later in 1595 there appeared *Pan's pipe: three pastorall eglogues in English hexameter, with other poetical verses delightfull*. The prose epistle 'To all youthful gentlemen, apprentises, favourers of the divine arte of sense-delighting poesie' is signed 'F. S.'. Greg described this work as the first attempt in English at writing original eclogues in the Virgilian metre, and added 'the injudicious experiment has not, I believe, been repeated' (W. W. Greg, *Pastoral Poetry and Pastoral Drama*, 1906, 114). Sabie's sources were Mantuan, Ovid, and Virgil, all books that were used in teaching at the time.

Sabie's third work, *Adams Complaint; The Olde Worldes Tragedie; David and Bathsheba*, contained three versifications of scripture written in popular secular genres. The first, 'Adams Complaint', took the form of a divine mirror, a genre popularized by the *Mirror for Magistrates* (1559) in particular, in which a ruler laments his fall from greatness and warns of the instability of human affairs. 'The Olde Worldes Tragedie' was a short epic, and 'David and Bathsheba' an erotic epyllion (short narrative poem about love), written in the same metre as Shakespeare's *Lucrece* (1594). The volume was dedicated to the Bishop of Peterborough, Richard Howland.

Sabie's son Edmond was apprenticed to Robert Cullen, a London stationer, on 12 June 1587 and was admitted a freeman on 5 August 1594.

SIDNEY LEE, *rev.* ELERI LARKUM

Sources Arber, *Regs. Stationers*, 2.146 · J. W. Bright and W. P. Mustard, 'Pan's pipe: three pastoral eclogues, with other verses by Francis Sabie (1595)', *Modern Philology*, 7 (1909–10), 433–64 · L. B. Campbell, *Divine poetry and drama in sixteenth-century England* (1959)

Sir Edward Sabine (1788–1883), by Stephen Pearce, 1850

Sabine, Sir Edward (1788–1883), army officer and physicist, was born in Great Britain Street, Dublin, on 14 October 1788, the last of the five sons (and nine children) of Joseph Sabine and his wife, Sarah Hunt, who died within a month of his birth. She was the daughter of Rowland Hunt of Boreatton Park, Shropshire.

Military career The males of Sabine's family had long served in the military. His great-grandfather Joseph *Sabine (1661–1739) had been a general in William III's campaigns in the Low Countries and elsewhere on the continent. Sabine's own military career began at fourteen when he entered the Royal Military Academy at Woolwich. He was commissioned as a second lieutenant in the Royal Artillery in December 1803, a reflection of the military need at the time. He was assigned to Gibraltar in 1804 and subsequently to various stations in England until 1813. He was then promoted second captain and sent to Quebec, where he served for three years and fought in the defence of that citadel, and in the Niagara campaign, against American incursions. Sabine ultimately achieved the rank of general in 1870, although he served in the field only once more, in Ireland in the 1830s. This military service, nevertheless, accustomed Sabine to discipline and provided him with important contacts in the government, both of which were most important in the career he developed in science.

With the end of fighting in North America and of the Napoleonic Wars in 1815, Sabine, like many British officers, turned his attention to science and exploration. He was introduced to London scientific society and to ornithology by his eldest brother, Joseph *Sabine (1770–1837), who had been a founding member of the Linnean Society in 1798 and who became an active officer of both the horticultural and zoological societies. Through his brother-in-law Henry Browne he met the surveyor and scientific instrument designer Captain Henry Kater FRS and others interested in sciences of the earth. Browne also provided Sabine with his first magnetic instruments and instruction.

Exploration With the recommendation of the Royal Society of London, Sabine was assigned in 1818 to serve as astronomer on John Ross's expedition in search of the north-west passage. Sabine's scientific assignments were broad. He was to determine latitude and longitude, to measure the direction and intensity of the earth's magnetism and the force of gravity, to observe atmospheric refraction and aurorae, and to make observations of tides, currents, temperature and salinity of seawater, and of bottom sediments, which might provide valuable clues to a seaway. He was also to assist in natural history. This voyage strongly affected the rest of Sabine's career. Although his first articles concerned Arctic birds and the Inuit, gravity, geomagnetism, and aurorae came to dominate his research. The expedition ended in a quarrel in print between John Ross and Sabine over the latter's assignments and over credit for the work he had done.

Sabine sailed to the Arctic again in 1819–20 under command of William Edward Parry on the first British expedition to overwinter, making magnetic observations all the while. In the Arctic Sabine made measurements with

Parry and James Clark Ross. His publications from Parry's expedition earned him the Copley medal of the Royal Society in 1821. His magnetic survey of the British Isles with J. C. Ross in the 1830s continued activities begun on the Arctic coast.

One other person he met in connection with these voyages became his long-term patron. John Barrow, then second secretary of the Admiralty and soon to be secretary, had endorsed the proposal that Sabine be elected a fellow of the Royal Society in 1818. After the first expedition Sabine and Barrow agreed in criticizing John Ross's leadership. Barrow thereafter supported Sabine and his projects both in the Admiralty and at the Royal Society. Indeed, Sabine, though still an army officer, enjoyed unusual access to naval facilities.

Geodesy Sabine continued his activity in expeditionary science in the 1820s with several geodetic projects. In 1821 to 1823 he sailed to locations in the south Atlantic Ocean and Caribbean and then as far north as Spitsbergen to measure variation in the gravitational force using a standardized (seconds) pendulum. The intent was to use the variation of gravity to derive a precise value of the ellipticity of the planet. Sabine obtained a value of 1/288.7, compared with 1/806 proposed by Pierre Simon de Laplace. Although Charles Babbage later severely criticized Sabine's observations as too good to be true, Sabine defended his measurements and procedures, and published his pendulum observations and calculations, along with hydrographic, meteorological, and magnetic intensity results, in 1825. Other results from these expeditions included water temperatures at depth, evidence of the Gulf Stream on European coasts, mountain height determinations, and the length of an arc of the meridian at Spitsbergen. Sabine received the French National Institute's Lalande gold medal in 1826 for the pendulum results in particular. Clearly, the central subject of his research had become the physical investigation of the earth.

In 1825 Sabine and John Herschel were commissioned, along with two French scientists, to measure the longitude difference between the Paris and Greenwich observatories. This datum was critical for standardizing both astronomical and geophysical researches. In 1827 and 1829 Sabine compared gravity pendulums and magnetometers at the Paris and Altona (Hamburg) observatories, in concert with François Arago and Heinrich Schumacher. This allowed scientists to correlate gravity and magnetic measurements based on different standards. It also put Sabine in direct contact with the most prominent earth scientists and astronomers in the world.

Simultaneously with these researches Sabine had begun to participate in the administration of science, especially at the Royal Society. As his brother had worked with other scientific societies Edward became a secretary of the Royal Society and a member of its council. He also strengthened his connections with prominent individuals in the army and Admiralty. His supporters now included Francis Beaufort, hydrographer to the Admiralty. Much of his work in the 1820s was supported by these

institutions. Sabine's ability to build support for his research projects in several organizations simultaneously was noteworthy.

Sabine, however, was no reformer. He accepted the paternalistic favouritism in the Royal Society against which Babbage railed, and to counter which John Herschel's friends mounted his presidential candidacy in 1830. When the board of longitude was eliminated in 1828 and replaced by a board of three scientific advisers, Herschel and Henry Kater declined appointment: Sabine accepted; where they saw unjustifiable patronage, he saw opportunity. He was moreover slow to see any value in the British Association for the Advancement of Science, joining only in 1835. His reputed charm and organizational ability, however, redeemed him. Once in, Sabine quickly established himself, published almost annually in the association's reports, attended annual meetings, served on committees, and became a general secretary in 1839, a post he held for twenty years, excepting 1852, when he was president. Meanwhile, his influence at the Royal Society grew apace. He had been secretary in 1827–9. In 1845 he became foreign secretary, acknowledgement of his widely distributed contacts from terrestrial research. In 1850 he was elected treasurer and vice president. The pinnacle of his institutional activity was his election to the presidency of the society, which lasted from 1861 to 1871. He resigned under allegation of autocratic behaviour.

The magnetic crusade Sabine's most ambitious organizational activity lay outside the individual institutions and societies in which he participated and drew on the resources of all of them: the magnetic crusade. In the 1830s Sabine began working towards an extensive co-operative project that was meant to yield a new level of understanding of the earth's magnetism. On one level this project required massive quantities of data. It was truly a global project. On another level the true cause of geomagnetism and the laws governing its phenomena were sought. On yet a third the magnetic crusade required investments for facilities, instruments, and personnel never before made for one scientific project. This required political support in the Royal Society, the British Association, the Admiralty and Ordnance, and in parliament. Sabine built this coalition beginning in 1835. Its culmination came in 1839 with the approval by the whig government of Lord Melbourne of J. C. Ross's Antarctic expedition and of a chain of geomagnetic observatories, primarily under Sabine's command and manned by the Royal Artillery and the navy. Sabine's extraordinary dedication to this project continued for thirty years.

Sabine's magnetic researches in the 1820s and 1830s had concentrated on discrete problems such as locating the magnetic poles. His vision, however, was becoming global. During his military posting to Ireland from 1830 to 1837 Sabine collaborated with J. C. Ross and Humphrey Lloyd in the first magnetic survey of the island in 1834. He extended this survey to Scotland in 1835 and to England in 1836. These efforts provided the foundation for a global magnetic survey, of which the magnetic crusade was a major component.

Geomagnetic theory was under serious discussion in Sabine's time. Although Sabine was not a significant theorist, he played a role. In 1835 he published the first account in English of Christopher Hansteen's theory that the earth's magnetism can be explained by means of two magnetic axes, both of which are in motion. Sabine carefully emphasized that Hansteen did not assert the physical reality of these axes. By 1839 Carl Friedrich Gauss had developed a radically different mathematical theory of the distribution of earth's magnetism which disavowed any and all thoughts of axes. Sabine distrusted Gauss's more advanced mathematics, but was assured by colleagues that it was sound. Both theories, in Sabine's estimation, served primarily as guides to further efforts to delineate what he termed the system of terrestrial magnetism.

One of Sabine's most important contributions was to publish an extended series of articles that laid out this system. This was a work of compilation, drawing on the work of many observers. His first entry in this series was a report on magnetic intensity measurements made around the world. Published in the British Association *Report* for 1836, these data were used by Gauss in his calculations. Between 1840 until 1878 Sabine published fifteen numbered (and several un-numbered) 'Contributions to terrestrial magnetism' in the *Philosophical Transactions of the Royal Society*. These drew specifically on the results of the British geomagnetic observatories and expeditions. That Sabine was able to accomplish such a feat before the advent of electronic computers was due to his management of an office of clerks at the Royal Military Academy at Woolwich. That he could maintain the funding for this office and manage its output speaks volumes for him as a scientific administrator. Although Sabine's preoccupation with data has been disparaged as naively inductive, in fact these 'Contributions' constitute the first global set of magnetic data with any claim to comprehensiveness. This effort provided a model for Sabine's successors in geomagnetic research, especially for Louis Agricola Bauer, who conducted a more extensive world magnetic survey through the Carnegie Institution of Washington in the twentieth century.

Sabine was also a pioneer in the analysis of data from the magnetic observatories, in an attempt to discover periodic phenomena. His methods sometimes did not meet later standards of statistical analysis, and his confidence in his results was sometimes exaggerated. Nevertheless, his investigations of atmospheric tides due to the moon, of periodicities in the occurrence of magnetic storms, and of periodicities in aurorae helped to open new problem areas in geophysics and in solar–terrestrial relations. Perhaps his best-known result of this type was his discovery that the eleven-year sunspot cycle is also seen in various geomagnetic phenomena.

Sabine's chief fault had the same origin as his major successes: his dogged pursuit of his goals and his urge to control the entire enterprise. His observers at the colonial observatories complained that he reduced them to mere data gatherers and allowed them no role in drawing conclusions from their researches. His colleague Humphrey Lloyd expressed the same concern as early as 1840. Moreover, once the observatory system was established, Sabine solidified his control. He attempted to exclude other scientists or tried to direct their research. George Biddell Airy at the Royal Observatory at Greenwich was a particular adversary to Sabine's activities. Sabine succeeded in having the original three-year duration of the colonial observatory network extended until the early 1850s, but could continue them no longer. To extend his control he redefined Kew observatory as the central geophysical observatory in his network. That made Kew a challenge to Airy, who had started a magnetic department in 1838, and been making continuous measurements since 1847. Worse, as president of the Royal Society, Sabine was chairman of the board of visitors to the Royal Observatory. Airy was used to dominating his visitors, and in 1862 had Sabine excluded from the board after Sabine had suggested that Kew's results compared favourably to Greenwich's (Airy, 248). In 1864, when Kew claimed its magnetometers as a standard model, Airy used his report to infer that its results derived from unfairly treated observations. Since the report was written without checking the allegation with Kew before the visitors were asked to endorse and share responsibility for it, Sabine appealed to John Couch Adams, as the only visitor whom Airy might heed, to intervene. When Adams did not reply Sabine chided him with his duty as a Royal Society council member (E. Sabine to J. C. Adams, 19 and 27 Sept 1864; 14 Nov 1864; G. B. Airy to J. P. Gassiot, 13 Nov 1864). Airy was obliged to agree to an exchange of observers which proved the long series of Greenwich observations flawed. He backed down via a grudging admission to his friend J. P. Gassiot, who, as a visitor, could mediate. Kew maintained its centrality.

Sabine had one significant partner who never wavered: his wife, Elizabeth Juliana Leeves (1807–1879), whom he married in 1826. Elizabeth translated two books by Alexander von Humboldt, whom Edward especially admired. Her translation of Humboldt's *Cosmos* appeared in four volumes between 1849 and 1858, for which Sabine wrote the introduction and notes. Her translations of Humboldt's *Aspects of Nature* (1850), of François Arago's *Meteorological Essays* (1855), and of Ferdinand von Wrangel's *Narrative of an Expedition to the Polar Sea* (1840) were also joint productions. The Sabines had no children.

Edward Sabine received many awards and honours for his scientific work. In addition to the Copley medal and the Lalande gold medal he received the Royal Society's Royal medal in 1849 for his geomagnetic writings. He was made DCL of Oxford and LLD of Cambridge (1855), and KCB in 1869. The Royal Society *Catalogue of Scientific Papers* lists 103 publications, but this does not include the hundreds of pages he wrote in the publications of the colonial magnetic observatories or the several books which he published. He, moreover, contributed far more than mere reporting of data and calculations. His occasional articles, his literature reviews, and his presidential addresses to the Royal Society and to the British Association kept others abreast of developments in terrestrial physics in the critical decades of the mid-nineteenth century when the earth sciences were taking form.

Sabine's involvement in scientific research and administration slowed considerably after his resignation from the presidency of the Royal Society in 1871. In 1876, in his eighty-eighth year, his mental capacities declined significantly. He died at his home, The Laurels, Queen's Road, Richmond, Surrey, on 26 June 1883. He was buried in the family vault at Tewin, Hertfordshire.

GREGORY A. GOOD

Sources [J. H. Lefroy], 'Memoir of General Sir Edward Sabine', *Minutes of the Proceedings of the Royal Artillery Institution*, 12 (1883), 381–96 · J. Georgi, 'Edward Sabine, ein grosser Geophysiker des 19. Jahrhunderts', *Deutsche hydrographische Zeitschrift*, 11 (1959), 225–39 · G. A. Good, 'Geomagnetism: theories in the nineteenth century', *Sciences of the earth: an encyclopedia of events, people, and phenomena*, ed. G. A. Good, 1 (1998), 350–57 · J. Cawood, 'The magnetic crusade: science and politics in early Victorian Britain', *Isis*, 70 (1979), 493–518 · N. Reingold, 'Sabine, Edward', *DSB* · *DNB* · G. B. Airy, *Autobiography of Sir George Biddell Airy*, ed. W. Airy (1896) · E. Sabine, letters to J. C. Adams, St John Cam., Adams MSS, Box 5 · G. B. Airy, letters to J. P. Gassiot, 1864, St John Cam., Adams MSS, Box 5 · *CGPLA Eng. & Wales* (1883) · election certificate, RS
Archives CUL, papers · Devon RO, corresp. · Meteorological Office, Bracknell, Berkshire, National Meteorological Library and Archive, corresp. relating to meteorological office and Kew observatory · Plymouth and West Devon RO, diary · PRO, corresp. and papers, BJ3 · RS, corresp. · Scott Polar RI, journal · Wellcome L., ornithological papers | Bin Castle Archives, Offaly, letters to third and fourth earls of Rosse · BL, letters to Sir Roderick Murchison, Add. MS 46128 · Castle Ashby, Northamptonshire, letters to Lord Northampton · CUL, corresp. with Sir George Airy · CUL, corresp. with Sir George Stokes, etc. · Inst. EE, letters to Michael Faraday · Inst. EE, corresp. with Sir Francis Ronalds · Mitchell L., Glas., Glasgow City Archives, letters to James Smith · NHM, corresp. with Sir Richard Owen and William Clift · NMM, Greenwich, Royal Observatory, George Biddell Airy MSS · NMM, Greenwich, Royal Observatory, Humphrey Lloyd MSS · PRO, corresp. with Balfour Stewart, BJ1 · Ransom HRC, corresp. with Sir John Herschel · RBG Kew, letters to Sir William Hooker · Royal Institution of Great Britain, London, letters to Sir William Grove · Royal Institution of Great Britain, London, letters to John Tyndall · RS, corresp. with Sir John Herschel · RS, corresp. with Edward Sabine · RS, Gassiot committee MSS · RS, Humphrey Lloyd MSS · RS, letters to Sir John Lubbock · Sci. Mus., corresp. with Thomas Andrews · Staats- und Universitätsbibliothek, Göttingen, letters to Göttingen Academy of Sciences · Trinity Cam., letters to William Whewell · U. St Andr. L., corresp. with James Forbes · UCL, letters to William Sharpey
Likenesses S. Pearce, oils, 1850, NPG [*see illus.*] · T. H. Maguire, prints, 1851, BM, NPG; repro. in T. H. Maguire, *Portraits of honorary members of the Ipswich Museum* (1852) · S. Pearce, oils, 1855, RS · J. Durham, marble bust, 1859, RS · G. F. Watts, oils, 1874, Royal Artillery Mess, Woolwich · S. Pearce, group portrait, oils (*The Arctic council, 1851*), NPG · W. Walker, photograph, NPG
Wealth at death £21,180 13s. 6d.: probate, 10 July 1883, *CGPLA Eng. & Wales*

Sabine, Joseph (1661–1739), army officer, came from a family of English settlers in Ireland. He was the second of the six sons (five of whom appear to have served with the army under William III) of Joseph Sabine, a landowner of Kilmolin, co. Wicklow, who married an English heiress by the name of Rawlins. On 8 March 1689 he was appointed lieutenant in Colonel Sir Henry Ingoldsby's regiment, raised that year for William's campaign in Ireland, and he was made captain of the grenadier company before 18 October 1689. Owing to losses the regiment was disbanded on 9 January 1690. On 13 July 1691 Sabine was made major in the late Colonel Charles Herbert's regiment of foot (later the Royal Welch Fusiliers, 23rd foot). The 23rd returned from Ireland to England in 1692 and did not see active service in Flanders until 1694. Sabine was promoted lieutenant-colonel on 6 July 1695, during which year the regiment played a prominent part in the siege of Namur, suffering heavy losses in the successful attack on the French counterscarp on the night of 17 July.

After the treaty of Ryswick (1697) the regiment was stationed in Ireland until the renewal of war, when the 23rd, under the command of Brigadier-General Ingoldsby, left from Carrickfergus on 1 July 1701. On 5 April 1700 Sabine married Hester, the daughter of Henry Whitfield, of Bishop's Stortford, Hertfordshire, in the church of St Peter and St Kevin, Dublin. They had three sons, all of whom died young. Sabine served with his regiment in Flanders throughout the War of the Spanish Succession, and was made brevet colonel in 1703. He was wounded in the attack upon the heights of Schellenberg on 2 July 1704, yet commanded the regiment at the following battle of Blenheim, on 13 August 1704. On 1 April 1705, following Ingoldsby's transfer to the colonelcy of the 18th Royal Irish regiment, Sabine was made full colonel of the regiment, which he commanded at Ramillies (1706). He was promoted brigadier-general on 1 January 1707 and in 1708 commanded the force of ten regiments which sailed from Ostend to Tynemouth to thwart the Pretender's plans to land on the Northumberland coast. Upon his return to Flanders, Sabine distinguished himself greatly in that year's campaign: first on 30 June, at the battle of Oudenarde, where at the head of his brigade he captured or destroyed seven Swiss battalions in the attack on the village of Heynem; and later at the siege of Lille, where on 27 August he commanded a force of 2000 men drawn from English regiments which suffered heavy losses in gaining a lodgement on the French counterscarp. Further assaults in early September caused the town to capitulate, and the citadel fell on 28 November.

On 17 March 1710 Sabine married Margaretta (1683–1750), the youngest daughter of Charles Newsham, of Chadshunt, Warwickshire; they had at least nine children, including twin daughters born in 1716.

On 1 January 1710 Sabine was made major-general and in July 1712 he was appointed to command the citadel of Ghent. During this time he was instrumental in crushing a mutiny which broke out among the garrison. On 9 July he received information which led him to send for Brigadier Sutton's dragoons, who together with loyal troops crushed the mutiny. Seven ringleaders were put to death after full evidence and the garrison was marched round the dead bodies. A general pardon was then read at the head of each regiment. Sabine remained at Ghent until some months after the peace of Utrecht in 1713. The magistrates of the town presented him with a silver basin and ewer in recognition of his office. His commission as major-general was renewed by George I in 1714 and his regiment, now reduced and renamed the Prince of Wales's Own Royal Welch Fusiliers, was stationed in Ireland. During the Jacobite rising in 1715 they were sent to Chester to relieve forces sent north, and thereafter were garrisoned at Hereford.

Sabine joined the duke of Argyll's staff as major-general at Stirling in early January 1716 and commanded a brigade of four regiments in the march towards the Pretender's army at Perth. The Jacobite forces withdrew and in the ensuing chase Sabine was ordered on 2 February, with three battalions of foot and supporting dragoons, to Aberbrothwick, and later, on 8 February, to Peterhead, in an attempt to intercept the retreating Jacobite cavalry. In the aftermath of the rising, following the return to London in April 1716 of the British commander-in-chief, Cadogan, Sabine was left in command of the army in Scotland. In July 1717 the duke of Atholl complained of 'the conduct of General Sabine and other officers in regard to rebel prisoners … and of the plundering and other impositions made by the troops' (*Atholl MSS*, 71). In 1719 Sabine was made governor of Berwick Castle.

In 1722, with Brigadier-General Thomas Stanwix, Sabine was appointed to examine the reduced officers and outpatients of Chelsea Hospital. In 1723, as honorary colonel, he carried out the annual review of his regiment at Inverness on its way to take up garrison duty at Fort William. His nephew Lieutenant-Colonel Newsham Peers, acting colonel of the regiment, succeeded to the full colonelcy upon Sabine's death.

In addition to the family's estate in Kilcullen, co. Kildare, in 1715 Sabine purchased the house and estate of Tewin in Hertfordshire. In the following year, at a cost of £40,000, he 'rebuilt the House and all the offices, in magnificent manner, and improved the gardens' (Salmon, 59); it was twice visited by George II.

From 1727 to 1734 Sabine was MP in the government interest for Berwick, where he also remained governor until 1730. In March 1727 he was made lieutenant-general and in July 1730 was promoted full general. During 1730 he was sent to Gibraltar as governor, and he died there on 24 October 1739, aged seventy-eight. His remains were buried at Tewin church, where a memorial stands to his name. He was survived by seven of his children; among his descendants were the natural historian Joseph Sabine and the army officer and physicist Sir Edward Sabine.

JONATHAN SPAIN

Sources W. H. W. Sabine, *Sabin(e): the history of an ancient English surname* (1953) • HoP, *Commons, 1715–54* • A. D. L. Cary, S. McCance, and others, eds., *Regimental records of the Royal Welch Fusiliers (late the 23rd foot)*, 7 vols. (1921–) • R. Cannon, ed., *Historical record of the seventh regiment, or the royal fusiliers* (1847) • D. Chandler, *Marlborough as military commander* (1973) • *Manuscripts of the duke of Atholl … and of the earl of Home*, HMC, 26 (1891), 71 • L. Melville, *The first George in Hanover and England*, 2 vols. (1905), 2.10 • N. Salmon, *History of Hertfordshire* (1728) • Venn, *Alum. Cant.* • *Old Westminsters*, vols. 1–2 • R. Clutterbuck, ed., *The history and antiquities of the county of Hertford*, 3 vols. (1815–27) • C. Dalton, ed., *English army lists and commission registers, 1661–1714*, 6 vols. (1892–1904) • P. Rae, *The history of the late rebellion* (1718) • J. Baynes, *The Jacobite rising of 1715* (1970) • IGI

Archives BL, corresp. with duke of Newcastle, Add. MSS 33770–33787 [copies] • BL, letters to the earl of Stafford, Add. MS 22211 • BL, corresp. with Lord Stafford, Add. MS 22211 • BL, letters to H. Watkins, Add. MS 33273 and MS 38852

Likenesses G. Kneller, portrait, 1711, repro. in Sabine, *Sabin(e)*; Christies, 1943 • J. Faber junior, mezzotint, pubd 1742 (after G. Kneller), BM, NPG

Sabine, Joseph (1770–1837), natural historian, eldest son of Joseph Sabine of Tewin, Hertfordshire, and brother of the astronomer Sir Edward *Sabine (1788–1883), was born at Tewin on 6 June 1770. He was educated for the bar, and practised until 1808, when he was made inspector-general of assessed taxes, a post which he retained until his retirement in 1835.

Sabine was one of the original fellows of the Linnean Society in 1798. He was elected fellow of the Royal Society on 7 November 1799, and in 1810 succeeded Richard Anthony Salisbury as honorary secretary of the Horticultural Society. He found the society's accounts in the greatest confusion, and for his success in the work of reorganization was awarded the society's gold medal in 1816. Sabine played a leading part in the establishment of the society's garden, first at Hammersmith and afterwards at Chiswick; in sending out David Douglas and others as collectors; in starting local societies in connection with the Horticultural Society; and in growing and distributing new and improved varieties of flowers, fruits, and vegetables throughout the country. He contributed forty papers to the *Transactions* of the society. These, among other subjects, dealt with paeonies, passion flowers, magnolias, dahlias, roses, chrysanthemums, crocuses, and tomatoes.

Sabine's management of the society's affairs, which he ruled despotically, ultimately became unsatisfactory. A too sanguine view of its future led him to incur debts of more than £18,000. In 1830 a committee of inquiry was appointed, a vote of censure was threatened, and he resigned. He afterwards took an active part in the work of the Zoological Society, of which he was treasurer and vice-president, adding many animals to their collection. He was a recognized authority on British birds, their moulting, migration, and habits.

Sabine died at his home in Mill Street, Hanover Square, London, on 24 January 1837, and was buried in Kensal Green cemetery on 1 February. His name was commemorated by de Candolle in the leguminous genus *Sabinea*. He contributed a list of plants to Clutterbuck's *History of Hertfordshire* (1815), a zoological appendix to Sir John Franklin's *Narrative* (1823), and four papers to the *Transactions of the Linnean Society*, one dealing with a species of gull from Greenland, and another with North American marmots.

G. S. BOULGER, *rev.* ALEXANDER GOLDBLOOM

Sources Desmond, *Botanists*, rev. edn, 602 • *GM*, 2nd ser., 7 (1837), 435–6 • *Catalogue of scientific papers*, Royal Society, 5 (1871), 354–5 • J. Britten and G. S. Boulger, eds., *A biographical index of British and Irish botanists* (1893) • S. Maunder, *The biographical treasury*, new edn, rev. W. L. R. Cates (1870)

Archives Devon RO, corresp. · Linn. Soc., letters | Royal Horti-
cultural Society, London, corresp. with David Don · Yale U., Bei-
necke L., Osborn collection, letters to Thomas Gibbs
Likenesses W. Drummond, lithograph (after E. U. Eddis), BM,
NPG; repro. in *Athenaeum Portraits* · W. Read, engraving (after E. U.
Eddis), RS · Miss Turner, lithograph (after E. Rigby), BM

Sabini, (Charles) Darby (1889–1950), gang leader, was a
prominent figure on racecourses during the 1920s and
1930s, but little is known about his origins. His father was
Italian and his mother was Irish, and he was born in Saffron Hill, Clerkenwell, London. When he was two his
mother was widowed, but she and her six sons continued
to live in London's Little Italy—Saffron Hill. At thirteen
Sabini left school and became involved with Dan Sullivan,
a boxing promoter. Sabini was a promising fighter but he
disliked the arduous training and became a bouncer at
Sullivan's promotions in Hoxton Baths. His reputation as
a hard man was established in 1920 in a bar brawl at the
Griffin public house in Saffron Hill. A notorious enforcer
for a gang from south London insulted an Italian barmaid:
Sabini knocked him out and gained status as the protector
both of Italians and women.

Protection rackets At this time the racecourses of southern
England were preyed on by gangs extorting money from
bookmakers. The main group was the Brummagem Boys,
led by **William Kimber** (*fl.* 1900–1930), known as Billy. He
described himself as a bookmaker and punter (better on
horse-races) from Bordesley in Birmingham, but he was
really a gang leader. Since the late 1800s 'roughs' from Birmingham had terrorized many racecourses, and especially those in the south of England, and in the early twentieth century it seems that they were joined by others
from south London.

The Birmingham gang was not a firm grouping under
the tight control of Kimber. From about 1916 'three low
blackguards, always more or less full of liquor' began to
terrify and blackmail a number of small-scale London East
End Jewish bookies (Divall, 183). After one of them was assaulted badly they turned for help to **Edward Emmanuel**
(*fl.* 1900–1930). He was regarded as 'a financial power' and
as 'the guv'nor before Darby Sabini' (Chinn, interviews
with Prince, 1). Little is known about Emmanuel's early
life but it is believed that he once worked as a market porter at Spitalfields, where he became involved in spieling
(illegal gaming activities). He came to notice in 1904 when
he threatened to shoot an Islington street trader and was
charged with possession of a loaded revolver. Emmanuel
stated he was a salesman but the magistrate declared that
he was 'a dangerous fellow' and imposed a high surety of
£250 or twelve months' imprisonment (Samuel, 316). Four
years later a John McCarthy attempted to kill Emmanuel
in east London. Both men were described as market porters. Over the next few years Emmanuel established himself as a proprietor of spielers and as a fixer of boxing
fights. It was also alleged that he was in collusion with certain police officers and that for a payment he could
arrange lighter sentences for Jewish criminals. By the
early 1920s he was regarded 'as in charge of the whole East

End underworld—or at least the Jewish part of it'
(ibid., 204).

Emmanuel 'was pally with the Italian push', Darby
Sabini's gang, and he recruited them to protect the Jewish
bookies (Chinn, interviews with Prince, 1). This action led
to protracted violence on many racecourses in southern
England, and as one Jewish bookie recalled, 'it was us
against them, the North against the South' (ibid., interview with S. Lewis, 1). On 25 March 1921 Sabini was
attacked by a mob of Brummies at Greenford Trotting
Park, and a few days later Kimber was shot when he went
to the Italian's flat to try to calm matters. The trouble
escalated and there were serious fights, but Kimber's position was weakened in June 1921 when the Brummagem
Boys attacked a coachload of bookies from Leeds, believing that the vehicle was actually used by the Sabini gang.
The Birmingham men were arrested in a pub nearby, and
the next month twenty-three of them were imprisoned. It
was believed widely that Sabini was bribing certain police
officers and by the summer of 1921 he had the upper hand
over Kimber.

Fearful of further trouble, on 23 August leading southern bookmakers formed the Bookmakers' and Backers'
Racecourse Protection Association (BBRPA; subsequently
a respected organization). The vice-president was Emmanuel, whose connection was explained by his interests in
credit betting away from the racecourses. At the inaugural
dinner of the association in December 1921 it was
explained that he was giving 'very valuable assistance'
(*Bookmakers' and Backers' Racecourse Protection Association*, 6).
This help consisted of finding eight stewards who were
each paid the large sum of £6 a week to protect bookies
who were members of the BBRPA. It seems that Edward
Emmanuel saw an opportunity to wrest control of the protection rackets on the southern racecourses from the
Brummagem Boys, and he became involved in providing
the lists of runners for various races. They were brought
out for as little as a farthing each but 'to the bookies they
were half a crown a set' (Greeno, 166).

Dominance of Sabini In 1922 Kimber acknowledged
Sabini's power on the racecourses of southern England,
but continued to operate his 'services' to bookies in the
midlands and the north, where he helped to minimize the
bullying of lesser gangs. Although Kimber's income was
gained from violence, he was called 'one of the best' by a
former chief inspector at Scotland Yard who was
employed by the racecourses to keep order at various
meetings and who was saved from a beating by Kimber
(Divall, 201). He was remembered by some Brummie
bookies as 'a game un', a fearless fighter who fought fairly
with his hands and did not use knives (Chinn, interview
with Green, 1). By the later 1920s the ageing Kimber was no
longer associated with bullying and coercion, and had
come to be 'greatly respected' by some well-known London bookmakers who had not been involved in the preceding gang wars (ibid., interview with Dell, 5–6;
Maskey, 9).

Sabini not only defeated Kimber but he also outmanoeuvred Emmanuel, forcing him to withdraw from the

racecourses—although the Jewish gangster later set up a profitable company which printed the tickets used by bookmakers as a receipt for their punters (customers). With no opposition, Sabini took over the protection rackets in the south of England which led the BBRPA to dispense with his services. However, he went on to become the leading gangster in southern England. Sabini's men provided a variety of 'services' to bookies, which they did not in fact need. These included payment for 'dots and dashes', whereby a racecard was marked to alert the bookmaker to the form of the horses and which told the bookie nothing more than he knew already; and the calling-out of the numbers allotted to the runners in a race. Bookmakers were also 'encouraged' to pay for the tools of their trade like lists of runners, stools to stand on, pieces of chalk with which to mark up the odds of the horses on a blackboard, and water with which to rub them out. Bookies were charged 2s. 6d. for each of these 'facilities', and at major meetings there could be as many as sixty bookmakers taking bets on up to eight races. In addition Sabini controlled the five or six best pitches (positions from which a bookie did business) at each meeting and put his own men on them on a 'ten bob in the pound basis' (Chinn, interview with Dell, 5). These protection rackets were highly profitable.

Racetrack controls From 1929 stringent controls by the Jockey Club and the Bookmakers' Protection Association stopped Sabini controlling the best pitches, while his other racecourse activities were combated by the police. Making less money, Sabini moved into protection rackets at greyhound tracks and at drinking and gambling clubs in the West End of London. In 1936 he lost a libel case with a newspaper and filed for bankruptcy. During the proceedings he denied that he earned at least £20,000 each year (Morton, 30). Sabini successfully thwarted challenges by other gangs, including the Cortesi brothers from within Saffron Hill and by the English Hoxton mob, but he lost his position of authority in the Second World War when he was interned as an alien on the Isle of Man. By then he had a penthouse flat in the Grand Hotel, Brighton, Sussex.

After the war Sabini settled in Hove, Sussex, and became a small bookie. Despite his wealth, in his heyday he was unostentatious. He wore a flat cap, collarless shirt, high-buttoned waistcoat, and dark suit. A later gangland boss stated that Sabini 'stood for no liberties', while a bookie remembered that 'he was the gentleman of the mob but he feared no one' (Hill, 5; Chinn, interview with Prince, 2). He was regarded by many as 'Uncle Bob', someone who was courteous to women and who was generous to children, the needy, and the local Catholic church. To others he was a ruthless gangster and extortioner. One policeman recalled that he 'and his thugs used to stand sideways on to let the bookmakers see the hammers in their pockets' (Greeno, 12). Sabini was said always to carry a loaded pistol, and he did not hesitate to order the vicious beating and razor-slashing of opponents. It is likely that he was the model for the gang leader Colleoni in Graham Greene's novel *Brighton Rock* (1938). When Sabini died at

Hove in 1950 he left little money, although his clerk was later found to have £36,000 and it was believed that this was Sabini's cash. CARL CHINN

Sources C. Chinn, *Better betting with a decent feller: bookmakers, betting and the British working class, 1750–1990* (1991) • J. Morton, *Gangland: London's underworld* (1992) • R. Samuel, *East End underworld: chapters in the life of Arthur Harding* (1981) • interviews with Sydney Lewis (Simmy Solomons), Lou Prince, Sam Dell, Charlie Maskey, Ali Harris, Dave Langham, Denny Green, Jackie Currigan, Mrs Gilliver, Mrs Lewis, Les Lewis, and Charlie Greenhill, U. Birm. L., special collections department, Carl Chinn bookmaking interviews • T. Divall, *Scoundrels and scallywags (and some honest men)* (1929) • *The Bookmakers' and Backers' Racecourse Protection Association* (1922) • E. Greeno, *War on the underworld* (1960) • 'Rival race gangs feud', *Glasgow Herald* (4 April 1921) • 'The racing feud sentences', *Glasgow Herald* (25 July 1921) • 'Blackmail charge', *Glasgow Herald* (11 Sept 1922) • B. Hill, *Boss of Britain's underworld* (1955) • 'Nutty' Sharpe, 'Fade out of the race gangs', *The Star* (4 Jan 1938) • 'Harry Sabini shot', *Daily Express* (21 Nov 1922) • 'Once again', *Banyan* [National Association of Bookmakers] (28 Nov 1936), 14 • E. T. Hart, *Britain's godfather* (1993) • 'Bookmaker shot', *The Times* (29 March 1921)

Likenesses photographs, London Borough of Islington Public Libraries Department, Local History Library

Sabran, Lewis (1652–1732), Jesuit, was born, probably in Paris, on 1 March 1652, the son of the marquis de Sabran, of the Saint-Elzear family, of the first nobility of Provence, for many years resident ambassador to the court of St James, and his English wife. He was educated in the college of the English Jesuits at St Omer, 1663–70, and entered the noviciate of the Society of Jesus at Watten on 17 September 1670. He studied at the Jesuit college at Liège from 1673 to 1675, and was ordained on 28 August 1679; he was admitted to the profession of the four solemn vows on 2 February 1688. On the accession of James II he moved to England and was appointed a royal chaplain and preacher, and on the birth of the prince of Wales on 10 June 1688 he became chaplain to the prince. At the outbreak of the revolution he was ordered (November 1688) to proceed to Portsmouth in charge of the royal infant but was afterwards directed to return to London. In endeavouring to escape to the continent, disguised as a gentleman in the suite of the Polish ambassador, he fell into the hands of a furious mob, was brutally treated, and committed to prison. He was soon liberated on the king's order, and escaped to Dunkirk.

As a result of a sermon preached by Sabran before the king at Chester on 28 August 1687 he became involved in a controversy with the anti-popish writer Edward Gee over the invocation of saints. With Gee as his chief antagonist he published three works on the subject in 1687–8. During his time in England he was also engaged in controversy with Dr William Sherlock, a prominent Anglican controversialist, then master of the Temple. Sabran has been considered the author of *Dr Sherlock Sifted from his Bran and Chaff* of 1687 (Oliver, 169) and in 1688 he published *An Answer to Dr Sherlock's Preservative* and *Dr Sherlocks Preservative Considered*. The controversy ended with the revolution, Sherlock's last word being *A Vindication: an Answer to the Cavils of Lewis Sabran* (1688).

Sabran was appointed visitor of the Jesuit province of Naples, and subsequently of the English province. On 23

June 1693 he was chosen at the triennial meeting of the province at Watten as the procurator to be sent to Rome. In 1699 the prince-bishop of Liège, by leave of the general of the order, appointed him president of the episcopal seminary in that city, since some of the staff had been accused of holding Jansenist views. He held the office until 1704, and was declared provincial of the English province. In 1712 Sabran was appointed rector (headmaster) of the college at St Omer, and about 1717 spiritual father at the English College, Rome. The letter-book which he kept as rector at St Omer is a source of much information about the college and the position of Catholics in England. He died in Rome on 22 January 1732.

THOMPSON COOPER, *rev.* GEOFFREY HOLT

Sources *The letter book of Lewis Sabran*, ed. G. Holt, Catholic RS, 62 (1971), vii–xv · Literae Annuae Societatis Jesu, Archivum Romanum Societatis Iesu, Rome, Anglia 35, fols. 114–120 · C. Dodd [H. Tootell], *The church history of England, from the year 1500, to the year 1688*, 3 (1742), 493 · H. Foley, ed., *Records of the English province of the Society of Jesus*, 5 (1879), 291–5, 1004–5; 7 (1882–3), 676 · G. Oliver, *Collections towards illustrating the biography of the Scotch, English and Irish members, SJ* (1838), 168 · A. de Backer and others, *Bibliothèque de la Compagnie de Jésus*, new edn, 7, ed. C. Sommervogel (Brussels, 1896), 358–60 · T. Jones, ed., *A catalogue of the collection of tracts for and against popery*, 2, Chetham Society, 64 (1865), 408–11, 457–8 · T. Jones, ed., *A catalogue of the collection of tracts for and against popery*, 1, Chetham Society, 48 (1859), 146 · G. Holt, *The English Jesuits, 1650–1829: a biographical dictionary*, Catholic RS, 70 (1984)

Archives Archives of the British Province of the Society of Jesus, London · English Convent, Bruges · Royal Library of Belgium, Brussels · Stonyhurst College, Lancashire · Ushaw College, Durham

Sacharissa. *See* Spencer, Dorothy, countess of Sunderland (1617–1684).

Sachellus (*fl.* 5th cent.). *See under* Connacht, saints of (*act. c.*400–*c.*800).

Sacher, Harry (1881–1971), Zionist and benefactor, was born on 3 September 1881 in London, the fifth son and the seventh child of Jacob Sacher (*b. c.*1841), a self-employed tailor, and his wife, Esther (*b. c.*1841), both of whom were Polish-born Jews and naturalized British subjects.

Sacher was educated at the Jews' Free School in Spitalfields; the Central Foundation School; University College, London; New College, Oxford, to which he won an exhibition and at which he gained a first in history; and at the universities of Berlin and Paris. From 1905 to 1909 he was a leader writer on the *Manchester Guardian* under the editorship of C. P. Scott. In 1909 he was called to the bar, but returned to the *Manchester Guardian* in 1913 and stayed until 1919.

During this period Sacher formed what was to prove one of the most important and enduring relationships of his life, a close and lasting friendship with Chaim Weizmann, the future Zionist leader who had settled in Manchester in 1904. Sacher had been a committed Zionist from the time he attended the Zionist Congress in Basel in 1903. Together with Simon Marks (later Lord Marks of Broughton) and Israel Sieff (later Lord Sieff), he formed a triumvirate that sustained Weizmann, both spiritually and financially, during the early days of Weizmann's struggle

to establish a Jewish homeland in Palestine, including funding his London office, a debt Weizmann warmly acknowledged in his autobiography, *Trial and Error* (1949).

Marks and Sieff married each other's sister, and were then engaged in building up the great business of Marks and Spencer stores. On 16 December 1915 Sacher married Miriam Marks (*b.* 1891/2), a sister of Simon Marks, and they had two sons, Michael and Gabriel, who also joined the business. Thus was created the Marks–Sieff–Sacher dynasty that not only came to make such an outstanding contribution to both British commerce and Zionist history, but was also a vital element in dislodging the leadership of the Jewish community from the reins of the 'grand dukes' to those of the 'merchant princes'.

Sacher introduced Weizmann to C. P. Scott and to another distinguished journalist colleague, Herbert Sidebotham. Scott knew many personalities of influence in English public life, and introduced Weizmann to them. Sidebotham collaborated with Sacher in publications promoting the Zionist movement, particularly in a monthly journal called *Palestine*, whose proclaimed aim was to 'reset the ancient glories of the Jewish nation in the freedom of a new British dominion in Palestine' (B. Litvinoff, ed., *The Essential Chaim Weizmann*, 1982). Sacher edited the journal, and Sidebotham wrote most of it, with occasional pieces from Sacher and Sieff.

Sacher took a prominent part in the conferences and negotiations that led to the Balfour declaration of 2 November 1917. Together with Lord Rothschild, Moses Gaster, Herbert Samuel, Sir Mark Sykes, James de Rothschild, Nahum Sokolow, Joseph Cowan, and Herbert Bentwich, Sacher was at the meeting held on 17 February 1917 at the Maida Vale home of Gaster, which Sokolow, in his *History of Zionism* (1919), called the turning point in the history of the movement. It was the first full-dress conference leading to the declaration.

In 1920 Sacher and his wife went to live in Palestine. He qualified and successfully practised at the local bar throughout the 1920s. Simultaneously, he rendered valuable service to the Zionist Organisation in Jerusalem and was editor of the *Palestine Weekly*. When, in 1927, one of the periodic crises in affairs of the Zionist Organisation arose, Sacher was appointed to the small executive set up to resolve the problem.

Upon his return to London in 1930 Sacher became a director of Marks and Spencer, a post he held until 1962. He continued to give wise counsel and generous support to the Zionist movement, and in 1948 took justifiable pride in the establishment of the state of Israel and in the election of Weizmann as its first president. Looking back on the triumph of the cause, he wrote *Israel, the Establishment of a State* (1952) and *Zionist Portraits and other Essays* (1959).

Sacher and his wife were munificent benefactors to a wide-ranging group of charities, particularly British and Israeli educational and cultural institutions. The Weizmann Institute of Science at Rehovot in Israel had his special sympathy, and in 1960 he established benefactions there in memory of C. P. Scott and Herbert Sidebotham. In 1963 the Sacher building at New College, Oxford, was opened, the first in Oxford to house graduates. Sir William Hayter, the warden of the college, described Sacher as 'the greatest benefactor the College has known since its founder, William of Wykeham' (*The Times*, 11 May 1971), and in a tribute in *The Times* Sir William said of him that 'he was the kind of benefactor that every institution would like to have, extremely generous and totally non-interfering' (13 May 1971). Many honorary university honours were bestowed upon him.

Sacher died at his London home, Flat 8, 37 Grosvenor Square, Westminster, on 10 May 1971, having suffered ill health for several years, and was survived by his wife and sons.
GERRY BLACK

Sources *The Guardian* (11 May 1971) · *The Times* (11 May 1971) · *Jewish Chronicle* (1 Sept 1961) · *Jewish Year Book* (1939–70) · C. Weizmann, *Trial and error* (1949) · I. Sieff, *Memoirs* (1970) · S. Brodetsky, *From ghetto to Israel* (1960) · A. Ruppin, *Memoirs, diaries, letters* (1971) · G. Rees, *St Michael: a history of Marks and Spencer* (1969) · WWW · m. cert. · d. cert.

Archives Marks & Spencer Company Archive, papers | Bodl. Oxf., letters to Sir A. Zimmern · JRL, letters to the *Manchester Guardian*

Wealth at death £140,867: probate, 22 June 1971, *CGPLA Eng. & Wales*

Sacheverell, Henry (*bap.* **1674**, *d.* **1724**), Church of England clergyman and religious controversialist, the third son of Joshua Sacheverell (*d.* 1684) and his wife, Susannah Smith, was baptized at St Peter's parsonage in Marlborough on 8 February 1674. Susannah was reputedly the daughter of a regicide, possibly Henry Smith, a signatory of the death warrant of Charles I. This could explain Sacheverell's later neglect of his widowed mother after he became a high-church champion of the 'king and martyr'. His paternal grandfather was also a skeleton in his cupboard, having been a Presbyterian minister ejected at the Restoration who had died in prison serving a sentence for defying the laws against nonconformist preaching. His father, however, had attended St Catharine's College, Cambridge, and entered the Church of England, and was rector of St Peter's, Marlborough, when Henry was born.

Education and early career On his father's death in 1684 Henry was adopted by his godfather, Edward Hearst, an apothecary, and his wife, Katherine. They sent him to Marlborough grammar school (1684–9) and after Hearst's death his widow sent him to Magdalen College, Oxford, where he was elected to a demyship in 1689. Although he had been officially reprimanded in his last year as an undergraduate for contumacy towards the dean of arts, he graduated with a BA in June 1693 and obtained his MA in May 1695, when the bishop of Oxford also ordained him deacon. In 1697, however, the bishop of Lichfield refused to ordain him a priest, claiming that his Latin was inadequate, a charge which Sacheverell vehemently denied. The high-church dean of Lichfield, Lancelot Addison, supported Sacheverell, who had become a friend of his own son Joseph, the writer, at Magdalen. On a second application for ordination he was successful, and took up the living of Cannock in Staffordshire. In 1701 he returned to Oxford to take up a fellowship at his old college. Despite being disliked by many of his colleagues he advanced in

Henry Sacheverell (*bap.* **1674**, *d.* **1724**), by Thomas Gibson, in or before 1710

the university, where he was granted a doctorate of divinity in 1708 at the unusually early age of thirty-four, and in Magdalen College, where he became senior dean of arts in 1708 and bursar in 1709. He was disliked for his overbearing arrogance and conceit, as well as for his drunken exploits.

Fiery preaching Sacheverell nevertheless was popular as a preacher who delivered fiery high-church sermons with a stentorian voice. One he preached at St Mary's, Oxford, in May 1702 was immediately printed as *The Political Union*. In it he urged Anglicans to have no truck with dissenters but instead to 'hang out the bloody flag and banner of defiance' (Holmes, 17). In print it circulated far from Oxford and attracted attention in London, not least that of Daniel Defoe who dubbed Sacheverell 'the bloody flag officer' and based his *Shortest Way with the Dissenters* (1702) on the style of the sermon (ibid.). Sacheverell also contributed a tract to the general election campaign of 1702, *The Character of a Low-Church-Man*. This was an attack upon the bishop of Worcester who was alleged to have published a pamphlet besmirching the character of Sir John Pakington, a tory candidate in Worcestershire. Sacheverell's defence of the knight earned him Pakington's backing for his attempt to be made chaplain to the speaker of the House of Commons, Robert Harley. Harley prudently declined the offer, the preacher's reputation as a high-church firebrand being too extreme for a moderate tory with dissenting connections. Sacheverell's anti-dissenting sentiments found expression in another pamphlet written in collaboration with two other Oxford dons in 1705: *The Rights of the Church of England Asserted and Proved*. He also continued to preach provocative sermons, including a version of his most notorious, 'In perils amongst false brethren', which he delivered in St Mary's on 23 December 1705.

While he confined his inflammatory harangues to Oxford University, a bastion of high-church toryism, Sacheverell was left alone. But when he started preaching outside the university he began to arouse more concern. In July 1706 he gave an assize sermon at Leicester, *The Nature, Obligation and Measures of Conscience*. Baron Price, informing Robert Harley of it, observed that 'Mr. Sacheverell … could not forbear giving the dissenters … a flurt' (*Portland MSS*, 4.321). In May 1709 he got a base in the capital by winning an election to a chaplaincy at St Saviour's, Southwark, in a campaign which brought his peculiar brand of invective to bear against his competitors. Ominously the doctor now had a pulpit near the centre of power. But it was another provincial assize sermon, *The Communication of Sin*, preached at Derby in 1709, that first led some whigs to consider taking proceedings against him. They took exception to a passage in the dedication to the high sheriff in which he referred to the age as one in which 'the principles and interests of our Church and Constitution are so shamefully betrayed and run down' (Madan, 18).

A sermon given to the lord mayor, aldermen, and council of London in St Paul's Church on 5 November 1709 was considered too subversive to be ignored. Such sermons normally took the opportunity to compare the Gunpowder Plot with the landing of William of Orange on 5 November 1688 as 'a double deliverance' from popery. Instead Sacheverell compared the plot not with the revolution of 1688 but with 30 January 1649, the day on which Charles I was executed; both were:

> indelible monuments of the irreconcilable rage and bloodthirstiness of both the popish and fanatick enemies of our Church and Government … These TWO DAYS indeed are but one united proof and visible testimonial of the same dangerous and rebellious principles these confederates in iniquity maintain. (Sacheverell, *The Perils of False Brethren*, 1974, 3)

He thus turned the anniversary of the Gunpowder Plot into an attack upon Catholics and dissenters. Indeed the bulk of his sermon was a rant against nonconformists. He dismissed the threat from Catholics in the first three minutes of a sermon which took about one and a half hours to deliver. The rest railed against 'sectarists and schismatics of whatsoever wild, romantic or enthusiastic notions so as to make the House of God not only a den of thieves but a receptacle of Legions of Devils' (ibid., 13). Above all it denounced the 'false brethren' who abetted them in the undermining of the constitution in church and state. When he did discuss the events of 5 November 1688 it was not to compare them with 1605 but to deny that there was any similarity. For the comparison to work it had to be assumed God's providence had condoned the right of the subjects of James II to resist him. But the doctrine of the Church of England denounced resistance. So Sacheverell instead sought to prove that the doctrine of non-resistance had not been violated in the revolution. James II had fled the country without a drop of blood being spilled. He had effectively abdicated, and William and Mary had succeeded peacefully. The church could therefore still uphold the scripture, 'touch not the Lord's anointed'. Moreover the Toleration Act of 1689, which removed penalties from protestant dissenters for not attending the established church, had been abused. It 'was never intended to indulge and cherish such monsters and vipers in our bosom, that scatter their pestilence at noon-day' (ibid., 25). Such toleration threatened to revive the fanaticism which had brought about the civil wars and the execution of Charles I: 'the old leaven of their forefathers is still working in their present generation and this traditional poison still remains in this brood of vipers to sting us to death' (ibid., 34).

Impeachment Sermons preached before the city fathers were generally printed with their agreement, but on this occasion they refused it because of its incendiary nature. Sacheverell nevertheless went ahead and published it, claiming that he had the permission of the lord mayor, Sir Samuel Garrard, to do so. Garrard denied giving it, but it was widely believed that he lied. The printer Henry Clements ran off 1000 in quarto at 1*s*. each and between 35,000 and 40,000 in octavo which sold for 2*d*. A second edition by Clements and many pirated editions, some selling for as little as 1*d*., swelled sales to about 100,000. This was a prodigious sale in the early eighteenth century, making copies available to at least a quarter of a million people, the equivalent of the entire electorate at the time.

The publication of Sacheverell's sermon caused a sensation. Whigs were outraged that so far from linking 5 November 1688 with the Gunpowder Plot it had actually denied that there was any such link by denying that there had been resistance in the revolution. The whig government determined to bring him to book. The lord treasurer, Godolphin, was particularly incensed against him since Sacheverell had referred to him by his nickname, Volpone, as one of the false brethren. Quite what to do with him was problematic. Some argued that he should be tried for seditious libel by the common law courts, but the tortuous prose of his sermon presented difficulties for the prosecution to prove seditious intent. Others thought he might be prosecuted in an ecclesiastical court, but that was regarded as too risky since the bishop of London, in whose jurisdiction the sermon had been preached, was a tory. The best suggestion in hindsight was that he should be brought before the bar of the House of Commons for contempt, since his sermon flagrantly contravened a resolution of the house in 1705 condemning those who claimed that the church was in danger. But at the time it was regarded as too lenient a procedure since the doctor would be released from confinement at the end of the parliamentary session.

So it was decided to impeach Sacheverell before the House of Lords. On 13 December a whig MP, John Dolben, rose and moved that the Commons should take into consideration two seditious pamphlets, and drew attention to the dedication to the sermon preached in Derby and some passages in *The Perils of False Brethren*. After the house had censured them Sacheverell was summoned to attend it the following day. When he did so he was impeached for high crimes and misdemeanours. The Commons then set up a committee to draw up articles of impeachment. This took until 9 January 1710 when four articles were laid on the table. The first and most important was that Sacheverell's sermon suggested that there had been no resistance in the revolution of 1688, so that 'the necessary means used to bring about the said happy Revolution were odious and unjustifiable' (Holmes, 280). The second accused him of suggesting and maintaining that the Toleration was 'unwarrantable' (ibid.). The third charged him with asserting 'that the Church of England is in a condition of great peril and adversity under her Majesty's administration' (ibid., 281). The fourth claimed that he suggested:

> that her Majesty's administration … tends to the destruction of the constitution; and that there are men of characters and stations in Church and State who are False Brethren, and do themselves weaken, undermine and betray and do encourage and put it in the power of others who are professed enemies to overturn and destroy the constitution and Establishment. (ibid., 281)

Trial On 12 January 1710 these articles were presented to the Lords. Sacheverell was then taken into the custody of the upper house, where he was bailed, he himself standing surety for £6000 and two Oxford dons (Dr Lancaster, the vice-chancellor, and Dr Bowes, fellow of All Souls) for £3000 each. At first Sacheverell was given until 18 January to give his reply to the articles, but later he was granted until 28 January. The answer was as intemperate as the sermon. It upheld the doctrine of passive obedience and the illegality of resistance and dismissed the Toleration as an 'indulgence'. So uncompromising was his response to the charges against him that two of his counsel resigned. But he was left with Sir Simon Harcourt, the ablest tory lawyer in England, and Constantine Phipps. They were joined by three others on 13 February. The groundswell of sympathy and support for the doctor became clearer each day that passed. Numerous pamphlets were published in his favour, prayers were offered for him in churches, and crowds began to gather on the streets on his behalf. The government began to realize that time was not on its side and tried to get the trial over with quickly. But the tories seized a chance to delay the proceedings, and gain maximum publicity, by successfully moving that the entire House of Commons should be accommodated in Westminster Hall for the trial. To convert the hall into an auditorium which could seat both houses of parliament and over a thousand spectators required a workforce of carpenters, directed by Sir Christopher Wren, to labour night and day for most of February. The opening day of the trial was thus delayed until 27 February 1710.

The whigs fielded their finest talents as managers of the articles, including Spencer Compton, Sir Peter King, Sir James Montagu, Sir Thomas Parker, and Robert Walpole. They vigorously spoke to the articles, resting their case on 2 March. The night before had witnessed riots in which several dissenting chapels were attacked and gutted, which seemed to confirm the fourth article's claim that

Sacheverell stirred people up to arms and violence. On 3 March Simon Harcourt opened the doctor's defence with a brilliant speech. He got Sacheverell off the hook of denying that there had been resistance in 1688 by defining the supreme power which could not be resisted as the king, Lords, and Commons and not the king alone. He then had to stand down, since he had been returned to the House of Commons in a by-election, and thus left his colleagues to conduct Sacheverell's defence to the last three articles. Sacheverell himself summed up his case in a carefully contrived speech probably written by Francis Atterbury. The managers of the articles then replied, leaving the verdict and sentence to the Lords. On 20 March they found the doctor guilty by sixty-nine votes to fifty-two.

Sentence and later life The Lords had to sentence Sacheverell on the following day. But whereas the government had wanted him to be incapacitated from preaching, fined, and imprisoned, the actual sentence was surprisingly lenient. He was only prevented from preaching for three years. This was mainly due to the influence of Queen Anne, who felt that he was guilty but should only be given a mild punishment. The verdict delighted tories, who celebrated it throughout the country, and dismayed the whigs. For the reaction foretold that were a general election to be called it would return a tory majority to the Commons. Although parliament was not dissolved until September electioneering had already begun in earnest. Sacheverell himself indulged in it by making a triumphal progress in June to Selattyn, a Shropshire living given him by an admirer at the time of the trial, and visiting eight counties and twelve parliamentary boroughs on his journey to and from his new parish, which took him six weeks to complete. His career after his triumph, however, was something of an anticlimax. Although he obtained the rectory of St Andrew's, Holborn, in 1713 it was not the high preferment he thought he deserved.

Sacheverell enjoyed a brief resurgence of fame in 1713 when the bar on his preaching was lifted. On Palm Sunday he preached a sermon in St Saviour's on the text 'Father forgive them for they know not what they do', which his enemies thought blasphemous. Published as *The Christian Triumph*, however, it sold only half the 30,000 copies printed. The House of Commons invited him to speak on 29 May, the anniversary of the Restoration, after which he was warmly received by the tory October Club. But when he went to St Paul's at the invitation of the Corporation of the Sons of the Clergy in December he was hissed by the crowd. The death of Anne in 1714 and the consequent triumph of the whigs under George I spelt the end of all hopes of preferment for high-church clergymen. Along with others Sacheverell turned to Jacobitism, but he soon withdrew from the cause, and there is no foundation to the claim that he left £500 in his will to Francis Atterbury. Instead he rather faded from the limelight after marrying, in June 1716, Mary (1664–1739), the widow of a relative, George Sacheverell, who had left him an estate in Derbyshire in 1715. In 1720 he acquired a house in Highgate. It was there that he slipped on the doorstep in January 1723, breaking two ribs. This and 'a complication of disorders' hastened his end. He died in Highgate on 5 June 1724, and was buried in St Andrew's, Holborn, on 11 June.

W. A. SPECK

Sources G. Holmes, *The trial of Dr Sacheverell* (1973) · F. F. Madan, *A critical bibliography of Dr Henry Sacheverell*, ed. W. A. Speck (1978) · H. Sacheverell, *The perils of false brethren, both in church, and state*, [another edn] (1710) · *The manuscripts of his grace the duke of Portland*, 10 vols., HMC, 29 (1891–1931), vol. 4, p. 321 · H. Sacheverell, *The perils of false brethren, both in church, and state* (1709); facs. edn (1974) · Venn, *Alum. Cant.* · *DNB*

Archives Bodl. Oxf., prayers for the sick, MS Don e.16 · CUL, papers relating to impeachment · Leics. RO, papers relating to impeachment · Magd. Oxf., prayers and devotions · Royal Institution of Great Britain, London, letters · Royal Institution of Great Britain, London, letters

Likenesses T. Gibson, oils, in or before 1710, Magd. Oxf. [*see illus.*] · A. Russell, mezzotint, 1710, AM Oxf. · P. Schenck, mezzotint, pubd 1710 (after T. Gibson), BM, NPG · silver medal, 1710, BM · G. Vertue, line engraving, pubd 1714 (after A. Russell), BM, NPG · A. Johnson, mezzotint (after T. Gibson), BM, NPG · J. Smith, mezzotint (after A. Russell, 1710), BM, NPG

Wealth at death approx. £1000 cash; also house at Highgate: will, Holmes, *The trial*, 266

Sacheverell, William (1637/8–1691), politician, was the only surviving son of Henry Sacheverell (1615/16–1662) of Barton, Nottinghamshire, and Joyce, daughter and heir of Francis Mansfield of Huggleston Grange, Leicestershire.

Early life and career Much about Sacheverell's early life is unclear, including his education. He was aged twenty-four on 25 August 1662. Before the death of his father, a Nottinghamshire landowner, he had married Mary (1632/3–1674), daughter of William Staunton of Staunton, Nottinghamshire. They had five sons (four of whom died before their father) and four daughters. In 1663, shortly after he succeeded his father, he was appointed a commissioner of assessment for Nottinghamshire, and in 1664 he was named a JP for the county. However, by 1664 his residence had shifted to Morley in Derbyshire, which his father had inherited in 1657 from a cousin. Sacheverell was an eyewitness to the Dutch attack on the Medway in 1666. At the age of about thirty, Sacheverell entered Gray's Inn on 30 December 1667, possibly in order to prepare for a political career. He never needed to practise at the bar as his landed income was about £1300 p.a. On 24 November 1670 Sacheverell won a hotly contested by-election, defeating George Vernon of Sudbury Hall, Derbyshire, 'besides all the dukes, earls and lords in the county' (Kerry, 48). As well as benefiting from a dislike of peers nominating candidates to county seats, he also had the support of the 'presbyterians'.

Court opponent, 1671–1679 Sacheverell was slow to attend at Westminster, being absent from a call of the House of Commons on 16 January 1671. Later in that session he made his first recorded speech to the house, supporting Thomas Lee, MP for Aylesbury, in an argument on 17 March with the speaker. Sacheverell quickly became a noted opponent of the court. In the session of 1672–3 he helped to draw up the Commons' answer to the king's message on the suspending power, and on 28 February he

William Sacheverell (1637/8–1691), by unknown engraver (after unknown artist, c.1656)

moved for the dismissal of recusants from military commands, a forerunner of the Test Act. His fear of 'the growth of popery' led him on 22 March to attack Lord Treasurer Clifford as 'a favourer of the Popish party', although he 'desired not the ruin of the man but the safety of the kingdom' (*Diary of Sir Edward Dering*, 149). Already a contributor to most debates, Sacheverell in the short next session attacked on 31 October 1673 'those villainous councillors that persuaded the king to make this war'. Attempts by the new lord treasurer, the earl of Danby, to gain his support failed, and in 1674 he resumed his attacks on the court. By now he was an acknowledged leader of the country opposition and, following the sudden prorogation on 24 February 1674, was one of those who took refuge in the City of London rather than attend a dinner at the Swan tavern, perhaps afraid that an arrest was imminent.

Sacheverell's first wife died on 19 August 1674, but this does not seem to have prevented his return to the fray at Westminster in 1675, including attending a number of conferences with the House of Lords on the *Shirley* v. *Fagg* case. In the second session of 1675 he evinced continued suspicion of the executive, suggesting on 4 November that the funds to build thirty warships should be appropriated from the customs revenue, and that the money should not be granted until other legislation had passed the house. Constituency interests led him to speak on 9 November on the need to prohibit the import of Irish cattle, which in Derbyshire 'has brought our cattle almost to nothing' (Grey, 3.435). In 1675 he was named a commissioner for executing the penalties against convicted recusants in Derbyshire. Sir Richard Wiseman's calculations of MPs gave no hopes to the court of changing Sacheverell's views, and the earl of Shaftesbury thought him 'thrice worthy'. Before parliament met again, Sacheverell had married, on 18 December 1676, Jane (*bap*. 1649, *d*. 1710), daughter of Sir John Newton, second baronet, of Culverthorpe, Haydor, Lincolnshire. They had three sons (two of whom died young) and three daughters.

When parliament reassembled, Sacheverell agreed on 15 February 1677 with the opposition claims that the length of the prorogation was illegal, but felt that to term it an adjournment would save the bills then under discussion. On 23 February he criticized the change in the nature of the judges' commissions, which had made them more willing to comply with the court as they could lose their patents if they did not. On the Lords' bill to repeal most of the penal laws he spoke on 4 April of his fears that after the king's death 'one inclinable to Popery will not execute the priests and jesuits', which was perhaps the first speech to hint at the future policy of exclusion. The bill itself was 'a bare toleration of popery and he would throw it out' (Grey, 3.335–6). In July 1677 Sacheverell appears to have been omitted from the Nottinghamshire commission of the peace 'at his own request' (*Finch MSS*, 2.46), and he was also omitted from the local assessment commissions. In the following session he noted on 6 February 1678 that 'when money is got, we may never have a parliament ever after', and on 2 May he appealed to the house not to be 'frightened with bugbears, prerogative, and 1641' (Grey, 5.101–2, 302–3).

In the last session of the Cavalier Parliament Sacheverell was alone on 9 November 1678 in moving explicitly for excluding the duke of York from the succession, noting that 'if we have no security that the successor shall be a Protestant, you sit down, and can do nothing effectually' (Grey, 6.172). On 18 November he produced a list of commissions of Roman Catholic officers, which the secretary of state, Sir Joseph Williamson, had countersigned, and for which Williamson was sent to the Tower. On 21 November Sacheverell opposed the amendment to the bill excluding Catholics from parliament, which exempted the duke of York. Since his election he had made over 170 recorded speeches in the Commons, and in the last session of the Cavalier Parliament he had made more recorded speeches and had more committee nominations than any other member. The French ambassador, Paul Barillon, also saw Sacheverell as an ally in opposing Lord Treasurer Danby and supplied him with 300 guineas.

The Exclusion Parliaments Sacheverell was elected unopposed to the new parliament on 6 February 1679, and Shaftesbury thought him 'worthy' in his assessment of the Commons. Sacheverell objected on constitutional grounds to the king's refusal to countenance Edward Seymour as speaker. He chaired the committee of secrecy into the Popish Plot. His pursuit of Danby centred on his belief that nothing would change unless ministers changed the way in which they governed. On 14 May he opposed supply, opining that 'once give your money, and fairly part, and the Lords in the Tower will not be tried,

and nothing done'. He clearly distrusted the king's policy of placing restrictions on a Catholic successor as an alternative to exclusion, and not surprisingly he voted on 21 May for the second reading of the Exclusion Bill. After parliament was dissolved, Sacheverell was re-elected unopposed for Derbyshire in the general election on 21 August 1679. On 12 November 1679 he was called to the bar of Gray's Inn, *ex gratia*. He did not support the Derbyshire petition calling for the new parliament to sit, believing the court to be not short enough of funds. In July 1680 Barillon still considered him one of the most influential MPs in the house.

When the new parliament sat Sacheverell entered the debate on 27 October 1680 to suggest a resolution that 'it is the undoubted right of the subject to petition the king to reform grievances and address by petition' (Grey, 7.370). Sacheverell proposed on 6 November that the Elizabethan statute against protestant dissenters be repealed (this bill passed both houses but the king ordered the clerk not to present it for the royal assent, so it fell). Sacheverell did not limit his analysis of the current crisis to popery alone, speaking on 27 November of the ministers that 'have a mind to have all in their own power and set up arbitrary government' (ibid., 8.100). However, the defeat of the Exclusion Bill in the Lords in November 1680 seems to have altered his political outlook. By December Sacheverell had stopped intervening in debates, and although elected again for Derbyshire on 3 March 1681, he did not contribute much to the Oxford parliament.

Tory reaction, 1682–1689 Outside parliament Sacheverell led the corporation of Nottingham in defence of its borough charter, proclaiming to Lord Chancellor Nottingham in May 1682 his 'great kindness for the town of Nottingham, in which I have lived several years' (*Finch MSS*, 2.169–70). In 1682 two mayoral elections were held, both claiming to act by a valid charter. In 1684 Sacheverell was one of twenty-two whigs indicted for riot, convicted, and fined 500 marks for his role in these elections. Even then he used his silence in the latter stages of the second Exclusion Parliament to declare his essential moderation. At the general election on 26 March 1685 Sacheverell's candidature for Derbyshire was disqualified as he was not resident in the county on the date of the writ. Although appointed a Nottinghamshire deputy lieutenant and JP in February 1688, he declined to act, apparently refusing 'a deputation and commission' (BL, Add. MS 36707, fol. 20). He was also appointed in March 1688 to inquire into recusancy fines in Nottinghamshire, Derbyshire, and Lincolnshire. Like many whigs in Nottinghamshire he became a 'collaborator' of James II, and was reported by the king's agents in September 1688 to be 'hearty to your majesty's interest' (HoP, *Commons, 1660–90*), and he was nominated by the court for Nottinghamshire in the elections designed for 1688. Sacheverell was not active in the revolution of 1688, and in the elections for the Convention Parliament in January 1689 he was defeated for Derbyshire, apparently being 'prejudiced by his not appearing for the prince' (BL, Add. MS 40621, fol. 3). Instead he accepted a seat from William Ashe at Heytesbury in Wiltshire.

Final years, 1689–1691 Sacheverell was an active participant in the convention debates, referring on 29 January 1689 to the mistake of previously granting 'an extravagant revenue' to the crown, and speaking of the opportunity to 'secure the right of elections and the legislative power' (Grey, 9.33). On 22 February he was named a lord of the Admiralty, no doubt because the court could use his extensive debating experience, but he was still minded to curtail the executive by granting revenue for only six months at a time. His most notable action, however, concerned the bill for restoring corporations, which was introduced in the second session of the Convention. Sacheverell presented a clause in January 1690 which sought to exclude from municipal office for seven years anybody involved in the surrender of a charter without the consent of the majority of the corporation. However, the 'Sacheverell' clause was amended in the full house to omit any reference to the majority, and he failed to vote for it himself at the third reading on 10 January 1690. On 22 January 1690 the new commission for the Admiralty omitted Sacheverell, who had rarely attended the board, not drawn his salary, and who was often in disagreement with government policy.

In the general election of 1690 Sacheverell was returned for Nottinghamshire. He attended the opening session of March–May 1690, exhibiting the same distrust of the executive in debates on supply, and on 15 May forcefully opposing the claim by the Lords to nominate their own commissioners for the Poll Bill. At the end of September 1690 some of William III's advisers saw Sacheverell as a key whig parliamentary manager, but as very difficult to bring over to the court because he 'is so full of himself' (Sydney and Coningsby to Portland, 27 Sept 1690, Portland (Bentinck) MS 299a).

Sacheverell was now in poor health and he did not attend the session of 1690–91. He died at Barton on 9 October 1691, just prior to the new parliamentary session, being buried at Morley on the 12th or 13th. He was succeeded by his son Robert, to whom he bequeathed his much prized collection of records on parliamentary affairs. Sacheverell's widow was buried at Morley on 24 March 1710. Sacheverell's monument paid tribute to his having 'served his king and country with great honour and fidelity in several parliaments' (Fox, 17). His eloquence in the House of Commons was long remembered, Speaker Arthur Onslow noting that his contribution to debate made him the 'ablest parliament man' (*Bishop Burnet's History*, 2.85).   STUART HANDLEY

Sources J. P. Ferris, 'Sacherevell, William', HoP, *Commons, 1660–90* · S. W. Handley, 'Sacherevell, William', HoP, *Commons, 1690–1715* [draft] · G. D. Squibb, ed., *The visitation of Nottinghamshire, 1662–4*, Harleian Society, new ser., 5 (1986), 28, 64 · J. J. Howard, ed., *Miscellanea Genealogica et Heraldica*, new ser., 1 (1874), 191 · S. Fox, *The history and antiquities of the parish church of St. Matthew, Morley* (1872), 17–19 · J. C. Cox, *Notes on the churches of Derbyshire*, 4: *The hundreds of Morleston and Litchurch* (1879), 339 · G. Sitwell, *The first whig* (1904), 4, 159–71, 190–91 · A. Grey, ed., *Debates of the House of Commons, from the year 1667 to the year 1694*, 10 vols. (1763), vols. 2–10 · BL, Add. MSS 36707, fol. 20; 40621, fol. 3; 6667, fols. 255–6 · *Report on the manuscripts of Allan George Finch*, 5 vols., HMC, 71 (1913–2003), vol. 2, pp. 46, 169–70 · M. J. Knights, *Politics and opinion in crisis, 1678–81* (1994) · C. Kerry, 'Leonard Wheatcroft, of Ashover', *Journal of the Derbyshire Archaeological and Natural History Society*, 18 (1896), 29–80 · J. Ehrman, *The navy in the war of William III, 1689–1697* (1953), 279–80, 297 · *The parliamentary diary of Sir Edward Dering, 1670–1673*, ed. B. D. Henning (1940), 149 · W. D. Christie, ed., *Letters addressed from London to Sir Joseph Williamson*, 2, CS, new ser., 9 (1874), 157 · M. Goldie, 'James II and the dissenters' revenge: the commission of enquiry of 1688', *Historical Research*, 66 (1993), 53–88 · *Bishop Burnet's History*, 2.85 · Lord Sydney and Thomas Coningsby to Portland, 27 Sept 1690, U. Nott. L., Portland (Bentinck) MSS, PwA 299a · D. H. Hosford, *Nottingham, nobles and the north: aspects of the revolution of 1688* (1976), 46, 71, 73

Likenesses engraving (after portrait at Renishaw in 1897), repro. in Sitwell, *First whig*, frontispiece · engraving (after portrait, *c.*1656), NPG [*see illus.*] · portrait (aged eighteen); at Renishaw, Derbyshire, 1897

Sachs, Edwin Otho (1870–1919), architect, the elder of two sons of Gustav Sachs (*d.* 1912), merchant of Hamburg and London, and his wife, Nanny Samson (*d.* 1941), was born at 16 Marlborough Hill, St John's Wood, London, on 5 April 1870. He attended University College School, London, before moving to Berlin to train as an architect. After a period as a government pupil there engaged on the imperial law courts, he studied at the famous Königliche Technische Hochschule and worked as an assistant with Ende and Böckmann, who were then designing their great scheme of government buildings for Tokyo. Early in his career Sachs conceived a passion for the relationship between architecture, fire prevention, and building legislation. To gain experience, he in 1890 enrolled as a 'ranker' in Berlin's Royal Police fire brigade, with which he claimed to have attended 3000 fires: 'for six weeks at a time I never had my boots off' ('On Fire!', 115). This was followed by a shorter stint with the fire brigade in Vienna, and possibly some weeks with the Paris brigade.

On returning to London about 1892, Sachs at first lived with his parents before in 1896 marrying Flora Jacobi (*d.* 1951), the daughter of another wealthy Hamburg merchant, Leopold Jacobi (*d.* 1895). He opened an office in Waterloo Place but at first had little architectural work, most of his time being taken up with the writing of *Modern Opera Houses and Theatres* (1896–8). This magnificent work, published by B. T. Batsford for subscribers, delineated playhouses all over the world to scrupulous standards of accuracy, and with particular emphasis (in an era of frequent theatrical fires) upon structure and stage machinery. The first volume was produced in collaboration with Ernest Woodrow, an expert in the theatres section of the London county council's architects' department, but the later ones appeared under Sachs's name alone. His means allowed him to travel widely, and he had visited both Russia and Egypt by 1895 in pursuit of material on theatres.

Sachs's career as a practising architect was most conspicuous for two important commissions for stages in existing London theatres, at Drury Lane Theatre (1898) and the Royal Opera House, Covent Garden (1899–1901). They followed from his patent of 1898 for an electrically operated 'stage bridge' to supplant unreliable, labour-intensive, and noisy timber stage contraptions. His work at Drury Lane supplemented hydraulic machinery recently imported from Vienna, but at Covent Garden Sachs installed an entirely new fly tower and stage with five enormous mobile bridges. These were in operation for nearly 100 years before their removal in 1997. He also re-equipped the flies on German principles devised by Fritz Brandt, installed a new type of safety curtain, and made various alterations front of house. Apart from these works, Sachs was not prolific as a designer, but he did design an important factory in Dalston, London, for The Shannon Ltd, office-furniture makers (1902); it was later used by the Marconi and Siemens companies.

In 1897 the much-publicized Paris bazaar fire, which cost 124 lives, followed by a costly conflagration in the Cripplegate district of the City of London, prompted Sachs to found the British Fire Prevention Committee. This voluntary body henceforward became the main focus of his work. 'Red books' analysing major fires and construction techniques and even a pamphlet containing cautionary stories for children were published between 1898 and 1912, many of which were written by Sachs himself. Europe's first fire-testing station was established in 1900, and soon found a permanent home in Porchester Road, Westbourne Park, London, and in 1903 Sachs hosted the first international fire congress at Earls Court and Caxton Hall, attended by notables from all over the world. He was quick to recognize the importance for fire prevention of reinforced concrete construction, whose take-up in Britain was tardy. In 1906, with the aim of improving the poor understanding and low quality of reinforced concrete, Sachs started the monthly periodical *Concrete and Constructional Engineering*, which he edited himself. Subsequently, in 1908, he helped to set up the Concrete Institute (later the Institution of Structural Engineers).

In 1911 Sachs became ill and was given a short lease of life. In the event he lived on until after the First World War, but his final years were overshadowed by the harsh consequences of the war for Anglo-German families and by grave money difficulties: his expenditure had always been lavish, the fire-testing station never paid for itself, and he maintained a large second home at St Margaret's Bay, Kent. He had always thought of himself as English, but had a high regard for German invention and organization. He died on 9 September 1919, aged only forty-nine, at his home, 5 Ulster Terrace, Regent's Park, London. He was cremated at Golders Green, where a plaque in the crematorium cloister commemorates him. He was survived by his wife and his only child, Eric Leopold Otho *Sachs (1898–1979).

Sachs was the British pioneer of scientific, disinterested building research: although not creative in the conventional sense (the only known theatre design that was exclusively his, for Alexandria in Egypt, was not built), he revolutionized attitudes and institutions across the construction industry. The founding of the building research station in 1920 owed much to his example. An assiduous networker and attender of international conferences, he was widely decorated by foreign organizations. But his energy and impatience sometimes caused friction with official bodies at home, notably the ill-managed London Fire Brigade. He served in the volunteer militia, was a member of the Institution of Naval Architects, fellow of the Royal Statistical Society and of the Royal Society of Edinburgh, and vice-president of the International Fire Service Council. Five feet ten inches in height, in his prime Sachs was a handsome, slender, and genial man, with wavy hair and a tidy moustache.

ANDREW SAINT

Sources D. Wilmore, ed., *Edwin O. Sachs, architect, stagehand, engineer and fireman* (1998) · Sir E. Sachs, unpublished memoir, priv. coll., chap. 3, 'My father' · 'On fire!: a chat with Mr. Edwin Sachs', *Builders' Journal* (2 April 1895), 115–16 · 'Reconstruction of the opera stage: a chat with Mr Edwin Sachs', *The Sketch* (3 April 1901), 426 · H. L. Childe, unpublished notes on life of Edwin Sachs, c.1960, Fire Research Station, Borehamwood · b. cert. · d. cert.
Archives Royal Opera House, London, archives
Likenesses photograph, repro. in 'On fire!: a chat with Mr. Edwin Sachs', 115 · photograph, repro. in 'Reconstruction of the opera stage'
Wealth at death £5231 6s. 6d.: probate, 26 Nov 1919, CGPLA Eng. & Wales

Sachs, Sir Eric Leopold Otho (1898–1979), judge, was born in London on 23 July 1898, the only child of Edwin Otho *Sachs (1870–1919), an architect and expert on fire prevention, and his wife, Flora Jacobi (d. 1951). His grandfather, a merchant, had emigrated to Britain from Germany. He himself was educated at Charterhouse School; he then joined the Royal Artillery, with which he served as a gunner officer from 1917 to 1919. He was seriously wounded in his left hand, which remained partially disabled throughout his life. On demobilization early in 1919 he immediately went to Christ Church, Oxford, where he read law (he was made an honorary student of Christ Church in 1971). He passed the shortened honours course in jurisprudence in 1920, after only five terms' residence.

Sachs was called to the bar by the Middle Temple in 1921 and became a pupil of Wilfrid Lewis, later junior counsel to the Treasury and subsequently a high-court judge. He joined the Oxford circuit and in due course acquired a first-class junior practice both in London and on circuit. On 12 May 1934 he married (Janet) Margaret (b. 1909), daughter of the future lord chief justice of England, Rayner *Goddard. They had a son and a daughter. His married and family life was one of great personal happiness.

In 1938 Sachs took silk and at the same time was appointed recorder of Dudley, his first judicial appointment. Characteristically, in 1939 he at once rejoined the army and served, at first as a very junior officer, in various departments of the War Office, under the control of the adjutant-general. His fierce courage in dealing with his military and civil superiors—they in their turn were somewhat frightened of a KC—did much to mitigate the mindless meanness over pay and allowances that did so much to damage service morale in the early stages of the war. He was appointed MBE in 1941.

In 1942 Sachs moved into the world of intelligence, in the political warfare department, and was promoted brigadier. To that body and to Sachs in particular was assigned the task of producing 'basic handbooks'. These were instructions for those who were to be responsible for the administration of territories still to be reoccupied. In due course Sachs presented a complete set of these volumes to the Middle Temple library.

On demobilization in 1945 Sachs returned to the bar. He had still to build a practice as a silk and it was not easy to start again. Stress of work during the war had not improved his health. In the ensuing years he was twice employed as a commissioner of assize, and in 1946 he was appointed special commissioner to inquire into allegations of serious corruption in the Gold Coast. From 1943 to 1954 he was recorder of Stoke-on-Trent, and for the last two of those years leader of the Oxford circuit. All these tasks he discharged admirably, while at the same time acquiring a substantial practice. He led the bar team that, in conjunction with the Law Society team headed by Sydney Littlewood, was responsible for the legal aid scheme later established by the Legal Aid and Advice Act of 1949. Sachs was in truth one of the principal architects of that great social reform. He did much to ensure the independence of both branches of the profession from its new paymasters.

In 1954 Sachs was appointed a judge of the High Court and knighted. He served in the Probate, Divorce, and Admiralty division of that court until 1960, when he was transferred to the Queen's Bench Division. After six further years he was appointed a lord justice of appeal in 1966, an office which he held until he retired in 1973; on appointment he was also sworn of the privy council. He never claimed profound knowledge of the law. His judicial qualities were great industry and an intense zeal to find the right answer and to prevent injustice wherever it might be found. His weakness was undue attention to detail, which occasionally led to over-complication of a simple case by concentration on inessentials. But the faults were in part due to his qualities.

Sachs's second great service was to his inn, the Middle Temple. He became a bencher in 1947 and treasurer in 1967. He transformed the government of that inn from an inefficient, oligarchical system to one suitable to the post-war era. The treasurership, which had too often been regarded as a post of honour rather than of obligation, thenceforth became an office to be held only by the active. He devised the committee system that not only made the burden of that office tolerable but also ensured proper financial control of the inn's limited resources. He also brought younger members of the inn into the machinery of its government. The subsequent strength of the Middle Temple, both financial and intellectual, is perhaps his best memorial.

Increasing deafness and a sense of duty requiring him not to remain too long on the bench combined to dictate Sachs's retirement in 1973. He moved from his flat in the Middle Temple to live entirely in east Sussex, but until afflicted by ill health he remained in contact with his many friends in London, and his lifelong interest in the law continued. But he never fully recovered from a serious

operation, and he died on 1 September 1979 at his home, Walland Oast, Wadhurst, Sussex. There is an indifferent portrait of him in the Middle Temple.   ROSKILL, *rev.*

Sources personal knowledge (1986, 2004) · private information (1986, 2004) · *The Times* (16 Nov 1979) · *Daily Telegraph* (3 Sept 1979) · *The Guardian* (3 Sept 1979) · Burke, *Peerage* (1967) · *CGPLA Eng. & Wales* (1979)
Likenesses portrait, Middle Temple, London
Wealth at death £164,393: probate, 30 Oct 1979, *CGPLA Eng. & Wales*

Sackville. For this title name *see* Germain, George Sackville, first Viscount Sackville (1716–1785); West, Lionel Sackville Sackville-, second Baron Sackville (1827–1908); West, Edward Charles Sackville-, fifth Baron Sackville (1901–1965).

Sackville [de Sackville] **family** (*per. c.*1066–*c.*1477), gentry, of southern England, is first represented by **Herbrand de Sackville** (*fl.* 1066–1086). Herbrand, who held the manor of Sauqueville in Normandy, in the Scie valley, was steward of Walter Giffard, lord of Longueville, a few miles to the south.

Sackville of Fawley In 1066 Giffard entrusted Herbrand with the care of his estates while he accompanied William, duke of Normandy, to England. So well did Herbrand perform his duties that he was offered, as a reward, a choice between the manors of Crendon and Fawley, Buckinghamshire, in England. Herbrand chose Fawley 'on account of its beauty' and was holding it in 1086 (*VCH Buckinghamshire*, 3.39). In the next generation the family acquired interests in Essex. **Robert de Sackville** (*d. c.*1154), Herbrand's second son and eventual successor, following the death of the elder son, Jordan [i], held property at Bergholt and Bures Mount, both in Essex; through his wife, Letitia, he also acquired an interest in Wickham Skeith in Suffolk. Robert may have prospered in the service of Stephen, count of Mortain, later King Stephen, for he attested one of the count's charters as his steward. Robert's identification with Essex is attested by his close relationship with St John's Abbey, Colchester. With his wife's consent he granted Wickham Skeith to the house, and in his final years he became a monk there.

Robert's eldest son, **Jordan** [ii] **de Sackville** (*d. c.*1175) gained the family its first interests in Sussex. Jordan's wife was Ela, daughter and eventual heir of Sir Ralph of Dean, of Buckhurst. The marriage brought Jordan half a dozen, mostly small, manors in east Sussex. It also brought him the patronage of the house of Premonstratensian canons which Ela's father had founded about 1182 at Otham near Hailsham. About 1208 the house moved to Bayham, near the Kent border, where it remained. It was in the choir of Bayham that the Sackvilles of Buckhurst were buried until the mid-fifteenth century, and their attachment to the house is attested by the lavish thirteenth-century rebuilding of that choir, to the cost of which they contributed.

At the beginning of the thirteenth century a number of settlements appear to have been made of the Sackville family estates. The first, probably made soon after the French conquest of Normandy, effected a division between the family's English and Norman interests: at intervals during the twelfth century references are encountered to the family's Norman interests; after about 1208 these cease. The second appears to have been a division between the family's lands in Buckinghamshire and Suffolk and those in Sussex and Essex. The circumstances and terms of this division are obscure, and the only evidence of it is the emergence by the early thirteenth century of two branches of the family—one at Fawley and the other at Buckhurst. The Fawley branch probably represented the senior line. In the 1230s Sir Bartholomew de Sackville (*fl. c.*1230), the head of the Fawley branch, was granted timber by the king for building 'a room' at his house. Jordan [iv] de Sackville (*d.* before 1302), probably his son, was in possession of the manor in 1284 and had been succeeded before 1302 by another Bartholomew de Sackville, an idiot. Sir Thomas [i] Sackville (*d. c.*1330) held the manor in 1316. **Sir Thomas** [ii] **Sackville** (*c.*1336–1406), Bartholomew's grandson, succeeded in 1358, when he came of age. This Sir Thomas, the most distinguished of his family, was active in the wars with France. In 1386, when he gave evidence in the *Scrope* v. *Grosvenor* dispute in the court of chivalry, he said that he had been 'first armed in 1354' and that he had served in all Edward III's later campaigns (Nicolas, 1.171). Sir Thomas was also active in his locality, twice serving as sheriff of Buckinghamshire, and fourteen times as member of parliament for that county. His son, Sir Thomas [iii] Sackville (*d. c.*1455), was also elected as a member of parliament. The last male representative of the line was this Thomas's son in turn, Thomas [iv] Sackville, esquire, who died before 1477.

Sackville of Buckhurst The fortunes of the branch of the family settled at Buckhurst were more chequered. **Sir Jordan** [iii] **de Sackville** (*d.* 1273), the son of Jordan de Sackville (*d. c.*1232) and Matilda de Normanville, was a supporter of Simon de Montfort against Henry III and was captured at the battle of Evesham. The cost of redeeming his forfeited lands was to place a strain on the family resources for a generation. Jordan's son Andrew [i] de Sackville (*d. c.*1290) was a minor when his father died and was brought up as a royal ward. This Andrew and his son and successor, Sir Andrew [ii] Sackville (*d.* 1316), were both active in royal service and fought in the Welsh and Scottish wars. On Andrew [ii]'s death there was another minority and the wardship of his son **Sir Andrew** [iii] **Sackville** (*c.*1306–1369) was granted to Sir John Beche, a royal household knight, who married his charge to his own daughter Joan. On Sir John's death without male children in 1336, there was a division of the Beche estates, and Joan was awarded the manors of Chiddingly, Claverham, Arlington, and Waldron. This substantial acquisition made the Sackvilles one of the richest landed families in east Sussex.

Sir Andrew [iii] was the most active of his line in the middle ages. Continuing a family tradition he took part in all the main military expeditions of the day. He fought in Scotland in 1336 and in the Low Countries in 1338, and in the following decade he was present at Crécy and Calais. He was also active in private and public administration.

He was employed by a succession of lords—Richard (II) Fitzalan, earl of Arundel, William Montagu, earl of Salisbury, Hugh, Lord Despenser, and Roger Mortimer, earl of March; the last he served in the capacity of household steward. In the 1360s, when his soldiering days were over, he served as sheriff of Sussex and was three times elected member of parliament for the county.

Sir Andrew [iii] married twice (his second wife being Maud Lovat), but his two recorded sons both predeceased him. Lacking a legitimate male heir, he settled his estates on a bastard **Sir Thomas** [v] **Sackville** (*d.* 1432), the son of his liaison with Joan Burgeys. In 1393, following the death of Sir Andrew's widow, Thomas [v]'s succession was challenged by Sir Thomas [ii] Sackville of Fawley, who claimed the Oxfordshire manor of Emmington, but the former's interests were upheld. Thomas [v]'s position in Sussex was strengthened by his alliance with the powerful Sir Edward *Dallingridge of Bodiam, whose daughter Margaret he married. In the 1380s he gave his backing to Dallingridge in a campaign of intimidation against the duke of Lancaster's officials in Ashdown, and in 1384, with his father-in-law, suffered brief imprisonment for his actions. In the next decade he was three times elected to parliament. Although he avoided involvement in the factional struggles of Richard II's reign, in 1400 he was arrested, apparently on suspicion of involvement in the 'Epiphany plot' against Henry IV. He was released when surety had been given for his appearance before the council. In 1407 he served as sheriff of Sussex and in 1418 and 1421 as a commissioner of array. He died in December 1432 and in his will left 100 marks to Bayham Abbey, where he was buried.

The Sackvilles' ascent into the peerage began in the next century when Thomas *Sackville, Queen Elizabeth's treasurer, was created Baron Buckhurst. The family's arms were quarterly, or and gules, a bend vair.

NIGEL SAUL

Sources C. J. Phillips, *History of the Sackville family*, 1 [1929] · H. M. Colvin, *The white canons in England* (1951), 109–18 · *VCH Buckinghamshire*, vol. 3 · N. H. Nicolas, ed., *The Scrope and Grosvenor controversy*, 2 vols. (privately printed, London, 1832) · HoP, *Commons, 1386–1421*, 4.271–4 · N. Saul, *Scenes from provincial life: knightly families in Sussex, 1280–1400* (1986) · *Chancery records* · CIPM, 5, no. 612 · E. Sussex RO, SAS/CH 258 · CPR, 1258–66, 461
Archives E. Sussex RO, SAS/CH 258
Wealth at death estates of Sackvilles at Buckhurst valued at least £200 by late fourteenth century: E. Sussex RO, SAS/CH 258

Sackville, Sir Andrew (*c.*1306–1369). *See under* Sackville family (*per. c.*1066–*c.*1477).

Sackville, Charles, **sixth earl of Dorset and first earl of Middlesex** (1643–1706), poet and politician, was born on 24 January 1643, probably at Copt Hall in Essex, the second of thirteen children of Richard *Sackville, Lord Buckhurst, later fifth earl of Dorset (1622–1677) [*see under* Sackville, Edward, fourth earl of Dorset (1590–1652)], and Lady Frances Cranfield (1622?–1687), daughter of Lionel *Cranfield, first earl of Middlesex. His mother was governess to the children of Charles I. In December 1658, following a year under Richard Busby at Westminster School, he and

Charles Sackville, sixth earl of Dorset and first earl of Middlesex (1643–1706), by Sir Godfrey Kneller

his younger brother, Edward, left to travel in Europe with a tutor. At the Restoration, although under age, he received a number of honours appropriate to his rank, including from 1661 a seat in the Commons as member for East Grinstead which he held until he entered the Lords in 1675, after inheriting the estates of his maternal uncle Lionel Cranfield, earl of Middlesex (d. 1674). On 9 April 1662, as a prisoner in Newgate, Sackville was tried for manslaughter after an attack on an alleged highwayman. The charge was later changed to murder, forcing him to plead the king's pardon. On 16 June 1663 his irreverent behaviour after a dinner at The Cock tavern in Bow Street with Sir Charles Sedley and Sir Thomas Ogle provoked a riot. Neither incident seems to have harmed him much: his friend Rochester complained 'my Lord Dorset might do anything, yet was never to blame' (Prior, br).

At court, Sackville witnessed the years, mythologized by Gramont, when not to participate in institutionalized hedonism was regarded as an insult to the royal brothers. Late in 1664 he went to sea as a volunteer against the Dutch but did not see action. In 1667 he was briefly the lover of Nell Gwynn before surrendering her to the king. On 26 December 1669 he was made a gentleman of the bedchamber. In 1669–70 he made three visits to France as Charles's representative on diplomatic matters.

Sackville came forward as a writer in 1662 by participating in a group translation of Corneille's *La mort de Pompée*, which was finally acted in October 1663. 'The first letter from B[uckhurst] to Mr. E[therege]', probably written about the same time, mixes nostalgia for the debaucheries of the town with a demand to be sent whatever new verse had appeared, however bad. In 1664 his 'To All ye Ladies now on Land', written at sea, gained lasting fame when it was reprinted as a broadside ballad. A burlesque commendatory poem on Edward Howard's *The British Princes* (1669) beginning 'Come on, ye critics! Find one fault who dare' was copied out many times in the manuscript miscellanies of the period. A few lyrics by Sackville appeared in printed anthologies of the early 1670s but most of the surviving verse circulated only in manuscript. His standing as a critic was confirmed when Dryden's *Of Dramatic Poesy* (1668) included him in an imaginary dialogue set on the Thames on 3 June 1665 in which, as Eugenius, he argues for the superiority of modern British drama and poetry over that of the Elizabethans and the ancients. He was an early admirer of *Paradise Lost*.

Sackville was also a patron in the mould established by William Cavendish, duke of Newcastle. He shared Newcastle's admiration for Ben Jonson and suspicion of the heroic play. Etherege and Shadwell were members of both circles. In effect, he took over Newcastle's role as Charles's unofficial minister of the arts, and in doing so consciously perpetuated the traditions of the Tribe of Ben, of which Newcastle had been a member. The 'poets' parlour' at Knole, its walls lined with portraits of writers, succeeded the Apollo tavern as a venue for literary socializing.

Known in his early years by the courtesy title Lord Buckhurst, Sackville was created earl of Middlesex on 4 April 1675, in recognition that he had inherited his maternal grandfather's estates, and on 27 August 1677 succeeded his father as earl of Dorset. About June 1674 he secretly married the widowed Mary Berkeley, countess of Falmouth (1645–1679), daughter of Colonel Hervey Bagot, of Pipe Hall, Warwick. At the time of his uncle Middlesex's death he was already at law with his parents about the inheritance and his mother's dowry. On 12 September 1679 his countess died in giving birth to a stillborn child. Although Harris presents the union as a genuine love match, Dorset acknowledged daughters, Mary (b. 1673) and Katherine (b. 1675), by Phillipa Waldegrave, and may also have fathered a son with her and another daughter with a woman named Lee. In March 1681, while in Oxford for the parliament, he suffered an apoplectic fit, and on 23 August left England to recuperate in France.

Dorset's political leanings were forged in the heyday of the Cabal ministry under the charismatic influence of his maternal relative the second duke of Buckingham. In July 1670 he and Sedley accompanied Buckingham on an embassy to Louis XIV, and in 1672 he accepted a captaincy in Buckingham's regiment of foot. Together with Rochester and Sedley, he supported Buckingham after the fall of the Cabal, adopting a moderate whig position on the succession. While Burnet may go too far in claiming that he 'hated the court, and despised the king' (*Bishop Burnet's History*, ed. Burnet and Burnet, 1.264), Dorset, like Sedley, was an anti-Yorkist during the later years of Charles's reign. In literary politics this meant championing Shadwell in opposition to Dryden and his patron, Dorset's relative John Sheffield, earl of Mulgrave. On James's accession in

1685, Dorset appears to have withdrawn from court as far as his offices permitted. If he is the author, which seems likely, of the lengthy satire 'A Faithful Catalogue of our most Eminent Ninnies', he must be numbered among the most vituperative critics of the regime. His second marriage, on 7 March 1685, to the seventeen-year-old Lady Mary Compton (1668–1691), daughter of James *Compton, third earl of Northampton, allied him to her uncle Henry Compton, the whig bishop of London. In January 1688 Dorset was deprived by James of the lord lieutenancy of Sussex. Although his indifference to religion was proverbial, he was one of the peers who gave their support to the seven bishops by their presence at the trial on 29 June.

At the revolution, Dorset and Compton were entrusted with assisting Princess Anne to abscond from Whitehall. During her flight from the palace she lost a shoe which Dorset immediately replaced with one of his white gloves. Appointed lord chamberlain on 14 February 1689, Dorset was one of the nine grandees who governed in the queen's name during William's absences overseas. On the queen's death in 1694 he became one of seven lords justices who performed the same function, but as regents rather than advisers. His wife died on 6 August 1691 having given him three children. In 1692 he received the Garter. With characteristic generosity Dorset privately compensated his political enemy Dryden for the loss of his laureate's salary.

Dorset's literary circle was now enlivened by two new protégés, Matthew Prior (whom he had rescued from his uncle's tavern) and Charles Montagu, later earl of Halifax. These three and Dorset's constant companion Fleetwood Sheppard are portrayed in 'On Mr Pr——r's letters to Mr Sheppard (not omitting the last one unown'd)' (1690) as conspiring to get a sinecure for Prior. Dorset's importance as a patron is visible through the number of works dedicated to him (Harris, 247–51, records 35) and begging letters preserved in the Sackville papers.

As a poet Dorset poses problems typical of aristocratic, occasional writers of the period in having circulated his work in manuscript rather than printed form, and in many cases anonymously. His court satires of the 1660s, including contributions to a series written against the earl of Chesterfield, have largely disappeared. In the mid-1670s he was approached by the scribe Robert Julian (Harris, 178–9), who from being a copyist of poems by Dorset and his friends became a trader in transcripts and manuscript anthologies, thus helping to ensure their survival. A further body of work was circulated in the 1690s in anthologies written from the archive of the 'Cameron' scriptorium (as it is known today), whose proprietor seems to have been in touch with Dorset. From these remains and unauthorized printings Brice Harris was able to assemble a 'collected poems' which is unlikely to be improved on without the discovery of new sources. While the case for his being the author of 'Ninnies' is much stronger than Harris concedes, Pickering's attribution to him of 'The Town Life' still awaits corroboration. His courtly and libertine lyrics are thoroughly deserving of the praise given to them by Dryden and Pope.

Dorset was often dilatory in carrying out his duties as lord chamberlain, and there was relief on both sides when on 19 April 1697 he surrendered the position to Sunderland. He remained a lord justice until the following year and was elected FRS in 1699. In 1704 he was recalled to the council to advise on the coronation of Queen Anne. A third marriage on 27 October of the same year to his housekeeper, Anne Roche, was seen as evidence of mental and physical decline. High living and benevolence had severely damaged his estate. He died at Bath on 29 January 1706 and was buried at Withyham, Sussex, on 17 February. He was succeeded by his son by his second marriage, Lionel Cranfield *Sackville, first duke of Dorset. His daughter by the same marriage, Mary, duchess of Beaufort, had died in the previous year. His illegitimate daughter Mary, countess of Orrery, survived him, as did his third wife, who died before May 1707. Prior paid a moving tribute to his old patron in the preface of his 1718 *Poems*, laying particular stress on his kind-heartedness.   HAROLD LOVE

Sources B. Harris, *Charles Sackville, sixth earl of Dorset: patron and poet of the Restoration* (1940) • *The poems of Charles Sackville, sixth earl of Dorset*, ed. B. Harris (New York, 1979) • HoP, *Commons, 1660–90*, 3.376–7 • J. H. Wilson, *The court wits of the Restoration: an introduction* (1948) • O. Pickering, 'An attribution of the poem "The town life" (1686) to Charles Sackville, earl of Dorset', *N&Q*, 235 (1990), 296–7 • G. de F. Lord and others, eds., *Poems on affairs of state: Augustan satirical verse, 1660–1714*, 7 vols. (1963–75) • C. J. Phillips, *History of the Sackville family*, 2 vols. [1930] • CKS, Sackville papers • M. Prior, *Poems on several occasions* (1718) • *Bishop Burnet's History of his own time*, ed. G. Burnet and T. Burnet, 2 vols. (1724–34) • GEC, *Peerage* • P. Beal and others, *Index of English literary manuscripts*, ed. P. J. Croft and others, [4 vols. in 11 pts] (1980–), vol. 2, pt 1, pp. 347–81
Archives CKS, corresp. and MSS • CKS, Sackville (Knole) MSS • PRO, state papers, work as lord chamberlain | Bodl. Oxf., letters to offices of the ordnance and Sir Henry Goodricke • Longleat House, Wiltshire, corresp. with Matthew Prior • Bath, corresp. with Matthew Prior
Likenesses G. Kneller, oils, c.1697, NPG • J. Faber junior, mezzotint, 1743 (after G. Kneller), BM, NPG • Clamp, stipple (after S. Harding), NPG • G. Kneller, oils, Knole, Kent [*see illus.*] • studio of G. Kneller, oils (version of portrait, Knole, Kent), NPG • attrib. G. Kneller, oils, Knole, Kent • J. Simon, mezzotint (after G. Kneller), BM, NPG • J. Smith, mezzotint (after G. Kneller), BM, NPG
Wealth at death very large but mortgaged: Harris, *Charles Sackville*

Sackville, Charles, second duke of Dorset (1711–1769), politician and impresario, was born on 6 February 1711 and baptized at St Martin-in-the-Fields, London, on 25 February, the eldest son of the six children of Lionel Cranfield *Sackville, first duke of Dorset (1688–1765), politician, and his wife, Elizabeth (1687–1768), the daughter of Lieutenant-General Walter Philip Colyear. He was styled Lord Buckhurst until 1720 and then earl of Middlesex until 1765. He was educated at Westminster School (1720–28) and at Christ Church, Oxford, where he matriculated on 27 November 1728 and graduated MA on 15 September 1730. From 1731 to 1733 he was on the grand tour, accompanied by the Revd Joseph Spence, and while in Florence in 1733 is said to have founded the English masonic lodge there.

Lord Middlesex had a long and bitter quarrel with his father, whom he actually opposed in his own boroughs, and he became an intimate friend of Frederick, prince of Wales. At the general election in April 1734 he unsuccessfully contested Kent, but was returned for the family borough of East Grinstead, which he continued to represent until his appointment as high steward of the honour of Otford on 26 May 1741. Politics, however, were not Middlesex's chief preoccupation. In 1737 and 1738 he took further extended trips to the continent and staged lavish entertainments for his friends in Italy. On his return to England in January 1739 he staged an opera, *Angelico e Medoro*, with music by Giovanni Battista Pescetti from a text by Metastasio; the opera was a showcase for the limited talents of Lucia Panichi, 'La Muscovita', Middlesex's mistress from about 1739 to about 1742, and also a sign of Middlesex's ambition to revive full-scale Italian opera seasons in London, recently abandoned by Johann Jakob Heidegger on the grounds of expense. Middlesex staged a season in 1739–40 at the Little Theatre, Haymarket, but was unable to raise enough subscriptions to follow it with another the next year. For the 1741–2 season he entered into partnership with seven other noblemen, and he was able to continue in business for three years at the King's Theatre, Haymarket. The opera proved socially prestigious but the costs of the enterprise exceeded income from subscriptions, and Middlesex had to finance operating costs from his own pocket and from loans. At the end of the 1743–4 season he and his colleagues sought to recover their deficits (of at least £3600) by filing a bill of complaint in chancery against their major subscribers. The case dragged on for three years and was probably eventually settled out of court. Middlesex then abandoned his career as an impresario. His extravagance in staging the operas brought derision from some. Although he maintained Italian opera's position as a socially exclusive form of entertainment, it was no longer as fashionable as it had been in earlier decades. After Middlesex's failure, opera producers looked increasingly to recoup their costs from box-office receipts rather than from advance subscriptions from the wealthy, as had previously been the case.

Middlesex's political career continued. From January 1742 to June 1747 he sat in the Commons for Sussex, where Newcastle had arranged to have him returned at a by-election. He was one of the lords of the Treasury in Henry Pelham's administration from 23 December 1743 to June 1747 and was the only member of the board not to resign in February 1746. He kept his place on Pelham's return to office, but in 1747 he joined the opposition party led by the prince of Wales. He was dismissed from his Treasury post when he was appointed master of the horse to Frederick. On 30 October 1744 he married the Hon. Grace Boyle (d. 1763), the only daughter and heir of Richard Boyle, second Viscount Shannon (1674–1740), and his second wife, Grace Senhouse. Walpole described her as 'very short, very plain, and very yellow: a vain girl, full of Greek and Latin, and music, and painting; but neither mischievous nor political' (Walpole, *Memoirs*, 1.76). However,

she was appointed mistress of the robes to Augusta, princess of Wales, in July 1745, and may have been influential in winning her husband over to the Leicester House party, especially as she was reputed to have been Frederick's mistress.

In 1747 Middlesex unsuccessfully contested by-elections in Queenborough and Seaford, but on 17 December 1747 he was returned for Old Sarum by Thomas Pitt, Frederick's election manager. He represented the borough until the dissolution of parliament in April 1754. After Frederick's death he remained in opposition, and he voted for a reduction of the army in November 1751, publishing in 1752 *A Treatise Concerning the Militia*. He had intervened against his father in East Grinstead in 1750, but in 1752 his friend George Bubb Dodington engineered a partial reconciliation between father and son. Dorset, however, refused to pay his debts or to provide him with a seat in the House of Commons, so Middlesex was without a place during the whole of the next parliament. At the general election in March 1761 he was again elected for East Grinstead. In the new parliament he was described by Bute as a 'doubtful' supporter of the government. In the three divisions on general warrants of February 1764, he voted with the opposition and followed his brother Lord George Sackville in opposing Grenville on this issue. But on 11 April 1764 his differences with Grenville were patched up, and he voted with the administration on Meredith's motion on general warrants on 30 January 1765.

Middlesex succeeded his father as second duke of Dorset on 9 October 1765, and took his seat in the House of Lords on 17 December. Although in July 1765 Rockingham had also regarded him as 'doubtful', Dorset usually supported the Rockingham party. On 10 February 1766 he was admitted a member of the privy council and sworn in as lord lieutenant of Kent. He spoke little or not at all in the House of Lords.

Dorset was a dissolute and extravagant man of fashion. According to Lord Shelburne, his appearance towards the close of his life was 'always that of a proud, disgusted, melancholy, solitary man', while his conduct savoured strongly of madness (*Life of … Shelburne*, 1.342). He died at his house in St James's Street, Piccadilly, on 6 January 1769, aged fifty-seven, and was buried at Withyham, Sussex, on 11 January. There were no children from his marriage and the title descended to his nephew John Frederick *Sackville (1745–1799).

G. F. R. BARKER, *rev.* MARTYN J. POWELL

Sources J. Brooke, 'Sackville, Charles', HoP, *Commons, 1754–90* · R. R. Sedgwick, 'Sackville, Charles', HoP, *Commons, 1715–54* · *The diary of George Bubb Doddington*, ed. H. P. Wyndham (1784) · H. Walpole, *Memoirs of the reign of King George the Second*, ed. Lord Holland, 2nd edn, 3 vols. (1847) · *The letters of Horace Walpole, earl of Orford*, ed. P. Cunningham, 9 vols. (1857–9) · *Life of William, earl of Shelburne … with extracts from his papers and correspondence*, ed. E. G. P. Fitzmaurice, 3 vols. (1875–6) · GEC, *Peerage*, new edn · J. E. Doyle, *The official baronage of England*, 3 vols. (1886) · A. Collins, *The peerage of England: containing a genealogical and historical account of all the peers of England* · J. Nichols, *Literary anecdotes of the eighteenth century*, ed. C. Clair, abridged edn (1967) · J. E. T. Rogers, ed., *A complete collection of the protests of the Lords*, 3 vols. (1875) · GM, 1st ser., 14 (1744), 619 · GM, 1st ser., 15 (1745), 333 · GM, 1st ser., 33 (1763), 257 · GM, 1st ser.,

39 (1769), 54 • C. Taylor, 'From losses to lawsuit: patronage of the Italian opera in London by Lord Middlesex, 1739–45', *Music and Letters*, 68 (1987), 1–25 • J. H. Lepper, 'The earl of Middlesex and the English lodge in Florence', *Ars Quatuor Coronatorum*, 58 (1947), 4–77

Archives CKS, family, political, and estate corresp. • priv. coll.
Likenesses G. Knapton, oils, 1741, Society of Dilettanti, Brooks's Club, London • stipple, pubd 1799 (after O. Humphry), BM, NPG • R. Carriera, two pastels, Knole, Kent • J. L. Natter, silver and copper medal, BM • F. Richter, oils, Knole, Kent

Sackville, Edward, fourth earl of Dorset (1590–1652), politician, was the younger surviving son of Robert *Sackville, second earl of Dorset (1560/61–1609), and Lady Margaret Howard (*c*.1560–1591). He was born in 1590, but the exact date and location are unknown. He was the younger brother of Richard Sackville, third earl of Dorset (1589–1624), and the two brothers both matriculated at Christ Church, Oxford, in July 1605. By 2 March 1612 he had married Mary (*bap*. 1586, *d*. 1645), daughter of Sir George Curzon and Mary Leveson. In August 1613 he incurred James I's displeasure when he killed Lord Bruce of Kinloss in a duel at Bergen-op-Zoom. Although he was officially pardoned, threats from Bruce's relatives induced Sackville to spend most of 1614–15 travelling abroad, principally in France and the Netherlands.

Political career to 1640 On his return to England, Sackville gradually regained favour at court, and was created a knight of the Bath on 3 November 1616. He sat for Sussex in the 1621 parliament and spoke frequently. He strongly supported granting aid to the Palatinate and took a clearly pro-French and anti-Spanish stance. While bitterly denouncing monopolists, he sought to absolve James I of any blame for monopolies or corrupt legal practices. He also warned the Commons not to encroach upon 'the privilege of princes' by advising on Prince Charles's marriage (E. Nicholas, *Proceedings and Debates in the House of Commons in 1620 and 1621*, 2 vols., 1766, 2.269). His supportive speeches brought him to the crown's attention, and rumours circulated that he would shortly be appointed ambassador to France, although in the end nothing came of this. Two years later a bitter row broke out within the Virginia Company regarding the conduct of the treasurer, Sir Edwin Sandys. Sackville, who had been a member of the company's council since 1620, forcefully took Sandys's side, and behaved so intemperately when the king heard the case in April 1623 that James 'was faine to take him downe soundly and rowndly' (PRO, SP 14/143/22) until Lord Treasurer Middlesex intervened on his behalf. However, Sackville once again found it prudent to go abroad, and he was at Florence when he learned that his elder brother had died on 27 March 1624, and that he was now earl of Dorset.

With his elevation to the peerage, Dorset's career soon gathered momentum. His pro-French, anti-Spanish views perfectly coincided with those of Charles and Buckingham, and preferment quickly followed: he was installed as a knight of the Garter in December 1625; he was appointed a privy councillor on 22 July 1626, and lord chamberlain of the queen's household on 16 July 1628; he also served as lord lieutenant of Sussex from 1624 and lord

Edward Sackville, fourth earl of Dorset (1590–1652), studio of Sir Anthony Van Dyck, *c*.1635

lieutenant of Middlesex from 1628. His appointment to the privy council was widely seen as a reward for loyalty to Buckingham during the 1626 parliament, and the following year Dorset publicly supported the collection of the forced loan. Behind the scenes, however, he adopted a more ambivalent attitude, telling Buckingham lukewarmly that these policies 'in all probability tend to happines' (PRO, SP 16/74/62). Dorset also assisted several loan refusers, including Sir Thomas Wentworth and Sir John Strangways, and came out against it in the 1628 parliament.

During the debates on the petition of right Dorset spoke regularly in defence of the royal prerogative, but within the bounds of the common law. For example: 'the King cannot commit for any cause triable at common law, but for reason of state he may … The King has as much right to *legem terrae* for matters of state as the subjects for their rights.' He advocated 'that a middle way be taken that his Majesty's right be preserved and the people's liberties' (M. F. Keeler, M. J. Cole, and W. B. Bidwell, eds., *Proceedings in Parliament, 1628*, 6 vols., 1977–83, 3.237, 324). He wished to preserve the prerogative, but also to avoid confrontations between the crown and the houses, and he disliked close definitions of their respective roles.

Throughout Charles I's personal rule Dorset remained a prominent courtier, and his wife was also appointed governess to the royal children, a position she continued to hold until shortly before her death in May 1645. Dorset's intense loyalty to the queen was particularly evident in February 1634 when he denounced William Prynne for making a veiled attack on her in *Histriomastix*. His speeches in other Star Chamber trials of the period revealed a similar concern with order, hierarchy, and authority. For example, when Henry Sherfield was tried in February 1633 for smashing a stained-glass window, Dorset blamed him for acting 'without the Bishop of the place', but opposed punishing him so as 'to avoyd the tumults of the rude ignorant people in the country where this gentleman dwelleth, where he hath been a goode governor' (Bodl. Oxf., MS Tanner 299, fols. 116v–117v). Such moderation brought Dorset into conflict with Laud, whom he described as 'the little man' (Dorset to the earl of Middlesex, 1 Oct 1636, CKS, uncatalogued Cranfield MSS). He gave assistance to several of Laud's enemies, including Bishop Williams of Lincoln and four young gentlemen of Lincoln's Inn who had drunk to Laud's confusion. He was sympathetic towards the godly minister John Cotton of Boston, yet was also close to a number of Catholics, notably Sir Kenelm Digby. He sought a church which tolerated diverse strands of opinion within a broad national framework: he admired the ecumenicism of Sir Thomas Browne's *Religio medici* and was wary of the Laudian insistence on unity through uniformity.

Relationship to Charles I These attitudes made for an intriguingly complex relationship with Charles I. There is no doubting Dorset's deep loyalty to the crown, and Clarendon later wrote of his 'most entire fidelity to the Crown' (Clarendon, *Hist. rebellion*, 1.76). Just as he had publicly endorsed the forced loan in 1627, so in the 1630s Dorset accepted ship money and even suggested that the king might revive scutage. Yet he remained equally devoted to constitutional propriety and gently tried to restrain some of Charles's more hasty actions. For example, in 1633, when Charles summarily dismissed Lord Keeper Coventry for refusing to issue pardons to various 'papists', Dorset declared that 'he knew the King would not condemne any man without hearing him', and Coventry was promptly reinstated (BL, Egerton MS 784, fol. 94r). Sometimes Dorset found Charles's behaviour baffling, and privately regretted episodes when the king acted 'for some reason best knowne to himselfe' (PRO, SP 16/355/65), or 'for what causes I know not' (PRO, CO 1/9, fol. 126r). By the later 1630s his influence was apparently waning, and he complained that he was excluded from the king's inner coterie of advisers. Never close to Laud, and on increasingly frosty terms with Strafford, Dorset was marginalized from what he called the 'Cabinett Counseyll' (Dorset to the earl of Middlesex, 20 Jan 1637, CKS, uncatalogued Cranfield MSS).

In the Short Parliament, Dorset supported the king by urging that supply should precede redress of grievances, and the following autumn he urged Charles to recall parliament. He served as one of the commissioners of regency during Charles's visit to Scotland in the summer of 1641, and he vehemently defended the right of bishops to sit in the Lords. At the end of November he tried to disperse the anti-episcopal demonstrators outside parliament by instructing the guards to open fire, an order which, although not obeyed, sharply divided opinion in both houses. He absented himself from the crucial vote on the Militia Ordinance on 5 March 1642, and ceased to attend the Lords on 23 March, when he surrendered his commissions of lieutenancy for Sussex and Middlesex. He probably joined the king at York some time in May.

Although he engaged to provide sixty horse for the king, throughout the summer of 1642 Dorset desperately hoped that an accommodation between Charles and the houses could be reached. For example, he begged the earl of Salisbury, who had initially gone to York but then returned to London, to 'study day and night, to keepe the more violent spiritts from passinge the Rubicon'. He stressed 'the tractable and councellable disposition of the King', while candidly admitting that Charles was 'apt to take extempore resolutions, upon the first impression', and hoped to find 'an easy and safe way' out of 'this darke and inextricable labyrinth' (BL, microfilm M 485, Hatfield House, Cecil MS, vol. 131, fols. 182v, 183r–183v). Dorset deeply regretted that 'there are to many hot headed people both heere and att London thatt advise and perswade desperate wayes', and he feared 'soe universall a change both in government and familyes as a victory must make, on which side soever it happens' (ibid., vol. 197, fols. 129v, 130r–130v). When the king raised his standard in August, Dorset lamented to the countess of Middlesex: 'Behold into whatt a sad condition blind zeale, pride, ambition, envy, malice and avarice … hath plunged the honor, quiet, safety, peace, plenty, prosperity, piety of this late, very late, most happy kingdome … All is lost, all is lost: soe lost as I wowld I weere quiet in my grave' (Dorset to the countess of Middlesex, August 1642, fols. 1r–1v, 3v, CKS, uncatalogued Cranfield MSS).

Dorset continued to promote a peace settlement throughout the years of civil war. On 25 August 1642 he joined Thomas Wriothesley, earl of Southampton, Sir John Colepeper, and Sir William Uvedale in conveying a message from Charles to the houses pledging his 'constant and earnest care to preserve the public peace' (Clarendon, *Hist. rebellion*, 2.304). The following month the earl of Essex wrote to Dorset asking if the king would receive the houses' terms and requesting safe conduct for peace commissioners. Dorset replied on Charles's behalf that the 'petitions of the houses shall never find his dower shutt against them', so long as they were not conveyed by 'those he hath by name accused of treason' (*JHL*, 5.380). The houses deemed this a breach of parliamentary privilege, and when Charles refused to give ground they resolved that he 'doth refuse all addresses and petitions from the Parliament' and broke off negotiations (ibid., 5.412). Essex, nevertheless, kept in touch with moderates at Oxford, and in May 1643 he 'sent to his confident the Earl of Dorset concerning the exchange of some prisoners' (BL, Add. MS 18980, fol. 60r). This initiative apparently bore fruit for, on 22 June, Essex was able to write to Prince Rupert proposing detailed arrangements for the exchange.

Lord chamberlain On 21 January 1644 Dorset was made lord chamberlain of the king's household, an appointment possibly intended to dignify the Oxford parliament, which opened the next day. Dorset sat in that parliament, and signed its conciliatory letter to Essex on 27 January, and at the end of the year he was actively involved in the preliminary negotiations that set up the treaty of Uxbridge (January–February 1645), although he did not himself participate in those talks. In a letter to the countess of Middlesex a few months later he summed up his view of the civil wars and the reasons for his royalist allegiance thus:

> I thank God my conscience wittnesseth unto mee, thatt in followinge my King, my master, my benefactor, I doe nothing butt whatt I am obliged to doe in honor, duty, piety and gratitude ... God and the King in my beleefe are both att stake, and if my life cann free them the one from beinge thrown out of his Church, and the other the State I will as hartely make itt a sacrifice as to wish my sinns in my last gaspe may bee forgiven mee. (Dorset to the countess of Middlesex, June/July? 1645, CKS, uncatalogued Cranfield MSS)

Yet, by the autumn of that year, Charles mistrusted even this loyal royalist. When the king returned to Oxford in November 1645, Dorset 'expressed in a speech full of affection for the King the joy they ought all to feel on his arrival', but the king 'replied to him coldly that he had the voice of Jacob, but that his hands were those of Esau' (Fotheringham, 1.60). In early December the earls of Dorset, Southampton, Hertford, and Lindsey again urged Charles to resume negotiations, but the king responded that he would defend his crown 'with his sword, if those of his friends failed him' (ibid., 1.70–71). Dorset remained at Oxford until the surrender, and on 20 June 1646 he was among those who signed the city's articles of capitulation.

Final years Dorset's role in public life became much more intermittent after June 1646. He continued to 'pray for peace and peaceable wayes of accommodation' (Dorset to the second earl of Middlesex, 1 Aug 1647, CKS, U269/C248, unfol.). In October 1647 he was one of a small circle of royalist peers whom the king summoned to Hampton Court to advise him. He apparently played no part in the second civil war, nor did he participate in the treaty of Newport. However, as late as 12 January 1649, eight days before the king's trial opened, it was reported that Dorset, together with Richmond, Hertford, 'and divers others of the King's party, have sent to the Councell of the Army to engage both their persons and estates that the King shall performe whatsoever he yeilds unto' (Bodl. Oxf., MS Clarendon 34, fol. 74r). However, the peers must have known that their chances of success were minimal, and this initiative came to nothing.

Dorset did not attend the king's funeral and, according to Sir Edward Walker, he never left his London house again after the regicide. By the early 1650s he was increasingly impoverished. In the autumn of 1646 Dorset had begged to compound under the Oxford articles; on 7 December he was assessed at the rate of one-tenth, or the value of two years' income from his estates, and fined £4360. After the settlement of impropriated rectories, his composition fine had been reduced to £775 in November 1647, although he was unable to pay this sum and secure his discharge until May 1650. Driven further and further into debt, Dorset was forced to borrow heavily, and in February 1652 he bemoaned his fate as 'a poore unsuccessefull Cavalier' (CKS, U269/C8). Five months later, on 17 July, he died peacefully at Dorset House. He was buried in the Sackville family vault at Withyham in Sussex.

Richard Sackville, fifth earl of Dorset (1622–1677), politician, the elder son of Edward Sackville, was born at Dorset House in London on 16 September 1622, and was styled Lord Buckhurst from 1624 until his father's death. In 1637 he married Lady Frances Cranfield (1622?–1687), daughter of Lionel Cranfield, first earl of Middlesex, and Anne Brett. He sat for East Grinstead, Sussex, in the Long Parliament, and was one of the fifty-nine 'Straffordians' in the Commons who opposed Strafford's attainder. He was officially disabled from sitting in the Commons on 5 February 1644, and the following July the committee for the advance of money fined him £1500. There is, however, no evidence that he took any part in the civil wars.

On his father's death Dorset inherited estates saddled with debts, and in 1657 lamented that he was 'one of the poorest earls in England' (Castle Ashby, Northampton, Compton MS 1084, fol. 21r). Impoverished and dispirited, he followed his father's example of retirement from public life, and apart from a brief visit to France lived quietly at his homes in London and Kent until the Restoration.

When the Convention assembled in April 1660, Dorset was appointed to the committee of safety, and was also chairman of the committee on the privileges of peers. The following month he chaired the committee charged with making arrangements for the king's reception. On 30 July Charles II appointed him lord lieutenant of Middlesex (an office which he held until 6 July 1662), and from 1670 until his death he was lord lieutenant of Sussex. He served on the commission for the trial of the regicides, and he was lord sewer at Charles's coronation on 23 April 1661. He was very active in the Lords, and proved himself an industrious and capable chairman of committees. Between 1661 and his death, he chaired no fewer than 84 (63 per cent) of the 133 meetings of the Lords committee for petitions. He also chaired numerous bill committees, especially those relating to economic and social matters.

By the mid-1670s Dorset had emerged as one of the 'country' peers, led by Shaftesbury. In particular, he staunchly defended the privileges and judicature of the Lords. His religious attitudes were apparently very similar to those of his father in their combination of commitment to episcopacy and acceptance of diversity. Dorset argued that the exclusion of the bishops in 1642, which his father had strongly resisted, had been contrary to the fundamental laws, and that all legislation passed in their absence was therefore technically illegal. Equally, about 1672–3 he wrote, in words reminiscent of his father's favourite work, Sir Thomas Browne's *Religio medici*, that 'no religion that is true can enjoin persecution of any person merely for being of another or different opinion, just because it is unreasonable for any man to be punished for what he cannot help' (CKS, U269/C20, fol. 86).

Dorset was a cultivated figure of wide interests. In 1638 he had contributed an elegy to a collection of poems, *Jonsonius virbius*, in Ben Jonson's memory, and according to John Aubrey he later translated Corneille's *Le Cid* into English. On 3 May 1665 he was elected a fellow of the Royal Society. He died at Knole on 27 August 1677 and was buried on 7 September in the Sackville family vault at Withyham.   DAVID L. SMITH

Sources CKS, Sackville papers, U269 · CKS, uncatalogued Cranfield MSS · Clarendon, *Hist. rebellion* · *JHL* · PRO, state papers domestic, Charles I, SP 16 · PRO, committee for compounding MSS, SP 23 · D. L. Smith, 'Catholic, Anglican or Puritan? Edward Sackville, fourth earl of Dorset, and the ambiguities of religion in early Stuart England', *TRHS*, 6th ser., 2 (1992), 105–24 · D. L. Smith, 'The fourth earl of Dorset and the personal rule of Charles I', *Journal of British Studies*, 30 (1991), 257–87 · D. L. Smith, 'The 4th earl of Dorset and the politics of the sixteen-twenties', *Historical Research*, 65 (1992), 37–53 · D. L. Smith, '"The more posed and wise advice": the fourth earl of Dorset and the English civil wars', *HJ*, 34 (1991), 797–829 · D. L. Smith, *Constitutional royalism and the search for settlement, c. 1640–1649* (1994) · C. J. Phillips, *History of the Sackville family*, 2 vols. [1930] · GEC, *Peerage*, new edn · J. G. Fotheringham, ed., *The diplomatic correspondence of Jean de Montereul and the brothers de Bellièvre: French ambassadors in England and Scotland, 1645–1648*, 2 vols., Scottish History Society, 29–30 (1898–9) · Foster, *Alum. Oxon.*

Archives BL, relation of his duel with Lord Bruce, Add. MS 18644 · CKS, corresp. and papers | CKS, Cranfield MSS

Likenesses attrib. W. Larkin, oils, 1613, Ranger's House, Blackheath, London · studio of A. Van Dyck, oils, *c.*1635, Knole, Kent [*see illus.*] · R. Dunkarton, mezzotint, pubd 1814 (after A. Van Dyck), BM

Wealth at death £2180 p.a. in 1646: PRO, SP 23/3, p. 318

Sackville, George. *See* Germain, George Sackville, first Viscount Sackville (1716–1785).

Sackville, Herbrand de (*fl.* 1066–1086). *See under* Sackville family (*per. c.*1066–*c.*1477).

Sackville, Herbrand Edward Dundonald Brassey, **ninth Earl De La Warr** (1900–1976), politician, was born on 20 June 1900 at the Manor House, Bexhill, Sussex, the only son and youngest of the three children of Gilbert George Reginald Sackville, eighth Earl De La Warr (1869–1915), and his wife, Muriel Agnes (*d.* 1930), daughter of Thomas, first Earl Brassey. His parents were divorced in 1902. Buck, as he was universally known, was educated at Eton College (1913–17), where he founded and became president of the Eton Political Society, and, briefly, at Magdalen College, Oxford. In 1918 he joined the Royal Naval Volunteer Reserve (trawler section), as he was a conscientious objector at the time. He had succeeded to the earldom in 1915 at the age of fifteen and was, perhaps, the only able seaman who sat, of right, on the steps of the throne in the House of Lords—the place reserved for peers who have succeeded as minors and so cannot take their place in the chamber until they are twenty-one.

After coming of age De La Warr actively supported the Labour Party in the House of Lords and was appointed lord-in-waiting in Ramsay MacDonald's government in 1924. In MacDonald's second Labour administration he was parliamentary under-secretary at the War Office, 1929–30, and at the Ministry of Agriculture, 1930–31. He followed MacDonald into the National Government in August 1931 and served successively as parliamentary secretary to the Ministry of Agriculture and deputy minister to the department of fisheries, 1931–5, and parliamentary secretary to the Board of Education, 1935–6. He was sworn of the privy council in 1936. He was appointed parliamentary under-secretary of state for the colonies, 1936–7 and was responsible for the De La Warr report on higher education in east Africa (1937), which has been regarded as an enlightened statement of policy for the creation of an indigenous university in tropical Africa. Under Neville Chamberlain he entered the cabinet as lord privy seal, May 1937 – October 1938. At this critical period he said in cabinet that he would face war to free the world from the constant threat of ultimatums. This may explain his demotion to the less prestigious offices of president of the Board of Education, 1938–April 1940, and first commissioner of works (not in the cabinet), April–May 1940. He was chairman of the National Labour Party, 1931–43.

De La Warr did not join Winston Churchill's government in May 1940, probably because National Labour was not acceptable to the Labour Party. He served in the Ministry of Supply as director of home flax production during much of the war.

In autumn 1951 De La Warr was appointed postmaster-general by Churchill, and held the post until Churchill resigned in April 1955. During his term of office there was trouble in Scotland with Post Office property which carried the royal emblem EIIR. On the positive side, several important developments were introduced, the most notable of which were the starting of the international telex service, the development of letter-sorting machines, the planning of the national telephone numbering scheme, and the laying of the trans-Atlantic cable from Scotland to Newfoundland. The public benefit of these became apparent only after he had left office. De La Warr, assisted by his wife, also took a personal interest in selecting the new high-value definitive stamps. His period of office was best remembered, however, by the introduction of commercial television, which met with virulent opposition firmly expressed in the House of Lords. It was only the calm, polite, and clear exposition of De La Warr which persuaded the house to accept the proposals.

De La Warr had thus served in the governments of four prime ministers—Labour, National, and Conservative. He was never a keen party politician, but was deeply and sincerely interested in the realities of politics; he had no love for dogmatic theories. He maintained a close interest in the welfare of the Commonwealth; besides holding the office of under-secretary of state for the colonies, he was a member of the Empire Marketing Board from 1930, chairman of the Royal Commonwealth Society (1960), and chairman of the Joint East and Central Africa Board from 1955 to 1958. He visited Africa most years.

De La Warr's constant and abiding affection lay in agriculture and land in general. He ran his farm in Sussex with ability and enthusiasm and was a pioneer in new agricultural ideas and practice. It was from these interests that he was appointed a member of the council of the duchy of Lancaster from 1931, chairman of the Agricultural Research Council from 1944 to 1949, and chairman of the National Trust estates committee (1950–51). As mayor of Bexhill, 1932–5, he persuaded the local council to finance an entertainments pavilion. Built to the design of Erich Mendelsohn and Serge Chermayeff, the De La Warr pavilion in Bexhill is regarded as a landmark in the history of modern British architecture. Opened in 1935, the pavilion was acquired by a charitable trust in 2000 with a view to its restoration. He served in government, off and on, over a period of thirty years and was an active member of the House of Lords for fifty years. His humility and simplicity of bearing tended to conceal his shrewd political judgement. He combined a warm heart and much personal charm. He was appointed GBE in 1956.

On 30 December 1920 De La Warr married (Helen) Diana (d. 1966), daughter of Captain Henry Gerard Leigh, 1st Life Guards, of Luton Hoo. They had two sons and a daughter who married F. T. R. Giles. Their second son was missing, presumed killed, on active service in 1943. On 1 March 1968 he married Sylvia Margaret, countess of Kilmuir DBE, widow of David Patrick Maxwell Fyfe, earl of Kilmuir, daughter of William Reginald Harrison, of Liverpool, and sister of Rex Harrison, the actor.

De La Warr died on the pavement outside St James's Palace while walking to the theatre on 28 January 1976. He was succeeded in the earldom by his son, William Herbrand Sackville (1921–1988). SELKIRK, rev.

Sources personal knowledge (1986) · private information (1986) · *The Times* (29 Jan 1976) · Burke, *Peerage* (1999)

Archives FILM BFI NFTVA, news footage

Wealth at death £175,678: probate, 26 July 1976, *CGPLA Eng. & Wales*

Sackville, John Frederick, third duke of Dorset (1745–1799), cricketer and courtier, was born on 25 March 1745 and baptized at St James's, Piccadilly, on 24 April, the only son of Lord John Philip Sackville (1713–1765), a politician, and his wife, Lady Frances, the daughter of John Leveson-Gower, first Earl Gower. He was educated at Westminster School and became member of parliament for Kent in the 1768 general election; however, he vacated his seat less than a year later, on succeeding his uncle Charles Sackville as third duke of Dorset (January 1769). A supporter of the Rockingham and Shelburne ministries, he was lord lieutenant of Kent (1769–97) and colonel of the West Kent militia (1778–99). He was sworn of the privy council on being appointed captain of the yeomen of the guard and master of the horse in 1782, but resigned these posts when he changed political allegiance to support Pitt the following year. From December 1783 until his recall in August 1789 he was an indolent and unremarkable ambassador to France.

Dorset's rank was the passport to public office, but he was also heir to the family cricketing tradition. He spent a great deal of time and money on the game, which attracted some criticism during the War of American Independence, though the *Morning Chronicle* of 1 July 1782 praised him for uniting 'the elegancies of modern luxury with the more manly sports'. He gave employment on his estate, Knole Park, near Sevenoaks, to men with cricketing ability, notably John Minshull, who in 1769 scored the first recorded century.

Dorset himself took part in 1774 in the first recorded partnership of a century when he made seventy-seven runs for Kent in an overwhelming defeat of Hambledon. Earlier in the same year he had served on the committee at the Star and Garter, in Pall Mall, which had revised the laws of cricket. He was one of the more talented of the aristocrats who played cricket in the eighteenth century, even if his record does not quite match up to the eulogy printed in the *Gentleman's Magazine* in 1773 by the poet John Burnby:

His Grace for bowling cannot yield
To none but Lumpy in the field.
He firmly stands with bat upright,
And strikes with his athletic might.
Sends forth the ball across the mead,
And scores six notches for the deed.
(Haygarth, 60)

To be compared with the Hambledon player Lumpy Stevens, whose portrait Dorset commissioned—the first ever of a paid cricketer—was high praise. Dorset himself played occasionally both for and against Hambledon and was the prime mover in the transfer in 1783 of the club's ground from Broadhalfpenny to Windmill Down. He played for England against Hambledon that year, when he was bowled by Stevens. Dorset had also been an early advocate of women's cricket and argued in his 'Letter to female cricket players': 'What is human life but a game of cricket and, if so, why should not the ladies play it as well as we' (Haygarth, xxii).

Dorset was widely known within the circles of the *ton* as a philanderer and had affairs with a succession of mistresses, including Elizabeth Bridget *Armitstead, Nancy Parsons, Elizabeth, countess of Derby, and Georgiana, duchess of Devonshire [see Cavendish, Georgiana]. His letters to Georgiana during his ambassadorship give a valuable account of the gathering crisis in France. In 1789 he allegedly asked his friend the earl of Tankerville to bring a cricket side over to France. The team (Lumpy Stevens included) assembled at Dover in August but was met there by the duke hastily retreating from the preliminary skirmishes of the French Revolution. Horace Walpole wrote of his ambassadorship: 'The French could not desire a man more qualified to be a dupe' (Foreman, 196).

After pestering Pitt with requests for a year, Dorset was created a knight of the Garter in 1788 and served as steward of the royal household from 1789 to 1799. On 4 January 1790 he married Arabella (1769–1825), the daughter of Sir

Charles Cope, second baronet, and his wife, Catherine Bishopp. They had two daughters and a son, George John Frederick, who succeeded to the dukedom on his father's death, at Knole Park on 19 July 1799. Dorset was buried at Withyham church in Sussex. In 1801 his widow married Charles Whitworth, Earl Whitworth.

Dorset, one of the founding members of the Marylebone Cricket Club in 1787, made a genuine contribution to cricket in the rural south-east, and in his will he left Sevenoaks Vine in Kent as a ground for cricket in perpetuity. Cricket apart, he was a patron of artists, notably Gainsborough, who painted him, and he was philanthropic to the poor of Sevenoaks—although, as the Sackville papers reveal, his expenditure on entertaining far exceeded such benevolence. Despite some savage satirization of him in the *Rambler's Magazine* (1 February 1783), he was generally liked for his sympathetic nature. He was, according to his steward, 'at all times the kindest in the world' (Einberg, 11).   GERALD M. D. HOWAT

Sources [A. Haygarth], *Frederick Lillywhite's cricket scores and biographies*, 1 (1862) · Lord Harris, ed., *The history of Kent county cricket* (1907) · R. D. Knight, *Hambledon's cricket glory*, 13 (1994) · D. Underdown, *Start of play* (2000) · J. Goulstone, *Hambledon: the men and the myths* (2001) · Lord Harris and F. S. Ashley-Cooper, *Lord's and the MCC* (1914) · F. S. Ashley-Cooper, *Hambledon cricket chronicle, 1772–1796* (1924) · *DNB* · E. Einberg, *Gainsborough's 'Giovanna Baccelli'* (1976) · *Rambler's Magazine* (1 Feb 1784) · C. J. Phillips, *History of the Sackville family*, 2 vols. [1929] · GEC, *Peerage* · M. M. Drummond, 'Sackville, John Frederick', HoP, *Commons, 1754–90* · A. Foreman, *Georgiana, duchess of Devonshire* (1998)
Archives CKS, corresp. and papers | Bakewell, Devonshire collection, letters to duke and duchess of Devonshire · BL, corresp. with Lord Carmarthen and William Eden, Add. MSS 34420–34428, *passim* · BL, corresp. with duke of Leeds, Add. MSS 28060–28065; Egerton MS 3499 · BL, corresp. with first earl of Liverpool, Add. MSS 38220–38227, 38309–38310, 38458, 38580 · Chatsworth House, Derbyshire, letters to duke and duchess of Devonshire · PRO, letters to William Pitt, PRO 30/8 · PRO, letters to Lord Stafford, PRO 30/29
Likenesses J. Reynolds, oils, 1769, Knole, Kent · O. Humphry, miniature, 1778, Knole, Kent · T. Gainsborough, oils, 1782, Knole, Kent · T. Hardy, mezzotint, pubd 1799 (after J. Reynolds, 1769), NG Ire. · O. Humphry, miniature, V&A · attrib. J. Reynolds, oils, Knole, Kent · S. W. Reynolds, mezzotint (after J. Reynolds), BM, NPG · J. Scott, mezzotint (after T. Gainsborough), BM, NPG · portrait, repro. in Ashley-Cooper, *Hambledon cricket chronicle*; priv. coll.

Sackville, Jordan de (d. c.1175). *See under* Sackville family (*per. c.*1066–c.1477).

Sackville, Sir Jordan de (d. 1273). *See under* Sackville family (*per. c.*1066–c.1477).

Sackville, Lionel Cranfield, first duke of Dorset (1688–1765), politician, was born on 18 January 1688 at Knole Park, Sevenoaks, Kent, the only son of Charles *Sackville, sixth earl of Dorset (1643–1706), and his second wife, Lady Mary (1668–1691), youngest daughter of James *Compton, third earl of Northampton (1622–1681), and sister of Spencer, earl of Wilmington. Sackville was educated at Westminster School and Oxford University. He succeeded his father as seventh earl of Dorset and second earl of Middlesex on 29 January 1706 and took his seat in the House of Lords on 19 January 1708. In January of the following year

he married Elizabeth (1687–1768), daughter of Lieutenant-General Walter Colyear and niece of David, first earl of Portmore. Elizabeth, then a maid of honour to Queen Anne, later became first lady of the bedchamber to Caroline both as princess of Wales and as queen. The couple had six children, three sons and three daughters: Charles *Sackville, second duke of Dorset (1711–1769); Lord John Philip Sackville (1712–1765), MP for Tamworth; Lord George Sackville *Germain, first Viscount Sackville (1716–1785); Lady Anne Sackville, who died young; Lady Elizabeth Sackville, who married Thomas, second Viscount Weymouth; and Lady Caroline Sackville, who married Joseph Damer, afterwards first earl of Dorchester.

An outspoken champion of the Hanoverian succession during the last years of Queen Anne, Dorset served the new dynasty in a variety of household and state offices. Elected knight of the Garter on 16 October 1714, he was created duke of Dorset on 17 June 1720, and re-entered the Lords on 8 October. On 30 May 1725 he was appointed lord steward of the household and acted as lord high steward of England at the coronation of George II. For years Dorset had aspired to go to Ireland as lord lieutenant, but an opportunity to do so did not arise until early 1730.

At that time Sir Robert Walpole abruptly turned out the serving chief governor of Ireland, Lord Carteret, and arranged Dorset's formal appointment on 23 June 1730. In the duke's entourage proceeding to Ireland as personal chaplain was a bright young clergyman with excellent English political connections, George Stone, brother of Newcastle's private secretary, Andrew Stone. George Stone was ambitious, industrious, and charming to a fault. Moreover, he was unmarried and later reputed to be more attracted to men than women. Once in Ireland, Stone decided to remain in that country and build a career in church and state, which he did with great rapidity and success.

Upon arriving in Dublin on 13 September 1731, Dorset quickly discovered that the English governments of that era had no consistent strategy for managing the Irish parliament or for governing the country. At that time Irish politics functioned in an unusually undirected state, and Dorset had to bargain with individual faction leaders to get the support necessary to pass the Irish money bills and to complete the rest of the king's business in a timely fashion. The duke socialized extensively with members of parliament in order to recruit supporters for the forthcoming session. One of those recruited was Thomas Carter, a gifted speaker and man of influence in the Irish House of Commons. Thus prepared and supported by Carter and others, Dorset found that his encounters with the Irish parliament were tolerably easy. In each of his three sessions the duke managed to complete most of the king's business expeditiously.

To be sure, Dorset did make several significant errors of judgement. In 1732 he missed an opportunity to obtain long-term debt funding. He played virtually no role in the election of Henry Boyle to the vacant speaker's chair in 1733, thereby receiving no gratitude or promises of future support for facilitating it. Also, he deeply distressed Walpole, first by failing to rally support for repeal of the Irish Test Act, and second by giving away an important Irish customs post to a friend of the new speaker.

Walpole had had enough of Dorset. The duke was replaced as chief governor of Ireland by William Cavendish, third duke of Devonshire, in March 1737 and then reappointed to his old post as lord steward of the household. Out of Ireland, Dorset refused to believe that he had been removed because of poor performance, and he never rid himself of a desire to return to Ireland as lord lieutenant.

The combination of an outbreak of war in Europe in 1740 and ministerial instability in England following the fall of Walpole in 1742 complicated Anglo-Irish politics for the next eight years. English ministers had no patience with and little time for Irish politics. During these years, English ministers were willing to pay reasonable prices for easy enactment of Irish money bills and short tranquil parliamentary sessions. Dorset's successors in Ireland between 1737 and 1750, the duke of Devonshire, the earl of Chesterfield, and especially the earl of Harrington, allowed men of influence in the Irish parliament to complete the king's business efficiently. Political faction leaders in the Irish House of Commons, including Henry Boyle, Thomas Carter, and Anthony Malone, all held office under the crown and yet demanded periodic gifts of additional patronage and favours to keep their factions intact and to provide the support needed to enact the money bills. Moreover, in time these men also gave political advice to Devonshire and Chesterfield, and virtually managed Lord Harrington, who lacked political allies in London.

Back in England, Dorset received regular reports about the state of Irish politics from George Stone who had risen spectacularly in the Church of Ireland from an appointment as dean of Derry in 1734 to that of archbishop of Armagh in 1747. Dorset continually pressed the king's ministers to allow him to return to Ireland. Persistence was rewarded in April 1750 when the king decided to endure Harrington no longer. On his reappointment Dorset chose his talented ambitious third son, Lord George Sackville, as chief secretary.

Dorset's second term was to prove far less harmonious than his first. Once installed in Dublin Castle, the chief secretary and Stone were appalled by the unreasonable patronage demands and unbridled power of Carter and Malone. Moreover, Stone had managed to offend both of those gentlemen severely. At the same time, Stone's intellectual arrogance and reputed homosexual lifestyle made a permanent personal and political enemy out of the earl of Kildare. Furthermore, Sackville and Stone engaged in a series of conversations with unattached members in the House of Commons suggesting that the time had come for Henry Boyle to retire as speaker. As the opening of parliament approached, relations between the principal persons in the Irish executive, Stone and Sackville, and the leadership in the House of Commons—Boyle, Malone, and Carter—as well as with the political friends of the earl

of Kildare had become so strained as to make confrontation unavoidable.

During the parliamentary session of 1751–2 the most serious contest between the Irish executive and the Boyle party occurred over the manner of applying a current revenue surplus to the national debt. Since part of that revenue surplus had been derived from the hereditary revenues, that is, moneys belonging to the king and not voted by parliament, crown law officers insisted that the Irish parliament could not dispose of such funds without royal consent. Therefore, any application of the surplus to the national debt would require phrasing in the Irish money bills which signified the king's previous agreement. The Boyle party argued and many members of the Irish parliament agreed that no such previous royal consent was necessary in order to appropriate a revenue surplus. However, in 1751, crown lawyers insisted that the king's right to dispose of his own money had to be protected from encroachment by the Irish parliament. They recommended including previous consent language in Irish money bills whenever revenue surpluses were intended to be appropriated for any purposes. Consequently, when Dorset transmitted the Irish money bills without previous consent language for approval in London in November 1751, the word 'consent' was added to the preambles of the bills. The Boyle party protested the alteration of the money bills but did not have enough votes in the Irish House of Commons to defeat them. In order to rally the votes needed to defeat the lord lieutenant on an issue as abstract and complicated as previous consent, Dorset's opponents began a major public relations campaign. This proceeded on two levels. First, there was a series of public and private condemnations of the Dorset administration culminating in a memorial prepared by the earl of Kildare and sent to the king in May 1753 urging the duke's removal as lord lieutenant of Ireland. On another level, there was a barrage of pamphlets attacking the arrogance and competence of Sackville and the character and lifestyle of Stone. Unintimidated by the scurrility of the attacks on his two principal advisers, Dorset returned to Ireland in October 1753, confident that he could cope successfully with a political situation made dangerous by another revenue surplus.

The situation further deteriorated after the session opened on 9 October. Dorset failed to obtain any formal recognition in the Irish House of Commons of the king's previous consent to dispose of another revenue surplus. In England, once again, the word 'consent' was inserted into the Irish money bills which were returned to Dublin for final enactment. However, this time the Boyle party had sufficient votes to reject an altered Irish money bill and it did so on 18 December 1753 by a vote of 122 to 117. Outside parliament the victory of the Boyle party was celebrated as the people's victory with demonstrations and bonfires. Dorset responded by proroguing parliament on 31 January 1754. Next, the duke recommended that George II order under his sign manual the appropriation of the revenue surplus to the same purposes intended by the rejected money bill. This the king undertook. Next,

Dorset recommended and achieved dismissal from crown offices presently held of Boyle, Carter, Malone, and other leaders of the majority who had voted against the money bill. On 10 May 1754 Dorset and Sackville took their leave of Ireland fully expecting to return.

In Dublin the pamphlet campaign against Stone intensified and made some important converts there as well as in London. More important, however, the policy of punishing the leaders of the Boyle party had failed. After five months of trying, Stone was unable to organize a party in the Irish House of Commons that could guarantee a working majority in the next session. Alarmed by a steadily deteriorating political situation in Ireland, the king and his English ministers decided to replace Dorset, make terms with Boyle and his political allies, and banish Stone at least temporarily from any role in the Irish government. Dorset was dismissed in early February 1755 and replaced by William Cavendish, marquess of Hartington.

In England Dorset was appointed master of the horse on 29 March 1755 and held that post until July 1757 when he was reinstalled as constable of Dover Castle and lord warden of the Cinque Ports for life, having previously held both offices on two separate occasions. During riots occasioned by the Militia Bill in 1757, Dorset was attacked by a mob at Knole Park but escaped serious injury by the timely arrival of a small cavalry force. The duke also suffered the great anxiety of Lord George Sackville's court martial and public disgrace for failing to act upon the orders of his commander-in-chief at the battle of Minden in 1759. A man widely noted for his conversation and his elegant and increasingly old-fashioned formality of manners, Dorset died at Knole Park on 9 October 1765 and was buried on 18 October at Withyham, Sussex. He was survived by his wife who died on 12 June 1768.

ROBERT E. BURNS

Sources DNB · R. E. Burns, *Irish parliamentary politics in the eighteenth century*, 2 (1990) · *The king's business: letters on the administration of Ireland, 1740–1761, from the papers of Sir Robert Wilmot*, ed. J. Walton (1996) · PRO, secretary of state MSS, SP63/392–414 · *Eighteenth century Irish official papers in Great Britain*, 1 (1973) · J. C. D. Clark, 'Whig tactics and parliamentary precedent: the English management of Irish politics, 1754–1756', *HJ*, 21 (1978), 275–301 · Derbys. RO, Wilmot MSS · PRO NI, Shannon MSS · C. L. Falkiner, ed., 'The correspondence of Archbishop Stone and the duke of Newcastle', *EngHR*, 20 (1905), 735–63
Archives CKS, corresp. and papers · Derbys. RO, papers relating to Ireland · PRO NIre., Irish papers · U. Mich., Clements L., corresp. and papers | BL, corresp. with Lord Hardwicke, Add. MSS 35585–35692, *passim* · BL, corresp. with Lord Holdernesse, Egmont MS 3435 · BL, corresp. with duke of Newcastle, Add. MSS 32556–32897, 33055, *passim* · PRO NIre., Boyle MSS, letters to Lord Shannon · V&A NAL, letters to Lady Sundon
Likenesses G. Kneller, oils, *c*.1695, Knole, Kent · G. Kneller, oils, *c*.1710, NPG · G. Kneller, oils, *c*.1717, Knole, Kent · J. Wootton, group portrait, oils, 1727 (*View of Dover castle*), Knole, Kent · J. Wootton, oils, 1727, Knole, Kent · attrib. R. Carriera, pastel drawing, Knole, Kent

Sackville, Lady Margaret (1881–1963), poet and children's writer, was born on 24 December 1881 at 60 Grosvenor Street, Mayfair, London, the youngest of two sons and three daughters of Reginald Windsor West, later

Sackville-West (changed to Sackville by royal licence), second Baron Buckhurst and seventh Earl De La Warr (1817–1896), rector of Withyam, Sussex, chaplain to Queen Victoria, and high steward of Stratford upon Avon, and his wife, the Hon. Constance Mary Elizabeth, *née* Baillie-Cochrane, Countess De La Warr (*d.* 1929), daughter of the first Baron Lamington. She was second cousin to Victoria (Vita) Sackville-*West (1892–1962). Lady Margaret's father died when she was fourteen, and her oldest brother Lionel drowned at twenty-one.

Sackville spent her youth in Sussex, holidaying in Scotland, and dedicated herself to poetry early in life, claiming that she dictated her first poem at six. Little is known about her education. At sixteen she was 'discovered' by the poet Wilfrid Scawen Blunt, who long remained a literary friend and admirer. In 1903 he gave her some of his verses for an Irish magazine she hoped to start, and in 1906 and 1907 she performed in plays he had written, singing and dancing much to his satisfaction. She published her poetry in periodicals such as the *English Review*, *The Englishwoman*, *Country Life*, *The Nation*, *The Spectator*, and the *Pall Mall Gazette*. Her published books, mainly poetry but also some prose, comprising twenty-one volumes in all, began with *Floral Symphony* (1900), followed by *Poems*, a volume of children's verse, in 1901. In 1909 she published *Fairy Tales for the Old and Young* with Ronald Campbell Macfie. In 1910 she edited *A Book of Verse by Living Women* (including her own); in the introduction she exulted in the fact that poetry was one of few arts in which women were allowed to engage without opposition. She further published dramatic poems in *Bertrud and other Poems* (1911). She was an officer of the Poetry Recital Society (founded in 1909), and retained its bardic sense of the poet as a counter-force to the modern world's disarray; her inaugural address, 'The art of speaking verse' (published in the *Poetical Gazette*, September 1912, 455), upholds the group's very traditional values. She published some lyrics in *Songs of Aphrodite* (1913).

In 1912 Sackville formed a friendship with the Labour leader Ramsay MacDonald that lasted many years. She sent him her poetry and wrote him letters sympathizing with his interest in social justice, but also deploring his attacks on the landed aristocracy. In June 1917 Lady Ottoline Morrell invited her to Garsington with MacDonald for a weekend at his suggestion, as he and Sackville were 'at the time great friends' (*Ottoline at Garsington*, 110). MacDonald had apparently unsuccessfully proposed to her in the past, but continued to arrange to see her when he came to Edinburgh because they 'remained friends' (Sackville, 'Whitehouse Terrace', 68).

During the First World War Sackville joined the anti-war Union of Democratic Control and published a collection of poems, *The Pageant of War* (1916), which denounced women who condoned war as betrayers of their sons:

> We spoke not, so men died …
> We mothers and we murderers of mankind
> ('Nostra culpa', repr. in *Literature and Society*)

Her other brother Gilbert died in the war.

In 1919 Sackville published her *Selected Poems*, in which

Wilfrid Scawen Blunt touted her in a preface as an exemplar of 'the classic tradition in form and dignity' (p. vi). Unimpressed by the modernists, she employed traditional forms and looked back to Swinburne, William Morris, and the Romantics; she wrote of beauty and happiness and classical myth. She published prose plays in *Three Fairy Plays* (1925).

Sackville spent much of her adult life in Midlothian and Edinburgh, where she was an accepted member of the Whitehouse Terrace salon of Marc-André Raffalovich and John Gray until their deaths. She was first president of the Scottish PEN and a fellow of the Royal Society of Literature. In October 1930 she presented 'Some aspects of modern Scottish literature' before the Royal Society, and spoke of herself occupying 'an amphibious position' between England and Scotland in which she could 'breathe in either with equal ease' ('Some aspects', 61). From 1936 Sackville lived at 22 Lansdowne Terrace in Cheltenham. She was principal reviewer for a local newspaper, active in local literary movements, and a champion of Gloucestershire poets. She served as first president of the North Gloucestershire (Cheltenham) Centre of Poetry (re-elected in 1942). Her collected poems were brought out in 1939.

During the Second World War Sackville gave talks on and recitals of Kipling and other poets, including herself, to aid the duke of Gloucester's Red Cross Fund and other charities. In the 1940s came three illustrated books in which poems are matched to pictures (such as *Lyrical Woodlands*, with drawings by Lonsdale Ragg, 1945), and *Miniatures* (1947), which were mainly single quatrains. In 1949 she was awarded the Schroeder Foundation's medal for her achievements in literature. In 1953 Georgina Somerville edited *Harp Aeolian*, a collection by Lady Margaret's admirers who admired her old-fashioned style. As late as 1960 came *Quatrains and other Poems*. Her final act of publication was contributing reminiscences to a volume of essays in 1963 on the Whitehouse Terrace salon.

Famous for her gracious manner and her classic beauty, Sackville was immortalized in a bronze bust fashioned by Scotland's sculptor royal, Pittendrigh Macgillivray, and her profile depicted in the muses surrounding Gladstone's statue in Atholl Crescent in Edinburgh. She never married and died of a heart condition at Rokeby Nursing Home in Cheltenham on 18 April 1963. In addition to her accomplishments, her obituaries credited her with generosity to other writers, kindliness, and a sense of humour. Sackville's popularity during her lifetime did not, however, survive her death. There has been no biography of her, or significant critical interest, and no modern editions of her works have appeared.

HARRIET BLODGETT

Sources *The Times* (20 April 1963) · *Gloucestershire Echo* (18 April 1963) · W. S. Blunt, preface, *Selected poems by Lady Margaret Sackville* (1919) · W. S. Blunt, *My diaries: being a personal narrative of events, 1888–1914*, 2 (1921) · D. Marquand, *Ramsay MacDonald* (1977) · *Ottoline at Garsington: memoirs of Lady Ottoline Morrell, 1915–1918*, ed. R. Gathorne-Hardy (1974) · M. Sackville, 'Some aspects of modern Scottish literature', ed. F. Younghusband, *Essays by Divers Hands,* being the Transactions of the Royal Society of Literature of the United Kingdom, new ser., 10 (1931) · M. Sackville, introduction, *A book of verse by living women* (1910) · M. Sackville, 'The art of speaking verse', *Poetical Gazette* (Sept 1912), 455 · M. Morrisson, 'Performing the pure voice: elocution, verse, recitation, and modernist poetry in prewar London', *Modernism/Modernity*, 3/3 (1996), 25–50 · Blain, Clements & Grundy, *Feminist comp.* · G. Somerville, ed., *Harp aeolian: commentaries on the work of Lady Margaret Sackville* (1935) · M. Sackville, *Collected poems* (1939) · M. Sackville, 'At Whitehouse Terrace', *Two friends*, ed. B. Sewell (1963) · b. cert. · d. cert.

Archives Indiana University, Bloomington, MSS · State University of New York, Buffalo, corresp. and literary papers · University of Wisconsin, MSS magazine | FM Cam., letters to W. S. Blunt · U. Edin. L., corresp. with Charles Sarolea · U. Leeds, Brotherton L., letters to Clement Shorter; letters to Alberta Vickridge · W. Sussex RO, letters to Wilfrid Scawen Blunt · Washington State University, Pullman, Washington, DC, letters to Francis Berry and Thomas Moult

Likenesses P. Macgillivray, bronze bust, Diploma Gallery, Edinburgh · photograph, repro. in Somerville, ed., *Harp aeolian*

Wealth at death £3534 17s.: probate, 25 June 1963, CGPLA Eng. & Wales

Sackville, Sir Richard (d. 1566), administrator, was the eldest son of John Sackville (c.1484–1557) of Withyham and Chiddingly, Sussex, and his first wife, Margaret (d. c.1533), daughter of Sir William Boleyn of Blickling. Through his father he had connections with the earls of Arundel, while on his mother's side he was cousin to Anne Boleyn. It is difficult to disentangle his early life from that of his uncle and namesake, Sir Richard Sackville of Westhampnett, but after early tuition by a schoolmaster who, he later reported, 'before he was fully fourteen years old, drove him with fear of beating from all love of learning' (HoP, *Commons, 1558–1603*, 3.314), he was probably educated at Cambridge and the Inner Temple. His family connections would have given him the entrée to the court but little is known of him before the 1540s. His first important public office was evidently as escheator of Surrey and Sussex in 1541–2. Thereafter, in 1544 he became steward of the archbishop of Canterbury's Sussex manors and took on various jobs such as the commission for chantries. Even the date of his marriage to Winifred (d. 1586), daughter of Sir John Brydges, or Brugges, lord mayor of London in 1520, is uncertain. They had three sons, of whom only Thomas *Sackville (later first earl of Dorset), born c.1536, survived and one daughter, Anne [*see* Fiennes, Anne], who married Gregory *Fiennes, tenth Baron Dacre of the South. He may have been on bad terms with his father, who cut him out of his testament in 1557, a move Sackville successfully challenged. If so, it may explain his involvement in the land market created by the sales of monastic property. His dealings, which were discreet but apparently widespread, enabled him to build up a private fortune, and also on occasion to extend his influence by lending money.

Sackville's appointment as chancellor of augmentations in August 1548 evidently resulted from his willingness to take over some of his predecessor's debts to the crown—for which he committed lands which he then rented back for £200 a year. He proved a competent and diligent administrator and by February 1549 had been knighted. He was sufficiently trusted to be given the custody of the twenty-fourth earl of Arundel's heir in 1551—an expensive undertaking since Lord Maltravers arrived with his entire household, which Sackville later itemized in attempting to recover his costs.

Another reason for Sackville's low profile under Henry VIII may have been his commitment to the reformed religion, which his wife did not share. He was described by Ascham in the introduction to *The Scholemaster* as 'an earnest favourer and furtherer of God's true Religion', a description supported by the preamble to his testament. He sat in the 1547 parliament for Chichester and in March 1553 for Sussex. He steered through the reefs and shoals of Edward VI's reign without alienating any of the powerful, perhaps because he was generally well liked. Ascham's encomium continues that he was a

> faithfull Servitor to his Prince and Countrie, a lover of learning and all learned men; wise in all doinges; Curtesse to all persons, showing spite to none, doing Good to many and as I well found, to me so fast a frend as I never lost the like before.

The financial resources which earned him the nickname of Fillsack may also have helped. He lent the duke of Northumberland £5000 for the venture to put Lady Jane Grey on the throne, with sufficient strings attached to enable him to recover the money later.

When the court of augmentations was dissolved in January 1554 Sackville made some attempt to argue for its continuation. Instead, he received an annuity of £300 a year. He also lost most of his paid local offices and retired to the life of a Sussex gentleman, serving as JP and *custos rotulorum* but taking no part in central government. Nevertheless, he was able to arrange a marriage for his son to the daughter of Sir John Baker, Mary's powerful councillor and under-treasurer of the exchequer.

The accession of his cousin Elizabeth to the throne saw an immediate revival of Sackville's fortunes. He was called to her first privy council meeting, appointed a privy councillor, and sat for Sussex in 1559 and 1563. On 5 February 1559 he was appointed under-treasurer of the exchequer. Proposals which he had made earlier for land revenue management were revived and implemented, and from then until his death he was involved in all the commissions set up to bring the kingdom's finances and financial courts into order. His personal commitment to this may be indicated by the £5000 he was willing to lend Elizabeth in 1561 to restore the exchange. He was also one of those given the sensitive job of investigating the position of the lord treasurer with regard to the secret treasury in the Tower. He was employed in various matters relating to securing the new church order, being appointed *inter alia* to see that the Acts of Uniformity and Supremacy were enforced. Margaret Stewart, countess of Lennox, who as Henry VII's granddaughter was close to the succession, was placed in his custody in 1562 and 1566. As the queen's cousin Sackville was acceptable as one of her surrogates when funeral services were held at St Paul's for foreign monarchs. Elizabeth trusted him but

she did not ennoble him—an honour his son received a year after his death.

Amid all his public duties, Sackville continued to deal in lands and to manage directly his extensive estates and ironworks. In 1564 he became a major London landowner, acquiring the whole of the land between Bridewell and Water Lane from Fleet Street to the water. By this time he was ailing. He left money to five physicians in his testament. His son was permitted to delay a diplomatic mission concerning the queen's proposed marriage to the Archduke Charles early in 1566. Sackville made his will on 22 March 1566, dying, he believed, substantially out of debt. He prudently left the queen a great table emerald with a mallet of diamonds, a great pearl and a hundred other great pearls, and a diamond brooch. He had made arrangements for three-quarters of his goods to be held in trust by his executors, who included Roger Manwood, fearing, he said, the alteration, undervaluing, and other devices used in relation to goods left only by testament. He died in London on 21 April and was buried at Withyham. His wife was handsomely provided for, and by 1568 had married again; her second husband was John Paulet, the son and heir of William Paulet, first marquess of Winchester and lord treasurer, who was one of the overseers of her first husband's will.

SYBIL M. JACK

Sources will, PRO, PROB 11/48, sig. 14 · W. C. Richardson, *History of the court of augmentations, 1536–1554* (1961) · *CSP dom.*, 1547–86 · Cooper, *Ath. Cantab.*, 1.241 · E. Hasted, *The history and topographical survey of the county of Kent*, 2nd edn, 12 vols. (1797–1801); facs. edn (1972) · T. W. Horsfield, *The history, antiquities, and topography of the county of Sussex*, 2 vols. (1835); repr. (1974) · *APC*, 1542–70 · R. Ascham, *The scholemaster*, ed. J. E. B. Mayor, [new edn] (1892) · HoP, *Commons*, 1509–58, 3.246–7 · HoP, *Commons*, 1558–1603, 3.314–15 · *CPR*, 1547–69 · *LP Henry VIII*, vols. 12–21 · R. Naunton, *Fragmenta regalia, or, Observations on the late Queen Elizabeth, her times and favorits*, 3rd edn (1653); repr. (1870)

Likenesses portrait, Knole, Kent

Wealth at death lent money so liquid assets perhaps considerable; £804 from offices; probably *c*.£1500 p.a. from lands: will, PRO, PROB 11/48, sig. 14; local histories; HoP, *Commons*, 1558–1603, 3.314–15

Sackville, Richard, fifth earl of Dorset (1622–1677). *See under* Sackville, Edward, fourth earl of Dorset (1590–1652).

Sackville, Robert de (d. *c*.1154). *See under* Sackville family (*per. c*.1066–*c*.1477).

Sackville, Robert, second earl of Dorset (1560/61–1609), politician, was the eldest son and heir of Thomas *Sackville, first Baron Buckhurst and first earl of Dorset (*c*.1536–1608), and his wife, Cicely Baker (d. 1615), daughter of Sir John *Baker of Sissinghurst, Kent. As the result of a conversation between his grandfather and the scholar and tutor Roger Ascham, when the court was at Windsor in 1563, he and Ascham's son received their early education from a schoolmaster chosen by Ascham. Sackville matriculated from Hart Hall, Oxford, on 17 December 1576, aged fifteen, and graduated BA and MA on 3 June 1579. In the following year he was admitted to the Inner Temple. He was, however, never called to the bar. In February the same year, 1580, Sackville married; his wife, Lady Margaret Howard (c.1560–1591), was the only daughter of Thomas *Howard, fourth duke of Norfolk and a devout Catholic. The marriage produced three sons (including the third and fourth earls, Richard Sackville and Edward *Sackville), and three daughters (including Anne, wife of Edward Seymour, Lord Beauchamp's eldest son, and Cicely, wife of Sir Henry Compton).

Sackville benefited from the prominence, prestige, and royal favour enjoyed by his father under Elizabeth I and James VI and I. Lord Buckhurst and Viscount Montague ensured his return to parliament as knight of the shire for Sussex in 1584 when he was twenty-three. In 1589 he represented Lewes, but thereafter (1593, 1597–8, 1601, and 1604–7) he sat for the county continuously. During that time he was named to parliamentary committees on the preservation of timber in Sussex (1584–5), the grant of subsidies (1584–5, 1588–9, 1592–3, 1597–8), the poor laws and a bill concerning country gentry (1592–3), armour and weapons, a poor law, enclosure, fen drainage, and highway maintenance (1597–8), 'weighty matters' and monopolies (1601), and wardships (1604).

Sackville served in county administration, as justice of the peace in Sussex and Kent (from about 1591–1592), deputy lieutenant for Sussex from June 1601, and joint lord lieutenant in 1608. In 1597 the council minutes noted that 'our lovinge freind and other Justices' had 'dyscovered and fownde out' a number of 'lewd dysposed persons' who were causing trouble and inciting others to do the same (APC, 1597, 56). Until 1604 he was also on the commission for causes ecclesiastical.

Robert Sackville also acquired a share of the profits from the patent for producing starch and, in particular, a patent for the export of ordnance. In 1602 he was reported as having a ship trading in the Mediterranean. Because of his trading activities he was in 1596 made a freeman of Southampton. He was, however, repeatedly accused of dishonest practice by a foreign merchant, Giles de Vischer. In complaints to the queen, privy councillors, and the whole council during the 1590s, Vischer claimed that Sackville lured him to his house and then 'spoiled him of his goods, place and patent, imprisoned him wrongfully, and now uses his patent to transport ordnance'. Sackville denied the 'false and slanderous accusations'. The council referred to him again as 'our lovinge freind' and refused to intervene on the grounds that the 'stranger' had bills of complaint against Sackville pending in the courts of chancery and requests (CSP dom., 1591–4, 156; APC, 1595–6, 301–2). In 1598 he was still engaged in the export of ordnance. There were also undated charges of corruption against Sackville and his father, by someone who wrote that he had been committed 'to cut me from my office and stop my mouth …' (Salisbury MSS, 12.565–7).

From 1604, when his father was elevated to the earldom of Dorset, Robert Sackville was styled Baron Buckhurst. On 19 April 1608 he succeeded to the earldom and to Knole, Buckhurst, and other extensive estates, especially in Essex, Kent, Middlesex, and Sussex. His first wife died on 19 August 1591; in his will he recalled Margaret as a lady

'of as great vertue and worthynes and indued with as many excellent properties of a good and sociable wief as is possible for any man to wish' (PRO, PROB 11/113, sig. 23; PROB 11/114, sig. 57). Fifteen months after her death, on 4 December 1592, Sackville married Anne (d. 1618), daughter of Sir John Spencer of Althorp and widow in turn of William, fifth Baron Monteagle and Henry, first Baron Compton. Their marriage was childless. It also ended in marital breakdown. In 1607 Anne protested to the privy council 'that he affords her neither meat, drink, apparel, fuel nor lodging'. He strenuously denied this, but he sought separation, partly because of her 'continual violent tempestuousness in domestical conversation, greater than flesh and blood could endure'. She also replied to his separation proposals with 'certain foolish rhymes of her own devising', which 'made him angry and the Countess merry' (Salisbury MSS, 19.341–2). She then proceeded to importune James I with such vehemence that, it was reported, 'he was locked up in his bedchamber to avoid her company' and 'she knocks at his chamber door when he is retired as if it were an inn' (ibid., 361–2). In 1608–9 Dorset negotiated with Lord Chancellor Ellesmere and Archbishop Bancroft on terms for a separation, but he would not approve an annual maintenance of £1400.

The matter was unresolved when Dorset died at Dorset House, Salisbury Court, Fleet Street, on 27 February 1609, aged forty-eight, only ten months after he had inherited the earldom. He was buried in the family chapel at Withyham, Sussex. His will made reference to his second wife's 'exceeding unkyndenes and intollerable evill usuage towards my selfe and my late deere … father'. He also made provision for his first wife's effigy on his tomb and for 'an hospitall or collidge' for thirty-one poor unmarried persons at East Grinstead, Sussex (PRO, PROB 11/113, sig. 23; PROB 11/114, sig. 57); Sackville College still survives and retains its function as an almshouse. The dowager countess survived her husband by more than nine years and died on 22 September 1618.   MICHAEL A. R. GRAVES

Sources GEC, Peerage, new edn, 4.422–3 • HoP, Commons, 1558–1603, 3.315–16 • CSP dom., 1591–7; 1601–10 • Calendar of the manuscripts of the most hon. the marquis of Salisbury, 6–8, HMC, 9 (1895–9); 11–13 (1906–15); 15–16 (1930–33); 18–19 (1940–65), esp. vols. 6, 12, 13, 19 • will, PRO, PROB 11/113, sig. 23; PROB 11/114, sig. 57 • APC, 1595–7 • S. D'Ewes, ed., The journals of all the parliaments during the reign of Queen Elizabeth, both of the House of Lords and House of Commons (1682) • R. Ascham, The schoolmaster, ed. L. Ryan, [new edn] (Ithaca, 1970), 7–8 • Foster, Alum. Oxon. • DNB • JHC, 1 (1547–1628)
Likenesses portrait, 1608, Knole, Kent
Wealth at death no value given: will, PRO, PROB 11/113, sig. 23; PRO, PROB 11/114, sig. 57

Sackville, Sir Thomas (c.1336–1406). See under Sackville family (per. c.1066–c.1477).

Sackville, Sir Thomas (d. 1432). See under Sackville family (per. c.1066–c.1477).

Sackville, Thomas, first Baron Buckhurst and first earl of Dorset (c.1536–1608), poet and administrator, was the son of Sir Richard *Sackville (d. 1566), MP, privy councillor, chancellor of the court of augmentations (1548–54), and under-treasurer of the exchequer from 1559 to 1566

Thomas Sackville, first Baron Buckhurst and first earl of Dorset (*c.*1536–1608), attrib. John de Critz the elder, 1601

(and a first cousin of Anne Boleyn), and Winifred Brydges of London (*d.* 1586) who seems to have remained a devout Catholic all her life. He had one sister, later Anne *Fiennes, Lady Dacre. Thomas was probably educated privately and, although there are no records of him as a student at either Oxford or Cambridge universities, in 1608 his chaplain, George Abbot, described him as Oxford educated. He is traditionally associated with Hart Hall. He was admitted to the Inner Temple in November 1554 and, according to Abbot, 'took the degree of Barrister' (Abbot, sig C2r). About 1554–5 he married Cicely (*d.* 1615), daughter of Sir John *Baker of London and Sissinghurst, Kent, MP, privy councillor, attorney-general (1536–40), and chancellor of the exchequer (1540–58). The marriage lasted for over fifty-three years, producing four sons and three daughters. In his will (dated 11 August 1607) Thomas appointed his wife joint executor with their heir, and made her substantial bequests as 'testimonye of [his] unspeakable Love, affection, estimacion and reverence, longe synce fixed and setled in [his] harte and soule towardes her' (PRO, PROB 11/113, fol. 2v).

Early life and writing Sackville entered public life from a double family tradition of experience in public finance and legal administration at the highest levels. In January 1558 he was elected to the House of Commons for Westmorland and for East Grinstead, sitting for Westmorland. Re-elected to Elizabeth's first parliament (January 1559) he sat for East Grinstead (his family's local borough); in 1563–6 he sat for Aylesbury. From 1559 he was a justice of

the peace in Kent and Sussex, and in 1561 he was appointed feodary for the crown's duchy of Lancaster lands in Sussex. (The *Dictionary of National Biography*'s statement that in 1561 Sackville became a grand master of the order of freemasons repeats a fiction, first generated in 1738, by James Anderson.)

Sackville's reputation as a poet was established by 1560, when Jasper Heywood mentioned him among notable English poets at the inns of court. The tragedy *Gorboduc* (written in blank verse with Thomas Norton of the Inner Temple) was first performed at the Temple's Christmas revels 1561–2, under the auspices of Robert Dudley, and then at court. (BL, Add. MS 48023, fol. 359v, contains an eye-witness account of this first performance which differed from the printed text.) The 1565 title-page attributed acts four and five, which contain the play's most affective and politically significant poetry, to Sackville. Both authors drew on English historical sources and Senecan drama to depict civil war as the consequence of a divided succession in Gorboduc's ancient British kingdom. (Philip Sidney's *Arcadia* and Shakespeare's *King Lear* later drew on *Gorboduc* as a narrative and dramatic source.) The politics of *Gorboduc* have been variously interpreted in the context of parliament's requests for Queen Elizabeth to marry or otherwise secure the succession to the throne by naming an heir.

Sackville's 'Complaint of Buckingham' and the prefatory verses known as the 'Induction' also show his interest in political lessons to be drawn from English chronicles. Both were printed in William Baldwin's second part of *The Mirror for Magistrates* (1563), and are presumed to have been unavailable for the first part (1559). The 'Induction', based on Virgil, *Aeneid*, vi, and influenced by medieval dream-vision poetry, created a series of allegorical images of human suffering, which provoke empathy in the poet's persona—named Sackville—and, by inference, his readers. The 'Complaint' generates a complex attitude to the voice and character of its ghostly complainant, Richard III's henchman, Henry, duke of Buckingham. By using English archaisms as poetic diction for heroic topics Sackville established an influential bridgehead between Chaucer and Spenser in verses accessible to a wide readership through numerous editions of the *Mirror* (1563–1609). Sackville wrote an English sonnet for publication with Sir Thomas Hoby's *Book of the Courtier* (1561), an English translation of Castiglione; he probably also wrote the English elegy inscribed on the Hoby tomb in Bisham church, Berkshire, which is signed with his initials. In 1571 he encouraged Bartholomew Clerke (then living at Sackville House, Fleet Street) to compose a Latin translation of *The Courtier* to which Sackville contributed a Latin epistle. The English Horatian verse epistle—'Sacvyles Olde Age'—(probably composed soon after September 1566), represents Sackville's farewell to poetry, as his persona recognizes that time is passing and his life has another course to run. Thereafter his literary talents were deployed in letter writing and in diplomatic or forensic oratory, but his contemporary reputation as a poet outlived his writing career. Spenser included a dedicatory sonnet in *The Faerie Queene*

(1590) to Sackville 'Whose learned Muse hath writ her owne record, In golden verse, worthy immortal fame'.

The purpose and status of Sackville's first known trip abroad remains uncertain. In December 1563 he was briefly imprisoned by the civil authorities in Rome on unknown charges (possibly for spying). Letters from the English College (19 January 1564) testifying to his birth and connections, secured his release, and two audiences with Pius IV followed, at which Sackville apparently discussed possible means for reconciling England and the papacy. It seems unlikely that he would have participated in such discussions and agreed to carry a message from Pius to Queen Elizabeth on his own initiative. In 1563 Vincent Parpaglia of the papal curia had initiated proposals for excommunicating the queen, and possibly Sackville's presence in Rome was connected with delaying this action. Thomas sent his father Parpaglia's memorandum of the meetings with Pius, which Sir Richard gave to the queen. As a result Thomas was warned not to proceed further because of the queen's displeasure. When he wrote to Rome with this news (20 November) his involvement with papal negotiations apparently ceased, perhaps because other approaches from Rome had been made in a letter to William Cecil in September.

Any royal displeasure was shortlived, because in February 1566 Sackville was appointed to negotiate a marriage treaty between Queen Elizabeth and Archduke Charles of Austria. However, his mission was cancelled when his father died in April. Thomas inherited property in London, Sussex, Surrey, and Kent, including livestock, and iron works at Sheffield, Sussex; also £400 of good creditors' debts and two wardships. The will also refers to separate deeds of gift.

At this period in his life Sackville recalled (in his own will) how, by the 'particular choise and liking' of the queen, he was 'selected to a contynewall privat attendance upon her owne person' (PRO, PROB 11/113, fol. 12r). Abbot cited Elizabeth's description of the young Sackville as 'a scholar, and a traveller and a Courtier of speciall estimation' whose discourse was 'judicious but yet wittie and delightfull' (Abbot, sig. C2v). On 8 June 1567 he was knighted and created Baron Buckhurst the same day. (His sponsors were Archbishop Parker and Lord Keeper Bacon.)

Lord Buckhurst's middle years, 1567–1599 Sidney Lee described how 'Rich, cultivated, sagacious, and favoured by the queen, [Buckhurst] possessed all the qualifications for playing a prominent part in politics, diplomacy, and court society' (DNB). In November 1569 Buckhurst was appointed a joint lord lieutenant of Sussex. In February 1571 he went to Paris, as the queen's personal envoy, to convince Charles IX that Elizabeth was genuinely resolved to marry and to elicit a proposal of marriage (from the king's brother, Henri, duc d'Anjou), which he succeeded in doing after secret negotiations with Catherine de' Medici. Buckhurst later escorted the official French negotiator in England and on a visit to the University of Cambridge (30 August) they were both made masters of arts.

In the following January Buckhurst was a commissioner at the trial of his Sussex neighbour, Thomas Howard, duke of Norfolk, and was later given powers to administer Norfolk's property in Sussex. About this time Buckhurst was also buying land to consolidate his own estates, and was engaged with such local issues as the drainage of Pevensey marshes, and acquiring wood from Ashdown Forest for his Sussex iron furnaces. In August 1573 he proposed, unsuccessfully, to marry his heir, Robert *Sackville, to Lord Burghley's younger daughter, and settle £2000 a year on them and their heirs. Robert later married Margaret Howard, daughter of the attained Norfolk (1580). Buckhurst's daughter Jane also married into a local Catholic family, her husband succeeding his grandfather in 1592 as the second Viscount Montagu. The presence of many old Catholic families in Sussex complicated local politics. As a magistrate or judicial commissioner Buckhurst only moved against recusants when forced by external pressures, not by personal incentive or zeal. His attitudes helped to maintain social and political stability. Even during the pre-Armada tensions of 1588 he rebuked his deputy lieutenants of Sussex for attempting to imprison a Catholic gentleman and warned them not to exceed their powers by assuming anyone's guilt before hearing his answers to charges. It is indicative of Buckhurst's local influence that in the contested election of 1584 both his nominees, Robert Sackville and Thomas Shirley (d. 1612), secured the parliamentary shire seats for Sussex. Buckhurst was not an armchair lord lieutenant. According to Holinshed's *Chronicles*, which emphasized his diligence and heroism, in 1586 Buckhurst stood guard all night, with a company of 1600 armed men on the Sussex downs, upon report of an invasion fleet of 50–60 ships sighted off Brighton. Next morning he sent out boats to investigate, which found some harmless Dutch merchants' ships seeking the wind.

In February 1586, during the earl of Leicester's absence, Burghley secured the appointment to the privy council of Archbishop Whitgift, Buckhurst, and Lord Cobham. Buckhurst undertook a full range of duties including foreign and legal affairs; he had a high rate of attendance, and gradually moved into the inner circle of the queen's advisers. He acquired a reputation for impartiality, courage, and plain speaking since his kinship with the queen largely enabled him to avoid factions at court. As a privy councillor Buckhurst was present in May 1586 at the Star Chamber interrogation of the earl of Arundel (another Sussex neighbour, and half-brother of Robert Sackville's wife) in connection with the Ridolfi plot. He also sat on the commission which tried Arundel for high treason (April 1589). In September Buckhurst was a commissioner for the trial of Anthony Babington and others accused of plotting to kill the queen. He was also nominated, with eighteen others, to the commission to try Mary Stewart. However, Buckhurst was absent from her trial and the Star Chamber meeting which condemned Mary unanimously. In November the queen sent him with Robert Beale, clerk to the council, to inform Mary of her sentence. Their instructions permitted either man to speak to Mary alone in case she wished to communicate secret matters to Elizabeth. His absence from her trial and execution would have enabled Buckhurst, as Elizabeth's kinsman, to appear neutral or even favourable to Mary. His reputation as a tactful bearer of bad news was exploited again in February 1587, when the queen, seeking a scapegoat for the privy council's action in sealing the warrant for Mary's execution and proceeding with it (before she could change her mind), sent Buckhurst to inform William Davison of her displeasure, and commit him to the Tower. Buckhurst, finding Davison was ill, left him in bed and wrote to his 'most sacred Queene' acknowledging himself more closely tied to her than others and therefore emboldened to 'manifest unto [her] those exceeding greate perills and mischiefes that are lyke to followe if that sever sentence … against Mr Secretarye should be putt in execucion' (BL, Add. MS 48116, fol. 151*r*). Although his actions did not prevent Davison's imprisonment, this attempt to prevail on his closeness to the queen in order to persuade her against injustice was characteristic of him.

A month later Buckhurst was sent on an 'expostulary mission' to the Netherlands, having been named by Leicester as best suited to aid his administration there. Two days after he arrived at Flushing, Buckhurst sent home a summary of Sir William Russell's account of the situation, and his own assessment. In writing to the queen he emphasized the pitiful complaints of her starving soldiers and warned, 'the kepinge of your majestes treasure in your cofers doth yeld no interest unto you … and shalbe the meane to preserve the liefes of … faithfull subjectes' (19 April; BL, Add. MS 48078, fol. 107). In every town he visited as the queen's representative, Buckhurst found that Leicester's administration had been high-handed, provocative of personal enmities, and disorganized. He therefore sought to reconcile differences among the Dutch, and to calm their fears about the queen's continued support. But, because of financial worries, the queen now wished to make peace with Spain. Buckhurst assured the privy council that, while he would not reject the queen's policy, he would only accept peace fully armed, in case it failed. He wrote repeatedly of the urgent need for £50,000 to pay serving troops, and sent the council his project advising how to establish good government in the United Provinces without Leicester, should he not return. When the money was refused he wrote thanking Sir Francis Walsingham for the warmth of his support, and regretting that the queen had condemned his actions unheard. He prayed that God would send her no worse meaning servants than himself: he was unable 'to prove worthy to be a skolar in the skole of so rare a mistress' (25 May; ibid., fol. 63). Seeing Walsingham as a collaborator, he circumvented the queen's order to report more fully to her than to the council, telling him that he had written to the queen, but put 'somwhat in ciphre so as I am sure you shalbe cald for to disiphre it' (13 June; BL, Cotton MS Galba Di, fol. 93). He also wrote to Burghley complaining about Leicester's many 'sinister informacions' which were

undermining his mission, asking again not to be condemned unheard:

> for if ever I did or shal do any acceptable servis to her m[ajesty] it was in the stay & apesing of thes countries here even redy at my coming to have cast all good respect towards us & to have entred even in to some desperat cours. (PRO, SP 84/14)

Buckhurst returned to London in July 1587, after handing over his administration to Leicester, but was refused access to the queen who, according to Abbot, ordered his house arrest. This disgrace was a dangerous crisis, because Buckhurst's relations with the queen had been the principal foundation of his career. He worked his way back into her trust by strenuously refuting Leicester's charges, point by point, in writing. He also wrote frequently to Burghley and to Walsingham, who became his advocates. On 15 September Buckhurst petitioned the queen directly: he lamented the effects of his 'restraint' from her presence, and protested at his ten weeks' banishment for the 'cause and quarrels of a private man', one who was 'but a subject' like himself. He assured the queen that sight of her princely face was the 'cheefest joy and comfort that this world could geve' him, and that 'only the consolation of a giltes consciens' had saved his 'afflicted minde' from 'an utter wrack and ruine' (Hatfield House, Cecil papers, 16.25). His early legal training, coupled with this literary language of courtship in pursuit of courtiership, enabled Buckhurst, eventually, to overcome Leicester's opposition. By January 1588 Leicester's friends were urging him to be reconciled with Buckhurst or lose the queen's favour. But it was not until 26 May, after a year of crisis, when Buckhurst attended the privy council, that his rehabilitation seems to have been complete. This Armada summer, when Buckhurst was busy organizing the defence of the strategically important Sussex coast— recruiting and training men, buying and stockpiling arms in Lewes—was no time for personal quarrels. Shortly before Leicester's unexpected death Buckhurst sent him a good-humoured note with a stag which he had killed with his own hand—'though I know you wilbe very hard of belefe in the opinion of my skill in hunting'—as testimony of his good will (Longleat, Dudley papers, II/259). However, three weeks after Leicester died Buckhurst's depression and disillusion remain evident in a letter to his cousin Francis Alford in London. Alford had written that Buckhurst was being considered for the lord chancellorship and urged his acceptance. Buckhurst replied promptly and firmly that he was getting old, the times were 'full of miserie, and daungers' and his 'mynde [was] quite aliened from that course of lief' (26 September; London, Inner Temple Library, Petyt MS 538.10, fol. 21*r*).

In April 1589 Buckhurst, as the council's Netherlands expert, was officially named for new negotiations with the Dutch states whose representatives he met at his London house together with Thomas Wilkes and Bartholomew Clerke, both senior Netherlands administrators who had shared Buckhurst's experiences in 1587, including disgrace. In the following November Buckhurst received instructions for a new embassy, but three Dutch leaders came to England, and, in 1590, Wilkes went to the Netherlands instead of Buckhurst who was thought too senior for the purpose. On 24 April 1589 Buckhurst was created knight of the Garter and installed on 18 December.

Throughout September 1589 Buckhurst was in Lewes and Rye organizing ships and stores for 2000 English soldiers to be sent from Sussex to aid Henri IV in France. He was also receiving intelligence from Dieppe, from his third son, William [see Sackville, Sir William], who was knighted by Henri IV but later killed in action in France. In 1591 Buckhurst was one of the queen's commissioners who signed a peace treaty with France. When Sir Christopher Hatton, lord chancellor, died in November Buckhurst was appointed one of four privy councillors charged with affixing the royal seal to acts of government until the appointment in June 1592 of Sir John Puckering as lord keeper, to whom he wrote letters of practical advice and reassurance.

Hatton had also been chancellor of the University of Oxford, and after a contested election in convocation, between Buckhurst and Robert Devereux, earl of Essex, Buckhurst was appointed chancellor (29 December), acknowledging his election as due to the queen's favour, the university's good will, and not his own deserts. He placated supporters of Essex by urging the university to be especially vigilant in 'the carefull seeking out suppressing & punishinge of all Jesuitt seminaries & recusants' within the university, which would otherwise be discredited, 'and the whole realme besyde' endangered (*Reg. Oxf.*, 2/1.241). He was to be an active representative and beneficiary of the university, giving £100, in March 1602, to the library restored and re-established by Sir Thomas Bodley; the money was spent on recently printed books, and 177 titles are listed in the benefactors' register under his name. During 1605 he also gave the university the bust of Bodley, displayed in Duke Humfrey's Library.

In 1593 Buckhurst was made a commissioner to investigate the activity of Catholics within a 10 mile radius of London, and at the end of February 1594 he was one of the commission which tried the queen's physician, Roderigo Lopez, for high treason. In August 1596 Buckhurst was one of several privy councillors charged with a defence review of London, against a possible new Armada threat. He had also been building up his business interests, besides land purchases, from a position of increasing power at the centre of government. In 1597 he was granted a lease on the farm of the pre-emption of tin, outbidding the earl of Oxford. In 1598, with Robert Cecil, he acquired a patent for the manufacture of starch; since production rose during the term of their monopoly it was probably very profitable. (His son-in-law, Henry Neville (d. 1641), and son, Thomas, had a monopoly on the production of iron ordnance.)

During July and August 1598 Buckhurst negotiated a revised treaty with Johan van Oldenbarnevelt in London, whereby the Dutch states promised to take over payment of English forces in the Netherlands and undertook to begin repayment of English military expenses since 1585. This action anticipates his larger financial responsibilities

after Burghley died in August, and demonstrates the queen's reliance on his experience in diplomacy. Court gossip assumed he would succeed Burghley as lord treasurer, the most senior minister of state with overall financial responsibility for government and defence. Elizabeth normally waited and reviewed her options before making major appointments. However, in his will Buckhurst stated that there had been opposition to his appointment, presumably from Essex. (In a letter to Essex of January 1599, about funds for Ireland, Buckhurst assured the earl of his 'faithful & friendly love' for him, 'howsoever malice or misreport may insinuate the contrarye'; Hatfield House, Cecil papers, 58.98.) After forty years of devoted service from such a conservative and prudent man as Burghley, the queen was unlikely to want a radical change of style, or personnel, in her government. She confirmed her choice of Buckhurst as lord treasurer on 15 May 1599. He was not just a safe pair of hands who had ably assisted Burghley over the last ten years, he was financially astute and an experienced councillor whom she had long trusted; he knew how the queen's mind worked and he shared her priorities in government.

Later years: lord high treasurer, 1599–1608 Buckhurst's treasurership occurred during a period of economic hardship for English governments beset by inflation, low income from fixed revenues, and high expenditure on war with Spain and in Ireland. Parliamentary subsidies and other forms of taxation were devalued by unrealistic assessment rates. However, there was little scope for radical reforms of direct taxation given the political upheavals these would cause, and the prospect of a new government after Elizabeth's death. Buckhurst's main problem was how to fund the Irish campaigns. But in July 1599 there was another Spanish invasion alert, and he stopped all payments from the exchequer, including £24,000 promised for winter supplies to 17,000 troops in Ireland. He considered that although Ireland was endangered, the exchequer only had funds sufficient for the defence of the realm and £12,000 for Ireland.

In September the government experienced difficulty appointing a controller for the royal mint. Buckhurst was worried that the moneyers—poor men—were out of work and a great deal of bullion was piling up. He cajoled Cecil into hurrying the queen's signature for a bill of appointment 'for to coine mony without a controller is to coin without warant, & and to coin without warant is Treason' (Hatfield House, Cecil papers, 73.86). Making and spending money were both urgent problems, but, in between crises, Buckhurst, informed by his Netherlands experience, sought to reform the fraudulent accounting of musters in Ireland and reduce costs. When Essex was first arrested, after leaving his post, it seems that there were plans for Buckhurst to visit Ireland to investigate relations between Essex and the Irish leader Tyrone, but Buckhurst objected to this mission. Later, on the eve of Essex's rebellion, he sent Robert Sackville to assess the situation at Essex House in the Strand and report on those present. In the immediate aftermath he wanted the queen to make an example of the 'principall actors' in 'the severity of justis': 'let her ma[jesty] no waies perswade her self that she is yet free from daunger'; he also urged Cecil, as principal secretary, to write with news of the conspirators' overthrow to every county, to stop rumour stirring up 'evell mindes' (9 February; ibid., 76.44). As lord high steward, Buckhurst presided at the trial of Essex and the earl of Southampton, before their peers at Westminster (19 February 1601). Both men were found guilty of treason; Essex was executed; Southampton was imprisoned; and their associate, the earl of Rutland, was fined heavily. The lord treasurer seems to have colluded in the non-payment of this fine: a politic decision, since both young men were strong supporters of James VI, who pardoned them in 1603.

During summer 1601 Buckhurst made a survey of trade monopolies; he found 'the number to be very grete & most of them so unfitt & so odious neither profitable to her majestie nor good for the comon wealth' (Hatfield House, Cecil papers, 87.70). He decided that some should be revoked, but not all, because that would damage the royal prerogative. He proposed a meeting of six councillors, including the lord chief justice, after which they would 'make a publik notification'. He thus anticipated the issues which dominated the 1601 parliament and cleared the way for a later more thorough review of trade revenues. In December 1601 Buckhurst, as a joint commissioner with the earls of Nottingham and Worcester, took on Essex's duties as earl marshal.

When a Spanish treasure ship was captured in June 1602, the lord treasurer wrote of his joy, envisaging some relief from 'our endles and exhausting expences'. He told Cecil that, even as he received the news, his chamber was full of barons, judges, and other officers: 'we all laboring to advauns her majesties revenues with the yerly profit of mainy thousandes' (Hatfield House, Cecil papers, 184.33). When the lord mayor of London offered to buy the carrack's goods Buckhurst thought the amount offered 'ridiculous', but this was not the time to 'exasperate things … nor to cast oile in to the flame'. The offer was an indication of 'how hard it will prove to draw any more water from this well, if necessitie come upon us': the corporation of London was unlikely to provide further funds for government (ibid., 96.164). This situation was to change after 1605.

During 1603 Buckhurst gained access to Knole, his great country house in Kent. (Although the queen had granted him the reversion of the manor in 1566 it had been subject to a lease previously granted by Leicester.) It is assumed that John Thorpe's earlier plans for renovating Knole were now executed. The work was supposed to have been finished in 1605 by 200 workmen, including craftsmen brought from Italy. Although the early records are lost, accounts for 1607–8 indicate vast expenditure still ongoing.

Buckhurst was appointed lord treasurer for life by James I on 17 April 1603. After attending Elizabeth's funeral, he met James, *en route* for London, at Broxbourne, Hertfordshire (2 May), and spent four days at Theobalds, Cecil's house nearby, briefing the new king and establishing his government. About this time Buckhurst asked Cecil to let him know, 'acording to true friendship' whether or not the king was satisfied with him: 'you have left me with child & in a longing' to know, he wrote, but '2 words by this bearer shall deliver me of my burden of longing' (Hatfield House, Cecil papers, 100.66). On 13 March 1604 Buckhurst was created earl of Dorset. James was eager to make peace with Spain and on 19 May 1604 the Somerset House conference opened in London, which culminated in a treaty, 18–19 August. (In a painting showing the negotiators at the table (1604; NPG), Dorset is depicted at the head of the English delegation on the right of the picture.) He received a pension from Philip III, also a ring and a chain, in recognition of his work for peace.

With the new reign safely established Dorset began to give serious consideration to planning more effective fiscal management, although James's profligacy became a new strain on scarce resources. Since direct taxation through parliament was limited by political concerns, and, since peace would boost trade, it was decided to focus on raising money by a new general system of farming the collection of customs revenues. In July 1604 negotiations began with London merchants, which extended over the summer and, simultaneously, a new book of rates was agreed and published in November. Several syndicates eventually made offers, and the so-called 'great farm' of the customs came into effect on 24 December. The farmers first agreed to pay the crown a rent of £112,000, raised in 1606 to £120,000 per annum for seven years, for which they were entitled to collect all customs due (at the new rates) on goods in and out of all English and Welsh ports, only excepting those already farmed by others, such as duties on wines, silks (Cecil's farm), iron ordnance, and tin (Dorset's farm). At a stroke the great farm established a regular and secure income for the crown with a centralized administration, but privatized administrative costs which were borne by the farmers who kept all income over £120,000. In turn the farmers became financiers with capital available to lend the government (using the customs as securities), which stimulated the growth of London as a financial market. The great farm system survived until Charles II's reign with new contracts issued for fixed terms, according to current trading conditions. Its establishment was Dorset's most important contribution as lord treasurer.

In 1606 Dorset heard the barons of the court of exchequer giving judgment on the constitutional test case of the merchant, John Bate, who had refused to pay impositions levied by royal proclamation. He supported the court's judgment for the crown, but delayed its publication, apparently to prepare thoroughly for any appeal, because he was aware of both the weakness of the legal case and the political implications of this decision which enabled the imposition of new customs duties without parliament's consent. Meanwhile government borrowing increased sharply in 1607–8 and some parcels of crown lands were sold; but the deficit continued to grow.

Death and reputation Dorset may be regarded as Robert Cecil's mentor, but their partnership was also central to

Dorset's work in James's government. In a note of 1605 Dorset begged God to restore Cecil's health: 'For when your hand is from the helm, God knows what I am resolved to do' (Hatfield House, Cecil papers, 191.128). Premature reports of Dorset's death circulated in early June 1607. As he approached threescore years and ten Dorset had detailed inventories of his possessions drawn up in chirograph as a prelude to making his will. In recent years he had also been occupied in preserving state papers for a national archive, and in building a collection of crown jewels.

Dorset died suddenly, as if he had fallen asleep, at the council table at Whitehall on 19 April 1608. His funeral service, at Westminster Abbey on 26 May, included the sermon by Abbot, printed later that year and dedicated to his widow, Cicely, who died on 1 October 1615. In his will Dorset thanked God for his creation as a man and a Christian; giving his soul to God—'trusting, beleving and freelie confessinge that by the Deathe and passion of his sonne … and by his onlie mercy meane and meadiation for me and by none other, and not by any good worke or merite of myne owne'—he hoped to be among the elect (PRO, PROB 11/113, fol. 2r). He was buried at Withyham, Sussex, beside his ancestors; the Sackville chapel containing his tomb, but not his remains, was destroyed by fire in 1663.

Thomas Sackville inherited a large fortune and bequeathed an even greater one. The fees available to a lord treasurer made it a lucrative office and, perhaps inevitably for a man in his position, he was libelled as a bribe taker by political enemies in his last years. He seems never to have lacked the material benefits of great wealth. But one recurring characteristic was an awareness of, and concern for, the misery of poverty, often associated in his experience with war or civil unrest. As a young man about the Inner Temple his poetry shows an imaginative empathy with depictions of human suffering. In his middle years his compassion for the English soldiers in the Netherlands helped to earn him not only the queen's sarcasm and Leicester's malice but also the approbation of those colleagues who recognized his common-sense humanity, and observed the successes of his sensitive diplomacy. In later years his political realism and courtly eloquence, coupled with his lifelong respect for due legal process, enabled him to avoid the troubles which undermined Cecil, his successor as lord treasurer. Finally, his bequest of £1000 to build a public granary at Lewes, with a further £2000 to stock it against times of scarcity or hardship, epitomizes his practice of Christian charity. (His will also specified the provision of one year's wages to all his servants, not otherwise remembered, with board and lodging for three months after his funeral.) Robert Naunton's assessment of Buckhurst's treasurership was that the queen 'might have had more cunning instruments, but none of a more strong judgment and confidence in his ways, which are symptoms of magnanimity and fidelity' (R. Naunton, Arcana aulica, 1641, repr. 1694, 229–30). His contribution to English history cannot equal Burghley's, but he was more versatile, and representative of his period and its culture as a renaissance man: poet, scholar,

traveller, courtier, statesman, a lover and patron of music and fine art. He was a religious man with the experience and pragmatism to tolerate his neighbours' (and his family's) freedom of conscience in private, and not only a loyal servant of the crown but also a discreet man of personal charm and moral integrity. RIVKAH ZIM

Sources will, PRO, PROB 11/113, sig. 1 • will of Sir Richard Sackville, PRO, PROB 11/48, sig. 14 • G. Abbot, *A sermon preached at Westminster, May 26, 1608, at the funerall solemnities of the right honorable Thomas, earle of Dorset* (1608) • *CSP dom., 1558–1610* • *CSP for., 1586–7* • *CSP Scot., 1586–88* • *CSP Spain, 1558–68* • *CSP Rome, 1558–71* • *Calendar of the manuscripts of the most hon. the marquis of Salisbury*, 24 vols., HMC, 9 (1883–1976), vols. 2–20 • C. J. Phillips, *History of the Sackville family*, 1 [1930], 128–242 • P. Bacquet, *Un contemporain d'Elisabeth I: Thomas Sackville, l'homme et l'oeuvre*, Travaux d'Humanisme et Renaissance, 76 (1966) • HoP, *Commons, 1509–58* • HoP, *Commons, 1558–1603* • R. Zim and M. B. Parkes, '"Sacvyles olde age": a newly discovered poem by Thomas Sackville, Lord Buckhurst, earl of Dorset (c.1536–1608)', *Review of English Studies*, new ser., 40 (1989), 1–25 • C. Wilson, 'Thomas Sackville: an Elizabethan poet as citizen', *Ten studies in Anglo-Dutch relations*, ed. J. van Dorsten (1974), 30–50 • C. G. Bayne, *Anglo-Roman relations, 1558–1565* (1913) • R. Zim, 'Dialogue and discretion: Thomas Sackville, Catherine de Medici, and the Anjou marriage proposal, 1571', *HJ*, 40 (1997), 287–310 • A. P. Newton, 'The establishment of the great farm of the English customs', *TRHS*, 4th ser., 1 (1918), 129–55 • F. C. Dietz, *English public finance, 1485–1641*, 2nd edn, 2 (1964) • *Reg. Oxf.*, 2/1.240–41, 353 • G. W. Wheeler, ed., *Letters addressed to Thomas James, first keeper of Bodley's library* (1933), 34–5 • F. Palgrave, ed., *The antient kalendars and inventories of the treasury of his majesty's exchequer*, RC, 2 (1836), 311–35 • R. B. Manning, *Religion and society in Elizabethan Sussex* (1969) • R. B. Wernham, *After the Armada: Elizabethan England and the struggle for western Europe, 1588–1595* (1984) • R. B. Wernham, *The return of the armadas: the last years of the Elizabethan war against Spain, 1595–1603* (1994) • P. Croft, 'Fresh light on Bate's case', *HJ*, 30 (1987), 523–39 • *Gould's History of freemasonry*, rev. H. Poole, 4 vols. (1951), vol. 2, pp. 44–6 • R. Schofield, 'Taxation and the political limits of the Tudor state', *Law and government under the Tudors: essays presented to Sir Geoffrey Elton*, ed. C. Cross, D. Loades, and J. J. Scarisbrick (1988), 227–55 • H. James and G. Walker, 'The politics of Gorboduc', *EngHR*, 110 (1995), 109–21 • R. Holinshed, *The chronicles of England, Scotland and Ireland*, 6 vols. (1807–8); facs. edn (New York, 1965), 4.901–2 [repr. 1965] • BL, Add. MSS 5702, fol. 89; 48023, fol. 359v; 48078; 48116, fols. 151–2; Cotton MSS Galba Cix; Di; Lansdowne MS 17, fols. 39–40; Stowe MS 399, fols. 1–36v • Hatfield House, Cecil papers, 16.25; 58.98; 71.98; 73.86; 73.89; 76.44; 87.70; 96.164; 100.66; 116.95; 184.33; 191.128 • Inner Temple Library, London, Petyt MS 538.10, fols. 18v, 21r

Archives BL, letters and papers • BL, papers relating to his mission to the Netherlands, Add. MS 48078 • CKS, corresp. and accounts • E. Sussex RO, letters and MSS • Hatfield House, Hertfordshire, letters and papers | BL, letters to Sir Julius Caesar, Add. MSS 11406, 12111, 12507

Likenesses attrib. J. de Critz the elder, oils, 1601, NPG [*see illus.*] • attrib. M. Gheeraerts, oils, 1601, Knole, Kent • group portrait, oils, 1604 (*The Somerset House conference*), NPG • engraving (after portrait at Buckhurst), repro. in *The works of Thomas Sackville, Lord Buckhurst*, ed. R. W. Sackville-West (1859) • oils, Bodl. Oxf.

Wealth at death vast wealth: will, PRO, PROB 11/113, sig. 1

Sackville, Sir William (1569/70–1592), soldier, was born in London, the third son of the poet Thomas *Sackville, earl of Dorset (c.1536–1608), and Cicely Baker (d. 1615). Like his elder brothers Robert *Sackville and Henry, he entered Hart Hall, Oxford, and graduated BA in 1585, aged fifteen. He followed Robert to the Inner Temple, as did their younger brother Thomas. In June 1589 his father urged

Henri of Navarre to accept William into his service, 'though he is inexperienced and has only just left school, as it were' (*CSP for.*, *1589*, 300). William went with Lord Willoughby's expedition to Normandy in support of the now declared Henri IV, and arrived from Dover in September 1589. In October, having been knighted by the French king, Sackville (described as 'Buckhurst') was with a group of gentleman-adventurers who distinguished themselves serving under François de La Noue in an attack near Paris. In July 1590 he suffered wounds and lost his horse at the siege of Paris; later that month he fought under the king in a skirmish at Meaux, and was present in August at Lagny when Parma forced Henri's troops to retreat. In the summer of 1591 he was ambassador to Prince Christian of Anhalt at a time when Queen Elizabeth was negotiating for an alliance with the German protestant princes.

On 8 February 1592 Sir Henry Unton, ambassador to Henri IV, recorded Sackville's loss that day during an attack on the village of Bures or Bure; his death and burial in a mass grave were confirmed five days later. Although Unton claimed that he was 'as towardlie a gentleman as ever came out of England', whose loss the king especially lamented, Burghley replied that Sir William's 'over great courage and forwardnesse wrought his owne destruction' (Unton, 327, 338). A fellow Inner Templar, John Ross, eulogized him in a long manuscript poem, mentioning his service at Rouen and a tournament victory fought in the king's presence. RICHARD F. HARDIN

Sources Foster, *Alum. Oxon.* · *The correspondence of Sir Henry Unton, knt: ambassador from Queen Elizabeth to Henry IV, king of France*, ed. J. Stevenson (1847) · J. Ross, 'Th'authors teares', *Poems on events of the day, 1582–1607*, ed. and trans. R. Hardin (1991) · *CSP for.*, *1589* · R. B. Wernham, ed., *List and analysis of state papers, foreign series, Elizabeth I*, 1–2 (1964–9) · letters from Queen Elizabeth to foreign dignitaries, 1591–2, BL, Add. MS 36774, fols. 15*v*, 19*v*

Sacleux, Charles Joseph (1856–1943), Swahili scholar, was born on 5 July 1856 at Enquin, Pas-de-Calais, France, the second of three children, all sons, of Auguste Sacleux, a tobacconist, and his wife Marie Firmine Bayart. His father died when he was five and it was his widowed mother who had the responsibility of bringing up the family. In 1869 he entered the junior seminary at Arras, and in 1874 he spent a year in the senior seminary. The following year he joined the Holy Ghost Fathers (Congregatio Sancte Spiritus) and was ordained priest in 1878 and made his profession in 1879, when he left for Zanzibar where his community had their east African headquarters. In due course he was posted to Bagamoyo, then an important coastal town. It was there that he began to study Swahili, the language of Swahililand, already the lingua franca for much of the east African interior and soon the chief local language of British administration. Altogether he was to spend nearly twenty years on the east African coast, devoting a great deal of his time to the Swahili language and to botany.

As a savant of exceptional ability (he was elected to membership of the Société Linguistique de Paris in 1894) Sacleux was fortunate to have studied Swahili before it was influenced by standardization and, later, by English language patterns. Two of his publications are outstanding: his *Grammaire des dialectes swahilis* (1909), still the best one-volume study of the Swahili dialects, and his *chef-d'œuvre*, *Dictionnaire swahili-français* (1939), which immediately became, and is likely to remain, the definitive Swahili lexicon.

Sacleux returned to France in 1898, and for the next forty years taught in the community's mother house at Chevilly. Just before the German occupation of Paris he was (with others) evacuated to Cellule and thence to Grasse, on the Côte d'Azur, where he died on 16 May 1943 and was buried. P. J. L. FRANKL

Sources Archives des Pères du St-Esprit, Chevilly · P. J. L. Frankl, 'Charles Sacleux: greatest of Swahili lexicographers', *Cahiers de Lexicologie*, 2/1 (1993), 201–8 · P. J. L. Frankl, *Dictionnaire de biographie française*, ed. J. Balteau and others (Paris, [forthcoming]) · b. cert.
Archives Archives des Pères du St-Esprit, Chevilly, France
Likenesses two photographs, repro. in *Annales Spiritaines*, 1 (1947), following p. 16

Sacrobosco, John de [John of Holywood] (*d. c.*1236), mathematician, was probably of British extraction, but the tradition that he came from Halifax in Yorkshire is unsupported. Contemporary records are silent about him and various accounts of his life rest only upon the arbitrary surmises of Leland, Bale, and later antiquaries. The date of his birth is unknown, and the only certainty is that he worked in Paris. He is not mentioned in the records of the university which, however, provided his tomb in the church of St Mathurin, with a monument on which an astronomical instrument was engraved, together with four lines of verse commemorating his fame as a *computista*, or calendar expert. These were copied before the monument was destroyed at the time of the French Revolution. In this situation the only clue to his life and achievement lies in his writings. In the course of time many works have been wrongly ascribed to Sacrobosco, but the following four books are authentic.

The *Algorismus* (in some manuscripts called *Algorismus vulgaris* or *Algorismus de integris*) has the incipit 'Omnia quae a primaeva origine rerum', and is a brief introduction (same 5600 words) to the new 'Arabic' numerals and the positional system of numbers. It explains all the elementary procedures of calculation from addition and subtraction to the extraction of square and cube roots. It is written in a dry and precise style, and demonstrates clearly the superiority of the new methods over the ancient Roman system. It was widely used and gave rise to several revised versions and commentaries, among which the great commentary by Peter Nightingale from 1291 occupies the first place. There were several printed editions between 1488 (Strasbourg) and 1582 (Antwerp). More recent printings by Halliwell (1838) and Curtze (1897) are now superseded by the critical edition by F. Saaby Pedersen (in Corpus Philosophorum Danicorum Medii Aevi, 10/1, 1983).

The *Tractatus de spera*, with the incipit 'Tractatum de spera quattuor capitulis distinguimus' is a longer work (some 9000 words) on elementary cosmology and astronomy. It is well organized in four chapters, describing respectively the general structure of the universe, the circles of the celestial sphere, the phenomena caused by the diurnal rotation of the heavens, and planetary motions and eclipses. The style is elegant and pleasant and, in the manner of the twelfth century, there are many quotations from both literary and scientific classical sources. Although it appears that the author was not familiar with the *Almagest* itself, he clearly aimed at making his students familiar with the elements of Ptolemaic astronomy, breaking away from the earlier tradition derived from Macrobius and Martianus Capella. No scientific work from the middle ages has ever enjoyed a similar popularity. The *Spera* is still extant in hundreds of manuscripts spread over all the major libraries of Europe, and there were at least 160 printed versions, from the *editio princeps* of 1482 (Ferrara) until 1673 (Antwerp). The Latin text is now available with an English translation in 'The *Sphere' of Sacrobosco and its Commentators* by Lynn Thorndike (1949).

Twice as long (some 19,000 words) is the *Compotus*, also called *De anni ratione*. It has the incipit 'Compotus est scientia considerans tempora', and deals with all aspects of time reckoning and calendaric problems. It is written in the same style as the *Spera*, but with even more references to earlier writers, and is of the same scope and importance as Bede's *De temporum ratione*, written 500 years earlier. Of particular interest is the discussion of the errors of the Julian calendar and Sacrobosco's proposal for eliminating them by methods essentially similar to those employed in the Gregorian reform of 1582: that is, by dropping ten days once and for all, and then leaving out one day with regular intervals. The *Compotus* was printed at least thirty-five times from Melanchthon's edition at Wittenberg in 1531 to the last edition at Antwerp in 1673. A modern, critical version is still a desideratum.

A fourth, brief treatise (about 2000 words) is usually called *De quadrante* and has the incipit 'Omnis scientia per instrumentum operative'. It describes the construction of the so-called 'old Quadrant' and its application as a sundial, and was critically examined by J. B. J. Delambre in 1819 (*Histoire de l'astronomie du moyen âge*, 243 ff.). Comparatively few manuscripts are preserved and no printed version seems to exist. For no obvious reason it has sometimes been reckoned among Sacrobosco's spurious works.

The dating of these works presents a very difficult problem. There is no evidence of when the *Algorismus* and the quadrant treatise were written. The *Spera* and the *Compotus* must be earlier than 1240, when they were both included in the same codex which is now in the Kongelige Bibliotek in Copenhagen (GKS 277, 2°). Internal evidence seems to indicate that the *Spera* is earlier than the *Compotus*, which is self-described as written in 1235; but in several manuscripts this year is given as 1232. The latter also ends with some verses pointing to the year 1234. In consequence it is natural to conclude that Sacrobosco's activity came to an end about 1235, in agreement with a notice in Miraeus that Sacrobosco died in 1236.

Sacrobosco's three principal works were often copied or bound together. Supplemented by a work on planetary theory and a set of astronomical tables, they formed the kernel of a *corpus astronomicum* on which the elementary teaching of astronomy was based for more than 300 years. This shows their inherent qualities, as does the fact that they were the subject of numerous later commentaries. They were brief, to the point, and contained very little that a student could afford to forget when passing on to a more advanced stage. It is also worth noticing that they were completely free from explicit astrological association. Despite their narrative form they contributed more than most other works to preserving the notion of science as the study of mathematical relationships between natural phenomena, in contradistinction to the Aristotelian view of science as a metaphysical quest for causal explanations.   OLAF PEDERSEN

Sources O. Pedersen, 'In quest of Sacrobosco', *Journal for the History of Astronomy*, 16 (1985), 175–221 • O. Pedersen, *The corpus astronomicum and the traditions of medieval Latin astronomy*, 3 (1975), 57–96 • *Petri Philomenae de Dacia et Petri de S. Audomaro opera quadrivialia*, ed. F. S. Pedersen (1983), 174–201 • 'The sphere' of Sacrobosco and its commentators, ed. L. Thorndike (1949) • J. B. J. Delambre, *Histoire de l'astronomie du moyen âge* (Paris, 1819) • A. Miraeus, *Rerum toto orbe gestarum chronica a Christo nato ad nostra usque tempora* (Antwerp, 1608) • G. Sarton, *Introduction to the history of science*, 2 (1931), 617–19 • L. Thorndike and P. Kibre, *A catalogue of incipits of mediaeval scientific writings in Latin*, rev. edn (1963) • P. Duhem, *Le système du monde: histoire des doctrines cosmologiques de Platon à Copernic*, 10 vols. (Paris, 1913–59), vol. 3, pp. 238–40
Archives Kongelige Bibliotek, Copenhagen, GKS 277, 2°

Saddington, John (d. **1679**), Muggletonian, was born at Arnesby, Leicestershire; the names of his parents are not known. According to the brief spiritual memoir with which he prefaced his *A Prospective-Glass for Saints and Sinners* (1673), as a child his love of learning was so great he was never content but when he was at school, and especially took more delight in reading the Bible and godly works such as Lewis Bayly's *The Practice of Piety* and prayer books 'than could be expected from one of my age' (Saddington, no pagination). Only his parents' (presumably financial) inability and unwillingness, he felt, had put a brake to his attaining as much human learning as could have been taught him by man, and he was evidently bound an apprentice to a member of the Merchant Taylors' Company in London. As an adult he was involved in the West India trade.

In the late 1640s and early 1650s Saddington continued to maintain a life of exemplary—and entirely orthodox—protestant piety. He learned the catechisms published by godly ministers, frequently attended sermons, and regarded the critics of the presbyterian establishment as 'false teachers that should come in sheep's cloathing, and daub with untempered mortar' (Saddington). His spiritual certainties were destroyed when, still 'not above 18 years of age', he read William Erbery's *The Sword Doubled to Cut off both the Righteous and the Wicked* (1652), with its fierce attack on his fellow ministers who took tithes as 'murderers, oppressors of the poor, and robbers of God' (Saddington). Disillusioned in the ministry which he had trusted, a disorientated Saddington continued to attend presbyterian services and ventured to Independent and Baptist meetings, redoubling his zeal in praying and attending sermons. Yet, he recalled, 'I could never find any difference in the foundation between the Presbyterians, Independents and the Baptists; for though they differ something in point of worship, yet they all own one God, and one Devil' (ibid.). Saddington first heard of the prophets Lodowick Muggleton and his cousin John Reeve and their commission from God in 1653, when a fellow apprentice shared a room with them in Bridewell prison. He then thought that they were just two more of the false prophets who would come in the last days. He heard of them again, and was convinced of their truth, late the following year when a friend lent him their *A transcendent spiritual treatise upon several heavenly doctrines from the Holy Spirit of the man Jesus, the only true God, sent unto all his elect as a token of his own love unto them* (1652). He was immediately convinced of their message. Fittingly for a man for whom books had been so central in shaping, and then shaking, his spiritual life, it was a book which now gave him certainty:

> Though there is no outward miracles done by the *Witnesses of the spirit*, yet that glorious language and heavenly matter which is written by them (which is the work of the spirit) maketh it appear that they are what they declare themselves to be. (ibid.)

Saddington's major contribution to the Muggletonian movement was the production of thirty-eight 'Articles of true faith' in 1675 (BL, Add. MS 60177). Since it was written 'to confound and disprove all Despisers that say wee know not what wee believe', the fact that it was not printed until 1830 must have lessened its impact. On the other hand, not until 1 January 1870 was it thought that believers needed a comparable work of synthesis in manuscript. That sums up the strengths and weaknesses of Saddington. He was no great polemicist and made little impact on the world outside; nor is his feeble poetic allegory on the Prophet Muggleton's sufferings in prison, 'The Wormes Conquest' (1677), strengthened by an epilogue spelling out for the reader that the 'worm' is actually Muggleton (BL, Add. MS 60203, fol. 15).

Yet internally Saddington's standing was very high. In a letter of 1665 Muggleton refers to his follower as 'a young man of the faith' to be trusted (Reeve and Muggleton, *Spiritual Epistles*, 191). In 1670 Muggleton referred inquiries about sugar imports from Antigua to Saddington, 'for I have not commerce with any men of the world' (ibid., 469). Nine years later—and six weeks after Saddington's death in London on 11 September 1679—the same correspondent was lamenting to Muggleton that there was nobody to take his place. Muggleton—a great hater of the water—was resolute, however, in his refusal to concern himself with maritime affairs, whatever the profit. The leading Muggletonian Thomas Tomkinson wrote a touching letter to Saddington's sister Lydia Brooks upon his death. He called it preaching his 'funeral sermon' to her. When he recalled a night at Loughborough on the way home with Saddington, tears fell on the paper he was writing: 'he was in the house of God long before

me, he hath taught me and been as a father to me' (BL, Add. MS 60183, fol. 2*v*). That very passage was quoted from Tomkinson's 'beautiful' letter in the anonymous *Faith and Practice of the Muggletonians* (1870). Tomkinson had pointed out that Saddington left behind him a widow (Elizabeth) and some learned works (he cited his *A Prospective-Glass*), but no young children. When the Victorian Muggletonian J. D. Aspland gave a funeral address on his fellow believer Joseph Gandar in June 1868 the highest compliment he could pay—across 200 years—was to compare Saddington 'in the Spirit' with Gandar 'in the flesh' (BL, Add. MS 60170, fol. 8).   WILLIAM LAMONT

Sources Muggletonian papers, BL, Add. MSS 60168–60256 · J. Saddington, *A prospective-glass for saints and sinners* (1823) · *The works of John Reeve and Lodowicke Muggleton*, ed. J. Frost and I. Frost, 3 vols. (1832) · L. Muggleton, *The acts of the witnesses*, ed. T. L. Underwood (1999) · C. Hill, B. Reay, and W. Lamont, *The world of the Muggletonians* (1983) · J. Reeve and L. Muggleton, *A volume of spiritual epistles*, ed. A. Delamaine (1755) · J. Reeve and L. Muggleton, *A stream from the tree of life*, ed. J. Peat (1758) · J. Reeve and L. Muggleton, *Supplement to the book of letters*, ed. J. Frost and I. Frost (1831) · J. Reeve and W. Sedgwick, *Sacred remains*, ed. J. Frost (1856) · will, GL, MS 9171/36, fols. 500*v*–501*v*

Archives BL, Add. MSS 60170, 60177, 60183, 60203
Wealth at death see will, GL, MS 9171/36, fols. 500*v*–501*v*

Saddler, John (1813–1892), engraver, was born on 14 August 1813. He was a pupil of George Cooke (1781–1834), the engraver of J. M. W. Turner's *Picturesque Views on the Southern Coast of England* (1827). Saddler received encouragement from the artist for his contribution to these plates, and on one occasion he was sent to Turner with the trial proof of a plate of which he had himself engraved a considerable portion. 'Scanning the plate with his eagle eye, Turner asked "Who did this plate, my boy?" "Mr. Cooke, sir," answered Saddler, to which Turner replied, "Go and tell your master he is bringing you on very nicely, especially in lying"' (*The Times*, 7 April 1892). While Saddler, in his later years, related many anecdotes of Turner, including those which recalled his secret acts of charity and benevolence, that recorded by *The Times* related to Saddler's youth. In 1846 Turner took a keen interest in Saddler's engraving of the vessels in the plate of his painting *The Fighting Téméraire*, the sky of which was the joint production of R. Dickens and James Tibbetts Willmore.

Saddler's earliest independent works on steel were mainly architectural book illustrations, among them Thomas Noble and Thomas Rose's *Counties of Chester* (1836), with plates after Thomas Allom. He then assisted John and Thomas Landseer in several of their engravings from the works of Sir Edwin Landseer, especially *The Twins*, *The Children of the Mist*, *Marmozettes*, and *Braemar*, and also in the plate of *The Horse Fair*, after Rosa Bonheur. Among works executed entirely by him are *The Lady of the Woods*, after John MacWhirter, published by A. Lucas; *The Christening Party*, after Albert Bellows, engraved for the *Art Journal* of 1872; two mezzotints published by H. Graves, *Shrimpers* and *Shrimping*, after the marine painter Hendrik Wilhelm Mesdag; and many book illustrations after John Everett Millais, Sir Edward Poynter, Sir John Tenniel, Gustave Doré, and others. He also engraved plates of *Christ Church*,

Hampshire, after Joseph Nash, and *Durham Cathedral*, after Henry Dawson, for the *Stationers' Almanack*, and some other views and portraits. At the time of his death he was engaged on the portrait of John Walter of *The Times*, from the picture begun by Frank Holl and finished by Hubert Herkomer. He exhibited a few works at the Society of British Artists, and twenty-one plates at the Royal Academy between 1862 and 1883. He earned a distinguished reputation for engraving the work of his contemporaries, specializing in landscape and architecture.

A well-respected and convivial man, Saddler was for many years the treasurer of the Artists' Fund, which brought him into contact with many of the artists of his time. In 1882 he left London for Wokingham in Berkshire, where on 29 March 1892 he committed suicide by hanging himself during an attack of temporary insanity.

R. E. GRAVES, *rev.* JOANNA DESMOND

Sources B. Hunnisett, *An illustrated dictionary of British steel engravers*, new edn (1989), 113–14 · R. K. Engen, *Dictionary of Victorian engravers, print publishers and their works* (1979) · Graves, *RA exhibitors* · Printsellers' Association, *Catalogue of registered engravings, 1847–1911* (1912), 101 · *Art Journal*, 34 (1872), 216 · *Art Journal*, 37 (1875), 332 · *Art Journal*, 38 (1876), 266 · *Art Journal*, new ser., 12 (1892), 160 · catalogue of prints and drawings, V&A, department of prints and drawings · *The Times* (7 April 1892) · d. cert.
Archives V&A
Wealth at death £545 10s. 5d.: probate, 13 May 1892, CGPLA Eng. & Wales

Sadington, Sir Robert de. *See* Sadyngton, Sir Robert (*d.* in or after 1361).

Sadleir [*née* Coke], **Anne** (1585–1671/2), literary patron, was born on 1 March 1585 at Huntingfield Manor, Suffolk, the second of the ten children of Sir Edward *Coke (1552–1634), judge and law writer, and his wife, Bridget (*d.* 1598), daughter and coheir of John Paston. In a short autograph poem on her life she writes that she was educated at Elsing, Norfolk, but gives no more details (Trinity College, Cambridge, MS R.13.74, fol. 97). After her marriage to Ralph Sadleir (1579–1661) on 13 September 1601 she lived at Standon Lordship in Hertfordshire, where her dowry was £3000. The suggestion that her childless marriage was not a happy one is found in the aforementioned poem: 'Standon Brought Affliction which Made Heaven my Meditation'. Sadleir was very close to her father and there are records of his visits to Standon in 1603 and again in 1616, after his dismissal from office. She was granted permission to visit him in the Tower in 1622, 'being a discrete woman, and likely to endeavour to bring him to more conformity' (*CSP dom.*, 1619–23, 347). At least two elegies on Coke were dedicated to Sadleir (BL, Add. MS 37484, and Harvard Law Library, MS 4060).

Several volumes of Sadleir's personal papers survive in the library of Trinity College, Cambridge, including religious and autobiographical meditations (MS R.13.74) and letters from leading Anglican divines and other correspondents (MS R.5.5). As a staunch supporter of the Church of England she continued to use the prayer book during its proscription in the 1650s and carried on vigorous epistolary disputes with her Roman Catholic nephew Herbert

Aston and the New England puritan divine Roger Williams. Sadleir gave large bequests to the libraries at Trinity College, Cambridge, and the Inner Temple, institutions attended by her father and by other family members. In 1649 and 1664 she presented Trinity with her letters and notebooks, her coins, and several illuminated manuscripts; in 1661 the Inner Temple Library received two portraits, thirteen manuscripts (Petyt MSS 530/A–F and 531/A–G), including a sermon dedicated to Sadleir by Andrew Marvell, father of the poet, and many books from her library. Standon Lordship passed to her husband's nephew on his death in 1661 but Sadleir continued to live there until her own death in late 1671 or early 1672.

VICTORIA E. BURKE

Sources C. W. James, *Chief Justice Coke: his family and descendants at Holkham* (1929) · J. C. Davies, ed., *Catalogue of manuscripts in the library of the Honourable Society of the Inner Temple*, 3 vols. (1972) · *The state papers and letters of Sir Ralph Sadler*, ed. A. Clifford, 3 vols. (1809) · *CSP dom.*, 1619–23 · *The letters of John Chamberlain*, ed. N. E. McClure, 2 vols. (1939) · *Calendar of the manuscripts of the most hon. the marquess of Salisbury*, 15, HMC, 9 (1930) · J. L. Chester and J. Foster, eds., *London marriage licences, 1521–1869* (1887) · C. D. Bowen, *The lion and the throne: the life and times of Sir Edward Coke (1552–1634)* (1957) · C. W. Johnson, *The life of Sir Edward Coke, lord chief justice in the reign of James I with memoirs of his contemporaries*, 2 vols. (1837) · F. A. Inderwick and R. A. Roberts, eds., *A calendar of the Inner Temple records*, 2 (1898); 3 (1901) · M. R. James, *The western manuscripts in the library of Trinity College, Cambridge: a descriptive catalogue*, 4 vols. (1900–04), vols. 1–2 · *Scots peerage* · Huntingfield parish registers · DNB
Archives Inner Temple, London, MSS, Misc. MSS 68, 82, 147; Petyt MSS 530/A–F, 531/A–G · Trinity Cam., MSS, R.5.5, R.5.6, R.13.74, R.16.2
Wealth at death £170 owed to her; £776 in legacies: Staffs. RO, D 1798/HM Aston/17/5

Sadleir, Franc [*formerly* Francis] (1775–1851), college head, youngest son of Thomas Sadleir (1753–1815), barrister, and his first wife, Rebecca (*d.* 1792), eldest daughter of William Woodward of Clough Prior, co. Tipperary, was born on 3 May 1775. He was admitted at Trinity College, Dublin, in 1790, becoming a scholar in 1794, and a fellow in 1805. He graduated BA in 1795, MA in 1805, and BD and DD in 1813, by when he had altered the spelling of his forename from Francis to Franc. On 17 July 1801 he married Letitia Abigail (*d.* 4 Dec 1850), daughter of William Grave of Ballynagar, King's county. They had four sons and two daughters. In 1816, 1817, and 1823 he was Donnellan lecturer at his college; his sermons and lectures preached in the chapel of Trinity College, Dublin, were published (3 vols., 1821–4). He was from 1824 to 1836 Erasmus Smith professor of mathematics, and from 1833 to 1835 regius professor of Greek.

In politics Sadleir was a whig, and his advocacy of Catholic emancipation was earnest and unceasing. In conjunction with the duke of Leinster, the archbishop of Dublin (Richard Whately), and others, he was in 1831 one of the first commissioners for administering the funds for the education of the poor in Ireland. He defended the work of the national board of education in a pamphlet (1835). He later supported the principle of the Queen's Colleges in Ireland. In 1833 he was appointed, with the primate, the lord chancellor, and other dignitaries, a commissioner to alter and amend the laws relating to the temporalities of the Church of Ireland, but resigned the trust in 1837.

On 22 December 1837, during the viceroyalty of the marquess of Normanby, Sadleir was made provost of Trinity College, a post which he held for fourteen years. He had a reputation as an academic pluralist and sinecurist, but was an efficient administrator and continued, at a more modest pace, the reforms of his predecessor, Bartholomew Lloyd. He is said to have declined a bishopric on more than one occasion. Sadleir died at Castle Knock Glebe, co. Dublin, on 14 December 1851, and was buried in the vaults of Trinity College on the 18th.

G. C. BOASE, rev. M. C. CURTHOYS

Sources GM, 2nd ser., 37 (1852), 193–4 · Burke, *Gen. Ire.* · *ILN* (27 Dec 1851), 763 · *Freeman's Journal* [Dublin] (16 Dec 1851), 2 · *Freeman's Journal* [Dublin] (17 Dec 1851), 2 · *Guardian* (17 Dec 1851), 867 · Boase, *Mod. Eng. biog.* · Burtchaell & Sadleir, *Alum. Dubl.* · R. B. McDowell and D. A. Webb, *Trinity College, Dublin, 1592–1952: an academic history* (1982)
Likenesses J. H. Nelson, portrait, TCD

Sadleir, George Forster (1789–1859), army officer and explorer in Arabia, was born on 19 January 1789 in Cork, the younger son of James Sadleir, a cotton manufacturer, and his wife, Joanna, daughter of George Forster of Cork. In April 1805 he was commissioned ensign in the 47th regiment of foot, being promoted lieutenant in 1806 and captain in 1813. In 1807 he was in the expedition that failed to take Buenos Aires and subsequently went with his battalion to India. Towards the end of 1812 Sadleir commanded a party sent to Tabriz to join a military mission engaged in training the Persian army. His services were recognized both by the shah, who presented him with a sword, and by the governor-general, Lord Hastings. After leaving Persia in 1815 Sadleir took part in campaigns in India on the political staff of Sir John Malcolm.

In the early nineteenth century the followers of Shaykh Muhammad ibn ʿAbd al-Wahhab troubled the British by preying on commerce in the Persian Gulf and raids off the Indian coast. In August 1818 Ibrahim, son of Mehmet Ali Pasha, viceroy of Egypt, captured the Saudi capital of Dirʿiyyah. Lord Hastings determined to send an envoy to Ibrahim to propose an alliance, together with Muscat, to destroy the Qawasim pirates. The envoy was also to present a letter of congratulations and a sword and gather military and geographical information. Sadleir was chosen, received formal instructions on 14 April 1819, and sailed at once from Bombay.

The first part of Sadleir's mission was a failure because Saʿid ibn Sultan, imam of Muscat, although receiving him affably, was unwilling to co-operate with the Egyptians. Sadleir arrived at Qatif on 21 June at a time when no European had been more than a few miles inland and no maps existed of the interior. He went inland to Hufuf, where he was informed that Ibrahim was near Dirʿiyyah, and decided to join a convoy that was going to his camp. He arrived to find that Ibrahim had recently departed and was at Rass, another ten days away in the very centre of the peninsula. At Rass he heard that Ibrahim was evacuating all but the Hejaz, and had withdrawn to Medina. Sadleir felt that he had done enough and wished to return to the coast. The Egyptian commander, however, said that the journey would need a large escort which he could not provide, so Sadleir had no choice but to continue. Near Medina he at last found Ibrahim, who expressed delight at the sword but declined to discuss politics. Sadleir then went down to the Red Sea coast at Yanbuʿ al-Bahr, which he reached on 20 September.

There was no other crossing of the peninsula until 1914, when Captain W. H. I. Shakespear travelled from Kuwait to ʿAqabah. Sadleir's *Diary of a Journey across Arabia* (1866) describes a critical period of history for which there are no other accounts in European languages and few in Arabic. It is a valuable geographical document, noting wells, compass readings, and periods on the march. In 1904 D. G. Hogarth wrote that it was still the only source for many places. Sadleir is unique among Arabian explorers, for his journey was involuntary and he loathed both the place and its 'turbulent barbarians'. He resolutely refused to conform to local customs and made not the slightest effort to understand the people. He showed himself stubborn, but also resilient, conscientious, brave, and not devoid of humour.

Sadleir continued to serve in India, took part in the First Anglo-Burmese War, and returned to England in 1828. He retired as a major in 1837 and became a sheriff of Cork in the same year. He married a Miss Ridings of Cork in 1847 or 1848 and then emigrated to New Zealand, where he died in Auckland on 2 December 1859.

ROBIN BIDWELL, rev.

Sources F. M. Edwards, 'Introduction', in G. F. Sadleir, *Diary of a journey across Arabia*, new edn (1977) · D. G. Hogarth, *The penetration of Arabia* (1904) · J. B. Kelly, *Britain and the Persian Gulf, 1795–1880* (1968)

Sadleir, John (1813–1856), politician and swindler, was born on 17 November 1813 at Shronell House in the parish of Shronell, co. Tipperary. He was the fifth of seven children of Clement William Sadleir, farmer and middleman, reputedly descended from Henry Sadeleyer of Hackney and the Sadleirs of Stratford upon Avon, who were in-laws of the Shakespeares. His mother was Joanna Scully, daughter of James Scully of Kilfeacle, a bank proprietor and wealthy farmer. As a Roman Catholic, Sadleir received his education in the prestigious, Jesuit-owned Clongowes Wood College from 1826 to 1831.

In 1831 Sadleir was apprenticed to his cousin's law practice in Tipperary, and he joined his brother William in his Dublin practice in the late 1830s. In 1839 he and his brother James founded the Tipperary Joint Stock Bank, which established nine branches in counties Tipperary, Carlow, and Kildare. Sadleir went to London in 1846, lived in the Albany Club for some years, and eventually moved to 11 Gloucester Square.

In his early years in London Sadleir established important social and business contacts and joined several clubs, including the Erectheum and the Reform Club. Not given to extravagant social activities, he confined himself to

John Sadleir
(1813–1856), by
unknown engraver

gambling occasionally at White's Club and hunting with the Gunnersbury hounds: he kept three hunters in Leighton Buzzard. Although an extant photograph shows him as a handsome man with dark hair and sallow complexion, Sadleir pursued a cautious romantic life. He remained a bachelor but courted Clara Morton, a member of a dancing troupe at Her Majesty's Theatre, and allegedly formed a liaison with the grass widow of an MP. Only when his financial situation deteriorated did he vainly pursue a Catholic heiress with serious matrimonial intent.

Sadleir concentrated most of his attention on business matters. Through his contacts he became a parliamentary agent and legal adviser to railway entrepreneurs. The experience and reputation thus gained enabled him to advance to participation in the management and ownerships of several new railway companies such as the Grand Junction Railway of France, the Rome and Frascati Railway, the Royal Swedish Railway Company, and the East Kent line. He also became chairman of the London and County Joint Stock Bank, which had sixty branches and 20,000 accounts.

An eminently successful businessman by 1847, Sadleir turned to politics and was elected MP for Carlow borough in that year. Within five years he was joined in Westminster by his brother James and his three Scully and Keating cousins, all five being grandsons of James Scully of Kilfeacle. They were the nucleus of the 'papal brigade', pledged to a policy of independent opposition, following the Ecclesiastical Titles Act of 1851, which declared ecclesiastical titles used by Catholic church dignitaries illegal and prohibited the wearing of canonicals in public. Opposition to the government's agrarian policy was also promoted. Sadleir was seen as betraying this pledge when he joined Lord Aberdeen's ministry in 1853 as junior lord of the Treasury and he was rejected by the Carlow electorate that year. Within months he was returned from the borough of Sligo, where he was initially greeted by a section of the local press as 'Carlow's vomit'. He resigned his ministerial position in 1854 when found guilty of being implicated in a plot to imprison a depositor of the Tipperary Bank because the individual in question had refused to vote for him.

By February 1856 the bank itself was insolvent, owing to Sadleir's overdraft of £288,000. His own financial affairs were beyond redress and in his efforts to solve his problems he milked the London Bank, ruined a small Newcastle upon Tyne bank, sold forged shares of the Swedish Railway Company, raised money on forged deeds, and spent rents of properties he held in receivership and money entrusted to him as a solicitor. He disposed of more than £1.5 million, mainly in disastrous speculations. Unable to face the consequences, he committed suicide near Jack Straw's Tavern on Hampstead Heath on 17 February 1856 by drinking prussic acid. He was buried in an unmarked grave in Highgate cemetery.

Sadleir's family and his Scully and Keating relations paid dearly for his delinquency. As the major shareholders, they were the prime targets of the enraged creditors. The entire estate of his brother James was sold; Emma Wheatley, James's wife, lost land given to her as part of her marriage settlement, and Sadleir's father, Clement, sold 500 acres to compensate depositors known to him. The Scullys suffered even greater losses. Vincent Scully was forced to sell 3000 acres to meet his compromise of £10,000 and James Scully had to mortgage property to the tune of £14,000.

The four MPs, once the nucleus of the Irish Independent Party, were also destroyed politically, and the shame of being connected with the swindles caused intense rancour within their families. James Scully fled for some time to Paris, from where he denounced James Sadleir as a 'notorious culprit'; the Scullys and the Keatings severed relations with each other; Frank Scully's marriage broke down and he died insane in a Paris asylum. James Sadleir fled to Geneva, where he was murdered in 1881, having lived alone there on an annuity provided by his in-laws, the Wheatleys.

While the memory of the swindles remained in people's minds for many years, the portrait of John Sadleir as the Prince of Swindlers is enshrined in the bizarre characters of some nineteenth-century novelists such as Merdle in Charles Dickens's *Little Dorrit* (1855–7), John Needham in Joseph Hatton's *John Needham's Double* (1885), Davenport Dunn in Charles Lever's 1857–9 novel of that name, and Jabez Morth in Mary Elizabeth Braddon's *Trail of the Serpent* (1861).   JAMES O'SHEA

Sources Burke, *Gen. Ire.* (1958) • Burke, *Gen. GB* (1958) • *Parliamentary Pocket Companion* (1846–56) • D. M. Evans, *Facts, failures, and frauds: revelations financial, mercantile, criminal* (1859); facs. edn (1968) • *Irish Genealogist* (1982) • *Bucks Herald* (1856) • *The Times* (1856) • *Freeman's Journal* [Dublin] (1847–58) • *Weekly Telegraph* (1850–56) • *Leinster Express* (1856) • *Railway Times* [England] (1856) • *Irish chancery and common law reports*, 17 vols. (1852–67), vols. 5–6, 9, 11 • *Dowling v. Lawler: a full report of the trial of the issues directed by the court of exchequer in Ireland ... before the Lord Chief Baron* (1854) • T. Corcoran, *The Clongowes Record, 1914–1932* (1932) • *Saunders Newsletter* (20 Feb 1856) • BL, Aberdeen MSS • NL Ire., Scully MSS • Diocesan archives, Dublin, Archbishop Patrick Murray MSS • Registry of Deeds, Dublin

Archives BL, letters to Lord Aberdeen, Add. MSS 43248–43253 · diocesan archives, Dublin, Archbishop Patrick Murray MSS · NL Ire., Scully MSS · registry of deeds, Dublin
Likenesses daguerreotype photograph, NL Ire. · engraving, NL Ire. [*see illus.*]
Wealth at death left debts of £1,500,000

Sadleir [*formerly* Sadler], **Michael Thomas Harvey** (1888–1957), bibliographer and novelist, was born in Oxford on 25 December 1888, the only child of the educational pioneer Sir Michael Ernest *Sadler (1861–1943), and his first wife, Mary Ann (*d.* 1931), daughter of Charles Harvey, linen factor, of Barnsley. He adopted an early variant of the family name, Sadleir, as a *nom de plume* to distinguish himself from his father, whom he called 'my best and wisest friend' and whose biography (1949) he wrote with affectionate understanding. Brought up in an atmosphere of scholarly cultivation and wide artistic interests, he was educated at Rugby School, and at Balliol College, Oxford, where he took second-class honours in history in 1912 and won the Stanhope prize for an essay on Sheridan which was published in the same year. Before that he had already written a novel, *The Anchor*.

In 1912 Sadleir entered the publishing firm of Constable, of which he became a director in 1920 and chairman in 1954. In 1914 he married Edith (Betty), daughter of Canon Darell Tupper-Carey. They had one daughter and two sons, the elder of whom was killed in action in the Royal Navy in 1942; Sadleir recorded his life in the privately printed *Tommy, 1916–1942* (1943). Sadleir served in the war trade intelligence department from 1915 to 1918. He was a member of the British delegation to the peace conference at Versailles in 1919, and for a brief period in the following year of the secretariat of the League of Nations.

Sadleir was an all-round man of letters who notably distinguished himself in each department of his activity. He was described as the most accomplished book collector of his time, and his collection influenced his success as a novelist and biographer and affected his policy as a publisher. He had begun to collect books as an undergraduate, specializing for some years in first editions of contemporary poets and novelists, of certain authors of the 1890s, and of the French symbolists and decadents. About 1918 he reverted to an early enthusiasm for the novels of Anthony Trollope which led him, in turn, to form an unrivalled collection of Victorian fiction of the three-decker period. This was developed into a sort of bibliographical museum illustrating the history of the novel during the nineteenth century, in which were included cheap editions, among them the famous 'yellow backs', and a variety of material on Victorian night-life. He also collected Gothic romances of the period of about 1780 to 1820, and this collection found its way in due course to the University of Virginia, just as his Trollopes eventually went to Princeton University and his great collection of nineteenth-century fiction (over 10,000 volumes) to the University of California at Los Angeles.

Sadleir revolutionized the bibliographical approach to books of the machine-printed and edition-bound era.

Michael Thomas Harvey Sadleir (1888–1957), by unknown photographer, pubd 1921

Excursions in Victorian Bibliography (1922) was followed by two books which pioneered the revival of interest in Trollope's novels: *Trollope: a Commentary* (1927) and *Trollope: a Bibliography* (1928), the latter a model of its kind to which he added notes on the literary history of Trollope's day. His *Evolution of Publishers' Binding Styles, 1770–1900* (1930) discussed the hitherto unwritten history of the book trade. His study of Victorian author–publisher relationships, distribution methods, and reading habits culminated in his two-volume *XIX Century Fiction: a Bibliographical Record* (1951). He was Sandars reader in bibliography at Cambridge University (1937) and president of the Bibliographical Society (1944–6).

In his introduction to *XIX Century Fiction* Sadleir confessed: 'I have never undertaken the intensive collection of any author or movement without the intention of ultimately writing the material collected into biography, bibliography or fiction'. His avowed practice, most strikingly exemplified in the case of Trollope, was continued in biography with *Bulwer: a Panorama* (1931), later renamed *Bulwer and his Wife, 1803–1836*, and its successor *Blessington–d'Orsay: a Masquerade* (1933). Both these books were sparkling original studies in the morals and taste of the early nineteenth century. As a biographer he combined a fluent and graceful style with an unusually discriminating sense of period.

While Sadleir's narrative gift imparted zest to his serious historical writing, his work as a novelist brought him popular fame. In his novels his understanding of period was markedly stronger than his imaginative impulse. *Privilege* (1921) chronicled the collapse of the old order which was accelerated by the First World War, and *The Noblest Frailty* (1925) had as its theme the decay in the ruling stock of mid-Victorian times. Meanwhile *Desolate Splendour* (1923) had emphasized Sadleir's weakness for melodrama and his absorption in the seamy side of nineteenth-century life, which he investigated with a sociological passion worthy of Henry Mayhew. He returned to fiction in 1937 with *These Foolish Things*, described by himself as 'a first-person experiment in emotional intimacy'. *Fanny by*

Gaslight (1940), his most successful novel, sold 150,000 copies at its original price in five years, was made into a film, and was widely translated. Both this novel and *Forlorn Sunset* (1947) depicted in authentic detail the vicious underworld of London in the 1870s, though the stories themselves were relatively artificial.

Although he spent much of his life in London, Sadleir lived for many years in Gloucestershire and latterly at Willow Farm, Oakley Green, near Windsor. Tall, distinguished in appearance, and alert in movement, he was by nature retiring but, overcoming his shyness, could dispense hospitality with great charm. He influenced the literary life and taste of his time not merely through his writing but also through his generous assistance to other authors, especially those whose nineteenth-century studies were published by his firm. The rare combination in his work of original research and creative exposition made him a figure of unique authority in his chosen sphere. Sadleir died at 20 Devonshire Place, London, on 13 December 1957 and was buried in Windsor parish churchyard.   DEREK HUDSON, *rev.* SAYONI BASU

Sources *The Times* (16–20 Dec 1957) • I. Elliott, ed., *The Balliol College register, 1900–1950*, 3rd edn (privately printed, Oxford, 1953) • private information (1971) • personal knowledge (1971)
Archives Harvard U., Houghton L., E. Verhaeren's Sadleir collection • NRA, corresp. and literary papers | BL, corresp. with Society of Authors, Add. MS 56797 • Bodl. Oxf., corresp. with Lewis Harcourt • Stanford University Library, California, letters to Anthony Newman • U. Leeds, Brotherton L., letters to Philip Fosse • U. Reading L., letters to R. L. Mégroz
Likenesses photograph, NPG; repro. in *The Bookman* (April 1921) [*see illus.*]
Wealth at death £78,359 15s. 9d.: probate, 3 June 1958, CGPLA Eng. & Wales

Sadler, Anthony (*bap.* 1602, *d.* 1643). *See under* Sadler, Anthony (*b.* 1610/11, *d.* in or after 1683).

Sadler, Anthony (*b.* 1610/11, *d.* in or after 1683), Church of England clergyman, was the son of Thomas Sadler of Chilton or Chitterne St Mary, Wiltshire. He matriculated from St Edmund Hall, Oxford, on 21 March 1628, aged seventeen. He graduated BA on 22 March 1632, having been ordained by Richard Corbet, bishop of Oxford, in 1631. For eleven years he acted as chaplain to 'Esquire Sadler in Hertfordshire', to whom he was related (Sadler, *Inquisitio*, 14). In 1643 he became rector of Bishopstoke in Hampshire upon the sequestration of the incumbent, Thomas Gawen. About 1647 he became domestic chaplain to Leticia, Lady Paget, and moved to Westminster where he preached 'both Practicall, and School Divinity' (ibid., 16).

In May 1654 Lady Paget presented Sadler to the rectory of Compton Hayway (Compton Abbas) in Dorset. On 10 June he submitted a certificate to the commissioners for approbation of publike preachers—the triers—attesting to his good character and godliness. This was signed by Lord and Lady Paget and four other prominent inhabitants of Westminster, but was returned to Sadler as unsatisfactory. On 1 July Sadler submitted a second certificate signed by five other people, including William Lenthall and Dr Thomas Temple. On the morning of 3 July Sadler

was examined by five of the commissioners. His answers to their questions were evidently unsatisfactory and he was re-examined later that same day by nine commissioners. The commissioners disapproved of Sadler, but apparently made no official decision on his case. On 14 August Sadler wrote to one of the commissioners, Philip Nye, asking for a decision but apparently received no reply. He then stated his case against the hectoring and inquisitorial style of the triers, in a pamphlet entitled *Inquisitio Anglicana*, which was dedicated to the lord protector and 'the high Court of Parliament'. In reply Nye's son John, clerk to the triers, penned a detailed refutation of Sadler's 'evil surmises, gross mistakes, and most notorious falshoods' (Nye, sig A2r). John Hall, bishop of Norwich, also objected to a passage in Sadler's 'strange Pamphlet' which he felt misrepresented his position on the Roman Catholic church (Hall, 1). *Inquisitio Anglicana* suggests that Sadler held Calvinist opinions on election and predestination, and demonstrates his uneasiness about answering questions concerning free will.

Sadler preached the funeral sermon of Lady Paget in 1655 and seems to have lived in some poverty in London until the Restoration, when he published a number of titles in a valiant attempt to assert his royalism and find a parish. *The Subjects Joy for the Kings Restoration*, a masque dedicated to General Monck, and the broadsheet poem *Majestie Irradiant*, can only be described as trite and banal. In the preface to *The Loyall Mourner*, Sadler attacked Oliver Cromwell and claimed that he had been arrested by troops in 1643. *The Loyall Mourner* consists of two separate items: an elegy on Charles I, which Sadler claimed had been 'Presented, to the Hands of many' in February 1649, and 'Mercy in a miracle', the text of a sermon which he preached at Mitcham in Surrey on 28 June 1660.

The patron of Mitcham, the London merchant Robert Cranmer, was so pleased with this sermon that he presented Sadler to the vicarage. Sometime during 1662, however, Sadler instigated a suit against Cranmer for dilapidations. When the case was heard in November 1664 Cranmer sued Sadler for libel and Sadler was imprisoned when he could not post bail. He was only released from prison once he had agreed to leave the vicarage after Easter 1665. Sadler reneged on the agreement by appealing against Cranmer to George Morley, bishop of Winchester. He published this appeal as *Strange News Indeed* (1664). The inevitable reply in defence of Cranmer, *Mr Sadler Sadled* (1665), contains some very serious accusations about his behaviour as vicar of Mitcham.

Sadler, it claimed, 'being very Poor, but well stockt with Wife and Children' had been very grateful to receive a living, even one as financially modest as Mitcham. But later in his 'Hot and Heady temper and Disposition' (*Mr Sadler Sadled*, 5), he had rejected the generous treatment that he had received from his patron by bringing the suit for dilapidations and had estranged the chief men of the parish. He harangued his parishioners from the pulpit: 'I was, and am for the Liturgie of the Church of England; You were, and are for the Covenant; I was and am for the Governance of the Church of England; You were, and are for

Presbytery' (ibid., 6). Yet this self-proclaimed dutiful son of the church was negligent in wearing the surplice, often did not turn up for Sunday services, and had failed to observe the fast day to commemorate the execution of Charles I on 30 January. On weekdays

> You shall finde this Anthony Sadler in the Ale-house Drinking, and Wantonly Discoursing of Women beyond all Bounds of Civility, or Railing against his Patron, or Enticing poor People to Subscribe their Hands, or set their Marks to some Stuff that Anthony Sadler hath prepared and drawn up before hand against his Patron. (ibid., 8)

According to Anthony Wood, Sadler later served as an extraordinary chaplain to the king and was created DD. He may have clung on at Mitcham as late as 1669. In 1671 he was instituted rector of Berwick St James in Wiltshire. There he performed clandestine marriages, denying the bishop's authority on the spurious grounds that Berwick as a royal manor was an exempt jurisdiction. In 1675 Sadler was suspended and excommunicated. The matter rumbled on even after Sadler was reinstated. In 1681 the bishop of Salisbury, Seth Ward, gave a damning account of Sadler's character to Archbishop Sancroft and accused him of debauchery. In the same year the church-warden of Berwick attempted to drag Sadler from his own pulpit. Sadler was last heard of in May 1683, suspended again and being advised to submit to Bishop Ward, but instead choosing to petition the archbishop against it. He died at an unknown date, 'leaving behind him the character of a rambling head, and turbulent spirit' (Wood, *Ath. Oxon.*, 3.1268).

His namesake, **Anthony Sadler** (*bap.* 1602, *d.* 1643), Church of England clergyman, was baptized at St Mary Woolchurch, London, on 28 October 1602, the son of Rowland Sadler (*d.* 1647) of St Nicholas Acon, London, haberdasher and vintner. He was admitted pensioner at Peterhouse, Cambridge, on 28 July 1620, matriculating the same year, graduating BA in 1623, and proceeding MA in 1627. He was presented to the rectory of West Thurrock, Essex, on 19 December 1628, and died there on 19 May 1643. His dying confession of faith was published in Thomas Fettiplace's *The Sinner's Tears, in Meditations and Prayers* (1653). JASON MᶜELLIGOTT

Sources DNB · *Walker rev.* · Foster, *Alum. Oxon.* · Wood, *Ath. Oxon.*, new edn, 3.1267–8 · W. Kennett, *A register and chronicle ecclesiastical and civil* (1728) · A. Sadler, *Inquisitio Anglicana, or, The disguise discovered* (1654) · J. Hall, *An apologeticall letter to a person of quality* (1654) · [J. Nye], *Mr Sadler re-examined* (1654) · A. Sadler, *Strange news indeed* (1664) · *Mr Sadler sadled* (1665) · A. Sadler, *Schema sacrum, vel, Forma uniformitatis* (1665) · D. Spaeth, *The church in an age of danger: parsons and parishioners, 1660–1740* (2001) · Venn, *Alum. Cant.* · IGI · T. Fettiplace, *The sinner's tears, in meditations and prayers* (1653) · R. Newcourt, *Repertorium ecclesiasticum parochiale Londinense*, 2 vols. (1708–10), vol. 2 · T. A. Walker, ed., *Admissions to Peterhouse or St Peter's College in the University of Cambridge* (1912) · Bodl. Oxf., MSS Tanner 38, 44, 138, 290

Sadler, Donald Harry (1908–1987), mathematician and astronomer, was born on 22 August 1908 at 10 St Mary's Place, Dewsbury, Yorkshire, the second son of James Wright Sadler, a master tailor, and his wife, Gertrude Jane Needham, formerly a schoolteacher. He attended the Wheelwright Grammar School in Dewsbury and won an open entrance exhibition to Trinity College, Cambridge, where he obtained first-class honours in mathematics in 1929. He spent a further year in Cambridge before joining the nautical almanac office, then based in the Royal Naval College, Greenwich, in October 1930.

Sadler became the seventh superintendent of the *Nautical Almanac* in July 1937, having served for a year in an acting capacity. Over the next few years he carried through successfully several projects that had been initiated by his predecessor, L. J. Comrie, including the publication in 1937 of the first British *Air Almanac*, for use by the Royal Air Force for astronavigation. During the Second World War the nautical almanac office was based in Bath, and additional staff were appointed to provide the computing centre of the Admiralty computing service; in addition to the navigational almanacs, Sadler planned in detail and supervised the production of many special tables and diagrams for use by the services. Of particular importance was the computation of co-ordinates for use in plotting hyperbolic lattices on charts for the newly developed top-secret DECCA navigation system, which was first used on D-day. Sadler's considerable wartime services were recognized by appointment as an OBE in 1948; he also received the Thurlow award of the American Institute of Navigation in the same year.

After the war Sadler's main efforts were first of all directed to the rationalization of the publication arrangements for the astronomical and navigational almanacs and tables that were produced by the nautical almanac office in co-operation with similar offices in other countries. He established a very good working relationship with Dr G. M. Clemence, the director of the nautical almanac office of the US Naval Observatory, and they eventually obtained agreement to the unification of the principal almanacs of the two countries. At the same time they introduced many improvements in their design. After the move of the nautical almanac office from Bath to Herstmonceux, Sussex, in 1949 to join the Royal Greenwich Observatory, Sadler, who was one of the chief assistants to the astronomer royal, became strongly involved in the administration of the observatory.

Sadler made contributions to several astronomical and navigational organizations. He was a secretary of the Royal Astronomical Society from 1939 to 1947, and played a major role in running the society during the war; he was president in 1967–9. He participated in the formation and activities of the Royal Institute of Navigation, served as its president in 1953–5, and was awarded its gold medal in 1957. He later contributed to the formation of the International Association of the Institutes of Navigation. Sadler was strongly involved in the activities of the International Astronomical Union, firstly in scientific matters in Commission 4 (ephemerides), of which he was president from 1952 to 1958, and later in its administration; he was general secretary from 1958 to 1964 and introduced many improvements to its procedures. He represented the union on the council of the Federation of Astronomical and Geophysical Services and served as its president (1968–70). He received an honorary doctorate from the

University of Heidelberg (1970) and several other foreign awards. In 1970 he gave up his day-to-day responsibility for the nautical almanac office in order to concentrate on the organization of the general assembly of the International Astronomical Union in Brighton in August. He was elected an honorary member of the American Institute of Navigation in 1979.

On 22 December 1954 Sadler had married Flora Munro McBain (1912–2000), who was a member of the staff of the nautical almanac office from 1937 to 1974; she served as a secretary of the Royal Astronomical Society from 1949 to 1954. He was a keen competitor and played a variety of outdoor and indoor games at a good standard. He retired from the Royal Greenwich Observatory in February 1972, but kept up his interests in time systems and in navigation and produced a series of papers for the *Journal of Navigation*. He wrote from memory a 'Personal history of HM nautical almanac office, 1931–1972' to supplement the formal record. Sadler suffered from angina, and he died at his home, 8 Collington Rise, Bexhill, Sussex, on 24 October 1987 and was cremated at Eastbourne crematorium on 2 November; he was survived by his wife.

GEORGE A. WILKINS

Sources G. A. Wilkins, *Quarterly Journal of the Royal Astronomical Society*, 32 (1991), 59–65 · M. W. R. [M. W. Richey], *Journal of Navigation*, 41 (1988), 139–41 · personal knowledge (2004) · private information (2004)
Archives CUL, papers | CUL, Royal Greenwich Observatory archives
Likenesses H. Hardy, photograph, repro. in R. J. Tayler, ed., *History of the Royal Astronomical Society*, 2: 1920–1980 (1987), facing p. 98
Wealth at death £89,251: probate, 16 Dec 1987, *CGPLA Eng. & Wales*

Sadler, James (*bap.* **1753**, *d.* **1828**), balloonist and chemist, was born in Oxford and baptized there on 27 February 1753. He was the elder son of James Sadler (1718–1791), cook and confectioner of (now 84) High Street, and his wife, Elizabeth (1718–1802), probably *née* Blakeney. Sadler followed his father into the family business at this shop, with brother Thomas (1756–1829) at another in St Clement's. On 7 July 1779 James was admitted a freeman of Oxford, by which time he had married Mary. Their son John Sadler [*see below*] was the eldest of four children born before 1785.

Sadler first released a 36 foot hydrogen balloon from Queen's College, Oxford, on 9 February 1784. On 4 October 1784 he made the first ascent by any English aeronaut with a 170 foot hot-air balloon he had constructed himself. He rose from Oxford to a height of 3600 feet, landing 6 miles away after a half-hour flight. The most remarkable aspect of Sadler's ballooning was that he was 'sole projector, architect, workman and chymist' in all his experiments (Cavallo, 176–7). In May 1785 he ascended with the statesman William Windham. A letter written soon afterwards noted that Sadler, 'a prodigy[,] … is oppressed, to the disgrace of the University … from pique and jealousy of his superior science' (Hodgson, *History*, 148).

Although Sadler abandoned ballooning for some years after this, he continued with other experiments and about 1785 was one of the first to use coal gas as an illuminant. By 1786 he was experimenting with driving wheeled carriages by steam engine. This brought early hostility from Boulton and Watt in Birmingham, who claimed a monopoly of such use. From about 1788 to 1790 Sadler was technical operator in the chemical laboratory at Oxford University. Whether he had held this post earlier (and thus whether his aeronautics were with or without the help of the university) is unknown. In 1789 and 1790 he gave public performances 'of philosophical fire-works' in Oxford town hall. A contemporary called him 'a clever, practical, and experimental manipulator in chemistry and as such … patronised … by the few scientific men then at the University' (Cox, 3).

From 1788 Sadler was closely involved with Thomas Beddoes, reader at Oxford University, who in April 1791 described his 'very valuable assortment of chemical apparatus … constructed by a pastry cook of this place, a perfect prodigy in mechanics' (Beddoes to Joseph Black, 15 April 1791, Edinburgh University Library). Beddoes and his friend William Reynolds encouraged Sadler to experiment further with his steam engine which, as it did not condense in the cylinder, laid it open to claims of infringement from Boulton and Watt. It worked at a pressure of 19 pounds per square inch and was self-contained and direct acting. Several Sadler engines were built and erected at Coalbrookdale, Shropshire, and in London from 1792 to 1799, despite threats of prosecution from Boulton and Watt from 1791. Because of these threats, Sadler's only patent (no. 1812 of June 1791) was for another, quite different, steam turbine.

Beddoes finally left Oxford in 1793. Sadler had intended to accompany Sir George Staunton as engineer to the Macartney embassy to China, but went with Staunton only to Italy in search of Chinese interpreters in 1792. Sadler's friend the Revd Dr Henry Peter Stacy was not appointed as Beddoes's replacement at Oxford as they both hoped, but was later involved with Sadler in gun boring experiments in London. In 1793 Beddoes sent Sadler to London to set up his Pneumatic Institution, but Bristol was soon chosen instead.

Sadler's technical skills were next put to use as barracks master at Portsmouth, at an annual salary of £300 in 1795. In 1796 he was appointed chemist to the board of naval works in London, at £400 a year. His first wife probably died in or after 1791; he settled in Pimlico, where his second wife, Martha Hancock, whom he had married on 24 October 1795 in the church of St Augustine the Less, Bristol, bore him (William) Windham *Sadler (1796–1824) in October 1796. Sadler also started a mineral water factory near Golden Square. In 1799 he erected the Admiralty's first steam engine at Portsmouth, having been from 1796 much involved in improving naval ordnance. Sadler researched copper sheathing of ships (with Humphrey Davy), distillation of sea water, seasoning of timber, and gunpowder combustion, and constructed air-pumps, signal lights, and apparatus for disengaging oxygen. Outside his naval work Sadler tried to improve alum making. He was elected a life subscriber to the Royal Institution in 1799.

Sadler's relationship with the inspector-general of the naval board, Samuel Bentham, was not happy. Sadler had had to build his own laboratory and by 1802 Bentham noted that he had in very few cases applied to Sadler, who thereafter disappeared from naval records. But Sadler continued in post, under great difficulties, until 1809, when he was dismissed without compensation and left deep in debt.

Sadler resumed aeronautics professionally in 1810 aged fifty-seven, soon using his balloon trademark to sell soda water. He was joined by his son John until 1814 and, from 1813, his youngest son, Windham. By 1815 Sadler had achieved his forty-seventh ascent. His ascents thereafter are impossible to distinguish from those of his youngest son. His second wife having died, on 3 April 1824 Sadler was nominated brother of the London Charterhouse by the king. These were gentlemen in decayed circumstances who received a civil resident pension. Sadler lived in the Charterhouse from the second quarter of 1824 to the end of 1827. He was much affected by the death of his son Windham in a ballooning accident in September 1824. Finally Sadler moved back to Oxford to live with his family (who received his Charterhouse allowance). There he died on 26 March 1828, in George Lane. He was buried four days later at St Peter-in-the-East, Oxford, where he had been baptized. His obituarist rightly noted that, as an aeronaut, he was 'architect, engineer, chemist and projector' (*Jackson's Oxford Journal*), as well as the pilot. He was honoured in Oxford in the twentieth century by a restored gravestone and two tablets, tributes to his pioneering and brave aerial exploits all over Britain and Ireland. John Coxe Hippesley noted in 1812 that Sadler 'has been harshly used … there is not a better chymist or mechanic in the Universe, yet he can hardly speak a word of Grammar' (BL, Add. MS 40221, fol. 270). Sadler's life was of deeds, not words, and left great problems for any biographer.

John Sadler (*bap.* 1779, *d.* 1838), chemist and metallurgist, was born in the High Street, Oxford, eldest son of James Sadler and his first wife, Mary, and was baptized at All Saints' Church on 9 March 1779. He made his first balloon ascent with his father in May 1785. By 1793 he was teaching chemistry at Beddoes's Bristol Pneumatic Institution. From 1800 he was chemical assistant at the Royal Institution, London, and assisted Humphry Davy until 1804 when he issued *An Explanation of Terms used in Chemistry*. By 1806 he was smelting lead at Thomas Richard Beaumont's Dukesfield smelt mill, near Hexham. He was active with the Newcastle Literary and Philosophical Society from 1806 to 1809 and consulting on metallurgy. In 1810 he moved to Hackney, Middlesex, to superintend the Beaufoy Chemical Works in Lambeth. Here he was active with the Hackney Literary and Philosophical Society as lecturer, and assisted John Clennell (1772–1822) with the new *Agricultural and Commercial Magazine*. His paper 'On the dislocation of mineral veins' was read to the Geological Society in 1814. He patented (no. 4524) a new

method of making white lead in 1821. Sadler and his wife, Mary, had four children. He died at Lavender Place, Wandsworth Road, Battersea, London, on 18 March 1838.

H. S. TORRENS

Sources J. E. Hodgson, *The history of aeronautics in Great Britain* (1924) • J. E. Hodgson, 'James Sadler of Oxford', *Transactions* [Newcomen Society], 8 (1927–8), 66–82 • J. E. Hodgson, 'The first English aeronaut', *Cornhill Magazine* (April 1928), 445–58 • Case of Mr James Sadler, 1810, BL, Add. MS 40221, fols. 272–9 • D. A. Stansfield, *Thomas Beddoes M.D., 1760–1808* (1984) • A. V. Simcock, *The Ashmolean Museum and Oxford science, 1683–1983* (1984) • L. T. C. Rolt, *The aeronauts: a history of ballooning, 1783–1903* (1966) • LMA, London Charterhouse archives, Ac. 1876 • T. Cavallo, *History and practice of aerostation* (1785) • J. C. Coad, *The Royal Dockyards, 1690–1850* (1989) • G. V. Cox, *Recollections of Oxford* (1868) • G. S. Davies, *Charterhouse in London* (1921) • J. L. Cranmer-Byng and T. H. Levere, 'Scientific apparatus in the Macartney embassy to China, 1793', *Annals of Science*, 38 (1981), 504 • parish register (baptism), Oxford, St Peter-in-the-East, 27 Feb 1753 • private information (2004) • *Jackson's Oxford Journal* (29 March 1828), 3 • *Oxford Times* (7 Nov 1986) • parish register (baptism), Oxford, All Saints, 9 March 1779 [John Sadler] • d. cert. [John Sadler] • J. Sadler, 'The process for refining lead … in England', *Nicholson's Journal of Natural Philosophy*, 15 (1806), 1–6 • J. Sadler, 'Explanation of a common impurity', *Nicholson's Journal of Natural Philosophy*, 15 (1806), 286–8 • J. Sadler, 'On smelting of lead', *New Agricultural and Commercial Magazine*, 1 (1811), 1–5, 177–9, 396–8, 469–74 • J. Sadler, 'On the dislocation of veins', 1814, GS Lond., John Sadler MSS • John Sadler, patent no. 4524, 1821 • *Annual Reports of the Newcastle Literary and Philosophical Society* (1806–22) • T. Monk-Mason, *Aeronautica* (1838) • J. E. Stock, *Memoirs of T. Beddoes MD* (1811) • R. W. Corlass, 'William Nicholson', *Reliquary*, 22 (1882), 42 • Royal Institution, *The archives of …, 1799–1810* (1971) • *Philosophical Magazine*, 38 (1811), 306–7 • IGI

Archives BL, Add. MSS • Cornwall RO, Davies Giddy MSS • Sci. Mus., Goodrich MSS

Likenesses E. Scott, engraving, pubd 1785 (after painting by J. Roberts), BM • B. Taylor, engraving, *c.*1815, AM Oxf., Hope collection • oils, *c.*1815, NPG • engraving, repro. in Hodgson, *History of aeronautics*, facing p. 141

Wealth at death very little

Sadler, John (*b.* 1512/13, *d.* in or after 1591), translator and music copyist, studied at Cambridge, perhaps as a scholar of Christ's College in 1536; he graduated BA in 1538 (possibly at Corpus Christi College). He was fellow of Jesus College from 1539 to 1546, graduated MA in 1540, and was made an original fellow of Trinity College by the charter of foundation in 1546. By 1548 he was master of the grammar school at Fotheringhay, Northamptonshire, where he remained until taking up a similar appointment at Oundle in 1555, doubtless at the instigation of his patron, Francis Russell, second earl of Bedford.

Sadler's musical interests manifested themselves about 1565 when he began copying Bodl. Oxf., MSS Mus. e. 1–5; this, one of the most important Elizabethan anthologies of vocal music, is prefaced by an instrumental In nomine of his own composition. On 11 June 1568 he was instituted to the Northamptonshire living of Sudborough, and about this time, at the suggestion of his neighbour Sir Edmund Brudenell of Deene, he embarked upon a translation of Vegetius's *De re militari*. This was published in 1572 as *The Foure Bookes of Martiall Policye*.

Preceded only by that by 'Walton' in 1408, Sadler's was the first English translation of Vegetius after the invention of printing. The 'Epistle Dedicatoryc', dated 1 October

1571 from Oundle (in whose rural deanery Sudborough was), states that Sadler had 'nowe manye yeares lately passed … received a liberall annuitye or stipende' of the dedicatee of the book, Francis (Russell), second earl of Bedford; this was presumably for scholarship in divinity, which Bedford, a devout protestant, supported (Thomson, 210).

Sadler also acknowledges the assistance he has received from Brudenell, 'not onlye wyth his good advyce, but also wyth Bookes which elsewhere I could not have had for the accomplishment of the saide translation' ('Epistle Dedicatorye'). Brudenell, whose historical studies attracted William Camden's praise (*Britannia*, 4th edn, 1594, 396), thought it was high time Vegetius's study of Roman military methods as the means to empire was made available to all Englishmen, his 'wyse and prudent counsels for all governours and Captaynes' having already been 'most diligentlye translated' by 'not onlye the Italians, Almaines and Frenchmen, but also many other Nations' ('Epistle Dedicatorye'). So inspired, perhaps, in 1582 Brudenell participated in a scheme for the discovery and colonization of America, in a colony where Roman Catholics could enjoy religious freedom (Finch, 151).

Sadler's translation is prefaced by commendatory lines by Christopher Carlile (a Hebraist and rector of Hackney, Middlesex), Thomas Drant (archdeacon of Lewes, Sussex), William Jacob (undergraduate, Trinity College, Cambridge), William Chark (fellow of Peterhouse, Cambridge), William Bulleyne (a London physician), and John Higgins (poet–scholar, from Oxford), all men with protestant or puritan affiliations. Sadler replied to them in Latin and English verses, shifting their praises onto Brudenell as prime mover of the book. Sadler himself, it appears, took no part in Northamptonshire puritanism.

During the years in which he was translating Vegetius, Sadler absented himself from his teaching responsibilities at Oundle, and in June 1573 the school governors, who were the wardens of the London Company of Grocers, informed him that he was thenceforth required to be resident. Although he undertook to comply, combining the duties of teacher and parish priest was evidently too much for an ageing man, and in March 1575 he resigned his schoolmastership. According to the 1576 survey of Peterborough diocese, Sadler was sixty-three at the time, married, and learned in Latin and theology. On 20 February 1584 he relinquished his Sudborough rectory.

Sadler was alive and seemingly well in 1591, the date of his other set of music partbooks, now sadly incomplete. No will has survived, and the date of his death is uncertain. Sadler had unusually antiquarian interests: nearly half of his personal anthology is of music for the Latin rite lately discarded and prohibited. His collection is also significant for having preserved the music of earlier composers not known to have survived in complete form elsewhere, especially some Taverner, Johnson, Aston, and Marbeck.　　　　　N. P. MILNER and DAVID MATEER

Sources H. I. Longden, *Northamptonshire and Rutland clergy from 1500*, ed. P. I. King and others, 16 vols. in 6, Northamptonshire RS (1938–52) · Venn, *Alum. Cant.* · diocese of Peterborough, clergy returns, 1576–7, LPL, MS CM XIII 56, fol. i · Bodl. Oxf., MSS Mus. e. 1–5 · Bodl. Oxf., MS Tenbury 1486 · Spetchley Park, Worcester, Willmott MS · Grocers' Company, orders of the court of assistants, GL, MS 11588/1 · Rymer, *Foedera*, 1st edn, 15.107 · G. Lester, ed., *The earliest English translation of Vegetius' 'De re militari' edited from Oxford MS Bodl. Douce 291* (1988) · G. S. Thomson, *Two centuries of family history* (1930) · M. E. Finch, *The wealth of five Northamptonshire families, 1540–1640*, Northamptonshire RS, 19 (1956) · M. St C. Byrne and G. S. Thomson, '"My Lord's books": the library of Francis, second earl of Bedford, in 1584', *Review of English Studies*, 7 (1931), 385–405 · J. A. Wisman, 'Flavius Vegetius Renatus', *Catalogus Translationum et Commentariorum*, ed. F. E. Cranz, 6 (1986), 175–84 · Wood, *Ath. Oxon.*, 2nd edn, 1.177 · J. Bridges, *The history and antiquities of Northamptonshire*, ed. P. Whalley, 2 (1791), 255 · D. G. Mateer, 'John Sadler and Oxford, Bodleian MSS Mus. e. 1–5', *Music and Letters*, 60 (1979), 281–95 · D. Mateer, 'John Baldwin and changing concepts of text underlay', *English choral practice, c.1400–c.1650*, ed. J. G. Morehen (1995), 143–60 · N. P. Milner, *Vegetius: epitome of military science* (1993)
Archives Bodl. Oxf., MS Tenbury 1486 · Spetchley Park, Worcester, Willmott MS

Sadler, John (1615–1674), political theorist and reformer, was born on 18 August 1615 at Patcham, Sussex, the eldest son of John Sadler (*d.* 1640), vicar of Patcham, and from 1627 of Ringmer, Sussex, and his wife, Mary, widow of Edward Fenner, late of Aubourne, Sussex. Admitted as a pensioner at Emmanuel College, Cambridge, on 13 November 1630, he matriculated in 1631, graduated BA in 1634, proceeded MA in 1638, and became a fellow in 1639, specializing in Hebrew and oriental languages. Archbishop William Sancroft attributed the masque *Masquarade du ciel: Presented to the Great Queene of the Little World* (1640) to Sadler. After studying law at Lincoln's Inn, Sadler was admitted master-in-ordinary in the court of chancery on 1 June 1644, a position he held until 1656. On 9 September 1645 he married Jane (*b.* 1625), fourth daughter and coheir of John Trenchard of Warmwell, Dorset; her share of the Trenchard estate was £10,000. The couple had fourteen children. An Independent in religion as well as politics, Sadler defended congregationalism against John Bastwick in 1645, and concurred with the Westminster assembly dissenting brethren on the need for an association of Independent churches.

A member of Samuel Hartlib's circle, Sadler helped him promote an office of addresses to co-ordinate projects for educational, ministerial, technological, and agricultural reform, and to facilitate correspondence between European scholars. He was instrumental in fostering links between the Cambridge Platonists (of whom he was one), the Hartlib circle, and experimental scientists such as Robert Boyle. Sadler facilitated William Dell's appointment as master of Gonville and Caius College, Cambridge (May 1649), and the following year, on 31 August 1650, Sadler was named master of Magdalene College after Edward Rainbow's deprivation. From 1649 to 1660 Sadler was town clerk of London, and was appointed commissioner for fen drainage in May 1649 and indemnity in June 1649. In December 1649 Cromwell wanted him to become chief justice of Munster, citing opportunities to render justice to the oppressed, but Sadler declined.

Sadler's principal political work, *Rights of the Kingdom*, a work replete with citations to mythical British monarchs, appeared the same year. In it he insisted the saints' rule would not be inaugurated by force, and he castigated shows of military might to awe parliament—a denunciation of Pride's Purge. Yet he also averred that parliaments should have limited terms, as the Long Parliament did not. His contention that parliaments should not be dissolved until all petitions had been considered later made the work relevant to the exclusion crisis, and it was reprinted in 1682. Sadler's general reformist interests are also evinced in *Rights of the Kingdom*, which includes complaints about lawyers' conduct and a call for prison reform.

Sadler was extraordinarily active in the 1650s. Appointed to the commission for the propagation of the gospel in Wales (February 1650), the high court of justice (March 1650), the admiralty court (November 1651), and the Hale commission (January 1652), he also served as an assessment commissioner for Cambridge town (November 1650, December 1652, June 1657) and a probate judge (April 1653, May 1659). One of the busiest members of the nominated assembly, Sadler sat on the committees for law reform, the advancement of learning, tithes, recusants' estates, St James's Library, the mentally ill, and foreign affairs. He chaired the grand committee on taxation and the committee to draft a declaration providing religious liberty to all but heretics, blasphemers, and the licentious. On 1 November 1653 he was elected to the council of state as a moderate, and later that month he was charged to investigate a murder by the Portuguese ambassador's staff. Sadler was named master of requests on 20 January 1654, and the same year he was appointed to the commission for the approbation of preachers (March), the commission to eject scandalous clergy (August), and the board of visitors of Cambridge University (September).

A proponent of toleration for the Jews, Sadler supported Manuel Dormido's petition of November 1654 to permit Jewish settlement in England, and helped them obtain permission to construct a synagogue in London. In January 1659 he urged Richard Cromwell to provide financial assistance to Menassah ben Israel's widow. As a member of Richard Cromwell's parliament for Yarmouth, Isle of Wight, he made prolix speeches, in one of which he ironically opposed tedious debate; the speaker once admonished him for posing a ridiculous question. At the Restoration Sadler lost all his offices.

A swansong of the interregnum, Sadler's *Olbia: the New Iland Lately Discovered*, was published in 1660 for Hartlib and John Bartlet. Couched as instructions from an elderly hermit to a shipwrecked voyager on a remote Atlantic isle, the book is an amalgam of theological discourse on law and grace; reflections on Christ's work, prayer, and spiritual counsel; an explication of the ten commandments; a discussion of the end times; and exhaustive, mind-numbing numerology. Sadler's religious experiences were at times unusual, as in July 1655 when he had a three-day vision, and in 1661 when he prophesied the great plague, the fire of London, three Dutch wars, and a dramatic event in 1688. Observers in 1661 thought he was mentally ill. In *Christ under the Law* (1664), Sadler predicted

Christ would return by 1680 or 1690, at which time believers would inherit the earth.

In 1666 the fire of London destroyed Sadler's £5000 house in Salisbury Court and other of his properties, and fire also claimed his country home in Shropshire. He received no compensation when the government seized crown properties he had acquired, including Vaux Hall and estates in the Bedford Level. A sometimes eccentric polymath and millenarian, he spent his final years at Warmwell, where he died in April 1674.

Sadler's second son, **Thomas Sadler** (*fl.* 1670–1689), studied law at Lincoln's Inn. Attracted to painting, Thomas became a pupil of Sir Peter Lely. He painted both miniatures, including one of the duke of Monmouth, and portraits. His much copied portrait of John Bunyan (1685) hangs in the National Gallery.   RICHARD L. GREAVES

Sources C. H. Firth and R. S. Rait, eds., *Acts and ordinances of the interregnum, 1642–1660*, 3 vols. (1911) • *CSP dom.*, 1651–2, 36; 1653–4, 229–30, 234, 267, 280, 287; 1658–9, 242 • Venn, *Alum. Cant.*, 1/4.3 • A. Woolrych, *Commonwealth to protectorate* (1982) • *Diary of Thomas Burton*, ed. J. T. Rutt, 4 vols. (1828), vol. 3, p. 279–81; vol. 4 • J. Hutchins, *The history and antiquities of the county of Dorset*, 3rd edn, ed. W. Shipp and J. W. Hodson, 1 (1861), 430, 435 • *The diary of Ralph Josselin, 1616–1683*, ed. A. MacFarlane, British Academy, Records of Social and Economic History, new ser., 3 (1976) • D. S. Katz, *Philo-Semitism and the re-admission of the Jews to England, 1603–1655* (1982) • *The writings and speeches of Oliver Cromwell*, ed. W. C. Abbott and C. D. Crane, 4 (1947) • C. Webster, *The great instauration: science, medicine and reform, 1626–1660* (1975) • D. Foskett, *Miniatures: dictionary and guide* (1987) • C. Hill, *The experience of defeat: Milton and some contemporaries* (1984)

Sadler, John (1720–1789), printer, was born in Aintree on 9 January 1720, the eldest son of Adam Sadler, printer and engraver, and his wife, Elizabeth Beeby. John entered the family printing business and learned the art of printing from his father, who owned a prosperous printing firm in the New Market in Liverpool. By 1740 he had established his own printing business in Harrington Street. Like his father, he was a great music lover and among the many works he published was a collection of over 300 songs set to music, entitled *The Muses' Delight* (1754). In 1757 he founded the *Liverpool Chronicle and Marine Gazetteer*, which he printed for two years.

More importantly John Sadler is credited with inventing a method of transfer-printing onto earthenware tiles, although it now seems unlikely that he was indeed the first to use this process. The idea apparently occurred to him from observing children sticking waste prints onto pieces of broken earthenware. It is not clear when his experiments began, but an affidavit made out by Sadler and his assistant Guy Green states that on 27 July 1756 they printed 1200 earthenware tiles of different patterns in six hours, and that the process had taken upwards of seven years to perfect.

Sadler, an astute businessman, did not proceed with the costly patent application, realizing that his process was safer if kept a closely guarded trade secret. In addition to his tile business, he also transfer-printed onto enamelled copper and porcelain, which he sold to other retailers and from his own shop in Harrington Street. From the middle of 1761 Guy Green became his business partner and in September of the same year Sadler entered into an agreement with Josiah Wedgwood to transfer-print the Wedgwood creamware.

In 1766 Sadler sold his presses and equipment to John Gore and William Everard, who had just begun to publish the *Liverpool General Advertiser*. Four years later, in September 1770, he retired, possibly because he was not in the best of health. However, his abiding passion for collecting recipes and formulas kept him experimenting for a further twenty years, perfecting the transfer-printing process.

In 1777 Sadler married Elizabeth Parker (*d.* 1842), the daughter of a business associate, a watchmaker who owned a toy shop in Seel Street, and the niece of Mr Fazackerley, silversmith of Pool Lane. They had three children, a daughter, Elizabeth Mary (*b.* 1782), and two sons: John Adam (*b.* 1778) and James (*b.* 1786). John Sadler died in Liverpool on 10 December 1789 and was buried in Sefton. J. M. STEPHENS, *rev.*

Sources E. S. Price, *John Sadler: a Liverpool pottery printer* (1949) · M. R. Perkins, ed., *The book trade in Liverpool to 1805: a directory*, Book trade in the north-west project, occasional publication, 1 (1981), 25
Archives Lpool RO, memorandum book

Sadler, John (*bap.* 1779, *d.* 1838). *See under* Sadler, James (*bap.* 1753, *d.* 1828).

Sadler, Sir Michael Ernest (1861–1943), educationist, was born on 3 July 1861 at Barnsley, Yorkshire, the elder child of Michael Thomas Sadler, medical practitioner, and his wife, Annie Eliza Adams of Lincolnshire. His great-great-uncle was Michael Thomas *Sadler, the Conservative factory reformer. He was educated first at the Winchester preparatory school and then at Rugby School, and was one of several Rugby old boys (R. H. Tawney, William Temple, and J. L. Stocks were others) who were to become important figures in the early twentieth-century educational landscape. The headmaster of Rugby School commented at the time that the school ran pretty well, so long as he took the advice that was proffered to him by Michael Sadler during his period as head boy of School House. Sadler's five years at Rugby did a great deal to mould his thinking. He commented, later in his life, that Rugby 'washed away from my mind, for a time, those old Winchester traditions'. He recalled the younger masters as being 'enthusiastically Liberal, not to say Radical politicians' (Higginson, 11). He remembered particularly warmly Arthur Sidgwick, Henry Lee Warner, and Canon James Wilson as teachers who were 'without knowing it … ardent propagandists of Liberal ideas' (ibid.). His schooldays left him also with a strong sense of the role of the Anglican church as 'a branch of the national machinery more sacred in its content … and more efficacious than the criminal law' (ibid.). A commitment to Liberal thinking and to the established church as one of the key organs of the state were to be the cornerstones of his thought and action in later life.

Sir Michael Ernest Sadler (1861–1943), by George Charles Beresford, 1914

University extension and secondary education From Rugby Sadler went to Trinity College, Oxford, in 1880 as a classical scholar and he took firsts in classical moderations (1882) and *literae humaniores* (1884). He attended the lectures of Arnold Toynbee, the historian, and John Ruskin. In June 1882 he was elected president of the union. As an undergraduate he became friendly with Austen Chamberlain and visited the Chamberlain family home at Highbury in Birmingham during vacations. He met Joseph Chamberlain, who liked him and offered him backing for a career in politics. But more significant to Sadler's future career was his growing friendship as a student with Arthur Acland, the Liberal MP. He joined Acland's 'inner ring' and through his friendship was drawn increasingly to 'the education question'.

In April 1885, when Acland returned full time to a political life, Sadler was elected unanimously to succeed him as secretary of the extension lectures sub-committee of the Oxford local examinations delegacy, which in 1892 was redesignated the delegacy for the extension of teaching beyond the limits of the university. His marriage, on 14 July 1885, to Mary Ann (*d.* 1931), who was nine years his senior, eldest daughter of Charles Harvey, a Barnsley linen manufacturer, influenced the direction of his career. He turned down the offer of an academic post in India and commented in his diary that 'the only alternative open to me is a schoolmastership, and my mind is set very strongly against that life' (Sadler, 61). He also refused the secretaryship of the Co-operative Wholesale Society since it would have meant leaving Oxford for London.

It was during Sadler's ten years as secretary to the Oxford extension delegacy that much of the direction of his future career was laid out. He was quickly identified as an extremely efficient administrator and was responsible for the very swift expansion of extension lecturing from within Oxford University. He was personally responsible for the establishment of extension summer schools from 1893 onwards and he edited the *University Extension Gazette*. In this connection he forged friendships and working relationships with young Oxford tutors who were to become some of the leading figures in English education during the following thirty years. In 1886 he was also appointed steward of Christ Church and this appointment enabled him to supplement his income during the early years of his marriage. He was determined not to become dependent on his wife's income and it was this consideration that led him to turn his back on a life in politics with its constant risk of loss of office. His views on the reform of secondary education, the need for a complete restructuring of the central administration of education, and the need for governmental support for the universities were all refined in a lengthy and regular correspondence with Acland.

In April 1891 Sadler visited America for the first time to lecture to the National Conference of University Extension, where he acknowledged the pressing need for the reform of secondary education in England. He met William Torrey Harris, whose reports for the United States bureau of education had proved influential, and became convinced of the need for a series of special reports to be available for educational policy makers and practitioners in Britain. This visit, together with his experience as administrator and tutor for Oxford University, forced him to the view, in the early 1890s, that without a more coherent system of secondary education it would be impossible to develop university adult education in a truly worthwhile form, and he believed that the necessary restructuring should be based on careful comparative research.

During a hiking tour in the Appenzeller Alps Sadler and Acland, together with Tom Ellis, the leader of the Welsh Nationalists in the House of Commons, formed the idea of, first, a conference on secondary education, and, following from that, of a royal commission to re-examine the secondary education issue in detail. Sadler wrote personally to leading figures within the University of Oxford calling for a conference to bring together representatives of the public schools, the universities, the charity commissioners, the school boards, and teachers' unions. The outcome was the 1893 Oxford Conference on Secondary Education, which led to the appointment of the royal commission on secondary education, chaired by James Bryce. Sadler was invited to sit on the commission and he became one of its most energetic members, arranging for questionnaires on the organization of national systems of education to be sent out worldwide. This anticipated his own research a few years later. Some contemporaries

thought him the principal author of the subsequent report.

Board of Education special inquiries and reports It was in the spirit of these ideas of Sadler's that Acland, determined to leave an educational legacy after the likely fall of the Liberal government, planned the office of special inquiries and reports. Consequently, in 1895 Sadler was announced as director of this research bureau, which was to be located in Whitehall. One of Sadler's contacts through the Oxford extension network was Canon Barnett, principal of Toynbee Hall, and it was Barnett who recommended to Sadler Robert Morant as his assistant director at the office of special inquiries. For four years Sadler and Morant worked closely on the *Special Reports on Educational Subjects*, eleven volumes of which were published before Sadler left the office. These constituted a thoroughgoing attempt to provide the hard evidence that Sadler thought necessary to inform the development of educational policy, and these reports remain an important source for educational researchers. From the beginning the approach was comparative, with visits being made to other European countries, Germany in particular, to enable systematic comparative accounts of the educational provision across the continent.

During Sadler's absences to gather research material Morant made himself politically useful to the new Conservative government and began to use the research bureau for the initial drafting of educational legislation. Although the two of them became involved in the drafting of the 1896 Education Bill, this development was resisted by Sadler, who, after Morant's departure in the autumn of 1899 to become personal private secretary to Gorst, sought to defend the ability of the office of special inquiries to carry out independent research with no imperative to become involved in day-by-day policy making. Sadler was sceptical of the direction of educational policy under the Conservative government and alarmed by Morant's willingness to become a pliant administrator of its policies.

Once Morant became permanent secretary of the newly established Board of Education in November 1902, he turned against his old colleague. Sadler posed a threat to the development of the educational policy of the Conservative government through his ability to bring into question the wisdom of what was being done. Morant starved Sadler's department of funds, and this resulted in Sadler's placing an anonymous letter in *The Times* (22 January 1903) and finally resigning in April 1903. The controversial circumstances of his resignation led to the publication in May 1903 of *Papers Relating to the Resignation of the Director of Special Inquiries and Reports*, and these were presented to parliament as a 'whitewash' of the circumstances of Sadler's resignation. One letter (3 April 1903) from Sadler to Morant at this time crystallized his views on the significance of this incident. Sadler argued:

> the true function of the Office of Special Inquiries and Reports is not limited to the promotion of the purely administrative purposes of the Board ... Its most important and responsible task is to undertake the dispassionate

examination of educational problems and to lay before the country an impartial and accurate survey of the facts *on both sides* of great educational questions, in order that readers may draw their own conclusions and that there may thus be formed, in regard to national education, that sound and enlightened public opinion, on the existence of which, far more than on Departmental control, the prospects of wise educational development depend.   (Sadler MS Eng. misc. C 552, fols. 57–8)

Manchester, Leeds, and return to Oxford Undaunted by this snub to his efforts to enshrine independent research at the heart of policy making in English education, Sadler accepted the post of professor of education at the University of Manchester. He refined his considerable public speaking technique, and his lectures on the history of education were invariably well attended and proved enormously popular with intending schoolteachers, stimulating his lifelong interest in educational history. At Manchester he proceeded to write a series of commissioned research reports for several of the new local education authorities, advising them on the best organization of secondary schooling in their respective areas. These reports emphasized two elements that were to become constant themes in his writing about education. On the one hand, he saw the need for some kind of balance between the power of central government and that of the local authorities in formulating educational policy, being suspicious of highly centralized systems but equally sceptical about the complete absence of governmental control. It was this constant tension between central and local that led Sadler to think in terms of what he called the 'two-mindedness' of England, and he returned to this theme frequently. Also prominent in his writing, and particularly emphasized in his reports, was his belief that secondary education needed to be organized into separate strands. In this respect Sadler is a very significant figure because he was, without it being realized at the time, reworking the tripartism that had surfaced in the 1868 Taunton report in a form that made it viable for the twentieth century. Without his advocacy, it appears unlikely that a system of grammar, technical, and secondary modern schools would have been adopted in the form it took in the years following the 1944 Education Act.

In 1911 Sadler was approached by the University of Leeds to become vice-chancellor, a post which he held for twelve years. He presided over a major expansion of the University of Leeds. Sadler Hall was named in his honour as a permanent testimony to his determination to expand on the Oxbridge model with sufficient halls of residence for students to become fully involved in the life of the university. During this period he wrote extensively about the comparison between English and German universities, reflecting the tensions between the two nations which were at their height during the First World War. Earlier in his career Sadler had commented that if the best sides of the English system of secondary education could be combined with the best sides of the German, the result would be the best system in the world. In this spirit he refused to become involved in crude propagandizing against Germany while the war was on. He also spent his time as vice-

chancellor building a significant art collection, and it was during this period of his life that his reputation as an art collector developed. His actions as vice-chancellor involved him in two public controversies. For permitting student volunteers to take the places of strikers during the Leeds municipal workers strikes of 1913–14 he was criticized by the local labour movement for compromising the university's independence. The unveiling, in 1923, of the war memorial at the university, which Sadler had commissioned Eric Gill to make, led to further public attacks, this time from business interests in the city offended by Gill's choice of design.

Sadler's long-term friendship with Austen Chamberlain, who had become secretary of state for India, resulted in his invitation in 1917 to participate in the Calcutta University commission. He served as president of that commission, and was in India from October 1917 to April 1919. His influence is evident throughout the thirteen volumes of report which it generated. He took particular pleasure in the chapter on the student in Bengal, which he wrote. Although he had grave reservations about the wisdom of imposing the British system of universities on a society such as India, his report was a significant landmark in the maintenance of a European model of education in the Indian subcontinent. For his work on the commission he was created KCSI in 1919. In 1923 he was a member of a Colonial Office committee, chaired by William Ormsby-Gore, which advised on education in tropical Africa. Sadler was responsible for the recommendation that a central training college for east Africa should be established at Makerere.

Sadler remained vice-chancellor of the University of Leeds until, in June 1923, he moved back to Oxford to take on the mastership of University College. As master he showed the same liberal traits as in the earlier posts he held. At the meeting held by the vice-chancellor during the general strike he voiced his college's view that there should be no official university contingent of volunteers, a view which prevailed. But for some fellows his liberalism and open-mindedness went too far; his invariable courtesy led him to be so eager at college meetings to ensure a full hearing for dissidents that proceedings were unduly prolonged. E. L. Woodward recalled that in university committees Sadler always preserved a certain rather disconcerting detachment, and 'would appear to change his mind suddenly and without regard to the immediate consequences or to his own reputation for consistency' (*Oxford*, summer 1944, 51–3). In this final phase of his career he played a significant part in beautifying the college and its chapel, where he became a daily worshipper. He was an advocate of modern studies at Oxford and he also worked for the extension of the Bodleian Library (lobbying unsuccessfully for its relocation to a new site). He was also involved in the Oxford Preservation Trust and was awarded the freedom of the city of Oxford in 1931. He retired in 1934, hoping to complete a major history of English education, and also to continue his studies of and writing about the examinations system, an interest he shared with Sir Phillip Hartog. He also continued to be a patron of the arts, collecting and exhibiting the work both of old masters as well as of numerous modern artists. His first wife, with whom he had a son, Michael Thomas Harvey *Sadleir, died in 1931 and in 1934 he married a teacher, Eva Margaret Gilpin (d. 1940), daughter of Edmund Gilpin, stockbroker. Sadler died at Old Headington, Oxford, on 14 October 1943.

Sadler's educational ideas Throughout Sadler's career there was a consistency in his thinking and writing about education. He remained committed to an essentially hierarchical view of secondary education but it was one which was well received in England. Arguing that different forms of knowledge were needed for differing callings in life, he advocated higher elementary, secondary, and higher secondary schools with contrasting curricula. These ideas were a well-developed part of his thinking by the time he was preparing reports on the needs of the new local education authorities in the early years of the century and were never greatly modified. In this respect he is of enormous historical importance as the figure who kept alive the ideas of the Taunton commission (which had advocated three distinct types of secondary school in 1868) and reworked them in a form acceptable to the twentieth century, although of course, for him, the selection of pupils and the reward of merit was a key element in this equation.

Second, Sadler's brush with Morant confirmed his instinctive dislike of over-centralized and over-bureaucratized systems. He commented in 1916 that 'there is something impalpably foreign in some of the bureaucratic developments of the last three generations of English life' (Higginson, 1). For Sadler a balance between the powers of central and local government was vital and this view was expressed repeatedly later in his life. The phrase he used most frequently to encapsulate this was 'the two-mindedness of England'. His religious views meant that he saw education as intrinsically spiritual: he thought it a grave danger to see an education system as nothing more than a system of schools. R. H. Tawney perceptively described him as 'more of a thinker than an administrator and more of a missionary than either' (ibid.).

Sadler remained committed to that ideal of educational research which saw it as essentially independent of the immediate needs of the bureaucratic machine but sensitive to changing economic and social circumstances. The question of which advice should influence educational policy reverberated throughout the twentieth century. Had Sadler's vision of an independent research bureau, so clearly articulated at the start of the century, been sustained in practice there might well have followed a more genuinely democratic debate on educational policy in twentieth-century Britain and the education system might not have lain so passive before a succession of educational ideologues.

Sadler had an exhaustive knowledge of education, an unquenching energy, and he wrote and worked tirelessly for educational causes throughout his long career. He is perhaps best remembered as one of that group of Oxford reformers whose deep and abiding interest in the education question was sparked by their involvement in extension lecturing during the 1880s and who subsequently played a central role in the development and systematization of education in England. Through his determination to provide a comparative perspective Sadler stands out from this group. Sadly, this strain of educational research, of which he was one of the founding fathers, was not sustained as one of the major lines of enquiry for educational researchers in twentieth-century Britain, and there can be little doubt that British universities and schools have been impoverished by the fact that the insights which he brought to bear have not been sustained.   ROY LOWE

Sources Bodl. Oxf., MSS Sadler · extension delegacy papers, Oxf. UA · J. H. Higginson, *Selections from Michael Sadler* (1979) · L. Grier, *Achievement in education: the work of Michael Ernest Sadler, 1885–1935* (1952) · M. Sadleir, *Michael Ernest Sadler … 1861–1943: a memoir by his son* (1949) · *The Times* (15 Oct 1943), 7 · O. S. Pickering, *Sir Michael Sadler: a bibliography of his published works* (1982) · R. Lowe, 'Personalities and policy: Sadler, Morant and the structure of education in England', *In history and in education*, ed. R. Aldrich (1996), 98–115 · E. Ashby, *Universities: British, Indian, African* (1966) · P. H. J. H. Gosden and A. J. Taylor, eds., *Studies in the history of a university, 1874–1974: to commemorate the centenary of the University of Leeds* (1975) · CGPLA Eng. & Wales (1944) · DNB · *The Times* (23 Oct 1943), 6

Archives Bodl. Oxf., commonplace books · Bodl. Oxf., corresp., diaries, and papers · Tate collection, corresp. and papers relating to art collection · University College, Oxford, corresp. and papers | BL, letters to Albert Mansbridge, Add. MS 65253 · Bodl. Oxf., corresp. with Gilbert Murray · Bodl. Oxf., corresp. with Sir Aurel Stein · Bodl. Oxf., letters to Sir Alfred Zimmern · JRL, letters to the *Manchester Guardian* · King's AC Cam., letters to Oscar Browning · LMA, corresp. relating to Toynbee Hall · NL Scot., corresp. with Sir Patrick Geddes · Oxf. UA, University of Oxford extension delegacy papers · U. Leeds, Thompson MSS · U. Leeds, Brotherton L., letters to Harriet Thompson · U. Reading L., letters to G. W. Palmer

Likenesses G. C. Beresford, photograph, 1914, NPG [*see illus.*] · M. Gertler, oils, 1914, U. Leeds · W. Rothenstein, drawing, c.1916, U. Leeds · J. Kramer, oils, 1917, U. Oxf. · W. Stoneman, photograph, 1921, NPG · L. Rey, bronze bust, 1933, U. Leeds · H. Lamb, oils, U. Leeds · F. H. Shepherd, group portrait, oils, University College, Oxford

Wealth at death £49,343 3s. 4d.: probate, 1944, CGPLA Eng. & Wales

Sadler, Michael Ferrebee (1819–1895), theologian, was born on 14 January 1819 in Leeds, the eldest son of Michael Thomas *Sadler, and Ann, daughter of Samuel Fenton, linen importer, of Leeds. Educated first at Sherborne School, he entered St John's College, Cambridge, after a short interval in business. He was elected Tyrwhitt's Hebrew scholar in 1846, graduating BA in 1847 and MA in 1850. He was ordained deacon in 1846 and priest in 1849. After holding curacies in Huntingdonshire and London, Sadler became perpetual curate of Hanover Chapel, Regent Street, in 1852. On 7 August 1855 he married Maria (d. 1873), daughter of John Tidd *Pratt, formerly registrar of the friendly societies in England. They had six sons and one daughter. He was vicar of Bridgwater from 1857 to 1864, and in 1863 was appointed to the prebend of Combe, thirteenth in Wells Cathedral. While incumbent of St Paul's, Bedford, from 1864 to 1869 he represented his archdiocese in convocation. In 1869 he refused on medical advice the bishopric of Montreal and the living of Brighstone, Isle of Wight, before accepting the rectory of Honiton, which he held until his death. A high-churchman, he wrote extensively on theological subjects, his widely circulated works doing much to popularize the Tractarian doctrines. Sadler died at Honiton on 15 August 1895.

M. E. SADLER, *rev.* ELLIE CLEWLOW

Sources Venn, *Alum. Cant.* · Boase, *Mod. Eng. biog.* · *The Guardian* (21 Aug 1895) · *The Churchwoman*, 1 (1895) · A. T. C. Pratt, ed., *People of the period: being a collection of the biographies of upwards of six thousand living celebrities*, 2 vols. (1897)
Wealth at death £2273 17s. 0d.: probate, 30 May 1896, *CGPLA Eng. & Wales*

Sadler, Michael Thomas (1780–1835), social reformer and political economist, was born on 3 January 1780 at the Old Hall, Doveridge, Snelston, Derbyshire. He was the youngest of the six children of James Sadler (*d.* 1800?), a gentleman farmer at Doveridge who claimed descent from Henry VIII's minister Sir Ralph Sadler, and his wife, Frances (*d.* 1797), the daughter of Michael Ferrebee, rector of Rolleston, Staffordshire, whose father was a Huguenot. Little is known of Sadler's childhood, save that between the ages of six and fifteen he was in the care of one Mr Harrison, a schoolmaster of considerable reputation at Doveridge. Sadler's father had meant for him to go to public school and, eventually, university. But Harrison, for some obscure reason, thought this ill-advised, and from the age of fifteen Sadler was practically self-taught, acquiring in his father's library a wide but desultory knowledge of classical and modern literature. Sadler's parents, though Anglican in name, were Methodists at heart. From his mother especially, Sadler inherited a tendency toward evangelical piety that remained with him all his life. His first published pamphlet (*An Apology for the Methodists*, 1797) was a vigorous and widely circulated defence of the new faith against the aspersions of the local vicar.

In 1800, shortly after the death of his parents, Sadler entered into partnership with his brother Benjamin, a linen merchant in Leeds. He had no head for business, however, and when not otherwise lost to fits of melancholic abstraction, he occupied himself with civic and philanthropic affairs. He was a frequent contributor to the *Leeds Intelligencer*, the leading tory newspaper in the north. A tireless patron of the sick and destitute, he was also for many years the superintendent of the largest Sunday school in Leeds and the treasurer of the parish overseers. In 1807, when William Wilberforce stood for election for the county of York, Sadler managed his campaign, and he remained thereafter a committed abolitionist. But he rose to prominence in the West Riding as an opponent of Catholic emancipation and parliamentary reform. His *First Letter to a Reformer*, a lengthy harangue against those who would tamper with the irregular genius of the constitution, went through two considerable editions in 1817 and established Sadler as a tory radical of some rhetorical reckoning.

In 1816 Sadler married Ann, the daughter of Samuel Fenton, a Leeds linen merchant with whose widow he and his brother had entered into partnership in 1810. They had

Michael Thomas Sadler (1780–1835), by William Robinson, in or before 1830

several children, among them Michael Ferrebee *Sadler (1819–1895), the high-church divine whose eventual Tractarianism suggests some immunity to his father's anti-Catholic influence. Sadler's public interests, meanwhile, increasingly turned on his own providential and violently anti-Malthusian understanding of the problems of public distress. From 1819 he read several papers on poverty and the poor laws to the Leeds Literary and Philosophical Society, of which he was a founder member. His evident intention, at this time, was to write a general treatise on 'the Law of Human Increase' (Seeley, 49), but the agitated state of Ireland—a country with which he and his brother, as importers of Irish linen, had considerable dealings—together with the (to his mind) misguided recommendations concerning Ireland of the 1827 emigration committee tempted him to detach his chapters on the sister kingdom and publish them separately in 1828. The first of his books, *Ireland: its Evils and their Remedies* (1828), was also his most successful. Against the individualist and Ricardian views that underlay most English thinking about Ireland, Sadler here proposed the establishment of an Irish poor law on the paternalist principle that in proportion to its means 'wealth should be compelled to assist destitute poverty, but that, dissimilar to English practice, assistance should in all cases, except in those of actual incapacity from age or disease, be connected with labour' (*Ireland: its Evils and their Remedies*, 1828, 193).

The warm reception of his views on the poor laws encouraged Sadler in his scholarly pretensions, and in

1830 he published his most ambitious work, *The Law of Population* (2 vols.). Here, against the dire forebodings of Malthus and his followers, Sadler advanced the original theory that 'the prolificness of human beings, otherwise similarly circumstanced, varies inversely as their numbers'. T. B. Macaulay promptly reduced this notion to absurdity in the *Edinburgh Review* (51, July 1830, 297–321), and Sadler was forced to concede that the problem of population was too complex to admit of earthly explanation. Meanwhile, in March 1829, with the help of the duke of Newcastle, Sadler had been returned to parliament from the borough of Newark. His maiden speech deploring the Roman Catholic Relief Bill earned him a reputation as an eloquent if over-earnest speaker. 'In his countenance there was such a seriousness and solemnity that a stranger might have mistaken him for a clergyman', one contemporary recalled. 'His voice was full and distinct, but it had a species of twange about it very much resembling that which is so often heard in the pulpit' (J. Grant, *Random Recollections of the House of Commons*, 1836, 102). A slight man in frequent ill health, Sadler was nevertheless said to be handsome and vigorous by nature. His dress was severe, his face intelligent.

In June 1830 Sadler moved for the first time his favourite resolution, calling for the establishment of a poor law for Ireland. Safely returned again for Newark at the general election in July, he then joined the ranks of those unreconciled to parliamentary reform. On 18 April 1831 he seconded General Gascoyne's motion to retain the existing number of members for England and Wales. His main interests remained social and economic, however, and in October 1831 he moved a resolution condemning commons enclosure and calling for the provision of parish allotments to the rural poor. To date he had taken little active part in the factory movement that his friend Richard Oastler had launched in Yorkshire a year earlier. But the idea of restricting by law the length of the working day in textile mills was bound to appeal to one of his paternalist disposition, and in October 1831, at Oastler's request, he succeeded the tepidly radical Sir John Hobhouse as parliamentary sponsor of the Ten Hours Bill.

Sadler's speech on moving the second reading of the bill on 16 March 1832 was by all accounts the greatest and most effective of his career. Against all current economic orthodoxies, he argued that employer and employed did not meet on equal terms in the market of labour and that some measure of legislative protection was therefore essential. Deeply moved by his description of the sufferings of factory children, the House of Commons was inclined to agree, but the government insisted on a committee of inquiry, which Sadler subsequently chaired. He was the featured speaker at the great public meeting that Oastler organized in support of factory reform at York on 24 April 1832, and on the publication of his committee's report the following August, he was fêted throughout the north as a delivering hero, the original factory child's friend. Together with the accompanying minutes of evidence, Sadler's report impressed the gravity of the factory

question on his contemporaries, and, though highly controversial, it remains a classic of industrial inquiry, the first of many of its kind.

Sadler's parliamentary constituency since 1831, Aldborough in Yorkshire, was one of those deprived of its seat by the Reform Bill, and on the dissolution of the last unreformed parliament in December 1832, Sadler declined other offers in order to stand for Leeds, where his chief opponent was that same Macaulay who had savaged his *Law of Population* two years earlier. The contest was correspondingly bitter, as economic interests—liberal and protectionist—lined up 'in textbook fashion' behind the candidates (Clive, 222). Macaulay and Sadler: one could hardly have asked for a better study in nineteenth-century contrasts, and when it was over, whig erudition had prevailed over tory piety by 388 votes. Sadler surrendered his leadership of the ten hours movement to Lord Ashley (later seventh earl of Shaftesbury) and retired to a family home at New Lodge, Belfast, where his firm had linen works. He stood once more for parliament, unsuccessfully, in 1834, but his health declined rapidly thereafter, and he died, probably of heart disease, at New Lodge on 29 July 1835. He was survived by his wife. He was buried on 4 August at Ballylesson churchyard.

'Sadler is a loss', Robert Southey had written to Lord Ashley after the Leeds election in words that anticipated Sadler's epitaph; 'he might not be popular in the house, or in London society, but his speeches did much good in the country, and he is a singularly able, right-minded, and religious man'. Lloyd Jones, another contemporary who knew Sadler well, bore similar testimony to his eloquence, marked ability, and 'modest honesty of purpose plain to the eye of the most careless observer in every look and action of the man' (*DNB*). Liberals thought him a romantic eccentric, and it is surely true that Sadler was too sanguine in his belief that the territorial aristocracy might yet rule Britain responsibly. At the same time, however, he had a precocious insight into the hurtful consequences of uncontrolled industry for which subsequent generations of British workers would have reason to be grateful.

STEWART A. WEAVER

Sources R. B. Seeley, *Memoirs of the life and writings of Michael Thomas Sadler* (1848) · *DNB* · C. H. Driver, *Tory radical: the life of Richard Oastler* (1946) · J. L. Clive, *Thomas Babington Macaulay: the shaping of the historian* (1973) · J. T. Ward, *The factory movement, 1830–1855* (1962) · A. Kydd [S. H. G. Kydd], *The history of the factory movement, from the year 1802 to the enactment of the Ten Hours' Bill in 1847*, 2 vols. (1857)

Archives BLPES, corresp. and pamphlets · Leeds Leisure Services, commonplace book | Leeds Leisure Services, diary of S. G. Fenton concerning life of Sadler · LUL, Goldsmith's Library of Economic Literature, Oastler collection · NL Scot., letters to William Blackwood · Notts. Arch., election returns (with Henry Willoughby) · U. Nott. L., Portland MSS · U. Nott. L., corresp. with the duke of Newcastle

Likenesses lithograph, pubd 1829, NPG · T. Lupton, mezzotint, pubd 1830 (after W. Robinson), BM, NPG · W. Robinson, oils, in or before 1830, NPG [*see illus.*] · engraving, 1832?, repro. in Driver, *Tory radical*, 116 · Park, statue, 1835, Leeds parish church · J. Doyle, caricature, BM · J. Doyle, two pencil drawings, BM · D. Maclise, lithograph, BM; repro. in *Fraser's Magazine* (1835) · portrait, repro. in Seeley, *Memoirs of … Michael Thomas Sadler*, frontispiece

Sadler, Sir Ralph (1507–1587), diplomat and administrator, was probably born in Warwickshire, the first son of Henry Sadler, administrator, of Warwickshire and Hackney, Middlesex. His father was a steward of Sir Edward Belknap until 1521, when he acquired a house in Hackney. He then became steward of Tilty, Essex, for Thomas Grey, second marquess of Dorset. Thomas Cromwell was Dorset's attorney by 1522 but his association with Henry Sadler probably predates this.

Education, early years, and early diplomatic career, 1507–1540

Ralph Sadler entered Cromwell's service by 1521. Although Sadler does not appear to have attended university his patron ensured that he had an excellent education, learning Latin, French, and Greek and acquiring familiarity with the law. The most valuable lessons of all, however, came when, at about nineteen, he began to serve Cromwell in a secretarial capacity, learning about counsel, administration, finance, and politics. He was involved in drafting and writing Cromwell's voluminous correspondence and gained valuable firsthand experience of great affairs from the late 1520s. He also took an increasingly prominent role in handling household business. Sadler was one of Cromwell's intimates by 1529, being appointed an executor of his will. People began to turn to him for favours, knowing his influence with his master.

Sadler also met his wife through his connection with the Cromwell household. He married Ellen, or Helen (d. after 1545), daughter of John Mitchell, of Much Hadham, Hertfordshire, by 1535. However, the marriage was bigamous because she was the wife of Matthew Barre, a London tradesman and a drunkard, originally from Sevenoaks, Kent, who had abandoned her and their two children. She enquired after Barre but eventually presumed him dead. She then found employment as a laundress in the Cromwell household, where she met Sadler, about 1530, and the couple married soon afterwards. Unfortunately Barre was not dead. Sadler was unaware until 1545 that his marriage was bigamous and that his children were illegitimate. There were seven surviving children in all: three sons, Thomas (c.1536–1607), Henry (c.1538–1618), and Edward, and four daughters, of whom the names of three are known, Anne (d. 1576), Jane (d. in or after 1587), and Dorothy (d. in or after 1578).

Sadler's duties as secretary to Cromwell, including involvement in the examinations of Sir Thomas More and John Fisher, bishop of Rochester, brought him to the attention of Henry VIII. In 1535 he became clerk of the hanaper of chancery. In the following year he was named a gentleman of the king's privy chamber and began his parliamentary career, being returned as MP for Hindon, Wiltshire, through Cromwell's patronage. He was well known as Cromwell's messenger at court and was placed in the privy lodgings as a means of countering the Boleyn party. He was entrusted in January 1537 with a diplomatic mission to Scotland, ostensibly to protect the interests of Margaret Tudor, the dowager queen. Beyond this aim the opportunity existed for Anglo-Scottish rapprochement, for a conciliatory approach from England might lessen French influence at the Scottish court. This appointment

Sir Ralph Sadler (1507–1587), by unknown sculptor

was to mark the beginning of Sadler's long association with Scottish affairs.

Travelling through the north of England in the wake of the Pilgrimage of Grace, Sadler wrote to Cromwell of sedition-mongers among the local gentry and of rebellious commoners, whose loyalty could be secured only by a show of royal force. His chief task while in the north was to secure the arrest of leading members of the Percy household, who were prime movers, in the king's mind, of the rebellion. This achieved, Sadler moved on to Edinburgh, arriving in mid-January. He was able to placate Margaret and to dissuade her from her ill-advised intention to flee to England. James V was in France at the time, busy with the final arrangements of his marriage to Madeleine de Valois. Sadler pursued the Anglo-Scottish rapprochement with the Scottish king himself, having an audience with him at Rouen on about 1 April, and then later in the year travelled once more to Scotland for further talks. For the time being James seemed well disposed towards Henry and the lingering threat of hostilities between England and Scotland receded temporarily. Yet this diplomacy had been only a partial success, failing to establish a basis for a lasting peace, and relations between the kings soon deteriorated.

Sadler was favoured by Henry and began to acquire patronage. In March 1536 he received the reversionary lease of Walthamstow, Essex, for forty years. He was elected knight of the shire of Middlesex in 1539. In January 1540 he returned to Scotland, with a gift of six geldings, charged with promoting the cause of religious reform and with denouncing David Beaton, cardinal and archbishop of St Andrews, as an instrument of Paul III and Charles V. The mission was particularly important to Cromwell, who desperately needed a foreign policy success to restore his battered credibility following Henry's dissatisfaction with his marriage to Anne of Cleves. The king's infatuation with Katherine Howard gave Thomas Howard, third duke of Norfolk, and Stephen Gardiner, bishop of Winchester, the opportunity they needed to engineer Cromwell's downfall. Sadler was made welcome in Edinburgh but found that the Scottish nobility was largely composed of young men. James, lacking such counsellors as served Henry, relied upon his bishops and clergy. The geldings, as Sadler was well aware, were unimpressive animals and a disappointment to the Scottish king when he presented them on 19 February. The advice Sadler was instructed to offer on how best to raise revenue on royal lands was tactless, since it implied criticism of James's ability to rule and reflected Henry's heavy-handed approach towards his nephew. The extent of Scottish anti-clericalism was wholly overestimated and James had no sympathy for the reformation. Improvising on his instructions Sadler proposed a personal meeting between Henry and James. He left Edinburgh in March, convinced that James had agreed to this, and conveyed that opinion to Henry. Yet James would not leave his realm; Henry travelled north to York in 1541, where he awaited James for two weeks before realizing that the meeting would not take place. Humiliated, Henry initiated military preparations on the border. Sadler's mission failed through a combination of unrealistic expectations and clumsy diplomacy.

Principal secretary and privy councillor, 1540–1547 Nevertheless Cromwell seems to have defended his position well for a time and this was to Sadler's benefit too. Sadler was knighted, probably on 18 April 1540, and was appointed, along with Sir Thomas Wriothesley, as principal secretary. Furthermore he was also a protonotary of chancery from 1537 and sat on the privy council, which gave him sufficient influence and security to survive his patron's fall. However, because of his association with the disgraced royal servant and his sympathies for religious reform, it is likely that in January 1541, in the wake of Cromwell's execution and Henry's marriage to Katherine, Sadler was briefly imprisoned in the Tower of London. Yet the king found him too valuable, for Sadler was capable and industrious. His habit of dating his letters by the hour as well as the day gives an insight into a gruelling schedule; he often rose by 4 a.m. and was rarely in bed before midnight. In order to be close to Henry, being the king's secretary as well as the principal secretary, and therefore working within the privy lodgings, he acquired a house at Hackney, Middlesex, and had accommodation at Hampton Court, Westminster Palace, and Whitehall Palace. Yet he remained politically marginalized for some time. He had not accompanied Henry and his favoured advisers as they travelled north in summer 1541. Dramatic revelations of Katherine's alleged adultery were, however, to transform his political fortunes once more.

Sadler was one of those who gathered enough evidence to ensure Katherine's execution in February 1542 and to discredit Norfolk and Gardiner before the king. He was a ruthless participant in this process, co-ordinating much of the inquiry into the queen's conduct and doing his utmost to transform a case of treason into a purge of those who had orchestrated Cromwell's downfall. In this, he and his allies, Thomas Cranmer, archbishop of Canterbury, being prominent among them, were unsuccessful. War now loomed with France and Scotland. Henry needed the services of both Gardiner, for his diplomatic talents, and Norfolk, a proven military commander, although their influence at court was diminished. Sadler, in contrast, was appointed master of the great wardrobe from 1543 to 1553. This meant that he was much concerned with the logistics of the royal household, giving him the necessary skill and experience for involvement in pay and supply during war. Additionally, he received other notable administrative appointments, becoming a recognized financial expert. He was a chamberlain or receiver of the court of general surveyors by 1545, commissioner of musters for Hertfordshire in 1546, and steward of Hertford and constable of Hertford Castle from 1549 to 1554. He was JP for Hertfordshire from 1544 and of the quorum for Hertfordshire and Gloucestershire from 1547.

James's death on 14 December 1542 provided the opportunity for achieving dynastic union between England and Scotland by the marriage of Edward, prince of Wales, and Mary, queen of Scots. Sadler was Henry's resident ambassador in Scotland, charged with engineering this union, and arrived in Edinburgh on 13 March 1543. His initial objectives were to have Mary removed to England and to persuade Scotland's governor, James Hamilton, second earl of Arran, to advance the reformation. The trust that Henry placed in Sadler is indicated by the king's desire that Lady Sadler be appointed as Mary's governess. This was entirely impractical, as Sadler tactfully informed him; having no experience of court life herself his wife could hardly be expected to provide a suitable upbringing for a queen. Discussions of such future arrangements were, however, soon irrelevant because of the situation that developed in Scotland. French ships were already delivering munitions on a regular basis, and a powerful party inimical to English interest was forming around Beaton. Sadler identified three main factions: Arran and his allies, whom he judged sympathetic to England and to the reformation; Beaton, Mary of Guise, and the clergy, who looked to France; and a body of neutrals, whose loyalties would ultimately lie with the strongest party. In this assessment Sadler erred. Unwilling to make concessions to Catholic interest, and placing far too much trust in those he believed to be religious allies, he proved unequal to the complexities of Scottish factional politics. Arran did, initially, give every indication of good faith. In order to win Sadler's support he claimed (probably falsely) that his own name headed a black list of prominent heretics drawn up by James. On 1 July at Greenwich his ambassadors agreed a treaty of peace and dynastic union through marriage. However, it was already apparent to Sadler that Arran's position was far from secure, with Cardinal Beaton's followers threatening to rebel. Henry urged him to give every encouragement to Arran to honour the treaty; he himself made offers of troops, money, and even the crown of Scotland itself in an effort to ensure the governor's continuing loyalty. Despite this, Arran was neither a champion of religious reform nor a servant of English interests. Sadler learned on 5 September that Arran had joined the cardinal in Stirling. Frustrated and furious, he railed against the Scots, 'under the sun live not more beastly and unreasonable people than here be of all degrees' (LP Henry VIII, 18/2.175).

There was much that was commendable in Sadler's conduct of affairs in Edinburgh. He favoured peace over war and argued that England's cause would be best served by the distribution of bibles and copies of the New Testament rather than by coercion. His position was made more difficult by Henry's aggressive posturing; talk of English garrisons in Scotland only confirmed the suspicions of many Scots that dynastic union would lead to subjugation. In the aftermath of Arran's defection the extent of Scottish hostility became all too apparent. Several attempts were made on Sadler's life and he was forced to flee Edinburgh on 10 November, first to the Douglas stronghold of Tantallon Castle, Haddingtonshire, and from there by sea to England on 12 December.

During the course of his long absence from London, Sadler was replaced, on 23 April 1543, in his office of principal secretary. He was, however, appointed treasurer for the war against Scotland and in this capacity accompanied Edward Seymour, first earl of Hertford, on a punitive expedition to Edinburgh in May 1544. This was well organized and brutally effective, delighting Henry but serving in the long term only to strengthen the Scottish will to resist. Sadler continued to work closely with Hertford, accompanying him once more across the border on a second bloody foray in September 1545. His transformation from diplomat to military administrator solidified his friendship with Sir William Paget, his replacement as principal secretary. Through Paget's endeavours he recovered some political influence at court, and in October 1545 took his place at the council board after an absence of over two years. Yet he was confronted with an unexpected crisis on his return to London. One of Wriothesley's servants overheard a drunken Barre boasting in November that he was Lady Sadler's husband. Barre was seized and interrogated, and the truth of his claims established. Sadler's only recourse was to parliament, of which he was MP for Preston, Lancashire. The experienced privy councillor had little difficulty securing passage of a private bill, passed on 24 December, that legitimized his children. Lady Sadler, however, remained legally Barre's wife and it may have been years before Sadler's marital status was regularized. Sadler was deeply attached to his wife and 'took his matter very heavily' (HoP, Commons, 1509–58, 251).

Sadler's position at court facilitated the purchase of crown lands and by 1547 he owned property in twenty-five counties in England and Wales. His annual income from land alone was £372 13s. 4d. by 1545–6. He was principally living at court or in London during these years. His estate

at Standon, Hertfordshire, acquired in 1544, where he built a great mansion, provided something of a refuge for his wife and himself, not only from the scandal of 1545 but also from the court's revels and masks, which they seemed to find distasteful. This distancing from court life, combined with his problematic marital status, may explain why Sadler never rose to the highest political office. He was, however, a trusted and efficient royal servant. In the final months of Henry's reign he worked alongside Sir Richard Rich in an examination of the procedure of the revenue courts and in the collection of debts due to the crown. He played a leading role in the reorganization of the courts of augmentations and of general surveyors and he was responsible for the systematic organization of the privy council's growing archive of documents.

Service under Edward VI and Mary I, 1547–1558 On Henry's death, on 28 January 1547, Sadler was one of the privy councillors deputed to arrange the late king's funeral in his capacity of master of the great wardrobe. Thereafter, and in accordance with Henry's instructions, he was appointed one of the assistants to the sixteen executors of the regency council who acted as guardians to Edward VI and were entrusted with the government of the realm. He received a £200 bequest in Henry's will. Sadler supported Hertford's elevation as duke of Somerset and lord protector, overthrowing the provisions of Henry's will, and was confirmed as a privy councillor in reward. He accompanied the English expedition under Somerset into Scotland in the capacity of high treasurer of the army in September. At the battle of Pinkie on 10 September he demonstrated that his role went beyond that of administrator. During the combat he was noted for his 'ready forwardness in the chiefest of the fray'. In the aftermath it was Sadler who, 'with much travail and great pains' restored order to the army (Pollard, 128). The experience seems to have made a lasting impression on him; his tomb was decorated with helmets, weapons, and a standard, all said to be trophies of Pinkie. Somerset personally created him a knight banneret on 28 September.

Although the war in Scotland dragged on Sadler returned to England. In March 1549 he signed the warrant for the execution of Thomas Seymour, Baron Seymour of Sudeley, lord admiral, and, in the summer, served against the rebels in Norfolk and was present during the expedition of William Parr, marquess of Northampton, to Norwich, which ended in disaster on 1 August. He backed John Dudley, earl of Warwick, during the October coup against Somerset. Although not a close adherent of Warwick, or a regular attendee at the council board, Sadler was clearly a trusted supporter of the new regime, partly because of his discretion and partly because he was a notable protestant. In late 1550 he was given command of a company of fifty men-at-arms maintained on a semi-permanent footing as *gendarmes*, a prestigious duty normally associated with a member of the nobility. Financial retrenchment led to the disbanding of this military force by the duke of Northumberland (Warwick) in 1552 and Sadler was then employed as a commissioner to survey crown revenues, having substantial influence over new fiscal policy. Sadler claimed to have suffered considerable financial loss through forced loans and sales to Northumberland, but he remained both wealthy and a supporter of the duke's regime. However, he rarely attended privy council meetings after May 1550, although he was re-elected for Hertfordshire in March 1553, when Northumberland wanted reliable people returned as MPs. Sadler's annual income from land alone was at least £400 by 1552, and probably more. He spent £4041 on purchasing crown lands in December 1550 but also sold property on a large scale. He signed the letters patent for the limitation of the crown, altering the succession, on 21 June 1553 and 'transacted affairs for' Lady Jane Grey in Hertfordshire (BL, Lansdowne MS 103, fol. 2v).

The failure of Northumberland's *coup d'état* and the subsequent succession of the Catholic Mary I saw Sadler marginalized politically. He lost most of his offices, including privy councillor and master of the great wardrobe, was removed from the commissions of the peace, and was briefly under house arrest from 25 to 30 July, before suing out a pardon on 6 October. For the remainder of the reign he retired quietly to Standon, although his hard work as a commissioner of the forced loan in Hertfordshire in 1557 was noted gratefully by the privy council. He did not sit in any Marian parliament.

Restored to favour, 1558–1571 Sadler's political career resumed at the accession of Elizabeth I and he was among the first to be admitted to her privy council on 20 November 1558. He was MP for Hertfordshire in 1559, 1563, 1571, 1572, 1584, and 1586. He was also restored to his place on the quorum for Hertfordshire in 1559 and was named *custos rotulorum* by 1562. In August 1559 he was a member of a commission ostensibly engaged in settling border disputes but actually working with reform-minded Scots to counter French influence. Later in that year he accepted that most burdensome post, warden of the east and middle marches, partly in order to monitor developments in Scotland, and provided Sir William Cecil, principal secretary, with detailed reports. Acting as paymaster to the lords of the congregation he distributed £3000 to further their cause, while controlling agents who infiltrated their ranks and surveyed the major French fortifications at Leith. Despite the strength of the *trace italienne* style defences constructed by the garrison Sadler urged that the port of Leith should be seized quickly, and in 1560 an English army was dispatched to aid in the expulsion of the French. In the aftermath of the siege Sadler travelled to Leith and helped arrange the treaty of peace and alliance between England and Scotland signed in Edinburgh on 6 July.

Sadler, now in his fifties, did not actively seek these onerous missions and he seems to have abandoned any commitment to the idea of a union between the two countries. In 1563 a debate took place in the House of Commons over the question of succession, Elizabeth's marital status, and the position of Mary, queen of Scots. Sadler was adamant that, just as the people of Scotland had refused to accept an English king, so the English would reject utterly a Scottish monarch. In the session of 1566 he spoke once more on the question of the succession and on the necessity of granting a subsidy in order that Ireland be made 'civil and obedient' (HoP, *Commons, 1558–1603*, 139). In 1579 the proposed Anjou marriage attracted Sadler's ire and he warned of the risk of English subordination to Catholic France. Besides the vexed question of the succession he busied himself with parliamentary business: administering the oaths at the commencement of parliament in 1571 and 1572; taking bills to the Lords; and serving on committees dealing with such matters as church attendance and abuses by collectors and receivers.

Cecil wrote to Sadler on 27 April 1568, advising him that 'as fishes are gotten with baits, so are offices caught with seeking'. The advice was well received and Sadler was appointed chancellor of the duchy of Lancaster the following month. This was the highest office he would hold during Elizabeth's reign and one for which he was considered to be particularly well qualified, being 'well affected in religion', 'well experienced and expedite in hearing and dispatching of causes', and 'of good spirit, countenance and credit' (Somerville, 325, 334). He retained the chancellorship for the remainder of his life, exploiting its tremendous opportunities for patronage. Allegations that he made extensive grants of lands and offices to his sons were strenuously denied in a letter to Lord Burghley (Cecil) in 1577. Yet he clearly used his influence in parliamentary elections. In 1584 Sadler found seats in parliament for no less than seventeen of his relatives and associates. One son, Henry, was MP for Lancaster in 1571, 1572, 1584, and 1586, and another son, Thomas, held the second seat for Lancaster in 1572. His three sons-in-law, Anne's husband, George Horsey, Jane's husband, Edward Bashe, and Dorothy's husband, Edward Elrington, were, at various times, returned for Aldbrough, in the East Riding of Yorkshire, and Clitheroe, Preston, and Wigan, all in Lancashire.

Mary fled to England on 16 May 1568. Sadler was immediately appointed as one of three commissioners who met with a Scottish delegation at York to discuss her plight. It was, for Sadler, a perplexing issue and he demanded to know whether or not the Scottish queen should be bound by the abdication that had been extorted from her. However, when the English commissioners were confronted by the contents of the casket letters, of which Sadler sent a précis to Cecil, suspicions of Mary's guilt were seemingly confirmed. In effect, the proceedings were to be a trial of Mary *in absentia* but the volatile situation in the north led to the conference reconvening at Westminster in November. There it was possible for Elizabeth, 'superior lady and Judg over the realm of Scotland' (Alford, 175), to invoke the imperial power of the English throne to confirm James Stewart, earl of Moray, as regent, the crowning of James VI, and to detain Mary.

It took almost twenty years to bring Mary to trial; Sadler was involved in her case throughout, not just in the complex legal proceedings but in the responses to the conspiracies that her presence in England engendered. He found himself serving in a military capacity once more in 1569, accompanying Thomas Radcliffe, third earl of Sussex, lord president of the council of the north, as he suppressed the northern rebellion. For most of 1570 Sadler enjoyed a brief respite at Standon from his public duties, assuring Cecil that he had no wish to play the courtier. Yet the following year he was active in the aftermath of the Ridolfi plot, arresting Thomas Howard, fourth duke of Norfolk, and investigating the extent of Mary's involvement in the conspiracy.

Final years, 1571–1587 Sadler concentrated on his parliamentary duties during the early 1570s. He sat not only on committees dealing with Mary but on others concerned with more mundane matters, such as the preservation of game, fraudulent conveyances, coining, and the fate of Arthur Hall of Grantham, Lincolnshire, whose presumptuous tracts were judged insulting to Elizabeth. Sadler was entrusted with the custody of Mary in August 1584, first at Sheffield, then at Wingfield, Derbyshire, and finally, in 1585, at Tutbury, Staffordshire. His attitude towards her was ambivalent. He had once held her in his arms when she was a baby and proved a sympathetic gaoler. He wrote to Elizabeth of Mary's integrity and loyalty in December 1584. The following year he allowed Mary to accompany him when he went hawking, a favourite pastime that alleviated the boredom of their situation to some degree. Yet in November 1586, having been discharged from his duties with Elizabeth's thanks, he spoke forcefully in parliament in favour of Mary's execution, denouncing her as the root cause of all conspiracies, who would, while she lived, never cease to be a threat to Elizabeth.

Sadler died on 30 March 1587, near his eightieth birthday, by repute one of the richest men in England. He bequeathed the bulk of his substantial landholdings, including Standon and Buntingford, Hertfordshire, to his eldest son and heir, Thomas Sadler. Henry Sadler received the manors of Hungerford, Berkshire, and Everley, Wiltshire. Jane Bashe was left a diamond ring and an annuity was arranged for an illegitimate son, Richard. Sadler himself was buried below a magnificent wall monument in St Mary's Church, Standon.   GERVASE PHILLIPS

Sources S. Alford, *The early Elizabethan polity: William Cecil and the British succession crisis, 1558–1569* (1998) · *CSP dom., 1547–53* · J. Cameron, *James V: the personal rule, 1528–1542*, ed. N. Macdougall (1998) · G. Dickinson, ed., *Two missions of Jacques De La Brose*, Scottish History Society (1942) · G. Donaldson, *Mary, queen of Scots* (1974) · *The chronicle and political papers of King Edward VI*, ed. W. K. Jordan (1966) · D. M. Head, 'Henry VIII's Scottish policy: a reassessment', *SHR*, 61 (1982), 1–24 · *HoP, Commons, 1509–58* · *HoP, Commons, 1558–1603* · D. E. Hoak, *The king's council in the reign of Edward VI* (1976) · C. P. Hotle, *Thorns and thistles: diplomacy between Henry VIII and James V, 1528–1542* (Lanham, Maryland, 1997) · *LP Henry VIII* · H. Matthews, 'Personnel of the parliament of 1584–1585', *BIHR*, 22 (1949), 52–4 · M. Merriman, *The rough wooings: Mary queen of Scots, 1542–1551* (2000) · J. E. Neale, *Elizabeth I and her parliaments, 1559–1581* (1953) · *DNB* · A. F. Pollard, ed., *Tudor tracts, 1532–1588* (1903) · M. B. Pulman, *The Elizabethan privy council in the fifteen-seventies* (1971) · will, PRO, PROB 11/70, sig. 23 · *The state papers and letters of Sir Ralph Sadler*, ed. A. Clifford, 2 vols. (1809) · A. J. Slavin, *Politics and profit: a study of Ralph Sadler, 1507–1547* (1966) · R. Somerville, *History of the duchy of Lancaster, 1265–1603* (1953) · *VCH Hertfordshire*, vol. 3

Archives BL, corresp. and MSS relating to embassies to Scotland, Add. MSS 31991, 32646–32657, 33591–33594 · BL, register of the signet, accounts, Add. MSS 35818, 35824 · NL Scot., corresp. as English ambassador in Scotland [copies] | BL, corresp. with Cecil relating to Scottish negotiations · East Riding of Yorkshire Archives Service, Beverley, wardrobe account · NRA, priv. coll., accounts relating to Mary, queen of Scots

Likenesses effigy on monument, St Mary's Church, Standon, Hertfordshire [*see illus.*]

Wealth at death by repute the the richest commoner in England

Sadler, Thomas [*name in religion* Vincent Faustus] (1604–1681), Benedictine monk, was born in Warwickshire, probably a younger son of Theodore Sadler of Fillongley, Warwickshire. He was converted to Catholicism by Father Augustine Baker through his Benedictine uncle Dom Walter Robert Vincent Sadler, alias Robert Walter (d. 1621), who had been aggregated to the community of Westminster Abbey in 1607. He was clothed in the Benedictine habit in September 1621 at St Lawrence's Priory, Dieulouard in Lorraine, and was professed there in 1622. He took the name in religion of Vincent Faustus. He was sent on to the English mission in the south province before 1637 and became *praepositus*, or superior, of Kent in 1649.

Sadler was highly connected and for many years served in London, where he became dean of the Confraternity of the Rosary which he helped to found probably at Cardigan House in Lincoln's Inn Fields. Many of his devotional writings were published for the use of this association, whose prefect, Robert Brudenell, second earl of Cardigan in 1663, wrote an address which forms the preface to Sadler's book, *Jesus, Maria, Joseph* (1657). In a number of such works, most of them translations of contemporary European spiritual classics, Sadler collaborated with another Benedictine, Dom Arthur Anselm Crowther or Crowder (1558–1666). Sadler's books went through innumerable editions, and their dedications, to Catherine of Braganza, William Sheldon of Beoley and Weston, and Sir Henry Tichborne, reveal the aristocratic character of the 'pious Rosarists' who were Sadler's patrons. The portrait of the Sheldons accompanying Sadler's dedication in *The Spiritual Conquest* (1651) and the mention of 'the great dole' yearly given out by the Tichbornes in his dedication in *The Dayly Exercise of a Devout Christian* (1662) suggest that Sadler was at one time chaplain to both these two households. James II was among those who derived some benefit from reading Sadler's translation of Pierre Lallemant's *The Holy Desires of Death* (1678). Some of the Benedictine items in the famed library of Ralph, William Sheldon's son, had come from Sadler, including the sole surviving copy of Sadler's *The Childe's Catechism* (1678), and the important manuscript of the monk Thomas Woodhope, 'Obital Book of Eminent Benedictines', which was continued by Sadler and which Sheldon gave to Anthony Wood.

The Confraternity of the Rosary seems to have been suspended during the difficult time of the Popish Plot, but information about its notable relics—part of the crown of thorns, originating from Glastonbury, and part of the true cross, from the relic at Westminster Abbey—probably came from Sadler. His published translations of spiritual works are of particular importance for their emblematic engravings, mostly by William Marshall, who copied engravings found in Francis Quarles's *Emblemes* (1643), which in turn derived from those in the Jesuit Herman Hugo's *Pia desideria*. This suggests that Benedictine authors were beginning to adopt a fashion already much exploited by the Jesuits, and which was acceptable to an Anglican readership, judging by the number of English editions of Sadler's books published.

Sadler became cathedral prior of Chester, and definitor of the south province in 1661. In 1669 he and John Huddleston were living in Oxford, at Amsterdam Court, adjoining Brasenose College—many of his books carry a false imprint, 'Amsterdam' instead of 'London'—and in 1671 they attended the solemnity of the act and graduation, making the acquaintance of Anthony Wood. Dodd describes him as 'a person of curiosity' (Dodd, 3.313). He continued writing devotional tracts into old age, the 1677 Benedictine general chapter, for instance, examined his manuscript *De vitis sanctorum* in 1677. Sadler died in retirement at St Lawrence's Priory, Dieulouard, on 19 January 1681.   GEOFFREY SCOTT

Sources Gillow, *Lit. biog. hist.* · H. Wansbrough and A. Marett-Crosby, eds., *Benedictines in Oxford* (1997) · T. B. Snow, *Obit book of the English Benedictines from 1600 to 1912*, rev. H. N. Birt (privately printed, Edinburgh, 1913) · T. H. Clancy, *English Catholic books, 1641–1700: a bibliography*, rev. edn (1996) · D. Lunn, *The English Benedictines, 1540–1688* (1980) · K. J. Holtgen, *Aspects of the emblem: studies in the English emblem tradition and the European context* (1986) · K. J. Holtgen, 'Emblem and meditation: some English emblem books and their Jesuit models', *Explorations in Renaissance Culture*, 18 (1992), 55–91 · B. Weldon, 'Memorials', Douai Abbey, Woolhampton, Berkshire, English Benedictine Congregation Archives · J. McCann and H. Connolly, eds., *Memorials of Father Augustine Baker and other documents relating to the English Benedictines*, Catholic RS, 33 (1933) · C. Dodd [H. Tootell], *The church history of England, from the year 1500, to the year 1688*, 3 vols. (1737–42)

Archives Ampleforth Abbey, Yorkshire, Allanson MSS · Bodl. Oxf., Wood MSS

Sadler, Thomas (*fl.* 1670–1689). *See under* Sadler, John (1615–1674).

Sadler, Thomas (1822–1891), Unitarian minister, was born at Horsham, Sussex, on 5 July 1822. His father, also Thomas Sadler (1777–1839), was born at Ditchling and became an agricultural labourer. Without ordinary schooling, he set about educating himself; he is said to have worn the Greek alphabet on his sleeve while working. Having attended the General Baptist Academy, London, in 1798–1800, he became assistant and then successor to the Revd John Dendy (1754–1814) at Horsham; he married Dendy's daughter.

The younger Thomas Sadler was educated at University College, London, studied for some months in Bonn, and proceeded to Erlangen University, where he received the degree of PhD in 1844. He entered the Unitarian ministry in November 1843 as assistant to the Revd Robert Aspland at the New Gravel Pit Chapel, Hackney. After Aspland's death on 30 December 1845 the congregation could not agree to make Sadler his successor. An imaginative plan was put forward for a joint ministry with the chapels in Little Portland Street, Marylebone, and in Hampstead, but

discussions came to nothing and a vote on Sadler's succession was lost by 27 votes to 24. Sadler then became minister at Rosslyn Hill Chapel in Hampstead, where he served for the remaining forty-five years of his life. A new chapel in Rosslyn Hill was opened on 5 June 1862; the opening sermon by James Martineau was printed together with Sadler's sermon on the closing of the old chapel. In 1849 he had married Mary (1821/2–1898), daughter of Charles Colgate (1792?–1873), who survived him; there were no children.

Sadler published *Gloria Patri: the Scripture Doctrine of the Father, Son, and Holy Spirit* (1859), a defence of the Unitarian position against the views expressed in *The Rock of Ages* (1859) by Edward Henry Bickersteth, later bishop of Exeter, but, though an explicit Unitarian, Sadler was not a doctrinal preacher. He was known and admired, rather, for his singular kindliness and sweetness of character; Mary Ann Evans (George Eliot), whose funeral sermon he was to preach in 1880, wrote after attending a baptism that he was 'a benignant-faced refined man whose voice and manner make the occasion such as affects one without any moral jar' (*George Eliot Letters*, 6.419–21). He did not parade his very considerable learning and, while a theological conservative, provided a valuable balance between adherents of the older, scriptural Unitarianism and of the new transcendentalist outlook associated chiefly with James Martineau. Sadler was a trustee of Dr Williams's Library and visitor of Manchester New College. He was especially interested in the history of the older English presbyterianism. His literary tastes and interests, together with his knowledge of German university life, led the trustees to make him editor of the diaries of Henry Crabb Robinson, which with other papers had come to the library. The work appeared in 1869, and a third edition was called for in 1872; but only a small portion of the diaries was used.

Sadler died at home at Rosslyn manse on 11 September 1891 and was buried in Highgate cemetery on 16 September. The funeral was conducted by James Drummond (1835–1918), who also delivered a memorial sermon at Rosslyn Hill on 20 September.   R. K. WEBB

Sources *The Times* (18 Sept 1891) · *The Inquirer* (19 Sept 1891) · J. Drummond, 'Memorial sermon', *Christian Life* (26 Sept 1891) · *Christian Reformer, or, Unitarian Magazine and Review*, 6 (1839), 992 [obit. of Thomas Sadler (1777–1839), father] · A. R. Ruston, *Unitarianism and early presbyterianism in Hackney* (1980), 27 · *The George Eliot letters*, ed. G. S. Haight, 6 (1956), 419–21 · *DNB* · d. cert. · m. cert. · *CGPLA Eng. & Wales* (1891)

Archives DWL, corresp. and papers

Likenesses F. Drummond, crayon drawing (after photograph), Harris Man. Oxf. · R. T., wood-engraving, NPG; repro. in *ILN* (19 Sept 1891) · photograph, DWL, Trustees Album

Wealth at death £23,580 10s. 5d.: resworn probate, Dec 1891, *CGPLA Eng. & Wales*

Sadler, (William) Windham (1796–1824), balloonist and gas engineer, was born on 17 October 1796 at 10 Stafford Row, Pimlico, London, the fourth, but second surviving, son of James *Sadler (*bap.* 1753, *d.* 1828), first English-born aeronaut, and his second wife, Martha Hancock. William was baptized on 30 March 1797 at St George's Church,

Hanover Square, and named after his father's early supporter and ballooning companion in 1785, the statesman William Windham.

Sadler is presumed to have been apprenticed to his father as both chemist and engineer. James Sadler was behind the formation of the first Liverpool Gas Light Company and, on 29 August 1817, Windham Sadler attended his first meeting of their committee. After successful canvassing he was appointed manager of this company on 21 September 1817 aged twenty. His engineering duties involved unremitting activity in obtaining gas supplies from retorted coal. His salary on appointment was £100 a year, increased to £130 from July 1819, and £150 from 1820. The rapid development of the company was undoubtedly due to Sadler's skill, energy, and enterprise, but towards the end of 1821 serious differences arose with the company's treasurer, John King, and on 3 June 1822 Sadler was paid off. In October he applied unsuccessfully for the post of engineer to the newly founded and rival Liverpool Oil Gas Company, sponsored by members of the Gas Light Company.

Sadler's first appointment had undoubtedly been helped by the publicity generated by his earlier exploits as a young aeronaut. Such aeronautics involved a detailed knowledge of the properties, generation, and control of different gases. Sadler had first ascended with his father in July 1810 at Oxford to celebrate the installation of the new chancellor of Oxford University. His first solo balloon ascent was made at Cheltenham on 7 September 1813, when, despite the consumption of nearly three tons of vitriolic acid and iron filings, insufficient gas was generated to lift the weight of his father, who disembarked, leaving his lighter son to go alone. After an hour's flight Sadler landed safely near Chipping Norton. He made a total of thirty successful balloon ascents all over Britain.

Since both Sadler's father and his brother were now also making balloon ascents, it is often impossible to tell which individual Sadler was involved in any particular flight. On 22 July 1817 Sadler succeeded, where his father had narrowly failed in 1812, in flying across the Irish Sea from Dublin to Holyhead, Anglesey, in a five-hour flight, using the 'counteracting Powers of Gas and Ballast' (Hodgson, *History*, 154–5). His first ascent using coal gas was recorded in September 1823. His ascents were helped on occasion, as appropriately on Ascension day, 27 May 1824, by the gift of gas from his former employers; Sadler had to pay only the cost of running a pipe from their gasworks to the site of his Liverpool ascent. Sadler also acquired a reputation in Oxford and Liverpool for lecturing between 1815 and 1819 on the new science of aerostation (ballooning).

Late in the autumn of 1822, when his employment as gas engineer had been terminated, Sadler and his wife, Catherine Richards (c.1794–1832), whom he had married in 1819, opened a warm vapour and medicated bath establishment at the corner of Hanover and Wood streets in Liverpool. This proved popular and was carried on after his death by his widow. They had two children, John Muncaster (c.1821–1912), a railway engineer who was for many years engineer to Liverpool corporation, and Catherine Windham, who died young. On 29 September 1824 Sadler made his thirty-first and fatal ascent at Bolton. In attempting to land near Blackburn, Sadler, aged twenty-seven, was thrown out of the balloon and died of his injuries the next day at the Fox Hill Bank inn. He was buried at Christ Church, Liverpool, on 4 October.　　H. S. TORRENS

Sources J. E. Hodgson, *The history of aeronautics in Great Britain* (1924) · J. E. Hodgson, 'James Sadler of Oxford', *Transactions* [Newcomen Society], 8 (1927–8), 66–82 · J. E. Hodgson, 'The first English aeronaut', *Cornhill Magazine* (April 1928), 445–58 · S. A. Harris, *The development of gas supply on north Merseyside, 1815–1949* (Liverpool: NW Gas Board, 1956) · 'Proposals for a subscription for the widow and orphan child', *Kaleidoscope*, n.s. 5/223 (5 Oct 1824), 116–20 · J. Gibson, 'Liverpool epitaphs', Lpool RO, vol. 2, Christ Church, fols. 107–22 · *GM*, 1st ser., 94/2 (1824), 364–6, 473–4 · D. E. Bick, *The Gloucester and Cheltenham tramroad* (1987) · 'Gas and bathing', *Liverpool Post* (11 Sept 1942) · G. J. Norman, *Aeronautica illustrata*, 10 vols. (1850–60) · *King's treatise on the science and practice ... of coal gas*, ed. T. Newbigging and W. T. Fewtrell, 1 (1878) · W. W. Sadler, *Aerostation: a narrative of the aerial voyage of Mr Windham Sadler across the Irish Channel* (1817) · parish register (baptism), London, St George, Hanover Square, 30 March 1797 · private information (2004) · parish register (burial), Liverpool, Christ Church, 4 Oct 1824 · IGI

Sadlington, Mark (d. 1647), Church of England clergyman and schoolmaster, matriculated as a pensioner from Christ's College, Cambridge, at Easter 1578. On 7 May 1580 he migrated to Peterhouse, where he graduated BA in 1581 and proceeded MA in 1584. A translation in 1583 of a work by Bartolomé de las Casas, *Chronicle of the Acts and Gestes of the Spaniard*, has been attributed to Sadlington. *The Arraignment and Execution of ... Eueralde Ducket, alias Hanns*, once attributed to him, is now thought to have been written by Anthony Munday. In 1583 a new fellowship was endowed at Peterhouse by Sir Richard Martyn, citizen and alderman of London, and on 15 February 1584 Sadlington became the first and only holder of the place, which was discontinued after his resignation on 19 October 1590. Sadlington contributed plate to Peterhouse and is listed as 'head lecturer' there in 1588.

Perhaps shortly after resigning his fellowship Sadlington married a wife, Jane, of whom nothing is known except that she survived him. He had already sought a position outside the university. On 2 October 1588 Sir Francis Walsingham wrote to the corporation of Colchester, strongly recommending Sadlington's appointment as master of the grammar school there, but despite his efforts and those of the retiring master, Samuel Harsnett (later archbishop of York), Samuel Bentley was preferred. On 25 June 1591, however, Sadlington secured the position of master of St Olave's Free Grammar School in Southwark, in succession to the former congregationalist and separatist leader, Robert Browne; the following year the vestry issued an instruction to 'convert the kitchen presently to a school house for the grammarians' (*VCH Surrey*, 2.185). He vacated the position before the appointment on 9 January 1595 of William Parys (d. 1609), also a fellow of Peterhouse. Sadlington had then just been admitted, on 18 December 1594, as perpetual curate of All Hallows-the-Less, London; he vacated that living before the institution of his successor on 28 May 1597. In 1599, on the presentation of the dean and chapter of St Paul's, he was instituted to the rectory of Holy Trinity, Guildford, Surrey, holding the benefice until 1633. On 11 March 1603 he was instituted to the vicarage of Sunbury, which he held until his death, at a very great age; he was buried at Sunbury on 27 April 1647. STEPHEN WRIGHT

Sources T. A. Walker, *A biographical register of Peterhouse men*, 2 (1930) · Venn, *Alum. Cant.* · Cooper, *Ath. Cantab.* · J. Peile, *Biographical register of Christ's College, 1505–1905, and of the earlier foundation, God's House, 1448–1505*, ed. [J. A. Venn], 1 (1910) · G. Hennessy, *Novum repertorium ecclesiasticum parochiale Londinense, or, London diocesan clergy succession from the earliest time to the year 1898* (1898) · *VCH Surrey*, vol. 2 · O. Manning and W. Bray, *The history and antiquities of the county of Surrey*, 1 (1804)

Sadyngton [Sadington], **Sir Robert** (*d.* in or after **1361**), justice and administrator, came of a family of minor Leicestershire gentry named from Saddington in that county. His father's name may have been John. Robert Sadyngton clearly trained for the law. First recorded in 1317, as an attorney in chancery, in 1327 he was a knight of the shire for Leicestershire, and in October 1329 he became a serjeant-at-law, thereafter appearing increasingly frequently as a pleader in the bench. He also began to act as a commissioner and justice, above all in the midlands. From February 1332 he was regularly appointed to commissions of the peace in Leicestershire and Rutland, and from 1334 was a justice on the midland assize circuit. His rise was certainly assisted by links with Henry, earl of Lancaster, whose tenant he was at Laughton. In 1334 he was a justice for forest pleas in Lancashire, and ten years later acted as the earl's attorney. But he also found favour at the royal court. Knighted in 1336, on 20 May 1337 Sadyngton was made chief baron of the exchequer. Appointed on 28 May 1338 to a commission to survey the lands of the king and queen north of Trent, from June 1338 he was regularly summoned to councils and parliaments.

On 25 June 1339 Sadyngton was made deputy treasurer of the exchequer, a promotion that heralded his involvement for several years in the highest levels of government. On 1 March 1340 he was appointed with the bishop of Lincoln to raise loans for the king, and on 2 May following became treasurer. Replaced by the bishop of Coventry on 21 June, he resumed the position of chief baron, and in the same year became a member of the king's council, and was made a member of the commission that Edward III set up to provide legal and administrative reform in return for a parliamentary grant of taxation. Sadyngton was one of the few prominent members of the government to survive the purge that followed Edward's dramatic return to England from the Low Countries at the end of November 1340. Indeed, he soon found himself employed in proceedings against former colleagues and associates, above all when as chief baron he presided over the trial in the exchequer in April–June 1341 of the financier Sir William de la Pole, a principal target for the king's wrath (and perhaps also Sadyngton's personal enemy). He acted as a trier of petitions in parliament in 1340, 1341, 1343, and 1347, and continued to act as a justice and commissioner, but

appears to have been preoccupied by government business, and on 29 September 1343 reached the height of his career, when he was appointed chancellor of the realm, an office he held for just over two years, until 20 October 1345.

After 1340 Edward III looked as much for compliance as competence in his government. During the 1330s the chancery had been in the hands of a succession of prelates. Sadyngton was one of a series of common lawyers who acted as chancellor in the early 1340s, laymen who could be better trusted than ecclesiastics to fulfil the king's wishes. He was not expected to be either independent or innovative in his conduct of business, and when he gave an unlooked-for show of initiative by countermanding a royal order concerning an advowson in 1344, the king at once slapped him down, suspending all the rights of patronage that he enjoyed as chancellor. The loss of favour was brief; in 1345 Sadyngton was employed in raising loans for the king, and served as a member of the regency council which governed England in the name of Lionel of Clarence when Edward was overseas. Following his replacement as chancellor he again became chief baron, on 8 December 1345, but although he remained a royal councillor, and continued to receive summonses to parliament, his services were less frequently called upon than previously, and on 1 February 1349 he was effectively licensed to retire, with an acknowledgement to his having 'served the king long time and without intermission' (*CPR, 1348–50*, 252).

Sadyngton was to enjoy a long retirement. He remained a JP for Leicestershire until at least 1357, and was last recorded on 25 April 1361, when he was the principal witness to a charter on behalf of Noseley chantry college. He may have been still alive in July that year, but it is likely that he died soon afterwards. Probably before 1334 he married Joyce Martival, perhaps a niece of Roger Martival, bishop of Salisbury, and a member of the family of the lords of Noseley, a few miles north-east of Saddington. No doubt his marriage led to Sadyngton's becoming a benefactor to the college at Noseley. He seems to have purchased the advowson of Noseley from the Norman abbey of St Evroult, and in 1336 petitioned for its appropriation to the college; his request was granted two years later. In 1344 he was once more a benefactor to the college, obtaining for it licence to acquire lands and rents worth £10 yearly. In the same year Sadyngton was himself the beneficiary of a royal grant, of free warren in his lands at Saddington, Laughton, Humberstone, Gilmorton, and Scraptoft, all in Leicestershire. His properties were inherited by his daughter and heir, Isabel, who married Sir Ralph *Hastings (*c.*1322–1397) of Allerton and Slingsby, Yorkshire [see under Hastings family]. HENRY SUMMERSON

Sources Chancery records · Sainty, *Judges*, 91–2 · Baker, *Serjeants*, 155, 535 · D. W. Sutherland, ed., *The eyre of Northamptonshire: 3–4 Edward III, AD 1329–1330*, 2 vols., SeldS, 97–8 (1983) · *Reports … touching the dignity of a peer of the realm*, House of Lords, 4 (1829) · *RotP*, vol. 4 · Tout, *Admin. hist.*, vol. 3 · *VCH Leicestershire*, vols. 2, 5 ·

J. Nichols, *The history and antiquities of the county of Leicester*, 2/2 (1798); 3/1 (1800) • G. F. Farnham and A. H. Thompson, 'The manor of Noseley', *Transactions of the Leicestershire Archaeological Society*, 12 (1921–2), 214–71 • B. Wilkinson, *The chancery under Edward III* (1929) • W. M. Ormrod, *The reign of Edward III* (1990) • E. B. Fryde, *William de la Pole, merchant and king's banker* (1988) • *CPR, 1330–34*, 516; *1348–50*, 252

Sæbbi (*d.* 693/4). *See under* East Saxons, kings of the (*act.* late 6th cent.–*c.*820).

Sæberht (*d.* 616/17). *See under* East Saxons, kings of the (*act.* late 6th cent.–*c.*820).

Sæward (*d.* in or after 617). *See under* East Saxons, kings of the (*act.* late 6th cent.–*c.*820).

Sæwulf (*fl.* 1102–1103), traveller, is known largely from the *Relatio* or written account he left of his pilgrimage to Jerusalem in 1102, shortly after its recapture by the crusaders. In his *Relatio* Sæwulf describes his journey from Monopoli, in Apulia, from where he sailed on 13 July 1102; as this was late in the season, he embarked on a trading ship (the only transport available). After being nearly wrecked just out of Monopoli, they sailed by way of Corfu and Corinth to Rhodes, stopping to trade at numerous ports along the way, and then on via Cyprus to Jaffa. There, when already disembarked, Sæwulf witnessed a violent storm in Jaffa Roads which he describes in vivid detail; he speaks movingly of the bodies of the drowned and the wreckage of ships cast up on the beach there. He visited Jerusalem and nearby towns such as Bethlehem and Jericho, going as far south as Hebron, and possibly also into the north, for he describes Nazareth and other places in Galilee. Although his descriptions of the holy places and other sites of pilgrimage are relatively impersonal, his account is clearly independent of those by other writers. Mentions of sites are usually accompanied by the conventional references to the relevant Old and New Testament passages, introduced by a Latin authorization; more unusually, on several occasions he guarantees his information by reference to the oral tradition of the 'Assirii' or Eastern Christians of Palestine.

On 17 May 1103 Sæwulf started the voyage home from Jaffa. The dromond in which he was sailing did not venture out into the open sea 'for fear of the Saracens' (Sæwulf, 75); nevertheless, they were attacked off the Syrian coast, just south of Acre, by a Fatimid squadron of twenty-six galleys coming out of Tyre and Sidon. The dromond's two companion ships, also galleys, escaped to Caesarea, 'leaving our ship alone. The Saracens, circling our ship and shooting arrows, delighted at such prey; but we, being ready to die for Christ, took up arms' (ibid., 76). They defended themselves for about an hour before the Saracens broke off the attack and sailed away. The ship crossed to Cyprus and continued towards Constantinople, but was attacked again by pirates off the coast of Asia Minor; but after describing the voyage through the Dardanelles, Sæwulf's narrative ends abruptly. Despite its

general terseness, Sæwulf's *Relatio* is the best Latin description of a sea voyage in the Mediterranean of the period, and gives a great deal of information about conditions of trade and travel; and it is enlivened by passages that vividly depict the hardships and dangers facing pilgrims to Jerusalem just after the first crusade.

Nothing certain is known about the rest of Sæwulf's life; however, he may be the same man as the merchant Seuulfus of Worcester mentioned in William of Malmesbury's *Gesta pontificum Anglorum*. After being frequently counselled by Wulfstan (*c.*1008–1095), bishop of Worcester, to embrace the monastic life, Seuulfus did indeed become a monk in Malmesbury Abbey in his later years.

PETER DAMIAN-GRINT

Sources Sæwulf, *Relatio de peregratione ad Hierosolymam*, ed. R. B. C. Huygens, *Peregrinationes tres: Sæwulf, John of Würzberg, Thodericus* (1994), 59–77 • J. H. Pryor, 'The voyages of Sæwulf', *Peregrinationes tres: Sæwulf, John of Würzberg, Thodericus*, ed. R. B. C. Huygens (1994), 35–57 • R. Sharpe, *A handlist of the Latin writers of Great Britain and Ireland before 1540* (1997) • Bede, *De locis sanctis*, ed. I. Fraipont, *Itineraria et alia geographica*, ed. P. Geyer and others, 1 (1965), 249–80 • Adamnan, *De locis sanctis*, ed. L. Bieler, *Itineraria et alia geographica*, ed. P. Geyer and others, 1 (1965), 175–234 • *Willelmi Malmesbiriensis monachi de gestis pontificum Anglorum libri quinque*, ed. N. E. S. A. Hamilton, Rolls Series, 52 (1870), 286–7 • *DNB*
Archives CCC Cam., MS 111

Saffery, Maria Grace (*bap.* 1772?, *d.* 1858), hymn writer and poet, was probably the child baptized on 30 November 1772 at Greenham, near Newbury, Berkshire, the daughter of James Andrews and his wife, Mary, according to the *IGI*; however, the *Dictionary of National Biography* identifies her father as William Andrews of Stroud Green, Newbury, Berkshire, while John Julian's *Dictionary of Hymnology* describes her as the daughter of Revd J. Horsey of Portsea. Under the influence of a literary-minded mother, at the age of fifteen she wrote a poem entitled *Cheyt Sing*; Chet Singh, the ruler of Benares, had fallen foul of Warren Hastings's administration in Bengal. Published in 1790, it was dedicated, with his permission, to Charles James Fox, one of Hastings's accusers. Early influenced by Thomas Scott, the biblical commentator, she moved to Salisbury and there attended the Brown Street Baptist Church. On 20 August 1799 she became the second wife of John Saffery, the Baptist minister; they had six children, the eldest of whom, Philip John Saffery, succeeded to his father's ministry after his death in 1825.

Maria Saffery wrote many hymns, often for special occasions and at the suggestion of her husband or son; they appeared in the *Baptist Magazine* and other periodicals, and in several collections, including John Leifchild's *Original Hymns* (1842). They include 'Fain, o my babe, I'd have thee know', 'Saviour, we seek the watery tomb', 'The Jordan prophet cries to-day', and ''Tis the great Father we adore'. Mrs Saffery later ran a successful girls' school in Salisbury, before retiring in 1835 to live in Bratton, Wiltshire, with her daughter, Mrs Whitaker. She died there on 5 March 1858, and was buried in the graveyard of the Baptist chapel.

ROSEMARY MITCHELL

Sources J. Julian, ed., *A dictionary of hymnology*, rev. edn (1907), 823–4 · *DNB* · E. F. Hatfield, *The poets of the church: a series of biographical sketches of hymn writers* (1884) · J. Miller, *Singers and songs of the church* (1869), 352–3 · *IGI*

Saffold, Thomas (*bap.* **1620**?, *d.* **1691**), astrologer and nostrum seller, was probably the son of Thomas and Mary Saffold who was baptized at West Hanningfield, Essex, on 14 September 1620; his brother James was living at Tillingham, 15 miles away in Essex, seventy years later. Thomas was apprenticed to the weavers' trade, though the *Grub Street Journal* of 1735 dubbed him 'the Heel-maker', possibly a term of opprobrium. His wife's name was Prudence, and there were no children living at the time of his death.

Saffold was one of the many astrologers practising during the seventeenth century. He claimed to be a disciple of William Lilly, yet Lilly does not appear to mention Saffold in any of his published works. Saffold certainly never achieved the prominence nor built up the royal and other influential connections enjoyed by Lilly. A practising astrologer for more than a quarter of a century, Saffold had his premises in Blackfriars, then a dog-legged thoroughfare south of Ludgate in London, near Blackfriars Gate. Close by were the shops of the puritan feathersellers who can scarcely have welcomed such an establishment as Saffold's on their doorstep. His sign was of the black ball and Lilly's head, the use of the latter proclaiming his professed links with the great man.

There Saffold sold the nostrums prepared by himself, the nature of which was made clear by the *Grub Street Journal*, which spoke of his having 'made Clap-curing his sole business'. He also took in residential patients, not restricting himself to curing venereal diseases; in his words, 'by God's blessing [he] cureth the sick of any age or sex of any distemper'. His success was shown by the imitators who set themselves up in the vicinity—he had to warn the public against mistaking his house, 'another being near him pretending to be the same'.

In 1674 Saffold received a licence from the bishop of London to practise as a doctor of physic, apparently not needing to show evidence of any study. Perhaps the knowledge of Lilly's licence, granted by the archbishop of Canterbury four years earlier, had encouraged Saffold to apply. Saffold publicized his nostrums through handbills graced with some exceptionally poor doggerel, a typical example reading:

> Here's Saffold's pills, much better than the rest,
> Deservedly have gained the name of best:
> A box of eighteen pills for eighteen pence,
> Tho' 'tis too cheap in any man's own sense.
> (*Grub Street Journal*, 263, 9 Jan 1735)

Other verses upbraided the 'conceited fools' and 'dark animals' who presumed to ask how he achieved the notable cures attributed to him and made such skilful predictions of future events.

In the spring of 1691 Saffold was taken ill; having allegedly refused all medicines apart from his own, he died in Blackfriars, London, on 12 May. His death evoked a number of satirical comments, one poet regretting the 'sad disaster' that 'sawcy pills at last should kill their master'. The *Grub Street Journal* observed that his 'exit' had taken place 'to the great Regret of the whoring Part of the Town'. These ribald remarks contrast piquantly with the pious sentiments he expressed in his will. He appointed his wife as sole executor and adequately remembered his brother and family, god-daughters, and friends. He bequeathed 40 shillings for poor relief in his parish church of St Martin Ludgate, and his residual estate was left to the churchwardens and overseers for parish needs.

Saffold's Ludgate premises and goodwill were acquired by the astrologer and physician John Case, who on his signboard kept Lilly's features but upgraded the ball to a golden one, informing the world:

> At the Golden Ball and Lillie's Head,
> John Case yet lives, though Saffold's dead.

His verses were little better than those of Saffold, and both men's nostrums disappeared from view early in the next century. None features in the list of 'nostrums and empirics' given in the *Gentleman's Magazine* for 1748 (*GM*, 18.348–50).   T. A. B. CORLEY

Sources *DNB* · *Grub Street Journal*, 263 (9 Jan 1735), 11 · D. F. Bond, ed., *The Tatler*, 3 (1987), 240 [see 21 Oct 1710, p. 234] · R. Porter, *Health for sale: quackery in England, 1660–1850* (1989) · PRO, PROB 11/404/89

Sage, John (**1652–1711**), Scottish Episcopal bishop and writer, was born in the parish of Creich, Fife, the son of a royalist captain in Lord Duffus's regiment. After a parish schooling he attended St Salvator's College, St Andrews, where he graduated MA on 24 July 1669. A keen student of classical authors and of logic and metaphysics, he continued to study while a schoolmaster at Ballingry, Fife, and Tibbermore, Perthshire. He entered trials before Perth presbytery on 17 December 1673, and received his testimonial for his licence on 3 June 1674. For several years he tutored the sons of James Drummond of Cultmalundie at school in Perth and then at St Andrews University. There he also studied further, and endeared himself by his 'piercing Wit, solid Judgment, and pleasant Temper' (Gillan, 4). After he left his post in 1684 his friend Dr Alexander Rose introduced him to his uncle, Archbishop Arthur Ross, who ordained Sage priest. He was presented to the east charge of the High Kirk, Glasgow, aged about thirty-four, soon becoming synod clerk, and being nominated for a divinity chair in St Andrews in 1688. A zealous preacher, he commanded the esteem even of the presbyterians. Nevertheless at the revolution he quit his charge after receiving threats, and carried off nine volumes of synod records. He busied himself in Edinburgh with the lengthy second and third letters in *An Account of the Present Persecution of the Church of Scotland* (1690), written with 'great Life and Spirit' (Gillan, 10), and further anonymous polemics in 1690–91. He also ministered in a well-patronized meeting-house, but after he and several brethren refused to undertake to pray for William and Mary, on 5 May 1692 the privy council banished them from Edinburgh.

John Sage (1652–1711), by unknown artist

Sage retired to Kinross, where he lived with his Jacobite friends, the architect Sir William Bruce and Henry Christie, deprived minister of Kinross. During this period he wrote his satirical *Account of the Late Establishment of Presbyterian Government* (1693). Responding to the calamitous loss of the church's episcopalian constitution, in his *Fundamental Charter of Presbytery* (1695, written by December 1693), he sought to demonstrate the error of the presbyterians' historical position and the falsehood of the article in the claim of right concerning prelacy as a grievance. In a rare mistake he denied John Knox's authorship of the *History of the Reformation*, relying on a corrupt edition of 1644. Next came *The Principles of the Cyprianic Age with Regard to Episcopal Power and Jurisdiction* (1695) in response to Gilbert Rule's challenge that the presbyterians would admit their schism if it could be proved that diocesan episcopacy existed in St Cyprian's day. A fuller version of the work appeared as *A Vindication … of the Principles of the Cyprianic Age* (1701). Convincing their opponents was a task beyond even Sage, but his masterly demonstration of the historic episcopalian order and its divine authority confirmed him as the nonjurors' leading apologist.

In 1695 Sage ventured to Edinburgh despite his banishment, only to be seized and forced to leave. He returned after Sir William Bruce was made close prisoner in the castle early in 1696. Smarting from Sage's stinging attacks, according to Gillan, the presbyterians hoped to imprison or force voluntary banishment on him. However, after a few days in hiding he escaped over the Forth and Tay to the Angus hills, where he lurked for several months under the name of Mr Jackson, taking the air and goat's milk for his health, before returning to Kinross.

Sage was next, about 1701 and 1702, chaplain to the countess of Callendar and tutor to James, fourth earl of Callendar, at Falkirk. Three works on toleration for the episcopalians followed between 1703 and 1705, and he went to serve as chaplain to John Stewart of Grandtully for several years. He remained a bachelor.

On 25 January 1705 Sage and John Fullarton were secretly consecrated at Edinburgh by Archbishop John Paterson and bishops Alexander Rose and Robert Douglas as the first bishops without diocesan jurisdiction. In November 1706 a partial paralysis confined him to bed in Kinross for nine months. In April 1709 he assisted in consecrating John Falconer and Henry Christie at Dundee, then went to Bath and London, 'his Company and Conversation very much courted' by nonjuring and established clergy (Gillan, 32). After returning to Edinburgh in November 1709, still in weak health, he nevertheless wrote a short life of Gavin Douglas and a critical introduction to the *History of the … Five King James's* by William Drummond of Hawthornden, and perhaps also a life of Drummond praising his royalism, for editions of their works published in 1710 and 1711. He died at Edinburgh on 7 June 1711, the same day as his friend Henry Dodwell, and was buried next day by Bishop Rose in Greyfriars churchyard.

TRISTRAM CLARKE

Sources J. Gillan, *The life of the reverend and learned Mr. John Sage* (1714) · *The works of the right rev. John Sage, a bishop of the church in Scotland; with memoir and notes*, 3 vols. (1844–6) · *Fasti Scot.*, new edn, vol. 3 · register of acta of privy council, 1693, 1696, NA Scot., PC 1/48, 50 · G. Grub, *An ecclesiastical history of Scotland*, 4 vols. (1861), vols. 3–4 · letters, 1702–11, NA Scot., CH 12/12 · H. Cowan, 'Bishop Sage and his argument against presbytery', *Historical papers submitted to the Christian Unity Association of Scotland* (privately printed, 1914) · D. Duncan, *Thomas Ruddiman* (1965) · letter, 1701, NA Scot., GD 29/2034 · accounts of countess of Callendar, c.1701–1702, NL Scot., MS 9636
Archives NA Scot., letters, CH 12/12
Likenesses drawing, Scot. NPG [*see illus.*]
Wealth at death books to be sold by executor Henry Christi: C. Littlejohn to A. Campbell, 3 July 1711, NA Scot., CH 12/12/1108

Saha, Meghnad (1893–1956), astrophysicist and nuclear scientist, was born on 6 October 1893 in the village of Seoratali in the district of Dacca, Bengal presidency, India, the fifth child in the family of five sons and three daughters of Jagannath Saha, shopkeeper, and his wife, Bhubaneswari Devi. A precocious student, he was equally good in mathematics and languages; in 1905 he received a government scholarship which enabled him to join the government collegiate school in Dacca but which he soon had to forfeit for his part in the boycott of a visit by the governor of the Bengal presidency. In 1911 he passed the intermediate science examination from Dacca College. He then moved to the Presidency College, Calcutta, where he obtained his BSc with honours in 1913 and the MSc degree in applied mathematics in 1915.

In 1916 Saha was appointed lecturer in mathematics in the newly established postgraduate University College of Science in Calcutta, where he was a colleague of C. V. Raman, the Palit professor of physics. Shortly afterwards he became deeply interested in relativity theory, following the discovery that light from the stars was deflected by the sun's gravitational field. This led him to his first original paper ('On Maxwell's stresses', *Philosophical Magazine*, 1917) and further investigations of the dynamics of the electron. In 1918 he married Shrimati Radha Rani Saha; they had three sons and three daughters.

Subsequently Saha became especially interested in the quantum theory of the atom being developed by Niels Bohr. It was fortunate that at about the same time he came across the popular books of Agnes Clerke on the sun and stars which gave him some idea of the outstanding problems in astrophysics. This background, in a sense, paved the way for his greatest contribution: the theory of high temperature ionization which marked the first effective step in linking the atoms and the stars together. In 1919 he obtained the equation of temperature ionization which goes by his name. His classic paper on the physical theory of stellar spectra appeared in 1921 (*Proceedings of the Royal Society*). Much of the later work in stellar spectroscopy has been dominated by Saha's theory and ideas. The theory has all the simplicity and inevitableness which characterize an epochal contribution. It is a direct consequence of the recognition that the laws of classical thermodynamics and kinetic theory of gases can be extended to a gas of free electrons. Apart from in astrophysics, the theory has found numerous other applications, as in the study of ionosphere, conductivity of flames, electric arcs, explosive phenomena, and shock waves.

Saha was awarded the Premchand Roychand scholarship of Calcutta University and spent two years travelling in Europe. He worked for some time in London in the laboratory of the spectroscopist Alfred Fowler, and spent about a year in W. Nernst's laboratory in Berlin. On returning to India he joined the University of Calcutta as Khaira professor of physics, but in 1923 accepted the professorship at the Allahabad University. A most conscientious and inspiring teacher, he completely reorganized the teaching in the department and developed a vigorous school of research in theoretical astrophysics and experimental spectroscopy. He himself concentrated on spectroscopy and the ionosphere. In 1927 he presented a paper 'On the explanation of complicated spectra of elements' at the Volta centenary celebrations in Como, and in 1936 he proposed photographing the solar spectrum at a height of 50 km, well above the ozone layer (*Records of Harvard Observatory*, 1936). In several papers about 1937 he discussed the possibility that the ultraviolet radiation from the sun may be several orders of magnitude above that corresponding to a black body at about 6500 K.

In 1938 Saha left Allahabad to take up the Palit professorship at Calcutta in succession to Raman and Bose. There he developed an extensive programme of work in nuclear physics. His own researches here were concerned largely with the beta-activity of atomic nuclei, with the propagation of electromagnetic waves in the ionosphere, and with the solar corona. Saha realized at an early stage the potential importance of nuclear physics for his country's scientific and industrial progress. It was due to him that the Institute of Nuclear Physics was established at Calcutta in 1948; after his death it was named after him. He took an active interest in the Indian Association for the Cultivation of Science and was largely responsible for its new laboratories. After the partition of India in 1947 he also gave a good deal of time and energy to the problems of refugees from East Bengal.

Saha's scientific work may be divided into three periods: 1918–25, when he was largely occupied with astrophysics; 1925–38, devoted mostly to spectroscopic and ionospheric studies; and 1939–55, when he was mainly concerned with nuclear physics. The most creative years belong to the first period, when he devoted himself almost completely to scientific work. Later his interests became more widespread. He was deeply involved in problems of national planning and the impact of science and technology on economic growth. He was an active member of the national planning committee (1939–41), and at the time of his death was an elected independent member of the Indian legislature.

Saha was the general president of the Indian Science Congress Association in 1934. In his presidential address he drew pointed attention to the problem of recurring floods in Indian rivers. It was due to his pioneering efforts that the multi-purpose Damodar River valley project was established, on the lines of the Tennessee Valley Authority in the United States. It served as the forerunner of several other multi-purpose river projects in India. As a member of the governing body of the Indian Council of Scientific and Industrial Research he played an active role in the establishment of several national laboratories, and he was a member of the Indian education commission appointed by the government of India in 1948 under the chairmanship of Dr S. Radhakrishnan.

In 1927 Saha was elected FRS. He was president of the National Institute of Sciences of India and of the National Academy of Sciences (Allahabad). He published about a hundred scientific papers in Indian and foreign journals and wrote extensively on scientific policy and national affairs in the journal *Science and Culture*, which he founded. He also published, in 1931 (with B. N. Srivastava), an internationally famous textbook on heat which has gone into several editions.

The life of Saha was an integral part of the scientific renaissance in India. He was fearless in his criticism of people and things, extremely simple in his habits and completely dedicated to his chosen vocation to the total disregard of his personal comforts. A detailed account of his work and life is given in the commemoration volume brought out by the Indian Association for the Cultivation of Science for his sixtieth birthday. Saha died suddenly of a heart attack in New Delhi on 16 February 1956.

D. S. KOTHARI, rev. ISOBEL FALCONER

Sources private information (1971) · personal knowledge (1971) · D. S. Kothari, *Memoirs FRS*, 5 (1959), 217-36 · S. N. Sen, ed., *Professor Meghnad Saha: his life, work, and philosophy* (Calcutta, 1954)
Likenesses photograph, 1954, repro. in Kothari, *Memoirs FRS*, facing p. 217

Saham, William of (c.1225–1292), justice, was the son of Ralph of Saham, who came from Saham Toney in Norfolk. His family name may have been Butler, for his heir was his brother John Butler and his executors included a William Butler who was also known as William of Saham. He also had a second brother, Richard, and possibly a sister, Alice. Saham's first appearance in the records seems to be in 1247, when he acted as essoiner for the future justiciar Philip Basset (d. 1271). By 1260 he had become a senior court clerk in the common bench, but by 1265 had transferred to the service of the Montfortian justiciar of England, Hugh Despenser (d. 1265). As justiciar Despenser presided over the court of the king's bench and Saham seems still to have been serving as a clerk there in 1269. His first judicial appointment was as a justice of the king's bench for a brief period during 1273. He also served as circuit assize justice in East Anglia in 1273–4, as a justice for the Worcestershire eyre of 1275, and as an associate of the king's bench while it sat in Kent in 1278.

Later in 1278 Saham was appointed as the second justice of the northern eyre circuit and served continuously on that circuit until 1287. He was its senior justice for only his final eyre in Gloucestershire in 1287. The surviving reports from the circuit show him active in hearing civil pleas, and it is likely that he regularly sat in a separate division of the court charged with hearing this kind of business. By the summer of 1288 he had returned to the court of the king's bench, and sat as one of its justices until the end of Hilary term 1290. From 1285 onwards he also acted as the head of an assize circuit covering four south-eastern counties and continued to receive assize commissions until early in May 1290. Saham was probably convicted of judicial misconduct not long after this, although he did not pay the first instalment of his 3000 mark fine until 21 November 1290. His status as a clerk in royal service had allowed him to hold several ecclesiastical livings in plurality and to remain in subdeacon's orders, but late in 1291 he obtained a papal dispensation for retaining his benefices on condition he became a priest. The dispensation may never have reached him. He died not long before 16 February 1292, when his executors found sureties to pay what was still outstanding of the fine owed to the king.

PAUL BRAND

Sources Chancery records · Court of king's bench, curia regis rolls, PRO, KB 26 · justice itinerant, eyre and assize rolls, PRO, JUST 1 · exchequer, queen's remembrancer's memoranda roll, PRO, E 159 · unpubd law reports of 1280s, BL; CUL · CEPR letters, 1.545–6

Sainsbury family (per. 1869–1956), food retailers, originated with **John James Sainsbury** (1844–1928), born on 12 June 1844 at 5 Oakley Street, Lambeth, the only son and youngest child of John Sainsbury (bap. 1809, d. 1863), ornament and picture frame maker, and his wife, Elizabeth Sarah, née Coombes (1817–1902). He was probably educated locally and is believed to have started work as a shop assistant to a grocer in the New Cut, Lambeth. Later he was working in Strutton Ground, Victoria, where he met his future wife, Mary Ann Staples.

Mary Ann Sainsbury (1849–1927) was born on 30 June 1849 at Little Charles Street, St Pancras, the eldest child

Sainsbury family (per. 1869–1956), by unknown photographer [John James Sainsbury (1844–1928) and Mary Ann Sainsbury (1849–1927)]

and only daughter of Benjamin Staples and his wife, Elizabeth, née Cant (c.1827–1909). Benjamin Staples was originally a woodcarver, but by 1864 he had become a dairyman and Mary Ann may have assisted him at his shop at 87 Chalton Street, Euston, before working for Tom Haile, another dairyman, in Strutton Ground. Tradition has it that John James and Mary Ann founded Sainsbury's on their wedding day, 20 April 1869. Their first shop was a dairy at 173 Drury Lane, Holborn, London, run by Mary Ann while John James worked out his notice; poverty obliged them to share the cramped accommodation over the shop with three other families. Mary Ann continued to play an active role in the business until the mid-1870s. Thereafter she devoted herself to the needs of her rapidly expanding family, which, by December 1890, comprised six sons and five daughters. In 1873 the couple moved their young family away from the tenements of Drury Lane to 159 Queen's Crescent, Kentish Town. About 1888 they moved to Bishopsfield, Broadlands Road, Highgate, Middlesex, where they lived thereafter.

The early success of the business was assured by offering in hygienic surroundings high-quality dairy products and fresh provisions at prices which even London's poor could afford. The slogan 'Quality perfect, prices lower', which appeared on early shop fascias, encapsulated this policy. John James was quick to exploit the expanding market for fresh foodstuffs in the railway suburb of Kentish Town and soon opened two further branches in the locality. By the early 1880s he had also taken over several shops from his wife's family and associates in established London market streets in Islington and Stepney. His most significant venture was to acquire in 1882 a shop at 6 (later 11) London Road, Croydon. This was Sainsbury's first branch outside London. It catered for a middle-class clientele by offering a wide range of provisions including foreign cheeses, poultry and game, and 'table delicacies' (cooked meats). This shop, which was more elaborately decorated than its predecessors, established the distinctive Sainsbury's house style.

John James Sainsbury's success lay in his ability to match the competitive pricing of the multiples while also offering higher standards of quality, service, and hygiene. This distinguished his shops from Lipton and Home and Colonial, which expanded more rapidly but offered a more limited product range. The slower rate of expansion of Sainsbury's suited John James's management style of closely supervised centralized control. His involvement in the detail of day-to-day business ensured that Sainsbury's retained its family character.

All the sons of John James and Mary Ann were appointed to senior positions in the firm. **John Benjamin Sainsbury** (1871–1956), the eldest, was taken into partnership on 27 March 1915. The other sons were given responsibility appropriate to their abilities. George, the second son, looked after the firm's accounts, office administration, and distribution, while Arthur and Alfred—the fourth and fifth sons—took on buying roles. Arthur also had responsibility for the production of cooked meats in the firm's 'kitchens'. The youngest son, Paul, was involved in building works and design. Frank, the third son, worked on the retail side of the business for a while, but in 1902 he became a farmer, and supplied his father's shops. He improved the quality of the products purchased for the shops by holding agricultural shows and setting up a breeding centre for prize pigs at Haverhill in Suffolk. He also introduced an egg collection scheme which provided a guaranteed market for local producers provided they conformed to specified quality controls.

J. Sainsbury Ltd was incorporated as a joint stock company on 10 November 1922 with an original share capital of £1.3 million. Only members of the Sainsbury family and their descendants were eligible to hold shares. John James became life chairman and governing director. At his death, six years later, his personal holding was reported to be about £300,000.

John James Sainsbury disliked personal publicity and there is little evidence of his private life. His devotion to the business was such that taking his wife for a drive invariably involved a round of branch visits. He continued to attend the office until a month before his death at Bishopsfield on 3 January 1928. Mary Ann had died six months earlier also at Bishopsfield, on 9 June 1927. They were buried at Putney Vale cemetery on 13 June 1927 and 9 January 1928.

John Benjamin Sainsbury succeeded his father as chairman of J. Sainsbury Ltd. He was born above the original Drury Lane shop on 8 January 1871 and educated in Kentish Town, close to his parents' second shop. As soon as he could count, he began to earn pocket money as an 'egg boy' and helped to drive his father's single-horse van. He progressed to salesman, learning the business alongside his father and, by 1915, was managing the day-to-day running of the firm's 122 branches. He married Mabel Miriam (1876–1941), daughter of Jacob Van den Bergh, the margarine magnate, in 1896; they had two sons, Robert James *Sainsbury and Alan John *Sainsbury, Baron Sainsbury, and a daughter.

John Benjamin was, like his father, a natural retailer who spent as much time as possible in the branches. He took the novel step of appointing female branch clerical staff to release managers from administration so that they too could devote themselves to trading matters. During his chairmanship the number of Sainsbury's branches increased from 180 to 248. He took an interest in the individual performance of each branch. Fred Salisbury, his former personal assistant and the first non-Sainsbury to become a director, described him as a 'benevolent dictator' who was known for his impetuosity and explosive temper.

John Benjamin's benevolence was most apparent in his concern for staff welfare. At a time when shop work was notoriously insecure and poorly remunerated, Sainsbury's wages were well ahead of competitors such as Lipton, Home and Colonial, and the Co-operatives. He introduced sickness payments, first through the 'good fellowship fund' on a discretionary basis in 1922, and subsequently through an insurance and pensions scheme twelve years later. The good fellowship fund also provided payments for employees in adversity. The purchase of a sports ground in 1922 and the setting up of libraries in each branch were further examples of John Benjamin's concern for his staff.

At a time when the alleged loss of skill in the grocer's art had led trade bodies to advocate increased professionalism and practical examinations, Sainsbury's was already providing a structured career progression for promising young men. John Benjamin had introduced a training school at the company's Blackfriars headquarters as early as 1915. This foresight was appreciated by competitors, who advertised for 'Sainsbury trained men'. John Benjamin Sainsbury built on his father's successful formula of offering a wide range of high-quality provisions to a broad spectrum of society. This policy provided a more secure basis for the business than the major national multiples could command and gave Sainsbury's an advantage in the inter-war years over Lipton, Home and Colonial, and the International Stores. He also foresaw the retailing opportunities provided by the expansion of London during the inter-war years. He spent hours observing possible locations for new branches and even took his family out at weekends on picnics looking for prospective sites. He was adept at negotiating favourable terms, even boasting that developers had 'given' him sites in order to attract Sainsbury's to their locations.

Under John Benjamin's management the business grew

in both scale and complexity. The product range expanded threefold over his period of management, with the most notable additions being fresh meat and groceries. However, fresh provisions remained its mainstay. John Benjamin retired at the age of sixty-seven in 1938 following a heart attack, and moved to the Thatched House, Little Common, Bexhill, Sussex. Although he recovered fully, he felt the time was right to pass executive control to his sons, Alan John *Sainsbury (1902–1998) and Robert James *Sainsbury (1906–2000), who became joint general managers. He retained the title of chairman until his death in 1956. He and his wife took a keen interest in the work of several charitable institutions, most notably the Pioneer Health Centre at Peckham, Queen Charlotte's Hospital, and the Mothercraft Training Centre at Highgate. His keen horsemanship was almost the only activity which would tear him away from the business. He rode with the Middlesex Farmers' Draghounds and the Whaddon Chase and, in his earlier days, drove tandems and phaetons. He continued to attend the office in later years and took an active interest in the firm's affairs. When the company ventured into self-service shopping in 1950 he instantly understood the potential of the new retailing method. After viewing the first self-service shop he demanded to know why every branch was not already undergoing conversion. John Benjamin Sainsbury died at the London Clinic, Marylebone, after injuries sustained in a fall, on 23 May 1956. He was cremated at Golders Green crematorium and his ashes buried at Putney Vale cemetery on 29 May; a memorial service was held at Southwark Cathedral on 5 June.

Alan and Robert Sainsbury, as general managers, each specialized in different aspects of the business: Alan on the retailing and trading side, Robert with responsibility for finance and general administration. After the Second World War, and the ending of both food rationing and the restrictions on new building, the brothers made Sainsbury's a leader in the introduction of self-service stores, supported by computerized stock control. Alan Sainsbury took over from his father as chairman in 1956, and served in that role until 1967; he was given a life peerage in 1962.

J. Sainsbury Ltd remained wholly in the ownership of its founding family until 1973, when it underwent public flotation. The Sainsbury family remained major shareholders, however, and retained executive responsibility until 1998. John Sainsbury, who served as chairman from 1969 to 1992, and his cousin David Sainsbury, who succeeded him and retired from the business in 1998, were great-grandsons of the founders. After the flotation the Sainsbury group, J Sainsbury plc, diversified into other retailing activities and operated four store chains in the UK and USA. Sainsbury's Bank, a joint venture with the Bank of Scotland, was established in 1997.

BRIDGET WILLIAMS

Sources B. Williams, *The best butter in the world* (1994) • [J. Boswell], ed., *J. S. 100: the story of Sainsbury's* (1969) • 'In memoriam', *JS Journal* (June 1956) [special no. of house magazine] • scrapbook of obituaries collected by Sir Robert Sainsbury, Sainsbury's Archives, London • Mrs D. Greig [H. S. Greig], *My life and times* (privately printed,

Bungay, [1940]) • *The Times* (5 Jan 1928) [J. J. Sainsbury] • *The Grocer* (7 Jan 1928) [J. J. Sainsbury] • *The Times* (25 May 1956) [J. B. Sainsbury] • *Grocer's Gazette* (1 June 1961) • *CGPLA Eng. & Wales* (1928) [J. J. Sainsbury] • b. cert. [J. J. Sainsbury] • b. cert. [M. A. Sainsbury] • b. cert. [J. B. Sainsbury] • m. cert. [J. J. Sainsbury] • m. cert. [J. B. Sainsbury] • d. cert. [M. A. Sainsbury] • d. cert. [J. B. Sainsbury] • IGI • order of service for funerals, Sainsbury's Archives [J. J. Sainsbury and J. B. Sainsbury]

Archives priv. coll., London, corresp. and papers relating to art collections

Likenesses photographs, 1890–1956 (of family), Sainsbury's Archives, London [see illus.] • H. A. Oliver, oils, 1903 (John James Sainsbury), Sainsbury's Archives, London • H. A. Oliver, oils (John Benjamin Sainsbury), Sainsbury's Archives, London • W. Soukop, bronze bust (John James Sainsbury), Sainsbury's Archives, London • Wartberg, bronze bust (John James Sainsbury), Sainsbury's Archives, London • bust (John Benjamin Sainsbury), Sainsbury's Archives, London • marble bust (John James Sainsbury), Sainsbury's Archives, London

Wealth at death £1,158,615 7s. 2d.—John James Sainsbury: probate, 13 Feb 1928, *CGPLA Eng. & Wales* • £38,847 0s. 9d.—John Benjamin Sainsbury: probate, 9 Aug 1956, *CGPLA Eng. & Wales*

Sainsbury, Alan John, Baron Sainsbury (1902–1998), food retailer and supporter of consumer rights, was born at 14 Avenue Road, Crouch End, London, on 13 August 1902, the elder son of John Benjamin *Sainsbury (1871–1956) [see under Sainsbury family (per. 1869–1956)] and his wife, Mabel Miriam, née Van den Bergh (1876–1941). His younger brother was Sir Robert James *Sainsbury (1906–2000). He was the eldest grandson of the founders of the family food-retailing business. He was educated at Haileybury College, after which he spent a period working in a mission in the East End of London. He joined the family firm in 1921, at the age of eighteen, as he later put it, 'chiefly because my mother said it would break my father's heart if I didn't'. He proved an instinctive retailer, however, and throughout his career demonstrated a profound sense of responsibility to the family business, its customers, and employees. He was known in the business as Mr Alan according to the custom of identifying family members by their Christian names or initials.

When Mr Alan joined Sainsbury's, it was a partnership owned by his father and grandfather. J. Sainsbury Ltd was formed as a private limited company in 1922, but share ownership remained restricted by the company's articles of association to lineal descendants of the founders and their spouses. His first job was with his uncles Arthur and Alfred, fourth and fifth sons of the founders, buying dairy produce for the shops, but he soon asked to be transferred to the retail side of the business. He worked incognito behind the counter of the shop at Boscombe under the alias 'Mr Allan' and although the experience was cut short when he was recognized by a family friend, it inspired him to continue with the firm. He returned to Sainsbury's Blackfriars headquarters and after a secondment with Buisman's, a butter supplier based at Leeuwarden in Holland, began to take increasing responsibility for buying and later for the retailing side of the business.

On 31 October 1925 Sainsbury married Doreen Davan Adams (1904–1985), with whom he had three sons: John (b. 1927), Simon (b. 1930), and Timothy (b. 1932), all of whom

Alan John Sainsbury, Baron Sainsbury (1902–1998), by Walter
Bird, 1963

later took prominent roles in the family business. This
marriage was dissolved in 1939. He married again on 12
September 1944; his second wife was Anne Elizabeth Lewy
(1916–1988), with whom he had a daughter, Paulette (*b.*
1946). Between the wars Sainsbury began to take an active
role in politics, his early interest in social issues fuelled by
concern about the widespread unemployment and poverty of the period. He stood as Liberal candidate for Sudbury, Suffolk, in 1929, 1931, and 1935, but the increasing
responsibilities of his business career led him to set aside
his political ambitions to concentrate on the family firm.
Between 1920 and 1939 Sainsbury's grew from a regional
chain of 129 shops with annual sales of £5 million to
become one of Britain's more important multiples, with
255 shops and sales of £12.6 million. Alan Sainsbury was as
demanding as his father in pursuit of 'Sainsbury standards' of quality and service with a 'hands on' style which
ensured that the family's centralized management was
undiminished as the business grew.

Sainsbury's father's sudden and unexpected retirement
in 1938 due to a heart attack led to the immediate transfer
of executive control to the third generation of the family.
John Benjamin retained the title of chairman until his
death in 1956, but Alan and his younger brother, Robert,
took on the management of the business. They became
joint general managers, with Alan taking responsibility
for trading matters and Robert for personnel, administration, and finance.

The brothers had barely a year before the Second World

War presented them with huge challenges. The introduction of rationing from January 1940 affected Sainsbury's
trade particularly badly because the high-quality fresh
foods in which the firm specialized were in short supply
and were very strictly rationed. In real terms turnover
halved between 1939 and 1943. The location of the firm's
trading heartland in London and the south-east also made
it vulnerable to loss of trade because many residents left
the region.

Despite these challenges Alan regarded the conduct of
the business during wartime as a national duty, an attitude which drew him into more public forms of service.
Before the war he had begun to advise the government on
the emergency distribution of foodstuffs; once war was
declared, he became increasingly involved in public service. He was recruited onto several Ministry of Food committees as chief representative of the multiple grocers. In
addition, he served as chairman of the ministry's import
committees for poultry and rabbits. He also encouraged
his employees to consider their work as service in the
national interest. Each was required to sign a declaration
acknowledging that they understood that breaches of the
rationing regulations would result in instant dismissal.
This document was headed 'Food is a munition of war'.
The points system which he introduced to ensure that
non-rationed goods in short supply were allocated fairly
to customers closely resembled the official points system
later introduced by the Ministry of Food for groceries.
Such measures, together with an advertising campaign
which provided general information to customers on coping with food shopping in wartime and urged them to be
public-spirited, contributed to the company's long-term
reputation for fair dealing.

Alan Sainsbury's role as an adviser to the government
continued after the war through his membership of the
Williams committee on milk distribution from 1947 to
1948. It also led him to initiate a watershed in the family
firm's history: the introduction of self-service. The post-
war government's enthusiasm for the application of new
food production methods and new sources of supply led,
in 1949, to the issuing of diplomatic visas to Alan Sainsbury and fellow director Fred Salisbury to allow them to
travel to America to study the frozen-food industry. While
they were in the USA they were inspired by the progress
made in America with self-service methods of food retailing. As Alan later put it, 'We came back so thrilled and
stimulated with the potentiality of self-service trading
that we became convinced that the future lay with what
we thought were large stores of 10,000 square feet of selling space'. He reported to Sainsbury's board on 6 April
1949 that 'We cannot afford to ignore the USA experience,
in spite of different circumstances.'

Immediate plans were drawn up to convert the store at
9/11 London Road, Croydon, into an experimental self-
service branch. Alan Sainsbury's determination to apply
the highest possible standards of service, hygiene, and
salesmanship quickly led to the Croydon shop becoming
regarded as a model not only for Sainsbury's, but for the
trade as a whole. Customers appreciated the increased

choice and convenience of self-service, and sales at the Croydon store almost trebled as a result of the conversion.

Alan Sainsbury perceived that the introduction of self-service demanded revolutionary changes in almost every aspect of the business, from store design and merchandising to food preparation methods, particularly for fresh foods. One of the most obvious signs of this new approach was in the design discipline he applied. In 1950 he appointed Leonard Beaumont as the company's design consultant. Together they created a radical new image for Sainsbury's self-service shops which was acclaimed for the attractiveness of its simple, clean lines and for its innovative approach to the use of design disciplines as a marketing tool. 'I wanted to get discipline into the look of things, and an avoidance of fussiness … it may be my reaction to Victorianism … Simplify, simplify!' he told *Design* magazine in 1967. The effect was to give graphic expression to his passion for fair dealing.

Alan Sainsbury became chairman of the company in 1956 on the death of his father. He and his brother retained their roles as joint general managers until 1962. Throughout his chairmanship Alan remained committed to preserving the firm's character as a family business. In the decade to 1965, total grocery turnover in the UK rose by almost 70 per cent, while Sainsbury's went up by more than 300 per cent.

In 1962 Sainsbury was created a life peer on the recommendation of Hugh Gaitskell, taking the Labour whip. The patent styled him Baron Sainsbury, of Drury Lane, after the location of his grandparents' first shop. Membership of the Lords allowed him to become a more active champion of consumers' rights. His opposition in the early 1960s to resale price maintenance, for example, was based on the conviction that the consumer had a right to expect retailers to pass on the cost savings made possible by scale and efficiency. He was chairman of the committee of enquiry into the relationship of the pharmaceutical industries with the National Health Service (1965–7) and of the food research advisory committee from 1965 to 1970, and served on the economic committee of the distributive trades (Little Neddy) from 1964 until 1968. His most powerful campaign, however, was directed against trading stamps in 1963–4. He regarded the stamps as a dishonest gimmick which benefited neither customers nor retailers, but merely added to the costs of distribution, which were ultimately passed on to consumers through higher prices. He led an energetic battle against trading stamps on three fronts: at Sainsbury's through an advertising campaign based on the slogan 'Honest to goodness value' which drew customers' attention to the hidden costs and misleading claims of trading stamp companies; through his chairmanship of the Distributive Trades Alliance, an industry body set up to oppose the spread of trading stamps; and in the House of Lords, where he sponsored a bill calling for controls on advertising and for stamps to be exchangeable for cash. It was a more limited bill which passed into law as the Trading Stamps Act (1964).

Sainsbury was also committed to industry groups dedicated to the exchange of information and the raising of standards in retailing. He was chairman of the Multiple Shops Federation from 1963 to 1965, of the Grocer's Institute from 1963 to 1966, and of the International Association of Chain Stores from 1965 to 1968. In 1967 he retired as chairman of Sainsbury's, accepting the title of life president. He continued to take an intense interest in the business but was disciplined in relinquishing full control to his successors: 'Now that I'm president, the rule is that nobody need ask my advice and if they do they needn't take it', he told *Director* magazine in 1982. Nevertheless, he retained an office at the firm's headquarters which he attended regularly until a few months before his death.

After his retirement from the business Alan Sainsbury remained active in politics, attending the House of Lords regularly. In 1981 he became a founder member of the Social Democratic Party. He was generous to a range of charities for underprivileged children, medical research, the furtherance of Jewish–Christian understanding and of civil liberties. One of his most loyal commitments was to the Pestalozzi Children's Village Trust, of which he became a founder trustee in 1957. He took a close interest in the trust's work and served on its council until 1993, for many years as its president. He died at his home, Hoses Farm, Toppesfield, Halstead, Essex, on 21 October 1998.

BRIDGET WILLIAMS

Sources B. Williams, *The best butter in the world* (1994) • [J. Boswell], ed., *J. S. 100: the story of Sainsbury's* (1969) • P. Johnson, 'Business heroes: Lord Sainsbury', *Director* (April 1984) • 'Happy birthday', *JS Journal* (Aug 1982) [profile of Lord Sainsbury] • *The Times* (23 Oct 1998) • *The Guardian* (23 Oct 1998) • *Daily Telegraph* (26 Oct 1998) • *The Independent* (26 Oct 1998) • WWW • Burke, *Peerage* • personal knowledge (2004) • private information (2004) • b. cert. • m. certs. • d. cert.

Archives Sainsbury's Archives, London, archives

Likenesses W. Bird, photograph, 1963, NPG [*see illus.*] • photograph, 1969, repro. in *The Guardian* • photograph, 1969, repro. in *Daily Telegraph* • photograph, 1969, repro. in *The Independent* • C. Drury, bronze bust, Sainsbury's head office, 33 Holborn, London • photograph, repro. in *The Times* • photographs, Sainsbury's Archives, London

Wealth at death £9,113,876: probate, 16 Dec 1998, CGPLA Eng. & Wales

Sainsbury, John Benjamin (1871–1956). *See under* Sainsbury family (*per.* 1869–1956).

Sainsbury, John James (1844–1928). *See under* Sainsbury family (*per.* 1869–1956).

Sainsbury, Mary Ann (1849–1927). *See under* Sainsbury family (*per.* 1869–1956).

Sainsbury, Sir Robert James (1906–2000), businessman and patron of the arts, was born on 24 October 1906 at Waverley, 33 Eton Avenue, Hampstead, London, the second son and the youngest of the three children of John Benjamin *Sainsbury (1871–1956) [*see under* Sainsbury family] and the grandson of the founder of the family food-retailing business John James *Sainsbury (1844–1928) [*see under* Sainsbury family]. His mother was Mabel Miriam Van den Bergh (1876–1941), of the Dutch food-

Sir Robert James Sainsbury (1906–2000), by Francis Bacon, 1955

manufacturing family of that name. He was educated at Haileybury College (1919–24) and Pembroke College, Cambridge (1924–7), where he read history. Although he loathed boarding-school he enjoyed university, where he gained an upper second while playing a lot of bridge. The most remarkable aspect of his Cambridge days, given what was to come, was the fact that while there he never entered any museum or art gallery. After Cambridge he studied accountancy (later becoming a fellow of the Institute of Chartered Accountants); then in 1930 he entered Sainsbury's, where, according to the custom of identifying family members by initials or forenames, he was known as Mr RJ. He became successively a director (1934), joint general manager with his brother (1938), deputy chairman (1956), chairman (1967), and joint president (1969). While his elder brother, Alan John *Sainsbury (later Baron Sainsbury of Drury Lane), was the dynamic retailer, Mr RJ was respected for his efficient running of the business and for his skills in managing personnel issues—for example, during the introduction of self-service in the 1950s. The firm pioneered improvements in staff conditions, and in 1935 Mr RJ introduced the company's own staff welfare schemes. During the Second World War the brothers supported the Beveridge report, which laid the foundations for the welfare state.

Despite his success as a businessman, which he always acknowledged was fundamental to his other interests, what really motivated Sainsbury was art, especially sculpture and drawings. He remained proud to the end that he had never received any formal art education, which he regarded as a blessing, as it allowed him to give free rein to his tastes. There was little family interest in art, and his own first experiences came in the form of private-press books, which he began to collect when at Cambridge. This interest in fine printing, in the appearance of metal type on quality paper, led him to frequent Zwemmers in London on Saturday mornings, and to buy two Jacob Epstein drawings in 1931. These were a stepping-stone to greater things, for at Leicester Galleries in 1933 he bought Henry Moore's major stone sculpture *Mother and Child of 1932* for £158, a sum equivalent to half a year's salary for the little-known art teacher, who became a lifelong friend. Also in 1933 Sainsbury started his own printing venture, the Gemini Press, with the engraver Blair Hughes-Stanton. It lasted for only two years, producing three short publications, but this experiment marked the beginning of his role as a patron of the arts.

On 3 March 1937 Sainsbury married Lisa Ingeborg Van den Bergh (*b.* 1912), a second cousin and the daughter of Simon Van den Bergh, professor of philosophy at the University of Paris. Shortly after their marriage they moved into 5 Smith Square, Westminster, their home until 1994, when they moved to Dulwich. Until the 1970s they also kept a house at Bucklebury in Berkshire.

From 1937 Bob and Lisa, as they were known in the art world, began what he referred to as a joint unplanned voyage of discovery in the world of art. He had already by then acquired works by artists unfashionable in England, such as Pablo Picasso, Amedeo Modigliani, and Charles Despiau, but, more importantly, he had encountered works from Africa on a trip to Paris in 1935. Thereafter 'primitive' art (as it was referred to then) became his greatest love. Objects were steadily acquired for the Sainsburys' relatively small London home, and their eclectic yet distinctive taste drew in pieces from many periods and regions—the Pacific, Africa, the Americas, and Asia. They agreed with Moore's dictum that the post-Renaissance European tradition (until modernism) was a diversion from the main course of human artistic production. Initially, pictures and objects were acquired from a number of dealers, including Pierre Loeb in Paris; after 1949 many things were brought to them by the London dealer John Hewett.

During the Second World War, Sainsbury co-ordinated the company's food supply activities as part of the war effort, while Lisa, with their eldest daughter, Elizabeth (1938–1978), sailed to Canada, where she gave birth to a son, David (later Lord Sainsbury of Turville and minister for science), in 1940. Leaving the children with friends, Lisa returned to London to work in St Thomas's Hospital. Another daughter, Celia, was born in 1945, followed by Annabel in 1948.

The company navigated difficult post-war trading conditions, and the first self-service store, forerunner of supermarkets, was introduced in 1950 in Croydon. In 1946 Sainsbury established a personal art account, which restricted annual purchases to a fixed amount, initially £1000, then £2000 (1953–6). During that period a remarkable range of high-quality material was acquired for what later seemed modest prices. Numerous works by Alberto Giacometti (who drew Elizabeth and David) were bought, and also paintings by Francis Bacon, who painted Bob and Lisa, and whose bank account Bob guaranteed in order to keep him painting. Close friendships developed with these two artists, to add to that enjoyed with Henry Moore.

During the 1960s the collection became internationally regarded, and there were exhibitions in New York (1963) and Otterlo (1966). It amused Sainsbury to see the shift in establishment opinion which had taken place. Whereas in the 1930s many had criticized him for buying ghastly monstrosities from Africa or by Henry Moore, now some of the same people lauded him for his taste and perspicacity. He served as a trustee of the Tate Gallery from 1959 to 1973, becoming vice-chairman in 1967 and chairman in 1969. He was also an early patron of the National Art Collections Fund. In 1967 he was knighted for services to the arts. In other areas, linked to his mother's and his wife's interests, he served as honorary treasurer of the Institute of Medical Social Workers (1948–71) and as a governor of St Thomas's Hospital (1939–68).

After his retirement in 1969 as chairman of Sainsbury's, Bob and Lisa embarked on a course of philanthropy barely rivalled in Britain in the twentieth century. Besides major donations to hospitals and Kew Gardens, they gave their collection of more than 400 works of art to the University of East Anglia (1973), commissioned the then little-known architect Norman Foster to design an art gallery on the campus, and worked with him to produce the Sainsbury Centre for Visual Arts, which opened in 1978. Sainsbury himself edited a catalogue to coincide with the opening exhibition. The building, and a Foster-designed extension completed in 1991, was funded by their son, David. After the initial gift they continued to acquire artworks for the university and to make endowments for running costs and for new departments specializing in non-Western arts. Sainsbury also supervised the production of a comprehensive three-volume catalogue of their collection, edited by Steven Hooper (1997), two volumes of which were set in hot metal, showing his abiding interest in fine printing and typography. 'As with a lot of things in my life,' he said, 'whether it be the layout of our garden, where I made a nuisance of myself with Lanning Roper, or the Sainsbury Centre, with Norman Foster, Lisa and I have never handed things over to people and just taken the consequences' (Hooper, 1.xxxii). He served on numerous committees and received several honorary degrees, as well as an honorary fellowship of the Royal Institute of British Architects. He left a bountiful legacy, including many fond memories of an exceptionally kind, generous, and elegant man. He died at his home, The Grange, Grange Lane, Dulwich, London, after a brief illness, on 2 April 2000, aged ninety-three, and was cremated in south London on 7 April; a memorial concert was held at St John's, Smith Square, on 3 October 2000. His wife survived him.

The life of Bob Sainsbury, in business and in art, was marked by a degree of creativity—an ability to bring things into existence through initiative, skill, and passion—which he perhaps never allowed himself to acknowledge. He admired artists, both those he knew and others from across centuries and continents whose faces he never saw, yet whose presence he felt through their works. Artists also admired him because of his eye and his confidence in buying when they were neither famous nor bankable. Acquiring for investment was never his way; he bought things which elicited a strong emotional reaction. His broad vision encompassed a passionate concern with detail—with the form of things, whether a column of figures, an ampersand, or a tiny carving. He especially liked small sculptures, which he arranged in a bedside display cabinet which his children referred to as 'the toy department'. He championed good display and exhibition lighting at the Sainsbury Centre gallery, although his father had once chided him for not being observant. In 1990 he conceded he had no sense of direction, but, 'On the other hand,' he said, 'I could describe in detail many of the dresses which my wife wore before the War, because that interested me and they were things of beauty' (Hooper, 1.xxx).

STEVEN HOOPER

Sources S. Hooper, 'Introduction: a history of the collection', *Robert and Lisa Sainsbury collection*, ed. S. Hooper, 3 vols. (New Haven and London, 1997), vol. 1, pp. xxv–lxxvii • R. Sainsbury, 'Foreword', *Robert and Lisa Sainsbury collection*, ed. S. Hooper, 3 vols. (New Haven and London, 1997), vol. 1, pp. xi–xiv • R. Sainsbury, ed., *Robert and Lisa Sainsbury collection* (1978) • B. Williams, *The best butter in the world: a history of Sainsbury's* (1994) • b. cert. • m. cert. • d. cert. • *The Times* (4 April 2000) • *The Independent* (8 April 2000) • *Daily Telegraph* (4 April 2000) • *The Guardian* (4 April 2000) • personal knowledge (2004) • private information (2004) [widow]

Archives priv. coll., corresp. and papers relating to art collections • Sainsbury's, Stamford Street, London, company archives • University of East Anglia, Norwich, Sainsbury Research Unit, incl. personal books and art-related papers • University of East Anglia, Norwich, collection | SOUND University of East Anglia, Norwich, Robert Sainsbury Library, Sainsbury Research Unit, taped art-related recollections: CD of memorial concert, incl. addresses

Likenesses F. Bacon, oils, 1955, University of East Anglia, Norwich, Robert and Lisa Sainsbury Collection [*see illus.*] • J. Davies, mixed media, 1973, University of East Anglia, Norwich, Robert and Lisa Sainsbury Collection • J. Davies, mixed media, 1973–4, University of East Anglia, Norwich, Robert and Lisa Sainsbury Collection • Lord Snowdon, photographs, repro. in B. Robertson, J. Russell, and Lord Snowdon, *Private view* (1965)

Wealth at death £1,154,413: probate, 20 July 2000, *CGPLA Eng. & Wales*

Sainsbury, William Noel (1825–1895), historian, third son of John and Mary Ann Sainsbury, was born at 35 Red Lion Square, Holborn, London, on 7 July 1825. Having entered the state paper office in 1848 as an extra temporary clerk, he was confirmed in the appointment, and was transferred to the record office when it absorbed the state paper office in 1854. He became an assistant keeper of the records in 1887.

Sainsbury chiefly devoted himself to calendaring the records relating to the history of America and the West Indies. In all, he published nine volumes of colonial state papers (1862–93). The value of his public work was matched by the private assistance he gave to historians and historical societies in the United States. In his early days he collected for George Bancroft, the American historian, those papers of the Board of Trade which related to the history of the American colonies. In recognition of his services to American historical writers he was made an honorary or corresponding member of the principal historical societies in the United States.

Sainsbury married twice: first, in 1849, Emily Storrs, second daughter of Andrew Moore, with whom he had two sons and eight daughters; second, in 1873, Henrietta Victoria, youngest daughter of John Hawkins, and widow of Alfred Crusher Auger, whom he also survived. He retired from the public service in December 1891, but continued, with the help of a daughter, to edit his calendar of colonial state papers up to the time of his death. He died on 9 March 1895 at 151 Sutherland Avenue, Maida Vale, London.   C. A. HARRIS, rev. G. MARTIN MURPHY

Sources *Proceedings of the American Antiquarian Society*, 10/1 (1895), 28 · *The Times* (14 March 1895)
Archives Herts. ALS, Lytton MSS
Wealth at death £6678 11s. 5d.: probate, 19 April 1895, CGPLA Eng. & Wales

St Alban. For this title name *see* Bacon, Francis, Viscount St Alban (1561–1626).

St Albans. For this title name *see* Burke, Richard, fourth earl of Clanricarde and first earl of St Albans (1572–1635); Jermyn, Henry, earl of St Albans (*bap.* 1605, *d.* 1684); Beauclerk, Charles, first duke of St Albans (1670–1726); Beauclerk, Harriot, duchess of St Albans (1777?–1837).

St Albans, Hugh [*called* Hugh le Peyntour] (*d.* **1368**), painter, is first noted in 1348–50, under the name of Hugh le Peyntour, painting flags or sails for Edward III's ships. He was then attached to the king's chamber. In March 1350 Hugh St Albans was named as master of the painters at St Stephen's Chapel, a royal foundation within the Palace of Westminster renewed by Edward I, the building and glazing of which were by then nearing completion. He was given a royal warrant to seek assistants in Kent, Middlesex, Essex, Surrey, and Sussex; he is also known at this time to have been working with two other master painters, John Athelard and Benedict Nightingale. Accounts of particulars for the chapel show that Hugh was employed as head painter at 1s. a day until 1354, and was certainly employed as late as 1358. In the decade 1351–61 he was also employed by Edward the Black Prince. In 1353 Hugh and his wife, Agnes, bought a house on Fore Street in the parish of St Giles Cripplegate, London, where he was also a churchwarden; in 1354 it is noted that Hugh St Albans was a resident of London but also owned property in Hertfordshire. In 1358 he was awarded an annuity of £10 for life.

Hugh St Albans's will of 1361, enrolled in 1368, is an exceptionally interesting document for the history of English medieval artists, since apart from indicating the size of his estate it includes a bequest to his wife, Agnes, of a six-piece Lombard panel painting (that is, a polyptych altarpiece) which cost him £20. This is an early example of the assimilation of Italian, probably Sienese, art in England. The work conducted under Hugh marked St Stephen's Chapel as one of the most richly adorned buildings in late medieval England, of importance for its early Perpendicular architecture and for the eclectic styles of its paintings. Although damaged in succeeding centuries,

and finally destroyed in the period 1800–34, fragments of the scheme created under Hugh, depicting biblical stories from the books of Job and Tobit, were rescued and are now in the British Museum. They mark Hugh's career as a landmark in the creation of an international Gothic style in England, bearing comparison with contemporary Italian and Flemish painting. Hugh died in London in 1368, and was buried at St Giles Cripplegate, where a light burned for the painters' trade.   PAUL BINSKI

Sources *Chancery records* · PRO, accounts various, E 101, exchequer, queen's remembrancer · R. R. Sharpe, ed., *Calendar of wills proved and enrolled in the court of husting, London, AD 1258 – AD 1688*, 2 (1890), 106–7 · J. H. Harvey, 'Some London painters of the 14th and 15th centuries', *Burlington Magazine*, 89 (1947), 303–5 · E. W. Tristram, *English wall painting of the fourteenth century* (1955) · R. Brown, H. M. Colvin, and A. J. Taylor, eds., *The history of the king's works*, 1 (1963), 518–19

St Albans, Nicholas of (*d.* in or before **1253**). *See under* Moneyers (*act. c.*1180–*c.*1500).

St Albans, Ralph of (*fl.* 1195×1214?), Benedictine monk and hagiographer, was probably a native of Dunstable and a monk of St Albans. By some writers he is called Robert. He is possibly to be identified with the Ralph who was prior of Wymondham, a cell of St Albans, at some point between 1195 and 1214. At the request of William, another monk of St Albans, he wrote a metrical life of St Alban, which amplified and versified William's Latin prose lives of St Alban and St Amphibalus. Copies of Ralph's work are in four St Albans manuscripts: BL, Cotton MS Julius D.iii, part 2, folios 125–58, and Claudius E.iv, folios 47–58v, and in Dublin, Trinity College, MS 177 (formerly E.i.40), folios 3–20, and Cambridge, Gonville and Caius College, MS 230, folios 172ff. (incomplete). In a treatise 'On the foundation and merits of the monastery of St Albans' composed probably by Thomas of Walsingham, Ralph is compared to Virgil.   MARY BATESON, rev. REBECCA READER

Sources R. M. Thomson, *Manuscripts from St Albans Abbey, 1066–1235*, 2 vols. (1982) · R. M. Thomson, 'Two twelfth-century poems on the *regnum-sacerdotium* problem in England', *Revue Bénédictine*, 83 (1973), 318–19 · W. McLeod, 'Alban and Amphibal: some extant lives and a lost life', *Mediaeval Studies*, 42 (1980), 407–30, esp. 412–16 · R. Vaughan, *Matthew Paris*, Cambridge Studies in Medieval Life and Thought, new ser., 6 (1958), 195–6 · T. D. Hardy, *Descriptive catalogue of materials relating to the history of Great Britain and Ireland*, 1, Rolls Series, 26 (1862), nos. 24–6 · D. Knowles, C. N. L. Brooke, and V. C. M. London, eds., *The heads of religious houses, England and Wales*, 1: *940–1216* (1972), 98 · *Annales monasterii S. Albani a Johanne Amundesham*, ed. H. T. Riley, 2 vols., pt 5 of *Chronica monasterii S. Albani*, Rolls Series, 28 (1870–71), vol. 2, p. 304
Archives BL, Cotton MS Claudius E.iv, fols. 47–58v · BL, Cotton MS Julius D.iii, pt 2, fols. 125–58 · Gon. & Caius Cam., MS 230, fols. 172ff. · TCD, MS 177, fols. 3–20

St Albans, Roger. *See* Alban, Roger (*d.* after 1461).

St Albans, William of (*fl. c.*1178), Benedictine monk and hagiographer, wrote a Latin prose *Passio S. Albani* at the request of Simon, from 1167 to 1188 abbot of St Albans, where William was a monk. Since the original version of the *Passio* does not mention the invention of Amphibalus in 1178, the probable date of its composition is between

1167 and 1178. In his work William made use of the writings of Bede and Geoffrey of Monmouth, but he claimed also to have translated from an Anglo-Saxon account of the martyrdom, dating from 590. The three earliest copies of his *Passio* are Oxford, Magdalen College, MS 53, and BL, Cotton MSS Faustina B.iv and Nero C.vii. William's *Passio* was the source of most of the medieval lives of saints Alban and Amphibalus, including those of Ralph of St Albans and Matthew Paris. He has been identified with William Martell the sacrist, who unsuccessfully challenged Warin for the abbacy of St Albans on the death of Abbot Simon, but there is no firm basis for this identification. MARY BATESON, *rev.* REBECCA READER

Sources R. M. Thomson, *Manuscripts from St Albans Abbey, 1066–1235*, 2 vols. (1982) · B. Gordon-Taylor, 'The hagiography of St Alban and St Amphibalus in the twelfth century', MA diss., U. Durham, 1991 · F. McCulloch, 'Saints Alban and Amphibalus in the works of Matthew Paris: Dublin Trinity College MS 177', *Speculum*, 56 (1981), 761–85 · W. McLeod, 'Alban and Amphibal: some extant lives and a lost life', *Mediaeval Studies*, 42 (1980), 407–30 · E. Uhlemann, 'Über die anglonormannische Vie de Seint Auban in Bezug auf Quelle, Lautverhältnisse und Flexion', *Romanische Studien*, 4 (1880), 543–626 · T. D. Hardy, *Descriptive catalogue of materials relating to the history of Great Britain and Ireland*, 1, Rolls Series, 26 (1862), nos. 8–31, pp. 4–17 · William of St Albans, 'Passio S. Albani', *Acta sanctorum: Junius*, 4, 149–59 · *Gesta abbatum monasterii Sancti Albani, a Thoma Walsingham*, ed. H. T. Riley, 3 vols., pt 4 of *Chronica monasterii S. Albani*, Rolls Series, 28 (1867–9), vol. 1, p. 195

Archives BL, Cotton Faustina B.iv, fols. 1–64r · BL, Cotton MS Nero C.vii, fols. 1–8 · Magd. Oxf., MS 53, pp. 19–50 | BL, Cotton MS Claudius E.iv, fols. 34–47 · TCD, MS 177, fols. 20–28v

St Aldwyn. For this title name *see* Beach, Michael Edward Hicks, first Earl St Aldwyn (1837–1916); Beach, Michael John Hicks-, second Earl St Aldwyn (1912–1992).

St Amand, Almaric, third Baron St Amand (1314–1381), justiciar of Ireland, was the son of John St Amand (d. 1330) and Margaret, daughter of Hugh *Despenser the elder, earl of Winchester. Having proved his age, on 16 March 1335 he did homage for his lands which lay mostly in southern England but included the Irish coastal manor of Gormanston, north of Dublin, which had been acquired from Henry III by his great-great-grandfather, the first Almaric. Already in 1332 he had been among the absentee lords summoned to go with Edward III on his projected Irish expedition. He had a long career in local government, chiefly in Berkshire and Oxfordshire, where he was frequently a commissioner of array, of oyer and terminer, and of the peace between 1338 and 1381. This was accompanied by a record of military service, which seems to have begun in 1335 when he went to Scotland with William Montagu, later earl of Salisbury. In 1337, by which time he had been knighted, he accompanied the earl overseas. He was at Crécy and Calais in 1346–7. In 1351, when he had attained the rank of banneret, he was granted an annuity of 200 marks 'for his stay with the king, for as long as he stays' (*CPR, 1350–54*, 41).

St Amand was appointed justiciar of Ireland on 14 July 1357, following the death of Thomas Rokeby, and served there from November 1357 to March 1359. The English colony was under heavy pressure from Irish raids. The justiciar spent his term on a war footing, travelling incessantly in Leinster and Munster, fighting and negotiating with Gaelic chiefs, and bargaining with the settler communities in the counties for grants of taxation. The retinue of 40 men-at-arms and 100 archers, for which he had contracted with the king, ate up a large proportion of the shrunken revenues of the Dublin exchequer, leaving little scope to raise paid armies locally. Early in 1359 he presided over a parliament which sent messages to the king about the dire state of Ireland. As he departed for France in October, Edward acknowledged the seriousness of the position; the embassy had helped to create the climate in which it was decided in 1361 that English resources should be devoted to the Irish wars.

After his return from Ireland, St Amand served again in France in 1359–60. In 1361 and 1362 he was among those ordered to prepare to go to Ireland with Lionel of Antwerp. In 1363 he sold his Irish property (which may have become less attractive as pressure mounted upon absentees to contribute to the defence of their lands) to Sir Robert Preston, chief justice of the Dublin bench, ancestor of the viscounts Gormanston; at the same time he paid £400 to a London citizen to redeem the manor of Grendon in Buckinghamshire. He held one further significant command, as keeper of Southampton in 1369, a time of danger from the French. During the last decade of his life he was regularly summoned to parliament. He died on 11 September 1381, when his son, Almaric, succeeded to his lands. The younger Almaric, with whom the direct male line of the St Amands ended, died in 1402, outliving by a year his only son, another Almaric. ROBIN FRAME

Sources *Chancery records* · PRO · J. Mills and M. J. McEnery, eds., *Calendar of the Gormanston register* (1916) · E. Tresham, ed., *Rotulorum patentium et clausorum cancellariae Hiberniae calendarium*, Irish Record Commission (1828) · A. J. Otway-Ruthven, 'Ireland in the 1350s: Sir Thomas de Rokeby and his successors', *Journal of the Royal Society of Antiquaries of Ireland*, 97 (1967), 45–59 · R. Frame, *English lordship in Ireland, 1318–1361* (1982) · A. J. Otway-Ruthven, *A history of medieval Ireland* (1968) · G. Wrottesley, *Crécy and Calais* (1897); repr. (1898) · GEC, *Peerage* · *CIPM*, 15, nos. 581–6

Wealth at death see *CIPM*

St Amand, Sir Amaury de (d. 1240/41), soldier and administrator, is first recorded in royal service in March 1217. Thereafter he served Henry III in various capacities. He went to Ireland on royal business in 1226, accompanied Henry on the Brittany campaign of 1230–31, and acted for him in Brittany in 1232–4 in diplomatic and military roles. In 1232 he was one of the wardens of the Channel Islands. In the Welsh marches, he emerged as a key royal agent in the 1230s: he was appointed constable or keeper of various castles, notably St Briavels (with the Forest of Dean), which he held from 1234 until his death; he negotiated with the Welsh in 1231, 1237, and 1238; and he held the post of high constable of the marches from January 1234. He was also sheriff of Herefordshire, 1234–40. This rise coincided with his appointment as one of the king's household stewards in 1233, when he is also first recorded as a knight. He enjoyed considerable influence at court thereafter. In 1239 he acted as one of the nine godfathers of Prince Edward, a mark of his closeness to the king. His service brought considerable reward, notably temporary grants of land in wardship at the king's pleasure, but in 1230 he was also granted seisin of the lands of Ralph, son of Walter de Verdun, his uncle. He married twice. His first wife is unknown; before December 1222 he had married Iseult, daughter of William Pantulf. In 1240 he went on crusade as one of the bannerets of Simon de Montfort, but it is unknown if he reached the Holy Land. He was dead by September 1241.   SIMON LLOYD

Sources *Chancery records* · Paris, *Chron.*

St Amand, James (1687–1754), classical scholar and book collector, was born in Covent Garden, London, on 7 April 1687 and baptized at St Paul's, Covent Garden, on 21 April, the son of James St Amand, apothecary to the family of James II, and his wife, Elizabeth. He matriculated from Hart Hall, Oxford, on 17 March 1703, the same day as his elder brother George matriculated from Corpus Christi College, Oxford. James does not appear to have taken up residence at Hart Hall and on 5 September 1704 he entered Lincoln College where he remained for one year as a gentleman commoner. His passion for classical literature, and especially his wish to collate manuscripts for a new edition of Theocritus, led him to travel to Italy in 1705, via Holland, Germany, and Austria. In Florence he made the acquaintance of the distinguished scholar Anton Maria Salvini, who furnished him with materials from the Laurentian Library and from the library of the Benedictine monastery of Santa Maria.

St Amand returned to England in 1710 and settled in a house in East Street, Red Lion Square, Bloomsbury, London, having amassed on his travels a valuable collection of books and manuscripts. He continued to collect for the rest of his life, but never completed his projected edition of Theocritus; his manuscript notes were later used by Thomas Warton for his edition of Theocritus, published in 1770.

St Amand died unmarried at his home on 5 September 1754 and was buried, according to instructions in his will, in the cloisters of Christ's Hospital, where a plaque was erected to his memory. He bequeathed to the school the residue of his estate, worth about £8000, and a portrait miniature of his grandfather John St Amand. This legacy was dependent on the condition that the school should never remove or destroy the portrait. He bequeathed his collection of books, coins, and prints to the Bodleian Library, but those items rejected by the Bodleian were to be given to Lincoln College. A catalogue of the library, which consisted principally of modern editions of classical works, was drawn up by Alexander Cruden in September 1754. William Stukeley was one of St Amand's executors and in May 1755 he brought the books to Oxford in twenty-seven cases; the coins and medals followed subsequently.

W. P. COURTNEY, *rev.* M. J. MERCER

Sources Foster, *Alum. Oxon.* · *N&Q*, 6th ser., 8 (1883), 425 · *GM*, 1st ser., 24 (1754), 434 · *GM*, 1st ser., 72 (1802), 493 · R. Brimley Johnson, ed., *Christ's Hospital: recollections of Lamb, Coleridge, and Leigh Hunt*

(1896), 142, 270n. · will, PRO, PROB 11/810, fols. 335v–340v · A. Chalmers, ed., *The general biographical dictionary*, new edn, 32 vols. (1812–17) · J. Ingamells, ed., *A dictionary of British and Irish travellers in Italy, 1701–1800* (1997), 834

Archives Bodl. Oxf., Adversaria, nos. 10725–10786

Wealth at death £8000; plus value of library: will, 1749, PRO, PROB 11/810, fols. 335v–340v

St André, Nathanael (1679/80–1776), anatomist and surgeon, was born in Switzerland and emigrated to England when he was young, probably as a servant in the household of a wealthy family. He was placed with a London surgeon, applied himself to the study of anatomy, and set up his own practice from his lodgings in Northumberland Court, near Charing Cross. He became the local surgeon at Westminster Infirmary. From 1719 to 1725 he gave public lectures in anatomy and in surgical operations. He published in 1723 *A Treatise of Chirurgical Operations*, a translation of the work of René-Jacques Garengeot, and in May of that same year he was appointed surgeon and anatomist to the royal household by George I.

Factual information about St André's life is scarce, and because he played suspicious roles in several notorious incidents, he became the object of rumours and accusations, many of which passed into the historical record as facts. He was widely considered a charlatan and a cheat. In truth, he almost certainly was neither. An anonymous friend and apologist (probably Thomas Tyers) admitted that St André loved praise, and more than praise he loved attention: 'so that people did but talk about him, he seldom seemed to care what they talked against him' (Nichols, 466). This and a penchant for self-promotion explain much of his behaviour and reputation. A cloud of notoriety often surrounded him, less because he did anything knavish than because, anxious to be in the public eye, he sought out promising situations, exploited them to draw attention to himself, and exploited them so brazenly that he provoked suspicions about his actions and motives.

It was said at the time that St André was appointed surgeon and anatomist to the royal household more because of his knowledge of German than his merit as a medical man. How qualified he was in his profession is difficult to ascertain, but the charge of incompetence implied in many attacks on him is groundless. In a paper on a herniated bowel he published in *Philosophical Transactions* in 1717 he showed himself to be a knowledgeable medical thinker (though, typically, he turned this scientific account into a panegyric on his own acumen). St André was an avid student of anatomy and is now considered a minor but significant pioneer in the preparation of anatomical specimens by means of wax injections. He probably was a proficient surgeon. In September 1726 Alexander Pope sought him out when he severely wounded his hand in a coaching accident, and the poet remained on friendly terms with him throughout his life. Charles Mordaunt, third earl of Peterborough, was a lifelong friend and patient.

St André first came to the public's attention in February 1725. By his account a stranger took him to a house, offered him a cordial, and asked him to examine a woman for venereal disease. Several hours later St André began to experience the effects of poisoning. On the king's orders his case was investigated by the privy council, which offered £200 for the detection of the offender. Neither the identity nor the motive of the assailant was discovered. The incident might have passed relatively unnoticed had St André not published a lengthy account recording in detail his day-by-day struggle against death and boasting how intimate he was with the king and members of the court. Some contemporaries considered the incident an egregious falsehood fabricated by St André to render himself an object of attention.

The next year St André became involved in his most notorious affair. On 15 November 1726 he accompanied his friend Samuel Molyneux, secretary to the prince of Wales, to Guildford to examine Mary *Toft, a young woman from Godalming, Surrey, who claimed to have given birth to fourteen rabbits. Within minutes of examining her St André delivered her of her fifteenth. He became a true believer. When Cyriacus Ahlers, a fellow surgeon, challenged him, St André staged an anatomical demonstration for George I to prove that the rabbits were 'praeternatural'. On the king's orders St André brought Mary Toft to London and lodged her in a bagnio in Leicester Fields. He orchestrated public viewings of the woman. The affair riveted the attention of all of London for nearly a month. Lord Hervey remarked, 'Every Creature both Men & Women have been to see & feel her' (Hervey to Fox, 3 Dec 1726). On 3 December St André published *A Short Narrative of an Extraordinary Delivery of Rabbets*, in which he proclaimed that the births were genuine. Three days later Mary Toft confessed that the whole incident was a hoax. On 8 December St André admitted that he had been duped and publicly apologized for his role in the affair.

It was generally assumed at the time that St André had conspired with Mary Toft to pass off the fraud on the public. But in her confession Mary Toft cleared him of complicity, and Richard Manningham and James Douglas, physicians who investigated the incident assiduously to expose the imposture, exonerated him of everything but credulity. In fact, St André's belief that Mary Toft's births were genuine is not as outrageous as it appears: it was a reputable medical theory of the time that a mother's imagination had the power to misshape her foetus. Many people—and many of them trained in medicine—entertained her claims seriously, though few argued for the truth of her story with the persistence and conviction of St André. Once again, he appears to have been the victim of his desire for attention. He probably believed Mary Toft, and he certainly promoted the affair relentlessly, because he saw in these births, perhaps unconsciously, something that could be parlayed into an uncommon incident with himself at the centre.

A little more than a year after the Toft affair St André gained additional notoriety. When his friend Samuel Molyneux, MP for Exeter, was seized with a fit in the House of Commons, St André was called in to treat him. Molyneux died several days later and, on the night of his death, 13 April 1728, St André eloped with Molyneux's wife, Lady Elizabeth, eldest daughter of Algernon Capel, second earl of Essex. He married her on 27 May 1730. The Revd Samuel Madden, Molyneux's cousin, openly accused St André of having poisoned Molyneux. Eventually St André won an action for defamation, but neither he nor his wife was able to live down the scandal. Lady Elizabeth lost her attendance on Queen Caroline and St André lost what remained of his public credit. They retired to the country and in the early 1750s settled permanently in Southampton. St André dabbled in gardening, architecture, and botany. He indulged himself in charitable activities, but so ostentatiously that he was accused of being motivated by sheer egocentricity. Lady Elizabeth had brought nearly £30,000 to the marriage, but the money went from St André on her death, and his circumstances became increasingly straitened because of unwise real estate investments. He lost many possessions, including much of his anatomical collection, in a fire. He died in Southampton in March 1776 at the age of ninety-six. He assigned his estate to William Henry and George Pitt, sons of Mary Pitt, his former servant, and rumoured at the time to be his own offspring.

St André was portrayed in three satirical engravings of 1726 occasioned by the Toft hoax: the anonymous *Doctors in Labour*, George and James Vertue's *The Surrey-Wonder: an Anatomical Farce*, and William Hogarth's *Cunicularii*. In all three he is pictured as thin, energetic, and very excitable.

DENNIS TODD

Sources J. Nichols, *Biographical anecdotes of William Hogarth, and a catalogue of his works chronologically arranged with occasional remarks*, 3rd edn (1785) · S. A. Seligman, 'Mary Toft: the rabbit breeder', *Medical History*, 5 (1961), 349–60 · N. St André, *A short narrative of an extraordinary delivery of rabbets* (1726) · J. Douglas, *An advertisement occasion'd by … Manningham's diary* (1727) · C. Ahlers, *Some observations concerning the woman of Godlyman* (1726) · R. Manningham, *An exact diary of … Mary Toft* (1726) · will, PRO, PROB 11/1019, fol. 8135 · *LondG* (23 Feb 1725) · *DNB* · S. Madden, *A letter from the Reverend Mr. M—D—N to the Hon. Lady M—n—x* (1730) · confessions of Mary Toft, U. Glas., James Douglas papers, D324, D327, D328 · Lord Hervey to Henry Fox, 3 Dec 1726, Suffolk RO, Hervey papers, 941/47/4, fols. 29–32

Likenesses W. Hogarth, engraving, 1726 (*Cunicularii, or, The wise men of Godliman in consultation*), Wellcome L. · J. Vertue, drawing, 1726 (*The Surrey-wonder: an anatomical farce as it was dissected at Theatre-Royal Lincolns-Inn-Fields*), BL · engraving, 1726 (*The doctors in labour: or a new whim wham from Guildford*), BL · R. Grave, line engraving, NPG, Wellcome L.; repro. in Caulfield, *Remarkable characters* (1819) · J. Vertue, engraving (after his drawing), BL

Wealth at death approx. £1500–£3000 expected value of real estate (sale may have realized less): will, PRO, PROB 11/1019, fol. 8135

St Aubyn, Catherine. *See* Molesworth, Catherine (1760–1836).

St Aubyn, Sir John, third baronet (1696–1744), politician, was born on 27 September 1696, the eldest son and heir of Sir John St Aubyn, second baronet (*bap.* 1670, *d.* 1714), landowner and politician, and his wife, Mary, the daughter and coheir of Peter de la Hay of Westminster. He matriculated as a gentleman commoner at Exeter College, Oxford, on 12 June 1718, and was created MA on 19 July

1721. In May 1722 he was returned to parliament for the county of Cornwall, a seat he held until his death.

St Aubyn established a reputation as a man of principle, and opposed successive measures by Walpole that seemed detrimental to the established church or appeared to embroil Great Britain in European conflicts. His independence was no doubt strengthened by his marriage on 3 October 1725 to Catherine (d. 16 June 1740), the daughter and eventual heir of Sir Nicholas Morice of Werrington, Devon. The marriage brought him several thousand pounds and the manor of Stoke Damerel, including the town of Devonport. The couple had one son and four daughters.

St Aubyn at least dabbled in Jacobitism; he sent reports of parliamentary debates to the historian Thomas Carte, who forwarded them to the Old Pretender. However, Carte may well have exaggerated when he told the chevalier in 1739 that St Aubyn could raise 8000 to 10,000 tin miners loyal to the Stuart cause. St Aubyn's real achievement lay in his always well-argued and never gratuitous interventions against the Walpole ministry, supporting the repeal of the Septennial Act when the matter was brought to the Commons in 1734, and resisting attempts to increase the size of the regular army. Following Walpole's fall on 9 March 1742 he seconded Lord Limerick's motion for a committee of inquiry into the twenty years of Walpole's ministry; when this was defeated by 244 votes to 242, he seconded Limerick's revised proposal for a secret committee of twenty-one to examine Walpole's official acts during the last ten years, which was carried by 252 votes to 245. In the polling for the committee he obtained the first place with 518 votes, a result pronounced by Speaker Onslow to be without precedent, but he declined to preside over the proceedings. He is said also to have declined a seat at the Board of Admiralty. West country fable credits Walpole with the remark, when speaking of the House of Commons, 'All these men have their price except the little Cornish baronet.' In 1743 the Old Pretender commended St Aubyn's abilities by appointing him to the 'council of regency' to act alongside Prince Charles Edward on his invasion. St Aubyn was also a friend, patron, and collaborator with Dr William Borlase, and a friend and correspondent of Pope. He died of fever at Pencarrow, Egloshayle, Cornwall, on 15 August 1744, and was buried alongside his wife, in a granite vault in Crowan church, Cornwall, on 23 August. W. P. COURTNEY, rev. MATTHEW KILBURN

Sources Boase & Courtney, Bibl. Corn. · G. C. Boase, Collectanea Cornubiensia: a collection of biographical and topographical notes relating to the county of Cornwall (1890) · E. Cruickshanks, 'St Aubyn, Sir John', HoP, Commons, 1715–54 · E. Cruickshanks, Political untouchables: the tories and the '45 (1979) · L. Colley, In defiance of oligarchy: the tory party, 1714–60 (1982) · The correspondence of Alexander Pope, ed. G. Sherburn, 4 (1956), 245, 392, 434, 520 · Nichols, Lit. anecdotes, 5.294 · Foster, Alum. Oxon.

Wealth at death large estate incl. several tin mines · inherited £20,000 from wife · inherited £10,000 from wife: DNB

St Aubyn, Sir John, fifth baronet (1758–1839), landowner and politician, born at Golden Square, London, on 17 May 1758, was the elder son of Sir John St Aubyn MP, fourth baronet (1726–1772), and Elizabeth, daughter of William Wingfield of Durham; Catherine *Molesworth, the painter, was his sister. He was admitted to Westminster School on 19 January 1773 and, in 1775, at the age of seventeen, he was reported to have induced a fellow pupil named Baker to lend him money. When the sum was not repaid, the case was put before the lord chancellor on 2 July 1777 and St Aubyn, despite a plea that he was under age, was ordered to repay the money with 4 per cent interest. St Aubyn at this time was abroad on the grand tour; he spent three years in France where, according to Joseph Farington, he 'formed a connection with an Italian woman, and by her had a daughter' (Farington, Diary, 11.3903).

St Aubyn succeeded to the baronetcy and to the family estates at Clowance, near Crowan, Cornwall, and Stoke Damerel, Devon, on 12 October 1772. He was sheriff of Cornwall in 1781, and on 6 February 1784 he entered parliament as MP for Truro. Six weeks later at the general election he was returned for Penryn together with his cousin, Sir Francis Bassett. He was a steadfast supporter of the opposition and he contested the county of Cornwall on their behalf in 1790, but was defeated after a very close and bitter campaign. From 1807 to 1812 he represented Helston and continued to support the opposition, although he never seems to have spoken in the house during his parliamentary career. In spite of his extensive interests in Cornwall, where he was provincial grandmaster of the freemasons from 1785 to 1839, St Aubyn chose to live in London or at his home at Short Groves, near Saffron Walden, Essex, or later at Woolmers, near Hertford. He conducted long-term relationships with two Cornish women: Martha Nicholls (d. 1829), the daughter of John Nicholls, a landscape gardener, and later Juliana Vinicombe (1769–1856), of Marazion, whom he eventually married on 1 July 1822 at St Andrew's, Holborn. Of his fifteen illegitimate children, he and Juliana had six sons and two daughters before their marriage; the other seven are thought to have been Martha's children. The painter J. B. Lane explained to Farington that St Aubyn's unorthodox lifestyle was due to the influence of a profligate clergyman who had led him at an early age 'into scenes of vice with women and familiarised him to this kind of intercourse' (Farington, Diary, 11.3903).

A lover of science and the arts, St Aubyn was a keen amateur mineralogist and in 1799 he bought the fossils and minerals of Richard Greene of Lichfield; his own collection of minerals, previously the property of the earl of Bute, was described by William Babington in his New System of Mineralogy in the Form of a Catalogue (1799). In May 1804 St Aubyn joined with others to raise £4000 for a mineralogical collection at the Royal Institution. He also subscribed to the fund for providing an annuity for Richard Porson. He was an early and constant patron and friend of John Opie and was a pallbearer at the artist's funeral in April 1807. Opie painted three portraits of St Aubyn and one of his wife. St Aubyn was a fellow of the Linnean Society, and was elected FSA in 1783 and FRS on 18 May 1797. He profited greatly from the development of the Royal Navy docks of Devonport on his estates at Stoke Damerel and he donated a site for the town hall together with a corporation mace, a cabinet of minerals, and two of Opie's paintings. After his death at Lime Grove, Putney, Surrey, on 10 August 1839, his body was conveyed through Devonport on 23 August, attended by the municipal authorities, on its way to Cornwall where it lay in state at St Austell, Truro, and Clowance. On 29 August he was buried, with great masonic ceremony, in the family vault in Crowan parish church. Although the baronetcy became extinct and the entailed estates passed to a nephew, the Revd John Molesworth of Crowan, the property at Devonport was inherited by his eldest son, James St Aubyn, with the proviso that he should set aside £130,000 for marriage settlements of £10,000 for each of his thirteen siblings. Another son, Edward St Aubyn (d. 1872), was created baronet on 31 July 1866, and was father of the first Baron St Levan.

W. P. COURTNEY, rev. HALLIE RUBENHOLD

Sources D. Hartley, *The St Aubyns of Cornwall, 1200–1977* (1977) · L. B. Namier, 'St Aubyn, Sir John', HoP, *Commons* · R. G. Thorne, 'St Aubyn, Sir John', HoP, *Commons* · Farington, *Diary* · GEC, *Baronetage* · Boase & Courtney, *Bibl. Corn.*, 1.222, 250, 264, 414; 2.509, 536, 613–16; 3.1209, 1332 · G. C. Boase, *Collectanea Cornubiensia: a collection of biographical and topographical notes relating to the county of Cornwall* (1890), 854, 857 · H. Walpole, *Journal of the reign of King George the Third*, ed. Dr Doran, 2 (1859), 126 · J. J. Rogers, *Opie and his works: being a catalogue of 760 pictures by John Opie … preceded by a biographical sketch* (1878), 153–4, 229 · J. Opie, *Lectures on painting* (1809), 48, 52, 68 · *GM*, 1st ser., 77 (1807), 387 · *GM*, 1st ser., 78 (1808), 172 · *GM*, 2nd ser., 12 (1839), 542
Archives Plymouth City Museum and Art Gallery, notes relating to Plymouth herbarium
Likenesses J. Reynolds, oils, 1757–9, Pencarrow House, Cornwall · N. Hone, oils, 1778, St Michael's Mount, Cornwall · J. Opie, oils, c.1785, Plymouth City Museum and Art Gallery · J. Reynolds, oils, 1786 · J. Opie, oils, c.1786–1790 (after J. Reynolds), St Michael's Mount, Cornwall · W. Beechey, oils, priv. coll. · J. Opie, three oils, Devonport Guildhall · J. Opie and son, oils, St Michael's Mount, Cornwall · S. W. Reynolds, mezzotint (after J. Opie), BM · J. S. C. Schaak, oils, priv. coll. · miniature, V&A

Saint Brides. For this title name *see* James, (John) Morrice Cairns, Baron Saint Brides (1916–1989).

St Calais [St Carilef], **William of** (c.1030–1096), administrator and bishop of Durham, was a Norman clerk and monk who became bishop of Durham and an influential counsellor of William I and his successor, William II. Probably a member of a clerical dynasty in the cathedral church of Bayeux, he was educated under Bishop Odo of Bayeux (1049–97), William the Conqueror's half-brother, who encouraged scholars. Symeon of Durham, William of St Calais's encomiast, considered him well read in the classical and religious authors; and by the time he became bishop he had acquired a useful knowledge of canon law. From the chapter of Bayeux, following the example of his father, he became a monk in the Benedictine abbey at St Calais in Maine, where he rose to the office of prior before his election as abbot of St Vincent-des-Prés, outside the walls of Le Mans. The county of Maine, disputed between Anjou and Normandy, was conquered by Duke William in 1063, and from at least 1081 his eldest son, Robert Curthose, was recognized as its titular ruler.

William of St Calais was a wholehearted monk, virtuous and deeply religious; but, like Lanfranc of Bec, with whom he was later to clash, he was no fanatic. Symeon considered him intelligent and subtle, possessed of an excellent memory, an eloquent speaker and a wise counsellor. He was from the beginning experienced in the way of the world. At St Calais and Le Mans, outposts of the Norman 'empire', secular politics were unavoidable, and, according to Symeon, his diligence in some very difficult matters so recommended him to the king that, on 9 November 1080, he appointed him to succeed the murdered bishop of Durham, Walcher, a Lotharingian clerk who had also been earl of Northumbria and become involved in the feuds that disturbed that anarchic province. That the king moved a monk from the marches of Anjou to hold a city and castle in the Scottish marches shows how much trust the monarch had in him. Except when exiled by William Rufus, the bishop was a member of the inner circle of the royal household, with one or two others regularly authorizing and witnessing royal writs and charters, and very much involved in the everyday conduct of affairs, a position that under the Angevin kings would be called 'chief justiciar'. His greatest achievement, it has been plausibly suggested, was to mastermind and organize the Domesday Survey of 1086, even serving as one of the commissioners. And he seems to have provided the main scribe of Great Domesday, as well as its corrector, from the Durham scriptorium. Moreover, he calmed affairs in the north and began to reform his church and diocese. Symeon also claims that because of his well-directed zeal William was regarded just as favourably by Philippe I, king of France, and Pope Gregory VII.

The events that followed the Conqueror's death in 1087, however, caused difficulties for all the aristocracy of the Anglo-Norman realm. With the eldest son, Robert Curthose, in exile and the half-brother, Odo of Bayeux, in prison, the second son, William Rufus—with the assent of Archbishop Lanfranc of Canterbury and the bishops, the approval of the English, and the acquiescence of most of the barons—was able to take possession of England. But the top stratum of Anglo-Norman society had been swayed mostly by immediate self-interest and political necessity; and when Robert secured Normandy and Maine, and, at Christmas 1087, Rufus allowed Odo to recover his earldom of Kent, men began to reconsider their allegiance and policy. St Calais had been Odo's protégé and may have preferred Robert Curthose to Rufus as a man. Moreover, his experience of diplomacy as well as his cleverness may have inclined him to intrigue. He must have been approached, and may have been tempted, when Odo began to recruit men who would welcome an invasion by the elder brother.

St Calais certainly behaved suspiciously. When Rufus, alerted to the conspiracy, rode with his household knights and the retinues of his companions—the bishop had seven knights with him—to reconnoitre Sussex and Kent, the bishop, although ordered to proceed, went off to Durham, apparently on the pretext of going to raise more troops, and did not return. St Calais was later prepared to swear that he had never violated his fealty to the king or been guilty of any other wrongdoing, that he had entered into no engagements with the conspirators, that he had informed the king of the plot and kept him in the picture, and that he had done his best to frustrate the rebels' schemes. All this may have been true, and Symeon believed that he had been destroyed by the machinations of his enemies. But, for some reason never explained, he had abandoned his lord in the face of the enemy, and, since he would not throw himself on Rufus's mercy, but instead behaved defiantly, indeed insolently, Rufus answered with unswerving malevolence. On 12 March 1088 he ordered the confiscation of St Calais's lands. But it was not until 2 November, and then under a safe conduct and on negotiated terms, that the bishop attended the king's court at Old Sarum to face the charges.

At the trial, which lasted no more than a brief winter's day, William of St Calais was charged as a baron with breaking his oath of fealty to the king and hence liable to the penalty of confiscation of the temporalities of his see. But, from beginning to end, he denied that a bishop was subject to the jurisdiction of the king's court, refused to plead to the charges, and demanded a trial in an ecclesiastical court according to canon law. He argued the jurisdictional and procedural matters brilliantly and may be thought to have outperformed Archbishop Lanfranc, a famous dialectician, who spoke for Rufus. But the king and archbishop likewise steadfastly answered that it was not the bishop but only the baron, who clearly held a secular fief, who was on trial, and that the court as constituted—archbishops, bishops, abbots, and barons—was competent to try him. And there was no overt sympathy among the suitors for a man who had first betrayed the conspirators and then deserted the king. In the end, after the bishop had appealed to the papal curia, the king's court condemned him to forfeit his fiefs, including the castle, for contumacy, in that he refused to answer the charges. In the following weeks the bishop, while making all the difficulties he could, bowed to *force majeure*, surrendered his castle and, probably in December, crossed to Normandy where he received such a warm welcome from Robert Curthose that he abandoned his projected journey to Rome and remained as the duke's principal adviser.

In February 1091 Rufus invaded Normandy, and within a short time the brothers came to terms. William of St Calais had taken part in the preliminary events and negotiations, and the rivals promised an amnesty to those who had been involved in the feud. The bishop recovered his fiefs and on 11 September, when the two brothers together invaded Scotland, he re-entered Durham. Thereafter, although the old intimacy may have disappeared, he was one of Rufus's most loyal vassals. He supported him consistently in his disagreements with the new archbishop of Canterbury, Anselm, so much so that Anselm's biographer, Eadmer, believed that he was aiming to replace him. From 25 to 27 February 1094 in the royal court at Rockingham, Northamptonshire, St Calais acted as prosecutor and leader of the bishops against the primate, who wanted to get the pallium from a pope Rufus had not recognized. It was an awkward matter, involving conflicting

rights and obligations and affecting the honour of both parties. Anselm was in the stronger legal position; the bishop of Durham was not only discomfited in court but also earned Rufus's reproaches for his failure.

If William of St Calais's career as a royal servant was not without some doubtful features, his record as a diocesan bishop seems to have been unimpeachable. He had two main problems: besides a disorganized church, there was a general lack of security due to Scottish ambition, the rivalry of Robert de Mowbray, earl of Northumbria, and the endemic disorder. He made friends with Malcolm, king of Scots, and attached the latter's whole family spiritually to St Cuthbert's Church. Nevertheless Malcolm invaded in May 1091, while St Calais was in Normandy, and for the fifth and last time in November 1093, less than three months after having been escorted by the bishop to the king's court at Gloucester. This time, however, he was ambushed by the earl and killed. After that Rufus and the bishop supported the claims to the throne of Malcolm's English-educated sons, first Duncan (*d.* 1094) and then Edgar (*d.* 1107), Queen Margaret's son. Neither the king nor the bishop was on good terms with the earl; and in 1095, when Mowbray rebelled, the bishop helped Rufus's successful campaign against him. By that time both the Scottish menace and local disorder had been brought under control.

The episcopal see had been established at Durham only in 995, and in 1080 was still served by secular, and usually married, 'clerks of St Cuthbert'. St Calais investigated the earlier history of the ancient church of Lindisfarne and decided to restore its monastic tradition. Accordingly, in 1083 he replaced the clerks with those monks from Evesham and Winchcombe who, under the patronage of Bishop Walcher, had recently resettled Benedict Biscop's old foundations at Monkwearmouth and Jarrow. And he acquired a copy of Lanfranc's *Consuetudines*, which described the arrangements he had made at Canterbury. Like Lanfranc he intended to be both bishop and abbot, the real and immediate head of his monks. And when he made the prior (his subordinate in the cloister) also his archdeacon (his subordinate in the diocese), he completed the integration. On 11 August 1093 St Calais, Prior Turgot, and King Malcolm laid the foundation stones of a new cathedral which was to become one of the architectural jewels of western Christendom. And in order to reduce the isolation of the community he entered into the wide-ranging network of confraternities that are recorded in Durham's *Liber vitae*. As well as the twinnings with houses in all parts of England except for East Anglia, there were bonds with Fécamp and Caen in Normandy, and with St Calais, though not St Vincent, in Maine. But, however loving a father of his monks he may have been, his arrangements were possibly incomplete and certainly unsatisfactory once he had been replaced by a non-monastic bishop. The Durham monks wanted a legally secured share of the church's lands, privileges, and revenues, instead of an informal division, and probably an elective prior. If St Calais had promised some of these things before he died, there was no written evidence. So the monks soon fabricated a series of charters to use in what proved to be a long-running struggle with the bishops for administrative independence.

After Rufus had captured Robert de Mowbray at Tynemouth in the summer of 1095, he decided to put him on trial at his Christmas court at Windsor. St Calais was there, but in poor spirits, for he had been warned by one of his knights, Boso, that he would shortly die. Boso when ill had had a terrible vision in which he was conducted through the purlieus of heaven and hell. Among those he met was the bishop. In a vast and horrible wilderness stood a lofty house made of iron, with a door which was always clanging open and shut. Suddenly St Calais stuck out his head and asked Boso where the monk Geoffrey was. 'He should be attending my court,' he said. Geoffrey was the bishop's steward; and Boso's guide told him that those two would soon die. In fact St Calais collapsed on Christmas day. Archbishop Anselm, always magnanimous, gave him spiritual comfort; and on 1 January 1096 Thomas of York, Walkelin of Winchester, and John of Bath, the physician, administered the last sacraments. St Calais expressed the wish to be buried not in St Cuthbert's Church but in the chapter house, where he would be a constant memento to his monks. He died at daybreak on the following day and was buried on 16 January in the place he had chosen.

Symeon, writing in the pontificate of William of St Calais's successor, Ranulf Flambard (d. 1128), a very different sort of man, remembered fondly that St Calais exemplified all the virtues of a monastic bishop. A good, religious, and abstemious man, wise and subtle and excellently educated, he was a father to his monks and a generous benefactor to his church. At his burial there was not one who would not have redeemed his life with his own, if that had been possible.   FRANK BARLOW

Sources H. S. Offler, ed., *Durham episcopal charters, 1071–1152*, SurtS, 179 (1968) • Symeon of Durham, *Opera* • [J. Stevenson], ed., *Liber vitae ecclesiae Dunelmensis*, SurtS, 13 (1841) • F. Barlow, *The English church, 1066–1154: a history of the Anglo-Norman church* (1979) • F. Barlow, *William Rufus* (1983) • W. M. Aird, 'St Cuthbert, the Scots and the Normans', *Anglo-Norman Studies*, 16 (1994), 1–20 • P. Chaplais, 'William of Saint-Calais and the Domesday survey', *Domesday studies: papers read at the novocentenary conference of the Royal Historical Society and the Institute of British Geographers* [Winchester 1986], ed. J. C. Holt (1987), 65–77

St Carilef, William of. *See* St Calais, William of (c.1030–1096).

St Clair, Rosalia. *See* Hall, Agnes C. (1775/6–1846).

St Clair, William, of Roslin (1700–1778), archer and golfer, was born at Roslin Castle, Roslin, in Edinburghshire, Scotland, one of seven children of Alexander St Clair of Roslin (1672–1706) and Jean Sempill, daughter of Robert, seventh Lord Semple. About 1723 he married Cordelia, daughter of Sir George Wishart of Cliftonhall, near Edinburgh; they had three sons and five daughters, all of whom, except one daughter, Sarah, died young. St Clair became a member of the Royal Company of Archers in 1723, in which year he won the Musselburgh arrow. His many successes continued over a fifty-year period, culminating in 1773 in

William St Clair of Roslin (1700–1778), by Sir George Chalmers, 1771

his winning the silver bowl trophy for the 180 yard competition.

In November 1736 St Clair was elected first grand master mason of the grand lodge of Scotland. His appointment proved something of a surprise since it was only in June of that year that St Clair had been admitted a member of Canongate Kilwinning lodge. Lord Home was generally expected to become the first grand master having been endorsed only five days before the election by one of the major organizing bodies, St Mary's Chapel lodge. However, on 22 November St Clair advanced with remarkable alacrity through a series of offices to qualify as a master. The subsequent election meeting was dramatic: Lord Home was not in attendance and St Clair renounced and discharged his purported hereditary grand mastership, whereupon he was appointed grand master. He maintained a lifelong involvement in Scottish freemasonry.

St Clair's golfing successes came later in life, the first evidence of his playing the game dating from 1751. He was the golfing champion, and thereby captain, of the Honourable Company of the Edinburgh Golfers in 1761, 1766, and 1771, and of the Gentleman Golfers of Fife (now the Royal and Ancient Golf Club of St Andrews) in 1764, 1766, and 1768. Until 1764 the champion was identified by the number of 'holes up' he was against other company members. St Clair's round in 1764 at St Andrews was the first medal, or stroke, round ever recorded in golf, calculated by the total number of strokes taken in the round. Over the course, then comprising twenty-two holes, his total of 121 strokes was a wonderful score with the clubs and balls of the time. In respect of his achievement, the very next day the number of holes was reduced to eighteen and that number was subsequently adopted from St Andrews as the standard for courses worldwide.

From 1766 until his death St Clair led the Royal Company of Archers as praesis of the council. At the introduction of each new member he announced, without justification, that the company had the right to form a bodyguard whenever the monarch visited Edinburgh. This claim proved the basis for the company's becoming the royal bodyguard during George IV's visit to Edinburgh in 1822 and on subsequent royal engagements. In later life St Clair was described by Sir Walter Scott as considerably above 6 feet, broad shouldered, with dark grey locks and handsome if somewhat exaggerated features. He died at his home at Liberton Wynd, Edinburgh, on 4 January 1778, and was buried in Edinburgh. The eulogy at his funeral by Sir William Forbes, then grand master mason of Scotland, bore ample tribute to one of the great Scottish sportsmen of his time.   STEVEN REID

Sources R. Douglas and others, *The baronage of Scotland* (1798) · J. B. Paul, *The history of the Royal Company of Archers* (1875) · A. MacKenzie, *History of the lodge Canongate Kilwinning no. 2* (1888) · *Grand Lodge of Scotland year book* (1952) · St Andrews, Lodge Canongate Kilwinning no. 2 minutes, 1735–78, U. St Andr. · W. Forbes, *Scots Magazine*, 40 (1778), 57–60 [funeral oration] · R. W. Saint-Clair, *The Saint-Clairs of the isles* (1898) · R. A. Hay, *Genealogie of the Sainteclaires of Rosslyn* (1835) · *The miscellaneous prose works of Sir Walter Scott*, 7 (1870) · J. Dickson, *Roslin Castle* (1879)

Archives NL Scot., minutes of the Honourable Company of the Edinburgh Golfers, Acc 11208, nos. 1–4 · U. St Andr. L., minutes of Lodge Canongate Kilwinning, no. 2, 1735–78

Likenesses G. Chalmers, portrait, 1771, Royal Company of Archers, Edinburgh [*see illus.*] · A. Ramsay, portrait (posthumous), Lodge Canongate Kilwinning no. 2, Edinburgh; copy, Grand Lodge of Scotland

St Davids. For this title name *see* Philipps, John Wynford, first Viscount St Davids (1860–1938); Philipps, Leonora, Lady St Davids (1862–1915).

Saint-Denis, Michel Jacques [*pseud.* Jacques Duchesne] (1897–1971), theatre director and broadcaster, was born in Beauvais, France, on 13 September 1897, the first of the two children (he had a younger sister) of Charles Saint-Denis, a salesman, and his wife, Marguerite Copeau, the sister of Jacques Copeau (1879–1949). Baptized a Roman Catholic, he was not in later life a practising Christian. His studies at the Collège Rollin, Paris, and the Lycée Hoche, Versailles, where he gained his *baccalauréat*, were disrupted by military service in the First World War, for which he was awarded the Croix de Guerre.

In 1919 Saint-Denis joined his uncle Jacques Copeau as actor, administrator, and secretary-general of the theatre at the Vieux-Colombier, Paris, and he later followed Copeau to a small Burgundian village, Pernand-Vergelesses, to work with an experimental theatre company, Les Copiaus (1924–9). When Copeau disbanded his

Michel Jacques Saint-Denis (1897–1971), by Gordon Anthony, *c.*1947

troupe Saint-Denis gathered around himself the most creative talents in La Compagnie des Quinze, which made its début at the Vieux-Colombier in January 1931 with *Noé* (Noah) by André Obey (1892–1975). The production was received enthusiastically by a small avant-garde coterie and hailed as a new renaissance of the French stage; but the general public did not follow. After a French and European tour, the Quinze were invited by the British Drama League to perform at the Arts Theatre Club in London. Their success was such that the season was extended at the New Theatre, and the Quinze returned to London four more times before their dissolution in 1934.

The overwhelming response of his British colleagues decided Saint-Denis to start afresh in London. In 1935 he directed John Gielgud in *Noah* at the New Theatre; and with Gielgud, Bronson Albery, and Tyrone Guthrie he founded his first school, the London Theatre Studio, in Islington. Concurrently he directed the foremost English actors (Laurence Olivier, Peggy Ashcroft, Michael Redgrave, Alec Guinness, Edith Evans, Gielgud) in a succession of ground-breaking productions in London: *The Witch of Edmonton* (Old Vic, 1936), *Macbeth* (1937), *The White Guard* (Phoenix, 1938), *Twelfth Night* (1938), and, most memorably, *The Three Sisters* (Queen's, 1938). The Second World War forced the closure of the school and interrupted Saint-Denis's directorial career.

At the start of the war, Saint-Denis was posted by the French as liaison officer with the British expeditionary force in France. After Dunkirk he was invited to run the BBC's Free French broadcast (July 1940 – October 1944) under the title 'Les Français parlent aux Français' ('the French speak to the French'). His pseudonym, Jacques Duchesne, refers to a symbolic popular character who, during the French Revolution, was the mouthpiece of the Parisian populace. *Le Père Duchesne* was also an extremist revolutionary paper (1790–94). Duchesne's daily opening statement, 'Today, the nth day of the French people's struggle for its liberation', introduced scrambled news items—censored in France—and a series of eagerly awaited coded 'personal messages', the main channel of communication between Free France in London and resistance movements on the ground. According to an obituarist, on 21 October 1940 Duchesne directed Sir Winston Churchill in his first broadcast in French to France, 'sitting on the Prime Minister's knee while announcing him at the microphone. "We have made history", said Sir Winston when it was over' (*The Times*, 2 Aug 1971).

From 1945 to 1951, in collaboration with Glen Byam Shaw and George Devine, Saint-Denis headed the Old Vic Theatre Centre and Old Vic School; he directed *Oedipus Rex* (Laurence Olivier), *A Month in the Country* (Michael Redgrave), and *Electra* (Peggy Ashcroft). In 1951 he supervised, with the architect Pierre Sonrel, the reconstruction of stage and auditorium at the Old Vic, and the two men were subsequently responsible for the building of the first post-war theatre in France, the Comédie de Strasbourg, which opened in 1957. In 1952 Saint-Denis had returned to France to take charge of the newly created Comédie de l'Est, in Colmar. On moving to Strasbourg, in 1954, he founded the first drama school outside Paris, the École Supérieure d'Art Dramatique, which remains an important training centre.

During the last fifteen years of his life Saint-Denis advised and inspired drama schools and theatre companies in France, Belgium, England, the United States, and Canada. He was involved in the setting-up of the Vivian Beaumont Theatre project and the Juilliard School at the Lincoln Center, New York (1957), the National Theatre School, Montreal (1960), and the Institut National Supérieur des Arts du Spectacle et Techniques de Diffusion (INSAS), Brussels (early 1960s). André Malraux, De Gaulle's minister for culture, appointed him *inspecteur général des spectacles* (1959–1964), and in 1962 Peter Hall invited him to become general artistic adviser and co-director of the Royal Shakespeare Company (RSC) in Stratford upon Avon and London. Saint-Denis directed *The Cherry Orchard* (1961) and *Squire Puntila and his Servant Matti* (1965). He was honoured in France (officier of the Légion d'honneur) and Britain (honorary CBE) and received honorary degrees from the University of Birmingham and Dartmouth College, New Hampshire.

Saint-Denis married in 1923 Marie Ostroga, Copeau's secretary, with whom he had a son (killed in action during the Second World War) and a daughter. The marriage was dissolved, and during the 1930s he had a liaison with Marie-Madeleine Gautier, an actress and designer in his own company, with whom he had a son. In December 1958 he was married a second time, to Suria Magito (1903–1987), a dancer, who was born Valia Maria Alexandra Grell

in Riga, Lithuania. He died at his home, 2 Bloomfield Terrace, London, on 31 July 1971.

In France, in the 1930s, Saint-Denis pioneered a new approach to the art of acting and directing. He laid great stress on respect for the text and on technical proficiency (physical skills, vocal control, mime, masks), and developed 'collective and ensemble creations'. In England he opened the way for new directors and companies like George Devine, Peter Brook, Peter Hall, the English Stage Company, and the RSC. Referring to Saint-Denis's influence upon British theatre over several generations, Peter Hall described him as an 'enemy of dead convention' and deeply suspicious of 'anything which inhibited challenge of change' (Hall, 160–61). After the war he inspired the French 'decentralization programme', which resulted in the creation of theatre spaces and companies in major cities. Ariane Mnouchkine's Théâtre du Soleil and Charles Joris's Théâtre Populaire Romand (French-speaking Switzerland) are two leading troupes which owe much to Saint-Denis's teaching: both are permanent professional companies with full-time apprentices, touring towns and villages, promoting theatrical activities in schools and associations, searching for and creating new styles of presentation, and performing a repertory of classics, new plays, and collective creations. But, as Jane Baldwin asserts, the name of Saint-Denis is rarely invoked, eclipsed by the aura of Jacques Copeau. When he was dubbed 'grand prêtre du théâtre anglais' ('high priest of the English stage') by the obituarist in *Le Monde* (3 Aug 1971), it was high praise indeed, but it also marked the start of a new, posthumous exile.

CLAUDE SCHUMACHER

Sources J. Baldwin, *Michel Saint-Denis and the shaping of the modern actor* [forthcoming] · *The Times* (2 Aug 1971) · *Le Monde* (3 Aug 1971) · *Who's Who en France* (1970) · dossier Saint-Denis, Bibliothèque de l'Arsenal, Paris, 4 Sw 13392 · *WWW, 1971–80* · *International dictionary of theatre*, vol. 3: *Actors, directors and designers* (1996), 677–8 · J. Baldwin, 'Chekhov, the rediscovery of realism: Michel Saint-Denis's production of *Three sisters* and *The cherry orchard*', *Theatre Notebook*, 53 (1999), 96–115 · J. Baldwin, 'The Compagnie des Quinze and the emergence of Michel Saint-Denis', *Theatre History Studies*, 14 (1994) · M. Saint-Denis, *Theatre: the rediscovery of style* (1960) · M. Saint-Denis, 'Mes années au Vieux-Colombier', *Review Europe*, 396–7 (1962), 62–70 · M. Saint-Denis, *Training for the theatre: premises and promises*, ed. S. Saint-Denis-Magito (1982) · P. Hall, *Making an exhibition of myself* (1993)
Archives Bibliothèque de l'Arsenal, Paris, MSS · BL, papers | FILM BFI NFTVA, performance footage
Likenesses G. Anthony, photograph, c.1947, Hult. Arch. [see illus.] · portraits, repro. in Saint-Denis, *Theatre*
Wealth at death £10,860: probate, 9 Aug 1972, CGPLA Eng. & Wales

Ste Barbe [Sancta Barbara], **William de** (c.1080–1152), bishop of Durham, had obscure antecedents. He was presumably a Norman from Ste Barbe-en-Auge in Calvados (*arrondissement* of Lisieux, canton of Mézidon). He occurs at York as clerk and canon during the 1120s in the entourage of Archbishop Thurstan (d. 1140); about 1135 he became dean of York, presiding as such in June 1141 when William Fitzherbert (d. 1154) was chosen to succeed Thurstan. The reforming monastic prelates in the province, convinced that royal interference had imposed an improper candidate, fiercely impugned Fitzherbert's election. In March 1143 Pope Innocent II (r. 1130–43) decreed that its validity was to depend on Ste Barbe's swearing that it had been canonical; he had not made this oath by February 1146, when Eugenius III (r. 1145–53) suspended Fitzherbert.

The political overtones to this imbroglio reflected the need of King Stephen to control the northern sees during the civil war, for David, king of Scots, the ally of the Empress Matilda, reinforcing his acquisitions in England north of Tyne, had in 1139 secured the earldom of Northumberland for his son Henry. When Bishop Geoffrey Rufus of Durham died on 6 May 1141, the Scots tried to intrude David's chancellor, William Cumin (d. 1160), as his successor, and Cumin immediately seized Durham Castle and the bishopric's temporal resources. But a pertinacious local opposition, headed by Prior Roger of Durham and Archdeacon Ranulf (the nephew of Bishop Ranulf Flambard) persuaded Innocent II to order a free election, and to enjoin David to stop supporting Cumin. Escaping to York, the Durham electors there chose William de Ste Barbe as bishop on 14 March 1143, while he was absent attending the legatine council in London that excommunicated Cumin. Ste Barbe was consecrated in Winchester Cathedral on 20 June, and in August made his way to his diocese. At first he was sheltered at Bishopton, north-east of Darlington, by Roger de Conyers, the constable of the bishopric, and then moved to St Giles's Church at Durham; but Cumin's men were too strong, and Ste Barbe withdrew, first to Bishopton, then to a fortress at Thornley, near Kelloe, a few miles south-east of Durham, and finally to Lindisfarne. His difficulties in his bishopric caused him to excuse himself from the consecration of Fitzherbert in late September. Only on 18 October 1144, after gradually winning over Earl Henry and the local lay barons, could Ste Barbe be enthroned in Durham by Fitzherbert; it had been a savage struggle, though lurid partisan denunciations of Cumin's atrocities are probably exaggerated.

Henceforward Ste Barbe depended on the sometimes exigent tolerance of the Scots, who still dominated the area politically. When it came to electing a successor to the deposed Archbishop Fitzherbert at Richmond in the North Riding on 24 July 1147, Bishop William opted for Henry Murdac (d. 1153), favourite of the Yorkshire reformers, against King Stephen's candidate, though his ability to involve himself in the York election dispute was limited by the depredations of Earl William of York (d. 1179). Ste Barbe's episcopacy was continuously troubled by local disorders, and he failed to attend the Council of Rheims, for which he was suspended by the pope. It was presumably Archbishop Murdac who released him from his suspension; grants to the Cistercians of Newminster and Augustinians of Guisborough, made 'at the intervention' of Eugenius III, show Ste Barbe opening his diocese to the influence of reformed monasticism, apparently to the alarm of the monks of Durham. Seventeen *acta* survive

from his episcopate, not all of them free from later tampering. Recording such acts as the settlement of a dispute over precedence between the prior and the archdeacon of Durham, a grant of land in Sherburn to the Durham hospital of St Mary Magdalen, and the dedication of the church of Finchale, they help to explain how, when he died on 13 November 1152, the bishop was in good repute for charity, learning, and prudence. However, a politically ineffective figure, Ste Barbe was less notable for those masterful qualities demanded by the circumstances of his exposed see.   H. S. OFFLER, rev. HENRY SUMMERSON

Sources Symeon of Durham, *Opera* · W. Holtzmann, ed., *Papsturkunden in England*, 2 (Berlin), Abhandlung der Gesellschaft der Wissenschaften zu Göttingen, 3rd ser., 14–15 (1935–6) · H. S. Offler, ed., *Durham episcopal charters, 1071–1152*, SurtS, 179 (1968) · A. Young, 'The bishopric of Durham in Stephen's reign', *Anglo-Norman Durham, 1093–1193*, ed. D. Rollason, M. Harvey, and M. Prestwich (1994), 353–68 · G. V. Scammell, *Hugh du Puiset, bishop of Durham* (1956)
Likenesses seals, repro. in Offler, ed., *Durham episcopal charters*, p. 1, no. 3

Ste Croix, Geoffrey Ernest Maurice de (1910–2000), ancient historian, was born in Macao on 8 February 1910; his father, Ernest Henry de Ste Croix, worked in the Chinese customs service, which had been put under foreign control in the aftermath of the Boxer uprising. On the death of his father in 1914 his mother, Florence Annie MacGowan, daughter of a prominent protestant missionary to China, John MacGowan, took him home to England. She was a fervently committed member of an extreme protestant group, the British Israelites, who identified the British with the lost twelfth tribe of Israel. A devoted only child, he acquired a profound knowledge of the Bible at his mother's knee; it may be supposed that he acquired there too his strong feelings about religion (in later life he often described himself as a 'politely militant' atheist), and a certain earnestness and missionary zeal that always marked him.

Ste Croix (who always spelt his name 'Ste. Croix', with a point after the 'Ste') went to school at Clifton College in Bristol, where he acquired a good grounding in Greek and Latin, and became eminent as a player of racquet games, tennis above all. He won the under-sixteen tennis championship of the south of England and later won several regional tournaments, and competed at Wimbledon in both singles and doubles in 1930, 1931, and 1932. His successes at tennis were mostly achieved in time off granted by an indulgent employer; he had left school at the age of fifteen to work in a solicitor's office in Worthing, eventually qualifying as a solicitor in 1932 and practising as such (latterly in London) until called up in 1940. On 17 September 1932 he married Lucile Hyneman (b. 1902/3).

The tennis-playing solicitor was shaken out of his political apathy by the rise of fascism and Nazism, and in the mid-1930s Ste Croix started to read about politics and became a socialist. He visited Russia for six weeks in 1935 or 1936, but broke with his Stalinist friends in Britain in 1938 and became a Labour Party activist in the Marylebone constituency. During war service in the RAF in the Middle East he resolved to abandon the law and seek a career in teaching. In 1946, encouraged and financially supported by his first wife, Lucile, he took up the Labour government's promise to provide a university education for veterans who desired one, and entered University College, London, as a freshman to read ancient history. In the same year A. H. M. Jones arrived in the department as professor, and the three years of close and constant contact with Jones (student numbers in the department being then tiny) were a decisive and often acknowledged influence. Jones's left-wing sympathies and interest in socio-economic and structural problems made him a congenial teacher, and his very broad chronological range, combined with a mastery of a huge range of primary evidence, was a crucial legacy to Ste Croix.

Ste Croix graduated in 1949 with a high first, and in 1950, through Jones's influence, he was elected to a new post as assistant lecturer in ancient economic history at the London School of Economics. Here he had great difficulty in finding any pupils to teach, but a cluster of masterly articles on disparate and technically challenging topics (Athenian taxation; the Athenian empire; Greek and Roman accounting; the great persecution) was essentially a product of his years at the school. The lucidity and analytical powers here displayed, the ability to ask vividly how particular institutions must have worked or what the consequences of particular practices must have been, were always among his greatest strengths. In 1953, again with Jones's strong support, he was elected tutor in ancient history at New College, Oxford. He failed in his campaign eleven years later to persuade New College to become the first Oxford men's college to admit women, but his article on the subject in the *Oxford Magazine* (15 October 1964, 4–6) helped to change attitudes within the university. He held his New College tutorship and the university lecturership that went with it until he retired in 1977. In 1959 his first marriage was dissolved and he married his second wife, Margaret Gladys Mary Knight, with whom he had two sons. Thenceforward his life was externally uneventful, and very happy except for one tragedy: the suicide in 1964 of his daughter, Carolyn, only child of his first marriage.

Ste Croix's influence in Oxford, as both tutor and lecturer, was enormous. His lecture courses entitled 'The economic background of Athenian politics' and 'The persecution of the Christians in the Roman empire' were famous for their learning, their professionalism (they were accompanied by long stencilled sheets of source references and bibliography, reputedly the first such to be seen in Oxford), their vigour, and their non-standard subject matter and iconoclastic perspectives ('too little too late' is the apophthegm always ascribed to him on the persecution of the Christians). His tutorial method was unorthodox: tutorials lasted two hours, for most of which he talked himself (essays having been handed in and very thoroughly corrected in advance); but prolonged exposure to a man so learned, so opinionated, so lively, and so profoundly committed to getting right every point whether great or small was for many an inspiration, as the string of pupils who went into academic life testifies.

Ste Croix devoted immense amounts of time to preparation for teaching (and also, as senior tutor for several years, to college administration), and, but for the new interests created by it, this socio-economic historian perhaps would not have taken the causes of a war as subject for a major book, *The Origins of the Peloponnesian War* (1972). The characteristic central claim—that responsibility for the war lay not with democratic Athens but with oppressive Sparta—has not been widely accepted, but all subsequent discussion of this topic takes its start from Ste Croix, and there are few issues in fifth-century history on which this very wide-ranging book does not make important observations. He never brought to completion the 'Essays in Greek history' (a set of interconnected studies mostly concerning the growth of the Athenian democracy) on which he was working simultaneously with *The Origins of the Peloponnesian War*, but these were published posthumously under the title *Athenian Democratic Origins*.

In 1973 Ste Croix delivered the three J. H. Gray lectures in Cambridge entitled 'The class struggle in the ancient Greek world', and from them eventually emerged (in 1981) the huge book of the same name. The subtitle 'From the archaic age to the Arab conquests' reveals the Jonesian sweep of the book, in consequence of which more space is devoted to what would conventionally count as Roman rather than Greek history. Conventionally too most people would regard what he wrote as an account of forms of exploitation in the ancient world, not of the class struggle or even of class struggles (about which rather little is in fact said); Ste Croix, however, argues that a proper reading of Marx establishes that for Marx himself 'class struggle' was defined by the fact of exploitation, not by any self-consciousness on the part of a struggling class. The book is a masterpiece (though some would say a theoretically flawed masterpiece, and certainly a very discursive one) of impassioned but always precise, and often wry and amusing, scholarship. Many specific analyses are indispensable reading even for those repelled by the Marxism or unpersuaded by Ste Croix's interpretation of Marx; and the whole has a gargantuan energy. *The Class Struggle* won him the Isaac Deutscher memorial prize for 1982, and international fame. He had already in 1972 been elected a fellow of the British Academy.

On completing *The Class Struggle*, Ste Croix set to work on what he planned to be two further books, both, revealingly, on themes relating to the Judaeo-Christian tradition, one on heresy, schism, and persecution in the later Roman empire and the other on early Christian attitudes to women, sex, and marriage. On the latter topic he delivered seven Townsend lectures at Cornell in 1988; very characteristically, he decided to take in pagan attitudes to women, sex, and marriage too, but this and other expansions of his original themes meant that neither project came near completion. (At one point he became preoccupied with the book of Job, the final editor of which he saw as being, like himself, a foe of Yahweh.) He died, three days short of his ninetieth birthday, on 5 February 2000 in the Churchill Hospital, Oxford, and was cremated at

Oxford crematorium on 14 February. His wife survived him.

Ste Croix combined political and social passion with great learning, great analytic power, and an old-fashioned belief in what he regarded as facts and objective truth. His two books are among the most remarkable achievements of ancient historical writing in the twentieth century.

R. C. T. PARKER

Sources private information (2004) · D. Kyrtatas, A. Matthaiou, and G. Pikoulas, 'Interview with Geoffrey de Ste Croix', *Horos*, 6 (1988), 123–33 · 'Biographical sketch', *Crux: essays presented to G. E. M. de Ste Croix on his seventy-fifth birthday*, ed. P. Cartledge and F. D. Harvey (1985); also pubd sep. as *History of political thought*, 6/2 (1985) · R. Parker, 'Geoffrey Ernest Maurice de Ste. Croix, 1910–2000', *PBA*, 111 (2001), 443–74 · *The Independent* (11 Feb 2000) · *The Guardian* (10 Feb 2000) · *The Times* (10 Feb 2000) · *Daily Telegraph* (11 Feb 2000) · *WW* (2000) · m. cert. [Lucile Hyneman] · d. cert.
Likenesses R. Sorrell, drawing, 1977, New College, Oxford · photograph, repro. in *The Times* · photograph, repro. in *Daily Telegraph* · photograph, repro. in *The Guardian* · photograph, repro. in *The Independent* · photograph, repro. in Parker, 'Geoffrey Ernest Maurice de Ste Croix, 1910–2000', 442

Ste Maure, Benoît de (*fl. c.*1160–*c.*1180), historian and poet, may have been a monk at the Benedictine abbey of Marmoutier. Virtually nothing is known about his life, except that he is more likely to have come from the town of Ste Maure in the Touraine region than from Ste Maure in Champagne. Two long narrative poems in octosyllabic rhymed couplets have been identified as his: the first, the *Roman de Troie* (*c.*1160), with certainty, and the second, the *Chronique des ducs de Normandie* (*c.*1174–1180), with certainty by a majority of scholars, but with hesitation (or not at all) by others. The identification of the Beneeiz de Sainte More of the *Roman de Troie* with the Beneeit of the *Chronique* is based upon linguistic and stylistic evidence, and not on biographical information in the *Chronique*, or on extratextual evidence (of which there is almost none). Although he was a contemporary of Wace who also wrote a poem containing a myth of Trojan descent, the *Roman de Brut* (1155), and a chronicle of the Norman dukes and Anglo-Norman kings, the *Roman de Rou* (*c.*1160–1174), Benoît de Ste Maure was much less forthcoming about his personal circumstances than the Norman poet; in that respect he was more typical of the majority of contemporary authors about whose lives very little is known.

Benoît de Ste Maure's practice of translation was also typical of contemporary practice: he considered the 30,316-line *Roman de Troie* a translation, though it is a lengthy adaptation of two short Latin prose works, the *De excidio Troiae historia* of Dares the Phrygian, and the *Ephemeridos belli Troiani* of Dictys of Crete, pseudo-histories dating from the fourth to the sixth centuries AD. One of the *romans d'antiquité* (French narratives based on classical authors), the *Roman de Troie* traces the legendary history of Troy from the Argonauts to the death of Ulysses upon his return home from the siege. In the *Roman de Troie* where Hector is the main hero rather than Achilles and the story of Troilus and Cressida (or as Benoît calls her, Briseida) is thought to appear for the first time, antiquity is depicted under the guise of twelfth-century feudalism, and the

element of love intrigue is considerable. The *Roman de Troie*, often thought to have been dedicated to Eleanor of Aquitaine based on Benoît's reference to a 'riche dame de riche rei', was extremely popular, widely translated and imitated. According to the scholars who accept the single identity of the author of the *Troie* and of the *Chronique*, it was probably the popularity of the *Troie* that brought the poet to Henry Plantagenet's attention.

Benoît de Ste Maure's chronicle of the Norman dukes, the 44,544-line *Chronique des ducs de Normandie*, was, however, less popular than the *Roman de Troie*. According to Wace, Henry II commissioned 'Maistre Beneeit' to write a history of the Norman dukes, leading Wace to break off the *Roman de Rou* before bringing the narrative up to the reign of Henry II. Although Benoît's chronicle of the Normans is more diffuse and less lucid than Wace's, and is considered by historians to be less reliable, possibly owing to the large amount of panegyric inserted for the benefit of the royal house, notable parallels exist between the *Rou* and the *Chronique* as regards circumstances of composition. Like Wace, Benoît de Ste Maure was at this point in his career writing for Henry's court. He also used the Norman histories of Dudo of St Quentin, William of Jumièges, and William of Poitiers as his primary sources; passages in the *Chronique* suggest that Benoît may have had Wace's *Rou* at hand as well. Again like Wace he did not complete his chronicle of the Norman dukes, ending with the death of Henry II's grandfather, Henry I, in 1135; towards the end of the work Benoît also expresses reservations about his patron's possible displeasure with the work, due perhaps to slow progress. Benoît de Ste Maure devoted less energy than Wace to the military aspects of the Normans' rise to power, and concentrated more on demonstrating the necessary interaction of chivalric with clerical values and interests. He is thereby thought to have made a significant contribution to the medieval theory of the three orders of social organization.

JEAN BLACKER

Sources B. de Sainte-Maure, *Le roman de Troie*, ed. L. Constans, 6 vols., Société des Anciens Textes Français (1904) · Benoît, *La chronique des ducs de Normandie*, ed. C. Fahlin, 4 vols. (1951–79) [vol. 3, O. Södergård, *Glossaire* (1967); vol. 4, S. Sandqvist, *Notes* (1979)] · C. Fahlin, *Étude sur le manuscrit de Tours de la 'Chronique des ducs de Normandie' par Benoît* (1937) · E.-D. Grand, 'Benoît de Sainte-Maure', *La grande encyclopédie*, ed. F. C. Dreyfus, 2 (1886) · H. Andresen, 'Über die von Benoît in seiner normannischen Chronik benutzten Quellen, insbesondere über sein Verhältnis zu Dudo, Wilhelm von Jumièges und Wace', *Romanische Forschungen*, 1 (1883), 327–412 · H. Andresen, 'Über die von Benoît in seiner normannischen Chronik benutzten Quellen, insbesondere über sein Verhältnis zu Dudo, Wilhelm von Jumièges und Wace', *Romanische Forschungen*, 2 (1886), 477–538 · G. Beckmann, *Trojaroman und Normannenchronik: die Identität der beiden Benoît und die Chronologie ihrer Werke* (1965) · J. Blacker, *The faces of time: portrayal of the past in Old French and Latin historical narrative of the Anglo-Norman regnum* (1994) · W. R. Schirmer and U. Broich, *Studien zum literarischen Patronat im England des 12. Jahrhunderts* (1962) · G. Duby, *Les trois ordres ou l'imaginaire du féodalisme* (1978) · P. Sullivan, 'Translation and adaptation in the *Roman de Troie*', *The spirit of the court: fourth congress of the International Courtly Literature Society* [Toronto 1983], ed. G. S. Burgess and R. A. Taylor (1985), 350–59 · P. Eley, 'The myth of Trojan descent and perceptions of national identity: the case of the *Eneas* and the *Roman* *de Troie', Nottingham Medieval Studies*, 35 (1991), 27–40 • J.-G. Gouttebroze, 'Henry II Plantagenêt, patron des historiographes anglo-normands de langue d'oïl', *La littérature angevine médiévale* (1981), 91–105 • *Le 'Roman de Rou' de Wace*, ed. A. J. Holden, 3 vols. (Paris, 1970–73) • P. Eley, 'History and romance in the *Chronique des ducs de Normandie', Medium Ævum*, 68/1 (1999), 81–95 • A. Petit, 'Benoît de Sainte-Maure', *Dictionnaire des littératures de langue française*, ed. J.-P. de Beaumarchais, D. Couty, and A. Rey, [2nd edn], 4 vols. (1994) • B. de Sainte-Maure, *Le roman de Troie: extraits du manuscrit Milan, Bibliothèque ambrosienne, D55*, ed. and trans. E. Baumgartner and F. Vielliard (1998)

Archives Bibliothèque Nationale, Paris, MSS

Ste Mère-Église, William de (*d.* 1224), administrator and bishop of London, took his name from the Norman ducal manor of Ste Mère-Église, where he and his mother had a royal pension in 1195. His family—which may have been connected to that of William de Revières (or Vernon), fifth earl of Devon (*d.* 1217)—was important to him: he bought marriages in England for four kinswomen; he provided for two nephews there; and in the chapter of St Paul's he made three men of his name canons of St Paul's. Presumably he had a clerical but not a university education, since he is never addressed as master. But at some time before 1182 he had won admission to the service of Henry II, and by 1183 he was being styled 'clerk of the chamber'. During Henry's last years he became one of the king's most trusted servants, even attesting royal writs. His power attracted gifts of land and ecclesiastical livings, including the prebend of Haydour-cum-Walton in Lincoln Cathedral. The king also rewarded him with the wealthy deanery of the collegiate church of Mortain.

William remained with Henry up until his death on 6 July 1189, but two months later he had followed Richard I to England. He soon obtained from the new king prebends in the cathedrals of York and London, as well as the prestigious deanery of St Martin's-le-Grand in London. During the ensuing months William was often at court, and seems to have taken up duties in the chamber again. He was supposed to have taken the cross, but accompanied Richard on his crusade only as far as Vézelay. They parted on 4 July 1190, and for nearly three years William's whereabouts are unknown. He is next to be found visiting the captive king in Germany in late March 1193. Hubert Walter, bishop of Salisbury, was also there on his way home from the crusade, and they returned to England together, William carrying Richard's letters nominating Hubert to the archbishopric of Canterbury. When Hubert had been elected, he returned the favour by making William archdeacon of Wiltshire, thus giving him a prebend in Salisbury Cathedral.

In one of Richard's letters William is called 'protonotary', but any connection he had with the chancery must have been brief, since he was soon involved in the raising of the king's enormous ransom. In that connection he made two or three more trips to Germany and accompanied Richard back to England in March 1194. He was in Richard's company almost constantly while the king was in England, including his solemn crown-wearing at Winchester. But when Richard went to France in May, William stayed in England, a very important figure in the government of Hubert Walter, now chief justiciar. For two and a half years William was keeper of the king's escheats in southern England, and during that same time he acted as one of the two justices of the Jews. In the great eyre of 1194 he led one of the circuits, and in the justiciar's court at Westminster he sat once in 1194, occasionally in 1195, and regularly in 1196, though rarely thereafter. William's principal sphere of activity was the exchequer, where he became a highly respected figure. In reward for his service Richard nominated him to the bishopric of London, ordering the election to take place at the royal court in Normandy on 7 December 1198. On 23 May 1199 William made his profession of obedience to Archbishop Hubert Walter and was consecrated in St Katherine's Chapel, Westminster, in the presence of thirteen other bishops.

By then King Richard was dead, and William's first major act as bishop was to participate in the coronation of King John on 27 May 1199. And until June 1208 William's talents were much used by John: he was one of the king's special counsellors; he was sent on diplomatic missions to Germany in 1204 and to Scotland in 1205; he served in the exchequer regularly; he authorized royal writs and assessed royal charters for confirmation; and he often witnessed the king's charters. Many royal gifts, both for himself and his church, showed how high he stood in the king's regard. At the same time, William was also active in the affairs of the church. He obtained a papal confirmation of the deanship of the province of Canterbury for the bishops of London, and three times in the illness or absence of the archbishop William consecrated bishops. He attended a provincial council held by Hubert Walter at Westminster on 19 September 1200. Newly elected abbots of Westminster sought William's blessing in 1200 and in 1213 (the latter while he was in exile in France). He appears to have conducted diocesan business himself, for no episcopal official is known for him. His relations with his canons were good, even with Peter of Blois, archdeacon of London, who presented William with his treatise *De amicitia Christiana*. William was also the recipient of several papal mandates to act as judge-delegate, indicating the pope's confidence in his abilities and integrity.

The death of Hubert Walter in 1205 precipitated a great struggle between King John and Pope Innocent III (*r.* 1198–1216), and William was placed squarely in the middle of it when the pope ordered him, along with the bishops of Ely and Worcester, either to obtain John's acceptance of Stephen Langton as archbishop of Canterbury or to impose an interdict upon the kingdom. After pleading with John for nearly eight months, the three bishops reluctantly proclaimed the interdict on 24 March 1208 and then fled the country. They were to remain in exile for five years, though they were invited back to England to negotiate with the king or the chief justiciar in the summer of 1208 for eight weeks, and twice again in 1209 for shorter periods. But the negotiations came to nothing, and the pope ordered them to excommunicate the king. When that also did not move John, in 1212 William and Eustace of Ely travelled to Rome with Stephen Langton to persuade the pope to authorize the king of France to invade

England. This threat did bring John to heel, and the exiles were able to return to England on 16 July 1213.

After John failed to reconquer his continental possessions in 1214, he returned to find England seething with conspiracies against his rule. Hoping to protect himself with the privileges of a crusader, he took the cross on 4 March 1215 at the hands of the bishop of London in his cathedral. When, in June, John was forced to come to terms at Runnymede, William is represented, along with others, as advising the king to grant the great charter of liberties to his people. William was one of eight bishops at Oxford a month later when John met the barons' representatives to implement Magna Carta. But thereafter William is conspicuous by his absence from all accounts of the baronial war and the French invasion. He may have attended the Fourth Lateran Council; on 29 September 1215 he was in France in the company of two prelates who are known to have gone to Rome. But he appears to have been in his diocese in October 1216 and April 1217; he may have taken up residence in Coggeshall Abbey, where some of his horses were commandeered by royalist troops. William did not attend the first coronation of Henry III nor his first great council at Gloucester in November 1216. But when peace had been made and another charter of liberties was issued on 6 November 1217, it was by the counsel and in the cathedral of the bishop of London. On or about that same date he was present at the reopening of the exchequer, and a year later he was one of the great council present at the inauguration of the new royal seal.

For another three years William served Henry III as he had served his grandfather, uncle, and father. He witnessed a royal document as late as 25 April 1220, and on 5 October he was asked to go to Llywelyn of Wales. But soon afterwards William obtained from the pope permission to resign his bishopric because of his great age. This he did on 25 or 26 January 1221, but retained his episcopal dignity and £100 of the revenues of the see for his maintenance. The custody of Colchester Castle, awarded to him in 1218, he also kept until at least December 1223. But at some point he took the habit of an Augustinian canon at the abbey of St Osyth on the east coast of Essex. There he built a chapel for his burial place, and he established a chantry for his soul, as he also did at St Paul's. He died at St Osyth's in 1224, probably on 27 March, and was buried there the following day. Many years earlier William had been denounced by Gerald of Wales as a mere follower of the court and a familiar of the king, but at his death he was remembered as a man of a great name and not a little authority, as one who had suffered great tribulation for the liberty of the church, and as an example of humility in his resignation of his see.   FRED A. CAZEL, JR.

Sources R. V. Turner, 'William de Sainte-Mère-Église, bishop of London', *Men raised from the dust: administrative service and upward mobility in Angevin England* (1988), 20–34 · R. W. Eyton, *Court, household, and itinerary of King Henry II* (1878) · L. Landon, *The itinerary of King Richard I*, PRSoc., new ser., 13 (1935) · *Selected letters of Pope Innocent III concerning England, 1198–1216*, ed. C. R. Cheney and W. H. Semple (1953) · *Radulphi de Coggeshall chronicon Anglicanum*, ed. J. Stevenson, Rolls Series, 66 (1875) · *Radulfi de Diceto … opera historica*, ed. W. Stubbs, 2 vols., Rolls Series, 68 (1876) · *Ann. mon.* · *Chronica magistri Rogeri de Hovedene*, ed. W. Stubbs, 4 vols., Rolls Series, 51 (1868–71) · *Chancery records* (RC) · *Pipe rolls* · PRO · BL · Bibliothèque Nationale · Canterbury Cathedral Library · Christ's College, Cambridge · M. Richter, ed., *Canterbury professions*, CYS, 67 (1973) · *The historical works of Gervase of Canterbury*, ed. W. Stubbs, 2 vols., Rolls Series, 73 (1879–80) · *The later letters of Peter of Blois*, ed. E. Revell (1993) · D. M. Smith, 'The administration of Hugh of Wells, bishop of Lincoln, 1209–1235', PhD diss., U. Nott., 1970

Saint-Étienne de La Tour, Agathe de (*b. c.*1690, *d.* in or after **1765**), landowner, was probably born in Cap de Sable in the French colony of Acadia (Nova Scotia), the third of the seven children of Acadian seigneur Jacques de Saint-Étienne de La Tour (*c.*1655–*c.*1698) and his wife, Anne (*c.*1668–1754), daughter of Charles Melanson and Marie Dugas. She spent her childhood in Port Royal, the small capital of the Acadian colony, where she was raised as a Roman Catholic. The British conquest of Nova Scotia in 1710 (made official by the signing of the treaty of Utrecht in 1713) encouraged her to abandon the faith of her youth and to become a member of the Church of England in 1712. In the winter of 1712–13 she married a military officer of the British garrison of Annapolis Royal (Port Royal), Edmund Bradstreet (*c.*1698–1718), with whom she had two sons, Simon and John. Widowed in 1718, she married about 1723 another British officer of Annapolis Royal, Hugh Campbell (*d. c.*1730).

Agathe de Saint-Étienne de La Tour had decided earlier on to profit from the British presence in Nova Scotia. In 1714 she convinced her mother, brother, sisters, aunts, and uncles to sign documents that gave to her their shares of their inheritance in the many seigniories of Acadia. By 1725 she was claiming to be the sole *seigneuresse* of all of Acadia, even though traditional French inheritance custom only recognized her claim to a fifth of the seigniorial estates. Many Acadian inhabitants of Nova Scotia, including influential members of her own family, did not recognize her to be the rightful lady of the manor and contested her right to collect seigniorial rents. Even Nova Scotia's British governor, Richard Philipps, thought that she had fraudulently laid claim to the entirety of the Acadian seigniories by misleading and tricking family members.

This opposition did not impress Agathe. Recently widowed, she sailed to England in the autumn of 1731 and personally petitioned the Board of Trade in London in early 1732, alleging that Governor Philipps was collecting for himself 'her' seigniorial rents. The British authorities took advantage of this situation to gain official possession of all seigniorial rights and land in Nova Scotia. Even if they recognized that Agathe de Saint-Étienne de La Tour's land titles were 'very oddly drawn in a way that might render a title here in England questionable' (Shaw, 2.572–3), the members of the Board of Trade agreed on behalf of the crown to purchase her supposed Acadian seigniorial rights for the sum of £2000 in 1734. This sale marked the end of the seigniorial system in Nova Scotia and the beginning of a more aggressive policy of trying to render the Acadian population of the colony real British subjects.

This policy tragically failed because of the refusal of the Acadians to swear an unconditional oath of allegiance to the crown. In 1755 the British colonial authorities of Nova Scotia ordered the expulsion of the Acadians.

Agathe de Saint-Étienne de La Tour went back to Nova Scotia for a short period of time after 1734, but by 1737 she was settled in Kilkenny, Ireland, where her first husband, Edmund Bradstreet, had rich and powerful relatives. She continued to look after the careers of her two oldest sons in the British army, especially John *Bradstreet (1714–1774), who became a major-general and played an important role in the Seven Years' War in North America. Very little is known of her later life except that she continued to receive a pension until 1765 as a widow of two British officers. The precise date and place of her death remain unknown. MAURICE BASQUE

Sources C. J. d'Entremont, 'Saint-Étienne de La Tour, Agathe de', *DCB*, vol. 2 · P. Delaney, 'The husbands and children of Agathe de La Tour', *Cahiers* [Société Historique Acadienne], 25/4 (1994), 263–84 · petitions of Agathe de Saint-Étienne de La Tour Campbell, 1733, PRO, CO, board of trade 8347/271, vol. 6, D:51, fols. 166–71; vol. 7, E:4, fols. 11–13 · W. A. Shaw, ed., *Calendar of treasury books and papers*, 2, PRO (1898) · C. J. d'Entremont, *Histoire du Cap-Sable de l'an mil au traité de Paris (1763)* (1981), vol. 4 · W. G. Godfrey, *Pursuit of profit and preferment in colonial North America: John Bradstreet's quest* (1982)

Archives PRO, petitions of Agathe de Saint-Étienne de La Tour Campbell, 1733, CO, board of trade 8347/271, vol. 6, D:51, fols. 166–71 and 217; vol. 7, E:4, fols. 11–13

Saint-Évremond, Charles de Marguetel de Saint-Denis de (*bap.* 1614, *d.* 1703),

soldier and writer, was baptized at St Denis-le-Gast, near Coutances, Normandy, on 5 January 1614, the third of six surviving children (all sons) of Charles de Saint-Denis (1566–1649), of a well-connected noble family of Basse-Normandie, and Charlotte de Rouville. From the age of nine he spent four years at the Jesuit Collège de Clermont in Paris, a year in Caen, then a further year at the Collège d'Harcourt in Paris. Although initially destined for the law, he had decided by the age of sixteen on a military career. In 1630 he served as an ensign in the attack on Piedmont, and thereafter lived the life of an aristocratic soldier, campaigning in the summer months and enjoying the social and literary pleasures of Paris in the winter. He was known as a brave soldier, a gourmet, and a wit, unconstrained by religious scruples, and independent-spirited to the point of imprudence. A noted swordsman, he developed a duelling thrust that was given his name, 'la botte Saint-Évremond'. He became a close companion of the duc d'Enghien, the future Grand Condé, and fought with distinction in his major battles, including Rocroi (1643), Freiburg (1644), and Nördlingen (1645), in which he was severely wounded in the knee. Shortly after the unsuccessful siege of Lérida (1647) he engaged in unwise private mockery of the great man's foibles, and an enraged Condé dismissed him from his service.

In the Frondes (1649–53) Saint-Évremond sided with the court, and ridiculed its opponents with satirical verve.

Charles de Marguetel de Saint-Denis de Saint-Évremond (*bap.* 1614, *d.* 1703), by Sir Godfrey Kneller, *c.*1693

The devastating satire of his *Retraite de M. le duc de Longueville en son gouvernement de Normandie* was a particular favourite of Cardinal Mazarin's, who was most probably unaware of its authorship. Mazarin was deeply suspicious of Saint-Évremond, and twice imprisoned him for three months in the Bastille (1653, 1658). The reasons are uncertain; but Saint-Évremond was very close to the increasingly powerful *surintendant des finances*, Fouquet, and many details of his life would be clarified if more were known about their relationship.

On 16 September 1652 Saint-Évremond was appointed *maréchal de camp* (roughly equivalent to brigadier), the highest rank that he attained, with a pension of 1000 écus. The post gave great opportunity for self-enrichment. In old age he told his editor Pierre Desmaizeaux that, serving under his friend the duc de Candale in Guyenne, he made the remarkable sum of 50,000 écus (150,000 francs) in one year (BL, Add. MS 4470, fol. 47: omitted from Desmaizeaux's biography); elsewhere his profits are given as 50,000 francs in two and a half years (Silvestre, sig. [b3]v). In 1659 he accompanied Mazarin to St Jean-de-Luz for the negotiations that led to the peace of the Pyrenees. Like many in the army he opposed this peace; he penned a brilliantly outspoken satirical attack on both cardinal and treaty, his notorious *Lettre sur la paix*, which circulated in manuscript. The following year he visited England with the comte de Soissons's embassy to congratulate Charles II on his restoration, and stayed on for six months, probably on a secret mission for Fouquet.

The great change in Saint-Évremond's fortune came with Fouquet's arrest on 5 September 1661. A copy of the

Lettre sur la paix was discovered, and its author's arrest ordered. The work alone does not fully explain the implacable hostility of Colbert, Fouquet's nemesis and successor: Saint-Évremond's real offences were his satirical talent and independence of mind, and probably some deeper implication in Fouquet's affairs. After some weeks in concealment he left France for Holland, moving on to London at the end of November 1661.

Saint-Évremond was well received by Charles II, and found in London a highly congenial society. He enjoyed terms of warm friendship with distinguished courtiers, including the dukes of Buckingham and Ormond, the earls of Bristol, St Albans, and Arlington, Louis Stuart, abbé d'Aubigny, and Lord Crofts. Literary friends included Abraham Cowley and, especially, Edmund Waller.

In 1665 Saint-Évremond moved to Holland on the pretext of ill health, hoping to facilitate his return to France, and perhaps acting as a political agent. He became familiar with both the grand pensionary De Witt and the young prince of Orange, and attended the negotiations for the treaty of Breda (31 July 1667). Otherwise his life was quiet, and he spent much time writing. Through Arlington, whom he had visited in London at least twice, Saint-Évremond was invited back by Charles in May 1670 for the celebrations accompanying the signing of the secret treaty of Dover. Thereafter, apart from one diplomatic mission to Holland in January 1672, Saint-Évremond spent the rest of his life in England.

Saint-Évremond's reputation derived principally from his short, informal critical essays, a form which he is often credited with having invented, and a model for the literary essay of the eighteenth century. The subjects are historical, moral, and literary, the tone that of a gentleman occupying his leisure hours, and writing for his friends. Much of their appeal comes from their personal tone: intelligent, judicious, and well read, Saint-Évremond is the very embodiment of taste, sound judgement, and the unprejudiced urbanity of the *honnête homme*. His intellectual position was essentially a broad-minded sceptical Epicureanism, with a sense of historical relativism and a ready curiosity for new ideas. Before his exile he had been strongly attracted to the Epicureanism of Gassendi; he admired Hobbes, and while in Holland sought out the acquaintance of Spinoza. His favourite authors included Montaigne, Cervantes, and Petronius, for whom, as both writer and man, he professed extraordinary admiration. He appreciated English comic drama despite his limited knowledge of the language, but always preferred French tragedy, especially that of Corneille.

Saint-Évremond produced one substantial historical study, *Réflexions sur les divers génies du peuple romain dans les divers temps de la République* (1665–70; seven chapters are missing from the middle, possibly lost but probably never written). His early reputation had been established by his witty satirical pieces; he also wrote three satirical comedies: the collaborative *La comédie des académistes* (1637, revised as *Les académiciens*, c.1680); *Sir Politick Would-Be* (1662–5), written probably with d'Aubigny and Buckingham, an entertaining study of national types, with the eponymous character and Venetian setting borrowed from Jonson's *Volpone*; and *Les opéra* (1676), inspired by new fashion for opera in France. His other literary remains consist of a considerable quantity of verse—mainly occasional, neatly turned, but scarcely deserving the admiration that his friends expressed—and his correspondence, of which 200 letters survive covering a period of more than sixty years. There was intense public demand for anything bearing Saint-Évremond's name. From 1668 onwards there were constant reprints in Paris and Amsterdam, and English translations, of unauthorized multi-volume editions of his *Œuvres meslées*, each including much that he had not written. His authentic works were collected by Desmaizeaux for the 1705 London edition, with a life by Silvestre. Many further editions followed over the next fifty years, with Desmaizeaux's own full but unreliable life of the author; he also published a collection of spurious works, *Mélange curieux des meilleures pièces attribuées à Mr de Saint-Evremond* (1706).

Saint-Évremond became the most celebrated and well-liked Frenchman in England, admired for his writings and sought after for his good company: he prized friendship and conversation (and good food) as the highest pleasures in life. He never felt the need to master the English language. He was able to give significant help to successive French ambassadors, but his own permission to return to France came only after the accession of William III, some time between 1688 and 1690. He replied to his old friend the comte de Grammont that he was now too aged, too out of touch, and too happy in England to accept.

Despite early difficulties Saint-Évremond lived comfortably enough in his exile, helped by generous friends and the goodwill of successive monarchs. In 1670 Charles II granted him a pension of £300 and named him governor of the ducks in St James's Park. Apart from this undemanding post he refused any official role: when James II offered him the position of secretary for the king's foreign correspondence he declined, using his age as an excuse. William III showed him marked favour, enjoying his company and (with a perhaps uncharacteristic touch of humour) renewing his governorship of the ducks and attendant pension.

The greatest friendship of Saint-Évremond's later years was that of the dazzling adventuress Hortense Mancini, duchesse de Mazarin, the cardinal's niece, who arrived in England aged twenty-nine in December 1675. Captivated by her beauty and wit, and especially her dynamic unconventionality, Saint-Évremond became one of her closest circle, celebrating her (not without some self-mockery) in hyperbolic verse and prose until her death on 2 July 1699. He then found another beauty to celebrate in Madame de La Perrine. He never married. Desmaizeaux wrote: 'M. de Saint-Évremond n'avoit pas un penchant extraordinaire pour le beau Sexe', although he engaged in a number of love affairs: he was one of the first lovers of the celebrated Ninon de Lenclos (1620–1705), and, typically, maintained the friendship throughout their long lives. There are suggestions in his writings of, at the least, an uncensorious acceptance of bisexuality in others.

Saint-Évremond's appearance was described by Silvestre:

M. de Saint-Évremond was well made. As he had in youth taken part in all manly exercises, he retained, even to a very advanced age, a natural and easy carriage. His eyes were blue, keen, and full of fire, his face bright and intelligent, his smile somewhat satirical. In youth he had had fine black hair, but though it had become quite white, and even very sparse, he never would wear a wig, and contented himself with wearing a skull-cap. More than twenty years before his death a wen developed at the root of his nose, and grew to a good size, but this did not disfigure him very much, at least in the eyes of those who saw him habitually. His conversation was gay and easy, his repartees lively and incisive, his manners good and polite; in a word, one can say of him that in all things he showed himself to be a man of quality. (Silvestre, sig. [c3]v; translation from *DNB*)

For all his social celebrity Saint-Évremond grew increasingly negligent of his personal appearance, and lived in conditions that were considered insalubrious even by seventeenth-century standards. His house in Pall Mall was full of animals of all kinds, dogs, cats, birds, and a monkey: he excused the mess by saying that as he grew old he needed to be surrounded by life and energy. In his ninetieth year he began to suffer from urinary problems, attributed by Silvestre to an ulcer in the bladder. He knew his end was near when he lost his appetite, and made his will on 24 August 1703. His estate was worth about £800. He left bequests to friends and servants; his books and manuscripts to his executor Lord Galway, son of his old friend the marquis de Ruvigny, and to Silvestre; and two sums of £20 to be distributed to impoverished Huguenot refugees and to the poor of the Roman Catholic 'or any other religion'.

Saint-Évremond died on 9 September 1703 at his home, alert to the last, and refusing to be attended by any minister of religion. He was buried in Poets' Corner in Westminster Abbey, despite the facts that he was French and wholly without religious belief, and that not a line of his undistinguished verse was written in English. Unsurprisingly this occasioned some criticism; but it appropriately reflects the exceptional status Saint-Évremond had attained, as almost a national institution.

RICHARD MABER

Sources P. Silvestre, 'Préface', in *Œuvres meslées de Mr de Saint-Évremond*, ed. P. Silvestre and P. des Maizeaux, 2 vols. (1705), sigs. [a3]–[c4]v • P. Desmaizeaux, 'Vie de Mr de Saint-Évremond', *Mélange curieux des meilleures pièces attribuées à Mr de Saint-Evremond* (1706) [rev. and expanded in successive eighteenth-century edns of the *Œuvres meslées*] • C. M. S. Saint-Évremond, *Œuvres en prose*, ed. R. Ternois, 4 vols. (Paris, 1962–9) • Q. M. Hope, *Saint-Evremond and his friends* (1999) • Q. M. Hope, *Saint-Evremond: the 'honnête homme' as critic* (1962) • H. T. Barnwell, *Les idées morales et critiques de Saint-Évremond* (1957) • *Lettres [de] Saint-Évremond*, ed. R. Ternois, 2 vols. (Paris, 1967–8) • *DNB*
Archives BL, notebook containing records of conversations, Pierre Desmaizeaux, Add. MS 4470
Likenesses G. Kneller, oils, *c*.1693, Althorp, Northamptonshire [*see illus.*] • attrib. J. Parmentier, oils, 1701, NPG • B. Arlaud, engraving (after portrait attrib. J. Parmentier, 1701), repro. in Saint-Évremond, *Œuvres meslées* (1705) • Edelinck, engraving (at eighty-five), repro. in [C. Cotolendi], *Saint-Evremoniana, ou, Dialogues des nouveaux dieux* (Paris, 1700) • P. van Gunst, line engraving (after portrait attrib. J. Parmentier), BM, NPG; repro. in *Œuvres meslées*, 2nd edn (1709) • P. van Gunst, sculpture (after portrait attrib. J. Parmentier, 1701), repro. in Saint-Évremond, *Œuvres meslées* • R. White, line engraving (after portrait by G. Kneller), BM, NPG; repro. in *The works of Mr de St Evremont*, 2 vols. (1700) • bust, Westminster Abbey, Poets' Corner • engraving (after portrait by Kneller), repro. in *The works of Monsieur de St Evremont*, 2nd edn, ed. and trans. P. des Maizeaux, 3 vols. (1728)
Wealth at death £800: Saint-Évremond, *Œuvres en prose*, ed. Ternois, vol. 1, pp. liii–liv; *DNB*

St Faith, Benedict (*d.* 1410). *See under* St Faith, John (*d.* 1359).

St Faith, John (*d.* 1359), Carmelite friar and theologian, was one of several distinguished members of his order bearing that name. However, there was no significant link between them except their surname, which may indicate that they were all born in, or could trace their ancestry back to, the villages of Horsham St Faith or Newton St Faith just north of Norwich. John joined the Carmelites at Burnham Norton, near the north coast of Norfolk, and incepted as a DTh at Oxford. Nothing is known about his life except that he returned to Burnham Norton, where he was prior until his death on 18 September 1359. Bale preserves the titles of sixteen of his compositions, many with incipits, including a postil and related works on St John's gospel, another on St Matthew, a commentary on Aristotle's *De coelo et mundo*, a concordance to the works of Thomas Aquinas, and sixty-three sermons. None survives, but one, 'In praise of John the Evangelist, on the vocation to poverty and its virtues', gives a glimpse of his approach.

The other Carmelites with this surname joined the order in Norwich. **Benedict St Faith** (*d.* 1410), Carmelite friar and diplomat, served Enrico Minutolo, cardinal-archbishop of Naples, and accompanied him when he went as legate to Bologna and Ravenna. He died in Naples in 1410. **Peter St Faith** (*d.* 1452), theologian and prior of Norwich, of noble birth, incepted as DTh at Cambridge and Paris (*c*.1425), where he was one of a group of English Carmelites sent to lecture in the Carmelite studium there while the city was under English control. In 1428 he was present in Norwich at the heresy trial of William White, and in 1429 for the trial of John Skylly. He was prior there in 1443 and a representative for the Norwich distinction at a meeting called to discuss reform in 1446. On 1 March 1449 he received a dispensation to hold a benefice, and on 10 March 1451 he was admitted as rector of Taverham, Norfolk. He died on 8 November 1452 and was buried in the Carmelite chapel, Norwich. **Robert St Faith** (*d.* 1386), Carmelite friar and papal official, worked in Rome and acted as a legate for Pope Urban VI (*r.* 1378–89) to England and Spain. He died in Spain in 1386, possibly accompanying the expedition of John of Gaunt, duke of Lancaster. **William St Faith** (*d.* 1372), Carmelite friar and theologian, incepted as DTh at Cambridge. He was there on 9 September 1337, when he was admitted to hear confessions in the diocese of Ely, and again on 4 April 1343. He died on 25

April 1372 and was buried in the Carmelite house, Norwich. Bale saw four of his works in the library there, a collection of *determinationes*, two *quaestiones*, and a collection of *benedictiones*. RICHARD COPSEY

Sources Bodl. Oxf., MS Bodley 73 (SC 27635), fols. 2, 20, 36, 51*v*, 58, 119, 120, 135*v*, 197*v*, 199*v*, 205*v* · Bodl. Oxf., MS Selden supra 41, fols. 168*v*, 173*v*, 373*v* · BL, Harley MS 3838, fols. 33*v*, 73–73*v*, 76*v*, 101*v*, 180, 183*v*, 208 · Bale, *Cat.*, 1.441, 478, 506, 593; 2.156–7 · *Commentarii de scriptoribus Britannicis, auctore Joanne Lelando*, ed. A. Hall, 2 (1709), 363–4 · J. Pits, *Relationum historicarum de rebus Anglicis*, ed. [W. Bishop] (Paris, 1619), 482–3, 510, 647–8, 826–7, 901 · C. de S. E. de Villiers, *Bibliotheca Carmelitana*, 2 vols. (Orléans, 1752); facs. edn, ed. P. G. Wessels (Rome, 1927), vol. 1, pp. 262, 597, 845–6; vol. 2, pp. 87–8, 691 · Tanner, *Bibl. Brit.-Hib.*, 51 · Emden, *Oxf.*, 2.1625 · Emden, *Cam.*, 502, 565

St Faith, Peter (*d.* 1452). *See under* St Faith, John (*d.* 1359).

St Faith, Robert (*d.* 1386). *See under* St Faith, John (*d.* 1359).

St Faith, William (*d.* 1372). *See under* St Faith, John (*d.* 1359).

St Faith's, John of. *See* St Faith, John (*d.* 1359).

St George, Sir Henry (1581–1644), herald, was born on 27 January 1581 at Hatley St George, Cambridgeshire, the fourth of eight children and third of five sons of Sir Richard *St George (1554/5–1635), Clarenceux king of arms, and his wife, Elizabeth, eldest daughter of Nicholas St John of Lydiard Tregoze, Wiltshire. Details of his education are unknown. He was created Rouge Rose pursuivant-extraordinary in May 1610, a warrant to deliver a tabard to him being dated 11 December 1609. The patent creating him Bluemantle pursuivant is dated 18 December 1611, and he accompanied his father in his visitations of Derbyshire (1611) and of Cheshire (1614).

On 15 May 1614 St George married at Lillingstone Dayrell, Buckinghamshire, Mary (*bap.* 1585, *d.* 1646), daughter of Sir Thomas Dayrell of that place. He was appointed Richmond herald by patent on 11 March 1616. On 3 March 1618 he was admitted to Gray's Inn, and he acted as William Camden's deputy for the visitations of Cambridgeshire in 1619, of Devon and Cornwall in 1620, and of Wiltshire, Dorset, and Somerset in 1623. In 1625 he and William Le Neve, Mowbray herald-extraordinary, were sent to France to bring Queen Henrietta Maria to England; the king of France was so pleased with the way in which they performed their mission that he gave them 1000 French crowns. In 1627 he was a member of a mission to invest the king of Sweden with the Order of the Garter. The king knighted him on 23 September 1627 in his military camp at Darsau in Prussia and gave him an augmentation to his arms of the royal arms of Sweden on a gold canton; this was one of the last cases of an augmentation of English arms by a foreign sovereign.

In 1628 James Balfour (1600–1657), subsequently Lyon king of arms, dined with the English heralds and noted their talents; Sir Henry St George's skills were given as genealogy and pedigree. Between 1633 and 1635 he acted as his father's deputy for the visitation of London, and on the promotion of William Le Neve to the vacancy created by the death in 1635 of his father, St George was created

Norroy king of arms by patent dated 24 June 1635. As Norroy he made no visitations. In April 1639 he was suspended and fined by the earl marshal for forging his father's signature on a faked grant of arms, but he was restored with a pardon under the great seal on 6 April 1640. During the civil war he accompanied the king to Oxford; Wood states that he was created doctor of medicine there on 9 May 1643.

Following the death at Oxford of Sir John Borough, Garter king of arms, on 21 October 1643, St George was appointed Garter, though his patent is dated as late as 6 April 1644. He died at Brasenose College, Oxford, on 5 November 1644 and was buried on 6 November at Christ Church Cathedral in that city. Letters of administration to his estate, in which he is described as of Lee Gardens, a manor which he purchased in 1635 in the parish of Hornchurch, Essex, were granted to his daughter Mary on 31 October 1646. His manuscript collections passed to his son Sir Henry St George the younger; some which were sold privately to John Percival, first earl of Egmont, are now in the British Library (Add. MSS 47170–47200) and others are in the Harley collection.

Sir Henry and his wife, Mary Dayrell, had eleven children. Four of their five sons survived childhood; two of them are noticed below. The second son, William St George (1620–1645), was a colonel in the royalist army killed at the storming of Leicester, and the fourth son, Richard St George (*d.* 1715), was Ulster king of arms from 1660 to 1683.

Sir Thomas St George (1615–1703), herald, the eldest child, lived at Woodford in Essex, but details of his education and early life are unknown. In or before 1646 he married Clara (*bur.* 14 November 1691 at Woodford), daughter of the Revd John Pymlowe, with whom he had six children. At the Restoration he was appointed Somerset herald by patent dated 10 August 1660. As deputy to Garter he went on a mission to Dresden and invested the elector of Saxony on 13 April 1669 with the Order of the Garter. He was knighted on 1 June 1669 and appointed Norroy king of arms by signet dated January 1680, in succession to his younger brother Henry, but did not receive a visitation commission. The seniority was reversed when, by patent dated 11 March 1686, he was appointed Garter. When William III invested the duke of Brunswick-Lüneburg with the Order of the Garter at The Hague on 8 April 1691 St George was in attendance. He married secondly in November 1692, at Wanstead, Essex, Anne (*d.* 14 Feb 1721), daughter of Sir John Lawson and widow of William Attwood. Their one daughter died in infancy. In 1693 he and his brother Sir Henry were appointed commissioners for the rebuilding of St Paul's Cathedral. He died at the College of Arms on 6 March 1703 and was buried on 11 March at Woodford. His manuscripts were purchased by Peter Le Neve, Norroy king of arms, and were dispersed with Le Neve's collections. According to Noble, 'he died more esteemed as a good, and more respected as an elegant man, than praised for his knowledge' (Noble, 332).

Sir Henry St George (1625–1715), herald, the eighth child and third son, was born in July 1625 in St Andrew's parish, Hertford. Nothing is known of his life before 1660. He was appointed Richmond herald at the Restoration by patent dated 18 June 1660, some weeks before his elder brother Thomas was appointed a herald, and was consequently senior to him. As deputy to Garter king of arms he went on a mission to Stockholm and on 29 July 1669 invested the king of Sweden with the Order of the Garter. He was appointed Norroy king of arms by patent dated 27 April 1677, was knighted on 25 May 1677, and was promoted Clarenceux king of arms by patent dated 28 January 1680. He received a visitation commission on 24 June 1680 and was responsible for visiting twelve counties south of the Trent between 1681 and 1700, giving the profits of six as a contribution towards rebuilding the College of Arms, which had been burnt in the great fire. Following his elder brother's death he was appointed Garter king of arms by patent dated 16 June 1703. He died at the College of Arms on 12 August 1715 and was buried in St Benet Paul's Wharf, London, on 18 August. He married at an unknown date Elizabeth Wingfield (d. 3 November 1704 at the College of Arms, and buried at Woodford) and had no children. The College of Arms recovered with difficulty from his executor certain books belonging to it. A large number of manuscripts were sold to John Percival, first earl of Egmont, for £500; a further 216 of his manuscripts together with thirty-three pedigree rolls were offered for sale in 1738 and 1739 by Thomas Osborne, a bookseller in Gray's Inn. The College of Arms was given fourteen volumes in 1846 and purchased a further fourteen (formerly Phillipps MS 13084) from Sir Anthony Wagner. His successor as Garter, John Anstis, called Sir Henry 'a timorous animal, governed by every creature, minding only his iron chest and the contents of it' (Noble, 354).

THOMAS WOODCOCK

Sources W. H. Godfrey, A. Wagner, and H. Stanford London, *The College of Arms, Queen Victoria Street* (1963), 50–51, 55–6 · M. Noble, *A history of the College of Arms* (1804), 234–5, 331–3, 352–4 · A. R. Wagner, *The records and collections of the College of Arms* (1952), 38, 39, 58, 60, 73, 80–82 · C. E. Wright, *Fontes Harleiana* (1972), 292–3 · Wood, *Ath. Oxon.: Fasti* (1820), 67 · *Miscellanea Genealogica et Heraldica*, new ser., 3 (1880), 77–84 · A. Wagner, *Heralds of England: a history of the office and College of Arms* (1967), 121, 231, 254, 264, 278, 281, 294, 295–9, 300, 308, 310–11, 315, 317, 320–21, 326, 330, 331–3, 335–6, 346–7, 544 · *Collectanea Topographica & Genealogica*, 6 (1840), 98 · *Heralds commemorative exhibition catalogue, 1484–1934* (1970), 61 · *IGI* · *VCH Essex*, 7.35 · J. Le Neve, *Monumenta Anglicana* (1717), 53, 90, 303 · J. L. Chester and J. Foster, eds., *London marriage licences, 1521–1869* (1887), 1175 · *N&Q*, 5 (1852), 252–3 · P. G. Begent and H. Chesshyre, *The most noble Order of the Garter: 650 years* (1999), 127, 207–8, 235, 237–8, 283, 375, 388 · A. Wood, *The history and antiquities of the colleges and halls in the University of Oxford*, ed. J. Gutch (1786), 509

Archives All Souls Oxf., heraldic MSS · BL, Add. MSS 47170–47200 · BL, genealogical notes and collection, Add. MSS 47171–47175, 47178–47179, 47182–47189, 47195 · BL, grants of arms, Add. MS 14295 · BL, heraldic and genealogical commonplace book, Add. MS 52801 · BL, treatise of honour, Harley MS 4145 · BL, visitation records, pedigrees, papers relating to creation of knights at coronation of Charles I, Add. MSS 4962, 27984, 34101, 47174, 47180, 47184, 52801 · Bodl. Oxf., heraldic notes made by him and his son, MS Eng. misc. c. 16 · Bodl. Oxf., memoranda and papers relating to Garter ceremonies, etc., MSS Rawl. statutes 31–33 · Coll. Arms [Sir Henry St George the younger] | BL, church notes made by him and Nicholas Charles, Lansdowne MS 874 · BL, Harley MSS 6148, 6213, 6238, 6250, 6589, 6591 · BL, Lansdowne MS 285 · BL, visitation of Hertfordshire, Stowe MS 615 [copy] · Bodl. Oxf., letters to A. Wood, MS Wood F44 · CUL, heraldic visitation of Cambridgeshire · Gon. & Caius Cam., John Knight collection, heraldic MSS, incl. ordinaries, pedigrees, and commonplace book, MSS 535, 539, 546, 550, 554, 564, 567

Likenesses N. Dixon?, miniature (Sir Henry St George the younger) · P. Lely, drawing (probably Sir Thomas St George and Sir Henry St George the younger), Albertina Gallery, Vienna; repro. in Wagner, *Heralds of England*, pl. xxiv

Wealth at death Sir Henry St George: will, Dec 1715, PRO, PROB 11/549, sig. 248 · Sir Thomas St George: will, PRO, PROB 11/469, sig. 58

St George, Sir Henry (1625–1715). *See under* St George, Sir Henry (1581–1644).

St George, James [*known as* Master James of St George] (d. 1306×9), military engineer, is first recorded as Master James, son of Master John *cementarius*, working in 1261 with his father on the castle of Yverdon for Count Peter of Savoy, earl of Richmond (d. 1268); by 1265 he was chief master mason. In the 1260s and 1270s he was concerned with works throughout Savoy, notably Aosta, Chillon, and St Georges-d'Espéranche. He worked with the count's military engineer, Sir John de Masoz, knighted by Henry III after the siege of Bénauges (1254). It is probable that James, and the brothers Tassin and Giles of St George, masons named in the building accounts of Saxon (Valais) in 1279/80, all sprang from the well-authenticated 'de sancto Jorio' family, originating at St Jeoire in Faucigny. But it is also possible that the surname by which he was known in England reflects his connection with the building of Count Philip of Savoy's castle of St Georges in the Viennois, which was nearing completion when Philip, who had succeeded his brother Count Peter in 1268, did homage there to his great-nephew, the as yet uncrowned Edward I, during Edward's return from crusade in 1273. Works were then also proceeding within a day's ride of St Georges at Voiron, La Cote, and St Laurent-du-Pont, visits to which might have occasioned Edward's first acquaintance with James's person and capabilities. Only for St Laurent, where the castle itself has disappeared, is there a substantial works account; in it 'tasks' are assigned 'per dominum J de Masout et Magistrum Jacobum' in the same terms as they are later authorized 'per dominum J de Bonovillario [deputy of Sir Otto Grandson] et Magistrum Jacobum' at Conwy.

James St George first appears in English records in March 1278, when as Master James *ingeniator* he travelled to Wales 'to ordain the works of the castles there' (*History of the King's Works*, 1.320). He thus assumed control of the works begun in July 1277, probably under the ageing Master Bertram *ingeniator* (d. 1284), at Flint, Rhuddlan, Ruthin, Aberystwyth, and Builth, at each of which the ground plan had been determined and building started several months before his arrival. By the outbreak of the second Welsh war in March 1282, Rhuddlan was complete and the others well advanced. St George proceeded to Aberystwyth 'ad castrum regis ibidem construendum'; in July 1282 he ordered the demolition of the old keep at Hope. Later, as James *machinator*, he was involved with works at

Ruthin and Denbigh. In January 1283 he was at the siege of the castle of Dolwyddelan, whose nodal position made its capture crucial to the English conquest of Snowdonia.

The programme of castle building which St George now directed as 'master of the king's works in Wales' marked the climax of his career. The castle and walled town of Conwy, adjudged together to be 'incomparably the most magnificent of Edward I's Welsh fortresses' (Taylor, 'Edward I's castle building', 38), were begun in March 1283 and virtually completed by late 1287. Harlech, started in May 1283, was finished in 1289. Caernarfon was begun in June, but not completed in St George's lifetime. With its polygonal towers and decorative banding in the imperial style of Constantinople, Caernarfon was envisaged as the state capital of a future dynasty of English princes of Wales, and was designed on an altogether grander scale than its contemporaries. Its creation has been attributed to Walter of Hereford, builder of Edward's abbey of Vale Royal, who took charge when construction was resumed after damage by the Welsh in 1294. Nowhere, however, is Walter named in connection with the initial, creative campaign of the 1280s, when Caernarfon was conceived as the visible embodiment of Macsen Wledig's dream of 'a mighty castle, the fairest man ever saw' (*Mabinogion*, 1.137). Realization of so special an assignment would surely be entrusted to the king's chief military architect.

In December 1280 St George was granted letters of protection for seven years, probably the estimated time for completing the works he took over in 1278. In 1284 his responsibility for the operations launched a year earlier was put on a permanent footing with the grant of 3s. a day for life and a future widow's pension of 1s. 6d. a day for his wife, Ambrosia, should she survive him. There is no further mention of Ambrosia in the records and possibly she is to be identified with the 'Dame Ambroise de Saint-Joire' named in 1288 among the first entrants to the Carthusian nunnery of Melan (Haute-Savoie), founded in 1282 by Beatrice de Faucigny. St George himself was appointed in 1290 to the constableship of his newly completed Harlech Castle.

The defeat of the Welsh rising of 1294 led to the inception in 1295 of St George's last great commission, Beaumaris Castle in Anglesey, Britain's most perfect example of the concentric castle plan. The first eighteen months saw phenomenal progress, with a labour force of 3000 men, 400 of them masons, and expenditure of over £10,000. Thereafter the more urgent demands of Gascony and Scotland reduced the average yearly outlay to a mere £300. From 1298 to 1305 St George was with the king in Scotland, where he executed works at Linlithgow and Kildrummy castles; in 1304 he was probably directing engineer of the siege works at Stirling. He resumed work at Beaumaris in 1306 but died before May 1309.

On any reckoning St George's achievement in the field of medieval military architecture was outstanding. His was the genius that enabled Edward I to raise great fortresses by threes and fours in the space of five or six summers. Unstereotyped, of striking beauty and enduring strength, the north Wales castles have survived as a unique and lasting monument to their age and their creator.　　　　　　　　　　　　ARNOLD TAYLOR

Sources records of wardrobe and household, PRO [especially exchequer accounts various, E101, and chancery miscellanea, C47] · Archivio di Stato, Turin · Archives Departementales de la Savoie, Chambéry · Archives Departementales de la Côte d'Or, Dijon · Archives Departementales de l'Isère, Grenoble · A. J. Taylor, 'Master James of St George', *EngHR*, 65 (1950), 435–57 · A. J. Taylor, 'Edward I's castle building in Wales', *PBA*, 32 (1946), 15–81 · A. J. Taylor, 'The king's works in Wales 1277–1330', *The history of the king's works*, ed. H. M. Colvin and others, 1 (1963), 293–408 · A. J. Taylor, 'Castle-building in thirteenth-century Wales and Savoy', *PBA*, 63 (1977), 265–92 · A. J. Taylor, 'Master Bertram, *ingeniator regis*', *Studies in medieval history presented to R. Allen Brown*, ed. C. Harper-Bill (1989), 289–304 · A. J. Taylor, *Studies in castles and castle-building* (1985), 88–97 · *The Mabinogion*, ed. T. P. Ellis and J. Lloyd, 2 vols. (1929), 1.137 · *CPR, 1281–92*, 137

St George, Sir John (1812–1891), army officer, born at Stafford on 18 January 1812, was the eldest son of Lieutenant-Colonel John St George of Parkfield, Birkenhead, and his wife, Frances, daughter of Archibald Campbell MD. He obtained a cadetship at the Royal Military Academy, Woolwich, in 1826, and was commissioned second lieutenant in the Royal Artillery on 19 May 1828. He became first lieutenant on 11 July 1829, captain on 1 April 1841, and lieutenant-colonel on 17 February 1854. He served in Canada, the West Indies, China, and Ceylon, and was for two years (1844–6) instructor in practical artillery at the Royal Military Academy.

In 1855 St George was ordered to the Crimea. He arrived there in March, and commanded the reserve artillery and later the siege train. Sir Richard Dacres, in his report of the artillery operations which preceded the fall of Sevastopol, said that he had rendered the greatest assistance. He was made brevet colonel and CB on 4 February 1856; he also received the Mejidiye (fourth class) and the Légion d'honneur.

St George commanded the Royal Artillery in Malta for two years, becoming colonel in the regiment on 29 August 1857. In 1859 he was made president of the ordnance select committee, and remained so until December 1863, when he was appointed director of ordnance. He held this office for five years, and he was thus for nearly ten years continuously at headquarters, in positions of the highest responsibility at a critical period in the development of artillery. He became major-general on 30 September 1865, having been given the temporary rank previously as director of ordnance.

In October 1868 St George went to St Petersburg as British delegate to the conference held there, at the instance of the Russian government, on the subject of explosive (dumdum) bullets. By the declaration of 11 December, the powers represented renounced their use. This was his last military employment. He was promoted lieutenant-general on 29 March 1873, and general on 1 October 1877, and was retired on 1 July 1881. He was made KCB on 2 June 1869 and GCB on 25 May 1889. He became a colonel-commandant RA, on 31 January 1872, and in 1884 he was appointed to the honorary office of master gunner of St James's Park.

St George was active in the order of the hospital of St John of Jerusalem, of which the English *langue* was reorganized in 1831. He was made a chevalier of justice in 1861, and was chancellor (1888–90) when the order received a royal charter. He was also a member of the order of the Friendly Brothers of St Patrick. St George married, on 15 August 1860, Elizabeth Marianne, daughter of Thomas Evans of Lyminster House, Arundel; she survived her husband and they had one son. St George died at his residence, 22 Cornwall Gardens, South Kensington, London, on 17 March 1891, and was buried at Brompton cemetery.   E. M. LLOYD, *rev.* JAMES FALKNER

Sources *Army List* · J. R. J. Jocelyn, *History of royal artillery — Crimean period* (1911) · *LondG* (2 Nov 1855) · *Hart's Army List* · *Minutes of the Proceedings of the Royal Artillery Institution*, 18 (1891) · Boase, *Mod. Eng. biog.* · Kelly, *Handbk*
Likenesses Maull & Fox, photograph, *c*.1880, priv. coll.
Wealth at death £13,435 10*s*. 7*d*.: probate, 16 April 1891, *CGPLA Eng. & Wales*

St George, Sir Richard (1554/5–1635), herald, was the second of two children, both sons, of Francis St George (*d.* 1584) of Hatley St George, Cambridgeshire, and his wife, Rose, daughter of Thomas Hutton of Dry Drayton, Cambridgeshire. The St George family had been of note in the county since the twelfth century, though land sales in the sixteenth century had somewhat reduced their standing. He matriculated at Cambridge from St John's College at Easter 1569. In 1575 he married Elizabeth, eldest of five daughters and one of the eight children of Nicholas St John (*d.* 1589) of Lydiard Tregoze, Wiltshire, MP. He and his wife also had eight children, all born at Hatley St George between 1577 and 1595.

St George entered the College of Arms as the result of dissensions among the kings of arms, which led to an inquiry in 1596 made on behalf of the commissioners for the office of earl marshal. The immediate result was the appointment on 23 October 1597 of William Camden (1551–1623) as Clarenceux king of arms after he had been made Richmond herald the previous day to qualify him. Camden and St George were two members of a Society of Antiquaries founded about 1586, and according to Noble (Noble, 236) the commissioners for the office of earl marshal wished to appoint St George Norroy king of arms, a position which in 1597 had been vacant for four years. Like Camden, St George had no previous service as a herald, and as a result of opposition from the other officers of arms William Segar, Somerset herald, was created Norroy on the same day as Camden was appointed Clarenceux. It was not until 22 April 1602 that St George was appointed Berwick pursuivant-extraordinary as a preliminary to being created Windsor herald on the same day.

The patent creating St George Norroy king of arms in succession to Sir William Segar is dated 24 January 1607. In that year he owned the roll of arms of *c*.1285, now known as St George's roll, and lent it to Nicholas Charles, Lancaster herald, to copy. As Norroy he carried out visitations of many of the northern counties in his province, going to Derbyshire (1611), Yorkshire (1612), Lancashire (1613), Cheshire, Nottinghamshire, and Staffordshire (1614), and Northumberland and Durham (1615). In 1615 he was responsible for providing the heraldic and genealogical information to enable his wife's nephew Sir John St John, bt (*d.* 1648), to erect the great painted triptych in Lydiard Tregoze church to his parents and ancestors, and St George also supplied the material for the St John heraldic window in Battersea church. John Weever, who had been travelling throughout England collecting inscriptions from funeral monuments, refers to him as 'a gentleman always ever ready to give me his best furtherance in this worke' (J. Weever, *Ancient Funeral Monuments*, 1631, 674).

St George was knighted at Hampton Court on 28 September 1616, and on 3 March 1618 he was admitted to Gray's Inn. By patent dated 17 December 1623 he was promoted to be Clarenceux king of arms in succession to William Camden, who had died on 9 November 1623. On 25 December 1633 a joint commission was issued to St George as Clarenceux and Sir John Borough, Norroy, for visiting the whole kingdom. Borough was created Garter by patent dated 27 December 1633 and obtained a confirmation of the commission. Between then and St George's death thirteen counties in Clarenceux's province and one in Norroy's were visited by deputies to Clarenceux and to Borough, Garter as Norroy.

Sir Richard died in his house at the eastern end of High Holborn on Whitsunday 17 May 1635 and was buried on 22 May in the chancel of St Andrew's Church, Holborn. A number of manuscripts both owned by him and in his hand are in the British Library and the College of Arms, including *A Historical and Heraldic Commonplace Book* (College of Arms, MS B.20) and his *Collectanea historica et genealogica*, written in 1606 (BL, Add. MS 10108).

Sir Richard St George's first two sons, William and John, were both killed in their father's lifetime in action in Ireland; Sir Henry *St George (1581–1644) was the third; the fourth, Sir George St George (1583–1660), was murdered in Ireland and was the father of Sir Oliver St George, first baronet; and the fifth and youngest, Richard St George (1590–1667), governor of the town and castle of Athlone in Ireland, was ancestor of the St George baronets of Woodsgift, co. Kilkenny, and of all surviving St Georges descended from Sir Richard. Two of Sir Richard's three daughters died unmarried in his lifetime.   THOMAS WOODCOCK

Sources W. H. Godfrey, A. Wagner, and H. Stanford London, *The College of Arms, Queen Victoria Street* (1963), 86–7 · A. Wagner, *Heralds of England: a history of the office and College of Arms* (1967), 226–9, 236, 248 · M. Noble, *A history of the College of Arms* (1804), 236–8 · A. R. Wagner, *The records and collections of the College of Arms* (1952), 38–9, 60, 73, 80–82 · A. Wagner, *Heralds and ancestors* (1978), 66 · L. Campbell, *A catalogue of manuscripts in the College of Arms* (1988), 492 · *VCH Cambridgeshire and the Isle of Ely*, vol. 5 · funeral certificate, Coll. Arms, MS letter 1, vol. 24, p. 32 · C. E. Wright, *Fontes Harleiana* (1972), 293–4 · Venn, *Alum. Cant.*
Archives BL, collections, Lansdowne MS 447 · BL, historical, heraldic, and genealogical papers and collections, Add. MSS 5937, 10108, 14305, 24278, 27982, 47195, 52800 · BL, Lansdowne MSS 861–863, 871 · BL, visitation of Yorkshire, Add. MS 18011 · Coll. Arms, 14 vols. · Queen's College, Oxford, heraldic MSS · St George's Chapel,

Windsor, papers of him and other members of his family · U. Durham L., records of visitation of Durham | BL, Lancashire visitation, Harley MS 1437 · Bodl. Oxf., copies and abstracts of wills, pedigrees, etc., by him and William Ferrers · Coll. Arms, Lancashire visitation, MS C 5, office copy · Staffs. RO, Wolseley family pedigrees

Likenesses Jameson, portrait (half length); sold at Christies, 4 April 1975

Wealth at death left house in Holborn to wife for life, with remainder to eldest surviving son, Sir Henry St George; mentioned two younger sons, and gave bequests to poor of St Andrew's, Holborn, and St Giles-in-the-Fields: will, PRO, PROB 11/168/53

St George, Sir Thomas (1615–1703). *See under* St George, Sir Henry (1581–1644).

St German, Christopher (*c.*1460–1540/41), legal writer, seems to have been the only son of Sir Henry St German of Shilton, Warwickshire, and Anne, daughter of Sir Thomas Tyndale of Hockwold, Norfolk. The family's history is obscure, but perhaps its modest fortunes were of mercantile origin. Christopher attended the Middle Temple, probably after an elementary legal education in one of the inns of chancery (as was usual at that time), and would have been in London by 1490 at the very latest—probably by 1480. He had been called to the bar before 1502, when he is mentioned in the inn records as an utter-barrister. However, apart from acting twice as auditor (in 1504 and 1509), he does not appear to have held office in the inn or to have become a bencher. He was described as being of the Middle Temple in 1508, which may indicate that he was still in residence; but it seems that he left the inn about 1511, the year of his last mention there. There is no hard evidence of his engagement in legal practice during or after this period: his name has not been found in any law reports and he is not named in commissions.

Clearly St German did not make a living from legal practice; and, although a knight's son, he gave up any pretensions to head a landed family. He lived modestly in the city of London and did not marry. His occupation between 1511 and 1528, the date of the first publication attributable to him, is even more obscure. He may have been engaged in legal publishing, working anonymously as an editor. A lawsuit of 1506 reveals that Richard Pynson retained St German as one of a committee of three barristers, all Middle Templars, to correct the proofs of his abridgement of statutes. Pynson's rival, John Rastell, also knew St German well as a contemporary Middle Templar from Warwickshire, and it was Rastell who printed the first edition of St German's first dialogue in 1528. In 1529 St German received his only public appointment, as a master of requests, but it is unlikely that he ever sat.

St German's first published work was the treatise commonly known as *Doctor and Student*, surely the most remarkable book relating to English law published in the Tudor period, and quite unlike any book to have come from the pen of an English lawyer before. Although it is stated in many works of reference that the first edition appeared in 1523, this is an error. The first known version appeared in 1528 under the imprint of John Rastell. The whole text was in Latin, with the title *Dialogus de fundamentis legum Anglie et de conscientia*. The title corresponds with the avowed object stated in the prologue (omitted from later editions), which was to explore the relationship between the principles of English law and conscience. There are twenty-four chapters, cast in the form of a dialogue between a doctor of divinity and a 'student' of the laws of England (that is, a barrister), and at the end a promise to pursue the discussion further. The promise was fulfilled in 1530 with the appearance of *The Second Dialogue*. This continuation was in English and with a different printer, Peter Treverys. In either 1530 or 1531 the first dialogue was printed in English translation, with considerable alterations, by Robert Wyer; and within twelve months Wyer had brought out a revised version 'with newe addycyons'. These additions expanded upon some questions relating to entails, which in their new form comprise eight chapters not in the Latin version. They are not to be confused with *A Lytell Treatise Called the 'Newe Addicions'*, a further thirteen chapters concerning the spiritual jurisdiction, which were printed in the same year by Thomas Berthelet as an addition to the *Second Dialogue*. The use of Latin for the 1528 dialogue suggests that St German had originally intended to address only learned readers, but it is evident that his project changed in character as the work progressed. By 1530 the king had formally raised the question of parliamentary competence in connection with his divorce. The intervention of Berthelet, the king's printer, for the *Newe Addicions* is doubtless explained by the political significance of such material for the government in the debate leading to the break from Rome a few years later.

In the introduction to the *Second Dialogue*, the student explained that he was speaking in English because French would have been understood only by lawyers, and they had 'least need' of the treatise because it was 'specially made' for those without legal knowledge. This was certainly no ordinary law book. Why the author should have chosen to explore the relationship between English law and conscience is a question with no received answer. A view widely held at one time was that it was essentially a defence of the equitable jurisdiction of the court of chancery as developed over the preceding century, while others have treated it as a treatise on abstract jurisprudence for its own sake. However, it seems unlikely to have been either, at any rate as it finally developed. St German set out to refute the notions that equity and conscience were outside or above the law, that because of their association with the law of God they belonged to the spiritual courts, and that therefore the canon law was somehow higher than the law of England. English law, he held, had exactly the same foundations in divine law as the canon law; it took due account of conscience and equity; and it was necessary for churchmen and ecclesiastical judges to know its contents in order to be able to act conscientiously.

It is hardly surprising that this obscure barrister soon found himself locked in controversy with Sir Thomas More. The Reformation may have been a theological movement, but the impending legislative break with

Rome was more concerned with legal than with theological difficulties, and some of the toughest opposition came from lawyers. In showing how those legal difficulties could be eased aside, St German must be reckoned one of the major intellectual forces behind the English Reformation. At the same time, however, his case method offered law students some deep insights into numerous basic points of English jurisprudence, not to mention the first attempt at listing elementary legal maxims. Although incidental to the author's main purpose, this pedagogic quality in the dialogues ensured them a lengthy afterlife in the profession which (in St German's modest disclaimer) had 'least need' of them. In fact *Doctor and Student* became a student primer. No substantial changes were made to it after the author's death. From 1541 onwards the two dialogues were published together in English as a single book, though until 1751 the thirteen *Newe Addicions* were omitted. The sheer number of subsequent reprints—about thirty, ending with a Cincinnati edition of 1886—shows just how popular the book remained and for how long, though its popularity in later times was within the legal profession rather than with the lay readership intended by the author.

St German's writing career continued with *A Little Treatise Concerning Writs of Subpoena* (not printed until 1787), which was indeed a defence of the equitable jurisdiction, by way of response to the somewhat indignant *Replication of a Serjeant at the Laws of England* to certain passages in *Doctor and Student* relating to that theme. It has been suggested that St German wrote the *Replication* as well, as a device to provide the opportunity for a reply, though the style is somewhat different and the matter is open to doubt. In 1531 he prepared a draft proposal for legislative reforms (PRO, SP 6/7, pp. 55–74), which shows that he was already in tune with Cromwell's policies. In the following year, the battle with More was opened with his *Treatise Concerning the Division between the Spiritualty and Temporalty*, which enlarged on the unstated premise of his earlier work. More responded with his *Apology*, St German immediately retaliated with *Salem and Bizance* (a dialogue between two imaginary Englishmen named after Jerusalem and Byzantium), and More rejoined with *The Debellation of Salem and Bizance* (all printed in 1533). The interchange ended with St German's *Additions of Salem and Bizance* (1534), published about the time of More's downfall. These pamphlets did not bear St German's name, but Bale's attribution of them to him (in 1559) is borne out by stylistic considerations. They were all published by the king's printer, probably under Cromwell's patronage. The principal topic of controversy was the treatment of heretics, though St German's underlying argument was that the clergy had arrogated to themselves unwarranted power, which they abused in their own interests to the detriment of the laity; that the laws which they had introduced—as distinct from the natural law of God—were no higher in nature than the common or statute law of England; and that the latter were in practice preferable. Although points were scored on both sides, St German succeeded in pushing More into some forced arguments

and disingenuous positions: allow heretics a fair trial, as St German suggested, and the streets would be swarming with them.

A number of anonymous pamphlets from 1535, on closely related themes, seem clearly to be by the same hand: *A Treatise Concerning the Power of the Clergy and the Laws of the Realm* (date conjectural, perhaps 1534), *A Treatise Concerning Divers of the Constitutions*, and *An Answer to a Letter*. These pursued the former argument that the only spiritual laws binding the king and his people were those pronounced by God. The church consisted not merely of the clergy but of all Christian people, and ecclesiastical matters—even scriptural exegesis—could as well be settled by parliament as by the clergy. These later pamphlets were published independently of the government, probably because St German was more theologically conservative than the king and held a more restrained view of the king's personal supremacy, which did not (as he argued) derive from the legislation of 1534 but was inherent in kingship. In his last years the author turned to more purely spiritual matters, and in 1537 wrote two unpublished theological tracts, one on the sacraments and the other on 'what we be bounde to byleve as thinges necessary to salvation, and what not', which repeats the device of a dialogue between a doctor and a student (PRO, SP 6/2, pp. 89–168). Bale attributed a number of other works to St German, including one on Mohammedanism and another on the teaching of St Bernard and St Bridget, but these have not survived.

A letter written by St German to Cromwell in July 1539, when he was nearly eighty, shows that he had become immobile but was still mentally active and keen to obtain books. According to Bale, he died on 28 September 1539 and was buried in the church of St Alphage, Cripplegate, not far from Thomas Lupset. However, his will is dated 10 July 1540—when he was living in a leased house in Old Fish Street near the Exchange—and was proved on 30 May 1541. His executor, Christopher Breteyn of the Middle Temple, was given the first choice of his books, but was to pay for them. The modesty of his bequests bears out Bale's statement that St German's library was the only valuable asset which he left. It must have been an impressive collection, though only one volume from it (Harvard law school, MS 155) has so far been found.   J. H. BAKER

Sources J. Guy, ed., *Christopher St. German on chancery and statute*, SeldS, suppl. ser., 6 (1985) · J. Guy, 'Thomas More and St German: the battle of the books', in A. Fox and J. Guy, *Reassessing the Henrician age* (1986), 95–120 · J. H. Baker, 'Introduction', in C. St German, *Doctor and student* (Birmingham, AL, 1988) · Bale, *Cat.*, 1.660–61 · will, PRO, PROB 11/28, sig. 29 · *St German's Doctor and student*, ed. T. F. T. Plucknett and J. Barton, SeldS, 91 (1974) · D. E. C. Yale, 'St German's *Little treatise concerning writs of subpoena*', *Irish Jurist*, new ser., 10 (1975), 324–33 · St Thomas More, *The apology*, ed. J. B. Trapp (1979), vol. 9 of *The Yale edition of the complete works of St Thomas More* · P. Hogrefe, 'The life of Saint Germain', *Review of English Studies*, 13 (1937), 398–404 · F. le V. Baumer, 'St German: the political philosophy of a Tudor lawyer', *American Historical Review*, 42 (1936–7), 631–51 · R. J. Schoeck, 'The most erudite of Tudor lawyers, Christopher St German', *Journal of the Rocky Mountain Medieval and Renaissance Society*, 4 (1983), 107–23 · J. H. Baker, *English legal manuscripts in the United States of America: a descriptive list*, 1 (1985), 31 · St Thomas

More, *The debellation of Salem and Bizance*, ed. J. Guy and others (1987), vol. 10 of *The Yale edition of the complete works of St Thomas More* • **Wealth at death** said to have consisted chiefly in books; also presses: will, PRO, PROB 11/28, sig. 29; Bale, *Cat.*

St Germans. For this title name *see* Eliot, Edward Granville, third earl of St Germans (1798–1877).

St Giles, John of (*d.* 1259/60), Dominican friar and physician, has often been confused with other persons. It is not clear whether he was identical with the Master John of St Giles who twice attested charters of Stephen Langton, archbishop of Canterbury, probably in the period 1220–28. Nor is it known where he began his studies, though Oxford seems the most likely. He was not, as is sometimes stated, the first master of the Oxford black friars and there is no evidence that he studied medicine in Montpellier. What seems certain is that in 1228 he was already master of theology in Paris, since Orlando da Cremona took his degree in this same year under him. In 1233 John of St Giles succeeded Orlando as lecturer in theology at Toulouse University. He had previously entered the Dominican order, perhaps on 22 September 1230, when, according to Nicholas Trivet, he interrupted for a while a sermon on voluntary poverty he was preaching, in order to don a friar's habit. This sermon and others, preached in the years 1230–31, have been preserved in two manuscripts (Paris, Bibliothèque Nationale, MS nouv. acq. lat. 338, fols. 9–11*v*, 43–5, 84–87*v*, and MS Lat. 12418, fols. 98*v*–101, 106*v*–107, 207*v*–210) and edited by M. M. Davy (*Les sermons universitaires parisiens de 1230–1231*, 1931, 271–98). Some questions disputed at Paris probably echo St Giles's teaching in theology. Attributed to 'magistro Io. An[glico]', they are found in a thirteenth-century manuscript (Douai, Bibliothèque Municipale, MS 434, fols. 103*v*, 107*v*–108, 115*v*–117*v*).

In the summer of 1235, after the dispersal of the Dominican convent of Toulouse, St Giles went to Mainz, where, according to Matthew Paris, he formed part of the suite of Isabella of England on the occasion of her marriage with the emperor Frederick II. On his return to England during the autumn, he is reported to have announced Isabella's pregnancy to her brother, Henry III. From this period he had links with the royal household. In September 1237 he joined Henry III at York, having been provided with good horses by the sheriff of Cambridgeshire. In 1238 he was an executor of the will of the king's sister, Joan, and in 1239 he was called to court as royal councillor. In 1242 he heard the confession of the pirate William Marsh, before the latter's execution in London.

John of St Giles probably belonged to the entourage of Robert Grosseteste, bishop of Lincoln, from the time of his return from Mainz to England. In a letter addressed in 1235 to the provincial prior of the English Dominicans, perhaps during John's stay at Mainz, Grosseteste expressed the wish that, when John returned to England, around Michaelmas, he would assist him in his episcopal duties. At approximately the same time, the bishop wrote to John, asking him to come and preach in his own country. In another letter, addressed in 1237 to Jordan of Saxony, prior-general of the Dominicans, Grosseteste requested that John be allowed to stay constantly by his side in order to advise him in his religious duties, for he did not know any assistant so efficient. St Giles seems to have remained in Grosseteste's entourage until the latter's death in 1253. He was summoned by the bishop in his last hours and heard his severe words denouncing the mendicants. John of St Giles died a few years after Grosseteste, probably in 1259 or 1260.

According to Matthew Paris, John of St Giles also acted as a skilled physician. Before the time of Grosseteste's last illness, John is reported to have treated the prelate when he was the victim of poisoning. He is likewise said to have treated the earl of Gloucester, allegedly poisoned in 1258; the earl recovered, though his teeth and nails fell out. Some medical recipes are found under the name Johannis de Sancto Egidio in two manuscripts: Oxford, Bodleian Library, MS Bodley 786, fols. 170–171*v*; Cambridge, Peterhouse, MS 222, fols. 10*v*–11*v*. These are the only medical works which can be securely attributed to him. Others have been mentioned, but they are either by the French physician Gilles de Corbeil or (*De formatione corporis*) by Giles of Rome.

John of St Giles is not to be confused with John of St Albans, an English physician who treated the French king Philip II in the Holy Land in 1191. Neither is he to be confused with Giovanni de Barastre, who gave to the Dominicans the site of the convent of St Jacques in Paris in 1218 and was subsequently dean of St Quentin. It would also appear that he is not to be confused with a contemporary namesake who, without being called master, attested charters of Robert Grosseteste in 1237–40. It was this man who was presented successively to the prebends of Banbury (1231/2) and Leighton Buzzard (1238) and had been appointed archdeacon of Oxford by July 1240.

DANIELLE JACQUART

Sources T. Kaeppeli, *Scriptores ordinis praedicatorum medii aevi*, 2 (Rome, 1975), 536–7 • J. C. Russell, 'Dictionary of writers of thirteenth century England', *BIHR*, special suppl., 3 (1936) [whole issue], esp. 73–5 • C. H. Talbot and E. A. Hammond, *The medical practitioners in medieval England: a biographical register* (1965), 178–81 • Emden, *Oxf.*, 3.1626 • K. Major, 'The *familia* of Robert Grosseteste', *Robert Grosseteste, scholar and bishop*, ed. D. A. Callus (1955), 220, 237 • *Roberti Grosseteste episcopi quondam Lincolniensis epistolae*, ed. H. R. Luard, Rolls Series, 25 (1861), 59–63, 70, 131–3 • R. W. Southern, *Robert Grosseteste: the growth of an English mind in medieval Europe* (1986), 74, 291–5 • *Paris, Chron.*, 3.324, 627; 4.196; 5.400–01, 705 • *Matthaei Parisiensis, monachi Sancti Albani, Historia Anglorum, sive … Historia minor*, ed. F. Madden, 3 vols., Rolls Series, 44 (1886–9), 3.293 • *F. Nicholai Triveti, de ordine frat. praedicatorum, annales sex regum Angliae*, ed. T. Hog, EHS, 6 (1845), 211–12 • O. Lottin, 'Quelques Questiones de maîtres parisiens aux environs de 1225–1235', *Recherches de Théologie Ancienne et Médiévale*, 5 (1933), 81–2 • K. Major, ed., *Acta Stephani Langton*, CYS, 50 (1950) • *Fasti Angl., 1066–1300*, [Lincoln]

Archives Bibliothèque Nationale, Paris [copies] • Bibliothèque Nationale, Paris, fonds lat. et nouv. acq. lat. [copies] • Bodl. Oxf., MS Bodley 786 • LPL, calendar of liberate rolls, 1226–40, MS 241 • LPL, close rolls, 1237–42, MS 241 • Peterhouse, Cambridge, MS 222

St Helens. For this title name *see* Fitzherbert, Alleyne, Baron St Helens (1753–1839).

St Helier. For this title name *see* Jeune, Francis Henry, Baron St Helier (1843–1905).

St John, Bayle Frederick (1822–1859), traveller and author, was born on 19 August 1822 in Kentish Town, London, the second of the eleven children (seven boys and four girls) of James Augustus *St John (1795–1875), author, from Laugharne, Carmarthenshire, and his wife, Eliza Caroline Agar Hansard (*c*.1798–1867), daughter of Alexander Hansard, surgeon and apothecary of Bristol. Percy Bolingbroke *St John (1821–1889) was his elder brother, and Sir Spenser Buckingham *St John (1825–1910), Horace Stebbing Roscoe *St John (1830–1888), and Vane Ireton Shaftesbury *St John (1839–1911) [*see under* St John, Sir Spenser Buckingham] were younger brothers. From 1829 to 1834 he lived with his family in France and Switzerland, and on their return to London was educated privately and by his father. His first article was accepted by a monthly magazine when he was thirteen. He had thoughts of becoming an artist and studied art until he was seventeen, but from 1838 to 1842 he served a literary apprenticeship by assisting his father, then partially blind, in the preparation of his *History of the Manners and Customs of Ancient Greece*. He then turned instead to writing, contributing to various periodicals, including the *Sunday Times*, the *Penny Magazine*, and the *Foreign Quarterly Review*. His first full-length publication was a novel, *The Eccentric Lover* (3 vols., 1845), written, as he said in the dedication to his father, as light relief from more serious studies.

From 1846 St John spent little time in England, travelling first to Egypt, where he stayed for two years, and then settling in Paris in June 1848. Ten years of intense literary production followed: his Egyptian experiences are described in *Adventures in the Libyan Desert* (1849), *Five Views in the Oasis of Siwah* (1850), consisting of lithographs of his own sketches and his map of the route he took across the desert, and *Two Years' Residence in a Levantine Family* (1850). In 1850–51 St John travelled up the Nile, and on returning to Paris published *Village Life in Egypt* (2 vols., 1852). *The Turks in Europe* (1853) considered the Eastern question on the eve of the Crimean War. *Purple Tints of Paris* (2 vols., 1854) is based on St John's first-hand knowledge of the Second Republic, the *coup d'état* of 1851, and the establishment of the Second Empire; *The Subalpine Kingdom* (2 vols., 1856) resulted from a visit to Piedmont in 1855. The most enduring of his works has been an abridged translation of the *Memoirs of the Duc de Saint-Simon* (4 vols., 1857), the first translation of the work into English. *Montaigne the Essayist, a Biography* (2 vols.) was published in 1858. During his time in Paris, St John was correspondent for the *Daily Telegraph*, edited and translated other works connected with Africa, and wrote a history of the Louvre. He wrote two further novels, *The Fortunes of Francis Croft* (3 vols., 1852), published anonymously, and *Maretimo* (1856). *Violet Davenant, or, The Blood-Marked Hand!* (n.d.), published in New York, is unambiguously attributed to him, but this may be spurious. He returned to London in 1858 for the last year of his life. By then suffering from consumption, he became too ill to work and had severe financial problems.

Bayle St John inherited many of his father's opinions and interests. Liberal, republican, egalitarian, his special field was foreign affairs, and he wrote on many of the momentous developments of the time. As a traveller and observer he was a reliable social commentator; his personal reminiscences are written in an entertaining, often humorous style, and his scholarly research was thorough. His writings were particularly esteemed in France, his adopted home, and met with some success in both Britain and America. He died at 13 Grove End Road, St John's Wood, London, on 1 August 1859, and was buried in Kensal Green cemetery on 6 August. At the time of his premature death he had a wife and two children, aged five and three; Queen Victoria and Prince Albert attended a charity theatrical performance in aid of his family.

S. V. SPILSBURY

Sources Royal Literary Fund papers, BL, Loan 96, case 1510 · *Men of the time* (1857), 665–7 · *The Athenaeum* (6 Aug 1859), 177 · census returns, 1841, PRO, HO 107/689, fol. 20 · *Wellesley index* · J. A. St John, *History of the manners and customs of ancient Greece*, 3 vols. (1842), v · Kensal Green cemetery records, 6 Aug 1859 · *DNB*
Archives BL, business transactions with Richard Bently, Add. MSS 46614, 46651
Wealth at death in straitened circumstances: Royal Literary Fund papers, BL, Loan 96, case 1510

St John, Charles George William (1809–1856), sportsman and naturalist, was the fourth son of General the Hon. Frederick St John (1765–1844), second son of Frederick, second Viscount Bolingbroke. His mother was Lady Arabella (*c*.1774–1819), daughter of William, sixth earl of Craven. Born at Chailey, Sussex, on 3 December 1809, Charles St John was sent to Midhurst School between 1821 and 1825. His particular interests first appeared at school, where he is reported to have been proficient in spinning for pike and catching eels in the River Arun. In 1828 he was appointed to a clerkship in the Treasury, but the regular work and confinement proved irksome.

St John left the Treasury in 1833. His uncle, Lord Bolingbroke, had lent him Rosehall, a shooting box in Sutherland, where he devoted himself to the study of animals and birds. On 20 November 1834 he married Ann (d. 1865), daughter of T. Gibson, a Newcastle banker. He afterwards spent much time in Moray, whose fine moors, studded with lochs, and the adjoining seaboard gave him exceptional opportunities for studying seabirds.

In 1844 some reminiscences by St John of his sporting experiences were incorporated by his friend Cosmo Innes, sheriff of the county, in an article which Innes published in the *Quarterly Review* (vol. 77). St John's contributions to the article included the story of 'The Muckle Hart of Benmore', which charmed Lockhart, the editor of the *Quarterly*. Thenceforth St John made careful and regular notes of all he saw. In 1846 he issued *Short Sketches of the Wild Sports and Natural History of the Highlands* (reprinted twelve times up to 1924 and again in 1981 and 1986). The work was recognized as that of an accurate observer and a writer of

Charles George William St John (1809–1856), by Whymper

talent. Other sporting books followed; but on 6 December 1853, when starting on a shooting expedition to Pluscardine, St John was struck with paralysis. He was moved to the south of England, but did not improve and died on 12 July 1856 at Hazeleigh, Woolston, Hampshire. He was buried in Southampton cemetery. The skull of a favourite retriever was buried with him. He left one daughter and three sons, including Colonel Frederick Charles St John (1835–1900), of the Madras staff corps, and Rear-Admiral Henry Craven St John (1837–1909).

As a sportsman St John was keen and persevering; as a field naturalist he was unrivalled, never accepting facts on hearsay and possessing great first-hand knowledge of the birds of Scotland. He possessed considerable skill as a draughtsman, and drew and painted his specimens; he even illustrated some of his books himself. His works retained some interest over a century later, as their republication in the 1980s shows; St John's reputation, however, suffered owing to such exploits as shooting 'probably the last ospreys in Sutherland' (Short Sketches, 100). He himself insisted 'though by habit and repute a being strongly endowed with the organ of destructiveness, I take equal delight in collecting round me all living animals and watching their habits and instincts' (ibid., author's introduction).   M. G. WATKINS, rev. JULIAN LOCK

Sources Boase, Mod. Eng. biog. • C. St John, Short sketches of the wild sports and natural history of the highlands, 9th edn (1893); pbk edn (1981); facs. edn with introduction by C. L. McKelvie (1986) • Burke, Peerage • private information (1897) • GM, 3rd ser., 1 (1856), 262 • A. Atha, ed., A Scottish naturalist: the sketches and notes of Charles St John (1982) • GM, 1st ser., 89/1 (1819), 589 [obit. of Lady Arabella St John]
Likenesses Whymper, engraving, repro. in St John, Short sketches (1893) [see illus.]

St John, Christopher Marie [née Christabel Gertrude Marshall] (1871–1960), writer, was born on 24 October 1871 at 38 High Street, Exeter, the youngest of the nine children of Emma *Marshall, née Martin (1828–1899), novelist, and Hugh Graham Marshall (c.1825–1899), manager of the West of England Bank. She changed her name on her conversion to Catholicism in adulthood, which may have contributed to a rift with her mother, whose protestant commitment and aversion to Roman Catholicism were evident in her writings. For whatever reasons, St John later claimed to have been illegitimate, and attempted (with some success) to conceal her origins. Educated from 1894 at Somerville College, Oxford, she developed skills as a historian and translator, before moving to London where she worked as temporary secretary to Lady Randolph Churchill and Winston Churchill.

After a relationship with the musician Violet Gwynne (later Gordon Woodhouse) in 1895, St John met Ellen Terry's daughter Edith Ailsa Geraldine *Craig (1869–1947), with whom she was to set up house at 7 Smith Square, Westminster. After moving to Adelphi Terrace House, they settled in the third-floor flat at 31 Bedford Street, Covent Garden, and when Ellen Terry bought the former port officer's house, at Smallhythe Place, Tenterden, Kent, they acquired a second home at nearby Priest's House. Their relationship became temporarily strained when Craig received a marriage proposal from the musician Martin Shaw and St John attempted suicide.

St John's first published book, The Crimson Weed (1900), an exploration of passion and revenge, was a novel concerning the illegitimate son of an opera singer. She had been attracted to the stage since childhood, giving her first performance at a drawing-room entertainment, where, in a man's dress suit, she sang the comic song 'The Frenchman'. She was a member of the Stage Society as Christabel Marshall, acting in Gilbert Murray's translation of Andromache at the Garrick Theatre in 1904. Her translation of The Good Hope performed by the Stage Society was published under her assumed name, Christopher St John. Through her association with Craig and Terry, she acted at the Imperial Theatre, first appearing in The Vikings in 1903; her first speaking part, under the stage name of Joanna Willett, was in Clo Graves's play The Mistress of the Robes.

St John had continued with her literary efforts, publishing several pieces in Pamela Colman Smith's magazine, the Green Sheaf, including an elegiac monograph, Henry Irving, on the actor's death in 1905. She also wrote the first of several biographies of Ellen Terry in 1907, during Terry's American tour.

Both St John and Craig were active in the women's suffrage movement. St John wrote plays and articles in support of the movement, and was arrested in 1909 for setting fire to a pillar box. Involved in the Women's Social and Political Union, she was a committee member of the Catholic Women's Suffrage Society and the Women Writers' Suffrage League. For the latter organization she was photographed holding a banner with Craig and Cicely Hamilton in a street procession of 1910. All three women acted in A

Pageant of Great Women (1909), a play devised by Hamilton and Craig, which was performed nationwide.

An understanding of the economic determinants of social inequalities was apparent in the plays St John translated and co-wrote. She translated from the Dutch plays by Herman Heijermans and co-wrote with Cicely Hamilton *How the Vote was Won* and *The Pot and the Kettle*, and with Charles Thursby, *The Coronation*. Her historical skills were also evident in her plays, especially *The First Actress*, *The Pageant of the Stage*, and *Macrena*.

When the Pioneer Players society was founded in 1911, with Edith Craig as director and Ellen Terry as president, Christopher St John contributed as dramatist, translator, and actor. She was also honorary secretary from 1915 to 1920, and a member of the advisory and casting committees. The Pioneer Players performed both St John's own plays and a number of her translations of works by Herman Heijermans, Isi Collin, and Jose Echegeray, including her most significant translation of a play by the first female dramatist, Hrotsvit. *Paphnutius* was given a world première by Craig for the Pioneer Players in January 1914.

During the First World War, St John continued to act and write plays. She wrote about her relationship with Craig in her journal, *The Golden Book* (1911), and in her anonymously published second novel, *Hungerheart: the Story of a Soul* (1915). In a hybrid form of *Bildungsroman* and *roman à clef*, this narrative represents the development of a lesbian or 'invert' whose sexuality is mediated through the self-abnegation of Roman Catholicism. In 1916 the artist Clare (Tony) *Atwood (1866–1962) joined Edith Craig and Christopher St John in their flat at 31 Bedford Street, Covent Garden. St John recalled Bernard Shaw's suggestion that she write about this *ménage à trois*, which was to be lifelong, disrupted only by Craig's death in 1947. To *Edy: Recollections of Edith Craig* (1949), edited by Eleanor Adlard, St John contributed an essay, 'Close-up', in which she noted that they achieved independence within their intimate relationships: Craig, Atwood, and St John, working respectively in the theatre, art, and literature, drew creative inspiration and support from each other.

After Terry's death in 1928, St John and Craig revised and edited *Ellen Terry's Memoirs* (1933). St John edited Ellen Terry's *Four Lectures on Shakespeare* (1932) and the *Shaw-Terry Correspondence* (1931). Craig raised funds to establish her mother's house as a memorial and on its grounds, the Barn Theatre, in which an annual memorial performance was given. St John acted there in *A Midsummer Night's Dream* in 1929 and subsequently in several other pieces. The Barn Theatre and Priest's House became the focus of a busy social and cultural life in Kent for women and actors in particular. Craig, St John, and Atwood, known as 'Edy and the boys', were close friends with Radclyffe Hall and Una Troubridge after the adverse publicity of the trial for obscenity in 1928 of Hall's novel *The Well of Loneliness*. The five spent Christmas together in 1931 and 1932. St John and Craig attended the Stage Society's production in 1930 of Colette's *Chéri*, organized by Gabrielle Enthoven and Una Troubridge. St John's journal documented her short-lived relationship with Vita Sackville-West in 1932; her difficulties in coming to terms with this rejection met with sympathy from Ethel Smyth but irritation from Virginia Woolf.

As music critic, St John wrote for *The Lady* under the initials C. M., and for *Time and Tide* from 1920 to 1931. She published her translations of Hrotsvit's plays (1923) and biographies of Christine Murrell MD (1935) and Ethel Smyth (1958); the latter, completed in spite of considerable ill health, was distinguished by the Book Society as book of the month. Some of her writings were apparently unpublished, such as the plays *What a Plague is Love* and *The White Room*.

St John died at West View, Tenterden, Kent, England, on 20 October 1960 after suffering pneumonia and heart disease. In response to the obituary in *The Times*, Vita Sackville-West wrote that 'she was in the grand tradition of English eccentrics' remembered as 'a Shakespeare character … roaringly rumbustious', while Dame Sybil Thorndike recalled her as 'vivid … too much an individual in her life and work to be one of the most popular'.

KATHARINE COCKIN

Sources E. Martell, L. G. Pine, and A. Lawrence, eds., *Who was who among English and European authors, 1931–1949*, 3 vols. (1978), 1240 · A. C. Ward, *Longman companion to twentieth century literature*, 3rd edn, rev. M. Hussey (1981), 469 · C. St John, 'Close-up', *Edy: recollections of Edith Craig*, ed. E. Adlard (1949), 16–34 · [C. St John], *Hungerheart* (1915) · N. Auerbach, *Ellen Terry: player in her time* (1987) · V. Glendinning, *Vita: the life of Vita Sackville-West* (1984) · M. Steen, *A pride of Terrys* (1962) · K. Cockin, *Edith Craig (1869–1947): dramatic lives* (1998) · J. Glasgow, 'What's a nice lesbian like you doing in the church of Torquemada? Radclyffe Hall and other Catholic converts', *Lesbian texts and contexts: radical revisions* (1990), 242–54 · S. Cline, *Radclyffe Hall: a woman called John* (1997) · R. Collis, *Portraits to the wall: historic lesbian lives unveiled* (1994) · J. Douglas-Home, *Violet: the life and loves of Violet Gordon Woodhouse* (1996) · b. cert. · d. cert. · *The Times* (25 Oct 1960)

Archives BL, corresp. with Society of Authors, Add. MS 63324 · Ellen Terry Memorial Museum, Tenterden, Kent, Edith Craig archive, letters, and plays · U. Cal., Los Angeles, 'The golden book', MSS

Likenesses Mrs Albert Brown, portrait, 1910, repro. in C. Hamilton, *Life errant* (1935), facing p. 80 · Thomson, photograph, repro. in C. Hamilton, *Life errant* (1935), facing p. 88 · photograph, repro. in V. Gardner, ed., *Sketches from the Actresses' Franchise League*, Nottingham Drama Texts (1985), facing p. 48 · photographs, Ellen Terry Memorial Museum, Tenterden, Kent

Wealth at death £817 19s. 1d.: probate, 24 Aug 1961, *CGPLA Eng. & Wales*

St John, Lady Diana. See Beauclerk, Lady Diana (1734–1808).

St John, Henry, styled first Viscount Bolingbroke (1678–1751), politician, diplomatist, and author, the son of Henry St John, Viscount St John (1652–1742), landowner, and Lady Mary Rich (d. 1678), second daughter of Robert Rich, third earl of Warwick, was born on 16 September 1678, very probably at Lydiard Tregoze, the family seat in Wiltshire, where his mother was buried on 2 October. He was baptized, however, at Battersea on 10 October. He was born into a family which liked to trace its ancestry as far back as the Norman conquest. The St John family had been divided by the civil war, but two junior branches

Henry St John, styled first Viscount Bolingbroke (1678–1751), attrib. Alexis-Simon Belle, 1712?

were reunited by the marriage of his paternal grandparents, when Sir Walter St John of Lydiard Tregoze of the cavalier branch married Johanna St John of Bletsoe, daughter of Oliver Cromwell's lord chief justice. Their son, Henry St John the elder, appears to have been a typical Restoration rake. He and his son, Henry, showed neither love nor respect for each other during the rest of their lives. Henry St John the younger was brought up by his paternal grandparents at their house in Battersea, probably until 1687 at least, when his father married Angelica Magdalena Wharton (*d.* 1736), daughter of George Pellissary, treasurer-general of the navy to Louis XIV. The young Henry was often a sickly child and had two serious illnesses which caused his grandfather considerable alarm. His grandmother is always reckoned to have taken a great interest in his education and is reputed to have hired leading dissenting ministers for the purpose. She may even have arranged for him to be educated at the dissenting academy at Sheriffhales in Shropshire, but there is no evidence to confirm this. It has been common practice to claim that St John was educated at Eton College and Christ Church, Oxford, but there is no evidence to support either claim, though he was awarded an honorary degree by the university in 1702.

The evidence for St John's early life does not become substantial until 1698, when he toured Europe, visiting France, Switzerland, and Italy before 1700. During these months he made friends with such young whigs as James Stanhope, but also corresponded regularly with the experienced and moderate tory Sir William Trumbull, who had recently been secretary of state to William III. Though St John undoubtedly enjoyed the pleasures of a young rake, his letters show that he also spent some time studying and that he took a considerable interest in politics and religion. He expressed his dislike of the absolutism of Louis XIV and considered that only the tyranny of the Catholic clergy was worse. He also noted the threatening situation in Europe, where the problem of the Spanish succession aroused considerable speculation and where it was strongly feared that France was preparing for war. On his return to England St John succeeded his father as one of the members for the family's parliamentary seat at Wootton Bassett, Wiltshire, for which he was elected in February 1701. His father, with whom he disagreed in politics, had sat in the Commons only for the duration of the previous parliament and he may have agreed to surrender his seat to his son, in return for the latter's agreement to marry Frances Winchcombe (*d.* 1718), an heiress with estates in Berkshire. It was to prove an unhappy and childless marriage. Though his wife supported his political career through all its vicissitudes, he treated her shamelessly. This shocked even his friends and damaged his reputation with Queen Anne in particular.

Character and abilities In the early years of his public career Henry St John gave evidence of those eminent qualities and defects of character that were to surround his name in controversy throughout his life and have done ever since. More than his talents and achievements, it was St John's personality that impressed contemporaries and has intrigued historians. A handsome, well-built man, with graceful manners and a ready wit, he also had a keen intellect, a quickness of perception, a vivid imagination, and a clarity and force of expression that together captivated some of the finest minds and most discerning critics of his age, including Jonathan Swift, Alexander Pope, Voltaire, and the earl of Chesterfield. At least for a time they were all seduced by the force and charm of his personality. Even St John's severest critics, anxious to reveal his faults, could not help acknowledging some of his personal qualities, even though they labelled them as specious or superficial. It was certainly widely accepted that there was a striking contrast between his virtues and his vices. His own professed models were Alcibiades and Petronius, and he earned and accepted the nickname Man of Mercury. The aspect of his character that attracted most contemporary comment in his early years was his flagrant debauchery. He took a positive delight in proving that he could live as a libertine, while also excelling in public affairs. He craved admiration for every facet of his character and achievements. This often led to accusations of affectation in its most obvious form. He never abandoned his image of a man of pleasure even after he had given up the practice.

A frequent and more damaging charge levelled at St John is that his immorality extended to a readiness to betray his friends in order to advance his own career. There is some justification for this charge. Particularly reprehensible was his treatment of his first wife, even though she appears to have been attractive in person and character, and remained devoted to him, even in his worst days in 1715. St John was also accused of basely betraying the duke of Marlborough, Robert Harley, and Alexander Pope, though they deserve to share some responsibility for his subsequent attacks upon them. Moreover, there is also another side of the coin. St John had attractive personal qualities which made him a stimulating and convivial companion, and he formed long attachments to such men as Sir William Wyndham, Lord Bathurst, Pope, and Swift. He also showed considerable devotion to his second wife, particularly during her long, final illness.

More striking was St John's early capacity for hero-worship. Though keen to excel in all things, he was also generous in his recognition of the talents of others. His first hero and model was Sir William Trumbull. He later witnessed and applauded the splendid talents of the duke of Marlborough. The third great influence on his public career was Robert Harley, whose political skills he learned to admire before he turned against him. In later life St John reversed these roles and expected younger men to hero-worship him. He loved to be at the centre of a circle of literary men and he certainly took a great interest in the education of the sons of his political and aristocratic friends.

In his frequent declarations of how much he loved study and learning, St John has been accused of striking a flattering pose. Contemporaries were justifiably suspicious of his frequent claims that he enjoyed the contemplative pleasures of his study as much as the cut and thrust of political life, but it is also true that, when he was debarred from politics, he did pursue his various studies most assiduously. Throughout his life he was genuinely attracted by learning and literary pursuits. From his earliest letters to the end of his life he showed a readiness to study seriously, a great pleasure in writing, and a delight in the company of writers and thinkers.

Affectation is a harmless enough flaw, but in St John's case it appears rooted in a condition of temperamental instability. In his early career he gave evidence of his lifelong conflict: a struggle between his reason and his passions. He had a cool, rational intelligence and a fierce, unbridled nature. While he always aspired to display the former, he was more often betrayed by the latter. Tense, sensitive, and highly strung, he reacted violently to criticism and came near to panic in a crisis. His attempts at philosophic indifference were numerous, but never carried conviction. There was always a contrast between what he hoped to feel and the emotions he actually experienced. The more he protested, the more he attracted attention and damaged his own case. He was undoubtedly a strange and paradoxical mixture of hypocrisy and candour. While not the bravest of men nor the coolest head in a crisis, he displayed immense physical and moral stamina. Though at times he quit the field, he never renounced the battle. He undoubtedly possessed great talents and substantial defects.

A man of wit, intelligence, and learning, it was St John's oratory which commanded most attention in his early political life and his polished written prose that brought him most fame in his later career. Unfortunately, while contemporaries frequently paid tribute to his oratory, no drafts of his speeches have survived and only a few short speeches have been recorded. We have to rely on contemporary testimony to gain some idea of his impact on his listeners. With his prose style we are much better served, since all his major political tracts have survived and we are reasonably sure which essays he contributed to *The Craftsman*. It is also clear that he could apply himself to business and that he had energy, industry, and organizational ability. His official letters reveal a minister with remarkable skill in instructing his subordinates, following the advice of his superiors, informing his colleagues, and negotiating with allies and opponents. He mastered the details of his official duties and displayed a positive relish for political power. He was always fascinated by politics and the pursuit of power, and sought it by his pen when he was denied access to cabinet and parliament. His frequent claims that he was not interested in power for its own sake do not carry conviction, though there is a streak of principle running throughout his career.

St John's political talents were accompanied by corresponding defects. His chief failing was his inability to manage men, other than his personal friends and closest adherents. He lacked the tact, persuasive arts, and conciliatory skills of which Harley and Robert Walpole were such masters. His imperious spirit could show the tory squires what game to hunt and his spoken and written arguments could sway backbenchers and informed opinion, but he found it difficult to negotiate support by personal contact and shrewd bargaining. While he could offer a bold lead, he could not ensure a large following. Nor was he able to devise a long-term strategy. He reacted to immediate events, but could not decide on his political priorities. Only the pressure of adverse circumstances forced him to develop a coherent political philosophy, but it was based on an interpretation which justified his own conduct and did not necessarily serve the interests of his allies or his party. His personal integrity was always suspect, which made it difficult to secure the unquestioning loyalty of others. In this respect his affectation was of less account than his lack of financial probity. Throughout his life he was dependent on his father or his wives for financial support and he was always anxious to free himself from such irksome restrictions. He several times sought financial gain by unorthodox means and he unwisely associated with men such as James Brydges and Arthur Moore, two experts in purloining government money. With such a record of debauchery, betrayal, and lack of financial probity, it is hardly surprising that he could never gain the full support of his sovereign or his party, however much his talents were admired.

St John's family background and education were probably more whig than tory. His father was reputed to be a whig and gained a peerage from George I in 1716, even though his son was then an attainted traitor. It was certainly claimed that the younger Henry St John joined the tories only because he believed he could more easily force himself to the forefront of that party, which lacked talent in the House of Commons. None the less, it is not true that he lacked all political principles. Whatever his motives for becoming a tory, he served the party for many years and tried to ensure it would hold power as much as possible. Even in his later career, when he tried to break free from the whig–tory disputes which had so long dominated political life, he was trying to serve the interests of toryism by clearing its adherents of the taint of Jacobitism and by advancing its platform by disguising it under country or patriot principles. Throughout his career he believed that the landed squirearchy was the backbone of the political nation and that its interests and those of the country as a whole were best served if such men dominated government at local and national level.

St John and the tory party St John's first years in parliament witnessed the strong revival of the tory party which had suffered so traumatically after the revolution of 1688–9. Dissatisfaction with the foreign policy of William III, with the rise of the financial interest, and with the threat to the privileged position of the Church of England rallied many of the squirearchy once more behind the tory party, while the accession of Queen Anne gave them the chance to renew their traditional allegiance to throne and altar. In view of the continued divisions within the party, however, St John could never be typically or consistently tory in all his attitudes and actions. He can nevertheless be identified with many tory prejudices and principles. Though opposed to the doctrine of divine right, he remained a staunch supporter of the royal prerogative. He never challenged the monarch's right to choose his or her own ministers and accepted that he or she would have a considerable role in the shaping of government policy. The doctrine of hereditary succession appealed to him only in so far as it had the utilitarian advantage of preventing disputes after the death of every monarch. He was never a Jacobite as a matter of principle, though he was at times tempted to support the Pretender, James Stuart, in order to secure office for himself and power for his party. In his religious policies he was never a pious Anglican like so many tories. He took communion only occasionally, perhaps to qualify himself for office, and in later life he could best be described as a deist. None the less, his private religious views never prevented him from defending the privileged position of the Church of England as the principal institution for the encouragement of private and public morality, and for promoting political harmony. He attacked the dissenters in Anne's reign and tried to restrict the concessions granted to them. When he courted the Pretender, St John insisted that, if he were to have any chance of gaining the throne, he must offer the strongest safeguards to the Church of England. During his years of opposition to Walpole, he avoided deliberately alienating the dissenters, but would countenance no attack on the special status of the established church.

In the disputes over the management of the War of the Spanish Succession (1702–13), St John did not adopt an intransigent tory line. During the early years of the war he showed a concern for the balance of power in Europe and was won over to the policy of supporting the duke of Marlborough's land campaigns in Europe. He did become increasingly concerned at the enormous cost of the war and at the gradual and unwarranted extension of the war aims of Britain and her allies, and he later came to share the landed interest's determination to achieve peace even at the cost of deserting Britain's European allies. His most rooted political belief was his conviction that the landed gentry were the backbone of the political nation and the natural leaders of society. This stemmed in part from his immense pride in the ancient lineage of his family, but he also shared the tory prejudice against the upstart financiers and stockjobbers, who were accused of corrupting the government, undermining the constitution, and ousting the landed élite from their position as the natural leaders in politics and society. While he was one of the new tories who had accommodated themselves to the revolution and the constitutional balance between crown and parliament, St John shared the widespread tory hostility to the other consequences of 1688–9. He did not, however, have a firm or consistent allegiance to any particular section of the tory party. His ambitions enabled him to swim confidently in tory waters, but to locate himself in different parts of the party at different times, depending on which section would best serve his own interests.

Early career, 1701–1710 St John first entered parliament in February 1701 and was soon engaged in those fierce political disputes which were such a feature of the last years of William III's reign. In these battles he ranged himself alongside the most partisan tory backbenchers. Although there is no evidence that he played a role in preparing the Act of Settlement of 1701, he was actively involved in the attacks on the conduct of the king's recent whig ministers and on their foreign policy in particular. He was returned to parliament without difficulty in the general election late in 1701, though the whigs tried to blacklist him. When Queen Anne succeeded to the throne in March 1702 he was among those tories who thought that her accession would enable the party to regain the political ground it had lost in William's reign. Again returned for Wootton Bassett in 1702, St John was soon prominent in the tory onslaught on the whigs. As a commissioner of accounts he helped investigate the whig misuse of exchequer funds in William's reign and helped to bring charges against Treasury officials. He played an even more important role in the religious disputes which the tories deliberately instigated. In 1702 and 1703 he helped to draft successive bills against the practice of occasional conformity, which allowed dissenters to qualify for office under the crown by taking communion occasionally in the Church of England. Both bills were defeated by the whig-dominated House of Lords. He also played a leading role in disputing with the whig peers over the Aylesbury election case and the investigation of the 'Scotch plot' in early 1704. Thereafter, however, St John began to trim his sails and to moderate his conduct in order to secure a government post.

The queen's chief political advisers, the triumvirate of Marlborough, Godolphin, and Harley, had all hoped to be able to secure the support of the moderate tories in parliament, while they endeavoured to prosecute the War of the Spanish Succession against France. They soon began to despair at the factious conduct of the tory majority in the Commons, however, and it was left to Harley, the speaker and the ministry's most able political manager in the lower house, to attempt to moderate their conduct. He had soon detected that St John was one of those partisan backbenchers who might be converted to being a supporter of the ministry's foreign policy and he set about courting him. For his part St John had begun to admire Marlborough's brilliant conduct of the war and he began to moderate his more factious behaviour. He refused to join his friends in obstructing the general's war efforts by delaying a vital money bill and he declined to be re-elected a commissioner of accounts in February 1704.

When the ministry was recast in April 1704 Harley became a secretary of state, St John was appointed secretary at war, and several of his tory friends also took minor office. Once he had accepted a ministerial place St John was anxious to end his association with the extreme tories and was determined to prove himself in office. He vigorously opposed tory plans to bring in a third bill against the practice of occasional conformity. When the tories proceeded with a new bill and even planned to tack this measure onto a money bill in order to drive it through the Lords, since the upper chamber did not usually oppose money bills, St John joined with Harley in defeating the threatened tack on 28 November 1704. This was one of the most crucial party votes of the reign and it rudely shattered the flimsy unity of the tory party. It took nearly six years to patch up this serious breach between the moderate and extreme tories.

St John did not desert his tory principles entirely. Like Harley he was determined that the ministry should not be dominated by the whigs but must continue to seek an accommodation with the more moderate tories. He was relieved when the general election of 1705 allowed the court and the moderate tory ministers to hold the balance between the two parties. Having cut himself off from the bulk of the tory party, he could only hope that Harley would win over more tory moderates and would successfully resist any drift by Marlborough and Godolphin towards the whigs, who were much more committed to the European war than were their tory rivals.

As secretary at war from 1704 to 1708 St John proved himself to be a vigorous and capable administrator in charge of recruitment, billeting, the supply of clothes and equipment, convoys, transport, the care of sick and wounded troops, and a whole complex of logistical details. In many of his tasks he had to work closely with Marlborough, Godolphin, or Harley. He impressed them all with his energy and diligence. Marlborough was particularly appreciative of his efforts, and the general's victories owed something to St John's efforts behind the scenes. The secretary spoke regularly on military affairs in the Commons as he piloted recruiting bills and army estimates through the house. He had a finger in many pies and this allowed him to see at first hand some of the intractable problems thrown up by the war. It brought home to him the enormous difficulties involved in reinforcing the armies overseas and in organizing a military expedition to a distant theatre of war. He certainly learned that the task of securing Spain for the Austrian claimant was beyond the resources of Britain and her allies.

Recruitment for the army began to break down when Britain was required to supply large forces for the war in Spain. By April 1707 the allied army that was defeated at Almanza was seriously undermanned. This was not due to any defect on St John's part as he had worked extremely hard to recruit troops for Spain, but he had to bear the brunt of explaining to an angry House of Commons why there were only 8660 active British troops at Almanza when parliament had arranged to pay for 29,395 men. Despite offering various excuses and explanations, St John was unable to provide a defence that satisfied the house. The ministry now recognized that it could not control the House of Commons without having the firm support of either the whig or the tory party.

Harley and St John had struggled for some time to persuade Marlborough and Godolphin that they needed to win over more tory supporters in the Commons. They had failed to prevent the tories raising the issue of 'the church in danger' in December 1705, opposing the Regency Act in 1706, or criticizing the Act of Union with Scotland in 1707. For their part Marlborough and Godolphin, preoccupied as they were with the war in Europe, saw the whigs as the more natural supporters of the ministry and its war policies. They had advised the queen to appoint the whig earl of Sunderland as Harley's fellow secretary of state in December 1706 and to advance a few other whigs to minor office in early 1707. In the parliamentary session of 1707–8, when both the whig and tory parties refused to give the ministry strong backing in the Commons, the leading ministers had to decide which party to buy off. Marlborough and Godolphin believed that it had to be the whig party, as it was more firmly attached to the war against France. Harley and St John had hoped the ministry would prefer to make concessions to the tories. When Marlborough and Godolphin won the battle of wills, Harley, St John, and their closest allies resigned in February 1708.

St John had not been forced to resign. He chose to follow Harley's lead because he accepted his interpretation of the crisis and he preferred to retain his strained links with the tories rather than sever them completely by capitulating to the whigs. His decision cost him dear in the short term. William Bromley and the high tories did not immediately welcome him back into the party fold with open arms. And in the general election of 1708 not only did the tory party suffer its only general election defeat in Anne's reign, but St John himself failed to be re-elected. A rift with his father prevented him contesting Wootton Bassett and he failed to find an alternative seat. He spent the next parliament largely on his wife's estate at Bucklebury in Berkshire, where he enjoyed the life of a rural squire and re-established his contacts with grass-roots toryism. He expressed himself content with his political retirement, but, given his energy, temperament, and ambition, his protestations had a hollow ring.

From his rural retreat St John learned to appreciate the tory discontent with the enormous financial burdens placed on the landed interest by the war, and he regularly urged Harley to ally himself with Bromley and reunite the tory party. Harley was already employed in this effort and after months of negotiations he established a working relationship with the bulk of the tory party. He was also active in winning over a number of moderate court peers, such as Newcastle and Shrewsbury, and in building an influence at court through the queen's new favourite, Abigail Masham. Meanwhile the Godolphin ministry ran into serious difficulties because of its failure to make peace and its unwise decision to impeach Henry Sacheverell for his high-church sermons and so unleash a powerful cry of 'the church in danger'. By August 1710 Harley had completed the piecemeal destruction of the Godolphin ministry, but he was most reluctant to create a ministry dominated by the high tories.

Secretary of state, 1710–1714 Because of his own usefulness and his adamant refusal to accept a lesser post, St John persuaded Harley to recommend him for promotion to secretary of state for the northern department in September 1710. While he envisaged making greater concessions to the tories than Harley desired, he was prepared for the moment to follow Harley's devious political strategy. A wish to catch the strong tide flowing in favour of the tories, however, persuaded him to write *A Letter to The Examiner* and to encourage the production and distribution of *The Examiner* as a party journal (and to enlist Swift as a regular contributor to it). His own strong desire to return to parliament also led him to urge Harley to call an immediate general election. The general election in the autumn of 1710 produced a large tory majority and saw St John elected for both Berkshire and Wootton Bassett. He preferred the more prestigious county seat.

In late 1710 St John had neither reason nor opportunity to challenge Harley's decision not to rely exclusively on the tory party for support. It was not until the spring of 1711 that he first saw an opportunity to strike out in a different direction from his mentor. He was influenced by the appearance of the October Club among tory backbenchers, a pressure group which demanded more partisan policies. He was also flattered with the popularity he gained on the tory backbenches after he had supported the Landed Qualification Act of early 1711 which ensured that candidates for seats in the Commons must possess substantial landed property. When Harley was severely wounded by Antoine de Guiscard, a French refugee, on 8 March 1711, and had to withdraw from politics for several weeks, St John saw an opportunity to direct the ministry's affairs. He proved inadequate to the task, however. He failed to control the tory backbenchers effectively and he secured the vote of adequate supplies only with some difficulty. His plan for an expedition against Quebec also came to grief. He had to admit that Harley was still indispensable to the success of the ministry and he was deeply jealous of the latter's elevation to the peerage, as earl of Oxford, and promotion to lord treasurer.

St John's breach with Oxford widened substantially when he discovered that he had been deliberately excluded from the ministry's tentative peace negotiations with France. These had opened as early as July 1710, but St John only belatedly learned what had been happening behind his back when the cabinet discussed the French proposals on 25 April 1711. Even then he was not allowed to play a major role in these negotiations for several more months. Oxford preferred to conduct all the important discussions himself, with both the allies and the French agents. St John deeply resented Oxford's inveterate secrecy, criticized his frequent contacts with the whigs, and was jealous of his monopoly of the queen's confidence. The strained relations between the two ministers gradually degenerated into bitter rivalry.

It took some time for St John to stamp his vigorous presence on the peace negotiations with France, but even then they never came under his direct control. By September 1711 he was dominating the discussions with French agents, he signed the peace preliminaries of that month, and he was much more prepared than Oxford to agree terms that might be rejected by Britain's allies. He struck out at domestic opponents of peace and he assisted Swift in his celebrated pamphlet *The Conduct of the Allies*, which claimed that Britain bore an unfair burden of the war. But, when the tory earl of Nottingham joined the whig peers in December 1711 in opposing any peace which allowed Spain to remain in Bourbon hands, it was again Oxford who came to the ministry's rescue. It was he who persuaded the queen to create twelve new tory peers to give the ministry a secure majority in the Lords. Marlborough and other officers were then dismissed from their army commands. Oxford had reasserted his dominance over the ministry, but only by making further concessions to the tories.

St John was aware that Britain could get advantageous terms from France if only the ministry could persuade the allies to reduce their demands. In February 1712 St John tried to intimidate the Dutch by launching an attack on the barrier treaty, by which the whigs had previously agreed to secure them a line of strong frontier fortresses against French aggression, and he also made it clear that he was ready to make a separate peace. In May he and Dartmouth, the other secretary of state, issued the new commander-in-chief of the British forces, the duke of Ormond, with the notorious 'restraining orders', which advised him to leave the confederate army and avoid any siege or battle. The French were made aware of these orders. St John's bold efforts received some reward. Several more tories were brought into the ministry and he himself was made Viscount Bolingbroke. He blamed Oxford, however, for what he believed to be an undeserved blow to his ambition and a slight to his family honour because he was not made an earl. It completed the personal breach between them.

Partly to soothe Bolingbroke's ruffled pride, Oxford

agreed to send him to France to speed up the peace negotiations. With the encouragement of the French ministers Bolingbroke sought to take a decisive step in the direction of a separate peace. Oxford refused to countenance his conduct. He upbraided Bolingbroke at a cabinet meeting on 28 September 1712 for going beyond his instructions and he put Dartmouth in control of correspondence with the French. He charged Bolingbroke with seeking a separate peace and with making the French such open-handed promises that they would be reluctant to make a general peace with all of the allies. Unsupported by his cabinet colleagues, Bolingbroke had to back down. Oxford also made it clear that he believed that Bolingbroke had met the Pretender in France (they had been to see the same opera) and had allowed the French to believe that the ministry sympathized with the Jacobite cause. Although he had no proof of his charge, Oxford made it clear that he regarded Bolingbroke's behaviour in France as the height of folly. The latter retired to Bucklebury for a few days to lick his wounds.

Although Bolingbroke gradually resumed his role of instructing the British agents negotiating terms in France and of corresponding with the French on the ministry's behalf, the final treaty signed at Utrecht in 1713 was still probably more Oxford's achievement than his. Only in the final stages did he make the running, threatening the French with a renewal of the war and securing the dismissal of more whigs still holding minor places in the government. In spite of some of its provisions and the perfidious nature of some of its implications, the peace proved extremely popular with parliament and with the nation at large. The tories were particularly delighted with it, but this did not prevent Sir Thomas Hanmer leading a revolt in June 1713 against the commercial treaty with France that Bolingbroke had worked so hard to negotiate. The scale of the revolt was so large that Bolingbroke unfairly saw Oxford's hand behind it. In fact the tory rebels feared that the treaty implied Jacobite sympathies within the ministry, and their revolt marked the emergence of a body of Hanoverian tories and heralded a major split in the party on the crucial issue of the succession to Queen Anne.

Bolingbroke's response to this crisis was to urge Oxford to greater boldness and to a more partisan tory party. He protested against Oxford's indecision and urged the removal of all whigs and moderates still in office. When Oxford did recast the ministry in August 1713, however, most of the new appointments went to his allies not Bolingbroke's. The general election which followed actually saw more tories returned than in the previous election, but the tories did not return to parliament as a united force. Bolingbroke strove to widen his own base of support within the party and again urged a vigorous, partisan policy on Oxford. He himself opened negotiations with the Pretender (as Oxford had also done, though more circumspectly) and he urged him to change his religion, warning him that the tories would never unite behind a Catholic claimant to the throne. He also tried to win over Abigail Masham, the queen's favourite, so that he might yet challenge Oxford's influence at court. Meanwhile, however, he had to co-operate with Oxford to resist whig attacks on the ministry's uncertain policy towards the succession.

In June 1714 Bolingbroke successfully curried favour with tory backbenchers by supporting the Schism Bill attacking the existence of dissenting academies, a measure Oxford would not support. His lack of leadership skills, however, was exposed by his failure both to prevent the whig opposition passing anti-Jacobite votes and to pilot votes of supply through parliament as the lord treasurer could do. He also found it difficult to combat Oxford's influence at court, as the lord treasurer warned the queen of the dangers to which she would be exposed if he were dismissed. There would be no money and no credit, and the whole church interest would believe she planned to bring in the Pretender. He could also stress Bolingbroke's notorious treatment of his wife and his lack of financial probity. The last charged gained weight when Bolingbroke narrowly escaped damaging disclosures in parliament when the terms of the commercial treaty with Spain, signed in November 1713, were discussed by parliament in the summer of 1714. Bolingbroke avoided further difficulties when the queen dissolved parliament on 8 July 1714.

Bolingbroke did not give up the struggle, and Oxford's neglect of business and his heavy drinking finally alienated the queen. She was persuaded to dismiss the lord treasurer on 27 July 1714, but there was to be no triumph for Bolingbroke. The queen fell mortally ill within hours of dismissing Oxford and she died on 1 August. Bolingbroke lost his nerve in this crisis. He had insufficient support in the cabinet and his negotiations with the Pretender were not far enough advanced. When Oxford threw his weight behind the Hanoverian tories Bolingbroke meekly followed his example and at once took the oath of allegiance to George I. There is no evidence that he considered declaring the succession of the Pretender. It was too late to model himself as a supporter of the incoming court, however. Bolingbroke was omitted from George I's list of regents or lords justices. At the end of August he was dismissed and his office was sealed up. He tried to put a brave front on his sudden reversal of fortune, and even turned up at George's coronation on 20 October in the hope that the new king would see the advantage of governing with the support of a united tory party. The party remained deeply split, however, and still lacked a generally recognized leader. They faced the general election in early 1715 more disunited than ever and saw the determined and loyal whigs, with firm crown support, win a very significant victory.

The Jacobite cause Bolingbroke did not immediately panic, but his alarm grew as the triumphant and vindictive whigs began dismissing the supporters of the previous tory administration and were clearly seeking evidence of political misconduct by the late ministers. Bolingbroke attended the new parliament in March 1715 in order to defend his past conduct. When the whig ministers ordered the seizure of Matthew Prior's papers in Paris (where he had helped Bolingbroke to negotiate the peace) and asked Bolingbroke to surrender his own papers, he feared for his life and decided to flee to France. He made his arrangements in great secrecy, borrowing money from James Brydges and conveying his lands to six loyal trustees, who were to hold them for his wife, who acknowledged his debt to Brydges and others. He then fled the country on 27 March, disguised as a servant of one of the French ministers. He was just in time to avoid arrest. He was later condemned in his absence by an act of attainder and lost his estates and title. His flight was an enormous blunder. Once again he had lost his nerve in a crisis and had made the situation worse. Oxford, by contrast, stood his ground, was imprisoned for a considerable time in the Tower, but was eventually released as the ministry failed to find sufficiently damaging evidence against him. The whigs were able to take Bolingbroke's flight as clear proof of his guilt, while the tories were demoralized and dismayed.

At first Bolingbroke sought to justify his actions and to lie low in Bellevue, near Lyons, hoping the storm would pass. He denied that he was intending to betray the Hanoverian succession or had ever planned to do so. When it was clear, however, that the whigs would take firm action against him he accepted an earldom from the Pretender in July 1715 and agreed to become his secretary of state. This was an even greater mistake than his original decision to flee, though he claimed that Jacobitism was the only refuge now that the tories had been virtually proscribed by George I and his ministers. Once Bolingbroke had joined the Pretender he set about his new duties with characteristic energy and enthusiasm. He soon realized that his optimism was misplaced. The whole Jacobite rising of 1715 was dogged by misfortune and mistakes. It was more difficult to gain financial and military assistance from the French than Bolingbroke had ever imagined. When Louis XIV died at the end of August 1715 a vital prop of the Jacobite cause collapsed. The duke of Orléans, the French regent for the young Louis XV, refused to commit himself to the cause, which was doomed by a complete failure to co-ordinate risings in various parts of the British Isles and reinforce them with professional troops from France. Bolingbroke was unable to harness the efforts and energies of the Pretender's various supporters and sympathizers. His own advice and counsel were frequently ignored or opposed in the Pretender's court and he regularly clashed with the Pretender's other advisers. He was adamant that the Pretender must put himself at the head of the tory party in England and he assured him that this could be achieved only if he gave the firmest of undertakings to preserve the privileged position of the Church of England. He also advised the Pretender to accept many of the major constitutional developments that had occurred in Britain since the revolution. He desired to preserve a limited monarchy and a constitution balanced between crown and parliament. Bolingbroke was not the type of Jacobite who had learned nothing and forgotten nothing since 1688.

When the Pretender's expedition to Scotland ended in disaster he blamed Bolingbroke for sending inadequate supplies and reinforcements. He dismissed his secretary of state in March 1716, a decision that soon resulted in mutual and unsavoury recriminations. Bolingbroke was made a scapegoat by other Jacobites for the fiasco of the 1715 rising. For his part, he quickly made contact with Lord Stair, the British ambassador to France, and sought to negotiate a pardon in return for betraying what he knew about the Jacobite cause. He desperately tried to make himself useful to the whig ministers in London. He recognized that the only card in his hand was his influence with some of the tory opposition. He argued that he could strengthen the ministry's position in parliament and the country by counteracting Jacobite propaganda and persuading some of the tories to moderate their opposition. He could not afford to betray his former Jacobite colleagues openly or he would lose all credit with the tories, but he was prepared to tell the king or Marlborough everything he knew and to trust to their discretion. He was concerned that his betrayal of the Jacobites should be secret, but he was willing to make it effective.

Bolingbroke warned Sir William Wyndham, in September 1716, that the Jacobite cause was desperate, its supporters on the continent were miserable wretches, and their measures weak and impractical. He himself was the subject of bitter denunciations by the Jacobites while the Pretender justified his dismissal of Bolingbroke in a personal letter to Wyndham. To combat this successful campaign of vilification, Bolingbroke redoubled his efforts to justify his whole conduct since 1710. He wrote letters to various tory friends and, by the end of 1717, he had prepared for circulation among them private copies of his *Letter to Sir William Windham*. In this, one of his most powerful works, he sought to justify his conduct since the tory triumph of 1710, to wean the tories from any commitment to Jacobitism, and to reduce the political temperature which threatened his own political future and that of the tory party. He insisted that the Pretender must be abandoned as a religious bigot or he would threaten to ruin the tory party and the Church of England. Yet he also strove to allay any whig suspicion that he was determined to revive the tory party so that it would become a serious rival to the whigs for political power. The tories proved deaf to his exhortations, however, and the whig ministers were not easily persuaded that he had really repented of his former actions. It was to take Bolingbroke several more years before he could work his passage home. Prolonged negotiations with various whig ministers failed to win any significant results for nearly a decade.

Exile and study During his enforced exile in France, Bolingbroke tried to resign himself to his fate and sought consolation in study. In 1716 he wrote his *Reflections upon Exile* (in imitation of Seneca). It was a false and puerile description of his state of mind as he stressed the virtue of a stoic resolve in the face of adversity and claimed a courage born of philosophy. He did, however, mix with French aristocrats interested in a wide range of studies, including Matignon, Torcy, and Madame de Ferriol, as well as with genuine scholars such as Voltaire, Pierre Joseph Alary, and

Lévesque de Pouilly. In such circles he came into contact with the ideas and notions of those who were playing a crucial role in the development of the French Enlightenment. He also met a widow, Marie-Claire de Marcilly, marquise de Villette (1675/6–1750), whom he married privately in early 1719, within a few months of the death of his first wife in England, though the public marriage ceremony was delayed until 1722. In December 1720 he and his second wife leased the Château de la Source, near Orléans, where he spent much of his time, apart from frequent visits to Paris, until his return to England in 1725.

While in exile Bolingbroke began making a serious study of history. His enlightened scepticism led him to doubt the historian's ability to recover the distant past. He repeatedly expressed his distrust of biblical and ancient history, which he regarded as little more than myths and fables. Nor did he have any patience with antiquaries who simply amassed facts and placed them in chronological order. On the other hand his humanist side led him to argue that the chief value of studying history was the constant improvement it encouraged in private and public virtue. History, he maintained, inculcated moral and practical lessons, promoted social virtues, and provided a guide to future action. It was philosophy teaching by example. This utilitarian view of history encouraged Bolingbroke to use the past for partisan purposes. By 1724 he was planning a study of European history from the mid-sixteenth century to the treaty of Utrecht in 1713. In trying to explain developments over this period, he vacillated between an emphasis on the actions of great men and a belief in the crucial influence of social structure and economic change.

Bolingbroke was also much attracted to the study of philosophy, which increasingly absorbed his attention from about 1720. He gave priority to experimental philosophy rather than to metaphysical speculation, and he rejected both Plato's philosophy and the Cartesian approach to deductive reasoning. He became a disciple of the intellectual approach of Locke and Newton, but he paid particular attention to the study of religion and morality. He was very interested in natural law and natural religion, and gradually developed into a deist. Professing a harmless rationalism, he came to believe in a supreme being, but one that was distinct, even remote, from the world. He rejected the notion of particular providence and of a God actively involved in the affairs of men. Not convinced that the Bible was the revealed word of God, he became critical of much of the Old Testament and he was not entirely satisfied with the New Testament either. He appears to have regarded Christ as a great religious teacher, but not as divine. He also rejected the doctrines of purgatory and eternal punishment, and remained unconvinced of the immortality of the soul. In his *Reflections Concerning Innate Moral Principles* (written in the early 1720s, but first published posthumously in 1752), he insisted that moral principles were not innate, but were the product of experience and instruction. Reason was not the same in all men and was never perfect in any man. In this and his other philosophical works, Bolingbroke borrowed heavily

(but often without acknowledgement) from greater thinkers, failed to create a coherent system of philosophy, and was frequently contradictory and inconsistent.

Although they did not appear until 1754, three years after his death, most of Bolingbroke's philosophical essays were the result of his studies started in France and continued after his return to England in 1725. While he gained in knowledge and experience, he did not radically depart from the views expressed in his earlier works. Nor did he ever lose his dependence on greater minds, though he tried to conceal his debt to particular scholars. His knowledge was large, but less extensive than he claimed and he never succeeded in developing a coherent philosophical system of his own. He strove in particular to erect an ethical and religious system based on reason and natural law. Although he was a critic of organized religion from a theological and philosophical standpoint, he remained convinced of its social and political utility. While he argued that men ought to be guided by reason as far as possible, he acknowledged that reason was never infallible and that it could often be overborne by passion. He confidently affirmed the existence of natural law, but never explained precisely what it was or how human reason derived such laws from the world of nature. The universe, he believed, was one vast linked design, the great chain of being, and man was only one part of this immense structure. There was an infinite gradation of forms of being, both above and below man; and it was impossible for man to realize the significance of them all. Man could not appreciate the entire pattern of the universe nor the significance of the role which good and evil played in it.

In his enquiries into civil government Bolingbroke rejected the doctrine of divine right and the social contract ideas of both Hobbes and Locke. He did not subscribe to the notion of a monarch chosen directly by God or elected by the free choice of all individuals. Nor did he favour a monarch imposed by conquest or outright force. Rather he favoured the notion that civil government was established by the heads of leading families and that rulers owed a duty to those who accepted their rule. Civil government was based on the implied consent of men of property, but must consult the interests of the people. Once established, civil government existed to promote law and order, to defend property, and to promote the welfare of all subjects. Bolingbroke undoubtedly admired England's ancient constitution, based on history, experience, and prescription. He always argued that the revolution of 1688–9 was justified in that it rejected absolute monarchy and restored the benefits of limited monarchy and a proper balance between the monarch and the landed classes through the latter's representatives in parliament.

Opposition to Walpole After years of uncertainty and bitter disappointment Bolingbroke was finally pardoned on 25 May 1723, but he was not released from all the penalties and forfeitures incurred under the act of attainder of 1715. Robert Walpole, the king's chief minister, refused to countenance further concessions and so Bolingbroke's estates, title, and seat in the Lords could not be recovered. Despite all his efforts to ingratiate himself with the Hanoverian court and the whig ministry, including a bribe to one of the king's mistresses, Bolingbroke failed to gain a complete restoration of his political rights. Walpole did not trust him not to stir up old party passions and so he would only support a reversal of the act of attainder to allow Bolingbroke to own and inherit property in England. This measure received the royal assent on 31 May 1725 and within weeks Bolingbroke had returned to England. He did not receive an ecstatic welcome, though Pope and Swift were delighted and so were a group of tories led by Wyndham and Bathurst. Other tories, especially the crypto-Jacobites and the friends of the late earl of Oxford, were not ready to welcome him with open arms and the whigs in power never trusted him.

Bolingbroke settled at Dawley, near Uxbridge, Middlesex, where he initially gave the impression of retiring from the political scene, but he very soon sought to rally the tory opposition in parliament and to ally it with the discontented whigs led by William Pulteney, who had recently resigned from Walpole's ministry. On 5 December 1726 there appeared the first issue of *The Craftsman*, a journalistic venture which heralded the birth of a formidable opposition to Walpole and the beginnings of a propaganda campaign of sustained brilliance and of rare political sophistication. Edited by Nicholas Amhurst and printed by Richard Francklin, *The Craftsman* attracted contributions from Bolingbroke, Pulteney, and other leading thinkers and writers in the opposition camp. Originally published twice weekly, *The Craftsman* became a weekly of more than twice the length from May 1727. During its period of greatest influence, from 1729 to 1732, at least 8000 copies of each issue were distributed and probably upwards of 12,000 copies in 1731. It was reprinted in several provincial towns, as well as in Amsterdam and New York, and collected editions appeared in 1731 and 1737. *The Craftsman* aroused such public interest and so embarrassed the ministry that Walpole spent large sums subsidizing a pro-ministerial press to reply to it (and to attack Bolingbroke and Pulteney in particular); and he had Francklin arrested on several occasions in an effort to silence it.

Bolingbroke opened his own political campaign in January 1727, with three essays in *The Occasional Writer* and 'The first vision of Camilick', his first contribution to *The Craftsman*. He set out to bring down Walpole as the necessary prelude to his own return to power. It was a daunting prospect as Walpole had the confidence of the king, an impregnable majority in the Lords, and a commanding influence in the Commons. To succeed, Bolingbroke had to forge a united and effective opposition from the most unpromising materials. The tories were still split along Jacobite and Hanoverian lines, and they were demoralized and disorganized after more than a decade in opposition. Some of the party's most able members had defected to the court or even joined the whigs and it now had fewer than 200 MPs in the Commons. The opposition whigs, led by William Pulteney, had a few men of talent,

but far fewer supporters in the Commons. Moreover these whigs did not differ from Walpole on any issue of basic principle and they had little in common with the tories, whom they suspected of harbouring Jacobite sympathies. Bolingbroke set about finding issues and exploring themes designed to embarrass Walpole and expose his methods of governing as corrupt and unconstitutional. He tried in particular to elaborate ideas and concepts of opposition that would justify his efforts to unite the disparate elements opposed to Walpole and his ministry.

Concerned with the interests of the landed gentry and conscious of the way Walpole abused his power, Bolingbroke devoted his pen to forging a political platform capable of uniting a majority of the political nation. He contributed nearly one hundred essays to *The Craftsman*. Many of these were individual polemical forays against the ministry that can be properly understood only by appreciating the specific context in which they were written and the debate with ministerial writers in which he was engaged. Some of his essays were part of a more coherent argument that delved below the surface of events and offered a sophisticated analysis of the political situation that resonated long after the death of the main protagonists. In 1730–31 Bolingbroke contributed twenty-two essays to *The Craftsman* using the persona of Humphrey Oldcastle. Together these formed his *Remarks on the History of England*. In 1733–4 he contributed a further series of essays which later formed *A Dissertation upon Parties*. In both of these series he laboured to destroy the old distinctions between whigs and tories and tried to forge a new country party able to defend the constitution and safeguard the liberties of the subject.

While Bolingbroke sensibly refrained from trying to revive the old cry of 'the church in danger' (though some of his tory allies still did so), as he knew this would drive a wedge between the tory and whig elements in the parliamentary opposition, he did seek to defend the interests of the landed gentry against the rising influence of the whole financial interest built around the national debt, the stock market, the Bank of England, and the great trading corporations such as the East India Company. He condemned the monied interest not only as a threat to the political influence and social status of the landed classes, but as a weapon which could be used by corrupt ministers to undermine the balance of the constitution, to subvert the liberties of the subject, and to weaken public morality in general. The money generated by the financial interest, together with the vast amount of crown patronage at the disposal of the crown, was condemned as the unconstitutional means by which Walpole and his ministerial cronies corrupted the electorate and influenced the behaviour of a majority of those sitting in both houses of parliament. By using crown patronage to pack parliament and destroy its political independence, Walpole was able to carry through his factious, corrupt, and unpopular policies. To combat this threat, Bolingbroke urged measures which would reduce crown patronage and make parliament more accountable to the landed classes by ending electoral corruption and ensuring more frequent general elections. Landed men alone, he believed, could be trusted to defend the true interests of the nation as a whole. As men of independent means, with a real stake in society, and as men of leisure, education, and the experience of commanding others, they were the natural governing élite of society.

Bolingbroke recognized that the opposition could never unite behind an effective programme while it remained divided by old whig and tory prejudices. He strove to counter the accusations that the tory party was still tainted with Jacobitism and, in the *Dissertation upon Parties* in particular, he tried to persuade parliament and public that the old whig and tory labels had lost all the real meaning they had once possessed. While admitting that there had once been real distinctions and genuine differences of principle between the two political parties, he now tried to maintain that the differences had all been settled at the revolution, when the two parties had combined to safeguard England's ancient, balanced constitution. It was absurd to continue using the same party labels when the real dispute was between a narrow and corrupt court faction and those honest, patriotic politicians trying to preserve the interests of the nation at large. The majority of the former whig and tory parties needed to unite in defence of liberty and the constitution, and in opposition to a handful of Jacobites on the one hand and Walpole's mercenary detachment on the other. Walpole and his hirelings were not upholding whig principles, as they claimed, but were simply feathering their own nests by corrupt and ignoble means. To defeat them, all men of good will with the true interests of the nation at heart must combine to save the nation. The opposition had to rise above the narrow spirit of the old party labels and create a new country party, which would embrace the interests of the whole nation and eject the corrupt faction now in power.

In his *Remarks on the History of England* Bolingbroke claimed that England had enjoyed an ancient constitution since time immemorial and that this constitution was based on a delicate balance between crown and parliament. English history had been a perpetual struggle between weak kings and their evil advisers on the one hand and the patriotic endeavours of brave parliamentarians on the other. Bolingbroke ransacked English history for examples of royal favourites and corrupt ministers undermining the constitution by corrupt methods, financial jobbery, crown patronage, continental alliances, and military adventures. The reader was always meant to equate Walpole and his methods with those of previous evil counsellors who had threatened the true interests of the people. The revolution of 1688–9, Bolingbroke insisted, had restored the balance of the constitution that had been disturbed by James II. It had not ushered in a new era of liberty. In recent years, however, Walpole had followed the example of earlier evil counsellors and had exploited crown patronage and the new financial interest in order to undermine the independence of parliament and the liberties of the subject. Walpole's defeat could be engineered only if the tories abandoned all attachment to the Jacobite cause and joined with the opposition whigs in a national, patriotic endeavour. A formed opposition of this kind was legitimate when it abandoned the corrupt aims of a particular faction and the vested interests of a specific party in order to promote the interests of the nation at large. Bolingbroke did not envisage and never advocated that this opposition needed to be a permanent feature of the parliamentary system, always criticizing the existing administration and standing by to replace it as the government at any time. His concept of opposition implied that once the united efforts of honest men had brought down a corrupt regime, then all abuses would be remedied and an age of harmony and virtue would ensue. Opposition would not be needed unless and until the constitution were again threatened by a corrupt faction that monopolized power and promoted its own narrow interests.

Bolingbroke's complaints against Walpole and his political methods were motivated by thwarted ambition and so they cannot be taken at face value. Despite Bolingbroke's claims, Walpole did not survive in power for so long solely because of his exploitation of crown patronage and his abuse of power, important to his success though these were. Walpole also possessed superb administrative abilities and rare powers of persuasion that were widely admired, and he promoted policies that were often willingly supported by independent backbenchers who owed him no particular allegiance. Bolingbroke never did his great rival justice. Nor did he find issues of sufficient gravity or arguments of sufficient weight to unite firmly the tories and discontented whigs into an effective opposition capable of ousting Walpole and replacing him with an entirely new administration based on different principles.

Bolingbroke did help to make *The Craftsman* the greatest opposition journal of the age and he was also at the centre of a literary circle (including Pope, Swift, and John Gay) that attacked Walpole in verse, plays, and imaginative prose fiction. It is a mistake, however, to see all the opposition writings of the age as being influenced by ideas emanating from the mind of Bolingbroke. There were many different strands in the opposition to Walpole, and Bolingbroke never controlled or inspired them all, and indeed never succeeded in his efforts to pull them together into a coherent political ideology or an agreed platform. Nor was he able in person to lead the opposition campaign within parliament or even to find a steady stream of issues that would enable his political allies to keep Walpole permanently on the defensive. Many leaders of the parliamentary opposition, even close allies such as Wyndham and Pulteney, were considerable political figures in their own right. They were not mere puppets manipulated by the scheming Bolingbroke. Jacobites and malcontent whigs might occasionally ally themselves with him while pursuing their own political agenda. Urban merchants in the opposition often acted quite separately from him, and even the tory party was never his to control and command. Only Wyndham and his followers in the Commons were amenable to his ideas, though they were never under his direct leadership.

All elements in the opposition to Walpole sought issues on which to attack the ministry. Bolingbroke played a significant role not only in condemning Walpole's political methods, but in challenging aspects of his specific policies. He particularly attacked the ministry's foreign policy and tried to drive a wedge between Walpole and Viscount Townshend, who already differed in their responses to the complex problems bedevilling the relations between the great powers of Europe. Bolingbroke encouraged the opposition to attack the treaty of Seville, signed by Britain in November 1729 and hailed by Walpole as a triumph, and also the ministry's employment of Hessian mercenaries. In the autumn of 1729 Bolingbroke toured the Netherlands and north-west France. This visit and his connections in France led him to suspect that the French were rebuilding the harbour and fortifications of Dunkirk, contrary to the terms of the treaty of Utrecht. At his own expense he organized further investigations of Dunkirk itself. He then persuaded Wyndham to open a surprise debate on the subject in the House of Commons in February 1730. The opposition at last had a major issue which temporarily embarrassed the ministry and seriously dented Walpole's large majority. The case of Dunkirk certainly rattled many independent backbenchers. To weaken their attachment to the opposition Walpole made great play of Bolingbroke's clandestine and suspicious role in bringing on the whole debate. He succeeded in turning the debate into a discussion on Bolingbroke's past conduct and he managed to discredit the opposition's legitimate criticism of ministerial negligence. Bolingbroke tried in vain to recover lost ground by writing *The Case of Dunkirk Faithfully Stated and Impartially Considered* (1730), and followed this up with a justification of his own conduct.

The opposition recovered strongly in 1732–3 as Walpole's plans to extend his excise reforms to wine and tobacco gave it a useful stick with which to belabour him. *The Craftsman* played a major role in whipping up considerable and widespread opposition to Walpole's proposals, particularly within the merchant communities. Bolingbroke himself was rather slow to join in this attack, but he eventually did see its significance and attempted to rally the landed interest behind the opposition to the excise scheme. Independent opinion in parliament became so alarmed that Walpole, seeing his majority steadily decline, abandoned his reforms in April 1733 before they were actually voted down. It was a major reverse for the ministry, nevertheless, but Walpole soon retrieved the situation. He skilfully exploited the divisions within the opposition and exposed it as an uneasy alliance between tories and discontented whigs. He again brought forward Bolingbroke's previous conduct and his Jacobite past, and quite easily extricated himself from the greatest crisis he had faced in ten years. Bolingbroke's *Dissertation upon Parties* failed to convince many politicians that the divisions between whigs and tories were obsolete, and his advice to

the electorate on how to vote for honest candidates, published in his pamphlet *The Freeholder's Political Catechism* (1733), failed to prevent Walpole securing a solid majority in the general election of 1734.

Worse for Bolingbroke's political ambitions and public reputation was his rash decision to establish a dangerously dependent relationship with Chavigny, the French ambassador in London. Together they regularly conferred on foreign affairs and domestic issues, and even freely discussed the Pretender's aims. Bolingbroke unwisely suggested ways in which the Pretender might revive the Jacobite cause in England and accepted French advice about the advisability of Britain remaining neutral during the War of the Polish Succession. Worse still, in the summer of 1733 he accepted a substantial pension from the French court in order to help finance the opposition to Walpole. He was clearly providing potentially damning evidence of his unbridled ambition and his political recklessness. In doing so he offered himself as a hostage to fortune. Walpole soon learned of his close relations with Chavigny, though not the precise details of his near treasonable conduct. Walpole used the information he had to set about demolishing Bolingbroke's already dubious reputation with the independent backbenchers. He found a convenient opportunity to attack Bolingbroke when the opposition brought in a bill to repeal the Septennial Act in the spring of 1734. Bolingbroke had recently opposed this act and sought a return to triennial parliaments in *The Craftsman Extraordinary; in which the Right of the People to Frequent Elections of the Representatives is Fully Consider'd*. Walpole ignored the details of the issue at stake and instead launched into a blistering attack on Bolingbroke in the House of Commons, accusing him of betraying the secrets of every court he had attended and every master he had ever served. This was followed by a savage press campaign designed to destroy the last vestiges of Bolingbroke's credit with the opposition whigs and to drive the wedge between opposition whigs and tories ever deeper. Bolingbroke's Jacobite past and his relationship with Chavigny were fully exploited in such pamphlets as *The Grand Accuser—the Greatest of All Criminals* (1734) and in a series of essays in the pro-ministerial *Daily Courant* from January 1735 that urged the necessity of driving Bolingbroke out of the kingdom. Bolingbroke even feared impeachment. This, his precarious financial situation, and his blasted reputation with the opposition whigs persuaded him that a return to France was his best strategy. He pretended to Wyndham that his second retirement from politics in late May 1735 was his own free choice. It was an unconvincing effort to camouflage his political failure. His departure from the political scene left the parliamentary opposition more prone than ever to a split along party lines. He had failed to create an effective country ideology and he had not succeeded in uniting the opposition into a potential governing party.

Patriotism In June 1735 Bolingbroke settled in Chanteloup, in Touraine, but within a year he had moved to Argeville, near Fontainebleau, where he lived until his final return to England in 1744. In between he did manage to pay several visits to England to settle his financial affairs and to keep in touch with his friends. From July 1738 to April 1739 he stayed with Pope at Twickenham, and he made further visits there in 1742 and 1743–4. In 1744, after the death of his father, he was able to resettle in the ancestral home at Battersea.

In his rural retreats in France, Bolingbroke once more lived the life of a country gentleman and the retired scholar. He hunted regularly and devoted himself again to his studies. He wrote *Of the True Use of Retirement and Study*, completed his *Letters on the Study and Use of History*, and revised his philosophical essays. He insisted that the true and proper object of the study of history was the constant improvement of private and public virtue. History should have a practical value to it and hence it was best to study recent history. He himself remained preoccupied with a study of European diplomacy from the sixteenth century to 1713.

Despite all his protestations to the contrary and all his efforts to renew his studies of history and philosophy, Bolingbroke was still captivated by the contemporary political scene in Britain. He did not entirely abandon his efforts to defeat Walpole or to destroy his system of government, even after the great minister had retired. He could never admit that Walpole had the confidence of parliament or of the political nation. Nor could he acknowledge that his own diagnosis of the country's political ailments was in any way at fault. The opposition to Walpole had failed because, he believed, it had refused to adopt the remedies he had prescribed. He tried once more to argue the case for a united opposition based on the patriotic desire to defend the balanced constitution and the liberties of the people. He addressed *A Letter on the Spirit of Patriotism* to Lord Cornbury in 1736, in which he urged all honest politicians to abandon their attachment to whig or tory notions and to unite against the ministerial abuse of crown patronage and the corrupting effects of the monied interest. Corruption must be destroyed by a revival of patriotism and public morality and by a regular, systematic opposition. Bolingbroke looked to a new generation of young politicians to follow his moral exhortations.

When Frederick, prince of Wales, openly quarrelled with his father in 1737, Bolingbroke was quick to see the political opportunity which this breach created. He hoped that the prince might remove Walpole from office when he succeeded his father and bring the opposition leaders into office. He therefore encouraged politicians and literary figures to gather around the heir to the throne and to promote an ideology of the patriot prince who would rescue the constitution from the corrupt gang in power. Bolingbroke himself was encouraged to write one of his most celebrated pamphlets, *The Idea of a Patriot King*, which was circulating in manuscript form by late 1738. This treatise has been more highly praised and more roundly condemned than any of Bolingbroke's other works. It probably does not merit all the attention lavished upon it. While it is the most philosophical of his treatises on politics and the most high-flown in style, it did not produce a really deep analysis of contemporary politics or an effective solution to the constitutional problems of the day. Bolingbroke confessed that Britain's balanced constitution could be preserved only if the monarch acted on patriot principles, ruling in the interests of the nation at large and choosing as his ministers men of property, probity, and public virtue. If he did so, all political abuses would be remedied, all differences of principle resolved, and the nation would unite in the pursuit of virtue and patriotic harmony. The spiritual and material welfare of the nation would be promoted and a regular, formed opposition in parliament would no longer be necessary. It has been suggested, though not convincingly, that the superficiality of Bolingbroke's political analysis in this tract masked a punitive satire that really urged an appeal to Charles Stuart, the Young Pretender, as the patriot king needed to safeguard the constitution.

Bolingbroke's appeal to the new patriots and to the supporters of Prince Frederick came just as Walpole was at last meeting considerable opposition in parliament and out of doors, and even within his ministry, to his conduct of foreign policy. War with Spain from 1739 and with France from 1740 led to the gradual disintegration of Walpole's administration, but the parliamentary opposition could still not heal the divisions between its whig and tory components or unite behind a country or patriot programme. Bolingbroke no longer had much credit with the opposition's leaders and this declined even further with the death of Sir William Wyndham in 1740. When Walpole finally resigned early in 1742 the opposition was still divided between Jacobites, Hanoverian tories, country whigs, and discontented whigs simply desperate for office. Walpole's political disciples, Henry and Thomas Pelham, easily bought off Pulteney and a handful of other opposition leaders, reconstructed the administration along essentially the same lines, and succeeded in keeping the bulk of the long-standing opposition to Walpole out of office. The fall of Walpole had failed to mark the triumph of a country or patriot programme for which Bolingbroke had striven for so long. His political analysis of the situation had been flawed and his political ideas had been rejected. Not surprisingly he blamed Pulteney's ambition and weakness for the failure to replace Walpole with an administration based on different principles and employing different methods.

Last years In the last decade of his life Bolingbroke had finally to acknowledge that his political career was over and that many of his cherished hopes had been dashed. He did play a minor role in helping to create a more broadly based administration in 1744, but this ministry failed to live up to the country or patriot ideals which he had been advocating for so long. During the 1745 Jacobite rising he wisely remained a mere spectator of events. Most of his time was now devoted to those writings of his which he hoped might instruct posterity and revive his name and cause in future generations. In 1749 he wrote his last political tract, *Some Reflections on the Present State of the Nation*, which expressed his frustration, his fears for the future of the country, and his lingering hope for a patriot king. Even this faint hope was dashed when Prince Frederick died in early 1751.

Under pressure from Alexander Pope, Bolingbroke did attempt to put his philosophical essays into some semblance of order, though he never completed this task. Four long essays were finished and were prefaced with a dedication to Pope (whose ideas they had influenced), but many of the others remained as mere fragments or minutes of essays. Bolingbroke did allow Pope to print private copies, for the use of their immediate circle of friends, of his *Letters on the Study and Use of History*, in 1738, and a volume containing *The Idea of a Patriot King*, *A Letter on the Spirit of Patriotism*, and *Of the State of Parties at the Accession of George the First*, in 1739. When Pope died on 30 May 1744 Bolingbroke was genuinely grief-stricken, but he was still shocked when he discovered that Pope had secretly printed some 1500 copies of *The Idea of a Patriot King*, a clandestine edition which Bolingbroke sought to destroy. Unfortunately not all copies were destroyed, because in January 1749 the *London Magazine* began publishing extracts from this text. Furious at the opening of old wounds, Bolingbroke published an official and revised volume containing the same three texts that had been privately printed in 1739. To this he unwisely attached an 'Advertisement', disclosing Pope's earlier betrayal of his confidence. It was the 'Advertisement' and not the text of this publication that caused a sensation when it appeared in May 1749. It provoked a storm of criticism as William Warburton and others rushed to defend Pope's reputation. Bolingbroke replied in kind with a scurrilous attack on Warburton and Pope. He failed to survive this unsavoury episode with credit.

Bolingbroke and his wife both experienced regular bouts of ill health during the 1740s. By the end of the decade he was a frustrated and embittered old man. Most of his friends and political contemporaries were dead, and his younger protégés had deserted the political cause to which he had devoted so much effort. After a long and painful illness his wife died on 18 March 1750, at the age of seventy-four. He was at once plagued by a lawsuit filed in France by her relatives seeking to inherit her estate. For the remaining months of his own life Bolingbroke was in almost constant physical pain. In the summer of 1751 a quack doctor failed to cure a painful cancer on his cheek bone. The cancer spread, the pain became intense, and he died in Battersea on 12 December 1751, at the age of seventy-three. He was laid to rest in the same vault as his second wife in St Mary's Church, Battersea. A mural monument records the epitaphs of both of them. This was almost certainly Bolingbroke's last composition. Since he had no children by either of his marriages, his title and property went to Frederick St John, the son of his half-brother, John. His personal estate, apart from a few minor bequests, went to his executors, John Taylor and William Chetwynd.

Bolingbroke's will allowed David Mallet to reprint any of his published works or to publish any of his manuscript works for the first time. In 1752 Mallet published a volume containing Bolingbroke's *Letters on the Study and Use of History*, *Of the True Use of Retirement and Study*, and *Reflections upon Exile*. The first of these tracts provoked a considerable critical reaction because of Bolingbroke's attacks on Old Testament and church history. In 1753 Mallet published a volume containing *A Letter to Sir William Windham*, *Some Reflections on the State of the Nation*, and *Letter to Mr Pope*, which was Bolingbroke's introduction to his philosophical essays. It attracted little critical attention. By contrast, when Mallet published the collected works of Bolingbroke in March 1754, the response was a positive flood of hostile comment. Bolingbroke was widely condemned, by Samuel Johnson among others, as a scoundrel for attacking religion and a coward for publishing his diatribes posthumously. His works inspired many substantial rejoinders, especially from clergymen. The most famous response was William Warburton's *A View of Lord Bolingbroke's Philosophy*, published in four parts in 1754–5. Even in France, Bolingbroke's prestige rapidly declined. Voltaire criticized his works, but also used Bolingbroke as a stalking horse for his own more trenchant criticisms of organized religion.

Bolingbroke's reputation as a philosopher was never substantial and, after the publication of his essays, it has never recovered. For nearly 200 years he was also widely condemned as an unprincipled political charlatan. Only in the late twentieth century did historians at last recognize him as a substantial, if flawed, political figure in Anne's reign and as a brilliant, if eventually unsuccessful, political writer in the age of Walpole. Although he supported a losing political cause, his career tells us much about the vicissitudes of the tory party and the divisions over fundamental issues of principle that cast them, a potential majority of the political nation, into the political wilderness after 1714. Although he failed to dislodge Walpole from office, he did write some of the most sophisticated and effective attacks on that great minister and his political methods. Bolingbroke's writings tell us much about the ideological divisions that persisted under the first two Hanoverian monarchs. Although he lacked good sense and political judgement, Bolingbroke was widely read, wrote well, and did make a sincere effort to provide the disparate elements of the parliamentary opposition with a coherent political ideology and a moral platform. All his life he supported the claims of the landed gentry to be the natural rulers of society and he defended the rights of parliament and the traditional features of England's ancient constitution.　　H. T. DICKINSON

Sources *The works of Lord Bolingbroke*, 4 vols. (1969) • H. St John, Viscount Bolingbroke, *The idea of a patriot king*, ed. S. W. Jackman (Indianapolis, 1965) • *Lord Bolingbroke: historical writings*, ed. I. Kramnick (Chicago, 1972) • *Lord Bolingbroke: contributions to The Craftsman*, ed. S. Varey (1982) • *Bolingbroke: political writings*, ed. D. Armitage (1997) • *Bolingbroke's political writings: the conservative Enlightenment*, ed. B. Cottret (1997) • *The letters and correspondence of Henry St John, Lord Viscount Bolingbroke*, ed. G. Parke, 4 vols. (1798) • *Lettres historiques, politiques, philosophiques et particulières de Henri Saint-John, Lord Vicomte Bolingbroke, depuis 1710 jusqu'en 1736*, ed. P. H. Grimoard, 3 vols. (1808) • *Lettres inédites de Bolingbroke à Lord Stair, 1716–1720*, ed. P. Baratier (Trévoux, 1939) • *Report on the manuscripts* of the marquis of Downshire, 6 vols. in 7, HMC, 75 (1924–95), vol. 1, pt 2 [letters of St John to Sir William Trumbull] · G. H. Rose, ed., A selection from the papers of the earls of Marchmont, 3 vols. (1831) · H. T. Dickinson, Bolingbroke (1970) · W. Sichel, Bolingbroke and his times, 2 vols. (1901–2) · S. Varey, Henry St John, Viscount Bolingbroke (Boston, 1984) · S. W. Jackman, Man of mercury: an appreciation of the mind of Henry St John, Viscount Bolingbroke (1965) · J. Hart, Viscount Bolingbroke: tory humanist (1965) · B. Cottret, Bolingbroke: exil et écriture au siècle des lumières, Angleterre–France (vers 1715 – vers 1750), 2 vols. (1988) · I. Kramnick, Bolingbroke and his circle (1968) · T. Macknight, The life of Henry St John, Viscount Bolingbroke (1863) · C. Petrie, Bolingbroke (1937) · D. Harkness, Bolingbroke: the man and his career (1957) · A. Hassall, Bolingbroke, rev. edn (1915) · S. Biddle, Bolingbroke and Harley (1975) · P. Baratier, Bolingbroke: ses écrits politiques (1939) · R. A. Barrell, Bolingbroke and France (1988) · B. S. Hammond, Pope and Bolingbroke: a study of friendship and influence (1984) · W. McIntosh Merrill, From statesman to philosopher: a study in Bolingbroke's deism (New York, 1949) · H. C. Mansfield, Statesmanship and party government: a study of Burke and Bolingbroke (1965) · A. Pettit, Illusory consensus: Bolingbroke and the polemical response to Walpole, 1730–1737 (1997) · D. G. James, The life of reason (1949) · M. R. Hopkinson, Married to mercury (1936) · G. S. Holmes, British politics in the age of Anne, rev. edn (1987) · H. T. Dickinson, Liberty and property: political ideology in eighteenth-century Britain (1977) · C. Gerrard, The patriot opposition to Walpole: politics, poetry, and national myth, 1725–1742 (1994) · B. A. Goldgar, Walpole and the wits: the relation of politics to literature, 1722–1742 (Lincoln, Nebraska, 1976) · W. S. Churchill, Marlborough: his life and times, 4 vols. (1934–8) · B. W. Hill, Robert Harley, speaker, secretary of state and premier minister (1988)

Archives BL, military papers, letter-books, diplomatic corresp., and dispatches, Add. MSS 22205–22207, 22264, 37272–37273, 49970–49971 · Longleat House, Wiltshire, corresp. and papers · LPL, corresp. · NYPL, corresp. and papers · Royal Arch., corresp. and papers | Alnwick Castle, Northumberland, letters to John Drummond · Birm. CL, Cobham MSS · BL, Berkshire estate papers, Add. MS 36243 · BL, letters to Lord Essex, Add. MSS 27732–27735 · BL, letters to Lord Hardwicke, Add. MSS 35585–35588, passim · BL, corresp. with Robert Harley, first earl of Oxford, loan 29 · BL, corresp. with T. Harley, Add. MS 40621 · BL, letters to Henrietta Knight, Add. MS 45889 · BL, corresp. with Lord Lexington, Add. MSS 46543, 46545 · BL, letters to Lord Luxborough and Lady Luxborough, etc., Add. MS 34196 · BL, letters to Lord Marchmont, Add. MS 37994 · BL, letters to earl of Orrery, Add. MS 37209 · BL, corresp. with Lord Strafford, Add. MS 70286 · BL, corresp. with Jonathan Swift, Add. MSS 4291, 4804–4806, passim · BL, corresp. with Sir William Trumbull · BL, corresp. with Charles Whitworth, Add. MSS 37358–37361 · CAC Cam., corresp. with Thomas Earle · Levens Hall, Cumbria, letters to James Grahme · Morgan L., letters to John Hynde Cotton · Petworth House, West Sussex, Wyndham MSS, letters to Sir William Wyndham and Charles Wyndham · TCD, corresp. with Shrewsbury and Stanley · Yale U., Osborn collection, letters

Likenesses G. White, mezzotint, c.1705 (after T. Murray), BM, NPG · attrib. A.-S. Belle, oils, 1712?, NPG [see illus.] · G. Kneller, 1715, Petworth House and Park, West Sussex · attrib. C. Jervas, oils, after 1723, Gov. Art Coll. · attrib. J. Richardson, oils, c.1730, NPG · oils, c.1730–1740, Lydiard Mansion, Wiltshire · J. M. Rysbrack, marble bust, 1737, Lydiard Mansion, Wiltshire · J. M. Rysbrack, marble bust, 1737, Petworth House and Park, West Sussex · enamel miniature, c.1740–1750, NPG · G. Kneller?, portrait, NPG · L. F. Roubiliac, relief portrait medallion, St Mary's parish church, Battersea, London · portraits, Hult. Arch.

St John, Mrs Horace Roscoe. See St John, Jane Elizabeth (1829–1906), under St John, Horace Stebbing Roscoe (1830–1888).

St John, Horace Stebbing Roscoe (1830–1888), author and journalist, was the son of James Augustus *St John

(1795–1875), author, from Laugharne, Carmarthenshire, and Eliza Caroline Agar Hansard (c.1798–1867), daughter of Alexander Hansard, surgeon and apothecary, of Bristol. He was born in Cormeille, near Caen, Normandy, on 6 July 1830 during his family's five-year stay (1829–34) in Europe and was educated by his father. Percy Bolingbroke *St John (1821–1889), Bayle Frederick *St John (1822–1859), and Sir Spenser Buckingham *St John (1825–1910) were elder brothers, and Vane Ireton Shaftesbury *St John (1839–1911) [see under St John, Sir Spenser Buckingham] his youngest brother. He married on 15 February 1855 Jane Elizabeth Roscoe [see below]; they had no children.

Following the family tradition, St John embarked on a literary career at a very early age, and over a period of thirty years was an assiduous contributor to the leading periodicals and newspapers of the day, including The Times, The Standard, and The Athenaeum, chiefly on politics and Eastern affairs. He published A Life of Christopher Columbus (1850), followed by A History of the British Conquests in India (2 vols., 1852). For his third work, The Indian Archipelago (2 vols., 1853), he used materials provided by his brothers Spenser Buckingham and James Augustus junior, both then living in the Far East. From 1857 until 1861 he was a political leader writer on the Daily Telegraph, his particular gift being 'to sit down at a table anywhere, and with the first writing implements that came to hand, dash off a leader in an hour's time' (Life and Adventures of George Augustus Sala, 1.398). In 1861 he was employed on the Morning Chronicle; when this failed in 1862 he had substantial debts and petitioned for bankruptcy, and he had financial difficulties for the remainder of his life. By 1873 overwork had broken his health, and he suffered, in addition, from rheumatism and epileptic fits which left him unable to write with any regularity. He died at 18 Thornsett Road, Anerley, Surrey, on 29 February 1888, and was buried at Highgate cemetery.

His wife, **Jane Elizabeth St John** [née Roscoe; known as Mrs Horace Roscoe St John] (1829–1906), author, was the daughter of Thomas *Roscoe (1791–1871), author, and Elizabeth Edwards. Born in London, she was the author of Audubon the Naturalist (1856), Englishwomen and the Age (1860), a pamphlet on the condition of women, and two historical works, Masaniello of Naples (1865) and The Court of Anna Carafa (1872). She died at 202 Croydon Road, Penge, on 11 March 1906.   S. V. SPILSBURY

Sources Royal Literary Fund papers, BL, Loan 96, case 1595 · The life and adventures of George Augustus Sala, 2nd edn, 2 vols. (1895) · The Athenaeum (10 March 1888), 310 · The Times (8 March 1888) · The Athenaeum (25 Aug 1860), 248–50 · census returns, 1841, PRO, HO 107/689, fol. 20 · Wellesley index · J. A. St John, Journal of a residence in Normandy (1831) · J. A. St John, There and back again, 2 vols. (1853) · m. cert. · d. cert. · d. cert. (Jane Elizabeth St John) · DNB

Wealth at death £451 0s. 3d.—Jane Elizabeth St John: probate, 29 March 1906, CGPLA Eng. & Wales

St John, James Augustus [formerly James John; pseuds. Greville Brooke, Horace Gwynne] (1795–1875), writer and traveller, was born James John, on 24 September 1795 in Laugharne, Carmarthenshire, the only son of Gelly John

(1749–1802), shoemaker, and his wife, Rachel William (1763–1828). He attended the Laugharne charity school and, after his father's death, received tuition in the classics and modern languages from the local vicar, John Williams. This was later supplemented by a programme of self-education in literature, philosophy, and politics. Childhood poverty and an artisan background at the time of the Welsh corn riots led him into radical politics. He went to London, probably about 1818, in the hope of publishing his political novel *Liberty, or, The Rights of Nations*. Adopting the name Julian Augustus St John, he contributed to *Sherwin's Weekly Political Register* and from August 1819 wrote for Richard Carlile's *Republican*, acting as editor in November and December of that year when Carlile was in gaol. On 22 December 1819 he married Eliza Caroline Agar Hansard (*c*.1798–1867), daughter of Alexander Hansard, surgeon and apothecary, of Bristol and sister of George Agar Hansard of Bath. They had seven sons and four daughters, of whom one son, Sir Spenser Buckingham *St John (1825–1910), became a prominent diplomat, and four others, Percy Bolingbroke *St John (1821–1889), Bayle Frederick *St John (1822–1859), Horace Stebbing Roscoe *St John (1830–1888), and Vane Ireton Shaftesbury *St John (1839–1911) [*see under* St John, Sir Spenser Buckingham], followed literary careers. From 1820 to 1822 he edited a radical newspaper, *The Patriot*, first in Plymouth and then in Exeter.

On his return to London, St John did not resume relations with his former associates and appears to have gone to some pains to conceal the facts of his early career. He dropped his adopted forename, Julian, in favour of his baptismal name of James, and, while remaining politically liberal, quietly became respectable. In 1824 he was employed on the new *Oriental Herald* as sub-editor (and resident poet under the name Bion) and published *Abdallah, an Oriental Poem* (1824) under the pseudonym Horace Gwynne. The lack of success of this work led him to relinquish his long-held ambition to dedicate himself to poetry. From 1827 to 1829 he edited the literary journal the *London Weekly Review*, which he had founded with David Lester Richardson. He left for Normandy in 1829 and with his family lived for three years in France and Switzerland, submitting regular work for publication in England, including *The Hindoos* (2 vols., 1834–5) for the Society for the Diffusion of Useful Knowledge, and *Journal of a Residence in Normandy* (1831). In 1832 he set out alone on a two-year trip to Egypt, recorded in *Egypt and Mohammed Ali* (2 vols., 1834).

St John returned to London in 1834 and for more than thirty years contributed to the leading periodicals, mainly on politics and foreign affairs. He also published numerous original works, novels, biography, and history among them. During the 1840s and 1850s he wrote a political column for the *Sunday Times* under the pseudonym Greville Brooke, and in the late 1850s, though by then blind, ran the political department of the *Daily Telegraph* with his son Horace. Among his other works mention may be made of *The History of the Manners and Customs of Ancient Greece* (3

vols., 1842), an impressive compilation taken from original sources; the novel *Sir Cosmo Digby, a Tale of the Monmouthshire Riots* (3 vols., 1843), which draws upon his childhood in Laugharne; and *Isis: an Egyptian Pilgrimage* (2 vols., 1853) and *There and Back Again* (2 vols., 1853), popular accounts of his trip to Egypt. He amassed no fortune from his considerable literary labours and died in relative poverty at 44 St John's Wood Terrace, London, on 22 September 1875, two days before his eightieth birthday; he was buried in Highgate cemetery.   S. V. SPILSBURY

Sources J. A. St John, 'journal, 1821–1822', priv. coll. · BL, Royal Literary Fund Archive, Loan 96, reg. case 1433 · J. H. Weiner, *Radicalism and freethought in nineteenth-century Britain: the life of Richard Carlile* (1983) · S. V. Spilsbury, 'The identity of "Horace Gwynne", author of *Abdullah*', *N&Q*, 224 (1979), 238–9 · *The life and adventures of George Augustus Sala*, 2 vols. (1895) · letter to Thomas Turton, 9 July 1840, Hunt. L., Carlile papers · *BL cat.* · *Men of the time* (1856) · R. Wedderburn, *High heel'd shoes for dwarfs in holiness* (1821) · *The Republican* (Nov–Dec 1819) · H. Hobson, P. Knightley, and L. Russell, *The pearl of days: an intimate memoir of the Sunday Times, 1822–1972* (1972) · BL, Bentley publishers archive, Add. MSS 46560–46632 · *Wellesley index* · parish records, St Andrew's, Plymouth · parish records, St Martin's, Laugharne · census returns, 1841, 1851, 1861 · *DNB* · private information (2004) [A. R. J. S. Adolph] · *CGPLA Eng. & Wales* (1876) · d. cert. · *IGI*

Archives NRA, priv. coll., journal while editor of *The Patriot* | BL, letters to Royal Literary Fund, Loan 96

Wealth at death he and all literary sons had constant financial difficulties; son Horace was paying father's rent in Oct 1873: BL, Royal Literary Fund Archive, Loan 96, reg. case 1433

St John, Jane Elizabeth (1829–1906). *See under* St John, Horace Stebbing Roscoe (1830–1888).

St John, Sir John de (*d.* 1302), soldier and diplomat, was grandson of William de Port, who had assumed the name of St John through his wife, Mabel, heir of Roger de St John of Halnaker, Sussex. John de St John's father, Robert, governor of Portchester Castle, died in March 1267, and he inherited the lordship of Halnaker and lands in Sussex, Hampshire, Herefordshire, Berkshire, Warwickshire, and Kent. His mother was Agnes, daughter of William (III) de Cantilupe. He married, before 29 June 1256, Alice, daughter of Sir Reginald fitz Peter, who survived him and with whom he had his eldest son, John, who succeeded to his lands.

John de St John was noted by contemporaries for his military abilities but, like other royal household knights of his time, he served the English crown in many capacities. He became a close associate and confidant of Edward I, who entrusted him with many important duties both at home and abroad. He had remained loyal to both Henry III and the Lord Edward during the disturbances of the 1250s and 1260s and, in 1269, was rewarded with a pardon for all excesses committed by him and his household. He was a member of the council that told Edward of his father's death when he was in Palestine in 1272. In 1277 and 1282 he served in Edward's two Welsh campaigns and in September 1283 he attended the Shrewsbury parliament at which Dafydd, brother of Llewelyn, prince of Wales, was tried. Between 1286 and 1289 he accompanied the king on his journeys through France and the duchy of Aquitaine, in which he was to see service for the next ten or so years.

Edward's role as mediator between the kings of Aragon and the Angevin house of Naples in their dispute over the title to Naples and Sicily led him to conduct negotiations from his south-western French duchy, and St John acted as a hostage for the fulfilment of the treaty of Canfranc between October 1288 and March 1289. He performed further diplomatic functions in 1290 and 1291–2, serving on missions to the pope (concerning a proposed crusade and the levy of a tenth to finance it) and to Tarascon, once more dealing with Edward I's mediation between the kingdoms of Aragon and Naples. His mission to Nicholas IV at Rome in February–March 1292 was also related to papal confirmation of the submissions offered by rival claimants to the Scottish throne, which Edward I was attempting to arbitrate at that time.

St John's career from 1290 until his death in 1302 was dominated by two major concerns: to defend the king's interests (as king–duke) in Aquitaine; and to serve his cause in Scotland and the northern marches. On 12 July 1293 he was appointed lieutenant of Edward I in Aquitaine, with an annual stipend of 2000 livres tournois. This fell at a particularly critical juncture in Anglo-French relations, as the men of Bayonne (subjects of Edward I as duke of Aquitaine) had recently attacked French shipping and sacked the port of La Rochelle. An Anglo-French confrontation over Aquitaine had been brewing for some time, but the storm only broke in 1293–4. Philippe IV of France declared the duchy forfeit and was to take possession, on a temporary basis, of certain Gascon strongholds and towns through an agreement reached at Paris with Edmund Crouchback, earl of Lancaster, Edward's brother. Both sides had been gathering forces and provisioning garrisons in the duchy, and St John was very active in this task. French commissioners were sent to take possession of the duchy in their king's name and on 20 February 1294 two of them confronted St John at the castle of St Macaire. Although Edmund of Lancaster had issued an order to surrender Gascon castles on 3 February, St John had evidently not received it by the time that the French envoys arrived. They were initially refused entry to the castle, but were eventually admitted and, after a long delay, received by St John in his chamber. Their attempts proved vain; he questioned their powers and sent them back to their master—the constable of France—with their mission unfulfilled. By 3 March 1294, however, St John had received Lancaster's instructions and, reluctantly, proceeded to deliver the fortified towns and castles to the French. He then returned, via Paris, to England.

Despite the terms of the agreement with Edmund of Lancaster, Philippe and his advisers refused to restore the duchy to Edward. Open war between England and France broke out when Edward renounced his homage to Philippe for his continental lands (Aquitaine and Ponthieu) on 20 June 1294. Soon after that date, on 1 July, he appointed his nephew John of Brittany as his lieutenant in Aquitaine, and St John as seneschal of the duchy. He was to act as the lieutenant's principal adviser on all aspects of Gascon affairs. An expeditionary force was assembled and sailed from Portsmouth in October. The strongholds of Macau, Bourg, and Blaye were recaptured from the French and Bordeaux became the force's next objective. Unable to take the city, they then divided: one contingent of the army sailed further up the Garonne, taking Rions and Podensac, while St John was dispatched with a force to Bayonne, journeying by sea and river. He took the town on 1 January 1295, expelled the French garrison, and captured the pro-French minority of Bayonne's *jurade* (town council), sending them to England as prisoners. French counter-attacks were launched against the duchy in 1295 and 1296, led by Charles de Valois and Robert (II) d'Artois. Plantagenet-held areas shrank to the more southerly parts of the duchy, around Dax, St Sever, and Bayonne. St John's task was to defend them and keep them supplied with provisions and munitions against French attack.

On 21 October 1295 John of Brittany was replaced as lieutenant of Aquitaine by Edmund of Lancaster, but St John still served as seneschal. Lancaster died of illness at Bayonne on 5 June 1296 and was succeeded by Henry de Lacy, earl of Lincoln. A near stalemate in the war had been reached, marked by desultory sieges and skirmishes, plundering expeditions by Anglo-Gascon forces from Bayonne into the Languedoc, and, on 2 February 1297, by an event which was to mark the end of St John's career in Aquitaine. He and Lacy were in command of a supply train and its escort which was bringing supplies to the besieged place of Bonnegarde, when they were ambushed by the troops of Robert d'Artois. Despite a brave resistance St John was captured by the French. The English chroniclers alleged that he was deserted by his Gascon troops, and that Lacy did not come sufficiently quickly to his aid. Whatever the case, he was captured with ten other knights, including some Gascon nobles. They were taken by their captors to Paris, Péronne, and elsewhere, and the *Flores historiarum* reported that just as the Philistines gloated over the capture of Samson, so the French gloated over that of St John.

His captors set a high price on their prisoner and St John was ransomed for £5000. This was a crippling sum for him and his estates to bear. Some assistance was, however, forthcoming and in September 1297 his son John, who had been serving with his father in Aquitaine, acknowledged receipt at Bayonne of sums of money from both the war treasurer and some Bayonne merchants to meet his father's expenses in the king of France's prison. But this did not suffice to meet his ransom. In May 1298 the abbot and monks of Westminster responded to his need by pledging £250 'pro utilitate regis et regni et reipublice Anglicane' ('for the utility of the king, kingdom, and English commonwealth'; Westminster Abbey Muniments, 12886) towards a sum of 20,000 livres petits tournois which had been advanced to Philippe IV in Edward I's name by the Frescobaldi and other Italian merchant bankers. This was intended to secure St John's release, which took place after the treaty of L'Aumône in the summer of 1299. But it was clearly insufficient to pay all the debts he had incurred during his captivity, for he was forced to pledge four manors to the Sienese Buonsignori in November of that year.

St John had already been involved in the king's Great Cause in Scotland in 1291–2 and had deputized for the infant earl of Fife at the enthronement of John Balliol in December 1292. After his return to England from captivity in 1299 he was to play an active part in Scottish affairs until his death. In January 1300 he was appointed Edward's lieutenant in Cumberland, Westmorland, Lancashire, Annandale, and the marches as far as the county of Roxburgh. He took part in the famous siege at Caerlaverock in July 1300, being entrusted with the care of Prince Edward (the future Edward II) at that—the prince's first—military engagement. The contemporary heraldic poem which celebrated the siege described him as 'li preus Johans de Seint Johan' ('the brave John de St John'; Wright, 18) and his son also served with him as the prince's companion. St John went on to serve in other border offices, including the wardenship of Galloway and sheriffdom of Dumfries. His diplomatic talents were again employed when he was appointed, with the earls of Warwick and Surrey, Aymer de Valence, and Hugh de Vere, to treat with envoys of Philippe IV for an Anglo-French peace and Anglo-Scots truce at Canterbury in March 1301. He was, as lord of Halnaker, among the hundred or so barons who sealed a letter to the pope in February 1301 that denied the pope's right to intervene in Anglo-Scottish and Anglo-French affairs. As a senior knight-banneret of the king's household, with a large retinue, he regularly received wages, gifts, and compensation (restaur) for horses lost or killed during his service in Scotland and the marches. The wardrobe records for 1300/01 contain many references to him and his retinue, including the payment of a large sum of 60 marks to his son for the loss of a particularly expensive black war-horse and for certain 'secret expenses' incurred by him on the king's service.

The inroads made by St John's French captivity into his landed income were to some degree repaired by grants of land in Scotland and the northern marches. But some of these were in war-torn areas, and not in his possession. In September 1300 he was therefore granted 1000 marks yearly for life on English lands until he obtained possession of lordships in Galloway. He had life annuities on the castles of Cockermouth and Skipton in Craven, and was appointed captain of the castle of Lochmaben. It was there that he died on Thursday 6 September 1302. He bore argent, on a chief gules, two mullets or, with a crest of a lion passant between two palm branches. These arms are depicted on some especially fine surviving specimens of his equestrian seal, which are the only extant visual records of him. MALCOLM VALE

Sources PRO, E.101 · PRO, SC.1 · PRO, C.61 · Westminster Abbey muniments · DNB · Chancery records · Rymer, Foedera, vol. 1 · F. Palgrave, ed., The parliamentary writs and writs of military summons, 1 (1827) · GEC, Peerage · F. Palgrave, ed., Documents and records illustrating the history of Scotland (1837) · E. L. G. Stones and G. G. Simpson, eds., Edward I and the throne of Scotland, 1290–1296, 2 vols. (1978) · H. R. Luard, ed., Flores historiarum, 3 vols., Rolls Series, 95 (1890) · J. Topham, Liber quotidianus contrarotulatoris garderobae: anno regni regis Edwardi primi vicesimo octavo (1787) · F. Michel, C. Bémont, and Y. Renouard, eds., Rôles Gascons, 4 vols. (1885–1962), vols. 1–3 · T. Wright, ed., The roll of arms of the princes, barons and knights who attended King Edward I to the siege of Caerlaverock (1864) · P. Chaplais, English medieval diplomatic practice, 1, PRO (1982), i–ii · R. Nicholson, Scotland: the later middle ages (1974), vol. 2 of The Edinburgh history of Scotland, ed. G. Donaldson (1965–75) · M. Prestwich, War, politics, and finance under Edward I (1972) · M. Prestwich, Edward I (1988) · M. Vale, The Angevin legacy and the Hundred Years War, 1250–1340 (1990)

St John, John (1745/6–1793), politician and fop, was the third son of John St John, second Viscount St John (c.1695–1749), landowner, and Anne Furnese (d. 1747), daughter of Sir Robert Furnese and Anne Balam of Waldershare, Kent. He was the nephew of Henry St John, first Viscount Bolingbroke, and the younger brother of Frederick St John, who succeeded as second Viscount Bolingbroke in 1751. He was educated at Eton College (1756–63) and he matriculated from Trinity College, Oxford, on 13 December 1763, aged seventeen, but did not take a degree. He entered Lincoln's Inn in 1765 and proceeded to the Middle Temple, from where he was called to the bar in 1770. He and his brothers, Frederick and Henry, were known to George Selwyn, who spoke well of St John's abilities but described 'the personal accomplishments of the most refined Macaroni' as the limits of his ambition (Jesse, 2.384).

In April 1773 St John entered parliament as MP for Newport, Isle of Wight. He voted with the administration and gave his maiden speech on 10 June in support of North's East India Regulating Bill. He was by common consent a dull and circumlocutory speaker, but he gained the lucrative office of surveyor of crown lands in 1775, which he held until 1784; in 1787 he published Observations on the Land Revenue of the Crown. St John was elected as MP of Eye in 1774 but was returned for his former seat of Newport at the 1780 general election. He continued to support North in his coalition with Fox but, after Pitt had come to power, did not stand for re-election in 1784. Although he published a vigorous pamphlet attacking Paine's Rights of Man in 1791, St John became more preoccupied with the theatre than with politics after retiring from the Commons, and he wrote two tragedies, Mary Queen of Scots and The Island of St Marguerite, which were performed at Drury Lane in 1789. The latter enjoyed some success largely because of its topical allusion to recent events such as the storming of the Bastille.

St John died, unmarried, at his home in Park Street, Grosvenor Place, London, on 8 October 1793. He was buried in the church of Lydiard-Tregoze, Wiltshire, where his brother General Henry St John erected a monument to him. G. LE G. NORGATE, rev. S. J. SKEDD

Sources L. B. Namier, 'St John, John', HoP, Commons · GEC, Peerage · Foster, Alum. Oxon. · GM, 1st ser., 63 (1793), 962 · J. H. Jesse, George Selwyn and his contemporaries, with memoirs and notes, 4 vols. (1843–4), vol. 2
Archives Bodl. Oxf., letters to Lord Guilford

St John, Oliver, first Viscount Grandison of Limerick (1559–1630), lord deputy of Ireland, was the second son of Nicholas St John (c.1526–1589) of Lydiard Tregoze, Wiltshire, sheriff of Wiltshire in 1579–80, and his wife, Elizabeth (d. 1587), daughter of Sir Richard Blount of Mapledurham, Oxfordshire. He matriculated from Trinity College,

Oxford, on 20 December 1577 as a commoner and graduated BA on 26 June 1578. On 14 November 1580 he was admitted as a student of Lincoln's Inn but did not proceed to be called to the bar because about 1584 he killed a George Best, probably the navigator and chronicler of Martin Frobisher, in a duel and was forced to flee abroad, where he became a soldier. He attained the rank of captain before 1591 and was present at the siege of Rouen under Robert Devereux, second earl of Essex. Upon his return to England in 1592 he was elected MP for Cirencester and served on a committee for the relief of maimed soldiers and mariners.

About 1592 St John married Joan (d. 1631), daughter and heir of Henry Roydon of Battersea and widow of Sir William Holcroft. They had no offspring. Early in 1600 he went to Ireland for the first time, bringing reinforcements to fight in the Nine Years' War against Hugh O'Neill. On 28 February 1600 he was knighted in Dublin by the new lord deputy, Charles Blount, Lord Mountjoy. In the following years St John served as a captain and colonel in the army in Ireland and made regular journeys to England with messages from the lord deputy.

There was a contemporary and kinsman of Sir Oliver St John, also called Oliver St John, and who also served in the English army on the continent and in Ireland. These two persons have sometimes been confused in the literature, including the *Dictionary of National Biography*. Questions about the two namesakes remain to be resolved, but it can be established without doubt that it was not the future lord deputy of Ireland who fought at the battle of Nieuwpoort in the Netherlands on 30 June 1600. In fact, Sir Oliver St John was campaigning in Ireland in the summer of 1600. In 1601 the future lord deputy left Ireland shortly before the battle of Kinsale in order to carry dispatches to Queen Elizabeth from Mountjoy, while his namesake, Captain Oliver St John, fought in the battle of Kinsale on 24 December. In 1618 Sir Oliver St John called Captain Oliver St John 'a poor kinsman' and tried to secure a pension for him 'in consideration of services in war here' (*CSP Ire.*, 1615–25, 208). A pension of £200 p.a. was then granted to Captain Oliver St John, who in 1625 was described as having been:

> the commander of two of the King's ships to the northern fishing, and when he was an officer, fought very valiantly at a sally at Kinsale; he is very strong of body and desirous of employment abroad; he was also at the battle of Newport. (ibid., 551)

In the English parliament beginning on 19 March 1604 Sir Oliver St John was a member for Portsmouth, and on 12 December 1605 he was appointed master of the ordnance in Ireland as the successor of Sir George Bourchier. He thus also became a member of the Irish privy council. Until his appointment as lord deputy in 1616, St John was a trusted adviser of the lord deputy, Sir Arthur Chichester, and frequently wrote to his English patron and secretary of state Robert Cecil on subjects such as the plantation of Ulster and the political, military, and religious situation in Connaught. As master of the ordnance he went to London

late in 1608 in order to urge an increase of military spending in Ireland, a request which was granted by the privy council. In 1608 and 1609 he was a commissioner for the plantation of Ulster, and as such accompanied Chichester on his journey through Ulster from 31 July to 30 September 1609. He became a planter in Ulster himself, obtaining 2500 acres in co. Armagh. In spite of this, however, St John repeatedly criticized plantation policy during Chichester's deputyship, initially arguing against a plantation in Ulster and repeatedly pointing to the negative effects of 'discoverers' and 'adventurers'. In 1610 St John became vice president of the province of Connaught, and he spent a lot of time in the province in the following years. He lobbied to become lord president of Connaught as successor to the earl of Clanricarde, but this office went to Sir Charles Wilmot in 1616.

Upon the incorporation of the town of Roscommon in 1612 St John became one of its burgesses. He was elected to the Irish parliament of 1613–15 as one of the knights of the shire for co. Roscommon. In this parliament, which began on 18 May 1613, he played a leading role in the conflict about the speakership between the 'recusant' and the 'protestant' parties. On 11 December 1614 he surrendered the mastership of the ordnance. In 1615–16 he was in England, and on 2 July 1616 he was appointed lord deputy of Ireland. This caused surprise at the English court and among the Irish councillors because the new lord deputy had not previously held a great office in Ireland. His appointment was certainly due to the influence of his new patron, George Villiers (later first duke of Buckingham), the rising favourite of James I, with whom St John was related through the marriage of his niece Barbara to Edward Villiers, Buckingham's half-brother. However, Francis Bacon, who was sceptical at first, became convinced of the new lord deputy's qualification for the office after discussing Irish affairs with him.

On 26 August 1616 St John was back in Ireland, and he received the sword of state on 30 August. His deputyship was dominated by two issues which had been in the forefront of Irish politics since Queen Elizabeth's time: the government's attitude to the recusants, and the plantations. On the first of these issues St John proved a hardliner who tried to repress Catholicism in Ireland. Besides issuing a proclamation ordering the banishment of priests educated abroad (17 October 1617), he attempted to enforce and collect the recusancy fines more effectively from 1618 onwards. In addition, Waterford was singled out to set a warning example to all towns that had repeatedly elected recusants to municipal offices: its charter was declared forfeit for that offence in 1618 and a governor installed. Lord Deputy St John was also much concerned with the second issue, namely plantations. Besides having to deal with the problems resulting from the plantation of Ulster, he was responsible for the land distribution in the plantation of Wexford, as well as for initiating the plantations of Longford from 1618 onwards and the plantation of Leitrim and other midland districts from 1621 onwards. It seems that he was torn between his earlier ideal of a plantation and the pressures created by the interest of his patron Buckingham.

St John's deputyship was marked by a constant lack of money for the army and, increasingly, by a strong opposition group against him in the Irish council. Although he did not lose the favour of the king, who raised St John to the rank of Viscount Grandison of Limerick on 3 January 1621, he was recalled on 18 April 1622 and departed for England on 4 May. His successor was Henry Carey, Viscount Falkland. Although at the instigation of the English parliament a commission to inquire into the ecclesiastical and temporal state of Ireland was appointed on 20 March 1622, St John was not to account for his deputyship. On the contrary, on 28 June 1622 he became a member of the English privy council, and in 1624 he was appointed to a commission considering the plantation of Ulster together with Sir Arthur Chichester and George Carew, earl of Totnes. After Chichester's death St John was appointed lord high treasurer of Ireland on 13 August 1625. He also received an English peerage, being created Baron Tregoz of Highworth on 21 May 1626. In May 1630 he returned once more to Ireland to assume his office as high treasurer and settle his estates there.

In many ways Oliver St John was a typical New Englishman, a crown official who rose steadily through his service in Ireland and who also became a planter. As such, he represents a whole class of people in sixteenth- and seventeenth-century Ireland. His advancement is typical of many New English in being not as spectacular as that of his contemporary Richard Boyle, earl of Cork, but still revealing the considerable opportunities service in Ireland afforded to the younger sons of the English gentry. He died on 29 December 1630 and was buried at Battersea on 12 January 1631. His wife, Joan, survived him less than two months and died in late February 1631, being buried at Battersea on 10 March. On St John's death the barony of Tregoz became extinct. The viscountcy of Grandison and his co. Leitrim estate passed to his great-nephew William, son of Sir Edward Villiers and Barbara Villiers, *née* St John. Apart from a bequest of £500 to his stepson Sir Henry Holcroft, the rest of his Irish and English property, in particular the manors of Battersea and Wandsworth, which St John had acquired in 1607, were bequeathed to his greatnephew and godson John St John, the second son of his nephew Sir John St John, who was the executor of his will. UTE LOTZ-HEUMANN

Sources CSP Ire., 1599–1632 · J. S. Brewer and W. Bullen, eds., *Calendar of the Carew manuscripts*, 3–5, PRO (1869–71) · V. L. Rutledge, 'Politics of Irish reform under Oliver St John, 1616–22', MA diss., McGill University, Montreal, Canada, 1976 · V. L. Rutledge, 'Court-castle, faction and the Irish viceroyalty: the appointment of Oliver St John as lord deputy of Ireland in 1616', *Irish Historical Studies*, 26 (1988–9), 233–49 · R. Bagwell, *Ireland under the Stuarts*, 1 (1909); repr. (1963) · V. Treadwell, *Buckingham and Ireland, 1616–1628: a study in Anglo-Irish politics* (1998) · DNB · GEC, *Peerage*, new edn, 6.74–5 · A. Harding, 'St John, Nicholas', A. M. Mimardière and P. W. Hasler, 'St John, Oliver III', HoP, *Commons, 1558–1603*, 3.322–5 · C. Arnold-Baker, ed., *The companion to British history* (1996), 1095 · 'Entry book of reports of the commissioners for Ireland, appointed by James I in 1622, and of letters from the king and council to the lord deputy, Oliver St John, and the Council of Ireland, 1616–1621', BL, Add. MS 4756 · will, PRO, PROB 11/159, fols. 1r–2r

Archives BL, entry book, Add. MS 4756 · Hunt. L., corresp. · TCD, MS 10949/4 | BL, warrants, Egerton MS 2126 · BL, orders to Sir A. Loftus, Add. MS 19839 · Bodl. Oxf., Smith MS 71 · Bodl. Oxf., Talbot de Malahide MSS c.5/44, c.5/45, c.6/59, c.6/60, c.7/35 · CKS, Cranfield papers, Official Ireland (U269/1 Hi) · LPL, Carew MSS

Likenesses C. Johnson, oils, c.1622, Lydiard Mansion, Wiltshire · print (of the council of war), S. Antiquaries, Lond.

Wealth at death estates in co. Armagh and co. Leitrim in Ireland; manors of Battersea and Wandsworth in England; bequeathed more than £1700 sterling plus household goods (incl. silverware): will, PRO, PROB 11/159, fols. 1r–2r; CSP Ire.; Treadwell, *Buckingham and Ireland*

St John, Oliver, first earl of Bolingbroke (c.1584–1646), politician, was the son and heir of Oliver St John, third Baron St John of Bletso (c.1545–1618), and his wife, Dorothy (d. 1605), daughter and heir of John Read of Boddington, Gloucestershire. His grandfather Oliver (d. 1582) had been created first Baron St John of Bletso in 1559; he was one of the judges who tried Thomas Howard, fourth duke of Norfolk, in 1572. His eldest son, John, who sat on the trial of Mary, queen of Scots, and died on 23 October 1596, succeeded him as baron. John's daughter Anne married William, eldest son of Charles Howard, second Baron Howard of Effingham and later first earl of Nottingham, but with no male heir the Bletso title passed to John's brother Oliver, who became third baron. Oliver St John (c.1598–1673), Hampden's counsel in the ship-money case, was a distant cousin, descended from the first baron's third son.

The third baron opposed the benevolence of 1614, and his son later identified himself with the 'popular party' in parliament. The younger Oliver St John is held to have matriculated at Peterhouse, Cambridge, in 1595, and then to have entered Gray's Inn in 1597. He was elected MP for Bedfordshire in 1601, although aged only about seventeen, and again in 1604. In the latter parliament he served on the committee appointed to discuss the change in the royal title. He married in April 1602 Elizabeth (d. 1655), daughter and heir of William Paulet of Somerset, and granddaughter of George Paulet, a younger brother of William Paulet, first marquess of Winchester. Their eldest son, Oliver *St John (bap. 1603, d. 1642), was baptized a year later. From 1609 St John was entrusted with managing the family estates by his ageing father. On 3 June 1610 he was made knight of the Bath at the creation of Henry, prince of Wales. He succeeded his father as fourth Baron St John of Bletso in September 1618 and the following year sumptuously entertained James I at his house; two years later he took his seat in the House of Lords. St John was created earl of Bolingbroke (a manor that had belonged to the Beauchamp family, from which he was descended) on 28 December 1624 and took his seat on 22 June 1625. In that parliament he was appointed to committees for reforming the ministry and for curbing the abuse of the sabbath. He was one of the lord lieutenants for Huntingdonshire from 1625 at least until 1630. In December 1626 he refused to contribute to the forced

Olivers, Iohn Earle of Bulling
brooke, Lord s, Iohn of Bletso,

Oliver St John, first earl of Bolingbroke (c.1584–1646), by
Wenceslaus Hollar

loan, and he was removed from the Bedfordshire commission the following year. In 1628 he was one of the majority of peers who supported the petition of right.

In 1639 Bolingbroke objected to the request that he contribute towards the expenses of the first bishops' war, and on 28 August 1640 he signed the petition of the twelve peers attributing the evils of the day to the absence of parliaments and urging Charles I to summon one forthwith. He and his fellow signatory Francis Russell, fourth earl of Bedford, jointly held the wardship of the daughters of Bolingbroke's brother-in-law Edward Bourchier, fourth earl of Bath. Bolingbroke remained with the Long Parliament in 1642 when King Charles retired to York, and in February 1643 was named by parliament as lord lieutenant of Bedfordshire; in this capacity he took an active part in raising the militia and providing for the safety of the county. In the same year he took the covenant and was appointed a lay member of the Westminster assembly. On 10 November 1643 and 19 March 1646 he was one of the commissioners named for the custody of the great seal. On 6 May 1644 he was excused attendance at the House of Lords. The transfer of his proxy during the debates on the formation of the New Model Army secured the passage of Sir Thomas Fairfax's commission as commander-in-chief, which by contrast with the earlier commission of the earl of Essex made no reference to preserving the king's person. Bolingbroke's estate of Bletsoe Park was exempted from all taxes on 23 June 1645. Men referred to in the *Journal of the House of Lords* as Bolingbroke's servants include Nicholas Cockaine, Samuel Boothouse, and John Barbier. Bolingbroke died in June 1646.   SEAN KELSEY

Sources M. Jansson and W. B. Bidwell, eds., *Proceeedings in parliament, 1625* (c.1987) · W. B. Bidwell and M. Jansson, eds., *Proceedings in parliament, 1626*, 4 vols. (1991–6) · *JHL*, 3 (1620–28), 3; 5 (1642–3), 164; 6 (1643–4), 542; 7 (1644–5), 577 · C. H. Firth and R. S. Rait, eds., *Acts and ordinances of the interregnum, 1642–1660*, 3 vols. (1911), vol. 1, p. 83 · *CSP dom.*, 1625–6, 139, 485; 1627–8, 221; 1629–31, 159; 1638–9, 465 · GEC, *Peerage*, new edn, 2.18–19, 203–4 · C. H. Firth, *The House of Lords during the civil war* (1910) · R. P. Cust, *The forced loan and English politics, 1626–1628* (1987), 102n. · A. Swatland, *The House of Lords in the reign of Charles II* (1996) · A. M. Mimardière, 'St John, Oliver II', 'St John, Oliver IV', HoP, *Commons, 1558–1603* · S. R. Gardiner, *History of England from the accession of James I to the outbreak of the civil war, 1603–1642*, 10 vols. (1883–4) · letters of Oliver St John to Sir Edward Scradling, BL, Add. MS 28852, fols. 30–37 · Clarendon, *Hist. rebellion* · *A true relation of the proceedings at Hereford by the Lord St. John* (1642) · *IGI* · Venn, *Alum. Cant.* · *The letters of John Chamberlain*, ed. N. E. McClure, 2 vols. (1939) · H. Ellis, ed., *The visitation of the county of Huntingdon ... 1613*, CS, 43 (1849) · S. R. Gardiner, *History of the great civil war, 1642–1649*, new edn, 4 vols. (1901–5) · letters of administration, PRO, PROB 6/21, fol. 82r; PROB 6/31, fol. 222v
Likenesses W. Hollar, engraving, BM, NPG [*see illus.*] · A. Van Dyck, group portrait, oils (with his family); in possession of the earl of Morley in 1897

St John, Oliver (c.1598–1673), lawyer and politician, was the eldest surviving son of Oliver St John (1562/3–1626) of Keysoe, Bedfordshire, and Sarah, daughter of Edward Buckley of Odell in the same county. He was the great-grandson of Oliver St John, first Baron St John of Bletso, but little is known of his parents or childhood.

Education and early career Oliver matriculated as a pensioner from Queens' College, Cambridge, in Lent 1616 and entered Lincoln's Inn on 22 April 1619. At Queens' he studied with John Preston, a leading puritan, and while he was at Lincoln's Inn, William Prynne was also a student there. He was called to the bar on 22 June 1626 and about 1629 made an advantageous marriage to Joanna (d. in or before 1639), daughter and heir of Sir James Altham of Markshall, Latton, Essex, and his wife, Elizabeth Barrington. Joanna was the niece of Sir Thomas Barrington, and her grandmother Joan, Lady Barrington, was the daughter of Sir Henry Cromwell and aunt both to Oliver Cromwell and John Hampden. The marriage took place despite the misgivings of the bride's family regarding St John's poverty and his prospects.

In 1629 St John was retained as a lawyer by the Russell family, the earls of Bedford. However, in that year he was imprisoned briefly for sending his patron, Bedford, a 'design of sedition'. This was the so-called 'Proposition for his majesty's service to bridle the impertinence of parliaments', an intemperate proposal for the establishment of military government and prerogative rule throughout England, written in 1614 by Sir Robert Dudley in an unscrupulous and rather ill-advised attempt to ingratiate himself with James I, who remained nonplussed. The paper had found its way, however, into the library of Sir Robert Cotton, where it was recognized as potentially devastating ammunition in the paper wars which had ensued with the establishment of new counsels by Charles I. Catching wind of the minor storm about to burst, the king and his principal new counsellor, Viscount Thomas Wentworth, acted swiftly, seeing an opportunity not only to punish their opponents but also to reaffirm their own

Oliver St John (*c.*1598–1673), by Pieter Nason, 1651

constitutionalist credentials. Those responsible for circulating the paper found themselves on the receiving end of a state prosecution. The charges were dropped eventually, but not before St John had been brought before Star Chamber and threatened with the rack. Writing many years later, the earl of Clarendon asserted that the episode shaped St John's future attitudes, since 'he never forgave the Court the first assault, and contracted an implacable displeasure against the Church purely from the company he kept' (Clarendon, *Hist. rebellion*, 1.246).

The connection with Bedford led to St John's association with the Providence Island Company. Bedford was the parliamentary patron of John Pym, who engineered St John's entrance into the company in 1630. The company's membership included many of the men, including Pym, Bedford, Rudyerd, and Hampden, who opposed or would later oppose aspects of Charles I's policies. By the 1630s St John was also closely connected to Oliver Cromwell. The two had been exact contemporaries at Cambridge and their friendship was strengthened by the role Joan, Lady Barrington, played in arranging both St John's first and second marriages, the second (on 21 January 1639) being to Elizabeth (*d.* in or before 1645), daughter and coheir of Henry Cromwell, Oliver's second cousin.

The ship money case and the Short Parliament In the mid-1630s the ship money case brought St John a national reputation. Charles I claimed that in national emergencies he could raise a rate for the navy—ship money—by prerogative action; and that he was the sole judge of what

constituted a national emergency. Charles began collecting the rate in 1634. St John served as legal counsel for Lord Saye and John Hampden in their challenge to the legality of ship money. In June 1637, shortly before the trial commenced, St John's rooms were searched by William Beecher, a clerk of the king's council, with a warrant provided by the king's council. The search was conducted, one contemporary surmised, because of St John's retention as Hampden's lawyer and because 'he had been a diligent searcher of records concerning forest bounds and laws' (Gardiner, *Prynne*, 77–8).

St John's arguments in the ship money case boiled down to one essential plea, namely that if the king was entitled to lay whatever charge he desired on his subjects, it would come to pass that their property was held entirely at 'the goodness and mercy of the king' (Rushworth, 2.508). Therefore, according to St John, by allowing the king to compel payments towards national defence, ship money threatened the foundation of property itself. In spring 1638 the judges began to return their opinions in the case, with the final tally in June being seven to five in favour of the king, two judges having found for Hampden on technical grounds, even though they upheld the legality of ship money. The most uncompromising decision was returned by Chief Justice John Finch, who denied that any acts of parliament intending to bind the king in any way made any difference.

Many regarded the closeness of the judges' decision as a victory for St John, giving him a new reputation as a spokesman, particularly for those who opposed the legal policies of Charles I. His enhanced stature became evident in the Short Parliament of 1640, in which he represented the Devon borough of Totnes, having almost certainly been elected on the interest of the earl of Bedford. At Westminster he quickly assumed a prominent role and, among other things, attacked those who claimed that Charles's dissolution of parliament in 1629 was legal, argued that no innovations in religion were binding unless they were approved by parliament, and asked on 4 May that the legality of ship money be overturned by a vote of parliament.

St John's separate attempt to have the judgment in Hampden's case overturned by a vote of parliament produced an uproar, since he was asking that parliament overturn a decision already rendered by the courts. The vote on the legality of ship money was never taken, because on 5 May, the day following St John's call for a vote, Charles I dissolved parliament. Clarendon recorded St John's reaction to the dissolution. Encountering him in the hallway and seeing that St John, normally a stern and reserved man, appeared to be happy, Clarendon asked him why. St John replied that the Short Parliament would never have done what was necessary. Things, he said, would have to get worse before they would get better. Indeed, he was not averse to accelerating the downward spiral. It was St John and Pym who were said to have composed the petition of the twelve peers, signed on 28 August—the same day as the victory of the Scottish army over the English at Newburn—calling for a new parliament. When military defeat and a lack of money forced the king to grant the petitioners their wish, St John was once again returned to Westminster as member for Totnes and resumed his place in the van of opposition to the personal rule of Charles I.

The early years of the Long Parliament, 1640–1642 In the Long Parliament St John was at the core of a group of men, including Pym, Hampden, Bedford, and Sir Henry Vane the younger, who were, according to Clarendon, hostile to many of the crown's policies and of a 'most intimate and entire trust'. In the early deliberations St John repeated his arguments that ship money was central to the case against Charles, and also objected to the idea that canons in religion could be imposed without parliamentary approval. In December 1640 he introduced articles of impeachment against Sir John Finch. Outraged at Finch's behaviour during the ship money case, St John believed that Finch had deliberately sabotaged the judges' decision. Even after Finch fled to the Netherlands to avoid proceedings, St John continued to inveigh against him and ship money itself; in St John's mind the two were inextricably linked. Not only had the judges been deceived by Finch, according to St John, but, if ship money were allowed to stand, 'our birthright, our ancestral right, our condition of continuing as free subjects is lost; that of late there has been an endeavour to reduce us to the state of villeinage, nay, to a lower' (St John, *Speech*, 2).

At the height of St John's fury against Finch and ship money Charles appointed him king's solicitor, on 29 January 1641. According to Clarendon, the enterprise was the work of the earl of Bedford, who hoped to solve the problem of evil counsellors by persuading Charles to appoint those who inspired parliament's trust in return for a favourable financial settlement. The 'bridge appointments' scheme collapsed, however, over the treason trial of Thomas Wentworth, now earl of Strafford. Strafford was one of Charles's most trusted advisers and to many members stood as a symbol of royal tyranny. As the trial unfolded, however, Strafford defended himself skilfully, capturing considerable support. With Strafford gaining ground daily, the Commons began to consider abandoning the impeachment trial and resorting to a bill of attainder by which Strafford could be convicted of treason by a vote of parliament. In defiance of Pym, who preferred a continuation of the trial, St John took up the case for attainder. On 21 April, by a vote of 204 to 59, the Commons approved the attainder.

It remained to justify the attainder to the Lords, a task that St John undertook on 29 April. In a famous speech he argued that attainder was the proper procedure for determining treason if doubts at law arose. If Strafford's actions were not treason, he contended, 'England's but a piece of earth wherein so many men have their commorancy and abode, without ranks or distinction among men, without property or anything further than possessions, no law to punish the murdering or robbing of one another'. St John concluded in almost scattergun fashion, by offering several other justifications, suggesting, among other things, that 'it was never accounted cruelty or foul play to knock foxes and wolves on the head as they can be found; because these be beasts of prey'. In conclusion he remarked that in matters of treason parliament was:

> both the physician and the patient. If the body be distempered, it hath the power to open a vein, to let out the corrupt blood for curing itself; if one member be poisoned or gangr[en]ed, it hath the power to cut it off for the preservation of the rest. (St John, *Argument*, 72)

The concept of parliament as physician and patient was the logical extension of St John's ship money doctrines. At various times between 1640 and 1642 he conferred on parliament the right to challenge the king's power of dissolution, the right to overturn decisions already rendered by the courts, the right to determine the nation's religious settlement, and the right to remove members of which it did not approve. His ideas emerged not from detached, theoretical reflection about the distribution of authority, but from specific objections to the exercise of that authority.

St John appeared to be most troubled by a king who, through the appointment of obsequious judges and by dismissing or intimidating independent judges, seemed determined to secure a judiciary amenable to his will. Moreover, by 1641 Charles I had displayed little inclination to consider, still less take, the advice of his representative body. With the evidence provided by the ship money case and during Strafford's trial, St John seemed to have decided that an alteration of government was not only in progress, it had already occurred, and that the courts were powerless to prevent it.

The position of St John as a parliamentary leader improved still further in the aftermath of Strafford's trial. Sir Symonds D'Ewes reported that his speech on the attainder gave 'satisfaction to all'. On 11 May 1641 the Commons had St John's speech, along with two of Pym's on the same subject, printed as part of a campaign to justify their actions.

The first evidence of St John's increased prominence can be glimpsed in his attempt to help reform the king's finances in May 1641. Until this point he had shown little interest in financial matters and had in earlier deliberations helped obstruct one of Pym's tonnage and poundage bills. Nevertheless, in late May he came forward with his own proposal for settling the king's finances. In March parliament had approved a two-month grant of tonnage and poundage, which expired in May. St John's proposal involved another two-month grant, but one which would turn the money over to the king directly. It also involved demanding a closer accounting from the customs farmers, whom many members regarded as delinquent. However, the proposal roused an outcry. Strode and Holles objected to it on grounds that the money should be controlled by commissioners appointed by parliament. Six days later the Commons gave a first reading to a bill that would debar members of the house from serving the king until they first obtained the consent of both houses of parliament, seemingly a direct attack on St John himself, who remained the king's solicitor.

St John also had another bombshell to drop. On 27 May Sir Edward Dering introduced a bill, drafted by St John, for the complete abolition of episcopacy. St John had in the past displayed some hostility toward the bishops, but he refrained from a larger attack on them, perhaps in deference to his friend and patron, Bedford, a decided moderate in religious matters. Bedford's death on 10 May, however, may have freed St John from this constraint. In the debates that followed he made no attempt to conceal his hostility toward the bishops. They, he stated, had usurped power that properly belonged to the civil magistrate (in England the crown) since the time of Augustine of Canterbury.

For the remainder of the summer of 1641 St John behaved more circumspectly, saying little and avoiding controversy. The rising in Ireland in late October 1641 drastically altered the situation. Fearing a Catholic invasion of England from Ireland, Pym urged members of parliament to accept a document called the grand remonstrance, which contained a list of all of Charles's errors and was drawn up by a committee of which St John had been a member. St John by contrast brought up a bill for a book of rates to cover the new Tonnage and Poundage Bill which expired on 1 December. In his proposal to help Charles financially at a time when members were suspicious of the king's motivations and loyalties, St John repeated a pattern of behaviour he had followed in May. After proposing a measure advantageous to Charles, he had another member introduce a bill which he had written, and which would be opposed by the king. On 7 December 1641 Sir Arthur Hesilrige introduced a bill written by St John, empowering a lord general to raise and command the militia, to levy money to pay it, and to execute martial law. The bill also specified an admiral's place, but blanks were left in the spaces provided for the admiral and lord general. The bill would in effect give parliament the right to choose the army's and navy's commander. Several members opposed it on the grounds that assembling the militia was the king's prerogative. St John undertook a vigorous defence, declaring that power ought to be entrusted to someone in the event of an invasion, and that parliament had every right to nominate persons of trust. These men, he continued, might well be the king's own men, and he hoped that they would be so.

St John's actions on the Militia Bill reflect his attempt to play a dual role in the autumn of 1641. As the king's solicitor, he had an obligation to promote the king's interests, which he tried on several occasions to do. On the other hand, Charles's government ran against the grain of St John's core political and legal beliefs. While his advocacy of the Militia Bill appears moderate, there was little chance that parliament was going to approve of the king's men unless they were also parliament's men. St John appears to have been trying to play both sides of the street.

St John evidently succeeded for the most part at his double game. In January 1642 when Charles decided to arrest those members of parliament he considered most odious, St John was not among them, yet he remained in parliament's inner councils. About the same time he proposed a lifetime grant of tonnage and poundage be given to the king, while dropping hints to D'Ewes that he had been compelled to do so by the king, and during the early months of the year he also seems to have become much more cautious in other aspects of his behaviour. He said little in the debates over the arrest of the five members and the Militia Bill, and even went so far as to plant the idea that, as king's solicitor, he could be absolved from action by parliament if he had acted on royal command. In June 1642, in another example of timidity, St John asked parliament if he should obey the king's order to join him in York. The Commons refused him leave, but posing the question to parliament seems yet another tactic by St John to give himself legal cover. If the rebellion failed and he was asked why he remained with parliament, he could reply that he had been ordered to stay.

The first civil war, 1642–1646 After the outbreak of civil war St John's career took another dramatic turn. He came gradually to be regarded as a member of the Independents, and he took a leading role in negotiating the solemn league and covenant with the Scots, and in persuading parliament to accept the agreement as a means of tipping the military balance of power in its favour. Moreover, with Pym seriously ill in the autumn of 1643, he, along with Sir Henry Vane the younger, assumed Pym's role as parliamentary leader.

At the time of his speech defending the solemn league and covenant St John also advocated aggressive pursuance of the war, suggesting he had begun to part company with the earl of Essex, parliament's chief military commander. For the next two years he devoted considerable time and effort to finding ways to replace Essex with more aggressive commanders, and tensions erupted between him and other members, such as Essex and Denzil Holles, who feared that a divisive victory over the king threatened the social stability of the realm. In his campaigns against Essex, St John resorted to his usual subterfuges, such as having his close associate Samuel Browne suggest that Essex should be impeached for treason. Essex countered that St John and Vane should be impeached instead, indicating that he knew that his real enemies were St John and Vane, not Browne. St John sought to undermine the peace party yet further by exploiting the revelations of the royalist defector Lord Savile concerning the surreptitious contacts with the court at Oxford established by Holles and Bulstrode Whitelocke in the run-up to the treaty of Uxbridge.

To break the deadlock over the conduct of the war St John supported several measures which appeared to be instruments intended to purge the parliamentary army of aristocratic commanders, to retain Scottish support without committing parliament to a presbyterian settlement in religion, and to install a more effective fighting force. Toward these ends, he promoted the self-denying ordinance, the ordinance's eventual exemption for Oliver

Cromwell, the creation of the New Model Army, and the treason trial of Archbishop Laud.

The proceedings against Laud were unusual. Because of his role in negotiating the solemn league and covenant, St John was regarded by the Scots and by most observers as one of the Scots' strongest friends. But his delaying taking the covenant himself, his support for Cromwell, and his share in the passage of the toleration order of 13 September 1644 were more than enough to arouse the Scots' suspicions. St John may have used the trial of Laud as a tool to keep the Scots in line. Laud had been arrested in early 1641 along with Strafford, but after the Strafford fiasco, parliament delayed the proceedings against him for several years while Laud languished in the Tower. St John was instrumental in reviving them in 1643, and Laud was brought to trial, convicted of treason, and executed on 10 June 1645. Several contemporaries thought Laud had been condemned to death for the Scots' benefit: 'The rebels have murdered the most reverend father in God, William Laud … Mr. St. John, Mr. Strode, Harbottle Grimston, and a few others undertake to dispatch him' (Palmer, 88). St John's true colours regarding the Scots emerged when the parliamentary army at last defeated the king, when he dumped them as ignominiously as he had dumped Essex.

Relations with the army, 1646–1648 But the army's victories came at a political cost. St John's long-time opponent Denzil Holles exploited fears of the army's radicalism to take control of parliament and to attempt to disband the army. St John appears to have done little to stop Holles and absented himself from the Commons when the crucial debates were in progress. This idleness earned him the ire of John Lilburne and other supporters of the army, who accused St John, Vane, Saye, and Wharton of standing in the way of liberty by refusing to oppose those who wished to bring down the army.

If, by absenting himself from the political stage, St John had shrewdly perceived Holles's ascendancy, he just as shrewdly perceived his fall. On 4 August 1647 St John subscribed to the Engagement, which pledged him to live and die with the army, as the army took control of parliament. Several observers remarked upon a council of 'Grandees', including St John, who now steered the affairs of the whole kingdom. He wanted to make Charles a limited monarch, and he served as a member of the committee which drafted the four bills, a moderate settlement presented to Charles.

Dreams of settlement vanished quickly in January 1648 with the news that Charles had escaped from parliamentary custody and that the Scots were raising an army to support him. But Cromwell's victory over them meant that new deliberations about a settlement had to begin. At this point St John possibly began to diverge from Cromwell, as part of a group led by Saye, which feared that the country was being forced to choose between a royal or military tyranny. The family ties between the two men might also have been temporarily weakened by the death of St John's wife, Elizabeth Cromwell; on 1 October 1645 St John had married as his third wife Elizabeth (d. 1680), widow of Caleb Cockcroft of London, and eldest daughter of Daniel Oxenbridge of Daventry, Northamptonshire, and London.

The Commonwealth St John's elevation to the bench in October 1648 as lord chief justice of the common pleas removed him from direct involvement in the revolutionary events which engulfed England after the second civil war. As one of the 'royal Independents' he undoubtedly abhorred the violence done to parliamentary privilege at Pride's Purge. Named as one of the king's judges in the abortive ordinance for the trial of Charles I which passed the Commons on 1 January 1649, he was not nominated in the act establishing the high court of justice a few days later on the 6th. However, he was nominated to the first council of state, set up in February, and retained this seat at the helm of Commonwealth affairs right down to 1653. Although he was not distinguished by his activity at the council board, it is mistaken to assume that he withdrew entirely from government and politics after the execution of Charles I. Although there is no evidence that he resumed his seat in the Commons before July 1651 (when an order barring judges from sitting as MPs was lifted), he certainly served on the committee which tried to persuade Fairfax not to resign his commission in June 1650.

In spring 1651 St John headed the extraordinary embassy sent by the Rump Parliament to the states general of the United Provinces at The Hague. The purpose of the mission was to seek 'a more strict and intimate alliance and union' in pursuit of mutual security, the protection of protestantism in Europe, and 'the just liberties, and freedoms of the people' (Pincus, 26). The real issue appears to have been a strong desire to seek the discontinuance of Dutch support for the Stuart cause, and the shipments of arms to Scotland from the United Provinces. St John and his fellow ambassador Walter Strickland were received warmly at The Hague. But the majority of their Dutch hosts, wedded to the interests of the house of Orange, could not stomach the kind of union they proposed, while the exiled supporters of the Stuarts domiciled in the Dutch capital made the lives of their retinue daily less comfortable. An attempt was even made on the life of St John himself. Diplomatically, the sticking point came with the English demand for the expulsion of the Stuart royal family and their supporters. Ideologically, the refusal of a clear majority of Dutchmen to countenance this demand was all the evidence some men needed to conclude that they were apostate.

It has been claimed that St John was powerfully motivated by a desire for protestant unity in defence of popular liberty, and that he set about personally to punish the Dutch when rebuffed. A tradition would have it that he took a leading role in the passage of a Navigation Act which was aimed directly at the Dutch monopoly in the carrying trade. However, it should be noted that he originally declined to lead the diplomatic mission to The Hague, whether through fear for his life or loss of profit from his judicial office, and that only a majority vote in the house was sufficient to change his mind. Moreover, when the two nations eventually came to blows in September 1652, St John was offered the chair of the council of state, the body responsible for organizing the war effort, but once again declined to become involved. In the interim he also played an extremely important role in the evolution of Anglo-Scottish relations. In the wake of the military conquest in the north he set out as one of the commissioners for the government of Scotland on 18 December 1651. He and his fellow commissioners arrived on 15 January 1652. He stayed until the spring, overseeing the establishment of courts of justice, and promulgating the Rump's declaration of an intention to open negotiations for the 'incorporation' of Scotland into the Commonwealth of England and Ireland. When these talks began in the autumn, St John was a prominent participant.

After the execution of Charles I, St John had continued to maintain close links with Cromwell, to whom he wrote frequently. It is not clear whether the lord general reciprocated, but it is highly likely that he did, valuing St John's support for some of his more daring attempts to placate moderate opinion in the wake of regicide. After the battle of Worcester on 3 September 1651, St John was in the delegation sent by parliament to meet Cromwell at Aylesbury. Whitelocke noted that the commissioners had 'much discourse' with the lord general over dinner, 'my Lord Chief Justice St John more than all the rest' (Underdown, 290). He and Cromwell were instrumental in finally persuading the Rump to set a date for its dissolution the following autumn. At the same time St John promoted the late return to parliament of several former middle-group associates, leading to the resumption of their seats in the house by men such as Thomas Westrow, John Stephens, and Saye's son-in-law Richard Norton. His influence has also been detected behind initiatives such as the Act of Oblivion, the Hale commission on legal reform, and Owen's proposals for church settlement. 'Cromwell and St John were out to reunite the "godly party" on lines similar to those proposed by the middle group before 1648, and in a way that strikingly anticipates much of the Protectorate' (ibid., 291).

In December 1651 it was St John who remarked that 'something of the monarchical power' was necessary to preserve 'the foundation of our laws and the liberties of the people', which Cromwell followed up by pointing out that a Stuart settlement was politically impossible. The closeness of their thinking on this crucial matter lends credibility to the later claim that St John was the *éminence grise* lurking behind Cromwell's throne. It may also account for his vehement dislike of the 'Instrument of government', fully evident when he angrily demanded of his former client and long-time associate secretary John Thurloe in February 1654, 'is this all the fruit the nation shall have of their war?', throwing the document aside in disgust (Aubrey, 40). The *Humble Petition and Advice* may have been more to his liking, and he was called to, but did not sit in, the other house, excusing his absence 'by reason of the busines of the Terme' (GEC, *Peerage*, 4.635n.). St John probably found it harder to swallow the protector's reluctance to adopt the full panoply of regality, but at Thetford assizes in the spring of 1658 he gave a firmly loyalist charge which took as its theme the large benefits enjoyed by Englishmen living under the law. There seems little doubting the depth of St John's commitment to 'old Oliver', nor indeed to his family. In March 1660 St John reportedly favoured restoring the protectorate of Richard Cromwell, an allegation which he fervently denied in the apologia for his actions during the civil war and interregnum which he published after the Restoration. Although it was on St John's own motion that the Long Parliament finally agreed to dissolve itself on 16 March 1660, it was reported a fortnight later that he was still all for Richard, and he withdrew from the council of state on 30 March, denouncing Monck as a rigid cavalier.

Last years On 14 May 1660 a bill of attainder was introduced against St John in the convention, but he escaped with nothing more serious than disablement from office for life. Advisedly he kept a very low profile during the Restoration. During the 1650s he had commissioned the construction of a country house at Longthorpe near Peterborough. Thorpe Hall became an exemplar of the country 'tower house', a style of building which almost became the norm for houses of the gentry built at the Restoration. The former lord chief justice retired there to compose his apologia, *The Case of Oliver St John*. A story is told that Clarendon sent for him to ask his advice in the matter of a building commission he had in mind. But St John had the presence of mind to reply that he 'had not the vanity to think his house, of five or six rooms on a floor, a fit pattern for his lordship' (Mowl and Earnshaw, 117). In 1662 he took ship for exile in Europe, and initially resided in Basel, France. Later he moved to Augsburg in Germany. He died on 31 December 1673. He was survived by his third wife, Elizabeth, who later married Sir Humphrey Sydenham of Chilworthy, Somerset, and died in 1680. From his first marriage he had four children: Francis (*c.*1634–1705), his heir, who first served in parliament as member for Tewkesbury in 1654 and was elected for the final time in 1698 as member for Peterborough; William (*b.* 1637); Johanna; and Catherine. A further two children, Oliver and Elizabeth, were born to his second wife.

Reputation In his personal manner St John was described by Clarendon as 'a man reserved, and of a dark and clouded countenance, very proud, and conversing with very few, and those, men of his own humor and inclination'. Yet elsewhere Clarendon says that St John was 'beloved' by parliament (Clarendon, *Hist. rebellion*, 1.246, 3.470). While St John was not primarily a writer, he did leave several speeches, including some on ship money, another on the attainder of the earl of Strafford, and numerous shorter speeches, as well as a brief personal memoir.

The career of Oliver St John represents the dilemma of the constitutional opponent of Charles I's policies and ministers. In most cases he sought a political system that could restrain the king's policies without threatening the social fabric of society. The ship money case provided him not only with a case he would plead many times, but also with a political philosophy about the distribution of power. There can be little doubt that St John considered

Charles's attempt to intimidate the judiciary and impose a new rate without parliamentary consent to be the most serious problem facing the nation in 1640. He was also a political realist, willing to sacrifice principles and dissemble in quest of political advantage. His arguments in Strafford's trial ran counter to his respect for the precise language of the law, and many of his associates who thought he was on their side found, to their sorrow, that he was not.

St John's religious views were cloudy. He was capable of speaking the language of the doctrinaire puritan and was, according to several sources, the author of the root and branch bill, as well as a supporter of religious toleration. But in his recorded comments on religion, he never approached the fervour of the true saint. There can be little doubt that the experience of alliance with the Scots brought out the Erastian strain in his thinking, repulsed as he was by the claims to *de jure* authority advanced by Scots presbyterians and their fellow travellers in the City of London. He sat on the Westminster assembly and was appointed to the parliamentary committees set up to decide what offences should be punished by sacramental exclusion. He has, in the past, been described as an Independent, but although he joined Isaac Penington, Sir Gilbert Pickering, and others in commending Roger Williams to John Winthrop and his associates in Massachusetts in 1644, he and his cousin Samuel Browne later installed Archbishop William Ussher, advocate of a more 'primitive' episcopacy, as preacher at Lincoln's Inn in 1647. There seems no reason to dissent from the view that St John was a man of 'orthodox Calvinist-inclined views which were as compatible with low-church Anglicanism as with classical Independency or Presbyterianism' who shifted his support among the denominations as circumstances required (Pearl, 'St John', 500–01).

St John was by no means a doctrinaire radical, and he tried repeatedly to reach compromises between Charles and parliament. In the months before the civil war he supported a compromise Root and Branch Bill, a compromise Militia Bill, and several grants of tonnage and poundage. As late as 1648 he was still working to reach a compromise by which Charles could retain his throne.

St John eventually came to fear the power of the army and the radicalism of the masses as much as he feared royal tyranny. As several of the participants in the civil war, such as Clarendon and Holles, came to reflect on the events of the 1640s, St John was perhaps unfairly vilified in their accounts, but he was the only one of the core leaders in 1640 who survived the course of the war. Despite this vilification by contemporaries, he was a moderate conservative, committed to traditional forms of political sociability, to parliament, to the law, and to the monarchy.   WILLIAM PALMER

Sources W. Palmer, *The political career of Oliver St John* (1993) • V. Pearl, 'Oliver St John and the "middle group" in the Long Parliament, August 1643 – May 1644', *EngHR*, 81 (1966), 490–519 • V. Pearl, 'The Royal Independents in the English civil wars', *TRHS*, 5th ser., 18 (1968), 69–96 • D. Underdown, *Pride's Purge: politics in the puritan revolution* (1971) • *DNB* • Clarendon, *Hist. rebellion* • *The journal of Sir Simonds D'Ewes from the beginning of the Long Parliament to the opening of the trial of the earl of Strafford*, ed. W. Notestein (1923) • *The journal of Sir Simonds D'Ewes from the first recess of the Long Parliament to the withdrawal of King Charles from London*, ed. W. H. Coates (1942) • W. H. Coates, A. Steele Young, and V. F. Snow, eds., *The private journals of the Long Parliament*, 3 vols. (1982–92) • S. Gardiner, *Documents relating to the proceedings against William Prynne in 1634 and 1637* (1876) • Venn, *Alum. Cant.* • B. Worden, *The Rump Parliament, 1648–1653* (1974) • A. Davies, *Dictionary of British portraiture*, 1 (1979) • S. R. Gardiner, *History of England from the accession of James I to the outbreak of the civil war, 1603–1642*, 10 vols. (1883–4) • *Diary of John Northcote*, ed. A. Hamilton (1877) • J. Rushworth, *Historical collections*, 5 pts in 8 vols. (1659–1701) • O. St John, *The case of Oliver St John* (1660) • O. St John, *The speech or declaration of Mr St John … concerning ship-money* (1640) • O. St John, *An argument of law concerning the bill of attainder of Thomas, earl of Strafford* (1641) • Foss, *Judges* • T. Wotton, *The English baronets*, 4 vols. (1741) • Thurloe, *State papers* • *JHC*, 2–8 (1640–67) • GEC, *Peerage*, 4.634–5 • E. R. Edwards, 'St John, Francis', HoP, *Commons, 1660–90*, 3.381 • C. Russell, *The fall of the British monarchies, 1637–1642* (1991) • P. Aubrey, *Mr Secretary Thurloe: Cromwell's secretary of state, 1652–1660* (1990) • S. C. A. Pincus, *Protestantism and patriotism: ideologies and the making of English foreign policy, 1650–1668* (1996) • T. Mowl and B. Earnshaw, *Architecture without kings: the rise of puritan classicism under Cromwell* (1995)

Archives BL, legal collections, incl. notes, Add. MSS 25142–25306, 26633–26651 • BL, religious commonplace book, Add. MS 25285 | BL, letters to Thurloe, Add. MSS 4156–4158, *passim* • Bodl. Oxf., MSS Rawl., letters to Thurloe

Likenesses P. Nason, oils, 1651, NPG [*see illus.*]

St John, Oliver, fifth Baron St John of Bletso (*bap.* 1603, *d.* 1642), politician and parliamentarian army officer, was baptized at Bletsoe in Bedfordshire on 2 April 1603, the eldest son of Oliver *St John, first earl of Bolingbroke (*c.*1584–1646), and his wife, Elizabeth Paulet (*d.* 1655). He was admitted a fellow commoner of Queens' College, Cambridge, on 3 November 1615, matriculated there in 1618, and was created MA by royal mandate in 1620. In May 1623 he married Lady Arabella Egerton (*d.* 1669), eldest daughter of John *Egerton, first earl of Bridgewater. At his father's elevation to the earldom of Bolingbroke in 1624 he was known by the courtesy title Lord St John, and in the same year was returned to sit as MP for Bedfordshire. He served in the same capacity in the parliament of 1625 (when among others he sat on committees to discuss the establishment of arithmetic and philosophy schools). He was knighted at the coronation of Charles I in February 1626. That year, having been returned to Westminster once again for the county of Bedfordshire, he sat on the Commons committee for the privileges of the house and the select committee which discussed Sir Dudley Digges's motion for a sea war with Spain. A participant in the debate that identified the duke of Buckingham as the 'cause of causes', he spoke in respect of the service of English ships against the Huguenots of La Rochelle, though to what effect it is impossible to determine from records of the debate. He was nominated to committees charged with investigating the inadequacies of food supplied to the Mansfeld mission, and the appointment of county muster masters. He also sat on a committee appointed to consider how best to intimate to the king the desires of the house 'for the rectifying and augmenting his revenue' (Bidwell and Jansson, 3.156). He entered Lincoln's Inn on 9 August 1627 at the request of the then reader, Richard Taylor, a step which helped confirm his membership of one of the leading political patronage networks of the early Stuart period.

In the parliament of 1628–9 St John was again nominated to the privileges committee of the House of Commons, but appears to have kept a lower profile than at his previous attendances at Westminster. In 1628 he was, however, one of the many who made a point of visiting Sir John Eliot during his imprisonment in the Tower of London. Clarendon criticized St John's licentious personal habits, which seem to have landed him in some acute financial difficulties, so much so that in December 1638 he attempted unsuccessfully to flee the country in order to evade his creditors. They, led by Sir Matthew Lister, Sir John Danvers, and others, petitioned the king in October 1639 that he not accede to St John's request for protection of himself and his sureties, that they might be able to recover what they were owed, which amounted to £5900. Presumably they were somewhat disappointed when the following month St John was summoned by writ under his father's barony to the House of Lords, making him immune from prosecution. Any hopes that such a summons might secure St John's loyalty were sorely mistaken, and at the outbreak of hostilities in England in 1642 he raised a regiment of horse in which Oliver Cromwell's eldest son, Oliver, served as cornet. St John occupied Hereford for parliament in October 1642, fortified the city, and refused admittance to the king when he pitched up before its gates on the 8th. Joining up with the rest of the forces under command of the earl of Essex, St John then fought at the battle of Edgehill on 23 October and sustained wounds from which he died, apparently in captivity, the following day. He left no heir and his widow died at Welby, Lincolnshire, in 1669 and was buried at Melton Mowbray.

SEAN KELSEY

Sources DNB · M. Jansson and W. B. Bidwell, eds., *Proceedings in parliament, 1625* (1987) · W. B. Bidwell and M. Jansson, eds., *Proceedings in parliament, 1626*, 4 vols. (1991–6) · R. C. Johnson and others, eds., *Proceedings in parliament, 1628*, 6 vols. (1977–83) · *CSP dom., 1638–41* · J. Peacey, 'Led by the hand: manucaptors and patronage at Lincoln's Inn in the seventeenth century', *Journal of Legal History*, 18 (1997), 26–44 · *IGI* · W. A. Shaw, *The knights of England*, 2 vols. (1906) · GEC, *Peerage*, 2.203–4 · Venn, *Alum. Cant.* · W. P. Baildon, ed., *The records of the Honorable Society of Lincoln's Inn: admissions*, 1 (1896), 203 · F. G. Emmison, *Bedfordshire parish registers* (1907)

St John, Sir Oliver Beauchamp Coventry (1837–1891), political officer in India and telegraph engineer, was born at Springfield House, Ryde, Isle of Wight, on 21 March 1837, the eldest son of Captain Oliver St John (1803–1844), of the Madras native infantry, and his wife, Helen (d. 1881), daughter of John Young and widow of Henry Anson Nutt. A great-grandson of the tenth Baron St John of Bletso, he was educated at Norwich grammar school and the East India Company's military college at Addiscombe, and in 1859 arrived in India as a lieutenant in the Bengal Engineers.

In October 1863 St John volunteered for the expedition led by Lieutenant-Colonel Patrick Stewart of the Royal Engineers to run a telegraph from India to Persia and across Turkey to the Bosphorus. Initially he took charge of the final Persian section, ranked by Stewart as the most

difficult, and from March 1866 until January 1867 superintended the whole line from Tehran to Bushehr. In May 1867 he went to Abyssinia as the director of the field telegraph and army signalling department of the Abyssinian field force commanded by Sir Robert Cornelius (Lord Napier). He carried the telegraph line 200 miles inland, for which he was mentioned in dispatches. After returning to England in 1868 he wrote a report on the military telegraphs of France, Prussia, and Russia. On 23 September 1869 he married Janette (d. 1921), fourth daughter of James Ormond, of Abingdon, Berkshire, but soon after the wedding returned to his telegraph duties in Persia.

In October 1871 St John was dispatched to Baluchistan as boundary commissioner of the Perso-Kalat frontier. A keen geographer, he afterwards wrote up a 'Narrative of a journey through Baluchistan and southern Persia', which was published in F. J. Goldsmid's *Eastern Persia* (1876). Back in England again in 1873–4 he was employed by the India Office to compile maps of Persia and Persian Baluchistan. These maps, which remained for decades the standard authority, were drawn using the longitudes of the principal Persian telegraph stations fixed by exchanging time signals between Greenwich, Karachi, and the stations themselves.

In January 1875 St John was appointed principal of the Mayo College, Ajmer, which educated the sons of Indian princes. It was a sedentary job, not much to his taste, and he was relieved in August 1878 when the Indian foreign secretary, Alfred Lyall, attached him to a diplomatic mission to Kabul. The Afghans refused to allow the mission beyond the Khyber Pass, a rebuff which provided the inflammatory Lord Lytton with sufficient excuse to launch the Second Anglo-Afghan War. St John was then appointed chief political officer to the staff of Sir Donald Stewart, commander of the Kandahar field force, and entered Kandahar with the force in January 1879. On 10 January an assassin's bullet missed him by a whisker, but he comforted himself that it was probably intended for Sir Robert Sandeman, a rival frontier specialist. Sandeman was of much broader girth than the thin, narrow-shouldered St John and would almost certainly have been killed by the shot.

St John was to remain in Kandahar until April 1881. In July 1879 he was made a CSI, but hoped for a better-paid career in the home diplomatic service. From Calcutta, Lyall attempted to placate him by getting him a brevet lieutenant-colonelcy and, early in 1880, appointing him political agent for southern Afghanistan, a job which required him to look after the new governor of Kandahar, Wali Sher Ali Khan, who was essentially a puppet installed by the British while they worked out what to do with Kabul in the north. In July 1880 a force under Brigadier-General Burrows set out from Kandahar to Girishk to support the wali's forces against the advance of Ayub Khan, a strong contender for the throne of Afghanistan. The wali's forces were riddled with disaffection, but Burrows fatally delayed attempting to disarm them and on 14 July 1880 they absconded with a battery of guns. St John took part in the pursuit to recover the guns but knew that neither he nor Burrows would come out of the affair well. A fortnight later, he was involved in another débâcle at the battle of Maiwand (27 July), in which Bombay infantrymen panicked before Ayub Khan's forces and fled haphazardly back to Kandahar. St John tried to redirect the soldiers onto a route which he knew to be well-watered but few would listen, and at the height of the Afghan summer many died of thirst.

Heads rolled after Maiwand, and St John was one of those fiercely criticized by Bombay army chiefs and the press. Lyall and the new viceroy, Lord Ripon, stood by him and once the furore had died down Lyall ensured that he was promoted to KCSI (1882). Even Lyall, however, privately believed that Calcutta had not been well served by their man in Kandahar, that he had put too much faith in the wali's competence and underestimated the destabilizing effects of Ayub Khan's advance southwards.

In April 1881, on the final evacuation of Kandahar, St John was transferred to Quetta as officiating agent to the governor-general for Baluchistan. A string of short-term political appointments followed in Kashmir, Hyderabad, Quetta again, and Baroda. In January 1889 he was appointed resident and chief commissioner of Mysore and Coorg. It was one of the top political jobs in the country but it was almost too calm for him and in May 1891 he responded instantly to Lord Lansdowne's request that he again officiate as the governor-general's agent in Baluchistan. Unfortunately, the sudden switch in climate proved fatal and on 3 June 1891, a fortnight after his return to Quetta, St John died of pneumonia. He was buried in the new cemetery at Quetta on 5 June.

St John had been a fellow of the Royal Geographical and Zoological societies for years and had frequently sent animals to the latter, including a Bactrian camel left behind in Kandahar by Ayub Khan. His publications included a paper in the Royal Geographical Society's *Journal* entitled 'On the elevation of the country between Bushire and Teheran' (1868), and a paper on Persia which won the gold medal of the Royal United Service Institution of India in 1879. As he had often feared, St John left his family poorly off and, on their behalf, Lord Lansdowne appealed to the secretary of state for a queen's cadetship for his son, Henry Beauchamp (1874–1954), and apartments at Hampton Court for his widow and daughters, Olive Helen (b. 1870) and Muriel (b. 1873).   KATHERINE PRIOR

Sources DNB · F. Goldsmid, *Proceedings* [Royal Geographical Society], new ser., 13 (1891), 434–7 · BL OIOC, Lyall MSS · BL OIOC, Lansdowne MSS · *The Times* (5 June 1891), 10 · military records, BL OIOC · Burke, *Peerage* (1959)
Archives BL, letters to Lord Ripon, Add. MS 43613 · BL OIOC, corresp. with Sir Alfred Lyall, MS Eur. F 132
Likenesses photograph, c.1882, repro. in F. Bremner, *Baluchistan illustrated* (1900)
Wealth at death £580 0s. 2d.: probate, 2 Feb 1893, CGPLA Eng. & Wales

St John, Percy Bolingbroke (1821–1889), journalist, the eldest son of James Augustus *St John (1795–1875) and his wife, Eliza Caroline Agar, *née* Hansard (c.1798–1867), was born in Plymouth. He accompanied his father on some of his travels, particularly to Madrid, when the latter was researching for his *Life of Sir Walter Raleigh*, and he also travelled in America.

St John began to write tales when a boy, and translated about thirty of Gustave Aimard's Indian tales into English (published between 1876 and 1879). He was Paris correspondent of the *North British Daily Mail* and *Lloyd's Weekly News*. In 1846 he edited the *Mirror of Literature*, and in 1861–3 the *London Herald*. As correspondent of various newspapers he sent numerous miscellaneous contributions to the press, though these were of no special note; he also frequently contributed to *Chambers's Journal* and other magazines. His publications included *The Young Naturalist's Book of Birds* (1838), *The Trapper's Bride, and Indian Tales* (1845), *Lobster Salad* (1855, with Edward Copping), *Quadroona, or, The Slave Mother* (1861), and other fiction. In 1841 he married his mother's younger sister—a prohibited degree of marriage—Mary Anne Agar Hansard (1806/7–1895), daughter of Alexander Hansard, surgeon and apothecary, with whom he had a son. In 1852, in circumstances which are unclear (his first wife was still alive), he married Frances Deane, with whom he had a son and a daughter. He died in London on 15 March 1889.

J. R. MACDONALD, rev. ROGER T. STEARN

Sources *Literary World* (March 1889) · BL cat. · Boase, *Mod. Eng. biog.* · census returns, 1881 · private information (2004) [Dr S. V. Spilsbury]

St John, Sir Spenser Buckingham (1825–1910), diplomatist, born in St John's Wood, London, on 22 December 1825, was third of the seven sons of James Augustus *St John (1795–1875), journalist and traveller, and his wife, Eliza Caroline Agar Hansard (c.1798–1867). Percy Bolingbroke *St John and Bayle *St John were elder brothers, and Horace Stebbing Roscoe *St John and Vane Ireton Shaftesbury St John [*see below*] were younger brothers. After education in private schools, Spenser wrote 'innumerable articles' on Borneo, to which the adventures of Sir James Brooke, raja of Sarawak, were directing public attention, and he took up the study of the Malay language. He was introduced to Sir James *Brooke on his visit to England in 1847. He was quickly caught by Brooke's charm and accompanied him as private secretary the next year, when Brooke became British commissioner and governor of Labuan. Lord Palmerston, an acquaintance of St John's father, allowed him 'in a roundabout way £200 a year' (St John, 130). Thenceforth St John and Brooke were closely associated, though St John's role was usually to tone down Brooke's extravagances. St John had a Malay mistress, Dayang Kamariah, and they had three children; the local Anglican bishop and others protested about his 'immorality'. St John was with Brooke during his final operations in 1849 against Malay pirates, and he accompanied Brooke to Brunei, the Sulu archipelago, and to Siam in 1850. Although St John thought some of his chief's dealings with the natives high-handed and ill-advised, in a letter to Gladstone he defended Brooke against humanitarian attack in the House of Commons. While the official inquiry into Brooke's conduct, which the home government appointed, was in progress at Singapore, St John acted temporarily as commissioner for Brooke (1851–5), and visited the north-western coast of Borneo and the north-eastern shore, ascending the principal rivers. Appointed in 1856 British consul-general at Brunei, he explored the country round the capital, and went further into the interior than any previous traveller. His habit of wearing native dress resulted in complaints to London. He supported Brooke's objective of an extension of power in Labuan, and had to be reined in by the Colonial Office. He thought the Bruneis 'totally unfitted for rule' (Tarling, 99ff.). He published his full and accurate journals, supplemented by other visitors' testimonies, in two well-written and beautifully illustrated volumes entitled *Life in the Forests of the Far East* (1862; 2nd edn, 1863). He used this book to exact revenge on the missionaries who had complained of his behaviour; the controversy went further with his *The Bishop of Labuan* (1862). He also wrote Brooke's biography in 1879, a sympathetic but not uncritical work, whose tone was softened by Charles Grant.

In November 1859 St John revisited England with Brooke, and after returning to Borneo in 1860 became chargé d'affaires in Haiti in January 1863. He remained in the West Indies twelve years. During his residence in the Haitian republic, there was a civil war and a war with the neighbouring state of Santo Domingo, and St John frequently took violent measures against native disturbers of the public peace. On 28 June 1871 he became chargé d'affaires in the Dominican Republic, and he was promoted on 12 December 1872 to the post of resident minister in Haiti. His leisure was devoted to a history of the country, finally published in 1884 as *Hayti, or, The Black Republic* (2nd edn, 1889; French trans., 1884), a savagely hostile account.

For nine years (from 14 October 1874 until 1883) St John was minister-resident in Peru and consul-general at Lima. In 1875 he went on a special mission to Bolivia, and in 1880–81 witnessed the war between Peru and Chile. With the ambassadors of France and Salvador he negotiated an armistice in January 1881, and by his diplomatic firmness helped to protect Lima from destruction after the defeat of the Peruvians by Chile. He was created KCMG on 20 March 1881. In May 1883 St John was sent to Mexico to negotiate the resumption of diplomatic relations with Great Britain. An agreement was signed at Mexico on 6 August 1884, and was ratified, not without much opposition, mainly through his tact. He was appointed envoy-extraordinary and minister-plenipotentiary to Mexico on 23 November 1884, and remained there until 1893. In 1886 a mixed commission was appointed to investigate British financial claims on the Mexican government, and in 1887 a long-standing dispute was successfully resolved under St John's guidance. From 1 July 1893 to January 1896 St John was at Stockholm as minister to Sweden. He was created GCMG in 1894.

After retiring from the diplomatic service in 1896, St John spent his last years writing. He wrote *Rajah Brooke* (1899) for the Builders of Britain series and drew upon his early experiences in the Malay archipelago in two vivacious volumes, *Adventures of a Naval Officer* (1905) and *Earlier Adventures* (1906), both of which he attributed to a fictitious Captain Charles Hunter RN. A final publication was a collection of sympathetic but rather colourless *Essays on Shakespeare and his Works* (1908), edited from the manuscripts and notes of an unnamed deceased relative.

On 29 April 1899, St John married Mary Augusta, daughter of Frederick Macnaghten Armstrong, lieutenant-colonel in the Indian army. She survived him. He had also continued to support Dayang Kamariah and his surviving son, Sulong, who had trained in England as a civil engineer. An ambitious, intelligent, but humourless man, St John died at his home, Pinewood Grange, Camberley, on 2 January 1910. He bequeathed his portrait of Brooke by Sir Francis Grant (1847) to the National Portrait Gallery.

Vane Ireton Shaftesbury St John (1839–1911), Sir Spenser's youngest and last surviving brother, pursued a literary and journalistic career. He was a pioneer of boys' journals, starting and editing the *Boys of England* and similar periodicals. He was also the author of *Undercurrents: a Story of our Own Day* (3 vols., 1860) and of many story books for boys. He died at Peckham Rye in poor circumstances on 20 December 1911. He was twice married, and had seventeen children.   G. Le G. Norgate, *rev.* H. C. G. Matthew

Sources R. H. W. Reece, introduction, in S. St John, *The life of Sir James Brooke: rajah of Sarawak*, ed. R. H. W. Reece, [another edn] (1994) · N. Tarling, *Britain, the Brookes and Brunei* (1971) · *The Times* (4 Jan 1910) · *Morning Post* (4 Jan 1910) · S. Baring-Gould and C. A. Bampfylde, *A history of Sarawak under its two white rajahs, 1839–1908* (1909); repr. with introduction by N. Tarling (1989)
Archives Bodl. RH, letters to C. T. C. Grant, J. B. Brooke, and C. J. Brooke · Lpool RO, corresp. with fifteenth earl of Derby
Likenesses photograph, RGS
Wealth at death £10,933 5s. 8d.: probate, 4 Feb 1910, CGPLA Eng. & Wales

St John, Vane Ireton Shaftesbury (1839–1911). *See under* St John, Sir Spenser Buckingham (1825–1910).

St Just. For this title name *see* Grenfell, Edward Charles, first Baron St Just (1870–1941).

St Laurent, Louis Stephen (1882–1973), prime minister of Canada, was born on 1 February 1882 at Compton, Quebec, Canada, the eldest of the seven children of Jean-Baptiste Moïse St Laurent (1840–1915), a storekeeper, an eighth-generation French Canadian, and his wife, Mary Ann Broderick (1852–1933), a schoolteacher, the daughter of Irish immigrants. He spoke English with his mother and French with his father before he knew he was bilingual. Compton is in the eastern townships, a tolerant world, where French and English intermingled and sometimes intermarried. Louis's residential church school at Sherbrooke was bilingual too. A bookish lad, he played chess rather than games, and with one of his philosophy teachers. He was an excellent student; his essay on Molière's *Le misanthrope* was the best in the school. In 1905 he graduated from Laval University's law school with the governor-general's gold medal. He took up practice in Quebec City

Louis Stephen St Laurent (1882–1973), by Yousuf Karsh

with C.-P. Pelletier, a well-established Conservative lawyer. Although St Laurent's political sympathies were Liberal, they made an excellent team. Pelletier cared little for legal research, while St Laurent enjoyed it.

In legal practice St Laurent's bilingualism was a major asset: French-Canadian lawyers whose English and English law were weak would retain him to plead for them; English-language lawyers who knew no French-Canadian civil law (which was modelled on the Code Napoléon) would engage him to do their French legal work.

St Laurent married on 19 May 1908 Jeanne Renault (1886–1966), from La Beauce, in the Chaudière valley 100 miles or so to the east; she was the daughter of P. F. Renault, a storekeeper. Their first child was born in 1909, and four more followed. St Laurent was always a good family man; if he worked hard at his law practice he seemed always to have time for his children. In 1909 he formed a legal partnership with Antonin Galipeault that progressed and expanded over the years. He was made professor of law at Laval in 1914, and took silk in 1915. By the 1920s he was a considerable power within the Quebec bar, and in 1928 he represented Ernest Lapointe, federal minister of justice, at the annual meeting of the Canadian Bar Association in Regina, Saskatchewan. It was his first trip west of Ontario. In 1930 he succeeded Richard Bedford Bennett as president of the Canadian Bar Association.

St Laurent was well liked. By the age of fifty he had acquired his mature style—a disarming mixture of modesty, charm, and quiet dignity; those who knew him were struck by his sincerity and honesty. There were few flights of fancy in his speeches: they tended to be dead straight, the way he was himself. He stressed the value of two languages, two legal systems in one country; Canada was the better for it.

In 1941, on the sudden death of Ernest Lapointe, minister of justice, the prime minister, Mackenzie King, needed a steady and able lawyer from Quebec. St Laurent was recommended by several senior Liberals. St Laurent had never been in politics; he had no wish now to be in politics, but in 1941 he felt he had no option. It was a duty, temporary no doubt, brought about by the war. He stood for by-election in Quebec East, Lapointe's constituency (once also Sir Wilfrid Laurier's). One major issue was conscription. St Laurent refused to oppose it unequivocally since he thought that conscription for overseas service might well become necessary. Despite this handicap he won his seat comfortably against a rabid nationalist.

In Ottawa, St Laurent worked a fifteen-hour day. His department of justice senior civil servants soon discovered a minister with remarkable capacity to absorb material, master the gist of it, and make decisions quickly. Gordon Robertson, secretary to the prime minister's office from 1945 to 1949, recalled that he had never served under a minister at once so deft, so sensible, and so reasonable.

The conscription crisis of late 1944 badly strained the Liberal government. Conscription already in force was for home defence. In 1944, however, it meant being sent overseas to fight in Europe. King had said that it would be brought in only 'if necessary', by which he meant necessary to win the war, not for some theoretical army requirements. St Laurent supported King in the bitter cabinet divisions that developed around this issue, always with an air of reasonableness and good sense. So much was he respected that his loyalty to the prime minister made it awkward for others to go against him. St Laurent never wavered, convinced that the army needed more men than were available by the volunteer system, and he and the prime minister managed to persuade most of the French-speaking members of the Liberal caucus to back the government.

Thus Mackenzie King found St Laurent indispensable, both then and later; St Laurent became minister of external relations in 1946, a portfolio to which King had clung for many years. When King retired from office in November 1948, St Laurent was not only King's choice as successor but the clear choice of the Liberal Party. He was sworn in as prime minister on 15 November 1948.

St Laurent played a leading role in negotiations for Newfoundland's entry into confederation, effected on 31 March 1949. It had been a long time in coming, having first been mooted in 1864. The Easter recess of 1949 St Laurent used as an opportunity to look at the west, where the Liberal Party was not as strong as he would have liked. His first speeches were starchy, a little like a geometry teacher dealing with dull pupils. But gradually he began to develop his own unique style, to mix with the crowds and chat comfortably—his English had an agreeable touch of Irish brogue in it—about crops and the weather, the way he used to do in French in his father's store in Compton, to pick up babies joyfully and talk with their parents. Watching him one reporter commented, 'Uncle Louis is going to be hard to beat' (Thomson, 465). He was right. St Laurent's style came from a remarkable combination of intelligence and suavity, and, be it added, his unabashed delight in children. He called an election for the summer of 1949 and was returned with a huge majority, larger than any that King had ever had. And he remained known as Uncle Louis to the end of his career.

St Laurent's nationalism was unobtrusive but effective: he was responsible for the appointment of a Canadian governor-general and the abolition of appeals to the privy council. He also wanted a much larger role for Canada in international affairs than King would ever have accepted, including membership in NATO and support for the United Nations in the Korean War (1950–53). St Laurent won the election of 1953; his majority was somewhat reduced, but he and the Liberals were quite unassailable. It looked indeed as if Uncle Louis would go on forever.

In 1954 St Laurent accepted the invitation of Nehru to visit India, and he decided to extend this to include the Far East. Jeanne, his wife, would not fly, so he was accompanied by two of his children plus a small technical staff. The group landed in New Delhi on 21 February 1955. It was a hard schedule. Indian food did not agree with him, and the pace and the heat were fierce. Then there were visits to Ceylon, Indonesia, the Philippines, and Korea to be got through. And Japan after that. St Laurent arrived back in Ottawa three weeks later worn out. He was, after all, seventy-three.

The summers at St Patrice on the lower St Lawrence had always restored St Laurent's vitality, and the summer of 1955 did something of that, but he did not soon recover his former vigour. In the rancorous pipeline debates of 1956 he seemed on the sidelines, while his dynamic and forceful minister of trade and commerce, Clarence Decatur Howe, ran the show. The trans-Canada gas pipeline was a good project, but there was a complex timetable to be met with both finance and construction. The legislation was managed in such a heavy-handed fashion that the merits of the project were obscured by the government's brutal tactics. Howe had never been a minister with much patience; as a rule he had got what he had wanted. That was useful in wartime, but not acceptable afterwards. As Howe rammed his legislation through, St Laurent seemed to be a prime minister no longer able to control his cabinet or his party.

St Laurent did better with the Suez crisis in early autumn 1956. He had a ductile and able minister of external affairs, Lester Pearson, who shared his views, though he was more diplomatic about expressing them. Neither man liked what the British and the French were threatening. The more St Laurent thought about it the less he liked it; the best service Canada could do for Britain and France was to dissuade them from what seemed a remarkable act of folly. After all attempts at persuasion had failed, and when Britain and France acted, St Laurent and Pearson could hardly believe it. St Laurent gave Pearson ample support in arranging the United Nations intervention.

By 1957, however, St Laurent was tired, and journalists' persistent questions made him testy. Both the pipeline debate and the Suez crisis had weakened Liberal appeal to English-speaking voters. St Laurent's government was appearing arrogant and impatient. Still, the polls were predicting another electoral victory when Canadians voted in June 1957. St Laurent himself was expecting a third mandate. The Liberals did indeed win a plurality of votes—42 per cent as against 39 per cent for the Progressive Conservatives—but seats in the Commons were another matter. The Progressive Conservatives won 112 (of 262) and the Liberals 106, with the socialist Co-operative Commonwealth Federation at 25, the Social Credit at 19, and a few others. Not all of St Laurent's party wanted him to resign; the Liberals had been in power since 1935, and were not pleased at having to give it up. Not a few Liberals felt they could somehow survive if only St Laurent did not resign. But he was too much a gentleman to cling to power under such circumstances. He gracefully handed power to John Diefenbaker, leader of the Progressive Conservatives; he then stepped down as leader of the Liberal Party, to be succeeded by Lester Pearson.

St Laurent did not enjoy retirement from politics as he should have done. At the age of seventy-six he felt dispirited and rejected. Finally his family persuaded him to have a comprehensive medical check-up. A prostate operation was overdue. That greatly helped, and when his son Renault had a heart attack shortly afterwards St Laurent was called back to the family firm. It was good to get back to legal work; he began to feel better. Perhaps the Canadian people might even forgive him his failings. The secret of good health, he roundly asserted, was to get defeated in an election. Jeanne, his wife, died on 14 November 1966, but St Laurent soldiered on for a few more years. He died of a heart attack in Quebec City on 25 July 1973 and was buried in St Thomas Aquinas cemetery, Compton.

In his best years St Laurent was a delightful man, a prime minister well liked. In spring 1949 he was walking on the campus of the University of British Columbia with its president, Larry MacKenzie, whom he was trying to recruit for the Liberal cabinet in Ottawa. The president stopped a 26-year-old graduate student he knew and introduced him to the prime minister. The young war veteran was polite but had a question. 'Sir,' he said to St Laurent, 'when is Canada going to get its own flag and stop flying the colonial version of the Union Jack?' St Laurent was quite unruffled. 'Young man,' he asked, 'is a flag a symbol of unity or disunity?' The graduate student replied, 'Unity, of course.' 'That', said St Laurent with a benign smile, 'is your answer.' And he sailed serenely on, beneath the red ensign (with the union jack in the corner) that flew over the university campus, towards his great electoral triumph of June 1949 (personal knowledge). The Canadian flag would come in time, of that he was confident. It did, in 1965. St Laurent was a man of considerable patience.

P. B. WAITE

Sources D. C. Thomson, *Louis St Laurent, Canadian* (1967) · J. W. Pickersgill, *My years with Louis St Laurent* (1975) · [L. B. Pearson], *Memoirs*, 2 vols. (1972–3) · G. Robertson, *Memoirs of a very civil servant* (2000) · personal knowledge (2004)
Archives NA Canada, papers | NA Canada, Mackenzie King papers; L. B. Pearson papers
Likenesses Y. Karsh, photograph, Camera Press [*see illus.*] · portrait, House of Commons, Ottawa

St Lawrence, Christopher, seventh Baron Howth (*d.* 1589), nobleman, was the third son of Sir Christopher St Lawrence, seventeenth lord of Howth (*d.* 1542), and Amy Bermingham, and younger brother of Edward and Sir Richard, eighteenth and nineteenth lords respectively. He was commonly called 'the Blind Lord' because of his defective eyesight. Educated at Lincoln's Inn in 1544, St Lawrence succeeded to the family estates on the death of Sir Richard in 1558, and the title of baron was confirmed to him in May 1561. Already experienced in local administration, the new lord became involved in affairs of state both as councillor and agent of government, and later critic of the regimes of successive chief governors of Ireland. The tempestuous relations of Shane O'Neill with the Dublin administration in the 1560s are reflected in the chieftain's abortive visit to London in early 1562, facilitated by Howth and Lord Slane among others, and in the series of military campaigns of Lord Lieutenant Sussex and Lord Deputy Sidney in Ulster in which Howth played a significant part. Together with Sir John Plunket, chief justice of the queen's bench, Howth travelled to London in late 1562 to present Elizabeth and her privy council with letters concerning these and other matters relating to the governance of her Irish realm. For his services during this period he was knighted by Sir Henry Sidney on 9 February 1570.

Howth became a leader of the 'country cause' against the cess, the government's policy of arbitrary taxation for the victualling of the army in Ireland. In his examination before the Irish council in 1577, Howth (whose knowledge of custom is attested to by his role in the compilation of the *Book of Howth*, a chronicle of medieval Ireland) argued that the imposition was unconstitutional. But after five months' confinement in Dublin Castle he affirmed that he had no intention 'to gainsay any part of the queen's prerogative', and acknowledged 'that, in times of necessity, the queen may lay charge upon her subjects here as fully as in England' (Brewer and Bullen, 1575–8, 133). Having been sharply reprimanded for his undutiful behaviour, he was set at liberty. The issue was revived, however, in 1586, and it was mainly due to the opposition of lords Howth, Slane, and Louth that an attempt by Sir John Perrot, the lord deputy, to persuade parliament to consent to a composition for cess was defeated. Howth once again retracted his criticism, and seems to have become reconciled to Perrot, to whom he sent, shortly before his death, an 'intermute gossawk'.

Howth's domestic life was turbulent, at least for a spell in the 1570s. He married first, in 1546, Elizabeth, daughter of Sir John Plunket of Beaulieu, co. Louth, with whom he had fourteen children, of whom only six survived to adulthood: Nicholas [*see below*], his successor, Thomas (*d.* 1600),

Leonard (*d.* 1608), Richard, Mary, who married Sir Patrick Barnewall of Turvey, and Margaret (*d.* 1620). The death of another daughter, thirteen-year-old Jane, was caused by the baron's own hand. In a case before the court of castle chamber in Dublin on 22 May 1579, Howth was charged with having beaten her so cruelly that she died within two days, and also with severely maltreating his wife, Elizabeth (who was confined to bed for two weeks with her injuries), and his butler, who attempted to comfort her. Having heard evidence of the assaults and of the baron's 'filthy conversation' and dissolute life with 'strange women', the court imposed a fine of £1000. Three years later the court reduced the fine to £500, having heard the baron's plea that he had already been punished to his 'intolerable charge and hindrance' by having spent nineteen weeks in prison. Elizabeth Plunket left her husband about 1579, and (probably in the following year) he married Cecily, daughter of Alderman Henry Cusack of Dublin, who, on the baron's demise, wedded first John Barnwell of Monkton, co. Meath, and second, John Finglas of Westpalston, co. Dublin. Lord Howth died on 24 October 1589 and was buried in Howth Abbey.

Nicholas St Lawrence, eighth Baron Howth (*d.* 1607), Howth's eldest son, who was knighted by Sir William Fitzwilliam in 1588, succeeded to the barony on his father's death. Taking advantage, like his father, of being the first to greet and play host to chief governors disembarking at Howth, he was commended for his service to the state at a critical time during the campaign against the earl of Tyrone. For his participation in an expedition against the insurgent Fiagh MacHugh O'Byrne in Wicklow in 1595, as well as for his reliability in marshalling the gentlemen of the pale and administering the region in the governor's absence in the later 1590s, he was nominated for membership of the Irish council by Lord Deputy Mountjoy in 1600.

While continuing to serve the Irish administration loyally, the eighth Baron Howth was a champion of the liberties of his fellow palesmen, as his father had been. As their envoy at court in 1600 he castigated the soldiery for plundering the pale, and in 1605 he campaigned against the imprisonment of Catholic dissidents. He demonstrated his independence in religious matters while the lord deputy, Sir Arthur Chichester, stayed at Howth during the plague of 1604–5 by accompanying the governor to the church door for Church of Ireland divine service and then withdrawing.

Howth's first marriage, about 1570, was to Margaret, daughter of Sir Christopher Barnewall of Turvey (whose son Patrick was husband to Nicholas's sister Mary), with whom he had Christopher *St Lawrence (*d.* 1619), his successor, Thomas, Richard, and Mary. His first marriage having ended in divorce, about 1575 he married Mary (*d.* 1607), daughter of Sir Nicholas White of Leixlip, with whom he had Edward, Richard, Almeric, Margaret, Elinor, and Alison. He died at Howth on 11 May 1607 and was buried in Howth Abbey ten days later. His widow died on 25 July the same year and was buried with him.   COLM LENNON

Sources F. E. Ball, *A history of the county Dublin*, 6 vols. (1902–20), vol. 5 · J. S. Brewer and W. Bullen, eds., *Calendar of the Carew manuscripts*, 6 vols., PRO (1867–73) · *Report on the manuscripts of the earl of Egmont*, 2 vols. in 3, HMC, 63 (1905–9), vol. 1/1 · *CSP Ire.*, 1509–92 · J. G. Crawford, *Anglicizing the government of Ireland: the Irish privy council and the expansion of Tudor rule, 1556–1578* (1993) · *DNB* · *Calendar of the manuscripts of the most hon. the marquis of Salisbury*, 2, HMC, 9 (1888) · V. J. McBrierty, 'Howth Castle and the St Lawrence family', *The Howth peninsula: its history, lore and legend*, ed. V. J. McBrierty (1981)

St Lawrence, Christopher, **ninth Baron Howth** (*d.* 1619), soldier and informer, was the eldest son of Nicholas *St Lawrence, eighth Baron Howth (*d.* 1607) [*see under* St Lawrence, Christopher, seventh Baron Howth], and his wife, Margaret Barnewall, daughter of Sir Christopher Barnewall. Most likely it was the young Christopher who, according to tradition, was kidnapped by the famous sea captain Grace O'Malley about 1576. Finding the gates of Howth Castle closed against her on a visit ashore to replenish her stores, Grace seized the young St Lawrence and took him back to her base in Clew Bay in co. Mayo. She agreed to his release only when Lord Howth promised to keep the castle gate open permanently to those seeking hospitality and that an extra plate would always be laid at the lord's table. These customs are maintained at Howth down to the present day.

A maverick who was more at home on military campaigns than in the council chamber, St Lawrence first gained distinction for his service during the Nine Years' War. He accompanied his father on an expedition into Wicklow against Feagh McHugh O'Byrne, during which he showed courage by capturing two of the chieftain's followers in April 1595. Subsequently he visited England where apparently he was knighted and, returning to Ireland with Sir Conyers Clifford in 1597, was given command of the garrison at Cavan. For almost two years he served there and in Leinster, chiefly employed against the allies of Hugh O'Neill, the earl of Tyrone, in King's and Queen's counties.

St Lawrence's service under the earl of Essex in 1599 went beyond merely campaigning with the new lord lieutenant in Leinster, Munster, and the north midlands. He demonstrated his bravery most notably at Athy by swimming across the River Barrow in order to recover some stolen horses, and at the siege of Cahir Castle, where, having repulsed a sortie of the garrison, he was one of the first to enter the place. He also accompanied Essex, who described St Lawrence as his 'dear and worthy friend' (*Salisbury MSS*, 9.287) on the earl's unwarranted and ill-fated return to England, and is said to have threatened the earl's enemies, including Sir Robert Cecil. Queen Elizabeth chose not to penalize St Lawrence but instead recommended him for continued service in Ireland. This pattern of turbulent interpersonal relationships interspersed with shows of royal favour continued to characterize his career.

Despite his persistent complaints about lack of preferment, St Lawrence enhanced his reputation for military valour during the last phase of the war. Lord Deputy Mountjoy employed him extensively from early 1600 against the O'Mores of Leix (Laois) and Tyrell of Westmeath in the midlands, and against the forces of Hugh O'Neill in the northern theatre where he was injured at Moyry in October 1600. On the arrival of a Spanish expedition at Kinsale in September 1601 he was dispatched into Munster, but his attempt, in conjunction with Sir George Carew, the president of the province, to intercept Hugh O'Donnell's southward march failed. At the siege of Kinsale he and the earl of Clanricarde were stationed to the west of the town to prevent a junction between the Spaniards and O'Donnell. Subsequently he was appointed governor of Monaghan where his rule elicited both popular acclaim and official disapproval.

Even before the submission of Hugh, earl of Tyrone, in 1603, St Lawrence had importuned the authorities in Dublin for permission to serve as a soldier overseas. The breakdown by autumn 1605 of his marriage to Elizabeth Wentworth (*d.* 1627), daughter of John Wentworth of Little Horkesley, Essex, with whom he had three children—two sons, Nicholas (his successor) and Thomas, and a daughter, Margaret—may have contributed to his restlessness and impecuniosity. By the terms of the separation agreement he had to pay Elizabeth £100 per annum. Eventually Lord Deputy Chichester wrote to the king in his favour and he was granted permission to recruit some troops from Monaghan, Fermanagh, and Cavan for the army of the archdukes, governors of the Spanish Netherlands. St Lawrence served as a captain in the regiment of Henry O'Neill from June 1606 until May 1607, joining thousands of his fellow Irish swordsmen, including his brother Thomas, who had migrated to the continent. In doing so he satisfied both his thirst for adventure and his need for an income, pending his entry into his inheritance.

St Lawrence's departure from the Low Countries was occasioned by the news of his father's death, but before returning to Ireland he journeyed to London to inform the privy council of a conspiracy of which he had become aware. It was supposed to entail an insurrection against the English administration in Ireland with Spanish assistance, and involved the earls of Tyrone and Tyrconnell and the baron of Delvin, among many others. The details were regarded with scepticism at first by the councillors, who dispatched St Lawrence, now Lord Howth, to Ireland for examination by Chichester. Assigned the initials A. B. to conceal his identity, Howth outlined the plot to the lord deputy, who remained only half-convinced by the story. Like the officials in London, Chichester was very well aware of Howth's reputation for instability and eccentricity. Far-fetched though the account of the conspiracy might have been, however, the London authorities were disposed in the later summer of 1607 to be wary of the dissident mood not only among the Gaelic leadership but also among the Old English population of the pale and the towns which had been subjected to a rigorous regime of religious repression in the previous two years by Chichester's administration. Thus the privy council prepared to compile evidence concerning the plot by calling Howth back to London while Hugh O'Neill would be in attendance at court.

The real significance of Howth's role as government informant, whether veracious or otherwise, lies in its helping to precipitate the departure of Tyrone and Tyrconnell to the continent in September 1607 in the famous flight of the earls. Recent evidence has shown that Tyrone did indeed have continuing and potentially treasonable diplomatic links with Spain, though it appears that the government was unable to prove the case. Howth was reluctant to implicate Tyrone directly and certainly unwilling to testify against him. Yet the very fact that the government was pursuing the matter and entertaining Howth's dubious tale gave substance to Tyrone's fears that he was about to be arrested and charged with treason. Accordingly he joined Tyrconnell on the ship to Flanders, and the subsequent course of Ulster history was changed.

When Howth was revealed as the government informer he became an object of distrust and contempt in Ireland, fearing for his life. His implication of the Old English Lord Delvin, who was briefly imprisoned, was particularly offensive to the sensibilities of many in the pale. Thus the years after 1607 were marked by personal vendettas and by several trips to England to attain vindication or support from the privy council. On every occasion, however, Howth managed to retain the goodwill of King James, a factor which made his position in Ireland all the more suspect.

Howth attempted to convince the authorities that Sir Garret Moore was implicated in the plot in revenge for Moore's description of him as 'an idle-headed lord, a speaker of untruths, one that would crack and brag much, yea, that would draw a man into the field, but when he came there would not and durst not fight him' (CSP Ire., 1606–8, 535). Although he failed to substantiate the charges, Howth returned from a sojourn in London with the highest testimony to his good faith. He then turned on Moore's brother-in-law, Sir Roger Jones, son of Archbishop Thomas Jones, chancellor of Ireland. Jones had dismissed him as a valiant man among cowards, and in revenge, in 1609 Howth assembled about a dozen followers armed with cudgels and led them to a court in Thomas Street, Dublin, where Jones and some friends were playing tennis. In the ensuing affray one of Jones's retainers was killed. Once again the Dublin councillors exasperatedly tried to investigate, being challenged by Howth for their partiality towards Jones. The more detached view of the English privy council was that 'most of Lord Howth's charges arose out of unkind speeches behind backs, and were grounded sometimes upon looks and sometimes on loose observations that men did not love him' (CSP Ire., 1608–10, 427). On repairing to England without authorization in May 1611, he nevertheless managed to retain the favour of the king who found 'his carriage unexceptionable' (CSP Ire., 1611–14, 291), and he returned to be reconciled with Chichester in 1612.

Howth's last years were more tranquil. He was a member of the Irish House of Lords in the parliament of 1613–15. In 1614 he took the lead in the raising of a free gift to the king by contributing £100. He died at Howth on 24 October 1619 and was buried at Howth Abbey, his obsequies being delayed until 30 January 1620.

COLM LENNON

Sources F. E. Ball, *A history of the county Dublin*, 6 vols. (1902–20), vol. 5 · *CSP Ire.*, *1592–1614* · J. McCavitt, *Sir Arthur Chichester, lord deputy of Ireland, 1605–1616* (1998) · V. J. McBrierty, 'Howth Castle and the St Lawrence family', *The Howth peninsula, its history, lore and legend*, ed. V. J. McBrierty (1981) · G. Henry, *The Irish military community in Spanish Flanders, 1586–1621* (1992) · *DNB* · A. Chambers, *Granuaile: the life and times of Grace O'Malley, c.1530–1603* (1983) · J. S. Brewer and W. Bullen, eds., *Calendar of the Carew manuscripts*, 5: *1603–1623*, PRO (1871) · J. S. Brewer and W. Bullen, eds., *Calendar of the Carew manuscripts*, 3: *1589–1600*, PRO (1869) · *Calendar of the manuscripts of the most hon. the marquis of Salisbury*, 9, HMC, 9 (1902)

St Lawrence, Nicholas, third Baron Howth (*d.* 1526), administrator, was the eldest son of Robert *St Lawrence, second Baron Howth (1435?–1486), administrator, and his second wife, Joan, daughter of Edmund Beaufort, first duke of Somerset. He was married three times: first to Genet, daughter of Christopher Plunket, third Lord Killeen, with whom he had a son, Christopher, who succeeded him as Baron Howth, and four daughters, Alison, Elizabeth, Ellenor, and Anne. His second wife was Anne Bermingham, daughter of Thomas Berford of Kilrow, co. Meath, with whom he had two sons, Amorey and Robert, and one daughter, Katherine. His third wife was Alison, daughter of Robert FitzSimons; they had a son named William or Walter, and a daughter, Marian.

Unlike the majority of English in Ireland, Lord Howth was a staunch Lancastrian. When Lambert Simnel early in 1487 personated the earl of Warwick, Howth refused to recognize his claims and apprised Henry VII of his designs. In 1488 he took the oath of allegiance and did homage before Sir Richard Edgcumbe at St Thomas's court in Dublin. Subsequently Henry summoned Howth along with other noblemen in Ireland to Greenwich, and rewarded him with 300 pieces of gold and confirmation to him of the lands of Howth by charter.

Howth attended the parliament held at Dublin in 1490 and the great council at Trim in September 1493. In January 1494 he was knighted and in 1497 he was appointed chancellor of the exchequer. In 1504 he attended the eighth earl of Kildare on an expedition against Clanricarde and O'Brien in Connaught. At Knockdoe in August they encountered a formidable Gaelic force. Lord Gormanston favoured retreating or negotiating with their Gaelic adversaries. However, Howth advocated immediate engagement, and led the billmen to the attack on foot, which ended in victory for the English forces. Although he opposed the earl of Kildare's support for Lambert Simnel, Howth later became a strong Geraldine supporter and even defied the earl of Ormond to mortal combat for speaking ill of Kildare. He was appointed lord chancellor in 1509, but after Kildare's death in 1513 Howth's political influence steadily diminished. In 1520 Lord Lieutenant Surrey excluded him from office, and in the same year he was replaced as chancellor of the exchequer by Patrick

Bermingham, though he remained a member of the council until his death. In 1524 he acted as witness to an indenture between the earls of Ormond and Kildare and was party to a dispute with Drogheda-based officials concerning payment of a rent of 40s. on property in the town. Howth died on 10 July 1526, and was buried in the family sepulchre at Howth.

E. I. CARLYLE, rev. MARY ANN LYONS

Sources J. S. Brewer and W. Bullen, eds., *Calendar of the Carew manuscripts*, 5: *1603–1623*, PRO (1871), 177, 182–3, 189–92 · *LP Henry VIII*, 1, no. 235; 3, no. 1242; 4, no. 558 · J. Lodge, *The peerage of Ireland*, rev. M. Archdall, rev. edn, 3 (1789), 188–92 · *State papers published under … Henry VIII*, 11 vols. (1830–52), 2.92, 108 · M. C. Griffith, ed., *Calendar of inquisitions formerly in the office of the chief remembrancer of the exchequer*, IMC (1991), 12, 16–18 · D. Bryan, *Gerald Fitzgerald, the great earl of Kildare* (1933), 104–5, 151, 177–8, 243–6 · S. G. Ellis, *Reform and revival: English government in Ireland, 1470–1534*, Royal Historical Society Studies in History, 47 (1986), 45, 155, 220, 223–4 · GEC, *Peerage*, new edn · J. R. O'Flanagan, *The lives of the lord chancellors and keepers of the great seal of Ireland*, 2 vols. (1870), 143, 157, 159–60 · T. W. Moody and others, eds., *A new history of Ireland*, 9: *Maps, genealogies, lists* (1984), 507 · J. Haydn, *The book of dignities: containing rolls of the official personages of the British empire* (1851) · S. G. Ellis, *Ireland in the age of the Tudors* (1998), 175, 308

Archives BL, Harley MS 1425, fol. 104

Wealth at death less than £100 p.a.: Griffith, ed., *Calendar of inquisitions*, 12, 16–18

St Lawrence, Nicholas, eighth Baron Howth (*d.* 1607). *See under* St Lawrence, Christopher, seventh Baron Howth (*d.* 1589).

St Lawrence, Robert, second Baron Howth (1435?–1486), administrator, was the eldest son of Christopher St Lawrence, first Baron Howth, and of Elizabeth Bermingham of Athenry. He served as sheriff of the county of Dublin in 1456, and, on his father's death about 1463, he succeeded to the title, reputedly at the age of twenty-eight. Apart from the manor of Howth, his scattered possessions, mainly in the county of Dublin, were of small value, and this may partly explain why Howth served in the minor exchequer office of chancellor of the green wax and clerk of common pleas, to which he was first appointed in February 1468. In 1474 and again in 1479 he was one of thirteen brothers of St George appointed to supervise the defence of the English pale, but from 1476 he also spent much time in England. Edward IV eventually rewarded him by appointment as lord chancellor in January 1483, but Gerald Fitzgerald, eighth earl of Kildare, who had meanwhile granted the office to his brother, refused to admit Howth, despite successive renewals of his patent in May and July and letters from Richard III in December.

St Lawrence married first, before 1459, Alice, daughter and heir of Nicholas White of Killester, Dublin, through whom he acquired the manor of Killester; and second, in June or July 1478 in England, Joan, second daughter of Edmund *Beaufort, first duke of Somerset, with whom he had four sons—Nicholas *St Lawrence, third Baron Howth, Thomas, Walter, and Christopher—and two daughters, Genet and Anne. He died in London and was buried there in the church of the Blackfriars in 1486; his widow afterwards married Sir Richard Fry.

STEVEN G. ELLIS

Sources H. F. Berry and J. F. Morrissey, eds., *Statute rolls of the parliament of Ireland*, 4 vols. (1907–39) · S. G. Ellis, *Reform and revival: English government in Ireland, 1470–1534*, Royal Historical Society Studies in History, 47 (1986) · *CPR, 1476–85* · GEC, *Peerage*, new edn, vol. 6 · F. E. Ball, *The judges in Ireland, 1221–1921*, 2 vols. (1926) · H. G. Richardson and G. O. Sayles, *The Irish parliament in the middle ages* (1952) · M. C. Griffith, ed., *Calendar of inquisitions formerly in the office of the chief remembrancer of the exchequer*, IMC (1991)

St Leger, Sir Anthony (1496?–1559), lord deputy of Ireland, was born at Ulcombe, Kent, the eldest of six sons of Ralph St Leger (*b.* in or before 1471, *d.* 1519), landowner, of Ulcombe, and his wife, Elizabeth or Isabel (*d.* 1517×19), daughter of Sir Richard Haut or Hart of Selvingbourne, Kent, and his first wife, Eleanor. He had at least three sisters. Robert St Leger (*fl.* 1517–1559) was one of his younger brothers. The St Legers were well-established and wealthy gentry from Kent, having lived at Ulcombe since the early twelfth century.

Early years and education St Leger was well educated, with royal service in mind, having been taught at home until he was twelve, when he 'was sent for his Grammar-learning with his tutor into France, for his carriage into Italy, for his philosophy to Cambridg, for his law to Grays-Inne; and for that which compleated all, the government of himself, to court'. He impressed Henry VIII with his urbane and easy manner and Cardinal Thomas Wolsey by his 'solidity and wisdome', and was granted Okington, Kent, in 1512 (Lloyd, 1.99). He attended the marriage of the king's sister Mary Tudor to Louis XII on 9 October 1514 as a servant of Thomas Wriothesley, garter king of arms, and the following year was in service to one of the leading noblemen in Kent, George Neville, fifth Baron Bergavenny. Despite this, he was not preferred at court, nor was local consequence forthcoming, because of his youth, when he succeeded his father on 26 October 1519. As Ralph St Leger's sole executor, he was responsible for providing for his siblings and for finding husbands for his younger sisters. St Leger married before 1525; his wife was Anne or Agnes (*d.* 1559), daughter of Hugh Warham of Croydon, Surrey, and niece and heir of William *Warham (1450?–1532), archbishop of Canterbury. The couple had five sons, including William (*b.* before 1525, *d.* in or after 1559), Sir Warham *St Leger (1525?–1597), Nicholas (*d.* c.1589), and Sir Anthony St Leger (*d.* 1613), and two daughters.

St Leger had to wait until about 1526 before being named JP for Kent. William Warham appointed him keeper of Langham Park, Kent, before 1528 and he participated more fully in court politics from the late 1520s, possibly playing some role in Wolsey's downfall, although David Lloyd is the only source and is generally unreliable. He entered the service of Thomas Cromwell, king's secretary and vicegerent in spirituals, and was involved in the dissolution of the monasteries, receiving the manor of Kingsnorth and the priory of East Bilsington, as well as other property in Kent on 8 July 1540 in reward (in February 1550 these were valued with other property as worth £110 8s. 8d.). He was a commissioner, with Sir William Fitzwilliam and George Paulet, to survey Calais in August 1535 and was sufficiently prominent to be on the grand jury in Kent that found against Anne Boleyn in 1536. St Leger was summoned on 7 October 1536 with his clientele (numbered at fifty men) to defend the king during the Lincolnshire rebellion and the Pilgrimage of Grace.

On 31 July 1537 St Leger was appointed to two commissions. The first, which included Paulet, Thomas Moyle, and William Berners, was:

> for an order and establisshment to be taken and made towching the hole state … our lande of Irelande and of all and every our affayres within the same bothe for the reduccion of the sayd lande to a due civilitie and obedience and thadvanncement of the publique weale of the same. (PRO, SP 60/4/33, fol. 99r–v)

This remit dominated St Leger's thinking for the rest of his career. The second commission included lord deputy Leonard Grey, Viscount Graney, Paulet, Moyle, Berners, the under-treasurer, William Brabazon, the chief justice Gerald Aylmer, and the master of the rolls, John Alen. Much of the land in the pale bordering the midlands was waste and Henry wanted to encourage settlement there by loyal Old English and New English planters. The need for order in the region was particularly acute in the aftermath of the rebellion of Thomas Fitzgerald, tenth earl of Kildare, and the commissioners were instructed to take the submissions of various rebels. They were also to reorganize finance and reduce the garrison to balance the books. The lord deputy entertained the English commissioners and treated them well, and St Leger was in a good position to observe his methods, especially his attempt to build a party among the Old English. Central to the reordering of the pale was the provision that any new tenants must speak English and adopt English customs. The commissioners worked rapidly, surveying the situation in counties Tipperary, Waterford, Wexford, Dublin, Meath, and Louth, and St Leger was particularly commended for his role, Thomas Agard commenting that 'Master Sentleger whom by reasson of his dyscreschion and indyffrensye towardes everye man is hylye comendyd here / and ryght well he is worthie' (PRO, SP 60/5/56, fol. 143r). St Leger returned to England with greater standing and the king showed his continued favour by making him a gentleman of the privy chamber about June 1538. He was knighted by 4 February 1539 and on 30 October was sent as special ambassador on £2 per day to Mary of Hungary, regent of the Low Countries, to obtain a safe conduct for Anne of Cleves to pass through Habsburg territory. St Leger then escorted Anne on her way to England. He was a commissioner to defend the Kent coast in 1539 and was sheriff of the county from 1539 to 1540—tense years owing to fear of invasion. He played a substantial role in local affairs and sat on other commissions during these years. Having attached himself to Thomas Howard, third duke of Norfolk, from June 1540 he actively supported Grey's recall in the hope of supplanting him and making his mark on Irish politics.

First period as lord deputy Although St Leger was appointed lord deputy of Ireland six times, reflecting the turbulent nature of mid-Tudor rule there, his career as chief governor can be broken into three periods: 1540–48, 1550–51, and 1553–6. He was first named lord deputy on 7 July 1540 with an annual salary of £666 13s. 4d. and arrived in Dublin on 5 August. The Kildare rebellion meant that the English government was 'forced to make policy' in Ireland because of the power vacuum left by the destruction of the Geraldines (Brady, *Chief Governors*, 55). The king's chief governor would no longer be a member of Old English society, royal authority was to be enforced by conciliation or coercion, and English land tenure and common law was to be more widely introduced, paving the way for the reduction of the whole island. St Leger understood that Ireland 'is moche easlyer wone then [than] kept' and focused on re-establishing royal authority in the pale and on securing the compliance of the Old English élite through persuasion and reward, before attempting to extend royal authority into Leinster and Munster (PRO, SP 60/6/1, fol. 1v). Prior to St Leger's arrival in Ireland, Cromwell's client, Brabazon, had advocated a more radical policy. However, in the 1540s, through his agent at Henry's court, Sir Thomas Cusack, master of the rolls from 1542 to 1550, St Leger was able to persuade the king to adopt a more gradual absorption of Ireland, hoping to make the country more tractable and financially self-sufficient. Like Grey, St Leger attempted to build up support among the local élite in order to give himself sufficient influence to govern on the king's behalf. He succeeded briefly in establishing a new party that was not based on coercion or faction but rather on mutual social and political interest, but sectional conflicts blighted long-term success.

Government income was small (only about Ir£4500 in 1540) and debts rose, despite subventions from England. Although revenue was increased to Ir£7450 in 1542–3, St Leger did not have a private patrimony in Ireland to rely on (something he sought to rectify) and could not attempt anything too ambitious. This suited his conciliatory methods. Unlike Grey, he was not a soldier but he embarked on a hosting against the Geraldine league, beginning with the Kavanaghs of Leinster from 16 to 26 August 1540 (forcing Cahir MacArt MacMurrough into submission), then the O'Mores of Leix. The most important submission St Leger received was that of James fitz John Fitzgerald, thirteenth earl of Desmond, at Cahir in co. Tipperary on 16 January 1541. Cusack later commented that 'the winning of the earl of Desmond was the winning of the rest of Munster with small charges' (Brewer and Bullen, 1515–74, 245). The lord deputy then set about building his party by offering the native Irish élite the opportunity to implement new terms of land tenure based on English copyholds and leaseholds and inheritance by tail male, rather than the existing Gaelic system of partable inheritance. Those who submitted were usually bound by indenture to recognize the king as liege lord, to attend parliament, and to resist papal authority. They were then granted a charter for their lands after careful negotiations that attempted to settle local disputes through arbitration with their kin, vassals, and neighbours, although exact details of tenure were left vague. It was hoped that this would pave the way for the wider adoption of common law in Leinster and

Munster and the eventual supplanting of Brehon law, the legal system used in Gaelic Ireland. The new policy of surrender and regrant was radical because it was meant to extend the system of government prevailing in the Irish lordship since the late fifteenth century into Gaelic Ireland. This was done in the hope that a more English socioeconomic structure would evolve there. Barnaby Mac Giolla Phadraig was among the first to surrender his traditional title to his land in return for elevation to the peerage, as first Baron Upper Ossory, and took the Anglicized name Fitzpatrick (11 June 1541). Conn Bacach O'Neill was forced to submit at Dundalk in co. Louth on 28 December, after a hard-fought campaign in Ulster during the autumn and early winter. He was sent to England and created first earl of Tyrone there on 1 October 1542.

The first of eight sessions of St Leger's parliament sat at Dublin from 13 June to 20 or 23 July 1541. It met there again on 7 November and 22 December, and enjoyed general support, with native Irish attending for the first time, and twenty-eight bills were passed, including an act for the suppression of Kilmainham and other religious houses (33 Hen. VIII sess. 2 c. 5). Like Grey, St Leger bypassed Poynings' law to allow parliament to initiate bills in Ireland. His most radical act was to persuade Henry to accept the kingship of Ireland by parliamentary statute (18 June 1541) on the grounds that it would make the Irish more obedient, clarify that he had always been sovereign in Ireland, and make surrender and regrant viable by recognizing all the Irish as royal subjects. Henry had misgivings, complaining that his lord deputy made too many concessions to the Irish, and the reform process was halted when parliament was dissolved on 19 November 1543, but not before he had accepted kingship in April 1542, albeit one suited to local conditions. This allowed St Leger to make individual agreements with Irish lords on the king's behalf rather than his own, making it harder for his critics to challenge him. In effect, his party was the king's party. He created stronger ties with the Old English and, because surrender and regrant involved many leading Irish landowners relinquishing their old titles and old system of land tenure in order to receive new English ones, a revolution occurred within the Irish polity and society. It was hoped that surrender and regrant would lead to the adoption in Gaelic Ireland of primogeniture over tanistry, or elective succession, and foster greater stability there. For example, Murrough O'Brien attended the new session of parliament at Limerick from 15 February to 7 or 10 March 1542 and renounced any claim to land east of the River Shannon. He became first earl of Thomond on 1 July 1543. This political and social change was tied to the religious reforms implemented since 1536 and the dissolution of the Irish monasteries provided the necessary rewards. By 1541 ex-monastic land worth about Ir£4070 per annum had been granted out at fairly low rents to leading figures on generous twenty-one year leases, reinforcing the financial and political dominance of established families and New English administrators. In turn, these men recognized the king's authority and the royal supremacy over the Church of Ireland. The three bishops provided to their sees by the papacy even surrendered their papal bulls, but the changes were not as deep as they first seemed. Visitations and surveys of Limerick, Cork, Youghal, and Kinsale and of counties Limerick, Cork, and Kerry between January 1541 and autumn 1542 were often only cursory and little was enforced. However, Henry was forced to commit himself to greater reform in Ireland than he had envisaged, beyond a short-term military solution; St Leger's policies worked well enough and the garrison level was reduced to 500 men in 1542, making Irish government cheap enough to keep the king happy.

St Leger was willing to use the new élite in government, especially through the Irish privy council (which predated the English privy council). He wanted Desmond and other leading Irish nobles to have a key role in royal administration but the king generally ignored this advice. St Leger's reason for this was, as he explained to the principal secretary, Sir William Paget, on 3 August 1545, 'the mocion I made for my retorne home whereby the kinges majestie may save x^{ml} [10,000] markes by yere and have the lande kept in the staye'. 'It is I suppose the overture pleased not orels I shulde have had some answer thereof / which maketh me half afearde to move it eftsones' (PRO, SP 60/12/16, fol. 38r). St Leger's other motivation for promoting Desmond was as a counterweight to the power of James Butler, ninth earl of Ormond and the leading magnate after the Kildare rebellion. Walter Cowley, Ormond's client and master of the rolls in Dublin, attacked the lord deputy as early as 26 August 1541, accusing him of aiming to revive the Geraldines, in order to 'say and doo whatever he wold … without feare of any answer', and of corruption (PRO, SP 60/10/28, fol. 106r). Cowley was a lone voice and was dismissed from office by May 1542. Other measures successfully advanced by St Leger included agreement by the king for creation of a council to administer Munster and Connaught under a lord president and admission of Irishmen to the inns of court, while he reconciled Tyrone and Manus O'Donnell before the Irish privy council on 14 July 1543, bringing a temporary respite to clan warfare in Ulster, and raised a contingent of 1000 kerne to serve during the Boulogne campaign from 19 July to 14 September 1544. St Leger promoted this last initiative himself (repeated again in 1545) to prove the success of his policies. Critics grumbled that the royal estate in Ireland would not realize the kind of income promised and expenditure outstripped Irish revenue. For example, in 1542 governing Ireland cost nearly £9700 while Irish revenue amounted to only £4967, but the alternative programmes advanced by St Leger's opponents looked less inviting and more expensive to Henry. Surrender and regrant was problematic, with difficulties over agreeing terms with chiefs in south Leinster, but St Leger's deputyship from 1540 to 1544 was one of the most vigorous and innovative in Irish history.

Problems About 10 February 1544, St Leger left for England, where he was elected a knight of the Garter on 25 April and installed on 18 May. He was reappointed lord deputy on 3 July with an addition to his salary of £200 and returned to Ireland on 11 August. His second term of office was marred by a quarrel with Ormond over the 2000 kerne the king ordered the Irish privy council to levy in September 1545. These were intended to assist Matthew Stewart, fourth earl of Lennox, against the Scottish regent, James Hamilton, second earl of Arran. Ormond believed he had been appointed on 5 September to lead this force as a ploy to remove him from Ireland and even claimed in mid-November that St Leger intended to assassinate him. St Leger and he were summoned to court in April 1546, where an investigation exonerated the lord deputy. St Leger was restored to office on 7 November and was back in Ireland the following month.

This conflict reflected tensions between men like Ormond and the New English over how Ireland should be governed. The former wanted their dominant position protected while the latter, a growing and vocal presence since the 1530s, were eager to reduce the whole island and to acquire wealth and land there. Such mutual hostility made the office of chief governor increasingly thankless. The problem was close to home for the lord deputy, who assisted Robert St Leger in encroaching on Butler interests, especially in co. Kilkenny. Between them Sir Anthony and Robert St Leger controlled a large proportion of the Irish military establishment, four officers and 200 cavalry costing Ir£113 8s. per month in 1542–3. Robert St Leger was appointed constable of Dungarvan, co. Waterford, from about August 1543, granted the manor of Kill, co. Kildare, on 5 January 1545, paying only a small rent, and was given custody of the castle and honour of Dungarvan on 7 April 1547. However, it is not always clear whether or not he was acting independently of his brother. He antagonized Joan Butler, dowager countess of Ormond, over land during 1547, forcing her to complain on 6 March that the 'grete part wrongfully gothe about to defeat my poore childrens title therunto' (PRO, SP 61/1/1, fol. 1r). This dispute went back to February 1546, when the earl and the St Legers were most at odds. Sir Anthony St Leger was not immune to this acquisitiveness himself and purchased under-valued estates at St Mary's in Trim, co. Meath, Grane in co. Kilkenny, and elsewhere.

During St Leger's absence in 1546 Cusack kept order in Ireland, reporting that 'those which woulde not be brought undre subjugacion with x thousannde men cometh to Dublin with a lettre' (PRO, SP 60/12/41, fol. 95r). However, in February Alen, the lord chancellor and a former ally of St Leger, launched his own attack, claiming that surrender and regrant was failing because it had been insufficiently advanced, the lord deputy's party excluded others from office, and Irish revenue was depressed through excessive use of land and office for patronage.

St Leger returned to Dublin on 16 December 1546, having been reconciled with Ormond and having defended himself successfully in August against Alen's charges by pointing out that he had brought relative peace to Ireland, no one else could offer a better alternative, and nobody was free from partisan interests. 'In such a dangerous area neither side was prepared to call the other's bluff' (Brady, *Chief Governors*, 43). Although few Irish state papers for 1547 are extant and it is difficult to trace his whereabouts,

it is unlikely that St Leger was present at Edward VI's coronation on 20 February with the other gentlemen of the privy chamber, although listed. He rarely attended court when not serving in Ireland, usually preferring to reside at Ulcombe between 1546 and 1548 and 1551 and 1553. He was not added to the commission of the peace in May 1547, having been reappointed lord deputy on 7 April (although initially named justiciar in March). However, he continued as a gentleman of the privy chamber under Edward Seymour, duke of Somerset, and lord protector. There was initial hesitation about reappointing him lord deputy, partly because of the fall of his patron, Norfolk. He did, however, get to exact revenge on his political opponents. Alen was removed from office in August 1546 and sent to the Fleet prison, while Cowley and William Cantwell were also deprived. These men were replaced by St Leger's supporters, principally Cusack, who became keeper of the great seal on 1 May 1546, and John Parker, but Piers Walshe, Oliver Nugent, and Owen White were also favoured. St Leger also advanced his own military clients, John Wakely and Francis Herbert. These changes did not alter policy but were part of the process whereby the lord deputy rebuilt his own party. However, constant alterations in personnel weakened the credibility of the administration and diminished its ability to promote reform, especially because such practice encouraged in-fighting.

St Leger found Ireland again in a state of rebellion. Before going to England in 1546 he had appointed Brabazon, the under-treasurer, to act as his deputy. In his absence open conflict broke out in the midlands with the O'Connor and O'More septs. This, the most serious midland revolt since the 1530s, was probably caused by Ormond's unexpected death in England on 28 October 1546, which created 'a sudden power vacuum' that Brian and Cahir O'Connor tried to take advantage of (Brady, *Chief Governors*, 57). The future of St Leger's policy of surrender and regrant was in doubt and it was important to deal effectively and cheaply with the native Irish through accommodation and conciliation, promising them the king's pardon, rather than through expensive military exercises. In May 1547 the privy council backed St Leger. Men were mustered and military equipment, including guns and munitions, was sent over in June with the new captain-general, Sir Edward Bellingham. The leader of the unrest, Brian O'Connor, co-ordinated his activities with other rebels, including the O'Byrnes and MacGeoghegans, who seized the opportunity to threaten the pale and burnt several towns. The revolt was serious enough to threaten St Leger's programme because the privy council became critical of his minimal response. As a result he took decisive action, succeeding in turning the MacGeoghegans against O'Connor, while the O'Tooles supported the English from the outset. During the summer Brabazon and he campaigned successfully against the O'Connors and O'Mores and by October seemed to have the situation under control. In this operation Desmond assisted St Leger. The earl was the lord deputy's most important supporter among the Old English, having been promoted lord treasurer by him on 29 March, and St Leger used him as his agent in the south-west, which he hoped to reform through an extension of surrender and regrant.

Despite placing the most experienced soldiers on the midland border and the privy council's order that the military retinues of Irish privy councillors and royal servants be made up of professional officers and men, not political allies, unrest rumbled on. On 2 November St Leger was ordered by the privy council to place himself and his retinue in close proximity to the border with Leix and Offaly in order to try to maintain personal control, as well as to set the Irish against one another. His problem was that the privy council was taking advice from those at court who 'have had experience in that Realme', but who did not have detailed knowledge of the situation on the ground, and from men in Ireland such as Alen (PRO, SP 61/1/8, fol. 20r). In his military client Bellingham, Somerset found an alternative to St Leger. Bellingham was in Ireland during the campaigning season but was recalled on 24 October to explain the situation there to the privy council. Through his influence an auditor was appointed in November to inquire into Irish finances and about December Brabazon attacked St Leger's policies, leading to the decision to recall the lord deputy. It is unknown why Brabazon turned on his former patron. Perhaps the negative nature of St Leger's fourth term as lord deputy was a factor. The deputyship turned out to be a holding operation. St Leger's policy of dealing with the midland septs by military means was paid for through substantial subventions from England, totalling £12,877 between 1547 and 1548. He attempted to secure the border by beginning work to repair the forts captured and garrisoned by Brabazon in summer 1546 at Dangan in Offaly and Ballyadams in Leix, renaming them Fort Governor and Fort Protector to please Somerset's ego. These were constructed using the system of cess, which St Leger adopted more fully than his predecessors had and which set a pattern for his successors. The forts did something to localize the midland rebellion but Brian and Cahir O'Connor and Patrick O'More continued to raid the pale during late winter and early spring 1548. However, St Leger's campaign proved successful and Brian O'Connor submitted in November. Bellingham finally replaced St Leger as lord deputy and Alen was reappointed lord chancellor on 22 April 1548. The new lord deputy took up office on 21 May.

Second period as lord deputy St Leger returned to England with Brian O'Connor and O'More, who were imprisoned in the Tower of London, then the Marshalsea prison. He mainly busied himself with county affairs. In July 1548 he was one of the commissioners to inquire into enclosures in Kent. They produced a memorandum for Somerset concerning popular protests against enclosures, reporting that the commons of Kent were dispersed with difficulty after the commissioners agreed to pass their grievances on to the privy council. St Leger continued to be employed to perform sensitive roles, including appointment on 20 April 1550 to meet the French hostages for the treaty of Boulogne, conducting them through Kent to London. Long-standing royal service had paid off. His English

estates were worth £375 per annum in 1545/6, a not insubstantial amount for a gentleman of his status, but had jumped in value to £600 per annum by 1549, giving credence to growing rumours that he lined his pockets while in Ireland. Between 1549 and 1552 he was favoured by a light tax assessment based on the value of his goods and made three payments averaging only £13 6s. 8d. St Leger conducted a series of land transactions during this period, conveying the Brookes and other property in Higham, Kent, to the king in 1550. On 4 August 1550 he was reappointed jointly with Warham St Leger constable of Leeds Castle and keeper of Langley Park in Kent (having been first appointed on 5 July 1540). Warham St Leger was recognized as his heir and William St Leger disinherited for his dissolute lifestyle. Nine days later Leeds Castle was granted outright in fee farm with other property valued at £58 7s. 7d.

Like his predecessor, Bellingham tried to build a party in Ireland and promoted surrender and regrant but his methods were often aggressive and expensive and did not bring the promised stability. By late February 1549 Wakely was telling whoever would listen 'that summe shulde saye we truste to have a merryi Ireland agayne', because St Leger was to be reappointed and Robert St Leger made admiral of Ireland (PRO, SP 61/2/21, fol. 43r). At first nothing came of it. However, Sir Anthony St Leger appears to have supported John Dudley, earl of Warwick, during the October coup against Somerset. On 4 August 1550 he was reappointed lord deputy, with a private military retinue of twenty-four men and an annual salary of £1000, and Cusack was named lord chancellor in the hope that peace could be brought to Ireland. St Leger arrived in Dublin on 10 September. There was no change of policy, however, although he was ordered to survey Leix-Offaly in preparation for its plantation with English settlers. This plantation would underpin surrender and regrant as well as acting, with the fortifications there, as a staging post for the steady reduction of the island. St Leger was given more soldiers and military supplies, while the policy of widespread fortification continued and loyal Old English and native Irish such as Desmond, Thomond, and Manus and Calough O'Donnell were to be persuaded through letters and gifts, 'wherby they shal the more diligentlie be inclynned', 'to sarve the king & not to embrace forren arguements' (PRO, SP 61/2/55, fol. 131r). By December a consortium of Irish privy councillors and New English had undertaken to plant Leix. It was the beginning of a new pattern in Ireland.

Despite initial support from London, good relations with William Cecil, and a growing political coherence among New English planters, St Leger's fifth deputyship was dogged by rumours concerning his recall and by continued efforts at court and in Ireland to oust him (White, 205). His difficulties were compounded by the antagonism felt by Andrew Brereton and Sir Nicholas Bagenal, marshal of the army, towards Tyrone, whom they accused, at Christmas 1550, of being a traitor. This directly challenged St Leger's conciliatory policy, and he told Cecil on 19 January 1551 that 'suche handeling of wylde men hathe don muche harme to Yreland'. The Leix-Offaly plantation was undermined by St Leger's opponents, led by Alen (who was bitter at his removal from the lord chancellorship), while his chaplain, James Bicton, and he were accused of being 'papist' (PRO, SP 61/3/3, fol. 9r–v). Cusack remained loyal and affected reconciliation between Desmond and Thomond and attempted to resolve the feud between Richard Burke, second earl of Clanricarde, and the Burkes of Clanricarde. Understanding that Brereton was working for his removal, St Leger wrote to the privy council and Cecil on 23 March to explain his actions and the Irish privy council supported him in a more detailed letter on 20 May. He had financial irregularities to hide, though, and appointed Andrew Wise joint under-treasurer with Brabazon on 20 January 1551 in order to cover his tracks. In late 1554 Sir William Fitzwilliam of Gaynes Park, Essex, first accused St Leger and Wise of defrauding the Irish accounts in order to purchase lands. Corruption and faction reached new levels in 1550–51. By late March 1551 the lord deputy engineered Brereton's removal from the Irish privy council for killing two of Tyrone's kinsmen. Brereton's dismissal backfired because he was a servant of one of Warwick's leading supporters, Sir William Herbert, and agitated for his restoration. This contributed to St Leger's growing isolation.

To make matters worse, St Leger was given the thankless task of introducing to Ireland the new English liturgy based on the Book of Common Prayer (1549) which was to be translated into Latin for general dissemination in counties Galway and Limerick. A printing press was established in Dublin to print English copies of the prayer book, of which there was a shortage, for the pale. On 1 March 1551 St Leger informed a convocation of the Irish clergy at Dublin of the impending religious changes, which they would be expected to accept under the royal supremacy. However, St Leger tried to be accommodating towards men such as George Dowdall, archbishop of Armagh, which offended protestants such as George Browne, archbishop of Dublin, who accused him of being Catholic. At the same time Henri II intrigued in Irish affairs, attempting to entice Tyrone into rebellion. From January the government response was to plan a large expeditionary force to the south coast of Ireland led by George Brooke, ninth Baron Cobham.

St Leger worked hard to instil order and security throughout Ireland, despite dearth, debasement, and inflation. He was supported in this by Thomond, Desmond, Tyrone, and Manus O'Donnell—testament to the continued efficacy of his conciliatory methods. By 24 February the privy council had abandoned Cobham's expedition, sending Sir James Croft to oversee the southern fortifications instead. St Leger achieved less than was hoped for because of growing and vocal opposition, economic and social disorder, and foreign interference in Ireland. He was replaced by Croft, a client of Warwick, on 29 April and recalled on 23 May. His lord deputyship had been neither less expensive nor more effective than Bellingham's had. The subventions during 1550–51 ran to £18,080. Also, he was suspect for religion in the new atmosphere at

court. His alleged Catholicism was investigated and he was banned from the privy chamber from 26 December 1551, being reinstated on 22 April 1552, when the charges could not be substantiated. St Leger was a commissioner to survey Calais and the marches from 12 June 1552 and to inquire into heresy. Despite having the favour of Warwick (now duke of Northumberland), he was in financial difficulties and sold Okington to Cobham in 1553. Although he signed the letters patent for the limitation of the crown on 21 June 1553, St Leger supported Princess Mary during the succession crisis and was appointed a privy councillor on 7 August. He was listed among gentlemen of the privy chamber to receive black mourning robes for Edward's funeral, which he attended on 8 August. He was then sent to France as special ambassador with Dr Nicholas Wotton and Sir Thomas Chaloner with the difficult task of justifying Mary I's accession to Henri, who had given tacit support to Lady Jane Grey. They received an audience with the French king on 15 August. St Leger ceased to be a gentleman of the privy chamber after 1553, as a consequence of the accession of a woman, who had no need for male attendants performing intimate body service. However, he continued to benefit from royal favour, including being reappointed JP for Kent on 18 February 1554.

Third period as lord deputy and final years St Leger was named lord deputy for the last time on 1 September 1553 and served in Ireland between 19 November 1553 and 26 May 1556. His instructions were to restore Catholicism, reduce the military establishment to 500 men, install a more formal presidential council in Munster, lease Leix-Offaly in small freehold plots for plantation, and end coign and livery. However, this term was hamstrung by the ever more vocal accusations against him of bribery and corruption, which had first emerged as early as 1538. The murder of Donough O'Brien, second earl of Thomond, by his brother Donald O'Brien, on 1 April 1553, created serious problems during the 1550s. The Butlers supported the earl's heir, Connor O'Brien, and disorder threatened to break out in Thomond as a result. The restoration of Gerald Fitzgerald as eleventh earl of Kildare on 13 May 1554 and the return of Thomas Butler, tenth earl of Ormond, to Ireland in the autumn caused the lord deputy even more difficulties because they were rivals and quickly set about re-establishing their local authority. Ormond was aggrieved at his failure to secure a position on the Irish privy council and Kildare effectively dominated the midlands, encouraged the revived power of the O'Connors and O'Mores, and supported Tyrone's tanist Shane O'Neill in Ulster. This meant that the garrison was not reduced below 1040 men, although military expenditure was cut by more than half and subventions fell to £12,000 in 1556–7 because St Leger held back from intervening too directly.

The Reformation had made little impact outside the pale, and Dowdall's restoration on 23 October 1553 and the deprivation of several Edwardian bishops caused St Leger little difficulty. On 7 June 1555 Paul IV issued a papal bull making Ireland into a kingdom and Cardinal Reginald Pole was named papal legate the following month. Yet Mary provided insufficient funds for St Leger to prosecute his reform programme and Irish revenue was low, especially as a result of land sales at reduced prices and further debasement in March 1555. Royal service was a severe drain on St Leger's personal finances and he left debts in Ireland amounting to almost Ir£5000, forcing him to sell land piecemeal. His health was poor and he suffered from sciatica. Fitzwilliam's investigations left him isolated, leading to dismissal and imprisonment of his leading supporters, including Wise, Bagenal, and Cusack (who was replaced on 7 August 1555 by Fitzwilliam himself). Fitzwilliam also attacked St Leger's policies, painting a picture of Ireland in crisis that was at odds with the lord deputy's laconic reports. When Thomas Radcliffe, Baron Fitzwalter, seeing 'Ireland's problems as a golden opportunity for glory and gain', agitated for appointment as St Leger's successor, the lord deputy probably welcomed it (Ellis, 271). St Leger was replaced on 21 April 1556.

St Leger was subject to two probing inquiries into his conduct as lord deputy, one under Mary and the other under Elizabeth I, but these were inconclusive and reflected the muddled nature of royal policy towards Ireland and the ambiguous role of the New English in the 1550s. He was returned as knight of the shire for Kent in 1559 but made little impression in the House of Commons because of rapidly deteriorating health. St Leger wrote his last will, with a Catholic opening formula, on 27 October 1558. It is short and vague, leaving detailed provisions to be carried out by his sole executor, Warham St Leger. He died at Ulcombe on 16 March 1559 and was buried in the parish church there after a magnificent funeral on 5 April. Agnes St Leger died on 24 March and was buried at Ulcombe the day before her husband. Warham St Leger inherited the bulk of his father's property but in an act of reconciliation he granted Bilsington and Belgar in Kent to his older brother on 3 May.

Sir Anthony St Leger's legacy as lord deputy has divided historians, as it did his contemporaries. While men such as Cusack and Cowley were highly critical of his partiality and corruption, John Hooker and even St Edmund Campion felt that he was a victim of local faction who attempted fundamental and necessary reform of the Irish polity to bring civility to the island. The late-Victorian historian Richard Bagwell admired his conciliatory policies and pragmatism, believing that St Leger understood Irish politics and society better than any other Tudor governor and tried to achieve realistic objectives. Early twentieth-century Irish historians were deeply critical of surrender and regrant, seeing it as a sell-out to the English. In recent years, however, Brendan Bradshaw and Steven Ellis argued that the early 1540s were an unprecedented but short-lived period of accord in Anglo-Irish relations that was terminated by the complexities of local politics, unexpected circumstances, and reformation conflict. Perhaps the programme was unfeasible but the alternatives of anarchy or conquest looked even less palatable. Ciaran

Brady has questioned St Leger's programmatic commitment to reform, seeing the new pattern in Ireland of conquest as inevitable in the wake of the Kildare rebellion. As well as establishing surrender and regrant, St Leger was clearly the driving force behind the foundation of the kingdom of Ireland, with its political and social consequences, and, having adapted Grey's methods, he set the pattern that later governors followed.   ALAN BRYSON

Sources AFM · APC, 1542–58 · R. Bagwell, *Ireland under the Tudors*, 3 vols. (1885–90) · B. Bradshaw, 'The beginnings of modern Ireland', *The Irish parliamentary tradition*, ed. B. Farrell (Dublin, 1973), 68–87 · B. Bradshaw, 'Sword, word and strategy in the Reformation in Ireland', *HJ*, 21 (1978), 475–502 · B. Bradshaw, *The Irish constitutional revolution of the sixteenth century* (1979) · C. Brady, 'Court, castle and country: the framework of government in Tudor Ireland', *Natives and newcomers: essays on the making of Irish colonial society, 1534–1641*, ed. C. Brady and R. Gillespie (1986), 22–49, 217–19 · C. Brady, 'The decline of the Irish kingdom', *Conquest and coalescence: the shaping of the state in early modern Europe*, ed. M. Greengrass (1991), 94–115 · C. Brady, *The chief governors: the rise and fall of reform government in Tudor Ireland, 1536–1588* (1994) · C. Brady, 'England's defence and Ireland's reform: the dilemma of the Irish viceroys, 1541–1641', *The British problem, c. 1534–1707: state formation in the Atlantic archipelago*, ed. B. Bradshaw and J. Morrill (1996), 89–117 · J. S. Brewer and W. Bullen, eds., *Calendar of the Carew manuscripts*, 6 vols., PRO (1867–73) · J. Morrin, ed., *Calendar of the patent and close rolls of chancery in Ireland for the reigns of Henry VIII, Edward VI, Mary, and Elizabeth*, 2 vols. (1861–2) · *CPR, 1547–58* · *CSP Ire., 1509–73* · S. G. Ellis, *Ireland in the age of the Tudors* (1998) · E. Hasted, *The history and topographical survey of the county of Kent*, 2nd edn, 12 vols. (1797–1801); facs. edn (1972) · Hatfield House, Hertfordshire, Cecil MSS, 144, fols. 1r–15v; 150, fols. 117r–118v; 151, fols. 14r–18v; 20r–21v; 231, fol. 33r–v · G. A. Hayes-McCoy, 'The royal supremacy and ecclesiastical revolution, 1534–47', *A new history of Ireland*, ed. T. W. Moody and others, 3: *Early modern Ireland, 1534–1691* (1976), 39–68 · G. A. Hayes-McCoy, 'Conciliation, coercion, and the protestant reformation, 1547–71', *A new history of Ireland*, ed. T. W. Moody and others, 3: *Early modern Ireland, 1534–1691* (1976), 69–93 · HoP, *Commons, 1558–1603*, 3.326–9 · *LP Henry VIII* · J. Lodge, *The peerage of Ireland*, rev. M. Archdall, rev. edn, 7 vols. (1789) · [D. Lloyd], *State-worthies, or, The statesmen and favourites of England from the Reformation to the revolution*, ed. C. Whitworth, 2 vols. (1766) · *DNB* · D. L. Potter, 'French intrigue in Ireland during the reign of Henri II, 1547–1559', *International History Review*, 5 (1983), 159–80 · exchequer, king's remembrancer, various accounts, PRO, E 101/248/22 · will, PRO, PROB 11/19, sig. 22; PROB 11/42B, sig. 25 · state papers, Ireland, Henry VIII, PRO, SP 60 · state papers, Ireland, Edward VI, PRO, SP 61 · state papers, Ireland, Mary I, PRO, SP 62 · *State papers published under … Henry VIII*, 11 vols. (1830–52) · D. G. White, 'The reign of Edward VI in Ireland: some political, social and economic aspects', *Irish Historical Studies*, 14 (1964–5), 197–211

Archives LPL, MSS 602–603, 611 · PRO, SP 60 · PRO, SP 61 · PRO, SP 62

St Leger, Francis Barry Boyle (1799–1829), novelist, was born in Ireland on 16 September 1799, the second eldest son of Richard St Leger (second son of the first Viscount Doneraile) and Anne, daughter of Charles Blakeney of Holywell, co. Roscommon. He was educated at Rugby School and in 1816 obtained a civil appointment with the East India Company. He resigned his post about 1821 and returned to England, where from 1822 onward he edited a fashionable annual called *The Album*. He printed privately in 1821 *Remorse and Other Poems*.

St Leger's best-known work, *Some Account of the Life of the Late Gilbert Earle, Esq.* (1824), was a romantic and moralizing novel in twelve 'fragments'. In 1826 he was editor of the *Brazen Head*, and published (anonymously) another novel, entitled *Mr. Blount's MSS, being Selections from the Papers of a Man of the World*. In 1829 he published *Tales of Passion*.

St Leger died unmarried, after an epileptic seizure, on 20 November 1829. A posthumous work, *Froissart and his Times*, appeared in 1832 (3 vols.).

D. J. O'DONOGHUE, rev. JOHN D. HAIGH

Sources F. B. B. St Leger, 'Preface', *Some account of the life of the late Gilbert Fade, Esq.* (1824) · *Annual Biography and Obituary*, 14 (1830), 450–51 · E. Lodge, *The peerage and baronetage of the British empire*, [new edn] (1896)
Archives NL Scot., letters to Blackwoods

St Leger, Sir Warham (1525?–1597), colonist, was the second of at least five sons and two daughters of Sir Anthony *St Leger (1496?–1559), lord deputy of Ireland, of Ulcombe, Kent, and his wife, Anne or Agnes (d. 1559), daughter and heir of Hugh Warham, of Croydon, Surrey. He was named co-feoffee of two Irish estates held by his uncle Robert St Leger of Carlow on 27 February 1546. He participated in the Scottish campaign in September 1547 and was captured and imprisoned at Edinburgh until January 1550, when he was ransomed for 100 marks.

St Leger became heir on the disinheritance of his brother William St Leger (d. in or after 1559), before August 1550. In recognition of his growing importance Edward VI appointed him, along with his father, constable of Leeds Castle, Kent, and keeper of Langley Park, Cumberland. He married Ursula (d. 1575), fifth daughter of George Neville, fifth Baron Bergavenny, and his third wife, Mary, probably about 1550. They had one son, Anthony (d. in or after 1597), and several daughters, including Anne (1555–1636). Early in 1554 St Leger fought against Sir Thomas Wyatt the younger in Kent. On the death of his parents in March 1559 he tried to restore family harmony by granting the manors of Bilsington and Belgar, Kent, to his eldest brother, who had taken up residence at nearby Hollingborne, on 3 May. These were inherited by his nephew Sir Warham St Leger (d. 1600) [see below]. St Leger was sheriff of Kent from 1560 to 1561.

St Leger took great pride in his ancestry, feeling that he was 'not inferior to eny man in Kent, the nobilitie onlie excepted' (PRO, SP 63/111/87(i)). Yet, he failed to secure substantial patronage, perhaps because of debt. Elizabeth I's government also expected him to act as a guarantor for money owed by his father to the crown since 1556. By the time of his knighthood (between October 1565 and February 1566) he had been forced to part with some of his inheritance. To improve his fortune he entered the Irish service.

When his fellow Kentishman Sir Henry Sidney was appointed lord deputy of Ireland in October 1565 St Leger was nominated to fill the most important new office in the country, as lord president of Munster. Based partly on the Welsh model, it was envisaged that the Munster presidency would impose formal royal authority on the Old English and Gaelic Irish lords, its judicial functions overriding their palatine liberties. Sidney anticipated that, as the son of Sir Anthony St Leger, who had greatly favoured the Fitzgeralds, Sir Warham St Leger was an ideal choice to win acceptance by the chief lord of the south-west, Gerald Fitzgerald, fourteenth earl of Desmond.

However, no sooner had St Leger arrived in the province than his nomination was withdrawn, following objections made in London by Elizabeth's Irish favourite, and Desmond's great rival, Thomas Butler, tenth earl of Ormond. The queen explained to Sidney on 14 May 1566 that St Leger's partiality towards Desmond—something she later described as 'notorious both in England and Ireland'—made him utterly unacceptable (T. Ó. Laidhin, ed., *Sidney State Papers*, Dublin, 1962, 50). How far St Leger may have acted as president before being forced aside has perplexed Irish historians. Yet, the fact is that he was paid for carrying out another government post, usually overlooked, that of 'general of the levies in the field … for the province of Munster' (*Irish Fiants*, Elizabeth I, no. 828), a position he continued to fill after his candidacy for the presidency had been rejected.

St Leger assisted Sidney's first Ulster expedition and led a detachment of southern lords—all members of the Fitzgerald party—on the royal hosting into Breifne, co. Cavan, in the autumn. Weeks later, having been reassigned 'for the gard of the Pale', he distinguished himself by helping to repel an attack on Drogheda by Shane O'Neill (Sidney, 3.41). His service went unrewarded. Late in 1566, in response to the queen's request, he relinquished his post. His role greatly reduced, he left Ireland at some time after 18 June 1567.

St Leger resided at his house in Southwark or at Leeds Castle but was fairly inactive during 1567–8. Following Desmond's imprisonment in the Tower of London, an opportunity arose for St Leger to return to Munster in a private capacity, as a colonial adventurer. Aware that Desmond was hugely in debt to the crown, St Leger and his nephew Sir Richard Grenville offered to improve the earl's income by leasing part of his territories in co. Cork. At some time before the summer of 1568 Desmond granted them Carrigaline Castle and other lands in the barony of Kerricurrihy. No evidence exists to support the view that the Kerricurrihy lease was a sham, and it would hardly have required a down payment if it had been. The lands actually belonged to Desmond's troublesome kinsman James Fitzmaurice Fitzgerald and the lease provided a convenient veneer of legality for what was otherwise a blatant act of theft. St Leger appears to have returned to Ireland by 14 June 1568, with Grenville arriving soon afterwards. Having instigated their first colony, they then sought permission to start a second. An undated document, belonging perhaps to autumn 1568, records that the two adventurers joined with several others, including Sir Humphrey Gilbert, to advocate the confiscation of all land belonging to the Gaelic lords west of Baltimore, co. Cork. Surviving evidence suggests they commenced putting the project into operation almost as soon as they had announced it. By the beginning of November the greatest Gaelic chieftain in the area, Donald MacCarthy More, earl of Clancare, was out in revolt, as was Fitzmaurice. Rather than stand his ground, St Leger returned to England. Despite his role in causing disturbances in Munster, Sidney praised St Leger as 'the greatest stay' in the region (Collins, 1.39).

Sidney's commendation to the privy council had little effect and official interest in St Leger's colonizing ventures quickly cooled in the wake of mounting problems in Munster. Even the appointment of St Leger and Grenville to a commission of martial law in March 1569 failed to quell unrest. In June Fitzmaurice attacked Carrigaline, forcing St Leger's family to seek Ormond's protection at Kilkenny. St Leger was forced to admit the imminent collapse of the Kerricurrihy colony when petitioning the privy council for a loan of £10,000 for three years and permission to raise 1500 men to 'evicte such rebells and traitors' (PRO, SP 63/28/19). Elizabeth refused his request.

His colony destroyed, it was several years before St Leger re-emerged as an important figure in Irish affairs. In November 1569 he was appointed JP for Kent and he mustered twenty-five men from his lands for the shire levy in 1573. As before, however, he was passed over for more senior positions in local government. In March 1571 he saw an opportunity to redevelop his Munster interests by volunteering to act as custodian of Desmond and his brother Sir John Fitzgerald on their release from the Tower. Within weeks he had antagonized both Desmond and the government by keeping three-quarters of the earl's daily allowance. Not allowed to profit from the arrangement, St Leger backed out of it in August 1572. He was included on a commission of oyer and terminer for co. Cork in March 1575 'yf he shalbe there' (APC, 1571–5, 354). He returned to Ireland and secured possession of Carrigaline. Significantly, it is recorded that Desmond menaced Carrigaline because St Leger reneged on the terms of the 1568 lease. Without holding any investigation, the government supported St Leger.

St Leger's efforts to breathe new life into the Kerricurrihy colony were temporarily delayed by the death of his wife in 1575 and his second marriage, by 1577, to Emmeline Goldwell (d. 1628). They had a son, Walter (d. in or after 1597). The colony was resurrected, although it incurred great costs, not least the rebuilding of Carrigaline Castle. St Leger was beset by financial difficulties. In November 1578 the government seized part of his Irish estate—ex-monastic holdings at Adare, co. Limerick, and Nenagh, co. Tipperary—after he defaulted on his crown rent, and it was during this period that he sold the Kent manors of Sturrey, Loyston, and Kingsnorth.

By 1579 St Leger's career was in free fall. In July 1578 Elizabeth angrily summoned him to Havering, Essex, to explain why he met Bertrand de Salignac de la Motte-Fénélon, the French ambassador, privately in London, and she considered ordering an official investigation. The fact that William Cecil, first Baron Burghley, lord treasurer, viewed him as having a dangerous 'appetite [for] glory and vain reputation' also damaged his prospects (PRO, SP 63/86/60). Hence, on the outbreak of the second Desmond rebellion St Leger was grateful for the opportunity to

regain some standing. Undeterred by the queen's choice of Ormond to lead the royal forces in Munster, St Leger immediately offered to serve under him. At first Ormond had cause to report well of St Leger's efforts, even though in January 1580 the latter's chronic insolvency created problems when purchasing victuals for the army from the merchants of the town of Cork. St Leger helped Ormond to guard the towns of Cork and Waterford and supplied him with information about enemy movements. Yet it was only a matter of time before old antagonisms resurfaced. Unable to secure a formal paid position under Ormond, St Leger stopped co-operating with the earl following the arrival of Sidney's friend Arthur Grey, fourteenth Baron Grey of Wilton, as lord deputy, in the autumn. To St Leger's great contentment, unlike Ormond, Grey of Wilton was willing to turn a blind eye to military profiteering. Early in 1581 St Leger combined with Walter Ralegh to plunder the estates of David Barry of Barryscourt, co. Cork, who fled their forces in fear of his life and consequently revolted. However, when Ormond reported the case to the lord deputy he dismissed the charges against St Leger and Ralegh. Thereafter Ormond became the target of a campaign of character assassination masterminded by St Leger. As he subsequently complained, St Leger was 'willinge to move styrres to the disturbance of his government [as general]', criticizing his tactics and suggesting he was soft towards the rebels (PRO, SP 63/106/56). Partly as a result of these allegations, Ormond was sacked as lord-general in June 1581.

St Leger was appointed colonel and commander of royal forces in Munster. However, he left his post and departed for court with his wife and family almost immediately, hoping to secure appointment as lord president of Munster. During his absence, which lasted from August 1581 to January 1582, he was replaced by John Zouche and was not reappointed on his return to Ireland. St Leger was granted the custodiam of the lands of the Catholic rebel William Nugent by Grey of Wilton. In September, St Leger was still holding out for appointment as lord president when Grey of Wilton departed. He stopped petitioning on learning that Ormond was to receive the office.

It was largely due to the patronage of Sir Francis Walsingham, principal secretary, and Robert Dudley, earl of Leicester, that St Leger survived Ormond's homecoming. Ormond made no secret of his hatred for St Leger, whom he derided as someone who 'tiples all day at [his] ale bench', doing nothing except 'write lies and breede needeles doubtes' (BL, Cotton MS Titus F. v, fol. 54r). Walsingham valued St Leger's 'doubtes', which confirmed his worst suspicions about the divided loyalties of the Catholic lords and gentry in Ireland. Thus encouraged, and determined to curb Ormond's growing influence following the earl's triumphant conclusion of the rebellion in November 1583, in February 1584 St Leger submitted secret information against him, alleging all manner of treason and misrule. With a melodramatic twist, he begged discretion of his reader, for 'I knowe if the Earle should knowe of this I shall die by his meanes' (PRO, SP

63/107/107). Ormond easily overcame the charges, yet could get no revenge on their author.

St Leger's greatest concern was to protect his title to Carrigaline as the crown prepared to set the Munster plantation in motion through the confiscation of all rebel land in the province. To prevent Carrigaline being recognized as former Fitzmaurice property, and so forfeit under the terms of the plantation as ex-rebel land without a lawful occupier, he maintained the fiction that he had 'leased' it from Desmond as part of the earl's inheritance. To secure his title the lease of 1568 suddenly became a mortgage acquired from Desmond to offset expenses of £2000 incurred while 'interteining' the earl 'at his owne houses in London and Kent' between 1571 and 1572 (PRO, SP 63/111/87(i)). He produced no documentation to substantiate this claim but his story was accepted by the plantation commissioners without question; Carrigaline became part of the Munster plantation, assigned to him as a seigniory.

St Leger next attempted to take possession of the entire barony of Kerricurrihy. He dismissed the native owners of these lands as the earl's tenants-at-will. The fact that he got away with such outrageous aggrandizement and misrepresentation is highly significant. By drawing attention to the chargeable lands, previously overlooked by the commissioners, he offered the crown a way of greatly increasing the plantation's scope by bringing much more land into play for confiscation and redistribution. However, by 1592 fifteen parcels of land annexed to St Leger's plantation seigniory as chargeable land—the greater part of Kerricurrihy—had had to be returned to their original owners. Far from lording it over a great colonial estate of perhaps 15,000 acres, he ended up with just 6000 acres.

St Leger spent the 1590s in virtual retirement, and died at Cork in 1597. At his death his English estates passed to his son by his first marriage, Anthony St Leger, his Irish lands going to his son by his second marriage, Walter St Leger. Emmeline St Leger died in 1628. A seventeenth-century copy of a 'funerall poem to the memorie of the truely noble Sir Warham St Liger, knight' can be found among the Troyte-Bullock MSS at Wiltshire County Record Office.

St Leger's nephew, also **Sir Warham St Leger** (d. 1600), soldier, was the eldest son of William St Leger, landowner, of Hollingborne, Kent. He first went to Ireland in 1574 as a servant of Walter Devereux, first earl of Essex, and pursued a moderately successful career in the queen's Irish army. As provost marshal of Munster he fought fiercely against the Fitzgerald rebels in the south between 1579 and 1583, and was responsible for executing Desmond's brother James Fitzgerald. Subsequently made governor of Leix (Laois), he earned great praise for his treatment of the rebel O'Mores, who loathed him 'in respect he houldeth a hard hand over them, not suffring any strangers to follow them' (NL Ire., MS 669, p. 134). He was knighted in 1597. St Leger was killed near the town of Cork on 18 February 1600 in a mutually fatal hand-to-hand struggle with Hugh Maguire. He was survived by his wife, Elizabeth Rothe of

Kilkenny (d. 1620), widow of Captain Humphrey Mackworth and of Henry Davells. His son and heir was Sir William *St Leger (d. 1642), the founder of the St Legers of Doneraile, co. Cork.   DAVID EDWARDS

Sources state papers Ireland, Elizabeth I, PRO, SP 63 · *Irish fiants of the Tudor sovereigns*, 4 vols. (Dublin, 1993) · M. MacCarthy-Morrogh, *The Munster plantation: English migration to southern Ireland, 1583–1641* (1986) · A. Sheehan, 'Official reaction to native land claims in the plantation of Munster', *Irish Historical Studies*, 23 (1982–3), 297–318 · P. J. Piveronus, 'Sir Warham St Leger and the first Munster plantation', *Éire-Ireland*, 14 (1979), 16–36 · N. P. Canny, *The Elizabethan conquest of Ireland: a pattern established, 1565–76* (1976) · D. Kennedy, 'The presidency of Munster, c. 1570–1625', MA diss., University College, Cork, 1973 · C. Brady, 'Faction and the origins of the Desmond rebellion of 1579', *Irish Historical Studies*, 22 (1980–81), 289–312 · S. G. Ellis, *Ireland in the age of the Tudors* (1998) · BL, Cotton MS Titus F. v · H. Sydney and others, *Letters and memorials of state*, ed. A. Collins, 2 vols. (1746) · H. Sidney, 'Memoir or narrative addressed to Sir Francis Walsingham, 1583', *Ulster Journal of Archaeology*, 1st ser., 3–5 (1855–8) · DNB

St Leger, Sir Warham (d. 1600). *See under* St Leger, Sir Warham (1525?–1597).

St Leger, Sir William (d. 1642), administrator, was born in Ireland, the eldest son of Sir Warham *St Leger (d. 1600) [*see under* St Leger, Sir Warham (1525?–1597)] and his wife, Elizabeth Rothe (d. 1620) of Kilkenny, widow of Humphrey Mackworth and Henry Davells. The family had a distinguished record of service in Ireland. His grandfather Sir Anthony St Leger was twice lord deputy of Ireland, and his father had been vice-president of Munster. In October 1607 William killed a man and was forced to flee Ireland in the company of Hugh O'Neill, earl of Tyrone, and Rory O'Donnell, earl of Tyrconnell. This was an ignominious turn of events for someone whose father had died fighting Tyrone's forces. St Leger appeared in Brussels in early November before travelling to the Netherlands, where he enlisted in the army and slowly rebuilt his career. Pardoned on 27 May 1610, he remained in the Low Countries and became the serjeant-major of the earl of Salisbury's regiment. In 1616 he married Gertrude de Vries, a Rhinelander, with whom he had a son and a daughter. He later married Gertrude Heywood, with whom he had two sons. His daughter, Elizabeth, married Murrough O'Brien, Lord Inchiquin, and his eldest son, William, died fighting for the royalists at the battle of Newbury. By the late 1610s he had attracted the attention of George Villiers, the future duke of Buckingham and royal favourite, through whose favour he was knighted on 25 April 1618 and received large grants of land in Ireland, principally in Queen's county, in summer 1619. He sold most of his land in Queen's county. Much in demand with the English government owing to his military experience, he now had interests in England, Ireland, and the Netherlands.

In 1623 St Leger commanded a royal ship, the *Bonadventure*, and he spent the first half of 1625 arranging the dispatch of an English army to fight in Germany. That autumn he commanded a regiment on the expedition to Cadiz, the failure of which led to bitter recriminations between the parties involved. Meanwhile, acting as Buckingham's agent in Ireland, he procured plantation lands for the duke in Ossory in November 1624. The duke handed over the administration of these estates to St Leger and demised some of his lands in Queen's county upon him. By the mid-1620s St Leger had lands in King's and Queen's counties, Clare, Westmeath, and co. Tipperary. In 1625 he was granted a company of foot in Ireland; he subsequently exchanged this for a troop of horse in June 1627. On 2 March 1627 St Leger was made lord president of Munster, also being sworn a member of the Irish privy council. However, despite his political pedigree, he had problems in imposing his authority as lord president. His chequered past told against him and the local settlers regarded him as an outsider imposed on the province by court interests, principally Buckingham. In response, he went out of his way to appease local interests, particularly Roger Boyle, earl of Cork, the most powerful landowner in Munster and an enemy of Buckingham's. In December 1627 St Leger was trying to mediate a settlement between Buckingham and Cork. The duke's assassination in autumn 1628 left St Leger politically isolated and largely dependent on Cork. Perhaps his greatest problem during his early years as lord president was the constant presence of pirates off the coast of Munster. St Leger felt he was not given enough resources to defend the coast and, in 1631, was forced humiliatingly to negotiate with a pirate called Nut who preyed off the coast of Munster with three ships.

In February 1630 St Leger purchased the Doneraile estate in north Cork for £1800. This represented an excellent deal, and during the 1630s he greatly increased the value of the estate, enabling him to accumulate more lands. However, the purchase also made St Leger a neighbour of Cork, who came to regard St Leger as a threat to his local hegemony. Late in 1630 St Leger was heavily involved in promoting plans for a plantation of Ormond in co. Tipperary, claiming to have information that would prove the crown's title to the area. Nothing came of this and St Leger appears to have blamed Cork, then lord justice of Ireland, for not giving his scheme enough support.

Given this growing tension with Cork, it is not surprising that St Leger rapidly switched his political allegiances following the arrival in Dublin in 1633 of Sir Thomas Wentworth, lord deputy of Ireland. Wentworth was determined to curb Cork's power, and St Leger, as governor of Munster, was the most obvious instrument for doing so. He played a leading role in Wentworth's efforts to end the tax exemptions enjoyed by corporations in Munster that were controlled by Cork, quartering his troops on the towns until they had paid in full. St Leger sat as MP for co. Cork in the 1634–5 and 1640–41 parliaments, acting as a government spokesman on both occasions. Wentworth thought very highly of St Leger, who was by all accounts an efficient administrator. In 1637–9 the lord deputy strongly supported St Leger in a dispute with Buckingham's widow over lands in Queen's county demised by the duke on St Leger. On 6 December 1639 St Leger became sergeant-major of the Irish army, in which capacity he oversaw the training at Carrickfergus, in summer 1640, of the largely Catholic troops raised by Wentworth to help put down the uprising of the Scottish covenanters.

However, events in England and Ireland swung dramatically against Wentworth and his supporters late in 1641. The lord deputy was overthrown, tried, and executed in London in spring 1641 and his enemies gained control of the Irish government. St Leger remained loyal to the end, testifying in April 1641 on Wentworth's behalf at his trial in London and taking care to look after his widow and children. Indeed, St Leger could count himself lucky to avoid being among those government ministers who were the subject of impeachment proceedings by the Irish parliament. Complaints against St Leger's governance of Munster were aired in London, but in March 1641 he was pardoned for any offences he might have committed while executing martial law. Crucially, Cork had made his peace with the king and did not press for St Leger's removal from office as he might otherwise have done. There is no doubting that St Leger was in a very vulnerable position and was hugely unpopular among the Munster settlers, who accused him of being pro-Catholic. However, the outbreak of the rising of October 1641 soon gave him the chance to prove these judgements wrong.

St Leger was highly critical of what he saw as the lords justices' timorous and panicked response to the initial reports of a rising in Ulster, believing that if the government had acted more resolutely, the rising would never have gained momentum. Determined to preserve Dublin at all costs, the lords justices denuded the rest of the country of forces, leaving St Leger with only three or four companies of foot and a troop of horse to maintain Munster. Moreover, they compounded this error by issuing a proclamation that spoke very generally of a Catholic rebellion, thereby driving more Catholics to take up arms. A further complication was the presence of an army of 1200 Catholics under Colonel Garret Barry at Kinsale. They had been raised as part of Wentworth's army and were awaiting shipment abroad. St Leger spent November organizing the province's defences, attempting to calm the now rather agitated Munster Catholics and sounding out Barry's intentions. In these extreme circumstances, Cork and St Leger set aside their long-running feud to face a common enemy.

By late November the rising was spreading to Munster, and St Leger responded in a ruthless and brutal fashion. On 1 December his troop arrived in Clonmel, co. Tipperary, to avenge robberies that had been committed there upon his brother-in-law William Kingsmill. His men appear to have terrorized Clonmel and its environs for several days, indiscriminately killing many local Catholics, including women. He also met with members of the local Catholic gentry, haranguing them for failing to prevent the growing disorders and declaring that all Catholics were untrustworthy. Generally, historians have criticized St Leger's tactics for driving more Catholics into rebellion. However, by then a general war throughout Ireland between the Catholics and the protestants was inevitable. From a purely military perspective, his actions probably delayed the spread of the rising to Munster by a few weeks. On 4 December he marched suddenly into Waterford and surprised and routed a group of rebels near Passage, killing 140 in battle and executing the fifty prisoners taken. He then returned to Clonmel, but realizing he did not have the numbers to hold an entire province, retreated back into co. Cork in mid-November.

A lull in the fighting followed as both the Catholics and the protestants tried to raise field armies. By mid-January 1642 St Leger had assembled 1500 foot and 400 horse. Meanwhile, a considerably larger rebel army under Richard, Viscount Mountgarret, marched south. In early February St Leger led his forces out to meet him, taking his stand at a pass leading from co. Limerick into co. Cork on the eastern end of the Ballyhowra Mountains. However, despite St Leger's attempts to provoke a battle, Mountgarret turned west and captured Kilmallock in Limerick. The protestant forces then camped at the Redshard Pass to block the rebels' route into Cork. Although Mountgarret had at least a two-to-one numerical superiority, his troops were poorly armed and he had no military experience. For his part, St Leger feared that the Catholics in Cork would rise up, trapping him. Hence, on 8 February, negotiations began between St Leger and Mountgarret, concluding two days later when both sides agreed to withdraw. This was a better deal for St Leger than it appears because the Catholic nobility in Kerry and Cork had been on the point of rebelling and were dismayed by Mountgarret's withdrawal. St Leger retreated to Cork city, before marching to Dungarvan, co. Waterford, which he captured from the rebels on 5 March. Meanwhile, the most powerful Catholic lord in Cork, Donough McCarthy, Viscount Muskerry, joined the rebellion, as did Barry's troops at Kinsale. St Leger hurried back to Cork, where he was besieged from mid-February by about 5000 rebels. The arrival in Cork city of some 1000 reinforcements from England at the start of March made the fall of the city unlikely, but St Leger was hampered by a lack of ammunition and money and by his own illness.

The months of campaigning had taken a toll on St Leger's health, and while he continued to direct the administration and general strategy of his forces, he did not participate in any more campaigns. The prosecution of the war fell to his officers, particularly his son-in-law Murrough O'Brien, Lord Inchiquin. On 13 April St Leger sent a detachment under Inchiquin and William Jephson to chase away some rebel scouts who were encroaching near to the city. However, this unexpected sally threw the rebels into a panic. The besiegers fell into disarray and were routed. Thereafter, St Leger's forces gradually regained control of co. Cork, but owing to a lack of ammunition, weapons, and money, he could not prevent the rebels from tightening their grip on much of the rest of the province.

Once the immediate threat posed by the rebels had dissipated, St Leger's uneasy alliance with Cork quickly broke down. By late May the two were quarrelling bitterly over what Cork alleged was St Leger's high-handed behaviour. Given the desperate circumstances in which St Leger found himself from late 1641 to early 1642, it is not surprising that he offended many people in trying to scrape together the men and resources to oppose the rebels. Cork certainly resented the manner in which St Leger tried to tap him for money, and the lord president's seizure of £4000 belonging to Sir Robert Tynt outraged many. There was the suspicion that through such actions, St Leger was settling personal scores as well as serving the king's cause. However, St Leger had gone deeply in debt in raising money for his men, and his bravery in battle and energetic conduct of the war had earned him the respect of the protestant forces in Munster. Even as his health deteriorated he continued to direct administrative affairs from his sickbed and made sure that Inchiquin, his political heir, was positioned to succeed him as commander of the protestant forces in Munster. During his last days St Leger was greatly depressed by the realization that the political deadlock in England between the king and parliament meant that there was little prospect of quelling the rebellion for the foreseeable future. He died at Doneraile on 2 July 1642 after a long sickness. TERRY CLAVIN

Sources BL, Egmont MSS, *passim* · V. Treadwell, *Buckingham and Ireland* (1999), 131, 239, 263, 275 · *CSP Ire., 1606–8; 1615–47* · *CSP dom.,* 1619–23, 1623–5, 1625–6 · A. B. Grosart, *Lismore papers*, 1st ser., 5.202, 205, 207, 209; 2nd ser., vol. 4, *passim*; vol. 5, pp. 26–7, 33–5, 41–4, 68–71, 73–9, 90 · C. Smith, *The ancient and present state of the county and city of Cork* (1818), 105–6, 108–9, 114–20 · *History of the Irish confederation and the war in Ireland ... by Richard Bellings*, ed. J. T. Gilbert, 1 (1882), 64, 67–8, 71–6, 244 · [T. Carte], *The life of James, duke of Ormond*, new edn, 6 vols. (1851), vol. 2, pp. 145, 147–52, 160–62, 300–04; vol. 5, pp. 259–61, 263–6, 271–2, 295, 311–12 · M. A. Hickson, *Ireland in the seventeenth century* (1884), vol. 2, pp. 240–43 · J. Lodge, *The peerage of Ireland*, rev. M. Archdall, rev. edn, 6 (1789), 111–18 · M. MacCarthy-Murrough, *The Munster plantation: English migration to southern Ireland, 1583–1641* (1986), 168, 283 · E. Borlase, *The history of the execrable Irish rebellion* (1680), 49, 83–5, 88–9, appx, 35–8 · *Calendar of the Irish patent rolls of James I* (before 1830), 173, 366, 402, 429, 543, 575

Archives BL, corresp. with Sir P. Perceval · Chatsworth House, Derbyshire, letters to earl of Cork

St Leger, William (1599–1665), Jesuit, was born in September 1599 in co. Kilkenny, the son of Thomas St Leger and Margaret Duignan. He studied classics at Antwerp and then philosophy at the Jesuit college at Douai in the Spanish Netherlands, graduating MA and doctor of philosophy. On 8 October 1621 he entered the Society of Jesus at Tournai. After his noviceship he spent a year teaching at the Jesuit college in Douai and then completed his ecclesiastical studies in the same city. He was ordained priest at Cambrai on 20 March 1627.

Recalled to Ireland in 1628, St Leger worked mainly in Kilkenny. He spoke English, Irish, and Latin fluently, and taught classics for many years. He became rector of the Jesuit residence and college in Kilkenny, director of the Sodality of the Blessed Virgin Mary, and consultor of the Irish province, which then numbered about fifty-six members. During the Irish confederate wars in the late 1640s he was among those who supported the truce of the supreme council of the confederation of Kilkenny with the protestant Lord Inchiquin which occasioned the issuing of an excommunication by the papal nuncio, Giovanni Battista Rinuccini, against all who accepted or supported the truce. Cities or towns which accepted or supported it were placed under interdict. Seventeen bishops, the majority of the secular clergy, the greater number of the Friars Minor, and most of the Jesuits of the 'old' Irish stock stood by the nuncio. Eight bishops, six Jesuits of Anglo-Irish background, including the superior of the mission, William Malone, and St Leger, some Friars Minor, Carmelites, and secular clergy supported the council in an appeal to Rome against the excommunication. Rinuccini, it was claimed, had exceeded his powers and had fomented division in the country. The supreme council claimed that pending the resolution of the appeal the censures did not apply. Many of the bishops who supported Rinuccini were unable to apply the censures in their dioceses because of opposition. Subsequently, when the Jesuit general, Vincent Caraffa, sent a representative, Mercure Verdier, to Ireland to investigate the charges against the Jesuits, mainly in Kilkenny, he declared the charges to be false and injurious. The general, having received a history of the controversy with the nuncio, judged the members of the order, in the circumstances, to have acted well. Verdier gave general absolution from the excommunication *ad cautelam* to the Jesuits concerned. St Leger was absolved later in Spain by the bishop of Leighlin, though presumably, like the other members of the Kilkenny community, he did not consider himself to have done wrong.

On 29 June 1652 St Leger was appointed superior of the Irish Jesuit mission in Ireland, but seven months later he had to leave the country. A government edict was published banishing all priests from Ireland within ten days. St Leger was lying ill at a friend's house when the news came in January 1653. He was transported on a stretcher to the nearest seaport and put aboard a ship for Spain. He arrived at San Sebastian in April, and thence moved to Santiago de Compostela. There he was appointed rector of the community and Irish College in 1654, and remained in the post until 1661, when he was again appointed superior of the Irish mission. Ill health prevented him from returning to Ireland, so for the next two years there were in practice two superiors of the mission: St Leger in Spain, and Father Richard Shelton in Ireland. While in Spain St Leger wrote a number of treatises on the state of religion in Ireland and on the Society of Jesus there, and in 1655 published at Antwerp a work in Latin on the life and death of Archbishop Thomas Walsh of Cashel (*De vita et morte illustrissimi domini Thomae Valesii archiepiscopi Casiliensis in Hibernia*). Walsh had been a good friend to the Jesuits, and had been imprisoned and humiliated in Ireland before being transported to Spain, where he died at Compostela in 1654. St Leger himself died at the Irish College of Santiago Compostela on 9 June 1665.

THOMAS J. MORRISSEY

Sources F. Finegan, 'Biographical dictionary of Irish Jesuits, 1598–1773', Irish Jesuit Archives, Dublin • J. A. Stephenson, 'Menology of the Irish province of the Society of Jesus', Irish Jesuit Archives, Dublin • B. O'Ferrall and D. O'Connell, *Commentarius Rinuccinianus de sedis apostolicae legatione ad foederatos Hiberniae Catholicos per annos 1645–1649*, ed. J. Kavanagh, 6 vols., IMC (1932–49), vol. 1, pp. 441, 525, 538; vol. 3, p. 48; vol. 4, pp. 59, 64, 219; vol. 5, pp. 229, 231ff., 216–19 • M. J. Hynes, *The mission of Rinuccini in Ireland: nuncio extraordinary to Ireland, 1645–1649* (Dublin, 1932), 131, 265n. • E. Hogan, 'Chronological catalogue of the Irish province S.J.', Irish Jesuit Archives, 30A

Archives Archives of the Irish Province of the Society of Jesus, Dublin, Irish Jesuit Archives

St Leofard [St Lifard], **Gilbert de** (*c*.1230–1305), canon lawyer and bishop of Chichester, was almost certainly a Frenchman, named from the college of St Liphard at Meung-sur-Loire near Orléans. He was in England by February 1254, probably an academic refugee from the University of Paris, which had been suspended the previous year. He was soon a regent master at Oxford but, perhaps because his talents were increasingly in demand in the ecclesiastical courts, he demised his schools to one of his former students in May 1256. In 1260 he was granted a pension of 10 marks by the dean and chapter of Wells, with the promise of a prebend whenever one came vacant, and by January 1263 he was probably employed in the bishop of Ely's liberty.

In the mid-1260s, however, St Leofard developed a connection with the diocese of Chichester (where he had become the most junior cathedral canon by December 1264), and there is strong evidence of his attachment to the baronial party, of which Bishop Bersted was a prominent member. Between the battles of Lewes and Evesham, while its patron was a Montfortian prisoner, St Leofard was presented to the valuable living of Petworth. Soon after Evesham, Gilbert was reportedly cured of painful and distressing symptoms by vowing a pilgrimage to the tomb of Simon de Montfort. He 'realised that for his cure a sufficient medicine was to think upon the suffering of Simon and the other knights who were martyred with him at Evesham' (Rishanger, *Chronicle*, 103).

At the end of March 1266 St Leofard was given protection to move his household to the court of the papal legate. Ottobuono granted a subsidy in favour of the disinherited in 1267, and St Leofard acted as its collector in the northern province. In November 1268 Archbishop Walter Giffard of York appointed St Leofard his official; he succeeded to a prebend of Beverley in the same year. He had, however, ceased to act as official at the end of 1272, and, although he was named as Giffard's vicar-general in 1274 and was collated as rector of Kirk Ella in the same year, his life until the end of the decade remains obscure. Giffard died on 22 April 1279, but St Leofard had probably already returned to the south; he was now treasurer of Chichester, and appointed Sussex men as attorneys when he went to Scotland in April and October that year.

John Pecham became primate in 1279; at the Easter synod of 1282 his bishops presented twenty-one *gravamina*, objecting to the extension of the appellate jurisdiction of the provincial court. St Leofard, who had also had experience of that court as a litigant in 1272 as rector of East Coker, was appointed to a commission headed by a former Canterbury official to arbitrate the dispute; its members were 'learned by long experience in the customs and rights of the church of Canterbury' (*Councils and Synods*, 2/2.932). The decisions of the arbitrators were moderate and, for the most part, favourable to the position of the bishops; they also established the church of St Mary-le-Bow as the permanent home of the provincial court. Metropolitan authority was assured, but so was diocesan organizational integrity. As an additional guarantee of peace St Leofard was appointed official of Canterbury.

One of St Leofard's first tasks as official was to settle a dispute between the prior of Canterbury and the majority of the convent. In 1285 the priory granted him a pension of 50 marks, together with a hall, chamber, and kitchen, with stabling for his horses and accommodation for his household, so often was he at Canterbury about monastic business; in that year Christ Church had twenty-one suits pending in different courts. He was also rewarded by Pecham with two Kent livings, and clearly enjoyed the full confidence of the archbishop. But Gilbert's forensic skills were not without their shady side. The Oxford Dominican Robert Holcot, writing a generation after St Leofard's death, repeats the boast of an anonymous bishop of Chichester that he had once taken £100 in a single day to keep his mouth shut when practising in the court of arches; the expensive piece of Persian cloth received by Gilbert from Bogo de Clare in 1283 looks suspiciously like an attempted bribe.

On 30 January 1288 St Leofard was elected bishop of Chichester in succession to Bersted. He received the temporalities on 24 June and was consecrated at Canterbury by Pecham on 5 September. Still in demand as a lawyer, in the month of his consecration he replaced the infirm bishop of Norwich as arbitrator between the archbishop of York and his dean. One of his first acts as bishop was the promulgation of a body of diocesan constitutions which, with four exceptions, had been in use in the northern province, but which may have travelled north with him from Wells. This was a brave move, given that the existing statutes were those of his saintly predecessor Richard, and less than forty years old. As a diocesan St Leofard was capable of resolute action—in 1292 he excommunicated the earl of Arundel for hunting in his woods—but in the affairs of others was frequently the subject of his provincial's impatient admonitions. For instance, he astonished the archbishop by his indulgent treatment of the prior of Hardham, a member of the family that had provided one of St Leofard's attorneys in 1279 and an esquire of his household in 1292.

St Leofard's energies were perhaps reserved, and indeed his character and training best suited, for a fight with the king over the right to present canons to the chapel in Hastings Castle, which the crown claimed as a free chapel, but over which successive bishops had long claimed jurisdiction as ordinary. St Leofard objected to collations made by the crown as early as 1290, while in October 1299 Archbishop Winchelsey sought the bishop of Durham's help in promoting St Leofard's business with the king. No doubt it was the same suit that brought St Leofard to Woodstock in August 1301, when he baptized the king's youngest son, Edmund. The bishop made lavish presents to Edward

whenever he visited St Richard's shrine, but the resolution of the dispute, which ultimately passed in Chichester's favour, was reserved for his successor. St Leofard's seems to have been the first register to have been kept at Chichester.

St Leofard used his prodigious wealth both to buy favour and to enhance his church. He loaned 500 marks to the king in 1290, and in 1294 Edward helped himself to £2000 which the bishop had deposited in St Paul's. He spent liberally to transform his cathedral from a comparatively small church to one 400 feet long; as well as adding two bays to the lady chapel, he heightened the building, reroofed it, and inserted a rose window in the east gable; he also rebuilt the hall and kitchen of the palace. The work was still in progress at his death, and he provided 1250 marks (£833 6s. 8d.) for its continuance. He spent over £400 in the purchase of manors, an annuity, and stock with which to endow the see, supplemented the endowment of the precentorship for the observance of his anniversary, and bequeathed his chapel, with its many jewels and ornaments, to the cathedral. He died on 12 February 1305 at Amberley, his preferred residence towards the end of his life, and was buried in his own lady chapel. His tomb fell victim to the commissioners sent to destroy that of St Richard in 1538; they evidently thought that both were being abused as shrines. His anniversary was kept both at Chichester and Beverley.

Gilbert de St Leofard left a reputation for sanctity at Chichester second only to that of St Richard. The bishop of Winchester, John de Pontoise, had died three months before him, but the chronicler who recorded the deaths of both prelates reserved his praise for St Leofard:

> the father of orphans, the consoler of widows, a pious and humble visitor at rough bedsides and hovels, the bountiful helper of the needy rather than the rich, the sanctity of whose life was attested by the large number of miracles worked at his tomb. (*Flores historiarum*, 129)

CHRISTOPHER WHITTICK

Sources Emden, *Oxf.*, 3.1628 · Chancery records · *The register of John le Romeyn … 1286–1296*, ed. W. Brown, 1, SurtS, 123 (1913) · M. Hobbs, ed., *Chichester Cathedral: an historical survey* (1994) · A. F. Leach, ed., *Memorials of Beverley Minster*, 2 vols., SurtS, 98, 108 (1898–1903) · W. D. Peckham, ed., *The chartulary of the high church of Chichester*, Sussex RS, 46 (1946) · PRO, exchequer, queen's remembrancer, memoranda rolls, E 159/60, m13d · PRO, special collections, ancient correspondence, SC 1/20/87, 28/21 · U. Durham L., archives and special collections, Durham Cathedral muniments, 2.2.Ebor.18 · PRO, court of common pleas, plea rolls, CP 40/75 · Canterbury Cathedral archives, ES Roll 208 · [W. Rishanger], *The chronicle of William de Rishanger, of the barons' wars*, ed. J. O. Halliwell, CS, 15 (1840) · H. E. Salter, W. A. Pantin, and H. G. Richardson, eds., *Formularies which bear on the history of Oxford*, 2, OHS, new ser., 5 (1942) · H. R. Luard, ed., *Flores historiarum*, 3 vols., Rolls Series, 95 (1890), vol. 3 · F. M. Powicke and C. R. Cheney, eds., *Councils and synods with other documents relating to the English church, 1205–1313*, 2 (1964) · W. Stubbs, ed., 'Annales Londonienses', *Chronicles of the reigns of Edward I and Edward II*, 1, Rolls Series, 76 (1882), 1–251 · B. Smalley, *English friars and antiquity in the early fourteenth century* (1960) · P. Hoskin, ed., *Chichester, 1215–1253*, English Episcopal Acta, 22 (2001) · P. Hoskin, ed., *Chichester, 1254–1305*, English Episcopal Acta, 23 (2001)
Archives PRO, letter to A. de Osegoteby, 22 Nov 1300, SC 1/28/21
Likenesses episcopal seal

Wealth at death account of the temporalities from 14 Feb 1305: PRO, E 404/481/10/3

St Leonards. For this title name *see* Sugden, Edward Burtenshaw, Baron St Leonards (1781–1875).

St Liz, Simon de. *See* Senlis, Simon (I) de, earl of Northampton and earl of Huntingdon (*d.* 1111x13).

St Lo, Edward (*c.*1682–1729), naval officer, was a son of Edward St Lo of Little Fontmell, Dorset, the elder brother of George *St Lo, commissioner of the navy. He entered the navy in March 1695 on the *Lichfield* with Lord Archibald Hamilton. In 1702 he was a lieutenant of the *Chichester*, one of the fleet with Sir George Rooke off Cadiz and at Vigo. On 9 September 1703 he was promoted to be captain of the *Pendennis* in the fleet under Vice-Admiral John Graydon in the West Indies and at Placentia. In 1704 he was again in the West Indies in the *Dolphin*, which in 1705 was employed in convoy service in the North Sea. In 1706 he was in command of the *Gosport* (32 guns), appointed to convoy a fleet of merchant ships to Jamaica. On 28 July they fell in with two French ships of war, one of which, the *Jason* (54 guns), engaged and took the *Gosport* after an obstinate defence. On 19 October St Lo was tried for the loss of the ship and fully acquitted. He was appointed shortly afterwards to the *Tartar* (32 guns), which during the following summer cruised from the channel, in the Soundings, and as far as Lisbon.

From March 1708 to August 1710 St Lo commanded the *Salisbury* prize in the North Sea, subsequently commanding the *Defiance* (64 guns) in the West Indies in 1711–12. On 25 December 1712, on her way home from Jamaica, the *Defiance* put into Kinsale in distress, being fifty men short of complement and having eighty sick. She did not reach the Downs until 26 March 1713. In 1720–21 St Lo was captain of the *Prince Frederick*, flagship of Rear-Admiral Francis Hosier in the Baltic, and he continued in her until 1723. In 1726 he went out to the West Indies in the *Superbe*, one of the squadron with Hosier, and he succeeded temporarily to the chief command on Hosier's death on 25 August 1727. He continued the blockade of Portobello until he was certain that the Spanish ships were all laid up owing to shortage of stores, and then returned to Jamaica, where Vice-Admiral Edward Hopson succeeded him in the command on 29 January 1728. The squadron returned to the coast of Spanish America in February, and St Lo succeeded to the chief command once more following Hopson's death on 8 May. He held the position until his own death on 22 April 1729 and was buried at sea the same day in Green Bay, Jamaica, as Hopson had been.

St Lo had been promoted rear-admiral on 4 March, but had not received the news. His last letter to the Admiralty, dated 25 March 1729 but not read at the board until five weeks after he was dead, stated that he had 'almost lost the use of my hands and feet by a violent cold, and finding myself worser, and despairing of any recovery here, I humbly beg their lordships will be pleased to recall me home' (PRO, ADM 1/230, St Lo to Burchett). St Lo never

married. His will, dated 2 May 1723, mentions a brother, John, a sister, Mary Smart, and an illegitimate son, Edward, for whom he placed £600 in trust.

J. K. LAUGHTON, *rev.* J. D. DAVIES

Sources R. D. Merriman, 'Captain George St Lo, RN, 1658–1718', *Mariner's Mirror*, 31 (1945), 13–22, 14–15 [see also corrective note in vol. 32 (1946), 186] · PRO, ADM 1/230 · will, PRO, PROB 11/630, fols. 305v–6 · NMM, Sergison MSS, SER/136 · J. Charnock, ed., *Biographia navalis*, 3 (1795), 284
Archives PRO, ADM 1/230
Wealth at death £600 placed in trust for his natural son: will, PRO, PROB 11/630, fols. 305v–6

St Lo, George (1658–1718), naval officer and official administrator, was the fourth of five sons of John St Lo of Little Fontmell, Dorset, and grandson of Edward St Lo of Knighton, Wiltshire. On the paternal side he was connected with the influential Hyde family, his great-grandmother Elizabeth being the granddaughter of Laurence Hyde (*d.* 1618) of Hatch, Wiltshire, grandfather of the first earl of Clarendon. This connection aided his rise in the navy with Laurence Hyde, earl of Rochester, acting as his patron. A further connection was established through St Lo's own marriage in November 1683 to Elizabeth Chiffinch (*b.* 1669), granddaughter of Thomas Chiffinch who, with his brother William, had been a companion in exile of Charles II and his brother James.

On 16 January 1678 St Lo was appointed lieutenant of the 42-gun *Phoenix*, then in the Mediterranean undertaking operations against the Barbary states. In 1680, while still a lieutenant, he was transferred to the *Hampshire*, a 46-gun ship commanded by Sir George Rooke. St Lo gained his own command on 11 April 1682 when he was promoted to the command of the ageing 22-gun *Dartmouth*. Ordered to the West Indies in 1686, he found the acting governor of the Leeward Islands, Sir James Russell, profiting from the activities of piracy. This set the pair at odds, with St Lo openly criticizing this abuse of authority. In 1688 St Lo, then captain of the 50-gun *Portsmouth*, brought the declaration of the prince of Orange to the fleet in the Downs, while in the following year he was present at the action against the French off Bantry Bay on 1 May. In August 1689 he lost his ship and was taken prisoner after a seven-hour engagement with the French 58-gun *Marquis*. Upon his release, following a general exchange of prisoners, he published the pamphlet *England's Safety, or, A Bridle for the French King* (1692). As well as an account of his own treatment as a prisoner, this contained observations on the manning and management of the French navy and how these might be applied to England. He indicated his belief that 20,000 men would be sufficient to man the fleet and that these could be gained without pressing provided they were paid, rather than given tickets, each time the fleet returned. A second pamphlet, *England's Interest, or, A Discipline for Seamen* was published in 1694 and gave further consideration to the more effective manning of the fleet.

The injuries St Lo had received in the sea fight with the *Marquis* probably left him unfit for further service at sea. Declining an offer to become governor of New York, he accepted a commissionership of prizes, before becoming an extra commissioner of the Navy Board in September 1693. His subsequent appointment to the dockyards as a resident commissioner, first at Plymouth (1695–1703) and then at Chatham (1703–12), encouraged him to take a close interest in the construction of dry docks, and he is credited with the design of a prototype entrance caisson (a floating dock gate) at Chatham. His desire for greater efficiency and his outspokenness soon brought him into conflict with both the civilian labour force and his own superiors, and he has been described as 'one of the most forceful if not to say irregular, of the outstation commissioners' (Coad, 21). On 4 October 1699 he was reprimanded by the Navy Board for expressing himself 'in such a manner as inferior officers ought not to do towards their superiors' (PRO, ADM 174/1, warrant 448). A further reprimand came in 1703 after he ordered away the guard ships from Winstanley's new Eddystone lighthouse, which led to its destruction by a French privateer and the capture of the workmen and architect. A third reprimand followed his move to Chatham, when St Lo took with him both the new dockyard yacht (appropriately named *St Lo*) and items of official correspondence. That he later threatened striking workers at Chatham with a drawn sword, chasing them out of the yard, provides a further illustration of his forthright character. His most lasting memorial at Chatham is the resident commissioner's grand house, built at his insistence. Upon his removal from Chatham, as a result of the omission of his name from the new patents for the Navy Board at the accession of George I, he served briefly as commander-in-chief at the Nore. He died in retirement at Northfleet on 20 September 1718 and was buried there, leaving at least one son, John, and two daughters, Elizabeth and Mary.

PHILIP MACDOUGALL

Sources J. Charnock, ed., *Biographia navalis*, 2 (1795) · G. St Lo, *England's safety, or, A bridle for the French king* (1692) · R. D. Merriman, 'Captain George St Lo, RN, 1658–1718', *Mariner's Mirror*, 31 (1945), 13–22 · J. G. Coad, *The royal dockyards, 1690–1850* (1989) · J. M. Collinge, *Navy Board officials, 1660–1832* (1978) · P. Dawson, *Commissioners in residence*, Chatham Dockyard Historical Research Paper (1998) · F. Majdalany, *The red rocks of Eddystone* (1959) · R. D. Merriman, ed., *Queen Anne's navy*, Navy Records Society, 103 (1961) · will, PRO, PROB 11/565, fols. 361v–364v · *DNB* · PRO, C 66/3379; ADM 1/3596, 1/174, 174/1
Likenesses J. Nutting, line engraving, BM, NPG · R. White, miniature, BM · oils, NMM
Wealth at death property in Kent: will, PRO, PROB 11/565, fols. 361v–364v

St Martin, Laurence de (d. 1274), bishop of Rochester, is first recorded in the early 1240s, when he is already styled *magister* and described as a royal clerk. Of his family origins and background little can be said, except that he was probably connected with the Wiltshire St Martins; and two of his brothers are found in association with him, Abel as his proctor in 1245 and William as archdeacon of Rochester from 1253.

St Martin probably began his career in the household of William de Valence, Henry III's half-brother, but in 1244 he became one of the king's chief advisers in ecclesiastical affairs, and as such was a member of the English delegation at the Council of Lyons in 1245. In his absence the king provided him with a prebend in Chichester Cathedral and collated him to the archdeaconry of Coventry during the vacancies of those sees; a prebend at Salisbury soon followed when that see, too, came into the king's hands in 1246. Then, on 19 October 1250, while St Martin was engaged on a diplomatic mission at the papal court, he was elected bishop of Rochester in succession to Richard Wendene. According to Matthew Paris, the king's influence was brought to bear upon the monastic chapter, but the monks' choice was probably also affected by the fact that the prior, Alexander de Glanville, was a close friend of St Martin, 'quem idem Alexander unice diligebat', in the words of the *Annales ecclesiae Roffensis* (*Flores historiarum*, 2.369). Archiepiscopal confirmation took place at Lyons on 9 February 1251, after the bishop-elect had there voiced his reluctance to give his homage to Canterbury, on the grounds that it might be construed as a slight upon the royal prerogative. His hesitation having been overcome by a statement issued by Archbishop Boniface that guaranteed the safeguarding of the king's rights, he made his profession and was consecrated by the archbishop at Lyons on Palm Sunday, 9 April 1251.

Two controversies for a time marred the new bishop's relations with his cathedral chapter and brought him into conflict with the see of Canterbury and with the crown. The monks protested against what they judged to be his interference in appointments to offices within the priory, and his claim to some of their manorial properties, which had the result, so the annalist reports, that the disillusioned prior fell ill and died. Disagreement with the archbishop and, indirectly, with the king arose when Henry III demanded payment of a feudal aid on the occasion of the knighting of his eldest son. St Martin's unease in this instance was based on the fact that his temporalities were held not of the king but of the archbishop as confirmed by King John's charter, which the bishop understood to have been a gift in free alms exempt from all secular dues and services. After lengthy discussions in the king's council and in parliament, and an appeal to the pope launched against the king's wishes, a settlement was agreed on 1 August 1259. This defined the rights and obligations of each to the other: the bishop was henceforth to have the return of all royal writs and pleas within his church and see, and the archbishop an annual payment of 12 marks for this concession.

St Martin's elevation to the episcopate did not bring an end to his employment in the royal service; he continued to make journeys to Rome and elsewhere as an envoy for both church and crown. In 1256, for example, he procured the canonization of an unfortunate Scot, William of Perth, murdered near Rochester on his way to the Holy Land; the offerings at the shrine of this new saint enabled the grateful monks to rebuild the choir of their cathedral church. He played no active part in the civil wars of the 1260s, but continued to be associated with the king; the sack of Rochester in 1264 was said to have been an act of revenge by the barons against the bishop. In 1268 St Martin was once more a royal envoy to Italy, dealing with Henry's remaining family interests in Sicily. He may have attended the opening session of the second Council of Lyons in May 1274, but he died about 3 June, and was buried in his cathedral on the north side of the high altar, in a tomb of Purbeck marble which boasts a fine effigy and canopy above.

As diocesan St Martin was greatly concerned to augment his own revenues, claiming that his see was the poorest in England. In 1251 he secured the pope's consent to his retaining for three years the benefices that he had held before he became bishop, and he also obtained papal licence to take for five years a fifth of the revenues of all the benefices in his diocese. To the same end he appropriated three churches to the bishop's endowment. In 1252 he conducted an inquest into the finances of Rochester Cathedral priory. But he achieved little. The priory's affairs remained in disorder, while the bishop's executor John de St Dionisius, archdeacon of Rochester by 1278, was at that date still pursuing the bishop's many debtors. St Martin's concern for administrative efficiency may also be apparent in his having kept an episcopal register. It was still available for consultation in 1347, but ultimately did not survive. However, two volumes of the writings of St Augustine and a 'Flores historii', all given by him to the Rochester monks, have survived in the British Library as Royal MSS 2 F. xi, 5 A. xv, and 5 B. vi.   JOAN GREATREX

Sources J. Thorpe, ed., *Registrum Roffense, or, A collection of antient records, charters and instruments … illustrating the ecclesiastical history and antiquities of the diocese and cathedral church of Rochester* (1769) · [J. de Westerham], *Custumale Roffense*, ed. J. Thorpe (1788) · H. R. Luard, ed., *Flores historiarum*, 3 vols., Rolls Series, 95 (1890) · *Paris, Chron.* · *Fasti Angl., 1066–1300*, [Monastic cathedrals] · *Fasti Angl., 1066–1300*, [Salisbury] · F. M. Powicke and C. R. Cheney, eds., *Councils and synods with other documents relating to the English church, 1205–1313*, 2 vols. (1964) · M. Richter, ed., *Canterbury professions*, CYS, 67 (1973) · *The historical works of Gervase of Canterbury*, ed. W. Stubbs, 2 vols., Rolls Series, 73 (1879–80) · W. H. St John Hope, *The architectural history of the cathedral church and monastery of St. Andrew at Rochester* (1900) · *Registrum Hamonis Hethe, diocesis Roffensis, AD 1319–1352*, ed. C. Johnson, 2 vols., CYS, 48–9 (1948) · J. R. H. Moorman, *Church life in England in the thirteenth century* (1945); repr. (1946) · E. U. Crosby, *Bishop and chapter in twelfth-century England* (1994) · N. R. Ker, ed., *Medieval libraries of Great Britain: a list of surviving books*, 2nd edn, Royal Historical Society Guides and Handbooks, 3 (1964), 299

Likenesses tomb marble effigy, Rochester Cathedral

St Maur [*formerly* Seymour], **Edward Adolphus**, **twelfth duke of Somerset** (1804–1885), politician and author, was born in London on 20 December 1804. He was the eldest son of Edward Adolphus *Seymour, eleventh duke of Somerset (1775–1855), and his first wife, Charlotte, daughter of the duke of Hamilton, and was educated at Eton College and Christ Church, Oxford, matriculating on 11 October 1823, but leaving the university without a degree. He then travelled abroad, visiting Russia among other countries. He married, on 10 June 1830, Jane Georgiana, the youngest of the three daughters of Thomas Sheridan (son of R. B. *Sheridan) and his wife, Caroline Henrietta, *née* Callender. Lord Seymour, as he was commonly called,

fought a duel in 1835 with Sir Colquhoun Grant, who challenged him because he would not deny having been privy to the elopement of Sir Colquhoun's only daughter and heir with Lady Seymour's brother, also called R. B. Sheridan. After shots had been exchanged without injury to either combatant, Seymour stated his ignorance of the transaction. His wife had helped her brother to obtain the hand of the heiress, and she did so without informing her husband. In August 1839 Lady Seymour presided as 'Queen of Beauty' over the tournament at Eglinton Castle. She had 'large deep blue or violet eyes, black hair, perfect features, and a complexion of lilies and roses' (*Songs, Poems and verses*).

Seymour entered the Commons as MP for Okehampton in 1830, and from 1834 to 1855 was MP for Totnes, sitting as a whig. In 1835 he was appointed a lord of the Treasury in Melbourne's administration. In 1839 he was promoted to be secretary to the Board of Control, and in 1840 he carried through the house a bill, which received the royal assent, for establishing a board of superintendence for railways. He was under-secretary for the Home department for two months in 1841. He voted for the repeal of the corn laws. Lord John Russell appointed him first commissioner of works in 1851, with a seat in the cabinet, but he was out of office for several years following Russell's resignation in 1852. During the campaign in the Crimea he served on the committee to inquire into the state of the army. When Totnes was disfranchised in 1855 he ceased to be a member of the Commons, but in the same year took his seat in the House of Lords, as duke of Somerset, on his father's death on 15 August. In Palmerston's government of 1859, Somerset was appointed first lord of the Admiralty. Although not personally popular, Somerset was an efficient administrator, and initially had some success, backed by Palmerston, in maintaining spending on the navy. He played an important part in the development of a programme of construction of iron clad ships, and from 1859 until 1862 he had public support. The rise of the economy movement in the Liberal Party led, however, to much criticism of the Admiralty as both expensive and inefficient, and from 1863 spending on the navy began to decline. After leaving office in 1866, Somerset defended his record anonymously in *The Naval Expenditure from 1860 to 1866, and its Results* (1866). He was created a knight of the Garter on 21 May 1862, and Earl St Maur of Berry Pomeroy on 17 June 1863, at which time he took the surname St Maur. He declined to join Gladstone's 1868 government; by 1872 Lord Granville thought him 'leader of a very formidable cave in the Lords'. He criticized government policy on the ballot and the *Alabama* affair, but voted for Irish disestablishment, and the abolition of army purchase.

Somerset's two sons died early, in 1865 and 1869, blighting his later life. Gladstone considered offering him the Indian governor-generalship but thought 'the recollection of his son's death might be an impediment' (though he also thought Somerset in 1872 'wonderfully strong and wiry'). In his grief Somerset worked on historical Christianity, and turned to theism, publishing *Christian Theology and Modern Scepticism* (1872). His wife died on 14 December

1884; he died on 28 November 1885 at Stover Lodge, near Newton Abbot, and was buried at Gerrards Cross. The dukedom devolved to the twelfth duke's younger brother, Archibald Henry Algernon (1810–1891). Somerset's first child, **Edward Adolphus Ferdinand St Maur** [*formerly* Seymour] (1835–1869), was born on 17 July 1835 and matriculated at Christ Church, Oxford, on 19 May 1853. Styled Lord Seymour and, from 1863, Earl St Maur, he attended the coronation of Alexander II as Lord Granville's attaché, and fought in Persia with Sir James Outram, and with Sir Colin Campbell in India in 1857. As 'Captain Sarsfield' he took part in Garibaldi's campaign in Sicily in 1860. He and Rosina Elizabeth Swan of Higham, a Gypsy and the daughter of a bricklayer, had two illegitimate children, Richard Harold (*b.* 1869) and Ruth Mary Cavendish-*Bentinck, the suffragist. St Maur died, unmarried, in Dover Street, London, on 30 September 1869. In 1872 Rosina married François Tournier of Bordeaux, but died shortly afterwards of consumption.

W. F. RAE, *rev.* H. C. G. MATTHEW

Sources GEC, *Peerage* · *Letters, remains, and memoirs of Edward Adolphus Seymour, twelfth duke of Somerset*, ed. W. H. Mallock and G. Ramsden (1893) · J. F. Beeler, *British naval policy in the Gladstone–Disraeli era, 1866–1880* (1997) · C. Baxter, 'The duke of Somerset and the creation of the British ironclad navy, 1859–66', *Mariner's Mirror*, 63 (1977), 279–84 · *The political correspondence of Mr Gladstone and Lord Granville, 1868–1876*, ed. A. Ramm, 2, CS, 3rd ser., 82 (1952) · Gladstone, *Diaries* · *Gladstone and Palmerston: being the correspondence of Lord Palmerston with Mr Gladstone, 1851–1865*, ed. P. Guedalla (1928) · *Songs, poems and verses by Helen, Lady Dufferin*, ed. Marquess of Dufferin and Ava (1894)
Archives Bucks. RLSS · Devon RO · Muncaster Castle, Cumbria | BL, Gladstone MSS, Add. MS 44304 · BL, Martin MSS, Add. MSS 41411–41412 · Borth. Inst., Halifax MSS · PRO, Russell MSS, PRO 30/22 · U. Southampton L., Palmerston MSS · U. Southampton L., Wellington MSS
Likenesses Ape [C. Pellegrini], caricature, NPG; repro. in *VF* (7 Aug 1869)
Wealth at death £202,423 8s. 0d.: probate, 28 Jan 1886, CGPLA Eng. & Wales

St Maur, Edward Adolphus Ferdinand, Earl St Maur (1835–1869). *See under* St Maur, Edward Adolphus, twelfth duke of Somerset (1804–1885).

Sainton, Prosper Philippe Catherine (1813–1890), violinist, was born on 5 June 1813 at Toulouse, the son of Jean Sainton, a merchant. He was educated at the college in Toulouse with the idea of ultimately becoming a lawyer, but his musical gifts led to his entering the Paris conservatory on 20 December 1831, where he studied under François-Antoine Habeneck (himself a pupil of Pierre Baillot), and won second and first prizes for violin playing in 1833 and 1834 respectively. After leaving the conservatory he was a member of the orchestras of the Société des Concerts and the Grand Opéra for two years. He then made a successful and extended concert tour on the continent, performing in Italy, Germany, Austria, Russia, Finland, Sweden, Denmark, and Spain, before returning to Toulouse in 1840 to fill the post of professor of the violin at the conservatory there.

Four years later Sainton appeared in England and played at a Philharmonic Society concert under the conductorship of Mendelssohn, of whom he was a close friend. He returned and settled in London on being appointed on 7 February 1845 professor of the violin at the Royal Academy of Music, a post he occupied until his death. In addition to his teaching duties and possibly a tour to Holland in 1848, Sainton was a very active performer in the capital and the provinces. Apart from leading the orchestras of the Philharmonic Society (1846–54) and the Sacred Harmonic Society (from 1848), he was involved with performances of the Musical Union, the Beethoven Quartet Society, and the Quartet Association (which he helped to found in 1852), and led (with Henry Blagrove) at the Bradford festival in 1853. He established a long association with the Three Choirs festival, and was leader for the evening concerts (Blagrove led for the morning) at Worcester in 1854. During one of the secular concerts at the same festival, Sainton and Blagrove performed a concerto for two violins and orchestra by Spohr. The first Leeds festival in 1858, during which Queen Victoria opened the new town hall, brought the two violinists together once more as leaders.

Sainton was one of the musicians who took part in 1859 in the experimental stages of the Popular Concerts, founded for the performance of chamber music. He was leader of the orchestra of the Royal Italian Opera (1847–71), sometimes acting as deputy conductor to Michael Costa, and leader at Her Majesty's Theatre (1871–80). From 1848 to 1855 he held the positions of conductor of the queen's band and chamber musician to the queen. On 4 February 1860 he married Charlotte Helen *Dolby (1821–1885), a well-known contralto, teacher, and composer. (Her obituary in the *Musical Times*, 1885, 145–6, mentions a son, Charles Sainton, who was a painter.)

Sainton continued to perform at the chief provincial festivals, and so busy was he as a teacher that it was his proud boast that, at the last Birmingham festival he was alive to see, all the violinists had been his pupils or had studied under his pupils. He taught, among others, Thomas Weist-Hill, A. C. Mackenzie, and Gabrielle Vaillant. In 1862 he conducted the music, including Sterndale Bennett's *Ode*, at the opening of the International Exhibition. His farewell concert took place on 25 June 1883, at the Albert Hall, at which his wife also made her last public appearance.

Among Sainton's compositions are two violin concertos, three romances for violin and piano (*c.*1875), several fantasias on operatic and other popular themes, and other virtuoso showpieces for the violin. A portrait in Carrodus's book (1895, 87) shows him as a fairly large, stocky man with prominent features and a beard and moustache. His obituary in the *Musical Times* describes him as 'one of the most eminent teachers of the violin of the present century' and as a man of 'affectionate disposition'. He died of a severe attack of bronchitis at 84 Westbourne Park Road, London, on 17 October 1890, and was buried in his wife's grave at Highgate cemetery.

DAVID J. GOLBY

Sources MT, 31 (1890), 665 · F.-J. Fétis, *Biographie universelle des musiciens, et bibliographie générale de la musique*, 2nd edn, 7 (Paris, 1864), 374 · A. Pougin, ed., *Biographie universelle des musiciens, et bibliographie générale de la musique: supplément et complément*, 2 (Paris, 1880), 474; repr. (1881) · J. T. Carrodus, *Chats to violin students on how to study the violin* (1895) · M. Campbell, *The great violinists* (1980) · m. cert. · G. Grove and R. J. Pascell, 'Sainton, Prosper Phillippe Catherine', *New Grove*
Likenesses C. Baugniet, group portrait, lithograph (*The Musical Union, 1851*), BM · portrait, repro. in Carrodus, *Chats to violin students*, 87
Wealth at death £1132 5s.: probate, 11 Nov 1890, CGPLA Eng. & Wales

St Oswald. For this title name *see* Winn, Rowland Denys Guy, fourth Baron St Oswald (1916–1984).

St Paul, John (d. 1362), archbishop of Dublin and administrator, was the son of Thomas St Paul of Owston in Yorkshire. His parents' clandestine marriage resulted in uncertainty as to his legitimacy, which was confirmed in 1339.

St Paul became a chancery clerk before 1318. He acted as keeper of the great seal during the chancellor's absence on several occasions from 1334 onwards. On 28 April 1337 he was appointed master of the rolls and on 7 June 1339 keeper of the Domus Conversorum. In 1340 he was among the officials appointed to open parliament in the absence of the keeper of the realm. He was attorney for various members of the nobility including Mary de St Pol, countess of Pembroke, who may have been related to him, and was counsel to the priory of Christ Church, Canterbury, which awarded him a pension in 1339. In 1326 he was presented to Kynton in the diocese of Hereford and subsequently acquired other benefices by presentation and exchange—Asshby David in the diocese of Lincoln (before 1329) and Sutton in the diocese of Salisbury (before 1335), and prebends in the free chapels of Hastings (1336) and Penkridge (1337) and in the cathedrals of Exeter (1338), York (before 1339), Wells (1339), Chichester, Lichfield, and London. He was provost of Wells in 1340.

St Paul was an associate of John Stratford, archbishop of Canterbury and chancellor of England, and in February 1340 was one of the royal officials imprisoned when Edward III took action against the Stratfords and their circle. He was released in response to Stratford's protest against imprisoning members of the clergy, but in December 1340 was replaced as master of the rolls. He returned to the chancery as a clerk and acted as keeper of the great seal in 1343 and 1349. In 1345 he was present as a member of the council when John, count of Montfort (d. 1345), did homage to the king. He acquired prebends in the collegiate church of Ledbury in the diocese of Hereford (1344), and in the cathedrals of Exeter (1344) and Dublin. He was archdeacon of Cornwall in 1346 and was created archbishop of Dublin by papal provision in 1349. He founded chantries in Owston, Yorkshire, and in the priory of Stratford-at-Bow and was involved in the formation of the Guild of St Katherine in Coventry.

As archbishop St Paul became involved in the dispute with the archbishop of Armagh, Richard Fitzralph, over the primacy, in which he had the support of the king. In November 1349 Edward III revoked his recognition of the primatial rights of Armagh and in the following year made representations to the papal curia in favour of Dublin and instructed his officials in Ireland to use the full rigour of the law against those who upheld Armagh's rights within the province of Dublin. In 1351 Armagh's rights were again revoked by the king but the papal curia delayed making a decision and the primacy was still unresolved in 1366.

In 1351 St Paul was appointed by Clement VI to proceed against certain heretics who had fled to Dublin from the diocese of Ossory and had been protected by Archbishop Bicknor, and in the same year he carried out a visitation of Ossory. He held a provincial council in Dublin in 1352 which forbade clandestine marriages, reasserted the right of sanctuary, and enjoined the observance of Good Friday and other feasts. He obtained a confirmation of the liberties and privileges of the see of Dublin in 1357 and a new royal grant of warren in 1360. In 1357 he received royal licence to appoint perpetual vicars to parish churches in the diocese of Dublin where this was necessary for the cure of souls. He was responsible for rebuilding the choir of the priory of the Holy Trinity (later Christ Church Cathedral) and for carrying out work to the chancel there.

John St Paul was appointed chancellor of Ireland on 20 July 1350, possibly at the request of Thomas Rokeby, the justiciar. This marked the beginning of an attempt to reform the Irish administration and to restore central control over local officials. The justiciar and chancellor were instructed to investigate deficiencies in the custody of the king's castles, to inquire into the activities of royal officials and to survey the state of the exchequer twice yearly. Rokeby and St Paul were responsible for sending petitions to the English council in 1350 and 1352 explaining the problems facing the Dublin government. St Paul was involved in further inquiries into the administration in 1355 which resulted in the discovery of malpractice on the part of the treasurer. He was rewarded for his good service with a grant of £100 from the Irish exchequer. As chancellor he attempted to improve the efficiency of the chancery by staffing it with English clerks. In 1350 he refused to seal charters of pardon on the grounds that the justiciar was not empowered to issue such charters. The Irish council affirmed that the justiciar had this power *ex officio* but had to agree to indemnify the chancellor for sealing them.

St Paul was replaced as chancellor in July 1356, as part of a reorganization of the personnel of the Irish administration, and possibly because of ill health. He continued to be a leading member of the king's council in Ireland for the remainder of his life. In 1359 James Butler, earl of Ormond, the justiciar, was ordered not to allow any important matters affecting the king to be brought to a conclusion without the archbishop's presence or consent and in July 1361 the indenture of Lionel, earl of Ulster, as the king's lieutenant in Ireland specified that he was to be advised by members of the king's council in Ireland, the first of whom to be mentioned was John St Paul. St Paul continued to carry out administrative functions, in 1360 being associated with the justiciar and treasurer in a search for mines in Ireland and in a wide-ranging inquiry into the behaviour of central and local officials. As a member of the council he was involved in making decisions relating to the defence of the Leinster marches.

John St Paul died on 9 September 1362 and was buried before the high altar in the priory of the Holy Trinity, Dublin, as directed in his will. PHILOMENA CONNOLLY

Sources *Chancery records* · *CEPR letters* · W. H. Bliss, ed., *Calendar of entries in the papal registers relating to Great Britain and Ireland: petitions to the pope* (1896) · A. Gwynn, ed., 'Provincial and diocesan decrees of the diocese of Dublin during the Anglo-Norman period', *Archivium Hibernicum*, 11 (1944), 31–117 · H. J. Lawlor, 'Calendar of the *Liber ruber* of the diocese of Ossory', *Proceedings of the Royal Irish Academy*, 27C (1908–9), 159–208 · J. C. Crosthwaite, ed., *The book of obits and martyrology of the cathedral church … Dublin*, Irish Archaeological Society, 4 (1844) · H. G. Richardson and G. O. Sayles, *The administration of Ireland, 1172–1377* (1963) · E. Tresham, ed., *Rotulorum patentium et clausorum cancellariae Hiberniae calendarium*, Irish Record Commission (1828) · Rec. Comm. calendars of memoranda rolls, NA Ire., RC8 · PRO, E 101 · *Adae Murimuth continuatio chronicarum. Robertus de Avesbury de gestis mirabilibus regis Edwardi tertii*, ed. E. M. Thompson, Rolls Series, 93 (1889) · J. B. Sheppard, ed., *Literae Cantuarienses: the letter books of the monastery of Christ Church, Canterbury*, 2, Rolls Series, 85 (1888) · R. Frame, *English lordship in Ireland, 1318–1361* (1982) · *The whole works of Sir James Ware concerning Ireland*, ed. and trans. W. Harris, 1 (1739), 332

St Pol, Mary de, countess of Pembroke (*c*.1304–1377), magnate and founder of Pembroke College, Cambridge, was the fourth daughter of Guy de Châtillon, count of St Pol (*d*. 1317), and of Mary of Brittany, granddaughter of Henry III. She had five sisters and two brothers, but nothing is known of her childhood. Both Philippe V of France and Edward II of England were involved in the negotiations for her marriage to Aymer de *Valence, earl of Pembroke, which took place in Paris on 5 July 1321; Mary entered London on 28 July. She was Aymer de Valence's second wife; his first wife, Béatrice de Clermont, died in 1320. No children were born of either marriage. The earl died suddenly in France on 23 June 1324 and Mary never remarried; in her will of 1377 she referred to her husband as 'her very dear lord' when she provided for commemorative masses at Westminster Abbey where he was buried.

After Aymer de Valence's death Mary suffered at the hands of the king and the Despensers. This may have been partly due to her husband's support of the Despensers' exile in 1321, but Mary's difficulties probably derived mainly from the lack of a direct heir, the younger Despenser's ambitions to build up his estates in south Wales, and Valence's financial problems. The king seized Valence's possessions, and refused to meet the payment of debts owed to the earl, while Mary and her fellow executor of Valence's will remained liable for the payment of debts due to the crown. Problems arose over the execution of Valence's inquisition *post mortem*. Mary had to relinquish certain wardships, and also her rights in Stamford and Grantham. Her dower was allocated in the winter and spring of 1324–5, with a valuation of about £700. There were further changes in her landholdings early in the reign of Edward III as a result of transactions with the crown and with her uncle, John, earl of Richmond.

Mary spent most of her widowhood in England, but it is likely that she was always regarded as French. In 1326 she

Mary de St Pol, countess of Pembroke (*c*.1304–1377), workshop of Jean Pucelle, *c*.1320 [kneeling, left, before St Cecilia]

was exempt from the royal order to arrest all people belonging to the dominion of the king of France, and she was again excepted when Edward III confiscated the lands of aliens in 1337. She had kindred ties with both the English and French kings, and seems to have been on good terms with Edward III; she was abroad on the king's business in 1331, and was in charge of his daughter Joan of Woodstock in 1337–8. She held lands in France in her own right as well as estates which had been held by her husband. Mary is known to have been in France in 1325, 1331–4, 1341, and 1352–7, but her French lands were confiscated by Charles V of France in 1372. Mary's attitude towards the Hundred Years' War was symbolized by her bequest in her will of a sword without a point to Charles V.

In England, Mary had residences at Anstey and La Mote in Cheshunt, Hertfordshire, Great Braxted in Essex, Fotheringhay, Northamptonshire, and London. She had her own chamber in the abbey at Denny, Cambridgeshire. She was well known for her piety, and her religious benefactions have much in common with those of her close friend Elizabeth de Burgh, Lady of Clare (*d*. 1360). Some of Mary's plans, such as that for a Carthusian foundation at Horne in Surrey in 1346, did not materialize. Her involvement with the Minoresses at Waterbeach, Cambridgeshire, dates from 1336 when she granted them the manor of Denny. Within three years she decided to transfer the nuns to Denny, but it was only in 1351 that Mary achieved her purpose. Mary received the royal licence to establish Pembroke College at Cambridge in 1347, and maintained her interest in the foundation throughout her life. The college statutes provided in detail for the organization of the college, and arrangements were made for the celebration of the anniversaries of Mary herself and her husband and parents. Mary's activities at Denny and in Cambridge show that she was both determined and authoritarian. Her will provided for bequests to other religious houses including the Minoresses at Bruisyard, Suffolk, and in London, and the Charterhouse at Hinton in Somerset. Provision was made for the poor. She bequeathed 100 marks to Edward III's Cistercian foundation of the abbey of St Mary Graces in London, and she asked the king as 'her gracious lord' to help her executors to carry out her will.

When James Nicholas of Denmark, who studied at Pembroke College, wrote his eulogy of Aymer de Valence, he described Mary in general terms as noble, wise, devout, and benevolent. Mary drew up her will on 20 February 1377, and added a codicil on 13 March; on that day she was at Braxted. She died on 16 or 17 March 1377; her will stipulated burial in the choir of the church at Denny, clothed in the habit of a Minoress. One of her books survives, a breviary written c.1320 in the Paris workshop of Jean Pucelle; it contains a conventional portrait of Mary kneeling before St Cecilia. Her dower lands reverted to Aymer de Valence's coheirs, who by the time of her death were John Hastings, earl of Pembroke, Gilbert Talbot, and the daughters of David, earl of Atholl, who both married into the Percy family.   JENNIFER C. WARD

Sources H. Jenkinson, 'Mary de Sancto Paulo, foundress of Pembroke College, Cambridge', *Archaeologia*, 66 (1915), 401–46 · J. R. S. Phillips, *Aymer de Valence, earl of Pembroke, 1307–1324: baronial politics in the reign of Edward II* (1972) · A. F. C. Bourdillon, *The order of Minoresses in England* (1926) · A. Du Chesne, *Histoire de la maison de Chastillon sur Marne* (1621) · *Chancery records* · W. Stubbs, ed., *Chronicles of the reigns of Edward I and Edward II*, 2 vols., Rolls Series, 76 (1882–3) · [T. Walsingham], *Chronicon Angliae, ab anno Domini 1328 usque ad annum 1388*, ed. E. M. Thompson, Rolls Series, 64 (1874) · *CEPR letters* · W. H. Bliss, ed., *Calendar of entries in the papal registers relating to Great Britain and Ireland: petitions to the pope* (1896) · Rymer, *Foedera* · Dugdale, *Monasticon*, new edn · *CPR, 1317–21*, 575 · *CIPM*, 6, no. 518; 14, no. 339
Archives CUL · LPL · Pembroke Cam. | PRO
Likenesses workshop of J. Pucelle, manuscript painting, c.1320, CUL, MS Dd.5.5 [*see illus.*]
Wealth at death £700, value of dower settlement in 1324–5

St Quintin, Sir William, second baronet (1661/2–1723), politician, was the second but eldest surviving son of William St Quintin of Harpham in the East Riding of Yorkshire (1632/3–1695) and his wife, Elizabeth (d. 1700), the youngest daughter of Sir William Strickland, bt, of Boynton, Yorkshire. In 1695 he was elected MP for the borough of Kingston upon Hull, which he served in eleven successive parliaments. In the following year he succeeded his grandfather Sir Henry St Quintin, becoming second baronet, of Harpham.

St Quintin was a commissioner of customs, with a salary of £1000 a year, from 22 November 1698 to 18 December 1701, when he resigned in obedience to an act banning holders of this office from sitting in parliament, preferring his seat to his salary. He was unsuccessfully challenged to a duel in March 1699 in a dispute at the committee of privileges over the Tamworth election, and on 24 December 1700 he was reported 'dangerously ill of a fever'. From April 1706 he was a commissioner of revenue

in Ireland, on the same salary as previously, until December 1710, when he was dismissed in the tory purge. As a supporter of the whigs, from 1714 to 1717 he held office again as a lord of the Treasury, but he resigned to follow Walpole into opposition. Evidently the break with the government was not irreconcilable, as he became a commissioner of the alienation office that July; on 16 June 1720 he was appointed to the lucrative office of joint vice-treasurer, receiver-general, and paymaster of Ireland, which he enjoyed until he died, unmarried, on 30 June 1723. He was buried in Harpham church. The loss of his abilities, probity, and patriotism was 'universally lamented'. A capable official, untouched by scandal, he was succeeded as baronet by his nephew Sir William, on whose son's death in 1795 the title became extinct.

TIMOTHY VENNING

Sources R. R. Sedgwick, 'St Quintin, Sir William', HoP, *Commons* · *VCH Yorkshire East Riding* · Venn, *Alum. Cant.* · *Dugdale's visitation of Yorkshire, with additions*, ed. J. W. Clay, 3 (1917) · T. Wotton, *The baronetage of England*, ed. E. Kimber and R. Johnson, 3 vols. (1771)
Wealth at death estate at Harpham, East Yorkshire

Saintsbury, George Edward Bateman (1845–1933), literary scholar and historian, was born in Lottery Hall, Southampton, on 23 October 1845, the second son (there were also two daughters) of George Saintsbury (d. 1860), then secretary and superintendent of Southampton docks, and his wife, Elizabeth Wright (d. 1877). His parents went to London, where, in 1850, his father became secretary of the East India and China Association. Saintsbury was educated at King's College School, London, and entered Merton College, Oxford, as a classical postmaster in 1863. He was awarded a first class in classical moderations (1865) and a second class in *literae humaniores* (1867). While at college his chief friend was Mandell Creighton. Having after several attempts failed to obtain a fellowship, he left Oxford in 1868, and on 2 June of that year married Emily Fenn King (d. 1924), daughter of Henry William King, surgeon, of Southampton; the couple had two sons.

Saintsbury became a schoolmaster, at first for a few months at Manchester grammar school and then as senior classical master at Elizabeth College, Guernsey (1868–74), where he read widely, especially in French literature, and sent his first reviews to *The Academy*. In 1874 he moved to Moray, Scotland, as headmaster of a new private foundation, the Elgin Educational Institute. It did not prosper, and he returned to London in 1876 to live by his pen, with a brief spell in 1877 on the staff of the *Manchester Guardian*.

Saintsbury's first essay of note, a signed article on Baudelaire, appeared in the *Fortnightly Review* (October 1875), and on the invitation of the editor, John Morley, it was followed in 1878 by eight essays on contemporary French novelists, reprinted as a volume in 1891. It was as a critic of French literature that he first made his name. He contributed over thirty articles on the subject to the ninth edition of the *Encyclopaedia Britannica* (1875–89; repr. as a separate volume, 1946) and wrote a *Primer* (1880) and a *Short History* (1881) of French literature. Together with his anthologies and further essays these provided the English reader with a sound factual introduction based on fresh

George Edward Bateman Saintsbury (1845–1933), by Walter Stoneman, 1919

and voluminous reading. His views often ran counter to the accepted verdicts of French critics.

Saintsbury was also hard at work in English literature, not just in reviewing but writing books and essays. His *Dryden* (1881), for the English Men of Letters series, was a much needed study of a favourite author; it was followed by an eighteen-volume reprint, with new introductions, of Sir Walter Scott's *Dryden*, which suffered through delays in publication (1881–93) and through using an unrevised text. By 1887, when Saintsbury's *History of Elizabethan Literature* was published, his main interests had turned from French literature to English, though he still oversaw, with his own critical introductions added, a forty-volume translation of Balzac (1895–8). From 1886 onward he contributed articles on English authors to *Macmillan's Magazine*; those which were collected in volumes of *Essays in English Literature, 1780–1860* (1890, 1895) and *Miscellaneous Essays* (1892) brought his name before a large reading public. In the 1880s and 1890s there was a flood of editions, anthologies, and selections, all with critical introductions which showed the breadth of his reading and the vigour of his opinions. He also contributed to most of the popular series of the time, including the short books *Marlborough* (for English Worthies, 1885), *Manchester* (for Historic Towns, 1887), and *Lord Derby* (for The Queen's Prime Ministers, 1892).

This great body of critical work had been exceeded in sheer bulk by Saintsbury's work as a journalist between 1876 and 1895. With Andrew Lang and Robert Louis Stevenson, he was a prominent contributor to *London* (1877–9) under W. E. Henley's editorship. He wrote for the *Pall Mall Gazette* while Morley remained its editor, and for the *St James's Gazette* and many other papers. His main work as a journalist, however, was on the *Saturday Review*, of which he was assistant editor from 1883 to 1894, when he left on a change of ownership. The independent toryism of the *Saturday Review* was never more vigorous than in the years when Saintsbury became a seasoned Fleet Street commentator. He made a speciality of the fight against Gladstone's Irish policy, and saved the paper from accepting Richard Pigott's forged 'Parnell letters', which duped *The Times* (G. E. B. Saintsbury, *Scrap Book*, 3, 1924, 274). 'In my twenty years of journalism', he wrote, 'I must have written the equivalent of at least a hundred volumes of the "Every Gentleman's Library" type—and probably more' (ibid., 1, 1922, x).

In September 1895 Saintsbury was able to withdraw from the precarious existence of a journalist and reviewer on appointment (in succession to David Masson) to the regius professorship of rhetoric and English literature at the University of Edinburgh. While obliged to face the disorder of a very large first-year 'ordinary' class, he could also take advantage of the small number of honours students to concentrate on substantial literary works. His influence grew steadily and he became a prominent figure in the university; the twenty years of his professorship form one of the most notable periods in the history of a famous chair.

Having conscientiously left off reviewing, Saintsbury's substantial books came out with notable rapidity. The *Short History of English Literature* (1898), wholly new in design and substance, was written in less than a year (and later revised to meet criticisms of detail). Thereafter he worked on *A History of Criticism and Literary Taste in Europe from the Earliest Texts to the Present Day* (3 vols., 1900–04), supplemented by *Loci critici* (1903), a collection of illustrative passages. Then came the three-volume *History of English Prosody from the Twelfth Century to the Present Day* (3 vols., 1906–10), with an illustrative *Historical Manual* (1910) and a natural but novel sequel in *A History of English Prose Rhythm* (1912). Before he was appointed to the chair he had planned a twelve-volume Periods of European Literature, and he contributed three volumes to the series: *The Flourishing of Romance and the Rise of Allegory* (1897), *The Earlier Renaissance* (1901), and *The Later Nineteenth Century* (1907). As well as writing or editing books on Scott (1897) and Arnold (1899), and *The English Novel* (1913), editions of the plays of Dryden (1904) and Shadwell (1912), a collection entitled *Minor Poets of the Caroline Period* (3 vols., 1905–21), and introductions to the *Oxford Thackeray* (17 vols., 1908), he delivered many major lectures to prominent learned societies. The main task of the later years of his professorship was his contribution of twenty-one chapters to the *Cambridge History of English Literature* (1907–16). When he retired from the chair in 1915, at the age of seventy, his unremitting energy had enabled him to accomplish much more than he had foreseen on his appointment. He signalled his retirement by writing *The Peace of the Augustans: a Survey of Eighteenth Century Literature as a Place of Rest and Refreshment* (1916), relaxed in manner and an antidote to wartime preoccupations, which long enjoyed popularity with a general readership.

On leaving Edinburgh, where he had resided at Murrayfield House (1896–1900) and 2 Eton Terrace (1900–15), Saintsbury sold up his cellar and much of his library and moved briefly to Southampton before settling at Bath in rooms at 1 Royal Crescent. A two-volume *History of the French Novel* (1917–19) was his last big book, but he continued industriously as an essayist. *Notes on a Cellar-Book* (1920), an allusive *causerie* on wine rather than a systematic treatise, brought him fame in gastronomic circles, and in 1931 a dining society, the Saintsbury Club, was founded in his honour. Three *Scrap Books* followed, in 1922–4, spicing his recollections (he forbade any biography of himself) with social and political observations. His strong and consistent conservatism, which in the first period of his journalism had necessarily been anonymous, showed itself unashamedly in his later general writings. His high-churchmanship, with a special reverence for Edward Pusey, was not much discussed, but he was a tory who gloried in the name and admitted that he would have opposed every great reform since 1832.

Saintsbury remained a voracious reader, and he could not abandon writing. 'The professor ceasing, the reviewer revives', he wrote in 1923. *A Letter Book* was published in 1922, and *Collected Essays and Papers* in 1923–4, in four volumes which presented only a selection from his total output. *A Consideration of Thackeray* (1931) gathered his writings on one of his most admired authors, and there were further *Prefaces and Essays* gathered (by Oliver Elton) in 1933, with *George Saintsbury: the Memorial Volume* (1945) and *A Last Vintage: Essays and Papers by George Saintsbury* (1950), both edited by his pupil Augustus Muir, adding to the many collections.

Saintsbury's long experience as a journalist gave him great facility in the composition even of learned commentary. His writing is generally vigorous and readable, but his literary output was too large for him to exercise full care with his prose style, which too easily became involved and densely allusive, or with factual details, where reviewers were ready to pounce. As a critic he was pre-eminently a 'taster', who said what it was he liked and why he liked it. He looked for the characteristic quality and found it in style rather than in form or substance. The true and only test of literary greatness, he said, was the *transport*, the absorption of the reader. Interested as he was in the lives of authors, as his many introductory memoirs show, his attention never strays from the primary importance of their works. His historical backgrounds are kept in their place as backgrounds; and he avoided a statement of any philosophy of literature. The *History of Criticism* is now seen to be weakened by its lack of a conceptual framework. As a historian of literature he had to deal with movements and tendencies, and here his remarkable knowledge made the task easy for him, and congenial. While never subordinating style to substance, he enjoyed tracing the fortunes of a literary form and showing the changes in its appeal to the reader. Yet even in his histories he is never better than when dealing with individual works or authors. He was the doyen of academic critics of his day, wide-ranging and with a gusto that had not been exceeded since Hazlitt.

In old age Saintsbury was much reverenced by the reading public as a sage, and he received many honours from his colleagues, including an address on his seventy-seventh birthday in 1922 from over 300 friends and admirers. He held several honorary doctorates and was elected a fellow of the British Academy in 1911. He appreciated above all his honorary fellowship (1911) of Merton College, Oxford. The college owns a characterful portrait of him (1923) by William Nicholson, which, with its skull-cap, large pondering brow, small spectacles, and long straggling beard, bespeaks the venerable savant. George Saintsbury died at his home in Royal Crescent, Bath, on 28 January 1933 and was buried in the old cemetery in Southampton, his birthplace.

ALAN BELL

Sources A. Blyth Webster, 'George Saintsbury', in *George Saintsbury: the memorial volume*, ed. A. Muir and others (1945), 23–64 • *A last vintage: essays and papers by George Saintsbury*, ed. A. Muir (1950) [incl. bibliography by W. M. Parker] • O. Elton, 'George Edward Bateman Saintsbury, 1845–1933', *PBA*, 19 (1933), 325–44 • *DNB* • D. Jones, *King of critics: George Saintsbury, 1845–1933* (1992) • J. Gross, *The rise and fall of the man of letters: aspects of English literary life since 1800* (1969) • H. Orel, *Victorian literary critics* (1984), 151–76 • b. cert. • m. cert. • d. cert.

Archives Merton Oxf., letters • NL Scot., corresp. and literary papers • NL Scot., account book • NRA, corresp. and literary papers | BL, corresp. with Macmillans, Add. MSS 55019–55020 • BL, letters to A. R. Waller, Add. MS 43681 • Bodl. Oxf., letters to Bertram Dobell • JRL, letters to W. E. Axon • LUL, letters to Austin Dobson and David Hannay • LUL, letters to Brenda E. Spender • Merton Oxf., letters to William Hunt and wife • NAM, letters to Earl Roberts • NL Scot., Blackwood MSS, MSS, letters • NL Scot., letters to D. N. Smith • Queen's University, Belfast, letters to Helen Waddell with anthology compiled for her • Royal Society of Literature, London, letters to the Royal Society of Literature • U. Edin. L., corresp. with Charles Sarolea • U. Leeds, Brotherton L., letters to Sir Edmund Gosse • UCL, letters to David Hannay

Likenesses W. Stoneman, photograph, 1919, NPG [*see illus.*] • W. Nicholson, oils, 1923, Merton Oxf.

Wealth at death £9655 19s. 5d.: resworn probate, 18 March 1933, *CGPLA Eng. & Wales*

St Victor, Achard of (*c*.1100–1171), abbot of St Victor and bishop of Avranches, was born in England and educated in France, as revealed in an early collection of Victorine epitaphs—'Huius oliva domus, Anglorum gloria cleri'—and in another, later, epitaph, which begins, 'Anglia me genuit, docuit me Gallia' (Bonnard, 1.204). He became an Augustinian canon at St Victor, Paris, probably in the lifetime of Master Hugh (*d*. 1141), the founder of the school of St Victor. As one of Hugh's successors in that school, Master Achard took part in the theological controversies of the 1150s, emerging as a sharp critic of Peter Lombard.

In 1155 Achard became abbot of St Victor: several letters and charters attest his financial vigilance and the practical support that he received from the English pope, Adrian IV (*r*. 1154–9). His election in 1157 to the see of Sées—which had an Augustinian chapter—was vetoed by

Henry II. But on 27 March 1161 Achard was consecrated bishop of Avranches, and in that capacity was on much improved terms with the king. He assisted at the baptism of Henry's daughter Eleanor in 1161, and at the translations of dukes Richard I and II of Normandy at Fécamp in 1162 and of Edward the Confessor at Westminster in 1163. As a diocesan bishop he was on good terms with his learned and active neighbour Arnulf, bishop of Lisieux (d. 1184). His later epitaph suggests that he had a good knowledge of canon law: 'legis doctorem tenuit illa' (namely Gallia). Achard died on 29 March 1171. He was a generous patron of Lucerne (in the diocese of Avranches), the Premonstratensian house in which his tomb and a fine, though damaged, contemporary effigy can still be seen.

Achard's two theological treatises, the *De Trinitate* and the *De discretione animae spiritus et mentis* (both ed. E. Martineau, 1987), probably belong to the 1140s or the early 1150s. They reflect the debates and use the terminology of contemporary Paris in a way that the work of Master Hugh does not; yet Achard is doctrinally conservative, and essentially unsympathetic to the drift towards organized secular schools and (within his lifetime) the University of Paris. His doctrinal position is further and usefully clarified in fifteen sermons (*Sermons inédits*, ed. J. Châtillon, Textes Philosophiques du Moyen Âge, 17, 1970), which presumably belong to his years as abbot and bishop.

Margaret Gibson, *rev.*

Sources Achard de St Victor, *De Trinitate*, ed. E. Martineau (1987) [incl. Fr. trans. of *De discretione animae spiritus et mentis*] · N. Häring, ed., 'Gilbert of Poitiers, author of the De discretione animae, spiritus et mentis, commonly attributed to Achard of Saint Victor', *Medieval Studies*, 22 (1960), 148–9 · Achard de St Victor, *Sermons inédits*, ed. J. Châtillon, Textes Philosophiques du Moyen Âge, 17 (1970) · F. Bonnard, *Histoire de l'Abbaye Royale et de l'ordre des Chanoines Réguliers de St-Victor de Paris*, 2 vols. (1907) · J. Châtillon, 'Théologie, spiritualité et métaphysique dans l'œuvre d'Achard de Saint-Victor', *Études de Philosophie Médiévale*, 58 (1969) · R. W. Hunt, 'English learning in the late twelfth century', *TRHS*, 4th ser., 19 (1936), 19–42

Likenesses effigy, repro. in Châtillon, 'Théologie', pl. 2

St Victor, Andrew of (c.1110–1175), biblical scholar and abbot of Wigmore, was born in England, but as a young man studied in Paris, where he became a canon of the Augustinian house of St Victor. There he explored the historical and literal sense of the Old Testament, in contrast to the allegorical exegesis of many of his contemporaries. He wrote commentaries, on the Heptateuch, Judges to 2 Chronicles, the wisdom literature, and the prophets. Several of these have now been published, in critical editions, in the Corpus Christianorum series. Among the Parisian masters Andrew was a pioneer in the serious study of the Hebrew text, available in bilingual form with a Latin interlinear translation. Although his linguistic command of Hebrew, spoken or written, was not extensive, he could communicate with contemporary Jewish scholars in French, learning much *viva voce*. Thus, in his own commentary, he was able to make apposite reference to Hebrew etymology and exegesis, and to Jewish tradition. In focusing so sharply on the literal meaning Andrew largely avoided the central issue for a Christian analyst of the Old Testament: in what ways was its interpretation affected by the life of Christ and the establishment of the Christian church? He was no theologian, neither a traditionalist maintaining the views of the fathers nor a scholastic systematizing a body of doctrine. Andrew remained a specialist within his own field.

In or after 1147 Andrew returned to England for a few troubled years as the first abbot of Wigmore, a daughter house of St Victor in Herefordshire. Although the Wigmore chronicle refers to him as prior of St Victor, he seems to have had no experience of monastic government, and showed no talent when the need arose. In 1154–5 he returned to his scholarly work in Paris. A few years later, however, he was recalled to Wigmore (1161–3), where he remained as abbot until his death on 19 October 1175 and where he was buried.

Andrew of St Victor was not a man of many pupils. Those whom he taught within St Victor provoked the criticism of a younger fellow canon, Richard, that they were 'judaizing'—that is, understanding the Old Testament primarily as Jews rather than as Christians. Andrew's own orthodoxy was never impugned. His greatest immediate influence was on another Anglo-Norman, Master Herbert of Bosham, a scholar of much greater linguistic competence but less of a historian. Andrew's commentaries remained available in Paris. They were used by the small group of masters who established the teaching credentials of the University of Paris, notably Stephen Langton. But it was the learned friars of the thirteenth century who discovered Andrew's work and used it extensively both in France and England. Andrew was a familiar author to Roger Bacon and to the circle of Robert Grosseteste.

Margaret Gibson, *rev.*

Sources B. Smalley, *The study of the Bible in the middle ages*, 3rd edn (1983) · F. Stegmüller, ed., *Repertorium biblicum medii aevi*, 11 vols. (Madrid, 1950?–1980), nos. 1295–1329 · *Adreae de Sancto Victore opera*, ed. C. Lohr and R. Berndt, 1 (1986) [other vols. pubd 1990–96 incl. Andrew's commentaries on the bks of Samuel and Kings, Wisdom literature, Ezechiel, and Daniel] · Dugdale, *Monasticon*, new edn, vol. 6

St Victor, Richard of (d. 1173?), theologian and prior of the abbey of St Victor at Paris, has been generally thought since the sixteenth century to have been a Scot. However, this must be regarded with reserve, for the earliest indications of his provenance suggest rather that he was English. The mid-thirteenth-century chronicle of Alberic of Trois-Fontaines describes him as 'English by nation' ('Chronica … a monacho novi monasterii Hoiensis interpolatum', 843). In conformity with, but hardly the origin of, this information is the nuance in a joint letter, probably to be dated 1166, of Ernisius, abbot of St Victor, and R. (Richard), prior of the same, to Robert de Melun, bishop of Hereford (d. 1167). The writers rejoice at Robert's promotion and the advantage thereby conferred on the English church, 'which, beyond the charity that we have towards all churches, we love with special affection, nature prompting [*natura suadente*]' (*Materials*, 5.457). While Ernisius's provenance is not otherwise directly known, his being English would be appropriate, in that he was one of two canons sent originally for the foundation of what became the abbey of Wigmore, Herefordshire, a daughter house of St Victor. Ernisius's being English might be enough to explain *natura suadente* but the consideration is presented as affecting both correspondents.

The consensus that Richard was a Scot was established severally by John Bale and by Jean de Toulouse, a seventeenth-century Victorine, whose life of Richard, based on several documents no longer available, is the major source of information. Jean de Toulouse presents two epitaphs on Richard, one in humanist Latin, ascribed to Jean Bordier, thirty-fourth abbot of St Victor, and another, by Guillaume de St Lô, twenty-second abbot, that he dates 1348. Jean de Toulouse's dating, 1531, of the later of these epitaphs may be correct for its engraving, but the epitaph itself is somewhat earlier since it is recorded by John Mair in his *Historia Maioris Britanniae* of 1521. Mair is Bale's source for Richard's provenance in both his edition of 1548 and that of 1557–9, which reproduces the later epitaph. This reads:

> Quem tellus genuit felici Scotica partu
> Te fovet in gremio Gallica terra suo
> (You [Richard] whom Scottish land brought forth in happy
>   birth
> Gallic soil fondles in its lap.)
> (*Patrologia Latina*, 196.xi–xii)

Though specific in its formulation, the later epitaph cannot be regarded as having a value on the point at issue independent of the first epitaph. This reads more simply:

> Scotus erat, devotus, magno temporis aevo
> Vixit canonicus
> (He was a Scot, devout: for a great period of time
> he lived a canon.)
> (ibid.)

The fourteenth-century Victorine perception of Richard as a Scot is confirmed—though not necessarily independently—by references to him in the *Memoriale historiarum* of Jean Bouin, a near contemporary of Guillaume de St Lô, as being *nacione Scotus* ('by nation a Scot') and as 'Magister Ricardus Scotus qui doctor subtilis et devotus fuit' ('Master Richard the Scot who was a teacher subtle and devout)'; Paris, Bibliothèque Nationale, MS Lat. 15011, fols. 380r, 384r).

It might be possible to reconcile these different indications by supposing that Richard's native place occasioned uncertainty as to how he described or regarded himself or was regarded by others. A plausible location would be the diocese of Carlisle, whose establishment was a point of contention between the bishop of Glasgow and the archbishop of York in the reign of Henry I. Carlisle was, moreover, unique among English cathedrals in having a chapter of Augustinian canons—the same rule as that of St Victor. Of the two provenances, however, the Scottish is the weaker. That the attestation is Victorine does not fully compensate for its relative lateness. Moreover, 'Scotus' could be mistakenly derived from 'sanctus' in abbreviation.

From the two epitaphs it has been deduced, uncertainly, that Richard became a canon in his youth and that he died relatively early. He entered St Victor under Gilduin, abbot

from 1113 to 1155. He refers to Hugh of St Victor (*d.* 1141) as 'the principal theologian of our time' (*Benjamin Maior*, book 1, chap. 4, *Patrologia Latina*, 196.67) though without specific indication that he had been his pupil. Richard himself is given the title of master: probably, but not certainly, his teaching was exclusively within St Victor. He was elected sub-prior by 1159, when he was party with Abbot Achard and Prior Nanterus to an agreement over tithes. In 1162 he succeeded Nanterus as prior, an office made difficult by the disordered rule of Ernisius, abbot from 1162 until his deposition in 1172. Richard's obituary was observed on 10 March and his death is deduced to have occurred on that date in 1173. The obit of his sister Matilda was observed on the same day.

Richard's works—over forty in all—may be broadly classified as exegetical and explanatory, as contemplative, and as theologically analytical. Within these three categories, the principal titles are listed below (the standard text remains that in *Patrologia Latina*, 196, unless otherwise noted).

Exegetical and explanatory works: 1 *Liber exceptionum*, ed. J. Châtillon (1958); plausibly dated 1153–9, and highly likely to have been written before 1162. 2 *In apocalypsim Joannis*. 3 *In visionem Ezechielis*. 4 *De Emmanuele*. 5 *Sermones centum*, *Patrologia Latina*, 177.901–1210; sermons 1–27 occur in series in book 10 of the second part of the *Liber exceptionum*, and sermons 28–30 and 88–90 in other books of the same; sermon 40 is datable to after 1153. 6 *Expositio difficultatum suborientium in expositione tabernaculi foederis*. 7 *Super exiit edictum*, ed. and trans. J. Châtillon, W. J. Tulloch, and J. Barthélemy, in *Richard de Saint-Victor, sermons et opuscules spirituels inédits: l'édit d'Alexandre ou les trois processions* (1951); internal reference may indicate that the work was written during the period of crisis under Ernisius.

Contemplative writings: 1 *De gratia contemplationis, seu, Benjamin maior*; perhaps written during the abbacy of Ernisius. 2 *De praeparatione animi ad contemplationem, liber dictus Benjamin minor*. 3 *Allegoriae tabernaculi foederis*. 4 *De quatuor gradibus violentae caritatis*, ed. G. Dumeige, in *Yves, Épître à Séverin sur la Charité: Richard de Saint-Victor, les quatre degrés de la violente charité* (1955). 5 *De eruditione interioris hominis*. 6 *Mysticae adnotationes in Psalmos*. 7 *In Cantica Canticorum*. 8 *De exterminatione mali et promotione boni*, after *Benjamin minor*, and probably datable to between 1159 and 1162.

Analytical theology: 1 *De Trinitate*, ed. J. Ribaillier (1958) and G. Salet (1959). 2 *De statu interioris hominis*, ed. J. Ribaillier, in *Archives d'histoire doctrinale et littéraire du moyen âge*, 42 (1967), 7–128; possibly written before 1159. 3 *De verbo incarnato*. 4 *De potestate ligandi et solvendi*, ed. J. Ribaillier, in *Richard de Saint-Victor, Opuscules théologiques* (1967), 77–110; written after *c*.1157 (the date of Peter Lombard's *Sentences*), and perhaps to be assigned to the years of Richard's priorate. 5 *De judiciaria potestate in finali et universali judicio*, ed. Ribaillier, 142–54. 6 *De spiritu blasphemiae*, 121–9. 7 *De tribus appropriatis personis in Trinitate*, 182–7.

There is evidence from the manuscript tradition that the last three treatises, along with the tract *De differentia peccati mortalis et venialis* (ed. Ribaillier, 291–3) and the minor exegetical *Declarationes nonnullarum difficultatum scripturae* (ed. Ribaillier, 201–14), were also works of Richard's priorate. Another short theological treatise, *Quomodo spiritus sanctus est amor Patris et Filii* (ed. Ribaillier, 164–6), dates from after *c.*1157. Of works formerly attributed to Richard *De gradibus caritatis* is inauthentic, while of *De superexcellenti baptismo Christi* only the prologue (*Patrologia Latina*, 196.1011–13A), which properly belongs with the minor exegetical *Adnotatio in psalmum 118*, is authentic.

With Hugh, by whose works, at least, he was much influenced, Richard typifies the school of St Victor. Three strands are incorporated in his work: the encyclopaedic tradition, represented principally in his *Liber exceptionum*, which also displays the historical interest prominent among the Victorines; the concern with a rationally argued theology epitomized in *De Trinitate*; and the profoundly mystical spirituality, characteristic of his theological writing in general but explicit and most specifically influential in *Benjamin Maior* and *Benjamin minor*. Many of his writings appear as having originated in spiritual discourses. Several were at the request of friends. At its best, his style charms.

As an exegete, Richard is less interesting than his fellow Victorine, Andrew (*d.* 1175), whom, in *De Emmanuele*, he criticizes for being unduly influenced by Jewish authorities. As a speculative theologian, a principal engine driving his thought, especially in his adventurous investigation of the mystery of the Holy Trinity, is the logic of 'necessary reasons'. With Richard, as with Anselm of Bec (*d.* 1109), from whom and the larger Augustinian tradition he inherited it, the concept had an overtly spiritual basis that helped to divert the hostility engendered by Peter Abelard's application of logic to theology. However, the web of affective and dialectical strands was already unravelling by the date of Richard's death, even in St Victor itself.

Largely no doubt because of this changing intellectual climate, Richard's influence, though important, is specialized. Within academic theology it affected deeply both a whole school and particular discussion beyond. It also contributed heavily to the intellectual foundations of late medieval mysticism. For the Franciscan school, both 'necessary reasons'—conceived as cogent argument at once underpinning and taking its cue from theological premises—and Richard's epistemology, which treated the created order as a world of signs pointing to the creator, had a potent dynamism. Alexander of Hales (*d.* 1245) and Bonaventure were variously and significantly indebted to him. When defining the relationship of scientific knowledge and faith, Bonaventure cites Augustine and Richard with undifferentiated respect. Particularly, Richard's concept of person as applied to Trinitarian doctrine had a wide influence, notably on Thomas Aquinas. Richard's dialectical theology was a source for Ramon Lull in the years round 1300. But chiefly important for mysticism were the two *Benjamins*, with their adaptation to an affective and voluntarist plane of the pseudo-Dionysian ascent and cloud of darkness as metaphors of the mystical quest.

It was Richard's repute as a contemplative that characterized him for Dante (*Paradiso*, canto 10, ll. 131–2). In England, the author of the late fourteenth-century *Cloud of Unknowing*, who rendered *Benjamin minor* into the vernacular, is a prime example of indebtedness. The continued appeal of Richard's writings into the early modern period is demonstrated by incunabula of *Benjamin minor* (Paris, 1489; Basel, 1494) and *Benjamin Maior* (Basel, 1494), and by an edition of his collected works at Venice in 1506. Between then and 1650 there were five other collected editions. MICHAEL HAREN

Sources Richardus S. Victori, *Patrologia Latina*, 196 (1855) · P. Scheffer-Boichorst, ed., 'Chronica Albrici monachi Triumfontium a monacho novi monasterii Hoiensis interpolatum', [*Chronica aevi Suevici*], ed. G. H. Pertz, MGH Scriptores [folio], 23 (Hanover, 1874), 631–950, 843, lines 44–7 · *Materials for the history of Thomas Becket, archbishop of Canterbury*, 5, ed. J. C. Robertson, Rolls Series, 67 (1881), 456–7 · J. Bouin, 'Memoriale historiarum', Bibliothèque Nationale, Paris, MS Lat. 15011, fols. 380r, 384r · A. Molinier, *Obituaires de la province de Sens* (1902), 1.546 · J. Châtillon, 'De Guillaume de Champeaux à Thomas Gallus', *Revue du Moyen Âge Latin*, 8 (1952), 247–82 · Richard de St Victor, *Liber exceptionum*, ed. J. Châtillon (Paris, 1958) · R. de St Victor, *Opuscules théologiques*, ed. J. Ribaillier (Paris, 1967) · Richard de St Victor, *De Trinitate: texte critique*, ed. J. Ribaillier (Paris, 1958) · Richard of St Victor, 'De statu interioris hominis', ed. J. Ribaillier, *Archives d'Histoire Doctrinale et Littéraire du Moyen Âge*, 34 (1967), 7–128 · J. Bale, *Illustrium Maioris Britanniæ scriptorum ... summarium* (1548), fol. 83v · Bale, *Cat.*, 2.211–13 · G. Teske, *Die Briefsammlungen des 12. Jahrhunderts in St Viktor / Paris: Entstehung, Überlieferung und Bedeutung für die Geschichte der Abtei* (1993) · J. Major [J. Mair], *Historia Maioris Britanniae tam Angliae quam Scotiae* (1521), 3.11, fol. 50r · J. C. Dickinson, *The origins of the Austin canons and their introduction into England* (1950)

St Vincent. For this title name *see* Jervis, John, earl of St Vincent (1735–1823).

Saker, Edward Sloman (1838–1883), actor and theatre manager, was born at 4 Waterloo Terrace, Bethnal Green, London, on 30 September 1838, one of several children of William Saker (*c.*1790–1849), a low comedian popular in London's minor theatres and later a tobacconist and newsvendor, and his wife, Eliza, *née* Hanbry. Having initially been articled to an architect, in 1857 he joined his elder sister and brother-in-law, Rosina Tyler and Robert H. Wyndham, at Edinburgh, where the latter had the lease of the Queen's Theatre and where Saker made lasting friendships with Henry Irving and Edward Sothern. His stage début, when he was twenty, was in the burlesque *Medea*. His first taste of management came when he undertook a three-week after-season at the Queen's in 1862. He harnessed the strength of the existing stock company and opened on 7 June with a triple bill including *The Lady of the Lake*. Among a remarkable range of productions, some starring the Irish comedian Gardiner Coyne, the highlight was the burlesque *Rob Roy*, advertised as 'klever, kuth, kean, komical, kwick, krotesque' (*Edinburgh Evening Courant*, 25 June 1862), in which Saker played Helen.

Saker went to Liverpool in 1864 as the principal low comedian at the Prince of Wales Theatre under the management of Alexander Henderson, to whom he had been recommended by Sothern. He achieved particular success there in F. C. Burnand's *Paris*, as Castor to the Pollux of Lionel Brough and with Henry Irving as Oenone. During a summer break the following year he went to Paris with Sothern to play in Tom Taylor's *Our American Cousin* at the Théâtre des Italiens.

In late 1868 Saker took over the lease of Liverpool's Alexandra Theatre in Lime Street, perhaps mistakenly 'built by the genteel for the genteel' (*Liverpool Courier*, 30 March 1883), where the two previous managers (one of them H. J. Byron) had failed, and where the pit had, unusually, been built above the stalls, which covered the whole ground floor, and there was an excess of boxes. In order to court a popular crowd at least as much as a more élite audience, Saker had the theatre adapted, reducing the stalls, creating a more conventional pit to seat 250, and providing an additional 'shilling' pit. He opened on 7 December with a stock company and his own production of *As You Like It*, in which he played Touchstone, and a farce, *His Last Legs*, in which the visiting Robert Wyndham starred.

In his years at the Alexandra, Saker provided a mixture of in-house productions, some of which were written specially for him, and shows by the leading companies on tour, including those of Charles Calvert (in which the young A. W. Pinero appeared), and Mrs John Wood. The theatre ranked 'as one of the city's cultural institutions comparable to the newly-built art gallery or the library' at a time when 'energetic cultivation of civic pride' was as necessary for a lessee as skilful house management and publicity (Jackson, 100–09). Especially notable were his pantomimes and, influenced by the productions of Charles Kean and Charles Calvert, his spectacular revivals of Shakespeare's plays. He rarely presented opera, evidently recognizing that this would not be to the taste of his more regular patrons.

On 16 February 1874 Saker married an actress whose stage name was Marie O'Berne (or O'Beirne). **Emily Mary Kate Saker** (1847–1912) was the daughter of John O'Brien, a printer, and became a comedian who could hold an 'irresistible sway over the gods and the elite' (*The Era*, 10 Feb 1912). After appearing in pantomime at the Theatre Royal, Hull, making her London début at the Court Theatre, and playing in May 1871 in H. J. Byron's *Daisy Farm* at the Olympic Theatre, she had joined Saker's Liverpool stock company in 1872. The pair appeared at the Alexandra for the first time after their marriage in Thomas Morton's farce *A Roland for an Oliver* on 2 March 1874. The couple, who 'had the entry to the best social circles in Liverpool' (*Daily Post*, 31 March 1883), had four sons and a daughter and were able to maintain a household staff of five, including a governess. A freemason and one of the founders of the Liverpool Dramatic Lodge, Saker otherwise preferred home life to any more 'promiscuous social intercourse' (*Liverpool Review*, 7 April 1883).

Described as an 'eccentric comedian', Saker was held to display a 'wonderful agility' in 'grotesque dances' and to have an inimitable power 'of mock conjuring and striking caricature' (*Daily Post*, 31 March 1883). Productions of original works were given 'as much care and completeness as

a London manager would bestow on a piece anticipated for a long run' (*Liverpool Review*, 7 April 1883).

Saker died at his home, 118 Bedford Street, Liverpool, on 29 March 1883 and was buried on 2 April in St James cemetery, Liverpool. His widow continued to run the Alexandra, albeit with a greater proportion of touring companies and less financial success than her husband, until April 1888, when Julia Neilson made her first appearance in Liverpool at her farewell benefit as Galatea in a production of *Pygmalion and Galatea* supervised by W. S. Gilbert. Marie Saker then returned to the London stage and later toured with Sir George Alexander's company. She died in London on 6 February 1912 and was buried at Chiswick.

Edward Saker's elder brother, **Horatio Saker** (1824/5–1861), also gained experience with the Wyndhams at Edinburgh before he and his wife, Ann, *née* Gamage, joined Charles Kean's company at the Princess's Theatre, London, in the early 1850s. They continued there under the management of Augustus Harris. Saker played a number of pantomime kings and such roles as Flute in *A Midsummer Night's Dream*, Launcelot Gobbo in *The Merchant of Venice*, and Pistol in *The Merry Wives of Windsor*, and appeared many times as one of the witches in *Macbeth*. He died at 23 Cardington Street, St Pancras, London, of smallpox on 3 April 1861.

C. M. P. TAYLOR

Sources J. C. Dibdin, *The annals of the Edinburgh stage* (1888) · R. J. Broadbent, *Annals of the Liverpool stage* (1908) · *Liverpool Courier* (30 March 1883) · *Liverpool Review* (7 April 1883) · *Liverpool Daily Post* (31 March 1883) · *The Times* (31 March 1883) · R. Jackson, 'Shakespeare in Liverpool: Edward Saker's revivals, 1876–81', *Theatre Notebook*, 32 (1978), 100–09 · M. G. Wilson, 'Edward Saker's revivals and Charles Kean: an addendum', *Theatre Notebook*, 34 (1980), 18–21 · *Edinburgh Evening Courant* (2 May 1862) [and following weeks] · *Daily Courier* [Liverpool] (2 Dec 1868) · *Daily Courier* [Liverpool] (17 Feb 1874) [notice of Saker's marriage] · playbills, London Princess's Theatre, 1853–60 · *The Era* (7 April 1861) [obit. of Horatio Saker] · *The Era* (10 Feb 1912) [obit. of Mrs Edward Saker (Marie O'Beirne)] · *The Era* (1 July 1849) [obit. of William Saker] · *Liverpool Citizen* (14 March 1888) · *Liverpool Citizen* (18 April 1888) · *Liverpool Citizen* (22 Aug 1888) · b. cert. [Edward Sloman Saker] · m. cert. [Edward Saker and Emily O'Brien] · m. cert. [Horatio Saker and Ann Gamage] · d. cert. [Horatio Saker]

Archives Liverpool Local History Collection, programmes and posters relating to the Alexandra Theatre

Likenesses J. E. Worrall, drawing, repro. in *Liverpool Town Crier album*, pl. 22, 23

Wealth at death £3504 3s. 3d.: resworn probate, Dec 1883, CGPLA Eng. & Wales

Saker, Emily Mary Kate (1847–1912). *See under* Saker, Edward Sloman (1838–1883).

Saker, Horatio (1824/5–1861). *See under* Saker, Edward Sloman (1838–1883).

Saki. *See* Munro, Hector Hugh (1870–1916).

Saklatvala, Shapurji (1874–1936), politician, was born in Bombay on 28 March 1874, the son of Dorabji Saklatvala, a merchant, and his wife, Jerbai Tata, a sister of J. N. Tata, the owner of India's largest commercial and industrial empire. The Saklatvala children were brought up alongside those of the Tatas, and they shared the same household. Both families were Parsi, and for many generations

Shapurji Saklatvala (1874–1936), by Bassano, 1922

his wife moved to London, where in 1907 he joined the Social Democratic Federation. Two years later he joined the Independent Labour Party (ILP), and it was through this organization that he became prominent in the labour movement.

For the first few years Saklatvala was little more than a passive supporter of socialist causes, but then the twin impacts of the First World War and the Russian Revolution galvanized him into activity. From 1916 onwards he was an active member of the ILP's City of London branch; on two occasions, in 1918 and 1919, he represented the branch at ILP national conferences. After the success of the Russian Revolution and the establishment of the Communist International, Saklatvala, along with others on the left in the ILP, began to agitate for the ILP to affiliate to the Communist International. Their efforts failed, and at the ILP national conference of March 1921 the delegates rejected affiliation. Following this defeat Saklatvala left the ILP and in June 1921 joined the newly formed Communist Party of Great Britain.

By then Saklatvala was a well-known figure in the labour movement, and in June 1921 he was adopted as the Labour parliamentary candidate for the London constituency of Battersea North. At the next two general elections Saklatvala, although a member of the Communist Party, was a nationally endorsed Labour Party parliamentary candidate. This was possible because, from 1920, the year of the Communist Party's formation, until 1924 there were no bans on communists being individual members of the Labour Party. At the general election of November 1922 Saklatvala won the seat for Labour, but he was defeated in the election of December 1923. During his short period as a Labour MP pressure was brought to bear on him to temper his revolutionary politics. Early in October 1924 the Labour Party annual conference passed a resolution expelling communists from the party. At the general election held later that month he stood as a Communist, supported by the Battersea Labour Party and Trades Council, and regained the seat. For most of his parliamentary career from 1924 to 1929 he was the sole Communist representative in parliament; in order to forge links between its parliamentary representative and the wider labour movement the Communist Party published some of his speeches as pamphlets. In 1925 his communist affiliations led to his being prevented from attending the Inter-Parliamentary Union Congress in Washington, DC, as the American secretary of state, F. B. Kellogg, revoked his visa. Following a May day speech which he delivered in Hyde Park, London, he was arrested at the start of the general strike (4 May 1926) and sentenced to two months' imprisonment for sedition.

In the House of Commons, Saklatvala constantly raised Indian issues and advocated Indian independence. He was a member of Annie Besant's Indian Home Rule League, founded in 1916. He was also a founder member in 1917 of the Workers' Welfare League; this was initially concerned with the working conditions of Indian seamen in London, but it widened its objectives to improve the position of all groups of Indian workers and was also the agent in Britain

had been Zoroastrians. Saklatvala attended St Xavier's School in Bombay, a private school run by Jesuit priests. At the age of nineteen he progressed to St Xavier's College, where he learned the art of public speaking and was one of the founders of the Gwalia Circle, a debating society.

In 1901, at the instigation of J. N. Tata, Saklatvala joined the family firm. The following year he led a prospecting expedition for iron and coal deposits in the jungles of Bihar and Orissa. The expedition's success led to the creation of Tata's iron and steel empire. Apart from his work for the company, Saklatvala also helped, in a voluntary capacity, during an outbreak of plague in Bombay in 1902. The prospecting work had taken its toll on his health and he suffered from malaria, so in 1905 he travelled to England to recuperate and to manage the Tata company's Manchester office. A further reason for his departure was a number of clashes with the British authorities in India, first during the search for minerals, and later over the administration of the plague relief work.

Saklatvala stayed first at the National Liberal Club in London, then convalesced at Matlock in Derbyshire, where he met Sarah Elizabeth Marsh (b. 1888), a waitress at the hydro where he was being treated. They married on 14 August 1907 and later had three sons and two daughters.

Saklatvala's political ideas began to develop in a socialist direction soon after his arrival in England. He rejected Liberalism, and during his stay in Matlock he attended meetings addressed by J. R. Clynes, one of the future leaders of the Labour Party. After his marriage Saklatvala and for the All-India Trade Union Congress. In January 1927 Saklatvala visited India, where he helped the nascent Indian communist movement and entered into a sustained dialogue with Gandhi about the direction of the independence movement. Back in England he was condemned by the Communist Party for having his children initiated at a Parsi ceremony in Caxton Hall, London; he accepted the censure but replied that it was a personal matter, done to meet the terms of a family trust. He was further criticized by the party for an overflattering speech which he made on the occasion of the retirement of the speaker of the House of Commons. Within the party he was one of the adherents, after 1928, with R. Palme Dutt and Harry Pollitt, of the 'class against class' position that denounced the Labour Party as reformist and held the Communist Party to be the only anti-capitalist party.

Saklatvala's period as a Communist MP came to an end at the general election of 1929, when he lost his seat. Battersea Labour Party and Trades Council, the focus of his support, was now virtually defunct, having been disaffiliated in 1926 for refusing to expel communists, and had been replaced by a new official Battersea Labour Party, whose candidate defeated him. Saklatvala was also resoundingly defeated at the Glasgow Shettleston by-election in June 1930, and he was unsuccessful again at Battersea in the October 1931 general election when his percentage of the poll dropped to 9 per cent and he lost his deposit. At the general election of 1935, in line with the Communist Party's united-front approach, he urged his supporters in the area to vote Labour.

Out of parliament Saklatvala remained prominent in the Communist Party. He was a popular speaker and addressed meetings throughout the country, and he was particularly active in the campaigns on behalf of the Meerut prisoners and the Scottsboro boys. In 1934 he visited the USSR and toured extensively in the Soviet Far Eastern republics, which he compared very favourably with India. During this trip he suffered his first heart attack. On his return he continued to speak at large indoor and outdoor rallies, and he was still addressing meetings up to a few days before his death. He died from a second heart attack at his home, 2 St Albans Villas, Highgate Road, London, on 16 January 1936, and was buried in the Parsi burial-ground, Brookwood, Surrey, on 21 January. He was survived by his wife. MIKE SQUIRES

Sources M. Squires, *Saklatvala: a political biography* (1990) · M. Squires, 'The life and influence of Shapurji Saklatvala', PhD diss., U. Leeds, 1987 · *DLB* · *DNB* · S. Saklatvala, *The fifth commandment: a biography of Shapurji Saklatvala* (1991)
Archives BL OIOC, corresp. and papers; unpublished biography, MS Eur. D 1173 | People's History Museum, Manchester, Communist Party archive | FILM BFI NFTVA, documentary footage
Likenesses Bassano, photograph, 1922, NPG [*see illus.*]

Sala, George Augustus (1828–1895), journalist, was born George Augustus Henry Fairfield Sala at 12 New Street, Dorset Square, London, on 24 November 1828, the youngest child of Henrietta Catherina Florentina Sala, *née* Simon (1789?–1860), a native of Demerara. His natural father was almost certainly Captain Charles Fairfield, who

George Augustus Sala (1828–1895), by Walery, pubd 1891

stood as his godfather assuming the forename Henry. Fairfield left the army and married in 1830; he inherited a life interest in his wife's estate in co. Kerry after her death. Sala's legal father, Augustus John James Sala (1792–1829), a dancing-master of Italian descent, died less than nine months after George's birth. Before and after her husband's death Henrietta Sala made a precarious living as a singer, singing teacher, and actress. From the age of twenty-one Sala ceased to use the names Henry and Fairfield, perhaps because his mother then told him who his father was.

Sala spent a year (1839–40) at a school in Paris, the Pension Hénon, where Dumas *fils* was a fellow pupil, then, after an interval, another year at a Pestalozzian school, Bolton House, in Turnham Green, Middlesex (1842–3). At fifteen he was briefly apprenticed to a painter of miniatures, Carl Schiller. He devoted himself to art for the next seven years, working as an assistant theatrical scene-painter and drawing illustrations for magazines and books, including Albert Smith's and Angus Reach's monthly *The Man in the Moon*, and several of Smith's shilling illustrated books. After learning to etch and engrave, he produced a number of comic illustrated guidebooks and panoramas for Adolphus Ackermann, the leading publisher of such works. Several of these, including *The House that Paxton Built* (1851), carried what was to become his familiar *nom de plume*, G. A. S., a household name.

Sala made his first significant foray into literary journalism in 1848–9, writing for *Chat*, a halfpenny weekly, which he later edited. But his real success began with the appearance of his article 'The key of the street' in *Household Words* on 6 September 1851. He quickly became one of the journal's most prolific and valued contributors, 'Dickens's young men' as they were called, his work being highly admired by Thackeray as well as Dickens. From an income seldom above £1 a week he rose to the affluence of £5 a week and set about establishing a reputation for drunkenness, quarrelsomeness, and financial and professional unreliability, which he never completely lost. In 1856, at Sala's own suggestion, Dickens removed him from bohemian temptations by sending him to Russia. This was the first of his many assignments as a 'special correspondent', a guise in which he later became famous. But Dickens considered the experiment costly and unsatisfactory, and a quarrel ensued after Sala's return as his Russian articles, 'A journey due north', belatedly trickled in. Although peace was later restored and he again became a prominent contributor to *Household Words*, and its successor, *All the Year Round*, his subsequent success owed little to Dickens. It was his friend and creditor Edmund Yates who introduced him to Edward Levy, one of the proprietors of the fledgeling *Daily Telegraph*, for which he wrote from June 1857 until just before his death; he became its best-known leader writer and special correspondent, the most readily identifiable of the 'young lions' ironically acclaimed by Matthew Arnold in *Friendship's Garland*. Earlier he had worked with Yates on Henry Vizetelly's *Illustrated Times*. Yates's column in that paper, 'The lounger at the clubs', no doubt helped give him the idea for 'Echoes of the Week', the column that he contributed, off and on, to the *Illustrated London News*, and later to the *Sunday Times*, from June 1860 until the year of his death, and which made his signature, G. A. S.

During his first years with the *Daily Telegraph*, Sala's best journalistic sketches (later published as *Twice Round the Clock*, 1859) appeared in Vizetelly's (later John Maxwell's) weekly, *The Welcome Guest*. Of the many other collections of his contributions to weeklies and monthlies, and special correspondent's reports from abroad, *My Diary in America in the midst of War* (1865), reprinted from the *Daily Telegraph*; *William Hogarth: Painter, Engraver, and Philosopher* (1866), reprinted from *Cornhill Magazine*; and *Paris herself Again in 1878–9* (1879), remain useful reference works. Besides taking him constantly to western Europe, Sala's journalistic duties entailed three visits to America and Russia, one to north Africa, and one to Australia. He was the first editor of *Temple Bar* (1860–63); he also edited *Banter* (1867–8) and *Sala's Magazine* (1892–3), neither of which succeeded. His five novels, although he belittled them himself and left one, *Quite Alone* (1864), to be completed by another writer (Andrew Halliday), retain some curiosity value as clever, though too self-indulgent, pastiches of Balzac. *The Seven Sons of Mammon* (1862) and *Margaret Forster* (1897), which was originally to have been written in collaboration with M. E. Braddon, are the most interesting. He was a friend of A. C. Swinburne, whose taste for flagellation he shared, and was part author of a pornographic tale, *The Mysteries of Verbena House* (1882).

Sala claimed that at the peak of his career his income never dropped below £2000 a year, but his bohemian improvidence precipitated frequent financial crises, some ending in bankruptcy or the forced sale of his possessions. He was imprisoned for debt in December 1858, but years later successfully sued James Hain Friswell for libel for stating that he had been. On several occasions he had to stoop to such hack work as writing commercial pamphlets in order to make ends meet. His monetary woes culminated in the last year of his life, when he was granted a civil-list pension of £100 a year. The flamboyance and disorder of Sala's life are reflected in his literary style, which never lost the exaggerated 'lightness and brightness' enjoined upon contributors to *Household Words*. Whatever the ostensible subject, most of his writing is about himself. His two avowedly autobiographical works, *Things I have Seen and People I have Known* (1894), and *The Life and Adventures of George Augustus Sala* (1895), are notably unreliable.

Sala's first wife, Harriett Elizabeth, *née* Hollingsworth, whom he married in 1859 (perhaps without benefit of clergy), died in Melbourne in December 1885 during one of his journalistic trips. He married his second wife, Bessie, daughter of Robert Stannard, who survived him, in 1890. He had no children. He was received into the Roman Catholic church in the month before his death, which occurred at 59 Norton Road, Hove, on 8 December 1895; he was buried on 12 December in Hove cemetery.

P. D. EDWARDS

Sources *The life and adventures of George Augustus Sala*, 2 vols. (1895) · P. D. Edwards, *Dickens's 'young men'* (1997) · R. Straus, *Sala: the portrait of an eminent Victorian* (1942) · F. Bywater, 'George Augustus Sala, 1828–1895' [paper presented to members of the Dickens Fellowship, 22 Feb 1990] · *Letters of George Augustus Sala to Edmund Yates in the Edmund Yates papers, University of Queensland library*, ed. J. McKenzie (1993)
Archives Hove Central Library, Sussex, commonplace book and notebook · Hunt. L., letters; literary MSS · Ransom HRC, papers · U. Leeds, Brotherton L., letter collection · Yale U., Beinecke L., papers | BL, letters to Royal Literary Fund, Loan 96 · Hove Central Library, Sussex, letters to Viscount Wolseley and Lady Wolseley · NL Scot., corresp. with Lord Rosebery · University of Queensland, Brisbane, Edmund Yates MSS
Likenesses photograph, 1850–55, NPG · Walery, photograph, pubd 1891, NPG [*see illus.*] · P. Vernay, ink drawing, 1894, NPG · Ape [C. Pellegrini], chromolithograph caricature, NPG; repro. in *VF* (25 Sept 1875) · H. Furniss, caricature, pen-and-ink sketch, NPG · S. P. Hall, two pencil drawings, NPG · P. Naumann and R. Taylor & Co., group portrait, wood-engraving (*Our literary contributors–past and present*), NPG; repro. in *ILN* (14 May 1892) · D. J. Pound, stipple and line engraving (after photograph by J. & C. Watkins), NPG · J. & C. Watkins, two cartes-de-visite, NPG · photograph, NPG · prints, NPG

Salaberry, Charles Michel de. *See* D'Irumberry de Salaberry, Charles-Michel (1778–1829).

Salam, Muhammad Abdus (1926–1996), theoretical physicist, was born on 29 January 1926 in Santokdas in the district of Sahiwal in the western Punjab, India (later Pakistan), the eldest of nine children of Muhammad Hussain (1891–1969), an educational official in the small market town of Jhang, and his second wife, Hajira Nabi Baksh

(1903–1977). Muhammad Hussain had high expectations of his eldest son. It is reported that he had a vision, when Hajira Begum was expecting her first child, that the child would be a son, who would bring glory to God by his intellectual prowess. He decided to name the child Abdus Salam ('servant of peace'). Salam added Muhammad in later life to make his name more distinctive and to emphasize his Muslim credentials. The young Salam certainly lived up to these high expectations. Growing up in Jhang, a hundred miles west of Lahore, he became a local celebrity when he was placed first in the whole Punjab in the matriculation examination. There is still extant a remarkable photograph of him in traditional Punjabi costume which appeared at this time in the local newspaper (reprinted in *TWAS Newsletter*, October–December 1996).

Salam was interested in science and mathematics from an early age. He recalled that his teacher in Jhang, telling the class about the forces of nature, had said that gravity was everywhere, even in Jhang, but that electricity had only reached Lahore, while the nuclear force lived only in Europe, so they should not worry about it—advice Salam certainly did not take! But he had much broader interests too. He was a fine literary scholar, and remained throughout his life a lover of poetry in several languages, including Persian, Punjabi, and English.

Cambridge, Princeton, and Lahore In 1946 Salam won a special scholarship to Cambridge, in remarkably fortuitous circumstances. The head of the Punjab government had some funds remaining that had been collected to aid the war effort, and had determined to use them to provide scholarships for overseas study, aimed specifically at the sons of small farmers. As it happened, Salam's father had acquired a small piece of land, making him eligible for the scheme. Moreover, at the last minute, Salam heard from St John's College, Cambridge, that another student had withdrawn, making it possible for him to take up his place immediately. The scheme was later cancelled, but leaving

Salam as the sole beneficiary, a piece of good fortune that he saw as a special gift of Allah.

In Cambridge, Salam first took a first in the mathematics tripos in two years and added a first in natural sciences in his third year; he found this particularly demanding because of his lack of previous experience of experimental work. After graduating he returned to his home in Pakistan, where, on 4 August 1949, he married his cousin, Amtul Hafeez Hussain (b. 1927). There were three daughters and a son of the marriage. He obtained an extension of his scholarship to allow him to do some postgraduate work, but since it was insufficient to support a wife he had to return alone to Cambridge. Initially he joined the Cavendish Laboratory and worked under Samuel Devons, but he rapidly came to the conclusion that experimental work was not for him. He then turned to Nicholas Kemmer, who suggested that he work with another student, Paul Matthews, who was just then completing a PhD thesis on renormalization theory. Recently developed by Julian Schwinger, Sin-Itiro Tomonaga, and Richard Feynman, this was a way round the long-standing problem of infinities in quantum electrodynamics (QED): any attempt to go beyond the lowest order of approximation had previously yielded nonsensical infinite answers, and renormalization theory provided a way of eliminating these infinities and extracting finite and meaningful answers. Matthews had been trying to extend these ideas to meson theory, then thought to describe the strong nuclear forces. He suggested to Salam that he try to fill in a gap in the proof by Freeman Dyson that renormalization works, and was amazed at the speed with which Salam returned with a complete answer. This was the beginning of a long and fruitful collaboration and close friendship between Matthews and Salam.

Following a very productive year with Matthews in Princeton, USA, Salam returned to Pakistan as professor of mathematics at both Government College and the University of Lahore. He wanted to continue his research while at

Muhammad Abdus Salam (1926–1996), by Ball, 1979

the same contributing to the development of his country, but he found poor facilities and no encouragement to do research. Finally in 1954 he decided to return to Cambridge as a lecturer and fellow of St John's. Another reason for his departure was the growing and violent antagonism towards the Ahmadiyya sect of Islam, to which he belonged. This sect, founded in 1889 by Mirza Ghulam Ahmad, who declared himself the Madhi, the rightful successor to Muhammad, was regarded by many orthodox Muslims as heretical.

Imperial College and Trieste Two years later Salam was offered the chair of theoretical physics at Imperial College, London (in succession to Hyman Levy). He arranged that Matthews join him as a reader. Together they built at the college one of the best theoretical physics groups anywhere. Salam was already famous for his work on renormalization, and in 1959 he was elected as the youngest fellow of the Royal Society, at the age of thirty-two. Initially the group was part of the mathematics department, but in 1960 Patrick Blackett persuaded Salam to move into the rapidly expanding physics department which had the advantages of a fine new building and easy interaction with experimenters.

Salam continued his close connections with Pakistan. In 1961 he was appointed scientific adviser by President Ayub Khan. He believed very strongly in the central importance of science and technology in development, and set about implementing these ideas, instituting laboratories for nuclear and space research, and research institutes for wheat and rice. He also tried to tackle the problem of waterlogging and salinity caused by irrigation, but the recommended solutions were never fully implemented. In 1974 Salam resigned in protest when, under Zulfikar Ali Bhutto, the Ahmadiyya were officially declared non-Muslim and deprived of civil rights. Nevertheless, though living mainly in Britain and Italy, Salam retained his Pakistani nationality throughout his life.

Salam deeply regretted having to leave his native country to pursue his chosen career, and determined to do what he could to help others faced with a similar dilemma. His opportunity came when he was appointed to represent Pakistan on the general council of the International Atomic Energy Agency (IAEA). He conceived the idea of an international centre with which scientists from developing countries could be associated, while retaining their links with their own countries. More or less single-handed, and against the opposition of most of the major powers, he persuaded the IAEA to back the idea, provided funds could be found from elsewhere. He found a suitable home for the centre in the city of Trieste, then seeking a new role after being separated from its natural hinterland by the post-war division of Europe. The International Centre for Theoretical Physics (ICTP) received generous backing from the Italian government and the city of Trieste, and was formally inaugurated in 1964; it moved to a new building on the outskirts of the city in 1968. Increasingly from then on, Salam came to spend more of his time in Trieste, though he retained his part-time professorship at Imperial College until his retirement in 1994.

Despite considerable initial scepticism in the scientific community, the ICTP was a great success, providing a lifeline for many thousands of scientists from developing countries. It was soon recognized as a world-class institute. It gradually broadened its scope, from high-energy physics to mathematics, materials science, and much else, and it organized workshops on more environmental topics such as soil science and oceanography. Similar institutes were set up in other subjects in several different countries. In 1997 it was formally renamed the Abdus Salam International Centre for Theoretical Physics.

Salam married twice. His second wife, whom he married on 11 November 1967, was Louise Napier Johnson (b. 1940), then a demonstrator in the zoology department of Oxford University, and later the David Phillips professor of molecular biophysics and a professorial fellow of Corpus Christi College, Oxford. There was one son and one daughter of the marriage.

Salam's research The basic aim of Salam's research was to find the theories describing the interactions of matter at the most fundamental level. By the early 1950s quantum electrodynamics had provided an excellent and increasingly well-verified theory of electromagnetic forces, and the search was on for similar theories of the strong nuclear forces that bind protons and neutrons in atomic nuclei, and of the weak forces responsible for the beta decay of radioactive nuclei.

Two main themes of Salam's work were symmetries and unification. As more and more fundamental particles were discovered, physicists tried to bring some order into the subject by grouping them together into multiplets related by various symmetries. For example, so far as the strong interactions are concerned, protons and neutrons behave similarly, and it seems reasonable to regard them as two different states of a particle termed the nucleon. The symmetry between the two (isospin symmetry) is not exact, because protons and neutrons do behave differently in regard to electromagnetism, since the proton has an electric charge while the neutron does not. Gradually, other approximate symmetries were discovered, which laid the foundations for the later formulation of the theory of the strong forces, quantum chromodynamics (QCD).

Salam played a significant role in this work, but his major contribution in the 1960s was in unification. He saw the newly discovered approximate symmetries not so much as important in themselves, but rather as clues to the structure of the underlying theory. From a very early stage he was convinced that the solution was to be found in a gauge theory. In gauge field theories, particle interactions are related in a special and intimate way to the basic symmetries. The best-known gauge example is quantum electrodynamics, but in a paper published in the *Physical Review* in 1954, Yang and Mills proposed a similar theory, based on isospin symmetry, as a possible theory of strong forces. Essentially the same theory was proposed independently by a student of Salam's, Ronald Shaw, though his work was published only as a Cambridge University PhD thesis.

The main focus of Salam's interest was on the weak forces. Over a decade, from the late 1950s, especially with his collaborator John Ward, Salam sought a theory that would describe them and, more ambitiously, a unified theory of weak and electromagnetic forces. There were serious obstacles to be overcome. Superficially, there are big differences between the two. In most field theories, forces between pairs of particles can be understood in terms of the exchange of other particles between them; in quantum electrodynamics these exchanged particles are photons, which have zero rest-mass. However, the weakness and very short range of the weak interactions show that in that case the exchanged particles (called W bosons) must be heavy, which is unnatural in a gauge theory. Another mysterious aspect of the weak interactions is parity non-conservation, or violation of mirror symmetry, first suggested by Lee and Yang in the *Physical Review* in 1956 and discovered experimentally by Wu and others the following year. How, then, could the theory be unified with QED, in which parity is strictly conserved?

It took more than ten years to solve these problems. To understand the large mass of the W particle, the key idea was 'spontaneous symmetry breaking', as first suggested in the context of the mass of the photon in a plasma by Philip Anderson, writing in the *Physical Review* in 1963. The resolution of the parity problem came only with the realization that another type of exchanged particle, besides the W, was needed, the Z boson, a suggestion that came from Sheldon Glashow writing in *Nuclear Physics* in 1961. But it still took several more years to put these two ideas together into a viable unified theory, which Salam called the 'electroweak' theory. It was first written down by Steven Weinberg (in *Physical Review Letters*, in 1967), and independently by Salam (in *Elementary Particle Theory*, edited by N. Svartholm, and published in Stockholm in 1968). The theory was triumphantly vindicated a few years later by the observation of Z-mediated interactions at the Conseil Européen de Recherches Nucléaires laboratory in Geneva. For this work, Glashow, Salam, and Weinberg shared the 1979 Nobel prize for physics.

The success of the electroweak unification encouraged many people to try to extend these ideas to incorporate other interactions. Writing in the *Physical Review, D (Particles and Fields)* for 1973, Salam, with Jogesh Pati, proposed one of the first grand unified theories, unifying strong, electromagnetic, and weak interactions. This theory made the very remarkable prediction that the proton is unstable. Whether this is true or not was still, at the end of the twentieth century, not known. Salam was also, writing in *Nuclear Physics, B (Particle Physics)* for 1974, with John Strathdee, one of early advocates of supersymmetry, which allows the unification of very different types of particles.

Science and technology in developing countries Salam was a passionate advocate of the importance of science and technology in development. He argued that only by building up an indigenous science base could the balance between the rich North and the poor South start to be addressed. As scientific adviser in Pakistan he pressed for 1 per cent of the gross national product to be devoted to this aim. He hoped to achieve the same kind of advance that was seen in Japan at the time of the Meiji restoration. But he failed to persuade his government to devote to science and technology anything approaching this figure. When he won the Nobel prize, President Zia ul Haq invited him to visit Pakistan, and awarded him the country's highest honour, the order of Nishan-e-Imtiaz. Salam then offered to donate his Nobel prize money of $66,000 to a fund to provide scholarships for young Pakistanis to study abroad, provided that the government itself would allocate $1 million to the fund. He was again disappointed by the meagre response, and in the end set up a fund independent of the government.

Salam was also very active on a wider international front. The award of the Nobel prize gave him enormous prestige throughout the developing world, particularly in Islamic countries—he was the first Muslim to win one of the science prizes. He received many honours and took every opportunity to argue the case for science in the 'third world', in particular urging on his co-religionists a return to the spirit of free enquiry that marked the golden age of Islamic science, when for 500 years the Arabs had led the world. He was fond of telling the story of Michael the Scot, who travelled to Spain in 1217 to study at the great Arab universities of Toledo and Córdoba and who translated Aristotle's works into Latin from Arabic texts. Salam wanted to perform a similar task in reverse, trying to inspire the Islamic world with the value of new knowledge and new ways of thinking.

One result of Salam's endeavours was the founding in 1981 of the Islamic Science Foundation, though with a much smaller budget than he would have liked. He was also the moving spirit behind the formation of the Third World Academy in 1983, with its base in Trieste and Salam as its first president. This was both active and influential, through its fellowship and associateship programmes, research grants, and prizes.

Later years In the mid-1980s Salam developed a degenerative neurological disorder, somewhat similar to Parkinson's disease, which made his life increasingly difficult. It was eventually diagnosed as progressive supranuclear palsy. Despite this affliction he remained cheerful and continued to travel and to work for as long as he could. Characteristically he branched out into new fields of research, writing papers on a new theory of high-temperature superconductivity with S. Randjbar-Daemi and J. Strathdee in *Nuclear Physics, B (Particle Physics)* in 1990, and on the problem of the origin of chirality in biology in the *Journal of Molecular Evolution* in 1991.

Towards the end of his life Salam was confined to a wheelchair, and he found communication difficult. He gave up the post of director of the ICTP in 1994, becoming instead its first president. In the same year he retired from his chair at Imperial College. He died peacefully at his home in Oxford on 21 November 1996, at the age of seventy. He was buried on 25 November at Rabwah in Pakistan, the traditional centre of the Ahmadiyya community.

The last prayers for him were attended by 35,000 people. Both his wives survived him, as did his six children.

Salam was a recipient of many honours, including the Atoms for Peace award (1968), the Nishan-e-Imtiaz (1979), an honorary KBE award (1989), membership of twenty-four academies, forty-five honorary doctorates from twenty-eight countries, the first Edinburgh medal and prize (1989), the Cataluña international prize (1990), and the Royal Society's premier award, the Copley medal (1990). He was scientific secretary of the Geneva conferences on the peaceful uses of atomic energy in 1955 and 1958, chairman of the United Nations advisory committee on science and technology in 1971–2 and of the UNESCO advisory panel on science, technology, and society in 1981, and a member of the South Commission. He was a warm and generous man, and an inspiration to many aspiring scientists throughout the world.   T. W. B. KIBBLE

Sources T. W. B. Kibble, *Memoirs FRS*, 44 (1998), 385–401 · J. Singh, *Abdus Salam: a biography* (1992) · C. H. Lai and A. Kidwai, eds., *Ideals and realities: selected essays of Abdus Salam* (1989) · *The Guardian* (22 Nov 1996) · *The Independent* (29 Nov 1996) · *Physics World* (Jan 1997) · *CERN Courier* (Jan/Feb 1997) · *News International* (24 Jan 1997) · *Daily Jang* (23 Feb 1997) [in Urdu] · *News* [Lahore] (26 Nov 1996) · P. Goddard, *The Eagle* (1997), 77–85 · *SUFI*, no. 33 (spring 1997) · *Daily Telegraph* (2 Dec 1996) · A. Ghani, *Abdus Salam* (1982) · *TWAS Newsletter* [newsletter of the Third World Academy of Sciences] (Oct–Nov 1996) · A. J. Roy, ed., *The Physicist, Bulletin of the Bangladesh Physical Society*, 17/1 (March 1997) · F. J. Dyson, 'Abdus Salam, 1926–1996', *Biographical Memoirs of the American Philosophical Society* · M. Kamran, 'Abdus Salam—soldier of science', *The Concept* [Islamabad] (April 1994), 9–38 · A. Ali and others, eds., *Selected papers of Abdus Salam* (1994) [incl. commentary] · *WWW* · private information (2004) [family]

Archives Abdus Salam International Centre for Theoretical Physics, Trieste, Italy · ICL

Likenesses photograph, 1961, ICL · photograph, 1978, RS; repro. in Kibble, *Memoirs FRS* · Ball, photograph, 1979, Hult. Arch. [see *illus.*] · N. Jackson, photograph, c.1979, ICL, Blackett Laboratory · Jorgethy, oils, c.1980, Abdus Salam International Centre for Theoretical Physics, Trieste, Italy · photograph, c.1980, priv. coll.; copies, priv. coll. · oils, c.1985, ICL · A. Buckley & Constantine, photograph, 1987, Abdus Salam International Centre for Theoretical Physics, Trieste, Italy · photograph, 1991, Abdus Salam International Centre for Theoretical Physics, Trieste, Italy · Gulgee, chalk on board, 1994, Abdus Salam International Centre for Theoretical Physics, Trieste, Italy · N. D. Vuong, oils, c.1997, Abdus Salam International Centre for Theoretical Physics, Trieste, Italy

Wealth at death £235,977: probate, 20 March 1997, *CGPLA Eng. & Wales*

Salaman, Charles Kensington (1814–1901), composer, was born on 3 March 1814 at 11 Charing Cross, London, the eldest son in the family of fourteen children of Simeon Kensington Salaman, from a Jewish family of German and Dutch origin, and his wife, Alice, an amateur pianist, the daughter of Henri Cowen. Julia *Goodman, the painter, was his eldest sister. Another sister, Rachel, married Sir John Simon, and a third, Kate (1821–1856), was a miniature painter, and exhibited at the Royal Academy. Salaman was educated privately, and had his first piano lessons from his mother. In 1824 he was awarded second place in the competition for admission to the new Royal Academy of Music, but decided to study the piano independently, first with Stephen Francis Rimbault and then, from 1826 to

1831, with Charles Neate, a friend of Beethoven. At Neate's house he met many distinguished musicians, and sometimes played at quartet parties. He also had lessons with Henri Herz in Paris in 1828. As a boy he played duets with Liszt and met Clementi.

Salaman's first public appearance was at Lanza's concert at Blackheath, in June 1828, and in 1830 he played in the Lenten concerts at Covent Garden Theatre, where he performed his own *Rondo brillant*. He composed the *Jubilee Ode* (with words by his uncle Isaac Cowen) for the Shakespeare festival at Stratford upon Avon on 30 April 1830. The following year he began his career as a piano teacher. In May 1833 he presented the first of an annual series of orchestral concerts at the Hanover Square Rooms, giving the first public performance of Mendelssohn's concerto in G minor by a player other than Mendelssohn himself. In November 1835 he was one of the founders of the Concerti da Camera, a chamber music organization. In 1838 he went on a European tour and performed in Vienna, Munich, Hamburg, and other places; he also met Schumann, Mozart's widow and son, Thalberg, and Czerny. He lived in Rome from 1846 to 1848 and conducted the first performance in Rome of Beethoven's symphony no. 2. In Rome he was elected an honorary member of the Accademia di Santa Cecilia.

In 1848 Salaman returned to London, and the same year married Frances (d. 1897), the eldest daughter of Isaac Simon of Montego Bay, Jamaica. They had three sons and two daughters. He started the first Amateur Choral Society in 1849. In 1855 he began a series of lectures with musical illustrations in London and the provinces, taking as his first topic 'The history of the pianoforte and its precursors'. He gave this lecture in front of Queen Victoria, Prince Albert, and their children at the Polytechnic Institution on 10 May 1855. In 1858 he founded the Musical Society of London, which lasted until 1868, and of which he was honorary secretary until 1865. In 1874 he was one of the founders of the Musical Association, of which he was secretary for three years and afterwards a vice-president. He gave his last concert in 1876.

Salaman's first compositions, piano pieces, dedicated to Charles Neate and Henri Herz, were published in 1828. In his later years he began an annual tradition of publishing a song on his birthday. The most famous is his setting of Shelley's 'I arise from dreams of thee', written at Bath in 1836 and published in *Six Songs* (1838). Some of his settings were to Hebrew, Greek, and Latin words. A deeply religious man, he composed and arranged in 1858 the choral and organ music for the psalms and service of the synagogue of the Reformed Congregation of British Jews; some of his settings of the psalms were used as anthems in cathedrals.

Salaman died at his home, 24 Sutherland Avenue, west London, on 23 June 1901, and was buried on 27 June in the Jewish cemetery at Golders Green.

J. C. HADDEN, rev. ANNE PIMLOTT BAKER

Sources *New Grove* · C. Salaman, 'Pianists of the past: personal recollections by the late Charles Salaman', *Blackwood*, 170 (1901),

307–30 • *The Times* (25 June 1901) • *WWW* • Brown & Stratton, *Brit. mus.* • *MT*, 42 (1901), 530–33 • *Jewish World* (28 June 1901)

Likenesses J. Goodman, oils, 1834; in possession of Malcolm Salaman, 1912 • R. J. Lane, lithograph, *c.*1834 (after S. A. Hart), BM, NPG; repro. in *MT* • Girometti, marble medallion, 1847 • S. Starr, oil sketch; in possession of Brandon Thomas, 1912

Wealth at death £5919 1s. 11d.: probate, 12 Oct 1901, *CGPLA Eng. & Wales*

Salaman, Raphael Arthur (1906–1993), collector and lexicographer of tradesmen's tools, was born on 24 April 1906 at Homestall, Barley, near Royston, Hertfordshire, the fourth of six children of Redcliffe Nathan *Salaman (1874–1955), physician and scientist, and his wife, Pauline Ruth (Nina), *née* Davis (1876/7–1925), writer, poet, and Zionist.

Salaman was the youngest son of prosperous Jewish intellectual parents. They had moved, just before his birth, from London to the unlikely surroundings of Barley in north-east Hertfordshire, where Redcliffe Salaman sought and found lasting relief from tuberculosis. In retrospect life in the country just before the First World War, and a long-postponed formal education, were keys to Raphael's later interests, for on walks and cycle rides with his tutor he came to know the many tradesmen then working in and around a large village like Barley. In 1975 he recalled over thirty trades there, including blacksmith, wheelwright, builder, cabinet-maker, butcher, and hurdle-maker. Even as a boy he was unable to pass by without stopping to watch men at their work.

Salaman was eventually sent to Bedales School in Hampshire (1918–25), and then read engineering and law at Emmanuel College, Cambridge (1925–8), although he had wanted to study archaeology. Drifting, and not in his own view a very good engineer, he worked briefly for a theatrical lighting firm and invented GEC's Salaman Control, a huge but very effective hydraulic dimmer used to simulate daybreak or nightfall on the stage. Partnership in a south London engineering firm followed (1929), and marriage to Miriam Polianowsky (*b.* 1914), on 10 May 1934. But the cancellation of a major order caused his firm to fail, and in 1938 he joined Marks and Spencer, where he made an impression through his organization of air-raid precautions and public safety during the Second World War.

On visiting his father at Barley in 1946 and seeking out old friends in their workshops Salaman suddenly realized that two wars, the depression, and the internal combustion engine had virtually wiped out their trades, although some of the old men lingered on doing repairs for a few customers. In the introduction to his first dictionary he looks back on the loss of local trades as 'one of the harsher changes of recent years'. He determined to collect—and save from oblivion—every tool of at least the major trades and to discover how they were used. Tools were generally to be had for the asking—£5 at most changed hands for substantial kits—and information was readily given. Forty years later he regretted never having taken a camera or tape recorder on his collecting expeditions.

By the early 1950s Salaman's collection had grown large, and the idea developed of an encyclopaedic work on tools.

He had the general inspiration of two unusual works: his father's *History and Social Influence of the Potato* (1949) and the Egyptologist Sir William Flinders Petrie's eccentrically ordered typological study, *Tools and Weapons* (1917; Petrie was a friend of the family and a boyhood hero of Salaman's). But in another sense there were no formal models for the work that Salaman contemplated, for the secondary literature was virtually non-existent and indeed tools and trades were not an accepted subject for academic study. He therefore took to the field rather than the library, eventually collecting tools and information from 400 workshops and tradesmen throughout Britain and supplementing this information with a thorough study of tool manufacturers' catalogues, ranging from the earliest (*c.*1800) to those of the 1960s (old tool catalogues were then among the least valuable of second-hand books). Work proceeded slowly, since by the 1950s Salaman was in charge of buildings and engineering (including refrigeration, air conditioning, and fire sprinklers) for all Marks and Spencer branches, but in 1963 he took early retirement to concentrate on study. In 1967 'Tools of the shipwright, 1650–1925' appeared (*Folk Life*, 5, 1967, 19–51), followed by the celebrated *Dictionary of Woodworking Tools* (1975) and *Dictionary of Leather-Working Tools* (1986). These are his monuments: substantial but concise, copiously illustrated, authoritative, thoroughly comprehensive, and unlikely to be superseded, now that the trades themselves are gone. Despite their success the two volumes were only part of Salaman's original plan, a survey of all the trades. Life proved too short for him to continue with the metalworking and engineering trades, which he knew well, and he was denied the pleasure of writing on farming and the agricultural trades, an early love.

During the gestation of the dictionaries Salaman found time for other expressions of his enthusiasm. He spoke on the radio, contributed a short but luminous overview of trade tools from 1500 to 1850 for the *History of Technology* (1957), and made collections of tools for the Science Museum, London (mainly wheelwrighting), and St Albans Museums (a general collection; St Albans was near Salaman's home at Harpenden). Where possible he arranged for their display in recreated workshop settings, and he oversaw the construction of a replica saw-pit and village carpenter's shop for successive building exhibitions at Olympia about 1950. It was very much in his mind, in these more public activities, to reintroduce its own past to a public hell-bent on progress and modernization.

'Raph' Salaman was a quietly-spoken, kindly, unassuming man, notably good with children (he had one son and three daughters), and much more interested in everyday things and ordinary people than conventional success. Away from work and study he joined the Labour Party and served as a councillor for Paddington while living in London, and as a governor of Bedales and of St George's School, Harpenden. From 1988 he suffered repeated strokes, which curtailed constructive work and left him increasingly disabled. He died at his home, 21 Kirkdale

Road, Harpenden, on 31 December 1993; he was cremated, and his ashes interred, at Golders Green Jewish cemetery, London, in January 1994.   CHRIS GREEN

Sources Raphael Salaman, interview, 24 March 1988, St Albans Museums [sound recording by Sam Mullins and transcript] · K. Ross, 'A study of Mr R A Salaman collector of tradesmen's tools', diss., 1990, St Albans Museums [copy] · D. Painter, 'Redcliffe and Raphael Salaman: a memoir', *History Workshop Journal*, 40 (1995), 276–82 · *Emmanuel College Magazine*, 76 (1993–4), 247–50 · *The Independent* (13 Jan 1994) · *The Times* (3 Feb 1994) · private information (2004) [family] · personal knowledge (2004)
Archives St Albans Museums, tools and materials used for the dictionaries │SOUND St Albans Museums, recorded interview (24 March 1988)
Likenesses photograph, repro. in *The Times*

Salaman, Redcliffe Nathan (1874–1955), geneticist and Jewish activist, was born Nathan Redcliffe Salaman, at 100 Redcliffe Gardens, Kensington, London, on 12 September 1874, the ninth of the fifteen children of Myer Salaman, a wealthy ostrich feather merchant, and his wife, Sarah Soloman, a relative of N. M. Adler, chief rabbi from 1844 to 1890. Salaman's schooling began on the classical side at St Paul's School. After passing the London matriculation he changed over to the scientific side, and eventually graduated top in his class. In 1893 he passed his preliminary examination for the MB (London), and obtained scholarships from both St Paul's and Trinity Hall, Cambridge. He entered Trinity Hall, sitting the natural sciences tripos and graduating in 1896 with first-class honours in physiology, zoology, and chemistry.

Salaman qualified in medicine at the London Hospital in 1900, and the following year went to Würzburg and Berlin to study morbid anatomy and pathology. In the same year, on 23 October, he married Pauline Ruth (Nina; 1876/7–1925), daughter of a retired mine engineer, Arthur Davis; she was a minor but distinguished poet. They had six children, one of whom, Myer Salaman, went on to become a renowned cancer researcher; another, Raphael Arthur *Salaman, became an authoritative collector and lexicographer. In 1903 Salaman was appointed director of the Pathological Institute at the London Hospital and began a series of investigations of cancerous tissues. The following year he obtained the MD. During the same year, however, he contracted tuberculosis and had to give up medical work. After six months in a Swiss sanatorium he bought a house in Barley, Hertfordshire, to rest in countryside. There he turned his restless mind to a different, but none the less related, set of scientific problems.

About 1905 William Bateson discussed with Salaman recent work in Cambridge by Rowland Biffen on the genetics of disease resistance in wheat. Salaman was very interested in this work and decided to pursue it further in his garden in Barley, working with the more manageable potato. By 1908 he had established the genetic nature of resistance to the notorious potato blight, *Phytophthora infestans*. This line of work was expanded and extended in collaboration with J. W. Lesley in the school of agriculture, at Cambridge. It eventually resulted in the introduction in crop potatoes of genes for resistance to the disease by crossing with the wild potato, *Solanum demissum*.

Redcliffe Nathan Salaman (1874–1955), by Walter Stoneman

Salaman's work on the potato was interrupted by the war, when he joined the Royal Army Medical Corps and served in Palestine, writing about his experiences there in *Palestine Regained* (1919). After the war, following the establishment of the National Institute of Agricultural Botany in Cambridge, Salaman was appointed chairman of the potato synonym committee. This committee was responsible for cataloguing the innumerable varieties of potatoes on the market and putting an end to the common practice of marketing old and unreliable varieties under new names. The results of his work at Barley and Cambridge were summarized in *Potato Varieties* (1926). In the same year, on 13 October, he married Gertrude (b. 1887/8), daughter of Ernest Lowy, stockbroker.

It was in 1926 that Salaman and his friend Daniel Hall convinced the Ministry of Agriculture to found an institute in Cambridge to investigate viral diseases of potatoes. Salaman was appointed director of the new unit—the Potato Virus Research Institute—a post which he retained until his mandatory retirement in 1939. Under Salaman's direction researchers in the institute did very important work to elucidate the nature of viruses, work which led to his election to the Royal Society in 1935. Salaman's persistent and driving interest was, however, in the potato and its role in history. Thus, after many years collecting material on the social history of this plant, he wrote his much reprinted *History and Social Influence of the Potato* (1949).

The humane concerns underlying *History and Social Influence of the Potato* were even more evident in Salaman's work to support the Jewish community. While at the London Hospital he also worked as a social worker among Jews in the East End. At the same time he was involved with the Zionist movement, and was elected in 1907 president of the English Zionist Federation. Later, Jewish scientists and scholars from Cambridge and elsewhere were invited to socialize in his home. In 1933 he was a founding member of the Academic Assistance Council (later the Society for the Protection of Science and Learning), which enabled academic refugees from Germany to find work in Britain. He also assisted other refugees by founding the Jewish Professional Committee. More important, he was the first chairman of the Jewish committee for relief abroad, which in 1945 set out to organize the task of rehabilitating any survivors of the extermination camps after the defeat of Germany. After the war Salaman was also involved in the establishment of the Hebrew University in Jerusalem, of which he then became an influential governor. He also served as president of the Jewish Health Organization of Great Britain and Jewish Historical Society of England.

Like many members of the Edwardian country gentry, Salaman was also closely involved in many local civic activities. Most prominent among these was his service as magistrate and chairman of the bench from 1927 until his retirement in 1950. He died at his home, Homestall, Barley, Royston, Hertfordshire, on 12 June 1955. He was survived by his second wife. PAOLO PALLADINO

Sources K. M. Smith, *Memoirs FRS*, 1 (1955), 239–45 · *The Times* (14 June 1955) · *The Times* (23 June 1955) · *The Times* (24 June 1955) · personal knowledge (1971) [*DNB*] · b. cert. · m. certs. · d. cert.
Archives Bodl. Oxf., Society for the Protection of Science and Learning, MSS · CUL, notes and papers · Herts. ALS, Smith End Farm accounts | CUL, corresp. with C. C. Hurst · Wellcome L., corresp. with Charles Singer
Likenesses C. Salaman, oils, National Institute of Agricultural Botany, Cambridge · W. Stoneman, photograph, RS [*see illus.*]
Wealth at death £86,287 10s. 5d.: probate, 24 Aug 1955, *CGPLA Eng. & Wales*

Sale [*alias* Neville], **Edmund** (1604/5–1647/8), Jesuit, was probably the son of William Sale and his wife, Anne Neville, and was born in his father's house at Holker, Lancashire. He named his uncle as a Jesuit, probably referring to the Edmund Neville SJ who died about 1646 and with whom, owing to his alias, he sometimes appears to be confused. After studying humanities at St Omer he entered the English College at Rome on 29 September 1621 aged sixteen. On 24 March 1626 he was admitted to the Society of Jesus at St Andrew's, Rome, where he served his noviciate, and after a period of theological studies at Liège and a stint on the English mission, in 1630 he was recorded as teaching humanities at St Omer. In that year he published *The Palme of Christian Fortitude*, a translation of João Rodriguez Giroa's account of recent martyrdoms in Japan and one of a number of works which reflected Jesuit pride in the 'heroism of their brethren and their converts in Japan' (Clancy, 24). He addressed the work to English Catholics 'who live in the happie danger of being partakers of the like crownes' (preface). He also composed works left in manuscript, including a life of St Augustine. Ordained

about 1632, in 1636 he was acting as socius to the provincial for what later became Belgium and in 1638 was reported to be collecting material for a history of the province. By 1639 he was resident in London and on 3 August 1640 was professed of the four vows there. He was noted as present in the residence of St Mary (Oxfordshire district) in 1641–3, the college of St Francis Xavier (south Wales and adjoining areas) in 1644–5, and in the house of probation of St Ignatius (London) in 1646. He died in 1647 (or possibly 1648), the date sometimes being given as 18 July.

THOMPSON COOPER, *rev.* R. M. ARMSTRONG

Sources H. Foley, ed., *Records of the English province of the Society of Jesus*, 7 vols. in 8 (1875–83) · T. M. McCoog, *English and Welsh Jesuits, 1555–1650*, 2 vols., Catholic RS, 74–5 (1994–5) · T. H. Clancy, *A literary history of the English Jesuits: a century of books, 1615–1714* (1996) · A. Kenny, ed., *The responsa scholarum of the English College, Rome*, 2 vols., Catholic RS, 54–5 (1962–3) · Gillow, *Lit. biog. hist.* · G. Oliver, *Collections towards illustrating the biographies of the Scotch, English and Irish members of the Society of Jesus*, 2nd edn (1845)
Likenesses J. G. Heinsch, group portrait, line engraving (after W. P. Kilian), NPG

Sale, Florentia, Lady Sale (1790–1853). *See under* Sale, Sir Robert Henry (1782–1845).

Sale, George (*b.* in or after **1696**, *d.* **1736**), orientalist, was the son of Samuel Sale, a London merchant, who may have been originally from Kent. The identity of his mother and his date of birth are unknown. Richard Alfred Davenport, his biographer, states that he was under forty at his death, which would place the time of his birth in or after 1696. On 24 October 1720 he started his study of the law at the Inner Temple, London. He was a solicitor by profession, but his practice never flourished due to his scholarly activities as an orientalist.

In 1720 the Society for Promoting Christian Knowledge (SPCK), whose offices were in the Middle Temple, took the initiative to publish an Arabic translation of the New Testament for the benefit of the Arab Greek Orthodox community of Syria and Palestine. Two Arab Christians were involved in the translation project: Salomon Negri from Damascus and, to a lesser extent, Carolus Dadichi from Aleppo. Most likely, George Sale received instruction in the Arabic language from these two scholars. On 30 August 1726 he consented at the SPCK's request to contribute to the project as a corrector. In 1727 the translation was published under the title *Al-ʿAhd al-jadid li-rabbina Yasuʿ al-Masih* ('The New Testament of our Lord Jesus Christ'), the original of Sale's Arabic calligraphy of the title-page being preserved in the SPCK papers at the Cambridge University Library. About this time he married Marianne d'Argent (*d.* after 1736), of French extraction, and their eldest son was born in 1728; the couple had six more children, three of whom died young. On 3 November 1726 Sale was elected a corresponding member of the SPCK and took an active part in the society's work through his attendance at the weekly general meetings of its standing committee. Occasionally he assisted in preparing the society's financial accounts and rendered various other services, mostly of a legal nature.

Translation of the Koran George Sale is best-known for his English translation of the Koran, which was published in London in 1734 under the title *The Koran, commonly called the Alcoran of Mohammed: translated into English immediately from the original Arabic; with explanatory notes, taken from the most approved commentators, to which is prefixed a preliminary discourse*. Sale made this translation 'at leisure times only, and amidst the necessary avocations of a troublesome profession', thereby doubtless referring to his regular work as solicitor (Sale, xii). To this translation he added a long 'preliminary discourse', a compendium of all that was known about the religion of Islam. The 1734 edition was the only one that was published during his lifetime, but the translation was reprinted in 1746, 1764, and many times afterward, most recently in 1984 (a list of mainly pre-1956 editions can be found in Binark and others). In 1746 a German retranslation was published in Lemgo by Theodor Arnold. Sale's 'preliminary discourse' was separately translated into several languages, first Dutch under the title *Verhandeling over de historie, stammen, zeden en godsdienst der Arabieren* ('Treatise on the history, tribes, traditions, and religion of the Arabs', 1742), and then French (*Observations historiques et critiques sur le Mahométisme*, 1751). Another, later translation of the discourse that deserves to be mentioned is the Arabic *Maqalah fi al-Islam* ('Essay on Islam', 1891).

Sale's translation of the Koran was only the second English version of the work, the previous one being the work of Alexander Ross (1649), itself based on a French version (1647) by André du Ryer, the French consul in Alexandria. Shortly before the turn of the century, in 1698, a Latin translation had been published in Padua by Ludovico Marracci, confessor to Pope Innocent XI. The title of this work, *Refutatio alcorani* ('Refutation of the Koran'), left no doubt as to the intentions of the translator. The work of the early twentieth-century orientalist Edward Denison Ross and after him G. J. Toomer have shown the extent of Sale's indebtedness to this latter translation, which goes much further than his own statement that he was 'much obliged' to Marracci's work. Sale used Marracci's numerous references to Arab commentaries on the Koran, and added to them by using a comparable exegesis by ʿAbdallah b. ʿUmar al-Baydawi (d. c.1286), the manuscript of which Sale borrowed from the Dutch Reformed church in Austin Friars, London. Sale's other references lead mainly to Latin translations of Arab historiographical works. Other frequently cited sources are Barthélemy d'Herbelot's *Bibliothèque orientale* (1697) and *De religione Mohammedica* ('On the Muhammadan religion') by Adriaan Reland (1705). Writing at a time when Europe no longer felt the military threat of Islam, Reland was the first scholar to refute Marracci's heavy-handed and controversial style by arguing that, if so many obviously reasonable and intelligent people had embraced a religion, it could not possibly be regarded as an easily detectable lie. In the same manner, Sale was convinced of the sincerity of Muhammad's intentions:

> His original design of bringing the pagan Arabs to the knowledge of the true GOD was certainly noble, and highly to be commended. ... Mohammed was, no doubt, fully satisfied in his conscience of the truth of his grand point, the unity of GOD.   (Sale, 'Preliminary discourse', 46)

Even so, Sale remained eager to secure the conversion of the Muslims to protestant Christianity: 'The Protestants alone are able to attack the Korân with success; and for them, I trust, Providence has reserved the glory of its overthrow' (ibid., iv).

Sale's presumed partiality to Islam earned him the criticism of his contemporaries. James Porter, ambassador to the Ottoman empire from 1746 to 1762, praised his translation but was 'sorry to say, that he frequently discovers an inclination to apologize for it [i.e. the Koran]; and rather endeavours to reconcile and palliate the numerous absurdities he meets with, than to expose them in the light they deserve' (*Observations on the Religion, Law, Government and Manners of the Turks*, 2nd edn, 1771, 55). However, his work found a more appreciative readership among the scholars and philosophers of the British and continental Enlightenment. Edward Gibbon, who knew no oriental languages, used Sale's translation and 'preliminary discourse' alongside Marracci's translation in his *History of the Decline and Fall of the Roman Empire* (1776–88), mainly in chapter 50, covering the history of the Arabian peninsula and the religion of Islam until the year 632 CE. While making ample use of Sale's work, Gibbon did not hesitate to call him 'half a Musulman'. Voltaire possessed a copy of the original 1734 edition of Sale's translation and the French version of the discourse. In his *Questions sur l'Encyclopédie par des amateurs* (1770–72) Voltaire referred to the work of 'Salles' in the articles 'Alcoran, ou le Koran' (1.127–35) and 'Arot et Marot' (2.172–84), in which he expressed his appreciation of the translation as 'une traduction fidèle de l'Alcoran' and 'une préface la plus instructive'. Although Sale never left his home country, Voltaire believed that he had 'lived for twenty-five years among the Arabs', or had 'lived twenty-four years near Arabia'. In Germany, Gotthold Ephraim Lessing declared that:

> we possessed no true knowledge [about Muhammad and his teachings] previous to the works of a Reland or a Sale; from which we have learned first and foremost that Muhammad is no senseless fraud and that his religion is not an entangled web of incoherent lies.   (K. Lachmann, ed., *Rettung des Cardan. Sämtliche Schriften*, 3rd edn, vol. 5, 1890, 325)

Sale's careful and unemotional approach in both his preliminary discourse and translation secured the fame of his work well into the twentieth century. In 1921 Edward Denison Ross claimed that Sale's version had not been superseded by any subsequent translation, and that his discourse still remained the best introduction in any European language to the study of Islam. More than fifty years later Sale's objectivity still guarded him from criticism in Edward Said's *Orientalism* (1978).

Although Sale's intentions were quite honourable from an orthodox protestant point of view, it is likely that his Koran translation influenced his relations with the SPCK, after all a Christian missionary society. No criticism of George Sale or his ideas can be found in the papers of the SPCK, but it is possible that they, like so many others, regarded his work as propaganda for the faith of Islam. After April 1733 the number of his visits to the society dropped dramatically, and he stopped attending its general meetings altogether after 10 September 1734. Thereafter his contacts with the society seem to have been limited to the occasional exchange of letters.

Sale's other scholarly activities were in the fields of ancient and oriental history and biography. Until his death he contributed the articles on oriental history to Thomas Birch's *General Dictionary, Historical and Critical* (10 vols., 1734–41), an encyclopaedia based on Pierre Bayle's *Dictionnaire historique et critique* (1697). For *An Universal History, from the Earliest Account of Time* (7 vols., 1736–44) Sale wrote the first chapters on the creation (in 4004 BC, according to Archbishop James Ussher's chronology) and most of the history of the world until the flood (in 2348 BC). Rumours about Sale's orthodoxy are reflected in the French study *Biographie universelle, ancienne et moderne* (begun in 1811 under Napoleon but finished in 1825 under the restoration), which states that the shareholders (*actionnaires*) of the *Universal History*, fearing Sale's heterodoxy and its effect upon the number of subscriptions, transferred its editorship from Sale to another contributor, George Psalmanazar (40.140–41). Sale's authorship of *The Lives and Memorable Actions of many Illustrious Persons of the Eastern Nations*, published posthumously in 1739, remains contested. Likewise it is improbable that the name Abdulla Mahumed Omar, the author of 'A defence of Mahomet, written in Arabick: a paradox' in *Miscellanea aurea* (1720, 165–88), is really the pseudonym of George Sale, as the British Library catalogue has it. Sale's manuscript memoranda and notebook, consisting mainly of oriental biographical material, are kept in the Victoria Art Gallery and Municipal Libraries of Bath.

Manuscript collection In the course of his life George Sale acquired a collection of Arabic, Persian, and Ottoman Turkish manuscripts, comprising eighty-seven items. About half of this collection is in Arabic, the other half being divided between Persian and Turkish. In contrast to the claim in the *Dictionary of National Biography* that he 'doubtless purchased [these] of the distressed orientals in London, whom he constantly recommended for employment or relief to the Society for the Promotion of Christian Knowledge', it is more probable that Sale used his contacts with Negri and Dadichi to acquire manuscripts. Besides, if charity had been Sale's only motive, his collection would not have been as coherent as it actually is, revealing the tastes and interests of a determined collector. The collection contains a number of texts by Ottoman historiographers; the fact that some of these were copied in Sale's own time suggests that they were specially made to order. The *Mir'at ül-ka'inat* ('Mirror of the universe') by Nishancızade Mehmet, for instance, was copied as late as 1727. The Persian texts in his collection belong mainly to the established literary canon, but his Arabic manuscripts betray the eye of the connoisseur, many of them containing post-classical poetry of the lightest possible kind, often humorous or sexually explicit, such as the autograph of the *Nuzhat al-nufus wa-mudhik*

al-'abus ('The recreation of the mind, bringing a laugh to a scowling face') by the fifteenth-century Egyptian author Ali ibn Sudun (Bodl. Oxf., MS Sale 13). The complete absence of religious texts, except for a Koran and a New Testament in Arabic, has been noted by Edward Denison Ross.

Not long before his death Sale was engaged in the establishment of a society for the encouragement of learning, whose aim was to subsidize the printing of books. One of the founders, he sat on the first executive committee. However, he did not live to see the results of this undertaking. Davenport describes Sale as having had a healthy constitution; none the less he contracted a fever and died at his home in Surrey Street, the Strand, London, on 13 November 1736, after an illness of only eight days. He was buried at the nearby church of St Clement Danes on 16 November. Moved by charity, the general meeting of the SPCK agreed to present his wife and children with 20 guineas as a benefit on the return of the society's Bible and lexicon.

After Sale's death his widow, Marianne, arranged for his manuscripts and books to be sold by William Hamerton, a London merchant. Hamerton printed a list of Sale's manuscripts under the title *A choice collection of most curious and inestimable manuscripts, in the Turkish, Arabic and Persian languages, from the library of the late learned and ingenious Mr. George Sale* (n.d.). In 1760 the complete collection was acquired by Thomas Hunt, Laudian professor of Arabic at Oxford, for the sum of £157 10*s*. They were at first placed in the Radcliffe Library, but in 1872 the collection was moved to Oxford's Bodleian Library. Sale's Persian and Turkish manuscripts were described in Sachau's and Ethé's *Catalogue of the Persian, Turkish, Hindûstânî, and Pushtû manuscripts in the Bodleian Library* (3 vols., 1889–1954), but there is no printed catalogue of the Arabic manuscripts other than Hamerton's list.   ARNOUD VROLIJK

Sources G. Sale, *The Koran, commonly called the Alcoran of Mohammed, translated from the original Arabic, with explanatory notes … to which is prefixed a preliminary discourse*, 2 vols., new edn (1836) • CUL, SPCK MSS • R. A. Davenport, 'A sketch of the life of George Sale', in G. Sale, *The Koran, commonly called the Alcoran of Mohammed*, new edn (1857) • E. D. Ross, *The preliminary discourse to the Korân by George Sale, with an introduction* [1921] • P. M. Holt, 'The treatment of Arab history by Prideaux, Ockley and Sale', *Historians of the Middle East*, ed. B. Lewis and P. M. Holt (1962) • I. Binark, H. Eren, and E. Ihsanoglu, eds., *World bibliography of translations of the meanings of 'The Holy Qur'an': printed translations, 1515–1980* (1986)
Archives Bath Central Library, memoranda and notebook | CUL, papers of the Society for Promoting Christian Knowledge (SPCK)
Wealth at death 'seems to have left his wife and children in necessitous circumstances': Society for Promoting Christian Knowledge MSS, CUL, general meetings, 30 Nov 1736

Sale, George Charles (1796–1869). *See under* Sale, John (1758–1827).

Sale, John (1758–1827), singer and conductor, was born in London, the son of John Sale (1734–1802). He was probably the John Sale baptized on 12 March 1758 at St Sepulchre, Holborn, London, son of John and Alice Sale. From 1767 to 1775 he sang as a chorister of St George's Chapel, Windsor, and also at Eton College, in both of which choirs he joined his father as lay vicar in 1777. By 1779 he had married a woman named Mary. Having been made a gentleman of the Chapel Royal in July 1788, a vicar-choral of St Paul's Cathedral in 1794, and a lay vicar of Westminster Abbey a year later, he thus found himself temporarily a member of no fewer than five choirs, and in December 1796 he duly resigned his Windsor and Eton appointments. In 1800 he succeeded the elder Richard Bellamy as almoner and master of the choristers at St Paul's, which post he held for twelve years.

Though principally an ecclesiastical musician, Sale was also much involved in the secular musical life of the capital. As a bass soloist with a particular forte for Handel, he sang for the Academy of Ancient Music in 1788–9 and in the Concerts of Ancient Music from 1789 to 1814 (as well as in many other London concert series and provincial musical festivals). His contemporaries seem to have been especially impressed by his clarity of articulation and 'energy of expression' (*Quarterly Musical Magazine and Review*, 9.544–6). A long-standing (honorary) member of the Noblemen and Gentlemen's Catch Club, he took over from Samuel Webbe as secretary and in effect treasurer in January 1812, and for the last three years of his life he was also conductor of the Glee Club. According to Sainsbury he was not only 'greatly esteemed and respected', but was patronized by George III and George IV, to some of whose family members he also taught singing. His few compositions—almost entirely vocal—are of no lasting importance. Sale died at his home in Marsham Street, Westminster, on 11 November 1827 and was buried with full musical honours in St Paul's Cathedral on the 19th. He was survived by his wife.

Sale's eldest son, **John Bernard Sale** (1779–1856), was born at Windsor on 24 June 1779 and was brought up as a chorister there from 1785. As a treble he sang in the chorus of the Concerts of Ancient Music and in 1794 as a soloist at the Three Choirs festival. His adult voice, like that of his father, was a powerful bass, and he too was said to have been 'a true disciple of the Handelian school' (Sainsbury). In 1801 he became a lay vicar of Westminster Abbey and in 1803 a gentleman of the Chapel Royal. Three years later he gained a second abbey appointment and in 1809 he added to this the post of organist of St Margaret's, Westminster. From 1821 to 1838 he once again sang at the Concerts of Ancient Music. In 1826 he was appointed teacher of piano and singing to the young Princess Victoria, and in 1838 organist also of the Chapel Royal (in succession to Thomas Attwood). He died at his home, 21 Holywell Street, Millbank, Westminster, on 16 September 1856, and left three daughters, one of whom, Laura, was married to the antiquary William *Thoms, founder of *Notes and Queries*. The other two, Mary Anne and Sophia, were both musicians. Sale's wife, Anne, probably died before him.

His younger brother **George Charles Sale** (1796–1869) was principally an organist. In 1817 he succeeded Thomas Busby as organist of St Mary's, Newington, and in 1826 was appointed organist of St George's, Hanover Square. He died on 23 January 1869 at his home, 1 Lomax Place,

Charles Street, Camberwell, London, and was survived by his widow, Frances. All three Sales were members of the Royal Society of Musicians.   H. DIACK JOHNSTONE

Sources [J. S. Sainsbury], ed., *A dictionary of musicians*, 2 vols. (1824) · *Quarterly Musical Magazine and Review*, 9 (1827), 544–6 [J. Sale] · Highfill, Burnim & Langhans, *BDA*, 13.177–8 · *The Harmonicon*, 5 (1827), 250 · *Annual Biography and Obituary*, 13 (1829), 466–7 · *GM*, 3rd ser., 1 (1856), 652 [John Bernard Sale] · J. D. Brown, *Biographical dictionary of musicians: with a bibliography of English writings on music* (1886) · Brown & Stratton, *Brit. mus.* · J. S. Bumpus, *The organists and composers of S. Paul's Cathedral* (1891) · Grove, *Dict. mus.* (1954) · B. Matthews, ed., *The Royal Society of Musicians of Great Britain: list of members, 1738–1984* (1985) · *GM*, 1st ser., 98/1 (1828), 90 · *CGPLA Eng. & Wales* (1869) [George Charles Sale] · *IGI* · J. Doane, ed., *A musical directory for the year 1794* [1794] · *Musical Gazette* (18 Oct 1856), 459

Wealth at death under £200—George Charles Sale: administration, *CGPLA Eng. & Wales*, 1869

Sale, John Bernard (1779–1856). *See under* Sale, John (1758–1827).

Sale, Sir Robert Henry (1782–1845), army officer, was born on 19 September 1782, the second son of Colonel Sale of the East India Company's service and his wife, daughter of Harry Brine of Buckden in Huntingdonshire.

Education and early military career Sale was educated with his brother George John (afterwards of the 17th and 4th dragoons) at Dr Nicholas's school at Ealing, and was commissioned as ensign in the 36th foot on 19 January 1795. He was promoted lieutenant on 12 April 1797 and, on 8 January 1798, was posted in the same rank to the 12th foot (later the Suffolk regiment) then stationed at Fort George, Madras. With that regiment he took part in General Harris's campaign against Tipu Sultan. He was present at the battle of Malavalli (27 March 1799) and in the siege and storm of Seringapatam, which fell on 4 May 1799 and for which he received the silver medal. Later he took part in the campaign by Colonel A. Wellesley (later duke of Wellington) against the freebooter Dhundia Wagh, and in the operations in Malabar and Wynaad.

The 12th foot spent more than four years at Trichinopoly, Sale being promoted captain on 23 March 1806. He accompanied his regiment in the operations against the raja of Travancore in 1809, and was present at the actions at Quilon and Killimanur in January and February 1809, before returning to Trichinopoly where, in the same year, he married Florentia [*see below*], daughter of George Wynch. In the following year Sale accompanied his regiment in the expedition against Mauritius, landing at Mapon Bay on 28 November 1810. He was involved in the storming of the French defences that resulted in the island's surrender on 3 December 1810. He remained at Mauritius for the next three years until the 12th foot were moved to Bourbon. Promoted regimental major on 30 December 1813, Sale returned to Mauritius after Bourbon was returned to France in April 1815. The 12th foot left Mauritius in July 1815, joining up with the 2nd battalion at Athlone in Ireland on 9 January 1818. There, as part of the reduction of the army, the 2nd battalion was disbanded and Sale, as a junior major, was placed on half pay on 25 March 1818.

Sir Robert Henry Sale (1782–1845), by George Clint, 1843

Service in Burma Sale returned to full pay on 28 June 1821 as major in the 13th foot (later the Somerset light infantry), joining at Dublin. On 1 January 1823 he sailed with his regiment to India, landing at Calcutta in May. In recognition of their distinguished record the 13th had been converted to light infantry in 1822 and, in 1824, the regiment formed part of the expedition against Burma, commanded by Major-General Sir Archibald Campbell. Sale commanded the 13th, his commanding officer having been promoted to command a brigade. Sale was an officer who led from the front and was, in consequence, frequently wounded. In the storming of the Burmese stockade at Kemmendine on 19 June 1824 he was the first man to appear on top of the works, and on 8 July he led his regiment in the storming of the seven stockades at Kamarut, engaging in personal combat the commander, whom he killed, acquiring thereby a valuable gold-hilted sword and scabbard.

At the end of November 1824 the Burmese commander-in-chief, Bundoola, as good a tactician as strategist, made a determined attempt to drive the British into the sea. There was much fighting around the Shwedagon Pagoda, the Burmese being driven off to Kokine where they constructed a strong stockade which Campbell attacked with two columns on 15 December 1824. Sale, as usual, was prominent in the assault and was severely wounded in the head. The 13th lost eleven officers and fifty-one men killed or wounded. General Campbell, in his dispatch, praised Sale as 'an officer whose gallantry has been most conspicuous' (*DNB*).

The Burmese army having retreated to Danubyu, Campbell decided upon an advance to Prome. Sale was sent with a column to reduce the province of Bassein. After successfully overcoming *en route* a succession of stockades Sale found Bassein abandoned and burning. He advanced for some 120 miles up the Irrawaddy without encountering any resistance, after which he re-embarked his troops and sailed back to Rangoon, where he arrived on 2 May 1825. On 2 June 1825 he was promoted regimental lieutenant-colonel. On the same day his brother George, in the 4th dragoons, was promoted lieutenant-colonel, and for some years their names were together in the *Army List*.

Sale rejoined Campbell at Prome on 25 August 1825. In the meantime the Burmese had been driven out of Danubyu on 2 April, when Bundoola was killed. Sale was given command of the 1st brigade and repulsed an attack by the Shans and Burmese at Simbike on 1 December. On the following day he stormed the position at Napadi and by the end of that month the Burmese were treating for a settlement. They were, however, dilatory and Campbell, losing patience, renounced the armistice and attacked the stronghold of Minhla. The place was taken by escalade from the Irrawaddy; Sale was again wounded while still embarked. The fighting continued, although the Burmese had lost heart. In February they accepted Campbell's terms, which included the surrender in perpetuity of the Arakan and Tenasserim provinces, and on 24 February 1826 a definitive treaty was signed and the First Anglo-Burmese War was over. Sale's name was made as a fine fighting leader, mentioned yet again in dispatches, and made CB for his services. In the middle of April he returned with the 13th light infantry to Calcutta.

Commanding Indian garrisons For the next ten years Sale commanded his regiment at a succession of Indian garrisons: Berhampore, Dinapore, Agra, and Karnal. On 28 June 1838, at Karnal, he was promoted brevet colonel. In October he was made commander of the 1st Bengal brigade in the army of the Indus, which was destined for the invasion of Afghanistan. Sale's brigade consisted of the 13th light infantry, now commanded by William Dennie, and the 16th and 48th regiments of Bengal native infantry. The aim was to overthrow the amir of Afghanistan, Dost Muhammad, and replace him by the supposedly pro-British former ruler Shah Shuja. In this the governor-general, Lord Auckland, was advised by Sir William Macnaghten, his foreign secretary, who accompanied the army as Auckland's envoy with Shah Shuja. Lieutenant-General Sir John Keane was the army commander.

Sale was sent with a force to Girishk, across the River Helmand, to dislodge the Kandahar chiefs who had taken refuge there, but he found Girishk deserted. He was back at Kandahar on 29 May, and on 27 June the march to Kabul was resumed. On 21 July the army was in front of Ghazni. It was taken by storm on 23 July. Sale commanded the storming party. He was brought to the ground by a sabre cut across the face but he wrestled with his assailant, whom he killed with the man's own sword. Ghazni was captured, the army replenished supplies, and Kabul was entered on 7 August 1839, almost a year since leaving

Karnal. Dost Muhammad had fled to Bukhara. On 23 July 1839 Sale had been given the local rank of major-general and was made KCB for his services. He was also given the second class of the order of the Durrani empire, which had been instituted by Shah Shuja.

In October 1839 General Keane handed over command to Major-General Willoughby Cotton and returned to India and elevation to a barony. The army of the Indus was broken up, and the troops remaining were much reduced in numbers. Sale spent Christmas at Jalalabad, where he was joined by his wife and their youngest daughter, Alexandrina. Lady Macnaghten joined her husband in Afghanistan, and she and the envoy also wintered at Jalalabad, where Shah Shuja had established his court. Macnaghten believed all was well in Afghanistan but he was greatly deceived; the Afghans bitterly resented Shah Shuja and the British.

Sale was now second in command to General Cotton. In the autumn of 1840 Dost Muhammad was back and raising the peoples. Soon Kohistan, north of Kabul, was ablaze and Sale was sent with a brigade to restore control. He had the 13th light infantry, the 17th native infantry, and two companies of the 37th native infantry, Abbott's 9-pounder battery, two of Shah Shuja's horse-artillery guns, a 24-pounder howitzer, two mortars, the 2nd Bengal light cavalry, and a regiment of the shah's horse. On 29 September he found the enemy strongly posted at Tutandara, and immediately attacked and routed them. There followed a succession of minor engagements as Sale tried to capture Dost Muhammad. His force was reinforced but Dost Muhammad remained elusive until 2 November, when Sale came up with him near the village of Parwan in Kohistan. In the cavalry charge that followed the British officers, out in front, galloped right into the enemy but the 2nd Bengal light cavalry failed to follow them, subsequently being disbanded for cowardice. Broadfoot of the engineers and Dr Lord, political agent, who accompanied the cavalry were, with the adjutant, killed, and several of the officers were severely wounded. The British infantry, advancing, recovered the lost ground and cleared the Parwandara, or pass of Parwan, the enemy, completely defeated, fleeing to the Panjshir valley. Dost Muhammad, seeing the hopelessness of further resistance, went to Kabul and surrendered to Macnaghten. He accompanied Sir Willoughby Cotton to India, leaving Kabul on 12 November 1840. Cotton had resigned on grounds of ill health and was succeeded by Major-General William George Keith Elphinstone, a Waterloo veteran with no previous experience of the East, prematurely aged and racked with gout.

Hardly a month passed without incident and yet the British garrison in Kabul settled to the quiet life of cantonments, in a false sense of security. Many of the married officers had sent for their wives and families. On 8 August 1841 Sale's daughter Alexandrina was married at Kabul to Lieutenant John Sturt of the engineers, in charge of public works at Kabul. The cantonment at Sherpur, outside the city, was ill sited and difficult to defend with the troops available. At an early stage Sale had protested against the position proposed, and had vainly advocated the occupation of the Bala Hissar where a British force could have held Kabul against any odds. But Shah Shuja would have none of it, and Macnaghten concurred. To add to the increasing unrest, the subsidies paid to the hill peoples to keep the passes open and refrain from plunder were withdrawn on government instructions for a paltry saving of £4000. The Ghilzai *sirdars* were informed at the beginning of October 1841, and soon afterwards the peoples occupied the passes and cut communication between Kabul and India.

Sale was under orders to return to India with his brigade, accompanied by Macnaghten, who had been appointed governor of Bombay, and by the debilitated General Elphinstone. Sale was ordered instead to clear the passes to Jalalabad. He had with him the 13th light infantry under Dennie and the 35th native infantry under Monteith. He had also a few Indian sappers, two field guns, and some Afghans armed with *jezails*. While forcing the Khurd Kabul Pass, Sale was wounded in the ankle, leaving Dennie to command the brigade. After a halt of nine days to allow for supplies and reinforcements Sale moved on and took the fort at Tezin on 22 October. Under Macnaghten the political officers were all-powerful and Macgregor, Sale's political officer, wasted days in fruitless negotiation with the Ghilzai chiefs. After sending back to Kabul some of his troops Sale advanced on 26 October, reaching Jagdalak after stiff fighting on 28 October. Gandamak was reached on 30 October and a halt was called to reorganize.

The rising of 1841–1842 On 2 November 1841 Sir Alexander Burnes, Macnaghten's designated successor, was murdered in his house at Kabul. The rising quickly became widespread. Sale received the news on 10 November, together with peremptory orders from Elphinstone to return to Kabul with his brigade. He called a council of war and, concurring with its advice, continued his march the following day towards Jalalabad, winning a successful action at Fatehabad *en route*. Since the 37th native infantry, which had been sent back by Sale, arrived at Kabul without serious loss either of personnel or of baggage, it is hard to understand why Sale could not have secured his sick and wounded, and his supplies, at Jalalabad and made a rapid march back to Kabul; but the arguments against doing so must have been compelling, bearing in mind that his wife, daughter, and son-in-law were still in Kabul.

Sale entered Jalalabad on 13 November. The town was deserted and practically defenceless, a collection of crumbling mud-brick houses huddled together round narrow stinking lanes. He had about 2000 men, 700 of them 13th light infantry of whom half were recruits, and 750 of the 35th native infantry. Broadfoot's sappers amounted to 150: 40 men of the shah's infantry, one squadron of the 5th Bengal cavalry and 90 sabres of the shah's cavalry, Backhouse's mountain train, and Abbott's battery—few enough for the perimeter to be defended—and Abbott and Broadfoot set to work to dig and erect defences. On 2 January 1842 Sale learnt of Macnaghten's murder on 23

December, and on 9 January he received orders from Elphinstone to evacuate Jalalabad and march to Peshawar. Akbar Khan, Dost Muhammad's son and Macnaghten's assassin, had promised a safe conduct although Sale had already been informed that Akbar was exhorting the peoples to attack him. On 13 January a solitary horseman, Dr Brydon, wounded and exhausted, arrived to tell of the annihilation of the Kabul force of 4500 men and thousands of followers. Ten days later they heard that an attempt to force the Khyber Pass had been abandoned, and the Jalalabad force was now isolated.

By now Sale knew that his wife and daughter, as well as officers, wives, and children, had been taken hostage, as had Elphinstone and his second in command, Brigadier Shelton. A letter of Shah Shuja to Macgregor inquired as to Sale's intentions and, at the council of war held the next day, Sale and Macgregor proposed to negotiate for evacuation. This was vehemently opposed by Broadfoot, who was supported by others, including Captain Henry Havelock of the 13th light infantry, who had accompanied the force in a supernumerary capacity. After heated discussion the shah was informed that, with his formal permission, Jalalabad would be evacuated, provided Akbar Khan was withdrawn, their safe conduct to India was guaranteed, and that hostages were given for the safety of the force. Further councils of war followed without reaching any firm conclusion.

These councils of war have been the subject of considerable discussion, not generally favourable to Sale and Macgregor. The surviving papers apparently show Sale too easily influenced by Macgregor to trust the treacherous Afghans, although he may have hoped to gain time by continuing negotiations. The credit for opposing evacuation belongs to George Broadfoot, supported by Havelock, who had Sale's confidence. The day after the council Sale received information that Sir George Pollock had arrived at Peshawar to command the force for his relief.

On 19 February there was a severe earthquake which virtually levelled Jalalabad's laboriously constructed defences. Broadfoot at once set to work to reconstruct them, ably seconded by Havelock. They provided the real inspiration for Jalalabad's defence. At the end of February and early in March, Akbar Khan made attacks which were repulsed. Provisions ran short but on 1 April in a sortie some 500 sheep were seized. Sale was determined to attack, and on 7 April moved out of Jalalabad in three columns commanded by Dennie, Monteith, and Havelock. Dennie was killed leading the 13th light infantry to victory. Akbar Khan's lines were carried and his camp, baggage, guns, arms, ammunition, and horses captured. Akbar fled towards Kabul, and the chiefs of the peoples in the Khyber direction hastened to submit to Sale.

Pollock forced the Khyber and arrived at Jalalabad on 16 April. The garrison, soon to be described by Lord Ellenborough, the new governor-general, as 'Illustrious', paraded to greet the relieving force, a hastily scratched together band playing the old Jacobite tune 'Oh! but ye've been lang o'coming'. Pollock remained at Jalalabad for several months, partly to collect transport but chiefly while arguments persisted between him and Ellenborough as to whether he should return to Peshawar or advance to Kabul to recover the hostages still in Akbar Khan's hands. During this time of indecision Sale was made GCB on 16 June 1842 for his defence of Jalalabad. Pollock determined on an advance, and towards the end of July Sale moved out with his brigade to Kabul, followed by Pollock on 20 August. Sale had a fierce fight on 12 and 13 September at the Jagdalak Pass, but gained a decisive victory and by 15 September was camped at Kabul.

On arrival at Kabul, Sir Richmond Shakespear with 600 Kuzzilbash horse was dispatched to rescue the British captives at Bamian. He was closely followed by Sale with his brigade. The captives, who had by bribery already effected their own release, met Shakespear on 17 September and the following day were safe in Sale's camp. He was greatly affected when greeting his wife, daughter, and grandchild. On 12 October, Sale led the advanced guard of Pollock's army on the return march to India, which was reached without opposition on 12 November. On 17 December, at the head of the Jalalabad garrison, Sale crossed the Sutlej by the bridge of boats at Ferozepore and was received with great honour and bungled ceremony by the governor-general. On 24 February 1843 the thanks of parliament were unanimously voted to Sale, moved in the Lords by Wellington and in the Commons by Peel. On the death of General Edward Morrison, colonel of the 13th, Sale received, on 15 December 1843, as a special promotion for distinguished service, the colonelcy of his old regiment—a most unusual distinction for so junior an officer.

Last years, death, and reputation After some time in England, Sale returned to India as quartermaster-general of the queen's troops in the East Indies. On the outbreak of the First Anglo-Sikh War in 1845 he served as quartermaster-general of the army under Sir Hugh (afterwards Lord) Gough. His left thigh was shattered by grapeshot at the battle of Mudki on 18 December, and he died from the effects of this on 21 December. He was buried in the field after the battle of Ferozeshahr on 22 December 1845. At Mudki he had been present as quartermaster-general and not as field commander. There was no reason for an officer of his rank and responsibilities to be in the forefront of the battle but, in Sale's case, it was unthinkable that he could have been anywhere else. In action intrepid, he lacked decision in council. His nickname, Fighting Bob, sums him up as a soldier but ignores his indecision off the battlefield. He was a brave but lucky, rather than good, general.

Lady Sale and her journal Sale had married Florentia Wynch [**Florentia Sale** (1790–1853)] in 1809. She was the daughter of George Wynch and proved herself to be a true 'soldier's wife', accompanying her husband on his numerous postings and bringing up their children in the arduous conditions of the East. Handsome rather than beautiful, she was forthright in her opinions and contemptuous of those she called 'croakers' during the siege of the cantonments that preceded the retreat of the Kabul garrison.

Taken hostage by Akbar Khan after the massacre in the Khurd Kabul Pass, along with her daughter Alexandrina Sturt and newly born granddaughter, she nursed her son-in-law, Lieutenant John Sturt, after he was mortally wounded, and made certain he received a Christian burial, the only one who did. When they were taken hostage their baggage had been looted and they had little more than the clothes they were wearing; in Lady Sale's case these were riddled with bullets. She was twice wounded and had a bullet in her wrist. Fortunately she had kept by her the diary she had begun at Kabul in September 1841, which provided a graphic account of the siege, retreat, and her imprisonment as a hostage.

The hostages consisted of nine women, twenty officers (who included General Elphinstone and Brigadier Shelton), and fourteen children, as well as seventeen European soldiers, two European women, and one child. They were not molested but were crowded together in cramped and freezing conditions and moved at frequent intervals from fort to fort to prevent their rescue. After Akbar Khan's defeat outside Jalalabad they were moved to near Kabul, leaving behind a few of the party, which included General Elphinstone, who died on 23 April 1842. His body was sent to Jalalabad, where he was buried with military honours. To avoid rescue by General Pollock's advancing troops Lady Sale and her companions were moved to Bamian on 3 September. There they discovered their gaoler, Saleh Mohammed Khan, was open to bribery, and he agreed to effect their release in return for 20,000 rupees down and a pension of 12,000 rupees per annum. On 16 September they started for Kabul from Bamian, meeting the next day, at the foot of the Kalu Pass, Sir Richmond Shakespear and the rescuing Kuzzilbash horsemen. On the following day they met Sale with his brigade just in time to prevent their recapture by an Afghan force sent for that purpose.

After the publication in 1843 of her *Journal of the Disasters in Affghanistan*, Lady Sale became the heroine of the hour, renowned for her courage. She was a woman of character and unafraid of speaking her mind. She had her defects: Lord Harding, the governor-general, wrote to his wife on 20 January 1845: 'She is a clever woman, shrewd enough to be on her guard in society … but from what I hear very coarse' (Singh, 44). Lady Sale continued to reside in India after her husband's death, and was granted a pension of £500 a year in recognition of her conduct as a prisoner and of her husband's services. In 1853 she visited the Cape of Good Hope for her health, and died at Cape Town on 6 July, only a few days after her arrival.   JAMES LUNT

Sources J. W. Kaye, *History of the war in Afghanistan*, 3rd edn, 3 vols. (1874) · J. A. Norris, *The First Afghan War, 1838–1842* (1967) · P. Macrory, *Signal catastrophe: the story of a disastrous retreat from Kabul, 1842* (1966) · G. Pottinger, *The Afghan connection* (1983) · V. Eyre, *The military operations at Cabul, which ended in the retreat and destruction of the British army, January 1842* (1843); repr. with an introduction by J. Lunt as *Journal of an Afghanistan prisoner* (1976) · Lady Sale, *A journal of the disasters in Affghanistan* (1843) · G. R. Gleig, *Sale's brigade in Afghanistan: with an account of the seisure and defence of Jellalabad*, 2nd edn (1861) · R. Cannon, ed., *Historical record of the twelfth, or the east Suffolk, regiment of foot* (1848) · R. Cannon, ed., *Historical record of the*

thirteenth, first Somerset, or the Prince Albert's regiment of light infantry (1848) · W. Broadfoot, *The career of Major George Broadfoot … in Afghanistan and the Punjab* (1888) · *GM*, 2nd ser., 26 (1846) · *GM*, 2nd ser., 39 (1853) · *Annual Register* (1845) · H. C. B. Cook, *The Sikh wars: the British army in the Punjab, 1845–1849* (1975) · *The letters of the first Viscount Hardinge of Lahore … 1844–1847*, ed. B. S. Singh, CS, 4th ser., 32 (1986) · W. Sale, *The defence of Jalalabad, engravings, with letter press at the end by Col. W. Sale* (1846) · *DNB*
Archives Somerset Military Museum, corresp. and papers
Likenesses G. Clint, portrait, 1843, Castle Museum, Taunton [*see illus.*] · R. J. Lane, lithograph, pubd 1846, BM, NPG · F. Holl, stipple (after H. Moseley), BM, NPG · T. Lupton, mezzotint (after G. Clint), NPG · engravings, repro. in Sale, *Defence of Jalalabad*, frontispiece

Saleeby, Caleb Williams Elijah (1878–1940), writer and eugenist, was born on 3 May 1878 at 1 Bedford Row, Worthing, Sussex, the only son of Elijah George Saleeby, the founder of the Mount Lebanon schools, and his wife, Frances Maria, daughter of the pioneering alienist Dr Caleb Williams of York. He was educated by his mother and then studied at the Royal High School in Edinburgh, after which he read medicine at Edinburgh University, where he was first in first-class honours for his MB ChB (1901). Saleeby briefly practised in Edinburgh as resident physician in the maternity hospital and in the Royal Infirmary, and then as a resident officer at the York City Dispensary, before moving to London in 1901 to work under Sir Jonathan Hutchinson (who had once been apprenticed to his maternal grandfather) at the Polyclinic, a postgraduate medical college in Chenies Street. On 24 June 1903 Saleeby married Monica Mary (*b.* 1880), eldest daughter of Wilfrid John Meynell and Alice Christiana *Meynell, the poet. Monica's father was related to Saleeby, being the nephew of Caleb Williams, while her brother was the poet and publisher Sir Francis Meynell. The couple had two daughters.

Saleeby soon abandoned clinical practice for the life of a freelance writer and journalist, applying his knowledge and experience to a wide range of social issues. A turning point in his career came in May 1904 when he attended the meeting of the Sociological Society at which Francis Galton delivered his famous lecture on eugenics. Saleeby set out to popularize this new creed, and played an influential role in the launching of the Eugenics Education Society, founded in 1907. However, Saleeby was soon at odds with the society's officers: in 1913 its council even declined his offer to lecture to the organization. The main quarrel centred around Saleeby's increasingly outspoken attacks on what he called the 'better dead' school of eugenists, whom he accused of discrediting the movement with their reactionary class prejudices. Saleeby also differed from most eugenists in combining a concern for heredity with an interest in post-natal care (the result of his training as an obstetrician) and with a desire to combat what he dubbed the 'racial poisons': venereal disease, insanity, and, in particular, alcohol. From 1907 to 1923 Saleeby regularly lectured on eugenics at the Royal Institution. But, although still playing his self-appointed role as 'counsel for the unborn', he gradually moderated his earlier confident belief in eugenics as the 'religion' upon which depended the salvation of the world. Saleeby's interest in

Caleb Williams Elijah Saleeby (1878–1940), by Lafayette, 1927

population questions never abated, but it is significant that when, during the First World War, he became chairman of the national birth-rate commission he seemed less concerned to emphasize the need for qualitative racial improvements, the main theme in his earlier writings, than to advocate policies designed to arrest population decline. The First World War provided other outlets for Saleeby's reforming energies. He acted as an unpaid adviser to Lord Rhondda, the minister of food, and vigorously argued the case for the establishment of a ministry of health as a national war priority. In addition, Saleeby developed an expertise in the design of protective body armour, and contributed to the invention of the steel helmet.

After the war Saleeby threw himself into the campaign for clean air and heliotherapy, or helio-hygiene, drawing his inspiration and many of his ideas from Dr A. Rollier's sanatorium at Leysin, Switzerland. In 1924 he founded the Sunlight League, of which he became chairman, and preached the gospel of sun worship in his regular column in the *New Statesman*, written under the *nom de plume* Lens. A keen temperance reformer, Saleeby continued his life-long attacks on alcohol, which he dubbed the 'most mortal abomination of our time' (Saleeby, *Modern Surgery*, 275), and in a stream of articles and pamphlets he also argued the case for smoke abatement, rational clothing, improved diets, and healthy exercise.

Saleeby's marriage to Monica had broken down by 1911.

On 30 July 1929 he married Muriel Gordon (*b.* 1879/80), elder daughter of the Revd Robert Burland Billinge; the couple shared many interests, especially a love of music—though, characteristically, he was keen to distinguish between 'healthy' and 'morbid' musical compositions (Saleeby, *Health*, 372–4). The couple were married by W. R. Inge, dean of St Paul's, who was himself a eugenist. At the start of the Second World War Saleeby moved his home from St John's Wood, London, to Appletree, Aldbury, near Tring, Hertfordshire, where he did unpaid consulting work in the local ante-natal clinic. He died from heart failure at his home on 9 December 1940. He was survived by his wife.

Throughout his life Saleeby waged war tirelessly against what he called the diseases of darkness, true to his family name, which in Arabic means 'crusader'. He was a tireless committee man, serving, *inter alia*, as vice-president of the Divorce Law Reform Union, the National Temperance League, and the National Council of Public Morals. Saleeby's handsome appearance and commanding manner made him an effective lecturer, and he addressed audiences all round the world in support of his favourite causes. He was equally fluent with his pen, contributing articles to a wide variety of coterie journals and popular newspapers as well as to the medical press. All his writings bear the same hallmarks: clarity of expression, polemical vigour, and the happy knack of supporting an argument with homely but apt illustrations.

It was perhaps as a pioneering eugenist that Saleeby exercised greatest influence, making that creed known to thousands who might otherwise never have heard of it. He boasted that he had invented the phrases 'positive' and 'negative eugenics' and 'racial poisons'. Yet even in this field he managed to fall out with many would-be collaborators. Karl Pearson was furious at Saleeby's habit of referring to Galton as 'My Master', and Galton himself came to feel that Saleeby's occasional outbursts of silliness made him more of a liability than an asset. Yet Saleeby was important, not just as a popularizer of science, but for his role in dissociating population questions from the prevalent conservative orthodoxy. Saleeby joined the Fabian Society in 1910, advocated the emancipation of women, and never tired of proclaiming his belief in the compatibility between eugenics and social and political progress. In so doing, he became a leading spokesman for what scholars later called 'reform eugenics'.

Although his name is not linked to any one outstanding work, Saleeby wrote over a dozen books and pamphlets, as well as innumerable articles. His earliest publications, *The Cycle of Life* (1904) and *Evolution: the Master-Key* (1905), are expositions of the cosmology of Herbert Spencer. His next book, *Health, Strength and Happiness* (1908), is very different in tone, demonstrating its author's skill at making scientific research relevant to the problems of everyday life. Saleeby then went on to write four of the most widely read popular expositions of eugenics, *Parenthood and Race-Culture* (1909), *The Methods of Race-Regeneration* (1911), *The Progress of Eugenics* (1914), and *The Eugenic Prospect* (1921). Among his other books are *Modern Surgery and its Making*

(1912), *Woman and Womanhood* (1912), *The Whole Armour of Man* (1919), and *Sunlight and Health* (1923).

Particularly in the earlier stages of his career, Saleeby struck unsympathetic contemporaries as a crank, but many of the causes he espoused had become widely accepted by the time of his death: for example, his advocacy of clean air legislation, his warnings of the dangers of tobacco, his commitment to preventive medicine, and his calls for the training of parenthood. As his obituarist in *The Times* observed, if people had heard little of Saleeby in his latter years, that was because so many of his crusades had succeeded.   G. R. SEARLE

Sources *The Times* (12 Dec 1940) · *The Lancet* (21 Dec 1940), 794 · R. A. Soloway, *Demography and degeneration: eugenics and the declining birthrate in twentieth-century Britain* (1990) · G. R. Searle, *Eugenics and politics in Britain, 1900–1914* (1976) · G. Jones, *Social hygiene in twentieth-century Britain* (1986) · R. A. Soloway, *Birth control and the population question in England, 1877–1930* (1982) · WW · b. cert. · m. certs. · C. W. Saleeby, *Modern surgery and its making* (1912) · J. Badeni, *The slender tree: a life of Alice Meynell* (1981) · C. W. Saleeby, *Health, strength and happiness* (1908) · CGPLA Eng. & Wales (1941)
Archives Eugenics Society, London, records · Keele University Library, LePlay Collection, corresp. and minute book entries as member of Sociological Society committees
Likenesses Lafayette, photograph, 1927, NPG [*see illus.*] · photograph, repro. in *The Lancet*
Wealth at death £284 14s. 6d.: probate, 13 Dec 1941, CGPLA Eng. & Wales

Salem witches and their accusers (*act.* 1692) were the participants in a witch panic that gripped Essex county, Massachusetts, in 1692. The witch hysteria began in Salem village but then spread rapidly throughout the region. The core group of accusers consisted of girls and young women in Salem village who had begun to suffer strange fits, diagnosed by the local doctor as symptoms of witchcraft. Once they were pressured to name their alleged tormentors other villagers began to come forward with accusations of their own. During that year formal charges of witchcraft were brought against 156 people (listed in Godbeer, 238–42). Many others were named informally. Over half of those indicted lived in two Massachusetts communities, Salem village and Andover, but the accused witches included women and men from twenty-four New England towns and villages.

The most obvious characteristic of those accused was that an overwhelming majority, about three-quarters, were women. On both sides of the Atlantic witchcraft was perceived as a primarily female phenomenon and this instance was no exception. Puritans did not believe that women were by nature more evil than men, but they did see them as weaker and thus more susceptible to sinful impulses. Ministers regularly reminded New England congregations that it was Eve who first gave way to Satan and then seduced Adam, when she should have continued to serve his moral welfare in obedience to God. Some women were much more likely than others to be suspected of witchcraft. Throughout the seventeenth century New England women became especially susceptible to accusation if they were seen as challenging their prescribed place in a gendered hierarchy that puritans held to be ordained by God. Women who fulfilled their allotted

social roles as wives, mothers, household mistresses, and church members without threatening assumptions about appropriate female comportment were respected and praised as the handmaidens of the Lord; but those whose circumstances or behaviour seemed to disrupt social norms could easily become branded as the servants of Satan. Especially vulnerable were women who had passed menopause and thus no longer served the purpose of procreation, women who were widowed and so neither fulfilled the role of wife nor had a husband to protect them from malicious accusations, and women who had inherited or stood to inherit property in violation of expectations that wealth would be transmitted from man to man. Women who seemed unduly aggressive and contentious were also likely to be accused; behaviour that would not have struck contemporaries as particularly egregious in men seemed utterly inappropriate in women. **Bridget Bishop** and **Susannah Martin**, both executed in 1692, exemplify these characteristics: both had been widowed; Bishop had assumed control of her first husband's property before remarrying; Martin had engaged in protracted litigation over her father's estate in an unsuccessful attempt to secure what she considered her rightful inheritance; both women had displayed an assertiveness and fiery temper that some of their neighbours found deeply troubling.

In addition a significant number of the accused in 1692, male and female, either had reputations for occult expertise or had at least experimented with magical techniques for divination or healing. Although ministers condemned any form of magic as diabolical, layfolk often appreciated being able to consult 'cunning folk' for benign purposes. Yet such individuals were vulnerable to allegations that they had also deployed their abilities to harm enemies. **Samuel Wardwell** (*d.* 1692), for example, was known to have told fortunes and had boasted of his abilities. One neighbour was reported as having declared that he must be 'a witch or else he could never tell what he did' (Boyer and Nissenbaum, *Salem Witchcraft Papers*, 3.787).

Other suspects in 1692 did not fit so obviously the witch stereotypes that had informed earlier accusations. These individuals became vulnerable during the panic because they were associated in people's minds with recent threats to the New England colonies that had created an intense sense of endangerment. American Indian attacks, political reforms imposed by the government in England that threatened to undermine the colonists' independence, the increasing visibility of religious dissenters, and the imposition of a new charter in 1691 that gave freedom of worship and the vote to previously disfranchised groups such as Quakers combined to leave the colonists feeling imperilled by alien, invasive, and malevolent forces. They described these threats in much the same language used to characterize witchcraft. Puritans believed, furthermore, that there was a close connection between heresy, heathenism, and witchcraft. A significant number of the accused had close Quaker associations and several suspects were linked by their accusers to American Indians. Samuel Wardwell had Quaker relatives; one of

John Alden's accusers claimed that he had sold gunpowder to Indians and had been sexually involved with their women. **Tituba**, an accused American Indian woman who had lived in the Caribbean before coming with her master to Salem village, was marked by her race as well as her reputation for occult skills. Many of the accused were clearly perceived as outsiders, either literally or figuratively. Eight of the Andover suspects were marginalized by ethnic affiliation: **Martha Carrier** (d. 1692), for example, was Scottish and had married a Welshman.

During the decades leading up to the witchhunt Salem village itself had become bitterly divided around a series of issues that paralleled crises in the region at large. The village was legally subordinate to Salem town and had no civil government of its own. Some villagers wanted independence from the town, partly because the latter had proven remarkably insensitive to their concerns and partly to separate themselves from the commercial spirit that increasingly characterized the town, which was flourishing as a seaport. Villagers who saw that way of life as spiritually suspect tended to distrust neighbours who lived near to or were associated with the town's interests. Factional division was shaped by disparate economic opportunity as well as by cultural values. Those farmers who lived closest to the town had land of a higher quality, enjoyed easier access to its markets, and tended to see the town's development as an opportunity; those living further west had poorer land, were less able to take advantage of the town's growth, and tended to resent those who could do so.

Proponents of separation from the town secured the establishment of an independent church in 1689 and the ordination of **Samuel Parris** (1653–1720), a failed merchant, as their pastor. Parris, whose position as pastor was under threat by 1692, fuelled hostilities by translating factional division into a cosmic struggle between the forces of good and evil. His daughter and niece, **Elizabeth Parris** [married name Barron] (1682/3–1760) and **Abigail Williams** (b. 1680/81), were among the initial accusers. **Ann Putnam** (1679–1715), daughter of the minister's close ally Thomas Putnam (1653–1699), was another member of that core group; **Mercy Lewis** [married name Allen] (b. 1672/3), a servant in the Putnam household, and **Mary Walcott** [married name Farrar] (b. 1674/5), a niece who lived with the Putnams, were also prominent accusers. The elder **Ann Putnam** [née Carr] (1662–1699), wife of Thomas, claimed that she too was afflicted.

Divisions within the village were reproduced in the pattern of accusations in 1692: most accused witches and their defenders lived on the side of the village nearest to Salem town, whereas most of the accusers lived on the western side. Many of the accused had personal histories or interests that either associated them with Salem town or otherwise marked them as threatening outsiders. In Salem village and in the county as a whole those individuals and families who had become identified with forces that seemed disorderly and immoral fell victim to accusations of witchcraft as the initial afflictions in the village ignited witch panic.

By early October, when the court proceedings were halted amid acrimonious controversy, nineteen people had been hanged: Bridget Bishop on 10 June; **Sarah Good**, **Elizabeth How**, Susannah Martin, **Rebecca Nurse**, and **Sarah Wilds** on 19 July; **George Burroughs**, Martha Carrier, **George Jacobs**, **John Proctor**, and **John Willard** on 19 August; and **Martha Corey**, **Mary Easty**, **Alice Parker**, **Mary Parker**, **Ann Purdeator**, **Wilmot Reed**, **Margaret Scott**, and Samuel Wardwell on 22 September. **Giles Corey** was pressed to death under interrogation on 19 September. Over one hundred individuals were in prison awaiting trial, four of whom died during their confinement (**Lydia Dustin**, died on 3 March 1693; **Ann Foster** (d. 1692/3); **Sarah Osborne**, died on 10 May 1692; and **Roger Toothaker**, died on 16 June 1692).

Many historians have recounted the events of 1692, offering explanations that range from cynical conspiracy and manipulation to collective food poisoning. Academic and popular interest in the Salem trials has often distracted attention from other persecutions for witchcraft in the region. The 1692 witch-hunt was exceptional in its scale and intensity, but belief in the existence of witches was part of everyday life in early New England; sixty-one witch trials are known to have taken place there during the seventeenth century, in addition to those at Salem. Three-quarters of those tried before 1692 were acquitted because the evidence against them, though compelling in the eyes of their accusers, proved unconvincing from a legal perspective. The Salem trials were halted primarily because of controversy over the court's reliance upon problematic testimony, which reaffirmed and intensified judicial concerns regarding evidentiary issues. Such concerns combined with embarrassment and distress over the deaths that resulted from the trials that year to discourage future prosecutions, though an end to witch trials in New England by the century's close did not signify an end to the belief in and fear of witches.

The panic that swept through Salem found a modern-day counterpart in the McCarthyist 'witch-hunt' in Washington in the early 1950s, as dramatized by Arthur Miller in his play The Crucible (1953). Miller, who was himself summoned before the House Un-American Activities Committee, drew inspiration from Charles W. Upham's two-volume study of the trials (1867). Miller took as the play's centre the relationship between the accused John Proctor and the accuser Abigail Williams, with Proctor emerging as the 'most forthright voice against the madness around him' (Miller, 'Why I wrote The Crucible'). When Miller later reworked the play for a film version released in 1997, he recognized the continued relevance of 'one of the strangest and most awful chapters in human history' (Miller, The Crucible).   RICHARD GODBEER

Sources P. Boyer and S. Nissenbaum, eds., The Salem witchcraft papers: verbatim transcripts of the legal documents of the Salem witchcraft outbreak of 1692, 3 vols. (1977) • P. Boyer and S. Nissenbaum, Salem possessed: the social origins of witchcraft (1974) • C. F. Karlsen, The devil in the shape of a woman: witchcraft in colonial New England (1987) • R. Godbeer, The devil's dominion: magic and religion in early New England (1992) • J. P. Demos, Entertaining Satan: witchcraft and the culture of early New England (1982) • E. G. Breslaw, Tituba, reluctant witch of

Salem: devilish Indians and puritan fantasies (1996) · E. Reis, *Damned women: sinners and witches in puritan New England* (1997) · A. Miller, *The crucible* (1953) · A. Miller, *Timebends* (1987) · A. Miller, 'Why I wrote *The Crucible*: an artist's answer to politics', asuaf. org/~gurujohn/drama/miller-crucible.html, 20 Dec 2002

Salesbury [Salisbury], **Henry** (*b.* 1560/61, *d.* in or after 1632), grammarian and lexicographer, displays in his background and in his work many of the most important features of Welsh Renaissance culture. He was the son of Robert Salesbury of Galltfaenan and Dôl Belydr in Henllan, Denbighshire, and of Margred, his wife, daughter of Gruffudd ap Llywelyn Fychan of Lleweni Fechan. (His lineage is described in BL, Harley MS 1971, 121d.) He was previously held to be the son of Foulke, son of Piers Salesbury of Bachymbyd and Rug, but this opinion is now discredited (Caerwyn Williams, 50–52).

Salesbury matriculated at St Alban Hall, Oxford, in December 1581, at the age of twenty, gaining the degrees of BA in February 1585 and of MA in June 1588. He settled in Denbigh, where he practised medicine; Dr John Davies refers to him as 'medicus etiam doctis annumerandus' in his preface to *Dictionarium duplex* (1632). The preface also makes clear that Salesbury was still alive at that time. His date of death is unknown.

Salesbury's geographical and family connections are significant. His father's house in Henllan, where Salesbury wrote the dedication to the reader of his *Grammatica Britannica* (1593), and his own home at Denbigh were at the heart of the area which is considered to be the cradle of Welsh Renaissance thought and activity: the Vale of Clwyd and its environs. Many of the leading figures of the scholarly humanist culture of sixteenth-century Wales lived here, in an area which was prosperous, traditionally Welsh, and also open to the enriching currents of new thought and influence. The several branches of the Salesbury (Salisbury, Salusbury, Salsbri) family were prominent in the area and produced many figures of note, including William Salesbury, translator of the New Testament into Welsh, and Thomas Salisbury of Clocaenog, who printed Henry Salesbury's grammar in London.

Salesbury's grammar is a typical product of Welsh humanism, which was profoundly concerned with the need to make the Welsh language a worthy vehicle for the new learning. In Wales, as in other countries, the producing of grammars and dictionaries of the vernacular and the devising of a suitable orthography were matters in the forefront of scholars' minds. Salesbury's *Grammatica Britannica*, written in Latin, is also intended to uphold the dignity and worth of the Welsh language, which, he says in his preface, could compete with the most ancient languages in grace, reasoning, and regularity. Salesbury's grammar followed hard on the heels of Siôn Dafydd Rhys's *Cambrobrytannicae Cymraecaeve linguae institutiones* (1592), but he was persuaded to publish it, he says, because of its concise nature and its different examples. It is dedicated to Henry, earl of Pembroke.

Salesbury's Welsh–Latin dictionary, 'Geirfa tafod Cymraeg' ('The vocabulary of the Welsh tongue'), probably written after the grammar, remained in manuscript

(the only copy is in the National Library of Wales, NL Wales, MS 13215). Parts of the work appear to have been incorporated into Ieuan Fardd's vocabulary in Jesus College, MS 10. The dictionary uses Salesbury's own revised orthography; the symbols he uses for various sounds are tabulated side by side with the traditional symbols. Like almost all the orthographical innovations of the day, Henry Salesbury's system did not receive general acceptance.

The dictionary includes, as well as a list of 'words from the old Welsh and their interpretation' ('Geiriau o hên Gymraeg ai deongliad'), neologisms of Salesbury's own invention. These new words appear to be based on the grammatical analyses previously made by the author. The dictionary also includes dialect words and words in popular use; these are described as 'voces barbarae' in contrast to 'voces genuinae, purae'. Salesbury's approach to vocabulary was therefore catholic and inclusive.

Salesbury's metrical version of Psalm 15, together with some commendatory verses in Latin and Welsh, is also extant. They were included in *Egluryn Phraethineb*, a work on rhetoric by Henry Perri (1595). BRANWEN JARVIS

Sources H. Salesbury, *Grammatica Britannica*, English Linguistics 1500–1800 (1969) · J. E. C. Williams, *Geiriadurwyr y Gymraeg yng nghyfnod y dadeni* (1983) · C. Davies, *Rhagymadroddion a chyflwyniadau Lladin, 1551–1632* (1980) · C. Davies, 'Y Berthynas rhwng *Geirfa tafod Cymraeg* Henry Salesbury a'r *Dictionarium duplex*', *BBCS*, 28 (1978–80), 399–400 · B. Jarvis, 'Welsh humanist learning', *A guide to Welsh literature*, ed. R. G. Gruffydd, 3: *c.*1530–1700 (1997), 128–53 · M. T. Burdett-Jones, 'Dau eiriadur Henry Salesbury', *National Library of Wales Journal*, 26 (1989–90), 241–50 · M. T. Burdett-Jones, '"Index auctorum" Henry Salesbury ac "Authorum Britannicorum nomina" John Davies', *National Library of Wales Journal*, 26 (1989–90), 353–60 · E. Poppe, 'Latin grammatical categories in the vernacular: the case of declension in Wales', *Historiographica Linguistica*, 18 (1991), 269–80 · E. Poppe, 'Henry Salesbury's *Grammatica Britannica* (1593) and Ramist linguistic method', *Studia Celtica Japonica*, 9 (1997), 35–49

Salesbury, John (*c.*1532–1580/81). *See under* Salusbury family (*per. c.*1454–*c.*1684).

Salesbury, Sir Robert (1566/7–1599). *See under* Salusbury family (*per. c.*1454–*c.*1684).

Salesbury [Salisbury], **William** (*b.* before 1520, *d. c.*1580), translator and humanist scholar, was born some time before 1520 at Cae-du, Llansannan, in Denbighshire. He was the second son of Ffwg Salesbury (*d.* 1520) and Annes, daughter of Wiliam ap Gruffydd ap Robin o Gochwillan; his father was of a cadet branch of the Salisburys of Lleweni, a family originally of yeoman stock of English provenance [*see* Salusbury family].

Early years and education By 1540 William Salesbury had moved to Plas Isa, Llanrwst, which had been his father's and latterly his brother's residence. Little is known of his boyhood except that on his own admission he was at one time in Lancashire. He was probably educated locally and certainly imbibed something of the rich literary traditions of the Vale of Clwyd, a region that was a veritable archive of medieval Welsh culture. Tudur Aled (*c.*1465–

*c.*1525), one of the greatest of the poets of the Welsh gentry, also born in Llansannan, had composed an elegy in honour of Salesbury's great-grandfather and a eulogy of his grandfather. One of Tudur Aled's pupils was Gruffudd Hiraethog (*d.* 1564) who was to be a major *cywydd* poet: Salesbury was to regard him as one of his staunchest allies in saving and nurturing the Welsh language.

Salesbury proceeded to Oxford, probably residing at Broadgates Hall: he would have got to know many of his fellow countrymen at the university. Salesbury was 'in tender age' nurtured in the Catholic faith: it was probably at Oxford that he witnessed the stirrings of the Reformation described in his *Baterie* as 'Christes seconde byrthe here in Englande'. It was at Oxford that he was caught up in the renaissance of learning: in the letter to Richard Colyngbourne at the start of *A Briefe and a Playne Introduction* (1550) he describes Erasmus as 'the head learned man of all our tyme'. Maybe at Oxford, too, he acquired a taste for other languages. In Sir Thomas Wiliems's annotated copy (Havod MS 26, Cardiff Central Library) dated 1574, of a word-list by Wiliam Llŷn, Wiliems claims: 'W.S. is the most learned Briton not only in British, but also in Hebrew, Greek, Latin, English, French, German, and other languages'. Perhaps it was there that he witnessed what the devotees of other languages were doing for their own. No record exists of his having taken a degree at Oxford or, indeed, of his having proceeded to one of the inns of court, though it is known that, in 1550, he was at Thavies Inn, the inn founded by a Welshman in the fourteenth century: Salesbury was serving Sir Richard Rich, the lord chancellor, that year. He was, himself, involved in lawsuits—one a family dispute. There is no evidence of his having travelled abroad, as so many of his contemporaries did, but he spent some considerable time in London supervising the printing of his work: he refers to 'soiourning' at the house of Humphrey Toy, the bookseller 'in Paules Churchyarde'. During the reign of Mary he was probably back in Llanrwst; certainly between 1564 and 1566 he was with Richard Davies, bishop of St David's, at Abergwili, Carmarthenshire. From 1555 to 1558 Davies had been an exile at Frankfurt am Main, a centre of protestant activity, of lively interest in learning and the power of the printing press—all concerns close to Salesbury's heart.

William Salesbury married Catrin Llwyd, sister of Ellis *Price (the Red Doctor). There is reference to their having been separated at one stage: she died about 1572 and an elegy notes how grave was the loss to her husband. There were three children.

Scholarship and writings Although there is no contemporary portrait or effigy or even elegy, Salesbury must in retrospect be regarded as one of the great benefactors of Wales. He was a protestant, loyal to the throne and to the administration, but above all he was Welsh, sensible of what he perceived to be the needs of his fellow countrymen. It was a combination of Renaissance curiosity, the protestant Reformation, and a regard for the literary traditions and language of his own country that shaped Salesbury's career. The advent of the mechanical device of

printing turned many of his interests and intentions into a reality.

The range of his writings is remarkable—the product of a Renaissance humanist scholar, lexicographer, and translator. There exist two examples of protestant polemic that were his—one a pamphlet in Welsh and English, *Ban wedy i dynny*, and another work, *The Baterie of the Popes Botereulx*, both of which appeared in 1550. His devotion to the protestant cause was demonstrated, palpably, in his translations into Welsh from scripture and liturgy—*Kynniver llith a ban* ('All the lessons and articles of holy scripture') of 1551, and the prayer book and New Testament of 1567. His participation in the spirit of the new learning is exemplified in his translation into English of a Greek original in Latin form—*The Descripcion of the Sphere or Frame of the Worlde* (1550). In Welsh, such participation bridged two consuming interests—learning and service to his own language, demonstrated in a series of publications: *A Dictionary in Englyshe and Welshe* (1547), a collection of proverbs (1547; repeated in 1567), and a treatise on pronouncing the letters of Welsh, *A Briefe and a Playne Introduction* (1550; with a revised edition in 1567). There remain a manuscript work on rhetoric of 1552 and maybe his last work, a paraphrase of the best-known contemporary herbals, of about 1569. The *œuvre* demonstrates that he was the example *par excellence* of Welsh protestant humanism.

Protestantism and prayer book Early in his career as a writer Salesbury declared his profound protestant sympathies. In 1550 he authored two short polemical works, both emanating from the press of Robert Crowley in London. *The Baterie of the Popes Botereulx, Commonlye called the High Altare* was a work of some fifty-four pages in which Salesbury engages in one of the great controversial issues of the time, debating the doctrine of the sacrifice of the mass as epitomized in the existence of stone altars in churches. The metaphor of *baterie* in the title continues as a motif, emphasizing the confrontational nature of the work: stylistically it demonstrates his command of English. The other work was a bilingual piece, published anonymously though clearly Salesbury's work, *Ban wedy i dynny air yngair allan o hen gyfreith Howel Dda … A certain case extract out of the auncient law of Hoel Da*: in the preamble to the appropriate section of the law Salesbury claims 'ye maie easely gather that priests at that time had maried wyues'. This was now 'the Kynges lawe also'. It attempts to justify the new permission for clerical marriage by recall to the past.

But there was a practical and Welsh side to his protestantism, too. In 1551 there appeared *Kynniver llith a Ban*, a version of the epistles and gospels for the Sundays and holy days throughout the year—Salesbury's first major contribution towards presenting the scriptures in Welsh. The work opens with a Latin address to five bishops (St David's, Llandaff, Bangor, St Asaph, and Hereford), issuing a gentle rebuke for their indifference to such a need and asking them to authorize his translation for use in the churches. His method of translation was to return *ad fontes*. The basis was the English Book of Common Prayer of 1549, but he augmented that with new sources available to provide what he regarded as an accurate translation, and his marginal glosses, on occasion, represent his effort at a best rendering. The work is marred by orthographical quirks and his concern for word derivation, and it has been said that his translation of the epistles is not as good as his gospel translations. But as a pioneering work it is remarkable.

The seed had been sown, and an act of parliament of 1563 ordered the bishops of Wales and Hereford to ensure that a Welsh translation of the whole Bible and Book of Common Prayer and administration of the sacraments be ready by 1 March 1567. It was what Salesbury wanted, and he embarked upon his next two ambitious ventures (though he was to fall short of producing the whole Bible). The Welsh prayer book, *Lliver gweddi gyffredin*, printed in London by Henry Denham 'at the costes and charges of Humfrey Toy. Anno 1567.6.Maij', reproduced the Book of Common Prayer in its revised form of 1564. It also included a translation of the Psalms indebted to various contemporary versions and Salesbury's own concern for fidelity to the original. His name does not appear, but textual analysis points incontrovertibly to him. Scholarship had advanced since his textual renderings of 1551 and he took advantage of that, too. Here, the orthographic quirks are slightly fewer, as are the English borrowings. There are Latinized forms bolstering the dignity and pedigree of Welsh and he uses more than one rendering, at times, to demonstrate the copiousness of the language. For him, accuracy was fundamental: all in all it is a work of extraordinary merit.

New Testament and new learning Within six months there appeared the Welsh translation of the New Testament, *Testament Newydd ein Arglwydd Iesv Christ*, published on 7 October 1567. It was a volume of 426 pages, and the title-page reads (in translation):

> drawn, as far as the different idioms allowed, word for word from the Greek and Latin … each word deemed to be unintelligible, either because of the local dialect, or because of the unfamiliarity of the matter, has been noted and explained in the margin of the same page.

There are three contributors to the translation noted in the text: Richard Davies, bishop of St David's (1 Timothy, Hebrews, epistle of James, 1 and 2 Peter); Thomas Huet, precentor of St David's (the Apocalypse); and Salesbury (all the rest, including the translation from the Geneva Bible of the 'arguments' and the 'contents', with the exception of the epistle of James). Much of the translation, therefore, is Salesbury's and he, clearly, is also 'editor'. Earlier versions, contemporary scholarship, and an instinctive feel for the genius of the language produced a masterpiece—despite the intrusion of Salesbury's philological and orthographic theories. There is an epistle to the Welsh people by Richard Davies, the acknowledged apologia for Welsh protestantism, and a dedication to the queen written by Salesbury in the style of Renaissance dedications. According to Sir John Wynn of Gwydir, Richard Davies and Salesbury were also collaborating on a translation of the Old Testament but they disagreed over

the use of one word: be that as it may, work on the Old Testament did not proceed and the intention of the act of parliament of 1567 was unfulfilled for the time being.

The new learning Salesbury was a product of the new learning, too. In 1550 appeared his work *The Descripcion of the Sphere or Frame of the Worlde*, a translation of *De sphaera* by Thomas Linacre, distinguished Renaissance scholar and friend of Colet, Erasmus, and More, itself a translation from the Greek of Diadochus Proclus. It is a treatise, in Salesbury's words, 'of the wonderfull goodly, and deuyne fabricature of the world'. The dedicatory letter 'To his verye lovynge Cosen Iohn Edwardes of Chyrcke' was written 'At Thavies Inne in Houlborne … 1550'. But for Salesbury the Renaissance ideal was married to an immediate, local, social conscience: the language of his fellow countrymen was Welsh and it was right that that language should meet the demands of the new spirit of enquiry.

Salesbury and the Welsh language The art of printing exposed the 'word', giving it sanction and definition, and among Salesbury's first printed books was *A Dictionary in Englyshe and Welshe*, printed by John Waley 'at London in Foster Lane' in 1547. Prefixed to the dictionary is 'a little treatyse of the englyshe pronunciacion of the letters', and there is a dedicatory letter to Henry VIII. The dictionary, probably compiled from contemporary dictionaries and Welsh manuscript vocabularies, has the appearance of a work-book, devised in the first place for Salesbury's own use. There are gaps and the work shows signs of haste. Though the title suggests an English–Welsh formula, the work is Welsh–English: this has caused scholars something of a dilemma. Maybe Salesbury's desire for his fellow countrymen to enjoy the fruits of learning and the benefit of biblical texts suggested that a knowledge of English was paramount and urgent. And he was a Tudor Welshman, too.

Salesbury was clearly fascinated by language and words. In 1550 he published what was, basically, a phonetic guide to Welsh: *A Briefe and a Playne Introduction …*, printed by 'Roberte Crowley, dwellyng in Elye rentes in Holburne'. It includes a short comparative study of Welsh sounds with Hebrew and Greek and a further examination of the Latin element in Welsh (first treated by him in the dictionary of 1547). A second edition appeared in 1567 under the title *A Playne and a Familiar Introduction*: the title-page reads 'This Treatise is most requisite for any man … who wyl be thorowly acquainted with anie piece of translation, wherein the sayd Salesbury hath dealed'.

But language was more than words for him: in 1547 there appeared *Oll synnwyr pen Kembero ygyd* ('The *summa* of a Welshman's wisdom'). It was printed 'at London in saynt Iohns strete by Nycholas Hyll' and was a collection of some 930 Welsh-language proverbs which Salesbury claimed he had taken by stealth from a manuscript copy in the hand of Gruffudd Hiraethog. In the letter to the Welsh reader that introduces it, Salesbury refers to Erasmus, John Heywood, and Polydore Vergil and their compilations of proverbs: he recalls the long tradition of proverb-collecting in Wales. Salesbury published the collection for several reasons—the fashion of the time, the fact that they represented the *sapientia* of the language and provided vocabulary ingredients necessary for other works. In his letter Salesbury begs those who possess manuscripts of all kinds to make them available: above all, such vocabulary would serve well in the task of scripture translation. A further edition, with corrections and additions, including the 'Triads of the island of Britain', appeared in 1567.

In 1552 Salesbury had compiled a translation and adaptation into Welsh of a work on rhetoric, *Tabulae de schematibus et tropis* by Petrus Mosellanus. The translation was not published and the original is to be found in Cardiff MS 21: at least nine copies were made. Although rhetorical devices were known, in part, to the Welsh poets and prose writers of an earlier age, Salesbury deemed it necessary to create a new vocabulary of rhetorical terms and to give them definition. It is his purpose to offer these figures of rhetoric as 'pillars, foundations and props' to support the language: Salesbury's illustrations are taken in the main from the Welsh poets though, occasionally, he resorts to Latin examples.

Last years Salesbury's last recorded work, *Llysieulyfr* ('Herbal'), belongs to the period 1568–74. It was not published and the original copy is lost, but a copy was made by Roger Morris of Coed y Talwrn in 1597: he claimed to have borrowed the original from Thomas Wiliems who referred to Salesbury in 1574 as 'phisicwr godidoc' ('a splendid physician [or mediciner]'). The *Llysieulyfr* is basically a paraphrase of some of the best-known herbals of the sixteenth century, in particular *De historia stirpium* by Leonhard Fuchs (whom Salesbury describes in his piece on 'Apiastrum' as 'the chief botanist of our age'; another source was William Turner's *A New Herball*, a complete edition of which appeared in 1568. The Welsh version betrays signs of a first draft: sometimes unidiomatic Welsh follows upon a hurried word-for-word translation. The entries normally follow the same pattern—the name(s) in Latin, English, Welsh, a description, where to find the herbs, the season of the year in which they appear, and what properties they possess.

In *The History of the Gwydir Family* by Sir John Wynn there is a suggestion that William Salesbury lived until 1599, but it is probable that he died about 1580. The place of his burial is not known and no elegy survives. He is the outstanding example of the Welsh Renaissance scholar, broad in his range and interests (language, law, theology, history, science, literature, medicine), inquisitive, and enquiring. Salesbury believed that, to prosper culturally, Wales had to become part of the new Europe, with the learning of the Renaissance within the grasp of his fellow countrymen. He had been converted to protestantism and was prepared to devote his very considerable energy and talents to providing the means by which his fellow countrymen 'shoulde participate and enjoy the incomparable treasure of Christes Evangelie' (W. Salesbury, *A Playne and a Familiar Introduction*, 1567). Salesbury's scholarship was formidable and his output immense. But perhaps his greatest contribution was that, grounded as he was in the indigenous literature of Wales, he was able to create a vibrant medium by grafting a new vocabulary and new forms of expression onto the richness of the language that he inherited. Bishop William Morgan virtually adopted Salesbury's version of the New Testament into his Bible of 1588 and that became not only the keystone to worship but also the canon of *bel usage* for the Welsh language. William Salesbury played no small part in preparing the way for it.   R. BRINLEY JONES

Sources R. G. Gruffydd, ed., *A guide to Welsh literature*, 3: *c.1530–1700* (1997) · I. R. Edgar, ed., *Llysieulyfr Salesbury* (1997) · R. Brinley Jones, *William Salesbury* (1994) · I. Thomas, *William Salesbury and his Testament* (1967) · I. Thomas, ed. and trans., *Y Testament Newydd Cymraeg, 1551–1620* (1976) · G. Williams, *The Reformation in Wales* (1991) · G. Williams, 'The achievement of William Salesbury', *Transactions of the Denbighshire Historical Society*, 14 (1965), 75–96 · W. A. Mathias, 'William Salesbury: ei fywyd a'i weithiau', *Y traddodiad rhyddiaith*, ed. G. Bowen (1970) · R. G. Gruffydd, 'The Renaissance and Welsh literature', *The Celts and the Renaissance*, ed. G. Williams and R. O. Jones (1990), 17–39 · G. Williams, *Recovery, reorientation and reformation: Wales, c.1415–1642*, History of Wales, 3 (1987) · NL Wales, MS 4581 · E. D. Jones, 'William Salesbury, a'i deulu 1546', *BBCS*, 7 (1933–5), 137–41 · W. Salesbury, *The baterie of the Popes Botereulx* (1550)

Archives NL Wales, copy of medicinal treatise in the hand of Roger Morris, MS 4581 · NL Wales, MS · NL Wales, treatise on rhetoric, Cardiff MS 21

Salesbury [Salisbury], **William** (1580?–1659/60), royalist army officer, was the third and youngest son of John *Salesbury (c.1532–1580/81) of Bachymbyd, Denbighshire [*see under* Salusbury family], and Rug, Merioneth, and Elizabeth (d. 1588), daughter of Sir John Salusbury of Lleweni. Salesbury, also known, in Welsh, as Hên Hosanau Gleision ('Old Blue Stockings'), matriculated from Oriel College, Oxford, on 19 October 1599. He appears to have turned shortly thereafter to a military life, gaining experience as a pikeman in the Netherlands and a privateer in the East Indies. He was shipwrecked on the way home, however, losing much of the wealth he had acquired. On his return to Wales he worked as a cattle dealer for a time until the death of his oldest surviving brother, John, in 1611, when he became head of this branch of the family. His brother had been in severe debt and had alienated much of the family estates of Bachymbyd and Rug, so William set about regaining and re-consolidating the estate, which he did with some success. He based his family at Rug and became a considerable figure in county politics, being appointed *custos rotulorum* in 1617, representing Merioneth in the 1620–21 parliament, and having some say in subsequent elections for the shire in the 1620s. He did not follow his father in the Catholic faith, but demonstrated a conservatism in his religion exemplified by the lavish decoration of the private chapel he built at Rug in the late 1630s.

At the outbreak of the civil war in 1642 Salesbury was nominated in the commissions of array for both Merioneth and Denbighshire, appointments that were confirmed in May 1643. It was Sir Thomas Salusbury, his relation at Lleweni and not, as sometimes suggested, William Salesbury, who was appointed colonel of the regiment of foot raised in north Wales in August 1642 and fought at Edgehill; Salesbury's own movements during this period are uncertain. Charles I appointed him governor of Denbigh in September 1643, and he began to fortify the dilapidated castle there at his own expense. The parliamentarian commander Sir Thomas Myddelton wrote from Wrexham on 14 November 1643 requesting Salesbury to surrender the castle, but he replied that to do so would be 'to betray so great a trust ... as in itself is abominable' (Phillips, 2.95–7). Myddelton shortly after retreated, and Salesbury remained relatively untroubled until 1645. After his defeat at Rowton Heath, Charles I stayed at Denbigh Castle from 25 to 28 September 1645 as his guest, on which occasion Sir Edward Walker stated that Salesbury 'under the cover of a countryman had more experience, courage and loyalty, than many that made far greater stress' (E. Walker, *Historical Discourses upon Several Occasions*, 1705, 141). After parliamentary advances in north Wales, on 7 April 1646 General Mytton asked Salesbury to yield his garrison, but he replied that he would discharge the king's command to keep the castle, and would 'endeavour to make good for him to my last gasp' (Smith, 163–4). Mytton thus began a siege of Denbigh on 17 April 1646, and issued a number of entreaties requesting Salesbury's surrender. The correspondence between the two men reveals Salesbury's complete commitment to Charles and his resoluteness in the king's cause. He was described as a 'very wilful man' by parliamentary commanders, and remained unyielding to Mytton's demands for surrender despite the increasingly desperate condition of the royalist cause in north Wales (Phillips, 2.307). He received a letter of thanks from Charles I on 13 September 1646 for his loyalty, and the next day the king ordered him to surrender. Accordingly, on 26 October 1646, Denbigh Castle, which was one of the last royalist strongholds to continue its resistance, surrendered on favourable terms. In remembrance of Salesbury's loyalty Charles I, on the eve of his execution, sent him an embroidered cap of crimson silk. Salesbury was fined at a tenth of £781 by the parliamentary authorities, though he was reported to be unable to attend the committee in London owing to 'a rupture in his body'; his fifth and twentieth were assessed at £3000 (Green, *Compounding*, 1723).

Salesbury married Dorothy Vaughan (*d.* before 1650), daughter of Owen Vaughan of Llwydiarth, Montgomeryshire, on 10 December 1611. It was at Salesbury's request that her near relative Rowland Vaughan of Caergai translated William Brough's *Manual of Prayer* into Welsh, Salesbury paying for copies to be distributed among the poor. Salesbury himself wrote religious poetry in Welsh. He was reported to have retired to a farm at Bodtegir and lived in 'obscurity and comparative indigence', though there are letters that show him living near Llanfwrog from 1653 (Lloyd, 6.28). A quarrel with his eldest son, Owen, over his marriage to Mary Goodman led Salesbury to split his estates into two, settling the greater part on his second son, Charles. In the event Owen predeceased his father, dying on 17 January 1658, transmitting the Rug estates to

his son, William. Salesbury made his will on 8 June in 1659 or 1660 and it was proved on 10 December; he was buried in the church at Llanynys, Denbighshire.

LLOYD BOWEN

Sources W. J. Smith, ed., *Calendar of Salusbury correspondence, 1553–circa 1700* (1954) · N. Tucker, 'Denbigh's loyal governor', *Transactions of the Denbighshire Historical Society*, 5 (1956), 7–34 · J. Williams, *Ancient and modern Denbigh* (1856) · [J. Ballinger], ed., *Calendar of Wynn (of Gwydir) papers, 1515–1690, in the National Library of Wales* (1926) · J. R. Phillips, *Memoirs of the civil war in Wales and the marches, 1642–1649*, 2 vols. (1874) · NL Wales, Bachymbyd papers · P. R. Newman, *Royalist officers in England and Wales, 1642–1660: a biographical dictionary* (1981), 325 · J. Y. W. Lloyd, *The history of ... Powys Fadog*, 6 vols. (1881–7) · M. A. E. Green, ed., *Calendar of the proceedings of the committee for compounding ... 1643–1660*, 5 vols., PRO (1889–92) · M. A. E. Green, ed., *Calendar of the proceedings of the committee for advance of money, 1642–1656*, 3 vols., PRO (1888) · Caernarvonshire RO, Newborough (Rûg) MSS, XD2/ · W. N. Yates, *Rûg chapel, Llangor church, Gwydir Ughaf chapel* (1993) · P. Yorke, *The royal tribes of Wales*, new edn, ed. R. Williams (1887) · NL Wales, Llansteffan MS 170 · Foster, *Alum. Oxon.*
Archives NL Wales, corresp. [transcripts] · NL Wales, papers as governor of Denbigh Castle | NL Wales, Bachymbyd MSS · NL Wales, Bagot (Bachymbyd) letters · Caernarvonshire RO, Newborough (Rûg) MSS, XD2/
Likenesses portrait, 1632, Blythfield House, Staffordshire; repro. in Tucker, 'Denbigh's loyal governor'
Wealth at death estates valued at £7810 in 1647 for the purposes of sequestration; Lady Elenor Salusbury's jointure of *c.*£2000 should probably be added to this figure: Smith, ed., *Calendar of Salusbury correspondence*, 15; Green, ed., *Calendar of the proceedings of the committee for compounding...* (1723)

Salgado, James (*fl.* 1666–1684), pamphleteer, was born in Madrid and educated in Spain, where he made his profession as a Dominican friar. According to his later published accounts he became unsettled in his religious views and in 1666 fled to France, where he found refuge with Charles Drelincourt, the minister of the protestant congregation at Charenton. There he renounced his Catholicism. After a short period in the Netherlands he returned to Paris only to be apprehended on the orders of Louis XIV's Spanish queen and extradited to Spain, where he was imprisoned by the Inquisition at Llerena. He escaped but was recaptured near Murcia and was sentenced by the Inquisition there to five years in the galleys. Released after one year on medical grounds he was sent to a house of correction in Murcia but escaped again, successfully, and reached London in 1678.

Salgado's arrival there coincided with the 'revelations' of Titus Oates, and he lent his support to the anti-papist cause in several publications denouncing Roman doctrine and practice, and recounting his sufferings at the hands of the Inquisition. These slim volumes were translated for him from the Latin or Spanish, since he never mastered English. His *The Romish Priest Turn'd Protestant* (1679) was prefaced by a testimonial from his fellow convert Andrew Sall, dated from Christ Church, Oxford, 26 December 1678, and dedicated to the University of Oxford in acknowledgement of its benevolence. *The fryer, or, An historical treatise wherein the idle lives, vitiousness, malice, folly and cruelty of the fryers is described in two parts, tragical and comical* (1680) was a more marketable collection of unedifying tales. *The*

Slaughter-House, or, A Brief Description of the Spanish Inquisition (1682), dedicated to Charles II, gave some account of Salgado's own experiences. He dedicated other brief works of controversy to the earl of Nottingham and to Prince Rupert, but poverty drove him reluctantly to seek more lucrative work. In the preface to *An impartial and brief description of the plaza, or sumptuous market-place of Madrid, and the bull-baiting there* (1683) he shamefacedly excused his recourse to popular print on the plea of 'pinching want'. It is the first account in English of the art of bull fighting, then in its formative stage, and a Spanish translation was published by the Unión de Bibliófilos Taurinos in 1962. The frontispiece is of historical value, depicting the plaza Mayor in Madrid as it was before its destruction by fire in 1672. Further evidence of Salgado's penury is to be found in the *Brief Description of the Nature of the Basilisk, or Cockatrice*, which he advertised about this time. The bird (presumably stuffed) had been brought back from Ethiopia by a Dutch physician who, out of pity, presented it to Salgado so that 'by showing this rarity to my honourable Benefactors, I might invite their Charity towards me'. The exhibit was not profitable. Salgado appears to have migrated soon afterwards to the Netherlands, since his last recorded work, a booklet of moral precepts entitled *Geraldus Lisardo de regimine morali*, was published from Amsterdam in 1684. Some of his rarer works, together with an autograph manuscript, are to be found in the Wiffen collection at Wadham College, Oxford, and in the Usóz collection in the National Library at Madrid. A copy of *Manners and Customs of the Principal Nations of Europe* (1684), based on his European travels, survives in Chetham's Library, Manchester.   G. MARTIN MURPHY

Sources J. Salgado, *The slaughter-house, or, A brief description of the Spanish Inquisition* (1682) · J. Salgado, *A confession of faith of James Salgado … with an account of his life and sufferings by the Romish party* (1681) · M. Menéndez y Pelayo, *Historia de los heterodoxos españoles*, 5 (1928), 191–4 · Wing, *STC* · D. Ruiz Morales, ed., *Jacobo Delgado y su descripción de la fiesta de toros* (1962) · A. Palau y Dulcet, *Manual del librero hispano-americano*, 2nd edn, 18 (1966), 384

Salisbury. For this title name *see* individual entries under Salisbury; *see also* Longespée, William (I), third earl of Salisbury (*b.* in or before 1167, *d.* 1226); Ela, *suo jure* countess of Salisbury (*b.* in or after 1190, *d.* 1261); Montagu, William, first earl of Salisbury (1301–1344); Montagu, Katharine, countess of Salisbury (*d.* 1349) [*see under* Montagu, William, first earl of Salisbury (1301–1344)]; Montagu, William, second earl of Salisbury (1328–1397); Montagu, John, third earl of Salisbury (*c.*1350–1400); Montagu, Maud, countess of Salisbury (*d.* 1424); Montagu, Thomas, fourth earl of Salisbury (1388–1428); Neville, Richard, fifth earl of Salisbury (1400–1460); Neville, Richard, sixteenth earl of Warwick and sixth earl of Salisbury (1428–1471); Pole, Margaret, *suo jure* countess of Salisbury (1473–1541); Cecil, Robert, first earl of Salisbury (1563–1612); Cecil, William, second earl of Salisbury (1591–1668); Cecil, James, third earl of Salisbury (*d.* 1683); Cecil, James, fourth earl of Salisbury (1666–1694); Cecil, Mary Amelia, marchioness of Salisbury (1750–1835); Stanley, Mary Catherine, countess of Derby [Mary Catherine Gascoyne-Cecil, marchioness of Salisbury] (1824–1900); Cecil, Robert Arthur Talbot Gascoyne-, third marquess of Salisbury (1830–1903); Cecil, James Edward Hubert Gascoyne-, fourth marquess of Salisbury (1861–1947); Cecil, Robert Arthur James Gascoyne-, fifth marquess of Salisbury (1893–1972).

Salisbury, Sir Edward James (1886–1978), ecologist and botanist, was born at Limbrick Hall, Harpenden, Hertfordshire, on 16 April 1886, the youngest of the nine children (six boys and three girls) of James Wright Salisbury, a businessman and company director, and his wife, Elizabeth Stimpson. His cousin was the portrait painter Frank O. Salisbury, and Edward and his sister Ethel were both skilled in drawing for botanical illustration. His early interest in living plants was maintained during his schooldays at University College School. Salisbury entered University College, London, in 1905 and, after graduating with second-class honours in botany, became a research student of F. W. Oliver, who had a lasting effect on his thought.

Salisbury gained his DSc in 1913 with a thesis on a fossil seed. In 1914 he moved to East London College (later Queen Mary College) as senior lecturer in botany. He returned to University College in 1918 and was appointed senior lecturer in 1919, reader in plant ecology in 1924, and finally Quain professor of botany in 1929. In 1917 he married Mabel (*d.* 1956), daughter of John Elwin-Coles; they had no children.

From 1908 onwards the woodlands of his native Hertfordshire increasingly engaged Salisbury's attention and he published a series of important papers on woodland ecology, and *Flowers of the Woods* (1946). He made numerous observations on light intensity in woods at different times of the year and studied the effect of this, together with coppicing and soil leaching, on the ground flora, thus revealing the importance of these hitherto somewhat neglected factors in woodland ecology. They led him to investigate the number of stomata on a square millimetre of leaf surface of different species and of the same species growing under different conditions and to establish a stomatal index for comparison. Studies involving laborious counting always fascinated Salisbury.

Of wider significance and the source of much financial gain were the textbooks jointly prepared by F. E. Fritsch and Salisbury: *An Introduction to the Study of Plants* (1914; 9th edn, 1928), *Elementary Studies in Plant Life* (1915; 8th edn, 1926), *An Introduction to the Structure and Reproduction of Plants* (1920; 2nd edn, 1927), and *Botany for Students of Medicine and Pharmacy* (1921; 3rd edn, 1928), followed by *Plant Form and Function* (1938) which combined the two *Introduction* volumes. Clearly written, well illustrated, and presenting information not readily available elsewhere, they were immediately appreciated. The title of the first chapter of the 1914 *Introduction*, 'The plant as a whole', epitomizes their approach. Salisbury himself was much interested in the quantity of seeds produced by individual plants of many species, notably weeds, which he rightly viewed as of great significance in relation to their spread and establishment. He painstakingly counted and weighed seeds belonging to over 240 species, and his calculation that individuals of some weed species produced on average 35,000 seeds indicates the labour involved. He reported these findings in *The Reproductive Capacity of Plants* (1942), *Downs and Dunes* (1952), *Weeds and Aliens* (1961), and a number of journal articles.

Salisbury was a keen and successful gardener all his life but little known before 1935 in horticultural circles. In an astute publicity act, Salisbury's attractively illustrated but scientifically sound *Living Garden* (1935) was presented to the council members of the Royal Horticultural Society, who were so impressed that they awarded him the Veitch memorial medal in 1936, invited him to deliver the Masters memorial lecture in 1937, and awarded him the Victoria medal of honour in 1953. This association, together with fellowship of the Royal Society, to which he was elected in 1933, served him well in 1943 when he was appointed director of the Royal Botanic Gardens, Kew, a position hitherto always filled by a taxonomic botanist. Salisbury received the then customary knighthood in 1946, having been appointed CBE in 1939.

The restoration of the war-damaged garden and the return to Kew of its collections and of staff members from the armed forces, together with inadequate funding, presented Salisbury with many problems in his new office. His service on a diversity of boards and committees occupied much time which some thought he should have devoted to Kew exclusively; frustrated staff members, unaware perhaps of the long hours he worked in the Kew office and his dedication to the institution as a whole, blamed him for deficiencies over which he had little control and inevitably there was much friction and discontent. The Australian house built in 1952 still stands but his chalk garden and clematis wall were later demolished. More important was post-war restoration, notably of the palm house, which he succeeded in getting the government to undertake. A further cause of unhappiness during Salisbury's Kew years was his wife's ill health.

Salisbury was a founder member and, from 1917 to 1931, honorary secretary of the British Ecological Society and the president in 1923, a vice-president of the Royal Society for 1943 and 1948–55 and the biological secretary from 1945 to 1955, vice-chairman of the Agricultural Improvement Council from 1945 to 1956, honorary secretary of the Hertfordshire Natural History Society from 1912 to 1922 and president from 1922 to 1925, president of the Norfolk and Norwich Naturalists Society for 1931, his *East Anglian Flora* (1932) being based on his presidential address, and a member of other councils, boards, and committees. On all these bodies his geniality, self-confidence, vitality, breadth of interest, and grasp of essentials made him a valuable member; he was, moreover, a popular lecturer. The Royal Society awarded him the royal medal in 1945 and he had honorary doctorates from Edinburgh (1950) and Glasgow (1956).

On Salisbury's retirement from Kew in 1956 he and his wife moved to a seaside house, Croindene, Strandway, Felpham, Bognor Regis, for the sake of her health. Tragically she died that year, but Salisbury continued to live at Felpham, returning to the investigation of fruit and seed production and publishing a further eighteen articles and notes. He died at home on 10 November 1978.

WILLIAM T. STEARN, *rev.*

Sources 'Profile: Sir Edward Salisbury, prophet and pragmatist of botany', *New Scientist* (11 June 1959), 1294–5 · *The Times* (14 Nov 1978) · *West Sussex Gazette* (24 Nov 1978) · A. R. Clapham, 'Sir Edward Salisbury', *Nature*, 279 (1979), 357–8 · P. Richards, *British Ecological Society Bulletin*, 10 (1979), 30–31 · J. P. M. Brenan, *Journal of Horticultural Science*, 54 (1979), 165–6 · A. R. Clapham, *Memoirs FRS*, 26 (1980), 503–41 · personal knowledge (1986)
Archives RBG Kew, notes, drawings, and papers | BL, corresp. with Sir Sydney Cockerell, Add. MS 52752 · CAC Cam., corresp. with A. V. Hill · Commonwealth War Graves Commission, Maidenhead, papers relating to work of Imperial War Graves Commission · NL Scot., corresp. with Sir George Taylor
Likenesses H. Coster, group photograph, 1937, NPG; *see illus. in* Field, (Agnes) Mary (1896–1968)
Wealth at death £202,531: probate, 1 Dec 1978, *CGPLA Eng. & Wales*

Salisbury, Enoch Robert Gibbon (1819–1890), barrister and book collector, eldest son of Joseph Salisbury, was born on 7 November 1819 at Bagillt, Flintshire. After working at Liverpool, he became prominent in the business and civic life of Chester. On 28 June 1842 he married Sarah (*d.* 1879), daughter of the Revd Arthur Jones, an Independent minister at Bangor. They had five daughters and one son, Philip Salisbury, who had an eventful military career.

On 7 January 1850 Salisbury became a student of the Inner Temple, and on 17 November 1852 he was called to the bar. He worked on the north Wales circuit, where he had a good practice, but he was most successful as a parliamentary counsel. He was elected Liberal MP for Chester in 1857, but he was unsuccessful in contesting the seat in 1859.

A keen and knowledgeable bibliophile, Salisbury built up a fine library, which now forms the Salisbury Library of the University of Wales at Cardiff, and which includes books and pamphlets in Welsh from the sixteenth century onward, books by Welsh authors, and books relating to Wales and the border counties, especially Cheshire and Shropshire. He published several works, including *A Catalogue of Cambrian Books at Glen-aber, Chester, 1500–1799* (1874) and *Border Counties Literature: a Catalogue of Border County Books in the Glen-aber Library* (1880). He died at his house, Glen-aber, Saltney, near Chester, on 27 October 1890, and was buried at nearby Eccleston.

ALBERT NICHOLSON, *rev.* BETI JONES

Sources *DWB* · J. Foster, *Men-at-the-bar: a biographical hand-list of the members of the various inns of court*, 2nd edn (1885), 410
Archives BL, corresp. with W. E. Gladstone, Add. MSS 44388–44475 · Ches. & Chester ALSS, letters to Thomas Hughes · East Riding of Yorkshire Archives Service, Beverley, Wintringham MSS · North East Lincolnshire Archives, Grimsby, letters to John Wintringham
Likenesses wood-engraving (after photograph by J. Watkins), NPG; repro. in *ILN* (May 1857)

Salisbury, Francis Owen [Frank] (1874–1962), painter, was born on 18 December 1874 at Harpenden, Hertfordshire, one of the family of five sons and six daughters of

Francis Owen Salisbury (1874–1962), self-portrait, 1937
[sketching in Westminster Abbey]

exhibited around the country. The government commissioned him in 1943 to paint *The Signing of the Anglo-Soviet Treaty* to present to the USSR.

Salisbury's gift lay not only in his able depiction of large crowds, for which he is principally remembered, but also in portraiture. His career as a portrait painter flourished, and he established a distinguished clientele in the United States as well as in Britain. Among his sitters he numbered five presidents of the United States, five British prime ministers, and three archbishops of Canterbury. He became a member of the Royal Society of Portrait Painters in 1917 and the Royal Institute of Painters in Water Colours in 1921.

Salisbury was deeply interested in religious subjects, having been brought up in a strictly religious household. For a portrait of John Wesley he asked the architect C. A. Voysey, a descendant of the Methodist leader bearing a close resemblance to him, to sit to him. Salisbury painted canvases of the prophets of Israel for the American Dr Parkes Cadman, and he designed stained glass for a number of churches, becoming master of the Worshipful Company of Glaziers in 1933–4. He was appointed commander in the Royal Victorian Order (CVO) in 1938 and received the honorary degree of LLD at St Andrews University in 1935. In 1936 he became cavaliere of the order of the Crown of Italy.

In 1944 Salisbury published his memoirs, *Portrait and Pageant* (revised as *Sarum Chase* in 1953). In the same year a large retrospective exhibition of his work, also called 'Portrait and Pageant', was held at the Royal Institute Galleries in Piccadilly, London. He was a man of great charm, and an enthusiastic gardener, for whom his garden in Hampstead was a great joy. A keen motorist, he took considerable pleasure in driving his Rolls-Royce. He dressed immaculately, 'like a Harley Street gout specialist', according to Kenneth Clark (Clark, 47), wearing an old-fashioned dark cravat and tie-pin. Salisbury died on 31 August 1962 at his home, Sarum Chase, 23 West Heath Road, Hampstead, London. His studio sale was held at Christies on 25 September 1985.

Henry Salisbury, plumber and glazier, and his wife, Susan Hawes. A delicate child, he was educated mostly at home by his sister, Emmie. When he was fifteen he was apprenticed to his eldest brother, James Salisbury, in his stained-glass works at St Albans. Later his brother took him to Heatherley's drawing academy in London, which he attended three days a week. At eighteen he won a scholarship at the Royal Academy Schools. He attended for five years, winning several medals and awards, including the Landseer scholarship which enabled him to travel to Italy in 1896.

Salisbury quickly acquired a considerable reputation exhibiting at the Royal Academy from 1899 until 1943, though he was never offered membership in the institution, which disappointed him very much. His first Royal Academy exhibit was a portrait of Alice Maude (*d.* 1951), daughter of C. Colmer Greenwood, whom he married in 1901; they had twin daughters. A year's study of his daughters sharpened his skills in portraiture and inspired a number of his pictures of children in subsequent years.

Heraldry and pageantry were also among Salisbury's interests. A very large composition, *The Passing of Queen Eleanor* (1907), led to a commission for the mural *The Trial of Katharine of Aragon* for the House of Lords. Other murals followed: *The Great Artists of Chelsea* for Chelsea town hall, and works for the Royal Exchange, Liverpool town hall, and elsewhere. Of great importance to him was his recording, in oils and generally on a large scale, of important national events and royal ceremonial. These paintings included *The Burial of the Unknown Warrior* (1921), the thanksgiving service for the silver jubilee of George V, and the coronation of George VI. Some of these were widely

MAURICE BRADSHAW, *rev.* CHARLES NOBLE

Sources F. O. Salisbury, *Sarum Chase* (1953) · *The Times* (1 Sept 1962) · B. A. Barber, *The art of Frank O. Salisbury* (1936) · F. O. Salisbury, *Portrait and pageant* (1944) · N. L. Silvester, 'The challenge to beauty: gleanings from a talk by Frank O. Salisbury, CVO, LLD, RI, RP', *Bulletin of the Russell-Cotes Art Gallery and Museum* (Dec 1942–March 1943) · K. Clark, *Another part of the wood* (1974), 47 · *CGPLA Eng. & Wales* (1962) · personal knowledge (1981) · NPG, Heinz Archive and Library, Salisbury papers · JRL, Methodist Archives and Research Centre, F. O. Salisbury MSS

Archives JRL, Methodist Archives and Research Centre · NPG

Likenesses F. O. Salisbury, self-portrait, oils, 1924, Russell-Cotes Art Gallery and Museum, Bournemouth · W. R. Dick, bronze bust, *c.*1927, repro. in *Royal Academy illustrated* (1927), 118 · photograph, *c.*1928, repro. in Salisbury, *Portrait and pageant* · F. O. Salisbury, self-portrait, oils, 1937; Christies, 25 Sept 1985, lot 240 [*see illus.*] · Bassano, photograph, 1939, NPG · A. C. Cooper, photograph, NPG · K. Pollack, photograph, NPG

Wealth at death £84,237 17*s.* 6*d.*: probate, 18 Oct 1962, *CGPLA Eng. & Wales*

Salisbury, Henry. *See* Salesbury, Henry (*b.* 1560/61, *d.* in or after 1632).

Salisbury, John of (late 1110s–1180), scholar, ecclesiastical diplomat, and bishop of Chartres, was born at Old Sarum in Wiltshire. From the fact that he began his studies in Paris in 1136, it is likely that he was born some time in the second half of the second decade of the twelfth century. On one occasion (*Letters of John of Salisbury*, no. 212) he writes that his name is 'little' or 'short' (*parvum nomine*), but to contemporaries he was usually known as John of Salisbury, and he refers to the people of Salisbury and Wiltshire as his own (*gens nostra*) in his *Policraticus* (John of Salisbury, *Policraticus*, 8.191; cf. ibid., 6.18) and to Salisbury Cathedral as his mother church (*mater mea*). The family also had connections with Exeter. John's mother, Gille Peche, had children by at least two husbands, one of whom may have been Richard fitz Serlo, prebendary of Teignton in Devon. John apparently had two half-brothers, Richard Peche, or Peccator ('Sinner'), and Robert 'son of Egidia' (or 'of Gille'). Richard was probably a canon of Exeter from at least 1143 until 1168 or later. Robert, who had a son and appears to have married, was a physician; he had the title of master and like John he shared his mother's looks. He became archdeacon of Totnes *c.*1170 and seems to have died in January 1186. John also had a full brother, Richard of Salisbury, with whom he seems to have got on well and who was much younger; he was probably a canon of Exeter, perhaps by *c.*1156, and he became an Augustinian canon at Merton Priory in Surrey by the spring of 1172. John himself may just possibly have been a canon of Exeter by *c.*1160, but he was treasurer by May 1173, and also came to acquire revenues from the dioceses of Salisbury, Canterbury, and Norwich. The family may have moved to Exeter when Robert of Chichester, dean of Salisbury since at least 1148, became bishop of Exeter in 1155. John's mother was still alive at Exeter in late 1170, but ill; on his return from exile on 15 November John made a final visit to her before returning to Canterbury by 19 December, ten days before Becket's murder.

Education John's early schooling, probably in Old Sarum, was provided by a priest who taught him the psalms and also sought unsuccessfully to involve him in sorcery and in crystal-gazing. In 1136 John went to Paris and, in his *Metalogicon* (2.10), he provides valuable sketches of the masters who taught him. He learned dialectic over two years on the Mont-Ste Geneviève, first from Peter Abelard, 'a clear and wonderful teacher' whose every word he drank 'with consuming avidity', then Master Alberic who was full of subtle questions, and next Robert de Melun who had more than one answer to them. In his later years John still called Abelard's pupils his friends (ibid., 2.17). He thought that both Alberic and Robert would have been better philosophers if they had read more widely in the Latin authors, and also that he himself, having plunged into dialectic, had become 'a young sage'. So to recover his senses, he writes, he transferred to William, 'the grammarian of Conches', with whom he remained for three years from 1138 to 1141 'during which I read widely. I shall

never regret the time thus spent' (ibid., 2.10). Then he passed to Richard, known as the Bishop, for a period of revision, including study of the quadrivium and rhetoric. He had also attended other teachers such as Hardwin the German, Master Theoderic, and Peter Helias; he had struck up a friendship with Master Adam, and started teaching the children of nobles, including William of Soissons, as a way of relieving his poverty.

After these three years John took up theology as well and briefly studied under Master Gilbert, who left Paris in 1142 on becoming bishop of Poitiers, then Robert Pullen, whom he admired but who also left Paris in 1144 on becoming papal chancellor, then Simon of Poissy, whom he found obtuse. John writes that the whole period spent in study amounted to twelve years. It is now thought unlikely that John spent any of this time at Chartres after leaving the Mont-Ste Geneviève in 1138. Although there is no direct evidence of where he was taught by William of Conches, his association with the other masters he mentions makes Paris far the likeliest place as four of these masters also taught William of Tyre, the future historian of the Latin East, when he came to Paris to study in 1145 or 1146. Finally, to compare his progress with that of his old associates, John revisited the Mont-Ste Geneviève, which was then physically and juridically outside the city of Paris, but he was disappointed to find that these dialecticians had not progressed as much as a hand's span. John counted himself (and was) exceptionally fortunate to have received an unhurried and wide-ranging education, and to have come to Paris at the time when its schools secured their pre-eminent position in Europe. He was also fortunate to come to the notice during these years of two notable figures in the monastic world: Peter of Celle, abbot of the Benedictine house of Montier-la-Celle in Champagne, who employed John as a clerk for a while, and Bernard, the Cistercian abbot of Clairvaux, later canonized, who provided the testimonial in 1147 that helped John to be appointed as a clerk at Canterbury. Bernard wrote that John was in penury and that he should carry Bernard's letter to Archbishop Theobald in person.

Canterbury, 1147–1163 For the next twelve years John was in the service of Theobald, archbishop of Canterbury, 'trifling away my time' as he wrote sardonically in the prologue to his *Policraticus*. He spent much of this time travelling to and from the papal court, and was apparently working for Eugenius III by March 1148 when the pope was at Rheims, possibly earlier too when the pope was in Paris between 20 April and 7 June 1147. Archbishop Theobald clearly saw in John a man who could move easily in ecclesiastical circles on the continent. In the late 1150s, as he was to recall in his *Metalogicon*, he had crossed the Alps ten times, twice travelled through Apulia, and many times crossed France as well as England (John of Salisbury, *Metalogicon*, 3, prologue). These journeys are as difficult to reconstruct as his movements while a student. Four datable crossings of the Alps occurred *c.*1149, early in 1154, in 1155, and in 1156, with another possibly in 1158–9. He was in Apulia with Pope Eugenius III in 1150 (and attended a feast given by Robert of Selby, chancellor of the king of

Sicily); at Ferentino between November 1150 and the summer of 1151; at Segni in spring 1152 when Frederick Barbarossa's election as holy Roman emperor was announced; at Rome in December 1153 with Pope Anastasius IV, and for three months at Benevento with the English pope, Adrian IV, between November 1155 and July 1156. On the latter occasion he obtained from the pope the grant of Ireland to Henry II as a hereditary fee. The form of this grant may well explain why John fell into disgrace with the king for a brief time after his return to England.

The first of the two collections of John's letters cover the years 1153–61. They contain in total 135 items, most of them written by John in Theobald's name. Theobald's consistent endeavour was to secure the liberty of the church during the anarchy of Stephen's reign, and co-operation with Henry II. One of John's principal tasks in writing Theobald's letters was to explain legal cases, offer advice, and present policy. The letters are relatively frequent for the years 1156–7 and 1159–61 but infrequent between 1158 and early 1159. The collection closes with the death of Theobald in 1161. John acquired in Theobald's court, as well as in that of the pope, a deep working knowledge of legal procedure, both in canon and in civil law. He coincided with the presence at Canterbury, between c.1148 and 1150, of Master Vacarius who had taught the Roman law at Bologna. Over half the letters are concerned with business touching the papal court and they provide evidence of some fifty appeals to it; others are addressed to the king, to his chancellor (from January 1155 this was Thomas Becket, who had been another of Theobald's clerks), to bishops, clergy, and laymen. The appeals to the pope include the case of Richard of Anstey which sheds much light on difficulties in the law of marriage as well as on the law's delays (*Letters of John of Salisbury*, no. 131). John also wrote playfully and affectionately to Peter of Celle (ibid., no. 112) and on one occasion (ibid., no. 33) he entertainingly wrote about wine, contrasting the renown of the English for hard drinking with the habit of the Gauls to send their guests away never dry but sober. Throughout he shows a rare gift for suiting his style to the person and the topic. Some of the last letters between 1159 and 1161 are concerned with the double election to the papacy in September 1159 which resulted in schism, and also with the difficulties surrounding the election of Bartholomew, another of Theobald's clerks, as bishop of Exeter shortly before Theobald died. This collection of letters appears to have been made by a colleague of John's at Canterbury in the early 1160s.

Although John complained on more than one occasion that his duties were inimical to study and that his only free time was that required for eating and sleeping, he managed in at least some of these years to write a great deal. In his early years at Canterbury he wrote an *Entheticus de dogmate philosophorum* which he dedicated to Becket as chancellor (and therefore finished in or after January 1155). This is a didactic satirical poem which, in ostensibly offering advice to an anonymous student who is about to leave Canterbury to study in the schools, develops thoughts about the right relationship between reason and

eloquence and directs satire against those who distort it. The student is encouraged to read as much as he can, to remember that there is always more to be read, and to prize the study of philosophy as well as of the Bible. John introduces into the poem some of the monks of Canterbury Priory, including his good companions Odo and William Brito, the sub-prior who loved cheese and loved books more. He also introduces dubious characters from the royal court who appear under made-up names, derived from antiquity, which render attempts at identification puzzling, if not deliberately futile: Hyrcanus (perhaps King Stephen or King Henry), Mandrogerus (Robert, earl of Leicester (*d.* 1168), or Roger de Pont l'Évêque), Antipater (Richard de Lucy), and Sporus (Richard du Hommet). John is gloomy about the state of his country, the royal court, indeed all courts and corrupt officials, including the archbishop's household. He presents a radiant picture of Thomas Becket, but he delivers warnings concerning Becket's ambiguous place on the royal scene. By 1159 John also completed the *Metalogicon* and the *Policraticus*; both works are dedicated to Becket.

Metalogicon The *Metalogicon* was written to defend the study of all the seven liberal arts from becoming streamlined and narrowly career-orientated. The work is the fruit of John's years of study during which he had learned the value of a broad education in which the powerful weapons of dialectic are mastered, but kept under control by a firm grounding in grammar and the other liberal arts. John offers general exhortation to his readers to 'reverence the words of the great authors … these words possess a certain majesty or prestige from the great names of antiquity with whom they are associated … they are very effective when used for proof or refutation' (John of Salisbury, *Metalogicon*, 3.10). John attacks the phantom figure of Cornificius and his followers, the Cornificians, who promoted a utilitarian or vocational approach to teaching and learning which led to a devaluation of the arts and to the invention of short cuts through them.

The *Metalogicon* conveys John's admiration for William of Conches, 'the most accomplished grammarian since Bernard of Chartres' (John of Salisbury, *Metalogicon*, 1.5), Bernard being William's master at the cathedral school of Chartres as well as the model (according to John) upon whom William based his own teaching. John had come to France too late to hear Bernard, who had ceased to be chancellor of Chartres by 1126, so it is probably from William that John gained the intimate knowledge of Bernard's methods and example as a teacher (ibid., 1.24). Bernard had made a famous comparison (also found in William's writings) of the moderns with dwarfs seated on the shoulders of ancient giants, only seeing a little further than the latter (ibid., 3.4). In his prologue John writes that he has not hesitated on occasions to prefer the opinions of the moderns to those of the ancients, and that he hopes that posterity will come to celebrate their glory, for many of his contemporaries have admirable qualities of mind and expression.

Policraticus On the *Policraticus* ('The statesman') more than on any other of his works, and on its innumerable allusions to the literature of pagan and Christian antiquity, rests John's reputation as a humanist scholar. It was very widely read later in the middle ages. John began it in 1156, while Becket was preparing for the siege of Toulouse, and he finished it in 1159. The dedication, which takes the form of a shorter version of the *Entheticus de dogmate philosophorum*, depicts John journeying to the chancellor's house to present his work and then returning to Canterbury where he catches sight on the horizon of the angel which topped the tower of Christ Church. In eight books John explores the opposition between the pursuit of philosophy and the habits of courtly life. The *Policraticus* seems to be at once a work of political theory, a manual of government, a mirror of princes, a moralizing critique of life at court; and also an encyclopaedia of letters and learning, a storehouse of *exempla* and *historiae*, and a didactic philosophical and ethical treatise. It recommends to lax, epicurean courtiers a wide programme of education in letters, philosophy, and law. Although it is certainly fat, the work is not in fact as loosely organized as it first appears: John seems to have started upon it when, in disgrace with the king, he meditated on the theme of fortune (book 7). Then he wrote a 'mirror of princess' (book 4), and then the books on courtiers. Finally in the summer of 1159 he expanded these essays, and bound them all together in eight books.

Books 1 and 2 deal with the perils created by success and fame—the extinction of reason and the withering of virtue. John especially makes fun of a wide range of frivolities including feasting and drinking at court, gambling, debauchery, dramatics, magic, astrology, auguries, the interpretation of dreams, and, above all, hunting. The crazy mania for hunting had led to a number of royal deaths, and although John avoids giving names, that of William Rufus springs to mind. England, he wrote, seemed to be governed by huntsmen. The frivolities are lambasted in a series of learned chapters. He had an endless supply of stories taken from his wide reading and often from memory. Had John lived in an age of newspapers he could have become a celebrated columnist writing both seriously and entertainingly as well as fast and frequently on any pastime. Occasionally he lifts the veil from current realities as when he criticizes (John of Salisbury, *Policraticus*, 2.27) Becket's recourse to soothsayers and to a palmist as the king's army prepared to advance into Snowdonia in 1157. He satirizes physicians for taking their fees while their patients are still in pain: they could not cure disease but they took the credit for time's kindly work, reviving with refreshing drinks and nourishment those whom they themselves had brought close to death through long fasting.

In the prologue to book 3 John mentions that his attacks on folly have gained him enemies, and he writes so again in the prologue to book 8, where he pleads that he has aimed to expose vice without hurting individuals. In book 3 he continues on the attack and writes at length on flatterers. He also briefly justifies the killing of a tyrannical

ruler. And he introduces the subject of philosophy by describing the first step that needs to be taken on the path to wisdom. This is to 'know thyself': the human heart carries within it a book of knowledge which may be opened by the exercise of reason.

In book 4 John turns to the ruler and portrays the differences between a prince and a tyrant, the prince being one who upholds law and equity and who serves the priesthood. In book 5 John draws upon a work which he says was written by Plutarch and given the title *On the Instruction of Trajan* (*Institutio Trajani*). Trajan is presented as the model of the good prince, Plutarch as the philosopher who taught and guided him. The work depicts an analogy between the commonwealth and a human body and soul. John focuses attention on the public, organic character of the state as distinct from personal lordship. To this end he employed classical legal concepts such as *aequitas, jus,* and *justitia.*

John's patriotism is best seen in book 6 where he criticizes the Welsh of Snowdonia for their raiding in English lands, and also berates his fellow Englishmen for slack military discipline which has enabled the Welsh to make inroads that they would not have made in the time of Edward the Confessor and Harold Godwineson. However, his admiration for the military skills of recent kings of England is very high; William Rufus and Henry I had been feared in France, and Henry II, still in the earliest years of his reign, was projected by John as destined to be the greatest king of his age; his titles form a continuous chain from the boundaries of the British Isles to the frontier of Spain. But of King Stephen, John was bitterly critical for usurping the throne, for exalting 'new men' and disinheriting others, as well as for his imprisonment of bishops. Of Stephen's son, Eustace, John wrote that all he wanted was to preserve the crown for himself. Though proud of his country and of its invincibility abroad, John accused his contemporaries of living lasciviously at home.

Books 6 and 7 contain comment on the state of the church. In book 6 John reports at length an intimate conversation he once had in Apulia with Pope Adrian IV, who was English and whom John had come to know well when he was Cardinal Nicholas Breakspear. The pope asked John for his candid assessment of the reputation of the Roman curia. At first John confined himself to an outline of the curia's reputation for venality, but the pope pressed him for a personal opinion. John made a show of reluctance for if he were to disagree with the common opinion he would be thought to be a flatterer, and if he were to agree with it he would be thought disloyal. So he balanced his answer by naming reforming critics within the curia itself as well as cardinals of obvious personal integrity. John was always loyal to the church and to its established institutions. One of the longest passages of criticism in the whole of the *Policraticus* is vigorously directed against charismatic and ascetical figures who, allegedly in the name of the free spirit, denounced the contemporary church. John does not name the objects of his criticism but they would have included dissenting preachers on the continent like Arnold of Brescia and Henry of Lausanne. True piety, John argues, is still to be found among the orders of monks and canons which, despite their shortcomings, uphold religion, whereas their critics are but ravening wolves dressed up in sheep's clothing. In book 7 John asks for free time and for domestic help to enable him to complete the work which Becket expects him to write. He plunges into a discussion of philosophy and expresses, as he did also in the *Metalogicon*, his own sympathy for the school of academics who, following Cicero, inclined to scepticism over the wide range of fundamental philosophical questions. He also provides a history of the development of philosophy from its beginnings with Pythagoras, through the Ionic school, Plato, and Aristotle, and then the Epicureans. The lives of the philosophers interest John as much as their doctrines, and in this he resembles Abelard. He upheld the example of Bernard—the 'old man of Chartres'—who told his pupils to renounce all and to live a humble life in pursuit of learning. John writes movingly of the exceedingly arduous lives chosen by the new monastic orders of Carthusians and Grandmontines. He admits that, as a secular priest, his own frugal life cannot be compared with even that of an indifferent monk who is confined within a cloister. He tells, however, a cutting story of the ambition of Gilbert Foliot who was then bishop of Hereford but who, as he had earlier risen up the ranks of monastic office, had always criticized the sloth of those immediately superior to him, only stopping (John was writing in the late 1150s) when he himself became a bishop.

John wrote the *Policraticus* in the early years of Henry's reign before Henry's positive achievements in statecraft, law, and administration had been put in place, but also before the king's quarrel with Becket. He was clearly disturbed by sleaze in courts and he gave a large array of *exempla* which illustrate both the paths followed by the wise and the fates which befall the foolish. Hence the subtitle which John added: *De nugis curialium et vestigiis philosophorum* ('Courtiers' trifles and philosophers' footsteps'). He lampooned the ambition of courtiers to acquire power, prestige, and wealth. He saw their self-indulgent excesses in the light of the warnings of scripture and of the church fathers as well as of the moral counsel found in classical writings. He attacked tyrants and advocated tyrannicide. On this topic John has been held to be inconsistent, though careful enquiry has shown that he in fact introduces in book 8 rather a series of qualifications to his doctrine than a *volte face*: he proposes that the tyrant should be slain, but proceeds to make it clear that God will do this, and that history shows that all tyrants have come to a bad end. He makes mention of a work on 'the Ends of Tyrants' which, if he ever wrote it, has not survived.

For John history was the guide of life (*historia magistra vitae*), and by history John meant stories from or about the past. He filled his *Policraticus* with series of examples of deeds and sayings which spur wise men to pursue virtue and to put aside vice, or which distract them from doing so. Examples in this sense (*historiae*) seemed often more useful than precepts. In the prologue to a later work, the *Historia pontificalis*, John was to cite Cato's *Distichs*: 'the lives of others are our teachers' (John of Salisbury, *Memoirs of the Papal Court*, 3). The outcome of present actions may be predicted from a knowledge of the outcome of similar actions in the past. Hence John writes that 'whoever knows nothing of the past hastens blindly into the future' (ibid.). Historical examples, however, can cut more than one way, and the lessons to be learned carry with them innumerable difficulties; John explores their ambiguities and their conflicts with relish and with a taste for controversy. They are topoi or *loci* which become lodged in the memory but from which the debaters may draw differing arguments. Faced, for instance, with the example of Brutus the elder—who had his sons executed for patriotic and republican reasons—John admits that the incident was infamous and the cruelty excessive, but he parades this and other examples of similar conflicts in order to illustrate the priority of the public interest over family loyalties.

John has been judged a reliable and accurate scholar in citing sources which he first read when a student in France. But he relied also on anthologies and excerpts, and much of his reading was pursued in English libraries such as those in Canterbury at Christ Church and at St Augustine's. He handled his materials very freely to suit his purposes and to provide good stories, introducing deliberate mistakes and even fabrications while asking his readers to accept that his fictions serve a good purpose. The most puzzling example of John's classical learning has been that of his reliance on the *Institutio Traiani* which John paraphrases in books 5 and 6. John attributes the work to Plutarch, but many scholars believe that John concocted it through cheerful cheating with other classical texts. John's scholarship is both grave and humorous, sometimes ambiguous, at times exasperating. But he did like to entertain. One playful display of *exempla* surrounds his parody of a candidate for ecclesiastical advancement (John of Salisbury, *Policraticus*, 7.19). The candidate has defects but they can all be excused: he is of low birth, but even St Peter was no patrician; he is under age, but so was St John the Baptist; he is slow in speech, but so was Moses for whom Aaron was found; he is illiterate, but so were the apostles; he consorts with prostitutes, but Hosea did the same and at God's command; he has been a soldier, but so was St Martin; he is accused of gluttony and drunkenness, but Jews said the same of Christ, and so on.

Exile, 1163/4–1170 After Becket's accession to the see of Canterbury in 1162 John continued his work as a clerk. There is little information on his life between Theobald's death and John's exile. He travelled to Montpellier in July 1162 to collect Becket's pallium and wrote a life of Anselm of Canterbury in support of the case for his canonization which may have been hoped for at the Council of Tours in May 1163. As clouds gathered over Becket because of his fight for ecclesiastical liberties, Anselm's own earlier struggles with Rufus and Henry I, as well as his two periods of exile, will have come to seem most pertinent. John left England late in 1163 or early in 1164. He first went to Paris, posing as a student and to make preparation for

Becket's possible flight from England, then to Rheims. Becket followed, after the Council of Northampton, in November 1164 and went to Sens to see the pope; then he settled at Pontigny. The quarrel between Becket and the king put a strain upon John's friendship: John would not abandon Becket's cause but he disagreed with what Becket did, and he was also short of money. The second collection of John's letters, covering the years 1163–80 and including 190 items, is largely filled with letters about the quarrel with the king.

John lived from 1164 to 1170 in Rheims as the guest of Peter of Celle, now abbot of St Rémi. He was joined twice by his brother Richard and he twice went on pilgrimage, to St Gilles in 1167 and to Vézelay in 1169. In these years the *Historia pontificalis* seems to have been written. It is a short and unfinished work, all but certainly written by John and addressed to Peter of Celle, abbot of St Rémi, 'my dearest friend and master'. It is presented as a continuation of the chronicle of Sigebert of Gembloux and contains 'memoirs of the papal court' between 1148 and 1152. Only one manuscript survives, from the abbey of Fleury. John narrates a number of events and draws fine vignettes of some of the leading personalities of the day who also often appear in his correspondence—of Bishop Henry, for example, buying old pagan statues in Rome to take back to Winchester, ostensibly to prevent the Romans from worshipping idols; of Pope Eugenius III reconciling King Louis of France and his wife Eleanor on their return from crusade in 1149 and getting them to sleep together in the same bed which he 'decked with priceless hangings of his own', or again of Eugenius III shrewdly dismissing the petition of the count of Molise for a divorce and then prostrating himself so totally before him that his mitre slipped off his head and rolled in the dust as cardinals and bishops struggled to lift him up.

But John writes first and at greater length about his former master Gilbert, now bishop of Poitiers but accused of heresy by Bernard of Clairvaux and others. Hearings had taken place at Rheims in 1148 before Pope Eugenius III and this was one of the earliest events which John had witnessed in the curia shortly after leaving the Parisian schools. John seems to have taken full notes of the arguments that were compiled as the basis for discussion and he discusses Gilbert's philosophy and theology in some detail. His portrayal of the characters of Bernard and Gilbert is memorable: both excelled in learning but in different branches of it. Gilbert could not be tripped; Bernard was filled with faith and charity in all he wrote, but the cardinals mistrusted him. John also writes about the refusal of Eugenius to allow Stephen's son Eustace to be crowned, and he discusses too the case brought by the Empress Matilda to Pope Innocent II in 1139 against King Stephen for his usurpation of the English throne. Of Stephen's advocate—Arnulf, bishop of Lisieux—John thought badly. He allows the venality of the papal court to appear and vividly portrays disagreements between popes and cardinals. He affirmed the greatness of Eugenius III but brought out his suspicious nature. He also sketches

the shortcomings of Henry, bishop of Beauvais and archbishop of Rheims, the brother of Louis VII of France. The *Historia pontificalis* is the most important extant source on several matters, and it is also informative on the Roman revolution of 1143 and on Arnold of Brescia.

In 1165 John learned that his property in England had been confiscated. As Becket lived at Pontigny, John corresponded with him there; there are numerous letters also to others, among them his friends John of Canterbury, formerly a clerk at Canterbury and now bishop of Poitiers, and Bartholomew, bishop of Exeter. John's hopes and fears, his advice to others, and the information he had gathered or required, are set forth. In 1165 and 1166 John held out little hope for Becket, and he sought his own reconciliation with the king. In letter 144 John reported to Becket on a discouraging meeting he had had with the king of France near Paris. He attended an abortive discussion between Henry II and Louis VII at Angers on about 24 April 1166, and in doing so wasted money and lost two horses (*Letters of John of Salisbury*, no. 167). In letter 168 John writes to Bartholomew about the conference held soon after at Chinon where Henry vented his resentment against the archbishop who had excommunicated John of Oxford and other royal counsellors. In letter 175 John identifies the writer of the poisonous letter, sealed with the seals of the bishops of London, Winchester, and Hereford (cf. ibid., no. 174), as Gilbert Foliot (Achitophel and Doeg). His efforts at mediation were not successful, but in 1167 his hopes were raised by news of the set-backs suffered by the emperor Frederick Barbarossa and the improvement of the position of Pope Alexander III. In letter 279 John gives an eyewitness account of the meeting between Becket and the English and French kings on 1–2 July 1168 at La Ferté-Bernard, and he mentions also the visit he made to Henry at Montmirail (cf. no. 288). The letter collection culminates in John's description, sent to Peter of Celle, of the fraught and dangerous atmosphere in England on the return there of Becket and his company following the patched-up peace agreed near Fréteval on 22 July 1170 (ibid., no. 304) and in his account, for his friend John, bishop of Poitiers, of the murder of the archbishop in Canterbury Cathedral on December 29 and of his burial in the crypt (ibid., no. 305). Of the murder itself John was not an eyewitness, for he had fled from the cathedral along with other companions of Becket.

Last years: bishop of Chartres John's letters continue after Becket's death until Becket's canonization and the election of his successor at Canterbury. He continued to do legal and other work for the bishop of Exeter and for Canterbury, increasingly so when Richard was consecrated archbishop in 1174. He also put together the materials he had been collecting for a life of Becket complete with Becket's letters. John's life of Thomas Becket, sometimes regarded as a disappointment, was meant to serve as an affirmation of the archbishop's sanctity as well as a brief introduction to the large collection of Becket's letters. It was not altogether a new life as it is modelled on the lives already written by William of Canterbury, and the Anonymous of Lambeth. Its only claim to uniqueness, the account of Becket's murder, was, word for word, the text of the letter (*Letters of John of Salisbury*, no. 305) earlier sent to Bishop John of Poitiers and here tacked on to the end of the short biography. The life was inserted as a preface to Alan of Tewkesbury's collection of Becket's letters.

The shortness of John's biography of Becket is also possibly due to John's election to the bishopric of Chartres in 1176 which led John to abandon his enterprise and to hand it over to Alan. No bishopric had come his way in England; indeed, John might neither have wished for, nor expected, one under Henry II. However, if Ralph de Diceto is to be believed, William of the White Hands, bishop of Chartres and archbishop of Sens, suggested to King Louis of France that he give up Chartres in favour of John, in honour of the martyred Becket (*Radulfi de Diceto … opera historica*, 1.410–12). William and John knew each other well, as John's letters show. On 22 July 1176 John received the news of his election to Chartres.

Little is known of John's activities as bishop. Letters written by Peter of Blois and by Peter of Celle show that his actions produced disappointment and that there were petty squabbles, but his years at Chartres are perhaps neither long enough nor sufficiently well documented for a firm assessment to be made. He died on 25 October 1180 and was buried in Chartres in the abbey church of Notre-Dame-de-Josaphat where his carved sarcophagus survives. John left books to the cathedral library; the list of these reflects his tastes and includes, for example, Cicero's *De officiis* and *De oratore*, Seneca's *Quaestiones naturales*, as well as the *Hierarchies* of Dionysius the Pseudo-Areopagite. He was succeeded in the bishopric by his friend Peter of Celle.

Assessment and reputation John's churchmanship, diplomacy, erudition, literary charm and skill, and his moral outlooks are among his most defining characteristics. He was steadfast in his loyalties, and for years paid a weighty price for supporting Becket. He was blunt as well as witty about those he disliked, whether they were scholars, bishops, or firebrands. He lives, and brings others to life, in his books and in his letters to a degree that is rare in the middle ages, but his was an age of cultivated personal expression, especially between friends when engaged in correspondence spiced with news and gossip. John's scholarly humanism is both literary and philosophical in its inspiration. It left its mark deeply, especially through the success of his *Policraticus*.

This work enjoyed a very considerable reputation during the middle ages and subsequently also as a gateway to knowledge of antiquity and as an anthology of moralizing and historical examples. Its stories found their way into later encyclopaedias and handbooks, such as those by Helinand of Froidmont (1227), Vincent of Beauvais, John of Wales, and, in the fourteenth century, into the *De vita et moribus philosophorum* of Walter Burley; and thence into sermons and into literature. Vital du Four (d. 1327), thinking that the work had been written in antiquity, believed that St Augustine had come across the story about the pirate's answer to King Alexander in the course of reading it. The *Policraticus* was known about by some of the barons in

the reign of Henry III; its political doctrines were drawn upon at this time by the English writer of a *Liber de tyrannis*. Italian jurists of the fourteenth and fifteenth centuries showed considerable interest in it. So did humanist scholars in early fourteenth-century France, including Jean de Montreuil, Nicolas de Clamanges, and Ambroise de Miliis. It was translated into French in 1372, at the request of Charles V, by Denis Foulechat, a Franciscan friar. Several Polish masters of theology are known to have possessed copies in the fifteenth century. Ben Jonson worked into his play *Timber, or, Discoveries* lengthy passages on flattery that he took from the edition of 1513, made in Paris, of *Policraticus*, book 3.   DAVID LUSCOMBE

Sources The letters of John of Salisbury, ed. and trans. H. E. Butler and W. J. Millor, rev. C. N. L. Brooke, 2 vols., OMT (1979–86) [letters cited are for this edn; Lat. orig. with parallel Eng. text] • *Ioannis Saresberiensis Metalogicon*, ed. J. B. Hall and K. S. B. Keats-Rohan (Turnhout, Belgium, 1991) • *Ioannis Saresberiensis episcopi Carnotensis policratici, sive, de nugis curialium et vestigiis philosophorum libri VIII*, ed. C. C. J. Webb, 2 vols. (1909) • *Ioannis Saresberiensis policraticus I–IV*, ed. K. S. B. Keats-Rohan (Turnhout, Belgium, 1993) • *The statesman's book of John of Salisbury: … Policraticus*, trans. J. Dickinson (1927) [bks 4–6, and pts of bks 7–8] • *Frivolities of courtiers and footprints of philosophers: being a translation … of the Policraticus of John of Salisbury*, ed. and trans. J. B. Pike (1938) [bks 1–3, and pts of bks 7–8] • John of Salisbury, *John of Salisbury's memoirs of the papal court*, ed. and trans. M. Chibnall, OMT (1986) [*Historia pontificalis*] • M. Wilks, ed., *The world of John of Salisbury*, SCH, Subsidia, 3 (1984) [incl. D. Luscombe, 'John of Salisbury: a bibliography, 1953–82', pp. 445–57] • F. Barlow, 'John of Salisbury and his brothers', *Journal of Ecclesiastical History*, 46 (1995), 95–109 • B. Smalley, *The Becket conflict and the schools* (1973) • R. W. Southern, *Scholastic humanism and the unification of Europe*, 1 (1995), 214–21 • J. Martin, 'John of Salisbury's manuscripts of Frontinus and of Gellius', *Journal of the Warburg and Courtauld Institutes*, 40 (1977), 1–26 • J. Martin, 'Uses of tradition: Gellius, Petronius, and John of Salisbury', *Viator*, 10 (1979), 57–76 • M. Kerner, *Johannes von Salisbury und die logische Struktur seines 'Policraticus'* (1977) • J. van Laarhoven, ed. and trans., *Entheticus maior et minor*, 3 vols., Studien und Texte zur Geistesgeschichte des Mittelalters, 17 (1987) [*Entheticus de dogmate philosophorum* and *Entheticus ad Policraticum*] • P. von Moos, *Geschichte als Topik: das rhetorische Exemplum von der Antike zur Neuzeit und die 'historiae' im 'Policraticus' Johanns von Salisbury*, Ordo, Studien zur Literatur und Gesellschaft des Mittelalters und der Frühen Neuzeit, 2 (1988) • K. Guth, *Johannes von Salisbury*, Münchener Theologische Studien, Hist. Abt., 20 (1978) • H. Liebeschütz, *Mediaeval humanism in the life and writings of John of Salisbury*, Studies of the Warburg Institute, 17 (1950) • J. B. Hall, 'Towards a text of John of Salisbury's *Metalogicon*', *Studi Medievali*, 3rd ser., 24 (1983), 791–814 • K. S. B. Keats-Rohan, 'The textual tradition of John of Salisbury's *Metalogicon*', *Revue d'Histoire des Textes*, 16 (1986), 229–82 • W. Ullmann, 'John of Salisbury's *Policraticus* in the later middle ages', *Jurisprudence in the middle ages: collected studies* (1980) [essay 6] • T. Struve, *Die Entwicklung der organologischen Staatsauffassung im Mittelalter*, Monographien zur Geschichte des Mittelalters, 16 (1978) • A. Duggan, *Thomas Becket: a textual history of his letters* (1980) • C. C. J. Webb, *John of Salisbury* (1932) • H. Hohenleutner, 'Johannes von Salisbury in der Literatur der letzten Jahren', *Historisches Jahrbuch der Görres-Gesellschaft*, 77 (1958), 493–500 • Joannes Saresberiensis, 'Vita S. Anselmi', *Patrologia Latina*, 199 (1855), 1009–40 • W. Fitzstephen, John of Salisbury, and others, *Vita sancti Thomae Cantuariensis archiepiscopi*, 2 vols. in 1 (1723), 301–22 • C. Schaarschmidt, *Johannes Saresberiensis nach Leben und Studien, Schriften und Philosophie* (1862) • *Radulfi de Diceto … opera historica*, ed. W. Stubbs, 2 vols., Rolls Series, 68 (1876) • *Cartulaire de Notre-Dame de Chartres*, ed. E. de Lépinois and L. Merlet, 3 vols. (1862–4), 1.5–6 • *The correspondence of Thomas Becket*, ed. and trans. A. J. Duggan, 2 vols., OMT (2000)

Wealth at death bequeathed books to cathedral library of Chartres: *Cartulaire*, ed. de Lépinois and Merlet, vol. 3, pp. 210–12; C. C. J. Webb, 'Note on books bequeathed by John of Salisbury to the cathedral library of Chartres', *Mediaeval and Renaissance Studies*, 1 (1941–3), 128–9

Salisbury, John (1501/2–1573), bishop of Sodor and Man, is of unknown parentage. A monk of Bury St Edmunds Abbey, he was sent to Gloucester College, Oxford (claims that he was a graduate of Cambridge were the product of confusion with a Robert Salisbury). There he was suspected of protestant leanings and, on Cardinal Wolsey's orders, was imprisoned for a year, probably between 25 February 1528 and 26 March 1529. Thereafter he returned to Bury where, he later claimed, he was 'little better than a prisoner' for five years (LPL, MS 113, fol. 79). Henceforth, however, he received rapid preferment. About 1534 he was made prior of St Faith's, Horsham, in Norfolk; in March 1536 he was consecrated suffragan bishop of Thetford, and the following year he was abbot of Titchfield, Hampshire, and archdeacon of Anglesey. He owed his swift advance to his links with Thomas Wriothesley (later first earl of Southampton), Cromwell's patronage manager, and to his compliance with the royal will. He bears responsibility for the surrender of two monastic houses, St Faith's in 1536 and Titchfield in 1537, and the ending of a third, helping to oversee the conversion of Norwich Cathedral priory in the spring of 1538. He was rewarded with a prebend in Norwich Cathedral in May 1538 and the deanery in August 1539, to which he added the rectories of North Creake, Norfolk (which he resigned in 1541), Claydon, Suffolk (1541), and North and South Lopham, Norfolk (1547).

By 1554 Salisbury had married Jane Barrett, and in the spring of that year he was therefore deprived of all his ecclesiastical preferments. His rehabilitation, however, was swift, owing to the support of the duke of Norfolk and the earl of Sussex: he was presented by the latter to the rectory of Diss, Norfolk, in May 1554, formally pardoned in October, and made chancellor of Lincoln in December. By the end of Mary's reign he had amassed a further four rectories, Redenhall and Trunch in Norfolk and Thorpe on the Hill and Caythorpe in Lincolnshire.

On Elizabeth's accession Salisbury was restored to most of his former preferments: the deanery of Norwich, the archdeaconry of Anglesey, and the rectory of North and South Lopham. Recognized formally as suffragan bishop of Thetford, he was one of the seven bishops charged with consecrating Matthew Parker as archbishop of Canterbury on 17 December 1559, and retained his episcopal status thereafter. He also received a further three rectories in 1559: Waltham and Bassingham in Lincolnshire and Blofield in Norfolk. Salisbury seems never to have visited his archdeaconry of Anglesey, but about 1562 he became involved in a sharp dispute with his diocesan, Bishop Rowland Meyrick of Bangor, who temporarily deprived him of the archdeaconry; the case was probably as much to do with a long-running jurisdictional and financial battle between bishops of Bangor and archdeacons of Anglesey

as with Salisbury himself or with his non-residence in the diocese.

By the mid-1560s Salisbury's religious conservatism was increasingly out of kilter with developments in the Norwich diocese. In 1564 Bishop John Parkhurst of Norwich gleefully supplanted Salisbury as the preacher at the funeral of the duchess of Norfolk, fearing that the dean of Norwich would expound only lukewarm protestantism on so public an occasion. Salisbury's links with the prebendary Miles Spencer and John Hoo, the chapter's receiver (whose father had been Salisbury's auditor at St Faith's), both of them at the centre of a network of religious conservatives in the diocese, were exposed in 1569. At the beginning of the year the royal commissioners entrusted with visiting Norwich Cathedral heard allegations of maladministration at the cathedral. It was claimed not only that Salisbury, Spencer, and Hoo were conspiring to defraud the cathedral by means of irregular leases of chapter estates, but also that they were embezzling the profits of the sale of lead from the cathedral; in addition it was said that Hoo was having an affair with Jane Salisbury, the dean's wife. The allegations cannot be substantiated, but the chapter estates were certainly disordered, with most of the best properties being let for ninety-nine years in possession and a further ninety-nine years in reversion, and much of the blame for the mismanagement must rest with Salisbury.

A third blow to Salisbury came at the end of 1569. On Advent Sunday he preached in the cathedral, attacking the ostentatiously godly as conceited and cruel and no better than papists (and incidentally giving his own age as sixty-seven). The sermon may also have been a veiled attack on his rival in the chapter and eventual successor as dean, George Gardiner, who had led the criticisms of his management of the cathedral earlier in the year. Parkhurst immediately, and with no little delight, suspended Salisbury from preaching until he explained himself, and he was forced to preach a recantation and explanation. None the less, Salisbury could still count on the effects of his own affability—Thomas Tusser, a lay clerk at Norwich, called him the 'gentle dean' (Tusser, 11)—and his powerful friends. Gardiner and his allies on the chapter were checked in 1570, while in March 1570 the earl of Derby, as hereditary overlord of the Isle of Man, nominated Salisbury as bishop of Sodor and Man; his appointment was confirmed by the queen in September. He was allowed to hold his deanery *in commendam* with the bishopric, and does not appear ever to have visited his diocese. Instead he seems to have continued to act as a suffragan in East Anglia, conducting ordinations for Parkhurst as late as 13 August 1573. He died, probably at Norwich, at the end of September that year and was buried in St Andrew's parish church there. His wife survived him.   IAN ATHERTON

Sources LPL, MS 113, fols. 69r–74r, 79r–83r • Norfolk RO, MS DCN 29/1, fols. 36, 38r • Emden, *Oxf.*, 4.501 • BL, Lansdowne MS 981, fols. 105–6 • *LP Henry VIII* • F. Blomefield and C. Parkin, *An essay towards a topographical history of the county of Norfolk*, [2nd edn], 11 vols. (1805–10) • *Fasti Angl., 1541–1857*, [Ely], 42, 59 • E. B. Fryde and others, eds., *Handbook of British chronology*, 3rd edn, Royal Historical Society Guides and Handbooks, 2 (1986), 273 • I. Atherton and others, eds.,

Norwich Cathedral: church, city and diocese, 1096–1996 (1996) • D. MacCulloch, *Suffolk and the Tudors: politics and religion in an English county, 1500–1600* (1986), 186–7 • J. R. Oliver, ed., *Monumenta de Insula Manniae, or, A collection of national documents relating to the Isle of Man*, 3, Manx Society, 9 (1862), 53–7 • *The acts and monuments of John Foxe*, ed. S. R. Cattley, 8 vols. (1837–41), vol. 5, p. 428 • will, PRO, PROB 11/55, fol. 240v • T. Tusser, *Five hundred points of good husbandry*, new edn, ed. W. Mavor (1812), 11 • *The letter book of John Parkhurst, bishop of Norwich*, ed. R. A. Houlbrooke, Norfolk RS, 43 (1974–5), 91–2 • J. Strype, *Memorials of the most reverend father in God Thomas Cranmer*, new edn, 2 vols. (1840) • A. Jessopp, *Diocesan histories: Norwich* (1884)

Archives LPL, two sermons, MS 113, fols. 69r–74r, 79r–83r

Wealth at death see will, PRO, PROB 11/55, fol. 240v

Salisbury [Salusbury; *alias* Parry], **John** (1575/6–1626), Jesuit, is described as a native of Merioneth, and may have been a member of the Rug branch of the Salisbury or Salusbury family of Bachymbyd and Lleweni in Denbighshire. The rector of the Jesuit College of St Alban, Valladolid, John Blackfan SJ, related how Salisbury was enticed from his home and carried to Ireland about 1588 (apparently by the earl of Thomond), where he was joined by a schoolfellow, William Robins, who persuaded him to become a Catholic. He entered St Alban's College on 22 June 1595, in the company of Robins, and was ordained priest on 21 November 1600. In 1602 the privy council was warned that Salisbury would be coming in the mission; he was described as 'yellow haired, sanguine, and of short stature, about the age of 26, and never will have a beard'. Blackfan described him as *pulchellus admodum puer* ('a very pretty boy'). In May 1603 he was sent to the English College at Douai, and thence to the English mission using the alias of John Parry. In 1604 he entered the Society of Jesus, being then described as a missioner in north Wales, and on 6 December 1618 he took the four vows. On the death of Father Robert Jones in 1615 Salisbury became superior of the united north and south Wales district, taking up his residence at Raglan Castle, where he also acted as chaplain to Lady Frances Somerset.

Salisbury oversaw the translation into Welsh, the publication, and the distribution of Bellarmine's catechism *Dichiarazione più copiosa della dottrina cristiana*, as *Eglurhad helaeth-lawn o'r athrawiaeth Gristnogawl*. The translation, in idiomatic Welsh, once thought to be Salisbury's work, was undertaken by Richard Vaughan of Bodeiliog, Denbighshire, and is said, in the colophon, to have been completed on 25 March 1618. It was printed anonymously at the English province press at St Omer in 1618.

In 1622 Salisbury established the college of St Francis Xavier, based at Cwm, in Llanrhyddol, Herefordshire, of which he became rector on 4 February 1623. He was appointed procurator of the English province to Rome, but died in England while preparing himself for his journey thither on 14 March 1626.

D. L. Thomas, *rev.* Ceri Sullivan

Sources A. F. Allison and D. M. Rogers, eds., *The contemporary printed literature of the English Counter-Reformation between 1558 and 1640*, 2 vols. (1989–94), vol. 1, p. 44, vol. 2, pp. 138, 148 • T. M. McCoog, *English and Welsh Jesuits, 1555–1650*, 2, Catholic RS, 75 (1995), 286 • E. Henson, ed., *The registers of the English College at Valladolid, 1589–1862*, Catholic RS, 30 (1930), 33–4, 46 • E. H. Burton and T. L. Williams, eds., *The Douay College diaries, third, fourth and fifth, 1598–1654*, 1, Catholic RS, 10 (1911), 53–4 • G. Anstruther, *The seminary priests*, 1 (1969), 298 • D. A. Bellenger, ed., *English and Welsh priests, 1558–1800* (1984), 104, 236 • Gillow, *Lit. biog. hist.* • DWB • H. W. Lloyd, 'Welsh books printed abroad in the sixteenth and seventeenth centuries, and their authors', *Y Cymmrodor*, 4 (1881), 25–69 • H. Foley, ed., *Records of the English province of the Society of Jesus*, 4 (1878), 335, 392, 471; 7/2 (1883), 681

Salisbury, John. *See* Digby, Sir John (1605–1645).

Salisbury, John (*fl.* 1695–1697). *See under* Salisbury, Thomas (1566/7–1622).

Salisbury, Patrick of, first earl of Salisbury [earl of Wiltshire] (*d.* 1168), baron, was a younger son of Walter of Salisbury (*d.* 1147), who may have been hereditary sheriff of Wiltshire under King Stephen, and Sibyl de Sourches. His inheritance included the Domesday honour of Chitterne in Wiltshire; in 1166 he reported more than forty knights enfeoffed on his patrimony, as well as sixteen on his mother's lands. He married Ela, daughter of Guillaume Talvas, count of Ponthieu, and widow of William (III) de Warenne, earl of Surrey (*d.* 1148); they had a son named William.

When his own elder brother William died in the mid-1140s, Patrick took his place as constable of Salisbury. Although William had been a supporter of the Empress Matilda in her bid to unseat King Stephen, Patrick was at least nominally loyal to the king in the early years of the war, while concentrating his energies on a local rivalry with John *Marshal, castellan of Marlborough. The two men eventually made a treaty whereby John married Patrick's sister, Sibyl (a union that produced the great William *Marshal, Patrick's nephew), and Patrick came over to the empress's side. By 1147 Matilda had made him earl of Salisbury (or Wiltshire). Ostensibly on her behalf he seized temporarily the bishop of Winchester's castle at Downton, a feat for which he and his men were excommunicated. Patrick seems also to have served as sheriff for the empress, and even to have accounted to an Angevin exchequer for the royal revenues of Wiltshire; he is the only baron for whom there is evidence of such a practice. He may also have coined his own money during the anarchy, as did a number of his contemporaries.

As earl, Patrick witnessed the peace treaty of 1153 between Stephen and Henry of Anjou. He retained his earldom when Henry II came to the throne the following year, and he served as sheriff of Wiltshire until 1160. A few years later he was sent to lead the king's troops in Aquitaine, where he died in 1168, of a spear wound delivered by a follower of the rebellious Lusignan family; he was buried at Poitiers. He was succeeded in his earldom and lands by his son, William (*d.* 1196).

Emilie Amt

Sources *Reg. RAN*, vol. 3 • R. Howlett, ed., *Chronicles of the reigns of Stephen, Henry II, and Richard I*, 4, Rolls Series, 82 (1889) • H. Hall, ed., *The Red Book of the Exchequer*, 3 vols., Rolls Series, 99 (1896) • P. Meyer, ed., *L'histoire de Guillaume le Maréchal*, 3 vols. (Paris, 1891–1901) • K. R. Potter and R. H. C. Davis, eds., *Gesta Stephani*, OMT (1976) • Pipe rolls • *Radulfi de Diceto ... opera historica*, ed. W. Stubbs, 2 vols., Rolls Series, 68 (1876)

Salisbury [*formerly* Markham], **Richard Anthony** (1761–1829), botanist and horticulturist, was born in Leeds on 2 May 1761, the only son (there were also two daughters) of Richard Markham, a Leeds cloth merchant. His mother was descended from Jonathan Laycock of Shaw Hill, brother-in-law of Henry Lyte, the translator into English of Dodoens's herbal. A connection with an old Yorkshire family of the same name and adherence to its Roman Catholic faith have been postulated but remain unproved.

All that is known of Markham's early years is that he was attending a school near Halifax at the age of eight and already by then had a passion for plants. Next heard of at Edinburgh University, he was one of the handful of students there whom James Edward Smith brought together in March 1782 as the Society for the Investigation of Natural History. In a letter home Smith described this recruit in some awe as 'a young man of large fortune from Leeds, who studies physic as an amusement, and is an excellent botanist; but has just left Edinburgh and 'tis uncertain whether he will return' (Smith MSS, Linn. Soc.). While it was normal at that period for students with expectations of an ample inheritance not to trouble to proceed to a degree, the absence of Markham's name from the class lists of the professor of botany, John Hope, seems to confirm Smith's impression of a shallow commitment to study.

It was about that time, according to Markham's own account, that he became acquainted with an elderly spinster, a distant relative of his mother, who shared his love of flowers. In 1785, being heirless, she settled on him a substantial fortune on condition that he took as his sole surname that of her ancient and illustrious Welsh family, Salisbury. His enemies were later to claim that he had admitted under pressure having made this story up, in order to justify his adoption of a status well beyond his means, and certainly it is strange that he was apparently unable to produce documentary evidence to rebut that accusation. Whatever the truth, however, Salisbury became his name thenceforward and he settled down to the leisured life of a country gentleman of wealth, living on one of his father's estates, Chapel Allerton, near Leeds. Here he indulged himself with a massive hothouse and mingled with landed neighbours who shared his horticultural enthusiasm. An invitation to redesign the grounds of Harewood House eventually followed. Concurrently he built up a correspondence with leading botanists, paid visits to London and Paris to examine herbaria (notably that of Banks, who was to remain a loyal friend), gained election to the Royal (1787) and the newly founded Linnean societies, and in 1796 published at his own expense a comprehensive list of the plants to be found on his estate (*Prodromus stirpium in horto ad Chapel Allerton vigentium*).

That Salisbury was a plantsman to the core is evident from his writings. His espousal of aristocratic values and behaviour, however, imparted an overlay of recklessness to a character that was basically that of a scholarly connoisseur. This was now to prove his undoing. The first

Richard Anthony Salisbury (1761–1829), by William John Burchell, 1817

casualty was his marriage. On 1 December 1796 he had married Caroline, younger daughter of John Staniforth, of Hull. After little more than a year she returned to her parents, taking their baby daughter with her. The separation was to prove permanent and lastingly bitter. According to Salisbury, she had been disappointed to find he was not the rich man she had supposed him to be but deeply in debt instead. Her family proceeded to harry him for the return of her dowry, obtaining a lien on his estate. Salisbury was forced to sell his valuable collection of rare exotics and seek refuge in nearby Wakefield with his unmarried sisters, who apparently also helped him financially. Turning his back on the north, soon after, in March 1800, he moved to Mill Hill in Middlesex, where he set up, again in style, in the former residence of Peter Collinson, Ridgway House, with its large and richly furnished garden. His wife's family, however, persisted in their legal harassment and he eventually escaped their clutches only by fraudulently declaring himself bankrupt. This necessitated his moving in 1806 to a small house off the Edgware Road, where, pathetically, his newly amassed collection of over 2000 species in pots had to be squeezed into a garden a mere 30 feet square. To round off this all-too-public sequence of embarrassments, he later successfully sued his wife for bribing three men to attack him in Hyde Park; one of the three had accused him of indecency. It may indeed be that a tendency to promiscuity on his part had been a deeper reason for the break-up of the marriage.

Certainly it was the relaxed attitude that Salisbury took to sexual behaviour that in 1802 abruptly terminated the friendship and mutual admiration that had prevailed until then between Smith and him. These had already been placed in jeopardy, however, by Salisbury's adoption for his 1796 *Prodromus* of the novel 'natural system' of classification, the rival to the artificial Linnaean one on which Smith had staked his reputation. Salisbury had then compounded this sin by extolling that rival scheme in his preface to the *Paradisus Londinensis* (1805–8), a forty-part series of coloured figures of plants in cultivation in and around the metropolis. By then his allegiance had largely transferred from Smith's Linnean Society to the Horticultural Society of London, which he played a leading part in founding in 1804 and of which he was elected honorary secretary a year later. Though this new body better reflected his interests, his position in the Linnean was in any case becoming untenable through his public differences with Smith, and in January 1806 he resigned as one of its vice-presidents (though retaining his fellowship). Two months later he created outrage at one of its meetings by accusing Smith of having extensively plagiarized Linnaeus in drawing up the generic descriptions for his *English Botany*, subsequently distributing his paper to this effect as a 34-page pamphlet.

Worse was to come. In 1809, by a shabbily underhand ruse, Salisbury robbed the much-respected Robert Brown of the necessary priority in print for various new names Brown had proposed in a lengthy paper on the difficult family Proteaceae read at four successive Linnean Society meetings—at which Salisbury had conspicuously been present. Apparently Salisbury regarded the Proteaceae as his preserve and resented this intruder who also dared to criticize his earlier work on it. Continuing to smart from this, in 1818 he further attacked Brown with a spiteful anonymous review of his account of the plants collected on Tuckey's Congo expedition. In reprisal, many of the Linnean fellows thenceforward ostracized Salisbury, and anyone else suspected of serving him as a stalking-horse. This resulted in the blackballing of the young John Edward Gray when he put up for election to the society in 1822, an event which was to lead that future keeper of the natural history department of the British Museum to lend his authority to the anti-Linnaean Botanical Society of London and thereby help to divide the capital's botanical community into two ideological camps.

Gray was to be one of several protagonists of the natural system whom Salisbury tried unsuccessfully to induce to take forward to publication a large-scale 'Genera plantarum' arranged on that system, on which he spent his later years. The bequest of his library and fortune was the bait offered in return. In the end the son of a Fulham florist, William John Burchell, afterwards a celebrated African traveller, became the chosen heir, but it finally fell to Gray after all, in 1866, to act as midwife to Salisbury's *magnum opus* and see its sole completed fragment into print.

Salisbury's association with the Horticultural Society, while much happier, was not without blemish. In 1816 its accounts were discovered to be in confusion, the paid assistant secretary was dismissed as a result, and Salisbury's eleven years as the key officer came to an end suspiciously abruptly. Though he remained a council member for another ten years, he took little part in the society's proceedings thereafter.

Regrettably, the estimable pioneer work Salisbury accomplished as a botanist largely fell victim to his waspish relations with Brown and the Smithians, whose attempts to consign it to lasting scientific oblivion proved all too successful. Many generic names which should rightly stand to his name today became overlooked and now cannot be revived without causing undue confusion. Salisbury died from paralysis on 23 March 1829 in London, a year after the death of his greatest enemy, Smith. His letters and other papers eventually passed to the Linnean Society and to the Natural History Museum in London. The substitution of *Salisburia* for Linnaeus's *Ginkgo* as the name of the maidenhair tree of China and Japan was a product of Smith's early admiration; flagrantly illegitimate, it has not been kept up. Lindley, a fellow antagonist of Robert Brown, later commemorated Salisbury afresh in a genus of Australian Myrtaceae, *Salisia*, but that has also been superseded.

D. E. ALLEN

Sources [A. Simmonds], 'The founders: Richard Anthony Salisbury, FRS, 1761–1829', *Journal of the Royal Horticultural Society*, 69 (1944), 58–65, 95–100 · D. J. Mabberley, *Jupiter botanicus: Robert Brown of the British Museum* (1985), 147–56 · Linn. Soc., Salisbury papers, MS 376 · J. Britten, 'Hookera v. Brodiaea', *Journal of Botany, British and Foreign*, 25 (1886), 49–53 · A. T. Gage and W. T. Stearn, *A bicentenary history of the Linnean Society of London* (1988), 27, 48, 155 · D. J. Mabberley, 'Generic names published in Salisbury's reviews of Robert Brown's works', *Taxon*, 29 (1980), 597–606 · J. E. Gray, 'Sowerby's *English botany*', *Journal of Botany, British and Foreign*, 10 (1872), 374–5 · G. S. Boulger, 'Richard Anthony Salisbury', *Gardeners' Chronicle*, 3rd ser., 35 (1904), 148 · J. Hunter, *Familiae minorum gentium*, ed. J. W. Clay, 1, Harleian Society, 37 (1894) · Desmond, *Botanists* · Linn. Soc., Smith papers

Archives Linn. Soc., corresp. and papers · NHM, drawings and MSS | NHM, letters to members of the Sowerby family

Likenesses W. J. Burchell, pencil sketch, 1817, RBG Kew [*see illus.*]

Salisbury, Roger of (d. 1139), administrator and bishop of Salisbury, was born of apparently humble stock, probably in Normandy, probably in the late 1060s.

Rise to greatness According to William of Newburgh, writing in the 1190s, Roger was a poor, unlettered priest, serving a church near Caen, when he attracted the attention of the future Henry I, then fighting in Normandy against his brother, William II. Henry and his men chanced upon Roger's church, where the soldiers were so impressed by his expeditious celebration of mass that Henry immediately summoned him into his service. Though not impossible, there is no contemporary support for this account, and the formal notification of Roger's election as bishop of Salisbury in 1102 describes him as a priest of Avranches, a noted intellectual centre in western Normandy. He certainly entered Henry's service as a chaplain, however, and probably became his steward. In 1101, soon after he had become king, Henry appointed Roger chancellor, possibly at Easter and definitely before 3 September. Nominated by Henry to the see of Salisbury, perhaps in September 1101, and elected by the chapter in 1102, Roger was invested by the king at Westminster in September 1102 and shortly afterwards resigned as chancellor. He attended Archbishop Anselm's Westminster council at Michaelmas 1102, but, the investiture dispute being then unresolved, the archbishop refused to consecrate him and two other recently invested bishops. When Henry asked Archbishop Gerard of York (d. 1108) to perform the ceremony, the other two openly refused to co-operate, but Roger prudently temporized so as to avoid either angering the king or injuring Anselm's cause. His consecration was delayed until 1107 when, following the formal end of the investiture dispute on 1 August, he and four other bishops were consecrated by Anselm at Canterbury on 11 August.

Roger was rapidly emerging as one of Henry's most trusted and important ministers. The king's confidence in him was demonstrated in 1106 when, after defeating and capturing Robert Curthose, duke of Normandy (d. 1134), at Tinchebrai in September, Henry entrusted his brother to Roger's custody at Devizes Castle. His administrative skills made him indispensable to the management of Henry's English affairs, and he was eventually given control of the whole government of the realm. Although contemporary chroniclers imply that Roger received such sweeping powers in a single grant, even as early as 1109, his authority probably increased gradually. His importance in royal government stemmed initially from his management of the king's finances, centred on the treasury at Winchester, in which he rose to a pre-eminent position by 1110 at the latest. In that year he was made responsible for collecting a major aid to the king, the documentation for which contains the earliest known reference by name to the exchequer, whose introduction as an improved means of accounting is generally attributed to Roger. It is likely that he was also behind the inauguration of the pipe rolls, the first apparent allusion to which occurs in 1114, and he served as a senior royal justice, especially in connection with financial matters. In the first two decades of Henry's reign, however, he was probably no more than a leading member of the group of ministers who governed the realm. During the king's absences in Normandy, Roger operated under the regency of Queen Matilda until her death in 1118, and then under that of Prince William until the latter's final departure from England in 1120. Thereafter he was the king's undoubted chief minister, and was himself appointed regent for Henry's absence in 1123–6.

In 1115 Roger attended the consecration of Theulf, bishop of Worcester, at Canterbury on 27 June and that of Bernard, bishop of St David's, at Westminster on 19 September. He officiated at the funeral of Queen Matilda at Westminster in May 1118, and was there for the consecration of David, bishop of Bangor, on 4 April 1120. In January 1121 he claimed the right to perform the marriage of Henry I and Adeliza of Louvain on the ground that Windsor was within his diocese, but was resisted by Archbishop Ralph d'Escures (d. 1122), who delegated the duty to the bishop of Winchester. On 2 October 1121 he was present at Lambeth for the consecration of Gregory, bishop of Dublin, and on 18 February 1123 he participated in the consecration at Canterbury of Archbishop William de Corbeil (d. 1136), whose election he had helped to engineer.

Chief minister of Henry I Notable among Roger's viceregal activities in 1123–6 was the mutilation and castration of the realm's corrupt moneyers carried out at Winchester during Christmastide 1124–5, in response to a royal order from Normandy. It is possible that he initiated a programme of judicial eyres about 1124 and introduced reforms of the sheriff's office. He appears also to have created the post of treasurer, to which his nephew, Nigel (d. 1169), was appointed c.1126. His authority may have suffered some diminution after Henry's return to England with his daughter, Empress Matilda (d. 1167), in September 1126, possibly owing to his doubts over the recognition of Matilda as heir to the kingdom and her betrothal to Geoffrey, count of Anjou, in 1127, both of which were carried forward by the king. But, whatever his private opinions, Roger played a major role in urging the nobles and prelates to swear acceptance of Matilda as Henry's heir at a royal council in London in January 1127, and himself took the oath second, after the archbishop of Canterbury. He was said to have claimed subsequently that his oath had been conditional on the king's not marrying his daughter to anyone outside England without consulting the nobility. In 1126 Robert, duke of Normandy, was removed from Roger's custody to that of Robert, earl of Gloucester (d. 1147), Matilda's half-brother. The bishop also faced concern over the administration of the royal finances in the later 1120s. A special audit of the treasury was held in 1128/9, not under his authority but that of the earl of Gloucester and Brian fitz Count (d. c.1149), both staunch allies of Matilda. Nevertheless, Roger retained Henry I's confidence, largely because he did not press his opposition to royal policies, and remained the king's chief minister, apparently serving in effect as regent during Henry's later absences abroad. In 1130 he attended the consecrations of Christ Church, Canterbury, on 4 May and of Rochester Cathedral on 8 May.

The accession of Stephen After Henry I's death in Normandy on 1 December 1135 Stephen of Blois quickly crossed to England and claimed the throne. Having gained recognition from the Londoners, he went immediately to Winchester where, either by his own persuasion or the efforts of his brother, Bishop Henry of Winchester (d. 1171), he secured acceptance from Bishop Roger, despite the latter's oath to Matilda, renewed as recently as 1131. Roger's action, explicable in part by his dislike of her Angevin marriage, was crucial to Stephen's success since it brought over to him the treasury and administrative establishment of the late king. Stephen rewarded Roger by granting him the borough and hundred of Malmesbury, and by appointing his son Roger chancellor and his nephew Adelelm treasurer. Roger was one of the three prelates who attended Stephen's coronation at Westminster at Christmas 1135, after which he accompanied the king to Henry I's funeral in Reading Abbey on 5 January 1136.

Roger was present at the archbishop of Canterbury's Easter council in London, at which Stephen promised to restore the church's liberties, and was among five English bishops who witnessed Stephen's charter to that effect at Oxford in early April, two of the others being his nephews, Alexander of Lincoln and Nigel of Ely. He was intermittently with Stephen during the siege of Exeter Castle (June–August 1136), and on 1 December he accompanied the widowed Queen Adeliza to the commemoration of Henry I's first anniversary at Reading. Stephen relied heavily upon Roger in the early years of his reign. When rumours of the bishop's death reached him at Portsmouth in May 1136 as he was about to embark for Normandy, Stephen at once postponed his expedition and hastened to Salisbury, where he found Roger alive and well. Nevertheless, although Roger probably acted as regent during the king's expedition to Normandy in 1137, and he and his family continued to direct the administration, his influence on political and ecclesiastical affairs declined once Stephen was firmly established on the throne, particularly relative to that of Bishop Henry of Winchester, appointed papal legate in 1139. Roger attended the legatine council of Alberic of Ostia in December 1138, at which Theobald, abbot of Bec (d. 1161), was elected archbishop of Canterbury, and assisted in Theobald's consecration at Canterbury on 8 January 1139. Although he had earlier successfully opposed the election of monks to the see of Canterbury, in 1114 and 1123, he chose not to object to Theobald's election. Soon afterwards Roger accompanied Stephen and the court to Oxford and attended the dedication of Godstow nunnery on about 13 January.

Decline and fall Clouds were beginning to gather over Roger's position, however. The ambitions of Matilda and her supporters, effectively quashed in 1136, now began to revive. In May 1138 Robert of Gloucester renounced his fealty to Stephen, and fears grew of an Angevin invasion. Against this background certain of Stephen's nobles, motivated primarily by jealousy of Roger's ostentatious wealth and ascendancy in government, raised suspicions that he and his family planned to transfer their power and castles to Matilda's allegiance. Whether or not this was true, Roger and his episcopal nephews certainly proceeded to strengthen and garrison their castles. In an atmosphere of growing uncertainty Stephen, persuaded especially by Waleran, count of Meulan (d. 1166), to make a pre-emptive strike, summoned Roger to attend his court at Oxford on 24 June. Accompanied by bishops Alexander and Nigel, and attended by an armed escort, Roger obeyed with a sense of foreboding. Though openly well received by the king, they fell victim to the strategy laid against them. An argument over accommodation between Roger's men and those of Alain de Dinan, count of Brittany, led to an ugly scuffle in which several were wounded and some killed.

According to Orderic Vitalis and the author of *Gesta Stephani*, the brawl was instigated by Waleran, count of Meulan, and others of the king's nobles, but William of Malmesbury, though ambiguous on who provoked the quarrel, blames Roger's men for starting the fighting. In any event, the bishops were summoned to Stephen to give satisfaction for the breach of his peace by surrendering their castles as a pledge of good faith. When they demurred, Roger and Alexander were arrested along with Roger's son, Roger the chancellor. Nigel, however, escaped to his uncle's castle at Devizes, then in the charge of Roger's mistress, Matilda of Ramsbury. The king at once marched against him, taking Roger and his son with him, and, lodging Roger in a cowshed and threatening to hang his son, secured Nigel's capitulation and the castle's surrender after a brief siege. This was followed by the surrender of Roger's other castles, at Sherborne, Malmesbury, and Salisbury, and the seizure of the weapons and treasure stored in them.

Bishop Henry of Winchester, the king's brother and papal legate, outraged at the attack upon episcopal privilege, remonstrated with Stephen and eventually summoned him to a council at Winchester on 29 August. However, despite the legate's forthright criticism of the king, the council turned into a trial of Roger, who proved unable adequately to rebut the charge of treason put by Stephen's nobles, or to refute the argument that he had been arrested not as a bishop but as a disloyal minister. Although Stephen promised to do penance, Roger gained nothing from this council and returned under the watchful eye of the king's agents to Salisbury. There, dejected and possibly abandoned even by his chapter, he died on 11 December 1139 of a quartan fever brought on by the mental anguish of his recent ill treatment. According to William of Malmesbury, he was mourned by very few owing to the envious hatred engendered by his excessive power. His sudden fall and wretched death were widely seen as divine retribution for overweening ambition. He was buried in the cathedral at Old Sarum, whence his remains were moved on 14 June 1226 to the new cathedral in the modern city of Salisbury. His memorial, though a matter of dispute, is possibly the Tournai marble grave-slab in the nave, carved with an episcopal figure in low relief and dating from the mid-twelfth century.

Bishop and minister In Roger the royal minister overshadowed the bishop, yet he proved as able and conscientious a diocesan as most of his contemporaries. According to William of Malmesbury, he carefully attended to his ecclesiastical responsibilities in the morning before dealing with other business. Of his thirty surviving charters, nine are purely episcopal in character, six relating to ecclesiastical affairs in the diocese and three to prebends of the cathedral. It was Roger, rather than his late eleventh-century predecessor, Osmund (to whom the credit is traditionally given), who established the framework of a prebendal system and endowed dignities at Salisbury. He encouraged learning in the chapter, and there is some evidence that diocesan inquiries into the patronage of parish churches began in his time. In 1122 he secured the annexation of Horton Abbey to Sherborne Priory, which he had controlled for twenty years as a dependency of his bishopric, and raised Sherborne to the status of an independent abbey. In the 1120s, both as diocesan and regent, he assisted in Henry I's foundation of Reading Abbey. He was also, however, a conspicuous pluralist in the diocese, annexing to his bishopric a number of Salisbury prebends, the abbeys of Abbotsbury and Malmesbury, and several churches. His acquisitiveness in other dioceses included the rich deanery of St Martin's-le-Grand in London, the collegiate church of Wolverhampton, and three churches belonging to St Frideswide's, Oxford (a house in whose foundation he appears to have been involved). In a mood of contrition when near to death he restored some of his unjustly held possessions to their rightful owners.

Roger's main sphere of activity was in secular government. His reform and reorganization of Henry I's financial administration marked the beginnings of a system of government separate from the royal household. His supervision of the government of England after 1120 was at the time unprecedented. Though often described as justiciar by later historians, he was never so styled in any official document, and it is now clear that no such distinctive office existed before Henry II's reign. Rather, he was the king's *alter ego* in an age of experiment in governmental techniques. His authority was personal and dependent on his consummate ability to serve the king's needs. Nevertheless, the later office of justiciar was clearly adumbrated in the concentration of power in Roger's hands. William of Malmesbury referred to him as having the governance of the whole kingdom, whether Henry was in England or Normandy, and Henry of Huntingdon described him as 'second to the king'. In two documents of *c*.1125 and soon after Roger styled himself '*procurator* of the kingdom of England' under the king (*Reg. RAN*, 2, nos. 1471, 1472), and in 1123 he was addressed by a religious house as 'vigorous *provisor* of the kingdom of England' (Kemp, 2, no. 771), both of which expressions were attempts to encapsulate his novel authority. He founded a powerful ecclesiastical and governmental dynasty whose members remained at the centre of affairs until the death of his great-nephew, Richard fitz Neale, in 1198. His influence secured the rich bishopric of Lincoln for his nephew, Alexander, in 1123, and the see of Ely for another nephew, Nigel the treasurer, in 1133, after he had seen to their intellectual training by sending them to study in the schools of Laon in northern France. He used his great wealth to indulge a passion for building. In addition to rebuilding the cathedral at Old Sarum on an enlarged and lavish scale and reconstructing the former royal castle there, he built castles at Sherborne, Malmesbury, and Devizes, the last, according to Henry of Huntingdon, being as splendid as any in Europe.

Roger Pauper [Roger le Poer] (*fl.* 1135–1139), administrator, was the son of Roger of Salisbury and Matilda of Ramsbury, and may have been called Pauper in contrast to his father's wealth. Through his father's influence he became King Stephen's first chancellor late in 1135, retaining the office until the arrest of the bishops in June 1139, when he was still a young man. A very active chancellor, he attested over sixty of Stephen's charters, the earliest in February 1136, and accompanied the king to Normandy in 1137. Following his unwilling involvement in the downfall of the bishops and the capture of Devizes Castle, described above, he was apparently exiled by the king, his career cut short. Nothing is known of his later history and death.

B. R. KEMP

Sources E. J. Kealey, *Roger of Salisbury, viceroy of England* (1972) • J. A. Green, *The government of England under Henry I* (1986) • D. M. Stenton, 'Roger of Salisbury, *regni Angliae procurator*', *EngHR*, 39 (1924), 79–80 • *Willelmi Malmesbiriensis monachi de gestis pontificum Anglorum libri quinque*, ed. N. E. S. A. Hamilton, Rolls Series, 52 (1870) • William of Malmesbury, *Gesta regum Anglorum / The history of the English kings*, ed. and trans. R. A. B. Mynors, R. M. Thomson, and M. Winterbottom, 2 vols., OMT (1998–9) • William of Malmesbury, *The Historia novella*, ed. and trans. K. R. Potter (1955) • Henry, archdeacon of Huntingdon, *Historia Anglorum*, ed. D. E. Greenway, OMT (1996) • Ordericus Vitalis, *Eccl. hist.* • K. R. Potter and R. H. C. Davis, eds., *Gesta Stephani*, OMT (1976) • *Eadmeri Historia novorum in Anglia*, ed. M. Rule, Rolls Series, 81 (1884) • *Reg. RAN*, vols. 2–3 • *Fasti Angl., 1066–1300*, [Salisbury] • B. R. Kemp, ed., *Reading Abbey cartularies*, 2 vols., CS, 4th ser., 31, 33 (1986–7) • C. W. Hollister, *Monarchy, magnates, and institutions in the Anglo-Norman world* (1986) • T. Webber, *Scribes and scholars at Salisbury Cathedral, c.1075–c.1125* (1992) • Symeon of Durham, *Opera* • B. R. Kemp, ed., *Salisbury, 1078–1217*, English Episcopal Acta, 18 (1999)

Likenesses funerary slab?, Salisbury Cathedral

Wealth at death see Kealey, *Roger of Salisbury*, 96–7; Green, *Government of England*, 273–4

Salisbury [*née* Pridden], **Sarah** [Sally] (1690×92–1724), courtesan, was born Sarah Pridden in Shrewsbury between 1690 and 1692; known as Sally she was the eldest of four daughters of Richard Pridden, bricklayer, and his wife, Mary. According to Adlard her father was the son of Thomas Pridden, a maltster, and was baptized on 8 November 1663. Sally's was a celebrated rags-to-riches story, as she rose from humble origins to become one of the most famous courtesans of her day at a time when courtesans were drawn from genteel stock. Her fame and beauty won her public affection and she was celebrated in popular songs and two full-length contemporary biographies.

When Sally was three the family moved to London, where they lived in an alley off St Giles High Street. At the age of nine Sally was apprenticed to a seamstress in Duke Street but ran away to make her living selling fruit around Covent Garden and even tried acting on the stage with the encouragement of the well-known actress Elizabeth Barry. By the time she was fourteen Sally had come to the attention of Drury Lane's famous brothel-keeper Mother Wisebourne; she later worked for another notorious procurer, Mother Needham. Sally's rise was meteoric; no longer did she need to supplement her income from selling pamphlets by whoring with apprentice boys for 2s. 6d. an hour.

Noted as a great and charismatic beauty Sally was in

survive her year's sentence and her deteriorating condition was the subject of bulletins in the *London Journal*. She died in Newgate, of gaol fever, 'almost reduced to a Skeleton' (*London Journal*, 15 Feb 1724), in February 1724, despite attempts made by John Finch to gain her early release on the grounds of ill health. She was interred in the vault of St Andrew's, Holborn.   BARBARA WHITE

Sources J. Adlard, *The softer paths of pleasure: a life of Sally Salisbury* (1980) · E. J. Burford, *Wits, wenchers and wantons: London's low life, Covent Garden in the eighteenth century* (1986) · *Authentick memoirs of the life, intrigues and adventures of the celebrated Sally Salisbury with true characters of her most considerable gallants by Capt Charles Walker* (1723) · *The genuine history of Mrs. Sarah Prydden, usually called Sally Salisbury, and her gallants* (1723) · *The effigies, parentage, education, life, merry pranks and conversation of the celebrated Mrs Sally Salisbury* (1723) · *An account of the tryall of Sally Salisbury* (1722) · *Sally Slisbury's* [sic] *garland, containing four excellent new songs* [n.d., 18th cent.] [incl. 'Sally Salisbury farewel to her sister'; a version of this ballad appears in *The bleach yard's garland* (1775)]
Likenesses J. Smith, engraving (after G. Kneller), NPG [*see illus.*] · print, priv. coll.; repro. in Burford, *Wits, wenchers and wantons*, 51 · woodcut, repro. in *The effigies, parentage, education, life, merry pranks and conversation of the celebrated Mrs Sally Salisbury*

Sarah Salisbury (1690×92–1724), by John Smith (after Sir Godfrey Kneller)

constant demand among the titled and powerful. Burford lists the elderly Lord William Bentinck, Lord Bolingbroke, George Brudenell, third earl of Cardigan, the duke of Buckingham, and the prince of Wales among those whom she claimed were her lovers. In such company she denied her humble origins: after hearing a passing remark that she bore a striking resemblance to Lady Salisbury, Sally adopted the name and claimed to be the natural daughter of one of the family. She was also famed for her ready wit and is credited with telling her clients, 'Ay, my lord! Whores and bastards are always lucky!' (Burford, 48).

Sally Salisbury was known for her quick temper and it was this which was to mark a turning point in her fortunes. At the Three Tuns tavern in Chandos Street, Covent Garden, on the evening of 22 December 1722, Sally picked up a breadknife and stabbed her lover the Honourable John Finch, third son of the second earl of Nottingham, in an angry argument over a theatre ticket. Although she immediately repented her action and Finch was not mortally wounded she was charged with attempted murder and sent to Newgate gaol to await trial.

Finch was involved in frantic efforts to have the charges dropped but the trial went ahead on 24 April 1723. *An Account of the Tryall of Sally Salisbury* describes the proceedings which took place in the sessions house of the Old Bailey. Sally pleaded not guilty and was acquitted of any intention to murder, but was found guilty of assault and wounding. She was fined, given a year's prison sentence, and a further two years' suspended sentence. Already in ill health from the appalling prison conditions, she did not

Salisbury [Salesbury], **Thomas** (1561×4–1586), conspirator, was born at Lleweni, Denbighshire, probably in 1561 (although the records of Oxford University imply that he was sixteen when he matriculated in 1580). He was the elder son of *Katheryn of Berain (c.1540–1591) and her first husband, John Salisbury (c.1542–1566), son and heir of Sir John Salisbury of Lleweni [see Salusbury family]. There is no doubt that sixteenth-century Welsh poets, heralds, and genealogists firmly (if mistakenly) believed that Katheryn's grandfather Sir Roland de Veleville was the son of Henry Tudor (later Henry VII) and a Breton lady, which would place Katheryn in the same blood relationship to Elizabeth I as Lady Jane Grey and Mary, queen of Scots, offspring of first cousins, while Thomas Salisbury and Ferdinando, Lord Strange (implicated in the conspiracy of 1593), would both be one step further removed.

Salisbury's father died in 1566, and by the arrangements made on 12 July and 14 September that year all his mother's estates were secured to descend to Thomas with remainder to his brother John. The 'mariadge and custodie of the bodie' of the two was given to their grandfather, and they remained at Lleweni when their mother accompanied her second husband to Antwerp in 1567.

The child-marriage settlement, drawn up on 20 September 1574, between Sir John Salisbury and his wife, Dame Jane, and Katheryn's third husband, Maurice Wynn of Gwydir, whereby Thomas was to marry Margaret, daughter of Maurice Wynn from his first marriage, may have been partly an attempt to lessen the tension between the two families concerning property, and partly to enable the Wynns to secure a hold on Katheryn's son; the marriage was to be solemnized before 25 March 1575. It was not a happy arrangement, with ill feeling and mistrust on both sides, while Thomas objected to the marriage. Thomas was still under age when his grandfather died in 1578; and Sir John, who was on friendly terms with the earl of Leicester, Baron Denbigh, made him Leicester's ward, an action fiercely resented by the rest of the Salisbury clan, by the Wynns of Gwydir, and by the lesser gentry families in north Wales who had, privately, no affection for the new religion of which Leicester was champion. There were well-known recusant families in north Wales who celebrated mass secretly, and many more suspects; while the coastal area, with easy access to Ireland, was regarded as a danger spot. Salisbury was at Oxford in 1578, but returned and was placed in the care of Maurice Wynn, Leicester promising to endeavour to get him to consent to the match with Wynn's daughter. A daughter, Margaret, was born of the marriage in February 1586; an older child, John, had died as an infant.

Salisbury matriculated at Trinity College, Oxford, on 29 January 1580. Here he joined a secret society, led by Anthony Babington, sworn to support the Jesuit priests entering the country. When he migrated to London, in Leicester's service, he moved in the same Roman Catholic society. He and Babington 'were bedfellows for a quarter of a year or more' (CSP dom., 1581–90, 346). Not surprisingly he joined Babington's conspiracy to assassinate Elizabeth, put Mary, queen of Scots, on the throne, and restore Roman Catholicism (though he himself would not consent to the assassination), a plan that had the support of Philip II of Spain. In March and April he and Edward Jones, of Plas Cadwgan, Wrexham, were named among those who would join Sir Edward Fyton for the peopling of Munster (CSP Ire., 1586–8, July, 42). On 8 June 1586 Salisbury pledged that he would raise a rebellion in Denbigh, and he and Jones discussed the matter.

From the beginning, however, the plot was known to Walsingham, head of Elizabeth's intelligence service, and by August 1586 the Babington conspirators were being hounded. Salisbury fled towards Wales, but was caught in Cheshire and taken prisoner to London. He received no support from his guardian, and with what seems to have been an inadequate trial, on 13 and 14 September, all involved were condemned for high treason and executed on the 21st. Salisbury admitted on the scaffold, 'I have lyved a catholique and so will I dye' (Kenyon MSS, 614).

A commission was sent to inquire about Salisbury's estate, and a jury empanelled, 'Whoe by some old estate to theires males of Lleweny saved the inheritaunce of Salesbury from forffecture' (Ballinger, Wynn Papers, 28–9). The Lleweni estate passed to his brother John. From then on no mention of Thomas is to be found in the numerous poems composed in honour of the family, in Welsh, English, and Latin (NL Wales, MS 6496, fols. 174–200). The execution of the head of the formidable Salisbury clan must have shaken all the north Wales gentry, and, in all probability, strengthened their acceptance, at least outwardly, of the new protestant religion. ENID ROBERTS

Sources J. Ballinger, 'Katheryn of Berain', Y Cymrodor, 40 (1929), 1–42 · [J. Ballinger], ed., Calendar of Wynn (of Gwydir) papers, 1515–1690, in the National Library of Wales (1926) · A schedule of the Lleweni collection (1971) [at NL Wales] · NL Wales, MSS 1553, 688 · NL Wales, Lleweni MSS 658 and 429 · NL Wales, MS 6496, fols. 174–200 · Chester City Archives, Combermere Abbey MSS, document 72/82/23/2 A · Foster, Alum. Oxon., 1500–1714 [Thomas Salisburie] · CSP dom., 1581–90 · CSP Ire., 1586–8 · J. H. Pollen, Mary queen of Scots and the Babington plot, Scottish History Society, 3rd ser., 3 (1922) · Calendar of the manuscripts of the most hon. the marquis of Salisbury, 24 vols., HMC, 9 (1883–1976) · CSP for., 1586–7 · The manuscripts of Lord Kenyon, HMC, 35 (1894), 614 · E. Roberts, 'Siôn Salsbri, Lleweni', Transactions of the Denbighshire Historical Society, 19 (1970), 66–102, esp. 68–78

Salisbury, Thomas (1566/7–1622), bookseller and Welsh-language poet, was the son of Pierce Salberye, a husbandman, of Clocaenog, Denbighshire. He was apprenticed, probably aged fourteen, to Oliver Wilkes, stationer, from 9 October 1581, and was admitted freeman of the Stationers' Company on 17 October 1588. His first known publication was a short catechism, in English, for children; in 1593 he published Henry Salisbury's Grammatica Britannica.

In 1603 Salisbury published, jointly with Simon Stafford, a version of the Psalms written in the strict Welsh metres by William Myddelton. Salisbury, who edited the work for the press, dedicated it to James I, and wrote in his address 'to the reader':

> I have also begun the printing of the Psalms in the like kinde of meeter in Brytish, as they are usually sung in the Church of England, and have prefixed apt notes to sing them withall, which I hope to see fully finished ere long.

A part of this free-metre psalter, which was of Salisbury's own composition, was published in the same year, with an introduction by Edward Kyffin; it was described as printed by Stafford for T. S. Salisbury's address continues:

> There are also divers other good things ready for the press, as namely, the Brytish Testament, lately corrected by the reverend Father in God, the Bishop of St. Asaphe [William Morgan]; a Treatise of the government of the tongue, and another Treatise of repentance, penned by Master Perkins; a preparative to Marriage and divers other sermons of Master Henry Smithes.

All the works published by Salisbury are of a decidedly protestant character.

Salisbury, who was married, received a pension from the Stationers' Company from 1608 to 1622. A letter (assigned to 22 June 1611) to Sir John Wynn of Gwydir, gives his address as Cloth Fair, West Smithfield, London. He probably died during the last quarter of 1622.

John Salisbury (fl. 1695–1697), printer, probably Thomas's grandson, was described by John Dunton (pp. 210–11) as 'a desperate hyper-Gorgonic Welchman' and 'a silly empty, morose fellow'. He was the first printer and editor of the Flying Post from Paris and Amsterdam which, denying competition with the London Gazette, claimed to supply the news missing from that journal. The first number was issued on 11 May 1695. Dunton says that Salisbury 'did often fill it [the "Post"] with stol'n copies'. In 1697 he published in it a false and malicious paragraph, evidently intended to throw suspicions on the exchequer bills, he being 'the tool of a band of stockjobbers in the city, whose interest it happened to be to cry down the public securities'. A warrant was issued against him by the speaker of the House of Commons, and a bill was immediately introduced to prohibit the publishing of news without a licence, which, however, did not succeed. Salisbury also went to law with the Stationers' Company, seeking to avoid the expense of being elected to the livery. He died, according to Dunton, before 1705.

D. L. THOMAS, *rev.* ANITA McCONNELL

Sources C. H. Timperley, *A dictionary of printers and printing* (1839), 417, 445, 578 · *STC, 1475–1640* · J. Williams, *The medieval history of Denbighshire*, 1: *The records of Denbigh and its lordship* (1860), 184 · J. Dunton, *The life and errors of John Dunton … written by himself* (1705); repr. (1974), 210–11 · N. Luttrell, *A brief historical relation of state affairs from September 1678 to April 1714*, 4 (1857); repr. (1969), 203–5 · *JHC*, 11 (1693–7), 765, 767 · *Commons Journal* (3 April 1697) · Arber, *Regs. Stationers*, vol. 2 · Stationers' Hall, poor book, fols. 4v–72r

Salisbury, Thomas. *See* Salusbury, Sir Thomas, second baronet (1612–1643).

Salisbury, William. *See* Salesbury, William (*b.* before 1520, *d. c.*1580); Salesbury, William (1580?–1659/60).

Salisbury, William (*d.* 1823/1829), nurseryman and botanist, has been erroneously described as a brother of Richard Anthony Salisbury. Nothing is known of his early life. In his *Botanist's Companion* (1816, 2 vols.) he states that from 1791 he was employed by the board of agriculture in conducting experiments on the growth of plants. Before then he may have been engaged as a nurseryman. In 1797 he was gardener to J. Symmons FRS at Paddington House, Paddington, and in the same year entered into partnership with nurseryman William Curtis (1746–1799) at his garden at Queen's Elm, Brompton. After Curtis's death he moved the garden to Cadogan Place, Sloane Street, where he held botanical classes. It is not clear whether he died in 1823, or in 1829, when David Ramsay acquired the Sloane Street nursery.

In addition to the *Botanist's Companion*, Salisbury published a number of other horticultural works. They included: *Hortus Paddingtonensis: a catalogue of the plants in the garden of J. Symmons, esq., Paddington House* (1797); *A General Catalogue of Trees, Shrubs, Flowers, etc., Cultivated in England* [n.d.]; *Hints to Proprietors of Orchards* [with] *the Natural History of American Blight* (1816); and *The Cottager's Companion, or, A Complete System of Cottage Horticulture* (1817).

G. S. BOULGER, *rev.* ALEXANDER GOLDBLOOM

Sources Desmond, *Botanists*, rev. edn, 603 · H. Trimen and W. T. Thiselton Dyer, *Flora of Middlesex* (1869), 395 · *GM*, 1st ser., 85/2 (1815), 103 · J. Britten and G. S. Boulger, eds., *A biographical index of British and Irish botanists* (1893)
Archives Linn. Soc., corresp. and papers · NHM, drawings and papers | NHM, letters to members of the Sowerby family

Salkeld, Henry (*bap.* 1584, *d.* 1645). *See under* Salkeld, John (1579/80–1660).

Salkeld [alias Dalston], **John** (1579/80–1660), Church of England clergyman and theologian, was the fourth of the five sons of Edward Salkeld of Morland, Westmorland, the younger brother of Sir George Salkeld of Corby Castle, Cumberland. According to Anthony Wood he was briefly at the Queen's College, Oxford, but of this there is no record. His father, a Catholic recusant, sent him abroad to be educated by the Jesuits, first at the University of Coimbra, Portugal, and then at the English College of St Gregory, Seville. From there in February 1602 he entered the

novitiate of the Andalusian province of the Society of Jesus at Montilla, near Córdoba, having by then completed three years of philosophy and four of theology; in January 1603 the records there listed him as aged twenty-three. He was subsequently ordained priest.

Salkeld remained in Andalusia until 1608, when he was sent on the English mission, using the alias John Dalston. In March 1612 he was apprehended in Cornwall by Sir William Godolphin, to whom he delivered 'papers relative to his conversion from Popery' (*CSP dom.*, *1611–18*, 124). Godolphin sent him on to London where he was interviewed by the lord treasurer and the archbishop of Canterbury. By July he was a house guest of John King, bishop of London, and had several theological conversations with James I who, impressed by his learning, presented him in November 1613 (when he was described as having a BD degree) to the living of Wellington, Somerset. In the same year he published *A Treatise of Angels*, styling himself on the title-page as 'sometime Fellow of the Jesuites Colledges in the universities of Conimbra, Corduba and Complutum [Alcalá], Assistant in Studies to the famous Jesuites Franciscus Suarius [Suárez] and Michael Vazquez'. The work was dedicated to the king, whom Salkeld praised as the angel who had rescued him from the dungeon of popery and enlightened him by the beams of his reasoning. Crammed with recondite learning, it was an attempt to expound the subtleties of Thomist angelology to the man in the English pulpit; a sequel, *A Treatise of Paradise, and the Principall Contents Thereof* (1617) was dedicated to Sir Francis Bacon. It is clear, however, that Salkeld's value to the Anglican establishment was not confined to the elucidation of esoteric doctrines. He was 'a real find' to the archbishop because of his 'effective anti-Romist preaching' and of major concern to his former co-religionists because, as Edward Bennett reported to Rome, he put 'devises in Canter[bury's] head to tak all the preste[s] in England' (Questier, 47). In November 1616 Salkeld reported his former neighbour Lord William Howard, of Naworth Castle, for recusancy.

In January 1634 Salkeld was instituted as rector of Churchstanton, Devon. During the civil war he was a committed royalist and as a result was deprived of his living about 1646. He settled at Uffculme, Devon, where he underwent examination by the county commissioners during the year 1651 to 1652. He died at Uffculme in February 1660 and was buried there on 16 March, survived by his wife, Susanna, who died about two months later, and by their son John.

His younger brother **Henry Salkeld** (*bap.* 1584, *d.* 1645) was baptized on 18 November 1584, the youngest son of Edward Salkeld. He was also a student at the English College of St Gregory, Seville, where in 1610 he contributed some Latin verses to a poetry festival held by the Jesuits to celebrate the beatification of Ignatius of Loyola. After ordination the same year he left for the English mission, travelling via Douai which he left on 6 October 1610. He, too, rapidly conformed to the Church of England and, along with his brother, on 17 March 1615 was granted a formal pardon under the sign manual for having attended a foreign seminary. With the patronage of James Montague, bishop of Winchester, he was instituted as rector of Wyke Without, Winchester, on 5 April 1617. The following year, on 22 August, he was instituted as rector of Milborne Port, Somerset, a living in the gift of Winchester College. He died at Milborne Port in September 1645 and was buried there on 12 September. G. MARTIN MURPHY

Sources M. Murphy, St Gregory's College, Seville, 1592–1767, Catholic RS, 73 (1992) · Report on the manuscripts of the marquis of Downshire, 6 vols. in 7, HMC, 75 (1924–95), vol. 3, p. 331 · F. W. Weaver, ed., Somerset incumbents (privately printed, Bristol, 1889), 462 · CSP dom., 1611–18, 124, 279 · Wood, Ath. Oxon., new edn, 2.315; 3.487–9 · H. Foley, ed., Records of the English province of the Society of Jesus, 5 (1879), 854 · H. Foley, ed., Records of the English province of the Society of Jesus, 6 (1880), 355 · C. B. Norcliffe, ed., The visitation of Yorkshire in the years 1563 and 1564, Harleian Society, 16 (1881), 272 · J. Salkeld, A treatise of angels (1613) · M. C. Questier, Conversion, politics and religion in England, 1580–1625 (1996) · Walker rev. · G. Anstruther, The seminary priests, 2 (1975), 276 · F. J. Baigent, History and antiquities of the parish church of Wyke (1825) · Foster, Alum. Oxon. · Archivum Romanum Societatis Iesu, Rome, Boetica 8 · parish register, Uffculme, Devon, Devon RO [burial], 16 March 1660, 16 May 1660 · parish register, Milborne Port, Somerset, Somerset RO [burial, Henry Salkeld], 12 Sept 1645

Archives Archivum Romanum Societatis Iesu, Rome, Boetica 8

Salkeld, William (1671–1715), serjeant-at-law and law reporter, was the eldest son of Samuel Salkeld (d. 1699) of Fallowden, Northumberland, from an old Cumberland family. He matriculated at St Edmund Hall, Oxford, on 22 April 1687, entered the Middle Temple on 2 May 1692, and was called to the bar on 3 June 1698. He settled in Dorset when he married, in 1700, Mary (c.1681–1723), only daughter of John Ryves of Fifehead Neville, Dorset. They had three sons and three daughters. As he had acquired part of the Fifehead Neville estate through his marriage in 1707 he sold the Fallowden estate he had inherited from his father.

Salkeld was created a serjeant-at-law in January 1715. In the same year he was appointed chief justice of the great sessions for the counties of Carmarthen, Cardigan, and Pembroke. On 24 January 1715 he was created a serjeant-at-law. He was well known for his legal reports, and his Reports of Cases in the Court of King's Bench, 1689–1712, published in 1717–18, became the standard work for that period. He was also one of the translators of the Reports of Sir Creswell Levinz in the King's Bench, 1660–1697, published in 1722. Salkeld died on 14 September 1715, and was buried in the church of Fifehead Neville.

W. R. WILLIAMS, rev. ANNE PIMLOTT BAKER

Sources Baker, Serjeants, 535 · W. R. Williams, The history of the great sessions in Wales, 1542–1830 (privately printed, Brecon, 1899), 181 · H. W. Woolrych, Lives of eminent serjeants-at-law of the English bar, 2 vols. (1869), 2.482–95 · J. Hutchins, The history and antiquities of the county of Dorset, 2 vols. (1774) · Foster, Alum. Oxon. · H. A. C. Sturgess, ed., Register of admissions to the Honourable Society of the Middle Temple, from the fifteenth century to the year 1944, 1 (1949)

Salkey, (Felix) Andrew Alexander (1928–1995), writer and broadcaster, was born on 30 January 1928 in Colón, Panama, the eldest son of Andrew Alexander Salkey (1895–1967), a worker in the canal zone, and his wife, Linda Gloria Marshall (1895–1967). His parents were both from Jamaica, and at two he was sent back there to his grandmother, later to be joined by his mother and a younger brother: he was not to see his father again for thirty years. The living popular traditions of the island instilled in him a strong affection for Caribbean folklore. He was educated at St George's and Munro colleges, and had his first poems published in the island newspaper, the Daily Gleaner. In 1952 he emigrated to England, where he was to read for a BA and MA in English at University College, London. To survive financially he took on a succession of odd jobs which brought him in contact with West Indians from various walks of life, and their living conditions drew him to Marxism and protest against colonialism. He joined the League of Coloured Peoples, and the Movement for Colonial Freedom.

On 22 February 1958 Salkey married Patricia June Verden (b. 1935), a teacher. In that year he also began secondary schoolteaching. However, he had discovered his talent for radio work while still in Jamaica, contributing to the BBC programme Caribbean Voices from 1948. He soon left teaching to become a full-time freelance broadcaster, continuing to write and present material for the Caribbean, but also working for the Pacific, African, and General Overseas services of the BBC. He also made it his especial business to make contact with Caribbean writers. Quietly persuasive, with a gift for friendship and an encyclopaedic memory for people, Salkey with his wife Pat made their Bayswater flat a meeting point for immigrant authors and artists in London. Through his personal contacts with publishers, in particular André Deutsch and Faber and Faber, he worked to get new West Indian writers published, and was responsible for persuading Faber to accept the work of the visionary Guyanese author Wilson Harris. He edited a series of anthologies, of which the most influential were West Indian Stories (1960), Stories from the Caribbean (1965), and a volume of poetry, Breaklight (1971). These collections showed remarkable insight in identifying the shape of an evolving Caribbean literary movement.

In 1966 the Barbadian poet and critic Edward Brathwaite was studying in England, and looked for a way to co-ordinate the creative arts of the Caribbean. He turned to Salkey and to John La Rose, a Trinidadian poet and publisher, with them launching the Caribbean Artists Movement (CAM), which remained active in Britain until 1972. Through its conferences, meetings, and publications, CAM helped create a cultural base for the Caribbean arts, and for black British writers generally. Salkey's interests continued to be international. His radical sympathies gave him great hopes of the revolution in Cuba, and his visit there in 1967–8 formed the basis for his travelogue Havana Journal (1971). He later edited Writing in Cuba since the Revolution (1977). After attending the seminal Caribbean Writers and Artists Conference at the founding of the Co-operative Republic of Guyana in 1970, he recorded his experiences in Georgetown Journal (1972). He had strong sympathies with Chile, and annually wrote the poems on the country's freedom cause which won him the 1979

Casa de las Americas prize, and were collected in *In the Hills where her Dreams Live* (1981).

Salkey's creative works included *A Quality of Violence* (1959), an account, partly drawing on his knowledge of Haiti, his mother's birthplace, of cultists in rural Jamaica at the time of the great drought of 1900. *Escape to an Autumn Pavement* (1960) began a series of picaresque novels, *The Late Emancipation of Jerry Stover* (1968), *The Adventures of Catullus Kelly* (1969), and *Come Home, Malcolm Heartland* (1976). These novels, set in England and the Caribbean, each focused on a young, deracinated black man seeking a meaningful identity in an increasingly bizarre and corrupt post-colonial world. The morally ambiguous careers of these anti-heroes may link them to the Caribbean folklore trickster figure Anancy the spiderman, who appears in character in Salkey's political parables, collected in *Anancy's Score* (1973), *One* (1985), and *Anancy, Traveller* (1992). Salkey also published four volumes of poetry, including the painstakingly researched historical epic of his homeland, *Jamaica* (1973), awarded the Thomas Helmore poetry prize. His children's story *Hurricane* (1964) won a Deutscher Kinderbuchpreis, and was the first of eight books for children. These featured young heroes as resourceful as the protagonists of his adult fiction were futile, facing, in the early stories, natural disasters and, in the later, political unrest.

A versatile and always professional writer, Salkey won literary honours which, in addition to those recorded above, included a Guggenheim award (1960) and the Sri Chinmoy award (1977). But he will be remembered in particular for his generosity of spirit and his tireless advocacy of the Caribbean arts. In a shifting world he kept his independent voice, remaining freelance as a broadcaster, and while most of his life an emigrant, staying a Jamaican citizen. In 1976 he left for the United States to become professor of creative writing at Hampshire College, Amherst, Massachusetts. He largely lived there until his death from a heart attack on 28 April 1995 at his home, 826 West Street, Amherst; he was survived by his wife and two sons. He was buried on 11 May in Paddington new cemetery, Mill Hill, London. A posthumous collection of his shorter pieces, *In the Border Country*, was published in 1998.

LOUIS JAMES

Sources A. Walmsley, *The Caribbean Artists Movement, 1966–1972* (1992) • D. C. Dance, 'Andrew Salkey', *Fifty Caribbean writers*, ed. D. C. Dance (1986), 418, 427 • F. Birbalsingh, *Frontiers of Caribbean literature in English* (1996), 2.29–41 • P. Nazareth, *In the trickster tradition* (1994) • personal knowledge (2004) • private information (2004) [Patricia June Salkey, widow]
Archives priv. coll., manuscripts and papers
Likenesses photograph, repro. in F. A. A. Salkey, *In the border country* (1998), cover • photograph, repro. in L. James, ed., *The islands in between: Essays on West Indian literature* (1968)

Sall, Andrew (*c*.1620–1682), Jesuit and Church of Ireland clergyman, was born in Cashel, co. Tipperary. The Salls (or Sauls) were an important Old English family of counties Tipperary and Waterford. His father was called John but nothing further is known about him. Sall has been confused with his older contemporary and kinsman Andrew FitzBennet Saul (1613–1686). Both were born in Cashel in the early seventeenth century and were educated abroad; both became Jesuits. The elder Sall remained a Catholic, whereas the younger converted publicly to Anglicanism. There is little difficulty in separating the two after Sall's conversion in 1674. They can be distinguished before that date by means of the autobiographical information in Sall's own works, in particular his *True Catholic and Apostolic Faith* (1676). It is also clear that the elder Sall had no connection with Spain.

The younger Sall asserts that before his conversion in 1674 but after his return from Spain he discussed theology for six years with Thomas Price, Church of Ireland archbishop of Cashel. This would put his return to Ireland about 1668. He also writes that he spent a total of twenty-six years in Spain but did not travel widely in the country. He says he passed his first two years (1642–4) in retreat in the exercise of devotion, the next seven (1644–51) being spent studying philosophy and theology. For seventeen years (1651–68) he taught in various Jesuit colleges: poetry, oratory, history, and cosmography in the colleges of Numacia and Villagaroia; philosophy, logic, physics, and metaphysics thereafter in the college at Pamplona. Finally he taught scholastic, moral, and polemic theology in the colleges of Pamplona, Palencia, Tudela, and Salamanca.

Sall himself states that he was rector of the Irish College in Salamanca in 1652, and letters survive from him in this capacity from 1650. For three years (1652–5) he was also *lector de la catedra de controversias contra herejes* ('reader of the chair of controversies against heretics') in the college and received an annual licence from Pedro Lopez de Brinnias, bishop of Palencia and inquisitor-general of Spain, to read prohibited books. Sall prints the text of the licence in the preface to *True Catholic and Apostolic Faith*. The prohibition was apparently so severe that he had little opportunity to read any proscribed works. The immoderation of Spanish piety, however, had already shaken his faith in Roman Catholicism. In Palencia in 1661 he heard a friar preach that a certain saint was inerrant, and his *obiter dicta* of equal authority with the Bible. Offended by this and similar excesses Sall complained to the inquisitor-general. He took the Jesuits' fourth vow of obedience to the pope in Valladolid in 1657 or 1658. While in Pamplona he became friendly with Diego de Benavides y la Cueva, count of Santistebán and governor of Navarre, who regarded Sall so highly that he printed a eulogy of him in his book *Horae succesivae* (Lyons, 1660).

Sall returned to Ireland and his native city about 1668 wishing, as he says himself, 'to spend the remnant of his days unknown to prepare better for the long day of eternity'. In Cashel he became acquainted with Price and other divines of the established church. He was greatly impressed by Price's kindness and learning and by the disciplined piety of the protestants. Early in 1674 some Catholic clerics falsely announced that Sall had already defected. So incensed were his former associates in Cashel and Clonmel that they sought to kill him. Hearing of the plot Price sent an armed guard to bring Sall to his own residence for protection. While in Price's house he wrote to his friends and the Catholic clergy in the city expressing the hope that he might still assuage his scruples and remain a Catholic. In May 1674 John Free, the superior of the Irish Jesuits and a personal friend, wrote to him assuring him that all his doubts would be eased. Further correspondence followed in which Sall tried to persuade his fellow Catholics that his problems were entirely theological and that he had no personal quarrel with anyone. His correspondents, however, seem not to have understood his difficulties.

On 17 May 1674 Sall made a public declaration in St John's Church, Cashel, of his adherence to the Church of Ireland before Archbishop Price, Bishop Hugh Gore of Waterford, and other clerics. Sall himself admits that he would not have converted so soon had it not been for the proclamation of the Lord Lieutenant Essex in 1674 banishing regular clergy from Ireland. His erstwhile ecclesiastical superiors continued to appeal by letter to him to desist and return to the fold, offering private discussions with him to that end. He was not deflected, and in a sermon preached on 5 July 1674 in Christ Church, Dublin, before the lord lieutenant and the Irish privy council he set out his reasons for having left the Church of Rome.

When he arrived in Dublin, Sall took up lodgings in Trinity College and was admitted there to the degree of doctor of divinity by thesis. In his dissertation he set out the two main conclusions he had reached: first, that there was salvation outside the Roman church, and second, that Anglicanism provided a safer route to salvation than Roman Catholicism. When his thesis was being disputed he invited many leading Catholics to attend. They were indeed present but remained silent. In 1675 he was presented by the crown to the prebend of Swords in St Patrick's Cathedral, Dublin. In 1676 he was made chancellor of Cashel. Two years later he was given the rectory of Kilfithmone in the diocese of Cashel, the rectory of Dungourney in Cloyne, and two livings in co. Meath. These Irish benefices were estimated at £300–£400 per annum.

In July 1675 Sall went to Oxford, where he was created doctor of divinity. He engaged in theological disputation there and was appointed domestic chaplain to Charles II. While he was in Oxford the Irish Catholics produced a number of books against him. The best known is *The Doleful Fall of Andrew Sall* (1675, reprinted 1749) by Nicholas French, a work more distinguished by its abusive tone than by any coherent argument. In 1676, as a final attempt to bring him back to the Roman church, Clement X published a bull which was delivered anonymously to Sall promising him pardon and restoration if he repented. Sall remained convinced of the truth of Anglicanism and answered all the calumnies and threats against him in very moderate language in *True Catholic and Apostolic Faith*. In this book he also defends the position of *Ecclesia Anglicana* with consummate erudition. In Oxford, he resided in Wadham College and then nearby in a house in Holywell Street. His health was poor and he moved to lodgings in the cloisters in Christ Church, staying there for three years. In October 1677 he was granted by the crown the chantorship of St David's Cathedral in Wales.

He published two further books in Oxford: *Votum pro pace Christiana* (1678) and *Ethica, sive, Moralis philosophia* (1680).

In Oxford Sall also met Robert Boyle, who hoped to publish the scriptures in Irish, and in 1680 returned to Ireland with the main purpose of promoting Boyle's enterprise. On arriving in Ireland he met Henry Jones, bishop of Meath, and Narcissus Marsh, provost of Trinity College, Dublin, since both were anxious to see the publication of the Bible in Irish. From November 1680 until his death he lived in Oxmantown, a part of Dublin north of the River Liffey. At the suggestion of Thomas Price the catechism from the Book of Common Prayer was translated into Irish and published in London in 1680. Sall urged Boyle and his helpers to imitate the Catholic catechism of Theobald Stapleton of 1639 and print the work in Roman characters. His wise counsel was ignored, however, for Boyle had had a new Gaelic typeface cast in London by Joseph Moxon. Boyle employed an Irish scholar, Hugh O'Reilly, in London to steer the book through the press. The catechism was a trial piece only, a reprinting of William Daniel's New Testament being the next step in Boyle's enterprise. Sall recommended to Boyle and Marsh that the new edition of the Irish New Testament contain an Irish version of the Jansenists' preface to their French New Testament. Marsh was unhappy with this preface on the grounds that it was too critical of protestantism. Sall therefore wrote his own preface in English and sent it to London, where it was translated into Irish by O'Reilly. Both English and Irish versions of the preface were printed at the front of the New Testament when it appeared in Moxon's type in June 1681. Although Sall's foreword was a new composition it was clearly based on the Jansenists, and in it, as in his other writings, Sall demonstrates the breadth of his learning.

The chief concern of both Sall and Boyle was the publication of the Irish translation of the Old Testament, which had been made at the insistence of William Bedell. The manuscript, unbound, torn, and in disarray, was in the possession of Henry Jones, who sent it to Sall in December 1681. With the help of Paul Higgins (Pól Ó hUiginn) he tidied up the manuscript and had it bound. Higgins, formerly a Catholic priest of the diocese of Killala, had converted to the established church and was teaching Irish in Trinity College. Sall immediately found as a scribe to write out a fair copy of the Old Testament 'one Denine; an Irishman who could both speak and write Irish very well' (Williams, 81). This seems to have been Uilliam Ó Duinnín, a well-known scribe and member of a celebrated Munster family of literati. Ó Duinnín's copy was sent in parts by Sall to Boyle in London. Early in 1682, however, Sall's health failed completely, and he was no longer able to assist the work of transcription. He died at Oxmantown on 5 April 1682 and was buried in St Patrick's Cathedral, Dublin. The Irish Old Testament, however, was eventually published in London in 1685.   N. J. A. WILLIAMS

Sources A. Sall, *True catholic and apostolic faith maintain'd in the Church of England* (1676) [incl. autobiographical material] · A. Breeze, 'Andrew Sall (†1682), Andrew Sall (†1686), and the Irish Bible', *Éigse*, 28 (1994–5), 100–02 · N. J. A. Williams, *I bprionta i*

leabhar (1987) · D. J. O'Doherty, 'Students of the Irish College, Salamanca (1595–1619) [pt 2]', *Archivium Hibernicum*, 3 (1914), 87–112 · F. Finnegan, 'The Jesuits in Dublin, 1660–1760', *Reportorium Novum*, 4 (1971), 43–100 · H. Foley, ed., *Records of the English province of the Society of Jesus*, 7/2 (1883), 681–2

Salmon, Cyril Barnet, Baron Salmon (1903–1991), judge, was born Barnett Cyril Salmon on 28 December 1903 at 232 Finchley Road, Hampstead, London, the son of Montagu Salmon, tobacco merchant, and his wife, Marian Nina Trevor, *née* Abrahams. His father's family co-owned J. Lyons & Co. Ltd, famous for its corner houses and tea shops until well after the Second World War. He was educated at Mill Hill School and Pembroke College, Cambridge, where he read law. Called to the bar by the Middle Temple in 1925, he was a pupil of Walter Monckton, who was already a prominent junior in distinguished chambers and 'a busy and prosperous man' (Lord Birkenhead, *Walter Monckton: the Life of Viscount Monckton of Brenchley*, 1969, 61). He then became a member of chambers at 5 Crown Office Row where the titular head was Robert Alderson Wright, Baron Wright, former master of the rolls and a legendary exponent of commercial law both as barrister and judge. He proceeded to build up his own practice covering a wide variety of (mostly civil) work, and by 1939 he was established as one of three leading common-law juniors in London, the others being Valentine Holmes, junior counsel to the treasury (the 'treasury devil'), and Gilbert Paul. Colin Sleeman, who was Salmon's pupil and became a member of his chambers in July 1939, later said: 'Cyril was a wonderful pupil master who really took trouble to instruct his pupils' (private information).

The outbreak of the Second World War in 1939 had immediate consequences, for Salmon and his chambers, which were even more catastrophic than for most others in London. He enrolled in the army and was commissioned in the Royal Artillery in 1940. Other members of the chambers were likewise dispersed on military and RAF service, and soon afterwards the chambers building itself was bombed to the ground. In the later part of his military service, from 1943, Salmon was on the headquarters staff of the Eighth Army as a judge advocate. He ended the war with the rank of major. When he returned to practice in 1945 the chambers were housed at 3 Paper Buildings, the senior clerk had retired, and nothing of his pre-war junior practice remained. In these circumstances, he took the courageous decision to apply for silk, and was appointed KC in April 1945.

Salmon had married, on 25 July 1929, Rencie Vanderfelt (*d.* 1942), daughter of Sidney Gorton Vanderfelt; they had two children, Gai Rencie (*b.* 1933) and David Neville Cyril (*b.* 1935). Rencie Salmon was remembered as 'a very attractive and charming young woman and a very kind and generous hostess' (private information). The loss Salmon suffered from her untimely death was matched by the happiness brought to him by his second marriage, to Jean Beatrice (Jeannie) Morris, Lady Morris (1912–1989), on 6 April 1946. She was the elder daughter of Lieutenant-Colonel David Edward Maitland-Makgill-Crichton, and

Cyril Barnet Salmon, Baron Salmon (1903–1991), by Lenare, 1946

the divorced wife of Michael William Morris, second Baron Morris, with whom she had had two daughters and twin sons. She was lively, intelligent, and attractive, and they were devoted to each other. They lived at 12 Wilton Street, London, a house which Salmon bought during the war years, and subsequently at 1 Melina Place, St John's Wood, London, and at the Old Drum, Sandwich, Kent. No reference to their home life during the 1950s and 1960s would be complete without a mention of Salmon's two long-haired dachshunds, Rudi and Mimi, who were his constant companions, on circuit as in London, and on some official as well as private occasions.

In the years after 1945 in the Temple, work was far from plentiful and the competition was intense. After a slow start, which perhaps was inevitable, Salmon acquired 'a large and varied practice' (*The Independent*, 14 Nov 1991), and during the 1950s became one of the acknowledged leaders of the bar. His practice included commercial cases, but he was too good a general advocate, and too much in demand, to become a specialist in that or any other field. His appointment as a judge of the High Court in 1957, with the accompanying knighthood, was presaged by the lord chancellor's invitation to travel the Wales and Chester circuit as commissioner of assize in 1955, which he did with considerable success. As a judge he achieved an even higher reputation than he had earned at the bar, both in the Queen's Bench Division and, from 1964, when he was appointed a lord justice of appeal and a privy councillor, in the Court of Appeal. It was said of him that 'the higher he went, the better he got' (private information).

As a judge Salmon was conspicuous both for his intellectual integrity and for his sometimes outspoken and fearless defence of liberal values and of the rights of the individual against intrusion by the state or by fellow citizens who failed to respect what became known as his, or her, human rights. At the same time, he retained the respect of more traditional common lawyers by recognizing the force of binding authority, even when it compelled a decision which was not necessarily in line with his personal sympathies for one or other of the parties in a particular case. At this time Lord Denning presided in the Court of Appeal as master of the rolls, and it was sometimes said, even by him, that the rules of precedent should give way, when justice demanded it, to the merits of the individual case as seen by the trial judge or appellate court. It is a mark of Salmon's intellectual distinction that he acquired a reputation which rivalled Denning's own for reconciling the justice of the case with the intellectual demands of the law. He received much favourable publicity, soon after his appointment, by reason of the tough prison sentences he imposed at the central criminal court in 1958 on the members of a gang of white youths who were convicted of attacking black victims during disturbances in the Notting Hill area of London, and his sentencing remarks were widely reported. They were credited with achieving their object of checking an incipient spread of racism at that time: 'Everyone, irrespective of the colour of their skin, is entitled to walk through our streets in peace, with their heads erect and free from fear. That is a right which these courts will always unfailingly uphold' (The Times, 9 Nov 1991). In 1966 he criticized the 'trial by television' of Emil Savundra, who was accused (and later charged and convicted) of insurance frauds and malpractice on a major scale: such a person was entitled to a fair trial and the protection of the law. Aptly, in the same year, Salmon was appointed chairman of the royal commission which inquired into the workings of the Tribunals of Inquiry (Evidence) Act, of 1921. The commission's report included recommendations which were designed to provide safeguards for witnesses and advocates appearing before tribunals of that kind. He also chaired a royal commission on standards of conduct in public life in 1974–6, following his appointment to the House of Lords. He set out his views on the subject of individual liberty in a lecture which he delivered at a public meeting of Justice in July 1967 and in his Haldane lecture at Birkbeck College, London, entitled 'The law and individual liberty' in December 1970.

Salmon's elevation to the House of Lords as Baron Salmon of Sandwich in 1972 was widely welcomed, and he remained an active and respected member of the appellate committee and of the judicial committee of the privy council until he retired in 1980. He began to suffer early symptoms of the ill health which increasingly marred the last decade of his life. Even during these later years, however, he spoke out against features of what became the Police and Criminal Evidence Act, of 1984, which he considered were unnecessarily restrictive of the legal rights of a criminal suspect in police custody. Characteristically, he supported in the House of Lords an early, unsuccessful, attempt to enact the European Convention on Human Rights as part of British law.

Salmon was a person of unique talents and charm, 'widely liked and admired for the breadth of his knowledge, his courtesy, humour and patience, and also for his strength of will' (The Times, 9 Nov 1991). He was of medium height and always immaculately dressed, with a demeanour which was modest and quiet, to the point where sometimes he might appear almost languid to a casual onlooker. But no one could doubt for long either his intellectual energy or his personal distinction, and the word 'elegant' perhaps best describes both his outward appearance and his manner, whether in conversation or as a speaker—or as an advocate. Indeed, it was because he was able to deploy these personal gifts in all aspects of his professional work that he not only achieved outstanding success but was held in high personal regard by all who came into contact with him. He was loyal to the Middle Temple, where he was elected a bencher in 1953 and treasurer in 1972; to Cambridge, where he became an honorary fellow of Pembroke College in 1965, an honorary doctor of laws (LLD) in 1982, and a commissary of the university in 1979; and to his adopted home county of Kent. He was recorder of Gravesend from 1947 until his appointment to the High Court bench ten years later, and in 1978 the University of Kent made him an honorary DCL. A keen and skilled golfer, he was captain of Royal St George's, Sandwich, in 1972–3 and a regular supporter of the Bar Golfing Society. He died on 7 November 1991 at Kenfield Hall Nursing Home, Petham, Canterbury, and was survived by the daughter and son of his first marriage, his wife Jeannie having predeceased him in 1989. He was commemorated at a memorial service in the Temple Church on 29 January 1992.

ANTHONY EVANS

Sources The Times (9 Nov 1991) · Daily Telegraph (9 Nov 1991) · The Independent (14 Nov 1991) · WWW · Burke, Peerage · personal knowledge (2004) · private information (2004) [Simon Brown; Colin Sleeman] · b. cert. · d. cert.
Likenesses Lenare, photograph, 1946, NPG [see illus.] · photograph, repro. in The Times · photograph, repro. in Daily Telegraph · photograph, repro. in The Independent

Salmon [née Munday; *other married name* Hinde], **Eliza** (1787–1849), singer, was born in Oxford. Her mother was a member of the Mahon family of professional musicians. She became a pupil of the singing master John James Ashley, and made her first appearance at Covent Garden in the Lenten oratorios on 4 March 1803, when she had an immediate success. She sang in the first performance of the *Messiah* at Covent Garden in 1805. She was gifted with a voice of beautiful tone, a charming manner, and a face 'of dazzling fairness', but her tendency to embellish her solos was criticized. On 11 February 1806 she married James Salmon, organist of St Peter's, Liverpool, who in 1813 joined the army out of financial difficulties; he went to the West Indies with his regiment, and died there. Mrs Salmon performed regularly at the Three Choirs festival, and at oratorios and concerts in London. She travelled extensively to fulfil her engagements, and in 1823 was said to have earned £5000. Her voice collapsed suddenly during one of the Concerts of Ancient Music in May 1825, and her career ended. She attempted, without success, to attract pupils, and married, as her second husband, a clergyman named Hinde. He died about 1840, leaving her destitute. She died in poverty at 33 King's Road, Chelsea, on 5 June 1849.

In her heyday, Eliza Salmon had a high, pure soprano voice of great agility, with a tone likened to that of musical glasses or a clarinet; however, she was deficient in imparting character to anything she sang.

L. M. MIDDLETON, *rev.* J. GILLILAND

Sources GM, 1st ser., 76 (1806), 180 · H. S. Wyndham, *The annals of the Covent Garden Theatre: from 1732 to 1897*, 2 vols. (1906) · J. E. Cox, *Musical recollections of the last half-century*, 2 vols. (1872) · C. Ehrlich, *The musical profession in Britain since the eighteenth century* (1985) · W. C. Russell, *Representative actors* (c.1875) · *New Grove* · Brown & Stratton, *Brit. mus.* · D. Baptie, *A handbook of musical biography*, 2nd edn (1887) · L. J. De Bekker, *Black's dictionary of music and musicians* (1924)

Salmon, Sir Eric Cecil Heygate (1896–1946), civil servant and local government administrator, was born at Newcastle upon Tyne on 3 July 1896, the eldest child and only son of Herbert John Salmon, businessman, and his wife, Edith Juliet, daughter of Frederick Lambert, of Garratts Hall, Banstead. In 1910 he went to Malvern College where he was senior classical scholar and Faber exhibitioner, and in 1915 entered Corpus Christi College, Oxford, as a classical scholar. On account of the First World War he did not proceed to a degree. His health having prevented earlier enlistment, he joined the Queen's Own Royal West Kent regiment in July 1916. The following April he was given command of the 41st divisional observation section, a group engaged in noting enemy movements and supplying information to commanders of fighting units. In September 1917 he was awarded the Military Cross. For a time, after the armistice, he was brigade education officer with the 123rd infantry brigade in the army of occupation in Germany.

Salmon took the examination for the administrative class of the civil service after the war and in 1919 entered the Ministry of Health. From 1925 to 1930 he dealt chiefly with local finance and legislation, work which taught him much about the ways of local authorities. He was secretary to a series of departmental committees, including those on smoke abatement (1920), rent restriction (1930), and housing (1933). In 1929 he married Hilda Marion, daughter of Canon Edward Ashurst Welch, and was for many years sustained and strengthened in his work by his domestic happiness. They had one son and one daughter.

For his last three and a half years in the civil service, from 1930 to 1934, Salmon was the principal responsible for the London section of the housing division of the Ministry of Health. The 1930s could be years of frustration in the civil service. Promotion was slow with little movement in the top ranks. By 1934 Salmon, at thirty-eight, was still a principal and despite an impressive background may have thought his prospects limited. So he took the unusual step—although from a position strengthened by

his work on London housing—of applying for the post of deputy clerk of the London county council (LCC). He was successful (out of 167 applicants).

The LCC had a reputation of being officer-run. Much of the business had been done behind the scenes at dinners and social meetings between the leading Conservative councillors and chief officers. But 1934 saw this all change with the election of a Labour council under the energetic leadership of Herbert Morrison. It must be one of Salmon's great achievements that as deputy clerk he handled much of the change not just of policy but of style of government which occurred in the LCC, even if the greater innovations happened in the technical divisions of the council. So well accepted was he that on 1 August 1939 he was appointed clerk to the council to succeed Sir George Gater, who had been appointed a permanent secretary in the civil service.

Local authorities, and especially the LCC, became particularly preoccupied with civil defence after the Air Raid Precautions Act (1937). Salmon was made personally responsible for co-ordinating those services—rescue, ambulance, fire, and welfare—which were functions of the London county council. His immediate task was to remove obstacles to co-ordinating the civil defence services. In this he worked closely with the London regional commissioners and their staff, and established such cordial contacts, although always safeguarding the LCC's interests, that the relationship between the commissioners and the council, in contrast to that prevailing in some regions, was one of friendly co-operation in a common effort.

This period was the undoubted climax of Salmon's career. Official records pay tribute to his considerable administrative skill in periods of great stress in wartime with many staff away in the forces. In 1943 he was knighted for his services to civil defence. In the mid-1940s the LCC was faced with enormous potential challenges in housing and other social issues. The council's own structure faced a period of reconstruction. Salmon took charge of this, by all accounts with a mastery of good staff relations. Meantime in the early 1940s he played a considerable part in the work which went into establishing the Administrative Staff College.

In 1942 Salmon received the honorary degree of MA from Oxford University. In 1944 he became a member of the council of Malvern College, his old school. He was appointed a deputy lieutenant of the county of London in 1945. All his life he loved outdoor sports, particularly shooting and cricket, in both of which he excelled. All memories of him pay tribute to his great sense of humour. His work for post-war reconstruction was cut short when he fell ill and died, after an operation, at St James's Hospital, London, on 9 July 1946, at the height of his powers and career. His wife and their two children survived him.

TOM CAULCOTT

Sources DNB · *The Times* (10 July 1946) · *The Times* (15 July 1946) · minutes of London county council, report of the general purposes committee, 15 July 1946 • Lord Morrison of Lambeth, *An autobiography* (1960) • personal knowledge (2004) • *CGPLA Eng. & Wales* (1946)

Likenesses W. Stoneman, photograph, 1945, NPG

Wealth at death £12,758 17s. 6d.: probate, 10 Oct 1946, *CGPLA Eng. & Wales*

Salmon, Frederick (1796–1868), rectal surgeon and founder of St Mark's Hospital, London, was born on 11 April 1796 in Bath, the son of Henry Salmon (1754/5–1827), attorney, and his wife, Denne (1762/3–1853). Salmon was the sixth of nine children, of whom three boys and four girls survived into adulthood. His brothers Edward and Henry were apprenticed in law, whereas Frederick was apprenticed on 27 November 1811 to Joseph Hume Spry (c.1778–1859), a member of a family of apothecary-surgeons in Bath. Salmon attended the Casualty Hospital in Bath for two years, possibly as a pupil to James Norman, to whose surgeon son, George, Salmon dedicated a book. Salmon was also associated with William White (1762–1826), surgeon to the City Infirmary and Dispensary and one of the few rectal disease specialists of the time.

Salmon became a licentiate of the Society of Apothecaries on 27 March 1817 and followed Spry to London to gain experience so that he could practise there. From October 1817 for six months he walked the wards at St Bartholomew's Hospital, Smithfield, as a pupil of John Abernethy. In 1818 Salmon was granted membership of the Royal College of Surgeons, and in 1820 he became Abernethy's house surgeon.

Between 1820 and 1827 Salmon attempted four times to gain an appointment at the General Dispensary in Aldersgate Street, in the City of London. In 1820 he declared that he would not, as usually happened, pay to create governors who would then vote him onto the staff. However, in 1824 he did pay out at least 200 guineas, but failed to match a competitor.

In 1827, on Abernethy's retirement, Salmon sought to succeed him at St Bartholomew's but discovered that Abernethy was supporting another applicant, Frederick Skey, who had promised to pass the position later to Abernethy's young son. The newly established reformist medical journal *The Lancet* took up the case, but to no avail. In 1827 Salmon finally secured an appointment to the General Dispensary after vote-buying had been banned there.

Salmon lived and practised in the City of London, from 1818 at 30 Bucklersbury, off Cheapside, and from 1828 at 12 Old Broad Street. He married Clara Breese (1805/6–1877), possibly the daughter of a clock manufacturer of 5 North Place, Gray's Inn Road, London, about 1828. They had three sons. The eldest, Frederick Breese Salmon (c.1832–1853), joined the 9th Bombay native infantry and died aged twenty-one on 17 January 1853 at Belgaum, in east India. The second son, Percy Howell Salmon, was born in Dulwich and died in Ostend on 1 June 1893. The third son, William Mayer Salmon (c.1837–1880), became a civil servant and magistrate in Bombay.

By the late 1820s Salmon was specializing in the treatment of rectal diseases. He published *A Practical Essay on Stricture of the Rectum* (1828) and *Practical Observations on Prolapsus of the Rectum* (1831). He also published in *The Lancet*. Salmon argued that stricture of the rectum was the cause of many rectal complaints. However, James O'Beirne (1786–1862), a Dublin surgeon, challenged him, arguing that what Salmon described as stricture was in fact part of the normal rectum. Later surgeons concurred with O'Beirne's interpretation.

Salmon associated himself with medical reformers. In 1833 he gave an oration to the Medical Society of London in which he lambasted the Royal College of Surgeons for promoting the lucrative interests of the few rather than supporting surgery generally or fighting quackery. Also in 1833 Salmon lost his position at the dispensary, when the staff resigned over perceived lay interference. If Salmon were to secure a hospital position again, essential for its contacts with well-off governors who might become patients, one possibility was to establish his own institution. By the 1830s a number of special hospitals were being established, despite opposition from leaders in the medical profession.

Salmon was a member of the City of London Club, whose chairman, John Masterman, a banker and later an MP, supported Salmon as he now established his own hospital. At least eight of the club's committee members and about twenty-five other members were among the founding benefactors when, in 1835, Salmon set up in Aldersgate Street the Benevolent Dispensary for the Relief of the Poor afflicted with Fistula, Piles and Other Diseases of the Rectum. Club member William Taylor Copeland, of the porcelain makers Copeland Spode, and lord mayor of London (1835–6), was its first president. Within its first year the dispensary became an infirmary with seven beds. Salmon was the only full (that is consultant) surgeon; he was assisted by a resident house surgeon and a matron.

In 1837 the infirmary moved to a 14 bed house in Charterhouse Square, off Smithfield. In 1853 it moved again, to a new building in the City Road near the Angel, Islington. The governors wished to name the hospital something suitable and unembarrassing, while Salmon wished to emphasize its specialty. It became St Mark's Hospital for Fistula and Other Diseases of the Rectum, and was officially opened by the lord mayor on St Mark's day, 25 April 1854. Salmon used his hospital position to good effect: he developed influential treatments, and his private practice flourished. Among his notable patients was Charles Dickens, treated in 1841 for fistula. By 1849 Salmon and his family had moved to 18 Lower Berkeley Street; afterwards he moved again, to Manchester Square, though he also continued to practise in Old Broad Street.

In 1857 Salmon retired from practice and from active surgical involvement at St Mark's. He moved to Woodfield Cedars, Ombersley, near Droitwich, Worcestershire, though retaining his house in Manchester Square. He retired as honorary surgeon in 1859, and to mark this the governors commissioned a portrait by Francis Grant RA, to hang in the hospital.

On 3 January 1868 Salmon died of acute bronchitis at Woodfield Cedars; he was buried on 10 January in Kensal

Green cemetery, in west London. His widow, Clara, died of cancer in Brighton, Sussex, aged seventy-one, on 23 November 1877. Following his death the *British Medical Journal* suggested that 'the course he took was prompted by difficulties in pursuing an useful and honourable career in a general hospital', and that his establishment of his hospital was 'contrary to the interests of the profession and the public', and had 'encouraged similar enterprises'. Nevertheless, it noted that he had 'influence in certain wealthy circles' and a 'lucrative practice', despite professional isolation (*BMJ*, 1.41–2).

However, it was specialization such as Salmon's which gathered in pace in the nineteenth century and took off in the twentieth. Staff at St Mark's increasingly came to play a key role at the top of the profession and in developing the fields of rectal, later colorectal, surgery, and also of gastroenterology. Salmon could thus be judged a successful medical entrepreneur at a time when entrepreneurial activity of all kinds was in the ascendant.

LINDSAY GRANSHAW

Sources L. Granshaw, *St Mark's Hospital, London: a social history of a specialist hospital* (1985) · d. cert. · F. Salmon, *Oration on the necessity for an entire change in the constitution and government of the Royal College of Surgeons, delivered before the Medical Society of London, March 8 1833* (1833) · MSS, St Bartholomew's Hospital, Bart's and the London NHS Trust, West Smithfield, London, St Mark's Hospital archive · *The Lancet* (11 Jan 1868), 68 · *BMJ* (11 Jan 1868), 41–2 · Bath City RO, freemen of the city of Bath documents 124, 164, 214 · Bath Abbey registers, christenings, 1569–1800, 1801–40; burials, 1599–1840 · annual reports of the Fistula Infirmary, later St Mark's Hospital · 'Vacancy at Bart's', *The Lancet* (30 June 1827), 399–400 · 'Vacancy at Bart's', *The Lancet* (14 July 1827), 474–5 · 'Resignation of the medical officers of the Aldersgate Street dispensary', *The Lancet* (2 Nov 1883), 214–19, esp. 218 · *The Lancet* (23 Nov 1833), 339–40
Archives London NHS Trust · St Bartholomew's Hospital, London, MSS · St Mark's Hospital Archive, London, MSS
Likenesses G. Brown, oils, 1837, repro. in Granshaw, *St Mark's Hospital* · F. Grant, oils, 1859, St Mark's Hospital, London · photograph, St Mark's Hospital, London
Wealth at death under £7000: administration with will, 4 April 1868, *CGPLA Eng. & Wales*

Salmon, George (1819–1904), mathematician and theologian, was born on 25 September 1819, probably in Dublin, the only son of Michael Salmon, linen merchant, and Helen, daughter of the Revd Edward Weekes. His family came from Cork, and he was educated there, at a private school, up to the age of fourteen. He entered Trinity College, Dublin, in 1833, was awarded a scholarship in classics in 1837, and afterwards turned to the study of mathematics. Eighteen months later, in 1838, he obtained his degree as first mathematical moderator (that is, the best student in his year). Scholars were expected to attend some theology lectures, which he did in 1839, and he was persuaded to take the fellowship examination in 1840, although he felt unprepared. To his astonishment he won Madden's prize, which was awarded to the candidate placed second. After another year of study he was elected to a fellowship.

Salmon settled down to the work of a college tutor and to the study of pure mathematics. The statutes of Trinity College required that he be ordained in the Church of Ireland, and he became deacon in 1844 and priest in 1845. His marriage to Frances Anne (*d.* 1878), daughter of the Revd J. L. Salvador of Staunton, Herefordshire, took place in 1844. They had four sons and two daughters, of whom the eldest son (Edward William) and younger daughter (Fanny Mary) survived him. Salmon began lecturing in theology as well as mathematics in 1845, and became devoted to both subjects. In 1858 he was appointed Donegal lecturer in mathematics and in 1859 he received the degrees of BD and DD. When, after about fifteen years, no professorship in mathematics was forthcoming at the university, Salmon, frustrated by the heavy teaching load, turned his attention more to theology. In 1866 he became regius professor of divinity and resigned his fellowship. He remained at Trinity College for the rest of his life, and in 1888 was appointed provost (an appointment made by the crown), with the unanimous approval of the fellows. He presided over the governing body of the college and exercised a wide and powerful influence over its affairs, and in 1892 led the tercentenary celebrations of Dublin University. His years as provost were characterized by consolidation rather than reform; the admission of women to university degrees, carried out in the last year of his life, was almost the only important change that he disliked.

Mathematical work The contributions to mathematics for which Salmon is chiefly remembered are his textbooks. They dealt, as did his original research, with geometry and algebra. He had the rare ability to present a theory as an organic whole and not as a series of disjointed propositions. After his death Horace Lamb remarked on the 'brilliant contrast which they [Salmon's books] exhibited with most of the current textbooks of that time' (Lamb, 421).

The best known of Salmon's textbooks was the first to be written, *A treatise on conic sections, containing an account of some of the most important modern algebraic and geometric methods* (1848). In this book he exhibited the power of Cartesian co-ordinates and drew together methods of analytic and descriptive geometry. It was translated, as were his other three textbooks, into many western European languages, and, like the others, ran to many editions. It was still a standard text in 1948, when the centenary of publication was remembered by an article in the *Mathematical Gazette*, and brought Salmon recognition from the leading mathematicians of his day. He followed up this success with *A Treatise on the Higher Plane Curves* (1852), a subject which was then little known and previously only accessible through the memoirs of scientific societies. By the simplicity of his methods he was able to minimize the difficulties of this subject; for example, he realized that the axes of a Cartesian co-ordinate system can be placed anywhere, and in this way the equation of a curve can be greatly simplified.

At this time the theory of the invariants of quantics was being investigated by Cayley and Sylvester in England, and by others on the continent. Salmon perceived the importance of this work and began to apply their results to geometrical theory. The result was *Lessons Introductory to the Modern Higher Algebra* (1859), a textbook containing much original material. He was a prodigious calculator: the second edition of this book (1866) contained a formula which ran to thirteen printed pages. His last textbook was *A Treatise on the Analytic Geometry of Three Dimensions* (1862), in which he applied the methods he had developed for conics to curves of three dimensions. He never dealt with four-dimensional space or non-Euclidean geometry; R. S. Ball 'heard him say, jestingly, that he reserved such themes for the next world' (Ball, xxvi).

In addition to textbooks Salmon published his own research in various journals, including the *Philosophical Magazine*, *Quarterly Journal of Mathematics*, *Cambridge and Dublin Mathematical Journal*, and *Proceedings of the Royal Irish Academy*. He published forty-one papers between 1844 and 1873, mainly on numerical characteristics of curves and surfaces. He corresponded with many mathematicians, and became a close friend of Cayley and Sylvester. When he approached Cayley to find a young mathematician to help with a second edition of *Higher Plane Curves*, Cayley offered to do the work himself; the discovery of the twenty-seven lines on a cubic surface was made by the two men.

Theological work From the time Salmon was ordained priest in 1845 he began to take part in the work of the divinity school at Trinity College, as assistant to the regius professor. His ability as a preacher was soon recognized; his first publication on a theological topic was a sermon on prayer in 1849, and he had many sermons published, all characterized by his vigorous common sense, originality, and bold but unaffected style. His contemporaries recorded that these addresses were better to read than to hear, because his delivery was bad, but that he was an excellent extemporaneous speaker, especially in synod.

In 1852 Archbishop Whately made Salmon an examining chaplain, and the archbishop's influence on Salmon's theological opinions seems to have been considerable. Both were strong protestants and deeply suspicious of the rise of the Oxford Movement. Responding to the publication of *Tracts for the Times* by the Oxford Movement, Whately, Salmon, and others issued their *Cautions for the Times* (1853). Salmon was a regular contributor to the *Catholic Layman* on the Roman Catholic controversy, and had three short stories published anonymously in 1854 dealing with the same subject. This material proved useful later when, as professor of divinity, he lectured on the points of debate between Roman Catholics and Anglicans. These lectures formed the basis of *The Infallibility of the Church* (1889), a brilliant display of polemic which exhibited his learning, humour, and critical abilities to the full.

When Salmon accepted the regius professorship of divinity in 1866 he embarked on theology and biblical criticism with the same enthusiasm and vigour which had characterized his mathematical studies. His *Introduction to the New Testament* (1885) is a criticism of the work of Baur and the Tübingen school on the origin and character of the books of the New Testament. Salmon's conservative views were influential throughout the United Kingdom. He became an authority on the Christian writers of the second century when he was asked to contribute articles

for the *Dictionary of Christian Biography* (1877–87). He was foremost a historian and did not care for textual criticism, but he revealed his considerable abilities in this area when he published *Thoughts on the Textual Criticism of the New Testament* (1897).

During the last ten years of his life Salmon devoted much time to the synoptic problem. His notes were edited after his death by a former pupil, N. J. D. White, as *The Human Element in the Gospels* (1907). In addition to pamphlets and several books of sermons, Salmon wrote academic essays for biblical commentaries and popular articles for magazines. He took part in current debates about the keeping of the sabbath, eternal punishment, and above all the continuing 'Roman Catholic question'.

The years after Salmon's appointment as regius professor were critical for the Irish church, which was disestablished and disendowed in 1869, and it was vitally important that the divinity school at Trinity College should be properly led. Salmon played an active part in the reconstruction of the church and held a unique and influential position in the general synod and as a member of the Representative Church Body. He managed the church's finances and investments with great skill and was involved in the revision of the prayer book. He was remembered by his colleagues as a formidable debater, able to hold the attention of his audience even in old age when his voice was failing.

Salmon's great strength as a theologian was his critical ability. He founded no school of theological thought, although he was greatly admired by his many pupils. His friend J. H. Bernard recorded that 'he was more anxious to train men to see clearly than to train them to see what *he* saw' (*PBA*, 314). Salmon tended towards a liberal evangelicalism, which distrusted more and more an appeal to any authority other than that of individual conscience. In politics he was strongly Conservative, and although he disliked political controversy, he considered it his duty to oppose Irish home rule, which he was convinced would be disastrous.

Honours and character Salmon received many academic honours in addition to those which his own university bestowed. He was a member of the Royal Irish Academy (1843), which awarded him the Cunningham medal in 1858. The Institut de France elected him a foreign member, and the royal academies of Berlin, Göttingen, and Copenhagen elected him honorary member. He was fellow of the Accademia dei Lincei of Rome (1885); he was made honorary DCL Oxford (1868), LLD Cambridge (1874), DD Edinburgh (1884), and DMath Christiania (1902). In 1863 he was elected fellow of the Royal Society, which awarded him the royal medal in 1868 and the Copley medal in 1889; he became FRS Edinburgh, and was on the founding list of the fellows of the British Academy (1902). He was president of the mathematical and physical section of the British Association in 1878. He was also chancellor of St Patrick's Cathedral (1871), and was presented with the freedom of the city of Dublin in 1892.

Salmon was a competent musician and an excellent chess player, and found time to pursue his love of music and chess throughout his career. He was an omnivorous reader (excepting metaphysics and poetry, which he disliked), described as 'an indefatigable devourer of fiction' (Stokes, 164). He was a well-known figure in Dublin, where his theological works were widely read and his jokes widely circulated, and was remembered by friends as a skilled impersonator with a fund of entertaining anecdotes. His hospitality was generous, although he himself lived in simplicity despite the luxuries available to him as provost. He was described by a contemporary as having strong and vigorous features, a well-set jaw, and massive forehead: 'His very body, mountainous in its bulk …, inspires a feeling of respect in smaller men' (ibid.). After several months of increasing physical weakness, he died at the provost's house, Trinity College, Dublin, on 22 January 1904, and was buried in Mount Jerome cemetery.

JULIA TOMPSON

Sources J. Ossory, *The Times* (23 Jan 1904) • *Nature*, 69 (1903–4), 324–6 • C. J. J. [C. J. Joly], *PRS*, 75 (1905), 347–55 • R. S. Ball, *Proceedings of the London Mathematical Society*, 2nd ser., 1 (1904), xxii–xxviii • *DNB* • J. H. Bernard, *New Liberal Review*, 7/38 (March 1904), 156–67 • G. T. Stokes, 'Leaders of religious thought and action: Rev. George Salmon, D.D.', *Review of the Churches*, 2/9 (15 June 1892), 159–64 • M. Noether, *Mathematische Annalen*, 61 (1905), 1–19 • J. H. Bernard, 'Dr George Salmon', *PBA*, [1] (1903–4), 311–15 • H. Lamb, *Report of the British Association for the Advancement of Science*, 74 (1904), 421 • H. Fehr, *L'enseignement mathématique*, 6 (1904), 232
Archives TCD, corresp. and papers | TCD, letters to Edward Dowden • TCD, letters to William Lecky • UCL, letters to Thomas Hirst
Likenesses S. Purser, portrait, 1888, TCD • Lawrence, photograph, before 1892, repro. in Stokes, 'Leaders of religious thought and action', facing p. 159 • photograph, 1892, RS • B. Constant, portrait, 1897, TCD, provost's house • A. B. Joy, bronze bas-relief, after 1904, St Patrick's Cathedral, Dublin • J. Hughes, marble statue, 1911, TCD • photograph, RS
Wealth at death £16,514 17s. 3d.: Irish administration with will sealed in London, 16 April 1904, *CGPLA Ire.* • £28,431 2s. 9d.: resworn administration, 8 March 1904, *CGPLA Ire.*

Salmon, John (*d.* 1325), administrator and bishop of Norwich, came from a family whose members had been hereditary goldsmiths to Ely Priory since the twelfth century. His parents were Salomon and Alice, and he had two younger brothers, both of whom he later promoted to archdeaconries. Probably born at Meldreth in Cambridgeshire, he became a monk at Ely and by 1291 had been elected prior. On 19 May 1298 a majority of the chapter elected him bishop, but on 12 July Edward I ignored this and gave his assent to the election of the minority candidate, his chancellor, John Langton (*d.* 1337). Appeals to the pope followed and both elections were quashed on 5 June 1299. However, Salmon was subsequently provided to the bishopric of Norwich, and was consecrated on 15 November 1299. That the pope then authorized Salmon to contract a 13,000 florin loan may demonstrate the expense of the dispute; it is also possible, however, that the loan was intended to cover the 'services' that a newly provided bishop was required to pay to the pope on his appointment.

Salmon came into conflict with Archbishop Robert Winchelsey (*d.* 1313) when the latter conducted a visitation of the diocese of Norwich in 1304 and opposed Salmon's claim to annates and first fruits of the churches in the diocese. In 1306 Salmon took his case personally to the papal curia, where the matter was eventually resolved in his favour.

Salmon was close to the government of Edward II. In November 1307 he was one of those appointed to make the final arrangements for the king's marriage and in March 1309 he was selected with Walter Reynolds (*d.* 1327) and others for an embassy to Pope Clement V (*r.* 1305–13) to obtain the revocation of Piers Gaveston's exile. His presence in July at the Stamford parliament, where Gaveston was formally reinstated, is a further indication of his support for the king. His election as one of the *lords ordainer in March 1310, and his appointment (with Hugh Courtenay) late in 1311 as an auditor of the accounts of foreign merchants, should not be read as indications of opposition to the king. In November 1310 he was permitted to pay £200 in commutation of service in Scotland, one of a select group so favoured. Also late in 1310 he was sent to Gascony, where he remained for a large part of 1311, participating in September in the important Anglo-French negotiations that comprised the Process of Périgueux. In March 1312 he was sent to explain the king's position on matters touching the ordinances to the meeting that Winchelsey arranged between the prelates and magnates in London, and in September he was ordered to prevent the earl of Lancaster attending parliament with a retinue. The following month his attention was reclaimed by legal business, when he was ordered to prepare defence briefs for royal officials from Aquitaine whose cases were to be heard at the Paris *parlement*.

Salmon remained a royal spokesman and was especially prominent in that role at the Lincoln parliament of 1316, where he was sworn of the king's council, served as an auditor of petitions for England, and was deputed (with three others) to act for the king during Edward II's absence. He sat on the committee established at that parliament, with the earl of Lancaster's agreement, to amend the royal household and the kingdom and to purge the royal administration. At the end of 1316 he was appointed to the mission to Avignon led by the earl of Pembroke. He participated in the negotiations between the king and Lancaster that led to the treaty of Leake in August 1318, and was one of the standing council appointed in conformity with that treaty, while in October of that year he was one of the king's nominees for the committee for the reform of the royal household.

In January 1320 Salmon succeeded John Hotham, bishop of Ely (*d.* 1337), as chancellor, being nominated in full parliament (albeit one boycotted by the earl of Lancaster), but with no mention of the baronial assent required by the ordinances. He accompanied the king on his visit to France in June. In January 1322 he was one of six councillors whom the king ordered to be constantly at his side, and he played a prominent role in government in the period after the battle of Boroughbridge (16 March 1322). In May 1323 he was one of those who negotiated a thirteen-year truce with the Scottish king, Robert I. Ill health forced his resignation as chancellor in early June 1323, but in July 1324, and again in November 1324, he was commissioned to negotiate with the French king in the aftermath of the outbreak of the War of St Sardos. He went to France on the king's behalf and helped negotiate the treaty of 31 May 1325, but on his return journey he died at Folkestone on 6 July. He was buried in Norwich Cathedral.

Only Salmon's register of institutions survives. John Salmon was distinctly unusual in his time, in being a monk who became a bishop and also a front-rank government official. Royal business inevitably necessitated frequent and often lengthy absences from his diocese. Yet he rebuilt the bishop's palace with its great hall on a grand scale, acquiring for the purpose some of the city's land adjacent to the cathedral close; and he built a two-storey charnel chapel, where he founded a chantry, in the west part of the cathedral cemetery in honour of St John the Evangelist. In 1309 he ordered the erection of what he specified should be a reliable clock, which had been built by 1325. The statutes of Clare College, Cambridge, of which he is reputed to have been a benefactor, stipulate prayers for his soul. M. C. Buck

Sources Chancery records · F. R. Chapman, ed., Sacrist rolls of Ely, 2 vols. (1907) · E. Fernie, An architectural history of Norwich Cathedral (1993) · E. H. Carter, Studies in Norwich Cathedral history (1935) · Fasti Angl., 1300–1541 · J. H. Denton, Robert Winchelsey and the crown, 1294–1313: a study in the defence of ecclesiastical liberty, Cambridge Studies in Medieval Life and Thought, 3rd ser., 14 (1980) · Rymer, Foedera, new edn · Special Collections, ancient correspondence, PRO, SC.1/33/136 · Exchequer, exchequer of receipt, receipt rolls, PRO, E.401/189 · W. Stubbs, ed., 'Annales Paulini', Chronicles of the reigns of Edward I and Edward II, 1, Rolls Series, 76 (1882), 253–370 · CEPR letters, vols. 1–2 · K. Edwards, 'The social origins and provenance of the English bishops during the reign of Edward II', TRHS, 5th ser., 9 (1959), 51–79 · J. C. Davies, The baronial opposition to Edward II (1918) Archives Norfolk RO

Salmon, John Drew (1802–1859), ornithologist and botanist, was born on 4 September 1802, the eldest of the surviving family of seven sons and two daughters of Thomas Salmon (c.1775–1852), a maltster and corn merchant, and Elizabeth, née Drew (1783–1836), both of Stoke Ferry, Norfolk. An upbringing on the edge of the fens gave Salmon a passion for collecting birds and their eggs and for natural history more generally. After probably training under his father, who superintended a group of Whitbread's maltings at Stoke Ferry, he moved to Thetford in 1833 to work in one of that town's breweries. He formed a herbarium of the rich flora of Breckland and contributed many notes on local birds to the Magazine of Natural History. Passage movements of birds increasingly became the dominant concern in these notes. In one published in 1834 (following visits to the Netherlands, Orkney, and other areas renowned for seabirds) he called for their study 'by the cooperative agency of naturalists residing near headlands on the coasts', anticipating by a century the chain of bird observatories eventually to emerge (Magazine of Natural History, 7). He was elected to honorary membership of Norfolk and Norwich Museum in tribute to the many specimens he had donated.

In 1837 Salmon moved to Surrey, where he worked in a brewery in Godalming. The move seems to have occurred at the same time as an estrangement from his father: he did not return to his parental home for several years. Now increasingly interested in botany, by 1843 he had joined the Botanical Society of London, become one of its local secretaries, and was regularly participating in its annual exchanges of herbarium specimens. He read an account of the flora of the Godalming district before the society in 1846; it was subsequently published in The Phytologist and reprinted as an appendix to The Letters of Rusticus (1849), a work by his friend and neighbour Edward Newman. Three years later, with a few helpers, he took on the major task of compiling a flora of Surrey, to which end he followed the relatively new practice of dividing the county into a series of botanical districts (the subject of a second lengthy contribution to The Phytologist in 1852). The work was published after his death, but, although his authorship is acknowledged on the title-page, the flora has since tended to be ascribed to its editor, James Alexander Brewer. Its progress was doubtless delayed by Salmon's move to London about 1851 to follow a new career as manager of the celebrated Wenham Lake Ice Company. In those days (before refrigerators) no London dinner party was complete without Wenham ice, imported from a lake in Massachusetts. Salmon resided over the firm's premises in the Strand. As a new arrival in the city he was at once put forward for the council of the Botanical Society of London by a faction battling to keep British field botany as that body's preponderating concern. He was also elected to the Linnean Society.

Some time after 1857 illness appears to have compelled Salmon to return to his childhood home in Stoke Ferry, where he died, unmarried and intestate, on 5 August 1859; he was buried four days later in Stoke Ferry church. His natural history papers and collections were the subject of a London auction in November 1861, at which most of those relating to Surrey went to the recently founded Holmesdale Club of Reigate (which had assumed responsibility for the much delayed flora), and those relating to Norfolk to Norwich Museum. The latter included a notebook of observations on bees, the product of yet another, almost lifelong, enthusiasm of his. D. E. Allen

Sources parish registers, Stoke Ferry, Norfolk RO · J. D. Salmon, diaries, Castle Museum, Norwich, 1825–37 · Transactions of the Norfolk and Norwich Naturalists' Society, 2 (1874–9), 420 · Pigot & Co., National commercial directory: Norfolk and Suffolk (1830) · D. E. Allen, The botanists: a history of the Botanical Society of the British Isles through a hundred and fifty years, St Paul's Bibliographies (1986), 54, 217 · register of deaths, St Catherine's House Archives Castle Museum, Norwich, diaries, notebooks, and MSS · Castle Museum, Norwich, main herbarium of British flowering plants | Holmesdale Natural History Club, Reigate, herbarium, Surrey MSS, and Surrey specimens Wealth at death all natural history collections and papers auctioned by Stevens, Nov 1861

Salmon, Joseph (fl. 1647–1656), Ranter, was briefly prominent as a Ranter between March 1650 and 1651 although his earliest work, Antichrist in Man (1647), indicates that he was first a Seeker in religion. His origins remain obscure:

he was known in Coventry and Wiltshire, and later in Kent. He may have come from Essex, as a Joseph Salmon led a riot in Great Burstead (Billericay) in the mid-1640s. Salmon served in the New Model Army, probably between 1647 and 1649, as a soldier and chaplain in the regiment of Commissary-General Henry Ireton. *A Rout, a Rout*, published in 1649, carries two dedications, one to the commanders and one to the soldiers—or 'the fellowship (of SAINTS scattered) in the ARMY' (Smith, *Collection*, 191). In it he expressed a belief shared by many others that the New Model was an instrument of God that would execute the 'beast' of monarchy and so herald the imminent second coming of Christ (Smith, *Collection*, 193).

Salmon preached in Coventry on 10 March 1650, where the Ranter Abiezer Coppe had been imprisoned since January. Salmon was imprisoned too, along with Andrew Wyke, and was released on condition that he publish a recantation, which appeared in August 1651 under the title *Heights in Depths*. During his imprisonment Salmon is purported to have preached through the gratings of the prison and to have composed his most Ranterish tract, *Divinity Anatomized*. The leading Quaker George Fox visited him and disputed with him. After his release Salmon lived in Kent, preaching regularly in Rochester Cathedral and laying the foundations for what became the Quaker community there. The parish registers of St Nicholas, Rochester, record the birth of his daughter, Hephzibah, on 10 September 1652. Salmon recommended Richard Coppin as his successor and emigrated to Barbados about 1655, where he may later have been investigated for organizing conventicles. He was listed for the receipt of tenement rates in the parish of Mary Magdalene, Old Fish Street, London, in February 1655.

Doubts have been raised concerning the precise nature of Salmon's religious identity and experiences, but the salient details are unproblematic. Like many radical religious figures in this period, Salmon 'crept out of the shell of Episcopacy' and, during the early and mid-1640s, passed through presbyterian, Independent, and Baptist forms of worship (Smith, *Collection*, 210). Eventually he found all forms of religion involving 'externals' and ordinances unsatisfying, and he describes how he became aware of the sufficiency of a personal and inward inspiration '(as one inspired with a supernatural life) sprang up farr above my earthly center, into a most heavenly and divine enjoyment' (ibid., 211). This sense of transcendence from earthliness coincided with his appreciation of the power of God, which had moved successively through monarchy, parliament, and New Model Army, each time effecting a further spiritual refinement of terrestrial life.

From these perceptions developed the inversions of accepted moral behaviour in the name of spiritual liberty which were labelled 'Ranter' by contemporaries. In Coventry Salmon is reported to have committed 'wicked Swearing, and uncleaness, which he justified and others of his way, *That it was God which did swear in them, and that it was their liberty to keep company with Women, for their Lust*' (Smith, *Collection*, 13). The reliability of this report has been questioned, and the situation has not been aided by

the fact that Salmon's one definitely Ranter publication does not survive. Nevertheless Salmon did know and correspond with other Ranters and sectarians associated with them, and he was imprisoned with Coppe and Wyke. Also, his writings dating from the Coventry period that do survive show the figural playfulness characteristic of Ranter discourse. Even if he was less transgressive than the more notorious Ranters Coppe and Laurence Clarkson, he was associated with them and expressed a form of their antinomianism at the height of Ranter activity. His later position was less socially provocative but no less mystical. It is not difficult to see from Salmon's publications why more orthodox contemporaries saw atheistical or extreme heretical ideas in them, although his four pamphlets, which were read widely in radical religious circles (*Antichrist in Man* went through four editions while *A Rout, a Rout* went through two), were really a highly personal attempt to articulate a nearly inexpressible sense of union with the divine.　　　　　　　　NIGEL SMITH

Sources J. F. McGregor, 'The Ranters: a study in the free spirit in English sectarian religion, 1649–1660', BLitt diss., U. Oxf., 1969 · N. Smith, ed., *A collection of Ranter writings from the seventeenth century* (1983) · N. Smith, *Perfection proclaimed: language and literature in English radical religion, 1640–1660* (1989) · J. C. Davis, *Fear, myth and history: the Ranters and the historians* (1986) · CSP dom., 1650, 45, 332; 1651, 258–9 · PRO, E121/3/4, no. 138 · PRO, CO 31/1/516 · annals of the life of Bulstrode Whitelocke, BL, Add. MS 37345, fols. 56v, 60r · RS Friends, Lond., Swarthmore MS 1.66 · Worcester College, Oxford, MS Clarke 18, fols. 23r–24r · parish registers of St Nicholas, Rochester, CKS, P 306/1/1 · *Report on the manuscripts of F. W. Leyborne-Popham*, HMC, 51 (1899), 57 · *A Perfect Diurnall* (11–18 March 1650), 128 · *A Perfect Diurnall* (18–25 March 1650), 141 · *A Perfect Diurnall* (1–8 April 1650), 175 · *A Perfect Diurnall* (29 April–6 May 1650), 218 · *The post-boy robb'd of his mail*, 2nd edn (1706), 431 · *The journal of George Fox*, ed. J. L. Nickalls, rev. edn (Philadelphia, 1985), 47 · W. Rosewell, *The serpents subtilty discovered* (1656), 1–2, 16 · E. Stokes, *The Wiltshire rant* (1652), 13–14, 21 · T. Tenison, *An argument for union from the true interest of those dissenters in England who profess and call themselves protestants* (1683), 9 · B. Whitelocke, *Memorials of the English affairs*, new edn (1732), 446, 448 · Essex RO, Chelmsford, Q/SR 327/12, 23, 76, 107; Q/SBa 2/59 · private information (2004) [A. Hessayon]

Salmon, Nathanael (1675–1742), antiquary, was born on 22 March 1675 at the rectory, Meppershall, Bedfordshire, the eldest son of the rector, Thomas *Salmon (*bap.* 1647, *d.* 1706), writer on music, and his wife, Katherine Bradshaw, daughter of Nathaniel Bradshaw. Thomas *Salmon (*bap.* 1679, *d.* 1767), historical and geographical writer, was a brother. Nathanael entered Corpus Christi College, Cambridge, on 11 June 1690, and graduated LLB in 1695. Having been ordained in 1699, he served at Westmill, Hertfordshire, as curate to the absentee rector, Daniel Price, who was also dean of St Asaph. He had taken the statutory oath of allegiance to William III, but refused to do so on Anne's accession in 1702, because the law now required him also to abjure James II's son, the 'pretended prince of Wales'. Having resigned his curacy, he practised medicine at St Ives, Huntingdonshire, and later at Bishop's Stortford, Hertfordshire. In 1710 he became an extra-licentiate of the Royal College of Physicians.

Salmon is said to have refused the offer of a Suffolk benefice worth £140 a year. In later life he eked out a living in London as a writer. His first two books (both 1726), which dealt with Roman antiquities to the north and east of London, were expanded into *A New Survey of England, wherein the Defects of Camden are Supplied* (11 parts, 1728–9), reissued with new title-pages in two volumes in 1731. Meanwhile he had been working on *The history of Hertfordshire, describing the county and its ancient monuments, particularly the Roman* (1728). This has been depreciated as merely an abridgement and continuation of Sir Henry Chauncy's *Historical Antiquities of Hertfordshire* (1700), but it was probably based on unpublished material left by Chauncy, augmented by Salmon's own research. Salmon's *Lives of the English Bishops from the Restoration to the Revolution* was published anonymously in three parts (1731–3), and reissued in 1733; it contains seventy-four biographies. His *Antiquities of Surrey* (1736) concentrates on Roman antiquities, adding some material overlooked by John Aubrey and Richard Rawlinson in their history of the county (1718).

In 1740, 'as his last shift to live' (Gough, ix), Salmon launched *The History and Antiquities of Essex*. This was based on the manuscript history compiled by the antiquary William Holman (1669–1730), which Salmon had bought for £60 in 1739. It was published in shilling numbers, nineteen of which appeared in 1740 and 1741, describing some 230 parishes in the west, south, and south-east of the county. Some 160 parishes in the centre and north, as well as the borough of Colchester, remained unpublished when Salmon died in London on 2 April 1742. He is said to have been buried in St Dunstan's Church; which of the churches so named is not known. He left three daughters.

Salmon's contemporaries tended to regard him as an eccentric hack. A fanatical nonjuror, he was outspoken in his loathing of those, such as Gilbert Burnet, who had conspired to overthrow the Stuart monarchy. He drew his material mainly from secondary sources or the unpublished work of others. He was given to perverse conjectures, and obstinate in defending them. Driven by poverty, he worked hastily, with little attempt at revision. One curious comment seems to cast doubt on his morals. William Holman was once advised by a friend, 'Pray strike out Salmon's name. He is such a rogue that his name is a scandal to your History. But let his words stand' (Nicholas Jekyll to Holman, 27 July 1730, Essex RO, Holman MSS, D/Y 1).

Yet Salmon had some admirable qualities. Hardworking, well read, and unconventional, he could turn a pungent phrase. He was no armchair topographer, but travelled widely, with an eye for landscape, an ear for local customs and folklore, and an interest in social and economic conditions. His work impressed Richard Gough, who rated his *History of Essex* above that of Philip Morant. Posterity has not agreed with Gough, but Salmon deserves credit, especially in Essex, for his energy in publishing useful material which had long lain in manuscript.

W. RAYMOND POWELL

Sources S. Doree, 'Nathaniel Salmon: Hertfordshire's neglected historian', *Hertfordshire in history*, ed. D. Jones-Baker (1991), 206–22 · E. A. Fitch, 'Historians of Essex, 2: Nathaniel Salmon', *Essex Review*, 2 (1893), 238–45 [incl. bibliography of Salmon's pubns] · C. E. Cobbold, 'The writing of Essex county history, c.1600–1768', *Essex Journal*, 8 (1973), 2–10 · R. G. [R. Gough], *British topography*, [new edn], 2 vols. (1780) · W. R. Powell, 'Antiquaries in conflict: Philip Morant versus Richard Gough', *Essex Archaeology and History*, 20 (1989), 143–6 · P. Morant, *The history and antiquities of the county of Essex*, 2 vols. (1768); repr. with introduction by G. H. Martin (1978) · Essex RO, Chelmsford, Holman MSS, D/Y 1 · *Calamy rev.*, 69–70 [Nathaniel Bradshaw] · *DNB*

Archives Bodl. Oxf., editions of *History of Essex* and *History of Hertfordshire* with MS additions · Essex RO, Chelmsford | Essex RO, Chelmsford, Holman MSS

Salmon, Robert (1763–1821), architect and mechanical engineer, youngest son of William Salmon, carpenter and builder, was born at Stratford upon Avon in Warwickshire. At an early age he entered the service of an attorney named Grey, residing near Leicester Fields, who aided him in his education. He soon displayed remarkable mechanical ability, and, being fond of music, made for himself a violin and other musical instruments.

A few years later Salmon obtained the appointment of clerk of works under the architect Henry Holland (1746?–1806), and was engaged in the rebuilding of Carlton House. In 1790 he was employed under Holland at Woburn Abbey in Bedfordshire, and, attracting the notice of Francis Russell, fifth duke of Bedford, he became in 1794 the duke's resident architect and mechanist. He was the first resident architect appointed by any English landowner. In this capacity he effected many reforms in the management of the property, and he designed several new farm buildings on the estate: Park Farm (1795–8); Tithe Farm, Eaton Socon (1797–8); Flitwick Wood Farm (1800–02); Crawley Mill Farm (1801); Speedwell Farm (1801); and Bidwell Farm (1802). The quality of design and construction was exceptional and the buildings were all models in their way, though Salmon was prepared to experiment. The farmhouse at Tithe Farm was octagonal because Salmon believed it would be cheaper to build, regardless of the practicalities of furnishing it. He had a liking for *pisé* construction; this was used for a number of his buildings and involved clay or earth being forced between boards, which were then removed as the infill material hardened.

Salmon's services in the improvement of agricultural implements proved of the highest importance, and his numerous inventions attracted much attention when exhibited at the annual sheep-shearings at Woburn. In 1797 the Society of Arts awarded him 30 guineas for a chaff-cutter, which was the parent of all later chaff-cutters. In 1801 Salmon exhibited his 'Bedfordshire drill', which had a system for keeping the drills level over uneven ground that in turn influenced the development of other drills. In 1803 he demonstrated a plough, where the slade (heel) was replaced by a skew wheel. It was intended to be drawn by one horse. In 1804 Salmon brought out an excellent 'scuffler', or cultivator, and two years later he exhibited a self-raking reaping machine, which embodied all the principles of the later reaping machines that became common from the 1860s and 1870s.

In 1814 Salmon patented the first haymaking machine, to which subsequent improvement added nothing but new details. The Society of Arts awarded him silver medals at various times for surgical instruments, a canal lock, a weighing machine, a humane mantrap, and a system of earthwalls. John Russell, sixth duke of Bedford, father of Lord John Russell, in 1806 conferred on him the stewardship of his Chenies estate, that he might improve the system of plantation. Salmon put the management of the woodlands on a more businesslike footing, with improved accounting. He paid great attention to the proper method of pruning forest trees, for which he invented an apparatus, and made numerous experiments to determine the best method of seasoning timber.

Salmon's wife, Ann, died in 1812. His daughter, Ann Maria, was born in 1803 and died in 1811. Salmon continued his duties at Woburn until September 1821, when failing health caused him to resign his offices and retire to Lambeth, in London. He died, however, within a month, while on a visit to Woburn, on 6 October 1821, and was buried four days later in Woburn church, where the sixth duke of Bedford placed a tablet commemorating his 'unwearied zeal and disinterested integrity'. Salmon was the author of *An Analysis of the General Construction of Trusses* (1807). He also contributed several papers to the *Transactions* of the Society of Arts.

E. I. CARLYLE, *rev.* JONATHAN BROWN

Sources J. M. Robinson, *Georgian model farms: a study of decorative and model farm buildings in the age of improvement, 1700–1846* (1983) · T. Batchelor, *General view of the agriculture of the county of Bedford* (1808) · J. Godber, *History of Bedfordshire, 1066–1888* (1969) · J. A. Ransome, *The implements of agriculture* (1843) · G. E. Fussell, *The farmer's tools* (1952) · *GM*, 1st ser., 91/2 (1821), 381 · Paul Smith, 'The landed estate as a patron of scientific innovation: horticulture at Woburn Abbey, 1802–1839', PhD diss., Open University, 1983
Archives Beds. & Luton ARS, R3, R5

Salmon, Thomas (*bap.* **1647**, *d.* **1706**), writer on music and Church of England clergyman, was baptized on 11 December 1647 at St John-at-Hackney, the second son of Thomas Salmon, merchant and alderman of London, and his wife, Elizabeth, *née* Okey. He matriculated at Trinity College, Oxford, on 8 April 1664, aged sixteen, graduating BA in 1667 and MA in 1670.

It is one of the ironies of history that perhaps the most interesting and controversial figure of seventeenth-century British music studied mathematics at university and was a musical amateur. Thomas Salmon's unique contribution to his times was primarily the *Essay to the Advancement of Musick* (1672), a work that advocated several innovations concerning musical notation and solmization. Salmon's revolutionary approach stands out even during a time when new ideas about music were commonplace in Britain. There can be no doubt that Salmon saw himself on a mission of sorts, to illuminate the arcane aspects of the musical art and, in so doing, to democratize and demystify practices which seemed to him intentionally obscure and illogical. Salmon's passion was born of his own frustrated attempt to learn more about music,

and his own difficulty in understanding its 'dark and tedious principles'. Thus he points out in the first chapter of his *Essay* that:

> the design of these papers is to take away the affrightening bug-bear terms, to reduce the confused cliffs into one established order, and if there be any faith had to reason and experience, to show a way for the attainment of Musick by Notes, in much less than the usual time required.

Salmon set the tone for his work during his discussion 'The gamut reformed' in the second chapter of the *Essay*, calling the 'Fardle of hard names and fictious words called the Gamut' a stumbling block to any beginner. He proposed that singing the note names themselves (such as G, A, B) would be far easier and, most important, would cut down on the inordinate time required to learn to read music. Another time-saving measure, and one which dominated the rest of the *Essay*, was Salmon's suggestion that a new clef system be used. Salmon advocated a single clef, its second line on G, and the various registers indicated by an initial (T = treble, M = mean, B = bass) placed before each staff. In the course of these discussions Salmon reiterated his belief that the musical beginner would, with the aid of this simplified system, be able to play or sing at sight much more rapidly than ever before. Finally, in chapter five of the *Essay*, matters relating primarily to instrumental music were discussed. After noting the advantages of the one-clef system for violinists and violists, such as the ability to read other music without transposing into new clefs, Salmon suggested a universal tuning, a subject to which he returned in his later writings. Salmon also argued that staff notation should replace the outdated tablature system for lute music then in use, noting that by doing so the student would have

> broke a Prison, and may by this use of Notes, come to arrive at perfection in composing for, as well as playing upon this supream Musick. None of which could in the least be done, though one practised an hundred years by letters.

While Salmon's suggested reforms may seem harmless enough, contemporary musicians viewed them with alarm, and the *Essay* inspired one of the most emotional and vicious pamphlet campaigns of the century. Salmon gave an indication of things to come in the final chapter of the *Essay*, where he responded to objections raised by 'some peevish piece of Antiquity' and those who 'continue obstinate, to maintain such needless difficulties'. The author's unnecessarily arrogant style and his searing condemnation of contemporary musical practices make the reaction of professionals to his theories understandable. The most notable critic of Salmon was Matthew Locke, who published his *Observations upon a Late Book, Entituled, 'An Essay to the Advancement of Musick'* (1672) soon after the appearance of the *Essay*. After dismissing Salmon as a mere schoolboy who once sought him out for musical instruction, Locke pointed out a number of the work's shortcomings: the *Essay* did not address sacred music, overlooked the need for maintaining the solfege system, and presented a clef system that was too unwieldy for actual practice. Locke finished off his opponent with the observation:

If I have us'd too much Gall in these lines, 'tis only to let him know that I can write with his Ink, and that I intend to vindicate the old Scale till I meet with a better, while I am capable of subscribing my self.

Unfortunately, Salmon felt the need to respond to Locke's objections, and his *Vindication of 'An Essay to the Advancement of Music'* (1672) appeared just a few months later. This merely incited yet another, and more obscene, response, *The Present Practice of Musick Vindicated* (1673) by Locke and his confederates, the composers John Phillips (the nephew of John Milton) and John Playford. Of these three, Playford's objections to Salmon's ideas are the most interesting and reasonable, and Playford's decision to henceforth publish his choral works using G clefs for both the soprano and tenor parts (a practice adopted by all later British composers) seems to have been inspired by his reading of Salmon.

In the same year that saw the publication of Locke's final barrage at Salmon, the erstwhile theorist became rector at Meppershall, formerly Mepsal, in Bedfordshire. He married Katherine (d. 1731), daughter of Nathaniel Bradshaw (not the regicide Sergeant John Bradshaw as formerly stated) in or before 1674, their eldest son, Nathanael *Salmon, being born at Meppershall on 22 March 1675. They had at least eight more children, including Thomas *Salmon, the historian. Salmon continued to publish on musical matters, however, producing the interesting *Proposal to Perform Musick in Perfect and Mathematical Proportions* (1688), where he revisited the temperament ideas already discussed in the *Essay*, as well as further works on musical tuning (including a Royal Society lecture in 1705 with musical examples performed by violists Frederick and Christian Steffkin) and ancient music. It should be noted that later musicians, including Alexander Malcom and Charles Burney, received Salmon's ideas more positively. He seems to have had no difficulty in accepting the new regime as he must have taken the oaths to William and Mary in 1689, remaining rector of Meppershall for the rest of his life. He died at Meppershall and was buried there on 1 August 1706. DONALD R. BOOMGAARDEN

Sources M. Tilmouth, 'Salmon, Thomas', Grove, *Dict. mus.* (1904–10) · L. M. Ruff, 'Thomas Salmon's "Essay to the advancement of musick"', *The Consort*, 21 (1964), 266–75 · O. Baldwin and T. Wilson, 'Musick advanced and vindicated', *MT*, 111 (1970), 148–50 · P. M. Gouk, 'Music in the natural philosophy of the early Royal Society', PhD diss., U. Lond., 1982 · R. E. Lawrence, 'The music treatises of Thomas Salmon (1648–1706)', MA diss., University of Calgary, 1991 · W. T. Atcherson, 'Symposium on seventeenth-century music theory: England', *Journal of Music Theory*, 16 (1972), 6–15 · D. Boomgaarden, *Musical thought in Britain and Germany during the early eighteenth century* (New York, 1989) · H. W. Forsyth Howard, ed., *The Genealogist*, new ser., 25 (1908–9), 201 · G. J. Armytage and J. P. Rylands, eds., *Pedigrees made at the visitation of Cheshire, 1623, Lancashire and Cheshire RS*, 58 (1909), 205 · F. A. Blaydes, ed., *Bedfordshire Notes and Queries*, 3 (1893) · IGI · Foster, *Alum. Oxon.*

Salmon, Thomas (bap. **1679**, d. **1767**), writer on history and geography, was born at Meppershall, Bedfordshire, and was baptized there on 2 February 1679, the son of Thomas *Salmon (bap. 1647, d. 1706), writer and rector of that parish, and Katherine, née Bradshaw. Nathanael *Salmon (1675–1742), antiquary, was his elder brother. Salmon kept a coffee house at Cambridge until limited trade forced him to move to London. Though he had no formal training for a profession he was said by the antiquary William Cole to have 'no small turn for writing, as his many productions show, most of which were written when he resided at Cambridge'. The best-known of his extensive and eclectic list of publications was *Modern History, or, The Present State of All Nations* (1739) which later appeared in Dutch and Italian translation. His many other historical works include *A Review of the History of England* (1722), an examination of Gilbert Burnet's *History*, published in 1724, and *The Chronological Historian* (1733), translated into French in 1751.

Salmon was said to have travelled extensively, residing in both the West and East Indies, and in several European countries; in 1739–40 he accompanied George Anson on his round-the-world voyage. His experiences formed the subject for a series of other titles, among them *A New Geographical and Historical Grammar* (1749), which ran to six editions by 1758, and *The Universal Traveller* (1752–3). In addition Salmon contributed surveys of the English, Scottish, and Irish peerages, guides for foreign visitors to Oxford and Cambridge, biographies of men who died in the service of their country, a review of state trials, and an essay on marriage. In 1725 he brought out an edition of his father's *Historical Collections of Great Britain*. He died on 20 January 1767. THOMPSON COOPER, rev. PHILIP CARTER

Sources R. Bowes, *A catalogue of books printed at or relating to the university, town and county of Cambridge from 1521 to 1893* (1894) · S. Halkett and J. Laing, *A dictionary of the anonymous and pseudonymous literature of Great Britain*, 4 vols. (1882–8) · W. T. Lowndes, *The bibliographer's manual of English literature*, 4 vols. (1834) · N&Q, 3rd ser., 3 (1863), 11 · GM, 1st ser., 37 (1767), 48 · Calamy rev.

Salmon, William (1644–1713), medical empiric and author, was born on 2 June 1644. Contemporaries claimed that as a boy Salmon was apprenticed to a mountebank, whom he served as a 'wachum' or 'zany', and amused audiences by 'tumbling through a hoop' or with 'tricks of legerdemain and slight of hand'; he also 'made speeches and wrote Panygyricks in praise of his master's Panaceas. He wrote Almanacks to direct the taking of his medicines, and made the stars vouch for their virtue' (Geshwind, 73–6). It appears he learned much of his craft accompanying his master in many travels, including some time spent in New England.

By 1671 Salmon had established a practice in London near the Smithfield gate of St Bartholomew's Hospital where, as was common among irregular types of practitioners, he offered his services to people denied admission to hospital. Using this location as his base, Salmon published *Synopsis medicinae, or, A Compendium of Astrological, Galenical & Chymical Physick* (1671), which had three further editions during the century. Another compendium, *Polygraphice, the art of drawing, engraving, etching, limning, painting, washing, varnishing, colouring, and dyeing*, appeared in 1672. Salmon's *Polygraphice* also discussed physiognomy, or the ways in which passions and emotions were represented on the faces of portraits. By 1679 Salmon had established his medical practice at the Red Balls tavern in Salisbury Court, off Fleet Street. Here he published *Horae mathematicae* (1679), *Iatrica, seu, Praxis medendi* (1681, 1684, 1694), and *Doron medicon, or, A Supplement to the New London Dispensatory* (1683, 1688).

In 1684 Salmon moved, after a brief residence in George Yard, near Broken Wharf, to the Blue Balcony by the ditch side near Holborn Bridge, where he remained until some time after 1692. In 1684 Salmon published the *London Almanac*, which later became known as 'Salmon's almanac'. In 1687 he published, together with Randal Taylor, *Select Physical and Chirurgical Observations*, and in 1689, with Edward Brewster, he produced a translation of the Utrecht physician Ijsbrand van Diemerbroek's *The Anatomy of Human Bodies*. Salmon also wrote on religious topics: *A Discourse Against Transubstantiation*, which featured a dialogue between a protestant and a papist, was published in 1690; his *Discourse on Water Baptism* appeared in 1700. It appears that he was a member of a sect that met at Leathersellers' Hall.

Salmon also compiled alchemical and metaphysical selections from the philosophical writings of Hermes Trismegistus, Kalid, Geber, Artephius, Nicholas Flammel, Roger Bacon, and George Ripley in his *Medicina practica, or, Practical Physick* (1692). *Seplasium, the Complete Family Physician, or, The Druggist's Shop Opened* appeared in 1693, and in 1696 Salmon published a widely read domestic manual entitled *The Family Dictionary or Household Companion*. In a style typical of these popular manuals, Salmon included sections on medicinal and surgical remedies in addition to 'domestic concerns' such as cookery and cosmetics. He offered a variety of remedies compounded from ingredients which were few in number, cheap, common, easily mixed, efficacious, safe, durable, and small in dose. Salmon's *Synopsis medicinae, or, A Compendium of the Theory and Practice of Physick* appeared in 1695 and was reissued in 1699. In 1698, giving his residence as the Great House by Black Friars' Stairs and signing his engraved frontispiece portrait as 'Medicinae Professor', Salmon published a surgical treatise, *Ars chirurgica: a Compendium of the Theory and Practice of Chirurgery*.

In 1699 Salmon joined in the controversy over the role of the Royal College of Physicians. The college leadership came under attack as it attempted to implement its own internal disciplinary actions against certain members, to prosecute impostors practising outside the bounds of the college, and to maintain control over the Society of Apothecaries through establishing a dispensary. Samuel Garth's *The Dispensary: a Poem* (1699) drew public attention to the dispute, while Salmon's *Rebuke to the Authors of a Blew-Book, Call'd The State of Physick in London* (1699) warned against the college's continuing monopolization of the profession. Salmon went on to publish *Collectanea medica: the Country Physician* (1703), and a translation of Thomas Sydenham's *Processus integri*, simply titled *The Practice of Physick* (1707). Salmon published *Botanologia: the English Herbal* in 1710–11, a work later recalled as 'the swan song of the great English herbalists'. Salmon's works are included in *Bibliotheca Salmonea* (1713), a somewhat inaccurate, incomplete, and

complicated work. This claims that Salmon helped to compile *Bibliothèque des philosophes* (1672) and that he contributed entries to *Dictionaire hermetique* (1695). Salmon also edited and translated at least portions of *Pharmacopoeia Londinensis* (1678, 1682, 1685, 1691, 1696, 1707, 1716) and *Pharmacopoeia Bateana* (1694, 1700), as well as compiling *Officina chymica*, *Systema medicinale*, and *Phylaxa medicinae*.

Salmon drew most of the information he incorporated into his writings from his extensive personal library. Indeed there is little evidence that he made any original contribution to medical knowledge. Salmon also created a cabinet of curiosities that included some items he brought back from his travels to the West Indies. He owned several Dutch paintings, two microscopes, and many mathematical and natural philosophical instruments, including a set of John Napier's 'bones'. Salmon died in London in 1713. His final compilation, *Ars anatomica, or, The Anatomy of Humane Bodies*, was published posthumously in 1714.

PHILIP K. WILSON

Sources M. Geshwind, 'William Salmon, quack-doctor and writer of seventeenth-century London', *Bulletin of the History of Dentistry*, 43 (1995), 73–6 · R. L. Meade-King, 'Notes from a seventeenth-century textbook of medicine', *BMJ* (25 Aug 1906), 433–5 · W. J. Bishop, 'Le Dr William Salmon (1644–1713) et sa bibliothèque', *Librarium*, 1 (1959), 79–83 · S. J. Childs, 'The ubiquitous Dr Salmon', *Canadian Medical Association Journal. Journal de l'Association Médicale Canadienne*, 66 (1970), 160–61 · DNB · W. Salmon, *Ars chirurgica: a compendium of the theory and practice of chirurgery* (1698), frontispiece

Likenesses W. Sherwin, line engraving, c.1671 (after his earlier works), BM, Wellcome L. · line engraving, 1686, NPG, Wellcome L. · R. White, line engraving, 1687 (after his earlier work), BM, Wellcome L. · R. White, line engraving, 1700 (after his earlier work), Wellcome L. · F. H. Van Hove, line engraving, 1714, Wellcome L. · L. Burnford, line engraving, BM, Wellcome L.; repro. in Salmon, *Synopsis medicinae* (1681) · Vandergucht, engraving · portrait, repro. in W. Salmon, *Ars chirurgica* (1699) · portrait, repro. in W. Salmon, *Ars anatomica* (1714)

Salmon, William (1701/2–1779), architectural writer, was probably born in Colchester, the elder of two sons of William Salmon (d. 1747) and his wife, Sarah (possibly Sarah Langham who married a William Salmon in the parish of St Giles, Colchester, in 1702). The elder Salmon, like his son, was a carpenter who lived and worked in Colchester. Salmon senior has previously been credited with authorship of a number of his son's books but no evidence to support this claim has so far come to light. Nothing is known of William Salmon's early career and education. Although he does seem to have practised as a carpenter, there are no known works by him and he does not appear to have served a formal apprenticeship. Instead he bought his freedom of the town of Colchester in 1728. He was married, but his wife died before 1774. They had no surviving children and on his death he left his few possessions to his nephew, William Salmon of Thorp.

Salmon wrote four manuals on building. His first, *The Country Builder's Estimator, or, The Architect's Companion*, first published in 1733, was a pocket price book giving details for measuring the various elements of a building and estimating total construction costs. It also provided calculations for estimating the size of windows required for lighting a room and the sizing of chimneys. An economic and useful tool for craftsman and client alike, it followed in a tradition of pricing books starting in 1659 with Thomas Willsford's *Architectonice*. In contrast *Palladio Londinensis, or, The London Art of Building, in Three Parts*, published in 1734, was a much more ambitious work, a quarto 'treatise' aimed at the aspiring architect. Its first part was devoted to geometry (to which was added a section on prices), the second to the orders, and the third to stairs and roof structures. A useful dictionary was added as an appendix. Two later works, *The Builder's Guide* (1736) and *The London and Country Builder's vade mecum* (1741), were both books of tables for estimating building quantities. A manuscript survives for a fifth work, 'The Vitruvian principles of architecture practically demonstrated', dated 1737 (and now located in Yale U. CBA), but this was never published.

Salmon's success lay in his ability to combine material from a number of sources into modestly priced books that appealed to the widest possible audience. In so doing they became highly influential: *Palladio Londinensis* was reprinted more times than any other book of its type and became the standard building manual for nearly forty years. Many of the elements such as doors and door-cases illustrated therein were repeated in buildings throughout the country, becoming standard forms in the eighteenth century. Its popularity can also be attributed to its numerous engravings, many of which were drawn not by Salmon himself but by Edward Hoppus, who worked as surveyor in the London Assurance Company from 1729 until his death in 1739. Hoppus may also have been an editor of, if not the source for, much of the information on London building prices. Salmon died in Colchester in March 1779 and was buried on the last day of the month at St Peter's Church, Colchester. A short obituary appeared on 3 April 1779 in the *Ipswich Journal*.　　J. W. P. CAMPBELL

Sources Colvin, *Archs.* · E. Harris and N. Savage, *British architectural books and writers, 1556–1785* (1990) · *Ipswich Journal* (3 April 1779) · Oath book, Essex RO, Colchester, MS D/B5 Gb7, fol. 245 · will, Essex RO, Chelmsford, MS D/abr 23/271 [William Salmon senior] · will, Essex RO, Chelmsford, MS D/abr 27/82 · parish register, St Peter's, Colchester, 31 March 1779, Essex RO, Colchester, MS D/P 178/1/3 [burial] · D. T. Yeomans, 'Early carpenters' manuals, 1592–1820', *Construction History*, 2 (1986), 13–33
Wealth at death see will, Essex RO, Chelmsford, MS D/abr 27/82

Salmond, Sir (William) Geoffrey Hanson (1878–1933), air force officer, was born on 19 August 1878 at Hougham, Dover, the elder son of Major-General Sir William Salmond (1840–1932), from Whaddon House, Bruton, Somerset, and his wife, Emma Mary, youngest daughter of William Fretwell Hoyle of Hooton Levet Hall, Yorkshire. Salmond had three sisters and a brother, John Maitland *Salmond. After private tuition in London, Geoffrey (as he was known) was educated at Aysgarth preparatory school near Bedale, Yorkshire, before attending Wellington College, Berkshire (1892–6).

Salmond entered the Royal Military Academy, Woolwich, on 24 September 1896, being commissioned second lieutenant in the Royal Artillery on 23 June 1898. He fought during the Second South African War at Venter's Spruit, Spion Kop, Vaal Krantz, Hussar Hill, Pieter's Hill, and the relief of Ladysmith before being wounded in June 1900. After recovery, he served in the China expeditionary force (1900–01) before returning to South Africa to the Transvaal, Orange River Colony, and Cape Colony between October 1901 and May 1902; he advanced to lieutenant on 16 February 1901. Salmond received the Queen's medal and seven clasps for the Second South African War and also received the China medal (1900).

Subsequently remaining in England until October 1905, Salmond then undertook a language course to become a Japanese interpreter (2nd class) in April 1907. Promoted captain on 2 December 1905, he was posted to the 110th battery Royal Field Artillery at Deepcut, Farnborough, in December 1907, acting as adjutant of the 24th brigade from 4 February 1908 until 22 January 1911. In autumn 1910 he married Margaret Mary, eldest daughter of William Carr of Ditchingham Hall, Norfolk, and they had a son and three daughters. Salmond attended the army staff college at Camberley between 23 January 1911 and 30 November 1912. On 18 February 1913 he gained a Royal Aero Club pilot's licence, and he was placed on the Royal Flying Corps (RFC) reserve of officers on 17 April 1913.

Salmond joined the directorate of military aeronautics at the War Office as a GSO3 on 31 July 1913. Seconded to the RFC, on 8 August 1914 he went to Amiens as GSO2 on Major-General Sir David Henderson's headquarters staff, where he helped to devise a method of pinpointing enemy artillery from the air using wireless signals and specially marked maps. He was promoted major on 30 August. Salmond took charge of 1 squadron on 26 January 1915, commanding it during the battles of Neuve-Chapelle, Aubers Ridge, and Hill 60 and being credited with further improving aerial wireless communication systems. Promoted temporary lieutenant-colonel on 18 August 1915, he returned to England before taking over 5 wing, RFC, in Egypt that November.

After advancing to brevet lieutenant-colonel on 3 June 1916, Salmond assumed command of the Middle East brigade of the RFC as a temporary brigadier-general on 1 July 1916 with responsibility for operations from the deserts of Mesopotamia to the mountains of Greece. He visited all his units in the Middle East to learn of the difficulties they faced and to bring about improvements in equipment and methods. His RFC units gave tactical support to army commanders in Salonika, east Africa, Egypt, and Palestine, spotting enemy artillery, pursuing retreating columns of enemy forces, and bombing Turkish transport behind the front lines. The arrangement of his principal air bases revealed the effectiveness of his strategic thinking; many of them remained in use until 1946. By the middle of 1917 his brigade was 'fully organized, well sited, and well served' (*DNB*). On 3 March 1917 he was awarded the DSO 'for conspicuous ability and devotion to duty when personally directing the work of the Royal Corps' in the Sinai in 1916 (*London Gazette*). In August 1917 Salmond briefly went to England to command a training brigade before returning to Egypt on 22 December 1917 to take over Middle East command, which embraced the area of his former brigade plus the Persian Gulf, east Africa, and India. In 1918 he received the CB, order of the Nile, and order of St Saviour of Greece. The following year he was created KCMG and made an honorary LLD by Cambridge University. A temporary major-general from 28 January 1918, made substantive on 1 April, he remained in the Middle East until 21 February 1922, when he became air member for supply and research on the Air Council, having secured a permanent commission in the RAF as an air vice-marshal on 1 August 1919.

Before leaving Egypt, Salmond planned a series of aerodromes from Cairo to South Africa, which were later developed by Imperial Airways for commercial flights. At the Air Ministry he realized that the vast responsibilities of his 'thorny and sprawling department' (Templewood, 180) were too onerous for one man and recommended a separate directorate of scientific research, which was eventually created. In 1926 Salmond was appointed KCB. Given command of RAF India on 27 December 1926, he set a precedent by flying out to Delhi. He displayed 'vivid imagination' (ibid., 212) in organizing the evacuation of 586 Europeans and members of the royal family by air from Kabul between 23 December 1928 and 25 February 1929 during a revolution in Afghanistan.

Promoted air marshal on 1 July 1929, Salmond left India on 28 February 1931 to become air officer commanding-in-chief air defence of Great Britain on 25 September 1931. He served as air chief marshal from 1 January 1933, and was appointed chief of the air staff on 1 April 1933 in succession to his brother John. Salmond was already suffering from terminal cancer, but 'temporary arrangements for the carrying on of the duties of the post' during his illness were optimistically announced with his brother returning to the Air Ministry (*The Times*, 5 April 1933). However, Salmond died in King Edward VII's Hospital, Grosvenor Crescent, London, on 27 April 1933. His wife and four children survived him. Salmond's funeral at St John's Church, Southwick Crescent, Hyde Park, and a memorial service at Ditchingham, Norfolk, took place on 1 May. It is moot whether John knew about his brother's grave medical condition: it has been suggested that his decision to stand aside was an act of sentiment on John's part; however, even Geoffrey's wife was evidently unaware of its severity.

Salmond was a member of the United Service and RAF clubs, and for some time in later years he lived at Woodlands, Stoke Poges, Buckinghamshire, and then in Hyde Park Gardens, London. Correspondents to *The Times* recalled his 'unostentatious sense of humour', 'boyish enthusiasm', and 'capacity for arousing the loyal devotion of all who came into contact with him' (29 April 1933).

JOHN SWEETMAN

Sources *Army List* · *Air Force List* · J. Laffin, *Swifter than eagles: the biography of marshal of the Royal Air Force Sir John Maitland Salmond* (1964) · Viscount Templewood, *Empire of the air: the advent of the air age, 1922–1929* (1957) · A. Boyle, *Trenchard* (1962) · Wellington College records, Wellington College, Berkshire · *The Times* (1 April 1933) · *The Times* (5 April 1933) · *The Times* (28–9 April 1933) · *The Times* (12 June 1933) · Royal Military Academy records, Royal Military Academy, Woolwich · *WWW* · H. St G. Saunders, *Per ardua: the rise of British air power, 1911–1939* (1944) · M. Smith, *British air strategy between the wars* (1984) · *DNB* · *CGPLA Eng. & Wales* (1933)

Archives SOUND IWM SA, oral history interview

Likenesses two photographs, 1914–25, repro. in Laffin, *Swifter than eagles*

Wealth at death £2804 19s. 3d.: probate, 8 June 1933, *CGPLA Eng. & Wales*

Salmond, James Bell (1891–1958), journal editor and writer, was born at 4 Gayfield, Arbroath, on 8 December 1891, the only son of James Boath Salmond (1860–1901), co-owner and editor of the *Arbroath Herald*, and his wife, Anne Duncan, *née* Bell (*b.* 1857), from Dundee. Salmond, known familiarly as J. B., had a younger sister, Georgina, known as Ina. His father wrote pawky stories in Arbroath dialect, collected under the title *My Man Sandy*. A popular figure, he died, aged forty, in August 1901, when his son was nine.

J. B. Salmond was to become a strapping six-footer who excelled at sport; he left Arbroath high school as dux medallist to study at St Andrews University, where he boxed, played rugby, was president of the gymnastic club, and edited the university magazine, *College Echoes*. Having graduated MA in 1912 he headed for Fleet Street. He wrote sporting articles for Northcliffe's junior magazines and collaborated with cricketer G. L. Jessop, known as The Croucher, in writing serials and *The Boys' Book of Cricket*. However, as his friend R. J. B. Sellar wrote, 'J B had a heathery streak … [and] was never at home in that vast Fleet Street emporium' (Sellar, 164).

In 1914 Salmond volunteered to serve with the Royal Highland regiment, the Black Watch; he gained his commission and served on the western front. By 1917 he was at Craiglockhart War Hospital, Edinburgh, where Siegfried Sassoon and Wilfred Owen were fellow patients. Assisted by Owen he edited the hospital's magazine, *The Hydra*. After the war he became a roving staff reporter on the *Dundee Advertiser* and the *People's Journal*, and in 1923 he married Margaret (Peggy) Chalmers (1889–1960) of Newport-on-Tay, Fife. Of tiny stature she was always described by Salmond as 'heart high'. It was a happy marriage, with holidays spent tramping the remoter parts of Scotland. They had no children.

By 1927 Salmond was editor of the *Scots Magazine*, a job tailor-made for his interests and abilities. Neil Gunn, Lewis Spence, Jessie Kesson, Eric Linklater, and Lewis Grassic Gibbon—among early contributors—were grateful for Salmond's counsel and encouragement and welcome guests at his home. Preferring a degree of anonymity for himself, his own articles were published under the pseudonyms Wayfarer and Alan Graham. Fascinated by General Wade's prowess in road building he published *Wade in Scotland* in 1934, which is still consulted. His poetry was published in *The Old Stalker* two years later, and his *Songs of Dundee* set to music by his sister-in-law Phoebe Chalmers.

During the Second World War Salmond was a major in the Home Guard, and in 1944 he was awarded an honorary LLD by his alma mater, St Andrews University. In that year he also published *Andrew Lang and St Andrews* and his first novel, *The Flower of the Flax*; a second novel, *The Toby Jug*, appeared in 1947. In 1948 he retired as editor of the *Scots Magazine* to be warden of St Salvator's Hall, where he became a good friend to students under his care. He was also made keeper of muniments at St Andrews, a challenge that he tackled with customary diligence. His *Veterum laudes*, written to mark the quincentenary of United College, appeared in 1950. Immensely proud of his regiment, the Black Watch, he wrote *History of the 51st Highland Division (1939–45)* (1953) and was then commissioned to write *The Story of the Royal & Ancient Golf Club* (1956), a painstakingly accurate account full of breezy anecdote.

Salmond was a founder-member of both the Scottish Youth Hostel Association and the Royal Scottish Country Dance Society, and president of the Grampian Club. He maintained links with his birthplace through Arbroath's abbey pageant. In demand as a speaker, he found it easy to communicate with the younger generation and often addressed schools. Though his speeches were written in full and kept in a pocket or sporran he rarely referred to them. When the Scottish PEN Club met in Edinburgh to mark the writing jubilee of Annie S. Swan, Salmond in his address said, 'Ma'am, this is a kind of waving to you of galley proofs from journalists all over Scotland, proud to think you are one of themselves' (private information). Described by a colleague as charming, but a rogue, Salmond was a man with boundless enthusiasm, generosity of spirit, and a great sense of humour, although at times he was excitable and quick of temper. Failing eyesight and ill health dogged his later years. 'When he was ill … He'd lie moaning if Peggy was around, sit up smiling as soon as her back was turned. The daylight shone out of his pants where Peggy was concerned' (private information). He died on 2 February 1958 at his home, Dhucraig, The Scores, in St Andrews, followed less than two years later by his beloved Peggy. He was cremated at Dundee on 5 February 1958.   SILVIE TAYLOR

Sources private information (2004) · R. J. B. Sellar, *Rothmill Quarterly* (spring 1959) · *IGI* · *Dundee Courier* · *Dundee Advertiser* · b. cert. **Archives** priv. coll., speeches **Likenesses** photographs, repro. in *St Andrews Citizen* · photographs, priv. coll. **Wealth at death** £9180 14s. 4d.: confirmation, 10 July 1958, *CCI*

Salmond, Sir John Maitland (1881–1968), air force officer, was born in London on 17 July 1881, the younger of the two sons among the five children of Lieutenant (later Major-General Sir) William Salmond (1840–1932), of the Royal Engineers, and his wife, Emma Mary (d. 1923), the youngest daughter of William Fretwell Hoyle of Maltby, Yorkshire. Jack was destined to follow in his father's martial footsteps. At the age of thirteen he went to Wellington College, and then, on his second attempt, passed the entrance examination to the Royal Military College at Sandhurst. Upon graduation he was gazetted to the King's Own Royal Lancaster regiment, which was in South Africa during the later stages of the Second South African War; after three years he was seconded to the West African frontier force in Nigeria. His years in Africa were exciting and challenging because he operated with a great deal of autonomy in a wild, colonial environment; he learned much about leadership, followership, administration, and politics.

After returning to England in 1907 Salmond rejoined his regiment at Colchester and in 1910 moved to Jersey. He became an avid observer of the developments in the new field of aviation, and in 1910 (by then a captain) he wrote an essay entitled 'Airships and aeroplanes in war'. Although it was unpublished, it is of interest for its farsighted predictions. Salmond opined that aircraft would play an increasingly important role in warfare through reconnaissance and the achievement of air superiority. He thought it inevitable that air combat would take place to allow friendly air forces unhampered access to the sky while denying the same opportunity for the enemy. He even speculated that aerial bombing would become a standard operation in war.

In 1912 Salmond applied for and was granted a transfer to the Royal Flying Corps (RFC); he learned to fly at the aviation company at Hendon set up by Claude Grahame-White. On 12 August 1912 he was awarded his Royal Aero Club certificate (no. 272) and was posted to the Central Flying School at Upavon as an instructor pilot. Promoted flight commander in November 1912 and squadron commander in May 1913, he was an excellent aviator, and in December 1913 set a British altitude record of 13,140 feet. On 11 August 1913 he married Helen Amy Joy Lumsden (d. 1916), the daughter of James Forbes Lumsden of Johnstone House, Aberdeen.

Upon the outbreak of war in 1914 Salmond went to France as commander of 3 squadron and then of 2 wing. As had been demonstrated in Africa, he was personally fearless and often flew in combat. After one particularly harrowing mission, in March 1915, he received a message from his superior, Colonel Hugh Trenchard: 'Dear Salmond: You are splendid, but don't do it again; I can't afford to lose you. It is really a magnificent example you set' (Laffin, 62). At the same time he showed great humanity to the men under his command. He did much to demonstrate to army commanders the value of aerial reconnaissance and artillery spotting. In April 1915, having been awarded the DSO, he was promoted lieutenant-colonel and for six months commanded the Royal Flying Corps wing at Farnborough before returning to France to command one of the three wings of the RFC in the field. He became particularly involved in developing air fighting tactics following the development by the Germans of fixed machine-gun firing through propellers.

Although it had quickly become apparent that aircraft were to play a far more important role in the war than many had anticipated, the RFC remained ill-equipped to expand rapidly to meet this challenge. It was clear that the situation would not improve at the front as long as it was disorganized at home. Promoted brigadier-general early in 1916, Salmond returned to Britain to command and reorganize the flying training system. Over the next year he laboured to increase the pilot output in response to crew shortages and inexperience. The results were dramatic: the number of training schools increased from forty-seven to seventy-eight, the pilot shortage abated, and new methods of instruction were pioneered at the Central Flying School, in association with Lieutenant-Colonel Smith-Barry, enabling pilots to master new manoeuvres and to understand the strengths and limitations of their aircraft. During this period of achievement he suffered personal tragedy when, on 8 May 1916, his wife died while giving birth to a daughter.

In October 1917 Salmond was promoted major-general and appointed to the army council as the director-general of military aeronautics. At the age of thirty-six he was the youngest officer ever to have served on the council. His leadership and organizational abilities, as well as his political acumen, were sorely needed to supply the growing RFC at a time when the war was putting increasing strain on the British economy. One of his schemes was to use newly arrived American maintenance personnel to fill slots in the RFC training stations, thus releasing British troops for France. Salmond was frustrated by the political intrigue endemic in London, however, and yearned to return to combat. He was soon granted his wish.

As a result of British fear over German bombing attacks, as well as continuous rivalry and inefficiency, the government decided to combine the air arms of the army and navy to form the Royal Air Force. Trenchard was recalled from France to become the first chief of air staff, and on 20 January 1918 Salmond was dispatched to take his place as commander of the air forces in France. He now had sixty-three squadrons at his disposal, and this at a time when the Germans were about to launch their massive and nearly successful spring offensives. British losses were heavy, but the front held, barely. This was perhaps the finest hour of the British air services, army or navy, in the First World War. The allies soon began the counter-offensives that led to the armistice and victory.

Salmond returned home as major-general (to which he had been promoted in April 1918) with a DSO, CMG, and CVO; he had also been mentioned in dispatches five times and received several foreign decorations. In 1919 he was appointed KCB and promoted air vice-marshal (1 August). Britain was exhausted by the war, and funds for defence were quickly and drastically reduced in its aftermath. It was not obvious that the Royal Air Force, less than a year old, would survive the budget cutters. The plight of the RAF in India was especially dire, and in early 1922 Salmond was sent there to investigate. What he found was alarming. The RAF, at the end of a very long supply train, was barely functional. Moreover, the local military authorities seemed unwilling or unable to do much about it. Salmond's scathing indictment of the situation generated quick action, which greatly improved the condition of the RAF forces and their aircraft. Soon after, he had a new challenge.

In an effort to fend off those wishing to disband the RAF, Trenchard came up with a clever and practical plan. He volunteered the RAF to conduct a portion of imperial policing duties. Although this had traditionally been performed by the army, Trenchard suggested that aircraft could assist in the function at dramatically less cost. Given the air of fiscal austerity then prevalent, this was an enticing offer. The RAF was given its chance, and over the next decade it had a great deal of success in the mission of 'air control'. One of the most impressive successes was in Iraq, where Salmond was sent in late 1922.

The Turks were moving towards Mosul, Iraq's major city in the north, and it was Salmond's job as the military commander of all British forces in Iraq to prevent this incursion, while at the same time subduing the Kurdish uprising that was in progress. Using a judicious blend of air attack, diplomacy, and the rapid deployment of his infantry regiments by air, he was able to manoeuvre the Turks out of Iraq and subdue the Kurds. Moreover, he was able to accomplish this feat at an astonishingly low cost in blood and treasure. In the Iraq insurrection of 1920, for example, the British army had suffered more than 2000 casualties: under Salmond, total British losses were a mere twenty-six. In addition, Winston Churchill stated that the annual cost of policing Iraq had dropped from £40 million to £5 million. The campaign gave the RAF a much needed boost in morale and credibility, and Salmond was promoted air marshal (2 June 1923). On 2 June 1924 he married again; his second wife was Monica Margaret Grenfell (1893–1973), the elder daughter of William Henry *Grenfell, first Baron Desborough. This marriage produced a son and a daughter.

In January 1925 Salmond became the air officer commanding-in-chief of the air defence of Great Britain, the forerunner of Fighter Command. Like Trenchard, Salmond was sceptical that an adequate air defence against a determined enemy was possible, and he subscribed to the belief that the best defence was a good attacking force. He therefore advocated the build-up of a powerful offensive striking arm as Britain's best hope for security. This belief in the deterrence value of airpower, especially before the development of radar, was not unreasonable, even though it was later proven inadequate. In 1928 Salmond visited Australia and New Zealand to inspect the air forces there, and in January 1929 he was appointed to the air council as air member for personnel.

When Trenchard retired at the end of 1929, Salmond was the obvious choice to succeed him as chief of the air staff. He had led the RAF in France during the First World War, he had brilliantly succeeded as an operational commander in Iraq, and he had also proven himself an adept administrator. Moreover, photographs and contemporary accounts show him as a handsome, suave, gregarious, and refined gentleman. He got on well with personnel of all ranks, and was expected to be more effective, or at least less incendiary, than Trenchard had been in his dealings with the other services. His work was cut out for him.

The economic situation in 1930 was, if anything, worse than it had been a decade earlier. The great depression meant that funds for defence were simply not adequate. Between the wars the RAF was always the poor stepsister to the other services, receiving on average only around 15 per cent of the annual defence budget. In times of fiscal austerity the demon of inter-service rivalry generally raises its head, and the early 1930s provided no exception. The RAF was once again fighting for its institutional life.

In 1932 disarmament talks opened in Geneva, and British politicians saw them as an opportunity both to enhance security and to cut the defence budget. Their main bargaining chip was to be the RAF. British diplomats suggested severe limitations on air forces, and proposals were soon made to ban aerial bombing altogether. Salmond was astounded that politicians could be so short-sighted and naïve. He was certain that such limitations would never be held to in war, but if Britain were to disarm in advance she would be particularly vulnerable. Britain's geographical position was unique—her main industrial, financial, political, cultural, and military centres were all located in London, a mere fifteen minutes' flying time from the English Channel. Thus she was far more vulnerable to an air attack than any other European country, all of whose vital centres were more widely dispersed and further inland. Only a strong RAF could serve as the nation's first line of defence. His government disagreed.

During the two years of the Geneva disarmament conference Salmond wrote strident letters to his civilian superiors, warning them that their aerial disarmament proposals were dangerous. It was to no avail. On one occasion Salmond was so exasperated that he went to the French and asked them to oppose his own government's policy. The prime minister got wind of this insubordination, but surprisingly took no action against him. In the end the RAF was saved so that it could save the nation in 1940, but this was not a result of the cogent logic and arguments of such airmen as Salmond; rather, it was due to the ascendancy of Adolf Hitler. When Hitler pulled Germany out of the Geneva conference in 1934, all talk of disarmament abruptly ceased; Britain began the slow military build-up that would prepare her for the Second World War.

Salmond was created GCB in 1931 and promoted marshal of the Royal Air Force in 1933. When he retired in March 1933, his elder brother, (William) Geoffrey Hanson *Salmond, was announced as his successor. However, Geoffrey was taken ill almost immediately and died within the month. Salmond remained as chief of air staff for a few weeks until Sir Edward Ellington could assume the duties of the post.

Upon his retirement Salmond became a director of Imperial Airways. In 1938, as war became imminent, he returned to RAF service as chairman of the Air Defence Cadet Corps, and on the outbreak of war he was appointed director of armament production at the Ministry of Aircraft Production under Lord Beaverbrook. As chairman of a committee appointed in September 1940 to inquire into the failure of fighter defences to cope with the German night bombing raids, he was a leading figure, along with Trenchard, in bringing about the removal of Cyril Newall as chief of air staff and Hugh Dowding from Fighter Command. Salmond himself disagreed with some of

Beaverbrook's methods, and he resigned from his position in March 1941. In August 1941 he was named director-general of flying control and air/sea rescue, a response to the heavy losses of aircrew and aircraft through inadequate rescue arrangements. His successful work in this area caused many lives to be saved. Ill health forced Salmond to retire again in 1943. For the next twenty-five years, however, he remained a popular and respected 'founding father' of the RAF who often participated in public celebrations and events. Typically, his notion of service and duty had him serving as president of the RAF Club for twenty-three years. He died at Eastbourne, Sussex, on 16 April 1968, survived by his wife and three children.   PHILLIP S. MEILINGER

Sources J. Laffin, *Swifter than eagles: the biography of marshal of the Royal Air Force Sir John Maitland Salmond* (1964) · H. Probert, *High commanders of the Royal Air Force* (1991) · H. M. Hyde, *British air policy between the wars, 1918–1939* (1976) · P. S. Meilinger, 'Clipping the bombers' wings', *War in History* (July 1999) · W. Raleigh and H. A. Jones, *The war in the air*, 6 vols. (1922–37) · D. Omissi, *Air power and colonial control* (1990) · *The Times* (17 April 1968) · *The Times* (20 April 1968) · *The Times* (25 May 1968) · J. Ferris, 'Fighter defence before fighter command', *Journal of Military History* (Oct 1999) · *DNB* · Burke, *Gen. GB* (1937) · J. P. Ray, *The Battle of Britain: new perspectives* (1994) · *WWW, 1961–70*
Archives PRO · Royal Air Force Museum, Hendon, corresp. and MSS | Herts. ALS, corresp., with extensive corresp. and papers of his wife · Royal Air Force Museum, Hendon, Geoffrey Salmond MSS; Trenchard MSS | FILM BFI NFTVA, news footage | SOUND IWM SA, oral history interview
Likenesses F. Dodd, charcoal and watercolour drawing, 1917, IWM · L. F. Roslyn, bronze bust, 1921, IWM · W. Stoneman, two photographs, 1928–53, NPG · H. Coster, photographs, 1929, NPG · L. F. Roslyn, sculpted head, exh. RA 1940 · C. J. Orde, portrait, Royal Air Force Club · M. Smith, portrait, priv. coll. · photographs, repro. in Laffin, *Swifter than eagles*
Wealth at death £10,244: probate, 1 Nov 1968, *CGPLA Eng. & Wales*

Salomon, Johann Peter (*bap.* 1745, *d.* 1815), violinist and impresario, was born in Bonn, where he was baptized on 20 February 1745. His father, Philipp Salomon, was a violinist at the court of the elector of Cologne. At the age of thirteen he joined the court orchestra, where his colleagues included Beethoven's father and grandfather. In 1764 he moved to Rheinsberg, north-west of Berlin, to become music director to Prince Heinrich of Prussia, a post he held until 1780.

Salomon arrived in London during the winter of 1780–81 and soon became a much sought after orchestral leader and occasional soloist in the increasingly cosmopolitan and competitive musical life of the city. During the summer months he took part in concerts in Dublin, Oxford, and Winchester. In the autumn of 1790 Salomon travelled to Vienna to persuade Joseph Haydn to visit London, where he was to compose an opera for the King's Theatre and be the central attraction in a new subscription series of concerts set up by Salomon. With Salomon's support and encouragement Haydn made two visits to London, in 1791–2 and 1794–5; however, contemporary plans to invite Mozart and Beethoven never came to fruition. Haydn's visits placed Salomon at the very centre of musical life in London and mark one of the most musically significant

Johann Peter Salomon (*bap.* 1745, *d.* 1815), by Thomas Hardy, *c.*1791

periods in the cultural history of the city. In 1791, 1792, and 1794 Salomon's concerts were held in the Hanover Square Rooms; in 1795 Salomon merged his patronage with that of the management of the King's Theatre to form the Opera Concert, held in the concert room that abutted the stage of the theatre. The principal legacy of these four seasons was the twelve 'London' symphonies, nos. 93–104, sometimes referred to as the 'Salomon' symphonies. As well as their unprecedented musical energy, wit, and brilliance, there is the occasional affectionate dig at the violinist and impresario who had effected their composition; for instance, Haydn writes a solo for Salomon in the trio section of symphony no. 97, but indicates that it should be played quietly ('Salomon ma piano'). Other major works by Haydn that were given their first performance in London by Salomon and his colleagues included the symphonie concertante and the six quartets, opp. 71 and 74. Towards the end of Haydn's second visit Salomon gave the composer a libretto for an oratorio, *The Creation*, which he hoped would be written for London; in the event, the work was composed and first performed in Vienna.

Although Salomon was to remain an influential figure in the musical life of London until the end of his life, he was never to recapture the pre-eminence of the early 1790s. Without the presence of Haydn or someone of equivalent stature, he found it difficult to organize successful subscription concerts and three attempts, in 1796, 1801, and 1808, were only moderately successful. In the 1801 season Salomon presented Beethoven's septet (op. 20) for the first time in London, played from manuscript parts supplied by the composer. He skilfully profited from his association with Haydn, hiring out the manuscript

parts of the 'London' symphonies, publishing small-scale arrangements of the symphonies before, finally, allowing the full orchestral parts to be published. However, his desire to present the London première of *The Creation* in 1800 was thwarted by his rival, John Ashley, who gave the work three weeks before Salomon managed to organize his performance.

Salomon was an occasional composer only whose output consisted of some stage works, songs, and violin music. His most ambitious work was *Windsor Castle*, an English opera written to celebrate the marriage of the prince of Wales in 1795.

In his old age Salomon preferred private music-making to the public arena and led the life of a society gentleman. He never married. In 1813 he was one of the founder members of the Philharmonic Society; he was also a leading figure in the attempt to establish a national academy of music in London. After a riding accident in the summer of 1815 he endured a painful illness of several months until his death from dropsy at 70 Newman Street, Oxford Street, London, on 25 November. He was buried on 2 December in the south cloister of Westminster Abbey.

DAVID WYN JONES

Sources Grove, *Dict. mus.* (1904–10) · [W. Ayrton], 'Memoir of Johann Peter Salomon', *The Harmonicon*, 8 (1830), 45–7 · H. Unverricht, 'Die Kompositionen Johann Peter Salomons: ein Überblick', *Studien der Musikgeschichte des Rheinlandes*, 3 (1965), 35–42 · H. C. Robbins Landon, *Haydn in England: 1791–1795* (1976), vol. 3 of *Haydn: chronicle and works* · A. Tyson, 'Salomon's will', *Studien der Musikgeschichte des Rheinlandes*, 3 (1965), 43–5

Likenesses W. Beechey, oils, 1784, U. Oxf., faculty of music · T. Hardy, oils, *c.*1791, Royal College of Music, London [*see illus.*] · G. Dance, drawing, *c.*1794, Royal College of Music, London · G. Facius, stipple, pubd 1807 (after W. Owen), NPG · W. Daniell, soft-ground etching, pubd 1810 (after G. Dance), BM, NPG · W. Lane, group portrait, chalk, Royal College of Music, London · W. Lane, group portrait, chalk study, Royal Collection · attrib. T. Lawrence, oils, Garr. Club

Wealth at death £1200—house, shares, and property: will, Tyson, 'Salomon's will'

Salomon, Sir Walter Hans (1906–1987), banker, was born in Hamburg on 16 April 1906, the elder son and second of three children of Henry Salomon, personal banker, and his wife, Rena Oppenheimer, from Vancouver. He was educated at the Oberrealschule, Eppendorf, Hamburg. He left at sixteen, partly because he upset its authorities by campaigning against a master active in extreme right-wing politics and partly to be independent of his father, who wanted him to sacrifice football to music.

Salomon joined Bachach & Co., a small private bank, and became a partner at twenty-eight. He studied part-time at Hamburg University but, disillusioned by philosophy asking but not answering questions, did not take a degree. Asked to train as a middle-distance runner for the Olympics, he declined lest it delayed his career progression. In 1935 he married Kate, daughter of Walter Jacoby, sugar merchant. They had a son and a daughter.

Quickly recognizing the full implications of Nazi policy for Jewish people, Salomon began in ingenious ways transferring funds for himself and his clients to London and New York. In 1937 he was investigated by the Gestapo and ordered to repatriate those funds. He immediately flew to London. His wife escaped across the Swiss border when security was slack at Christmas, and her parents joined them in London. Salomon's family escaped to Chile.

In London Salomon formed Walter H. Salomon & Co., a private banking company, largely servicing other refugees. When war began he was interned near Liverpool and spent his time learning Spanish. If hard at work, he skipped roll-calls, asking a friend to answer for him since 'they're English, not German'. He was soon released and spent the rest of the war combining banking and helping to run a wartime factory. In 1946 he obtained British citizenship.

In 1948, by reverse take-over, Salomon merged his business with the small merchant bank Rea Brothers, which became the hub of all his business activities for the rest of his life. He quickly became dominant in it, being its chairman from 1950 to 1984. He ran it on traditional German private banking lines, emphasizing confidentiality, personal commitment, and detailed control from the top. As well as accepting business from England, he built strong links with clients in Germany and Brazil. In 1971 he became a commander of the Southern Cross of Brazil and in 1979 Germany gave him an officer's cross of the Order of Merit.

Over the years, Salomon became closely involved as adviser, director, or chairman with many other companies, particularly Furness Withy, Ocean Wilsons, Canal-Randolph, and Scottish and Mercantile.

In 1967 Rea Brothers was accepted into the prestigious Accepting Houses Committee, the only bank for generations to obtain this status without taking over an existing member. In the committee Salomon showed little newcomer's diffidence, quickly becoming its most vociferous member. Frequently he hectored and irritated, but his views were never ignored. When talking, he often raised his left shoulder, turning his head to the right; many in the committee affectionately copied this gesture while passing on his latest *obiter dicta*.

In 1963 Salomon demonstrated his belief in practical education by founding Young Enterprise, to teach young people business. Thirty years later 28,000 youngsters of school age throughout Britain were involved in 2000 Young Enterprise companies. For this he was knighted in 1982.

As his status in the City grew, Salomon became a prolific writer and commentator on public affairs, passionately proselytizing for individual freedom and against interference by government in business. His views were contained in his *One Man's View* (1973) and *Fair Warning* (1983), the latter a collection of essays. Although actively involved with the Liberal Party in the 1950s, he later became an ardent supporter of Margaret Thatcher, who valued his advice and individuality. Nevertheless, he fought bitterly against her government's imposition of new regulatory bodies on financial companies. He believed 'fonctionnaires' could not understand banking and threatened its cornerstone of secrecy.

Salomon was immensely proud of winning in 1964 a three-year battle in the courts with the customs, recovering £15 18s. excess duty on a camera. In private life, he was devoted to his family. He was an active club man, master of the Pattenmakers' Company in 1977–8, keen on tennis and snooker, and excellent at bridge. He skied until late in life, enjoyed his large yacht, and built an outstanding collection of paintings, mainly of French Impressionists. He was slim, trim, and well proportioned, with an air of confident distinction. In town he always wore a bowler hat and a red carnation in his buttonhole. He died at his home in London, Flat 1, Castlemaine House, 21–2 St James's Place, on 16 June 1987, and was buried at Ohlsdorf in Hamburg. George Blunden, *rev.*

Sources *The Times* (20 June 1987) · *The Independent* (19 June 1987) · private information (1996) [wife, son, son-in-law] · personal knowledge (1996) · *CGPLA Eng. & Wales* (1987)

Wealth at death £9,706,549 in England and Wales: probate, 19 Nov 1987, *CGPLA Eng. & Wales*

Salomons, Sir David, baronet (1797–1873), banker and politician, was born in London on 22 November 1797, the second son of Levy Salomons, a stockbroker whose family was of Dutch Ashkenazi Jewish (German and Polish) origin, and Matilda de Metz, of Leiden.

At the age of twenty-six Salomons joined the London stock exchange, becoming in time an authority on joint-stock banking, and one of its chief exponents. At that period (and since the early eighteenth century) banks could only operate on the partnership principle. However, in 1826, in response to a campaign in which Salomons played a prominent part, the government permitted joint-stock banks to operate beyond a 65 mile radius from London; subsequently, at Salomons's suggestion, joint-stock banks were permitted to operate in the capital, but lost the right (subsequently restricted to the Bank of England) to issue notes. The consequent flourishing of joint-stock banks in London was due in no small measure to Salomons's efforts. In 1832 he became one of the founders of the London and Westminster Bank (of which he was chairman from 1859 to 1867), the first joint-stock bank in the capital; two years later he commenced business as an underwriter. By then he had acquired a well-deserved national reputation as an expert on currency and banking matters.

On 18 April 1823 Salomons married Jeanette Cohen (d. 1867), a niece of both Nathan de Rothschild and Sir Moses *Montefiore (1784–1885). To his own family's wealth, therefore, was added that brought by his wife. Salomons thus found himself at the very heart of the 'cousinhood'—the coterie of exceedingly wealthy, interrelated families which constituted the lay leadership of Anglo-Jewry during the struggle for legal and political emancipation in the mid-nineteenth century. At its heart sat Moses Montefiore, whose religious fundamentalism was not at all to Salomons's liking. Montefiore supported Chief Rabbi Solomon Hirschell and his successor, Nathan Marcus Adler, in giving priority to the survival of Orthodox Jewish practice, and in attempting to suppress the movement for the establishment of Reform Judaism in England; Jewish

Sir David Salomons, baronet (1797–1873), by Charles Turner,
pubd 1837 (after Mary Martha Pearson)

emancipation they viewed as of secondary importance. Salomons put emancipation—by which he meant absolute equality before the law—top of the agenda. He was opposed to the establishment of Jewish schools, arguing that these hindered the process of acculturation, a necessary prerequisite of emancipation. In October 1838 he was elected as the first Ashkenazi president of the London Committee (later Board) of Deputies of British Jews, but resigned less than a month later in protest against the policy (orchestrated by Montefiore) of excluding Reform Jews from membership of it: Salomons argued that the Jews could not demand equality with the gentiles while denying it to fellow Jews who happened to be reformers.

Salomons had, meanwhile, commenced on his own account a highly idiosyncratic campaign to achieve emancipation. In 1830 the common council of the City of London had permitted professing Jews to become freemen of the City, and thus members of the City livery companies. In recognition of his charitable work Salomons was admitted liveryman of the Coopers' Company, and in 1835 he was elected one of the two City sheriffs, obliging parliament to legislate to enable him to enter office without having to take a Christian form of oath. In 1838, together with Moses Montefiore and J. M. Montefiore, he became one of the first Jewish magistrates, and the following year he was appointed high sheriff of Kent without having to take the prescribed declaration. He had meanwhile, made two attempts to gain admittance to the court of aldermen of the City of London (1835 and 1844), but, although elected in the Liberal interest, was denied his seat because

he objected to the form of oath. In 1845 parliamentary opponents of Jewish emancipation permitted the passage into law of Lord Lyndhurst's Act enabling professing Jews to hold municipal office, hoping thereby to deflect the campaign for admission to parliament. Salomons was at once admitted as a City alderman, becoming in 1855 the first Jewish lord mayor of London.

In 1847 five professing Jews, of whom Salomons was one, stood for election to parliament. Salomons had contested Shoreham, unsuccessfully, in 1837, and Maidstone, unsuccessfully, in 1841. In 1847 he again stood, without success, at Greenwich, but his cousin, Lionel de Rothschild, was elected for the City of London. Between 1847 and 1857 Rothschild was elected MP for the City no fewer than five times; on each occasion he refused to swear the oath of abjuration 'on the true faith of a Christian', and was thus unable to take his seat in the Commons. Salomons employed a very different tactic. In June 1851 he was returned for Greenwich at a by-election. Far from refusing to take the oath he merely omitted the offending words, took his seat, voted in three divisions during the debate which followed, and only then agreed to withdraw.

This conduct led to the imposition of a severe statutory fine on Salomons as well as various civil penalties, but he had succeeded in having the issue of principle brought to the forefront of political debate. Although he lost his Greenwich seat at the general election of 1852, the minority Conservative government led by the earl of Derby and Benjamin Disraeli sponsored an act relieving him of the civil disabilities the courts had imposed. More importantly, Conservative moderates searched for ways of meeting Jewish claims for political equality, while satisfying the die-hards. In 1858 another Derby–Disraeli minority government legislated to permit each house of parliament to decide for itself the form of oath to be administered to a Jewish politician. Lionel de Rothschild took his seat in the Commons on 26 July 1858. At the general election of 1859 Salomons was also returned to parliament, for the Greenwich constituency which he continued to represent until his death. He sat as a Liberal (from 1868 with W. E. Gladstone as his co-member) for what was an increasingly radical borough.

Salomons's first wife died in 1867. On 23 September 1872 he married Cecilia, daughter of Samuel Moses Samuel and widow of P. J. Salomons. There were no children of either marriage. He was created a baronet in 1869. He died at his house at 26 Great Cumberland Place, Hyde Park, London, on 18 July 1873, and was buried at the West Ham cemetery of the United Synagogue on 23 July.

GEOFFREY ALDERMAN

Sources A. M. Hyamson, *David Salomons* (1939) · C. Bermant, *The cousinhood: the Anglo-Jewish gentry* (1971) · G. Alderman, *The Jewish community in British politics* (1983) · *Jewish Chronicle* (25 July 1873), 277–9 · *The Times* (23 July 1873), 5 · d. cert. · *DNB*
Archives NRA, priv. coll., books, mementoes, papers | BL, letters to W. E. Gladstone, Add. MSS 44379, 44400, 44406, 44416, 44420, 44422, 44428, 44432 · BL, corresp. with Sir Robert Peel, Add. MSS 40414–404609 · W. Sussex RO, letters to duke of Richmond

Likenesses C. Turner, mezzotint, pubd 1837 (after M. M. Pearson), AM Oxf., BM, NPG [*see illus.*] · engraving (after portrait), U. Southampton, Anglo-Jewish archive, MS 187 · photograph, repro. in Bermant, *The cousinhood* · woodcuts, NPG

Wealth at death under £160,000: probate, 27 Aug 1873, *CGPLA Eng. & Wales*

Salomons, Sir David Lionel Goldsmid-Stern-, second baronet (1851–1925), mechanic, was born on 28 June 1851, at 18 Brunswick Terrace, Hove, Sussex, only son of Philip Salomons (1796–1867), gentleman-at-arms, and his wife, Emma Abigail (1830–1859), daughter of Jacob Montefiore, merchant of Sydney, New South Wales. He had two younger sisters. He was educated privately at Brighton, and attended University College, London, before reading the natural science tripos at Gonville and Caius College, Cambridge (BA 1873). In 1873 he succeeded by special remainder (dated 1869) his uncle, Sir David *Salomons, as second baronet, and inherited the Broomhill estate near Tunbridge Wells. In 1874 he was called to the bar at the Middle Temple and was unsuccessful Liberal parliamentary candidate for Mid Kent. He contested St George-in-the-East as a Liberal in 1885, but seceded from that party in 1910 and was a convinced tariff reformer by 1912. He was active in Kentish affairs, as a magistrate (1874), high sheriff (1881), and mayor of Tunbridge Wells (1895), and serving for fifteen years on the county council. He succeeded another Kentish landowner, Lord Brabourne, on the board of the South Eastern and Chatham Railway (1895), and was a director of its successor, Southern Railway (1922). Salomons's life was, however, notable less for his public and official services than for the distinction of his private avocations.

From the earliest age Salomons played with clockwork engines, building blocks, and tools. In adolescence he wandered around Clerkenwell and Soho looking into tool shops. At the age of fourteen he befriended a working watchmaker who taught him practical mechanics: he retained a lifelong interest in watchmaking, became a member of the Clockmakers' Company, and published a monograph in 1921 on the French watchmaker Breguet, of whose work he amassed a large collection. After his succession to the baronetcy he installed private workshops, laboratories, and electricity at Broomhill in 1874, and investigated electromotive force and electric conductors in association with Sir Charles Wheatstone. In 1876 he built a waterworks at Broomhill and fitted a telescope to its water-tower. Within a few years he had thousands of tools in his workshop and was constantly devising experiments. He took out patents for railway signalling, electric lamps, current meters, electric circuits, electric magnets, pressure gauges, vacuum tubes, electric torches, and electromotor apparatus. He was one of the founders of the Institution of Electrical Engineers, serving as vice-president and treasurer, but, as a non-professional electrical engineer, he was judged ineligible for its presidency. His textbook, *Electric Light Installations*, passed through eleven editions during the 1880s and 1890s. Salomons was first chairman of the City of London Electric Lighting Company established in 1891 with an electric-lighting franchise for the City of London and the St Saviour's district of Southwark.

As well as his lifelong delight in gadgetry Salomons enjoyed tandem and four-in-hand driving. In 1874 he built a tricycle powered by a 2 hp electric motor, and later imported from France the second petrol-driven car to appear in England. He organized trial demonstrations of early automobiles from 1895 (Lord Salisbury was nervous on a joyride with Salomons at Crystal Palace), and as president of the Self-Propelled Traffic Association was instrumental in removing the legal restrictions which until 1896 compelled horseless carriages to be preceded by a man waving a red flag. Salomons was a founder of the Royal Automobile Club and wrote pamphlets, articles, and lectures on motor cars, including a chapter 'The motor stable and its management' in the volume on motoring edited by Lord Northcliffe for the Badminton Library series. He later developed a comparable interest in aviation.

Salomons had a practical as well as theoretical interest in radium, and made donations of radium and radioactive equipment to several hospitals. He gave monetary or other endowments both to Cambridge colleges and to learned societies. He served on the jury of the Universal Exhibition at Paris in 1900 and donated the pavilion to exhibit contemporary British art at the Venice Exhibition of 1909.

The versatility of Salomons's interests is attested to by the many learned societies that honoured him. He was a fellow of the Royal Astronomical, Chemical, and Geological societies and of the Physical Society of London. He was a gold medallist of the Royal Photographic Society, an associate member of the Institution of Civil Engineers, an honorary member of the International Society of Electricians, president of the Society of Engineers (1901), and honorary colonel of the Kent (fortress) Royal Engineers. He was master of the Coopers' Company in 1893. His sponsors for the Athenaeum in 1901 were Lord Alverstone, Lord Avebury, A. J. Balfour, Joseph Chamberlain, and Lord James of Hereford.

Salomons married in 1882 Laura Julia (1855–1935), younger daughter of Hermann de Stern, a London banker and Portuguese baron, and sister of the first Baron Michelham. He assumed by royal licence the surname of Goldsmid-Stern-Salomons in 1899. He had one son (Reginald, who died at Gallipoli) and four daughters. He died after an operation on 19 April 1925, in a nursing home at 4 Dorset Square, St Marylebone, and was buried in his family's private chapel ground at Lower Green, Tunbridge Wells. His baronetcy became extinct. His will included bequests to Gonville and Caius College, to Cambridge University, and to the Bibliothèque Nationale in Paris.

RICHARD DAVENPORT-HINES

Sources *The Times* (21 April 1925) · *The Times* (25 April 1925) · A. M. Hyamson, *David Salomons* (1939) · D. Salomons, *Breguet* (1921) · D. Salomons, *Catalogue of the library at Broomhill* (1909) · D. Salomons, *Motor traffic* (1897) · *CGPLA Eng. & Wales* (1925) · b. cert. · Burke, *Peerage*

Archives Salomons, Broomhill Road, Southborough, Kent, notebooks, papers | LUL, Simms corresp. · Veteran Car Club of Great Britain, letters to F. R. Simms and papers

Likenesses photograph, *c.*1920, repro. in Hyamson, *David Salomons*, facing p. 109

Wealth at death £388,412 19s. 6d.: probate, 19 June 1925, *CGPLA Eng. & Wales*

Salomons, Edward (1828–1906), architect, was born in London, the sixth of fourteen children, seven sons and seven daughters, of German-Jewish cotton merchant Henry Moses Salomons (1794–1874) and his wife, British-born Priscilla Lucas (1801–1886). Salomons's parents were married on 27 January 1819. The family moved from London to 54 Plymouth Grove, Chorlton-on-Medlock, Cheshire, in 1837 and the name of Edward Salomons later became identified with the city of Manchester, where he lived and worked for the rest of his life.

Salomons was educated by tutors at home and may also have attended school in Manchester. After a short spell working in his father's warehouse, from 1850 he studied architecture at the Manchester School of Design, a rare career option for a Jewish boy in the period immediately before Jewish political emancipation (1858). While still a student he played a conspicuous part in creating an elaborate 'Cosmorama' of scenery and sculpture at the Free Trade Hall in 1850—judged by the *Manchester Guardian* to be the first attempt 'to render a place of amusement attractive to the higher and purer resources of genuine art' (Williams, 199). In 1851–2 Salomons was articled to the Scottish architect John Edgar Gregan (1813–1855), an exponent of the newly fashionable 'Italian' *palazzo* style for the warehouses springing up all over the city. Afterwards he was a draughtsman in the office of Henry Bowman (1814–1881) and Joseph Stretch Crowther (1832–1893) and drew and lithographed many illustrations for their *The Churches of the Middle Ages*.

Salomons became an associate of the Royal Institute of British Architects (RIBA) on 28 April 1851. He set up his own practice in King Street about 1853 and was elected a fellow of the RIBA on 19 March 1860. He worked in flexible partnerships with John Philpot Jones, John Ely (1848–1915), Ralph Selden Wornum (1847–1910), Alfred Steinthal (1859/60–1928), and Nathan S. *Joseph. As well as being active on the RIBA council in London, Salomons was deeply involved in the cultural life of 'Cottonopolis'. He was a founder of the Manchester Society of Architects and served twice as its president. He was a member of the council of the Royal Manchester Institution and for nearly twenty years was its honorary secretary. He was on the council of Manchester School of Art and on the City Art Gallery committee, set up to promote the establishment of a free public art gallery. He was elected to the Manchester Academy of Fine Arts in 1859. Salomons relaxed by painting watercolours and exhibited accomplished topographical British and continental scenes at the Manchester City Art Gallery, Mosley Street (1901), Messrs Grundy and Smith's Gallery, Exchange Street (1902), and at the Royal Academy in London.

Salomons's architectural practice was successful and wide-ranging; it embraced numerous commercial warehouses, some banks, shops, and theatres. He was an acknowledged expert on theatre building, and delivered a paper on the subject before the RIBA in March 1871. He also built villas for wealthy clients in both town and country. His best-known building in Manchester is the Reform Club, King Street (1870–71; with John Philpot Jones); the Art Treasures Exhibition Hall, Old Trafford, of 1857, owing an obvious debt to Crystal Palace, was somewhat more ephemeral. Salomons won competitions held for these and other projects; by contrast, he came nowhere in the important competition for Manchester town hall, won by Alfred Waterhouse in 1867. Salomons never went in for full-blooded Gothic. Notwithstanding the opinion of *The Builder* that 'this gentleman seems to go in for a new style in every building he erects' (Stewart, 52–3). Salomons was most at home in the Italianate and the Romanesque.

As the son of an acculturated German Jew, Salomons became a founder member of the Manchester Reform Synagogue and, indeed, was responsible for the congregation's so-called 'Byzantine' building on Park Place, Cheetham (1857–8), destroyed in the blitz in 1941. He collaborated with Nathan Joseph on the Bayswater Synagogue in London (1862–3). He designed the Manchester Jews' School in Derby Street (1868–9), which replaced an Italianate predecessor (1850–51) by J. E. Gregan, and it is quite possible that Salomons, as his pupil, had had a hand in this earlier work. In 1873–4 he designed the delightful Spanish and Portuguese Synagogue, York Street (now Cheetham Hill Road), in appropriate Moorish style, which survives as the Manchester Jewish Museum.

Jewish commissions notwithstanding (he is only known ever to have designed one church, Hope Congregational Church, at Denton in 1876), Salomons in his personal life moved away from Judaism. He married two gentile women in succession. First, in 1863 he married Carlotta Marion Montgorry (or Montgarry), of Liverpool, with whom he had two sons, both of whom died of typhoid in 1894. After her death he married Gertrude Bruce Roberts on 11 September 1877, with whom he had three more children, a daughter and two sons, the youngest of whom, Gerald (also an architect), changed his name to Sanville and joined the local parish church. After Edward Salomons died at his home, Ireton Bank, Platt Lane, Rusholme, Manchester, on 12 May 1906, he was cremated according to Christian rites at the southern cemetery, Manchester, the impressive Romanesque chapel of which he had also designed (1891–2). His second wife survived him. The *Jewish Chronicle* did not honour him with an obituary, merely noting, with some exaggeration: 'Mr Edward Salomons, FRIBA, who died on Saturday in Manchester was born a Jew, but never identified himself with the Jewish community'. SHARMAN KADISH

Sources biography file, RIBA BAL · *Dir. Brit. archs.* · R. H. Harper, *Victorian architectural competitions: an index to British and Irish architectural competitions in The Builder, 1843–1900* (1983) · *The Builder* (19 May 1906), 560 · *Jewish Chronicle* (18 May 1906) · *Manchester City News* (19 May 1906) · *Manchester Guardian* (15 May 1906) · *RIBA Journal*, 3rd ser., 13 (1905–6), 393–4 · R. Beenstock, 'Edward Salomons, 1828–1906: Manchester architect', BA diss., Manchester Metropolitan University, 1993 · R. Beenstock, 'Edward Salomons: a sociable architect', *Manchester Region History Review*, 10 (1996), 90–95 · E. Jamilly, 'Anglo-Jewish architects, and architecture in the 18th and 19th centuries', *Transactions of the Jewish Historical Society of England*, 18 (1953-5), 127-41 · J. J. Parkinson-Bailey, *Manchester: an architectural history* (2000) · C. Stewart, *The architecture of Manchester: buildings and their architects, 1800-1900* (1956) · W. B. Tracy and W. Pike, *Contemporary biographies: Manchester and Salford at the close of the 19th century*, 2 (1899), 219 · B. Williams, *The making of Manchester Jewry, 1740-1875* (1976)

Archives RIBA BAL, biographies file

Likenesses photograph, 1899, repro. in Tracy and Pike, *Contemporary biographies*, vol. 2, p. 219

Wealth at death £4243 8s. 6d.: probate, 10 July 1906, CGPLA Eng. & Wales

Salomons, Sir Julian Emanuel (1835-1909), lawyer and politician in Australia, born at Edgbaston, Birmingham, on 4 November 1835, was the only son of Emanuel Solomons, a Jewish merchant of that city, and his wife, née Levien. After emigrating to Australia in 1853, he obtained clerical employment in Sydney before becoming secretary of the Great Synagogue there. Sydney's Jewish community assisted his return to England to read for the bar. He changed the spelling of his name and entered at Gray's Inn on 14 October 1858. He was called to the bar on 26 January 1861 and, on returning to New South Wales, was admitted to the colonial bar on 8 July 1861. On 17 December 1862 he married his cousin Louisa (d. 1912), the fourth daughter of Maurice Solomons of Lower Edmonton, Middlesex.

Salomons practised with success, especially at common law, often being counsel for the crown. A brilliant lawyer, he amalgamated analytical reasoning with aggressive advocacy, masterly cross-examination, and witty and prompt repartee. His successful application in 1866 that Henry Louis Bertrand be granted a new trial on his conviction of the murder of a bank clerk established Salomons's reputation in criminal cases. But in all matters, civil or criminal, he worked to the point of physical exhaustion and mental prostration.

Salomons was an appointed member of the legislative council from 5 August 1870 until he resigned on 15 February 1871. He was reappointed on 7 March 1887, and took a prominent part in debates until 21 February 1899, when he again resigned. He was solicitor-general from 1869 to 1870, and representative of the government in the council with a seat in cabinet from 11 August to 15 December 1870. From 7 March 1887 to 16 January 1889 he was vice-president of the executive council and representative of Henry Parkes's ministry in the upper house; he held the same office in George Dibbs's ministry from October 1891 to January 1893. In all these positions he showed little interest in factional politics. He took a prominent part in the Australian federation campaign, but opposed the Commonwealth Enabling Bill.

Salomons took silk on 18 February 1881. In that year, as royal commissioner inquiring into the Milburn Creek Copper Mining Company scandal, he reported that trustees had defrauded their co-shareholders—as a result of which report the responsible minister was expelled from parliament. In 1886 Salomons accepted appointment as, and was gazetted, chief justice on the death of Sir James Martin; but owing to some public hostility, the resistance

of the bar, and the reservations of fellow judges who questioned his stability of mind he resigned without sitting or being sworn in.

Knighted by patent on 13 July 1891, Salomons was from 1899 until his death a bencher of Gray's Inn. He acted in London as agent-general for New South Wales from 25 March 1899 to 13 May 1900, and on his return to Australia he built up a substantial practice in the new high court from 1903, including holding a general retainer from the commonwealth government. He was intellectually equal, if not sometimes superior, to the foundation high court justices. His recreational interests included travel, collecting paintings, and studying natural history. He was a trustee of the National Art Gallery of New South Wales and a member of the local Linnean Society. He died at his home, Sherborne, in Woollahra, Sydney, on 6 April 1909, survived by his wife and two daughters, and was buried in the Jewish part of Rookwood cemetery.

CHEWTON ATCHLEY, rev. J. M. BENNETT

Sources J. M. Bennett, 'Sir Julian Salomons: fifth chief justice of New South Wales', *J. Royal Aust. Hist. Soc.*, 58 (1972), 101 and annotations · S. Edgar and B. Nairn, 'Salomons, Sir Julian', *AusDB*, vol. 6 · J. M. Bennett, *Portraits of the chief justices of New South Wales, 1824-1977* (1977) · *New South Wales parliamentary record*, New South Wales Parliament (1905) · P. Serle, *Dictionary of Australian biography*, 2 vols. (1949) · R. Travers, *The amorous dentist* (1977) · *The Times* (7 April 1909) · *Sydney Morning Herald* (7 April 1909) · *Sydney Mail* (7 April 1909) · *Sydney Daily Telegraph* (7 April 1909) · *Sydney Daily Telegraph* (9 April 1909) · d. cert., Registrar-general of New South Wales · *DNB*

Archives Mitchell L., NSW, Sir William Windeyer MSS

Likenesses P. Bigland, portrait; formerly in possession of his daughter, Mrs J. T. Wilson · oils, Supreme Court of New South Wales

Wealth at death £34,813: probate, New South Wales · £160 11s. 2d.: administration with will, 29 Dec 1909, CGPLA Eng. & Wales

Salote Mafile'o Pilolevu Tupou III (1900-1965), queen of Tonga, was born on 13 March 1900 in Nuku'alofa, Tonga, the first daughter and eldest legitimate child of King Taufa'ahau Tupou II (1874-1918), king of Tonga, and his wife, Lavinia Veiongo (1879-1902). Salote's father was the great-grandson and successor of the founder of the modern kingdom of Tonga, Siaosi Taufa'ahau Tupou I (1797-1893). Salote's mother was descended from the Tongan aristocracy, being the granddaughter of the noble Fotofili and great-granddaughter of Laufilitonga, the last tu'i Tonga (1797-1865), the highest-ranking Tongan male under the former dispensation. From 1900 Tonga was a British protectorate.

Salote was baptized in the Free Church of Tonga which had emerged from the Wesleyan Methodist mission in the reign of Tupou I. Although her mother died when Salote was two, she was given a traditional upbringing suitable for an aristocratic woman, rather than the training that might fit her for the monarchy. After her father remarried in 1909, a marriage which also produced only daughters, Salote was sent to be educated in Auckland, New Zealand, where she remained until she was fifteen. By this time her father's declining health highlighted the question of Salote's marriage. Although by the Tongan constitution Salote would succeed her father, the general presumption was that whoever she married would become king. The

Salote Mafile'o Pilolevu Tupou III (1900–1965), by Thurston Hopkins, 1953

choice of husband was of paramount importance, and the selection fell on Viliame Mailefihi (William) Tuku'aho (1887–1941), who had inherited the title of Tungi, and represented one of the senior lineages in the Tongan ranking system. He was indeed third in line of succession to the throne after Salote herself and her surviving half-sister. Tungi and Salote married on 19 September 1917. Tupou II died on 5 April 1918 at the age of forty-three, a few weeks after Salote's eighteenth birthday. She succeeded her father as Tu'i Kanokupolu (installation 9 October 1918) and was crowned queen on 11 October 1918. Contrary to earlier expectation, her husband became not king but prince consort.

The most pressing problem facing the new queen was securing the stability of the dynasty and the nation, and some years elapsed before she developed the political acumen to control the dissident nobles. There were critics also among the small resident European population, among whose leaders were expatriate civil servants whose loyalty to both the government and the crown were slight. Her strongest political assets for the first twenty years of her reign were the aristocratic fear of British annexation in the event of serious instability, combined with the moral support and advice of the successive holders of the position of British consul and agent, Islay McOwan and James Scott Neill. Her position became somewhat more secure after 1923 when her husband became premier.

With the fear of British annexation limiting how far her inherited enemies would attempt to destabilize the dynasty, Salote's strategy was to avoid confrontation with the dissidents while cultivating the next generation. This she did by arranging strategic marriages which bound them more closely to the dynasty, and by offering educational opportunity. Her outlook was not democratic: she believed that those who were entitled to lead by breeding and rank should be made fit to rule by education. This principle was applied to her own family pre-eminently. Both surviving sons were sent to Australia for secondary schooling, like selected other well-born Tongans, but the princes alone went on to tertiary education. The elder son, Taufa'ahau (b. 1918), studied for degrees in arts and laws at the University of Sydney, and the younger, Ngu (1922–1998), studied agriculture in Queensland.

This strategy of élite education had a secondary purpose: to free Tonga in general, and the monarchy in particular, from reliance on expert advice from expatriate employees. Some of the previous reign's political difficulties had arisen from expatriate interference, and Salote herself found some of her senior expatriate officials uncooperative and critical. The last serious challenge to her authority was made by a new chief justice, W. H. Stuart, in 1939 and 1940.

The unwavering support and guidance of consuls McOwan and Neill had confirmed in Salote's outlook a firm loyalty to the British crown, a sentiment reinforced in 1932 by her appointment as a dame commander in the Order of the British Empire. On the outbreak of war in 1939 she pledged Tonga's support for Britain, placing all Tonga's resources at British disposal. The queen and her consort took an active part in organizing a Tongan defence force and nursing training in case battle casualties should occur in or be brought to Tonga. Salote personally sponsored fund-raising campaigns for the St John Ambulance, Red Cross, and the 'Sponsor a Spitfire' scheme. From her own resources she gave £200 a year to such causes. Her loyalty was recognized in her elevation to dame grand cross in the Order of the British Empire in 1945.

The Second World War was a watershed in Salote's reign. After her husband's premature death on 20 July 1941 and her elder son's return from Sydney at the end of 1942, there was a perceptible increase in Tongan political energy. Taufa'ahau inherited his father's title and was known as Tungi until he ascended the throne in 1965. He immediately became the driving force in cabinet for more progressive development policies, and for greater investment in education and public health. By this time also, many of the old enemies of the dynasty had died, and their successors were the beneficiaries of Salote's policies of reconciliation of the 1930s.

Queen Salote came to international notice most prominently during her attendance at the coronation of Elizabeth II in London in June 1953. Later that year she was appointed dame grand cross in the Royal Victorian Order. She was tremendously popular with the British press and public, and travelled extensively in Britain and Europe before returning home.

In her old age Salote continued to perform her royal duties, which included an active role in the affairs of government, but she concerned herself mostly with matters of public welfare. Public appearances were rare from the mid-1950s, perhaps because of her declining health. She was diagnosed with diabetes at that time, and in 1964 was found to have cancer. She died at the Aoetea Hospital, Epsom, Auckland, on 16 December 1965. Her body was taken back to Tonga and buried in the royal cemetery (Mala'e Kula) at Nuku'alofa on 23 December. A few weeks before her death she received a further British honour, dame grand cross in the Order of St Michael and St George.

The length of Queen Salote's reign, forty-seven years, permitted her to overcome the opposition both to her dynasty and to her own accession, and during the final third of her life she was looked on as the mother of her country, to which she had brought unity, stability, and peace. Salote was also passionately devoted to the survival of Tongan culture which she saw as a vehicle for a limited form of modernization. She was herself an authority on all aspects of Tongan culture, especially of genealogy and history, and was a poet and composer of the highest order. She was survived by two sons (her second son, Tuku'aho, having died at the age of sixteen in 1936), the elder succeeding her as King Taufa'ahau Tupou IV.

I. C. CAMPBELL

Sources E. Wood-Ellem, *Queen Sālote of Tonga: the story of an era, 1900–1965* (1999) · M. Hixon, *Sālote, queen of paradise* (2000) · I. C. Campbell, *Island kingdom: Tonga ancient and modern*, 2nd edn (2001) **Archives** Palace Office Archives, Nuku'alofa, Tonga · University of Auckland Library, Bott-Spillius collection | FILM BBC Film and Video Archives | SOUND BBC Sound Archives **Likenesses** T. Hopkins, photograph, 1953, Hult. Arch. [*see illus.*] · photographs, repro. in Wood-Ellem, *Queen Sālote* · photographs, repro. in Hixon, *Sālote*

Salt, Dame Barbara (1904–1975), diplomatist, was born at Oreville, California, on 30 September 1904, the second of three daughters of Reginald John Salt, banker, and his wife, Maud Fanny, daughter of Robert Wigram, of Broomfield, Weybridge, Surrey. Her grandfather was Sir Thomas Salt, chairman of Lloyds Bank and member of parliament for Stafford. The family returned to England shortly after her birth and settled at The Close, North Place, Headington, Oxford. She was educated privately and at the Downs School, Seaford, Sussex. She then studied at the universities of Cologne and Munich, where she obtained a diploma in psychology and a fluent command of the German language.

From 1933 to 1938 Salt worked as a secretary in England. In 1940, still as a secretary, she joined the Special Operations Executive (SOE), where her ability was soon recognized. From 1942 to 1946 she served in the SOE office in Tangier, first as assistant head and from 1944 as head. She was appointed MBE following her retirement from SOE, in 1946.

In November 1946, armed with an introduction from Sir Charles Peake, British ambassador in Athens, which Lord Gore-Booth later described as containing 'the highest praise and enthusiasm for the bearer as I have ever seen, before or since' (*The Times*, 6 Jan 1976), Salt secured an appointment as temporary first secretary in the United Nations department of the Foreign Office. In 1949 she passed second in the open competition for principals in the home civil service. She was invited to join the Treasury, but she chose instead to join the foreign service. In 1950 she was appointed first secretary (commercial) in Moscow, but her post was soon abolished, as an economy measure, and Salt herself returned to England with infectious hepatitis. In July 1951 she was appointed first secretary in Washington, and in 1955 she was promoted counsellor *sur place*. In 1956 she was offered, but declined, the post of head of the United Nations department in the Foreign Office.

In 1957 Salt was appointed counsellor and consul-general at Tel Aviv, acting on a number of occasions as chargé d'affaires. This was the case when the Iraq crisis broke in 1958 and it was decided to send British troops to Jordan. On 17 July she was instructed to obtain immediate permission for the Royal Air Force to overfly Israel. Her handling of this delicate negotiation earned her a message of thanks and congratulation from Harold Macmillan. She was promoted CBE in 1959.

In 1960, with the rank of minister, Salt was appointed deputy head of the United Kingdom combined disarmament and nuclear tests delegation to the United Nations at Geneva. A year later she was appointed United Kingdom representative to the Economic and Social Council of the United Nations in New York. In these two posts she suffered severely from migraine but coped with the work admirably.

It was decided in April 1962 that Salt should be appointed ambassador to Israel. This was the first time that a woman was appointed to a British ambassadorial post. Sadly, shortly after the announcement of her appointment, she developed thromboses which did not respond to treatment. In 1963, in successive operations, both her legs were amputated. Her appointment to Israel was cancelled, although she was able to draw some small comfort from her advancement to DBE in June 1963.

Salt bore pain, disablement, and disappointment with fortitude. She resumed work as soon as she had made herself mobile, serving on civil service selection boards and updating the handbook on etiquette for young diplomats. She took a particular interest in the training of new recruits to the diplomatic service. In 1963–4 she led the United Kingdom delegation in financial negotiations with Israel, and in 1966 she led the United Kingdom delegation to the Anglo-Romanian negotiations. From 1967 to 1972 she was head of the SOE section of the Foreign and Commonwealth Office, engaged in historical research covering the period of the Second World War.

Salt was the first woman in the history of the British diplomatic service to become counsellor, minister, and ambassador-designate. Although her diplomatic career was interrupted by ill health, her achievements were by any reckoning considerable. In particular, she did much to break down the prejudice against women which imbued the diplomatic and other services. Colleagues frequently recalled her strength of character, her determination and (especially after the tragedy which prevented her becoming Britain's first woman ambassador) her courage.

Salt retired from the Foreign Office in early 1973, and devoted herself to various good causes. She died at her home, 17B Montagu Square, London, on 28 December 1975. A memorial service was held in her honour in the crypt chapel, St Paul's Cathedral, on 28 January 1976.

ALEX MAY

Sources *DNB* · *The Times* (31 Dec 1975) · *The Times* (6 Jan 1976) · *WWW* · private information (1986) · *FO List* · personal knowledge (1986) [*DNB*] · *CGPLA Eng. & Wales* (1976)
Wealth at death £51,348: probate, 3 Feb 1976, *CGPLA Eng. & Wales*

Salt, Henry (1780–1827), traveller and collector of antiquities, was born at Lichfield, Staffordshire, on 14 June 1780, the youngest of the eight children of a Lichfield surgeon, Thomas Salt, and his wife, Alice, *née* Butt. He was educated at schools in Lichfield and Market Bosworth, and under the tutelage of his brother John Butt Salt MD in Birmingham. Having decided to be a portrait painter he studied first in Lichfield under John Glover, the watercolour artist, then, from 1797, in London under Joseph Farington, then under John Hoppner. However, despite a talent for catching likenesses, his skills were not sufficient to gain him the success he craved.

On 20 June 1802 Salt left England on an eastern tour, as secretary and draughtsman to Viscount Valentia (later the earl of Mountnorris). He visited India, Ceylon, and the Red Sea, and in 1805 was sent by Valentia on a mission into Abyssinia, to the ras of Tigré, whose affection and respect he gained, and with whom he left one of his party, Nathaniel Pearce. The return to England in 1806 was made by way of Egypt, where he first met the pasha, Mehmet Ali. Lord Valentia's *Travels in India* (1809) was partly written and completely illustrated by Salt, who published his own *24 Views in St Helena, India and Egypt* in the same year.

On 2 March 1809 Salt sailed on a mission from the British government to Abyssinia, to carry presents to the king and report on the state of the country. Owing to factious unrest, he was prevented from going to the king at Gondar and was obliged to deliver the presents instead to the ras of Tigré. While in Abyssinia he made many observations on the geography, the customs of the people, and the flora and fauna. He brought back many specimens, including a previously unknown dik-dik. Another member of Salt's party, William Coffin, chose to remain in Abyssinia when Salt returned to England in 1811. In 1812 Salt became a fellow of the Royal Society and of the Linnean Society, and a correspondent of the Institut de France. In 1812 he was elected one of the very few honorary members of the African Association in acknowledgement of information he

Henry Salt (1780–1827), by unknown engraver (after John James Halls)

had procured in its interest. In 1814 he published *A Voyage to Abyssinia*, which was received with some acclaim.

In June 1815 Salt was appointed consul-general in Egypt; leaving England in August, he made a tour through France, Switzerland, and Italy before arriving at Alexandria in March 1816. He formed a good relationship with Mehmet Ali, the viceroy of Egypt, and was able on many occasions to influence his conduct, not least in persuading him not to invade Abyssinia in 1820, and in 1826–7 to consider withdrawing his forces from the Morea during the Greek uprising. The pasha made no final decision and the Egyptian and Turkish fleets were destroyed ignominiously in Navarino Bay.

Salt did much to further knowledge of ancient Egypt through excavation and studying inscriptions. In 1816, together with John Lewis Burkhardt, he employed Giovanni Belzoni to remove the colossal bust of Rameses II (the 'young Memnon') from Thebes. They presented the bust to the British Museum, where it still dominates the Egyptian gallery. In 1817 he employed Belzoni to open the great temple of Abu Simbel. In 1818 Salt and William Bankes discovered and copied down a very early Greek inscription on the legs of one of the colossi before that temple. With others he funded Captain Caviglia's researches in connection with the great pyramid, the sphinx, and the surrounding tombs. He made drawings at the sites, particularly of the sphinx, excavated from the sands possibly for the first time in at least 1500 years and then re-covered to protect it from the elements. After 1819, when Belzoni returned to England, Giovanni d'Athanasi became Salt's chief agent in the collection of antiquities.

In June 1818 Salt enclosed in a private letter to William Richard Hamilton of the Foreign Office a list of a collection he wished to offer to the British Museum, unfortunately with tentative (as he stressed) prices attached. Thoughtlessly, Hamilton showed the priced list to Sir Joseph Banks, who had previously encouraged Salt to collect for the nation. Although Salt's prices now appear modest, Egyptian antiquities were not then highly valued, and he was accused of being 'a second Lord Elgin'. The British Museum trustees avoided making a decision to purchase for several years. Salt reckoned the collection had cost him £3000 to assemble, but eventually, on 13 February 1823, Salt's agent, Bingham Richards, felt obliged to accept £2000, excluding an alabaster sarcophagus discovered by Belzoni in the tomb of Seti I in the Valley of the Kings. This was later bought by Sir John Soane for a further £2000, and is now in the Soane Museum in Lincoln's Inn Fields, London. Salt felt that he had been treated shabbily by the British Museum trustees. He was prepared to present his second collection of some 4000 objects directly to the British government in return for a pension, but, on receiving a generous offer from the French government, sold it to them for £10,000 in April 1826. This collection was, like all Salt's collections, of 'exceptional variety and quality', and included the great sphinx of Tanis, and the painted male bust, probably of the reign of Amenophis IV, but often dated some 1000 years earlier, to the Egyptian Old Kingdom, known as the 'Salt head', which remains a prized possession of the Louvre.

In 1824 a lengthy and rather pedestrian poem by Salt, entitled *Egypt*, was published in Alexandria, the first book in English to be published in Egypt. He published in 1825 an *Essay on Dr Young and M. Champollion's Phonetic System of Hieroglyphs*. Although some of his conclusions are now known to be erroneous, Champollion, who was working along the same lines, expressed his respect for the work of 'an English savant' who was advancing 'an impartial and reflective view', using 'the entire monuments of Egypt'. He praised Salt's important contribution of three further letters in the hieroglyphic alphabet. Experts still have a high regard for the accuracy of Salt's reproductions of hieroglyphs.

Henry Salt was 6 foot tall, a personable man, cultured, a good conversationalist, and possessed of a dry sense of humour. He is remembered in many contemporary accounts as a kind and helpful host to British travellers and scholars in Egypt. He married, in Alexandria, in October 1819, the daughter of Signor Pensa, a merchant of Leghorn. Only one of the four daughters born to them survived his wife's death on Good Friday 1824; this child was sent to Italy to be brought up by her grandmother. Salt himself, who had suffered periodic ill health for a large part of his life, died of disease of the spleen at the village of Desuke, on the Nile near Alexandria, on 29 or 30 October 1827. He was buried in Alexandria in the garden of his house.

A third collection of antiquities formed by Salt was sold, under the direction of d'Athanasi, at Sothebys in 1835, and realized £7168 16s. 6d., of which £4500 was for artefacts purchased by the British Museum.

DEBORAH MANLEY and PETA RÉE

Sources J. J. Halls, *The life and correspondence of Henry Salt*, 2nd edn, 2 vols. (1834) · H. Salt, *A voyage to Abyssinia* (1814) · G. d'Athanasi, *Brief account of the researches … in Upper Egypt* (1836) · R. Hallett, ed., *Records of the African Association, 1788–1831* (1964) · C. Ziegler, *The Louvre: Egyptian antiquities* (1990) · *GM*, 1st ser., 98/1 (1828), 374 [or 21/1 new ser.] · D. Manley and P. Rée, *Henry Salt: artist, traveller, diplomat, Egyptologist* (2001) · R. R. Madden, *The infirmities of genius* (1833)
Archives BL, corresp. and papers, Add. MSS 19338, 19419–19420, 19343, 54195 | BL, Annesley MSS, Add. MS 19347 · CUL, African Association MSS · NL Scot., corresp. with Archibald Constable · PRO, corresp. with Straford Canning, FO 352 · PRO, FO MSS, 78/various
Likenesses J. Hoppner, portrait, *c.*1800, priv. coll. · drawing, 1815, priv. coll. · drawing, *c.*1826, priv. coll. · stipple (after J. J. Halls), BM, NPG [*see illus.*]

Salt, Henry Shakespear Stephens (1851–1939), classical scholar and publicist, was born in Naini Tal, India, on 20 September 1851, the son of Thomas Henry Salt, lieutenant in the Bengal artillery, and his wife, Ellen Matilda *née* Allnat. He was a king's scholar at Eton College (1866–71) and went in 1871 to King's College, Cambridge, where he was a Browne's medallist (Greek epigrams) in 1874 and gained a first in the classical tripos in 1875 (BA 1875). From 1875 to 1884 he taught classics at Eton.

In 1884, disenchanted with his life at Eton—he alleged Eton masters 'were but cannibals in cap and gown' (Venn, *Alum. Cant.*)—Salt decided to live at Tilford in Surrey and concentrate on a simple vegetarian life, following his many interests in the field of humanitarianism. For the next thirty-five years he published a spate of pamphlets and books on the subjects about which he felt strongly and the authors whom he admired deeply or disagreed with emphatically. In 1888 he published *Flesh or Fruit? An Essay on Food Reform* and in 1892 *Animals' Rights Considered in Relation to Social Progress. The Ethics of Corporal Punishment* appeared in 1907 and he returned to this theme in 1916 in *The Flogging Craze: a Statement of the Case Against Corporal Punishment*.

In 1891 Salt published a pamphlet entitled *Humanitarianism*, a subject on which he frequently lectured, since it embraced all those matters about which he held strong opinions. In that year he founded the Humanitarian League, which became a channel for the promotion of his ideas. He worked as its honorary secretary until its demise in 1919 when, according to his own view in his *Seventy Years among Savages* (1921), 'It ended as it began in its character of Forlorn Hope; we had the good will of the free-lances, not of the public or the professors'. Salt in his care for natural beauty and condemnation of the spoliation of the countryside was in advance of his time.

In politics Salt was a socialist and became a member of the Fabian Society shortly after it was founded in 1884. He had a wide variety of friends, including J. Ramsay MacDonald, W. H. Hudson, and M. K. Gandhi. In one of his letters to Salt Gandhi wrote that he had become a confirmed vegetarian after reading Salt's essays published under the title *The Logic of Vegetarianism* (1897).

In the preface to Stephen Winsten's *Salt and his Circle* (1951) G. B. Shaw said that 'Salt was a born naturalist and never went out of doors without a binocular to watch the birds'. Salt himself expressed his love of natural beauty in books such as *On Cambrian and Cumbrian Hills: Pilgrimages to Snowdon and Scawfell* (1908) and *Our Vanishing Wild Flowers* (1928).

Salt's biographies and works of literary criticism include *The Life of Henry David Thoreau* (1890), *Tennyson as a Thinker: a Criticism* (1893), *Percy Bysshe Shelley: Poet and Pioneer* (1896), and *De Quincey* (1904). He could not resist the urge to criticize the Eton of his time; hence *Eton under Hornby: some Reminiscences and Reflections* (1910) and *The Nursery of Toryism: Reminiscences of Eton under Hornby* (1911). He also continued to demonstrate his early understanding of classical authors by translations of Lucretius (1912) and his masterly verse translation of Virgil's *Aeneid* (1928).

In 1879 Salt married Catherine Leigh Joynes (*d.* 1919), author of studies of Shelley, De Quincey, and Richard Jefferies, the daughter of the Revd James Leigh Joynes, a master at Eton. According to Salt's friend George Bernard Shaw, she refused to sleep with her husband and had a number of affairs with her women friends. In 1927 Salt married Catherine, daughter of Frederick Mandeville of Brighton. Salt died at Brighton Municipal Hospital, Elmgrove, Brighton, on 19 April 1939, survived by his second wife. H. F. OXBURY, rev.

Sources *The Times* (20 April 1939) · S. Winsten, *Salt and his circle* (1951) · Eton, archives · H. S. Salt, *Company I have kept* (1930) · H. S. Salt, *The nursery of toryism: reminiscences of Eton under Hornby* (1911) · H. S. Salt, *Seventy years among savages* (1921) · Venn, *Alum. Cant.* · BL OIOC

Archives NRA, corresp. and literary papers | BL, letters to George Bernard Shaw, Add. MS 50549 · Bodl. Oxf., letters to Bertram Dobell · JRL, letters to W. E. A. Axon · Lincs. Arch., corresp. with R. W. Goulding relating to botanical subjects · Sheff. Arch., letters to Edward Carpenter

Wealth at death £1761 1s. 9d.: probate, 7 July 1939, CGPLA Eng. & Wales

Salt, Samuel (*d.* 1792), lawyer and benefactor of Charles Lamb, was a son of John Salt, vicar of Audley in Staffordshire. He was admitted at the Middle Temple in 1741 and at the Inner Temple in 1745, and was duly called to the bar in 1753. In 1782 he was raised to the bench at the Inner Temple, and became reader in 1787 and treasurer in 1788. Charles Lamb says that he had:

> the reputation of being a very clever man, and of excellent discernment in the chamber practice of the law. I suspect his knowledge did not amount to much … It was incredible what repute for talents Salt enjoyed by the mere trick of gravity. (HoP, *Commons*)

Through the influence of the family of Eliot, whose legal agent he was, Salt was returned to parliament in 1768 for their pocket boroughs of St Germans and Liskeard, Cornwell, and preferred to sit for the latter constituency. He represented Liskeard during the three parliaments from 1768 to 1784 (having from 1774 to 1780 Edward Gibbon as his colleague), and sat for Aldeburgh in Suffolk from 1784

to 1790. In politics he was a whig. 'He was a shy man', says Lamb, 'indolent and procrastinating', very forgetful and careless in everything, but 'you could not ruffle Samuel Salt'.

Salt's wife died in 1747 and he never remarried, although Lamb claimed that 'he was pursued unsuccessfully by Susannah Pierson, a sister of one of his fellow benchers' (Prance, 299).

John Lamb, father of Charles Lamb, the 'Lovel' of the essay on the Inner Temple benchers, was Salt's clerk for nearly forty years. Charles was born in Crown Office Row, where Salt 'owned two sets of chambers', and it was the home of the Lamb family until 1792. He procured the admission of Charles to Christ's Hospital, and made himself answerable for the boy's discharge, giving a bond for the sum of £100. Through Salt's influence as a director of the South Sea Company, Charles and his elder brother obtained clerkships under the company, and in his will Salt made provision for his old clerk and his wife. Salt was also a governor of Christ's Hospital and other hospitals, including the Foundling Hospital.

Salt died at his chambers at 2 Crown Office Row, Inner Temple, on 27 July 1792, and was buried in a vault of the Temple Church. A shield with his coat-of-arms was placed in the sixteenth panel (counting from the west) on the north side of the Inner Temple hall.

W. P. COURTNEY, rev. MICHAEL BEVAN

Sources C. A. Prance, *Companion to Charles Lamb: a guide to people and places, 1760–1847* (1983) · HoP, *Commons, 1754–90*, vol. 3 · GM, 1st ser., 62 (1792), 678

Wealth at death £500 in South Sea stock to John Lamb; £200 to Mrs Lamb; legacies to Susannah Pierson: Prance, *Companion*

Salt, Sir Titus, first baronet (1803–1876), textile manufacturer and politician, was born on 20 September 1803 in the Old Manor House, Morley, near Wakefield, Yorkshire, the eldest of the five surviving children of Daniel Salt (1781–1843) and Grace Smithies. Daniel was a man of considerable business experience who in 1822 moved to Bradford, where he set up as a wool-stapler. It was at that time that Bradford was becoming pre-eminent as the international centre of the worsted trade. Titus Salt was educated at Batley grammar school and Wakefield, where he displayed the talent for hard work and the reticence which were characteristic of him throughout his life. At the age of seventeen he was apprenticed to a wool-stapler in Wakefield. After moving to Bradford he studied the textile trade for two years with William Rouse & Sons, and in 1824 joined his father's firm, which became known as Daniel Salt & Son. He remained with his father for ten years, and then started his own business. In 1829 he married Caroline, the youngest daughter of George Whitlam, a wealthy sheep farmer of Grimsby. They had eleven children, of whom two died in infancy and one at the age of twenty; of the survivors, the most important was Titus junior, who took over the family business and died at the early age of forty-five.

While Salt was in partnership with his father the firm successfully specialized in the sale of *Donskio* wools from

Sir Titus Salt, first baronet (1803–1876), by William Holl (after Appleton & Co.)

eastern Europe, a product which, until then, was considered unsuitable for the worsted industry. However, the chief problem for the Bradford manufacturers in the 1830s was the production of mixed rather than all-wool fabrics. Salt concentrated on material made from alpaca and mohair combined with cotton or silk. Working in secrecy, he overcame the technical difficulties by 1839. The resulting cloth proved very popular for women's dress fabrics. With two or three others, Salt effectively dominated the alpaca market and made a fortune.

By 1850 Salt had five separate mills and employed large numbers of outworkers. He was widely respected as a good employer and an outstanding, occasionally ruthless, businessman, as well as one of the most prominent of Bradford citizens. A devout member of the Congregational church, he contributed generously to many charitable causes. As one of the leading radical Liberals in a notably politicized town, Salt occupied every leading public office except that of poor-law guardian. He was Bradford's second mayor in 1848–9 and in 1859 was elected one of its members of parliament. He was MP for two years but never spoke in a debate, having a reputation as a poor public speaker. Nevertheless, his contemporaries deferred to him for his quickness of perception and intelligent pragmatism, qualities which were needed as Bradford passed through the painful processes of urbanization and industrialization, gaining a national reputation for its environmental squalor and propensity to riot and as a centre of radical politics.

In 1850 Salt decided to transfer his business to a new mill and build a model village for the workforce. He called the site Saltaire. It was 3 miles from Bradford on the bank of the River Aire, adjoining the Leeds and Liverpool Canal and the Leeds–Bradford–Skipton railway. The mill, covering acres, was the largest of its kind in the world when it was opened in 1853, and was an integrated works combining on a single site all the manufacturing processes which would turn alpaca into cloth. The village was constructed when the mill was complete. By 1871 there were 4300 inhabitants living in 824 houses, all, directly or indirectly, reliant on Salt for their livelihoods. None of the houses were back-to-backs, they were generally slightly bigger than the norm, all were connected to mains drainage, and nearly all had their own lavatory. Each house had sun and light, and the streets were open-ended. Generous amenities were also provided. There was a school; an institute, which served as a mechanics institute and community centre; almshouses; a Congregational church and a Methodist chapel; baths and a wash-house; and a park. The Salt family also encouraged sporting and recreational activities in the village.

Saltaire caught the Victorian imagination, and Salt came to personify the best of contemporary capitalism. The enterprise was considered a remarkable experiment in industrial and social relations. Laudatory articles appeared in numerous papers and magazines, where the community was seen as a practical solution to the pressing social concern of the day: the relationship between labour and capital. Salt was eulogized; he was decorated by Emperor Napoleon III and in 1869 was created baronet. A few commentators were derogatory. Of contemporary critics John Ruskin was the most damning, and others suggested that the village provided Salt with a captive labour force, or that he was doing no more than a good employer should.

Salt's motives in building Saltaire remain obscure. They seem to have been a mixture of sound economics, Christian duty, and a desire to have effective control over his workforce. There were economic reasons for moving out of Bradford, and the village did provide him with an amenable, handpicked workforce. Yet Salt was deeply religious and sincerely believed that, by creating an environment where people could lead healthy, virtuous, godly lives, he was doing God's work. Perhaps, also, diffident and inarticulate as he was, the village may have been a way of demonstrating the extent of his wealth and power. Lastly, he may also have seen it as a means of establishing an industrial dynasty to match the landed estates of his Bradford contemporaries. However, Saltaire provided no real solution to the relationship between employer and worker. Its small size, healthy site, and comparative isolation provided an escape rather than an answer to the problems of urban industrial society.

A few years after the completion of Saltaire, on 29 December 1876, Salt died at his house, Crow Nest, Hipperholme, Halifax. His funeral was one of the great civic events of Victorian Bradford, with over 100,000 people lining the streets as the procession moved to his burial place in Saltaire Congregational Church. It was a remarkable demonstration of the respect in which he was held by all his contemporaries. DAVID JAMES

Sources J. Reynolds, *The great paternalist: Titus Salt and the growth of nineteenth-century Bradford* (1983) · R. Balgarnie, *Sir Titus Salt, baronet, his life and its lessons* (1877); repr. (1970) · R. Reynolds, 'Reflections on Saltaire', *Model industrial communities in mid-nineteenth century Yorkshire*, ed. J. A. Jowitt (1986), 43–71 · J. Styles, *Titus Salt and Saltaire: industry and virtue* (1990) · W. Alderson, *Salt and Saltaire* (1988) · I. Bradley, 'Titus Salt, the enlightened entrepreneur', *History Today*, 37/5 (1987), 30–36 · *Saltaire: an introduction to the village* · J. Reynolds, *Saltaire: an introduction to the village of Sir Titus Salt* (1977) · R. W. Suddards, ed., *Titus of Salts* (1876) · B. Allsopp, *The late Sir Titus Salt bart., founder of Saltaire, a brief resumé of his life and works* (1887) · [W. Cudworth], *Saltaire, Yorkshire, England: a sketch history with brief description of its origin and later developments* (1895) · A. Holroyd, *Saltaire and its founder, Sir Titus Salt bart.* (1873)
Archives University of Bradford, J. B. Priestley Library, daybook · W. Yorks. AS, Bradford, Salt and Saltaire MSS
Likenesses J. Adams-Acton, statue, Lister Park, Bradford · J. Adams-Acton, marble bust, Bradford City Art Gallery · W. Holl, stipple (after photograph by Appleton & Co. of Bradford), NPG [*see illus.*] · F. D. Wood, statue, Roberts Park, Saltaire, Yorkshire · chromolithograph, NPG · medallion, Bradford Wool Exchange · wood-engraving (after photograph), NPG; repro. in *ILN* (2 Oct 1869)
Wealth at death under £400,000: probate, 27 Oct 1877, *CGPLA Eng. & Wales*

Salt, William (1808–1863), antiquary, born on 29 October 1808, was the third son of John Stevenson Salt (1775–1845) of 9 Russell Square, London, and Weeping Cross, Stafford, a member of the firm of Stevenson, Salt & Co., bankers in London and Stafford, and his wife and cousin, Sarah Stevenson (*d.* 1848). He was educated at Dr Morris's school at Brentford, Middlesex, from 1815 until 1825, when his father took him into the family bank. He later became a junior partner.

From the early 1830s Salt devoted much of his spare time to antiquarian pursuits. He became a fellow of the Society of Antiquaries in 1842 and a member of the British Archaeological Association in 1844. He amassed a large collection of printed royal proclamations, broadsides, and private acts of parliament, from which he made extensive gifts to the library of the British Museum and that of the Society of Antiquaries. The only work he published was *A list and description of the manuscript copies of Erdeswick's survey of Staffordshire; which, after a careful inquiry, have been traced in public libraries, or private collections* (1842–3). Only twenty copies were issued, but it was included by Thomas Harwood in the preface to his second (1844) edition of Erdeswick's *Survey*. Salt spent thirty years collecting books, pamphlets, maps, drawings, and manuscripts illustrative of the history of Staffordshire; he also commissioned work in the county from topographical artists such as John Buckler and employed researchers to transcribe or calendar Staffordshire items in some of the major national collections. Shortly before his death he arranged for the sorting and indexing of the wills in the probate office at Lichfield. On 29 October 1854 he married Helen, daughter of Thomas Black; the marriage was childless. The Salts lived in Park Square East, Regent's Park, London, where William died suddenly, apparently after a heart attack, on 6 December 1863. He was buried in Highgate cemetery.

In 1868 Salt's widow put his collection up for auction at Sothebys but was persuaded to cancel the sale and instead to offer the collection to Staffordshire as a gift. In 1870 an appeal was launched in the county for funds to house and endow it, and in 1872 the William Salt Library was established at Stafford in a house given by Salt's nephew, Thomas Salt MP. The collection has since been greatly augmented by gifts and purchases.

In Salt's memory the William Salt Archaeological Society was established at Stafford on 17 September 1879, with the object of editing and printing original documents relating to the county of Stafford in a series of volumes of 'Collections for a History of Staffordshire'. The society remains in existence as the Staffordshire Record Society.

D. A. JOHNSON

Sources T. J. Pettigrew, *Journal of the British Archaeological Association*, 20 (1864), 186–8 · M. W. Greenslade, *The Staffordshire historians*, Staffordshire RS, 4th ser., 11 (1982), 136–50 · Coll. Arms, Salt MSS · *The Examiner* (12 Dec 1863) · *The Times* (9 Dec 1863) · m. cert.
Archives Coll. Arms · William Salt Library, Stafford, corresp. and papers | Ches. & Chester ALSS, banking corresp.
Likenesses watercolour, William Salt Library, Stafford
Wealth at death under £30,000: will, 1 Aug 1864, *CGPLA Eng. & Wales*

Salter [*née* Brown], **Ada** (1866–1942), socialist and pacifist, was born on 20 July 1866 at Raunds, Northamptonshire, the second daughter of the three daughters and a son of Samuel Brown, a farmer, and his wife, Sarah Ekins, both of them Wesleyan Methodists. In her late twenties she left her comfortable home to join the West London Mission, at first out of a spirit of religious evangelism, but once there she developed a sense of serious social purpose. In 1897 she transferred to the Bermondsey settlement, recently founded by John Scott Lidgett, as the worker in charge of girls' clubs. The girls were 'rough and tough'—ragpickers, wood-choppers, tin smiths in the local factories, who sometimes arrived drunk at the club. Her gentleness and affectionate concern for them won many of them over to her own values of kindness and a responsiveness to beauty, even in their grim world.

In 1899 Ada Brown startled her friends and family by becoming engaged to a revolutionist five years younger than she—the settlement's militant socialist, pacifist, agnostic teetotaller, Dr Alfred *Salter (1873–1945). Very soon she was as enthusiastic as he for radical political, social, and economic change in a Britain of poverty and chronic unemployment. On 22 August 1900 they were married. As the wife of a poor people's doctor, who charged only 6*d.* (or even nothing) for a consultation, Ada Salter willingly led a life of altruistic self-denial herself. They first lived in two rooms above the surgery in Jamaica Road, and later moved to 5 Storks Road, Bermondsey, whose unlovely situation and aspect Ada so startlingly transformed that thirty years later she was invited to write in *The Lady* in 1940 about her garden in Bermondsey. Dr Alfred Salter worked from early morning until late at night—seeing up to sixty patients in an evening; meanwhile Ada did unpaid social work among the poorest families he discovered in his practice as well as continuing her work with the settlement girls and beginning her political life with the then reformist Liberal Party, becoming president of the Rotherhithe Women's Liberal Association.

The Salters began their lifetime practice of reserving the hours between 11 p.m. and 1 a.m. for their quiet time together, Alfred's ebullient idealism that could suddenly sink into acute depression being balanced by Ada's steadiness and serenity. They had one child, Joyce, born in June 1902. Very soon they were faced by the supreme challenge to their social conscience: should they protect their only child from the dirty, verminous, sick children of Bermondsey and eventually send her away to a Quaker boarding-school? They felt they could not give her the chance denied to the unprivileged slum children around them and Joyce attended the local Keeton's Road School. Twice she caught scarlet fever. In 1910 Joyce was attacked by the disease for a third time and on 10 June she died. 'Ada's sadness never quite left her' (Brockway, 43). Thereafter both parents dedicated themselves with even more commitment to the needs of the poorest parents and children in London.

In May 1908 the Salters gave up their promising political career prospects with the Liberal Party in order to found the first branch of the young Independent Labour Party (ILP) in Bermondsey, and in November 1909 Ada Salter was the sole ILP candidate returned and the first woman borough councillor to be elected in London. Though widely expected to support the Progressive (radical Liberal) bloc on the council, she declined to vote with the Progressives 'unless my conscience or my own [ILP] organization so direct' (*Southwark and Bermondsey Recorder*, 12 Nov 1909). Her refusal to support the Progressive aldermanic slate at the first meeting of the elected councillors allowed the Conservatives to retain control of the finely balanced council and ensured her ostracism from the Bermondsey Liberals, who denied her election to the housing and public health committees. She none the less developed her own municipal agenda: she hoped one day to introduce gardens and beautiful parks as well as maternity and child welfare centres into Bermondsey. In August 1911, when the whole working population of Bermondsey went on strike for decent employment conditions, it was Ada Salter who organized free meals for the women and children (as she would again in the 1926 dockers' strike, when she served as treasurer to the London Dock Strike Fund). Her first spell as a Bermondsey councillor ended with defeat in the 1912 elections.

The First World War was a second tragic challenge to the Salters. As declared pacifists they had to witness the destruction not only of their idealistic vision of the international working class but also of much of their own welfare work for the London poor. They also had their house attacked by enraged stone-throwing mobs and Ada had to give long hours of work as trusted treasurer of the maintenance department of the No-Conscription Fellowship, supporting impoverished families of imprisoned conscientious objectors. The Salters purchased and used Fairby Grange in Kent as a convalescent home for released, weakened conscientious objector prisoners. One such ex-prisoner, the Jamaican carpenter Isaac Hall,

reduced by mistreatment to a skeleton, was nursed by the Salters themselves and housed for nine months in their own home. In 1915 Ada Salter was accepted into the Religious Society of Friends, remaining a Quaker to the end of her life. At the end of the war she represented the British section of the Women's International League for Peace and Freedom in Zürich and Vienna, bringing back hungry Austrian women and children to recuperate at Fairby Grange.

Ada Salter returned to Bermondsey council in 1919, one of many Labour and Progressive beneficiaries of a leftward swing that overturned the long-established Conservative control of the borough. Re-elected three years later, she was chosen to be the first woman Labour mayor both in London and in the British Isles. (Dr Garrett Anderson had been the first woman mayor, of Aldeburgh, in 1908.) She refused to wear the mayoral robes or chain of office or to impose chaplain-led prayers on the council, instead starting meetings with a Quaker-style service. The interwar years saw Bermondsey council fall under virtually unchallenged Labour control, but the wider social ambitions of the Labour majority were generally thwarted by the inadequate resources of an exclusively working-class borough. The most enduring feature of Labour Bermondsey would prove to be the environmental politics pioneered by Ada Salter. A lifelong gardener, she created the council's beautification committee (chairing it between 1923 and 1925) to promote the 'greening' of Bermondsey. In due course it planted 9000 trees and 60,000 plants in the hitherto dreary borough, and created two unlikely sounding species of dahlia—the 'Bermondsey Gem' and the 'Rotherhithe Gem'. She struggled to convert churchyards into the only open spaces for children's recreation and to substitute cottage housing for the worst slums. The Wilson Grove estate, on the site of the Salisbury Street slum, displayed silver birches, cottages, and climbing roses within yards of Tower Bridge. Wilson Grove was intended to be the first instalment of a wider programme to replace slums with cottages. The project was given a fair wind by the short-lived Labour government of 1924, but in the long run this attempt to apply environmentalism to housing policy implied residential densities so low as to create major rehousing problems. It was consequently unacceptable both to the London county council (LCC) and to the Ministry of Health, which dispensed the housing subsidies on which a poor borough depended: no subsequent cottage-estate proposals in the borough would be endorsed by Whitehall, and Bermondsey would instead be covered by tenement blocks.

Ada Salter's other principal council work was in the field of public health: together with her husband and other Labour colleagues she introduced several health clinics and a solarium to fight tuberculosis. These resulted in a drop in infant mortality and an even greater fall in maternal mortality in the borough. Though she remained a borough councillor until her death, Ada Salter also served as a Bermondsey guardian in the 1920s and as a London county councillor from 1925. She was elected first for the southern division of Hackney, where the local Labour

Party was run by Herbert Morrison, once a protégé of Alfred Salter in the pre-war ILP, but in 1928 she moved to home territory in West Bermondsey, the only constituency of the LCC to be represented by two women. This was also Alfred Salter's seat in parliament, but by now the charge once levelled against Ada that she was her husband's puppet carried no weight. She saw herself as 'not a militant feminist or a pioneer or anything like that' (*Evening News*, 25 July 1939), but she had been prominent, with Margaret MacDonald and Mary McArthur, in early attempts to found women's branches of trade unions and had served on the executive of the Women's International League. Her municipal programme in 1934, when Labour finally gained control of the LCC (and she secured the highest Labour vote), was marked by an emphasis upon domesticity characteristic of female local politicians of the period—'in the affairs of State is needed the unselfish spirit of the good mother who considers the happiness and well being of all the members of her household rather than the aggrandisement of some' (*South London Press*, 8 Dec 1942). She laid an equally characteristic stress upon the personal social services, calling for the humane administration of relief and a unified medical service for London separate from the poor law. She appealed to the female voter, hoping to 'induce the home-loving woman to serve the community as she serves her family by helping to secure a Labour majority' (*Daily Herald*, 28 Feb 1934). As vice-chair of the LCC's parks committee, she continued to pursue her environmentalist objectives, identifying herself with the Labour advocates of a green belt policy, eventually secured in 1938.

The Second World War was a tragic horror to both the Salters. Once again isolated as pacifists, even within the Labour Party, they lost many of their Bermondsey friends in the blitz, as well as their lifelong home. But worse still was the descent of the world into competitive barbarism once more. Ada struggled to hold her faith—and to convince her despairing husband—that the ultimate victory must, one day, be that of the forces of creativity and kindness. She died in Balham, London, from cerebral thrombosis on 5 December 1942, and was cremated at Camberwell crematorium five days later. Alfred was overwhelmed by the hundreds of written tributes to her from all over Britain. The Quaker James Hudson wrote:

> by her faith in the people for whom she laboured [she brought] ennoblement of spirit. ... They revered her. ... They often saw her frail figure threading its way on cycle through their streets. ... They knew of her investigations, her encouragements, her committees without end. ... Socialism in action; that is what she was. (*Friends' Quarterly Examiner*, 1 March 1943, 12)

Over forty years earlier Alfred Salter had written to his wife: 'You and I ... are living and working for the same goal—to make the world, and in particular this corner of the world, happier and holier for our joint lives' (Brockway, 16). The Old English Garden in Southwark Park, the railings of which she had vainly attempted to save from being turned into Spitfires, had been commonly known as 'Mrs Salter's Garden' during her lifetime and was formally renamed the Ada Salter Garden in 1958. In 1960 the ashes of Ada and Alfred Salter were moved to a vault in a children's playground in Coxon Place, Bermondsey.

SYBIL OLDFIELD

Sources F. Brockway, *Bermondsey story: the life of Alfred Salter* (1949) • *The Friend* (18 Dec 1942) • J. F. Hudson, *Friends' Quarterly Examiner*, 77 (1943), 11–14 • J. Vellacott, *Bertrand Russell and the pacifists in the First World War* (1980) • b. cert. • m. cert. • P. Hollis, *Ladies elect: women in English local government, 1865–1914* (1987) • S. Goss, *Local labour and local government: a study of changing interests, politics and policy in Southwark, 1919 to 1982* (1988) • *South London Press* (8 Dec 1942)

Likenesses photograph, c.1938, repro. in Brockway, *Bermondsey story*

Salter, Alfred (1873–1945), medical practitioner and politician, was born at 23 South Street, Greenwich on 16 June 1873, the son of Walter Hookway Salter and Elizabeth Jester. His father was an administrative officer with the Metropolitan Gas Company. Salter's childhood and adolescence were economically secure; his family's growing prosperity was indicated by a move to Lewisham Hill. His early experiences were also deeply religious. Initially the family were Wesleyans but later joined the Plymouth Brethren. At the age of nine Salter joined the Band of Hope; his commitment to temperance would be lifelong. Educated at the Roan School in Greenwich, Salter became a medical student at Guy's Hospital in 1889. His student career was outstanding. In 1895 he took triple first-class honours in the MB and was awarded the gold medal. The following year he came first in the MD examination and again took the gold medal. In 1897 he became house physician and resident obstetric physician at Guy's, and Joseph Lister appointed him bacteriologist to the British Institute of Preventive Medicine. His talent was apparent in a range of research papers published in British and German journals. He seemed destined for a prestigious and lucrative career.

Salter's strong ethical sense drove his career in a very different direction. During his student years he had been attracted to socialism and had joined the Social Democratic Federation. This had been accompanied by a shift to agnosticism. As a student he had also visited homes in working-class Bermondsey. The poverty in this southeastern London riverside borough had left a lasting impression. In 1898 he went to live in the Bermondsey settlement, a centre for social service with a strongly Christian ethos. His evenings were spent organizing activities for the settlement's programme.

The most decisive influence on Salter came from Ada Brown (1866–1942), the daughter of a comfortably-off family in Raunds, Northamptonshire [see Salter, Ada]. She lived in Bermondsey and ran the girls' club at the settlement. Her involvement was inspired by a blend of religious zeal and social concern. Together with the settlement's head, the Revd John Scott Lidgett, she brought Salter back to Christianity. They were married on 22 August 1900; both joined the Peckham meeting of the Society of Friends. They decided to devote their lives to the people of Bermondsey, where Salter established a general medical practice which provided the core of his identity within the community. Driven by his sense of mission, Salter worked prodigiously long hours. His political activities, influenced by Scott Lidgett, became focused on the Liberal Party, which seemed congenial to his religious and ethical beliefs. He was elected to the Bermondsey borough council in 1903, and two years later became a member of the Progressives on the London county council (LCC). But his discontent with the Liberals grew. On 5 May 1908 he was one of a small group that formed the Bermondsey branch of the Independent Labour Party (ILP).

The party was relatively weak in London. Working-class Liberalism was strong and socialists tended to join the Social Democratic Federation. Yet the ethical style of the ILP was obviously attractive to Salter. The initial membership included two other partners in his practice and some working-class activists. In October 1909 the branch faced its first serious test. Bermondsey's Liberal member died and Salter contested the by-election. The ILP depended heavily on Salter's local reputation as a doctor; Liberals responded that a vote for him was a wasted vote. Especially in the context of the deepening crisis over the people's budget and the Lords, this was a powerful weapon. Salter finished bottom with 1435 votes. Subsequent socialist growth in Bermondsey was slow. Neither general election was fought in 1910; Salter, fighting for his new party, lost his LCC seat. When the ILP ran a slate in the borough elections, only Ada Salter was successful. Salter's austere and principled politics was complemented by an immense capacity for organizational work. He and his colleagues courted trade-union branches to build Bermondsey Labour Party; on a wider canvass he was heavily involved in the creation of the London Labour Party. His activism was accompanied and perhaps heightened by a personal tragedy. Alfred and Ada Salter's only child, Joyce, had died in 1910, a victim of scarlet fever in a borough where child mortality rates were appallingly high.

Salter's response to the outbreak of the First World War was based on his interpretation of Christianity. His 'Faith of a pacifist' was unequivocal: 'I believe that all killing is murder and is wrong' (*Labour Leader*, 24 Sept 1914). He participated vigorously in the anti-war propaganda of the ILP and played a significant role in the No-Conscription Fellowship. At wartime ILP conferences Salter repeatedly moved a resolution pledging the ILP to press the Socialist International to oppose any future war. Sidelined in 1915, passed but ignored by the party leadership the following year, the proposal was adopted firmly as party policy at the 1917 conference. In moving the resolution Salter emphasized a principle that shaped his political choices: 'There is no greater fallacy than to think that you can secure good results by using bad means' (*Independent Labour Party Conference Report 1917*, 56).

Labour's electoral progress in post-war London was at first uncertain. Salter predictably polled poorly in the new Bermondsey West seat in 1918, but four years later, in November 1922, he entered the Commons, aided by the division of the anti-Labour vote between three candidates. The fragility of his position was clear in December 1923, when he lost to a Liberal in a straight fight. But in the 1924

election Salter won the seat back and retained it until he retired in 1945. By the mid-1920s Bermondsey was a solidly Labour borough at every level, parliamentary, LCC, borough council, and the board of guardians. The local Labour Party was well organized, and the ILP branch was the centre of the labour movement's social activities. The Labour majority on the borough council pioneered an ambitious programme of housing construction, environmental improvements, and welfare provision, of which Salter as an alderman was typically viewed as the principal inspiration.

In parliament Salter was characteristically assiduous in dealing with constituents' problems. His pacifism strengthened his commitment to parliament as the only instrument for a better society. But his austere and often inflexible principles made him an outsider. One of his early Commons interventions was in support of a bill to introduce prohibition. In October 1926 he was found guilty of a breach of privilege. He had commented at a temperance meeting on drunkenness in the Commons, and had repeated the claim when the issue was brought before the house. In congenial company Salter could be relaxed and humorous; in the formality of the Commons his style could be bleak. One seasoned observer captured him as 'a stern man of granite quality quite unused to the melting mood' (cited in Brockway, 150).

Salter's attachment to the ILP was shaken by that party's radicalization in the late 1920s. He remained a supporter of MacDonald and was thoroughly hostile to the leadership of James Maxton. Salter took a leading role in the manoeuvres that produced two meetings of the ILP parliamentary group in December 1928. The purpose was to mobilize against the ILP left, but the strategy provoked opposition, not just from supporters of Maxton, but also from many who saw Salter and his allies as needlessly divisive. Nevertheless, Salter's views were endorsed by many within the Bermondsey ILP and the branch strongly opposed the national party's disaffiliation from the Labour Party in 1932.

Within the small post-1931 Parliamentary Labour Party Salter felt unusually comfortable. He admired Lansbury's leadership, and on international issues the party seemed closer to his own position. In the Commons he led effectively for the parliamentary party on a variety of issues. However, the Italian invasion of Abyssinia and the Labour Party's debate over sanctions marked the beginning of a deepening political isolation. At the party's conference in 1935 he supported Lansbury's pacifist position. Subsequently he was a leading figure in the parliamentary pacifist group. He remained close to Lansbury as the latter embarked on his crusade for peace. Much of Salter's energy was devoted to the Peace Pledge Union. His pacifism and distaste for the Versailles settlement made him a supporter of appeasement. After the Munich agreement he insisted that 'the average German will withdraw his backing from Hitler if we show willingness to be just' (A. Salter, *Reconciliation*, November 1938, 352). Even in Bermondsey Salter could seem isolated. He quarrelled fiercely with the trades council in 1937 over its organization of a counter-demonstration against Sir Oswald Mosley. He told delegates that their behaviour made them indistinguishable from the Fascists. At the end of 1938 his disillusion was severe: 'I am very distressed about the moral and spiritual condition of the Labour Party' (Salter to Arthur Creech Jones, 30 Dec 1938, Creech Jones MSS).

Salter's residual optimism was destroyed by the outbreak of war. His health was deteriorating; his political allies were few; bombs devastated much of Bermondsey. Salter made his last Commons speech in November 1941, a pacifist plea for an armistice. But within two weeks Pearl Harbor would herald a vast extension of hostilities. Ada Salter's death in December 1942 left Salter effectively dependent on his links with the Peace Pledge Union. Yet he and another Labour politician, James Hudson, broke with them not over policy but over the alleged sexual libertarianism of some union employees. He remained a moral absolutist.

Salter died in Guy's Hospital, London, on 24 August 1945 and was buried at Peckham Friends' meeting-house. Bermondsey had been physically and socially battered by the war. His uncompromising pacifism had been rejected by almost all of his former political associates. Yet to many in Bermondsey he remained The Doctor, a man whose medical and municipal achievements far outweighed disagreements with his austere politics.

DAVID HOWELL

Sources F. Brockway, *Bermondsey story: the life of Alfred Salter* (1949) · M. Caedel, *Pacifism in Britain, 1914–1945: the defining of a faith* (1980) · P. R. Thompson, *Socialists, liberals and labour: the struggle for London, 1885–1914* (1967) · *The political diary of Hugh Dalton, 1918–1940, 1945–1960*, ed. B. Pimlott (1986) · *WWW* · b. cert. · d. cert.
Archives Bodl. RH, letters · Mitchell L., Glas., speeches, accounts of parliamentary group meetings | BLPES, Francis Johnson corresp., corresp. on Bermondsey | SOUND IWM SA, oral history interviews
Likenesses photograph, repro. in Brockway, *Bermondsey story*
Wealth at death £8919 7s. 5d.: probate, 15 July 1947, *CGPLA Eng. & Wales*

Salter, (James) Arthur, Baron Salter (1881–1975), politician and university professor, was born on 15 March 1881 at Oxford, the eldest of the four sons of James Edward Salter, a member of a well-known Oxford firm of boat builders, who served as a member of the city council for many years and became mayor of the city, and his wife, Julia Maria Millin, the daughter of an Oxford draper. Salter was educated at the Oxford City High School and at Brasenose College, Oxford, where he won a scholarship in classics. He gained a first class both in classical honour moderations (1901) and in *literae humaniores* (1903). His college elected him after graduation to a senior scholarship, enabling him to spend a further year reading widely in history, law, and economics.

In 1904 Salter entered the civil service, spending at first seven frustrating years in the transport department of the Admiralty. Then came a great opportunity. In 1911 he was transferred to the staff set up first to plan and later to administer the national insurance scheme introduced by Lloyd George. He found himself a member of a *corps d'élite*,

including such men as N. F. Warren Fisher, J. S. Bradbury, and John Anderson, all destined to reach the highest positions in the public service. Within a year he was appointed private secretary to C. F. G. Masterman, the minister in charge of health insurance, and in 1913 he was promoted to be assistant secretary of the Insurance Commission.

Then came the First World War. Salter found himself recalled to the transport department of the Admiralty, where he soon achieved a key position. As director of ship requisitioning, at first in the Admiralty and subsequently in the Ministry of Shipping, he was in charge of the allocation of all merchant shipping, and as losses mounted and demands both civil and military increased shipping became the vital central point in the supply system both of Britain and of its allies.

The entry of America into the war brought new demands for shipping and inevitably increased the pressure on Britain's dwindling resources. Salter was sent to Washington to urge upon the Americans the vital need to build ships on the largest practicable scale. In this he was successful, and the American programme of new construction soon exceeded the most optimistic estimates. At the same time losses were reduced through the convoy system; and the system of allocation and programming which had been so successfully built up in Britain was extended to cover the needs of all the allied powers. To achieve this Salter with John Anderson and with Jean Monnet, then a young man in his twenties, drew up a plan for an allied maritime transport council which was adopted at an allied conference in Paris. The council was served by an allied maritime transport executive of which Salter became the chairman in 1918, retaining at the same time his position in the ministry in London.

The ending of the war brought new problems, such as the repatriation of demobilized forces and the sending of relief supplies to starving and disorganized countries in Europe. Salter played a prominent part in the handling of these, serving in 1919 as one of the secretaries of the supreme economic council in Paris. It was natural therefore that when the League of Nations was set up Salter should have been chosen to head (June 1919 – January 1920) the economic and financial section of the secretariat. For two years he was diverted to a position much higher in status though not, as it turned out, in importance, as general secretary of the reparations commission. But in 1922 he was glad to return to his position in the league secretariat in Geneva.

The next nine years were spent in stimulating and constructive work in which much progress was made in the financial and economic reconstruction of Europe, notably in the stabilization of the currencies of Austria and Hungary, and the resettlement of refugees in Greece and Bulgaria. In all this work Salter added greatly to his already high reputation and other governments, including those of India and China, sought his advice in framing their policies.

In 1930 Salter left the league secretariat and returned to London. There followed years of varied activity as a journalist and author (among his books were *Allied Shipping*

Control, 1921, and *Recovery*, 1932), as a member of the Economic Advisory Council, and as chairman of the road and rail conference whose unanimous recommendations were passed into law in 1933. In 1934 he was appointed to the Gladstone professorship of political theory and institutions at Oxford, a chair which carried with it a fellowship of All Souls. He made many friends there, and the college continued to be his academic home until almost the end of his life.

In 1937 Salter was elected with support from all three parties as MP for Oxford University. He continued to hold this position until the university seats were abolished in 1950. In the years before the Second World War Salter was active both in and out of parliament in pressing upon the government a more vigorous policy of defence preparations, particularly in the building up of reserve stocks of food and raw materials, about which, from his experience of shipping control in the First World War, he could speak with special authority.

After the outbreak of war Salter was appointed in November 1939 as parliamentary secretary to the Ministry of Shipping set up by Neville Chamberlain's government, and he held a similar position in Winston Churchill's coalition government. In the earlier months of the war he worked closely with his old friend Jean Monnet, becoming vice-chairman of the Anglo-French co-ordination committee of which Monnet was chairman. Together they did important work in placing contracts for war supplies in North America. In March 1941 he was summoned to Chequers by Churchill and invited to head a British shipping mission to Washington. Once more, as in the First World War, shortage of shipping had become a growing threat to Britain's survival. Again Salter had to press upon the US administration the urgent need for a vast programme of new construction, in a country where shipbuilding had virtually ceased between the wars. In his work in Washington, Salter was greatly helped by his wife, whom he had married in June 1940. She was Ethel Mather, daughter of John Sherman Bagg, doctor, and widow of Arthur Bullard, who had been one of Salter's colleagues in Geneva. American by birth but cosmopolitan in education and experience, she had a house in Washington and knew well many of the leading figures in the administration. She died in 1969. There were no children.

The crisis in shipping was at its most acute not only in the spring of 1941 but also in 1942 after the entry of the United States into the war. But by the middle of 1943 Salter had the satisfaction of seeing this danger overcome thanks to a shipbuilding programme in the USA which reached the staggering total of 20 million tons a year, all of which was made available for the war effort of the allies as a whole.

With his work in Washington successfully accomplished Salter returned to London, and after a brief and unsatisfactory period of service in 1944 as deputy director-general of United Nations Relief and Rehabilitation Administration he joined Churchill's caretaker government as chancellor of the duchy of Lancaster 'with special responsibility for questions affecting European relief'. In

February 1951, after a year without a seat in parliament, he was invited to stand for Ormskirk at a by-election as a Conservative. He was re-elected at the general election in October, and appointed to be minister of state for economic affairs in the Treasury. He served there for a year during which he found himself in strong disagreement with the policy of making sterling convertible at a floating rate of exchange advocated by the Treasury and the Bank of England. The proposal was rejected by the cabinet and the prime minister subsequently acknowledged to Salter, as he himself recounts, the importance of the part he had played in opposing it. He was appointed in November 1952 to be minister of materials, with responsibility for supervising the orderly winding up of the department. In October 1953 he left the government and was elevated to the peerage, as Baron Salter of Kidlington.

Many other honours had been conferred upon Salter in his long career. He was appointed CB in 1918, KCB in 1922, PC in 1941, and GBE in 1944. By foreign governments he was appointed officer of the Couronne Belgique in 1919, commander of the Légion d'honneur in 1920, and *commendatore* of the Crown of Italy in 1922, and he received the Chinese decoration of the Brilliant Jade in 1937. He was made an honorary fellow of his old college, Brasenose, and after relinquishing his professorial fellowship at All Souls in 1974 was immediately re-elected to an honorary fellowship. He received honorary doctorates from Oxford, Manchester, Vienna, Harvard, Columbia, McGill, California, and Amherst. Salter died at his home, 35 Glebe Place, London, on 27 June 1975, and the peerage became extinct.

DENIS RICKETT, *rev.*

Sources A. Salter, *Memoirs of a public servant* (1961) · A. Salter, *Slave of the lamp: a public servant's notebook* (1967) · *The Times* (30 June 1975) · *The Times* (5 July 1975) · *The Times* (22 July 1975) · personal knowledge (1986) · *CGPLA Eng. & Wales* (1975)

Archives NRA, corresp. and papers · PRO, private office papers, MT 62/95–123 | BL, corresp. with Lord Cecil of Chelwood, Add. MS 51113 · BL, letters to Albert Monabridge, Add. MS 65253 · BLPES, letters to Violet Markham · BLPES, corresp. with Royal Economic Society · Bodl. Oxf., corresp. with L. G. Curtis · Bodl. Oxf., corresp. with Gilbert Murray · CAC Cam., corresp. with Sir E. L. Spears · JRL, letters to *Manchester Guardian* · King's AC Cam., corresp. with A. E. Felkin · NA Scot., corresp. with Lord Lothian · University of Cape Town Library, letters to J. N. Thompson · Welwyn Garden City Central Library, corresp. with Sir Frederic Osborn

Likenesses W. Stoneman, two photographs, 1930–45, NPG

Wealth at death £36,348: probate, 3 Sept 1975, *CGPLA Eng. & Wales*

Salter, Sir Arthur Clavell (1859–1928), judge and politician, was born in London on 30 October 1859, the eldest son of Henry Hyde Salter MD FRS, of Harley Street, London, and his wife, Henrietta Laura, eldest daughter of the Revd Edward Powlett Blunt, vicar of Spetisbury, Dorset. He was educated at Wimborne grammar school and at King's College, London, where he graduated in arts and law. He was called to the bar by the Middle Temple in 1885, and joined the western circuit in 1886. He took silk in 1904, and was recorder of Poole from 1904 to 1917.

Salter unsuccessfully contested West Southwark as a Conservative candidate at the general election of January 1906, but was elected at a by-election in the same year for the Basingstoke division of Hampshire, which he represented until 1917, when he was appointed a judge of the King's Bench Division of the High Court and knighted. He was appointed chairman of the railway and canal commission in February 1928.

Salter was married twice: first in 1894 to Mary Dorothea (*d.* 1917), daughter of Major John Henry Lloyd, Royal Artillery, with whom he had one son, who was killed in action in the First World War; second in 1920 to Nora Constance, eldest daughter of Lieutenant-Colonel Thomas Heathcote Ouchterlony, of The Guynd, Arbroath, Forfarshire.

Salter took the view that the sole function of a judge was to adjudicate. There was never a word that was superfluous or out of place in his judgments, but they were not notable for their brilliance or originality. Nor did Salter see any point in citing a long string of precedents and judicial authority. Having considered a problem, he was content with a brief statement of his decision, delivered without circumlocution or lengthy discussions on the chain of his reasoning.

Salter's most sensational criminal trial was that of Horatio Bottomley for fraudulent conversion (1922). The case was difficult, involving a search into complex facts and figures. Salter's summing-up was masterly, lucid, and concise, yet complete. In criminal cases he similarly abstained from attempting to edify the prisoner or the public with moral aphorisms.

Salter's civil judgments were not to everybody's taste. Their brevity is explained by his desire to advance the law. He was seldom reversed, and where he was, much can be said in favour of his opinion. In *Blundell-Leigh* v. *Attenborough* (1921) Salter held that the bailor in the particular circumstances of the case was entitled to the unconditional return of the chattel, but was reversed by the Court of Appeal on a different view of the facts. A considerable body of contemporary learned opinion regarded Salter's reasoning as the more convincing. Previously, in *Whiteley* v. *Hilt* (1918), a case about the law of hire purchase, Salter said a hirer who sold goods before paying all instalments due ended a bailment, so that the buyer had no right to the goods. The Court of Appeal regarded it as an assignment of a chose in action, entitling the purchaser to keep the goods provided he paid the instalments as the hirer should have done. In general, however, the Court of Appeal and the court of criminal appeal regarded Salter's decisions with the utmost respect. He died in London on 30 November 1928.

H. G. HANBURY, *rev.* HUGH MOONEY

Sources *The Times* (3 Dec 1928) · CGPLA Eng. & Wales (1929)
Wealth at death £64,138 4*s.* 3*d.*: resworn probate, 2 Feb 1929, CGPLA Eng. & Wales

Salter, Herbert Edward (1863–1951), historian of Oxford, was born in Harley Street, London, on 6 February 1863; he was the second son of a physician, Henry Hyde Salter FRS, and his wife, Henrietta Laura, *née* Blunt, and the younger brother of Sir Arthur Clavell *Salter. His father died when he was only eight years old, and his mother, daughter of the Revd Edward Powlett Blunt, took him to live with her family at Spetisbury in Dorset. He attended Wimborne

grammar school. From it he won, in 1876, a scholarship at Winchester College, where he became eventually prefect of hall. At school he developed an enduring fascination with sports statistics, particularly athletics. From Winchester he went, again with a scholarship, to New College, Oxford. He took a second class in classical moderations in 1883, a first in *literae humaniores* in 1886, and a first in theology in 1887. He then went to Cuddesdon College, was ordained deacon in 1888, and took priest's orders in 1889. After serving as curate at Sandhurst, Berkshire (1888–91), he was appointed vice-principal of Leeds Clergy School. He left Leeds in 1893 when he married and became vicar, first of Mattingley in Hampshire, and then, in 1889, of Shirburn in south Oxfordshire.

It was during the ten years which he spent at Shirburn, and when he was nearing forty, that Salter first began historical work by collecting material for the history of his parish. In 1904 he offered to edit the *Eynsham Cartulary* for the Oxford Historical Society. This was the first of thirty-four volumes which he brought out for that society, and he paid for the cost of producing eleven of them. The *Eynsham Cartulary* was straightforward editing and in that respect differed from the *Cartulary of the Hospital of St. John the Baptist* (3 vols., 1914–17) and the yet more elaborate six-volume edition of the *Oseney Cartulary* (1929–36) both of which were based primarily upon the original deeds. In them and in other works—*Oxford Balliol Deeds* (1913), *Oxford City Properties* (1926), and *Oriel College Records* (1926)—he adopted the plan of arranging his documents under parishes and, within the parish, under tenements, and of carrying down the history of each tenement through subsequent leases to the nineteenth century. The abundance of his sources enabled him to construct a detailed history of house-sites in a manner which had not been attempted for any other English city. The results are recorded in his *Survey of Oxford*, published posthumously by the Oxford Historical Society (1960, 1969). His *Munimenta civitatis Oxonie* (1920) contained the transcripts by Brian Twyne of the lost city deeds. Salter published documents from Oxford's colleges and from the university archives, most notably *Mediaeval Archives of the University of Oxford* (2 vols., 1920–21) and the chancellor's register for 1434–69 (2 vols., 1932).

Salter did more than edit. He contributed articles on ecclesiastical history and on religious houses to volume 2 of the *Victoria county history of Oxfordshire* (1907) and in 1933 was appointed to edit, and planned, a further volume on the history of the university and city. His *Medieval Oxford* (1936) was a publication of the Ford's lectures which he gave in 1934. His *Early History of St. John's College* (1939) was compiled from materials left by his friend, W. H. Stevenson. And although he disclaimed having studied history of any kind except the medieval history of Oxford, he edited for the Canterbury and York Society (1922) the *Chapters of the Augustinian Canons* and collaborated with G. J. Turner in the publication, for the British Academy, of the *Register of St. Augustine's Abbey, Canterbury* (2 vols., 1915–24).

Salter's rich store of transcripts, largely from Oxford

college muniment rooms, contained in nearly a hundred notebooks, along with many copies of plans of property in Oxford, were deposited in the Bodleian Library. Transcribing made him expert in diplomatic, as may be seen from the fine volume of *Facsimiles of Early Charters in Oxford Muniment Rooms* which he printed privately in 1929. He was led on to a special study of the royal charters of Henry I, Stephen, and Henry II, lending liberally from his collections both to H. W. C. Davis and to Leopold Delisle, and contributing short articles to the *English Historical Review*.

Salter came to be recognized as the leading authority on Oxford history since Anthony Wood. Magdalen College elected him to a research fellowship in 1918, and this he held until 1939, devoting his stipend to the cost of publications. He was made a fellow of the British Academy in 1930 and, in the same year, an honorary freeman of the city of Oxford. In 1933 he received from his university the honorary degree of doctor of letters.

Salter was twice married; first, in 1893, to Beatrice Eva (d. 1932), daughter of the Revd James Steuart Ruddach, with whom he had a son and three daughters. Their son died when still a boy at Winchester College. He married second, in 1933, Gladys Nina, daughter of Douglas Dewar, who survived him. Giving up parochial duties in 1909, he went to live nearer to Oxford at Dry Sandford, and later at Frilford; but in 1942 he returned to Dorset, the county in which he had spent his boyhood, and died there, on 23 April 1951, at his home, Broad Oak, Sturminster Newton.

Salter was happy in the countryside; was given to the keeping of bees and ferrets, to the growing of fruit and vegetables, and, up to the last year of his life, to felling trees and sawing logs. Physically active, he was a good walker; when he was at Shirburn he used to cycle the 15 miles into Oxford two or three times a week to work in Oxford libraries, and he still went out with the beagles when he was seventy-five. He had an excellent memory, alike for the personnel of medieval Oxford and for the details of cricket matches played seventy years before. He shared to the full the qualities of industry and accuracy with which he credited an earlier Oxford antiquary, Thomas Hearne. To great modesty he united shrewd common sense, and, though full of a quiet reserve, he was kindly and liberal in the help he gave to younger students of medieval history, a number of whom united to publish in his honour in 1934 a volume entitled *Oxford Essays in Medieval History*. The work contains a good photograph of Salter and a list of his published writings up to 1933.

EDMUND CRASTER, rev. H. C. G. MATTHEW

Sources *The Times* (2 May 1951) · W. A. Pantin, 'Herbert Edward Salter, 1863–1951', *PBA*, 40 (1954), 219–39 · personal knowledge (1971) · private information (1971)
Archives Bodl. Oxf., Berkshire, Oxfordshire, and Hampshire collections, photographs of charters, seals, and other documents; tracings of early maps | LUL, letters to J. H. Round | SOUND BL NSA, oral history interview
Likenesses Elliott & Fry, photograph, repro. in Pantin, 'Herbert Edward Salter', 219 · photograph, repro. in *Oxford essays in medieval history: presented to Herbert Edward Salter* (1934)
Wealth at death £17,610 7s. 8d.: probate, 14 July 1951, *CGPLA Eng. & Wales*

Salter, James (*fl.* 1665). *See under* Salter, James (1649/50–1718).

Salter, James (1649/50–1718), Church of England clergyman, was born in 1649 or 1650, the 'son of a father of both his names of the city of Exeter' (Wood, *Ath. Oxon.*, 4.600). It is unclear whether the father or son (as an Oxford student) is the **James Salter** (*fl.* 1665) who wrote *Caliope's cabinet opened, wherein gentlemen may be informed how to adorn themselves for funerals, feastings, and other heroick meetings* (1665; 2nd edn, 1674), 'an heraldic work of little worth' addressed to Thomas Clifford and Henry Ford, justices of the peace for Devon, the author's friends in adversity (Lowndes, 2180). The Salters claimed descent from Edward I through the Bullers, a Somerset family that settled in Cornwall through marriage with the coheiress of Trethurffe, a cousin and coheiress of the first earl of Devon.

Salter entered Magdalen College, Oxford, on 24 July 1668, aged eighteen; he was a clerk during 1668–71 but left without taking a degree, presumably returning to his native Devon. In 1671 Salter was among the fifty-four 'exhausted verse writers of University' who contributed to a memorial volume for Anne, duchess of York (Madan, 249). He was ordained deacon on 17 July 1672 and priest on 4 June 1674, by which date he was in Cornwall, serving as curate of the parishes of South Hill and St Ive near Launceston. Subsequently he was vicar of Lostwithiel in 1674 and apparently also vicar of Lesnewth in 1678–9. On 4 March 1684 he was appointed master of the free grammar school at Exeter until his 'removal' on unspecified grounds by the chamber of the city of Exeter on 19 January 1690, when he was succeeded by Zachary Mayne. While master Salter wrote *Compendium Graecae grammatices chatichisticum* (1685) for the benefit of his students.

Salter, at one time a prebendary of Exeter Cathedral, was (contemporaneously, it seems, with the last years of his mastership) vicar of the church of St Mary the Virgin (St Mary Church), St Marychurch, Devon, near Torbay. According to church rolls he was appointed vicar there on 4 September 1688 and served for thirty years. He had married Katherine Fathers, daughter of the Revd John Fathers of Saltash, Cornwall, and his wife, Cordelia (*née* Parker), with whom he had three sons (John, Joseph, and James [see below]) and five daughters (twins Mary and Martha, born on 15 November 1690; Ann, Elizabeth, and Katherine). In 1692 Salter published *The triumphs of the holy Jesus, or, A divine poem of the birth, life, death, and resurrection of our Saviour*, a work in heroic couplets dedicated to Richard Ansley, dean of Exeter. During Salter's incumbency, in 1713, St Mary Church suffered severe fire damage amounting to £1300. Salter died on 24 March 1718, and was buried three days later in the old chancel; the administration of his property was granted in 1719. Katherine Salter's will, dated 18 October 1721, was probated (her son James as executor) on 20 February 1753.

Salter's younger son, **James Salter** (1696–1767), Church of England clergyman, was born on 8 January 1696 at St Marychurch, matriculated at Magdalen College, Oxford, on 29 April 1713 aged seventeen, and graduated BA in 1717.

Like his father, he became vicar of Lesnewth, Cornwall. On 2 March 1718, during his father's last illness, he became vicar of St Mary Church. He wrote two exegetical treatises: *An Exposition, or, Practical Treatise on the Church Catechism of the Church of England* (1753), and *The pious and well-dispos'd Christian instructed how to make his prayers and supplications to almighty God* (1765). Improvements to the church during his long incumbency included an entrance gallery put up in 1732, described a century later by a London architect as being in a 'tottering state' (Edmonds, 50). Salter died early in March 1767 and was buried on 8 March in the chancel. He and his wife, Mary Adams of Totnes (whom he had married on 30 July 1728 at Upton Pyne near Exeter), had one child, Mary, baptized on 13 January 1729, who married Jacob Bartlett of Westhill House on 6 February 1758 and was buried at St Mary Church on 23 June 1791.

PAGE LIFE

Sources private information (2004) [K. Davies, Hereford] · Wood, *Ath. Oxon.*, new edn, 4.600 · Foster, *Alum. Oxon.* · F. S. Edmonds, *Chronicles of St. Mary Church: with notes on Babbacombe, Ilsham, Shiphay Collaton, Kingskerswell and Coffinswell* (1925) · N. Carlisle, *A concise description of the endowed grammar schools in England and Wales*, 1 (1818); repr. (1972), 317 · W. D. Macray, *A register of the members of St Mary Magdalen College, Oxford*, 8 vols. (1894–1915), vol. 4, p. 92 · E. A. Fry, ed., *Calendars of wills and administrations relating to the counties of Devon and Cornwall proved in the court of the principal registry of the bishop of Exeter, 1559–1799* (1908); repr. (1968), 181 · E. A. Fry, ed., *Calendar of wills and administrations relating to the counties of Devon and Cornwall proved in the consistory court of the bishop of Exeter, 1532–1800* (1914); repr. (1968), 200 · C. Worthy, *Devonshire parishes, or, The antiquities, heraldry and family history of twenty-eight parishes in the archdeaconry of Totnes*, 2 vols. (1887–9) · *Pedigree of the family of Bartlett of St. Mary Church, co. Devon*, 2nd edn (1891) · Burke, *Gen. GB* (1965), 1.95–7 · W. T. Lowndes, *The bibliographer's manual of English literature*, ed. H. G. Bohn, [new edn], 4 (1864), 2180 · F. Madan, *Oxford literature, 1651–1680* (1931), vol. 3 of *Oxford books: a bibliography of printed works* (1895–1931); repr. (1964), 249–50

Salter, James [called Don Saltero] (d. *c.*1728), coffee-house proprietor, is said to have come from Ireland and settled in Chelsea about 1673. He was at one time a servant of Sir Hans Sloane, whom he accompanied on his travels. He opened his first coffee house in Lawrence Street about 1695, moving a few years later to Danvers Street, and finally settling at 18 Cheyne Walk, Chelsea, in 1717. Sloane and other collectors made him a present of various curiosities; both Rear-Admiral Sir John Munden and Richard Steele are credited with bestowing on him the title of Don Saltero. Don Saltero's coffee house, as it was known, became a favourite meeting-place for men like Sloane, Richard Mead, and Nathaniel Oldham. In 1709 Steele described 'the ten thousand gimcracks' at Don Saltero's in *The Tatler* (28 June 1709; Bond, 1.252). As one of the sights of Chelsea, it was visited by Thoresby in 1723 and by Benjamin Franklin about 1724, and it features in a passage of Fanny Burney's *Evelina* (1778). The don himself was—according to Steele—'a sage of a thin and meagre countenance' (ibid.). He was famous for his punch, could play a little on the fiddle, and, for no charge, would shave, bleed, and draw teeth.

Salter's museum was an astounding assemblage of oddities, including a petrified crab from China, medals of William Laud, Gustavus Adolphus, and the seven bishops who resisted James II's declaration of indulgence, William the Conqueror's flaming sword, Henry VIII's coat of mail, Job's tears (of which anodyne necklaces were made), a bowl and ninepins in a box the size of a pea, Madagascar lances, and the root of a tree in the shape of a hog; the last object was presented as a 'lignified hog' by John Pennant, great-uncle of the traveller and naturalist Thomas Pennant. The curiosities were placed in glass cases in the front room of the first floor, and weapons, skeletons, and fishes covered the walls and ceiling. Salter printed (price 2*d*.) 'A catalogue of the rarities to be seen at Don Saltero's coffee house in Chelsea'; extant editions range from 1729 to the 'forty-eighth' version in 1795. The donors listed in the catalogues include Sir Robert Cotton, Martin Folkes, the earl of Sutherland, and Sir John Cope. A poetical autobiography and account of his 'Museum Coffee House' appeared in the *British Apollo II* (4 May 1709) and in *Mist's Journal* (22 June 1723).

Salter died at home about 1728. It is not known whether he was married, although records exist for the baptism in Chelsea of two of his children, May in 1682 and John in 1687. The coffee house and museum were carried on until about 1759 by his daughter May, now Mrs Hall, and the collection, or a considerable part of it, remained on the premises until 7 January 1799, when the house and its contents were sold by auction. The sale of the curiosities—distributed in 121 lots—realized only about £50, the highest price for a single lot being £1 16*s*. for a model of the holy sepulchre, which appeared as the first item in all editions of the catalogue. In its later days the house became a tavern. It was pulled down in 1866 and a private residence (18 Cheyne Walk) built on the site.

W. W. WROTH, *rev.* P. E. KELL

Sources B. Lillywhite, *London coffee houses* (1963) · J. Timbs, *Curiosities of London* (1855) · D. F. Bond, ed., *The Tatler*, 3 vols. (1987) · *GM*, 1st ser., 69 (1799), 160 · *GM*, 1st ser., 82/1 (1812), 207 · R. Blunt, *The lure of old Chelsea* (1922) · H. B. Wheatley and P. Cunningham, *London past and present*, 3 vols. (1891)

Salter, James (1696–1767). *See under* Salter, James (1649/50–1718).

Salter, John Henry (1841–1932), sportsman and general practitioner, was born on 14 July 1841 at Arundel, Sussex, the son of Henry Salter (1809–1849), surveyor, of Arundel, and his wife, Catherine Alexandrina, *née* Wilson (1814–1909). His diary was kept from 1849 to 1932. He remembered Balaklava and saw the rise of Hitler. He was educated at Grix's School, Littlehampton, and from 1856 to 1858 at King's College School, then in the Strand. In 1858 he started to study medicine at King's College Hospital, London, and he qualified in 1863. His medical career is mentioned scantily in the diary ('Feb.3. Repulse of Austro-Prussian army by the Danes after a fight of six hours. Over to the College of Surgeons to hear Huxley—magnificent'). He often records cricket, rowing, cock-fights, dogfights, prize-fights, and scraps he got into with 'ruffians', as he was very handy with his fists. On Derby day 1862 he lost an eye in a brawl with prize-fighter Jack Sullivan and others, which caused him to decline the offer of a staff appointment at King's College Hospital. He witnessed the public hanging of a woman and his description of the drunken, brawling crowd is sickening.

On 12 October 1864 Salter married Laura Mary (d. 1904), daughter of John Duke of Court Wick, Sussex, and on 29 October the Salters moved to a rural medical practice at Tolleshunt D'Arcy in Essex, where they remained for the rest of their lives. There were no children.

Dr Salter was a prolific accumulator of records, not least through his diary which covers a remarkably long period (eighty-three years). He bred 2123 dogs, and owned a total of 2696; out of forty-four breeds he produced champion pointers, greyhounds, retrievers, Sussex spaniels, and Gordon and Irish setters, as well as training thirty-one Waterloo cup winners. He won 611 prizes at dog shows, including 199 firsts and 30 silver cups. A vice-president of the Kennel Club, he was president of Cruft's in 1925. He won 1400 prizes for his own fruits and vegetables. He ranked with lords De Grey and Walsingham as one of England's finest shots. Between 1865 and 1925 he shot 62,504 head of game, including eleven wolves and a lynx shot in Russia as guest of the tsar and Russian princes. In spite of having only one eye, he was also a skilled boxer. His game book is a remarkable document. In 1902 he bred a blood-red alstroemeria (named after his wife), which won the award of merit from the Royal Horticultural Society. Salter's large collection of stuffed birds and animals once occupied the Doctor Salter Room in Chelmsford Museum.

Salter became a distinguished freemason and grand deacon of England. He was involved in many local activities, including politics (he was a high tory), and sat as a county JP for Essex, but in spite of all this and his travels and sporting exploits his proudest boast was to have brought over 10,000 Essex babies into the world. He died at his home, D'Arcy House, Tolleshunt D'Arcy, Essex, on 17 April 1932, and was buried four days later in Tolleshunt D'Arcy churchyard. After his death his friend James Wentworth Day wrote:

> I saw him lying in his coffin … with two huge, gaunt, grey wolves sitting gazing glassily at the old hunter who had slain them more than thirty years before. So passed a man who epitomised all that is most admirable in the character of the English country gentleman. (Day, 2249)

It is the voluminous diaries, a remarkable record of social history, which make Salter immortal. After his death they were acquired by Alderman John Ockelford Thompson, proprietor of the *Essex Chronicle*, who published a small selection prefaced with 'An appreciation' by the fifth earl of Lonsdale. The bulk of the diaries was destroyed by a flying bomb during the Second World War. In addition to the diary extracts are fifty-nine short, amusing, amazing, and informative reminiscences. James Wentworth Day considered Salter, as a diarist, the equal of Woodforde, Kilvert, and Gilbert White. The diary reveals a man of extraordinary stamina. Even when old he would

rise very early, spend three hours duck shooting in freezing weather on the marshes, and after breakfast and a whole morning on his rounds he would garden all afternoon, walk several miles to a dinner, return late, and be up again at dawn. ROBERT INNES-SMITH

Sources Dr Salter of Tolleshunt D'Arcy in the county of Essex, medical man, freemason, sportsman, sporting-dog breeder and horticulturalist: his diary and reminiscences from the year 1849 to the year 1932, ed. J. O. Thompson (1933) · J. W. Day, 'The amazing Doctor Salter', Country Life, 116 (1954), 2248–9 · R. Innes-Smith, 'A doctor digresses', Country Life (20 April 1989), 212 · private information (2004) [archivist, King's School, Wimbledon] · R. Innes-Smith, The charge of the right brigade (1998) · J. Thorogood, Margery Allingham: a biography (1991) · b. cert. · d. cert. · The medical who's who (1914)
Archives NL Wales, diary and notes · NMG Wales, notebooks
Likenesses G. Earl, oils · photograph (as deputy grand master of Essex) · photograph · photograph, priv. coll. · photographs, repro. in Thompson, ed., Dr Salter of Tolleshunt D'Arcy · portrait, Essex RO
Wealth at death £24,785 11s. 3d.: probate, 16 June 1932, CGPLA Eng. & Wales

Salter, John Henry (1862–1942), naturalist and diarist, was born on 5 June 1862 at Westleton, Suffolk, the son of William Henry Salter (d. 1869/70) and his wife Lucy, formerly Appleton. His Quaker parents were shopkeepers. He had one brother, William. His father died when he was seven, and the family then moved to Scarborough. He attended the Quaker school at Ackworth, Yorkshire, studied botany at Flanders College and Owens College, Manchester, and taught at Quaker schools in Lisburn in Northern Ireland, in Yorkshire, and in Birmingham. He was briefly on the staff of University College, London, before going to the University College of Wales, Aberystwyth, in 1891 as assistant lecturer and demonstrator in biology. He initiated the College Scientific Society in 1892. In 1896 he had leave of absence for nine months at Bonn University in Germany where he worked on starch grains, and for this work he gained his DSc from University College in 1897. In that year he spent three months at Marburg University in Germany, working on the relationship between the algal and fungal components of lichens.

Salter was appointed first professor of botany at Aberystwyth in 1899, and on 15 August the same year he married Adah Sophia (1862/3–1917), the daughter of Henry Freeman, a Birmingham tea blender. They had two sons, Arnold and Ronald. He resigned his chair in 1903, but held minor posts as curator of the University Museum and lecturer in bacteriology and entomology in the agricultural department until 1908, when because of his wife's deteriorating health he retired completely and in December took her and their sons to Güimar on Tenerife. In February 1910 they moved to south-east France, staying at a variety of health resorts including Arcachon, Bagnères-de-Bigorre, and Capbreton. They moved to Verwood in Dorset in 1916 and after Adah's death there in 1917 and the completion of his sons' education, Salter returned to Aberystwyth in 1923, living for the rest of his life at Fairview, Llanbadarn Fawr, on the outskirts of the town.

Throughout his life Salter made extensive collections of plants and insects which are now in the National Museum and Gallery of Wales. He published many papers and notes, chiefly in the *North Western Naturalist*. One of his chief interests was in discovering the height above sea level at which plants could grow, and this resulted in a paper, *The Altitudinal Range of Flowering Plants and Ferns in Mid Wales* (1928). He wrote a *List of the Flowering Plants and Ferns of Aberystwyth and Neighbourhood* [1901], followed by *The Flowering Plants and Ferns of Cardiganshire* (1935) which is still the only flora of the county. His stay in the Canaries resulted in a paper *Regional Distribution of the Native Flora in Teneriffe* (1918), and he is commemorated in the name of a Tenerife moss *Brachythecium salteri* Cardot & Dixon. His herbarium, now at the National Museum and Gallery of Wales, Cardiff, comprised some 3000 specimens, including 700 plants that he grew in his own garden at Fairview, the flowering dates of which he meticulously recorded in his diaries.

Ornithology was Salter's other main interest, also resulting in many short articles, *List of the Birds of Aberystwyth and Neighbourhood* (1900), and a popular book, *Bird Life throughout the Year* [1913]. Although he was an enthusiastic egg collector (it is not known whether his collection has survived), he was not a shooter and often deplored the activities of those who were. He was very much a conservationist in his concern for birds as well as for plants and wild places, and in 1903 he initiated through the British Ornithologists' Club the red kite protection scheme that led to the revival of the fortunes of this species in mid-Wales. The scheme is still in existence.

Salter's greatest legacy is probably his natural history diaries, now in the National Library of Wales. They contain entries covering sixty-eight years and are immensely readable, carefully composed (presumably mostly from field notebooks that have disappeared), and give a vivid picture of his days in the field especially in Cardiganshire, Tenerife, the western Pyrenees, and Dorset. As a descriptive source for the state of plant, bird, and other animal life of the countryside in his time they are invaluable, and they contain much still unpublished information of importance. Although his correspondence has not been preserved, he copied much relevant material from it into his diaries. In Cardiganshire he frequently walked 20–30 miles a day and never owned a car. He was a tall, quietly spoken, shy and retiring man, a Quaker, a vegetarian, a teetotaller and a non-smoker. In spite of his academic career, it is as a local naturalist who was the main source of information on the natural history of Cardiganshire and the neighbouring parts of mid-Wales for over fifty years that he is best remembered. He was found dead after a fall in his garden on 5 August 1942, never having fully recovered from a prostate operation in March of that year. He was buried with a Quaker funeral on 8 August in Llanbadarn Fawr churchyard.   A. O. CHATER

Sources J. H. Salter's natural history diaries, 1875–1942, NL Wales, MSS 14429B–14453B · *North Western Naturalist*, 17 (1942), 265–70 · *Cambrian News* (14 Aug 1942) · *Welsh Gazette* (13 Aug 1942) · *Nature*, 150 (1942), 314–15 · *The Calendar of the University of Wales* (1892–1908) · *University College of Wales Magazine* [Aberystwyth], 15–28 (1892–1906) · personal knowledge (2004) · private information (2004) · b. cert. · m. cert. · d. cert.

Archives NL Wales, natural history diaries · NMG Wales, herbarium, entomological collections, and notebooks · U. Wales, Aberystwyth, botanical drawings

Likenesses photographs, *c*.1930–1940, priv. coll. · photograph, *c*.1940, repro. in *North Western Naturalist*

Salter, John William (1820–1869), palaeontologist, was born on 15 December 1820 in Kentish Town, London, the son of John Salter (1779–1837), a banking clerk, and his wife, Hannah. His early education was at a private boarding-school, but in 1835 he bound himself as an apprentice to palaeontologist and scientific illustrator James de Carle Sowerby. Salter contributed to Sowerby's *Supplement to the English Botany* (1831–63), the *Mineral Conchology of Great Britain* (1812–46), and Roderick Murchison's *Silurian System* (1839), among many other works. In 1836 he read a paper on entomology to the Camden Literary Society, but his interests soon turned to the fossils of the older rocks.

Salter's enthusiasm, artistic skill, and unrivalled knowledge of these obscure fossils served him in good stead as his apprenticeship drew to a close. From 1842 to 1846 he organized the Palaeozoic remains in the Woodwardian collection at Cambridge, spending some months each year in Cambridge and north Wales with Adam Sedgwick. Sedgwick hoped to employ Salter to produce a full catalogue, but in 1846 he was offered a better-paid position as Edward Forbes's assistant on the expanding Geological Survey. His future now secured, on 7 July 1846 at St Pancras Old Church, he married Sowerby's second daughter, Sarah (1819–1892), known as Sally. At the museum of the survey, first in Whitehall and after 1851 in Jermyn Street, Salter identified and put on display tens of thousands of specimens. He contributed palaeontological appendices for memoirs on the Malvern hills by John Phillips and on north Wales by Andrew Ramsay, and undertook private commissions. These included the palaeontology for Murchison's *Siluria* (1854), Charles Lyell's *Manual of Elementary Geology* (5th edn, 1855), and major Arctic expeditions.

By the early 1850s Salter was the country's leading general expert on Palaeozoic fossils. His favourite study was trilobites, and he published descriptions of the survey collections and a monograph (in collaboration with T. H. Huxley) on the giant eurypterid *Pterygotus*. He commenced a comprehensive memoir on British trilobites for the Palaeontographical Society, of which four parts and thirty plates were completed. Salter became one of the first to apply Charles Darwin's gradual theory of evolutionary change to the invertebrate fossil record; but, like most palaeontologists, he believed Darwin had explained species but not the origin of larger taxonomic groups.

Salter was never a good lecturer or administrator, and it was only reluctantly that he was appointed chief palaeontologist after Forbes left the survey in 1854. Despite his new title, Salter continued to work almost exclusively with the Palaeozoic collections, other responsibilities being taken by Huxley, Robert Etheridge, and William H. Baily. Salter's erratic temperament increasingly led to complaints from his colleagues, many of whom also objected to his self-righteous piety (he was an evangelical

John William Salter (1820–1869), by unknown photographer

Anglican who distributed tracts and took his Bible on field trips). Salter was shocked by Huxley's 'bold infidelity' and thought Murchison could not 'look forward to a blessed future' (Secord, 'Salter', 67).

In 1862 Huxley forced the issue: he would quit unless Salter did. Salter resigned in 1863, only to discover that he was not eligible for a pension. The family (now with seven children) struggled to make ends meet, moving from a large house in Kentish Town to a country cottage in Finchley. While waiting for a permanent position, Salter identified fossils in provincial collections, attempted (unsuccessfully) to give public lectures, contemplated emigration, and pressed wealthier naturalists for 'loans'. Sedgwick was his most faithful supporter, and to repay his debt Salter undertook a supplementary catalogue of the Lower Palaeozoic fossils in the Woodwardian Museum, published in 1873. Salter hoped for a post in the British Museum, but his difficult reputation effectively blocked any appointment in London.

By the mid-1860s Salter's awkward temperament gave way to insanity, and he spent substantial periods in the country undergoing the 'moral therapy' of contemporary psychiatry. 'They may lock me up if they like;' Salter said, 'I shall take my Bible and my palaeontological books, and then I don't much care where I am' (Secord, 'Salter', 70–71). During stays in Pembrokeshire, Salter collaborated with his physician and asylum-keeper Henry *Hicks on important papers on the ancient rocks of St David's,

including one read before the British Association for the Advancement of Science which christened the Menevian as a stratigraphical subdivision. Salter's physician at Malvern, the temperance advocate Ralph B. Grindrod, also had an interest in fossils. It was shortly after a visit to Grindrod, on 2 August 1869, that Salter threw himself into the Thames and drowned, while travelling with his son William on a steamer from Margate to London. His body was recovered and buried in Highgate cemetery.

J. A. SECORD

Sources J. A. Secord, 'John W. Salter: the rise and fall of a Victorian palaeontological career', *From Linnaeus to Darwin* [London 1983], ed. A. Wheeler and J. H. Price (1985), 61–75 · J. A. Secord, *Controversy in Victorian geology: the Cambrian–Silurian dispute* (1986) · NHM, Sowerby MSS (including Salter archive) · *Geological Magazine*, 6 (1869), 477–80 · IGI

Archives NHM, corresp. and family MSS · NHM, papers, incl. autobiographical notes, prints, and drawings · Oxf. U. Mus. NH, papers relating to mollusca, brachiopoda, and trilobites | BGS, letters to Henry De la Beche · CUL, Sedgwick MSS · Hergest Trust, Kingston, Hertfordshire, corresp. with R. W. Banks · ICL, letters to Sir Andrew Ramsay · U. Edin. L., corresp. with Sir Charles Lyell

Likenesses carte-de-visite, BGS; repro. in Secord, 'John W. Salter', 64 · photograph (in old age), NHM · photograph, BGS [*see illus.*]

Wealth at death under £100: probate, 5 Aug 1870, *CGPLA Eng. & Wales*

Salter [*formerly* Sulzer], **Lionel Paul Sydney** (1914–2000), musician and music administrator, was born in London on 8 September 1914, the son of Morris Mortimer Sulzer, a schoolmaster, who changed the family surname to Salter, and his wife, who worked for a small record company. His father was a descendant of the Viennese cantor Salomon Sulzer (1804–1890), the synagogal composer and friend of Beethoven and Schubert. Salter began his musical training young, studying with Stanley Chapple and Yorke Trotter between 1923 and 1931. He showed exceptional musical ability, and at twelve made his first professional appearance as an accompanist. At the age of fourteen, having won a piano as junior prize in a competition sponsored by the *Daily Express*, he made a recording of Mussorgsky's *Ein Kinderscherz*. After spending a year at the Royal College of Music, London, he entered St John's College, Cambridge, in 1932; he studied there with Edward Dent, gaining his BA in 1935 and his MusB in 1936 with first-class honours in music and modern languages. His time at Cambridge was spent in a whirl of activity, for, in addition to studying the harpsichord with Boris Ord and playing in some 100 concerts, he worked as a music critic for *Granta*, the student magazine, and helped to found the University Gramophone Society. He then returned to the Royal College of Music for a further year to take piano lessons from James Ching and the Australian composer Arthur Benjamin and to study conducting under Malcolm Sargent and Constant Lambert. His other musical studies included viola and organ tuition with Arnold Goldsborough and orchestration tuition under Gordon Jacob.

After leaving the Royal College of Music, Salter moved to the London Film Studios, Denham, where he worked under the music director, Muir Matheson; his tasks included editing Arthur Bliss's score for Alexander Korda's film *Things to Come* (1935) and the orchestration of film scores by composers such as Richard Addinsell. He also acted as chorus master and realized piano parts performed by actors on the screen, gaining valuable insight into film techniques. Although he was offered employment in Hollywood in 1936 he declined, preferring to take up the post of station accompanist for BBC television, with which he remained associated for most of his life. He subsequently held BBC posts as chorus master, répétiteur, and general assistant. On 11 October 1939 he married Christian Edgar Fraser (1915/16–1989), with whom he had three sons.

With the advent of the Second World War, Salter was seconded to intelligence, though he continued his work as conductor and performer. In 1943 he was sent to Algiers, where from 1943 to 1944 he was guest conductor of the Radio France Symphony Orchestra during its exile in north Africa. In 1945 he rejoined the BBC as assistant conductor of the BBC Theatre Orchestra. Over the following decades Lionel Salter continued to combine his practical musical skills with his gifts as performer, administrator, and writer. Possessing phenomenal abilities as a sight-reader, he played the piano part in Stravinsky's *Petrushka* for Ernest Ansermet without any preparation. In 1948 he was appointed to the BBC gramophone department as a producer, with special responsibility for the Third Programme (in 1970 renamed Radio 3). He began to review records for *Gramophone*—he continued doing so for the next fifty-one years—and participated regularly in the BBC's programme *Music Magazine*, later named *Record Review*. In the same year he became BBC European music supervisor, with responsibility for forty-two different language sections, for which he himself wrote many talks. Salter also held posts as head of music productions (1956–73) and head of opera (1963) for BBC television; the camera techniques that he established in the broadcasting of music became standard practice. In 1967 he was appointed assistant controller of music under William Glock. He retired from the BBC in 1974.

But Salter's musical interests were not narrowly confined to the BBC. From 1972 to 1976 Salter worked as opera co-ordinator and producer for the European Broadcasting Union. From 1948 he was harpsichordist of the London Baroque Ensemble, and he also played with the Vienna Capella Academica. He is said to have been the first person to play a fortepiano in the Royal Festival Hall. As an accompanist, he once visited the cellist Pablo Casals at his home in Prades and persuaded him to make recordings for the BBC, which would form part of a series of twenty-six programmes on Spanish music. He wrote several books, including the popular *Going to a Concert* (1950), *Going to the Opera* (1955), *The Musician and his World* (1963), and *The 'Gramophone' Guide to Classical Composers and Recordings* (1978, 2nd edition 1984), in addition to countless notes for records and articles for periodicals, dictionaries, and encyclopaedias. He edited many programme notes for the Promenade Concerts and the Edinburgh Festival, as well as working as an examiner for the Associated Board of the Royal Schools of Music and an international adjudicator.

Apart from incidental music, he wrote music for educational purposes and edited the scores of many baroque operas, including Cavalli's *Erismena* and Lully's *Alceste*. He translated many lieder and the librettos of 126 operas. Throughout his life Lionel Salter was a person of immense energy, integrity, and determination. Always seeking the highest standards, he was of a kind and generous disposition. He was a powerful force on the British musical scene, not least in the field of broadcasting. He died from cancer on 1 March 2000 at the home of one of his sons, 25 Hampstead Lane, Camden, London.   G. R. SEAMAN

Sources S. Sadie, 'Salter, Lionel (Paul)', *New Grove*, 432 • S. Sadie, 'Salter, Lionel (Paul)', *New Grove*, 2nd edn, 178–9 • *The Times* (10 March 2000) • *The Independent* (6 March 2000) • *The Guardian* (6 March 2000) • m. cert. • d. cert.
Likenesses G. Salter, photograph, repro. in *The Guardian* • G. Salter, photograph, repro. in *The Independent* • photograph, repro. in *The Times*

Salter, Samuel (*c*.1680–1756), Church of England clergyman, was born at Dedham, Essex, the son of Samuel Salter and his wife, Ann. He was educated at Corpus Christi College, Cambridge (1697–1701), where he graduated BA in 1701, MA in 1704, and later DD in 1728. He was ordained deacon at Norwich on 19 September 1703; he was vicar of Thorpe Market from 1705 to 1708 and, from 1708 to 1728, of the city living of St Stephen's, Norwich, with which he briefly held the rectory of Earlham (1712–14). He married Anne Penelope, daughter of John Jeffrey, archdeacon of Norwich from 1694 to 1720. On 13 March 1728 Salter was appointed to a prebend, sixth stall, in Norwich Cathedral, and in 1734 he became archdeacon of Norfolk; he was to hold the archdeaconry jointly with the prebend, the living of Bramerton, and the Norwich curacies of St George-in-Colegate and St Saviour until his death in 1756. In April 1733, as a prebendary, he stood proxy for the new bishop, Robert Butts, at his enthronement. One uncorroborated source records that he was also chaplain to the king at the time.

About 1750, however, Salter's life took a new turn. J. Hawkins, one of Samuel Johnson's biographers, tells us that Salter left Norwich at the age of seventy because of undisclosed disagreements with his children, and settled in London. Here he became a member of Johnson's Rambler Club, which met regularly at the King's Head in Ivy Lane. Apart from Johnson himself, Hawkins, and Salter, the nine members of the club included the writer John Hawkesworth, whose wife ran a boarding-house, to which Salter eventually retired, and where he died in 1756. In Hawkins's eyes Salter was 'a man of general reading, but no deep scholar'; he was 'courteous and affable, and enlivened conversation by his relation of a variety of curious facts of which his memory was the only register' (Hawkins, 220). His only known publication was a sermon, which, taking the eighteenth verse of Psalm 132 as his text, he preached in Norwich Cathedral on 20 October 1714, the day of George I's coronation. Clearly supporting the Hanoverian succession, he appealed to the people to 'heal our wide breaches, to cement and make up our unhappy divisions, and to engage us all to be of one heart and mind' (*A Sermon Preach'd at … Norwich*, 1714, 24).

Salter's son, **Samuel Salter** (*bap.* 1713, *d.* 1778), Church of England clergyman, was born in the parish of St Stephen, Norwich, and baptized there on 8 December 1713. He was educated at the free school in Norwich, the Charterhouse in London (1728–30), and, like his father, at Corpus Christi College, Cambridge, from where he matriculated in 1730. Here he graduated BA in 1734 and MA in 1737, and was a fellow from 1735 to 1738. About 1734, on the recommendation of Thomas Herring, then dean of Rochester, he became tutor to Philip Yorke (later second earl of Hardwicke), the son of Lord Chief Justice Hardwicke. In 1737 Hardwicke became lord chancellor and Salter quickly benefited from his patronage. Hardwicke appointed Salter his domestic chaplain and had him preferred to a prebend in Gloucester Cathedral in 1739, and to the rectory of Burton Coggles, Lincolnshire, in 1740. Salter married Elizabeth Secker, a relative of Thomas Secker, the future archbishop, in November 1744; they left two daughters and a son, Philip, who later became vicar of Shenfield in Essex. In 1751 Herring, now archbishop of Canterbury, awarded Salter a Lambeth DD. Eventually Hardwicke saw that he also acquired, in 1756, the rectory of St Bartholomew by the Exchange, which he held jointly with his Charterhouse appointments.

Salter's Norwich connections also yielded fruit. In 1745 his father personally installed him to a prebend in Norwich Cathedral, which he held until his death, and he was for a time (1750–54) vicar of Great Yarmouth. By 1778 he was also the official to the archdeacon of Norfolk. A scholar versed in the classics, his publications included a contribution to *Athenian Letters* (1741–3), principally the work of his pupil Philip Yorke, and editions of Richard Bentley's *Dissertation upon the Epistles of Phalaris* (1777) and Benjamin Whichcot's *Moral and Religious Aphorisms* (1753). His published sermons include one preached before the lord mayor of London on 2 September 1740, the anniversary fast commemorating the great fire of London.

Salter began his Charterhouse years in 1754, first as preacher but in effect as deputy master; and then, in 1761, he became master. Here he tried to regularize inefficiencies perhaps too pedantically; he soon developed acrimonious relationships with his registrars and officials over bureaucratic minutiae. He died on 2 May 1778 at the Charterhouse, where he was buried two days later, as he wished, in the common burial-ground, without slab or monument to his memory. His wife survived him.

WILLIAM MARSHALL

Sources Venn, *Alum. Cant.* · *Fasti Angl., 1541–1857,* [Ely] · F. Blomefield and C. Parkin, *An essay towards a topographical history of the county of Norfolk,* [2nd edn], 11 vols. (1805–10), vols. 3–5, 8 · J. Hawkins, *The life of Samuel Johnson, LL.D.,* 2nd edn (1787) · will of Samuel Salter the elder, PRO, PROB 11/825, sig. 261 · will of Samuel Salter the younger, PRO, PROB 11/1042, sig. 218 · B. Marsh and F. A. Crisp, eds., *Alumni Carthusiani: a record of the foundation scholars of Charterhouse, 1614–1872* (1913), 92 · G. Harris, *The life of Lord Chancellor Hardwicke,* 3 vols. (1847) · parish register, Dedham, Essex RO, D/P26/1/2 · bishop's register, Norfolk RO, DN/REG/22, bk 30A, fol. 189*r* · ordination subscription books, diocese of Norwich, Norfolk RO, DN/Sub/3/2
Archives BL, letters to first and second earls of Hardwicke and to Charles Yorke, Add. MSS 35586–35658 · BL, corresp. with duke of Newcastle, Add. MSS 32934–32980
Likenesses H. Bromley, etching, 1714, repro. in H. Bromley, *Catalogue of engraved British portraits* (1793), 227 · Vivares, etching, NPG

Salter, Samuel (*bap.* 1713, *d.* 1778). *See under* Salter, Samuel (*c.*1680–1756).

Salter, Thomas (*fl.* 1579–1581), author, was probably the Thomas Salter, schoolmaster of Upminster, Essex, who married, on 14 March 1584, Johanna, daughter of John Welshe, yeoman of Thurrock in the same county. In 1585 Thomas Salter with the same profession and from the same parish was a witness in a case concerning tithes. Apart from these unsubstantiated details Salter is known only through two works first published in London in 1579 and 1581.

A Mirrhor Mete for All Mothers, Matrones, and Maidens, Intituled the 'Mirrhor of Modestie' was licensed to Edward White on 7 April 1579 and dedicated to Anne, wife of Sir Thomas Lodge and mother of Thomas Lodge the poet. It has been identified as a version of Bruto's *La institutione di una fanciulla nata nobilmente*, which was first published with a text in both Italian and French in Antwerp in 1555. The book consists of advice to parents regarding the upbringing and training of their daughters. Using the popular Elizabethan literary device of the mirror to reflect and illuminate the inward mind rather than the letter format of the original, Salter takes a conservative view of the nature of girls' education. Emphasizing the importance of character over intellectual training, he stresses the usual desirable feminine virtues of chastity, silence, and humility. Salter permits learning for girls provided that it is tightly focused on appropriate material which will inculcate these virtues, and he includes needlework and other domestic activities: 'I suppose there is no Manne of reason and understandyng, but had rather love a Mayden unlearned and chast, then one suspected of dishonest life, though never so famous and well learned in Philosophie' (Salter, *Mirrhor,* sig. B8v). It was written for a popular audience in black type, and advocated a less extensive education than the original, which was designed for an aristocratic audience. A translation of Bruto finally appeared in English in 1598 as *The Necessarie, Fit, and Convenient Education of a Yong Gentlewoman,* translated by W. P.

Salter's other known work, *A contention betwene three bretheren, that is to say, the whoremonger, the dronkarde, and the diceplayer to approve which of them three is the worste,* first appeared in 1580, licensed to Thomas Gosson on 3 October. Further editions were published in 1581 and 1608. The work is a translation of Philippus Beroaldus's *Declamatio de tribus fratribus* which was first published in 1499 and was translated into German (1530) and French (1556). Salter appears to have worked from the French version. It is a moral debate, dramatized by personifying the three sins of drunkenness, lechery, and gambling in the persons of three sons, each of whom puts forward the arguments for being the least of three evils in the hope of inheriting his father's wealth. Salter's preface explains his purpose to the reader: to teach men to be careful of themselves, to avoid hypocrisy, and not to judge their neighbours—in biblical terms, 'Judge not, that ye be not judged' (Matthew 7: 1).   CAROLINE M. K. BOWDEN

Sources T. Salter, *A mirrhor mete for all mothers* (1579) • T. Salter, *The contention betweene three brethren* (1608) • J. B. Holm, ed., *A critical edition of Thomas Salter's 'The mirrhor of modestie'* (1987), vol. 32 of *The renaissance imagination* • D. Cressy, *Literacy and the social order: reading and writing in Tudor and Stuart England* (1980) • R. Kelso, *Doctrine for the lady of the Renaissance* (1956)

Salter, Thomas Frederick (*b.* 1762/3, *d.* in or after 1820), writer on angling, carried on business as a hatter at 47 Charing Cross, London. He began angling as a child, accompanying his father on fishing expeditions, and until the age of fifty-two (1815) he used to fish wherever possible in the vicinity of London, remaining at favourite stations for weeks together. When, owing to declining health, he retired from business, he lived for a long time at Clapton Place, Hackney, and put into writing his observations on angling. He called himself 'gent.' in the title of his first book, *The angler's guide, or, Complete London angler in the Thames, Lea, and other waters twenty miles round London*, which was published in 1814. A popular, practical book, it went to nine editions, as did an abridged version, first issued in 1816. His *The Troller's Guide* first appeared in 1820; the second edition (1830) advertised the author's last corrections.   M. G. WATKINS, *rev.* WRAY VAMPLEW

Sources T. F. Salter, *The angler's guide*, 9th edn (1841) • [J. Watkins and F. Shoberl], *A biographical dictionary of the living authors of Great Britain and Ireland* (1816)

Salter, William (*bap.* 1804, *d.* 1875), portrait painter, son of William and Sarah Salter, was born in Honiton, Devon, and baptized there on 26 December 1804. He moved to London in 1822 and became a pupil of James Northcote. Salter studied with Northcote until 1827. He then went to Florence, where in 1831 he exhibited his *Socrates before the Judges of the Areopagos*. The success of this work led to his election as a member of the Florentine Academy of Fine Arts; he was appointed professor of history. While in Italy, he visited Rome and Parma, where he was also elected to their respective academies of fine arts. Salter returned to England in 1833, where he began his best-known work, *The Waterloo Banquet at Apsley House* (Apsley House, London). He took six years to complete the work, which features eighty-four portraits of the officers who served with the duke of Wellington at Waterloo, as well as portraits of Wellington himself, William IV, and the king of Holland. The publisher F. G. Moon exhibited the work in 1841 at his London gallery in Threadneedle Street, and it immediately earned public interest and admiration. A popular large engraving by Greatbach was published by Moon in 1846. In 1852 a proposal was made to purchase the picture by subscription and present it to the duke of Wellington, but the project faltered owing to the duke's death. It was subsequently purchased by G. Mackenzie, who owned other works by the artist.

Salter also painted religious, mythological, and historical subjects, exhibiting chiefly at the British Institution. He became a member of the Society of British Artists in 1846, and he exhibited regularly with them, contributing 101 works in all. He later became vice-president of the society. He was a prolific portraitist, his subjects including the duke of Wellington, Wilberforce, and Sir Alexander Dickson. Many of his portraits served as preparatory works for *The Waterloo Banquet at Apsley House*, and they are now in the collection of the National Portrait Gallery, London. Contemporaries praised the quality of his portraits, which were often engraved for public consumption. In 1838 Salter presented an altarpiece, the *Descent from the Cross*, to the new parish church of his native town of Honiton. He died of bronchitis at his home, Devon Lodge, Portland Place, Fulham, London, on 22 December 1875, and was buried at Kensal Green cemetery. He left a widow, Mary.   F. M. O'DONOGHUE, *rev.* MORNA O'NEILL

Sources G. Pycroft, *Art in Devonshire: with the biographies of artists born in that county* (1883), 128–9 • Redgrave, *Artists* • *Art Journal*, 38 (1876), 80 • Bryan, *Painters* (1876) • Wood, *Vic. painters*, 3rd edn • d. cert. • C. E. Clement and L. Hutton, *Artists of the nineteenth century and their works: a handbook containing two thousand and fifty biographical sketches*, rev. edn, 2 vols. in 1 (Boston, MA, 1884) • 'Mr Salter's Waterloo Banquet', *The Athenaeum* (1 May 1841), 342 • 'Salter's picture of the Waterloo Banquet', *Art Union*, 3 (1841), 90 • Graves, *Brit. Inst.* • J. Johnson, ed., *Works exhibited at the Royal Society of British Artists, 1824–1893, and the New English Art Club, 1888–1917*, 2 vols. (1975), 410–11
Likenesses wood-engraving, BM; repro. in *ILN* (22 Jan 1876)
Wealth at death under £7000: probate, 22 Feb 1876, *CGPLA Eng. & Wales*

Salthouse, Thomas (1630–1691), Quaker preacher and writer, probably born at Dragley Beck, near Ulverston, Lancashire, was the third son of William Salthouse. His parents were possessed of 'a good estate in the outward' and from this 'he had been supplied' (Besse, 1.579). After a brief education he became a bailiff or land steward to Margaret and Judge Thomas Fell of Swarthmoor Hall, and was convinced of the Quaker message following George Fox's visit there in 1652. His contemporary John Whiting described him as 'a pleasant man in conversation, which rendered him acceptable to many others as well as Friends', and added that he also had 'a large capacity as a man, and an excellent gift of the ministry' (Whiting, 216).

After his convincement Salthouse travelled widely disseminating the Quaker message, mainly in the south-west of England, keeping in close contact with Margaret Fell through letters. In 1655 he set off from London towards Plymouth with Miles Halhead, stopping on the way at Reading and Bristol to hold meetings. At Honiton in Devon they were imprisoned for fourteen days on suspicion of being cavaliers and were then sent back home, being passed from officer to officer as vagrants. After their release they arrived in Plymouth in May 1655 and held many meetings, but soon after were re-arrested and imprisoned at the Guildhall for denying the Trinity. Later deemed innocent on this charge they were detained instead for refusing the oath of abjuration. On 28 May they were sent to gaol in Exeter Castle for disturbing the public peace and were later taken to the bridewell at Exeter, where they were incarcerated for several months.

Salthouse continued his work in the south-west in 1656. He was imprisoned in Ilchester gaol shortly after a meeting at Thomas Budd's 'as a dangerous, idle, wandering person' (Whiting, 214). Brought up at the general quarter sessions at Taunton, he was tendered the oath of abjuration, but, refusing to swear, was fined and returned to prison until payment was made, where he remained for about a year.

Following his release Salthouse travelled to many parts, including Gloucestershire and Reading, as well as returning to the north and 'divers other places' (Whiting, 215). He was back in the south-west about 1660, 'which by long imprisonments in it, as at Exeter and Ivelchester, was become naturaliz'd to him … and where his service pretty much lay' (ibid.). Letters from local Quakers to George Fox and Margaret Fell suggest that his itinerating work in Devon and Cornwall was highly valued; one Friend, writing in 1660, related how Salthouse had ridden up and down to Friends' meetings and been of great help (Braithwaite, 344; RS Friends, Lond., Swarthmore MSS, vol. 1, 140, MS vol. 351). About this time he was imprisoned at Plymouth for meetings and refusing to swear. In 1661 at the sessions at Ilchester, he and John Scafe were desired to 'return into their own country, in a month, and to come no more for the space of three year, into the county of Somerset', which he refused, subsequently being returned to the common gaol at Ilchester, where he was released by the king's proclamation in May 1661 (Whiting, 215).

Salthouse met George Fox at Topsham in Devon in 1663 and continued to suffer in the Quaker cause: he was imprisoned on a number of occasions in 1665; at Barking, Kingston, and seven weeks in the White Lion prison at Southwark. In 1668 he was evidently back in the south-west, for he wrote from there to Margaret Fell of the Quaker resolve 'to meet, preach and pray, in public and private, in season and out of season, in city, town, or country', and noted that Friends in the region 'were preparing [their] minds for prison' (Barclay, 245–6).

On 10 November 1670 Salthouse married Anne Upcott of St Austell, and appears to have settled there. He continued to travel in this area, though it was noted that 'he went to London to the yearly meetings, as he often did while at liberty' (Whiting, 216). In 1681 he was fined £20 for preaching at a funeral, and later, in 1683, was praemunired along with Thomas Lower for refusing the oath of allegiance and imprisoned in Launceston gaol, remaining there for three years until the general pardon of James II in 1686.

Salthouse's literary output, much of which was produced during periods of incarceration, was valued by Friends, and his contemporary the Quaker bibliographer John Whiting observed that Salthouse wrote 'some notable books, and divers excellent epistles to Friends', and lamented that they 'were never yet collected together as they deserve' (Whiting, 216). His early writings include a number of tracts concerning disputes with Baptists, such as *An Epistle to the Churches of the Anabaptists* (1657) and The

Line of True Judgement (1658), the latter being partly by him. Other tracts concern Quaker sufferings, such as *A Candle Lighted … from the Altar*, in which he warns 'the king, and all you in authority' not to set themselves up as 'Lords over Gods heritage by making laws or prescribing ways of worship to impose upon those tender consciences and those righteous souls contrary to the spiritual law of God' (p. 5), and *To both the Houses of Parliament, the General, and the Officers of the Army* (1660), which was signed by Salthouse and other Quakers, including Richard Hubberthorne and Edward Billing. In *A Loving Salutation*, written with Richard Farnsworth, Friends were urged to keep up their 'public testimony, whether it be by doing, or suffering' (p. 9). In 1665 he also wrote *A Brief Discovery of the Cause for which this Land Mourns*, which lamented the use of general fast days.

Thomas Salthouse died at his own house in St Austell, Cornwall, on 29 January 1691, leaving no children, and was buried on 1 February at Tregangeeves, Cornwall, where his wife was later interred with him after her death on 5 July 1695. Although the will of neither Thomas nor Anne Salthouse makes any reference to children, Thomas acknowledged three brothers and a sister still living. The inventory of 'Thomas Salthouse merchant', listing a personal estate of £18 18s. 0d., was taken in May 1695, so long after the Quaker's death that it most probably refers to the goods of another man. The inventory of Anne's estate, taken a fortnight after her death, showed a personal estate of £77 6s. 0d., of which £40 was accounted for by goods in her shop.　CAROLINE L. LEACHMAN

Sources J. Whiting, *Persecution expos'd: in some memoirs relating to the sufferings of John Whiting and many others of the people called Quakers* (1715) · *The Friend*, 2 (1844), 145–8 · T. Salthouse and M. Halhead, *The wounds of an enemy in the house of a Friend* (1656) · J. Besse, *A collection of the sufferings of the people called Quakers*, 1 (1753) · A. R. Barclay, ed., *Letters, &c. of early Friends* (1841) · J. Smith, ed., *A descriptive catalogue of Friends' books*, 2 (1867) · W. C. Braithwaite, *The beginnings of Quakerism*, ed. H. J. Cadbury, 2nd edn (1955); repr. (1981) · 'Dictionary of Quaker biography', RS Friends, Lond. [card index] · B. Y. Kunze, *Margaret Fell and the rise of Quakerism* (1994) · *The journal of George Fox*, ed. N. Penney, 2 (1911) · wills and inventories, Cornwall RO, AP/5 1950/1, 2, and 3 [Thomas Salthouse and Anne Salthouse]

Archives RS Friends, Lond., Caton MS 3, vol. 581, 74, 102–3, 109–11, 114, 116, 120–26 · RS Friends, Lond., letters to Margaret Fell and others · RS Friends, Lond., Swarthmore MS 3, vol. 354, 155–8, 162–71, 174, 179, 181–3, 185, 189–90

Wealth at death personal estate of a Thomas Salthouse, merchant, valued at £18 18s. but this was in May 1695, four years after subject's death; value of widow's personal estate, taken in July 1695, fourteen days after her death, was £77 6s., of which shop goods accounted for £40: wills and inventories of Thomas Salthouse and Anne Salthouse, Cornwall RO, AP/5 1950/1, 2, and 3

Salting, George (1835–1909), art collector and benefactor, was born in Sydney, Australia, on 15 August 1835, the elder son of Danish parents, Severin Kanute Salting (1805–1865), merchant, and Louisa Augusta Fiellerup (d. 1858), who had married in London in 1833 and emigrated to Sydney in July 1834. Severin prospered as a marine merchant, and in 1842, with Philip William Flower (1809–1872), son of a City of London merchant, he formed a partnership called Flower, Salting & Co., in Hunter Street, Sydney, which was involved in the highly profitable import-export business, principally shipping wool from Australia but also investing in sheep stations, sugar plantations, and other businesses in the young colony. George and his younger brother, William (1837–1905) lived at the family home of Greenknowe, at Potts Point, and were educated locally. In 1848 the two boys were taken to England—their parents joined them two years later—where George was sent to Eton College; a contemporary described him as 'a pale, lean, tall, eccentric person' (*DNB*). On account of George's poor health the Salting family returned to Sydney in 1853. In the following year George enrolled at the recently founded University of Sydney, where he excelled in classics and graduated BA in 1857. After his two sons had graduated Salting senior established the Salting exhibition at the University of Sydney, for pupils of Sydney grammar school.

On his father's retirement in 1858 Salting's family returned to England, where his mother died on 24 July. George attended Balliol College, Oxford, for one term but then left to accompany his grieving father to Rome. There he absorbed the city's rich artistic and architectural heritage over the winter of 1858–9, even taking up photography, at that time an unwieldy task involving pushing a cart with equipment, and black tent to develop the plates, through the streets of Rome. This experience proved pivotal in determining his future career as an art connoisseur, although his father remained sceptical of his son's interest, confiding to a Sydney friend, 'my greatest difficulty is to choose a pursuit for George' (Salting). Following a brief trip to Australia the Salting family settled in Silverlands, a house near Chertsey, Surrey. On 14 September 1865 Salting senior died, leaving his two sons joint heirs to his considerable fortune, valued at £90,000 in England and £85,000 in Australia. Though George, at the age of thirty, had an annual income estimated at £30,000 he chose to live very simply in two large rooms above the Thatched House Club, at 86 St James's Street, London, where he paid a yearly rent of £210 for the rest of his life.

On entering his inheritance Salting began his career as a passionate collector. On 9 April 1867 he was elected to the Burlington Fine Arts Club (BFAC; founded 1866), an exclusive association of gentlemen collectors, where he became a regular and important lender to its exhibitions. His first area of collecting was Chinese porcelain, principally the fashionable blue-and-white, *famille verte*, and *famille rose* varieties, to which he was introduced by his collector friend Louis Huth (1822–1905), a founding member of the BFAC. Rapidly outgrowing his bachelor rooms, from 1874 Salting began to place his oriental porcelain and other collections of *objets d'art* on deposit at the South Kensington (now Victoria and Albert) Museum, where they were displayed in the galleries, his oriental porcelain eventually filling some twenty-nine showcases at his death. He went on to form magnificent, wide-ranging collections of Italian Renaissance bronzes and maiolica, Limoges enamels, Palissy ware, Persian and Syrian ceramics, carved Renaissance furniture, and other classes of the decorative arts before turning to old master pictures,

drawings, and prints later in his career. In every category of object Salting developed an extraordinary eye for exquisite quality, fine detail, and high finish that informed everything he collected, whether it was Renaissance *objets d'art*, English miniatures, early Flemish and Dutch seventeenth-century old masters, or presentation Turner watercolours. He refined his collections by constantly trading up pieces, which earned him the epithet 'the prince of weeders' by R. H. Benson, the Italian picture connoisseur (Benson, vii). Every afternoon for more than forty years he visited the Bond Street dealers, where he became notorious for his protracted haggling, involving the part-exchange of objects weeded from his collection; yet he rarely failed to secure an object at the price he had in mind. He sought the opinions of fellow collectors and museum curators, notably Charles Hercules Read and Augustus Wollaston Franks, of the British Museum, and Dr Wilhelm Bode, director-general of the Berlin museums. A regular bidder at the London salerooms, Salting also attended the heroic Frédéric Spitzer sale of medieval and Renaissance *objets d'art* held in Paris over seventy days in 1893, where he bid in person, much to the fury of the professional dealers; he spent over £35,000, dispatching his purchases (almost one-tenth of the 3369 lots) directly to the South Kensington Museum. A compulsive collector to the end, Salting crowned his collection of English miniatures with Nicholas Hilliard's masterpiece *Young Man among Roses* a few months before his death.

On 12 December 1909, aged seventy-four and unmarried, Salting died of pneumonia in his rooms at 86 St James's Street. He was buried four days later at Brompton cemetery. Speculation as to the fate of his priceless collections was settled by the discovery of his simple, 400-word will, made on 14 October 1889, in which he gave 'unto the Nation my Art Collections' (will). The trustees of the National Gallery were allowed to select his pictures, and those of the British Museum his prints and drawings, while the Victoria and Albert Museum was the recipient of all his other collections (more than 2500 objects), provided that these were 'not distributed over the various sections but kept all together according to the various specialities of my exhibits' (ibid.). In keeping with his sensibility and taste the National Gallery bequest (192 pictures) concentrated on small, finely detailed works, particularly by northern artists, such as Memling's *A Young Man at Prayer*, Robert Campin's *Virgin and Child before a Fire Screen*, and Vermeer's *A Young Woman Seated at a Virginal*. The British Museum bequest (291 drawings, 151 prints) comprised a small but choice cabinet; it included such famous sheets as the Rembrandt red-chalk sketch *Two Women Teaching a Child to Walk* and Watteau's delicate study for the *Departure for the Island of Cythera* (Louvre Museum, Paris). The splendour and richness of Salting's bequest to the nation was celebrated in three special exhibitions held by the National Gallery, the British Museum, and the Victoria and Albert Museum in 1910–11.

A frugal and private man, Salting avoided the public eye throughout his life. Yet his extraordinary wealth and his personal miserliness gave rise to many stories of his having 'paid sixpence for his tea, or three shillings for a dinner on the same day that he had bought a picture for £5,000' (Read, 250). Despite his father's misgivings Salting possessed a sharp business mind. He had multiplied his capital inheritance by shrewd investments in stocks and shares as well as property developments in London (the Park Town Estate, Battersea) and Australia. At his death his estate was valued at some £1.3m.

Salting's ambition as a collector was aesthetic rather than scholarly. However, shortly after his death the *Burlington Magazine* (in March, April, May, and August 1910) published a series of four articles by the leading scholars G. F. Hill, Claude Phillips, C. J. Holmes, and Sidney Colvin on different aspects of his collection. Charles Hercules Read, president of the Society of Antiquaries, paid tribute to Salting as 'a great collector of the most catholic sympathies [who] stood almost alone, and [who] has unquestionably left his mark on the connoisseurship of our day … By his magnificent legacy he has made England's position in the art world immeasurably stronger' (Read, 251).

STEPHEN COPPEL

Sources S. Coppel, 'George Salting (1835–1909)', *Landmarks in print collecting: connoisseurs and donors at the British Museum since 1753*, ed. A. Griffiths (British Museum Press, 1996), 189–210 [exhibition catalogue, Museum of Fine Arts, Houston, TX, 1996, and elsewhere] · S. Coppel, 'George Salting and his Turner watercolours', *Apollo*, 151/457 (March 2000), 41–7 · will · *The Times* (14 Dec 1909), 10 · 'Wills and bequests: Mr Salting's estate', *The Times* (26 Jan 1910), 11 · R. H. Benson, *Catalogue of Italian pictures at 16, South Street, Park Lane, London and Buckhurst in Sussex collected by Robert and Evelyn Benson* (privately printed, London, 1914) · *DNB* · 'Salting, Severin Kanute', *AusDB*, 2.415 · S. K. Salting, letter to Edward Knox, 26 Jan 1859, Mitchell L., NSW, Knox family MSS, ML MSS 98/3, pp. 479–85 · C. H. Read, 'George Salting', *Burlington Magazine*, 16/83 (Feb 1910), 250–51 · 'The Salting collection', *The Times* (25 Dec 1909), 6 · 'The Salting bequest: the display at South Kensington', *The Times* (23 March 1911), 7 · Foster, *Alum. Oxon.*, 1715–1886, 4.1247
Archives National Gallery, London, notebooks | GL, P. W. Flower and Sons archive, business papers · Mitchell L., NSW, Knox family papers, corresp. with his father, Severin Kanute Salting
Likenesses J. Oppenheimer, pencil drawing, 1905, NPG · O. Rosenheim, two photographs, BM
Wealth at death £1,332,760 7s. 3d.: resworn probate, 1910, *CGPLA Eng. & Wales*

Saltmarsh, John (d. 1647), preacher and religious controversialist, came from Saltmarsh in the East Riding of Yorkshire. Having matriculated as a pensioner from Magdalene College, Cambridge, in 1627, he graduated BA in 1633 and proceeded MA in 1636. His first published writing was a collection of Latin and English poems on scriptural subjects, *Poemata sacra* (Cambridge, 1636). Among the dedicatees are Henry Smith, professor of theology and master of Magdalene; his tutor John Pullen; Sir Thomas and Lady Metham, prominent but recusant East Riding gentry; and George Butler, one of the council of the north. The poems themselves are mostly short and epigrammatic, with some extended conceits in the manner of the late metaphysicals. There is nothing in this volume and its evidence of early contacts which suggests the political and theological radicalism for which Saltmarsh later became

known. Ordained deacon at Durham in 1637, he became rector of Heslerton, Yorkshire, about 1639. His *Holy Discoveries and Flames* (1640), dedicated to Charles I, is indebted to the aesthetics of George Herbert and a process of meditation found widely in the Church of England in the period.

Saltmarsh's adoption of more radical ideas was signalled in 1643 by his resignation from Heslerton owing to scruples about taking tithes. In the same year he published an attack on Thomas Fuller, *Examinations, or, A Discovery of some Dangerous Positions*, in which he accused Fuller of being so moderate that the work of reformation would not proceed any further. Fuller replied in *Truth Maintained* (Oxford, 1643); Saltmarsh responded with *Dawnings of Light*. Questions were raised in the House of Commons about Saltmarsh's apparently derogatory remarks about the royal family in the first pamphlet; he was defended vigorously by Henry Marten, so much so that Marten was expelled and imprisoned in the Tower of London. In the meantime Saltmarsh had been preaching around Northampton and had become vicar of Cranbrook, Kent. In 1645 Saltmarsh was appointed rector of Brasted, also in Kent, by the committee for plundered ministers. He refused the annual income of £200, choosing instead to live on voluntary contributions; later, according to his own account, in an argument about tithes with the presbyterian John Lay, he gave up those as well, and in 1646 a successor was instituted at Brasted.

Saltmarsh came to prominence as a chaplain to Sir Thomas Fairfax and the parliamentary army, where he served from May 1646 to November 1647. In June 1646 he preached at St Mary's after Oxford had been taken by the army. According to Richard Baxter, who was shocked by his influence, Saltmarsh and William Dell were the dominant voices in the army's move to a more radical protestantism, particularly the doctrine of free grace (the title of a 1646 book that went into ten editions by the end of the century). Sometimes associated with antinomianism by its critics, free grace is an extension of orthodox Reformed doctrines on the supremacy of grace over law, while, in Saltmarsh's version, departing from Calvinist election in the direction of universalism, 'The Law is now in the Spirit' is a representative phrase. On the title-page of *Free Grace* he alludes to a spiritual crisis he had experienced some twelve years previously (about 1634), now resolved because his conscience has been relieved of the burden of the Mosaic law. Saltmarsh would have thus experienced a typically Lutheran conversion; what marked him out from many of his contemporaries was his insistence that grace should not be mixed with the law at all in the Christian life. With such views he attracted the attention of the presbyterian heresiographers of the 1640s. Samuel Rutherford's *Survey of the Spirituall Antichrist* (1648) singles out 'the Antichristian doctrine of John Saltmarsh and Will. Dell' on its title-page, and Thomas Edwards accused him of allowing a woman to preach at Brasted in the second volume of *Gangraena* (1646). Edwards also complains that 'Master Saltmarshes saints' do not keep fasts or thanksgivings. Rutherford is inaccurate in labelling Saltmarsh a Seeker; in *Sparkles of Glory* (1648) Saltmarsh criticizes Seekers for waiting for what is already there and available in Christ and his saints. In *Groanes for Liberty* (1646) Saltmarsh also attacked the presbyterians, especially Edwards, for opposing toleration when only a few years earlier they had pleaded for it on their own behalf when Smectymnuus were attacking the bishops. Saltmarsh, like Dell, denied that Oxford and Cambridge degrees, or ordination, should be the qualification for ministry. His plea for 'the infinitely abounding Spirit of God' as the only giver of prophecy in *Sparkles of Glory* is charismatic in its theology. His popular works (mostly published by the radical Giles Calvert) accordingly ignore the paraphernalia of scholarship, such as marginal notes or Latin quotations, for a clean page and adopt simple, accessible language.

During his time as army chaplain, Saltmarsh was active in the promotion of toleration and freedom of speech. 'The interest of the people in Christ's kingdom', he argued, 'is not only an interest of … submission, but of consultation, of debating, counselling, prophesying, voting' (Hill, 59). While never part of the Leveller organization, he supported many of their aims, and was cited by them in the Putney debates. He requested that a letter of his to the council of war (written from Laystreet in Essex, 28 October 1647) be read out, berating the army, as a friend, for mismanaging 'that glorious principle of Christian liberty' (Woodhouse, 438–9). There is no record of his having preached in London, and he denied making 'state-business' the subject of sermons. However, he did dedicate his *Sparkles of Glory* to the House of Commons; its emphases on the spiritual rather than organizational unity of Christians, freedom of conscience, and 'the spirituality of God's people, raising them from the love of worldly Interests and Ingagements' (p. 168) address crucial matters before parliament at the time. About this time he attended a meeting at John Duppa's Independent church in London to debate the question of whether Christians should meet in the 'high places', the old Church of England buildings. As the objections to this were unanimously voted down, Saltmarsh's position is clear.

On 4 December 1647, already seriously ill, Saltmarsh told his wife that he had a vision from God to give to the army. According to a number of sources, he went from his house in Essex to Windsor, where he spoke to Fairfax and then Cromwell with his hat on, explaining that he could no longer honour them because they had imprisoned the saints, by which he meant the Levellers who had been arrested at Corkbush Field. He had a similar meeting with the officers, explaining that, though God was angry with them, He still had a great work for the army to do. The respect with which his criticism was heard is a measure of his reputation, as well as the army's attitude to potentially prophetic messages. He then returned home to Laystreet near Ilford and died on 11 December 1647. He was buried at Wanstead on 15 December.

Eighteen months after his death his widow, Mary, published three letters from Saltmarsh to the army under the title *Englands Friend Raised from the Grave* (1649). Other publications in the Commonwealth period which cite him testify to his continued prestige. William Penn recommended him as one of the few pre-Quaker writers that young Friends should read. Although Saltmarsh is often described in more recent studies as a mystical writer, actually a more illuminating comparison is with pentecostal or charismatic Christianity. His defences of toleration, of lay ministry, and of movements towards democracy all seem to come from his emphasis on the spirit of God in that brief period in the mid-1640s when he was one of the most influential radical preachers and writers in England. ROGER POOLEY

Sources L. F. Solt, *Saints in arms* (Stanford, 1959) · A. L. Morton, *The world of the Ranters: religious radicalism in the English revolution* (1970) · A. Laurence, *Parliamentary army chaplains, 1642–51* (1990), 170 · Venn, *Alum. Cant.* · N. T. Burns, 'Saltmarsh, John', Greaves & Zaller, *BDBR* · A. S. P. Woodhouse, ed., *Puritanism and liberty* (1938) · T. Cooper, *Fear and polemic in seventeenth-century England: Richard Baxter and antinomianism* (2001) · W. C. Braithwaite, *The beginnings of Quakerism*, ed. H. J. Cadbury, 2nd edn (1955) · G. F. Nuttall, *The Holy Spirit in puritan faith and experience* (1946) · *Walker rev.*, 209, 211 · J. T. Cliffe, *The Yorkshire gentry from the Reformation to the civil war* (1969) · C. Hill, *The world turned upside down* (1972)

Saltonstall, Charles (*bap.* 1607, *d.* 1665), naval officer and teacher of navigation, was baptized on 27 January 1607 at St Dunstan-in-the-East, Middlesex, the third of five children of Sir Samuel Saltonstall (*d.* 1640). In November 1627 Saltonstall was the owner, sole merchant, and captain of a merchant ship which arrived at St Kitts, 'who brought with him good store of all commodities to relieve the plantation'. However, he found that some Dutch had been there before and carried away all the tobacco, so 'he was forced to put away all his commodities upon trust until the next crop'. In the meantime he decided to stay at St Kitts 'and employ himself and his company in planting Tobacco, hoping thereby to make a voyage'. But before he was ready to sail for England 'a Haricon' [hurricane] hit the island and 'his ship was split to his great loss, being sole Merchant and owner himself' (*Travels and Works of Captain John Smith*, 2.902). In 1629 Saltonstall commanded the *Susan and Ellen*, of nearly 300 tons, and sailed to Barbados, with Sir William Tufton, governor, 'and divers gentlemen, and all manner of commodities fit for a plantation' (ibid.).

It was probably in the early 1630s that Saltonstall served with the Dutch West India Company in the Caribbean. He seems to have returned to England by 1636, the year he published his navigational textbook based on wide reading and his own experience; he was then living near the Postern Gate on East Tower Hill, calling himself 'A Public Professor of Mathematics' and teaching the art of navigation. In 1642 he was appointed captain of the *Swallow* as part of the fleet commanded by Captain William Jackson on his privateering voyage, during which he captured Cartagena de las Indias and held it for eighteen months. In 1648 when the fleet revolted Saltonstall, who was captain of the *Hind*, signed the pledge of loyalty to parliament.

In 1649 Saltonstall was appointed captain of the *John* (30 guns) and in 1650 was part of the fleet under Robert Blake which pursued Prince Rupert and his fleet of privateers to Lisbon. When Blake learned in October that Rupert was at Alicante, he went after him. On 4 November Saltonstall chased the *Black Prince* and overhauled her. To avoid capture the ship ran ashore off Cartagena and the captain blew her up. On 9 November Blake sailed in pursuit of the rest of Rupert's fleet and left Saltonstall at Cartagena as commander-in-chief with the *John* and two French prizes. Saltonstall also told Robert Cotymor, the admiralty committee secretary, on 22 November 1650:

> the Lord hath proved us exceedingly since we have had little of the arm of flesh amongst us ... since our great and powerful fleet ... were reduced only to a little squadron of ten ships, for ... we have taken the Brazil fleet, and ... our squadron being now but three ships and four frigates ... we have taken three French ships and destroyed all Rupert's ships ... and thus hath God owned us in the midst of our implacable enemies, so that the terror of God is among them. (*Letters of Robert Blake*, 90–91)

In January 1652 Saltonstall was appointed captain of the hired merchant ship *Lion* and served under Blake at the battles of Kentish Knock (28 September) and Dungeness (30 November 1652). Saltonstall was then arrested and committed to the Fleet 'in order to his trial for his defect and neglect of his duty ... for not engaging in the last fight against the Dutch' (Gardiner and Atkinson, 3.163–4). He was later freed after giving a personal bond with two sureties. On 2 April 1655 he married Elizabeth Howell at St Brides's, Fleet Street; they had two sons, Thomas and Charles. Saltonstall probably went back to teaching navigation. He issued the third, enlarged, edition of his book on navigation in 1660. He died in 1665, by which time 'he had instructed many expert navigators, some of them now officers in the Navy' (Taylor, 211). He was survived by his wife.   PETER LE FEVRE

Sources E. G. R. Taylor, *The mathematical practitioners of Tudor and Stuart England* (1954), 211 · *Travels and works of Captain John Smith*, ed. E. Arber and A. G. Bradley, 2 vols. (1910), 2.902 · D. W. Waters, *The art of navigation in England in Elizabethan and early Stuart times* (1958), 446, 474 · V. T. Harlow, 'The voyages of Captain William Jackson, 1642–5', *Camden miscellany, XIII*, CS, 3rd ser., 34 (1924), 11 · *The letters of Robert Blake*, ed. J. R. Powell, Navy RS, 76 (1937), 90–91 · S. R. Gardiner and C. T. Atkinson, eds., *Letters and papers relating to the First Dutch War, 1652–1654*, 3, Navy RS, 30 (1906), 163–4 · B. Capp, *Cromwell's navy: the fleet and the English revolution, 1648–1660* (1989), 298 · IGI

Likenesses W. Marshall, line engraving (aged twenty-nine), BM, NPG; repro. in C. Saltonstall, *The navigator*, 2nd edn (1642)

Saltonstall, Gurdon (1666–1724), colonial governor and Congregationalist minister in America, was born on 27 March 1666 in Haverhill, Massachusetts, the eldest of the five children of Nathaniel Saltonstall (*c*.1639–1707), gentleman and magistrate, and his wife, Elizabeth (1647–1741), daughter of the Revd John Ward of Haverhill and his wife, Alice. A third-generation member of one of New England's most prominent families—his father and grandfather served simultaneously on the governor's council of Massachusetts from 1680 to 1683—Saltonstall

was eighteenth-century Connecticut's most unusual, talented, and successful governor.

Named after his great-grandfather, Brampton Gurdon, a staunch Suffolk puritan and politician, Saltonstall showed signs of genius and future greatness at an early age. At fourteen he entered Harvard College, where he was ranked third of nine in social distinction, and distinguished himself as an undergraduate, showing a 'vast proficiency in all the parts of useful learning', as one professor said of him (Sibley, 277). Having been selected to stay on as a tutor after graduating in 1684, Saltonstall earned an MA degree in 1687 and then made the career decision that was expected to fix his place in New England life. He accepted an invitation from the First Society of New London, Connecticut, to preach on probation in the late winter of 1687 and received a unanimous call from the parish in May of the following year to be its permanent minister. New London selected Major-General John Winthrop, grandson of the founding governor of Massachusetts, to be 'the mouth of the town' at Saltonstall's ordination (ibid.). Winthrop and Saltonstall formed a friendship that turned into a political partnership and changed the lives of both men and the history of the colony of Connecticut.

Almost immediately after settling in New London, Saltonstall earned renown as a great preacher and distinguished scholar. At the same time he developed a reputation—unique among New England's clergy, with the possible exception of Increase Mather—as a political statesman of great ability. New England magistrates often consulted ministers on matters of state because they respected the clergy's great learning. Usually, however, politicians sought advice on general policy: customarily, ordained ministers did not serve in any formal political office, or act in an administrative capacity. But through the urging of Winthrop and other Connecticut leaders, Saltonstall was repeatedly drawn into day-to-day political decision making. When Connecticut sent Winthrop to England in 1693 on a difficult mission to sort out the colony's legal position after the collapse of the dominion of New England, the general assembly asked Saltonstall to accompany him. Realizing that he might have to abandon his ministerial career, and also mindful of his duties to his two daughters and wife, Saltonstall declined the offer and attempted to devote himself full-time to his clerical duties.

When Winthrop returned from England in early 1698 with guarantees of Connecticut's semi-autonomous status within the empire, he was regarded as a hero for saving the Connecticut charter of 1662: within a few months the freemen elected him governor. Winthrop again prevailed upon Saltonstall for assistance, and he quickly became known as the new governor's most influential adviser. In his seventeen years as governor, Winthrop frequently travelled outside Connecticut, was embroiled in personal feuds and financial difficulties, and suffered from chronic ill health. His governorship was not a happy or peaceable time for either himself or for Connecticut, and increasingly other leaders turned to Saltonstall, who functioned as the governor's secretary. Although he held no elective office, Saltonstall served directly on a number of boards and commissions, and acted as the colony's agent several times in negotiations with England and with other colonies. In light of all this activity, the Connecticut general assembly's request that Saltonstall assume the governorship in 1707 on Winthrop's death is less surprising. Nevertheless, it was unprecedented in puritan New England's history for a minister to become a magistrate, and it was unprecedented in Connecticut's history for anyone to become a governor without having been an experienced office-holder. Saltonstall resigned his ministry, accepted the temporary appointment, was formally elected the following year, and was re-elected every year for the rest of his life.

Saltonstall's governorship was characterized by his unswerving devotion to traditional puritan values, his defence of the Connecticut charter of 1662, and his commitment to imperial military co-ordination. A natural conservative, who believed in ceremony, deference, and authority to a degree that could easily be construed as haughty, Saltonstall none the less remained immensely popular with all classes of society throughout his tenure. His accomplishments include securing the adoption of the Saybrook platform (1708), which created a quasi-presbyterian structure to help preserve religious order; moving Yale College to New Haven in 1716, and putting the fractious school on a secure footing; working smoothly with the Board of Trade on matters of trade, finance, and boundaries; and ending the vicious battles between rival companies of land speculators that had plagued New London and Windham counties. Connecticut was far more peaceful and harmonious under Saltonstall's governorship than it had been during Winthrop's term in office.

Saltonstall was married three times: about 1689 to Jerusha Richards (1665–1697) of Hartford, with whom he had five children; in 1699 to Elizabeth Rosewell (c.1676–1710) of Branford, with whom he also had five children; and in 1712 to Mary Whittingham (d. 1730) of Lawrence, Massachusetts, the widow of William Clarke of Boston, with whom he had no children. Saltonstall died suddenly, aged fifty-eight, on 20 September 1724, at New London, and was buried there two days later. The tributes paid reveal him to have been a governor held in particularly high regard. The *Boston News-Letter* thought him 'peculiarly formed for the benefit and delight of mankind; he had a wonderful quickness of tho't, and yet as strange an attention and closeness … he was as great a Christian as he was a man' (Sibley, 281). Cotton Mather published a commemorative essay which concluded: 'We will not call him a star, but even a constellation … when he stood among the people he was higher than any' (Labaree, 318).

Puritan New England is often mislabelled a theocracy, which historians know it emphatically was not. A delicate balance existed between a church and state that were legally separated in structure but morally and politically joined in a common bond of mutual support. Reverend/ Governor Saltonstall proved uniquely able to serve on both sides of the balance. At the time of his death, Connecticut enjoyed the greatest equilibrium of its colonial history.

BRUCE C. DANIELS

Sources J. H. Trumbull and C. J. Hoadly, eds., *The public records of the colony of Connecticut*, 15 vols. (1850–90), vols. 5–6 · R. S. Dunn, *Puritans and Yankees: the Winthrop dynasty of New England, 1630–1717* (1962) · J. L. Sibley, *Biographical sketches of graduates of Harvard University*, 3 (1885), 277–86 · L. W. Labaree, 'Saltonstall, Gurdon', *DAB* · R. L. Bushman, *From puritan to Yankee: character and the social order in Connecticut, 1690–1765* (1967) · F. Caulkins, *History of New London, Connecticut* (1852) · J. M. Poteet, 'The lordly prelate: Gurdon Saltonstall against his times', *New England Quarterly*, 53 (1980), 483–507 · R. Saltonstall, *Ancestry and descendants of Sir Richard Saltonstall* (1897) · T. W. Jodziewicz, 'Saltonstall, Gurdon', *ANB*

Archives Connecticut Historical Society | Connecticut State Library, Hartford, Connecticut State Archives · Mass. Hist. Soc., Winthrop papers

Likenesses portrait, Yale U. · portrait, Museum of Connecticut History, Hartford

Wealth at death £1547: inventory of estate, Connecticut State Library, Hartford, probate district, New London, file 4674

Saltonstall, Sir Richard (1521?–1601), merchant and local politician, was born in Halifax, Yorkshire, the second son of Gilbert Saltonstall, a yeoman, and was apprenticed to Richard Stanfield, a prosperous member of the Skinners' Company, of which he became free in 1551. By 1571 he was well established as one of the leading exporters of cloth to the Low Countries, but his activities extended beyond their traditional bilateral trade with northern Europe, making it serve broader multilateral interests. He became one of the largest traders with Spain, and elbowed his way into membership of the Spanish Company in 1577. His partnership's imports from Iberia were valued at £2956 in 1584, but he continued to import large quantities (as much as £6000-worth from Hamburg and Stade in 1587–8) from northern Europe in the later 1580s. Saltonstall was also a member of the regulated companies trading to Turkey (1580), Russia (1586), and the Levant (1592), although it is not clear whether he was an active trader in these areas. In later years he became involved in customs administration, securing the lucrative post of customer of London by 1598, in which he was assisted by his son Samuel. His subsidy assessments suggest that he was numbered among the top seventy-five citizens in terms of his wealth, and he was reported to be worth £20,000 in the 1590s.

From 1573 until 1599 Saltonstall dwelt in a property in Mincing Lane, in the parish of St Dunstan-in-the-East, rented from the Grocers' Company, although he seems to have been residing in the parish from at least 1564. He also enjoyed a suburban estate at South Ockendon, Essex, purchased from Edward Tyrell in 1576, and owned the manors of Ledsham in Yorkshire and Moorhall in Yardley, Essex. He was active in both the management of the Company of Merchant Adventurers and the Skinners' Company and in the government of the city. He assisted John Marsh, governor of the merchant adventurers, in negotiations with Alva's government in the Netherlands in 1570, and was himself acting as governor of the company by 1585, and undertook the delicate negotiations with Stade and Hamburg over the location of the English staple in 1587 and 1588. First elected warden of the Skinners' Company in

1568, he served as its master four times (1589–90, 1593–4, 1595–6, and 1599–1600), though on the last occasion he required a deputy because of his deteriorating health. He was a common councillor from 1571, and served as a governor of St Thomas's Hospital from 1571 to 1578 and as its treasurer from 1575 until 1577. His business acumen ensured that he was frequently called on by the privy council to arbitrate commercial disputes and (especially in the 1590s) to assist in the provision of exchange facilities for the crown. He also served as MP for the city of London in 1586. He was elected alderman of Aldgate ward on 26 September 1588 and moved to Tower ward in 1592, where he served until his death. He held the office of sheriff in 1588–9 and of lord mayor in 1597–8. By the time of his mayoralty the worst of the difficulties of the 1590s had passed, and he oversaw the implementation of the new poor law legislation which led to a doubling of the rates in London. However, the war in Ireland continued to make demands on the city's resources, and much of the administration's energies during this time was consumed in the pursuit of tax defaulters. In 1598 Saltonstall was knighted.

Saltonstall married Susanna (d. 1613), the daughter of Thomas Poyntz, a gentleman of North Ockenden, Essex. They had seven sons and nine daughters, for whom favourable marriages into gentry or leading mercantile families were arranged. Three of his daughters, for example, married prominent members of his own livery company, Richard Wyche, John Harvie, and Thomas Myddleton, all of whom acted as overseers of his will. The large size of his family perhaps explains the modesty of his charitable bequests (only £265): one-third of his estate was destined for his wife, another third was to be divided among his sons after a bequest of £1000 to his as yet unmarried daughter Martha, and the residue of the remaining third after the bequests for charity and specified family members was to be divided equally between his wife and his children still in their minorities. Saltonstall died on 17 March 1601 at South Ockendon and was buried there in the parish church, where an alabaster monument to him remains. In 1602 the terms of the will were disputed by a natural daughter, Abigail Baker, and later by his sons.   IAN W. ARCHER

Sources HoP, *Commons* · M. Benbow, 'Index of London citizens involved in city government, 1558–1603', U. Lond., Institute of Historical Research, Centre for Metropolitan History · R. G. Lang, 'The greater merchants of London in the early seventeenth century', DPhil diss., U. Oxf., 1963 · wills, customs accounts, subsidy assessments, inquisitions post mortem, PRO, PROB 11/97, sig. 31 · repertories of the court of aldermen and journals of common council, CLRO · freedom lists and court minutes, Skinners' Company, London · CSP dom., 1547–1650 · A. B. Beaven, ed., *The aldermen of the City of London, temp. Henry III–[1912]*, 2 vols. (1908–13) · G. E. Cokayne, *Some account of the lord mayors and sheriffs of the city of London during the first quarter of the seventeenth century, 1601–1625* (1897) · sentence to will, PRO, PROB 11/100, sig. 51

Likenesses alabaster effigy on monument, 1700–40, church of St Nicholas, South Ockendon, Essex

Saltonstall, Sir Richard (*bap.* 1586, *d.* 1661), colonist in America, was baptized at Rookes Hall, Highcliffe in

Sir Richard Saltonstall (*bap.* 1586, *d.* 1661), by unknown artist, 1644

Hipperholme, Halifax, Yorkshire, on 4 April 1586, the eldest son of Samuel Saltonstall (1562–1613) and his wife, Anne (1564–1589), daughter of John Ramsden of Almondbury, Yorkshire. The Saltonstalls had grown wealthy as Tudor clothiers, and Richard's uncle Sir Richard Saltonstall was lord mayor of London in 1597–8. After education at Clare College, Cambridge (1603–5), and the Middle Temple (1606–7), he was married in 1609 to Grace (c.1590–1625), daughter of Robert Kaye of Almondbury, Yorkshire, and lived from 1609 to 1626 at Huntwick Hall, Wragby, Yorkshire, where their six children were raised. He was knighted at Newmarket on 23 November 1618, and was a justice for the West Riding in 1625 and 1626. As a widower he sold most of his Yorkshire estate (over 3000 acres worth some £15,000) and moved to the puritan parish of St Stephen's, Coleman Street, London.

Saltonstall joined the Massachusetts Bay Company on 4 March 1629 and was elected assistant (though, despite his rank, not governor) in 1629 and 1630. He lent the company £500, sent cattle and servants ahead, and financially assisted his fellow passengers in the 1630 *Arbella* fleet. He led the settlement of Watertown, where he was granted 588 acres. He returned permanently to England with his two daughters in April 1631. By 1632 he had married Elizabeth West (*b.* 1599), daughter of Thomas West, third baron

De La Warr; at Isleworth, Middlesex, they had twins, who soon died. His colonizing interests switched to the Saye and Sele–Brooke ventures on the Connecticut and Piscataqua rivers, but his 1632 expedition failed with a loss of over £500 and the 1700 acre Saltonstall Park north of Windsor, Connecticut, cost a further £1000 but was not 'improved' from wilderness. About 1640 he married his third wife, Martha Wilsford (*née* Cammock) (*bap.* 1587, *d.* 1662), a cousin of the puritan second earl of Warwick. Much of the rest of Saltonstall's estate was lost in schemes in Ireland and commercial ventures in the Netherlands, which he visited in 1643 and 1644, when his portrait was painted.

Saltonstall opposed the crown in the civil wars, and his fortunes recovered with the parliamentarian victory. In March 1650 he was appointed a commissioner of the high court of justice, set up to punish opponents of the regime. From 1649 he held lucrative posts controlling the sales of crown property, and by 1658 he could afford to buy Brymbo Hall, near Wrexham, Denbighshire. After the Restoration, however, he was forced to flee arrest as a 'seditious person', and died at Crayford, Kent, in 1661, probably in September.

In 1651 Saltonstall sent a remonstrance to Boston's ministers castigating them for the violent persecution of Baptists and advocating liberty of conscience. Members of his family continued in Massachusetts regularly performing public service; their posterity has followed in this tradition to the present day.   ROGER THOMPSON

Sources J. G. Bartlett, historical genealogy of the Saltonstall family, 1931, Connecticut State Library, Hartford, 203–46 · R. E. Moody, ed., *The Saltonstall papers*, 1 (1972), 3–24 · R. C. Anderson, ed., *The great migration begins: immigrants to New England, 1620–1633*, 3 (Boston, MA, 1995), 1618–21 · *CSP dom.*, 1660–61, 123 · C. H. Firth and R. S. Rait, eds., *Acts and ordinances of the interregnum, 1642–1660*, 3 vols. (1911) · Venn, *Alum. Cant.*
Archives Mass. Hist. Soc., family papers
Likenesses oils, 1644, Peabody Essex Museum, Salem, Massachusetts [*see illus.*]

Saltonstall, Wye (*bap.* 1602, *d.* after 1640), translator and poet, was baptized on 3 October 1602 at St Dunstan-in-the-East, London, the son of Sir Samuel Saltonstall (*d.* 1640), and grandson of Sir Richard *Saltonstall, lord mayor of London in 1597. The Saltonstall family originally came from Halifax. The poet reveals something of his family's history in 'Funeral elegies in English, Latin, and Greek, upon the death of his father' (BL, Harley MS 509). Sir Samuel was imprisoned for some unknown reason for thirteen years until he was released following the intervention of his brother-in-law, Sir Thomas Myddelton. In the same poem Saltonstall describes the earlier death of his mother (*d.* before 1640), of whom nothing else is known.

Saltonstall entered Queen's College, Oxford, as a commoner in Easter term 1619, but did not graduate. Although he is said to have studied law at Gray's Inn his name does not appear on the register. In 1625 he returned to Oxford, where he remained for several years, apparently working as a tutor in French and Latin. Little is known of his later life, although it seems he was 'living in good repute for his

learning in sixteen hundred and forty, and after' (Wood, *Ath. Oxon.*, 2.677).

Saltonstall published a variety of works. These include *Picturae loquentes* (1631), a collection of satirical portraits in prose of various social and professional types including 'a young heir' and 'a scholar in the University'. Further portraits were added to subsequent editions; 'A Maid', a poem in rhyming couplets, is also included in the volume, which was dedicated to 'suo C.S.', probably his brother Charles *Saltonstall.

Saltonstall was particularly drawn to the works of Ovid. In the epistle to the reader which prefaces his translation of the *Tristia* (dedicated to Sir Kenelm Digby), he describes Ovid's banishment and lonely death with great feeling, fancying that 'the Muses, together with Venus and a hundred little Cupids [were] mourners at his funeral' (*Tristia*, epistle to the reader, 1633). He went on to publish the *Epistolae ex Ponto* in 1639. A translation of Ovid's *Heroides*, dedicated 'to the virtuous ladies and gentlewomen of England', was published in 1637 (2nd edn). Saltonstall is not a particularly distinguished poet; his rhyming couplets are halting and unpolished:

> Having lost my credit and virginity;
> To lose a few words a small loss will be;
> For thy poor Dido thou mean'st to forsake,
> And unto sea wilt a new voyage make.
> Aeneas thou wilt needs depart from me,
> To find strange kingdoms out in Italy.
> (Saltonstall, *Heroides*, epistle 7, ll. 5–10)

Saltonstall also translated Jodocus Hondius's *Historia mundi, or, Mercator's atlas* (1635). In his dedicatory epistle to Sir Henry Marten he makes oblique reference to personal difficulties: 'Let the authors, and your own worthiness mitigate my presumption, that I whose life hath been all *Tristia*, have presumed to offer up the whole world at so high an altar'. Saltonstall went on to translate Eusebius's *Life of Constantine* (1636), which he dedicated to Sir John Lambe, Sir Henry Marten's successor as dean of the arches court of Canterbury.

Saltonstall's date of death is unknown, though it is probable that it predates the publication of *Somnia allegorica* (2nd edn, 1661), a novel, no copies of which survive, which Wood believed he had written (Wood, *Ath. Oxon.*, 2.678). It is also unlikely that he was responsible for *Poems of Ben Johnson Junior* (1672), 'by W. S. gent.', another work sometimes attributed to his pen.

SARAH ANNES BROWN

Sources Wood, *Ath. Oxon.*, new edn, 2.676–9 · Foster, *Alum. Oxon.* · J. Foster, *The register of admissions to Gray's Inn, 1521–1889, together with the register of marriages in Gray's Inn chapel, 1695–1754* (privately printed, London, 1889) · *N&Q*, 2nd ser., 11 (1861), 409, 434, 513 · *N&Q*, 2nd ser., 12 (1861), 372 · *N&Q*, 3rd ser., 1 (1862), 350, 418 · *N&Q*, 3rd ser., 11 (1867), 68 · *DNB* · *IGI*

Saltoun. For this title name *see* Fraser, William, twelfth Lord Saltoun of Abernethy (1654–1715); Fraser, Alexander George, sixteenth Lord Saltoun of Abernethy (1785–1853).

Saltrey, H. [Henry] **of** (*fl. c.*1184), writer and Cistercian monk, whose initial is usually extended as Henry, was a member of the abbey of Saltrey, Huntingdonshire. In 1184, at the request of Abbot H(ugh) of Warden, Bedfordshire (1173–85), the mother house of Saltrey, he wrote the *Tractatus de Purgatorio sancti Patricii*; a second version followed before 1190. He claims to relate what he heard from **Gilbert of Louth** (*fl. c.*1148–*c.*1180), who was sent *c.*1148 by Gervase, the first abbot (1139–55) of Louth Park, Lincolnshire, to an Irish king (Diarmait Mac Murchadha of Leinster) in order to build a monastery (Baltinglass) on land that the king had donated. As Gilbert could not speak Irish, the king gave him as interpreter the knight Owein. During their time together (1148–51) the knight told Gilbert what he had seen and suffered in St Patrick's Purgatory (a pit situated on Station Island, Lough Derg, Donegal). Gilbert then returned to England and became abbot of Basingwerk, Flint (1155–79). He often related the knight Owein's experience, and it was when Gilbert was no longer abbot of Basingwerk that Saltrey heard him and subsequently was asked to write this story. Gilbert's authorship has often been suggested, since Saltrey denies being the author and Gilbert is named in the title in one manuscript (Vatican City, Biblioteca Apostolica Vaticana, MS Barberini 270).

In this story reality and fiction are intertwined. The tale is centred on Owein's journey to the other world to which the pit is the entrance, and is clearly influenced by the third-century 'Vision of St Paul', the 'Vision of Dryhthelm' in Bede's *Historia ecclesiastica* (Bede, *Hist. eccl.*, 5.12), and Honorius Augustodunensis's early twelfth-century *Elucidarium* (ed. Y. Lefèvre, Bibliothèque des Écoles Françaises d'Athènes et de Rome, 170, 1954, 3.14–15). But the introduction to this physical journey to the land of torments and to earthly paradise is the sole historical record of the transformation of a pilgrimage for life in the tradition of the recluse into a short-term penitential pilgrimage, the main exercise of which was to be locked for twenty-four hours in a pit (apparently a souterrain). From the mid-thirteenth to the sixteenth century the pilgrimage attracted many overseas pilgrims who left their own accounts; it still exists but the incarceration has been replaced by a vigil in the church. While Saltrey is partly right in declining authorship, he nevertheless gave to the story its written form and, besides the dedication and epilogue, added the long prologue, the anecdote of the prior, the two homilies, and the various testimonies (in the long version); moreover in the long version he mentioned that he had divided the work into chapters and 'interspersed it with the exhortations of the Holy Fathers' (*St Patrick's Purgatory*, trans. Picard, 78). There are some 150 manuscripts containing the *Tractatus*, and none is the original manuscript. This story has been translated into most European languages; such translations constitute a further large corpus of manuscripts. The origin of the sudden popularity of the *Tractatus* after the 1180s can only be explained by Anglo-Norman activity in Ireland. One of the earliest translations was into Norman-French by a Marie de France (*c.*1190) who may have been Marie de Beaumont de Meulan, of whose first cousins one had married the

founder of Saltrey, another the son of the founder of Basingwerk, and a third the daughter of the founder of Baltinglass.   Yolande de Pontfarcy

Sources J.-M. Picard, trans., *St Patrick's Purgatory: a twelfth-century tale of a journey to the other world* (Dublin, 1985) · *St Patrick's Purgatory: two versions of 'Owayne Miles', and 'The Vision of William of Stranton' together with the long text of the 'Tractatus de Pugatorio Sancti Patricii'*, ed. R. Easting, EETS (1991) [incl. list of MSS] · Marie de France, *L'Espurgatoire Seint Patriz*, ed. and trans. Y. de Pontfarcy (1995) [incl. short version of *Tractatus* and the additions to the long version, and a large bibliography] · R. Easting, 'Owein at St Patrick's Purgatory', *Medium Aevum*, 55 (1986), 159–75 · M. Haren and Y. de Pontfarcy, eds., *The medieval pilgrimage to St Patrick's Purgatory* (1988) · K. Warnke, ed., *Das Buch vom Espurgatoire S. Patrice der Marie de France und seine Quelle* (Halle, 1938); repr. (Geneva, 1976) · Y. de Pontfarcy, 'Si Marie de France était Marie de Meulan', *Cahiers de Civilisation Médiévale*, 38 (1995), 353–61 · J. T. Gilbert, ed., *Chartularies of St Mary's Abbey, Dublin: with the register of its house at Dunbrody and annals of Ireland*, 2 vols., Rolls Series, 80 (1884) · D. Knowles, C. N. L. Brooke, and V. C. M. London, eds., *The heads of religious houses, England and Wales*, 1: 940–1216 (1972)

Saltwood, Robert (*fl.* 1518–1538), author and Benedictine monk, was born in the last decade of the fifteenth century, probably at Saltwood, Kent. He was professed at St Augustine's Abbey, Canterbury, before 1518 and was sent to study at Gloucester College, Oxford, where he received the bachelor's degree in theology in 1526.

After returning to Canterbury Saltwood continued to pursue his scholarly interests, probably in association with the circle of scholars surrounding the abbot, John Essex (or Foche), which included the musician John Dygon and the antiquarian John Twyne. In 1535 he collaborated with Twyne in the production of an English edition of the Old French text, the *Hystory and Questyons of Kynge Boccus and Sydracke* (STC 3186). Saltwood may have contributed to the text, and he certainly funded the printing of the book, which is described in its colophon as having been produced in London 'At the coste and charge of dan Robert Saltwode monk of saynt Austens Cantorbury'. The following year he published his own composition, *A comparyson bytwene iiii byrdes, the larke, the nyghtyngale, the thrushe & the cucko, for theyr syngynge who shuld be chauntoure of the quere* (STC 21647), an allegory of the virtues and vices of man in English verse. The *Comparyson* was printed at Canterbury by John Mychell, the town's first printer. Mychell also printed at least one other book for the monks of St Augustine's, *A Goodly Narration how Augustine Raysed Two Deed at Longcompton* (now lost), based on a verse by John Lydgate, with which Saltwood may also have been involved.

In the same year that the *Comparyson* was published, Saltwood was implicated in a case concerning another monk at the abbey, William Winchelsea, who was accused of slandering Archbishop Cranmer and speaking openly against the recent changes in the church. Saltwood was summoned to testify before Cranmer, and confirmed several of the charges against Winchelsea.

Saltwood remained at the abbey until its suppression on 30 July 1538, at which time he held the office of warden of the chapel of St Mary. Nothing further is known of him.   James G. Clark

Sources Emden, *Oxf.*, 4.503 · J. G. Clark, 'The Benedictines and printing in early Tudor England', *The uses of script and print, 1300–1700*, ed. J. Crick and A. Walsham [forthcoming] · PRO, state papers domestic, Henry VIII, general series, SP 1/88, fols. 19r–20v · Dugdale, *Monasticon*, 1.124 · *LP Henry VIII*, 13/1, no. 1503

Salusbury [Salesbury] **family** (*per. c.*1454–*c.*1684), gentry, were one of the most prominent families in north Wales in the sixteenth and seventeenth centuries. The origins of the family are obscure (they claimed descent from one Adam of Salzburg, who was alleged to have come to England in 1066), but they may have come originally from Herefordshire, and had settled at Lleweni in the lordship of Denbigh by 1334. Thomas Salusbury Hen ('the old'; *d. c.*1490) was constable of Denbigh Castle in 1454. Most accounts of the family have stated that he was killed at the battle of Barnet on 14 April 1471 but contemporary poetry suggests that he died in 1490. Lleweni was inherited by his eldest son, Sir Thomas Salusbury (*d.* 1505), who was knighted for his service at the battle of Blackheath on 17 June 1497. Sir Thomas Salusbury was succeeded by his eldest son, Sir Roger Salusbury (*d.* 1530). Sir Roger Salusbury was one of Henry VIII's bodyguard in 1509, in which year he was appointed steward of the lordship of Denbigh and constable of the castle. He married twice, his second wife being Elizabeth, daughter of John Puleston of Hafod y Wern. His heir, according to his inquisition post mortem, was his son Thomas, but by 1538 Lleweni was in the possession of another son, **Sir John Salusbury** [Salesbury] (*b.* in or before 1520, *d.* 1578). Sir John Salusbury was MP for Denbighshire six times between 1545 and 1558. On 22 February 1547 he was knighted and he was chamberlain of north Wales from 1547 to 1578. He was a member of the quorum of the peace for Denbighshire from 1543 to 1578, sheriff of Denbighshire from 1541 to 1542 and again from 1574 to 1575, and for Flintshire from 1548 to 1549, and held numerous lesser offices. Salusbury was *custos rotulorum* from 1558–9 to 1564 or after. His career shows the level the family had now reached and he continued to add to its wealth. According to tradition he was known as Siôn y Bodiau (John of the Thumbs) because of a physical deformity, although the nickname has also been attributed to his uncle, John Salusbury, of Holt, Denbighshire, who was active in the service of Henry VIII in both Wales and Ireland. He married Jane (*d.* in or after 1578), daughter and coheir of David Myddelton of Chester. His son John Salusbury (*d.* 1566) was the first husband of Katherine (*d.* 1591), daughter and heir of Tudur ap Robert of Berain, Denbighshire, famous for her four successive marriages to members of the north Wales gentry. Sir John Salusbury died by 11 June 1578 and was buried in St Marcel's Church, Denbigh. He was succeeded by his grandson and heir, Thomas *Salisbury or Salusbery (1561x4–1586), conspirator.

Thomas Salisbury married Margaret (*d.* in or after 1586), daughter of his stepfather, Morris *Wynn [see under Wynn family], landowner, of Gwydir in Caernarvonshire, between 1 January and 25 March 1575. Educated at Oxford University, he entered the service of Robert Dudley, earl of Leicester, his former guardian. The Salusburys seem generally to have conformed with the new order in religion. However, Thomas Salisbury had gone over to Rome by 1580 and was a member of the Catholic Association, a secret society established to further the work of Jesuit missionaries in England and Wales. He became a close friend of Anthony Babington, who in 1586 became involved in a plot to assassinate Elizabeth I and replace her on the throne with Mary, queen of Scots. Salisbury's part in the conspiracy was to organize a rising in Denbighshire and another friend, Edward Jones of Plas Cadwgan, Denbighshire, was also one of the conspirators. However, the plot was infiltrated from the start by Sir Francis Walsingham's agents and Babington was arrested in August 1586. Salisbury fled from London to Cheshire but was soon apprehended, and Jones and he were among the conspirators executed on Tower Hill on 21 September 1586. Babington and six others had been hanged, drawn, and quartered the previous day, but their treatment caused such public revulsion that Salisbury and his companions were left to die on the gallows.

Some leaders of north Wales society may have flirted with Catholicism but Salisbury's execution brought home to them the implications of open recusancy and they were forced to think seriously about their loyalties. Salisbury's brother and heir, Sir John Salusbury (1566/7–1612), was able to hold on to his inheritance, thanks to a providential entail. He matriculated at Jesus College, Oxford, on 24 November 1581, when he was fourteen, and was a student of the Middle Temple in 1594. He had to tread carefully for several years but was of the quorum of the peace for Denbighshire by 1592 and in 1595 he was made an esquire of the body to the queen and he proved his loyalty during the revolt of Robert Devereux, second earl of Essex, in 1601; he was knighted as a result. On 16 December 1601 he was returned to parliament for Denbighshire following a bitter struggle between local factions in the wake of Essex's fall. He was deputy lieutenant of Denbighshire by about 1602. Like his predecessors he was a major patron of the Welsh poetic tradition; the Salusburys were praised and mourned by most of the leading poets of the sixteenth century. However, Sir John Salusbury's interests spanned two cultures; he was himself a poet in English, and Robert Chester's *Loves Martyr*, published in 1601 and dedicated to him, includes William Shakespeare's poem 'The phoenix and the turtle' and a poem by Ben Jonson. During the last decade of the sixteenth century he was frequently in London but James I did not show him the favour that he had enjoyed under Elizabeth and he spent the rest of his life on his estates. He married Ursula, the illegitimate (but acknowledged) daughter of Henry Stanley, fourth earl of Derby, and Jane Halsall. The couple had seven sons and three daughters. Salusbury died on 24 July 1612. The Lleweni estate was by now one of the largest in north Wales, being worth about £1500 per annum. However, Sir John Salusbury's lavish lifestyle meant that he died heavily in debt. He was succeeded by his son Sir Henry Salusbury, first baronet (1589–1632), who married Hester (*d.* 1614), daughter of the wealthy London merchant and native of

Denbigh Sir Thomas *Myddelton (1549x56–1631). Henry Salusbury made over much of the estate to Myddelton in return for the settlement of his own and his father's debts. Myddelton had already lent him £1000 for the same purpose and the marriage might well have been part of the same transaction. Salusbury received a baronetcy in 1619 and died in July 1632. His son Sir Thomas *Salusbury, second baronet (1612–1643), was, like his grandfather, a poet, much of whose work survives in manuscript. He died in August 1643 and the baronetcy was inherited by two of his sons in turn. On the death of the fourth baronet, Sir John Salusbury, in 1684 the direct male line came to an end and the estate passed to his sister and her descendants.

The fourth son of Thomas Salusbury Hen, John Salusbury or Salesbury (this branch of the family usually used the latter spelling), was the ancestor of the Salesburys of Bachymbyd near Ruthin. His son Piers Salesbury married the heiress of Rug in Merioneth and this added substantially to the estate. Piers Salesbury was succeeded by his son Robert Salesbury (d. 1551). Robert Salesbury married Katherine, daughter of John ap Madog of Bodfel and Llannor, Caernarvonshire. Their son and successor, **John Salesbury** (c.1532–1580/81), was MP for Merioneth in October 1553 and increased the standing and influence of the family in Denbighshire through his land purchases. Salesbury was MP for Denbigh Boroughs in April 1554 and 1558 and for Denbighshire in 1559. His marriage to Elizabeth (d. in or after 1581), daughter of his kinsman Sir John Salusbury (b. in or before 1520, d. 1578), of Lleweni, by 1566, was the only match between the two branches of the family. He died by 6 February 1581. His eldest son, **Sir Robert Salesbury** (1566/7–1599), was MP for Denbighshire in 1586 and for Merioneth in 1588 and was knighted in 1593 for his military service in Ireland. He was educated at Brasenose College, Oxford, matriculating on 31 January 1584, aged seventeen, and entered Gray's Inn in 1586. His wealth and social status gave him local consequence. He was JP and, by 1587, deputy lieutenant of Denbighshire, JP of Merioneth by 1591, and deputy lieutenant from about 1592. Salesbury was *custos rotulorum* of Merioneth by about 1594. He married Elinor, daughter of Sir Henry Bagnall of Norley Castle and Stoke, Staffordshire, and his wife, Eleanor. He had one son, John Salesbury (d. 1608), and an illegitimate daughter, probably by his mistress, who was the daughter of his steward. Salesbury died on 14 July 1599. His father built up the estate, but he, like his contemporary at Lleweni, had expensive tastes, and died in debt. His son John Salesbury (d. 1608) did not live to adulthood and the estate passed to Sir Robert Salesbury's younger brother, Captain John Salesbury (d. 1611), who had also served in Ireland as well as on the continent along with his kinsman Owen Salusbury of Holt, who had fought a duel with John Salusbury of Lleweni in 1593. Relations between Bachymbyd and Lleweni were bad in the 1590s and the duel may have been connected with this. John and Owen served with Essex at Cadiz in 1596 and in Ireland in 1599 and joined his rebellion in 1601. John Salesbury was lucky to survive Essex's fall with only a fine of £40 and a brief spell in prison, but Owen Salusbury was killed. John Salesbury

was as extravagant as his brother and was obliged to mortgage Bachymbyd to the London-based Welsh goldsmith John Williams. He had no children and the estate was inherited by another brother, William *Salesbury (1580?–1659/60), a royalist army officer. William Salesbury, known as Hen Hosanau Gleision (Old Blue Stockings), was the antithesis of his brothers, being sober and hardworking and of a somewhat puritanical cast of mind. By his efforts he raised enough money to redeem the mortgage and to remove all the other encumbrances on the estate. He is best known for his epic defence of Denbigh Castle during the civil war, only surrendering it to the parliamentary forces when ordered to do so in 1646 by Charles I, and marching out with all the honours of war. He died by 10 December 1659 or 1660.

The fifth son of Thomas Salusbury Hen, Robert, was the grandfather of one of the greatest Welshmen of the sixteenth century, William *Salesbury (b. before 1520, d. c.1580). Salesbury was one of a group of young Welsh humanists, some protestant and some Catholic, who took an intense pride in their language and culture and he and his fellow protestants were anxious to make the new Anglican liturgy and the scriptures available in Welsh. He published his first book, a Welsh–English dictionary, in 1547; in the same year he produced *Oll synnwyr pen Kembero ygyd*. He published several other books and in 1551 translated the gospels and epistles appointed to be read at the communion service on Sundays and feast days into Welsh. On the accession of Mary I he probably remained at home in Denbighshire, although he may have continued his biblical translation. Following the accession of Elizabeth a number of Welsh clerics and humanists like Richard Davies, the new bishop of St Asaph, and Salesbury began a campaign to have the Bible and the Book of Common Prayer translated into Welsh. This was authorized by an act of parliament in 1563 and the Welsh prayer book and the New Testament both appeared in 1567. Salesbury and his fellow humanists saved the Welsh language and ensured its survival as a medium of culture as well as of communication.   A. D. CARR

Sources W. J. Smith, ed., *Calendar of Salusbury correspondence, 1553–c.1700* (1954) · D. Mathew, *The Celtic peoples and Renaissance Europe* (1933) · *Poems by Sir John Salusbury and Robert Chester*, ed. C. Brown (1913) · *Gwaith Siôn Tudur*, ed. E. Roberts (1980) · A. H. Dodd, 'North Wales in the Essex revolt of 1601', *EngHR*, 59 (1944), 348–70 · E. Roberts, 'Ymryson y Salsbriaid, 1593', *Transactions of the Denbighshire Historical Society*, 17 (1968), 108–46 · E. Roberts, 'Siôn Salsbri, Lleweni', *Transactions of the Denbighshire Historical Society*, 19 (1970), 66–102 · J. Gwynfor Jones, *The Welsh gentry, 1536–1640* (1998) · HoP, *Commons, 1509–58*, 3.261–6 · HoP, *Commons, 1558–1603*, 3.333–4, 336–7
Archives NL Wales, Bachymbyd MSS · NL Wales, Lleweni MSS

Salusbury, Hester Lynch. See Piozzi, Hester Lynch (1741–1821).

Salusbury, Sir John (b. in or before 1520, d. 1578). *See under* Salusbury family (*per. c.*1454–*c.*1684).

Salusbury [Salisbury], **Sir Thomas**, second baronet (1612–1643), poet and politician, was born in March 1612, the eldest son and heir of Sir Henry Salusbury, first baronet (1589–1632), of Lleweni, Denbighshire, and Hester (d. 1614), daughter of Sir Thomas Myddleton. He matriculated as a gentleman commoner of Jesus College, Oxford, but did not graduate. He entered the Inner Temple in November 1631, but on the death of his father in late July 1632 left London to take charge of the Lleweni estate. Shortly afterwards he concluded a marriage with the widowed Hester La Marie (fl. c.1590–1655), daughter of Sir Edward Tyrrell of Thornton, Buckinghamshire. After attaining his majority in March 1633 he became a member of the commission of the peace in both Flintshire and Denbighshire. He became a burgess of Denbigh corporation in September 1632, achieving election to the common council a few months later. He represented Denbighshire in the Short Parliament of early 1640 but was inconspicuous in its debates. He does not appear to have attempted to gain the seat in the Long Parliament, when the place was taken by his relation, Sir Thomas Myddleton. However, when Myddleton's election was in danger of being voided, Salusbury did demonstrate an interest in securing the seat at the prospective by-election, though this did not come to pass.

Salusbury viewed the estrangement of king and parliament with concern, and attended the king's court at York in the summer of 1642. After returning to Denbighshire in July he wrote his sister, Lady Ursula Lloyd, a letter detailing his conviction to support Charles I against the increasingly hostile parliament. He was concerned that opposing God's anointed leader would unleash forces of social and religious upheaval. As a consequence, he determined to support the king, stating 'if all the men of the earth were of another opinion, in this I am resolved to live and die' (NL Wales, MS 5390D, 251–3). He was soon involved in securing hands to a loyalist petition from the freeholders of north Wales. He was appointed a commissioner of array in his native Denbighshire and by 6 August 1642 had been elected colonel of a royalist regiment raised in north Wales. He was also elevated to *custos rotulorum* of the county bench. His actions caused the Commons to accuse him of treason and demand that he be sent for as a delinquent.

Salusbury's regiment fought at Edgehill, and he received the honorary degree of DCL from the king at Oxford a few days later. After this 'early and effectual adhering' to the king he was to play no further part in the war effort as he fell ill at Worcester; he was buried in the family vault at Whitchurch near Denbigh on 13 July 1643 (Lloyd, 661; Thomas, 208; NL Wales, Lleweni MS 766). As his heir, Thomas, was still in his minority, Salusbury's estate was placed in the hands of his widow, Hester.

Wood states that Salusbury was 'a most noted poet of his time', but only one of his pieces was published during his lifetime, *The History of Joseph* (1636) (Wood, *Ath. Oxon.*, 3.56). A number of his poetic and dramatic works survive in manuscript, however (NL Wales, MS 5390D; C. C. Brown, 'The Chirk Castle entertainment of 1634', *Milton Quarterly*, 11, 1977, 76–86).   LLOYD BOWEN

Sources W. J. Smith, ed., *Calendar of Salusbury correspondence, 1553–circa 1700* (1954) · NL Wales, Lleweni MSS · N. Tucker, *Denbighshire officers in the civil war* (1964) · NL Wales, MS 5390D · D. R. Thomas, ed., *Y cwtta cyfarwydd* (1883) · [J. Ballinger], ed., *Calendar of Wynn (of Gwydir) papers, 1515–1690, in the National Library of Wales* (1926) · Wood, *Ath. Oxon.*, new edn · D. Lloyd, *Memoires of the lives … of those … personages that suffered … for the protestant religion* (1668) · J. R. S. Phillips, ed., *The justices of the peace in Wales and Monmouthshire, 1541 to 1689* (1975) · W. H. Cooke, ed., *Students admitted to the Inner Temple, 1547–1660* [1878] · J. Williams, *The medieval history of Denbighshire*, 1: *The records of Denbigh and its lordship* (1860) · JHC · GEC, *Baronetage* · W. H. Rylands, ed., *The visitation of the county of Buckingham made in 1634*, Harleian Society, 58 (1909) · PRO, PROB 6/21, fol. 114

Archives NL Wales, Lleweni MSS

Likenesses portrait, repro. in P. Gaunt, *A nation under siege: the civil war in Wales, 1642–48* (1991)

Wealth at death allegedly spent £2000 on royalist war effort, 1642–3

Salvador, Joseph (1716–1786), merchant, was born on 21 January 1716 in London, the eldest son of Francis Salvador (c.1685–1754), merchant of Lime Street, and of his wife, Rachel Mendes da Costa (c.1690–1758). Joseph Salvador served as a warden of London's Portuguese Synagogue in 1746, 1751, 1755, and 1765. He was active in founding its infirmary, the Beth Holim, and is portrayed in an engraving attacking its committee entitled *The Jerusalem Infirmary: alias a Journey into the Valley of Jehosaphat*.

On 15 October 1738 Salvador married Leonora (Rachel; 1716–1766), eldest daughter of Antonio Lopes Suasso, third baron d'Auvernes le Gras. They had two sons, who died in infancy, and five daughters. He traded in partnership with his younger brother Jacob with a joint capital of £58,000. In 1749 Jacob died, leaving two sons. Salvador realized that if they too were to die their land would be forfeit to the crown, because Francis Salvador was Dutch-born. He therefore petitioned the duke of Newcastle in January 1753 for an act of parliament to enable Jews to be naturalized. He published two pamphlets in favour of this measure under the pseudonym Philo Patriae. In these he gave an interesting summary of the activities of London's Jewish merchants, arguing that it was in the national interest to encourage their residence and trade. The 'Jew Bill' was duly enacted, but the opposition launched a fierce campaign against the measure and won a by-election in Oxfordshire. The act was repealed, and Salvador's ill-judged initiative set back the improvement of Jewish civil status for many years.

When Salvador inherited his parents' fortune, he spent £2000 on buying 100,000 acres of land in South Carolina, extended his country estate at Tooting, and in 1757 built a handsome town house in White Hart Court, Bishopsgate. In 1759 he was elected a fellow of the Royal Society, and in 1764 a fellow of the Society of Antiquaries. He was the secretary of the London Committee of Deputies of British Jews on its foundation in 1760, and its president in 1778. Like his father he was, to use his own phrase, a merchant 'of the most extensive Trade and plumb Capitals' (Philo Patriae, *Further Considerations*, 35–6): he owned ships and was a major importer of rough diamonds and bullion. In 1761 Newcastle procured Salvador's advice on floating a government loan. Under Lord Bute's ministry Salvador continued to advise the Treasury and to underwrite its new issues. He was active in mustering support for Robert Clive in the power struggle within the East India Company, and Clive employed him to market his diamonds. As he prospered, Salvador spent money on 'protecting' expensive mistresses, first Catherine Maria *Fischer (Kitty Fisher) and then Margaret Caroline Rudd. He had a natural son, Joseph Salvador de Moriencourt, by the comtesse de Moriencourt.

In 1763 financial failures in Amsterdam caused Salvador heavy losses. George Clive wrote to Robert Clive that Salvador's capital was then reduced from £200,000 to £80,000. At the same time his insolvent son-in-law, Joshua Mendes da Costa, sued him over his daughter Judith's marriage contract. In 1773 another financial crisis in both Amsterdam and London destroyed most of his fortune. He sent his nephew Francis Salvador to South Carolina to manage and develop their American plantation. Francis was elected to the general assembly and then to the provincial congress and was active in the colony's struggle for independence. In 1776, leading a unit against British-armed Cherokees, Francis was shot and then scalped to death. His widow, Joseph's daughter Sarah, and their children were baptized in 1780. Joseph Salvador sold his property in England and half of his American estate and then settled on his 50,000 acre plantation at Coronaca Creek, South Carolina, in 1784. He died there on 29 December 1786 and was buried in the Da Costa Sephardi cemetery in Charleston. Joseph Salvador was an articulate, able, and ambitious merchant. Active as a Jewish leader and government adviser, he met his reverses of fortune with courage.   EDGAR SAMUEL

Sources M. Woolf, 'Joseph Salvador, 1716–1786', *Transactions of the Jewish Historical Society of England*, 21 (1962–7), 104–37 · E. R. Samuel, 'The Jews in English foreign trade: a consideration of the *Philo Patriae* pamphlets of 1753', *Remember the days: essays on Anglo-Jewish history presented to Cecil Roth*, ed. J. M. Shaftesley (1966), 123–43 · G. Yogev, *Diamonds and coral: Anglo-Dutch Jews and eighteenth-century trade* (1978) · L. Hühner, 'Francis Salvador, a prominent patriot of the revolutionary war', *Publications of the American Jewish Historical Society*, 4 (1901), 107–22 · L. Hühner, 'The Jews of South Carolina from the earliest settlement to the end of the American Revolution', *Publications of the American Jewish Historical Society*, 12 (1904), 39–61 · Philo Patriae [J. Salvador], *Considerations on the bill to permit persons professing the Jewish religion to be naturalized by parliament. In several letters from a merchant in town to his friend in the country. Wherein the motives of all parties interested therein are examined; the principles of Christianity, with regard to the admission of Jews, are fully discussed; and their utility in trade clearly proved* (1753) · Philo Patriae [J. Salvador], *Further considerations on the act to permit persons professing the Jewish religion, to be naturalized by parliament, in a second letter from a merchant in town to his friend in the country; in this part, the utility of the Jews in trade, their situation in other nations, and the expediency of continuing them on the present footing, are fully considered and proved* (1753) · R. D. Barnett, 'Dr Jacob de Castro Sarmento and Sephardim in medical practice in 18th-century London', *Transactions of the Jewish Historical Society of England*, 27 (1978–80), 84–114 · R. D. Barnett, ed., *The burial register of the Spanish and Portuguese Jews, London, 1657–1735* (1962) [repr. from *Miscellanies of the Jewish Historical Society of England*, vol. 6] · L. D. Barnett, ed., *Bevis Marks records, 1: The early history of the congregation from the beginning until 1800* (1940) · L. D. Barnett, ed., *Bevis Marks records, 2: Abstracts of the Ketubot or marriage contracts of the congregation from earliest times until 1837* (1949) · R. D. Barnett, ed., *Bevis Marks records, 4: The circumcision register of Isaac and Abraham de Paiba (1715–1775)* (1991) · M. Rodrigues-Pereira and C. Loewe, eds., *Bevis Marks records, 6: The burial register (1733–1918) of the Novo (New) Cemetery of the Spanish and Portuguese Jews' Congregation, London* (1997) · D. Verdooner and H. J. W. Snel, *Handleiding bij de index op de Ketuboth van de Portugees–Israëlietische gemeente te Amsterdam van 1650–1911* (Netherlands, 1990) · *GM*, 1st ser., 57 (1787), 181
Likenesses caricature, 1749, repro. in Woolf, 'Joseph Salvador'
Wealth at death main asset was 50,000 acre plantation at Coronaca Creek, South Carolina

Salvesen, (Salve) Christian Fredrik (1827–1911), shipowner and whaling entrepreneur, was born on 8 March 1827 at Mandal, Norway, the eighth of nine children of Thomas Salvesen, merchant shipowner, and Johanna Ross. He was trained as a shipbroker in Stettin and Glasgow before joining his father's firm in 1846. Five years later, he married Amalie Georgina Salome Andorsen, daughter of Gulow Andorsen, a leading Mandal shipbuilder, and they had four sons and three daughters. Salvesen then moved to Leith, where his brother Theodor, a broker in nearby Grangemouth, financed a partnership (Turnbull and Salvesen, 1853–1872) with George Turnbull, whose sister Jane married a third brother, now running the Mandal firm. After a slow start in broking, they prospered, importing timber from Salvesen's extended family and exporting coal from Turnbull's Scottish connections.

Shipbroking was also interwoven with part ownership of vessels (chiefly German) and ship management. Their first ship, *Syria*, was purchased in 1855, with support from Norway, where tramp shipowning was developing rapidly. Like his compatriots, Salvesen bought cheap wooden vessels, though it was a dispute over losses incurred with a more valuable ship trading to Australia that ended the partnership. Salvesen, trading alone (Christian Salvesen & Co.), began buying steamers seriously in the 1880s, and in 1886 started a line to Stavanger. Its success was followed by runs along the Norwegian coast and to the Mediterranean; in the early twentieth century Salvesen owned sixteen vessels of assorted size and type.

Christian Salvesen, though cautious about trading ventures which might upset his agency customers, always used his family connections to find new ways of feeding his agency and filling his ships. He bought shares in Finnish forests, Norwegian copper, and Lofoten coal. The failure of his Paraffin Oil Company to process coal in Mandal led to promising oil exports from Scotland in 1866, when he travelled the Norwegian coast adding oil to his coal distribution network. However, oil exports turned to imports two years later when Svend Foyn established the modern whaling industry in Finnmark, and Salvesen, who supplied his coal, became the leading Scottish agent for his and subsequent whalers' oil.

In 1883 Salvesen, though still in control until his health failed in his eighties, delegated management of shipping operations to his eldest sons, Thomas Johan and Frederick Gulov, both trained in Germany, as partners. The third son, Edward Theodore Salvesen, became a distinguished maritime lawyer and judge (Lord Salvesen), but a new dynamism entered the firm in 1889 with the fourth son,

Theodore Emile, educated in Norway and trained in Hamburg and Paris, who took on the timber and oil trades. It was Theodore who persuaded Christian to risk oil agency business by going into whaling in 1906, with Norwegian-type shore stations in Faeroe, Iceland, and especially Olna Firth in Shetland, where the company began total carcass utilization, which raised profitability and became a Salvesen hallmark. As interest moved to the Antarctic, work began in 1909 on Leith harbour in South Georgia, which cost over £118,000 and produced £35,000 profit in 1911, the year in which Christian died.

Although based in Britain, Salvesen and his family spoke—and ate—Norwegian at home and spent much time in Norway, maintaining those cordial family connections on which their success depended as their two countries grew closer in economic and social interdependence. Before his sons joined him, Christian Salvesen worked long hours in his office; but in later life he had time for public service in Leith and served the Dock commission and chamber of commerce. In 1859 he became a naturalized British citizen. However, he was made a knight of St Olav (first class) for public services in Norway, in 1891. He began his career indebted to his brother Theodor but, branching out on his own, founded a successful business, and expanded it through flexible entrepreneurship and careful innovation. By the time of his death Christian Salvesen & Co. was the largest whaling company in the world, and for the next half century was best known as the leading single operator in Antarctic whaling.

Salvesen died on 15 January 1911 at his home, Mayfield House, East Trinity Road, Leith. His wife predeceased him. GORDON JACKSON

Sources H. F. Andorsen, ed., *Memoirs of Lord Salvesen* (1949) · W. Vamplew, *Salvesen of Leith* (1975) · W. Vamplew, 'Salvesen, Salve Christian Fredrik', *DSBB* · J. N. Tønnessen and A. O. Johnsen, *The history of modern whaling* (1982) · G. Jackson, *The British whaling trade* (1978) · *The Times* (18 Jan 1911)
Archives priv. coll. | David Geddes & Co., Basingstoke, Geddes MSS · U. Edin. L., Christian Salvesen & Co. MSS, Handlist H36 · Unilever Legal Department, Blackfriars House, London, Southern Whaling Company records
Likenesses group photograph, repro. in Vamplew, *Salvesen of Leith* · photograph, repro. in Andorsen, ed., *Memoirs of Lord Salvesen* · photographs, priv. coll. · portrait, repro. in Vamplew, *Salvesen of Leith*
Wealth at death £209,383 17s. 6d.: confirmation, 16 Aug 1911, *CCI*

Salvetti, Amerigo. *See* Antelminelli, Alessandro (1572–1657).

Salveyn, Sir Gerard (d. 1319/20), landowner and administrator, was the son of Robert Salveyn of North Duffield, Yorkshire, and his wife, Sybil, daughter of Nicholas Wake. In March 1295 Salveyn was enfeoffed with Croom and Sledmere by his namesake Gerard Salveyn, who died in 1296. For about twenty years Salveyn was active in a wide range of local administrative commissions. On 26 December 1298 he was appointed a commissioner 'de walliis et fossatis' (embankments and ditches) on the Ouse, and on 24 October 1301 an assessor and collector of the fifteenth

for Yorkshire; he held both types of commission again in later years. He was a knight of the shire for the county of York at the parliaments of February 1305 and January 1307, and was appointed to a variety of judicial commissions, as a justice of trailbaston (23 November 1304), of oyer and terminer in specific instances (for example 4 March 1307), and for the trial of forestallers in Yorkshire (6 July 1311). On 23 May 1308 he was appointed escheator north of the Trent, and held the office until 10 December 1309. On 11 September 1309 he was appointed a commissioner of array, to lead the levies against the Scots. Military service against the Scots had been required of him in 1300 and continued to be required periodically until 1319. He was appointed sheriff of Yorkshire on 5 March 1311, being succeeded on 1 October 1314.

Salveyn was, however, more than merely a Yorkshire county administrator. He was employed on missions overseas by both Edward I and Edward II, for example in September 1304, May 1310, and March 1311. He was one of the royal officials whom the ordainers removed from office and access to the king in 1311; their animosity probably reflects the fact that Salveyn had by this time became a household banneret, and as such was close to the king, since it probably fell to him to escort Piers Gaveston to the continent late in 1311, and to bring him back to the king early in the following year. Moreover, various complaints were made about 1313–16 concerning his oppressions as sheriff and escheator, and several commissions were appointed to investigate. As a consequence he was imprisoned in York Castle, but was released on bail in June 1315, and in October 1316, by ceding to the king the manor of Sandhall, near Skelton in Howdenshire, Yorkshire, and a (remitted) fine of £2000, he obtained pardon. This he subsequently cited in king's bench in the Hilary term of 1319. In 1316 he was returned as lord or joint lord of a number of lordships in Yorkshire, including Ottringham, North Duffield, Harswell, and Croom. He had pardon as an adherent of Thomas of Lancaster in the York parliament in November 1318. He died before 13 March 1320.

Salveyn's wife's name was Margery. In 1312 Salveyn and Margaret, wife of Sir Robert Percy, cleared themselves of adultery by process of compurgation. Salveyn apparently had at least three sons: John, who predeceased him, Gerard, who fought for Thomas of Lancaster at Boroughbridge, and George, described as a king's clerk when presented to the prebend of Newthorpe by the king in June 1311. George and his father fell into dispute with Sir Henry Percy over the church at Wharram; sentences were passed against them in 1315. At his death Salveyn was succeeded by his heir, another Gerard, who was a minor aged twelve, the son of John Salveyn and Margaret, daughter of Robert de Ros (d. c.1270) of Wark. This Gerard, variously described as Salveyn's grandson and as his nephew, subsequently became a knight of the shire and sheriff of Yorkshire.

C. L. KINGSFORD, rev. HELEN M. JEWELL

Sources *Chancery records* · W. Brown, ed., *Yorkshire inquisitions of the reigns of Henry III and Edward I*, 3, Yorkshire Archaeological Society, 31 (1902), 41 · F. Palgrave, ed., *The parliamentary writs and writs of military summons*, 2 vols. in 4 (1827–34) · *The register of William Greenfield, lord archbishop of York, 1306–1315*, ed. W. Brown and A. H. Thompson, 1, 3, SurtS, 145, 151 (1931–6) · *RotP*, 1.316, 325 · *RotS*, 1.73 · F. H. Slingsby, ed., *Feet of fines for the county of York from 1272 to 1300*, Yorkshire Archaeological Society, 121 (1956), 89, 140 · G. O. Sayles, ed., *Select cases in the court of king's bench*, 7 vols., SeldS, 55, 57–8, 74, 76, 82, 88 (1936–71), vol. 4, pp. 86–8 · W. Stubbs, ed., *Chronicles of the reigns of Edward I and Edward II*, 1, Rolls Series, 76 (1882), 200; 2, Rolls Series, 76 (1883), 40 · [W. Illingworth], ed., *Placita de quo warranto temporibus Edw. I, II, et III*, RC (1818), 219 · J. R. Maddicott, *Thomas of Lancaster, 1307–1322: a study in the reign of Edward II* (1970) · *VCH Yorkshire East Riding*, vols. 2–3 · P. Chaplais, *Piers Gaveston: Edward II's adoptive brother* (1994) · *CIPM*, 6, nos. 223, 458

Salvidge, Sir Archibald Tutton James (1863–1928), political organizer, was born on 5 August 1863 at 54 Park Street, Birkenhead, Cheshire, the second son of Archibald Tutton Salvidge (*d.* 1906), wine and spirit merchant, and his wife, Sarah (*d.* 1871), daughter of William Croxton of Hoylake, Cheshire. There were five children altogether; Sarah Salvidge died in giving birth to her second daughter, also Sarah, who later married the champion amateur golfer H. H. Hilton. The youngest son, Edward, a Cheshire county rugby player, died in the Second South African War. Salvidge's father, whose family came from Bleadon, Somerset, had struggled in business as a mineral water manufacturer before discovering profit in the provision of alcohol. His eldest son, Willie—a boyhood friend of F. E. Smith, who later owed his parliamentary seat to Archibald Salvidge's management—succeeded as head of the firm. Archibald Salvidge set out in a similar trade, starting as a publican and rising to be managing director of Bent's brewery; and his marriage, on 31 August 1885, was to the daughter of a publican, Alice Margaret McKernan (*b.* 1863/4). After elementary education at a Wesleyan school, he had transferred to the Liverpool Institute. His record there was undistinguished; however, an interest in amateur theatricals, amplified by membership of the Toxteth Parliamentary Debating Society in his early twenties, made him confident about addressing audiences. Speaking up and out, rather than oratory, was the Salvidge style; but he was most effective as a party organizer. The power base that made Salvidge 'the king of Liverpool' (so tagged by Warden Chilcott, MP for Liverpool Walton, 1918–29) was the Working Men's Conservative Association (WMCA), which had membership of all committees of the Liverpool Constitutional Association. It was crucial to the Conservatives' domination of Liverpool's municipal and parliamentary representation, a singular outcome in an age of extended franchise when first the Liberals and then Labour tended to win urban working-class seats.

In 1914 Salvidge, who had become the WMCA's chairman in 1892, explained the importance of 'lectures, dances, concerts, picnics, anything and everything, to keep our men, *our workers*, together and at fighting pitch' (Waller, 142). Under him the number of WMCA branches increased to twenty-six and the membership to over 8000 by the early 1900s. One secret of Salvidge's success was his willingness to muck in. When he first joined the Granby branch, he pushed a handcart round the ward to collect donations of books and furniture to improve the club's fittings. Salvidge's common touch was an electoral asset, but

his trade was a potential liability when the temperance movement proclaimed that alcohol debased the working classes and corrupted political life. Certainly, the drink interest exerted power on the Liverpool licensing bench, and Salvidge's party opponents charged that most pubs acted as tory committee rooms. It was even said that in the January 1910 general elections in Liverpool a thousand barmen were sent by brewers from Manchester to act as canvassers, reciprocating Salvidge's services during a famous by-election there in 1908, when the president of the Board of Trade, Winston Churchill, was defeated. Salvidge, however, sought publicly to separate his trade and politics. Remarkably, the WMCA clubs were 'dry'; and when Salvidge was knighted in 1916 it was in recognition of his assistance in smoothing the acceptance of wartime licensing restrictions.

How was it, then, that Salvidge mobilized the WMCA as an electoral force? According to A. G. Cameron, defeated Labour candidate in Liverpool Kirkdale in 1910, Salvidge 'turned a somersault from a brewery into the pulpit' (Waller, 245). Although Salvidge was not an Orangeman, he had declared on the Glorious 12th (of July) 1891 that his principles were identical to those of the Orange order, because the WMCA's cardinal rule required a member 'to be a sound Protestant'. He forced the pace on this issue, which had three important applications in Liverpool. First, sectarianism galvanized local opposition to Irish home rule, which was perceived as endangering the faith and livelihood of protestant Ulster. Liverpool was the city in England where this question most mattered, owing to the presence of a large immigrant Catholic Irish population which sustained a separate Irish nationalist party and won both municipal representation and a parliamentary seat. Second, sectarianism involved the promotion of church discipline bills to preserve the vitality of protestantism as an evangelical, Bible-based religion by rooting out from the Church of England so-called Romanizing clergy who adopted ritual, the mass, and confessional. Third, sectarianism promised to resuscitate democratic toryism in Liverpool by furnishing it with a popular base in place of the active social programme with which Arthur Forwood had been associated and which had alienated traditional Conservative interests both locally and nationally.

On the back of popular protestantism Salvidge attained the ascendancy over Liverpool Conservatism. Until 1919 he was not the nominal leader. Following Forwood's death in 1898, the presidency of the Constitutional Association was held successively by Sir Edward Lawrence, T. B. Royden, and Sir Charles Petrie; but it was Salvidge who called the tune. He understood the difference between office and power. He became a city councillor in 1896 and alderman in 1898 and, though in 1899 he also became chairman of the Hoylake and West Kirby urban district council, on the Cheshire side of the Mersey, where he lived, he refused the lord mayoralty of Liverpool in 1910 and never sought the parliamentary seat which was his for the asking. Instead, he unseated MPs who would not toe the line, as was the fate of the cabinet minister Walter

Long, who was deselected in Liverpool West Derby in 1899, when he would not subscribe to church discipline. Such brutal methods brought Liverpool Conservatism close to anarchy around the turn of the century, as the WMCA equated 'ritualists' and 'aristocrats' and Salvidge was accused of 'too often getting at the upper ten' (Waller, 178). His own sectarian credentials were subject to critical inspection when it was discovered that his wife was a Catholic, though they had been married according to Anglican rites by a clergyman of unimpeachable evangelical persuasion, and their two sons and daughter were raised as protestants. A beleaguered Salvidge swore that 'no Roman Catholic priest had ever crossed the threshold of his door' (ibid., 179); but the movement he essayed to direct was naturally fissiparous, and a separate protestant party emerged on the Liverpool city council and sectarian violence disturbed many wards.

Salvidge held on to the protestant card and made up to the firebrand preacher George Wise, leader of the Protestant Reformers' Memorial Church; but in the Edwardian period he also needed to take account of extraneous factors, the tariff reform controversy, and the rise of organized labour. While professing tariff reform to be 'a great ideal' (Salvidge, 126), he recognized that local shipping interests, and working-class consumers generally, were reluctant to abandon free trade and to forfeit cheap food. Salvidge dished up protection as an anti-foreigner crusade, designed to maintain full employment; he also emphasized that Conservatives should not 'endanger the Ulster cause for the sake of insisting on the full gospel of Tariff Reform' (ibid., 125–6). His success in preserving the Conservatives' control of Liverpool in 1906, when their party elsewhere suffered crushing defeat, and again in 1910, ushered him into national prominence. He was consulted by Arthur Balfour and other leading Conservatives about policy and electoral strategies, and was chairman of the National Union of Conservative and Unionist Associations in 1913. The new party leader, Bonar Law, came into line with the position promoted by Salvidge and the earl of Derby, reducing the commitment to tariff reform while presenting an uncompromising stand against Irish home rule.

This was brinkmanship, not statesmanship. Salvidge feared that Liverpool 'might easily turn out to be a second Ulster' (Waller, 268), as local volunteers for both sides in the Irish dispute were recruited and drilled. The First World War—in which Salvidge's younger son, Archie, fought and was taken prisoner—overlaid that; and the war's dislocations cumulatively transformed the political context. In 1918 F. E. Smith told the prime minister, Lloyd George, that Salvidge and the WMCA were '*Pivotal*. The Tory Party cannot refuse what they endorse' (ibid., 281). Salvidge was now leader of the council and in, 1919, chairman of the Constitutional Association; but the WMCA's membership was half its pre-war peak, and the branches appeared 'skeletons'. Salvidge was almost continuously on the retreat in Liverpool politics at the same time as his profile nationally was raised. His intervention at the national union conference in 1921, lambasting die-hard

posturizing and backing an Irish settlement, won him plaudits; and Lloyd George rewarded his support for the coalition with the KBE in 1920 and elevation to the privy council in 1922. A peerage was offered and refused. Salvidge calculated that coalition represented the best bulwark against Labour–socialism. His disappointment at the coalition's collapse turned to fury against Baldwin and the Conservative central office in 1923, when a general election mandate for protection was sought. Speaking for the Liverpool Constitutional Association in conjunction with Lancashire and Cheshire unionist associations, Salvidge asserted that they had 'an undoubted right to have a say on policy' (ibid., 294); and Baldwin, like Bonar Law ten years before, was compelled to demote the tariff cause.

Labour won its first parliamentary seat in Liverpool in 1923. This, combined with economic recession, caused Salvidge to refurbish a tory democrat image. He deferred still to the protestant party, opposing Sunday music-playing in the corporation parks in deference to sabbatarians; but he declared that governments had a duty 'not to reduce the income tax, but to carry out their social programme of housing and widows' pensions and other measures for the relief of the under-dog' (Waller, 296). Salvidge promoted the Mersey Tunnel, in recognition of which he received the freedom of Liverpool in 1925; and he was circumspect in response to serious industrial disputes, such as the Liverpool police strike in 1919 and the general strike in 1926, in this following the pattern set by the transport strikes in 1911, when he stood out for reinstatement of dismissed workers after the employer victories. Nevertheless, the cracks in the Liverpool Conservative organization became a breach in 1927–8 when Leslie Scott led a revolt of seven of the eight MPs against Salvidge's authority and methods. Scott first tilted against Salvidge in 1917–18 during the suffrage debates, when he advocated proportional representation to counter party caucuses; now he proposed a decentralization, enabling MPs to appoint full-time constituency agents with independent fund-raising powers. Salvidge accused the MPs of wanting 'to abrogate the powers of a democratic organization' (ibid., 304). 'M.P.s come and M.P.s go', he liked to boast, 'but the organization goes on for ever' (Salvidge, 294). For Salvidge, the Conservative Party was doomed if it kowtowed to wealth and status as previously it had done to birth and rank: he would not salute men

> merely because they had been to public schools. They must share the dust as well as the palm. I had never had any use for the old Tory prayer, 'God bless the Squire and his relations and keep us in our proper stations'. (ibid., 301)

The popular voice channelled by Salvidge's organization was, however, too frequently crude and sectarian, a Frankenstein's monster; and the democratic structure was threadbare, masking an autocratic executive. The MPs received support from Baldwin and the central office and from Lord Derby, who was invited to mediate; but Salvidge made no concessions by the time he died on 11 December 1928, at his home, Braxted, King's Gap, Hoylake, from blood poisoning caused by a pelvic abscess, compounded by diverticulitis of the sigmoid colon. His effects were probated at £14,385 11s. 4d., but this was bogus because creditors waived claims either from sympathy for Salvidge's family—both his wife and his elder son, Stanley, who was a haemophiliac, required medical treatment—or from a determination to conceal how Liverpool Conservatism had been run by a virtual bankrupt. Questions about Salvidge's use of moneys raised for party and election purposes were smothered too, although the national party chairman, J. C. C. Davidson, recorded that Salvidge confessed to misappropriation. In 1929 Lord Derby strived to raise a testimonial fund of £10,000 to support Salvidge's family. It reached £8700, with Derby subscribing £1000; but the shortfall was interpreted as a sign not just of economic recession but of resentments which Salvidge's rule had left. History was ransacked for parallels to describe this democratic dictator. A cross between Cardinal Richelieu and Field Marshal Lord Kitchener was proposed, but Lloyd George provided the best analogy: 'the nearest to a Tammany boss that we have in this country' (T. Jones, *Whitehall Diary*, ed. K. Middlemas, 1971, 3.168). Stanley Salvidge completed a political biography of his father shortly before his own death in August 1933. Salvidge himself had initiated it by compiling his reminiscences during the 1920s, and it is probably best read as a veiled autobiography. Most of the archive on which it was based has disappeared, presumed destroyed; but a few surviving letters cast doubt on Stanley Salvidge's procedures, because words are changed or omitted from quotations without notice. It is thus an appropriate monument, being deeply machiavellian. PHILIP WALLER

Sources S. Salvidge, *Salvidge of Liverpool: behind the political scene, 1890–1928* (1934) · P. J. Waller, *Democracy and sectarianism: a political and social history of Liverpool, 1868–1939* (1981) · Lpool RO, seventeenth earl of Derby MSS · b. cert. · m. cert. · d. cert. · *DNB*
Archives NRA, corresp. · priv. coll., MSS | HLRO, corresp. with Andrew Bonar Law · Lpool RO, seventeenth earl of Derby MSS | FILM BFI NFTVA, news footage
Likenesses J. A. Grant, portrait, 1926–1929?, Constitutional Club, Liverpool · photographs, repro. in Salvidge, *Salvidge of Liverpool*
Wealth at death £14,385 11s. 4d.: probate, 12 Feb 1929, *CGPLA Eng. & Wales*

Salvin, Anthony (1799–1881), architect, was born on 17 October 1799 at Sunderland Bridge, Durham, co. Durham, the only child of General Anthony Salvin (1758–1844), soldier, and his second wife, Elizabeth (Eliza), daughter of Colonel Henry Mills of Willington, near Newcastle upon Tyne. His parents had married on 11 September 1798 at Brancepeth, Durham. After education at Durham School Salvin was placed as a pupil with John Paterson of Edinburgh during the latter's restoration work on Brancepeth Castle. In November 1821 he moved to London with his cousin William Andrews Nesfield and took lodgings at 52 Newman Street. Although carrying an introduction to Sir John Soane from Rowland Burdon, he did not enter Soane's office. According to his nephew William Eden Nesfield, Salvin entered the office of John Nash (*The Builder*, 31 Dec 1881, 809–10); however, there is scant other evidence for this. He was elected fellow of the Society of Antiquaries on 4 March 1824, and shortly after this he embarked on a lengthy sketching tour of Great Britain. He

married his cousin Anne Andrews Nesfield (d. 1860) on 26 July 1826, and they had six children, including Osbert *Salvin, two of whom died in infancy.

Early commissions Salvin's first major commission was Mamhead Park (1825–38) in Devon, for Robert William Newman, begun in 1826. Newman was senior partner in a general merchants' firm trading with Portugal and Newfoundland. Sited above the Exe estuary, the house, in the Tudor style, is symmetrically planned. The plan was retained from a design by Charles Fowler for a classical house, restricting the ability to create variety in the elevations. At Moreby Hall (1828–33), Escrick, East Riding, for Henry Preston, Salvin was free to create a complete design in the Tudor style. While still symmetrically balanced, the building was a compact design with the main reception rooms grouped round a central double-height hall and the main service rooms grouped round a courtyard separated by a linking wing. Both houses were included by Charles Eastlake in his *A History of the Gothic Revival* (1872) as important early examples of the use of the Tudor style in a 'correct' manner. At Scotney Castle (1835–43), Lamberhurst, Kent, for Edward Hussey, Salvin produced a powerful asymmetrical design in the Tudor style.

Salvin's most important early domestic work is Harlaxton Manor, Lincolnshire, for Gregory Gregory. The patron, originally named Gregory Gregory-Williams, inherited the estate in 1822 and Harlaxton was intended to house a collection amassed after the end of the Napoleonic wars. Design work started in 1831. Salvin's initial design combined elements of Montacute House, Somerset, with Hengrave Hall, Norfolk. Building work started on a revised design in 1832. Salvin was replaced as architect by 1838, and work subsequently continued under the supervision of William Burn. The authorship of the interiors remains undecided. Salvin spent five weeks in Germany in 1835, including visits to Munich and Nuremburg. It is possible that this was to gain inspiration for the baroque-inspired interiors at Harlaxton, but by the time work had started on these Salvin had been dismissed.

Because of the destruction of much of Salvin's archive by his youngest son, Osbert, when he inherited his father's property, Hawksfold, Fernhurst, Sussex, it is difficult to be certain how Salvin gained many of his commissions. However, it is clear that he had a reputation as an expert on medieval buildings at an early age, as evinced by his election to the Society of Antiquaries. This expertise and its demonstration in his early works probably led to many of his commissions relating to the restoration and improvement of castles. Certainly by the end of his career he was regarded as the expert on such restoration work. Much of his country house work may have come by personal recommendation from contented clients. It is also possible that some clients may have been recommended by the Nesfields. Salvin also exhibited some of his work at the Royal Academy, and the accomplished and attractive perspective views of Scotney Castle and Harlaxton clearly indicate his skill in composing a building. Salvin does not appear to have courted publicity in the contemporary building press: few of his major works were engraved for publication.

Salvin was among the many unlucky entrants to the competition for the new Palace of Westminster in 1836. Although not a premium winner, his design attracted attention in the contemporary press. A Tudor design, the building is articulated by large square towers with projecting balconies and elaborate octagonal cupola roofs. The model for these appears to be the palace of Aschaffenburg (1605–14), Unterfranken, which Salvin had possibly seen on his trip to Germany in 1835. He also failed to win the competition for the Ashmolean Museum, Oxford (built to the designs of C. R. Cockerell). He won the competition for the design of the Carlton Club, Pall Mall, London, but the club decided not to proceed with his scheme. After losing the competition to design the Army and Navy Club, St James's Square, London, in 1847 Salvin evidently decided not to enter any further competitions.

Major works Salvin designed Keele Hall (1854–60), Staffordshire, for Ralph Sneyd. Sneyd, like Gregory at Harlaxton, was a bachelor and this is reflected in the planning: the Tudor-style house contained a suite of rooms for Sneyd and his male guests, including a smoking room and a billiard room. The success of Keele Hall may have gained Salvin the commission for Thoresby Hall (1864–76), Nottinghamshire, for Sydney Pierrepont, third Earl Manvers. The earl had inherited a house designed by John Carr of York and sought its replacement with something far larger. Thoresby does not have the decorative embellishments of Harlaxton, but is similarly massive in scale. It is in the Tudor style of Salvin's earlier work that was by the 1860s rather out of date.

Most of Salvin's other country house work was in the Tudor style. The exceptions, which include Penoyre (1846–8), Brecon, an Italian villa-style house for Colonel John Lloyd Vaughan Watkins, and Oxon Heath (1846–8), West Peckham, Kent, in the French empire style for Sir William Geary, bt, are rare but are still well-handled designs. It would appear that Salvin could design in the Italianate style but preferred, and was known for, the Tudor and medieval style of much of his work.

Salvin did considerable work restoring, refitting, and creating castles. He refaced Norwich Castle, Norfolk (1835), and he repaired the ruins of Newark Castle, Nottinghamshire (1844), and of Carisbrooke Castle on the Isle of Wight (1845). After the collapse of the Queen's Gate he was called in to examine Caernarfon Castle in 1844 and repaired the gate and rebuilt some masonry of the Eagle and north-east towers. In 1851 he surveyed the Beauchamp Tower of the Tower of London, and following work on this he restored many parts of the complex, including the Salt Tower (1856–7) and the Wakefield and White towers, and finishing with the chapel of St Peter ad Vincula, London, for which unexecuted designs were drawn up in 1867. Salvin's final work at the tower, commenting on plans by the Royal Engineers, took place in 1876. Salvin was instructed by Prince Albert to carry out restoration work at Windsor Castle. Work started in 1856 and continued in stages until 1867. This included the removal of

sash windows and their replacement with lancets and mullioned windows and the rebuilding of Clewer Tower to a design based on Viollet-le-Duc's Tour du Trésor at Carcassonne in France.

In 1844 Salvin began work on Peckforton Castle (1844–52), Cheshire, for the first Baron Tollemache. This was a new castle, built as a re-creation of an Edwardian one. Sir Gilbert Scott, in his criticism of the fashion to build new castles, described it as

> not a sham fortress, such as those of twenty years back, whose frowning gateway is perhaps flanked on either side with a three foot clipped hedge,—but it is a real and carefully constructed medieval fortress capable of standing a siege from an Edwardian army,—a bulwark against the inroads of a Llewelyn or a Glendower. (G. Scott, *Royal Institute of British Architects Papers*, 1857, 23)

However, there may have been need for the defence that Salvin provided. Peckforton was close to Manchester, the centre of major civil unrest in 1842, and Tollemache may have feared that such riots would recur.

In 1852 Salvin started work on Alnwick Castle in Northumberland, for Algernon Percy, fourth duke of Northumberland. The castle, medieval in origin, had been remodelled by James Paine and Robert Adam for Sir Hugh Smithson. Salvin's work was to remodel the castle, replacing a tower with the much larger Prudhoe Tower and creating a *porte-cochère* in the central courtyard. As at Windsor, later windows were removed and replaced with lancets or mullions. The interior was replanned, with a new main staircase and improved circulation for the main reception rooms. Much of the Italianate decoration of the interior, criticized at the time by Gilbert Scott and others, was supervised by Salvin, although it was clearly not to his taste. Salvin's own wish had been to create medieval decoration, as he made clear in a speech to the Royal Institute of British Architects.

Church repair work Salvin repaired and reordered many churches. His work was often not restoration, as it is now understood, but rather an attempt to return the church to some previous ideal state. He was made an honorary member of the Cambridge Camden Society in November 1841, early in his church designing, because of his work on Holy Sepulchre, Cambridge (1841–4). This included the rebuilding of the south aisle, the removal of the upper stage of the central tower and the construction of a conical roof, the removal of wall monuments from the interior, and the introduction of a stone altar table. This work, carried out at the society's expense, was removed by the incumbent, the Revd R. R. Faulkner, after a court of arches decision in his favour.

Salvin's other ecclesiastical repair work included the removal of buildings around the south transept of Norwich Cathedral (1830); he also reordered the choir, removing box pews and restoring the choir stalls. He repaired the south transept of Durham Cathedral in 1842 and also altered the 1665 choir stalls, placing the tabernacle work above a row of stalls set between the piers of the choir. Salvin also removed the organ screen, creating a view from the west door to the high altar. At Wells Cathedral

Salvin took over from Benjamin Ferrey in 1847 to redesign the choir, retaining only the misericords of the choir stalls. Salvin's organ case was evidently much criticized and some regarded it as the ugliest in the country.

Salvin's ecclesiastical work does not give a definite indication of his religious beliefs. His early churches derived from the commissioners' model and were economical both financially and in their use of architectural detail. His later designs for new churches could be more elaborate where money permitted, and he had no evident sympathy with the philosophy of the Society for the Protection of Ancient Buildings: his ruthless removal of unwanted fabric has led Dr Allibone to state that Salvin 'must bear part of the responsibility for the rape of the English parish church in the nineteenth century' (Allibone). Salvin's church work, in common with his other work, shows a determination to achieve a structurally satisfying result, repairing and rebuilding rather than retaining fabric. This attitude was to be questioned by Morris and others subsequently, but Salvin was held in high regard at the end of his career. His character matched his work, pragmatic and practical, financially careful, and conservative.

Later years Salvin had a considerable practice, covering a geographically wide area and involving a considerable variety of building types. The range of work, from cathedral restoration to new country houses, also included works for the universities. At Durham he was approached in 1834 to increase the accommodation of the new university. These proposals came to nothing, but in 1839 he rebuilt the castle keep as accommodation. In 1843 he altered the Red Lion Hotel, which had been bought by the university, to accommodate poor students. At Cambridge he worked on Trinity College, restoring the master's lodge (1841–2), rebuilding the Trinity Street façade (1856), and constructing the first and second master's courts (1857 and 1865).

Given the scale of this work, it is little surprise that in 1857 Salvin suffered a stroke while working at Warwick Castle. After his recovery in 1858 he returned to London, and rented 11 Hanover Terrace, Regent's Park. However, the death of his wife in June 1860 prompted his purchase, in 1862, of 145 acres at Fernhurst in Sussex, where he designed a new house, Hawksfold, a rare essay in the vernacular style. The following year Salvin was awarded the royal gold medal of the Royal Institute of British Architects. In 1879 he retired from formal practice.

Some important Victorian architects gained their initial training in Salvin's office. These included his nephew William Eden Nesfield, who joined the office in 1853–7, Richard Norman Shaw, who joined in 1856–8, and John Loughborough Pearson, who joined in 1842 for six months. None of these, however, can be said to have been influenced by Salvin's style. Salvin's son, also Anthony, was in the office, but retired before his father because of ill health.

Salvin died at Hawksfold on 17 December 1881. His daughter Eliza Anne gave the cause of death as 'old age'. He was buried beside his son Anthony, who had died in the same year, in the new graveyard at Fernhurst. Some of his drawings are in the British Architectural Library at the Royal Institute of British Architects, London; others are in the Victoria and Albert Museum, London.

RICHARD HOLDER

Sources J. Allibone, *Anthony Salvin: pioneer of Gothic revival architecture* (1988) · *CGPLA Eng. & Wales* (1882) · A. Bonney, *Dear Mr Salvin* (1999) · J. M. Crook, *The rise of the nouveaux riches: style and status in Victorian and Edwardian architecture* (1999) · IGI
Archives London Borough of Barnet Archives and Local Studies Centre, diaries, journals, and sketchbooks of him and his daughters · London Borough of Barnet Public Libraries, MS reminiscences · U. Durham, MSS, legal documents · University of Toronto, Thomas Fisher Rare Book Library, architectural drawings of churches and houses and catalogue of his library | Bloxham School, Banbury, letters to Lord Leconfield · Norfolk RO, letters to George Pellew · NRA, priv. coll., accounts and papers relating to Longford Castle · Sheff. Arch., corresp. relating to renovation of Silkstone parish church · Som. ARS, letters relating to Dunster Castle · U. Durham L., letters relating to Naworth Castle · Warks. CRO, letters and accounts relating to restoration of Warwick Castle
Wealth at death £78,484 18s. 5d.: probate, 2 March 1882, *CGPLA Eng. & Wales*

Salvin, Francis Henry (1817–1904), field sports enthusiast, born at Croxdale Hall, co. Durham, on 4 April 1817, was fifth and youngest son of William Thomas Salvin (1768–1842), of Croxdale Hall, and his wife, Anna Maria, daughter of John Webbe-Weston, of Sutton Place, near Guildford, Surrey. The Salvins were a Roman Catholic landed family, and Francis was educated at Ampleforth College. He served for several years in the militia, joining the 3rd battalion of the York and Lancaster regiment in 1839 and retiring with the rank of captain in 1864. In 1857 he inherited from his uncle Thomas Monnington Webbe-Weston the family seat, Sutton Place, a fine old Tudor mansion, but he usually lived at Whitmoor House, another residence on the estate near Guildford.

Salvin's early love of hawking was stimulated by an acquaintance with John Tong, a one-time assistant falconer to Colonel Thomas Thornton (1757–1823). In the manner of Thornton, he made a highly successful hawking tour of northern England in 1843 with John Pells (then in the pension of the hereditary grand falconer of England). When serving with his regiment in Ireland in 1855, Salvin used to fly peregrine falcons at rooks and tiercels at magpies. After returning to counties Cork and Kildare in 1857 with his falconers John and Robert Barr, he continued in a similar and successful vein. He also kept goshawks and trained them for flights at mountain hares, rabbits, and pheasants. From 1870 he was a prominent member of the old Hawking Club, which met on Salisbury Plain.

Salvin also practised the old sport of fishing with cormorants. His famous cormorant Izaak Walton, brought from Rotterdam, was mounted after its death in 1847 and was exhibited in the Newcastle upon Tyne Museum. Another, known as Sub-Inspector, was the first known instance of a cormorant bred in captivity (*The Field*, 27 May 1882), and was sent after Salvin's death to the London Zoological Gardens, where it survived until 1911.

Salvin had a great understanding of animals. He tamed

two young otters to follow him like dogs and sleep in his lap, and at one time kept a wild boar with collar and bell. For his time he possessed a remarkably developed sense of conservation. He was active in numerous field sports when past seventy, but falconry remained his first love. He died, unmarried, on 2 October 1904, at the Manor House, Sutton Place, and was buried in St Edward's cemetery, Sutton Place.

Salvin, who was a frequent contributor to *The Field*, collaborated in two works on falconry. The first, *Falconry in the British Isles* (1855; 2nd edn, 1873), written in conjunction with William Brodrick of Chudleigh, is considered to have been the best English work on the subject written during the nineteenth century, and has been reprinted (1971). The figures of hawks, drawn by Brodrick, are said to bear comparison with the work of Josef Wolf, the animal painter. The text of the second edition is to be preferred, but the illustrations are inferior to those of the original (*Quarterly Review*, July 1875). Salvin also assisted Gage Earle Freeman in *Falconry: its Claims, History, and Practice* (1859); the 'Remarks on training the otter and cormorant' appended to it are wholly his. In the early part of the nineteenth century falconry had a small but active following. Salvin's nineteenth writings represent an aspect of its limited revival in the middle decades of the century, although it never became more than a minority interest. None the less, Salvin's work was significant in maintaining the practice and tradition of falconry as a field sport both in the British Isles and throughout the British empire.

G. Le G. Norgate, *rev.* Gordon T. Mellor

Sources Burke, *Gen. GB* · *The Field* (8 Oct 1904) · *The Times* (4 Oct 1904) · *The Ibis*, 8th ser., 5 (1905) · J. E. Harting, *Bibliotheca accipitraria: a catalogue of books … relating to falconry* (1891) · G. Lascelles, *The art of falconry* (1892) · C. H. Fisher, *Reminiscences of a falconer* (1901) · F. H. Salvin and W. Brodrick, *Falconry in the British Isles* (1855); facs. edn with introduction by P. Glasier (1971) · R. Upton, *O for a falconer's voice* (1987) · R. Upton, *A bird in the hand* (1980)
Archives Durham RO, family and estate MSS · U. Durham L., family and estate MSS
Likenesses J. C. Hook, group portrait, exh. RA 1873 (*Fishing by proxy*) · F. W. Frohawk, drawing, repro. in *The Field* · Hinks, portrait; in possession of Mr Charles Sibeth, Kensington, London, 1912 · photograph, repro. in Upton, *A bird in the hand*, 26 · photograph, repro. in Upton, *O for a falconer's voice*, 30 · portrait, repro. in Fisher, *Reminiscences of a falconer*
Wealth at death £80,131 5*s.* 6*d.*: administration with will, 12 Nov 1904, *CGPLA Eng. & Wales*

Salvin, Osbert (1835–1898), naturalist, second son of Anthony *Salvin (1799–1881), an architect, and his wife, Anne Andrews Nesfield (*d.* 1860), was born at Elmshurst, Finchley, Middlesex, on 25 February 1835. He was educated under the Revd Charles Worsley at the Manor House, Finchley, and from 1846 at Westminster School. In 1853 he entered Trinity Hall, Cambridge, where he took a scholarship at the end of his first year and graduated BA as senior optime in the mathematical tripos of 1857. He proceeded MA in 1860, and was elected an honorary fellow of his college in 1897.

As befitted an architect's son, Salvin was very good with his hands, particularly as a carpenter. While still at Westminster he and his elder brother built and fitted two small steamers, which were ultimately bought for use on some of the Indian rivers. Salvin was also interested in natural history, especially ornithology, entomology, and palaeontology, and devoted much of his leisure time at Cambridge to the subject. After taking his degree he joined his second cousin by marriage, H. B. Tristram, in a five-month natural history exploration of Tunis and eastern Algeria; their detailed accounts of this excursion were published in *The Ibis* in 1859 and 1860.

In the autumn of 1857 Salvin visited Guatemala with George Ure Skinner, the discoverer and importer of new orchid species. In the middle of the following year he joined Edward Newton in the Antilles, but returned after a few months to Central America, where he proved himself an unsurpassed collector. After returning to England in May 1860 he set off again in the autumn of 1861, in company with his old college friend, F. Du Cane Godman, for Guatemala, twice ascending the Volcán de Fuego near the capital. They returned in January 1863. Salvin was then induced to undertake the management of some engineering works in the north of England, but he found this employment unrewarding and it did not last long.

On 24 May 1865 Salvin married Caroline, daughter of W. W. Maitland of Loughton, Essex, and in 1873 they both travelled to Central America, returning by way of the United States, in order to inspect collections in the principal museums. Salvin had by this time decided to embark on a curatorial career. In 1874 he became the first holder of the Strickland curatorship of ornithology at the University of Cambridge; he remained there until 1882. He became a fellow of the Zoological Society in 1860, of the Linnean Society in 1864, and of the Royal Society in 1873, frequently serving on their councils; he joined the Royal Geographical Society in 1883, and was also a fellow of the Entomological Society. He was a founder member of the British Ornithologists' Union and edited its journal, *The Ibis*, in 1871–82; he was also author or co-author of many other important ornithological works. His best-known work is probably *Biologia Centrali-Americana*, co-edited with Godman; the two friends contributed the sections 'Aves' (1879–98) and 'Lepidoptera Rhopalocera' (butterflies), begun in 1879. Salvin was also co-author with P. L. Sclater of *Exotic Ornithology* (1869), *Synopsis of the Cracidae* (1870), and *Nomenclator avium neotropicalium* (1873). Also with Sclater he contributed sections to the *Reports of the Scientific Results of the Challenger Expedition* (*Zoology*) (1881). He wrote *Catalogue of the Picariae* (*Upupae and Trochili*) in the British Museum, London (1892) and *Catalogue of the Tubinares in the British Museum, London* (1896). Salvin also contributed 'On some Venezuelan birds' to Spence's *Land of Bolivar* (1878); 'On collecting and preserving reptiles and fish' to the Royal Geographical Society's *Hints to Travellers* (1889; 1893); and descriptions of Lepidoptera Rhopalocera to Whymper's *Travels among the Great Andes of the Equator* (1891). He completed Lord Lilford's *Coloured Figures of the Birds of the British Islands* (1885–97). As well as editing *Ibis*, Salvin compiled an index to series one to three, and for the Willoughby Society he edited Sir A. Smith's *Miscellaneous Ornithological Papers* (1880) and Leach's *Systematic catalogue of the specimens of the indigenous mammalia and birds in the British Museum* (1882). He was also author, or joint author with Godman or Sclater, of upwards of 120 papers on ornithology or the Lepidoptera Rhopalocera that appeared in various scientific journals or transactions of learned societies from 1856.

Salvin devised a simple method, later widely adopted, of constructing cabinets for natural history specimens whereby deep and shallow drawers are interchangeable, thus enabling species to be kept in taxonomic order rather than filed by size. It is therefore fitting that the larger part of his immense bird collections was later stored in cabinets descended from his prototypes at the Natural History Museum at Tring and in the Liverpool Museum.

Salvin's opinion was widely sought by fellow natural historians because of the soundness of his advice and the breadth of his interests, as well as the fact that he was a kindly and unassuming man. His knowledge in all branches of his favourite science was extensive, though he was particularly involved in studies on the birds of tropical America (on which he was an acknowledged authority) and on butterflies. Having succeeded to his father's property in 1882, Salvin moved to Hawksfold, Fernhurst, near Haslemere, Sussex, where he died, from heart disease, on 1 June 1898. About thirty bird species or subspecies, including an albatross, a parrot, a curassow, two antbirds, and several humming-birds, now bear the name *salvini*.   CLEMENCY THORNE FISHER

Sources A. N. [A. Newton], *PRS*, 64 (1898–9), xiii–xvii · *DNB* · University of Cambridge, *Reports of the museums and lecture rooms syndicate for 1874–1882* · *The Ibis*, 9th ser., 2 (1908), 127–8 · *The Ibis*, 7th ser., 4 (1898), 626–7 · H. M. Whittell, *The literature of Australian birds: a history and a bibliography of Australian ornithology* (1954)
Archives NHM, corresp., notebooks, and papers · RGS, notes on Guatemala · U. Cam., department of zoology, letter-book and papers | NHM, letters to Albert Gunther and R. W. T. Gunther · U. Cam., corresp. with Alfred Newton · U. Oxf., department of zoology, Francis Jourdain collection, notes taken from Salvin
Likenesses photograph, repro. in *Ibis* (1908), facing p. 127 · portrait, repro. in *Challenger expedition reports: portraits of the contributors* (1897) · portrait, repro. in F. Du Cane Godman, *Biologia Centrali-Americana*, introductory volume (1915)
Wealth at death £8312 12s. 11d.: probate, 30 June 1898, CGPLA Eng. & Wales

Salway, Thomas (*d.* 1743), singer, was singing as a treble in the musical establishment of James Brydges, first duke of Chandos, at Cannons, Edgware, by January 1721. Johann Christoph Pepusch was in charge of the music both at Cannons and for John Rich's theatre company at Lincoln's Inn Fields, where Salway sang in pantomime afterpieces and appeared as an entr'acte singer in spring 1724 and from December 1724 to May 1725. Salway still had a room at Cannons in June 1725, but from that September he sang as a regular member of the theatre company in musical afterpieces and was frequently advertised as singing music by Henry Purcell. In October 1726 Salway played a prudish nymph in Johann Ernst Galliard's masque *Pan and Syrinx*, and a month later he took the role of the ageing

court lady, Tullia, in the comic sub-plot of the English version of Giovanni Bononcini's *Camilla*, where he sang opposite the bass Richard Leveridge. He and Leveridge were soon performing comic female–male dialogues together, particularly Purcell's 'Since times are so bad' and 'No kissing at all'. In April 1729 Salway played the young hero, Friendly, in *Flora*, the first afterpiece role in which he both spoke and sang. During the summer vacations he appeared in theatre booths at Bartholomew fair between 1729 and 1734, and at the theatre in Richmond, Surrey, in 1730 and 1731.

On 26 March 1731 Salway sang the second tenor role of Damon in the first public performance of Handel's *Acis and Galatea* for Gaetano Filippo Rochetti's benefit at Lincoln's Inn Fields, and he was one of the singers who accompanied Handel to Oxford in July 1733 to sing in his oratorio performances there. The *Daily Post* for 28 August 1732 reported that Salway had been appointed to the choir of Salisbury Cathedral, but there are no references to him in the Salisbury records and he sang throughout the 1732–3 theatre season, moving with the company to Rich's new Covent Garden Theatre in December. The rest of his career was spent at that theatre, apart from two seasons at Drury Lane in 1734–6 in a very similar repertory. He was primarily a singer in musical pieces, but took a few minor speaking roles, such as Albany in *King Lear*. In February 1733 he created the title role in John Gay's posthumously produced ballad opera *Achilles*, where the young hero is in female disguise throughout. Its risqué humour aroused some controversy, but the piece received nearly twenty performances before the end of the season and gave Salway his best petticoat role.

On 7 January 1735 at St George's, Hanover Square, Salway married Sarah Odum (*bap.* 1712?), 'the Niece of the late Mr. *Westall*, a considerable Tallow-Chandler near *Smithfield*, a Fortune of 5000l' (*London Magazine*). At the Haymarket Theatre that summer he sang the hero, Gaylove, in Henry Carey's ballad opera *The Honest Yorkshireman*, and he later created three further leading roles for Carey. He was the gallant Moore of Moore-Hall in the runaway success *The Dragon of Wantley* (26 October 1737), a burlesque opera with words by Carey and music by John Frederick Lampe, where, resplendent in spiked armour, he won the heroine Margery by killing the dragon with a kick on the backside. He also sang Moore in Carey's sequel, *Margery, or, A Worse Plague than the Dragon* (9 December 1738) and the following year created the hero, True-Blue, in another Carey piece, *Nancy, or, The Parting Lovers*. Carey's poem *The Beau's Lamentation for the Loss of Farinelli* cited three English singers as attractive alternatives to the castrato: 'There's Beard, and there's Salway, and smart Kitty Clive' (*Poems*, ed. Wood, 110). Salway was a freemason and one of the original members of both the Beefsteak Club and the Royal Society of Musicians. He continued to appear regularly at Covent Garden until winter 1741–2, when he missed several weeks, presumably because of illness. His last stage appearance was as the Chasseur Royal in Edward Phillips's pantomime *The Royal Chace*, and he died six weeks later, on 6 April 1743, leaving everything to his widow, whom he made his sole executor; he was buried at St Pancras, Middlesex, on 10 April.

OLIVE BALDWIN and THELMA WILSON

Sources E. L. Avery, ed., *The London stage, 1660–1800*, pt 2: *1700–1729* (1960) · A. H. Scouten, ed., *The London stage, 1660–1800*, pt 3: *1729–1747* (1961) · G. Beeks, 'Handel and music for the earl of Carnarvon', *Bach, Handel, Scarlatti: tercentenary essays*, ed. P. Williams (1985), 1–20 · account books of Lincoln's Inn Fields Theatre, Sept 1724–June 1725; and Sept 1726–June 1727, BL, Egerton MSS 2265–2266 · S. Rosenfeld, *The theatre of the London fairs in the eighteenth century* (1960) · *Daily Post* [London] (28 Aug 1732) · *Mist's Weekly Journal* (17 Dec 1726) · *London Magazine*, 4 (1735), 46 · B. Matthews, ed., *The Royal Society of Musicians of Great Britain: list of members, 1738–1984* (1985) · W. Arnold, *The life and death of the Sublime Society of Beef Steaks* (1871) · 'The beau's lamentation for the loss of Farrinelli', *The poems of Henry Carey*, ed. F. T. Wood (1930) · parish register, St George's, Hanover Square, London, 7 Jan 1735 [marriage] · *GM*, 1st ser., 13 (1743), 217 · will, GL, MS 9171/68 · parish register, London, St Pancras, 10 April 1743 [burial]

Likenesses engravings (to songs from *The dragon of Wantley*), repro. in G. Bickham, *The musical entertainer*, 2 (1738)

Wealth at death whole estate left to wife: will, GL, MS 9171/68

Salwey, Humphrey (*c*.1575–1652). *See under* Salwey, Richard (*bap.* 1615, *d.* 1685×8).

Salwey, Richard (*bap.* 1615, *d.* 1685×8), politician, was baptized on 22 October 1615 at Stanford-on-Teme, Worcestershire, the fourth son of Humphrey Salwey and Anne Littleton (*bap.* 1581). **Humphrey Salwey** (*c*.1575–1652), politician and lawyer, was the son of Arthur Salwey, lawyer, and Mary Serle, or Sherley. He matriculated from Brasenose College, Oxford, on 8 November 1590 and was admitted to the Inner Temple in 1591. He married Anne, daughter of Sir Edward Littleton of Pillaton Hall, Staffordshire. In 1630 he was fined £25 for failing to take a knighthood at the coronation of Charles I. Elected as MP for Worcester in 1640, in the civil war he took the side of parliament, and on its behalf endeavoured to prevent the execution of the king's commission of array in Worcestershire. On 5 August 1644 parliament appointed him king's remembrancer in the court of exchequer and on 12 June 1643 a member of the Westminster assembly of divines. In 1645 he was one of four commissioners sent by parliament to the Scottish army in England. In January 1649 Salwey was appointed one of the king's judges, but refused to sit, though he resumed his seat in the Commons not long after the regicide. He died in December 1652 and was buried in Westminster Abbey on 20 December. At the Restoration his body was exhumed and removed by an order of 9 September 1661.

Richard Salwey was apprenticed to a London tradesman. In September 1641 he obtained a licence to marry Anne (*bap.* 1618, *d.* in or after 1688), daughter of Richard Waring, in which he is described as a citizen and grocer of St Leonards, Eastcheap, London. He is said to have been the spokesman of the apprentices in some of their tumultuous petitions to the Long Parliament. In October 1645 Salwey was elected to the Long Parliament for Appleby in Westmorland with Henry Ireton as his colleague. He is mentioned as taking part in the siege of Worcester in June 1646. In October 1646 parliament appointed him one of

the five commissioners sent to Ireland to negotiate with Ormond for the reception of parliamentary garrisons in Dublin, and other strongholds—a mission which, after three months' futile negotiations, ended in failure. Like his father Salwey refused to sit in the high court of justice, and he steered clear of Westminster for a time after the execution of the king, apparently not resuming his seat until 14 May 1649. He was a member of the third and the fourth councils of state elected during the Commonwealth. He was also appointed on 23 October 1651 one of the eight commissioners sent to Scotland to prepare the way for its union with England, and on 10 December 1652 was appointed one of the commissioners for the regulation of the navy.

On 13 September 1650 Salwey had been selected as one of the commissioners for the civil government of Ireland, but on 20 November his resignation was accepted. According to Edmund Ludlow he opposed the dissolution of the Long Parliament when it was first debated by army officers, and again expressed his disapproval after Cromwell had dissolved it, withdrawing from all dealings with the interim council of state on 3 May 1653. He was called to, but refused to sit in, the nominated assembly. But he remained on friendly terms with Cromwell, and in August 1653 was offered the post of ambassador to Sweden, which he declined 'on account of his unfitness through want of freedom of spirit and bodily health' (*Westmorland MSS*, 410). He likewise refused in June 1657 the invitation of the lord mayor and corporation of London to go to Ulster to settle the city estates. Nevertheless, on 14 August 1654 he was appointed English ambassador at Constantinople, and some of his letters to the Levant Company on his mission are among the state papers.

On the fall of the Cromwellian protectorate in April 1659 Salwey came once more to the fore. He took part in the negotiations between the army and the members of the Rump which led to the re-establishment of the Long Parliament, and was appointed a member of the committee of safety (7 May 1659) and of the council of state (14 May 1659). He also became once more one of the committee which managed the navy. When the army officers turned out the Long Parliament again Salwey was nominated one of the committee of safety erected by them, but refused to sit. Nevertheless he complied with them much too far for his reputation among parliamentary republicans, as he consented to take part in their discussions about the future constitution, and continued to act as navy commissioner. Fear lest the officers should attempt, if left to their own devices, to restore Richard Cromwell seems to have been one of his motives. He consented to act as one of the mediators between the army and the fleet (18 December 1659), when the latter declared for the restoration of the parliament. The restored Long Parliament consequently regarded him as a traitor, and on 17 January 1660 ordered him to be sent to the Tower; but, on the plea of ill health, he was on 21 January allowed to retire to the country instead.

At the Restoration Salwey escaped unpunished, though William Prynne made an effort to have him excluded from the Act of Indemnity. In July 1662 Lord Newport arrested him in Shropshire on suspicion of conspiring against the new regime, but Clarendon ordered his release (on 11 August) as there was no information against him, and several persons of unquestionable integrity had given bail for him. On 2 November 1663 Salwey was again committed to the Tower in connection with what was known as the Farnley Wood plot, but was released on 4 February 1664. In 1678 Charles II ordered him to absent himself beyond sea for some time, and he was again under suspicion at the time of Monmouth's rising. He died, distracted by commercial losses, some time between signing his will on 9 December 1685 and 20 May 1688 when the will was proved. He was survived by his wife, Anne, with whom he had at least one son, John.

C. H. FIRTH, *rev.* SEAN KELSEY

Sources D. Underdown, *Pride's Purge: politics in the puritan revolution* (1971) · B. Worden, *The Rump Parliament, 1648–1653* (1974) · A. Woolrych, *Commonwealth to protectorate* (1982) · T. Liu, 'Salway, Richard', Greaves & Zaller, *BDBR*, 139–40 · *CSP dom., 1645–60* · IGI · Burke, *Gen. GB* (1833–8), 1 · W. P. W. Phillimore, ed., *The visitation of the county of Worcester made in the year 1569*, Harleian Society, 27 (1888) · Foster, *Alum. Oxon.* · will, PRO, PROB 11/391, fol. 185 · E. A. Andriette, 'Salway, Humphrey', Greaves & Zaller, *BDBR*, 3.138–9 · *The manuscripts of the earl of Westmorland*, HMC, 13 (1885); repr. (1906)
Archives NRA, priv. coll., letters | BL, letters to cousin, W. Charleton, Sloane MS 3962, fols. 191, 301
Likenesses portrait; in possession of Mr Alfred Salwey, 1897
Wealth at death see will, PRO, PROB 11/391, fol. 185

Salzman [*formerly* Salzmann], **Louis Francis** (1878–1971), antiquary and historian, was born on 26 March 1878 at Brighton, Sussex, the younger son of Frederick William Salzmann, a physician, and his wife, Clara Sinnock. He was educated at Haileybury School and Pembroke College, Cambridge, where he read, though ingloriously, the natural sciences tripos. Having inherited a small private income while still young, he lived for a while in Hailsham, Sussex, and there exchanged medicine for history, publishing *The History of the Parish of Hailsham* in 1901, the first of some twenty books that he wrote or edited.

Through indifferent health Salzman escaped military service in the First World War and instead taught at St George's School, Harpenden, Hertfordshire. In 1918 he moved to Cambridge and coached and supervised history students. In 1904 he had married Maud Elizabeth, daughter of George Monro Russell, then vicar of Upper Dicker, Sussex; they had three sons, the youngest of whom died in 1943, and two daughters. The marriage was dissolved in 1934 and Salzman thereupon left Cambridge for London.

When Salzman's literary career began, English economic history was still comparatively unexplored. Some of Salzman's earliest essays were in that field, for he contributed the articles on all the Sussex industries then identified to the second of the volumes devoted to Sussex (1907) in the Victoria History of the Counties of England, which had been founded at the turn of the century and itself pioneered economic history. Those articles were complemented by *English Industries in the Middle Ages* (1913),

and *English Trade in the Middle Ages* (1931), learned textbooks which were indispensable to students at a time when little of the kind was readily available. The first had originally excluded building but the enlarged edition of 1923 supplied the lack. That in turn was replaced in 1952 by *Building in England Down to 1540* (2nd edn, 1967), which deals with the early organization of the trade, technique, and materials, and prints many documents, notably contracts. This was Salzman's permanent contribution to scholarship. An outcome was the Vernacular Architecture Group, of which Salzman was a founder and whose meetings he still attended in his eighties.

The Victoria History of the Counties of England, after wartime discontinuance and painful resuscitation, was eventually acquired by William Page, its editor, who in 1932 presented it, though unendowed, to the University of London. The university entrusted it to its Institute of Historical Research. In 1934 Page died and Salzman became editor. The moment was inauspicious, for the History was doubtfully popular and the university had little money for its support. Nevertheless, Salzman resumed the Oxfordshire and Warwickshire series and started Cambridgeshire, without halting Sussex. Before retiring in 1949 he had brought out fifteen volumes; for eleven of them he was the sole editor. Some of the general chapters that he commissioned were attractively original but the volumes of parish histories continued the Page convention. Given contemporary calamities, that conservatism was prudent, for extravagant innovations could have killed the History or hampered its later evolution. As an editor Salzman justifiably condemned both verbosity and procrastination, and, if always fair, could express his displeasure forcefully.

Sussex was a leading beneficiary of Salzman's industry. He joined the council of its archaeological society in 1903 and became president in 1954 and 1955. He edited forty-five volumes of its transactions, from 1909 to 1959, and published its history in 1946. He helped to excavate Pevensey Castle and Alfriston's Saxon cemetery in youth, and Robertsbridge Abbey in 1935. He was a founder of the Sussex Record Society and its joint or sole literary director from 1905, himself preparing for it ten texts. For these and other services to learning he was appointed CBE in 1955 and made an honorary DLitt of the University of Sussex in 1965.

Salzman's knowledge of antiquities was deep, versatile, and generously shared. He had widely explored the public records, as his book called *Medieval Byways* (1913) and two others descriptive of English social life (medieval and Tudor, both 1926) reveal. He also wrote biographies of Henry II (1917) and, less successfully, Edward I (1968). His prose was clear and easy and he seldom altered his first drafts. He thought out many of his serious works on long walks. Latterly his personality seemed somewhat forbidding and he could be devastatingly outspoken, but there was a far lighter touch: he wrote plays and verses for children and he commemorated in verse occurrences in the Institute of Historical Research. He was sparely built and to the last retained his abundant locks and eyebrows. From about 1938 he lived at Lewes, Sussex, and died there on 4 April 1971.   RALPH B. PUGH, rev.

Sources *The Times* (6 April 1971) · *The Times* (15 April 1971) · *VCH General introduction* · *West Sussex Gazette* (11 March 1954) · F. W. Steer, 'Louis Francis Salzman', *Sussex Archaeological Collections*, 109 (1971), 1–3 · private information (1986) · *CGPLA Eng. & Wales* (1971)
Archives S. Antiquaries, Lond., corresp., notebooks, and papers, incl. many published works · Sussex Archaeological Society, Lewes, research notes and papers | LUL, letters to J. H. Round · Sussex Archaeological Society, Lewes, letters to G. P. Burstow
Likenesses photograph, 1970, repro. in Steer, 'Louis Francis Salzman'
Wealth at death £39,499: probate, 17 May 1971, *CGPLA Eng. & Wales*

Samber, Robert (*bap.* 1682, *d. c.*1745), writer and translator, was baptized on 20 April 1682 at Lymington, Hampshire, the son of Samuel Samber (*d.* 1716) of Lymington, surgeon, and Susannah Legg of Fawley. The Samber 'clan' was affluent and influential (a number of seventeenth-century Sambers became mayors of Lymington). Given this social milieu it is rather surprising to find that Robert, unlike his elder brother Samuel, was brought up as a Roman Catholic (perhaps because of his mother's religion). While Samuel went to Gonville and Caius College, Cambridge, Robert had to go abroad to acquire an education. On 11 July 1705 he entered the English College at Rome, presumably after spending some time at the English College at Douai—he might be the Robert Samber who received a pass to visit Holland on 17 September 1703. He left again on 15 April 1706 without taking orders.

Back in England Samber started on a literary career by publishing a meditation in verse entitled *On the Passion of our Blessed Saviour* (1708). In the preface he talks about religious experiences during his stay at the English College at Rome and laments 'the new fashionable humour of squaring mysteries of Christianity by human reason'. Very quickly life must have taught him that the only way to make a living by writing was to adapt to the taste of the time. Most prominent in his next extant publication, *Poems on Several Subjects* (1714), are imitations of Horace and epigrams in the true Augustan manner. Subsequently Samber engaged in all kinds of other literary activities that one associates with 'Grub Street'. The range is extensive: from religious verse, medical handbooks, plays, books on architecture and economic history, devotional treatises, and pornography to wedding odes. He used his knowledge of Roman Catholic literature in adapting a popular tract of Jeremias Drexelius for the English market (*A Devout Christian's Hourly Companion*, 1716, and subsequent editions), cutting out all the too obviously Roman Catholic elements. He introduced England to two of the most advanced books on midwifery of his time (by Henry van Deventer).

As one of Edmund Curll's hack writers Samber translated Jean Barrin's *Venus dans le cloître, ou, La religieuse en chemise* (again using his inside knowledge of things Catholic) and thus became involved in the major obscenity case of the century: in 1725 Curll was accused of publishing obscene books among which was Samber's translation.

After lengthy legal proceedings Curll was fined 25 marks for each offence in February 1728, but, Curll being Curll, *Venus in the Cloister* was again advertised in 1735. Samber instigated the publication of the correct text of Herman Boerhaave's *Methodus discendi medici* by publishing a garbled version; he was the adapter and translator of literary 'curiosities', such as Charles Ançillon's *Traité des eunuques*; and he was responsible for the English text of Charles Perrault's fairy tales which has never been out of print from 1729 to date. Many of his works, such as *The Courtier*, translated from the original by Castiglione, demonstrate that he was a very competent translator—having French, Latin, and Italian—and that he was highly interested in the problems posed by editing and translating. In the preface to *The Courtier* he shows an intimate knowledge of the English publishing history of Castiglione, and discusses past and present English versions.

Samber's papers, preserved in the Bodleian Library, also give an impression of all the numerous projects that did not reach publication, such as a number of plays and translations of Ovid's *Metamorphoses* and the homilies of Pope Clement XI. Among the papers are many draft letters to Samber's patrons (notably to John, duke of Montagu, and to members of the Catholic Howard dynasty) that give a unique insight into the day-to-day reality of the patronage system in the early eighteenth century. In order to ingratiate himself with Montagu Samber dedicated books to him, among them *Long Livers* (1722; a translation of a work by Harcouet de Longville); in the preface Samber presents himself as an eager proselyte to the fraternity of freemasons, of whom Montagu was grand master. Furthermore, among both his published and unpublished works there are 'poetic congratulations' on births and weddings in the Montagu family and some of Samber's letters suggest that he was engaged by Montagu to act on his behalf in complicated legal issues. It is interesting to speculate why, in another pseudonymous publication (a translation, published in 1723 of *L'éloge de l'yvresse* by A. H. de Sallengre), Samber mercilessly ridicules the drinking habits of the fraternity of which his patron was a prominent member. Robert Samber died about 1745.

J. BLOM and F. BLOM

Sources Bodl. Oxf., MSS Rawl. poet. 11, 131, 132, 133, 134a, 134b, 135; C. 640 · BL, Stowe MS 658; Add. MS 38728 · J. M. Blom, 'The life and works of Robert Samber (1628–±1745)', *English Studies*, 70 (1989), 507–50 · R. Straus, *The unspeakable Curll* (1927) · D. Foxon, *Libertine literature in England, 1660–1745* (1963) · P. M. Hill, *Two Augustan booksellers: John Dunton and Edmund Curll* (1958) · *ESTC* · A. J. Willis, *Hampshire marriage licences, 1669–1680* (1963) · *VCH Hampshire and the Isle of Wight* · Venn, *Alum. Cant.*, 1/1–4 · E. Armitage, 'Robert Samber', *Ars Quatuor Coronatorum*, 9 (1898), 30 · R. F. Gould, 'Introduction', *The preface to long livers* (1892) · W. Kelly, ed., *Liber ruber venerabilis collegii Anglorum de urbe*, 2, Catholic RS, 40 (1943), entry 1204, p. 137 · *CSP dom.*, 1703–4, 340
Archives BL, literary MSS and financial papers, Stowe MS 658; Add. MS 38728 | Bodl. Oxf., MSS Rawl. poet. 11, 131, 132, 133, 134a, 134b, 135; MS Rawl. C 640

Samble, Richard (*bap.* 1644, *d.* 1680), Quaker minister, was baptized at Penhale in the parish of St Enoder, Cornwall, on 24 July 1644, the son of William Samble and his wife,

Christobell, and was brought up in the Church of England. He joined the Quakers around 1666, having been 'convinced' by Christopher Bacon, 'the first public Friend that ever [he] heard' (*Richard Samble's Testimony Concerning Christopher Bacon*, sig. A). He became a Quaker minister, travelling throughout England and Wales for about six years, after which time he returned home to work as a tailor. Even then he was 'much pressed in spirit to travel' and spread the Quaker message, for as his contemporary Thomas Salthouse remarked in his preface to Samble's *A Handful after the Harvest Man* (1684), 'he had a gift for the work of the ministry, and did impose it with great diligence' (Salthouse).

Samble married Jane Voyte of Creed, Cornwall, on 15 November 1668 and they had a number of children, many of whom died in their childhood years. In her testimony to her husband she said, 'since I have been his wife … I do not remember that ever I heard an unsavoury word come from his mouth' (J. Samble, 'Testimony').

Samble was fined £20 for preaching at Plymouth on 5 April 1677, and a further £40 a few days later for breaches of the Conventicle Act. He was also heavily fined for absence from the Anglican church.

Not a prolific writer, Samble produced few tracts. As well as the aforementioned work, he wrote *A Testimony unto the Truth* (1676) and *A Testimony to the Plainness and Simplicity of the Truth* (1679), the latter being a discussion of baptism in which he puts forth the Quaker view that 'no baptism short of the baptism of the Holy Ghost will prepare the soul for the Lord, for outward water cannot wash away sin' (p. 13).

Towards the close of his life, Samble lived in Falmouth and continued to travel from there. About March 1680 he was taken sick at Poole, but having recovered sufficiently after some weeks he set off for home, only to suffer a relapse at Clampet, near Moreton (Moretonhampstead) in Devon, where he died on 15 May 1680. He was buried at Kingsbridge, Devon, three days later.

CAROLINE L. LEACHMAN

Sources W. Evans and T. Evans, eds., *The Friends' Library*, 14 vols. (1837–50), vol. 12 · T. Salthouse, 'Preface', in R. Samble, *A handful after the harvest man* (1684) · Boase & Courtney, *Bibl. Corn.*, vol. 2 · J. Besse, *A collection of the sufferings of the people called Quakers*, 1 (1753) · J. Smith, ed., *A descriptive catalogue of Friends' books*, 1 (1867) · J. Samble, 'A testimony for my dear husband Richard Samble', in R. Samble, *A handful after the harvest man* (1684) · *Richard Samble's testimony concerning Christopher Bacon* [n.d., 1678?] · R. Samble, *A testimony to the plainness and simplicity of the truth* (1679) · *The Friend*, 2 (1844), 121–3 · *IGI* · *DNB* · Quaker digest registers, RS Friends, Lond.

Sambourne, (Edward) Linley (1844–1910), cartoonist and illustrator, was born on 4 January 1844 at 15 Lloyd Square, Pentonville, London, and baptized at St Philip's Church, Clerkenwell, the only surviving child of Edward Mott Sambourne (1802–1866) and his wife, Frances Linley (1811–1892), a member of the family to which Elizabeth Linley, wife of Richard Brinsley Sheridan, belonged. His paternal grandfather had left England for the United States and had been naturalized an American citizen but his father, born at Easton, Pennsylvania, returned to England as a

child and eventually carried on a wholesale furrier's business in St Paul's Churchyard, London.

Linley Sambourne was educated at the City of London School (1855–6) and afterwards at Chester Training College (1857–60). His talent for drawing was encouraged by his father's sister, Mrs Barr, herself an accomplished artist. At the age of sixteen he attended the School of Art at South Kensington but left after a brief period to become an apprentice at the marine engine works of John Penn & Son, Greenwich. In his spare time he amused himself by drawing caricatures and fanciful sketches. A friend showed some of these to Mark Lemon, editor of the weekly satirical magazine *Punch*, who included a small drawing in the issue for 27 April 1867 and then asked for further contributions.

Linley Sambourne's career with *Punch* lasted nearly forty-three years. His first contributions show ingenuity, if little artistic merit, but he soon developed the strength of conception and firmness of touch which characterizes an outstanding draughtsman. His early predilection was for the grotesque and fanciful, and in 1871 he was put to illustrating a regular feature, 'The essence of parliament'. His convoluted decorations around the initial letter of the article were well received and over time were gradually extended until they almost filled the page. In 1878 he was appointed 'cartoon junior', second in rank to John Tenniel, who had been cartoonist-in-chief since 1851. Sambourne decided to abandon grotesquerie and for twenty years supplied the required full-page cartoon in a vigorous realistic style. Produced in two days to meet the printing deadline, these drawings comprise the bulk of his mature output. Well thought out, with strong contrasts of light and shade, they are masterfully executed but lack the quirky charm of his other work, such as the series of 'Fancy Portraits' which appeared throughout the 1880s. Here personalities of the day were gently mocked, either garbed in fancy dress and sporting their appropriate emblems, or cleverly disguised as the animals, birds, and insects which were the artist's particular passion. His gifts for pattern making and design are manifest in the extra Christmas number, *Punch's Almanack*, especially in those editions at the turn of the century when his imaginative powers reached new heights.

Sambourne found drawing true to life difficult without regular recourse to a model, so as an aid he built up a reference collection of commercially available photographs, augmented with pictures cut from magazines. In 1882 he took up photography and from 1884 onwards regularly posed his family and servants in the attitudes required for the cartoons. He did his own developing and printing and then drew directly from these images. In 1893 he joined a camera club which provided nude models, photographs of which became the basis for the classically draped figures often featured in his later work.

Most of Sambourne's drawing was done for *Punch* but he had the occasional commission from other magazines and also illustrated several books, the best-known being the 1885 edition of Charles Kingsley's *Water Babies*. His most outstanding work is the large diploma card for the

1883 Fisheries Exhibition. Bordered with fish, birds, and water-loving creatures, all beautifully observed, it shows penmanship of the highest order.

From 1885 onwards Sambourne exhibited nearly every year at the Royal Academy and held a successful one-man show at the Fine Art Society in 1893. He was appointed one of the royal commissioners of the fine arts at the Paris Exhibition of 1900, being sole juror for Great Britain in class 7. At the end of 1900, when Tenniel retired after fifty years with *Punch*, Sambourne was the natural choice to fill the post. This he did to general public acclaim until his death ten years later.

Linley Sambourne married on 20 October 1874 Mary Ann (Marion; 1851–1914), eldest daughter of Spencer Herapath FRS of Westwood Lodge, Broadstairs, Kent. With her he had a son, Mawdley Herapath (always known as Roy) and a daughter, Maud Frances, who married Leonard Messel in 1898 [*see* Messel, Oliver]. Sambourne enjoyed a happy marriage and was much loved by his children and grandchildren. Energetic and gregarious, fond of all kinds of outdoor exercise, and tireless in the pursuit of social pleasures, he made a delightful companion and was noted for his fund of good stories.

Linley Sambourne died at his London home, 18 Stafford Terrace, Kensington, on 3 August 1910. He was cremated at Golders Green, Middlesex, and the ashes were buried in the graveyard of St Peter's Church, Broadstairs, Kent, on 8 August 1910.

Furnished and decorated in the aesthetic manner by the Sambournes during the 1870s and 1880s, 18 Stafford Terrace was preserved by their descendants almost unaltered. The house and its extensive collection of artworks, including many of Sambourne's own drawings and several thousands of his photographs, passed into the public domain in 1980, and was opened as a museum named Linley Sambourne House.

R. C. LEHMANN, rev. SHIRLEY NICHOLSON

Sources *The Times* (4 Aug 1910) · *The World* (24 March 1886) · *Pall Mall Gazette* (8 Nov 1889) · *Westminster Budget* (2 June 1893) · *ILN* (28 Jan 1893) · *The Sketch* (16 Jan 1901) · R. G. G. Price, *A history of Punch* (1957) · Linley Sambourne's diaries, 1882–1910, Central Library, Royal Borough of Kensington and Chelsea, London [microfilm and MSS] · *CGPLA Eng. & Wales* (1910) · S. Nicholson, *A Victorian household* (1988) · D. Low, *British cartoonists, caricaturists and comic artists* (1942), 21–4 · *Public artist, private passions: the work of Edward Linley Sambourne* (2001) [exhibition catalogue, Leighton House, 27 Sept 2001–13 Jan 2002] · b. cert. · d. cert.
Archives Central Library, Royal Borough of Kensington and Chelsea, London, drawings, diaries, letters, photographs · Linley Sambourne House, London, drawings, photographs · priv. coll., archive, papers | *Punch* archive, London, vols. 52–138 · BL, corresp. with Macmillans, Add. MS 55233
Likenesses G. Reid, oils, 1882, Aberdeen Art Gallery · L. Sambourne, self-portrait, pen-and-ink drawing, 1891, NPG · photograph, 1893, Central Library, Royal Borough of Kensington and Chelsea, London · Elliott & Fry, photographs, NPG · H. Furniss, pen-and-ink caricatures, NPG · B. Partridge, drawing, Linley Sambourne House, London · L. Sambourne, self-portrait, pen-and-ink drawing, Athenaeum, London · Spy [L. Ward], chromolithograph caricature, NPG; repro. in *VF* (1892)
Wealth at death £16,150 2s. 5d.: resworn probate, 21 Oct 1910, *CGPLA Eng. & Wales*

Samelson, Adolphus (1817–1888), ophthalmic surgeon, was born on 6 September 1817 in Berlin to Jewish parents; his father, whose forename is unknown, died in 1830 and his mother, born Maria Ann Hartog, lived to an advanced age. Samelson was educated in the Berlin Gymnasium primary classes, by a minister at Wusterhaus for two years, and at the Friedrich-Wilhelm Gymnasium, Berlin. In 1836 he proceeded to Berlin University and he graduated MD in 1840. After qualifying in the state medical examination in 1841, he settled in practice at Zehdenick, in Brandenburg.

A staunch liberal, Samelson served on Zehdenick town council and was instrumental in founding a friendly burial society and a co-operative loan society. In 1848 he was elected a member of the electoral colleges for the Prussian national assembly and the German Reichstag. The following year he lost to an ex-minister in district elections to the Prussian second chamber. He became an active contributor to a new local liberal newspaper, *Die Neue Zeit*. For an article critical of the role of the Prussian soldiery in the suppression of the Dresden insurrection, he was imprisoned for six months and deprived of his position on the town council and of his civil rights. His medical licence was withdrawn but he managed to practise in Zehdenick until 1852.

After returning to Berlin, and barred from official courses of instruction, Samelson turned to the study of eye disease, becoming a pupil and friend of Dr Albrecht von Graefe. Subsequently forced by the authorities to leave the country, he went to Paris and attended the leading hospitals there. His intention was to join the French military medical service in the Crimea, but he became seriously ill during a cholera epidemic. While recovering at Champigny he was invited to the Netherlands by friends. From there he went to Liège and Brussels, where he had relatives, but he was refused permission to practise in Belgium.

In June 1856 Samelson went to London. He spent several months at general and specialist eye hospitals, before moving in 1857 to Manchester, home of a prosperous German community, where he settled in practice. Although his civil status in Germany and his medical licence were restored in 1859, Samelson chose to remain among his new friends in Manchester. He never married. In 1862 he became a surgeon at the Manchester Eye Hospital, which he served conscientiously, bringing to the post an extensive knowledge of the specialist literature and a passion for organization. In 1867 the hospital relocated to larger accommodation in St John Street, a fashionable medical area. Samelson, who moved opposite the hospital, frequently took the names of poor-looking elderly patients and unobtrusively sent them food and clothing.

Samelson was a member of the Manchester Medical Society, to which he regularly presented interesting cases, and he contributed to British and German medical journals. During 1865 he went to Berlin for treatment by Von Graefe for 'granular lid' eye infection. His 'Reminiscences' of his four months' stay contain the first account in English of Von Graefe's method of linear extraction of cataract. In 1867 he translated Von Graefe's essay 'The study of ophthalmology'. He resigned from the Manchester Eye Hospital in 1876 after his relationship with the management deteriorated, following changes he disliked.

Reduced professional commitment meant more time for the many organizations with which Samelson was involved. These included the Manchester Statistical Society, the District Provident Society, the Education Aid Society, the Art Museum, the Provident Dispensaries Association, Henshaw's Blind Asylum, Manchester Ratepayers' Association, and the Schiller Anstalt—an Anglo-German gentleman's club which attracted a number of political refugees. Samelson frequently attended the meetings of the Manchester Literary Club, where his extensive reading and critical acumen were much appreciated. His most important contribution was 'The temple at Pergamus', in 1881. From 1862 he was active in the Manchester and Salford Sanitary Association, promoting open spaces and school playgrounds, day nurseries, and the provision of vital statistics. His paper 'Dwellings and the death rate of Manchester' was published in the *Health Journal* in 1883. For the Dramatic Reform Association he presented a paper, later published, entitled 'The education of the drama's patrons', at the Social Science Congress in Nottingham in 1882.

Samelson was motivated by a zealous public spirit and a strong sense of duty. He was extremely conscientious but became bogged down in detail. His lack of patience also caused problems. But for those who knew him, such failings were outweighed by his sterling character. In later life, suffering from failing health and persistent insomnia, he sought relief at Bournemouth, then at Cannes, where he died at the Hotel Richemont, on 12 January 1888. His funeral at the protestant cemetery the following day was attended by many English residents and fellow hotel guests. The bulk of his property was bequeathed to old servants, friends, and charitable institutions, in Manchester, London, and Berlin.

JOAN MOTTRAM

Sources W. E. A. Axon, *In memoriam Adolph Samelson* (1888) · 'Adolph Samelson MD', *Health Journal* (March 1887), 152–4 · *Manchester Guardian* (14 Jan 1888) · *Manchester Guardian* (20 Jan 1888) · *Manchester Guardian* (12 March 1888) · F. S. Stancliffe, *The Manchester Royal Eye Hospital, 1814–1964* (1964) · *London and Provincial Medical Directory* (1857–69) [see also various years, 1870–83] · census returns for Manchester, 1861 · JRL, Samelson MSS, Manchester medical collection, estate account · *Annual Report* [Manchester Art Museum] (1888), 10 · *Papers of the Manchester Literary Club*, 2–14 (1876–88) · *Annual Report* [Manchester and Salford Sanitary Association] (1862–86) · *Statuten*, Manchester Schiller Anstalt [and reports] · *Medical Register* (1859) · *DNB*
Archives JRL
Likenesses Meisenbach, photograph, repro. in *Health Journal*, 153
Wealth at death £4870 2s. 1d.: probate, 9 March 1888, *CGPLA Eng. & Wales*

Sammes, Aylett (*c.*1636–*c.*1679), antiquary, was born at Kelvedon in Essex, the son of Thomas Sammes, gentleman, and his wife, Mary Jeffrey. His father's younger brother, Edward, married into the Aylett family of Rivenhall, and presumably one of the Ayletts was his godfather. In 1648 he entered Felsted School, where his master was John Glascock, a fellow of Christ's College, Cambridge.

Sammes proceeded to Christ's College, being admitted as a fellow-commoner on 3 July 1655, and graduating BA in 1657. He was admitted to the Inner Temple on 28 October 1657, and was incorporated MA at Oxford on 10 July 1677.

In 1676 Sammes published, at his own expense, *Britannia antiqua illustrata, or, The antiquities of ancient Britain, derived from the Phoenicians*. The volume was licensed by Roger L'Estrange in March 1675, printed by Thomas Roycroft, and dedicated to Heneage Finch, the lord chancellor, who was also of the Inner Temple. Sammes's book, which traces British history from earliest times to the Saxons of the eighth century, is one of the odder antiquarian productions of the seventeenth century, for it maintains that Britain was originally settled by the Phoenicians, who established a flourishing culture there:

> Not only the name of Britain itself, but of most places therein of ancient denomination are purely derived from the Phoenician Tongue, and ... the Language itself for the most part, as well as the Customs, Religions, Idols, Offices, Dignities of the Ancient Britains are all clearly Phoenician, as likewise their instruments of war. (A3v)

Much of the evidence Sammes offers is philological, and the book is full of misleading etymologies. Nowhere does Sammes look for evidence in the field, or produce a single object of Phoenician origin to substantiate his claims. His opinions are initially derived from his reading of Strabo's *Geography*, and they echo the views of the Tudor historian John Twyne that were published in *De rebus Albionicis* (1590). The largest influence on the book was the work of the French scholar Samuel Bochart, whose *Geographia sacra* (1646) gave an extravagant account of the voyages and colonies of the Phoenicians.

Sammes's authorship was doubted by Anthony Wood, who noted that 'the common report was, that not he, but his quondam Uncle was the Author; and to confirm it, was his great ignorance in matters and books of Antiquity'. Wood gives a cutting picture of Sammes:

> I was several times in his company when he spent some weeks this year [1677] in Oxon, and found him to be an impertinent, girning and pedantical coxcomb, and so ignorant of authors, that he never heard of, before I mentioned it to him, of the great antiquary John Leland, or of his printed or manuscript works, nor any thing of Baleus, nor could he give any account of authors that are quoted in the said *Britannia antiqua illustrata*. (Wood, *Ath. Oxon.: Fasti*, 2.363)

Thomas Hearne corroborated this view: 'Mr Collins Schoolmaster of Magd. Coll. Schoole tells me that knew Aylett Samms, and that he was a very ignorant, silly fellow, not at all qualify'd to write *Britannia antiqua*' (*Remarks*, 3.231, 16 Sept 1711). The question remains unresolved, but the absence of Sammes's name from contemporary correspondence among antiquaries leads one to believe that he was not a serious scholar. Sammes died 'in the year 1679 or thereabouts, perhaps in the Inner Temple, where he had a Chamber' (Wood, *Ath. Oxon.: Fasti*, 2.363). It is not known whether he married or had children.

GRAHAM PARRY

Sources Wood, *Ath. Oxon.: Fasti* (1820), 363 · *Remarks and collections of Thomas Hearne*, ed. C. E. Doble and others, 3, OHS, 13 (1889) ·

DNB · P. Morant, *The history and antiquities of the county of Essex*, 2 vols. (1768) · W. Nicolson, *The English, Scotch and Irish historical libraries*, new edn, 3 pts in 1 vol. (1776) · M. Davies, *Athenae Britannicae*, 6 vols. (1716–19) · G. Parry, *The trophies of time: English antiquarians of the seventeenth century* (1995)

Sammons, Albert Edward (1886–1957), violinist and composer, was born on 23 February 1886 in Fulham, London, the son of Thomas Sammons (*b*. 1863), a street musician, and his wife, Annie Jackson (*b*. 1875). He attended the Edinburgh Road School, Barlby Road, London. Without academic training, his only violin lessons were from his father (an amateur violinist) in childhood, and from two orchestral colleagues early in his career. He played in restaurants and theatres from the age of twelve, and in 1909 was heard playing at the Waldorf Hotel by Thomas Beecham, who offered him a place in the Beecham orchestra. A few months later he became leader, and he subsequently learned the symphonic, opera, and ballet repertory as he went along. In later years the conductor commented that Sammons was the finest leader he ever had. Sammons married Laura Molly Tomkins on 31 October 1907; the marriage ended in divorce in 1920, and on 5 December 1921 he married Olive Hobday.

Sammons founded the London String Quartet and led it from 1910 to 1919, but it was a performance of Elgar's violin concerto in 1914 that launched his solo career. The composer avowed that no other violinist could match his performances: 'Sammons gets to the heart of it' (private information). In 1915 Sammons began a musical partnership with the Australian pianist William Murdoch which lasted until the latter's death in 1942, and together they made many fine recordings of the classical repertory and of English music.

Always keen to encourage British composers, Sammons gave first performances of, and recorded, chamber works by Ralph Vaughan Williams, Frank Bridge, John Ireland, Elgar, Delius, Herbert Howells, Granville Bantock, Eugene Goossens, and Edmund Rubbra, and concertos by Delius and George Dyson. Notable performances included the première of John Ireland's second sonata in March 1917; and he also took part in the first performance of Elgar's piano quintet in 1919. Delius dedicated his violin concerto to Sammons, who also made the first complete recording of Elgar's violin concerto in 1929, with Sir Henry Wood.

In 1919 Sammons formed the Chamber Music Players, a group of flexible instrumentation that could perform programmes containing anything from three to seven players. This, together with a sonata repertory with Murdoch and concerto playing, was the basis of a career that lasted until the onset of Parkinson's disease in 1946. Sammons was appointed professor of violin at the Royal College of Music in 1939 and was remembered with affection by the many pupils who entered the musical profession after his careful guidance. At the same time he would joke that he himself had never received a prize for violin playing. He was the composer of a number of light pieces for violin and piano, written mostly during his early career as a café

Albert Edward Sammons (1886–1957), by Olive Edis

musician. They show an instinctive grasp of musical structure in spite of his total lack of tuition in any branch of musical theory. More significantly, he won the Cobbett prize in 1915 with a 'Phantasy' quartet. He also published sets of violin studies.

Sammons had a modest, friendly, and humorous personality which endeared him to his pupils, and his magnificent tone, astonishing technique, and faultless intonation never ceased to be a wonder to them. Sammons was obliged to give up concert work by 1948 as his illness progressed, and finally gave up teaching in 1954, by which time he could walk only with difficulty. A benefit concert was given in his honour at the Albert Hall in December 1954; he attended it confined to a wheelchair. He was appointed CBE in 1944 and died at Middleton-on-Sea, Sussex, on 24 August 1957; he was cremated in Brighton.

Sammons's good humour and resilience never left him. While attending a rehearsal of the BBC Symphony Orchestra in his final years, on walking in the break with great difficulty to the canteen with an acquaintance, he held up his left hand, now shaking in the manner characteristic of Parkinson's disease, and said with a smile, 'Look Harry, I've got the best vibrato in the world now' (private information).

Sammons was one of the finest of English violinists, though his fame was limited by circumstances. He was shy, diffident, and because of a fear of flying always refused offers of work abroad. Nevertheless, his performances and recordings were held in high esteem by violinists the world over. J. Heifetz, F. Kreisler, J. Szigeti, and

Mischa Elman were friends and devotees, and younger players as diverse as I. Perlman, P. Zukerman, and Nigel Kennedy have acknowledged their debt to his recorded performances. ERIC WETHERELL

Sources E. Wetherell, *Albert Sammons: violinist* (1998) · G. Tankard and others, 'Albert Sammons', *RCM Magazine*, 52/3 (1956), 94–7 · J. Ireland, 'Albert Sammons: a tribute', *MT*, 98 (1957), 548 · H. Rutland, *MT*, 98 (1957), 571 · H. Howells, 'For Albert Sammons', *Musical Opinion*, 81 (1957–8), 171 · J. Creighton, *Discopaedia of the violin, 1889–1971* (1974) · private information (2004) · *New Grove*
Archives SOUND BL NSA, documentary recordings · BL NSA, performance recordings
Likenesses P. Blundell, bronze bust, 1928, Royal College of Music, London · F. Man, photograph, 1943, Hult. Arch. · A. Akerbladh, oils, 1950, Royal College of Music, London · M. Wrightson, bronze bust, 1952, Royal College of Music, London · O. Edis, photograph, NPG [*see illus.*] · photographs, priv. colls.
Wealth at death £9498 15*s*.: probate, 31 Oct 1957, CGPLA Eng. & Wales

Sampson. *See also* Samson.

Sampson, Agnes (*d*. 1591). *See under* North Berwick witches (*act*. 1590–1592).

Sampson, George (1873–1950), literary scholar, was born at Greenwich on 6 April 1873, the fourth and youngest child of Thomas Sampson, mariner, and his wife, Sarah Ann Hows, both from Jersey, though Thomas's father had come from Cornwall. In his earliest years, afterwards described in 'A boy and his books' (*Seven Essays*, 1947), his eldest sister taught him to read, and he became an omnivorous reader, especially of poetry. Poor health prevented him from going to school until nearly eleven and circumstances compelled him to leave before he was sixteen. He was then set to work for London matriculation and was trained as an elementary schoolteacher at Southwark Pupil Teacher School and Winchester Training College. On 14 December 1907 he married Grace (1880/81–1953), daughter of Frederick Lewis Alldis; they had no children. He taught for twelve years in elementary schools in Poplar and Rotherhithe. At thirty-seven he became headmaster of a higher-grade school and in 1925 he was appointed a district inspector by the London county council.

As a schoolmaster Sampson worked for the improved teaching of English in the spirit of a crusader. In May 1919 he was appointed a member of the distinguished departmental committee on the teaching of English and served as general secretary of the English Association. In 1921 he published *English for the English*, a passionate plea for better teaching based on two principles: first, that 'it is the purpose of education not to prepare children *for* their occupations, but to prepare children *against* their occupations', and second, that 'a sound educational system must be based upon the great means of human intercourse— human speech in spoken and written word'. The book was a tract for the times, but became a minor classic, its memorable dictum that 'every teacher is a teacher of English' being widely quoted (Thompson, 44). After many reprints, it appeared in a new edition in 1952.

With this pioneering work as a teacher Sampson combined a continuous activity as editor and critic. He edited George Berkeley's works in 1897–8, and this was followed by editions of many authors, including Edmund Burke, J. H. Newman, Thomas More, George Herbert, Ralph Waldo Emerson, John Keats, William Wordsworth, and William Hazlitt. Some of these were designed for use in schools and universities, but all bore the mark of an individual critical mind. This was recognized by the University of Cambridge, which made him an honorary MA in 1920. The width and catholicity of Sampson's reading, supplemented by a pungent style, qualified him in a notable way as a literary historian. His supplement (1924) to Stopford Brooke's *Primer of English Literature* was a brilliant and epigrammatic survey. In 1941 he triumphed on a much larger scale. Twenty years before, he had been invited to write a one-volume epitome of the *Cambridge History of English Literature*. Its completion was delayed by ill health, but when it was published it was rightly hailed as a *tour de force*. It was designed primarily as a handbook for students, but Sampson was one of nature's scholars, and the book is as readable as it is informing. Throughout the long labour of condensation he retained an individual freshness, and his supplementary chapter on the post-Victorians is a powerful piece of criticism. Sampson also had a profound and scholarly interest in music and drama. His 'Bach and Shakespeare' was chosen by the first earl of Birkenhead as one of the *Hundred Best English Essays* (1929), and Sampson in his *Seven Essays* (1947) included a spirited defence of Henry Irving. His opinions were strongly held and he did not aspire to be an essayist of gentle charm. But he was a warm-hearted friend and a good clubman. At the Reform Club, where he was a member of the library committee, he was a familiar figure in the group which gathered round T. E. Page, Arnold Bennett, H. G. Wells, and other literary men of his time. After his retirement Sampson went to live at Hove where his later years were darkened by persistent insomnia. He died on 1 February 1950 at 10 Eaton Gardens, Hove, of a coronary thrombosis.

SYDNEY C. ROBERTS, *rev.* JOHN D. HAIGH

Sources personal knowledge (2004) [S. C. Roberts] · *The Times* (4 Feb 1950), 1, 8 · G. Sampson, 'A boy and his books', *Seven essays* (1947) · D. Thompson, 'Introduction', *English for the English: a chapter on national education, George Sampson*, first printed (1921); new edn (1952); repr. (1970), 1–15 · *WWW*, 1941–50 · m. cert. · d. cert.
Wealth at death £11,996 8*s*. 7*d*.: probate, 10 July 1950, CGPLA Eng. & Wales

Sampson, Henry (*c*.1629–1700), ejected minister and historian of dissent, was born at South Leverton, Nottinghamshire, the eldest son of William Sampson (*c*.1590–*c*.1636), the poet and dramatist, and Helen (1603–1687), the daughter of Gregory Vicars (or Viccars) of Treswell, Nottinghamshire, and the sister of John Vicars (1604–1660), the biblical scholar. His father died about 1636, and on 25 December 1637 his mother married, second, Obadiah *Grew (*bap*. 1607, *d*. 1689), ejected from the vicarage of St Michael's, Coventry, at the Restoration. Nehemiah *Grew (*bap*. 1641, *d*. 1712), the future secretary of the Royal Society, was a younger stepbrother. Sampson was educated at Atherstone grammar school under his stepfather and at King Henry VIII School, Coventry, under Phinehas White; in 1646 he went up to Pembroke College, Cambridge, where his tutor was William Moses. He was elected to the Watts scholarship in Greek in December 1646. He graduated BA in 1650 and MA in 1653. Elected a fellow of the college in 1650, he was lecturer in Greek in 1651, junior bursar in 1652, and lecturer in philosophy in 1653. In 1654 he was appointed one of the commissioners for Suffolk, and in the same year his college presented him to the living of Framlingham, Suffolk, in the place of Richard Goltey, who refused to take the engagement to be loyal to the Commonwealth. As an intruding minister Sampson was displaced from Framlingham in 1660 on the return of Goltey, and ejected from his college fellowship on his refusal to conform.

After his ejection Sampson at first remained in Framlingham preaching privately at nonconformist meetings and gathering an Independent congregation which still exists, though now Unitarian. According to his stepbrother, Nehemiah Grew, Sampson resolved to qualify himself to practise medicine because he was never ordained. He entered Padua University on 27 August 1666 but then moved to Leiden, where he graduated MD on 12 July 1668. His thesis, published in 1668, opposed the practice of curing by the use of opposites, *Contraria contrariis curari*. He developed an extensive medical practice in London which included many fellow nonconformist ministers and the young Edmund Calamy. In 1680 he became an honorary fellow of the Royal College of Physicians with Grew. Grew was encouraged in his botany by Sampson, to whom he remained very close. Sampson published a number of papers on morbid anatomy in the *Philosophical Transactions* of the Royal Society between 1674 and 1697. In 1657 he had published Thomas Parker's *Methodus gratiae divinae* with a Latin preface. His will records a noted collection of early printed English bibles and common prayer books, some of which he had inherited from the father of his first wife and many of which he left to his brother William *Sampson, the rector of Clayworth, Nottinghamshire, who had conformed.

Sampson's major scholarly interests were antiquarian and historical. As early as 1663 he had written an account of Framlingham Castle, with a description of the interior destroyed in 1656, which Thomas Hearne subsequently published in his edition of Leland's *Collectanea*. Sampson was for many years engaged in preparing a history of puritanism and nonconformity in which he sought to represent the nonconformists 'as a Considerable, an injured & misjudged people' by examining their lives, learning, and usefulness to the church (H. Sampson to R. Thoresby, 9 May 1699, Yorkshire Archaeological Society, MS 7). He therefore drew up a list of ejected ministers for each county, and 'there were few Counties in which he did not add some Characters of the Ejected, (either from his own Knowledge, as particularly in Warwickshire; or from the Information of others)' (Calamy, *Abridgement*, 2.xxiii, 752). Ralph Thoresby, the Leeds antiquary, was among those who assisted him. He also co-operated with Roger Morrice, who was engaged in a similar project. The history was never published, as Sampson himself admitted the undertaking proved too great for him: 'Onus impar humeris'

(H. Sampson to R. Thoresby, 9 May 1699, Yorkshire Archaeological Society, MS 7). Calamy when preparing his own account of the ejected ministers relied greatly on Sampson's manuscript collections, particularly in his *Account* (1713) and the *Continuation* (1727).

Sampson remained a nonconformist. He was a member of Lazarus Seaman's congregation and that of Seaman's successor, John Howe. An original contributor to the Common Fund established to support provincial dissent, Sampson subscribed £50. He was listed as one of the gentleman managers of the reconstructed fund in February 1695, having care of the meetings in Leicestershire, Lincolnshire, and Suffolk.

Sampson married three times. The first marriage, on 3 March 1662, to Margaret, the daughter of another ejected minister, Oliver Bromskill, lasted but a short time, as she died in 1663. Their only son, Nathaniel, baptized at Loughborough in 1662, died in April 1669. Sampson's second wife was Esther, who died in November 1689; John Howe published a funeral sermon for her. Sampson married Anne Culling, of the parish of St Andrew's, Holborn, on 16 December 1690. Sampson at his death is said to have left an estate of between £8000 and £9000, but his nonconformist contemporaries were scandalized that he

> should not leave one penny to pious and charitable uses. All that can be said is, his wife made, or forced him to make a new will … and if she can be made a lady by it, she will think it as much for his honour. (Hunter, ed., *Letters of Eminent Men*, 1.400)

His will was made 'before my journey to Clayworth' (PRO, PROB 11/456, fol. 286r), where he died on 23 July 1700 and was buried in the parish church, where his brother was incumbent.

The importance of Sampson's historical collections was recognized by his contemporaries, and after his death there was considerable anxiety as to their fate. His widow 'has been spoken to once and again, and she promises they shall be all preserved safe' (Hunter, ed., *Letters of Eminent Men*, 1.400). Unfortunately, she sent them to William Tong at Coventry, who had little leisure to give them any attention. By January 1709 Sampson's collection had been split; part was with Calamy, the remainder still with Tong but in much confusion. Both parts of the collection were lost and of the original only Thoresby's notes from Sampson's daybook now survive.   DAVID L. WYKES

Sources J. Howe, *A discourse relating to the expectation of future blessedness with an appendix, containing some memorial of Dr Henry Sampson, a late noted physician in the City of London* (1705), 77–90 • R. B. Aspland, *Brief memoirs of Mr Richard Frankland, one of the ejected clergy in 1662 by the Act of Uniformity, and of Dr Henry Sampson, ejected on the Restoration from the living of Framlingham in Suffolk. To which are added, extracts from Dr Sampson's day-books, taken from the MSS of Thoresby in the British Museum* (1862) [orig. pubd as 'Some account of Dr Henry Sampson, one of the clergy ejected at the Restoration', *Christian Reformer*, new ser., 18 (1862), 154–66; 'Dr Henry Sampson's daybook', *Christian Reformer*, new ser., 18 (1862), 235–47] • F. Packard, 'Henry Sampson, 1629–1700: nonconformist minister & physician', *Suffolk Review*, 4 (1977), 256–63 • D. L. Wykes, 'Manchester College at York (1803–1840): its intellectual and cultural contribution', *Yorkshire Archaeological Journal*, 63 (1991), 207–18 • *Calamy rev.*, 236, 425 • will of Henry Sampson, Clapham, Surrey, dated 13 July, proved, 23 Aug 1700, PRO, PROB 11/456, sig. 119 • A. Gordon, ed., *Freedom after ejection: a* review (1690–1692) of presbyterian and congregational nonconformity in England and Wales (1917), 162–8, 345 • Walker rev., 335–6 • J. Hunter, Hunter's pedigrees: a continuation of Familiae minorum gentium, ed. J. W. Walker, Harleian Society, 88 (1936), 44, 83 • Ralph Thoresby's extracts from Sampson's day-books, BL, Add. MS 4460; pubd in 'The day-books of Dr Henry Sampson', GM, 2nd ser., 35 (1851), 381–8; 2nd ser., 36 (1851), 11–17 • [J. Hunter], ed., Letters of eminent men, addressed to Ralph Thoresby, 1 (1832), 400 • H. Sampson, Surrey, to R. Thoresby, 9 May 1699, W. Yorks. AS, Leeds, Yorkshire Archaeological Society, Thoresby correspondence, MS 7 • E. Calamy, ed., An abridgement of Mr. Baxter's history of his life and times, with an account of the ministers, &c., who were ejected after the Restauration of King Charles II, 2nd edn, 2 vols. (1713), vol. 1, p. 118 • E. Calamy, A continuation of the account of the ministers … who were ejected and silenced after the Restoration in 1660, 2 vols. (1727) • Disputatio medica inauguralis de celebri indicationum fundamento, Contraria contrariis curari quam, Deo O. M. auxiliante, ex auctoritate magnifici D. Johannis Cocceji, S.S. theol. doct. ejusdemque facultatis in illustri Lugd. Bat. professoris, nec non amplissimi senatus academici consensu, & almae facultatis medicae decreto, progradu doctoratûs, summisque in medicinae honoribus & privilegiis ritè consequendis, publico examini subjicit Henricus Sampson, L.A.M. Cantabr. aulae Pembrochinae pridem socius ad diem Julii, loco horsique solitis (1668) • J. Howe, A funeral sermon for Mrs. Esther Sampson, the late wife of Henry Sampson, Dr. of physick, who died Nov. 24. MDCLXXXIX (1690) • parish register, Loughborough, 3 March 1662, Leics. RO, DE 667/2 [marriage] • parish register, Loughborough, 3 March 1663, Leics. RO, DE 667/2 [burial]

Archives BL, diary, Sloane MS 4460

Wealth at death approx. £8000–9000: Letters of eminent men, ed. Hunter

Sampson, Henry (1841–1891), newspaper proprietor and editor, the son of David Sampson, a schoolmaster and journalist, and his wife, Belelia Egan, was born at Lincoln on 29 January 1841. He may have been born into a Catholic family or he may have converted later. At the age of twelve he entered a printing office in London, and became successively a compositor and proof-reader. From youth he was devoted to sport, and excelled as a boxer, runner, and sculler until he was twenty-three, when he was disabled by an accident to his left foot. In 1866 he was engaged by Samuel Orchart Beeton to contribute sporting leaders to The Glow-Worm and the Weekly Dispatch. Afterwards he joined the staff of the Illustrated Sporting News and Theatrical Review, and early in 1869 was appointed editor of that journal. On its collapse on 19 March 1870 he became the first editor of the Latest News, a penny Sunday paper of sixteen pages, which ran from 29 August 1869 to 25 September 1870, when it folded after fifty-seven issues. In 1870 he was engaged as a leader writer on the Morning Advertiser, and commenced contributing to Fun. The former role inspired him to compile a substantial History of Advertising (1874). During the illness of Thomas Hood the younger he acted as sub-editor of Fun, and he was its editor from Hood's death, in 1874, until February 1878. In 1875, 1876, 1877, and 1878 he edited the Fun Comic Annual. Early in 1872 he commenced sending to the Weekly Dispatch, under the signature of Pendragon, letters of general criticism on sport, especially boxing; he later published Modern Boxing by Pendragon (1878). On 19 August 1877, as part proprietor and editor, under the same pseudonym of Pendragon, Sampson started a weekly sporting paper, The Referee, on which he concentrated for the remainder of his life. By 1881 he

was married to Julia (b. 1850/51). He died at his home, 6 Hall Road, St John's Wood, London, on 16 May 1891, of influenza or 'a cold caught at Kempton Park' (ILN).

G. C. BOASE, rev. JULIAN LOCK

Sources Boase, Mod. Eng. biog. • ILN (23 May 1891), 667 • CGPLA Eng. & Wales (1891) • H. Sampson, History of advertising (1874) • b. cert. • census returns, 1881

Likenesses engraving, repro. in ILN, 671 • portrait, repro. in Sporting Mirror (April 1881), 72–4 • portrait, repro. in Entr'acte Annual (1882), 22

Wealth at death £37,420 9s. 2d.: probate, 1 July 1891, CGPLA Eng. & Wales

Sampson, John (1862–1931), librarian and Romani scholar, was born on 25 February 1862 at Schull, co. Cork, the eldest son and third of the six children of James Sampson (1813–1871), a chemist and mining engineer of Cornish stock, and his wife, Sarah Anne Macdermott (1829–1907), an Irishwoman of Huguenot descent. Ralph Allen *Sampson was his brother. His father died in 1871 in Liverpool, where the family had recently settled in straitened circumstances. Sampson was apprenticed at the age of fourteen to a Liverpool lithographer and engraver. His formal education had been brief—in Ireland he was instructed by his mother, in Liverpool at a school kept by a family friend—and he was largely self-educated. In 1888 he started a printing business but continued to extend his scholarship with unusual self-discipline, particularly in the linguistic domain. Influenced by what he called the 'glowing romances' of George Borrow, he cultivated the society of Gypsies and mastered their language. He was also among the first to investigate the secret speech, known as Shelta, of the Irish tinkers.

Remarkably, these esoteric studies secured Sampson's future when his printing business collapsed after four years, for they brought him into contact with Kuno Meyer, lecturer in Teutonic languages at the University College (afterwards the University) of Liverpool. In 1892, through Meyer's mediation, Sampson became the college's first full-time librarian. In that capacity he sat on the senate, and in academic affairs always sided with the progressive party. For thirty-six years he developed and enriched the library; and while firm in maintaining discipline, encouraged all genuine study. On his arrival he found gifted and inspiring friends, among them Walter Alexander Raleigh. Later Augustus John joined in Sampson's Gypsy pursuits when he came to teach at the art school affiliated to the college.

Though the stipend was modest, the library gave Sampson a firm scholarly base, and also enough security to marry Jessie Margaret (1871–1947), daughter of David Sprunt, on 21 April 1894. Shortly afterwards he encountered Edward Wood, a Welsh Gypsy harpist and fiddler, from whom he first heard a miraculously preserved and richly inflected Romani dialect that constituted an Indian language spoken in the heart of Wales. After this, Sampson devoted the better part of his life to further study of Romani and its speakers, roaming among them and noting their sayings, tales, and customs. He drew them out sympathetically, and became par excellence the Romano rai (scholar Gypsy). In July 1906 a daughter was born of his relationship with one of his assistants, Gladys Imlach (*d.* 1931). Sampson spent successive holidays with the child and her mother, unknown to his family and the university. He managed to preserve the secret during his lifetime, but never resolved the contradictions in his domestic life. In 1909 he established a base near his Gypsy friends in north Wales by renting a cottage at Betws Gwerful Goch in Denbighshire. The house became a convivial centre for helpers and like-minded visitors. His wife lived there, with their younger son and their daughter. During term time Sampson himself occupied spartan rooms in Liverpool.

Sampson's status as a scholar grew steadily. He amassed a mountain of Romani material; extended his grasp of phonetics, Sanskrit, and comparative philology; and published many articles, chiefly in the *Journal of the Gypsy Lore Society*. The final fruit of thirty years' labour was his massive *The Dialect of the Gypsies of Wales* (1926), hailed by experts as a masterpiece. In the words of one, it was a 'splendid volume, epoch-making in Gypsy and in Indo-Aryan studies' (J. Bloch, 'La première personne du présent Kaçmiri', *Bulletin de la Société de Linguistique*, 28, 1928, 1–6). Its lexicon abounded with examples taken straight from the unlettered speakers, rich in entertainment even for the layman, and redolent of the Gypsy way of life. Sampson's other publications in the same field were more compact but no less scholarly, among them *The Wind on the Heath* (1930), an attractive Gypsy anthology in prose and verse from many tongues. Posthumously, his *Welsh Gypsy Folk-Tales* (1933) provided a sampler from the rich store he had recorded over the years, and his Shelta material was printed in R. A. S. Macalister's *The Secret Languages of Ireland* (1937).

Sampson's other great scholarly contribution was the restoration of the text of William Blake's lyrics, long overlaid and 'improved' by editors. In the *Poetical Works* (1905) he established the definitive text, with much critical and bibliographical apparatus, and in the edition of 1913 included 'The French Revolution', never before published, and long selections from the 'prophetic books'. Partly for his work on Blake, but more for his linguistic studies, he was awarded an honorary DLitt at Oxford in 1909.

The First World War devastated Sampson's life: his younger son Amyas was killed and his elder son Michael was wounded several times. And his family existence was dissolving. Already, before the war, he was mostly apart from his wife; in 1920 she went to live with her parents. His work as librarian continued, but he felt less closely in touch with the post-war university. He retired from office in 1928 and moved first to Shrewsbury and then, in poor health, to West Kirby in Cheshire. There he died at his home, 38 Brookfield Gardens, of heart failure on 9 November 1931. Brought up as a Roman Catholic by his mother, he had become an agnostic, and stipulated that there should be no religious ceremony at his funeral. By his own wish his ashes were scattered on Foel Goch, above the hamlet of Llangwm near Corwen, to the sound of Gypsy music. A Romani elegy, which he had long before written on another *Romano rai*, Francis Hindes Groome, was declaimed by Augustus John.

To his contemporaries Sampson seemed at first very shy and, despite his courtesy, somewhat formidable and even overbearing; but among his friends he was a great companion and free-minded humorist. Equally at home in a college and in the nomad camp, he carried a breath of the 'wind on the heath' into every atmosphere.

OLIVER ELTON, *rev.* ANGUS FRASER

Sources A. Sampson, *Scholar Gypsy: the quest for a family secret* (1997) • Andreas [R. A. Scott Macfie], 'John Sampson, 1862–1931', *Journal of the Gypsy Lore Society*, 3rd ser., 11 (1932), 3–23 • D. Yates, *My Gypsy days* (1953) • personal knowledge (1949)

Archives U. Lpool L., corresp. and papers | CUL, letters to J. N. Keynes • Princeton University Library, New Jersey, letters to Arthur Symons • U. Lpool L., corresp. and papers relating to the Gypsy Lore Society • U. Reading L., Chatto and Windus corresp.

Likenesses A. John, sepia drawing, *c.*1903, priv. coll.

Wealth at death £2407 7s. 2d.: probate, 19 Dec 1931, *CGPLA Eng. & Wales*

Sampson, Margaret Phoebe [*name in religion* Mary Clare] (1906–1988), Anglican nun, was born on 5 June 1906 at 11 Rawlinson Road, Oxford, the only daughter of Charles Henry Sampson (*d.* 1936), fellow and later principal of Brasenose College, Oxford, and his wife, Margaret Caroline Sophie Bolckow (*d.* 1946). She was baptized on 2 July 1906 at St Margaret's Church, Oxford, and confirmed on 9 December 1919. She had three older brothers: Reginald, who was killed in the First World War (1918); Ronald, who died after the second (1948); and Christopher, who was ordained as an Anglican priest and died in 1967. Educated at Felixstowe, she read politics, philosophy, and economics as a home student in Oxford, spending time in the vacations in voluntary work in the East End of London and becoming deeply involved with the Anglo-Catholic movement in the Church of England. When she graduated she immediately entered the active Anglican sisterhood of St Margaret at East Grinstead, where she was professed on 14 September 1932 as Sister Margaret Clare. She taught in their school, and during the war was at their house in Cardiff. Impressed by the needs of the times, she felt called by God to a deeper commitment to prayer and reconciliation, so in 1941 asked for transfer to the enclosed contemplative community of the Sisters of the Love of God in Oxford; on 6 August 1943 she was received as Sister Mary Clare of the Precious Blood. On 3 April 1954 she was elected as the reverend mother. With the support of the community of St John the Evangelist and later working closely with the warden of the community, the Revd Gilbert Shaw, she began her life's work within the enclosed order.

A woman full of energy and humour, one of Mary Clare's first priorities was the practical dimension: the buildings, food, clothing, customs, and timetable of the sisters were all firmly updated, while the finances of the community were put on a sound basis. At Bede House in Kent a new style of community was created, with hermitages for those called to solitude—both sisters and others—alongside a small group of sisters offering accommodation for visitors.

With the interior life of the sisters Mary Clare emphasized prayer as a channel of the love of God for the world. With this in view, she evoked a revival of hermit life in the Church of England and in Wales, giving opportunities for those who felt called to a life of complete solitude, as well as emphasizing solitary prayer for each sister within the convents. She inspired a renewal in the corporate prayer of the community: the music for the office was revised, English being used with Gregorian chant, and a total revision was undertaken of the material used both for mass and for the day and night offices. She also took a keen interest in the life of the mind as a basis for prayer, by encouraging personal study as well as by teaching exacting courses on spirituality within the convents. Because of her conviction that the energy of love within contemplative prayer was not a cloistered matter only, she accepted many opportunities for teaching about prayer and the contemplative life. She explored different ways for men and women living outside the cloister to be formally associated with the order, and also allowed non-members to live in the community at times. A printing press was installed to publish literature concerned with Christian spirituality. She encouraged and participated in ecumenical dialogue, especially with the Roman Catholic and Orthodox churches. Her personal ministry was primarily towards the sisters, but included visitors of all kinds who came for counsel. She was consulted by church leaders and participated in important meetings and conferences. She helped many other religious communities in their search for ways of reconstruction.

The written record of Mary Clare's teaching remains mainly in her unpublished conferences, but between 1969 and 1988 SLG Press published ten pamphlets containing her teaching on prayer; a longer book, *Encountering the Depths*, was published by Darton, Longman, and Todd in 1981 and reprinted by SLG in 1993. Though she retired as reverend mother in 1973, Mary Clare's personal ministry continued unabated. She died at the Convent of the Incarnation, Fairacres, Oxford, on 14 August 1988 and was buried four days later at Rose Hill cemetery in Oxford.

BENEDICTA WARD

Sources Archives of Sisters of the Love of God, Oxford · b. cert. **Likenesses** photographs, Convent of the Incarnation, Fairacres, Oxford · portrait, Convent of the Incarnation, Fairacres, Oxford

Sampson, Ralph Allen (1866–1939), astronomer, was born on 25 June 1866 at Skull, co. Cork, the third son in the family of six children of James Sampson (1813–1871), metallurgical chemist, and his wife, Sarah Anne Macdermott (1829–1907). He was the younger brother of John *Sampson. When he was five years old the family moved to Liverpool, where his father, who was a Cornishman, lay ill for two years. At his death the income had fallen to £50 a year. Sampson had little education until he was fourteen, when it became possible to send him to the Liverpool Institute: there he soon came to the front, and in June 1884 he was admitted as a sizar of St John's College, Cambridge, going into residence the following Easter, and being elected

scholar of the college at the end of his first term. In 1888 he graduated as third wrangler. In the spring of 1890 he was awarded the first Smith's prize, and in November was elected into a fellowship at St John's.

From 1889 to 1891 Sampson held a lecturership in mathematics at King's College, London, and during this period he published a hydrodynamical investigation on Stokes's current-function in the *Philosophical Transactions of the Royal Society* (182, 1891). In 1891 he returned to Cambridge as the first holder of the newly founded Isaac Newton studentship in astronomy and physical optics. For two years he worked on astronomical spectroscopy with H. F. Newall, and in 1893 he published a memoir, 'The rotation and mechanical state of the sun' (*Memoirs of the Royal Astronomical Society*, 51), which is notable as being the first treatment of the subject in which prominence was given to the effects of radiation and absorption (as compared with convection) on the sun's internal temperature. In 1893 Sampson married Ida, daughter of Hudson Atkinson Binney, of St Helens, Lancashire. They had a son and four daughters.

In the autumn of 1893 Sampson left Cambridge on his election to the chair of mathematics in the Durham College of Science at Newcastle upon Tyne. In 1896 he moved to Durham itself, as professor of mathematics in the university, where he concurrently held the revived chair of astronomy from 1908 to 1910. In the latter year he was appointed professor of astronomy in Edinburgh University and astronomer royal for Scotland. Failing health led to his resignation from these posts in 1937. He died suddenly at Bath on 7 November 1939.

Sampson's most important contributions to science, which occupied most of his time and energy from 1900 to 1920, are his *Tables of the Four Great Satellites of Jupiter* (1910) and his theory of these satellites (*Memoirs of the Royal Astronomical Society*, 63, 1920). He was elected FRS in 1903, was awarded the gold medal of the Royal Astronomical Society for his work on the satellites of Jupiter in 1928, and received honorary degrees from the universities of Durham and Glasgow.

E. T. WHITTAKER, rev. ISOBEL FALCONER

Sources E. T. Whittaker, *Obits. FRS*, 3 (1939–41), 221–6 · *The Times* (11 Nov 1939) · personal knowledge (1949) · *CGPLA Eng. & Wales* (1940)
Archives Royal Observatory, Edinburgh, corresp. and papers · U. Durham L., corresp. and papers relating to his work on the satellites of Jupiter | RAS, letters to Royal Astronomical Society · St John Cam., letters to Sir Joseph Larmor
Likenesses photograph, repro. in Whittaker, *Obits. FRS*, facing p. 221
Wealth at death £5818 19s. 1d.: confirmation, 27 Dec 1939, *CCI*

Sampson, Richard (d. 1554), bishop of Coventry and Lichfield, was probably born in Berkshire, one of three sons of Robert Sampson and Anne Chatterton. His brother Robert was clerk of the council to Henry VII and Henry VIII, but little is known about his other brother, Nicholas. Richard Sampson was educated in law initially at St Clement's Hostel and later at Trinity Hall, Cambridge, and graduated BCL about 1505–6. He then studied abroad for almost six years, at Paris, Perugia, and Siena universities, before returning to Cambridge, where he graduated DCL (1513) and DCnL (1520). He was admitted an advocate on 20 March 1515.

Sampson's skills, education, and experience came to make him practically indispensable to both Wolsey and the king, although initially he denounced politics as 'odious' (PRO, SP 1/19, fols. 77–8). Possibly because of his membership in the lawyers' circle known as Doctors' Commons, he was recruited into Wolsey's household as a chaplain. In 1513, when Wolsey became bishop of Tournai, Sampson was placed there as his chancellor, vicar-general, and as a member of the council, giving him valuable experience in European affairs. Indeed, he was assigned to an embassy to treat with Lady Margaret at Brussels in September 1514, and was named to the famous trade commission to Burgundy with Sir Thomas More, Cuthbert Tunstall, and others (7 or 8 May 1515). On 1 October 1515, with the earl of Worcester and Lord Mountjoy, Sampson negotiated with the French for the custody of Tournai. Later, with Thomas Cromwell and Richard Mayhew, bishop of Hereford, he was named in a commission to treat for the peace of Europe. Despite a desire to pursue further legal studies, however, he remained at Tournai as royal proctor to the old bishop, until finally he took an important part in the negotiations to return custody to the French in 1517. He declined Wolsey's offer to head his household, opting instead to carry on legal studies. Shortly thereafter, however, he found himself back on royal business.

In 1521 Sampson was incorporated at Oxford and named to a commission dealing with suspected heretical books. In October 1522 he was included in an embassy to the emperor at Bilbao with Sir Thomas Boleyn. The embassy then proceeded to Valladolid, where Sampson stayed on as resident ambassador, working with such men as Sir Richard Jerningham (who took Boleyn's place in June 1523) and Robert Wingfield (who replaced Jerningham in 1525), and was involved with the treaty negotiations of late June–early July 1523 which aligned England with the Habsburgs against the French. As resident he moved with the imperial court, visiting Madrid (March 1525) and Toledo (June 1525). He was recalled to England in October 1525, but did not return to court before early 1526. In the meantime his clerical career had been proceeding apace, his early association with Wolsey no doubt leading to many preferments, and helping to account for his having often been dismissed as a mere time-server.

In 1516 Sampson was made dean of St Stephen's, Westminster, and of the Chapel Royal, and also a royal chaplain. Thereafter he was presented to a number of livings in the neighbourhood of London, and at various times held prebends in Lincoln, Lichfield, York, and St Paul's cathedrals. On 14 November 1523 he became dean of Windsor. By then already archdeacon of Cornwall he resigned this office in 1528, but became archdeacon of Suffolk early in 1529, and of Taunton some six years later. He was made dean of Lichfield in April or May 1533, and treasurer of Salisbury on 16 March 1535. On 3 June 1536 he was elected bishop of Chichester on the king's nomination; royal assent was given on 11 June, the day of his consecration,

and he was enthroned by proxy on 15 August. He held the see *in commendam* with the deanship of St Paul's, having resigned his position in the Chapel Royal. In 1543 he was translated to Coventry and Lichfield (election 19 February, confirmation 9 March).

Sampson supported the king's efforts to obtain a divorce, often speaking officially on his behalf, and consequently returned to the diplomatic stage. On 15 July 1527 Henry ordered him to reply to the Hungarian ambassador, Laski, and sent him on an embassy to the emperor and the pope (8 October 1529) with Sir Nicholas Carew. Later, in 1536, he represented the king as his proctor against Anne Boleyn. In that same year he was described as 'in great favour with the king' (*LP Henry VIII*, 10, no. 1147), and also enjoyed the friendship of Thomas Cromwell, to whom he owed his bishopric. He was also a supporter of the royal supremacy, opining against papal authority, while remaining largely conservative in other religious matters, although somewhat ambiguous on the idea of royal 'spiritual' power. In 1533 he published a Latin oration in favour of the supreme headship. Sampson's *Oratio* was hotly disputed by Cardinal Reginald Pole in his *Pro ecclesiasticae unitatis defensione* (*c*.1537) and by Joannes Cochlaeus in his *Defensio Joannis episcopi Roffensis et Thome Mori, adversus Richardum Samsonem Anglicum* (Leipzig, 1536).

In 1537 Sampson took part in drawing up *The Institution of a Christian Man*, but he did so without enthusiasm, and increasingly aligned himself with the conservatives among the bishops. The next year he was on a commission against Anabaptists, and took part in the show trial of the supposed heretic John Lambert. Despite doubts about his reliability (and his opposition to Cromwell in the 1537 debates over the Bishops' Book), the king assigned him to Cranmer's commission to treat for religious agreement and mutual defence with the German theologians Franz Burkhardt, Georg von Boineburg (a Hessian scholar), and Friedrich Myconius (a high-ranking churchman of Gotha), who arrived in England on 31 May 1538. He was never able to satisfy Cromwell fully of his support, however. In July 1539 Hugh Latimer, who had just been obliged to resign his see of Worcester, was entrusted to Sampson for safe keeping, but in the following month Sampson himself lost his place on the privy council. He was not disgraced, for he became involved in plans for the creation of new dioceses, and was himself proposed for one of them, intending to exchange Chichester for a see at Westminster. He was also a member of the committee appointed to meet Anne of Cleves at Dover in February 1540. But as the faction fighting precipitated by the king's disastrous marriage intensified, Sampson's position weakened, and on 26 or 27 May, as part of Cromwell's drive against his conservative rivals, he was arrested and sent to the Tower, to be replaced as preacher at Paul's Cross by Thomas Cranmer. He either resigned or was deprived of his deanery at St Paul's. This action may have been justified by reference to Sampson's having sent alms to a priest named Abel, who had been imprisoned for opposing the royal supremacy. The French ambassador did not expect Sampson to leave the Tower alive, but he was saved by

Cromwell's fall, and was eventually pardoned in August 1540. In 1543 not only did he become bishop of Coventry and Lichfield, but he was also, in a demonstration of the conservatives' growing strength, appointed president of the council for the marches of Wales, a position he held until 1548.

Sampson had been an ineffective and absentee bishop of Chichester. His employment in the Welsh marches seems to have led to his being largely absent from Lichfield as well. In 1546 his see lost five manors in return for a number of advowsons, and he disposed of the presentations to no fewer than nineteen stalls in his cathedral. Early in Edward VI's reign, moreover, he granted manors and advowsons in Warwickshire to Thomas Fisher, an agent of the duke of Somerset, presumably in a bid for the new protector's friendship. In 1548 he was replaced in his presidency by John Dudley, earl of Warwick, but managed to retain his bishopric, remaining vague on religious questions but supportive of royal policy. He endorsed Cranmer's first prayer book and routinely implemented religious reforms in his diocese (once these were passed into law). Some historians have suggested that Sampson was rather more radical in his thinking, having developed a bizarre view on the eucharist termed 'transmutation'. None the less, in April 1551 he was appointed a commissioner to treat with Scotland in regard to border disputes and settlements. His religious views and political knowhow were such that he managed to survive long enough to see the succession of Queen Mary, subsequently acting energetically against married priests. He died on 25 September 1554 at Eccleshall, Staffordshire, and was buried on the north side of the altar of the parish church there.

Sampson's scholarly output is interesting and varied. Besides writing the *Oratio* he was probably the composer of two sacred choral pieces, written about 1516, and was the author of three folio collections entitled: *In priores quinquaginta psalmos Daviticos familiaris explanatio* (1539); *Explanatio in D Pauli epistolam ad Romanos atque in priorem ad Corinthos* (1546); and, *Explanationis psalmorum secunda pars* (1548). Other works survive in manuscript only. *Contra quasdam positiones Wiclevi* and *The answer or declaration of Richard, bishop of Chichester, in the presence of the king's majesty, against the sixth reason or argument of John Lambert, concerning the most holy and blessed sacrament of the altar*, were published by Strype. ANDREW A. CHIBI

Sources A. A. Chibi, 'Richard Sampson, his "Oratio" and Henry VIII's royal supremacy', *Journal of Church and State*, 39 (summer 1997), 543–60 · J. Strype, *Ecclesiastical memorials*, 3 vols. (1822) · *LP Henry VIII*, vols. 2, 6, 9–10 · J. Strype, *Memorials of the most reverend father in God Thomas Cranmer*, 2 vols. (1848) · J. J. Scarisbrick, 'The conservative episcopate in England: 1529–1535', PhD diss., U. Cam., 1963 · A. A. Chibi, *Henry VIII's bishops: administrators, scholars and shepherds* [forthcoming] · L. B. Smith, *Tudor prelates and politics, 1536–1558* (1953) · S. Thompson, 'The pastoral work of the English and Welsh bishops, 1500–58', DPhil diss., U. Oxf., 1984 · *Literary remains of King Edward the Sixth*, ed. J. G. Nichols, 2 vols., Roxburghe Club, 75 (1857) · J. S. Block, *Factional politics and the English Reformation, 1520–1540* (1993) · P. O'Grady, *Henry VIII and the conforming Catholics* (1990) · Emden, *Cam.*, 805–6 · T. F. Mayer, 'On the road to 1534: the occupation of Tournai and Henry VIII's theory of sovereignty', *Tudor political culture*, ed. D. Hoak (1995), 11–30 ·

P. Hughes, *The Reformation in England*, 3 vols. (1950–54) · F. A. Gasquet and E. Bishop, *Edward VI and the Book of Common Prayer*, 2nd edn (1891) · G. Burnet, *The history of the Reformation of the Church of England*, rev. N. Pocock, new edn, 7 vols. (1865) · G. Redworth, 'A study in the formulation of policy: the genesis and evolution of the Act of Six Articles', *Journal of Ecclesiastical History*, 37 (1986), 42–67 · J. S. Brewer, *The reign of Henry VIII from his accession to the death of Wolsey*, ed. J. Gairdner, 2 vols. (1884) · R. Sampson, *Oratio quae docet hortatur admonet omnes potissimum Anglos regiae dignitati cum primis ut obediant* (1534) · *VCH Staffordshire*, vol. 3 · F. Heal, *Of prelates and princes: a study of the economic and social position of the Tudor episcopate* (1980) · D. MacCulloch, *Thomas Cranmer: a life* (1996)
Archives BL, diary of his embassy to the emperor kept by T. Wall, Egerton MS 3315 · Lichfield RO, episcopal registers, B/A/I/14iv, fols. 40v–60r; B/A/I/15, fols. 1r–7r · Staffs. RO, accounts · W. Sussex RO, episcopal registers, EP I/1/6, fols. 1r–8r | BL, letters to Thomas Wolsey and Henry VIII, etc., Cotton MSS · BL, letters from Cardinal Wolsey and papers, Add. MS 5860 · BL, letters from Cardinal Wolsey and papers, Sloane MS 3839

Sampson, Thomas (*c*.1517–1589), Church of England clergyman and reformer, is said to have been born at Playford, Suffolk, but possibly came from Binfield in Berkshire. He studied at Cambridge, graduating in 1542 and proceeding MA in 1549; in 1548 he became a fellow of Pembroke College. In February 1547 he was also admitted to the Inner Temple. He was already a committed religious reformer, and during 1547–8 was given a royal licence to preach. He may have contributed to John Bradford's conversion; he was certainly close to Bradford, and the two men were ordained deacon together by Bishop Nicholas Ridley on 10 August 1550. The ordination was held up by Sampson's objection to the prescribed vestments—a harbinger of troubles to come; Ridley eventually excused him from using them. He clearly made an impression on Ridley, who asked after him from prison in 1555. In 1551 Sampson was collated to the London rectory of All Hallows, Bread Street, and in 1552 he was considered for a prebend in St Paul's. When Bartholomew Traheron resigned the deanery of Chichester in December 1552, he recommended Sampson to succeed him, calling him 'a preacher … of such integrity as I would be glad to see placed here' (*CSP dom.*, 1547–53, no. 791); and he was duly preferred to the post the following February.

Sampson was never installed: Mary Tudor's accession intervened. It is testament to his rising reputation that his arrest was ordered as early as August 1553, and he had a narrow escape. However, he did not actually fly the country until May 1554, apparently in the company of Edmund Grindal and Richard Cox. In the interim he is said to have been involved in a scheme to raise funds for evangelical students at the universities. During his exile he travelled almost ceaselessly, prefiguring the restless discontent which was to characterize his later life. From a base in Strasbourg, he journeyed repeatedly to Frankfurt and Zürich, and at least once to Geneva and to Lausanne. He published a letter to his former flock in Bread Street, urging them to faithfulness; he studied with the Hebraist Immanuel Tremellius; he translated a work by Rudolf Gwalther; and he was involved in the early stages of John Foxe's martyrological project. There does not, however, seem to be any foundation for the tradition that he was one of the translators of the Geneva Bible, as he cannot be placed in Geneva during the relevant period. In 1555 he was drawn into the acrimonious split in the English congregation in Frankfurt over the 1552 prayer book. Sampson had urged his Bread Street parishioners to observe that book's order, and when he wrote to Calvin in February 1555 about the matter he still leaned the same way. Indeed, when the 'advanced' minority withdrew from the Frankfurt congregation later that year, Sampson supported those who remained. However, he and others took this decision only because the majority had abandoned some of the book's ceremonial: Sampson picked out, as particularly objectionable, the practice of kneeling and the use of the surplice.

Within weeks of Mary's death in November 1558 Sampson returned to England, and had he wished to do so he might have resumed his promising career. In May 1559 he was being considered for bishop of Hereford, and in November for bishop of Norwich. He preached at Paul's Cross on Low Sunday 1559, and continued to preach both there and at court over the following two years. However, his experience of the purer life of exile made him wary of the half-reformed Elizabethan church. In a series of letters written to his somewhat reluctant mentor Pietro Martire Vermigli (known as Peter Martyr) in 1559–60, Sampson agonized about the compromises which he feared might be forced upon him. He was consumed by scruples regarding the royal supremacy, the queen's crucifix, the office of bishop and, again, 'the vanity, not to say the unseemliness of their superstitious dresses' (Robinson, *Zurich Letters*, 1.1). Martyr felt that Sampson's scruples were excessive, and advised him that vestments were a matter of indifference. In the end, however, Sampson refused episcopal office, apparently causing some offence in the process. He did accept a prebend at Durham, where he was installed in September 1560. Yet he continued his peripatetic ways. A visit to Bishop Thomas Bentham at Lichfield in the same year only deepened his worries; he fell out with Bentham over the latter's perceived failure to discipline his clergy.

An acceptable major appointment finally came Sampson's way in 1561. Christ Church, Oxford, faced with a prospective dean of unacceptably Catholic views, proposed Sampson instead, praising both his religion and his scholarship. Lord Robert Dudley's intervention secured the appointment. Sampson was presented as dean on 11 April, and installed on 5 September, having probably been admitted BD and DD on the basis of his studies elsewhere. He quickly made his presence felt. Within a week of his installation he oversaw the destruction of all images, missals, and other relics of Catholicism within the college. In November he settled his conscience for the time being by winning the reluctant permission of the university to preach in a doctoral habit rather than the surplice and square cap. And he was indeed one of the most regular preachers in early 1560s Oxford, together with his like-minded colleague Laurence Humphrey, president of Magdalen College. Yet he did not neglect his administrative

duties, and won praise for halting his college's slide into debt while continuing to maintain learning.

Sampson continued to agitate for further reform of religion. In the convocation of 1563 he was at the forefront of the radical party's protests against ceremonial. Yet these protests failed, and the nonconformity of such prominent men as Sampson and Humphrey could not go unnoticed. In December 1563 Secretary Cecil ordered Sampson to use the prescribed vestments: he refused, justifying his stance at some length. Both sides agreed that vestments were, strictly, a matter of indifference: but the regime held that a Christian government could require conformity in matters of indifference for the sake of order, while Sampson and Humphrey insisted that tender consciences should not be compelled—especially when the ceremony in question was redolent of popery and might lead the simple into error. Moreover, nonconformity over vestments was of necessity a public act, and as such impossible for the regime to ignore. In December 1564 Archbishop Parker conducted lengthy but fruitless negotiations with Sampson and Humphrey over the issue. In January 1565 the queen instructed Parker to enforce the use of the surplice and cap; in March, Sampson and Humphrey were again summoned to Lambeth, together with four London nonconformists. When they again refused to conform, Parker refused to allow the two heads of house to return to Oxford. On 20 March Sampson and others begged forbearance from the ecclesiastical commissioners, but Parker was now pressing for both men to be deprived if they would not conform. They still had influential friends: remarkably, both men preached at Paul's Cross at Easter 1565. Parker was inclined to blame Sampson's old friend Grindal, who had been bishop of London since 1559, for this, but Dudley, now earl of Leicester, may also have had a hand in it. On 29 April, however, Parker formally required both men to choose between conformity and resignation; Grindal, too, urged them to give in. They refused; and while Humphrey was protected by Magdalen's statutes, Sampson was deprived on 26 May 1565, a move whose doubtful legality was overridden by royal command. He was the first minister of the reformed Church of England to be deprived for nonconformity.

Sampson was confined, but quickly released, in part thanks to Parker's intercession on his behalf, and slowly reassembled a living for himself. In 1567 he was permitted to preach in London without the surplice; in 1568 he was made master of Wigston's Hospital in Leicester, probably at the suit of the third earl of Huntingdon; in 1570 he was collated to the prebend of Pancratius in St Paul's Cathedral; and before 1573 he became master and lecturer in theology at Whittington College, London. He also continued to agitate for the cause of which he had become a symbolic leader, trying with mixed success to win support for his stand from Zürich, Geneva, and Scotland. However, while his preaching remained influential, by the late 1560s Sampson was losing friends. The more radical puritans were leaving him behind; by 1569, the separatists were labelling him a semi-papist, and he openly opposed them in return. Archbishop Bancroft's later claim that

Sampson was involved in the 1572 *An Admonition to Parliament* cannot be substantiated. Yet Sampson claimed that even natural sympathizers such as Anthony Gilby misunderstood his views. Bullinger wrote in 1567 that Sampson was 'a man of a captious and unquiet disposition … The man is never satisfied; he always has some doubt or other to busy himself with' (Robinson, *Zurich Letters*, 2.152). When Grindal tried to effect a reconciliation with Sampson in 1574, he was met with a vicious rebuff and with mockery for his episcopal lordliness. By then, Sampson was seriously ill. He suffered a series of strokes late in 1573, which left him paralysed on one side and with a severe speech impediment. Relinquishing his mastership of Whittington College, he withdrew to Leicester, where he clearly expected to die. In March 1574 he sent Cecil, now Lord Burghley, what seems to have been intended to be a final testament. He lamented that the Church of England was still 'governed by such canons and customs as by which Antichrist did rule his synagogue' (Strype, *Annals*, 2/1.393), and urged Burghley to pursue reform along the lines of Bucer's *De regno Christi*. In the same year, writing a preface to a newly published sermon by his old friend John Bradford, he recalled the glory days of Edward VI's reign, and commented bitterly that 'all states and sorts of persons in England are now more corrupt than they were then' (*Writings of John Bradford*, 1.37).

In the event, however, Sampson made a partial recovery and lived for another fifteen years. During this last period of his life, he produced a few books, most notably a response to the Catholic John Fowler's *Psalter of Jesus*, and he continued occasionally to press the regime for reform of the church; but the bulk of his efforts were devoted to the care of Wigston's Hospital. With the earl of Huntingdon he worked on a major revision of the hospital's statutes which obliged him, as master, to preach thrice weekly in the town. Moreover, after his predecessor's improvident administration, Sampson secured the hospital's financial position, in part by choosing to relinquish some of his own allowances. After his death, on 9 April 1589 in Leicester, he was buried in the hospital's chapel.

Sampson probably married during Edward VI's reign; his wife's name is unknown, but she is said to have been a niece of Hugh Latimer. She joined him in exile and lived at least until January 1560, when she was ill with ague. Their children included two sons, Nathaniel and John, and a daughter, Joanna, who was perhaps born in 1558.

ALEC RYRIE

Sources J. Strype, *Annals of the Reformation and establishment of religion … during Queen Elizabeth's happy reign*, new edn, 4 vols. (1824) • H. Robinson, ed. and trans., *The Zurich letters, comprising the correspondence of several English bishops and others with some of the Helvetian reformers, during the early part of the reign of Queen Elizabeth*, 2 vols., Parker Society, 7–8 (1842–5) • H. Robinson, ed. and trans., *Original letters relative to the English Reformation*, 1 vol. in 2, Parker Society, [26] (1846–7) • J. Strype, *The life and acts of Matthew Parker* (1853) • P. Collinson, *The Elizabethan puritan movement* (1967) • C. M. Dent, *Protestant reformers in Elizabethan Oxford* (1983) • C. H. Garrett, *The Marian exiles: a study in the origins of Elizabethan puritanism* (1938) • Venn, *Alum. Cant.*, 1/4.12 • *Correspondence of Matthew Parker*, ed. J. Bruce and T. T. Perowne, Parker Society, 42 (1853), 42 • *VCH Leicestershire*, vol. 4 • *The writings of John Bradford*, ed. A. Townsend, 1 vol. in 2 pts, Parker Society, 31 (1848–53), pt 1 • *CSP dom.*, 1547–53

Sampson, William (*b.* 1599/1600, *d.* in or after 1655), playwright and poet, may have been related to the Sampsons of Nottinghamshire, but he cannot be identified certainly with any of the William Sampsons born in England around that time. His education is unknown, and no William Sampson was at Oxford or Cambridge at the appropriate period.

Sampson first appears as the co-author, with Gervase Markham of Nottinghamshire, of the tragedy *Herod and Antipater*, printed in 1622. This play had apparently been written years before by Markham alone (who refers to it as his *Herodius* in the epistle to *The English Husbandman*, 1613), and was revised by Sampson shortly before publication. Most surviving copies contain prefatory verses by the publisher, Matthew Rhodes, but a few incorporate instead a fawning dedication by Sampson to Sir Thomas Finch of Eastwell, Kent (later Viscount Maidstone and earl of Winchilsea). The play tells the well-known story of tyrannical King Herod, his bastard son Antipater, and their plots against various innocent parties and each other. The title-page states 'According to Josephus, the learned and famous Jew', but the playwrights' more immediate source was Peter Morwyng's English translation (1558) of a sixteenth-century Latin version of Josephus's story. Numerous echoes of Shakespeare also appear throughout the play.

Around 1624 Sampson wrote a play for Prince Charles' Men called *The Widow's Prize, or, The Woman Captain*. On 25 January 1625 Sir Henry Herbert licensed this play, 'which containing much abusive matter, was allowed of me, on condition, that my reformations were observed' (Bentley, 5.1046). In 1653 it was entered in the Stationers' register with an attribution to 'Mr. Wm. Samson', but it was never printed and is now lost. A 1656 publisher's list included 'Loves labor lost C Will. Sampson' (ibid., 5.1043), but this almost certainly involves confusion with Shakespeare's play.

By 1628 Sampson was a retainer in the household of Sir Henry Willoughby of Risley, Derbyshire, who had also employed the poet Phineas Fletcher from 1616 to 1621. In 1636 Sampson dedicated his play *The Vow Breaker, or, The Fair Maid of Clifton* to Willoughby's daughter Anne, writing that 'This infant received breath, and being under your noble Fathers roofe … it properly prostrates it selfe to you for a patronesse'. Sampson states in the prologue that this is a true story, and its two plots are based on stories then current in Nottinghamshire. The first plot, based on Holinshed, concerns the Scottish–French military action around Leith in 1560, with the Nottinghamshire knight Sir Gervase Clifton playing a prominent part. The second plot, based on a ballad known as early as 1603, tells the story of Ann Boote, the fair maid of the title. She breaks her engagement to young Bateman to marry another man, causing Bateman to commit suicide and come back as a ghost, leading to Ann's own death. In the final gratuitous scene the queen visits Nottingham and grants privileges to the town. The Nottinghamshire orientation of the play, along with the vague title-page statement that it had been 'divers times Acted by severall Companies', suggests that it had only been acted provincially in Nottinghamshire.

Also in 1636 Sampson published a volume of poetry entitled *Virtus post funera vivit, or, Honour Tryumphing over Death*, with three dedications: one to William Cavendish, earl of Newcastle; one in prose to Christian, dowager countess of Devon; and one in verse to Charles Cavendish, Viscount Mansfield, the earl of Newcastle's son. The volume contains thirty-two poems in heroic couplets commemorating various prominent people, including Elizabeth Talbot, countess of Shrewsbury (Bess of Hardwick), and William Cavendish, earl of Devonshire. There also exists a manuscript poem by Sampson, 'Love's Metamorphosis, or, Apollo and Daphne' (BL, Harleian MS 6947, no. 41, fols. 318–36), dedicated to Margaret Cavendish, marchioness of Newcastle. It is strongly influenced by Shakespeare's *Venus and Adonis*. Sidney Lee, in the *Dictionary of National Biography*, noted another manuscript poem by Sampson, 'Cicero's Loyal Epistle According to Hannibal Caro', dedicated to Lucy Hastings, wife of Ferdinando, Lord Hastings, but its present whereabouts are unknown.

In 1653 Sampson served as one among three executors of the will of his master, Sir Henry Willoughby, in which he received black cloth to make cloaks. Willoughby entrusted the dispersal of many of his goods to a Hanna Sampson, presumably some relation of the playwright, possibly a daughter or wife. Sampson is last traceable in 1655, when he petitioned the lords commissioner concerning Willoughby's will, describing himself as 'late of Risley in the County of Derby' (Wallrath, 6).

DAVID KATHMAN

Sources H. Wallrath, 'Einleitung', *William Sampson's 'Vow breaker'* (1914), 1–58 · G. E. Bentley, *The Jacobean and Caroline stage*, 7 vols. (1941–68), vol. 5, pp. 1042–7 · G. N. Ross, 'Introduction', *A critical edition of the true tragedy of Herod and Antipater by Gervase Markham and William Sampson* (1979), iii–xxxiii · DNB · F. N. L. Poynter, *Bibliography of Gervase Markham, 1568?–1637* (1962)

Sampson, William (*bap.* 1635, *d.* 1702), Church of England clergyman, was born at South Leverton, Nottinghamshire, where he was baptized on 14 June 1635, a younger son of William Sampson (*c*.1590–*c*.1636) and his wife, Helen (1603–1687), daughter of Gregory Vicars (in December 1637 she married the puritan minister Obadiah *Grew). The family were Nottinghamshire yeomanry who achieved literary and academic success. The younger William's brother was the eminent dissenting minister and medical lecturer Henry *Sampson, his stepbrother Nehemiah *Grew, FRS, the celebrated botanist. At the age of eighteen William Sampson went up to Pembroke College, Cambridge, in the Lent term 1654; he graduated BA in 1657, and proceeded MA in 1660, in which year he became a fellow of the college. As treasurer Sampson was an able administrator at Pembroke, and his financial accounting system instituted in 1667–8 lasted until the nineteenth century.

Sampson was presented to the rectory of Tilney, Norfolk, in 1669, and subsequently to the rectory of Clayworth, Nottinghamshire, in 1672. He was a prebendary of Lincoln for Clifton from the same year. Sampson was appointed president of Pembroke College in 1672 (the second most senior position), and left Clayworth in the hands of a curate for the next three years before returning to Nottinghamshire, in a final protest against the validity of the fellowship of Nathaniel Coga, who had been elected in 1658 and confirmed by royal mandate after the Restoration. Coga was elected master of Pembroke in 1677, and Sampson had little more to do with the college although he was one of the subscribers to the work on the new library in 1690. When Sampson was himself brought news in January 1694 by two fellows that he had been elected master of Pembroke following Coga's death, he declined the office and stayed in Clayworth.

Sampson continued as rector and prebendary until his own death on 30 October 1702. He was buried in Clayworth nine days later. He bequeathed to Pembroke the advowson of Earl Stonham, Suffolk. Meanwhile Henry Sampson had left his Clapham, Surrey, home a sick man in mid-July 1700 to stay with his brother at Clayworth, and died there later that month; William's nephew and intended heir Nathaniel, who lived with him, had died the previous year.

One of Sampson's early acts at Clayworth was to purchase a vellum book as his parish and personal record, for 'A Register is so useful and necessary a thing that the places of learning, wisdom and business could never be without one.' This earns Sampson his particular place in posterity: most aspects of parish life and work are reflected in it. Sampson recorded his own farming account and profit, with frequent disputes about tithes and piecemeal enclosure of the former common fields. He noted extreme weather conditions, pursued attempts to educate and reform the manners of the poor, was pleased by the extent of religious conformity in the parish, and recorded reactions to the extraordinary political and religious events of the revolution of 1688–9. In 1676 and again in 1688 he listed the population of the parish, household by household—on the former occasion alphabetically, on the latter topographically beneath the principal household of Mr Thomas Wawen, 'Lord of the Soil'.

Sampson's *Rector's Book*, published in 1910, has been used to illustrate many aspects of parochial life, religious conformity, and agricultural history. In 1963 it formed a building block of the new social history pioneered by Peter Laslett, who used Sampson's population counts in 1676 and 1688 to measure turnover of population. Far from being rooted to the soil the inhabitants were mobile; twenty-three of the ninety-one households in the later year were new formations, ten households were 'entirely novel'. Yet population size changed little overall, at a shade over 400, and the family structure—small, nuclear, two-generational households with servants living in—remained identical. Study since has served to underline rather than undermine the broad picture of village family and social structure Laslett painted using this almost unique source.

DAVID SOUDEN

Sources H. Gill and E. L. Guilford, eds., *The rector's book, Clayworth, Notts* (1910) [original in Notts. Arch., ref. PR 5229] · Venn, *Alum. Cant.* · *DNB* · A. L. Attwater, *Pembroke College, Cambridge: a short history*, ed. S. C. Roberts (1936) · *Fasti Angl., 1541–1857*, [Lincoln] · W. A. Tate, 'The Clayworth manorial map', *Transactions of the Thoroton Society*, 44 (1940), 105–12 · N. Sykes, *From Sheldon to Secker: aspects of English church history, 1660–1768* (1959) · P. Laslett and J. Harrison, 'Clayworth and Cogenhoe', *Historical essays presented to David Ogg*, ed. H. W. Bell and R. L. Ollard (1963) · P. Laslett, *The world we have lost* (1965); 2nd edn (1971) · F. West, *Sparrows of the spirit*, 2nd edn (1961), 45–62 · W. T. Lancaster, ed., *Letters addressed to Ralph Thoresby FRS*, Thoresby Society, 21 (1912), 84–6 · *IGI* · K. S. S. Train, *Lists of the clergy of North Nottinghamshire*, Thoroton Society Record Series, 20 (1961), 44

Archives Notts. Arch., rector's book, Clayworth, PR 5229 · Pembroke Cam., archives

Sampson, William (1764–1836), Irish nationalist and jurist, son of a Presbyterian minister of the same name, was born at Londonderry on 17 January 1764. At the age of eighteen he enrolled himself among the Irish Volunteers. Later that year he entered Trinity College, Dublin, but he did not graduate. In 1790 he kept his terms at Lincoln's Inn, and in the same year he married a lady named Clarke, with whom he had several children.

On his return to Ireland Sampson took up his residence at Belfast. He was called to the Irish bar, and obtained a good practice on the north-eastern circuit. He took some part in nationalist politics, although his connections were all with the government party. At Belfast he wrote for the radical *Northern Star*, and some of his contributions were circulated as pamphlets. When the proprietors of the *Northern Star* were indicted for libel, in May 1794, Sampson acted as junior counsel, with John Philpot Curran as his senior. The prosecution of the newspaper led Sampson to write *The Trial of Hurdy Gurdy*, a satire on the increasing numbers of prosecutions for seditious libel. Also in 1794, with Thomas Russell, he composed the *Review of the Lion of Old England*, a satirical epic on the British constitution and contemporary political issues. Subsequently he was engaged with Curran in the defence of William Orr for administering the oath of the United Irishmen. Sampson himself, like Thomas Addis Emmet, took the oath in open court, 'because I hated dissimulation'.

In 1796, in a pamphlet entitled *Advice to the Rich*, Sampson predicted the Irish union, and tried to show that the government was stimulating rebellion with a view to bringing it about. At public meetings held in Belfast on the receipt of the news of the approach of the first French expedition to Ireland, Sampson gave proofs of his loyalty. At the second meeting, on 2 January 1797, he took the chair and put resolutions in which it was declared that a reform in parliament, 'without distinction on account of religion', would satisfy the public mind. To these moderate resolutions there was appended a request to government for permission 'to arm, in like manner as the volunteers', against the French.

But Sampson's attitude failed to satisfy the Irish administration. He was known to be the writer of letters signed Fortesque in *The Press*, the Dublin organ of the United Irishmen. He was a prime mover in a society formed for obtaining authentic information concerning outrages by the military in Ireland. The society met chiefly at Lord Moira's house in Dublin, and all the leading members of the Irish parliamentary opposition were members of it. Some of the documents collected by the society were privately printed in London.

On 12 February 1798 an abortive charge of high treason was brought against Sampson by the aldermen of Dublin for attempting to protect from the army the house of his client Stockdale, printer of *The Press*. In March a false report was circulated that he held a French general's commission, and an attempt was made to arrest him. He escaped, but wrote offering to surrender on promise of a fair trial. He received no answer and fled to England on 16 April, but was arrested at Whitehaven and sent to Carlisle gaol. On 5 May he was taken back to Dublin, where he was confined for several months, first in The Castle tavern, and afterwards in the Bridewell. He was never brought to trial.

Sampson was now approached on behalf of the Irish administration, with a view to mediating between it and the other state prisoners. He declined the proposal, but in order to save the life of his friend Oliver Bond he agreed, with the other prisoners, to give all information concerning their organization and go into voluntary exile, on condition that Bond's life were spared. Sampson's release was delayed for some time; but early in 1799, in accordance with the agreement, he arrived at Oporto. After living quietly for some time there, Sampson was arrested on 12 March 1799, by order of the English ministry, on suspicion of writing *Arguments for and Against a Union Considered*, a pamphlet against the union. This was in fact by Edward Cooke, the Irish under-secretary. In May he was shipped on board a Danish dogger at San Sebastian, and obtained a passport to Bayonne. From there he proceeded to Bordeaux, near which place he remained under the close surveillance of the municipality for some eighteen months. From the winter of 1800 until May 1805 he was in Paris, and after spending nearly a year at Hamburg, he obtained from the British minister there a passport for England. On his arrival in London, in April 1806, he was placed under arrest, and on 12 May he was sent, at the government's expense, to New York. His family followed him four years later.

Sampson soon attained a high position at the American bar. He acted as legal adviser to Joseph Bonaparte when he arrived in America. Wolfe Tone's son entered his office, and subsequently married his daughter. In 1823 he delivered before the Historical Society of New York a lecture on the common law, which led to much discussion. It was published in 1824 and republished, with additions by Pishey Thompson, in 1826. Sampson was a great promoter of legal amendment and codification in America. He took a prominent part in all meetings concerning Irish affairs held in America, and in 1831 was invited to Philadelphia to defend some of his countrymen charged with riot. In his last years he vainly endeavoured to obtain leave from the British government to revisit Ireland. Besides various reports of American trials and pamphlets dealing with law reform, Sampson published his *Memoirs* (1807).

Sampson had a high forehead, a large nose, and an oval face, and, in his youth, brown hair. He died in New York on 28 December 1836.

G. Le G. Norgate, rev. Gerard McCoy

Sources W. Sampson, *Memoirs of William Sampson*, 2nd edn (1817); repr. with introduction and notes by W. C. Taylor (1832) · R. R. Madden, *The United Irishmen: their lives and times*, 2nd ser., 2 vols. (1843) · H. Grattan, *Memoirs of the life and times of the Rt Hon. Henry Grattan*, 5 vols. (1839–46) · *Correspondence of Charles, first Marquis Cornwallis*, ed. C. Ross, 3 vols. (1859) · A. J. Webb, *A compendium of Irish biography* (1878) · N. J. Curtin, *The United Irishmen: popular politics in Ulster and Dublin, 1791–1798* (1994), 181–5 · Burtchaell & Sadleir, *Alum. Dubl.*
Archives L. Cong., corresp. and papers [copies]
Likenesses F. Gimbrede, engraving (after Jarvis), repro. in W. Sampson, *Memoirs of William Sampson*, American edn (1817), frontispiece · mezzotint (after C. S. Tone), NG Ire., NPG; repro. in Madden, *United Irishmen* (1846)

Sams, Joseph (1784–1860), bookseller and dealer in antiquities, was born on 26 February 1784 at Wellington, Somerset, the son of Joseph Sams and his wife, Esther, both members of the Society of Friends. He was educated at Ackworth School, Yorkshire, from 1794 to 1798, and was a teacher there from 1804 to 1810. He married at Doncaster on 15 September 1808 Mary Brady (1787–1834); they had seven children, of whom five predeceased their parents.

Sams left Ackworth in 1810 to start a Friends' school at Paradise Row, Darlington, but resigned in 1816 and opened his own school adjoining the Bull Wynd in Darlington in 1817. He closed it in the summer of 1824 to open a bookseller's shop at Darlington's Prospect Place. He published *A descriptive catalogue of a valuable collection of books in various languages and almost every branch of science and literature etc.* (1822–6), which contained 8071 entries. From 1826 to 1828 Sams travelled over the continent of Europe and the Near East in search of antiquities, forming a valuable collection of Egyptian papyri, mummies, and sarcophagi. He was said to have visited every site mentioned in the New Testament that could then be identified. On his travels he carried with him religious books and tracts in Italian, Arabic, and other tongues. When granted an interview with Mehmet Ali at Alexandria he gave him a copy of the Bible and he deposited another in the monastery at the foot of Mount Sinai.

In 1831 Sams moved his bookshop to Prebend Row in Darlington; he also had premises in London at 56 Great Queen Street, Lincoln's Inn. The bulk of his Egyptian collection was offered to the British Museum and was purchased by that institution in late 1834 for £2500; it formed a valuable addition to the museum's growing collection. Sams formed a second Egyptian collection from the remainder of his antiquities, to which were added purchases from the sale of the collection of the consul Henry Salt in 1835 and the acquisition of the collection of Charles Bogaert of Bruges. He published *Ancient Egypt: objects of antiquity forming part of the extensive and rich collections from ancient Egypt, brought to England by, or now in the possession of J. Sams* in 1839. The British Museum declined to purchase this second collection, and it was acquired about 1850 by Joseph Mayer, who exhibited it with his own collection in Great Colquitt Street, Liverpool, until in 1867 he

presented it to the city museum. Thus Sams's collections enriched two important British institutions.

Sams was somewhat eccentric; he wore a 'three-decker' hat, and on his travels he secreted the money for which his circular notes were changed in a screw ferrule at the end of a walking-stick. He had a reputation for miserliness and sharp practice, and was described as 'a plausible old hypocrite and unmitigated old rogue' (*N&Q*, 8th ser., 8, 1895, 499). Sams died at Prebend Row, Darlington, on 18 March 1860 and was buried in Darlington. His books, pictures, tapestries, and manuscripts were sold by Messrs Puttick and Simpson in London on 2 November 1860.

M. L. Bierbrier

Sources 'Dictionary of Quaker biography', RS Friends, Lond. [card index] · N. Penney, 'Joseph Sams: schoolmaster, bookseller and virtuoso', *Journal of the Friends' Historical Society*, 20 (1923), 24–7 · H. Spencer, *Men that are gone from the households of Darlington* (1862), 135–45 · W. H. D. Longstaffe, *The history and antiquities of the parish of Darlington* (1854), 343–5 · *N&Q*, 8th ser., 8 (1895), 499–500 · *N&Q*, 8 (1853), 521–2 · BM · J. S. Hodgson, *Superintendents, teachers, and principal officers of Ackworth School from 1779 to 1894* (1895), 8 · J. H. Nodal, *The bibliography, biographical and topographical, of Ackworth School* (1889), 27 · *GM*, 1st ser., 102/1 (1832), 451 · *GM*, 1st ser., 102/2 (1832), 65–6 · *GM*, 1st ser., 103/1 (1833), 257, 312–15 · d. cert. · *CGPLA Eng. & Wales* (1860)
Likenesses B. R. Haydon, group portrait, oils (*The Anti-Slavery Society convention, 1840*), NPG
Wealth at death under £6000: resworn administration, 16 May 1860, *CGPLA Eng. & Wales*

Samson [St Samson] (*fl.* 561/2), bishop (possibly of Dol in Brittany), was born in south-west Wales, probably in the early sixth century. His parents, Amon and Anna, are reputed to have come from families with a tradition of service in the courts of the British kings and to have placed him in Illtud's monastery at Llantwit Major for his education. Not tied to this community, Samson moved around Wales, Ireland, and Cornwall in search of greater ascetic rigour, converting pagans wherever he encountered them. In association with his parents and other relatives, he also founded several new monastic settlements. Identifiable monasteries with which he was associated are, in addition to Llantwit Major, a community on Caldey Island and a house at Docco (now Lanow) in Cornwall.

According to Samson's earliest life, he was ordained deacon, priest, then bishop in Wales by St Dyfrig (Dubricius). At some point after his episcopal consecration he crossed to Brittany where he founded the monastery of Dol. He seems to have visited the court of the Frankish king Childebert I, who gave him the site for a monastic community on the banks of the lower Seine, now St Samson-sur-Risle. He is almost certainly to be identified with the 'Samson, sinner and bishop' who attended the Synod of Paris which took place in 561 or 562. He died and was buried at Dol.

Samson's relics were moved from Dol at the height of the viking attacks on Brittany in the 920s. Taken first to Paris, some relics reached Orléans and others England. William of Malmesbury records that Æthelstan gave relics of Samson to Milton Abbas; in all probability these were the arm and crozier of Samson noted at Milton Abbas in the early eleventh-century Old English list of saints' resting places (*De gestis pontificum*, chap. 249; Liebermann, 19). In addition to the dissemination of Samson's relics, his cult spread widely on both sides of the English Channel. His feast day (28 July) is first mentioned in the Hieronymian martyrology of the late eighth century and occurs in over forty martyrologies, calendars, and sacramentaries from Brittany, Normandy, and the Île-de-France from the ninth to the fifteenth centuries. In the British Isles, his feast is noted in the earliest surviving Welsh martyrology, that of Rhigyfarch (late eleventh century), and is common in English calendars from the late tenth century onwards. It was observed in Ireland from the twelfth century, and in Scotland by the thirteenth. In addition, churches are dedicated to him throughout Brittany and Normandy. There is only a handful of dedications in Cornwall and southern Wales and one in south-eastern Ireland. His cult in Ireland cannot be proven to predate the Norman invasions, though it is possible that earlier evidence of devotion to him there was conflated with the cult of the Irish saint Santán.

Samson was the subject of several Latin lives. The earliest life was written at Dol probably, though not indisputably, in the late seventh century. Its author had informants in several of the British monasteries associated with Samson, and is the source for the biographical data provided above. It is of prime significance for the history of early monasticism in Wales and Cornwall and exercised considerable literary influence over later Welsh and Breton hagiography. Subsequent versions of the life are noteworthy for the political contexts from which they emanated. Although it remains open to dispute whether Samson established an episcopal see in the monastery of Dol, Dol was certainly a bishopric by the early ninth century. Efforts to claim archiepiscopal status for its incumbent in the 860s prompted a new life which claimed that Samson was archbishop. The status of the see of Dol again became a bone of contention after 1050, causing a further version of the life to be written by Baudri of Bourgeuil (archbishop of Dol, 1107–30). Dol remained a notable cause of friction between Henry II and Louis VII.

The ninth-century Breton claims that Samson had been an archbishop became central to the jurisdictional quarrels between the Welsh church and Canterbury in the twelfth century. Elaborating on the purported dispatch of a Christian mission to Britain by Pope Eleutherius, the community of the see of St David's wrote to Honorius II, probably early in 1129, claiming that St David's had been an archbishopric ever since the first arrival of Christianity in Britain and that Samson had been consecrated archbishop in the church at St David's, but that he had fled to Brittany during a plague, taking his pallium with him (*De invectionibus*, pt 2, chap. 10). This claim was picked up by other writers: Geoffrey of Monmouth borrowed the idea that Samson had been one of the earliest British bishops, but transformed him into 'archbishop of York' in his *Historia regum Britanniae* (8.12, 9.8). Gerald of Wales found the claims of Samson's Welsh archiepiscopate of value to his fight in the papal courts in 1199–1203 to vindicate St

David's metropolitan claim; he argued that Samson was the twenty-fifth archbishop after David, that he fled to Dol with his pallium during the pontificate of Gregory the Great, but that succeeding bishops of St David's had nevertheless enjoyed full archiepiscopal status. In an effort to counter the claims of St David's, the see of Llandaff reproduced a version of the earliest life of Samson, which at no point attributed archiepiscopal rank to the saint. Both the Welsh and the Breton archiepiscopal claims were definitively quashed by Innocent III. After Samson's reputation ceased to be of political significance, no new life was composed. John Tynemouth included an epitome of the Llandaff life in his *Sanctilogium Angliae, Walliae, Scotiae et Hiberniae*.　　　　　　　JULIA M. H. SMITH

Sources *Bibliotheca hagiographica latina antiquae et mediae aetatis*, 2 vols. (Brussels, 1898–1901) [suppls., 1911 and 1986] · M. Lapidge and R. Sharpe, *A bibliography of Celtic-Latin literature, 400–1200* (1985) · R. Fawtier, *La vie de Saint Samson: essai de critique hagiographique* (1912) · F. Duine, *Inventaire liturgique de l'hagiographie bretonne* (1922) · V. Leroquais, *Les sacramentaires et les missels manuscrits des bibliothèques publiques de France*, 3 vols. (1924) · F. Wormald, ed., *English kalendars before AD 1100*, 1, HBS, 72 (1934) · F. Wormald, ed., *English Benedictine kalendars after AD 1100*, 2 vols., HBS, 77, 81 (1939–46) · J. C. Davies, ed., *Episcopal acts and cognate documents relating to Welsh dioceses, 1066–1272*, 2 vols., Historical Society of the Church in Wales, 1, 3–4 (1946–8) · P. O'Riain, 'Samson alias San(c)tán?', *Peritia*, 3 (1984), 320–23 · E. G. Bowen, *Saints, seaways, and settlements in the Celtic lands*, 2nd edn (1977) · O. Pontal, *Die Synoden im Merowingerreich* (1986) · L. Olson, *Early monasteries in Cornwall* (1989) · C. N. L. Brooke, 'The archbishops of St David's, Llandaff and Caerleon-on-Usk', *The church and the Welsh border in the central middle ages* (1986) · F. Dolbeau, M. Heinzelmann, and J.-C. Poulin, 'Les Sources hagiographiques narratives composées en Gaule avant l'an mil (SHG): inventaire, examen critique, datation. Annexe: le dossier de saint Samson de Dol', *Francia*, 15 (1987), 715–31 · *Willelmi Malmesbiriensis monachi de gestis pontificum Anglorum libri quinque*, ed. N. E. S. A. Hamilton, Rolls Series, 52 (1870) · F. Liebermann, *Die Heiligen Englands* (1889) · Giraldus Cambrensis, 'De invectionibus', ed. W. S. Davies, *Y Cymmrodor*, 30 (1920), 145 · *The Historia regum Britanniae of Geoffrey of Monmouth*, ed. A. Griscom, trans. R. E. Jones (1929)

Samson (d. 1112), bishop of Worcester, born at Douvres, near Caen in Normandy, was the son of Osbert and Muriel, members of the Norman aristocracy. *Thomas (I) of Bayeux (d. 1100), archbishop of York, was his brother. Samson was sent to study philosophy at Liège by Odo, bishop of Bayeux, and at Angers he was a pupil of Marbod, afterwards bishop of Rennes. He became a clerk in William I's chapel. In 1073 William offered him the bishopric of Le Mans, but he refused it on the ground that his character was not irreproachable. In 1082 he was treasurer of the church of Bayeux, of which he was also a canon and probably dean. Although, on the basis of a correction to the entry for Samson's estate at Templecombe, Somerset, in Exon Domesday, it had been suggested that he may have been the man behind the Domesday survey, more recent research has shown this to be unlikely.

On 8 June 1096 Samson was consecrated bishop of Worcester at St Paul's, London, by Archbishop Anselm and by his own brother, Archbishop Thomas. He had been admitted to priest's orders at Lambeth on the preceding day. On 15 July 1100 he assisted at the dedication of Gloucester

Abbey church, and in 1102 was present at a council held by Anselm at Westminster. Samson made rich grants to the prior and monks of Worcester, and brought ornaments for the church from London; but he offended the whole monastic order by removing the monks from Westbury, putting secular canons in their place. He corresponded with Anselm, Ivo of Chartres, and Marbod of Rennes and he was probably the inspiration behind the compilation of Worcester documents known as Hemming's cartulary.

Samson was married before he took orders. In 1109 he was required to oppose his son *Thomas (II) (d. 1114), archbishop of York, who had refused obedience to Anselm. His younger son Richard became bishop of Bayeux (1108–33) and his daughter, Isabella de Douvres, is said to have been mistress of Robert, earl of Gloucester (d. 1147). Samson died at Westbury on 5 May 1112, and was buried in Worcester Cathedral, at the bottom of the steps going up into the choir.	MARY BATESON, rev. MARIOS COSTAMBEYS

Sources P. Chaplais, 'William of Saint-Calais and the Domesday survey', *Domesday studies: papers read at the novocentenary conference of the Royal Historical Society and the Institute of British Geographers* [Winchester 1986], ed. J. C. Holt (1987), 65–77 · V. H. Galbraith, 'Notes on the career of Samson, bishop of Worcester (1096–1112)', *EngHR*, 82 (1967), 86–101, esp. 86–97 · F. Barlow, *The English church, 1066–1154: a history of the Anglo-Norman church* (1979) · Ordericus Vitalis, *Eccl. hist.*, 4.11 · *Willelmi Malmesbiriensis monachi de gestis pontificum Anglorum libri quinque*, ed. N. E. S. A. Hamilton, Rolls Series, 52 (1870) · *Patrologia Latina*, 165, 171 (1854) · W. H. Hart, ed., *Historia et cartularium monasterii Sancti Petri Gloucestriae*, 1, Rolls Series, 33 (1863) · Symeon of Durham, *Opera*, vol. 1

Samson (1135–1211), abbot of Bury St Edmunds, was born at Tottington in Norfolk. His life and personality are known in a detail exceptional among medieval English monks, thanks to the chronicle of the Bury monk Jocelin of *Brakelond, who became Samson's chaplain and subsequently held other offices in the monastery.

Early career Jocelin records that when Samson was nine, his mother took him to St Edmund's shrine after he had had a dream that St Edmund, standing at the gates of the abbey cemetery, saved him from the devil's clutches. Samson's education was as a poor clerk, first in the school of William of Diss, and then at the University of Paris, where he apparently graduated as a 'master of arts and medicine'. He became a schoolmaster in Norfolk, but in 1159 the monks of Bury St Edmunds Abbey sent him to Rome with an appeal to Alexander III (r. 1159–81) for the restoration of a pension from their church of Woolpit, Suffolk. His mission was successful, but on the journey home, although disguised as a Scot, he was seized and robbed by adherents of Victor IV, the schismatic pope. He saved the papal letter by hiding it under his drinking cup which he held above his head, but for some reason Hugh, abbot of Bury St Edmunds, was angry with him on his return. Samson took refuge under St Edmund's shrine, but was seized, fettered, and exiled to Castle Acre. Nevertheless he professed as a monk of Bury St Edmunds in 1166 under Abbot Hugh. His ability was soon apparent. He became novice master; Jocelin of Brakelond, his future biographer, was among the novices. Later Samson held a series of offices—guestmaster, pittancer, third prior, and

sub-sacrist—but, since he was often uncompromising (Jocelin remarks that flattery could never bend him), his career was far from peaceful.

Abbot Hugh died on 14 November 1180, and the process for the election of a new abbot began early in 1182. Samson was one of the twelve monks chosen by the convent to go to Henry II, then at Bishop's Waltham, Hampshire, to elect an abbot in the king's presence, and he was one of the three monks previously nominated by the convent as suitable for election. The choice fell on Samson. At this his bearing was so dignified and self-confident that Henry exclaimed, 'By God's eyes, this elect thinks himself worthy to be guardian of his abbey!' (*Chronicle of Jocelin of Brakelond*, 23). Samson reached Bury St Edmunds on 21 March 1182. After his installation he almost immediately ordered a new seal to be made, bearing the image of a mitred abbot, although no previous abbot of Bury St Edmunds had been thus represented.

Reforming abbot Hugh had left a legacy of debt and maladministration. To rectify his own ignorance of secular affairs Samson studied law books, but also appointed well-qualified men to advise and serve him. To prevent obedientiaries raising unauthorized loans he called in individual seals, and ordained that henceforth conventual business should be transacted in chapter, and documents sealed with the convent's seal. As soon as practicable he recovered from lessees the management of the eight and a half hundreds that constituted the liberty of Bury St Edmunds Abbey, and of his and the convent's estates, and instituted an inquiry into all the abbey's manors and their revenues.

Under Samson the previous development towards the keeping of written records gained momentum. Apparently he inherited from his predecessors only 'one small sheet with the names of the knights of St Edmund, and the names of the manors and rents due from each tenancy' (*Chronicle of Jocelin of Brakelond*, 29). There survives a copy (of c.1265) of his survey, of c.1186–91, of the eight and a half hundreds (CUL, MS Add. 6006). Samson 'called this book … his *Kalendar*, and consulted it almost daily, as though he could see therein the image of his own efficiency, as in a mirror' (*Chronicle of Jocelin of Brakelond*, 29). Jocelin's new year's gift to him in 1191 was a list of the abbot's churches. There also survives a list of St Edmund's knights made in 1200. The purpose of these records was financial: Jocelin claims that 'within four years of his election no one could deceive him concerning the abbey's revenues to a single pennyworth' (ibid., 29). Probably Samson also commissioned the compilation of the abbey's first register, the Black register, a handsome book containing copies of papal bulls and royal charters, enshrining the abbey's privileges and liberties (CUL, MS Mm.4.19).

Samson's reforms resulted in many conflicts with the convent, principally with the cellarer, who incurred the worst debts. Besides trying to reduce the debts by imposing unpopular economies on the monks' food consumption, Samson twice deposed the cellarer (in 1198 and 1200) and put in his own clerks to oversee or run the cellary. Because such acts eroded the division of the convent's property from the abbot's, the monks feared that during a vacancy of the abbacy the king would take custody of their property as well as the abbot's barony. A quarrel in 1199 reached such a pitch that Samson forbade the cellarer food and drink, and stayed away for a week because, he said, the monks plotted 'to kill him with knives' (*Chronicle of Jocelin of Brakelond*, 119). Another confrontation took place early in 1202, on the eve of Samson's departure to visit King John in Normandy. Samson was in a dilemma, whether to please the king or the pope, and he was in poor health and worried about leaving the abbey. The monks seized the opportunity to press their claims. Eventually Samson conceded that on his return 'he would do everything with their counsel, make just arrangements and restore to every man his due' (ibid., 137). Possibly it was then that a detailed statement was written of the monks' rights that had been 'usurped'; a thirteenth-century copy, with additions, survives in a late fourteenth-century hand, made from 'a very old roll of the abbot' (Gransden, *Customary*, 100).

Relations with the townsfolk The town of Bury St Edmunds was an especial bone of contention between Samson and the convent. The abbot was lord of the town, and the sacrist, as his deputy, held the portmann-moot and had charge of the town gaol, while the cellarer was lord of the manor of Bury St Edmunds and held the manorial court. The result could be not only injustice to suitors at the manorial court, which was less privileged than the portmann-moot, but also disorder, since the sacrist prevented the cellarer using the gaol. Samson, in the interests of justice and public order, virtually deprived the cellarer of his court. In general, Samson was more favourable to the burgesses than were the monks. Unlike the convent (and later abbots) he was sympathetic to the burgesses' aspirations and in 1193 confirmed their charter of liberties. One of his particular concerns was the market. A prosperous market was in the interests of all parties, since it was the chief source of supplies for both his and the convent's buyers. He refused the monks' request to destroy the shops and stalls erected by the burgesses without the convent's consent, saying correctly that long tenure gave the burgesses prescriptive right. When, some time in Richard's reign, the Londoners claimed by charter of Henry II to be quit of toll in the market, Samson stoutly resisted them.

Samson made important contributions to poor relief and education in the town. About 1184 he founded the hospital of St Saviour, the largest and best endowed of the six medieval hospitals in Bury St Edmunds, for the poor and sick, and obtained papal protection for it in 1192. He also made the town one of the earliest places in England where grammar school education was subsidized. In 1190 he gave to the schoolmaster stone houses to provide poor scholars with free lodgings, and in 1198 he granted him £2 per annum from the revenues of Wetherden church to provide free tuition.

Secular affairs Good relations with the king were essential for the protection of the regalian liberties of Bury St Edmunds Abbey. Samson was trusted by, and conspicuously loyal to, the Angevins. At a meeting of magnates in London in 1192, assembled to discuss the problem of Richard I's capture, Samson declared that he would go personally to find and identify the king, 'for which men called him a man of high spirit' (*Chronicle of Jocelin of Brakelond*, 55). In 1193 he, wearing armour, led the knights of St Edmund to the siege of Windsor which was being held by supporters of Count John of Mortain (the later king). And in 1194 Samson visited the captive Richard at Worms, 'bearing many gifts' (ibid., 55). The fact that Samson bequeathed his palfreys and jewels to King John suggests that he was on friendly terms with him as well. The kings' veneration for St Edmund probably helped to make them well disposed towards the abbey. When in 1208 John confiscated ecclesiastical property in retaliation for the papal interdict on England, he restored to Bury St Edmunds the administration of its estates within three weeks. Nevertheless Samson had problems in his dealings with successive kings. For instance, in 1196 Richard I ordered him to send four knights of St Edmund to Normandy. The knights refused to go, saying that they had no obligation to serve abroad. Samson therefore went himself, and persuaded Richard to accept four mercenaries instead, at the abbot's expense.

Jocelin relates that Samson was 'a wise judge and proceeded according to the forms of law' (*Chronicle of Jocelin of Brakelond*, 34). He was appointed a justice on eyre in September and October 1194, to serve on a circuit in East Anglia, with Cambridgeshire, Huntingdonshire, Essex, and Hertfordshire. But his legal ability was exercised most frequently in defending the abbey's liberties. For example, on the death of one of the knights of St Edmund, Robert of Cockfield, in 1190, his heir, Adam of Cockfield, tried to establish his right to hereditary tenure of the half hundred of Cosford, part of the abbey's liberty. Samson successfully fought his claim, and the case was finally settled in the abbot's favour in the royal court by assize of mort d'ancestor. A dispute in 1196–7 with the knights of St Edmund was likewise settled in the royal court. The knights claimed that they owed service for forty knights, Bury St Edmunds' original quota. But Samson claimed that the ten extra knights subsequently enfeoffed also owed service. He won his case, and took the knights, their wives, and heiresses to London to make recognition of their service in the king's court.

Samson's disputes with Christ Church, Canterbury, and Ely Cathedral arose because of incompatible royal charters. Christ Church owned the manor of Monks Eleigh which lay within the liberty of Bury St Edmunds Abbey. Archbishop Baldwin claimed rights of jurisdiction over it in accordance with a charter of liberties granted to Christ Church by Henry II. In 1186–7 dispute broke out over a homicide. Baldwin refused to allow those accused of the crime to be tried in the abbey court at Bury. Samson, therefore, 'put himself in seisin of his liberty' by arresting the culprits (*Chronicle of Jocelin of Brakelond*, 50). The dispute came before Henry II, who admitted the incompatibility of the charters but stamped out of the meeting, angered by the wrangling. When Jocelin wrote his chronicle, the matter was still unresolved. A dispute with Ely in 1201, over the latter's market at Lakenheath, was similar. Samson likewise had to defend the exemption of the abbey and its immediate surroundings from any ecclesiastical authority except the pope or his legate a latere. In 1195–6 he heard that Archbishop Hubert Walter intended to hold a legatine visitation of Bury St Edmunds. Samson said that if the archbishop tried to enter the chapter house he would meet him with the abbey's charters of privilege. He appealed to Celestine III who reminded Hubert of Bury St Edmunds' exemption, and forbade him to visit exempt houses.

Spiritual concerns Samson was an excellent canon lawyer and received numerous commissions to act as a papal judge-delegate. The latest known dated commission to him was issued by Innocent III (r. 1198–1216) on May 1205. A number of his cases arose from appeals to Rome by monks in England complaining of oppression by ecclesiastical authorities. He was one of the three commissioners appointed by Clement III in 1197 to reinstate in their priory the monks of Coventry, whom Hugh de Nonant, bishop of Coventry and Lichfield (d. 1198), had ejected. When the monks were put in seisin in Oxford Samson feasted both them and the masters of the schools, and, according to Jocelin, 'he never seemed happier in his life than then, such was his zeal for the re-establishment of the monastic order' (Chronicle of Jocelin of Brakelond, 95). Although not of outstanding spirituality, Samson was a man of strong religious feeling. After the fall of Jerusalem in 1187 he began to wear drawers and shirt of haircloth, and to abstain from meat. And, when Henry II visited Bury St Edmunds in 1188 to pray before leaving on crusade, Samson 'secretly made a cross of linen and holding the cross and needle and thread, asked the king's leave to take the cross' (ibid., 53–4)—the request was refused. No doubt it was partly for religious reasons that Samson expelled the Jews from Bury St Edmunds in 1190. But since the expulsion followed the massacre of Jews by the town's inhabitants on Palm Sunday, the need to keep public order was probably a contributory motive.

Possibly it was Samson who composed the revised version of the De miraculis sancti Eadmundi, attributed to Hermann the archdeacon (BL, Cotton MS Titus A. viii). Samson certainly owned a copy. From it he would have learnt that the abbey church had never been consecrated; his great ambition was to make good this omission: according to Jocelin, Samson 'claimed that once that was done he would die content, and was prepared to spend 2000 marks in silver, provided the king was present and all was performed with due ceremony' (Chronicle of Jocelin of Brakelond, 47–8). This objective spurred on Samson's enthusiasm as a builder. He completed much of the west end of the church and built the great west tower. He had started beautifying the shrine, where lay the 'incorrupt' body believed to be St Edmund's, when on 22 June 1198 it was badly damaged by fire. Lest the shrine should lose its attraction to pilgrims, hasty repairs were carried out. To verify that the body had survived intact, Samson had the coffin opened in the presence of a few monks. The body was unwrapped and Samson 'touched the eyes and nose, the chest and arms, … the fingers and toes, counting the toes as he touched them' (ibid., 114). Later that year he applied to Innocent III for licence to dedicate the church. This was issued on 1 December 1198, but for some reason the dedication never took place.

The man and his achievement Jocelin of Brakelond depicts Samson's character and appearance in a brilliant set piece. For example he writes:

> [Samson] was eloquent in both Latin and French, having regard rather to the sense of what he had to say than to ornaments of speech. He read English perfectly and used to preach in English to the people (but in the speech of Norfolk) … and for this he had a pulpit set up in the church for the benefit of his hearers

In appearance Samson 'was of medium height, his face was neither round nor long, his nose was prominent, his lips thick, his eyes clear as crystal and of penetrating glance'. On election he had 'a few white hairs in a red beard and just a few in the hair on his head which was black and curly, but within fourteen years he was as white as snow' (Chronicle of Jocelin of Brakelond, 39–40). Jocelin also reveals much about Samson's character in his narrative: he appears as a forceful, determined, and emotional man, quick-tempered but a loyal friend, austere in his habits, of great integrity, and with a just pride in his office. The monastic annalist records Samson's death, on 30 December 1211, with a fitting tribute:

> He had ruled the abbey successfully for thirty years (less two months), freed it from manifold debts, enriched it with most ample privileges, liberties, possessions and buildings, and put religious observance within and without the church on a proper footing.   ('Annales S. Edmundi', 150)

ANTONIA GRANSDEN

Sources The chronicle of Jocelin of Brakelond: concerning the acts of Samson, abbot of the monastery of St Edmund, ed. H. E. Butler (1949) · 'Annales S. Edmundi', Ungedruckte anglo-normannische Geschichtsquellen, ed. F. Liebermann (1879) · The kalendar of Abbot Samson of Bury St. Edmunds, ed. R. H. C. Davis, CS, 3rd ser., 84 (1954) · The letters of Pope Innocent III (1198–1216) concerning England and Wales, ed. C. R. Cheney and M. G. Cheney (1967) · 'Cronica Buriensis', Memorials of St Edmund's Abbey, ed. T. Arnold, 3, Rolls Series, 96 (1896), 1–73 · 'Gesta sacristarum', Memorials of St Edmund's Abbey, ed. T. Arnold, 2, Rolls Series, 96 (1892), 289–96 · W. Holtzmann, ed., Papsturkunden in England, 3 (Berlin), Abhandlung der Gesellschaft der Wissenschaften zu Göttingen, 3rd ser., 33 (1952) · M. D. Lobel, The borough of Bury St Edmunds (1935) · A. Gransden, 'A democratic movement in the abbey of Bury St Edmunds in the late 12th and early 13th centuries', Journal of Ecclesiastical History, 26 (1975), 25–39 · A. Gransden, 'The question of the consecration of St Edmund's Church', Church and chronicle in the middle ages: essays presented to John Taylor, ed. I. Wood and G. A. Loud (1991), 59–83 · R. M. Thomson, 'Two versions of a saint's life from St. Edmund's Abbey', Revue Bénédictine, 84 (1974), 383–408 · A. Gransden, 'The alleged incorruption of the body of St Edmund, king and martyr', Antiquaries Journal, 74 (1994), 135–68 · C. Harper-Bill, ed., Charters of the medieval hospitals of Bury St Edmunds, Suffolk RS, Suffolk Charters, 14 (1994) · A. Gransden, ed., The customary of the Benedictine abbey of Bury St Edmunds in Suffolk, HBS, 99 (1973) · BL, Cotton MS Titus A. viii · CUL, MS Mm. 4.19 · CUL, Add. MS 6006

Archives CUL, MS Add. 6006 · CUL, MS Mm.4.19

Samson, Charles Rumney (1883–1931), air force officer, was born at Manchester on 8 July 1883, the second son of Charles Leopold Samson, solicitor, and his wife, Margaret Alice Rumney. He was educated at Locker's Park, Hemel Hempstead, and Greenwich, and passed into HMS *Britannia*, joining his first ship as a midshipman in 1898. He served in the *Pomone* during the Somaliland operations of 1903–4, and as first lieutenant in the cruiser *Philomel* he took part in the suppression of gun-running in the Persian Gulf in 1909–10.

In 1911 Samson was selected by the Admiralty as one of the first four naval officers to be trained to fly. He qualified for his Royal Aero Club aviator's certificate, no. 71, on 25 April after only six weeks of flying, much of it in bad weather. From then onwards his life was devoted to flying, and he helped to establish the first naval flying station, at Eastchurch, in October 1911. By December that year he had persuaded the Admiralty to equip the *Africa* with a launching platform which projected over the bows, and in the following year, with similar apparatus, he took off in a Short biplane from the *Hibernia* while the ship steamed at full speed. This was the first flight from a ship's deck to be made in Europe and marked the beginning of the idea of the aircraft-carrier: Samson contributed largely by experiment and demonstration to the growth of this project. He collaborated with Horace Short in designing a seaplane and was a pioneer in aerial wireless communication and in bomb dropping. On the formation of the Royal Flying Corps he was given command of the naval wing, and as commandant of Eastchurch from 1912 to 1914 he practised cross-country flying and night flying as exercises in air navigation. He had undertaken so much advanced naval flying during the early months of 1912 that he and four of his officers were allowed to fly over the naval review at Portland in May. However, during naval manoeuvres in August 1913 Samson and his observer were forced to ditch in the North Sea after the engine suddenly cut out. It was a sobering reminder of how hazardous the business of sea flying could be.

On the outbreak of war in 1914 Samson was given charge of aerial patrols operating over a section of the east coast from a base at Skegness. Soon afterwards he was given work more suited to his temperament when his squadron was sent to Dunkirk with a brigade of marines. When the brigade was withdrawn to England a week later, he contrived to keep his planes behind. Using the slightest appearance of fog as an excuse not to cross the channel, he succeeded in getting an attachment to the French forces in northern France. He then fitted out some of the squadron's motor cars and lorries with machine-guns, and subsequently with a 3-pounder gun, and proceeded to help the French with a mixture of cavalry operations, infantry attack, and air reconnaissance. Self-reliance, dash, and ingenuity gave an air of buccaneering to these operations, which delighted the French and produced results that, although on a small scale, could not be ignored by the British authorities. His mixed collection of aircraft also bombed the Zeppelin sheds at Düsseldorf and Cologne; and by the end of the year, when mobile warfare ended and trench warfare took its place, his squadron had won four DSOs, among them his own, and he was given special promotion and the rank of commander. He spent the next few months bombing gun positions, submarine depots, and seaplane sheds on the Belgian coast.

In March 1915 Samson's unit was moved to the Dardanelles, and he was allotted a base made out of vineyards on the island of Tenedos. He was later moved to Imbros, where he rejected the existing aerodrome and made a new one, using seventy Turkish prisoners as labourers. His squadron patrolled the straits, spotted for the battleships, attacked the Turkish communications, including railway bridges, and ultimately covered the allied evacuation. He even made his own brand of large bomb out of a 26 gallon petrol tank, when he considered the regulation 20 lb bombs inadequate. At Gallipoli and elsewhere 'Samson was more interested in adventure than in the duller work of adhering to the routine of reconnaissance and ordered bomb-dropping for the army' (*The Times*). While his bravery was admired, this penchant for freelancing ultimately had an adverse effect on his career, and at Gallipoli he was passed over for the position of overall commander of air operations, a great disappointment to him.

At the end of this campaign Samson's unit was disbanded and he was given command of the *Ben My Chree*, a former Isle of Man passenger steamer fitted out as a seaplane carrier, and attended by two slower ships as escorts. Based on Port Said, he ranged the coasts of Palestine, Syria, and Arabia, sometimes bombarding Turkish positions, sometimes sending his seaplanes on reconnaissance and offensive tasks, and always demanding more work from the naval and military commanders. In January 1917 he sailed to Kastelorizo to carry out some operations with the French, and in the harbour there the *Ben My Chree* was sunk by Turkish gunfire. His two escort ships, already equipped to carry a few seaplanes, were now fitted out for independent air operations, and from Aden and later Colombo he searched among the islands and over the expanses of the Indian Ocean for enemy raiders.

From November 1917 to October 1918 Samson was in command of the aircraft group at Great Yarmouth which was responsible for anti-submarine and anti-Zeppelin operations over the North Sea. He remained in this position until the end of the war and during that time his group shot down five Zeppelins. In order to bring fighter aircraft into action near the enemy coasts, he devised lighters to be towed behind naval ships and used as take-off platforms by fighter aircraft. Samson insisted on using skids rather than wheels for his undercarriage, running the risk that if these dislodged from their runners they would foul on the deck. When he attempted his first take-off in a trial off Orfordness, on 30 May 1918, this is exactly what happened. His Camel tumbled over the port bow, the lighter passing over both aeroplane and pilot at over 30 knots. With Samson jammed in the wreckage under water, it seemed impossible, as one eye-witness later recalled, that he 'could avoid being battered to atoms'

(Snowden Gamble, 393). In fact he emerged unhurt, and upon regaining the deck of the towing destroyer exclaimed: 'Well! ... I think it well worth trying again' (ibid.). He afterwards modified the design of the aeroplane and platform so that it served satisfactorily, and the system later led to the destruction of a Zeppelin by one of Samson's team. In October 1918 the group at Great Yarmouth became 73 wing of the new 4 group based at Felixstowe, under the control of the RAF; Samson became commanding officer of this group, and in August 1919 he gave up his naval commission and received a permanent commission in the RAF with the rank of group captain.

During 1920 Samson served in the Coastal Area as chief staff officer, and in August 1921 he became air officer commanding RAF units in the Mediterranean, with headquarters at Malta. In 1922 he was promoted air commodore and given command of 6 fighter group at Kenley. At this period his domestic affairs caused him much grief and anxiety and seemed to shake the buoyant self-assurance which was part of the secret of his success. He had married in 1917 Honor Oakden Patrickson, the daughter of Herbert Storey, of Lancaster; they had one daughter. The couple were divorced in 1923. Samson did excellent work a few years later, but the incident left its mark and probably had some influence on his early retirement from the service. In 1924 he married Winifred, daughter of Herbert Kempson Reeves, solicitor, of Leatherhead; they had a son and a daughter (who was born after his death). In June 1926 he became chief staff officer, Middle East command, and in that position he did the last of his pioneering work. He organized and led the first flight of an RAF bomber formation over Africa from Cairo to the Cape. This involved making and supplying the necessary bases and surveying an undeveloped route. The flight, made by four Fairey III.Fs, succeeded. Where Samson had led, other formations followed, and later on commercial air transport for the most part used the trail which Samson had blazed in 1926. He remained with the Middle East command until August 1927, but the great flight through Africa was his last big task.

Samson's chief qualities were his energy, his skill in improvisation, his personal courage, and his ability to pick the right men and to inspire them to intense and efficient effort. He was short and thick-set, and continued to wear a pointed beard after his transfer to the otherwise beardless RAF. To contemporaries he was a real-life Captain Kettle, the fictional hero of Charles John Cutliffe Hyne's pre-war novels, and this dashing temperament accorded with his appearance. His superiors, continually bombarded with well-thought-out if advanced proposals, were never allowed to forget his existence for long. He resigned his commission in 1929 and died suddenly of heart failure at his home, Red House, Cholderton, near Salisbury, Wiltshire, on 5 February 1931. He was buried at Putney on 10 February. Samson was awarded the DSO (1914) and bar (1917), the AFC (1919), and the French Croix de Guerre with palm (1914), and was appointed CMG (1919) and chevalier of the Légion d'honneur (1915). He was the author of the autobiographical *Fights and Flights* (1930) and also of *A Flight from Cape Town to Cairo and Back* (1931), which was published only days before his untimely death.

E. C. SHEPHERD, rev. MARK POTTLE

Sources *The Aeroplane*, 40 (11 Feb 1931), 234–5 · *The Times* (6 Feb 1931) · C. F. Snowden Gamble, *The story of a North Sea air station* (1928) · C. R. Samson, *A flight from Cape Town to Cairo and back* (1931) · C. R. Samson, *Fights and flights* (1930)
Archives IWM, papers
Likenesses C. R. Fleming-Williams, watercolour drawing, 1916 (*An "OK" bombing Chikaldir Bridge*), IWM · D. Maxwell, pen and watercolour drawing, c.1916, IWM · photograph, repro. in *The Times*
Wealth at death £4406 1s. 3d.: probate, 26 March 1931, CGPLA Eng. & Wales

Samthann ingen Díaráin (d. 739). *See under* Meath, saints of (act. c.400–c.900).

Samuda, Isaac [Ishac] **de Sequeira** [formerly Simão Lopes Samuda] (bap. **1681**, d. **1729**), physician and poet, was baptized in Lisbon in 1681. He was the second son of Rodrigo de Sequeira, merchant, and his wife, Violante Nunes Rosa, who were both of Jewish origin. He was named after his maternal grandfather, Simão Lopes Samuda, a Lisbon physician. Samuda graduated from Coimbra University as a bachelor of medicine on 21 May 1702. Like his friend Dr Samuel Nunes, whose wife was his first cousin, and two of his maternal uncles, he was arrested on 23 August 1703, tortured and convicted *de vehemente* of Judaizing, at an *auto da fé* held in Lisbon on 19 October 1704. This made him liable for the death penalty if convicted a second time; his maternal grandfather's widow was burnt at the stake in Lisbon in 1706, and so was his only sister Maria de Melo Rosa in 1709. He, his mother, one uncle, and five aunts escaped to London, where his elder brother, Abraham de Almeida (Gaspar de Almeida de Sequeira), was one of the twelve Jewish sworn brokers on the royal exchange. He joined the Spanish and Portuguese Synagogue in London in October 1709 and changed his name to Ishac de Sequeira Samuda.

In March 1722 Samuda was examined by the Royal College of Physicians and admitted as a licentiate. In February 1723 he translated a description of a whale stranded in the Tagus, from a Portuguese gazette for the Royal Society. On 27 June 1723 he was elected a fellow of the Royal Society; he was proposed by its secretary, James Jurin, and supported by Sir Hans Sloane, who obviously valued him as a contact with Portuguese scientists. In April 1724 he delivered a paper to the society giving a detailed description by a Lisbon physician (possibly Dr Diego Nunes Ribeiro) of the yellow fever epidemic, which had devastated Portugal in 1723. Samuda was also physician to António Galvão, the Portuguese envoy in London.

Astronomers at this time were interested in measuring longitude by using Galileo's method of comparing the exact time of the eclipses of the satellites of Jupiter as observed in different places. Samuda contributed six reports in Latin from Lisbon, from the Neapolitan Jesuit astronomer João Baptista Carbone, which were published in the Royal Society's *Philosophical Transactions*. These detailed the observations made by Portuguese Jesuits in Paris, Lisbon, Rome, and Peking (Beijing), in order to compare them with the times of similar observations made in London. These were then used to calculate the longitude of each place, with the most erratic results. The Jesuits also described the sighting of a comet and the times of eclipses of the sun and the moon.

As well as these scientific interests, Samuda was respected as a poet. In 1720 he contributed an introductory poem in Latin hexameters to Daniel Lopes Laguna's *Espejo fiel de la vida*. In 1724 he wrote a poem of 415 stanzas in Portuguese *ottava rima*, arranged in thirteen cantos, entitled 'Viridiadas', after Viriato, the hero who secured Lusitanian independence from Rome in the first century BC. After Samuda's death, Jacob de Castro Sarmento added a further fifty stanzas to the poem and presented the manuscript to King João V of Portugal, whence it gravitated into the library of the dukes of Palmela. This poem has never been published. It was said 'to show great ingenuity and poetical imagination' (Innocêncio, *Diccionario bibliographico Português*, 3.233). In the 1960s A. Rosenthal Ltd of Oxford bought and resold the manuscript. Samuda also wrote a polemic reply to an attempt 'to reduce the Jews to Christianity', which featured in the catalogue of the sale of Salomo Jessurun's books in Amsterdam in 1811. The present location of these two manuscripts is unknown. When David Nieto died in 1728, Samuda delivered a memorial address in Portuguese in his praise, which was printed. He also composed the eight-line epitaph in Portuguese verse, which was engraved on Nieto's tombstone.

From 1714 to 1723 Samuda held over £500 of Bank of England stock. He died unmarried on 20 November 1729, in the parish of St Botolph without Bishopsgate, London, and was buried in the Portuguese Jews' old cemetery at Mile End Road, Stepney, Middlesex. Administration of his estate was granted to his paternal uncle Joseph Rodrigues (Andre de Sequeira), who was described as his principal creditor, with the consent of his maternal uncle, Dr Abraham Samuda (António Manuel Henriques), and five aunts.

Isaac de Sequeira Samuda is best-known as the first Jew to be elected a fellow of the Royal Society, despite the religious discrimination which was then normal in other fields. Sir Hans Sloane laboured successfully to build up the society's scientific standards by recruiting foreigners and promoting international correspondence. Samuda helped this process by bringing in scientific information from Portugal. As a Portuguese writer, his main work remains hidden in two lost manuscripts.

EDGAR SAMUEL

Sources *Processo de Simão Lopes Samuda: inquisição de Lisboa 2,784*, Instituto dos Arquivos Nacionais, Torre do Tombo, Lisbon · 5469 Nedaboth, Archives of the Spanish and Portuguese Jews' Congregation, London, MS 378 [offerings made in 1709] · letter of administration, March 1730, PRO, PROB 6/106, fol. 40*r* · 'The burial register of the Spanish and Portuguese Jews, London, 1657–1735', *The Jewish Historical Society of England miscellanies part 6*, ed. R. D. Barnett (1962), 1–72 · A. D'Esaguy, 'A short note on Isaac de Sequeira Samuda', *Bulletin of the Institute of the History of Medicine*, 4 (1936), 783–8 · D. I. Lopes Laguna, *Espejo fiel de la vida, que contiene los Psalmos de David en verso, obra devota, util y delectable compuesta por Daniel Israel Lopes Laguna* (1720) · Munk, *Roll* · E. R. Samuel, 'Dr Meyer Schomberg's attack on the Jews of London, 1746', *Transactions of the Jewish Historical Society of England*, 20 (1959–61), 83–111, esp. 86–7 · I. Solomons, 'David Nieto and some of his contemporaries', *Transactions of the Jewish Historical Society of England*, 12 (1928–31), 1–101, esp. 58–9, 93, 99 · R. D. Barnett, 'Dr Jacob de Castro Sarmento and Sephardim in medical practice in 18th-century London', *Transactions of the Jewish Historical Society of England*, 27 (1978–80), 84–114 · R. D. Barnett, 'Dr Samuel Nunes Ribeiro and the settlement of Georgia', *Migration and settlement*, ed. A. Newman (1971) · I. de Sequeyra Samuda, *Sermam funebre para as exequias dos trinta dias* (London, 1728) · J. A. Giuseppi, 'Early Jewish holders of Bank of England stock [1694–1725]', *Jewish Historical Society of England miscellanies part 6* (1962) · *The record of the Royal Society of London*, 4th edn (1940)
Archives RS, journal book copy XII
Likenesses portrait, repro. in D'Esaguy, 'A short note'

Samuda, Joseph D'Aguilar (1813–1885), engineer and shipbuilder, was born in London on 21 May 1813, the second son of Abraham Samuda, a broker and East and West India merchant of Portuguese Jewish origin, and his wife, Joy, daughter of H. D'Aguilar of Enfield Chase, Middlesex. The family lived at 10 South Street, Finsbury. Joseph studied as an engineer under his brother Jacob, with whom he entered into partnership in 1832. He married, in 1837, Louisa, daughter of Samuel Ballin of Holloway, London; they had five children. Between 1832 and 1842 the firm of Samuda Brothers was principally concerned with the building of marine engines. From 1842 to 1848 the brothers also constructed tracks for atmospheric railways at Dalkey in Ireland, at Croydon, and in Paris; but operational difficulties ultimately led to the abandonment of this method of traction.

In 1843 the firm commenced a shipbuilding business, working from premises at Bow Creek. Their first vessel was the *Gipsy Queen*, but during the trial trip on 12 November 1844 Jacob Samuda, along with six others, was scalded to death when an expansion joint of the engine gave way. From 1843 onwards the firm was uninterruptedly engaged in the construction of iron steamships for both the war and merchant navies, the passenger and mail services of England and other countries, besides royal yachts and river boats. Among ships built for the British navy were the *Thunderer*, the first armour-cased iron vessel; the *Prince Albert*, the first ironclad cupola ship; and the first iron mortar vessel ever constructed. Under Samuda's personal control they later built the *Riachuelo* and the *Aquidaban*, two ironclads, for the Brazilian government, and also three channel steamers, the *Albert Victor*, the *Louise Dagmar*, and the *Mary Beatrice*, for the service between Folkestone and Boulogne. Samuda introduced into his yard on the Isle of Dogs all the efficient time- and labour-saving machines of the day. Among these was a hydraulic armour-plate bending machine, capable of exerting a working pressure of 70 cwt per square inch, or a total pressure of 4000 tons.

In 1860, in co-operation with Sir Edward Reed and

others, Samuda established the Institution of Naval Architects, of which he was elected the original treasurer and a member of council. He subsequently became one of its vice-presidents. His contributions to its *Transactions* were numerous, and there were few discussions at its meetings in which he did not take part. He was a member of a committee appointed by the Admiralty in 1884 to inquire into the condition under which contracts were invited for the building and repairing of HM ships and their engines, and into the practical working of the dockyards.

On 6 May 1862 Samuda became a member of the Institution of Civil Engineers, and he frequently spoke at their meetings. He was a member of the Metropolitan Board of Works from 1860 until 1865, in which year he entered parliament in the Liberal interest for Tavistock. He sat for that constituency until 1868, when he was returned for Tower Hamlets, which he continued to represent until 1880. He failed to secure re-election owing to his support of Lord Beaconsfield's foreign policy. He spoke frequently in the house, particularly on naval subjects. He was captain in the 2nd Tower Hamlets rifle volunteers from 6 April 1860, and major from 10 November 1863 to 4 December 1867, and lieutenant-colonel of the 1st Tower Hamlets rifle volunteers from 4 December 1867 to June 1869. He died at his home, 7 Gloucester Square, Hyde Park, London, on 27 April 1885, and was buried on 2 May at Kensal Green cemetery. G. C. BOASE, *rev.* ANITA McCONNELL

Sources PICE, 81 (1884–5), 334–7 • GM, 2nd ser., 23 (1845), 321 • *The Times* (29 April 1885), 5 • *Iron* (1 May 1885), 384 • *East End News* (1 May 1885), 3 • *East End News* (5 May 1885), 3 • VF (15 Feb 1873), 55 • CGPLA *Eng. & Wales* (1885)
Likenesses chromolithograph caricature, NPG; repro. in *VF* (15 Feb 1873), 55
Wealth at death £199,350 19s. 11d.: resworn probate, Nov 1886, CGPLA *Eng. & Wales* (1885)

Samuel, Edward (1674–1748), Church of England clergyman and translator, was born at Cwt-y-Defaid in the parish of Penmorfa, Caernarvonshire, the son of Edward Samuel. His parents were poor, and he owed his education to the interest of Bishop Humphrey Humphreys of Bangor. On 19 May 1693, aged nineteen, he matriculated as a 'pauper puer' from Oriel College, Oxford. After taking holy orders, he became on 4 November 1702 rector of Betws Gwerful Goch, Merioneth, a position he exchanged on 12 January 1721 for the rectory of Llangar in the same county.

Samuel was a facile writer of Welsh verse and prose. Several of his poems were published: *Blodeugerdd Cymru* (1759) contains four carols and a lyrical piece, all of which are characterized by his loyalty to the church and the house of Hanover. An ode to the poet Huw Morys was included in *Eos Ceiriog* (1823) and other verses were printed in 1798. He was more celebrated, however, as a translator into Welsh of religious works, including Grotius's 'De veritate religionis Christianae' and Richard Allestree's *The Whole Duty of Man*. His own sermons appeared in 1731 and 1766.

Samuel was married and had at least two sons: Edward (1710–1762), rector of Llanddulas, and William Samuel (1713–1765), rector of Nantglyn. The poet David *Samwell (1751–1798) was his grandson. Edward Samuel died on 8 April 1748 and was buried at Llangar.

J. E. LLOYD, *rev.* S. J. SKEDD

Sources Foster, *Alum. Oxon.* • *DWB* • preface, H. Grotius, *Gwirionedd y Grefydd Gristiongol*, trans. E. Samuel, 3rd edn (1854) • D. R. Thomas, *Esgobaeth Llanelwy: the history of the diocese of St Asaph*, new edn (1874)

Samuel, Frank (1889–1954), gramophone manufacturer and industrialist, was born on 19 January 1889 at 20 Marlborough Place, London, the youngest of three children in the Jewish family of Nelson Samuel and his wife, Harriett Hymans. Nelson headed the prosperous family business of Barnett Samuel, an old established firm of London piano manufacturers and musical instrument dealers. Frank Samuel was educated at Clifton College and subsequently studied in Lausanne and Berlin.

In 1904, Samuel, together with his brother Edgar and two cousins, entered the family business, then undergoing a transformation caused by the new recording industry. A decade later, the four—by this time presiding over one of the largest record wholesalers and dealerships in London—patented the first portable gramophone which they called the Decca Dulcephone. This major breakthrough in the technology of recorded sound gave good-quality reproduction and the convenience of portability: the Decca could be carried around like a briefcase.

Poor eyesight excluded Samuel from war service in 1914, and he ran the business with his father while the other partners went off to fight. The essentially static nature of trench warfare meant that gramophones and records quickly became a feature of life on the western front. As a consequence, there was a brisk trade in Barnett Samuel's 'Trench' model Decca, which allowed the company to prosper during these difficult years. The death of Edgar Samuel on active service in Flanders in 1916 meant that on his father's death in 1920 Frank Samuel became head of the company. He married Esther Marie, daughter of A. D. Benjamin on 20 December 1916, but the marriage did not produce any children.

During the ensuing decade sales of the Decca range of gramophones rocketed to become the most profitable area of the business. By 1928 turnover was seven times its pre-war level. In that year, Frank Samuel calculated that sales of Decca gramophones had probably peaked, and that in order to remain competitive his company had to expand and diversify. In addition, he and his family wanted to realize a part of their company fortunes. This led Samuel and the other directors to take Barnett Samuel to a successful flotation on the London stock exchange in 1928. In those boom days, the shares were over-subscribed by a factor of twenty, with Samuel's own share in the new business, renamed the Decca Gramophone Company Ltd, worth over £100,000. At this juncture, Samuel sold his shares and severed his links with the business.

Freed from the demands of day-to-day management of a large concern, Samuel embarked on a world cruise. However this was cut short when he accepted the offer of a position as joint managing director with the United Africa

Company (UAC), a commodity trading subsidiary of Unilever. Over the next decade, Samuel nursed this business through the ravages of the depression, diversifying its interests into heavy industry, motor vehicles, refrigerated food, and cargo shipping (the origins of the Palm Line). However, by 1938, although UAC remained in a poor financial condition, it had gained a reputation for exploitation and monopolistic practices, and Samuel's own expansionist aims of creating manufacturing and trading organizations from within the local African population themselves had foundered upon problems of capital and resource scarcity.

The coming of war in 1939 saw Samuel left to run the business while his colleagues went to war. The Second World War provided him with the opportunity to transform the company's fortunes. Also at this time other responsibilities came his way, specifically his appointment in 1940 to the main Unilever board. Like many other companies, UAC was co-opted by the Ministry of Food into the business of commodity requisition. Although this move deprived UAC of its usual speculative trading business, the company was able to shrug off its exploitative image; it also expanded its retailing, processing, and manufacturing sectors, opening up factories and stores across west Africa. Meanwhile, Samuel was recruiting younger men such as Arthur Smith and George (later Lord) Cole, both of whom went on to be chairmen of UAC and Unilever respectively.

Ironically, the Tanganyika groundnut scheme of 1946–51 proved to be Samuel's major career failure and the first venture to bring him into the public eye. Born out of the worldwide shortage of edible oils and fats and Britain's own shortage of hard currency in the mid-1940s, the scheme saw Samuel uncharacteristically back a venture without sufficient investigation of the enormous risks involved. It all but collapsed in 1948, overburdened by soaring costs and local difficulties of labour procurement and transportation. Nevertheless, Samuel became chairman of UAC in 1953 and continued to establish new industries in west Africa. Under his direction UAC was transformed from a loss-making liability to a corporation with pre-tax profits of over £14 million. Samuel's colleagues later praised his 'strong sense of justice' and 'intensity of concentration', together with his 'great gift for developing subordinates, always seeking to give them confidence in their own powers' (DBB, 42).

Samuel died suddenly at his home, 25 Harley House, Regent's Park, Marylebone, London, on 25 February 1954, while still active in business life. He was survived by his wife. PETER MARTLAND

Sources F. Pedler and D. Fieldhouse, 'Samuel, Frank', DBB · *The Times* (1 March 1854) · C. Wilson, *The history of Unilever: a study in economic growth and social change*, 2 vols. (1954) · D. K. Fieldhouse, *Unilever overseas: the anatomy of a multinational, 1895–1965* (1978) · m. cert. · d. cert. · *CGPLA Eng. & Wales* (1954) · D. K. Fieldhouse, *Merchant capital and economic decolonization: the United Africa Company, 1929–1987* (1994)
Archives Museum of Jewish History, London
Wealth at death £130,893 4s. 2d.: probate, 17 July 1954, *CGPLA Eng. & Wales*

Samuel, George (d. c.1823), landscape painter and topographical draughtsman, practised in both oils and watercolours. No details of his birth or parentage are known. He received an award from the Society of Arts in 1784, and afterwards exhibited annually at the Royal Academy from 1785 to 1822, and at the British Institution from 1807 to 1822. Samuel's works depict views across rural England, as well as fashionable sites in and around London, such as Greenwich and Hampstead Heath. His landscapes are as notable for their carefully delineated fashionable and rustic figures as for their contribution to the contemporary aesthetic of the picturesque. Samuel's view of the Thames from Rotherhithe during the great frost of 1789 attracted much attention when exhibited at the Royal Academy in that year. He also made drawings of buildings, from cottages to royal palaces, which were engraved and published throughout his career, appearing in volumes such as Angus's *Select Views of Seats*, the *Copperplate Magazine* (1792), Walker's *Itinerant* (1799), Robert Wilkinson's *Londina illustrata* (1819), and Pyne's *Royal Residences* (1819). In 1799 he illustrated Thomas Maurice's *Grove Hill*, a poem describing the seat of Dr Lettsom.

Samuel was a member of Thomas Girtin's small and select sketching club which aimed to establish a school of historic landscape. He was one of the first artists to produce lithographs. He died in or soon after 1823, when an old wall fell on him while he was sketching.

F. M. O'DONOGHUE, *rev.* ROSIE DIAS

Sources R. Redgrave and S. Redgrave, *A century of painters of the English school*, 2 vols. (1866) · M. H. Grant, *A chronological history of the old English landscape painters*, rev. edn, 8 vols. (1957–61) · Graves, *RA exhibitors* · Graves, *Brit. Inst.*

Samuel, Harold, Baron Samuel of Wych Cross (1912–1987), businessman, was born on 23 April 1912 at 8 Fawley Road, Finchley, Middlesex, the second of three children and younger son of Vivian Samuel, master jeweller and later property developer, and his wife, Ada Cohen. He was educated at Mill Hill School and the College of Estate Management, Lincoln's Inn Fields. He was then articled to surveyors and qualified as a fellow of the Chartered Surveyors' Institution in 1933. He set up as an estate agent in London, but subsequently decided to become a property developer and investor, and promptly ceased to practise, in order to avoid any conflict of interest.

In 1944 Samuel acquired the shares of an insignificant company, the Land Securities Investment Trust, which owned three properties with total assets of under £20,000. He foresaw that the key to the success of a property investment company was a strong base, a sound reputation, and the provision of fixed long-term finance at low interest rates. In 1947 profits from the Land Securities Investment Trust enabled him to provide the financial backing to secure bomb sites in provincial cities devastated during the Second World War. The associate company, which he formed for this purpose with colleagues and subsequently merged into Land Securities, succeeded in rebuilding the city centres of Plymouth, Exeter, Hull, Coventry, and Bristol.

Samuel adopted a revolving development policy, acquiring new sites to improve the portfolio and refurbishing or rebuilding existing holdings. His aims were to provide high-quality building in first-class locations, tenants of good standing, and architects' open competition to ensure innovative designs. He assembled throughout Britain a fine collection of income-producing commercial buildings of all types. He developed the financial muscle of his company, which enabled him to take over control of the United City Property Trust, Associated London Properties, the shares and assets of City Centre Properties, with its vast holdings and subsidiary companies, and the City of London Real Property Company, with its exceptional portfolio of outstanding buildings. In 1953 he failed to gain control of the Savoy, an episode which ended in public acrimony. Eventually his company accounts showed assets of £3 billion. He donated generously to many charities, but liked to remain anonymous. Among others, he supported the Royal College of Surgeons and the universities of Cambridge and London. He was president of the Central London Housing Trust for the Aged, an honorary fellow of Magdalene College, Cambridge (1961), and University College, London (1968), and vice-president of the British Heart Foundation. He was knighted in 1963 and became a life peer in 1972.

In 1936 Samuel married Edna, daughter of Harry Nedas, outfitter, of Manchester. They had three daughters, one of whom died in 1968. In 1947 the family moved from Hampstead to a house with extensive gardens in Regent's Park. There their love of horticulture and art was nurtured, and Samuel assembled an outstanding personal collection of paintings, which included works by Pieter Brueghel and Frans Hals. In 1952 he acquired an estate in Ashdown Forest, Sussex, which provided more room for his growing art collection. He also completely renovated the mansion there and cultivated magnificent flower gardens. Samuel bequeathed his private art collection to the corporation of London, where it hangs in the Mansion House.

Samuel was 5 feet 10 inches tall, clean shaven, and with good regular features. He dressed immaculately, in formal and conservative style. He was a perfectionist, extremely precise, and a deep thinker with high standards of integrity. A shy man, he avoided public speaking. He died on 28 August 1987 at his home, Wych Cross Place, Forest Row, Sussex, survived by his wife and two daughters.

EDWARD ERDMAN, *rev.*

Sources E. L. Erdman, *People and property* (1982) · *The Independent* (4 Sept 1987) · *The Times* (1 Sept 1987) · personal knowledge (1996) · *CGPLA Eng. & Wales* (1987) · b. cert.
Wealth at death £26,227,352: probate, 8 Dec 1987, *CGPLA Eng. & Wales*

Samuel, Harold Solomon (1879–1937), pianist, was born on 23 May 1879 at 37 Bristol Gardens, Paddington, London, the son of Moses Samuel, an auctioneer, and his wife, Victoria Mallaw. At seventeen he entered the Royal College of Music, where he studied piano with Edward Dannreuther and composition with Charles Villiers Stanford. At first he was known mainly as a brilliant player of Liszt, but soon

he became interested in a wider range of music and virtually abandoned the virtuoso repertoire. Typically, he became one of the coaches in the opera class at the college, and was involved in the earliest English performances of Verdi's *Falstaff*, given by students of the college under the direction of Stanford.

Samuel gave his first piano recital on 14 March 1900 at the Steinway Hall in Wigmore Street. The main part of his programme was devoted to the hour-long 'Goldberg' variations by J. S. Bach. Today this would cause little surprise; but at that time Bach's keyboard music was rarely heard other than in transcriptions by Liszt, Tausig, or Busoni. In spite of the recital's success, Samuel was forced to abandon the hazardous career of a soloist for the early death of his father had left him with unexpected financial responsibilities. Instead he turned to the more secure if less glamorous work of accompanying and teaching.

At the comparatively late age of forty Samuel took the courageous step of giving up accompanying entirely and devoting himself to solo work. Two years later he gave a series of six daily Bach recitals at the Wigmore Hall (30 May – 4 June 1921), thus establishing himself in the public mind as a Bach specialist (a term he disliked intensely). In all, Samuel gave six of these 'Bach weeks' in London, and one in New York in 1928. In later years he restricted himself to single recitals, partly because the mental and physical strain of the 'weeks' was excessive, and partly because he felt that his missionary work in establishing Bach's keyboard music had already been accomplished.

Samuel was also a notable chamber music player, and in the 1930s formed a partnership with violinist Isolde Menges, with whom he gave many concerts in the Netherlands and elsewhere. In 1924, at the invitation of Mrs Elizabeth Sprague Coolidge, he gave the first of many tours in the USA. He was an important influence, both personally and musically, on another and considerably younger composer, Howard Ferguson (1908–1999).

During the twenty years before he became a soloist, Samuel wrote songs and piano pieces, and a musical comedy, *The Hon'Able Phil*, which had a London run. But by far his greatest success in this field was merely acknowledged on the printed cover as 'arranged by H. S.'. It was the piano accompaniment to Frederick E. Weatherly's sentimental words, 'Danny Boy', written to the tune of the 'Londonderry Air'.

In 1936 Samuel toured South Africa for the last time. On the homeward journey in November he had a severe coronary attack on board ship, and spent six weeks in a nursing home in Southampton. When he finally reached London by ambulance in December his condition was seen to deteriorate, and gradually it became apparent that he had had a secondary attack—probably when being moved from the ship—and that his brain was being affected. On 15 January 1937 Samuel died at his home, 34 Willoughby Road, Hampstead, London; although he was never a practising Jew, a memorial service was held for him three days later at the West London Synagogue. His remains were cremated at Golders Green crematorium.

HOWARD FERGUSON

Sources *New Grove* · H. Ferguson, *Music, friends and places* (1997) · b. cert. · *CGPLA Eng. & Wales* (1937) · S. Banfield, *Gerald Finzi: an English composer* (1997) · d. cert.
Archives SOUND BL NSA · BL NSA, 'Harold Samuel', 23 Jan 1979, T2418W/R C1 · BL NSA, oral history interview · BL NSA, performance recordings
Likenesses H. Lambert of Bath, photograph, *c.*1922
Wealth at death £7078 1*s.* 4*d.*: resworn probate, 19 March 1937, *CGPLA Eng. & Wales*

Samuel, Herbert Louis, first Viscount Samuel (1870–1963), politician, was born on 6 November 1870 at Claremont, Belvedere Road, Sefton Park, Liverpool, the youngest of five children of Edwin Louis Samuel (1825–1877), a banker, and his wife, Clara, *née* Yates (1837–1920). His ancestors, of German-Jewish origin, had settled in England in the eighteenth century. Edwin Samuel was a partner with his younger brother Montagu (in adulthood known as Samuel Montagu, later first Baron Swaythling) in the banking firm of Samuel and Montagu, which the younger brother had established in the City of London in 1853. In December 1871 Edwin Samuel moved with his family to London to take an active partnership in the firm. The business prospered, and by the time Edwin died suddenly in 1877 he was able to leave his wife and children enough for them to have no worldly cares for the rest of their days.

Education and Liberalism Herbert Samuel enjoyed an untroubled, pampered childhood, brought up mainly by his gently protective mother in a substantial house in South Kensington, a few doors away from Samuel Montagu and his large family. Samuel grew up in close contact with his Montagu cousins. His domineering uncle exercised a general guardianship but was a distant figure who had little influence on his development. Samuel was educated as a day boy at a nearby preparatory school and at University College School (1884–8), then in Bloomsbury. In 1889 he entered Balliol College, Oxford, where he read modern history, emerging in 1893 with a first-class degree.

In January 1889, before going up to Oxford, Samuel had become involved in politics as a campaigner for his elder brother Stuart, a Progressive candidate for the Whitechapel ward in the election to the newly established London county council. This was a working-class area with a significant Jewish immigrant population. The encounter with extreme poverty deeply affected Herbert Samuel, and from that point he determined on a political career in the Liberal Party.

While at Oxford Samuel took an active part in university Liberal activity and joined Tom Mann, George Bernard Shaw, L. T. Hobhouse, and others in weekend forays into the Oxfordshire countryside to unionize agricultural labourers. In early 1893, while still an undergraduate, he was adopted by the South Oxfordshire Liberal Association as their prospective parliamentary candidate. He fought two energetic elections for this Conservative-held constituency, in 1895 and 1900, and achieved creditable results, but lost on both occasions.

During the 1890s Samuel developed the radical Liberal

Herbert Louis Samuel, first Viscount Samuel (1870–1963), by Olive Edis, *c.*1932

outlook to which he clung for the rest of his life. Greatly influenced by the progressive social ideas of Graham Wallas and Sidney and Beatrice Webb, he wrote some Fabian pamphlets and joined J. Ramsay MacDonald, J. A. Hobson, Charles Trevelyan (his closest friend), and others in a radical discussion group, the Rainbow Circle. This sought to define a 'new Liberalism' (the title of a paper read by Samuel to the circle in November 1895) with a reformist and interventionist social agenda. In 1902 Samuel produced a comprehensive formulation of his political philosophy, *Liberalism: its Principles and Proposals*, in which he provided an intellectual foundation for many of the social reforms subsequently enacted by the Liberal governments after 1905.

Marriage and parliament On 17 November 1897 Samuel married his first cousin Beatrice Miriam (1871–1959), daughter of Ellis Abraham Franklin, a banker. They had three sons and one daughter. Although Samuel had a wide range of political contacts, he and his wife, unlike his cousin Edwin Montagu, did not mix much in high society. They remained most at home in the 'cousinhood', the Anglo-Jewish patriciate.

In November 1902, aged thirty-one, Samuel finally secured election to parliament at a by-election at Cleveland, an ironstone-mining constituency in which he ran with some Labour support. He developed a strong following among the miners, and his relations with leaders of the nascent Labour Party prevented any Labour opponent challenging him until 1918. In spite of his interest in social problems, Samuel's early parliamentary reputation was forged mainly on imperial issues. A moderate supporter of the Second South African War, Samuel had visited Uganda in 1902 and developed a special expertise in African affairs. As a back-bencher over the next three years he attacked the inhuman regime of Leopold of the Belgians in the Congo, endorsing the charges of the former British consul there, Roger Casement, whom he called (to his later embarrassment) 'a gentleman of the highest standing and reliability' (Wasserstein, 73). He was one of the leaders of opposition to so-called 'Chinese slavery' (the importation from China of indentured labourers to the goldmines of the Transvaal), using the issue as an effective stick to beat the dying Balfour government.

Political office, 1905–1916 When the Liberals took office in December 1905, Samuel was appointed under-secretary at the Home Office. He was given wide latitude by the home secretary, Herbert Gladstone, and succeeded in securing passage of several measures of social reform. His most significant achievement was the Children Act of 1908 (the 'Children's Charter'), which extended state responsibility to all children, ended child imprisonment, restricted corporal punishment, and instituted the first countrywide system of juvenile courts. A related measure in the same year established the 'Borstal' system of reformatory schools for juvenile offenders—Samuel claimed paternity of the neologism (so called after the first such institution at Borstal, in Kent). He was also responsible for the 1907 Probation of Offenders Act which, for the first time, created a national system of probation.

In 1909 Samuel was promoted to the cabinet as chancellor of the duchy of Lancaster (in effect, minister without portfolio). He showed his mettle by hard labour on the unrewarding task of chairing a parliamentary committee on theatrical censorship—in which post he had some memorable exchanges of fireworks with Shaw. His administrative capacity was given broader scope in February 1910 when he was appointed postmaster-general. During the four years that he held the position, Samuel presided over some major changes. Paradoxically, given his opposition in principle to extension of public ownership, he presided in 1911 over the first major nationalization of a British industry—the telephone system. In the same year he was responsible for approving the world's first experimental air mail service (it was judged a failure).

Samuel's efficiency and reliability were recognized but he was not popular. H. G. Wells satirized him mercilessly in *The New Machiavelli* (1911) as 'Lewis, a brilliant representative of his race, able, industrious and invariably uninspired' (Wasserstein, 127). More dangerously, he was the victim of unfair criticism during the long-drawn-out Marconi scandal, in which he was falsely accused by Hilaire Belloc and others of insider trading in Marconi Company shares. The campaign (in which Rufus Isaacs and Lloyd George were more justly impugned) was pursued with a virulent edge of antisemitism. Samuel won a libel suit over the issue in 1913 (he was represented by Sir Edward Carson and F. E. Smith, who were assisted by Raymond

Asquith, son of the prime minister), but although he was exonerated some of the mud inevitably stuck in the public mind.

In early 1914 Samuel was moved to the presidency of the Board of Trade, a post that afforded little room for legislative radicalism. In the crisis of July 1914 he was a moderate member of the war party in cabinet and in this capacity devised the formula on 2 August that became the basis for British entry to the European war two days later.

Although Samuel moved further up the political ladder until December 1916, the war years were frustrating for him. He was placed in charge of the reception of Belgian refugees and given other uninspiring administrative tasks. When the coalition government was formed in 1915 he was temporarily dropped from the cabinet, returning to his old job at the Post Office, but upon Churchill's resignation in November he was restored to the cabinet and in January 1916 became home secretary. Conditions of war, however, were held to preclude the introduction of any reformist measures: the only notable innovation was the introduction of daylight saving time and the related unification of British and Irish time (until then Irish was twenty-five minutes earlier than British). As home secretary Samuel was obliged to deal with a number of delicate civil liberties issues. He made several decisions that posterity judged illiberal. After the Easter rising in Dublin, he was briefly responsible for Irish affairs and for the heavy-handed repression that followed. In England conscientious objectors were maltreated, and Bertrand Russell and Fenner Brockway were imprisoned for anti-war propaganda. Sir Roger Casement was hanged after landing in Ireland from a German submarine—Samuel declined to recommend mercy for his former ally in the Congo agitation. Other former allies such as Graham Wallas bitterly criticized what they considered Samuel's betrayal of his earlier principles.

High commissioner of Palestine In the political crisis of December 1916 Samuel was a consistent supporter of Asquith—and paid the price in self-exclusion from office under Lloyd George. At the general election of 1918, he was opposed for the first time by a Labour candidate and as a result lost his seat to a coalition Unionist. There was some talk, nevertheless, of his appointment to an executive position, but he rejected the humiliating offer of the post of controller of disposal of surplus stores (huts and hutting material section) as well as other, hardly more tempting, proposals.

Meanwhile, however, an opportunity arose to serve in a quite different capacity—as head of the civil government of Palestine. Samuel's support for Zionism came as a surprise to those who knew him. He was not a believing Jew, although, partly out of deference to his wife, he observed the basic outward forms of the religion. Before the war he had evinced no public interest in Zionism. Yet in November 1914, immediately after the entry of the Ottoman empire into the war, he took the initiative, without prior contact with the Zionist Organization, in proposing to the cabinet that Britain sponsor the establishment of a Jewish state in Palestine after the war. He promoted the idea both informally with fellow ministers and in a formal paper that was circulated to the cabinet (in which, however, the idea of a Jewish state was modified to a 'Jewish centre' under British protection). In December 1914 he met the Zionist leader Chaim Weizmann, inaugurating a political relationship that, while sometimes stormy, yielded rich fruit. Although out of office at the time of the Balfour declaration (whereby Britain undertook to facilitate the establishment of a Jewish national home in Palestine) in November 1917, Samuel's advocacy was an important element in the Zionists' success—particularly as against the fierce anti-Zionism of his cousin Edwin Montagu, secretary of state for India. In the spring of 1920 Samuel visited Palestine for the first time, and at the San Remo conference that April Lloyd George approved his appointment as first high commissioner in charge of the new civil administration to be established in Palestine under a League of Nations mandate.

Samuel's five years in Palestine were the most politically constructive of his career and, in a sense, its highest point. He had been knighted prior to his departure from England, but on arrival in Palestine on 30 June he was greeted by the small Jewish community as a veritable prince. He assumed authority from the military administration headed by General Sir Louis Bols, who demanded that he sign a receipt for 'one Palestine, complete': Samuel complied but added the common commercial escape clause, 'E&OE' (errors and omissions excepted).

One of Samuel's early acts as high commissioner, in August, was to visit Transjordan (at that time a political vacuum, owing to the French ejection of the emir Faisal from Damascus). Without authority, and rather against the spirit of Foreign Office instructions, he effectively annexed the territory, quadrupling the area under his control. The foreign secretary, Curzon, initially repudiated Samuel's action. That December, however, the region passed under the aegis of the Colonial Office and in March 1921 the colonial secretary, Churchill, visited Jerusalem and confirmed the addition of Transjordan to the mandatory area—with the proviso that it would be under the nominal rule of the emir Abdullah and would not form part of the Jewish national home established west of the River Jordan.

Samuel's main efforts as high commissioner were devoted to seeking the acquiescence of the Arab majority of the population in the implementation of the Balfour declaration. He proposed unsuccessfully a number of constitutional devices towards that end: a nominated advisory council that would include Arab and Jewish members, an elected legislative council with limited powers, and a representative Arab Agency after the model of the Jewish Agency established by the Zionists. None of these succeeded in damping down Arab nationalist opposition to Jewish immigration. Samuel sought to co-opt Arab nationalists by appointing some to official positions, most notably Haj Amin al-Husseini, whose election as grand mufti of Jerusalem was arranged in 1921 by the attorney-general, Norman Bentwich (Samuel's wife's nephew). In

May that year violent anti-Jewish riots at Jaffa and elsewhere led Samuel to suspend Jewish immigration—an action bitterly criticized by the Zionists as a surrender to violence. Henceforward Zionist approbation turned to hostility and accusations that Samuel bent over backwards to accommodate Arab nationalism. A white paper issued in June 1922 (sometimes known as the Churchill white paper, but largely drafted by Samuel and Sir John Shuckburgh of the Colonial Office) tried to reassure the Arabs, but at the same time reaffirmed the commitment to the Balfour declaration and stressed that the Jewish national home meant that the Jews were 'in Palestine as of right and not on sufferance' (Wasserstein, 260). The policy statement laid down the principle of economic absorptive capacity as the governing criterion for Jewish immigration. Over the following three years Samuel succeeded in calming the political atmosphere. By mid-1925, when his period of office ended, the Jewish national home was firmly established, Jewish immigration and land purchase were growing, and Arab nationalism seemed for the moment dormant.

Aged fifty-four, Samuel wanted to remain in Palestine, live in a house on Mount Carmel, and devote the rest of his life to writing philosophy. This wish was vetoed by his successor as high commissioner, Lord Plumer, who feared Samuel's presence would hamper his administration. Effectively expelled from the national home he had brought into being, Samuel found himself drawn back into the hurly-burly of British politics.

The coal industry and the general strike In August 1925 the prime minister, Baldwin, invited Samuel to chair a royal commission on the coal industry, which was in a state of acute crisis, with 60 per cent of its output being produced at a loss and its million-strong workforce threatening to strike. At first reluctant, Samuel eventually agreed. The commission completed its work within six months and, together with William Beveridge, who served as one of the four members of the commission, Samuel wrote or drafted most of its report. The commission recommended nationalization of mineral royalties, though not of the industry itself. Voluntary amalgamation of smaller units was favoured, and a number of reforms in miners' conditions of work were proposed. On the burning immediate issues, the commission urged an end to the government's temporary subsidy for the industry and supported the owners' demand for a reduction in wages. The report, published on 11 March 1926, became a best-seller, but neither owners nor miners welcomed the recommendations. Positions hardened, and a lock-out (or strike, depending on the point of view) began on 1 May 1926. The miners enjoyed the reluctant support of the TUC, which called a general strike beginning on 4 May.

Samuel was holidaying on the continent but decided to return to London to try to mediate unofficially in the conflict. He held lengthy meetings with government ministers and TUC leaders, and by 12 May succeeded in securing TUC adhesion to a formula that would serve as a basis for calling off the general strike. Samuel won many plaudits for his peacemaking efforts, though in the event neither the government nor the TUC honoured Samuel's formula; the miners refused to regard themselves as bound by it, and did not return to work until they were starved into submission in November 1926.

Return to Liberal politics The wretched state of his old party, depleted in parliament and still deeply divided between the followers of Asquith and Lloyd George, now persuaded Samuel to return to active politics as the Liberals' chairman early in 1927. He took charge of the arthritic party machine and succeeded in reviving it as an effective political force. Although personally repelled by Lloyd George's nonchalant amoralism and troubled by wrangles over the 'Lloyd George Fund' (allegedly secured in payment for honours) Samuel faithfully served under Lloyd George's leadership. He joined J. M. Keynes, Walter Runciman, and others in producing the Liberal 'yellow book', *Britain's Industrial Future* (1928). In 1929 he returned to the Commons as MP for the Lancashire seat of Darwen and over the next two years served, in effect, as deputy leader of the party. The Liberals' difficult balancing role in this parliament accentuated internal rifts. Samuel was closely involved in discussions with the Labour government over proposals for proportional representation, but these dragged on without result.

In the financial and political crisis of the summer of 1931 Samuel suddenly found himself thrust into a leading role by Lloyd George's temporary absence due to illness. In spite of his work with Keynes on the 'yellow book', Samuel remained wedded to orthodox doctrines of public financial prudence. He urged a balanced budget and reduction in unemployment benefits as the necessary price of maintaining the value of sterling. In a conversation with the king on 23 August Samuel suggested a national government and expressed Liberal readiness to support it, and the next day he joined MacDonald's national cabinet.

Home secretary in the National Government Samuel's second stint as home secretary was no happier than his first. Again adverse circumstances were held to preclude significant measures of social reform. The *raison d'être* of the coalition, defence of the currency, disappeared within a few weeks when the gold standard was abandoned and sterling devalued. In the election of October 1931 the Liberal vote declined by half from 1929. The party in the Commons was now divided into three groups: the thirty-three Samuelites were outnumbered by the thirty-five followers of Sir John Simon; Lloyd George's 'family party' numbered four, but made up for size by its leader's return to activity in full rhetorical flow and acrid resentment of Samuel's presumption in seizing the party leadership.

The most difficult issue facing Samuel in government was tariffs: the Conservatives were determined to force through 'imperial preference'—and with their overwhelming majority within the coalition could do so with or without Liberal support. For a time the Samuelites salved their conscience with the 'agreement to differ', a constitutional innovation by which the convention of collective cabinet responsibility was relaxed. But over the

next few months Samuel found himself the butt of criticism from all sides, and a few weeks after the Ottawa agreements of August 1932 he resigned. 'So the Jews have left the land of Gos[h]en for the wilderness. May their bones rot there!' (Wasserstein, 360) was Lloyd George's reaction.

Over the next three years Samuel struggled unavailingly to hold the remnants of his party together. Lloyd George did not help. He mocked Samuel in public and cursed him in private. In November 1933 Samuel led his thirty remaining supporters across the floor and into opposition. The party suffered further defections to right and to left. Samuel tried with dogged determination to carve out a distinctive policy—'vomit of a sick dog' (Wasserstein, 366) Lloyd George called it. In the 1935 election the Liberals declined to only nineteen seats, Samuel losing his to a Conservative. This marked the end of Samuel's leadership and of his role in front-rank politics.

Peerage, broadcasting, and philosophy Samuel's removal from the House of Commons nevertheless hardly reduced the tempo of his political activity. On 8 June 1937 he was raised to the House of Lords as Viscount Samuel, taking the territorial designations of Mount Carmel and Toxteth (the latter after the district of Liverpool in which he had been born). He still hoped for office and was disappointed not to be offered the viceroyalty of India. Unlike many in his party, he supported the Munich agreement in 1938 but shortly afterwards declined Chamberlain's offer of a cabinet seat as lord privy seal. During the early part of the Second World War he still hoped to be able to serve in some capacity, but Churchill (*b.* 1874) considered him too old and he was never again offered public office.

Meanwhile, with the rise of Nazism, Samuel had become increasingly involved once again in Jewish issues. He headed the Council for German Jewry, which sought to raise money in Britain and the United States to facilitate Jewish refugee migration from Germany. Before and during the war he lobbied the British government to give effective succour to Jews in Europe threatened by the Nazis. He also renewed his involvement in Palestine affairs, opposing the proposals of the 1937 royal commission under Earl Peel for the partition of the country into separate Jewish and Arab states. He maintained his opposition to partition after the war but welcomed the establishment of the state of Israel in 1948. The following year he was received there as an honoured guest and crossed the armistice line to visit his old colleague, Abdullah, now king of Jordan.

In old age Samuel won a wide audience as a writer, broadcaster, and sage. He was a frequent member of the radio programme *The Brains Trust* in its wartime heyday and later also appeared on its television successor. On 15 October 1951 he became the first British politician to deliver a party political broadcast on television. His 1947 Romanes lecture at Oxford, 'Creative man', was broadcast on the BBC Third Programme to general acclaim. He continued to speak at public meetings and in the House of Lords into advanced old age. He was elected visitor of

Balliol College in 1949 and in 1958 was admitted to the Order of Merit.

Throughout his life Samuel poured out books and articles. His memoirs, which appeared in 1945, were characteristically discreet. He hoped to be remembered as much as a philosopher as for his political work, and in private reveries of self-esteem liked to compare himself with Francis Bacon. His best-known philosophical work, *Belief and Action*, first published in 1937, appeared in two paperback editions and sold nearly 100,000 copies. Perhaps his most attractive book was *An Unknown Land*, published in 1942, a utopian novel inspired by Bacon's *New Atlantis*. Samuel's theories on the philosophy of physics earned a testimonial from as high an authority as Einstein. But few professional philosophers took his work so seriously. Intellectually self-confident, hard-working, and well read, Samuel was undaunted and remained active until the end. His last book, *A Threefold Cord*, a philosophical dialogue with Professor Herbert Dingle, appeared to indulgent reviews in 1961 when he was aged ninety.

Of medium height, with a good head of hair and a moustache, Samuel was undemonstrative in his emotions and to the outward world a cold fish. Yet he could be warmly affectionate towards his family and close friends and sometimes displayed a rather naïve sense of humour, delighting in puns, practical jokes, and conjuring tricks. His relationship with his wife, who died in 1959, was one of easy companionability: the marriage 'had a certain "cousinly" element', as his daughter recalled it. Political contemporaries tended to underestimate him as an unimaginative workhorse. In part this was the disdain of the amateur for the professional, the gentleman for the player, the dunce for the swot. Samuel was a formidable administrator and a well-organized speaker who, when he cared deeply about a subject, could achieve impressive rhetorical effects—for example, in a speech on Zionism at the London Opera House in 1917, or another in the House of Lords in 1960 denouncing a proposed road across Christ Church meadow, Oxford. In his later years the Anglo-Jewish community regarded him as its elder statesman, though Zionists tended to remember him unfairly as a backslider. As he surveyed in old age a career in Liberalism that stretched from the era of Gladstone to that of Jo Grimond, he deeply regretted the decline of his party: his lasting achievement, none the less, was the preservation of historic Liberalism as a significant current in British political life. Samuel died at his London home, 32 Portchester Terrace, Bayswater, on 5 February 1963, and was buried in Willesden Jewish cemetery.

BERNARD WASSERSTEIN

Sources HLRO, Samuel papers · Israel State Archives, Samuel MSS · Home Office papers, PRO · Post Office Archives · Viscount Samuel [H. L. S. Samuel], *Memoirs* (1945) · B. Wasserstein, *Herbert Samuel: a political life* (1992) · WW **Archives** Brandeis University, Waltham, Massachusetts, MSS · HLRO, corresp. and MSS · Israel State Archives, corresp. and papers relating to Palestine and Zionism · St Ant. Oxf., Middle East Centre, corresp. [copies] · U. Southampton L., family corresp. | BL, corresp. with Lord Gladstone, Add. MS 45992 · BL, corresp. with Albert Mansbridge, Add. MS 65253 · BL, corresp. with Society of Authors, Add. MS 63324 · BLPES, corresp. with Lord Beveridge · BLPES, letters to the Fabian Society · BLPES, corresp. with E. Morel · Bodl. Oxf., corresp. with Viscount Addison · Bodl. Oxf., corresp. with Herbert Asquith · Bodl. Oxf., corresp. with L. G. Curtis · Bodl. Oxf., corresp. with Gilbert Murray · Bodl. RH, corresp. with Lord Lugard · CAC Cam., corresp. with A. V. Hill · CUL, corresp. with Lord Hardinge · HLRO, letters to David Lloyd George · King's AC Cam., letters to Oscar Browning · NA Scot., Lothian MSS · NL Wales, corresp., mainly with Clement Davies · NL Wales, corresp. with Sir J. H. Lewis · Nuffield Oxf., corresp. with Lord Mottistone · Rehovot, Israel, Weizmann MSS · U. Durham L., corresp. with Sir G. F. Clayton · U. Newcastle, Robinson L., corresp. with Walter Runciman · U. Newcastle, Robinson L., corresp. with C. P. Trevelyan · U. Southampton L., corresp. with Cecil Roth · Welwyn Garden City Central Library, corresp. with Sir Frederic Osborn | FILM BBC WAC · BFI NFTVA, documentary footage · BFI NFTVA, news footage · BFI NFTVA, party political footage · BFI NFTVA, propaganda footage (Hepworth Manufacturing Company) | SOUND BBC WAC · BL NSA **Likenesses** E. Kapp, drawing, 1920, Barber Institute of Fine Arts, Birmingham · W. Stoneman, three photographs, 1928–48, NPG · H. Coster, photographs, 1930–39, NPG · O. Edis, photograph, c.1932, NPG [*see illus.*] · F. O. Salisbury, oils, 1949, National Liberal Club, London · F. Rederer, oils, 1953, NPG · P. Vincze, silver bronze medallion, 1960, NPG · A. Aroch (*The high commissioner*), Israel Museum, Jerusalem · W. Salisbury, portrait, Balliol Oxf. · photograph (as high commissioner), Israel State Archives · photographs, HLRO · photographs, Israel State Archives · photographs, repro. in Wasserstein, *Herbert Samuel* **Wealth at death** £28,919 6s. 0d.: probate, 3 April 1963, CGPLA Eng. & Wales

Samuel, Howard (1914–1961), property developer and publisher, was born on 2 February 1914 at 1 Maisemore Mansions, Canfield Gardens, Hampstead, London, one of at least two sons of Henry Samuel, jeweller, and his wife, Grace Jacobs. He was educated at St Paul's School, where he became interested in rare books and while still very young acquired sufficient expertise to contribute to trade catalogues. His business career put a stop to his book collecting activities, but after he had amassed his fortune he resumed this interest and assembled what his *Times* obituary called 'an important and highly individual collection'.

Samuel went into surveying after leaving school, founding the agency Basil and Howard Samuel with his brother Basil. Their cousin, Harold Samuel, was also active in the commercial property market; he eventually became Britain's most successful post-war property developer and founder of Land Securities, the country's largest property company. Howard Samuel served in the army in the ranks throughout the Second World War and turned to property dealing during the post-war property boom, and with his brother formed a company which acquired extensive properties in London. Great Portland Estates Ltd was subsequently formed to hold these interests and rapidly grew into a major concern. The firm obtained some of its initial mortgage finance from the church commissioners and later took part in the redevelopment of the commissioners' Hyde Park estate. Samuel's property interests formed the core of a considerable business fortune, worth almost £4 million at his death.

Howard Samuel was said to be a man with a strong social conscience, which a long friendship with Aneurin Bevan and Jennie Lee served to develop, and was an active supporter of the Labour Party. He was able to develop his political interests via a close association with the left-wing newspaper *Tribune*—he joined its board in 1952 and was an active contributor—and the *New Statesman*. While visiting the Bevans he met his wife, Jane Lane, the artist. They married in 1944 and later divorced, but remarried in 1959. The couple had a son and a daughter.

In addition to his property interests, Samuel's other main area of business activity was publishing, which allowed him to further his enduring interest in books. By the beginning of the 1960s he controlled a number of publishing houses, and shortly before his death he had made an unconditional offer for all the outstanding ordinary shares of Associated Publishers. In addition to his interest in books, Samuel was also recognized as a discriminating connoisseur of painting.

Samuel was found dead in shallow water off Glyfada, near Athens, on 6 May 1961, having drowned after a heart attack. He was survived by his wife.   PETER SCOTT

Sources *The Times* (8 May 1961), 17 · *Estates Gazette* (20 May 1961), 513 · 'Mr Samuel's death by accident', *The Times* (9 May 1961), 11 · O. Marriott, *The property boom* (1967) · *The Times* (25 May 1961) · E. L. Erdman, *People and property* (1982) · b. cert. · *CGPLA Eng. & Wales* (1961)
Wealth at death £3,848,222 6s. 5d.: probate, 23 May 1961, *CGPLA Eng. & Wales*

Samuel, Marcus, first Viscount Bearsted (1853–1927), petroleum entrepreneur, was born in Whitechapel, east London, on 5 November 1853, the second son of Marcus Samuel, a merchant, and his wife, Abigail, daughter of Abraham Moss, both of London Jewish families. He was educated privately, and began his commercial career as the owner of a small business in Houndsditch, trading principally in painted shells. Other lines were afterwards added, such as curios of all kinds, general produce, and rice. On 9 January 1881 he married Fanny Elizabeth, only daughter of Benjamin Benjamin, and they had two sons and two daughters. The younger son was killed in the First World War.

It was during a visit to Japan on behalf of his business that Samuel first became acquainted with the petroleum industry. He decided to commence the shipping of oil, and in 1890 he was approached by the French Rothschilds with a scheme to export oil from their Russian oilfields to the East. Having secured permission for oil tankers to use the Suez Canal in 1892, Samuel was able to sell this Russian oil cheaper than its American competitor in Asia. This coup, which challenged Standard Oil's hold on the Asian markets, laid the basis for a successful oil business. Subsequently, Samuel sought to locate a source of oil nearer his markets. In 1897 his drillers found oil in Borneo. Soon afterwards, in October 1897, the Shell Trading and Transport Company was formed, the name being taken from Samuel's original business. The company began with a capital of £1.8 million; at the time of Samuel's death thirty years later this had increased to more than £26 million.

For a time the British company encountered a serious

Marcus Samuel, first Viscount Bearsted (1853–1927), by Sir William Orpen, 1921

rival in the Royal Dutch Petroleum Company, which obtained its oil from Java and Borneo. Samuel was primarily a merchant, and he lacked the organizational skills to manage a large integrated oil company. As a result, he proved no match for the dynamic leader of Royal Dutch, Henri Deterding, who was determined to build a world oil company which could match J. D. Rockefeller's Standard Oil. During the 1900s Samuel, increasingly distracted by civic duties, made a series of costly business misjudgements. These included an ill-fated contract in 1901 to buy a large quantity of oil from the newly discovered Spindletop field in Texas and ship it to Europe. When the oil stopped flowing, Samuel was left with a critical shortage of oil as well as a fleet of oil tankers which had to be converted into cattle boats. In 1903 Samuel merged his Eastern marketing activities with those of Royal Dutch and the Rothschilds. This arrangement did not work in Shell's favour. By 1906 the position of Shell was so weak that Samuel was obliged to accept a full merger offer from Deterding, under which the combined Royal Dutch–Shell was created with 60 per cent Dutch control. Under Deterding's leadership, this became and remained one of the world's biggest oil companies.

Samuel was knighted in 1898 for services rendered in the salvage of HMS *Victorious*. In February of that year this vessel was grounded near Port Said, and she was pulled off by two of the Shell company's tugs. After the merger, Deterding retained Samuel as the figurehead of the Shell group in Britain. During the First World War Samuel and

Shell were very active in the war effort (though his pomposity and outspoken views earned him the dislike of many government officials and politicians): not only was every form of petroleum made available wherever it was required either for the land or the sea forces, but a petroleum distillate, which formed the basis of the high explosive TNT (trinitrotoluene), was provided in large quantities. A refinery was established near Bristol for this purpose, the erection of the works being carried out, owing to Samuel's energy, in a few weeks.

Although he was one of the first to appreciate the value of oil fuel as a substitute for coal, Samuel's contention was that the burning of oil under boilers was a waste of power. He was always an advocate of the internal combustion engine for ships, and his efforts were directed to proving that this type of propulsion could be made suitable for large vessels. During the war he formed a company to test this possibility by experiment and enquiry.

Samuel was at one time a prominent figure in the life of the City of London. His municipal career began in 1891 when he was elected alderman for Portsoken ward. He was chosen as sheriff in 1894, and was lord mayor of London in 1902–3. In this capacity he presided over the committee which formulated the scheme for the Port of London Authority. He carried out his duties as lord mayor with zest, paying a state visit to Brussels and other places, as well as entertaining the French president at the Guildhall. When his year of office came to an end he was created a baronet for his municipal and other services.

Samuel's benefactions to hospitals and other philanthropic schemes were considerable. In 1895 he bought for his residence The Mote, near Maidstone. When war broke out in Europe he turned this house into a hospital for noncommissioned officers, continuing to live there and interesting himself in the welfare of the patients. In 1921 Samuel was raised to the peerage as Baron Bearsted, of Maidstone, and in 1925 was advanced to a viscountcy. He received the freedom of Sheffield and of Maidstone, and was awarded honorary degrees from the universities of Sheffield and Cambridge in 1924 and 1925 respectively.

Samuel's wife died on 16 January 1927, and he survived her by only a few hours, dying at his home, 3 Hamilton Place, Park Lane, London, on 17 January 1927. His estate, valued at £4 million, was one of the highest cash values then recorded. His elder son, Walter Horace *Samuel, succeeded his father as second viscount.

ALFRED COCHRANE, rev. G. JONES

Sources R. D. Q. Henriques, *Marcus Samuel: first Viscount Bearsted and founder of the Shell Trading and Transport Company* (c.1960) · D. Yergin, *The prize: the epic quest for oil, money and power* (1991) · G. Jones, *The state and the emergence of the British oil industry* (1981) **Archives** GL, diary as lord mayor of London | London, Shell Archives · The Hague, Shell Archives **Likenesses** London Stereoscopic Co., photograph, c.1902, NPG · W. Orpen, oils, 1921, Guildhall Art Gallery, London [see illus.] · W. Stoneman, photograph, 1921, NPG **Wealth at death** £4,000,000: probate, 3 Feb 1927, *CGPLA Eng. & Wales*

Samuel [Samuels], **Moses** (1795–1860), watchmaker and Hebrew scholar, was born in London, the youngest of three sons of Emanuel Menachem Samuel (c.1755–c.1800) and Hanna (Hinde). Emanuel Samuel, who bore the Hebrew title 'the learned', had left his birthplace, Kempen in the province of Posen, and settled in London about 1775. At the age of ten Moses moved with his mother to Liverpool where his brothers had already settled. He lived there for the rest of his life, residing for the longest period in Paradise Street. He seems to have received little formal education but was an outstanding autodidact and is said to have mastered twelve languages, including Chinese. Samuel set up in business as a watchmaker and silversmith. In 1821 he married Harriet (1793–1843), daughter of Israel Israel of Bury Street, St Mary Axe, London. They had two daughters and three sons; the latter all married daughters of Schreiner Wolfe of Great Yarmouth, first mayor of Kimberley in the northern Cape Colony.

Samuel's main source of literary inspiration was the philosophy of Moses Mendelssohn, whom he called 'the grand luminary of science and knowledge' (*Memoirs of Moses Mendelsohn*, 1825, vi). Samuel became his chief English interpreter and translator; he published English editions of Mendelssohn's *Jerusalem* (1838) and of the celebrated correspondence between Mendelssohn and Lavater, published as part of *Memoirs*. Samuel praised the 'inimitable mellifluence' of Mendelssohn's style and the 'pleasing ductility of his most exquisite cogitations'. Samuel favoured 'a plain, almost literal, flowing, easily comprehended translation' (*Address on the Position of the Jews in Britain*, 1844, 11). His renderings of Mendelssohn succeeded in conveying the charm and lucidity of the original and remained the standard English versions for more than a century.

Samuel also translated into English the pseudepigraphical Book of Jasher, a supposedly ancient Hebrew text, which Samuel persuaded himself was authentic. He sold his translation for £150 to the American-Jewish newspaper owner Mordecai M. Noah, who published it in New York in 1840. Samuel's name was not mentioned, since the two men differed over the authenticity of the work. The translation was accepted as accurate but the publication provoked criticism by scholars who rejected the claims made on behalf of the text. It won acceptance, however, by the Mormon prophet Joseph Smith.

Samuel was a determined foe of Christian proselytization among the Jews and published anti-missionary pamphlets in 1819, 1822, and 1827. A liberal in politics, he was a vigorous campaigner for Jewish emancipation. In 1840, while attending a meeting on the subject, he collapsed and in 1845 he became paralysed. 'My doctor informed me that if I did not give up my abstruse calculations I should have another attack', he later wrote to Lord Brougham (Samuel to Brougham, 24 Feb 1850, UCL, Brougham MSS). Samuel nevertheless persisted in his literary activity and attributed his partial recovery to the embrace of total abstinence. During the later part of his life he earned a living as a teacher of languages.

Like his hero Mendelssohn, Samuel combined strict orthodoxy with attraction to the ideas of the Enlightenment. While opposed to the incipient Reform movement in Judaism, he favoured modest innovations in synagogal practice, such as the institution of lectures in English. In 1846–7, with D. M. Isaacs, minister to the Liverpool Jewish community, Samuel edited *Kos Yeshuot* ('Cup of Salvation'), a monthly magazine 'devoted to the advocacy of Orthodox Jewish principles'. Many of the contributions appeared in Hebrew with English translations. The magazine's publication of original articles in Hebrew on secular subjects, for example, one by Samuel celebrating the railway engine, was unusual for the period, particularly in England.

Unlike his brother Louis (1794–1859), who died a rich man, Samuel remained poor to the end. He nevertheless acquired a library of rare Hebrew books. Samuel's business prospered in the hands of his descendants. By the turn of the century it developed into the first multiple shop jeweller in Britain. Trading as 'H. Samuel' it became the most successful retail watch and jewellery chain in the country. Moses Samuel's great-grandson, Gilbert Samuel Edgar, served as chairman from 1935 to 1978. Moses Samuel died at Ranelagh Place, Mount Pleasant, Liverpool, on 17 April 1860 and was buried in the Liverpool Jewish cemetery. He left 'effects under £100'. His descendants included a Roman Catholic priest, Father Edward Hill, and a Metropolitan Police magistrate, Geoffrey George Raphael. His great-nephew was Herbert Louis Samuel, first Viscount Samuel.					BERNARD WASSERSTEIN

Sources *Jewish Chronicle* (27 April 1860) · *Voice of Jacob* (7 June 1844) · *Voice of Jacob* (5 July 1844) · L. Wolf, ed., *The history and genealogy of the Jewish families of Yates and Samuel of Liverpool* (1901) · A. Franklin, ed., *Records of the Franklin family* (1935) · R. D'A. Hart, *The Samuel family of Liverpool and London from 1755 onwards* (1958) · B. L. Benas, 'Records of the Jews of Liverpool', *Transactions of the Historic Society of Lancashire and Cheshire*, 51 (1899), 45–84 · J. Picciotto, *Sketches of Anglo-Jewish history* (1875) · M. Margoliouth, *History of the Jews of Great Britain*, 3 vols. (1851) · T. M. Endelman, *The Jews of Georgian England, 1714–1830* (1979) · J. Sarna, *Jacksonian Jew: the two worlds of Mordecai Noah* (1981) · A. A. Chiel, 'The mysterious book of Jasher', *Judaism*, 26/3 (1977), 367–74 · W. Rosenstock, 'Lord Samuel's Ancestry', *AJR Information* (Oct 1958) · Liverpool poll books, U. Lond., Institute of Historical Research · Liverpool poll books, Liverpool Public Library · Liverpool directories · d. cert.

Likenesses double portrait (with his wife), repro. in Hart, *The Samuel family*, pl. 3

Wealth at death under £100: probate, 8 Aug 1860, *CGPLA Eng. & Wales*

Samuel, Raphael Elkan (1934–1996), historian, was born on 26 December 1934 in the Elizabeth Garrett Anderson Hospital, London, the son of Barnett Samuel (1906–1971), a solicitor, and Minna Nerenstein, later Keal (1909–1999) [*see* Keal, Minna], a composer. Raphael was the only child of Jewish parents who separated when he was six and later divorced. He was brought up in Hampstead Garden Suburb and subsequently around Parliament Hill by his mother; she taught the piano and was also a partner in the family business Shapiro Valentine, a bookshop specializing in Hebraica. She became a communist activist and much of Samuel's childhood was spent with his aunt and uncle Miriam and Chimen Abramsky, who provided a second home.

Samuel's particular combination of political activism

Raphael Elkan Samuel (1934–1996), by Stefan Wallgren, early 1990s

and passionate interest in history was first nurtured by his uncle Chimen Abramsky, a renowned Judaic scholar, book collector, and historian of socialism. In 1939 Raphael and his school were evacuated to Aspley Guise in Bedfordshire, while his mother became an aircraft factory worker in Slough, where she met her second husband, Bill Keal. Between 1945 and 1952 Samuel attended the progressive King Alfred's School in Hampstead and from there, inspired by his history teacher John Handford, he won a scholarship to Balliol College, Oxford. Between 1952 and 1956 (with a year off for medical reasons) he read history under another political mentor and lifelong friend, the seventeenth-century historian Christopher Hill.

Even as a dedicated communist at the height of the cold war, Samuel (then known as Ralph) made a considerable impact on a broad range of his Oxford contemporaries, both intellectually and practically. Practically, he revived the moribund socialist society as a novel forum for discussion between socialists and communists, and a seedbed of the future new left. Intellectually he arrived in Oxford, already well versed in Marxist historical debate through his schoolboy membership of the Communist Party Historians' Group (which included Hobsbawm, Thompson, Hill, Hilton, and others). He himself drew no distinction between his political and historical work. It was allegedly on party orders that he devoted his final year exclusively to academic work and gained a first-class degree. This total dedication to communism was shattered in 1956 by Khrushchov's revelations about Stalin and the Soviet invasion of Hungary. Samuel left the Communist Party, and—together with his Oxford contemporaries Stuart Hall, Charles Taylor, and Gabriel Pearson—founded the *Universities and Left Review*, one of the starting points of the new left movement in Britain and a forerunner, together with Edward Thompson's *New Reasoner*, of the *New Left Review*, founded in 1960.

Although briefly an editor of *New Left Review*, Samuel's dissociation from communism provoked in him a crisis of confidence, which lasted well into the 1960s. After Oxford he joined Michael Young's Institute of Community Studies to study youth and housing in Bethnal Green. Attachment to the institute also led him to share a house at 19 Elder Street, Spitalfields—once a Huguenot and weaving quarter in the oldest part of the East End on the edge of the City—which he later bought and made his permanent home. In the early 1960s, however, a near breakdown led him to seek refuge and even consider settling in Ireland. A gradual re-engagement with Britain was prompted by Christopher Hill, who in 1962 secured for him a part-time tutorship in sociology at Ruskin College, a trade-union-supported Oxford college which prepared working people who had left school without qualifications for university. He continued to work at Ruskin until the last year of his life, when he became professor at the University of East London and the director of a centre for London history.

In 1966 Samuel put on the first of the annual 'history workshops' at Ruskin. Not content with the existing diploma course, he encouraged students to pursue historical research projects which built on their own experiences, and to present their findings alongside established academics at the yearly workshops. These workshops also signalled a renewal of political engagement sparked, in particular, by his alarm about the condition of Britain around the time of Enoch Powell's 'rivers of blood' speech. The workshops lasted until the 1980s and regularly attracted over 1000 participants, mainly students and teachers from Britain and abroad and a wide spectrum of unaffiliated 1960s-style radicals. It was at the workshop of 1969 that the National Women's Liberation Conference was first proposed. Samuel published the best of these Ruskin research essays in a series of history workshop booklets.

In 1976, together with a number of new left, Oxford, and Ruskin friends, Samuel founded the *History Workshop Journal*, and he remained one of its most active editors until his death. His impact was clearly to be detected in the journal's initial sources of inspiration: the experimentalism of Joan Littlewood's Theatre Workshop, the commitment to accessibility pioneered in adult education, echoes of a popular front politics uneasily combined with more anarchist notions of history from below.

From this time Samuel also began to publish more of his own work. After his early sociological work in Bethnal Green, Samuel's interests switched to Ireland. It was archival work on the famine and the nineteenth-century Irish poor which rekindled his passion for history. But he published nothing until the early 1970s, when collaborative work with his students and a growing interest in oral history resulted in a study of quarry labourers in Headington, *Village Life and Labour* (1975), and a pioneering investigation of manual work in Victorian England, 'The workshop of the world' (*History Workshop Journal*, 3, 1977). Six years of interviews also resulted in an extraordinary autobiographical account by Arthur Harding of the East London Edwardian and inter-war criminal underworld, starting out from childhood in Arthur Morrison's notorious 'Jago' in Shoreditch, published as *East End Underworld* (1981).

In the 1980s political change produced a substantial shift in the direction of Samuel's writing. Mrs Thatcher's defeat of organized labour and her mobilization of patriotic support for the Falklands War, the demise of Marxism, the growth of feminist and post-colonial criticism, and the linguistic turn strongly affected both Samuel and the *History Workshop Journal*. Most important for him was the fading of a politics of class. In a book-length essay for the *New Left Review* he put his own communist childhood and beliefs into a historical perspective, in 'The lost worlds of British communism' (1985–7). He also attempted to set the split between Labour and the SDP in a longer-term social-historical context, initially ascribing the disintegration of pre-1950 class identities to the emergence of a new consumerist middle class. By the end of the 1980s, however, he had become convinced that this political shift was only one component of a larger set of social and cultural changes involving all groups in the population.

Samuel tried to grasp this process through an examination of changing attitudes towards the past. He actively participated in the political debate about the place of history in the national curriculum, but always stressed that historical awareness was as much a product of 'unofficial' knowledge (myth, ritual, childood memory, fiction, fantasy) as of formal schooling. In his contributions to the three volumes he edited on *Patriotism* in 1989 he noted that in the preceding thirty years there had grown up an 'extraordinary and ever-growing popular enthusiasm for the recovery of the national past'. He defended this development as a phenomenon which drew as much on radical as on conservative or nationalist roots. By 1994, in his last book, *Theatres of Memory*, intended as the first volume of a trilogy, this interest had been elaborated into a major research study of 'memory work' and the changing role of history in late twentieth-century Britain. He argued against detractors, especially on the left, that the expanding historical culture from 'theme parks' and 'living museums' to 'heritage' and 'retro-chic' was not only more democratic but also more inclusive of minorities of all kinds. Shortly after the publication of *Theatres of Memory* Samuel developed cancer of the lung, from which he died at his home at 19 Elder Street, Spitalfields, on 9 December 1996. He was buried in Highgate cemetery on 18 December. A second volume of the trilogy, *Island Stories*, was published posthumously in 1998.

In his personal life, Raphael Samuel actively sustained a

wide range of friendships dating from different periods in his life: from his early Oxford days, Stuart Hall, Dennis Butt, and Peter Sedgwick; from his Ruskin years, Tim Mason, Gareth Stedman Jones, Alun Howkins, Sally Alexander, Sheila Rowbotham, Jerry White, Barbara Taylor. His adult life was also punctuated by a series of important and intellectually creative relationships with women, including Jean McCrindle, Lydia Howard, Hannah Mitchell, and Miranda Chaytor. Particularly important were the years 1970–76, during which he lived in Elder Street with Anna Davin and her children. On 3 July 1987 he married university lecturer Alison Elizabeth Light (*b.* 1955). It was a close and happy relationship, reinforced by shared passions and commitments, and it was an enormous source of strength throughout his last illness.

No account of Samuel's writings or of his publishing and political activity could convey the extraordinary impact he made on all who met him or saw him speak. His physical appearance was in itself arresting. It conveyed intensity, energy, singularity of purpose, and drivenness, but lightened by considerable charm, an infectious sense of humour, and a never diminished boyish enthusiasm. He was slightly built, with a thin angular face, a sallow complexion, burning black eyes, and a mop of black hair which in middle age was sustained by the substitution of a long side-lock swept precariously across the crown of his head to conceal a bald pate. His dress, like his appearance, was singular, indefinably French, bohemian—even slightly dandyish—but harking back several decades, like a denizen of a left-bank café in a film from the 1940s or 1950s.

In his youth a memorable political orator (who reputedly even addressed workers in languages other than his own), Samuel brought an equally theatrical talent to the delivery of academic papers. He never wrote out lectures, but instead brought thick files bulging with clippings, dog-eared photocopies, and pasted pieces of paper, each containing a few lines of typescript. Characteristically in his talks a few propositions were thickly elaborated with a mosaic of connected quotations, retrieved with a touch of suspenseful uncertainty from the bulging files and accompanied by a frequent sweeping back of the thinning mop of hair. The effect at its best was electrifying. Few who attended ever forgot the 'paper' he delivered to the Oxford Stubbs Society on the Irish famine: an eloquent, fiercely indignant, and witheringly contemptuous yet scholarly denunciation of whig attitudes. At their most powerful, these rhetorical powers introduced a passion into historical debate matched only by Edward Thompson.

As in all memorable theatrical performance, power of delivery was inseparable from risk. A precise sense of time and timing was essential, if audience and speaker were to share the suspense of locating the right quotation from the jumble of manuscripts—a suspense which could easily turn into impatience or exasperation if the hunt went on too long. This happened spectacularly in Oxford on the occasion of a special Ford lecture which Samuel delivered

on 'The conservative view of history' in 1994. There, nervous and perhaps exhilarated by being honoured by Oxford, for which he felt long-standing affection, he spent so much time on preliminaries and paper-sorting, that he barely reached the substance of the lecture at all.

Samuel's importance, therefore, cannot be measured solely by his writing or even by his organizational achievements. From his time in the Communist Party, through the foundation of the new left, to the establishment of annual history workshops and the development of the *History Workshop Journal*, Samuel was a brilliant and tireless, if eccentric, inspirer of events and creator of institutions which would not have come into existence without his energy and his ability to inspire others.

GARETH STEDMAN JONES

Sources S. Hall, S. Rowbotham, and R. Blackburn, 'Raphael Samuel 1934–1996', *New Left Review*, 1221 (Jan–Feb 1997) · *Raphael Samuel, 1934–1996: tributes and appreciations* (1997) · A. Light, 'A biographical note on the text', in R. Samuel, *Island stories* (1998) · R. Samuel, 'The lost world of British communism', *New Left Review*, 154 (1985) · R. Samuel, 'The lost world of British communism', *New Left Review*, 156 (1985) · R. Samuel, 'The lost world of British communism', *New Left Review*, 165 (1987) · *The Times* (11 Dec 1996) · *The Guardian* (10–11 Dec 1996) · *The Guardian* (21 Dec 1996) · *The Independent* (11 Dec 1996) · *Daily Telegraph* (12 Dec 1996) · b. cert. · m. cert. · d. cert. · personal knowledge (2004) · private information (2004) [widow]
Archives Bishopsgate Institute, London · priv. coll.
Likenesses S. Wallgren, bromide fibre print, 1990–94, NPG [*see illus.*] · photograph, repro. in *The Guardian* (10 Dec 1996) · photograph, repro. in *The Independent* · photograph, repro. in *Daily Telegraph* · photograph, repro. in *The Times*
Wealth at death £298,659: probate, 3 March 1997, *CGPLA Eng. & Wales*

Samuel, Richard (*d.* 1787), portrait painter, of whose parents nothing is known, entered the Royal Academy Schools on 1 October 1770. He twice obtained the gold medal of the Society of Arts for the best original historical drawing, and in 1773 was awarded a premium for an improvement in laying mezzotint grounds. He showed five works there and became assistant secretary in 1779, a post he held until his death. Samuel contributed to Royal Academy exhibitions, between 1772 and 1785, sixteen paintings comprising small whole-lengths, with an occasional conversation or subject-piece, and in 1779 his *Nine Living Muses of Great Britain* (National Portrait Gallery, London). He painted somewhat in the style of Gainsborough a large portrait of the engraver Robert Pollard (National Portrait Gallery, London; 1784). In 1786 he published a short pamphlet *Remarks on the Utility of Drawing and Painting*. Engravings after his work are represented in the National Portrait Gallery and the British Museum. Samuel died at his home in Beaufort Buildings, London, on 26 July 1787. Very few examples of his paintings are known.

L. H. CUST, *rev.* TINA FISKE

Sources R. Samuel, *Remarks on the utility of drawing and painting* (1786) · B. Stewart and M. Cutten, *The dictionary of portrait painters in Britain up to 1920* (1997) · Waterhouse, *18c painters* · D. Foskett, *A dictionary of British miniature painters*, 2 vols. (1972) · S. C. Hutchison, 'The Royal Academy Schools, 1768–1830', *Walpole Society*, 38 (1960–62), 123–91, esp. 136 · Graves, *RA exhibitors* · Graves, *Soc. Artists* · K. K. Yung, *National Portrait Gallery: complete illustrated catalogue, 1856–*

1979, ed. M. Pettman (1981) • Redgrave, *Artists* • Graves, *Artists* • *Engraved Brit. ports.* • *GM*, 1st ser., 57 (1787), 646

Samuel, Walter Horace, second Viscount Bearsted (1882–1948), art collector and philanthropist, was born on 13 March 1882 in London, the eldest child and only surviving son of Marcus *Samuel, first Viscount Bearsted (1853–1927), and his wife, Fanny Elizabeth Benjamin (1857–1927). Educated at Eton College and at New College, Oxford, Walter Samuel's childhood coincided with the rapid expansion of his father's family trading business, M. Samuel & Co., into the sale of petroleum. In 1904 he joined the staff of the Shell Transport and Trading Company (founded by his father and uncle in 1897), becoming a director in 1907 and succeeding his father as chairman in 1921, a post which he held until his own retirement in 1946. Samuel's marriage on 23 July 1908 to Dorothea (Dorothy; 1882/3–1949), daughter of Edward Montefiore Micholls, gave him a family of three sons: Marcus Richard, subsequently third Viscount Bearsted (1909–1986), Peter Montefiore, who became fourth Viscount Bearsted (1911–1996), and Anthony Gerald (b. 1917). In the First World War, Samuel served with the West Kent yeomanry on the general staff, ending the war as a captain with the Military Cross. In the Second World War he served in the intelligence corps with the rank of colonel.

His position and great wealth gave Samuel the opportunity to pursue the interests for which he is best remembered: philanthropy and art collecting. An observant Jew of the United Synagogue, he supported many Jewish charities, including the Bearsted Memorial Hospital at Stoke Newington and the Bearsted maternity home at Hampton Court, both in London. He worked for the emigration of Jews from Nazi Germany in the 1930s and, although no Zionist himself, for a peaceful accommodation in Palestine. He was an art collector and public benefactor even before succeeding to his father's titles in 1927. The first viscount had financed a new wing for Maidstone Museum to house his son's Japanese collection, which reflected the family's oriental trading activities. Samuel had started collecting paintings by European old masters before the First World War and purchases, inspired by his fine eye and personal tastes, continued unabated until the year of his death, forming one of the most important collections of the century. In 1927 he acquired Upton House on Edge Hill in Warwickshire where he could indulge his passion for hunting. He transformed the house into a suitable setting for his growing collection, which included the original versions of *The Haymakers* and *The Reapers* (both 1783) by George Stubbs, El Greco's *Disrobing of Christ*, and *The Dormition of the Virgin* by Pieter Bruegel the elder; works by other masters such as Hogarth, George Romney, Giovanni di Paolo, Guardi, Steen, and Metsu also featured. Acquired individually, mainly through dealers and with the benefit of advice from such experts as Sir Alec Martin of Christies, the paintings chosen by Samuel also included masterpieces by lesser known artists. Combining his philanthropy with his love of art, in 1948 he gave this internationally important collection, together with Upton House, its fine garden, and a large endowment, to the National Trust.

Samuel was chairman of the trustees of the National Gallery, a trustee of the Tate Gallery, a major benefactor of the Ashmolean Museum, Oxford (with a donation of £18,000 in 1938), and in the last years of his life chairman of the Whitechapel Art Gallery in London. Reserved and private in character, Samuel spoke in the House of Lords only on the subjects of petroleum and Jewish affairs. He died at Upton House on 8 November 1948.

OLIVER LANE

Sources R. Henriques, *Bearsted* (1961) • S. Howarth, *A century in oil* (1997) • *The Times* (10 Nov 1948) • *Jewish Chronicle* (12 Nov 1948) • private information (2004) [V. Tonge, Maidstone Museum and Art Gallery; family] • National Trust, *Upton House* (1990) • Burke, *Peerage* (1959) • m. cert.

Likenesses J. Lavery, oils, 1917, priv. coll. • photographs, NPG

Wealth at death £863,573 7s. 1d.: probate, 2 Dec 1948, *CGPLA Eng. & Wales*

Samuel, William (*fl.* 1551–1569), poet, was the author of an important example of scriptural literature in the reign of Edward VI. Nothing of Samuel is known except from the printed copies of his works. In 1558 and 1569 he is described as 'Minister'. Although the *Dictionary of National Biography* mentions connections with Samuels in Northampton or Cornwall, the surviving works imply residence in London. On the title-page of *The Abridgemente of Goddes Statutes in Myter* (1551) he calls himself 'servaunt to the duke of Somerset hys grace' and appends a dedicatory letter to Seymour's wife, Anne Stanhope. The dedications place Samuel at the centre of Edwardian religious patronage. *The Abridgemente* promised to encourage piety by reducing every chapter of the Old Testament to a single, memorizable stanza in fourteeners. A mnemonic device makes each stanza begin with a consecutive letter of the alphabet, with a key using the five fingers to help readers remember where they are. The 1551 edition (printed by Robert Crowley) contained the Pentateuch. Successive editions took the work up to Kings in 1558, and in 1569 completed the canonical books of the Old Testament. The abridgement can be brutal: Psalm 119 is reduced to eight lines. Samuel's promise to add the Apocrypha, if death did not intervene, was left unfulfilled.

Samuel's signature is also found at the end of three other undated works in verse. *The Practice of Prelates* is a mock confession in verse by the pope, cheerfully admitting the loss of England to the protestant cause. *A Warnyng for the Cittie of London*, which refers to Edward VI as still living, paints a picture of the city in the midst of religious conflict, urging further reformation. Humfrey Powell printed both these works. *The Love of God* carries no notice of printer or date, but refers to Queen Mary as mercifully dead.

BRIAN CUMMINGS

Sources W. Samuel, *The abridgemente of goddes statutes in myter* (1551) • J. N. King, *English Reformation literature: the Tudor origins of the protestant tradition* (1982) • DNB

Samuelson, Sir Bernhard, first baronet (1820–1905), ironmaster and promoter of technical education, was the eldest of the six sons of Samuel Henry Samuelson (1789–

1863), merchant, and his wife, Sarah Hertz (*d.* 1875). He was born at Hamburg on 22 November 1820 during a visit of his mother to the city. In his infancy his father settled at Hull. Educated at a private school at Skirlaugh, Yorkshire, Samuelson left at fourteen to enter his father's office. At home he developed a love of music and a command of modern languages. He was soon apprenticed to Rudolph Zwilchenhart & Co., a Swiss firm of merchants, at Liverpool, where he spent six years. In 1837 he was sent to Warrington by his masters to purchase locomotive engines for export to Prussia. The experience led him to seek expert knowledge of engineering, and it suggested to him the possibility of expanding greatly the business of exporting English machinery to the continent. In 1842 he was made manager of the export business of Sharp, Stewart & Co., engineers, of Manchester, for whom he travelled abroad, but owing to the domestic railway boom of 1845, the firm gave up the continental trade.

He married in 1844 Caroline (*d.* 1886), daughter of Henry Blundell of Hull, with whom he had four sons and four daughters. In 1846 Samuelson went to Tours, and established railway works of his own, which he carried on with success until the revolution of 1848 drove him back to England.

In 1848 Samuelson purchased a small factory producing agricultural implements at Banbury, which the death of the founder, James Gardner, brought into the market. Samuelson developed the industry energetically, and the works, which in 1872 produced no less than 8000 reaping-machines, rapidly became one of the largest of its kind. A branch was established at Orléans. The business, which was turned into a limited liability company in 1887, helped to convert Banbury from an agricultural town into an industrial centre.

Meanwhile in 1853 Samuelson had met, at the Cleveland agricultural show, John Vaughan, who had discovered in 1851 the seam of Cleveland ironstone, and now convinced Samuelson of the certain future of the Cleveland iron trade. Samuelson erected blast furnaces at South Bank, near Middlesbrough, within a mile of the works of Bolckow and Vaughan at Eston. These he worked until 1863, when they were sold, and more extensive premises were built in the neighbourhood of Newport. Samuelson, who was keenly interested in the practical applications of science, studied the construction of blast furnaces, and resolved to enlarge their cubic capacity at the expense of their height. By 1870 eight furnaces were at work, most of them of greater capacity than any others in the district. In 1872 between 2500 and 3000 tons of pig iron were produced weekly. In 1871 a description of the Newport iron-works, which he presented to the Institution of Civil Engineers, was awarded a Telford medal. His first wife having died in 1886, he married in 1889 Lelia Mathilda, daughter of Chevalier Leon Serena and widow of William Denny, shipbuilder of Dumbarton.

In 1887 the iron-working firm of Sir B. Samuelson & Co. Ltd was formed with a nominal capital of £275,000. Samuelson was chairman of the company until 1895, when he handed over the chairmanship to his second son,

Francis. The blast furnaces were in 1905 producing about 300,000 tons of pig iron annually, and the by-products from the coke ovens started in 1896 averaged about 270,000 tons of coke, 12,000 tons of tar, 3500 of sulphate of ammonia, and 150,000 gallons of crude naphtha.

An important extension of Samuelson's commercial energies took place in July 1870. He then built the Britannia ironworks at Middlesbrough, his third manufacturing enterprise (which subsequently came under the ownership of Dorman Long & Co.). The Britannia works housed the largest plant then in operation with a vast output of iron, tar, and by-products. One of Samuelson's endeavours which bore tribute to his mechanical ambition came to nothing. He was anxious to make steel from Cleveland ore—an effort in which no success had yet been achieved. He learned on the continent of the Siemens-Martin process, and now spent £30,000 in experimenting with it. In 1869 he leased for the purpose the north Yorkshire iron-works at South Stockton; but the attempt proved unsuccessful, though the trial taught some useful lessons to ironmasters.

Samuelson took part in developing the Middlesbrough and Cleveland districts, identifying himself with such local institutions as the Cleveland Institution of Engineers and the Cleveland Literary and Philosophical Society. But his home was at Banbury, and he was prominent there in public affairs. In politics Samuelson was a committed Liberal, and supporter of Gladstone. He first stood as the parliamentary representative for Banbury in February 1859, winning the seat by a majority of one vote. However, he was defeated at the general election two months later. In 1865 he was again elected, and an allegation that he was not of English birth, and therefore ineligible, was examined and confuted by a committee of the House of Commons. He retained the seat in 1868, 1874, and 1880. In 1885, when the borough was merged in the North Oxfordshire division, he was returned for that constituency, and he sat for it until 1895, when he retired and was made a privy councillor. While supporting home rule for Ireland, he lost sympathy with the more radical sentiments which increased in the party during his last years. Although for most of his life a convinced believer in free trade, in his last years Samuelson reached the conclusion that 'a departure from free trade' was 'admissible with a view to widening the area of taxation'. In a paper read before the Political Economy Club in London on 5 July 1901, the chief conclusions of which he summarized in a letter to *The Times* (6 November), he urged a 'tariff for revenue', and sketched out the cardinal points of the tariff reform movement before they had been formulated by Joseph Chamberlain.

In the House of Commons, Samuelson, who gave expert advice on all industrial questions, was best known for his strenuous advocacy of technical instruction. His chief public services were identified with that subject. He believed in the importance for all Englishmen of a rigorous scientific training. In 1867 he investigated personally the conditions of technical education in the chief industrial centres of Europe and made a valuable report (*Parl.*

papers, 1867–8, 54). He was in 1868 chairman of a committee of the House of Commons to inquire into the provisions for instruction in theoretical and applied science for those engaged in industry; and he was a member of the duke of Devonshire's royal commission on scientific instruction (1870), being responsible for that part of the report which dealt with the Department of Science and Art. In 1881 he was made chairman of the royal commission on technical instruction. He was also a member of Viscount Cross's royal commission on elementary education in 1887, and the following year of the parliamentary committee for inquiring into the working of the Education Acts.

Samuelson's activity in other industrial inquiries is evidenced by the series of reports which he prepared in 1867 for the Foreign Office, on the iron trade between England and France, when renewal of the commercial treaty between the two countries was under consideration. He was chairman of parliamentary committees on the patent laws (1871–2) and on railways (1873). He was a member of the royal commission for the Paris Exhibition of 1878, and received from France in that year the cross of the Légion d'honneur. In 1886 he was chairman of the Associated Chambers of Commerce of the United Kingdom.

Samuelson was elected a fellow of the Royal Society in 1881, becoming a member of the council in 1887–8. He joined the Institution of Mechanical Engineers in 1865, and the Institution of Civil Engineers in 1869. He was one of the founders of the Iron and Steel Institute in the latter year, and was president of that body in 1883–5. He was also first president of the Association of Agricultural Engineers.

In 1884 Samuelson established, at Banbury, a technical institute, which was opened by A. J. Mundella on 2 July 1884. Mundella then announced that a baronetcy had been conferred on Samuelson for his services to education.

Samuelson published at Gladstone's request a memoir on Irish land tenure (1869), and a report on the railway goods tariffs of Germany, Belgium, and the Netherlands, presented to the Associated Chambers of Commerce (Birmingham, 1885). Besides his presidential address (1883), he contributed to the *Journal of the Iron and Steel Institute* papers on the Terni steelworks and on the construction and cost of blast furnaces in the Cleveland district (1887).

Samuelson, who was long an enthusiastic yachtsman, died of pneumonia at his residence, 56 Princes Gate, London, on 10 May 1905, and was buried at Torre cemetery, Torquay. He was succeeded in the baronetcy by his eldest son, Henry Bernhard, formerly MP for Frome.

W. F. SPEAR, rev. IAN ST JOHN

Sources *Journal of the Iron and Steel Institute*, 67 (1905), 504–8 · *The Times* (11 May 1905) · *Banbury Guardian* (11 May 1905) · *Yorkshire Post* (11 May 1905) · *The Engineer* (12 May 1905) · *Engineering* (12 May 1905) · Burke, *Peerage* · *CGPLA Eng. & Wales* (1905)
Archives Oxon. RO, personal, business, and educational corresp. and papers
Likenesses H. von Herkomer, oils, 1884 · Fantachiotti of Florence, bronze bust, priv. coll.; replica, Queen Victoria Memorial Hospital Annex, Mont Boron, Nice · Gelli of Florence, oils, priv. coll.
Wealth at death £756,100 17s. 4d.: resworn probate, April 1906, *CGPLA Eng. & Wales*

Samuelson, George Berthold [Bertie] (1889–1947), film producer and director, was born on 6 July 1889 at 41 Nevill Street, Southport, the youngest of the five children of Henschel Samuelson, formerly Metzenberg (1829–1889) and his wife, Bertha (1854/5–1918), daughter of Solomon Weile and his wife, Rahle. The Metzenberg family were Jews from Lissa, Prussia. Members emigrated to Ireland and about 1846 changed the family name to Samuelson. Henschel Samuelson, a tobacconist, died seven weeks after Bertie Samuelson's birth, and the children were brought up in Southport by their mother. The three boys of the family who survived infancy all went on to flourishing careers in the arts: Julian Wylie (as he became known) became famous as a producer of pantomimes, Lauri Wylie wrote for the theatre, and Bertie Samuelson rose high in the film trade. He was educated at University School, Southport, but left at the age of fourteen. After several attempts to found a career, he became interested in the emergent film industry, and initially ran a cinema in Southport, before turning to film rental and establishing in 1910 the Royal Film Agency, which he moved to Birmingham at the end of that year.

The business was a success, and provided Samuelson with the capital to realize his idea of a grand feature film on the life of Queen Victoria. In 1913 he approached producer Will Barker to make the film *Sixty Years a Queen* at Ealing, which Samuelson financed and distributed. The film, a bold patriotic pageant, was a triumph and made his fortune. It persuaded him to expand into production, which he did in 1914, by purchasing Worton Hall, Isleworth, which he converted into studios, and hiring the skilful George Pearson as director. Their first production, an adaptation of the Sherlock Holmes mystery *A Study in Scarlet*, was a noteworthy success, and set the pattern for Samuelson Film Company productions: well-made dramas, generally based on literary properties, with a preference for sentimental scenes from the past.

The war years were Samuelson's finest and saw such productions as *The Great European War* (1914), made within days of the declaration of war (a typically bravura action), *John Halifax, Gentleman*, *Little Women*, *Hindle Wakes*, and his probable masterpiece, *Milestones*, based on the Arnold Bennett and Edward Knoblock play, which employed the kind of multiple-story narrative that he often favoured. Pearson left him after fifteen months, unable to keep up with his ceaseless energy, and subsequent Samuelson productions were directed by Alexander Butler, Fred Paul, and others, including Samuelson himself. A flurry of good productions in 1919 seemed to offer much post-war promise, but the competition of lavish American product, the iniquities of the block-booking system, which held up the release of British films, and the poverty of both budgets and imagination in too many British films spelt doom for Samuelson and his kind. He was more enterprising than most, however, and took a company of British actors and technicians to Hollywood in 1919–20 to make six features that were somewhat too hastily produced. A hoped-for cross-Atlantic exchange agreement with an American production unit never materialized. In 1923 he married Marjorie Vint (1901–1989). Their four sons also went into the film industry.

Samuelson had a fearless approach to film-making, and took on such bold subjects as venereal disease, in his version of Eugene Brieux's *Damaged Goods* (1919), and birth control, in *Married Love* (1923), with a scenario by Marie Stopes. He also diversified into the coach business, at the time of a threatened rail strike. The Samuelson Transport Company, offering trips to seaside resorts, opened in May 1921 and was immediately swamped by business. Samuelson's coaches rapidly became famous, but the venture was heavily dependent on vehicles purchased on credit, and a public flotation was a failure. The strike did not materialize, the fine summer ended, and Samuelson was left with little but debts. He returned to film-making, but the British film industry was now in a slump. In 1922 he started a new company, British Super Films, which lasted only a few months, then formed Napoleon Films, when he made an ambitious drama about Napoleon, *A Royal Divorce* (1923), his last success. Further production floundered in the industry's mid-1920s depression, and a bold move to film Rider Haggard's *She* in studios in Berlin became a singularly ill-fated and costly venture that effectively ruined him. He was made personally bankrupt in 1929. Thereafter he could remain only on the fringes of the film industry, directing cheap 'quota quickies' during the 1930s. He tried other enterprises, including a circulating library, and eventually took a job as a clerk in the offices of film producers British Lion. During the Second World War he was superintendent of two nitrate film depots outside Birmingham, where his film career had properly begun. In his latter years he was afflicted by diabetes.

In his heyday G. B. Samuelson was an unmistakable figure. He was large in frame, dynamic and unstoppable in his enthusiasm, generous and trusting, a lover of all that the cinema could show, but in the end not hardhearted enough to survive long-term in the tough film business. In the 1910s his films were a beacon for the native film industry; those of the 1920s increasingly suffered from poor judgement and poorer budgets, and he in any case belonged to a more innocent age of film-making.

Samuelson died on 17 April 1947 at Crook House, Crook Lane, Great Barr, Aldridge, Staffordshire. His body was cremated. Sadly, he did not live to see the Samuelsons become virtually the first family of the British film industry. He told his sons, 'If you must go into the film industry, be a technician and not a producer' (Dunham and Samuelson, 394). They followed this sound advice. Sydney Samuelson trained as an editor and cameraman, then as a director of documentaries, before founding Samuelson's Film Service, where he was later joined by brothers David (heading the technical side), Michael (operations), and Anthony (finance). The business grew into the Samuelson group to become the world's largest supplier of audio-visual equipment. Sydney Samuelson, beneficiary of many film industry awards, became CBE in 1978 and was knighted in 1995. Between 1991 and 1998 he was the first British film commissioner. David became a noted news and documentary cameraman and his manuals for film technicians are used the world over. Michael, made a CBE in 1989, became a specialist in sports documentaries. Succeeding generations of Samuelsons also took up work behind and in front of the camera, honouring further a distinguished name.   LUKE MCKERNAN

Sources H. Dunham and D. Samuelson, 'Bertie: the life and times of G. B. Samuelson', 1989–96, priv. coll. [unpubd biography] · R. Low, *The history of the British film*, 4: *1918–1929* (1971) · R. Low, *The history of the British film*, 3: *1914–1918* (1950) · R. Low, *The history of the British film*, 2: *1906–1914* (1949) · G. Pearson, *Flashback: the autobiography of a British film-maker* (1957) · G. B. Samuelson, 'From 15/- to £100,000 and back to 15/-', 1938, priv. coll. [typescript] · W. Macqueen-Pope, *Shirtfronts and sables* (1953) · W. J. Macqueen-Pope, *Ghosts and greasepaint* (1951) · d. cert.

Archives NRA, priv. coll. | FILM BFI NFTVA, performance footage

Likenesses cartoon, priv. coll. · photographs, priv. coll. · portrait, repro. in Dunham and Samuelson, 'Bertie', frontispiece

Samuely, Felix James (1902–1959), civil engineer, was born on 3 February 1902 in Vienna of a Jewish family. His father was in the medical profession and he had a younger sister. Matriculating in science at the Kaiser Friedrich Gymnasium, Berlin, in 1919, Samuely gained a Dipl.Ing. degree at the Technische Hochschule Berlin-Charlottenburg in 1923. The thesis he submitted as part of his studies dealt with the design of reinforced concrete bridges, and he remained in Berlin for a year, working with a firm of contractors, Held and Francke. This was followed by further experience with a consulting engineer, a Dr Bauer, in Vienna. Returning to Berlin in 1925, he spent four years with the contractor, Trägerlagergemeinschaft GmbH, on steel buildings and was introduced to the new technique of welding steel.

In 1929 Samuely set up in practice with Stephen E. Berger, with whom he had been at university, as Berger and Samuely Consulting Engineers, attracting young architects as clients. His commissions at this time included the construction of a factory and offices for Fromms Act Köpenick with Arthur Korn and he was also one of those who worked on the design (unbuilt) for the Josty Haus, a skyscraper in Potsdamerplatz. The firm also built the first welded-steel building in Berlin, an office block in Georgenkirchenplatz. After the 1931 July slump in the German stock market and the resulting depression, Samuely, in some despair for the future, accepted an offer from the Russian government to go as a specialist to work on the design of a large steel production plant in Sverdlovsk. Lack of professional help and unacceptable living conditions prompted a move to Moscow where he designed heavy steel industrial buildings and later carried out further research on welding.

In 1932, while he was in Moscow, Samuely married Henny Pfingst, who came from Berlin. The following year he left Moscow and travelled with his wife to Manchuria and China looking for any suitable professional opening,

Felix James Samuely (1902-1959), by unknown photographer

but without success, and they eventually returned to Berlin. Later in 1933 he was invited to London; he managed to obtain a monthly extendable permit to stay, and Henny joined him at the end of the year. He was introduced to Ove Arup (1895-1988), then chief engineer of J. L. Kier & Co., who appointed him to carry out the structural calculations for the spiral ramp of the penguin pool designed by the architect, Berthold Lubetkin (1901-1990), for the London Zoo. Samuely showed his mastery of calculation by completing this task over a weekend, and he subsequently joined J. L. Kier & Co. on a permanent basis. During this time he also wrote a number of articles on welded steelwork and a book in German on welding which was never published.

In 1934 the architects Serge Chermayeff and Eric Mendelsohn, who had recently come from Berlin, won the competition for the Bexhill Pavilion. They invited Samuely to become their structural engineer, and this led to his going into partnership with Cyril Helsby and Conrad Hamann to form the firm of Helsby, Hamann, and Samuely. Although Bexhill Pavilion was conceived in reinforced concrete, Samuely, for reasons of economy, persuaded the architects to change to welded steelwork, on which he had become a leading expert. The building was the first public welded steel building in Britain and as such was studied by many bodies, including the district surveyors of the London county council who would not, at that time, accept such a construction. Two years later they relented, when Samuely, in association with the architect Joseph Emberton, built a new department store in welded steel for Simpson's of Piccadilly. The firm flourished doing further work first for Mendelsohn and Chermayeff and then for Chermayeff alone, as well as helping many leading Modern Movement architects such as Wells Coates, A. V.

Pilchowski, Denys Lasdun, Connell Ward Lucas, and Frederick Gibberd. Samuely's imaginative structures were not only in welded steelwork but in sheet metal, reinforced concrete, timber, and brickwork.

In 1935 Samuely went to live in Hampstead, London, where he rented a flat in Highfield Court, remaining in Hampstead for the rest of his life. In 1937 he became senior lecturer in structural engineering at the Architectural Association School of Architecture, a position he held until his death. His interest in architecture led him to become a member of the MARS (Modern Architectural Research) Group of architects and in 1939 he studied air-raid precautions with Conrad Hamann, writing a book on civil protection. When war broke out, his application for citizenship had not been completed and he was classified as an alien and prohibited from working on projects of national importance. By then Helsby had left the partnership, Hamann had joined a government agency, and Samuely became a consultant to Scaffolding, Great Britain (SGB), designing some outstanding lightweight welded steel tube and rod roof structures.

Samuely's workload was sufficiently low to allow him time to study privately for UK qualifications. In 1941 he passed the Royal Aeronautical Society's examination to become an associate member and later in 1943 gained a BSc (Eng.) degree in structural engineering with first class honours from London University. The following year he was accepted as an associate member of the Institution of Civil Engineers and a member of the Institution of Structural Engineers. During the war years he was also very active with the MARS Group in planning studies for the future. His particular interest lay in transport and in June 1942 he edited, with Arthur Korn, the group's *Master Plan for London*. He wrote and lectured on economic construction and became a great influence on architects in the early post-war reconstruction with his pioneering structures and by stimulating better understanding and co-operation between members of the building team.

Because of the shortage of steel and timber and the trend for building technicians to seek stable employment in factories, Samuely began his studies into the use of pre-cast and pre-stressed concrete. He wanted to minimize timber formwork and maximize crane handling on site, and his solution was to promote composite construction made up from expensive pre-cast concrete and relatively cheap *in situ* concrete. Samuely's first major, and perhaps best, building using such techniques was a factory at Malago, Bristol (architect J. E. Collins), for E. S. and A. Robinson in 1949. This was followed by Hatfield Technical College and a host of other educational buildings. He developed the use of external pre-cast concrete load-bearing frames for office construction, such as the National Dock Labour Board in London (architect Frederick Gibberd) of 1953 and for the US embassy (architect Eero Saarinen in association with Yorke, Rosenberg, and Mardall), also in London, in 1958. For long-span construction Samuely quickly moved from curved concrete shells with their large on-site labour costs to folded plates of composite construction. Where appropriate he used lightweight steel lattices and timber folded plates and on occasion pre-stressed the roofs further to reduce weight and cost. For the British pavilions at the Brussels International Exhibition in 1958 he used a timber folded plate construction for the government pavilion and a latticed steel folded plate roof for the industrial pavilion which was taken down at the end of the exhibition and re-erected in Hilversum in the Netherlands.

Samuely will be remembered, above all, as the engineer of the Skylon (for which the architects were the firm of Powell and Moya) at the Festival of Britain in 1951. To provide the necessary restraint against wind oscillation he pre-tensioned the main cables of the Skylon, a measure which meant that two of the three proposed bracing cables to each pylon could be omitted. The resulting, widely acclaimed, streamlined design was thus brought about by a brilliant collaboration of architect and engineer.

Samuely's extensive writings include *Welding* (1935) and *Steel Economy* (1939), as well as the MARS plan for London (1942). He gave important lectures on force and form (1950) and on space frames and stressed skin construction (1952) at the Royal Institute of British Architects; and others on structural prestressing (1955) at the Institution of Structural Engineers and composite construction (1952) at the Institution of Civil Engineers. He was awarded the Telford premium by the Institution of Civil Engineers for his lecture and paper on the Skylon (1952). In June 1960 the Architectural Association devoted the whole issue of its journal to his life, listing his buildings and his writings and giving a clear picture of his outstanding contribution to engineering and the built environment.

Samuely had a unique gift for the conception of structural forms. He was consulted by many architects and, as he wished to be personally involved with each project from concept to completion, he always kept his office small. He was an energetic, cheerful, small, rotund man with a quizzical smile known affectionately to colleagues, architects, and friends as Sammy, and generations of architectural students have an enduring memory of his lectures on lettuce girders. He and his wife had a long and happy marriage and enjoyed travelling together. They had no children. He died on 22 January 1959 in the London Clinic, 20 Devonshire Place, London, following a heart attack, leaving his wife and his mother, and was cremated at Golders Green crematorium in Middlesex.

FRANK NEWBY

Sources F. Newby, 'A Tribute to Felix J. Samuely', *Architects' Journal* (12 March 1959) · M. Higgs, *Architectural Association Journal*, 76 (1960), 2–31 · d. cert.
Archives F. J. Samuely and Partners, London
Likenesses photograph, priv. coll. [*see illus.*]
Wealth at death £16,944 7s. 8d.: probate, 19 May 1959, *CGPLA Eng. & Wales*

Samwaies [Samways], **Peter** (1615–1693), Church of England clergyman, was born at Eltham, Kent, reputedly the son of a 'person about the court' (*DNB*). He was educated at Westminster School and elected in 1634 to a scholarship at Trinity College, Cambridge, where he was admitted on 10 April 1635. He graduated BA in 1637, was elected fellow in 1640, and proceeded MA in 1641. He was ordained a deacon of Rochester on 28 May 1643. During his residence at Cambridge he contributed verses to the university collections of poems on the birth of the Princess Elizabeth in 1635, on the birth of Charles I's fifth child in 1637, on the birth of a prince in 1640, and on the king's return from Scotland in 1641.

Samwaies was to show further evidence of his loyalty to the monarchy: the parliamentarian visitors of Cambridge charged him with having sent plate to Charles during the civil war. He survived the visitors' first purge of the university and continued to work as a college tutor until 28 August 1650 when he was ejected for refusing to answer a summons to take the engagement of loyalty to the Commonwealth. Despite his evident commitment both to the monarchy and to the Anglican church, he was none the less admitted by the triers to the vicarage of Cheshunt, Hertfordshire, on 28 February 1655. He was ejected from this living in March 1656, apparently on the ground that he persisted in reading the liturgy of the Church of England, and the Independent divine John Yates was admitted in his place. In spite of this, Samwaies appears to have served as rector of Maulden in Bedfordshire in or before 1657. In 1658 he successfully petitioned Cromwell for another living and was presented to the rectory of Wath, in the North Riding of Yorkshire by Thomas, earl of Elgin. He had stayed with the earl's family following his ejection from Cheshunt and had composed a funeral elegy for one of his servants, *The Wise and Faithfull Steward* (1657). In 1659 he was chaplain to Elizabeth, countess of Peterborough.

With the restoration of the monarchy Samwaies was created DD at Cambridge by royal mandate on 5 September 1660. As well as retaining his living at Wath, where he built and endowed a school, he was presented by Charles II to the neighbouring rectory of Bedale, worth £600 per annum. On 27 May 1668 he was made prebendary of Barneby in the church of York. Samwaies was a staunch supporter of the Church of England and an implacable opponent of both Catholic recusants and protestant dissenters. In December 1661 he wrote against proposals for the comprehension of nonconformists within the national church. In an earlier work, *Devotion Digested: in Severall Discourses and Meditations* (1652), he had attacked the doctrine of transubstantiation and it is even alleged that he argued the point with the duke of York (later James II). In 1663 he published *The Church of Rome not Sufficiently Vindicated from Apostacie, Heresie and Schism*. He refused to read King James's declaration of indulgence in 1688, and it is claimed that he printed a letter persuading the clergy of his neighbourhood to take the oaths to William and Mary. In return he was said to have been offered the bishopric of Bath and Wells, which he later declined. However, no pamphlet attributed to Samwaies or published by him exists relating to this subject.

Samwaies corresponded with Thomas Comber, later dean of Durham, and listed Isaac Barrow and archbishops Ussher and Sancroft among his intimate friends. He died on 6 April 1693 at Bedale, and was buried in the church there. In his will, dated 28 November 1690, he left £10 to Sir Robert Darcy, in whose house he had stayed while vicar of Cheshunt, and £5 to the poor of his birthplace, Eltham. He also established a scholarship at Westminster School.

EDWARD VALLANCE

Sources J. Welch, *The list of the queen's scholars of St Peter's College, Westminster*, ed. [C. B. Phillimore], new edn (1852), 106–7 · Venn, *Alum. Cant.*, 1/4.12 · *DNB* · *Walker rev.*, 203 · J. Twigg, *The University of Cambridge and the English Revolution, 1625–1688* (1990), 151, 303 · *The autobiography of Mrs Alice Thornton*, ed. [C. Jackson], SurtS, 62 (1875), 108 · *Fasti Angl., 1541–1857*, [York], 24 · *Calamy rev.*, 551 · *The autobiographies and letters of Thomas Comber, sometime precentor of York and dean of Durham*, ed. C. E. Whiting, 1, SurtS, 156 (1946), xxvii · *The autobiographies and letters of Thomas Comber, sometime precentor of York and dean of Durham*, ed. C. E. Whiting, 2, SurtS, 157 (1947), 125–6 · M. Goldie, 'The revolution of 1689 and the structure of political argument', *Bulletin of Research in the Humanities*, 83 (1980), 473–564 · P. Samwaies, *The wise and faithfull steward, or, A narration of the exemplary death of Mr Benjamin Rhodes* (1657) · BL, Add. MS 5880, fol. 154 · LPL, Lambeth MSS 997, 3, 65 · BL, Sloane MS 1823, fol. 43 · BL, Royal MS 12 A XIII, fol. 8; Royal MS 12 A LVIII, fol. 46

Archives BL, Add. MS 5880, fol. 154 · BL, Royal MSS 12 A XIII, fol. 8; 12 A LVIII, fol. 46 · BL, Sloane MS 1823, fol. 43 · LPL, Lambeth MS 997, 3, 65

Wealth at death see will, *Autobiography*, ed. Jackson, 108 n.

Samwell, David [Dafydd Samuel; *pseud.* Dafydd Ddu Feddyg] **(1751–1798)**, naval surgeon and poet, was born on 15 October 1751 at Nantglyn, Denbighshire, the second son of William Samuel (1713–1765), vicar of the parish, and his wife, Margaret (1708?–1780). He was the grandson of Edward *Samuel (1674–1748), poet and translator. Evidence of Samwell's early years is fragmentary, but there is reason to suppose that he attended Ruthin grammar school and was thereafter apprenticed to John Crosier, a naval surgeon. By 1771 Samwell was serving at sea near Greenland and living in London during his periods ashore, participating in the rich cultural life of the city's Welsh societies. A fellow member of the Gwyneddigion Society, of which Samwell was a founder, described him as: 'tall, stout, black-haired, pock-marked, fierce-looking, wondrous friendly in company and very fond of the cup' (Jenkins and Ramage, 107).

On 5 October 1775 Samwell qualified as second mate, third rate, with the Company of Surgeons of London and, during the following year, on Crosier's recommendation, he was appointed surgeon's first mate to the *Resolution*, on Captain James Cook's third voyage of exploration. When William Anderson, surgeon to the *Resolution*, died at sea in August 1778 Samwell succeeded John Law as surgeon to Cook's second ship, the *Discovery*. Samwell's journal (*Journals*, pt 2, 987–1300) is a distinguished account of the voyage, containing the first written record of the Maori language and valuable observations on the culture and topography of New Zealand, Alaska, and the Pacific islands. Samwell revered Cook, and his journal contains an exhaustive description, scrupulously gathered from eye-witnesses, of the murder of his hero in Hawaii in 1779. Samwell later revised and published it as a pamphlet entitled, *A narrative of the death of Captain James Cook … and observations respecting the introduction of the venereal disease into the Sandwich Islands* (1786). In contrast with other surviving journals, Samwell's is often racy and irreverent, giving glimpses of the more frivolous aspects of the voyage, particularly in his rakish preoccupation with the attractions of the local women.

Samwell was also an ambitious and dedicated surgeon and on his return from the Pacific in 1780 he attended William Hunter's anatomy classes in London. Between April 1781 and November 1786 he served on three ships: the frigate *Crocodile* under Captain James King, followed by *Le Pegaze* and the cutter *Kite*. The next six years, with the exception of a brief period on the *Tremendous* in 1790, were spent ashore practising medicine in London, frequenting meetings of the Gwyneddigion, of which he was appointed secretary in 1788, and pursuing his literary interests. Samwell became an authority on the work of the seventeenth-century Welsh-language poet Huw Morys, and later published an account of his researches ('A sketch of the life and writings of Hugh Morris', *Cambrian Register*, 1, 1795, 426–39). He assisted with the important 1789 edition of the poetry of Dafydd ap Gwilym (*Barddoniaeth Dafydd ab Gwilym*, ed. Owen Jones and William Owen) and took a keen interest in the local eisteddfods, which the Gwyneddigion did much to foster during the late eighteenth century. By temperament Samwell was manic and often violent. At an eisteddfod in Corwen in 1789, incensed at the failure of his protégé, Thomas Edwards, to be awarded a poetry prize, he challenged an adjudicator to a duel. The incident ended harmlessly. Samwell was himself a skilful poet in both Welsh and English, claiming that composition at sea alleviated the dullness of shipboard life. He had a gift for satire, perhaps best displayed in his squib, *Padouca Hunt*, which contains caricatures of some of his fellow London Welshmen engaged in debate at the Caractacan Society in 1791. The following year, assuming the bardic name Dafydd Ddu Feddyg (Black David the Doctor), Samwell played a leading role in the pseudo-druidic gorsedd ceremonies devised by his friend Edward Williams (Iolo Morganwg), and performed at Primrose Hill in London.

In March 1793, following the outbreak of war with revolutionary France, Samwell returned to sea, serving on the *Marlborough*, his earlier enthusiasm for the ideals of the revolution now tempered by patriotism. Between September 1794 and July 1796 he was appointed surgeon to the *Unicorn* and saw active service in the Irish sea. By now, however, his health was in decline; disenchanted with naval life and frustrated at his failure to secure a more lucrative post, he resorted increasingly to alcohol and opium. In March 1798 he accepted a position at Versailles, attending to British prisoners of war. In September 1798 Samwell returned to London, where he died on 23 November at his house at 117 Fetter Lane. He was buried on 2

December at St Dunstan-in-the-West, Fleet Street. An elegy on him by Thomas Edwards was printed in *Diliau barddas* (1827).   GERAINT PHILLIPS

Sources D. Samwell, 53 letters to Matthew Gregson, 1772–98, Liverpool Central Library, Gregson corresp., 17 · W. Ll. Davies, *Transactions of the Honourable Society of Cymmrodorion* (1926–7), 70–133 · *The journals of Captain James Cook*, ed. J. C. Beaglehole, 3/1–2, Hakluyt Society, 36a–b (1967) · D. Samwell, commonplace book, 1789–98, NL Wales, Cwrtmawr papers, MS 35B · R. T. Jenkins and H. M. Ramage, *A history of the Honourable Society of Cymmrodorion* (1951) · W. Ll. Davies, 'David Samwell's poem *The Padouca hunt*', *National Library of Wales Journal*, 2 (1941–2), 141–52 · W. Ll. Davies, 'David Samwell: a further note', *Transactions of the Honourable Society of Cymmrodorion* (1938), 257–8 · E. G. Bowen, *David Samwell (Dafydd Ddu Feddyg)* (1974) · *DNB*

Archives NL Wales, volume of memoranda, verse, etc. | BL, journal of James Cook's last voyage, Egerton MS 2591 · Liverpool Central Library, Gregson corresp.

Likenesses M. Gregson?, silhouette, *c*.1782, BL, Egerton MS 2591, fol. 1 · Chretien, engraving (after portrait by Fouquet, 1798), BL

Samwell, William (*bap.* **1628**, *d.* **1676**), architect, was baptized at Westminster on 14 September 1628, the eldest son of Anthony Samwell (*bap.* 1604, *d.* 1656) of Dean's Yard, Westminster, and his wife, Anne Heynes. He was the grandson of Sir William Samwell of Upton Hall, Northamptonshire. He was admitted to the Middle Temple in 1648, and lived in chambers until 1656, but he never practised law. After the Restoration he bought the manor of Watton in Norfolk, and remained its owner until his death. Samwell was a gentleman architect of considerable accomplishment, whose achievement has been undervalued, although John Aubrey considered him 'an excellent architect, that has built several delicate howses' (*Brief Lives, Chiefly of Contemporaries, Set Down by John Aubrey, between the Years 1669 and 1696*, ed. A. Clark, 1898, 1.293). These were distinguished by the sophistication of their planning, in which a balance was struck between the grand public rooms and convenient private ones. In their exploitation of spatial possibilities, his designs are at least as accomplished as those of the better-known gentleman architects Sir Roger Pratt and Hugh May.

Samwell's first authenticated building, the King's House in Newmarket (1668–71), designed for Charles II, was partly demolished in 1814: the south-east block survives as Palace House Mansion. It was criticized by John Evelyn, visiting in 1670, as 'mean enough', apart from the cellars, '& hardly capable for a hunting house' (Evelyn, *Diary*, 542). At Grange Park, Hampshire, built about 1670 for the lawyer Sir Robert Henley, Samwell's house was swallowed up by the neo-classical remodelling by William Wilkins, but despite alterations and the threat of demolition, the shell of his house substantially survives, concealed within the later work. It is on this building, and on his long-demolished Eaton Hall, Cheshire (1675–82), built for Sir Thomas Grosvenor, that any assessment of his work must rest. In both designs he brought to the Restoration house an unexpected elegance of arrangement, combining corner suites in the French manner, comprising bedchamber and closets, the private suites linked with each other by corridors which opened onto grand, formal staircases and provided access directly to the major public rooms. In this sophisticated satisfaction of complex spatial and social requirements, Samwell achieved a synthesis premonitory of the great houses of the eighteenth century. Although at Grange Park Samwell did not introduce to England the Imperial staircase of three open flights, there is little doubt that his was grander than its precursor at Gunnersbury by John Webb.

Samwell's other work included the doubling of the central range of Ham House, Surrey, for John Maitland, first duke of Lauderdale, and his wife, Elizabeth Murray, in 1672–4, to create a plan more in keeping with contemporary expectations of convenience and grandeur, and the addition of a wing for William Windham at Felbrigg Hall, Norfolk (1674–86); both these works survive. Roger North considered the reforming of Ham to be:

> the best of the kind I have seen … For I doe not perceive any part of the old fabrick is taken downe, but the wings stand as they were first sett, … joyned with a strait range intirely new. And there are all the rooms of parade, exquisitely plac'd. (*Of Building: Roger North's Writings on Architecture*, ed. H. M. Colvin and J. Newman, 1981, 144)

This new range was innovative in incorporating the first large-scale use of the sash-window in England. Samwell was also responsible for the design of a coach house (1673–4; dem.) in the Royal Mews, Charing Cross, commissioned by George Villiers, second duke of Buckingham, master of the horse.

Samwell married Anne (1648–1720), daughter of Sir Denner Strutt of Little Warley, Essex; they had two daughters. He died in London in 1676 and was buried on 23 May at Upton, Northamptonshire, as he had directed in his will.   JOHN BOLD

Sources Colvin, *Archs.* · J. Geddes, 'The Grange, Northington', *Architectural History*, 26 (1983), 35–48 · J. G. Dunbar, 'The building-activities of the duke and duchess of Lauderdale, 1670–82', *Archaeological Journal*, 132 (1975), 202–30 · G. Baker, *The history and antiquities of the county of Northampton*, 1 (1822–30), 225 · H. M. Colvin and others, eds., *The history of the king's works*, 5 (1976) · E. Mercer, 'William Samwell and the Grange', *The country seat*, ed. H. Colvin and J. Harris (1970), 48–54 · J. Redmill, 'The Grange, Hampshire [pts 1–2]', *Country Life*, 157 (1975), 1166–8, 1242–5 · P. K. Thornton and M. F. Tomlin, *The furnishing and decoration of Ham House* (1980) · R. W. Ketton-Cremer, *Felbrigg: the story of a house* (1962) · H. J. Louw, 'The origin of the sash-window', *Architectural History*, 26 (1983), 49–72

Archives BL, Lauderdale MSS · Hants. RO · Leics. RO, Tollemache MSS · NA Scot., Bruce of Kinross MSS · Thirlestane Castle, Berwickshire, Maitland MSS

Sancho, (Charles) Ignatius (**1729?–1780**), author, was born on the middle passage, on a slave ship crossing the Atlantic Ocean *en route* for the West Indies. His mother soon died of disease in the Spanish colony of New Granada, where the bishop had baptized her son, naming him Ignatius. His father shortly thereafter committed suicide rather than endure slavery. Barely two years old, the orphan slave was taken by his owner to England and given to three maiden sisters in Greenwich, who believed that keeping the pudgy child ignorant would render him submissive. They surnamed him Sancho because they thought that he resembled the fictional Don Quixote's squire. He remained overweight throughout his life.

(Charles) Ignatius Sancho (1729?–1780), by Thomas
Gainsborough, 1768

Fortunately for the young slave, John, second duke of
Montagu, had a house in nearby Blackheath and met Sancho by accident. Montagu was so impressed by his intelligence that he frequently brought him home, encouraged
him to read by giving him books, and unsuccessfully tried
to get his mistresses to support his education. Shortly
after the duke's death in 1749, Sancho fled from Greenwich and sought protection from the duke's widow. He
considered suicide when the duchess at first rejected his
appeal, but she soon relented and hired him as her butler,
a very responsible position in a noble household. At her
death in 1751 the duchess left him an annuity of £30, an
ample income to support a single man, as well as a year's
salary. The bequeathed salary, combined with his own savings, gave him a sum of £70 beyond the annuity. Unsupervised, he soon squandered his money on gambling,
women, and the theatre, where he spent his last shilling
to see David Garrick play the role of Richard III. An
attempt at a stage career playing Othello and Oroonoko
failed because of a speech impediment. In 1766 he sought
service in the household of the late duke's son-in-law
George, first duke of Montagu of the new creation, who
made him his valet. While in Montagu's employ, Sancho's
portrait was painted by Thomas Gainsborough at Bath on
29 November 1768. The new duke proved to be as good a
master to him as the old duchess had been.

Illness and obesity aggravated by gout eventually rendered Sancho unfit to continue in Montagu's service.
Aided by the duke, Sancho and his wife, Ann(e) Osborne
(1733–1817), whom he married on 17 December 1758 in St
Margaret's Church, Westminster, established a grocery
shop on 29 January 1774 at 20 Charles Street, Westminster.

They had seven children, three of whom died before the
age of six and none of whom left a record of ever having
married. All the children—the 'Sanchonettas' (I. Sancho
to Mrs H——, 9 Feb 1774, Letters, 50)—were baptized in St
Margaret's. Some time between the baptism of his third
child in 1766 and his fourth in 1768 he stopped using his
first name, Charles. Despite the apparent success of his
shop, he often complained of financial problems. To supplement his income he published compositions of music,
a Theory of Music, and two plays (all now lost). His financial
independence as a male householder in Westminster
qualified him to become the only eighteenth-century
Afro-Briton known to have voted in parliamentary elections in 1774 and 1780 for the representatives of Westminster. Many of his letters discuss public affairs, and he
published newspaper essays, serious and comic, under
both his own name and the pseudonym Africanus, in
which he expressed his allegiance to the monarchy and
his support for the British in the war against the rebellious
Americans led by 'General Washintub' (I. Sancho to
M. Cockredge, 5 Nov 1777, Letters, 106). Sancho's constant
concern for his friends and his country enabled him to
keep his own problems in perspective, using humour to
avoid sounding self-indulgent even when talking of discrimination, illness, political disappointment, and death.
He gained widespread celebrity when one of his letters
appeared in the posthumously published Letters (1775) of
Laurence Sterne, with whom he had initiated a correspondence on 21 July 1766, encouraging Sterne to continue
writing to alleviate the oppression of Sancho's fellow
Africans. The first African to be given an obituary in the
British press, he died on 14 December 1780 from complications associated with gout. He was buried on 17 December
in St Margaret's chapel and burying-ground, Westminster.

In 1782, motivated by 'the desire of shewing that an
untutored African may possess abilities equal to an European' (Letters, 4), Frances Crewe, one of Sancho's younger
correspondents, edited and published the two-volume Letters of the Late Ignatius Sancho, an African, sold by subscription. An engraving by Francesco Bartolozzi after the
Gainsborough portrait served as frontispiece to the first
volume, and the anonymous brief prefatory biography by
Joseph Jekyll remains our main source of information
about the first thirty years of Sancho's life. The subscription list for the first edition of the Letters reflects the great
range of Sancho's social circle: men and women, aristocrats, servants, artists, businessmen, country squires, and
prominent politicians. The ease and respect with which
he communicates with his correspondents, no matter
how much they differ from him in age or social status,
account for much of the appeal of the tone of his letters.
Even though his own status rose, he never lost contact
with those who had been his fellow servants, some of
whom were also fellow Afro-Britons.

Sancho's more famous friends included the duchesses
of Queensberry and Northumberland; the artists John
James Barralet, William Henry Bunbury, Matthew and
Mary Darly, Daniel Gardner, John Hamilton Mortimer,

Joseph Nollekens, and William Stevenson; the actors Garrick and John Henderson; the banker John Spink; and the booksellers John Ireland and John Wingrave. Mortimer frequently consulted Sancho about his paintings. Others sought his literary advice. For example, the aspiring author George Cumberland read some of his works to Sancho because 'he is said to be a great Judge of literary performances' (BL, Add. MS 36492, fol. 204). He treated as protégés the much younger John Meheux, an amateur writer and artist, John Highmore, an aspiring author, and Julius Soubise, black servant of the duchess of Queensberry and man about town. Sancho's relationships with Meheux and Highmore make him the only known black patron of aspiring white artists and writers during the century. Sancho was also the first black literary critic of Phillis Wheatley, the contemporaneous African-American poet, 'a Genius in bondage' (I. Sancho to J. Fisher, 27 Jan 1778, *Letters*, 112).

Sancho's surviving letters reveal a religious and patriotic man of feeling and sentiment and an avid reader of eighteenth-century literature, with enough education to imitate Sterne's prose style, punctuation, Shandean multilingual jokes, and word play. Sancho's interest in the theatre suited him for playing the roles demanded of a correspondent who, at appropriate times, assumes the voice of the sober, older sage advising the young Jack Wingrave or the irresponsible Julius Soubise; the flirtatious married voice addressing the unmarried Margaret Cocksedge; the voice of the loving and affectionate father relating the joys and sorrows of family life; the official voice of the representative of the Montagu family announcing the death of its heir, or of the humble supplicant acknowledging Daniel Braithwaite's rejection of his petition to allow him to open a post office; the playful voice swapping literary jokes and Shandean imitations with John Meheux; the serious voice reporting the Gordon riots to John Spink; or the stoical voice in the later letters facing approaching death. Although Stevenson tells us that he had 'often witnessed [Sancho's] patient forbearance, when the passing vulgar have given vent to their prejudices against his ebon complexion, his African features, and his corpulent person', he recounts an incident in which Sancho demonstrated 'his manly resentment' in the face of such prejudice. Insulted by a 'fashionable' man in the street with the shout, 'Smoke Othello!' Sancho,

> immediately placing himself across the path, before him, exclaimed with a thundering voice, and a countenance which awed the delinquent, 'Aye, Sir, such Othellos you meet with but once in a century,' clapping his hand upon his goodly round paunch. 'Such Iagos as you, we meet with in every dirty passage. Proceed, Sir!' (Nichols, *Lit. anecdotes*, 8.682–3)

Sancho's widow received over £500 from the more than 1200 subscribers to his *Letters* and a fee paid by the booksellers for permission to publish a second edition. The literary quality of his *Letters* was frequently cited by opponents of slavery as evidence of the humanity and inherent equality of Africans, and even Thomas Jefferson felt compelled to acknowledge, albeit begrudgingly, that 'we

admit him to the first place [as an author] among those of his own colour' (*Notes on the State of Virginia*, 1787, Query xiv).　　　　　　　　　　　　　　　VINCENT CARRETTA

Sources Letters of the late Ignatius Sancho, an African, pbk edn, ed. V. Carretta (1998) · J. Wright, ed., Ignatius Sancho (1729–1780), an early African composer in England: the collected editions of his music in facsimile (1981) · R. King, ed., Ignatius Sancho: an African man of letters (1997) · Nichols, Lit. anecdotes, 8.682–3 · BL, Add. MS 36492
Likenesses caricature, 1746 (possibly Sancho; after Hogarth) · T. Gainsborough, oils, 1768, National Gallery of Canada, Ottawa [see illus.] · F. Bartolozzi, stipple, pubd 1802 (after T. Gainsborough), repro. in Carretta, ed., Letters, frontispiece

Sancroft, William (1617–1693), archbishop of Canterbury and nonjuror, was born at Fressingfield, Suffolk, on 30 January 1617, the second son of Francis Sandcroft (*d.* 1649) of Fressingfield and his first wife, Margaret, daughter and coheir of Thomas Butcher (or Boucher) of nearby Wilby. He belonged to a loving and closely knit family of yeoman farmers, long settled at Fressingfield and Stadbroke, to the south-east of Diss. Though their pedigree was traceable to Angevin times, and they commanded a comfortable standard of living, they were not armigerous. Besides an elder brother, Thomas, Sancroft had six sisters. He remained on cordial terms with them for the rest of his life. He continued to spell his surname indifferently, Sandcroft or Sancroft, well into middle age. He was educated at the grammar school of Bury St Edmunds, a thriving establishment which catered for the sons of local landowners, and left school a proficient classicist, as the Latin and Greek juvenilia offered to his father and uncle testify. He proceeded to Emmanuel College, Cambridge, an Elizabethan foundation then at the height of its academic fame as a puritan seminary under his uncle, Dr William Sandcroft, master from 1628 to 1637. The second son of a religious family, it is probable that he was destined for the ministry, though he entered Emmanuel for reasons of family connection rather than confessional orientation.

Emmanuel College, Cambridge Sancroft was admitted to the college, with his brother, on 10 September 1633, and matriculated on 3 July 1634. His tutor was Ezekiel Wright, to whom he became devoted. He studied hard and showed an aptitude for languages and literature, classical and modern. He took a particular delight in poetry, philosophy, history, and geography, thus laying the foundation of a lifetime's pursuit of multifarious knowledge. He graduated BA in 1637 and MA in 1641. Thereafter he concentrated on divinity in preparation for his ministerial calling. 'I am perswaded', he wrote in September 1641, 'that for this end I was sent into the world; and therefore, if God lends me life and abilities, I shall be willing to spend myselfe, and be spent, upon this worke' (Bodl. Oxf., MS Tanner 66, fol. 180). Elected a fellow in 1642, he was made a tutor and assigned pupils by the master, Dr Richard Holdsworth, chaplain-in-ordinary to Charles I and vice-chancellor of Cambridge. He held a variety of college offices, including those of Greek and Hebrew praelector and bursar, and was drawn into the wider arena of university life.

Barely had Sancroft embarked on an academic career

William Sancroft (1617–1693), attrib. Bernard (I) Lens, *c.*1650–55

and taken holy orders than the 'great rebellion' broke out. He deprecated the descent into uncivil war, and criticized the 'arbitrariness' of the rebel Long Parliament. The progressive remodelling of the university under parliamentarian and sectarian auspices made collegiate life difficult for him. While remaining entirely passive in the face of armed conflict, his allegiances were never in doubt. A Church of England loyalist who reverenced the established laws, he held to the conjoint rule of king and bishop, and adhered to the Book of Common Prayer. Ineluctably he found himself isolated in a college and university shorn of its Anglican royalist governors. Having avoided taking the covenant in 1643, he lamented the fate of the leading royalist clergy, believing that they had 'sufferd ever since buffe and steele hath swaggerd abroad in the world with soe much authority'. For him, the power of the sword could not abrogate the dictates of conscience, which were, he confessed, 'God's voyce in my soule', and absolutely binding on him (Bodl. Oxf., MS Tanner 62, fol. 641v; 61, fol. 161).

A non-combatant, Sancroft sat still and attended the verdict of providence. His survival in the fellowship was attributable to timely absences from Cambridge (excused on the grounds of ill health), natural caution, scrupulous passivity, and, more importantly, to the intercession of friends on both sides of the conflict. The ejected royalist master, Holdsworth, to whom he remained attached, prevailed on his intruded presbyterian successor, Anthony

Tuckney, to protect Sancroft, which he did through his interest in Adoniram Byfield, erstwhile scribe to the Westminster assembly. Meanwhile Sancroft disdained the *Directory for the Publique Worship of God*, and applied himself to theological studies, drawing on the best available scholarship, biblical and patristic. He graduated BD in 1648.

Regicide, ejection, and retirement Parliamentarian negligence preserved Sancroft's fellowship beyond Charles I's execution, though not for long. To him regicide, the ultimate 'black act' of rebellion, meant more than 'the martyrdome of the best Protestant in these kingdomes'; it betokened the killing of the Lord's anointed (Bodl. Oxf., MS Tanner 57, fol. 525). The event, which occurred on Sancroft's thirty-second birthday, hastened the death of his distressed father. Having automatically transferred his allegiance to Charles II, Sancroft was expelled from his fellowship in July 1651 for refusing the engagement to the newly proclaimed Commonwealth.

The rest of the 1650s Sancroft spent in retirement, partly in Fressingfield and partly with friends in London and elsewhere. A confirmed valetudinarian who enjoyed adequate financial means, he made no attempt to exercise his ministry publicly, and repeatedly refused offers of private chaplaincies. His correspondence reveals him to have been at the centre of a growing circle of like-minded partisans, mostly deprived royalist clergymen and their lay patrons. His intimacy with the ejected bishop of Exeter, Ralph Brownrigg, introduced him to James Ussher, the learned archbishop of Armagh. He formed valuable friendships with some of the luminaries of episcopalian resistance: Henry Hammond, Herbert Thorndike, Timothy Thurscross, Peter Gunning, and George Wilde. Among his dearest friends were two former pupils, John and Robert Gayer, the well-to-do sons of a lord mayor of London. He often stayed with them in Lincoln's Inn Fields and at Stoke Poges, in Buckinghamshire. They shared his loyalties, welcomed his company, and indulged his love of books.

Sancroft's studies gathered apace in the years of his enforced leisure but, though forward to aid the labours of others, he shrank from publication. His aversion sprang less from prudential motives than from personal modesty. It is noteworthy that his acknowledged publications after 1660 were printed either at the command of his superiors, or were official pronouncements made by him as primate. The titles traditionally ascribed to him in the 1650s cannot stand. The authorship of the anti-Calvinist dialogue *Fur praedestinatus* was not his. It first appeared in 1619 in Dutch as *Den gheprestineerden dief*, a work now assigned to Henricus Slatius. Albeit Sancroft was an accomplished Latinist and a gifted translator, the grounds for his having published the Latin translation at London in 1651 are infirm. The attribution of the similarly anonymous diatribe, *Modern Policies, Taken from Machiavel, Borgia, and other Choise Authors by an Eye-Witnesse* (1652) is also doubtful, resting on little more than a likely dedication to Bishop Brownrigg. Sancroft's own copies of both treatises betray no signs of his involvement in either work. The crediting him with the Latin preface fronting John Boys's

Veteris interpretis cum Beza aliisque recentioribus collatio, in quatuor evangeliis et actis (1655) depends on an unidentified and unsupported manuscript note in H. J. Todd's copy, which his nineteenth-century biographer, George D'Oyly, examined.

Exile Late in 1657 Sancroft made an extended visit to the United Provinces, then a subsidiary centre of fugitive royalism closely connected with the court of the exiled Charles II at Cologne. In all probability his reputation had preceded him for, before quitting England, he was in correspondence with John Cosin, chaplain to the protestants in Queen Henrietta Maria's household in Paris. Cosin, a grateful recipient of Sancroft's pecuniary charity, rejoiced to know 'how firm and unmoved' he continued 'in the midst of these great and violent storms … raised against the Church of England' (BL, Harleian MS 3783, fol. 102). On arriving in the Netherlands Sancroft befriended the ejected Anglican clergy residing in Amsterdam, Utrecht, and The Hague—most notably Bishop Bramhall of Derry, Thomas Browne, George Morley, and Michael Honeywood. He preached before the king's sister, Mary, princess of Orange, and there were moves to make him her chaplain.

In the autumn of 1658 Sancroft was joined by his younger friend, Robert Gayer, who had recently arranged an annuity of £60 for him. Moved by the plight of the more poverty-stricken royalist clergy, they gave money to John Earles at Brussels and Robert Creighton at Utrecht, as well as renewed subsidies to Cosin in Paris: all these men were to become Church of England bishops. After a stay of two years Sancroft left the Netherlands in August 1659 and, accompanied by Gayer, journeyed up the Rhine to Basel and passed into Italy from Geneva. In addition to the obligatory sightseeing in Venice, Padua, and Rome, Sancroft took every opportunity to converse with foreign scholars and to collect books for his library. Among his purchases were a number of art and architecture publications, indicating a burgeoning aesthetic dimension to his personality. News of Charles II's restoration summoned him home.

Restoration preferment Sancroft returned too late in 1660 to obtain suitable preferment for one who was esteemed 'a good scholar, a good preacher, and a pious man' (BL, Harleian MS 3784, fol. 202). Aware of his worth, Bramhall, now archbishop-nominate of Armagh, offered him the place of chaplain to the marquess of Ormond, lord steward of the king's household, and, with it, the prospect of promotion in Ireland. He opted instead to serve as domestic chaplain to Cosin, whom the king had named bishop of Durham, thereby enabling the bishop to repay the charity of his former benefactor. On 2 December he preached at Cosin's consecration, with six other bishops, in Westminster Abbey. His sermon on Titus 1: 5, printed at his patron's command, was admired as an authoritative exposition of the divine origin and apostolic character of the episcopal order which lay at the heart of the re-establishment of the Church of England in that year.

He took no part in the Savoy Conference called to reconcile the presbyterians to episcopacy but, by Cosin's means, was employed in expediting the revision of the Book of Common Prayer made by convocation. Besides rectifying the calendar and rubrics, which governed the use of the liturgy, he saw the entire book through the press, a laborious task which earned him the gratitude of king and bishops.

Cosin gave Sancroft the valuable rectory of Houghton-le-Spring, outside Durham, on 7 December 1661. Detained by his superiors in London, it was not until 13 August 1662 that he was inducted. On 4 March he was collated prebendary of the ninth stall in Durham Cathedral, and installed by proxy on 11 March. On entering the ranks of the dignified clergy he obtained a grant of arms to his brother and himself on 26 January 1663. In only one respect did he resist Cosin's overflowing bounty. As a celibate resolved 'to live single', he courteously, yet firmly, declined to wed the woman whom the bishop had marked out for him. Once in residence he began to repair his ruinous parsonage house and prebendal lodgings. He found temporary shelter in the deanery with Dr John Sudbury, his fellow countryman and collegian. Despite the brevity of his time at Durham, and his regular assistance at the worship of the cathedral, he used his leisure hours to investigate the antiquities of the county palatine. His manuscript collections were to prove helpful to subsequent local historians.

Master of Emmanuel College and dean of York Sancroft's loyal record and obvious talent for business attracted the patronage of the most powerful figure in the Restoration episcopate, Gilbert Sheldon, dean of the Chapel Royal and bishop of London. Sheldon brought Sancroft into the royal household, obtaining for him appointment as chaplain-in-ordinary to Charles II in 1661; January was the month stipulated for Sancroft's attendance at court. The first fruits of Charles's favour came shortly afterwards when he received a DD from Cambridge *per literas regias*, dated 15 March 1662. Intent on making the most of his protégé's abilities, Sheldon took advantage of the removal of the nonconformist William Dillingham from the mastership of Emmanuel College on 24 August 1662 to place Sancroft at the head of the foundation which had spawned so many of the rebellious clergy in 'the late iniquitous times'. His procurement of the king's letter of 27 August, recommending the election of Sancroft, was part of a concerted cavalier Anglican strategy to bring the college into line with the rest of the church and university by putting an end to its infamous 'singularity'. He silenced Sancroft's misgivings over the stringency of the founder's statutes by stressing the importance of his duty to his alma mater, and promising to obtain from the king whatever dispensations were necessary to ease his lot and secure the conformity of the society. In obedience to Charles's recommendation the fellows unanimously elected Sheldon's candidate on 30 August.

At his return to Emmanuel, Sancroft faced considerable problems. Not only was his acquaintance 'wholly worn out', but the old 'singularities' persisted—an unconsecrated chapel, the form and furnishing of which were unlike any other in the university, meagre stipends, and Mildmay's harshly restrictive statutes. These defects were aggravated by a lack of qualified gremials with which to strengthen the fellowship, a drop in admissions, dwindling tutorial incomes, and the parlous state of the corporate revenues. In typical fashion the new master accepted the challenge.

In between discharging his ecclesiastical commitments Sancroft displayed determination and assiduity in the management of college affairs. He turned for advice and assistance to tried friends: to Sheldon, Dean Sudbury of Durham, his old tutor Ezekiel Wright, and his former travelling companion, Sir Robert Gayer, who had been knighted in the coronation honours. Using a bequest from his royalist predecessor, Richard Holdsworth, he set about converting the existing unsatisfactory chapel into a library (in the hope also of retrieving Holdsworth's books from the university), and commissioned the design of a new chapel, conformable to Anglican worship, from Sheldon's Oxford client, Christopher Wren. He sought, and received, funds from well disposed Emmanuelists. Gayer responded generously, giving £1000, which with Sancroft's donation of almost £600 got his building projects off to a promising start. In the quest for fellows of the right intellectual calibre and churchmanship from outside the college Sheldon proved as good as his word, obtaining the royal dispensations requisite for their election. Under Sancroft's short invigorating mastership, and that of his two successors, John Breton and Thomas Holbech, who constantly consulted him in realizing his aims, Emmanuel was transformed from a 'trouble church' puritan seminary into a pillar of Anglican respectability and a reliable prop of the protestant establishment.

Royal favour knew no bounds where Sancroft was concerned. On 8 January 1664 Charles nominated him dean of York. Elected on 23 January, he was installed by proxy on 26 February, and held the deanery barely nine months. During the time snatched from Cambridge duties he made a rental of the dean and chapter lands and brought the accounts of the minster into tolerable order. Having a good head for business, he appreciated how essential financial recovery was to rehabilitating cathedral life after so disruptive a break. He was beginning to settle into the northern metropolis and make friends there when the king, anxious to have his nearer attendance, summoned him permanently south to London. Sancroft lost heavily by the deanery, expending more than he received. As at Durham and Houghton-le-Spring, his major item of expenditure was on dilapidations.

Dean of St Paul's, London On 8 November 1664 Charles nominated his chaplain dean of St Paul's, with the blessing of Archbishop Sheldon and Dr Humfrey Henchman, bishop of London. Elected on 10 November, Sancroft was installed in the prebend of Oxgate on 9 December and in the deanery the next day. He resigned his rectory, and the mastership of Emmanuel, a few months later, but kept his stall in Durham Cathedral. It was a measure of Charles's

confidence in Sancroft's loyalty and devotion to duty that he put him in charge of the cathedral of his capital—the city where the rebellion had begun in 1642, and in which, for all Sheldon's exertions, nonconformity and disaffection were still rife. Sancroft succeeded his friend, Dr John Barwick, who had begun the arduous process of reviving cathedral worship with its distinctive liturgical and choral ethos. It was a form of worship in which Sancroft delighted to bear his part.

The new dean was somewhat overawed by receiving two deaneries in the space of one year, but grateful that his 'long and tedious journeys' were over. Sancroft's response to the king's prodigality was predictable: 'I will', he told his brother, 'study to deserve by the best service I can do'. The revenue of St Paul's was ampler than that of York, yet he feared it would be 'much harder to gain' the affection of the Londoners, 'there being such diversity of humours, and those so nice, too, amongst them' (Bodl. Oxf., MS Tanner 47, fol. 205). Again he applied himself to the shaky finances of his church. He produced an exhaustive review of its income, identifying arrears, and writing off those which were desperate, in an effort to establish a sound basis for future accounting. His husbanding of decanal revenues did not inhibit his charity. He augmented the small vicarage of Sandon in Hertfordshire and endowed the rectory of St Paul's, Shadwell, a new parish erected out of overpopulous Stepney by his promotion of an act of parliament in 1670.

A more intractable problem—one which the king was keen to address—was posed by the fabric of the cathedral. Despite Inigo Jones's classicization of St Paul's in the 1630s it was badly out of repair, having deteriorated in the interregnum. Recurrent bouts of illness and the great plague of 1665 kept Sancroft from giving his mind to the question of repairs until the summer of 1666. On 27 July he, Henchman, and a group of architects inspected the cathedral. The experts were divided on what to do. Sir Roger Pratt and John Webb were for 'patching up' the decrepit central tower, whereas Wren and John Evelyn favoured the raising of a 'noble cupola' of the kind as yet unknown in England. Sancroft, who in Venice had seen Palladio's domed churches and in Rome Michelangelo's St Peter's, sided with Wren, who was ordered to provide a design and estimates. Further progress was halted by the great fire of September 1666, which devastated the city and reduced Old St Paul's to a shell.

The conflagration was widely interpreted as a divine judgment on a licentious age. In a specially appointed fast sermon, preached before Charles on 10 October and published as *Lex ignea*, Sancroft turned the catastrophe into a call for national repentance. Rather than blame foreign enemies for the disaster, he bade his august audience to look to their 'own opposition, direct and diametrical to God and his holy law' (D'Oyly, 2.372). The complacent king altruistically commanded him to publish his sermon for the benefit of lesser mortals.

After attempting to renovate the west end of the cathedral, which exposed Jones's defective work, Sancroft concluded in April 1668 that reparation was impractical.

Following a meeting on 1 July of the rebuilding commission, on which Sheldon and Henchman sat, he gave Wren the go-ahead 'to frame a design, handsome and noble', answerable to the needs of the church and 'the reputation of the city and the nation' (Bolton and Hendry, 13.49; Wren, 279). The commissioners rejected Wren's suggestion that they should set a budget. Sancroft, who endorsed Charles's desire for 'magnificence', believed that funds would be forthcoming. The clerical input to the design process was decisive. While Wren's predilection favoured a centrally planned Renaissance church in the manner of the 'great model' of 1673, Sancroft objected that it was unsuited to protestant worship and made building by stages impossible, thus preventing the early reintroduction of services. The outcome was an architectural compromise between the Vitruvian requirements of 'Use' and 'Beauty'. By taking advantage of Charles's licence to vary the agreed 'warrant design' of 1675 Wren was able to combine the traditional Latin cross plan demanded by the clergy with a baroque dome over the crossing and a classical elevation.

From 1668 onwards Sancroft directed his energies to realizing the projected cathedral. Money was a prime concern. He gave £1400 himself, over and above what was spared from capitular revenues, and raised large outside contributions. His involvement in the project was such that, in dispensing with Sancroft's statutory residence at Durham in 1670, Charles stated that the commission required his 'perpetual and close attendance' in London, nothing being done 'without his presence, no materials bought, nor accounts passed without him' (PRO, SP 44/35B, fol. 10; SP 29/280, nos. 92, 93). Nor was the cathedral the sole building to occupy him. He built a new deanery at a cost of £2500, and oversaw the design and erection of the houses of the three residentiary canons. He was also instrumental in soliciting the passage of the Coal Act, which funded the rebuilding of the burnt parish churches and cathedral through a tax levied on coal imported into London.

On a wider front Sancroft worked with Sheldon, Henchman, and successive lord mayors in drafting parliamentary legislation for the rebuilding and uniting of the city churches, and settling the maintenance of their incumbents. His shouldering the heavy administrative legacy of the great fire was all the more impressive in the light of his refusal of higher preferment. Though he held the archdeaconry of Canterbury from 1668 to 1670, again on the king's presentation, he twice refused bishoprics—Chester in 1668 and Chichester in 1669. His standing among the clergy was declared by his election in 1667 as prolocutor of the lower house of the convocation of Canterbury, a platform he used to canvass proposals for liturgical and ecclesiastical reform.

Primate of all England Sheldon's death on 9 November 1677 allowed Charles to nominate Sancroft to the archbishopric of Canterbury on 30 December over the heads of the entire episcopate. The dean and chapter of Christchurch, Canterbury, elected him on 10 January 1678 and royal assent followed on the 14th and the restitution of the temporalities of the see on 23 January. He was consecrated in Lambeth House chapel on 27 January and took his seat in the House of Lords the next day and in the privy council on 6 February. His overtaking the rumoured front runners, Compton of London and Crewe of Durham, the clients respectively of Lord Treasurer Danby and James, duke of York, the king's brother, was much commented on, and came as a surprise to him. Dryden noted the determining factor in his appointment, his lack of personal ambition:

Zadock the Priest, whom, shunning Power and Place,
His lowly mind advanc'd to David's Grace.
(J. Dryden, Absalom and Achitophel, lines 864–5)

Unencumbered by aristocratic connections, Sancroft was what he had always been—the king's man. His years of service in both provinces of the church under Cosin, Sheldon, and Henchman had equipped him with the necessary experience to be primate of all England, and Charles knew he could depend on him to rule the church on his behalf. His nomination to Canterbury announced the king's resolution to make the most of the Church of England's traditional role as a bastion of monarchy.

Throughout his primacy Sancroft, as the first servant of the crown, rewarded the claims of loyalty in others, an acknowledgement that the trust reposed in him was justified. Confident of the political benefits that flowed from Sheldon's reconciliation to the court under Danby's cavalier Anglican administration, he saw it as his duty to support the king's ministers, Danby in parliament, and Lauderdale in Scotland, both of whom were upholders of the protestant establishment in church and state. Notwithstanding gossip that he owed his elevation to Canterbury to Roman Catholic influence at court, he was well aware of the threat which the conversion of the heir presumptive posed to the protestant establishment. A dogmatic anti-Catholic by education and conviction, Sancroft believed that the Church of Rome taught 'doctrines destructive of salvation' (Singer, 2.71). With Charles's approval he therefore attempted to reclaim James, duke of York, for protestantism. On 21 February 1678 he and Bishop Morley of Winchester waited on the king's brother. Sancroft's speech, in which he reminded the duke of his martyred father's injunction never to forsake the established religion, proved unavailing. It served as a prelude to James's banishment. Fortunately, once in exile, James chose to construe their effort as a mark of their abiding regard for him, which, indeed, it was. As such it offered a basis for future co-operation.

From Popish Plot to tory reaction Animated by the same anti-popery prejudice as the rest of his countrymen, Sancroft swallowed the existence of the bogus Popish Plot of late 1678, but responded to it cautiously. In a sermon before the House of Lords on 13 November he tried to allay the heats generated, even inside Westminster, by Oates's feigned 'discoveries', and counselled the peers to attend the king's commands. He was, in fact, no better prepared than was his master for the political turbulence which followed. Charles's dissolution of the Cavalier Parliament in January 1679 robbed him of what had been Sheldon's greatest support in times of political adversity. It also plunged the realm into the fever of three general elections within as many years. The result was the repeated election of an aggressive whig-dominated House of Commons, which between 1679 and 1681 strove to exclude James from the succession and to modify the Restoration church settlement in favour of the whigs' electoral allies, the protestant dissenters. The archbishop was fundamentally opposed in principle and interest to whig innovation. He distrusted the whigs' manipulation of popular hysteria, knowing of old what harm could come of it. As a veteran Anglican royalist, who had lived through the ordeals of the 1640s and 1650s, he was quick to see the parallels between the rise of the puritan and whig factions.

With the fall of Danby in 1679 Sancroft had perforce to seek new allies. These he found in the younger generation of the Hyde family—Henry, second earl of Clarendon, and Lawrence, earl of Rochester, the Anglican former brothers-in-law of the duke of York. Together they and their clients became the pivot of an increasingly influential 'Yorkist' reversionary interest, pledged, with Charles's active connivance, to maintaining James's succession as part of the lawful, legitimist, Anglican scheme of things. Crippling as his defection to Rome was to them, they insisted that it did not, and could not, negate the inheritance which was his by divine right.

In the struggle against whiggery Sancroft was unsparing in James's cause. He attested Charles's disavowal of his rival Monmouth's legitimacy; he promoted propaganda on his behalf; he advanced Yorkist stalwarts within the Anglican hierarchy; he prosecuted his enemies, the dissenters especially; and he encouraged the integration of Scottish episcopalians into James's Edinburgh administration after his recall from exile, and published to protestant England the reassuring news of the duke's exemplary patronage of its sister church north of the border. In parliament he was unwavering. He voted against the Exclusion Bill on 15 November 1680, along with thirteen other bishops, and, again with them, opposed a Comprehension Bill to reunite dissenters to the established church. In return both princes were warmly appreciative of the episcopate's stand. Charles, who had long since abandoned his independent pursuit of toleration, refused to countenance any statutory relaxation of the penal laws against dissent, while James from Edinburgh instructed Clarendon to assure Sancroft and the bishops that 'I have ever stuck to them, whatsoever my own opinion is [in religion], and shall continue to do so' (Bodl. Oxf., MS Clarendon 87, fol. 331). At the dissolution of the third Exclusion Parliament in 1681 the stage was set for the tory reaction.

Charles led the way with his declaration of 8 April, a ringing affirmation of the laws on which church and state, religion, and property rested. Sancroft moved in council that it should be read from the pulpit of every church, and arranged for it to be done throughout the provinces of Canterbury and York. The nationwide propaganda coup turned opinion invincibly against the whigs. A stickler for law and order, Sancroft launched a two-pronged assault on the adversaries of his church; the dissenters and the papists. Against the latter he insisted that the king had sanctioned a wholesome severity, that they might be either reduced to submission, or driven out of the kingdom. The competence of the ecclesiastical courts was reinforced by a parallel campaign in the secular courts, as Charles put an intolerant Anglican tory magistracy in charge of local government. The combined efforts of church and state unleashed the last great religious persecution seen in England, one which considerably boosted outward conformity.

Pastoral objectives Sancroft's high concept of the sacred ministry made him call for improved standards in admissions to holy orders. In 1678 and 1685 he drew up instructions aimed at tightening ordination procedures and keeping better central records. This he complemented with a paramount care over the bestowal of preferment. His influence and that of his Hyde allies, exercised initially through the commission for ecclesiastical promotions (1681–4) and afterwards through their standing at court, ensured that the majority of clerical appointees were dedicated pastors and staunch loyalists committed to James's succession. The choice of bishops was particularly distinguished and provided Sancroft with some of his ablest colleagues. In 1680 he tackled the diminished 'patrimony of the church'. Recalling Charles's directives from the 1660s and an act of parliament of 1676, he urged the bishops and cathedral clergy to do more to augment the small livings in their patronage. Not content with exhortation, he set them an example by augmenting the ministerial stipends of those poor livings for which he was officially responsible in Kent, Lancashire, and Suffolk. He denounced simony, strove to minimize the evils stemming from pluralism, and endeavoured to free All Souls College, Oxford, and Dulwich College, of which he was visitor, of corrupt practices. He promoted monthly communions in cathedrals, and the reprinting of the proclamations and statutes ordered to be read annually in church. He lent his authority to the regulation of hospitals and the curtailing of clandestine marriages.

Sancroft's regard for the episcopal office was such that he chose to invite, rather than command, the co-operation of his bishops. However, when he detected shortcomings in episcopal administration he did not flinch from his duty to correct them. He was one of the last archbishops of Canterbury to exercise the superior authority of his see by conducting metropolitical visitations. He visited three dioceses in his province: in 1685 Lichfield and Coventry, where he had already suspended the unsatisfactory Thomas Wood for gross negligence in 1684; in 1686 Salisbury, where the ultra-tory dean, Thomas Pierce, was locked in controversy with his senile diocesan, Seth Ward; and, also in 1686, Lincoln, where the scholarly Thomas Barlow had succumbed to age. He did not visit in person, but deputed reliable bishops to act for him, while reserving to himself the meticulous supervision of each operation. Freed from the duty of parliamentary attendance, he began in the prosperous later years of the tory reaction to think anew of the cause of ecclesiastical reform and to make plans for implementing it.

Though political and primatial duties detained him in London, the government of the diocese of Canterbury rarely left Sancroft's thoughts. From Lambeth he ran his diocese by remote control, which he did by a combination of industry and resourcefulness. Visitations and confirmation tours he delegated to trusted suffragans, who functioned alongside his diocesan officials. In a bid to improve archiepiscopal oversight, and to circumvent his obstreperous archdeacon, Samuel Parker, he inserted his own chaplain, George Thorp, recruited from Emmanuel College, into the chapter of Christchurch, and, with his help, began the revival of ruridecanal discipline. He worked systematically through the detailed reports he received weekly at Lambeth, making pastorally informed judgments and issuing clear instructions to his agents on the ground. Always accessible to his clergy, he personally vetted all preferments in the diocese. He supported local charities, overhauled hospital statutes, checked clerical nonconformity, punished dissent, and befriended magistrates visiting the capital. That he coped so well was a real achievement for a man rising sixty, who might reasonably have found primatial administration a full-time occupation in itself.

James II Cast down by the death of Charles II and his rejection of the protestant sacrament, Sancroft's spirits were raised by James's declaration of support for the legal establishment. On 7 February 1685 he congratulated his accession, and reiterated the Church of England's 'holy boast, that she hath been always loyal to her kings' (Bodl. Oxf., MS Tanner 32, fol. 214). Its loyalty would, he hoped, provide a basis for continuing co-operation. The retention in office of Clarendon and Rochester reassured him. Nevertheless James's accession meant that the church had a Catholic supreme governor, who no longer attended its services and went openly to mass. The change was underlined by a command to shorten the coronation rite and omit the communion, which Sancroft did. His alterations betrayed a lack of understanding of pre-Reformation liturgy. As was his right, the archbishop crowned the king and queen on St George's day.

Lambeth was soon inundated by complaints from the dioceses, as dispensations to individual papists and the royal pardon of 19 March began to blight the operation of the church courts against recusancy and dissent. The political break came in the November session of James's parliament, when there was outspoken opposition to the king's request to retain Roman Catholic officers commissioned to put down the rebellions of Monmouth and Argyll. In the Lords twenty bishops, including Sancroft, joined the opposition. James promptly prorogued parliament, which never again met. The uncertain honeymoon in church and state was over. An early casualty of the break was the archbishop's influence over episcopal appointments. In July 1686 his recommendations of Robert South for Oxford and James Jeffreys for Chester were

ignored in favour of Samuel Parker and Thomas Cartwright, two maverick ultra-tories. The year also saw the dismissal of Clarendon and Rochester from office.

Condemned to the wilderness of royal disfavour Sancroft had to pick a precarious middle way as best he could between compliance and truculence. Burnet's malicious assertion that 'he lay silent at Lambeth', and was 'so set on the enriching his nephew, that he showed no sort of courage', is a travesty of the truth (*Bishop Burnet's History*, 4.109, and Swift's explosive footnote: 'False as hell'). His declining to order the clergy to cease afternoon catechising; his refusal to sit on the ecclesiastical commission, which he judged illegal and an encroachment upon his primatial jurisdiction, and consequent banishment from court; his sympathetic reception of the aggrieved dons of Oxford and Cambridge; and his joining the governors of Charterhouse in refusing James's mandate to admit a papist—all indicate his opposition, not to James's person, but to James's Catholicizing policies.

Unwilling to abandon his Roman Catholic subjects, James pressed on towards his ultimate goal of liberty of conscience. By an exercise of the prerogative his declaration of indulgence of 4 April 1687 established religious toleration in the parishes. It completely undermined the official Anglican monopoly. His removal of Anglican tories from local government pushed them and their clerical dependants further into opposition. So severe was the impact on the church of the loss of royal patronage, so consuming its hatred of popery, and so fearful were its bishops of a court allied to dissent, that Sancroft inaugurated conversations with dissenters with a view to forming a united protestant front against Rome. The promulgation of James's second declaration of indulgence on 4 May 1688, attended by an order to read the declaration in church, provoked a crisis of unforeseen magnitude.

Caught unawares, Sancroft summoned his suffragans to Lambeth, consulted Clarendon and other noblemen, and authorized a poll of clerical opinion in London. Though these soundings revealed disagreement on what to do, he decided not to obey the order—not from 'any want of tenderness towards Dissenters', but from the apparent illegality of the declaration, it 'being founded on such a dispensing power as may at pleasure set aside all laws ecclesiastical and civil' (Bodl. Oxf., MS Tanner 28, fol. 35). He based his non-compliance on a resolution of the House of Commons in 1672. The petition, signed by him and six other bishops, was presented to James by Sancroft's co-signatories, he being still forbidden the court. The king saw it as raising 'a standard of rebellion'. On their declining to enter into recognizances the seven bishops were committed to the Tower, which triggered widespread demonstrations of sympathy in London and the country at large. They were subsequently charged with having made and published a seditious libel. Released on bail on 15 June, they were tried in the court of king's bench on 29 June. Their acquittal the next day occasioned universal rejoicing, a sign that the nation emphatically rejected James's Catholicizing policies. Emboldened by their legal victory Sancroft designed a medal to commemorate the occasion.

The revolution of 1688–1689 Freed from imprisonment, Sancroft instructed his bishops and clergy to collaborate with the gentry, to resist 'popish emissaries', meaning the vicars apostolic sent from Rome, and to cultivate their 'brethren', the dissenters. Significantly, he also insisted on dutifulness to the king. Anxious to revive Anglican tory fortunes at court, he pressed James on 3 October to reverse his domestic policies, which he soon began to do. On 22 October he attended an extraordinary meeting of the council to clear the legitimacy of the prince of Wales from partisan doubt. As news of William of Orange's invasion circulated, the archbishop denied having invited him over, but refrained from repudiating his manifesto on behalf of protestantism. On 17 November he urged the summoning of 'a free parliament' to settle the disordered state of the kingdom. The attempted Anglican tory counter-revolution, in which he played a prominent part, and which by December had brought about the opening of formal negotiations between the king and prince, was well under way when it was disrupted by James's flight from London and William's soaring ambition, backed by an unexpected whig resurgence.

Responding to a summons from Sancroft and Rochester, twenty-seven peers assembled at Guildhall on 11 December and, under the archbishop's chairmanship, formed a provisional government to secure the capital from mob violence. They issued orders halting hostilities against William, whom they asked to assist them in obtaining a parliament. They deliberately avoided inviting him either to London, or to assume the reins of government. Notwithstanding the assembly's success in reimposing order in the capital, the meeting revealed the presence of a party violently opposed to James's kingship. Sancroft, alarmed at this development, absented himself thereafter, and, on learning that the king was in Kent, declined to take further action. He demonstrated his loyalty by waiting on James when he returned to London on 16 December. William's expulsion of the king from Whitehall caused Sancroft to withdraw permanently from public affairs. On 18 December the University of Cambridge elected him chancellor, setting aside the king's letter nominating Lord Dartmouth. He refused the election outright.

During the interregnum—the second he had experienced in his lifetime—Sancroft discussed the emergency with his friends and minutely examined the pros and cons of dynastic revolution. He refused to attend the irregular Convention Parliament, even to vote in favour of the regency project. He spurned the proclamation of William and Mary, maintaining that 'while King James lived, no other persons could be sovereigns' of England (D'Oyly, 2.137). He looked on William as a second Cromwell. He ignored the summons to crown the usurpers, and refused to consecrate Gilbert Burnet a bishop, but issued on 15 March 1689 a commission virtually empowering his suffragans to proceed. Meantime he continued to administer the church.

Deprivation, ejection, and schism Having solemnly sworn allegiance before God to King James, on whose head he had set the crown, Sancroft did not think himself free, in conscience, to transfer his loyalty to another. Refusing to recognize James's supplanters, he was suspended on 1 August, and deprived on 1 February 1690, with five bishops and about 400 clergy in England. Their deprivation, and replacement by Williamite bishops, gave rise to the nonjuring schism, which weakened still further a church that had already lost its legal monopoly of national religion by the passage of the 1689 Toleration Act. Unjustly assailed in the press for intriguing with France, the country to which James had withdrawn, Sancroft published *A Vindication of the Archbishop and Several other Bishops* (1690). On 23 April 1691 John Tillotson was named his successor. Sancroft defied Mary's order of 20 May to vacate Lambeth within ten days, and, on removing to the Temple on 23 June, left his steward behind to contest the writ of intrusion. On 3 August he left London for Fressingfield, where he lived out the remainder of his days. Visitors apart, he kept himself private, and devoted long hours to his books and papers.

Remaining true to his passive principles, Sancroft refused to be drawn into political conspiracy, albeit an ardent Jacobite. Believing the Williamite church to be schismatic, he refused to communicate in its prayers and sacraments, and officiated as his own chaplain. He took great pains to continue the remnant of 'the true Church of England' loyal to James II and the house of Stuart. On 9 February 1691 he delegated his archiepiscopal powers to William Lloyd, the deprived bishop of Norwich, and gave his wholehearted support to the consecration of new bishops, whose names were dutifully submitted to the exiled king for approval. While preparing Laud's diary for publication—a task which had been imposed on him by Sheldon in the 1660s—he fell ill of a fever, and died at Fressingfield on 23 November 1693. On his deathbed he prayed 'with great zeal and affection' for the restoration of James II, his queen, and the prince of Wales (Bodl. Oxf., MS Tanner 25, fol. 108; *A Letter Out of Suffolk*, 36). To avoid recognizing the testamentary jurisdiction of his supplanter, Tillotson, Sancroft made no will; he asked to be interred outside the walls of Fressingfield parish church, the vicarage of which he had re-endowed. He was buried by a nonjuring parson on 27 November. The inscription on his tomb, composed by himself, expressed total resignation to the divine will.

Slightly built, self-effacing in manner, and, with age, increasingly deaf, Archbishop Sancroft was not an imposing figure. Yet, upon acquaintance, his quiet goodness, sterling sense of duty, and great learning impressed his contemporaries. While presiding over a large household and dispensing hospitality to all comers, he remained the gentle obliging character he naturally was. He was especially happy in the conversation of scholars. He was regular at prayer, attending chapel four times a day. He inspired devotion in many of his bishops and clergy, and admiration in not a few of the leading laity. He was esteemed by Charles II, and respected by James II. Standing in the tradition of Reformation ecclesiology, he rejected a party label, seeing himself as a Christian whose duty it was to honour the king and fear God. That his primacy coincided with the advent of party strife, in which the divine nature of hereditary monarchy was disputed, inevitably exposed him to whig detraction. From Burnet to Macaulay, Sancroft has been portrayed as a cold, timorous, ineffectual prelate, but the reality was much otherwise. It is probable that his role as an Anglican *érudit*, who collected, conserved, and transcribed historical documents, and assisted and rewarded scholars to the utmost of his ability, will ensure him lasting fame. The bulk of the archbishop's manuscript collection was purchased from his nephew, William Sancroft, his former steward, by the well-known antiquary, Dr Thomas Tanner, bishop of St Asaph, and by him bequeathed to the Bodleian Library in Oxford. A number of stray items were subsequently donated by the nonjuring bishop Richard Rawlinson. Sancroft's prize possession, his library of 6000 volumes, he gave to Emmanuel College, not to Lambeth.

R. A. P. J. BEDDARD

Sources G. D'Oyly, *The life of William Sancroft, archbishop of Canterbury*, 2 vols. (1821) [incl. his three printed sermons] · R. A. Beddard, 'William Sancroft as archbishop of Canterbury, 1677–1691', DPhil diss., U. Oxf., 1965 · *Familiar letters of Dr. William Sancroft … to Mr. North … to which is prefixed some account of his life and character* (1757) · *A letter out of Suffolk to a friend in London* (1694) · *The proceedings and tryal … of … William lord archbishop of Canterbury … in the court of Kings-bench at Westminster, in Trinity-term … 1688* (1716) · H. Cary, ed., *Memorials of the great civil war in England from 1646 to 1652*, 2 vols. (1842) · E. Cardwell, ed., *Documentary annals of the reformed Church of England, and other proceedings connected with the revision of the Book of Common Prayer*, 2 vols. (1839) · E. Cardwell, ed., *A history of conferences and other proceedings connected with the revision of the Book of Common Prayer*, 2nd edn (1841) · R. Beddard, ed., *A kingdom without a king: the journal of the provisional government in the revolution of 1688* (1988) · R. A. Beddard, 'The unexpected whig revolution of 1688', in R. A. Beddard, *The revolutions of 1688* (1991), 11–101 · F. Stubbings, *Emmanuel College chapel, 1677–1977* (1977) · *The correspondence of Henry Hyde, earl of Clarendon, and of his brother Laurence Hyde, earl of Rochester*, ed. S. W. Singer, 2 vols. (1828) · *The life of James the Second, king of England*, ed. J. S. Clarke, 2 vols. (1816) · J. Gutch, ed., *Collectanea curiosa*, 2 vols. (1781) · W. Kennett, *The complete history of England*, 2nd edn, 3 vols. (1719), vol. 3 · N. Sykes, *From Sheldon to Secker: aspects of English church history, 1660–1768* (1959) · *The copy of a letter from Scotland, to his grace the lord archbishop of Canterbury* (1682) · *Bishop Burnet's History* · *A supplement to Burnet's History of my own time*, ed. H. C. Foxcroft (1902) · R. A. Beddard, 'Observations of a London clergyman on the revolution of 1688-9', *Guildhall Miscellany*, 2 (1960–68), 406–17 · R. A. Beddard, 'The commission for ecclesiastical promotions, 1681–4: an instrument of tory reaction', *HJ*, 10 (1967), 11–40 · *DNB* · A. T. Bolton and H. D. Hendry, eds., *The Wren Society*, 20 vols. (1924–43), vols. 1, 5, 13 · S. Wren, *Parentalia* (1750) · C. J. Cuming, ed., *The Durham book, being the first draft of the revision of the Book of Common Prayer in 1661*, Alcuin Club (1975) · J. H. Overton, *The nonjurors: their lives, principles, and writings* (1902) · [W. Sancroft], *A vindication of the archbishop and several other bishops* (1690) · [W. Sancroft], *Articles of visitation and enquiry … in the ordinary visitation of … William … lord archbishop of Canterbury* (1682) · A. J. van der Aa, P. O. van der Chij, and W. Eekhoff, eds., *Biographisch Woordenboek der Nederlanden*, 21 vols. (1852–78), 17 (Haarlem, 1874) · D. Wilkins, ed., *Concilia Magnae Britanniae et Hiberniae*, 4 (1737), vol. 4 · W. Dugdale, *The history of St Paul's Cathedral in London*, 2nd edn (1716) · Bodl. Oxf., MSS Tanner · Sancroft papers, Bodl. Oxf., MSS Tanner · Sancroft registers, LPL · PRO,

SP 29, SP 44 · college archives, Emmanuel College, Cambridge, esp. COL 9.10, nos. 10, 16, 21; COL 14.1, pp. 71–6; CHA 1.1; CHA 1.2 · dean and chapter archives, U. Durham L., archives and special collections, Palace Green section [esp. diocesan registry books, 1, 4; dean and chapter institution book 1] · dean and chapter archives, York Minster archives · St Paul's dean and chapter archives, GL, esp. W.C. 45, fols. 68–75, 77; W. C. 50; W. B. 78, fols. 35–83*v* · Canterbury Cathedral Library, Reg. 29, fols. 363*v*, 404

Archives BL, corresp. and collections, Harley MSS 3783–3798 · Bodl. Oxf., corresp. and papers · CUL, corresp. and papers · St John Cam., papers on forms of prayers and services | BL, letters to William Dillingham, Sloane MS 1710 · LPL, letters to William Lloyd, bishop of Norwich

Likenesses attrib. B. (I) Lens, oils, *c*.1650–1655, Emmanuel College, Cambridge [*see illus.*] · D. Loggan, line engraving, 1680, BM, NPG · G. Bower, silver medal, 1688, NPG · E. Lutterel, drawing, chalks, *c*.1688, NPG · group portrait, oils, *c*.1688 (*The seven bishops committed to the Tower in 1688*), NPG · P. P. Lens, oils, 1754 (after D. Loggan, 1680), Emmanuel College, Cambridge; version LPL · F. H. van Houg, line engraving (after effigy), NPG · R. White, line engraving, BM, NPG · tomb effigy, St Peter's and St Paul's Church, Fressingfield, Suffolk

Sandale, John (*c*.1274–1319), administrator and bishop of Winchester, may have been the son of William of Wheatley, who held the manor of Wheatley within Long Sandale by Doncaster, Yorkshire. Sandale inherited this property, and in 1301 was licensed to have free warren there and ten years later to crenellate his residence. He also held the manor of Great Coates, near Grimsby, Lincolnshire, for which in 1313 he likewise received a grant of free warren. He can be shown to have had three younger brothers, William, Robert, who became steward of his episcopal household, and Thomas, who was with him in Scotland in 1306–7, and whom Sandale, as bishop, appointed constable of Farnham Castle. On his sister Margery he settled his Wheatley property. William had two clerical sons, William and John, of whom the latter was to be his heir and one of his executors. Gilbert Sandale, probably a nephew, was a canon of Auckland (1313–15). Two unnamed nephews were taken prisoner by the Scots at Bannockburn and the king granted Sandale a Scottish prisoner to exchange for them.

Sandale was a clerk both of Henry de Lacy, earl of Lincoln (*d*. 1311), for whom he acted as executor, and of Edward I and Edward II. He began his administrative career in the royal wardrobe, as controller to the keeper (1295), but soon migrated to the exchequer. In May 1297 he was controller of receipts in Gascony, having accompanied Edmund, earl of Lancaster (*d*. 1296), there. Two years later he made a return journey. He was appointed keeper of the royal mints on 15 October 1298, from the issues of which he was in 1300 paid large sums for his service in Scotland at the siege of Caerlaverock in that year. At the parliament of 1305 he was appointed to hear and respond to Gascon petitions, and was made chamberlain of Scotland, where, in February 1306, he became one of the deputy guardians. On 26 October 1305 he received custody of Berwick Castle, being granted £40 a year for the office, and was also entrusted with the collection of burgage rents in the town.

With Edward II's accession in 1307 Sandale became chancellor of the exchequer (20 August) and rented a house at Aldgate in London, but on 20 May in the following year he was dismissed, allegedly because of royal hatred for the earl of Lincoln. But he succeeded Walter Reynolds (d. 1327) as treasurer on 6 July 1310, and served until 23 October 1311, when he may have been seriously ill, since a false report of his death triggered the sequestration of his goods. He was lieutenant of the treasurer between 4 October 1312 and 26 September 1314, and in 1312 a writ of privy seal directed him, together with the elder Hugh Despenser (d. 1326) and Aymer de Valence, earl of Pembroke (d. 1324), to carry out a reform of the household, though this was not effected. At the end of his period as acting treasurer he again succeeded Reynolds, this time as chancellor, and continued in office until 9 June 1318. He attended the burial of Piers Gaveston (d. 1312) at Langley in January 1315 and was one of those appointed to secure the return of his goods. He resumed the treasurership on 16 November 1318 and held it until his death a year later. Another of his responsibilities was that of principal collector of the papal sexennial tenth, which was diverted to Edward II's use.

A notable pluralist, Sandale was at one time chancellor of St Patrick's, Dublin, treasurer of Lichfield, and dean of St Paul's with prebends in Dublin, Beverley, Wells, Lincoln, London, York, and Glasgow, as well as ten rectories from Chalk in Kent (worth £20) to Dunbar in Scotland (worth £240). Murimuth regarded his accumulation as having caught the eye of John XXII as a ready source of papal patronage—a cynical interpretation of the bull *Execrabilis* (1317), which limited to two the number of benefices which could be held in plurality. At the king's insistence, with the personal intervention of the earl of Pembroke, Sandale was elected bishop by the Winchester chapter on 26 July 1316. The temporalities were restored on 23 September and he was consecrated at Canterbury on 31 October by Archbishop Reynolds. Sandale none the less retained the great seal for a further two years, apart from intervals when he was engaged in missions at a distance from Westminster, on pilgrimage to Canterbury (February 1318), or during short bursts of activity in his diocese.

Sandale's status as bishop ensured his involvement in the political turmoil over the observance of the ordinances following their enactment in 1311. They were adopted by the Leicester assembly of April 1318, at which, according to the Bridlington chronicler, Sandale was present and swore acceptance. He was also one of the bishops who endorsed the political agreement of the following June. He was therefore an active participant in the negotiations leading to the treaty of Leake (9 August 1318) and was at York for the parliament of October, where he was nominated an auditor of petitions and his name was added to the permanent council established at Leake to oversee the government of the realm. So far as can be judged he was a competent administrator loyal to the king and not, as Conway Davies thought, 'too closely associated with Lancaster' to be acceptable to what he termed the 'middle party'. In September 1318 Sandale was at St Paul's to participate in the process against Robert I, king of Scots, and in March 1319 he was there again, with the earls

of Pembroke and Norfolk, to resolve a dispute between the mayor and citizens of London. It is not possible adequately to evaluate his work as a diocesan, but his register is an interesting one, with details of action taken in response to *Execrabilis*. Not until 30 August 1319 did he visit his cathedral priory, but apparently he carried out all recorded ordination ceremonies in person.

On 17 March 1317 Sandale was granted papal licence to choose a confessor, possibly because of increasing infirmity. He died on 2 November 1319 at his manor of Southwark and was buried in St Mary Overie there on the 11th. The king seized his chattels, though allowing expenses for his funeral (which in the event included an extensive meal for a large number of mourners), and pursued his executors for more than twenty years to recover alleged arrears in his accounts. ROY MARTIN HAINES

Sources Chancery records · Rymer, *Foedera* · W. Stubbs, ed., *Chronicles of the reigns of Edward I and Edward II*, 2 vols., Rolls Series, 76 (1882–3) · *RotP* · H. G. Richardson and G. O. Sayles, eds., *Rotuli parliamentorum Anglie hactenus inediti, MCCLXXIX–MCCCLXXIII*, CS, 3rd ser., 51 (1935) · F. J. Baigent, ed., *The registers of John de Sandale and Rigaud d'Asserio, bishops of Winchester*, Hampshire RS, 8 (1897) · T. Madox, *The history and antiquities of the exchequer of the kings of England*, 2nd edn, 2 vols. (1769); repr. (1969) · J. C. Davies, *The baronial opposition to Edward II* (1918) · Tout, *Admin. hist.*, vols. 2, 6 · J. G. Edwards, 'The negotiating of the treaty of Leake, 1318', *Essays in history presented to Reginald Lane Poole*, ed. H. W. C. Davis (1927), 360–78 · R. A. Roberts, ed., 'Edward II, the lords ordainer, and Piers Gaveston's jewels and horses', *Camden miscellany, XV*, ed. R. A. Roberts, CS, 3rd ser., 41 (1929) · J. R. Maddicott, *Thomas of Lancaster, 1307–1322: a study in the reign of Edward II* (1970) · J. R. S. Phillips, *Aymer de Valence, earl of Pembroke, 1307–1324: baronial politics in the reign of Edward II* (1972) · R. M. Haines, *The church and politics in fourteenth-century England: the career of Adam Orleton, c. 1275–1345*, Cambridge Studies in Medieval Life and Thought, 3rd ser., 10 (1978)

Sandars, John Satterfield (1853–1934), political secretary, was born on 15 January 1853 at Foleshill, Coventry, one of five children, and the only son, of Charles Sandars (d. 1877), an estate and colliery agent, and his wife, Agnes, née Patterson. The family lived at Mackworth, Derbyshire, where they had been established for five generations, and Sandars attended nearby Repton School. In 1871 he went up to Magdalen College, Oxford, where he took a third class law degree in 1875 and a second class BCL in 1876. In 1885 he submitted a dissertation on the Roman doctrine of *culpa* for a DCL, which was subsequently published. In 1877 he was called to the Lincoln's Inn bar, serving on the midland circuit until 1886 when he was appointed private secretary to the home secretary, Henry Matthews. Part of his work involved liaising with the Irish Office, which brought him into contact with A. J. Balfour, then chief secretary for Ireland and the brother of one of his first friends at Oxford, Cecil Balfour.

In the general election held in July 1892 Sandars stood unsuccessfully as the Conservative candidate for Mid-Derbyshire and in the following month he married Harriet(te) Grace Mary, daughter of Sir William Don, seventh baronet, of Repton, and relative of the painter Millais. When she died in 1947 her estate included a number of paintings by her family and two by Rubens. 1892 also saw

John Satterfield Sandars (1853–1934), by Sir Benjamin Stone, 1897

Sandars's appointment as private secretary to Balfour (leader in the Commons and first lord of the Treasury) and the beginning of over twenty years at the hub of British political life.

Sandars's influence extended into many areas including party organization and patronage but it found its chief expression in his role as one of Balfour's closest advisers and the main channel between Balfour and senior members of the Conservative and Liberal sections of the Unionist Party. Balfour's indifferent health, detached political style, and frequent absences from London increased the scope for Sandars's involvement. He played a central role during Balfour's premiership from 1902 to 1905, performing many of the functions which would later be allocated to the cabinet secretariat. He remained with Balfour until 1911 when the latter resigned as party leader. His letters to Balfour blended information, cogent political advice, gossip, and travel arrangements in a format designed to suit Balfour's temperament—the obsequious tone in these, and in letters to other colleagues and friends, sitting oddly with the firm views strongly expressed. Sandars had a 'genial' personality but he was also enigmatic and 'secretive' and some of his contemporaries objected to the extent of his authority. His posthumous significance stems from his archival legacy—the correspondence with leading political figures and accounts of such key events as Balfour's resignation.

Sandars's relations with Balfour ended abruptly. When the coalition government was formed in May 1915 Sandars initially supported Balfour's decision to return to office as first lord of the Admiralty but broke with him when Balfour refused to accept his advice that it would be unwise to allow Churchill (whom Sandars detested) to continue to live in Admiralty House and keep an office there. The break in relations was permanent: Sandars refused Balfour's invitation to lunch in 1916.

In retirement Sandars continued to follow national politics and as one of those who nominated Lord Cane for the chancellorship of Oxford University in 1925, he delighted in the defeat of Asquith. Sandars wrote a number of books between 1884 and 1928, mainly on legal and political matters. His leisure pursuits were chiefly racing, golf, and classical literature. In 1905 he was sworn of the privy council and created CVO. He died from pneumonia at his home at Eastley End, Thorpe, Chertsey, Surrey, on 29 March 1934.

HELEN LANGLEY

Sources *The Times* (31 March 1934) · J. E. Sandars, *The Sandars centuries* (privately printed, 1971) · M. Egremont, *Balfour: a life of Arthur James Balfour* (1980) · C. Petrie, *The powers behind the prime minister* (1958) · J. Ramsden, *The age of Balfour and Baldwin, 1902–1940* (1978) · A. Gollin, 'Balfour, 1902–1911', *The conservative leadership, 1832–1932*, ed. D. Southgate (1974), 151–70 · S. H. Zebel, *Balfour* (1973) · *WWW* · J. S. Sandars, *Studies of yesterday* (1928)

Archives Bodl. Oxf., corresp. and papers | BL, corresp. with A. J. Balfour, Add. MSS 49760–49768 · BL, corresp. with Lord Northcliffe, Add. MS 62153 · Bodl. Oxf., Asquith MSS · Bodl. Oxf., Dawson MSS · Bodl. Oxf., letters to Lady Milner · Bodl. Oxf., corresp. with Lord Selborne · CKS, letters to Aretas Akers–Douglas · Durham RO, letters to Lady Londonderry · HLRO, letters to Ralph Blumenfield · IWM, corresp. with H. A. Gwynne

Likenesses B. Stone, photograph, 1897, NPG [*see illus.*]

Wealth at death £17,742 7*s.* 5*d.*: probate, 8 June 1934, *CGPLA Eng. & Wales*

Sandars, Thomas Collett (1825–1894), jurist, was the eldest son of Samuel Sandars of Lochnere, near Hemel Hempstead, Hertfordshire. He matriculated at Balliol College, Oxford, on 30 November 1843, was a scholar from 1843 to 1849, and graduated BA in 1848, having taken first-class honours in *literae humaniores* and the chancellor's Latin verse prize. He became fellow of Oriel in 1849, and proceeded MA in 1851. On 25 May that year he married Margaret, second daughter of William Hanmer of Bodnod Hall, Denbighshire.

Sandars was called to the bar in 1851, and was reader of constitutional law and history to the inns of court from 1865 to 1873. He was one of the earliest contributors to the *Saturday Review*, and an intimate friend of James FitzJames Stephen, judge and legal historian. He interested himself in commercial affairs in later years, and went twice to Egypt, in 1877 and 1880, to represent the Association of Foreign Bondholders. He was also chairman of the Mexican Railway Company.

Sandars died on 4 August 1894 at his home, Queen Anne's Mansions, Westminster. He was survived by at least one child. Sandars was remembered chiefly for his *Institutes of Justinian*, a translation with notes and an introduction, which first appeared in 1853. A new edition appeared as late as 1970.

W. A. J. ARCHBOLD, *rev.* ERIC METCALFE

Sources Foster, *Alum. Oxon.* · *The Times* (9 Aug 1894) · L. Stephen, *The life of Sir James Fitzjames Stephen* (1895), 152, 178, 197 · J. Foster, *Men-at-the-bar: a biographical hand-list of the members of the various inns of court*, 2nd edn (1885) · d. cert.

Wealth at death £35,489 11s. 0d.: probate, 20 Sept 1894, CGPLA *Eng. & Wales*

Sanday, William (1843–1920), biblical scholar, the eldest son of William Sanday, a sheep and cattle breeder, and his wife, Elizabeth Mann, was born on 1 August 1843 at Holme Pierrepont, Nottinghamshire, where his family had been settled for more than a century. He was educated at Repton School from 1858 to 1861 and matriculated at Balliol College, Oxford, in 1862; in the following year he switched colleges after winning a scholarship at Corpus Christi College. He was awarded a first-class degree in 1865 and was elected a fellow of Trinity College, Oxford, in 1866. He taught at Trinity for three years until, having been ordained priest, he left Oxford in 1869. He held successively the college livings of Navestock, Essex; St Nicholas, Abingdon (1871–2); Great Waltham (1872–3); and Barton on the Heath, Warwickshire (1873–6). Sanday was appointed principal of Bishop Hatfield Hall, Durham, in 1876, and on 10 July 1877 he married Marian Charlotte Amelia Woodman Hastings (1855?–1904), daughter of Warren Hastings Woodman Hastings, of Twining, Tewkesbury, Gloucestershire. They had no children, and she died in 1904.

Sanday left Durham in 1882 upon being appointed Dean Ireland's professor of exegesis of holy scripture, a post which he held in conjunction with a fellowship and tutorship at Exeter College, Oxford, from 1883. From 1895 to 1919 he was Lady Margaret professor of divinity and canon of Christ Church. He was made one of the original fellows of the British Academy, in 1903, and an honorary doctor of several universities, including Edinburgh, Durham, and Dublin.

Sanday's academic career was dedicated to the critical study of the New Testament and especially of the gospels. His first books, *The Authorship and Historical Character of the Fourth Gospel* (1872) and *The Gospels in the Second Century* (1876), were representative of his later work. As Lady Margaret professor he instituted, in 1894, a seminar which met to discuss New Testament textual critical questions such as the relationship between the gospel according to Mark, the hypothetical source Q, and Matthew and Luke. These were considered in minutiae, the findings being published in 1911 as *Oxford Studies in the Synoptic Problem*. In 1886 he published a work *Portions of the Gospels According to St Mark and St Matthew from the Bobbio MS*, which asserted the importance of the close examination of the primitive Western authorities for the text. Such examination of textual critical questions prepared the way for later synthesis by others, but also demonstrated the need for more detailed specialization within the field.

In some sense the *Critical and Exegetical Commentary on the Epistle to the Romans* (1895), written in collaboration with A. C. Headlam, was a diversion from the exegetical studies which, as professor of exegesis, he felt a duty to publish. He therefore began to lecture and publish in the field of historical criticism. In his work *The Criticism of the Fourth*

William Sanday (1843–1920), by Leonard Campbell Taylor, 1908

Gospel (1904), a series of lectures delivered at the Union Theological Seminary in New York city, he argued against the reductionist approach towards St John's gospel and claimed that it had some historical uses. But he devoted much of his intellectual energy to the study of the life of Jesus. His article 'Jesus Christ' in James Hastings's *Dictionary of the Bible* (vol. 2, 1899) was highly regarded by the critical school, and Sanday was pressed to develop a substantial work on the life of Christ. But his awareness of the complexity of the critical issues surrounding the subject was a constraint. Although he went on to disseminate the views of continental critical scholars, such as A. Schweitzer, in *The Life of Christ in Recent Research* (1907), and published short works on the subject, such as the popular *Christology and Personality* (1911), he never wrote his own life of Christ.

The article 'Jesus Christ' was later published separately as *Outlines of the Life of Christ* (1905). Its significance lay more in its reflection of the movement in Anglican thought towards an acceptance of critical study of the text than in its radicalism. Sanday's view of Christ did not depart very far from earlier nineteenth-century portrayals, but his critical premises questioned the authenticity of the infancy narratives, the genealogies, and some miracle stories, and they expounded the implications of the synoptic relationship between Matthew, Mark, and Luke.

Sanday's later courses of professorial lectures illustrated his conception of the 'praeparatio evangelica' as rooted in the history of religion in the East, far back in the centuries before Christ and not only of the Jews. While maintaining an orthodox theological position Sanday was regarded, at the turn of the century, as one of the leading gospel critics, following B. F. Westcott and F. J. A. Hort in Cambridge. His cautious attitude and conservative theology contributed to the acceptance of the critical principle by Anglican clergymen and scholars. His support of Charles Gore in the *Lux mundi* controversy helped rather than hindered the critical school precisely because Sanday was recognized as a moderate, even if occasionally he was a little impetuous or pontifical.

When the First World War broke out in 1914 Sanday found a new subject for his writings. His political standpoint was rather conservative (just as in his economic views he supported the middle classes), and the armed forces always had a curious fascination for him. He threw himself wholeheartedly into the business of a pamphleteer, publishing *The Deeper Causes of the War* (1914); *The Meaning of the War for Germany and Great Britain: an Attempted Synthesis* (1915); *In View of the End: a Retrospect and a Prospect* (1916); and *When Should the War End?* (1917). Having all but abandoned theological controversy and biblical research, the summary of the results, as he saw them, of the critical study of the gospels was published in 1918 as *The New Testament Background*.

Sanday held an unusual position among British biblical scholars as the interpreter *par excellence* of the immense strides in New Testament studies which were being made abroad, particularly by German scholars. He was acquainted with some of the most influential scholars abroad. He respected the encyclopaedic scale of German literary output and for many years he kept up with almost everything that was being written in his field in German or English. He also donated more than 900 bound volumes of pamphlets to the library of Queen's College, Oxford. Although not original in his research and slow to arrive at conclusions, he was capable of absorbing large quantities of reading, to challenge hypotheses, and to defend his own positions. It was in part because of these qualities that he was trusted as a critic in both British and Anglican circles.

Through Sanday's work, sober and cautious, the critical study of the New Testament became a less fearful pursuit among Anglican clergy and scholars. Sanday died at Christ Church, Oxford, on 16 September 1920.

Joanna Hawke

Sources *Church Times* (24 Sept 1920) · *Oxford Magazine* (22 Oct 1920), 27–9 · A. S. Peake, 'Dr Sanday', *Expositor*, 8th ser., no. 119 (Nov 1920), 321–34 · A. Souther, 'William Sanday', *Expositor*, 8th ser., no. 119 (Nov 1920), 335–48 · 'William Sanday, the man and his message', *Expositor*, 8th ser., no. 120 (Dec 1920), 415–31 · A. Plummer, 'William Sanday and his work [3 pts]', *Expository Times*, 32 (1920–21), 151–5, 199–203, 247–52 · *Journal of Theological Studies*, 22 (1920–21), 97–104, 194–205 · W. Sanday, *Novum Testamentum S. Iranaei* (1923), preface · S. Neil and T. Wright, *The interpretation of the New Testament, 1861–1986* (1988) · D. L. Pals, *The Victorian lives of Jesus* (1982) · O. Chadwick, *The Victorian church*, 1 (1966)
Archives Bodl. Oxf., corresp.
Likenesses L. Campbell Taylor, oils, 1908, Christ Church Oxf. [*see illus.*] · W. Stoneman, photograph, 1917, NPG · C. H. Shannon, portrait, Christ Church Oxf., chapter house
Wealth at death £9308 14s. 7d.: probate, 26 Oct 1920, *CGPLA Eng. & Wales*

Sandbach, Francis Henry [Harry] (1903–1991), classical scholar, was born on 23 February 1903 in an Edgbaston nursing home, the elder son of Francis Edward Sandbach (1874–1946), lecturer and subsequently professor of German in the University of Birmingham, and Ethel Bywater (1874–1949), a teacher. From 1914 to 1921 he was at King Edward's School, Birmingham, where he was captain of the school, which he represented at rugby football. In 1920 he was elected to a major scholarship in classics at Trinity College, Cambridge, where he began in 1921 a residence that lasted with only short intermissions until his death. His university distinctions included first classes in both parts of the classical tripos, the Browne and Craven scholarships, the first chancellor's classical medal, and the Charles Oldham scholarship. Rejecting the civil service, he embarked on research for a Trinity research fellowship, to which he was elected in 1927 for a dissertation on Plutarch. This he took up in 1928, having from 1926 to 1928 held an assistant lectureship at Manchester.

In 1929 Harry Sandbach (as he was always known) was appointed to college and university lectureships in classics, in 1951 to a Brereton readership, and in 1967 to a personal chair in classics, the first such appointment in his faculty. That this distinction, and election to the British Academy in 1968, came so late in his career is not wholly attributable to the distractions from scholarship arising from the Second World War and the demands of college administration, engrossing though these were. From 1939 to 1943 Sandbach remained in Cambridge, where in addition to a heavy teaching programme he served as junior proctor, air raid warden, and Home Guard. From 1943 he worked in the economics section of the topographical department of the Admiralty in Oxford. He was released in 1945 to take up a Trinity tutorship, and from 1953 to 1956 he was senior tutor. As a loyal Trinity man he never begrudged these commitments, and such external factors are not the whole story.

The cast of Sandbach's mind was deliberative. His entry in the *Trinity Who's Who* when he was an undergraduate read 'Well, it depends'; and many students and colleagues were disconcerted by his habit of thinking for some time before he spoke. Before the war he published many reviews and short notes which attest the range of interests, literary as well as philosophical, embraced by his wide and discursive reading. There being then no pressure on academics to 'produce', he was free to pursue what interested him. The first solid results of these explorations began to appear in the 1960s, in his substantial contributions to the edition of Plutarch in the Loeb Classical Library, for the last volume of which, the fragments, he was solely responsible. He was also working on Menander, having in 1959 accepted an invitation from the Clarendon Press to complete a comprehensive commentary begun by A. W. Gomme. This was published in 1973, and together with the Oxford Classical Text of Menander (1972) constitutes Sandbach's *chef d'oeuvre*. His international standing in this field was signalled by his election in 1977 to the Royal Society of Arts and Sciences of Göteborg. Two short books for the student and general reader that came out at this time, *The Stoics* (1975) and *The Comic Theatre of Greece and Rome* (1977), were warmly appreciated by their intended readership. The former reflected an interest in Stoicism which had originated in his Plutarchan studies, and which was the occasion of his last substantial work, *Aristotle and the Stoics* (1985). This questioned received ideas on the subject and provoked a lively controversy, issuing in a special conference to debate its findings. A natural bent to literature had received little encouragement from the classical tripos as it was in Sandbach's day and for long afterwards, but he also made a number of distinctive contributions to the interpretation of Latin poetry; in particular, a lifelong and fruitful interest in Virgil, the subject of his first publication, had been stimulated at Manchester by R. S. Conway's notorious 'Virgil Discussions'.

On 9 July 1932 Sandbach married Mary Warburton Mathews (1901–1990), later to become a distinguished Swedish scholar and translator of Strindberg. They had two children, a daughter born in 1940 and a son in 1943. Sandbach was of medium height and build, wiry, a good walker, and to the end of his life a strong swimmer. His face, scarred by adolescent acne and with a prominent chin and large nose, was redeemed from ugliness by benevolent eyes of a deep grey-blue, the true reflection of an amiable and modest character. Though his scholarly standards were high and severe, his criticisms were always expressed with courtesy and moderation. As in his scholarship, so in his teaching and lecturing all rhetoric and display were foreign to his nature. He was generous in sharing his learning with others, as many prefaces testify. His upbringing was agnostic, and before leaving school he had come to disbelieve the central tenets of Christianity. Sandbach died of diabetes mellitus in Cambridge at 2 Hedgerley Close, his home since 1936, on 18 September 1991, and was cremated at Cambridge on 30 September. His ashes were scattered at the crematorium.

E. J. KENNEY

Sources autobiographical notes, British Academy · E. J. Kenney, C. F. L. Austin, D. A. F. M. Russell, and M. Schofield, 'Francis Henry Sandbach, 1903–91', *PBA*, 84 (1994), 485–503 · personal knowledge (2004) · private information (2004) [C. Sandbach-Dahlström] · W. G. Arnott, *The Guardian* (27 Sept 1991) · R. D. Dawe, *The Independent* (27 Sept 1991) · *The Times* (5 Oct 1991) · R. D. Dawe, *Gnomon*, 64 (1992), 473–4
Likenesses photograph, 1927, Trinity Cam. · J. Minton, charcoal drawing, 1953, Trinity Cam. · photograph, 1968?, British Academy, London · P. Gaskell, photograph, 1971, Trinity Cam.
Wealth at death £702,384: probate, 11 Dec 1991, *CGPLA Eng. & Wales*

Sandbach [*née* Roscoe], **Margaret** (1812–1852), poet and novelist, was born in Liverpool on 28 April 1812, the granddaughter of William *Roscoe (1753–1831), the historian, and the daughter of Edward Roscoe (1785–1834), merchant, and his wife, Margaret Lace (1786/7–1840), his second cousin and author of *Floral Illustrations of the Seasons* (1829). The Roscoes were a prominent Unitarian intellectual family of Liverpool. Margaret had two brothers, one of whom died in infancy. She grew up very close to the other, Edward Henry Roscoe (1813–1866), dedicating her

first publication, *Poems* (1840), to him, 'beloved companion' of her youth. The volume contains one of her best and most spirited poems, 'The Appeal of the Wounded Amazon', inspired by the work of the sculptor John Gibson, a Welshman whose early career had been helped by her grandfather. On 4 May 1832 she married Henry Robertson Sandbach (1807–1895), of Hafodunnos, Denbigh, JP for Caernarvonshire and from 1855 high sheriff of Denbigh; but the major focus of her writing remained fixed on the relation between brother and sister. This is true of her tragedy *The Amidei* (1845), as well as of *Hearts in Mortmain* (1850), probably the best of her several prose fictions. Her strengths as a writer, however, lay rather in poetry, for which she had a fine ear, if not the 'gifts of genius' ascribed to her by Lady Eastlake (p. 11). She published *Aurora and other Poems* in 1850, dedicated to John Gibson; in 1851 she began writing his autobiography from his dictation while he was a guest at their house at Hafodunnos. But the death of his brother took him back to Rome, where she and her husband had first made friends with him in the late 1830s (their long correspondence was to be a key source for Lady Eastlake's *Life of John Gibson*, 1870), and her own increasing illness from breast cancer halted her work. Margaret Sandbach died at Hafodunnos after much suffering on 23 June 1852, and was buried at Llangernyw, near Hafodunnos.　　　VIRGINIA H. BLAIN

Sources F. W. Dunston, *Roscoeana: being some account of the kinsfolk of William Roscoe of Liverpool and Jane (née Griffies) his wife* (privately printed, 1907) · Lady Eastlake [E. Eastlake], ed., *Life of John Gibson, R.A., sculptor* (1870) · *GM*, 2nd ser., 38 (1852), 322 · E. Taylor, *Memories of some contemporary poets* (1868)

Sandberg, Samuel Louis Graham (1851–1905), Tibetan scholar, born on 9 December 1851 at Oughtibridge in Yorkshire, was the fifth child in a family of five sons and two daughters of Paul Louis Sandberg (*d.* 1878), then vicar of Oughtibridge, and his wife, Maria (1815–1903), daughter of James Graham of the diplomatic service and granddaughter of Dr James Graham (1745–1794), a London doctor. Both parents were distinguished by their linguistic talents. Paul Louis Sandberg, whose ancestors had come to England from Sweden, won the Tyrwhitt Hebrew scholarship and had other successes at Cambridge, and was conversationally acquainted with as many as thirteen languages, including Arabic, Syriac, and Hindustani. He was in India as a missionary from 1843 to 1849, becoming principal of Jai Narayan's College at Benares. From 1874 until his death he was rector of Northrepps in Norfolk. Maria Sandberg, a writer of devotional works and a philanthropist, received the exceptional title of honorary life member of the Church Missionary Society. She was acquainted with seven languages, including Hindustani (*The Times*, 27 April 1903).

Samuel Sandberg, after attending Liverpool College (1861–3) and Enfield School, Birkenhead (1863–7), graduated BA from Trinity College, Dublin, at nineteen in 1870. His tastes were linguistic and mathematical, with a leaning towards Asiatic languages, such as Chinese and Japanese. He developed an aversion for the medical profession, for which he was originally destined, and on leaving Trinity College he was admitted a student at the Inner Temple on 9 June 1871, was called to the bar on 30 April 1874, and joined the northern circuit. His practice was insignificant, and he mainly divided his time between journalism, the preparation of an elaborate treatise entitled 'The shipmaster's legal handbook', which he failed to publish, and private tuition. A year's prostration by Maltese fever (1877–8), contracted while travelling with a pupil, was followed in 1879 by his ordination as a clergyman. He was curate of St Clement's, Sandwich, from 1879 to 1882, and chaplain of the Seckford Hospital, Woodbridge, Suffolk, from 1882 to 1884. In the latter year he married Mary Kempson Grey (d. 1910); they had no children.

In 1885 Sandberg went to India as chaplain on the Bengal establishment, where he held numerous different charges. When on a holiday at Darjeeling he made his first acquaintance with the Tibetan language, and in 1888 he published at Calcutta a *Manual of the Sikkim-Bhutia Dialect* (2nd edn, enlarged, 1895). He learned much of the secret explorations of Tibet in progress during the next seventeen years, and wrote in the press and the magazines about the topography of Tibet and routes through the country. In 1901 he issued at Calcutta *An Itinerary of the Route from Sikkim to Lhasa, together with a Plan of the Capital of Tibet*. On the eve of the British expedition in 1904 he published a systematic treatise, *The Exploration of Tibet: its History and Particulars from 1623 to 1904*. Sandberg drafted the letter from Lord Curzon, the viceroy, to the 'grand lama', the rejection of which precipitated Younghusband's expedition of 1904.

To Tibetan philology Sandberg's contributions were equally notable, for example his *Manual of Colloquial Tibetan* (1894). But his most important philological work was his collaboration in *A Tibetan–English Dictionary* (1902), which he was commissioned in 1899 by the Bengal government to prepare in conjunction with the Revd A. W. Heyde, from materials collected by Sarat Chandra Das. At the time, this was the most complete work of its kind.

One of his more important and lasting contributions to Tibetan studies was his posthumously published book *Tibet and the Tibetans* (1906) which he was in the final stages of preparing for publication at the time of his death in 1905. The book is a mine of information and, among other things, provides a good deal of ethnographic and economic detail about the life of Tibetan nomads, including trade and livestock herding. One of the more complete and informative books on Tibet in its day, it remains, almost a hundred years later, a work of scholarly value. In it the author pays tribute to the work of the 'secret native agents of the Transfrontier Survey' who provided the information, remarking that they were on the whole 'more exact in their narratives than the English visitors'.

Sandberg illustrated the width of his interests by publishing articles on the Armenian language, and the state of Bhutan (in the *Calcutta Review*, 1891 and 1898). He also espoused the cause of the Eurasians in 'Our outcast cousins in India' (*Contemporary Review*, 1892). Another of

his attainments was a thorough knowledge of Italian language and literature.

In August 1904 Sandberg was attacked by tubercular laryngitis, and was invalided home. He died at his home at 6 Carlton Road, Bournemouth, on 2 March of the following year.   F. W. THOMAS, *rev.* SCHUYLER JONES

Sources Crockford · *The Times* (6 March 1905) · *Homeward Mail* (11 March 1905) · *Liverpool Albion* (1878) [obit. of father] · *The Times* (27 April 1903) [obit. of Maria Sandberg] · private information (1912) · *CGPLA Eng. & Wales* (1905)

Wealth at death £584: probate, 5 May 1905, *CGPLA Eng. & Wales*

Sandby, Paul (*bap.* 1731, *d.* 1809), painter and engraver, was almost certainly born in Nottingham and was baptized there in St Peter's Church, on 12 January 1731, the younger son of Thomas Sandby (1686–1742), framework knitter and sometimes associated with property at Babworth in Nottinghamshire, and his wife, Ruth Ash (1686–1766).

Early career Little is known about the early life of Paul and his elder brother Thomas *Sandby; the brothers appear to have been apprenticed to the Nottingham land surveyor Thomas Peat, and in 1742 Thomas began his career in the south when he was engaged as military draughtsman in the Ordnance office in the Tower of London. It seems likely that Paul Sandby learnt his early skills as a draughtsman and watercolour artist from his elder brother, but nothing definite is known about his movements before March 1747, when he submitted specimens of his work to the Board of Ordnance (eight of the drawings are in the British Museum and one in the Victoria and Albert Museum, London). Soon after the establishment of the military survey in Scotland in September 1747, Paul was appointed draughtsman to the survey. This was set up under Lieutenant-Colonel David Watson to make maps of the highlands, as part of the campaign to restore peace in the area after the rising of 1745.

Sandby was with the survey for some five years, and during this time he made numerous landscape drawings and figure studies, some of the former and most of the latter already remarkably able and mature, which are to be found in many public collections. The impressive maps on which he was principally employed—as well as working on some of the initial surveys he was largely responsible for the colouring of the many sheets of the fair copy—show the very high standards achieved by Sandby and his colleagues. In his Scottish landscape watercolours, as in the contemporary landscape studies of Thomas Sandby, the influence of late seventeenth- and early eighteenth-century Netherlandish landscape drawing is evident, while in many of Sandby's figure drawings, especially those in pencil and chalk, eighteenth-century French examples come to mind. Dutch and French influences are also seen in the elegant landscape etchings that Sandby executed while in Scotland and immediately after his return to London, though most were not actually published until 1765. While in Edinburgh he was apparently instructed by an engraver named Bell, and was said (in the memoir written by his son) to have 'etched a number of scenes in the neighbourhood, which were done on the spot on the copper' (Oppé, 'Memoir', 145).

Paul Sandby (*bap.* 1731, *d.* 1809), by Francis Cotes, 1761

Sandby returned to London for some months in 1751, spending the summer with Thomas at Windsor, and left Scotland permanently in the autumn of 1752. For a time he shared lodgings with his brother in Poultney Street, where they gave sketching classes, and in the next few years he probably continued to live with his brother and his growing family. Proof of the brothers' close collaboration at this time is found in the series of eight engraved views of Windsor Great Park, published privately in 1754 and reissued by John Boydell in 1772. All are inscribed as drawn by Thomas, but it is likely that Paul, who engraved three of the plates, was responsible for the figures and staffage and perhaps also some of the landscape. The brothers produced a further set of engravings, *Six London Views*, in the later 1750s, though this was not published until 1766, in which the drawing is ascribed to both of them. During the 1750s and 1760s it is often difficult to differentiate between the landscape work of Thomas and of Paul, but there is no doubt of the younger brother's superiority in the depiction of figures.

Satires and other early work Sandby's skills in drawing figures are seen in his series of eight remarkably powerful satirical etchings published in 1753–4 under the title *The Analysis of Deformity*. These constitute an attack on William Hogarth, whose influential book *The Analysis of Beauty* was published in 1753. There is no convincing explanation why the young Sandby should so viciously have burlesqued his renowned senior, though it has been suggested that Thomas Sandby's attachment to William Augustus, duke of Cumberland, the butt of the satire in Hogarth's much publicized painting of 1749–50, *The March*

to *Finchley*, motivated Paul in his own attack (Herrmann, 19). A few years later, in 1760, Sandby published his *Twelve London Cries*, which actually show something of the influence of Hogarth, especially in the crowded title-page. Though only twelve etchings were issued, there are many more Sandby drawings of street characters, of which large collections are in the Yale Center for British Art and in the Museum of London.

It is possible that Sandby published no more of these etchings because he was increasingly occupied with painting landscape both in gouache and watercolour, as well as in oils. In 1760 he showed two oils, including the fine *View of Lord Harcourt's Seat at Newnham* (one of a pair of views of the earl's new house at Nuneham Courtenay, Oxfordshire, now priv. coll.), and three watercolours at the first exhibition of the Society of Artists. In the following year Sandby's lost *Historical Landskip Representing the Welsh Bard in the Opening of Mr. Gray's Celebrated Ode* was shown at the Society of Artists, where it was well received. This was his only recorded major historical landscape, probably painted in response to Richard Wilson's acclaimed *The Destruction of the Children of Niobe* of the previous year. Until 1768, when the Royal Academy was founded, Sandby showed annually at the Society of Artists, and though only a few of his canvases of this period survive it seems likely that many of his exhibits were oil paintings. In 1768 Sandby became a founder member of the Royal Academy, and he showed four works at the first exhibition in 1769 and then up to nine works almost every year until the year of his death.

Years of success Sandby's early work in oils has been largely forgotten as so few examples are now known, but these few prove him to have been a gifted and skilful landscape painter. It is likely that when Thomas Gainsborough wrote to Lord Hardwicke in 1764 declining a commission to paint 'real Views from nature in this Country', and recommending Paul Sandby as 'the only Man of Genius … who has employ'd his pencil that way' (Herrmann, 23–5), the senior artist was thinking of Sandby's work in oils. There is no doubt that it was also in the 1760s that Sandby was at the height of his powers as an artist in watercolour and bodycolour and produced some of the best of his great series of drawings of Windsor Castle and its surroundings. An outstanding group of these, many formerly in the collection of Sir Joseph Banks, is in the Royal Collection at Windsor. There is no record that George III himself acquired any works by Paul Sandby, and the foundations of the Windsor Sandby collection were laid by the considerable purchases of George IV when prince of Wales. In his Windsor compositions, many of them panoramic views, Sandby combines delicacy of colour and meticulous detail to provide informative and telling records of the scenes he is depicting, and it was probably the high quality of these drawings and others like them, as, for instance, the set of views of the marquess of Bute's Luton Park in Bedfordshire (ex Christies, 3 July 1996), that earned Paul Sandby the description of 'father of English watercolour'. Though he is best-known for his watercolours, in the earlier and final decades of his career Paul Sandby regularly used bodycolour, both on its own, most frequently in strongly coloured imaginative and often romantic compositions, as well as in conjunction with watercolours.

From early in his career Sandby was also busy as a drawing master, counting several of his patrons, such as Lord Harcourt and Sir Watkin Williams Wynn, among his pupils. In 1768 he was appointed chief drawing master at the Royal Military Academy, Woolwich, at a salary of £150 per annum, a post that he retained until his retirement in 1796, and when there he lived in lodgings at Old Charlton in Kent. Officers in the Royal Artillery and the engineers were trained at Woolwich, and Sandby was able to introduce a wide range of the sons of the aristocracy and gentry to the practice and appreciation of landscape drawing. Through some of his Woolwich pupils Sandby's influence spread as far afield as Canada.

Another way in which Sandby helped to popularize the art of watercolour and the appreciation of landscape was by his pioneering use of the recently developed printing technique of aquatint, which is especially suited to the reproduction of watercolour drawings. Though it can no longer be claimed that Sandby was the first British artist to use the new process, it was he who named it and popularized it. In 1775 he published *XII views in Wales in aquatinta from drawings taken on the spot in south-Wales dedicated to the Honourable Charles Greville and Joseph Banks esquire*, and a similar set of views in north Wales, dedicated to Sir Watkin Williams Wynn, followed in 1776. Sandby had collected the material for these series on sketching tours in 1771 and 1773 in the company of his dedicatees. In his depiction of the Welsh landscape in the mid-1770s Paul Sandby was breaking new ground not only from the point of view of technique but also of subject matter, for it was not until the end of the 1770s and the following decades that Wales became a popular area among travellers and artists in search of the picturesque and the romantic. Sandby published two more series of aquatints of Welsh subjects in 1777 and 1786, and in all he was responsible for over one hundred prints in that medium, most of them after his own landscape designs.

Sandby also continued to make drawings for engraving on copper, and his major series of landscape and topographical engravings, the 108 plates of *The Virtuosi's Museum*, was published in parts, each containing three small engravings, between 1778 and 1781. During the same years Sandby made drawings for numerous plates in the *Copperplate Magazine*, of which forty-two were added to the *Virtuosi's Museum* plates, which were reissued by John Boydell in 1783 as *A Collection of one Hundred and Fifty Select Views in England, Wales, Scotland and Ireland*, with texts in both English and French. Thus in the 1760s and 1770s Sandby was the master of several media and was in the van of British landscape art, for the development and growing appreciation of which this period was of great importance. He was an active member of the Royal Academy, and a popular, knowledgeable, and influential figure in London's artistic and literary society. In 1772 he and his family moved to his final London home, 4 St George's Row, Bayswater, close to the Bayswater turnpike on the Oxford Road

and with fine views over Hyde Park. A studio at the end of the garden, probably designed by his brother, was used for teaching and for his weekly *conversazioni*. Sandby:

> drew round him a circle of intellectual and attached friends, comprising the most distinguished artists and amateurs of the day. His house became quite a centre of attraction … when, on each Sunday, after Divine Service, his friends assembled, and formed a conversazione on the arts, the sciences and the general literature of the day.   (*Life of James Gandon*, 39)

The final years The three final decades of Sandby's long career were far less auspicious than the first three, though he maintained his active London life for much of them. In June 1780 many of the troops called in to deal with the anti-Catholic Gordon riots were encamped in Hyde Park, and Sandby made numerous studies of the encampments. In 1781 he exhibited seven views of the various encampments at the Royal Academy, and he also issued four large aquatints and two sets of small aquatints of these scenes. Some of Sandby's encampment drawings are rather crude and loose in detail, both in the rendering of figures and of trees and other landscape features. This change and apparent decline in his manner was probably deliberate, and may be associated with a conscious policy to produce landscape rather than topography, for despite their weaknesses many of the encampment compositions retain a good overall effect. In his later years Sandby worked mostly in this freer style, which he combined with greater fluency in the rendering of light and shade. He also worked more frequently in bodycolour and at the end of his life he returned to painting in oils, usually somewhat vacuous compositions on a small scale, in this case because he could no longer afford the high cost of the glass needed when framing watercolours. Perhaps because in his old age he could not travel in search of subject matter, much of Sandby's later work consists of imaginary compositions, many of the grander ones reminiscent of Rubens's landscape paintings. In 1793 he completed an unusual commission from Sir Nigel Gresley for the decoration of the dining-room (distemper on plaster) at Drakelow Hall in Derbyshire. The house was demolished in 1934 and only one end wall survives (V&A). The central scene in this is reminiscent of Welsh mountain scenery, and the whole composition is in a mood of harmonious tranquillity, showing that the artist could work with complete authority on this large scale.

Most of what we know about Sandby's closing years comes from the frequent references to him in Joseph Farington's invaluable *Diary*. Many of these are concerned with Sandby's active involvement in the affairs of the Royal Academy, others with the artist's poor health and failing eyesight and his financial difficulties. In 1794 Farington noted that some of Sandby's watercolours were exhibited in Poggi's saleroom, priced from 24 to 2 or 3 guineas, and that 'they are admired but do not sell' (Farington, *Diary*, 1.220, 26 July). Five years later Sandby was anxious to succeed the Royal Academy librarian, Edward Burch, who was ill, as 'he had no business now as a teacher & the income would be an object to him' (ibid., 10 Dec

1799); a few days later he was appointed deputy librarian. On 11 July 1801 Farington noted that 'P. Sandby it is probable will come upon the Academy,—so much has his fortune been reduced by expenses incurred for his Children', and on 20 January 1808 he recorded that Sandby's son Tom informed the president, Sir William Beechey, 'that His Father was in such circumstance as to stand in need of assistance from the Royal Academy'; Sandby was granted a pension of £60 per annum. During these difficult final years there were, however, only three, 1803–5, when Sandby did not take part in the academy's summer exhibitions.

Family, character, death, and reputation On 5 May 1757 Sandby married Anne Stogden (d. 1797), and they lived in Dufours Court, Broad Street, Carnaby Market. They had three children, two sons and a daughter. The elder son, Paul, was an officer in the army and died at Barbados in 1793. The second son, Thomas Paul (d. 1832), also became an artist and succeeded his father as drawing master at Woolwich. In 1766 Sandby took a house in Poland Street, but at this time and throughout his life he and his family spent much time at Windsor, with his brother, Thomas. In 1782 Thomas Paul married Harriot, Thomas Sandby's second surviving daughter, and had a large family.

There are several records of Paul Sandby's friendliness and generosity. He had a strong sense of humour and wrote and conversed fluently and effectively. That he was also good-looking is shown by several portraits, especially that of 1761 by Francis Cotes (Tate collection), in which he is shown seated at a window and sketching. Sandby died at home at 4 St George's Row on 8 November 1809, and was buried at St George's, Hanover Square. His will, drawn up in November 1797, made Thomas Paul his sole heir and executor, but gives no details of his estate. It was Thomas Paul who arranged several sales of his father's collections and work, the first at Christies on 2–4 May 1811, and three more in 1812, 1817, and 1824. Before the first of these T. P. Sandby had written to his Bristol friend George Cumberland, indicating his difficulties 'in getting into something like an arrangement, the mass of papers he [Paul Sandby] has left of every kind, and indeed it appears that, the more I sort them, the more I confuse myself, and them too' (BL, Cumberland papers, Add. MS 36516, fol. 257). The sale catalogues are imprecise and uninformative; it is impossible to identify specific lots and it is certain that the work of the two brothers was often conflated. Sandby also had a considerable collection of paintings, drawings, and prints by other artists of all schools, including many of his British contemporaries. Most significant among these were his drawings by Richard Wilson, many of them purchased to help his older fellow artist when in financial difficulty, and a large number of works by Marco Ricci.

In the last years of Paul Sandby's long life his mature work was very influential on the next generations in the development of the British watercolour school. Since then his reputation as a pivotal figure in that development has never been disputed, and in the vast literature on the subject he has always been regarded as a leading figure. At the close of the twentieth century his standing was as high as ever, and his drawings fetched record prices in the salerooms, one of the Bute views of Luton selling for £340,000 in 1996.

Paul Sandby's work is represented in numerous museums, galleries, and private collections in Britain and abroad. The outstanding collection is in the Royal Collection at Windsor, and the next most notable assembly of both prints and drawings is at the British Museum, with important work also in the map library of the British Library. There is a large collection at the Castle Museum in Nottingham, the artist's assumed birthplace, which is, however, of rather mixed quality. Representative groups of Paul Sandby drawings are in the Victoria and Albert Museum, London, the Ashmolean Museum, Oxford, the Fitzwilliam Museum, Cambridge, the National Museum and Gallery of Wales in Cardiff, and the National Gallery of Scotland, Edinburgh, which includes an important selection of his early Scottish drawings. The outstanding collection of Sandby drawings in America is in the Yale Center for British Art at New Haven, and in Australia there is an important group of Paul Sandby's later gouache drawings in the City of Hamilton Art Gallery, acquired in Australia in 1971.   LUKE HERRMANN

Sources L. Herrmann, *Paul and Thomas Sandby* (1986) · P. Oppé, *The drawings of Paul and Thomas Sandby in the collection of his majesty the king at Windsor Castle* (1947) · W. Sandby, *Thomas and Paul Sandby* (1892) · J. Ball, *Paul and Thomas Sandby, Royal Academicians* (1985) · J. Roberts, *Views of Windsor: watercolours by Thomas and Paul Sandby* (1995) · B. Robertson, *The art of Paul Sandby* (1985) · P. Oppé, 'The memoir of Paul Sandby by his son', *Burlington Magazine*, 88 (1946), 143–7 · *The life of James Gandon, esq.*, ed. T. J. Mulvany (1846) [repr. 1969] · Farington, *Diary* · J. Roberts, *Royal landscape: the gardens and parks of Windsor* (1997) · BL, Cumberland papers, Add. MS 36516

Archives BL, corresp. and papers, Add. MS 36994

Likenesses F. Cotes, oils, 1761, Tate collection [*see illus.*] · E. Fisher, engraving, 1763 (after F. Cotes) · P. E. Falconet, chalk and wash drawing, 1768, BM · W. Beechey, oils, 1789, NPG · G. Dance, watercolour drawing, 1794, RA · W. Beechey, oils, RA · R. Dagley, stipple (after R. Cosway), BM, NPG; repro. in Arnold, *Library of the fine arts* (1831) · P. Sandby, group portrait, etching (with his family), BM · H. Singleton, group portrait, oils (*Royal Academicians, 1793*), RA · J. Zoffany, group portrait, oils (*Royal Academicians, 1772*), Royal Collection

Sandby, Thomas (bap. 1723, d. 1798), architect and draughtsman, was almost certainly born in Nottingham and was baptized there in St Peter's Church on 8 December 1723, the elder son of Thomas Sandby (1686–1742), framework knitter and sometimes associated with property at Babworth in Nottinghamshire, and his wife, Ruth Ash (1686–1766).

Early career Nothing is known about the early life and education of Thomas Sandby and his younger brother, Paul *Sandby, and there are few definite facts for much of Thomas's career. The brothers appear to have been apprenticed to the Nottingham land surveyor Thomas Peat, but when his father died in 1742 Thomas moved to London, and, probably through the good offices of John Plumptre, MP for Nottingham and treasurer of the Board of Ordnance, he was engaged as military draughtsman in the Ordnance office in the Tower of London, a post that he retained, but without any activity after 1746, for the rest of his life. By this time Sandby was a member of the household of William Augustus, duke of Cumberland, who became captain-general of British land forces in 1745. He was paid as draughtsman to the duke from 1746 at an annual salary of £80. Sandby had spent some months in Scotland in 1743, and returned there during the duke's 1745–6 campaign; several drawings made at this time are in the Royal Collection at Windsor. Sandby was also in the Netherlands with Cumberland during the final stages of the War of the Austrian Succession, as is demonstrated by his drawings of encampments at Meldart, Zeeland, and elsewhere, dated 1747 and 1748, at Windsor and in the British Library. These military drawings are of a high standard with fluent and effective use of watercolours, and prove Thomas already to have been a gifted topographical and landscape artist. There is no record of his receiving any artistic training other than in the Tower drawing school. The strongest influence to be found in these early military drawings is Dutch rather than British, though they also display the meticulous attention to recording details which would have been learnt in the Ordnance office.

Work at Windsor In 1746 George II appointed the duke of Cumberland, his third and favourite son, as ranger of Windsor Great Park, and for the next twenty years he and his large household spent much time in Windsor. The Great Lodge, later known as Cumberland Lodge, was quickly repaired and altered to house the duke and his retinue and remained his principal residence at Windsor. The architect was the duke's former tutor in architecture, Henry Flitcroft, an important figure in the office of works, and it has been plausibly suggested that Sandby worked as one of his assistants. While there is no firm evidence for this surmise, there are numerous surviving drawings and prints which demonstrate Sandby's activities in recording the buildings and landscape of Windsor in the 1750s. Outstanding among these is the set of five large, detailed, and atmospheric panoramic views in Windsor Great Park, two of which are dated 1752 (Royal Collection). Here the watercolour and bodycolour are meticulously applied, while in other drawings of this period and later Thomas's use of watercolour is often much more fluent.

Though Paul Sandby provided the figures in several of these early Windsor views it seems certain that at this time the younger brother was learning the skills of landscape drawing from Thomas, who may well be more worthy than his brother of the title of 'father of English watercolour', which is usually given to Paul. Support for that theory is found in Benjamin West's comment, recorded by Joseph Farington in his *Diary* on 29 March 1807, 'that a style of drawing had been practised in this country such as had not been seen in any other, and that with Thomas Sandby it originated'. Throughout their careers it is often difficult to distinguish between the work of the two brothers, who were holding joint sketching classes in London early in 1753. They collaborated in the series of eight engraved views of Windsor Great Park, four of them of Virginia Water, dedicated to the duke and probably published privately for him in 1754, and reissued by

Boydell in 1772. All are inscribed as drawn by Thomas, but it is likely that Paul, who engraved three of the plates, was responsible for the figures and staffage and perhaps also some of the landscape. Another collaborative undertaking by the brothers was a further set of engravings, *Six London Views*, initiated in the later 1750s but not published until 1766, in which the drawing is ascribed to both of them.

As well as topographical and landscape compositions Thomas Sandby produced many architectural drawings, some of them very precise and detailed and others more rapid and sketchy. It seems that from 1757 he was in charge of a second extensive building campaign at the Great Lodge, which resulted in the considerable enlargement of the house by the addition of a new wing in Palladian style. Sandby also prepared plans for the re-erection of the Holbein gate from Whitehall, bought by the duke in 1759, but these were not executed, though in later years he produced designs for the reuse of masonry from the gate at Windsor. The details of Sandby's role in the other improvements and additions carried out in Windsor Great Park by the duke, who died in 1765, and by his successor as ranger and as duke of Cumberland, his nephew Prince Henry Frederick, are uncertain. The first duke's main concern was the creation of Virginia Water, with which Sandby's name is usually associated. However, it is now thought that he only became closely involved with the lake after the damage caused by serious floods in 1768 and again in 1782, after the second of which he drew up new schemes, and made his numerous plans and drawings of the lake, its rockwork, and the like.

In 1764 Thomas Sandby became steward to the duke and also acted as deputy ranger of Windsor Great Park, with a salary of £400. He was retained in that post by the new ranger, and was in charge of the park's management and finances. When Henry Frederick died in 1790, George III himself took over as ranger and again retained Sandby, whom he had already employed in the restoration of St George's Chapel, Windsor, as deputy. Immediately after his accession the king had in fact appointed Sandby 'His Maj: Steward and Superintendant of Works in Windsor Great Park', but that position had then long overlapped with his work for the dukes of Cumberland, before being cancelled in 1788.

Other architectural activities As well as his work in the park, Sandby designed a number of private houses in the Windsor area, including St Leonard's Hill for Maria, duchess of Gloucester, and Holly Grove (now Forest Lodge), later incorporated in the Great Park, for Colonel Deacon. Further afield he competed for the Royal Exchange in Dublin in 1769, winning the third premium, and he designed the imposing Freemasons' Hall, built in 1775–6 in Queen Street, Lincoln's Inn Fields. This was greatly altered a century later, then damaged by fire and finally demolished in 1932. About 1785 Sandby was the architect of the Bleach Works at Lleweni in the Vale of Clwyd, near Denbigh, for the Hon. Thomas Fitzmaurice. Towards the end of his life he designed a stone bridge over the Thames at Staines, which was built in 1792–7 but failed in 1799 and was replaced by an iron bridge a few years later. A codicil in his will reveals that Sandby prepared plans for the rebuilding of Cliveden House in Buckinghamshire, after its partial destruction by fire in 1795, for Mary, countess of Orkney.

Little of Thomas Sandby's executed architectural work has survived, and his achievements have to be judged very largely by his drawings, which reveal him to have been an elegant neoclassical designer in the mode of Sir William Chambers. He exhibited large architectural drawings at the Society of Artists in 1767 and at the Royal Academy each year from 1769 to 1773 and again in 1781 and 1782. Collections of his drawings are in the British Museum and British Library, the Victoria and Albert Museum, Sir John Soane's Museum, London, the Bodleian Library, Oxford, and, principally, the Royal Library at Windsor Castle.

Professional life in London Thomas Sandby was active in the artistic world of London; he served on the committee of the newly formed Society of Artists in 1759, and in 1768 was a founder member of the Royal Academy, of which he was appointed the first professor of architecture. In 1770 he gave his first series of six annual lectures, the last of which was illustrated with his drawings, and continued to do so until the end of his life, though the final two series had to be read for him. The manuscripts of Sandby's lectures are in the Royal Institute of British Architects library, and another copy is in Sir John Soane's Museum. His ability may also be judged from the other high architectural offices that marked his career. In April 1777 he was appointed architect of the king's works in succession to Sir Robert Taylor, and in 1780 he was promoted to the titular office of master carpenter, with which came a seat on the board of works, but which was abolished only two years later. On its foundation in 1791 Sandby was elected an honorary member of the Architects' Club.

Private life and death Thomas Sandby was twice married, on 2 December 1746 in London to Margaret Bowes, who died within a few years, and on 26 April 1753 to Elizabeth Venables, who died in 1782. They had ten children, to two of whom royal dukes stood as godparents. She held the appointment of sempstress and laundress to the duke of Cumberland from 1758 to 1763. Three of the children died young, and Thomas was survived by one son and four daughters. In 1753 the Sandby brothers were living in Poultney Street; subsequently Sandby and his family divided their time between Windsor and different houses in London. In 1764 Thomas Sandby settled in Windsor, where he lived for the rest of his life, from about 1770 in the Dairy House close to the Great Lodge, which became known as the Deputy Ranger's Lodge (now Royal Lodge). It was there that he died on 25 June 1798 after some years of illness, and he was buried in the churchyard at Old Windsor. There is no monument, but a memorial plaque was put up in 1883, giving his birth date as 1721.

Thomas Sandby's last will was drawn up in April 1797 and proved in London on 8 November 1798. It divides his estate, including £3500 'vested in the ffunds in the three pr. Cent reduced Annuities in the Bank of England',

equally between his four surviving daughters, and leaves only a token £10 and two drawings to his son, Major William Keppel Sandby, whom he had already provided for when he helped to purchase his majority. A codicil bequeaths a group of seven drawings and plans of Clifton (presumably Cliveden) House in Buckinghamshire, 'on the proposed idea of rebuilding that noble edifice', to the countess of Orkney. In the months after Thomas Sandby's death there are several entries in Joseph Farington's *Diary* referring to the possible purchase of the one hundred drawings that he had made to illustrate his lectures as professor of architecture, for which the president, Benjamin West, thought that not more than £200 should be paid, though initially 300 guineas was mentioned. This sale did not take place and many of these sheets were included in the auction of Sandby's library and drawings at Messrs Leigh and Sothebys in July 1799, which realized £570.

Thomas Sandby was very much a family man, and it appears that despite moving in high court circles he remained modest and unpretentious, as witnessed by the instructions in his will for the simplest of funerals, 'without the pageantry of an hearse'. The obituary in the *Gentleman's Magazine* described him as 'one of the gentlest and best of human beings'.   LUKE HERRMANN

Sources L. Herrmann, *Paul and Thomas Sandby* (1986) · J. Roberts, *Royal landscape: the gardens and parks of Windsor* (1997) · W. Sandby, *Thomas and Paul Sandby* (1892) · P. Oppé, *The drawings of Paul and Thomas Sandby in the collection of his majesty the king* (1947) · J. Roberts, *Views of Windsor: watercolours by Thomas and Paul Sandby* (1995) · H. Hudson, *Cumberland Lodge* (1989) · J. Ball, *Paul and Thomas Sandby, Royal Academicians* (1985) · Colvin, *Archs.* · will, PRO, PROB 11/1315, sig. 73b · IGI

Archives BL, corresp. and papers, Add. MS 36994

Likenesses G. Dance, chalk drawing, 1779, RA · W. Beechey, oils, 1792, NPG · G. Sanders, mezzotint, pubd 1878 (after T. Gainsborough), BM, NPG · H. Singleton, group portrait, oils (*Royal Academicians, 1793*), RA · J. Zoffany, group portrait, oils (*Royal Academicians, 1772*), Royal Collection

Wealth at death £3500 in the 'ffunds'; plus proceeds of sales of drawings, etc.: will, PRO, PROB 11/1315, sig. 73b

Sandeman, Albert George (1833–1923), port and sherry producer, was born at 31 Highbury Place, Highbury, Middlesex, on 21 October 1833, the eldest of the four sons (there were also four daughters) of George Glas Sandeman (d. 1868) and his wife, Elizabeth, the daughter of Albert Forster. His great-great-grandfather was the Revd John Glas, founder of the Glasites, a nonconformist sect which became the Sandemanians after Albert's great-great-uncle Robert Sandeman married Glas's daughter. Albert was also a cousin of Sir Robert Groves Sandeman.

George Glas Sandeman was the nephew of George Sandeman, who in 1790 had become a wine merchant in London and had built up agencies with port and sherry exporters in Portugal and Spain respectively. Albert, having completed his education at Eton College, about 1851 joined his father in the firm. His business links with Portugal brought him in contact with Maria Carlota Perpetua de Moraes Sarmento (d. 1923), the daughter of Visconde Da Torre de Moncorvo, one-time Portuguese minister in London, whom he married in 1856; they had two sons and four daughters. In 1866 he was appointed a director of the Bank of England, the bank with which the firm had had an account since 1812. He retained that directorship until 1918.

On his father's death in 1868, Sandeman became head of George G. Sandeman, Sons & Co. Two years later the firm was the main shipper of port from Portugal, and Sandeman sought to achieve a comparable leadership in sherry, which then accounted for over two-fifths of the wine drunk in Britain. In 1879, therefore, he purchased a bankrupt sherry business at Jerez, and a decade later built up the firm's stock of fine sherries by making a purchase from another producer of 800 casks of unblended wines. This dramatic step helped to ensure supplies, which could be in danger from poor harvests and diseases such as phylloxera.

Sandeman was very active in public life. In 1872 he was appointed high sheriff of Surrey, and later became a commissioner of lieutenancy and commissioner of income tax for the City of London. He also served as major of the 12th Middlesex (Prince of Wales's Own Civil Service) rifle volunteers. Sandeman was elected to the board of the London Assurance Company, and in 1898 he held the presidency of the London chamber of commerce.

For twenty-five years, from 1893 onwards, Sandeman served on the Bank of England's influential committee of treasury; he was deputy governor in 1894–5 and governor from 1895 to 1897. His period of office as governor was also a time of extra-cheap money, when the bank's earnings and reserves fell sharply. Having as deputy governor been responsible for supervising the bank's branches, he actively prodded the branch agents into seeking new and profitable business. Moreover, he rebuffed attempts by the chancellor of the exchequer, Sir Michael Edward Hicks Beach, to investigate the bank's management system following the sacking of its chief cashier for irregularities.

As the Victorian era drew to its close, the cartoonist 'Spy' featured Sandeman as a worthy in *Vanity Fair*. Portrayed as a genial, moustached, and slightly rotund figure, immaculate in green-grey frock coat and buff spats, with monocle at the ready and a gardenia in his buttonhole, he typified the shrewd city magnate who contributed commercial expertise to the not over-demanding but highly prestigious task of directing the world's leading financial institution. In 1902 he had the family firm registered as a private limited company, but ensured that its direction and shareholding remained entirely in family hands. With two sons and three grandsons then in the company, Sandeman was merely its nominal head when he died, of bronchitis, at his home, Greylands, Hastings Road, Bexhill, Sussex, on 6 January 1923. He was survived by his wife.   T. A. B. CORLEY

Sources N. Halley, *Sandeman: two hundred years of port and sherry* (1990) • R. S. Sayers, *The Bank of England, 1891–1944*, 3 vols. (1976) • Burke, *Gen. GB* (1925) • *WWW*, *1929–40* • d. cert. • *The Times* (24 Oct 1833) • private information (2004) [archivist, Bank of England]
Archives Bank of England Archive, London • Segram Company archives
Likenesses Spy [L. Ward], cartoon, repro. in *VF* (12 Sept 1895) • photograph, repro. in *The Times* (10 Jan 1923), ix

Wealth at death £85,732 19s. 1d.: probate, 2 March 1923, *CGPLA Eng. & Wales*

Sandeman, Robert (1718–1771), promoter of the Glasite church, was born in Perth on 29 April 1718, the eldest son and second of the twelve children of David Sandeman, linen weaver, and his wife, Margaret. After being apprenticed in the family linen-weaving business, he attended Edinburgh University for a few terms between 1734 and 1736, hesitating between medicine and the church. In the city he came under the influence of the teachings of John Glas. He returned to the family business in Perth in 1736, and the following year he married Glas's daughter, Katharine (d. 1746). In 1744 he was elected an elder of the Glasite church in Perth. More forceful than his father-in-law, Sandeman ensured that the Glasite church spread through Scotland and beyond, so that the denomination became known outside Scotland as Sandemanian. His wife died, childless, in 1746.

In 1756 Sandeman returned to the Glasite church in Edinburgh, and in 1757 entered theological controversy by publishing, under the pseudonym of Palaemon, *Letters on Theron and Aspasio*, in which he took issue with the devotional writer James Hervey, attacked the doctrine of imputed righteousness, and propounded the Glasite intellectualist view of faith. He attacked the so-called popular preachers, the evangelicals, for adding works to faith and for not following the example of the apostles. These sharply written letters appeared at a time when there was a flourishing interest in Calvinistic teaching, and drew responses from John Wesley and John Brine, among others. Several Independent ministers in London and in the north of England embraced his principles, and in 1760 Sandeman 'set in order' a church in London which continued until the 1970s, and whose most celebrated member was Michael Faraday.

In 1760 Sandeman's *Letters* was published in New England, and in 1764, at the invitation of some Congregational ministers, Sandeman and a fellow elder, James Cargill, visited America, where his teaching led to the formation of some small fellowships in Connecticut and Nova Scotia. He was a fervent loyalist, and this, combined with his exclusive ideas on church fellowship, kept his following small. In March 1770 he was arrested in Danbury, Connecticut, for refusing to leave the town, and he died in Danbury on 2 April 1771. On his tombstone are inscribed words which summarize his creed: 'he long and boldly contended for the ancient faith that the bare work of Jesus Christ, without a deed or thought on the part of man is sufficient to present the chief of sinners spotless before God'.

The churches whose foundation can be traced to Sandeman were few in number and small in size, but had remarkable tenacity, and the Sandeman family has continued to be represented in the eldership until the end of the twentieth century. Their exclusiveness, nonevangelical stance, and the cold regularity of their liturgy are factors in their decline, and also in their survival, and

Sandemanian influence on other bodies such as the Campbellites, or Disciples of Christ, and the Christadelphians has been acknowledged.   DEREK B. MURRAY

Sources G. N. Cantor, *Michael Faraday: Sandemanian and scientist* (1991) · L. A. McMillon, *Restoration roots* (1983) · J. F. Riley, *The hammer and the anvil: a background to Michael Faraday* (1954) · D. M. Lewis, ed., *The Blackwell dictionary of evangelical biography, 1730–1860*, 2 vols. (1995) · *DNB* · F. Stanley, 'The life and work of Sandeman in Scotland and New England', DPhil diss., U. Oxf., in preparation
Likenesses portrait, repro. in R. Sandeman, *Discourses on passages of scripture* (1857)

Sandeman, Sir Robert Groves (1835–1892), army officer in the East India Company and political officer in India, was born on 25 February 1835 in Perth, Scotland, the second of four sons in a family of ten children of General Robert Turnbull Sandeman (1804–1876) of the East India Company's army and his wife, Jane, *née* Barclay. He was educated at Perth Academy and St Andrews University.

Sandeman obtained a direct appointment to the East India Company's army. He briefly served in a British regiment and then joined his father's regiment, the 33rd Bengal native infantry, as an ensign in 1856. When the mutiny broke out in 1857 the regiment remained loyal, although it was disarmed as a precautionary measure. Sandeman volunteered for active service with the 2nd Bengal fusiliers outside Delhi and, following the successful assault on the city, fought with them during the capture of Jhajjar. In February 1858 he was appointed a lieutenant in the 1st Sikh cavalry (Probyn's Horse), and served as adjutant during the assault on the Dilkusha palace, the final capture of Lucknow, and the pursuit of the rebels; he was severely wounded twice. He was then selected to carry dispatches for Sir John Lawrence, the chief commissioner of the Punjab, who later offered him a place in the Punjab commission, which had originally been appointed in 1849 to administer the region when it was occupied by the British.

Sandeman was gazetted an assistant commissioner in the Punjab in 1859, and served in a succession of posts there and in the trans-Indus areas bordering on independent tribal territory. Following a brief furlough in England, during which he married in 1864 Catherine Grace (*d.* 1868), daughter of John Allen, of Kirkby Lonsdale, he led a force of a thousand tribal levies protecting the line of communication during the 1863 Ambela campaign. In 1866 he was selected as deputy commissioner of Dera Ghazi Khan, near the border with Sind. In this post he was responsible for local judicial and administrative arrangements as well as managing tribal relations. For the first time he dealt with Baluch tribesmen, whose social organization was very different from that of the Pathans who inhabited the more northern territories where he had previously served. Sandeman pioneered the highly successful 'tribal service' system for the political management of the local Baluch tribes. He dealt directly with their hereditary chieftains, who were made responsible for maintaining order among their own people. By this means Sandeman re-established the authority of the chiefs, stopped inter-

tribal fighting, and, by employing levies to protect communications, opened the country to trade. His handling of the Marris and Bugtis, however, brought him into conflict with the commissioner of Sind, who disapproved of his breaches of the official policy of non-intervention. But Sandeman was supported by the government of the Punjab in his border-crossings and in his extension of British influence among the tribes; he was promoted captain in 1868. When the policy of non-intervention was finally dropped by the viceroy, Lord Lytton, Sandeman (who was promoted major in February 1876) made further efforts to secure the goodwill and support of other Baluch tribes. Later that year he secured a settlement between the khan of Kalat and his rebellious Sirdars, and negotiated a treaty that secured the Bolan Pass between Afghanistan and India, extended British influence to Quetta, and secured the right to station troops in this strategically important khanate. On 1 January 1877 Sandeman's important work was recognized at the imperial assemblage at Delhi, held to proclaim Queen Victoria empress of India, when he was made CSI. On 21 February he was gazetted as the governor-general's agent in Baluchistan, which made him responsible for the administration of the area.

Sandeman's efforts in the region bore fruit when the Second Anglo-Afghan War broke out in November 1878. British troops moved through Baluchistan and the Bolan Pass without incident, and the local inhabitants willingly provided supplies and transport animals. Sandeman initially accompanied General Sir Michael Biddulph's advance force into Pishin, and reconnoitred the route to Kandahar through the Khojak Pass. Despite his wish to serve as Sir Donald Stewart's political officer at Kandahar, Sandeman's presence in Baluchistan was judged indispensable during the war. He was made KCSI in 1879 for his work in organizing supplies and maintaining order among the Baluchis during this campaign. The loyalty of the Baluch tribes was severely tested, however, when news of the British defeat at Maiwand (27 July 1880) spread. While further operations in Afghanistan were under way, Sandeman quickly restored order in Baluchistan, Pishin, and Sibi when several tribes revolted. He commanded the line of communications while Kandahar was occupied, and, thanks to his efforts, further quantities of transport animals and supplies were collected in Baluchistan.

In 1881 Sandeman returned to Britain on furlough, where on 17 January 1882 he married Helen Catherine (*d.* 1912), daughter of Lieutenant-Colonel John William Gaisford of Clonee, co. Meath. They had a daughter, Florence Mary. Sandeman returned to the subcontinent at the end of 1882 and resumed work in consolidating the British administration in Baluchistan and the two new assigned districts of Pishin and Sibi. He oversaw the peaceful settlement of tribal disputes and the construction of roads, railways, dispensaries, and irrigation schemes. In June 1887 Baluchistan was elevated to the prestigious status of a first-class residency, and on 1 November Sandeman was appointed *ex officio* chief commissioner of the former assigned districts, which were now designated British

Baluchistan. He also extended his system of tribal management northwards into the area between British Baluchistan and the Punjab. A new protectorate was established in the Zhob valley in December 1889; its headquarters were renamed Fort Sandeman and the Gomal Pass was opened to trade. He also prepared plans for administering Makran and Panjgur in the south. Sandeman died from influenza on 29 January 1892 while on a tour of Las Bela, a small state on the Sind frontier. He was buried there with full military honours on 1 February.

T. R. MOREMAN

Sources T. H. Thornton, *Colonel Sir Robert Sandeman: his life and work on our Indian frontier* (1895) · A. L. Tucker, *Sir Robert G. Sandeman, K.C.S.I., peaceful conqueror of Baluchistan* (1921) · R. I. Bruce, *The forward policy and its results, or, Thirty-five years' work amongst the tribes on our north-western frontier of India* (1900) · T. A. Heathcote, 'British policy and Baluchistan, 1854–1876', PhD diss., U. Lond., 1970 · C. C. Davies, *The problem of the North West Frontier, 1890–1908* (1932) · Lord Roberts [F. S. Roberts], *Forty-one years in India*, 2 vols. (1897) · C. E. Buckland, *Dictionary of Indian biography* (1906) · H. Ram, *Sandeman in Baluchistan* (1916) · DNB · Burke, *Gen. GB* (1937) · b. cert. · *CGPLA Ire.* (1892)
Archives BL, letters to Lord Ripon, Add. MS 43613
Likenesses F. Bremner, photograph, repro. in F. Bremner, *Baluchistan illustrated* (1900) · F. Bremner, photograph, BL OIOC · Walker and Boutall, photograph, repro. in Thornton, *Colonel Sir Robert Sandeman* · woodcut, NPG
Wealth at death £13,207 5s. 5d.: probate, 4 June 1892, *CGPLA Ire.*

Sander [Sanders], **Nicholas** (c.1530–1581), religious controversialist, was born in Charlwood, Surrey, the son of William Saunders and his wife, Elizabeth Mynes. His usual signature in English was simply Sander. He enrolled in Winchester College in 1540 and came to know well its warden, John White. In 1548 he was made a fellow of New College, Oxford, where he proceeded BCL in 1551. At the visitation of the university in 1557 he gave the welcoming oration, especially praising the chancellor, Cardinal Pole. He was also Shagling professor, or extraordinary lecturer, in canon law that year. In 1558 he is said to have read the Hebrew lecture. He witnessed the Westminster conference of 31 March and 4 April 1559. When Sander left England for Rome is a matter of dispute. At some point he is alleged to have been asked to serve Elizabeth I as Latin secretary, but he may already have gone to Rome in company with Thomas Butler in the spring of 1559. Perhaps this first visit was brief, and Sander returned to England for a time. Not later than 1560 he resigned his fellowship rather than take the oath of supremacy, although he appears to have witnessed Bishop Horne's visitation in 1560, which he alleged had to be stopped lest the entire college be emptied. Sander's escape from England was largely due to Sir Francis Englefield.

When Sander reached Rome, he was probably lodged in the English Hospice through the patronage of Cardinal Morone, the protector of England. Sander appeared as one of its auditors in early 1561 and as a chamberlain in May 1563. Rome impressed him greatly, especially the numerous sites associated with martyrs. Some time in 1561 Thomas Goldwell ordained Sander, certainly in Rome, perhaps to the title of a benefice provided by Morone. It is likely to have been about then that he wrote a report to the cardinal on the state of English Catholics; some of its proposals for filling episcopal sees were taken into a memorandum probably drawn up at Trent in the middle of 1561. Shortly thereafter Sander appeared at Trent, serving Cardinal Stanislaus Hosius as a theologian. Anthony Wood claimed that he 'shew'd himself to be a man of great parts by his several disputations and arguings' (Wood, *Ath. Oxon.*, 1.469), and he may have been involved in the decision that English Catholics could not attend protestant services. At the council's conclusion he accompanied Hosius to his diocese of Ermland, where he met Gianfrancesco Commendone. In one of their conversations Commendone outlined for Sander the plan of what became *De visibili monarchia ecclesiae*, a reply especially to the protestant church history put forward by the Magdeburg centuriators. In 1564 Sander and three other Englishmen received 'archiepiscopal power in the forum of conscience' (Meyer, 475) from Michele Ghislieri, the inquisitor-general, which they were to use to absolve Catholics of schism.

Louvain Shortly after this grant Sander went to Louvain, where he matriculated in the university on 12 November 1564. He defended three theses in January 1565 which were published in Antwerp in the following year; two of them concerned points disputed at Westminster. In March 1566 he accompanied Commendone at the Diet of Augsburg for four months. Rather ironically, he advised Commendone not to press Ferdinand I for the adoption of Trent's decrees lest this worsen the German Catholics' position. Soon after his return to Louvain he received an apostolic delegation to publish the decision about English Catholics and protestant services. In June 1567 he arranged for its circulation in England.

Sander became a chief cog in the exile community of Louvain, taking a leading role in the reply to Bishop Jewel and, as a stipendiary professor in the university, distributing charity to many needy Englishmen and -women. He wrote three works against Jewel, all published in Louvain by John Fowler: *The Supper of Our Lord* (1566), *The Rocke of the Churche* (1567; republished, 1642), and *A Treatise of the Images of Christ and of his Saints* (1567). *The Rocke of the Churche* contained in embryo Sander's theory of resistance to political authority, although at that point he denied that priests exercised dominion and that the pope in particular lacked sovereignty. It may be that his *Briefe Treatise of Usurie*, also published by Fowler in 1568, arose from concern that some exiles were taking advantage of others. He took a line at odds with many other Louvainists by praising the duke of Alba's savage repression of the iconoclasm of 1568 in his *De typica & honoraria imaginum adoratione* (1569), dedicated to Alba.

Sander did what he could to assist the northern uprising of 1569, especially through Nicholas Morton's mission to England, which Sander claimed was intended to inform English Catholics that Elizabeth had been deposed as a heretic. When Pius V officially did this in *Regnans* (1570), Sander defended the pope's action, to the horror of many of his fellow exiles, notably William Allen, who persuaded him to suppress the book after publication. No copy is known to survive.

De visibili monarchia The point is of small importance, since in 1571 in *De visibili monarchia* (dedicated to Hosius, Morone, and Commendone) Sander printed the papal bull in full and praised as a martyr John Felton, the man who nailed it up in London. Sander argued that the rising had failed only because its leaders had not known of the bull. He was unique among English Catholics in holding a resistance theory that saw the world as one church under a single head, the pope, whom other rulers were bound to obey. His view was singled out for particular attention by the English government in the 'bloody questions' of 1581 put to suspected priests. *De visibili monarchia* also contained an English martyrology, drawing on lists similar to those in his report to Morone, with similar inaccuracies. The book's central argument was the divine establishment of papal monarchy. Sander made a somewhat more original point by structuring his argument round St Augustine's two cities, renamed the city of God and the city of the devil; the constant struggle between them Sander represented graphically by facing-page treatment of their histories. The work rested on wide reading, Sander showing no concern for possible heterodoxy on other matters of doctrine if a writer defended papal primacy. Thus Pole figured prominently; Sander narrated his role in the reconciliation of England, taking his account from Andras Dudic's biography of Pole, published in 1563. The work's final book attempted to name Antichrist as a specific individual in order to refute the protestant identification of him with the papacy. Sander tried to disseminate his book to British Catholics, sending a copy to William Maitland of Lethington, for instance, but it was intercepted.

De origine ac progressu schismatis anglicani On 25 January 1572 Sander left Louvain, summoned to Rome. He had a very good relationship with Pius V, who had helped him financially, and it was widely expected that the pope would make him a cardinal. Shortly after Sander's arrival in Rome, Pius died and Sander failed to gain the red hat from his successor, Gregory XIII, despite efforts on his behalf by Englefield in October 1572 and the Carthusian Maurice Chauncy in early 1573. Sander may now have considered joining the Jesuits, but was dissuaded on grounds of age. He certainly thought highly of the society. Soon after Sander's arrival in Rome, Allen and other English Catholics in the Low Countries sent a memorial to Pope Gregory which suggested that he consult Goldwell, Sander, and Morton about England. Sander composed his differences with Allen and made common cause, as Robert Persons later observed. In 1579 Allen called Sander 'my special friend' (Renold, 10).

Almost as soon as Sander arrived in Rome he began to write his most influential work, *De origine ac progressu schismatis anglicani*. Its textual history is complicated. Sander left it unfinished. Only one incomplete manuscript is known, partially annotated by Persons. The first edition, nominally published in Cologne in 1585, actually appeared from the press of Jean Foigny at Rheims. Its editor, Edward Rishton, reworked at least book 3. Rishton's account of his edition includes a number of mysteries, chief among them the identity of the 'Jodochus Skarnhert of Cologne' who had pressed him for a copy of *De origine* and who had taken responsibility for its publication. It has been suggested that Skarnhert may have been Persons, who is also said to have seen the expanded second edition (1586) through the press. Against these two points is Persons's treatment of *De origine* and its author in his 'Certamen ecclesiae anglicanae', which refers to the writer as 'a most famous man for learning, talent and piety' (*Robert Persons*, 31), together with Persons's claim that book 2 was Allen's work. It seems likely that Allen had a large hand in the whole of the text as printed, both the original and the revised editions.

The revised *De origine* proved very popular; there were further editions in Ingolstadt (1586, 1587, and 1588) and Cologne (1610 and 1628), the last with extensive additions by the Spanish Jesuit Pedro de Ribadeneira, whose frequently reprinted *Historia ecclesiastica del scisma del reyno de Inglaterra* was one of the many adaptations of Sander's book. The catalogue of the British Library lists fifteen editions of *De origine* before 1700, and that is certainly not the total. Others who incorporated Sander's material were Girolamo Pollini (first edition 1591, but a much bigger book than *De origine*), Bernardo Davanzati (1602), and Andrea Sciacca (1597). Nearly all of these support Rishton's (or his printer's) conversion of the work into a martyrology. In addition, there were two French translations by 1587, one of which had three printings, and a German version of 1594. In the seventeenth century François Maucroix's adaptation in *Histoire du schisme d'Angleterre* (1676; 1678; 1715) served as the proximate cause of Gilbert Burnet's *History of the Reformation* and thus launched modern historiography of the English Reformation. Burnet solidified the protestant attitude to Sander which had already produced Peter Heylin's label 'Dr Slanders', mainly for the aspersions he cast on Anne Boleyn.

De origine has a very simple plot: Henry VIII's desire for a divorce caused the Reformation. The villains other than Henry are drawn with broad strokes, especially Cardinal Wolsey. Most of the second edition's interpretation and substance descend from Pole, particularly his *Pro ecclesiasticae unitatis defensione*, which is frequently quoted, his letter congratulating Mary I on her accession, and perhaps some unpublished and possibly lost works, including a letter about Henry's tomb. Pole figures as the hero: book 2 concludes with his death, not that of Mary Tudor, and he is praised as 'the hope of England, great ornament and light of the church of Rome' (N. Sander, *De origine ac progressu schismatis anglicani, libri tres … aucti per Edouardum Rishtonum*, 1586, 308–9). Among other sources was a lost life of John Fisher that contained the bishop's witticism on the way up the scaffold (suspiciously reminiscent of Thomas More's): 'Feet, do your job, and the rest of my journey will take care of itself'; Richard Hilliard's mainly lost history of the English Reformation; and Johannes Cochlaeus's attack on Richard Morison's *Apomaxis calumniarum*. Sander put his legal training to good use in long discussions about the validity of Henry's marriage to Katherine of Aragon and the invalidity of that to Anne Boleyn.

Ireland Ireland was already much on Sander's mind, as he singled out English oppression of and papal concern for it. After about a year and a half in Rome Gregory dispatched Sander to the court of Spain in late 1573 and ordered the nuncio Nicolò Ormanetto, once Pole's datary, to assist him. Sander's mission was to induce Philip II to support the invasion of England. He spent almost six years on that goal. Philip gave him initial encouragement, most tangibly in the form of a pension of 300 ducats, which Sander had the usual difficulties collecting. Beyond that Philip would not go. The pope, exasperated with Philip's delays, finally launched his own invasion project commanded by the adventurer and veteran of Lepanto, Sir Thomas Stuckley. Stuckley apparently tried to involve Sander in the planning, along with Englefield and Allen, who were summoned to Rome in late 1575. Ormanetto thought Sander should not go, and the pope approved his remaining in Madrid. It proved wise to keep his distance from Stuckley, although, notwithstanding his reservations, Sander wrote a manifesto for him. When the expedition finally left in 1578, despite Sander's efforts to stop it, Stuckley diverted it at Portuguese request to north Africa, where it was destroyed. Sander tried to get compensation from the Portuguese without success.

Sander did not relax his pressure on Philip and the pope regarding England, even if he was sometimes prepared to give up on the king. No matter by what means, as he told Allen on 6 November 1577, 'the state of Christendome dependethe uppon the stowte assaillinge of Englande' ('Some letters', 13–14). Yet just a few months later Sander sounded much less optimistic, writing that 'God rewards not so much the event as good advice' (Bellesheim, 2.705), which might almost stand as his epitaph. The pope continued to support Sander financially, and late in 1578 another expedition was mounted. Sander, who had submitted a detailed plan for it in August, emphasizing the necessity of a nuncio to accompany it, pressed hard to be allowed to go. His request was granted, although he was not made nuncio, and he asked and received special faculties for the Irish bishops to reconcile schismatics. Yet when the expedition sailed in June 1579, Sander wrote to the cardinal secretary of state that he did not hope for much and was going mainly out of gratitude to the pope. Before he departed Sander gave the manuscript of his *De clave David*, a reply to attacks on *De visibili monarchia*, to the nuncio in Madrid, Filippo Sega, who published it at Rome in 1588 with Allen's approval; another edition followed in 1592. Sander also left the manuscript of *De iustificatione contra Colloquium Altenburgense*, with a preface dated 9 September 1578. Some of the printed editions contain an anonymous 'De vita et scriptis Nicolai Sanderi'.

The end The small force under the command of James Fitzmaurice landed at Smerwick in late July 1579, and Sander promptly opened a campaign for reinforcements. He immediately wrote a proclamation for the earl of Desmond, claiming war against England was just and based on the natural law right of resistance to the 'she-tyrant' (Veech, 262). Sander acted as treasurer to Fitzmaurice and wrote at least one of his appeals to other Irish nobles. When such covert assistance proved inadequate, Sander wrote to other potential allies in his own name, especially Ulick Burke, telling him that his father's capture was a warning from God that heretics must be destroyed. By early October 1579 Sander had changed his mind about the invasion's prospects and become wildly optimistic. On 28 October Desmond was ordered to surrender Sander. When he claimed, three days later, never to have promised to comply, it became one of the principal charges in his outlawry, in which Sander was described as an 'odious, unnatural, pestiferous traitor' (Brewer and Bullen, 2, no. 146).

Sander dangled various blandishments in front of Desmond and—after Desmond's death—before his brother Sir John of Desmond, and tirelessly urged on the other rebels, promising repeatedly that Spanish help was about to arrive. At one point he pledged himself 'to be massacred' if it did not come soon (Brewer and Bullen, 2.199). He included an interesting report on Irish customs in a letter to Sega of January 1580. Among other points, Sander observed the prevalence of barter, the numerous kinds of drink, dress, manners at table, and especially the strength of Irish religion. Rumours circulated in May 1580 that Sander had gone to Spain, but he was seen in Desmond's camp on the 20th. In June he was almost captured by English forces, and again when Desmond suffered another reverse in August. Sander was excluded from the offer of parley thereafter. Further letters asking for aid went off to Philip and the pope in October, at which time Sander was back at Smerwick. He left the fort ten days before it fell, dooming the invasion. Tangible military aid from Spain never arrived, but in April and May 1581 Philip put his diplomatic machinery to work seeking a cardinalate for Sander.

Sander, however, may already have been dead. The circumstances of his death are obscure. The date seems to have been between March and June 1581, although the Spanish ambassador to Elizabeth reported that she received confirmation of his death only in November, a claim repeated on 3 January 1582. At this point observers were unanimous that he had died of illness, probably dysentery, and the Spanish ambassador added that Sander had been found with his Bible and breviary under his arm. A few years later Sir William Cecil told a more lurid story of Sander's end. In his *Execution of Justice* (1583) Cecil alleged that Sander, 'wandering in the mountains in Ireland without succor, died raving in a frenzy' (ed. Kingdon, 30). William Camden later incorporated Cecil's allegations in his version of Sander's death, quoted in Wood. Wood also drew on the most circumstantial account in O'Sullivan Beare's *Historiae catholicae Iberniae compendium* (1621). It claimed that once Sander knew he was terminally ill he asked the bishop of Killaloe to administer last rites and he died at dawn the following day. He was buried in an unmarked grave near Clonlish by four Irish knights.

T. F. MAYER

Sources T. M. Veech, *Dr Nicholas Sanders and the English Reformation, 1530–1581* (1935) · Wood, *Ath. Oxon.*, new edn, 1.469–70 · A. F. Allison and D. M. Rogers, eds., *The contemporary printed literature of the English Counter-Reformation between 1558 and 1640*, 2 vols. (1989–94), vol. 1, pp. 135–40; vol. 2, pp. 138–9 · J. H. Pollen, ed., 'Dr Nicholas Sander's report to Cardinal Moroni', *Miscellanea, I*, Catholic RS, 1 (1905), 1–47 [from a transcript of Archivio segreto vaticano, Armaria 64:28, fols. 252r–274r] · 'Some letters and papers of Nicholas Sander, 1562–1580', *Miscellanea, XIII*, Catholic RS, 26 (1926), 1–57 · *CSP Rome, 1558–78* · J. S. Brewer and W. Bullen, eds., *Calendar of the Carew manuscripts*, 2: *1575–1588*, PRO (1868) · *CSP for., 1560–61* · *CSP Ire., 1574–85* · A. O. Meyer, *England and the Catholic church under Queen Elizabeth*, trans. J. R. McKee (1916); repr. with introduction by J. Bossy (1967) · A. Kenny, 'From hospice to college', *The Venerabile*, 21 (1962), 218–73 [sexcentenary issue: *The English hospice in Rome*] · *CSP dom., addenda, 1566–79* · J. M. Cleary, 'Dr Morys Clynnog's invasion projects', *Recusant History*, 8 (1965–6), 300–22 · C. G. Bayne, *Anglo-Roman relations, 1558–1565* (1913) · J. H. Pollen, 'Dr Nicholas Sanders, 16th century Catholic controversialist', *EngHR*, 6 (1891), 36–47 · Robert Persons, SJ, 'Certamen ecclesiae anglicanae', ed. J. S. F. Simons (1965) · T. M. McCoog, *The Society of Jesus in Ireland, Scotland, and England, 1541–1588* (1996) · 'The execution of justice in England' by William Cecil and 'A true, sincere, and modest defense of English Catholics' by William Allen, ed. R. M. Kingdon (1965) · J. Strype, *Ecclesiastical memorials*, 7 vols. (1816), vol. 2, pp. 472–3 · A. Bellesheim, *Geschichte der katholischen Kirche in Irland, von der Einführung des Christentums bis auf die Gegenwart*, 3 vols. (1890–91) · *Letters of William Allen and Richard Barret, 1572–1598*, ed. P. Renold, Catholic RS, 58 (1967) · P. Heylin, *Ecclesia restaurata, or, The history of the Reformation of the Church of England*, 2 (1661); repr. J. C. Robinson, ed. (1849), 310 · P. O'Sullivan-Beare, *Historiae Catholicae Iberniae compendium* (1621)

Sanders [*formerly* Carter], (**Orrell**) **Alexander** [Alex] (**1926–1988**), promoter of the Wicca religion, was born Orrell Alexander Carter, at 56 Church Road, Tranmere, Birkenhead, on 6 June 1926, the son of Orrell Alexander Carter, labourer and musician, and Hannah Jane Bibby, a domestic servant who later became a professional foster mother. Although his parents never married, Alex was the first of thirteen children. The family soon moved to Manchester, where he lived for about forty years. On moving to Manchester his father adopted the surname Sanders, with which Alex grew up and which was formally granted to him by deed poll on 22 October 1970. Though he was an able schoolboy, practical considerations curtailed his formal education at fourteen, and he subsequently worked for a pharmaceutical company and for the John Rylands Library, as well as being adopted for a time by a wealthy stockbroker. On 17 July 1948 he married Doreen Stretton (*b.* 1928/9), a packer of surgical plasters and the daughter of a foundry labourer, Joseph Herbert Stretton. They had a son and a daughter, but were divorced in 1953.

Sanders's religious inheritance was complex. He was brought up and confirmed as an Anglican, and attended a Church of England school (St George's, Hulme). A major childhood influence, however, was his maternal grandmother, a Welshwoman from Caernarvonshire who was skilled in traditional folk magic. His mother, moreover, introduced her sons to a spiritualist church, and all became mediums. In the 1950s, working under the name

of Paul Dallas, Alex acquired fame as one, with a special talent for healing; it is remembered that when in trance he could take burning coals in his bare hands. His work at the library gave him access to the classic texts of ritual magic, and on 9 November 1961 he wrote to the main local leaders of the pagan witch religion of Wicca, saying that he had seen them on a television programme and had always wanted to be a witch.

These Wiccans, however, took a lasting dislike to Sanders, and his first attempt to extol pagan witchcraft to the Manchester press, in September 1962, cost him his job at the library. He was apparently formally initiated into Wicca on 9 March 1963 by a priestess in Derbyshire, and acted as high priest of a coven in Nottinghamshire later that year. This group had dissolved by 1964, and later that year he got to know a fellow Mancunian, a strikingly beautiful seventeen-year-old called Arline Maxine (*b.* 1946), usually known as Maxine, the daughter of a club steward, Herbert Victor Morris. By mid-1965 they were running a coven together in Manchester, and they celebrated a witches' wedding to each other that December. By June 1965 their coven had been discovered by a local newspaper, and thereafter they encouraged and manipulated the attention of the mass media with such skill that by 1966 the couple were the best-known, and certainly the most photographed, witches in the world. They were now at the centre of a burgeoning network of covens. This attention confirmed the enmity of longer-established Wiccan leaders, who denounced Sanders as a charlatan. He responded with the claim that he had been initiated by his grandmother at the age of seven, and allowed his followers to invest him with the title of King of the Witches.

In June 1967 Sanders and Maxine moved to Clanricarde Gardens, London, which became their base for the next six years. They were formally married at Kensington register office on May day 1968, and had two children, Maya (already born in 1967) and Victor (*b.* 1972). On his marriage certificate, Sanders gave his rank or profession as 'lecturer in comparative religion'. Sanders's London period brought his fame to its apogee, and established his tradition of Wicca as the largest and fastest-growing branch of the time. It was broadly based upon that established in the 1950s, and was associated with Gerald *Gardner, but differed in three important points of detail. First, it had a greater component of the ritual magic which Sanders had studied at the John Rylands Library, taking images and conjurations from the Cabbala, the Enochian system of the Elizabethan occultist John Dee, and (above all) the rites of the main order of Victorian magicians, the Golden Dawn. Second, it had a more eclectic attitude to divinity, adding Hebrew angels and spirits to the unequivocally pagan deities of Wicca and suggesting at times that its beliefs might be compatible with Christianity. Third, it laid a more overt emphasis on hands-on magical healing, the alleged power to aid the sick or troubled by an energy transferred to the latter by touch. In 1969 a journalist, June Johns, published a biography of Sanders, *King of the Witches*, and in 1971 another journalist, Stewart Farrar, brought out a study of his tradition, *What Witches do*.

Farrar was initiated and subsequently became a major author on Wicca.

Portraits of Sanders at the height of his fame reveal a slim balding man standing 5 feet 7 inches tall, with a quick smile, soft voice, and often sad brown eyes. He could by turns be generous and unscrupulous, protective and exploitative, kind and abrasive, boastful and modest. He was at once an outrageous showman and a genuine and gifted healer. His partnership with Maxine broke down in 1973, and they divorced on 11 November 1982, although they remained friends and he frequently proposed remarriage. In 1986 he contracted a third legal union, with a woman called Jill, but this did not outlast the year. On separating from Maxine, Sanders left London for the Sussex coastal town of Bexhill, later settling at St Leonards nearby. There he continued to practise and teach Wicca, expanding his network of initiates far into continental Europe, but had effectively retired as a public figure. The recordings and transcripts taken of his meditations during his last years breathe a spirit of humility and piety. He died of lung cancer in St Helen's Hospital, Hastings, on 30 April 1988, and his pagan funeral took place at that town's crematorium on 11 May. The death certificate gave his occupation as 'occultist'.   RONALD HUTTON

Sources R. Hutton, *The triumph of the moon: a history of modern pagan witchcraft* (1999) · private information (2004) [Sanders family] · J. Johns, *King of the witches: the world of Alex Sanders* (1969) · S. Farrar, *What witches do* (1971) · private archive, Wiccan Church of Canada, Toronto, Canada, Gardner MSS · file of meditations by Sanders, Museum of Witchcraft, Boscastle · *The Cauldron* (1976–88) · *Manchester Evening News and Chronicle* (15 Sept 1962) · *Manchester Comet* (23 June 1965) · P. Crowther, *One witch's world* (1998) · private information (2004) [Doreen Valiente newspaper cutting collection] · m. certs. · b. cert. · d. cert.
Likenesses photographs, 1965–6, repro. in Johns, *King of the witches*

Sanders, Francis (1648–1710), Jesuit, was born in Worcestershire, pursued his humanity studies in the English College at St Omer, and went through his higher course in the English College, Rome, which he entered as a convictor, or boarder, on 6 November 1667. He took the college oath on 27 January 1669 and was ordained as a secular priest on 16 April 1672. He was admitted into the Society of Jesus at Rome by the father-general, Oliva, on 4 January 1674, and left for Watten to make his noviceship on 5 April or 4 June 1674. He was professed of the four vows on 15 August 1684. A catalogue of the members of the society, drawn up in 1693, states that he took the degree of DD at Cologne and had been prefect of studies and vice-rector of the college at Liège, and of the College of St Ignatius, London.

In 1692 Sanders was called to St Germain-en-Laye to replace Father John Warner as the confessor of the exiled James II. It is not clear when he took up his new post, for he was already at St Germain when Warner died in November of that year. Sanders remained at St Germain for the rest of his life, serving as confessor to James II until his death in September 1701 and then to his son James

Francis Edward Stuart (James III) until February 1710. Sanders lived in a small mezzanine room in the king's apartment of the château of St Germain. He seems to have exercised considerable spiritual influence in sustaining James II and reconciling him to his new circumstances, particularly after 1696. The king's *Papers of Devotion* probably reflect this influence.

Surviving documents show that Sanders was active in obtaining charity money and distributing it among the Jacobite community in and around St Germain. He was consulted by James II over the contents of his declaration of April 1693, but it is unlikely that he exercised much political influence. When, in 1694, he was accused of contributing to the fall of John Drummond, titular duke of Melfort, the latter's private secretary, David Nairne, defended him: 'Fr. Sanders is a very different man, has a good caractere, and does not appear to meddle more that he should'. A report in the state papers that he was encouraging people to assassinate William III in 1701 can probably be dismissed as a fabrication. Sanders was with James II when he lay dying in September 1701. His 'narrative of the reading of the will to the King' was later published (*Stuart Papers*, 2.518–19).

Sanders is best remembered for his involvement in the publication of two books. The first was *The practice of Christian perfection. Written in Spanish by Rd. Father Alphonsus Rodriguez of the Society of Jesus*. Sanders's translation of the French version was published in three volumes in London and St Omer in 1697–9. The second was *Abrégé de la vie de Jacques II, roy de la Grande Bretagne, & Tiré d'un écrit anglois du R. P. François Sanders, de la Compagnie de Jésus, confesseur de sa majesté*, published in Paris in 1703. This short life of James II was widely circulated, and quickly translated into Italian (Milan, 1703; Ferrara, 1704), English (London, 1704), and Spanish (Cadiz, 1707). In fact Sanders was only partly responsible for the original English text, which was written mainly by John Caryll (styled Lord Caryll), David Nairne, and Lewis Innes between November 1701 and March 1702. The completed text was sent to Père Bretonneau by July 1702, then modified by Charles, Lord Middleton. Bretonneau later admitted that he had lost the original English version of the text attributed to Sanders, but a copy of the first few pages has survived in the Bodleian Library (MS Carte 180, fol. 51).

It is not clear if Sanders accompanied James III when he was away from St Germain during the military campaigns of 1708–9, but the king was at St Germain when Sanders died there on 19 February 1710. He was buried the next day in the parish church beside the château and was replaced as confessor by another Jesuit, Father Thomas Eyre.

THOMPSON COOPER, *rev.* EDWARD CORP

Sources E. Corp, 'The Jacobite Chapel Royal at Saint-Germain-en-Laye', *Recusant History*, 23 (1996–7), 528–42 · E. Corp, 'An inventory of the archives of the Stuart court at Saint-Germain-en-Laye', *Archives*, 23 (1998), 1–29 · Bodl. Oxf., MS Rawl. D. 21 · BL, Gualterio MSS, Add. MSS 20310 and 31258 · Scottish Catholic Archives, Edinburgh, BL 1/181 · *Calendar of the Stuart papers belonging to his majesty the king, preserved at Windsor Castle*, 7 vols., HMC, 56 (1902–23), vols.

1–2 · Royal Arch., Stuart papers, Misc. 7 · *CSP dom.*, *1700–02* · Archives départementales du Val d'Oise, Pontoise, France, 68/H/5 · D. A. Bellenger, ed., *English and Welsh priests, 1558–1800* (1984)
Archives Bodl. Oxf., letters to Edward Meredith, MS Rawl. D. 21
Likenesses R. Westall, portrait, 1807 (earlier version of *The death of King James*) · R. Westall, oils, exh. RA 1833 (*The death of King James the Second at the Palace of St Germains en Laye, 1701*)

Sanders, Francis Williams (1769–1831), lawyer, was the eldest son of John Williams Sanders of the island of Nevis, West Indies. On 30 April 1787 he was admitted to Lincoln's Inn, where, after some years of pupillage to John Stanley, attorney-general of the Leeward Islands, and MP for Hastings from 1784 to 1801, he began to practise as a certificated conveyancer. He was called to the bar on 29 January 1802. He gave evidence before the real property law commission appointed in 1828, and was afterwards added to the commission, for which he signed the second report in 1830.

Sanders was best known as a legal writer. His works included not only the edited *Reports* of John Tracy Atkyns, but also a much admired treatise entitled *An essay on uses and trusts, and on the nature and operation of conveyances at common law, and of those which derive their effect from the Statute of Uses* (1791). It reached its fifth edition in 1844, and became a standard work in its field. Sanders died at his house, 5 Upper Montagu Street, Russell Square, London, on 1 May 1831, never having recovered after the death of his wife shortly before.

J. M. RIGG, *rev.* JOANNE POTIER

Sources *GM*, 1st ser., 101/1 (1831), 475 · Allibone, *Dict.* · 'Sketches of the bar, no. IV: Mr Humphreys and Mr Sanders', *Legal Observer*, 2 (1831), 33–4 · J. G. Marvin, *Legal bibliography, or, A thesaurus of American, English, Irish and Scotch law books* (1847) · [R. W. Bridgman], *A short view of legal bibliography* (1807) · *Browne's General Law List* (1795) · W. P. Baildon, ed., *The records of the Honorable Society of Lincoln's Inn: the black books*, 4 (1902)

Sanders, George (1774–1846), portrait painter, was born on 21 April 1774, at Kinghorn, Fife, the son of John Sanders and his wife, Jean, *née* Bruce. His surname is sometimes given as Saunders and he has often been confused with the painter George Lethbridge Saunders (1809–1863), who also painted portraits in miniature. The miniature painter Christina *Robertson, *née* Saunders (1796–1854), whom Sanders later taught, was his niece. He was educated in Edinburgh and afterwards apprenticed there (together with William Allan) to a coach painter named Smeaton or Smiton, 'a man of considerable taste' (Conolly, 390). He then practised as a drawing-master, a painter of miniature portraits, and a designer of book illustrations. According to Irwin and Irwin (p. 80), his frontispiece to Zimmerman's romantic study *Solitude, with Respect to its Influence upon the Mind and Heart* (Edinburgh edn, 1797) shows a contemplative young man by a stream. He also painted a panorama of Edinburgh 'taken on board ship lying in the River Forth [which] was rather a seaview than a landscape. Many vessels were introduced and the whole ... had as good an effect as those of Barker in Leicester Fields' (Farington, *Diary*, 24 Oct 1801). At least fifteen pencil sketches by Sanders survive in an unpublished sketchbook of drawings by various artists compiled by Francis, eighth earl of

Wemyss (priv. coll.); these depict landscape and figure scenes at Inveresk and in Haddingtonshire.

On 18 June 1806 Farington noted in his diary:

> Saunders, Miniature Painter, I called on & saw Him. He told me He came from Edinburgh abt. a year ago and is now so overwhelmed with business as to be obliged to refuse sitters.—He has 30 guineas for a miniature about 3 inches high by 2 inches ½ wide,—for the size (abv.) that 40 guineas—for the next size 50 guineas & for the largest 70 guineas.—I saw portraits of Lord & Lady Fitzharris (Miss Dashwood) and of Sir Stephen Glynn,—Lady Francis Ponsonby &c.—He said that being of a robust constitution He requires Exercise & suffers from close application, having pains in his breast &c. (Farington, *Diary*, 7.2787)

On 9 November 1806, after referring in his diary to David Wilkie, who had himself come to London in 1805, Farington noted that:

> He [Wilkie] spoke of Saunders the Miniature painter who He sd was encouraged to come to London by Sir Walter Farquar. He sd. Saunders had great ability and finding that miniature painting hurts his eyes proposes to practise *in large*. (ibid., 8.2900–01)

A fellow Scot, Farquar was physician-in-ordinary to the prince of Wales, a position that would have enabled him to introduce his protégé to Scottish and English nobility in London. On 2 August 1811 Farington noted further:

> Sir Wm. Beechey has given an acct. of Saunders, the Scotch painter, who after having been very popular as a miniature painter at great prices, has given up that practise & now paints portraits, size of life in oil. He has 250 guineas for a whole length. He applies with great industry; rises at 4 oClock in the morning & goes to bed at 8 oClock at night. (ibid., 11.3979)

Sanders suffered increasingly from ophthalmia; despite having given up painting miniatures he was obliged to paint for only six months of each year.

Remarkable for its prefiguring of Byron as an icon of the Romantic movement, Sanders's double portrait of him and Robert Rushton, which includes in the background a yacht at anchor and wild mountain scenery (1807–8; Royal Collection), is undoubtedly his masterpiece. Byron (who had not yet 'awoke[n]' to find myself famous') commissioned the portrait from his fellow Scot in anticipation of a voyage. But it was Sanders who drew on his knowledge of Reynolds's celebrated *Commodore Keppel* (1753–4)—based on the *Apollo Belvedere* (and, possibly, Allan Ramsay's *Norman, 22nd Chief of Macleod*, 1748)—of Scottish scenery, and of yacht design, as well as his own sensitive ability to render Romantic mood and atmosphere, to produce *avant la lettre* an image of the author and hero of *Childe Harold's Pilgrimage*, a conflation that Byron was later both to contribute to and to deny. Sanders's experience as a miniature painter is evident in the detailed and highly finished rendering of Byron's head; the smooth quality of the thinly applied paint conveys the beauty of a face that Scott compared to an alabaster vase lit from within (Guiccioli). When Byron wrote to his mother from Constantinople to ask whether she had 'receive[d] a picture in oil by *Sanders* in *Vigo Lane* London' (*Byron's Letters and Journals*, 1.251) he eventually received her reply that she had 'received your Picture about three weeks ago after a *great* deal of trouble,

Saunders said he left it to show as an honor and credit to him, the countenance is *angelic* and the finest I ever saw and it is very like' (Peach, 31). The portrait was engraved by William Finden and reproduced as the frontispiece to Thomas Moore's *Letters and Journals of Lord Byron with Notices of his Life* (1830); via this and subsequent engravings it became perhaps the most widely known portrait of Byron in the nineteenth century.

Before going abroad in 1809 Byron also commissioned Sanders to paint miniatures of himself (prime version, priv. coll.) and several of his 'most intimate [Harrow] Schoolfellows' (*Byron's Letters and Journals*, 1.197), including William Harness and Lord Clare. On his return Byron sat again to Sanders (*c*.1812; prime version, priv. coll.). The several versions of each of these miniatures of Byron were much sought after by his female acquaintances. After the return of the later miniature to John Murray, following its theft from his house by Lady Caroline Lamb, it was engraved for Byron's publisher by Henry Meyer as the intended frontispiece to a new edition of *Childe Harold's Pilgrimage*. Byron made 'a *very strong objection* to the engraving' (ibid., 2.224), however, commenting that 'Sanders would not have survived the engraving' (ibid., 2.234). While it gives no indication that Sanders's reputation would have suffered, the apparently unique surviving impression (priv. coll.) from Meyer's engraving (all except two were burnt, according to Byron's wishes) is testimony both to the extraordinarily powerful effect that both Byron and his publisher realized that the publication of his portrait could have on his public, and to Sanders's sensitive and sophisticated ability to capture this effect in his portraits of Byron. That his portraits succeeded in conveying to Byron, to his inner circle, and to contemporary and modern viewers a poetic likeness of one who remains a figurehead for Romanticism gives a clear indication of Sanders's important status as a Romantic painter.

Sanders's portraits of John, fourth earl of Rosebery, and of his first wife, Harriet, in 'Van Dyck' dress (*c*.1808; both priv. coll.); his double portrait of Walter and Lady Eleanor Campbell of Islay landing from a boat in a stormy sea (priv. coll.); and his large equestrian portrait of Charles, third marquess of Londonderry (priv. coll.), for which he was said to have been paid £800, are further examples of Sanders's blend of portraiture with romantic scenery and / or dress. His portraits appealed to the Scottish nobility and the fashionable world of Regency London; other sitters included Admiral George Elphinstone, Viscount Keith (miniature, 1807); Margaret, countess of Wemyss (oils, priv. coll.); William Cavendish, sixth duke of Devonshire, in 'Van Dyck' dress (oils, priv. coll.); and Admiral Sir Charles Rowley (oils; engraved J. Richardson Jackson, 1848). Of his miniature of Princess Charlotte (Royal Collection) the preparatory pencil drawing made during sittings in 1813 is in the Scottish National Portrait Gallery, Edinburgh. Engravings by John Burnet, Charles Turner, and Henry Meyer record further portraits. Sanders exhibited only once at the Royal Academy, in 1834, when he showed five portraits. Conolly (p. 390) records that he 'declined being a candidate for academic honours'.

That several of his sitters were naval officers suggests that Sanders maintained his early knowledge of shipping; in his will he bequeathed his entire estate to two friends, Robert Dryburgh Menzies and Thomas Menzies, shipbuilders at Leith. His male sitters are usually portrayed either in ceremonial naval or military dress, highland dress, or masquerade costume. The latter also enhances several of his portraits of women; Margaret Mercer Elphinstone (later comtesse de Flahault) sat to Sanders in oriental dress (*c*.1814; priv. coll.). She appears, brightly lit in a darkened interior, in a life-size portrait that is richly coloured, exotic, and sensuous: the warm amber and brown of her dress, and her gorgeous floral turban of gold, red, yellow, and green form a luxuriant setting for the portrayal of her face; her dark eyes and dreamy expression suggest an air of private reverie heightened by the romantic mood of the painting.

Sanders travelled frequently to the continent; twenty-six of his watercolour copies after Dutch and Flemish paintings, including works by Rembrandt, are in the National Gallery of Scotland, Edinburgh. He died, unmarried, at his home in Allsop Terrace, New Road, Middlesex, on 26 March 1846. His will was proved on 21 April 1846 before William Tassie and 'oil and colorman' John Page. Tassie, a noted modeller of gems and seals, of 8 Upper Phillimore Place, Kensington, and his nephew William Hardy Vernon, of the rectory, Sutton, Surrey, also a modeller, were the executors. Of Scottish descent, Tassie was a cultivated man whose studio in Leicester Square was a meeting place for artists and literary men, including Moore and Byron. Though details of Sanders's personal life are few his friendships with Farquar and Tassie, and his acquaintance with Wilkie, together with his predominantly Scottish clientele, suggest that throughout his life in London he maintained close contact with the highly successful Scottish group of artists working in London in the early part of the nineteenth century.

ANNETTE PEACH

Sources A. Peach, 'Portraits of Byron', *Walpole Society*, 62 (2000), 1–144 · Farington, *Diary* · G. Wills, 'A forgotten Scottish painter', *Country Life* (8 Oct 1953), 1120–21 · *IGI* · will, PRO, PROB 11/2035, sig. 306 · *The Times* (26 March 1846) · M. F. Conolly, *Biographical dictionary of eminent men of Fife* (1866) · photographs, papers, correspondence, NPG, Heinz Archive and Library · R. Walker, *The eighteenth and early nineteenth century miniatures in the collection of her majesty the queen* (1991) · D. Irwin and F. Irwin, *Scottish painters at home and abroad, 1700–1900* (1975) · T. Guiccioli, *My recollections of Lord Byron & those of witnesses of his life*, trans. H. Jerningham, 2 vols. (1869), 1.66 · Graves, *RA exhibitors* · private information (2004) [Stephen Lloyd] · *Byron's letters and journals*, ed. L. A. Marchand, 12 vols. (1973–82)
Likenesses A. Geddes, oils, 1816, NG Scot.

Sanders, George (1906–1972), film actor, was born on 3 July 1906 at 6 Petroffski Ostroff, St Petersburg, Russia, one of two sons and a daughter of Henry Sanders (*b. c*.1870), a rope manufacturer, and his wife, Margaret Kolbe, a horticulturist and a fair musician. Although born in Russia, his parents had retained their British identity, being of Scottish ancestry. With the revolution in 1917 the family fled to England. Sanders was educated at a Russian grade school, Dunshurst preparatory school, Bedales School near Petersfield in Hampshire, Brighton College, and Manchester Technical College. In Manchester he studied textiles, a profession he pursued for a year, followed by three years as a salesman with tobacco companies in Argentina and Chile. When this was terminated he returned to Britain where, in the early 1930s, after a brief spell as an 'account executive' with Lever Brothers in London, Sanders turned to the stage, encouraged by Greer Garson. He appeared in a revue, *Ballyhoo*; acted in more than fifty radio plays for the BBC, where he received voice coaching; appeared in the play *King's Ransom*; he also did night-club work and appeared in Noël Coward's *Conversation Piece*, going to Broadway with it (where he was Coward's understudy); he took the lead in the play *Further Outlook* on his return.

Sanders's film début was *Find the Lady* (1936). He was the leading actor in only his second film, *Strange Cargo*, the same year. Other films quickly followed before he decided to try his luck in Hollywood when the studio with which he had a long-term contract burnt down. His first American film was *Lloyds of London* (1937) for Twentieth Century Fox, which had taken over his contract. Several featured roles followed before the RKO studio negotiated for him to play Leslie Charteris's smooth adventurer, the Saint, in their 'B' series of films, which he did five times between 1939 and 1941. Through the war years Sanders often portrayed Nazis, such as in Fritz Lang's *Man Hunt* (1941). However, he also undertook other roles, in *Rebecca*, as the caddish cousin, Jack Favell, and also in *Foreign Correspondent*, both in 1940 for Alfred Hitchcock; and, especially, as Charles Strickland (modelled on the painter Paul Gauguin) in *The Moon and Sixpence* (1942) from W. Somerset Maugham's novel. He also played Michael Arlen's debonair troubleshooter, the Falcon, four times (1941–2) in another RKO 'B' series, before passing the role to his brother in the series and in real life, Tom Conway. Offsetting this were more prestigious roles in *This Land is Mine* (1943) for director Jean Renoir, *The Lodger* (1944), and *The Picture of Dorian Gray* (1945) as Lord Henry Wotton, the evil influence on Gray. This last role was a cynical, world-weary portrayal, the prototype of the character for which he would be best remembered, the suave and sophisticated, mocking, almost sneering, cad. It seemed he wished to imply this image was his real-life self: 'for an elegant assumption of superiority over the other cast-members, George wins hands down' (Shipman, 484). However, he was remembered also as a 'kind and emotional person … a somewhat lost and overgrown schoolboy' (Ogden).

After the Second World War the films Sanders made were mixed. *Hangover Square* (1945) was his last under contract at Twentieth Century Fox. He subsequently played the title role in *The Private Affairs of Bel Ami* (1947); he was good in *The Ghost and Mrs Muir* and better as Charles II in *Forever Amber* (both 1947). With *All about Eve* (1950), though, as 'that venomous fish-wife Addison de Witt', as Bette Davis's character calls him, he excelled, winning an Academy award as best supporting actor for his portrayal of the cynical drama critic. Of the award he wrote 'Apart from

making my already large ego one size larger it did absolutely nothing for me' (Sanders, 69). He had another excellent role opposite Ethel Merman, in the Irving Berlin musical *Call me Madam* (1953). His solo 'Marrying for Love' showed he could more than carry a tune. With a rich bass-baritone voice he did make some commercial recordings; he was even signed by Rodgers and Hammerstein to replace Ezio Pinza on stage in *South Pacific*, a commitment he backed out of.

Call me Madam was Sanders's last important leading role. Thereafter he appeared in mediocre productions, although a few films rose above generally indifferent programmers: *Witness to Murder* (1954), *While the City Sleeps* (1956), *Death of a Scoundrel* (1957). In 1958 he hosted *The George Sanders Mystery Theatre*, a series for television. In 1960 he published his autobiography, *Memoirs of a Professional Cad*, referring to acting as unnecessary hard work: 'it takes up a lot of time that might be more profitably employed' (Sanders, 58). But if his films in the 1950s were uninspired, those of the 1960s were worse. These were mostly shot in Britain or on the continent and Sanders was usually 'his old tired self', even in better films such as *The Quiller Memorandum* (1966), often relying on his image of languid indifference and articulate disdain. 'He so practised the sneer that eventually he required no words' (Thomson, 663). His mellifluous tones, though, were used to excellent effect when he provided the voice of Shere Khan the tiger in Disney's cartoon version of *The Jungle Book* (1967). In John Huston's *The Kremlin Letter* (1970) he was seen, sadly, as a drag queen. Final films, in Britain, out of a lifetime total of 110, included *Psychomania* (1971) about a motor cycle gang brought back from the grave by the devil, and *Doomwatch* (1972), based on the television series.

Away from film-making, Sanders had put his name to two ghost-written Inner Sanctum Mystery novels, *Crime on my Hands* (1944), and *Stranger at Home* (1946), the basis of the film *The Unholy Four* (1954). He was also a director of Cadco Developments Ltd, a piggery firm which marketed sausages, with a factory in Sussex and an extension in Scotland. It was a financial disaster. Following its collapse in 1964, a Board of Trade investigation strongly criticized his behaviour.

Sanders married four times, three of his marriages ending in divorce. His first marriage (1940–48) was to the actress Susan Larson (real name Elsie M. Poole). His second (1949–54) was to the film actress Zsa Zsa Gabor. What Sanders described as 'the best thing that has happened in my life' (Sanders, 142) was his marriage in 1958 to the actress Benita Hume (1906–1967), widow of Ronald Colman, which lasted until her death. His brief final marriage in 1970 to Magda Gabor (1921–1997), sister of his second wife, lasted only a few months.

Sanders suffered a stroke in 1969, and several small strokes during the next year. David Niven, in his second volume of autobiography, *Bring on the Empty Horses*, recalled Sanders saying in 1937 'I will have had enough of this earth by the time I am 65 … So I shall commit suicide' (Walker, 365). Sanders died in his hotel room at

Castelldefels near Barcelona on 25 April 1972 from an overdose of sleeping pills. Shortly before he had sold his house in Majorca. His suicide note read 'Dear world, I am leaving you because I am bored. I feel I have lived long enough …' (ibid.). His brother had died in 1967; Sanders was survived by his sister, Margaret. He was buried in England.   ROBERT SHARP

Sources R. Vanderbeets, *George Sanders: an exhausted life* (1991) · G. Sanders, *Memoirs of a professional cad* (1960); new pubn with introduction, epilogue, and filmography by T. Thomas (1992) · B. Aherne, G. Sanders, and B. Hume, *A dreadful man* (1979) · D. Niven, *Bring on the empty horses* (1975) · D. Shipman, *The great movie stars: the golden years* (1970) · E. Katz, *The international film encyclopedia* (1980) · D. Thomson, *A biographical dictionary of film*, 3rd edn (1994) · *The international dictionary of films and filmmakers*, 3: *Actors and actresses*, ed. J. Vinson (1986) · *The Times* (26 April 1972) · W. G. Ogden, *The Times* (5 May 1972) · J. Walker, ed., *Halliwell's film-goer's companion*, 12th edn (1997) · *DAB*
Archives FILM BFI NFTVA, performance footage |SOUND BL NSA, performance footage

Sanders, Henry (1727–1785), antiquary, the son of Henry Rogers Sanders, apothecary, and Rebecca Hawkes, was born at Dudley where he was baptized on 16 January 1727. His father's mother, Sarah, was the daughter of Thomas Rogers, a Stourbridge glassmaker and ancestor of Samuel Rogers the poet. His father, who invented a locally popular medicine, had a large family and seems to have relied partly on financial help from the Rogers family and from his elder brother, Thomas, a surgeon. Sanders attended Dudley grammar school and entered Oriel College, Oxford, as a servitor in 1746. The college subsequently awarded him an exhibition and employed him to read prayers at St Bartholomew's Hospital at Cowley, just outside Oxford. He graduated BA in 1750.

After some delay Sanders found a poorly paid curacy at Wednesbury, Staffordshire, and was ordained. On 30 November 1754 at St Bartholomew's, Wednesbury, he married Elizabeth Butler (d. 1760), the eldest daughter of John Butler of Wednesbury. Her father disapproved of the match because of Sanders's poverty, but was reconciled when Sanders became curate of Shenstone, Staffordshire, in 1755 and immediately obtained the patronage of one of the leading parishioners, Samuel Hill of Shenstone Park. Hill died in 1758 and Elizabeth Sanders in 1760 but Sanders remained at Shenstone until early 1770, combining his curacy with some private tutoring and antiquarian pursuits. He then spent a period as usher at King Edward VI School, Birmingham. Through the influence of Lord Lyttleton, who was the patron of his uncle, Thomas Sanders, he was appointed in 1771 master of Halesowen School in Shropshire. Pynson Wilmot, vicar of Halesowen and a former master of Dudley grammar school, also granted him the cure of Oldbury.

Sanders seems to have compiled much of *The History and Antiquities of Shenstone* while living in Shenstone but made major additions in 1773–4. The book was finally published by John Nichols in 1794; it was prefaced by a short account of the author by his son and contained an appendix of additions and corrections supplied by the Staffordshire historian Stebbing Shaw and by Shaw's friend Samuel Pipe Wolferstan. It is the first published Staffordshire parish history and is a long, detailed work, containing elaborate accounts of the local manors, hamlets, farms, genealogies, and topography, although its usefulness is impaired by the lack of an index.

Sanders died at Halesowen in January 1785 and was buried by his special request at Shenstone on 4 February. His wife had been buried at Wednesbury. Their only child, John Butler Sanders (1755–1830), spent most of his adult life as curate in various London parishes and was an untiring supporter of the Royal Humane Society.
THOMAS SECCOMBE, rev. D. A. JOHNSON

Sources J. B. Sanders, 'Biographical memoir', in H. Sanders, *History and antiquities of Shenstone* (1794) · Foster, *Alum. Oxon.* · *GM*, 1st ser., 100/1 (1830), 473–4 · Wednesbury parish register, William Salt Library, Stafford · Shenstone parish register, William Salt Library, Stafford · Dudley parish register, Dudley Archives and Local History Service · private information (1897) [C. L. Shadwell] · *IGI*

Sanders [Saunders], **John** (1750–1825), painter, was born in London, the son of John Saunders, a pastel painter, who practised at Norwich, Stourbridge in Worcestershire, and elsewhere. Sanders was a student at the Royal Academy Schools in 1769 and obtained a silver medal in 1770. He first appears as an exhibitor at the Royal Academy in 1771, when he sent a portrait and *A Philosopher*. In 1772 he exhibited *St. Sebastian* and a portrait; in 1773 *Jael and Sisera* and three portraits; and he continued to exhibit pictures in oil and crayon, and drawings, for some years. During these years he was resident in Great Ormond Street, London, and in 1775 appears in the catalogue of the Royal Academy as John Saunders junior. Possibly some of the works mentioned above were exhibited by his father, with whom he is often confused. In 1778 he moved to Norwich, but continued to contribute to the Royal Academy portraits, including one of William Crotch the musician, and views of Norwich Cathedral. On 9 July 1780 he married at St Martin-in-the-Fields, Westminster, London, Rebecca Arnold of Norwich; they had five daughters and one son. Mrs Sanders was noted for her beauty and sat as model for many of Sanders's paintings. In 1790 he settled in Bath, where he practised for many years with success as a portrait painter. A portrait of Judith, countess of Radnor (1821; Longford Castle, Wiltshire), is a very good example of his work and shows stylistic similarities to the work of Sir Thomas Lawrence. He is mentioned by Frances Burney in her *Diary and Letters of Madame D'Arblay* (1842–6) as painting a portrait of Princess Charlotte of Wales. Sanders died at Clifton, near Bristol, in 1825. His son, John Arnold Saunders (b. c.1801), born at Bath, also pursued an artistic career and practised with some success as a landscape painter in London; he was popular as a drawing master before emigrating to Canada in 1832.
L. H. CUST, rev. HALLIE RUBENHOLD

Sources B. Stewart and M. Cutten, *The dictionary of portrait painters in Britain up to 1920* (1997) · Waterhouse, *18c painters* · Redgrave, *Artists* · Graves, *Artists* · *N&Q*, 7th ser., 6 (1888), 462 · *N&Q*, 7th ser., 7 (1889), 96–7, 184–5 · private information (1897) [P. E. Clark] · *IGI*

Sanders, Nicholas. *See* Sander, Nicholas (c.1530–1581).

Sanders, Robert (*c*.1727–1783), compiler of biographies and writer, was born in or near Breadalbane, Perthshire, the son of Thomas Sanders. He was apprenticed to a comb maker for seven years, during which time, having a passion for reading and 'a prodigious memory', he spent most of his nights studying Latin, Greek, Hebrew, mathematics, and history. He seems to have worked as an usher in various schools in the north of England before going to London about 1760, where he made his living as a hack writer. According to the *Gentleman's Magazine*, about 1764 Sanders began compiling the criminal biographies that were published first in numbers, and then as *The Newgate Journal, or, Malefactor's Bloody Register* (5 vols., 1773). In 1769 he was employed by George Lyttelton, first Baron Lyttelton, to correct for the press the third edition of his *History of the Life of King Henry II*, which was published in six volumes (1769–73) with nineteen pages of errata. Under the pseudonym of Nathaniel Spencer he published in weekly numbers *The complete English traveller, or, A new survey and description of England and Wales, containing a full account of what is curious and entertaining in the several counties, the isles of Man, Jersey, and Guernsey ... and a description of Scotland* in 1771. This travel guide was partly based on his own travels but also drew on the travel writings by John Ray, Daniel Defoe, and John Pennant.

Sanders, who had a wife and five children to support, was always impoverished; he was described by the bookseller Henry Lemoine as 'one of the sons of misfortune, who, with a share of learning that might have entitled a less voluminous writer to a name among the literati, never emerged from obscurity' (*GM*, 311). He made good use of his Hebrew for his next work, a learned annotated edition of the Bible, which first appeared in numbers and was reissued as *The Universal Family Bible, or, Christian's Divine Library* (2 vols., [1773]). Aware that he had no literary reputation Sanders published this work under the name of Henry Southwell DD, rector of Asterby in Lincolnshire, to whom he paid a fee of 100 guineas. By contrast Sanders was paid 25*s*. per sheet for this work. In 1774 he published anonymously four volumes of *The Lubracations of Gaffer Graybeard*, a satire on dissenters, in which leading dissenting ministers of London are roundly mocked; Dr John Gill is portrayed as Dr Half-pint, Dr Thomas Gibbons as Dr Hymn-maker, and others in equally transparent nicknames. A manuscript note on the British Library copy by the historian of dissent, Walter Wilson, suggests that Sanders may have been a student at an Independent academy in Hackney from where he was ignominiously expelled but this story remains uncorroborated.

Sanders, who styled himself DD, was working on a general chronology of all nations under the patronage of Lord Hawke when he died of a pulmonary disorder on 24 March 1783.   THOMAS SECCOMBE, *rev.* R. D. E. EAGLES

Sources *GM*, 1st ser., 53 (1783), 311–13, 400, 482 • Nichols, *Lit. anecdotes* • J. Lackington, *Memoirs of the forty-five first years of the life of James Lackington, bookseller. Written by himself* (1827)

Sanders, Robert Arthur, **Baron Bayford** (1867–1940), politician, was born at 27 Norfolk Square, Paddington, London, on 20 June 1867, the eldest son in the family of three sons and one daughter of Arthur Sanders (1826–1886), barrister, of Fernhill, Isle of Wight, and his wife, Isabella (*d*. 1907), daughter of John Synge of Glenmore, co. Wicklow. He was educated at Harrow School and at Balliol College, Oxford (1886–90). Despite leading an active social life at Oxford and hunting regularly, he surprised contemporaries by achieving a first-class degree in law.

Sanders was called to the bar by the Inner Temple in 1891 but seems never to have practised, preferring the life of a country gentleman which his private means allowed. He married on 3 August 1893 Lucy Sophia Halliday, daughter of William Halliday Halliday, a landowner, of Lynton, north Devon, and lived initially in Leicestershire for the hunting, and later at Exford, Somerset. Lucy Sanders became the active supporter of his public life, one of those wives who did much to establish Conservative organizations for women after 1918. He was master of the Devon and Somerset staghounds (1895–1907), a Somerset county alderman, JP, and later deputy lieutenant, and a yeomanry officer.

Sanders was blooded as Conservative candidate for Liberal East Bristol in 1900, but then lost in 1906 by just seventeen votes in the more favourable Conservative territory of Bridgwater. Known only in the west country, he could not hope for a better constituency elsewhere, so he actively nursed Bridgwater in a manner unusual for the time (though typical of his own professionalism under the gentleman amateur's appearance). He won easily in January 1910, and held the seat until 1923. He was always bored by back-bench life, but from early 1911 found an outlet for his energies in the whips' office. He now thoroughly enjoyed himself in the Conservative campaign to obstruct Liberal legislation between 1911 and 1914, and his diary shows how keenly he entered into the team-game side of Westminster life.

On the outbreak of war, Sanders rejoined the North Devon yeomanry, of which he had been lieutenant-colonel since 1911, and commanded the regiment at Gallipoli, subsequently in Egypt and Palestine. It was characteristic that he rarely ever referred afterwards to this part of his life. He returned to Westminster early in 1917, when the chief whip asked him to 'come for duty in the House', where the new Lloyd George coalition was already a worry to the party managers. He became unofficial party whip, working sometimes with and sometimes against coalition whips, and did much to protect party interests, for example in the Representation of the People Act (1918). Largely as a result of Sanders's efforts, franchise extensions harmful to Conservatives were balanced by extensions of the business vote and a favourable redistribution of constituency boundaries. In this he had to co-operate closely with Conservative central office, and early in 1918 became deputy party chairman under George Younger, in which capacity he helped adapt the party to the new electoral system and ironed out difficulties over 'coupons' for government candidates during the 1918 general election. Thereafter he remained a senior party manager, in 1927 chairman, and in 1934 president, of the National Union of

Conservative Associations, and from 1933 chairman of the Association of Conservative Clubs.

Although Sanders formally entered the Lloyd George coalition government as treasurer of the household in 1919, and was created a baronet in January 1920, he remained committed to the party, a partisanship which ensured that he did not become government chief whip when the post fell vacant. He was, however, under-secretary at the War Office in 1921–2, and thereby helped lead the 'under-secretaries' revolt' in 1922 against Lloyd George. He was the rebels' first speaker at a meeting with Austen Chamberlain on 3 August 1922. At the end, hating to be in conflict with his leaders, Sanders offered his resignation, which was not accepted. Unsurprisingly, he helped Younger to orchestrate the opposition that necessitated the Carlton Club meeting ten weeks later and there voted with the majority against another coalition election.

Sanders had his reward when Bonar Law made him minister of agriculture, but almost lost Bridgwater a month later at the general election held in November 1922. Sanders, who had been appointed a privy councillor when he took office in October 1922, found it a congenial cabinet, most of whose members were friends, happily reflecting that it was 'a real old Tory cabinet' (*Real Old Tory Politics*, 192). He seems not to have been consulted in the leadership crisis that followed Bonar Law's enforced retirement in May 1923, but carried on as instructed under Baldwin, his Harrow contemporary. Sanders was not, however, an effective minister, even with a lifetime's interest in agriculture. He had no imaginative scheme to mitigate the prevailing depression, and had trouble with the Beaverbrook press over imported Canadian cattle. Most importantly, he did not produce a plausible policy to counter opposition parties' claims that 'food taxes' would be introduced when Baldwin called an election over protection in autumn 1923.

In that election Sanders lost at Bridgwater to a Liberal, and this ended his ministerial career, for although re-elected to the Commons for Wells in 1924, the world had moved on during his absence, and the return of former coalitionists to the party fold made his ministerial re-employment impossible. He did not complain, but found back-bench life tedious, standing down in 1929. In June 1929 he was raised to the peerage as Baron Bayford. During the 1930s he increasingly kept to Somerset, where he was chairman of the county council, and was increasingly unhappy with modern political trends. A former party colleague noted after his death that in his last letter in August 1939 Bayford had concluded that 'all recent news seems very beastly' (*Real Old Tory Politics*, 8). He died at his home, Bayford Lodge, Stoke Trister, Somerset, on 24 February 1940, and since he had no living son (his only son had committed suicide in 1920) the barony became extinct. He was survived by his wife and two daughters.

Peter Sanders (a universal nickname) was a well-set up man whose ruddy complexion and strong voice indicated the outdoor life—even when in cabinet he tried to hunt several days a week. He was regarded by opponents as a 'delightfully Tory' gentleman, a man difficult to dislike but who seemed to represent a dying breed in the party. He felt much the same himself, admiring most as his political heroes the squires Harry Chaplin, Walter Long, and 'the Pink 'un', Acland-Hood of Somerset, another whipper-in, both inside and outside the house.

JOHN RAMSDEN

Sources *Real old tory politics: the political diaries of Robert Sanders, Lord Bayford, 1910–35*, ed. J. Ramsden (1984) · *WW* · *WWW*, 1941–50 · *The Times* (27 Feb 1940) · *Somerset County Gazette* (18 July 1914) · *Bridgwater Mercury* (9 Dec 1903) · *Daily Telegraph* (27 Feb 1940) · private information (2004) [Vera Butler, daughter] · GEC, *Peerage* · b. cert. · d. cert.
Archives Bodl. Oxf., notebooks and diary | HLRO, corresp. with A. B. Law

Sanders, Ruth Vernon Manning- [*née* Ruth Vernon Manning] (1888–1988), writer and folklorist, was born on 21 August 1888 in Swansea, the youngest of three daughters of John Edmondson *Manning (1848–1910), Unitarian minister, and his wife. Brought up in a book-loving, play-acting household and moving to Sheffield, then to Manchester, Ruth won a Shakespeare scholarship to Manchester University, where she hoped to gain a degree in English literature and become an actress. A serious illness, however, ended her studies at the university, and a period of convalescence and travel then followed.

Ruth met George Rawlings Sanders (1884/5–1952), then a painter, in Devon. The pair married in Totnes on 22 May 1911, joined their surnames with a hyphen, and took to the road together—literally: in a horse-drawn caravan—and spent two exciting, unorthodox, and thoroughly enjoyable two years travelling with the well-known tenting circus known as Count Rosaire's, owned by Freddie Ross. A photograph shows Ruth in boots and breeches, whip in hand, seated on the knee of a crouching elephant—which she apparently rode through the streets as part of the circus parade. With the birth of their daughter Joan in 1913 the circus period ended, and more conventional quarters were established in Bude, Cornwall. The caravanning influence must have persisted, however, because between 1914 and 1927 the Manning-Sanders household (augmented by a son, David, born in 1915) lived in Newlyn (Cornwall), Midhurst (Sussex), Catchal (Cornwall), Grasse (near Cannes), Catchal again, and Sennen Cove.

In 1919 Ruth's first work was published: *The Pedlar, and other Poems*. Two years later she submitted a narrative poem, *Karn*, to the Hogarth Press in hopes of publication. Virginia Woolf was enthusiastic: 'She sent a long poem, which seems to have a good deal of merit, and we are going to bring it out this Spring … its rather exciting and altogether most unexpected' (*Letters*, 2.495). By early 1922 the publishing process was well under way: 'We are … busy printing a new long poem by a short fat poetess, who came to correct her proofs the other day … She was very nice, and very modest' (ibid., 2.502). To herself (in her diary, 6 February 1922) Woolf described the author: 'Mrs Manning-Sanders is a bob haired, wide mouthed woman, dressed in a velvet dressing gown, plump, sandy-haired with canine brown eyes far apart. We liked her' (*Diary*, 2.160).

Karn did not sell, nor did its successors *Martha Wish-You-Ill* (1926) and *The City* (1927)—though the latter was awarded the Blindman international poetry prize. Ruth Manning-Sanders turned her hand to prose with the novel *The Twelve Saints* (1925); this was followed by more fiction for adults and for children, a biography of Hans Andersen, a book about Devon and Cornwall, and *The English Circus* (1952). This title and her children's books *Circus Boy* and *Luke's Circus* drew upon her earlier experience of life with Count Rosaire's travelling troupe—and Ruth Manning-Sanders is credited in the *Oxford English Dictionary* with the earliest use of the term 'strong woman', which is quoted from *The English Circus*.

George, confined to a wheelchair as the result of illness, abandoned painting for writing, and produced two or three novels of his own during the thirties. He died after a road accident in 1952, and it was in the aftermath of her bereavement that Ruth Manning-Sanders, in her late sixties, found her literary métier in the telling or retelling of folk-tales and legends for children. *Peter and the Piskies: Cornish Folk and Fairy Tales*, illustrated by Raymond Briggs, which happily united the author's lifelong interest in folk-lore and her abiding love for her adopted county, was published by Oxford University Press in 1958 and was an immense success. This was followed by the popular series of works entitled *A Book of …*, which was brought out by Methuen in twenty-two volumes between 1962 (*A Book of Giants*) and 1984 (*A Book of Magic Horses*). The timeless quality of her subject matter meant that the fact that the author was now in her nineties did not detract from her appeal to the children of the 1980s; the uncluttered style of her vigorous narrative and her lack of sentimentality were as appropriate to that decade as they had been when she first became a best-seller in the early fifties.

Manning-Sanders continued to work with the aid of her daughter Joan, who shared her house in Penzance, until 1988, when her last book, *A Cauldron of Witches*, was published six months before her 100th birthday. On 12 October 1988, two months after her birthday, this hard-working and professional writer died at Penzance, with more than ninety titles to her credit.

VERONICA HURST

Sources *The letters of Virginia Woolf*, ed. N. Nicolson, 2 (1976), 495, 502, 507 · *The diary of Virginia Woolf*, ed. A. O. Bell and A. McNeillie, 2 (1978), 160 · J. Manning-Sanders, 'Introduction', *Drawings and paintings* (1929) · A. Bell, 'Manning-Sanders, Ruth', *Twentieth-century children's writers*, ed. D. Kirkpatrick (1978) · *The Independent* (18 Oct 1988) · *The Guardian* (17 Oct 1988) · Blain, Clements & Grundy, *Feminist comp.* · *An Baner Kernewek* [The Cornish Banner] (Nov 1989), 22 · m. cert.

Likenesses photograph, pubd 1961, Oxford University Press

Wealth at death £131,257: probate, 12 Jan 1990, *CGPLA Eng. & Wales*

Sanders, William (1799–1875), geologist, was born on 12 January 1799 in Bristol, one of the sons of Thomas Sanders (1768–1854), seed and hop merchant of 2 Bridge Parade, Bristol. Educated at the private school of Thomas Exley (1774–1855), he joined the family business and, after his father's retirement, continued in partnership with his brother Edward (c.1801–1872). He was a founder member in 1835 of the Bristol Institution for the Advancement of Science, Literature and the Arts, to which he devoted much energy during the rest of his life. Others of his family were members and benefactors, notably his father and his uncle John Naish Sanders FGS (c.1777–1870), who were active members of the institution's building committee from 1809.

Sanders's knowledge of geology led to his accompanying John Phillips (1800–1874) and Henry De la Beche (1796–1855) in surveying north Devon and Cornwall in 1835 and he was elected a fellow of the Geological Society in 1839. Encouraged by De la Beche, in 1835 he began, at his own expense, a detailed geological survey of 720 square miles around his native city on a scale of 4 inches to the mile. Sanders had to produce much of the base map from parish surveys, and an enormous amount of fieldwork was needed before he completed and finally published the map (in 19 sections) in 1862. In recognition of this work he was elected a fellow of the Royal Society in 1864.

Sanders contributed five papers to the British Association and, from his interest in a clean water supply for Bristol, he contributed to the health of towns commission (1844–5), to the report of the General Board of Health in 1850, and he became a director of the Bristol waterworks in 1865. He retired from business in 1856 to become the honorary curator of the Bristol Institution and, before he retired in 1872, saw through its merger with the Bristol Library Society and the opening of a new Bristol Museum and Library in 1871. In 1862 he was elected the first president of the Bristol Naturalists' Society and remained in that position until his death. He was of a quiet and retiring nature and, like his brother Edward with whom he lived, he never married. He died in Clifton, Bristol, on 12 November 1875, and was buried at Arnos Yale cemetery, Bristol, on 18 November.

R. D. CLARK

Sources E. B. T[awney], *Proceedings of the Bristol Naturalists' Society*, 2nd ser., 1 (1876), 503–6 · R. E. [R. Etheridge], *Geological Magazine*, new ser., 2nd decade, 2 (1875), 627–8 · J. Evans, *Quarterly Journal of the Geological Society*, 32 (1876), 85–6 · *Daily Bristol Times and Mirror* (22 Nov 1875) · news cutting, 1875?, Bristol Museum Historical File, 78 · *Mathews' Bristol Directories* · M. Neve, 'Science in a commercial city: Bristol 1820–60', *Metropolis and province: science in British culture, 1780–1850*, ed. I. Inkster and J. Morrell (1983), 179–204 · H. E. Meller, *Leisure and the changing city, 1870–1914* (1976) · *DNB*

Likenesses photograph, 1870–79, Bristol City Museum and Art Gallery, Geology Department

Wealth at death under £20,000: probate, 13 Dec 1875, *CGPLA Eng. & Wales*

Sanders, William Rutherford (1828–1881), physician, was born in Edinburgh on 17 February 1828, the son of James Sanders, physician. His education began at Edinburgh high school, but was interrupted when, in September 1842, the family went to Montpellier for the sake of James Sanders's health; he died there in 1843. Sanders's education was completed at Montpellier University, where he took with distinction the degree of bachelier-ès-lettres in April 1844. He returned to Scotland in June that year, and began to study medicine at Edinburgh University. He took his MD in 1849, obtaining a gold medal for his thesis, 'On the anatomy of the spleen', which laid the foundation for some of his later pathological studies.

After two years in Paris and Heidelberg, Sanders returned to Edinburgh. While occupying the interim position of pathologist in the Royal Infirmary in 1852 he was able to pursue his study of certain degenerations affecting the liver and spleen. He acted as tutorial assistant to the clinical professors and contributed numerous papers to the medical journals. In 1853 Sanders succeeded John and Harry Goodsir as conservator of the museum of the College of Surgeons of Edinburgh, and when required he delivered lectures and gave demonstrations to make the museum's holdings more widely known to medical students. From 1855 he also delivered in the extra-academical school of Edinburgh a six-month course on the institutes of medicine, including physiology and histology, with outlines of pathology. In 1861 he was appointed physician to the Royal Infirmary, and soon gained a considerable and well-founded reputation as a clinical teacher, accurate and perceptive in diagnosis, and with great power of lucid exposition. Sanders married, on 24 December 1861, Georgiana Bridget (b. 1841/2), daughter of George Woodrow of Norwich, auctioneer.

Sanders's first major paper was 'Case of an unusual form of nervous disease, dystaxid, or pseudo-paralysis agitans, with remarks' (*Edinburgh Medical Journal*, 10, 1865, 987–97). It was followed in the same year by 'Paralysis of the palate in facial palsy' (*Edinburgh Medical Journal*, 11, 1865, 140–54) and 'Facial hemiplegia and paralysis of the facial nerve' (*The Lancet*, 1865/2, 452–4, 478–80). Later he took up the subject of aphasia, in connection with Broca's researches, and that of 'the variation or vanishing of cardiac organic murmurs', and contributed articles to John Russell Reynolds's *System of Medicine* (1866) on some subjects connected with nervous disease. Although he never published his own medical memoirs, such was his reputation that in 1869, when the chair of pathology in the university became vacant by the death of Professor Henderson, Sanders was appointed. He immediately introduced new methods of teaching, which were then generally adopted. For some years he was assisted by Professor Hamilton of Aberdeen.

At the same time Sanders built up a reputation as a consulting physician in Edinburgh. 'He was known among us', wrote Matthews Duncan, one of the most distinguished of his associates:

> as an unassuming, genuine man, on whom we could rely for a sound diagnosis and candid opinion; and, even before he rose into prominence with the public as a consultant, he was one to whom his professional brethren, when suspecting that all was not right with themselves, would prefer to go for an opinion. (*The Lancet*, 26 Feb 1881, 352–3)

A chronic abscess, which formed in January 1874, temporarily interrupted Sanders's professorial work and private practice. Although he resumed both, his health was not restored. In September 1880 he had an attack of right hemiplegia or palsy, together with loss of speech so complete as to prevent him communicating either by speech or by writing, although his mental faculties remained almost, if not quite, intact. His biographer in the *Edinburgh Medical Journal*, a close friend as well as a medical colleague, remarked upon the touching coincidence that one who had so largely and intelligently occupied himself with this very disease should have become, more than five months before his death, an example of that curious affliction, whereby a living, breathing, and in many respects normal and intelligent man, was absolutely cut off, by physical disease of one portion of the cerebral hemisphere, from communication with his kind. He died at Charlotte Square, Edinburgh, on 18 February 1881 after a sudden attack of apoplexy, coupled with complete loss of consciousness. He was survived by his wife and five children. His eldest son followed him in the medical profession.   W. T. GAIRDNER, *rev.* ANITA McCONNELL

Sources *The Times* (19 Feb 1881), 10d · *Edinburgh Medical Journal*, 26 (1880–81), 939–49 · *The Lancet* (26 Feb 1881), 352–3, 968 · private information (1897) · *BMJ* (26 Feb 1881), 321–2 · m. cert. · *CGPLA Eng. & Wales* (1881)

Sanderson. For this title name *see* individual entries under Sanderson; *see also* Furniss, Henry Sanderson, Baron Sanderson (1868–1939).

Sanderson, (Julia Sarah) Anne Cobden- (1853–1926), socialist and suffragette, was born on 26 March 1853 at Westbourne Terrace, London, the fifth of the six children of Richard *Cobden (1804–1865), radical politician and statesman, and his wife, Catherine Anne (1815–1877), daughter of Hugh Williams, timber merchant, and his wife, Elinor. Her early years were spent at Dunford House, Midhurst, Sussex, but after her father's death she attended schools in London and Germany. Her mother having moved to Wales in 1869, she spent lengthy periods among a loyal circle of family friends, most formatively with the poet and novelist George MacDonald, then residing at The Retreat (later, as Kelmscott House, the home of William Morris). In 1874 with her sister Ellen she accompanied Sir Robert Lambert Playfair on his expedition to the Aures Mountains, Algeria. In 1877 she set up home in London with her sisters, taking up social work in the East End, enjoying amateur theatricals, and continuing to travel abroad. In April 1881 at Siena in the company of her sister Jane [*see* Unwin, (Emma) Jane Catherine Cobden], and of Jane Morris, she met the briefless and unworldly barrister Thomas James *Sanderson. They were engaged in February and married on 5 August 1882, when they both took the surname Cobden-Sanderson. The early years of their marriage were marked by travel, reading, philanthropy, theosophy, vegetarianism, and a keen interest in the ideas of Henry George and of their friend William Morris. Annie, somewhat dissatisfied with Sanderson's metaphysical search for the Absolute, encouraged him to take up the craft of bookbinding. Through their own manual work, they identified with the wider cause of the working class, joining Morris's Hammersmith Socialist Society in 1890. With Annie providing energy and funds as

(Julia Sarah) Anne Cobden-Sanderson (1853–1926), by unknown photographer

well as a ready needle, Thomas set up the Doves Bindery in 1893. He played a leading part in the arts and crafts movement, while at their Hampstead home Annie was hostess to a wide array of political and artistic friends. However, she spent the years 1897 to 1898 with their children Richard (1884–1964) and Stella (1886–1979) in Lausanne. There Thomas recorded 'the freedom of her life suits her', although her absence was part of a joint plan of 'renunciation … the better way for ourselves *and* our children' (*Journals of Thomas James Cobden-Sanderson*, 1.370, 378). After their return, Sanderson set up the Doves Press in 1899, but with Thomas much given to self-doubt as well as cosmic yearning, Annie's role was a vital one in sustaining his business and artistic ventures.

After 1900 Annie played a more active part in the socialist movement, organizing in 1902 an important series of lectures for the Independent Labour Party (ILP) in London and serving as treasurer of the Metropolitan ILP. She took a special interest in the needs of children, supporting the pioneering Bow Children's Clinic, set up by Margaret MacMillan, with whom Annie campaigned for school meals and compulsory medical inspection. She was also prominent in the right to work campaign. More dramatically, in 1905 she joined the Women's Social and Political Union (WSPU) and, following its Westminster protest in October 1906, she was imprisoned in Holloway, gaining the women's suffrage movement a high profile with this notorious mistreatment of 'the daughter of him who gave you bread', 'one of the nicest women in England suffering from the coarsest indignity' as George Bernard Shaw wrote to *The Times* (31 October 1906). Released in November, Annie continued to campaign for women's suffrage but in 1907 seceded from the WSPU to help form the Women's Freedom League. In late 1907 and early 1908 she and Thomas travelled to the United States, where Thomas was lionized in 'arts' circles, she in suffrage ones. On their return, Annie remained a prominent advocate of women's rights, attending suffrage congresses abroad, supporting the 'Great Watch' on Asquith's home in

December 1909 (she was sentenced to a week's imprisonment but avoided this through the intervention of a third party), leading the procession to the Commons on 'black Friday' (18 November 1910), and escaping arrest in the 'Downing Street raid' a week later only through Winston Churchill's intervention. (She had been a guest at his wedding in 1908.) But she now turned primarily to the tactic of tax resistance, helping to set up in October 1909 the Women's Tax Resistance League and speaking widely on its behalf until it suspended activities in August 1914. However, by 1909, her husband, a fervent admirer of Annie's courage and selfless devotion to others, noted 'The Labour Party, and especially the "right to work" is Annie's field. She has contributed her unit to the Women's Cause' (*Journals of Thomas James Cobden-Sanderson*, 2.134–5). She was also interested in land reform, enrolling her father's name in the socialist cause in her pamphlet *Richard Cobden and the Land of the People* (ILP, *c.*1909).

Annie's increasing concern with unemployment led naturally to a close interest in the poor law, and having become publicly embroiled as a critic of its operation locally, she was elected on a reform platform to the Hammersmith board of guardians in March 1910. Her scope for influence proved limited, but through long service (until 1922) 'a dear old lady still ever young', she achieved much, especially for the women and children among 'her *Pauperibus*' (*Journals of Thomas James Cobden-Sanderson*, 2.348, 326). Thomas suffered severe mental anguish during the First World War, and they mixed largely in pacifist circles. After the war, Annie resumed her involvement in Labour politics in Hammersmith, campaigning for the unemployed in both the *Hammersmith Pioneer* and on the board of guardians. Following Thomas's death in 1922, Annie settled at great personal cost a lawsuit brought against her by Sir Emery Walker, seeking compensation for the typeface her husband had thrown into the Thames on closing the Doves Press in 1917. More happily in June 1926, she undertook the visit they had long planned to California, where she was fêted by their many friends and admirers, and in July she saw published by her son the heavily self-censored *Journals* of her husband. She died at 15 Upper Mall, Hammersmith, on 2 November 1926 and was buried on 6 November. Her work 'in the service of humanity' was commemorated by the Anne Cobden-Sanderson Fund organized by Sir Nigel Ross Playfair, reviver of the Lyric Theatre, Hammersmith, and nephew of her travelling companion in Algeria half a century earlier.

A. C. HOWE

Sources *The journals of Thomas James Cobden-Sanderson*, 2 vols. (1926) · W. Sussex RO, Cobden papers · *Four lectures by Thomas James Cobden-Sanderson*, ed. J. Dreyfus (1969) · A. Cobden-Sanderson, MS prison diary, BLPES, Kelley MSS · *The collected letters of William Morris*, ed. N. Kelvin, 4 vols. (1984–96) · Women's Tax Resistance League, minute books, 1909–14, Women's Library, London · minute books and records, 1908–22, LMA, Hammersmith board of guardians archives · A. Cobden-Sanderson, press cuttings and miscellanea, Hammersmith and Fulham Archives and Local History Centre, London · *Hammersmith Pioneer* (May 1921) · *Hammersmith Pioneer* (Oct 1921) · *Hammersmith Pioneer* (Jan 1922) · notes on Annie

Cobden-Sanderson, Museum of London, Suffragette Fellowship MSS · *The Times* (Oct–Dec 1906) · *The Times* (4 Nov 1926) · 1902–10, BLPES, Independent Labour Party Archive · *DNB* · M. Tidcombe, *The Doves Press* (2003)

Archives Stanford University, Morgan A. and Aline D. Gunst Memorial Library, *L'Avenir* commonplace book · W. Sussex RO, corresp. and MSS | BLPES, corresp. with Independent Labour Party · BLPES, Kelley MSS

Likenesses photograph, 1881, NPG · oils, Dunford House, Midhurst, West Sussex · photograph, NPG [*see illus.*] · photographs, W. Sussex RO · photographs (at Doves Bindery), Hammersmith and Fulham Archives and Local History Centre, London

Wealth at death £21,722 6s.: probate, 6 Dec 1926, *CGPLA Eng. & Wales*

Sanderson, Edgar (1838–1907), historian, born at Nottingham on 25 January 1838, was the son of Edgar Sanderson and his wife, Eliza Rumsey. His father, a direct descendant of Bishop Robert Sanderson, was a lace manufacturer at Nottingham, who later kept private schools in London at Stockwell and Streatham. Sanderson was educated at the City of London School and at Clare College, Cambridge. After graduating in 1860 in the second class of the classical tripos he was ordained deacon in 1862 and priest in 1863. He married in 1864 Laetitia Jane (*d.* Oct 1894), elder daughter of Matthew Denycloe, a surgeon of Bridport; they had two sons and four daughters. Between 1870 and 1881 he was successively headmaster of Stockwell, Macclesfield, and Huntingdon grammar schools. Thenceforth he lived at Streatham Common, and occupied himself in writing educational manuals and popular historical works. Sanderson's digests of world history enjoyed a wide circulation, and his *History of the British Empire* (1882) went into twenty editions in his lifetime. He died at his home, 23 Barrow Road, Streatham Common, on 31 December 1907.

G. LE G. NORGATE, *rev.* G. MARTIN MURPHY

Sources *The Times* (1 Jan 1908) · *The Guardian* (8 Jan 1908) · R. Ingpen, Introduction, in T. Carlyle, *Life of Frederick the Great*, ed. E. Sanderson (1909), xxii–xxiii

Sanderson, Frederick William (1857–1922), headmaster, was born at Brancepeth, co. Durham, on 13 May 1857, the youngest son of Thomas Sanderson and his wife, Margaret Andrews. His father worked on the estate of Viscount Boyne. He was educated at the village school at Brancepeth and then became a pupil teacher at Tudhoe national school. In 1876 he entered Durham University as a theological student, and obtained first-class honours in mathematics and physical science in the BA examination in 1877, being elected a fellow of the university in 1881. In 1879 he won an open mathematical scholarship at Christ's College, Cambridge, and was bracketed eleventh wrangler in 1882.

Sanderson remained at Cambridge, lecturing at Girton College, until 1885 when he was appointed by J. E. C. Welldon to an assistant mastership at Dulwich College. His initial instructions were to develop the teaching of chemistry and to introduce the study of physics. In 1886 he established the engineering side of the school, with a syllabus that included applied mechanics and physics, workshop practice, and mechanical drawing. This was to prove one of his most successful educational innovations. Its distinctive feature was that the boys used actual working engines, dynamos, and testing machines rather than models for their experiments.

In 1892 Sanderson was elected headmaster of Oundle School, which was then at a low ebb with only ninety-two pupils. Oundle's governors, the Grocers' Company, wished to introduce the teaching of modern subjects, and this he was well qualified to do. His appointment was, however, a controversial one and his early years brought him into contention with both old boys and masters. Unlike most public school headmasters of the period, he was not a clergyman, and his theological leanings were of a modernist kind, which raised suspicions as to his orthodoxy. In politics he was a Liberal. Not educated at a public school himself, he was held to lack experience of boarding education, while his strong Durham accent and irregular attire emphasized his doubtful social credentials, which were unredeemed by any record of athletic achievement. Within seven years of his appointment, he had forced out all but three of the staff of assistant masters whom he had inherited from his predecessor; one dismissal led to critical correspondence in the *Journal of Education* (October 1899).

Prosperity came after 1900. By 1909 there were 323 pupils and all the houses were full. Soon after Sanderson's appointment new science and engineering sides were established, and laboratories and workshops fitted up. Oundle boys gained open scholarships in science at the universities. Although those boys who went on to become engineers valued the work they had done at school, Sanderson did not promote applied science as primarily a type of technical education, seeking instead to establish it as an integral part of a public-school education. Large numbers of boys were attracted to the workshops, which undertook ambitious projects, notably the construction in 1905 of a reversing engine for a 4000 hp marine engine. During the First World War the school made metal parts for munitions. The methods replicated those of an engineering factory. 'Each boy had his job for which he alone was responsible; but the result of his efforts had to be combined with that of all the others, and the final success depended upon the independent work of each individual' (*DNB*). These practices were extended to other areas of school life, including the library. 'A subject for study was chosen, the boys in a form were divided into small groups each of which studied one aspect of the subject, and the results of their work were combined and collected into one whole' (*DNB*). The school provided extensive courses, still unusual at that time, in modern humanities subjects. Geography and history were taught by encouraging boys to adopt the methods of an original researcher.

In 1885 Sanderson married Jane (*d.* 1944), daughter of L. T. Hodgson, of Broughton Hall, Cumberland. They had two sons and a daughter. His wife ran the boarding-house for Oundle's preparatory department, which opened in 1893. To her Sanderson owed his love of the Lake District, and his enthusiasm for climbing, which he valued as an activity demanding co-operative rather than competitive effort.

Under Sanderson, Oundle gained a reputation for being in the forefront of modern education, and this attracted H. G. Wells, who sent his sons there in 1914. The two men formed a friendship and Wells encouraged him to pursue what some of Sanderson's colleagues evidently regarded as rather visionary projects. At Oundle a 'Temple of Vision' was erected with funds provided by Sir Alfred Yarrow, who had lost a son in the war. It was dedicated as a monument to the progress of science and human achievement. Sanderson, whose own eldest son had been killed in the war, became prominent in promoting ideas about the role of education in national reconstruction. He contributed a chapter on modern education to *Natural Science and the Classical System in Education* (1918), edited by E. Ray Lankester, and wrote the preface to F. J. Gould's *History the Teacher* (1921). A frequent public speaker, he collapsed and died in the old Botanical Theatre, University College, London, on 15 June 1922, having delivered an address to a meeting of the National Union of Scientific Workers, chaired by Wells, on 'The duty and service of science in the new era'. His body was cremated on 23 November and his ashes placed in the war memorial chapel at Oundle.

Contemporaries were divided about Sanderson's significance. Two accounts of his life appeared shortly after his death: one, by members of staff at Oundle, gave a record of his work; another, by Wells, who deplored the neglect into which the Temple of Vision fell after Sanderson's death, laid more emphasis on his ideals. It was acknowledged that the facilities at Oundle for science and engineering were second to none; but few headmasters in the inter-war period followed Sanderson's wholehearted promotion of science education. Although he was not mentioned by name, many of Sanderson's ideas were identifiable in the Board of Education report, *The Education of the Adolescent* (1926).   M. C. CURTHOYS

Sources *Sanderson of Oundle* (1923) · H. G. Wells, *The story of a great schoolmaster* (1924) · H. G. Wells, *Experiment in autobiography*, new edn, 2 vols. (1984) · *Times Educational Supplement* (24 June 1922) · *Times Educational Supplement* (22 July 1922) · *Nature*, 109 (1922), 822 · W. G. Walker, *A history of the Oundle schools* (1956) · R. J. Palmer, 'The influence of F. W. Sanderson on the development of science and engineering at Dulwich College', *History of Education*, 6 (1977), 121–30 · R. J. Palmer, 'F. W. Sanderson, Oundle, and games', *Durham and Newcastle Research Review*, 8 (1977), 35–42 · *DNB*
Likenesses oils, *c*.1907 (after photograph), Oundle School, Peterborough · E. H. Lacey, bronze bust, 1937, Oundle School, Peterborough · Messrs Speaight, photograph, repro. in Walker, *History of the Oundle schools*
Wealth at death £28,041 8*s*. 7*d*.: probate, 9 Aug 1922, *CGPLA Eng. & Wales*

Sanderson, James (1769–*c*.1841), composer and instrumentalist, was born at Workington, Cumberland, and baptized on 23 April 1769. From earliest childhood he showed musical talent, and at the age of fourteen, although he had received no tuition, was engaged as a violinist at the Sunderland theatre. In 1784 he established himself in South Shields as a teacher of violin and piano, and in 1787 became leader at the Newcastle theatre. He went to London in 1788, and led the orchestra at Astley's Amphitheatre and appeared as a violinist in the Philharmonic Orchestra. His first dramatic composition was an illustrative instrumental accompaniment to William Collins's 'Ode on the Passions', which G. F. Cooke was to recite during his benefit at Chester in 1789. A drama entitled *Harlequin in Ireland, or, Apollo and Daphne* was subsequently produced at Astley's Amphitheatre on 17 September 1792.

In 1793 Sanderson was engaged at the Royal Circus (from 1806 the Surrey Theatre) as composer and musical director. He remained there for many years, producing the incidental music for numerous dramas as well as several vocal and instrumental pieces. It is reported that between 1792 and 1820 he wrote 154 melodramas, burlettas, and pantomimes for the minor theatres, and received a salary of 8 guineas a week for much of that time as musical director. He worked mainly with J. C. Cross, who wrote most of the words and contrived the scenic effects. In addition, he composed violin duets (1800–07), a piano sonata (*c*.1810), and *A Celebrated Study for the Bow and Fingerboard of the Violin*, op. 41 (2nd edn, *c*.1825). The accepted tune of 'Comin' thro' the Rye' was adapted from Scottish collections by Sanderson for London use and included in his *Harlequin Mariner* (Royal Circus, 28 May 1796). The most successful of his acknowledged compositions was a ballad, 'Bound 'Prentice to a Waterman', sung in the drama *Sir Francis Drake* (1800); it was regularly introduced into nautical plays for half a century. Two of Sanderson's ballads were reprinted in the *Musical Bouquet* as late as 1874. He died *c*.1841.

HENRY DAVEY, *rev.* DAVID J. GOLBY

Sources Grove, *Dict. mus.* · [J. S. Sainsbury], ed., *A dictionary of musicians*, 2 vols. (1824) · Brown & Stratton, *Brit. mus.*

Sanderson, John (*b.* in or before 1540, *d.* 1602), Roman Catholic priest, was born in Lancashire. In 1579 he was said to be about thirty-eight which would place his birth about 1540 or 1541, although an earlier year seems more likely. He matriculated at Trinity College, Cambridge, in May 1554, and graduated BA in 1558 and MA in 1561, having in the meantime been elected a fellow of the college. In 1562 he became logic reader in the university. In September of that year he created a scandal when delivering a commonplace, an exposition of a particular thesis in the form of a sermon, in the college chapel. His words gave great offence to the master of the college, Robert Beaumont, and to the other fellows, since what he said displayed Roman Catholic and profane tendencies. Sanderson maintained that the biblical rules with regard to fasting ought to be judged according to the spirit rather than to the letter of the law. The 'profane' author Plato was cited as one of his authorities. Sanderson refused to recant and, as a result, was expelled from his fellowship. Both Sanderson and his opponents appealed to Archbishop Parker, and a debate ensued about the question under whose authority the case ought to be tried. The correspondence makes clear that the dispute was not simply seen as an internal college affair. Alexander Nowell, the dean of St Paul's and a prominent clergyman, observed in a letter to Archbishop Parker: 'It is not onlie in hande whether John Sanderson shalbe felow of Trinitie College, or noo felow; but whether ther shalbe … enie redresse or reformation in religion in that hoole Universitie or noo: whether the truthe shall obteine, or papistrie triumph' (MS Parker, 106, fol. 534).

Sanderson lost his case and soon afterwards went to the continent, first to Rome and then to France and Flanders. He matriculated at Louvain on 17 August 1568. Two years later, in 1570, he arrived at the English College, Douai, where he completed the first part of his theological studies on 6 November 1571. He is next found at the hospice in Rome (the precursor of the English College) in August 1577. It was probably there that he was ordained priest and was awarded the degree of doctor of theology. On 5 July 1579 Charles Sledd, an English government spy in Rome, gave a description of Sanderson as being 'about 38 yeares of adge, short of stature & slender—the heare of his bearde blacke & thicke, cute short & and the heare of his hede thin before as yf he were balde. His face is full of wrinkles & verye talkative' (Talbot, 207). In 1580 Sanderson travelled back to France in the company of Cardinal Allen and arrived on 2 April at the English College, Rheims. Five days later he left Rheims, probably for Cambrai of whose cathedral church he had been made a canon while still living at Rome. The English College records show that he returned to Rheims for the period 29 August 1582 to 13 May 1583, during which time he may have taught theology. He appears to have lived quietly at Cambrai until his death there in 1602. His only substantial work is a textbook on logic entitled *Institutionum dialecticarum libri quatuor*. It was first published at Antwerp in 1589, dedicated to Cardinal Allen. The book proved to be very popular in England with other editions (without the dedication) appearing at Oxford in 1594, 1602, and 1609.   F. BLOM and J. BLOM

Sources J. Pits, *Relationum historicarum de rebus Anglicis*, ed. [W. Bishop] (Paris, 1619), 799–800 • T. F. Knox and others, eds., *The first and second diaries of the English College, Douay* (1878) • G. Anstruther, *The seminary priests*, 1 (1969) • C. Talbot, ed., *Miscellanea: recusant records*, Catholic RS, 53 (1961) • T. Fuller, *The church history of Britain*, ed. J. S. Brewer, new edn, 6 vols. (1845); vol. 5 • Venn, *Alum. Cant.* • M. R. James, *A descriptive catalogue of the manuscripts in the library of Corpus Christi College, Cambridge*, 2 vols. (1912) • CCC Cam., Parker MS 106, pp. 529–45 • R. Churton, *The life of Alexander Nowell, dean of St Paul's* (1809) • A. F. Allison and D. M. Rogers, eds., *The contemporary printed literature of the English Counter-Reformation between 1558 and 1640*, 1 (1989)

Sanderson, Sir **John Scott Burdon**, baronet (1828–1905), pathologist and physiologist, was born at Jesmond, near Newcastle upon Tyne, on 21 December 1828, the second son and fourth child of Richard Burdon Sanderson (1791–1865), at one time fellow of Oriel College, Oxford; originally surnamed Burdon, his father had taken the additional surname of Sanderson on his marriage in 1815 to Elizabeth Skinner Sanderson (1797–1864), only daughter of Sir James Sanderson, first baronet, MP. His father's mother, Jane, daughter of William Scott of Newcastle upon Tyne, was sister of John Scott, first earl of Eldon, and William

Sir John Scott Burdon Sanderson, baronet (1828–1905), by Walter William Ouless, 1886

Scott, Lord Stowell. His sister Mary Elizabeth married Robert Haldane of Cloanden, and her children included R. B. Haldane, J. S. Haldane, and E. S. Haldane. Burdon Sanderson was raised in an atmosphere of intense and rather unworldly evangelicalism, and was educated at home. His father expected him to study for the law, in which two great-uncles had won distinction. But Burdon Sanderson was drawn to a career in medicine, and he persuaded his parents to accept this decision.

Medical training Burdon Sanderson entered the University of Edinburgh in 1847, and graduated MD in 1851 with the gold medal for his thesis on the metamorphosis of the red blood corpuscles. While at Edinburgh he was particularly impressed by the teaching of John Hughes Bennett and John Goodsir, both of whom were vigorously advancing the view that the new laboratory sciences would lead to improvements in the knowledge and practice of medicine. He took their arguments to heart, and after graduating he went on to study in Paris, initially in the chemical laboratories of Charles Gerhardt and Adolf Wurtz. Subsequently he devoted himself to physiology under Claude Bernard, attending Bernard's lectures and conducting experiments in his laboratory. He also attended clinical classes in the Paris hospitals, but these did not fire his enthusiasm in the way that Bernard's teaching did.

Burdon Sanderson returned to Newcastle late in 1852. By that time he had become engaged to Ghetal (1832/3–1909), eldest daughter of Ridley Haim *Herschell and sister of Farrer *Herschell, later first Baron Herschell, lord chancellor. They were married at Trinity Chapel, Marylebone, London, on 9 August 1853. Burdon Sanderson had hoped to pursue a career in medical research, but scientific posts were rare in British medicine at that time. Now, faced with the need to support a household, he decided to go into private practice in London. Patients were slow to consult him, but his abilities were recognized towards the end of 1853, when he was appointed medical registrar to St Mary's Hospital, Paddington. The following year he began lecturing at the hospital's medical school, first in botany and then in medical jurisprudence. In 1856 he was selected to fill the newly created part-time post of medical officer of health for Paddington. The post carried a proper professional salary, and for the first time Burdon Sanderson found himself comfortably off.

Medical officer of health Like others of the first generation of London medical officers of health, Burdon Sanderson faced the difficulty of working largely with the owners of the dwellings and businesses in which he was supposed to enforce sanitary standards. He fulfilled his contract with tact and diplomacy, managing to effect modest improvements without antagonizing his employers. He used his chemical skills to investigate the adulteration of bread and milk, and took a special interest in the ventilation of workplaces, including St Mary's Hospital, which was located in the parish. He approached his work from a sanitarian perspective, looking for improvements primarily in environmental conditions, but he was also keen to apply new scientific techniques to the investigation and promotion of public health. In 1857 he began an investigation into the incidence of diphtheria, looking for but failing to find evidence that it was caused by environmental factors.

Early in his appointment Burdon Sanderson had struck up a correspondence with John Simon, the chief medical officer of the privy council. Simon was impressed by Burdon Sanderson's scientific acumen, and especially by his work on diphtheria, and in 1860 appointed him an inspector to the privy council. Burdon Sanderson's first duty was to take part in a nationwide investigation into vaccination practices, a task which lasted until 1864. In 1865 he was sent to Danzig to investigate an epidemic of cerebrospinal meningitis. Later that year he began research for the royal commission that had been set up to deal with the cattle plague. Burdon Sanderson was commissioned to investigate the natural history of the disease with a view to improving early recognition of its onset. But he went beyond his remit to demonstrate also that the disease could be transmitted by inoculation, and that it involved some contagious agent that multiplied rapidly in infected animals. The extent to which disease in general might be caused by some kind of transmissible germ, and the implications that such transmission might have for public health practice, were at that time being hotly debated, and Simon was eager to sponsor research into the subject. Consequently he engaged Burdon Sanderson to undertake other investigations into the causes of infectious disease. The work, conducted between 1865 and 1870, included investigating whether tuberculosis could

be passed on by inoculation, carrying out feeding experiments to determine what influenced the infective virulence of the intestinal discharges of cholera, and isolating and studying the contagious constituents of lymph in cowpox and smallpox. Burdon Sanderson concluded that these diseases were transmitted by some form of particulate contagium that was present in the body fluids and discharges of infected organisms. His findings were published in the *Reports of the Medical Officer of the Privy Council*. In the course of this work, Ghetal contracted a mild case of smallpox, probably from material her husband brought home for his research.

Burdon Sanderson resigned his post as inspector to the privy council in 1865 or 1866, but he continued to augment his income from private practice and from his work as medical officer of health, with fees for the research he undertook for Simon. On his father's death he came into an inheritance that enabled him to resign his remaining post and to devote the extra time to research work. In 1872 his growing reputation as an experimental pathologist secured his appointment as the first professor-superintendent of the Brown Institute at the University of London, established by an endowment to conduct research into veterinary diseases. There he investigated foot-and-mouth disease and anthrax, and, with funds provided by Simon, he performed research into inflammation, fever, and tuberculosis, concluding that the last is an infectious rather than a constitutional disease. By such means Burdon Sanderson did much to advance the acceptance of germ theory in Britain. His own work was marked by a deep reluctance to theorize beyond his immediate empirical findings, however; throughout, he refused to draw firm conclusions about whether infectious diseases should be attributed to the agency and transmission of minute living organisms. Nor was he particularly original in his pathological research, preferring to replicate the experiments of continental researchers. Nevertheless, he was a moving force in the establishment of experimental pathology as a field of scientific and medical enquiry in Britain. He also preached the relevance of the new discipline to medical education, contributing the chapters 'Inflammation' to T. Holmes's *System of Surgery* (1883) and 'Fever' to T. C. Allbutt's *System of Medicine* (1896). For his efforts he was honoured by the medical profession. He was elected a fellow of the Royal College of Physicians in 1863, was Harveian orator at the college in 1878, was awarded the Baly medal in 1881, and in 1891 delivered the college's Croonian lectures, when he surveyed the progress of discovery relating to the origin of infectious diseases. By that time he was no longer active in pathological research. In 1878 he had resigned from his post at the Brown Institute, burdened by ill health and suffering from depression, which was exacerbated by the death of his uncle and two nieces in a train crash in 1876.

Physiological investigation Burdon Sanderson's resignation from the Brown Institute by no means marked his withdrawal from scientific life. For some time he had nurtured a parallel career as a physiologist, which now became his main occupation. As a medical practitioner he was interested in applying new physiological methods and techniques to the elucidation of problems in clinical medicine. Late in 1859 he was appointed assistant physician to the Brompton Hospital for Consumption (he became full physician in 1867), and in 1863 he also took the post of assistant physician to the Middlesex Hospital, London; these appointments afforded him the opportunity to pursue his physiological interests. In 1862–3 he undertook an investigation on behalf of the Royal Medico-Chirurgical Society into the best methods of resuscitating the apparently drowned, which led him to recommend the Sylvester method of artificial respiration. He went on to research the relationship between the movements of respiration and the circulation of the blood, and thence to an interest in the clinical use of the sphygmograph to reveal subtle variations in the pulse. This work won Burdon Sanderson recognition as a physiologist as well as a pathologist. He was elected a fellow of the Royal Society in 1867, and in the same year he delivered his first Croonian lecture to the Royal Society, outlining his research on the relations between breathing and circulation. He also won the support of William Sharpey, the professor of anatomy and physiology at University College, London. In 1870 Burdon Sanderson succeeded Michael Foster as professor of practical physiology and histology at University College, whereupon he was able to give up his private practice and his hospital appointments. Four years later, on Sharpey's retirement, the chair of anatomy and physiology and the chair of practical physiology and histology were merged to create a new post, the Jodrell chair of human physiology, with Burdon Sanderson as its first incumbent. He did much to introduce continental methods of physiology teaching to Britain, organizing practical courses in physiological chemistry and in the electrophysiological properties of muscle and nerve.

In 1873 Burdon Sanderson embarked on a new line of research when Charles Darwin wrote to ask whether the movements of the leaf of *Dionaea* (Venus flytrap) were accompanied by electrical activity. In effect Darwin was asking whether excitatory processes in plants could be regarded as fundamentally identical with nervous activity in animals, and Burdon Sanderson determined to answer the question by adapting electrophysiological methods to the study of plant life. He soon confirmed the presence of electrical excitation in *Dionaea* and went on to describe the underlying processes in considerable detail. He also investigated the electrical activity of the frog heart. Burdon Sanderson was an adept experimenter, particularly skilled in devising or modifying the sophisticated measuring and recording apparatus that characterized the developing field of electrophysiology, and the results of his experiments were published in numerous contributions to the *Philosophical Transactions* and the *Proceedings* of the Royal Society between 1877 and 1889 and to the *Journal of Physiology* between 1880 and 1900. As a result of this work, in 1877 he was chosen to deliver the Croonian lecture to the Royal Society for a second time, and in 1883 he was awarded the society's royal medal.

Professor at Oxford In November 1882 Burdon Sanderson heard that he had been elected to the new Waynflete chair of physiology at the University of Oxford, with a professorial fellowship at Magdalen College. The following year the university conferred on him the degree of MA. In Oxford he continued to pursue his electrophysiological research, broadening his project to include a study of the electromotive changes in skeletal muscle, and later investigating the electrical sense organs of the skate. In 1889 he was for the third time selected by the Royal Society to deliver the Croonian lecture; his subject was 'The relation of motion in animals and plants to the associated electrical phenomena'. Meanwhile he endeavoured to build up physiology teaching at Oxford, and to revive the moribund medical school there. He lent his weight to efforts to reform the organization of the honours degree, with the aim of reducing the amount of non-scientific study imposed on would-be scientists before they specialized at honours. By such means he hoped to make Oxford more attractive, especially to medical students, many of whom were deterred from training at the university by the excessive length of the curriculum. He was only partially successful in securing these aims. To his credit he could claim the creation of the faculty of medicine in 1886, and a reduction in the minimum length of the medical degree from eight to seven years—though this still compared badly with the minimum of five years for the Cambridge degree. He was also instrumental in establishing first a lectureship and then a chair in human anatomy. But his efforts at reform were hindered by the opposition of the existing Oxford medical graduates, who feared that Burdon Sanderson's plans to shorten the curriculum and increase the technical content would devalue the cultural currency of their own qualifications. This, together with the difficulty of securing funding for research within the peculiar financial organization of Oxford University, prevented Burdon Sanderson's school from growing to rival Cambridge as a producer of either medical graduates or career physiologists.

In September 1894 Burdon Sanderson learned from his brother-in-law, Lord Herschell, then vice-chancellor of Oxford University, that he had been elected to the university's regius chair of medicine. He was officially appointed to the chair on 2 January 1895. He now devoted himself to building up teaching and research in other subjects, most notably pathology, bacteriology, and pharmacology, that he considered necessary to establish a proper school of pre-clinical medical science in Oxford. He was instrumental in securing a private gift to establish a pathology laboratory for the university, and in his will he bequeathed £2000 for the support of the university's pathological department and especially to provide for the expenses of research in pathology conducted in its laboratory or elsewhere.

Throughout his career Burdon Sanderson also pursued other strategies to advance the interests of medical science. In 1868 he was instrumental in establishing the Clinical Society, which he hoped would foster a more physiological and systematic approach to clinical problems than that adopted by the Pathological Society, which at that time was the main forum for debate among scientifically minded medical practitioners. He was editor and one of the main contributors to the *Handbook for the Physiological Laboratory* (1873), which was intended to introduce advanced methods of physiological investigation into the medical curriculum and into research. His involvement in this project led to his being singled out for attention by the anti-vivisection movement. In 1875 Burdon Sanderson gave evidence to the royal commission on the practice of subjecting live animals to experiments for scientific purposes. It supported the introduction of legislative controls, which he argued would outlaw the practice of amateur vivisection while preserving the academic freedom of legitimate researchers. His reputation as a vivisectionist would later be used against him by those who opposed his efforts to reform the science teaching at Oxford. On 28 March 1876, two months after the royal commission submitted its report, Burdon Sanderson invited a number of the country's most eminent medical scientists to his home to discuss the formation of a society—subsequently named the Physiological Society—to represent the interests of the new discipline of experimental physiology. He was also involved in setting up the British Institute of Preventive Medicine (later the Lister Institute) in 1891, and took an active part in shaping the programme of research that developed over the first decade or so of the institute's life. He served on three royal commissions: on the provision of smallpox and fever hospitals in London (1881–2), on the effects on humans of consuming food from tuberculous animals (1890–95), and on the University of London (1892–4).

These activities earned Burdon Sanderson a reputation in science and medicine that extended far beyond the confines of his chosen disciplines of physiology and pathology. In 1889 he was president of the biological section of the British Association for the Advancement of Science at Newcastle, and there delivered an address entitled 'Elementary problems in physiology'; he was president of the entire association at Nottingham in 1893, when his subject was 'The origin of biology and its relations to other branches of natural science'. In 1900 he was elected a vice-president of one of the sections of the thirteenth International Medical Congress in Paris; his address, 'Cellular pathology', appeared in *The Lancet* of 25 August 1900. On 10 August 1899 he was created a baronet. Many other honours fell to him. He became honorary LLD of Edinburgh, honorary DSc of Dublin, and a corresponding member of the Institut de France and of the Academy of Science, Berlin. He carried these honours well. In public his striking features and dignified bearing gave him a commanding presence, but he also displayed a rare charm of manner which endeared him to his friends, colleagues, and students.

Burdon Sanderson's health had never been robust, and early in 1904 it began to decline markedly. Later that year he resigned his professorship. After several months of increasing physical weakness, he died from 'cardiac degeneration' at his home, 64, Banbury Road, Oxford, on 23 November 1905, and was buried nearby at Wolvercote cemetery on 28 November. His widow, whose support for her husband's career had extended to helping him draft his reports and papers, survived him until 5 July 1909. They had no children, and the baronetcy became extinct at Burdon Sanderson's death. STEVE STURDY

Sources G. Burdon Sanderson, J. S. Haldane, and E. S. Haldane, eds., *Sir John Burdon Sanderson: a memoir, with selections from his papers and addresses* (1911) • T. M. Romano, *Making medicine scientific: John Burdon Sanderson and the culture of Victorian science* (2002) • *PRS*, 79B (1907), iii–xviii • R. D. French, *Antivivisection and medical science in Victorian society* (1975) • R. G. Frank, Jr., 'The telltale heart: physiological instruments, graphic methods, and clinical hopes, 1854–1914', *The investigative enterprise: experimental physiology in nineteenth century medicine*, ed. W. Coleman and F. L. Holmes (1988), 211–90 • *DNB* • m. cert. • d. cert. • Munk, *Roll* • *The Times* (29 Nov 1905), 9f

Archives CUL, annotated authorial copy of his contribution to *Handbook for the physiological laboratory* • NL Scot., corresp. and papers • Oxf. U. Mus. NH, letters and papers to Sir E. B. Poulton • RS • UCL, corresp. and papers • University of British Columbia, Woodward Biomedical Library • Wellcome L., letters to Sir Edward Sharpey-Schafer | Bodl. Oxf., letters to Sir Henry Wentworth Acland • CUL, letters to Charles Darwin • NL Scot., corresp. mainly with Sir Patrick Geddes • PRO, privy council documents, file series PC8 • UCL, corresp. with Sir Francis Galton • Westminster City Libraries, Marylebone Reference Library, Paddington sanitary committee minutes and reports of the medical officer of health

Likenesses J. Collier, oils, 1883, Oxford Physiological Laboratory • W. W. Ouless, oils, 1886, NPG [*see illus.*] • W. H. Hunt, group portrait, oils, 1891 (*May Day, Magdalen tower*) • R. Lehmann, pencil sketch, 1893, BM • C. W. Furse, oils, 1901, Magd. Oxf. • Bassano, photograph, repro. in Sanderson, Haldane, and Haldane, eds., *Sir John Burdon Sanderson*, facing p. 112 • H. R. Hope Pinker, marble bust, Oxf. U. Mus. NH • Maull & Fox, photograph, Wellcome L. • Spy [L. Ward], chromolithograph cartoon, NPG; repro. in *VF* (17 May 1894) • photograph, repro. in *PRS*, facing p. ii

Wealth at death £35,255 19s. 6d.: probate, 1906

Sanderson, Robert (1587–1663), bishop of Lincoln, was born in Sheffield on 19 September 1587, the second son of Robert Sanderson of Gilthwaite, Rotherham, and his wife, Elizabeth Carr of Butterthwaite, Eccleston, both in Yorkshire. He attended Rotherham grammar school. Izaak Walton, in his life of Sanderson, wrote that his father considered placing him at Eton or Westminster for a year before sending him to Oxford, but that a learned friend interviewed the boy and pronounced him 'so perfect a Grammarian' that he should go straight to Oxford (Walton, 'Life', 3). He matriculated as a clergyman's son (Foster, *Alum. Oxon.*) from Lincoln College, Oxford, on 1 July 1603, graduated BA on 23 January 1605, and proceeded MA on 20 October 1607 and BD on 19 May 1617. A fellow of Lincoln from 1606 until 1619, he was a chaplain to the bishop of London (and former bishop of Lincoln), George Montaigne, to whom he dedicated his first published sermons in 1622. The date of his marriage to Ann Nelson, daughter of a Lincolnshire clergyman, is uncertain, but probably came soon after he resigned his fellowship at Lincoln in 1619; their son Thomas (who matriculated from Lincoln in 1639) was born in 1622 or 1623.

Sanderson spent the rest of his career based in Lincolnshire, first as rector of Wyberton (1618–19) and vicar of Heckington (1618), and then from September 1619 until

Robert Sanderson (1587–1663), by unknown artist, 1662

1660 as rector of Boothby Pagnell. During his long parochial service he promoted neighbourliness by mediating disputes between landlords and tenants, denounced those who initiated lawsuits, and opposed engrossing, rack renting, enclosing, and other violations of the traditional moral economy. In 1629 he received a prebend at Lincoln. He also preached at the assizes, at visitations (including Laud's metropolitical visitation in 1634), at Paul's Cross, and at the royal court. Charles I, encouraged by Laud, made him one of his chaplains in November 1631. 'I carry my ears to hear other Preachers', said the king, 'but I carry my Conscience to hear Mr. Sanderson, and to act accordingly' (Walton, 'Life', 15). Sanderson proceeded DD in 1636, and the following year, through the earl of Rutland's favour, gained the rectory of Muston, Leicestershire. A member of the 1640 convocation, he expressed his willingness to take the 'et cetera' oath, yet urged the king to either forbear 'the pressing of the Oath' or issue an explanation which would end the ambiguities that had given rise 'to cavill and misconstruction' (Works, 6.361). He received a prebend at Southwell in 1641 and a canonry of Christ Church, Oxford, in 1642. During the Oxford treaty negotiations early in 1643 he was among a group of clergymen named to assist a committee established by the House of Lords to design a religious settlement. Although the attempt failed, Sanderson's reputation for judiciousness (and doubtless his theological stance) led to a seat in the Westminster assembly, which he never occupied.

A doctrinal Calvinist, Sanderson had tried to resolve the controversy created by Richard Mountague's books in the mid-1620s by offering a slight alteration of the sublapsarian doctrine of predestination. Nevertheless, he insisted that the Church of England held that divine act of election was entirely gratuitous and to suggest otherwise was 'quarter-Pelagian and Arminian novelty' (Works, 5.277). Marginal notes condemning the Arminians and 'their Semipelagian subtilties' continued to appear in all editions of his sermons until 1657, and vigorous efforts in the late 1650s by Henry Hammond, Thomas Pierce, and others to change his mind had little success. Sanderson's soteriology, his denunciations of usury and idleness, and his support for the reformation of manners show that he had much in common with puritans. Izaak Walton's biography of Sanderson wholly ignores his Calvinism, his agreement with puritans on many issues, and his quarrels with Hammond and the churchmanship that Hammond and his friends represented. However, throughout his long career he rejected puritan arguments against ceremonies, probably in part because of his observation of the actions of John Cotton and his followers at nearby Boston. Sanderson, deeply concerned to retain protestant unity against Rome, was an anti-puritan in the Whitgiftian mould, an excellent example of the way 'that even men who shared great tracts of ideological terrain with the Puritans could end up hating them with a passion' (Lake, 115). In 1655 and 1657 he wrote strongly worded prefaces to collections of his sermons that accused presbyterians and Independents of having opened the door first to sectarianism and thus to 'popery' or atheism. Acknowledging that this had not been their intention, he nevertheless concluded that 'The Master in the Fable did not well to beat his Maid for serving him with thin Milk, when it was his own Cow that gave it' (XXI Sermons, 1681, sig. a1r).

Sequestered from his living in 1644, Sanderson was seized by parliamentarian soldiers and briefly imprisoned in Lincoln while an exchange for a puritan minister held by the royalist garrison at Newark was negotiated. Each was to regain his living and be left alone, so Sanderson returned to his family, books, and parishioners at Boothby Pagnell. In 1646 he went to Oxford to take up the regius professorship of divinity to which the king had appointed him in on 1 July 1642. The following year he wrote most of the university's negative response to the Long Parliament's demand that its members take the covenant and accept the new religious order. Deprived of his professorship in June 1648, he was permitted by the House of Commons to attend the king on the Isle of Wight. There Charles either translated himself or ordered the translation into English of seven lectures Sanderson had given during Michaelmas 1646. Published as De juramento (1655), they were among the casuistical works on which his fame as the Church of England's 'best Casuist' was based, and Sir Robert Boyle arranged to pay a salary to Sanderson so that he could continue such work after his deprivation from his post in Oxford (Lloyd, 533, 535). Back at home Sanderson, who had taken the engagement, found his services interrupted by soldiers who objected to the Book of Common Prayer, a problem faced by other Anglican clergymen. He infuriated Henry Hammond, Herbert Thorndike, and their circle by modifying the liturgy that he used in his parish. He transposed 'the very same words and phrases' in such a way that the service 'might appear not to be, and yet to be the same' (*Works*, 5.40).

On 28 October 1660 Sanderson was consecrated bishop of Lincoln. That year he was a member of a committee of eight bishops appointed by convocation to recommend revisions for the prayer book. The revised Book of Common Prayer of 1661 embodied his willingness—up to a point—to meet puritan concerns. The new preface and several of the changes, including parts of the burial service and the prayer of humble access, are certainly his, and the prayer for 'all conditions of men' probably is. He was 'the outstanding figure of the revision' (Cuming, 192). Despite his advanced age, Sanderson also administered his diocese energetically, working hard to fill vacancies quickly and to augment the stipends for the poorest livings. Yet he remained hostile to those puritans who rejected the restored church. In the House of Lords on 3 February 1661 he joined his fellow bishops Gilbert Sheldon, Edward Reynolds, George Morley, and John Gauden in a successful effort to block Commons' amendments to the act for settling ministers that would have allowed some nonconformist clergy to retain their livings.

Sanderson died on 29 January 1663 and was buried at Buckden, his episcopal seat. In his will he wrote that he and his wife had lived nearly forty-three years 'in perfect amity and with much comfort'. She and their three sons, Thomas, Robert, and Henry, survived him; two daughters, Katherine and Mary, had predeceased him. The will also specified a simple funeral, one without the flattering sermon, black hangings, and other mourning gear that had become 'the mode of these tymes'. Rejecting a 'costly monument' in favour of a 'faire flatt marble stone', he expressed his hope that his example would encourage others to employ their wealth in charitable works rather than 'funerall solemnities and entertainements' (Novarr, 437). Thus the man who revised the burial service made his own funeral a sermon, and his sermons placed him in 'the highest and first rank of English writers' (Wood, *Ath. Oxon.* 3.627). According to *The Spectator*, Sanderson's sermons, along with those of Bull, South, Barrow, and Tillotson, continued to guide preachers in the eighteenth century (Spurr, 392). J. SEARS MCGEE

Sources I. Walton, 'The life of Dr. Sanderson', in R. Sanderson, *XXXV sermons*, 7th edn (1681) • P. Lake, 'Serving God and the times: the Calvinist conformity of Robert Sanderson', *Journal of British Studies*, 27 (1988), 81–116 • *The works of Robert Sanderson*, ed. W. Jacobson (1854) • D. Lloyd, *Memoires of the lives ... of those ... personages that suffered ... for the protestant religion* (1668) • Foster, *Alum. Oxon.* • Venn, *Alum. Cant.* • G. C. Cuming, 'The prayer book in convocation, November 1661', *Journal of Ecclesiastical History*, 8 (1957), 182–92 • J. Spurr, *The Restoration Church of England, 1646–1689* (1991) • J. Walker, *An attempt towards recovering an account of the numbers and sufferings of the clergy of the Church of England*, 2 pts in 1 (1714) • Walker rev. • I. M. Green, *The re-establishment of the Church of England, 1660–1663* (1978) • D. Novarr, *The making of Walton's 'Lives'* (1958) • R. S. Bosher, *The making of the Restoration settlement: the influence of the Laudians, 1649–1662* (1951) • Wood, *Ath. Oxon.*, new edn, 3.623 • C. Holmes, *Seventeenth-century Lincolnshire*, History of Lincolnshire, 7 (1980) • J. S. McGee, *The godly man in Stuart England* (1976) • R. S. Paul, *The assembly of the Lord: politics and religion in the Westminster assembly and the 'Grand debate'* (1985) • *Izaak Walton: selected writings*, ed. J. Martin (1997) • J. W. Packer, *The transformation of Anglicanism,*

1643–1660 (1969) • T. Wood, 'A great English casuist', *Church Quarterly Review*, 147 (1948), 29–45
Archives BL, collections relating to history of England, Add. MSS 17992–17997 • BL, texts for sermons and treatise on predestination, Add. MS 5783, 20066 • Bodl. Oxf., genealogical and church notes, sermons, and other papers • Lincoln Cathedral, survey of the monuments of Lincoln • Lincs. Arch., Lincolnshire collections • St George's Chapel, Windsor, MS book of arms, prayer book, and life of Matthew Palmery
Likenesses oils, 1662, Christ Church Oxf. [*see illus.*] • Hollar, portrait • W. Polle, line engraving (after portrait attrib. J. Riley), BM, NPG, V&A; repro. in R. Sanderson, *Sermons* (1662) • White, portrait • engraving, repro. in Holmes, *Seventeenth-century Lincolnshire*, pl. VIII • portrait, episcopal palace, Lincoln
Wealth at death significant: Novarr, *Making of Walton's 'Lives'*, 437

Sanderson, Robert (1663?–1741), archivist, was born, almost certainly on 26 July 1663, at Eggleston Hall, co. Durham, a younger son of Christopher Sanderson (*d.* 1693), landowner and JP, and his second wife, Margaret (*d.* 1667), daughter of Robert Webster of Hartlepool. Among his cousins were members of the families of Mickleton and Spearman, including the antiquary James Mickleton. After schooling in Brignall, North Riding of Yorkshire, Sanderson was a student at St John's College, Cambridge, where he matriculated in July 1683; his contemporary Matthew Prior was to be a lifelong friend. He proceeded BA in 1686/7.

At some point in the 1690s Sanderson was appointed a clerk in the Rolls Chapel, the archival repository for the records of the principal courts of common law; there he worked as an assistant to Thomas Rymer, editor of the *Foedera*, a vast collection of state records relating to foreign affairs. In 1704 he published a volume entitled *Original letters from King William III, then prince of Orange, to King Charles II, Lord Arlington &c., translated; together with an account of his reception at Middleburgh, and his speech upon that occasion*. He also wrote a history of the reign of Henry V, a detailed narrative of which six volumes survive, covering the years 1416–22 (BL, Add. MSS 19979–19984). This elaborate compilation was never published, but the sources that he cites demonstrate a wide range of reading in printed and manuscript materials.

On 3 May 1707 Sanderson's name was joined with that of Rymer in Queen Anne's warrant for the search of archival offices for the purposes of compiling the *Foedera*; on 15 February 1718 a warrant was issued to Sanderson alone. Rymer had got into financial difficulties, and Sanderson gradually assumed direction of the enterprise. On 1 July 1719 he was sworn in as (joint) clerk of the rolls. Ultimately, in 1725, Rymer became a paid transcriber for Sanderson, in a reversal of their former roles. As the title-pages of successive volumes of the *Foedera* indicate, Sanderson was responsible for editing volume 16 (1715), and was wholly responsible for volumes 17 to 20 (1717–35).

In his diary Sanderson recorded his gift of volume 18 to George I: 'I presented the Booke open upon my Knee, his Majesty accepted it with a Smile and reach'd his Right Hand to me, which I kissed' (St John's College, Cambridge,

MS Aa.3.64, 26 Jan 1725). Carelessly, however, Sanderson had overlooked the fact that in flagrant breach of parliamentary privilege the volume included the text of a journal of both houses from the first year of Charles I's reign, and in 1729 the Lords ordered the remaining stock of the book to be seized and this part (pp. 335–565) to be taken out and burnt or destroyed.

As an editor Sanderson is open to criticism on two counts. He was no more accurate than Rymer, and George Holmes found many errors to correct for a second edition. He also lost sight of the Leibnizian conception of the *Foedera* as a collection of treaties and similar instruments:

> seldom pursuing his researches beyond documents which came easily to his hand … he went far, in the volumes for which he was responsible, towards transforming the *Foedera* into a collection of materials for domestic history in which documents relating to foreign affairs were but sparsely intermingled. (Douglas, 230)

Sanderson was a member of the Society of Antiquaries almost from its beginning, being proposed at its sixth meeting, on 16 January 1708, by Peter Le Neve, and he was a founder member of the revived society, from July 1717. His diary shows him to have collected medals: on 7 February 1727 'the key of our Medal Cabinet dropped off Deare Spouse's Key Ringe' (St John's College, MS Aa.3.65), and a week later he bid unsuccessfully for a gold medal of the king and queen of Denmark.

Sanderson had an account at Child's Bank and was perhaps always prosperous—certainly after 1726, when he was appointed an usher in the court of chancery (entitling him to 4s. for every cause), and 1727, when he inherited his elder brother's estates in Cumberland, co. Durham, and the North Riding of Yorkshire. He now had a country seat, Armathwaite Castle, near Carlisle, though he continued to spend most of the year in London, principally at his house in Chancery Lane. He married four times. The names of two of his wives are unknown, but his wife in April 1706 was Elizabeth Nutting, whom he had married at St Matthew's, Friday Street, London, on 22 February 1697; his fourth wife was Elizabeth Hickes (*d*. 1753), whom he married at St Pancras on 6 February 1727. He died on 25 December 1741 at his home in Chancery Lane, and was buried in Red Lion Fields, London. He had no surviving children, and on his widow's death in 1753 his estates passed to his great-nephew William Milbourn.

NIGEL RAMSAY

Sources diary, 1706–32, St John Cam., MSS Aa.3.61–66 · Rymer, *Foedera*, 1st edn · T. Duffus Hardy, *Syllabus … of the documents … in the collection known as 'Rymer's Fœdera'*, 1 (1869) · Venn, *Alum. Cant.* · J. Evans, *A history of the Society of Antiquaries* (1956) · BL, Add. MSS 19979–19984, 38525 · *JHL*, 23 (1726–31), 422 · D. C. Douglas, *English scholars, 1660–1730*, 2nd edn (1951) · *Calendar of the manuscripts of the marquis of Bath preserved at Longleat, Wiltshire*, 5 vols., HMC, 58 (1904–80), vol. 3, p. 433 · J. Hunter, *Familiae minorum gentium*, ed. J. W. Clay, 3, Harleian Society, 39 (1895), 872 · *IGI* · *DNB* · Nichols, *Lit. anecdotes*, 1.477 · J. E. B. Mayor, ed., *Admissions to the College of St John the Evangelist in the University of Cambridge*, pts 1–2: Jan 1629/30 – July 1715 (1882–93), pt 2, p. 93 · M. M. Condon and E. M. Hallam, 'Government printing of the public records in the eighteenth century', *Journal of the Society of Archivists*, 7 (1982–5), 348–88

Archives BL, collections and papers relating to English history, Add. MSS 17992–17997, 38525 · St John Cam., diary

Wealth at death 'always prosperous'; owned estates in Cumberland, co. Durham, and North Riding, incl. Armathwaite Castle near Carlisle

Sanderson, Thomas (1759–1829), poet, was born at Currigg in the chapelry of Raughtonhead, Cumberland, and baptized at Castle Sowerby, Cumberland, on 25 August 1759, the fourth son of John Sanderson (1723–1776) and his wife, Sarah, *née* Scott, of Caldbeck. Sanderson's father did much to improve the well-being of the locality by promoting the enclosure of wastelands and the making of turnpike roads, but died in poor circumstances. A mural tablet to his memory and that of his wife and deceased children was placed in Sebergham church in 1795 by his sixth son, with an inscription by the poet.

Thomas Sanderson was educated first by his father, and afterwards at Sebergham School. He was a good classical scholar, and in 1778 he became master at a school at Greystoke, near Penrith. Afterwards he was a private tutor in the neighbourhood of Morpeth, and this was the only period in his life when he crossed the borders of his native county. He soon returned to his mother's house at Sebergham, and lived in seclusion, but occasionally met, at a spot overlooking the River Caldew or Caudu, Josiah Relph, the Cumbrian poet. On his mother's death he resumed work as a schoolmaster, first at Blackhall grammar school, near Carlisle, and afterwards at Beaumont, where, in 1791, he became acquainted with Jonathan Boucher. Boucher thought well of some verses which Sanderson had contributed under the signature Crito to the *Cumberland Packet*, and induced him to contribute an 'Ode to the Genius of Cumberland' to William Hutchinson's *History of the County of Cumberland* (1794).

In 1799 Sanderson wrote a memoir of Josiah Relph, with a pastoral elegy, for an edition of the Cumbrian poet's works. In 1800 he published a volume of *Original Poems*. Owing partly to their success, but principally to legacies from some relatives, he gave up teaching and retired to Kirklinton, 9 miles north-east of Carlisle, where he boarded with a farmer, and spent the remainder of his life in literary work. He published only two poems after 1800, although he contemplated a long one on benevolence.

In 1807 Sanderson issued a *Companion to the Lakes*, a compilation from the works of Thomas Pennant and William Gilpin, supplemented by his own knowledge. Specimens of Cumbrian ballads are given in the appendix. He defended the literary style of David Hume against the strictures of Gilbert Wakefield in two essays in the *Monthly Magazine*. His other friends included Robert Anderson (1770–1833), the Cumbrian ballad-writer, to whose *Works* (1820 edn) he contributed an essay on the character of the peasantry of Cumberland, and John Howard, the mathematician. Sanderson died on 16 January 1829, from the effects of a fire which broke out in his room while he was asleep. Some of his manuscripts perished in the flames. Unlike his friends, Sanderson never wrote in dialect, but his rhymes occasionally showed the influence of local pronunciation. In 1829 appeared *Life and Literary Remains of Thomas Sanderson*, by J. Lowthian (rector of Sebergham, 1816–18).

G. LE G. NORGATE, *rev.* M. CLARE LOUGHLIN-CHOW

Sources J. Lowthian, *The life and literary remains of Thomas Sanderson* (1829) · [J. Watkins and F. Shoberl], *A biographical dictionary of the living authors of Great Britain and Ireland* (1816) · *IGI* · Watt, *Bibl. Brit.*

Sanderson, Thomas Henry, Baron Sanderson (1841–1923), civil servant, was born on 11 January 1841 at Gunton Park, Norfolk, which had been rented by his father from Lord Suffield. He was the second son of Richard Sanderson (1783/4–1857), Conservative MP for Colchester from 1832 until his defeat in 1847, and his wife, the Hon. Charlotte Matilda (d. 1898), elder daughter of Charles Manners-Sutton, first Viscount Canterbury, speaker of the House of Commons from 1817 to 1835. The Sandersons were a Yorkshire farming family from Armthorpe, near Doncaster. Richard Sanderson, an East India proprietor, voted against the repeal of the corn laws in 1846. Thomas Sanderson was sent to Eton College, but had to leave in 1857 when only sixteen; in October of that year his father died, and his business failed shortly afterwards. Two years later, in 1859, on passing the recently instituted qualifying examination, he entered the Foreign Office as a junior clerk and remained there, steadily progressing through the grades, until his retirement in 1906 as permanent under-secretary of state.

For a large part of his life Sanderson was very close to the fifteenth earl of Derby. As a young Foreign Office clerk he became his private secretary in July 1866, and in August 1867 received from him a special allowance of £100 a year in addition to his salary in some recompense for his services. By the end of 1868 he was described by Derby on his departure from the office as 'the best of the juniors' (Vincent, *Disraeli, Derby and the Conservative Party*, 338). At the same time he was becoming a member of Derby's household, most notably as his walking companion. He was also a potential son-in-law: Derby encouraged Sanderson's courtship of Lady Margaret Cecil, his stepdaughter. Although this suit came to nothing (Sanderson never married), his place in the household became ever more secure, and after Derby left the office finally in 1878 he continued as a close adviser. Like some other Foreign Office clerks in straitened financial circumstances he received financial support from Derby, even becoming his eventual co-executor: he received a legacy of £10,000. A century afterwards, the editor of Derby's diaries speculated that Sanderson 'may have been the son Derby and Lady Derby never had' (*Diaries of E. H. Stanley … 1869–78*, 6). Sanderson himself published an edition of Derby's speeches in 1894, having persuaded his widow to agree to it in preference to commissioning a biography.

Sanderson was again private secretary to Lord Derby during the latter's second spell at the Foreign Office (1874–8), and was appointed to the same post by the second Earl Granville in 1880. In 1885 he was appointed senior clerk, rising to assistant under-secretary in 1889. He had only two short missions abroad. In December 1863 he accompanied Lord Wodehouse (later first earl of Kimberley) to Berlin and Copenhagen on his special mission during the Schleswig-Holstein crisis, and in 1871 he was sent to Geneva during the arbitration between the United Kingdom and the USA on the *Alabama* claims. Sanderson's work there merited great admiration from Lord Chief Justice Cockburn, the British arbitrator, and he was mentioned in a dispatch.

Having been promoted permanent under-secretary of state at the Foreign Office in 1894, Sanderson spent almost all his period in post working with Lord Salisbury and, from 1900, with Lord Lansdowne as foreign secretary. He was an able administrator, pressing to maintain standards of efficiency in the office: he insisted on good and clear drafting by the clerks, even circulating Wellington's dispatches as a model. In 1891 he issued *Observations on the Use and Abuse of Red Tape* to his juniors. He was the last of a long line of conservative civil servants working with strong chiefs at the Foreign Office, a relationship which had been established between the permanent secretary and the foreign secretary since the role of the former was extended during the tenure of Edmund Hammond. The Northcote–Trevelyan report of 1854 recommended the marking of a distinction between 'intellectual' and more mechanical civil service clerical grades and formed the basis for an 1870 order in council, but this only slightly penetrated the Foreign Office before Sanderson's retirement. He attempted to improve the system for keeping the office's papers by the appointment in 1898 of two additional clerks, but their efforts failed to reduce the chaos as the flow of business was steadily increasing. Sanderson was generally regarded as a conservative on the issue of civil service reform, but eventually gave way to pressure from Francis Villiers and, supported by Lansdowne, began to take steps which would lead to a division of responsibilities between different levels of clerks. In 1903 he appealed to the Treasury for additional second-division clerks, as well as two assistant clerks, to help with parliamentary papers in the planned blue book department and to act as secretaries to the committee of imperial defence. He authorized the reallocation of mechanical work such as the making up of the dispatch bags to the office keepers, and consented to the appointment of an interdepartmental committee of inquiry into the record-keeping systems in other major government departments. This reported in 1904 that the best way forward lay in the creation of a general registry system. Sanderson was eventually persuaded to accept these findings and, despite Treasury resistance, the system was sanctioned in December 1905 and came into operation on 1 January 1906, just before his retirement. Thus the door was opened for the transformation of the first-division clerks into advisers engaged in the policy-making process. Sanderson's successors as permanent secretary lost their specific departmental responsibilities and instead undertook the general supervision of the office and assumed a co-ordinating advisory role for the foreign secretary.

Sanderson's last years in office were clouded by ill

health and deteriorating eyesight. His strong spectacles meant he was widely known in the Foreign Office as Lamps. He was raised to the peerage as Baron Sanderson of Armthorpe on 20 December 1905. This was the first such elevation for a permanent under-secretary who had not been an ambassador, and who had spent virtually all his career in London, since that of his predecessor Edmund Hammond, who had been created Lord Hammond of Kirk Ella, Kingston upon Hull, in 1874. In retirement Sanderson served as chairman of the committee on Indian emigration to the crown colonies (1909–10) and of the council of the Royal Society of Arts (1911–13). His increasing blindness prevented him from undertaking further public work. He was a member of three clubs, the Athenaeum, the Travellers', and the St James's. He wrote many of the articles on late Victorian and Edwardian diplomatists for the *Dictionary of National Biography*. Sanderson died on 21 March 1923 at his home, 65 Wimpole Street, London, after four days of influenza.   VALERIE CROMWELL

Sources Z. S. Steiner, *The foreign office and foreign policy, 1898–1914* (1969) · R. Jones, *The nineteenth-century foreign office: an administrative history* (1971) · *Disraeli, Derby and the conservative party: journals and memoirs of Edward Henry, Lord Stanley, 1849–1869*, ed. J. R. Vincent (1978) · *The diaries of E. H. Stanley, 15th earl of Derby, 1869–1878*, CS, 5th series, 4 (1994) · *The later Derby diaries … selected passages*, ed. J. Vincent (privately printed, Bristol, 1981) · A. Ramm, 'Lord Salisbury and the foreign office', *The foreign office, 1782–1982*, ed. R. Bullen (1984), 46–65 · d. cert.
Archives PRO, corresp. and MSS, FO 800/1–2 | BL, corresp. with Arthur James Balfour, Add. MS 49739, *passim* · BL, letters to W. E. Gladstone, Add. MSS 44172–44678 · Bodl. Oxf., corresp. with Lord Kimberley · Bodl. Oxf., corresp. with Lord Selborne · CAC Cam., corresp. with Sir Cecil Spring-Rice · CUL, letters to Lord Acton · CUL, corresp. with Lord Hardinge · LMA, corresp. with Sir Willoughby Maycock · NA Scot., corresp. with A. J. Balfour · NL Scot., corresp., mainly with Lord Rosebery · PRO, corresp. with Sir Arthur Nicholson, PRO 30/81 · PRO, letters to Lord Odo Russell, FO 918 · U. Leeds, Brotherton L., letters to Sir Edmund Gosse
Likenesses Spy [L. Ward], watercolour, 1898, NPG; repro. in *VF* (10 Nov 1898)
Wealth at death £34,587 10s. 2d.: probate, 28 April 1923, CGPLA Eng. & Wales

Sanderson, Thomas James Cobden- (1840–1922), bookbinder and printer, was born Thomas James Sanderson on 2 December 1840 at Alnwick, Northumberland, the only son of James Sanderson (c.1813–1895), a district surveyor of taxes, and his wife, Mary Ann Rutherford How (1800–1891). James Sanderson's career took his family from place to place, and his son was educated in Worcester, Hull, Pocklington, and Rochdale. From 1857 to 1859 he studied at Owens College in Manchester, and in 1860 he went to Trinity College, Cambridge. He lost his Christian belief at Cambridge, and left in 1863 without taking a degree.

To describe Cobden-Sanderson as a bookbinder and printer is to identify him with the things for which he is known, but it gives a false impression of the man. It would be truer to describe him as 'thinker, bookbinder, and printer', not because his thoughts were original or profound, but because he lived on such a high intellectual plane. As a young man he read Carlyle, Goethe, Spinoza,

Thomas James Cobden-Sanderson (1840–1922), by Sir William Rothenstein, 1916

Wordsworth, and the pioneering geographer and scientist Alexander von Humboldt; these were lifelong intellectual companions. But he was also anguished and lonely, thinking high thoughts to turn away the pain. He limped through the 1860s, not knowing what to do with his life, suffering long periods of depression, sometimes talking of suicide. German idealism and romantic poetry simply magnified his unhappiness, giving it a heroic dimension.

Towards the end of the decade Sanderson felt stronger and took up the law, practising as a barrister in London from 1871 to 1883. He was involved in making 'a kind of Code of all the powers, rights, and obligations of the London & North-Western Railway Company' (Cobden-Sanderson, *Cosmic Vision*, 114). Shifting this mass of legal details was like mining, he recalled, but at the end there was no gold and his health was broken. He went to Italy to recuperate.

In the 1860s Sanderson had got to know Edward Burne-Jones and William Morris, perhaps through his Cambridge friend George Howard, later ninth earl of Carlisle. In April 1881, outside the duomo in Siena, he met Morris's wife, Janey, with Annie and Janie Cobden, daughters of the radical MP Richard Cobden. In the following year, on 5 August, he married Julia Sarah Anne (Annie) Cobden (1853–1926), changing his name to Cobden-Sanderson out of respect for her father. He was forty-one and she was twenty-nine. He wrote later that 'her active and practical mind gave to my own that feeling for reality which it had long been in want of' (Cobden-Sanderson, *Cosmic Vision*, 115). This was a turning point. Nearly a year later he was again with Janey Morris. He was eager to do work with his hands, in the spirit of the arts and crafts movement, and she suggested bookbinding. Two days later he went to the bookbinding workshop of Roger de Coverley, and asked to be taught. This was another turning point.

De Coverley's was one of a number of firms in the London bookbinding trade which bound individual books for customers using traditional methods. Cobden-Sanderson spent about six months there and then set up on his own in 1884, working first in Covent Garden and then from home in Hendon and Hampstead. He also bound individual books, but he chose what he bound, which was not the usual practice in the trade. From 1886 onwards he bought books, rebound them, and took them to the bookseller James Bain in Haymarket, where they sold enough to earn him a modest living. (Annie had brought a small inheritance to the marriage.) From the late 1880s many of his bindings were sold to American customers, and the two principal modern collections of bindings designed by Cobden-Sanderson are American: the Strouse Collection at the University of California at Berkeley and that of J. Paul Getty junior.

Cobden-Sanderson thought of bookbinding as the clothing of fine literature, and Shakespeare, the English romantic poets, Tennyson, and Morris were the writers whose works he bound most. The more he admired a work the more sumptuously he bound it. He worked in gold on leather, using simple, mainly floral tools of his own design, and his rich effects brought a kind of springtime to the French and English binding traditions on which he drew. He seemed to have found his métier. He worked as a binder for only about ten years, but he started a tradition of fine binding in Britain which continues to the present day.

Cobden-Sanderson had found his métier late in life, and he had never been strong. By the early 1890s he no longer had the strength for heavy work. In 1893 he took a lease on 15 Upper Mall, Hammersmith, a small house with a garden running down to the Thames, near William Morris's own Kelmscott House. Here he started the Doves Bindery, employing three professional binders and naming it after a nearby pub. At first the bindery worked as he had, binding individual books to his designs, and selling them through Bain. But when he started printing books at the Doves Press in 1900, it began to do more repetitive work, binding whole editions of Doves Press books in plain vellum.

Four years after starting the Doves Bindery, the Cobden-Sandersons moved with their two children, Richard and Stella, from Hampstead to 7 Hammersmith Terrace, a short walk from Upper Mall, and from this date Cobden-Sanderson lived and worked among the houses, wharves, and workshops that lined the river's edge at this point. Other luminaries of the book arts—Morris himself, the process engraver Emery *Walker, the calligrapher Edward Johnston—lived near by.

In 1900 Cobden-Sanderson set up the Doves Press at 1 Hammersmith Terrace, in partnership with Emery Walker. This was as distinct from trade printing as his

bookbinding had been, a private press on the lines of Morris's Kelmscott Press. He and Walker wanted to print great literature in monumental form, and to see if they could make a book beautiful with type alone. Goethe, Wordsworth, Milton, and Shakespeare were among the chosen authors and, as their masterpiece, the Bible. Some fifty titles were printed between 1900 and 1917. They are similar in layout and they all employ the Doves type, which Walker derived from a fifteenth-century Venetian model. There are no illustrations and no ornaments, apart from some initials drawn by Edward Johnston and Graily Hewitt; just the words printed with care on handmade paper. As with his sumptuous bindings, this austerity expressed Cobden-Sanderson's reverence for the canon of western literature. In the early twentieth century it was a visual model for the reform of typography in Britain, Europe, and America.

In photographs of the 1880s Cobden-Sanderson looks much younger than he was, shrimp-like, unformed, clean-shaven. In those of *c*.1900, on the other hand, he has a fine beard and moustache and looks his sixty years. He sits the very image of the artist-craftsman in an embroidered sky-blue smock, his normal dress at this time. He had come into his own. It was partly that he had married, but perhaps more that he had picked up his binder's tools. After all the *Weltschmerz* of his early years, it was little humble things, leather and type, that had shown him what to do. He was now a leader of the arts and crafts movement in England. The course of his life ran more smoothly. And his speculative mind came happily into play around the practical world of printing and binding. He saw the history of the world as a God-filled process of physical and spiritual evolution, and the history of man as its dialectical complement. He felt as though the work of his hands kept time with the movement of the universe. Unfortunately this 'cosmic vision', as he called it, was not easy to convey. In lectures he talked persuasively about bookbinding or typography, but as he moved towards his larger theme he became childlike and rhetorical; the words came too easily. When he told his audience that the ideal book was 'a symbol of the infinitely beautiful in which all things of beauty rest and into which all things of beauty do ultimately merge', they were not always sure what he meant (Cobden-Sanderson, *The Ideal Book*, 9). Arts and crafts colleagues admired his work, but did not always understand him.

Towards the end of his life Cobden-Sanderson did one mean-spirited thing in the name of his cosmic vision. He was restless in partnership with Walker at the Doves Press, because he put more into the work of the press than Walker, who had his own business to run. The partnership was dissolved in 1908, but Walker claimed part-ownership of the Doves type. In 1909 Cobden-Sanderson (the older man) signed an agreement whereby the type would be his for life, and would pass to Walker at his death. But he did not trust Walker to use the type in the spirit of his vision. During the war he brought the printing to an end. On many evenings in the autumn and winter of 1916, under cover of darkness, he took the Doves type and threw it into the Thames off Hammersmith Bridge. It was a dedication (he had been reading the book of Leviticus); a symbolic act (giving his work back to the river of life); an old man's act of folly; and a betrayal. In May 1917 he wrote to Walker's lawyers explaining what he had done, and his letter was published in the *Times Literary Supplement*.

The Doves Press closed down in 1917. At this point the Cobden-Sandersons went to live at 15 Upper Mall, where two binders continued working in a small way until 1921. Cobden-Sanderson died at home on 7 September 1922, and following his cremation at Golders Green on 11 September the urn containing his ashes was placed in the garden wall of 15 Upper Mall. Annie Cobden-Sanderson died in 1926 and her urn was placed with his. Two years later there was a severe flood and the Thames overflowed its banks. It seems that both urns were washed away.

ALAN CRAWFORD

Sources *The journals of Thomas James Cobden-Sanderson, 1879–1922*, 2 vols. (1926) · M. Tidcombe, *The Doves Bindery* (1991) · M. Tidcombe, *The bookbindings of T. J. Cobden-Sanderson* (1984) · T. J. Cobden-Sanderson, *The ideal book or book beautiful* (1900) · T. J. Cobden-Sanderson, *Cosmic vision* (1922) · W. Ransom, ed., *Kelmscott Doves and Ashendene: the private press credos* (1952) · J. H. Nash, ed., *Cobden-Sanderson and the Doves Press* (1929) · T. J. Cobden-Sanderson, *Amantium irae: letters to two friends, 1864–1867* (1914) · B. Middleton, 'English craft bookbinding, 1880–1980', *Private Library*, 4/4 (winter 1981), 139–69 · C. Franklin, *Emery Walker: some light on his theories of printing and his relations with William Morris and Cobden-Sanderson* (1973) · *CGPLA Eng. & Wales* (1922)

Archives BL, working diary · BL, binding work book · Hunt. L., pattern books · Ransom HRC, photograph album · Smith College, Northampton, Massachusetts, corresp. and MSS · U. Cal., Berkeley, Strouse Collection, binding patterns, corresp. and MSS, photographs | BL, corresp. with S. Cockerell, 52710 · Castle Howard, North Yorkshire, corresp. with G. Howard · Hammersmith and Fulham Archives and Local History Centre, letters to W. Bull

Likenesses W. Crane, sketch, 1881, repro. in W. Crane, *An artist's reminiscences* (1907), 221 · P. Lombardi, photograph, 1881, NPG · group portrait, photograph, 1881, NPG · photograph, c.1890, U. Cal., Berkeley, Bancroft Library · A. Legros, etching, 1898, repro. in *Catalogue raisonné of books printed & published at the Doves Press, 1900–1916* (1916) · photograph, c.1900 (with Emery Walker), repro. in *Philobiblon* [Vienna], 9 (1932) · photograph, c.1905, V&A · photograph, c.1910, Hammersmith and Fulham Libraries, London · W. Rothenstein, drawing, 1916, repro. in W. Rothenstein, *Twenty-four portraits* (1920) · W. Rothenstein, engraving, 1916, NPG [*see illus.*] · group portraits, photographs (with his family), Ransom HRC

Wealth at death £12,988: probate, 30 Oct 1922, *CGPLA Eng. & Wales*

Sanderson, Wilfrid Ernest (1878–1935), composer and organist, was born on 23 December 1878 in Christ Church Street, Ipswich, the third son of Thomas Sanderson, Wesleyan minister, and his wife, Emily Collinson. His father's work took the family from East Anglia to Launceston, in Devon, and later to the London area, where Wilfrid was educated at St Dunstan's College, Catford, and at the City of London School.

Though initially intended for a business career, Sanderson had early demonstrated his musical ability, and by the age of seventeen was organist at St Stephen's, Walthamstow. He began a career as music teacher and organist at All Hallows, Bread Street, in 1897 and at St James's, Hampstead Road, from 1899 to 1904. At the same time he had become a pupil of (and later was assistant to) Frederick Bridge, organist at Westminster Abbey. During his association with the abbey, from 1897 to 1904, he sang tenor in the abbey choir for Queen Victoria's funeral, in 1901, and for the coronation of Edward VII, in 1902. He became a bachelor of music at Durham University, a licentiate of the Royal Academy of Music, and a fellow of the Royal College of Organists.

On 25 October 1904 at St Gabriel's, Willesden, Sanderson married Mary Elizabeth (b. 1877/8), daughter of Alfred Buck Petch, manufacturer, with whom he had a son and a daughter. He had taken up the position of organist and choirmaster at St George's, Doncaster, on 1 May of that year, and retained it until 1923, while operating from teaching rooms in the town, in South Parade. In 1910 he supervised a major renovation of the church's Schulze organ and organized a series of organ recitals by various performers to mark the event. He conducted the Doncaster Musical Society in major choral and orchestral works from 1911 to 1924, as well as helping to found the Amateur Operatic Society in 1909 and continuing to conduct it even after he had left the town.

Sanderson's early years in Doncaster were also the years in which, encouraged by music publisher Arthur Boosey of Boosey & Co., he came to the fore as a prolific composer of ballads. These were soon being accepted by popular singers of the day such as Harry Dearth and Flora Woodman for performance at the immensely popular Saturday afternoon Boosey ballad concerts. Some of the songs were unashamedly sentimental, others rousing and forthright in their melodic richness, and all provided rewarding material for singers. The earliest to achieve big success was 'My Dear Soul' (1906; words by May Byron), which was popularized by Dame Clara Butt. Later came 'Drake Goes West' (1910; words by P. J. O'Reilly), 'Until' (1910; words by Edward Teschemacher), 'Friend o' Mine' (1913; words by Fred E. Weatherly), 'Up from Somerset' (1913; words by Weatherly), 'Shipmates o' Mine' (1913; words by Teschemacher), 'Break o' Day' (1915; words by O'Reilly), 'Captain Mac' (1915; words by O'Reilly), 'The Glory of the Sea' (1916; words by Weatherly), 'Longshore' (1917; words by Bernard Moore), 'God be with you Tonight' (1917; words by Fred G. Bowles), 'The Company Sergeant-Major' (1918; words by P. H. B. Lyon), 'Devonshire Cream and Cider' (1919; words by Theodore Curzon), and 'The Stars have Eyes' (1920; words by Bowles). He also composed various piano solos, hymns, and other church music.

During the First World War Sanderson took leave of absence from his duties in Doncaster. Being classed unfit for active service, he took his family south to Egham, in Surrey, and secured a post as senior clerk with the Ministry of Works. In 1923 he moved permanently from Doncaster to a house in Nutfield, near Redhill, Surrey, for the sake of his wife's health. He became an examiner for Trinity College of Music, and in that capacity travelled widely, visiting South Africa in 1933.

Tall, bespectacled, and distinguished in appearance,

Sanderson's somewhat stern exterior hid a kindly nature and a keen sense of humour. His non-musical interests included cricket, golf, tennis, and motoring. He continued to compose songs up to the time of his death, on 10 December 1935 at his home, Lone Oak, Cormongers Lane, Nutfield. His wife survived him. His son, Wilfrid Guy Sanderson, was later Anglican bishop of Plymouth.

ANDREW LAMB

Sources P. L. Scowcroft, *British light music* (1997) · private information (2004) [grandson] · *CGPLA Eng. & Wales* (1936) · b. cert. · m. cert. · d. cert.
Likenesses photograph, repro. in Scowcroft, *British light music*
Wealth at death £51,045 12s. 3d.: probate, 5 Feb 1936, *CGPLA Eng. & Wales*

Sanderson, William (1547/8–1638), merchant, was the eldest son of William Sanderson (d. 1570) and his wife, Jane, formerly Wall. The Sanderson family had moved from Pontefract to London in the person of the younger William's grandfather Stephen Sanderson (d. 1495). Sanderson learnt the merchant's trade under Thomas Allin, and travelled widely in Denmark, Poland, Germany, France, and the Low Countries. At some time before 1592 he joined the Fishmongers' Company and was on the court of assistants until he moved from London in 1595, although he was a member until his death. He was well known in Elizabeth's court, and to the duke of Norfolk, and lords Burghley and Leicester.

His travelling days over, Sanderson was a wealthy man; in addition to his trading profits, he had inherited property in several counties of England and in Ireland. His first London house was in the parish of St Magnus the Martyr, by London Bridge. He married, probably about 1584–5, Margaret, daughter of Hugh Snedale of Cornwall and his wife, a sister of Sir Walter Ralegh. The names of a daughter and seven sons are known, the eldest being Sir William *Sanderson (1586–1676), while three others bore the names of his friends: Ralegh, Cavendish, and Drake. Sanderson was eager to invest in new ventures. Henry Lane of the Muscovy Company compiled for him an account of voyages to the Russian Arctic between 1553 and 1583, but Sanderson seems to have rejected this route in favour of a north-west passage to the riches of the Orient. He funded Martin Frobisher's three voyages towards Greenland and Baffin Island. The family connection with Ralegh was supported by Sanderson's purse: he several times stood bond for Ralegh, for sums said to exceed £100,000, and indemnified Ralegh's exploits in Virginia between 1584 and 1590. He provided the majority of the money that, supplemented by the merchants of Exeter, funded John Davis's voyages of 1585–7, and Sanderson's own ship *Sunshine*, with his servants travelling as supercargo, accompanied Davis on all three voyages. Although China eluded him, Davis brought back from Greenland a profitable cargo of sealskins, and on his last voyage reached 72°41′ N, where he named two prominent features, Sanderson's Tower on Baffin Island and, on the Greenland side, Hope Sanderson.

Sanderson also supported Emery Molyneux, the first English globe maker. His large terrestrial and celestial globes were published in 1592 and presented to Queen Elizabeth at Greenwich. A second terrestrial globe, bearing Sanderson's newly bestowed arms and a declaration of his patronage, was presented to the queen at an entertainment at Sanderson's house in Newington Butts, to the south of London. As a farmer of the Mines Royal, Sanderson visited Derbyshire, Worcestershire, and Devon; in 1600 he was among the company shareholders accused of misbehaviour at the Isleworth brassworks and in 1602 he was named in an action in Star Chamber.

In the latter days of Queen Elizabeth Sanderson was involved in an examination of the mechanism of foreign exchange; his report survives as BL, Harley MS 5208, fols. 50–52. He also oversaw the business of goods coming into Leadenhall during the years about the accession of James I. In 1594 Sanderson was in Devon making final arrangements with Ralegh and his associates for a voyage to Guiana. In view of the hazardous nature of this enterprise, Sanderson presented Ralegh with an account of the expenses, a release was signed and then altered, to operate in the event of Ralegh's death. But Ralegh accused Sanderson of dishonest accounting and Sanderson thought the altered release a forgery. They parted in anger; the matter eventually went to Star Chamber in 1613, although there is no record of the outcome. When Ralegh was executed in 1618 Sanderson was obliged to go to law in order to recover the considerable sums owing to him.

In the early decades of the seventeenth century Sanderson was beset by troubles, probably caused by unwise investments in voyages and properties, as well as expensive litigation. He spent at least seven years in prison between 1613 and 1622, at first in the Gatehouse at Westminster, then in the Fleet. The evidences given by his enemies at the Star Chamber hearings present him as a ruined and broken man. In 1656 his son, Sir William Sanderson, published *A compleat history of the lives and reigns of Mary queen of Scotland, and of her son King James, of Great Britain, France and Ireland, the sixth* in which he blackened Ralegh's actions and character; in reply, Ralegh's son Carew Ralegh published, anonymously, a pamphlet attacking the author and his father, in which he stated that William Sanderson had died in a debtors' prison. This in turn led Sir William Sanderson to issue *An Answer to a Scurrilous Pamphlet Intituled 'Observations …'*, which presented his father in a better light. This account reveals that Sanderson died at his house in the Strand, Westminster, in 1638, aged ninety, and that his body was embalmed for several months before being buried in the parish church of the Savoy. The Savoy Chapel was at this time serving the parishioners of St Mary-le-Strand, their church having been demolished about 1548. He was said to have left lands to his children, but no will has been found. Of his sons, Drake Sanderson and another son pursued Ralegh in his last voyage, Drake dying at San Domingo in the West Indies. A third son died while on Captain Weymouth's voyage to the Arctic in 1602, and a fourth, possibly Hugh (d. 1624), in the East Indies. A fifth, Thomas (*d.* 1635), fought with the Dutch against the Portuguese, in the East Indies, eventually taking over 2000 men by sea to Russia to fight at Smolensk.   ANITA McCONNELL

Sources R. A. McIntyre, 'William Sanderson, Elizabethan financier of discovery', *William and Mary Quarterly*, 13 (1956), 184–201 · J. W. Shirley, 'Sir Walter Ralegh's Guinea finances', *Huntington Library Quarterly*, 13 (1949–50), 55–69 · BL, Harley MS 5208 [examination of mechanism of foreign exchange], fols. 50–52 · *The voyages and works of John Davis*, ed. A. H. Markham, Hakluyt Society, 59 (1880) · Coll. Arms, Vincent MS 119, p. 292 · 'A letter of M. Henrie Lane to the worshipfull M. William Sanderson, conteining a briefe discourse of that which passed in the north-east discovery for the space of two and thirtie yeares', in R. Hakluyt, *The principal navigations, voyages, traffiques and discoveries of the English nation*, 3, Hakluyt Society, extra ser., 3 (1903), 330–36 · J. W. Shirley, *Thomas Hariot: a biography* (1983), 218–22 · records of the Fishmongers' Company, vol. 1, and court ledger of the Fishmongers' Company, vol. 1, GL

Sanderson, Sir William (1586–1676), historian, was born in Lincolnshire according to Wood, the son of William *Sanderson (1547/8–1638), merchant, and his wife, Margaret, daughter of Hugh Snedale of Cornwall, who had married a sister of Sir Walter Ralegh. The elder Sanderson had business dealings with Ralegh until they fell out in 1594, which accounts for the animus towards Ralegh apparent in the writings of the younger William, his eldest son. William the younger's formal education is unknown, and he is not the William Sanderson who was at Cambridge in the early seventeenth century according to Venn, though Wood thought that he was a graduate of that university. Sanderson's friend James Howell later described Sanderson as having been bred up at court and as being employed both at home and abroad; Sanderson himself spoke of having been 'beyond seas' (Howell, address to author in W. Sanderson, *A Compleat History of the Life and Raigne of King Charles*, 1658; W. Sanderson, *Graphice*, 1658, author's preface). Sanderson served as secretary to Henry Rich, earl of Holland, when the latter was appointed chancellor of Cambridge University in 1628 (Wood, *Ath. Oxon.*, 3.565). He married, about 1626, Bridget (1592/3–1681/2), daughter of Sir Edward Tyrrell, baronet, of Thornton, Buckinghamshire, who later served as the ceremonial 'mother of the maids', that is the maids of honour to Catherine of Braganza.

According to his own epitaph, commissioned by his widow, Sanderson suffered in the royalist cause during the civil war (Dart, 2.125), and at the Restoration he was knighted by Charles II and made a gentleman of the privy chamber. The king also confirmed a previous grant to Sanderson, by the earl of Holland, of the Paddock Walk, Windsor Park, which he surrendered for a payment of £1100 in 1671 (*CSP dom.*, 1660–61, 242; *1671*, 348, 500). On 7 June 1671 Sanderson and his wife were jointly granted an annual pension of £200 (ibid., *1671*, 500). They appear to have had no children.

Sanderson's major achievement lay in his historical writing, which was partial and polemical, but no more so than the works to which he responded. In 1650 there appeared, posthumously, a libellous memoir, *The Court*

and *Character of King James*, by Anthony Weldon, a disaffected former Jacobean courtier and member of the Kentish parliamentary county committee, who had died a year earlier. This was one of several historical works, critical of the Stuart monarchs, inspired by the virtual elimination of censorship and the advent of civil war, and it immediately stirred up controversy. Sanderson felt obliged to write a defence of James I's memory and to vindicate him from Weldon's criticism of the person, court, and conduct of the king. His defence was published as *Aulicus coquinariae* in 1650 and addressed Weldon's accusations point by point. Though the *Aulicus* appeared anonymously, and was once misattributed to Peter Heylyn, it is unquestionably by Sanderson, who in any case avowed his authorship in the preface to his *Compleat History of the Lives and Reigns of Mary Queen of Scotland, and of her Son James* (1656)—a more substantial work in which Sanderson now took aim at a more respectable, if equally damning, history of James I published by Arthur Wilson in 1653. The section on James was based at least in part on his personal knowledge of court life. The same personal acquaintance is less evident in Sanderson's third historical work, *A Compleat History of the Life and Raigne of King Charles from his Cradle to his Grave* (1658), with a portrait of Sanderson himself at the age of sixty-eight. Derived principally from newsbooks and from second-hand sources such as *Eikon basilike* it has little value as an independent authority. It remains, however, an important example of the early attempts by royalists to manage the memory of the martyred king, and therefore a significant work in the development of later seventeenth-century history writing, which was notably more controversial, even polemical, than that of the pre-civil war decades.

It was an interesting feature of the controversial historical writing of the 1650s and 1660s that opponents were often, nominally, on the same side. Although Sanderson's original targets had been parliamentarian historians such as Weldon and then Wilson, he had shifted by the history of Charles I to attacking other royalist writers such as Hamon L'Estrange, who had penned a moderate account of the king's life, and especially Peter Heylyn, author of some of the most vehemently royalist histories of the period. In 1658 Heylyn published *Respondet Petrus* in answer to a book entitled *The Judgment of the Late Primate of Ireland*, including an appendix criticizing parts of Sanderson's *King Charles*, in particular his account of the attainder of Strafford. Sanderson's original work had itself criticized both L'Estrange and Heylyn's earlier response to the latter, and relations between Sanderson and Heylyn, who said that their previous relations were civil, deteriorated (*Examen historicum*, 2.41). Sanderson replied in *Post Haste: a Reply to Dr Peter Heylyn's Appendix* (25 June 1658). Heylyn in turn responded in his *Examen historicum* (1659), which criticized Sanderson's histories of Mary Stuart, James, and especially Charles; the criticisms are largely over matters of factual detail rather than interpretation. Sanderson himself had the last word in the controversy in his *Peter Pursued, or, Dr Heylin Overtaken* soon after.

In a separate controversy Sanderson's account of the

imprisonment, Guiana expedition, and death of his great-uncle, Sir Walter Ralegh, was criticized by Ralegh's son, Carew Ralegh, in *Observations upon some particular persons and passages, in … 'A compleat history of the lives and reignes of Mary Queen of Scotland, and of her son James'* (1656), to which Sanderson responded in *An Answer to a Scurrilous Pamphlet Intituled, 'Observations upon a compleat history of the lives and reignes of Mary, Queen of Scotland, and of her son, King James'*.

Sanderson's final work, published in June 1658, was *Graphice: the Use of the Pen and Pensil* on the history of various forms of painting. During the Restoration he lived in retirement, dying in London, at the age of ninety, on 15 July 1676. John Evelyn, who attended his funeral on 19 July, described him as 'author of two large but mean histories' (Evelyn, 4.94). He was buried in Westminster Abbey (Dart, 2.125); his widow was buried alongside him in January 1682 (Luttrell, 1.159). D. R. WOOLF

Sources J. Dart, *Westmonasterium*, 2 vols. (1723) · D. R. Woolf, *The idea of history in early Stuart England* (1990) · N. Luttrell, *A brief historical relation of state affairs from September 1678 to April 1714*, 6 vols. (1857) · Evelyn, *Diary* · Wood, *Ath. Oxon.*, new edn · Venn, *Alum. Cant.* · *DNB*
Archives LUL, MS treatise of State Merchant
Likenesses W. Faithorne, line engraving (after G. Soest), BM, NPG; repro. in W. Sanderson, *Graphice, or, The use of the pen and pensil* (1658) · engraving, repro. in W. Sanderson, *A compleat history of the life and raigne of King Charles* (1658)

Sandford. *See also* Sanford.

Sandford, Daniel (1766–1830), bishop of Edinburgh, was the second son of the Revd Dr Daniel Sandford (*d.* 1770) of Sandford Hall, Shropshire, and Sarah, daughter of the Reverend John Chapone. His mother's sister-in-law was Hester Chapone, the essayist. He was born at Delville, near Dublin, in the house of Dean Delaney. Educated privately, he matriculated at Christ Church, Oxford, on 26 November 1783, aged seventeen. He graduated BA in 1787 and MA in 1791. On 11 October 1790 he married Helen Frances Catherine (*d.* 1837), the eldest daughter of Erskine Douglas, a staunch Jacobite, whom he had met at Bath, to where his mother had removed at his father's death. He was ordained as a deacon in the same year. In 1792 he resigned as curate of Hanworth, near Sunbury, Middlesex, to take up an invitation from English Anglicans in Edinburgh to open an Episcopal chapel. His congregation first worshipped in West Register Street, then Rose Street, and from 1818, at St John's, a prominent church at the west end of Princes Street. The last move signalled the rising fortunes of Episcopalians, at least in Edinburgh.

Sandford was awarded a BD and a DD from Oxford in 1802. Through his connections with the primus, Bishop John Skinner of Aberdeen, and leading Anglican high-churchmen, he became a leading advocate of the union of the so called 'English chapels' with the Scottish Episcopal church through Episcopalian acceptance of the Thirty-Nine Articles of the Church of England. This was agreed at the Laurencekirk convention in 1804, and Sandford brought his congregation into communion with the Episcopal church in November of the same year.

In January 1806 Sandford was elected bishop of Edinburgh, the first Englishman to become a Scottish Episcopalian bishop. It was a move strongly supported by Bishop Skinner as a means of placating English and Anglophile Scottish discontent, which persisted in spite of the reunion of most of the English chapels. Bishop Abernethy Drummond had purposely resigned the Edinburgh portion of his united southern dioceses to permit the election of a bishop appealing to southern Episcopalians. Sandford was consecrated on 9 February 1806 by bishops Skinner, Watson, and Jolly. In 1807 his diocesan responsibilities were enlarged when the five clergy of Fife, impressed by Sandford's qualities, voted to be included in his jurisdiction. In 1809 the clergy of the diocese of Glasgow similarly petitioned to be placed under his jurisdiction following the death of Drummond, whom he thereby emulated in having under his episcopal care all the small congregations of Episcopalians in Scotland south of the River Tay.

Sandford was one of the few bishops at that time who resided in his diocese, as incumbent of St John's, Edinburgh. He retained a congregation out of necessity, as his episcopal income reflected the extreme poverty of the Episcopal church after the penalties suffered during the eighteenth century. Compared with many of his elderly colleagues he was an energetic bishop, holding regular visitations of the clergy, and annual confirmations, largely in Edinburgh. In establishing the mechanisms for diocesan administration, he laid the foundations for growth in the diocese of Edinburgh on which his successors were able to build. In addition to the erection of more prominent buildings, the higher public profile of Scottish episcopacy at this time was signified by Sandford's adoption of full episcopal dress outdoors, with short cassock and buckled shoes. His unspectacular administration saw the growth in the number of congregations in southern Scotland largely owing to immigration from the north, England, and Ireland into the central industrial belt. He died in Edinburgh on 14 January 1830, and was buried on 21 January in the eastern side of the cemetery attached to St John's Church, Princes Street, Edinburgh. He was survived by his wife, three daughters, and three sons, including John *Sandford (1801–1873) and Sir Daniel Keyte *Sandford (1798–1838). ROWAN STRONG

Sources J. Sandford, 'Memoir', *Remains of Bishop Sandford*, 1 (1830), 1–75 · R. Foskett, 'The episcopate of Daniel Sandford, 1806–30', *Records of the Scottish Church History Society*, 15 (1963–5), 141–52 · G. F. Terry, *Memorials of the church of St John the Evangelist* (1911) · R. Keith and J. Spottiswoode, *An historical catalogue of the Scottish bishops, down to the year 1688*, new edn, ed. M. Russel [M. Russell] (1824) · J. P. Lawson, *History of the Scottish Episcopal church* (1843) · W. Walker, *The life and times of John Skinner, bishop of Aberdeen* (1887) · *DSCHT*
Archives Shrops. RRC, family corresp. | Linn. Soc., corresp. with Richard Pulteney · NA Scot., Episcopal church records
Likenesses W. Walker and S. Cousins, mezzotint, pubd 1829 (after J. W. Gordon), BM, NPG
Wealth at death £895 15*s.* 3*d.*: inventory, NA Scot., SC 70/1/44, fols. 825–6

Sandford, Daniel Arthur (1882–1972), army officer and adviser in Ethiopia, was born at Landkey vicarage, south Devon, on 18 June 1882, one of the seven sons and two daughters of the Revd Ernest Grey Sandford (1839–1910) and his wife, Ethel M. R. Poole. His father, who had been an Oxford athlete, and was later canon and archdeacon of Exeter, had served as chaplain to Archbishop Frederick Temple. As a result of this connection young Daniel, on attending St Paul's School, lived with the Temples at Fulham Palace. On finishing school he adopted a military career. He attended the Royal Military Academy at Woolwich and was commissioned in 1900 in the Royal Artillery. Transferred to India, he served in Bombay and Karachi until 1906. He was then posted to Aden, took a gunnery course in Britain, and returned to Aden in 1909. There, as a young subaltern, he took leave, sailed across the Gulf of Aden, and, entering Ethiopia, hired mules at Diredawa, and rode across the country to Sudan. These travels greatly enamoured him with Ethiopia, and made him determined to return to the country. This he did in 1910 when, joining the Sudan civil service as a contract officer, he was posted to the British legation in Addis Ababa.

Dan Sandford, as he was generally known, rejoined the army in 1913. He served in France, where he was wounded, mentioned in dispatches, and was made a member of the French Légion d'honneur and DSO and bar. On 14 November 1918 he married Christine (1893–1975), daughter of Hubert Stanley Lush, a solicitor. The marriage, which was to last fifty-four years, was a happy one. Throughout her life Christine identified herself closely with her husband's career and interests. They had two sons and four daughters.

In 1919 Sandford accompanied Lord Lugard on the latter's visit to Addis Ababa to inspect the work of a private British company, the Abyssinian Corporation, and was appointed its general manager. He held this post until the company's liquidation in 1921. By then deeply attracted by life in Ethiopia, he retired from the army in 1922 and leased a piece of land at Mulu, 30 miles north of Addis Ababa. Until the world slump of 1931, from which Ethiopia suffered greatly, he farmed at Mulu, grew strawberries for local sale, exported, mainly coffee and hides and skins, and for two years practised as an advocate.

In 1935, after Emperor Haile Selassie's accession to power and ensuing efforts to suppress slavery and the slave trade, the Ethiopian ruler appointed Sandford adviser to the Ethiopian governor of Maji. This territory, on the Kenyan border, was a major centre of the slave trade which the emperor wished to suppress, and was planned by him to become a model province. However, not long after Sandford's arrival there, fascist Italy began its brutal invasion of Ethiopia. Learning of the emperor's defeat and departure for Europe, Sandford made his way south to Kenya, and returned to England where, through his Church of England connections, he became appeals secretary for Guildford Cathedral.

At the outbreak of the Second World War Sandford joined the officers' emergency reserve, and was shortly afterwards sent to Cairo as a member of the Middle East intelligence centre. There, as an expert on Ethiopia, he was involved in planning British support for the Ethiopian patriots, who had been resisting the Italians for over four years. After Mussolini's declaration of war on Britain and France in June 1940, Sandford, then aged fifty-eight, entered Ethiopia's Gojjam province on 12 August with the rank of colonel as head of the British 'Mission 101'. Its object was to encourage and unify the efforts of the Ethiopian patriots, and thereby tie down the Italian forces. The latter then enjoyed considerable numerical superiority over the British and for a time seemed to threaten the entire British position in east Africa. Sandford's mission, though sometimes almost forgotten by the British higher commands in Cairo and Khartoum, was a considerable success: it laid the basis for the subsequent visit of another British officer, Colonel Orde Wingate, who was flown into Gojjam on 20 November 1940, and hence also for the emperor's arrival in the province from Sudan on 30 January 1941.

After Haile Selassie's return to Addis Ababa on 5 May 1941, and Wingate's departure shortly afterwards, Sandford became, unofficially, the emperor's principal foreign adviser. This was a difficult position in that the interests and policies of the British and Ethiopian governments often greatly diverged. Sandford's brother-in-law, Brigadier Maurice Lush, was then deputy British political officer for British-occupied Ethiopia, and Sandford's loyalties were inevitably divided. His position as adviser was, however, formalized in May of the following year when, following the signing of the Anglo-Ethiopian treaty of 31 January 1942, he was officially appointed adviser to the Ethiopian ministry of the interior. He was in 1945 made director-general of the Addis Ababa municipality, a position which he held until 1948.

Sandford retired from Ethiopian government service in 1948, devoting his energies thereafter to his farm at Mulu, which after the emperor's restoration had once again been leased to him. He also took an interest in Addis Ababa's English School (later the Sandford School), which his wife Christine had founded in 1942, and which was reckoned the best private secondary school in the country. He died on 22 January 1972 at his home, Mulu Farm, Ethiopia, and was buried on 24 January at the Commonwealth war cemetery in Addis Ababa, in the presence of the emperor.   RICHARD K. P. PANKHURST

Sources E. Casbon, *The incurable optimists: Chris and Dan Sandford* (1993) · D. Shirreff, *Bare feet and bandoliers: Wingate, Sandford, the patriots and the part they played in the liberation of Ethiopia* (1995) · A. Del Boca, *The Ethiopian war, 1935–1941*, trans. P. D. Cummins (1965) · K. Tasamma, *Ya-tarik mastowasha* (1970) [in Amharic] · A. Mockler, *Haile Selassie's war* (1984) · L. Mosley, *Haile Selassie: the conquering lion* (1964) · R. Pankhurst, 'The Ethiopian patriots and the collapse of Italian rule in east Africa', *Ethiopia Observer*, 12 (1969), 92–127 · C. Sykes, *Orde Wingate* (1959) · C. Sandford, *Ethiopia under Hailé Selassié* (1946) · C. Sandford, *The Lion of Judah hath prevailed, being the biography of His Imperial Majesty Haile Selassie* (1955) · M. Lush, *A life of service* (1992) · J. H. Spencer, *Ethiopia at bay: a personal account of the Haile Selassie years* (1984) · H. Boustead, *The wind of the morning: the autobiography of Hugh Boustead* (1971) · G. L. Steer, *Sealed and delivered: a book on the Abyssinian campaign* (1942) · D. Wright, 'Daniel Arthur Sandford', *Ethiopia Observer* (1972), 202–3 · personal knowledge (2004) · W. Thesiger, *The life of my choice* (1987) · m. cert. · d. cert. · *The Times* (24 Jan 1972) · WWW

Archives SOUND IWM SA, recorded talk

Sandford, Sir Daniel Keyte (1798–1838), classical scholar, born at Edinburgh on 3 February 1798, was the second son of Daniel *Sandford, bishop of Edinburgh, and his wife, Helen Frances Catherine, *née* Douglas (*d.* 1837); he was brother of John *Sandford. After a distinguished career at the high school and the University of Edinburgh, he entered Christ Church, Oxford, in 1817, graduating BA in 1820 with a first class in *literae humaniores* and MA in 1825; he was made an honorary DCL in 1833. In 1821 he won the chancellor's prize for an essay on the 'Study of modern history'. Having been unsuccessful in the open competition for a fellowship at Oriel College, he made some ill-judged criticisms of that college's elections in the *Edinburgh Review* (July 1821), which attracted an effective rejoinder from Augustus Hare.

In September 1821, in defiance of the test law—he was an Episcopalian—Sandford was appointed to succeed Professor Young in the Greek chair of Glasgow University. There he was identified with the controversial policy of enforcing the classics as a requirement for all students. He was considered an inspiring teacher of the senior classes: 'although only twenty-three years of age, he succeeded by skill and enthusiasm in awakening a love for Greek literature far beyond the bounds of his university'. In 1823 he married Henrietta Cecilia (*d.* 12 Feb 1878), only daughter of John Charnock.

During the controversy about Catholic emancipation Sandford hurried to Oxford in 1829 to vote for Sir Robert Peel, and was rewarded with a knighthood on 27 October 1830. At the time of the Reform Bill he abandoned Greek for politics, and made many brilliant speeches in the bill's favour at public meetings. On the passing of the bill he contested Glasgow City unsuccessfully in December 1832; but in March 1834 he was elected MP for Paisley. His appearances in the House of Commons were failures, his rhetoric, which had won admiration at the university, exciting only derision there. 'His politics were not self-consistent; he was a disciple of Hume in finance, and of Goulburn in antipathy to Jewish claims.' In January 1835 he resigned his seat and returned to Glasgow, where he died of typhus fever, after a week's illness, on 4 February 1838. He was buried at Rothesay.

Sandford wrote numerous Greek translations and brilliant papers in *Blackwood* and articles in the *Edinburgh Review*. He was a colleague of Thomas Thomson MD, and Allan Cunningham in the editorship of the *Popular Encyclopaedia*. Besides *Greek Rules and Exercises* and *Exercises from Greek Authors*, written for the use of his class, and *Introduction to the Writing of Greek* (1826), he translated *The Greek Grammar of Frederick Thiersch* (1830), and reprinted from the *Popular Encyclopaedia* an essay *On the Rise and Progress of Literature* (1848).

Sandford had three sons and seven daughters. The eldest son was Francis Richard John *Sandford; the third, Daniel Fox Sandford (1831–1906), was bishop of Tasmania from 1883 to 1889. **Sir Herbert Bruce Sandford** (1826–1892), army officer, the second son, was born on 13 August 1826. He entered Addiscombe College in 1842, and received a commission in the Bombay artillery in 1844, of which he became colonel in 1865. He proceeded to India, and was appointed (9 April 1848) assistant resident at Satara and first assistant commissioner there (1 May 1849). During the Indian mutiny his services were of great value. He was a special commissioner for the suppression of the mutinies (1857–8), and became the close associate and lifelong friend of Sir Bartle Frere. In 1860–61 he acted as special income-tax commissioner at Satara. He returned to England in 1861, and in 1862 he married his cousin Sarah Agnes, third daughter of James Edward Leslie of Leslie Hill, Antrim. Sandford was closely associated with the International Exhibition of 1862, English commissioner for the International Exhibition at Philadelphia in 1875, for that at Melbourne in 1881, and for that at Adelaide in 1887. His services on all these occasions won for him high opinions both in England and in the colonies, and he was knighted in 1877 and created a KCMG in 1889. He was assistant director of the South Kensington Museum in 1877–8. He died at his home, West Hill House, St Leonards, Sussex, on 31 January 1892.

GEORGE STRONACH, *rev.* M. C. CURTHOYS

Sources GM, 2nd ser., 9 (1838), 543 · Anderson, *Scot. nat.* · J. F. Waller, ed., *The imperial dictionary of universal biography*, 3 vols. (1857–63); new edn (1877–84) · R. D. Anderson, *Education and opportunity in Victorian Scotland: schools and universities* (1983) · 'Sandford, Herbert Bruce', *AusDB* · Boase, *Mod. Eng. biog.* [Herbert Bruce Sandford] · *CGPLA Eng. & Wales* (1892) [Herbert Bruce Sandford]
Archives Shrops. RRC, corresp. | BL, corresp. with Lord Holland, Add. MS 52014 · BL, letters to Macvey Napier, Add. MSS 34614–34618 *passim* · BL, letters to Sir Robert Peel, Add. MSS 40404–40423 *passim* · Lpool RO, letters to Lord Stanley · NL Scot., corresp. with Blackwoods
Likenesses A. Edouart, silhouette, 1830, Scot. NPG · portrait (Herbert Bruce Sandford), repro. in *ILN*, 69 (1876), 109, 110 · portrait (Herbert Bruce Sandford), repro. in *ILN* (13 Feb 1892), 197 · portrait (Herbert Bruce Sandford), repro. in *The Graphic*, 13 (1876), 552
Wealth at death £5511 0s. 6d.—Herbert Bruce Sandford: will, 1892

Sandford [*née* Poole], **Elizabeth** (1797/8–1853), domestic moralist, was the daughter of Richard Poole. In the early 1820s she married John *Sandford (1801–1873), who became archdeacon of Coventry in 1851. They had at least five sons, the eldest of whom was Henry Ryder Poole Sandford (1826–1883), an inspector of schools. Elizabeth Sandford died on 15 September 1853 at the rectory at Dunchurch, near Rugby, where her husband was then vicar.

In 1831 Sandford published *Woman in her Social and Domestic Character*, an advice book 'written exclusively for her own sex' (*Woman*, advertisement). Believing that 'domestic comfort' was the chief source of female influence, Sandford argued that women, inferior by nature to men, should devote themselves to the duties of the domestic sphere, fortifying themselves with religion and the cultivation of an elegant mind. The book was reviewed in the *London Evangelical Magazine* and the *Christian Examiner* and sold well, reaching a sixth edition by 1839. Her next work, *Female Worthies* (1833), was intended to be the first of a series of volumes containing biographies of virtuous women from English history who exemplified Sandford's ideal of womanhood. However, only the first volume, which contained the lives of Lady Jane Grey and Lucy Hutchinson, ever appeared. *Female Improvement* (1836), another advice book, was an expanded version of her first work: Sandford not only included chapters on subjects such as temper, taste, and study but also reflections on stages in women's domestic lives, including courtship, early marriage, and motherhood. The critic of *The Spectator* viewed the work with cool approbation, commenting that Sandford's observations appeared to be 'the result of experience and mature reflection, and [were] distinguished by amiability and good sense, pervaded by strong religious feeling' (*The Spectator*, 636). Elizabeth Sandford's advocacy of a primarily domestic role for women and her support for the ideology of the separate spheres makes her a significant precursor of Sarah Stickney Ellis and other female writers of advice works in the 1830s and 1840s.   ROSEMARY MITCHELL

Sources Boase, *Mod. Eng. biog.* • *GM*, 2nd ser., 40 (1853), 538 • Allibone, *Dict.* • review, *The Spectator* (2 June 1836), 636 • d. cert.

Sandford, Francis (1630–1694), herald and genealogist, was born at Carnow Castle, co. Wicklow, Ireland, the third son of Francis Sandford of Sandford, Shropshire, and his wife, Elizabeth, daughter of Chalcot Chambre of Williamscot, Oxfordshire. Although his ancestors had long been seated in Shropshire his birthplace and childhood home belonged to his maternal grandfather. In 1641 Sandford fled from the rebellion in Ireland to Shropshire, where 'he had no other education than what the grammar schools afforded' (Wood, *Ath. Oxon.: Fasti*, 2.288). He may have returned to Ireland in the late 1640s or 1650s, as he apparently graduated BA from Trinity College, Dublin. By 1662 he was married to Margaret, widow of William Kerry and daughter of William Jokes of Buttington, Montgomeryshire, with whom he had at least five children.

On 6 June 1661 Sandford became Rouge Dragon pursuivant in the College of Arms, an office he purchased from William Crowne. In this capacity he acted as a deputy for Dugdale, travelling the realm to make visitations that corrected and extended those compiled before the civil wars. His first book appeared shortly after his appointment as a herald, being *A Genealogical History of the Kings of Portugal* (London, 1662), a translation of the French text of 1623 by Scevole and Louis de Saincte-Marthe. The first of his published tributes to the royal family, it celebrated the marriage of Charles II and Catherine of Braganza in May 1662 and included a detailed account of the new queen's arrival and wedding. At the command of the king Sandford next produced *The order of ceremonies used for, and at, the solemn interment of the most high, mighty and most noble Prince George duke of Albemarle* (London, 1670). This was a detailed account of Albemarle's death, lying-in-state, funeral, and burial, and was chiefly composed of twenty folio engravings depicting the long funeral procession, including a portrait of Sandford himself.

From 1670 to 1673 Sandford was occupied by planning the rebuilding of the College of Arms in the wake of the great fire of London. He had earlier made a survey of the destroyed city with Wenceslaus Hollar at the king's

Francis Sandford (1630–1694), by George Vertue (after unknown artist, *c*.1680)

request. On 16 November 1676 he was appointed Lancaster herald, shortly before his major scholarly work was published, *A genealogical history of the kings of England and monarchs of Great Britain … from the conquest, anno 1066, to the year 1677* (London, 1677; reissued 1683; 2nd edn with continuations by Samuel Stebbing, 1707). Although the *History* contained no new information it brought together the bulk of royal genealogical knowledge and provided illustrations of royal tombs and portraits, becoming the key reference work on the subject.

Following the accession of James II, Sandford worked for two years with his fellow herald Gregory King to produce a record of the coronation rituals, published as *The History of the Coronation of … James II … and of his Royal Consort Queen Mary* (London, 1687; CD-ROM edn 1999). This magnificent work incorporated twenty-seven lavish engravings of the sumptuous feasts, processions, and fireworks in a style previously unseen in the British Isles. To Sandford's misfortune the book appeared on the eve of the revolution, and despite a gift of £300 from James II the authors barely cleared their expenses. Sandford conscientiously refused to attend the new monarchs William and Mary, and in 1689 sold his office as Lancaster herald to Gregory King for £220. John Gibbon claimed that King attempted to deceive a number of heralds into so doing by playing on the uncertainty of the times.

Throughout his life Sandford was dogged by financial

problems, despite occasional royal gifts of money, yet he managed to produce some of the most beautifully illustrated and systematically organized works of the late seventeenth century. He died on 17 January 1694 in Newgate prison where he had been imprisoned for debt, and was buried in St Bride's churchyard, Fleet Street.

PETER SHERLOCK

Sources A. Wagner, *Heralds of England: a history of the office and College of Arms* (1967) · M. Noble, *A history of the College of Arms* (1804), 322–4 · Wood, *Ath. Oxon.: Fasti* (1820), 288
Archives BL, Shropshire pedigrees, Add. MS 28616 · CUL, genealogy of Lord Yarmouth, Add. 6968 · Shrops. RRC, additions to a pedigree of the Sandford family
Likenesses G. Vertue, pencil drawing (after unknown artist, c.1680), NPG [*see illus.*] · engraving, repro. in F. Sandford, *The order and ceremonies used for … the solemn interment of George, duke of Albemarle* (1670)

Sandford, Francis Richard John, Baron Sandford (1824–1893), civil servant, was born in Glasgow on 14 May 1824, the eldest of the three sons and seven daughters of Sir Daniel Keyte *Sandford (1798–1838), professor of Greek at the University of Glasgow, and his wife, Henrietta Cecilia (d. 1878), *née* Charnock. After attending Glasgow high school and the privately run Grange School at Sunderland he entered Glasgow University, and went from there, as a Snell exhibitioner, to Balliol College, Oxford. Having matriculated in 1842, he took a first in Greats in 1846. After one year teaching privately and a second at the Grange School, the close links between Jowett's Balliol and the education department of the privy council office secured his appointment as an examiner there at the end of 1848. His marriage to Margaret (d. 1905), fourth daughter of Robert Findlay, followed on 1 August 1849.

Almost all Sandford's civil service career was spent at the education department. In 1854 he was promoted assistant under-secretary. After brief secondment to serve as organizing secretary to the International Exhibition 1861–2, he went as assistant under-secretary to the Colonial Office in November 1868, but returned to the education department in January 1870 as permanent secretary. There he remained until 1884, adding to his responsibilities for elementary education in England and Wales parallel responsibilities for Scotland in 1873, and taking charge also of the Department of Science and Art at South Kensington from 1874. In January 1884 he became a charity commissioner and from 1885 to 1887 served as the first permanent under-secretary to the newly created Scottish Office. With these posts went appropriate honours. Knighted in 1863, Sandford became CB in 1871 and KCB in 1879; he was sworn of the privy council in 1885. He entered the Lords as Baron Sandford of Sandford in January 1891, but his title died with him, as he and his wife, who survived him, had no children.

Sandford's career trajectory is a perfect early example of that of the successful civil servant—a highly competent administrator, carefully neutral and expecting to serve successive governments whatever their political hue. The education department proved a particularly testing environment. Formally it had two political masters, the lord president of the council and the vice-president of the

committee of council on education. In addition, the period following 1870 was one of unprecedented expansion but also one of intense controversy. Less abrasive than his fellow Balliol man and predecessor as permanent secretary, R. R. W. Lingen, Sandford negotiated both personal and administrative minefields with considerable skill, his meticulous, almost fussy, attention to detail serving him well.

The 1870 Education Act represented the first commitment to a national network of elementary schools in England and Wales. Previously the grants administered by the education department had gone to support pre-existing local voluntary schools. These schools were overwhelmingly denominational in character, the largest single group being schools affiliated to the Anglican National Society. The act allowed voluntary schools to continue; but in areas where there were no such schools or a majority of rate-payers wanted further school provision, new directly elected local authorities—school boards—were created, with powers to draw on the rates to build and run additional schools. It was a complex dual system, complex not only to set up but also to run, entailing vastly increased expenditure and an enlarged central government bureaucracy; the system was, in addition, perpetually beset by the hostility of nonconformists to the pretensions of the established church and the anxieties and suspicions of Anglicans towards the competition of the new boards and their schools.

Leaving office in February 1874 the Liberal vice-president, W. E. Forster, wrote of Sandford's excellent work in implementing the 1870 act, adding 'if my successor be not specially moderate and sensible, education will come to grief … Sandford would be a check to that' (Forster to W. E. Gladstone, 13 Feb 1874, BL, Add. MS 44157). While at the education department Sandford conducted himself with great circumspection. But once he left in 1884 his commitment to the protection of Anglican voluntary schools, and thus to their staunch defenders within the Conservative Party, emerged. It marked all of his contributions to the work of the royal commission on the Elementary Education Acts chaired by Lord Cross 1886–8, on which he served, and he was conspiratorially eager to share advance intelligence about policy with others, such as the third Earl Harrowby, who felt as passionately about church schools as he did. In the Lords Sandford spoke only on educational issues, and was prominent in the attack on the Liberal government's efforts to bring about the upgrading of voluntary school buildings in 1893. He died at his home in London, 26 Gloucester Terrace, Hyde Park, on 31 December 1893, and was buried at Sandford in Shropshire on 5 January the following year.

GILLIAN SUTHERLAND

Sources *DNB* · G. Sutherland, *Policy-making in elementary education, 1870–1895* (1973) · R. Johnson, 'Administrators in education before 1870: patronage, social position and role', *Studies in the growth of nineteenth-century government*, ed. G. Sutherland (1972), 110–38 · *The Times* (2 Jan 1894), 3 · *The Times* (6 Jan 1894) · Burke, *Peerage* · W. H. G. Armytage, 'Francis Richard John Sandford, first Baron Sandford, 1824–1894', *Bulletin of the John Rylands University Library*, 31 (1948), 110–19 · H. J. Hanham, 'The creation of the Scottish office, 1881–7',

Juridical Review, new ser., 10 (1965), 205–44 · BL, Gladstone MSS, Add. MS 44157, fols. 106–7
Archives NRA Scotland, priv. coll., corresp. and family papers · Shrops. RRC, family papers | Sandon Hall, Staffordshire, Harrowby MSS · University of Sheffield, Mundella MSS
Likenesses Dalziel, woodcut, BM; repro. in *What do you think of the exhibition* (1862) · R. T., wood-engraving, NPG; repro. in *ILN* (17 Jan 1891) · wood-engraving, repro. in *ILN*, 40 (22 March 1862), 282, 296
Wealth at death £2931 9s. 5d.: probate, 23 Feb 1894, *CGPLA Eng. & Wales*

Sandford, Fulk of [Fulk Basset] (d. **1271**), archbishop of Dublin, was the nephew of Sir Philip *Basset (d. 1271), and therefore the son of either Fulk *Basset (d. 1259), bishop of London, or of Gilbert *Basset (d. 1241). He was occasionally called Basset but more often referred to as Fulk of Sandford, the toponym also applied to his brother John. In 1244 he was appointed to the archdeaconry of Middlesex by his episcopal relative, the bishop of London. This date would imply that Fulk was probably born before 1225, since the minimum canonical age for a deacon was nineteen. Fulk was also prebendary of Ealdland in St Paul's Cathedral and held the treasurership there from at least 1252 until he was appointed archbishop of Dublin in 1256.

Unlike his English predecessors in Dublin who owed their promotion to their good standing with the king, Fulk owed his elevation to his influence at the papal curia. He was in Rome in 1256 when Pope Alexander IV quashed the election of Ralph of Norwich who had been chosen by the two Dublin chapters. Fulk was informed on 19 July 1256 of his election to the see of Dublin and a week later Pope Alexander wrote advising the two chapters that he had provided the treasurer of St Paul's to the see, and describing him as a noble, lettered, and honest man, circumspect in both spiritual and temporal affairs.

Fulk arrived in Dublin in late October or early November 1256 and was consecrated almost immediately. His first action was to undertake a visitation of the Dublin province. It is likely that this was the first such visitation and it resulted in a flood of litigation. This set the tone for Fulk's episcopacy for he was an active and contentious ecclesiastic who took his pastoral responsibilities towards his province seriously. He was the first of the English archbishops of Dublin who, when resident, devoted virtually all his time and energy to diocesan affairs. He was also the first archbishop of Dublin to have been provided by the Holy See. He retained close links with Rome, receiving constant support both from Alexander IV and Urban IV. The archbishop realized early in his episcopacy that certain of his actions were likely to provoke hostility and in the summer of 1257 he asked Pope Alexander to allow him to choose a confessor who would be allowed to absolve him if necessary from sentences of excommunication that he might incur. The pope granted Fulk this privilege in July 1257.

In 1259 Fulk had to return to Rome in connection with a dispute with the Cistercian prior and convent of Baltinglass who objected to the archbishop's visitation of their chapels. While in Rome the archbishop also complained to the pope that his ecclesiastical jurisdiction in Dublin was being infringed by the secular authorities, chiefly the justiciar of Ireland and his officials. Pope Alexander wrote three letters to ecclesiastics in Ireland asking them to intervene in Dublin and protect the archbishop's rights. After Fulk returned to Ireland his case was taken up by the new pope, Urban IV, who in November 1261 wrote to King Henry and the Lord Edward repeating the charges levelled by Fulk against the Irish justiciar. Urban also wrote to prominent English churchmen asking them to intervene. There is no evidence that a settlement was reached, and in the following years the papacy responded to continuing complaints from Fulk concerning encroachments of his spiritual jurisdiction.

Given his poor relations with the secular authorities it is surprising to find that in 1265, during the period of crisis in Irish affairs that followed the capture of the justiciar Richard de la Rochelle, Fulk was asked to take over custody of Ireland, either by Henry III or by the Montfortian council. He appears to have held this office for a short period. It is the only recorded duty that he performed on behalf of the royal administration in Ireland.

Shortly after this Fulk became embroiled in perhaps the most serious dispute of his episcopacy. The conflict was with the mayor and citizens of Dublin and concerned the amount of customary payments to be made to the Dublin church as well as attempts by the citizens to limit the archbishop's exercise of spiritual jurisdiction. In 1266 Fulk excommunicated the mayor and citizens and laid an interdict on Dublin before leaving to consult with the papal legate Cardinal Ottobuono in London. Ottobuono supported his action and confirmed his sentence. The interdict was probably in effect for the best part of a year. There is no record of its lifting but nine months after the papal legate's letter, in November 1267, an agreement was reached between the archbishop (represented by his attorney John of Sandford) and the citizens over one of the matters at issue, namely the limitation of public penance.

In April 1267 letters of protection had been issued to Fulk to cover his pilgrimage to Santiago de Compostela. During his absence from Dublin his brother John of Sandford acted as his official. The archbishop was back in his diocese by August 1270 when he was granted the privilege by the king that after his decease his executors might have easements in the manors and pastures of his see for six months. Fulk died early in 1271, before June, and was buried in St Patrick's Cathedral. A late thirteenth-century tomb effigy in St Patrick's has been identified as belonging to either Fulk or John of Sandford.

Many of the records of Fulk's episcopacy deal with arrangements and agreements concerning the sale and rental of lands of his see and the collection of debts. This activity was no doubt connected with the archbishop's efforts to pay off a large debt to Italian merchant bankers which he may have contracted before coming to Dublin or during his long stay at the papal curia. In 1266 Fulk paid £100 to one merchant and 550 marks to another.

Fulk's episcopacy was contentious but there is no doubting this archbishop's energy or concern for spiritual affairs. It is likely that the majority of the undated synodal canons transcribed into the thirteenth-century register

Crede mihi belong to his episcopacy. One third of the collection of statutes has been positively ascribed to his episcopacy and the case for including the rest appears to be strong. Taken together they form a most important source for religious practice in the Dublin diocese and province in the thirteenth century and provide evidence for the attempts Fulk of Sandford made to raise the religious standards of the lower clergy and dispense instruction to them.   MARGARET MURPHY

Sources M. Murphy, 'The archbishops and administration of the diocese and province of Dublin, 1181–1298', PhD diss., TCD, 1987 · M. P. Sheehy, ed., *Pontificia Hibernica: medieval papal chancery documents concerning Ireland, 640–1261*, 2 vols. (1962–5) · H. S. Sweetman and G. F. Handcock, eds., *Calendar of documents relating to Ireland*, 5 vols., PRO (1875–86) · C. McNeill, ed., *Calendar of Archbishop Alen's register, c.1172–1534* (1950) · M. Murphy, 'Ecclesiastical censures: an aspect of their use in thirteenth century Dublin', *Archivium Hibernicum*, 44 (1989), 89–97 · *DNB* · J. T. Gilbert, ed., *Historic and municipal documents of Ireland, AD 1172–1320, from the archives of the city of Dublin*, Rolls Series, 53 (1870) · A. Gwynn, ed., 'Provincial and diocesan decrees of the diocese of Dublin during the Anglo-Norman period', *Archivium Hibernicum*, 11 (1944), 31–117 · C. R. Cheney, 'A group of related synodal statutes of the thirteenth century', *Medieval studies presented to Aubrey Gwynn*, ed. J. A. Watt, J. B. Morrall, and F. X. Martin (1961), 114–32 · J. Hunt, *Irish medieval figure sculpture, 1200–1600*, 2 vols. (1974)

Sandford, Sir Herbert Bruce (1826–1892). *See under* Sandford, Sir Daniel Keyte (1798–1838).

Sandford, James. *See* Sanford, James (*fl.* 1567–1582).

Sandford, John of (*d.* 1294), administrator and archbishop of Dublin, was of illegitimate birth and has traditionally been regarded as the brother of Fulk of *Sandford, archbishop of Dublin, although he was not described as Fulk's brother in any contemporary source. This connection, if true, would have linked him with the Basset family of High Wycombe, Buckinghamshire. He was the only thirteenth-century archbishop of Dublin whose career before his elevation to the see was firmly rooted in Ireland, and who had experience in the administration of the Dublin church.

Having obtained a master's degree (probably at Oxford), John appeared in the service of Fulk of Sandford in Dublin as early as November 1267 when he was described as the vicar-general of the diocese. Fulk left his diocese in John's charge when he was on pilgrimage in Santiago de Compostela and John continued to represent the archbishop up to the latter's death in 1271. In these years John collected an impressive list of benefices which were detailed in a papal document of 1284. Although still in sub-deacon's orders he held a prebend in St Patrick's, Dublin, the treasurership of the cathedral of Ferns, and the churches of Cavendish in Suffolk and Loughborough in Leicestershire. Because his illegitimacy stood in the way of ecclesiastical advancement, he had obtained a dispensation from Pope Gregory X which allowed him to hold benefices to the value of £500 and be promoted to the episcopate. On accepting the deanery of St Patrick's in 1275 he resigned the treasurership of Ferns.

It was also during these years that Sandford began his long and illustrious career in the Irish administration. His first position was as escheator of Ireland, an office which he held from September 1271. As escheator Sandford was one of the most important ministers. He was a leading member of the king's council and the immediate representative of the king in relation to the Irish church. His duties took him all over Ireland and he fulfilled them faithfully for almost fourteen years. With very few breaks the records show him continually involved in the business of taking into the king's hand, administering, and restoring lands and ecclesiastical temporalities. Sandford's period as escheator was very successful and when he handed over the office to his successor in August 1285 there had been a sharp rise in the issues. Further evidence of his efficiency can be inferred from the 1284 inquiry into the Irish administration, when the escheatorship was the only office which was stated to be functioning properly and in no need of reform.

During this period Sandford showed himself to be particularly successful at raising money for the king in other ways. In 1282 he was appointed to find funds for the Welsh campaigns, and succeeded in raising £1000. He also helped the citizens of Dublin to charter ships and transfer victuals and supplies to the king's camps at Flint and Rhuddlan in Wales. In the meantime he was also acquiring estates for himself. In April 1279 John de Bohun enfeoffed him with the manor of Ballymaden (in what is now co. Dublin) and lands and a castle in Castlecomer (Kilkenny), and in November of the same year Bohun was given licence to sell all his Irish lands to Sandford. By virtue of a royal licence to make grants of 'wastes', the justiciar Robert Ufford granted to Sandford land in Roscommon amounting to 35 carucates. About the same time, he obtained other Connacht lands from Richard fitz John, son of the former justiciar John fitz Geoffrey.

When Sandford was promoted to the deanery of St Patrick's in 1275 the chapter was involved in the most persistent of its disputes with Holy Trinity over the election of an archbishop to succeed Fulk of Sandford. Both chapters had sent candidates to Rome and neither was prepared to stand down. Sandford does not appear to have taken any part in the dispute, which ended in 1279 with the provision of the Dominican John of Darlington. However, during his ten-year tenure of the deanship he succeeded in establishing cordial relations with Holy Trinity, and it was under his guidance in 1284 that the two chapters came together to appoint a joint custodian of the spiritualities of the newly vacant see of Dublin. Having received licence to elect a new pastor in 1284, the two chapters were in unique agreement and elected Sandford. Canons from both chapters accompanied him to Rome and stood by him in the face of papal objections to his illegitimacy, re-electing him and finally receiving papal confirmation on 30 May 1285. He was consecrated in Dublin on 7 August 1286 in Holy Trinity.

Sandford held the archbishopric until his death in 1294, but the records contain little evidence of his ecclesiastical preoccupations. In truth, spiritual matters could have taken up only a small proportion of his time between 1285 and 1292 when he was resident in Ireland. It was during these years, however, that he became the most important figure in Irish politics and the person around whom the Irish administration revolved.

On the death of the justiciar Stephen of Fulbourn in July 1288, Sandford and Geoffrey de Geneville declared themselves guardians of the country and a little later Sandford was appointed keeper of Ireland, a position which he accepted 'out of reverence for the king and the people'. The archbishop's tenure of the office was brief but notably successful. He was faced with two pressing problems: first, the increasing rebelliousness of the Irish in various parts of the country, which was threatening the stability of the colony, and second, the growing inefficiency and corruption of local government, which was causing distrust and dissatisfaction among the populace. He set about tackling these problems with remarkable vigour and his efforts can be fully appreciated by the fortunate survival of a long account detailing his journeys to different parts of Ireland and his expenses during the years 1288–90.

The account shows Sandford and his retinue constantly on the move, traversing the country on military and diplomatic missions. This was a period of great instability, when the Gaelic revival was beginning to take hold of areas close to the heart of colonial Ireland. Particularly worrying for the governor was the resurgence of conflict in Laois and Offaly, where his ally John fitz Thomas Fitzgerald, the new lord of Offaly, was coming under increasing pressure. In 1288 Sandford called a royal service and launched a massive attack upon the midlands Irish, beginning a war which lasted for more than a year. In the course of the campaign he set up a vast warding system, which at its greatest stretched from Athlone to Kilkenny. It has been suggested that the archbishop's attempts to maintain stability in this critical region, which frequently went beyond a chief governor's usual response to an emergency, were partly motivated by his personal commitment to Fitzgerald. However, it is undeniable that the midlands Irish had become a considerable threat, one which could only be met by expenditure of a great deal of time and money. Alongside his military activities Sandford was addressing the problem of discontent with local officials, by proclaiming that all complaining of the king's ministers were to come before him at appointed places 'to receive justice'. The chief governor's ability to execute his decisions with speed and efficiency was facilitated by the fact that during the years 1289 to 1291 he also held the office of chancellor.

In 1290 Sandford held parliaments in Dublin and Kilkenny, and it is clear that the strains of his office were beginning to show. After eighteen months of campaigns he wrote to the king, begging him to take counsel concerning the affairs of Ireland and complaining that he had received no money for his expenses, with the result that he was in debt to Italian merchants. Edward replied that he had no time at present to devote to Irish affairs and that the justiciar would be reimbursed as soon as possible. However, shortly afterwards, a new justiciar, William de

Vescy, was appointed, although Sandford continued to act as chancellor until March 1291.

There is no reason why Sandford should have been replaced in these offices unless he had requested it himself; his loyalty to the king was unquestioned, as was the success of his campaigns. In a short space of time he had managed to stem the tide of rebellion which threatened to engulf the colony. To his contemporaries it seemed that he had permanently established peace in the critical midland region. This was not to prove the case, however: the chief governor's warding system could only continue to work by massive inputs of cash. This financial help was not forthcoming, and in the 1290s the 'land of peace' continued to be eroded. Sandford attempted to warn the crown about the consequences of continued inaction towards Ireland, but quickly realized that his pleas were falling on deaf ears.

Having been relieved of his duties in Ireland, Sandford travelled to England. He was in Reading in June 1292, when he granted an indulgence of forty days to all who visited and subscribed to the church of St Mary and St James there. Later that year he was present at the proceedings concerning the future of the Scottish crown; he attended the final judgment at Berwick and witnessed Balliol's oath of fealty to Edward at Norham. In May 1293 Sandford was present at the consecration of William March as bishop of Bath and Wells, and his servants were involved in a brawl with the men of the bishop of Ely on their way back from the festivities.

In September 1293 Sandford officiated at the marriage of the king's daughter Eleanor. The following year he was sent with Antony (I) Bek, bishop of Durham, to seek an alliance with Adolph von Nassau against the French. The ambassadors were successful and a treaty was signed at Nuremberg. On arriving back in England, Sandford contracted a fatal illness and died in Great Yarmouth on 2 October 1294. The canons of St Patrick's, Dublin, asked for his body, which was conveyed to Ireland and buried in 1295 in St Patrick's Cathedral.

John of Sandford spent in all about six years of his episcopacy in Ireland and the majority of this time he spent outside his diocese of Dublin. It is clear that the demands of his secular office left him little time for the spiritual concerns of his diocese. He did exert himself to obtain privileges from the pope, so that the ills which his diocese had suffered because of the conflicts in Ireland were remedied, but the day-to-day running of his church he left in the hands of his officials. The long vacancy which followed Fulk of Sandford's death, followed by the absenteeism of Archbishop Darlington, meant that the ecclesiastical administration of the diocese and province had for a long time been in the hands of such officials. Sandford himself had been a part of this administrative machine, and he presumably felt confidence in its abilities to ensure that the spiritual concerns of the diocese were being attended to.

James Ware described John of Sandford as a prelate with a great reputation for learning and wisdom, but the records which survive suggest that his most noteworthy qualities were his organizational ability and his loyalty and zeal in pursuing the affairs of the king in Ireland.

MARGARET MURPHY

Sources M. Murphy, 'The archbishops and administration of the diocese and province of Dublin, 1181–1298', PhD diss., TCD, 1987, chap. 6 • T. W. Moody and others, eds., *A new history of Ireland*, 2: *Medieval Ireland, 1169–1534* (1987) • exchequer, queen's remembrancer, accounts various, PRO, E 101/231/9 • C. Ó Cleirigh, 'The problem of defence: a regional case-study', *Law and disorder in thirteenth-century Ireland*, ed. J. Lydon (1997), 25–56 • Emden, *Oxf.*, 3.2213 • H. G. Richardson and G. O. Sayles, *The administration of Ireland, 1172–1377* (1963) • H. S. Sweetman and G. F. Handcock, eds., *Calendar of documents relating to Ireland*, 5 vols., PRO (1875–86), vol. 3 • G. J. Hand, 'The rivalry of the cathedral chapters in medieval Dublin', *Journal of the Royal Society of Antiquaries of Ireland*, 92 (1962), 193–206 • *Ann. mon.*, 3.389 • J. T. Gilbert, ed., *Chartularies of St Mary's Abbey, Dublin: with the register of its house at Dunbrody and annals of Ireland*, 2 vols., Rolls Series, 80 (1884)

Archives PRO, account of his expenses while chief governor of Ireland, E 101/231/9

Sandford, John (*c.*1565–1629), poet and grammarian, was the son of Richard Sandford, gentleman, of Chard, Somerset, where he was born. He entered Magdalen College, Oxford, as a commoner about 16 October 1581, and graduated BA from Balliol on 17 December 1586 and MA on 27 May 1595. In 1592 he acted as 'corrector Typograph' to the press at Oxford. In 1593 he became rector of Guildford Holy Trinity, and was elected chaplain of Magdalen College, a post he retained until 1616, but more than once he was censured for absenting himself from public worship.

Sandford obtained a reputation as a writer of Latin verse within and without the university. John Lane reckoned him on a level with Daniel, describing them jointly as the 'two swans' of Somerset, and John Davies of Hereford eulogized him in a sonnet appended to *The Scourge of Folly* (1611, p. 215). Sandford's earliest publication, *Appolinis et Musarum Euktika Eidyllia in serenissimæ Reginae Elizabethae … adventum*, was published in Oxford in 1592 by his most frequent printer, John Barnes. It describes in Latin verse the banquet given by the president and fellows of Magdalen to Queen Elizabeth's retinue on the occasion of her visit to Oxford on 22 September 1592.

Sandford also contributed the Latin hexameter verse 'In obitum clarissimi herois, domini Arthuri Greij' to a funeral sermon by Thomas Sparke on Lord Grey of Wilton in the winter of 1593, and 'In funebria nob. et praest. equitis D. Henrici Unton' (1596), printed in *Academiae Oxoniensis funebre officium in mort. Eliz. Reginae* (1603, sig. E3). Sandford's Latin and French commendatory verses preface John Davies's *Microcosmos* (1603, sig. A4v); Thomas Winter's translation of Du Bartas, *The Third Dayes Creation* (1604) and *The Second Day of the First Weeke* (1603); and Thomas Godwin's *Romanae historiae anthologia* (1614).

Sandford's prose works include an exploration of the afflictions exercised by God upon his children and of contemporary weaknesses in faith, a sermon which Sandford was prevented from delivering by a recurrent infirmity. In 1610 he printed a translation, corrected and reviewed by the author himself, of Pierre du Moulin, titled *A Defence of the Catholicke Faith*. After dedicating the text to King James,

Sandford urged readers that du Moulin's expressions of fidelity and zeal were worthy of sustained 'study and Meditation' (sig. A4v). Less problematically, he also produced French, Latin, and Italian grammars: *Le guichet fran-çois, sive, Janicula et brevis introductio ad linguam Gallicam* (1604); *A briefe extract of the former Latin grammar, done into English for the easier instruction of the learner* (1605), dedicated to his former pupil William, son of Arthur, Lord Grey of Wilton; and *A Grammar, or Introduction to the Italian Tongue* (1605). The last of these was dedicated to Magdalen College, Oxford.

In 1610 Sandford travelled as chaplain to Sir John Digby, later first earl of Bristol, during his embassy to Madrid. Hopeful of obtaining an acceptable settlement for English merchants and negotiating a marriage between Prince Henry and the infanta Anne, the party departed on 20 March 1611. Possibly it was not Sandford's first visit, since he prepared *Propylaion, or, Entrance to the Spanish Tongue* (1611) for the use of the ambassador's party: 'I have added this Grammar … chiefly for such whose company and conversation I am likely to have into Spaine' (Sandford, 64). The Bodleian Library copy is dedicated to Lady Beatrice Digby, though William Langton is the most usual addressee. Sandford corresponded with Sir Thomas Edmondes from 6 March 1610 to 21 April 1613 on the progress of the embassy, its controversial adherence to Calvinism, and Jesuitical activities in Spain (BL, Stowe MSS). He had previously resided in his household.

On 2 December 1614, when Sandford wrote to Edmondes, ambassador at Paris, to console him on Lady Edmondes's death, he was at Lambeth, acting as domestic chaplain to George Abbot, Calvinist archbishop of Canterbury. The latter soon after (1615) presented him to a prebend in Canterbury Cathedral and to the rectories of Ivy-church, in Romney Marsh, and Blackmanstone (June 1614), also in Kent. On 27 October 1621 Sandford was presented to Snave in the same county, which he held until his death on 24 September 1629. He was buried in Canterbury Cathedral.

CHARLOTTE FELL-SMITH, *rev.* ELIZABETH HARESNAPE

Sources STC, 1475–1640 • Foster, *Alum. Oxon.*, 1500–1714 [John Sanforde] • F. Madan, *The early Oxford press: a bibliography of printing and publishing in Oxford, 1468–1640*, OHS, 29 (1895), vol. 1 of *Oxford books: a bibliography of printed works* (1895–1931), 34, 35, 60, 62, 63, 96 • CSP dom., 1611–18, 261 • *Catalogue of the Stowe manuscripts in the British Museum*, 1 (1895) [Stowe MSS 171, fol. 370, 172, fols. 154, 226, 173, fol. 188, 174, fol. 19] • P. A. Welsby, *George Abbot, the unwanted archbishop* (1962) • J. Sandford, *The Spanish grammar, or, An entrance to the undertaking of the Spanish tongue* (1633), 64 • J. Le Neve, *Fasti ecclesiae anglicanae* (1716), 53–4 • E. Hasted, *The history and topographical survey of the county of Kent*, 3 (1790), 432, 497, 500; 4 (1799), 613 • [T. Birch and R. F. Williams], eds., *The court and times of James the First*, 1 (1848), 105–6 • BL, Lansdowne MS 984, fol. 120 • C. Plummer, ed., *Elizabethan Oxford: reprints of rare tracts*, OHS, 8 (1887), 275–300 • J. R. Bloxam, *A register of the presidents, fellows … of Saint Mary Magdalen College*, 8 vols. (1853–85), vol. 2, pp. lxxxiii, lxxxv, 129–32

Sandford, John (1801–1873), Church of England clergyman, born on 22 March 1801 in Alvechurch, Worcestershire, was the third son of Daniel *Sandford, bishop of Edinburgh, and his wife, Helena Frances Catherine, *née* Douglas (*d.* 1837). Sir Daniel Keyte *Sandford was an elder brother. He was educated at the high school, Edinburgh, and Glasgow University, before matriculating from Balliol College, Oxford, in 1820. He graduated BA in 1824, with a first class in *literae humaniores*, and proceeded MA in 1841 and BD in 1845. Ordained in 1824, he was appointed chaplain to the marquess of Queensberry in the following year. On 23 August 1825 he married, at Wells, Elizabeth, daughter of Richard J. Poole of Sherborne. Elizabeth *Sandford became a notable author of tracts on domestic morality. Sandford was appointed successively to the vicarage of Chillingham, Northumberland (1827), the chaplaincy of Long Acre, London, and the rectories of Dunchurch (1836) and Grimley with Hallow (1853). He held the rectory of Alvechurch near Bromsgrove from 1854 until his death. In 1844 he was named honorary canon of Worcester, and was warden of Queen's College, Birmingham, from 1853. In 1851 he became archdeacon of Coventry in the same diocese, being also examining chaplain to the bishop of Worcester from 1853 to 1860. Following the death of his first wife in 1853 Sandford married in 1856 Anna, widow of Lord David Erskine (*d.* 1855) and eldest daughter of William Cunninghame Graham of Gartmore, Stirling. In 1861 he delivered the Bampton lectures at Oxford, published as *The Mission and Extension of the Church at Home* (1862). Besides sermons, lectures, and charges Sandford published *Remains of Bishop Sandford* (1830) and works on aspects of theology, church life, and social reform.

Sandford was an active member of the lower house of convocation, and was chair of its committees on intemperance and on the preparation of a church hymnal. His report on the former subject was the first step towards the formation of the Church of England Temperance Society. In 1863–4 he was a member of the commission for the revision of clerical subscription, being himself an advocate of relaxation. He served on the committee of the lower house that in 1865 produced a report on the subject matter and means of theological training. He praised the work of the theological colleges, but advocated his practice of placing graduate candidates under the superintendence of an incumbent. In politics he was a Liberal. Among his close friends was Archbishop Tait.

Sandford died at Alvechurch, Worcestershire, on 22 March 1873, leaving five sons and two daughters. His eldest son, Henry Ryder Poole Sandford (1827–1883), an inspector of schools from 1862, wrote pamphlets dealing with labour and education in the Potteries, and married a daughter of Gabriel Stone Poole, a cousin of Thomas Poole; she published *Thomas Poole and his Friends* (2 vols., 1888). The second son, Charles Waldegrave Sandford (1828–1903), became censor of Christ Church, Oxford, and bishop of Gibraltar in 1874; the third, John Douglas Sandford (1833–1892), became chief judge in Mysore. The fifth son, Ernest Grey (1839–1910), was archdeacon of Exeter from 1888 to 1909.

G. LE G. NORGATE, rev. ELLIE CLEWLOW

Sources Boase, *Mod. Eng. biog.* · Foster, *Alum. Oxon.* · F. W. B. Bullock, *A history of training for the ministry of the Church of England* (1955) · Ward, *Men of the reign* · *The Times* (23 March 1873) · *GM*, 1st ser., 95/2 (1825), 270

Likenesses W. Gordon, portrait · W. Green, portrait
Wealth at death under £12,000: probate, 4 April 1873, *CGPLA Eng. & Wales*

Sandford [*née* Poole], **Margaret Elizabeth** (1839–1903), headmistress and author, was born on 20 March 1839 at Bridgwater, Somerset, the daughter of Gabriel Stone Poole, solicitor, and his wife, Maria Westmacott. Nothing is known of her schooling or early life, though in 1867 she contributed a short article on the Abbot's Way, Turf Moor, Somerset, to *Macmillan's Magazine* and published in 1870 *Pictures of Cottage Life in the West of England*. On 23 May 1872 she married her distant cousin, Henry Ryder Poole Sandford (1827–1883), son of John *Sandford, archdeacon of Coventry, and his first wife, Elizabeth Poole, who was Margaret's second cousin. Margaret's sister, Ethel Maria Ruscombe Poole, married Henry's brother, Ernest Grey Sandford, archdeacon of Exeter and biographer of Frederick Temple.

Margaret and Henry Sandford settled in Sheffield, where Henry, a clergyman, was a schools' inspector. Margaret Sandford was the originator and first honorary secretary of the Sheffield branch of the Union of Women Workers and with her husband took an active interest in education in the city. Following visits to German schools in 1872, she contributed an article on the education of German girls to *Macmillan's Magazine* in 1874. Both her husband and father-in-law supported Emily Davies in her work for the higher education of women and girls, and had been signatories to her memorial to open the Cambridge local examinations to women (1864). On the death of her husband in 1883 Margaret Sandford was appointed assistant mistress at Sheffield high school, run by the Girls' Public Day School Company, where she taught divinity, history, and literature, having also been considered in that year for the post of mistress of Girton College. She was described by Mrs Woodhouse, headmistress of Sheffield high school, as a brilliant conversationalist, bright and full of humour, and a woman who gave good advice, permeated by a deep spirituality.

In 1886 Margaret Sandford was appointed headmistress of the Queen's School, Chester, where she remained until her death. On taking up the post she reorganized the school along high school lines and introduced into the curriculum mathematics, modern languages, chemistry, gymnastics, and the Ablett system of teaching art. She also placed the school under university inspection. During her period as headmistress a number of scholarships were founded enabling girls in Chester to progress from the elementary schools to higher education. Pupils recalled her as a calm and understanding woman, who knew them individually and who always dressed in a black satin dress.

Margaret Sandford's educational philosophy and writing were influenced by her second cousin and mother-in-law, Elizabeth *Sandford, the well-known writer on girls' education. Margaret Sandford frequently quoted her maxim 'be on your guard against imperfect attainment'. She believed that competition was to be avoided in girls' education and was of value only in so far as it encouraged girls to strive for excellence. Her aim was to prepare girls for 'the varied responsibilities of Christian womanhood, for the duties of family life, for the larger duties of useful citizenship, and above all, for the faithful service in the Kingdom of our Lord Jesus Christ' (Woodhouse). In *What is the Use of a Liberal Education?* (1887) Margaret Sandford noted that although the Queen's School aimed to provide a path to higher education for girls, she would be happy if the education in the school fitted a girl to serve others. Her contributions to contemporary educational literature include reading books for girls, and articles on girls' education, religious education, and on pedagogy. In 1901 she addressed the Association of Headmistresses on the subject of religious education. She was a supporter of women's involvement in the administration of education. In her capacity as manager of Hunter Street Girls' School, Chester, she was the only woman member of the central board of managers of church schools in Chester, and in 'Woman's duty as citizen', posthumously published in *Have Mynde* (1903), she discussed the role that women might play in the future as members of the education committees of county councils.

Margaret Sandford was an ardent anti-suffragist and publicly debated the women's suffrage issue with Mrs Fawcett at the conference of the National Union of Women Workers in 1895. Her father-in-law, Archdeacon Sandford of Coventry, had spoken in 1868 with Lydia Becker at the inaugural meeting of the Manchester National Society for Women's Suffrage and again at a public meeting in Birmingham in 1868 in support of women's suffrage. Her brother-in-law, Archdeacon Sandford of Exeter, however, held similar views to Margaret Sandford. He campaigned within the Church of England to exclude women from office, believing that women should work for the church but not take part in any activity that impinged on the governance of the church. His daughters lived with Margaret Sandford at the Queen's School, where they were educated. One daughter, Ethel Sandford, continued the family's female tradition of interest in education, becoming headmistress of Beverley High School for Girls in 1933.

Margaret Sandford was keenly interested in literature, publishing in 1888 a two-volume work entitled *Thomas Poole and his Friends*, an account of the life of Coleridge, with whom her family were acquainted. In 1893 she addressed the Chester Society of Natural Science and Literature, and her paper, 'The Chester mysteries and their connection with English literature and the English drama', was reprinted. She also contributed articles on the Chester mystery plays to contemporary magazines and the local press, and published a novel, *Pamela's Bequest* (1881).

On 7 January 1903, while still in post at the Queen's School and busy with arrangements to open a new wing there, Margaret Sandford underwent an operation for breast cancer from which she did not recover. She died at 17 Upper Wimpole Street, London, on 9 January 1903, and was buried on 14 January at the old cemetery, Chester, after a service at Holy Trinity Church, Chester, where she had been a regular worshipper. JOYCE GOODMAN

Sources G. Phillips, *A short history of the Queen's School, Chester* (1987) · *The way we were: a century of recollection of the Queen's School, Chester* (1987) · E. Woodhouse, 'In memoriam: Mrs Henry Sandford', *Have Mynde* [Queen's School annual] (1903), 5–7 · *Wellesley index* · b. cert. · m. cert. · d. cert. · *Chester Chronicle* (17 Jan 1903)
Archives Som. ARS, collection
Likenesses T. W. Price, portrait, 1899, Queen's School, Chester · G. W. Webster, photograph, Queen's School, Chester
Wealth at death £8577 0s. 8d.: resworn probate, 6 March 1903, CGPLA Eng. & Wales

Sandford, Samuel (*fl.* 1661–1698), actor, 'proceeded from the *Sandfords* of *Sandford*, that lies between *Whitchurch* and *Newport*, in Shropshire', according to Aston (Aston, 306). Nothing is known of Sandford's education or occupation before he entered the theatre. Aston reported that Charles II considered Sandford 'the best Villain in the World', the speciality for which he was best known. Despite a long career, only in his last years did he rise above the third rank in salary, from £2 10s. a week to £3. Few traces of his life off the stage survive.

Sandford joined the Duke's Company in its second season, 1661–2, but appears never to have owned a share in either the company or the theatre it later built. He helped other actors hold prisoner a messenger from the master of the revels on 4 July 1662, for which he was fined 3s. 4d. An arrest order of 9 December 1669 declared that he had 'beene refractory & disorderly contrary to the Rules of [the] house' (PRO, LC5/187, fol. 187), but no further details are known. In June 1670 one Leonard Blofield claimed that Sandford owed him £50 in rent (PRO, LC5/188, fol. 14).

Three unexplained gaps occur in Sandford's career. In the 1673–4 season he is invisible but may have been present. He is again untraceable between September 1679 and November 1682, during the Popish Plot, which might mean that he was a Roman Catholic. He reappeared at an awkward time, when the Duke's Company had just absorbed the remnants of the rival theatre and, with a surplus of personnel, were de-emphasizing new plays. Because old plays were not reprinted with new casts, records are minimal, and Sandford is again invisible from December 1682 until February 1688. Whether or not he continued to perform in London is impossible to say.

Sandford may also have lost some time in the 1692–3 season. In act V of the Dryden–Lee *Oedipus*, Adrastus (played by George Powell), disarmed except for a poignard, stabs Creon (played by Sandford). Narcissus Luttrell reported that on 13 October 1692, 'by mistake of a sharp dagger for one that runs the blade into the handle', Powell was wounded '3 inches deep', but if Luttrell identified the play correctly, Sandford was the one wounded (Luttrell, 2.593). In the cast printed with the Bancroft–Mountfort *Henry the Second*, Sandford was listed for a major role, the wicked Abbott, which would have put him back on stage early in November. However, on 24 December 1692 Anthony Wood noted without explanation that Sandford was 'dangerously ill' (*Life and Times*, 3.412).

Late in 1694 Sandford joined fourteen colleagues in

complaining to the lord chamberlain about new management policies. The patentees replied that his salary was under scrutiny because of 'Indisposition' and because 'his voice often failing he is able to Act but seldom' (PRO, LC 7/3, fol. 19). On 22 February 1695 he was sworn as a royal servant with other actors who joined the breakaway company led by Thomas Betterton, specially licensed to perform at Lincoln's Inn Fields (PRO, LC 3/31, p. 108). Little of the repertory of this venture is known, leaving Sandford's place in it unclear, except that his salary increased. According to an incoherent anecdote from Aston, Sandford 'would not be concern'd … as a Sharer' but preferred to continue as a hireling, saying: '*This is my Agreement.—To* Samuel Sandford, *Gentleman*, Threescore Shillings a Week' (Aston, 306–7). Cave Underhill twitted him for accepting lower status, to which Sandford merely replied, 'Go, you Sot'. His retirement occurred at some time between 1697 and 1698, but achieved no contemporary notice, nor are the time and circumstances of his death known.

All accounts of Sandford's talent are posthumous. In *The Tatler* (no. 134, 16 February 1710), Richard Steele questioned the decorum of 'publick Executions' in English tragedy, since violence was kept offstage elsewhere: 'When poor *Sandford* was upon the Stage, I have seen him groaning upon a Wheel, stuck with Daggers, impaled alive' to please the audience, 'who were wonderfully delighted with seeing a Man in Torment so well acted' (implying roles in Thomas Otway's *Venice Preserv'd*, Charles Hopkins's *Boadicea*, and Thomas Porter's *The Villain*). Colley Cibber reinforced this view in his *Apology*, using Sandford to exemplify the actor who could develop a speciality despite limited gifts. He claimed that Sandford's 'bodily Defects were too strong to be admitted into great or amiable Characters', but he was excellent 'in disagreeable Characters' and became a 'Stage-Villain' not 'by Choice, but from Necessity' (Cibber, 1.130–31). Aston questioned whether Sandford was a principal actor, but agreed with most of Cibber's description of the niche he occupied, naming Iago in *Othello*, Foresight in William Congreve's *Love for Love*, and the title role in *The Villain* as typical.

These accounts shortchange Sandford. He undoubtedly played more than the sixty-one roles which are listed in order of acquisition in the Highfill–Burnim–Langhans *Biographical Dictionary*. In fact, a variety of comic old men make up a slight majority of that list. Some are troublemakers who get their come-uppance, comic villains easily foiled, and the emphasis is on their ineptitude rather than wickedness. Many are heavy fathers who come round; some are just gulls. Sandford's comic gifts were overshadowed by those of Cave Underhill and James Nokes, and he was fortunate to have the option of playing villains, though he did not automatically receive those roles, particularly if they were principal characters. He played not the Cardinal but Cassonofsky in John Crowne's *Juliana*, and while Cheatly, his role in Thomas Shadwell's *Squire of Alsatia*, leads Belford senior astray, Cheatly's henchmen have more time onstage than he does. Sandford may have attempted Gloucester in *Richard III* as early

as 1672 and as late as 1692, but appears not to have been successful in the role. His best villains were energetic secondary characters, often given to sword fighting: Benducar in Dryden's *Don Sebastian*, Tissaphernes in Otway's *Alcibiades*, Lycungus in Elkanah Settle's *Conquest of China*.

A possible description of Sandford as a braggart soldier comes from Abraham Cowley's comedy *Cutter of Coleman Street* (1661): 'Little' Worm is rallied concerning his 'Ember-week face', 'Razor' of a nose, and thinness so extreme that his 'cheeks begin to fall into [his] mouth'; he is compared to a 'very Lath, with a thing cut like a face at top, and a slit at bottom' (pp. 8, 9). Cibber speaks of 'a long and crooked Person', and Aston mentions a figure 'diminutive and mean (being Round-shoulder'd, Meagre-fac'd, Spindle-shank'd, Splay-footed, with a sour Countenance, and long lean Arms)', adding that Sandford 'acted strongly with his Face' (Cibber, 1.131; Aston, 302).

Cibber, who reported extensively on Sandford, noted the 'acute and piercing Tone' of his voice, which made every syllable count (Cibber, 1.138). He alerted the audience to important passages by 'a peculiar Skill in his Look'. He was willing to sacrifice 'Harmony' to gain 'Force', particularly in issuing commands. He tried to avoid 'the Jingle' of rhymed heroic drama, 'rather chusing, when the Sense would permit him, to lose it, than to value it'. These skills explain why Sandford's characters often have long expository or ceremonious speeches (Bishop of Arras in Roger Boyle's *History of Henry the Fifth*; Sir Arthur Oldlove in Thomas D'Urfey's *Madam Fickle*; Nicias in Otway's *History of Timon of Athens*; Hamilcar in Crowne's *Regulus*). Aston acknowledged that Sandford's 'Energy was, by his Voice and Action, enforc'd with great Soundness of Art, and Justice', but felt that his appearance sometimes worked against what he said (Aston, 306). Despite Cibber's anecdote about the audience that damned a play in which Sandford unexpectedly played a good character, roles like Priamus in John Banks's *The Destruction of Troy*, Sir Thomas Credulous in Crowne's *English Frier*, and Lieutenant-General Dareing in Aphra Behn's *Widow Ranter* must have been largely sympathetic.

Although Sandford played both comic and tragic roles throughout his career, he never moved beyond the level of a supporting actor. His time onstage was usually brief: seldom did more than two or three scenes in a play depend chiefly upon him. While he was performing, however, his skills left a vivid impression on perceptive commentators as different as Steele, Cibber, and Aston.

JUDITH MILHOUS

Sources C. Cibber, *An apology for the life of Mr. Colley Cibber*, ed. R. W. Lowe, 2 vols. (1889); repr. (New York, 1966) • A. Aston, *A brief supplement to Colley Cibber, esq.: his 'Lives of the late famous actors and actresses'* [1747]; repr. in C. Cibber, *Apology for the life of Mr Colley Cibber*, new edn, ed. R. W. Lowe, 2 (1889), [297]–318 • J. Milhous, 'United Company finances, 1682–1692', *Theatre Research International*, 7 (1981–2), 37–53 • Highfill, Burnim & Langhans, *BDA* • H. Ross, 'Samuel Sandford: villain from necessity', *Publications of the Modern Language Association of America*, 76 (1961), 367–72 • J. Milhous, *Thomas Betterton and the management of Lincoln's Inn Fields, 1695–1708* (1979) • J. Downes, *Roscius Anglicanus*, ed. J. Milhous and R. D. Hume, new edn (1987) •

L. Hotson, *The Commonwealth and Restoration stage* (1928); repr. (New York, 1962) • N. Luttrell, *A brief historical relation of state affairs from September 1678 to April 1714*, 6 vols. (1857) • *The life and times of Anthony Wood*, ed. A. Clark, 3, OHS, 26 (1894)

Sandham, Andrew (1890–1982), cricketer, was born at Kelso, High Road, Streatham, London, on 6 July 1890, the son of George Sandham, a domestic gardener, and his wife, Jane Laurence. Baptized at the Roman Catholic church of the English Martyrs, Streatham, he was educated locally and played his early cricket for Streatham United. He later played for Mitcham, a nursery for the Surrey county side, whose staff he joined in 1910. A year later he made a half-century on his début in first-class cricket and he was hailed as a batsman 'from whom much may be expected' (*Wisden*, 1912, 83). Yet by 1914, despite making 196 against Sussex at the Oval in 1913, he had not secured a regular place in the side. He had been successful for the second eleven and Surrey paid him a retainer of 15s. a week during his service with the Royal Fusiliers in the First World War. He reached the rank of lance-corporal before being invalided out in 1918. In the same year, on 27 July, he married Kathleen Louise O'Callaghan (1891–1953), a jeweller's assistant; they had two daughters.

Sandham had always aspired to be an opening batsman and, with the retirement of Tom Hayward in 1914, Surrey needed a post-war partner for Jack Hobbs. With 175 not out against Middlesex in 1919 he virtually secured his position, though he conceded it occasionally to the amateur D. J. Knight. An innings of 292 not out against Northamptonshire in 1921 was the first of ten scores of over 200 in his career, and in nine days that season he accumulated 640 runs.

In 1924 Sandham topped the national averages with 2082 runs at 59.48; *Wisden* declared he scarcely knew 'what failure meant' (*Wisden*, 1925, 231) and the cricket historian Harry Altham believed he played 'as well as anyone in England' (Altham, 361). When he opened for Surrey with Hobbs, with whom he would share sixty-three century partnerships (a few of them for the Players against the Gentlemen), there was little to choose between the two men statistically. In 1926 they set a Surrey first-wicket record of 428, and Sandham also shared in what are still the county's sixth- and tenth-wicket records.

Sandham seemed to play second fiddle to Hobbs but the latter's absence through test match duties and illness allowed him to call the tune himself, and in the 1920s and 1930s he became Surrey's principal run-getter. As late as 1934 and 1937 he could make double centuries against the Australians and Glamorgan respectively.

It is a commentary on England's batting strength in the inter-war period that Sandham was seldom selected to play against Australia or South Africa. There was no challenger to Herbert Sutcliffe as Hobbs's opening partner. What gave him, in fourteen tests, the very respectable average of 38.21 was achieved by a tour of the West Indies in 1929–30, when innings of 152 and two fifties were themselves eclipsed by 325 not out at Sabina Park, Kingston, Jamaica, in April 1930. England, for the only time ever, had

sent two sides of parallel ability abroad (the other to New Zealand) and matches against the full overseas' opposition were styled 'representative' ones. Subsequently, they were accorded test match status. While history would see Sandham as the first man to score a triple century in a test match, contemporaries gave the accolade to Don Bradman for his 334 for Australia at Leeds three months later.

Sandham, in his youth, had watched Hayward and emulated the straightness with which the latter played, together with his ability to force the ball away off his legs. Short in height and nimble of foot, he was an unflinching player of fast bowling, and excelled in cutting and hooking. He had a powerful throw from long-on or deep third man and was seldom beaten in the field. He ended his career with the modesty he had displayed throughout it. After a century in the last match of 1937, 'without any fuss or bother' (*Wisden*, 1938, 498) he announced his retirement.

Sandham had always been content to let Hobbs take the plaudits of the crowd and to be on the shadow side of the spotlights, a man whose personality matched his technique—'quiet, neat, crisp [with] restraint, dignity and self discipline' (Robertson-Glasgow, 133). He 'set himself and expected of others a high standard of behaviour' (*Wisden*, 1983, 1255).

Sandham spent the two seasons before the Second World War as coach at Beaumont College, whose 1939 season, under his tutelage, 'was one of the most successful ever' (*Wisden*, 1940, 634). These skills were also displayed in the coaching school which he and Herbert Strudwick established. He returned to Surrey as coach (1946–58) and as scorer (1959–70) to add to his career record of 41,284 runs (average 44.82), of which 33,312 were made for the county. He made 107 centuries and, in an age of great batsmen, by all but the benchmark of performances against Australia and South Africa, he was among the best of them. He was one of the twenty-six professionals elected to honorary membership of MCC in 1949 and became a vice-president of Surrey in 1979. He died at the Middlesex Hospital, London, on 20 April 1982 and was buried seven days later in Streatham Park cemetery.

GERALD M. D. HOWAT

Sources *Wisden* (1923) • *Wisden* (1928) • *Wisden* (1936) • *Wisden* (1972) • *Wisden* (1983) • R. C. Robertson-Glasgow, *Crusoe on cricket* (1966) • H. S. Altham, *A history of cricket* (1926) • J. Arlott, *Jack Hobbs* (1983) • P. Bailey, P. Thorn, and P. Wynne-Thomas, *Who's who of cricketers* (1984) • private information (2004) [Joan Sandham, daughter] • b. cert. • m. cert. • d. cert.
Likenesses double portrait, photograph, *c.*1920–1929 (with Hobbs), Hult. Arch.; repr. in R. Mason, *Jack Hobbs* (1988) • Narraway, portrait, 1967, Surrey CC Pavilion, London
Wealth at death under £25,000: probate, 2 Sept 1982, *CGPLA Eng. & Wales*

Sandham, Henry (1842–1910), painter and illustrator, was born on 24 May 1842 in the Griffintown area of Montreal, Quebec, Canada, the youngest of the three sons of John Sandham, house painter, and his wife, Elizabeth, *née* Tate.

Both parents had emigrated from England. At the age of fourteen Sandham decided to become an artist, working as an errand-boy at the Montreal studio of the photographer William Notman before becoming assistant to the artist John Arthur Fraser, who was in charge of the art department, in 1862. It was here that he learned how to draw, as there was no art school in Montreal, and he had lessons from some of the other artists who worked there, including the German painter Otto Reinhold Jacobi. In 1865 he married Fraser's sister, Agnes Amelia Fraser. They had six children, four of whom died in infancy.

When Fraser went to Toronto in 1868 to open a branch of Notman's studio, Sandham became head of the Montreal art department. In the 1870s he worked on the large composite photographs for which the Notman studio became famous, winning a silver medal at the Paris Universal Exhibition of 1878 for his photograph of the 300 members of the Montreal Snow Shoe Club on the slopes of Mount Royal. He also specialized in the painting of winter scenery as a background against which the clients could pose. A partner in Notman's firm, which became Notman and Sandham, from 1877 to 1882, he went to Saint John, New Brunswick, in 1879 to open a new branch.

At the same time, Sandham was painting landscapes of the St Lawrence River and Canadian scenery and became known as a watercolourist. His paintings were very literal, strongly influenced by the photograph, and several, including *Hunters Returning with their Spoils* (1877), were acquired by the National Gallery of Canada. He began to paint portraits, including that of Sir John A. Macdonald, the first prime minister of the dominion of Canada, which was hung in the parliament buildings in Ottawa. A regular exhibitor in Montreal and Toronto, he was a founder member of the Royal Canadian Academy in 1880. He also began to illustrate books and magazines, doing work for *Scribner's Monthly* (later *Century Monthly Magazine*) in New York, including a four-part series 'The dominion of Canada' (1879).

After a visit to England in 1880, Sandham decided to emigrate to the United States, and settled in Boston, where he remained for twenty years, working as an illustrator and painting portrait commissions and large historical paintings, including *The Dawn of Liberty* (1886) for the town hall in Lexington, Massachusetts, and *The March of Time* (1890). He exhibited regularly at the Boston Art Club, and the American Water Colour Society of New York. Among his illustrations were those for four articles on the Mission Indians of southern California for *Century Magazine* in 1883, *Ramona* (1900), the best-selling novel by Helen Maria Jackson, and a series of drawings for Theodore Roosevelt's books on ranch life and the west.

Sandham left Boston in 1901 to live in London, and he exhibited paintings at the Royal Academy between 1905 and 1908. He died at his home, Quinta Lodge, South Parade, Bedford Park, Middlesex, on 21 June 1910 and was buried at Kensal Green cemetery in London. A memorial exhibition of his major paintings was held in London in June 1911.   ANNE PIMLOTT BAKER

Sources P. B. Landry, 'Sandham, Henry', *DCB*, vol. 13 · D. Reid, *A concise history of Canadian painting* (1973), 83–4 · W. Jenkins, 'A Canadian artist in the Azores', *The Studio*, 27 (1902–3), 173–7 · J. R. Harper and S. Triggs, eds., *Portrait of a period: a collection of Notman photographs* (1967) · R. H. Hubbard, *The development of Canadian art* (1963), 64–7 · A. H. Robson, *Canadian landscape painters* (1932) · d. cert. · private information (1912) [daughter] · *DNB* · *WWW* · Graves, *RA exhibitors*
Likenesses group portrait, photograph, 1880 (with artists including Henry Sandham), repro. in Harper and Triggs, eds., *Portrait of a period*, fig. 39 · portrait, repro. in *New England Magazine*, new ser. 4 (1891), 165

Sandhurst. For this title name *see* Mansfield, William Rose, first Baron Sandhurst (1819–1876); Mansfield, Margaret, Lady Sandhurst (*bap.* 1827, *d.* 1892).

Sandilands, James, of Calder, **first Lord Torphichen** (*d.* **1579**), nobleman, was the second son of Sir James Sandilands of Calder (*d.* 1559) and Margaret or Marion (*d.* 1562), daughter of Archibald Forrester of Corstorphine. The family originally owned the lands of Sandilands in Lanarkshire and through marriage acquired the barony of West Calder in Edinburghshire. Before 1537 Sandilands entered the order of the hospital of St John of Jerusalem. On 5 April 1540 he obtained permission from James V to travel to Malta, the order's headquarters, where he remained until 1542. On 17 February 1541 he acquired the right to succeed to the preceptory of Torphichen on the recommendation of the preceptor and head of the order in Scotland, Sir Walter Lindsay, whom he succeeded as Lord St John of Jerusalem. The appointment was not confirmed, however, by either Pope Paul III or Juan d'Omedes, the grand master of the order, until 29 March and 3 June 1547 respectively. In 1556 Sandilands was granted a licence to travel to Malta, where in the following year he was authorized to reclaim possessions of the order which had been misappropriated by neighbouring landowners. During his absence his affairs were handled by John Spottiswoode, the family parson at Calder and subsequently superintendent of Lothian.

James Sandilands and his father were strong supporters of the Reformation, and patrons of two leading Scottish reformers, George Wishart and John Knox. As preceptor of the hospitallers, Sandilands was a long-serving member of parliament and privy councillor, alike during the reigns of Mary and James VI and during the regencies of Mary of Guise and the earls of Arran and Moray. In 1550 he accompanied Mary of Guise to France, but later joined the protestant lords of the congregation and fought against her at Cupar Muir in 1559. In the following year he again visited France, this time on the orders of parliament, in order to give Queen Mary an account of its proceedings, but returned to Edinburgh having failed to obtain ratification of its legislation. Mary later complained to the English ambassador, Nicholas Throckmorton, about the size of the delegation sent to her compared with that sent to Elizabeth. To the ambassador's explanation that Sandilands was a prior of the hospitallers she replied, 'I do not take him for Great Prior for he is married' (Tytler, 6.194). Sandilands was a signatory of the act of 27 January 1561 approving the first Book of Discipline.

On account of debts owed to his friend Timothy Cagnioli, a Genoese banker living in Scotland, Sandilands was forced to sell some of his lands. On 24 January 1564 he resigned the possessions of the hospitallers to Mary in return for a payment of 10,000 crowns, an annual pension of 500 merks, and the temporal lordship of Torphichen. The grant did not include the title of Lord Torphichen, but in 1606 it was accepted as evidence of the creation of the lordship and the right to use that title. In 1565 his wife, Janet, daughter of William Murray of Polmaise, whom he had married in 1559, renounced to him her interest in various properties. He was later accused of forging the renunciation, but in 1577 obtained a declarator absolving him.

Torphichen was involved in the downfall of Mary, joining the rebel army which forced her to surrender at Carberry Hill on 15 June 1567. On 25 July he attended the coronation of James VI, but thereafter played a lesser role in national affairs. His health declined, and on 31 May 1570 he obtained a licence from Elizabeth to travel to England to visit the baths to cure his ailments. In 1572 an action was raised against him to recover items formerly belonging to Queen Mary, including a number of books. He returned the books to the privy council, but denied having any other item. Later in the year he was granted another licence to travel to the continent and was probably in France on 25 November 1575, when Henri III made him a gentleman of his chamber. Torphichen died on 29 September 1579 of a 'deidlie seikness of apoplexie, quilk tuk the haill strenth of his body and use of his speiche frome him' (*Reg. PCS*, 3.238), and was survived by his wife, Janet, from whom he had been separated since 1571. Following his death she successfully raised an action against the regent, the earl of Morton, to regain possession of Hallbarns and Hallyards to which he claimed to be infeft. In 1586 she was also successful in an action against George Dundas of that ilk, who was ordered to deliver to her a box of Torphichen's personal effects, including amounts of gold and silver, less the funeral expenses. She lived until 1596. Torphichen and his wife had no children and the title passed to his grandnephew, also James Sandilands of Calder.   MICHAEL J. YELLOWLEES

Sources NA Scot., Torphichen writs, GD 119 · inventory of Torphichen writs, NA Scot. · *Reg. PCS*, 1st ser., vols. 1–3 · M. Livingstone, D. Hay Fleming, and others, eds., *Registrum secreti sigilli regum Scotorum / The register of the privy seal of Scotland*, 8 vols. (1908–82), vol. 4, nos. 882, 3191, 3314; vol. 6, no. 1717 · J. M. Thomson and others, eds., *Registrum magni sigilli regum Scotorum / The register of the great seal of Scotland*, 11 vols. (1882–1914); facs. repr. (1984), vol. 4, no. 1499 · P. F. Tytler, *History of Scotland*, 6 (1837), 190–95 · T. Thomson, ed., *A diurnal of remarkable occurrents that have passed within the country of Scotland*, Bannatyne Club, 43 (1833), 280 · *Scots peerage* · CSP *Scot.*, 1547–63, 463ff. · F. J. Grant, ed., *The commissariot record of Edinburgh: register of testaments*, 1, Scottish RS, old ser., 1 (1897), 243 · I. B. Cowan, P. H. R. Mackay, and A. Macquarrie, eds., *The knights of St John of Jerusalem in Scotland*, Scottish History Society, 4th ser., 19 (1983), 201 · A. Macquarrie, *Scotland and the crusades, 1095–1560* (1997), 117–18, 133
Archives NA Scot., Torphichen writs, GD 119
Likenesses G. Jameson, *c.*1635–1637, priv. coll.
Wealth at death see NA Scot., inventory of Torphichen writs, GD 119, appx IV

Sandilands, James, seventh Lord Torphichen (*d.* 1753), army officer, was the second but eldest surviving son of Walter Sandilands, sixth Lord Torphichen (*bap.* 1629, *d.* 1696), and his fourth wife, Christian (*b.* 1647), daughter and heir of James Primrose, clerk of the council. In 1702 he was commissioned a captain in the earl of Mar's foot. In 1703 he married Jean (1683–1751), youngest daughter of Patrick Hume, first earl of Marchmont. They had eight sons and three daughters. He took his seat in the Scottish House of Lords on 6 July 1704, where he followed the squadrone and its allies. He voted for the first article of the Union with England on 4 November 1706 and for the ratification of the treaty on 16 January 1707.

Torphichen was serving in Lord Polwarth's dragoons (later Lord Kerr's and known as the 7th hussars) before 2 April 1709, and was promoted major on 15 February 1712 and lieutenant-colonel in April 1713. He fought at Sheriffmuir on 13 November 1715. He appears to have retired from the army in 1720, and in 1722 was appointed a lord of police, a position he held until his death. He died at Calder House, near Edinburgh, on 10 August 1753. He was succeeded by his second son, Walter, his eldest son, James, having died in 1749 of wounds received four years previously at the battle of Prestonpans.   STUART HANDLEY

Sources GEC, *Peerage* · *Scots peerage* · C. Dalton, *George the First's army, 1714–1727*, 1 (1910), 111 · C. Dalton, ed., *English army lists and commission registers, 1661–1714*, 5 (1902), 212; 6 (1904), 209–10 · P. W. J. Riley, *The Union of England and Scotland* (1978), 334 · J. S. Shaw, *The management of Scottish society, 1707–1764: power, nobles, lawyers, Edinburgh agents and English influences* (1983), 61
Archives NA Scot., corresp. with Thomas Shairp
Likenesses A. Hay, oils, 1710, Mellerstain House, Scottish Borders

Sandile (*c.*1820–1878), chief of the Ngqika Xhosa, son of Chief Ngqika and his great wife, Sutu, was born in independent Xhosa near the later Fort Beaufort in South Africa. He was installed as chief in 1842 and led the Ngqika Xhosa until his death in battle in 1878. In accordance with Xhosa custom he had several wives and many children. His great wife was Nopasi, the daughter of the Mpondomise chief Myeki and the mother of his great son and heir, Gonya. Although the elder son of the great wife, Sandile was not the eldest son of his father. On Ngqika's premature death in 1828 Sandile was still a minor and the regency was assumed by Maqoma, his elder brother by a junior wife of Ngqika. Relations between the brothers were never good. Maqoma was more forceful both intellectually and physically, but he was also very erratic, and Sandile gradually managed to assert his authority. Shortly before Sandile was born Ngqika was dispossessed of his ancestral lands around the Kat River by Governor Lord Charles Somerset. This grievance gave rise to the 1834–5 Cape Frontier War during Maqoma's regency, and to the 1846–7 Cape Frontier War (known as 'the war of the axe') shortly after Sandile had assumed power. This war ended abruptly when Sandile, who had voluntarily entered the British camp to conduct negotiations, was treacherously imprisoned. His country was annexed to the British crown under the name of British Kaffraria, and the new governor, Sir Harry Smith, embarked on a policy of humiliating the Xhosa chiefs and taking over their powers.

A crisis erupted in 1850 with the emergence of a Xhosa prophet and witch-finder named Mlanjeni. Sandile refused to attend a meeting called by Smith for fear of being imprisoned a second time, and was immediately deposed by the British. This triggered the 1850–53 Cape Frontier War, the longest and most brutal ever fought on that frontier. Sandile lost more territory, and these losses were compounded as a result of the prophecies of *Nongqawuse in 1856–7. Sandile wavered for a long time, but finally committed himself to the prophecies and slaughtered the last of his remaining cattle. The starvation which followed reduced the population of British Kaffraria by two-thirds, from 105,000 to 37,500. Although Sandile escaped imprisonment, his power was broken, and for nearly twenty years he existed as a mere cipher, drinking heavily and clinging ever harder to traditional customs. But in 1877, when King Sarhili of the Gcaleka branch of the Xhosa became embroiled in a war against the British, Sandile rallied to his cause. He entrenched himself in the Isidenge forests near the town of Stutterheim and refused to give up, even after Sarhili himself had surrendered. Sandile was wounded in a skirmish on 29 May 1878, and died of his wounds a few days later. He was buried in the forest on 9 June. Some controversy has arisen concerning the fate of his body, more especially because Lieutenant F. Carrington returned to Britain with a skull reputed to be that of Sandile. It is probable, however, that his body was buried intact. In 1972 a memorial was erected over the grave site.

Sandile was physically not a strong man, having been born with a club foot. Colonial sources portray him, moreover, as weak-willed and unintelligent. Xhosa oral tradition, however, remembers Sandile with respect and affection. He was one of the few Xhosa chiefs to consistently resist the colonial occupation, and the only one to actually die in battle. As a chief he was generous and unassertive, sensitive to the will of his people and always articulating their aspirations rather than his own.   J. B. PEIRES

Sources J. B. Peires, *The house of Phalo* (1981) · J. Milton, *The edges of war* (1983) · C. Brownlee, *Reminiscences of Kafir life and history*, 2nd edn (1916) · J. Maclean, ed., *A compendium of Kafir laws and customs* (1858) · [J. Crealock], *The Frontier War journal of Major John Crealock, 1878*, ed. H. C. Hummel (1988)
Likenesses F. I'ons, oils, Africana Museum, Johannesburg; repro. in Milton, *Edges of war* · photograph, repro. in Brownlee, *Reminiscences*

Sandow, Eugen (1867–1925), strongman and physical culturist, was born Friedrich Wilhelm Müller in Königsberg, East Prussia, on 2 April 1867. According to conflicting sources he had an older brother or half-brother, and his father was either a prosperous jewel dealer or a greengrocer. His mother was Russian, or of Russian descent, and her maiden name, Sandov, is the likely origin of the stage name, Eugen Sandow, by which he was universally known. Sandow may have had some medical training, but he showed no inclination to become a doctor or Lutheran

Eugen Sandow (1867–1925), by Henry van der Weyde, 1889

minister, as his parents wished. Instead he was drawn to circus strongman acts. He frequented the local gymnasium, or *Turnhalle*, and developed the physique of a wrestler and acrobat. When he left Prussia to avoid military service, around 1885, it was probably with a travelling circus. About two years later he visited the Brussels gymnasium of the renowned strongman Louis Durlacher, known as Professor Louis Attila. After being coached by Attila in a programme of heavy weightlifting, Sandow began to develop the Herculean physique for which he became world famous.

Sandow combined great strength with natural athleticism: he perfected the trade-mark stunt of turning a somersault from a standing start with a 55 lb dumb-bell in each hand. He nevertheless struggled to make his mark as a novice strongman, and supplemented an uncertain income by working as a life model for medical students and artists. He worked briefly with Attila in London before travelling through France as one half of an imaginative circus act, Les Frères Rijos. After working as a professional wrestler in northern Italy he arrived in London, with Attila as his interpreter, to challenge the strongman 'Samson' at the music-hall in the Royal Aquarium, Westminster. Samson offered £100, a sum much greater than the average yearly earnings of a working man, to anyone who could perform the feats of his protégé, Cyclops, and a further £1000 to anyone who could match his own. When Sandow accepted the challenge, on 29 October 1889, the

Royal Aquarium was packed in anticipation. His appearance in evening dress provoked laughter, but this stopped when he stripped to the waist revealing his powerful frame. After much controversy the contest was decided when Sandow lifted overhead two weights totalling 250 lbs—not twice, as Cyclops had done, but seven times, to thunderous applause.

On 2 November, before another packed house, Sandow faced Samson himself. The contest was judged by the marquess of Queensberry and Lord De Clifford. Sandow equalled each of Samson's specially chosen feats. He bent a large iron bar across his neck, lifted a 280 lb dumb-bell with one arm, and won the judges' verdict after lifting a 220 lb dumb-bell and breaking a chain around his chest before lowering it. The crowd cheered him all the way back to his lodgings in Leicester Square. Although he never received the prize money promised by Samson, the Royal Aquarium management gave him £350, and he was soon engaged at the Alhambra for £150 a week. After a three months' run there he toured the provinces. Sandow had an acute sense of theatre and was 'cool, confident and an artist in everything he did' (Trevor, 29). His 'geniality and gentlemanly bearing … made him a popular idol of the music-hall', and he settled in London, becoming a naturalized British subject (ibid.).

With blue eyes and fair hair Sandow was the epitome of Teutonic manhood. Although revered as an originator of modern body-building, his physique does not compare with that of the steroid user of the late twentieth century. To Victorian audiences, however, it was awe-inspiring. A little over 5 feet 9 inches tall he weighed 14 stone 6 lbs in his prime, and boasted biceps of 19 inches, an 18 inch neck, and a 62 inch expanded chest. By exposing his body to public gaze he helped to change attitudes to the male physique and to athleticism in general. He was often photographed in a classical pose, naked except for a strategically placed fig leaf, or else pictured as a hunter with leopard-skin trunks, sandals, and club.

In 1893 Sandow embarked on a successful tour of New York and Chicago and from 1894 to 1896 he spent long periods in America, where he found lucrative work in circuses and vaudeville. Between tours he married, in Manchester on 8 August 1894, Blanche Brookes, daughter of a photographer; they had two daughters.

Sandow's constant search for novelty sometimes backfired, and in San Francisco he unwisely accepted the challenge to fight a fairground lion, heavily gloved and muzzled. His own account glorifies the contest, but newspaper reports showed that the lion was aged and infirm. Sandow emerged from an unedifying spectacle with the crowd against him, having been 'made to look very foolish' (Chapman, 87). By late 1896 the strain of constant performances, as well as of a hectic social life, had begun to tell. Amid signs that the American public was tiring of his act he returned to England close to a physical and nervous breakdown.

Sandow recuperated in London and re-emerged as the leading exponent of 'physical culture'—the systematic training of the muscles to preserve and restore bodily health. He later wrote: 'My aim is to raise the average standard of the race as a whole. A stupendous task, no doubt, but one from which I do not shrink' (Sandow, Body-Building, 8). To this end he campaigned for a system of national physical education in schools and improved nutrition for the masses. He also pioneered exercise programmes for women. His advocacy of national health complemented the Victorian ideal of muscular Christianity. It also coincided with growing concern over national physical deterioration, accentuated by the poor quality of army recruits for the South African War.

But whatever Sandow advocated was likely to be of benefit to himself, as well as to the nation. In 1897 he opened his first 'institute of physical culture' at 32A St James's Street, near Piccadilly. It was geared to the needs of a wealthy clientele and Sandow himself interviewed many of those who attended. After initial diagnosis they were coached by trained instructors in a range of calisthenic exercises and light weightlifting. The institute proved highly successful and he opened five such centres in London and one in Manchester. At the other end of the social scale were the Sandow physical-culture clubs that sprang up in hundreds of towns and villages. He stimulated interest with local contests to find the best developed contestant. These culminated in a great competition at the Royal Albert Hall, in September 1901, watched by 15,000 spectators. He also wrote a popular training manual Strength and How to Obtain It, first published in 1897. And in July 1898 he began the monthly magazine Physical Culture, through which readers could subscribe to a correspondence course of Sandow exercises, another valuable source of business.

As Sandow's own strength declined his stage act relied more on posing and elaborate tricks. A high point came at the London Hippodrome in September 1900 when, as 'Tommy Atkins' in the khaki of the South African War, he formed a human bridge over which a stage British army travelled to safety, to the tune of 'Rule Britannia'. From 1901 to 1905 he toured extensively, promoting physical culture and consolidating his reputation as the world's most famous strongman. He visited the United States, Australia and New Zealand, South Africa, and India. When finally he returned to England, in September 1905, the craze for physical culture was dying out. He closed all but the Piccadilly institute and in June 1907 Physical Culture magazine ceased from lack of interest. To compensate for the loss of earnings Sandow put greater emphasis on the mail-order sale of health products, such as his 'wonderful ringing dumb-bells' and 'health and strength cocoa'. He also developed the Symmetrion, an exerciser specially designed to enhance feminine grace. He pointedly welcomed the greater physical freedom enjoyed by women: equally pointedly he presented his system as the one perfectly suited to their needs.

He also continued his efforts to improve the fighting strength of the nation. When in 1909 Lord Esher appealed for 11,000 recruits for the territorial regiments, Sandow provided at his own expense the physical training necessary to raise some volunteers to the required standard. In

1911 he was honoured with a royal warrant appointing him 'professor of scientific physical culture to the king', George V having followed his teachings. The warrant was symbolic recognition of his services to the nation as a whole. During the First World War he again trained army recruits, enabling thousands to pass fit for active service. So closely had he integrated with his adopted country that he escaped the intense anti-German feeling evoked by the war. After the conflict he renewed his campaign for national health as a means of effecting national regeneration with the ambitious work *Life is Movement* (c.1920).

Sandow's detractors claimed that his many feats of strength had injured his internal organs and they predicted an early death. In return he accused them of envy and publicly boasted of a life insurance policy worth £20,000 with Norwich Union. But on 14 October 1925 he died at fifty-eight, at his home, 61 Holland Park Avenue, Kensington, London. The cause of death was given in the press as a burst blood vessel in the brain, attributed to the strain he received when lifting his motor car out of a ditch after an accident two or three years previously. But there was no post-mortem and the official cause of death, aortic aneurysm, is consistent with syphilis, from which it is thought that Sandow may have been suffering. He had been unfaithful to his wife and so far did their relations deteriorate that she refused to erect a marker on his grave, in Putney Vale cemetery, where he was buried on 16 October.

Sandow combined the egotism and domineering traits of a circus strongman with the open-minded zeal of a genuine enthusiast for national health. He looked back to a Greek ideal of bodily perfection, and forwards to an age where science, medicine, and physical culture counteracted the more corrupting effects of civilization. Today he is remembered chiefly as a bodybuilder, although to contemporaries he was equally an entertainer and an educator. MARK POTTLE

Sources D. L. Chapman, *Sandow the magnificent: Eugen Sandow and the beginnings of bodybuilding* (1994) • C. T. Trevor, *Sandow the magnificent: his life of adventure, amazing feats of strength, and exploits as a strongman* [n.d., 1946?] • E. Sandow, *Strength and how to obtain it* [n.d., c.1922] • E. Sandow, *Strength and how to obtain it*, rev. edn [1911] • E. Sandow, *Body-building, or, Man in the making: how to become healthy and strong* (1911) • E. Sandow, *The construction and reconstruction of the human body: a manual of the therapeutics of exercise* (1907) • E. Sandow, *Life is movement: the physical reconstruction and regeneration of the people* (*a diseaseless world*) [n.d., 1920?] • *The Times* (28 March 1911), 8c; (16 Oct 1925), 17b; (15 Oct 1925), 16c; (12 Nov 1925), 12d; (31 Dec 1925), 13d • *Cornhill Magazine* (1901), vols. 10, 11 • *CGPLA Eng. & Wales* (1925)
Likenesses H. van der Weyde, photograph, 1889, NPG [*see illus.*] • photographs, repro. in Sandow, *Body-building*
Wealth at death £9565 4s. 6d.: probate, 1925, *CGPLA Eng. & Wales*

Sands. For this title name *see* Johnston, Sir Christopher Nicholson, Lord Sands (1857–1934).

Sands, Ethel (1873–1962), painter and hostess, was born at Newport, Rhode Island, USA, on 6 July 1873, the eldest of the three children of Mahlon Day Sands (1842–1888) and his second wife, Mary Morton Hartpence (1853–1896), whom he had married in 1872. The success of his father's business as a manufacturer of patent medicines had allowed Mahlon Sands to retire from work in 1865 on his first marriage, to Edith Minturn (1844–1868). The only child of the first marriage, Mabel, died in 1890 of puerperal fever following the birth of her son, Archibald Henry Macdonald *Sinclair (later first Viscount Thurso).

Ethel Sands grew up in England where, from 1874, her parents spent much time. Nothing is known of her childhood education. The beauty of Mary Morton Sands (painted by John Singer Sargent) and the wealth of her husband won them an assured place in society. They settled permanently in England in 1879. In 1888 Mahlon Sands died as a result of a riding accident; his widow died of a heart attack in 1896. Ethel was left to care for her two younger brothers, Alanson (1878–1936) and Morton (1884–1959).

The inheritor of her mother's grace and intelligence, but not of her looks (*Portrait of Ethel Sands* by Walter Sickert, priv. coll.), Ethel Sands went to Paris in 1894 to study art. There she met her lifelong companion, the American painter Anna Hope (Nan) Hudson (1869–1957). From 1896 until 1901 they attended the studio of Eugène Carrière and admired the work of Édouard Vuillard. Until 1907, when Sickert introduced them to a new circle in London, their artistic life was based in Paris. Ethel had shown work at the Salon d'Automne since 1904 and was elected *sociétaire* in 1909. It was, however, a view of Venice by Nan, hung at the 1906 Salon d'Automne, which prompted Sickert to seek closer acquaintance with its painter and thereby begin an association crucial to the life and art of both women. In 1907 he invited them to join the Fitzroy Street Group which, under the formula 'Mr Sickert at Home', rented premises at 19 Fitzroy Street to discuss, exhibit, and sell to discriminating patrons. In 1913 they became founder members of the London group, with whom they exhibited until their deaths. Despite Sickert's campaign, often conducted by letter, to induce Ethel towards a more rigorous approach to construction, drawing, and handling, her paintings—domestic in scale, informal in content, and bright in colour—changed little over her lifetime. She painted interiors (either of her own elegant homes or those of her friends) with and without figures, portraits, and still lifes of flowers and *objets d'art*. *The Chintz Couch*, a work of this type, is in the Tate collection.

In 1898 Ethel Sands had bought Newington House in Oxfordshire as a base for her young brothers. In later 1906 or 1907 she rented a London house, 42 Lowndes Street, in Belgravia, before buying 15 Vale Avenue in Chelsea in 1913, where she commissioned mosaics from Boris Anrep and paintings from Sickert. The war, during which she and Nan ran a hospital in Normandy at Veules-les-Roses, outside Dieppe (1914–19), disrupted the pattern of her life, so that in 1920 she was prepared to sell Newington House. In its place Nan bought the Château d'Auppegard, outside Dieppe, where in 1927 Duncan Grant and Vanessa Bell painted the walls of a loggia. In Newington, London, and Auppegard, Ethel provided exquisite and congenial settings for her friends, writers and artists, Chelsea and Bloomsbury, old and young, established and aspiring, in which to congregate. Under her roof Lytton Strachey met Gertrude Stein and George Moore; Henry James (a long-standing friend of Ethel's mother) and his brother William met Lady Ottoline Morrell; Virginia Woolf met Arnold Bennett and Bennett met Sickert.

In 1939 Ethel Sands and Nan Hudson again became nurses in France, only just escaping the German advance in 1940. The Château d'Auppegard was occupied and its garden used as a launching pad for flying bombs. In 1941 a bomb gutted Ethel's new house at 52 Chelsea Square, London. In 1957, following a long illness, Nan Hudson died. Ethel Sands died of heart failure at her home, 18 Chelsea Square, on 19 March 1962. WENDY BARON

Sources W. Baron, *Miss Ethel Sands and her circle* (1977) · priv. coll., Sands MSS
Archives Tate collection, corresp., family papers, and photographs
Likenesses W. Sickert, oils, *c.*1913, priv. coll.
Wealth at death £74,372 8*s.*: probate, 9 July 1962, *CGPLA Eng. & Wales*

Sands, Robert Gerald [Bobby] (1954–1981), Irish republican and hunger striker, was born in Abbot's Cross in Newtownabbey, a northern suburb of Belfast, on 9 March 1954, the son of John Sands, a Post Office worker, and his wife, Rosaleen. The eldest of four children, he was educated at Stella Maris primary school and the local Catholic secondary school. He left school in June 1969 and attended Newtownabbey Technical College for nine months before getting a job as an apprentice coach builder. Sands, who was a keen and able sportsman, played football for a local team with a mixed membership and was also a member of Willowfield Temperance Harriers, a well known and predominantly protestant running club. His family moved into the Rathcoole housing estate in Newtownabbey when he was seven. Rathcoole was a new public authority estate, the largest in western Europe, and until the outbreak of the troubles in August 1969 it had a substantial number of Catholic tenants. By the time Sands left school the deepening political crisis was generating tense intercommunity relations and the beginning of the ugly process of intimidation of minorities in housing estates and workplaces throughout Belfast. Catholics were the minority in Newtownabbey and Rathcoole, and from 1969 onwards there was a growing exodus to areas such as the Catholic Twinbrook estate in west Belfast, where Sands's family was forced to move in June 1972.

There was no history of republican involvement in his family, and Bobby Sands was typical of a generation of young working-class Catholics whose republicanism was born out of the sectarian conflagration of August 1969 which brought British troops onto the streets of Belfast and Londonderry. Sands joined the provisional Irish Republican Army (IRA) in 1972 and was arrested for the first time in October 1972. While on remand he married on 3 March 1973 Geraldine Noade, a seventeen-year-old shop assistant. They had a son. Geraldine Sands moved to England after Sands was imprisoned in 1977. Charged with possession of four handguns and sentenced to five years in April 1973, he was sent to Long Kesh prison (renamed the Maze in 1976) near Lisburn. Granted special category status by the British government in June 1972, the paramilitary groups controlled their own compounds inside the prison. Sands was in cage 11. It was here that Sands and other young republicans acquired a political education that was a mixture of traditional republicanism and revolutionary theories then current in the developing world. Sands became 'officer commanding' one of the huts in the compound and took a leading role in organizing political education and Irish language classes as well as beginning his own attempts at political analysis and politicized verse.

Released in April 1976, within six months Sands was involved in an IRA attempt to bomb a furniture showroom in south-west Belfast which was interrupted by the Royal Ulster Constabulary. Sentenced to fourteen years in September 1977, he was sent back to Long Kesh (as republicans continued to call it). In the interim special category status had been abolished for all new paramilitary offenders and Sands was put in the new cellular accommodation known as the H blocks. Republican prisoners had launched a campaign for the restoration of special category status which involved the refusal to wear prison uniforms: the 'blanket protest'. This developed into the 'dirty protest' as, refused permission to leave their cells to go to the toilet unless they wore prison uniform, they began to smear their cells with excrement. By late 1980 there were 837 republican prisoners in Long Kesh, of whom 341 were on the dirty protest. Frustrated by the failure of the protest to shift the British government and the lack of active support in the Catholic community for their demands, seven prisoners began a hunger strike on 27 October 1980. It ended after fifty-three days with an ambiguous understanding between the government and the leadership of the republican movement. This soon broke down and a second hunger strike began on 1 March 1981. Ten men had been chosen to follow one another in a phased process, with Sands, who was now the IRA leader in Long Kesh, the first.

Sands had now become the prisoners' most effective literary voice, with a stream of prose pieces and poems smuggled out for publication under the pseudonym of Marcella. These were written during his involvement in the prison protests, which he had joined as soon as he entered Long Kesh in September 1977. They reveal a literary talent wedded to a romantic–fatalist acceptance of death rather than compromise. He died on 5 May 1981 after sixty-six days without food (the government rejected the possibility of force-feeding the prisoners), and nine more prisoners were to die before the hunger strike was called off. More than 100,000 people attended his funeral at Milltown cemetery, Belfast, on 7 May. Even before his death he contributed powerfully to the emergence of Sinn Féin, the IRA's political wing, as a significant political force in Northern Ireland. Sinn Féin organized for him to be nominated as H block candidate in a by-election for the Fermanagh and South Tyrone seat at Westminster. His victory on 9 April 1981 was a powerful impetus for the group of republican revisionists around Gerry Adams who, while still wedded to the armed struggle, believed that it could be defeated unless assisted by a political breakthrough. The victory of Sands allowed Adams to persuade the traditionalists in the movement that Sinn Féin's involvement in electoral politics would complement and not undermine armed struggle.   HENRY PATTERSON

Sources D. Beresford, *Ten men dead* (1987) · B. Sands, *Writings from prison* (1997) · L. Clarke, *Broadening the battlefield: the H-blocks and the rise of Sinn Féin* (1987) · P. Taylor, *Provos: the IRA and Sinn Fein* (1997) · M. Thatcher, *The Downing Street years* (1993) · m. cert.
Archives FILM BFI NFTVA, *World in action*, 23 April 1991
Likenesses photograph, 1981, Hult. Arch.

Sandsbury, John (1575/6–1610), Latin poet and Church of England clergyman, son of John Sandsbury, 'plebeius', was born in London. He was probably educated at St Paul's School, then admitted at Merchant Taylors' School in May 1587, and matriculated, aged seventeen, as scholar of St John's College, Oxford, on 6 July 1593. On 7 February 1597, at the request of Alderman Bennet, he was granted an exhibition of £5 per annum (from St Paul's School funds for poor university scholars); this exhibition was continued for a further three years in 1600, and presumably also in 1603; in 1606 it was ended, with a final gift of 5 marks to commence BD (McDonnell, 89). He became BA on 5 December 1597, MA on 25 June 1601, and BD on 13 July 1608. In 1608 he became vicar of St Giles's, Oxford, and published *Ilium in Italiam*, in which the arms of the university and colleges are each accompanied by nine descriptive Latin hexameters. Bliss commends Wood's research in establishing Sandsbury's authorship, from a catalogue in St John's that calls him 'poeta ingeniosissimus, cuius praeter tragaedias multas apud nos actas, etiam libellus prodit de insignibus collegiorum, additis epigrammatis' ('A most ingenious poet, from whom (apart from many tragedies performed among us) there also appeared a little book on the arms of the colleges, with epigrams added.'; Wood, *Ath. Oxon.*, 2.58–9). The Latin tragedies that he wrote for performance in St John's, and that were, according to Wood, performed many times there, appear to be lost.

Sandsbury's interest in tragedy is confirmed by his introductory verses in *Nero* (1603) by another member of St John's, Matthew Gwinne. There, in twelve neat iambics addressed to Justus Lipsius, he offers Gwinne's work as a superior alternative to the pseudo-Senecan *Octavia*, and a match for anything by Gager, Buchanan, or Beza (Binns, 136). The dedication of *Ilium in Italiam* to James I shows that the poems were composed in 1606, as a demonstration of the university's loyalty. Sandsbury also contributed to the university's verse collections in these years, including the manuscript of 1606 for Christian IV of Denmark. His poem on the death of Elizabeth (*Funebre officium*, 1603, 51–3) is an extended iambic lament, with sixty-six lines of his own (and a half-line quoted from Virgil), praising her charity, in the maundy dole to 'paupercularum turba mulierum' ('a crowd of poor women'), and touching for the queen's evil:

> Strumosa turba quis tibi Princeps opem
> Feret? Quis aurum collo amuletum dabit?

Transfusa nisi sint in Iacobaeum manum

Unless James can inherit the magic, there are poor prospects for the scrofulous. Elizabeth's myriad virtues make her, if not a 'Deipara virgo', at least 'Dei nutrix' (if not 'the virgin who gave birth to God', then 'the nurse of God') ; there is both a clever pun and a sharp rebuke for any reader who confesses boredom: 'Manibus Elisae, non tuis manibus dedi'—this is for her shade, not your hands. When Oxford's poets welcomed James, Sandsbury sent seven separate poems, one of forty-four iambics to the king himself, and shorter offerings to the queen, princes, and princesses (*Pietas*, 1603, 188–90). James comes as a 'Gazophylax' ('a guardian of treasure') to save protestant wealth, 'Papae spes non pias / lusisti' ('you have mocked the pope's impious hopes'), the prince's tennis and dancing give playful hints of his future glory as Henry IX, hopes that Sandsbury himself was not to see dashed. He died in January 1610, and was buried in St Giles's Church on 10 January 1610.   D. K. MONEY

Sources Wood, *Ath. Oxon.*, new edn, 2.58–9 · M. McDonnell, ed., *The registers of St Paul's School, 1509–1748* (privately printed, London, 1977) · J. W. Binns, *Intellectual culture in Elizabethan and Jacobean England: the Latin writings of the age* (1990) · D. K. Money, *The English Horace: Anthony Alsop and the tradition of British Latin verse* (1998) · Foster, *Alum. Oxon.* · M. Gwinne, *Nero* (1603)

Sandwich. For this title name *see* Montagu, Edward, first earl of Sandwich (1625–1672); Montagu, John, fourth earl of Sandwich (1718–1792); Montagu, John, fifth earl of Sandwich (1744–1814); Montagu, (Alexander) Victor Edward Paulet, tenth earl of Sandwich (1906–1995).

Sandwich, Henry of (*b.* before 1205, *d.* 1273), bishop of London, was the son of Sir Henry of Sandwich, a Kentish knight. He spent much of his adult life at Oxford, where he was a master of arts by 1238, and was incepted as doctor of theology in 1256. His outlook may also have been influenced, while he was rector of Helpringham, Lincolnshire, after 1227, by the views of his bishop, Robert Grosseteste. By 1259 Sandwich was archdeacon of Oxford, canon of St Paul's, and prebendary of Weldland, but he gave up these appointments after he was elected bishop of London on 13 November 1262. He was consecrated in Christ Church, Canterbury, on 27 May 1263, by John Gervase, bishop of Winchester, assisted by the bishops of Worcester, Chichester, and Lincoln. All were prominent supporters of the provisions of Oxford and Simon de Montfort, and Sandwich at once emerged as a leading negotiator for the barons in their dealings with Henry III. At their behest, in June 1263, he joined other bishops in urging the king to observe the provisions of Oxford, and expel aliens, except those acceptable to the barons, terms which were incorporated in the peace agreed between the opposing sides on 16 July. Where his sympathies lay was also shown by his decision to pass over the prior claims of a papal chaplain, and present two vacant prebends at St Paul's to Montfort's youngest son, Amaury, and to Thomas de Cantilupe, the nephew of Montfort's long-standing friend, Walter de Cantilupe, bishop of Worcester. On 13 December 1263 Sandwich and Cantilupe were the two bishops who subscribed to the baronial letter agreeing to the arbitration of

Louis IX, and in March 1264, after the king had condemned the Provisions, Sandwich, together with the bishops of Chichester, Winchester, and Worcester, represented the barons in negotiations at Brackley in which they agreed to accept the mise of Amiens, provided that the king expelled aliens and promised to rule through natives. This mission ended in failure, as did another led by Sandwich and Cantilupe, on the eve of the battle of Lewes, in which, with the approval of Montfort and the clergy, they offered Henry £30,000 in compensation for the ravaging of his kingdom.

In June 1264, when the government was reconstructed following Montfort's victory, Sandwich was the only bishop appointed to the new baronial council of nine set up to advise the king. In September, as part of a delegation that also included Cantilupe, sent to the papal legate, Guy Foulquois, cardinal-bishop of Sabina, at Boulogne, he made clear that the king would be required to accept councillors not of his own choosing, and would have to carry out their decisions. The two bishops promised in return that they would try to secure the release of the Lord Edward, and that if they failed, they would oppose the barons. When they returned to England on 3 October, reluctantly carrying bulls of excommunication against the Montfortians, they were intercepted by men of the Cinque Ports who tore up the offending documents. Sandwich was also a member of a committee set up in December to take action against the perpetrators of attacks on church property—earlier in the year he had written to Gilbert de Clare, the earl of Gloucester, reproving him for such depredation. He was summoned to the parliament of January 1265, and in the following March, when Edward was formally released, he was probably among the nine bishops who excommunicated transgressors against Magna Carta and the charter of the forest and the scheme of government agreed in the previous year.

After the fall of Montfort, Sandwich was one of the bishops cited to appear *coram rege* to answer for unspecified offences against the peace and transgressions against the king. He was temporarily suspended by Cardinal Ottobuono, the new legate, in December 1265, and ordered to appear at London on 15 March 1266, when he was accused of treating the previous legate with contempt, acting disloyally towards the king, and celebrating divine offices for excommunicated Montfortians. Although Sandwich complained that he could not prepare his defence out of fear of the king, he was formally suspended and ordered to go to Rome, where he remained, living on a small allowance from his diocese, until, having 'shown his humility and devotion' (*CEPR letters*, 1.441), and at the request of the Lord Edward, he was reinstated by Gregory X on 31 May 1272. He returned to St Paul's on 31 January 1273, but his health was already failing. He was unable to attend Archbishop Robert Kilwardby's consecration on 26 February, and he died on 15 September at the manor of Orsett, Essex. He was buried in St Paul's, at the spot he had selected at the time of his enthronement. His chalice of silver gilt and some of his vestments were long preserved, and his tomb

survived until the Reformation. His executors included Archbishop Kilwardby, and two former Kentish rebels, Nicholas of Lenham and Roger of Tilmanstone.

CLIVE H. KNOWLES

Sources *Chancery records* · T. Stapleton, ed., *De antiquis legibus liber: cronica majorum et vicecomitum Londoniarum*, CS, 34 (1846) · *The historical works of Gervase of Canterbury*, ed. W. Stubbs, 2: *The minor works comprising the Gesta regum with its continuation, the Actus pontificum and the Mappa mundi*, Rolls Series, 73 (1880) · F. N. Davis and others, eds., *Rotuli Ricardi Gravesend, diocesis Lincolniensis*, CYS, 31 (1925) · Emden, *Oxf.* · *Fasti Angl., 1066–1300*, [St Paul's, London] · F. M. Powicke and C. R. Cheney, eds., *Councils and synods with other documents relating to the English church, 1205–1313*, 2 vols. (1964) · W. Dugdale, *The history of St Paul's Cathedral in London*, new edn, ed. H. Ellis (1818) · *Ann. mon.*, vol. 4 · *CEPR letters* · [W. Rishanger], *The chronicle of William de Rishanger, of the barons' wars*, ed. J. O. Halliwell, CS, 15 (1840) · J. R. Maddicott, *Simon de Montfort* (1994)

Sandwich, **Sir Ralph** (*c*.1235–1308), justice and administrator, was a younger son of Sir Simon of Sandwich (*d. c*.1270) of Preston, near Wingham, in Kent, and his wife, Gillian (*d.* in or before 1255), and nephew of Henry of *Sandwich, bishop of London from 1262 to 1273. He belonged to a family with strong Montfortian connections, and his uncle's participation in Earl Simon's administration no doubt brought Ralph into government. He had become part of the captive king's household by September 1264, and was appointed keeper of the wardrobe, and the king's effective gaoler, on 1 January 1265. On 7 May the chancellor delivered the great seal to Sandwich, but with authority for its use only for routine writs; otherwise the presence of Peter de Montfort and two others was necessary. Although Sandwich was no more than keeper of the seal, the chronicler Thomas Wykes nevertheless expressed astonishment that it should be in lay hands.

Sandwich was captured at Evesham, and his property granted to the Kentish magnate Roger of Leybourne, while his father's property at Preston went to Leybourne's son William. However, Sandwich was pardoned in November 1266, and thereafter maintained close connections with the Leybourne family. In 1272 he acted as attorney for Roger of Leybourne's widow, the countess of Winchester, and was to serve as her executor four years later. When the bishop of London died on 15 September 1273, the temporalities of his see were committed to Sandwich, who had possibly been involved in their administration during his uncle's long exile in Rome. He was by this time also steward of the lands of the archbishop of Canterbury, and in November 1273 was appointed to audit the accounts of the constable of Dover Castle. In 1274 he was summoned to attend Edward I's coronation. He sat in several southern counties as commissioner for the inquiry of 1274, and the following year was appointed on several occasions to determine the king's claims on those who had fought against his father at Evesham; his rehabilitation was complete.

In November 1275, in a financial innovation that lasted until 1282, three men were appointed as stewards of the king's demesnes; Sandwich was given responsibility for the counties of the south and west. The post, which exhausted one of his colleagues, involved Sandwich in constant travel, the management of huge sums of money—over £7000 between 1277 and 1279—and the superintendence of major building-works at Devizes, Banstead, and Odiham. He also acted as keeper of the port of Dover (where he was receiver of customs), of the Forest of Dean, and of the temporalities of the see of Canterbury during the vacancy of 1278–9. In 1280 he was appointed to begin negotiations for the acquisition of the site of New Winchelsea. A regular member of the king's council, in February 1278 Sandwich was appointed a justice *coram rege* for as long as the king was in Kent, and was present with the judges when Alexander III, king of Scots, did homage at Westminster in October; he was summoned to the Shrewsbury parliament in September 1283.

In June 1285 Edward I took London into his own hands, and on 1 July Sandwich was appointed warden of the city, with a house on Cornhill; he became constable of the Tower on 10 September. Apart from two interruptions, Sandwich was effectively mayor of London until 1295. He presided in its court of hustings, and in 1285 promulgated a series of ordinances for the administration of the city. At the beginning of the Michaelmas law term of 1289 it was to Sandwich that the king turned for a replacement for the fugitive chief justice, Thomas Weyland, on 24 September appointing him a justice in Weyland's place 'until the king makes further provision' (*CPR, 1281–92*, 324). Sandwich not only sat for at least part of the term, but seems to have been accorded Weyland's precedence, although his appointment had been simply as a justice. Sandwich remained as constable of the Tower, with a brief interlude, from 1285 until weeks before his death. In 1287 the Tower was used to detain the heads of the London Jewish community. There he not only had the charge of Welsh and Scottish political prisoners, but also received into his custody a lion and a leopard sent by the king from Gascony in 1288.

Sandwich sat every year between 1286 and 1307 as a justice at Newgate, where notorious criminals from the whole country as well as London suspects were tried. In that role he issued writs under his own seal, and amerced sheriffs who quite properly refused to execute them; in 1303 the sheriff's oath was altered to permit Sandwich's pragmatic innovation. He also sat at more spectacular trials, including that of William Wallace at Westminster Hall in 1305. He continued to be involved in the governance and mercantile life of London, and was frequently given responsibilities in Kent. The Leybourne family continued to rely on him: in 1297 he was called on to stand surety for his great-nephew, the miscreant Henry Leybourne. In the same year Sandwich was a member of the regency council during the king's absence in Flanders.

In 1306 Sandwich petitioned the crown for repayment of the money he had spent as constable of the Tower, chiefly on building-works (including the reconstruction of the chapel of St Peter ad Vincula between 1285 and 1287) and the custody of prisoners, and also for arrears of his annual fee of £100, which had never been paid. After an investigation over £1750 was eventually allowed by the

king 'in consideration of his free and praiseworthy service to him and his father' (PRO, E 159/79 m21d).

Sandwich can be counted among the many Montfortians who were rapidly reabsorbed into public life. Edward I quickly became willing to entrust him with crucial public positions, and in private regularly employed him to browbeat his adversaries—on two occasions he was sent to convocations to protect the king's rights, and in 1304 was directed to admonish a papal collector 'out of the hearing of his household and with no notary present', seize his money, and banish him (*CClR, 1302–1307*, 334). Yet he seems to have performed the delicate task of managing London for the king to the satisfaction of at least some of its citizens. In 1303 Peter Berneval said in his presence (and unfortunately for himself that of the mayor) that 'he wished to God that Sandwich was still warden of the city as he used to be, because business was dealt with speedily under him' (Thomas, 146).

Sandwich was summoned to attend the coronation of Edward II on 8 February 1308, and on 24 March delivered the custody of the Tower to John Cromwell, who had married the younger Roger Leybourne's widow. He was dead by 20 August 1308 and was buried in the nave of the Greyfriars Church near Newgate, where he had so long presided.   CHRISTOPHER WHITTICK

Sources Chancery records · C. Moor, ed., *Knights of Edward I*, 4, Harleian Society, 83 (1931) · L. B. Larking, 'On the heart-shrine in Leybourne church', *Archaeologia Cantiana*, 5 (1863), 133–93 · J. R. Planché, *A corner of Kent* (1864) · A. H. Thomas, ed., *Calendar of early mayor's court rolls preserved among the archives of the corporation of the City of London at the Guildhall, AD 1298–1307* (1924), 146 · BL, Harley MS 6033, fol. 15v [cited in C. L. Kingsford, *Grey Friars in London*, 1915, 11] · R. B. Pugh, ed., *Calendar of London trailbaston trials under commissions of 1305 and 1306* (1975) · G. O. Sayles, ed., *Select cases in the court of king's bench*, 7 vols., SeldS, 55, 57–8, 74, 76, 82, 88 (1936–71), vol. 2, p. cxlvii · R. Brown, H. M. Colvin, and A. J. Taylor, eds., *The history of the king's works*, 1–2 (1963) · I. J. Churchill, R. Griffin, F. W. Hardman, and F. W. Jessup, eds., *Calendar of Kent feet of fines to the end of Henry III's reign*, 5 vols., Kent Archaeological Society Records Branch, 15 (1939–56) · PRO, exchequer, lord treasurer's remembrancer, pipe rolls, E372/120 m23, 124 m23, 128, 159 m39 · PRO, exchequer, king's remembrancer; accounts various, E 101/4/10, 11, 25; 6/1, 34; 7/27; 24/10; 349/28, 350/3 · PRO, exchequer, king's remembrancer, memoranda rolls, E 159/47–61 · *Ann. mon.*, 4.168
Archives PRO, E 101/24/10

Sandwith, Humphry (1822–1881), army physician and author, was born and baptized at Bridlington, Yorkshire, on 12 April 1822, the son of Humphry Sandwith (*d.* 1867), a physician, and his wife, Jane, the daughter of Isaac Ward, a shipping merchant. His schooling included two years (1832–4) at Horncastle grammar school, Lincolnshire, and in 1834 he went to King's College School, London, when his father assumed the position of editor of the *Watchman*, a Wesleyan Methodist newspaper. From 1838 to 1843 he was unhappily apprenticed to his uncle, Dr Thomas Sandwith of Beverley, which was followed by six months of medical study in Hull, where his father had established a medical practice after leaving his editorial position. The younger Sandwith then enrolled in University College,

Humphry Sandwith (1822–1881), by Camille Silvy, 1862

London, and prepared for the examinations of the Royal College of Surgeons, which he passed in 1846.

A voyage taken in 1847 to recuperate from a knee injury gave Sandwith his first glimpse of the Near East. On his return he took employment as staff surgeon at the Hull Infirmary, but resigned after recurrent bouts of illness. When his efforts to open a practice in London failed, Sandwith decided to seek his career abroad. With financial assistance from his father and a cousin and a letter of introduction to Sir Stratford Canning, the British ambassador to the Ottoman court, Sandwith departed for Constantinople in early 1849. It proved to be a decisive turning point in his life.

Sandwith soon gained *entrée* to British embassy circles in Constantinople. In August 1849 he was invited to accompany an archaeological expedition under the command of Austen Henry Layard that sought to excavate Nineveh in Mesopotamia. He spent the next two years trekking across Asia Minor and providing medical care for the expedition members as well as local peoples. Sandwith was much taken by the experience: he spent much of his time hunting and travelling, enthralled by his exotic surroundings. He described the rugged, arid country as a 'fairyland'. On his return to Constantinople in September 1851 he was placed in charge of the British hospital, which provided him with a modest, but secure practice.

When the Crimean crisis arose in 1853 Sandwith took

up his pen as local correspondent for *The Times*, but his strong defence of the Turkish cause soon caused the newspaper to terminate the relationship. At the outbreak of war in 1854 he joined the irregular force organized by General Beatson as staff surgeon and upon its disbandment he became the chief military officer for British and Turkish forces at Kars. His medical and organizational skills were pushed to the limit when the Russian siege of Kars led to starvation and rampant cholera among the besieged troops. After the fall of Kars in 1855 Sandwith was the sole British captive to be released by the Russians, in appreciation of his services to the sick and wounded among their forces as well as to his own.

With little to cheer about in the Crimean campaign, the British welcomed Sandwith as a hero. He found himself the toast of the country on his return in 1856: he had a private interview with Queen Victoria and Prince Albert; was made CB and received an honorary degree from Oxford University; lectured before the Royal Geographical Society; and was elected a member of the Athenaeum. He accompanied the official British delegation to the coronation of Tsar Alexander II. Sandwith wrote an account of his experiences, *A Narrative of the Siege of Kars* (1856), which showed the first signs of his shift to a more critical opinion of the Ottoman government and the Turkish peoples. The book proved a commercial and critical success, and Sandwith launched a lecture tour that benefited from his celebrity. On 29 May 1860 he married eighteen-year-old Lucy Ann Hargreaves (1842–1882), daughter of Robert Hargreaves; the couple honeymooned in Egypt, Damascus, Rhodes, and Constantinople.

Despite offers to join lucrative medical practices Sandwith decided to abandon his medical career, accepting instead an appointment as colonial secretary of Mauritius, in January 1867. His career as a colonial official was short-lived, however: he took a leave of absence from his post in September 1869, returned to England, and resigned his office in Mauritius, and although he hoped for a more favourable posting none was forthcoming.

Over the next few years Sandwith was drawn into Cobdenite political circles by his wife's uncle, William Hargreaves, and in 1862 he was offered the opportunity to stand for the parliamentary seat at Wycombe. He declined, and instead became an adviser to Cobden and others on the so-called 'Eastern question'. He visited the Balkans in 1864 and returned a critic of the Ottoman government's treatment of its Christian subjects. His novel, *The Hekim Bashi* (2 vols., 1864), is a loosely autobiographical account of a doctor in the Turkish service who becomes disillusioned with Ottoman rule. Sandwith took an increasingly active role in other radical liberal causes, joining John Stuart Mill on the Jamaica committee that sought to prosecute Governor Eyre in 1865, and participating in the popular agitation for parliamentary reform in 1866. With support from Mill, Goldwin Smith, and other liberals, he made an unsuccessful bid to enter parliament for Marylebone in the 1868 election.

During these years Sandwith lived in Wales, first at Llanrhaeadr Hall near Denbigh, then near Llandovery. His family soon grew to five children, with the first, Catherine Sinclair, born in 1862. The outbreak of the Franco-Prussian War in 1870 led him to France, where he used his expertise in military medicine as a volunteer for the National Society for the Sick and Wounded. After his return to Britain he moved his family to Old House, Wimbledon, in Surrey, and published another novel, *Minsterborough: a Tale of English Life* (3 vols., 1871), which was evidently based on memories of his youth.

The last decade of Sandwith's life saw him increasingly involved in Serbian–Ottoman affairs. In 1872 he attended the coronation of Prince Milan of Serbia and established close ties with Serbian leaders. In the following year he returned to seek a Serbian railway concession for some London financiers, but was unsuccessful. When Serbia declared war on the Ottoman empire in 1876, he sped to Belgrade to provide assistance to Serbian refugees and wounded soldiers. He appealed to English charities for relief funds and wrote a series of letters to *The Times* and other British newspapers in support of the Serbian cause.

In January 1877 Sandwith returned to Britain to mobilize public opinion and collect financial aid for Serbia; his lecture tour (one of the lectures being chaired by Gladstone) and his partisan pamphlet, *Shall we Fight Russia? An Address to the Working Men of Great Britain* (1877), provided a preview of the strategies and themes that Gladstone would use in his famous Midlothian campaign against the pro-Turkish foreign policy of Benjamin Disraeli. When Sandwith went back to Serbia in March 1877 he carried with him £7000 in relief funds, but his own health began to break under the strain of his efforts. Twice he was forced from Serbia for medical reasons, the second time permanently. He continued, however, to voice his objections to Disraeli's policies in articles for the *Daily News* and other periodicals. Once so enamoured by the exotic appeal of the Ottoman empire, Sandwith had become one of its fiercest British critics.

In 1876 Sandwith had moved his family to Tours, France, probably because its climate was considered better suited to the needs of his tubercular wife and third daughter. Sandwith was in Paris when he died of heart disease on 16 May 1881. He was buried at Passy in south Paris.

DANE KENNEDY

Sources DNB · T. H. Ward, *Humphry Sandwith: a memoir, compiled from autobiographical notes* (1884) · *The Times* (17 May 1881) · H. Sandwith, *A narrative of the siege of Kars* (1856) · *BMJ* (28 May 1881), 868 · *The Lancet* (21 May 1881) · m. cert. · Gladstone, *Diaries*
Archives BL, letters to Sir Austen Layard, Add. MSS 38979–38988 · DWL, letters to Henry Allon · W. Sussex RO, letters, incl. by his wife, Lucy, to F. A. Maxse
Likenesses C. Silvy, photograph, 1862, NPG [*see illus.*] · D. J. Pound, stipple (after photograph by Watkins), NPG · portrait, Wellcome L.
Wealth at death £5937: probate, 24 Aug 1881, *CGPLA Eng. & Wales*

Sandys. For this title name *see* individual entries under Sandys; *see also* Hill, Mary, marchioness of Downshire and *suo jure* Baroness Sandys of Ombersley (1764–1836).

Sandys, Charles (1786–1859), antiquary, born in Canterbury on 26 October 1786, was the second son of Edwin Humphrey Sandys, solicitor, of Canterbury, and his second wife, Helen, daughter of Edward, Lord Chick. Sandys became a solicitor in 1808, and practised in Canterbury until 1857. He married Sedley Frances Burdett at Bromley, Kent, on 27 May 1815; they had several children.

As a native of Kent, Sandys took a keen interest in Kentish archaeology and antiquities. He joined the newly founded British Archaeological Association in 1844, and contributed a paper on the Dane John Hill at Canterbury to the Gloucester congress volume of that association in 1846. In the same year he was elected a fellow of the Society of Antiquaries on 18 June, and published *A Critical Dissertation on Professor Willis's 'Architectural History of Canterbury Cathedral'*. A concise history of Reculver, Kent, from the time of the Romans to that of Henry VIII, compiled by Sandys, was included in C. Roach Smith's *History and Antiquities of Richborough, Reculver, and Lymne* (1850). His principal work, published in 1851, was *Consuetudines Kanciae: a history of Gavelkind and other remarkable customs in the county of Kent*. Sandys died in 1859, after two years spent abroad because of financial difficulties at home.

SHIRLEY BURGOYNE BLACK

Sources C. Vivian, *Some notes for a history of the 'Sandys' family*, ed. T. M. Sandys (1907) · Burke, *Gen. GB* · DNB
Archives BL, corresp. and papers, Add. MS 45866 · Canterbury Cathedral, archives, charters, and extracts mainly compiled for books on Clerici-Laici and history of Canterbury Cathedral · LPL, collections relating to liberties of Canterbury

Sandys, (Edwin) Duncan, Baron Duncan-Sandys (1908–1987), politician, was born on 24 January 1908 at the Manor House, Sandford Orcas, Dorset, the only child of Captain George John Sandys (1875–1937), army officer and politician, and his wife, Mildred Helen, *née* Cameron, daughter of Duncan Cameron, of Canterbury, New Zealand. His father served with the second Life Guards in the Second South African War, and again with the British expeditionary force in France in 1914, when he was wounded at Ypres. He was Conservative MP for Wells from 1910 to 1918.

Churchill's son-in-law Sandys was educated at Eton College and Magdalen College, Oxford, where he served in the Oxford cavalry Officers' Training Corps and the Oxford University air squadron. After graduating with a second-class degree in modern history in 1929, he was called to the bar by the Inner Temple, but decided in 1930 to join the Foreign Office. He served briefly in Berlin before returning in 1933 to London. He represented the Foreign Office in negotiations for commercial treaties with the Scandinavian countries, and was a member of the British delegation to the abortive world economic conference of 1933.

Sandys's political career began in 1935: in March that year he was elected Conservative MP for Norwood at a by-election, and on 16 September he married Diana Bailey (1909–1963), former wife of Sir John Milner Bailey, second baronet, and eldest daughter of Sir Winston Leonard

Spencer *Churchill, politician. They had one son and two daughters. Sandys's political fortunes during the 1930s were very tied up with those of his father-in-law. Although Sandys's reputation as a critic of appeasement was sometimes later overstated, he did use the knowledge gained as a member of the Territorial Army to attack the poor state of readiness of UK air defences—a tactic which in 1938 saw him threatened with a court martial but exonerated by the parliamentary select committee of privileges.

Sandys's wartime roles fell into two main phases. In 1940–41 he was in active service, first in Norway and then in Wales as commander of an anti-aircraft regiment. This second posting was cut short by a serious car crash which left him with injuries to both feet that continued to trouble him for the rest of his life. Then from 1941 onwards he resumed his full-time political career and began his rise into ministerial ranks. His appointment as financial secretary to the War Office in July 1941 was initially criticized by the 1922 committee as an example of nepotism. His subsequent effectiveness in office, however, suggested that this complaint was largely unjust. In February 1943 he was made parliamentary secretary to the Ministry of Supply and asked to chair the cabinet committee responsible for devising countermeasures to the V-weapons. In this capacity he displayed the activism and attention to detail for which he became renowned, holding his own with the service chiefs in their discussions of how to stop the German weapons, reportedly suggesting the extremely effective step of moving many anti-aircraft batteries to the south coast, where V1s were easier to shoot down, and persisting despite strong cabinet opposition, notably from Herbert Morrison, with a disinformation campaign towards the Germans about where their rockets had landed. He was also responsible for co-ordinating the intelligence effort which identified Peenemunde as the launch site for the unstoppable V2s and opened the way for the base to be bombed. He was sworn of the privy council in 1944.

In November 1944 the dire state of Britain's house rebuilding effort persuaded Churchill to move his son-in-law to the Ministry of Works. Here Sandys proved able to revitalize the reconstruction drive, once more demonstrating a remarkable ability both to push forward policy despite bureaucratic and logistical obstacles and to immerse himself in the details of his brief. It is claimed that Sandys himself came up with the idea of producing prefabricated houses in 'left-hand' and 'right-hand' models, designed to ensure that the living-room would receive afternoon sunlight regardless of the building's exact location.

The European movement Given the political importance of the house-rebuilding effort such success might have been expected to produce a rapid political reward. Instead, Sandys's rising ministerial career was brutally interrupted by the general election of 1945 at which he, like so many other prominent Conservatives, lost his seat. Churchill would have liked to have placed him in charge

of the Conservative Research Department—a role to which Sandys's capacity to think radically would have been well suited, but which might have led the Conservatives' post-war policy rethink in a much more right-wing direction than was actually the case under Rab Butler's guidance—but this was blocked. As a result, Sandys channelled his considerable energies into the organization of Churchill's post-war campaign for European unity.

Sandys's impact as an organizer of pro-European activity was considerable. He and Churchill had been discussing ideas for European co-operation since the final stages of the war. But it was Sandys who persuaded the leader of the opposition to voice these ideas publicly and to use a speech which he was due to give in Zürich in September 1946 as an occasion to launch an inspirational call to the nations of Europe, and to France and Germany in particular, to unite. This rhetorical appeal was followed up, again as a result of Sandys's prompting, by the establishment of an organized campaign. The 'United Europe Committee' was formally established in January 1947 with Churchill as the figurehead and Sandys as the general secretary and driving force. It was the latter who drafted most of Churchill's April 1947 Albert Hall speech, which marked the UK launch of the campaign. Likewise it was to Sandys that the tasks fell of recruiting support within the Conservative Party—Robert Boothby, Harold Macmillan, Lord Cranborne, and others were soon signed up—and of forging those trans-European links without which the campaign could not hope to succeed. To this end Sandys attended the Gstaad and Montreux meetings of European federalists and then, in concert with Joseph Retinger, decided to organize a large-scale 'Congress of Europe', a plan which culminated in the 1948 meeting in The Hague attended by a stellar roll-call of European politicians. He also became chairman of the international executive of the European movement, a role which allowed him to ensure that pressure for European unity did not fall away after delegates had left The Hague.

Britain's rather ambivalent attitude towards European unity soon began to undermine Sandys's efforts, however. Already at The Hague representatives of the Labour government had been notable by their absence. But Sandys's difficulties were not confined to the opposite side of the House of Commons; within his own party, too, several prominent front-benchers—Anthony Eden and Butler, for instance—and probably the majority of back-benchers, regarded Churchill's and Sandys's Europeanism with suspicion and mistrust. Continental hopes that Britain's aloof attitude and its self-willed exclusion from such early integration efforts as the 1950 Schuman plan were attributable to Labour and would end once the Conservatives returned to power, were therefore dashed in 1951 when the peacetime Churchill government adopted an attitude of benevolent neutrality towards the efforts under way on the continent—an attitude which differed little from that of Ernest Bevin and the post-war Labour cabinet. The self-styled 'Europeans' such as Macmillan, Boothby, and Sandys himself, who had returned to parliament as MP for

Streatham in 1950, could do no more than watch in frustration as the tone and substance of British European policy was shaped by Eden's views and attitudes rather than their own.

Ministerial career In personal terms Sandys's disappointment was tempered by the resumption of his own ministerial career. His first post-war portfolio, held between October 1951 and October 1954, was as minister of supply. Here his most pressing task was to undo Labour's nationalization of the steel industry, a step which he carried out with a degree of moderation. He also had a first opportunity to think about the way of adapting Britain's world role (and more specifically its military role) to its economic capacity, a question that was central to his later stint as secretary of state for defence. Then between October 1954 and January 1957 he became minister for housing and local government, planning a modernization of local government (which became the 1958 Local Government Act), overseeing a reform of the rental system, introducing slum clearance allowances, and championing pedestrianized city centres.

The apogee of Sandys's political career was reached under Harold Macmillan. Eden's successor did not have an easy personal relationship with Sandys—he spoke often of his 'cassant' manner—but he appreciated Sandys's forcefulness, hard work, and capacity to get things done. As Macmillan later put it to his official biographer, Sandys was 'a very tough man—he wouldn't have any nonsense … and was—quite simply—good at any job you gave him to do' (Horne, 2.48). He therefore employed Churchill's son-in-law in a succession of demanding posts where an abrasive and forthright hatchet man was seen as being necessary.

The first of these was as secretary of state for defence. Britain had inherited armed services still bloated from the Second World War—a nonsense at a time of steady decolonization and the recasting, if not the disappearance, of Britain's global role. Sandys was thus entrusted by Macmillan with the job of radically pruning Britain's military capacity and adopting a defence posture more in keeping with a medium-size power. This was something the need for which Macmillan had become aware of during his own brief tenure of the defence portfolio in 1954–5. It was also a task, however, which had to be carried out in the face of strong opposition from the armed forces themselves and from many within the Conservative Party, not least Anthony Head, Sandys's immediate predecessor. Sandys threw himself at the challenge with his customary vigour. Both the nature of his mission and the manner in which he approached it quickly won him enemies—he is said to have literally come to blows with Sir Gerald Templar, chief of the Imperial General Staff—but he was able to strike up a surprisingly effective working relationship with Lord Mountbatten, the first sea lord, and produced a wide-ranging and radical defence white paper in 1957 which mapped out a defence strategy for the following decade and cut back much of the UK's surplus military capacity. In order to reach agreement with the service chiefs, Sandys had to drop some of his more radical ideas:

his plan to replace all fighters with missiles was abandoned, while Mountbatten was able to win a reprieve for the notion of a navy with global reach. His proposed reorganization of the decision-making structures of British defence policy—with the institution of a powerful Ministry of Defence in place of the multiple service ministries—generated such opposition that it was temporarily disowned by Macmillan (although it was revived later on in Macmillan's premiership). But to have achieved as much as he did, given the entrenched opposition of the military and the emotive nature of the subject, was a tribute to his combative character and an achievement of lasting significance.

In October 1959 Sandys was shifted back to Supply, this time with the brief of breaking up the ministry and forming a new Ministry of Aviation. This bureaucratic reorganization was accomplished, although the second aspect of the job, that of revitalizing Britain's ailing aircraft industry, had barely begun when the minister was once more on the move, this time to the Commonwealth Relations Office. Macmillan had two reasons for moving Sandys. The first was that he was already planning his application to the EEC and used the July 1960 reshuffle to move reliable pro-Europeans into those posts which would be most sensitive during an EEC membership bid. Relations with the Commonwealth clearly fell into this category. The second was that, at a time during which the 'winds of change' were blowing strongly through Britain's empire and Africa in particular, the prime minister wanted to counter-balance the liberal instincts of the colonial secretary, Iain Macleod, with someone whose views were less difficult for the bulk of the Conservative Party to swallow. As John Ramsden put it, Sandys was to 'act as brake to Macleod's accelerator in Africa' (Ramsden, *Winds of Change*, 147).

Macmillan's complicated calculations worked in part. On the EEC front Sandys proved an effective operator, listening to Commonwealth grievances during the months before the July 1961 application but then playing them down during cabinet debates, and contributing to the skilful management of the September 1962 Marlborough House conference, in the course of which grudging Commonwealth acquiescence was obtained in the entry terms so far agreed in Brussels. But on Africa his partnership with Macleod was a stormy affair, especially over Roy Welensky and the planned Central African Federation. The colonial secretary threatened to resign over the issue on several occasions and for over a year co-operation between the two ministers was only sustained by dint of frequent intervention by the premier. By October 1961 it had all become too much and Macleod was replaced by Reginald Maudling. This partnership worked no better—Maudling shared his predecessor's liberalism—and in March 1962 the whole central African issue was taken from the two ministers and given to Butler, the deputy prime minister. The most difficult issue of the period had proved beyond Sandys, although his lack of success had much to do both with Macmillan's over-clever attempt to divide responsibility for Africa between two incompatible ministers and the inherent difficulties of an affair which would continue to torment successive British governments until 1979. Central Africa apart, Sandys retained responsibility for Commonwealth issues until October 1964, when the Conservatives lost office. His offer to resign in 1963, when his name became entangled with the Profumo affair, was rejected by Macmillan.

Later career Despite his seniority, Sandys did not follow ministerial responsibility with a lengthy stint as a shadow spokesman. In 1965 he did help shape the opposition's European policy—an easy task given the similarity between his instincts and those of the new party leader, Edward Heath—but in 1966, after Labour's new electoral triumph, he was dismissed. Quite why is unclear. Heath's ostensible reason was that he wanted fresh faces after the election defeat; others speculate that Sandys was either too right-wing, or somewhat tainted in Heath's eyes by his colourful private life.

Controversy continued to dog Sandys even after 1966. Two years later he became involved in a very public row with Macleod over whether or not the Kenyan Asians, increasingly discriminated against in east Africa, should be able to settle in Britain. In keeping with his very strong views on the subject, Sandys was strongly against immigration being allowed and supported the restrictive measures taken by the home secretary, James Callaghan. And in 1973, the year before Sandys ended his lengthy Commons career and accepted a peerage, as Baron Duncan-Sandys, and the year in which he was made CH, he faced renewed criticism from Heath for the way in which he had been given a very large tax-free payment in the Cayman Islands as chairman of Lonrho at a time when British residents were not allowed to hold overseas accounts. The affair was famously denounced by the prime minister in parliament as 'the unpleasant and unacceptable face of capitalism' (Heath, 418). Sandys's first marriage broke down in the late 1950s, and the divorce was finalized in 1960. (His former wife resumed her maiden name, Diana Churchill, by deed poll in 1962, and committed suicide in 1963.) On 19 April 1962 Sandys married Marie-Claire Hudson (*b*. 1928/9), daughter of Adrien Schmitt, industrialist, of Paris, and former wife of Robert William Hudson, second Viscount Hudson. The marriage was happy, and they had one daughter. Marie-Claire nursed her husband through a long final illness, which necessitated a move from their house in Vincent Square, London, to a flat at 12 Warwick Square. It was there that Sandys died on 26 November 1987, of cancer. He was survived by his wife, their daughter, and the three children of his first marriage. A memorial service was held on 10 February 1988 at St Margaret's, Westminster.

Assessment Despite a somewhat tawdry end to his career, Sandys was a remarkable politician. A man of immense energy, he showed himself to have both a creative mind and great doggedness in overcoming obstacles. Lord Orr-Ewing summed up his characteristics well: 'the man was a steam-roller—he would grind away in first gear and nothing could stand in his path' (Onslow, 18). Both Churchill

and Macmillan made good use of this tenacity. He was also an effective parliamentary speaker, if a little prone to excessive detail, and a conscientious minister whose civil servants came to respect his sheer hard work and attention to the minutiae of policy making. The 1957 defence white paper, perhaps his most significant peacetime achievement, was typical in being substantially drafted by Sandys himself. But while these characteristics made him a very able lieutenant to a political master who knew where he wanted to go, Sandys himself at times lacked the judgement, the tact, and the political flair to rise to the highest office. N. PIERS LUDLOW

Sources *DNB* · *The Times* (27 Nov 1987) · *The Independent* (28 Nov 1987) · Burke, *Peerage* · *WWW* · S. Onslow, *Backbench debate within the conservative party and its influence on British foreign policy, 1948–57* (1997) · A. Horne, *Macmillan*, 2 vols. (1988–9) · J. Ramsden, *The age of Churchill and Eden, 1940–1957* (1995) · J. Ramsden, *The winds of change: Macmillan to Heath, 1957–1975* (1996) · S. Ball, 'Harold Macmillan and the politics of defence: the market for strategic ideas during the Sandys era revisited', *20th century British history*, 6/1 (1995) · R. Hansen, 'The Kenyan Asians, British politics, and the Commonwealth Immigrants Act, 1968', *HJ*, 42 (1999), 809–34 · E. Heath, *The course of my life* (1998) · H. Evans, *Downing Street diary: the Macmillan years, 1957–63* (1981) · K. Young, 'The party in English local government', *The conservative party since 1900*, ed. A. Seldon and S. Ball · b. cert. · m. certs. · d. cert.

Archives CAC Cam., corresp. and papers · PRO | Bodl. Oxf., corresp. with L. G. Curtis · Bodl. RH, corresp. with R. R. Welensky · CAC Cam., corresp. with Sir E. L. Spears · European University Institute, Florence, Historical Archives of the European Communities, European Movement archives · HLRO, corresp. with Lord Beaverbrook · King's Lond., Liddell Hart C., corresp. with Sir B. H. Liddell Hart · Nuffield Oxf., corresp. with Lord Cherwell · U. Leeds, Brotherton L., corresp. with Sir Harry Legge-Bourke · Welwyn Garden City Library, corresp. with Sir Frederic Osborn

Likenesses photograph, repro. in *The Times* · photograph, repro. in *The Independent*

Wealth at death £209,010: probate, 25 April 1988, *CGPLA Eng. & Wales*

Sandys, Edwin (1519?–1588), archbishop of York, was probably born in 1519: he believed himself to be sixty-three in 1582, while in 1588 Tobie Matthew, his successor but two as archbishop, reported that Sandys now claimed to be sixty-six and was reckoned by his own brother to be 'seventy at the most' (BL, Cotton MS Titus B vii, fols. 424–6).

Origins and early academic career Sandys and Archbishop Edmund Grindal were thus exact contemporaries, and both came from present-day Cumbria. Whether they shared their childhood and early education, perhaps at Rottington Hall, on the coast within Grindal's native parish of St Bees, the seat of a senior branch of the Sandys family, is less certain than has sometimes been thought. Sandys was looking for someone who would vouch for his good character when he wrote, as bishop of Worcester, that Grindal and he had lived 'familiarlye' and 'as brothers' (PRO, SP 12/28/40), but he appears to be saying that their friendship began only when he was twelve, and that they were separated from his thirteenth to his eighteenth year, Sandys having gone up to Cambridge before Grindal (but not as much as five years ahead). Sandys was

Edwin Sandys (1519?–1588), by unknown artist, 1571

born at Esthwaite Hall near Hawkshead, then in Lancashire, where he would later found the grammar school attended by William Wordsworth. He was the fifth of the seven sons of William Sandys (d. 1548) and his wife, Margaret, daughter of John Dixon of London and sister to a merchant tailor, which may explain the choice of school for the archbishop's second son, Sir Edwin *Sandys. In 1578, as archbishop of York, Sandys took steps to make Hawkshead a parish in its own right and rebuilt the north aisle of the church to create a sort of shrine for his parents, erecting a table-tomb of ostentatious antiquarianism. William Sandys is depicted in full armour, his feet resting on a lion, and his wife with a lapdog and in attire which would have been fashionable in the fourteenth century. The inscription, spelling out in antique characters the father's service to the crown and the son's academic and ecclesiastical achievements, is not suggestive of Christian humility. But in his great dispute with Sir John Bourne, Sandys did not claim that his father was a gentleman, only that he was 'an honest man' and a JP (PRO, SP 12/28/40).

Since John Foxe records that Sandys's 'schoolmaster' was the martyr John Bland, vicar of Adisham in Kent, and since Bland was a native of Sedbergh and may have taught at Furness Abbey, it has been assumed that that is where Sandys had his grammar schooling. But it is more likely that Sandys became Bland's pupil at St John's College, Cambridge, which he entered in 1532 or 1533, graduating BA in 1539 and proceeding MA in 1541 and BTh in 1547. In 1542 he was proctor and in 1547, without having held a fellowship at St John's, became master of St Catharine's College. He proceeded DTh in 1549, and in 1552, at little more than thirty, was vice-chancellor. There is no record of his ordination, but from later controversies it is clear that this was not performed according to the protestant ordinal. He occurs on an Edwardian list of licensed preachers and accumulated a small portfolio of benefices: the Buckinghamshire vicarage of Haversham (1548) and prebends at Peterborough (1549) and Carlisle (1552). He married a remote cousin, Mary Sandys, who brought to the marriage the manor of Edwardes Hall at Woodham Ferrers, Essex, which was rebuilt in the archbishop's time and renamed Edwins Hall. It was there that the second Mrs Sandys would spend her widowhood and be buried.

Sandys was a protestant from the time that anything is known about his religion. In Cambridge he was said to have been one of the extended family circle of the Strasbourg reformer Martin Bucer. His Elizabethan sermons were robustly anti-Catholic, insistent on the most salient of protestant doctrines. 'This doctrine of justification by faith in the death and resurrection of Christ Jesu', he proclaimed at the Spittle in London, 'is no new doctrine, but old' (Ayre, 291). And in another sermon, preached in St Paul's: 'This grace of God which saveth, hath appeared to all men: this heavenly food, Christ Jesus, by preaching the gospel is offered to all' (ibid., 11). It would be anachronistic to call Sandys an Arminian, but there is no trace in his preaching of the Calvinist stress on exclusive election, and in 1575 he contributed a commendatory preface to a translation of Luther's commentary on Galatians, which may have been intended by John Foxe, its promoter, as a prophylactic against the anxieties associated with extreme Calvinism.

Prison and exile With the death of Edward VI in July 1553, it becomes possible to put flesh on the bare bones of Sandys's curriculum vitae, thanks to a circumstantial narrative which first appeared in the 1583 edition of Foxe's *Acts and Monuments*, which Sandys presumably supplied. When John Dudley, duke of Northumberland, came into East Anglia to proclaim Queen Jane and apprehend the Lady Mary, Sandys as vice-chancellor was forced to preach in support of this *coup d'état*. He was about to dispatch a fair copy of his sermon for publication when Mary was proclaimed in London, and Northumberland was obliged to follow suit in Cambridge. He told Sandys that Mary was merciful and that he was likely to survive. Sandys told him not to count on it, and later observed in an Elizabethan sermon that justice ought not to spare 'mighty men … for their sins are mighty sins. If such offend, their fall draweth down others with them' (Ayre, 227).

That was said from bitter experience. Sandys had been prepared to fight for his vice-chancellorship, threatening to use his dagger against those sent to depose and arrest him. This was not the first time that he had drawn his weapon in public, and it was evidence of a violent temperament, even of what his enemies called 'phrensye' (PRO, SP 12/28/38). On 25 July he was among alleged traitors, including Northumberland and other nobles, who were escorted to the Tower by an army of 4000 men. Sandys confirms that he was 'the first prisoner that entered in that day' (*Acts and Monuments*, 8.593).

Yet Foxe headlined the narrative 'God's Providence in

Preserving Dr. Sands in Queen Mary's Days'. Apart from divine providence, how had it been managed? Sandys spent twenty-nine weeks in the Tower, sharing a cell with the future martyr, John Bradford. When Sir Thomas Wyatt rose in arms the Tower was cleared, supposedly to make room for new traitors, and Sandys was moved to the Marshalsea in Southwark, where his cell-mate and 'sworn stakefellow' was another martyr, Lawrence Saunders. But after nine weeks political wires were pulled, particularly by Sir Thomas Holcroft, knight marshal of the Marshalsea and a protestant sympathizer, and Sandys was more or less a free man. In his own account he was anxious to emphasize that his offence had not been treason, and that his release had been both legal and without any concessions on his part. After a series of picaresque adventures, and with the assistance of Edward Isaac of Well Court, Ickham, a prominent Kentish protestant and a supporter of Sandys's tutor John Bland (which perhaps explains the connection), he got away to Antwerp, and eventually to Strasbourg, where his wife joined him after a year. He soon buried her, and a son, and was himself gravely ill for nine months. Nevertheless in one of his Strasbourg sermons he was ecstatic. 'We have lost the saving truth at home, and found it abroad: our countrymen are become our enemies, and strangers are made our friends' (Ayre, 296). The experience left a permanent mark. Later Sandys would beg Archbishop Matthew Parker, a close Cambridge colleague who had stayed at home, not to condemn 'all Germanical natures' (Bruce and Perowne, 125).

The Marian exiles can be roughly divided into public and private figures. Sandys had arrived in company with Richard Cox, who with Grindal fits into the first category, and Cox and Grindal were now to be embroiled in the troubled affairs of the exiled congregations, which had significance for the ecclesiastical future in England. Sandys played an active part in both rounds of 'the Troubles of Frankfort'. But like John Jewel he devoted himself mainly to study, particularly to Hebrew, which would later qualify him to handle the translation of the books of Kings and Chronicles for the Bishops' Bible. When their mentor, Pietro Martire Vermigli (known as Peter Martyr), withdrew from Strasbourg to Zürich, Sandys and Jewel followed him.

At dinner with Peter Martyr when the news arrived of Mary's death, Sandys found that he could not join in the general rejoicing. 'It smote into his heart, that he should be called to misery' (Acts and Monuments, 8.598). Years later, he would confess to Heinrich Bullinger some nostalgia for his life at Zürich 'as a sojourner and private person' (Robinson, 295). Meeting with Grindal in Strasbourg, they travelled back together, starting out on 21 December 1558 and reaching London on the day of Elizabeth's coronation, 15 January 1559. Sandys celebrated his return by remarrying, on 19 February, in defiance of what was then the law. His new wife was Cicely (d. 1611), daughter of Sir Thomas Wilford of Cranbrook, Kent, whose brother Thomas had been a fellow exile. Both Cicely's brothers were to be knighted and both her sisters married knights. Cicely, described even by Sandys's enemy Bourne as 'faier,

well nurtured, sober and demure' (PRO, SP 12/28/38), was destined to be the mother of seven sons, including the writer and traveller George *Sandys, and two daughters.

The Elizabethan religious settlement and politics The Germanically natured Sandys was disappointed with the Elizabethan religious settlement. On 30 April 1559 he wrote wearily to Parker of 'these tossings and griefs, alterations and mutations' (Bruce and Perowne, 66). The causes of grief included the clause in the Act of Uniformity, with its corresponding rubric in the prayer book, which required use of the 'ornaments', such as vestments, stipulated in the first Edwardian prayer book. Sandys thought that the intention was not that the clergy would be obliged to use these things, but that the queen would be able to help herself to items of considerable value before they found their way on to the second-hand market. He was wrong, and his entire episcopal career was to be compromised by the royal imperative to achieve obedient uniformity in respect of what Jewel called trifles. When Sandys came to write his will, he declared that the controverted ceremonies were neither ungodly nor unlawful, but remained adamant that 'some of them be not so expediente for this churche nowe but ... they may better be disused by litle and litle then more and more urged'. While the English ecclesiastical polity 'in some poyntes may be bettered', he utterly misliked what came to be called presbyterianism, for 'the state of a smale private Churche and the fourme of a large christian kingdome neither woulde longe like nor can at all brooke one and the same ecclesiasticall governmente' (PRO, PROB 11/75, fol. 233r). These remarks were remembered, and a bone of contention, as late as 1679. It is unfortunate that historians have reported that Sandys's funeral effigy in Southwell Minster shows him vested in a chasuble with a mitre, which would indeed have been unique for an Elizabethan bishop. In fact the bare-headed Sandys is arrayed in a rochet and chimere, standard academic and episcopal attire.

Sandys had ministered in 'a small private church', but now he was to be a bishop in a large Christian kingdom, not an easy transition to make. From August to November 1559 he was employed in the royal visitation of the northern province, a punishing circuit which took him from Nottingham through York to Chester, via Durham and Carlisle. He shared the preaching with fellow émigrés and future bishops James Pilkington and Edmund Scambler, occupying the pulpit at Nottingham, York, Hull, Newcastle, Richmond, Kendal, and Manchester. At Bishop Auckland he preached so strongly against the real presence that his kinsman Bernard Gilpin, who was to preach the visitation sermon at Lancaster, had difficulty in subscribing. Sandys took pride in the fact that everywhere the visitors went 'images of every kind' were removed and burned, and especially the cross, or 'rood'. Hence his discomfiture when later in the year the queen countermanded what he supposed to have been done by public authority, ordering the general restoration of crosses. Sandys claimed to have been 'rather vehement in this matter', to have incurred the royal displeasure, and to have been in danger of removal from the episcopal bench even before he got there (Robinson, 74).

Sandys had been first offered the see of Carlisle but turned it down, as did Gilpin, Sandys's preferred candidate for that see. Sandys claimed to have been almost as reluctant to accept Worcester, but protested to Peter Martyr that he could not have refused it without incurring Elizabeth's displeasure, 'and in some measure deserting the church of Christ' (Robinson, 73). Whether Sandys owed his episcopal promotion to the queen, or to William Cecil, or to Robert Dudley, may be a *question mal posée*. Sandys claimed more than once to have enjoyed Elizabeth's favour and seems to have had easier access to court than other bishops. But it is doubtless significant that he and Cecil had been contemporaries at St John's. In 1563 Sandys sent Cecil a new year's gift, describing him as 'the meane to bringe me into the place of honestie' (BL, Lansdowne MS 6, no. 88, fol. 204). Whenever he found himself in a hole, which was often, Sandys always looked to Cecil to dig him out. But he also counted on Dudley, from 1564 earl of Leicester, assuring him that 'your lordship nedith not to be a suetor unto me … but rather to commande me' (BL, Add. MS 32091, fol. 185). When he tried to turn down the bishopric of London, he explained himself to Cecil but not to Leicester, and Leicester was furious. However, once installed, Sandys made the earl steward of his lands. That more letters survive to Cecil than to Leicester may be an archival accident.

Moves to improve the settlement in the convocation of 1563 were led by the bishops rather than by 'Puritans' in the lower house, and Sandys seems to have drafted a paper which proposed the abolition of the sign of the cross in baptism and baptism by midwives. More than twenty years later, as archbishop of York, he would claim never to have allowed women to baptize in his diocese, and that he had spoken to the queen about the matter 'very earnestly' (Peel, 1.281). It is likely that Sandys was subsequently involved in the abortive parliamentary reform programme which followed defeat and frustration in convocation.

Certainly Sandys seems to have been one of the most active parliamentarians on the episcopal bench. In particular, he was in the van of the campaign to bring Mary, queen of Scots, to book. In a letter to Cecil he called her the root of England's troubles and he was one of the first to demand her head. In the parliament of 1572, the bishops confronted the queen with arguments urging her to proceed with severity against Mary, and came as close as they dared to threatening Elizabeth herself with deposition, citing the Old Testament precedent of Saul whom God had deprived of his kingdom for sparing the life of Agag. There are good reasons for identifying Sandys as the author of this ultimatum. In a sermon preached at Paul's Cross at the time of the Babington plot, he again cited the example of Saul and Agag, and in an undated parliament sermon (perhaps preached in 1572) he reminded his hearers that it was Samuel, a role model for Elizabeth, who had made it his business to hew Agag in pieces. Here he spoke of 'foolish pity', a phrase used in the marginal note which

he himself had composed for the Bishops' Bible, to accompany the story of good King Asa failing to put to death his wicked mother, Maachah, in 2 Chronicles. This was the 'bitter note' which so offended James I when he found it in the Geneva Bible, partly prompting him to order the Authorized Version: where the same comment still appeared. Although Sandys is not known to history as a resistance theorist, it is significant that he had called Mary Tudor 'Bloody Mary', an expression usually said to have been invented in the nineteenth century, and 'Mary Marall', or even plain 'Mary' (PRO, SP 12/28/38).

Elizabeth was not amused by Sandys's politics. In her response in 1566 to the petition of the Lords and Commons that she marry and limit the succession, she singled out the bishops for harsh criticism, almost pointing at Sandys when she recalled that some of them, after Edward VI's death, had openly preached that she and her sister were bastards. Yet this may not be the whole story. If a letter from Sandys to the earl of Shrewsbury is to be believed, the queen took him into her confidence in 1579 about the Anjou match: a rare glimpse of an Elizabethan bishop as courtier.

Worcester Sandys was consecrated bishop of Worcester at Lambeth on 21 December 1559. On 24 March 1560 he preached at St Paul's in his episcopal rochet and in April left for his diocese, where there began to appear another and less spiritual side to his nature, quarrelsome and acquisitive. But Sandys was a most energetic bishop, claiming to have preached once or twice every Sunday and holy day, besides visitation sermons and 'wourk daye sermons' (PRO, SP 12/28/40). His diocesan visitation in 1569 was based on no less than forty-seven articles, with thirty-four articles for the cathedral. He made his first visitation of the cathedral within two or three weeks of his arrival in Worcester, and on 17 May the great cross and image of Our Lady, which had somehow escaped the holocaust of 1559, were burned in the precincts. The newly restored Marian choir was wrecked, and the great organ, 'being one of the most solempne instrumentes of this realme', was demolished, allegedly to make pewter dishes and bedsteads (PRO, SP 12/28/35). Sandys's precipitate visitation soon became the occasion of a falling out with the archbishop, who had tried to prevent it in order not to overburden the parishes, and who now accused him of doing it to make money, 'before I was lukewarm in place', which Sandys vehemently denied. 'My private gain was £24 loss.' Then came the familiar *nolo episcopari*: 'Such joy have I of this office, that I could wish to be dispatched; and I have often wrestled with myself for keeping it thus long' (Bruce and Perowne, 126–7). He had served a mere eighteen months!

What this blustering letter suggests is that Sandys had stirred up a hornets' nest, through depriving two prominent prebendaries on his own say-so and falling out with the numerous conservatively minded JPs. One quarrel in particular was to dominate his Worcester episcopate. Sir John Bourne had become a powerful local magnate, having served the Marian regime as secretary of state, and had profited from his connections with the cathedral priory, and later chapter, which had made him its high steward. Given their religious differences, Bourne and Sandys were bound to find each other intolerable. In particular, Bourne was unable to stomach what he called priests' whores ('I must confess my continuall misliking of preestes mariage, specially his'), alleging that ecclesiastical property had been misappropriated to build a washhouse, 'necessarye for his wyeffes laundrye', and to provide a nursery, 'his wyef beinge of good fecundytye and a very frutefull woman' (PRO, SP 12/28/36). Some of this bad blood went back to the bishop's misadventures in the days of Queen Jane and Queen Mary, in which Bourne had played a part.

If Sandys comes out of this unedifying affair as the aggrieved party, he was unwise to allow himself to be dragged into the insults and injuries mutually inflicted by the families and servants of the two warring factions. And some of the dirt stuck, especially allegations of the misuse of episcopal property, forcing Sandys to protest: 'I was never charged before with covetousnes: ... for my gredie getting is suche, that I am in debt a good somme' (PRO, SP 12/28/40). But the evidence is clear that he was already making use of the opportunity to advance his children, and even to settle his brother Miles Sandys in Worcestershire. As for Bourne, he was subjected to the humiliation of imprisonment in—ironically—the Marshalsea, but his letter of abject apology seethes with indignation, and not long before his translation to London in 1570 Sandys described him as a constant and cruel enemy who continued to make his life hell. And Bourne was evidently not the only adversary. At the time of the northern rising of 1569, Sandys told Cecil: 'Religion is liked as it may serve their owne turne: not one that is earnest and constant, they are but as waveryng reedes' (BL, Lansdowne MS 11, no. 70, fol. 156). For spite, 'they' had mustered the bishop's tenants for military service, sparing their own people.

London London was to be no more comfortable. Parker could have been thinking of Sandys when he told Cecil, with some sarcasm, that the only reason for wanting London would be to change one misery for another, while Grindal, Sandys's predecessor, could write: 'But surely ... the bishop of London is always to be pitied' (Nicholson, 347). Sandys did all that he could to resist promotion, but only succeeded in alienating the queen, Cecil, and Leicester, and even 'the people of London', who were said to have voted for him 'with an universall consent' (BL, Lansdowne MS 12, no. 82, fol. 179). His reasons may have included his plans to settle his family in Worcestershire, and also the desire to avoid the punitive tax of first fruits. Perhaps it helped to change his mind that the queen decided to waive her rights in this respect (a cool £1000), on the grounds that Sandys had kept good hospitality at Worcester. His translation was confirmed on 13 July 1570.

Sandys's tenure began with a dangerous illness from which he was not expected to recover, and which left him 'almost worn away like a clout' (Ayre, 333). And now his past caught up with him, with Bourne's serious charges once again filed away by members of the privy council. In one of many letters which might nowadays justify a diagnosis of paranoia, Sandys complained to Leicester of 'the malice of my enemy', a pretended friend (Bourne?), who could 'kisse and kill', covering up 'that chest full of golde which he hath miserably and wickedly scraped together' (BL, Add. MS 32091, fol. 238). The queen's mind had been poisoned against him. Yet when he left London in 1577, Sandys's farewell sermon sounded an almost sentimental note, comparing himself with St Paul as he took leave of Corinth. 'My dear and faithful flock, farewell: my joy and my crown, farewell: again (with grief I speak it) farewell' (Ayre, 420).

As bishop of London, Sandys added to his reputation for precipitate and misguided zeal. He ordered a raid on the Portuguese embassy, interrupting a celebration of mass attended by many Englishmen. This was a grave breach of diplomatic immunity, but in the bishop's view such idolatry was not to be suffered. If the queen were to tolerate this, 'she can never answer God for it' (BL, Lansdowne MS 16, no. 25). With as it were his other hand, Sandys was the principal prosecutor of a congregation of Dutch Anabaptists, two of whom lit the fires of Smithfield for the first time for seventeen years, a very controversial sentence which Sandys pronounced and which was deplored by Foxe.

But when Grindal wrote that the bishop of London was to be pitied, he had one specific problem in mind: puritanism. It had dogged his own footsteps and it would nearly break Sandys. And it almost took the form of one man, the most admired preacher of the day, Edward Dering. At first Sandys extended his patronage to several notorious nonconformists, including Thomas Sampson and George Withers, whom he placed as archdeacon in the puritan heartland of Colchester. In 1571 some leading preachers, Dering included, offered an olive branch, a 'kinde of agreement' (Peel, 1.82), proposing a compromise on the disputed ceremonies. At this point Archbishop Parker feared that Sandys was not to be relied upon. Indeed, Dering reported to his brother that the bishop was 'a good man', whom he reverenced and would serve in Christ 'all wayes that I may' (Dering, sig. A3v). Sandys now appointed Dering to the prestigious divinity lecture in St Paul's Cathedral.

But a little later everything changed with the publication in 1572 by John Field and Thomas Wilcox of the radical manifesto *An Admonition to the Parliament*. With Field and Wilcox in prison, a section of public opinion was polarized, and crystallized, against the bishops. The St Bartholomew's day massacre, with which the *Admonition* coincided, stirred up religious opinion to fever pitch, not least in the sermons preached at Paul's Cross, and the ministers of the French church in London were what Sandys called 'medlers in these matters' (BL, Lansdowne MS 17, no. 33, fol. 67). Sandys was now attacked in printed libels cast in the streets, one of them the work of Robert Johnson, a prisoner in Westminster Gatehouse, who addressed him as 'superintendent of popish corruptions in the Dioces of London' (*A Parte of a Register*, 101). Sandys complained to Burghley: 'Our estimacion is litle, our autoritie is lesse, so we are become contemptible in the eies of the basest sorte of people' (BL, Lansdowne MS 17, no. 43, fol. 96).

Dering was supported not so much by the basest sort of people as by much of the ruling establishment and their wives, to the extent that neither the politicians nor the bishop dared to be seen to be his accusers. When Dering, Field, and Wilcox were examined before the privy council in May 1573, with Sandys and Parker in attendance, the councillors protested that they must give the dissident ministers a fair hearing. According to Sandys, the rumour was rife that the queen and the council favoured Dering (the queen certainly did not) and that it was 'only the malitiouse proud bishops that sought his trouble'. Things reached a hysterical pitch when Dering told Sandys that he would obey his order not to preach, 'lest some disordered fellow byd youe come of your horse when as youe shal ryde down Cheape syde', and Sandys defied him by deliberately taking that route (BL, Lansdowne MS 17, fol. 100). Sandys told Burghley and Parker that the crisis was so serious that it called for a national council of the church.

Yet Sandys was still on the side of the evangelical angels, which once again set him at odds with Parker. In 1574 the queen began to complain of the preaching exercises known as 'prophesyings', and through the archbishop ordered their general suppression. This was the issue which would later unseat Grindal as archbishop of Canterbury. But Sandys obtained the political backing of the council in evading, even ignoring, the order, claiming that to suppress the exercises would only breed unquietness. As archbishop of York he would preside over the extension of a modified form of clerical exercise throughout his province, to which the queen's direct prohibition of 1577 did not extend.

On 17 May 1575 Parker died, still suspicious of Sandys, to be replaced at Canterbury by Grindal. Sandys, who was the principal mourner at Parker's funeral, would now succeed Grindal at York, sped on his way by letters from Burghley intended to ensure that his houses at Cawood and Bishopthorpe would be ready and waiting for him, sufficiently provided with wood and other provisions. His translation was confirmed on 8 March 1577. He left London to John Aylmer.

York Sandys's zealously implemented policies were a promising continuation of Grindal's attempts to protestantize a conservative and even recalcitrant region. On the one hand he promoted clerical synods, conferences, and exercises, attempting to turn the Bedern at York into a new college of preachers, and initiating at Southwell a synod which continued to be held into the late eighteenth century, while providing for weekly lectures. 'I have set the preachers on worke to give to every market and greate towne every seconde Sunday a sermon' (BL, Lansdowne MS 27, no. 11, fol. 18). When Tobie Matthew came north in 1584 as dean of Durham, Sandys brought fifty leading clerics to Bishopthorpe to meet him, arranging a learned conference which was alleviated by hunting: Sandys rode

at a gallop and shot a stag which he presented to Matthew.

On the other hand, Sandys conducted a vigorous campaign against 'popish' recusancy and all aspects of Catholic 'survivalism', following Grindal's example in employing the high commission as his principal weapon. He presided over it on 127 occasions in twelve years (compared with Grindal's 157 days spent in the commission in an active archiepiscopate of less than five years); unlike Grindal, he concentrated on the ingrained Catholicism of the leading citizens of York itself, and especially on that of their wives, calling even lord mayors to account for their wives' recusancy. So it was Sandys who was primarily responsible for bringing Margaret Clitherow to her hideous death, and for the executions of another fourteen Catholics. He also sent commissioners into the countryside to convene local juries to detect recusancy. Consequently Sandys began by sharing Grindal's misplaced optimism that the problem of the old religion was near its final solution. 'We shall in short time clear all this country of perverse papists and reduce it to good conformity' (BL, Lansdowne MS 30, no. 54). But his efforts were in reality counter-productive and responsible for a critical transition from mere survivalism to hardline recusancy. In 1577 only 178 recusants were returned for the entire northern province. But by 1582 there were 329, and by 1590 587.

Six or seven years into his archiepiscopate what may be called Sandys's other side, aggressive and on the make, had begun to tarnish a reputation which might otherwise have been as blameless as Grindal's. First there was the affair of Dean William Whittingham of Durham and his supporters—Dean Matthew Hutton of York and the president of the council of the north, Henry Hastings, earl of Huntingdon—who were now to be ranged against Sandys. It began with Sandys's attempt, resisted by Whittingham, to conduct a visitation of Durham Cathedral during the vacancy of the see. Sandys responded by excommunicating the recalcitrant parties. The lawyers were clear that Sandys was legally in the wrong but a special commission was now secured under letters patent to investigate alleged malpractice at Durham. This turned into a personal vendetta against Whittingham, with Sandys alleging that his orders were irregular. Anglican historians have supposed that this case concerned the legitimacy or otherwise of non-episcopal orders, since Whittingham had been ordained in Geneva. However, Sandys's actual point was not that presbyterian ordinations were invalid but that Whittingham had been made a minister in a mere conventicle and not according to Genevan public practice.

The case became a *cause célèbre* and soon involved Hutton, who told Sandys that Whittingham's orders were better than his, since Sandys had been priested under the old dispensation, and that for that matter, 'my orders are better than yours … What, said tharchbushop, dost thow call me a papist. Yf I be a papist thow art a puritaine' (BL, Add. MS 33207, fols. 5, 7). This quarrel outlasted Whittingham, who died surrounded by scandal in 1579. On one occasion

Sandys was observed at dinner, neither eating nor drinking and silent until the servants had withdrawn, whereupon he exploded and declared that he would never again sit with Hutton on the high commission. Sandys begged Burghley that Hutton might be moved upstairs—'The Bishoprik of Litchfeld wold next serve the turne'—and to succeed him as dean proposed Tobie Matthew to the queen, 'of whome hir Majesty liked well' (BL, Lansdowne MS 28, fol. 175). Nothing came of the proposal, and two years on Hutton 'spitteth out his venome still' (BL, Lansdowne MS 50, no. 33, fol. 72). In the archbishop's ever suspicious mind, Hutton and Huntingdon had banded against him, Huntingdon having moved out of Bishopthorpe to make way for the archbishop. But when Burghley and Leicester attempted to effect a reconciliation with Huntingdon, Sandys professed not to know what they were talking about. Sandys knew that he was being compared unfavourably with Grindal, who could do no wrong. In his later years he chose to visit York as seldom as possible, spending most of his time at Southwell or Bishopthorpe, and in 1586 he retired from the council of the north.

One of the more substantial bones of contention between Sandys and Hutton concerned usury. Sandys had always been against it, and while he was probably most concerned with extortionate usury he made no distinction between that and the taking of what was regarded as reasonable interest in the business community (up to 10 per cent), and in sticking to this hard line he was supported by an act of parliament of 1571. In his sermons at York he repeatedly returned to this theme, and prosecuted some of York's most prominent citizens in high commission, taking bonds from eighteen businessmen that they would in future avoid 'the vyle and destestable cryme of usury' (Ellis, 'The archbishop and the usurers', 40). Hutton, who was himself a 'usurer', in that he took interest on his investments, was opposed to Sandys's hard and strictly legal line, in part because it threatened to bring the jurisdiction of the high commission into disrepute. But in the archbishop's perception it was the dean who had damaged the credibility of the commission by making a public demonstration of his dissent.

All this was small beer compared to the great Stapleton scandal of 1581–4. This probably had it roots in the designs of the court on two most desirable pieces of archiepiscopal real estate in Nottinghamshire, Southwell and Scrooby, which Sandys had repeatedly resisted, playing the old resignation card, 'and my resignation shall be absolute', whether the queen gave him 'ought or nought' to live on (BL, Lansdowne MS 36, no. 54, fol. 63). To lose these manors and houses would effectively exclude the archbishop from Nottinghamshire, where he now spent much of his time.

Leicester seems to have been behind this, alleging that Southwell was a concealed royal manor, but there were also manoeuvres on the part of Sir Robert Stapleton, a young but impecunious Yorkshire gentleman whom the queen liked. Stapleton at last resorted to blackmail. While Sandys was on visitation, sleeping in a Doncaster inn, Mrs Sysson, the innkeeper's wife, crept into bed with him, only to be 'surprised' by her husband. Stapleton (a fellow high commissioner and sheriff of the county) intervened, and at his suggestion Sandys was foolish enough to hand over £50 in gold to the innkeeper, later paying him £200 more. His anxiety to end the matter in this way was sharpened by the embarrassing fact that the Syssons had been his servants at Bishopthorpe, where there had already been a whiff of scandal. Sysson was soon demanding £800, while Stapleton wanted £1000 and the leases of Southwell and Scrooby. Sandys now had no choice but to go public, complaining to Burghley and the privy council. The upshot was that under insistent pressure from Sandys, Stapleton was taken to Star Chamber, fined £300, ordered to make restitution, and imprisoned, with the lesser accomplices suitably punished. But the sad consequence for Sandys was that he became a figure of fun in his own diocese, 'arraigned … in all tavernes and alehouses' (BL, Lansdowne MS 38, no. 73, fol. 172), and a convenient target for Catholic polemicists. Insult was added to injury when Dean Hutton, required to examine Sysson's wife, took salacious pleasure in the story she had to tell—or so Sandys alleged. That Sandys's credit was damaged in more exalted circles may be indicated by the fact that when the privy council demanded that he surrender his house at Battersea to be used as a prison for papists, he gave way.

Property and family The capacity of Sandys to fall out with those around him is impressive, and tempts the historian to make some kind of clinical diagnosis. Only weeks before his death in summer 1588 he had even managed to quarrel with one of his closest friends, Tobie Matthew, dean of Durham, complaining to Burghley of Matthew's 'manifest wronges' and 'indirect dealinges' (BL, Lansdowne MS 57, no. 73, fol. 164). But if Sandys had not been obliged to provide for seven sons and two daughters his career would not have been so compromised. It is not that he was corrupt. He constantly defended himself against charges of having alienated ecclesiastical property, and it was ostensibly out of concern for the good of his see that he refused to surrender Bishopthorpe and resisted designs on York House, only reluctantly giving way over Battersea. The inscription on Sandys's funerary monument in Southwell Minster credits him with saving 'this church in which you now lie, itself lying prostrate'.

But in granting leases of episcopal manors and rectories, not to speak of profitable offices and cathedral dignities and prebends in his gift, Sandys favoured his family, including sons-in-law, to an extent which constituted nepotism. Of this he made no secret, saying that since someone had to benefit it might as well be his sons as anyone else. He even admitted granting a reversion of the office of diocesan registrar to one of his younger sons, then only fourteen and still at grammar school. Four weeks after denying Scrooby to the queen, he granted the lease to his eldest son, Samuel, for twenty-one years (whereas the queen had demanded seventy, which was tantamount to alienation). He admitted that he had granted all his sons leases (Samuel six, Miles five, Edwin four, the others two each), but asserted that this had cost the archbishopric nothing. It was Hutton who leaked incriminating information and forced Sandys into these disclosures, and it was Burghley who carefully annotated the long (but by no means complete) list, estimating their total value at £1549.

Recalling in his will that he had preferred and advantaged all his children with leases, patents, and annuities, Sandys asked that they content themselves with that and make no further demands. The boys all did exceptionally well. Samuel built up a large estate in Worcestershire, served as an MP, and was sheriff of the county. Himself knighted, he had a son who was elevated to the peerage. Miles settled in Cambridgeshire, eventually becoming a baronet. History records what became of Sir Edwin Sandys. In 1620 five of the brothers were members of the Virginia Company. And all this was done out of church revenues.

But the simple fact that on death or translation episcopal temporalities passed back to the crown and then to the next incumbent meant that the constant need for money, which the bishops shared with the whole land-owning class, led to conflicts of interest and public rows which were scarcely compatible with the Christianity of which the bishops were the leading representatives. And the very worst of all these acrimonious affairs happened after Sandys's translation to York. It concerned dilapidations. When Sandys succeeded Grindal in London he had neither claimed nor received any dilapidations, knowing that his predecessor had had to bear much of the immense cost of repairing St Paul's after the fire of 1561. But in his successor's perception that was negligence rather than generosity. Sandys claimed to have recommended John Aylmer to the queen, and to have participated in his consecration when it proved hard to find enough bishops from the southern province to do the job. In return, Sandys alleged, Aylmer had undertaken to forgo any claims upon him, a promise which Sandys's brother Miles thought he should have secured in writing. In fact Aylmer demanded hundreds, then thousands of pounds—'So soone as the bishop of Yorke had holpen him on with his rochett he was transformed and shewed him selfe in his own nature' (PRO, SP 12/112, 45.1). Sandys was now forced to make belated demands against Grindal for dilapidations at both London and York. Aylmer reacted by obtaining a special royal commission to hear what was now a tripartite suit, which ensured that this dirty and very complicated linen would be thoroughly washed in public for several years to come.

One occasion when this happened was a service of ordination conducted by Aylmer at Fulham on Ascension day (16 May) 1577. The sermon was preached by a young client of Aylmer, a Trinity graduate and Essex minister named John Keltridge. Keltridge departed gratuitously from the edifying commonplaces appropriate for the occasion to attack ministers of the church who, like Eli, were only interested in using their livings to advance their 'jolly' sons. 'There is some in Englande that have good and large stipends for serving the Lorde, and they spende it as

liberally on their sonnes to make them Courtiers. Well, Aaron did not so' (Exposition, 236–7). This could only have been heard as criticism of Sandys's nepotism.

Another way of realizing the assets of a bishopric for short-term advantage was to sell off the scarce resource of timber. Aylmer's notorious opportunism in this regard, which won him the nickname of 'Marelm', led to a full-scale privy council inquiry into the management of episcopal woods. During this investigation, it was alleged that, at Worcester, Sandys had made £2000 out of timber, some of it sold to his brother Miles, and Aylmer accused him of destroying 400 acres of woodland in his time as bishop of London.

The judgment of history Edwin Sandys died on 10 July 1588 and was buried in Southwell Minster. That combination of expediency and graft which has come to be called sleaze might appear to sound an appropriate note on which to end the life of an archbishop who has gone down in history as a model of grasping episcopal nepotism. He had come a long way, and perhaps in the wrong direction, since those quiet and scholarly days in Zürich. When he wrote to that city as an archbishop in 1579, it was in reply to letters received in London three years earlier. Zürich knew nothing of his translation, and no one in London had thought to send the letters on.

But it has to be said that by the end of the twentieth century Sandys had never attracted a biographer equipped to find and make a case for his rehabilitation. Even John Strype, who wrote lives of Parker, Grindal, Aylmer, and Whitgift, and who called Sandys 'a man of great note for his piety and learning', a 'truly primitive bishop' (Strype, 2/2.41–2, 44), was not attracted to the subject. Sandys's spiritual activity as a diocesan and metropolitan, in preaching, visitation, and justice, has yet to be thoroughly investigated. When this is done, he may yet emerge as one of those 'prelates as pastor' celebrated by Kenneth Fincham in the Jacobean period. There is grist for this mill in the volume of *Sermons* (1585) published, perhaps, with the object of redeeming a tarnished reputation, the only substantial collection of sermons by any Elizabethan bishop to have survived. Sandys is also the victim of archival lacunae which, for example, have probably concealed for ever an extremely active role as a spiritual peer in the House of Lords. What the more accessible documentation in state papers and the Cecil archive in the Lansdowne manuscripts draws to attention is the unedifying spectacle of the 'frenzied' Sandys who quarrelled so violently with Bourne, Whittingham, Hutton, Huntingdon, Stapleton, and Aylmer.   PATRICK COLLINSON

Sources E. S. Sandys, *History of the family of Sandys* (1930) · *The sermons of Edwin Sandys*, ed. J. Ayre, Parker Society, 2 (1842) · *The acts and monuments of John Foxe*, ed. S. R. Cattley, 8 vols. (1837–41), vol. 8 · *A commentarie of M. Doctor Martin Luther upon the epistle of S. Paul to the Galatians* (1577) · I. P. Ellis, 'Edwin Sandys and the settlement of religion in England, 1558–1588', BLitt diss., U. Oxf., 1962 · S. Storer, 'The life and times of Edwin Sandys, archbishop of York', MPhil diss., U. Lond., 1973 · *Correspondence of Matthew Parker*, ed. J. Bruce and T. T. Perowne, Parker Society, 42 (1853) · L. M. Hill, 'The Marian experience of defeat: the case of Sir John Bourne', *Sixteenth-Century Journal*, 25 (1994), 531–49 · PRO, state papers domestic, Elizabeth I,

SP 12/28, 12/40, 12/112 • BL, Lansdowne MSS 6, 11, 12, 16, 17, 27, 28, 30, 36, 38, 50, 57, 989 • J. Strype, *Annals of the Reformation and establishment of religion … during Queen Elizabeth's happy reign*, new edn, 4 vols. (1824) • exchequer, first fruits and tenths office, composition books, PRO, E334/8, fol. 223v • BL, Add. MSS 32091, 33207 • P. Collinson, *Archbishop Grindal, 1519–1583: the struggle for a reformed church* (1979) • P. Collinson, 'A mirror of Elizabethan puritanism: the life and letters of "Godly Master Dering"', *Godly people: essays on English protestantism and puritanism* (1983), 288–324 • P. Collinson, *The Elizabethan puritan movement* (1967); pbk edn (1990) • *A parte of a register* [1593] • P. Tyler, *The ecclesiastical commision and Catholicism in the north, 1562–1577* (1960) • P. Tyler, 'The ecclesiastical commission for the province of York, 1561–1641', DPhil diss., U. Oxf., 1965 • R. Eades, 'Iter boreale', Bodl. Oxf., MS Rawl. B. 223 • *The correspondence of Dr Matthew Hutton, archbishop of York*, ed. [J. Raine], SurtS, 17 (1843) • I. P. Ellis, 'The archbishop and the usurers', *Journal of Ecclesiastical History*, 21 (1970), 33–42 • N. Jones, *God and the moneylenders* (1989) • F. Heal, *Of prelates and princes: a study of the economic and social position of the Tudor episcopate* (1980) • will, PRO, PROB 11/75, sig. 30 • BL, Cotton MS Tib. B vii • LPL, MS 2003 • T. E. Hartley, ed., *Proceedings in the parliaments of Elizabeth I*, 1 (1981) • L. Womock, *The late proposal of union among protestants, review'd and rectifi'd* (1679) • E. Dering, *Certaine godly and verie comfortable letters, full of Christian consolation* (1590?) • H. Robinson, ed. and trans., *The Zurich letters, comprising the correspondence of several English bishops and others with some of the Helvetian reformers, during the early part of the reign of Queen Elizabeth*, 2 vols., Parker Society, 7–8 (1842–5) • W. Nicholson, ed., *The remains of Edmund Grindal*, Parker Society, 9 (1843) • A. Peel, ed., *The seconde parte of a register*, 2 vols. (1915) • M. C. Fowler, 'Edwins Hall and the Sandys family', *Transactions of the Essex Archaeological Society*, new ser., 18 (1925–7), 216–21 • *The exposition and readynges of Iohn Keltridge … upon the wordes of our saviour Christe, that be written in the xi of Luke* (1578)

Archives BL, biographical papers, Add. MS 45866 • LPL, corresp. and papers | Arundel Castle, West Sussex, corresp. with earl of Shrewsbury

Likenesses oils, 1571, priv. coll. [*see illus.*] • S. de Passe, line engraving, BM, NPG; repro. in H. Holland, *Heröologia* (1620) • alabaster tomb effigy, Southwell Minster, Nottinghamshire • double portrait, oils (with his wife; after type, 1571), NPG; version, Bishopthorpe Palace, York

Sandys, Sir Edwin

Sandys, Sir Edwin (1561–1629), politician and colonial entrepreneur, was born on the morning of 9 December 1561 and was baptized at Hartlebury, Worcestershire, five days later, the second son and also the second of nine surviving children of Edwin *Sandys (1519?–1588), then bishop of Worcester, and his second wife, Cicely Wilford (d. 1611), a member of a prominent Kentish family.

Education and early career At the age of nine, in the same year as his father's translation to the bishopric of London, Sandys entered Merchant Taylors' School. Its headmaster, Richard Mulcaster, was known for his love of the classics, the English language, and public speaking—preoccupations that were to mark Edwin's career. Among his schoolmates were Lancelot Andrewes, Edmund Spenser, and the young man who became his best friend for the next thirty years, George Cranmer, the great-nephew of Archbishop Thomas Cranmer.

When Sandys was fifteen his father was made archbishop of York, and Sandys was sent, along with his friend Cranmer, to Corpus Christi College, Oxford, to study with Richard Hooker. Hooker had been a protégé of John Jewel, bishop of Salisbury, an old friend of the archbishop, who had become Hooker's patron when Jewel died in 1571. At

Corpus there developed what Izaak Walton called 'a sacred friendship' that bound Sandys, Cranmer, and Hooker 'by a similitude of inclinations to the same recreations and studies' (I. Walton, *The Life of Mr. Richard Hooker*, ed. C. H. Dick, 1899, 134). Although Hooker left Corpus in 1584, to enter the Middle Temple in the following year, the connection continued. Sandys graduated BA from Oxford in 1579 and proceeded MA in 1583, but then the trail vanishes. He must have left the university when he married, at some point in the mid-1580s, but there is an otherwise unexplained reference to his returning to Oxford in April 1589, nine months after his wife died, when he 'did supplicate for the degree of batch. of law [in civil law], but was not admitted' (Wood, *Ath. Oxon.: Fasti*, 1.247). Soon thereafter he went to London, where he was reunited with Hooker and Cranmer at the Middle Temple.

As he approached thirty Sandys hardly seemed destined for a major public career. His stint at Oxford had been uneventful, and his first marriage had left little mark. His wife, Margaret Eveleigh of Devon, had died in childbirth in July 1588, leaving Edwin with a baby daughter, Elizabeth, who eventually married one of her Kentish Wilford cousins. The only other information that has survived from the 1580s is the first hint of a parliamentary connection. Edwin may have served in the 1586 session, though the MP was probably his cousin and namesake, the son of Sir Miles Sandys. It is more likely that he was elected in 1589, representing Plympton, a Devon borough not far from his wife's family home, but there is no record of his participation in its affairs.

Sandys lived mainly in London between 1590 and 1596, although for a while he moved to Yorkshire, where his father had bestowed on him the revenues of the prebend of Wetwang and the lucrative patent for the chancellorship of the diocese of York, plus four leases worth £322 per annum. The move coincided with his second marriage, to Anne Southcote of Devon, a cousin of his first wife, who died shortly thereafter, possibly in childbirth, since the couple had no children. Returning to London early in 1593, after her death, Sandys resumed his previous interests. He renewed his associations at the Middle Temple; sponsored the publication of the first five books of Hooker's *Laws of the Ecclesiastical Polity*; and again entered parliament as MP for Plympton. It was in this 1593 session that he made his first known interventions in debates, strongly supporting government efforts to repress the 'seditious sectaries' known as Brownists and Barrowists. This was Sandys's first significant public activity. It reflected not only the conservative religious sentiments that he shared with Hooker but also his emerging adherence to the Cecils. The first surviving description of Sandys is in a 1586 letter from his father to Lord Burghley, which captured him quite accurately as a 25-year-old who was 'a great deal older in discretion, sobriety and learning' (Rabb, 12). Burghley had met the archbishop's son and had thought well of him, and in the following decade Sandys continued the relationship with Burghley's son, Robert Cecil. Indeed, one of Sandys's 1593 speeches immediately followed and seconded an assault on the sectaries by Cecil.

A *Relation of the State of Religion* In 1596 the connection with the court yielded appointments for Sandys and Cranmer to a brief diplomatic mission to Germany, with permission 'afterwards to travel into other foreign parts' (*APC*, 1595–6, 496–7). For the next three years the two friends undertook what was later called a grand tour, spending time in Geneva (where they registered at the academy), Italy, and France. About the time that he returned home in 1599 Sandys completed his one major piece of writing, *A Relation of the State of Religion*. Dedicated to Archbishop John Whitgift, the book was a survey of the various faiths Sandys had encountered on the continent. It focuses mainly on Catholicism, assessing strengths and weaknesses in the manner of an official report after a factfinding mission. Full of shrewd insights—including a careful calculus of the number of clerics at the disposal of the papacy—and notable for its even-handedness (there is even praise for the devoutness of Pope Clement VIII), the book combines political analysis with moral pronouncement. For Sandys, calm and sobriety were major virtues, and he applied them in the book's remarkable conclusion.

The question Sandys posed was whether reconciliation, Christian unity, might be possible. After going through a succession of possible solutions, he left this 'honesthearted desire' for God to effect, because it was inconceivable in practical terms (p. 206). Contacts had to continue, he argued, but they would not break down the confessional barriers that had arisen. This was probably the first comprehensive justification for peaceful co-existence in Reformation Europe, a call for pragmatic tolerance that reflected its author's sober temperament.

Published in June 1605, *A Relation* was ordered to be burnt by the court of high commission in November, possibly because of Sandys's obstreperous behaviour in the 1604 parliament, or perhaps because its tolerant comments about Catholics might have seemed dangerous in the wake of the Gunpowder Plot. But over the next eighty years it went through fourteen editions, and was translated into Italian, French, and Dutch, attracting the attention of Paolo Sarpi, Hugo Grotius, and other leading intellectuals of the time. The story that Sandys himself demanded the suppression of the first edition was almost certainly an attempt to save face. The book's long-term success should be seen, rather, as testimony to the reasonableness he brought to bear on the emotional and divisive religious issues of his day.

As Sandys entered his forties, his life began to change in a number of ways. In 1601, a few months after the deaths of both Hooker and Cranmer, he moved to Kent, obtaining a manor that had once belonged to Cranmer's family. He married his third wife, Elizabeth Nevinson, from Eastrey in Kent. They had a daughter, Anne, but since she apparently did not survive to adulthood, he may again have had to endure a childbirth death. In any case, by 1605 he had a fourth wife, Katherine Bulkeley (*d.* 1640) of Anglesey, daughter of his fellow MP Sir Richard Bulkeley. Now

at last Sandys became a true paterfamilias, for she gave birth to twelve children over the next two decades. And it is a description of a stillbirth in 1620 that offers one of the few personal glimpses of Sandys: a harrowing letter he wrote his friend John Ferrar describing the 'dolor and anguish' the family suffered over a three-day period as Katherine agonizingly lost her child (Rabb, 49).

The parliament of 1604–1610 By the time he married Katherine, Sandys had moved unmistakably onto the public stage. He may have been working in Scotland on Cecil's behalf during Elizabeth I's last days, and early in the new reign, in May 1603, he was knighted by James I and soon thereafter appointed to the queen's council. A quiet official career seemed in the making. But in 1604 Sandys returned to parliament as MP for Stockbridge, and a month into its meeting he made a speech that was to send his career, at the age of forty-two, in an entirely new direction.

In the early weeks of the session the Commons had focused on the disputed Buckinghamshire election. A few days after that quarrel was resolved, the house took up the king's proposal for a union of England and Scotland. This proceeded smoothly until Sandys's speech, on 19 April, which called the entire scheme into question. This, he said, was 'the weightiest cause' parliament had ever considered, and he outlined a series of objections. Most remarkable was his assertion that 'The King stands not alone' and that 'England sits here representatively only' (*JHC*, 1547–1628, 950–51). This demand for delay and consultation with constituents transformed the debate. After a week of stalemate, Sandys summed up the problems, and the union was postponed until the next session.

In one stroke Sandys had established himself as a dominant figure in the house. Over the next few weeks, moreover, he took command of the fight for free trade that was to become a signature issue both for him and for other gentry seeking to break England's commercial monopolies. And his prominence continued in the discussions of wardship and the preparation of the famous 'Apology' of the Commons, the two issues that dominated the last days of the session. In all these areas, his position as an opponent of the king's wishes was unmistakable. Although it is possible that Cecil may have encouraged the objections to the union and to wardship, the attacks went beyond anything he could have countenanced, culminating in an insolent lecture to the king about English political forms. To the extent that, more than anyone else, Sandys had led the Commons down this path, he was indeed at the start of an entirely new career.

Over the next twenty years the role Sandys assumed in April 1604 established his place in English political history. He became the quintessential 'Commons man' in that crucial moment between the privy councildominated sessions under Elizabeth and the turbulent, assertive sessions under Charles I and Oliver Cromwell. In James I's reign the Commons gained, for the first time, a significant influence on royal policy, sometimes by confrontation, but more often through negotiation. This was not yet an age of parties, and Sandys guided debates by putting into calm, reasoned speeches the concerns of his fellow gentry. Even on a fraught issue like the union, he went through numbered points, accumulated arguments, and very rarely succumbed to inflammatory rhetoric. He also used house committees, which he regularly chaired, effectively; he made shrewd alliances with like-minded MPs; and, together with these colleagues, he planned his tactics carefully. Recesses, for instance, were often followed by initiatives that had clearly been prepared in advance. Yet it was above all his calm demeanour, and the concern for England's welfare that he articulated, that enabled Sandys so often to sway the house. Again and again his intervention would bring a debate to an end and the house would follow his recommendations.

The results were noticeable in all the sessions Sandys attended. In 1606, relieved at the happy conclusion of the Gunpowder Plot, the Commons voted generous subsidies. But Sandys gained an exemption for northern counties, and then intervened decisively in a contentious issue, an assault on the royal prerogative of purveyance. A fellow MP, John Hare, had been reprimanded by the Lords for his stand on purveyance, and Sandys insisted that the house defend its privileges—a repeated concern that was crucial to the Commons' growing self-confidence. From this intervention he moved on to a major speech on 8 March. This was an issue, he said, in which the MPs' obligation to the 'country' had to be taken as seriously as their obligation to the king. They were 'populars'—that is, they had to take into account the view of their constituents—because 'from hence we return to our private' selves. There was a difference between king and state, between government and governed, and they could not approve a 'composition' for the abolition of purveyance, because they had to ensure that the king 'not meddle with the possessions of the people' (*Diary of Robert Bowyer*, 68–72; Rabb, 117–19). In the end the attack on purveyance came to naught, but the view of England's polity that it had inspired Sandys to expound was a milestone in the application of natural rights theories to politics.

The house reconvened late in 1606 and again after a recess in early 1607. Now the major issue was the union, and in these debates Sandys's tactics determined the outcome. The only part of the king's initiative that became law was the repeal of laws hostile to Scotland. His other aims, equal commercial rights and common nationality, succumbed to Sandys's manoeuvring. In 1604 Sandys had warned of 'a deluge of Scots' (*JHC*, 957), and cited the prediction that, within forty years, English daughters would 'be married into Scotland and the Scots inhabit here' (*JHC*, 973). Now he argued that, to please James, they should enact a 'perfect Union' (*JHC*, 1027–8)—that is, a complete unification of all laws and institutions, with the Scots accepting English law and thus able to 'participate all benefits with us' (*Diary of Robert Bowyer*, 218–24). The disingenuousness was unmistakable, because it was obvious that suspicion of the Scots rendered a perfect union impossible. And there the proposal languished, prompting a final tongue-lashing from the king at the 'fanatical

spirits' (*JHC*, 366–8) who had spoken 'against duty, almost against allegiance' (*Diary of Robert Bowyer*, 287–8).

By the time parliament reassembled for its final sessions in February 1610, Sandys was clearly in command of the Commons. He chaired its major committees, notably the committee on grievances, and he was the chief negotiator with the Lords and the crown in discussions of the great contract, Cecil's offer to surrender the king's financial prerogatives, such as wardship, in return for a guaranteed income. This far-sighted effort to modernize royal revenues eventually foundered on opposition within the court, which scuttled the project by raising, over the summer, the £200,000 price that had been agreed, after long haggling, in late July. In the process Sandys parted company with his former patron, Cecil, partly because he was making consideration of abuses and grievances central to proceedings. Yet this was one means of maintaining his hold on the house. Another, as he had shown over the previous sessions, was to master procedure; thus, Sandys had led the way in insisting that the journal of the House of Commons be kept in more regular fashion, and he had helped establish the committee of the whole house as a way of allowing MPs to speak more than once on an issue. His mastery of the chamber may often have brought him into opposition to crown wishes, but that, too, was coming to be the mark of the 'Commons man'.

As Sandys approached his forties, other interests began to come to the fore. He bought a 'moiety' of the manor of Northbourne, near his other estate in Kent, in 1611 for £850. This land, near Sandwich, had also once been owned by the Cranmer family, and on it Sir Edwin built one of the first Italianate villas in England. The construction became a major drain on his finances, but it reflected a fondness for the new style of villa that, like his friend Sir Henry Wotton, he acquired during his stay in Italy. The ground plan, with two wings connected by a loggia, has been reconstructed, but the house itself was torn down by a descendant in the 1750s. And the town house he owned by 1608 on Aldersgate was also a financial burden. This was one of London's most fashionable streets—Sandys had four earls as neighbours—but it doubtless proved most convenient as his parliamentary and colonial interests increasingly drew him to the capital.

In these years, too, Sandys was probably preparing his second book, *Sacred Hymns*, a collection of fifty psalms, produced in collaboration with the playwright Robert Tailor, 'to be sung in five parts'. Published in 1615, the book reflected a love of singing that he inherited from his father and that was to reappear in his will. It reflected, too, a devoutness of which there are hints but never sustained evidence. After the major statement in *A Relation*, Sandys said nothing explicit about his religiosity, except for the conventional sentiments in his last will and his oft-repeated demands for legislation against swearing. His connections with Hooker, Lancelot Andrewes, and, through his close friends John and Nicholas Ferrar, the Laudian piety of their eventual home, Little Gidding, all suggest a persistent high Anglicanism. But no credo from Sandys himself has survived.

Colonial ventures and the Addled Parliament Another growing interest, perhaps derived from his immersion in the issue of free trade in parliament, was overseas colonization. Already in *A Relation* he had noted how 'superior to their Northern adversaries' were the Catholic countries that engaged in 'traffic to all parts of the world' (pp. 197–8). That sense of competition had fuelled the founding of the East India Company in 1600 and the Virginia Company in 1606, to both of which he was to make a notable contribution. He was named to the council of the Virginia Company in 1607, and he may well have helped draw up the company's second charter in 1609. By 1611 he was signing official letters in his capacity as councillor, and he had also appeared as an investor in the East India Company. In 1612 he was a founder of the Somers Island Company that was settling Bermuda, and over the next decade he emerged as a major promoter of overseas enterprise.

First, however, came a return to politics, the 'Addled' Parliament of 1614. Sandys was elected from Rochester, and quickly resumed his leadership of the house. Sir Francis Bacon told the king that 'Sandys is fallen off' and would be pliable, and indeed the issue of 'undertaking'—MPs following patrons' instructions—became an issue in the session (*The Letters and the Life of Francis Bacon*, ed. J. Spedding, 7 vols., 1861–74, 4.370). But there is no evidence that Sir Edwin pursued any but his own independent course which, while trying to organize the house's business in orderly fashion, also led him into conflict with the crown.

Sandys's main interests in 1614 were with the privileges of the Commons; with grievances; and above all with impositions, the royal prerogative of raising customs duties and other dues on goods. Conflicting visions of England's welfare were coming to a head, and on 18 May, denouncing impositions, Sir Edwin quoted Juvenal in a denunciation of tyrants; one diarist quoted him as saying 'it is come to be almost a tyrannical government in England' (Jansson, 316). Comments like these were driving a wedge between court and parliament, and it was small wonder that James angrily dissolved the gathering, calling it 'nullum Parliamentum'; sending four MPs to the Tower; and requiring Sandys and seven of his colleagues to bring their papers to Whitehall, where they were summarily burned.

Parliament did not meet for another seven years, and during this interim Sir Edwin became more deeply involved in his overseas interests. His close associate in these enterprises was Henry Wriothesley, earl of Southampton, a distant kinsman. Sandys was reputed to have converted the younger man from Catholicism in the 1590s, and they may have worked together to oppose the union. By the mid-1610s they also shared commitments to Virginia, the East India Company, and Bermuda. In 1616 Sir Edwin was elected an assistant (essentially a director) of the Virginia Company, and in the following year plunged into the negotiations with the Leiden puritans that led to the journey of the *Mayflower* and the Pilgrim Fathers in 1620. Both he and Southampton already owned significant plantations in Bermuda, and the two men extended their investment in Virginia in 1618, arranging for 310 settlers to travel to the dwindling colony.

This was a low point in the Virginia Company's fortunes. Early in 1618 there were only 400 people in the colony, almost as few as at any time since its earliest days. There seems little reason to doubt that the burst of activity by Sandys was intended, as he himself said, to ensure that this 'great action' would not 'fall to nothing' (Kingsbury, 1.350). At first the treasurer (essentially chairman) of the company, Sir Thomas Smythe, welcomed Sir Edwin's interventions, notably reforms that rationalized company procedures and, famously, created a representative 'general assembly' in Virginia. But soon, as Sandys launched an investigation of company finances, relations soured, and in April 1619 Smythe stepped down as treasurer. His successor was Sir Edwin Sandys, the first non-merchant to take on such a responsibility in a major commercial and colonial venture.

Sir Edwin also sought the governorship of the Bermuda Company, and possibly also the East India Company, in 1619. Smythe prevailed at both elections, but Sandys did become a director of the latter. His lasting contribution, however, was in Virginia. If his hope to diversify the colony's economy failed, his relentless transportation of settlers over the next five years was probably the single most important reason that England's foothold at Jamestown survived. For despite his shipment of some 4000 people across the Atlantic in these years, attrition was so intense that the colony was only a few hundred people larger in 1624 than it had been in 1618. Without the emigration, the native American attack of 1622 might well have destroyed the young settlement.

The immigrants encountered considerable hardship in Jamestown, and at home Sandys antagonized a leading investor, Robert Rich, earl of Warwick, as well as Smythe. They prevailed upon the king, already irritated with the troublesome MP, to forbid Sandys's re-election in 1620: 'choose the Devil if you will but not Sir Edwin Sandys', he is reputed to have said (A. Brown, *The First Republic in America*, 1898, 367). Southampton took over as treasurer, but the direction of company affairs remained with Sandys and his friend, the London merchant John Ferrar, for the next four years.

The parliament of 1621 Troubles mounted in 1621 as various economic initiatives failed, but for most of that year Sandys was distracted by a new parliament. Elected by Sandwich, Sandys continued in his role as a manager of Commons business, though it is clear that he worked closely with Sir Robert Phelips and Sir Edward Coke, drawing in particular on the latter's massive legal learning to justify the MPs' positions. During the first session, in the spring, Sandys's skills as a manager were inescapable. He helped pass with remarkable speed a grant of subsidies to counter the Habsburg expulsion of the king's son-in-law, the Elector Frederick V, from the Palatinate; he smoothed the way out of a contentious discussion of free speech; and he brought a nasty dispute over abuses at court, exacerbated by Coke, to a harmonious conclusion. In the words of John Chamberlain, 'Sir Edwin Sandys turned the tide and brought them all about' (Notestein, Relf, and Simpson, 2.235n.). Moreover, his own interests, bills on fishing and tobacco that were designed to help the Virginia colony, and a renewal of the 1604 campaign for free trade, also moved steadily ahead. All of this, however, was merely part of an almost ubiquitous involvement in debates: he spoke at least twenty-two times in the last two weeks of April, and made over fifty speeches in May.

It was in May that the harmony began to disintegrate. A nasty dispute with the Lords over how to punish Edward Floyd, a Catholic who had disparaged the ousted rulers of the Palatinate, was an ominous portent, especially as it opened a breach between Sandys and his friend Sir Lionel Cranfield, soon to be lord treasurer. Tempers were rising. The revived process of impeachment had brought down Bacon, the lord chancellor; attacks on corruption at the court had focused increasingly on George Villiers, marquess of Buckingham, but royal support kept him impervious to attack; and there were further outbursts of anger when the house heard that Buckingham had threatened his enemies and that James seemed to know exactly what was being said in debates. As these distractions mounted, the king decided to prorogue parliament. The reaction was passionate, full of concerns about constituents who would complain about the lack of legislation and high-flown oratory about England's dire economic condition. Even Sandys displayed uncommon emotion. In a speech on 29 May he denounced the monopolies that enriched the few at the expense of the many, lamented the decay of agriculture and trade, and justified his grim assessment: 'I had rather speak now than betray my country with silence' (Notestein, Relf, and Simpson, 3.345).

The denouement was swift. On 31 May Sandys had heated words with Cranfield, first over the state of trade and then because he suggested that the house pass no more bills. It was becoming clear that MPs might be called to account for their actions, and on 1 June Sir Edwin had the house clear him of blame for his behaviour. But it was to no avail. On 4 June parliament was adjourned, and on 16 June he was arrested, together with his friend Southampton. He was questioned about the behind-the-scenes planning of tactics, in which he had doubtless engaged with Southampton and a number of others; about his actions in the last days of the session; about his views on foreign policy; and about some papers found when his Aldersgate home was searched. The results of the interrogation, though unknown, were apparently inconclusive because on 20 July Sandys was ordered to be released from the sheriff's custody and confined to Northbourne until early November.

Sandys remained in Kent, however, when parliament reconvened on 14 November. Despite denials from courtiers and the king, the MPs were sure he had been arrested for his behaviour in parliament, and in December Sandys returned to London to try to bring the affair to a close. Two members, Sir Peter Heyman and William Mallory, came to see him 'at ten of clock at night, the servants being put out' (Rabb, 268), and they reported the conversation to the Commons, but it is not known what was said. Just before

parliament was dissolved on 19 December their report was ordered to be burnt by the house, and both men suffered royal displeasure, which suggests that Sandys may have confirmed that his parliamentary privilege had indeed been breached, but had insisted that nothing further be done.

The failure of the Virginia Company and the parliament of 1624 Sandys's troubles in 1621 also extended to Virginia. The company was losing money; the flow of new settlers was multiplying the strains; and he had uneasy relations with such powerful figures as Smythe, Cranfield, and Warwick. When the native Americans attacked the colony on 22 March 1622, killing 350 people, the prospects seemed utterly bleak. But Sandys had one more remedy to offer: over the next few months, he and Southampton negotiated a contract with Cranfield that gave the company a monopoly over tobacco imports. This achievement, however, triggered a confrontation that eventually destroyed Sandys's regime. When the terms by which the contract would be administered were announced in November 1622, it appeared that Sandys and his allies would receive handsome salaries for their work. For a company in financial straits, this seemed entirely inappropriate, and over the next few months accusations of financial impropriety and mismanagement mounted. By April 1623 Cranfield was openly sympathetic to the complaints. The contract was dissolved, and in May the privy council launched an inquiry into Sandys's administration. It soon discovered that conditions in Virginia were indeed parlous, and that the truth had been withheld from the London investors. In July the king demanded that the charter be revoked and ten months later the company was dissolved.

By that time, however, the pendulum of success and failure had swung yet again. A new parliament met in February 1624, and it fulfilled many of the aims long sought by Sandys, who sat as knight of his shire, Kent. Unlike 1614, when not one bill, or 1621, when only two bills, became law, in 1624 more than seventy became law, thirty-eight of which were public statutes. About half of the latter had been passed in earlier parliaments, but had not received royal assent. For a manager of business like Sandys, it was the triumph of a legislative programme that for twenty years had foundered on tensions between court and Commons.

The reason for the turnaround was the campaign by Prince Charles and Buckingham for war with Spain. To pressure the reluctant king they joined forces with house leaders to ensure that all treaties with Spain were broken off, and that subsidies were provided for the ensuing hostilities. Sandys played a central role in this campaign, and in return won approval for much of the house's legislative agenda, notably a major bill to free trade for which he had been arguing since 1604, and the securing of the tobacco monopoly for Virginia—a crucial final gift for the colony he had served.

Sandys could also take personal satisfaction from the impeachment of the man who had been so largely responsible for the debacle in the Virginia Company, Cranfield. It was in Buckingham's interest to have the independent-minded lord treasurer disgraced, but Sandys's animosity was more deeply felt, and his speech of 12 April, an emotional exception to his usual common-sense sobriety, was a decisive moment in the campaign against the minister. As he examined trade, he said, he kept finding restraints and burdens newly imposed by Cranfield. He would have wanted to 'suppress all acerbity of speech', but he was 'commanded contrary by the anguish' of the merchants, who 'compared the suffering under his Lordship's rigour to the Israelites' brick making in Egypt' (Rabb, 293). Once unleashed, the process was inexorable, and soon after Sandys presented the house's charges to the Lords the minister was disgraced.

Last years Because of his association with Buckingham, there were rumours that Sandys might gain high office when Charles became king in March 1625. But he was approaching his mid-sixties, an advanced age at the time, and in his remaining years he suffered more frequently from illnesses (never defined) that had been interrupting his public career with growing frequency since 1607. Despite Buckingham's influence, moreover, he failed to win election in Kent in either 1625 or 1626. Instead, he had to depend on the patronage of a Cornish friend to represent the borough of Penryn, which, he reportedly admitted, he 'had never seen … nor knew the name of it' (Rabb, 306). In 1628 all influence failed, and his parliamentary career came to an end. Even in 1625 and 1626, however, he was a shadow of his former self. He started strongly in both years—drawing up a petition against Catholics with John Pym, addressing trade and impositions, and playing a moderating role in 1625, and discussing trade, religion, and the subsidy in 1626—but then faded from the scene. Tainted by his connection with Buckingham, the old 'Commons man' was no longer a dominant figure in the house.

In his last years Sandys remained active in East India Company affairs, and was nominated for the governorship in 1628. But he had little energy left for public office, and withdrew his name. On 25 August 1629, less than six months after his last appearance at a company meeting, he completed his will. He died in the second half of October, and the will was probated on 30 October 1629. That his finances were shaky was clear from the fate of his bequests, which included £2500 for Oxford and Cambridge universities that was never paid. And his widow, Katherine, who survived until 1640, had to fight both Sir Edwin's brother George *Sandys and the archbishop of York to maintain her resources.

Events were to sweep aside the kind of moderate gentry politics that Sandys embodied. It is suggestive that in the 1640s two of his sons became parliamentarians, and another son and his most prominent son-in-law became royalists. Sir Edwin had been able to straddle court and country, but his firm yet accommodating approach to the issues of his day held little appeal in the increasingly divided England of the next generation.

THEODORE K. RABB

Sources T. K. Rabb, *Jacobean gentleman: Sir Edwin Sandys, 1561–1629* (1998) • *JHC*, 2 (1640–42), 91a, 236a • *JHL*, 2–3 (1578–1628) • IGI • S. M. Kingsbury, *The records of the Virginia Company of London*, 4 vols. (1906–35) • *The parliamentary diary of Robert Bowyer, 1606–1607*, ed. D. H. Willson (1931) • E. R. Foster, ed., *Proceedings in parliament, 1610*, 2 vols. (1966) • M. Jansson, ed., *Proceedings in parliament, 1614* (*House of Commons*) (1988) • W. Notestein, F. H. Relf, and H. Simpson, eds., *Commons debates, 1621*, 7 vols. (1935) • M. Jansson and W. B. Bidwell, eds., *Proceedings in parliament, 1625* (1987) • W. F. Craven, *Dissolution of the Virginia Company: the failure of a colonial experiment* (1932) • R. E. Ruigh, *The parliament of 1624: politics and foreign policy* (1971) • C. J. Sisson, *The judicious marriage of Mr Hooker and the birth of 'The laws of ecclesiastical polity'* (1940) • W. Notestein, *The House of Commons, 1604–1610* (1971) • E. S. Sandys, *History of the family of Sandys* (1930) • A. Brown, *The genesis of the United States*, 2 vols. (1890)

Archives Magd. Cam., Ferrar papers

Likenesses V. Green, mezzotint, BM; repro. in Nash, *History of Worcestershire* (1781) • portrait, Graythwaite Hall, Cumbria; repro. in Rabb, *Jacobean gentleman*

Sandys, Emma (1843–1877). *See under* Pre-Raphaelite women artists (act. 1848–1870s).

Sandys, (Anthony) Frederick Augustus (1829–1904), painter and illustrator, was born in Norwich on 1 May 1829 to Anthony Sands (*bap.* 1804, *d.* 1883), a minor local artist who was originally a dyer, and his wife, Mary Ann Brown (*d.* 1883). He was baptized at St Stephen's Church, Norwich, as Antonio Frederic Augustus Sands. His sister was Emma *Sandys (1843–1877) [*see under* Pre-Raphaelite women artists], who also became an artist. In 1853 the family added a 'y' to their surname, implying (wrongly) a connection to an ancient Cumbrian family.

Sandys was a precocious artist, and as early as 1839 his father exhibited his work locally. In 1842 he attracted a commission from the banker and ornithologist John Henry Gurney (1819–1890) of Yarmouth, to paint watercolours of birds in his collection; these are now in the Norwich Castle Museum. He attended Norwich grammar school, and then the newly founded Norwich School of Design from 1846. While there he competed for prizes at the Society of Arts in London, winning their silver medal in 1846 for a portrait in chalk and in 1847 for an oil painting of wild ducks painted from nature. On the latter occasion, the young John Everett Millais was being examined at the same time: this was their first meeting.

In 1845 Sandys started work for his most important early patron, the Revd James Bulwer (1794–1879), an amateur watercolour artist and keen antiquary. Sandys was employed to illustrate a number of Bulwer's articles in *Norfolk Archaeology* with etchings, as well as to make some 220 pencil and watercolour drawings of local antiquities, medieval church furnishings, and architectural details for Bulwer's extra-illustrated version of Francis Blomefield's *Topographical History of the County of Norfolk* (11 vols., 1805–10). In addition he painted portraits of James Bulwer and his family.

For a few years after 1849 Sandys and his father collaborated in reproductive work for the Norwich publisher Charles Muskett. This provided him with experience that was to serve him in future jobbing work for London printsellers and their engravers. Sandys's first lodgings in London seem to have been at 2 Osnaburgh Street in 1848, where he continued to live periodically until about 1853.

(Anthony) Frederick Augustus Sandys (1829–1904), by Percy Wood, late 1890s

In London he studied by copying works of art in the National Gallery and British Museum. On 20 May 1853 Sandys married Georgiana Creed at St Pancras Church, London. However, the marriage did not last, and thereafter Mrs Sandys seems to have vanished. There was an unrealized attempt to obtain a divorce from her about 1864.

The year 1857 brought Sandys to prominence in the London art world when he published, anonymously, a caricature print entitled *A Nightmare*. Employing a newly invented autographic lithographic process, the print was a parody of J. E. Millais's painting *Sir Isumbras at the Ford* exhibited at the Royal Academy that year, and was an outsider's joke at the expense of the Pre-Raphaelites and their supporter John Ruskin. The mounted knight, Sir Isumbras, had the face of Millais, and the two children riding pillion had the faces of Rossetti and Holman Hunt. The horse was transformed into a braying donkey branded 'J. R.' (John Ruskin). It caused much amusement and speculation about the name of the artist—which quickly emerged. Robert Ross wrote that in order to get a likeness of Rossetti, Sandys called on the artist and that this was the start of their friendship.

Sandys first exhibited at the Royal Academy in 1851; thereafter he exhibited about once every two years until 1886, and in the winter of 1905, after his death, a retrospective exhibition was held there. His first oils shown in London, *Queen Eleanor* (1858; National Museum and Gallery of Wales, Cardiff) and *Mary Magdalen* (c.1859; Delaware Art

Museum), were exhibited at the British Institution gallery in 1860. The former is his first known subject picture in oils. A new friend and patron bought both pictures, the lawyer James Anderson Rose (1819–1890). In 1862 Rose accompanied Sandys on a short trip to the Netherlands to look at Flemish and other northern European old master paintings. The notebook Sandys kept showed his admiration for Holbein and Rubens portraits. This appears to be his only trip abroad.

Sandys's most active and creative period was undoubtedly the 1860s which he spent between London and Norwich. His chief friend and supporter was the Norwich industrialist William H. Clabburn (1820–1889) who commissioned at least eight family portraits and was the owner of many other pictures painted by Sandys during this productive period, including *Oriana* (1861; Tate collection) and the large drawing *Spring* (c.1860; Norwich Castle Museum). He apparently discovered in Norfolk and subsequently brought to London the handsome Gypsy Keomi, who became his model and reputedly his mistress for a time. She can be recognized in a number of paintings by Sandys, for example *Medea* (1866–8), and in Rossetti's *The Beloved* (1865–6). 1860 probably marks the beginning of Rossetti's influence on Sandys's work, in the painting of poetic-erotic representations of women in various guises. In fact, the rift in their friendship during 1869–74 was caused by Rossetti's perception of this influence, which he saw as plagiarism.

The majority of Sandys's portraits also dates from the 1860s, and includes *Mrs. Susanna Rose* (1862; Cleveland Museum of Art, Ohio) and *Mrs. Jane Lewis* (1864; Los Angeles County Museum, California). In the manner of Holbein, Sandys invariably preceded his painting with a precise drawing on paper, in which he fixed the likeness and pose, which was then transferred to the support. These drawings came to be admired in their own right and patrons were often satisfied with a drawing, avoiding the considerable expense an oil painting entailed, not to mention the many hours of wearisome sittings that Sandys required for his painstaking technique.

These portrait drawings became more detailed, often with floral backgrounds, and the best examples date mostly from the 1870s, such as *Mrs. Howell* (1873; Birmingham Art Gallery) and *Cyril Flower* (1878; Norwich Castle Museum). These crayon or chalk portraits were, in their time, an original development in the art of the portrait and proved to be a success with Sandys's wealthy, middle-class clients.

Also in the 1860s, like many of his contemporaries, Sandys designed illustrations for the new literary magazines—the *Cornhill Magazine*, *Good Words*, and *Once a Week*. These drawings were reproduced by professional wood-engravers including the Dalziel brothers and Joseph Swain. He designed only a relatively small number, twenty-six between 1859 and 1866, but, such was the care that he put into them, they can be counted among the finest of this genre, and show the influence of Dürer, Holbein, and Rethel.

In London, Sandys moved frequently owing to his inability to pay the rent during financial crises. In one such an emergency Rossetti took him in at 16 Cheyne Walk where he lived from May 1866 to July 1867, playing a lively part in Rossetti's bohemian dinner parties. Sandys enjoyed a wide circle of friends in the 1860s: fellow artists such as J. A. M. Whistler and Frederic Leighton, but also writers, actors (he was a member of the Garrick Club), journalists, lawyers, and the entrepreneur C. A. Howell, who began to act as Sandys's agent. In the late 1870s he was very intimate with the architect Edward Godwin.

In 1873 a new patron, Cyril Flower (later Lord Battersea), whose family was developing parts of Westminster, offered Sandys a studio and apartment in Westminster, but he became a bankrupt in 1876 and the studio was repossessed. Meanwhile, he had already started on a development of large draped figure drawings with titles such as *Danae* (1867; Bradford Art Gallery), *Fate* (1868; Ferens Art Gallery, Hull), *Lethe* (1874; William Morris Gallery), *Persephone* (1878; priv. coll.) in response to the taste for neo-classicism.

An increasing blandness characterizes Sandys's portrait drawings in the 1880s, notable for the series of eleven authors made for the publisher Alexander Macmillan (1881 to 1885, and two later ones, unfinished; Macmillan Ltd) to be engraved for frontispieces. These crayon works in portraiture and those with anonymous female heads enhanced by a veneer of symbolism, such as *Iris* (1898; Rhode Island School of Design), *Poppies* (1898; Wightwick Manor), *Peace and War* (1902), and replicas of earlier work, gave him a bare living as his powers waned towards the end of his life.

Sandys's problems stemmed from his attempt to live the life of a fashionable man about town, keeping up appearances and mixing with the wealthy, who were his patrons, while at the same time trying to support a large family. His gambling, and other unwise and extravagant habits, also help to account for his being so often penniless (and a notorious borrower), in spite of good prices paid for his work. He was tall and distinguished in appearance; Robert Ross described Sandys in old age as somewhat resembling Don Quixote. His common-law wife, Mary Emma Jones (1845–1920), an actress known as Miss Clive, whom he met about 1862 when she modelled for *The Magdalen* (Norwich Castle Museum) and to whom he was devoted, bore an increasing flock of children (ten of whom survived him), who lived under the name of Neville in a London suburb. Mary was the original inspiration for his *Proud Maisie* (1867; V&A). Such was its attraction that he made at least eleven replicas, the last in 1904.

Late in life Sandys suffered much from ill health, although financial difficulties ensured he continued to work. He died at 5 Hogarth Road, Kensington, on 25 June 1904, and was buried at Brompton cemetery on 30 June.

The largest collection of his work is at the Birmingham City Art Gallery, which is due to its preservation by Charles Fairfax Murray and to the body of local citizens who bought Murray's collection. There are some early works at the Fitzwilliam Museum, Cambridge, given by Murray, and Norwich Castle Museum has a good collection accumulated by gift and bequest. Other works are held in the British Museum, the Victoria and Albert Museum, the Tate collection, the Ashmolean Museum, Oxford, the Delaware Art Museum, Wilmington, the Yale Center for British Art, New Haven, and the National Gallery of Canada.   BETTY ELZEA

Sources B. Elzea, *Frederick Sandys, 1829–1904: a catalogue raisonné* (2001) · B. O'Looney, *Frederick Sandys, 1829–1904* (1974) [exhibition catalogue, Brighton Museum and Art Gallery] · J. M. Gray, 'Frederick Sandys', *Art Journal*, new ser., 4 (1884), 73–8 · E. Wood, 'A consideration of the art of Frederick Sandys', *The Artist, Photographer and Decorator, an Illustrated Monthly Journal of Applied Art* [special winter number] (1896) · DNB · Bryan, *Painters* (1903–5) · *Winter exhibition* (1905) [exhibition catalogue, RA] · P. Bate, 'The late Frederick Sandys: a retrospect', *The Studio*, 33 (1904–5), 3–17 · G. White, *English illustration, 'the sixties': 1855–70*, another edn (1903) · G. C. Williamson, *Murray Marks and his friends* (1919) · W. S. Talbot, 'A Victorian portrait by Frederick Sandys', *Bulletin of Cleveland Museum of Art*, 67 (Dec 1980), 298–309 · *The Owl and the Rossettis: letters of Charles A. Howell and Dante Gabriel, Christina and William Michael Rossetti*, ed. C. L. Cline (1978) · m. cert. · d. cert.

Archives Delaware Art Museum, Wilmington, Bancroft collection, corresp. with Samuel Bancroft and related material · JRL, Fairfax Murray collection, corresp. · Norwich Castle Museum, art department archives · University of British Columbia, Angeli-Dennis MSS

Likenesses A. Sandys, oils, 1848, NPG · F. Sandys, self-portrait, oils, 1848, Norwich Castle Museum · A. Sandys, etching, c.1848–1849, FM Cam. · P. Wood, photograph, 1896–9, NPG [*see illus.*] · A. Sandys, miniature, drawing (as a child), FM Cam. · F. Sandys, self-portrait, oils, Uffizi Gallery, Florence · photograph, BM

Wealth at death seemingly left family impoverished; partner, Mary Sandys, attempted to sell remaining drawings; there were also other fund-raising attempts

Sandys, George (1578–1644), writer and traveller, was the ninth child and youngest son of Edwin *Sandys (1519?–1588), archbishop of York, and his second wife, Cicely (1536–1611), daughter of Sir Thomas Wilford, and was born at the episcopal palace at Bishopthorpe on 2 March 1578. One of his godfathers was George Clifford, third earl of Cumberland. He probably attended St Peter's School in York, but the first documented evidence of his education is his admission to St Mary Hall, Oxford, on 5 December 1589, one year after the death of his father. Sandys is said to have transferred shortly afterwards to Corpus Christi, which his brothers Sir Samuel Sandys, the eldest, and Sir Edwin *Sandys had previously attended. In 1596 George transferred to the Middle Temple, where his uncle Myles Sandys had until recently been treasurer; no less than four brothers and four cousins had preceded him there. No evidence of his having qualified either from Oxford or the Middle Temple exists.

At some point before 1602 George Sandys was married to one of Archbishop Sandys's wards, Elizabeth (*fl.* 1587–1662?), daughter of John Norton of Ripon; the Nortons were a noted Catholic family. It was an arranged marriage, Archbishop Sandys and John Norton having stipulated terms for the marriage in their wills as early as November 1584. George Sandys was said to have gained lands to the value of £3000 by this marriage, and after leaving the Middle Temple he resided in Ripon, surrounded by Norton

George Sandys (1578–1644), by Cornelius Johnson, 1632

relatives. But in 1606 he moved to southern England, deserting his wife. In 1609 the Nortons entered into a lawsuit against Sandys, accusing him of having entered into 'a wasteful course of spending', and neglecting his estates (Davis, 38). They blamed his brother Sir Myles Sandys for the breakup of the marriage. In the same year George Sandys was mentioned as resident in Canterbury, close to his brother Sir Edwin, who was established near Folkestone.

Sir Edwin Sandys was a leading member of the nascent Virginia Company, and in 1609 George Sandys's name appeared among the list of persons to whom the second Virginia charter was granted by James I. But his first travels lay to the east. In 1610 Sandys set out for Europe and the Levant; in May of that year he arrived in Paris, in the tense aftermath of the assassination of Henri IV. Later in the same year Sandys embarked at Venice for the long voyage to Constantinople, entering the Sea of Marmora on 27 September. In his subsequent description of the Ottoman empire, he makes one of the first references to coffee, which Francis Bacon and Robert Burton both reproduced. In January 1611 Sandys took a ship to Alexandria, reaching Cairo on camelback. He later presented some figurines of the Egyptian gods to John Tradescant. From Cairo he travelled overland to Jerusalem, beating off an assault by desert Arabs on the way, and arrived in the city for the great Easter celebrations; he was probably back in England by March 1612, returning via southern Italy.

The completed narrative of his travels was published as *A Relation of a Journey Begun an. Dom. 1610* (1615); like all of Sandys's subsequent writings, it was dedicated to Prince Charles. Sandys was an observant, inquisitive traveller and his description of the foreign cultures he encountered is remarkable for moderation and tolerance. In this work he became the first English writer to discredit the medieval belief that Jews emit an unsavoury odour (D. S. Katz, *Philo-Semitism and the Readmission of the Jews to England, 1603–1655*, 1982, 170). He also evinces something of the ecumenical interests which had formed the burden of his brother Sir Edwin's earlier *Relation of the State of Religion in the Western Partes of the World* (1605): George Sandys's description of the gathering of Christian sects from all corners of the Old World for the Easter festivities of 1611 celebrates a brief moment of Christian unity in a divided world. *A Relation of a Journey* was widely influential as a source of information on the Near East; it was used by Ben Jonson, Francis Bacon, Robert Burton, Sir Thomas Browne, Abraham Cowley, and John Milton among others.

After his return to England, Sandys took a renewed interest in the Virginia Company; in 1619 he narrowly failed in an attempt to be appointed governor of the Bermudas, and in 1621 the Virginia Company, now controlled by Sir Edwin Sandys and the earl of Southampton, appointed him treasurer for the colony, member of the council of state in Virginia, and member of his majesty's council for Virginia in London. He sailed in July 1621, arriving in Jamestown, Virginia, in October; with him was another Sandys kinsman, the newly appointed governor, Sir Francis Wyatt. As treasurer, Sandys was granted 1500 acres in Virginia, but these turned out to be virgin forest, and on his arrival he was forced to purchase 200 acres of cleared plantation where he could grow the crops necessary for the survival of his tenants. Wyatt and Sandys pursued a moderate and tolerant approach to colonization in Virginia, in the belief that the Virginian natives were about to convert to Christianity. Their hopes were shattered on 22 March 1622 by a great Indian uprising, in which over 300 of the colonists died. Sandys himself led the first English counter-attack against the Indians and a popular ballad celebrating this exploit has survived. Sandys's remarkably frank letters to friends and relatives about the appalling conditions in the colony after the uprising had the misfortune to be impounded in London and used as evidence of Sir Edwin's mismanagement of the company. After the crown dissolved the Virginia Company and assumed direct control of the colony in 1624, Sandys was reappointed to the colony's council (26 August), but in 1625 he returned home, narrowly escaping from Turkish pirates on the way.

Before leaving for Virginia, Sandys had published a verse translation of the first five books of Ovid's *Metamorphoses* (1621). Two further books were completed on the voyage to Virginia, 'amongst the roreing of the seas, the rustling of the Shrowdes, and Clamour of Saylers' as Sandys later wrote (Kingsbury, 4.66); the remaining books were completed during the long evenings in the colony. On 24 April 1626 Sandys was granted a patent from the king for exclusive rights to print and sell the work for twenty-one years, and the completed *Ovid's Metamorphosis*

Englished was published in the same year. In 1632 a magnificent edition appeared which included elaborate panegyrics to Charles I and Henrietta Maria, engravings designed by Francis Clein and executed by Salmon Savery, and extensive neo-Platonic allegorizations of Ovid's mythology, occasionally interspersed with personal anecdotes. Some of the comments, especially those derived from Bacon, reveal a sceptical approach to contemporary politics. Michael Drayton addressed a poem to Sandys before his departure for Virginia, encouraging him to continue with the Ovid translation, and later praised the completed work for 'sweetnesse and unusual grace' (Davis, 222).

Many parallels with Sandys's *Ovid* have been traced in Milton's work, and Sandys's use of the heroic couplet and his poetic diction were particularly influential on Dryden and Pope. In 1693 Dryden denigrated the work, but later he declared that Sandys was 'the best versifier of the former age' (Davis, 224); his own translations of Ovid are heavily indebted to Sandys. Pope praised Sandys as 'one of the chief refiners of our language' (ibid.). The style of Sandys's *Ovid* is ornate, compressed, and highly Latinate in grammar and syntax; some of Ovid's wit and pace is lost. More successful as translation is his version of Book One of Virgil's *Aeneid*, not published until 1632 but probably completed before the outward voyage to Virginia. Previous Virginian adventurers had drawn parallels between themselves and Virgil's empire-building Trojans, and through this translation Sandys was able to express many of the emotions of early colonization.

On his return from Virginia, Sandys became a gentleman of the privy chamber of Charles I. He became acquainted with Lucius Cary, second Viscount Falkland, who held a similar post, and became a member of the Great Tew circle, moderate ecumenical scholars and divines for whom Falkland held open house. Sandys's niece Anne was married to Sir Francis Wenman, and Sandys often stayed with them, at Carswell, near Falkland's residence at Great Tew in Oxfordshire. Falkland became an ardent supporter of Sandys's Caroline religious verse. Sandys's *Paraphrase upon the Psalmes* (1636) was prefaced by a long commendatory poem by Falkland, as were all but one of his subsequent publications. Sandys's psalm poetry is anti-Calvinist in theology, and at its best effectively combines a formal delight in 'the beauty of holiness' with personal devotion. A second edition of the *Psalmes* appeared in 1638, which also included fine translations of the book of Job, Ecclesiastes, and Lamentations, and commendatory poems from brother-poets Henry King, Sidney Godolphin, Thomas Carew, and Edmund Waller. The mood of this second edition is more sombre: several of the poets, including Sandys himself, meditate upon the growing troubles of the kingdom. Musical settings of the *Psalmes* by Henry Lawes were also included, probably for performance by the Chapel Royal.

Sandys's final religious work was a translation of *Christus patiens*, a Latin verse drama by Hugo Grotius published in 1608. This work shows that Sandys was directly influenced by the thinking of Falkland and William Chillingworth, for whom Grotius's eirenic, rational theology represented a moderate alternative to the increased polarization of the country between puritans and high Anglicans. Although loyal to the crown, the leaders of Great Tew were dismayed by Archbishop Laud's persecution of religious dissent, and Sandys's translation of Grotius, *Christ's Passion* (1640), dramatizes the dangers of such persecution. In the figure of Caiaphas, Sandys portrays a persecuting, over-powerful priest who attacks Christ for being an 'Innovator', and leads astray a moderate Roman leader, Pilate: an unmistakable parallel with Laud is created. The work was prefaced with a lengthy poem by Falkland eulogizing Grotius and Sandys. Sandys's final publication was *A Paraphrase of the Song of Solomon*. This had been completed several years earlier but fallen foul of the Laudian censorship for its excessive sensuality; it was only published after the demise of that system, in 1641.

Sandys remained involved with Virginia after his return from the colony. Despite his absence in England, he was reappointed to the colony's council in 1626, and again in 1628, presumably in the expectation that he would return. But he remained in England, serving on a royal commission which advised on the state of the colony in 1631 and at some time before 1638 he was appointed to the subcommittee for foreign plantations under the Laud commission. When Sir Francis Wyatt returned for a brief spell as governor (1639–42), one of his first actions was to appoint Sandys as the colony's agent in London. Sandys was twice directly involved in attempts to revive the Virginia Company, first in 1631, and second in 1640, when he presented a petition to the House of Commons for the restoration of the company's former constitution. This was done in collaboration with John Pym, and presumably reflected Wyatt's wishes. However, in 1642 Wyatt was replaced as governor by William Berkeley, who disowned the petition. From 1639 Sandys spent much of his time at Boxley Abbey in Kent, the family seat of the Wyatts. In 1641 Thomas Fuller met Sandys at the Savoy, describing him as 'a youthful soul in a decayed body' (Fuller, *Worthies*, new edn, 1840, 3.434); in 1642 Sir Francis Wyatt returned from Virginia, and the two seasoned campaigners spent their last years together, both dying at Boxley in 1644. Sandys was buried in Boxley church on 7 March of that year. Some years after Sandys's death, Richard Baxter was shown a summer house in the garden at Boxley with the inscription that in that place '*Mr. G. Sandys after his Travels over the World, retired himself for his Poetry and Contemplations*' (Baxter, 'To the reader'). Sandys never remarried and there were no children. In his latter years he appears not to have been wealthy, describing himself as 'content with little' (Hooper, 2.406). None the less, recent attempts to identify him as the 'Sir George Sandys' who was tried and acquitted of highway robbery in 1616 are implausible: the record probably refers to Sandys's cousin of the same name, who was indeed knighted, and who died in 1618.

JAMES ELLISON

Sources R. B. Davis, *George Sandys: poet adventurer* (1955) · R. Hooper, *The poetical works of George Sandys*, 2 vols. (1872) · M. A.

Rogers, 'Materials towards an edition of George Sandys's *A relation of a journey begun anno. dom. 1610* (1615)', DPhil diss., U. Oxf., 1976 · J. Ellison, 'George Sandys: religious toleration and political moderation in an early Anglican', DPhil diss., U. Oxf., 1998 · S. M. Kingsbury, *The records of the Virginia Company of London*, 4 vols. (1906–35) · E. S. Sandys, *History of the family of Sandys* (1930) · R. R. Cawley, 'Burton, Bacon, and Sandys', *Modern Language Notes*, 56 (1941), 271–3 · R. Baxter, *Poetical fragments: heart-imployment with God and it self* (1681) · J. Haynes, *The humanist as traveller: George Sandys's 'Relation of a journey begun an. dom. 1610'* (Cranbury, NJ, 1986) · D. Rubin, *Ovid's Metamorphoses Englished: George Sandys as translator and mythographer* (1985) · K. E. Schmutzler, 'George Sandys's paraphrases on the Psalms and the tradition of metrical psalmody: an annotated edition of fifty selected psalms, with critical and biographical introduction', PhD diss., Ohio State University, 1956 · *Reg. Oxf.*, 2/1–4 · E. A. Jones, *American members of the inns of court* (1924) · J. Cave-Brown, *History of Boxley parish* (1892) · *DNB* · Archbishop Sandys's copy of the Bishops' Bible, Hawkshead grammar school, Lancashire

Archives PRO, letters, nos. 318, 319, 320, 321, 326; C.O.1, vol. 2, nos. 27, 35

Likenesses C. Johnson, portrait, 1632, priv. coll. [*see illus.*] · G. Powle, etching, 1781 (after C. Johnson), BM; repro. in T. Nash, *Collections for the history of Worcestershire*, 1 (1781) · W. Raddon, line engraving, pubd 1824 (after C. Johnson), BM, NPG; repro. in B. W. Procter, *Effigies poeticae, or, The portraits of British poets* (1824) · C. Johnson, portrait (when older), repro. in Davis, *George Sandys*; priv. coll.

Sandys, Sir John Edwin (1844–1922), classical scholar, was born at Leicester on 19 May 1844, the fourth son of the Revd Timothy Sandys, of the Church Missionary Society, Calcutta, and his wife, Rebecca, daughter of Joseph Swain, of Leicester. He spent his earliest years in India, but returned to England at the age of eleven and was educated first at the Church Missionary Society School in Islington and then at Repton School, where he came under the influence of the reforming headmaster S. A. Pears. He remained devoted to the school and later wrote its Latin *carmen*. In 1863 he won a scholarship to St John's College, Cambridge, where he had a distinguished academic career. He obtained a Bell scholarship (1864) and a Browne medal for Greek ode (1865), was twice Porson prizeman (1865, 1866), twice Members' prizeman for Latin essay (1866, 1867), and in 1867 was senior classic. In the same year he was elected fellow of his college and he was also appointed to a lecturership there which he held until 1907. Sandys's official connection with St John's was always close, for he was appointed to a tutorship in 1870, and held the office until 1900. In the university, his scholarship was early recognized by election to the post of public orator in 1876 and, after his retirement in 1919, he was given the title of *orator emeritus*. In 1880 Sandys married Mary Grainger, daughter of the Revd Henry Hall, vicar of St Paul's Church, Cambridge; there were no children of the marriage.

In the academic world, Sandys was accorded a full share of honours, including honorary doctorates of Dublin (1892), Edinburgh (1909), Athens (1912), and Oxford (1920). From Cambridge, where he had already taken the LittD degree in 1886, he received the honorary degree of LLD in 1920. Added to these distinctions was a fellowship of the British Academy (1909), and a commandership in the order of the Saviour (1914)—an honour which gave him

especial pleasure, as a recognition by modern Greece of his services to classical literature and archaeology.

Sandys produced a number of books, including important editions of several speeches of Demosthenes and other Greek orators, as well as of Cicero's *Orator* (1885) and the recently discovered Aristotelian *Constitution of Athens* (1903). His largest work, however, was the *History of Classical Scholarship* (3 vols., 1903–8), a valuable reference guide which remains the only substantial work to cover the history of classical learning from the sixth century to the year of publication.

Although Sandys's main interests lay in Greek oratory and poetry, he emphasized, both in his lectures and editions, the importance of Greek art. He was active in the establishment of the British School at Athens and was one of those who successfully prevented the handing over of the British Museum to a department of war service during the First World War. He enjoyed travel and left several diaries recording visits to Mediterranean countries: in 1887 he published *An Easter Vacation in Greece*.

It was as an orator that the academic public knew Sandys best. In over forty years he presented close on 700 distinguished men for honorary degrees, with speeches which, of their kind, were almost perfect. His style was modelled on Cicero, and could well pass the most stringent test of Latinity both in rhythm and language; but his speeches were as remarkable for their matter as for their manner. However eulogistic, Sandys went straight to the point, picking out the real merits of the person presented. He himself was honoured by a knighthood in 1911.

Sandys was known to many, but intimate, perhaps, with few. His pupils were apt to think of him as 'donnish', cold and impassive, unapproachable, and unsympathetic. This was largely a form of self-protection: he was extremely shy, and never able to take, or simulate, any great interest in the daily life and amusements of the average undergraduate. But beneath a rather frigid exterior, his friends and many of his pupils recognized the generosity of the man, and his warmth of affection for those whom he liked and trusted.

Sandys died on 6 July 1922 after collapsing in the third court of St John's in his robes on the way to a presentation of honorary degrees. By his will, he left over £8000 to Cambridge University for the purpose of founding a studentship for research in the language, literature, or other branches of classical study. He was also, in various ways, a benefactor of his college, to which he was loyally devoted.   E. E. SIKES, *rev.* RICHARD SMAIL

Sources J. S. Reid, 'Sir John Edwin Sandys, 1844–1922', *PBA*, 10 (1921–3), 545–51 · N. G. L. Hammond, *Sir John Edwin Sandys* (1933) · *The Eagle*, 43 (1923–4), 15–18 · *The Times* (7 July 1922)

Archives St John Cam., papers | BL, corresp. with Macmillans, Add. MS 55123 · King's AC Cam., letters to O. Browning

Likenesses W. Stoneman, photograph, 1917, NPG

Wealth at death £44,252 15s. 2d.: probate, 15 Aug 1922, *CGPLA Eng. & Wales*

Sandys, Samuel, first Baron Sandys of Ombersley (1695–1770), politician, was born on 10 August 1695, and baptized the following day at Greenwich. He was the elder son of Edwin Sandys (*bap.* 1659, *d.* 1699) and his wife, Alice (or Elicia), daughter of Sir James Rushout, first baronet, of Northwick Park, Brockley, Worcestershire. Sandys's immediate forebears had emerged over the course of the previous century as one of Worcestershire's premier gentry families. The family estates centred on the manor of Ombersley which had been granted initially as a lease in 1594 to Sir Samuel Sandys, eldest son of Archbishop Edwin Sandys of York (*d.* 1588). Succeeding generations represented the county and its boroughs in parliament and Sandys's father, Edwin, served as knight of the shire during 1695–8 but predeceased his own father in 1699. The bulk of the estate, having already been transferred to Edwin Sandys at his marriage in 1694, was consequently inherited by Samuel when he was barely four years of age, and in 1701 he inherited the remainder of the estate on the death of his grandfather and namesake. In April 1711 the young Samuel matriculated at New College, Oxford, and in due course travelled abroad.

Despite Sandys's possession of an estate which even during the 1690s was reckoned to yield £1125 annually, the comforts of provincial society held little attraction to his serious-minded temperament, and in March 1718, aged only twenty-two, he seized the opportunity of a by-election at Worcester to enter parliament. He was returned for the city without opposition, and retained the seat until he was made a peer in 1743. Sandys quickly attached himself to Robert Walpole, whom he evidently perceived as the key to his own political aspirations, and by 1722, when Walpole was back in power, he numbered among the ministry's most prominent backbench adherents. Described as 'a tall, thin young man' (*Egmont Diary*, 3.256), he applied himself industriously to all kinds of parliamentary business, and became something of a procedural expert. On his feet he was capable but dry and said to possess little humour. A government henchman, Giles Earle, once observed of him 'that he never laughed but once, and that when his best friend broke his thigh' (Walpole, *Corr.*, 17.249–50). His expectations of high office matured during the early years of the Walpole administration, but when in March 1724 he was passed over for secretary at war in favour of Henry Pelham he felt the affront keenly. The following session he took his place among the small but vociferous group of whig opponents of the ministry whose leading light, William Pulteney, had likewise been disappointed of ministerial office.

Sandys was married on 9 June 1725 to Laetitia (or Laetithea; *bap.* 1699, *d.* 1779), the eldest daughter and coheir of Sir Thomas Tipping, first baronet, of Wheatfield, Oxfordshire. Her fortune was said to have amounted to £170,000. The marriage subsequently produced seven sons and three daughters. In close association with William Pulteney (whose chief lieutenant he became) and other discontented whigs, Sandys contributed to the strategic aim of co-ordinating, expanding, and unifying the disparate sources of opposition to Walpole in the Commons. Initially the ministry's active whig opponents consisted mainly of the Pulteneyites, numbering only a dozen or so

MPs, but in the years immediately after George II's accession in 1727 the group presented an increasingly plausible patriot challenge to the ministry, and through the rhetoric of country principles exposed ministerial shortcoming in many areas of policy and government. Their ultimate aim, to oust Walpole and secure their own appointment to office, remained for many years a remote prospect given the ministry's numerical superiority in parliament and the king's unwavering esteem for his minister. None the less, the upsurge and intensity of opposition during the early 1730s was a phenomenon that had been absent from the political scene for many years, and many whigs were attracted to the opposition critique of overblown Walpolian power. The working relationship which the patriot whig leadership forged with the previously inert tory rump produced an opposition which in numerical terms began to assume the capacity to usurp Walpole's majority. An important factor behind the rapid emergence of 'formed opposition' to Walpole was its organizational clout, much of which was due to Sandys. Pulteney regarded him highly, and spoke of him as 'a very particular friend of mine' (W. Pulteney to Colman, 1 June 1732, BL, Add. MS 18915, fol. 10). Although Sandys lacked Pulteney's debating panache and vigour, and may even have been overshadowed by other patriot speakers such as Pulteney's able but inebriate cousin Daniel Pulteney, his speeches bear the hallmarks of clarity and precision. His own distinctive contribution to proceedings, of tabling debating motions that frequently sought to needle the ministry on some particular aspect of policy or conduct, earned him the epithet of 'the motion-maker'.

Government supporters were quick to denigrate Sandys as a man of 'republican' sentiment. His espousal of old whig principles concerning the necessity of preserving parliament from executive entrenchment, featured prominently in the country campaign against the ministry, and was given particular attention in the sequence of bills he presented to disable elected MPs who possessed pensions or offices of profit from taking their seats in the house. These measures helped to publicize the reality behind Walpole's apparent unassailability in the Commons, that it was buttressed by Treasury largesse, and that this 'corruption' of the constitution prohibited the inauguration of a truly just and patriotic administration. Sandys's pension bills, of which the first, presented in 1730, helped to aggravate the independent whig revolt in the Dunkirk crisis, were followed by similar bills in the parliamentary sessions of 1731, 1732, and 1733, followed by bills against placemen in 1734, 1735, 1736, 1740, 1741, and 1742. Although each bill was defeated, their appeal to 'independent' whigs provided proof of the opposition's capacity to draw off support from the government's usual rank-and-file adherents on popular points.

In 1732 Sandys chaired the opposition-dominated inquiry proceedings into the financial frauds concerning the Charitable Corporation, a torrid affair in which the whiff of ministerial guilt was much exploited. The following year, as Walpole prepared to unveil his excise scheme, Sandys warned of the marginalization of parliament that would arise from abolishing the annually imposed land tax in favour of an expanded system of excise duties. At the height of the ensuing crisis Sandys was designated as speaker in a new ministry which the patriots planned in anticipation of Walpole's fall. After the 1734 general election the opposition leadership seriously considered opening the new parliament with an attempt to elect Sandys to the speaker's chair in place of Arthur Onslow. In 1737, at the time Pulteney first considered the possibility of coming to terms with the ministry, it was understood that Sandys, too, was prepared to follow him into office as a manager for the court and probably as speaker. The long years of frustrated hopes were taking their toll and the commitment to attritional opposition had begun to wane. Though Pulteney's negotiations on this occasion came to nothing, the patriot leaders' real motives were thereafter increasingly suspect. Sandys maintained the veneer of opposition in a way that may have seemed more credible than Pulteney. In March 1739, following narrow defeat in a vote concerning the breakdown of Britain's relations with Spain, he joined in the patriots' 'secession' from the house for the remainder of the session in protest at Walpole's continuing abuse of parliament.

Sandys's most famous motion, for an address to the king demanding the removal of Walpole from his counsels, was debated at length on 13 February 1741. However, its outcome revealed it to be a gross tactical miscalculation. The tories, strongly disapproving the question as a slight upon the king's prerogative, withdrew beforehand *en masse*, leaving the malcontent whigs isolated in a division of 290 against 106, and revealing the unpleasant truth that collaboration between opposition whigs and tories had foundered on growing suspicions concerning the patriot whigs' leaders and their contact with the ministry. The chief patriots' determination to come into office, seemingly at any cost, became more widely apparent to those in political circles after the general election in May 1741, apprehensions which rang true when Walpole's resignation early in February 1742 was quickly followed with Sandys's appointment as chancellor, and of fellow Pulteneyites, his uncle Sir John Rushout and Phillips Gybbon, to the Treasury board. The speed with which this was accomplished clearly suggested the existence of a pre-arranged deal between Pulteney, who himself chose not to accept office, and the ministry. Sandys kissed the king's hand for the chancellorship on 11 February and was sworn of the privy council on the 16th. At a large meeting of opposition peers and MPs on the 12th at The Fountain tavern in the Strand, both Pulteney and Sandys faced angry insults for their apostasy, and Sandys was particularly abused for having accepted his office 'privily' and without due consultation with other opposition chiefs. In self-justification he told the gathering that:

the business of the public must go on; the king had removed the chancellor of the exchequer, and if somebody did not accept the office, his Majesty must employ the same person again, which he supposed they would not choose. And that they ought not to think ill of him till he had done something amiss.   (S. Taylor and C. Jones, eds., *Tory and Whig: the*

Parliamentary Papers of Edward Harley, Third Earl of Oxford, and William Hay, MP for Seaford, 1716–1753, 1998, 178)

When privately asked how he would deal with the 'popular bills' he had formerly championed:

he said that all men knew that parties attempted many things of this kind in opposition which they never meant to carry, but it was necessary to amuse the people. But that these [popular measures] in general he should oppose, and so must every minister, and that as Sir Robert used to say, they were but the flurries of a day.   (Sedgwick, 2.407)

For a while, however, Sandys retained the respect of country MPs mainly on account of his avowed support for a 'committee of secrecy' to inquire into Walpole's conduct in office, and was unanimously voted one of its members. But these good opinions soon began to fade when in April he voted against key motions calling for the repeal of the Septennial Act and for protesting against the peers' rejection of a bill indemnifying witnesses who might testify against Walpole. He also spoke in defence of his new colleague the Treasury secretary John Scrope for refusing to reveal information about Walpole's disposition of secret service money.

With Treasury business now fully occupying his attention, Sandys had completed his transformation into a fully-fledged ministerialist. When the new session opened in December 1742 he strenuously resisted reopening the proceedings against Walpole, and was constantly vilified by many former rank-and-file friends in opposition. Moreover, he angered his Worcester constituents by opposing a new place bill, defying their instructions to support it. Like Pulteney and his Treasury board associates, Sandys found increasing difficulty in maintaining credibility in the Commons. Full advantage of this situation was taken by Henry Pelham, Walpole's favoured heir who had succeeded Lord Wilmington as first lord of the Treasury in July 1743, and moves were initiated for Pelham to replace Sandys as chancellor. Although willing to stand down, Sandys at first pressed to be made paymaster-general in succession to Pelham, but when this was resisted, he settled instead for a peerage and the post of cofferer of the household. Matters were finalized in December and on the 12th Sandys relinquished the chancellorship to Pelham. On the 20th he was created Baron Sandys of Ombersley, taking his seat in the Lords on the 22nd. A year later, Sandys and other members of the Pulteney–Carteret group were removed altogether from the administration as part of the project to form a 'broad-bottom' administration.

Sandys's demotion consigned him to the outer fringes of politics for the rest of his career. He remained an active if largely inconspicuous figure in the Lords, and briefly enjoyed office once more during the Newcastle and Bute ministries. In December 1755, on the recommendation of his friend Lord Hardwicke, he was appointed chief justice in eyre south of the Trent, resigning in November 1756 to become speaker of the House of Lords, which role he fulfilled until July 1757. He was chief justice in eyre north of the Trent from February 1759 to March 1761. The duke of Newcastle then brought him into more substantive office as first lord of trade in March 1761 and he was retained by Lord Bute until February 1763.

Sandys died on 21 April 1770 from injuries received when his carriage overturned on Highgate Hill, and was buried at Ombersley. He was succeeded in the barony by his eldest son, Edwin, who had entered parliament in 1747.   A. A. HANHAM

Sources DNB · R. R. Sedgwick, 'Sandys, Samuel', HoP, *Commons, 1715–54* · A. A. Hanham, 'Whig opposition to Sir Robert Walpole in the House of Commons, 1727–34', PhD diss., University of Leicester, 1992 · GEC, *Peerage* · *Manuscripts of the earl of Egmont: diary of Viscount Percival, afterwards first earl of Egmont*, 3 vols., HMC, 63 (1920–23), vol. 3, p. 256 · W. Coxe, *Memoirs of the life and administration of Sir Robert Walpole, earl of Orford*, 3 (1798), 516–20, 579–81 · J. B. Owen, *The rise of the Pelhams* (1957), 203 · Walpole, *Corr.* · *The manuscripts of the earl of Carlisle*, HMC, 42 (1897) · J. C. D. Clark, *The dynamics of change: the crisis of the 1750s and English party systems* (1982), 223, 289 · *The correspondence of the dukes of Richmond and Newcastle, 1724–1750*, ed. T. J. McCann, Sussex RS, 73 (1984), 93, 110 · H. Walpole, *Memoirs of King George II*, ed. J. Brooke, 3 vols. (1985), vol. 1, p. 47 n. 6; vol. 2, p. 10 · W. Pulteney to Colman, 1 June 1732, BL, Add. MS 18915, fol. 10 · *The parliamentary diary of Sir Edward Knatchbull, 1722–1730*, ed. A. N. Newman, CS, 3rd ser., 94 (1963), 115–22 · IGI · 'Sandys, Edwin', HoP, *Commons, 1690–1715* [draft]

Archives Bodl. Oxf., corresp. and papers · Worcs. RO, corresp. and papers | BL, corresp. with Lord Hardwicke, Add. MSS 35586–35596 · BL, corresp. with duke of Newcastle, Add. MSS 32708–32904

Wealth at death duke of Richmond described him in 1743 as 'immensely rich' and worthy of peerage: *Correspondence of the duke of Richmond*, ed. McCann, 110

Sandys, William, first Baron Sandys (c.1470–1540), soldier and courtier, was born at Sherborne St John, Hampshire, the second, but eldest surviving, son of Sir William Sandys (d. 1496) and Margaret, the only daughter of Sir John Cheney of Shurland, Kent. His family had long been respected members of the Hampshire gentry.

The younger William Sandys began his career in 1492 as a soldier fighting in Flanders, and attended the knighting of the future Henry VIII in 1494. Some time between May 1495 and February 1497 his fortunes dramatically improved with his appointment as a knight of the body to Henry VII. That promotion was probably connected to his marriage, before 26 October 1496, to Margary (d. 1539), the daughter and heir of John Bray and the niece and heir of Sir Reginald Bray, a prominent member of Henry VII's government; ultimately Sandys inherited the fortunes of both Bray brothers. The couple produced three sons: the eldest son, and heir, Thomas (d. 1560); John, a soldier at Guînes; and Reynold, a priest; there were also several daughters. Sandys proved his mettle against the Cornish rebels at Blackheath on 17 June 1497, and appointments to the commissions of the peace for Hampshire in 1498 and Wiltshire in 1501 followed, as did lucrative local offices such as constable of Christchurch Castle in 1499. In 1501 Sandys was appointed to receive Katherine of Aragon, on her arrival in England, and in August 1503 he accompanied Margaret Tudor when she went to Scotland to marry James IV.

The accession of Henry VIII in 1509 further advanced Sandys's career. He continued as a knight of the body, and the young king developed a great and lasting affection for him. On 12 January 1510 Henry VIII made him constable of Southampton Castle, a position he held for the rest of his life. Later in July the king honoured him with a visit to his Hampshire home, The Vyne, and on 9 November selected him to be sheriff of Hampshire. During 1512 he served as treasurer of the earl of Dorset's expedition to Gascony, and blamed Thomas Wolsey for its failure. He commanded 100 men in the king's retinue during the invasion of France in 1513 and did the same in the next year's invasion. During October 1514 Henry VIII entrusted him with accompanying Mary Tudor on her journey to marry Louis XII of France. As constable of Southampton Castle he suppressed a riot in that city during May 1517 and earned the praise of Richard Fox, bishop of Winchester. Later that year, on 6 October, Henry VIII made him treasurer of Calais, a post he held until 6 April 1526. He became a knight of the Garter on 16 May 1518, a sure sign of Henry VIII's favour, and probably about this time began attending the king's council. During June 1520 he participated in the Field of Cloth of Gold. Meanwhile Sandys and Cardinal Wolsey had patched up their earlier differences and in 1521 Wolsey proposed the competent but relatively low-ranking Sandys to command the next expedition against France. It was a suggestion that the status-conscious Henry VIII flatly rejected. More military and diplomatic assignments followed, however, and on 27 April 1523 Henry VIII created him Baron Sandys, which made him the only baron serving on the council. Although still not entrusted with command of an army, he ably assisted the duke of Suffolk during his invasion of France in August 1523. A lifetime appointment as captain of Guînes followed on 21 September 1523. Sandys's cordial relations with Bishop Fox and Cardinal Wolsey also continued. Wolsey would later confess that Sandys, along with the duke of Suffolk and the marquess of Exeter, had persistently encouraged him to ruin the duke of Norfolk. During 1524 Sandys and Fox founded the Guild of the Holy Ghost at Basingstoke, Hampshire. Some years later, on 15 February 1528, Fox would make Sandys a supervisor of his will. During the late 1520s Sandys completed a beautiful chapel at The Vyne, modelled on the chapel of the Holy Ghost and built in a style characteristic of the late middle ages in England. These connections and activities underline the extent to which he was, and remained, a conservative in matters of religion.

Sandys's duties as treasurer of Calais largely kept him out of England between 1517 and 1526. This situation changed during the latter year, however, when Henry VIII made him lord chamberlain. Sandys assumed the office on 15 April and became resident at court, relinquishing the office of treasurer of Calais. The Eltham ordinances name him as one of the people who were to attend and advise the king. His diplomatic duties and friendship with Henry VIII continued unabated, and during August 1531, as a prelude to a trip to Calais in October, the king visited him at The Vyne, where between 1518 and 1528 Sandys had built a magnificent new house. Sandys attended the coronation of Anne Boleyn on 1 June 1533. During 1534 and 1535 the imperial ambassador Eustace Chapuys reported that Sandys was conspiring against Henry VIII's religious changes. The king and Anne Boleyn, however, visited him at The Vyne during October 1535. A few months later, in May 1536, he served as one of the jurors at the trial of Anne Boleyn. On 27 June 1536 the king gave him Mottisfont Priory and its lands in Hampshire in exchange for Chelsea manor, making Sandys, John Russell, and Thomas Cromwell the only barons who received gifts of monastic land from Henry VIII between 1536 and 1539. Sandys was present at the baptism of Edward VI on 15 October 1537 at Hampton Court, while a month later, on 12 November, he witnessed the funeral of Queen Jane Seymour at Windsor. During December 1538 he served as a juror at the trial of those involved in the so-called Exeter conspiracy, while avoiding being himself drawn into the matter because of his alleged connections with the marquess. His wife died in late March 1539.

Now in his sixties, Sandys during his last years withdrew from court affairs, although he continued to attend some council meetings up to a few weeks before his death. That occurred between 3 and 7 December 1540, either at The Vyne or at Mottisfont, and he was buried in the Chapel of the Holy Ghost, Basingstoke. In the course of his life Sandys had been fortunate to secure a series of influential friends—Bray, Fox, Wolsey, and especially Henry VIII—who helped him to rise to the peerage and become a leading figure in Hampshire. Sandys's career also demonstrates the limits of Henry VIII's friendship and generosity. Sandys never advanced beyond baronial rank, nor were the king's gifts of land and offices so excessive as to arouse jealousy and resentment. He seems to have been respected for his military prowess and generally liked, no mean achievement in the backbiting environment of Henry VIII's court.   RONALD H. FRITZE

Sources GEC, *Peerage*, new edn, 11.441–4 · H. Miller, *Henry VIII and the English nobility* (1986) · *Letters of Richard Fox, 1486–1527*, ed. P. S. Allen and H. M. Allen (1929) · *DNB* · *Hampshire and the Isle of Wight*, Pevsner (1967)
Archives BL, papers and dispatches, Cotton MSS

Sandys, William (1792–1874), writer on music and antiquary, eldest son of Hannibal Sandys (1763–1847) and his wife, Anne (d. 1850), daughter of William Hill, was born at 5 Crane Court, Fleet Street, London, on 29 October 1792. He was educated at Westminster School from 1800 to 1808, and in January 1814 qualified as a solicitor. From 1861 to 1873 Sandys was head of the firm of Sandys and Knott, Gray's Inn Square; he was also commissioner of affidavits in the stannary court of Cornwall, and a fellow of the Society of Antiquaries. He married on 13 January 1816 at Constantine, Cornwall, Harriette, eldest daughter of Peter Hill of Carwythenack, Cornwall. After her death on 3 August 1851 he married on 6 September 1853 Eliza, daughter of Charles Pearson of Ravensbourne House, Greenwich. She survived him.

An enthusiastic musical amateur from youth, Sandys studied the cello under Robert Lindley, thought by many to have been the greatest cellist of his day. Sandys was also a keen antiquary. His first works, on freemasonry (1829) and macaronic poetry (1831), were of little importance. Of

much greater value were his writings on music. Sandys's most important work was his *Christmas Carols Ancient and Modern* (1833), which, together with Davies Gilbert's earlier but smaller collections and his own *Christmastide; its History, Festivities and Carols* (1852), laid the foundations for the discovery of the ballad carol which was then in danger of disappearing and becoming forgotten. The carols were not originally unique to Cornwall but they had died out in most other parts. In Cornwall the ballad carol, a popular form used for narrative and entertainment and characterized by dance rhythms, had survived as part of a vigorous tradition of singing in the home but was increasingly under threat from the carol hymn, a form composed in the eighteenth and nineteenth centuries specifically for church purposes to proclaim dogma. Realizing that the ballad carol was under threat, Sandys collected examples from oral and manuscript sources and published his collection, which included some music and more words, there being at the time no fixed relation between particular sets of words and particular tunes. He also wrote a long scholarly introduction. His transcriptions of the tunes are considered accurate, though his harmonizations are sometimes clumsy. Among the carols in his collection which have subsequently gained wide currency are 'God rest ye merry, gentlemen', 'I saw three ships', and 'A child this day is born', while others such as 'Tomorrow shall be my dancing day' have gained their place in the more specialist repertory. The collection, in which there is 'a barely concealed link between conviviality and theology' (McGrady, xxvii), also had an impact on subsequent scholarly collections, notably the 1928 edition of *The Oxford Book of Carols*. Sandys also wrote a volume of old *Festive Songs* for the Percy Society (1848). Another important work, written with Simon Andrew Forster, of the famous Forster family of instrument makers, was a *History of the Violin* (1864). Sandys was mainly responsible for the earlier part of the work, which is an important mid-nineteenth-century treatise. In 1846 he published a work on Cornish dialect.

In 1873 Sandys retired, and on 18 February 1874 he died at his residence, 10 Torrington Square, London. He was buried at Kensal Green cemetery on 23 February.

    HENRY DAVEY, rev. ELIZABETH BAIGENT

Sources R. McGrady, *Traces of ancient mystery: the ballad carols of Davies Gilbert and William Sandys* (1993) · P. Dearmear, R. Vaughan Williams, and M. Shaw, eds., *The Oxford book of carols* (1928) · E. Routley, *The English carol* (1958) · W. H. Husk, 'Sandys, William, FSA', Grove, *Dict. mus.* (1878–90) · *The Times* (18 Dec 1874) · *Law Journal* (7 March 1874), 134 · *CGPLA Eng. & Wales* (1874) · *DNB*
Archives NL Wales, journal of a walking holiday through south Wales with his brother Sampson Sandys
Wealth at death under £450: administration, 9 May 1874, *CGPLA Eng. & Wales*

Sanford, George Edward Langham Somerset (1840–1901), army officer, was born on 19 June 1840, the son of George Charles Sanford. After attending the Royal Military Academy, Woolwich, he entered the Royal Engineers as lieutenant on 18 October 1856, when little over sixteen. As a subaltern he saw much service in China, where he arrived in 1858. He took part in the occupation of Canton (Guangzhou), in the expedition to the River Peiho (Beihe), and in the demolition of forts at the mouth of the river and advance to Tientsin (Tianjin). He served in the campaign in north China in 1860. In 1862 Sanford joined Charles George Gordon in the operations against the Taipings. He did useful survey work during the campaign, and assisted Gordon in drafting *Military Plan of the District Round Shanghai under the Protection of the Allied Forces* (1864). Gordon described him as the best officer he had ever met. He was promoted second captain on 8 February 1866 and captain on 5 July 1872. He had married in 1867 Maria Hamilton (*d.* 1898), daughter of R. Hesketh of Southampton.

On returning to England, Sanford served in the Ordnance Survey there until 1872. In 1873 he went to India as executive engineer in the public works department, becoming major on 10 December 1873. In 1878 he served in the Afridi expedition as assistant quartermaster-general, Peshawar district. Later, in 1878–9, he took part in the Second Afghan War, and was present at the capture of Ali Masjid. He was mentioned in dispatches and received the brevet of lieutenant-colonel (22 November 1879). Sir Frederick Roberts rewarded his efficiency by appointment as assistant quartermaster-general of 1st division in the Peshawar valley field force. Thenceforth his work lay long in the quartermaster-general's department. In 1880 he was deputy quartermaster-general of the newly formed Indian intelligence department, and during the absence of Sir Charles Macgregor he officiated for a year (1882–3) as quartermaster-general in India. He showed his ability in dispatching the Indian contingent to Egypt in 1882, becoming lieutenant-colonel on 26 April 1882. He had previously prepared excellent intelligence reports on Egypt as a possible theatre of war, and the success of the transport arrangement was largely due to him.

On completion of his term as deputy quartermaster-general at headquarters in December 1885 Sanford, who was promoted colonel on 22 November 1883, saw service as commanding royal engineer in the Burmese expedition of 1885–6. He was made CB on 25 November 1886.

From March 1886 until 1893 Sanford was director-general of military works in India, and held office during a period of great activity in connection with frontier defences. On 1 January 1890 he was made CSI. On leaving the military works department he commanded the Meerut district until 1898. He had been made major-general on 1 January 1895, and became lieutenant-general on 1 April 1898. He was mentioned in 1898 for the Bombay command, when it fell to Lieutenant-General Sir Robert C. Low. A first-rate soldier and an accomplished man, he died, while still on the active list, at his home, 41 St Peter's Street, Bedford, on 27 April 1901.

H. M. VIBART, rev. JAMES LUNT

Sources *The Times* (11 May 1901) · *Hart's Army List* · *General Gordon's private diary of his exploits in China*, ed. S. Mossman (1885), 209 · *WWW* · *CGPLA Eng. & Wales* (1901)

Wealth at death £1843 4s.: probate, 20 May 1901, *CGPLA Eng. & Wales*

Sanford [Sandford], **James** (*fl.* 1567–1582), translator, may have been a native of Somerset: one of his earliest publications was addressed to a Somerset man, Sir Hugh Paulet.

The visitation of London made in 1568 records a family of Sanfords at Milverton, Somerset, within a few miles of Paulet's house at Hinton St George; one of this family was named James. Another Sanford family was situated at Chard, also in Somerset; one of its members was John, born *c.*1565, a poet and grammarian who was probably related to James. Another possible relative was James Sandford of Devon, who entered the Inner Temple in 1566.

Information about Sanford's education is equally scarce, there being no record of his admission to Oxford, Cambridge, or the inns of court. Sanford's expertise in French and Italian suggests that he was educated abroad, and his ability to translate from Greek and Latin indicates that he also had a good classical education, possibly at home from a private tutor.

James Sanford began his career as a translator in 1567, noting that one of his earliest attempts, the *Manuell of Epictetus*, was a 'triall in the true trade of interpreting' (sig. A2*r*); this was a translation from the Greek via a French translation, and is dedicated to Queen Elizabeth. Another translation dating from the same year, *Amorous and Tragicall Tales of Plutarch*, was dedicated to Paulet, whom Sanford describes as 'a valiant warlike noble man' (sig. A5*r*). Two years later there appeared one of Sanford's most substantial translations, *Henrie Cornelius Agrippa, of the Vanitie and Uncertaintie of Artes and Sciences*, an important philosophical and satirical work which was popular enough to merit a second edition in 1575. Sanford's next translation, *The Garden of Pleasure* (1573), was addressed first to Robert Dudley, earl of Leicester, and second, revised and retitled *Houres of Recreation* (1576), to Sir Christopher Hatton. Sanford's last translation, in 1582, was of a religious nature and dedicated again to Dudley.

In addition to translation Sanford produced some fairly uninspiring verses, the most attractive of which are to be found in 'A ternarie given to the *Queens Moste Excellent Maiestie on New Yeeres Day*' included in *Houres of Recreation*, and some verses addressed to the poet George Turberville and prefaced to one of the latter's translations (1568). Sanford's verse is very conservative, employing as it does the alliterative metre, archaic vocabulary, and Latin scansion applied to English verse which were characteristic of earlier sixteenth-century poetry.

Although Sanford had few merits as an original writer, as a translator he was one of the most prolific, skilled, and conscientious of his generation; he deserves to be far better known and valued as a translator in the present day.

VIVIAN SALMON

Sources J. J. Howard and G. J. Armytage, eds., *The visitation of London in the year 1568*, Harleian Society, 1 (1869) · R. Hovenden, ed., *The visitation of Kent, taken in the years 1619–1621*, Harleian Society, 42 (1898)

Sanford, John Langton (1824–1877), historian, was born at Upper Clapton, London, on 22 June 1824, the son of Henry Sanford and his wife, Lucy Langton. He studied at University College, London, and afterwards entered Lincoln's Inn. He read in the chambers of John Richard

Quain, and was called to the bar in 1855, but never practised law, devoting himself to literary and historical research. From 1852 to the end of 1855 he was joint editor of *The Inquirer*, a unitarian paper established in 1842, and from 1861 until his death he contributed to *The Spectator*.

Sanford published several works of history, including *Studies and Illustrations of the Great Rebellion* (1858), parts of which appeared originally in the *Christian Reformer* under the signature of Sigma, and *The Great Governing Families of England* (2 vols., 1865), which was written in conjunction with Meredith Townsend and which originally appeared in *The Spectator*. Sanford's *Estimates of English Kings* (1872) was also reproduced from *The Spectator*.

On points of genealogy and of topographical and parliamentary history Sanford's knowledge was minute and full; his ability to characterize historical figures showed a wide range of sympathies. Among his closest friends were Walter Bagehot and the poet and essayist William Caldwell Roscoe. Gradually Sanford's eyesight began to fail, and early in 1875 he became totally blind. He was unmarried and after the death of his sister Lucy he retired, in May 1876, from London to Evesham, Worcestershire. He died at Evesham on 27 July 1877 and was buried in the graveyard of Oat Street Chapel on 31 July.

ALEXANDER GORDON, *rev.* NILANJANA BANERJI

Sources *The Inquirer* (4 Aug 1877) · *Law Times* (4 Aug 1877) · Allibone, *Dict.* · personal knowledge (1897)
Wealth at death under £3000: administration, 7 Sept 1877, *CGPLA Eng. & Wales*

Sanford [Sandford], **Joseph** (*bap.* 1691, *d.* 1774), antiquary and bibliophile, was baptized at Topsham in Devon on 3 August 1691, the son of George Sanford, a gentleman who was buried there a year later, and his wife, Elizabeth (*d.* *c.*1740). He had a much older brother, George Sanford (*c.*1670–1734), who became rector of Stokeinteignhead in Devon, but no other siblings are mentioned in the will their mother made in 1735. He invariably wrote his name Sanford, but his contemporaries often spelt it Sandford, and the confusion persists. He entered Exeter College, Oxford, on 19 March 1709, graduated BA from there in 1712, and then migrated to Balliol College as a commoner. Elected a probationer fellow of Balliol in 1714, he lodged initially at Mrs Clerke's in the Turl but moved into college before he became an actual fellow in 1715. He was in residence for nearly sixty years, fifty-two of them as senior fellow, in which capacity he convened the controversial 1726 election of Theophilus Leigh (1693–1785) to the mastership. Sanford was ordained priest on 14 June 1719 in the nick of time: he had taken his MA on 16 June 1715, and the college's statutes allowed only four years' grace. It was said that he avoided officiating in the college chapel, but he graduated BD in 1726, and Balliol presented him in 1722 to the rectory of Duloe in Cornwall, which he held until his death, and in 1739 to the rectory of Huntspill in Somerset, which he resigned in 1767.

Sanford—Old Joe or Honest Joe Sanford to his contemporaries—was a regular Bodleian reader and a familiar figure in Fletchers, the Turl bookshop. His manner was unpolished, tending to eccentricity, and his attire was sometimes unconventional. Although he published nothing of his own, he was well known for his erudition and helpfulness—often in tandem with his colleague Charles Godwyn—to other antiquaries. Thomas Hearne frequently mentions Sanford with approval, and he earned the warmly recorded gratitude of John Hutchins, Richard Polwhele, and Richard Chandler. He also helped Benjamin Kennicott, an intimate acquaintance from 1750, with his work on Hebrew manuscripts. Sanford was an avid book collector, and made occasional gifts to the Bodleian—notably in 1753 a copy of *De antiquitate Britannicae ecclesiae* (1572). His most prized possession was a very rare Hebrew Bible printed at Soncino in 1488, discovered by him in a London bookshop and snapped up for a trifle in 1767.

Sanford died unmarried and intestate on 25 September 1774 in college and was buried three days later in St Mary Magdalen Church, Oxford, where there is an effusive Latin epitaph. He had kept to his rooms in Balliol for several months, latterly paranoid and confused. But in a relatively lucid interval on 6 September 1774 he had attempted to order the disposition of his library; he dictated to the bookseller James Fletcher the elder (*c.*1707–1795) his instruction that Exeter College should have his printed books, which numbered some thousands, and his manuscripts, most of which were on historical, antiquarian, and legal topics and had belonged to Sir William Glynne (*d.* *c.*1691), baronet, of Ambrosden. Although Sanford had dated the resulting paper, he had then thrown it aside unsigned and lapsed into delirium. It was nevertheless accepted as a valid testamentary schedule after protracted litigation. Evidence was given that he had often said while *compos mentis* that he did not want his collection (valued at about £1500) sold, and that he would bequeath it to Exeter College, whose library had suffered a catastrophic fire in 1709. This was unsuccessfully disputed by Sanford's nephew William Sanford DD (*c.*1711–1783), rector of Hatherop in Gloucestershire and formerly fellow of All Souls College, who was heir under intestacy law, jointly with his sisters Elizabeth Cheeke and Margaret Sanford. Exeter College still has Sanford's library, including his Hebrew Bible, and his portrait, which was given in 1814 by William Sanford's son-in-law John Eveleigh, provost of Oriel.

JOHN JONES

Sources J. Jones, *Balliol College: a history*, 2nd edn (1997), 155 n.2, 156, 168, 169, 170 · *GM*, 1st ser., 86/2 (1816), 212–13, 338, 488 · *Remarks and collections of Thomas Hearne*, ed. C. E. Doble and others, 11 vols., OHS, 2, 7, 13, 34, 42–3, 48, 50, 65, 67, 72 (1885–1921), vols. 7–11 · Nichols, *Lit. anecdotes*, 8.224–60 · J. Hutchins, *The history and antiquities of the county of Dorset*, 2nd edn, ed. R. Gough and J. B. Nichols, 4 (1815), xii–xxii · Nichols, *Illustrations*, 3.705–6 · depositions concerning the Balliol mastership election of 1726, Balliol Oxf., D.3.19b, esp. fols. 297–341 · R. Chandler, *Marmora Oxoniensia* (1763), preface · R. Polwhele, *The history of Cornwall*, 7 vols. (1803–8), vol. 5, p. 179 · J. Hutchins, preface, *The history and antiquities of the county of Dorset* (1774) · A. G. Watson, *A descriptive catalogue of the medieval manuscripts of Exeter College, Oxford* (2000) · H. O. Coxe, ed., *Catalogus codicum MSS qui in collegiis aulisque Oxoniensibus hodie adservantur*, 1 (1852), 24–45 · I. Philip, *The Bodleian Library in the seventeenth and eighteenth centuries* (1983), 82 · W. D. Macray, *Annals of the Bodleian Library, Oxford*, 2nd edn (1890), 234 · *Jackson's Oxford Journal*

(22 July 1775) • estate litigation MSS concerning the subject's library, Exeter College, Oxford, E.V.2 • PCC documentation concerning the subject's estate, and voluminous MSS, PRO, PROB 6/150, fol. 11v; PROB 11/1016, sig. 94; PROB 18/86; PROB 31/621 • will, PRO, PROB 11/703, sig. 184 [Elizabeth Sanford] • *DNB* • parish register, Topsham, Devon [baptism], 3 Aug 1691 • parish register, Topsham, Devon [mother's burial], 1740 • parish register, St Mary Magdalen, Oxford [burial], 28 Sept 1774 • Foster, *Alum. Oxon.*

Archives Balliol Oxf., notebook, MS 459 • Exeter College, Oxford, autograph catalogue (2 drafts) of his library | Balliol Oxf., contributor's file concerning Sanford, misc 292 • Balliol Oxf., depositions concerning Balliol mastership election of 1726, D.3.19b, esp. fols. 297–341 (subject's own deposition) • Exeter College, Oxford, litigation MSS concerning subject's estate, E.V.2

Likenesses J. Orson, oils, Exeter College, Oxford • engraving (after J. Orson), repro. in Jones, *Balliol College*

Wealth at death approx. £13,000; incl. c.£1500 (est. value of subject's library): estate litigation MSS, Exeter College, Oxford, E.V.2

Sang, Edward (1805–1890), mathematician and civil engineer, was born on 30 January 1805 at Kirkcaldy, the sixth of eleven children of Edward Sang (1771–1862), nurseryman and sometime provost of Kirkcaldy, and his wife, Jean Nicol (b. 1773) a sister of William Nicol (b. 1768) who invented the Nicol prism. He attended a subscription school founded by his father and others under a gifted headmaster, Edward Irving. At Edinburgh University during 1818 to 1824 he impressed professors William Wallace and John Leslie in mathematics and natural philosophy, despite periods of illness. Small for his age, he was first mocked by fellow students, then admired for his precocious talent.

Sang first worked in Edinburgh as surveyor, civil engineer, and mathematics teacher, and lectured on natural philosophy. During 1841 to 1843 he was professor of mechanical sciences at the nonconformist Manchester New College, then went to Constantinople to establish engineering schools, plan railways and an ironworks. He lectured (in Turkish) at the Imperial School, Muhendis-hana Berii and gained fame by predicting the solar eclipse of 1847, thereby dispelling superstition. He resigned against the sultan's wishes, returning to Edinburgh in 1854 to teach mathematics.

An active fellow of the Royal Scottish Society of Arts and the Royal Society of Edinburgh, Sang received awards from both and from the Institution of Civil Engineers, London (1879). He was a founder member and first official lecturer of the Faculty of Actuaries in Scotland, a corresponding member of the Royal Tunis Academy, an LLD of Edinburgh University, and an honorary member of the Franklin Institute, Philadelphia. In 1832 he married Isabella Elmslie (b. 1805?) and they had one son and four daughters.

Mainly in Edinburgh-based journals, Sang wrote extensively on mathematical, mechanical, optical, and actuarial topics including vibration of wires, a theory of toothed wheels, an improved lighthouse light, railways, bridges, manufacturing, and life insurance. He published actuarial, annuity, and astronomical tables, books on elementary and higher arithmetic, and much used tables of 7-place logarithms (1871). But his most remarkable achievement is his massive unpublished compilation of 28- and 15-place logarithmic, trigonometric, and astronomical tables, filling forty-seven manuscript volumes. Compiled over forty years, latterly with assistance from two daughters, Flora and Jane, these surpass in accuracy the (also unpublished) French Cadastre tables of 1801. They were given to the nation in 1907 by Anna and Flora Sang. Sang died at his home, 31 Mayfield Road, Edinburgh, on 23 December 1890. **A. D. D. CRAIK**

Sources D. B. Peebles, 'Edward Sang', *Proceedings of the Royal Society of Edinburgh*, 21 (1895–7), xvii–xxxii [incl. list of writings] • NL Scot., Sang MS Acc. 10780 [89 vols. incl. items of tables, correspondence, etc. previously held by the Royal Society of Edinburgh] • C. G. Knott, 'Edward Sang and his logarithmic calculations', *Napier tercentenary memorial volume*, ed. C. G. Knott (1915), 261–8 • A. R. Davidson, *The history of the Faculty of Actuaries in Scotland, 1856–1956* (1956) • [C. G. Knott ?], 'Dr Edward Sang's logarithmic, trigonometrical, and astronomical tables', *Proceedings of the Royal Society of Edinburgh*, 28 (1907–8), 183–96 • U. Edin. L., Edward Sang MSS, Gen. 310–349 [40 vols.] • W. Swan, 'Presidential address for 1882', *Transactions of the Royal Scottish Society of Arts*, 11 (1887), 1–7 • C. D. Waterston, 'Notes on portraits in oils, busts and statuettes, the property of the Royal Society of Edinburgh, displayed in the rooms of the society', *Year Book of the Royal Society of Edinburgh* (1992–3), 83–117 • microfiche index of old parish records, Scotland • *Catalogue of scientific papers, 1800–1900, subject index*, Royal Society, 1 (1908) • d. cert. • A. Craik, 'Edward Sang (1805–1890): calculator extraordinary', *Newsletter of the British Society for the History of Mathematics* (2002) • A. Craik, 'The logarithmic tables of Edward Sang and his daughters', *Historia Mathematica* (2003)

Archives NL Scot., corresp., mathematical notes and tables • NL Scot., corresp. and papers by and relating to him • U. Edin. L., papers | NL Scot., corresp. with the Scottish Society of Arts

Likenesses A. R. Moffatt?, oils (after photograph), Royal Society of Edinburgh • photograph, NL Scot., Canon of Sines Part 1, Acc 10780 [frontispiece] • photograph, Royal Society of Edinburgh; repro. in Davidson, *History of the Faculty of Advocates in Scotland*, facing p. 28

Wealth at death £115 0s. 6d.: confirmation, 14 March 1891, CCI

Sangar, Gabriel (1608–1678), clergyman and ejected minister, was born at Sutton Mandeville, Wiltshire, in May 1608, the son of Thomas Sangar, the vicar of the parish. He attended school at Gillingham, Dorset, where Edward Hyde, afterwards earl of Clarendon, is said to have been among his fellow pupils. Sangar matriculated from Magdalen Hall, Oxford, on 20 October 1626, graduated BA from Magdalen College on 22 October 1629, and proceeded MA from Magdalen Hall on 5 June 1632. Ordained by Bishop Davenant of Salisbury, he was admitted to the rectory of Sutton Mandeville in 1630. The drift of religious policy in the 1630s was not to his taste. Imprisoned at Salisbury for refusing to read the Book of Sports in 1633, he was cited before high commission on 29 April 1635.

On 5 May 1642 Sanger was one of those nominated by parliament to preach a lecture at Warminster, Wiltshire. In 1645 he resigned from the rectory of Sutton Mandeville, and moved to that of Havant, Hampshire, and from thence, 'the air of that place not agreeing with the health of his family', to Chilmark in Wiltshire (Calamy, *Abridgement*, 2.27). From there he signed the presbyterian petition, *The Concurrent Testimony of the Ministers of Wiltshire* (June 1648). Before the end of 1648 Sangar, who had experienced great difficulties collecting the tithes, decided to sue for them in London, and was soon afterwards invited by the parishioners of St Martin-in-the-Fields to serve as their rector; according to the Fifth Monarchist John Rogers, who sought to displace him in 1653, Sangar was at that time simultaneously holding another, rural, living worth £100 per annum. In 1654 Sangar acted as an assistant to the London and Middlesex commissioners into the ministry, and on 4 February 1656 the London provincial assembly, in a renewed attempt to make classical organization a reality, sought to persuade Thomas Case, Thomas Manton, Sangar, and others 'to associate themselves for the making up or renewing of the 11th classis, to settle the Presbyterial government' (Shaw, 2.111). Little was achieved in this regard, but a series of twenty-five morning exercises was set up at St Martin's, each led by a different minister, including Sangar's friend Case, who contributed a preface to the published series, *A Word of Faith* (1656). Sangar was one of the delegates at the tenth session of the London province on 24 August 1657. In March 1660 parliament appointed him a commissioner for approbation of ministers.

In October 1660 Sangar was ordered by the magistrates at Middlesex sessions to hand over possession of St Martin-in-the-Fields to Nathaniel Hardy. He was successful in gaining admission (24 May 1661) to the vicarage of Steeple Ashton, Wiltshire, but the respite was temporary. The best efforts of his old acquaintance Clarendon were insufficient, Calamy reports, to persuade Sangar of the virtues of conformity; he was ejected and a successor was instituted to Steeple Ashton on 27 May 1663. Sangar moved to Brompton, where he narrowly escaped arrest in 1665 when the troops declined to enter after being told that plague had visited his refuge. Other moves quickly followed, to Ealing and from thence to Brentford, Middlesex. But Sangar had wealthy protectors. In her will Lady Mary Armyne, widow of the former councillor of state Sir William Armyne of Osgody Hall, Lincolnshire, left £20 to Gabriel Sangar, 'under whose ministery I sometime lyved' at St Martin's (quoted in Cliffe, 47). In a will proved on 27 April 1668 Sir William Waller entrusted £200 to Sangar and Case to be distributed to charitable causes, leaving each man £10 for himself. The following year Sangar was in correspondence with Lord Wharton. In 1669 Sangar was reported to be preaching in the Strand, close to his old church of St Martin-in-the-Fields, probably to members of his former auditory; he was licensed as a presbyterian teacher there on 16 May 1672. Sangar was a signatory with Henry Hurst of *The Judgement of Nonconformists of the Interest of Reason in the Matter of Religion* (1676). He died a few days after his seventieth birthday in May 1678.

STEPHEN WRIGHT

Sources Calamy rev., 427 · J. T. Cliffe, *The puritan gentry besieged, 1650–1700* (1993) · W. A. Shaw, *A history of the English church during the civil wars and under the Commonwealth, 1640–1660*, 2 vols. (1900) · E. Calamy, ed., *An abridgement of Mr. Baxter's history of his life and times, with an account of the ministers, &c., who were ejected after the Restauration of King Charles II*, 2nd edn, 2 vols. (1713) · Foster, *Alum. Oxon.* · CSP dom., 1635

Sanger, George [*known as* Lord George Sanger] (1825?–1911), circus proprietor and showman, was born at Newbury, Berkshire, on 23 December probably in 1825, the sixth of ten children of James Sanger (d. 1850), a naval pensioner who served on board the *Victory* at Trafalgar and afterwards became a showman. His mother, a native of Bedminster, was named Elliott. In keeping with the tradition of intermarriage within the itinerant performing community, in Sheffield on 1 December 1850 George married Ellen *Chapman (1830/31–1899), who, as Madame Pauline de Vere, was an accomplished lion tamer; they had two children.

Sanger's chief claim to fame was in the mid- to late nineteenth century when the commercialized entertainment market expanded, his enterprise evolved from a small fairground type to a large-scale exhibition. This evolution helped to distance his entertainment from the traditional perception of the itinerant performance world as 'low'. Starting off with his brother, John *Sanger, he ran various travelling exhibitions in the 1840s and 1850s throughout Britain. By 1854 he had taken over a large piece of ground in 'Paddy's Market' in Liverpool where he constructed a 'semi dramatic *cum* circus sort of entertainment' (Sanger, *Seventy Years*, 138). It was around this time that Sanger became aware of the competition posed by American companies, such as Howes and Cushing's Great American circus which was said to have 'eclipsed all English circuses' (ibid., 141) with its display of Native Americans. In many respects, the Howes and Cushing show was an early example of the influence of American popular culture on Britain's emerging mass leisure market, a trend that affected not only the circus, but also the theatre and later, film. By 1860, at Plymouth, Sanger's show had grown to even larger proportions: 'I collected about a hundred of the smaller shows to make a fair,' Sanger recalled, 'giving them their standings free. I had three circus rings, and two platforms going at the same time with a gate admission to the whole show' (Sanger, *Seventy Years*, 158). It was small wonder, then, that two decades later, when P. T. Barnum made his appearance in London with his three-ring circus, Sanger insisted that the American's attempt at grandeur was nothing new. Sanger's rivalry in this period with another American showman, the 'Honorable' William Cody, otherwise known as Buffalo Bill, led to his adopting the title Lord.

The period between 1860 and the late 1880s was a time when Sanger expanded and consolidated his enterprise. By purchasing Astley's Amphitheatre in 1871 for £11,000, he and John effectively 'arrived' in London's legitimate theatrical world. The building had had a formidable reputation in the capital since the late eighteenth century, being one of the first of its kind to offer equestrian exhibitions. The Sanger brothers also maintained exhibitions at the Agricultural Hall, Islington, and erected circus buildings in many provincial towns, notably Ramsgate and Margate, at the latter of which they had their headquarters at Hall by the Sea. Despite their success, the brothers broke up their partnership in 1884. George remained at Astley's until 1893 when the London county council ordered the theatre to be closed because of his failure to make necessary improvements to the house.

In consequence of his professional interests, Sanger sought to protect the rights of showmen, especially in the late 1880s when the latter were under attack by George Smith (1831–1895), of Coalville, who considered them to be dirty and lacking in decency. Smith drafted the Moveable Dwellings Bill to parliament, a bill designed to ensure that showmen, Gypsies, and other itinerants obeyed the public health acts and registered their children with local school board authorities. Although nine versions were brought before parliament (1884–1894), it never reached the statute book. However, in response to the threat, Sanger founded the Showmen's Guild, a society which flourished from the early 1890s well into the twentieth century. It united small and large showmen alike in a campaign which resulted in the eventual defeat of the proposed legislation in 1894. Sanger also involved himself politically with the Conservative Party at a time when its machinery was developing at grass roots level. It was said in 1898 that he had practically established the Margate Beaconsfield Working Men's Association, of which he was president for over twenty years (*East Kent Times*, 24 Aug 1898, 8).

By 1905 Sanger had disposed of his circus and retired to Park Farm, East End Road, East Finchley, later publishing his highly readable autobiography, *Seventy Years a Showman*, in 1910. One year later, on 28 November 1911, he was murdered at Park Farm by Herbert Charles Cooper, an employee, who attacked him with a hatchet for reasons that were unclear, and then committed suicide. The event, as one might expect given Sanger's fame, received sensational attention from the press. He was buried with municipal honours on 4 December by the side of his wife in Margate. According to Sanger's great-grandson who travelled to the funeral from London by a crowded special train, 'the occasion was almost like a national event' ('Sanger's circus', Mander and Mitchenson theatre collection).   BRENDA ASSAEL

Sources G. Sanger, *Seventy years a showman* (1910); repr. with introduction by C. MacInnes (1966) · 'Our portrait gallery no. 88 Mr George Sanger', *East Kent and District Advertiser* (24 Aug 1898), 8 · Circus Friends Association, Blackburn [various articles relating to the murder of Lord George Sanger] · *DNB* · 'A showman's tricks revealed', *Tit-Bits* (3 April 1926), 158 · 'Sanger's circus', Jerwood Library of the Performing Arts, London, Mander and Mitchenson theatre collection · 'Sanger's circus', *The Clipper* (14 Sept 1923), 13 · Boase, *Mod. Eng. biog.* · 'The last of "Old Astley's": a chat with Mr George Sanger', *The Sketch* (22 March 1893), 493–4 · G. Sanger, letter to lord chamberlain, 15 Oct 1889, PRO, LC1 526 · T. Murphy, *History of the Showmen's Guild, 1889–1948* [1949], 12–27, 68–70 · G. S. Coleman and J. Lukens, *The Sanger story: being George Sanger Coleman's story of his life with his grandfather, 'Lord' George Sanger* (1956) · G. B. Burgin, 'The oldest circus', *Some more memoirs* (c.1925) · E. Hodder, *George Smith (of Coalville)* (1896)
Archives Circus Friends Association, Blackburn, Lancashire · Theatre Museum, London | SOUND BL NSA, call nos. LP27597, LP27280
Likenesses photographs, Circus Friends Association, Blackburn, Lancashire

Wealth at death £29,348 13s. 1d.: probate, 6 Feb 1912, CGPLA Eng. & Wales

Sanger, John (1819/20–1889), circus proprietor, was born at Chew Magna, Somerset, the eldest son of James Sanger who was supposedly seized by the press gang and fought as a sailor at the battle of Trafalgar, and later became a showman. It has been commonly asserted that after witnessing equestrian performances of Andrew Ducrow at Astley's, Sanger, with his brother George *Sanger, began in 1845 a conjuring exhibition on a small scale at the Onion Fair, Birmingham. Perhaps they had performance in their blood, as one descendant of the family claimed that 'the Sangers came to England as court jesters in the time of King John' (Coleman and Lukens, 78). Little is known about their movements in the 1840s and 1850s but like many other showmen, they probably found permanent quarters for the winter season. Few of these accommodations could have been as curious as Enon Chapel in London. It was reported that beneath the chapel floors were buried hundreds of bodies, 'in a space 60 feet long and 30 feet wide and 6½ feet deep', many of which were not yet excavated when the Sangers staged a pantomime with the macabre title, *The Ice Witch, or, The Frozen Hand* shortly before Christmas 1850 (Coleman and Lukens, 88–9).

The Sangers' chief claim to historical notice, however, came in the 1870s when they took over the lease of Astley's Amphitheatre, London's permanent circus establishment. By this time they were already staging spectacular performances such as that during the Christmas season of 1866–7 when they produced the *Congress of Monarchs* at the Agricultural Hall in Islington, which was said to have been seen in one day by 37,000 spectators. According to the contract between Messrs Sanger and P. T. Barnum, the properties and paraphernalia of the *Congress of Monarchs* were purchased in 1874 by Barnum for £33,000.

Throughout the 1870s, however, the Sangers were associated with Astley's, although during the summer they also travelled through the country with a large establishment—a pattern which was typical of commercial circuses in Britain. The partnership lasted throughout the decade but by 1884 the brothers dissolved their concern, each taking his share of the company and giving separate circuses and fairground entertainments, with George Sanger remaining at Astley's until the building was demolished in March 1893. John never became as widely known or respected within the profession as his brother George, although he continued in the business.

> To John, each audience was a business deal, a mass of heads which could be counted to see how much money the house held … [whereas to George] each audience was a section of that vast public which wanted to be entertained. (Coleman and Lukens, 23)

While on tour at Ipswich, John contracted a cold and soon afterwards on 22 August 1889, at 42 Princes Street, Ipswich, he died of pneumonia at the age of sixty-nine. On 27 August he was buried in Margate cemetery in the family's new vault, where a costly white marble monument, part of which represented a mourning horse, was placed above his grave. In his will, dated 4 March 1882, he left his wife, Elizabeth, the right to carry on the business and £1000, a part of his estate, as well as 'his furniture and household effects, and the income for her life of all his residuary estate' (Liverpool, Circus Friends Association, scrapbook clipping). She assumed the management of the company—not atypical of the role that circus proprietors' wives played—for several years, dying on 29 December 1892 at the age of sixty-seven in Manchester, where her circus was performing. John Sanger was survived by three sons, John jun., William, and George, as well as one daughter, Lavinia.   BRENDA ASSAEL

Sources G. Sanger, *Seventy years a showman* (1910); repr. with introduction by C. MacInnes (1966), 158 · P. T. Barnum, *Struggles and triumphs: sixty years' recollections of P. T. Barnum* (1889), 290 · article, source unknown, Circus Friends Association, Liverpool, scrapbook no. 604, 121 · 'Death of John Sanger', *Ipswich Journal and Suffolk, Norfolk, Essex and Cambridgeshire Advertiser* (30 Aug 1889), 5 · *The Era* (24 Aug 1889), 10 · *The Era* (31 Aug 1889), 14 · 'The last of "Old Astley's": a chat with Mr George Sanger', *The Sketch* (22 March 1893), 493–4 · 'Sanger's Circus and Hippodrome at the Agricultural Hall', *The Era* (13 Jan 1867), 11 · G. S. Coleman and J. Lukens, *The Sanger story: being George Sanger Coleman's story of his life with his grandfather, 'Lord' George Sanger* (1956), 88–9 · 'Funeral of Mrs John Sanger', *The Era* (7 Jan 1893), 8 · d. cert. · Boase, *Mod. Eng. biog.*
Archives Circus Friends Association, Liverpool | SOUND BL NSA, LP 27280 · BL NSA, LP 27597
Wealth at death £40,747 17s. 10d.: probate, 12 Nov 1889, *CGPLA Eng. & Wales*

Sanger, Sophy (1881–1950), internationalist and labour-law reformer, was born on 3 January 1881 in Westcott, near Dorking, Surrey, the youngest of the three sons and three daughters of a wealthy London businessman, Charles Sanger, and his wife, Jessie Alice Pulford; Sophy was the sister of C. P. Sanger (1871–1930), the legal authority on wills and friend of Bertrand Russell. She was educated at Dr Elizabeth Dawes's school, Weybridge, and at Newnham College, Cambridge, where she read mathematics (1899–1902) and then moral sciences, narrowly missing a first in 1903. She was converted to pacifism by the Quaker Hilda Clark while at university during the Second South African War.

From 1903 to 1909 Sophy Sanger worked with Mary Reid Macarthur (later Anderson) and Margaret Bondfield for the Women's Trade Union League, setting up its legal advice bureau while studying labour law at University College, London, mastering insurance regulations for workers' compensation and interviewing women factory inspectors on conditions in the workplace. At the age of twenty-three she was called to give evidence on workmen's compensation before a parliamentary commission in the House of Lords and she also helped Labour MPs prepare their case for the Shops Bill.

Sophy Sanger soon realized that many of the worst evils of working life—occupational disease, industrial injury, and sweated labour—could be combated only by effective international action. Therefore, in 1905, she set up a British section of the International Association for Labour

Sophy Sanger (1881–1950), by unknown photographer

Legislation, and soon, with the help of volunteer translators, was bringing out an English edition of its French and German *Bulletin*. Between 1909 and 1919 Sophy Sanger edited and largely wrote the quarterly *World's Labour Laws*, which campaigned internationally on such issues as the abolition of child labour, the prohibition of the use of white phosphorus and lead, and the prevention of anthrax. It was Sophy Sanger's belief that by co-operating internationally for such practical, specific reforms, human beings might evolve into peaceful internationalists. The First World War, therefore, came as a terrible blow, but she persevered in keeping alive both the British section of the International Association for Labour Legislation and the *World's Labour Laws*—to such effect that in February 1919 it was she who wrote the draft to the Paris commission on the basis of the International Labour Office to be established by the Versailles treaty. When the ILO was set up in Geneva, Sophy Sanger was appointed chief of its legislative section, a post she held until 1924, when she was edged out of the organization by Albert Thomas, the director.

On her return to Britain in 1924, Sophy Sanger read for the bar at Gray's Inn, qualifying in June 1928. However, she never practised, and neither did she publish more than an (authoritative) article on labour law for the *Encyclopaedia Britannica*. She had been an exemplary, modest public servant, hoping to build a more just world. Her life's motto was Goethe's 'Law alone can give us freedom.' She died on 7 December 1950 in Cambridge, nursed by her lifelong companion, Maud Allen. She was unmarried.

SYBIL OLDFIELD, *rev.*

Sources A. M. Allen, *Sophy Sanger: a pioneer in internationalism* (1958) · A. M. Allen, *Newnham College Roll Letter* (1951) · b. cert. **Likenesses** photograph, repro. in Allen, *Sophy Sanger* [*see illus.*] **Wealth at death** £11,870 6s. 2d.: probate, 13 Sept 1951, CGPLA Eng. & Wales

Sangster, John Young [Jack] (1896–1977), motor cycle manufacturer, was born on 29 May 1896 at Northfield, King's Norton, near Birmingham, the second of three sons of Charles Thomas Brock Sangster, a Birmingham engineer and businessman of Scottish origin and his wife, Louisa, *née* Wicks. He was educated at Hurstpierpoint College in Sussex. Then it is believed he underwent apprenticeship in French and German cycle and car factories, where he acquired linguistic ability. The outbreak of war terminated this training and he served in the City of Birmingham battalion of the 14th Royal Warwickshire regiment from 1914 to 1918.

About 1896, Sangster's father had joined the Cycle Components Manufacturing Company in Birmingham, becoming managing director in 1897. This firm acquired the Ariel Cycle Company, also in Birmingham, and the first Ariel motor tricycle was exhibited in 1898, followed by a car in 1900 and a motor cycle in 1905. After the war, Jack Sangster, as he was known, developed a motor quadricycle at a factory in Tyseley belonging to his father's company. The design was taken over by the Rover Company in Coventry and became the Rover Eight car, a 'simple, yet efficient, little air-cooled, flat-twinned' 1000 cc or 8 hp car (Holliday, 63). Rover gave Sangster a job in Coventry producing the car where 'he won a good name for himself' (*The Times*, 29 March 1977). He left in 1923 to join his father at Components and by 1930 was its joint managing director with his father. The Ariel Nine and Ten cars were his idea though inappropriate for a firm already doing badly in the depression and facing competition from Morris and Austin.

A better future appeared to lie with motor cycles. Edward Turner, Val Page, and Bert Hopwood were on the design staff at this time. However, Components was driven into receivership in 1932, and Sangster was able to buy the machinery and part of the premises in Grange Road, Selly Oak, beside the university, to form Ariel Motors. He was the chairman and main shareholder, assisted in a minor way by his brother Harvey; his father died in 1935. Ariel went on making motor cycles, for the army during the war, until Sangster sold out to the Birmingham Small Arms Company (BSA) in 1944 for £376,257. The factory closed in 1963.

Sangster's ambition led him to acquire other, bigger, interests. In 1935 he bought the Triumph motor cycle business (not the car side) and its Priory works in Coventry for £50,000 from the receiver. He was chairman from 1936 to 1964. He brought across Edward Turner and Bert Hopwood from Ariel as manager and designer. Sangster drove the Triumph Engineering Company hard: staff either left or took a pay cut, sales managers were pushed out on to the road to sell, and new models were produced, including the famous Speed Twin and the Tiger. One model, in 1937, could do 90 m.p.h. In 1936, the New Imperial motor cycle company was absorbed. Success was achieved.

The war brought changes. Priory works was only 200 yards from Coventry Cathedral and was destroyed during the same air raid in November 1940. Production continued in temporary premises and a new works was built at Meriden on the edge of Coventry in 1942. Peace brought a modest expansion at Meriden and the firm went from strength to strength. Triumph produced 5000 motor cycles a year very profitably (in contrast to BSA which produced 50,000 much less profitably).

However, Sangster became concerned at the impact his death duties could have on the firm and he and Turner decided to sell out to BSA in 1951 for £2.5 million. Sangster became a director, bringing much needed motor cycle expertise to the BSA board, then chaired by Sir Bernard Docker and managed by James Leek. Sangster and Leek led the attack on Docker's mistaken emphasis on the Daimler car side and his (and his wife's) flamboyant extravagances. As a result, Sangster became chairman from 1956 until 1961, retiring when he reached sixty-five. Although he guided BSA through a period of good profitability, he failed to update the technology in production and design or to expand production sufficiently to meet demand, let alone the potential demand that subsequent new models and sympathetic marketing generated in the 1970s. As a result, BSA and Triumph gradually yielded their place as world leaders to France and Italy (in mopeds and scooters) in the 1950s and to Japan (in under-350 cc and finally the 500–1000 cc motor cycles) in the 1960s. The failure seems to have lain with the main board and not with middle management. Apart from Sangster, Edward Turner and Sangster's successor, Eric Turner, have a great deal to answer for in this decline to extinction in the early 1970s. Sangster remained as a director of BSA until he was seventy-two. However, he had been living in London from about 1953 and so was seldom seen at either BSA's works at Small Heath or Triumph's at Meriden.

Bob Holliday described Sangster as having a 'clever head for business with a trained mechanical mind, attributes that enabled him to select the right men as his lieutenants and to evaluate the potentialities of a good design when he saw one' (Holliday, 63). Even Hopwood considered him 'needlesharp' (Hopwood, 13) and *The Times* called him 'a formidable leader of design and production teams'. Subsequent history casts some doubt on whether this acumen continued into the late 1950s. A rather different impression is given by the *Birmingham Mail*'s 'shy millionaire' dictum of 1 June 1956.

Motorcycling was one of Sangster's recreations, along with motoring, skiing, and yachting. He married three times, first in 1923 to Kathleen Burns; they had one daughter, Heather. His second marriage was in 1951, to Phyllis, daughter of Frederick K. Hamer, a retired colonel, and the third, in 1963, to Margery, daughter of Robert Cheney Hart, a company director. Margery and Heather survived him. He died of cancer at his home, 34 Ennismore Gardens, Westminster, London, on 26 March 1977.

BARBARA M. D. SMITH

Sources B. M. D. Smith, 'Sangster, John Young', *DBB* · B. M. D. Smith, *The history of the British motorcycle industry, 1945–75* (1981) · B. Holliday, *The story of BSA motor cycles* (1978) · B. Hopwood, *Whatever happened to the British motorcycle industry?* (1981) · B. Ryerson, *The giants of Small Heath: the history of BSA* (1980) · P. Hartley, *The Ariel story* (1980) · I. Davies, *It's a Triumph* (1980) · H. Louis and B. Currie, *The story of Triumph motorcycles*, 2nd edn (1978) · *BSA Group News* (April 1958) · *BSA Group News* (7 June 1961) · *Birmingham Mail* (1 June 1956) · *The Times* (29 March 1977) · *The Times* (13 Dec 1977) · *Stock Exchange Year Book* · *WW* · d. cert.
Archives priv. coll. | Birm. CL, BSA material · U. Warwick Mod. RC, BSA board minutes
Wealth at death £651,538: probate, 1 Dec 1977, *CGPLA Eng. & Wales*

Sangster, Samuel (1804/5–1872), engraver, was a pupil of William Finden and worked in the line manner. Several of his earlier plates were engraved for *The Amulet* and other annuals, then at the height of their prosperity. His earliest independent steel plate, dated 1 October 1828, was *Beatrice*, after Henry Howard, engraved for *The Anniversary* of 1829, and is a good example of his work. *Don Quixote*, after Richard Parkes Bonington, was engraved for *The Keepsake Français* (1831), and *The Death of Eucles*, after Benjamin Robert Haydon, *The Lute*, after Henry Liverseege, *The Festa of Madonna dei Fiori*, after Thomas Uwins, and *No Song, No Supper*, after Kenny Meadows, were engraved for *The Amulet* of 1832 and succeeding years. He contributed one plate to the *Literary Souvenir* (1835), and two engravings were included in S. C. Hall's *Book of Gems* (1838)—*Sleeping Beauty* (an octagonal picture), after W. Meadows, and *Child and Flowers*, after Richard Rothwell. Two oval pictures, *The Pilgrims Overtaken by Evangelist* and *The Pilgrims Passing through the Valley of the Shadow of Death*, after Thomas Stothard, were engraved for editions of Bunyan's *The Pilgrim's Progress*, and *Thankful Children*, after Thomas Uwins, appeared in *The Casquet of Literature*, ed. Charles Gibbon (6 vols., 1873–4). Sangster engraved some larger plates, of which the best are *The Gentle Student* and *The Forsaken*, both from pictures by Gilbert Stuart Newton and published by H. Graves, and *Neapolitan Peasants Going to the Festa of Piè di Grotta*, after Thomas Uwins and published by F. G. Moon for *Finden's Royal Gallery of British Art* (1838–49). This latter plate was regarded as one of his best. In 1842 he engraved *The Young Mendicant's Noviciate*, after Richard Rothwell, and in 1844 *Belisarius*, after Martin Shee, for the Royal Irish Art Union. For the *Art Journal* he engraved in 1850 *A Syrian Maid*, after H. W. Pickersgill, in 1851 *The Victim*, after Augustus Egg, in 1852 *Juliet and the Nurse*, after H. P. Briggs, and in 1853 *The Sepulchre*, after William Etty, all from pictures formerly in the Vernon collection and now in the Tate collection. These were published in *The Vernon Gallery of British Art*, edited by S. C. Hall (3 vols., 1854). Sangster also engraved *A Scene from Midas*, after Daniel Maclise, and *First Love*, after

J. J. Jenkins, from pictures in the Royal Collection. In addition he painted some fancy subjects in oils.

Sangster died, apparently unmarried, at his home, 83 New Kent Road, London, on 24 June 1872, in his sixty-eighth year, having retired some years earlier.

R. E. GRAVES, rev. JOANNA DESMOND

Sources B. Hunnisett, *An illustrated dictionary of British steel engravers*, new edn (1989), 115–16 · R. K. Engen, *Dictionary of Victorian engravers, print publishers and their works* (1979) · *Art Journal*, 34 (1872), 204 · Redgrave, *Artists* · C. E. Clement and L. Hutton, *Artists of the nineteenth century and their works: a handbook containing two thousand and fifty biographical sketches*, 2 (1879), 233 · *CGPLA Eng. & Wales* (1872)
Wealth at death under £12,000: administration, 13 July 1872, *CGPLA Eng. & Wales*

Sangster, Vernon Edmund (1899–1986), football pools promoter, was born at 69 Orient Street, Cheetham, Manchester, on 25 June 1899, the son of Alfred Edmund Sangster and his wife, Robina Kate, *née* Burgess. His father was a wholesale draper operating from a number of warehouses in Manchester. Sangster manifested little interest in pursuing the family business. Following the First World War, during which Sangster spent a brief period of service as a teenage soldier of the Manchester regiment in the 55th West Lancashire division, he and his father noticed the growing interest in football betting in the north-west of England. They drew up a plan based on the principle that large prizes for a little outlay would appeal to the gambling instinct, and that enough stakes pooled could generate large prizes. They launched their scheme, based on coupons, in 1923 in Manchester.

The scheme was successful, and in 1925 the Sangsters moved their operation to Liverpool, where Littlewoods and other pools companies were based, giving as their reason the spur of competition. The business prospered during the 1920s, and boomed during the 1930s, causing Vernons, as the company was known, to invest in new plants throughout the Liverpool area. A wealthy man, Vernon Sangster purchased West Lodge on Meols Drive, Hoylake, in the Wirral. Within commuting distance of his various workplaces in the north-west, it was to be his lifelong home, shared with his wife, Margaret Martha (Peggy), with whom he had one son, Robert, born in May 1936. The house was also conveniently next door to a golf course: golf was Sangster's favourite hobby.

Sangster was a paternalistic employer, pioneering a house magazine from 1935, with a variety of features and a regular contribution from himself. He was known as the 'Guv'nor' to his 6000 employees. The works-based singing group, the Vernons Girls, sang their way to national fame during the war. Sangster thus developed both formal and informal techniques of securing good working relations in his pools-checking plants, as well as publicity for his company. Most of his workforce were women, largely employed on a part-time and seasonal basis.

During the 1930s Sangster engaged in public philanthropy, donating large sums to local charities at a time when there was considerable national concern over the health and morale of the unemployed in poorly-off areas.

In particular, he donated thousands of pounds to Liverpool city council to found the Vernon Sangster Sports Centre at Stanley Park. Set alongside his paternalism and philanthropy, however, was his oft-repeated maxim to his son that there was no room for sentiment in business.

Vernons, in common with other pools companies, faced difficulties despite its prosperity. During the 1930s a strong anti-gambling lobby wanted to stamp out pools betting. The Irish Hospitals' Sweepstake raised the spectre of a national lottery. A few tricksters attempted fiddles by infiltrating coupons into the system after the football results were published. As a consequence, Sangster was a leading founding member of the Pools Promoters' Association (PPA), formed in 1934 to articulate and lobby for the interests of his company. Through the PPA, Sangster also opposed the imposition of a pool betting duty by the Labour government in the later 1940s.

Sangster ran the business until his retirement in the early 1970s. By then, Vernons's market share had decreased in competition with Littlewoods. Sangster appears to have been upset about, and to have resisted, the attempts by his son, Robert, to sell the company. In retirement Sangster lived with his wife and a number of house servants. He died at his home on 17 December 1986 from cardiac failure and arteriosclerosis. His funeral took place at St Hildeburgh's Church, Hoylake. Survived by his wife, he left an estate worth almost £3 million.

MARK CLAPSON

Sources R. David, *Robert Sangster: tycoon of the turf* (1991) · *The Times* (19 Dec 1986), 5a · R. Munting, *An economic and social history of gambling in Britain and the USA* (1996) · b. cert. · d. cert. · *CGPLA Eng. & Wales* (1987)

Wealth at death £2,713,905: probate, 29 Jan 1987, *CGPLA Eng. & Wales*

Sangster, William Edwin Robert (1900–1960), Methodist minister and writer, was born on 5 June 1900 at 3 Edmund's Place, near City Road, in London, one of the five children of Henry George Sangster (1872–1931), foreman at a collar-box factory, and his wife, Martha Deal (1871–1954). His parents did not attend church; 'they were', as Sangster stated, 'devoted Church of England, but just stayed away' (P. Sangster, 26). He received his early education at Holy Trinity church school (1903–9), before obtaining a scholarship for Shoreditch secondary school, where he was a pupil until 1915.

From 1909 Sangster began to attend the Methodist mission hall on Radnor Street, London, where he underwent an evangelical conversion experience in 1913 and met Margaret Conway, whom he later married in 1926. On leaving school at the age of fifteen he commenced work as an office boy at a London accountancy firm. In 1917 he became a fully accredited local preacher.

In June 1918 Sangster joined the army and began serving with the Queen's Royal West Surrey regiment, quickly gaining the rank of corporal and sergeant. In 1920 he attended Handsworth College, Birmingham, and later Richmond College, in Surrey, to train as a Methodist minister. He served as a probationer minister at County Road Methodist Church, Liverpool, in April 1923, and then,

William Edwin Robert Sangster (1900–1960), by Walter Stoneman, *c.*1950

three months later, at Littlehampton, Sussex. On 27 July 1926 he was ordained in Wesley Chapel, Priory Street, York. Sangster served as minister at Conwy and Rhos-on-Sea, north Wales (1926–9), during which time his wife gave birth to twins. He gained an external London University degree in philosophy, and then ministered at Fazakerley and Aintree, Liverpool (1929–32). In 1931, due to overwork and doubts about his sincerity as a Christian, he experienced a spiritual crisis culminating in a total commitment to God and his first publication, *Why Jesus Never Wrote a Book*. Now more effective as both a preacher and a pastor, he was appointed minister at the Queen Street Central Hall, Scarborough (1932–6), and Brunswick Church, Leeds (1936–9). While at Leeds he worked also on the BBC northern region religious advisory committee and as a British representative to the General Conference of the Canadian Churches. From 1939 he was the minister of the Westminster Central Hall, regularly sharing pulpits with Dr Leslie Weatherhead and Donald Soper. During the war years Sangster supervised the air-raid shelters in the Westminster area, using the basement of the hall as a centre of both social and evangelistic activities. He was awarded a doctorate by the University of London in 1942 for his thesis on Christian perfection, later published as *The Path to Perfection* (1943).

In the post-war period Sangster travelled to America on several occasions and made a world tour, rapidly becoming one of the most influential preachers of his day, his reputation reaching far beyond denominational barriers at home and abroad. As an ecumenicist he served on the Methodist delegation which met to discuss closer relations with the Anglican church, and was involved in the Free Church Federal Council and the National Sunday School Union.

A regular contributor to the *Empire News*, the *Daily Sketch*, and other newspapers, Sangster criticized the 'moral rottenness' of the nation, calling for a 'new penitence' among the people. In 1953 he made headline news with a sermon entitled 'What would a revival of religion do for Britain?', in which he argued that faith in Jesus Christ was the ultimate panacea for the problems of modern Britain.

Sangster served as president of the Methodist conference in 1950 and was involved in the work of the Evangelical Alliance, various evangelistic campaigns with Billy Graham and other speakers, and, with the Africa Bureau, in taking a stand against apartheid. He helped found the Christian Publicity Organisation, which attempted to use advertising as a means of evangelism. He was also involved in the formation of the Prayer Life Movement: this set out to establish prayer groups throughout Britain and other countries, with a view to religious revival.

After leaving Westminster Hall in 1955, Sangster worked as general secretary of the Methodist home mission department. He was also for several years a member of the senate of London University. A prolific writer, he was best known for his two books on preaching: *The Craft of Sermon Illustration* (1946) and *The Craft of Sermon Construction* (1949), later republished in one volume as *The Craft of the Sermon* (1954). His numerous devotional books include *God does Guide Us* (1934), *He is Able* (1936), and *The Secret of Radiant Life* (1957). His two-volume *Westminster Sermons* (1960–61) proved to be of use to both minister and lay person alike. Throughout the 1950s he published the Westminster Pamphlets, a series of tracts aimed at providing the 'spiritual check-up of ourselves and our churches'.

Although at times Sangster could appear domineering and imperious, he was a man of piety, dignity, and vitality, possessing 'a colourful and dynamic personality' (*Minutes of Conference*). In appearance he had 'a strong, erect figure' and, especially in later life, had a 'striking mane of grey-white hair' (*Sangster of Westminster*, 28). From 1957 Sangster's health was steadily deteriorating. He was diagnosed as suffering from progressive muscular atrophy. He died at his home, 52 Lyford Road, Wandsworth, London, on 24 May 1960. He was survived by his wife.

SIMON ROSS VALENTINE

Sources P. Sangster, *Doctor Sangster* (1962) · *Methodist Recorder* (June 1960) · letters, papers and notes, JRL, Methodist Archives and Research Centre · Sangster ephemera, Westminster College, Oxford, Wesley and Methodist Studies Centre · *Sangster of Westminster* (1960) · M. Sangster, *A daughter's tribute* (1960) · H. Davies, *Varieties of English preaching* (1943) · S. R. Valentine, *William E. Sangster* (1998) · *The Times* (25 May 1960) · *CGPLA Eng. & Wales* (1960) · WWW · *The minutes of the annual conference of the Methodist church* (1960), 202–3

Archives JRL

Likenesses W. Stoneman, photograph, c.1950, NPG [*see illus.*] · photographs, repro. in Sangster, *Doctor Sangster* · photographs, repro. in Valentine, *William E. Sangster* · photographs, NPG

Wealth at death £15,858 14s. 8d.: probate, 1 Sept 1960, *CGPLA Eng. & Wales*

Sankey, Ira David (1840–1908). *See under* Moody, Dwight Lyman (1837–1899).

Sankey, John, Viscount Sankey (1866–1948), lord chancellor, was born in Moreton in Marsh, Gloucestershire, on 26 October 1866, the son of Thomas Sankey, a grocer specializing in dry goods, and his second wife, Catalina, daughter of James Dewsbury, clerk, of Manchester. Sankey's father died when he was still a child and his mother moved to south Wales to be near her husband's brothers. There Sankey attended a local Church of England school and, through the generosity of an Anglican clergyman, was sent to Lancing College. He went on to Jesus College, Oxford, where he was a scholar, and was placed in the second class in honour moderations (1887) and modern history (1889) and in the third class in the bachelor of civil law in 1891. He was called to the bar by the Middle Temple in 1892.

Sankey began his practice in south Wales and, with local connections, relatively rapidly developed a common-law practice, later specializing in workmen's compensation cases. He became a king's counsel in 1909 and in 1914 was promoted to the King's Bench. In 1915 he was chairman of the Enemy Aliens Advisory Committee, dealing especially with Irish cases, and for his services was appointed GBE in 1917, having been knighted on his appointment to the bench.

In 1919 Sankey took on the role with which his name first achieved prominence, becoming chairman of the commission appointed under the act of that year to inquire into the conditions of the coal industry. From his background and practice he had developed a sensitivity to the problems of the coal industry, although he still thought of himself as a political Conservative. Following a long inquiry, in which he found the mine owners even more intransigent than the miners, Sankey recommended nationalization of the coal mines. The owners and miners voted along 'party' lines. Sankey's courage in standing by his convictions was resented by some of his old Conservative friends, but it was much appreciated by the Labour Party, and especially by Ramsay MacDonald.

It was thought by some that Sankey would be the first Labour lord chancellor, but in 1924 the claims of Lord Haldane were preferred. Instead, in 1928, Sankey was promoted to the Court of Appeal and made a member of the privy council. He assumed his political career was over, although he had by then various political contacts, including a vigorous correspondence with Professor Harold Laski of the London School of Economics. When Labour came to power for a second time in 1929, he was offered and accepted the Woolsack. Thus at the age of sixty-three he entered into a new and demanding career in which he achieved remarkable distinction, being one of the most

John Sankey, Viscount Sankey (1866–1948), by Olive Edis

important and innovative lord chancellors of the twentieth century.

Sankey was made a baron in 1929 and a viscount in 1932. On the formation of the 'national' government in 1931, he was one of the few ministers who elected to stay with Mac-Donald, although he attracted less opprobrium than most, because he still had something of the non-political aura and his claim to be acting out of a concern for the national interest was more plausible than similar claims. He remained lord chancellor until 1935, when Baldwin became prime minister and preferred to recall Lord Hail-sham who had served previously as Conservative lord chancellor. Many have explained the move in terms of the need to find a place for Malcolm MacDonald, the son of the outgoing prime minister. Whatever the reason, it was a blow from which Sankey never fully recovered.

In the early years of Sankey's chancellorship, much of his work was political and it was fortunate that one so sensitive to Commonwealth issues was in his position. In retrospect, the 1930 Imperial Conference was probably the most important such gathering in the history of the empire and Commonwealth. In preparing for it, the Lord Chancellor's Office played a surprisingly important role and, in some ways, Sankey was at least as vital as J. H. Thomas, the dominions secretary. Sankey could live with the equality of Commonwealth members more easily than Thomas and he was, in so many ways, the father of the Statute of Westminster (1931). The lord chancellor saw no reason why the dominions should not abolish appeals to the judicial committee of the privy council as part of

the proposed statute, which was the basis of the new concept of the Commonwealth. Thomas had doubts, particularly where Éire was concerned, and persuaded the House of Commons that such appeals were protected by the Irish treaty of 1921 and thus outside the Statute of Westminster.

Sankey did not share such imperialist views and he actually presided in the judicial committee of the privy council, when it upheld the right of the Irish Free State to abolish appeals (*Moore* v. *Attorney-General of the Irish Free State*, 1936). He also presided in the appeal where the judicial committee upheld the right of Canada to abolish criminal appeals (*British Coal Corporation* v. *R.*, 1935). Indeed, Sankey was one of the few English judges, sitting in the privy council as the final court of appeal for Canada, who understood the nature of a constitutional court. He accepted that:

> the British North America Act planted in Canada a living tree capable of growth and expansion within its natural limits. Their Lordships do not conceive it to be the duty of this Board—it is certainly not their desire—to cut down the provisions of the Act by a narrow and technical construction, but rather to give it a large and liberal interpretation.   (*Edwards* v. *Attorney-General for Canada*, 1929)

It was in this spirit that Sankey held air navigation (*In re Regulation and Control of Aeronautics in Canada*, 1932) and broadcasting (*In re Regulation and Control of Radio Communication in Canada*, 1932) to be exclusively federal matters. It was all a long way from the narrow, technical approach of lords Watson and Haldane, who had done so much to turn a federal state into a confederation and it is a reminder about the damage that was done when Sankey, still sulking from his dismissal as lord chancellor, refused to preside in the cases testing the constitutionality of the Canadian new deal. Instead, Lord Atkin, who had a largely undeserved reputation in the constitutional field, presided in five related appeals in December 1936. Atkin, who did not approve of the Statute of Westminster, struck down the new deal (*Attorney-General for Canada* v. *Attorney-General for Ontario*, 1937) and Canadian politicians began the process of abolishing appeals to London, finally completed in 1949.

Sankey's judicial work was not limited to constitutional law. He gave at least one imaginative decision in international law (*In re Piracy jure gentium*, 1934) and he showed considerable elegance in the criminal law. *Maxwell* v. *Director of Public Prosecutions* (1935) was important with respect to the admission of previous bad conduct. *Woolmington* v. *Director of Public Prosecutions* (1935) ended the Blackstonian heresy that, after a finding of unlawful death, the burden of innocence passed to the accused. Sankey's elegant prose has passed into legal literature:

> Throughout the web of the English criminal law one golden thread is always to be seen, that is the duty of the prosecution to prove the prisoner's guilt. No matter what the charge or where the trial, the principle that the prosecution must prove the guilt of the prisoner is part of the common law of England and no attempt to whittle it down can be entertained.

On the borders of law and politics, Sankey also proved

an effective lord chancellor. With Lord Hanworth he was a powerful mediator in the dispute between the judges and the cabinet over cuts in judicial salaries made by order in council under the National Economy Act of 1931. Legally the judges may well have been in the right. At the very least, the cuts themselves should have been made by act of parliament. The reaction of the judges was, however, pretentious and was seen by the outside world as unpatriotic. Sankey, with infinite patience, managed to coax the judges into a reasonable position. Equally importantly, in 1934, he established a Law Revision Committee which, although on a small scale, recommended a series of changes in substantive law and may legitimately be considered to be the forerunner of the Law Commission.

Despite Lord Hailsham's scepticism, Sankey was a distinguished lord chancellor and lawyer on the borders of law and politics; but what of politics itself? There is something naïve about his surprise that his Conservative friends should be shocked by his recommendation of nationalization for the coal mines. It was perhaps that same naïvety that left him a little out of touch with reality about the reaction of his Labour friends when he stayed with the National Government in 1931. In that National Government he became something of a figure of fun. He was a bachelor who lived with his sister Edith, a spinster, and wrote all his letters on black bordered paper after the death of his mother. He was a keen high-churchman. He took an atlas to cabinet meetings so that he could follow discussions on foreign affairs. When dropped, he burst into tears and refused to sit as a judge for several years. These were sad elements in the character of a man who was a superb judge and lawyer, a reformer and a radical, and one of the few English judges of the twentieth century who understood Commonwealth and constitution.

Sankey was a bencher of his inn, an honorary fellow of Jesus College, Oxford, and high steward of the university, from which he received the honorary degree of DCL (1930). He also had an honorary LLD from the universities of Wales (1929), Cambridge (1932), and Bristol (1933). He died in London on 6 February 1948 and the peerage became extinct. ROBERT STEVENS

Sources R. F. V. Heuston, *Lives of the lord chancellors, 1885–1940* (1964) · R. Stevens, *Law and politics: the House of Lords as a judicial body, 1800–1976* (1979) · R. Stevens, *The independence of the judiciary: the view from the lord chancellor's office* (1993) · DNB

Archives Bodl. Oxf., corresp., diaries, and papers | BL OIOC, letters to Lord Reading, MSS Eur. E 238, F 118 · Bodl. Oxf., corresp. with Lord Ponsonby · NA Scot., corresp. with Lord Lothian · NL Scot., letters to Lord Haldane · PRO, MSS, Lord Chancellor's office | FILM BFI NFTVA, documentary footage

Likenesses W. Stoneman, two photographs, 1918–39, NPG · O. Birley, oils, 1930, Middle Temple, London · H. Lister, photographs, 1930–39, NPG · E. Walters, oils, 1937, NMG Wales · I. Opffer, sanguine drawing, 1938, NPG · O. Birley, oils, Jesus College, Oxford · O. Edis, photograph, NPG [*see illus.*]

Wealth at death £85,588 13*s.* 2*d.*: probate, 8 April 1948, CGPLA Eng. & Wales

Sankey, Sir Richard Hieram (1829–1908), army officer, was born at Rockwell Castle, co. Tipperary, on 22 March 1829, the fourth son of Matthew Sankey, barrister, of Bawnmore, co. Cork, and Modeshil, co. Tipperary, and his wife, Eleanor, daughter of Colonel Henry O'Hara JP, of O'Hara Brook, co. Antrim. Educated at the Revd D. Flynn's school in Harcourt Street, Dublin, he entered the East India Company's military seminary, Addiscombe College, in February 1845. A talented artist, he won a silver medal at a Dublin Society exhibition in 1845, and the prize for painting on leaving Addiscombe at the end of 1846. Commissioned second lieutenant Madras engineers on 11 December 1846, after the usual Chatham course he arrived in Madras in November 1848.

After serving with the Madras sappers at Mercatur, Sankey officiated in 1850 as superintending engineer, Nagpur subsidiary force; but owing to ill health he was at home for three years (1853–6). Promoted lieutenant on 1 August 1854, he was appointed, on returning to Madras in 1856, superintendent of the east coast canal. In May 1857 he was called to Calcutta as under-secretary of the public works department under Colonel William Erskine Baker.

On the outbreak of the Indian mutiny Sankey was commissioned captain of the Calcutta cavalry volunteers, but in September was sent to Allahabad for field duty. Besides completing the defensive works along the Jumna River, he levelled the whole of the Aliganj quarter of the city, employing some 6000 workmen to clear the front of the entrenchments of obstructions and to construct a causeway across the muddy bed of the Ganges. He established a bridge of boats, and having to provide shelter for the advancing troops all along the grand trunk road in the North-Western Provinces, he arrived at Cawnpore, in the course of this duty, the day before it was attacked by the Gwalior force under Tantia Topi. He acted as assistant field engineer under Lieutenant-Colonel McLeod, the commanding engineer of General Windham's force, and when that force fell back on the entrenchments was employed in strengthening the defences; noticing that the whole area as far as an outpost some 600 yards away was swept by the enemy's fire, he effectively connected the outpost with the entrenchment by a simple screen of mats fixed during one night.

After the rebels were defeated by Sir Colin Campbell on 6 December, Sankey was transferred as field engineer to the Gurkha force under Jang Bahadur. He organized an engineer park at Gorakhpur and procured material for bridging the Gogra and Gumti rivers for the march to Lucknow. Alone he reconnoitred the Gogra, which was crossed on 19 February 1858, when the fort Mowrani on the other side of the river was seized. Next day he took part in the action of Phulpur, where he constructed a bridge of boats 320 yards long in two and a half days, and made 3 miles of road. The Gurkha army, 20,000 strong of all arms, then crossed into Oudh, and Sankey received the thanks of his commander and of the government of India for 'his great and successful exertions'. While on the march on 26 February, Sankey's conspicuous gallantry in forcing an entry into a small fort at Jamalpur occupied by the rebels was highly commended by the commander in his dispatch, and he was unsuccessfully recommended for the Victoria Cross.

Sankey was at the action of Kanduah Nulla on 4 March,

and was mentioned in dispatches. He constructed the bridge to pass the troops over the river to Sultanpur and received the thanks of government. At Lucknow the Gurkha army was posted in a suburb south-east of the Charbagh, which it attacked on 14 March. Next day Sankey was with the Gurkhas when they carried all before them to the gate of the *kaisarbagh*, which General Thomas Franks had captured. Sankey was also engaged with the enemy on 15, 18, and 19 March, and on the final capture of the city made arrangements for establishing the bridge over the canal near the Charbagh.

Soon after the fall of Lucknow, Sankey returned to Calcutta in ill health, and was sent to the Nilgiris to recover. For his services he was promoted second captain on 27 August 1858, and brevet major the next day. During 1859 he was executive engineer, and also superintendent of the convict gaol at Moulmein in Burma. In 1860–61 he was garrison engineer at Fort William, Calcutta.

Promoted first captain in his corps on 29 June 1861, and appointed assistant to the chief engineer, Mysore, he held the post with credit until 1864. In 1864 he succeeded as chief engineer and secretary to the chief commissioner, Mysore, and during the next thirteen years managed the public works there. He originated an irrigation department to deal scientifically with the old Indian works; the catchment area of each valley was surveyed, the area draining into each reservoir determined, and the sizes and number of reservoirs regulated accordingly. He also improved the old roads and opened up new ones. Government offices were built, and the park around them laid out at Bangalore.

In 1870 Sankey spent seven months on special duty at Melbourne, at the request of the Victorian government, to arbitrate on a question of works for supplying water to wash down the gold-bearing alluvium of certain valleys. He was promoted brevet lieutenant-colonel on 14 June 1869, regimental lieutenant-colonel on 15 October 1870, and brevet colonel on 15 October 1875.

In 1877 he was transferred to Simla as under-secretary to the government of India, and in September 1878, when war with the amir of Afghanistan was imminent owing to the rebuff to the Chamberlain mission, was appointed commanding royal engineer of the Kandahar field force under Lieutenant-General Sir Donald Stewart. Sankey arrived with the rest of his staff at Quetta on 12 December, and being sent forward to reconnoitre recommended an advance by the Khawga Pass, leaving the Khojak Pass for the 2nd division under Major-General Michael Biddulph. On 30 December 1878 he was promoted regimental colonel. On 4 January 1879 Sankey was with the advanced body of cavalry under Major-General Palliser when a cavalry combat took place at Takht-i-Pul. Stewart's force occupied Kandahar, and advanced as far as Kalat-i-Ghilzai, when the flight of the Amir Sher Ali ended, for a brief period, the war. While Sankey was preparing winter quarters for the force at Kandahar he was recalled to Madras to become secretary in the public works department. For his role in the Kandahar expedition he was mentioned in dispatches and made a CB.

During almost five years at Madras, Sankey became member of the legislative council, and a fellow of Madras University. He helped to form the Marina and to beautify the botanical gardens and Government House grounds. On 4 June 1883 he was promoted major-general. He retired from the army on 11 January 1884, with the honorary rank of lieutenant-general. He had previously received the distinguished service reward in India.

Sankey returned to England in 1883 and from 1884 to 1896 was chairman of the Irish board of works. In May 1892 he was made KCB. After his retirement in 1896 he resided in London, but his activity was unabated. He visited Mexico and had much correspondence with President Diaz. Sankey was twice married: first in 1858, at Ootacamund, to Sophia Mary (*d.* 1882), daughter of W. H. Benson, Bengal civil service, and they had two daughters; second in 1890, at Dublin, to Henrietta, widow of Edward Browne JP, and daughter of Pierce Creagh; she survived him. Sankey died at St George's Hospital, London, on 11 November 1908, and was buried at Hove, Sussex.

R. H. VETCH, rev. ROGER T. STEARN

Sources BL OIOC · *The Times* (12 Nov 1908) · H. M. Vibart, *Addiscombe: its heroes and men of note* (1894) · H. M. V., 'Lieut.-Gen. Sir Richard Hieram Sankey', *Royal Engineers Journal*, new ser., 9 (1909), 469–74 · WWW · C. Hibbert, *The great mutiny, India, 1857* (1978) · B. Robson, *The road to Kabul: the Second Afghan War, 1878–1881* (1986) · T. A. Heathcote, *The military in British India: the development of British land forces in south Asia, 1600–1947* (1995) · E. W. C. Sandes, *The military engineer in India*, 1 (1933)
Wealth at death £2447 7s. 5d.: probate, 12 Dec 1908, CGPLA Eng. & Wales

Sansetun, Benedict of. *See* Sawston, Benedict of (*d.* 1226).

Sansom, Sir George Bailey (1883–1965), diplomatist and Japanese scholar, was born at 20 Farrance Street, Limehouse, London, on 28 November 1883, the only son of George William Morgan Sansom, naval architect, of Little Thurrock, Essex, and his wife, Mary Ann Bailey, from Yorkshire. He was educated at Palmer's School, Grays, and the *lycée* Malherbe, Caen, and later attended the universities of Giessen and Marburg. He passed a competitive examination for the British consular service in September 1903 and was attached to the British legation in Tokyo to study the Japanese language. He served as private secretary to Sir Claude Macdonald, ambassador to Japan, from 1905 to 1912, and also in consulates around Japan. In these posts, he acquired great proficiency in the Japanese language, including local dialects. In 1915 he was in London on home leave and, being unfit for military service, was lent by the Foreign Office first to the Admiralty and then to the War Office for political intelligence work, which took him to Archangel. On 22 December 1916 he married Caroline, daughter of Godfrey Weston, from whom he obtained a divorce on 20 June 1927. On 29 May the following year he married, at the British embassy in Tokyo, Katharine, former wife of Stephen Gordon, and daughter of William Cecil Slingsby, landowner and naturalist, of Carleton in Craven, Yorkshire. She was a writer on Japanese topics and published in 1972 a memoir of her husband. There were no children of either marriage.

Sir George Bailey Sansom (1883–1965), by Walter Stoneman, 1935

After his return to Japan in January 1920, Sansom worked as secretary to the ambassador, Sir Charles Eliot, a post in which he made the acquaintance of many Japanese leaders and scholars. Eliot, for whom he had unbounded admiration, encouraged him to devote the spare time which was available to him in the relatively relaxed pace of official life to the study of Japan, her language, culture, and history. In 1928 he published his first work, *An Historical Grammar of Japanese*, a pioneer study. Already regarded as an authority on the early history of Japan, he published in 1931 *Japan: a Short Cultural History*, which was based on primary materials in Japanese and added a new dimension to the English-language literature on the subject. While he was dissatisfied with aspects of the work and wanted to revise it, it was reprinted as it stood in 1936 and on countless occasions thereafter. It became the standard and most reliable text for the university courses on the subject which were growing up in the United States and elsewhere. Sansom then edited the monograph *Japanese Buddhism* (1935) which Eliot had left incomplete at the time of his death in 1931 and added a chapter of his own. His scholarship was recognized when, during leave in 1935, he spent half a year in New York, lecturing at Columbia University.

From the 1920s Sansom was responsible for the commercial work of the embassy. He was appointed commercial secretary in September 1923 and then commercial counsellor in January 1930. In this capacity he travelled to the Philippines in 1932 and then to India in the autumn of 1933, where he played an important negotiating role in resolving the difficult Indo-Japanese cotton dispute in a dual capacity as representative of both the Indian and British governments. He was made a KCMG in June 1935, having been appointed CMG in January 1926.

The contradiction between the diplomatic and scholarly sides of his career came to the fore while Sansom was on leave in London at the onset of the Second World War. While his commercial work in Tokyo was universally respected and his political advice was highly regarded in the Foreign Office, Sansom felt that he was being sidelined at the Tokyo embassy. Deciding to leave the service and devote himself to writing, he took retirement on a pension which was to take effect in September 1940. Before then, however, he agreed in the abnormal circumstances of war to go on a special mission to Japan. Thereafter he was free to teach the winter semester at Columbia University. In the following year he volunteered for war service and was sent to Singapore to act as adviser to the Far East mission of the Ministry of Economic Warfare. He then became the civilian representative on the Far East war council, Singapore, in 1941–2. Moving to Java after the fall of Singapore, he was attached to the united command headquarters under General Archibald Wavell, as political and diplomatic adviser. Evacuated through Australia, he reached the United States and was appointed adviser to the ambassador in Washington from 1942 to 1947 with the local rank of minister-plenipotentiary. For the rest of the war years he had special responsibility for aspects of the Asia-Pacific War, especially for influencing British thinking on allied post-war policy towards Japan. In 1946 he was appointed as the British representative on the Far Eastern commission, the international body which had a nominal responsibility for the allied occupation of Japan. In this capacity he was able to revisit Japan in 1946. He finally retired from the Foreign Office in 1947, and was appointed GBE.

From 1947 to 1953 Sansom was professor of Japanese studies at Columbia University and from 1949 to 1953 he was the first director of its East Asian Institute. It was during this period that he wrote *The Western World and Japan: a Study in the Interaction of European and Asian Cultures* (1950), in which he emphasized the influence of Western thought as it reached Japan down the centuries. He was able to make another academic visit to Japan in 1950 and to publish the seminal lectures he gave on that occasion under the title *Japan in World History* (1951). In 1955 he decided on health grounds to move to California, where he was given an honorary 'consultant professorship' at Stanford University. There he spent much of the last ten years of his life, freed from routine work, working on his three-volume *History of Japan* (1958–64). Considering the exacting standards that he set for himself, it was a marvellous publication, but the strains of age and illness affected the final volume. He had built up over half a century a range of intellectual contacts in Japan unusual for a diplomatist; and he was able to plough into his writing the richness of Japanese material towards which he was guided by a network of academic friends. He became an honorary fellow of the Japanese Academy in 1951.

Although Sansom's official career was distinguished in its own right, it is as an interpreter of Japan that he will be remembered. His writings, originating in linguistic and Buddhist studies, gradually moved away from cultural history and in later works tended towards social and political history. He was the bridge between Japanese scholars who were anxious to have their country understood abroad and a western readership who appreciated the style and wit of his writing. He died on 8 March 1965 during a visit to Tucson, Arizona. He was survived by his wife, who died in 1998.   IAN NISH

Sources *The Times* (10 March 1965) · *DNB* · K. Sansom, *Sir G. Sansom and Japan* (1972) · G. Daniels, 'Sir G. Sansom (1883–1965): historian and diplomat', *Britain and Japan, 1859–1991*, ed. H. Cortazzi and G. Daniels (1991) · R. Buckley, *Occupation diplomacy: Britain, the United States and Japan, 1945–52* (1982) · F. S. G. Piggott, *Broken thread: an autobiography* (1950) · G. Sansom, address presented at the annual ceremony, 1956, SOAS · 'The reminiscences of Sir George Sansom', 1957, Col. U., Oral History Research Office · C. Hosoya, 'George Sansom: diplomat and historian', *European studies on Japan*, ed. I. H. Nish and C. Dunn (1979) · W. N. Medlicott and others, eds., *Documents on British foreign policy, 1919–1939* [various vols.] · *CGPLA Eng. & Wales* (1966) · b. cert. · m. cert.

Archives Col. U., papers · St Ant. Oxf., Middle East Centre, corresp. and papers | JRL, letters to the *Manchester Guardian* · UCL, G. C. Allen MSS

Likenesses W. Stoneman, photograph, 1935, NPG [*see illus.*]

Wealth at death £1878 effects in England: probate, 2 Dec 1966, *CGPLA Eng. & Wales*

Sansom [née Fowke], **Martha** (1689–1736), poet, was born on 1 May 1689 at Hertingfordbury Park, Hertfordshire, the eldest child of Major Thomas Fowke (d. 1708), of a Staffordshire gentry family, and his third wife, Mary Chandler, *née* Cullen (d. c.1705). She was educated at home by tutors, and subsequently at boarding-school. She was brought up a Roman Catholic, but later became a non-practising Anglican. Her autobiographical *Clio* (written in 1723 but not published until 1752) records her early passion for French romances and love poetry, and a literary ambition discouraged by her mother but nurtured by her father. On her mother's death and her father's return to the army in 1705 she moved in with friends in London. Her father's murder in 1708 proved a devastating blow.

Fowke's earliest published verse appeared in *Delights for the Ingenious* (1711). She first achieved public fame in 1720 with verse published in Anthony Hammond's *New Miscellany* and with *Clio and Strephon*, an important Platonic poetic correspondence with William Bond prefaced by a critical essay by John Porter, which went through several editions. She enjoyed wide-ranging literary friendships, particularly with the poet and critic Aaron Hill, and the poet John Dyer, whose career she encouraged, as well as earning the enmity of others, notably Eliza Haywood, who attacked her in *The Injur'd Husband* (1723) and the *Memoirs … of Utopia* (1725–6). Nine poems by Clio, and verses addressed to her, feature in Richard Savage's *Miscellaneous Poems* (1726).

By 1721 Fowke's younger brother Thomas had persuaded her to regularize her relationship with Arnold Sansom, a lawyer some years her senior. The marriage proved miserable. Martha left London for East Anglia in 1730, when her husband took up a political post there. He died of alcoholism four years later. She subsequently joined her brother in Leicestershire, where she died on 17 February 1736 at the early age of forty-six. She was buried at St Martin's Church, Leicester.

During her lifetime Martha Sansom's poetic reputation was blackened by the moral aspersions cast on her character by Haywood and subsequently echoed by Dr Johnson. Recent scholarship has discovered in her work a strongly individual female voice, passionate in quest of literary renown, personal liberty, and a marriage of true minds. Her poetic self-portrait, 'Clio's Picture', consciously opposes contemporary conventions of femininity with a wry account of her own unconventional dark looks. In her poetry she frequently registers her contempt for the narrow confines of female domesticity:

> I was, oh hated Thought! a Woman made;
> For household Cares, and empty Trifles meant.
> (Savage, *Miscellaneous Poems*, 209–10)

Much of her writing was first circulated in manuscript, and recent evidence has considerably enlarged the known corpus of her poems, including some fine amatory verse first printed in the *Barbados Gazette*, subsequently collected in *Caribbeana* (London, 1741).

                                                        CHRISTINE GERRARD

Sources *Clio: the autobiography of Martha Fowke Sansom, 1689–1736*, ed. P. J. Guskin (1997) · R. Lonsdale, ed., *Eighteenth-century women poets: an Oxford anthology* (1989); pbk edn (1990), 520 · P. J. Guskin, '"Not originally intended for the press": Martha Fowke Sansom's poems in the *Barbados Gazette*', *Eighteenth-Century Studies*, 34 (2000–01), 61–91 · B. Overton, ed., *A letter to my love: love poems by women first published in the Barbados Gazette, 1731–1737* (2001) · *The works of the late Aaron Hill*, 4 vols. (1753), vol. 1, p. 338; vol. 2, p. 180; vol. 3, pp. 6, 41, 45–6, 50; vol. 4, pp. 96–8 · A. Hill, *The dramatic works of Aaron Hill*, 2nd edn, 2 (1763), 389–92 · *GM*, 1st ser., 51 (1781), 22 · G. Jacob, *Historical account of our most considerable English poets* (1720), 326 · C. Tracy, *The artificial bastard: a biography of Richard Savage* (1953) · K. Davis, 'Martha Fowke: "A lady once too well known"', *English Language Notes*, 23/3 (1986), 32–6 · [E. Hatton], *A new view of London*, 2 vols. (1708) · J. L. Chester and J. Foster, eds., *London marriage licences, 1521–1869* (1887) · *Report on the manuscripts of the earl of Egmont*, 2 vols. in 3, HMC, 63 (1905–9), vol. 1, p. 97

Archives Bodl. Oxf., material relating to family tree, MS Rawl. B130

Sansom, William (1912–1976), writer, was born on 18 January 1912, at 51 Pickwick Road, Dulwich, London, the third son of Ernest Brooks Sansom, naval architect, and his wife, Mabel May, *née* Clark, of Barrow. He was registered as Norman Trevor but adopted the name William at a later date. After being educated at Uppingham School, he studied German in Bonn and he spent some time travelling on the continent with his father. These youthful peregrinations developed a taste for foreign countries which resulted in several distinguished books which apply fictional methods to the travel genre—notably *South* (1948) about the Mediterranean and *The Passionate North* (1950) about Scandinavia.

Sansom had been writing since the age of seven, but before adopting it as a career he had a number of jobs. He worked for the National Provincial Bank and as an advertising copy-writer for J. Walter Thompson, and played piano in a night-club, an experience which provided the background for one of his best books, a sardonic romance titled *The Cautious Heart* (1958). During the Second World War he joined the National Fire Service and began contributing short stories to *Penguin New Writing* and *Horizon*. He appeared (playing the piano) in Humphrey Jennings's film *Fires were Started* (1943), collaborated with his fellow fireman Stephen Spender on a book about the service, *Jim Braidy: the Story of Britain's Firemen* (1943), and published an authorized and well-documented account, *Westminster in Wartime* (1947). More important, however, was his first volume of short stories, *Fireman Flower*, published to considerable acclaim in 1944. For two years, from 1946 to 1947, he received an annual bursary of £200, arranged by the Society of Authors in co-operation with Hodder and Stoughton, during which time he took up writing full-time. His second work of fiction was *Three* (1946), a volume of 'two short novels and a story', (publisher's description on dust jacket of *Goodbye*). Thereafter he wrote prolifically until the mid-1960s, publishing at least one book a year, and occasionally more.

In the first story of Sansom's first collection, a man in a café observes the world through the quinquina glass from which he is drinking and finds it curiously altered. This might stand as a metaphor for Sansom's own writing. His subject matter was ordinary (usually London) lives, but his prose has an almost visionary quality which transforms the quotidian into something altogether rich and strange. Suburban gardens become jungles, and perfectly normal human behaviour takes on a sinister or melodramatic colouring. The intensity of Sansom's own gaze is reflected in the obsessively voyeuristic plots of two of his most highly regarded novels, *The Body* (1949) and *The Loving Eye* (1956), and it is no surprise that he should have given 'watching' as his recreation in *Who's Who*. His early work shows the influence of Kafka, and it is significant that he edited a volume of Edgar Allan Poe's tales (1948). Despite their sometimes menacing or macabre subject matter, Sansom's books are shot through with humour of a dry, ironic sort, a trait which reached its apotheosis in *Goodbye* (1966), a black comedy in which a man attempts to prevent his wife from leaving him. Sansom also had a gift for dialogue that seems naturalistic but is in fact highly stylized, and he was particularly adept at reproducing the speech patterns of the pub and the workplace. Indeed, his work has much in common with that of his friend Henry Green.

As well as novels, travel books, and short stories, Sansom wrote children's books, song lyrics, revue sketches, an unproduced screenplay of *The Loving Eye*, an illustrated study of Proust, and a volume of 'Prose Ballads', *Lord Love Us* (1954), with illustrations by Lynton Lamb. This last led John Betjeman to observe: 'He makes prose live again' (dust jacket of *The Loving Eye*), and his writing always drew the praise of fellow writers, including Elizabeth Bowen, who wrote an admiring introduction to his 1963 volume of collected stories.

Sansom's rate of production was considerable, and in later years the quality of his work became variable, but almost everything he wrote bore the inimitable stamp of his quirky vision. He lived in London for a time in Warwick Square, Victoria, before moving to a ground-floor flat opening on to a lush garden in Buckland Crescent, Swiss Cottage, during which period he conducted a semi-detached relationship with the fashion artist Ruth Sheradski, who designed the dust jacket for *The Body* and in whose Chelsea home Sansom spent his weekends. This relationship ended abruptly when Sansom failed to return from a shopping expedition, subsequently announcing that he was going to marry Ruth Evelyn Blake (1918/19–1983), the divorced daughter of Norman Dennis Grundy, chartered accountant. They were married on 23 April 1954. Having worked as an actress under her maiden name, Ruth subsequently moved to a job finding plays and books for several European publishers, which caused her husband to joke that he was 'one of the few heterosexuals married to a scout' (Sansom, *Living in London*, 61). For some years they lived at 42 Acacia Road, St John's Wood, London, where their son was born; Ruth's son from her former marriage also lived with them. They subsequently moved to a large Victorian mansion nearby at 135 Hamilton Terrace, 'the nearest thing in London to a boulevard' (ibid., 60, 55). The house was 'fairly-well furnished in a roughly Early Victorian style' (ibid., 60), and had a large garden, which Sansom described as 'high-walled, screened by a dozen tall trees, and otherwise laid out as a kind of deerless park, planted only with things that need a minimum of care' (ibid., 54). In good weather he liked to write outdoors, which may explain why gardens play so prominent a role in several of his books. He particularly enjoyed watering the roses, which he felt 'somehow assuages the thirst, and thus retards the aperitif hour' (ibid., 54). This became increasingly necessary, since Sansom and his wife were both heavy drinkers, and the quiet of the boulevard was frequently disturbed by noisy altercations.

Despite this, Sansom continued to pursue a strict working regime in the house's former billiards room. 'To the soundless click of ghostly balls I do the writing part of work every morning from ten until half-past one, seven days a week', he claimed in the last decade of his life (Sansom, *Living in London*, 61). Bearded, of medium height, and affecting Edwardian clothing ('checked, waisted suits, high-cut, lapelled waistcoats, elastic-sided boots' and a brown bowler), he was likened by his friend Alan Ross to 'a character out of Chekov'—though on bad days 'he could be taken for a bookmaker drowning his sorrows' (Ross, 119). His suits were originally made up to a pattern worn by his father, but he later claimed: 'I always buy dead men's suits—brand new Savile Row stuff resulting from a coronary or some bankrupt death of the purse' (Sansom, *Living in London*, 56).

Sansom's marriage endured, but relations with his wife deteriorated along with his health, and while hospitalized he received a note from her to say (incorrectly) that she had destroyed all his papers, 'so if you ever come out you won't find anything' (Ross, 115). He died of cancer in St Mary's Hospital, Paddington, London, on 21 April 1976, and was cremated at Golders Green crematorium.

PETER PARKER

Sources *The Times* (21 April 1976) · A. Ross, *Coastwise lights* (1988) · W. Sansom, 'William Sansom', *Living in London*, ed. A. Ross (1974), 53–65 · private information (2004) · W. Sansom, *The loving eye* (1956) · W. Sansom, *Goodbye* (1966) · b. cert. · m. cert. · d. cert. **Archives** BBC WAC, corresp. with BBC staff · Mormon University, Utah, MSS · U. Leeds, letters to the *London Magazine*; letters to Norah Smallwood · U. Reading L., corresp. with Hogarth Press · University of Bristol, editorial corresp. relating to publication of *South*, *Selected short stories*, and *The body* | S O U N D BL NSA, recordings of readings from his own work
Wealth at death £28,995: probate, 7 June 1976, *CGPLA Eng. & Wales*

Sansum, Robert (*c.*1626–1665), naval officer, a native of Ipswich, Suffolk, was probably the son of Robert Sansum (*d.* 1650), master and part-owner of the *Alexander* of Ipswich, hired by the state in 1649–50 to help with the Irish invasion and drowned when the ship was wrecked in the spring of 1650, leaving a widow, Elizabeth. The younger Robert was bred to the sea, and in 1649 was serving as master of the *Tiger's Whelp*, formerly the *Mary of Antrim*, which had been captured by James Peacock in the *Tiger* on 14 February 1649 and fitted out at Plymouth as a warship. Peacock was also an Ipswich man, and it is very likely that Sansum had been serving with him in the *Tiger*, perhaps as a mate. The *Tiger's Whelp* captured another Irish privateer near Dublin in June, but was wrecked on Dublin bar in October.

In the autumn of 1651 Sansum was appointed commander of the sixth-rate *Bryher*. The ship was too small to be of use in fleet actions, and Sansum spent 1652 and 1653 on convoy duties in the North Sea, a region he knew well. In January 1653 he captured a Flushing man-of-war of fifteen guns off Newcastle. In June he brought three French ships laden with tar and hemp into the downs, part of a campaign to persuade France not to allow the royalists to sell prizes in their ports. Members of his crew were alleged to have been selling ropes, casks of beef, and barrels of gunpowder from the ship at Newcastle, 'which some here conceive … the captain was not ignorant of' (Capp, 232 n.). The accusation did not prevent Sansum's promotion to the fourth-rate *Adventure* in December 1653. The war was drawing to a close, and his main activity in 1654 was to challenge the French by interrupting their trade in the channel. Sansum was appointed to the fourth-rate *Portsmouth* in April 1655, commanding her until 1660. He was mainly employed in the North Sea and channel in the dull but essential task of protecting shipping from the depredations of Ostend privateers, several of which he captured. His only foreign expedition was with Mountagu's fleet to the sound in 1659.

Following the Restoration Sansum was laid aside as an 'Anabaptist' and resumed a mercantile career. On the outbreak of the Second Anglo-Dutch War he was recalled to naval service and appointed rear-admiral of the white in *Resolution* under Prince Rupert, a position reflecting his experience and seniority. Sansum was killed in the great battle off Lowestoft on 3 June 1665, and was buried at St Clement's, Ipswich, on 24 June. He left a widow, Mary, and four children. Mary was awarded a grant of £500 by the crown but found difficulty in securing its payment. In 1667 she petitioned Lord Arlington for help, explaining that most of her husband's estate had been tied up in Surinam at the outbreak of the Anglo-Dutch War, and that the merchant to whom he had entrusted his affairs was evading payment. In 1670 she complained to the navy commissioners that, despite many tedious journeys to London, she had still only received £320 of the £500 promised by the king.

MICHAEL BAUMBER

Sources *CSP dom.*, 1649–70 · B. Capp, *Cromwell's navy: the fleet and the English revolution, 1648–1660* (1989) · Bodl. Oxf., MSS Carte 73, 74 · Pepys, *Diary* · BL, Add. MS 9305 · J. Charnock, ed., *Biographia navalis*, 1 (1794) · S. R. Gardiner and C. T. Atkinson, eds., *Letters and papers relating to the First Dutch War, 1652–1654*, 6 vols., Navy RS, 13, 17, 30, 37, 41, 66 (1898–1930) · *The journal of Edward Mountagu, first earl of Sandwich, admiral and general at sea, 1659–1665*, ed. R. C. Anderson, Navy RS, 64 (1929) · PRO, HCA 13/62 · PRO, SP 25/123, 353–4 · Bath papers, Coventry MS 98, fol. 67 · A. G. E. Jones, note, *Mariner's Mirror*, 39 (1953), 135–6

Sant, James (1820–1916), portrait and genre painter, was born on 23 April 1820 in Croydon, Surrey, the son of William Sant (1787–1850), and his wife, Sarah Maria Baker (1793–1868). During the 1830s Sant studied with John Varley and Augustus Wall Callcott, and from 1842 to 1846 at the Royal Academy Schools. He exhibited his first painting at the academy in 1840. On 15 July 1851 he married Eliza (1833–1907), daughter of Dr R. M. M. Thomson, staff surgeon in Bengal. He gained popular acclaim for his idealized depictions of childhood (occasionally modelled on his own son and four daughters), which were widely disseminated through engravings. His most successful paintings include *The Children in the Wood* (1854) and *Little Red Riding-Hood* (1860).

Later in his career Sant became a fashionable painter of social and political luminaries. The extensive series of portraits that he produced for Frances, Countess Waldegrave, was exhibited at the French Gallery in 1861. In that same year Sant was elected an associate of the Royal Academy, becoming a full academician in 1869. In 1877 he was elected a corresponding member of La Regia Accademia Raffaello in Urbino. On 19 January 1871 Queen Victoria appointed Sant her principal painter, but his inability to capture an acceptable likeness made her refuse to sit to him. State portraits for Japan and the embassies of Turkey and Madrid were among the few he completed. He had far greater success with sweetly sentimental paintings of the queen's children and grandchildren.

Although Sant's best-known works are executed in a carefully polished style, he experimented with the loose brushwork and outdoor lighting effects of impressionism in works such as *Miss Martineau's Garden* of 1873 (Tate collection). In a lecture of 1871 Sir Coutts Lindsay named Sant among the contemporary painters who were influencing the direction of English art. He later invited Sant to exhibit at the progressive Grosvenor Gallery. Although Sant described himself as shy, he was not without daring. When a new client arrived at his studio heavily made up with rouge and powder, he reportedly remarked, 'I see we both paint' (Ward, 283). A prolific artist with an exceptionally long career, he exhibited over 300 paintings at the Royal Academy from 1840 to 1916. He was appointed CVO in 1914 and resigned from the academy that year, 'wishing to afford an opportunity of full membership to an Associate' (*The Times*, 13 July 1916, 11). Sant died at his home, 43 Lancaster Gate, Hyde Park, London, on 12 July 1916 and was buried three days later at Kensal Green cemetery, leaving a large estate valued at £35,981.

ROBYN ASLESON

Sources W. W. Fenn, 'Our living artists—James Sant, R. A.', *Magazine of Art*, 3 (1880), 128–33 · *The Times* (13 July 1916), 11 · Graves, *RA exhibitors* · O. Millar, *The Victorian pictures in the collection of her majesty the queen*, 2 vols. (1992) · *Men and women of the time* (1899), 965 · *The Cosmopolitan* (21 Sept 1897), 641 · *ILN* (18 Feb 1861) · H. M. A. Ward [Mrs Humphry], *Memories of ninety years* (1924) · *Great Victorian pictures: their paths to fame*, Arts Council of Great Britain (1978) · J. Maas, *Victorian painters* (1978) · R. Ormond, 'Ceremonial royal groups', *The Connoisseur*, 195 (June 1977), 88–9 · *WWW*, 1929–40
Likenesses Negretti and Zambra, photograph, *c*.1880, repro. in *Magazine of Art*, 3 (1880), 128 · R. W. Robinson, photograph, 1891, NPG · photograph, *c*.1895, repro. in 'Studios of English Royal Academicians', *Monthly Illustrator and Home and Country* (3 Feb 1895), 224 · Elliott & Fry, carte-de-visite, NPG · Lock & Whitfield, woodburytype, NPG; repro. in T. Cooper, *Men of mark: a gallery of contemporary portraits* (1877) · G. G. Manton, group portrait, watercolour (*Conversazione at the Royal Academy*), NPG · J. Russell & Sons, photograph, NPG · J. Sant, self-portrait, oils, NPG · J. Sant, self-portrait, oils, Aberdeen Art Gallery · J. & C. Watkins, carte-de-visite, NPG · woodcut, NPG; repro. in *The Graphic* (7 May 1870)
Wealth at death £35,981 16s. 7d.: probate, 31 July 1916, CGPLA Eng. & Wales

Sir Charles Santley (1834–1922), by Barraud, pubd 1890

Santley, Sir Charles (1834–1922), singer, was born in Liverpool on 28 February 1834, the elder son of William Santley, an official of the city corporation, an organist and woodwind player, and a teacher of piano and singing, and his wife, Margaret, *née* Fletcher. He was educated at the Liverpool Institute, and as a boy sang alto in the choir of the Unitarian Ancient Chapel, Toxteth Park. He passed the examination for admission to the second tenors (he later transferred to the basses) of the Liverpool Philharmonic Society on his fifteenth birthday, and in the same year took part in the concerts at the opening of the Philharmonic Hall. He also studied the piano and later the violin, and became leader of the second violins in a local orchestra. While working in the bookkeeping department of large wholesale provision and leather merchants' houses in Liverpool he devoted all his spare time to music, and his voice developed early into a fine baritone. Urged by the cellist Joseph Lidel, his father eventually allowed him to take up a career as a singer, and after giving a farewell concert on 15 October 1855 he went to Milan to study with Gaetano Nava, who subsequently bequeathed him his library.

Santley made his début in opera in Pavia in 1857, in the bass role of Doctor Grenvil in *La traviata*, and in the same year appeared at the Santa Radegonda Theatre in Milan. Here he met Henry Chorley, on whose advice he returned to England that October. In London he was engaged by John Pyke Hullah to sing the part of Adam in Haydn's *The Creation* at St Martin's Hall, Long Acre, on 16 November 1857; though nerves caused him to break down at one point, he made an impression, which he followed up in *Messiah* on 16 December. He then sang for the Sacred Harmonic Society. After further vocal study with Manuel García and some acting lessons from Walter Lacy, he embarked on a career exceptional in its length, versatility, and distinction. He made his English operatic début at Her Majesty's Theatre on 1 October 1859 as Hoël in Meyerbeer's *Dinorah* (*Le pardon de Ploërmel*) with the Pyne-Harrison company, with whom he remained until 1863 and created leading roles in operas by Wallace, Balfe, Glover, and Benedict. In 1862 he sang the Conte di Luna in *Il trovatore* in the Royal Italian Opera season at Covent Garden, and later that year joined Mapleson's company at Her Majesty's and sang the count in *The Marriage of Figaro* and Nevers in *Les Huguenots*. He also performed in Manchester and elsewhere in England, in Dublin, in Milan (La Scala), in Barcelona, and in America (1871 and 1891), lending distinction to the Carl Rosa and Pyne-Harrison companies, as well as to that of John Hollingshead in an important English season at the Old Gaiety Theatre in 1870.

Among Santley's most notable appearances was Valentine in the English première of *Faust* (in Italian) on 11 June 1863 at Her Majesty's. This was so successful that he managed to persuade Gounod, reluctant because of business difficulties in England and never to accept it into French scores, to write for him the cavatina 'Even the bravest heart', arranged from music in the instrumental introduction to words by Chorley; this he sang at the English-language première on 23 January 1864. He sang the title role in Thomas's *Hamlet* at its English première (in Italian) at Covent Garden on 19 June 1869, and the title role in *The Flying Dutchman*, given at Drury Lane on 23 July 1870 as *L'Olandese dannato* (the first Wagner opera in England). He also sang with an English company at the Gaiety Theatre in London, and in 1872 toured America under Carl Rosa. Later operatic appearances were with the newly formed Carl Rosa Opera Company in 1875, when he sang Mozart's Figaro on the opening night of the opera's first London season on 11 September at the Princess's Theatre. His last operatic performance was as the Flying Dutchman in 1876.

Santley thereafter sang only in concert. His first festival engagement had been in 1858 in Leeds (where he performed regularly until 1886), followed by Norwich from 1860, Birmingham from 1861 to 1891, and the Three Choirs from 1863 to 1894. He was a popular figure at many other festivals, especially in Handel and in the title role of Mendelssohn's *Elijah*: he sang this for over half a century, and was generally accepted as supreme in his day. He sang at the Handel festivals at the Crystal Palace from 1862, and at the opening of the Albert Hall on 29 March 1871. He also toured Australia (1889–90), New Zealand, South Africa (1893 and 1903), and Canada. His repertory embraced Italian arias (with Giovanni Mario and Giulia Grisi), German lieder (with Clara Schumann), and English, Irish, and Scottish ballads. In 1871 he was awarded the gold medal of the Royal Philharmonic Society. He was received into the Roman Catholic church in 1880, and in 1887 Pope Leo XIII made him knight commander of the order of St Gregory the Great. At the Albert Hall on 1 May 1907 he celebrated his jubilee as a singer, and that year he was the first singer ever to be knighted. He made his farewell at a Covent Garden benefit on 23 May 1911. When more than eighty he sang with much of his old mastery at a Mansion House concert in February 1915 in aid of the Belgian Refugees' Fund.

Santley dominated the last four decades of Victorian England as, in George Bernard Shaw's words,

> the best baritone singer with whom the London public is familiar. He has a voice; he knows how to produce it; he [has] acquired the art of managing his breath properly; and he conscientiously interprets the works which he sings without adding or subtracting a note.

His voice was described by some as of great beauty, by others as lacking in natural beauty but of great expressive powers. His technique in scales and roulades was remarkable, his enunciation in various languages and in dialect clear, and his declamation, which showed complete understanding of the meaning of the text, eloquent. Shaw added that he was 'neither a great nor a poetic artist', and found his stage bearing 'congenial and familiar, but quite unsuited for characters requiring dignity or refinement' and that 'acting is evidently no part of his vocation'. However, Hermann Klein praised 'the profound unforced

pathos of his portrayal' of the Flying Dutchman. His platform presence included a nervous shaking of the hands, which audiences sometimes found distracting. While outspoken where efficiency or integrity were concerned, he was a loyal and generous friend. He published three books, two on singing and one of memoirs. He also composed some works for Roman Catholic services, including a mass in A♭, first performed at the pro-cathedral, Kensington, on 25 December 1892, an offertory and an Ave Maria, as well as a berceuse for orchestra (performed in Sydney in 1890) and some songs under the name of Ralph Betterton. He was a keen amateur painter. He married first, on 9 April 1859, Gertrude, daughter of the historian John Mitchell *Kemble and granddaughter of Charles Kemble, who had sung as a soprano, and with whom he had two sons and three daughters; she died on 1 September 1882, and he then married, on 7 January 1884, Elizabeth Mary, daughter of George Rose-Innes, with whom he had one son. He died at his home in London, 13 Blenheim Road, St John's Wood, on 22 September 1922. His eldest daughter, Edith, made her stage début in Cherubini's *Les deux journées* (*The Water Carrier*) at the Theatre Royal, Birmingham, on 19 May 1876, and also appeared as a concert singer, notably with the Philharmonic Society. She married the Hon. R. H. Lyttelton on 14 July 1884, then retired to Warwickshire and sang only for charity concerts.

JOHN WARRACK

Sources J. M. Levien, *Sir Charles Santley* (1930) · Brown & Stratton, *Brit. mus.* · C. Santley, *Reminiscences of my life* (1909) · G. B. Shaw, *Music in London, 1890–94*, 3 vols. (1932) · G. B. Shaw, *How to become a musical critic*, ed. D. H. Laurence (1960) · H. Klein, *Thirty years of musical life in London* (1903) · *The Mapleson memoirs: the career of an operatic impresario, 1858–1888*, ed. H. Rosenthal (1966) · J. F. Barnett, *Musical reminiscences and impressions* (1906) · H. Rosenthal, *Two centuries of opera at Covent Garden* (1958) · private information (2004) · m. cert. · d. cert.
Archives Lpool RO, corresp. and papers
Likenesses Barraud, photograph, NPG; repro. in *Men and Women of the Day*, 3 (1890) [*see illus.*] · W. & D. Downey, woodburytype photograph, NPG; repro. in W. Downey and D. Downey, *The cabinet portrait gallery* (1894) · Elliott & Fry, photograph, NPG · Spy [L. Ward], chromolithograph caricature, NPG; repro. in *VF* (27 Feb 1902) · cartes-de-visite, NPG · chromolithograph, NPG · group photograph, repro. in Barnett, *Musical reminiscences*, facing pp. 84, 286 · photograph, repro. in Rosenthal, ed., *Mapleson memoirs*, facing p. 62 · photograph, repro. in B. Palmer, *Musical recollections* (1904), 77 · photograph, repro. in *New Grove*
Wealth at death £13,335 2s. 11d.: administration with will, 2 Nov 1922, *CGPLA Eng. & Wales*

Santlow, Hester. *See* Booth, Hester (*c.*1690–1773).

Saphir, Adolph (1831–1891), Free Church of Scotland minister, was born at Pest, Hungary, in 1831, the youngest son in a family of two sons and three daughters of Israel Saphir, a Jewish merchant, and his second wife, Henrietta Bondij (*d.* 1879). His father's brother, Moritz Gottlieb Saphir, was well known as a Hungarian poet and satirist.

In 1843 the Saphir family, including Adolph, were converted to Christianity by the Jewish mission of the Church of Scotland. At the close of the same year his father sent him to Edinburgh that he might be trained for the Free

Church ministry. Thence in the following year he proceeded to Berlin, where he attended the *Gymnasium* until 1848. In the autumn of that year he entered Glasgow University, graduating MA in 1854. In 1849 he proceeded to Marischal College, Aberdeen, and in 1851 he became a student of theology in the Free Church college, Edinburgh.

In 1854 Saphir was licensed by the Belfast presbytery and appointed a missionary to the Jews. In the same year he married Sara Owen, from a Dublin family, and they had a daughter (who died in the late 1850s). His first post was at Hamburg, but, as the Austrian government was desirous of obtaining his extradition for non-performance of military service, he resigned his appointment and, returning to Great Britain, settled in South Shields in 1856. He moved after five years to London, first to Greenwich, and thence in 1872 to Notting Hill. In 1878 he received the honorary degree of DD from the University of Edinburgh. In 1880 he left Notting Hill, and two years later he accepted a call from the Belgrave Presbyterian Church, where he remained until 1888.

Like his friend Dr Alfred Edersheim, Saphir threw much light on biblical study by his intimate knowledge of Jewish manners and literature. As early as 1852 Charles Kingsley wrote to him: 'To teach us the real meaning of the Old Testament and its absolute unity with the New, we want not mere Hebrew scholars, but Hebrew spirits—Hebrew men' (Carlyle, 102). In later life Saphir took much interest in the endeavour of rabbis Lichtenstein and Rabinowich to convert to Christianity the Jews of Hungary and southern Russia; and in 1887 he was chosen president of an association formed in London to assist them, under the title of the Rabinowich Council. Saphir was a theologian of the evangelical school, and many of his pamphlets and lectures were intended to controvert the rationalistic theories of German critics. One of his earliest publications was *From Death to Life: Bible Records of Remarkable Conversions* (1880); this was described by a reviewer as 'Harsh, dogmatic, and ingeniously disagreeable' (Allibone, *Dict.*, 2, 1930). Another was *Christ and the Scriptures* (1867). Saphir also published his lectures on the Lord's prayer (1870), on Corinthians 2 (1873), and on the epistle to the Hebrews (1874–6). An account of *Rabinowich and his Mission to Israel* appeared in 1888. A final work, *The Divine Unity of Scripture*, appeared posthumously.

Adolph Saphir died on 4 April 1891 at his home, 19 Lansdowne Road, Kensington Park, Notting Hill, London; he was survived by his sister. His wife had died four days earlier.
E. I. CARLYLE, rev. ROBERT BROWN

Sources G. Carlyle, *Mighty in the scriptures: a memoir of the Rev. Adolph Saphir*, 2nd edn (1894) · Boase, *Mod. Eng. biog.*, vol. 3 · P. Schaff and S. M. Jackson, *Encyclopedia of living divines and Christian workers of all denominations in Europe and America: being a supplement to Schaff-Herzog encyclopedia of religious knowledge* (1887) · *CGPLA Eng. & Wales* (1891) · Allibone, *Dict.*
Likenesses E. Seeley, carte-de-visite, NPG · process print (after photograph by T. Rodger), NPG
Wealth at death £16,157 11s. 10d.: administration (with will), 1891

Sapper. *See* McNeile, (Herman) Cyril (1888–1937).

Sapru, Sir Tej Bahadur (1875–1949), Indian nationalist and political mediator, was born in Aligarh on 8 December 1875, of a Kashmiri Pandit family, the son of Ambika Prasad Sapru, and grandson of Radha Khrishen Sapru, of the Indian provincial service. He married Durga Devi Madan in 1888; the couple had two daughters and three sons: Prakash Narain Sapru, later a judge of the Allahabad high court, Anand Narain Sapru, of the Indian Civil Service, and Triyugi Narain Sapru, later professor of law at Allahabad University. Sapru's wife died in 1910, and thereafter he remained notoriously shy with women. Much influenced by Professor Andrews, a close follower of John Stuart Mill, he took first-class honours in English at Agra College, in both his bachelor's (1894) and his master's degrees (1895). He also took an LLM at Allahabad University (1895) and an LLD (1902)—only the second person to do so.

Sapru began practising law in Moradabad in 1896, but in 1898 moved to Allahabad where, at 19 Albert Road, he spent the rest of his life. There in 1906 he was admitted as an advocate, making him the equal of members of the English bar. In due course he became arguably the most distinguished lawyer in India, appearing not only in Allahabad and Lucknow, but in Calcutta, Madras, and Lahore, and was in frequent demand by Indian landlords and princes too. He was at the same time a considerable scholar in Persian, and a leading devotee of Urdu poetry, language, and literature.

From an early age Sapru was interested in the Indian National Congress, and by his own lights remained a staunch Indian nationalist. He first spoke at the Madras Congress in 1908, and was closely involved with the 1910 Congress in Allahabad. In 1913 he was nominated to the United Provinces' legislative council and there led a campaign for a governor-in-council to bring the province into line with Bengal, Madras, and Bombay. In 1914 he became president of the United Provinces' provincial political conference, and in 1916 played a major part in the Lucknow pact between Congress and the Muslim League which sought to reconcile Hindu and Muslim political interests. In that year he was elected to the central legislative council. By now he was seen by some younger nationalists such as Jawaharlal Nehru as their potential leader. Energetic in seeking further constitutional reforms, he was incensed at the government's treatment of Annie Besant. He was, however, substantially assuaged by the Montagu declaration of 1917 promising India eventual self-government, and by the Montagu–Chelmsford reforms which ensued. While vehement in his opposition to the Rowlatt Acts of 1919, he joined with other leading 'moderates' to break away from the Congress in 1918 to form what became the National Liberal Federation to work the Montagu–Chelmsford reforms to the full. By the time of M. K. Gandhi's accession to Congress's leadership he was thus no longer a member.

While always retaining a high personal regard for Gandhi, the deep commitments he had now developed to the rule of law, and to pursuing British precedents for the attainment of self-government without revolutionary

Sir Tej Bahadur Sapru (1875–1949), by Walter Stoneman, 1935

upheaval, Sapru found it impossible to join Gandhi in non-co-operation and civil disobedience. Instead he served on the Feetham committee on the allocation of governmental functions, appeared before the joint select committee of the British parliament on Indian reforms in 1919, and in 1920 accepted appointment as law member of the viceroy's council. There, apart from instituting some notable reforms, for example by removing racial distinctions in the criminal procedure code, he not only successfully urged the viceroy, Lord Reading, not to arrest Gandhi until he had called off his non-co-operation campaign, but late in 1921 played the pivotal role in persuading Reading to call a round-table conference which, if Gandhi had been more adroit, could well have initiated further reforms that did not come for another fifteen years.

Sapru retired from the viceroy's council in 1922 and was made a KCIE. In 1923 he was a delegate to the Imperial Conference (where he had a notable clash with General Smuts over the rights of South Africa's Indian minority) and became (as again in 1927) president of the National Liberal Federation. During the 1920s he was more intimately involved than anyone else in discussions about Indian constitutional reforms, and became as he remained the greatest constitutional expert on either the Indian or the British side. Closely involved with Besant's commonwealth of India proposals in 1923, he served in 1924 on the government-appointed Muddiman reforms inquiry committee and contributed to its important minority report.

Along with so many others Sapru was outraged by the appointment of the all-white Simon commission on Indian constitutional reforms in 1927, and not only supported its boycott, but played a large part in drafting the Indian riposte, the Nehru report of 1928. He was then foremost in persuading the next viceroy to make the Irwin declaration of October 1929 promising further constitutional reform and a round-table conference in London. Despite an initial success he was twice frustrated, however, in persuading Congress's leaders to attend the conference, first by their launching of civil disobedience in March 1930, and then, in association with M. R. Jayakar, in the Yeravda gaol discussions with Gandhi and the Nehrus the following summer. He and a good many others none the less went to London, where Sapru was pre-eminent in winning the Indian princes' support for an Indian federation, thereby securing the British government's support for further constitutional reforms. On returning to India he and his associates were rewarded by the Gandhi–Irwin pact of March 1931 under which civil disobedience was suspended and Gandhi agreed to attend a second round-table conference in London later that year. That conference, however, was fruitless, deeply riven by communal issues (which led Sapru to resign from the Liberal Party for its involvement in these), and upon Gandhi's return to India civil disobedience was renewed.

During 1932 Sapru played a principal part in negotiating the Poona pact with Gandhi and a range of Hindu orthodox and untouchable leaders that sought to resolve the constitutional position of India's untouchables. He was to the fore, too, among those successfully denouncing the apparent decision of the British to abandon the conference method for framing constitutional reforms, and attended both a third conference and the discussions of the joint select committee on Indian constitutional reforms, which finally led to the Government of India Act of 1935. For his major contributions to these Sapru was sworn of the privy council, but in India found himself relegated to the political sidelines. From there he was brought back in 1941, not least by Gandhi, to act as a mediator between Congress and the Muslim League, and between Congress and the viceroy, Lord Linlithgow. His principal instrument was a series of non-party conferences over which he presided for several years. He failed in 1941 to persuade Linlithgow to countenance an Indian national government which for the duration of the Second World War would be 'responsible to the Crown', but by dispatching an open telegram to Churchill early in 1942 he succeeded brilliantly in precipitating Sir Stafford Cripps's mission to India and its accompanying promise that India would have independence at the end of the war. He was considerably less successful with Jinnah and the Muslim League, despite one final effort through the Sapru report of 1945 which epitomized all his constitutional expertise.

Sapru appeared briefly in 1946 for the defence in the Indian National Army trials, but by then had Parkinson's disease. Had he been well he would very probably have chaired the Indian constituent assembly. Although he had for many years been spurned by Jawaharlal Nehru, they were touchingly reconciled at the end. With India independent under the rule of law and a parliamentary democracy, Sapru died well content, despite his dismay at India's partition, in Allahabad on 20 January 1949.

D. A. Low

Sources M. Kumar, *Sir Tej Bahadur Sapru: a political biography* (1981) • *Commemoration volume compiled and published by the bar council of Delhi on the birth centenary of Dr. Tej Bahadur Sapru* (1976) • D. A. Low, 'The government of India and the first non-co-operation movement, 1920–1922', in R. Kumar, *Essays on Gandhian politics* (1971) • D. A. Low, 'Sir Tej Bahadur Sapru and the first Round Table Conference', *Soundings in modern South Asian history*, ed. D. A. Low (1968), 294–329 • D. A. Low, 'The mediator's moment: Sir Tej Bahadur Sapru and the antecedents to the Cripps mission to India, 1940–1942', *Perspectives on imperialism and decolonisation: essays in honour of A. F. Madden*, ed. R. F. Holland and G. Rizvi (1984), 145–64 • R. Hooja, *Crusader for self-rule: Tej Bahadur Sapru and the Indian national movement: life and selected letters* (1999)
Archives National Archives of India, New Delhi • National Library of India, Calcutta | BL OIOC, letters to Lord Reading, MSS Eur. E 238, F 118 • Bodl. Oxf., corresp. with Lord Sankey • Bodl. Oxf., letters to E. J. Thompson • PRO, corresp. with Sir Stafford Cripps, CAB127/149
Likenesses W. Stoneman, photograph, 1935, NPG [*see illus.*]

Saravia, Adrian (1532–1613), Church of England clergyman and theologian, was born early in January 1532 at Hesdin in Artois, the son of Christopher de Saravia (*d.* 1572), a native of Spain, and Elisabeth Boulengier (*d.* 1578) from Artois. Saravia probably entered the Franciscan convent in Hesdin, and moved with the friars to St Omer when the former town was razed. About 1553 he was influenced by Lutheranism through German officers stationed in St Omer, and by Calvinist ideas through contact with Jacques Taffin. Calvinism prevailed, and Taffin was accused of assisting Saravia's flight from his convent in 1557. Saravia crossed to England early in 1559 but later returned to the Netherlands and in July saw Philip II's entry into Ghent. In 1561 Saravia married Catherine d'Allez from St Omer, whose father had been executed for his beliefs; they had one son, Thomas (burial recorded on 28 December 1588), and an unknown number of daughters.

On 22 June 1561 Saravia joined the Dutch church in London. As a member of the consistory, he played a prominent role in the community, preached, and was involved in a theological dispute. However, he retained his links with the Netherlands; by January 1562 he was minister to the Walloon congregation in Antwerp, and with Jean de Marnix, lord of Toulouse, he founded the Walloon church in Brussels. Saravia seems to have been well acquainted with the *Confessio Belgica* of Guy de Biès at an early stage, and in the spring of 1562 used his family connections to draw it to the attention of William of Orange and the high nobility.

When Elizabeth College was founded on Guernsey in September 1563, Saravia took up the post of headmaster, and in October 1565 he was appointed to assist Nicolas Baudouin as a minister in St Peter Port. But he continued to spend time in the Netherlands: he attended a synod at Antwerp in May 1566 and probably remained there until the iconoclastic fury of August and September led him to return to Guernsey with his parents. However, with William of Orange's attack on the Netherlands in 1568, Saravia returned to serve as his chaplain and in September published *A Heartfelt Desire*, which attacked Alva's tyranny.

Saravia had received letters of denization in February 1568 and at the end of 1571 became headmaster of the grammar school in Southampton. He may have arrived in the town earlier, as his parents were admitted to the Lord's supper of the French church in 1569. Saravia's students in Southampton included the linguist Robert Ashley, the Hebraist Nicholas Fuller, Francis Markham, Edward Reynolds, and the poet Joshua Sylvester; he probably also assisted Walerand Thevelin, the minister of the French church. However, he retained his links with the Low Countries and in 1572 served as a minister at Flushing, probably arriving in August, a few months after the Sea Beggars captured the town.

During the summer of 1578 Saravia resigned his headmastership as a result of appeals for his services from the continent. He was reluctant to take up a post at Kortrijk, and by October 1580 was living in Ghent. Catholicism had been banned there in July 1578, leaving Calvinism as the dominant force. Saravia served as one of the inspectors of the newly established theological school and played an active role in the religious affairs of Flanders and the presbyterian classis of Ghent; he was the chairman of the provincial synod which met in Ghent in March 1582. With Ghent threatened by Spanish forces, however, in November 1582 Saravia took up a post as minister in the relative safety of Leiden.

During his time at Leiden, Saravia continued to play an active role in the affairs of the Reformed church and in debates over church orders and the issue of the ownership of church goods. He was also involved in the disputes with Caspar Coolhaes and Dirk Volckertsz Coornhert. He was active with the Walloon congregation in Leiden and in 1584 chaired the meeting of the classical assembly of the Walloon congregations of Walcheren and Holland. Saravia had matriculated at the University of Leiden in February 1583 and on 13 August 1584 was given a permanent appointment at the university, as professor of theology. In February 1585 he became rector magnificus and was reappointed in 1586.

In January 1586 Saravia welcomed the earl of Leicester, who had been appointed governor-general in the Netherlands following the treaty of Nonsuch. Saravia was a keen supporter of Leicester and frequently advised him on church matters, and by May 1586 there were complaints that he was too frequently absent at the earl's headquarters at Utrecht. Saravia also provided information and advice on political issues, and having become implicated in an abortive scheme to deliver Leiden into Leicester's hands, in November 1587 was dismissed from his post as professor. Although Saravia pleaded his innocence, in January 1588, with eight others, he was sentenced to death *in absentia* and his goods were confiscated; however, he had already escaped to England. He was embittered by his treatment as well as by the lack of support he received, and attempted through his correspondence during 1588 to seek redress and to clear his name. But there is no evidence that he returned to the Netherlands again.

On 24 January 1588 Sir Francis Walsingham appointed Saravia rector of Tatenhill in Staffordshire. This rural parish provided a contrast with the academic life of Leiden, but in the spring of 1590 he nevertheless published his *De diversis ministrorum evangelii gradibus*, a treatise defending episcopal church government on the grounds of being divinely instituted, and attacking the advanced Calvinism of Theodore Beza. He argued that episcopal government had been ordained by God and was confirmed by scripture. However, Saravia was forced to admit that there might be exceptional circumstances, such as he had experienced in the Netherlands, where the bishops had been necessarily overthrown. In 1592 Beza responded to Saravia's attack, but in his *Defensio tractionis de diversis ministrorum evangelii gradibus* (1594) Saravia elaborated further upon his original arguments. As an apologist for episcopacy, he joined such divines as Richard Bancroft, Thomas Bilson, and Matthew Sutcliffe in asserting the apostolic origins of English church government against the challenges of the presbyterians. Saravia had also defended the political establishment against the views expressed in Beza's *Du droit des magistrats*, publishing his own *De imperandi authoritate et christiana obedientia* in 1593. He launched a further attack on Beza in his *Examen tractatus de episcoporum triplici genere*, published with other of his works in 1610.

Saravia was appointed a prebendary at Gloucester Cathedral on 22 October 1591, but did not attend a chapter meeting until March 1595 and resigned later that year. At the end of 1595 he left Tatenhill, having been collated on 6 December to the sixth prebend in Canterbury Cathedral by Archbishop Whitgift; he had also been appointed vicar of Lewisham. His theological views initially gave rise to controversy, but he proved to be an active member of the cathedral chapter, regularly attending meetings and serving for a period as vice-dean. He also took an interest in the affairs of the French church in Canterbury, which his wife had joined, and occasionally preached at their services.

In December 1601 Saravia took up his appointment to a canonry in Westminster Abbey, the reversion to which he had originally been granted in 1594, and was able to play an active role in chapter affairs while retaining his position at Canterbury. Following the 1604 Hampton Court conference, he was one of the team of scholars at Westminster under Lancelot Andrewes, charged with the new translation of the Bible. This work kept Saravia in London during 1608 and 1609. He also worked on other theological projects in his later years, writing *De sacra eucharistia* about 1605–6 and a tract against the Jesuit Jacob Gretser in 1610. He relinquished Lewisham about 1604 and in February 1610 became rector of Great Chart, Kent.

Saravia's wife died on 1 February 1606 and was buried in Canterbury Cathedral. At the end of 1606 he married Marguerite (1575/6–1615), the daughter of John Wijts. After his death, on 15 January 1613 at Canterbury, Saravia was buried on the 19th with his first wife, and his widow erected a memorial inscription. The inventory of his goods records that he left £1366 3s. 1d., £100 of books, and 'upon bonds and bils, is it shalbe received: £914' (Nijenhuis, 369).

Andrew Spicer

Sources W. Nijenhuis, *Adrianus Saravia (c.1532–1613): Dutch Calvinist, first reformed defender of the English episcopal church order on the basis of jus divinum* (1980) · A. Spicer, *The French-speaking Reformed community and their church in Southampton* (1997) · H. M. Godfray, ed., *Registre des baptesmes, mariages et mortz, et jeusnes de léglise wallonne et des isles de Jersey, Guernesey, Serq, Origny, etc.*, Huguenot Society of London, 4 (1890) · P. Lake, *Anglicans and puritans? Presbyterianism and English conformist thought from Whitgift to Hooker* (1988) · P. Collinson, 'The protestant cathedral, 1541–1660', *A history of Canterbury Cathedral, 598–1982*, ed. P. Collinson and others (1995), 154–203, esp. 179–80
Wealth at death £1366 3s. 1d., plus books with shelves, value £100, also 'bonds and bils' of £914: Nijenhuis, *Adrianus Saravia*, 368–9

Sargant, Sir Charles Henry (1856–1942), judge, was born in London on 20 April 1856, the son of Henry Sargant, a barrister and conveyancer of Lincoln's Inn, and his wife, Catherine Emma, daughter of Samuel Beale, at one time member of parliament for Derby. Both his parents came from families well known in the midlands.

According to family legend, Sargant was said to have been a precocious child, who taught himself to read at the age of three. Throughout life he remained a great reader, and had an exceptional memory. On entering Rugby School he was placed in the lower fifth, where he soon began to shine, being equally good at classics and mathematics. He became head of the school, won most of the open prizes, and gained a leaving exhibition and an open scholarship at New College, Oxford. There, in spite of his uneven health, he was placed in the first class of the honours list in classical moderations (1876), in the second class in mathematical moderations (1877), and the first class in *literae humaniores* (1879). His delicate health meant that he could not take part in robust sports, but he played billiards for Oxford, and became a keen fisherman and a steady golfer.

After leaving university, he spent a year with Beale & Co., solicitors of Birmingham and London, who were afterwards regular clients, and then read as a pupil in the chambers of the well-known conveyancer Edward Parker Wolstenholme. He was called to the bar by Lincoln's Inn in 1882. After building up a conveyancing practice he began to engage in court work. Although in his later years at the bar he refused conveyancing work, he nevertheless regarded it as an indispensable part of a chancery barrister's training, and was a fine draftsman himself. Two of his pupils, Frederick Liddell and William Graham-Harrison, attained the office of first parliamentary counsel to the Treasury.

Sargant did not look like a typical lawyer, with his large tawny moustache, full complexion, and benevolent blue eyes. Behind these, however, lay a quick and accurate brain, and a retentive memory, all allied to common sense and breadth of view. 'Looking at the matter broadly' was a phrase he often used. He never took silk—perhaps wisely.

Not being particularly ambitious, nor particularly industrious, he never allowed his legal work to overwhelm him; there were other things in life for which a reasonable amount of leisure was desirable.

In 1900, in middle age, Sargant married Amelia Julia, eldest daughter of Dion Gambardella, civil engineer; they had one son and two daughters. In 1908 he was appointed junior counsel to the Treasury in equity matters. This made life more strenuous; but in the same year he was made a bencher of Lincoln's Inn. He did not have to wait long for promotion. In 1913 he was appointed a judge of the High Court. He made an admirable Chancery judge, having the necessary learning and the rarer qualities of common sense and quickness of mind. His judgments stood the test of review in the Court of Appeal, which he joined in 1923. He was knighted in 1913 and sworn a member of the privy council in 1923. In 1919 he was elected an honorary fellow of New College, Oxford.

Soon after the First World War Sargant was appointed chairman of a royal commission to make awards to inventors whose work had been useful in the war. The commission's first report, which Sargant drafted himself, laid down the principles on which such awards should be made. He regretted that his appointment to the Court of Appeal made it necessary for him to give up this work. In 1928, at the age of seventy-two, he resigned as a lord justice of appeal. He served for a while as chairman of the Board of Trade committee on patent law and practice, and sat occasionally on the judicial committee of the privy council. Towards the end of his life he became increasingly lame through arthritis, and, as in his earliest days, he found his chief resource in books. He died at his home, 21 Madingley Road, Cambridge, on 23 July 1942. He was survived by his wife.

P. W. B. WILBRAHAM, rev. HUGH MOONEY

Sources The Times (28 July 1942) · CGPLA Eng. & Wales (1942)
Likenesses Elliott & Fry, photograph, NPG · W. Rothenstein, chalk drawing, New College, Oxford · photograph, repro. in The Times
Wealth at death £39,514 19s. 10d.: probate, 14 Nov 1942, CGPLA Eng. & Wales

Sargant, Ethel (1863–1918), botanist, was born at 45 Regent's Park Road, London, on 28 October 1863, the third daughter in the family of three daughters and three sons of Henry Sargant, barrister and conveyancer of Lincoln's Inn, and his wife, Catherine Emma (d. 1912), daughter of Samuel Beale, MP for Derby. One of her brothers was Sir Charles Henry *Sargant. She was educated at North London Collegiate School and, from 1881, at Girton College, Cambridge. She obtained a second class in part one of the natural sciences tripos (1884) and a third class in part two (1885).

Ethel Sargant spent one year (1892–3) at the Jodrell Laboratory at Kew Gardens, studying under D. H. Scott. There she gained valuable training in research methods, especially in plant anatomy. From 1893 onwards she worked at home, first in a laboratory built in the grounds of her mother's house in Reigate, and later at her home in Girton village, Cambridge. For some years she took care of her mother and an invalid sister. From time to time she acted as research adviser to the Cambridge students who came to her laboratory for instruction. She was elected to an honorary fellowship of Girton College in 1913. Ethel Sargant carried out research in two separate areas—cytology and anatomical morphology. Her earliest work in cytology concerned the presence of centrosomes in higher plants; she then moved to a general study of oögenesis and spermatogenesis in Lilium martagon. Her most important results, demonstrating the existence of the synaptic phase in living cells, were published in the Annals of Botany in 1896 and 1897.

Constant use of the high power microscope proved a strain on Sargant's eyes, and this was part of the reason that she began to concentrate on anatomical and phylogenetic questions. Her best-known work concerned the anatomy of seedlings. Her theory of the origin of monocotyledons, put forward in 1903, was based on her extensive investigations of the anatomical structure of very young monocotyledonous seedlings. She offered a new interpretation of the relationship between monocotyledons and dicotyledons, suggesting that both had evolved from a common ancestral stock, and that the single seed-leaf in the monocotyledon was homologous to the pair in the dicotyledon. The implications of these findings were discussed in three major papers published between 1903 and 1908.

Ethel Sargant was elected a fellow of the Linnean Society in 1904, and was the first woman to serve on its council. At the 1913 Birmingham meeting of the British Association for the Advancement of Science she was elected president of section K (botany), thus becoming the first woman ever to preside over a section. Though primarily a research botanist, she gave a course on the ancestry of the angiosperms at the University of London in 1907. She published over twenty papers. All her writings are characterized by an outstanding clarity and vigour of presentation, a reflection of her keen interest in English literature. As president of the Federation of University Women she gave much time near the end of her life to compiling the register of university women for war work. She died, unmarried, on 16 January 1918 at 4 Clifton Place, Sidmouth, Devon, after a short illness, and was buried at Sidmouth.

MARY R. S. CREESE, rev.

Sources Nature, 100 (1917–18), 428–9 · E. N. Thomas, Proceedings of the Linnean Society of London, 130th session (1917–18), 41–2 · Annals of Botany, 32 (1918), i–v · New Phytologist, 18 (March–April 1919), 120–28 · CGPLA Eng. & Wales (1918) · M. R. S. Creese, Ladies in the laboratory? American and British women in science, 1800–1900 (1998) · R. Schmid, 'Agnes Arber, née Robertson (1879–1960): fragments of her life', Annals of Botany, 88 (2001), 1105–28
Wealth at death £31,932 6s. 10d.: probate, 14 May 1918, CGPLA Eng. & Wales

Sargant, Thomas (1905–1988), law reformer, was born in Highgate, Middlesex, on 17 August 1905, the fourth child in the family of five daughters and three sons of Norman Thomas Carr Sargant, commodity merchant, and his wife, Alice Rose, daughter of William Davies Walters, a Methodist minister. Tom (as he was always known) was brought up in a household committed to devout Methodism, progressive politics (his father was four times a Liberal candidate), and high moral principles. He inherited all these commitments. He was educated at Highgate School, where he became head boy, won the public schools' mile, and gained a scholarship to Cambridge. However, his father got into financial difficulties and Sargant offered to join him in the family business instead of taking up his place at Cambridge. Eventually the business collapsed and Sargant went to work in the Royal Mint refinery, where he later became commercial manager. He left the refinery in 1947 and held various jobs in the metal trade until at the end of 1955 he became ill with tuberculosis.

In 1941 Sargant had published *These Things Shall Be*, a plea for a new and more just social order. The book came to the attention of Sir Richard Acland, who invited Sargant to join the Christian socialist movement, Common Wealth, which Acland was launching. Sargant stood for Common Wealth in a by-election in 1943 and in the general election of 1945. He then joined the Labour Party, for which he stood in the 1950 and 1955 elections, again without success.

On his recovery from illness, Sargant found himself with no qualifications, no job, and no wish to return to the City. In November 1956 Peter Benenson, then a young barrister, asked Sargant to help in setting up an all-party group of lawyers to send observers to the trial of the leaders of the Hungarian uprising and to the treason trial in South Africa. Benenson persuaded leading lawyers from the three main political parties to convert their *ad hoc* group into a permanent organization for the protection of human rights and the rule of law, which was formally established under the name Justice in June 1957, and became the British section of the International Commission of Jurists. Sargant's offer to act as the part-time secretary of Justice, at a salary of £500 a year, was accepted.

Sargant remained the secretary of Justice for twenty-five years, until 1982. He had no legal training, but his concern with the legal process had been stimulated by his own experiences as a defendant in a libel action, in which he eventually succeeded, in the face of great difficulties, against a plaintiff supported by the General Medical Council. His sympathy for the underdog led him to begin taking up—contrary to instructions—the cases of individual prisoners who wrote to Justice complaining of wrongful convictions. His disregard of orders proved fortunate both for the prisoners whom he helped (he was able to secure the release of some twenty-five of them) and for Justice. Sargant's casework kept Justice firmly involved with the practical realities of the legal system and gave it an unrivalled expertise in the causes of miscarriages of justice and the problems of correcting them. He helped to make miscarriages of justice a matter of public concern through his co-operation with the BBC in producing a series of television programmes on the subject under the title *Rough Justice*.

Sargant was also actively involved in Justice's work on law reform. This was mainly achieved through reports prepared by expert committees, but he was influential in choosing the subjects, selecting the chairmen and members of the committees, and sometimes guiding their discussions. He was in no way overawed by the very distinguished lawyers, such as Lord Gardiner, Sir John Foster, and Lord Shawcross, who chaired the council of Justice. He was particularly proud of the part which Justice reports and his own efforts had played in the creation in 1967 of the post of ombudsman (parliamentary commissioner for administration) and the extension of the ombudsman system into other fields; in the setting up of the Criminal Injuries Compensation Board; and in reforming the system of appeals in criminal cases. He also wrote, jointly, *More Rough Justice* (1985) and *Criminal Trials: the Search for Truth* (1986). He was appointed OBE in 1966, was awarded an honorary LLM by Queen's University, Belfast, in 1977, and sat for many years as a JP in Hampstead.

Sargant looked like a shabby eagle. Tall, angular, and untidy, he was usually covered in cigarette ash. On 7 September 1929 he married Marie Anna Hlouskova (1899–1991), daughter of František Hloušek, shoemaker. They were divorced in 1942, and in that year he married Dorothy (*b.* 1903), daughter of William Lattimer, headmaster. Sargant had two daughters from his first marriage and a son from his second. He died of lung cancer in Highgate on 26 June 1988 and was buried in Highgate cemetery. A memorial service was held at the Temple Church, London, in October 1988.   WILLIAM GOODHART, *rev.*

Sources autobiography, priv. coll. · *The Times* (28 June 1988) · *The Times* (21 Oct 1988) · *The Independent* (28 June 1988) · personal knowledge (1996) · private information (1996) · *CGPLA Eng. & Wales* (1988)
Archives Amnesty International, London, transcription of interview · U. Hull, Justice archive
Likenesses S. Schmolle, portrait, 1970, priv. coll.
Wealth at death under £70,000: probate, 17 Oct 1988, *CGPLA Eng. & Wales*

Sargant, William Lucas (1809–1889), educational reformer and political economist, was born at King's Norton, Worcestershire, the son of William Sargant and his wife, Elizabeth. He was baptized at St Philip's, Birmingham on 25 January 1810. His father was a military arms manufacturer in Edmund Street and Whittall Street, Birmingham, supplying the 'African trade'. He had two sisters, Sarah and Elizabeth. Sargant was educated at the Hazlewood School, Edgbaston, which was run for many years by Thomas Wright Hill, and subsequently by his sons Rowland Hill and Matthew Davenport Hill. In 1832 he entered Trinity College, Cambridge, but left within two years to join his father's business. On 11 November 1835 he married, at Edgbaston, Maria Redfern, with whom he had a son, William Sargant (*b.* 1839), who was admitted to Trinity College, Cambridge in 1858, and two daughters. Sargant took an active interest in local affairs in Birmingham, becoming a JP in 1849, serving on the town council, and as a governor of King Edward's School, Birmingham, where he helped to open up the oligarchy which governed the school. He was especially prominent in schemes to improve elementary education, including the Birmingham Education Association, founded in 1857. In the same year he encouraged the establishment of university local examinations in the city. In 1867 he published an account of the progress of elementary education, exposing regional variations in literacy (*Journal of the Statistical Society*, 30, 1867, 80–137). In 1870 he helped to promote the National Education League, of which he became chairman. He was chairman of Birmingham school board from 1870 to 1873. As a churchman he advocated religious teaching in elementary schools, and found himself bitterly opposed by an energetic minority of the members of the league; but he held his own in a long and severe struggle. In 1879 he retired from business, and he died at his home, 1 Rotton Park Road, Edgbaston, Birmingham, on 2 November 1889, leaving a widow (presumably a second wife), Theodosia.

Sargant studied intelligently all political and economic questions, and brought to their examination the practical experience drawn from business. In his published writings those who agreed and those who disagreed with his views alike recognized his sagacity and fairness. His chief publications were: *The Science of Social Opulence* (1856); *Economy of the Labouring Classes* (1857); *Social Innovators and their Schemes* (1858); *Robert Owen and his Social Philosophy* (1860); *Recent Political Economy* (1867); *Apology for Sinking Funds* (1868); *Essays by a Birmingham Manufacturer* (4 vols., 1869–72); *Taxation Past, Present, and Future* (1874); and *Inductive Political Economy* (vol. 1, 1887). He also made many contributions to the proceedings of the Statistical Society.

SAMUEL TIMMINS, *rev.* M. C. CURTHOYS

Sources Boase, *Mod. Eng. biog.* · Venn, *Alum. Cant.* · G. R. Searle, *Entrepreneurial politics in mid-Victorian Britain* (1993) · D. I. Allsobrook, *Schools for the shires: the reform of middle-class education in mid-Victorian England* (1986) · *CGPLA Eng. & Wales* (1889) · *IGI* · A. Munden, 'Sarah Sargant's diary', *Warwickshire History* (2000) · census returns, 1851
Wealth at death £1420 4s. 10d.: probate, 19 Dec 1889, *CGPLA Eng. & Wales*

Sargant, William Walters (1907–1988), psychiatrist, was born at Bryanston, The Bank, Highgate Hill, Highgate, Middlesex, on 24 April 1907, the fifth child and second son in a family of eight. He was the son of Norman Thomas Carr Sargant, a devout Methodist and a wealthy metal broker who later lost his money, and his wife, Alice Rose Walters. Five of his uncles were Methodist preachers and his younger brother became bishop of Bangalore in India. Sargant lost his faith early but retained the evangelical zeal. He attended St Wilfrid's School, Seaford, and the Leys School, Cambridge, where he spent most of his time playing football. Academically he was above average but not outstanding. Sargant read medicine at St John's College, Cambridge, where he used his sporting talents to meet influential people. He became president of the Cambridge University Medical Society and kept a file called 'Autograph letters of eminent medical men'. He won a 'football' scholarship to St Mary's Hospital, London, where he became captain of rugby and expanded his list of distinguished acquaintances.

Sargant qualified MRCS and LRCP in 1930 and obtained his Cambridge MB degree in 1933; he also held various

William Walters Sargant (1907–1988), by Edward Irvine Halliday, 1967

house jobs at St Mary's. At the age of only twenty-five he was appointed medical superintendent of St Mary's with 'complete control' over admissions, beds, junior doctors, and nurses, and seemed likely to be appointed to the staff as a consultant physician, which was his ambition. To do this he needed to conduct research and publish papers, a venture which brought further success and then disaster. Sargant developed a largely spurious idea about the treatment of recalcitrant cases of pernicious anaemia and published papers recommending it in both *The Lancet* and the *British Medical Journal* (with both of whose editors he had become friendly). His work was praised by uncritical seniors but was eventually discredited by the real experts in the field. About 1934 Sargant became depressed to the point of being mentally ill, spent time as a patient in a mental hospital, and became unacceptable as a future teaching-hospital physician. Sargant suffered from depression all his life, and treated himself with a variety of drugs.

In the mental hospital Sargant became angry about the state of patients with chronic mental illness who were housed in the back wards of the hospital—untreated, uncared for, and ignored. He turned to psychiatry and was probably the only prominent psychiatrist in the twentieth century to express concern about the suffering of chronically mentally ill people, though he confined his interest largely to those of 'previously good personality'; his autobiography, *The Unquiet Mind* (1967), reveals the zeal with which he set about his mission. He obtained a post at the Maudsley Hospital, London, under Edward Mapother, and devoted the rest of his life to trying to prove that psychiatry was a branch of clinical medicine, not a 'metaphysical' exercise. Sargant was enthusiastic in using the new physical treatments in psychiatry—lobotomy (leucotomy), electro-convulsive therapy (ECT), and psychoactive drugs. He always disliked and despised any form of 'talking cure', though he often practised psychotherapy quietly and skilfully himself. His philosophy did not include self-exploration either for himself or for his patients.

In 1938 Sargant was awarded a Rockefeller travelling fellowship to study in the United States. He returned to Britain at the outbreak of the Second World War, which he spent working on the outskirts of London at Sutton Emergency Hospital (later the Belmont Hospital), a centre for psychologically disturbed and injured servicemen. Here he used leucotomies, ECT, acute sedation with Pentothal and Amytal, and ether abreactions to treat patients. The clinical director, Eliot Slater, approved of Sargant's ideas and added many of his own. Together they wrote *An Introduction to Physical Methods of Treatment in Psychiatry* (1944), which became a standard textbook and ran into five editions. However 'the early extravagant claims for the efficacy of these methods, particularly in schizophrenia, failed to be substantiated' (*BMJ*, 24 Sept 1988, 789). Sargant was largely unsupervised in what he did and during these years he worked out and refined the techniques of physical treatments in mental illness for which he became both famous and infamous. On 10 August 1940 Sargant married Dorothy Margaret Katz Heriot Glen (*b.* 1919/20), daughter of Heriot Riddock Glen, a company director; there were no children.

After the war Sargant returned to the United States and was impressed by Walter Freeman's new modified leucotomy technique. He also became deeply and permanently interested in the 'brainwashing techniques' he saw in some of the churches in the south, which he related to the process of religious conversion. Over many years he made a series of films on the subject. These were later lodged in the Museum of Mankind in London. In 1948 Sargant was appointed consultant psychiatrist to St Thomas's Hospital, London, where he remained until his retirement, apart from a period of illness from tuberculosis. He spent his convalescence in Majorca, where he became friends with Robert Graves, who encouraged him to write his influential best-seller about brainwashing, *Battle for the Mind* (1957). Graves corrected the book and also contributed to it.

Determined to be a physician rather than a psychiatrist, Sargant called himself a 'physician in psychological medicine'. He believed passionately that mental illness was a form of physical disorder and he promoted the cause of physical treatments in psychiatry. He always extolled the virtues of dramatic and often extreme treatments and denigrated psychoanalysis and psychotherapy: 'an ounce of phenobarbitone, or rather some modern tranquilizers, may be worth more than a hundredweight of persuasive talk' (*BMJ*, 24 Sept 1988, 789). Much of Sargant's success may be attributed more to his therapeutic fervour and dominating personality than to his methods of treatment.

He boasted that he could cure cases of schizophrenia, believed strongly in ECT and leucotomy, did everything he could to ensure that psychiatry was part of general (internal) medicine, and predicted that by the year 1990 mental illness would have ceased to exist. In 1956–7 he was president of the section of psychiatry at the Royal Society of Medicine. He gave long service to the Royal Medico-Psychological Association as its registrar but was opposed to its proposed transformation into the Royal College of Psychiatrists because he wanted psychiatry to remain part of the Royal College of Physicians. However, once the establishment of the new college had become inevitable, he was eager to be its first president and was deeply disappointed when he was not elected.

Sargant was described as 'the most important figure in post-war psychiatry … huge by any standards in stature and charisma' (Munk, *Roll*). Of all twentieth-century psychiatrists he was one of the best loved and most hated. He died on 27 August 1988 at Cobley House, East Woodyates, Wiltshire, and was buried on 2 September at St Rumbold's Church, Pentridge, Salisbury. He was survived by his wife. A thanksgiving service was held at St Marylebone parish church, London, on 10 November 1988.   ANN DALLY

Sources W. Sargant, *The unquiet mind: the autobiography of a physician in psychological medicine* (1967) · personal knowledge (2004) · private information (2004) [Peggy Sargant] · *The Times* (31 Aug 1988) · *The Independent* (5 Sept 1988) · *The Guardian* (2 Sept 1988) · *BMJ* (24 Sept 1988), 789–90 · *The Lancet* (24 Sept 1988) · *St Thomas's Hospital Gazette*, 65 (1967), 18–23 · *World Medicine* (18 June 1975) · Munk, *Roll* · b. cert. · m. cert. · d. cert. · *Medical Directory* (1962)
Archives Wellcome L., corresp. and papers | FILM Wellcome L., videos
Likenesses E. I. Halliday, oils, 1967, priv. coll.; repro. in Sargant, *Unquiet mind*, frontispiece [*see illus.*]
Wealth at death £753,558: probate, 30 Jan 1989, *CGPLA Eng. & Wales*

Sargeaunt, John (1857–1922), classical scholar and teacher, was born at Irthlingborough, Northamptonshire, on 12 August 1857, the eldest son of John Barneby Sargeaunt, barrister, and his wife, Elizabeth, daughter of the Revd William Drake, curate-in-charge of St Giles's Church, Northampton. He was educated at Bedford grammar school under James Surtees Phillpotts, and in 1876 went up with a classical exhibition to University College, Oxford, of which George Granville Bradley was then master and Samuel Henry Butcher senior classical tutor. He obtained a first class in classical moderations (1878) and a second class in *literae humaniores* (1880). He was president of the Union Society in 1881.

On leaving Oxford, Sargeaunt went as a master to Inverness College, and in 1885 became master of the classical sixth form at Felsted School, in Essex. Five years later, on the recommendation of Dr Bradley, then dean of Westminster, Dr William Gunion Rutherford, headmaster of Westminster School, offered Sargeaunt a place on his staff, and in January 1890 Sargeaunt began his work there as master of the classical sixth form. That form was not the highest division in the school, for Westminster preserved the seventh form of Dr Busby's day. Sargeaunt held his post for nearly twenty-nine years with a distinction which made him one of the select company of schoolmasters who enjoy a reputation and a memory far wider than the field of their main work. On his death he was the subject of a leading article in *The Times* (24 March 1922).

Sargeaunt's exceptional capacity as a teacher was founded not only upon the versatility of his learning but also upon the breadth of his tastes. Fisherman, mountaineer, botanist, and gardener, he was also archer, amateur actor, and devotee of the chessboard and bridge table. He was an antiquary and an ardent genealogist. He had a wide and thorough command of Greek and Latin literature, a lifelong passion for poetry, and a skilled and sensitive appreciation of English letters. He was most at home in the eighteenth century. It almost follows that he was first and foremost a Virgilian. The chief of his familiars was Dr Johnson, whose distaste for music he shared, though not his toryism. All Sargeaunt's resources were at the command of a masterly memory, and all contributed copiously to his teaching. It was true in a narrow sense that he taught without method or discipline. He could afford to indulge his unpedagogic aversion from penalties, for he enjoyed an effortless hold upon boys and their interest, and boys were eager to justify his quiet assumption that they were responsible fellow learners. The method was equally free. Sargeaunt taught by digression: there was no saying where the play of illustration, quotation, and parallel, not without dramatic impersonation and declamation at times, might not carry a lesson. It was not a system at work, but a personality, and the end was attained when a boy became fired with the determination to seek out Sargeaunt's treasures for himself.

Sargeaunt was a bachelor and, with his easy, humorous temperament, a clubbable man. He availed himself fully of the social and literary opportunities which London offered. He was a member of the Literary Society, sometime 'prior' of the Johnson Club, and an original member of the Pepys Club. Claiming that 'boys have a right not to be taught by a sexagenarian', he retired at Christmas 1918 to a small house which he had built near Fairwarp in Sussex. He died at Hove on 20 March 1922, and was buried in Brighton cemetery.

Sargeaunt's published output, like that of many who have given their lives to teaching, left too scanty a memorial of his scholarship. His principal works were the *Annals of Westminster School* (1898), an excellent example of lightly borne erudition, and an edition of the restored text of Dryden's *Poems* (1910). His observation of the annual Latin play on the Westminster stage was reflected in the translation and edition of the plays of Terence, which he contributed to the Loeb Classical Library in 1912. He contributed two essays to the Johnson Club *Papers* in 1899, and was joint-editor with George Whale of two volumes of these papers, in 1899 and 1920. He was also the author of *Virgil's Pastorals in English Verse* (1900), an edition of Pope's *Essay on Criticism* (1909), a little book on the *Trees, Shrubs and Plants of Virgil* (1920), a tract on *The Pronunciation of English Words Derived from the Latin* (1920), and of various school textbooks of the

Latin and English classics. At the time of his death he had completed a selection of his poems, posthumously published under the title of *Westminster Verses* (1922), and a translation of the *Odyssey* into English hexameters.

R. M. BARRINGTON-WARD, *rev.* M. C. CURTHOYS

Sources *The Times* (23 March 1922) · *The Times* (24 March 1922) · J. Gow, 'memoir', in J. Sargeaunt, *Westminster verses* (1922) · *The Elizabethan* [magazine of Westminster School] (April 1922) · *The Elizabethan* [magazine of Westminster School] (Nov 1922) · personal knowledge (1937) · L. E. Tanner, *Recollections of a Westminster antiquary* (1969) · J. D. Carleton, *Westminster School: a history* (1965)
Likenesses F. W. Pomeroy, relief panel sculpture, *c.*1924, Westminster School, London

Sargent, Sir (Sidney) Donald (1906–1984), civil servant, was born at Hydes Road, Wednesbury, Staffordshire, on 11 December 1906, son of Sidney George Sargent, who later became manager at the Stewarts and Lloyds steelworks in Wolverhampton, and his wife, Edith Elsie Cox. He was educated at King Edward's School, Birmingham, and at Trinity College, Cambridge, where he held a scholarship and took firsts in both parts of the classical tripos (1926, 1928) and an upper second in part two of the historical tripos (1929). He entered the civil service in 1929 and joined the General Post Office (GPO) as an assistant principal. Here he remained for most of his career. He served as private secretary to the director-general from 1935 to 1937, when he became a principal. Between 1938 and 1941 he was transferred to supervise staff training in the air raid precautions department. However, he returned to the GPO to serve as principal private secretary to the postmaster-general in 1941–4, and was made an assistant secretary in 1944. On 7 October 1944 he married Dorothy Mary (*b.* 1904/5), formerly the wife of James Basil Foster Earle, and daughter of Edward Raven CB, second secretary of the GPO; they had a son.

In 1946 Sargent was transferred to be deputy chief administrative officer in the Allied Control Commission for Germany, but he returned to the GPO again in 1949. He subsequently undertook a series of senior positions in the GPO: director of personnel and accommodation from 1949 to 1953; director of postal services from 1953 to 1955; and deputy director-general from 1955 to 1959. In 1959 he left the GPO for the last time on becoming secretary of the National Assistance Board. In 1966 he became deputy secretary of the newly created Ministry of Social Security and continued as secretary of the National Assistance Board's successor, the Supplementary Benefits Commission. He was made a CB in 1951 and a KBE in 1961, and retired from the civil service in 1968.

Sargent's work in the GPO was always focused on postal services as opposed to communications, and much of his life's work was spent in adapting the service to the enormous expansion of postal trade during this period. He was noted by his colleagues for being thorough and hardworking, and creating a work climate that was inspirational. He was also celebrated for his many personal kindnesses.

At the National Assistance Board, Sargent entered the

more politically sensitive world of administering assistance benefits that provided the safety net for those ineligible for contributory insurance benefits. The sensitivity arose from the fact that assistance benefits were heavily stigmatized in the eyes of the public because they were the direct successor of poor-law relief and were means-tested. He was to play a key role in a major reorganization and destigmatization of this system of social provision. In 1966 the Labour government established a Ministry of Social Security. This brought together the administration of the insurance and assistance systems for the first time in an attempt to lend the respectability of insurance benefits to assistance benefits. The renaming of assistance benefits as supplementary benefits under the administration of the Supplementary Benefits Commission was then accompanied by a new approach which stressed the legal right to benefit, greater publicity to encourage the take-up of these rights, and the simplification of application procedures. He was the key official in the implementation of this major change of policy in the post-war welfare state, and despite his long service at the GPO it is for this phase of his career that he became best-known. He was widely praised for his transformation of the character of the National Assistance Board and in particular its attitude towards claimants; his steely observance of the politically neutral role of the civil servant on an issue which was hotly debated by the political parties; and his conscientiousness in implementing the change in a period of growing economic crisis.

In his private life Sargent was similarly a man of principle, vigour, and generosity. He converted from the Plymouth Brethren to the Church of England, a matter which caused some family upset but upon which he held firm. He loved outdoor pursuits. In his earlier years he was a skilled sailor and mountaineer and he was an enthusiast for driving, golf, and cricket. He lived in Croham Valley Road, South Croydon. His wife was unwell and bedridden for much of their marriage but the family was close and the house remained a fulcrum of endeavour. Family holidays were full of walking, swimming, and winter skiing. He remained throughout his life a man of classical learning, widely read, and a passionate lover of music and the arts. After leaving the civil service he continued to feel a strong sense of public service, chairing the civil service retirement fellowship (1968–74) and the Society of Pension Consultants (1970–81). He was also director of the Abbeyfield Society (1968–70) and a vice-chairman of the Hospital Saving Association from 1970. He died in the Mayday Hospital, Croydon, on 15 April 1984. His memorial service was packed with former colleagues.

JONATHAN BRADBURY

Sources WW · British imperial calendar and civil service list (1929–68) · The Times (24 April 1984) · The Times (16 Aug 1984) · private information (2004) [Anthony Sargent, son] · R. Lowe, The welfare state in Britain since 1945 (1993) · J. Veit-Wilson, 'The national assistance board and the "rediscovery" of poverty', Welfare policy in Britain: the road from 1945, ed. H. Fawcett and R. Lowe (1999) · Burke, Peerage (1967) · b. cert. · m. cert. · Trinity Cam.
Likenesses portrait, priv. coll.

Wealth at death £94,585: probate, 1 Aug 1984, CGPLA Eng. & Wales

Sargent, John (1714–1791), merchant and politician, was born on 12 June 1714, in St Dunstan-in-the-East parish, London, the younger of the two children of John Sargent (1690–1762), a grocer from Plymouth who had moved to London to become the navy's accountant for stores at Deptford, and his wife, Mary Arnell (b. 1694), the daughter of John Arnell of Plymouth (1658–1703). With their father always on the move with the navy, Sargent and his sister spent their childhood in Lisbon, Sheerness, Chatham, and Deptford, where their father worked as a clerk of the survey. Settling in Deptford in 1729, the Sargents apprenticed their son to the firm of Mary Sargent's first cousin George Arnold (1685–1751), a London linen draper.

In Cheapside, Sargent served an apprenticeship from 1729 to 1735, received the freedom of the City in 1735, and for the next sixteen years traded as Arnold's junior partner. In 1749 he married Rosamund (1722–1792), the daughter of John and Elizabeth Chambers. During the 1740s, Sargent brought to the cloth trade an extensive knowledge of naval supply and a desire to enter new geographical regions such as India and Africa, which were opening up to private traders. Prodded by Sargent, the firm became a large wholesaler of India goods and a large supplier to the Company of Merchants Trading to Africa. In addition the firm provisioned Bance Island, a slave trans-shipment factory in Sierra Leone, which Sargent had purchased with Richard Oswald, John Mill, Augustus and John Boyd, and Alexander Grant in 1748.

After Arnold's death in 1751 Sargent continued the business as Sargent, Birch & Co. and, after 1754, as Sargent, Aufrere & Co. when he joined forces with the Huguenot George Aufrere. Thereafter, Sargent's firms were always marked by a large number of partners, having three or four more partners than the typical London two- or three-man firm of the day. Yet, despite these changes, the basic thrust of enterprise persisted. Secure in the inheritance he had received from Arnold and the growth in his African and Indian business, Sargent pushed into new areas in the 1750s. Company politics was one. In 1753 he was elected to the directorate of the Bank of England and, for the next fifteen years, he helped to manage its affairs. Two years later, when the government decided to reinstate the private provision of packet services between England and the Caribbean, Sargent and Richard Stratton (1704–1759) moved into contracting. Reaching an agreement with the Treasury and General Post Office, they signed formal articles on 6 November 1755. As the contract evolved they furnished five boats to carry the mail between Falmouth in Cornwall and the West Indies. From beginning to end, for eight years, the enterprise earned on average a profit of £785 per month, in addition to the money made from other freight.

National parliamentary service was likewise a draw. In 1753, the same year as he joined the bank, Sargent was introduced to Lord Montagu, the patron of Midhurst, Sussex. After proffering Montagu a much needed loan of

£1500, he secured Montagu's recommendation to the constituency. After a contest over the results of the election, Sargent took his seat in the Commons in 1754. In parliament, he cared for the Montagus' business, and he sided with Henry Legge, Thomas Pelham, Thomas Walpole, Charles Yorke, and Richard Stratton, voting with them in support of the government. In 1760, when the Montagus decided to handle their own parliamentary affairs, Sargent found himself without a patron. Unsuccessful in his approaches to the duke of Newcastle and the earl of Bute, he was forced to step down. Not until 1765 did he again take a seat, this time as the representative of West Looe, Cornwall, and with the help of George Grenville. Throughout this term in the house, he remained loyal to Grenville, even after the minister's fall from power in June 1765. He was considered an expert on financial and colonial matters, and used his access to information to apply pressure behind the scenes. He advised administrative departments needing information on the intricacies of commercial practice, like the handling of bills of credit, and served as the agent of both Pennsylvania (1760–66) and New York (1765–6). Ultimately, however, Sargent disliked the work of a party politician and, unwilling to succumb to 'the venality of the times', he voluntarily stepped down in 1768.

The last years of his public service were dominated by a large-scale speculation in American lands, a fitting preoccupation for one of Benjamin Franklin's closest friends in Great Britain. Almost from its inception in 1766, Sargent was involved in the Illinois Company, which came to be called the Walpole Company, a concern for settling lands west of the Appalachian crest which he was lured into by Franklin. It took two years to organize the company and even more time to win a grant for 2.4 million acres. Not until August 1772 did the privy council issue the Walpole Company with an order for establishing such a colony west and south of Pennsylvania, but completion of the project was cut short by American independence.

The American War of Independence shattered Sargent's dreams of overseas speculation, in much the same way as it made his American cloth trade less profitable and attractive. As one of the oldest and most respected merchants in the transatlantic shipping community, Sargent struggled to keep his business intact through the calamitous 1770s, but it was an uphill fight. Before the end of the war, he expected to remain 'in the track', but his plans changed as he began to realize the significance of the geographical shift in transatlantic trade. He wound up his adventures in overseas shipping and turned over the affairs of the firm to his younger partners. He died at Tunbridge Wells on 20 September 1791. His wife died the following year, and was buried alongside him in St Margaret's churchyard, in Halstead. He left his business and one-third of his personal estate to his younger son, John *Sargent; the residue he bequeathed to his older son, George.   DAVID HANCOCK

Sources D. Hancock, *Citizens of the world: London merchants and the integration of the British Atlantic community, 1735–1785* (1995) • H. Wagner, 'Pedigree of Sargent, afterwards Arnold, and Sargent', *The Genealogist*, new ser., 33 (1916–17), 189–97 • *The papers of Benjamin Franklin*, ed. L. W. Labaree and others, [35 vols.] (1959–) [esp. vols. 7–] • *Pennsylvania Archives*, 8th ser., 6, 7 (1934) • W. M. Acres, *The Bank of England from within, 1694–1900*, 2 (1931) • *Journal of the votes and proceedings of the general assembly of the colony of New York from 1766 to 1776*, 2 (1776) • E. B. O'Callaghan, ed., *Documents relating to the colonial history of the state of New York*, 7 (1856) • K. P. Bailey, ed., *The Ohio Company papers, 1753–1817* (1947) • R. H. D'Elboux and W. Ward, eds., *The registers of St Dunstan in the East, London*, 4–5, Harleian Society, register section, 86–7 (1958), 34 • will, PRO, PROB 11/1210, sig. 483
Archives BL, Newcastle MSS • BL OIOC, East India Company MSS, B84, B86 • CKS, Halstead deeds and records • CLRO, London, Freedom MSS • Hunt. L., Grenville MSS • PRO, navy board minutes • PRO, Company of Merchants Trading to Africa MS, T70 • Sheffield Central Library, Sheffield, Wentworth-Woodhouse MSS • West Looe, Cornwall, Buller MSS
Likenesses A. Ramsey, oils, *c.*1749, Holburne Museum, Bath

Sargent, John (1750–1831), politician, was the younger of the two sons of John *Sargent (1714–1791), draper and MP, of May Place, Kent, and his wife, Rosamund Chambers (1722–1792). He was educated at Eton College (1760–67), where he contributed to the *Musae Etonienses*, and then entered St John's College, Cambridge (1767), and Lincoln's Inn (1770). Introduced to his future wife by his friend the poet Thomas Hayley, on 21 December 1778 he married Charlotte (1754–1841), the daughter of Richard Bettsworth of Petworth and his wife, Charlotte Orme. Through her mother she inherited Woollavington in Sussex, which was rebuilt as their marital abode; they had six sons and four daughters. Sargent, like his father, was a director of the Bank of England (1778–9), and he was also appointed a gentleman of the bedchamber. In 1785 he published a poem, *The Mine*, celebrating fossil life in quicksilver mines; to the third edition of 1796 he appended poems on Stonehenge and Mary Queen of Scots.

Sargent's neighbour in Sussex, the duke of Richmond, secured his return to parliament for Seaford in 1790, despite a disputed election. Sargent supported Pitt's administration, first speaking in favour of the bank's appropriation of unclaimed dividends on 15 December 1790. In 1791 he joined the public revenue committee, and from 1792 he was a ministerial division teller. He became clerk of the ordnance under the duke of Richmond in November 1793 and exchanged Seaford for Queenborough on the ordnance interest on 15 February 1794. He mostly spoke on departmental matters in the house but occasionally addressed other matters. For example, he introduced a Poor Law Amendment Bill on 12 November 1795 and chaired the committee on the Seditious Meetings Bill on 27 November. Pitt then recommended him warmly, but in vain, to Lord Camden as his chief secretary at Dublin. He secured tax exemption for physicians on 22 December 1797 and chaired the income tax committee in March 1799. Retaining office under Addington, Sargent became junior secretary to the Treasury on 8 July 1802, but he was defeated in the general election. He came in for Bodmin on Lord De Dunstanville's interest on 17 December 1802, but ceased debating to concentrate on managing government bills through the house. In 1803 he joined the board of agriculture. Despite Pittite overtures, he went into opposition in May 1804 with Addington, who procured an annual pension for his wife of £616 to reward his public services. He supported Addington when he joined forces again with Pitt in 1805 and, like him, seceded from Pitt's government that summer. His support for Grenville's administration of 1806 won him a commissionership of public accounts, on condition that he resign his seat. Sargent held office until 1821, and served as chairman of quarter sessions in Sussex for more than forty years. He died on 9 September 1831 and was buried in Lavington, Sussex.   ROLAND THORNE

Sources R. G. Thorne, 'Sargent, John', HoP, Commons, 1790–1820 · R. A. Austen-Leigh, ed., The Eton College register, 1753–1790 (1921), 62 · Venn, Alum. Cant. · H. Wagner, 'Pedigree of Sargent, afterwards Arnold, and Sargent', The Genealogist, new ser., 33 (1916–17), 189–97 · D. Elwes and C. Robinson, A history of the castles, mansions and manors of western Sussex (1879), 273 · T. W. Horsfield, The history, antiquities, and topography of the county of Sussex, 2 (1835), 171 · The later correspondence of George III, ed. A. Aspinall, 5 vols. (1962–70), vol. 2 · W. P. Baildon, ed., The records of the Honorable Society of Lincoln's Inn: admissions, 1 (1896), 465 · IGI · Boyle's Court Guide · Sargent pedigree, Society of Genealogists, London
Archives Devon RO, Sidmouth MSS

Sargent, John (1780–1833), Church of England clergyman, was the eldest son of John Sargent (1750–1831), banker and politician. The latter published in 1784 *The Mine* and other poems; he married at Woollavington, Sussex, on 21 December 1778, Charlotte (d. 1841), only daughter and heir of Richard Bettsworth of Petworth, Sussex. Their son John, born on 8 October 1780 at Woollavington, was educated at Eton College, where he was a king's scholar. In 1799 he proceeded to King's College, Cambridge, where he was elected to a fellowship and graduated BA in 1804 and MA in 1807. At Cambridge he was influenced by Charles Simeon, a friendship which shaped his career. Sargent trained for law and was admitted to the Inner Temple in 1803, but he was ordained deacon in 1805 and priest in 1806. On 29 November 1804, at Carlton Hall, Nottinghamshire, he married Mary, only daughter of Abel Smith, banker, niece to Lord Carrington, and a first cousin of William *Wilberforce.

Sargent was presented by his father to the family living of Graffham in Sussex on 11 September 1805; from 5 June 1813 until his death he held with it a second family rectory, that of Woollavington. On his father's death he became the squire of the district. He was regarded as a model country pastor by evangelicals, in the same way that Keble was revered by high-churchmen. Lavington rectory, rebuilt by Sargent, was at the centre of a network of the Sumner, Ryder, Manning, and Wilberforce families, based upon evangelical and familial ties. Sargent died at Woollavington on 3 May 1833, and was buried there. Sargent's widow died on 6 July 1861, aged eighty-two, having lived for many years with her son-in-law, Bishop Wilberforce, and was buried at Woollavington. John and Mary Sargent had seven children: two sons, John Garton and Henry Martyn, who predeceased their father, and five daughters. The second daughter, Emily (d. 1841), married in 1828 Samuel *Wilberforce, later bishop of Oxford and Winchester; Mary married in 1834 the Revd Henry William *Wilberforce and died in 1878. Caroline married in 1833 Henry

Edward *Manning, who had previously lived with the Sargents as a curate, and died on 24 July 1837; Sophia Lucy married in 1834 George Dudley Ryder, second son of the bishop of Lichfield, and died in March 1850.

Sargent wrote a memoir of the missionary the Revd Henry Martyn in 1819 at Simeon's suggestion. Samuel Wilberforce edited Martyn's journals and letters, publishing them with a memoir of Sargent. Simeon also prompted Sargent to write a life of Revd T. T. Thomason in 1833.

W. P. COURTNEY, *rev.* ELLIE CLEWLOW

Sources S. Wilberforce, 'introduction', in Journals and letters of the Rev. Henry Martyn, ed. S. Wilberforce, 2 vols. (1837) · Venn, Alum. Cant. · D. Newsome, The parting of friends: a study of the Wilberforces and Henry Manning (1966) · GM, 1st ser., 103/1 (1833), 636–7 · E. S. Purcell, Life of Cardinal Manning, 2 vols. (1896) · A. R. Ashwell and R. G. Wilberforce, Life of the right reverend Samuel Wilberforce … with selections from his diary and correspondence, 3 vols. (1880–82)
Archives Bodl. Oxf., corresp. · W. Sussex RO, family papers

Sargent, John Grant (1813–1883), founder of the Fritchley Friends, the youngest son of Isaac Sargent (1782–1871) and his wife, Hester, *née* Sturge (d. 1836), was born at Paddington on 30 July 1813. His parents, who were members of the Society of Friends, moved to Paris in 1823, leaving their sons to be educated in boarding-schools at Islington and Epping. In April 1830 Sargent was apprenticed to John D. Bassett, a Quaker draper, at Leighton Buzzard, Bedfordshire. Having served his time, in October 1834 he joined his father, a coach-builder and brick maker, at Paris. In both these businesses he engaged, having Auguste Charlot as his partner in the brickyard. In 1835 he discarded the distinctive Quaker costume and attended Wesleyan services. Early in 1838 a Friends' meeting, promoted by his father, was begun at 24 faubourg du Roule, the residence of Ann Knight. Sargent regularly attended it: he resumed the other usages of Friends early in 1839, and held his ground, though not infrequently he was the only worshipper in the meeting-room. He would not sell bricks for fortifications. In 1842 he disposed of his businesses, intending to take up farming in England. He took part in 1843 and 1844 in religious missions to the south of France. He studied farming with Thomas Bayes at Kimberley, Norfolk, and on 23 December 1846 he married Catherine (1813–1888), the daughter of George and Elizabeth Doubell of Reigate. After managing Bregsells Farm near Dorking, Surrey (1846–51), he moved to Ireland in 1851 to superintend Hall Farm, near Moate, co. Westmeath (1851–4).

Sargent first spoke in a Friends' meeting at Clonmel on 23 November 1851. His first publication, *An Epistle of Love and Caution* (1853), was directed against the growing influence of the evangelical views of Joseph John Gurney. The visit to England in that year of an American Friend, John Wilbur (1774–1856), who had been disowned by the New England yearly meeting for his opposition to Gurney, led Sargent to identify himself with the advocates of the older, quietist type of Quakerism. His frequent business journeys were made occasions of urging his views on Friends, both in Britain and on the continent.

In 1854 Sargent returned to England and took a wood-turning mill at Cockermouth, Cumberland, where he made bobbins. It was from here in April 1860 that he issued a manuscript circular letter suggesting the assembling of conferences. The first took place in London on 17 October 1862, and was attended by seventeen persons; similar conferences were held, about three in a year, until 15 October 1869. After his removal, in 1864, to Fritchley, Derbyshire, where he took over another bobbin mill, he accompanied other Quakers in May 1868 in visiting America to confer with the groups of primitive Friends, known as the 'smaller bodies'; they returned with the idea of separating themselves from the London yearly meeting. In January 1870 a general meeting was initiated at Fritchley. It met twice a year, and its members came to be known as the Fritchley Friends and sometimes as Wilburites. Sargent was clerk of the meeting and its leading spirit. In 1882, after two business journeys on the European continent in the previous year, he was specially 'liberated' by the Fritchley meeting for a second visit to America. On his return his health began to fail. He died at Fritchley on 27 December 1883, and was buried on 29 December in the Quaker burial-ground at Toadhole Furnace, near Alfreton, Derbyshire. His widow died on 20 September 1888. They were survived by several children. The Fritchley Friends were officially reconciled with the London yearly meeting of Quakers in 1967.

ALEXANDER GORDON, rev. TIMOTHY C. F. STUNT

Sources *Selections from the diary and correspondence of John G. Sargent* (1885) · J. Smith, ed., *A descriptive catalogue of Friends' books*, suppl. (1893), 297 · W. Lowndes, *The Quakers of Fritchley* (1986), 3–36 · J. Wilbur, *Journal* (1859), 547 ff. · W. Hodgson, *The Society of Friends in the nineteenth century*, 2 (1876), 379ff. · *Modern Review* (Oct 1884) · W. Hodgson, *Correspondence* (1886), 316 ff. · *The Friend* [Philadelphia, PA] (1909), 134
Likenesses photograph, repro. in Lowndes, *The Quakers of Fritchley*, 4
Wealth at death £825 5s. 11d.: probate, 4 March 1884, *CGPLA Eng. & Wales*

Sargent, John Neptune (1826–1893), army officer, was born on 18 June 1826, at sea, on board the East India Company's ship *Atlas*. He was by descent an Irishman and a soldier. One of his ancestors had served under William III at the Boyne. His father, John James Sargent (d. c.1844), was an officer of the 18th Royal Irish, who, after more than thirty-one years' service as subaltern and captain, obtained a brevet majority for his conduct at the capture of Canton (Guangzhou) in 1841, and died about three years afterwards from the effects of the climate of Hong Kong. His mother, Matilda, born Fitzgerald, died in 1841.

Sargent obtained a commission by purchase in the 95th foot on 19 January 1844, joined his regiment in Ceylon, and went on with it to Hong Kong in March 1847, having become lieutenant on 11 December 1846. His company was sent to Canton to protect the factories after violence broke out in December 1847, and he later acted as assistant engineer at Hong Kong. He returned to England in 1850 with his regiment, of which he was adjutant from 11 November 1851 to 18 November 1853, when he was promoted captain. In 10 March 1852 he married Miss R. S. Champion, who died on 26 July 1858.

In 1854 the regiment was ordered to Turkey, and by great efforts Sargent escaped being left behind as junior captain. While the troops were at Varna he went on leave to the Danube, and was under fire there with General W. F. Beatson. At the Alma, in command of the leading company of the right wing of his regiment, he led the advance with 'determined bravery', as his immediate commanding officer reported. He was wounded in the leg, but refused to be struck off duty, which was at that time heavy, as eighteen officers of the regiment were killed or wounded at the Alma. He took part in the repulse of the Russian sortie on 26 October, and served with distinction at the battle of Inkerman. He also served throughout the siege of Sevastopol, and was wounded in the final attack on the Redan on 8 September 1855. He was praised by his colonel as 'a most zealous, meritorious, and brave officer', and mentioned in dispatches. He was awarded a brevet majority on 2 November 1855, the Mejidiye (fifth class), and the Légion d'honneur (fifth class). He was appointed one of a committee of three officers to examine the equipment of other armies in the Crimea and suggest improvements to the British equipment.

Sargent was on half pay from 29 February 1856 to 25 August 1857, when he was given a majority in the 2nd battalion of the Buffs. On 29 July 1859 he became second lieutenant-colonel in the 1st battalion, and served with it in the Second Opium War in 1860. He was appointed to command a provisional battalion for the garrison of Hong Kong, but was allowed to accompany his regiment when the expedition went north to take Peking (Beijing). He had charge of the advanced guard in the attack of Sinho on 12 August, and was present at the affair of Tangku (Tanggu); during the storming of the north Taku (Dagu) forts on the 20th he commanded a mixed detachment which diverted the fire of batteries that would otherwise have taken the attacking troops in flank. When the army advanced on Peking he was appointed British commandant at the Taku forts, and succeeded in establishing a market there which supplied the fleets. He was made a CB on 27 January 1862.

On the voyage home the transport *Athleta*, with some companies of the Buffs under Sargent's command, touched at the Cape, where the crew tried to desert and refused to work the ship. Under his orders his soldiers guarded the crew and sailed the ship for a week, after which time the crew resumed work.

Sargent commanded the 2nd battalion of the Buffs at Malta until July 1862, when he was given the command of the 1st battalion in England. This he held until 6 December 1864, when he sold out of the regiment to half pay. On 28 July 1863 he remarried; his new wife was Alice May, second daughter of Thomas Tredwell of Lower Norwood, Surrey. They had several children.

Sargent had become colonel in the army on 29 July 1864, and for some years he commanded the Inns of Court Volunteers. On 1 April 1873 he was appointed to a brigade depot at Milford Haven, and in the following year was transferred to Oxford, where he remained until promoted major-general on 1 October 1877. Much objection had been made to a military depot at Oxford, but he worked cordially with the university and civic authorities, and helped to gain acceptance for the army there. He commanded the troops in China and Malaya for three years from 1 April 1882, his tenure being shortened by his promotion to lieutenant-general on 7 October 1884.

Sargent retired on 1 April 1890, and was made colonel of the 1st battalion Inniskilling fusiliers on 17 January 1891. He died at his residence, Mount Mascal, near Bexley, on 20 October 1893, survived by his wife and several children.

E. M. LLOYD, *rev.* JAMES LUNT

Sources Fortescue, *Brit. army*, vol. 13 · A. W. Kinglake, *The invasion of the Crimea*, 8 vols. (1863–87), vols. 2, 5 · *The Times* (24 Oct 1893) · *LondG* (4 Nov 1860) · G. Blaxland, *The buffs: royal east Kent regiment* (1972) · M. Mann, *China, 1860* (1989) · G. J. Wolseley, *Narrative of the war with China in 1860* (1862) · *Hart's Army List*
Wealth at death £2634 17s.: probate, 29 Nov 1893, *CGPLA Eng. & Wales*

Sargent, John Singer (1856–1925), portrait and landscape painter and muralist, was born probably on 12 January 1856 in Florence, in the Casa Arretini, next to the Palazzo Sperini, in the Lungarno Acciaioli on the left bank. The family celebrated his birthday on that date but some family letters give his date of birth as 10 January. He was the eldest surviving child of American parents, Dr Fitzwilliam Sargent (1820–1889), who came from a New England shipping family, and his wife, Mary Newbold Singer (1826–1906), the only daughter of John Singer and Mary Newbold, prosperous merchants in Philadelphia.

Early years Fitzwilliam Sargent had trained as a doctor and practised in Philadelphia; he wrote and edited medical textbooks, had begun to make investigations into the disorders of the eye, and had been appointed attending surgeon at the Wills Hospital, Philadelphia. In 1854, after the death of their first child, Mary Newbold Sargent (1851–1853), the Sargents travelled to Europe and began an expatriate existence, returning to America only for visits. Their other surviving children were Emily (1857–1936) and Violet (1870–1955). The Sargents led a cultivated, itinerant life on a modest income, spending winters in apartments or pension houses in Nice, Rome, or Florence, and summers in cities and resorts in Switzerland, France, and Germany. Sargent's education was informal, even haphazard, but it was intensively cultural and cosmopolitan. He grew up speaking French, Italian, and German, in addition to English, was widely read and an accomplished pianist, and he developed a passionate interest in art and architecture.

Paris: art education and the Salon Mrs Sargent, a keen watercolourist, ardent Europhile, and cultural romantic, encouraged her son's precocious artistic talent. Sargent studied briefly at the Accademia delle Belle Arti in Florence, but in May 1874 went to Paris, then the undisputed capital of the art world, in search of professional artistic training. He entered the independent atelier of the fashionable portrait painter Charles-Emile-Auguste Durand, styled Carolus-Duran (1838–1917), at 81 boulevard Montparnasse, and enrolled at the École des Beaux-Arts to study drawing from casts and from life. Carolus-Duran was a friend of Edouard Manet and of Claude Monet, and was regarded by his contemporaries as a progressive. He was an advocate of direct, realistic painting and taught his students to work *au premier coup* (at the first touch), working with a loaded brush, applying wet paint into wet paint, a technique that encouraged a broad, painterly style. Sargent passed the *concours des places* (the exams in perspective and anatomy, ornament, and life drawing) and

John Singer Sargent (1856–1925), by unknown photographer, *c.*1886 [in his Paris studio]

matriculated at the École des Beaux-Arts in October 1874, and again in January 1875 and March 1877. By August 1875 he was sharing a rented studio on the Left Bank, 73 bis rue Notre Dame des Champs, near the Luxembourg Gardens, with the American artist James Carroll Beckwith.

Sargent made his début at the Paris Salon in 1877 with a portrait of a family friend, Frances Sherburne Ridley Watts (Philadelphia Museum of Art). In the same year Carolus-Duran invited him to assist with work on a commission for a ceiling decoration for the Luxembourg Palace. The finished ceiling, *Gloria Mariae Medicis*, which includes portraits of Carolus-Duran by Sargent and vice versa, was shown at the Salon in 1878 and is now installed in the Musée du Louvre. The ceiling project also led Carolus-Duran to agree to sit to Sargent, and Sargent exhibited a formal portrait of Carolus-Duran at the Salon in 1879 (Sterling and Francine Clark Art Institute, Williamstown, Massachusetts), a painting that performed the dual function of paying homage to his master and declaring independence from him. Like Manet and other artists of his generation, Carolus-Duran had travelled to Spain and fallen under the spell of the seventeenth-century Spanish master Diego de Silva Velázquez. Sargent made the journey to Spain himself in 1879 and copied works by Velázquez in the Museo del Prado in Madrid, an experience that proved to be a lifelong inspiration. In the following year he travelled to Holland, as many contemporary artists had done, going to Haarlem to see at first hand the expressive brushwork and inflected surfaces of paintings by Frans Hals.

In Paris, Sargent exhibited a deliberate balance of portraits and subject pictures and achieved critical attention and success quite remarkable for a young foreign painter. He was regarded as an innovator challenging the conventions of Salon taste and of traditional representation, without entirely overturning them. He was awarded an honourable mention at the 1879 Salon for his portrait of Carolus-Duran and a second-class medal in 1881 for that of a young Chilean woman, Madame Ramón Subercaseaux (priv. coll.). His subject pictures—inspired by travels to Brittany, Capri, Spain, north Africa, and Venice—embraced contemporary themes, but were distinguished by a technical modernity and a sensitivity to light and atmosphere: a group of Breton peasants on a luminous stretch of beach, *Oyster Gatherers of Cancale* (three versions: exh. Paris Salon, 1878; Corcoran Gallery of Art, Washington, DC; exh. Society of American Artists, New York, 1878; Museum of Fine Arts, Boston; and untraced); a poetic study of a young Capri model in an olive grove, *A Capriote* (three versions: exh. Paris Salon, 1879, and Society of American Artists, New York, 1879; Museum of Fine Arts, Boston; and priv. coll.); *Fumée d'ambre gris* (exh. Paris Salon, 1880; Sterling and Francine Clark Art Institute, Williamstown, Massachusetts), an oriental study of a woman perfuming herself with ambergris, painted in white on white—a work of exquisite refinement. His large-scale, ambitious *El jaleo* (Isabella Stewart Gardner Museum, Boston), an electrifying evocation of Spanish dance, was one of the sensations of the 1882 Salon. It was followed by his

study of four children dispersed in the shadows of a hushed interior, *The Daughters of Edward D. Boit* (exh. Paris Salon, 1883; Museum of Fine Arts, Boston), a homage to Velázquez's mysterious royal group portrait, *Las meninas* (Museo del Prado, Madrid).

Sargent was professionally and personally in touch with a literary circle of advanced tastes: he knew the aesthete and connoisseur Dr Samuel Pozzi and the orientalist and writer Judith Gautier, both of whom he painted (1881; Armand Hammer Museum of Art and Cultural Center, Los Angeles; and three oils, *c*.1883–5; Detroit Institute of Arts, priv. coll., and Musée Jean Faure, Aix-les-Bains; a watercolour, *c*.1883–5; untraced; and two wash drawings, *c*.1883–5; priv. coll. and Royal Collection), the poet Robert de Montesquiou, and the novelist Paul Bourget. He also painted portraits of the Polish-born novelist Charles Edmond (*c*.1882; priv. coll.), the poet and essayist Charles Frémine (*c*.1880; priv. coll.), the writer Madame Allouard Jouan (*c*.1882; Petit Palais, Paris), and the art critic Louis de Fourcaud (1884; Musée d'Orsay, Paris). He knew the work of the impressionists and attended their exhibitions; he bought paintings by Manet at his studio sale in 1884 and would acquire several paintings by Monet. He associated with a number of figures who occupied the artistic middle ground: Jean Charles Cazin, Albert Besnard, Ernest Duez, and Giovanni Boldini, with whom he exhibited at progressive venues, most significantly at the 'Société Internationale des Peintres et Sculpteurs: Première Exposition' in the Galerie Georges Petit in December 1882. His friendship with the artists Paul Helleu and Albert de Belleroche, formed during his early years in Paris, lasted throughout his life.

In 1883 Sargent moved into his own studio, 41 boulevard Berthier opposite the fortifications, beyond Batignolles, and seemed to be settling in Paris. During 1883 and the early months of 1884 he was preoccupied by his portrait of a contemporary celebrity, Madame Pierre Gautreau (*Madame X*, exh. Paris Salon, 1884; Metropolitan Museum of Art, New York), an American woman living in Paris, who was famous for her striking, if eccentric, beauty and whom he had requested to paint. It was a painting in which he had invested a great deal, but its formal sophistication perplexed the Parisian public and the majority of French critics when exhibited at the Salon of 1884, where it was a *succès de scandale*. Its largely hostile reception was one factor spurring his decision to leave Paris for London. Sargent had already been asked to paint members of the Vickers family (connected with the famous armaments firm) in England, and he had met the novelist Henry James. James was impressed both by the man and his work. He described Sargent as 'civilised to his fingertips' (James, *Letters*, 3.32), and made strenuous efforts to introduce and promote him in London society. His essay on the young Sargent for *Harper's New Monthly Magazine*, which was published in October 1887, is one of the most illuminating discussions of the artist's early work.

England: Broadway and London In late summer 1885 Sargent was on a boating holiday on the Thames with his friend the American artist Edwin Austin Abbey. After a swimming accident at Pangbourne, Abbey took Sargent to Broadway in Worcestershire to stay with the American artist Frank Millet and his wife, which marked the introduction to a brief pastoral interlude. Sargent spent the autumn months of 1885 and 1886 at Broadway, first at Farnham House and then at Russell House, with a group of Anglo-American artists, including Abbey, Frank Millet, Alfred Parsons, Frederick Barnard, and the writers Henry James and Edmund Gosse. The atmosphere was relaxed, convivial, and familial, with games, music, plays, and high spirits very much the order of the day. It was an intensely creative period, and it was at Broadway that Sargent painted his English nocturne *Carnation, Lily, Lily, Rose* (Tate collection), which was an astonishing success at the Royal Academy in 1887 and was bought for the nation under the terms of the Chantrey Bequest for £700. In the absence of portrait commissions, Sargent turned to landscape and to his own experiments with impressionism.

Sargent was in touch with Monet by this time, though the date of their first meeting is yet to be established. Towards the end of his life, Monet told Sargent's biographer Evan Charteris that they had met 'vers 1876'; they certainly exhibited together in Paris, at the Cercle des Arts Libéraux on the rue Vivienne in 1881 and again at the 'Quatrième Exposition Internationale de Peinture' at the Galerie Georges Petit in May 1885. They seem to have been professionally at their closest in the late 1880s: Sargent visited Monet in Giverny in 1887 and began to acquire works by him around the same time; Monet visited Sargent in England in the following year, and in 1889 they were both involved in the campaign to purchase Manet's *Olympia* for the Louvre. Sargent twice painted Monet's portrait, in 1885 and again in 1888 (Tate collection and National Academy, New York). Monet did not regard Sargent as an impressionist painter: 'Il n'était pas un Impressioniste, au sens où nous employons ce mot, il était trop sous l'influence de Carolus-Duran' (Charteris, 130); but he retained a personal affection for him, writing of his death to their mutual friend Paul Helleu: 'Nous perdons un viel ami. C'est bien triste et de suite ma pensée va vers vous' (priv. coll.). Sargent's sketch *Claude Monet Painting by the Edge of a Wood* (c.1885; Tate collection), which shows the French artist sitting at his easel painting a landscape, seems to illustrate the creed of late nineteenth-century *plein-air* painting.

Sargent spent the summers of 1887, 1888, and 1889 in the English countryside, at Henley, Calcot, and Fladbury, respectively. Between the years 1885 and 1889 he produced a significant corpus of open-air studies—landscapes, figure studies, river scenes, and still lifes. He had come from France, bringing with him a breath of the 'new painting', which had both animated and divided the contemporary art world. Sargent's relationship with impressionism is a complex one. While many of his paintings show a preoccupation with the effects of natural light and deploy a high-keyed palette and broken brushwork, he never carried his experiments with light and colour as far as the impressionists: he does not lay on his pigment in strokes of pure colour, and his figures remain solidly and realistically defined. He was an honoured member of the New English Art Club, a society of artists who supported the exhibition of French art in England, and he exhibited at their opening show in 1886 and in subsequent years. The paintings he showed there and in various American venues in the late eighties and early nineties helped to disseminate French-inspired painting abroad.

America: portraiture and the murals Sargent made the decisive move to London in 1886, taking James McNeill Whistler's old ground-floor studio at 13 (later renumbered 33) Tite Street, in Chelsea; but patronage, which had apparently declined in Paris, was slow to develop in England. His first sustained success as a portrait painter came in America on two successive trips in 1887–8 and 1889–90. He travelled to New York in September 1887 to paint the wife of the prominent banker and collector Henry G. Marquand at their summer home in Newport, Rhode Island. He was welcomed and lionized, especially in Boston, where he was given his first one-man show at the St Botolph Club in 1888, and where he already had friends: the artist Edward Boit, whose daughters he had painted, the banker Charles Fairchild, who had commissioned a portrait of Robert Louis Stevenson and who would manage Sargent's financial affairs, and the redoubtable Isabella Stewart Gardner, who was to build up one of the great American collections of European art, which she installed in a Venetian-inspired palace, Fenway Court, which still, as the Isabella Stewart Gardner Museum, bears her name. In New York Sargent's technical modernity and the general aura of European chic that surrounded him were very seductive and attracted a raft of commissions from the upper echelons of society, among them four portraits of the super-rich Vanderbilts. His friendships with the architects Stanford White and Charles McKim were probably behind several of these commissions and certainly led to his appointment in 1890 as a muralist for the new Boston Public Library, which they had designed.

Sargent's mural decorations reveal the profound influence of the French tradition in which he had been educated, which placed history painting and mural decoration at the head of the hierarchy of art, and they represent what he regarded as his artistic legacy. Sargent hall on the second floor of the library depicts the history of religion, using imagery from ancient, Egyptian, Hebraic, and Christian iconography in a decorative scheme which incorporates ornamental borders, enrichments, and sculpted reliefs. The murals were his grand project, an intellectual and aesthetic adventure which posed huge imaginative, logistical, and technical challenges and which preoccupied and taxed him for thirty years. He worked on them in a large iron studio at Morgan Hall, Fairford, in Gloucestershire, which he shared with Edwin Austin Abbey from 1891 until 1895, when he took a twenty-one year lease on two studios in the Fulham Road, which were suitable for larger pieces and conveniently close to Tite Street. Two further mural commissions followed. Between 1916 and 1925 Sargent produced a decorative scheme, designed as a homage to the arts and the classical tradition, for the rotunda and grand stairway of the Museum of Fine Arts in Boston, and in 1922 he painted *Death and Victory* and the *Coming of the Americans* as a First World War memorial for the Widener Library, Harvard University. The relief work for the library mural scheme introduced him to the technical demands of a different medium and he made some forays into sculpture. A full-size bronze cast of the crucifixion, which hangs on the south wall of Sargent hall, was presented by Sargent's sisters to St Paul's Cathedral as a memorial to their brother and was unveiled in the crypt on 1 January 1926. Sargent produced only a few sculptural works independent of his decorative scheme: a large bronze of a turkey and some small bronze figurative pieces.

London: recognition and public life The 1890s were dominated by portraiture and the murals. Sargent became, in effect, the portraitist of an international élite. In America in 1890 he painted some forty portraits in nine months, including a whole-length of the Spanish dancer La Carmencita (Musée d'Orsay, Paris), which was bought by the French state for the Musée du Luxembourg in 1892. In England recognition was slower in coming but in summer 1893 his *Lady Agnew of Lochnaw* (NG Scot.), with its beguiling synthesis of impressionism, aestheticism, and realism, and his nervously alert *Mrs Hugh Hammersley* (Metropolitan Museum of Art, New York) were triumphs at the Royal Academy and the New Gallery, respectively. It was a pivotal season for him and, by the mid-1890s, he was in such demand as a portraitist that he was painting three sitters a day. He was recognized by the artistic establishment when he was elected an associate of the Royal Academy in 1894, and a full member in 1897. His portrayals continued to command attention by their daringly oblique compositions and immediacy of characterization. In 1897 his flamboyant and fantastic *Mrs Carl Meyer and her Children* (exh. RA, 1897; priv. coll.) led Henry James to wonder at his 'knock-down insolence of talent' ('London', *Harper's Weekly*, 5 June 1897; James, *The Painter's Eye*, 257). In the following year he painted portraits of the Bond Street dealer Asher Wertheimer and of his wife in celebration of their silver wedding. Wertheimer became Sargent's friend and his greatest patron, commissioning a further ten portraits of his wife and children and bequeathing all but two of them to the National Gallery in London (now in the Tate collection).

In August 1900 Sargent leased the house next door to his own in Tite Street, no. 31. It was an arts and crafts building designed by Colonel Sir Robert Edis, and in it he installed a second studio where he arranged his French furniture and *objets d'art*, his piano, a Japanese lacquer screen, a Brussels tapestry, and a panel of carved boiserie on wheels, objects which served as studio props. By the turn of the century he began to be approached by the aristocracy, whose forebears had been painted by Van Dyck, Sir Peter Lely, Sir Godfrey Kneller, Sir Joshua Reynolds, and Sir Thomas Lawrence, against portraits by whom his own works would hang in some of Britain's grandest country houses. His inventiveness, fluency, and painterly *élan* was reanimating the international tradition of portraiture. In adapting his style to a new typology, he created images of Edwardian nobility which have become definitive, like those of the attenuated and ultra-refined Lord Ribblesdale (exh. RA, 1902; National Gallery, London); the young patrician Lord Dalhousie (exh. RA, 1900; priv. coll.), an embodiment of Edwardian gilded youth; the remarkable, eccentric conversation piece of the Sitwell family; and the grand manner group portrait of the duke of Marlborough and his family (exh. RA, 1905; priv. coll.). In England he painted many of the prominent figures of his day, including Ellen Terry in her role as Lady Macbeth (1889; Tate collection); Octavia Hill, founder of the National Trust (1899; NPG); the poet Coventry Patmore (1894; NPG); and statesman Joseph Chamberlain (1896; NPG). Among his American sitters were actors Joseph Jefferson, Edwin Booth, and Ada Rehan; architect Richard Morris Hunt and garden designer Frederick Law Olmsted; politicians Thomas Brackett Reed, Joseph Choate, and Calvin Brice; and the president Theodore Roosevelt (1903; White House, Washington, DC). At the Royal Academy in 1902 it was Auguste Rodin who produced the definitive phrase to describe his achievement: Sargent was 'le Van Dyck de l'époque' ('M. Rodin in London', *Daily Chronicle*, 16 May 1902, 6).

Although Sargent painted so many figures in the establishment, he was never part of it, retaining both a personal privacy and an artistic independence of spirit. With critical and popular recognition came the responsibilities of public life. He was diligent, acting as a regular visitor at the Royal Academy Schools and teaching and advising students, including a young Vanessa Bell; but it is entirely in character that, when he was approached about the presidency of the Royal Academy in 1918, he refused absolutely. His public profile also brought with it administrative duties. For example, when two of his painter friends, Charles Furse and Robert Brough, died, it was he who was called in to assist in the sale and exhibition of their work, and in 1911 he selected 322 works for a memorial exhibition of the work of his friend Edwin Austin Abbey at the Royal Academy. He wrote a preface to the catalogues of an exhibition of the watercolours of his friend Hercules Brabazon held at the Goupil Gallery, London, in 1892 and a foreword to the catalogue of an exhibition of the work of the Spanish artist Ignacio Zuloaga, which toured Boston, New York, and several other American cities in 1916 and 1917. The honours began to roll in. He was made chevalier of the Légion d'honneur in 1889, an associate of the National Academy of Design in 1891, and a full member in 1897; he was awarded the French order of merit and the Belgian order of Leopold in 1909, and received honorary degrees from the universities of Pennsylvania (1903), Oxford (1904), Cambridge (1913), Harvard (1916), and Yale (1916).

The landscape painter The demands of portraiture and the murals had kept Sargent studio-bound in the 1890s, though he travelled abroad to do mural research, to Italy, Spain, and the Middle East. In the early 1900s a freer pattern developed whereby he spent the summer and autumn of each year painting landscapes in Switzerland, Italy, and Spain. He would spend August in the Alps, before moving down to Italy or Spain. In the Alps he was usually accompanied by his sisters, Emily and Violet, and by the latter's family and a group of close friends, who frequently acted as his models. About 1907 he attempted to give up both formal portraiture and the social commitments that it generated. He shifted his emphasis to landscape and produced a huge output of figure studies, architectural paintings of parks and gardens, fountains and statues, scenes of local life, boats and animals, streams and waterfalls, rocks and boulders. He painted a series of alpine studies of his nieces and friends dressed in Turkish costume or wrapped in cashmere shawls, fantastic caprices expressed in rhythmic, cursive lines and executed with bold, painterly freedom. He returned to Venice, his favourite city, almost annually, painting her canals, palace façades, and campi from different angles and under varying conditions of light. Sargent had worked in watercolour from childhood, and he painted a small body of delicate studies in the 1870s and 1880s, but it was in the 1900s, when he was travelling so much and it became practical to explore a portable medium, that he devoted real artistic energy to it and developed a distinctive bravura style. The apparent ease of execution and beguiling fluency of his work in watercolour are deceptive in that they mask a thorough command of sophisticated techniques. The claims of portraiture never entirely ceased. He compromised by drawing charcoal portraits—he did between twenty and thirty a year—in the space of a sitting or two; and he painted portraits of close friends like Sybil Sassoon (1913 and 1922; priv. coll.) and Henry James (1913; NPG).

Personal life and interests Sargent was tall, over 6 feet in height, with dark hair and, from early adulthood, a full beard. Slightly bulging eyes, his most striking feature, seemed to become more pronounced with age. He dressed formally, even in the studio, in well-cut, bespoke suits made by Henry Poole & Co. of Savile Row, London, smoked cigars, and possessed a huge appetite, which has become the stuff of legend. He complained to the artist William Rothenstein that he could not get enough to eat at the Chelsea Arts Club, and so had recourse to 'the Hans Crescent Hotel, where, from the table d'hôte luncheon of several courses, he could assuage his Gargantuan appetite' (W. Rothenstein, *Men and Memories*, 1931, 244). He became corpulent in middle age—the massive figure defined by the caricatures by his friend Henry Tonks and Sir Max Beerbohm—though he retained a certain grace and speed of movement. His physical bulk was matched by huge reserves of energy. Evan Charteris wondered at a mental and physical stamina that seemed to protect him from normal human fatigue, recalling that: 'at the end of a long day's work his mind would be serene and cool, his temperament buoyant; he would show up no sign of fag either in brain or limb' (Charteris, 227). There are several self-portraits of Sargent in oil, showing him at different stages of life: 1886 in the Aberdeen Art Gallery; 1892 (his diploma work) in the National Academy (formerly the National Academy of Design), New York; 1906 in the Uffizi Gallery, Florence.

The impression that emerges from descriptions by his sitters is of a vigorous, decisive, and driven artist. There are stories of Sargent's rushing to and from the easel, totally absorbed, placing his brushstrokes in gestures of absolute precision, of the cries of frustration as he rubbed out, scraped down, reworked, and grappled with the problems of representation, cries punctuated by his mild expletives 'demons, demons'. Occasionally, he would dash to the piano and play as a brief respite from painting. He was single-minded about what he wanted to achieve and would brook no interference—an approach born of professional self-belief rather than personal arrogance, from which he was remarkably free. He insisted on the right to select his sitters' costumes and accessories, and took brisk exception to comments from his sitters and their families about the truth of the likenesses and characterizations he created. While working on his decorative scheme for the Museum of Fine Arts, he demanded that significant architectural changes be made to the building to accommodate his plans. It is an indication both of his supreme confidence and of the esteem in which he was held that his views were accepted and the changes made.

The immense energy channelled into Sargent's work is expressed in an output of some 1200 oils, 1000 watercolours, three mural cycles, and an untold number of drawings—a production made possible by his personal discipline and by a precise daily routine. His household in Chelsea was run by a cook and housekeeper and by a manservant, Nicola D'Inverno, who assisted him in the studio and occasionally modelled for him. It was Sargent's practice to rise at seven, breakfast at eight, bathe, and then dispatch his correspondence before starting work in the studio at ten. He broke for an hour and a half at lunch and worked on until five in the afternoon. He received many invitations, but his correspondence is interspersed with polite refusals for he was not a naturally social creature. Cynthia Asquith described him as a:

> curiously inarticulate man, he used to splutter and gasp, almost growl with the strain of trying to express himself; and sometimes, like Macbeth at the dagger, he would literally clutch at the air in frustrated efforts to find, with many intermediary 'ers' and 'ums', the most ordinary words. (C. Asquith, *Haply I may Remember*, 1950, 88)

Sargent was most at ease with his family and close friends, with whom he could prove to be a warm and witty companion and a keen mimic and story-teller. He was a generous and supportive friend and an unstinting and self-effacing supporter of struggling artists and musicians.

Sargent's industry in the studio was evident when he travelled abroad on sketching expeditions. Eliza Wedgwood, a friend of the artist and his sister Emily, wrote an account of memorable holidays in Florence and Frascati, Majorca and Corfu, which were characterized by Sargent's ceaseless activity:

> Every autumn we spent together the routine was the same—breakfast generally 7.30, afterwards work literally all day till the light failed. At rare intervals an excursion—if very hot a siesta after the midday meal, but work was the order of the day—when possible, a bathe the end of the morning. After

dinner duets and chess—& early to bed. I was the drone of the party, but allowed to sit and watch John for hours at a time; I don't think he was conscious of my presence, or if he were he didn't mind, but I incline to the first—he was so absorbed in his work that he was oblivious of all else. (Wedgwood, 6–7)

Sargent has remained elusive to his biographers, but there are glimpses from those who knew him well which strike a true note. In 1881 his childhood friend the writer Vernon Lee described the then twenty-five-year-old Sargent as:

very stiff, a sort of completely accentless mongrel … rather French, faubourg sort of manners. Ugly, not at all changed in feature, except for a beard. He was very shy, having I suppose a vague sense that there were poets about … I think John is singularly unprejudiced, almost too amiably candid in his judgements … He is just what he was, only much more serious, without spirits or humour. He talked art & literature, just as formerly, and then, quite unbidden, sat down to the piano & played all sorts of bits of things, ends & middles of things, just as when he was a boy.   (Vernon Lee's Letters, 61, 63)

Sargent never married. There was a brief romance with Louise Burckhardt, a young American woman living in Paris, whom he painted (Lady with the Rose, exh. Paris Salon, 1882; Metropolitan Museum of Art, New York), and some talk of marriage, but the relationship settled down into friendship. He had few strong attachments outside his family and a close circle of friends, was devoted to his two sisters, to Violet and her six children and particularly to Emily, his junior by a year, who suffered from a spinal deformity and to whom he was a beloved and heroic figure. When his father died in 1889 he assumed the role of head of the family and, after their mother's death in 1906, though Emily maintained an independent household in Chelsea, in reality her life revolved completely around his. There has been much discussion about Sargent's private life and sexual orientation. It has been argued that a homosexual charge fuels some of his work, and homosexual readings have been proposed, but in the absence of substantive biographical evidence the speculation is necessarily inconclusive.

Sargent moved in a very sophisticated milieu, but he remained a strangely unworldly, ingenuous character. His portraits commanded high prices—he received £2100 for The Ladies Alexandra, Mary, and Theo Acheson (exh. RA, 1902; priv. coll.); £3000 for his group of medical doctors Professors Welch, Halsted, Osler and Kelly (exh. RA, 1906; Johns Hopkins University medical school, Baltimore); and 2500 guineas for his group of the Marlborough family. He was less than businesslike with the mechanics of payment, and there are a number of touchingly diplomatic letters to patrons asking whether they had paid him. He was unforthcoming about either his religious feelings or his political opinions. Vernon Lee described the young Sargent as 'quite emancipated from all religious ideas' (Vernon Lee's Letters, 63), and it is difficult to discern a powerful religious impulse behind the grand intellectual and aesthetic framework of his history of religion mural scheme.

His first biographer, Evan Charteris, who knew him well, summed up his position vis-à-vis the contemporary world:

He read no newspapers; he had the sketchiest knowledge of current movements outside art; his receptive credulity made him accept fabulous items of information without question. He would have been puzzled to answer if he were asked how nine-tenths of the population lived, he would have been dumbfounded if asked how they were governed. (Charteris, 202)

Sargent's intellectual interests were diverse and sometimes recherché. He had read widely since childhood, in biography, history, and poetry; whenever he travelled his luggage was crammed with books. His education had inclined him to French tastes and his large library was particularly strong in the classics of French literature: Molière, Montaigne, Balzac, Voltaire, Diderot, Flaubert, Stendhal. He enjoyed the orientalist literature then very much in vogue, the newly translated Arabian Nights, William Beckford's Vathek, and Charles Doughty's Arabia deserta—all literary expressions of themes that inspired his own late subject pictures. He approached preparation for the Boston Public Library murals with the intellectual curiosity and dedication of a scholar, and his extensive research involved mastering a wide range of complex and recondite sources.

Music played a central role in Sargent's life. He was anything but a musical dilettante. After the Madame X débâcle in Paris, when his future career as a painter seemed uncertain, he considered making a volte face and pursuing a career in music; the composer Percy Grainger declared that Sargent might have had a brilliant musical career had he chosen to pursue it professionally (J. Bird, Percy Grainger, 1976, 72–3). Sargent's tastes were eclectic and uninfected by snobbery: he was an ardent Wagnerian—an advanced taste at the time—and admired the raw energy of Spanish folk music. A gifted pianist, he specialized in the virtuoso technique demanded by composers like Albeniz, whose technically dazzling and difficult Iberia he played with considerable flair. Sargent's closest musical association was with the French composer Gabriel Fauré, whom he had known since his Paris years, and whom he painted (c.1889; Musée de la Musique, Paris). He frequently played Fauré's piano pieces, and helped to promote his career in London. When Fauré was struggling financially, Sargent negotiated the sale of several of his musical scores to Harvard University and, as a gesture of his gratitude, Fauré gave the artist the manuscript of his second piano quintet (op. 114). Sargent painted a number of contemporary singers and musicians: Elsie Swinton (1896; Art Institute of Chicago), Mabel Batten (1895; Glasgow Museums and Art Gallery), Sir George Henschel (1889; priv. coll.), Charles Martin Loeffler (1903; Isabella Stewart Gardner Museum, Boston), Joseph Joachim (1904; Art Gallery of Ontario, Toronto), and Manual Garcia (1905; Rhode Island School of Design, Providence, Rhode Island). He was an enlightened and influential advocate of contemporary composers and new forms of music, and he counted many musicians and patrons of music among his friends. Percy Grainger contributed a short memoir to Evan Charteris's biography of Sargent, in which he asserted: 'However, remarkable as his playing was, intense as his delight in active music-making was, I consider his greatest contribution to music, lay in the wondrously beneficent influence he exerted on musical life in England' (Charteris, 149).

Although America was never Sargent's home, and indeed he did not visit it until he was twenty-one, when he went to see the Centennial Exhibition (1876) in Philadelphia and meet members of his family, his American ancestry and identity remained important to him. He took seriously his role as a member of a national artistic community, and was involved in American exhibition groups, serving for example on the first jury of the Society of American Artists in 1878. He exhibited regularly in Boston, New York, and Philadelphia, and was represented in exhibitions in cities across America—San Francisco, Chicago, Pittsburgh, St Louis, Buffalo, Cleveland, Cincinnati, Washington, and Worcester. He advised several American museums on important old master purchases and acted personally in negotiations to sell large blocks of his own watercolours to American institutions.

The placing of his watercolours was linked to two important watercolour shows at Knoedler & Co., New York, held jointly with his friend Edward Boit in 1909 and 1912. Of the eight-six watercolours in the 1909 exhibition, eighty-three were bought by the Brooklyn Museum of Art, while the Museum of Fine Arts in Boston bought forty-five watercolours exhibited in 1912. The Metropolitan Museum followed suit and acquired a cache of watercolours direct from the artist in 1915. In steering these works to important American museums, Sargent seems to have been looking to the future, to posterity, to protecting his reputation and his status as a national artist. The emotional and ancestral bonds with America seemed to strengthen with time and, as Sargent grew older, he referred more frequently, and with greater feeling, to his New England antecedents and his 'puritan' disposition. When, in 1907, he was recommended to Edward VII for a knighthood, he declined on the grounds that his American citizenship rendered him ineligible.

Sargent was essentially a cosmopolitan figure with international instincts and allegiances. As a painter he was part of a pan-European movement which encompassed artists like the German Max Liebermann, the Swede Anders Zorn, and the Spaniard Joaquin Sorolla y Bastida, with whom he exhibited at international venues in Paris, Rome, Venice, Berlin, and in major American cities. They were bravura painters, masters of bold and fluid brushwork, immediate impressions, and striking light effects, who expressed an essentially romantic, nostalgic vision in their portraiture and in their painterly descriptions of landscape and rural life. The artistic tide was, however, turning towards modernism and, to a new generation, Sargent seemed to represent a lost world. When he did not support the 'Manet and the post-impressionist' exhibition at the Grafton Galleries in London in 1910, the art critic Roger Fry was roused to a fierce attack on his work. The dispute, and the aesthetic divisions it appeared

to crystallize, cast a shadow from which Sargent's reputation is only just emerging.

The late years Sargent was in the Austrian Tyrol at the outbreak of the First World War, and was trapped there without a passport and regarded as an alien: it was his last visit to continental Europe. The society whose unofficial chronicler he had been was fractured by the war. He turned to America, where he spent two years from April 1916 to May 1918, installing the third phase of his library decorations and working on his mural scheme for the museum. While in America he also painted portraits of two great American figures, the oil magnate John D. Rockefeller (1917; Kykuit, National Trust for Historic Preservation, New York) and President Woodrow Wilson (1917; NG Ire.), the latter on behalf of the Red Cross. He painted a series of lyrical, light-drenched watercolours in Florida, and responded to the grandeur and sublimity of the Canadian Rockies in paintings that are dramatic and romantic in feeling. On his return to England, he accepted a commission as an official war artist, travelling to the western front to work out a subject for a painting to commemorate the sacrifice of war for a planned hall of remembrance. His monumental *Gassed* (exh. RA, 1919; IWM), which represents a frieze-like line of soldiers blinded by mustard gas queuing outside a dressing station, stands in eloquent contrast to the images of Edwardian glamour and *dolce far niente*, which are his popular signature. He was not personally untouched by the war: his young niece Rose-Marie, who is the model in some of his most ravishing figure studies, was killed in the church of St Gervais during a German bombardment of Paris in 1918.

The South African financier and statesman Sir Abe Bailey also commissioned Sargent to commemorate the war by painting a group portrait of the twenty-two general officers who had helped secure victory, *Some General Officers of the Great War*, 1920–22; two further groups of naval officers and statesmen were painted by Sir Arthur Cope and Sir James Guthrie, respectively (all three, NPG). Sargent struggled with a composition in which a line of uniformed officers stand side by side, and the finished work is a more prosaic representation than he had envisaged.

Sargent intended to travel to Boston to supervise his final mural installations but died in his sleep on 15 April 1925 at home in Tite Street having suffered a heart attack. He was buried in Brookwood cemetery, Woking, Surrey, on 18 April, and a memorial service was held at Westminster Abbey on 24 April. His estate sale, held at Christies in London on 24 and 27 July, and consisting of 237 of his own works and some 100 works by other artists, realized £175,000. Memorial exhibitions were held at the Museum of Fine Arts, Boston, the Royal Academy in London, and the Metropolitan Museum of Art in New York. Sargent's sisters were generous and disinterested custodians of his memory: they gave collections of his work to various institutions, principal among them the Harvard University Fogg Art Museum, the Museum of Fine Arts in

Boston, the Metropolitan Museum of Art, New York, and the Tate Gallery, London.

At the time of his death, Sargent was regarded as the outstanding portrait painter of his generation on both sides of the Atlantic, but in reality his reputation was already waning, tainted by the label of fashionable portrait painter which was attached to him. In both aesthetic and social terms he has suffered from the polarities of the modernist debate. His sheer technical skill and virtuosity damned him to some critics. His portraiture has sometimes been regarded as an affirmation of the Edwardian *status quo* and its values; and it has taken a historical perspective to recognize that he was painting at a time of social transformation and that his pictorial interpretations may represent a more subtle and intelligent analysis of a society in transition than has sometimes been allowed. It now seems possible to define Sargent in broader artistic terms: to appreciate him in the round. The landscapes and figure studies, which had limited public exposure in his lifetime, have become the object both of popular acclaim and of art-historical scrutiny, and the mural schemes, to which he attached such importance, though long neglected and sometimes derided, are themselves the subject of serious and revisionist scholarship.

ELAINE KILMURRAY and RICHARD ORMOND

Sources E. Charteris, *John Sargent* (1927) • S. Olson, *John Singer Sargent: his portrait* (1986) • C. M. Mount, *John Singer Sargent: a biography* (New York, 1955) [abridged edn 1957; repr. 1969] • E. W. Sargent, ed., *Epes Sargent of Gloucester and his descendants* (Boston and New York, 1923) [biographical notes by C. S. Sargent] • R. Ormond and E. Kilmurray, *John Singer Sargent: the early portraits* (1998) • R. Ormond and E. Kilmurray, *John Singer Sargent: the later portraits* [forthcoming] • W. Adelson and others, *Sargent abroad: figures and landscapes* (New York, 1997) • E. Kilmurray and R. Osmond, eds., *Sargent* (1998) • W. H. Downes, *John S. Sargent: his life and work* (Boston, MA, 1925) • H. James, 'John S. Sargent', *Harper's New Monthly Magazine*, 75 (Oct 1887), 683–91 [reprinted in *Picture and Text*, New York, 1893, 92–115] • *Henry James: letters*, ed. L. Edel, 3: *1883–1895* (1980) • H. James, *The painter's eye: notes and essays on the pictorial arts* (1956) • I. C. Willis, preface, in *Vernon Lee's letters with a preface by her executor* [*Miss I. C. Willis*] (privately printed, London, 1937) • T. Fairbrother, *John Singer Sargent and America* (New York, 1986) • T. Fairbrother, *John Singer Sargent* (New York, 1994) • R. Ormond, *John Singer Sargent: paintings, drawings, watercolours* (1970) • C. Ratcliff, *John Singer Sargent* (New York, 1982) • D. McKibbin, *Sargent's Boston: with an essay and a biographical summary and a complete check list of Sargent's portraits* (Boston, MA, 1956) • M. Simpson, *Uncanny spectacle: the public career of the young John Singer Sargent* (1997) [with essays by R. Ormond and H. B. Weinberg] • M. C. Volk, *John Singer Sargent's 'El Jaleo'* (Washington, DC, 1992) [with an essay by W. Adelson and E. Oustinoff] • D. Wildenstein, *Claude Monet: biographie et catalogue raisonné*, 2–3 (Lausanne, 1979) • P. Hills, ed., *John Singer Sargent* (New York, 1986) [with essays by L. Ayres and others] • J. Lomax and R. Ormond, *John Singer Sargent and the Edwardian age* (1979) • J. R. Rolfe, *The portrait of a lady: Sargent and Lady Agnew, National Gallery of Scotland, Edinburgh* (1997) [with essays by D. Cannadine, K. McConkey, and W. Mellers] • L. S. Ferber and B. D. Gallati, *Masters of color and light: Homer, Sargent and the American watercolor movement* (1998) [exhibition catalogue, Brooklyn Museum of Art, Washington and London] • S. W. Reed and C. Troyen, *Awash in colour: Homer, Sargent and the great American watercolor* (1993) • A. Stokes, 'John Singer Sargent, RA, RWS', *Old Water-Colour Society's Club*, 3 (1925–6) • S. Promey, *Painting religion in public: John Singer Sargent's 'Triumph of religion' at the Boston Public Library* (Princeton, 1999) • 'Sargent Hall',

A new handbook of the Boston Public Library and its mural decoration (Boston, MA, 1916), 37–58 • M. Kingsbury, 'Sargent's murals in the Boston Public Library', *Winterthur Portfolio*, 2 (1976), 153–72 • R. Fry, 'J. S. Sargent as seen at the Royal Academy exhibition of his works, 1926, and in the National Gallery', *Nation* (1926) [repr. in *Transformations: critical and speculative essays on art*, 1926, 125–35] • M. Birnbaum, *John Singer Sargent, January 12, 1856: April 15, 1925: a conversation piece* (New York, 1941) • N. Pousette-Dart, *John Singer Sargent* (New York, 1924) [with an introduction by L. W. Zeigler] • E. Wedgwood, 'Memoir' [in the form of a letter to Sargent's biographer, E. Charteris, 22 Nov 1925] • *Catalogue of pictures and water colour drawings by J.S. Sargent, R.A. and works by other artists, the property of the late John Singer Sargent, R.A., D.C.L., L.L.D. … which … will be sold by auction by Messrs. Christie, Manson & Woods … on Friday July 24, and Monday, July 27, 1925* [with nineteen illustrations] • *Catalogue of paintings and sketches by John S. Sargent, R.A.* (Boston, MA, 1899) • *Catalogue of the memorial exhibition of the works of the late John Singer Sargent* (1925) [exhibition catalogue, Museum of Fine Arts, Boston] • *Exhibition of works by the late John S. Sargent, R.A.* (1926) [exhibition catalogue, RA] • *Memorial exhibition of the work of John Singer Sargent* (1926) [with an introduction by M. G. Van Rensselaer; exhibition catalogue, Metropolitan Museum of Art, New York] • C. L. Hind, *Hercules Brabazon Brabazon, 1821–1906: his art and life* (1912) [repr. of Sargent's preface to the catalogue of the 1892 Brabazon exhibition at the Goupil Gallery, London] • A. de Belleroche, 'The lithographs of Sargent', *Print Collectors' Quarterly*, 13 (Feb 1926), 30–45 • R. H. Getscher and P. G. Marks, *James McNeill Whistler and John Singer Sargent: two annotated bibliographies* (New York, 1986)

Archives American Academy of Arts and Sciences, Cambridge, corresp. • priv. coll., family papers | Bodl. Oxf., letters to Lewis family, incl. some drawings • Boston Atheneum, Boston, letters to Mrs Charles Hunter • Colby College, Waterville, Maine, letters to Isabella Stewart Gardner • Harvard U., Fogg Art Museum, letters to Mrs Charles Hunter • Isabella Stewart Gardner Museum, Boston, letters to Isabella Stewart Gardner • Metropolitan Museum of Art, New York, letters to Mrs Charles Hunter • Museum of Fine Arts, Boston, letters to Mrs Charles Hunter • priv. coll., Catalogue Raisonné archive, letters to Isabella Stewart Gardner • RA, letters to Royal Academy • Smithsonian Institution, Washington, DC, Archives of American Art, letters to Mrs Charles Hunter • Tate collection, letters to Isabella Stewart Gardner • U. Birm. L., letters to M. H. Spielmann • U. Leeds, Brotherton L., letters to Sir Edmund Gosse

Likenesses A. Saint-Gaudens, bronze medal, 1880, American Academy of Arts and Letters, New York; copies Metropolitan Museum of Art, New York, Museum of Fine Arts, Boston, Salle du Jeu de Paume, Paris • Bassano, photograph, 1882, NPG • J. S. Sargent, self-portrait, oils, 1886, Aberdeen Art Gallery • photograph, c.1886, Smithsonian Institution, Washington, DC, Archives of American Art [*see illus.*] • J. S. Sargent, self-portrait, oils, 1892, National Academy of Design, New York • W. Rothenstein, lithograph, 1897–8, BM, NPG • M. Beerbohm, caricatures, c.1900, Tate collection • G. Boldini, drypoint, 1902, Museo Boldini, Ferrara • J. E. Purdy of Boston, photograph, 1903, NPG • J. S. Sargent, self-portrait, oils, 1906, Uffizi Gallery, Florence • A. L. Coburn, photogravure, 1907, NPG; repro. in A. L. Coburn, *Men of Mark* (1913) • H. von Herkomer, group portrait, oils, 1908 (*The council of the Royal Academy*), Tate collection • M. Beerbohm, caricature, drawing, 1911 (*Mr Sargent in Venice*), Johannesburg Art Gallery • M. Beerbohm, caricature, drawing, c.1912 (*The strong man of the Royal Academy*), AM Oxf. • M. Beerbohm, caricature, Hentschel-colourtype (*A great realist*), NPG; repro. in *VF* (24 Feb 1909) • M. Beerbohm, caricature, drawing, V&A • B. Partridge, pen-and-ink caricature, NPG; for *Punch*, 1925 (unpublished) • photographs, priv. coll.

Wealth at death £25,703 7s. 2d.: probate, 1925 • £23,793 15s. 6s.: further grant: 1925

Sargent, Sir (Harold) Malcolm Watts (1895–1967), conductor, was born in Ashford, Kent, on 29 April 1895, the

Sir (Harold) Malcolm Watts Sargent (1895–1967), by Sir Gerald Kelly, exh. RA 1948

only son of Henry Edward Sargent of Stamford, Lincolnshire, and his wife, Agnes Marion Hall, daughter of a Hertfordshire landscape gardener. Henry Sargent, employed in a coal merchant's business, was a keen amateur musician, an organist, and choirmaster, who carefully fostered his son's talent from the beginning. The most important early influence, however, was that of Frances Tinkler, an inspiring local teacher who greatly helped Sargent and, some years later, Michael Tippett. At Stamford School, Sargent was soon noted for irrepressible high spirits and quick intelligence. But his interests were never academic, and other possibilities were elbowed aside in the determined drive towards a career in music.

On leaving school in 1912 Sargent was articled to Haydn Keeton, organist of Peterborough Cathedral, and was one of the last to be trained in that traditional system, so soon to disappear. The discipline involved daily contact between master and pupil in a severe but balanced curriculum, and Keeton was an exacting tutor, old-fashioned perhaps, but highly professional. He taught the counterpoint of Fux, organ-playing in the style of Samuel Sebastian Wesley, and piano-playing in that of Mendelssohn and Sir W. Sterndale Bennett. Score-reading and continuo-realization were learned not as academic subjects but in the daily practice of cathedral music, performed from the scores of William Boyce and Samuel Arnold. It was hard

work, and Sargent loved it all. 'We had no money', he said in later years, 'and our future was quite uncertain: but it was music, music, music all the way.'

By the end of his articles Sargent was already recognized as a fine player, a composer of marked talent, and a well-equipped professional whose charm, vitality, and technical accomplishment were outstanding. But his ambitions, though ample, were not yet defined. Sometimes he thought of being a solo pianist and, like a Rakhmaninov, playing his own compositions all over the world. He could probably have done this. After a performance of *The Dream of Gerontius* in 1912, however, he told a group of friends about his intention to be 'a second Elgar'. For that destiny he was less well suited.

In 1914 Sargent was appointed organist of Melton Mowbray, and found himself among people able to appreciate his talent and to give him substantial help. It was made possible for him to have piano lessons from Benno Moiseiwitsch; a good orchestra was created for him to conduct in Leicester; opportunities were offered generously. In his Leicester concerts he appeared as pianist, composer, and conductor, and won the approval of Sir Henry J. Wood, who invited him to conduct, in the 1921 Promenade Concert season, his tone-poem *Impressions of a Windy Day*. The performance was a triumph: but it was as conductor rather than composer that the young man was acclaimed, and on that evening the pattern of his career was settled. For a time he continued to work from his base in the midlands, but in 1923, invited to join the staff at the Royal College of Music, he moved to London, where in the following year he married Eileen Laura Harding Horne; they had two children, a son, Peter, and a daughter, Pamela. The marriage ended in divorce in 1946.

The ten years after 1923 were decisive in Sargent's career, and were a time of unremitting hard work and social activity. He was a restless man, for whom dancing until dawn after a concert seemed a necessary relaxation. With no private income and increasing responsibilities, as well as a natural inclination to spend freely, he was obliged to undertake whatever work was offered; his schedule involved much travel, with varied programmes on limited rehearsal time. Only a musician of great talent and resilience could have done what he did. But he might have been wise to be more selective, even if the experience made him a general-purpose conductor of extreme efficiency, sometimes criticized for not being fastidious but also admired for being totally reliable.

Sargent's responsibilities at this time included the Robert Mayer concerts (1924), the Diaghilev Ballet (1927), the Royal Choral Society (1928), including the spectacular productions of *Hiawatha*, the Courtauld–Sargent concerts (1929–40), and the D'Oyly Carte Opera Company (1930). He conducted many performances of the British National Opera Company and numberless concerts in cities outside London. Among the works entrusted to him for first performance were *Hugh the Drover* by Ralph Vaughan Williams, William Walton's *Belshazzar's Feast*, and Walton's opera *Troilus and Cressida*.

Success so brilliant and an enjoyment of its glamour so

uninhibited were bound to provoke hostility and to 'excite the common artifice by which envy degrades excellence'. There began to be troubles with orchestras which Sargent tried to discipline. Methods that delighted his devoted choralists were less acceptable to experienced orchestral players: harsh things were said on both sides. Some critics described his performances as brash and superficial, and purists objected to adjustments that Sargent made in the scoring of well-known works, even though these were always effective and generally less drastic than those made by other conductors. Sargent seemed to disregard these attacks: in fact he was deeply hurt, and they added to the strain under which he worked, a strain that was beginning by 1930 to affect the quality of his performances and his health.

In 1932 Sargent suffered a complete breakdown, and there was doubt whether he would recover from the tubercular infection that involved serious abdominal operations. For two years he was out of action, but when he did reappear his performances had all the old zest and a new depth.

In 1944 a fresh blow fell when Sargent's much loved daughter, Pamela, was smitten with polio and died. For months he was almost a broken man, but music saved him, and he seemed in time to draw inspiration from the experience. There were, however, works that he never conducted again except as a kind of memorial to Pamela, and not a few of his many generous but strictly private benefactions to other sufferers were really an offering to her.

In 1950 Sargent was chosen to follow Sir Adrian Boult as conductor of the BBC Symphony Orchestra and entered the final, most influential, stage of his career. With that orchestra, the BBC Chorus, the Royal Choral Society, the Huddersfield Choir, the Promenade Concerts, and many appearances as guest conductor with other ensembles, he enjoyed unrivalled opportunities for music-making on a great scale. Old prejudices had largely evaporated, and his interpretations were now seen to be equal to those of any conductor in the world; as an accompanist he was regarded by many exacting soloists as pre-eminent.

Sargent's influence in these years was extended by appearances on *The Brains Trust*, where he effectively represented the common sense and decency of the ordinary citizen, and proved himself more than a match for the plausible intellectuals who often appeared with him. In this as in other activities he used his gifts of personality and showmanship to spread the love of music and to insist upon its place in a good life.

Sargent was now accepted as a valuable ambassador for music, and especially British music, in many parts of the world, and it was on one of his numerous foreign tours that he was taken ill. There was a temporary recovery, and he returned to conducting, but again collapsed in Chicago in July 1967. On his return he was seen to be dying. During the months that remained he continued to present himself with courage and something of the old panache, and made an unforgettable farewell visit to his devoted audience on the last night of the Proms. He died a day or two later at his home in London, 9 Albert Hall Mansions, on 3 October 1967.

Sargent's death provoked a remarkable demonstration of public sorrow and admiration. During a career in which social success had played no small part he had won the affection and loyalty of countless ordinary music-lovers who recognized his sincerity and came to share his buoyant love of life and music. He once said in jest that his career had been based on the two Ms, *Messiah* and *Mikado*, and there was an element of truth in the comment, which was a characteristic example of his unguarded spontaneity. But he could have added that it also rested on a long record of fine performances, an unfailing devotion to music, and natural endowments of exceptional brilliance.

Sargent's character was a strange blend of simplicity and sophistication, of apparent self-confidence and a deep sense of insecurity. He was an extremely generous man, but could sometimes appear vain and arrogant, displaying a frank enjoyment of fame and success which more cautious persons would have concealed, not from modesty but from fear of ridicule.

The circumstances of Sargent's early life had permanently influenced him. If he had enjoyed the privilege of attachment to a great professional orchestra and its conductors he might have become a different musician but not necessarily a better one. As it was, in the tough campaign to make his own way, he won the equipment necessary for the work he had to do, a work that greatly forwarded the interests of British music. After Sir Henry Wood's death in 1944 there was nobody except Sargent who could carry on his particular task, and when Sargent himself passed from the scene his place was not filled. Sargent was appointed honorary DMus (Oxford) in 1942 and honorary LLD (Liverpool) in 1947, the year in which he was knighted. Among his many other honours were appointment as an honorary member of the Royal Academy of Music, honorary fellow of the Royal College of Organists, fellow of Royal College of Music, honorary fellow of Trinity College of Music, and fellow of the Royal Society of Arts.

THOMAS ARMSTRONG, *rev.*

Sources C. Reid, *Malcolm Sargent* (1968) · R. Aldous, *Tunes of glory: the life of Malcolm Sargent* (2001) · *The Times* (4 Oct 1967) · R. Crichton, 'Sargent, Sir (Harold) Malcolm (Watts)', *New Grove* · personal knowledge (1981) · private information (1981) · *CGPLA Eng. & Wales* (1967) · d. cert.

Archives FILM BFI NFTVA, current affairs footage · BFI NFTVA, documentary footage · BFI NFTVA, propaganda film footage | SOUND BL NSA, performance recordings

Likenesses E. Kapp, drawing, 1930, U. Birm. · H. Wiener, pencil drawing, c.1935, Royal College of Music, London · R. Reeve, chalk drawing, 1939, Royal College of Music, London · W. Stoneman, photograph, 1943, NPG · E. Kapp, drawing, 1946, U. Birm. · G. Kelly, oils, exh. RA 1948, Royal College of Music, London [*see illus.*] · W. Stoneman, photograph, 1955, NPG · G. Davien, caricature, plaster bust, 1964, NPG · C. Beaton, photograph, NPG · K. N. Collins, photograph, NPG · H. Coster, photograph, NPG · J. Gilroy, oils, Garr. Club; version, Royal Albert Hall, London · D. Low, pencil caricature, NPG · W. E. Narraway, bronze bust, Royal Festival Hall, London · A. W. Rissik, lithograph, NPG · W. Timyn, bronze bust, Royal Albert Hall, London

Wealth at death £43,657: probate, 3 Nov 1967, *CGPLA Eng. & Wales*

Sargent, Sir (Harold) Orme Garton (1884–1962), diplomatist and civil servant, was born Giles Orme Sargent on 31 October 1884 at 2 Elvaston Place, Kensington, London, the only child of Harry Garton Sargent, a gentleman of independent means, and his wife, Henrietta Sarah Finnis Stud Mackinnon, whose sister married the fifteenth duke of Somerset. His parents changed his name subsequent to registering his birth. He had an unhappy childhood, both parents being elderly, strict, and possessive. 'Moley', as he was known from childhood, was educated at Radley College, and then spent some time in Switzerland preparing for the diplomatic service, which he entered in March 1906. He passed on examination in public law in May 1908, was promoted third secretary in October 1911, and served as secretary to the British delegates at the international sanitary conference in Paris, from November to December 1911.

During the early stages of the First World War, Sargent worked in the department of the Foreign Office dealing with the blockade, which gave him a good grounding in commercial and economic affairs. In October 1917 he was promoted second secretary and transferred to Bern; he was promoted first secretary in April 1919. In July that year he was seconded to the British delegation to the peace conference at Versailles. Following the signature of the treaty of Versailles and the disbandment of the British delegation in December 1919, he remained in Paris to work with the conference of ambassadors, which continued to meet to discuss the problems of European security and reconstruction. He finally returned to London in November 1925. Thereafter he refused to attend conferences or to go abroad for any purpose; it was thought that he suffered from claustrophobia in ships and aircraft. Contemporaries believed that this was perhaps for the best: he had few of the qualities necessary for a great ambassador. Intelligent, informed, and passionate about defending British interests, he was nevertheless reserved and somewhat aloof; he had little time for the social life which was so important a part of an ambassador's job; and he had none of the political skills of colleagues such as Sir Robert Vansittart. Indeed, the latter observed, with some truth, that 'Orme Sargent was a philosopher strayed into Whitehall. He knew all the answers; when politicians did not want them he went out to lunch' (Vansittart, 399).

In October 1926 Sargent was promoted counsellor and put in charge of the Foreign Office's central department, which covered Italy, Austria, Hungary, Yugoslavia, and the Balkans. In August 1933 he was promoted assistant under-secretary, with additional responsibility for relations with Germany, France, and Poland. Apart from official minutes, he never wrote about his time in the Foreign Office. Nevertheless, from the diplomatic record it emerges that he was conscious of Britain's proximity to the European continent, and of the need to prevent any single power from dominating that continent, be it Nazi Germany or communist Russia.

There is evidence that as early as the beginning of 1930 Sargent was anxious lest Germany adopt a forward foreign policy, and welcomed internal wrangles in Germany that could limit this. On 13 November 1934 he wrote to Winston Churchill arguing against Churchill's view that Hitler was plotting a war of aggression in the immediate future. Sargent's analysis was that Hitler hoped to achieve his purpose by playing off one power against the other, and isolating each power in turn, rather than by force. Although Britain was probably the last power on Hitler's agenda, its turn would come. At this stage, however, Sargent's opposition to 'appeasement' was by no means clear-cut. In June 1935 he blamed the French for refusing to make a bargain with the Germans when it had been possible in April 1934; and in a memorandum of 21 November 1935 he and Ralph Wigram of the central department set out the case for coming to terms with Germany. They argued that Britain had a choice of three policies: it could do nothing; it could encircle Germany; or it could come to terms with Germany. Despite the immense obstacles involved, they concluded that an agreement was desirable and hinted that concessions over the Rhineland as well as in the colonial sphere could pave the way for an overall settlement. This was one of the classic statements of appeasement, and, in effect, outlined the policy later followed by Neville Chamberlain when he was prime minister. Nevertheless, Sargent found himself increasingly opposed to this policy, especially after Hitler's re-militarization of the Rhineland in 1936.

When at the end of 1937 Neville Chamberlain considered the issue of colonial compensation for Germany as a means of removing the differences between Britain and Germany, Sargent felt the need to raise the matter with the dominions. He now argued that in this matter Britain should keep the initiative, and saw advantages in a conference of the League of Nations mandatory powers. This device would have the incidental merit of forcing South Africa to justify its policy of reconciliation with Germany alongside its refusal to hand back former South-West Africa, and the veto it had placed on Britain handing back Tanganyika. In March 1938 his paper on the *Anschluss* reflected his changing view of Hitler's intentions: Hitler would advance his conquests, reduce the whole Danube basin to vassal status, and dismantle Czechoslovakia. If the western powers did nothing central Europe would be lost, Italy would be forced to side with Germany, and Hitler would arrange for Mussolini to secure a controlling hand in Spain. To counter this Britain needed to mobilize its diplomatic resources, hold staff conversations with France and Belgium and elaborate a common policy for central and south-eastern Europe, strengthen its ties with Greece and Turkey, cultivate Poland and Russia, and restore good relations with Japan. Above all, Sargent emphasized the need for Britain to cultivate, interest, and educate the United States. The Munich agreement, and the enthusiastic reception accorded Chamberlain on his return, he regarded as a disgrace; indeed, he is alleged to have remarked that it might have been thought that Britain had won a great victory rather than betrayed a small country. Perhaps because of his now well-known opposition to appeasement, it was only with difficulty that Sir

Alexander Cadogan was able to secure Sargent's promotion to the post of deputy under-secretary of state in September 1939.

Following the outbreak of the Second World War, Sargent was increasingly concerned at the prospect of the Soviet Union dominating a devastated post-war Europe. In November 1940 he advanced ideas about taking over the anti-Comintern pact and so attracting Italy, Japan, and Spain to the allied cause. Even after Hitler's attack on Russia, he was determined to limit the power of the Soviet Union: when considering post-war planning in 1942–3 he favoured an Anglo-French alliance in the west, and two large confederations in middle Europe which could maintain a balance of power and control a united Germany. As the Soviet Union established puppet governments in eastern Europe, Sargent became increasingly alarmed and was responsible for drafting Churchill's telegrams to President Truman urging the Americans to make a stand over this. He was particularly concerned when any chance of an American thrust on Prague, in May 1945, was lost through General Eisenhower's self-denying ordinance. On 26 July 1945 Cadogan recorded him as predicting a communist avalanche over Europe, and the reduction of Britain to a second-class power.

Sargent was acutely aware of the fundamental weakness of Britain as a great power, in comparison with the United States and the Soviet Union. Thus in October 1945 he observed that Britain's position in relation to the two latter powers was 'Lepidus in the triumvirate with Mark Antony and Augustus' (Ovendale, The English-Speaking Alliance, 18). In July 1945 he produced an influential memorandum, 'Stocktaking after VE-day', in which he argued that the only way 'to compel our two big partners to treat us as an equal' was for Britain to assume the leadership of western Europe as well as of the empire or Commonwealth (Rothwell, 145). Such ideas chimed well with those of Ernest Bevin, foreign secretary in the new Labour government, and there was little surprise when Sargent was appointed permanent under-secretary at the Foreign Office in succession to Cadogan, in February 1946. He continued to urge a positive British approach to western European integration, defining Britain's 'primary objective' in December 1946 as being 'by close association with our neighbours to create a European Group which will enable us to deal on a footing of equality with our two gigantic colleagues, the USA and the USSR' (ibid., 435). As permanent under-secretary, Sargent was also increasingly involved with the Middle East. In April 1946 he expressed reservations about the defeatist attitude of the British delegation negotiating the withdrawal from Egypt. He was also concerned that American Zionist propaganda endangered Anglo-American relations at the time of the joining of the cold war, and in May 1947 was responsible for reports being sent to the Americans about the links between funds collected in the United States and the Irgun.

Sargent retired in February 1949 and moved to Bath, living in a restored Georgian home, Bathwick Hill House, and cultivating an interest in antique furniture. He was

created GCMG in 1948, having been appointed CB in 1936, KCMG in 1937, and KCB in 1947. He was made a justice of the peace for Bath in 1949 and a church commissioner in 1952. He was a devout Christian. He died, unmarried, in the Lansdown Nursing Home, Bath, on 23 October 1962 after a long illness; the funeral service was held in Bath Abbey on 27 October and a memorial service at St Margaret's, Westminster, on 16 November.

RITCHIE OVENDALE

Sources H. M. G. Jebb [Lord Gladwyn], The memoirs of Lord Gladwyn (1972) • M. Gilbert, Winston S. Churchill, 5: 1922–1939 (1976); 6: Finest hour, 1939–1941 (1983); 7: Road to victory, 1941–1945 (1986) • R. A. C. Parker, Chamberlain and appeasement: British policy and the coming of the Second World War (1993) • V. Rothwell, Britain and the cold war, 1941–1947 (1982) • R. Ovendale, 'Appeasement' and the English speaking world: Britain, the United States, and the policy of 'appeasement', 1937–1939 (1975) • R. Ovendale, The English-speaking alliance: Britain, the United States, the dominions and the cold war, 1945–1951 (1985) • R. Ovendale, Britain, the United States, and the end of the Palestine mandate, 1942–1948 (1989) • DNB • The Times (24 Oct 1962) • FO List • WWW • Burke, Peerage • b. cert. • CGPLA Eng. & Wales (1962) • The diaries of Sir Alexander Cadogan, ed. D. Dilks (1971) • P. Dixon, Double diploma: the life of Sir Pierson Dixon, don and diplomat (1968) • N. Rose, Vansittart: study of a diplomat (1978) • A. Roberts, 'The Holy Fox': a biography of Lord Halifax (1991) • Lord Vansittart [R. G. Vansittart], The mist procession: the autobiography of Lord Vansittart (1958) • H. Nicolson, Diaries and letters, ed. N. Nicolson, 2 (1967) • A. Eden, earl of Avon, The Eden memoirs, 3: The reckoning (1965) • A. Bullock, The life and times of Ernest Bevin, 3 (1983) • The diplomatic diaries of Oliver Harvey, 1937–40, ed. J. Harvey (1970) • The war diaries of Oliver Harvey, ed. J. Harvey (1978) • T. T. Hammond, ed., Witnesses to the origins of the cold war (1982) • W. J. Mommsen and L. Kettenacker, eds., The fascist challenge and the policy of appeasement (1983) • J. L. Gormly, The collapse of the grand alliance, 1945–1948 (1987)

Archives NRA, priv. coll., diaries and papers • PRO, Foreign Office papers, corresp., FO 800 series | BL, corresp. with P. V. Emrys-Evans, Add. MS 58238 • Bodl. Oxf., corresp. with Sir Horace Rumbold • CAC Cam., corresp. with Sir Eric Phipps

Likenesses W. Stoneman, photograph, 1941, NPG • photograph, repro. in The Times • photograph, Foreign Office, permanent under-secretary's room

Wealth at death £71,466 16s.: probate, 19 Dec 1962, CGPLA Eng. & Wales

Sargrove, John Adolph (1906–1975), electrical engineer, was born at 25 Delamere Terrace, St Pancras, London, on 23 May 1906, the son of Arpad Szabadi, an electrician, of Hungarian origin, and his wife, Cissie Lily, née Solomons. He was baptized John Adolph Szabadi but changed his name to Sargrove in 1938. Soon after his birth he was taken to Budapest, the home of his parents, and received his early schooling in that city. After returning to London in 1920, he studied at the polytechnic in Regent Street, while undertaking an apprenticeship with several small engineering firms in the London area. In 1930 he was employed by Tungsram Electric Lamps Ltd (later British Tungsram Radio Works Ltd) as a patent researcher. This provided a valuable background for the innovator he was to become, his importance being marked by the large number of British and foreign patents filed under his names. In 1933 he became chief technical engineer of British Tungsram, a post which he held until 1940. During this time he contributed much to the development of new and improved types of thermionic valves. His technical interests, already broadened by experience as a patent researcher, extended into what was later known as electronics with his appointment in 1940 as chief engineer with Electro-Physical Laboratories and with Mervyn Sound and Vision Ltd. He spent the war years (1939–45) mainly with these companies, developing photoelectric devices. Towards the end of this period he began to make contributions in special research on electronic automation equipment for the armaments industry, which led directly to his post-war plans in automatic production equipment for the radio industry.

Sargrove's wide interests in radio, electronic, and production techniques at this time determined his professional involvement, and led him in the technical direction that dominated his later career. The professional interests of most engineers are served by membership of an appropriate organization; Sargrove gained membership of and contributed fully to four of these institutions. In 1939 he became a member (and later a fellow) of the Institute of Radio and Electronic Engineers, to the activities of which he contributed for the rest of his life; from 1965 to 1968 he served on its council, and in 1966 he was elected vice-president. He was also accepted as a member of the Institution of Electrical Engineers in 1942 (he became a fellow in 1949). Finally, he gained membership of both the Institution of Mechanical Engineers and the Institution of Production Engineers. He showed much talent in the technical direction of projects involving electronics allied with automation within a number of specialized companies, several of which he founded himself. This culminated in Electronic Circuit Making Equipment (ECME), which aroused enormous interest in 1946–7 and gained Sargrove the first Clerk-Maxwell premium of the Institution of Radio and Electronic Engineers.

The basic idea of ECME was to eliminate the conventional assembly and wiring of a multitude of individual components mounted on a metal chassis, which was the common method of receiver construction at that time. Instead, Sargrove proposed to make the wiring and components an integral part of a moulded plastic panel, with only the valves, loudspeaker, and electrolytic capacitors inserted as plug-in elements. In this way he was to produce the complete radio receiver in a single production machine with very little assembly-line labour. This brilliant invention, ahead of its time and dogged by political problems, was never taken up generally. It was, however, the first modern approach to automatic operation in electronic manufacture and was acknowledged as 'the first automatic factory' by the Stanford Research Institute in a leading article under this title in the magazine *Fortune* in 1948.

In 1955 Sargrove moved on to introduce automation into many industries, and founded his own company, Automatic Consultants and Associates, of which he became technical director and, later, chairman. While with this firm he made major contributions to the new and growing field of automation technology and assisted in the work of organizations such as the joint services technical committee, the technical committee of the British Standards Institution, and the United Kingdom Automation Council. Sargrove can justifiably be considered as one of the pioneers of automation in the United Kingdom. He foresaw the immense advantages that the application of electronics would give to machine control and applied his ideas successfully to a number of automatic production processes. Many of his ideas found common acceptance, particularly in the automatic production of electronic equipment, such as computer systems, which became an essential part of twentieth-century technological infrastructure.

Sargrove died of cancer on 9 January 1975, at the Nuffield Home, Shores Road, Woking, Surrey, leaving a widow, Mildred Rose Sargrove. They had made their home at Flat 3, The Leys, Esher Road, Hersham.

K. G. BEAUCHAMP

Sources G. W. A. Dummer, C. Brunetti, and L. K. Lee, *Electronic equipment design and construction* (1961) · R. L. Henry and H. H. Rosen, 'A Fortune round table, the automatic factory', *Fortune* (Oct 1953) · *Journal of the Institution of Electronic and Radio Engineers* (March 1975) · A. Hope, 'How Britain lost its lead in automation', *New Scientist* (24 April 1980) · J. A. Sargrove, 'New methods of radio production', *Journal of the British Institution of Radio Engineers*, 7 (1947), 2–33 · J. A. Sargrove and D. L. Johnson, 'Automatic inspection as the key control element in full automation', *Journal of the British Institution of Radio Engineers*, 17 (1957), 529–35 · K. G. Beauchamp, 'John Sargrove — inventor of the first PCB', *Electronics and Power: the Journal of the Institution of Electrical Engineers*, 27 (1981), 477–83 · b. cert. · d. cert. **Archives** Sci. Mus., artefacts produced by the Sargrove method of automatic radio receiver production (ECME) | FILM Technograph and Telegraph Ltd, Easthampstead Road, Bracknell, Berkshire, a short film about the ECME production process **Wealth at death** £12,768: probate, 30 April 1975, *CGPLA Eng. & Wales*

Saris, John (1580/81–1643), sea captain, was probably born in London, one of the two children of Thomas Saris (*d.* 1588) and his first wife, Katherine Lovell. His family originated in Tickhall, Yorkshire, and had been armigerous for at least three generations. His mother died when he was an infant or young child, and his father married Katherine Chevall, with whom he had three further children. When John was eight years old his father also died, and was buried in the church of St Andrew Undershaft, London. We know nothing of his apprenticeship, only that, when he was twenty-four, the East India Company took him into service for the second voyage to Asia, under the command of Henry Middleton. Saris was one of eight factors who remained behind in Bantam on the island of Java, when Middleton returned to England in October 1605, and they formed, under the chief factor, Gabriel Towerson, the first English factory there. Saris advised the company on the commodities of Asia, and he in turn became chief factor in December 1608 when Towerson returned home. In a letter to the directors of the company, while serving in that capacity, he wrote a comprehensive description of trading patterns in south-east Asia, centred on Bantam. He included information about customs and port charges at Bantam, the seasonal arrivals of Gujarati and Chinese merchant ships, and the conditions under which commodities might be obtained, such as the diamonds of Borneo, the sandalwood of Timor, the cloves of the Moluccas, the mace and nutmeg grown on the islands around the Banda Sea, or the pepper of Java and Sumatra. Saris served for a further ten months, until October 1609, before he too returned to England, where he arrived in May 1610.

Plans proceeded quickly for Saris to return to Asia in command, at the age of thirty-one, of the eighth voyage, consisting of three ships, the *Clove*, the *Hector*, and the *Thomas*, which sailed in April 1611. Investors to the voyage subscribed £55,947. By the instructions issued by the company, Saris's initial objective was to obtain a return lading for the *Hector* and the *Thomas*, first at Surat and then at Bantam. Should he not arrive to catch the monsoon winds the following winter, he was also to seek out opportunities in the Red Sea, and primarily at Mocha. In establishing commercial priorities, the directors made ample use of Saris's intelligence, relating in almost his exact terms, for example, the difference between raw silk from Nanking (Nanjing) and Canton (Guangzhou). In this case they indicated their exclusive preference for the better quality silk from Nanking, a sample of which Saris had provided for them, and 'is here well requested' (Birdwood, 286).

Saris reached Socotra, an island off the Horn of Africa, in February 1612, too late for him to proceed eastwards. While Middleton, who was in command of the sixth voyage, had had great difficulty with the sanjakbeyi of Mocha the previous winter, Saris had the advantage of a change in office and a pass of safe conduct issued in Constantinople by Ahmed I (r. 1603–17). Any opportunities to trade were, however, cut short after three weeks by the return of Middleton from Surat, where he had also been rebuffed, seeking revenge. Saris and Middleton made an uneasy and sometimes acrimonious arrangement to divide the goods taken from Indian merchant ships in the Red Sea by a combination of forced trade at fixed prices and piracy. Organized under separate capital subscriptions, the trade each of the commanders was able to transact or the plunder each of them was able to take determined the relative success of the two voyages. The competition between Saris and Middleton and whatever personal animosities may have developed as a result led to a growing rivalry between them.

This rivalry continued as both commanders sailed east for Bantam in August 1612 in order to procure a more ample return lading. Saris arrived a month before Middleton, and, against the backdrop of rising prices for pepper with the anticipation of further demand, he laded the *Hector* and the *Thomas* with 14,000 sacks. These two ships sailed for England in December 1612 and January 1613 respectively.

It had been the directors' intention, expressed in the instructions, that Saris and the *Clove* should proceed to explore new opportunities in the Moluccas and in Japan once an assured lading had been procured for the other two ships. For nearly a decade the directors had known, by Dutch and Portuguese word of mouth, that William Adams had been living in Japan, recently with notable preferment from the shogun, Tokugawa Ieyasu. Saris also knew from his time in Bantam of a Dutch expedition that arrived in Japan in the summer of 1609 with the aim of establishing a factory, although not of its outcome. Evidence of Adams's willingness to facilitate commercial contact came with a letter he wrote in October 1610 to the English factory at Bantam, which Saris read to his crew before sailing in mid-January 1613.

Before making the voyage to Japan, Saris sought to trade for cloves in the Moluccas, sailing first for Batjan Island, now known as Pulau Bacan. At several places in and around the islands off the west coast of Halmahera, including Tidore and Ternate, he attempted to circumvent Dutch control, recently won from the Spanish in all but a few places, but was able to obtain only small quantities of the spice in clandestine exchanges. War had visibly devastated large tracts of land; Dutch intimidation, moreover, kept local producers from selling cloves to Saris or from assisting him in other ways. 'They were inquisitive to know who piloted us to ride in this place, seeing it could not be one of the naturals', wrote Saris in his journal, 'and if they knew him they would cut him to pieces before our faces' (Satow, 34). In mid-April he gave up the attempt, and sailed for Japan having procured 3690 lb. He arrived at Hirado on 11 June 1613.

Accompanied by William Adams, Saris embarked on a diplomatic mission to obtain legal standing for a factory at Hirado, which was to last for three months, from August to November 1613. Although Tokugawa Ieyasu (r. 1603–5), the founder of the dynasty which bore his name, had abdicated the title of shogun in favour of his son Hiretada (r. 1605–23), he still controlled most important features of the government; and it was for the purpose of presenting King James's letter and legal terms for English trade to Ieyasu that Saris travelled to Sumpu (Shizuoka). He followed this visit with a journey to meet Hiretada at Edo (Tokyo), a return to Sumpu to receive official copies of the approved terms, and finally a journey to Kyoto, where he received Ieyasu's gift to James of five folding screens. Saris's contempt for Adams's assimilation of and apparent preference for Japanese manners, which he privately expressed after the journey's end, resulted in muted tension, although they maintained a working relationship. Adams was officially part of the factory of eight at Hirado, headed by Richard Cocks, that Saris established before departing for Bantam in early December.

Saris's return to England with valuable commodities ensured the success of the eighth voyage, although the private trade he conducted while in Asia dampened recognition among directors of the company. In Bantam he took six weeks to lade a cargo of pepper and reorganize the factory before setting out on his return voyage of eight months' duration. He arrived in Plymouth at the end of September 1614. Auditors brought in by the company immediately assessed the profit to investors in the voyage to be 200 per cent; and in 1617, after the sale of goods had been completed, these investors realized a further return of 11 per cent, producing a 66 per cent profit per annum and making it, in absolute terms, the second most profitable of the first twelve voyages. In addition, Saris had extended the scope of the English trade in Asia and the company's knowledge of commercial opportunities.

Brazilwood from Siam, raw silk from China, and pepper from Java, Saris reported to the directors, could all be sold at high profit in Japan for silver specie, which then could be used to purchase returns at Bantam. A significant minority of the company nevertheless believed, despite these successes, that Saris should be punished for trading with his own capital and for his attempt to unlade his goods clandestinely at Plymouth. In a compromise exemption from the prohibition against private trade, the directors agreed to buy these goods for £2000.

Despite rumours of a second voyage to Japan, Saris retired from active service with the company. Approximately a year after his return he married Anne, the daughter of William Migges. For several years afterwards they resided in London, and when Anne died in February 1622, at the age of twenty-one, she was buried in the parish church of St Botolph. By 1629, when he first appeared in assessments for the poor law, Saris had moved to Church Row, Fulham, to a house called Goodriche's, which had been built in the early fifteenth century. There he remained until his death, on 11 December 1643 at the age of sixty-three; eight days later he was buried at the contiguous parish church, marked by a black stone in the floor of the choir.

Saris bequeathed just over £2000, including notably large gifts to two servants. The chief beneficiary was his nephew George Saris, the son of his half-brother, who inherited whatever had not been specifically bequested, as well as two houses in London, including one situated in St Mary Axe. He also left £30 for the poor of Fulham to be distributed in the form of thirty two-pence loaves each Sunday.   J. K. LAUGHTON, rev. TREVOR DICKIE

Sources E. M. Satow, ed., *The voyage of Captain John Saris to Japan, 1613*, Hakluyt Society, 2nd ser., 5 (1900) · C. J. Fèret, *Fulham old and new: being an exhaustive history of the ancient parish of Fulham*, 1 (1900) · PRO, PROB 11/197, fols. 352v–353v · S. Purchas, *Hakluytus Posthumus, or, Purchas his pilgrimes*, bk 3 (1625); repr. Hakluyt Society, extra ser., 16 (1905) · K. N. Chaudhuri, *The English East India Company: the study of an early English joint-stock company* (1965) · G. Birdwood, ed., *The register of letters … of the governour and company of merchants of London trading into the East Indies, 1600–1619* (1893) · T. Rundall, *Memorials of the empire of Japan in the XVIth and XVIIth centuries*, Hakluyt Society, 8 (1850) · T. K. Rabb, *Enterprise and empire: merchant and gentry investment in the expansion of England, 1575–1630* (1967) · W. R. Scott, *The constitution and finance of English, Scottish and Irish joint-stock companies to 1720*, 2 (1912); repr. (1968) · *The journal of John Jourdain, 1608–1617*, ed. W. Foster, Hakluyt Society, 2nd ser., 16 (1905)

Wealth at death over £2000 plus two houses in London and one in Fulham: PRO, PROB 11/197, fols. 352v–353v

Sarkar, Sir Jadunath (1870–1958), historian, the third son of Raj Kumar Sarkar and Hari Sundari, was born on 10 December 1870 at Karachmaria in the Rajshahi district of Bengal. His father belonged to a Barujibi (betel-grower) *zamindari* family. Educated at the Rajshahi and Calcutta collegiate schools and at the Presidency College, Calcutta, in 1892 he stood first in the first class in the University of Calcutta's MA examination in English. In 1893 he married Kadambini, daughter of Madhusudan Chaudhuri; they had two sons and three daughters. From 1893 to 1896 he taught English at Ripon College before serving as professor of English at Vidyasagar College. Winning the

Premchand Roychand scholarship in December 1897, Sarkar entered the provincial educational service in June 1898. After a year at Presidency College he was transferred in 1899 to Patna College, where he served as professor of English and then as professor of history until his retirement from government service in 1926, with an interval (1917–19) as head of the department of history at the new Hindu University of Benares and as professor of history and English literature at Ravenshaw College, Cuttack (1919–23). In 1918 he was promoted to the Indian educational service.

From 1926 to 1928 Sarkar was vice-chancellor of Calcutta University. From 1929 to 1932 he served as a nominated member of the Bengal legislative council. He was appointed CIE in 1926, and knighted in 1929. He was a founder member of the Indian historical records commission (1919), an honorary member of the Royal Asiatic Society (1923), Campbell gold medallist and honorary fellow of the Bombay branch of the Royal Asiatic Society (1926), and a corresponding member of the Royal Historical Society (1935).

As a historian Sarkar found the study of the history of the later Mughals uncertainly dependent on European travellers' accounts and late Persian histories in challengeable English translations. He left it resting firmly upon rich resources of contemporary letters, news reports, official documents, and histories in Persian, Marathi, French, and Portuguese. Holding that Indian historiography at the beginning of the twentieth century stood where European historiography had stood at the beginning of the nineteenth, Sarkar was indefatigable in search of material hidden away in libraries and private collections in India. He drew attention to the Jaipur archives and had a large share in the publication of the Poona residency correspondence. As president of the Indian historical records commission Sarkar inspired, led, and directed a generation of Indian archivists and historians in the salvaging of historical evidence. Sarkar himself was ever most generous in granting access to his own fine collection of manuscripts, particularly to young and humble scholars.

In his own work on Aurangzeb and his successors—*History of Aurangzib* (5 vols., 1912–24), *Fall of the Mughal Empire* (4 vols., 1932–50), and his edition and continuation of W. Irvine in *Later Mughals* (2 vols., 1922)—Sarkar narrated meticulously the fortunes and misfortunes of the Mughal dynasty. Although he recognized the importance of economic, social, and cultural history, he felt that, for his lifetime, the establishment of a detailed and accurate political chronology must be given priority. But in his choice of subject and in its treatment within the framework of general history, Sarkar was very much the child of his time. Proud of the Bengali renaissance of the nineteenth century, which he attributed largely to the stimulus and protection afforded by British rule, Sarkar wrote from the premiss that in the late seventeenth and eighteenth centuries the history of India was moving in the right direction and that the passing of Muslim rule was not to be regretted, as under it India had lain inert. Believing that 'history when rightly read is a justification of Providence a revelation of a great purpose in time', Sarkar did not always avoid anachronistic judgements and a certain lack of sympathetic awareness of the dilemmas facing the peoples of India in the eighteenth century. He regretted that they failed to form, and the Mughals failed to foster, 'a compact nation with equal rights and opportunities for all'. He described his historical research as 'literary work', and his writings often achieved great literary excellence, for instance in his account of the last days of Aurangzeb.

Sarkar's study of Aurangzeb led him on to Maratha history and to more than fifty years of friendship and co-operation with the doyen of Maratha history, Dr G. S. Sardesai. The outcome, for example, his *Shivaji and his Times* (1919) and *House of Shivaji* (1940), did not altogether please Maratha sentiment since Sarkar was critical of what he regarded as the mercenary shortsightedness of eighteenth-century Maratha leadership.

Sarkar's acquisition of Persian, Sanskrit, Portuguese, Hindi, Urdu, Marathi, and French did not prevent him from venturing into general history as his *India through the Ages* (1928) and *Military History of India* (1960) demonstrate. His two contributions to the history of Bengal were a biography of the sixteenth-century saint Chaitanya, *Chaitanya: Pilgrimages and Teachings* (1913) and his *History of Bengal*, vol. 2 (1950), sponsored by Dacca University, which he edited and partly wrote. Sarkar was moreover a voluminous writer in Bengali, popularizing the findings of his scholarly work in his mother tongue. He was also one of the first translators of Rabindranath Tagore into English. In numerous articles for the *Modern Review* and other English-language periodicals and newspapers he often drew contemporary morals for India from her past history. He was a severe critic of Indian education, calling for the establishment of higher academic standards and for reforms of the examination system.

Sarkar was a stern Victorian moralist and a staunch patriot, but critical of the generation which brought India to independence and partition. He himself practised what he preached—habits of regularity, frugality, punctuality, self-discipline, and devotion to his calling. Reserved and taciturn, sharp and outspoken, not a clubbable man, Sarkar lived up to his own conceptions, expressed in his *Economics of British India* (1919; 1st edn, 1909), of the Englishmen of his earlier days as 'methodical, cool-headed, strenuous and thorough in all they undertake, self-confident and filled with a divine discontent with things as they are'. His later years were overcast with personal tragedy, but he bore his misfortune with stoic fortitude and refused to abstain from his scholarly pursuits even for a single day. He died at his home, 10 Lake Terrace, Calcutta, on 15 May 1958, and was cremated at the Keoratala burning ghat, Calcutta, the same day.

PETER HARDY, *rev.* TAPAN RAYCHAUDHURI

Sources H. R. Gupta, ed., *Life and letters of Sir Jadunath* (1957) · S. Sengupta and A. Basu, eds., *Samsad Bangali charitabhidhan* (1971) · S. P. Sen, ed., *Dictionary of national biography*, 4 vols. (1972–4) [India] · *The Times* (21 May 1958) · Centre for Social Studies, Calcutta, Jadunath Sarkar MSS · private information (1971, 2004)

Archives Centre for Social Studies, Calcutta

Likenesses photograph, Asiatic Society of Bengal, Calcutta, India · photograph, National Library of India, Calcutta

Sarmento, Jacob de Castro [*formerly* Henrique de Castro] (1692?–1762), physician and scientific writer, was born at Bragança, Portugal, as Henrique, the third son of Francisco de Castro de Almeida (*b.* 1651/2), tobacco merchant (*estanqueiro*), and his second wife, Violante de Mesquita. His parents settled in Mértola, where they were arrested in 1708 by the Evora Inquisition and accused of Judaizing. Henrique de Castro's mother died in prison and in 1710 his father was sentenced to imprisonment and the confiscation of his property. In 1711 he graduated from Evora University as a licentiate in the arts, and in 1717 from Coimbra as bachelor of medicine.

Henrique de Castro and his wife arrived in England in 1721 and converted to open Judaism. They were remarried at Bevis Marks Synagogue in London on 10 March, as 'Jacob and Rahel de Castro, arrivals from Portugal'. In the same year, as Jacob de Castro, he published a pamphlet entitled *A dissertation on the methods of incubating the small pox, with critical remarks on the several authors who have treated the disease*, followed by editions in Latin and German. In May 1724 he was appointed physician to the synagogue's poor, but was dismissed in September for writing and riding in his coach on festivals. Accused by Daniel de Flores of having betrayed Jews to the Inquisition in Beja, Jacob de Castro, who had by now added Sarmento to his name, was investigated by the synagogue elders, who exonerated him. In recompense, he was given the honour of giving three discourses in the synagogue on the Day of Atonement; these were published in 1724 as *Exemplar de penitencia*. In 1725 Sarmento was admitted as a licentiate of the Royal College of Physicians and the following year published *Siderohydrologia*, on drinking mineral waters. In 1728 he preached a sermon at the funeral of David Nieto MD, the rabbi of the London Portuguese Synagogue. Despite a malicious campaign against his candidacy by Meyer Schomberg, he was elected a fellow of the Royal Society in 1729. From then on he engaged in correspondence with Portuguese scholars and statesmen and in publishing and translating works of natural philosophy, in an attempt to improve the state of scientific knowledge in Portugal. Sarmento also reported to the Royal Society on the discovery of diamonds and on the Jesuits' detailed observations of eclipses in Brazil. He gave the medical faculty of Coimbra University its first microscope, and offered to help it to establish a botanical garden with seeds and cuttings from the Chelsea Physic Garden. He tried unsuccessfully to persuade the Portuguese government to publish a Portuguese translation of Francis Bacon's *Novum organum*. Sarmento published books in Portuguese about Newton's discovery that the moon's gravity controls the tides, about smallpox inoculation, and about British advances in surgery. Isaac de Sequeira Samuda FRS died in 1730, leaving an incomplete manuscript of a Spanish epic poem of 1415 stanzas, entitled *Viriadas*; Sarmento added another fifty stanzas

Jacob de Castro Sarmento (1692?–1762), by Richard Houston (after Robert Edge Pine)

and a dedication to the king of Portugal. In 1735 he secured the election to the Royal Society of Marco António de Azevedo Coutinho, the Portuguese ambassador, and dedicated to him his *Materia medica: physico-historico-mechanica reyno mineral*: in the dedication, he professed strong loyalty to Portugal. The book included a puff for the quinine water agoa de Inglaterra which he made to a secret recipe, bottled, and exported to Portugal as a cure for all fevers. In 1738 Sarmento was appointed staff physician to the Portuguese embassy. He also arranged the election of the conde de Ericeira and the new Portuguese ambassador, Sebastião Carvalho e Melo (Pombal), to the Royal Society. During the same year Sarmento complained to the Royal College of Physicians about Meyer Schomberg's attempt to prevent his treatment of a patient, Benjamin Mendes da Costa. Schomberg was reprimanded and fined.

Sarmento was granted an MD by Marischal College, Aberdeen, in 1739, on the recommendation of Sir Hans Sloane and others. In 1747 he proposed and founded a small infirmary (Beth Holim), for London's Portuguese Jewish community, and wrote a pharmacopoeia for its out-patients' dispensary.

Sarmento's wife, Isabel, died on 27 January 1756, and was buried as Sarah; it seems likely that she was the Rahel who married Sarmento in 1721, and that she had undergone a ritual name change in illness. Sarmento then married his mistress, Elizabeth, with whom in 1748 he had had a son, Henry de Castro (later a general in the East India Company's service); their second son, Charles, was born and baptized on 20 March 1758. In October the *Annual Register* announced Sarmento's renunciation of Judaism.

Sarmento died at his home in King's Road, Holborn, London, in 1762 and was buried on 20 September in the churchyard of St Andrew's, Holborn.

Sarmento was a scholar of distinction. As a refugee he was unusual in maintaining friendly contacts with Portuguese scholars and statesmen. It is possible that he influenced Pombal's determination to end the persecution of the New Christians in Portugal.　EDGAR SAMUEL

Sources R. D. Barnett, 'Dr Jacob de Castro Sarmento and Sephardim in medical practice in 18th-century London', *Transactions of the Jewish Historical Society of England*, 27 (1978–80), 84–114 · A. D'Esaguy, *Jacob de Castro Sarmento, notas relativas a sua vida e à sua obra* (1947) · A. D'Esaguy, 'Uma carta do Dr Jacob de Castro Sarmento à Diogo de Mendonça Corte Real (O terremoto de 1 de Novembro de 1755)', *Imprensa Médica* (19 March 1955) · A. Rubens, *Anglo-Jewish portraits* (1935) · E. R. Samuel, 'Dr Meyer Schomberg's attack on the Jews of London, 1746', *Transactions of the Jewish Historical Society of England*, 20 (1959–61), 83–111 · I. Solomons, 'David Nieto and some of his contemporaries', *Transactions of the Jewish Historical Society of England*, 12 (1928–31), 1–101, esp. 83–8 [appx II; incl. text of his will and of his defence against Schomberg's attack] · F. M. Alves, *Os judeus no distrito de Bragança* (1925) [incl. bibliography and details of Sarmento's father's sentence by the Evora Inquisition] · A. D'Esaguy, 'Da quina quina as agoas de Inglaterra inventadas pelo Dr Jacob de Castro Sarmento', *A Medicina Contemporanea*, 50 (1930) · 'Une lettre de Manuel Teles da Silva, marquis d'Alegrete, secrétaire de l'Académie Royale Portugaise à Jacob de Castro Sarmento, médecin et membre du Collège Royale de Londres', *Revue d'Histoire de la Médecine Hebraïque* (1957) · 'Uma carta inedita do Dr Jacob de Castro Sarmento', *Imprensa Médica* (1953) · A. M. Hyamson, *The Sephardim of England: a history of the Spanish and Portuguese Jewish community, 1492–1951* (1951) · J. Jacobs and L. Wolf, eds., *Magna bibliotheca Anglo-Judaica: a bibliographical guide to Anglo-Jewish history*, rev. C. Roth, rev. edn (1937) · *The record of the Royal Society of London*, 4th edn (1940) · parish register, Holborn, St Andrew's, GL, MS 6673/11 [burial]

Archives Biblioteca Nacional, Lisbon

Likenesses A. Miller, mezzotint, 1737 (after H. Stevens, 1729), repro. in J. de C. Sarmento, *Theorica verdadeira das marés, conforme à philiosophia do incomparavel cavalheiro Isaac Newton* (1737) · caricature, 1749, repro. in Rubens, *Anglo-Jewish portraits*, 122 · R. Houston, mezzotint (after R. E. Pine), BM, NPG, Wellcome L. [*see illus.*]

Sarmiento de Acuña, Diego, count of Gondomar in the Spanish nobility (1567–1626), diplomat, was born on 1 November 1567 in Astorga in Leon, Spain, where his paternal uncle was bishop. Rightly has it been said that his family possessed more breeding than money. Through his father, Don García Sarmiento de Sotomayor (d. 1579), a minor courtier under Charles V, he was closely connected to the Sotomayor counts of Salvatierra; through his mother, Doña Juana de Acuña y Enríquez (d. 1600), he could claim two kings among his ancestors, Pedro I of Portugal and Enrique II of Castile.

Early years Gondomar's early life was spent in the small seignorial house across the river from the town of Gondomar, the lordship of which his father, a younger son, had bought about the time of his marriage. Despite the death of his father when he was only twelve, Gondomar retained the most profound affinity for his eponymous home. His mother continued to live there until her death, and Don Diego constantly returned, adding to the house and estate whenever he could. Gondomar was conspicuously proud of where he had been brought up, and was

Diego Sarmiento de Acuña, count of Gondomar in the Spanish nobility (1567–1626), by unknown artist

unusually fond of enumerating its produce in his many nostalgic letters. In 1614 he wrote from London to a friend about spending a summer in Galicia, mentioning 'a small house and a fine little mountain of mine which I think of every day here, and that is what keeps me going' (Real Biblioteca, Madrid, MS II-2168, fol. 229).

Virtually nothing is known of Gondomar's education, despite the fact that he became the greatest private collector of books in Spain, with his library in the city of Valladolid cited as one of the wonders of the age. He may have received some formal instruction in the nearby episcopal cities of Tuy or even Toro. In addition to his native Galician and Castilian, Gondomar probably acquired early on a firm grasp of French and Latin, the languages in which he conducted diplomatic business in London. French he may have practised with the merchants who frequented the various Galician ports, notably Bayona. Though perfectly able to converse in Latin, he never claimed a classical mastery. It is likely that his Sotomayor cousins oversaw his education, not only because his father had decreed that this branch should always be regarded as head of the family, but also because Gondomar was married to his cousin, Doña Beatriz Sarmiento de Mendoza (d. 1586), on 27 December 1581, when he had just turned fourteen.

As a first-born son Gondomar was marked out for a life of action. He may have fought on the Portuguese border at about the time of his first marriage, and it is probable that he was in Italy when his first wife died, childless, in 1586. During his absence his mother arranged his second marriage in 1588, to Constanza de Acuña y Avellaneda (d. in or after 1626). She was another if more distant cousin, whose father had seen distinguished service in Italy and in the duke of Alba's army in Flanders, where he probably met Constanza's Netherlandish mother. According to the prenuptial agreement, Gondomar was to live with his wife in the northern Castilian city of Valladolid and be absent from her for no more than two months in the year, unless he was at court. The union proved blissfully happy, producing three daughters and four sons, though one son died shortly after birth.

The early days of Gondomar's second marriage were interrupted by possibly his first encounter with the English. As lord of Vincios and Gondomar, and with responsibilities for the soldiers of the bishopric of Tuy, either he or an older cousin of the same name was obliged to return to Galicia to defend the coasts from any attack from Sir Francis Drake, who set sail in the spring of 1589 to support a pro-English pretender to the Portuguese throne. He must soon have returned to Valladolid, where on 6 December his first child, Lope Ambrosio (d. 1618), was born, father of Diego, second count of Gondomar. Soon afterwards Gondomar undertook his first role at court. On 31 March 1590 he carried a motto during a joust attended by Philip II. It read: 'The torments which afflict me, stronger and firmer do they leave me'. This was prescient. For the next seven years Gondomar achieved little. He continued to oversee the defence of the Galician coasts and was rewarded with the perpetual governorship of the fortress of Monte Real in Bayona. He was also active in the church, joining the confraternity of Santa María de Esgueva, and later became a member of the military order of Calatrava, after proving that he was untainted by Jewish blood.

Administrator, 1597–1612 Early in 1597 Gondomar was appointed *corregidor* or royal representative in the city of Toro. He undertook a programme of modernization, including repairs to the bridge and to the highways, as well as securing supplies of wheat for the inhabitants. He also saw to it that the city acceded most readily to the crown's demands for taxation. All this made him an ideal choice for the much more important position of *corregidor* of Valladolid, which in 1601 had once more become the capital of Spain and the principal residence of the royal court. He took up office on 14 September 1602, after declining various other posts, including the governorship of the Philippines. In addition to running the city Gondomar was intimately involved in arranging numerous royal festivals. This may have given him especial pleasure because it brought him into contact with numerous artists and poets, including Quevedo and Góngora, with the latter satirizing the tight watch Gondomar maintained over the comings and goings from the city. Less welcome was the fact that his new-found prominence also brought him to the attention of the duke of Lerma, Philip III's chief minister and the prime mover in translating the court from Madrid to his own city. The duke seems for some reason to have taken against Gondomar, and for as long as he remained in power prevented him from coming too close to the king and court. In 1605 Gondomar lost the position of *corregidor* to the duke's twenty-year-old son, the count of Saldaña. He followed the court on its return to Madrid in 1606 but failed to achieve any significant reward other than a place on the *consejo de hacienda*, which looked after the crown's finances. Early in 1612 he wrote an impassioned letter to Lerma asking to be made *corregidor* of Madrid. It was no secret, however, that he hoped to become head of the council of Castile, the kingdom's main administrative body, in succession to one of his own cousins.

Though Gondomar had consistently refused to consider an overseas posting in Spain's vast empire, Lerma's response was to engineer his appointment on 21 August 1612 as permanent ambassador to London. There had been rumours to this effect as early as June, and it was taken as a further sign of continued ducal hostility, though Gondomar was probably also offered a post in Seville, which too would have kept him away from the court. Perhaps the fact that if he undertook the ambassadorship he would be allowed to keep his seat in the *consejo de hacienda* tipped the balance in favour of London. He finally embarked for England on 9 July 1613. Meanwhile, he had drawn up plans for the decoration of his family crypt in the church of St Benedict the Old (San Benito el Viejo), next to his house in Valladolid. He commissioned a final judgment, to include figures of Christ and the saints, and with images of Doña Constanza and of himself under the protection of Benedict, his patron saint.

For all Lerma's wish to be rid of an irritating suitor, a new Spanish ambassador was being appointed at a crucial time for relations between London and Madrid. Since the ending of the Anglo-Spanish war on the accession of the Scottish king to the English throne, relations between the two dynasties had been good, despite occasional tensions in Ireland and the New World. But by 1612 the British king's friendship could no longer be taken for granted, especially as his children were all of or approaching marriageable age. James I's daughter, Elizabeth, was about to marry the foremost Calvinist prince in Germany, the elector palatine, Frederick V, whereas his heir, Prince Henry, was looking for a bride, possibly French. A renewal of protestant or anti-Spanish solidarity threatened Habsburg interests in the Low Countries and in Germany and Austria.

First embassy to England, 1613–1618: connections and intelligence Gondomar's motto was 'Osar morir da la vida' ('Risking death gives life'). His arrival in Portsmouth on 21 July 1613 was evidence of that as well as an auspicious beginning for an embassy based on his willingness to play for high stakes. When the captain of the English escort ordered him, in accordance with English custom, to lower the flags of King Philip III in salute to those of King James, Gondomar seized the opportunity to make his presence felt. He was told that the present king of Spain's father had done the same when he landed in 1554 to marry Mary

Tudor. If Gondomar refused to strike his colours, the captain warned him, he would blow him out of the water. Fortunately, James was hunting nearby, and Gondomar wrote that day to explain his refusal, asking that he be allowed merely to return to Spain:

> because I was born of a good and honourable family, and I wish to emulate them; all of which obliges me to die, as I will, to defend my honour and duty, which is that these ships should enter and then return from this kingdom in the state that they left Spain.

The letter was passed to the king as he was about to kill a stag and, captivated by the swagger of the new ambassador, James made an exception for his entry into the country (*Correspondencia oficial*, 3.71–86).

Gondomar was accompanied to London by Doña Constanza. They kept on the embassy in a house just outside the city walls at the Barbican, taking over the lease at a cost of 720 ducats a year from John Egerton, earl of Bridgewater. Together they enhanced its existing reputation as the principal centre of Catholic worship in the city. From its chapel a bell rang out to announce mass or even give warning of a raid by the authorities. Many committed Catholics took up residence in the vicinity for protection. Gondomar described it as 'the parish and cathedral church for London' (Fernández, 260). This was not simply his accustomed hyperbole. At the start of 1614 he reported that seventy-two people were either living in the embassy or were being fed there on a daily basis. Numbers were so great that on Sundays two services were held, one for his staff and the other a public celebration. The leading Catholic laywoman in London, the 48-year-old Doña Luisa de Carvajal, received up to 500 reales a month until her death on 23 December 1613. Her funeral in the ambassadorial chapel was determinedly ostentatious. In addition, Gondomar rented a house in the country. This he justified as necessary for his country's reputation, and his generosity as a host, not least with the products of his native Galicia, was duly noted.

There can be no question of Gondomar's diligence as an ambassador. In the first year of his embassy he wrote over 100 letters to Philip III and almost half as many to the king's chief minister, the duke of Lerma. He also maintained an active intelligence network. He supplemented his many friendships at court with an impressive list of pensioners, often disguised in his accounts with names taken from romances of chivalry. Many of these pensioners he inherited from previous ambassadors; indeed, soon after he arrived in London he wrote to Philip III warning that, 'times being what they are and given what these people are like' he would doubtless be expected to expend more money (*Correspondencia oficial*, 3.88). Despite C. H. Carter's suggestions to the contrary, the Spanish pensions were paid, albeit erratically. To scrutinize one of the many accounts Gondomar sent back to Madrid, in November 1617 he paid to 'Priam' (Katherine Howard, countess of Suffolk) 4000 ducats; to 'Socrates' (Admiral William Monson) and to 'Florian' (Lady Drummond) he handed over a total of 2250 ducats each. He usually reckoned that there were 4 ducats to the pound sterling, and these were all pensions established before he had arrived. Among the pensioners he had himself recommended, Secretary Sir Thomas Lake received his annual pension of 2000 ducats backdated for one and a half years, making 3000 ducats in total. Among other high-placed recipients, George Villiers's name appears for the first time when he received full payment of the annual pension of 6000 ducats which he had been awarded in August 1616, the month he was created Viscount Villiers. Even so, Gondomar was becoming disenchanted with the pensions he was expected to pay out, and he suggested to the king that the money might be better spent on Spain's armies. Really useful information, he said, came either from those who 'were devoted to the service of God' or those who could be induced by occasional gifts or demonstrations of friendship. Villiers's pension none the less increased as he made his way up the ranks of the English peerage as earl and then marquess of Buckingham (*Correspondencia oficial*, 1.128–31).

Gondomar's informants were not confined to the royal court. In September 1613 he announced that in the French ambassador's house there was 'someone extremely well placed and his confidant, who has offered to tell me what is going on and even pass me copies of his papers' (*Correspondencia oficial*, 3.122). He also had his spies in the English parliament. During his second embassy an unnamed source provided him with a daily account of activities in the first session of the parliament of 1621, which he had translated into Spanish. His best sources of information were often the king and his ministers, however. Especially during the parliamentary crisis of late 1621 and the concomitant threats to the Rhineland, Gondomar was given copies of James's correspondence with his son-in-law or even with the House of Commons. On one occasion Gondomar was allowed to copy for himself a letter from General Mansfeldt in the Palatinate, even if the original had to be returned to Buckingham's safekeeping. Perhaps in terms of espionage Gondomar was most successful in exercising a watching brief over Ireland. Many Irish Catholics sought temporary refuge in the embassy before being provided with money and the necessary contacts in Flanders or Spain, and in this respect Gondomar was merely continuing his interest in the welfare of Irish exiles in Spain, the vast majority of whom had first landed in Galicia.

First embassy: the fall of Ralegh and the beginnings of the Spanish match In political terms Gondomar's principal task as ambassador was to smooth over the rough edges of the treaty of London, by which James had established peace with Spain shortly after arriving in his new kingdom. English trade in the New World, even as far north as Bermuda and Virginia, seemed to Spain to be no more than a continuation of the piracy that had typified Elizabeth's reign. Gondomar reiterated Spain's promise not to interfere in Ireland, in return for sterner treatment of the more notorious corsairs of the age. The most notable example of this involved Sir Walter Ralegh. Imprisoned in the Tower of London since 1605, Ralegh was released in 1616, principally because of an offer he made to sail to the

Guyanas and discover the legendary source of gold known as El Dorado. In a *démarche* worthy of the greatest ambassadors, Gondomar quietly referred the scholarly king of Great Britain to folio 584 of the third part of Antonio de Herrera's *History of Philip II*. It confirmed that this now invaluable source of gold had already been visited by Ralegh some twenty years earlier. Not only that, it proved that the area was legitimately claimed by Spain and, to top it all, that the stories about the mine were 'laughable' (*Correspondencia oficial*, 1.54–7). Gondomar extracted promises from James that if Ralegh were allowed to sail then an absolute guarantee would be given that no harm would befall Spanish settlements. Instead, Ralegh raided the Canary Islands before launching attacks in the New World, including upon San Tomé in the Guyanas, where the governor, a relative of Gondomar, was killed. In June 1618 the ambassador had been given permission to return to Madrid, but Philip III ordered him to remain until Ralegh had been brought to justice. Gondomar kept up a barrage of complaints to the privy council and, in a letter of 13 July, he informed his king that he had personally told James that 'Ralegh and those who went with him should be sent as prisoners to your majesty so that you may order them to be hanged in the square in Madrid' (Cantón, 125). Ralegh was duly taken prisoner on his return. News of his execution on 29 October 1618 reached Gondomar after he had left for Spain. Henceforth the ambassador was stigmatized by many English protestants for his marked role in the death of one of their heroes.

The issue that came to dominate Gondomar's first embassy was the Spanish match. With the death of Henry, prince of Wales, in 1612, eyes focused on the marriage of Prince Charles. An anti-Spanish marriage, either to the house of Bourbon or with Savoy, seemed the most likely choice, but there remained the possibility of reviving plans to marry the heir to the British throne to Philip III's daughter, the Infanta María. In England one of Gondomar's closest allies in promoting this alliance was James's consort, Queen Anne. She had a particular fondness for the ambassador not only on account of her own Catholicism and of the Habsburg blood which, she liked to point out, ran through her veins, but also because both Gondomar and the queen viewed the match as a counterbalance to the protestant marriage of her daughter, Elizabeth, to the elector palatine. In 1614 the British minister in Madrid, Sir John Digby, raised the matter with Lerma, though firmly 'insinuating that it was of his *motu proprio*' (Madrid, Ministerio de Asuntos Exteriores, MS 243, fol. 1v). By the time Gondomar's first embassy was over the terms of a possible marriage were being negotiated, though without a sense of urgency on either side.

The close links between Gondomar and James were apparent by the time of his first departure for home. Though he had secured his recall by citing evidence of his deteriorating health, Gondomar was feasted by the greatest nobles, including the lord chancellor, Francis Bacon, with whom he had enjoyed many a philosophical conversation, and by the earl of Arundel, who had passed on many titbits in return for his pension. His farewell from the king was memorable. Not only were 'the two James'— the king and Diego—in tears, but the former granted Gondomar a series of historic concessions. He was given the right to take out of England 'horses, dogs and falcons' (Madrid, Biblioteca Nacional, MS 9408). Further evidence of improved relations with Spain came from the fact that seventy Catholic priests were released from prisons all over England. (When the previous ambassador had left, shortly after Gondomar's arrival in 1613, a mere dozen had been released.) It fell to Gondomar to send for the priests, take them to London, and feed them, all at his own expense, before they marched out of the city with him in July 1618. Finally, in the most symbolic gesture of all, Gondomar was presented with the Spanish artillery captured by Drake and other English corsairs as a token of esteem of a quite exceptional magnitude. The departure of the countess of Gondomar was also marked, but in a less formal way. She also received many letters from fellow Catholics thanking her for all she had done, including one particularly ornate sheaf dated Channell Row, 1 October 1618, from Francis of Kildare (no doubt Frances Fitzgerald, countess of Kildare) promising her 'constant love' and saying how pleased she would be 'yf you would commaund any thing in this cuntrey' that was in her power to grant. (Real Biblioteca, Madrid, MS II-2160, fol. 45). The apprentices of London, however, had a different attitude to his departure and gave him a rowdy send off, much to James's disgust. Gondomar was informed that the king had taken the rare step of appointing members of his council to act as judges in the matter within the jurisdiction of the City of London.

Gondomar, King James, and Prince Charles Gondomar had achieved a degree of intimacy with his royal host rarely paralleled in diplomatic history—on occasion members of the English court called upon him to intervene on their behalf with King James. In 1619 William Lake wrote to him, even though he was now in Spain, in the hope that he would intercede for the release of his namesake and master Sir Thomas Lake and his family, who were imprisoned in the Tower of London. The family, Gondomar was told, had done nothing to dishonour either James or even Buckingham, and that the cause of the family's downfall (and William's loss of the office of Latin secretary to the king) was that James had received written reports from Brussels claiming that Lake was there being prayed for as 'the friend and protector of Catholics'. Gondomar was told that they were like 'lakes without fishes' (Real Biblioteca, Madrid, MS II-2160, no. 4a). Indeed, such was the perception of Gondomar's influence that even Buckingham sought his help, as at Christmas 1621 when he asked him to press James to be firm with his enemy, the earl of Oxford. Gondomar was listened to by the king (but by no stretch of the imagination was what he said always followed) because of their interest in a common goal, a marriage between the prince of Wales and the infanta. A union with the foremost Catholic power would greatly enhance James's claim to be a peacemaker among Christian princes, just as much as it would advance Gondomar's

career at home. Yet there was also something entirely personal about their relationship. Gondomar's scholarship and bibliophilia attracted and flattered the king, as did his mannered Castilian sense of deference. These attributes the ambassador spiced with an agile wit. An example of this combination is that Gondomar said to the monarch that he, Gondomar, spoke Latin badly, like a king, whereas James spoke Latin well, like a scholar. His sense of humour also worked with the royal favourite. When Buckingham was raised from an earldom to the rank of marquess, Gondomar, who had himself been made a count on 12 June 1617 NS, congratulated him, as he said, most genuinely, even though it pained him to see him leaving the rank of count. After his return to England, Gondomar consolidated an easy relationship with Prince Charles, thus making himself a friend to king, prince, and favourite at one and the same time. His way with words did not endear him to everyone, however. In January 1614 he had confessed to Juan Hurtado de Mendoza, his confidant at the Spanish court and the king's secretary, that complaints had come back to him about the brevity of some ambassador's letters and 'the longwindedness of my own' (Real Biblioteca, Madrid, MS II-2168, fol. 67r).

Despite Gondomar's personal triumph at the court of St James he was not oblivious to the underlying rivalry between Spain and Great Britain. He never forgot that he was the servant of the Spanish crown. In fact, his early dispatches as ambassador were marked by a barely concealed belligerence towards a protestant monarchy which he believed had imposed its religion against the will of the majority of its subjects. In November 1616 he composed a long dispatch dealing with all aspects of Hispano-British relations. If war were again advisable (and he felt that peace allowed England to build up her commercial wealth and naval prowess at Spain's expense), then he suggested that invasion should take place through Ireland or Scotland, where Catholic uprisings were to be expected. If through the latter, which he considered defenceless, it would take only eight days to reach London, 'because all is totally flat, and without a single castle or fortress anywhere' (*Cinco cartas*, 66).

During Gondomar's absence from England relations between Madrid and London deteriorated along with the situation in central Europe. James's son-in-law, the elector palatine, had accepted election to the Bohemian crown which the Habsburgs of Vienna felt belonged to them. In October 1619 Gondomar wrote to James to announce his return, saying that only the death of his eldest son, Lope Ambrosio, had detained him. In fact, his son had died twelve months earlier, and Gondomar was doing his utmost to avoid being sent as ambassador to Paris, let alone London. In the following month he wrote to Secretary Ciriza from Casarrubios, the village between Madrid and Toledo where he was staying, protesting yet again that he was 'of no use, since the matter of England requires someone who is healthy and robust' (*Correspondencia oficial*, 2.240). His unwillingness to leave Spain and Doña Constanza accounts in part for the sentiments he expressed when consulted about James's protestations that he neither supported the elector Frederick's actions nor was in favour of an alliance with the Dutch. Like all heretic kings, he said, James would say anything to please, and the danger was that Spain would allow herself 'to be taken in by his words, while each year he took money from Seville and Lisbon in such abundance, only to build up his navy and support Spain's enemies' (ibid., 2.228).

Second embassy to England, 1620–1622 Gondomar left Spain in January 1620. This time he left Doña Constanza behind and travelled overland through France before reaching London on Wednesday 8 March. Lodgings were provided for him in the former residence of the bishops of Ely, in Hatton Gardens. He had his first audience with James the following Sunday at the royal mansion Theobalds in Hertfordshire. There a beam gave way and he took shelter in a stone doorway, while others, including the earl of Arundel, fell through a hole in the floor. Gondomar reported that this was nothing more than an unfortunate accident involving old wood and, in a rare rejection of his normal fears for his safety, he discounted the fact even though 'the puritans have tried and are trying to have me killed' (*Correspondencia oficial*, 2.263–4). James's welcome for the ambassador was enthusiastic, and he announced in French to all that he looked just like an old friend of his, the count of Gondomar. In the subsequent discussions the king wanted to know if the war would spread out from Bohemia with the emperor pursuing his son-in-law and his family into their hereditary lands in the Upper and Lower Palatinate. Gondomar replied that this was the same as asking him what James would do if someone seized London. The ambassador faithfully reported what he called the puritan pressures on James to act decisively in defence of his grandchildren's inheritance. When a parliament was summoned in 1621 he advised Madrid that James was responding to pressures to be seen as doing something; it did not necessarily mean that war with Spain was imminent. Gondomar sent back to Madrid detailed accounts of events at Westminster. This included transmitting a copy of the Commons' declaration of June 1621. Madrid was left in no doubt that, if James ever did decide to break with Spain, then MPs at least claimed they were willing to offer up their lives and their money in defence of the Palatinate.

The military situation became still more acute during the autumn, when the last fortresses loyal to Frederick in the Palatinate were under threat from pro-Habsburg forces, despite the token presence of English garrisons commanded by Sir Horace Vere. James's daughter and grandchildren fled to the Netherlands and the calls for intervention increased. With the return of Digby (now Lord Digby) from Brussels after the failure to achieve a ceasefire from the emperor and the elector, Gondomar was informed that James had no alternative but to recall parliament and ask for further supply, in order to be seen to be ready to go to his family's defence. Buckingham went to see Gondomar in Hatton Gardens. The favourite revealed the divisions within the king's innermost counsels. He poured scorn on Digby, saying he just wanted to make himself immortal with the puritans as the restorer of the Palatinate. Nothing would be done in the parliament without Buckingham's knowledge and approval, since 'the king trusted no one so entirely as him and myself', the ambassador related, 'because he knew that we had no other goal but peace and the common good' (Archivo General de Simancas, MS Estado 374, fol. 308ff.). Gondomar was summoned to see the king on the following day, Friday 2 November 1621. Anxious to transmit to Spain his keenness to maintain peace, James reminded Gondomar how even Digby had spoken warmly of the Spanish king's efforts to induce the emperor to call a halt to hostilities, but he also said he was determined to help Elizabeth 'recover and hold onto the state that she had married into'. James then uttered some of the most contested words of his reign. He would go to Newmarket and Gondomar was not to worry about what he might hear in parliament. He would leave Prince Charles to attend, 'with a secret commission … and if the parliament wanted to meddle in anything other than aid for the Palatinate, the Prince would dissolve it' (Pursell, 436). Money for the defence of the Rhineland was the sole reason why he was recalling the parliament, the king explained, and he himself was going to be far away so this could be undertaken without peers and MPs coming to him with their complaints and remedies. The ambassador was being reassured, nothing more. Buckingham then joined in, sniggering that they would not even send the money to the elector but use it against the common enemy. The king laughed and, taking the ambassador by the arm, said he was wrong if he thought the common enemy was the Turk. Rather it was the solemn burghers of Holland. Gondomar was asked to react coldly to the recall of parliament, so that the king's subjects would believe that a rupture with Spain was a distinct possibility. Digby, whom the royal trio blamed for the recall of parliament, also came in for some undignified mockery. Gondomar quaintly asked the king where he would think of putting the images which the puritans were making of Digby.

James's words to Gondomar have been portrayed as indicating that the king deliberately 'sabotaged the parliament of 1621' (Pursell, 428). This is hard to believe, since towards the end of the parliament James struggled to come to a compromise which would enable him to extract some taxation from MPs. Certainly Gondomar feared that the parliament might pressurize the king into breaking with Spain and pursuing an anti-Catholic policy throughout the Stuart dominions as well as abroad. After hearing reports that his king had been disrespectfully spoken of during debates in the Commons, Gondomar informed Madrid that he had written at the end of November reminding James of the promise he had made before the parliament began. The ambassador apparently said that, had he not trusted 'the word and goodness of the king that he would punish and set things right with the speed and severity that was called for, I would have left his kingdoms within three days' (ibid., 440). Gondomar added that if only he had an army with him he would punish those responsible himself. That his threats were real enough is shown by the fact that he certainly wrote directly to the duke of Alburquerque, the Spanish ambassador in Rome, advising him that no further action should be taken on the dispensation for Charles's marriage, 'because though the king's intention is without doubt good, it is not known what he will choose to do, as he is not here', he being still at Newmarket. Gondomar's audacity meant that he had to write separately to his king, justifying why he had sent instructions to a fellow ambassador (Archivo General de Simancas, MS Estado 2558, nos. 17 and 16). In January 1622 parliament was formally dissolved. Gondomar was shown the draft of a proclamation announcing its failure, and he successfully lobbied for direct references to the abuse of the king of Spain to be removed on the grounds that this would be highly disrespectful to a prince with whom James claimed to enjoy amicable relations. James now needed the Spanish match more than ever, and Gondomar intensified his efforts to bring about a marriage on Spanish terms. He felt that if the prince of Wales could be induced to come to Madrid to collect his bride then it would be possible to persuade him to convert to Catholicism.

The failure of the Spanish match and the death of Gondomar
Gondomar left England for the last time at the end of May 1622. With James's full approval he was recalled to Madrid in order to negotiate with Lord Digby, who had arrived in Spain to finalize details of the marriage between Charles and María. Before he left Gondomar had concentrated his efforts on persuading Charles that it might be necessary for him to travel to the court of Philip IV (who had succeeded his father in March 1621). In an astonishing aside, Charles apparently told him that if he were to send word from Madrid that he should come to collect his bride, he would travel in disguise, with just two servants in attendance, to 'place himself in the hands' of his most Catholic majesty (Redworth, 406). Negotiations carried on apace in Madrid, and in September 1622 Gondomar penned a letter to Buckingham, claiming that 'the decision has already been taken, and with enthusiasm, that the Prince of Wales should mount Spain'. Charles was advised to come to Madrid 'post haste' (BL, Harley MS 1583). Though Gondomar was premature in his advice, by December a final marriage treaty was sent to England, and confirmed early in January 1623. Gondomar's endorsement and the subsequent treaty helps explain Charles's decision to leave for Madrid the following month; he travelled in the belief that his bride was waiting for him. When he arrived in Madrid, Gondomar was the first Spaniard to be informed. His comment was 'Nunc dimittis' ('Lord, now let your servant depart in peace'). He duly reported the prince's arrival to Philip IV's favourite, the count-duke of Olivares. Gondomar was immediately promoted to the council of state. Both Gondomar and Olivares initially assumed that Charles had come to convert to Catholicism before taking his bride. By the time Charles left Madrid at the end of August 1623, Gondomar's advice was to wait until James actually carried out his promises to grant full toleration of Catholics before dispatching the infanta. As it turned out, Charles and Buckingham had irrevocably turned against

the Spanish match. Within a year war seemed inevitable with Great Britain, and Gondomar was ordered at the end of October 1624 to return to London. Again he cited ill health and his departure was postponed until March 1625. He travelled as far as Irún, at which point news of James's death reached him. This he used to delay his journey further. After a stay in France, where ironically he was obliged as ambassador-extraordinary to offer his congratulations on the news of the prince of Wales's marriage to a French princess, he reached Brussels in October 1625. He drew up his will in January 1626; despite his deteriorating health he managed to commence his return to Spain. He died on 2 October 1626 NS in Casa de la Reina in Logroño; he was survived by his second wife. His body was transferred to the family vault in San Benito el Viejo in Valladolid and remained there until it was disturbed by French invaders in the nineteenth century. In 1990 the crypt of the church was restored to allow the count's remains to be returned to where he had always wished to be buried.

Gondomar's notoriety during his time in England ensured that, for more protestant writers, he was the incarnation of the Machiavellian diplomat. Thomas Scott caricatured him in *Vox Populi, or, Newes from Spayne* (1620) and in *The second part of Vox Populi, or, Gondomar Appearing in the Likeness of Matchiavell in a Spanissh Parliament* (1624). In the following year he was again lampooned in Thomas Middleton's *A Game at Chesse*, which ran for nine nights before packed audiences at the Globe Theatre before being taken off, the playwright imprisoned, and the actors fined.

GLYN REDWORTH

Sources Real Biblioteca, Madrid · Archivo General de Simancas, Estado MSS · Ministerio de Asuntos Exteriores, Madrid · Biblioteca Nacional, Madrid · *Correspondencia del conde de Gondomar*, ed. M. L. López-Vidriero (Madrid, 1999–) [vol. 1 and continuing] · Gondomar, *Correspondencia oficial, Documentos inéditos para la historia de España*, ed. A. Ballersteros Beretta, vols. 1–4 (Madrid, 1936–45) · Gondomar, *Cinco cartas político-literarias*, ed. P. de Gayangos y Arce (Madrid, 1869) · J. G. Oro, *Don Diego Sarmiento de Acuña, conde de Gondomar y embajador de España (1567–1626)* (La Coruña, 1997) · C. Manso Porto, *Don Diego Sarmiento de Acuña, conde de Gondomar (1567–1626): erudito, mecenas y bibliófilo* ([Santiago de Compostela], 1996) · L. T. Fernández, *Gondomar y su triunfo sobre Ralegh* (Santiago de Compostela, 1974) · F. Francisco de Jesus, *El hecho de los tratados del matrimonio pretendido por el principe de Gales con la serenissima infante de España, María / Narrative of the Spanish marriage treaty*, ed. and trans. S. R. Gardiner, CS, 101 (1869) · S. Cantón, 'Como se enteró el conde de Gondomar de la ejecución de Sir Walter Ralegh', *Bolitín de la Real Academia de la Historia*, 113 (1943), 123–9 · B. Pursell, 'James I, Gondomar and the dissolution of the parliament of 1621', *History*, 275 (2000), 428–45 · G. Redworth, 'Of pimps and princes: three unpublished letters from James I and the prince of Wales relating to the Spanish match', *HJ*, 37 (1994), 401–9 · Ó. R. Morales, 'Irlanda en la estrategia política de la monarquía hispánica (1602–1649)', PhD diss., University of Alcalá, 2000 · A. de Herrera y Tordesillas, *Segunda parte de la historia general del mundo, de XV. años del tiempo del señor rey don Felipe II. el Prudent, desde el año de M.D. LXXI hasta el de M.D. LXXXV*

Archives Archivo General de Simancas, Estado MSS · Biblioteca Nacional, Madrid · Ministerio de Asuntos Exteriores, Madrid · Real Biblioteca, Madrid

Likenesses portrait, Ministry of Foreign Affairs, Madrid [*see illus.*]

Sarolea, Charles Louis-Camille (1870–1953), political writer and French scholar, was born on 25 October 1870 in Tongres (Tongeren) in eastern Belgium, one of the six sons of Jean-Pierre Sarolea, a doctor, and his wife, (Marie) Félicité Vrindts. He was to describe himself in 1912 as 'a Fleming by birth and a Dutchman by origin' (*The Anglo-German Problem*, 1912, 16). He was educated at the Royal Athénée, Hasselt, and at the University of Liège, graduating in classics and philosophy. He then studied in Paris, Palermo, and Naples, and travelled in north Africa, America, and the Near East. Subsequently he listed his recreations in *Who's Who* as 'travelling and learning languages'; a committed cosmopolitan, he is said to have known some twenty languages.

At the age of twenty-two Sarolea was private secretary and literary adviser to a former Belgian liberal prime minister, Walthère Frère-Orban, and was offered (but declined) the editorship of the liberal journal *La Liberté*. At about the same time he was, he claimed, offered a chair of philosophy at Brussels University, but withdrew, as he put it in *Who's Who*, owing to the 'organized opposition' and 'riotous disturbances' of socialists and in 1894 he moved to the University of Edinburgh, where he was the first head of the department of French. In 1918 he became professor of French, a post he retained until his resignation in 1931.

Residing at times in Belgium and subsequently Paris, Sarolea made Edinburgh his permanent home, living for nearly fifty years at 21 Royal Terrace, and taking British nationality in 1912. In 1895 he married Martha, daughter of Professor van Cauwenberghe, rector of the University of Ghent. She died in 1901, and in 1905 he married Julia Frances (*d.* 1941), daughter of Charles Dorman, and sister-in-law of Ernest Shackleton, the explorer. He had two sons from his first marriage.

Sarolea wrote more than once of the failings of modern-language teaching in Britain, and he sought to remedy these. He was at first an active head of department, creating the Edinburgh French course from scratch, lecturing on all aspects of the subject, and establishing a full year abroad as an integral part of the degree. He published some works on French literature, philosophy, and history, including the essays contained in *The French Renascence* (1916), a clarion call in defence of French culture and society, and in addition published on various literary subjects, including Ibsen, Newman, and Tolstoy.

But being a French professor was not central to his life; Sarolea was often in conflict with the university authorities, and claimed, according to the *Edinburgh University Journal* (1953) that his work made him feel 'like a racehorse between the shafts of a coal cart'. Most of his energy went into attempts to influence a broader public. His papers show him to have been a person of enormous energy, travelling, writing thousands of articles, lecturing, campaigning, and cultivating a very wide circle of acquaintances from President Masaryk of Czechoslovakia to the Nobel prize winner Maurice Maeterlinck. His activities were rewarded by a variety of civic and academic honours in several countries.

From 1901 until his death in 1953, Sarolea was Belgian vice-consul and then (from 1908) consul in Edinburgh, where he was also consul for the Congo Free State from 1903 to 1908. Being on friendly terms with many important compatriots, including the royal family, he took a sometimes controversial part in Belgian affairs, accompanying King Albert as political adviser in 1920 on a visit to Brazil and west Africa. He claimed to have addressed over 200 mass meetings during the First World War in Britain and America, raising over £100,000 for Belgian refugees.

Sarolea also threw himself into publishing and journalism. From 1909 to 1912 he was the editor primarily responsible for the Collection Nelson, the very successful French-language publishing venture by Nelsons of Edinburgh, which eventually reached 500 titles. In 1913 he began to direct the similar, but short-lived, Collection Gallia for Dent and created a new publishing house with the Paris publisher Georges Crès. Between 1912 and 1917 he was the founding editor of *Everyman*, a large-circulation literary and political journal of eclectic liberal tendencies.

Sarolea's early liberalism was to evolve rightwards under the influence of international politics, always his greatest concern. Russia was particularly important to him. He spoke the language and visited the country before the revolution, meeting Tolstoy, on whom he published *Count L. N. Tolstoy: his Life and Work* (1912). Fiercely hostile to the Bolsheviks, he wrote in 1924 a highly partisan account of a recent visit, *Impressions of Soviet Russia*, which was translated into several languages. It was primarily his anti-communism which later led him to frequent extreme right-wing circles. In *The Anglo-German Problem* (1912), written with the aim of helping to avert war, he had denounced the 'military Junkertum' of a Prussian-dominated Germany, but in the late 1930s, in the face of the Bolshevik threat, he sympathized actively with the national socialism and antisemitism of Hitler's Germany and with German policy towards Czechoslovakia and Poland. Similarly, his *Daylight on Spain* (1938), a vitriolic riposte to the duchess of Atholl's pro-republican *Searchlight on Spain*, presents Franco's rule as a bulwark of Catholic Christendom against 'the deadly menace of communism'. On such topics he wrote innumerable articles and letters to newspapers (often *The Scotsman*) and was a tireless, voluble, and controversial speaker. Although his views did not essentially change, he was less active after 1940, but remained a well-known figure in Edinburgh society.

Contemporaries and colleagues were often irritated by Sarolea's impulsive and self-important behaviour, but an article of January 1923 in the *Evening Dispatch* claims that his students found him 'an awfully decent soul'. The same article notes that 'he is tall and seems to walk like a sprinter' and that 'the upward tilt of the chin and beard tell us something of the man who was forever chasing butterflies'. One of his dominating passions was that of the collector; he famously amassed one of the largest private libraries in Europe, estimated by himself as 'over 200,000 volumes' by 1930. He had to buy a second house in Royal Terrace to accommodate these; after his death at his home in Edinburgh, on 11 March 1953, his books were dispersed, about half of them going to the library of the future University of Keele.   PETER FRANCE

Sources U. Edin. L., Sarolea MSS [234 files in 81 boxes] · *The Scotsman* (12 March 1953) · *The Times* (12 March 1953) · *WW* · *University of Edinburgh Journal*, 16 (1951–3), 271 · *Evening Dispatch* (Jan 1923) [source for quotations in entry: article in Sarolea MSS 223] · private information (2004) · S. T. Johnson, 'A good European and a sincere racist: the life and work of Professor Charles Sarolea, 1870–1953', PhD diss., University of Keele, 2001 · F. Stockmans, 'Sarolea', *Biographie nationale*, 39, suppl. 2 (Brussels, 1976) · d. cert. · *CGPLA Eng. & Wales* (1953)

Archives U. Edin. L., corresp. and papers | NL Scot., Clark MSS, corresp. with publishers

Likenesses W. L. Calderwood, oils, 1924, U. Edin., Talbot Rice Gallery · photograph, repro. in *The Scotsman* · photographs, U. Edin. L., file Photo ill.SF

Wealth at death £5733 4s. 1d.: confirmation, 27 May 1953, *CCI*

Sarony, Leslie [*real name* Leslie Legge Frye] (1897–1985), songwriter and entertainer, was born at Denman Villa, Tolworth, Surbiton, Surrey, on 22 February 1897, the youngest of the three sons and three daughters of William Rawstorne-Frye, portrait painter, and his wife, Mary Sarony. He first appeared in talent shows at the age of twelve. At fourteen he took his mother's maiden name and became a professional entertainer with Park's Eton Boys and Girton Girls and other juvenile variety acts.

When the First World War began Sarony lied about his age, joined the London Scottish regiment, and saw service on the Somme at Vimy Ridge and in Salonika and Macedonia. He contracted malaria and dysentery and, during recuperation in Malta, wrote his first lyric, a parody of a popular song called 'Three Hundred and Sixty Five Days'. His version was about the surfeit of cheese the troops were served.

On being demobilized Sarony resumed his career in variety, pantomime, revue, and musical comedy. An excellent dancer, in 1926 he played the juvenile lead, Frank, in the original Drury Lane Theatre production of *Show Boat*. His West End shows in the 1920s included appearances in *The Peep Show*, *Dover Street to Dixie*, *Brighter London*, and *The Whirl of the World*. His songwriting and recording careers also started in the 1920s. Between 1926 and 1939 he worked for every recording company in the country. He made over 350 records under his own name and dozens more under assumed ones. Many of his recordings, as featured vocalist, were with Jack Hylton and his band.

In 1935 Sarony formed, with Leslie Holmes, the variety act the Two Leslies. For eleven years they appeared on radio and topped variety bills all over the country. In 1938 they appeared in the royal variety performance. Holmes retired in 1946 and Sarony continued the act for three years with Michael Cole. He became a solo variety act in the late 1940s. He had married, on 3 April 1939, an actress, Anita (*b.* 1914/15), daughter of Frederick Charles Eaton, a dairy owner, auctioneer, and racehorse owner. They had three sons, but the marriage ended in divorce in 1953. In the 1970s he was much in demand as a character actor, playing everything from Samuel Beckett's *Endgame* and *As*

You Like It to film roles in *Chitty Chitty Bang Bang* and *Yanks* as well as, on television, *I Didn't Know you Cared*.

Sarony was a tiny, dynamic, ebullient, aggressively forthright and hard-working, dyed-in-the-wool professional to whom entertaining was a job of work. Yet his songs were special. 'I lift up my finger and I say tweet tweet', 'Jollity Farm', and 'Ain't it grand to be bloomin' well dead' were all enormously popular, as was his recording of the folk-song 'The Old Sow'. His stirring march 'When the Guards are on Parade' reflected his love of the military life. The titles of a few of his 150 published songs recall the England of the 1930s—'Tune in', 'Teas, light refreshments, and minerals', 'I like riding on a choo choo choo', and 'Mucking about in the garden' (written, incidentally, under the pseudonym Q. Kumber).

Off stage Sarony was a keen golfer and his 'men only' parodies, written and performed for the Vaudeville Golfing Society, are masterpieces of Rabelaisian doggerel. In the 1980s he was made a member of the Grand Order of Water Rats and president of the Concert Artistes' Association, and was presented with the gold badge of merit by the Songwriters' Guild of Great Britain. In 1983 he appeared in his second royal variety performance. Sarony died of cancer on 12 February 1985 in St George's Hospital, Tooting, London.   ROY HUDD, *rev.*

Sources personal knowledge (1990) · private information (1990) · *The Times* (14 Feb 1985) · D. Robinson, 'Leslie Sarony: going straight at 78', *Times Saturday Review* (23 Aug 1975), 9 · b. cert. · m. cert. · d. cert.

Likenesses group portrait, photograph, 1931, Hult. Arch. · double portrait, photograph, 1937 (with Leslie Holmes), Hult. Arch.

Wealth at death £93,945: probate, 19 July 1985, *CGPLA Eng. & Wales*

Sarratt, Jacob Henry (1772/3–1819). *See under* Dufour, (Elizabeth) Camilla (*d.* 1846).

Sarsfield, Patrick, Jacobite first earl of Lucan (*d.* 1693), army officer, was the second son of Patrick Sarsfield of Tully Castle, co. Kildare, and Anne O'More, a daughter of the confederate leader Sir Rory *O'More. The family estates were confiscated in the Cromwellian settlement, but Tully was restored to his father in 1661, and it is there that Sarsfield was brought up.

The Catholic soldier His eldest brother, William (*d.* 1675), married Mary Walter, the sister of James Scott, duke of Monmouth, and Sarsfield began his military career in Monmouth's regiment which was then serving in Flanders in French pay. In 1678 he went to London where he took a captain's commission in a new regiment to be raised in Ireland by Thomas Dongan. When news of the Popish Plot broke, Sarsfield was arrested and held at Chester on his way to take up his new post. The regiment was never formed and, as a Roman Catholic, he was barred from pursuing a military career. For the next seven years he led a dissolute life in London where he lost at least three duels, was involved in two abductions of young widows, and was arrested for threatening Ford, Lord Grey, who had made a supposedly anti-Irish remark. The duke of Berwick described Sarsfield as 'a man of huge stature, but without sense, very good natured and very brave' (Wauchope, 93).

The accession of James II in 1685 brought about a change in Sarsfield's fortunes. During Monmouth's rebellion he served as a gentleman volunteer in Theophilus Oglethorpe's reconnaissance party which dogged the rebels in their progress through the west country. He was wounded in the skirmish at Keynsham and was clubbed from his horse and left for dead during the battle of Sedgemoor (5 July 1685). After the rebellion had been crushed he was rewarded with a commission in an English regiment of horse. He was one of those Catholics exempted by the king from taking the oaths of allegiance and supremacy and in 1686 was the lieutenant-colonel under John Churchill of the 4th troop of Life Guards. He was promoted colonel when James's reign was brought to crisis in 1688, and in September was sent to Dublin on an urgent but fruitless mission to Richard Talbot, earl of Tyrconnell, to get Irish troops sent to England.

When the prince of Orange invaded England, Sarsfield was the only officer of his rank to strike a blow for James. On 20 November 1688 he led his Horse Guards in a successful but bloody skirmish at Wincanton. After James fled to France, Sarsfield was approached by the new government to persuade Tyrconnell to relinquish power in Dublin and thereby avoid civil war. Sarsfield refused and William was advised that as he 'was a man of a desperate and daring nature it might be advisable to secure him for fear he might assassinate his person' (Wauchope, 43). Sarsfield's troop was disbanded in January 1689, and he was allowed to join King James in exile.

With James II in Ireland In March 1689 Sarsfield sailed with James's fleet to Ireland, where he was promoted brigadier. His first task was to reform the oversized, newly raised regiments that could be neither paid nor equipped. He was chosen as one of the members for co. Dublin in King James's Dublin parliament which opened on 7 May 1689, although it is doubtful that he ever took his seat. After Lord Kingston abandoned Sligo in April, Sarsfield was sent with 2000 men to secure the town against the Williamite garrison at Enniskillen. He occupied Sligo in early May and on 4 May he laid siege to Ballyshannon. To prevent its relief he detached some of his troops along the Enniskillen Road. This detachment was scattered by a larger force led by Thomas Lloyd at the 'break of Belleek' (7 May 1689), forcing Sarsfield to raise the siege and withdraw to Manorhamilton. He entered into negotiations with Gustavus Hamilton, the governor of Enniskillen, for the exchange of the Sligo leader, Terence McDonogh, and others captured at Ballyshannon. Having no prisoners of war to hand over, he resorted to rounding up those Sligo protestants who had stayed behind and taken protection, and holding them in Sligo gaol. This tactic enraged Hamilton, but nevertheless forced him to allow the exchange. Following this Berwick addressed Sarsfield in correspondence as 'Deare Notorious'.

Sarsfield successfully kept the enemy out of Connaught for the next three months, boasting from his camp in co. Leitrim that 'I am so well posted that I do not fear them

were they double the number' (Wauchope, 69). Plans were laid for him to mount a joint attack on Enniskillen with Justin MacCarthy, but before they could join forces MacCarthy was defeated at Newtownbutler on 31 July 1689, the same day on which the siege of Londonderry was raised. Finding himself isolated in the north-west, Sarsfield abandoned Sligo to the Enniskilliners. He arrived in Dublin in mid-August to report to James, and was given command of a further force with which to retake Sligo. He reached Roscommon on 12 October 1689 and by forced marches quickly retook Jamestown and Boyle, and chased Thomas Lloyd and the Enniskillen troops out of Sligo on 15 October 1689. Six hundred Huguenot troops stranded in the stone fort held out against him for six days, during which Sarsfield made the last use of a mobile siege tower in the British Isles. Articles of surrender were signed on 21 October 1689 and Sarsfield entertained the officers to dinner before allowing them to march to Enniskillen. As they crossed the bridge out of Sligo, he stood on the parapet with a bag of gold in his hand in an unsuccessful attempt to lure their men into James's army. Leaving Henry Luttrell as governor of Sligo, he returned to Dublin.

The French ambassador, the comte d'Avaux, approached James in the hope that Sarsfield would be released to command a proposed Irish brigade in France. Sarsfield's reputation in Ireland, wrote d'Avaux in October 1689, 'is greater than that of any man I know. He is brave but above all he has a sense of honour and integrity in all that he does'. James refused: 'When I asked him for Sarsfield ... he stormed around the room three times in a temper' (Wauchope, 93). The difficulty was eventually overcome by the appointment of Justin MacCarthy. About this time, probably at the end of 1689, Sarsfield married Lady Honora Bourke [see below], a fifteen-year-old daughter of William Bourke (or de Burgh), seventh earl of Clanricarde (d. 1687), and Lady Helen MacCarthy (d. 1722).

In the spring of 1690 Sarsfield was posted to guard the frontier, first at Cavan and then at Finnea. In late June he joined forces with the main army, which took up a position on the Boyne River. At the battle of the Boyne (1 July 1690), the main body of the Jacobite army, including Sarsfield's brigade, marched 4 miles west of the crossing point to prevent a flank attack. In consequence he took no part in the fighting at Oldbridge where King William forded the river and defeated that part of the army commanded by Tyrconnell and Richard Hamilton. After the battle King James fled to France and the Irish army re-formed at Limerick where the senior officers were called to a general council of war. Tyrconnell told the meeting that he was persuaded that Limerick could not withstand a siege and that he proposed to bring the war to an end by negotiating a treaty. In the consequent uproar, Sarsfield was established as the leader of the no surrender party. Confident that the overwhelming majority of the officers were intent on fighting on, Sarsfield plotted to overthrow the viceroy. In order not to alienate King James, he intended to replace him with the duke of Berwick, James's son. The conspiracy failed when Sarsfield approached Berwick, who threatened to expose the conspirators if they continued.

The Ballyneety raid and the defence of the Shannon On 28 July, while Limerick was being prepared for the coming siege, Sarsfield led an expedition to relieve Athlone. The besieging forces retreated on hearing rumours of his approach, and Sarsfield returned to Limerick on 8 August 1690, the same day that King William arrived outside the walls and summoned the city to surrender. On receiving intelligence that the Williamite siege train was some two days behind the main army, Sarsfield resolved to save the city by destroying the artillery. He set out on his celebrated raid with 600 horsemen on the evening of 10 August, crossed the Shannon at Killaloe, and led his men into the Silvermine Mountains. Two nights later, in the early hours of 12 August 1690, he attacked the siege train while it camped at Ballyneety, near Cullen, co. Tipperary, some 12 miles from Limerick. Tradition records that the password for the night was 'Sarsfield'. He is said to have answered the sentry 'Sarsfield is the name, and Sarsfield is the man!' (Wauchope, 134). The wagons were burnt and the artillery pieces were crammed with gunpowder, jammed muzzle first into the ground, and discharged. Although only two of the eight siege guns were split, the general destruction of stores and gunpowder proved fatal to King William's attempt on Limerick. Sarsfield told a prisoner that if he had failed he would have considered the war lost and would have returned to France. He escaped with the horses and recrossed the Shannon at Portumna. The siege was delayed while fresh supplies were brought to Limerick. The weather deteriorated, and William was obliged to attack a too narrow breach in the walls which allowed the Irish a victory (27 August 1690) in which he lost 2000 men. 'The ill success at Limerick was well known to be owing to the want of ammunition occasioned by Sarsfield falling upon the artillery', wrote George Clarke, William's secretary at war (ibid., 153). The siege was raised on 31 August, and William left Ireland on 5 September. Tyrconnell also left Ireland in September to report to King James in France and to beg for French aid for the coming campaign. He left the government to Berwick and a council of twelve, one of whom was Sarsfield.

As the Williamites withdrew into winter quarters Sarsfield was involved in the scramble for the forts on the Leinster side of the Shannon. In mid-September he took part in Berwick's unsuccessful attempt on Birr. Sarsfield's winter was spent in improving his strongholds along the Shannon, frustrating the Williamite attempts to get a toehold in Connaught, and in encouraging his irregulars, the 'rapparees', to plunder the Williamite garrisons scattered in winter quarters. Meanwhile his struggle against Tyrconnell flared up in the viceroy's absence. Berwick was compelled to allow a delegation to travel to King James in France to counter whatever might be said by Tyrconnell and to get the king to replace him. Sarsfield forced the removal of several of Tyrconnell's appointees, including Thomas Nugent, the secretary of state for war. Berwick felt obliged to make Sarsfield governor of Connaught, the only province in Jacobite hands, and of Galway, the principal port, allowing him control of all communication with France. When Berwick fell ill in the winter, Sarsfield became the *de facto* ruler of Jacobite Ireland. His administration was not a happy one, 'for he was so easy that he would not deny signing any paper that was laid before him' (Wauchope, 176). Sarsfield's delegation to James failed to get Tyrconnell replaced, and the viceroy returned from France on 14 January 1691, bearing a patent elevating Sarsfield to the earldom of Lucan. Lucan was confirmed in his rank as major-general and ordered to re-form the Irish army in readiness for the coming campaign. Nevertheless, there was no stop to the bickering in the army between the Lucan and Tyrconnell factions.

According to Berwick, after the Ballyneety raid, Lucan 'considered himself to be the greatest general in the world' (Wauchope, 154), and was reported to have boasted: 'There are two factions here, Lord Tyrconnell's and mine; he can do whatever he wants, I do not care. I will always be stronger than him' (ibid., 195). Of Tyrconnell, Lucan wrote:

> He is very jealous and he despairs of the influence I have over the army. This perfidious and ungrateful man knows full well that during the siege of Limerick he would have been massacred without me, and he is not ignorant of the fact that I prevented and resisted the pressing entreaties of the whole army who adamantly wanted to remove him and proclaim me general in his place.   (ibid., 194)

Tyrconnell, aware of Lucan's hold over the army, governed from Limerick and sent him back to Athlone to oversee the defence of the Shannon. Lucan and his faction eagerly awaited the arrival of a French commander who they hoped would put an end to Tyrconnell's interference in military matters. General Charles Charlmont, marquis de St Ruth (or St Ruhe), arrived in Limerick on 19 May 1691.

The fall of Athlone and the second siege of Limerick St Ruth correctly anticipated that the enemy's first move of the campaign would be on Athlone. He gave the command of the town to one of his French lieutenant-generals and posted Lucan to the camp on the Roscommon side of the town. The Williamite general Ginckel began his attack on Athlone on 19 June 1691. During the siege Tyrconnell visited the army outside Athlone. Lucan was determined that he should neither interfere nor stay. 'I was shocked to discover', wrote Tyrconnell, 'that while the enemy was within cannon shot of us, these men: Lord Lucan, Purcell and Luttrell: were spending all their time and effort taking round a petition calling for my resignation from the army' (Wauchope, 208). Lucan's partisans circulated the rumour that Tyrconnell was receiving French gold in exchange for the Irish recruits who were to be sent to France, and one colonel went so far as to threaten to cut the ropes on Tyrconnell's tent if he did not return to Limerick. Athlone fell on 30 June 1691 in a way that brought severe criticism on St Ruth. Forced to withdraw the army westwards, he decided, against Lucan's advice, to meet Ginckel's army in a pitched battle rather than retreat to the fortifications of Limerick and Galway. At the battle of

Aughrim (12 July 1691), Lucan commanded the right wing of the Irish army which was positioned along Kilcommodon Hill so as to block the road to Galway. Successive attacks on the Irish positions were beaten off but, late in the battle, St Ruth was killed by a cannon-ball. In the confusion that followed the left wing collapsed and as the day turned to dusk the battle became a rout. Lucan's cavalry covered the retreat, but he was unable to prevent the greatest slaughter of the war.

The remnants of the Irish army again fell back to the safety of Limerick's walls. While Ginckel first concentrated his efforts on Galway, which surrendered on 28 July 1691, Lucan led a force into Tipperary to destroy the forage and the stores between Cashel and Limerick in anticipation of a second siege. On 2 August, with Ginckel's army still three weeks away, Lucan discovered correspondence from the enemy addressed to his old friend and ally Henry Luttrell. Lucan had him arrested, to the delight of the French, who hoped that this signalled a reconciliation between Lucan and Tyrconnell. Their joy was short-lived. Within a fortnight Tyrconnell was dead. Although the civil government was nominally vested in the hands of three lords justices and the army was commanded by two French lieutenant-generals, Lucan was once again the power in the land.

The siege of Limerick began on 25 August, though it took Ginckel until 22 September to drive the Irish away from their positions on the co. Clare side of the river so that Limerick could be invested from both sides. Even then, Ginckel accepted that he did not have the means to storm the city and settled down to a blockade. His only fear was that Limerick would be relieved from the sea in the same way that Londonderry had been two years previously. Nevertheless, it was to the surprise of both the garrison and the besieging forces that Lucan sued for peace on 23 September 1691. The promised French supply fleet had not arrived and the Irish army was for the first time to be forced to winter within the city walls. Lucan demanded and was granted terms of surrender that would allow his men to travel to France. The treaty of Limerick was signed on 3 October 1691. It formed two separate sets of articles: the military articles which principally provided for the shipping to France of the Irish army, and the civil articles which sought, so far as the Jacobite negotiators were concerned, to safeguard the rights of the Irish until the return of the army, and to secure the property rights of those who swore allegiance to William and Mary. According to Bishop Burnet, during the cease-fire Lucan told some English officers: 'As low as we are now, change but kings with us and we will fight it over again with you' (Wauchope, 268).

Last years Lucan left Ireland for the last time on 22 December 1691, having succeeded in getting over 12,000 Irish soldiers transported to France to join King James. He was rewarded with the colonelcy of the 2nd troop of Horse Guards and kept the rank of major-general in King James's army of exiles which was gathered in Normandy in preparation for an invasion of England. After the destruction of the French navy at the battle of La Hogue (19–24 May 1692) King James's army was amalgamated into that of Louis XIV and Lucan was given the equivalent rank of *maréchal de camp*. He joined the French army in Flanders and served as a volunteer at the battle of Steenkerke (3 August 1692). He was noted both for his bravery on the field and for his humanity after the battle in arranging passes so that English surgeons could tend to the prisoners of war. In the spring of 1693 he took up his command in the French army and was fatally wounded at the battle of Landen (29 July 1693). He died a few days afterwards in Huy.

> In a continental context Sarsfield's military achievements were not great, but they threatened to change the history of his country at a time when the balance of Europe could well have been altered by events in Ireland. … By the time of his death Sarsfield was by far the best known and most loved of all Irishmen. With the exception of the early saints, none of his predecessors or his contemporaries have been written about as much as he has been, and no Irish leader until the times of Wolfe Tone a century later. (Wauchope, 1)

Lucan's wife, Honora [**Honora Fitzjames**, duchess of Berwick upon Tweed (1675–1698)], born at Portumna, co. Galway, had been evacuated to France during the war in Ireland before being joined by her husband in early 1692 at the Jacobite court in exile at St Germain-en-Laye. She was outlawed for her adherence to James II. Admired for her beauty, she was credited with the introduction of 'les contradanses anglaises' to the French court. With Lucan, she had one child, James Francis Edward (the Jacobite second earl), born in April 1693, three months before she was widowed. She married second, on 26 March 1695, James II's natural son James *FitzJames, duke of Berwick (1670–1734). Her second son, James Francis (the second duke), was born on 19 October 1696. After suffering a miscarriage, she died of tuberculosis on 16 January 1698 in Pézenas in Languedoc and was buried in the English convent at Pontoise. Her widower had her heart removed and encased in a silver box. James Francis Edward Sarsfield, second earl of Lucan (1693–1719), served in both the French and Spanish armies. He died unmarried in St Omer aged twenty-six. PIERS WAUCHOPE

Sources P. Wauchope, *Patrick Sarsfield and the Williamite war* (1992) [incl. comprehensive bibliography] · J. C. O'Callaghan, *History of the Irish brigades in the service of France* (1886) · GEC, *Peerage*, new edn, vol. 3 · C. Petrie, *The marshal duke of Berwick: the picture of an age* (1953) · C. Petrie, *The duke of Berwick and his son* (1951) · *The manuscripts of his grace the duke of Rutland*, 4 vols., HMC, 24 (1888–1905), vol. 2, p. 128

Likenesses J. Riley, oils, *c*.1685, NG Ire.; repro. in Wauchope, *Patrick Sarsfield* · oils, *c*.1690, repro. in Wauchope, *Patrick Sarsfield*; priv. coll. · M. Tilliard, line engraving, BM · oils (Honora FitzJames), repro. in Petrie, *Marshal duke of Berwick* · oils (Honora FitzJames), Kilkenny Castle; repro. in Wauchope, *Patrick Sarsfield*

PICTURE CREDITS

Rowland, Daniel (1711?–1790)—by courtesy of the National Library of Wales

Rowland, Roland Walter [Tiny] (1917–1998)—© Jane Bown

Rowlandson, Thomas (1757–1827)—The Metropolitan Museum of Art, The Elisha Whittelsey Collection, The Elisha Whittelsey Fund, 1959. (59.533.963) All rights reserved, The Metropolitan Museum of Art

Rowntree, Joseph (1836–1925)—© reserved; Rowntree Archives; photograph National Portrait Gallery, London

Rowntree, (Benjamin) Seebohm (1871–1954)—Jane Bown / Camera Press

Rowse, (Alfred) Leslie (1903–1997)—© National Portrait Gallery, London

Roxburgh, John Fergusson (1888–1954)—© National Portrait Gallery, London

Royce, Sir (Frederick) Henry, baronet (1863–1933)—Royal Aeronautical Society Library

Royden, (Agnes) Maude (1876–1956)—© National Portrait Gallery, London

Rubens, Sir Peter Paul (1577–1640)—The Royal Collection © 2004 HM Queen Elizabeth II

Ruck, Amy Roberta (1878–1978)—by permission of the E. O. Hoppé Trust, Curatorial Assistance, Inc., Los Angeles

Rucker, Sir Arthur Nevil (1895–1991)—© National Portrait Gallery, London

Rudd, Charles Dunell (1844–1916)—© reserved

Rue, de la, family (per c.1820–1923) [Rue, Thomas de la (1793–1866)]—photograph National Portrait Gallery, London

Rue, Warren de la (1815–1889)—© National Portrait Gallery, London

Rumbold, Sir Horace George Montagu, ninth baronet (1869–1941)—© National Portrait Gallery, London

Runcie, Robert Alexander Kennedy, Baron Runcie (1921–2000)—Snowdon / Camera Press

Runciman, Hilda, Viscountess Runciman (1869–1956)—© National Portrait Gallery, London

Runciman, Walter, first Baron Runciman (1847–1937)—© National Portrait Gallery, London

Runciman, Walter, first Viscount Runciman of Doxford (1870–1949)—© National Portrait Gallery, London

Runcorn, (Stanley) Keith (1922–1995)—© Nick Sinclair; collection National Portrait Gallery, London

Rupert, prince and count palatine of the Rhine and duke of Cumberland (1619–1682)—The Royal Collection © 2004 HM Queen Elizabeth II

Rushbrooke, James Henry (1870–1947)—© National Portrait Gallery, London

Rushton, William George (1937–1996)—Apex Photo Agency Ltd

Ruskin, John (1819–1900)—private collection

Ruspini, Bartholomew (1730–1813)—Ashmolean Museum, Oxford

Russell, (Muriel) Audrey (1906–1989)—BBC Picture Archives

Russell, Bertrand Arthur William, third Earl Russell (1872–1970)—© National Portrait Gallery, London

Russell, Charles Arthur, Baron Russell of Killowen (1832–1900)—© National Portrait Gallery, London

Russell, Dora Winifred (1894–1986)—© Jane Bown

Russell, Edward, earl of Orford (1652–1727)—© National Maritime Museum, London

Russell, Francis, fifth duke of Bedford (1765–1802)—The Royal Collection © 2004 HM Queen Elizabeth II

Russell, Francis Xavier Joseph, Baron Russell of Killowen (1867–1946)—© National Portrait Gallery, London

Russell, George William (1867–1935)—National Gallery of Ireland

Russell, George William Erskine (1853–1919)—© National Portrait Gallery, London

Russell, Sir (Sydney) Gordon (1892–1980)—© Gordon Russell Trust; collection National Portrait Gallery, London

Russell, Henry (1812x14–1900)—private collection; photograph National Portrait Gallery, London

Russell, Herbrand Arthur, eleventh duke of Bedford (1858–1940)—Getty Images - Hulton Archive

Russell, James Burn (1837–1904)—© National Portrait Gallery, London

Russell, John, first earl of Bedford (c.1485–1555)—The Royal Collection © 2004 HM Queen Elizabeth II

Russell, John, fourth duke of Bedford (1710–1771)—© National Portrait Gallery, London

Russell, John (1745–1806)—© National Portrait Gallery, London

Russell, John, sixth duke of Bedford (1766–1839)—by kind permission of the Marquess of Tavistock and the Trustees of the Bedford Estates

Russell, John [Lord John Russell], first Earl Russell (1792–1878)—© National Portrait Gallery, London

Russell, John [Jack] (1795–1883)—© National Portrait Gallery, London

Russell, John, Viscount Amberley (1842–1876)—© National Portrait Gallery, London

Russell, Sir (Edward) John (1872–1965)—© National Portrait Gallery, London

Russell, Katharine Louisa, Viscountess Amberley (1842–1874)—© reserved

Russell, (Edward Frederick) Langley, second Baron Russell of Liverpool (1895–1981)—© National Portrait Gallery, London

Russell, Lucy, countess of Bedford (bap. 1581, d. 1627)—National Museum of Fine Arts, Sweden

Russell, Odo William Leopold, first Baron Ampthill (1829–1884)—© National Portrait Gallery, London

Russell, (Arthur) Oliver Villiers, second Baron Ampthill (1869–1935)—© National Portrait Gallery, London

Russell, Rachel, Lady Russell (bap. 1637, d. 1723)—© National Portrait Gallery, London

Russell, Richard Drew (1903–1981)—private collection

Russell, Thomas (1767–1803)—photograph reproduced with the kind permission of the Trustees of the National Museums & Galleries of Northern Ireland

Russell, Sir Walter Westley (1867–1949)—© Royal Academy of Arts, London

Russell, William, Lord Russell (1639–1683)—© National Portrait Gallery, London

Russell, Sir William Howard (1820–1907)—V&A Images, The Victoria and Albert Museum

Rust, William Charles (1903–1949)—by permission of the People's History Museum

Rustat, Tobias (bap. 1608, d. 1694)—Jesus College, Cambridge; photograph © National Portrait Gallery, London

Rutherford, Daniel (1749–1819)—© National Portrait Gallery, London

Rutherford, Ernest, Baron Rutherford of Nelson (1871–1937)—Estate of the Artist / © The Royal Society

Rutherford, Dame Margaret Taylor (1892–1972)—© Photographer's Estate; collection National Portrait Gallery, London

Ruthven, Alexander Gore Arkwright Hore-, first earl of Gowrie (1872–1955)—© National Portrait Gallery, London

Ryan, Sir Edward (1793–1875)—Dilettanti Society, Brooks' Club. Photograph: Photographic Survey, Courtauld Institute of Art, London

Rycaut, Sir Paul (1629–1700)—© The Royal Society

Ryder, Sir Dudley (1691–1756)—private collection / National Portrait Gallery, London

Ryder, Dudley, first earl of Harrowby (1762–1847)—private collection; photograph © National Portrait Gallery, London

Ryder, Dudley Francis Stuart, third earl of Harrowby (1831–1900)—© National Portrait Gallery, London

Ryder, Henry (1777–1836)—private collection; photograph © National Portrait Gallery, London

Ryder, John Nicholas Robins (1814–1885)—© National Portrait Gallery, London

Ryder, Robert Edward Dudley (1908–1986)—© National Portrait Gallery, London

Ryder, (Margaret) Susan, Baroness Ryder of Warsaw (1924–2000)—Snowdon / Camera Press; collection National Portrait Gallery, London

Ryland, John (1753–1825)—© National Portrait Gallery, London

Ryland, William Wynne (bap. 1733, d. 1783)—© National Portrait Gallery, London

Ryle, Gilbert (1900–1976)—© National Portrait Gallery, London

Ryle, John Charles (1816–1900)—© National Portrait Gallery, London

Rymer, Thomas (1642/3–1713)—© National Portrait Gallery, London

Ryrie, Sir Granville de Laune (1865–1937)—© National Portrait Gallery, London

Rysbrack, (John) Michael (1694–1770)—Yale Center for British Art, Paul Mellon Collection

Ryves, Bruno (c.1596–1677)—The Royal Collection © 2004 HM Queen Elizabeth II

Sabine, Sir Edward (1788–1883)—© National Portrait Gallery, London

Sacheverell, Henry (bap. 1674, d. 1724)—The President and Fellows of Magdalen College Oxford

Sacheverell, William (1637/8–1691)—© National Portrait Gallery, London

Sackville, Charles, sixth earl of Dorset and first earl of Middlesex (1643–1706)—private collection. Photograph: Photographic Survey, Courtauld Institute of Art, London

Sackville, Edward, fourth earl of Dorset (1590–1652)—National Trust Photographic Library / John Hammond

Sackville, Thomas, first Baron Buckhurst and first earl of Dorset (c.1536–1608)—© National Portrait Gallery, London

Sadleir, John (1813–1856)—courtesy of the National Library of Ireland

Sadleir, Michael Thomas Harvey (1888–1957)—© National Portrait Gallery, London

Sadler, Sir Michael Ernest (1861–1943)—© National Portrait Gallery, London

Sadler, Michael Thomas (1780–1835)—© National Portrait Gallery, London

Sadler, Sir Ralph (1507–1587)—St Mary's Church, Standon; photograph © National Portrait Gallery, London

Sage, John (1652–1711)—Scottish National Portrait Gallery

Sainsbury family (per. 1869–1956)—Sainsbury's Archives

Sainsbury, Alan John, Baron Sainsbury (1902–1998)—© National Portrait Gallery, London

Sainsbury, Sir Robert James (1906–2000)—© Estate of Francis Bacon 2004. All rights reserved, DACS. Collection of Robert & Lisa Sainsbury, University of East Anglia, Norwich. Photograph: James Austin

St Clair, William, of Roslin (1700–1778)—Collection Royal Company of Archers, Edinburgh; © reserved in the photograph

Saint-Denis, Michel Jacques (1897–1971)—Getty Images - Gordon Anthony

Saint-Évremond, Charles de Marguetel de Saint-Denis de (*bap.* 1614, *d.* 1703)—Althorp

St John, Charles George William (1809–1856)—© National Portrait Gallery, London

St John, Henry, styled first Viscount Bolingbroke (1678–1751)—© National Portrait Gallery, London

St John, Oliver, first earl of Bolingbroke (*c.*1584–1646)—© National Portrait Gallery, London

St John, Oliver (*c.*1598–1673)—© National Portrait Gallery, London

St Laurent, Louis Stephen (1882–1973)—Karsh / Camera Press

St Pol, Mary de, countess of Pembroke (*c.*1304–1377)—by permission of the Syndics of Cambridge University Library

Saintsbury, George Edward Bateman (1845–1933)—© National Portrait Gallery, London

Saklatvala, Shapurji (1874–1936)—© National Portrait Gallery, London

Sala, George Augustus (1828–1895)—© National Portrait Gallery, London

Salam, Muhammad Abdus (1926–1996)—Getty Images – Ball

Salaman, Redcliffe Nathan (1874–1955)—Godfrey Argent Studios / Royal Society

Sale, Sir Robert Henry (1782–1845)—Somerset County Museums Service

Saleeby, Caleb Williams Elijah (1878–1940)—© National Portrait Gallery, London

Salisbury, Francis Owen (1874–1962)—© Estate of the Artist; unknown

collection / Christie's Images Ltd. (2004)

Salisbury, Richard Anthony (1761–1829)—© Royal Botanic Gardens, Kew: reproduced by kind permission of the Director and the Board of Trustees

Salisbury, Sarah (1690x92–1724)—© National Portrait Gallery, London

Salmon, Cyril Barnet, Baron Salmon (1903–1991)—© National Portrait Gallery, London

Salomon, Johann Peter (*bap.* 1745, *d.* 1815)—Royal College of Music, London

Salomons, Sir David, baronet (1797–1873)—Ashmolean Museum, Oxford

Salote Mafile'o Pilolevu Tupou III (1900–1965)—Getty Images – Hulton Archive

Salt, Henry (1780–1827)—© National Portrait Gallery, London

Salt, Sir Titus, first baronet (1803–1876)—© National Portrait Gallery, London

Salter, John William (1820–1869)—reproduced by permission of the British Geological Survey. © NERC. All rights reserved. IPR/44-24CW

Saltonstall, Sir Richard (*bap.* 1586, *d.* 1661)—photography courtesy Peabody Essex Museum

Sammons, Albert Edward (1886–1957)—© National Portrait Gallery, London

Samuel, Herbert Louis, first Viscount Samuel (1870–1963)—© National Portrait Gallery, London

Samuel, Marcus, first Viscount Bearsted (1853–1927)—Guildhall Art Gallery, Corporation of London

Samuel, Raphael Elkan (1934–1996)—© Stefan Wallgren; collection National Portrait Gallery, London

Samuely, Felix James (1902–1959)—private collection

Sancho, (Charles) Ignatius (1729?–1780)—National Gallery of Canada

Sancroft, William (1617–1693)—by permission of the Master, Fellows, and Scholars of Emmanuel College in the University of Cambridge

Sandars, John Satterfield (1853–1934)—© National Portrait Gallery, London

Sanday, William (1843–1920)—© courtesy the Artist's Estate / Bridgeman Art Library; collection Christ Church, Oxford

Sandby, Paul (*bap.* 1731, *d.* 1809)—© Tate, London, 2004

Sanderson, (Julia Sarah) Anne Cobden-(1853–1926)—© National Portrait Gallery, London

Sanderson, Sir John Scott Burdon, baronet (1828–1905)—© National Portrait Gallery, London

Sanderson, Robert (1587–1663)—Christ Church, Oxford

Sanderson, Thomas James Cobden-(1840–1922)—© Estate of Sir William Rothenstein / National Portrait Gallery, London / private collection

Sandford, Francis (1630–1694)—© National Portrait Gallery, London

Sandow, Eugen (1867–1925)—© National Portrait Gallery, London

Sandwith, Humphry (1822–1881)—© National Portrait Gallery, London

Sandys, Edwin (1519?–1588)—© National Portrait Gallery, London / Country Life Picture Library; private collection

Sandys, (Anthony) Frederick Augustus (1829–1904)—© National Portrait Gallery, London

Sandys, George (1578–1644)—private collection; © reserved in the photograph

Sanger, Sophy (1881–1950)—© reserved; photograph National Portrait Gallery, London

Sangster, William Edwin Robert (1900–1960)—© National Portrait Gallery, London

Sankey, John, Viscount Sankey (1866–1948)—© National Portrait Gallery, London

Sansom, Sir George Bailey (1883–1965)—© National Portrait Gallery, London

Santley, Sir Charles (1834–1922)—© National Portrait Gallery, London

Sapru, Sir Tej Bahadur (1875–1949)—© National Portrait Gallery, London

Sargant, William Walters (1907–1988)—© reserved; photograph National Portrait Gallery, London

Sargent, John Singer (1856–1925)—Archives of American Art, Smithsonian Institution

Sargent, Sir (Harold) Malcolm Watts (1895–1967)—© reserved; Royal College of Music, London

Sarmento, Jacob de Castro (1692?–1762)—© National Portrait Gallery, London

Sarmiento de Acuña, Diego, count of Gondomar in the Spanish nobility (1567–1626)—© reserved